C000216555

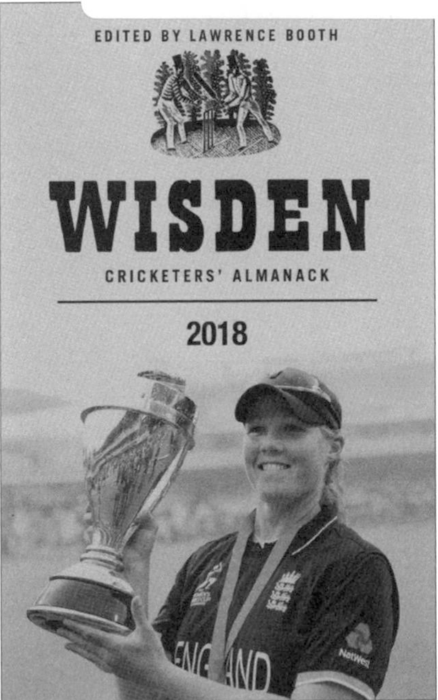
EDITED BY LAWRENCE BOOTH
WISDEN
CRICKETERS' ALMANACK
2018

WISDEN

CRICKETERS' ALMANACK

2018

EDITED BY LAWRENCE BOOTH

WISDEN

CRICKETERS' ALMANACK

2018

155th EDITION

John Wisden & Co

An imprint of Bloomsbury Publishing Plc

WISDEN
Bloomsbury Publishing Plc
50 Bedford Square, London, WC1B 3DP, UK

First published in Great Britain 2018

WISDEN CRICKETERS' ALMANACK
Editor **Lawrence Booth**
Co-editor **Hugh Chevallier**
Deputy editors **Steven Lynch** and **Harriet Monkhouse**
Digital editor **James Gingell**
Contributing editor **Richard Whitehead**
Production co-ordinator **Peter Bather**
Chief statistician **Philip Bailey**
Proofreader **Charles Barr**
Database and typesetting **Gary Holmes** and **Laura Earl**
Publisher **Charlotte Croft**
Consultant publisher **Christopher Lane**

Reader feedback: almanack@wisdenalmanack.com
www.wisdenalmanack.com
www.wisdenrecords.com
Follow Wisden on Twitter @WisdenAlmanack
and on Facebook at Wisden Sports

A catalogue record for this book is available from the British Library

Library of Congress Cataloguing-in-Publication data has been applied for

Hardback 978-1-4729-5354-4 £55
Soft cover 978-1-4729-5357-5 £55
Large format 978-1-4729-5355-1 £75
Leatherbound 978-1-4729-5356-8 £290
The Shorter Wisden (eBook) 978-1-4729-5358-2 £8.99

2 4 6 8 10 9 7 5 3 1

Typeset in Times New Roman and Univers by David Lewis XML Associates, Bungay NR35 1EF
Printed and bound in Italy by Grafica Veneta S.p.A., Trebaseleghe (PD)

A Taste of Wisden 2018

It started with the arrival of Heston, a charming curate from Cape Town, who smote the ball through the off-side ring like Samson wielding the jawbone of an ass through the Philistines.

The Power and the Glory, page 80

* * *

He was the Egon Ronay of fish and chips.

Obituaries, page 187

* * *

It was also the highest score by a medical practitioner, beating W. G. Grace's 344 in 1876.

Obituaries, page 229

* * *

Gunaratne all but sealed it with another six, an audacious sweep off Bumrah towards the gas-holder, where the Sri Lankan *papare* band was by now drowning out the Indian drummers.

Champions Trophy, page 279

* * *

There was little about a long, slow walk back to his mark to make South African hearts flutter: he bore the sagging shoulders of an accountant returning home from a commute.

England v South Africa, page 312

* * *

Was it elite international sport, or ritual sacrifice? A Technicolor window into cricket's future, or a marketing exercise dressed up as innovation?

England v West Indies, page 329

* * *

Four times Sangakkara cued the pink for six in a dazzling masterclass which proved that, whatever colour the ball, whatever the conditions, he remained – in his 40th year – one of the world's best.

Yorkshire v Surrey, page 645

* * *

Twelve months in Vietnam was good training to be in Ian Chappell's dressing-room.

Cricket Round the World, page 1092

LIST OF CONTRIBUTORS

Timothy Abraham
Andrew Alderson
Tanya Aldred
Zafar Ansari
Matthew Appleby
Chris Aspin
Philip August
Vaneisa Baksh
Greg Baum
Benedict Bermange
Edward Bevan
Paul Bird
Paul Bolton
Daniel Brettig
Liam Brickhill
Gideon Brooks
Colin Bryden
Andy Bull
Ian Callender
Nazvi Careem
Brian Carpenter
Adam Collins
Tom Collomosse
James Coyne
Jon Culley
John Curtis
Shamya Dasgupta
Debashish Datta
Geoffrey Dean
William Dick
George Dobell
Paul Edwards
Vithushan Ehantharajah
Mark Eklid
Matthew Engel
Peter English
John Etheridge
Melinda Farrell
Fidel Fernando
Warwick Franks
Alan Gardner
Mark Geenty
Richard Gibson
Haydn Gill
Gideon Haigh
Kevin Hand
David Hardy
Tom Harrison
Shahid Hashmi
Douglas Henderson
Andrew Hignell
Paul Hiscock
Tristan Holme
Jon Hotten
Steve James
Nishant Joshi
R. Kaushik
Abid Ali Kazi
Jarrod Kimber
Malcolm Knox
Richard Latham
Geoff Lemon
Jonathan Liew
Will Macpherson
Neil Manthorp
Vic Marks
Mazher Arshad
Kalika Mehta
Suresh Menon
Peter Miller
Mohammad Isam
R. Mohan
Benj Moorehead
Raf Nicholson
Andrew Nixon
Harry Pearson
Mark Pennell
Dileep Premachandran
Andrew Radd
Paul Radley
Richard Rae
Charles Reynolds
Osman Samiuddin
Neville Scott
Mike Selvey
Kamila Shamsie
Utpal Shuvro
Rob Smyth
Richard Spiller
Fraser Stewart
Andy Stockhausen
Bharat Sundaresan
Pat Symes
Bruce Talbot
Matt Thacker
Sa'adi Thawfeeq
Alan Tyers
Anand Vasu
Telford Vice
Phil Walker
John Ward
David Warner
Tim Wellock
Isabelle Westbury
Tim Wigmore
Freddie Wilde
Simon Wilde
Marcus Williams
Dean Wilson
Andy Zaltzman

Photographers are credited as appropriate. Special thanks to Graham Morris. **Cartoons** by Nick Newman. Contributors to the **Round the World** section are listed after their articles.

The editor also acknowledges with gratitude assistance from the following: Robin Abrahams, Enid Bakewell, Derek Barnard, Mike Bechley, Martin Briggs, Tony Brown, Derek Carlaw, Andrew Carr, Adam Chadwick, Henry Cowen, Brian Croudy, Stephen Cubitt, Prakash Dahatonde, Nigel Davies, Charles Davis, Lizzy Ewer, Gulu Ezekiel, M. L. Fernando, Martin Fiennes, Ric Finlay, Alan Fordham, David Frith, Nagraj Gollapudi, Chris Haynes, Clive Hitchcock, David Kendix, Patrick Kidd, Rajesh Kumar, Tim Lamb, David Lamming, Edward Liddle, Katherine Macpherson, Nirav Malavi, Mahendra Mapagunaratne, Bob Marsden, Peter Martin, Clayton Murzello, Michael Owen-Smith, Francis Payne, Peter Pollock, Mick Pope, Qamar Ahmed, Danny Reuben, Giles Ridley, Andrew Samson, Clare Skinner, Mike Smedley, Steven Stern, Richard Sydenham, Chris Tavaré, George Thomas, Chris Walmsley, Charlie Wat, Oliver Webb Carter, Andy Wilson.

The production of *Wisden* would not be possible without the support and co-operation of many other cricket officials, county scorers, writers and lovers of the game. To them all, many thanks.

PREFACE

The gender of the figure on the cover, and of three Cricketers of the Year, should not obscure the bigger picture. Look left, and you see few women. Reflecting press boxes around the world, most of our contributors are men; so too the entrants for our writing and photography competitions. But things are beginning to change, thanks in no small part to the careers of two of the most significant figures in the obituary pages – Rachael Heyhoe Flint and Jan Brittin. *Wisden* is determined to continue their good work.

This year's edition includes another shift of emphasis. A new section, Part Six, covers overseas domestic Twenty20 cricket, a form of the game which may not be to everyone's taste but is now a fixture on the menu. It seemed the natural moment to start an award for the Leading Twenty20 Cricketer in the World: the first winner is Afghanistan leg-spinner Rashid Khan.

Three items of housekeeping. With the exception of matches involving English touring teams, we no longer run short reports for games that descend into 15-a-side farces. We are tweaking our abbreviation for the rarest type of bowler: SLC (slow left-arm chinaman) becomes SLW (slow left-arm wrist-spin). And there is an alteration to the overseas section; Afghanistan and Ireland are now more prominent in Part Five after being given Test status.

Back in print after an absence of 14 years is *Wisden Cricket Monthly*, under the editorship of Phil Walker; accompanying it is a fully fledged wisden.com website. This means more editorial voices bearing the Wisden name: we hope you'll find them as distinctive as the Almanack. Two other voices have moved on. This is Andrew Radd's 30th and last season as Northamptonshire correspondent, making him our longest-serving current county reporter; just up the M1, Leicestershire's Paul Jones had already stepped down, after 13 years. Both leave with our gratitude for their dedication and professionalism.

In the editorial team, special thanks go to co-editor Hugh Chevallier, who has chalked up 20 years at Wisden, and has never been less than a pleasure to work with. Without him, or the diligence of Harriet Monkhouse, Steven Lynch, James Gingell and Richard Whitehead, these pages would not be possible. Thanks, too, to Chris Lane, our consultant publisher, to Peter Bather, our production co-ordinator, to Alan Williams for his legal advice, to Charles Barr for his proofreading, and to our typesetting team at DLXML.

We were sorry to see the departure from Bloomsbury of Charlotte Atyeo, who was always so supportive. Since then Charlotte Croft has backed us all the way. And I'm grateful to colleagues at the *Daily Mail* and *The Mail on Sunday* – in particular Lee Clayton, Alison Kervin and Mike Richards – for giving me breathing space as the Wisden deadline approached.

My wife, Anjali, could have been forgiven for wanting a little more of my time this year: our first child, Aleya, was born in October. They are both wonderful.

LAWRENCE BOOTH
Barnes, March 2018

CONTENTS

Part One – Comment

Part Two – The Wisden Review

Part Three – English International Cricket

Part Four – English Domestic Cricket

Statistics

Specsavers County Championship

One-Day County Competitions

Other English Cricket

Part Five – Overseas Cricket

Cricket in Afghanistan

Cricket in Australia

Cricket in Bangladesh

Cricket in India

Cricket in Ireland

Cricket in New Zealand

Cricket in Pakistan

Cricket in South Africa

Cricket in Sri Lanka

Cricket in the West Indies

Cricket in Zimbabwe

World Tables, Rankings and Averages

Other Overseas International Cricket

Part Six – Overseas Domestic Twenty20 Cricket

Part Seven – Women's Cricket

Part Eight – Records and Registers

RECORDS

Part Nine – The Almanack

SYMBOLS AND ABBREVIATIONS

*	In full scorecards and lists of tour parties signifies the captain. In short scorecards, averages and records signifies not out.
†	In full scorecards signifies the designated wicketkeeper. In averages signifies a left-handed batsman.
‡	In short scorecards signifies the team who won the toss.
MoM/PoM	In short scorecards signifies the Man/Player of the Match.
MoS/PoS	In short scorecards signifies the Man/Player of the Series.
DLS	Signifies where the result of a curtailed match has been determined under the Duckworth/Lewis/Stern method.

Other uses of symbols are explained in notes where they appear.

FIRST-CLASS MATCHES

Men's matches of three or more days' duration are first-class unless otherwise stated. All other matches are not first-class, including one-day and Twenty20 internationals.

SCORECARDS

Where full scorecards are not provided in this book, they can be found at Cricket Archive (www.cricketarchive.co.uk) or ESPNcricinfo (www.cricinfo.com). Full scorecards from matches played overseas can also be found in the relevant *ACS Overseas First-Class Annuals*.

In Twenty20 scorecards, the second figure in a bowling analysis refers to dot balls, and not maidens (as in first-class or List A games).

RECORDS

The entire Records section (pages 1183–1315) can now be found at www.wisdenrecords.com. The online Records database is regularly updated and, in many instances, more detailed than in *Wisden 2018*. Further information on past winners of tournaments covered in this book can be found at www.wisden.com/almanacklinks.

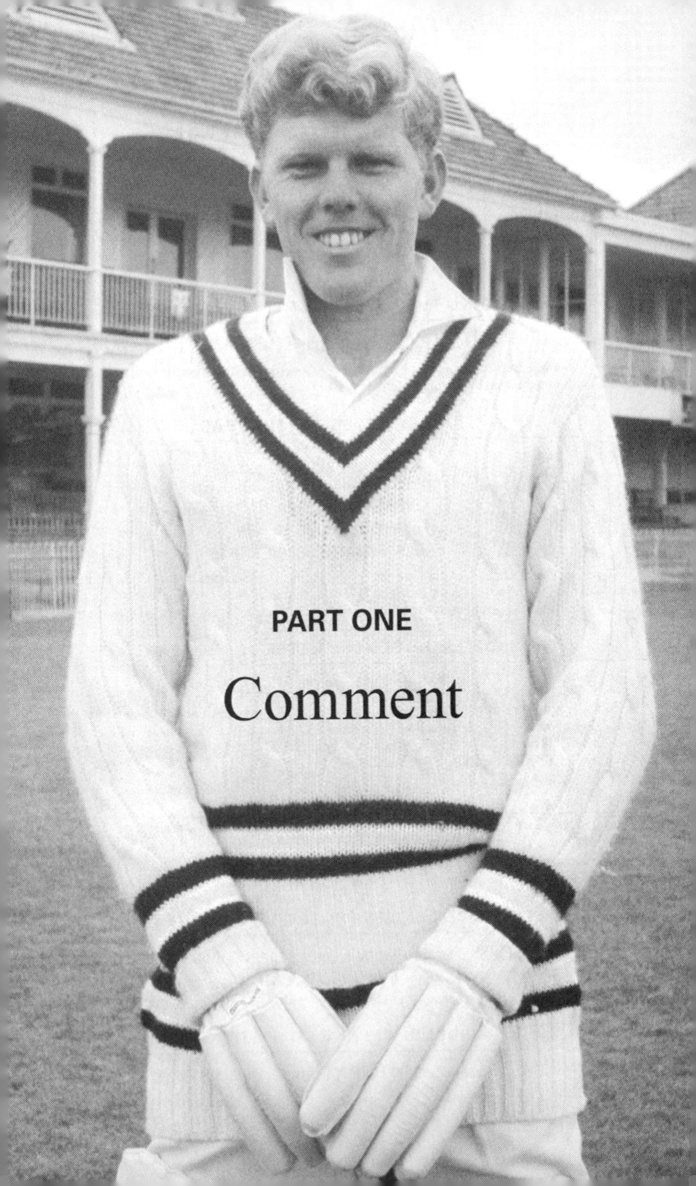

PART ONE

Comment

Wisden Honours

THE LEADING CRICKETERS IN THE WORLD

Virat Kohli (page 78)
Mithali Raj (page 1120)

The Leading Cricketers in the World are chosen by the editor of *Wisden* in consultation with some of the world's most experienced writers and commentators. Selection is based on a player's class and form shown in all cricket during the calendar year, and is merely guided by statistics rather than governed by them. There is no limit to how many times a player may be chosen.

THE LEADING TWENTY20 CRICKETER IN THE WORLD

Rashid Khan (page 1098)

This new award exactly mirrors those above, but is based solely on performances in Twenty20 cricket – and may be won by a male or female player.

FIVE CRICKETERS OF THE YEAR

Shai Hope (page 87)
Heather Knight (page 89)
Jamie Porter (page 91)
Natalie Sciver (page 93)
Anya Shrubsole (page 95)

The Five Cricketers of the Year are chosen by the editor of *Wisden*, and represent a tradition that dates back to 1889, making this the oldest individual award in cricket. Excellence in and/or influence on the previous English summer are the major criteria. No one can be chosen more than once.

WISDEN SCHOOLS CRICKETER OF THE YEAR

Teddie Casterton (page 751)

The Schools Cricketer of the Year, based on first-team performances during the previous English summer, is chosen by *Wisden's* schools correspondent in consultation with the editor and other experienced observers. The winner's school must be in the UK, play cricket to a standard approved by *Wisden* and provide reports to this Almanack.

WISDEN BOOK OF THE YEAR

A Clear Blue Sky by Jonny Bairstow and Duncan Hamilton (page 135)

The Book of the Year is selected by *Wisden's* guest reviewer; all cricket books published in the previous calendar year and submitted to *Wisden* for possible review are eligible.

WISDEN–MCC CRICKET PHOTOGRAPH OF THE YEAR

was won by Stu Forster (whose entry appears opposite page 64)

The Wisden–MCC Cricket Photograph of the Year is chosen by a panel of independent experts; all images on a cricket theme photographed in the previous calendar year are eligible.

WISDEN'S WRITING COMPETITION

was won by Robert Stanier (page 80)

Wisden's Writing Competition is open to anyone (other than previous winners) who has not been commissioned to write for, or has a working relationship with, the Almanack.

NOTES BY THE EDITOR

Three days before the Boxing Day Test at Melbourne, chief executive Tom Harrison sat down to outline the ECB's "five pillars of strategy". Was he about to reveal plans for a mystery spinner or a reliable No. 3? He was not. Instead, with England on their way to a 4–0 defeat, and their supporters looking for answers, we got bullet points: "More play. Great teams. Inspired fans. Strong finance. Good governance."

An old rule of journalism says a headline is not worth the ink if its polar opposite – less play, rubbish teams, bored fans, penury, corruption – is more startling. But this is an age when matters other than the cricket need trumpeting. The ship may be going down, but feel the quality of the lifejackets!

Harrison is presiding over a make-or-break era for English cricket, and the board have made some brave calls. But to claim 2017 was a "very good year" suggested a changed landscape – either that, or he couldn't see the wood for the eucalypti. Time was when a thrashing by Australia might have provoked questions in Parliament, which was barmy but strangely reassuring: Test cricket was part of the national debate. Now, it sounded like an inconvenience. It sounded as if surrendering the Ashes was being taken for granted.

The 2017-18 edition, it's true, was a stinker: one-sided, often boorish, and dulled by pitches stripped of their old character. Even Cricket Australia's marketing hashtag (#BeatEngland) smacked of the back of an envelope as executives watched reruns of the Big Bash. When giant hands – one holding up four fingers, the other none – appeared on the podium at the SCG to confirm the score for those who had lost count, or interest, or possibly both, one of sport's oldest rivalries felt more like *It's a Knockout!*

The gimmicks are in keeping with a format that still talks a good game but is no longer sure of itself. Once, the Ashes needed neither explanation nor justification: they simply were, because they always had been. People do care. But, one suspects, not as much as they did.

In late January, Michael Vaughan asked his Twitter followers whether they would rather England won the next World Cup or Ashes, both in 2019. This might not have been the most rigorous of polls, but the result was startling: of more than 21,000 who responded, 58% said the World Cup. A decade ago, this would have been heresy. It then emerged that BT Sport's viewing figures for the Big Bash were higher than for the Ashes. Again, this merits caution. For BT's audience, the Ashes were mainly on in the middle of the night, the Big Bash at breakfast. But it all left an uncomfortable feeling. Time is moving on, faster than Test cricket realises.

Perhaps you shouldn't blame the marketeers for manufacturing some of the fun, because the story has grown stale: only once in the last nine Ashes have the visitors won. In the other eight, stretching back to 2002-03, the Test ledger reads 28 home and five away wins – only three in live matches. Not since 1982-83 have the teams arrived at the venue of the final (usually Sydney, one of the game's great theatres) with the urn still at stake. Though the crowds flocked in, there was a curious sense that these were the most invisible Ashes of the modern era. People came for an event: the floodlights in Adelaide, the farewell to the WACA, the festive spirit in Melbourne. But did they come for the cricket?

As a contest, the Ashes need shaking up. The world game needs it too: if England v Australia sleepwalks towards the retirement home, what chance South Africa v Pakistan? The administrators continue to protest that Test cricket is inviolate. Yet the ICC's proposed Test championship for 2019 is essentially the current one, with a couple of tweaks. The inclusion of Afghanistan and Ireland will generate feelgood stories for a while, but the absence of promotion and relegation – an indictment of the more powerful Full Members' instinct for self-preservation – has deprived Test matches of the context they badly need.

There is another problem. It's not so much that the ECB and their fellow boards have taken their eye off the ball – just that the ball has changed colour. How else to explain the continued marginalisation of the County Championship, shoved mainly into April, May and September to accommodate the new Twenty20 tournament? There will be more seaming pitches, less incentive for counties to produce fast bowlers and spinners, and even less hope of England competing overseas. And despite the reduction of the Championship programme, there is still too much cricket. When Steven Finn complained that the county circuit grinds down young quicks, the alarm should have rung. Louder still, when Adil Rashid, whose leg-breaks had earned 30 wickets in seven subcontinental Tests in 2016-17, opted out of four-day cricket for Yorkshire this summer.

Overseas, England's Test team are already going backwards. Too many games at the wrong time of year will only hasten the process. By the end of the Ashes, they had taken 20 wickets just once in ten Tests abroad – at Visakhapatnam, where India, momentarily stunned, won easily. That sequence includes the highest total they have ever conceded, plus two of their three highest in Australia. Not since the first decade of the 20th century have they lost four Tests on successive tours; back then they even won a game or two. This was a new low.

Selection, too, suggested a shrug of the shoulders and a roll of the dice. Moeen Ali was the first-choice spinner in Australia, despite a mauling in India, and has now paid 81 per wicket across two tours. His inability to penetrate or contain meant England in effect had four bowlers, not the five they had touted as an advantage. Nathan Lyon, by contrast, attacked as expertly as he defended; by doing so in long spells, he gave Australia five bowlers for the price of four.

When Hampshire's Mason Crane, a promising 20-year-old leg-spinner, took one for 193 in the Fifth Test, we were almost pathetically grateful. James Vince, meanwhile, got a second chance in the team on the flimsiest of evidence, having averaged only 32 in the Championship. Gary Ballance used up a place that might more profitably have gone to Jos Buttler, and was never seen at all. A lack of red-ball cricket would have made Buttler's selection a risk, but since when has playing safe succeeded in Australia? England fell back on their old conservatism, with predictable results.

They will take part in their 1,000th men's Test this summer, and deserve a slap on the back for leading the way. But if they refuse to address their inadequacies on pitches that don't help 82mph right-arm seamers, and if the ECB treat another away Ashes defeat like a spot of bother in the colonies, fans will look elsewhere long before they reach 2,000.

Blinded by the white

The one-day series that followed the Tests provided more proof that the English game has had its head turned. This need not be a concern per se: the ritual underperformance at World Cups has made England a laughing-stock, grandads at the rave. But their thrilling 50-over progress has come at a cost. The Ashes left them with only 15 wins from 38 Tests under coach Trevor Bayliss, and 18 defeats – a losing percentage of 47. During Peter Moores's two (often derided) spells in charge, that percentage was 28. The one-day numbers tell a different story: Moores won 40% of his games, Bayliss – after the 4–1 win in Australia – an impressive 70%.

To make matters more delicate, no one can say where the one-day game is heading after the next World Cup. And concerns that it will become the black sheep of the white-ball family grew even more acute over the winter, when the Emirates Cricket Board – presumably bored with the uneventful middle overs in Twenty20 – sanctioned a T10 tournament in Sharjah. England, then, are mastering a tongue threatened by extinction – all the while forgetting the vocabulary of Test cricket.

They are hardly alone. In early September, Rupert Murdoch's Star India paid nearly £2bn for the worldwide rights to the Indian Premier League until 2022, and changed cricket for good, or possibly ill. The value of a single IPL game now surpassed that of an Indian home fixture – a decisive moment in international cricket's battle to hold back the tide of franchise T20. A couple of months later, with the Ashes fast approaching, Cricket Australia's chief executive James Sutherland put it another way: the value to the all-important Indian market of a Twenty20 international was the same as a Test. The financial hierarchy could not be clearer.

Nor could the players. When Australia's vice-captain David Warner warned his board that their pay dispute could endanger the Ashes, he did so – symbolically – from the IPL. When South Africa's former captain A. B. de Villiers attempted to relocate his *joie de vivre*, he briefly gave up Test cricket, at a stroke devaluing the quality of last summer's series in England. When West Indies named their squad for the World Cup Qualifiers in March 2018, four of their biggest names – Darren Bravo, Sunil Narine, Kieron Pollard and Andre Russell – were absent, preferring the lure (and lucre) of the Pakistan Super League

Back home, no sooner had Sam Billings been named captain of Kent than it emerged he would miss their first few Championship matches because of the IPL. Rashid's decision to concentrate on white-ball cricket was then taken by Alex Hales – with others, no doubt, to follow.

The cricketers are entitled to their slice of the pie. But without making Test matches more financially attractive for those outside England, Australia and

India, the claim that the three formats can harmoniously coexist rings hollow. For all the talk of pink balls (a good idea) and four-day games (the jury's out), Test cricket looks like the frog in the saucepan of boiling water: it won't react until it's too late.

A winter of ifs and butts

One figure lay in a street in Bristol, another in the dressing-room at the SCG. Each was flat on his back, and neither – it's fair to assume – was thinking happy thoughts about Ben Stokes. "Supine" and "English cricket" have often featured in the same sentence, usually as a metaphor-cum-insult. This time it was a statement of fact.

When Stokes allegedly punched a man to the ground in the small hours one Monday morning, it was as if he had starred in the opening exchanges of a Netflix box set which would end – 10,000 miles away and three months later – with Joe Root downed by gastroenteritis and wrapped in towels. If it hadn't been the England cricket team, you wouldn't have believed it possible.

In between, we had the weird sight of Stokes taking part in a quiet net session with Canterbury in the New Zealand backwater of Rangiora, only hours before England embarked on the first floodlit Ashes Test, in Adelaide. The sky was pure blue, the picket fence virgin white, and the TV crews less chippy than their Australian cousins. When Stokes asked them to move from behind the bowler's arm, they actually apologised.

Back in England, two days before Bristol, he had media coverage of a different kind, glaring out through his helmet's grille on the cover of the *Times* magazine, the better to convey his billing: "The hit man. Don't mess with Ben Stokes – he's fast and furious." When he did appear to hit a man, it was unclear whether life had imitated art, or vice versa. In February, he pleaded not guilty to affray.

The ECB had already lost control. To suspend Stokes while he awaited the decision of the Crown Prosecution Service was reasonable. To lift the suspension the moment he was charged was perverse. And the story took another twist when he was summoned to attend Bristol magistrates' court on February 13, the date of his planned international comeback in New Zealand. And for what? A few beers and a night out. It was all so sad.

The chances are England would have lost the Ashes with or without Stokes. But the Bristol brawl burdened an already difficult tour with an impossible load. It meant Jonny Bairstow's harmless – if odd – headbutt on Cameron Bancroft could be used as further evidence of a team with behavioural problems. When, in the same bar in Perth, Ben Duckett poured a pint of beer over James Anderson, the outcry suggested he had emptied a vat of boiling oil. And when one of England's few teetotallers was spotted sprinting back to the team hotel in Adelaide minutes before a new midnight curfew, it told of a trip dancing to the tune of media outrage. It's traditional for England captains to collapse in a heap, but Root may have done so in record time.

Quirk of history

None of this detracts from the performance of Steve Smith, who attached his name to the Ashes as surely as Ian Botham in 1981 or Mitchell Johnson in 2013-14. Only under lights in Adelaide did he look anything less than what he is: the best Test batsman since Don Bradman. If Virat Kohli is the more complete all-format package, Smith has mastered the rhythms of the five-day game.

His value lay not just in his runs – only Bradman, in 1930, has averaged more across a full Ashes series than his 137 – but in their impact. On the third day of the series, England limited him to 17 before lunch by keeping the ball out of his reach, and felt they had done their job. They had merely delayed the inevitable: Smith made 141 not out. From there, they had no obvious plan, leaving Root to cling to an old piece of sportsman's logic. Without his opposite number, he pointed out, things would have been closer.

And it made you wonder. Would Smith have enjoyed the same success had he opted to throw in his lot with England, the country of his mother's birth? He began his Test career as a lower-order leg-spinner. His first Ashes series, in 2010-11, brought mainly mockery. He didn't score a Test century until 2013. But between that game, at The Oval, and the end of the 2017-18 Ashes, he averaged 73, with a conversion-rate – 23 hundreds, 18 fifties – to make Root drool. Through it all, he has maintained the quirkiest technique in world cricket. He was lucky he didn't choose England, where they would soon have squeezed the originality out of him. Smith didn't just see off his opponents. He exposed the difference between two sporting cultures.

Textual criticism

It is only 12 years since Leicestershire chairman Neil Davidson sent a gloating text message to his Somerset counterpart Giles Clarke after a one-day win: "I can see why Somerset is the home of girls' cricket." To the criticism that ensued, a Leicestershire spokesman responded with weasel words typical of the time: "It was meant as a light-hearted comment and not an insult to women." Of course it was…

As Anya Shrubsole – from Somerset, naturally – tore in at Lord's last July and wrenched the World Cup from India, Clarke might have been enjoying the last laugh. Thanks to the broadcast deal with Sky Sports, his subsequent chairmanship of the ECB had coincided with huge investment in the women's game, and paved the way for a world in which sentiments such as Davidson's belong in the Mesozoic Era. Clarke and Sky have not always featured favourably in these pages, but for this they deserve credit.

Of the 26,500 who turned up at the women's World Cup final, an estimated 60% were attending cricket for the first time. Champagne and Pimm's yielded to coffee and cake, and the crowd were happy to spectate, not make a spectacle. Only the long queues – Lord's is not flush with ladies' toilets – harked back to the days when dinosaurs roamed St John's Wood.

Shrubsole is *Wisden's* cover star, and one of three women – with England captain Heather Knight and all-rounder Nat Sciver – among the Five Cricketers. When the cover was unveiled in January, it generated seven times as much social media interest as its predecessor, which depicted Virat Kohli, the most marketable player of the world's best-supported team. *Wisden* shouldn't be too smug: we have often been slow to acknowledge the women's game. But, thanks to Shrubsole and her team-mates, the case has become unanswerable. There were few cries of tokenism.

Partly, this was because there is more to enjoy. There were 111 sixes at the 2017 World Cup, hit by 38 different players; in 2013, it was 67 by 28 – and in only six fewer games. Sciver, who hit four against Pakistan alone, also played the most memorable stroke of the summer: a deliberate flick between her legs, once called the draw, and widely considered extinct. Resurrected, it was rechristened the Natmeg, and even brought Sciver to the attention of readers of *The Sun*. These are the things that happen when boards invest properly in both halves of the population.

But there are constant reminders that more must be done. Recently, to no clear purpose, a senior journalist asked his Twitter followers: "Do you like having female commentators on men's cricket?" And in a heartfelt piece in this Almanack about sexism in the sport, Tanya Aldred points out another sin of omission: the absence, as far as we know, of a meaningful monument anywhere in the world to a woman cricketer. The Sporting Statues Project lists 58 connected to the game, including six to Don Bradman alone. But if Barnsley and Hobart can honour Dickie Bird and David Boon, Lord's can find room for Rachael Heyhoe Flint – preferably in the Coronation Garden behind the Pavilion, casting a mischievous eye in the direction of WG.

Great expectations

If the city-based tournament in 2020 follows the lead of the women's World Cup and unearths droves of new fans, all other objections to the ECB's revolution will be null and void. It is a big if – yet the board had little choice. Cricket is withering in the public consciousness: privileged and venerable, rich but invisible, British sport's Miss Havisham. When Sky lost the Ashes rights to BT, splitting the pay-to-view market, the problem was magnified. Despite the traditionalists' objections, the new tournament really is the ECB's last chance to see if there is anyone else around willing to join the fun.

One incident last summer ought to give critics pause for thought. It came when Worcestershire's Ross Whiteley hit Yorkshire's Karl Carver for six sixes in an over during a T20 Blast group game at Headingley on July 23, providing a fresh take on the old question about a tree falling in a wood and no one being around to hear it. Because unless you were in the crowd at Leeds that afternoon, the chances are the noise escaped you altogether. It's true that it was the day Shrubsole roared at Lord's. But, more to the point, six other Blast games were on at the time. For the casual fan – and how the sport needs casual fans – Whiteley's feat was lost in a sea of other cricket. He should have been waving, not drowning: Yorkshire v Worcestershire had to be the only show in town. The new tournament will address this problem by staging 36 games in 38 days. As at the IPL and the BBL, each can leave its mark.

The Asian equation

There has been widespread delight that 21 Twenty20 matches, including internationals, will be broadcast by the BBC from 2020. That figure should be higher but, since we have been told for years by men in suits that the free-to-air debate was dead, we should be pleased the corpse has twitched. This alone will not reverse cricket's decline, but the good news is the ECB know there are other vital matters – which is why, after years of neglect, they are treating English cricket's South Asian question seriously.

This is about more than doing the right thing, and bringing a passionate group in from the cold. It is a matter of survival. A report commissioned last year by the board confirmed discrepancies cricket can no longer tolerate. While less than 5% of the British population is of South Asian ethnicity, the figure among recreational players rises to 30%. Then, at first-class level, it drops back to 4%. The ECB are so concerned that they want to provide "unconscious bias awareness training" for recruitment within the game. Unpack the jargon and there is an overdue acknowledgment that Britain's South Asian cricketers have not always been made to feel welcome. That's putting it generously.

There is something else. While 39% of this demographic say they support an IPL franchise, only 8% support a county in the T20 Blast. And while crowd figures for the Blast have been on the rise, this suggests there is room for improvement. One other point. The ECB's report underlined the love of big names among fans of Asian extraction: 40% were more likely to attend domestic matches featuring international stars (the national average is 16%). Since the new tournament – down from 18 teams to eight – will spread the talent more thickly, the appeal is obvious. If it can make this country's most passionate fans believe English cricket is for them too, the ECB will have earned our thanks.

Home comforts

For the second time in less than a year, Pakistan's cricketers left The Oval smiling from ear to ear. In 2016, they squared the Test series. This time, even more improbably, they won the Champions Trophy, having made the transition from hopeless to irresistible in a fortnight, thrashing India in the final after India had thrashed them in the group stages. As if to underline Pakistan's penchant for boom or bust, their next two 50-over outings produced a 5–0 win against Sri Lanka, and a 0–5 defeat in New Zealand.

It was all very Pakistani, and utterly uplifting – rather like the euphoria that greeted three events in Lahore either side of the Champions Trophy: the final of the Pakistan Super League, a Twenty20 series against a World XI, and a one-off 20-over game against Sri Lanka. The security bill was huge, but for

Pakistan's long-suffering fans – deprived of major home fixtures following the terrorist attack of 2009 – it was money well spent. In one way or another, Pakistan still tug at the heartstrings like no one else.

A flutter each way

Ever since 1694, when a "wagger" of two shillings and sixpence was placed on a match in Lewes, cricket and gambling have snuggled together. Yet as the ICC step up their fight against corruption, the game seems unable to kick its addiction.

Click on ESPNcricinfo, as millions do every day, and you see that the page is "presented by bet365". Drag the cursor over the potted score of each match, and there are two options: a "summary" of the game, and a chance to "bet now". Cricket's most visited website is in good company. During BT Sport's Ashes coverage, no ad break was complete without the actor Ray Winstone encouraging viewers to have a flutter, but urging them with a straight face to "gamble responsibly". And spectators at major matches in this country do well to find their seat without walking past an in-stadium bookie or two. This is all legal, but so is tax avoidance.

Last year, the UK's betting industry took a record £13.8bn off the public, and the Gambling Commission estimated that two million Britons were either "problem gamblers" or at risk of addiction. Cricket is guilty of cakeism, ostensibly policing the game, while at the same time encouraging the one-armed bandits. And when, in late January, footage went viral of dodgy goings-on in a UAE tournament calling itself the Ajman All Stars, some of the reaction brought to mind Captain Renault in *Casablanca*, who was "shocked – shocked! – to find gambling is going on in here", before pocketing his winnings.

At least the All Stars helpfully showcased the latest threat to the game: matches made for bookies and (mainly gullible) gamblers, and broadcast back to the subcontinent for a brisk trade. The ICC are on to it. In the meantime, cricket feels like an enabler.

Hungry for more

Some believe over-rates are a media obsession. So what if a county team bowls only 94 in a day? Worse things happen at sea. But last season two sides did pay a price. Middlesex, the 2016 champions, were relegated by two points, the size of their penalty for bowling their overs slowly against Surrey at The Oval. And Northamptonshire missed out on promotion by five – the size of theirs after transgressing at Trent Bridge. Nottinghamshire, their opponents, went up instead.

Middlesex earned some sympathy because a crossbow bolt had been fired on to the outfield, ending the game and depriving them of the chance to up their rate. On the other hand, spectators were spared the sight of bowlers hurrying through meaningless overs simply to avoid punishment. They shouldn't have fallen behind the (reasonable) demands in the first place.

There was a wider issue. Had the penalties been more immediate, Middlesex and Northamptonshire might have been less inclined to dawdle. Losing the odd point here or there over the course of a long season does not focus the mind. Monetary fines and occasional suspensions make no difference at international level – the players are sometimes quietly thankful for a breather – while the application of penalty runs during a match has had some success in limited-overs cricket, but can produce bad blood and chaos.

The answer has to be to hit players – and umpires, who bear some responsibility – where it hurts. Make them stay out there for as long as it takes, every session, until the overs have been bowled. If that means shorter lunches, so be it: the fielding side will soon get a move on. And it will spare us the hard-luck stories come September.

Bridging the divide

There was a whiff of charm in the air at Chelmsford, where the new county champions drew extensively on local talent: the Essex averages on page 445 tell us that ten of their players in 2017 are from the county, and five born in Leytonstone alone. At last, Alfred Hitchcock and David Beckham are in good company.

It wasn't long ago that Essex were the protagonists of a dismal tactic: prepare a greentop, win the toss, unleash the medium-pacers. But the new regulation, giving the visiting side the chance to bowl first, has kept that in check. And besides, Essex's 2017 record at home and away was identical: five wins, two draws. Just as gratifyingly, they won the title by a landslide in their first season back in Division One, which encouraged the thought that the gap between the two tiers was not the chasm many feared. It was quite a story.

Yet there is work to be done on English pitches – and prejudices to address. Old-timers noted, for instance, that surfaces at The Oval were once so hard that boot spikes were more hindrance than help; Sylvester Clarke would bowl in flats. The bounce provided some of the best cricket in the country. In 2017, by contrast, Surrey won only two Championship matches, yet still finished third, over-rewarded for being hard to beat, and by an archaic bonus-point system that places too much emphasis on the first innings at the expense of the match as a whole.

When Somerset produced turning pitches that won Taunton an unexpected nickname – Ciderabad – opponents were up in arms. The argument has been made here before, but it needs restating: unless we allow one or two counties to become havens for spin, we will never produce world-class slow bowlers, or batsmen capable of flourishing in Asia. And an 18-team tournament will become even harder to justify. That is the last thing defenders of the status quo are after.

Would you credit it?

It was, screamed a commentator, "the best catch you'll ever see". For once, Twenty20's ingrained hyperbole sounded about right. When Dwayne Bravo launched Rashid Khan towards deep extra cover at Melbourne's Etihad Stadium in January, the best the fielder Ben Laughlin could surely hope for was a run-saving interception. But he clung on with two hands, before flicking the ball back into play as he tumbled over the rope. Jake Weatherald was running from cover point, though his initial aim, he admitted, had been to congratulate Laughlin. Instead, he found himself diving forward to complete the kind of relay catch that makes you wonder what cricketers will be capable of in the years ahead.

The scorecard could not possibly capture the excitement. Yet cricket fans are good at interpreting this list of names and numbers to assess a game, so why not make things even more vivid? Football has used the assist to reward the player who has dribbled round three opponents before setting up a simple tap-in – and the assist should become part of cricket's lexicon too. The scorecard would read: Bravo a Laughlin c Weatherald b Rashid Khan 4. Fielding has long bent the knee to bowling, and especially batting. Twenty20 urges us to reconsider.

Age concern

December 31 threw up one of those dates that splits the world. On that day, and that day alone – with apologies to the sticklers who regard 2001 as the first year of the millennium – anyone born in the 20th century was an adult, and anyone in the 21st a child. As so often, however, cricket had got there first, thanks to a more complex method of making some of us feel old.

Against Glamorgan at Cardiff in June, Hamidullah Qadri – a 16-year-old off-spinner born in Kandahar, Afghanistan – took a second-innings five-for on his first-class debut for Derbyshire. He also became the first county cricketer born in the 21st century. If that didn't instantly add a wrinkle to your brow, worse was to follow in September, when Nottinghamshire captain Chris Read called it a day, aged 39, signing off with a promotion-clinching century at Hove. Read's claim to fame? He was the last remaining English first-class cricketer to have played a Test in the 1990s. The baton is passed again.

JAMES ANDERSON TAKES 500 TEST WICKETS

Numerical duckling to statistical swan

ANDY ZALTZMAN

Kandy, December 2007. Sri Lanka were slowly building their second innings after trailing England by 93, with Sanath Jayasuriya, in his final Test, on 31. James Anderson, 25 years old and in his 20th, more than four and a half years after his first, had bowled three overs for eight. Six balls later, Jayasuriya was on 55, and Anderson had bowled four overs for 32. For only the fourth time in Tests, a batsman had hit six fours in an over – two slapped over extra cover, one slashed through Ian Bell's fingertips at slip, a square-drive, a pull and a thick edge.

Sri Lanka declared at 442 for eight, with Anderson conceding 128 in 23 overs, for the wicket of Michael Vandort. It was his third mauling in consecutive Tests, after figures of one for 134 at Trent Bridge and four for 182 at The Oval, both against India. In those three games, he had conceded 90 boundaries – one every nine balls. England lost at Kandy, and Anderson was dropped, again. His previous 13 caps had come in seven different stints, spread over 50 Tests. And he had a bowling average of 39. Among England seamers, only Chris Lewis (52 wickets at 39), Phillip DeFreitas (48 at 42) and Andrew

THE FIVE PHASES OF ANDERSON

		T	*O*	*M*	*R*	*W*	*BB*	*5I*	*10M*	*Avge*
1	May 2003 to Dec 2007 .	20	648.3	136	2,431	62	5-42	3	0	39.20
2	Mar 2008 to Jan 2010 . .	26	923.1	186	3,000	94	7-43	5	0	31.91
3A	May 2010 to Apr 2012. .	22	866.4	235	2,352	102	6-17	4	1	23.05
3B	May 2012 to Jan 2014 . .	24	953.2	231	2,739	85	5-47	3	1	32.22
3C	Jun 2014 to Jan 2018 . . .	42	1,541.4	451	3,811	180	7-42	10	1	21.17
		134	**4,933.2**	**1,239**	**14,333**	**523**	**7-42**	**25**	**3**	**27.40**

Flintoff (32 at 46) had worse averages after 20 Tests (though Stuart Broad and Ben Stokes have since joined the club). His economy-rate of 3.74 was, at that point, the fourth-worst of anyone who had bowled more than 500 overs. There had been flashes of quality, but the Great Selectorial Scrapheap of English Cricketing Hopes must have been gurgling in anticipation, ready to receive the tattered, abbreviated career of yet another wasted talent.

Lord's, September 2017. Anderson bowls West Indies opener Kraigg Brathwaite with a fizzing inswinger. It is his 500th Test wicket, and reminiscent of his first – Zimbabwe's Mark Vermeulen – at the same ground 14 years and more than 28,000 deliveries earlier. He is the first Englishman, the third seamer, and the sixth bowler of any genre to reach the landmark. He goes on to take a career-best seven for 42 in 20 overs of unremitting mastery.

Clive Mason, Getty Images

Down and out in Kennington, London: Anderson struggles against South Africa at The Oval in 2003. Five years later, he claims his 100th Test wicket – Jacques Kallis.

Somewhere in the world, Jayasuriya checks YouTube to confirm the 24-run over did in fact happen, and that the bowler was the same James Anderson. In Downing Street, a disappointed Chancellor of the Exchequer wakes up in the middle of a cheese-addled dream in which, as that Kandy Test ended, he had slapped a £100bn bet on Anderson becoming the first Englishman to 500 Test wickets. Donald Trump, watching on admiringly while padding up for his daily blast on the White House bowling machine, thinks to himself: "Truly, we live in an age when the unexpected has become normal."

At the end of that game at Lord's, Anderson had taken his last 100 Test wickets, in 23 matches, at an S. F. Barnesian average of 17, with an economy-rate of 2.34. It is a staggering sequence, even in the context of the career he has carved since Kandy (461 wickets at 25 in 114 Tests since 2008, including the 2017-18 Ashes). Admittedly, statistics concerning best 23-Test sequences are seldom the subject of animated conversation in pubs, playgrounds or late-night kebab shops these days. But since 1960 – and assuming a minimum of 30 wickets – only Imran Khan, Richard Hadlee, Malcolm Marshall, Waqar Younis, Shaun Pollock and Muttiah Muralitharan have averaged less over a 23-match span. Even more remarkably, the Cannon-Fodder of Kandy has completed the second-most economical 23-Test sequence since 2005, surpassed only by his old friend, Indian left-arm spinner Ravindra Jadeja.

Anderson's Test record tells a tale of transformation, endurance and skill. A numerically ugly duckling has mutated into a beautiful statistical swan – one of the best bowlers of all time in English conditions and, during the first half of this decade, one of the best of his generation anywhere.

His career can be broadly broken into three distinct phases: that largely unsuccessful beginning, up to and including Kandy; two years of marked improvement but continued inconsistency; and an elongated peak, from the 2010 English summer onwards, within which there are three sub-phases, two purple patches sandwiching a slump.

ANDERSON AGAINST THE WORLD

Opponents	*T*	*O*	*M*	*R*	*W*	*BB*	*5I*	*10M*	*Avge*
Australia	31	1,171.1	282	3,594	104	6-47	5	1	34.55
Bangladesh	2	84	21	223	9	4-78	0	0	24.77
India	22	822.3	208	2,423	86	5-42	3	0	28.17
New Zealand	12	413.1	98	1,410	52	7-43	3	0	27.11
Pakistan	13	456.4	145	999	54	6-17	2	1	18.50
South Africa	24	923.2	194	2,753	84	5-63	3	0	32.77
Sri Lanka	11	408.1	111	1,136	51	5-16	4	1	22.27
West Indies	17	590.2	162	1,572	72	7-42	4	0	21.83
Zimbabwe	2	64	18	223	11	5-73	1	0	20.27
	134	**4,933.2**	**1,239**	**14,333**	**523**	**7-42**	**25**	**3**	**27.40**

In **Phase 1** (20 Tests, 62 wickets, average 39, economy-rate 3.74), his promise was undermined by injuries and the tinkering of coaches and selectors. There were moments of unignorable quality that ensured he was never fully discarded – five wickets in his debut innings, against Zimbabwe in 2003; seven in the match in a taut victory over South Africa at Trent Bridge in 2003 (when he became the only man to bowl Jacques Kallis twice in a Test); six in England's memorable win at Mumbai in 2005-06; five for 42 against India at Lord's in 2007, including Dravid, Tendulkar and Ganguly. Generally, however, he was a project which showed only intermittent signs of reaching fruition, a luxury who interspersed brilliance with profligacy.

Phase 2 (26 Tests, 94 wickets, average 31, economy-rate 3.24) lasted from the Wellington Test in early 2008, when he replaced Matthew Hoggard and promptly dismissed New Zealand's top five, to the end of the tour of South Africa in 2009-10. That series was trademark Phase 2 Anderson: crucial interventions and prolonged bouts of ineffectiveness. He was now a fixture in England's side, but ups mingled with downs. After Wellington, he took one for 153 in 24 overs at Napier. He took seven for 43 against New Zealand at Trent Bridge in 2008, then averaged over 40 in his next nine Tests. An eight-wicket Test at Cape Town in January 2010 preceded none for 111 at Johannesburg. The definitive breakthrough remained elusive.

It arrived in **Phase 3** (88 Tests, 367 wickets, average 24, economy-rate 2.64), which began in the summer of 2010. **Phase 3A** (22 Tests, 102 wickets at 23 up to the end of the tour of Sri Lanka in April 2012) saw Anderson finally establish himself as one of the world's best. He took 23 wickets at 13 at home against Pakistan, then 24 at 26 in the 2010-11 Ashes, dismissing Michael Clarke and Ricky Ponting three times each for a total of 61 runs as England won in Australia for the first time in 24 years.

Phase 3B (24 Tests, 85 wickets at 32 from the start of the 2012 summer to the end of the 2013-14 Ashes disintegration) encompassed a relative decline. Perhaps, at times, the volume of multi-format cricket hampered Anderson. South Africa largely blunted him in 2012. He was superb in India, then toothless on some flat pitches in New Zealand, in 2012-13. He did put in arguably his most important performance, five wickets in each innings at Trent

Bridge in the nerve-shredding First Ashes Test of 2013. But he had no influence on the rematch that winter, as the era of Kevin Pietersen, Matt Prior, Graeme Swann and Jonathan Trott came to a stroppily calamitous, controversial-book-generating end.

Phase 3C (42 Tests, 180 wickets at 21) has been the most fruitful of all, in which four years of brilliance, especially at home, have produced numbers to rank with the greats. Fred Trueman's best 42-Test sequence (in terms of average) brought 194 wickets at 20; Ian Botham's 211 at 20; Brian Statham's 162 at 21. Anderson's current streak is similar, in wickets and average, to the best of Michael Holding, Ray Lindwall and Alan Davidson. This remarkable success has been aided by the end of his one-day international career in 2015, reducing his workload and enabling undiluted focus on the lines, lengths and skills required for five-day cricket. There have been striking disappointments even in this most pomp-filled section of his career, notably in helpful conditions at Lord's against India in 2014, on a wicketless final day at Leeds against West Indies last summer, and in the first innings of the day/night Test at Adelaide over the winter. There were also three quiet Tests in India – his first failure in Asia since he returned identical figures (four for 214) in a two-Test series in India in 2008-09.

The difference between Anderson's records at home and away has led to suggestions he is not the complete bowler. Overall, his record outside the UK – 58 Tests, 188 wickets at 32, and with only five of his 25 five-wicket hauls – is unspectacular (Dale Steyn, by comparison, has 176 wickets at 24 in 39 Tests outside South Africa). But this conceals the same improvement as his overall statistics, as well as his performances abroad during the first half of this decade.

His first 19 away Tests (in Phases 1 and 2) brought 52 wickets at 43. The next 28, from the 2010-11 Ashes to the end of the Pakistan series in the UAE in late 2015, brought 108 at 27, including 43 at 23 in 12 Tests in Asia. These

TOP OF THE PILE

The leading Test wicket-takers since Anderson made his debut on May 22, 2003:

	T	*O*	*M*	*R*	*W*	*BB*	*5I*	*10M*	*Avge*
J. M. Anderson (E)	**134**	**4,933.2**	**1,239**	**14,333**	**523**	**7-42**	**25**	**3**	**27.40**
D. W. Steyn (SA)	86	2,898.3	628	9,354	419	7-51	26	5	22.32
H. M. R. K. B. Herath (SL)	86	4,047.5	757	11,384	409	9-127	33	9	27.83
S. C. J. Broad (E)	114	3,922.1	901	11,706	399	8-15	15	2	29.33
M. Muralitharan (SL/World)	53	2,820.2	607	7,579	350	8-46	30	11	21.65
M. G. Johnson (A)	73	2,666.5	514	8,891	313	8-61	12	3	28.40
R. Ashwin (I)	57	2,752.3	558	7,951	311	7-59	26	7	25.56
M. Morkel (SA)	83	2,659	580	8,256	294	6-23	7	0	28.08
M. Ntini (SA)	70	2,523.4	502	8,403	290	7-37	16	4	28.97
N. M. Lyon (A)	74	2,988.1	566	9,178	290	8-50	12	2	31.64
Harbhajan Singh (I)	70	3,312.3	544	9,707	273	7-62	14	3	35.55
A. Kumble (I)	56	2,843.2	561	8,587	270	8-141	15	4	31.80
G. P. Swann (E)	60	2,558.1	493	7,642	255	6-65	17	3	29.96

As at February 10, 2018.

numbers made him one of the world's most proficient bowlers away from home. In the five English summers between those series, Anderson took 130 wickets at 26. Home or away, then, there was little difference.

Since Christmas 2015, however, when England began their victorious series in South Africa, there has been a divergence – 69 wickets at an astonishing 14 at home, 28 at 35 away. He struggled with form and fitness in South Africa and India, while in Australia a decent series haul camouflaged a lack of match-shaping interventions with the new ball. In the first 30 overs of the first innings of these three series, Anderson took just two for 198 – a significant factor in England's failures in India and Australia.

LANDMARKS ON THE ROAD TO 500

Wkt	*T*	*I*	*Batsman*	*Opposition*	*5I*	*Avge*
50	17	31	M. S. Dhoni	India at Lord's, 2007	3	35.45
100	29	54	J. H. Kallis	South Africa at The Oval, 2008	5	34.36
150	45	81	G. C. Smith	South Africa at Cape Town, 2009-10	8	34.13
200	55	101	P. M. Siddle	Australia at Perth, 2010-11	10	31.76
250	67	123	H. D. R. L. Thirimanne	Sri Lanka at Galle, 2011-12	12	30.15
300	81	148	P. G. Fulton	New Zealand at Lord's, 2013	13	30.26
350	93	173	A. D. Mathews	Sri Lanka at Lord's, 2014	15	30.40
400	104	194	M. J. Guptill	New Zealand at Leeds, 2015	17	29.33
450	115	216	H. M. K. R. B. Herath	Sri Lanka at Chester-le-Street, 2016	21	28.33
500	**129**	**242**	**K. C. Brathwaite**	**West Indies at Lord's, 2017**	**24**	**27.39**

Figures for five-fors and averages are to the end of the innings in which he reached the milestone.

As with any cricketer of such longevity, there are quirks and fascinations lurking within the stats, especially in his head-to-head numbers against leading opponents. Anderson enjoyed extraordinary success against Tendulkar, dismissing him a record nine times in 58.2 overs for just 208 runs. By contrast, he has extracted Hashim Amla only twice in 131 overs for 398 runs. Collectively, Tendulkar, Clarke, Kallis, Kumar Sangakkara, Virender Sehwag, David Warner, Virat Kohli and Kane Williamson have averaged 27 against Anderson. But Amla, Mike Hussey, A. B. de Villiers, Graeme Smith, Steve Smith and Ponting have averaged 76. Yet of his 523 wickets, 310 have been top-five batsmen; only Muralitharan (355 out of 800) and Glen McGrath (325 out of 563) have dismissed more.

Unusually, he has been almost equally effective in all four innings, averaging 28 in the first, 27 in the second (when he has taken 13 of his 25 five-wicket hauls), and 26 in the third and fourth. He also averages 27 against both right-handers and left-handers. And while the figure is 41 against No. 3 batsmen, it drops to 24 against No. 4s, in an era when that position has tended to produce the highest average. His record at Trent Bridge is wonderful, with 60 wickets in nine Tests at 18, and seven five-wicket hauls. At Brisbane, by contrast, four Tests have yielded seven wickets at 75. The Oval has been his least successful English ground: 39 at 33.

Where you place Anderson in the pantheon is a matter of preference. In 2013, David Saker, then England's bowling coach, upset many South Africans by describing Anderson as the "most skilful bowler in the world", and it's true

Home stretch: Anderson flies in against South Africa once more, here at Old Trafford in 2017.

that over a prolonged period Steyn had a significantly better record. But in terms of an ability to manipulate the motion of five and a half ounces of stitched leather at high speed, peak-Anderson stands comparison with anyone.

Few bowlers have possessed such capacity to make the ball talk. Early in his career, what the ball said was not always pleasant listening for England supporters. "Please hit me for four" were evidently the words Jayasuriya heard it yelp in Kandy. Yet for all that the West Indian batsmen could decipher it at Lord's last summer, the ball might as well have been speaking ancient Sumerian.

The course of Anderson's career has been one of cricket's most striking upward curves. Of the 42 bowlers who have taken 250 or more Test wickets, only two have had a worse average after 20 Tests – Broad and Zaheer Khan (both 40). Since then, Anderson has averaged 25, a 34% decrease – the only other bowlers in that list to have improved by a greater margin after their first 20 Tests are Hadlee (40%) and Imran (37%).

In a less patient era, Anderson might have been discarded after Kandy. Before central contracts, he might have been worn down by the grind of first-class cricket, rather than preserved and prepared for the international game. Instead, the sport has been treated to a decade of a supreme craftsman and competitor, honing and perfecting his art, achieving feats and creating statistics that even the most ardent Lancastrian would not have thought conceivable as Jayasuriya peppered the boundary, and another promising England bowler seemed destined to fall hundreds and hundreds of Test wickets short of 500.

Andy Zaltzman is believed to be the first to achieve the double of being both a stand-up comedian and a scorer-statistician for Test Match Special.

CRICKET AND SEXISM

"Too ugly to be raped"

TANYA ALDRED

Cricket's first global event: the 1973 women's World Cup. The first player to score a double-century in a one-day international: Belinda Clark. The first player to take ten wickets and score a century in the same Test: Betty Wilson. Don't blush, baby.

For over 200 years, cricket has had an unapologetically male gaze. Its public face – players, umpires, scorers, writers, photographers, advertisers, commentators, cameramen, producers – has been almost exclusively male, and its product has been tailored for a male audience.

So when Chris Gayle made a pass at journalist Mel McLaughlin on live television in January 2016, he felt safe. When the commentators in the studio snorted with laughter, and when Ten Sport's Twitter account chuckled "#smooth", they felt safe. It was fine to judge McLaughlin on how she looked, to humiliate her in her place of work. Why? Because it was banter. It was the way the world worked.

Then something happened. The public didn't like Gayle's behaviour. Commentators backtracked furiously. Andrew Flintoff, Chris Rogers and Ian Chappell all criticised him. He was fined $A10,000 by Melbourne Renegades, his franchise, and reprimanded by Cricket Australia. "Those sorts of comments border on harassment," said James Sutherland, CA's chief executive, "and are completely inappropriate in cricket."

Gayle has not found another Big Bash franchise since – but he has played in the Indian Premier League, the Bangladesh Premier League, the Pakistan Super League and for Somerset in the NatWest T20 Blast. Indian condom company Skore thought it was a good idea to make an advertisement referencing the McLaughlin incident. And yes, there were still people who believed his behaviour was OK, even when a young woman had been harassed in plain sight. The world has turned, but there are many revolutions to go.

Records of women playing cricket go back to the 18th century. Matches between married women and their single sisters were popular spectacles, often attracting large bets, though regarded by many as grotesque. In 1890, a crowd of 15,000 turned up in Liverpool to watch the Original English Lady Cricketers, the first professional women's side. They were forced to disband after their (male) manager ran off with the money.

But cricket grounds remained bastions of male privilege. On April 11, 1913, the suffragettes burned down the pavilion at The Nevill ground in Tunbridge Wells, part of a year's campaign against sporting institutions, best remembered because Emily Wilding Davison threw herself to her death in front of King

PA Photos

Wind in their sails: a 1913 suffragette march arrives at Hyde Park.

George V's horse at the Derby. But why The Nevill? One story has a Kent official saying: "It is not true that women are banned from the pavilion. Who do you think makes the teas?" The people of Tunbridge Wells were pleasingly disgusted, and the pavilion was rebuilt. There was, though, some male support for the movement within sport, and playwright Laurence Housman claimed Jack Hobbs "startled the clubs of Piccadilly" by walking in the male section of a suffragette march.

Two years before the introduction of universal suffrage in 1928, the Women's Cricket Association were set up, and by 1930 the *Women's Cricket* magazine was being published under the editorship of Marjorie Pollard, a WCA founder member, who later had a column in *The Cricketer*. England women embarked on their first Test tour, of Australia, in late 1934, and returned home broke after funding the trip themselves. *Wisden* chose not to report the tour until 1938. Six decades later, the Almanack moved the venue for its annual dinner from the East India Club in St James's Square after the editor's wife was refused a drink at the bar.

Women continued to play the game they loved but, for the international cricketers among them, there were choices with consequences. Betty Wilson, who won 11 Test caps for Australia between 1948 and 1958 – averaging 57 with the bat and 11 with the ball – chose cricket over marriage and children. Everyone had to take unpaid leave to play, and the women were stuck on a merry-go-round of fund-raising for flights and kit. Enid Bakewell, one of

England's finest, used to sell chocolate on the boundary at Trent Bridge to raise a few pennies. Women's games were tolerated, but not taken seriously by the wider public, the media, or the authorities. Len Hutton was not alone when he harrumphed: "Ladies playing cricket – absurd. Just like a man trying to knit." Socially and economically disenfranchised, female cricketers had little power.

Between the wars, cricket-watching had been popular with both sexes, but their experiences were very different. In 1930, Lancashire had 1,387 female members and 4,055 male, but women could neither become full members nor enter the pavilion. At Yorkshire, a woman could sit in the pavilion, but not become a full member with voting rights.

At Lord's, things had even further to go. In 1929, the WCA wrote to MCC to ask if they would stage a women's match. The answer was an incredulous "no". In 1948, the WCA tried again. The reply read: "The chances of being able to fit in a game for the Association are so remote that it would be best to abandon the idea at once." The Association persisted. MCC again said no in 1973, this time to hosting the deciding match in the first World Cup. But in 1976, after intense lobbying from Rachael Heyhoe Flint, they relented, and agreed to a one-day game between England and Australia – provided Middlesex did not reach the quarter-finals of the Gillette Cup. They did not but, as a joyful Heyhoe Flint led her team on to the field, single women still needed a chaperone to get into the Warner and Tavern Stands. It would be two decades before women – typists, barmaids and the Queen excepted – would be let into the Pavilion.

That bastion fell in 1998, after club president Colin Ingleby-Mackenzie forced through two votes on women membership in seven months, and *Wisden Cricket Monthly* persuaded Isabelle Duncan, a Surrey club cricketer, to wear an MCC sweater on their front cover. Men voted against the motion for a variety of reasons: from not wanting to see "knitting needles in the Pavilion" to the worry of finding lacy lingerie in egg-and-bacon colours in the MCC shop; from the possibility of breastfeeding in the Long Room, to the social confusion that would occur if a man reserved his spot with a copy of *The Daily Telegraph*, yet had been raised to give his seat to a lady.

Eventually the sands of time caught up with even the Pavilion doorman – that, and the threat of missing out on Lottery money. Since then, MCC have been transformed – Duncan herself now sits on the

767

WOMEN'S CRICKET

ENGLAND—AUSTRALIA TEST MATCHES

If, ten years ago, anyone had suggested that Test Matches between women cricketers would take place in England, and that one day's play in such a game would attract five thousand spectators, the idea would have been laughed to scorn. Yet this ideal of women cricketers was realised in 1937 when people of the Midlands and elsewhere flocked to Northampton to witness the opening of the first Test Match in England between women's teams representing England and Australia.

Important occasion as was the 12th of June last summer, the historian must state a date shortly after Christmas in 1934 as the commencement of women's international cricket. On December 28 in that year England met Australia in a women's Test Match, the game taking place at Brisbane, Australia, and ending in victory for England by nine wickets. Thus last year's visit of the Australian side completed a chapter in the development of women's cricket.

For the success of this phase of the game, the Women's Cricket Association has been largely responsible. Founded in 1926, the W.C.A., besides organising the tours, has helped to form clubs and county associations and has set up a complete organisation for the furtherance of women's cricket.

Women play under the M.C.C. Laws of Cricket with the exception of that relating to the ball. For women's cricket in England the weight of the ball varies between $4\frac{15}{16}$ ounces and $5\frac{5}{16}$ ounces compared with the M.C.C. specification of not less than $5\frac{1}{2}$ ounces and not more than $5\frac{3}{4}$ ounces. In no other respect does the material used for women's cricket differ from that for men. Of course women employ bats, pads and gloves of suitable weight. There is a regulation mode of dress in white.

The growth of women's cricket in England was closely matched by the progress of the women's game in Australia, and

Sin of omission: in its report of the 1937 England–Australia women's Tests, *Wisden* hints at its earlier silence.

general committee – though the number of women members remains small, and there is still no female statue to compete with the bronze WG in the Coronation Gardens. In fact, there is no well-known statue of a female cricketer anywhere.

In 1998, the WCA were subsumed into the newly formed ECB, a move that would be copied around the cricketing world, and an era came to an end. The women's game would benefit hugely from more funding and greater professionalisation. However, as journalist Raf Nicholson has pointed out, the merger also meant that a women's sport run by women was now a women's sport run by men – with mainly male umpires and male coaches. The women who used to volunteer quietly vanished. A women's cricket seat on the ECB board, requested by the disbanded WCA, was granted only in 2010. But with that loss of identity came something precious: money. And with money, at last, came opportunity.

The ECB, together with Chance to Shine, produced the first (semi-professional) contracts for women in 2008; full professionalisation came in 2014. Other countries followed, though with vastly different pay schemes for men and women. Then, in August 2017, after prolonged wrangling, Cricket Australia announced a new pay deal, christened the biggest windfall in women's sport. A new memorandum of understanding covered men and women in the same agreement for the first time, with players earning the same hourly rate of pay. "This agreement is a huge step for sport in Australia," said their former captain Jodie Fields, "because for the first time it considers male and female players as one entity." The ground was shifting.

In fact, since 2015 women's cricket in Australia has moved from being almost invisible unless you were a committed fan – the Women's Big Bash League didn't even have a marketing budget in its first year – to attracting impressive crowds. The opening weekend of the tournament's third edition, last December, produced viewing figures far in excess of the second. CA aim to sell out a major stadium for the final of the women's World T20, to be held on International Women's Day 2020. And the commercial case continues to grow. "The 2017 World Cup built a bigger and stronger business case for the women's game," said Clare Connor, England's director of women's cricket. "There has to be a correlation between what has happened here and investment. We know it isn't a saturated market."

At administrative level, too, things are changing: the new ECB independent board has to be at least 30% female, and in Australia the target is 40% by 2022. In India, the BCCI have largely ignored women's cricket, despite the huge commercial potential – though the 2017 World Cup may be a tipping point. Diana Edulji, a former player and now part of the Supreme Court-appointed Committee of Administrators managing the affairs of the BCCI, has called the Indian board "a very male chauvinist organisation". She quoted their former president N. Srinivasan as saying, "If I had my way I wouldn't let women's cricket happen." In February 2018, it was announced that Indra Nooyi, chairman and CEO of PepsiCo, would be appointed as an independent director. But until she takes her place in June, there will be no woman on the main ICC board.

There has also been a small but significant shift in the use of language: we now have the "Australian men's team" and the "Australian women's team", not "Australia" and "Australia women". It is the same for England and West Indies, while New Zealand's men are the Black Caps and their women the White Ferns. In Australia, the Belinda Clark Award was redesigned as a medallion to match the Allan Border Medal. Just as symbolic was the decision to fly women cricketers business-class to the 2017 World Cup; for the World T20 the previous year in India, they had flown economy, unlike their male counterparts.

Historically, it has been difficult to know where sexism ended and homophobia began. But attitudes to homosexuality have changed rapidly over the last decade, and six of the countries that have played women's Test cricket have now legalised gay marriage. Even so, Australia's Alex Blackwell has spoken about the unhelpful assumption that male athletes are straight, female athletes gay. "Sports have tended to focus on feminine attributes when promoting their female teams, perhaps to compensate for this public perception," she said. But she was pleased that, at the 2016 Allan Border Medal night, she and her wife, the former England international Lynsey Askew, "were correctly referred to as a married couple. Having Cricket Australia proudly show us as a couple in a photo on their website made me feel included, and is a small but strong example of action being taken to become a more LGBTI-inclusive sport."

Cover point: where *Wisden Cricket Monthly* goes in 1998, the Almanack follows in 2018.

But if there has been a revolution at the top, sex still sells. As recently as 2013, Neeraj Vyas, the business head of the Sony Max network in India, explained away the rolling cast of models he employed on his cricket show by saying they must be "younger and fresher" each year. The IPL persists with its lavish use of mostly eastern European cheerleaders. And in October last year, after the Indian women's captain Mithali Raj appeared on the cover of *Vogue India*, the ICC posted a tweet drawing attention to her looks. It was quickly deleted. Such a view of women is not merely unfunny: it becomes insidious.

Sexual harassment exists within cricket as it does in life – perhaps more so, given the sport's male domination. A number of women working in the game have experienced inappropriate behaviour. Sleazy emails. Revolting comments. Rape jokes. Accusations of sleeping with the boss to get a job. Bottom pinching. Professional interviews that become awkward when a player chances his arm. A young Indian television reporter was asked by a prospective

Dennis Oulds, Central Press/Getty Images

All-rounder, but on men's terms... Betty Wilson (batting against Kent at Sevenoaks in 1951) had two strings to her cricketing bow, but had to choose between sport and a family.

employer if she was prepared to have a boob job. Twenty years ago, I was casually groped by an international cricketer. It would be nice to think things have changed, but still certain men are excused – because of their power, always their power. Most of the time, women let it lie because they are young or scared or unsure of their rights, or worried about jeopardising their reputations. Sometimes, they find the courage to speak out. Recently, one male journalist was sacked for inappropriate conduct with female workmates. Another was reported to CA for assaulting a female colleague in the press box. He was accredited for the following home season, and when the two worked at the same match, CA seated the perpetrator in the main press box, and the woman in the secondary, overflow area. Asked for comment, CA said the matter was confidential.

"The incident was horrible and humiliating and unexpected in the press box, because the other journalists are incredibly respectful," said the woman involved. "When females come in, we want to be part of the gang, valued for what we do. We don't want special treatment, or to have anyone fight our battles for us. Privately, I had a lot of support, but publicly everyone carried on as if nothing had happened, because generally people don't like confrontation or awkward situations, which I completely understand. At the same time it would have meant a lot to me had any of my colleagues told him what he did was disgusting and unacceptable, refused his invitations to events because of it, rather than accept them or make polite excuses. But I didn't see anyone do that. If he'd done the same thing to their partners or daughters, I can't help thinking social awkwardness wouldn't have stopped them. It's hard not to feel less valued by that thought. The only way things will really change is when the perpetrators feel they're the ones who are not accepted."

The point is a serious one. In 2013, five women accused two officials at the Multan Cricket Club in Pakistan of sexual harassment. At the PCB enquiry, three changed their statements, and the two others didn't appear, amid speculation they had been pressurised into standing down. Club chairman Maulvi Sultan Alama brought a defamation case against the players. After the case collapsed, all five were banned for six months. One of them, Haleema Rafique, 17, later took her own life.

On social media, female writers come in for particularly vicious attacks. Lizzy Ammon of *The Times* says she gets sexist abuse four or five times a week. "It can batter you down: you ugly old hag, you deserve to be raped, she's too ugly to be raped – there's no way that doesn't seep through."

Cricket is not alone. Another woman who worked in a different sport spoke of the existence of "wank tapes" – slow-motion video footage of cheerleaders, close-ups of tits and arse, specially edited by men who worked on the programme, and played in the outside broadcast truck.

Revolting. Depressing. Criminal.

Cricket should want to be the best it can – to employ the best men and the best women, to appeal to everyone, regardless of gender, colour or sexuality. That must mean dismantling barriers wherever they exist.

So, stop judging women on how they look. Ensure women working in a cricket environment – from the television presenters to the cleaners – are treated as equals. Call it what it is if you see harassment. Educate the male players, teach young men about consent. Give a woman the first question in a press conference – it makes a difference. Stop television's cringe-making lascivious lingering over attractive women in the crowd. Use the correct language – Ireland's Test against Pakistan in May will be the country's first *men's* Test: Ireland's women played a Test 18 years ago. Get rid of those cheerleaders from the IPL, or use an equal number of male dancers. Treat women's cricket with respect. Cover it. Fund it. Value it. Enjoy it for what it is, rather than resent it for what it isn't. Stop the constant comparisons with the men's game. Cricket has continually evolved, shaken off the past and tried innovation on for size. Sexism has no place here any more – by kicking it out, there is everything to be gained.

Tanya Aldred is a freelance writer, and co-editor of The Nightwatchman.

FIFTY YEARS OF OVERSEAS PLAYERS

The past is a foreign county

HARRY PEARSON

The summer of 1967 was one of tumultuous cultural change. Jimi Hendrix set his guitar alight at the Finsbury Park Astoria, The Beatles released *Sgt Pepper*, and the musical *Hair* brought full-frontal nudity to mainstream theatre. English cricket appeared untouched by the turmoil. While the rest of the world gave off heady and exotic scents, county grounds smelled of mildew and wintergreen ointment. Even on the sunniest days, the game was played with a sense of impending chill; every batsman seemed to have a dewdrop forming on the end of his nose. The cricket was dour and attritional, victories ground out with all the grace of Ray Illingworth chewing a day-old chunk of gum. Attendances slumped like a teenager's shoulders during double maths. Summer of Love? Not in Scarborough, Taunton or points in between it wasn't.

Yet change was coming. That autumn, after the BBC had launched Radio One to a mix of groovy elation and purse-lipped disapproval, a move by the Advisory County Cricket Committee was greeted by similar measures of excitement and tutting across the shires: they agreed to Nottinghamshire's proposal that the rules on county qualification, first established way back in 1873, should be relaxed to allow the immediate registration of one overseas player per team.

For historians, May 1968 might best be remembered for the Paris student riots, but – 50 years on – county cricket fans of a certain age probably recall the first regular sightings of Majid Khan, Asif Iqbal and Rohan Kanhai. Beneath the outfield, the beach, as the *soixante-huitards* might have put it. The relaxation was overdue. Overseas professionals had been drawing crowds to league cricket in northern England for generations, and had already made an impact on the county game, despite the various obstacles posed by the complex residency qualifications.

Several overseas players had already opted for the security of county cricket over the uncertainty of the international game. The dynamic batting of Barbadian Roy Marshall helped Hampshire win their first Championship, in 1961. Pakistan's Khalid "Billy" Ibadulla had been a fixture at Warwickshire for a decade, and was joined at Edgbaston in 1967 by Guyana's Lance Gibbs. Mushtaq Mohammad was playing for Northamptonshire, while his fellow Pakistani Younis Ahmed had gone to Surrey. Kenyan Basharat Hassan and West Indies wicketkeeper Deryck Murray were on Nottinghamshire's books; the apparently ageless Australian all-rounder Bill Alley had spent a feisty decade with Somerset; John Shepherd was with Kent; and his fellow Bajan, the flamboyant all-rounder Keith Boyce, was on his way to making Essex one of the most entertaining sides on the circuit. Add to that Ron Headley and Tony Cordle, two West Indians who made their careers with Worcestershire

Patrick Eagar, Popperfoto/Getty Images

County commitment: Mike Procter of Gloucestershire and Hampshire's Barry Richards meet at Southampton in the semi-final of the 1977 Benson and Hedges Cup.

and Glamorgan, and county cricket wasn't quite the Little England some traditionalists might have wanted.

Even so, the rule change sparked a genuine frisson. Only Derbyshire, Leicestershire, Middlesex and, inevitably, Yorkshire remained unmoved. Yorkshire had vehemently opposed overseas players ever since Lancashire employed Australian fast bowler Ted McDonald in the 1920s and, to the snorting disgust of Lord Hawke, won a hat-trick of Championships.

The biggest furore surrounded the battle for the services of the world's greatest all-rounder. Garry Sobers had been playing for Radcliffe in the Central Lancashire League, but it was his heroics for South Australia, where he had nearly doubled gate receipts, that were perhaps at the forefront of committeemen's minds as three counties engaged in a bidding war. Lancashire and Gloucestershire eventually lost out to Nottinghamshire's offer of a salary of up to £7,000, a flat and a car. He repaid them by hitting six sixes in an over off Malcolm Nash at Swansea.

Lancashire settled on the dashing Indian wicketkeeper-batsman Farokh Engineer, who was soon happily ensconced there. Asked about the 1971 Indo–Pakistan War, he said he would worry only if the fighting reached his home village. And where was that? "Oswaldtwistle."

Gloucestershire, meanwhile, turned to a young all-rounder who had impressed them during a season with their Second XI in 1965. Natal-born Mike Procter had fair hair, a barrel chest and the beefy, determined look of a man you might have seen driving cattle in a Saturday-night western. He would stay for 14 seasons, captain them for five, score over 14,000 runs, take more than 800 wickets and help Gloucestershire win their first piece of silverware –

the 1973 Gillette Cup, when Procter thrashed 94 against Sussex in the final, and picked up a couple of wickets in a parsimonious spell.

Like Sobers, he brought a panache and dynamism that lit up the grey county game like a lightning bolt. He surged to the wicket stiff-jawed, as if straining against a leash. His front-on delivery was such a whirling blur of arms and knees that most observers thought he delivered off the wrong foot. His killer delivery was a booming inswinger. To watch clips of him again is to realise that the vigour of his run-up and the brutal muscularity of his action made him look quicker than he actually was. It certainly worked on batsmen, who had palpitations at the sight of Procter galloping towards them like a bullock down a bank, to a chorus of "Prawk-taaar! Prawk-taaar!". He grabbed four hat-tricks in the Championship, and his haul of 109 wickets in 1977 – when Gloucestershire won the Benson and Hedges Cup – took them to within a nose of their first title.

The immediate effect of overseas players is hard to gauge, but a brief study of the Championship tables from 1967 and 1968 suggests it was considerable. Inspired by Sobers, Nottinghamshire – who had not won a match in 1967 – rose from joint-15th to fourth. Hampshire, for whom Procter's South African team-mate Barry Richards scored over 2,000 runs, went from 12th to fifth; Lancashire climbed from 11th to sixth. Perhaps the greatest impact, however, was in Wales.

> Asif Iqbal's flares and billowing silk shirts hinted at disco nights to come

Majid Khan had impressed Wilf Wooller when he hammered 13 sixes in 147 not out for the Pakistani tourists at St Helen's in 1967. Majid raced to a century in 61 minutes and struck five sixes in an over off Roger Davis. Bubbling over with grace and flair, he arrived at a team that had just finished 14th. In his first season, Glamorgan bounced to third; in his second, they won the title. One highlight was his superb 156 out of 265 on a beast of a pitch at Sophia Gardens: the subsequent win over Worcestershire helped secure the trophy.

If the new overseas players scored runs and took wickets, they also brought glamour and style: at Kent, Asif Iqbal's flared trousers and billowing silk shirts hinted at disco nights to come. But, more than that, they brought an attacking attitude that drew spectators and was better suited to a time when one-day cricket was on the up: the Sunday League was launched in 1969, the B&H Cup in 1972.

Yorkshire might blame other factors, but it is surely no coincidence that 1968 was the last time they won the Championship in the 20th century. By the time they won it again, in 2001, they had abandoned the Yorkshire-only policy established by Lincolnshire-born Lord Hawke, and their batting was led by Darren Lehmann, a pugnacious Australian.

The number of overseas players a county could field remained at two, but some of the first wave of signings soon qualified by residency, and many teams grew associated with double acts – players whose names became as linked to each other in the minds of cricket lovers as Laurel and Hardy or Morecambe and Wise. At Hampshire, Barry Richards was joined by Gordon Greenidge,

Sunday best: Garry Sobers bats and Farokh Engineer keeps as Nottinghamshire take on Lancashire at Manchester in the John Player League in 1970.

and the title won for a second time; Clive Lloyd paired up with Engineer at Lancashire and helped them dominate the one-day game. At Somerset, Joel Garner and Viv Richards inspired Somerset to the Gillette Cup and John Player League in 1979, the B&H Cup in 1981 and 1982, and the NatWest Trophy in 1983 – easily the most successful spell in their history. Richard Hadlee and Clive Rice, meanwhile, were Nottinghamshire's most famous couple since Larwood and Voce, driving them to the Championship in 1981 – their first in 52 years – and again in 1987, when they also won the NatWest Trophy.

Despite the obvious benefits overseas players brought to the circuit, some felt they were having a detrimental effect on England's Test team. The naysayers tended to focus on youngsters such as Viv Richards and Andy Roberts, who both played county cricket before Tests. In saloon bars across the land came mutterings that the counties were fifth columnists, training up England's enemies so they could defeat the mother country. As Devon Malcolm later summarised in a manner as elegant as his run-up: "We are preparing these guys to come back and one day bite the hand that once fed them."

In 1982, a new rule allowing the counties to field just one overseas player in Championship matches was introduced. In 1991, that was tightened to one *per squad*. But things had changed, and Ole "Eric Bloodaxe" Mortensen, a towering Danish seamer who joined Derbyshire in 1983, took action. Citing the Treaty of Rome, which guaranteed equal employment rights to all European Union citizens, he won his case. This helped ruddy-cheeked Dutch medium-pacer P-J. Bakker and his compatriot Roland Lefebvre to prolong their stay in county cricket, and was also the reason Dieter Klein (a South African with a German passport) could play for Leicestershire last season.

The notion that the Treaty of Rome might see hordes of European cricketers flooding into the UK did not cause the administrators any lost sleep. At least not until 2003, when Maroš Kolpak, a handball goalkeeper from Prešov in Slovakia, appeared in the European Court of Justice. Kolpak argued that, since he was a citizen of a country that had a free-trade agreement with the EU, he should not be categorised as a foreigner by the German Handball Union. The court found in his favour. From then on, citizens of any country with a free-trade agreement with the EU were eligible to work within it, and that included Jamaicans, Zimbabweans and South Africans.

The sudden influx of Kolpak players sent county cricket into a spin, culminating – or so it might be hoped – in an infamous game between Leicestershire and Northamptonshire at Grace Road in 2008, when less than half the players were England-qualified. There was little glamour; drama had given way to farce.

Overseas cricketers were increasingly looked on not as a long-term solution but a quick fix. Wayne Daniel had spent 12 seasons with Middlesex, Courtney Walsh 11 with Gloucestershire, Allan Donald 11 with Warwickshire. They, and many like them, had forged bonds with team-mates and supporters. In the wake of Kolpak, the stars and even the journeymen seemed unwilling to stick around – they were guns for hire. And the rise of Twenty20 leagues meant better money could be made more quickly elsewhere.

In May 2015, Wahab Riaz flew in to London, played two T20 matches for Surrey in two days, then departed, like a ringer in a pub match. Dwayne Bravo's career with Essex had been even shorter, consisting of a lone T20 game in 2010 (he was run out for five and leaked 11.5 an over). And in 2017, David Miller travelled over 6,000 miles from Potchefstroom to Cardiff, by aeroplane, helicopter and car, to get back for Glamorgan's T20 quarter-final against Leicestershire – and didn't even bat.

Time moves on, and cricket – usually several paces behind – moves with it. Rock musicians destroying their instruments is no longer headline news, and few worry that Radio One is undermining the morality of the nation. In the age of YouTube, the tingling thrill of seeing great cricketers in the flesh for the first time cannot be reproduced. For those of us who grew up in the decade or so following the relaxation of the qualification laws, it looks like a golden era of county cricket, dappled with sunlight, speckled with sixes and splintered stumps – a game of heroes. The world changes, cricket changes, but nostalgia is always waiting.

Harry Pearson is a writer from Yorkshire. Despite strenuous efforts to maintain a modern outlook, he sounds increasingly like his dad.

CALLING IT A DAY AT 25

Left-field decision

ZAFAR ANSARI

As I walked off The Oval in April 2017, bowled by Lancashire's left-arm spinner Simon Kerrigan for three, I knew the time had come to end my professional career. I texted my girlfriend and my brother, then spoke to my parents. They all suggested I should allow the normal feelings of embarrassment that come with a low score to subside. Quickly, however, they realised I had done all the thinking I needed.

This was not the first time I had confided in those closest to me about retiring. In the year leading up to the Lancashire game, I had returned to the subject with tedious regularity. I had also spoken sporadically with colleagues at Surrey about the possibility over the seven years I held a contract there. And it was, at least partly, for this reason that Alec Stewart, Michael Di Venuto and Gareth Batty – the club's director of cricket, head coach and captain – were so supportive when I explained my reasoning during a Championship match at Edgbaston the following week. As Alec later said, I was "never going to be a county cricketer at 30 or 35 – or even 28".

I begin with this not to indulge in mawkish narrativising but to emphasise that this was not a kneejerk decision, nor even one made over a period of months. Rather, both through design and accident, I had never reconciled myself to life as a professional cricketer. Throughout my career, retirement was almost perpetually imminent. So why had I never allowed myself to settle into this unique existence? This question implicitly emerged in some of the more sceptical reactions, which largely fell into two categories.

On the one hand, there was a struggle to comprehend why someone would give up something for which so many would sacrifice so much: by calling it a day at 25, I was doing these people a disservice. I can only respond that, from my experience last summer, watching cricket – even avidly – is different from playing it for a living. To assume that a passion for the sport as a spectator or club player translates into a love of the lifestyle of a professional cricketer is naive. It fundamentally misses the point. More simply, I could not base such an important personal decision on the dreams of others. Playing cricket was no longer for me, and I wanted to do something else.

On the other hand, there was an assumption that the only common-sense reason to stop playing would be to go into the City and make more money than cricket could offer. But this neither captured my lingering trouble with the professional game, nor explained my desire to change paths: money is very good as a county cricketer, and played no part in my thinking.

These analyses, though, were in the minority. In general, reactions were considered and sympathetic, and a third narrative developed: that the problem was an intellectual gap between me and my team-mates. While this was

Jordan Mansfield, Getty Images

Out and over: Zafar Ansari falls to Lancashire's Simon Kerrigan, a fellow left-arm spinner, and his cricket career is at an end.

flattering, once again I felt it missed the mark: there are lots of intelligent cricketers, many cleverer than I am.

Instead, I would argue that, if there *was* a separation, it arose out of my struggle to come to terms with a set of seemingly prosaic ethical demands – values and principles governing everyday conduct – that professional cricket threw up. The need to be permanently competitive, for example, was something I found difficult. In Bangladesh and India in 2016-17, I would watch Ben Stokes, Joe Root and Alastair Cook with admiration and alienation as they conjured up a hypercompetitive spirit, whether on the cricket field or at the hotel ping-pong table. It goes without saying that competition is a foundation of sport: to be competitive is clearly an advantage, providing the mental framework to maximise the chances of success. Yet as my career progressed, I felt uncomfortable conducting myself in this way.

This feeling emerged, in part, from a broader left-wing perspective, which informed my approach to life, and was both a cause and an effect of my studying Social and Political Sciences at university, and of my choice of master's thesis: African-American self-defence during the Civil Rights era. Against this background, I grew wary of a professional culture that treated the uncompromising pursuit of victory as essentially virtuous.

I had not always been such a sceptic. I revelled in my competitiveness as I was growing up. I'm sure it contributed to any success I did achieve. But as the years passed, I tired of the effort it required, and carried my growing suspicion of the merits of competition into my cricket. I would try to subvert this drive in small ways – such as taking pleasure in the success of an opponent – and avoid competition outside work. But I could not maintain it. The sight at close quarters of Virat Kohli living every ball as if it were his last highlighted an absence that had been building within me.

I also wrestled with, and eventually started to resent, the individualising tendency of the professional game. Like the will to compete, this is a defining feature of cricket. Indeed, what distinguishes cricket from many team sports is the productive tension between the individual and the group. Yet this was supplemented by an *ethos* of individualism to which I responded grudgingly.

The mantra of personal responsibility and a no-excuses culture that went with every act, for instance, were distortions of the reality confronting me every day. And, however glib it may sound, the fact that dependency – on others, on luck, on privilege – represented the rule rather than the exception made the pervasive logic of the individual steadily more jarring. Put plainly, I feel cricketers are heavily reliant on their circumstances and the people around them. Yet this cannot be acknowledged, for fear it would suggest they lack the toughness to take responsibility for their actions.

This perspective may have been a defence mechanism designed to compensate for my limits as a cricketer. And I'm aware of the virtues of this ethic – it drives players to see themselves as the principal authors of their own destiny, and to work harder to improve. Still, as I developed an aversion to it, the problem of my long-term motivation grew in equal measure.

Other factors played into my dissatisfaction. Like many cricketers, I struggled with the way the job pulled me away from friends and family. Similarly, the cycle of scrutiny, failure and judgment, occasionally in the public domain, was a challenge that never quite let up. While neither led me to end something to which I had dedicated most of my life, their accumulation created the circumstances in which retirement – even at a young age – felt right.

The tour of Bangladesh and India was a moment of crystallisation. Reading through old letters and watching home videos of me as a young boy, I was reminded that playing Test cricket had always been my ambition. My three caps still fill me with pride and joy. Even so, it was through touring that the factors I have described coalesced. Being in the presence of other players with an insatiable appetite to compete and better themselves as cricketers was disarming and revealing, since it forced me to challenge my own position.

The trip also raised questions I had not, until then, had to confront. I had avoided social media, for example, because I felt neither qualified to try to influence others casually with my views, nor comfortable with the self-promotion it inevitably involves. At the same time, I am committed to advancing social and economic justice, and the chance to do so by harnessing the exposure of an England tour was something with which I had to grapple.

I remember having a long, stimulating conversation during the trip with Mark Ramprakash, our batting coach, and coming away with a sense of the potential that a successful cricketing career might provide. Equally, I was aware that this potential was constrained by the need to avoid any controversy in relation to non-cricketing matters, as the ICC's decision to ban Moeen Ali from wearing a "Save Gaza" wristband in 2014 exemplified. In short, playing for England provides cricketers with a great opportunity to make themselves

Philip Brown, Getty Images

Test of commitment: Zafar Ansari in action against Bangladesh, in Mirpur, October 2016.

heard, but limits what they can say. I concluded that, even in the unlikely scenario of a long international career, this trade-off between exposure and authenticity was not one I wanted to make.

Of course, other jobs come with trade-offs, frustrations and constraints, which in part explains why I agonised so much. I say "in part" because for the previous seven years I had also taken huge pleasure in being a cricketer. I could not have given it up lightly. I'm sure I will miss the feeling of bowling an unplayable delivery, the satisfaction of winning a Championship match, and the excitement of taking part in a Twenty20 game at a packed Oval. I will miss even more the feeling of being a small part of something with a long, powerful history, such as Surrey, and of being a large part of a team, with its friendships and shared moments.

It is telling that in the weeks and months after retiring, I went back to The Oval many times to catch up with old team-mates, and watch them play, as a Surrey supporter. But it is equally significant that I did not feel the urge to do so as a player.

Zafar Ansari played 68 first-class matches for Cambridge, Surrey and MCC, and three Tests and a one-day international for England. He works for the charity Just for Kids Law, and is completing a law conversion degree.

ENGLAND 1,000 NOT OUT

Test of stamina

SIMON WILDE

On August 1, against India at Edgbaston, England will notch up one of cricket's worthier endurance records. Barring mishap, it will be their 1,000th Test, homage to a nation's commitment to one of sport's more ambitious ideas: a game that spans several days and, in the age of timeless matches, spanned many. Whether the contest was done and dusted before lunch on the second (Old Trafford in 1888, England's Test No. 30), or stretched over ten (Durban 1938-39, No. 240), they have remained true to a concept that would surely have died without their devotion. Next in the list is Australia, who by the end of the 2017-18 Ashes had played 808 (including 346 against England alone), followed by West Indies, far behind on 530.

By August 1947, when Test cricket was almost precisely halfway through its 141 years so far, 257 of its 289 matches – or 89% – had involved England. Even today, the percentage stands at around 43. A game that has always been too long for Americans, and increasingly appears too long for many of us, has

Popperfoto/Getty Images

The pioneers: James Lillywhite's team the day before their departure for Australia in 1876, where they would play the first Test. *Standing:* Harry Jupp, Tom Emmett, Richard Humphrey, Allen Hill and Tom Armitage. *Seated:* Ted Pooley, James Southerton, James Lillywhite (captain), Alfred Shaw, George Ulyett and Andrew Greenwood. *On the grass:* Henry Charlwood and John Selby.

not yet been abandoned by the English administrators. Far from it. Other countries may not be that interested in playing Test cricket against each other, but they still queue up to play England – and preferably beat them, though only Australia and West Indies, who will have accounted for exactly half of England's 1,000 Tests, have beaten them more often than they have lost.

For much of those first 70 years, England Tests did not have significant radio or television coverage, which meant the fact they were captained by an amateur – as it almost always was – escaped the scrutiny it merited. The first live radio commentary of a home Test came at Lord's in 1934 (No. 208), and the first TV broadcast, also at Lord's, four years later (No. 233). The first time

ENGLAND'S TEST RECORD, 1877–2018

	T	*W*	*L*	*D*	*%W*	*W/L*	
v Australia	346	108	144	94	31.21	0.75	1877–2018
v West Indies	154	48	55	51	31.16	0.87	1928–2017
v South Africa	149	61	33	55	40.93	1.84	1889–2017
v India	117	43	25	49	36.75	1.72	1932–2016
v New Zealand	101	48	9	44	47.52	5.33	1930–2015
v Pakistan	81	24	20	37	29.62	1.20	1954–2016
v Sri Lanka	31	12	8	11	38.70	1.50	1982–2016
v Bangladesh	10	9	1	0	90.00	9.00	2003–2016
v Zimbabwe	6	3	0	3	50.00	–	1996–2003
	995	**356**	**295**	**344**	**35.77**	**1.20**	

As at January 8, 2018. This table does not include England's five abandoned Tests.

every Test of a summer was shown on television, even if only in parts, was when India toured in 1952, and Len Hutton became the first professional to lead them at home. Alec Bedser and Fred Trueman marked England's 300th Test, at The Oval, by reducing the tourists to six for five.

It had taken them 32 years to notch their 100th, at Headingley in 1909, and another 24 for their 200th, at Auckland. But after the Second World War, the tempo picked up. Newly independent India and Pakistan were hungry for fixtures, and West Indies were developing into a major force. Air travel was making touring easier: by the mid-1960s, voyages by sea were at an end. England were soon maintaining a rate of around ten Tests a year: their 400th was at Madras in 1964, and the next three century landmarks came in 1974 (Headingley), 1984 (Lahore) and 1994 (Bridgetown). Since then, they have been getting through 100 Tests every eight years: Brisbane 2002 and Trent Bridge 2010 staged their 800th and 900th.

Michael Vaughan, who played the first of his 82 Tests at Johannesburg in 1999 (No. 762), believes it was this hectic fixture list – also incorporating a heavier programme of one-day and, from 2005, Twenty20 internationals – that led to a transformation in the way the team operated. Central contracts, for instance, were introduced in 2000. "Clearly they helped," he says. "But England were only doing what others already were. The biggest change was the amount of cricket they played. It turned you into an England cricketer, rather than a county player who happened to represent England. When I went back to Yorkshire, it was almost like England were leasing me."

It was not always thus. In the early days, the teams for home Tests were chosen by the committee of the host county. Was it bias, or the need for a wicketkeeper equipped with local knowledge, that led to Dick Pilling of Lancashire playing all three of his home Tests at Old Trafford? Surrey's Harry Wood, meanwhile, appeared in his only home Test at The Oval. Lancashire's decision in 1896 to pick Sussex's brilliantly gifted Indian-born batsman Ranjitsinhji against Australia (No. 51), after MCC had overlooked him for the previous match at Lord's, was key to centralising the process: Ranji made 62 and 154 not out.

For much of the 20th century, the England team were run as an arm of MCC. A Board of Control for Test Matches in England, created in 1898 and largely made up of MCC aristocracy, arranged home Tests and appointed a panel of selectors; from 1903, the MCC committee oversaw the management of overseas tours.

In 1968, under pressure to reform in order to receive government funding, English cricket replaced this system with a new entity, the Test and County Cricket Board, to run the professional game; not without ructions, the TCCB's influence grew over the next 20 years at MCC's expense.

On the field, however, a lack of cohesion remained. "We were a group of individuals, never a team," recalls Keith Fletcher, who made his England debut at Headingley in 1968 (No. 448). "It wasn't a collective effort. It was a wing and a prayer. If you had two bad Tests, there was a fair chance you'd be left out. The senior batsmen weren't nasty, but they didn't come forth and say: 'This bowler swings it out – look for his straight one.' There was none of that. They weren't keen on somebody taking their place."

Ken Kelly, Poppertoto/Getty Images

Halfway there! England's team v Pakistan at Leeds in 1974 (No. 500). *Standing:* David Lloyd, Chris Old, Tony Greig, Mike Hendrick, Geoff Arnold, Dennis Amiss, Jack Birkenshaw (twelfth man). *Front row:* Keith Fletcher, Alan Knott, Mike Denness (captain), John Edrich and Derek Underwood.

The profile of Test cricket was lower then, especially when England toured, and less TV footage found its way into front rooms and newspaper offices back home. That changed only when Sky TV began showing overseas Tests live, starting in Jamaica in 1990 (No. 658). "Test matches then weren't such a big thing," says Fletcher. "You just went and played for England. Even for Australia Tests, it wasn't like it is now. There's no comparison. In 1970-71, it was sort of, 'Oh, we won the Ashes.' It wasn't hyped up as tremendous. In fact, it *was* tremendous to win the Ashes out there. If we'd have done it now, we'd have been heroes and gone up to the Palace and got OBEs." Once, the team largely operated in the shadows; now every detail grabs the limelight.

Mike Brearley, who led England in 31 Tests between 1977 and 1981, reinforces this impression, recalling how the national team fought for space within a busy domestic programme. "We'd gather on a Wednesday – sometimes even in the afternoon, having driven up from London to, say, Headingley – have a net and then dinner with the chairman of selectors. There was virtually no coaching. Who ran the nets? Good question. Perhaps Ken Barrington, if he was there. The physio Bernard Thomas would be helping Bob Willis stretch his hamstrings, dealing mainly with the bowlers.

"There was not much chance to savour the result, because after the Test ended on a Tuesday afternoon you usually had to drive halfway across the country to play for your county next day. It felt normal, though, and I don't think it diminished Test cricket. Your loyalty was as much to your county as your country, and in a way more so because you were contracted to them. We were serving two masters, whereas today they serve one."

Brearley, who led England to three Ashes wins, also presided over another high-water mark, at Birmingham in 1979 (No. 549), when an innings defeat of India left their win–loss record at +72 (210 won, 138 lost). That is the healthiest margin it has been, though it also reached +72 by the end of the home series against New Zealand in 1983. The nadir since then has been +34, after Cape Town 2000 (No. 765) and Melbourne 2002 (No. 803). At the end of the 2017-18 Ashes, it stood at +61.

England players didn't begin gathering two full days before a Test until Micky Stewart, their first cricket manager, found himself being interrogated by journalists ahead of the Old Trafford Test in 1989 (No. 655) as to why Ian Botham had not taken a full part in Wednesday practice; Botham had driven from Hove, having bowled 40 overs on the Monday and 25 on the Tuesday. An extra day of preparation, free of county cricket, paved the way for England to fall into line with a trend for playing five-day Tests straight through, without a rest. The first time they had done this was at Old Trafford in 1981 (No. 571); their last Test with a rest day was at Nottingham in 1996 (No. 726). The change demanded greater fitness and resilience, especially from fast bowlers.

Stewart was appointed in 1986 after it became clear over a number of losing tours that players needed closer management, and that only some were capable of providing pastoral care. "Micky was very much ahead of his time," says Medha Laud, who was brought by Stewart to the TCCB from The Oval, and remains involved in the planning and preparation of England sides. "What were later regarded as new ideas originated with him. They were claimed as

TEST RECORDS FOR ENGLAND

Record	Figure	Player	Years
Most runs	12,005	A. N. Cook	2006–2018
Most hundreds	32	A. N. Cook	2006–2018
Most double-hundreds	7	W. R. Hammond	1927–1947
Highest score	364 (v Aus)	L. Hutton	1938
Most runs in a calendar year	1,481	M. P. Vaughan	2002
Most sixes	†81	K. P. Pietersen	2005–2014
Most fours	1,380	A. N. Cook	2006–2018
Most ducks	24	J. M. Anderson	2003–2018
		S. C. J. Broad	2007–2018
Best batting average (1,000 runs)	60.73	H. Sutcliffe	1924–1935
Most wickets	523	J. M. Anderson	2003–2018
Most five-fors	27	I. T. Botham	1977–1992
Most ten-fors	7	S. F. Barnes	1901–1914
Best innings figures	10-53 (v Aus)	J. C. Laker	1956
Best match figures	19-90 (v Aus)	J. C. Laker	1956
Most wickets in a calendar year	†67	S. J. Harmison	2004
Best bowling average (50 wickets)	10.75	G. A. Lohmann	1886–1896
Most catches (wicketkeeper)	250	A. P. E. Knott	1967–1981
Most stumpings	46	T. G. Evans	1946–1959
Most dismissals	269	A. P. E. Knott	1967–1981
Most dismissals in a calendar year	70 (66 ct, 4 st)	J. M. Bairstow	2016
Most catches (fielder)	156	A. N. Cook	2006–2018
Most Tests as captain	59	A. N. Cook	2010–2016
Most appearances	152	A. N. Cook	2006–2018

As at January 8, 2018.

† *A. Flintoff (1998–2009) hit 82 sixes in his Test career, including four for the ICC World XI; in 2005, he took 68 wickets, including seven for the ICC World XI.*

---

novel, but I remember typing them up as things being discussed years earlier. The frustration was that the finance wasn't there to put them in place. I sometimes wonder just what Micky would have done if he'd had the money the game is awash with now."

Thanks to enhanced broadcast deals, the delisting of home Tests – a crucial but controversial move, allowing wealthy satellite channels to enter the bidding – plus sponsorships by the likes of Whittingdale, Tetley and Vodafone, that money gradually became available. Central contracts, long an ambition, became a reality under Lord MacLaurin, the first chairman of the ECB, the TCCB's successor body. "Simon Pack came on board as international teams director because the team needed a defined management structure," says Laud. "David Lloyd [head coach 1996–99] pushed for a larger support staff, more specialist coaches and various other positions. The TV rights deals created the finance to put things on a professional footing. When people say the team weren't professionally run, I'd disagree. It was just that the money wasn't there."

Mindsets did have to change, though. Duncan Fletcher, who took over from Lloyd, recounted how he felt he had to educate some ECB officials "to think only of making decisions which would help England win cricket matches". And when Vaughan became captain four years later, his first ambition was to make the team fitter. "I realised the standard in international cricket was rising, and also I believed fitness drives an ethic of hard work," he says. "It worked,

Jason O'Brien, PA Photos

New model army: the England squad sport pink caps (in aid of Glenn McGrath's breast cancer charity) at Sydney, January 2018 – the venue for Test No. 995. *Standing:* Mason Crane, Gary Ballance, Dawid Malan, Jake Ball, Craig Overton, James Vince, Ben Foakes, Tom Curran and Mark Stoneman. *Seated:* Chris Woakes, Alastair Cook, James Anderson, Joe Root (captain), Stuart Broad, Jonny Bairstow and Moeen Ali.

though I had to fight to get a masseuse. The ECB didn't want to pay for one, so I said, 'Not a problem, we'll pay for it ourselves.' The ECB realised this would come out. All of a sudden they paid for it."

Finding the funds for support staff and players had long been a problem. Only in 1954-55 did MCC agree to pay for a physio to accompany an Ashes tour. Essex's Harold Dalton immediately proved his worth by keeping Frank Tyson and Brian Statham strong enough in the heat to rout the Aussies. Previously, local Australian masseurs had been recruited to rub away hours spent on overnight trains. Today, England's top players, nurtured through national age-group sides, have their every need met by technical advisers, strength and conditioning coaches, physios, psychologists and data analysts. They are handsomely rewarded too, but for long periods the players' remuneration was derisory, highlighted when two went on strike at The Oval in 1896 (No. 52) and the defections to Kerry Packer hatched in Melbourne during the Centenary Test in 1977 (No. 525). The match fee for professionals rose from £10 to £20 as a result of that 1896 protest, but had gone up to only £210 by the time of Packer's intervention. Today, the figure is around £12,500.

The poser is how many more Tests England will play in a world obsessed with Twenty20. The next broadcast deal covering the English seasons 2020–2024 has built into it only a modest reduction, nothing to suggest imminent Armageddon. One suspects that if anywhere has the will to keep the Test flag flying, it is here.

By the end of the 2017-18 Ashes, Simon Wilde had reported on 245 of England's Tests as cricket correspondent of The Sunday Times. *His history of the England team is published in the summer.*

A BRIEF HISTORY OF THE HAT-TRICK

What will the valet think?

JON HOTTEN

Technology was at the heart of last summer's most joyous moment. Moeen Ali's match-clinching hat-trick at The Oval against South Africa was Test cricket's 43rd, and the second in succession confirmed by DRS's all-seeing eye. Somehow, the delay built the tension rather than deflating it: the England players huddled together to watch the big screen, then hoisted Ali up, battle-weary but smiling blissfully.

Like most hat-tricks, it was a banquet for statisticians: of the 43, it was the first at The Oval, the first for 79 years by an England spinner, the first for 60 to win a Test and the first to comprise three left-handers. The summer also had plenty of near misses. South Africa's Chris Morris was on a hat-trick at Trent Bridge, and so too Ben Stokes and Toby Roland-Jones, on Test debut, at The Oval. Against West Indies, it was the turn of Stuart Broad (at Edgbaston), James Anderson (Headingley) and Stokes again (Lord's, where he was joined by the tourists' captain Jason Holder). And two Tests finished with two wickets in two balls – Duanne Olivier at Trent Bridge, Ali at Old Trafford – though convention dictates that the feat cannot be spread across games. Still, cricket rarely offers more drama than the split-second the hat-trick ball is mid-air. In 2017, fans were spoiled.

The hat-trick is one of the game's oldest markers, a quirk that stretches back to the mists of its early years. It remains rare and mysterious. The name has extended beyond cricket, and beyond sport, yet it is in cricket that it undeniably began. What is it about a sequence of three that makes it magical? Who alighted on it as a frequency both special and achievable, even on the village green?

Cecil Fiennes's hat sits inside a glass case at Broughton Castle in Oxfordshire. Broughton was built around 1300, and has been in the Fiennes family since 1451. It has a moat, a great hall, a bedroom used by James I, and another by Anne of Denmark. History enshrouds it, and perhaps overshadows Cecil's hat, too, which sits surrounded by cannonballs from the Civil War and other ephemera. Nonetheless, it is almost certainly the oldest surviving and verifiably genuine hat presented to a taker of three wickets in a row.

The Hon. Cecil Brownlow Twisleton-Wykeham-Fiennes turned out for I Zingari, the aristocratic amateur wandering side, which in 1859 toured Ireland. At Dublin's Phoenix Lodge, they met "The Military, With Lawrence And Doyle". The scorecard, recorded in club scrapbooks now at the MCC library, shows Cecil taking the wickets of P. Ducane Esq. (Scots Guards), J. Aldridge Esq. (20th Regiment), Captain Glyn (1st Dragoons), and the Hon. Major Fiennes (no known relative). The order is not clear, and the card somewhat confusing, but in there somewhere is Cecil's mighty achievement.

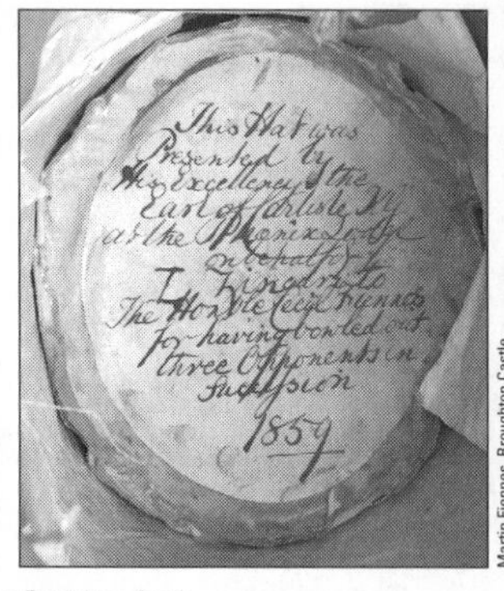

Martin Fiennes, Broughton Castle

Trick of the light? Cecil Fiennes's hat is on display at Broughton Castle.

Great banter followed. The scrapbooks go on to report: "The Hon. Cecil Fiennes accomplished what is called 'the hat-trick' in one of our matches. After breakfast one morning, Lord Carlisle addressed him in the most precise and appropriate terms, and then presented to him an enormous, rough whitewash hat! As Fiennes was later going to his bedroom he turned around and said: 'The joke may be a very amusing one to you fellows, but what on earth am I to do with this hat? When my valet comes into my room and sees it, he'll think I'm mad.'"

Lord Carlisle may have been the kind of guy who would start a parody Twitter account, yet Cecil's hat – although enormous and rough, and apparently a tremendous joke – is rather beautiful, and made of white beaver-skin. He received it the year after H. H. Stephenson, Surrey's feared round-arm bowler, had taken three in three at Sheffield for All-England against Twenty-Two of Hallam and Staveley; the customary collection from the crowd for a notable deed was used to buy him a hat, the first such recorded instance. As Stephenson's headwear appears to have fallen foul of time, Cecil's beaver-skin remains the oldest tangible link to the tradition.

Stephenson took two other hat-tricks in 1858, but neither came with a hat, nor the suggestion of one – evidence, perhaps, that the phrase was not yet widely known. It was not until 1868 that it first appeared in print (outside the I Zingari scrapbooks, at least), and it took another two decades to pass into common usage.

Even then, its origins were disputed. A letter attributed to "An Old Harrovian" and published in *Cricket: A Weekly Record* in August 1900 suggested the custom stretched back to Lord Frederick Beauclerk, the volcanic and vindictive Doctor of Divinity whose appointment as a vicar in St Albans served as cover for his career as player, gambler and autocratic administrator. Maybe significantly (or maybe not), Beauclerk, who retired from the game in 1825, liked to sport a white beaver-skin hat while batting.

Through all the game's changes, from Broadhalfpenny Down to the IPL, the hat-trick has retained its scarcity and significance. The frequency does not seem to vary. After Ali at The Oval, it had happened in 1.89% of Tests, or once every 52 games. In limited-overs cricket, preserving a wicket can be meaningless, yet at the time of Ali's hat-trick there had also been 42 in one-day internationals, one every 93 games. So, allowing for the extra two innings in almost every Test, they occur roughly as often in both forms (Kuldeep Yadav took the 43rd, for India against Australia at Eden Gardens in September, just to even up the score again).

Generally, they happen how and when they want to. Wasim Akram picked up two in a Test career that bridged three decades, but these came within nine days of each other, in March 1999. Alok Kapali took Bangladesh's first, yet he was primarily a batsman, never claimed another Test wicket, and finished with six in all at 118 apiece; by contrast, Muttiah Muralitharan's tally of 800 did not include a hat-trick. So complex was Merv Hughes's, against West Indies at Perth in 1988-89, he didn't realise it had happened. He dismissed Curtly Ambrose with the last ball of one over, and Patrick Patterson with the first ball of his next, ending West Indies' first innings. Hughes then trapped Gordon Greenidge with his first ball of their second. He might have been more alert: in the previous game, at Brisbane, Courtney Walsh had become the first bowler to split a Test hat-trick across two innings. After more than 1,100 Tests without such an occurrence, two arrived in the space of a couple of weeks. And shortly before last winter's Ashes, nothing said England were heading for trouble quite like the two hat-tricks Australia's left-arm seamer Mitchell Starc took in the same game for New South Wales against Western Australia.

Back at The Oval, it transpired that Ali's hat-trick was not just his first in Tests, but – football aside – his first anywhere, ever. Like Cecil, he probably deserved a hat.

Jon Hotten is the author of The Meaning of Cricket.

CRICKET'S DATA REVOLUTION

The geeks who inherited the earth

JARROD KIMBER

While travelling around Australia in his dual role as commentator and selector, Mark Waugh carries a form guide on thoroughbred racing. Among other details, it gives each horse's jockey, trainer, parentage – and if it wears blinkers. When Waugh commentates on the Big Bash, he doesn't always seem as well prepared.

He has been a lifelong racing fan: he has owned horses, is married to a trainer and, when it's time to place a bet, wants all the information going. That's not how most cricket selectors work. There is a big community of former players in the game whose decisions – despite the sport's evolution – are often based on biases, anecdotal evidence and their own experiences.

But there is a new breed, who claim to be doing the cricket equivalent of *Moneyball* – Michael Lewis's book on how data changed baseball. Usually, that means they have seen the film, starring Brad Pitt. Few, it emerges from one conversation after another, have actually read the book; fewer still have read anything by Bill James, who invented sabermetrics – an acronym of the Society for American Baseball Research – and inspired Lewis.

There is a third group, using advanced cricket metrics. They watch more cricket than anyone, study it closely, analyse the data, and create complex algorithms. They are following cricket like Wall Street brokers, technology consultants and professional gamblers – because that is what they are. And they are changing the way teams play.

It is 2014. At their team hotel in Mohali, the Barbados Tridents are watching a briefing about tactics ahead of their Champions League match against Kings XI Punjab. Among them are Jason Holder, Ravi Rampaul, Ajantha Mendis, James Franklin and coach Desmond Haynes. They listen to ground information, strategy, strengths, weaknesses and tips. The man leading the presentation tells them Mohali has short straight boundaries, which they should target. He tells them about left-arm spinner Akshar Patel, who had dominated that year's IPL, with an economy-rate of 6.13. People try to play him square, says the man; if you play straight or fine, you can score runs. Mohali, he concludes, is the perfect ground to take on Patel.

The man is Gaurav Sundararaman. He is 32, has a degree in computer science and an MBA in marketing, and spent three years in technology consulting before moving into green energy. On the field, his favourite memory is an unbeaten 43 that won him the match award and 100 rupees (just over £1). He is no one's idea of a cricketer, yet here he is telling a bunch of internationals and a retired legend how to play. It turns out he has a point: the Tridents attack the straight boundaries, and Patel goes for more than ten an over.

Jason O'Brien, Action Images/Reuters

Finding an edge: spinners Moeen Ali and Adil Rashid do their homework.

There are others like Sundararaman. Dan Weston, who played village cricket in Kent to no acclaim, is a professional gambler. He started with slot machines, moved into online poker, then became a sports trader. Through posts written for sportsanalyticsadvantage.com, he was discovered by a county – he declines to say which – and asked to help in their recruitment. "There is more flawed thinking in cricket than in other sports," he says. "You will hear a commentator praise a strike-rate of 80 in an ODI, or 150 in T20, even if both are below the average rate in a given situation. This happens all the time." Weston, now 38, sells his advanced analytics to cricket fans, traders and the media.

Mohammad Khan, born in New Jersey to Pakistani parents, has a finance background, and was once an American football quarterback. He didn't much care for cricket, until he saw how Pakistan's defeat by India at the 1996 World Cup affected his family. He got his start by working in sports sponsorship – and force of personality. "After one defeat, I texted one of the Jamaica Tallawahs' owners: 'If I was responsible for building that team, you wouldn't be losing games like this.'" Having spent years keeping his own data on players from around the world, Khan soon became the Tallawahs' general manager. In 2016, his first year, they won the Caribbean Premier League.

T. A. Adhishwar had enough talent to appear in age-group cricket – his father, T. A. Sekhar, played two Tests and four one-day internationals for India in the 1980s – but his career as a tech entrepreneur took off more quickly, and he founded a company called Hotel for Dogs. While Sekhar was employed by Delhi Daredevils, Adhishwar concentrated on his own business, but his analytics skills meant he offered tips to Delhi about the best players to pick, and led to work with St Kitts & Nevis Patriots and Jo'burg Giants. He is 23.

Nathan "Numbers" Leamon, one of England's team analysts, is a Cambridge maths graduate who was at the forefront of former coach Andy Flower's Moneyball tactics. Under his data reign, England went top of the Test rankings, overhauled their approach to one-day cricket, and came within an over of winning their second World T20. Hassan Cheema and Rehan Ulhaq, once bloggers and podcasters, are now in charge of squad selection at Islamabad United, who won the inaugural Pakistan Super League in 2016. Richard Barker, previously an American Football journalist, has helped turn Northamptonshire into one of the most unlikely T20 powerhouses in modern cricket.

With cricsheet.org offering free ball-by-ball data, statisticians Ric Finlay and Andrew Samson providing analysis for a fee, and CricViz releasing more of their product, there has never been easier access to cricket knowledge. Unlike former players, this new breed of outsider cannot rely on personal experience, so they watch more cricket – and look for any advantage along the way.

In T20's early days, Chris Pickett (now the Hong Kong team analyst) worked for Sussex. Inspired by sabermetrics, he examined where the bowler could stand to make the batsmen travel further for each run. Before Pickett came Krishna Tunga, who played low-level cricket for many years. He was a merchandiser for an export house and a designer in women's fashions, before trying his hand at acting and modelling. He collected Australian cricket magazines, and was obsessed with stats. Soon he was back-watching all the games he could, creating the most advanced set of ball-by-ball data the sport had seen. He knew each bowler's lines and lengths, and each batsman's typical choice of shot, which he would code from A1 to D2.

Tunga was introduced to Australian coach John Buchanan at the team hotel during their tour of India in 2000-01. Buchanan found what he had always wanted: someone following cricket as if it were binary code. Cricket Australia had no data or video analysts, so Tunga became an integral part of the team: "We emailed almost daily." Buchanan called him cricket's Bill James. Much of his early work was unpaid, but that changed; he has also been employed by the BCCI and – again through Buchanan – New Zealand Cricket. At a time when no country had video analysis, and data wasn't even a sporting term, Tunga – now 52 – was ten years ahead of the game. His findings are on his blog: allthatcricket.com.

Data is now a significant part of cricket – for better, and occasionally worse. Australian fast bowlers are managed using the latest scientific methods, yet remain injury-prone. Northamptonshire don't worry about fitness levels, as long as players possess the necessary skills with bat and ball. There is, however, still no adequate way of measuring how much fielding is worth. Nothing proves this

---

KRISHNA TUNGA'S CODE FOR STROKES

A1 off side, front foot, defensive
B1 off side, back foot, defensive
C1 leg side, front foot, defensive
D1 leg side, back foot, defensive

A2 off side, front foot, attacking
B2 off side, back foot, attacking
C2 leg side, front foot, attacking
D2 leg side, back foot, attacking

Ryan Pierse/Getty Images

Seeing to it: West Indies' Carlos Brathwaite launches Ben Stokes for a C2 six in the final over of the 2016 World Twenty20.

more than wicketkeeping, where even the most advanced data advocates throw up their hands in despair. Many sides count the runs each drop allows, but that has obvious flaws. Durham's Chris Scott dropped Brian Lara 18 runs into his unbeaten 501 in 1994, but that didn't make him a terrible keeper. And what is a chance, what is a half-chance? No one is sure.

While former players often complain that the game is overrun with data and sports science, most analysts believe there's nowhere near enough. When one up-and-coming tech company met an IPL franchise, they were shocked by the team's lack of data. Even the sides with good-quality data often don't know how to use it. There are 45-year-old coaches who can't remember their Hotmail password, yet are thrust into a whole new world. As Weston says: "You're asking someone using an abacus to use a supercomputer, when they've never even used a calculator."

The current craze is match-ups: for instance, a batsman may strike at 150 against right-arm seam but 110 against left-arm spin, so on comes the part-time left-arm spinner. T20 leads the way in this respect, but Tests are catching up. No Test team, for example, should be without at least one bowler who specialises in taking out the tail. You won't want an attack in which your three seamers take wickets only with the new ball. But you will want a detailed analysis of when wickets fall at a particular ground. Some have a problem with numbers in cricket, despite averages being around since the 1700s. Yet analytics allow modern selectors to show due diligence.

The career of slow left-armer Michael Beer is a perfect example of what can go wrong if they don't. When he was chosen in Australia's 2010-11 Ashes squad for the Perth Test, head selector Andrew Hilditch said he would "bowl very well against the English on his home ground". At that point, Beer had played three first-class games at the WACA and one List A match. In the Big Bash, by contrast, he has long been one of the premier bowlers, yet he's never played a T20 international, nor been signed by an overseas team. Cricket is a billion-dollar industry that uses advanced algorithms to decide on social-media strategy, promote the game and invest money. But when picking its best resources – the players – it often goes on hunches.

They used to say that, if you were out of the game for five years, your playing days counted for nothing. That is probably less now. In 2009, Merv Hughes made the news for his role on the Australian selection panel. It turned out he did not have a pay-TV subscription, which meant – the Ashes aside – he could hardly see them play overseas. Sometimes he was at the cricket, as a selector or as the leader of a spectators' tour party, but he was seeing less of Australia than a fan with a credit card. "I think I follow the game closely enough anyway," he claimed. "To me there is no substitute for actually being there live."

In 1932, Douglas Jardine sat down and watched clips of Don Bradman, searching for a weakness. What he saw led to Bodyline. It took another 80 years for video analysis to become a staple of all the top teams.

After working with Sundararaman, Desmond Haynes became a fan, insisting Phil Simmons – then West Indies coach – hire him. Sundararaman eventually became a consultant for the team at the 2016 World T20. Money was tight, so he didn't travel with them, instead chatting to Simmons for an hour a day on the phone. While other sides had a higher activity rate (scoring from a higher percentage of balls), West Indies knew they hit more boundaries. If you wanted to take a risk, they calculated, it was better on a big hit than a quick single.

After the final in Kolkata, Carlos Brathwaite talked about boundary percentage. But in that last over against Ben Stokes, he wasn't just trying to slog: he was using information fed by his coaches. "Looking at the field and their plans from before, England are usually a good-yorker death-bowling side," he said. "I knew it would be that plan, or they would go into the wicket and force me to hit towards square leg, midwicket, cow corner, which was the bigger side of the ground. I guessed they didn't want to bowl a wide yorker, since the short side of the ground was on the off side."

Brathwaite went C2, C2, A2, and C2. It was he who hit the sixes. But it was Sundararaman who provided the measurements.

Jarrod Kimber is the global writer for ESPNcricinfo.

CRICKET MANNERISMS

"I like to annoy them a bit"

GIDEON HAIGH

Few batsmen in history have had such an idiosyncratic technique as Steve Smith, with his backlift more of a sidelift, his trigger movements as elaborate as loading a bolt-action rifle. Fewer still can have had such a repertoire of habitual gestures: the tactile preliminary inventory of his pads, gloves, helmet and trousers, bat held upright; the stiff-legged double tap; the bent-knee double dip. Then, after each stroke, the signature followings-through, including – when he leaves the ball – a gesture of the bat as if bestowing a knighthood, and a movement of the right arm as though slipping it into a sleeve.

Far from random, it has a hint of the robotic; Smith admits to being fussy and controlling, obsessed with his gear, superstitiously averse to anyone touching his bat during breaks in play, insistent on taping his laces tight to his shoes for neatness's sake. But it also follows in traditions well-worn. A game of repetition and repose, cricket offers ample scope for different methods and manners, quirks and quiddities.

Who has not picked up a bat and flourished it in the manner of a personal favourite? Who has not fancied themselves in the mould of champion bowler or fielder? It is an expression of wonderment and allegiance to mimic Dhoni's helicopter shot or Pietersen's switch hit, as it was to emulate Ranji's glance or Hammond's cover-drive. It might, though, simply be the way a player stands, moves, occupies space, that detains us. There is a T-shirt of a broad-backed figure, leaning on his bat at the non-striker's end with legs crossed. The face is obscure, but you know at once that the jaws would have been chewing gum implacably, because it is unmistakable as Viv Richards.

Observation and emulation start in childhood, where the discovery of sport intersects with the world of make-believe. In *The Return of the Ashes*, Mike Brearley describes the three-year-old son of friends who, by shaping left-handed, tugging a cap low and swinging vigorously to leg, made himself into a facsimile of Australia's wicketkeeper Rod Marsh. He had a commentary to match: "I'm Rommarsh. Square cut."

Sometimes the homage leads to greater things. It was Richards's lounging prowl and Sunil Gavaskar's studious control that Sachin Tendulkar used to imitate in his games of tennis-ball cricket; it was Ian Chappell, with that upturned collar, and Dennis Lillee, with his spread-eagling appeal, whom Shane Warne favoured in backyard Test matches against his brother. They matured into players with their own catalogue of tics, notably Tendulkar's helmet tug and bow-legged squat, and Warne's languid hand-to-hand roll of the ball and adjustment of the shoulder of his shirt. But mostly we go on living in our own heads, wondering what it feels like as we grow familiar with what it looks like, noting the similarities and differences, continuities and originalities.

Stephen Blackberry, Action Plus/Getty Images

Serious side-effects: Steve Smith lifts the bat in his own, productive, style.

In *How to Watch Cricket*, John Arlott argued that cricket's "immense imaginative quality" was rooted in the habits of youth, never quite outgrown, of discerning character in distinction. "Hero-worship is expected to disappear with maturity, and at its most idolatrous it is not a good thing for a man," he wrote. "But in watching a cricket match, only a sheer dullard will fail to realise that he is not watching 11 identical and drilled dummies. All men are different, and their differences show on the cricket field. Cricketer after cricketer reveals his essential nature at this game."

It was, perhaps, ever thus. John Nyren's *The Cricketers of My Time* rejoices in the foibles of its characters. Billy Beldham had "a peculiar habit of bringing his hand from behind his back immediately previous to his delivering the ball", the Duke of Dorset "when unemployed, of standing with his head on one side". Noah Mann was "short in stature" and "swarthy as a gypsy", and "always played without his hat"; David Harris prepared to bowl by "standing erect like a soldier at drill"; Lumpy Stevens celebrated wickets with a "little grin of triumph". These are cameos that vault cultures: C. L. R. James read them as a boy in Port-of-Spain and "began to tingle".

While there is little directly descriptive writing about W. G. Grace, and next to no footage, one idiosyncrasy is mentioned almost invariably: the way he cocked his front toe. As Arthur Conan Doyle noted, Grace would "slowly raise himself up to his height and draw back the blade of his bat, while his left toe would go upwards until only the heel of the foot remained upon the ground". It conveyed a cocky readiness, an imperious disdain. It was, perhaps, the Edwardian embrace of style, with its premium on appearance and deportment. Victor Trumper was known by the neatness with which he folded his sleeves beyond the elbows – you can see it in George Beldam's sublime photograph. Generations of Sydney grade cricketers did the same, including Alan Kippax, who in his boyhood followed Trumper to every local game, with a scorebook in which he recorded only his hero's runs.

Jack Hobbs's custom of spinning the bat in his hands before facing was immortalised in a cartoon by Arthur Mailey. Cecil Parkin's trick of flicking the ball from boot to hand was regarded as so novel as to feature in its own Pathé newsreel, helping cement his reputation as cricket's great jester. As the distinctive grows familiar, in fact, the familiar turns suggestive. Philip Mead's range of cap tugs, bat pats, wiggles and shuffles encouraged R. C. Robertson-

Glasgow to see "the air of a guest who, having been offered a weekend by his host, obstinately decides to reside for six months". Walter Hammond's walk to the wicket was in J. M. Kilburn's opinion "the most handsome in all cricket", a flow "linking stillness to stillness", inherently regal: "He came like a king and he looked like a king in his coming." Recalling the blue handkerchief that protruded from Lala Amarnath's trouser pocket, Vijay Hazare thought he displayed "showmanship that would have been the envy of an advertising expert". Citing Richie Benaud's plunging neckline and unrestrained appealing, Ray Robinson referred to him as "the spectator's best friend".

After the Second World War, television and the age of mass reproduction brought appearance into sharper focus. The Brylcreemed locks of Keith Miller and Denis Compton in the 1940s savoured of masculinity and sophistication; the probity of the 1950s, wrote Simon Rae, was somehow "guaranteed by Peter May's immaculate parting"; the swing of the 1960s was caught in Ted Dexter's seigneurial bearing, and the glint of the gold chain round Wes Hall's neck. By the 1970s, there were cricketers with a set of moves that would not have been out of place on the dance floor. Lillee choreographed his walk back so superbly that he needed only a casually outstretched right hand to accept the ball, and a single right forefinger to flick the sweat from his brow.

Long careers leave deep traces on the memory. Graham Gooch took guard proprietorially by presenting the full face of the bat in front of middle and leg; David Gower took his leave by nonchalantly tucking it beneath his arm, as though that was enough elegance for the day; Derek Randall jerked and twitched as if on a puppeteer's strings. A generation of Indians imitated Mohammad Azharuddin's upturned collar. Sri Lankans were intrigued by Sanath Jayasuriya's preparatory check of all his gear. In the last couple of years in club cricket, I have seen batsmen fiddling with the Velcro on their gloves every bit as pedantically as M. S. Dhoni, and setting fields from the crease in the mode of Michael Clarke. In the case of 18-year-old Austin Waugh, the likeness is more than skin deep; he is the spit of his father, Steve, in motion and at rest.

Popperfoto/Getty Images

Left foot forward: an edition of *The Mask* from 1879 caricatures Grace's cocked toe and "Monkey" Hornby's restless energy.

The gesture can also convey the autobiographical. It might tell us something of a cricketer's upbringing: Morne Morkel undertakes his anti-clockwise twirl at the end of his run because there was a lack of room in his local nets when he was growing up. It may relate something of their technical contemplations: Shane Watson's nervous adjustment of his back pad before every delivery is a little memento mori of lbw. It may reveal a belief system: Lasith Malinga applies a kiss to the ball before bowling because as "a good Buddhist" fortunate enough to lead a comfortable existence, he feels obliged to "worship what helped me get here". In a recent interview concerning that fashionable notion of batting with intent, David Warner proposed a wide definition: "Intent can be leaving the ball, and your mannerisms around the crease. Those things bring a spark to my eye when I am at the other end. You know when your partner is on as well." Warner's little limbo after taking guard, his loosening of the shoulders before he takes strike, and of the wrist bands on his gloves when he is off strike, are fundamental to his ringcraft.

His captain now intuits that he is being watched too. When Smith played and missed during his Test century at Pune in February 2017, Ravindra Jadeja cheerfully imitated his head toss, eliciting from Smith a smile of recognition. When he was beaten by a ball that kept low at Bangalore, Ishant Sharma responded with a range of grimaces, which Smith met with an insouciant head wobble, and the next ball an almost self-parodic leave. All part of the plan, he has said: "I like to try and annoy them a little bit with some of my mannerisms rather than anything I say."

James Anderson adjusts his forelock after each delivery

Yet there remains a pleasing sense at such moments that we are seeing the player unguarded, free – whether it's Joe Root's warning against a run by holding his bat vertically in his left hand like a stop sign, Stuart Broad's trio of jumps and scratches before bowling his first ball, or James Anderson's adjustment of his forelock after each delivery. For all his experience, Alastair Cook still embarks on a single with a sudden ungainly lope, as though still a schoolboy slightly surprised to have made a good hit.

To enjoy these little glimmers of imagined personality is also to express our freedom as spectators. Cricket is growing obsessed with action and spectacle to the exclusion of the game, as though any pause for reflection or digression is against the spirit of entertainment. Where television was once about conveying the live experience, the role of the live match now is to be more like television, a narrated whirl replete with replays and advertisements. To watch players be themselves is to appreciate cricket's compounding of human material, its space and its scope. During his 239 at Perth against England in December, Smith faced 399 balls over 20 minutes short of ten hours, while 505 runs were added. That's a lot of pads touches, bat taps and knee bends, but they all in their way played a part.

Gideon Haigh's latest book is A Scandal in Bohemia: The Life and Death of Mollie Dean.

Stu Forster

THE WISDEN–MCC CRICKET PHOTOGRAPH OF 2017 Stu Forster wins the award for his image of Katherine Brunt taking a photo of herself and the triumphant England team after the women's World Cup final, at Lord's on July 23.

David Rowe

THE WISDEN–MCC CRICKET PHOTOGRAPH OF 2017 David Rowe is one of two runners-up, for his photograph of Surrey's Sam Curran being comprehensively bowled during the NatWest T20 Blast match at The Oval on July 19. The unseen bowler is Essex's Paul Walter.

The eighth Wisden–MCC Cricket Photograph of the Year, attracted over 650 entries. First prize was £2,000; the two runners-up received £1,000, and the eight other shortlisted entries £250 each. Any image with a cricket theme taken during 2017 was eligible. The independent judging panel, chaired by former *Sunday Times* chief photographer Chris Smith, comprised award-winning photographers Patrick Eagar, Adrian Murrell and Kevin Cummins, broadcaster Ali Mitchell, and Nigel Davies, the former art director of *The Cricketer*. For more details, go to www.lords.org/photooftheyear

Stu Forster

THE WISDEN–MCC CRICKET PHOTOGRAPH OF 2017 The second runner-up is another image by Stu Forster. Also taken during the women's World Cup in July, it shows New Zealand's Hannah Rowe hidden behind a mane of hair.

Philip Brown, Getty Images

THE LEADING CRICKETERS IN THE WORLD In the men's game, the award is won by Virat Kohli; in the women's, by Mithali Raj. Both captain India.

Nigel French, PA Photos

Matthew Impey, Wired Photos

GREEN LANDSLIDE… GREEN LANDSCAPE Pakistan, led by Sarfraz Ahmed, celebrate their unexpected triumph in the Champions Trophy, while MCC set an attacking field in their match on Alderney, in the Channel Islands.

Archie Brooksbank

Cameron Spencer, Getty Images

EVENING SCORES The sun sets on the Second Ashes Test at Adelaide in December; in the third, at Perth, Steve Smith hits a double-hundred, and Australia are about to snatch back the urn.

Ryan Pierse, Getty Images

Graham Morris

Graham Morris

THE SPICE OF LIFE – VIVACIOUS, VITAL, VIBRANT Henry Blofeld bids farewell to admirers; a supporter in traditional *pakol* welcomes Afghanistan's appearance at Lord's; and Indian fans come prepared for the British weather during the Champions Trophy.

Kieran Galvin, NurPhoto/Getty Images

Courtesy of Marylebone Cricket Club

SOURCE OF INSPIRATION? The batsman, keeper and umpire in this detail from *Cricket at Christchurch* seem to reappear in Eric Ravilious's sketch for the wood engraving now synonymous with Wisden.

Courtesy of the Ravilious family

THE WISDEN WOOD ENGRAVING

A mystery with history

MATT THACKER

In the front room of Don Bradman's childhood home hangs a print of *Cricket at Christchurch*. Andrew Leeming, who has restored the house, at 52 Shepherd Street in Bowral, suggests a closer look at the figures of the Victorian batsman and wicketkeeper. "Where have you seen them before?" he twinkles. It's like a *University Challenge* question: the answer must be there, somewhere. Leeming holds up a *Wisden*, the Eric Ravilious wood engraving on its cover. Eureka: an 80-year-old mystery solved at a stroke.

Ravilious – famed for illustrations, ceramics and South Downs watercolours – had been commissioned to produce a retro-style artwork for the redesign of the Almanack in 1938 to mark the 75th edition. His engraving sat on the front cover until 2003, when editor Tim de Lisle replaced it with a photograph; it was moved to the back and the spine. The change caused a stir. In 2004, the engraving reappeared on the front, though it has remained on the spine ever since.

"In 2015, I was reading Robert Winder's *The Little Wonder*, the history of *Wisden*, and the question of Ravilious's inspiration found its way into my mind," says Leeming. "Looking at the painting, I was struck by the poses of the batsman and keeper, as well as the umpire's top hat. I felt sure I had seen this vignette before. Then it hit me: the cover of *Wisden*. What put the discovery beyond reasonable doubt, though, was Ravilious's original concept sketch, which had been reproduced in Winder's book."

Ravilious, who didn't earn a fee for his labours, may have copied an image from an existing pub sign, perhaps The Bat and Ball at Hambledon. This discovery appears to quash that notion. But Adam Chadwick, MCC's curator of collections, is not wholly convinced that *Cricket at Christchurch* (see opposite), attributed to Thomas Musgrave Joy, is quite what it seems. In 1947, Lord's was gifted a number of paintings by Sir Jeremiah Colman – he of the mustard – and Chadwick has suspicions about the authenticity of several. In any case there are many artworks featuring similar configurations of batsman and keeper. *Cricket at Christchurch* is tentatively dated between 1845 and 1855, but Chadwick believes it could have been painted up to a century later. Until tests are done, we shall remain in the dark.

Yet how else to explain the striped top, the top hats and the positioning of the umpire – common to the painting and Ravilious's preparatory sketch? As Winder says: "If he did base his emblem on a pub sign, he may not have known that the sign was based on this painting. He turned a scene into an icon by simplifying it to its basics. And I guess he wanted the top-hat period feel to capture the book's Victorian origins more than the game's."

Matt Thacker is managing editor of The Nightwatchman.

THE EVOLUTION OF THE GAME

Laying down the Laws

ALAN GARDNER

To mark the introduction of a new Code of the Laws of Cricket in October 2017, *Wisden* names the ten most significant changes to the way the game has been played.

The size of the bat

MCC used the new Code of Laws to restrict the depth of a bat (as well as the thickness of edges), though its width was standardised almost 250 years ago. The earliest model was curved, resembling a hockey stick, to deal with balls bowled along the ground. But the advent of the pitched delivery led to the adoption of today's shape – pioneered by John Small, 18th-century batting's nonpareil. Small was present when cricket's first great laws controversy flared, between Chertsey and Hambledon in 1771. Chertsey's Thomas "Daddy" White walked out with a bat as wide as the wicket. Synonymous with the game's development, Hambledon quickly passed a resolution limiting bats to 4¼ inches wide, a stipulation written into the 1774 Code, and still unchanged. An iron gauge was used to test bats suspected of being too broad, which led to one of W. G. Grace's scrapes with officialdom. In 1884, during a match against the Australians at Sheffield Park, he accused Alick Bannerman and Percy McDonnell of using illegal bats. Bannerman was not guilty, though McDonnell was. More to the point, so was WG.

The third stump

They say the modern game favours the batsmen – but until the late 1770s there were only two stumps to defend. In the mid-18th century, the average wicket cost less than eight; pitches were rough (no mowing or rolling), and selected by a member of the visiting team, usually the best bowler. Still, when in 1775 Edward "Lumpy" Stevens whistled one through the defences of John Small (him again), between the stumps and beneath the single bail three times in the same innings, the bowlers submitted a complaint. Hambledon intervened once more, although use of a third stump was not written into the Laws until 1838, which suggests not everyone sympathised with Lumpy. The size of the wicket has also increased, from 22 inches by six to 28 by nine, with the stumps now a set diameter. But in a Test at Faisalabad in 1997-98, Pakistan's Mushtaq Ahmed slipped a googly between South African Pat Symcox's middle and off stumps. An incredulous Symcox survived, and *Wisden* reported: "Umpire Dunne gave his spectacles a disbelieving wipe, but the bail was found to be badly cut".

Popperfoto/Getty Images

Early days: much has changed since this late 18th-century engraving, yet it is recognisably cricket.

Overarm bowling

The very word – Laws with a capital L, rather than rules – seems to warn against transgression, and the sense of a moral dimension is especially apparent in the ball's delivery. Back in 1833, when bowling was underarm – propelled from below the elbow – John Nyren, the great Hambledon chronicler, fulminated against "the modern innovation of throwing, instead of bowling the ball". John Willes of Kent had supposedly hit on a round-arm style after seeing the action of his sister, Christina, whose hooped skirt got in the way. But he was no-balled at Lord's in 1822, and reacted by riding off on his horse and "out of cricket history", as H. S. Altham put it. Or into it, perhaps: MCC, by now administering the Laws, legalised Willes's method in 1835. The ball was supposed to be released from no higher than the shoulder, though this was inevitably hard to police and, come 1864, MCC sanctioned the style we know today. That wasn't the end of the matter. Throwing of a different kind – straightening the arm at the elbow – became another crusade for the purists, resulting in various crackdowns and, in 2004, the ICC's introduction of 15 degrees of tolerance in recognition that most bowlers naturally flex their arm during delivery.

The introduction of boundaries

In the limited-overs age, a boundary means a four or a six. Yet there was a time when, if a boundary was there at all, it was to keep the crowd off the field. As cricket became more of a spectator sport during the 19th century, tents were sometimes pitched around the field; hits that reached them were called "booth balls", and earned an allotted number of runs. Not until the 1884 Code were boundaries mentioned in the Laws, and it was up to the umpires to arrange them. At Lord's, in the early days of Grace's career, all scoring strokes were run, though as time wore on WG probably enjoyed not having to expend so much energy. There is a story from the 1860s (possibly apocryphal) of the ball getting caught in a sheep pen on the edge of a pitch: around 100 runs were added as fielders battled to retrieve it. Sixes took even longer to become standardised, with most venues requiring the ball to be hit out of the ground; Albert Trott may have cleared the Lord's Pavilion in 1899, but it was worth only four, as many as a shot that trickled into the gate. Finally, in 1910, the six as we know it landed with a thud beyond the rope.

The end of Bodyline

The tactics adopted by England during the 1932-33 Ashes, intended as a means of neutralising Don Bradman, have reverberated down the ages. What the English referred to as "fast leg theory", the Australians called "Bodyline bowling", as Harold Larwood and Bill Voce implemented Douglas Jardine's plan of peppering batsmen, to a leg-side cordon of catchers. The Australian board sent a cable to MCC deploring the tactic as "unsportsmanlike", and hinting at a diplomatic incident. Although there was an initial reluctance to legislate, the sight of West Indies' Learie Constantine enthusiastically bouncing England the following summer encouraged MCC to pass a resolution calling "any direct attack" on a batsman an offence against the spirit of the game. This was followed after the Second World War by the introduction of a section of the Laws covering unfair play that banned "intimidatory bowling". However, the real body blow for Bodyline came via a different law – that of unintended consequences. Concerned by the tedious practice of medium-pace inswing to defensive fields, MCC in 1968 trialled a playing regulation that had applied in the County Championship since the late 1950s, preventing more than two fielders behind square on the leg side. It was inked in to the Laws two years later. Bodyline was no longer viable in practice, though not for the reasons many assumed.

The vexed matter of lbw

A bit like explaining football's offside rule, knowing your lbw is a key test for any aspiring cricket fan. "No dismissal has produced so much argument," wrote Gerald Brodribb in his history of the Laws. In the days of curved bats, being leg-before was not considered enough of a problem to exercise the rule-makers, since batsmen generally stood to the side of the wicket. As playing straight took over, the possibility of obstructing the path of the ball (without pads) became an issue. However, the decision to include a clause in the 1774 Code that would see a batsman dismissed if he did so "with design" handed umpires the task of determining intent. That was soon removed, but the new wording – "the ball must pitch straight" – was also vague. Eventually, by the 1830s, it was made clear the ball had to pitch wicket-to-wicket (and be hitting the stumps), a situation that persisted until the 1930s, when the fun really

Central Press/Getty Images

Count them! At Brisbane in the 1932-33, Douglas Jardine places six close fielders on the leg side. Harold Larwood is the bowler; Bill Woodfull, the Australian captain, takes evasive action.

began. In response to the rise of "legging play" came an initial experiment with the snicking rule, whereby a batsman could still be lbw after edging the ball. This was soon followed by a change to the Law allowing for dismissals to deliveries pitching outside off stump – initially recorded by scorers as "lbw (n)". Further legislation against padding up was introduced in 1972: a batsman could be out if struck outside the line of off, but only when not playing a shot. Simple? Wait until we get to DRS…

The front-foot no-ball

During the 1947-48 Australian summer, Movietone cameras recorded Ray Lindwall side-on in his action. Stopped at key moments, the footage (viewable on YouTube) illustrated the problem of dragging. For more than 200 years, the bowler merely had to land a foot behind the bowling crease (and inside the return crease). But this allowed canny operators such as Lindwall – and many others, including Fred Trueman – to perfect the skill of dragging their back boot along the turf after grounding, and releasing the ball from well in front of the popping crease. After Gordon Rorke exploited the method to Australia's advantage in the 1958-59 Ashes (advised to play forward, Colin Cowdrey said he was afraid Rorke would tread on his toes), MCC began experimenting with the front-foot no-ball Law in 1963, and fully sanctioned it in 1969. This caused different problems for the umpire, who has a more restricted view of front foot than back, and less time to adjudicate before focusing on the delivery itself. It has also been suggested that the Law has led directly to the increase in fast bowlers suffering stress fractures of the back, as they now jump to land on the popping crease.

Declarations

What would the latter stages of a Test match be like without the Declaration Speculation Game? Probably quite pleasant, but still… For a long time, scores were not high enough to make the matter a concern, but by the late 19th century it was obvious the option was required to avoid farce. At The Oval in 1887, Surrey's tailenders were ordered to sacrifice their wickets, but Thomas Bowley's attempts to get stumped were foiled by Sussex, who had no desire to bat. By the time Bowley stood on his wicket, it was too late for Surrey to win. A couple of years later, MCC legalised declarations, but only on the final day of a match; in 1900, when three-day games were the norm, that became "any time at or after lunch on the second day". Further tweaks followed – you can't rush good Law-making – with MCC as worried about "freak" declarations as facilitating bold captaincy. Only in 1957 were all restrictions removed. County captains can be punished for making "extraordinary declarations" – those which prevent the opposition from acquiring bonus points "without enhancing the batting side's prospects of winning or saving the match".

Covered pitches

Here we step outside the strictures of the Laws, which are universal, and into the realm of Playing Conditions, which are specific to a country or a competition. Given cricket's reputation for eccentricity, it is perhaps unsurprising that the administrators were initially more concerned with ensuring pitches *weren't* covered. Until the 2017 revision, the Laws stated that "the pitch shall not be completely covered during the match unless provided otherwise by regulations or by agreement before the toss". That is partly because the art of batting on a sticky dog was highly regarded: Victor Trumper was a master, and you may have heard Geoffrey Boycott mention the subject. It was also an opportunity for spinners to clean up. However, the desire to get on with things after the rain had stopped slowly won out. Sheffield Shield matches saw covering mandated during the 1930s, and it became common practice in Tests in Australia in the 1950s, but local regulations varied. Counties often breached them in England, either by accident or design, and it wasn't until after a series of trials during the 1960s and '70s that the TCCB finally decided all home Tests from 1979 would be played on covered pitches.

The Decision Review System

For a long time, the use of technology meant little more than a mechanical mower. In 1992, TV replays were first used to help determine run-outs in international matches (Sachin Tendulkar was the first victim). But it took more than a decade for the authorities to go further, by which time TV viewers were getting decisions dissected via a multitude of camera angles. This again lay outside the Laws and, for those who view the umpire's decision as final, was inimical to the essence of the game. But in 2008, the ICC introduced the Umpire Decision Review System. The first Test series to use it, Sri Lanka

Ben Radford, Corbis/Getty Images

No hiding place: giant screens reveal umpiring misjudgments to spectators at the ground; smaller ones tell the same story to viewers at home.

against India, revealed numerous problems, and set India against the system for several years after Anil Kumble's side managed just one successful review out of 21. But the seeds had been sown. There have been numerous controversies: over the accuracy of ball-tracking, the use of Vaseline to fool infra-red cameras, the availability and cost of equipment, the question of what constitutes conclusive evidence, the umpire's call. But one of the main effects of DRS was seen in adjudicating lbw appeals against spin; Ray Illingworth reckoned he would have taken 520 more first-class wickets had the technology been used in his day.

Alan Gardner is an associate editor at ESPNcricinfo, with a keen appreciation of the Lord's library archives.

ENGLAND'S NEW T20 TOURNAMENT: FOR

Harnessing the millennial bug

TOM HARRISON

It is a privilege to present my views in these pages, in an edition whose cover is graced by Anya Shrubsole, one of the stars of last year. Anya is pictured on that unforgettable Sunday in July, when England won the ICC women's World Cup in such thrilling style at Lord's. For everyone building towards the start of a new domestic competition in England and Wales in 2020, the atmosphere at Lord's as she turned the match on its head was as significant as the result itself.

Lord's was different that day. The ECB and the ICC had worked hard on spreading the word about the tournament, and taking the final, in particular, to a new audience. The focus was on women and girls, families, and diverse groups with affiliations to countries other than England. It was not a traditional crowd. The match was sold out long before England had reached the final, and the day itself made a statement about where the game can grow.

Tea, coffee and bottled water were the biggest-selling drinks, and the atmosphere was intoxicating. Families and youngsters were there in abundance: women and men, girls and boys, all savouring their big day out, many new to the game and Lord's. They were transfixed by the drama. TV audiences, digital-clip downloads and social media all confirmed something special was happening.

As a taste of what we're trying to achieve in 2020, it is the perfect place to start. It shows that, if we are prepared to present and promote the game differently, then a younger and more diverse audience, so crucial if cricket is to keep thriving, will be attracted to the sport we all love.

Cricket is rightly proud of its history and traditions. Test matches matter just as much to the game's future as newer formats. We must never lose sight of that. Equally, we have to recognise that we are confronted by major challenges in attendance, participation and relevance; sometimes our structures can be a straitjacket, making it difficult to attract new followers and holding back important changes. To stay relevant to the millennial audience, it is essential we reach outside the game and listen to the wider world.

The growth of T20 since it was devised in England and Wales in 2003 shows how cricket is constantly evolving. The shortest format helps demystify it and make it more accessible, easier to follow and wider in appeal. It has reminded us that cricket can have mass appeal. We need to strip away the tag of privilege and elitism which the sport in this country still carries, unfairly. Accessibility at all levels of the game, for all communities, must remain a priority – and will be under our leadership.

A successful new tournament will benefit our more established competitions at both domestic and international level. We will invest in these, promoting

Darrian Traynor, Getty Images

Numbers game: the Big Bash League match between Melbourne's Stars and Renegades at the MCG in January 2016 attracted a record attendance for a domestic fixture in Australia.

them and ensuring each has a big role. If we are creating something to which more people can feel connected, then the long-term health of the whole game will benefit, at all levels and across all counties and boards. The new fans we attract can and will become the Test fans of the future, but in order to achieve that goal we need to broaden the base of those introduced to cricket.

Some question why we need a new competition in addition to the T20 Blast – which has already done a great job for county cricket, getting big audiences back into our domestic grounds. That will still be the case after 2020: outside the high-summer window we have identified as ideal for the new competition, the Blast will continue to take T20 to all corners of the country. But you only have to look at the huge success of the Indian Premier League and Australia's Big Bash in different markets, with a format invented here, to see the potential, and need, for us to go to another level. There is a way we can do this, while ensuring that other competitions, all formats and the counties have an opportunity to thrive – and continue to be the breeding ground for talent.

Let me also be clear about why we need a step change. Within the thorough research on which all plans are being developed, we did seriously investigate repackaging the T20 Blast. But it is only by thinking more radically, by getting outside the cricket bubble, and even beyond sport, that we've been able to deliver new investment of well over £1bn into our game from our new broadcast partnerships.

That means harnessing the combined pulling power of Sky Sports and the BBC in an innovative way, ensuring live cricket's return to free-to-air television. These are partnerships that will drive participation and the first live free-to-air exposure for T20 – domestic and international, women's and men's. There should be optimism about cricket's future in this country. These are exciting times. I know that is felt around the game, and there is a sense we are making real progress, while understanding the challenges we need to address, particularly at recreational level.

What will the new competition look like? For five weeks of the season, we're going to target a different audience, and promote the game in different ways. There will be 36 matches in 38 days, ensuring a strong daily narrative that's easy to follow. I've seen the tournament described as – and criticised for – being a city T20. That's true, in that the venues will be based around our major cities, so we can draw the biggest crowds. But the appeal of the teams themselves must be nationwide, reflecting the globalised world we live in.

Spectators will get a completely different match-day experience from anything we've previously offered. The young in particular will feel connected to the game, the players, the teams and the cricket in a way they have not felt before. You won't have to be a first-class county member to come and watch the new competition – although you will be very welcome if you are. You won't need to know the ins and outs of the lbw Law, or even how many balls are in an over. You'll be attracted to the competition because you love cricket presented in this way: you enjoy watching sixes fly and fielders pull off stunning catches – brilliant skills with bat and ball.

Because we're creating a fresh competition aimed at a different audience, we're introducing a new financial model too – to make sure it's sustainable and serves the game's best long-term interests. The ECB will retain ownership of the eight teams, but not control how they operate on the field. The key is that any money generated remains in cricket, for the good of all sections of the game – with at least 10% directly funding our participation programmes. This is why we have not sold equity stakes to private enterprise, and why this is not franchise cricket.

There has been plenty of interest from private entities in the UK and abroad wanting stakes in teams. We have resisted those approaches because we must maintain control of the tournament's objective, keep investment within our game and focus on the long-term strategic purpose. This is about creating more fans and building a bigger following. That is our guiding philosophy. By getting this right, we will attract long-term riches in attendance and participation – new fans, new players and the growth of the whole game.

We make no apologies for doing things differently, or for having our eyes firmly on the future. We want to keep our game front and centre of the national conversation, making sure cricket means as much to the next generation of *Wisden* readers as it does to this.

Tom Harrison is chief executive officer of the ECB.

ENGLAND'S NEW T20 TOURNAMENT: AGAINST

A needless risk

GEORGE DOBELL

As another Ashes tour slipped away, the ECB's chief executive Tom Harrison held a press conference in Melbourne in which he insisted cricket in England and Wales was "in extremely good shape". He provided several reasons for his optimism, but key was the recent conclusion of a broadcasting deal worth £1.1bn. It seemed to confirm the suspicion of many: what matters to administrators is not the size of the trophy cabinet, but of the bank account.

To be fair to Harrison – who earns over £600,000 a year – he didn't just cite the broadcast deal. There was the success of the women's team at the World Cup (though he didn't mention their failure to regain the Ashes), the success of the men's white-ball teams (though he didn't mention they fared less well at the 2017 Champions Trophy than in 2013), the launch of a participation programme for children and – laughably – the suggestion that changes to the ECB's corporate governance provided some sort of compensation for Ashes defeat.

Harrison and his ECB colleagues deserve credit for acknowledging the need for change. Cricket in this country has, by most measures, been ebbing in public relevance. Sure, this was a problem of the board's making: their predecessors had sold the TV rights to subscription broadcasters, after all. They were right to conclude that Twenty20 is the vehicle to inspire a new generation of players and supporters, and right to explore ways to exploit its potential. But, as Captain Scott might have told them, not all explorations end happily. And while that broadcast deal is a lot of money, there's a good chance it will turn out to be fool's gold.

The problem with the ECB's plans is that we stand to lose far more than we gain. Yes, the new competition could inspire new followers, but so could a rebranded T20 tournament involving all the counties – especially if it were broadcast free to air – and it wouldn't carry the inherent risks.

Play T20 in a block? We did that. And after one wet summer (2012) led to a 50% fall in ticket sales (admittedly, there were fewer fixtures), it was abandoned. Playing games in a window demanded too much of spectators – their time and money – and left the competition vulnerable to being eclipsed by rival events, such as the Olympics or football tournaments. Market research undertaken by the ECB suggested spectators were confused by different start times: in 2010, there were 19 variations in the group games alone. They desired predictability, or "appointment to view", as it was called in the Morgan Report into county cricket. All that seems to have been forgotten.

Meanwhile, to make space for a white-ball window, the County Championship will be squeezed ever more into the margins of the summer. With so many games played in April, May or September (when matches start

Harry Trump, Getty Images

Good intent? The T20 Blast game between Gloucestershire and Kent in July 2017 sold out – but what does the future hold for smaller grounds such as Cheltenham?

at 10.30, making dew a factor), the need for fast bowlers and spinners is negated. Medium-pacers, gaining movement they can rarely replicate on international surfaces, proliferate and dominate. Don't be surprised when England struggle for wickets in India and Australia.

Other formats will suffer, too. Current plans indicate the 50-over tournament will be played at the same time as the new T20 competition – and some Test matches – which means the best 100 or so England-qualified cricketers won't be available to play in it, and the best eight or so venues won't be able to host it. Surely that doesn't give England the best chance of winning 50-over World Cups? And what message are we sending to the next generation of players if the glamorous new competition overlaps with England Tests?

There are many other questions. What evidence is there to suggest spectators will warm to teams with new identities? They certainly didn't when Welsh rugby attempted something similar. Will they travel to what have long been considered rival grounds to support the team based there? What will happen to attendances for Tests – or domestic 50-over matches – if the new competition is played simultaneously, and marketed more aggressively? What will happen to those counties who don't host games? Isn't it likely they will, in time, be impoverished and marginalised? Isn't this an attempt to cut the number of first-class counties by stealth?

The ECB have, at various times, claimed the new tournament – with its influx of broadcast money – will enable them to pump funds into grassroots cricket. But Jim Wood, who has served on the ECB board for years as the voice of the recreational game, accepts that's unlikely. The start-up costs of the competition (£1.3m a year has been promised to each first-class county, before we even consider marketing costs and players' pay demands) mean there will be no such surplus. Wood supports the competition on the entirely reasonable basis that it will inspire new followers. But actual cash? The ECB have already spent a chunk of the reserves they built up over many years preparing the ground.

Were such risks necessary? The number of spectators attending the current domestic T20 tournament – the Blast – had grown by 63% in four years, and is expected to exceed a million in 2018. The format is starting to reach a new audience, with 69% of T20 ticket-buyers at The Oval having never attended a cricket match before the competition started. Imagine how much higher those figures could have been if the ECB had invested in marketing it. Imagine how much higher it could have been with promotion and relegation, and some free-to-air broadcasting. Imagine how the game could have grown with an FA Cup-style knockout tournament.

Instead they have been seduced by an Australian example (the Big Bash) that cannot simply be transposed to England – the nations have different holiday patterns, climates and city densities, for a start. And they have undermined a successful competition, threatened a key revenue stream of the counties and pushed more than half towards irrelevance. Several of those counties, bound by gagging orders and intimidated by fears they would lose their funding or hosting rights, have been pulled along kicking and screaming. The most brittle of agreements holds it all together.

We needed evolution not revolution. We needed context and free-to-air coverage. But whether or not the prospective start date of the new competition – July 24, 2020 (or 24/7, 2020) – is a Freudian slip, it underlines the impression the ECB have prioritised one format at the expense of all others, and are prepared to sacrifice the long-term success of the Test and one-day sides in pursuit of the T20 dollar.

There are still reasons for optimism. Cricket remains a terrific game and, if we can only find a way to get more people to see it, there's no reason it should not thrive. But the ECB's plans are a monumental, unnecessary risk.

George Dobell is the senior correspondent at ESPNcricinfo.

THE LEADING CRICKETER IN THE WORLD IN 2017

Virat Kohli

SURESH MENON

In a year India topped the Test and 50-over rankings, Virat Kohli was the most prominent player across the formats – and seventh in the Forbes list of sporting brands, ahead even of Barcelona's Lionel Messi. Contemporary cricketers have averages, strike-rates and brand value, and Kohli was doing rather well in all three.

In Tests, his 1,059 runs came at 75; among those with 1,000, only Steve Smith had a better average (by one). Three of his five centuries were doubles; the other two were unbeaten. In one-day internationals, he scored most runs (1,460), and had the best average (76) of anyone who played more than ten innings; his strike-rate was nearly 100. In 46 internationals overall, he totalled 2,818 – more than 700 clear of the next best, Joe Root, and more than 1,000 ahead of Smith. It all contributed to India winning seven of their 11 Tests, 21 of 28 completed ODIs, and nine of 13 Twenty20s. And Kohli became *Wisden's* Leading International Cricketer for the second year in a row, emulating Virender Sehwag in 2008 and 2009.

But statistics are only part of the story. The year began with his one-time mentor Anil Kumble as national coach, and ended with Ravi Shastri in charge, having replaced Kumble at Kohli's behest. With the BCCI reduced to a shambles following Supreme Court rulings that took power from the hands of a few and placed it in the hands of even fewer, Kohli was monarch of all he surveyed.

His marriage in December to Bollywood star Anushka Sharma seemed to confirm his royal status. By leading his side to nine Test series wins in a row, comfortably an Indian record, between August 2015 and December 2017, Kohli became the most powerful man in Indian cricket. No matter that six were at home, and two in Sri Lanka: the success helped turn public focus away from the BCCI.

If Sachin Tendulkar was the symbol of India's economic liberalisation and greater disposable income for the middle classes, Kohli – who turns 30 this year – is an icon of a country that is getting younger. More than 65% of India's population is under 35, with all the self-confidence and in-your-face attitude that brings. Perhaps this is merely a synonym for passion, something Kohli has in everything he does.

At Bangalore in March 2017, he suggested Australian skipper Steve Smith was being dishonest ("I don't want to use the C-word") when he looked up to the dressing-room for advice on a referral. Smith dismissed it as a "brain fade", but Kohli had made his point – as he did while gesturing, conducting the cheers of the crowd, telling an opponent off, or showing his disappointment when things were going wrong. If you were to watch a telecast focused exclusively on Kohli's reactions, you could write a convincing report of the flow of the game. His face mirrors events.

The finest all-round batsman of the year is, in his heart, an old-fashioned Test player, conscious of the sport's folklore, and his role in keeping the format alive. There is no contradiction in his energetic and innovative displays in white-ball cricket. In the 50-over format, he is the finest chaser in history: by the end of 2017, he averaged 93 when India won batting second, with 17 centuries. His 32 hundreds overall were topped only by Tendulkar's 49. Both have scored more centuries than their age, like golfers carding a round in fewer strokes than theirs. And in Twenty20 internationals, Kohli has extended the limits of the possible by scoring at 137 per 100 balls, without any apparent strain or ugly strokeplay.

Rahul Dravid summed him up: "He has to do what he has to do to get the best out of himself. I would have been inauthentic if I had tried to wear tattoos and behaved like Kohli."

Kohli's psychological influence as captain has also been significant. In his first Test in charge, at Adelaide in December 2014, India were set 364 on the final day, and decided to go for it. Despite the second of his two centuries in the game, they fell short by 49 runs. Not since Tiger Pataudi had an Indian captain been so willing to risk defeat in pursuit of victory. Since then, Kohli has taken ownership of Indian cricket, bringing to it a rare energy and an even rarer focus on physical fitness. His big scores are tribute as much to the state of his technique as the state of his body. "I will not ask anyone to do anything I will not do myself," he has said.

At the midpoint of his career, he is the only batsman with an average above 50 in all three formats, though his legacy as captain may be settled in 2018, after tours of South Africa and Australia, where India have never won a Test series, and England, where they have won one since 1986. As a batsman, England is Kohli's last frontier; he averaged 13 on his previous visit, in 2014, some 40 below his career figure. There is more than one score to settle.

THE LEADING CRICKETER IN THE WORLD

2003 Ricky Ponting (Australia)
2004 Shane Warne (Australia)
2005 Andrew Flintoff (England)
2006 Muttiah Muralitharan (Sri Lanka)
2007 Jacques Kallis (South Africa)
2008 Virender Sehwag (India)
2009 Virender Sehwag (India)
2010 Sachin Tendulkar (India)
2011 Kumar Sangakkara (Sri Lanka)
2012 Michael Clarke (Australia)
2013 Dale Steyn (South Africa)
2014 Kumar Sangakkara (Sri Lanka)
2015 Kane Williamson (New Zealand)
2016 Virat Kohli (India)
2017 Virat Kohli (India)

A list of notional past winners from 1900 appeared in Wisden 2007, *page 32.*

WISDEN WRITING COMPETITION WINNER IN 2017

The power and the glory

ROBERT STANIER

Each year, the clergy of the Church of England compete in an inter-diocesan cricket competition, the *Church Times* Cup; each year, hope springs up in the souls of the participants; each year, for all of us except those in London diocese, the season ends in defeat. If you can remember Surrey in the 1950s or Yorkshire in the 1970s, you can imagine London in the 2010s. The other finalist changes, but London are always there, with a seemingly endless stream of virile curates.

I was ordained not in London, but in Southwark. We are a middling diocese, who win and lose in roughly equal measure, but what follows is the tale of our one great triumph. Some may think of 2012 as the year of the Olympics, but for those of us involved it will always be the year of Southwark's glory.

It started with the arrival of Heston, a charming curate from Cape Town, who smote the ball through the off-side ring like Samson wielding the jawbone of an ass through the Philistines. St Albans did not know what had hit them when we chased down 270 in 40 overs.

On to a quarter-final against Exeter, which we won – though not before Heston top-edged a pull into his face, and ended up in casualty. With our Samson out, we were destined to lose the semi-final to a strong Lichfield side. But it was rained off: Southwark went through by a quirk of run-rate in the earlier rounds so obscure that even Duckworth, Lewis or Stern's algorithmic excellence would have been hard put to understand it.

And so to Southwark's first *Church Times* final since 1975 – against our nemesis, London. Heston was fit again, though his wife insisted on his wearing a helmet. By happy chance the Petertide ordinations also brought us Susikaran, brought up in Chennai, bowling the sort of nibbling medium-pace you associate more naturally with the Lancashire leagues. Armed with these two men from the remoter outposts of the Anglican Communion, we stood a chance.

London set us 232. In reply, we limped along; Heston, in his helmet for the first time, simply could not time the ball. We still needed 35 from four overs when the Reverends Coulson and Jelley came together. They had a combined age of 122, but the determination displayed only by Shackleton in the Antarctic – or Southwark clergy beaten by London every year for the previous two decades. They ran like demented rabbits, and brought us home with two balls to spare.

The victory has not been repeated. Heston and Susikaran have departed for Leeds and Portsmouth dioceses. Before we played London in 2017 (a 125-run defeat), I overheard one of their players say to another in the changing-rooms: "We don't have to worry about this lot, do we? They hardly ever beat us."

"No, but when they do," said the other, "they go on about it for years." He was right: we do. And I have just done it again.

Robert Stanier is vicar of St Andrew and St Mark, Surbiton.

THE COMPETITION

Wisden received 120 entries for its sixth writing competition, more than ever before. They poured in from Ireland, Italy, India and, if not Indonesia or Israel, then from many other countries – and an array of counties. The standard was astonishingly high, and Wisden remains hugely appreciative of the industry, imagination and inventiveness of all entrants. All were equally welcome, and all were read by the editorial team. The business of judging, however, becomes no easier. The prize is as ever: publication, adulation, and an invitation to the launch dinner, held at Lord's in April.

The rules are also unchanged. Anyone who has never been commissioned by Wisden can take part. Entries, which should not have been submitted before (and are restricted to a maximum of two per person), must be:

1. the entrant's own work
2. unpublished in any medium
3. received by November 30, 2018
4. between 480 and 520 words (excluding the title)
5. neither libellous nor offensive
6. related to cricket, but not a match report.

Articles should be sent to almanack@wisdenalmanack.com, with "Writing Competition 2018" as the subject line. (Those without access to email may post their entry to Writing Competition 2018, John Wisden & Co, 13 Old Aylesfield, Golden Pot, Alton, Hampshire GU34 4BY, *though email is much preferred.*) Please provide your name, address and telephone number. All entrants will be contacted by the end of 2018, and the winner informed by the end of January 2019. (Please contact Wisden if your entry has not been acknowledged by the end of December.) Past winners of this competition, Bloomsbury staff and those who in the editor's opinion have a working relationship with Wisden are ineligible. The editor's decision is final.

THE 2017 ENTRANTS

Lee Ashton, Matthew Atkins, Dwarkesh Bagri, Austin Baird, Jim Barclay, Simon Barton, Anik Basu, Mike Battrum, Will Baxter, Mike Bechley, Andrew Beech, Jonathan Belbin, Ian Bennett, Rob Blackhall, Gary Brampton, Nick Brown, Paul Bullman, Andrew Carr, Paul Caswell, Mohit Choudhary, Paul Clifford, Richard Conway, John Cooper, Alex Crouch, Tim Curtis, Geoffrey Easton, Tom Evans, Shahrukh Faisal, David Fanthorpe, David Fraser, Gareth Frith, Deborah Gahan, Mark Gannaway, James Gardener, Allan Garley, Jim Gibb, Nick Gormack, Steve Green, Gary Hansman, Philip Hardman, Michael Hill, Adam Hopkins, Keith Horsley, Andrew Jefford, Janani N, Jamie Keir, John Kirby, John Kirkaldy, Simon Lamb, Pete Langman, Andrew Leeming, George Lillywhite, Richard List, Roger Long, Alan Lovell, Karen Lowther, Mark McCaughan, Carolyn McCrae, Hamish McDouall, Don McLaren, Ian Marshall, Thomas Maslona, Patrick Medhurst-Feeney, Martin Mellors, Kevin Menhinick, Rob Minto, Anthony Morrissey, David Moyes, Colin Norton, Graham Parker, Stephen Pickles, David Potter, Gordon Price, Paajivs Punter, Rajiv Radhakrishnan, Richard Reardon, John Rigg, Ken Rignall, Mark Sanderson, Abhijato Sensarma, Christopher Sharp, Oliver Sigsworth, David Sim, John Sleigh, Chris Smith, Chris Sowton, Robert Stanier, Richard Staniforth, Peter Stone, Thomas Stuttard, Seth Thomas, Ian Tier, Jain Vedant, Peter Vousden, Andrew Walker, David Walsh, Rick Walton, Stephen Ward, Peter Warwick, Ben Watson, Simon Wilson, Ashley Wren and Tom Young.

WINNERS

2012	Brian Carpenter
2013	Liam Cromar
2014	Peter Casterton
2015	Will Beaudouin
2016	John Pitt
2017	**Robert Stanier**

FIFTY YEARS OF THE PCA

Part of the union

MATTHEW ENGEL

Long before the start of play, the autograph collectors were there in force outside the big marquee. These were not, I thought to myself, the dressing-room johnnies of my era. Now the huntsmen were as old as their quarry. And then I realised. That's precisely who they were: the boys of half a century ago, still following the hobby of their youth, politely accosting the ageing cricketers as they walked – often stiffly – from the car park to join their comrades.

It was day two of the Cheltenham Festival, the day the Professional Cricketers' Association held their annual gathering – the national version of the counties' old players' lunches which have become a yearly fixture on the circuit. This reunion, however, was special: the 50th anniversary of the PCA, founded in 1967 when Fred Rumsey, then of Somerset, summoned a representative from each county to London. The players met the leaders of the football equivalent, Jimmy Hill and Cliff Lloyd, and diffidently began to formulate and articulate their views on cricket's future. Some at Lord's thought it was the beginning of the end: a small-scale mutiny that might lead to insurrection.

Alex Morton, Getty Images

Founding fathers: Mike Smedley, Don Shepherd, Fred Rumsey, Eric Russell and Harold Goldblatt.

Rumsey had been plotting for over a year. He would ask Somerset's opponents if he could address their players; surprisingly, most agreed. Less surprisingly, Rumsey had received a phone call from Warwickshire's Jack Bannister, one of the most energetic and lateral-thinking of players. Bannister was to hold every office in the association over the next three decades. He died in 2016. But four of those present at that first meeting made it to Cheltenham, all still recognisable. Rumsey, as dominant and burly as in his youth; the others as smiley and slim as one remembers – Mike Smedley of Nottinghamshire, Eric Russell of Middlesex, Don Shepherd of Glamorgan.

Shep was a month short of 90, just behind Roy Booth of Worcestershire as senior man in the tent. He was a most improbable revolutionary: "I hardly knew what a union was, or anything." And indeed he was the most uncomplaining of cricketers – more wickets than anyone who never played a Test, but a man who could still say: "I was a very lucky boy." Yet he shared the general sense that cricketers were not treated fairly. So did Russell, who took the practical step of roping in Harold Goldblatt, an accountant whose clients included most of the Middlesex and Surrey teams, not that they had much money to count. Goldblatt in turn brought in the lawyer Lawrie Doffman, and the infant body – then known as the Cricketers' Association – had the back-up expertise it desperately needed. Goldblatt, rabbinically bearded, was an honoured guest at Cheltenham.

Rumsey identified three burning issues: money, health and registration. The last proved simple, because the traditional practice of imposing a year's ban on players who wished to move counties turned out to be unlawful and had to be scrapped. Other issues took a little longer. "It was a voice, that was all," said David Graveney, whose uncle Tom was infamously banned for a year in 1961 after leaving Gloucestershire. "In the era when my father [Ken] and uncle played, there was no question of medical insurance, no pension." In 1998, David became the PCA's first full-time chief executive.

In the late 1990s, two cricketers suffered terrible off-field injuries. One, Winston Davis, a former West Indies and Northamptonshire fast bowler, had recently retired; the other, Yorkshire's Jamie Hood, had barely started. Both were left as tetraplegics, and initially the system was not geared to help them. "The condition of both Winston and Jamie presented new challenges for the organisation," said Graveney. "We didn't have enough resources to make a meaningful difference. Over time we have been able to do a great deal."

At Cheltenham, a smiling Davis steered into the tent in his wheelchair, having organised the trip on his specially adapted computer and travelled to the ground in his specially adapted vehicle, both provided by the PCA. Hood was not there, but Graveney said: "There can be no more humbling experience than to visit Jamie at his converted bungalow in Marske and admire his courage and optimism." The PCA have become an enveloping organisation, dealing with everything from mental health to motor insurance. "I feel very fortunate to be playing in this era," said Daryl Mitchell of Worcestershire, the current chairman. "I think what Fred and the boys did 50 years ago has stood us in good stead."

The 20-wicket men: Ray Bailey and Brian Crump.

And yet. It didn't seem to me as though envy of the young was the overwhelming mood of the gathering. For a start, as is traditional in all hospitality tents and boxes, the sport laid on for them was not a primary concern. It was hardly a dull game. Twenty-five wickets had fallen on the first day, and it was over around teatime, to the consternation of Gloucestershire officials – as two days' festival takings crumbled to nothingness – and the complete indifference of the old pros. "Have you watched a single ball?" I asked Chris Old. "No," replied Chilly firmly. "I've seen two balls. Two wickets." He captured the old pro's pride in knowing precisely when to watch.

Old was just one of a crowd of Test players scattered round the tent – there was MJK and Giff and Shutt (hair jet-black still) and Steely (hair steel-grey still, though I think if anything he looks a bit younger) and Proccy and Foxy (whose beard is more George V than rabbinical), dear old Chat and Percy and more*… Nearly all were as instantly recognisable – except Foxy – as in their heyday. And that was true not only of the Test players. Because up to the 1980s, county cricketers quickly got established both in the community of the circuit and in the minds of its distant followers.

"There was no money, no security, no central contracts. So the camaraderie was much stronger. It wasn't about money. It was about playing a game of cricket. Now it's a livelihood." My notes suggest it was Neal Radford, a quite intense man, who said that. But, you know, it was a long day and I had a lot of

* M. J. K. Smith, Norman Gifford, Ken Shuttleworth, David Steele (his brother John was also there), Mike Procter, Graeme Fowler, Bob Taylor and Pat Pocock.

conversations, and the notebook ended up more illegible than usual. It might have been blithe Pat Pocock. Or Kevin Emery. They were both part of the same group, still lingering after tea. It could have been anyone, really. Because they all seemed to feel the same: yes, they were treated badly; but by crikey they were great times. As Don Shepherd put it: "When you went for a win and there was a two quid bonus on it, you never thought of the money, you just wanted to win the game."

Back together were men for ever linked on the field. D. H. K. Smith and P. J. K. Gibbs, the watchful Derbyshire openers from days of greentops and mordant humour; a trio of umpires – Ken and Roy Palmer and David Constant – in echelon round the same lunch table, more like a slip cordon. And then there was little Brian Crump and Ray Bailey. For them it was another 50th anniversary: in 1967, the summer Rumsey was finalising his plans, the pair bowled unchanged for Northamptonshire against Glamorgan at Sophia Gardens, taking all 20 wickets.

Neither looked much older. I wandered with them round the ground for an ice cream – not, we all agreed, quite as good as the Gallone's sold at Northampton. Then they moved on to 1965, the year they coulda-woulda-shoulda won the Championship, but got done on the line by Worcestershire. "Second in the Championship! I got a ballpoint pen," recalled Bailey. Crumpy was outraged. "I never got a ballpoint pen!" he wailed.

At lunch the roll was read of newly absent friends, those who had died since the last gathering. Not everyone had heard each item of news. Jaws dropped from time to time; some guests stared for a moment or two into space as they digested a loss; there was the odd sotto voce "bloody hell". The undercurrent of sadness never quite went away, but nor did the sense of continued renewal. Chris Old told me of how he sat at home one day watching a Yorkshire and England batsman smack it through the covers. "'I've just seen David hit a four,' I shouted. 'You mean Jonny,' came an exasperated female voice from the other room. 'No, I don't. It was *exactly* like his dad.'"

But as tea was served and the on-field players vanished towards their fancy cars, the late-stayers turned to what has been lost from the game. It was all about comradeship, and the effect on the cricket itself. County pros now might go years without playing against some teams, except perhaps in a Twenty20. They hardly ever come up against any England stars. And, between the warm-downs and the ice baths and the rest of it, they might never even have a friendly conversation with their opponents, let alone a pint.

"Spin bowling has gone down and down and down," said Pocock. "There's a lack of experience and knowledge being passed on." The Surrey seamer Graham Monkhouse said: "I'm still involved with club cricket and it's just the same in that. One team's over *here* and the other's over *there*. And they never chat." Monkhouse added that the best advice he ever had came in the bar from Jack Birkenshaw, when he was umpiring. "He said, 'Son, if you ever want LBs, get closer to the stumps.' " That sort of conversation happens less too.

The last of the autograph seekers were still there as I left. At the start, a fair-sized group of kids had been on the far side of the ground. They were long gone now, not much interested in the players, past or present. They had been

Alex Morton, Getty Images

On the hunt: M. J. K. Smith obliges a line of admirers.

in the nets doing cricket-related exercises, which offered far more inclusive fun than just watching, or sticking them on the field with a hard ball, and few having anything to do. But they were learning cricket as a foreign language; maybe they will fall in love with its grammar and vocabulary, as my generation – gifted or not – did with our peers through our games in the back gardens and back alleys of England, and as kids still do in Karachi, Kolkata and Kandy. But probably not.

So I wondered about them. And I wondered too about Daryl Mitchell. Will he be back at Cheltenham for the centenary gathering, an elder statesman of the game, reminiscing with his contemporaries about the good times, the fun he had, what's wrong with cricket in 2067, and how this lot don't know they're born? I do hope so, because that's the way it should be.

Six weeks later, a week after his 90th, the news broke that Don Shepherd had died. In 2018, his name will be read out, and there will be sadness at his absence. But he lived the contented life of a fulfilled county cricketer. And, as he said to me in that tent last summer, he was a very lucky boy.

Matthew Engel began collecting cricketers' autographs before the invention of the PCA, but gave up when he started reporting the game in 1972.

FIVE CRICKETERS OF THE YEAR

The Five Cricketers of the Year represent a tradition that dates back in Wisden *to 1889, making this the oldest individual award in cricket. The Five are picked by the editor, and the selection is based, primarily but not exclusively, on the players' influence on the previous English season. No one can be chosen more than once. A list of past Cricketers of the Year appears on page 1412.*

Shai Hope

DEAN WILSON

First come the strains of calypso music – maybe "Island in the Sun" by Harry Belafonte – then the camera pans from a radiant sun in a blue sky to its reflection in gently lapping waves. The waves meet a sandy beach, where palm trees peer over some boys playing cricket. This is the Hollywood opening to a film set in the Caribbean, and the picture-postcard start to life enjoyed by Shai Hope, and his older brother Kyle, on their path to international cricket.

"We lived about five minutes' walk from the beach," says Shai. "After school we would go down there and play with a tennis ball or soft ball. That helped my flexibility and my movement from a young age."

Fast forward a decade and a half, and the brothers are still batting and chasing a ball around, this time on the green grass of Headingley. The sun is hidden behind cloud, and there are no gentle waves – just the dripping from the plastic glasses that form the beer snake along the White Rose Stand. But in late August last year, Shai Hope seemed in his element.

Headingley has been home to Herbert Sutcliffe, Len Hutton, Geoff Boycott, Michael Vaughan and Joe Root, yet by the end of the Second Test between England and West Indies, Hope had become the first cricketer to score two hundreds in a first-class game there. This was the 534th, spread across 127 years. Either it was a statistical anomaly, or Hope – finally fulfilling the potential spotted by various selectors and coaches – was quite a player.

SHAI DIEGO HOPE, born in Saint Michael, Barbados, on November 10, 1993, made his bow in Test cricket against England in May 2015 at his home ground, the Kensington Oval – a game West Indies would unexpectedly win to square the three-match series. He had long been earmarked for international cricket, but many wondered whether, at the age of 21, he was ready. No matter: a double-hundred for Barbados against the Windward Islands at the same venue seven weeks earlier had caught the selectors' attention, and soon he was facing James Anderson and Stuart Broad. It didn't go well – Hope made five and nine – but he was picked for the subsequent home series against Australia, falling three times out of four to Mitchell Johnson, then for a tour of Sri Lanka. The scores were yet to flow, but his Test career was up and running.

Hope had been spotted in Barbados by former Sussex and England batsman Alan Wells, and included in the first draft of a programme run in conjunction with the Barbados Cricket Association. The scheme sent a student on a scholarship to Bede's School near Hailsham on the edge of the Sussex Downs, where Wells was in charge of cricket. Hope captained the first team in 2011, aged 17, and 2012, following in the footsteps of Middlesex off-spinner Ollie Rayner and Sussex batsman Luke Wells, Alan's son. And he was grateful for what he learned.

"I would say that was a life-changing experience. At Bede's, I mixed with 16 different nationalities under one roof. Being able to adjust to certain people's lifestyles, and how they do things, was a real experience off the field. On the field, the incredible facilities helped me develop my game and make the most of the ability I had."

Hope appeared to be made of the right stuff. His dad Ian was a decent club cricketer who stopped playing to watch his boys, while mum Quinta played netball and cricket, enjoying bowling more than batting, to her sons' amusement. The reports from England and in Barbados were of a dedicated individual. Those who know him well say he is not demonstrative, but focused on meeting challenges. His coach at the West Indies high performance centre, Graeme West, was struck by his commitment: "It was always a case of when Shai made it, rather than if."

And yet that first foray into Test cricket suggested it did indeed come too soon: in his first 16 innings, he failed to pass 41. A breakthrough came in a win over Pakistan in May 2017, again at Bridgetown, where he made a patient second-innings 90 to scrape together a target of 188. The Pakistanis were skittled for 81.

Even so, on arrival in England shortly after, expectations were low, and lower still after West Indies lost the day/night Test at Edgbaston by an innings. At that point Hope, who made 15 and four as they lost 19 wickets in a day, was averaging 18 from 21 Test innings. With Kyle making 25 and 12, there were concerns that West Indies might soon be without a Hope.

Leeds changed all that. First, Shai made 147, putting on 246 with Kraigg Brathwaite to earn West Indies a lead of 169. Then, with his team chasing a distant 322, he took them to victory with an unbeaten 118, his alliance with Brathwaite this time worth 144. He conducted a series of post-match interviews with such unflustered dignity one wondered whether he quite realised what he had achieved.

A classy 62 at Lord's, where England resumed normal service, confirmed he was now the wicket the opposition craved most and, when he began a two-Test series in Bulawayo against Zimbabwe with scores of 90 not out and 44, his average reached a respectable 35. But the memories of Leeds lingered.

"No one expected us to win at Headingley," says Shai. "That was a huge motivation for us. Why shouldn't we compete and win? We have pride in the badge and we are proud of where we come from. There's an expectation now, and I'm happy with that."

Heather Knight

VITHUSHAN EHANTHARAJAH

Heather Knight was unwell. She had drunk only one beer, so it couldn't be that. It might have been some dodgy chicken. The changing-rooms were too far away, so she made a beeline for the Grace Gates. "I had to run around the corner from Lord's," she remembers. "I was sick next to a very expensive car. Luckily no one saw!" She *was* lucky: she was still in her England kit, and more than 26,000 were at Lord's that day, most of them still there, reeling from one of the summer's great finales. Knight composed herself, returned to the ground and rejoined the celebrations.

India had needed 38 off 44 balls with seven wickets in hand to win the World Cup, but Knight maintained her cool, as she had all tournament. She had managed the last throes of the three-run group-stage win over Australia, and spent the denouement of the semi-final against South Africa calming a nervous Alex Hartley, England's No. 11, on the balcony; Hartley wasn't needed, but that wasn't the point. Now, in the final, Knight handed the ball to Anya Shrubsole, who charged in from the Pavilion End and took care of the rest.

Knight's contribution to England's triumph extended beyond the armband. A maiden one-day international hundred, against Pakistan, and two fifties meant a personal tally of 364 runs at 45 – despite her preparation being stunted by a stress fracture of the foot in March. She carried the injury with her to the end of the year, through the Kia Super League, where she led Western Storm to glory, and through the Ashes in Australia, where England battled back to draw the multi-points series 8–8. Another scan showed the problem had worsened: a period of rest was prescribed. She deserved it.

HEATHER CLARE KNIGHT was born in Rochdale on December 26, 1990. Her parents, Mike and Becky, moved to Plymouth and encouraged their two children to pursue their passions and, aged eight, Heather followed her older brother Steve to Plymstock Cricket Club. A year later, she excelled in her first hard-ball boys' game, finding herself on a hat-trick. "It was filthy seamers back then, not filthy off-spin," she says. "It gave the boys a bit of a shock and I absolutely loved it."

Knight quickly earned a place in the Devon side, but their third-division status meant higher honours proved elusive. So she joined Reading, and a year later became eligible for Berkshire – a Division One county. Knight was now testing herself against England players; Berkshire team-mates included Isa Guha and Claire Taylor. Even so, thanks to the taxi of mum and dad, Knight remained in Plymouth. She would play men's cricket in Devon on Saturday, get driven to Berkshire, play club or county cricket, then head back to Plymouth on Sunday. It was a 400-mile round-trip. "I'd revise for my GCSEs in the car. Then on Monday I'd go to school, and my parents would go to work. They didn't have much of a social life." Still, the grind paid off.

In 2008, Knight had made the England Academy, and impressed Mark Lane, then the national coach. Higher education beckoned at one of the MCCUs, and in 2009 Knight turned down Cambridge to read biomedical science and physiology at Cardiff. In her second term, playing for the university in an indoor tournament at Lord's, she got a surprise call: she had been drafted on to England's tour of India as a replacement. This time, she drove herself: from London to Cardiff, then back to Heathrow for a flight next morning. There was only one problem.

"I had enjoyed my freshers' week a lot, so I was a little bit podgy. I turned up overweight and jet-lagged, while my team-mates had been there for two or three weeks already, and hadn't had a great time of it. I'm not sure I made the best first impression." Despite the excess baggage, Knight opened the batting in the fifth one-day international and top-scored with 49; England won by two wickets. From then on, she knuckled down.

Soon she became a woman for all occasions, able to bat anywhere in the top six in all formats. But it was Test cricket that put her name in lights. Two and a half years after her Ashes debut at Sydney, Knight was saving her side's skin at Wormsley with a seven-hour 157. England went on to regain the Ashes. By now, the management knew she was captaincy material. Appointed deputy to Charlotte Edwards in 2014, she was the obvious candidate to replace her after England crashed out of the 2016 World Twenty20 in India.

All the same, she had to work on her personal skills, speaking in front of others and – with the help of the team psychologists – developing an appreciation of different personalities and their motivations. "We've got such a range of interesting characters," she says. "Previously, we had swept things under the carpet – like how we have reacted under pressure. Going into the World Cup, you felt a shift. Everyone was more honest and open. Suddenly there were ten people talking in meetings instead of two or three."

It showed. Rarely have an England side been so free-wheeling and self-assured; Knight's own transformation has been one of the best examples. Between her debut in 2010 and the end of 2015, she averaged 28 in ODIs with a strike-rate of 61. Since then, those figures have been 50 and 76, and she has hit 12 of her 13 sixes.

She is still striving to improve. Between winning the KSL and heading out to the Ashes, she worked two or three times a day with batting coach Alastair Maiden on her backlift, so she could hit harder on slower wickets. A fortnight before leaving for Australia in October, it clicked. She scored 335 runs in the series at 55, and became the second to register a half-century in all formats on a women's international tour, after Karen Rolton for Australia in England in 2005. "Cricket is always about trying to master the game," she says. "You never do, but it's fun along the way."

Jamie Porter

WILL MACPHERSON

During the Ashes whitewash of 2013-14, Jamie Porter was a 20-year-old recruitment consultant in London who believed his cricket career was all but over. He had been on the books of Middlesex and his native Essex, spent three years with the MCC Young Cricketers, and time at the Darren Lehmann Cricket Academy in Adelaide and in the Australian grades. But there he was, unwanted, working at a medical recruitment specialist in Enfield.

"I felt a bit unlucky," he says. "I felt I'd been messed around a bit in cricket. I really enjoyed the job, but I always wanted to be a cricketer and would take any avenue possible to get there. I never quite gave up."

Four years on, England were off to Australia again, and this time Porter's only visit to his London office was to see old colleagues and his sister Nicole, who still works there. After a season in which his 75 wickets helped Essex romp to their first Championship title in 25 years, he was being mentioned as a potential Ashes tourist. He was named Championship Player of the Year by the Cricket Writers' Club (even in the summer of Sangakkara), and Young Player of the Year by the PCA. Then came a stress fracture to his back, ruling him out of his first tour with England Lions, and ending any Ashes dreams. "I was brought back down to earth pretty quickly," he smiles.

JAMES ALEXANDER PORTER was born in Leytonstone on May 25, 1993, the son of Steve, who also works in recruitment, and Debbie, a teaching assistant. From a young age, he was all about East London, West Ham and seam bowling. He played Essex age-group cricket until he was discarded at 15; mates at Middlesex asked if he wanted a trial. It worked, but not permanently, and he was once more on the outside, looking in.

From that point, Porter's ascent was rapid. In 2014, he performed well for Chingford – where he played with his best friend and future county team-mate Dan Lawrence – and earned a place with Essex Seconds. He promptly quit recruitment, a decision he calls "a bit rogue", adding: "I'd have looked a right muppet if I'd asked for the job back at the end of the week." There was no need: he played three Championship games in September 2014, then took 115 first-class wickets across the next two seasons.

In 2017, everything changed. At the age of 23, he found himself Essex's key bowler: his mentors David Masters and Graham Napier had retired after the club achieved promotion. He was joined by South African off-spinner Simon Harmer, who raced him all season for Championship wickets (Porter won by three), as well as by the overseas pace of Neil Wagner and Mohammad Amir, and a revolving door of locally sourced seamers. But Porter was the fulcrum, and missed just one match, when he was called up by the Lions to face South Africa A – and took three wickets in each innings.

His success was built on a rubbery right wrist that extracted seam movement even on the flattest surfaces, and an unerring ability to locate a length that appeared drivable, but was not. He had spent a quiet off-season building his strength and working on bowling round the wicket, providing him with another option against Division One's glut of top-order left-handers.

"My job is to take wickets with the new ball," he says. "It's the best time to bowl. You won't see me bowl short with it – I feel like bouncers are a waste when the ball's new. Top of off, stand that seam up. I'm asking more questions that way.

"I realised early on last summer there was pressure on me. We always had one raw bowler in the side, and I was both the strike threat and the guy who had to keep it tight. My role quickly became helping younger bowlers, just like Napes and Hoddy [Masters] did for me, which is weird at my age. But I relished it. And I received a great bit of advice from Graham Gooch. He said, when you're in form, train harder, play more. I did that."

Of Porter's 75 wickets, 27 came in the first ten overs of an innings (no one else took more than 13 in that period), and 56 were top-six batsmen (the next highest in Division One was 38). He believes that his own slightly convoluted path, and the similar stories of some of his team-mates – such as opening batsman Nick Browne, who fought his way up through the local league system – contributed to Essex's remarkable triumph. For most of the year, eight of the XI were home-grown, while captain Ryan ten Doeschate was in his 15th season with the county.

"We're all great mates, and we loved our success," he says. "I truly believe we have something no other club have. When we were celebrating after the last win over Yorkshire, it was the only time I've felt like a celebrity. I was about ten metres away from my family, and I couldn't get to them! Everyone wanted a photo. For a good hour I moved about five metres. Insane. Carnage. The best day of them all."

Time outside cricket's bubble, he says, has made him hungrier. "I appreciate what I've got, but I also play with no fear, because if it does end I'm not scared of the real world. I know I can go out and work and be happy. That gives me a bit of an advantage over many of the guys I play against. I know what the real world is like."

Natalie Sciver

ISABELLE WESTBURY

Pick a stroke to define last summer, and few would quibble with "Natmeg". Pick a player, and you won't go far wrong with its exponent, Natalie Sciver, the linchpin of the England side which earned World Cup glory in front of a full house at Lord's. If the tournament proved a turning point for women's cricket, it was a coming of age for Sciver.

Her early international career had shown promise with bat and ball across all three formats – a true, and natural, all-rounder – but consistency had been elusive. Then, after four years without a hundred for England, two came along at once in 2017. Already boasting an ODI strike-rate of over 100, Sciver smashed 137 off 92 balls against Pakistan at Leicester. It was an innings described by captain Heather Knight as the best she'd seen – better even than Sciver's 80 off 33 balls against the Pakistanis at Worcester the previous summer. Two weeks after Grace Road came 129 off 111 against the fancied New Zealanders at Derby. To prove it wasn't all brute force, she then made a well-crafted fifty against India in the final to help deliver the World Cup.

"I feel I can now produce that kind of innings," she says. "Before, I had gone in, and just wanted to score quickly. But Robbo [England coach Mark Robinson] and the coaching staff have taught me a little bit of patience – taking the easy runs when they're on offer, but learning how to build an innings."

For someone who has spoken about the difficulty of overcoming the self-doubt and batting demons she feared would plague her game – "Am I going to get out? Am I even good enough?" – Sciver has flourished. It helps that under Robinson's guidance, England are more relaxed and assured than ever. In a team of quietly spoken individuals – Sciver among them – she is able to channel her energy straight on to the pitch.

While it's futile to compare women with men, the players themselves look to what they know. Growing up, Sciver dreamed of emulating David Beckham or Andrew Flintoff, while England team-mate Jenny Gunn says of her batting: "She hits balls so hard, she hits like a man." Meanwhile, Knight had no qualms after that hundred against Pakistan in hailing her "our Ben Stokes", though Sciver is quick to point out that this is confined to the field.

The Natmeg, a deft clip between the legs, initially arose to overcome a technical defect: her stance is so wide she struggles to adjust her feet quickly enough against the yorker, finding it easier to flick her wrists instead. She was playing the shot during the inaugural women's Big Bash in Australia in 2015-16, so the attention that came with it last summer took her by surprise. "I'd just scored a hundred against New Zealand, but no one asked me about that," she says. "They only wanted to know about the shot through the legs."

Sciver's story is so compelling because it mirrors the game itself. Just as the World Cup did more to raise the profile of women's cricket than years of hard graft by those before it, the Natmeg elevated Sciver on to a platform almost overnight. Richard, her father, tried to persuade his daughter to copyright the term. Typically self-effacing, she refused.

NATALIE RUTH SCIVER was born in Tokyo on August 20, 1992. If variety is the spice of life, Sciver's is a dish full of flavour. Her mother, Julia, is a diplomat, so the family travelled in Nat's early years, from Japan to the Netherlands, then to Poland. She didn't reach England until she was 14. She was raised amid an eclectic mix of sports, depending largely on what was on offer at the time: tennis (she couldn't stop hitting the ball out of the court), basketball, football, and only later cricket, which she finally settled on because she "got on more with the girls at the cricket club in Stoke D'Abernon". Sciver quickly made her way up the ranks from school (Epsom College) to county (Surrey). By the age of 20, she was playing for England.

She made her international bow as a skiddy, exciting bowler who could also drive the ball hard, very hard. And she showed early promise, taking three for 28 to win the match award in only her second game, a one-day international against Pakistan at Loughborough in July 2013. A few months later, against New Zealand in Bridgetown, she became the first – and so far only – English cricketer to take a Twenty20 international hat-trick.

Despite cementing a regular spot in the England side, there was a sense Sciver had more still to offer. Katherine Brunt – her team-mate, best friend and, of late, her landlord – has witnessed her growth. "For Nat, it has been a bit of a learning curve," she says. "She came into the squad while at Loughborough University and you know what that can be like – you're young, immature and having fun, not taking anything too seriously. But Nat was just going about it her way; being able to express herself has made her the player she is today. It's not like it didn't work for her previously, but it was a case of putting that all together and learning when to play shots and when to take risks."

A contract with Melbourne Stars saw her billed as one of the big names at the 2016-17 WBBL. She struggled with the bat, but the added responsibility and expectation meant that, by the time the World Cup came around last summer, Sciver knew exactly what she was capable of. As her father points out, it was her all-round package – as much as the batting feats and Natmegs – which did the job: three for three against West Indies, an athletic catch to prevent a near-certain six by Australia's Ellyse Perry, then the run-out of Indian captain Mithali Raj in the final. In years to come, perhaps the next Ben Stokes will be taking tips from Nat Sciver's highlights reel.

Anya Shrubsole

TANYA ALDRED

Anya Shrubsole folds up five foot ten into the large marshmallow doubling as a chair in an ECB meeting room. It is lunchtime, and already she has done a couple of interviews to camera, been to the gym, grabbed a paper bag of food from Pret. This evening it is frock up and away, off to another December awards dinner.

It has been quite a year, one in which women's cricket in the UK was catapulted from semi-obscurity to front page – and Shrubsole with it. She was the face of England's World Cup success, belting the winning boundary in the semi-final against South Africa, then conjuring the best bowling figures – six for 46 – in a final.

That extraordinary Lord's Sunday in July, when the stands were packed with colour – vivid anoraks, brazen umbrellas – and women and children were everywhere; when the noise was swelling into every elbow and every knee, so that the players were deaf to each other; when, from the gloaming, with India ticking towards victory, Shrubsole produced her spell. Heather Knight had brought her back for the 43rd over, and her first two balls disappeared for four, but with her fifth she trapped the dangerous Punam Raut. It was the first of her five wickets for 11 in 18 legal deliveries.

In the penultimate over, so nearly there, India needed ten with one wicket in hand, and Poonam Yadav ladled to mid-off, where Jenny Gunn put down the catch. A ghastly silence descended, but Shrubsole was phlegmatic. "I had the ball in my hand, and I knew the No. 11 was on strike. I'd just got four quick wickets, and if you're not confident at that stage, I don't think you ever will be." Next ball she charged up, her fluid policeman-plod action at full surge, and yorked Rajeshwari Gayakwad. Lord's erupted. Shrubsole ran down the pitch and roared, arms outstretched, body arched, hazel ponytail hanging down, a symbol of female power echoing out to those watching girls: this game, this game is for you too.

ANYA SHRUBSOLE was born in Bath on December 7, 1991, and spent her childhood in the same city, in the same house, until she moved to Loughborough University to study psychology. She is the middle child of three, squeezed between older brother Tom and sister Lauren. Their postage-stamp garden was the setting for hours of football, tennis, rugby and cricket – with four for a hit to the back wall, and one for hitting the cage of the guinea pigs, Joey and Chandler. Sam, her mum, looked on in resignation as her older daughter and husband Ian competed over absolutely everything, with sulks to match. Anya was an all-round sportswoman, swimming for her club and playing football for Bristol Rovers, but cricket came calling first, offering a clear pathway for progression.

By 12, she was playing for Somerset's first team, and age-group cricket for Somerset boys. There were comments, of course there were, but luckily she is "a water-off-a-duck's-back kind of person". She was the first girl to be selected for the Somerset Academy at 13, picked by Kevin Shine, now the ECB's lead fast-bowling coach: "She was so much better than any other girl – it wasn't even close. She was quicker, had more control, knew what she wanted to do and was incredibly dedicated." Education was at Hayesfield, a local state school. She loved the work, but didn't fit in. "I was leading a different life, because I was playing for England while others were worrying about fake ID." There was a World Cup tour just before her A-levels, but she still managed an A and two Bs.

Her England debut came in 2008 as a 16-year-old, and she won the match award in her first Twenty20 international nine days later, but injury slowed her progress. The fitness required by England was a shock, and she struggled. But in early 2012 she had a good tour of New Zealand, topping the Twenty20 averages with ten wickets at 4.80. Things started to fall into place.

The most important phase of her development, though, came on a whim during the World Cup in India the following year. It was February, and England were playing West Indies in Mumbai. The morning dew was still wet on the ground, and Shrubsole was trying her usual awayswing to two left-handers, but the ball wouldn't deviate a stubborn inch. Despondent, she turned it round: "It hooped!" She took four for 21, then three for 24 in the next match, against Australia, and five for 17 against South Africa. "I bowl quite front on, so naturally I'm the inswing side of the ball. I fought it for years. What a waste of time!" She didn't look back: her 70mph induckers have become her most potent weapon.

The biggest slump came just before the biggest triumph – the early stages of the 2017 World Cup. In her first four games, she took a single wicket. She convinced herself she was going to be dropped, and it was only when coach Mark Robinson called her in and told her firmly that "she hadn't become a bad bowler over a few games" that the tide turned.

At 26, the years ahead are rich with possibility. Her standing could hardly be higher. She won the 2017 CMJ Spirit of Cricket Award for her compassion in victory in that World Cup semi-final; was nominated for the BBC's Sports Personality of the Year award, coming top of the female contenders (who all finished in the bottom four – women's sport still has a way to go); and earned an MBE in the New Year's honours list.

If last winter's Ashes tour didn't go to plan, this winter brings the World Twenty20, not her favourite suit but her best: she was Player of the Tournament in 2014. She's intrigued by what the future will bring women's cricket, the new players that will emerge, the changes to come. She relishes the vice-captaincy, and she and Knight make a terrific pair: the hey-hold-on-a-minute details woman and the action skipper.

Shrubsole is not one for fuss. Her broad shoulders tether her to the things that matter: family, the team. The attributes that kept her going as a girl in a boys' team, a teenager in a women's team, an introvert in a team of extroverts, have helped her cope with the sudden fame, the nominations, the media. The future? Bring it on! But with a cup of tea first. She smiles, content to be a square peg, whatever shape the hole.

Nathan Stirk, Getty Images

FIVE CRICKETERS OF THE YEAR Anya Shrubsole

Stu Forster, Getty Images

FIVE CRICKETERS OF THE YEAR Shai Hope

Richard Heathcote, Getty Images

FIVE CRICKETERS OF THE YEAR Heather Knight

Nathan Stirk, Getty Images

FIVE CRICKETERS OF THE YEAR Jamie Porter

Stu Forster, Getty Images

FIVE CRICKETERS OF THE YEAR   Natalie Sciver

Mohammad Ismail, Reuters

ALTITUDE SICKNESS December snow is no barrier to a game of cricket in the mountains near Kabul – unlike the winter smog that mars the Delhi Test between India and Sri Lanka.

Pankaj Nangia, India Today Group/Getty Images

Stu Forster, Getty Images

Md Zakirul Mazed Konok

THE FRIENDLY GAME Anya Shrubsole commiserates with South Africa's Dane van Niekerk after England win a tense World Cup semi-final; children near Dhaka make do with a cracked pitch; and a coaching session in Srinigar, Kashmir.

Saqib Majeed

Rajesh Dhar

SILENT... SOLENT The stillness of a Kolkata morning, and the madness of the annual Bramble Bank match (see *Wisden 2007*, page 65).

Andrew Matthews, PA Photos

INDIGENOUS AUSTRALIAN CRICKET

Scrubbing away the whitewash

GEOFF LEMON

When you research Aboriginal Australian cricket, you find 1868. Then you keep finding it. You cast around for the next thing, and grasp empty air. But this one story, it tumbles along, a hundred retellings dressed in the same trimmings of novelty. A team from western Victoria who sailed to England and caused a sensation, having done the same at home. The extra narrative sauce that Tom Wills, the lionised founder of Australian Rules football, ran the team for a time. Here a book, there a thesis, a documentary, surely a feature film to come. Cricket Australia are running a 150th anniversary tour in 2018. Increasingly, there's a willingness to grasp the story as a foundation myth. But if this is a massif in the subject's landscape, it ends in a cliff.

Australian cricket is all about whiteness. It's the glare of sun washing out TV screens. Pitches baked to chalk by January heat. Picket fences and fresh uniforms and smears of zinc across the nose. Blank scorecards and high summer cloud, new Kookaburras for night games. Our Test history is rich in whitewashes, from Armstrong to Johnson, but the history itself is a whitewash. Scan the list of players to find a barely broken white line, uphill on a highway. A parade of Anglo monikers – Hassett to Bradman to Harvey, Chappell to Walters to Waugh – with the odd O'Reilly or McCool. Through a century and more, only Nitschke, Meuleman and Benaud even cross the Channel. Cricket remains the island of Robert Menzies's fantasy: "Where Great Britain stands, there stand the people of the entire British world."

It's not as if Australia was short on Europeans, even before the post-war flood. They started businesses, invigorated cuisine, and soon came through in football codes. But even domestic cricket took until the 1980s and beyond to include the odd Zoehrer, Noffke, Manou, Clingeleffer, Jaques. From then, we saw Italians and Greeks: Di Venuto, Veletta, Stoinis. Some Slavic names: Katich and Kasprowicz and Krejza. Very recently, Asia: Khawaja, Sandhu, Fawad.

But compared with Aussie Rules, elite cricket has never had a Wirrpanda or Cockatoo or Wanganeen. Of course colonialism left most Indigenous footballers with settler names, but traditional ones signalled the normality of Indigenous presence. A teamsheet in the newspaper became political affirmation. Cricket, conversely, has a great absence. A silence. Which tallies with so much other Indigenous experience, being removed from the reckoning, from families, from land, from being counted. *Terra nullius*, reinstated time and again.

So here we are: ten years on from Federal Parliament's apology to the Stolen Generations, 150 from that England tour, and a proud and excited Indigenous team set to retrace it. This, at the end of a season where half a dozen Indigenous players were making their way professionally; where an Aboriginal batsman

The Aboriginal team of 1867, at Sydney's Albert Ground. *Back row:* Tarpot, T. W. Wills, Johnny Mullagh. *Front:* King Cole, Jellico, Peter, Red Cap, Harry Rose, Bullocky, Cuzens and Dick-a-Dick.

from Darwin named D'Arcy Short hit the Big Bash League from what seemed like nowhere to be the sensation of the summer. In 2015, the Australian National University delivered *For the Love of the Game*, an independent report commissioned by CA on cricket's relationship with Indigenous people. Its conclusions were brutal, and have changed the sport's administration.

At the same time, Australia remains a country where columnists with byline photos supposed to convey gravitas still write that Aboriginal people should be grateful for being hauled out of the Stone Age. Grateful for dispossession, the loss of so many lives, of histories and languages, as though these can be assessed as a trade for the electric toothbrush. Being honest about this history, and the advantage we migrants derive from it daily, draws accusations of negativity. Let go of the past, people say, then demand respect for the 100-year dead of Gallipoli.

A vocabulary note for unfamiliar readers: "Indigenous" is the broad term including mainland Aboriginal people and Islanders from the Torres Strait, which lies between Australia and New Guinea. Within those categories are hundreds of nations, tribes and language groups across the breadth of an enormous country. That country is now deeply multicultural, while wrestling with racism like an aberrant subconscious. Yet its fractious relationship with each new migrant group is managed better and settled sooner than its inability to reconcile with Indigenous Australians. Case in point: when invited to write this piece, I thought someone else should take the space. But while I looked and asked and wrote around, I couldn't find a cricket writer who publicly identifies as Indigenous.

"Aboriginal people have not been in charge of the stories other people tell about us," says Alexis Wright in *Meanjin*, an Australian literary journal. "It would be fair to say that we are the country's troubling conscience and managed by its most powerful power brokers through a national narrative. I saw the fallout of this changing negative narrative in our communities, and in the lifetime of hard work our people do to fight against each political story-making trend."

Here is a sport that has so efficiently excluded a people that we can't find a voice to tell of that exclusion. So round we go again, another white reflection on black experience. Acknowledging it doesn't make the problem go away. But the problem is part of cricket's legacy.

Archives suggest Indigenous involvement with cricket as early as 1795, and matches are fully recorded by the 1850s. Livestock stations were nuclei. The 1880s New Norcia team would walk 80 miles into Perth to thrash white city sides. The 1868 players were mostly Jardwadjali men from three stations. They had toured Victoria and New South Wales in 1866-67, and would have seen England a year earlier had their white manager not embezzled profits.

When CA say they will "commemorate 150 years since an Aboriginal XI toured the UK", it makes that long-ago team sound official. We marvel at the players' feats, especially of Unaarrimin (Johnny Mullagh). But while the tour was voluntary, compulsion surely played a part once it was under way: matches squeezed back to back, 99 days in the field out of 125, Unaarrimin's absurd tally of 1,877 overs in 43 games. These weren't players sitting out with tightness in the quad. One died and two were sent home sick; as a result of the 1866-67 tour, four had died.

Some accounts exaggerate the team's exploits, a common presentation where Aboriginal ability is exoticised as mystical rather than skilful. You'll still hear Indigenous AFL players described as "magic" far more than the average. But nor were the tourists a sideshow: historian Anthony Condon's research suggests several matched the contemporary standard of first-class cricket, while others were athletically brilliant. The touring party was padded with less adept cricketers, whose job was to entertain: all were given comic English nicknames, and matches were followed with exhibitions of boomerang throwing, whip cracking, and sprinting backwards.

"In many ways, the team represented an oddity from the colonies, a spectacle to be viewed, an entertainment driven by notions of the 'savage' cloaked in the trappings of the gentleman's game," says the ANU report. "Without the trappings of the novelty provided by Indigenous cultural displays, such a tour would not have been commercially viable. In sum, the 1868 tour – when viewed through such a prism – can be seen as a commodified product of colonisation." You can bet your vintage *Wisden* collection nobody Aboriginal got much of the proceeds.

The tour remains a contested historical site. Where some accounts depict it as a rosy chapter in race relations, *For the Love of the Game* notes that it was "bookended by major massacres of Aboriginal people by pastoralists", and Victoria passing the Aboriginal Protection Act. For a century to come, Australia's colonies and Commonwealth asserted control over Indigenous lives. The tour was probably a partial catalyst. The team had left Victoria clandestinely to avoid interception, faking a fishing expedition before sailing to meet a steamer bound for Sydney. Politicians were uneasy about what might transpire in England beyond their control, and the cricketers were mentioned in parliamentary debate. Welfare was the excuse for curtailing movement but, with depredations unchecked in a rapidly expanding colony, it was surely more about concealing violence.

"The signing of the Act virtually ended Indigenous participation in cricket in Victoria, as similar acts would in other colonies," writes Condon in a forthcoming essay for *The International Journal of the History of Sport*. "Some notable exceptions played first-class cricket… However, they never became full members of the team, and required permission to be able to travel with other team members. This was a story repeated across Australia until the restrictive laws governing the lives of Aboriginal people were removed in the 1960s and '70s."

Those exceptions were few. Of the UK tourists, Murrumgunarrimin (as Twopenny) played once for New South Wales, Unaarrimin once for Victoria. After that, 100 years saw three names: Albert Henry and Jack Marsh between 1900 and 1905, even dismissing each other when Henry made his first-class debut for Queensland against New South Wales; and Eddie Gilbert in the 1930s. All three were properly fast, enough to impress the luminaries of their day. All had idiosyncratic actions. All excelled in a handful of state matches before being no-balled out of the game. No wonder there were echoes of something other than the Laws of Cricket when Darrell Hair and Ross Emerson stretched out an arm to Muttiah Muralitharan.

Murali had the last laugh on his detractors, a chuckle 800 wickets high. Marsh was bashed to death outside a pub aged 42. Henry was exiled to a mission a thousand miles from his home, and died of tuberculosis at 29. Gilbert spent his last three decades in a psychiatric ward.

And so the great whiteness set in. Faith Thomas played one Test in 1958, in an era when administrators regarded women's cricket as an embarrassment. Ian King bowled a domestic season for Queensland in 1969-70. As his career was ending, so were the laws that created the Stolen Generations, the Indigenous children taken from families by government agencies to be assimilated into white society.

For the current Australian all-rounder Dan Christian, this is more than an episode in a history book. "Dad's side of the family have all been very vocal and active in the Aboriginal community," he says. "He's mellowed now, but he was always pretty passionate as a young bloke about standing up for Aboriginal rights. He went through… I wouldn't say a rough childhood, but he had times when the welfare officers would come, and him and his brothers and sisters would have to run off and hide in the bush so they wouldn't take them away. It was pretty heavy stuff for a kid."

Michael Mainhardt played six scattered games for Queensland in the 1980s. Jason Gillespie was almost a double take. He first played for Australia in 1996, but his heritage didn't come up until 2000. "What did people expect me to do once I started playing for Australia?" he wrote later. "Call a press conference and announce I am an Aboriginal?" That he was already established in the team defused any hype. The milestone had slipped by.

That the milestone took until the turn of the millennium only emphasises the empty decades before. Evonne Goolagong won seven tennis Grand Slam

Exceptionally fast: Eddie Gilbert in 1934.

singles titles, Lionel Rose was a world boxing champion, Cathy Freeman took Olympic gold in the 400m and ran her lap of honour flying the Aboriginal flag. The National Rugby League and AFL were rich with Indigenous players, from trailblazers in the 1900s to stars by the 1980s. The 1993 on-field image of Nicky Winmar pulling up his jumper and pointing to the colour of his skin forced a largely effective AFL push against racial abuse. By 2009, AFL numbers peaked with 82 Indigenous players out of about 600. In 2017-18 came the second AFL Women's season and the third Women's Big Bash: football had 11 Indigenous players, cricket one.

There are plenty of hypotheses about why football codes have flourished among Indigenous Australians. Those about cricket needing space or expensive equipment don't account for the street games of India and Pakistan. Perhaps football welcomed rebels, and cricket was the Establishment: the 1972 *Illustrated History of Australian Cricket* had a foreword by Menzies, and omitted the 1868 tour entirely. Whatever the initial cause of connection or disconnection, representation soon becomes circular.

John Blurton was New Norcia's star in the 1880s, and his great-grandson John McGuire played first grade in Perth a century later. "Let's be honest about it, cricket hasn't been a game for all Australians," McGuire told ESPNcricinfo. "Aboriginals think cricket is a whitefella's sport, because we don't see black players in the team." McGuire's youthful affection went to West Indies.

It all tallies with Test batsman Usman Khawaja's memoir for the PlayersVoice website, where he recalls racial abuse from opponents and parents in primary school. He and his Asian friends supported "West Indies, Pakistan, India, Sri Lanka. Anyone else… Everything that was going on in our childhood and around us built up this resentment of the Australian cricket team. I mean, none of them looked like us… By high school I was a diehard Australian team supporter. But the damage had been done… it's no surprise it has taken Australian cricket so long for coloured players to come through the system."

As McGuire told *The Guardian*: "There wasn't a match I wasn't racially abused in when I went out to bat." Even as his race held him back, white cricketers called him a coconut: black on the outside, white on the inside. "That's one of the worst things you can say to an Aboriginal, but I was called much worse. I was called a black cunt so many times."

Less blunt racism, he said, existed at higher levels. "Cricket has this unfortunate trait: cultural bias sits there, and it's unconscious." The numbers support him: of 24 Perth batsmen who topped 7,000 grade runs, one never played for Western Australia. No prizes for guessing who. McGuire now sits on CA's National Indigenous Cricket Advisory Committee. But tensions remain. The Western Australian Cricket Association refused to comment for the *Guardian* piece. And when McGuire was quoted in another outlet last year, a WACA official telephoned to berate the writer, calling McGuire an "extremist". It's a familiar appellation for anyone protesting against racial injustice.

Gillespie's ascent didn't open the floodgates, which probably added to the frustration that unfairly spilled in his direction. "I've known since I was a young kid that our family was of Aboriginal heritage," he told *The Final Word* podcast in 2017. "It's obviously something we're incredibly proud of. There was a bit of criticism in some quarters that I wasn't embracing my culture, which couldn't be further from the truth. My late father was CEO of the Aboriginal Legal Rights Movement for a long time; my brother still works there. Our family's got a strong connection." His era saw the first state advisory committees and diversity officers, but they were under-resourced and ineffective. Gillespie retired in 2008, passing the torch to Christian, who has played limited-overs formats for Australia and hovered near Test selection. There was plenty of talk of inclusion – and little progress.

The 2015 ANU report was the watershed: "It is evident that the damage resulting from a legacy of exclusion, racism and disastrous public policy by government, particularly during the period between the late 1890s and the 1950s, has been instrumental in the causation of a disconnect between cricket and the wider Indigenous community.

"This has been compounded by poor practices and ignorance at many club and district levels when it comes to providing an open, welcoming and safe space for Indigenous engagement to occur… We all need to ensure that this is not replicated in the eras that stretch in front of us."

Bluntness was met with willingness. All the major recommendations were instituted, and the new national committee given clearer authority and direction. Specialist Indigenous officers were recruited, rather than having generalists fail at combined portfolios. In short, CA got serious, as they have about women's cricket.

Paul Stewart is the head of their Indigenous programme, and speaks enthusiastically about helping teenagers with schooling, and spreading the game as broadly as he can. "We know where Indigenous people live in the regions we're in, and we're making sure we're not just going to the schools that might have been an easy choice. We're getting out to remote communities and taking cricket to them. It's not a day trip."

Mark Kolbe, Getty Images

D'Arcy Short in Australia cap, February 2018.

There's also the false impression that all Indigenous communities are remote. "It's just perceived, maybe what people see on TV. We've got a coined phrase: I'm a city black. Australian Bureau of Statistics data says there's a significant amount of Aboriginal people living in the city."

The Imparja Cup, contested by teams of Indigenous cricketers, has gone from a local Alice Springs knockabout to the marquee event of the year, and many have responded. "They grew up with not many Indigenous players taking part," says Short, "and suddenly there's five or six of us playing state level cricket. They get a pride and sense of enjoyment in seeing other Indigenous players as well, and coming together in a tournament is always good for us. It's a sense of self-pride in the community."

In the last couple of years, Scott Boland has broken through for 17 internationals as a death-overs seamer, Short has made Australia's T20 side as a power-hitting opener, and Ashleigh Gardner has flipped between off-spin for Australia and smoking sixes in the WBBL. Brendan Doggett and Carly Fuller are making their way for Queensland, and Josh Lalor for New South Wales, while Hannah Darlington was a development signing for Sydney Thunder.

They are all of partial Indigenous descent, which two of them raise in interview. On racial abuse, Short says: "I don't get it as much as a lot of others – obviously because of my skin colour not being the same – but definitely when I was younger I got a bit."

Christian echoes him: "I'm fair-skinned, so I never had to deal with anything particularly discriminatory. You come across a lot of casual racism, as a kid and even now. There are kids and cousins I grew up with who were subjected to that sort of racism, and missed out on opportunities they otherwise could have gotten."

McGuire, dark in complexion, supports those players, but makes an additional point. "It's easier to pick a white-skinned Aboriginal person because they fit in," he said to ESPNcricinfo. Later, in *The Nightwatchman*: "The Aboriginal guys that have been in the teams look white, unless they say they're Aboriginal. A kid in Hermannsburg is not going to know they're blackfellas. They are great guys, but I want to see a black Aboriginal playing cricket. Then there will have been real change."

It's a deeply complex subject, with the potential for hurt. A favourite strand of Australian racism, next to abusing those deemed Indigenous, is the abuse and denial of identity of those deemed not Indigenous enough. Efficient racists can even double-dip. Sections of white Australia seem obsessed with arbitrating Indigenous identity, effectively writing fractions on slips of paper to pin to people's shirts.

This is based on the narrow conception of what a white society thinks Indigenous people are supposed to look like. Aboriginal academic Anita Heiss named her memoir *Am I Black Enough For You?* Actors Nakkiah Lui and Miranda Tapsell host a podcast called *Pretty For An Aboriginal*. In one episode, the rapper Briggs pursues the issue: "I've got cousins with red hair, who look super white. I've got another cousin who's as black as Wesley Snipes. You put us three in a room and you might not even know that we're related. But we're all family." Lui responds: "My mum calls them crayons. Different group of blackfellas in a room: box of Crayolas."

Paul Stewart says: "I'm as fair as Dan Christian, but Dan's a Wiradjuri man and I'm a Taungurong man, and this is what we do in the Imparja Cup. We write our club against the fixture, and we write who our mob is, our date of birth, whether we're a left-hand bat or a right-arm off-spinner."

Christian elaborates. "I grew up part of an Aboriginal family and Aboriginal culture. My dad's one of nine – huge family – so I've got lots of cousins and very close second cousins. I loved my upbringing, and it's nice to be able to represent them now as I've gotten older."

Short has experienced "people saying I wasn't Aboriginal. But that's just out of people being idiots, or maybe a bit of jealousy in terms of where I was with my cricket." There are grimmer historical undertones, though: the 1937 Commonwealth State conference concluded that "the destiny of natives of aboriginal origin, but not of the full blood, lies in ultimate absorption". Short is part of a movement that rejects this, embracing and amplifying his descent.

While McGuire's point could be twisted into an attack, it reflects the need for breadth in representation. In another episode of *Pretty For An Aboriginal*, (white) actor Yael Stone explains it in terms of the series *Orange is the New Black*, hailed for its nuanced depiction of inmates in a women's prison. "Once you have more than one person of colour, there's a reason to go into deeper complexity of characters, and have interactions that are multilayered. I walk around the streets of New York, and that's what the streets of New York look like. For a long time we've had a very strange popular culture reflection back at us. Maybe, for a lot of white people, we say: 'Oh yeah, that's my life, that

Exception to the rule: Faith Thomas was the first Indigenous Australian to play Test cricket. Here she meets Dainira Papertalk, captain of the Western Australian women's Imparja Cup team.

feels accurate – cool, cool, cool.' But for anyone else, it's like a weird fairytale that's not recognisable, that you can't connect with. Even if you're not insulted by it, it's completely isolating."

With CA's reform, that sort of representation may be possible. "It's a step in the right direction, let's put it that way," says Christian. "I think it's a long, long way from a finished product." The same is true in a broader social sense. Personal abuse is one thing, systemic discrimination another: barriers of economy and access, time and transport, perception and safety and encouragement.

This is still a country whose national celebration is January 26, the anniversary of colonisation. It's a country suspicious of accountability, lashing out when told of problems. Aboriginal AFL champion Adam Goodes spoke about racial inequality late in his career, and spent his final season being booed around the country. On Australia Day in 2018, politicians raged against a young Aboriginal activist, Tarneen Onus-Williams, for rhetorical fire in a speech, while media outlets made her a target on front pages and bulletins, knowing threats and abuse would follow.

It's also a country where tens of thousands marched in protest; a country where Briggs had a hit with the scathing track "January 26". Appetite for progress is undiminished. Onus-Williams said she hoped Australia burns to the ground. "It was a metaphor," was her weary explanation. "I just want everything, all the governments, to fall apart, because our people are dying and nobody cares and the whole system needs to change."

That's not hyperbole. Indigenous Australians are disadvantaged on every conceivable measure: life expectancy, health, income, employment; more arrests, jail time, deaths in custody, suicide, institutional abuse. In 2018, Melbourne's *Age* newspaper was still saying "the greatest failing of Australia, one of the most prosperous nations, is the gulf between the situation of Aboriginal and Torres Strait Islander people and that of the rest of the population". The same day, online clips of Olympic ice skater Harley Windsor were trolled with slurs: he was both Aboriginal and not Aboriginal enough.

Problems this big can be addressed only by a million small actions. Cricket can be part of it. Asked what he hopes the future holds, Short says: "I'd like to see that it's just the norm having Indigenous people picked in Australian sides, all the time. It would still be a massive thing, but not like 'He's the third or fourth to be playing for Australia.'"

For Christian: "I'd like there to be more than five guys playing first-class cricket with Aboriginal heritage. I'd love to see a full Indigenous round next year, like we see in the AFL and NRL. To have an Indigenous squad that's together for a lot of the year, and can go on tours and play against state teams, and make it a viable goal for kids growing up and coming through. Something you aspire to – to grow up and play for the National Indigenous team."

Next, that team tour England in June. Even for those who see symbolism as toothless, and even if the pace is glacial, it's some kind of movement. Far from the dubious aspects of 1868, this team will visit in a completely different way, respected from the outset, and clear in what they represent. There's reason to hope that this time it's the start of something, not the end.

Geoff Lemon is an Australian writer and broadcaster, on cricket and otherwise.

THE NEW-BALL PARTNERSHIP

Marriage or myth?

MIKE SELVEY

December 17 in Western Australia brought another pristine summer's morning, and a relentless sun to knock the temperature into the thirties. The crowd had come in force to the WACA to witness more Australian dominance. This was not to be a day of celebration for England – and yet, briefly, it was. The old Perth scoreboard, overseeing its final Ashes Test before the switch to the vast new stadium across the Swan River, was groaning under the weight of runs: 560 for five, with the Australian captain Steve Smith 239 to the good and set for a whole load more. Then Jimmy Anderson delivered the first ball of the 157th over. It was full, with a hint of reverse swing. Smith sensed another leg-side boundary, but instead played all round it. Anderson shrieked his appeal, to no avail, and England opted for DRS. A good move: the delivery met all the criteria for lbw and, after more than nine and a half hours, Smith was on his way.

This was Anderson's second wicket of the morning, and his tenth of the series. It was also the 763rd that had fallen either to him or Stuart Broad in the 100 Tests they had played together since joining forces, nearly a decade before, at Wellington's Basin Reserve, following the culling of Matthew Hoggard and Steve Harmison.

WITH OR WITHOUT YOU

	T	*O*	*M*	*R*	*W*	*BB*	*5I*	*10M*	*Avge*
Anderson (with Broad)	102	3,847.4	1,007	10,675	416	7-42	22	3	25.66
Anderson (without Broad)	32	1,085.4	232	3,658	107	5-42	3	0	34.18
Total	134	4,933.2	1,239	14,333	523	7-42	25	3	27.40
Broad (with Anderson)	102	3,535.1	800	10,614	360	7-44	13	2	29.48
Broad (without Anderson)	12	387	101	1,092	39	8-15	2	0	28.00
Total	114	3,922.1	901	11,706	399	8-15	15	2	29.33
Anderson and Broad (together)	102	7,382.5	1,807	21,289	776	7-42	35	5	27.43

As at January 8, 2018.

The significance of the moment had its roots at The Oval more than 17 years earlier, on September 3, 2000. When the West Indies giant Courtney Walsh removed Mike Atherton, it took to 762 the Test wickets he and Curtly Ambrose had claimed in harness. The day before, Ambrose, that other goliath of an attack that had sustained West Indies through the 1990s, had dismissed Marcus Trescothick – the 405th and last wicket of a wonderful Test career. They were such a distance ahead of the nearest pair of pacemen that it seemed improbable they would ever be overhauled.

Gareth Copley, Getty Images

Striding ahead: Stuart Broad and Jimmy Anderson do what they do best.

Yet Broad and Anderson – doesn't it scan better that way round? – have done just that. Only the spin–pace combinations of Shane Warne and Glenn McGrath (1,001 wickets in Tests together) and Muttiah Muralitharan and Chaminda Vaas (895) lie ahead. The intense nature of international cricket and the rise of the franchise T20 leagues mean the demands on pace bowlers are increasing. Longevity such as that shown by McGrath, Walsh and Anderson (who in the 2017-18 Ashes delivered more overs in a series than ever before) will become unsustainable. The collective haul of Broad and Anderson will almost certainly never be beaten.

Broad and Anderson, Curtly and Courtney: the names fit together like sausage and mash, or gin and tonic. It is how followers of the game like to view bowlers, as a collective rather than individuals, singularly brilliant though they may be (only opening batsmen are accorded the same co-operative status). Curiously, these pairings will refer almost exclusively to pacemen. Mention McGrath, for example, and the reaction is not to invoke Warne, but Jason Gillespie or Brett Lee. Outside India, the great quartet of spinners from the 1960s and '70s – Bedi, Prasanna, Venkat and Chandra – are remembered individually, rather than as part of a group.

To appreciate this, there has to be a more general understanding of the nature of cricket. It has become a cliché that it is an individual game played within a team contest. But that is a simplification: the essence of cricket is collaboration. It may be bowler against batsman, but where would the bowler be without the wicketkeeper or fielders? And if batsmen rely on partnerships, does this apply to bowlers too? Do the most successful teams contain bowling partnerships in which the sum of the collective, because of its symbiotic nature, is greater than the constituent parts? Or is that a romantic ideal?

In his book *In Tandem*, Patrick Ferriday argues persuasively that, while there are a number of exceptional and familiar pace-bowling pairs, in many cases the individuals within them actually had better overall records, and produced their best performances, when the other half was missing. Furthermore, some alliances were so short-lived within the context of an individual career as to be almost irrelevant – a transient relationship, in other words, rather than the long-term marriage of mythology.

An example might be Dennis Lillee and Jeff Thomson, ferocious as a duo and morphed in our minds into the harridan Lilian Thomson. Lillee played 70 Tests and Thomson 51, but – as Ferriday points out – only 26 were together.

MOST WICKETS TAKEN TOGETHER BY PACE BOWLERS

		For	*T*	*Avge*
776	**J. M. Anderson (416) and S. C. J. Broad (360)**	**E**	**102**	**27.43**
762	C. E. L. Ambrose (389) and C. A. Walsh (373)	WI	95	22.67
559	Wasim Akram (282) and Waqar Younis (277)	P	61	22.12
547	S. M. Pollock (377) and J. H. Kallis (170)	SA	93	25.99
538	M. Ntini (350) and J. H. Kallis (188)	SA	93	30.45
522	**D. W. Steyn (305) and M. Morkel (217)**	**SA**	**62**	**24.88**
490	M. Ntini (255) and S. M. Pollock (235)	SA	63	26.24
484	G. D. McGrath (274) and J. N. Gillespie (210)	A	58	23.01
476	I. T. Botham (254) and R. G. D. Willis (222)	E	60	25.18
424	D. W. Steyn (335) and J. H. Kallis (89)	SA	65	25.46
397	A. A. Donald (208) and S. M. Pollock (189)	SA	47	21.84
371	G. D. McGrath (194) and B. Lee (177)	A	45	25.31
367	M. J. Hoggard (200) and A. Flintoff (167)	E	49	29.11
345	R. R. Lindwall (195) and K. R. Miller (150)	A	51	23.00

Wickets shown only for matches in which both players appeared.

In these, Thomson took 98 wickets at 28, and Lillee 119 at 26. Apart, Thomson took 102 at 27, and Lillee 236 at 22. So while Thomson was much the same either way, Lillee enjoyed more success without him, a statistic offset only to a degree by the possibility that Lillee on his own may have been able to hog more of the pickings.

In any case, for a partnership to be effective there has to be a balance. Bowlers, in terms of skills and temperament, need to be complementary, rather than duplicates. Take Fred Trueman and Brian Statham, inextricably linked in the annals. Precisely half Statham's 70 Tests were played with Trueman (who played 67). Individually, their averages were better apart, Trueman's by almost eight. But Trueman, a fast outswing bowler, appreciated Statham's nagging seam movement and different length as a counterpoint.

Or consider Wasim Akram and Waqar Younis, even more inextricably linked. Wasim was the finest left-arm paceman the game has seen, a magician with a pitter-patter run who could manipulate the ball to his will at a pace

Business partners: Waqar Younis and Wasim Akram fly in.

beyond waspish, delivered with a blurringly fast action. Waqar was right-arm, skiddy and muscular, galloping in to deliver low-slung, ridiculously late-swinging yorkers at high velocity, as near unplayable as fast bowling can get. Both were masters of reverse swing, an art form which made a virtue out of dreary subcontinental pitches.

So, do bowlers genuinely feed off the presence of a close collaborator at the other end? In 11 seasons with the new ball for Middlesex, I had three regular partners. First, for a couple of years, came John Price, genuinely fast, though nearing the end of his career. Next was the peripatetic Allan Jones, another capable of good pace. Finally, The Diamond – Wayne Daniel – with whom I had the most enduring relationship. In each case, we were a partnership in the sense that we had complementary skills, particularly when it came to the specific demands of Lord's. Yet it was with Jones, for a couple of years until his back gave in, that I had a properly close alliance: we travelled, socialised and planned together.

The reality, though, was that in terms of his career I was a transitory part: only 135 of his 549 first-class wickets were for Middlesex, and 71 of them in the summer of 1976 (when I managed 90). Was he a more productive bowler with me? I suspect the change of environment – he had just left Somerset – had as much to do with his success as any contribution on my part, while my own success was a product of natural maturity. It is just that, for one season, the stars were in alignment. In retrospect, it was the closest I came to understanding Anderson's relationship with Broad.

With Daniel, again our skills dovetailed: he was brutally quick, I was fast-medium swing – and it was fun. But his success wasn't contingent on anything I did, for he was a wonderful bowler, come what may. And my best match figures – 12 for 160 against Nottinghamshire at Trent Bridge in 1975 – occurred in a game where none of that trio was playing.

The great West Indies pacemen of the 1970s and '80s hunted in a pack, but we still think of pairs within it, such as Andy Roberts and Michael Holding. For Holding, representing his region was his paramount motivation, but he drew inspiration from bowling with Roberts, with whom he played 30 of his 60 Tests. "I don't think you could want a better bowling partner than him," says Holding. "Andy knew the game, and probably the fact that we were good friends before we even started playing for West Indies enhanced the situation. We roomed together. He was always helpful, always telling me what to look for, what to exploit in batsmen. But as a group we knew each other's game, so if one was off, we would notice and have a word. With Andy, though, I always knew he was the senior. He would do what he wanted, and I would do the rest. In 1981, Clive Lloyd asked me which end I wanted, and I just said: 'The end Andy doesn't.'"

There is something of the Anderson–Broad dynamic in this: Anderson is the senior and decides what he wants, from the choice of ball to the choice of ends. Yet it was at Trent Bridge in 2015, when he was absent, that Broad produced his finest spell – eight for 15 to destroy Australia and all but clinch the Ashes.

With Wasim and Waqar, it is clear from the statistics that each benefited from the other. They played 61 Tests together, Wasim taking 282 wickets at 21, and Waqar 277 at 22. When apart, the difference is significant: in 43 games without Waqar, Wasim managed 132 wickets at 28; in 26 without Wasim, Waqar managed 96 at 25. A curiosity is that their personal relationship was terse, so this was strictly business. But what a blue-chip business.

Only three of Ambrose's 98 Tests were without Walsh, so he scarcely knew what it was like to don his maroon cap without him. Not so Walsh, who had already played 17 matches in three years, and taken 71 wickets, before the pair first came together, at Georgetown in April 1988. Walsh also continued for ten matches after Ambrose retired.

Like Wasim and Waqar, they shared their wickets and workload virtually equally, with 389 to Ambrose and 373 to Walsh; Ambrose sent down just 27 more deliveries in that time. "On my good days he would support me, and on his good days I would support him," Walsh told *All Out Cricket*. "And when we both had good days batsmen were in trouble. We were more than cricketing friends, we were brothers." Ambrose agreed: "There was never any rivalry between us – ever. If it was his day to take wickets then my job was to keep the pressure on at the other end. If it was my day, he would do the same."

Until the arrival of Broad to join Anderson, only Walsh and Ambrose had come close to an enduring bowling marriage. Now the England pair have taken it further: by the end of the 2017-18 Ashes, they had played 102 matches together. In that time, Broad had delivered 3,535 overs for 360 wickets, and Anderson 3,847 for 416. There may have been a time when a pace bowler disappeared for a break between overs to fine leg or third man. But every

Anderson over sees Broad at mid-off or mid-on, chatting, talking tactics, cajoling; and for every Broad over, there is Anderson doing the same. If they are not quite psychic, they are joined umbilically.

There were signs in Australia, though, that their alliance might be starting to fray at the edges. Anderson, even at 35, was indefatigable, but Broad, four years his junior, had lost his spark; injury is beginning to play an intrusive part. With a summer of cricket in England to come, it would be foolish to write him off. It is just that the signs are there. Already thoughts will be turning to the next generation. An era may be coming to an end. We may never see another like it.

Mike Selvey played 278 first-class matches between 1968 and 1984, taking over 1,100 wickets across formats. He was The Guardian's *cricket correspondent for 30 years.*

AFGHANISTAN AND IRELAND JOIN THE TEST FOLD

Status upgrade

TIM WIGMORE

Taj Malik spent the 1987 World Cup, held in Pakistan and India, at the Kacha Garhi refugee camp in Peshawar. Every day, he and other Afghans huddled around a grainy television, falling in love with cricket. He was 12. "There was a lot of drama in the game, so that's why I got interested," he says. When England returned to Pakistan at the end of 1987, Malik grew enthralled by Test cricket too. But watching was not enough. Pop-up games started being played at the camp, using a stick and – if no tennis ball was available – scrunched-up plastic bags.

For Brían O'Rourke, the penny had dropped as a teenager in 1983. He grew up in Carlow, a sleepy town in south-east Ireland, where the sport was Gaelic – football or hurling. Gaelic speakers themselves, none of the O'Rourkes had played cricket. "It just wasn't the in thing," says Brían, before using an old Irish insult: "It was seen as a West Brit sport." That year, his family moved to Dublin. Serendipitously, their new house was next to Pembroke Cricket Club, one of Ireland's oldest and proudest, founded in 1868, a forgotten age when cricket was the nation's most popular game and thrived across all 32 counties. "I remember looking over the wall and thinking: 'Cricket – not sure about that.'" Then someone asked him if he wanted to join in. He was hooked.

From the start, Malik believed Afghanistan would "one day play at the highest level". Yet the dream was out of kilter with reality. The camp's ground was covered with stones, and there was no proper gear, let alone protective equipment, and little organisation. That began to change in 1996. Now 21, Malik was still a refugee, since the Taliban were making a return home increasingly dangerous. But a ground sprang up at Kacha Garhi, and Malik formed the Afghan Cricket Club. They took on teams in Peshawar, including first-class players. It was here that the nucleus of the side who would help Afghanistan to their first World Cup learned cricket.

O'Rourke's love of the game had led him to become Leinster's first cricket development manager, in 1997. As he went into primary schools with basic kit and tried to spread the gospel – normally through Kwik Cricket – he encountered the usual prejudice: the sport was too slow, too boring and, above all, too English. But O'Rourke's Gaelic was useful. Many of the teachers he first approached about offering sessions were Gaelic speakers from the countryside: a few words went a long way.

At the time, cricket in Ireland was still a niche activity. It had been 50 years since a local had enjoyed a significant professional career in the county game: Maurice Robinson represented Glamorgan and Warwickshire between 1946 and 1952. O'Rourke was a one-man team; his office was his car. But his enthusiasm gave thousands of children an experience they might otherwise

Cloud nine: Malahide will stage Ireland's first men's Test – against Pakistan in May.

have been denied. Slowly, cricket became less obscure. In 2000, *The Irish Times* reported: "Brían O'Rourke is doing his damnedest to ensure that as many kids as possible are given a start in one of the world's great games. And who can say what brilliant talents will emerge in time thanks to his efforts?"

The answer was the best generation of cricketers Ireland has ever produced. In 2004, O'Rourke coached the Under-19s at the World Cup in Bangladesh, where a side including Eoin Morgan, Kevin O'Brien, William Porterfield, Boyd Rankin and Gary Wilson lost to West Indies by just six runs, and gave Australia a scare, too. Three years later, all but Wilson were in the Ireland squad at their first men's World Cup, in the Caribbean. As they took the field at Sabina Park on St Patrick's Day, they were greeted by derision from a group of Pakistan fans: "You should be back in the pub, drinking Guinness. You don't play cricket." By the day's end, no one was mocking Ireland: on a green pitch, they won by three wickets. Combined with their tie against Zimbabwe, it meant they qualified for the Super Eights, where they defeated Bangladesh. Irish cricket was a secret society no more.

Malik also built the game in his homeland from the ground up. In December 2001, after the ousting of the Taliban, he returned home, having been a refugee in Pakistan ever since his family fled almost 16 years earlier during the occupation of Afghanistan by the Soviet Union. Yet even in this uncertain and perilous time, Afghan cricket had a semblance of organisation and infrastructure. In 1995, Allah Dad Noori had formed the Afghan Cricket Federation in Kabul and registered it as a national sport with the Afghan Olympic Committee. Cricket was one of the few games permitted by the Taliban, who approved of the conservative dress code. It helped that cricket was the national sport of Pakistan, one of only three other states – along with

Afghan nursery: the Chaman-e-Huzuri ground in Kabul hosts countless games.

Saudi Arabia and the United Arab Emirates – to recognise the Taliban as Afghanistan's official government; some Taliban teams even played matches in Pakistan. Cricket also bore some resemblance to the old Afghan game of *top danda*, which involves hitting a round object with a wooden bat. In June 2001, the ACF were registered with the ICC, who awarded Afghanistan affiliate membership.

When Malik returned to Afghanistan – first to Jalalabad, then Kabul – he became embroiled in a tussle. In their different ways, both he and Noori regarded themselves as the father of Afghan cricket. They hit upon a compromise: Malik would become national coachand general secretary, Noori board president. Charities and foreign governments faced obstacles, but sensed cricket's power. They sent second-hand bats, stumps and balls, which went a long way.

Malik was the very essence of Afghan cricket's early years. From their first official matches in the 2004 Asian Cricket Council Trophy, he was unstinting in his enthusiasm and unyielding in his standards. Yet he was also temperamental and bombastic, reacting to the merest whiff of a batting collapse by reaching for his cigarettes. His bluster could seem absurd. In Jersey in 2008, when Afghanistan were playing in World Cricket League Division Five, he boasted they would score 400 against Japan (they managed 179, but still won easily), and could beat England. He threatened to throw himself into the Atlantic if his side failed to win the tournament; they spared him the ordeal.

Yet Afghanistan now believed they needed more than Malik's passion. Ruthlessly, they replaced him with Kabir Khan, a former Pakistan Test seamer. Under Kabir, they continued their ascent up the WCL ladder, all the way to the qualifiers for the 2011 World Cup, held in South Africa in 2009. There, for the first time, they met the leading Associate nation: Ireland. The Irish easily won a warm-up game, skittling Afghanistan for 86, but when the sides met in the Super Eights at Krugersdorp, a brilliant spell from Hamid Hassan, a headband-wearing purveyor of late-swinging yorkers honed in Kacha Garhi, turned the tables. Their inconsistency meant they failed to join Ireland at the World Cup, but a captivating rivalry was born: Ireland's efficiency and orthodoxy against Afghanistan's audacity and aggression.

For all their on-field battles – in recent years, Afghanistan have surpassed Ireland – the two have also been allies. They confirmed that nations outside the cosy cartel of the old ten Full Members had huge talent, and weren't getting the chance to show it. And it helped that they came from different regions: promoting both would maintain the balance of power within the ICC.

Cricket served a wider purpose in each nation. In Ireland, it had once been a symbol of division: the Gaelic Athletic Association maintained The Ban, prohibiting their members from playing, or even the watching, foreign sports from 1902 until 1971. But it has become a unifying force. The team have included all strands of modern Ireland, from both sides of the border: Protestants and Catholics, unionists and republicans, as well as immigrants from Australia, South Africa and India. Sinn Fein's Martin McGuinness was a devoted fan, once dressing up as W. G. Grace for charity. And all Ireland could unite around toppling England at the 2011 World Cup in India.

"The biggest thing that broke down the idea of cricket being English was witnessing an Irish team beat England at what they call their own sport," says John Mooney, who struck the winning runs that night in Bangalore. "Hopefully it will continue to break down the barriers between North and South, and continue to integrate young Catholics and young Protestants."

Sometimes in Afghanistan every week seemed to bring new catastrophe, and cricket was not immune: Rahmat Wali, a former Afghan player, was shot by American forces in 2008 after being suspected of helping build improvised explosive devices. And the women's game has been suppressed, unlike in Ireland, where it has developed in line with the men's (in 2000, the Irish women thrashed Pakistan in a Test, though they have not played another). But social and religious conservatism has got in the way in Afghanistan, with female players threatened and called prostitutes.

Ahmad Masood, Reuters

Guiding light: Taj Malik in Kabul, 2006.

Yet the Afghan men's national side – easily the most successful sports team in a country boasting only two Olympic medals, both bronze, both in taekwondo – swiftly became one of

Father figure: Brían O'Rourke presents Paul Stirling – after twin Under-19 hundreds against Denmark – with a new bat in 2006.

the few institutions cherished by the Taliban, by Afghanistan's national government, and by foreign donors: Germany, for instance, funded a cricket ground in Khost, in the east of the country. Their first appearance at an ICC global event came in the Caribbean in 2010, at the World Twenty20 – Malik was there as assistant coach, although he ceased working for the Afghan board soon after. In October 2013, when the players returned home after securing qualification for the 2015 World Cup, both the Taliban and the army shot in the air to celebrate their success. "It brings peace to every tribe," said Mohammad Nabi, who played with Malik for the Afghan Cricket Club in Peshawar, and later became the national captain and the first Afghan signed up by the IPL.

Such jubilation would be rivalled four years later, in the boardroom: at The Oval on June 22, 2017, Afghanistan and Ireland gained Full Member status, becoming the 11th and 12th Test nations.

Unlike Malik, O'Rourke thought it would never happen, calling the idea of Ireland playing a men's Test "pie in the sky". Yet if Test status is a symbol of their ascent – despite their struggles since the 2015 World Cup – the sport's grassroots transformation has been just as significant. O'Rourke, now the head of Leinster's development team, takes particular pride in the Leprechaun Cup, a T20 hard-ball competition that launched in 2007 and now involves almost 50 primary schools in Dublin. After all the hours spent working with Morgan and

Rankin, he believes Ireland's new-found status means he will never again nurture a player who goes on to represent England. Ireland's first Test, against Pakistan on May 11 at Malahide, a genteel coastal town north of Dublin, will be a proud moment.

Malik is back working for the Afghanistan board, as a technical adviser helping preparations for his country's first Test, scheduled to take place against India at Bangalore on June 14. It will be the realisation of a dream he hatched crowding around TVs in a refugee camp. Thirty years on, he is more convinced than ever of what cricket can achieve: "Sport is an ambassador for peace and friendship."

The contrasting ascents of Afghanistan and Ireland stand as a totem of cricket's ability to regenerate, captivate new fans and overcome differences in country or creed. Long after their inaugural Test matches, this will endure.

Tim Wigmore writes for The Daily Telegraph, *ESPNcricinfo and* The Economist. *He is co-author of* Second XI, *a book on Associate cricket.*

PART TWO

The Wisden Review

CRICKET BOOKS IN 2017

Wickets of surprising truthfulness

KAMILA SHAMSIE

"What is art?" asked C. L. R. James in order to assert that cricket, more than any sport, is art, even if we aren't exactly sure what art is. If we go along with his claim, as we certainly should, then Christian Ryan's **Feeling is the Thing that Happens in 1000th of a Second: A Season of Cricket Photographer Patrick Eagar** might be taken as a paean to the art of capturing art. The book focuses on one season, 1975, in which England hosted the first World Cup and an Ashes, all captured by Eagar's lens.

There are 43 photographs reproduced in *Feeling* (as it's necessary to call it, the title being one of the few clumsy elements of the whole enterprise), and the book is part Ryan's meditations on them, part his interviews with Eagar about them. Eagar's contributions are mostly instructive for revealing how wide the gap can be between practitioner and commentator – or perhaps they simply reveal his natural diffidence, his unwillingness to claim too much for his own work. "It's only luck" is a common refrain when Ryan asks him how he managed to achieve something extraordinary. Ryan believes Eagar is mis-steering him by suggesting that everything in his photographs is a happy accident, and Eagar responds: "That's all. And then later, you can look back. That's the strength of photography."

What makes this book so wonderful, and so unlike anything else, is Ryan's ability to communicate what he sees in the photographs, which is often beyond the moment itself – character, symmetry, inevitability, foreshadowing. The bowling action of Thommo, the Chappell brothers walking out to bat, a young Botham square-driving – Ryan lets us see the pictures, then shows us what he sees in them, communicating his joy in the coming together of two great passions: cricket and photography. Or make that three: cricket, photography and writing. There is a photograph of Ken Wadsworth leaping to field a ball behind the stumps, three other players also in the shot. "Wadsworth was dead from cancer 15 months later. Glints of sunlight splash on his closed eyes. Ball's beyond reaching, which we know, he doesn't yet, however high he jumps his jumping is futile, both ball and photograph are a pre-glint: of what was to come. See Wadsworth's shadow, thinner than the others' three shadows – a sliver, a trapdoor."

This is the sort of thing Ryan can do, and convincingly. He can also meditate intelligently on different players, on different aspects of the game, and on photography itself (a good sports photographer must be almost preternaturally responsive – like a slip fielder or wicketkeeper, he senses "a kind of shimmer and starts pre-twitching"). There is, though, one great shortcoming to this little book (impossible-to-remember title aside), and that's its shoddy appearance. What should have been a gorgeous volume with wonderful reproductions, fine paper and thoughtful layout has none of them. Those glints of sunshine splashing on Wadsworth's eyes – we can't see them.

At some point in the autumn, a ladybird hauled itself on to my copy of Duncan Hamilton's **The Kings of Summer** and entered a state of dormancy. Wise. What finer way to get through the winter months than to attach yourself to this beautifully told account of the last days of the 2016 English county season. The last four days, to be exact, with Middlesex, Yorkshire and Somerset all in contention for the title. Some might raise an eyebrow at the manner in which Somerset were removed from the equation on the final day – it would have taken a Middlesex–Yorkshire draw for them to win, but the two captains at Lord's contrived to ensure a result. Hamilton is cheerfully approving of the "gerrymandering" that produced a thrilling last session.

He's a man who appreciates the theatre of cricket – in both its interludes and its climaxes – and he writes about each change of pace and mood with equal elegance. There is a particular pleasure in reading him on the long stretches of the game when nothing much happens: "… as the sun drops, the shadows become fantastically long and lamp-black, but the pitch remains in intense sunshine, like a lit stage… One moment passes into the next, peacefully seductive. Someone bowls. Someone bats. Someone fields." Glorious.

Charlie Campbell would probably argue that the captains of that Lord's game had it easy. All they had to worry about was winning a match and raising the trophy. In **Herding Cats: The Art of Amateur Cricket Captaincy**, he suggests, with a charmingly indistinct relationship of tongue to cheek, that it is the captain of an amateur side who has the hardest time. As leader of the Authors XI, he should know. His book, which uses Mike Brearley's *The Art of Captaincy* as a guide, is replete with humour, anecdote, seriousness and insight.

At times, life can be straightforward – when it comes to selection, the amateur captain's aim is to get 11 players. At others, things are more complicated. In Campbell's view, the amateur's primary responsibility is not to win but to make cricket into as much of a team sport as possible – even if some players have little discernible ability (declaration of interest: I played twice for the Authors, and have scores that range from a duck to nought not out). And yet winning is not entirely irrelevant. So the amateur captain must try to work out how to win, while keeping the gap in performance between the best and worst players to a minimum, and being sporting towards opposition who prove hopeless but must never, if possible, lose by too wide a margin. Everything is complicated by the fact that "in cricket, things are usually about to go wrong".

There are times when *nothing* seems to go wrong. In **On Form**, Mike Brearley investigates the phenomenon. But form is not just a matter for cricket, and his interests have always ranged far beyond the pitch. Within a dozen pages, he invokes Tolstoy, Tony Greig, Malcolm Gladwell, Donald Winnicott, Joseph Conrad, J. L. Carr, Icarus, Othello and David Hume. All have a place and a purpose in the introduction, and helpfully make it clear that this is not a book about cricket per se – rather it's a book about a concept that we may all recognise but don't properly understand, and which exists in myriad contexts. Cricket just happens to be the context in which Brearley has closest acquaintance with the concept.

So far, so fine, but alarm bells may start to ring at the sentence: "There is, however, no simple narrative logic to this book." Several chapters in, you start to query the adjective "simple". For me, this happened in chapter 11 – entitled "Why Sport?" In the first four pages alone, Brearley's references include: Jonathan Smith, author of *The Learning Game*; Dadie Rylands, theatre director and academic; Albert Camus; Usain Bolt; the philosopher G. E. Moore; Johan Huizinga, author of *Homo Ludens;* and the psychotherapist Julia Stone. There may well be a narrative logic here, but it's drowned by the denseness of anecdote and reference, which can leave you struggling to find the point.

Unexpectedly convincing links between canoeing and brain surgery

The book undoubtedly contains a great deal of interest, whether it's the distinction between being "in the zone" and "on form" (the first can lead to excessive risk-taking and arrogance, the second is a more balanced state), or Brearley's discussion of why Kevin Pietersen might have fared better for Australia than England (being blunt and upfront was probably the best way to handle him). And there are unexpectedly convincing links between canoeing and performing brain surgery (in both, the greatest chance of success comes from attempting solid performances and avoiding "glory shots", though that summary doesn't convey the complexity of Brearley's ideas).

But at one point I attempted to track my own responses, and they ended up looking like this: *This is interesting… Oh, that's a fascinating cricket nugget… Wait, what does this have to do with the other thing?… This is smart… That's a fascinating cricket nugget… Help – a compressed tour of the works of Aristotle, Plato, Sartre and Wittgenstein!… This is interesting… Haven't we been over this already?… Where am I?* One theory of writing says a book should resemble an iceberg – the reader must feel there's a great deal under the surface, known to the writer but out of sight. In *On Form*, Brearley did the hard work of shaping the iceberg, but forgot to add the water.

For those of us who grew up watching cricket in India or Pakistan, Henry Blofeld came to our attention in the 1980s, commentating on one-day internationals at Sharjah. His fascination with women's earrings, and his need to talk at length about them whenever the camera found a pair, became a fond joke across the subcontinent. But it is with *Test Match Special* that Blofeld is

most closely connected in England, where he eschewed earrings and instead became "the head public-relations man for pigeons, seagulls, helicopters".

What you think of **Over and Out: The innings of a lifetime with Test Match Special** will depend entirely on what you think of Blowers on *TMS*, for it is the same voice and character that come through in these pages. So, many of us will find the book high on entertainment and amusement, if a little lower on revelation. We skip easily from one passage of his life to another – the schoolboy cricketer who never regained his cricketing talent after being knocked down by a bus (which could explain his lifelong fascination with them), the young broadcaster, the foreign tours, the departure from *TMS*, and the return. He is generous to colleagues he admires, often quoting passages of their commentary. It's the likes of Arlott, Cozier and Trueman he writes about in those glowing terms. Current practitioners can attract muttered asides, such as "it sometimes seems that conformity rather than individuality is the order of the day".

There are points when he is being so amusing, so clever with words, so very Blowers, it's hard not to feel some regret that individuality such as his is now deemed old-fashioned. Then you come to the earring explanation: among the spectators at Sharjah were Bollywood stars "who had delicious boobs of every size". As he couldn't be too explicit to the largely Muslim audience in Pakistan, he developed a code – there were the "small, delicate and fetching" earrings, the "wonderful pair of large and robust earrings", the "medium-sized danglers, and on it went". Ah.

It's a pity there are no commentary archives to allow us to relive the moment Albert Trott cleared the Lord's Pavilion, a feat no one has emulated, though not for lack of trying. Even so, one shot seems a flimsy reason to write a biography, and a reviewer might pick up a copy of Steve Neal's **Over and Out – Albert Trott: The Man Who Cleared the Lord's Pavilion** with trepidation. The book starts in 1899 with the scene of The Great Shot, and it doesn't take long to realise there is a great deal more to the story. In fact, it becomes clear at the very moment Trott, playing for MCC, faces up to Monty Noble – "the man who occupies Trott's true place in the Australian team".

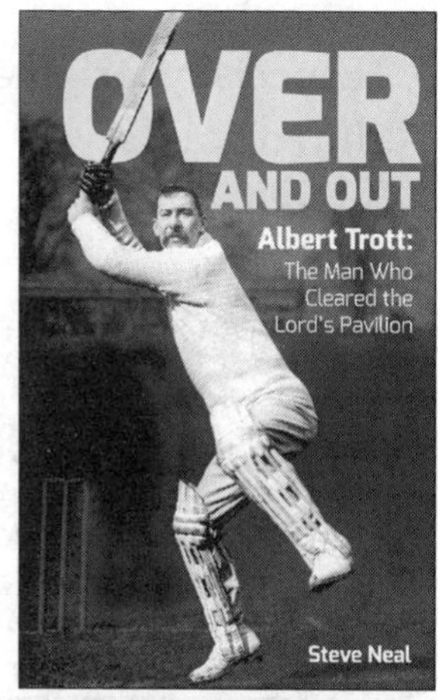

Neal has a fine way of introducing a plot twist. In cricketing terms, he makes a persuasive case for why Trott needs to be better recognised: in addition to That Shot, he was the first player to take 200 wickets and score 1,000 runs in a season in England, and his figures on Test debut (eight for 43, for

Australia against England) have yet to be bettered. But really it is the story of Trott's life, and Neal's telling of it, that makes this book so compelling.

Trott's family arrived in Australia from Antigua in 1855 – the oldest member was his great-grandmother, who had been born a slave. His grandfather Adolphus passed as white, and set about establishing the family's fortune. Within four decades, the Trotts had not one but two players in the Australian Test side – Albert and his older brother, Harry. Albert made his record-setting debut against England, but a year later was left out of the side, captained by Harry, which toured England. Even so, Albert sailed with the team in order to play for MCC, hoping he might be called up at some point. He wasn't, and decided his future lay in England – which is how, a few years later, he came to clear the Pavilion.

"A perversity of genius prevented him from being the best all-rounder in the world"

Trott played two matches for England against South Africa which were retrospectively given Test status, but never again for either England or Australia, in part due to MCC restrictions that made it impossible for him to appear for both Middlesex and Australia, but also because of his inconsistency. Plum Warner wrote that "a certain perversity of genius prevented him from being the best all-round cricketer in the world", and Neal is stellar at capturing both the perversity and the genius that made "the Albatrott" such a great draw at Middlesex.

The book is peppered with tiny details that bring Trott's world to life – from the cabbage leaves Australian players wore under their hats to counter the sun's effects, to Albert's coaching of women cricketers, including one Millie Finkelstein, author of the anti-feminist dystopian novel *The Newest Woman: The Destined Monarch of the World.* But the greatest success of Neal's book is how it brings its subject to life – so much so, that when we come to Trott's death, this line is heartbreaking rather than melodramatic: "He had shot himself in the temple, with a Browning pistol still resting in his right hand – the great hand that had bowled 71,459 balls in first-class cricket, the hand that had gripped the bat and hammered the ball over the Lord's Pavilion."

Mike Procter's autobiography – co-written with Lungani Zama – should provide at least as much interest as the life of Trott, if not more. Here is a man whose career has included years in South Africa during the boycott, their return to international cricket, a bomb blast next to the hotel in Pakistan where he was staying on his first outing as an ICC match referee, and "Monkeygate". And yet **Caught in the Middle: Monkeygate, Politics and Other Hairy Issues** starts disappointingly, managing to make the explosion feel mundane, and follows up with details of an Indian tour during which he's full of praise for Mother Teresa and the Taj Mahal.

It's only when he arrives at Monkeygate, the controversy that tarnished India's "Bollyline" tour of Australia in 2007-08, that we begin to understand that this appreciation of Indian icons might be there to try to ward off accusations of bias against another Indian icon, Sachin Tendulkar. Procter found Harbhajan Singh guilty of racist abuse against Andrew Symonds after a hearing in which – according to Procter – Tendulkar claimed he hadn't heard what Harbhajan, his batting partner at the time, had said. On appeal, though, Tendulkar changed his story, and the guilty verdict was overturned. (This is in contrast to Tendulkar's own account of the initial hearing: he insists he heard what Harbhajan said and recounted it to Procter, of whom he's very critical.) This is the only point in his autobiography when Procter cuts loose, making clear his feelings towards the Indian press, Tendulkar and Cricket Australia, and the book is all the livelier for it, even if it won't put an end to the "he said, he said" arguments. But mostly it's hard to avoid feeling that Procter either doesn't have much to say or doesn't want to say it. On the matter of South Africa's enmeshed cricketing and political history, he's particularly hard to pin down, at one point calling the boycott "a necessary sacrifice", and a few pages later insisting "sport and politics should never mix".

Precisely this mix forms the basis of the magisterial **Cricket & Conquest: The History of South African Cricket Retold, 1795–1914**. The four authors – André Odendaal, Krish Reddy, Christopher Merrett and Jonty Winch – successfully set about dismantling the idea that Africans never took to cricket, and that it was this, rather than discrimination, that caused the marginalisation of black players. Drawing on a range of sources, they recast the history of South African cricket, most notably by bringing to light all the teams and tournaments that included African players in the 19th and early 20th centuries. Not only did Africans play cricket from the mid-1800s, but there were intercommunity matches, and many victories over white teams.

Part of the book's explicit purpose is to return the names of those black players to the "whitewashed" official records. As such, there are sections here that the writers acknowledge a reader may want to skip, consisting as they do of statistics and scorecards that are important to history but less than riveting to the layperson. Admittedly, little of the book is light reading, though that does nothing to diminish its value, both as an analysis of the entwining of Empire and cricket, and as a corrective to accepted history. It is frequently gripping on a human level, never more than in the case of "Krom" Hendricks. He was considered the fastest bowler in South Africa in the 1890s, and – because of his skin colour – his selection, or not, for their first tour of Britain in 1894 became a hot political issue: he was often called "Malay", but the authors are clear he was black, with a Dutch father and a mother from St Helena. Cecil Rhodes played an important role in his eventual omission from the team.

Hendricks's story, the authors contend, "was a microcosm for the tragedy of thousands of black South Africans at the time". This is even more evident if you look back just 25 years to a newspaper report in *The Free Press* of a game between a black team from St Mark's Mission and the white Queenstown club: "We were surprised to hear intelligent men… speak as though they thought the Europeans were demeaning themselves in playing such a game. We cannot see it, and must attribute such feelings to the abominable prejudice which would raise impassable barriers between one race and another."

Cricket and race inevitably form much of the backdrop to Harry Pearson's **Connie: The Marvellous Life of Learie Constantine**. Pearson is adept at detailing the background of race and racism in Trinidad, where Constantine grew up, and at pinpointing historical ironies: there were greater barriers involved in being a black cricketer in the West Indies than in England, though readers may feel they've been taken through all this more thoroughly in *Beyond a Boundary*. C. L. R. James thought the racial attitudes of the Caribbean shackled Connie's talents, which were finally able to break free when West Indies toured England. Whether that's true or not, his performance in England was enough to secure him a contract playing Lancashire League cricket in Nelson, where he became a beloved local hero. (Pearson robustly defends League cricket against accusations of being second-rate.)

Bradman's wish that England might get a dose of Bodyline themselves

Constantine continued to play for West Indies, and was part of the attack that fulfilled Don Bradman's wish that the England players might get a dose of Bodyline themselves. Wally Hammond, who had always opposed the tactic, told his team-mates: "We started it, and we had it coming to us." He must have known that he in particular might face hostile stuff from Constantine, who had long disliked him after a perceived snub on an earlier tour. At Old Trafford, Hammond was bloodied by a ball that smashed into his face, and had to leave the ground for treatment. When he returned, his chin bandaged up, he "walked down the field to Connie and offered his hand". The two became firm friends – one of the many stories in the book that illuminate Constantine's appreciation for the kind or gracious gesture, an appreciation that was especially important in his relationship with the people of Nelson.

But not everything about his life in England was marked by graciousness. His stature as a cricketer didn't prevent his being turfed out of a hotel room in London during the Second World War, because the manager thought the presence of a black man would upset the American army officers staying there. The case he brought against Imperial Hotels would be a legal milestone on the way to the establishment of the 1965 Race Relations Act. Pearson acknowledges that "his actions on the cricket field would fade from memory, but those few days in court would be his lasting legacy". And yet Pearson's real talent is in retelling Constantine's actions on the cricket field, with crackle and fizz. "Connie was a man not of days, but of brief golden moments… a cartwheeling catch, a lightning-fast yorker that splintered a stump, a lofted back-foot drive that cannoned off the pavilion fence." His descriptions of Connie's fielding heroics are a particular delight – reading them, it's easy to understand why Bradman called him "the greatest fieldsman I have ever seen".

Sometimes, what is most straightforward can be most affecting. **The Coming Storm: Test and First-Class Cricketers Killed in World War Two** is precisely what it says on the tin. Nigel McCrery has already compiled books of rugby players, Olympians and cricketers killed in the First World War, and moving on to the Second has done nothing to lessen the poignancy of his project. The form is simple: biographical entries, ordered by date of death, of 152 first-class cricketers (including 12 who played Tests).

One of the first entries, from May 20, 1940, is Captain Patrick William Rucker, who played seven first-class matches for Oxford University, and "took the honour of bowling the first first-class ball following the 1919 Armistice". It is moving enough to read this, knowing he lost his life in the war that followed – and even more moving to learn that his brother Robin, also a cricketer, died in action in 1918 while serving with the RAF. One of the final entries is Lance Corporal Paul Wilson Brooks. As a 16-year-old member of the Lord's groundstaff, he had the chance to bowl to Bradman in the nets – and knocked over his middle stump. In his only first-class match, for Middlesex, he scored an unbeaten 44 while batting with Denis Compton. He died, aged 24, of wounds received in the last months of the war.

The Second World War provides the opening image of **Wisden at The Oval: An Anthology**. In his introduction, Micky Stewart recalls his first memory of the ground, covered in barbed wire while converted to a prisoner-of-war camp. Soon enough though, normal service commences with the first chapter, entitled "The Greatest Match" – no prizes for guessing the final Test of the 2005 Ashes. Who could fail to resist an anthology which returns you, via *Wisden's* coverage, to that passage of play when "Pietersen reeled off shots outrageous in any circumstances, unimaginable in these".

Jon Surtees has edited the anthology, and his shot selection is very fine, if neither outrageous nor unimaginable. The 19 chapters range across such topics as "The Birth of the Ashes", "Hutton at The Oval", "Surrey's Magnificent Seven" and "Visitors from the East" (given how much of the East there is in cricket, perhaps a single chapter is a touch skimpy). It is deeply satisfying to revisit *Wisden's* coverage of some of The Oval's most significant and memorable matches, but no less a delight to find unexpected gems such as the obituary of Surrey's royal patron, George VI, who was remembered for the hat-trick achieved on the grounds below Windsor Castle – his victims were King Edward VII, King George V and the Duke of Windsor. One of the delights of the anthology is in tracking how *Wisden's* writing style has changed over the years, a fine balancing act of respecting tradition and keeping up with the times. Though a forward movement is always necessary, a case might be made for bringing back such phrases as "wickets of surprising truthfulness" (from a Gentlemen v Players match report in 1870).

So much more was expected than delivered from Chris Lewis. What was true of his career is as true of his memoir. **Crazy: My Road to Redemption** begins after the end of his playing days, when he's arrested for smuggling drugs into Gatwick. It's a gripping start, and yet much of the memoir is superficial and unrevealing. His explanation for the ups and downs of his cricket life is that he made mistakes along the way, but too often people took against him for no reason. It's all surprisingly dull from a sportsman who was anything but.

It's Swann chatting, like someone in a pub getting stuck into his favourite subject

If you give a few months of your life to reading cricket books published in England, it becomes clear, if it wasn't already, how the Ashes occupy the cricketing brain of the nation, with all other Test teams attracting only a sliver of attention between them. As long as this remains the case, the question "Do we need another book about the Ashes?" will remain redundant. And who can complain when reading **The Cricketer Anthology of the Ashes**? It is intelligently organised, with sections such as "All-Time Ashes XI" and "Diplomacy, Politics, Controversy". And, in the case of Simon Hughes's picks for the Ashes XI, it is also bracingly controversial. Is Allan Border really the best No. 5? Each chapter is a nicely judged mix of contemporary writers and excerpts from past issues of *The Cricketer*, which allows the reader to savour Plum Warner alongside Christopher Martin-Jenkins and Gideon Haigh. If constructing an Ashes Writers XI, you could do worse than start here.

Graeme Swann's **The Ashes: It's All About the Urn** is harder to pin down. Is it a history? A personal reflection? Or an analysis of some aspect of the contest – and, if so, which? Really, it's Swann chatting, in the manner of someone in a pub getting stuck into his favourite subject. Covering the entire history of the Ashes, with many comments about convicts thrown in for the amusement of those who like that sort of thing, it veers between match summaries, gossip, tangents about his own career, his opinion on one bit of one series. He's good on some subjects (the invention of the googly), bad on others (the role of class in Bodyline). A discussion about Sydney Barnes responding to being heckled by spectators in the 1911-12 Ashes can veer into "that is exactly the kind of thing my dad Ray would have done"; a comment about alcohol consumption by players on that same tour becomes occasion for Swann to air his objections to isotonic sports drinks.

You read through it all, skimming the rapid summaries of one series after another, waiting to get to the Ashes tours Swann played in, at which point the gossip and opinions and off-field stories and tactical analysis are bound to come together in more interesting fashion. And then they don't. He is, strangely, more reticent about the matches he's played in than those from a hundred years ago. You end up with no real sense of the players, the dressing-room, the mental game. His fractious relationship with Kevin Pietersen is barely mentioned, and what he does say is not revelatory: "Kev and I never liked each other. But we had to form a professional relationship… Basically, we rubbed along because it was in both our interests to do so."

For a far more revealing take on life with England, turn to Steve Harmison's autobiography **Speed Demons**. He pulls no punches, whether talking about his own mental struggles, his feelings about other players and administrators, dressing-room politics, or any other subject he touches. He is kind about those he loves (Andrew Flintoff, Rob Key) or admires (Michael Vaughan, Nasser Hussain, Shane Warne), and scathing about those he dislikes (Brian Lara, Geoffrey Boycott, Duncan Fletcher).

His insights into player morale – the importance of central contracts to make individuals feel secure, and of a non-elitist cricket team, as in 2005 – are valuable. And he doesn't hesitate to point the finger of blame at younger players, led by Swann, in the KP affair, even if you get the feeling Harmison's loyalty to people he likes (and he clearly likes Pietersen) may matter more than who was actually at fault.

But the most significant and moving parts of the book centre on the mental health issues he's lived with since his earliest days as a player. To start with, it was touring that brought on depression and anxiety, but his account of the summer of 2004, when he became the No. 1 bowler in the game just as he was being smothered in "a cloak of darkness", is raw and terrifying. "The demons hadn't bothered to travel, they'd come to get me at home." He writes compassionately about most of the other players who suffered mental health problems, though not Jonathan Trott, whose description of his own plight leads Harmison to conclude he was "mentally not very strong, not mentally poorly". Being mentally poorly is a state Harmison doesn't pretend he can conquer. The final chapter, covering life after retirement, is honest about both the struggle and the victory that is survival. *Speed Demons* is always readable, and at its best it's far more than that: it's vital.

If the professional help available to Harmison and others had been around in the days of David Bairstow, would it have saved him? It's a question his son Jonny touches on in **A Clear Blue Sky**, written with Duncan Hamilton, though he focuses more on the need for greater understanding of mental health than circling around the what ifs of his father's suicide. Early on there is a clear statement of intent – a man should be remembered by his life, not his death. So though the book doesn't shy away from addressing David's death, and is painful and detailed about the day it happened, it is the man's

life – as father, cricketer, friend, Yorkshireman – that Jonny wants to celebrate. And how gloriously he does it.

It's a difficult balancing act to write about both your life and the life of a man who wasn't there to witness most of it. But Hamilton's touch is evident in their successful juxtaposition. There is rarely an achievement by Jonny that isn't occasion for him to pivot towards his father and some key moment in his life. So Jonny's maiden Ashes Test leads to David's maiden Ashes Test, Jonny's experience of being whitewashed by Australia in 2013-14 leads to David's horrendous tour of the West Indies in 1980-81. It is as if the two men are running between the wickets together, rotating the strike, taking pleasure in each other's success, and sharing the pain of failure.

Jonny's certainty that his father would have enjoyed his achievements, his almost palpable sense of his presence when he's out in the middle – these are what make this richly rewarding autobiography so affecting. It is not a book of grand declarations, but of small details that break your heart. Such as Jonny, on Test debut, knowing he's the 13th son to follow his father into the England team, but also knowing one other fact: "I was the only son whose dad wasn't there to see him play." Or Jonny as a boy putting on his father's wicketkeeping gloves: "When I had them on, it was like holding hands with him." There are, though, other moments when the book strikes a wrong note – such as when it quotes J. B. Priestley's description of 1930s Bradford. It's one thing for Hamilton to choose not to attempt literary ventriloquism, but quite another to make us feel his imprint to the exclusion of Bairstow. At its finest, though, this production has cricketer and writer working together – Hamilton the runner, Bairstow the batter.

And for the most part, that's precisely how it works. Wonderfully written, always thoughtful, this is a book of two cricketing lives – and also of love and grief. It's a reminder, too, that there is a world beyond cricket, and that cricket contains within it a microcosm of that world. *A Clear Blue Sky* is *Wisden's* Book of the Year.

Kamila Shamsie is a novelist. Her most recent book is Home Fire.

> "Gunaratne all but sealed it with another six, an audacious sweep off Bumrah towards the gas-holder, where the Sri Lankan *papare* band was by now drowning out the Indian drummers."
>
> Champions Trophy in 2017, India v Sri Lanka, page 279

WISDEN BOOK OF THE YEAR

Since 2003, *Wisden's* reviewer has selected a Book of the Year. The winners have been:

2003 *Bodyline Autopsy* by David Frith
2004 *No Coward Soul* by Stephen Chalke and Derek Hodgson
2005 *On and Off the Field* by Ed Smith
2006 *Ashes 2005* by Gideon Haigh
2007 *Brim Full of Passion* by Wasim Khan
2008 *Tom Cartwright: The Flame Still Burns* by Stephen Chalke
2009 *Sweet Summers: The Classic Cricket Writing of JM Kilburn* edited by Duncan Hamilton
2010 *Harold Larwood: The authorized biography of the world's fastest bowler* by Duncan Hamilton
2011 *The Cricketer's Progress: Meadowland to Mumbai* by Eric Midwinter
2012 *Fred Trueman: The Authorised Biography* by Chris Waters
2013 *Bookie Gambler Fixer Spy: A Journey to the Heart of Cricket's Underworld* by Ed Hawkins
2014 *Driving Ambition* by Andrew Strauss
2015 *Wounded Tiger: A History of Cricket in Pakistan* by Peter Oborne
2016 *The Test: My Life, and the Inside Story of the Greatest Ashes Series* by Simon Jones and Jon Hotten
2017 *Following On: A memoir of teenage obsession and terrible cricket* by Emma John
2018 ***A Clear Blue Sky*** **by Jonny Bairstow and Duncan Hamilton**

OTHER AWARDS

The Cricket Society Literary Award has been presented since 1970 to the author of the cricket book judged best of the year. The 2017 award, made by the Cricket Society in association with MCC, was won in April by Mark Nicholas for **The Beautiful Game: My Love Affair With Cricket** (Allen & Unwin); he received £3,000. In June, Nicholas also won the cricket category at the British Sports Book Awards.

BOOKS RECEIVED IN 2017

GENERAL

Brayshaw, Ian **Lillee & Thommo** The Deadly Pair's Reign of Terror (Hardie Grant, paperback, £14.99)

Brearley, Mike **On Form** (Little, Brown, £20)

Campbell, Charlie **Herding Cats** The Art of Amateur Cricket Captaincy Foreword by Mike Brearley (John Wisden, £16.99)

Cawkwell, Tim **The Tale of Two Terriers and the Somerset Cat** The scrap for cricket's County Championship 2016 between Middlesex & Somerset & Yorkshire (Sforzinda Books, paperback, £12.50, ebook £5.50)

Down, Michael **Calling the Shots** Correspondence over fifty years between Don Bradman and Jim Swanton (Boundary Books, £40)

Hamilton, Duncan **The Kings of Summer** How cricket's 2016 County Championship came down to the very last match of the season (Safe Haven, £9.99)

Harman, Jo, ed. **Cricketing Allsorts** The good, the bad, the ugly (and the downright weird) Foreword by David Lloyd (John Wisden, £14.99)

Lazenby, John **Edging Towards Darkness** The story of the last timeless Test (John Wisden, £16.99)

Lonsdale, Jeremy **A Game Taken Seriously** The Foundations of Yorkshire's Cricketing Power (ACS, paperback, £20)

McCrery, Nigel **The Coming Storm** Test and First Class Cricketers Killed in World War Two (Pen & Sword Military, £25)

Midwinter, Eric **Class Peace** An Analysis of Social Status and English Cricket 1846–1962 (ACS, paperback, £15)

Odendaal, André; Reddy, Krish; Merrett, Christopher and Winch, Jonty **Cricket & Conquest** The History of South African Cricket Retold, 1795–1914 (BestRed, paperback, £27.95)

Overson, Chris **All Ten** The Ultimate Bowling Feat (ACS, paperback, £20)

Rigg, John **Still An Ordinary Spectator** Five More Years of Watching Sport (SilverWood, paperback, £16.99)

Ronayne, Michael **A Guide to the Memorials of Cricketers** (ACS, paperback, £20)

Ryan, Christian **Feeling is the Thing that Happens in 1000th of a Second** A Season of Cricket Photographer Patrick Eagar (Riverrun, £20)

Shimwell, David **Cricket and Cannons** Witness of the Game during the Crimean Campaign (ACS, paperback, £15)

Sullivan, Paul **Keeping Secrets** A Wicketkeeper's Handbook (Book Guild, paperback, £8.99)

Swann, Graeme **The Ashes** It's All About the Urn (Hodder & Stoughton, £20)

BIOGRAPHY

Burns, Michael **Endean** A South African Sportsman in the Apartheid Era (Nightwatchman, £15)

Chalke, Stephen **In Sunshine and in Shadow** Geoff Cope and Yorkshire cricket (Fairfield Books, £16)

Cozier, Tony **Sir Everton Weekes** An Appreciation (J. W. McKenzie, paperback, £20)

Murtagh, Andrew **Gentleman and Player** The Story of Colin Cowdrey, Cricket's Most Elegant and Charming Batsman Foreword by Sir John Major (Pitch, £18.99)

Musk, Stephen **George Raikes** 'Muscular Christianity?' (ACS, paperback, £14)

Neal, Steve **Over and Out** Albert Trott: The Man Who Cleared the Lord's Pavilion (Pitch, paperback, £12.99)

Pearson, Harry **Connie** The Marvellous Life of Learie Constantine (Little, Brown, £20)

Popplewell, Mike **Maurice Leyland** (ACS, paperback, £15)

Rowe, Mark **Brian Sellers** Yorkshire Tyrant (ACS, paperback, £15)

Thompson, Mike **The Lord of Lord's** The Life and Times of Lord Frederick Beauclerk (Christopher Saunders, paperback, £10)

AUTOBIOGRAPHY

Bairstow, Jonny and Hamilton, Duncan **A Clear Blue Sky** (HarperCollins, £20)

Blofeld, Henry **Over and Out** The innings of a lifetime with Test Match Special (Hodder & Stoughton, £20)

Harmison, Steve **Speed Demons** My Autobiography Foreword by Andrew Flintoff (Sport Media, £20)

Lewis, Chris **Crazy** My Road to Redemption (The History Press, £20)

Procter, Mike and Zama, Lungani **Caught in the Middle** Monkeygate, Politics and Other Hairy Issues; the Autobiography of Mike Procter (Pitch, £16.99)

ANTHOLOGY

Surtees, Jon **Wisden at The Oval** An Anthology Forewords by Micky Stewart and Alec Stewart (John Wisden, £20)

Turbervill, Huw, ed. **The Cricketer Anthology of the Ashes** (Allen & Unwin, £20)

ILLUSTRATED

Elliott, Robert **Changing Rooms 2** The Cricket Pavilions of Hampshire and the Isle of Wight Foreword by Tim Tremlett (George Mann Publications, £20)

POETRY

Aspin, Chris **Just a few extras** Some no-balls and wides (The Tor Press, paperback, £3.99, from the author, 21 Westbourne, Helmshore, Rossendale, BB4 4QD)

STATISTICAL

Bailey, Philip, comp. **First-Class Cricket Matches 1952** (ACS, acscricket.com, paperback, £32)
Bryant, John, ed. **First-Class Matches India 2003/04 and 2004/05** and **First-Class Matches India 2005/06 and 2006/07** (ACS, paperback, £20 each)
Percival, Tony **Dorset Cricketers 1845–2016** (ACS, paperback, £13)

HANDBOOKS AND ANNUALS

Bailey, Philip, ed. **ACS International Cricket Year Book 2017** (ACS, paperback, £30)
Bryant, John, ed. **ACS Overseas First-Class Annual 2017** (ACS, paperback, £70)
Full scorecards for first-class matches outside England in 2016-17.
Bryden, Colin, ed. **South African Cricket Annual 2017** (CSA, www.sacricketshop.co.za, R200 plus p&p)
Clayton, Howard, ed. **First-Class Counties Second Eleven Annual 2017** (ACS, paperback, £13)
Colliver, Lawrie, ed. **Australian Cricket Digest 2017-18** (paperback, $A30 plus p&p; more from lawrie.colliver@gmail.com)
Marshall, Ian, ed. **Playfair Cricket Annual 2017** (Headline, paperback, £9.99)
Moorhead, Benj, ed. **The Cricketers' Who's Who 2017** Foreword by Marcus Trescothick (Jellyfish, £19.99)
Payne, Francis and Smith, Ian, ed. **2017 New Zealand Cricket Almanack** (Upstart Press, $NZ55)
Piesse, Ken, ed. **Pavilion 2018** (Australian Cricket Society, paperback, £19.95 inc airmail; more details from www.cricketbooks.com.au)

REPRINTS AND UPDATES

Haigh, Gideon **The Cricket War** The Story of Kerry Packer's World Series Cricket (John Wisden, £12.99)
Wilson, James **Court & Bowled** Tales of Cricket and the Law (Wildy, Simmonds & Hill, paperback, £14.99)

PERIODICALS

The Cricketer (monthly) ed. Simon Hughes (The Cricketer Publishing, £4.95; £44.99 for 12 print issues, £44.99 digital, £49.99 print & digital. Subscriptions: www.thecricketer.com)
The Cricket Paper (weekly) ed. David Emery (Greenways Publishing, £1.50; £20 for ten issues inc p&p, from www.thecricketpaper.com)
The Cricket Statistician (quarterly) ed. Simon Sweetman (ACS, £3 to non-members)
The Journal of the Cricket Society (twice yearly) (from D. Seymour, 13 Ewhurst Road, Crofton Park, London, SE4 1AG, £5 to non-members, www.cricketsociety.com)
Wisden Cricket Monthly ed. Phil Walker (Cricket Properties, £4.95; £41.99 for 12 print issues, £17.99 digital. Subscriptions: www.wisdensubs.com)

CRICKET IN THE MEDIA IN 2017

There's always next year

ALAN TYERS

Michael Vaughan used his 2017 New Year's Day column in *The Sunday Telegraph* to suggest it would be "the most important year ever in English cricket". His *annus importantissimus* saw the sport and its scribes deal with a variety of subjects. Some were familiar, such as Twenty20's unfolding patricide of Test cricket. Some were surprising, though not unforeseeable, such as England's women carrying all before them at Lord's. And some, such as the introduction of the "headbutt greeting" into the sport's lexicon, were unknown unknowns.

In *The Times*, Mike Atherton warned of the development of a "two-speed cricketing economy" – Tests in one lane, Twenty20 in the other – and predicted a "divergence likely to end in tears for Test and international cricket". It remained the issue of issues for newspapermen, perhaps because it mirrored print's fears about its own death by a thousand clicks.

As with much in British life, change was both embraced and feared. A few wanted to call the whole thing off and return to the 1950s, where Denis Compton was always sweeping the ball dreamily into a gap, the beer was warm, and foreigners knew their place. Matthew Engel told *Guardian* readers that "everything worthwhile about cricket is being destroyed", but another former *Wisden* editor, Scyld Berry, was more measured. "Everyone agrees that Test cricket needs context," he wrote in *The Sunday Telegraph.* And a context of sorts finally arrived when the ICC approved a nine-team structure, to begin in 2019.

Whether the move helps save Tests remains to be seen, but the game cannot be accused of a reluctance to tinker. The *Daily Telegraph's* Nick Hoult reported in September that the ECB were "leading the push for Test matches to be reduced to four days after the 2019 Ashes. They are confident they have the support of broadcasters and host grounds."

One broadcaster keen to get back into cricket, if not Tests, was the BBC, who will show live matches once more from 2020 – and Twenty20 is what it will be, international and

THE Sun
WIN £100K
6 MONTHS OF CHAOS
EXCLUSIVE: ENGLAND ACE BRAWL
HIT FOR SIX
Vid catches Ben Stokes in punch-up
Cricketer's right hook floors clubber

Courtesy of *The Sun* and Getty Images

Decisive blow: Ben Stokes's Bristol antics reach the national press.

domestic. With the ECB casting envious eyes at the Big Bash League and the IPL, those domestic matches will involve eight city-based teams. "What we are doing here is future-proofing county cricket," ECB chief executive Tom Harrison told BBC sports editor Dan Roan. In that piece of seemingly harmless management guff was contained much of the challenge facing the game outside India: an attempt to hold back the tide.

Some of us will be glued to the Manchester JD Sports Meerkats against the London Subway Vodafones in 2020, and some of us won't, but English cricket can at least point to the BBL as proof that a televised, city-based T20 tournament can indeed capture a nation's interest. While it would be lovely if ten hours of BBC1 were given over to uninterrupted Test coverage of England routing Sri Lanka on an Orkney greentop in March, perhaps we should recognise that something is better than nothing.

From complicated deals involving impossibly divergent interests to Theresa May, who was a guest on *Test Match Special* as part of its 60th birthday celebrations. She revealed an admiration for a certain strong and stable Yorkshireman. "I have been a Geoff Boycott fan all my life," said the PM, who in 2017 often seemed likely to be run out by a team-mate herself. "It was just that he kind of solidly got on with what he was doing." May also recorded a goodwill message for another *TMS* institution: "Can I just say, Blowers, my dear old thing, we wish you all the best in your well-earned retirement."

Jonathan Liew used that retirement as a launchpad for a thoughtful piece in *The Daily Telegraph* about privilege and opportunity: "Was Henry Blofeld the best man for the job over his 45 years? How many potential commentary greats from less privileged backgrounds never enjoyed his fortune, never knew the right people?" There was a kerfuffle online and in the readers' letters, with Liew taking some fearful tap. Some wrongly construed the piece as a personal attack on Blofeld, rather than an examination of a wider theme.

One group who did get an opportunity in the summer were second-rank West Indies cricketers. With their big names choosing to rally round their bank balances by earning T20 cash, they got a pasting in the First Test at Edgbaston. Hence Boycott in the *Telegraph*: "This West Indies lot are the worst Test match team I have seen in more than 50 years. They can't bat and can't bowl. The gulf between [England and West Indies] was as wide as the Grand Canyon." A week later, West Indies won at Headingley. If you cannot enjoy that, what else is there?

The fury directed at Liew over Blofeld was as nothing compared with the vitriol unleashed on the unfortunate developers of ESPNcricinfo. To better serve mobile users, who make up 80% of its audience, cricket's leading website was redesigned, apparently by the criminally insane. But Cricinfo did continue to produce diverse, freewheeling reportage, with writers not so bound by space or the news cycle as their inky colleagues.

The way people convey and receive ideas and information about cricket has already undergone huge change; in a few years' time, perhaps the concept of reporters trekking to a sporting event, and readers consuming their thoughts shortly after the close of play, will seem quaint. If we really all have had enough of experts, and if technology – legal or otherwise – means we can

watch the live action and bark out our opinions, then it will be up to writers to tell us something new, dazzle us, unearth the unique and true and beautiful. Oh, and preferably to do it online for free.

Miraculous moment: *Wisden Cricket Monthly* is reborn.

This post-authority world has not yet fully come to pass, and there was even an old-school rustling in the magazine undergrowth. *All Out Cricket* retired, and the same team were relaunched as *Wisden Cricket Monthly*, returning the title to the news stands after a 14-year hiatus. Simon Briggs of the *Telegraph* wrote: "A long-standing conflict will be resumed in the land of bats and balls. Not England v Australia, but *Wisden Cricket Monthly* v *The Cricketer*. For cricket tragics, this is a miraculous moment."

Talking of moments, the presence of women's cricket in every national paper after England's World Cup win in July marked a dramatic step change, and a *Times* leader described their triumph over India as "one of the best games of recent times". Not everyone, though, was prepared to take the happy occasion at face value. The *Daily Mirror* couldn't resist ho-ho comparisons with the men's team: "Here's How To Win A World Cup, Boys". But when *The Sun* are running a spread on the Natmeg, something is afoot. One or two columnists saw an opportunity to sneer: Dominic Lawson told *Daily Mail* readers that coverage of women's sport was "propaganda", which owed "very little to objective assessment of sporting quality and excitement". He "burst out laughing" when Jenny Gunn dropped a sitter in the final. Lawson's loss.

The incident involving Ben Stokes in Bristol received major coverage when it first broke, and again when *The Sun* published a mobile-phone video of the "shocking street brawl". He was even papped at his wedding. Cricket hadn't seen anything like this since mid-1980s Botham. Two men subsequently came forward to tell the newspaper that Stokes had been defending them from homophobic abuse. "We were so grateful to Ben for stepping in to help," said Billy O'Connell. "He was a real hero." His friend Kai Barry added: "We couldn't believe it when we found out they were famous cricketers. I just thought Ben and Alex [Hales] were quite hot, fit guys." The endorsement came too late to get Stokes on the plane to Australia.

With Sky being outbid, the Ashes were now being broadcast to the UK by BT Sports. The signing of Ricky Ponting was a coup: he is well on his way to being a pundit of the first rank. Damien Fleming (quirky) and Adam Gilchrist (enthusiastic) were welcome, less-familiar voices and, unlike Michael Slater (Aussie Aussie Aussie), avoided the tub-thumping, all-bloody-good-mates-together shtick that pervades Australian cricket broadcasting. Alison Mitchell, a class act on radio and TV alike, had an excellent series. But Giles Smith of *The Times* said Graeme Swann's "contrived humour and platitudes are starting to grate". And if Swann wants a comedy mentor, he need look no further than anchor Matt Smith, who inadvertently produced the funniest moment of the winter, referring to the Australian national anthem "Advance Australia Fair" as "Waltzing Matilda".

Charlie Sale of the *Daily Mail* turned his pitiless eye on BT's viewing figures: "The paltry averages for the five days in Brisbane were 100,000, 106,000, 80,000, 89,000 and 73,000 for the last rites on the fifth morning." Attacking the same cracks but from a different angle on the crease, the *Guardian's* Marina Hyde noted that subscription TV had brought an end to the-era of the genuinely famous cricketer: "Most of the England squad enjoy the sort of obscurity you'd expect from one of the better witness-protection programmes."

In Australia, however, Jonny Bairstow and Ben Duckett both found themselves persons of interest. Bairstow had essayed an innocent but ill-judged headbutt greeting on Cameron Bancroft when they met in a Perth bar. During the Brisbane Test, Australia's brains trust made sure mention of this was picked up by their obliging media via on-field stump mikes; Bairstow said in his *Daily Mail* column he had been "stitched up", and it was just a case of "boys being boys". Chris Tremlett, a veteran of the two previous Ashes tours, used his *City AM* column to call it "an unwanted and unnecessary furore",

Class acts: BT's Alison Mitchell interviews Alastair Cook at the end of the Melbourne Test.

while the *Mirror* lamented Duckett's "beer antics" after he poured a pint over Jimmy Anderson. Given the Stokes backdrop, England's players and handlers had a tin ear for the sort of story that gets in the papers and helps destabilise a tour party.

On the first day of the Perth Test came an unexpected front page: "*The Sun* has smashed a multi-million pound plot to fix today's third Ashes cricket Test". But everyone was reassured when the *London Evening Standard* and others promptly quoted "world cricket's anti-corruption boss Alex Marshall" as saying "there is no evidence, either from *The Sun* or via our own intelligence, to suggest the current Test has been corrupted". If fixing remained a constant niggle, the absence of any significant names to English eyes meant it could be just about ignored, like a man not wanting to bother his GP about a persistent cough.

Maybe it's because the sport is less in the mainstream, maybe because defeat in Australia is no longer seen as a disgrace, but press reaction to the Ashes hammering was relatively mild compared with the frothing spite of the past. The *Daily Express* said the team had "meekly surrendered", but that was generally as strong as it got. Scyld Berry opted for humanity: "The fundamental fact is that Root's squad does not contain enough good players to beat Australia away."

And so Vaughan's most important year came to an end, with widespread newspaper resignation – stop me if you've heard this one before – that the English system was not preparing a Test side to win away from home. Was 2017 the most important year for English cricket? Or is that always the year to come?

Alan Tyers is a sportswriter for The Daily Telegraph.

CRICKET AND BLOGS IN 2017

From Friedrich Nietzsche to Martin Peters

BRIAN CARPENTER

It is a basic human need to seek something to hold on to in times of flux or crisis. In 2017, the temptation was to insulate oneself from the events of the wider world. Cricket has a role to play and – though we shouldn't overstate it – following the game can act as a conduit for many feelings: of belonging, possession and, as the sport's evolution leads to mutations many don't like, loss and nostalgia. There are different ways of meeting these challenges, and of writing about them.

Pure nostalgia was provided by Peter Hoare's recreation of Kent's 1967 season, 50 years on. With a montage of references to cricket and the news of the day, he immersed his readers in a pivotal time both for him and Kent. It was the year Hoare first owned a *Wisden* and visited Lord's; it also marked the start of a golden era for the club. In his post "The First of the Great Days" (**mylifeincricketscorecards.blogspot.co.uk**), he evoked the atmosphere at the St Lawrence Ground during the Gillette Cup semi-final against Sussex that July. Kent would go on to win 11 trophies in 12 years, while Hoare began a lifetime's intoxication with cricket.

The sport's rich history, too, offers ballast against the vicissitudes of modern life. This was illustrated well by the brief return to the blogosphere of one of its finest writers, Jon Hotten, at **theoldbatsman.blogspot.co.uk**. Hotten's series on the psychogeography of cricket evocatively recounted the exploits of David Harris, Silver Billy Beldham and Lord Frederick Beauclerk on the grounds of east Hampshire and west Surrey, where Hotten himself learned the game. He chronicles cricket's history, and charts his own small place in it. In uncertain times, these things matter.

Of course, cricket cannot continue to exist in a backward-looking bubble, and there is, at least in England, an awareness of the need to attract new followers. Two regular bloggers – Chris Smith, who coaches the juniors at Sale CC, and Rick Walton, an award-winning community coach in Pembrokeshire – were involved in All Stars Cricket, the ECB's latest attempt to do this. Smith (**chrispscricket.wordpress.com**) pointed to the ambivalence the devoted fan may feel about the initiative, while acknowledging the game must expand beyond its exclusive confines. "Its ambition is substantial," he writes of All Stars Cricket. "It aims to make cricket the popular choice of young children and their families. And if it succeeds, cricket will be popular, and my slightly eccentric obsession will be ordinary. I will be part of the mainstream."

Central to any devotee's love of the game are the sights and sounds of the *form* of cricket they most enjoy. For the ever wry Nick Slough (**newcrimsonrambler.wordpress.com**), it is the County Championship at Grace Road, where a bouncer flies "as far over Lewis Hill's head as a lecture

CRICKET AND TWITTER IN 2017

Viral Kohli rules the world

NISHANT JOSHI

In its infancy, Twitter was lauded as a platform for democracy, amplifying the voice of the people, and allowing truth to prevail. In 2017, these hopes were debunked.

Cricket is a public-relations curiosity, since the ratio of fans to household names is bigger than in most other team sports. Any misstep tends to draw a disproportionate media reaction: on slow news days, tabloid fodder can inspire 24/7 rolling coverage, with talking heads shouting over one another about the effect of Virat Kohli's marriage on his back-foot punch through the covers.

The game's biggest and best-paid star is often the centre of online attention, and his influence was typified by the reaction to an innocuous interview in which former Australia batsman Brad Hodge commented on Kohli's injury-enforced absence during the India–Australia Test series: "If you miss one game of Test match cricket and you're fronting up the next week for RCB versus whoever at Bangalore… you'd be pretty dirty if he didn't front up to a Test match and try and win a valuable series against Australia. You would think that your captain would get out there and get among the fight."

Hodge soon regretted his lese-majesty. Kohli's army of fans demanded an apology, and Bollywood megastar Amitabh Bachchan, another social-media powerbroker, raged: "Brad Hodge says 'Virat skipped 4th to play IPL'. RUBBISH! He did it to tell you that his team can wallop you even without him!"

The Indian media sensed blood, and Hodge was forced into a humiliating climbdown, tweeting a sweet-as-saccharine image of his typed apology: "I take this opportunity to apologise to the people of India, cricket fans, the Indian national cricket team, and particularly Virat Kohli for my previous comments."

You would have thought Hodge had committed a felony in public office. His letter was four paragraphs long, and contained several phrases highlighted in bold. But Kohli's aura was now so large that another man's minor comment had given way to a grovelling apology – all without Kohli typing a word in anger. In unrelated news, Hodge later earned a three-year contract as coach of Kings XI Punjab.

At the less exalted end of the spectrum, a spat between Alex Hales and former West Indies quick Tino Best kept Twitter users amused. Before a one-day international at Old Trafford, Best questioned Hales's ability against fast bowling, saying he would have "enjoyed cracking that nut". Hales responded: "I faced you in 2010, mate, in your peak. You literally couldn't land it on the cut strip #90mphDross". When another user complimented Hales on his riposte, he landed another blow: "It was a wide long hop to be fair, unsurprisingly."

In an unexpected intervention, comedian John Cleese waded in to the end-of-season debate about the turning pitch Somerset laid out for Middlesex in a crucial Championship game. "I see Middlesex are squealing about the pitch at Taunton," he tweeted. "Bit rich, after they created last year's fiasco against Yorkshire at Lord's."

One user's suggestion that someone "should ask for answers" was accompanied by an image of Cleese's *Monty Python* colleagues Terry Jones, Michael Palin and Terry Gilliam cloaked in red as part of their Spanish Inquisition sketch. The things that end up on Twitter…

Nishant Joshi used to tweet @AltCricket but, after a series of unfortunate tweets involving an unnamed Indian superstar, the account is currently suspended.

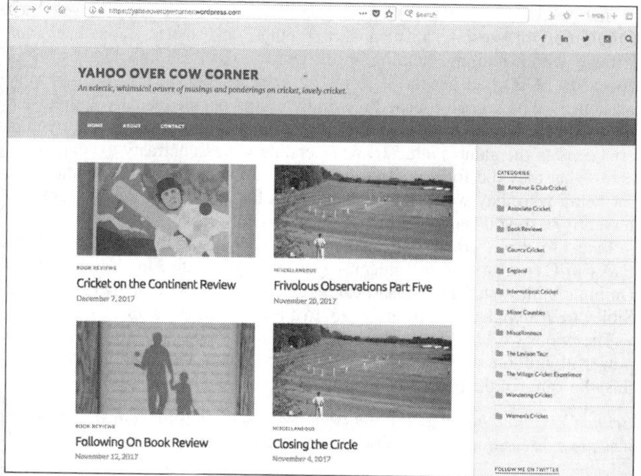

on Hegel". But the comfort of the familiar is rarely without a strong sense of wistfulness and incipient loss: "It has sometimes occurred to me that the ideal reader of this blog has not yet been born. This is not because, like Friedrich Nietzsche or Martin Peters, I imagine myself to be ahead of my time, but because, I hope, it may serve as a record of a way of life that, I suspect, will have long since ceased to exist."

For Hector Cappelletti (**yahooovercowcorner.wordpress.com**), it is largely the game below first-class level that sustains him against the winds of change. During 2017, his blog was enriched by a series of posts paying tribute to a section of English cricket which rarely receives its due, but to which those of us who know it well keep coming back. In response to an article in *The Guardian* by Matthew Engel about disillusionment with the modern game, Cappelletti enumerated the many virtues of Minor Counties cricket: "The culture of the umpire's decision being final? No problem, as there are no television cameras or DRS… the first innings is restricted to 90 overs… pitches are not rolled within an inch of their life, spin bowlers are hugely valuable assets and regularly bowl the lion's share of overs, while centuries are still a reasonably rare commodity and a landmark achievement."

Some bloggers resist the urge to retreat into nostalgia's warm embrace. **Beingoutsidecricket.com** feels deeply uneasy about the way the game is going, and comes out swinging. This was best encapsulated by the unwaveringly angry Dmitri Old's dissection of the experience of watching a T20 Blast match at The Oval. Chris Crampton, another contributor to the blog, writes with wisdom and elegance, as illustrated by "Community Service" and his truly exceptional "Standing on the Shoulders of Giants", which offered a refreshing contrast to Old's confrontational approach.

The first of these posts lauded the contribution to cricket at all levels by a certain sort of person, "this band of brothers and sisters… the backbone without whom nothing, nothing at all, would exist". He concludes with an appeal to ECB chief executive Tom Harrison to "thank them for their very existence". The second touched movingly on the people, usually appreciated only with the lucid retrospect conferred by middle age, who introduce young cricketers to the game's ethical values, ending with an entreaty to "express to them what they did for you. Tell them how important they were, thank them for being who they were and what they did. Before it's too late. Before you fervently wish you had taken just a moment to do so."

Like life itself, cricket constantly changes. When Cappelletti visited the Parks in Oxford to see the students play Surrey in late March, he watched Dominic Sibley and Zafar Ansari bat together. By August, both had moved on: Sibley to Warwickshire; Ansari, at 25, to a life outside the game.

The wider world is a complex and concerning place, and cricket can be a powerful antidote to its madness. While playing and watching are central to this, the value of the pen and the keyboard should not be underestimated.

Brian Carpenter blogs at differentshadesofgreen.blogspot.com. In 2013, he was the inaugural winner of Wisden's *writing competition.*

RETIREMENTS IN 2017

The superhero with red corkscrew curls

STEVE JAMES

It is easy to judge **Chris Read's** career by an early mistake. Back in 1999, aged just 20 and in only his second Test, he ducked under a slower ball from New Zealand's Chris Cairns at Lord's, and was unceremoniously bowled. Easy, but unfair. It's also unfair to judge him simply on his international career. He played 15 Tests and 36 one-day internationals, making a total of 97 dismissals. His batting record was similar in both, averaging a little above 18 in Tests, a little below in ODIs. That was one reason former England coach Duncan Fletcher did not rate him, preferring a more vocal and ebullient wicketkeeper – and one more reliable with the bat.

It's also true that Peter Moores, Fletcher's successor, ignored Read. And yet he was a magnificent county cricketer, one of the purest glovemen of recent decades. In an era of Adam Gilchrist-style wicketkeeping packages – code for scoring runs heavily and quickly – he was a throwback to a time when keeping was valued as an art in itself. Not that Read was a mug with the bat: he improved enormously, ending with 26 first-class centuries and an average of 37. Many frontline batsmen would be happy with that.

He played briefly for Gloucestershire in 1997 where Jack Russell had the gloves, then settled at Trent Bridge, where he spent 20 seasons. In all, he made 1,104 first-class dismissals; no other current keeper has 900. At the time of his retirement, only Marcus Trescothick among England contemporaries (375 matches) had played more than Read's 349. He was a shrewd captain, too, leading Nottinghamshire from 2008, and winning the Championship in 2010. Just as importantly, he was one of county cricket's gentlemen.

A prominent member of Read's Championship-winning side was left-arm seamer **Ryan Sidebottom**, who spent seven summers at Nottinghamshire before finishing his career where he had started it, at his native Yorkshire. He too was one of the game's most popular players, as an end-of-season/career celebration proved: his county colleagues all dressed as Sidebottoms – complete with mops of curly ginger hair – as they did the Otley Run, a Leeds pub crawl. His team-mates had told him the theme was superheroes…

The reverence was justified. Sidebottom took 762 first-class wickets at under 24, and was a part of five Championship-winning teams – twice with

MOST FIRST-CLASS GAMES AS NOTTINGHAMSHIRE CAPTAIN

	M	*Span*		*M*	*Span*
A. W. Carr	397	1914–34	R. T. Robinson	174	1987–97
A. O. Jones	282	1897–1914	G. F. H. Heane	165	1928–46
R. T. Simpson	249	1948–61	**C. M. W. Read**	**159**	**2008–17**
C. E. B. Rice	174	1979–87	J. A. Dixon	158	1889–99

Standing back: Chris Read bows out of county cricket, at Hove in September.

Nottinghamshire, thrice with Yorkshire. He also had a fine England career, which looked unlikely after he went wicketless on Test debut against Pakistan in 2001, and fell out of the reckoning. But he had gathered extra pace by the time he was recalled in 2007 against West Indies, his left-arm inswing now especially dangerous to right-handers. In 2008, he tormented New Zealand away and home, taking 41 wickets in six Tests at 18 each, including a hat-trick at Hamilton. Injuries limited his career to 22 caps, but he became an integral part of the side in the shorter formats, notably when England won the World Twenty20 in the Caribbean in 2010, their first global tournament.

Also in that side was **Michael Lumb**. His selection was a surprise: he and Craig Kieswetter had proved such an effective opening pair when England Lions beat their senior counterparts in a warm-up match in Dubai that they were instantly promoted. The left-handed Lumb's role was simple: get the team off to a flyer. His top score at the World T20 was only 33, but an upright, muscular method, honed in his native South Africa, helped him do the job superbly; a strike-rate of 141 was England's highest.

Lumb had played 20 T20 internationals before making his ODI debut against West Indies in February 2014, and he hit the ground running with a hundred on debut. But three games in the Caribbean was the sum of his 50-over England career. He played seven more T20s, all in March, then returned to county cricket. Like Sidebottom, whose father Arnie was a Headingley stalwart of the 1970s and '80s, Lumb was the son of a Yorkshire regular, Richard. And, like Sidebottom, he left Leeds to play for Nottinghamshire – though in Lumb's case via Hampshire.

Kumar Sangakkara was a different left-hander, all elegance and style. He had already established himself as one of the game's greats by climbing to fifth on the list of Test run-scorers. Yet his insatiable desire at the lower level was equally spectacular: he enjoyed three seasons at Surrey, none more dazzling than 2017, when he made 1,491 Championship runs at an average of 106. He scored eight centuries, including five in a row; two came at Lord's in the week his portrait was unveiled in the Pavilion. The county game was blessed by his presence.

It was no surprise **Jacques Rudolph** – another left-hander – could not match those figures. But he had a successful four-year stint at Glamorgan, after appearing for Yorkshire and, briefly, Surrey. He played 48 Tests for South Africa, and there was nothing shabby about his average of 35. In first-class matches, he racked up 51 centuries, though his strongest suit was the one-day game: more than 10,000 runs at a remarkable 48, with 18 hundreds.

Ian Westwood, who made 159 first-class appearances for Warwickshire, was – like Lumb and Rudolph – a left-handed opener. He might not have had a wide range of strokes, but was nuggety enough to score 16 centuries. He captained Warwickshire for two seasons, and was part of their Championship-winning teams of 2004 and 2012.

The decision of **Zafar Ansari** to retire came as a shock, since he stepped down less than six months after his Test debut, aged 24, in Bangladesh. He was a solid, useful cricketer – a developing batsman and left-arm spinner – even if he owed his elevation more to England's desperate search for slow bowlers than to outstanding performances for Surrey.

Glamorgan's wicketkeeper-batsman **Mark Wallace** had a longer career. He made his debut as a 17-year-old in 1999, and became established in the side two years later, after being summoned from a second-team game at Abergavenny by his captain, the writer of this piece. The regular keeper, Adrian Shaw, was ill, and Wallace held eight catches and hit an unbeaten 80.

Hair today, gone tomorrow. A musclebound superhero and 21 Ryan Sidebottoms on the Otley Run.

To say he did not look back is an understatement: it was the first of 230 consecutive appearances in the Championship, a run ended by a calf injury in 2015. He did not play in 2017, having taken up a role with the Professional Cricketers' Association.

Tom Smith did not appear last season either: a back injury forced his retirement in January. A useful all-rounder, he played a central role in the Lancashire side that won a long-awaited title in 2011. He was appointed captain in 2015, but fitness allowed him to lead them in just one Championship match.

Others to hang up their boots included two who turned out for Kent. **Fabian Cowdrey**, who announced his retirement two weeks before the season began, is the son of Chris and grandson of Colin; he played 12 first-class matches. **Charlie Shreck**, a beanpole swing bowler from Truro, started his first-class career at Nottinghamshire, joined Kent in 2011, then Leicestershire three years later. He claimed 577 first-class wickets, but managed only a couple in 2017 before he was claimed by injury.

CAREER FIGURES

Players not expected to appear in county cricket in 2018

(minimum 40 first-class appearances)

BATTING

	M	*I*	*NO*	*R*	*HS*	*100*	*Avge*	*1,000r/ season*
J. Allenby	153	240	30	7,784	138*	10	37.06	1
Z. S. Ansari	71	116	15	3,009	112	3	29.79	1
Azharullah	111	149	76	968	58*	–	13.26	–
W. D. Bragg	111	196	8	5,673	161*	6	30.17	3
A. N. Kervezee	97	164	9	4,621	155	6	29.81	1
M. J. Lumb	210	352	18	11,443	221*	21	34.26	3
M. W. Machan	44	67	4	2,089	192	5	33.15	–
D. Murphy	78	105	22	2,205	135*	1	26.56	–
C. M. W. Read	349	526	87	16,361	240	26	37.26	3
J. A. Rudolph	294	508	31	19,825	228*	51	41.56	4+1
K. C. Sangakkara	260	430	31	20,911	319	64	52.40	2+1
A. Shahzad	97	128	31	2,237	88	–	23.06	–
C. E. Shreck	175	211	109	801	56	–	7.85	–
R. J. Sidebottom	230	284	91	2,684	61	–	13.90	–
G. P. Smith	105	194	10	4,963	158*	8	26.97	–
T. C. Smith	107	160	25	3,972	128	3	29.42	–
S. J. Thakor	51	80	12	2,571	134	5	37.82	–
M. A. Wallace	264	422	36	11,159	139	15	28.90	1
I. J. Westwood	159	266	22	8,077	196	16	33.10	–

2+1 indicates two seasons in England and one overseas.

BOWLING

	R	*W*	*BB*	*Avge*	*5I*	*10M*	*Ct/St*
J. Allenby	7,902	298	6-54	26.51	5	1	165
Z. S. Ansari	4,592	128	6-30	35.87	6	–	31
Azharullah	10,345	362	7-74	28.57	17	2	23
W. D. Bragg	459	5	2-10	91.80	–	–	46/1
A. N. Kervezee	378	8	3-72	47.25	–	–	46
M. J. Lumb	260	6	2-10	43.33	–	–	118
M. W. Machan	103	1	1-36	103.00	–	–	18
D. Murphy	43	1	1-40	43.00	–	–	207/19
C. M. W. Read	90	0	0-2	–	–	–	1,051/53
J. A. Rudolph	2,696	61	5-80	44.19	3	–	244
K. C. Sangakkara	150	1	1-13	150.00	–	–	372/33
A. Shahzad	8,709	249	5-46	34.97	4	–	16
C. E. Shreck	18,353	577	8-31	31.80	23	2	49
R. J. Sidebottom	18,138	762	7-37	23.80	31	4	64
G. P. Smith	73	1	1-64	73.00	–	–	86
T. C. Smith	6,882	241	6-46	28.55	7	–	112
S. J. Thakor	2,452	57	5-63	43.01	1	–	11
M. A. Wallace	3	0	0-3	–	–	–	707/56
I. J. Westwood	337	7	2-39	48.14	–	–	83

CRICKETANA IN 2017

Tall tales from Bodyline?

MARCUS WILLIAMS

"O my Hornby and my Barlow long ago!" is the refrain from Francis Thompson's nostalgic 1907 poem "At Lord's", as he harked back to youthful days watching Lancashire's opening pair at Old Trafford. Wind forward to 2017, and it might have been a case of "OMG!! Barlow £45k!!!! #AshesWinner" after the huge interest in a silver trophy presented to Dick Barlow for his match-winning performance at Sydney in 1882-83. This was the Test, after all, that spawned the Ashes: Australia needed 153 to take the series 2–1, but were destroyed by Barlow's seven for 40.

As well as his prowess on the field, he was a keen collector of memorabilia, which he kept on display in his Blackpool home. In his autobiography, *Forty Seasons of First-Class Cricket*, he also mentioned a £20 purse that accompanied the cup, so he might have been intrigued to learn that, at a Knights auction in Leicester last May, a bidder paid £45,436 (a hammer price of £37,000, plus buyer's premium and VAT) for his trophy. This was far in excess of the estimate of £7,000–10,000.

The cup is an elaborate, if unofficial, match award – the precursor of today's medallions and motorbikes, jeroboams and jumbo cheques – and is richly decorated. The main bowl rests on two bats and a stump, there are balls on the base and handles, while the lid sports the figure of a batsman. According to its inscription it was presented to Barlow "by a few friends in Australia for his excellent batting & bowling against the Australian Eleven. January 29th 1883". In all, he took eight wickets, and hit useful scores of 28 and 24.

Knights

Barlow sets the bar high: the cup that fetched over £45,000.

Following the match, a group of Melbourne women reputedly burned a bail and placed the ashes – representing the death of Australian cricket, after *The Sporting Times* had the previous September carried a mock obituary for the English game – in the urn before presenting it to the victorious England captain, Ivo Bligh.

Barlow features in the verse fixed to its side:

When Ivo goes back with the urn, the urn;
Studds, Steel, Read and Tylecote return, return;
The welkin will ring loud,
The great crowd will feel proud,
Seeing Barlow and Bates with the urn, the urn;
And the rest coming home with the urn.

Nearly a century later, in 1981, came another celebrated Ashes series. The Headingley Test, where Ian Botham and Bob Willis inspired England to victory after they followed on, was the high-water mark. At the same Knights auction, the ball with which Willis took eight for 43 was offered for sale, together with two of his medals: a one-off presented by the sponsors, Cornhill Insurance, for his Headingley exploits (Botham was the official Man of the Match), plus another for being part of the Ashes-winning team. Between them, they fetched £13,508 – around ten times more than when sold in 1988. Even allowing for inflation that was a huge advance.

Like many modern cricketers, Willis was unmoved by memorabilia, and in 1988 said: "I've never been one to make my home into a shrine to myself. I always kept the trophies and things in a suitcase. Now I've moved from Birmingham to Clapham, and I've got less space." As for the ball: "I've never taken it out of its box." Collectors, on the other hand, thrive on the vicarious thrill of owning items used in top-level sport.

A different motive prompted Dermot Reeve, another Warwickshire and England cricketer, to sell one of his valuable possessions. He had lost a TV commentary job, and his marriage, because of a well-publicised issue with cocaine, and the leatherbound *Wisden* he was given for being one of the Five Cricketers of the Year in 1996 offered a source of cash. "I wouldn't want anyone to think I'm being disrespectful to Wisden," he said. "The award was very special to me and my family, and I have cherished it. But I live in Perth, and my kids are in Sydney, and if this pays for a couple of flights so I can see them more often, it will be worth it."

The book, No. 5 in an edition of just 150, eventually sold for £3,000 on wisdenauction.com. (This was close to the sum paid in 2016 for a leatherbound *Wisden 2011*, never presented because of the previous summer's spot-fixing scandal.) The purchaser of Reeve's volume, he disclosed, was a friend and former team-mate from his birthplace, Hong Kong, who showed great generosity by immediately returning the book to its owner. A friend indeed.

There was another intriguing tale earlier in the year. In February, stories appeared in the press about a "secret weapon" that might have helped England win the 1932-33 Bodyline series. A set of mechanical stumps had surfaced on which, it was suggested, Douglas Jardine's fast bowlers might have honed their skills while journeying to Australia. There was even a label stating "1933 tour" (though the squad sailed in September 1932). Brass bails were permanently attached to the off and leg stumps, and the whole contraption, which could be screwed to a wooden surface such as the deck of a ship, was intriguingly ten inches taller than regulation. All three stumps slotted into a base housing a tilting mechanism. At the foot of each was a set of numbers from one to six: the greater the force of the impact, the higher the number.

Had Harold Larwood, Bill Voce and others used this device on board the SS *Orontes*? In response to press speculation, Knights Auctioneers went on record "to state categorically that there is no evidence to support the theory that the stumps were used for bowling practice during the MCC Bodyline tour of Australia in 1932-33". A brass plate identified the patentee and manufacturer as J. G. S. Pullen of Footscray in Kent, but research failed to unearth more information. There was even a suggestion it might have been a fairground attraction from the 1940s or 1950s. Whatever its history, it was an unusual piece of equipment, and the mystique surrounding its origins helped bump up the price from an estimated £250–350 to £1,842.

The year's sales also threw up two small and extremely rare items. The first was a cigarette card issued in 1900 by Glasgow tobacco manufacturers D&J Macdonald, and it depicted the Yorkshire side, newly crowned county champions. This is one of the rarest of all cards produced in the UK. It is about twice the usual size (reflecting the large decorated tins in which the tobacco was sold) and was printed in colour.

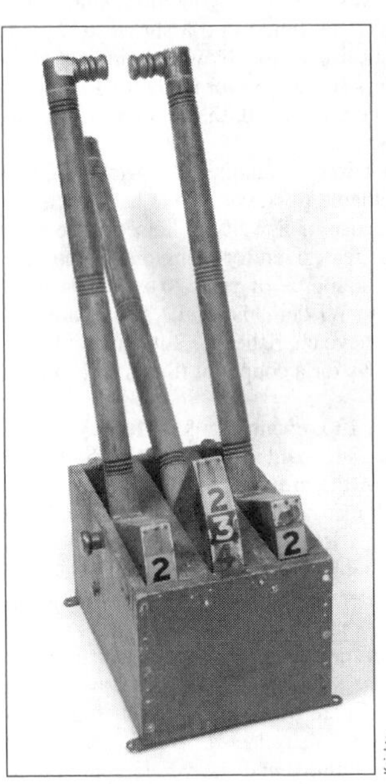

Weapons training – or fairground attraction? These mystery stumps realised £1,842.

The auction was held by the London Cigarette Card Company (long since based in Somerset), and bidding reached £2,700, more than the forecast £2,000. Only ten such cards are believed to remain in existence: even with cracked and slightly rounded corners, as well as brown stains on the back, it attracted fierce competition. LCCC director Ian Laker said: "This is the first one I have seen in 47 years with the firm. It is potentially a once-in-a-lifetime opportunity."

Macdonald's Winning Team cigarettes were so called, the reverse of the card states, "out of compliment to the Yorkshire County Cricket team, and, like them, are INVINCIBLE". Macdonald's had a point, of sorts. Yorkshire were champions in 1901 and again in 1902, when Macdonald's (later subsumed into Imperial Tobacco) issued a further 11 cricket team cards – including another of Yorkshire – and 25 cards of cricketers. All are scarce.

The second small item was a 30-page book, *The Log of the "Old Un" from Liverpool to San Francisco*, an account of an 1886 tour undertaken by a team of English amateur cricketers, several with first-class experience. It was organised by E. J. Sanders, a significant figure in Devon cricket. The book calls itself "a plain unvarnished log, a simple tribute… in recollection of many pleasant days on land and sea".

The "Old Un" was another Devonian, William Clulow Sim, who wrote the account on his return to England. Officially, he was the scorer, though the trip also proved a handy opportunity to visit his son in California. The slim volume was printed for private circulation, and only four copies are thought to have survived, including one in the MCC library at Lord's. Given that none has appeared at auction in living memory, it was hard to gauge what it might fetch. In the end, it sold for £30,700, far beyond an estimate of £8,000–12,000. Another case of small is beautiful.

CRICKET AND THE WEATHER IN 2017

The end of the Lord's rain?

ANDREW HIGNELL

Overall, 481 hours' play were lost in the Championship, down almost 47 on 2016. Midland counties tended to fare best, with interruptions for Northamptonshire 49 lower. The exception was Derbyshire, whose match against Kent at Chesterfield in September was abandoned because of a saturated outfield. It had been little better at Derby a fortnight before: barely two sessions of the Glamorgan match survived the rain. The wettest weather, though, came in late June, badly disrupting the round of floodlit Championship games. In all, 80 hours disappeared – roughly 37% of playing time – with northern games worst hit. At Headingley and Chester-le-Street, only eight of the scheduled 24 hours saw cricket; Durham had lost only 17 during their seven previous games.

From a meteorological perspective, this was high summer. But variations in the jet streams over the North Atlantic brought a heatwave to southern Europe – and damp to the UK. Frontal systems played havoc with the T20 Blast. On July 28, there were washouts at Birmingham, Derby and Manchester, interruptions at Leicester and Hove, and contrasting fortunes either side of the Severn: no play at Cardiff, but a home win on DLS at Bristol. On August 8 and 9, a total of eight scheduled days were washed out of the Championship programme.

Such disruption may become a thing of the past. MCC are interested in trialling a fine mesh, suspended from pylons and a central balloon, that admits light – but not rain.

HOURS LOST TO THE WEATHER IN THE 2017 CHAMPIONSHIP

	Home	*Away*	*2017*	*2016*	*Difference*
Derbyshire	**67.50**	19.25	**86.75**	78.25	8.50
Durham	36.75	14.00	50.75	53.75	–3.00
Essex	22.50	25.00	47.50	40.75	6.75
Glamorgan	16.25	22.25	38.50	44.75	–6.25
Gloucestershire	18.75	34.50	53.25	42.25	11.00
Hampshire	40.75	30.50	71.25	63.50	7.75
Kent	13.75	**55.75**	69.50	80.25	–10.75
Lancashire	28.50	25.75	54.25	**31.00**	**23.25**
Leicestershire	23.75	15.50	39.25	61.00	–21.75
Middlesex	28.75	38.75	67.50	64.25	3.25
Northamptonshire	26.00	24.75	50.75	**99.75**	**–49.00**
Nottinghamshire	23.75	26.75	50.50	57.25	–6.75
Somerset	27.50	33.75	61.25	57.25	4.00
Surrey	15.25	45.25	60.50	46.25	14.25
Sussex	19.25	**9.50**	**28.75**	49.75	–21.00
Warwickshire	25.75	11.75	37.50	65.75	–28.25
Worcestershire	**10.25**	33.75	44.00	64.25	–20.25
Yorkshire	36.00	14.25	50.25	55.50	–5.25
Total	481.00	481.00	962.00	1055.50	–93.50

CRICKET PEOPLE

Climbing the mountain

JAMES GINGELL

"I'm anonymous in the Mumbles," says **Richard Madley**, a proud South Walian. "But famous in Mumbai." It's not for his role as an auctioneer on the BBC's *Bargain Hunt*, either. One wet Tuesday in early February 2008, he received an email from Andrew Wildblood, an old friend who was now working for IMG, the company responsible for delivering the IPL. "Heard about the auction of cricketers, Madley?"

It was a new concept, and Wildblood realised they needed someone who knew what they were doing. In Madley, he saw a safe pair of hands – in more ways than one. The two had played together at Sherborne School in the early 1970s, with Wildblood opening the bowling, and Madley ("I never dropped a catch off him") keeping wicket.

Every year since, he has supervised the auction, which runs over two days from ten to six in a hotel ballroom, and is broadcast to 100 million across the globe. Despite the scrutiny, Madley does not get nervous. "It's no different from going out to bat for Lacock Second XI." Though one imagines rather fewer watch Division Seven of the Wiltshire League.

The dimensions of the room make things tricky. "In cricketing terms, I have to scan the field from deep square leg to deep backward point. I'm expected to be able to see everything that happens in that 180 degree arc." It can lead to the occasional argument, most memorably when Vijay Mallya, billionaire owner of Royal Challengers Bangalore, reported Madley to the BCCI after a disputed bid. These are people who are used to having their wishes granted; it is often Madley's job to refuse them.

Of those cricketers he has helped make rich, some are more appreciative than others. At the second IPL, held in South Africa for security reasons, he bumped into two of his biggest sales: Andrew Flintoff bought him a pint, and was humble and gracious; Kevin Pietersen didn't recognise him.

In July, as the women's World Cup final wound to its thrilling conclusion, **Clare Connor** took her seat in the Tavern Stand. She had performed the duties expected of the ECB's director of women's cricket, and now got to enjoy the occasion with her best friend, her brother and her dad. She cherishes that last hour as "one of the greatest afternoons of drama there's ever been".

Afterwards, she was invited into the dressing-room to enjoy a few drinks. While some of the players continued revelling through the night, Connor crashed out in her hotel bed around midnight. Then, in the morning, she switched back from fan to administrator, and travelled once more to Lord's for meetings from 8.30. If some of her colleagues were nursing sore heads, she was still buzzing, eager to build on the success of the tournament.

Connor, who captained England during her playing years, also sits on the ICC's chief executives committee. She is one of two women among a panel of 20, along with Betty Timmer of the Netherlands. Yet she does not feel outnumbered. "Almost with every set of meetings, there is less reliance on me to drive the women's cricket conversation." The penny is beginning to drop. "It isn't just about women *playing* cricket: it's about cricket's broad engagement with females – how does the game have a relationship with 100% of the population, rather than just 50? The committee realise it makes business sense."

But cricket is more than business to Connor. After the final, a picture emerged of her hugging England captain Heather Knight tight. "I told her how immensely proud I was," says Connor. "We have a special bond." And not just because they have both led the national side: in 2014, they shared a tent for a week when they climbed Kilimanjaro. And what did they do when they got there? Played a game of cricket, of course, on a crater just below the summit.

Colin Maynard remembers what it was like when women were first allowed membership of MCC. In his 42 years at the club – beginning in the accounts department and working up to assistant secretary – nothing generated as much interest. "I had 700 *letters*," he said. "Not emails or phone calls."

With the men's World Cup staged in England in 1999, the time had come for a vote. "What would the club have looked like if no women were allowed into the Pavilion during the final?" says Maynard. But the motion to grant women membership was defeated in February 1998, and he was despatched to the provinces to work out the sticking points.

"Most of them were sensible; members tend to be intelligent and persuasive," he says. "But there were some spurious arguments – that we would spend a fortune putting in new lavatories, that sort of thing." In September, the second vote passed. If it had not, Maynard thinks that would have been that. "You can't keep voting on the same subject: it's like punishing people for not doing what they're told."

Maynard joined MCC in 1975, appointed by the pipe-smoking Group Captain W. R. Ford. One of his responsibilities was paying the England players' wages, which were little more than the stewards received: around £200 a head, a bit more for the captain. Then came the Packer Revolution. "It hit everyone like a steam train." In the days before an international governing body, MCC were intimately involved. Club secretary Jack Bailey was regularly in court, while Packer's defence lawyer, Robert Alexander, later became president. "What hurt the club more than anything was that Tony Greig was clearly doing underground work while captain of the MCC team in India and Australia in 1976-77, in particular the Centenary Test in Melbourne, which was a celebration of Test cricket."

Maynard, who was in his last year before retirement, has seen enormous change. And though MCC have earned a reputation as a home for reactionaries, he is insistent they have a forward-looking position, citing the radical architecture of Lord's. "The big question," he says, "is how to progress without tearing up what makes the club unique." They are clearly doing something right: few clubs have a waiting list of 28 years.

CRICKET IN THE COURTS IN 2017

Indecent exposure – and a cockatoo

GAYLE WINS DEFAMATION CASE

A jury in Sydney found in favour of West Indies star Chris Gayle after he sued Australian publishers Fairfax Media for claiming he had exposed himself to a masseuse. Leanne Russell told the court Gayle had dropped his towel and displayed part of his penis during a training session at the 2015 World Cup.

Gayle said he had not seen Russell that day, had been fully dressed throughout and had not worn a towel at any stage. On October 30, the jury decided the claims were untrue and that the reports – which appeared in three major Australian newspapers – were motivated by malice. "It will cost the company a lot of money unless we can reverse it on appeal," said Fairfax solicitor Peter Bartlett. Gayle later said on Twitter that bidding for an exclusive interview would start at $US300,000.

GAMBLING RUINS CONTROVERSIAL UMPIRE

Darrell Hair, who umpired 78 Tests, admitted stealing over $A9,000 (£5,000) from an off-licence where he worked. Hair, 65, took the money from D'Aquino's Liquor in the New South Wales country town of Orange over a three-month period in early 2017 to fund his gambling habit. Magistrate Michael Allen called it "a monumental fall from grace".

But after Hair admitted sample charges of theft and embezzlement on October 24, Allen decided not to record a conviction; instead he sentenced him to an 18-month good behaviour bond. Allen noted that Hair had repaid the money, written letters of apology, and was in counselling for depression and addiction. Hair's umpiring career included controversy: at the MCG in 1995-96, he no-balled Muttiah Muralitharan, and at The Oval in 2006 his penalising of Pakistan for ball-tampering led to the game's abandonment.

EX-COUNTY PLAYER JAILED FOR CHILD GROOMING

Richard Sladdin, 48, who played for Derbyshire and Somerset in the 1990s, was jailed for a year after he admitted trying to meet someone he thought was a 14-year-old girl called Claire for sex. He was in fact meeting a group of vigilante paedophile hunters who posted their encounter online; it was reportedly viewed two million times. Sladdin had the username trickydicky69. Jailing him at Bolton Crown Court on April 13, Judge Timothy Clayson said: "The messages demonstrate you were asking the witness you believed to be a teenage girl to engage in various forms of penetrative sex." The judge said he accepted Sladdin was remorseful and had pleaded guilty at an early stage.

UMPIRING? NO, PLANNING A MURDER!

A former TV producer who worked on *The Bill* was sentenced to 17 years in jail for plotting to kill his partner. David Harris, 68, of Amberley, Sussex, told Hazel Allinson he spent his days umpiring matches for Arundel Castle CC. In fact he was going to London to see a 28-year-old Lithuanian prostitute, and was planning to kill Allinson, his partner of 28 years, so he could inherit her house and fortune. Harris approached two separate men, offering them £200,000 to murder her in what would look like a car-jacking or mugging gone wrong. Harris admitted running up huge debts on presents for his lover, but said he had approached the possible hitmen only as research for a novel.

FIRST-CLASS PLAYER JAILED FOR 18 YEARS

South African-born Dion Taljard, 47, who played 25 first-class matches for Border, was convicted of 19 counts of rape at Minshull Street Crown Court, Manchester. Taljard also played for several clubs in the Lancashire leagues. The case involved a single woman who said she was attacked more than 150 times over a ten-year period before reporting him in 2015. Taljard was also convicted of two cases of indecent assault and one of witness intimidation. He denied all wrongdoing.

GROUNDSMAN'S REVENGE ENDS IN COURT

Chris Hallam, a former member of the groundstaff at Derbyshire, caused £3,000 worth of damage at the County Ground when he returned shortly before the Twenty20 match on August 18. He was caught on CCTV slashing the covers and pouring liquid into the fuel tank of the blotting machine. Security cameras had been installed after Hallam was dismissed earlier in the summer. Derby magistrates, who heard this was an act of revenge, gave him an eight-week suspended sentence after he admitted criminal damage.

SNORTING IN THE STANDS

A spectator at Trent Bridge was fined £475 after pleading guilty to using cocaine while watching the Test match against South Africa. Daniel Wilton, 37, was seen to have "a white powder residue in stubble at the side of his mouth", Nottingham magistrates were told on July 31.

TEST PLAYER THREE TIMES OVER LIMIT

New Zealand all-rounder Doug Bracewell, 27, was sentenced to 100 hours' community work on May 25 after his third drink-driving offence in nine years. Bracewell was three times over the legal limit. His lawyer, Ron Mansfield, told Hastings District Court that he had responded to a panicky call from his partner after the couple's pet cockatoo had been killed by dogs. "The cockatoo was of some significance to his partner and she was quite distraught," said Mansfield.

COUNTY PLAYER GUILTY OF EXPOSING HIMSELF

Derbyshire player Shiv Thakor was guilty of exposing himself to women on two occasions in June, Southern Derbyshire magistrates court decided on November 15. Thakor, who had also played for Leicestershire and England Under-19s, had been jogging when he exposed himself through a gap in his tracksuit. He denied the offences, telling the court: "I have got a tendency, that is almost a running joke, that I tend to rearrange myself both at the front and back during games." He was given a three-year community order and told to pay more than £1,000 costs. The county later terminated his contract.

BALL-STEALER FAILED – THEN JAILED

A man who removed a safe from a cricket pavilion was caught after trying to drag it across the pitch into a waiting car. However, the club steward at East Lancashire CC, Blackburn, said all he would have found inside, had he managed to open it, was a single ball: the safe was heavy because it was attached to a concrete base. The club had lost the key two years earlier and never got round to obtaining a replacement. Andrew Robert Smith, 39, who broke into the pavilion at around 4am, was sent to prison for 12 weeks by magistrates on October 9. The offence took place while he was out on licence.

CRICKET AND THE LAWS IN 2017

Alive and kicking

FRASER STEWART

The new Code of Laws came into effect on October 1, and one of the changes was immediately put to the test. In a match between a Cricket Australia XI and Queensland at the end of September – the Code was backdated to the start of the Australian domestic programme, to avoid having two sets of Laws in the same season – Queensland's Marnus Labuschagne tried to stop a drive from Param Uppal. He dived to his right at extra cover, before standing up and faking a throw, even though the ball had passed him and was heading towards another fielder at long-off. Uppal hesitated before completing a single.

The umpires awarded five penalty runs to the CA XI, ruling that Labuschagne had tried to deceive the batsman, a violation of Law 41.5, which now states: "It is unfair for any fielder wilfully to attempt, by word or action, to distract, deceive or obstruct either batsman after the striker has received the ball." Some fielders had been pretending to be in possession of the ball, hence the introduction of the concept of deception. This practice was unfair, and becoming increasingly common. It does not matter if the batsmen are actually deceived: the umpire must decide if there has been an *attempt* to deceive.

Soon after that incident, there was a thrilling finish to a game in Pakistan's Quaid-e-Azam Trophy, with WAPDA, nine down, needing four runs to beat Peshawar. Noticing that Mohammad Irfan, the non-striker, had left his ground early, Peshawar bowler Taj Wali ran him out. The appeal was upheld, and Peshawar celebrated victory. WAPDA's captain, Salman Butt, argued the dismissal had "spoiled" the game, claiming it was against the Spirit of Cricket. Did he have a point?

In short, no. Running out the non-striker is enshrined in the Laws, and has long been part of cricket. The revised Law (41.16) states that the run-out of the non-striker can be attempted up to the instant the bowler would be expected to deliver the ball; the old Law 42.15 stated that the attempt could be made by a bowler only "before entering his delivery stride". The revision is aimed at keeping non-strikers in their ground for longer, and to re-emphasise that it is for the batsman, not anyone else, to ensure he/she is not dismissed in this manner. The title of the Law has also been changed, from "Bowler attempting to run out the non-striker" to "Non-striker leaving his/her ground early." It is often the bowler who is criticised for attempting such a run-out; India's Vinoo Mankad had the method of dismissal informally named after him, after running out Australia's Bill Brown at Sydney in 1947-48. But it is the batsman who is attempting to gain an advantage.

As Don Bradman said of Mankad's act: "For the life of me, I can't understand why [the press] questioned his sportsmanship. The Laws of cricket make it quite clear that the non-striker must keep within his ground until the ball has been delivered. If not, why is the provision there which enables the bowler to run him out? By backing up too far or too early, the non-striker is very obviously gaining an unfair advantage."

Bradman was not the first great to defend the tactic. W. G. Grace once wrote: "Some people argue that to put a batsman out in this way is sharp practice on the bowler's part, but I take the opposite view very strongly. If there is any sharp practice in the matter, I think it is on the part of the batsman who tries to gain an unfair advantage by leaving his crease before the ball is bowled. When a batsman is run out in this way I always think he has got his deserts." MCC agree.

Another match to end in confusion took place in the Women's Big Bash League, between Melbourne Renegades and Sydney Sixers early in 2018. Requiring three from the final delivery, and two for a super over, the Sixers' Sarah Aley skewed to short fine leg and scampered a single as the ball was returned to the Renegades wicketkeeper, Emma Inglis. That should have been that – but it wasn't. Without removing the bails, and believing the ball was dead, Inglis threw it up in celebration, and some team-mates celebrated too. But Aley concluded it might still be in play. She called her partner, Angela Reakes, for a second, which Aley completed with a dive as Amy Satterthwaite, the bowler – belatedly alive to the situation – tried to run her out.

After much deliberation, the umpires concluded the second run should count, forcing a tie and a super over (which, fortunately for Inglis, the Renegades won). The decision was correct. Law 20 states that, once the ball is dead, no further runs can be scored – though it isn't always clear if the ball is dead or in play. Law 20.1.1.1 says it is dead when "it is finally settled in the hands of the wicketkeeper or of the bowler". And a further clause, Law 20.1.2, clarifies: "The ball shall be considered to be dead when it is clear to the bowler's-end umpire that the fielding side and both batsmen at the wicket have ceased to regard it as in play."

At the point she started celebrating, Inglis believed the ball was no longer in play, even though Aley was turning and looking for a second run. Furthermore, Satterthwaite gestured to her team-mates to pick the ball up and started running towards it: clearly at least one member of the fielding side believed the ball was live. Aley did not set off for her second run until Satterthwaite was halfway down the pitch. The umpires rightly decided the ball was not finally settled, and so allowed the run. The Renegades learned a valuable lesson: it's never over until the call of "Time".

MCC launched a new Laws of Cricket eLearning portal in 2017, which provides users with an in-depth explanation of the new Code. It uses video clips, photos, animations and diagrams to educate the users on all 42 Laws. There are also tips from five ICC elite panel umpires. The resource can be used by players and officials to check a specific point of Law, and there is an option of working through the entire course, then taking a test. It is free to access and available at the Laws section of www.lords.org.

Fraser Stewart is Laws Manager at MCC.

CRICKET AND THE ENVIRONMENT IN 2017

Time for a sea change

TANYA ALDRED

It was the year plastic pollution of the oceans finally rose up the public – and cricket's – agenda. The raw figures are shocking enough: 8–12m tonnes are dumped in the sea each year, more has been produced in the last ten years than in the entire 20th century, and plastic fibres have been found inside the creatures who live in the deepest trench on earth. But the emotional hit was almost as bad. It came during the final episode of the BBC's *Blue Planet 2*, when a mourning whale carried the carcass of her calf, poisoned by polluted milk, and albatrosses unwittingly fed plastic to their young. The message from Sir David Attenborough, who as controller of BBC2 first brought one-day cricket to British screens, was stark: "The future of humanity, and indeed all life on earth, now depends on us."

Cricket is as guilty as any sport in its use of disposable plastics. *Wisden* asked all 18 first-class counties for feedback on their environmental strategies, especially efforts to reduce single-use plastics. We heard back in detail from Glamorgan, Kent, Somerset, Surrey and Warwickshire, plus MCC.

Focusing on waste: at The Oval last July, Surrey and Sky Ocean Rescue handed out reusable water bottles – the start of a campaign to reduce single-use plastic products.

At The Oval, Surrey teamed up with the Sky Ocean Rescue Campaign, and aimed to become free of single-use plastic by 2020; before 2018 is out they hope to be using plastic-free bottles, straws, plates, crockery and coffee-cup lids. During last summer's Third Test against South Africa, 20,000 reusable water bottles were given away, and fans encouraged to fill them from the 20 fountains around the ground. Glamorgan, Warwickshire and MCC have also been working to install more water points.

Surrey hold a Green Tourism Award, and employ a clean technology company to recycle their 11 tonnes of coffee waste into biofuels and bio-chemicals. They also use eco-burners, far more efficient than the industry standard, to keep food warm at events. Kent's club shop was upgraded with unwanted fittings from West Ham's old shop at Upton Park, the footballers' claret and blue close enough to the cricketers' maroon and navy for no one to notice. "We wouldn't have been able to afford it, without reusing what would otherwise have been destroyed," said Kent's then chief executive Jamie Clifford. At Taunton, Somerset concentrated on improving waste and recycling.

The parkland setting of Sophia Gardens has helped Glamorgan encourage their staff and spectators to use active modes of transport: capacity for bicycles has doubled. The club have become a beacon of green action and, through partnerships with the Carbon Trust and Amber Energy, have reduced their carbon footprint and energy usage.

At Edgbaston, Warwickshire are working towards ISO 50001, which certifies efficient energy use. They are installing sensor-controlled lights across the stadium, have installed new bike racks, and introduced biodegradable packaging across all catering units on major match days. Nearly 95% of all food is now prepared on site and locally sourced, with meat supplied by a Shropshire organic farm.

MCC are still the only club to employ a full-time sustainability manager, Russell Seymour. Electricity at Lord's comes from 100% wind power, and the new Warner Stand is powered by solar panels, solar thermal and a ground-source heat pump. The ground's buggies, and appliances such as leaf blowers, are electric, and all new equipment is low-energy rated. There is strict waste separation, and light sensors are used in most toilets and corridors. As at The Oval, food is seasonal, locally sourced and organic where possible, and anything uneaten is distributed to local charities. Lord's have been working on a closed-loop recycling scheme to turn plastic waste from catering back into food-grade plastic items.

Progress is considerable, if uncoordinated and piecemeal. There is still no central environmental strategy, nor specific funding for carbon-saving projects. The ECB facilities team provide useful advice, but there is no dedicated expert to help clubs navigate an area as complex as sustainability. Even something as seemingly uncontroversial as a reusable pint pot, which MCC are considering, and the five counties mentioned earlier have already addressed – Surrey returned an excellent 91% of its 589,694 reusable cups to the supplier during the 2017 season – has complications.

"Replacing single-use plastics isn't as straightforward as it seems," says Seymour. "Even though they might look and behave the same, the type of

CRICKET AND GARDENING

Green fingers turn Indian blue

MATTHEW APPLEBY

What do iridescent blue meconopsis flowers and Sachin Tendulkar have in common? Not much, you may think. But an unlikely partnership was due to take shape at the Royal Horticultural Society's Chelsea Flower Show in May – in the form of the first cricket-themed garden in the event's 105-year history.

Every show garden needs a concept to impress the judges, and this one takes as its inspiration the UK–India Year of Culture, which began in 2017. Above all, it is a homage to cricket. The garden came about when the RHS suggested to Swati Piramal, an Indian industrialist and organiser of the Vaikunth Flower Show, which took place in Mumbai in January 2018, that she might like to sponsor a garden at Chelsea. Piramal knew the direction it should take: "Everyone is cricket mad in India. Having it as a theme would quickly gain the attention of ordinary people who have not been to the Chelsea Flower Show but know about cricket."

An initial problem was that Indian plants are not allowed into the UK because of customs rules. So Piramal focused on plants that had already been imported – in particular the meconopsis, or Himalayan blue poppy. In 1922, mountaineer George Mallory discovered the plant during an unsuccessful attempt on Everest; it was introduced to England at the RHS spring show in 1926.

To plan the garden, the society teamed Piramal up with designer Sarah Eberle, who has won a record 15 gold medals at Chelsea but says she knows nothing about cricket, which is "a good thing". Her design features a set of stumps, a pitch of sorts and the meconopsis, which are the same shade of blue as India's one-day shirt, and will sit in oversized leather planters resembling half a cricket ball. It could look kitsch, but gets away with it. Blue vanda orchids, marigolds, roses, and meconopsis, says Eberle, "collectively represent the bold colour and vibrant energy of Indian urban living".

Eberle relates the cricket crease and contained space of the pitch to the formal gardens of the Islamic tradition. Indeed, the overall design has clear links to the Mughal gardens of northern India, with the crease replacing the rill, and the carved, oversized stumps recalling mosques. Indian artisans have produced *pietra dura* marble work, and paintings. The IPL is on during Chelsea Show week (May 24–28), which could limit the number of Indian cricket figures who come over, but Eberle and Piramal say Tendulkar knows about the garden, and plans are afoot for celebrity guests to attend.

Cricket and gardening, two quintessentially English pastimes, have long had a connection. A fine example is the oeuvre of Gerry Wright, an artist who in 1985 produced a book called *Cricket's Golden Summer: Paintings in a Garden*. His canvases – collected by Mick Jagger, Tim Rice, Michael Parkinson and others – depict blooming paradise gardens as backgrounds for colourful portraits of Golden Age cricketers. They include Kent and England amateur Jack Mason in a symbolic Kentish blossomy orchard, and Arthur Shrewsbury and Tibby Cotter in red poppy fields. Wright consulted archivists at Lord's and Melbourne to get the colours of the rainbow blazer right. But what gives the paintings such vitality are their summer-garden settings. In 2017, the year after Wright's death, the Lord's museum mounted an exhibition of his work. "He always loved gardens, and painting trees and flowers," said his widow, Sylvia. "The shapes and colours, too. So two of his great loves were married together."

Outside the museum, the connection is more poignant. Some MCC members ask to have their Ashes scattered in the Harris Garden, while groundsman Mick Hunt says he has turned a blind eye when the families of famous cricketers scatter ashes on the outfield.

Hunt, who has been on the Lord's staff since 1969, shares his bugbears with many gardeners: the weather and unwanted wildlife. Foxes, which invade from the nearby churchyard, are a particular nuisance. Lord's uses contractors to trap them, releasing the healthy ones. "There are quite a few," says Hunt. "More than you'd think. They're holed up in nooks and crannies, and they come from everywhere. They're brazen." Pigeons are pests too, as they eat the grass seed. Hunt says a kestrel that nests on top of some adjacent flats occasionally takes one out, which stops the rest becoming too brave. Lord's has more flowers than most grounds, he says: "Trouble is, there are 30,000 people here for the Tests, and there are a few pinch points where people just tread on them."

Are any cricketers interested in gardening or groundsmanship? "Not really. They tend to moan about it, using their own code. For 'the pitch is too dry', they say: 'You got water restrictions on at the moment?' Too much grass, and they want more taken off: 'Has your mower broken down?'"

John Rodgers runs landscaping company Quality & Service, and has looked after the gardens and floral displays at Lord's for 25 years. There are up to 4,000 blooms planted in hanging baskets and borders, and in homage to MCC's egg-and-bacon colours Rodgers uses yellow and pink bedding plants – geraniums, begonias, and busy lizzies – underpinned by box hedges. In 2018, spectators can also look at a design in the Harris Garden featuring plants from all the Test-playing countries. Sunnier beds will be filled with tropical species, such as South African proteas, while shadier areas will have plants such as silver ferns from New Zealand; more tender flowers from the subcontinent will be added later in the season. Most of the traditional roses will go.

The Lord's connection extends further than the 1934 Harris Garden. An advertisement in *The Gardeners' Chronicle* in 1861 promoted a catalogue of "new flowers, florists' flowers and vegetables" from Messrs E. G. Henderson & Son, a nursery based in St John's Wood. After ten years of talks, MCC eventually bought Henderson's Nursery in 1887 for £18,500, and turned it into the Nursery Ground.

Even further back, the sport's link with horticulture can still be seen outside grand country houses: many an 18th-century aristocrat had a pitch within their demesnes. The lawn or hay meadow at the front was often ideal, and a space for cricket was as much a status symbol as grounds designed by Lancelot "Capability" Brown, the pioneer of landscape design. Viscount Palmerston, the Duke of Bedford, the Earl of Northumberland and the Duke of Marlborough – all commissioned Brown, and all staged their own games. In 2016, the National Trust's Wimpole Estate hosted a Georgian cricket match between a Wimpole XI and the Cambridgeshire County Cricket Board to celebrate Brown's 300th birthday.

Betting was essential to cricket in its early days, and it was only in the mid-19th century, when horse racing took over as the favoured gambling sport, that cricket's ties with the country house and its gardens started to fade. The link has not vanished, though: Sir Paul Getty laid out a glorious ground at Wormsley Park in the 1990s, and in 2018 there may just be the sight of Sachin Tendulkar – at Britain's premier show devoted to the art of the garden – standing next to some oversize stumps and flanked by flowers of Indian-cricket blue.

Matthew Appleby is deputy editor of Horticulture Week *and a gardening writer. He is a former cricket journalist.*

The scale of the problem: cricketers on a beach near Mumbai have to clear the sand of jetsam before a game can start.

plastic makes a difference. Most plastics are recyclable, in theory, but you have to ask a practical question: do we actually recycle *this* type of plastic, either in the UK or elsewhere? It also depends on the market for the recycled product. So there is a much bigger issue the government need to deliver on.

"A single-use plastic pint pot that is segregated from other waste and recycled back into another plastic pint pot in a closed-loop system will have less of an impact than a reusable cup, six times its weight, that is taken home initially as a souvenir but gets thrown away months later. The plastic problem may simply be dispersed from the ground into the community where, once discarded, it is less likely to be recycled.

"Any system should be right both operationally for the venue and in how it impacts the environment. Reuse, though, is usually better than recycle."

The ECB's Cricket Unleashed initiative promised much on the environment, but a year down the line no money has been committed. Pilot studies at Old Trafford and Derby have suggested that an initial investment in energy efficiency, LED lighting and solar panels would reduce carbon emissions and save money. Funding decisions for 2019–24 were due in the spring.

Air pollution was set to be discussed at an ICC meeting in February 2018 after high levels interrupted the Delhi Test between India and Sri Lanka in early December. As a heavy cloud of smog roosted over the city, Sri Lankan fielders wore masks, players vomited on the pitch, and the game was suspended three times on the second day. Oxygen cylinders were placed in both dressing-rooms.

The air-quality index reading in Delhi that day was "very poor", while the concentration of dangerously polluted particulate matter – an airborne mixture of solid particles and liquid droplets – was in some cases more than six times higher than recommended levels. Breathing polluted air has been linked to eye irritation and reduced stamina, and can contribute to pneumonia, heart disease, strokes and some cancers. It poses particular risks for sportspeople, who breathe more often and more deeply: the *Hindustan Times* suggested that Suranga Lakmal, the Sri Lankan seamer, would typically have been exposed to four times more pollution than a spectator.

"This match should not have taken place," said the Indian Medical Association president K. K. Aggarwal. "It is time the ICC come up with a policy on pollution." The Laws currently permit umpires to suspend play if "conditions of ground, weather or light" pose a risk, and the ICC have said air pollution should be "considered by the medical committee for guidance should the situation arise in future".

Air pollution in Delhi in the last three months of the year is notoriously bad, as the burning of arable crops in nearby states coincides with cooler air which traps particulates closer to the ground. The IMA had unsuccessfully appealed to the Delhi High Court to postpone the city's half-marathon because of air so toxic they called a public health emergency. Greenpeace had also warned against the levels of atmospheric pollution in Delhi and other cities hosting football's Under-17 World Cup in October. The BCCI, who initially accused the Sri Lankan players of making a "big fuss", said they would consider air cleanliness when arranging matches. That may be bad news for Delhi.

CRICKET AND FILM IN 2017

More sugar than spice

HUGH CHEVALLIER

The major surprise of the 2017 biopic of Sachin Tendulkar is that it took so long. M. S. Dhoni released his a year earlier, and he was still playing; Virat Kohli's must surely be in production. Perhaps the reason why *Sachin: A Billion Dreams* was not released until three and a half years after his retirement was because they had to work out how to cram the logos of the myriad commercial, media and technology partners on to the opening screens.

No cricketer has endured such public scrutiny, yet there are still one or two revelations in this slick, 140-minute window on the Sachin world. For a week after India flopped at the group stages of the 2007 World Cup, he dared not leave his Mumbai flat – two commandos moved in to protect him. Otherwise, the exposés are limited: Tendulkar is a Dire Straits obsessive and, though he aimed to be a hands-on parent, he drew the line at changing nappies.

Father–son relations form a central – sometimes moving – strand of the film. The beginning shows the birth of his son, Arjun, in 1999, and it is clear Sachin judges himself by how he matches up to his own father, Ramesh, who had died four months earlier. Centuries scored before then were dedicated to God; afterwards to Ramesh.

The Little Master and Sir: Sachin Tendulkar and Ramakant Achrekar.

The film – made by the British director, James Erskine – has a broadly chronological structure, and recreates episodes from Sachin's childhood. It looks idyllic, the young lad playing practical jokes on friend and foe, before being taken under the wing of Ramakant Achrekar, or "Sir", as he always called him. This was a serious business, and he left his beloved parents, and moved in with his uncle, to be nearer Sir. It must have been tough – not that you'd think it from what we see. There is a glib syrupiness the film never shrugs off.

And when the Indian captaincy later shifts back and forth between our hero and Mohammad Azharuddin, there is no mention of the corruption that would bring Azharuddin's world crashing down.

Nor of the allegations of ball-tampering by Tendulkar that threw India's tour of South Africa into crisis in late 2001.

Yet an unspoken sadness does seep into the retirement years, when the focus of Sachin's energy is Arjun or, more accurately, Arjun's batting. The son's body language does not radiate the father's confidence. Years before, Donald Bradman's son John had found the burden of his surname too much, and changed it to Bradsen. It is too soon to tell what Arjun can achieve, though he will be aware of what his father had done by his age.

There are, of course, countless shots of balls elegantly and violently despatched to all corners of the cricket-playing universe. A very enjoyable sight they are too, even if the repetitive overdubbed thwack of bat on ball starts to grate. Will the film's core audience worry about that, or the clunky product placement? Probably not. It is, on one level, decent entertainment. But there is also a danger that the idol of a billion dreams has been reduced to a saccharine Sachin. He must be more than that, though not on this evidence.

CRICKET IN THE FILM ARCHIVES IN 2017

A warm soak in a long bath

RICHARD WHITEHEAD

In the shadow of a sun-scorched Italian mountain, a group of men wander among neat rows of gleaming gravestones. Their dress – Sunday-best smart – suggests respect. They find the stone they are seeking, carefully lay a bunch of white roses, and stand back in contemplation. The camera focuses on the inscription: "Captain Hedley Verity. The Green Howards. 31st July 1943. Age 38."

It is September 1954. Alongside the England captain, Len Hutton, are Yorkshire team-mates Vic Wilson and Bob Appleyard, and a group of journalists, including the former fast bowler Bill Bowes, Verity's close friend. Bowes, now a writer for the *Yorkshire Evening News*, spent three years in a North African prisoner of war camp. It is hard to imagine how painful this moment must be.

The man behind the cine camera at the Caserta military cemetery is a Bedser, though whether it is Alec or Eric, who accompanied his twin on every tour, is uncertain. The MCC party en route to Australia had first called in at Naples, 45 minutes south of Caserta. The 1954-55 Ashes was to be Alec's final tour, and proved a chastening experience, but he (or Eric) kept the camera rolling

Pulling a fast one: Percy Chapman (far right) leads an early version of the bleep test after some bare-faced cheating.

throughout one of the most celebrated of all England series. The twins would have intended the footage for private use, or to give friends back in Woking a glimpse of far-off lands. They would have been astonished to discover that, more than six decades on, those flickering images are available to millions.

The British Film Institute have digitised hours of precious footage from all aspects of British life at player.bfi.org.uk. Cricket features prominently, with scores of films – long and short, silent and soundtracked – available for free. Never has it been so easy to take a long soak in the warm bath of nostalgia.

The collection is rich and diverse. There are Test stars, county toilers, pioneering women, flinty northern league pros, village enthusiasts. Some clips last a few seconds, some several minutes, some up to an hour; many are beguiling. Cine films such as the Bedsers' are an irresistible draw – an opportunity to see cricketing greats amid relaxed informality. As well as the travel, the social events and the golf, "Alec Bedser Cricket Home Movies" – as the BFI call them – give us a chance to study the bowling of Brian Statham, Frank Tyson, Johnny Wardle and Bob Appleyard. There is also slow-motion footage of Alec's own famously muscular action.

An earlier cinematic tour diary, shot by Maurice Allom on the 1930-31 trip to South Africa, captures all the japery, including captain Percy Chapman blatantly cheating in fitness drills on the ship's deck. Perhaps inspired by the Bedsers, Wardle wielded his own camera on another trip to South Africa, in 1956-57 – one of three Wardle productions available at the BFI site. He confirms what a leisurely business it was: the next cocktail party or tourist outing seldom seems far away. And he gives a glimpse of the ugly truth of 1950s South Africa, photographing a segregated beach.

Later, Wardle – recently sacked by Yorkshire and dropped by England, and now working as a columnist – performs a service for cricket historians by filming some of the Australians' dubious actions during the controversial 1958-59 Ashes. He also has footage of his old team-mate and rival Tony Lock's questionable quicker ball; by way of antidote comes the thrilling purity of Fred Trueman's run-up and delivery.

Trueman crops up several times in an amble around the archive, poignantly so in a short black and white film of Yorkshire's final game in the 1968 Championship, against Surrey at Hull's Circle Ground. There is some priceless action: captain Brian Close fielding inches from the bat with his usual cavalier regard for health and safety; slow left-armer Don Wilson's bouncing, balletic stride; and Trueman, with a shorter approach than in his pomp but still a stirring sight. There is no sound, and it requires a glance at *Wisden* to reveal that Yorkshire's win in the dying minutes completed a hat-trick of titles. Nor do you learn that Trueman, who bowled six wicketless overs in each innings, retired at the end of the season.

After women's cricket enjoyed unprecedented exposure in 2017, there is evidence of the struggles it has had to overcome. An Anglia TV film from 1971 sees the England women taking on a men's works XI at Hull, with a reporter doing his best to cope with the concept: "What happens to your husband when you go off on tour?" Captain Rachael Heyhoe Flint is by turns patient, gutsy and eloquent: "Nobody asks if women can play tennis or golf."

Sin of the times: apartheid rears its head in South Africa, 1956-57.

Longer films include a stunning 1970 documentary called *The Summer Game*, narrated in reverential tones that do justice to some evocative images: "Cricket, the ever changeful, changeless game." There are shots of West Indies at Lord's in 1969; of the Sussex team arriving by coach at New Road, with Tom Graveney waiting in the car park to welcome them; and of county action at Southampton's old Northlands Road and at Bath.

Cricket on Test, made in 1965 as part of the Rank Organisation's *Look at Life* series, is narrated by Richie Benaud and, though just nine minutes long, contains gorgeous footage of the men of Nettlebed CC in Oxfordshire preparing for, and playing in, a Saturday fixture. The club president – arriving on horseback to add a whiff of glamour – is the travel writer Peter Fleming, brother of Ian. Benaud's attention then switches to Lord's and the rituals of a county match against Yorkshire. If flats were to be built on these prime acres of London real estate, he reveals, it could produce an instant windfall in the region of £2.5m, "before collecting the rent".

From the earliest film (Ranji in the nets at Melbourne in 1897) to Ian Botham discussing his poor form in the summer of 1980 at Taunton ("Does Lester Piggott ride a winner every day?") the archive offers a richly contrasting perspective on cricket. There are few better ways to lose an afternoon.

OBITUARIES

AIZAZUDDIN, FAQIR SYED, who died on May 8, aged 81, played three unofficial Tests for Pakistan in 1963-64 against the Commonwealth XI, scoring 72 at Karachi and an undefeated 62 at Dacca. He had started his first-class career while studying economics at Cambridge, but in five matches in 1957 never passed 18. He had more luck when he returned to Fenner's in 1963 with the Pakistan Eaglets (a precursor of today's A-Team), hitting 187 – which remained his highest score – against the university, captained by Mike Brearley. Aizazuddin was chosen for the 1967 tour of England, despite having played little recent domestic cricket, but did not make the Test side; his best score was 74 against the Minor Counties. He wrote occasionally about cricket, and was manager of the Pakistan team that toured New Zealand in 2000-01.

ALLOM, ANTHONY THOMAS CARRICK, who died on September 26, aged 78, was thought to be the tallest English county cricketer: 6ft 10in, according to *Wisden 1958*. A fast bowler, Allom played five first-class matches, taking six wickets in the third, for MCC against Cambridge University at Lord's in 1960. Not long after, he made what turned out to be his only Championship appearance, for Surrey: Warwickshire's openers Norman Horner and Billy Ibadulla put on 377 at The Oval without being separated, still a county record. Allom later captained Charterhouse Friars in the 1971 Cricketer Cup final. His father, Maurice – a mere 6ft 6in – played five Tests for England.

ALTER, THOMAS BEACH, died on September 29, aged 67. An Indian actor of American descent, Tom Alter featured in more than 300 Bollywood films and many stage productions. Passionate about cricket, he wrote newspaper columns on the subject and, in 1988, undertook the first filmed interview with Sachin Tendulkar, then 15. Alter wrote in the 2016 *Wisden India Almanack* of the time in 1983 when Sunil Gavaskar asked him to make up the numbers for an Indian XI against the United States in New Jersey, as he was filming nearby. He took a wicket, and "was embraced by Gavaskar and Kirmani and Madan and Mohinder and Ravi and Roger – and the entire universe..." His son, Jamie, worked for ESPNcricinfo and later became sports editor of *The Times of India*.

AMBROSE, MILLIE OTTO, died on December 7, 2016, aged 84. "Hillie" Ambrose was famous for going out of her house in Swetes Village, Antigua, and ringing a bell every time her son took a Test wicket. It became a well-worn path: Curtly Ambrose finished with 405 victims, behind only his long-time new-ball partner Courtney Walsh (519) for West Indies. Hillie always loved cricket – unlike Curtly, who was initially keener on basketball, but admitted his mother "steered me towards cricket at every possible opportunity".

AMROLIWALA, HOSHANG DADIBA, died on December 29, aged 86. A consistent scorer for Bombay, Hoshie Amroliwala hit 139 against Bengal in the Ranji Trophy final in March 1959, after entering at 80 for five. Bombay went on to win the first of what became 15 successive Ranji titles. Amroliwala had also made 84 not out in the semi-final against Services, sharing a partnership of 144 with the 17-year-old Ajit Wadekar. He was considered for the tour of England that followed, but missed out, possibly because Bombay already had several representatives in the side. In March 1960, in the inaugural Irani Trophy match, between the Ranji champions and the Rest of India, Amroliwala dismissed five Test players with his leg-breaks on the way to six for 44, then made 76 not out. He scored another century against Maharashtra later that year, but never did win a Test cap. "Hoshie was one of the finest batsmen at that time," said the former Indian captain Nari Contractor, a fellow Parsi. "He never played in the air, and was fantastic with the square cut and pull."

ASHER, KIRAN PRATAPSINH, who died on May 27, aged 69, was a wicketkeeper-batsman from Bombay whose seven first-class matches produced one century – 105 for

Hampshire CCC

Cheque mates: Tony Baker (far left) at Northlands Road in 1987, when Hampshire won £2,000 for coming fifth in the Championship. Also there are Eric Hood (Britannic Assurance), Donald Rich (chairman), Tim Tremlett, Mark Nicholas, Chris Smith, David Turner and David Carter (Britannic).

the Associated Cement Company in a Moin-ud-Dowlah Cup semi-final against Hyderabad in 1971-72, when he shared an opening stand of 183 with Sunil Gavaskar. Five years later, on Asher's Ranji Trophy debut for Bombay, he and Gavaskar put on 199 to set up a semi-final victory over Tamil Nadu. He later became a coach, often teaching underprivileged children for free.

AUSTIN, RICHARD GRAHAM PAUL, died of cancer on May 16, aged 55. Graham Austin spent several years on the Lord's groundstaff, appearing for various county Second XIs. But he never quite cracked a first team, to the vexation of MCC's head coach, Don Wilson, who felt Austin could have followed him as Yorkshire's slow left-armer. He was briefly plagued by a case of the yips, which was cured by the young Martin Crowe, at Lord's on a scholarship from New Zealand. Crowe made him bowl in the indoor school with the lights off, and the old fluid action returned. Austin went back to league cricket in Yorkshire, playing for a variety of clubs around his native Morley, including Hanging Heaton and Gildersome, where he was a familiar – and immensely popular – figure behind the bar.

BAGGETT, DAVID JACK, who died on May 19, aged 84, was for many years Derbyshire's official statistician, and edited their yearbook; he was president of the Association of Cricket Statisticians from 2004 to 2007. He was also a qualified umpire, standing in numerous Second XI Championship games between 1987 and 2000, and in one Benson and Hedges Cup match at Derby in 1984.

BAKER, ANTHONY FRANK, died on October 13, aged 77. Tony Baker was the man charged with the epic task of moving Hampshire from their ramshackle historic home at Northlands Road to the spanking new Rose Bowl in 2001. He was working from an almost blank sheet of paper: Glamorgan had relocated to Sophia Gardens from the Arms Park at the end of the 1960s, and Durham had opened Riverside in 1995, though with no permanent base from which to move. That Hampshire completed the transition smoothly was down to Baker's calm efficiency and logistical skills. "Over the two decades that I knew him, I don't recall him ever raising his voice," said Hampshire chairman Rod Bransgrove. Baker had been an outstanding club cricketer in the Southampton area. He opened the batting and bowling for Old Tauntonians in the 1960s and '70s, and in a local cup final in 1972 took all ten. He honed his administrative skills as chairman of the Southern League, before becoming Hampshire treasurer, then moving up to chief executive in 1986. One of his early jobs was to look into the possibility of redeveloping Northlands Road, Hampshire's home since 1885. He found that unworkable, and set about identifying a site for a new ground. It took 13 years, and needed a late injection of funds from Bransgrove to prevent the club going into liquidation, but on May 9, 2001, the Rose Bowl hosted its inaugural first-class fixture, against Worcestershire. Baker retired that year as Hampshire were restructured, but he remained in a part-time capacity until 2005, by which time the Rose Bowl had hosted its first one-day internationals and a memorable victory over Australia in England's first game of Twenty20.

BANERJEE, TAPAN JYOTI, who died on May 29, aged 73, was a seamer who played 17 matches for Bengal – and one for East Zone – over 17 years from his debut in December 1965. He took 15 wickets in his first two games, and in 1966-67 claimed six for 58 against Assam at Jorhat. Banerjee later coached the Bengal women's team to the national title. "He was the only coach who told us: 'Eat sweets, it won't harm you,'" remembered India's leading wicket-taker Jhulan Goswami. "But he was strict on the field and had a clear knowledge of the game."

BARTHOLOMEW, PRINCE CHARLES SMITH, who died on April 25, aged 77, was a tall fast bowler and handy batsman who played for Trinidad & Tobago for 11 seasons, and captained them to a share of the regional title in 1975-76, when his 53 and six wickets helped swing the match against Guyana at Port-of-Spain. Five years earlier against Guyana he had hit 95 and 53 – both not out – to guide T&T to a draw after following on. Bartholomew's best bowling figures were eight for 27, for North & East Trinidad in 1975-76 – a record for the Beaumont Cup, which was then first-class. Dinanath Ramnarine, the former Test spinner, called him "the Glenn McGrath of his time".

BECKER, DANZEL FRANK, died on April 20, aged 69. Danny Becker was a fast bowler whose height helped him generate good bounce during 35 matches for various Transvaal sides. His best figures were six for 23 for North Eastern Transvaal against the South African Universities in Pretoria in November 1970, although a better performance was his five for 49 for Transvaal against Rhodesia at the Wanderers in 1972-73. Earlier that season he had been the last man out in Bulawayo as Mike Procter completed victory for Rhodesia with moments to spare by taking a career-best nine for 71. Becker became an umpire, and stood in 16 one-day internationals between 1997 and 2001. His uncle, Syd Burke (see below), played two Tests for South Africa in the 1960s.

BHANDARI, PANAMBUR NARASIMHA, died on November 17, aged 83. "Bab" Bhandari made 102 on first-class debut, for Bihar against Assam at Jamshedpur in 1959-60. He never improved on that, and played only six more matches, the last for East Zone in the Duleep Trophy in October 1961.

BORE, MICHAEL KENNETH, died on May 2, aged 69. Mike Bore was the central character in perhaps the most dramatic conclusion to a County Championship. At Taunton in 1984, Nottinghamshire needed to defeat Somerset to pinch the title off Essex and, after a generous declaration from Ian Botham, set off in pursuit of 297 in 60 overs. But they were down to the last pair when Bore – who finished with a first-class average of 8.24 – was joined by Andy Pick, with 14 needed off the final over, bowled by slow left-armer Stephen Booth. Bore hit the first two balls for four and the third for two, then blocked the next. "Andy came down the track and said: 'What did you do that for?' I replied: 'It wasn't in the right place.'" With four needed off two, Bore launched Booth towards long-off. "As soon as I hit it, I thought: 'That's it, we've won!'" Instead, substitute fielder Richard Ollis,

Bob Thomas, Getty Images

Life and soul: Mike Bore (far right) celebrates Nottinghamshire's 1981 Championship triumph at Trent Bridge. Clive Rice, Bruce French and Richard Hadlee join in.

ten yards in from the boundary, extended his 6ft frame to deny Bore his place in history, and ensure the trophy stayed at Chelmsford.

Bore – always Noddy to his team-mates – drove home with his friend Paul Johnson, who remembered: "He was so upset, he barely stopped crying." In 2006, Bore told the writer Simon Lister: "No matter how many times I lie in bed and replay that ball, I never score those four runs." But there were compensations. He won the title twice during his ten seasons at Trent Bridge, perhaps reward for a frustrating nine-year stretch with his native Yorkshire, where he never commanded a regular place. Bore bowled left-arm medium-pace, later changing to brisk orthodox spin, in the manner of Derek Underwood. "Like Deadly, he was very dangerous on a damp pitch," said Derek Randall.

He was born in Hull and made his debut for Yorkshire in 1969. His best season for them was 1971, when 44 wickets at 26 included six for 63 against Gloucestershire at Bramall Lane, while he took seven for 63 against Derbyshire at Scarborough in his final first-class appearance for Yorkshire, in 1977. But he was instantly more at home at Trent Bridge, often bowling with Eddie Hemmings, and told to keep the game tight, which suited him. He took 61 wickets in his first season with Nottinghamshire, and 36 at 29 in 1981, the first of his two title-winning summers. In the second, 1987, he managed 13 at 26.

"On the field he was probably our least lively player, and off it the most lively," said Randall. "He was the life and soul of the party, a very funny man. He was intelligent, too – he was the only one in our dressing-room who could do the crossword." Bore stepped down to captain the Second XI at the end of 1984, having taken 210 first-class wickets for Nottinghamshire in 85 matches, and 89 in 92 one-day games. His best performance was eight for 89 against Kent at Folkestone in 1979. He became a popular and respected coach with both his former counties, and worked with the young Michael Vaughan at Headingley's indoor school.

He was also a valued companion on away trips. Johnson said: "He gave people directions via fish and chip shops: 'Down there, and left at the Wetherby Whaler…' And he had his own code for the size of the portion. If it was just a normal bagful, he would say it was an OTA – off the arm, meaning he could carry it. Anything bigger was an OTB – on the bonnet, meaning he'd need to rest the bag on something. He was the Egon Ronay of fish and chips."

BOSE, SREERUPA, who died on November 30, aged 66, opened the bowling in two one-day internationals for India's women against New Zealand in 1984-85, without taking a wicket. She captained Bengal for many years, and managed the Indian team at the 1993, 1997 and 2000 World Cups. She also commentated on sport for Doordarshan and All India Radio.

BRADLEY, ROGER ROBERT ANDREW FRANCIS, who died on March 24, aged 54, played one first-class match for Northern Districts in his native New Zealand in 1990-91, before moving to the Netherlands, where he made several appearances for the national side. He was part of the team that won the ICC Trophy in Canada in 2001, although he made a golden duck in the final against Namibia. That was a rare failure: Bradley amassed almost 10,000 runs in Dutch senior club cricket. He suffered from a hereditary heart condition, eventually undergoing a transplant.

BRITTIN, JANETTE ANN, MBE, died of cancer on September 11, aged 58. There was much more to the gilded career of Jan Brittin than the statistics that identify her as one of the greats of the women's game. Team-mates held her in awe, and opponents were often lost in admiration for her relaxed, classical technique. "I loved watching her bat – even when she was getting runs against us," said the former New Zealand captain Debbie Hockley. Brittin's 19-year England career – 1979 to 1998 – bridged two distinct eras: in her first Test, Rachael Heyhoe Flint was a team-mate; in her final series, she opened with Charlotte Edwards.

Although Brittin scored high marks for artistic impression, it did not compromise her competitiveness. "She looked after herself, when the rest of us were happy to eat rubbish and have a few drinks," said England team-mate Jackie Court. "She was a professional in an amateur era." Brittin held two records that, given the reduction in women's Tests, may never be beaten. She is the leading scorer in the format, with 1,935 runs at just under 50 in 27 matches, and the leading centurion, with five. She made 2,121 runs at 42 in 63 one-day internationals, also with five hundreds.

Cover point: Jan Brittin graces the October 1984 edition of *The Cricketer*.

And she was a magnificent fielder. "She was a wonderful athlete," said Enid Bakewell. "She would field at mid-off or cover and nobody ever took a run to her. She watched the angle of the bat intently to see where the ball would go." Her electric work led to a landmark moment: because her legs were so often grazed and bloody from sliding stops or diving catches, it was decided to switch from skirts to trousers.

Brittin came from a sporting family. Her father Kevin played cricket for Surrey and football for Tottenham Hotspur at junior levels, and ran a sports shop in Surbiton. She excelled at hockey – she played three indoor internationals for England in 1987 – but at the age of 12 attended a steam fair with her grandparents, and performed impressively on a catching machine. The woman running it recruited her instantly

Patrick Eagar, Popperfoto/Getty Images

A cut above: Jan Brittin guides England towards World Cup glory at Lord's in 1993. The New Zealand keeper is Sarah Illingworth.

for Tadworth Cricket Club. Her progress was rapid. While a student at Chelsea College of Physical Education in Eastbourne, she made her Test debut, aged 19, against West Indies in 1979; her scores were modest, her potential huge.

By the time of New Zealand's visit in 1984, she was a mature talent and poised for a summer of extraordinary dominance. Now in her preferred position of opener, Brittin made 338 runs at 112 in the three Tests, and 258 at 128 in the ODIs. *Wisden* said: "She used her feet well and despatched the ball elegantly to all quarters of the field, bringing back memories of a former outstanding England batsman, Molly Hide." She ended the season on the cover of *The Cricketer*. Her exploits won her a crate of champagne, which she happily shared with team-mates before they went to Australia that winter. "It would never be allowed now," said Brittin. "But it certainly added to team bonding." She made her first overseas century in the First Test at the WACA, but Australia won the Ashes 2–1.

She regarded the 1993 World Cup as her career highlight. She had been part of the team that had lost to Australia at Christchurch in February 1982, and in December 1988 had top-scored for England in the final with 46 not out, only for Australia to knock off the runs at the MCG. "The ground seemed a very large and a very lonely place," she said. Five years later she began the tournament with a hundred against Denmark at Banstead, and made another against India at Finchampstead. She found the final an emotional occasion: she was reduced to tears when she and her opening partner Wendy Watson were given a rousing reception as they walked through the Lord's Long Room on their way out to the wicket. But the tears soon dried, and she again top-scored, with 48 in England's 195 for five. New Zealand folded in reply, and Brittin took the catch that won the World Cup, running back to cling on to Catherine Campbell's slog. "Dropping it was never an issue," wrote Mike Selvey in *The Guardian*. "Up went her arms – the ball was last seen heading aerially towards Swiss Cottage." Brittin described it as "the stuff of dreams". By the time England lost in the semi-finals in Chennai in 1997, she was the leading run-scorer in women's World Cups, with 1,299 at 43 in 36 matches, a record that passed to Hockley in the final.

Against New Zealand at Guildford in 1996, Brittin opened with the 16-year-old Edwards, old stager and tyro putting on 63. "To know I was going to open the batting with my hero Jan Brittin – wow," said Edwards. "It was four days I'll never forget." Brittin's valedictory season in 1998 was a personal triumph. In three drawn Ashes Tests she scored 450 runs at 112, including 146 at Guildford and 167 at Harrogate, batting more than 24 hours in all. After that she concentrated on her golf handicap, coaching at her former county Surrey, and beginning a new career in teaching, after working for British Airways for most of her cricket career. "For girls of my generation she was our first female role model," said the former England captain Clare Connor. "She was so beautiful to watch."

BURKE, SYDNEY FRANK, died on April 3, aged 83. The South African swing bowler Syd Burke made a startling Test debut at Cape Town in 1961-62, taking 11 wickets – but was made twelfth man in the next match. New Zealand had won that game at Newlands – their first Test victory over South Africa – and so the home selectors, feeling extra pace was needed, recalled Neil Adcock and Peter Heine for Johannesburg (it worked: they won by an innings). Burke had toiled through 81 overs to take six for 128 and five for 68: "He

BEST MATCH FIGURES ON TEST DEBUT

16-136	N. D. Hirwani	India v West Indies at Madras	1987-88
16-137	R. A. L. Massie	Australia v England at Lord's	1972
12-102	F. Martin	England v Australia at The Oval	1890
12-358	J. J. Krejza	Australia v India at Nagpur	2008-09
11-82	C. V. Grimmett	Australia v England at Sydney	1924-25
11-96	C. S. Marriott	England v West Indies at The Oval	1933
11-112	A. E. Hall	South Africa v England at Cape Town	1922-23
11-130	Mohammad Zahid	Pakistan v New Zealand at Rawalpindi	1996-97
11-145	A. V. Bedser	England v India at Lord's	1946
11-196	**S. F. Burke**	**South Africa v New Zealand at Cape Town**	**1961-62**
11-204	A. L. Valentine	West Indies v England at Manchester	1950

Marriott was playing in his only Test; Burke, Krejza and Martin played only one more. J. J. Ferris took 13-91 on his debut for England, against South Africa at Cape Town in 1891-92, but had already played for Australia.

was overbowled and, but for his gallantry and phenomenal stamina, must have fallen in his tracks," wrote journalist R. S. Whitington. Three years later Burke played another Test, against England, also at Cape Town, and this time failed to take a wicket. He had begun his first-class career with North Eastern Transvaal in December 1954, but made little impression before moving to Orange Free State: he took seven for 11 for them – six bowled and one lbw – against Eastern Province at Port Elizabeth on New Year's Day in 1959. It was another ten-wicket haul against EP that earned Burke (by now back with NE Transvaal) his Test recall in 1964-65.

BURT, VERA ESTHER (*née* Robinson), MBE, who died on September 21, aged 90, had been New Zealand's oldest Test cricketer, a distinction that passed to 89-year-old John Reid. Burt had a remarkably long international career, although she won only three Test caps. After playing against Australia and England in the late 1940s, she had to wait nearly 20 years for another chance, against England at Wellington in March 1969, when she was 42. A batsman who sometimes bowled left-arm spin, she made 84 for Auckland against Wellington in 1951-52. Burt also played hockey for New Zealand, and was a hockey umpire for 34 years.

CAMERON, JOHN DANIEL, OAM, died on April 7, aged 93. During his 50 years as the Australian Broadcasting Corporation's scorer at the MCG, it was as if Jack Cameron had taken a vow of silence: he believed he should be a discreet support to the commentators. When plied with questions from the likes of Alan McGilvray and Lindsay Hassett, his answers came promptly, accurately and quietly – and their "Thanks, Jack" made him one of the most well-known yet opaque presences on Australian radio. His children said he broke his rule only once, when he told the family he would contact them at 4.50pm; right on cue they heard a cough in the background. Cameron did the job for half a century from 1954, and was the official scorer for Richie Benaud's side in England in 1961.

CHAMBERS, JOHN LINDSAY, who died on September 12, aged 86, was an attractive left-hander, who caught the eye of Keith Miller while still at school. In his first two Sheffield Shield matches for Victoria, in 1951-52, Chambers hit 54 against Western Australia at Perth, then 114 against South Australia at Adelaide. Known as "Cocky" because of a crown of wavy fair hair and a jaunty approach to batting, he was touted as a possibility for the 1953 Ashes. The commentator Johnnie Moyes warned he was "a bit impetuous", but thought he would "get plenty once he learns restraint". Chambers did play a few more bright knocks, including another hundred against South Australia, but restraint continued to be a problem. He dropped out of the Victorian team after 1954-55, in part to attend to his family's property and auctioneering business.

CHAMPNISS, LAURENCE JOHN, died on September 17, aged 78. The sight of the balding Laurie Champniss bustling in to bowl his tricky leg-breaks was common in club cricket north of London in the 1960s and '70s. He had captained Harrow School in 1957, went on to represent Buckinghamshire, and played one first-class match, on an MCC tour of East Africa in 1973-74 under the captaincy of Mike Brearley. He later established a successful bridge club in Burnham, near Slough.

CHEVALIER, GRAHAME ANTON, who died on November 14, aged 80, was an economical slow left-armer whose first-class career with South Africa's Western Province did not begin until he was almost 30, when he took four for 29 against Border in November 1966. Before that, his path had been blocked by Harry Bromfield, who played nine Tests. But with South Africa casting around for spinners, Chevalier put his name in the frame with four-fors in successive matches against Natal and Eastern Province in November 1969, and was called up for the First Test against Australia, at home in Cape Town. He did well enough, removing Paul Sheahan with his fifth ball, and finished with five wickets in the match. His other victims included Ian Chappell in the second innings, after taking a smart catch to dismiss him in the first, as South Africa started what would become a 4–0 whitewash with a 170-run victory. But off-spinner John Traicos, ten years younger and a better fielder, was preferred for the subsequent Tests, and that was the end of Chevalier's brief international career. "He was a very decent chap, quiet and reserved," said Peter Pollock, part of their destructive pace attack. "The reason he only played one Test was that he would have been regarded very much as a Newlands specialist. It was his home ground and, in those days, the only pitch that was spin-bowler friendly." Chevalier was selected for the tours of England and Australia that were due to follow, but they were cancelled as South Africa's long excommunication from the world game began. He played on for Western Province, taking a career-best seven for 57 against Currie Cup champions Transvaal at the Wanderers in 1970-71, and rolled out figures of 22–11–23–6 against Natal at Newlands a few weeks later.

CLARKE, SIMON JOHN SCOTT, who died on October 12, aged 79, was a small but nimble scrum-half who won 13 England rugby caps, the first while at Cambridge University in 1963. He rejoiced in the nickname "Steptoe", after a perceived resemblance to Wilfrid Brambell, who played the older rag-and-bone man in the TV sitcom. Clarke's final act in international rugby came at Twickenham in 1965, when he started the late move that led to Andy Hancock's 80-yard try, which tied the match against Scotland. He also played cricket for Cambridge, although he had little success and failed to win a Blue. His highest first-class score was just 19, but in 1958, while doing national service, he made 81 at Edgbaston and 70 at The Oval, for the Navy against county Second XIs. Those two innings sandwiched an inglorious first-class debut, for Combined Services against Lancashire at Old Trafford, where he was bowled for a duck in the first innings, then dropped down the order in the second after pulling a shoulder muscle. His team-mate Tony Lewis recalled that Clarke told their unamused captain: "Did the damn thing shaving."

CORBETT, EDWIN FAWDRY, died on August 9, aged 82. Ted Corbett arrived in Australia in inauspicious circumstances in 1982-83 as the newly appointed cricket correspondent of the *Daily Star*. He had been promoted from covering snooker to replace the popular Derek Hodgson (see below) and was seen by several colleagues, quite unjustly, as a usurper. Corbett was in fact an affable man – but also shrewd, capable and determined enough to remain on the Test circuit long after most of his critics had vanished, by which time he was regarded within the press box as a sort of universal uncle. He was particularly skilful in building subcontinental contacts. This led to his finest hour: he secured an interview with the controversial umpire Shakoor Rana after his row with Mike Gatting during the infamous Faisalabad Test of 1987-88. Rana and Corbett were apparently ensconced in the umpires' room when the England manager Peter Lush marched in. Lush was made even more furious by the sight of Ted, calmly taking both notes and tea. Corbett left the *Star* in 1989, but continued to freelance on cricket, travelling the global circuit with his partner, the scorer Jo King, until 2008. He wrote columns for *The Hindu* newspaper and its associated magazine *Sportstar* until he was past 80.

COSH, STEPHEN HUNTER, MBE, died on March 15, aged 97. The hard-hitting Ayr wicketkeeper-batsman Hunter Cosh played in 36 of Scotland's 38 first-class matches in the 1950s, captaining them from 1956; they beat a county for the first time in his final game, against Warwickshire at Edgbaston in 1959. Cosh, who once hit a six off Fred Trueman through Yorkshire's dressing-room window at Scarborough, was run out for 99 against Derbyshire in 1954, and two years later made 81 not out – with 64 in boundaries – in the annual match against Ireland. During the war he was a major in the Royal Scots Fusiliers, and received an MBE. He and his wife Betty were married for 75 years.

COUSINS, RICHARD JOHN, died when a seaplane crashed into the Hawkesbury River, north of Sydney, during a sightseeing flight on December 31. He was 58, and visiting Australia for the Ashes. Four members of his family and the pilot were also killed. A successful businessman, Cousins built up the Compass catering group, from which he was about to retire. He was passionate about cricket, a member of all 18 first-class counties, and had been linked with a role as a non-executive director of the ECB.

CRAWFORD, GEOFFREY DOUGLAS, CVO, died on September 27, aged 66. Sydney-born Geoff Crawford was the Queen's press secretary at a difficult time: he started as an assistant in 1992, which she termed her *annus horribilis* after the Prince of Wales's divorce and a fire at Windsor Castle, and was in the top job when Princess Diana was killed in a car crash in 1997. His Australian directness made him popular at Buckingham Palace, and he once greatly amused the Queen by telling her how he knew when she was irritated: "It's that silent stare, ma'am." Crawford left the Palace in 2000, and returned to Australia to work for the ABC. Latterly he lived in Bowral where, a keen cricket fan, he busied himself writing player biographies for the Bradman Museum.

CUMBERBATCH, CLYDE ELLIOT, who died on December 29, aged 81, was a tall (6ft 6in) umpire from Trinidad who stood in 63 first-class matches, 12 of them Tests, as well as 26 one-day internationals. His first Test, England's visit to Port-of-Spain in 1980-81, had an unusual start: it was delayed for four hours after the pitch had been damaged by locals upset at the omission of Trinidad wicketkeeper Deryck Murray. Cumberbatch was well respected in the Caribbean, although he might have ended one famous career almost before it started, by no-balling Curtly Ambrose for throwing when the Leeward Islands visited Trinidad in January 1988. The Leewards players asked why Cumberbatch had made the call, but he did not reply; some started to walk off, before their manager persuaded them to continue. Ambrose, who played the first Test of a glittering career a few weeks later, said: "If you're going to call someone for throwing, you have to explain yourself." After retiring, Cumberbatch headed the training committee for West Indian umpires for 12 years.

CURRAN, KEVIN PATRICK, who died on August 23, aged 88, was the father of the late Zimbabwe all-rounder Kevin, and grandfather of the Surrey brothers Sam and Tom. Kevin senior had six first-class matches for Rhodesia, never surpassing the unbeaten 52 he made on debut against Western Province in 1947-48. He also played for a South African XI against the Australian tourists in Salisbury (now Harare) in November 1949.

DAVIDSON, THOMAS REX, died on January 11, aged 89. Wicketkeeper Rex Davidson's defiant 71 in a total of 120 against the West Indian tourists on his home ground at Launceston in 1951-52 persuaded the Tasmania selectors to make him captain for the following season. He added twin fifties against the Australian touring team en route for England in 1953.

DAVIES, HUGH DANIEL, who died on December 2, aged 85, was a fast bowler who showed great promise for Glamorgan before knee trouble curtailed his career. Davies took five for 35 against the 1955 South African tourists in one of his early games, and the following summer demolished Gloucestershire at Newport with five for 32. In 1957 he collected 52 wickets, with a career-best six for 85 in a rare victory over Yorkshire at Sheffield – but then injury struck, and he played only nine matches over the next three seasons. He became a PE teacher, and occasionally commentated in Welsh on cricket for BBC Radio Cymru. Davies later joined Glamorgan's committee, eventually becoming their chairman of cricket, and was also the chair of Cricket Wales. His son, Adam, was on the Glamorgan staff for a time.

DAVISON, IAN JOSEPH, who died on January 2, aged 79, was a lively opening bowler who collected more than 500 wickets for Nottinghamshire, including 111 in 1963. The previous summer he had taken seven for 28 against Derbyshire. "He was tall, quite pacy, and swung it in," remembered team-mate Mike Smedley. "He was also a lookalike for Keith Miller, which amused him." Davison was signed from Bedfordshire, not long after taking seven for 17 as they skittled Lincolnshire for 46 in 1958, and made his first-class debut in 1959, claiming a distinguished maiden scalp in Brian Close. He formed an effective new-ball partnership with the Jamaican left-armer Carlton Forbes but, still only 28, decided to retire after the 1966 season because of injury problems. Smedley recalled an incident that year, against Northamptonshire: "Davo bounced Colin Milburn, who hooked him down to long leg. Barry Stead took the catch, and threw the ball up in glee – but in his excitement he threw it over the boundary, so it was a six. That was the year the first innings in the Championship was limited to 65 overs – Milburn scored a hundred in 77 balls, and Northants got 355." Davison continued to play at club level, helping Ockbrook & Borrowash become a force in the Derbyshire League.

DE GRANDHOMME, LAURENCE LEONARD, who died on December 13, aged 61, was an off-spinner and handy batsman who played several representative matches for Zimbabwe in pre-Test days, and toured England with them in 1985. In the first match of the trip, against Oxford University, his 32 not out was dwarfed by the 19-year-old Graeme Hick's 230. Zimbabwe had no domestic first-class cricket at the time, so de Grandhomme's senior opportunities were limited to visits from touring teams: in September 1985 he captained Zimbabwe B against a strong Young Australia side, which included Steve Waugh. Three years later he played the last of his 16 first-class games, taking three wickets against Sri Lanka B, but bagging a pair. His son, Colin, played for Zimbabwe A, before moving to New Zealand and making his Test debut for them in November 2016; he scored a maiden Test century against West Indies at Wellington little more than a week before his father's death.

DELLOR, RALPH, who died on September 1, aged 69, was a journalist and broadcaster of great versatility and apparently tireless energy. He was just as at home commentating

True gentleman: Ralph Dellor reports from an India–Pakistan match in Sharjah in 1999.

for *Test Match Special* from a broiling subcontinental ground as for Five Live Sport from a freezing Premier League press box. He embraced the arrival of the internet with more gusto than some of his contemporaries, and was an early editor at ESPNcricinfo. He wrote books, hosted stage shows and was a polished after-dinner speaker. There was nothing, it seemed, to which he could not turn his hand.

Still, it took him a while to find his métier. He worked for a fur company and in insurance before getting his break: reading the football results for Radio London. But cricket was his great love. He was an ECB coach, and took charge of the Norway team which won the European Cricket Council Trophy in 2003, 2005 and 2006. He also coached Oxford University and Berkshire, where he was heavily involved in the county's restructuring.

He covered three overseas Tests for *TMS*, including England's nine-wicket win in Chennai in 1984-85 and the incendiary Faisalabad match of 1987-88, famous for Mike Gatting's confrontation with Shakoor Rana. On the day when there was no play because of the developing stand-off, he managed to secure an interview with the aggrieved umpire. He was also part of the *TMS* team for the 1983 World Cup. On television he introduced BBC2's coverage of the Sunday League, and since 2014 had been the voice on the PA at Lord's. Dellor covered cricket for *The Daily Telegraph*, wrote and edited a string of books, including *The Cricketers' Who's Who* from 1984 to 1988, and provided *Wisden* with reports on university cricket from 2000 to 2016. He also conducted a series of interviews with former players that were released as audio tapes under the title *In Conversation*. Through it all he played whenever possible, usually opening the bowling at a nippy medium-pace. Fellow writer John Etheridge remembered an inexhaustible seamer, and "the first journo with his name on a sponsored car!"

When he left Cricinfo, Dellor expanded Sportsline Media Limited with Stephen Lamb, providing video and audio content for websites. The Cricket Writers' Club chairman Mark Baldwin called him "a true gentleman of our profession, and a great servant of cricket in many capacities". *TMS* producer Adam Mountford added: "He had an ageless voice and an incredible enthusiasm for cricket."

DERRICK, JOHN, who died of a brain tumour on March 22, aged 54, was arguably Glamorgan's most successful coach. After more than 200 first-class and one-day appearances for them, he moved into coaching, taking over the senior role on a full-time basis from Jeff Hammond in 2002. Though genial, he was not afraid to deliver a few stinging words, such as when his team were bowled out for 144 that summer on a good pitch at Northampton. But they did win the 45-over competition, a year after gaining promotion. Glamorgan captain Steve James recalled: "I wasn't sure he was the right man, and I don't think John was either – he felt better suited to working with the second team and younger players. But the club didn't have much money, and John was very good about taking on a role he didn't feel suited for."

Even better followed in 2004 when, under the inspirational captaincy of Robert Croft, Glamorgan won promotion in the Championship, and added another 45-over league title. The team, said *Wisden*, "thought hard about the peculiar requirements of the cricket, and honed them close to perfection". There was also a first appearance at Twenty20 finals day, where they were beaten in the semi-final by Leicestershire. But from those highs, the fortunes of both Glamorgan and Derrick went downhill. They found it harder to win Championship matches and, after being relegated in 2005, finished second-bottom of Division Two. While their Cardiff headquarters were extensively redeveloped to become a Test ground, there was no money for overseas players. When they found enough cash to sign Brendon McCullum for the 2006 Twenty20 campaign, no one thought to tell Derrick. "That really put my back up," he said. He lost his job in the winter of 2006, and joined Cricket Wales, where he became national performance director.

Stu Forster, Getty Images

"That big grin": John Derrick in 2000.

Derrick was born in the former mining village of Cwmaman near Aberdare, and played for Wales Under-15s alongside Hugh Morris, who became a close friend. He was on the groundstaff at Lord's, and made his first-class debut for Glamorgan against Cambridge University at Fenner's in 1983. His first Championship match followed a few weeks later. Solidly built, he bowled medium-pace, batted down the order and was a fine close fielder. His best season was 1988, with 47 wickets at 32, including a career-best six for 54 against Leicestershire at Grace Road. His best return with the bat was in 1986, when he made 569 runs at 35, including 78 not out against Derbyshire at Abergavenny, his highest first-class score.

Derrick went straight into coaching after retiring in 1991, briefly taking charge of the first team later in the decade. Among his Cricket Wales graduates to progress to first-class cricket were Aneurin Donald, Kiran Carlson and Lukas Carey. When he was taken ill in August 2016 and underwent brain surgery, a dinner to raise funds to convert his house was three times oversubscribed. "He had a profound influence on so many young Welsh cricketers," said Morris. "Whenever you saw him he had that big grin." Former Glamorgan batsman Mike Powell said: "He was a mentor for me beyond cricket. He went deeper than that. How I behaved, how I conducted myself, was all from John."

DHAROD, RAMJI PREMJI, who died on March 27, aged 77, was a well-known swing bowler in club cricket in Bombay. He never played first-class cricket, but made a mark during the first Test played at the Wankhede Stadium, against West Indies in January 1975. Crowd trouble flared after a spectator intent on congratulating Clive Lloyd on his double-century was manhandled by police, but Dharod and a friend jumped over the fence from the members' enclosure – risking arrest themselves – and successfully persuaded the protesters not to damage the pitch. Play was able to resume next morning. Karsan Ghavri, who opened the bowling for India in that match, attended Dharod's funeral.

DOGGART, SIMON JONATHON GRAHAM, who died on July 23, aged 56, followed his father Hubert, the former Sussex captain, in representing Cambridge University. An off-spinner who batted left-handed, he made 35 first-class appearances and played in the Varsity Match four times. His highest score and best figures both came against Nottinghamshire at Fenner's in 1983: 70, and three for three. He also played ten times for Combined Universities in the Benson and Hedges Cup, and a handful of Second XI games for his father's old county, but went into teaching, becoming headmaster of Caldicott School in Berkshire. He retired two months before his death.

EVANS, RUSSELL JOHN, died on November 30, aged 52, from complications after routine surgery. Evans joined his older brother, Kevin, on the Nottinghamshire staff in 1985, but made a solitary half-century – against the Sri Lankan tourists in 1988 – in six first-class games before being released in 1992. He then turned out for Lincolnshire, and in one further first-class appearance for the Minor Counties, against the South Africans at Torquay in 1994, increased his highest score to 59 not out. After working for a time as a bat-maker – and arranging Joe Root's first equipment deal – Evans was promoted to the English first-class umpires' panel in 2015, and proved an able and popular official. "I always enjoyed bowling at his end," said Essex's Jamie Porter, the leading wicket-taker of 2017. Local umpire Martin Briggs added: "He attended every local umpires' training session at Trent Bridge, answering questions with unlimited patience, deep knowledge and no little wit." The England team wore black armbands in his honour on the first day of the Ashes Test in Adelaide.

FARR, BRYAN HENRY, who died on May 20, aged 93, was a 17-year-old schoolboy at Harrow when he made his debut for Nottinghamshire, in a wartime match against the RAF in 1941. He also scored 35 for Cambridge against Oxford at Lord's in 1943, in a one-day game that replaced the usual Varsity Match. After the war he played six Championship matches, saving his best for New Road in 1951 when, armed with the new ball, he took five for 96 to add to scores of 32 not out and 37, although his efforts were in vain as Worcestershire sprinted to a victory target of 131 in 40 minutes with five to spare (Farr 3–0–32–0). In his next match he finished with none for 160 as Derbyshire made hay, and did not appear for Nottinghamshire again, although he did play one further first-class match the following year for the Free Foresters. He later ran the Worksop Manor Estate and stud farm.

FENIX, PETER, who died on January 11, aged 77, was a talented all-round sportsman – he also played rugby, hockey, squash and polo to a high level in South Africa – and a long-serving batsman for Border and Eastern Province. He scored 166 for EP against Transvaal at the Wanderers in November 1966, and 102 in the next match – his side's first century against an Australian touring team – in Port Elizabeth. Fenix later ran a financial company and bred horses.

FERRANT, JEAN GERMAIN, died on December 3, aged 83. Born in South Africa to French parents, John Ferrant played 43 first-class matches as a seamer, mainly for Eastern Province, in a long career that stretched to 1970-71. "He bowled better with the old ball," said his team-mate Geoff Dakin, "and he could analyse a batsman's faults better than any bowler I knew." Ferrant took six for 45 against Rhodesia at Port Elizabeth in 1957-58. The previous season, in one of his early matches for EP, he found the edge of the touring

England side's best-known batsman, only for Dakin to shell a simple chance at slip. "I'll go to my grave thinking of how you dropped Denis Compton," said Ferrant. A pharmacist, he served on Eastern Province's board; his son, David, also played first-class cricket.

FIDLER, CECIL THOMAS ALBERT, died on July 5, aged 82. "Sam" Fidler was a popular Kent groundsman for more than 20 years from the late 1970s. "His was one of the best-known faces in Canterbury," said the Kent historian Derek Carlaw. "Walking with him through the town centre was akin to a Royal progress." Called for his initial interview by secretary Les Ames, Fidler arrived at the St Lawrence ground on a tractor.

FISHWICK, ROBERT, died on March 29, aged 82. Left-hander Bob Fishwick scored 3,346 runs and took 342 wickets with his slow left-armers in over 20 years for Church in the Lancashire League. He was a member of their 1962 title-winning side – when their professional, the West Indian fast bowler Chester Watson, took 117 wickets at 7.58 – and went on to captain them.

FRANCIS, ALBERT, MBE, who died on June 19, aged 89, was head groundsman at Sophia Gardens in Cardiff for many years, after a spell at the nearby Arms Park. The first Championship matches were played at the new ground in 1967, and Francis helped stabilise the pitches after some early problems. "His death is especially poignant," said Glamorgan's chief executive Hugh Morris, "when we are celebrating 50 years of county cricket at Sophia Gardens."

GAUTAM, SHUBAM, died on June 19 after collapsing on a bus taking his side to a cricket tournament in Bangalore. He was 22, and had been playing for the Hubli Cricket Academy. Gautam reportedly fell off his seat during the journey, and was declared dead on arrival at hospital. Mourners at his funeral protested that he had been murdered, but initial police enquiries drew a blank.

GHAI, SHARAD, who died on May 20, aged 64, was closely involved with the Kenyan Cricket Association (later Cricket Kenya) from 1996 to 2005, latterly as chairman. He was credited with modernising it, especially in marketing. When one reporter joked that he must have made a million dollars from an ICC tournament in Nairobi in October 2000, Ghai shot back: "No, I didn't. I made 1.6 million." He was hailed as a hero when Kenya reached the semi-finals of the 2003 World Cup, but that high point preceded a rapid decline; starved of resources and players, they have hardly won an important match since, and lost one-day international status in 2014. By then Ghai was long gone, sacked by the government amid allegations of financial misconduct on a grand scale. In 2006, he was cleared of stealing $3.3m from the old board, but was still frozen out by the new.

GLENN, JACK, drowned in the River Foyle, near Londonderry in Northern Ireland, on February 2. He was 23, and had apparently been depressed after losing his job a few weeks earlier. A leg-spinning all-rounder for Creevedonnell, he had represented Ireland's age-group teams, taking four for 18 for the Under-15s against Denmark in 2009.

GOLDSTEIN, FREDERICK STEVEN, died on December 3, aged 73. A Rhodes Scholar from Bulawayo who played for Oxford University for four years, captaining them in the last two, Fred Goldstein was an aggressive opening batsman, strong on the leg side. He made an immediate mark in the Parks, with 65 and 78 on his first-class debut, against Gloucestershire in 1966; later that season he hit 211 against the Army in a non-first-class game at Aldershot. He continued to attack, and in the 1968 Varsity Match hammered 155 (including all 53 runs as the total moved from 125 to 178) before he was dismissed at 206. Although that was his only hundred for Oxford, Goldstein added 21 half-centuries, including twin 87s in 1969, when he also launched Lancashire's usually parsimonious off-spinner Jack Simmons for three successive sixes in an innings of 76. He played a few matches for Northamptonshire, making 90 against Glamorgan in August 1969.

After leaving Oxford, Goldstein moved to South Africa, eventually becoming a professor at the University of Cape Town. He played for Transvaal and Western Province,

GREAT WAR OBITUARY – 100 YEARS ON

A thousand pities

GOODWIN, 2ND LT HAROLD JAMES, died on April 24, 1917, aged 31. To his contemporaries at Cambridge it must have seemed as if Harold Goodwin could have had his choice of sporting careers. He was an outstanding cricketer and a fine hockey player – he won an England cap against Scotland in 1908 – and also excelled at tennis, the 120-yard hurdles and throwing the hammer. Somehow he had also found time between studying mathematics to play in goal in college football matches. But he chose the life of a Birmingham solicitor, making a handful of appearances for Warwickshire when business commitments allowed.

It did not prevent him captaining the county ten times in the summer of 1910, and *Wisden* lamented: "It was a thousand pities that he could not find time to play more regularly. Whenever he appeared, the side played up with a dash and vigour worthy of all praise for Goodwin." That said, the results were not outstanding, Warwickshire winning just twice under his leadership. He made a smattering of useful contributions: 81 from No. 9 against Sussex at Leamington Spa, and 64 against the same opponents at Hove. His leg-breaks earned him six wickets against Worcestershire at New Road. The following season, now under Frank Foster, Warwickshire were champions for the first time.

Jesus College, Cambridge

Harold Goodwin at Cambridge.

Goodwin was born in Edgbaston, and his father was the county's treasurer. He went to Marlborough and, in the Colours' Match against Rugby at Lord's in 1904, he took five for 46 in a nine-wicket win; a year later, he made 193 against the Free Foresters. (In a house match he once scored 365 and took 15 wickets.) He went up to Jesus College, but did not secure a regular place in the Cambridge team until his second year – winning Blues in 1907 and 1908, and making contributions to successive victories at Lord's. His best year was 1908, which brought 467 runs at 26, and 35 wickets at 27. It included his only first-class century, 101 for Warwickshire against Sussex at Hove.

He was the star of a stirring victory for the university over Lancashire in May 1907. After Cambridge made 366 on the first day – Goodwin 47 – the second was washed out. Then on the last he bowled unchanged to take a career-best seven for 33 in the first innings and five for 29 in the second. Lancashire were dismissed for 97 and 65, and Cambridge won by an innings and 204. "None of the batsmen was able to cope with his leg-breaks," said *The Times*.

Goodwin was commissioned in the Royal Garrison Artillery in December 1916, and died during the Battle of Arras just a few weeks after reaching the front. He was survived by his wife and one-year-old son; his daughter was born four months after his death.

Wisden *first published an obituary for Goodwin in 1918. Until 2019, an updated appreciation of a player who died in the Great War will appear 100 years after the original notice.*

PA Photos

"Thrilling cricket": Fred Goldstein, 1968.

where he often opened with Eddie Barlow. He made 104 – his second and last first-class century – for them against Natal in November 1973, sharing a second-wicket stand of 174 with Hylton Ackerman, with whom he had opened at Northampton. John Ward, *Wisden's* long-serving Zimbabwe correspondent, said: "The most thrilling cricket I ever saw were the times I watched Goldstein take on Mike Procter with the new ball."

GORRINGE, HARRISON REGINALD, died on June 25, aged 89. Harry Gorringe was one of a posse of Western Australian fast bowlers who often made life miserable for visiting batsmen on the pacy WACA pitch of the 1950s. He generated genuine speed from a long, loping run – but away from Perth tended to bowl short, and could be easy pickings for batsmen strong off the back foot. Gorringe had a spectacular afternoon at the WACA in December 1952, when he took four Queensland wickets for none in his first three overs, then returned to demolish the tail, finishing with eight for 56. His bag included four Test players – Ken Archer and Wally Grout for a single apiece, and Colin McCool and Don Tallon for nought. Gorringe wasn't much of a batsman: in 42 first-class innings he reached 25 only once, and bagged 11 ducks.

GRAHAM, SIR DAVID JOHN, KNZM CBE, died on August 2, aged 82. John Graham lived the dream of every young New Zealander, captaining the All Blacks in three of his 22 rugby internationals, in which he scored 11 tries as a loose forward. But he also made a huge mark in education, first as a teacher, then as headmaster of the prestigious Auckland Grammar School for 21 years from 1973. Not long after retiring, he was a left-field choice as manager of New Zealand's cricket team, a position he held from 1997 to 1999. "John was a very good leader, fair and honest," wrote Martin Crowe. "It was a masterstroke to lure him into the cricket ranks."

GRANT, CHRISTOPHER ROBERT WELLESLEY, died on October 22, aged 81. Chris Grant played three first-class matches for Nottinghamshire in 1968, earning a chance to open with Brian Bolus after a century for the Second XI. Diminishing returns set in after he made 48 and 32 on debut against Derbyshire at Trent Bridge, and he was not called up again. Grant returned to teaching in his home town of Newark, where he later ran a sports shop and had a term as mayor.

GREAVES, WILLIAM, died on November 28, aged 79. Yorkshireman Bill Greaves was a journalist who spent 20 years with the *Daily Mail*, writing entertainingly on travel and general subjects. In retirement he co-founded the Capital Kids Cricket charity, after discovering that in 1990 only 20 of London's 800 state schools were playing cricket. His "Greaves's Guide" to the etiquette of ordering a round of drinks hangs behind the bar in many a pub.

GREETHAM, CHRISTOPHER HERBERT MILLINGTON, died on March 13, aged 80. Chris Greetham was a powerful all-rounder who played 205 matches for Somerset over a decade from 1957, after first representing the second team as a 16-year-old in 1953. Bristol Rovers were also interested, but he chose cricket over football and cemented a county place in 1959, when he followed 151 not out against the Combined Services (which remained a career-best) with his first Championship century, against Derbyshire, during a big stand with Peter Wight. Greetham passed 1,000 runs in 1962, when he received his county cap, and did so again in 1963, when 1,186 was his best return. He was also a handy medium-pacer: in 1962, he took seven for 56 against Glamorgan at Swansea and ten for 48 in the match against Lancashire at Old Trafford, and finished the season with 69 wickets. After leaving Somerset, he played briefly for Devon – and, in his last Minor Counties Championship match for them, scored 92 *against* Somerset Seconds at Taunton. David Foot wrote that "he would have been made for one-day cricket." Team-mate Ken Palmer agreed: "He could certainly hit the ball around. If he was about today he would be worth quite a bit of money in the Twenty20 and 50-over competitions." Greetham had been a handy amateur boxer, although it didn't affect his looks – he earned money in the winter as a film extra – and latterly turned to golf.

GUPTE, MAHENDRANATH YESHWANT, died on May 7, aged 86. Mahendra Gupte had a long career as an umpire in India, standing in 26 first-class matches from 1970-71 – including one Test, against England at Madras in 1984-85. He had little to do while Graeme Fowler and Mike Gatting were amassing double-centuries in a total of 652. His son, Vineet, also became an umpire, and stood in two one-day internationals in 1999.

HAMPSHIRE, JOHN HARRY, died on March 1, aged 76. Tall, powerful and destructive, John Hampshire was one of the most watchable batsmen in county cricket in a career spanning three decades, and a mainstay of the Yorkshire team that won five Championships in seven years in the 1960s. "In three-day cricket you had to make time to bowl teams out twice, and John was crucial to our plans in doing that," said Ray Illingworth. But Hampshire was much more than a middle-order hitter: his 21,979 runs put him tenth on Yorkshire's all-time list, and he made 43 first-class hundreds.

Yet the feeling persisted that Hampshire might have been even better. "I never thought I was as good as some people believed me to be," he said. Some of those doubts could be

Player of substance: John Hampshire bats for Yorkshire in 1979.

traced back to an incident at Middlesbrough in May 1963, when he was hit on the head by a ball from Charlie Griffith that he did not believe was legal. He collapsed twice at the crease before being helped off and, although he batted bravely against Griffith in a second tour match later in the summer, he could never quite forget the incident. From then on, he never got more than four hours' sleep a night.

As Yorkshire's fortunes faded in the 1970s, Hampshire became an unwilling central combatant in their prolonged civil war. The powerful group supporting captain Geoff Boycott felt he was in the enemy camp; it was a painful period for a man who played hard but still wanted to enjoy his cricket. "He hated it," said team-mate Geoff Cope. At Northampton in 1978, Hampshire staged an extraordinary protest against Boycott, scoring 11 runs in the last ten overs of the day and costing a bonus point. Yorkshire disciplined him but, when Boycott was sacked at the end of the season, Hampshire took over. The wounds were too deep to heal, however, and after two rancorous summers – "the worst years of my cricketing life" – he gave up the job, and later departed for the calmer waters of Derbyshire. The title of his autobiography was *Family Argument*.

He had made a sensational start to his Test career, becoming the first England batsman to score a century on debut at Lord's, against West Indies in 1969, an achievement he typically played down. "I nicked my way to a hundred over four hours," he said. "I've never been so embarrassed. God, it was terrible." It did not unduly trouble him to be dropped after one more match, and he made just eight Test appearances in all, scoring 403 runs at 26.

Patrick Eagar, Popperfoto/Getty Images

Calm authority: John Hampshire in 1990.

Hampshire later became a respected international umpire, bringing calm authority to such tense encounters as Pakistan's two-wicket win over England at Lord's in 1992, and England's over West Indies in 2000, also by two wickets at Lord's. At the request of Imran Khan, he and John Holder took charge of the entire Pakistan v India series in 1989-90. Hampshire called it "one of my best experiences". Barry Dudleston, a friend and regular umpiring partner, said: "He was very principled and he would not let anything go by, but he had a way of dealing with situations. He commanded respect." Hampshire was coach of Zimbabwe when they first acquired Test status, instilling common-sense principles. "He was a very important part of our early years," said Andy Flower.

He also played a central role in the development of cricket in Tasmania, spending several winters there as player-coach from the mid-1960s, and laying the groundwork for the state's move into the Sheffield Shield. Hampshire particularly relished an innings of 92 against a West Indian attack including a fired-up Griffith at Launceston in 1968-69. And when Tasmania played their first Shield match in 1977-78, he top-scored in both innings against Western Australia.

Hampshire was born in Thurnscoe, a mining village between Barnsley and Doncaster. His father, Jack, was a colliery blacksmith who made three Championship appearances for Yorkshire in 1937 (Denis Compton was the last of his five first-class victims), and in the winter played for Manchester City, where Matt Busby and Frank Swift were among his team-mates, and Bristol City. John also played both sports and thought himself a better footballer, until the moment came to decide: he opted for cricket because the pay was better. Within a few years, the abolition of football's maximum wage tipped the balance permanently in the other direction.

In his teens, he played for Rotherham Town as a leg-spinner who came in at No. 11. But his batting progressed, and he was recommended to the county by the former Yorkshire batsman Charlie Lee, by then with Derbyshire, who lived in Thurnscoe and regaled the youngster with tales from the county circuit during his paper round. Hampshire had already played for Yorkshire Schools in a team that included Boycott, Jack Birkenshaw, Chris Balderstone and Duncan Fearnley. Meanwhile, a hundred for a Yorkshire Federation team at Edgbaston led to a contract offer from Warwickshire. He was tempted, believing he would never leapfrog the talent at Yorkshire. But they refused to release him: Headingley had recognised his potential.

He made his Second XI debut in 1959, and at Jesmond two years later hit a century for Minor Counties against the Australians. By then, he had already made his first Championship appearance, scoring 61 at Grace Road. But a turning point came at Taunton in 1962, when Fred Trueman was dropped by captain Vic Wilson for arriving late.

MOST FIRST-CLASS RUNS FOR YORKSHIRE

		M	*Avge*	*100*	
38,558	H. Sutcliffe	602	50.20	112	1919–45
33,282	D. Denton	677	33.38	61	1894–1920
32,570	G. Boycott	414	57.85	103	1962–86
32,035	G. H. Hirst	717	34.74	56	1891–1929
31,098	W. Rhodes	883	30.04	46	1898–1930
26,220	P. Holmes	485	41.95	60	1913–33
26,181	M. Leyland	548	41.03	62	1920–46
24,807	L. Hutton	341	53.34	85	1934–55
22,650	D. B. Close	536	31.94	33	1949–70
21,979	**J. H. Hampshire**	**456**	**34.61**	**34**	**1961–81**
20,548	J. V. Wilson	477	31.66	29	1946–62
20,306	D. E. V. Padgett	487	28.55	29	1951–71

Hampshire had expected to be left out, but kept his place for the rest of the season, and scored the winning runs when the Championship was secured against Glamorgan at Harrogate. "Hampshire, a young batsman with abundant talent, led the final burst to victory," wrote John Woodcock in *The Times*.

Starting in 1963, he passed 1,000 runs in nine successive summers. "He was capable of taking an attack apart," said Illingworth. Cope added: "He was powerful but orthodox. He had a lot of grace. When you bowled to him in the nets you thought, 'I'm glad I don't have to bowl at this fella very often.'" With wicketkeeper Jimmy Binks, Brian Close and Phil Sharpe, Hampshire also formed part of Yorkshire's formidable close-catching unit. And at Cardiff Arms Park in July 1963, he revived his schoolboy leg-spin to take seven for 52.

The fact that he and Boycott had progressed through Yorkshire's junior sides at the same time meant frequent comparisons. "He certainly had more natural ability than Boycott," said Illingworth. "But he was never a great technician – he just played his natural game throughout his career." The pair shared car journeys in their early days in the team, but in the 1970s Hampshire came to believe that Boycott's captaincy was harming Yorkshire's fortunes. Yet he did not enjoy his own two years at the helm, and stepped down when his wife and children suffered verbal abuse. He spent a summer back in the ranks under Chris Old, but chose to leave when Boycott was dropped for an end-of-season game against Northamptonshire at Scarborough, and the match took place in an atmosphere of poisonous recrimination.

He decamped to Derbyshire, and at first was taken aback by the serene atmosphere in the dressing-room. Early in the summer of 1982, his new county faced Yorkshire in a

Benson and Hedges group game at Chesterfield, and Hampshire made a match-winning unbeaten 66, finishing with a six into the Queen's Park lake. "I didn't particularly enjoy hitting that one," he wrote. "I didn't feel delight or exhilaration at the victory."

But he had long made his peace with the county, and it gave him enormous satisfaction to be Yorkshire's president in 2016. Michael Vaughan and Joe Root tweeted tributes on his death, and Yorkshire opener Alex Lees said: "It didn't matter who you were. John would always take time out of his day to speak to you."

HANSELL, THOMAS MICHAEL GEOFFREY, died on November 14, aged 63. A left-hander who often opened, Tom Hansell played 14 first-class matches for Surrey between 1975 and 1977, but managed only one half-century – 54 against Nottinghamshire at The Oval in 1976. He later emigrated to Perth, in Western Australia, and became a stalwart of the Willetton club, where the practice area was named after him. Among the players he coached there was Cameron Bancroft, who made his Test debut against England at Brisbane shortly after Hansell's death.

HEALD, BRIAN, who died on October 8, aged 79, was one of the founder members of the Association of Cricket Statisticians in 1973, and edited several of their early publications. A Yorkshireman who was also keen on rugby league, he was Essex's official statistician for many years, and had a large collection of cricket ties, as well as a well-stocked library.

HECTOR, AUCKLAND, who died on December 31, aged 72, was a wicketkeeper from St Kitts who played 29 matches in West Indian domestic cricket for the Combined Islands team and the Leeward Islands. He top-scored on his debut, with 37 against the 1964-65 Australian tourists, but was disappointing with the bat after that, although he did make two undefeated half-centuries against Guyana at Basseterre in February 1969. A banker, he was later president of the Leeward Islands cricket board, and a director of the West Indian governing body.

HEYHOE FLINT, BARONESS (RACHAEL), OBE, DL, died on January 18, aged 77. Rachael Heyhoe Flint did not live to see the match that best summed up her devotion to women's cricket: England's World Cup final victory over India in front of a packed and enthralled Lord's, and a vast global television audience. Next morning, the celebrations featured on five national front pages.

It was light years from the first women's international there, in 1976, when – after years of lobbying to use the ground – she captained England in a one-day international against Australia, and was unsure whether she would be allowed to lead her team out through the Long Room. When she eventually did, it was with an uncharacteristic show of emotion. Fittingly, she was at the crease when England completed an eight-wicket win – thanks to an act of self-sacrifice. "I got myself out so that she could bat," recalled opener Enid Bakewell. "I said, 'You've done so much to get us here you deserve to bat.' Chris Watmough, our No. 3, went mad at me."

In the tributes that followed her death, the word that frequently cropped up was "pioneer". Through her talent as a batsman and a successful England captain, but also via her relentless energy, engaging personality and flair for publicity, she became the world's best known female cricketer. Scyld Berry in *The Daily Telegraph* and Jarrod Kimber on ESPNcricinfo compared her impact to W. G. Grace. For some years in the 1970s, she ranked alongside Mary Peters and Virginia Wade as Britain's most familiar sportswoman, even while playing a game with virtually no public profile.

She led the fight to allow women to join MCC, setting the ball rolling when Tim Rice and Brian Johnston proposed her for membership under the name "R. Flint" in 1991. "I've played cricket all my life, I got to the top, and I just wanted to be a member of this club," she said. Against implacable opposition, she was prepared to play the long game. It was a campaign that encapsulated Heyhoe Flint. She was not strident, nor did she harangue those in authority; instead, she used charm, humour and gentle powers of persuasion. In the end

Net benefit: Rachael Heyhoe in the nets in 1960 and, now Heyhoe Flint, at Buckingham Palace in 2008 to receive her OBE.

the ban was shown to be a ridiculous anachronism. It took two votes in 1998 but, at the second, almost 70% of members voted in favour of the change. She was among the first group of women admitted, and in 2004 became the first on the MCC committee. She still slapped down anyone who called her a feminist.

Sport had always been central to her life. Her parents were PE teachers, and she soon showed a talent for hockey (she won four caps as England's goalkeeper in 1964), netball and rounders. Saturday afternoons in the winter were spent at Molineux watching the Wolverhampton Wanderers team that won three League Championships in the 1950s. But cricket was confined to back-garden games with her father, brother and his friends. She was allowed only to field, useful for retrieving the ball from the jaws of the neighbour's dog and being "the preserver of the flowerbeds". When finally given a chance she batted for three days and totalled "about 380". She loved to tell the story of a street game that was abandoned when a policeman arrived to take down the names and addresses of the players. He ignored Rachael, who persisted: "But I was playing too. Don't you want to take my name down?" The officer replied: "Girls don't play cricket."

But girls *could* play cricket. In 1954, she was in a party from Wolverhampton Girls' High School that went to Edgbaston to see the touring New Zealand women take on Warwickshire & South Midlands. She was enthralled. "I came away with an image of an exciting, challenging life, travelling the world playing cricket, meeting people," she wrote. "It seemed everything I wanted out of life." She was fortunate that the new head of PE at her school was Mary Greenhalgh, a keen cricketer. A school team was started soon after the Edgbaston visit, and the first team photo featured two other future England players – Jackie Elledge and Ann Jago.

Intent on qualifying as a teacher, she went to Dartford College of Physical Education, where the England captain Mary Duggan was among the staff. Heyhoe – Flint was not added until 1971, when she married Derrick, a former Warwickshire leg-spinner – began to play for Staffordshire and other representative sides in the late 1950s, and took up her first teaching appointment. In 1960-61, she asked for leave of absence when she was selected for England's tour of South Africa. She enjoyed the experience immensely but, apart from a first international fifty in the Second Test at the Wanderers, her performances did not stand out. She also made little impact at home against Australia in 1963, although in the third match at The Oval she had the satisfaction of hitting the first six in a women's Test. She called it the Heyhoe heave-ho – and attributed it to an irritated groundsman, who had prepared a pitch at the edge of the square with a correspondingly short boundary.

She came of age after replacing Duggan as captain for the series against New Zealand in 1966, making 356 runs at 71, including her first Test hundred, in the opening match at Scarborough. In the winter of 1968-69, she took her team to Australia and New Zealand for a six-Test tour. It had been announced 18 months in advance to allow time for fundraising: Heyhoe was a one-woman PR machine, organising matches against men's teams, fighting for column inches and securing a sponsorship deal with Marks & Spencer for the squad's blazers. It was a four-month trip – spirits were kept up with team singalongs – and a successful one. England retained the Ashes after drawing all three Tests in Australia, then beat New Zealand 2–0, Heyhoe scoring 503 runs at 45. She had already given up teaching to become a journalist, and was writing regularly for the *Telegraph.* After each day's play she went back to her hotel room and filed copy, appearing as "A Special Correspondent". She did not tell them she was also filing for the *Daily Express*, PA and Reuters. "If I had a bad day, I didn't mention myself," she said.

She struck up a lasting friendship with the businessman Jack Hayward, a fellow Wulfrunian with shared passions in cricket and Wolves; he funded two non-Test tours to the Caribbean, which were beyond the meagre funds of the Women's Cricket Association. She was staying at Hayward's house in Sussex one evening in 1971 when he came up with the idea of a women's World Cup – and offered to provide the finance. Heyhoe Flint's memory was that several glasses of brandy were involved. Relishing the challenge, she organised the first tournament in 1973, two years before the first men's World Cup, selling tickets and putting up posters in the host towns. There were seven teams, including an International XI and Young England, and a round-robin format. Lord's turned down the chance to host the last game, which proved to be the decider, so it was held at Edgbaston. England beat Australia by 92 runs; Heyhoe Flint made a typically pugnacious 64, and put on 117 with Bakewell, before receiving the trophy from Princess Anne.

Her ambition of appearing at Lord's was finally realised in 1976 (earlier in the year she had, perhaps only half-jokingly, threatened to take MCC to the Equal Opportunities Commission). Australia were again the opponents. England won the one-day series 2–1, and retained the Ashes after three drawn Tests. Her leadership was always aggressive. "She was phenomenal," said Bakewell. "She was always trying to make something happen. If the batsmen looked set she would do something different with the field placings. You would think 'Why has she done that?' but it was just to make the batsmen think. Often it got us a wicket." In the final Test of the Ashes at The Oval, Australia scented victory but, defying her instincts, Heyhoe Flint made 179 in eight hours 41 minutes. The high point of her captaincy, though, was also the end of it. In 1977, the WCA replaced her with Mary Pilling, despite an unbeaten record in 12 Tests in charge. "No one has a divine right to be England captain, but after 11 years in the job I think I deserved a reason for my sacking," she said. "I've definitely not signed for Kerry Packer so I just don't know why." She not only lost the captaincy, but her place in the team for the second World Cup in India.

The outcry was such that the WCA were forced to call an extraordinary general meeting. Hayward withdrew his financial support. Heyhoe Flint believed some officials had become resentful of her profile and thought the good work of others was going unnoticed. She had been rapped over the knuckles for being photographed with her baby son at Lord's. Another suggestion – not made public – was that the money she earned from writing contravened her amateur status. The WCA were so desperate to avoid the taint of commercialism that Heyhoe Flint had to white out the manufacturer's green stripes on her cricket shoes.

In 1979, she was back in the England team, scoring 162 runs at 40 in a three-match series against West Indies, but it marked the end of her Test career. In all, she played in 22 Tests, scoring 1,594 runs at 45, with three centuries, and taking three wickets with her

Patrick Eagar, Popperfoto/Getty Images

Equal to the task: in a 1971 game between England Women and Hampshire, Rachael Heyhoe top-scored with 83. Geoff Keith is at gully, Michael Hill keeps wicket.

occasional leg-spin. It was not, however, the end of her international career. Aged 42, she was recalled for the 1982 World Cup in New Zealand, making 76 against the hosts, 61 against an International XI, and 29 in the final against Australia, which England lost. In 23 one-day internationals, she scored 643 runs at 58, with one hundred.

Retirement did not mean putting her feet up. She campaigned on behalf of women's sport, and became an award-winning after-dinner speaker, a director of Wolves, a charity fundraiser and a regular panellist on Radio Four. "My husband said it is like being married to a whirlwind," she said. She joined the ECB board in 2010, when she became the first woman inducted to the ICC Hall of Fame. The following year, she was made a Conservative life peer, and liked to tell visitors that she had the highest Test average of the six international cricketers to have sat in the Lords. After her death, the ICC renamed their Player of the Year award in her honour. The first winner was Ellyse Perry.

Part of her popularity with the media was her gift for a soundbite. She said women referred to their boxes as "manhole covers", and cheerfully repeated the Duke of Edinburgh's question about whether her team wore coconut shells in their bras for protection. Women played three-day Tests, she explained, because "we get on with it more than the men". But the jokes did not hide her deep satisfaction at the development of the women's game. "Now the mums and the daughters have their own cricket," she said, "instead of making cucumber sandwiches every weekend."

HILL, ROBERT GRIBBEN, died on November 19, aged 79. A left-hander from Kilmarnock, Bobby Hill played six first-class matches for Scotland in the 1960s, making 50 against Warwickshire at Edgbaston in 1964. He later managed the national side, and was in charge when Scotland qualified for the 1999 World Cup via the ICC Trophy in Malaysia. He ensured that, come the tournament proper, the team were appropriately kitted out in tartan trews.

HOAR, NEWMAN RONALD, who died on January 11, aged 96, was an opening bowler who played four matches for Wellington in 1944-45. His best return was three for 68 – including New Zealand Test batsman Merv Wallace – in his last match, against Auckland. In the previous game, against Canterbury, he had top-scored with 76 from No. 8. Hoar was a handy lower-order hitter, who cracked 158 (and took eight wickets) in Wairarapa's Hawke Cup match against Rangitikei in January 1946, and also made a century against the Fijian tourists in 1954. He later ran his family's long-standing business making headstones.

HODGSON, DEREK, who died on June 10, aged 87, was a highly professional and versatile sportswriter who, in a long career, covered cricket for a remarkable range of newspapers. He moved from being northern cricket correspondent of the *Daily Express* to the No. 1 job on the *Daily Star* when it launched in 1978. Such a febrile paper was not the ideal berth for his refined prose and gentle temperament, but he lasted four years and – satisfyingly – made a rapid return to touring in 1983-84, as stand-in for John Woodcock as the *Times* correspondent for England's series in New Zealand. Hodgson joined *The Independent* when it started in 1986, and covered county cricket for them for 11 years – the happiest phase of his career. He also became secretary of the Cricket Writers' Club and, in an 18-year term of office, played a crucial role in its transformation from an organisation that held one-minute AGMs into a serious representational body. He was then elected president, a sign of his colleagues' unanimous affection for "Hoddy". He was a Yorkshire member for 62 years, and for 21 of them edited their much-admired annual; he also wrote an official history. Somehow he also fitted in two years as assistant manager (effectively head of PR) at Stoke City, and had a stint as a publisher. He revelled in jazz, books and conversation, and enjoyed enviable contentment from his 65-year marriage to Doreen. His sons Guy and Myles both became sports journalists, Myles serving as cricket correspondent of the Press Association and *Wisden's* representative in Lancashire.

HOLLAND, ROBERT GEORGE, OAM, died on September 17, aged 70. Late-blooming leg-spinner Bob Holland gave hope to a generation of thirtysomethings by making his Test debut for Australia in 1984 at the age of 38. He took ten wickets in his third match, to end a winning streak by West Indies, and in his next claimed a five-for at Lord's, which would prove beyond Shane Warne. Holland was an unlikely destroyer: greying at the temples, he sent down his teasing leg-breaks and googlies from an almost mincing run,

OLDEST TEST DEBUTANTS FOR AUSTRALIA

Yrs	*Days*			
46	253	D. D. Blackie	v England at Sydney	1928-29
46	237	H. Ironmonger	v England at Brisbane	1928-29
38	**35**	**R. G. Holland**	**v West Indies at Brisbane**	**1984-85**
37	290	E. J. Gregory	v England at Melbourne	1876-77
37	290	N. F. D. Thomson	v England at Melbourne	1876-77
37	184	H. S. B. Love	v England at Brisbane	1932-33
37	163	J. Harry	v England at Adelaide	1894-95
37	154	R. K. Oxenham	v England at Melbourne	1928-29
36	359	B. E. McGain	v South Africa at Cape Town	2008-09
36	148	A. J. Richardson	v England at Sydney	1924-25
35	242	A. C. Voges	v West Indies at Roseau	2015
35	127	J. B. Iverson	v England at Brisbane	1950-51

with a twirl of the wrist just before he began the upswing of his delivery. Leg-spin was an endangered species at the time, especially in Australia, but Holland had old-fashioned virtues – seductive flight, disciplined length, a well-disguised top-spinner and a sparingly used wrong'un – all dispensed with a ready smile.

That smile might just have derived from the unlikeliness of it all. Although he was born near Sydney, "Dutchy" Holland lived most of his life in more remote parts of New South Wales, and played his club cricket around Newcastle, 100 miles north of Sydney. Rick McCosker, another Australian Test player who grew up away from the bright lights, said:

Dutchy original: Bob Holland is watched by Dickie Bird at Old Trafford in 1985.

"Dutchy loved his family – he lived for them and his cricket, and he was the epitome of a good Aussie bloke."

Holland had made his way to the Baggy Green by skill and persistence. From the mid-1960s he was a regular for representative teams in Newcastle. One of his earliest outings was against M. J. K. Smith's England tourists of 1965-66 – but none for 58 in six overs hardly hinted at a rosy future. He did not play in the Sheffield Shield until January 1979, when he was 32, and his progress was steady but unspectacular until 1984-85, when he took seven wickets in NSW's match against the West Indian tourists at the spin-friendly SCG. A week later, at Brisbane, Holland became Australia's third-oldest Test debutant.

He had a quiet start, dismissing Larry Gomes and Jeff Dujon at the Gabba, where defeat spelled a tearful end for Kim Hughes's captaincy. But he ensured selection for the next Test with a career-best nine for 83 against South Australia at Sydney, and claimed two more wickets in Allan Border's first Test in charge, although West Indies won heavily again to take an unbeatable 3–0 lead. Holland sat out the Melbourne Test, but returned for the finale, on familiar turf at the SCG. After Australia batted solidly for 471, he got to work on a helpful, dark-tinged pitch. He took six for 54 – including Viv Richards for 15 – as West Indies collapsed for 163, then claimed four more in the follow-on to finish with ten for 144. It was West Indies' first Test defeat for more than three years, and their first by an innings since 1968-69. John Benaud wrote: "Bob came out to the fence after a particularly successful over. The crowd rose to him as one, some leaning over the fence, reaching out. Bob took it all in that graceful, dignified, modest way, flashing a grin with a slight wave of the hand that had on it the golden spinning finger."

In the 1985 Ashes, Holland's five for 68 at Lord's contributed to Australia's only victory of the series. Wicketless in the first innings, he twirled down 32 tight overs in the second and, after the early dismissal of Tim Robinson, later claimed the last four, including top-scorer Ian Botham for 85. "It was a weird tableau," wrote Matthew Engel of this cat-and-mouse battle. "A grey-haired leg-spinner from the Nursery End bowling to our bare-headed hero, while fielders in Baggy Green caps hovered and an airship progressed serenely over Regent's Park. At tea one half-expected the teams to be presented to George V."

The strength of the home batting saw Holland reduced to a containing role, which blunted his effectiveness as England won 3–1. But back in Australia he grabbed another ten wickets at Sydney, to square the series against New Zealand. Two more caps followed before he bowed out with 34 wickets at 39. Holland finished his first-class career in 1987-88 with a season for Wellington in New Zealand: he was 41, but claimed 31 victims in seven matches, including seven for 69 at Auckland.

He was associated with the Southern Lakes District Cricket Club on New South Wales's northern coast – as player, administrator, fundraiser, groundsman, junior coach and general organiser – for more than 50 years. Two days before his death from an aggressive brain tumour, the club organised a tribute night, compered by the former Australian captain Mark Taylor. Helped by the camaraderie of family and friends, Holland was able to defy his illness and enjoy one last hurrah.

IMBERT, LORD (PETER MICHAEL), KT, CVO, QPM, DL, died on November 13, aged 84. Peter Imbert became a policeman in 1953, and rose to become Commissioner of the Metropolitan Police for six years from 1987, after achieving prominence as the chief negotiator during the Balcombe Street siege in London in December 1975. He was knighted in 1988, and ennobled 11 years later. A regular visitor to The Oval, he was asked after retirement to investigate the way Surrey CCC were run: his 1995 report suggested widespread changes, and preceded a successful time for the club.

INSOLE, DOUGLAS JOHN, CBE, died on August 5, aged 91. A glance at the list of positions held by Doug Insole reveals the depth of his lifelong commitment to cricket. From humble beginnings at a Walthamstow grammar, he became captain of Cambridge University and Essex, vice-captain of England, chairman of selectors, chairman of the Test and County Cricket Board, manager on two Ashes tours, a long-serving MCC committee member and later their president. He remained a proud president of Essex, and was at Chelmsford just a few days before he died. "He was a really great man of English cricket," said Graham Gooch.

To every role Insole brought common sense, an affability which did not prevent him being firm when required, and an unobtrusive diplomacy perfectly suited for life at the heart of the game's establishment. "Had he become the head of MI5 or MI6, never would there have been a leak," wrote Scyld Berry in *The Daily Telegraph*. In all his jobs he held a constant belief: that the interests of cricket, and the obligation to entertain the paying public, were paramount. He also had a sharp, dry sense of humour. When Tony Lock's notorious quicker ball demolished his stumps, he asked the umpire: "Was I run out or bowled?" Players on the tours he managed, in 1978-79 and 1982-83, referred to him as "Inspector", after he appeared at their Christmas fancy-dress parties as Peter Sellers's bumbling detective Clouseau.

Rather than his 25,000 first-class runs and 54 centuries, it was his long period as an administrator – in particular his central role in the crises involving Basil D'Oliveira and Kerry Packer – that came to define him. Chairman of selectors when D'Oliveira was left out of the England party to tour South Africa in 1968-69, Insole bore the brunt of the outrage. When the squad was announced to widespread opprobrium, he said: "I think we

In form: at Romford in 1954, Doug Insole hit 48 and 64, but Essex lost by eight wickets; Roy Booth is Yorkshire's keeper.

have got rather better than him in the side." A *Guardian* editorial retorted: "Anyone who would swallow that would believe the moon was a currant bun." Insole's quote has endured, when his longer, nuanced explanation of the decision on cricketing grounds is less often cited. But of the three other selectors – joined by England captain Colin Cowdrey – only Don Kenyon, D'Oliveira's former captain at Worcestershire, supported his selection, despite his 158 against Australia at The Oval a few days earlier. When interviewed by Peter Oborne for his 2004 biography of D'Oliveira, Insole described the furore around his omission, subsequent selection, and finally the cancellation of the tour, as the worst few months of his life. The Labour MP Derek Wyatt said Insole broke down in tears when talking to him about the affair.

Insole was in the middle of three years as chairman of the TCCB when the Packer storm broke early in the summer of 1977. The International Cricket Conference and the TCCB issued a threat to ban all players who had signed for him. Insole said the game was in a "war situation", adding: "We must make sure this thing does not get off the ground." Privately, he and secretary Donald Carr had received legal advice that a ban would be hard to enforce, but the ICC and the counties were determined to adopt a hard-line stance. The High Court verdict, delivered as the first World Series Cricket matches were about to begin in Australia, found decisively in favour of Packer and his players. "We were well and truly stuffed," Insole told TV reporters.

He was born in Clapton, but grew up in Highams Park and played for London Schools and Essex Schools while a pupil at Sir George Monoux Grammar School in Walthamstow. He spent the war in an outpost of Bletchley Park, taking down German messages for decoding. Although he scored runs in schools cricket, he received no formal cricket instruction – for which he remained eternally grateful – and his arrival in the nets at Fenner's drew a scathing verdict from the coaches, who told captain Guy Willatt that he hit across the line too frequently to prosper in first-class matches. Undeterred, he forced his way into the Cambridge team, and made 44 on debut against Yorkshire in 1947. By the end of a summer in which he also made his first appearances for Essex, he had passed

1,200 runs and scored a century for the university against Hampshire at Portsmouth, and another for Essex against Lancashire at Clacton.

Insole's technique remained unapologetically idiosyncratic. He had an open stance and, using his bottom hand, worked almost everything to leg. It succeeded because he had an excellent eye and dogged determination. "He was the only man I knew who used to play forward with his back foot," said Essex opener Dickie Dodds. Insole was also a fine slip fielder, and – reluctantly – Cambridge's regular wicketkeeper in 1948. He became captain in 1949, and made headlines against Essex in May, when John Dewes and Hubert Doggart put on 429, an English record for the second wicket. At the close on Saturday, they were 27 short of surpassing the world record, only for a posse of pressmen to arrive on Monday morning and discover Insole had declared. Later that summer, he led his team to an unexpected seven-wicket victory over Oxford.

He topped the Essex averages in 1949, and was their leading run-scorer in 1950, having taken over the captaincy from Tom Pearce in mid-season. He set about transforming the county from perpetual also-rans, and in his first full summer in charge Essex moved from last to eighth, not least because of Insole's emphasis on fielding, which included practice every morning before play. When the *News Chronicle* launched a Brighter Cricket Table in 1952, designed to reward counties for playing positively, Essex were the winners; they repeated that success in 1953. It was a happy but competitive team, even if there was a minor complaint: Insole's driving. Working his way through copious supplies of fruit, he would test the speed limits. Dodds, a committed Christian, was one of the few who would travel with him. "I like having Dickie with me," Insole said. "He prays while I drive."

He did not enjoy his first exposure to international cricket – a single Test against West Indies at Trent Bridge in 1950, when he made 21 and nought. "I didn't feel I was part of a team," he said. In 1955, a golden summer in which he was the country's leading run-scorer, with 2,427 at 42, he was given a chance, against South Africa at Headingley, but got dropped after making 47 in the second innings.

After another one-off appearance, against Australia in 1956 – when he was named a Wisden Cricketer of the Year – he might have assumed his Test career was over, but in recognition of his sparky leadership of Essex he was named as Peter May's vice-captain for the tour of South Africa that winter. It proved a shrewd choice, in terms of *esprit de corps* – and, less predictably, batting. Insole led the Test averages with 312 runs at 39, and in the third match at Durban helped stave off defeat with 110 not out in more than six hours, his only Test hundred. He reached three figures with last man Brian Statham at the crease, and only after surviving a torrid examination from Neil Adcock; *Wisden* saluted his "splendid temperament and fighting qualities". But after failing twice against Sonny Ramadhin in the First Test of the following summer, he was dropped for the last time. "Is Test cricket enjoyable?" he later wrote. "I must say I believe that very few players do enjoy it." In nine matches, he finished with 408 runs at 27. He was the oldest England player at a dinner for past and present internationals at Lord's early in 2017, and was given a commemorative cap by Joe Root.

In 1956, Insole also achieved the peak of a distinguished amateur football career when he played on the right wing for Corinthian-Casuals against Bishop Auckland in the FA Amateur Cup final at Wembley, setting up the goal in a 1–1 draw (they lost the replay at Middlesbrough's Ayresome Park). After becoming a Test selector in 1959, he gave up the Essex captaincy, handing over to his great friend Trevor Bailey in 1961. He played on until the end of 1963, retiring with 20,113 runs for the county, the eighth-highest in their history. He passed 2,000 in a season three times.

Insole worked in marketing for the construction industry, but it did not curtail his involvement in cricket. He became chairman of selectors in 1965, and was plunged almost immediately into controversy when the panel dropped Ken Barrington for scoring too slowly during a seven-and-a-quarter-hour 137 against New Zealand at Edgbaston. "We have agreed that we have to show the younger players, in particular, that we are prepared to leave out and discipline a man whatever his status if he does not play in the proper manner," Insole said. *Wisden* endorsed the decision: "At last positive action has been

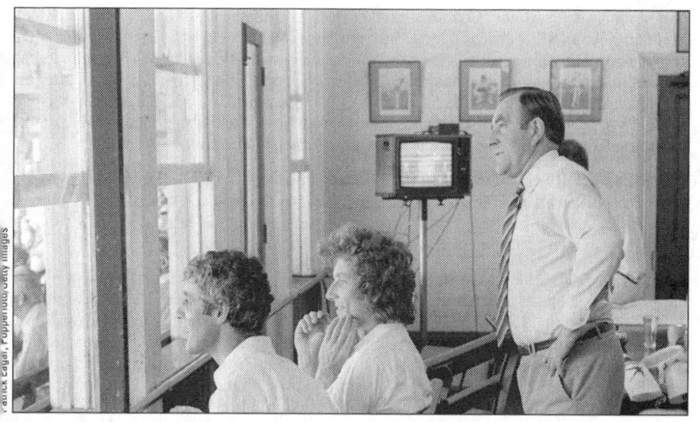

In control: England team manager Doug Insole watches play at the SCG in January 1979 with Mike Brearley and Bob Willis. They won 5-1.

taken to make cricket more entertaining." The same fate befell Geoff Boycott after an undefeated 246 against India at Headingley two years later. Insole stood down as chairman in 1969.

He served on the MCC committee from the 1950s to the 1990s and was president for 2006–07. He was also chairman of Essex for three years in the late 1970s, and president from 1994 until his death. It was a cause of deep regret that he did not live to see them complete their Championship triumph last summer. Their captain Ryan ten Doeschate said: "He will be so missed around the place. He was a great storyteller and very comfortable around the younger lads in the dressing-room." The pavilion at Chelmsford was named in his honour. "He embodied everything that is good about Essex cricket," said Gooch. "The whole club is built on his values."

JENNER, ANDREW KEITH, died on February 20, aged 71. The 6ft 6in Andy "Jungle" Jenner was an instantly recognisable figure in Essex club cricket, mainly for Gidea Park & Romford. He also played for the county's over-age sides, and toured with MCC and the XL Club. Jenner once brought W. G. Grace to mind: after being bowled through a textbook forward defensive, he rebuked the umpire for giving him the wrong guard.

JICHKAR, AMOL MANOHAR, hanged himself in Nagpur on April 25, while depressed about financial problems. He was 38. An off-spinner, Jichkar played six first-class and eight List A matches for Vidarbha, with a best of four for 45 – including Test batsman Mohammad Kaif – in what turned out to be his last game, a one-dayer against Uttar Pradesh at Udaipur in December 2001.

KEMP, JOHN WESLEY, who died on May 9, aged 64, was an all-rounder who played three matches for Border in the mid-1970s. His father had also represented Border, while his son, Justin, played four Tests and 79 one-day internationals for South Africa, and also appeared for Worcestershire and Kent.

KIPPAX, PETER JOHN, who died on January 17, aged 76, took five for 74 with his leg-breaks and googlies on the first day of his second Championship match, at Leicester in July 1962. It seemed as if Yorkshire had unearthed a sensation – but they already had Ray Illingworth and Don Wilson to do the slow bowling, and had historically been suspicious of leg-spin. Kippax played only twice more before decamping for a long career as a league professional, and Minor Counties cricket for Northumberland and Durham. Ralph Middlebrook, a fellow coach, likened him to Shane Warne: "He bowled in a similar style at that pace, and he fizzed it." Another former team-mate, Peter Chadwick, reckoned he "turned his googly more than any other bowler I played against". Some 25 years after his previous matches, Kippax made a fifth first-class appearance, for MCC against Yorkshire at the 1987 Scarborough Festival and, now 46, took four wickets in a victory. By then he had started a bat-making business, using willow grown in and around Leeds.

KRISHNAMURTHY, Dr SUBBARAO, who died on December 7, aged 79, was a wicketkeeper-batsman who sometimes captained Mysore (now Karnataka). His highest score of 95 came in his third match, opening against Andhra at Bangalore in November 1959. He was later chairman of Karnataka's selectors.

LATHAM, HUBERT JOSEPH, died on May 22, aged 84. Seamer Bert Latham played ten first-class matches for Warwickshire as an amateur in the 1950s. He took six for 49 against the Combined Services at Edgbaston in 1958, when his victims included the future Test players Peter Parfitt and Barry Knight, then four for 33 in the next game, against Sussex. But Warwickshire had a well-stocked pace department, and Latham returned to club cricket with Moseley, taking over 1,000 wickets in the Birmingham League. He twice claimed all ten in an innings, both times against Kidderminster.

LAVER, JACK FRANCIS LEE, died on October 3, seven months after his 100th birthday. Born in Victoria, he moved to Tasmania in 1940, but spent the next four years as a military policeman. He represented Tasmania and its combined teams in 13 matches between 1946-47 and 1951-52, bowling quickish off-spinners and occasionally wielding a pugnacious bat. Laver made his presence felt twice against MCC touring teams. In 1946-47 he took five for 34, including Denis Compton, Bill Edrich and Norman Yardley. Four years later, batting at No. 9, he made 59 of the 72 scored while he was in.

LEWINGTON, PETER JOHN, who died on July 31, aged 67, was a tall off-spinner who took 19 wickets in his first four matches for Warwickshire, in 1970. But there was a snag: he was playing only because Lance Gibbs was with the Rest of the World XI and, when Gibbs returned to Edgbaston, Lewington was limited to occasional appearances, stepping up with six-fors against Yorkshire and Oxford University in 1973 while Gibbs was touring with West Indies. Two years later, with Gibbs gone, he claimed 66 wickets, including a career-best seven for 52 at Worcester. But now he faced a new rival: Eddie Hemmings had switched from medium-pace to off-spin. "Eddie got the nod because he was the better bowler when conditions were in his favour," said M. J. K. Smith. Lewington left Edgbaston after a few matches in 1976, returning briefly in 1982 when Hemmings received a Test call. In the interim Lewington had become a consistent wicket-taker for his native Berkshire: in all he claimed 607 in the Minor Counties Championship. He became a well-respected cricket professional and groundsman at Wellington College.

LOWE, DOROTHY MEGAN, died on May 16, aged 101. Medium-pacer Megan Lowe played in all four of England's Tests in Australasia in 1948-49, taking three for 34 – the top three in the order – in the drawn Second Test at Melbourne. She had taken time off from her job as a teacher (she later became a headmistress) to make the long tour. Aged only 14, Lowe had collected six for 39 for a Women's Cricket Association XI against Torquay and South Devon in 1929. Her 100th birthday in 2015 was marked with a card from the Queen, and a signed England shirt.

LUCAS, DANIEL THOMAS, died of undiagnosed coronary heart disease on March 12, aged 31. Dan Lucas was a cricket and rugby writer for *The Guardian*, best known for his sparkling live blogs, which were cultured, trenchant and unashamedly nerdy. He also wrote about music. "It's a devastating reminder of quite how short and fragile life is," said the *Drowned in Sound* editor Sean Adams. "One minute you're writing a live blog and tweeting about Batman, the next someone is sharing the news that you're gone."

We'll drink to that! Peter Lewington (back right) toasts the selection of Warwickshire team-mates John Jameson, Bob Willis and Dennis Amiss (front row) for the 1973-74 tour of the West Indies, together with Jim Cumbes (then of Worcestershire), David Brown and Bill Blenkiron.

McGUINNESS, JAMES MARTIN PACELLI, MP, died on March 21, aged 66. Martin McGuinness was an unlikely cricket lover: a former IRA commander who played a key role in the Northern Ireland peace process and became the province's deputy first minister, he might have been expected to be immune to the charms of something so English. Yet he became bewitched after chancing upon BBC highlights in the late 1960s. "It was a game where discipline was required," he recalled. "I became very interested in the different techniques and strategies." He never played, apart from holiday matches with his children on the beaches of County Donegal, but he maintained that a love of cricket among Northern Ireland's Catholic community was more common than might be supposed; Raymond McCartney, a former hunger striker who is now a Sinn Fein politician, is also a fan. McGuinness supported England during the 2005 Ashes, but delighted in Ireland's World Cup win over them in 2011. He was especially fond of a tie presented to him by Ireland's 2007 World Cup squad. He did not live to see their first men's Test, scheduled for May 2018, but hoped it would boost participation levels. "All over the north, we have people from the Catholic tradition who play," he said. "And I have to say I'm very proud of that."

MANTELL, DAVID NORMAN, who died on January 26, aged 82, was a wicketkeeper from Haywards Heath who played 26 matches for Sussex in the 1950s. Most of them came in 1957, when he briefly supplanted Rupert Webb behind the stumps, but Webb returned in 1958, before Jim Parks – who had already played for England as a specialist batsman – claimed the gloves. Mantell was a polished keeper but no batsman, and reached double figures in only three of his 34 first-class innings. "There was a move away from pure wicketkeepers to players who were or could become batsmen," he said. "I think that was the birth of that era."

MARJORIBANKS, HUGH LYNCH, who died on May 3, aged 83, played four first-class matches for New South Wales in 1958-59, even though he never appeared in grade cricket in Sydney. He was selected after the prolonged success of his leg-breaks in Newcastle, 100 miles to the north. Marjoribanks took five wickets in NSW's match against South Australia at Adelaide, bowling with Richie Benaud, who collected four. He also played rugby league, eventually becoming secretary/manager of the South Newcastle club.

MARSH, ERIC, died on November 9, aged 77, two days after Brian Perry (see below), a fellow member of the Shropshire side that won the Minor Counties Championship in 1973. Marsh was an attractive batsman, who usually opened; a good all-round sportsman, he was the national Rugby fives champion for four years from 1960. After representing Kent Second XI while still at school, he played ten matches for Oxford University as a postgraduate student in 1962, scoring 50 against the Free Foresters and 49 against Hampshire, but was not selected for the Varsity Match. He became a maths teacher, and a stalwart of the Oswestry club. He played for Shropshire between 1962 and 1974, and later captained their Over-50 side.

MARTIN, WILLIAM TREVOR, MBE, died on August 4, aged 92. Trevor Martin turned to umpiring after a back operation meant he could no longer play club cricket, and enjoyed a long career in New Zealand, standing in 49 first-class matches from 1958-59, including 15 Tests. "He used to umpire a lot in Wellington, which can get pretty miserable with the weather," said his son, Graeme. "He used to come home wind-burnt and red in the face. But he just loved it."

MAVALWALA, SOLI, who died on February 22, aged 90, had the unique distinction of playing for Sind in both India's Ranji Trophy and, after Partition, in the inaugural Quaid-e-Azam Trophy match in Pakistan. Unusually in Pakistan cricket at the time, he was a Parsi. A slow left-armer, he took five for 96 against Punjab at Lahore in 1947-48 – the first first-class match in independent Pakistan – when his victims included four future Test players.

MILKHA SINGH, AMRITSAR GOVINDSINGH, died on November 10, aged 75. The beturbanned Milkha Singh was a consistent performer for Madras and South Zone throughout the 1960s, scoring five centuries – the highest 151 against North Zone at Madras in 1961-62. An aggressive left-hander, he had made his Test debut the previous season, just days after turning 18, but struggled at the top level: his best score in four appearances for India was 35, against Pakistan at Delhi in 1960-61. "I bowled to a lot of world-class left-handers, including Garry Sobers, but Milkha was up there," said the Test leg-spinner V. V. Kumar, a former team-mate. "He could play any shot against any type of bowling." Milkha's father, Ram Singh, took 11 wickets in the inaugural Ranji Trophy match in November 1934, while his brother Kripal Singh played 14 Tests, making a century on debut against New Zealand at Hyderabad in 1955-56. They played together against England in Bombay in 1961-62.

MORGAN, DEREK CLIFTON, died on November 4, aged 88. Of all the record 540 matches Derek Morgan played for Derbyshire between 1950 and 1969, none better demonstrated his value than the extraordinary victory over Hampshire at the Ind Coope ground at Burton-on-Trent in August 1958. Only 20 minutes were possible on the first day, on which just one wicket fell, and the teams returned on the second to find a soaking pitch drying under a hot sun: Derbyshire were bowled out for 74 – and Hampshire for 23. When Morgan walked out to bat in Derbyshire's second innings, they were 25 for three. Survival was hazardous. A ball from Derek Shackleton reared up and hit him on the forehead. He slapped a plaster on the wound, and went on to make 46 – a remarkable display of guts and technique, when the next-highest score on either side was 19. But Morgan was not finished. After Derbyshire were all out for 107, he took three for four as the game's first bowling change, and Hampshire were skittled for 55. Thirty-nine wickets had fallen in the day.

It was typical Morgan. He rarely earned headlines, and no one would have selected him on artistic grounds, but he became one of Derbyshire's greatest servants. His 17,842 runs placed him third on their all-time list, while 1,216 wickets put him fifth. He also held 563 catches, the highest by an outfielder for the county. With Donald Carr and Alan Revill, he was a member of the formidable leg trap that snaffled wickets for Cliff Gladwin and Les Jackson, and he was a brilliant ground fielder, his swooping stops and bullet throws responsible for dozens of run-outs: he was selected as England's twelfth man five times. In another era he might have earned a Test cap. "He was a very fine all-rounder, and unlucky that he played when England had an abundance of them," said wicketkeeper Bob Taylor.

Serendipity took Morgan to Derby. He was born in north London but completed his national service seven miles from the County Ground in the village of Etwall, where his feats in club cricket brought him to Derbyshire's attention. As they assembled a team for the new decade, he made his debut against Northamptonshire in May 1950, and stayed in the side for 19 years, as captain for the last five. With Gladwin and Jackson in their pomp, Derbyshire were usually in the top half of the table in the 1950s, and in 1954 finished third. Against Yorkshire that July, he made 66 and took ten wickets as Derbyshire won at Headingley for the first time since 1895. Briefly, it looked as if they might win the title, but they were hampered by rain, and Surrey stormed through the pack.

Derbyshire CCC photo archive

All-round good egg: Derek Morgan made 540 first-class appearances for Derbyshire.

Consistency was a byword. Morgan passed 1,000 runs eight times, including six times in seven seasons in the 1960s. It was widely thought he had more shots in his armoury, but reined in his instincts in the team cause. He made 1,669 runs at 46 in 1962, his most productive summer, while his highest score was 147 against Hampshire at Bournemouth in 1964. He frequently exceeded 50 wickets with his fast-medium outswingers, and his best summer with the ball was 1957, when he took 94 at 23. His best bowling was seven for 33 against Glamorgan at Chesterfield in 1965, the first year of his captaincy.

Life became more difficult for Derbyshire as the decade wore on, with the rumbling controversy over Harold Rhodes's action a regular distraction. In Morgan's final season in charge they finished second-bottom of the Championship, and there was criticism of his leadership. Now 40, and finding the county grind a strain, he announced his retirement. He was denied a fitting send-off when his team lost to Yorkshire in the Gillette Cup final. "His contribution to Derbyshire cricket has been immense," said *Wisden*. He served as club president between 2011 and 2013. "He was one of the nicest people you could ever wish to meet," said Taylor. "A true gentleman."

MORPHETT, ANDREW KENNETH, OAM, died on August 25, aged 69, after watching an Australian Rules football match on television. Drew Morphett had an extensive career in sports commentary on TV and radio, mostly covering cricket and football but also six Olympic Games. Jim Maxwell, a colleague for many years, said "his passion for sport and life allowed him to connect with the audience, and those he met on the job". Morphett exuded an infectious and genuine enthusiasm for his work, and a wide knowledge. Many sportsmen and broadcasters attended his memorial service at the MCG.

MOTLEY, KEVIN GEORGE, who died on March 30, aged 58, was a combative batsman from Johannesburg whose 97 helped Northern Transvaal save their match against Eastern Province at Port Elizabeth in January 1980; his only other half-century, a round 50, came in the next game, also against EP. Motley's father, Arthur, also played first-class cricket.

MUNILALL, CHIMWALA, died on April 12, aged 68. Lall Munilall hailed from Port Mourant in Guyana, like Rohan Kanhai and Alvin Kallicharran, but unlike them failed to do justice to his batting talent: some felt he did not take cricket seriously, others hinted he was too fond of a drink. Munilall did play alongside Kalli for Guyana, although his highest score of 77 came in 1972-73 for Berbice against Demerara (captained by Lance Gibbs) in the final of the Jones Cup, which then had first-class status.

NARAYANAN, PERUNGULAM SUNDARESAN, who died on May 18, aged 75, played one first-class match for Madras (later Tamil Nadu) in 1969-70 against Andhra, bowling one over and not batting. A consistent scorer at lower levels, he was part of a famous cricket family: cousins V. Sivaramakrishnan and V. Ramnarayan both played more regularly for Tamil Nadu. He was later the publisher of *Sruti*, a Chennai cultural magazine, while his brother P. N. Sundaresan edited the *Indian Cricket* annual, and also contributed to *Wisden.*

NORMAN, BARRY LESLIE, CBE, who died on June 30, aged 83, was a journalist and television presenter best known for a long stint at the helm of the BBC's *Film…* programme from 1972 to 1998 (minus a short spell in 1982 while he fronted *Omnibus*). *The Guardian* said Norman "perfected a flair for talking beguilingly about cinema to a mass audience, but in a way that did not make true aficionados wince". The silver screen had a rival for his affections, however. "Cricket is my great passion," he once said, "right up there with the movies." He was often seen at Lord's, was *Wisden's* book reviewer in 2004, and five years later produced *The Bumper Book of Cricket*, a lavish and entertaining compendium.

And why not: Barry Norman at Lord's in 2001.

OSTLERE, Dr GORDON STANLEY, died on August 11, aged 95. Under the pseudonym Richard Gordon, he wrote the successful "Doctor in the House" books (later turned into films and a TV series), based on his time as a medical student. He had a lifelong interest in cricket, his other works including *Fifty Years a Cricketer* (1986), a light-hearted memoir. It contained an account of a visit to a Soho strip club during a rain break at Lord's, while still wearing his MCC tie ("Still not playing, then?" asked the cashier), and a list of the prudent cricket-watcher's equipment: "Binoculars, lunchbox, drinks cooler, thermos flask, corkscrew, ballpoint, newspaper, scorecard, paperback, mackintosh, umbrella, sun hat, dark glasses, pullover, transistor and *Wisden*."

PANDYA, HARESH, jumped from a bridge in his home town of Rajkot on November 11. He was 53, and had been troubled by health issues. An English teacher, Pandya was also passionate about cricket: he wrote long letters to many players and journalists, and eventually became a freelance himself, contributing to many publications at home and abroad, once writing on Indian music for the *New York Times*. His correspondence with Don Bradman formed the basis of a feature article in the 2017 *Wisden India Almanack*.

PATHMANATHAN, GAJANAND, died on August 29, 2012, aged 58. An attacking batsman who often opened, Gajan Pathmanathan was one of only five to play on both sides in the Varsity Match: after winning Blues for Oxford between 1975 and 1978 (and scoring four half-centuries), he popped up as a postgraduate for Cambridge in 1983, and hit 64. His highest first-class score was 82, for Oxford against Northamptonshire in 1976, when team-mate Chris Tavaré made 104. "Gajan liked to play his wide array of strokes

TWO SHADES OF BLUE

Players who appeared for both sides in the Varsity Match:

D. W. Jarrett	Oxford 1974–75; Cambridge 1976
S. M. Wookey	Cambridge 1975–76; Oxford 1978
G. Pathmanathan	**Oxford 1975–78; Cambridge 1983**
J. A. Lodwick	Oxford 2010; Cambridge 2012
A. D. J. Kennedy	Cambridge 2010–12; Oxford 2013–14

Kennedy's five successive Varsity Matches constituted his first-class career; he captained Oxford in 2014. P. M. Sankey (an Oxford Blue in 1852), C. J. Saunders (Oxford 1964) and M. E. D. Jarrett (Cambridge 1992–93) all played first-class cricket for the other university as well, but not in the Varsity Match. J. E. Poulson (Cambridge 2017) had one match for Oxford MCCU in 2014. G. S. Seaton played for Cambridge (1946–47) and Oxford (1957), but not in a Varsity Match. H. E. Knatchbull, an Oxford Blue in 1827 and 1829, played for Cambridge in 1837 after they turned up a man short against MCC at Lord's.

from the outset, and being caught at mid-off on several occasions did not deter him," remembered Tavaré. "In 1976, the Combined Universities travelled to Barnsley in the Benson and Hedges Cup. Yorkshire scored 185 on a sluggish wicket, still a daunting target for a young, inexperienced team – but Gajan opened the batting with Peter Roebuck, and took England's Chris Old apart with a series of fine drives and hooks. He made 58 out of 82, and we went on to win: Gajan got the Gold Award." Pathmanathan might have featured in some of his native Sri Lanka's early internationals after they gained Test status in 1981-82 – he had played a few representative matches in the early 1970s – but had already embarked on a business career in which he was headhunted by the World Bank. He worked in Kenya and India, and at the time of his death was running a department in Washington DC.

PATKAR, SUDHIR VITHAL, died on May 16, aged 78. As a schoolboy in December 1953, he scored 431 not out, with 83 boundaries, in a Harris Shield match on the Bombay

Gymkhana. This remained a record for the long-running schools' tournament – it started in 1897 – until Sarfaraz Khan amassed 439 in November 2009 (the record has changed hands twice since).

PERRY, BRIAN JAMES, who died on November 7, aged 74, was a handy all-rounder for Shropshire for 17 seasons from 1970. A left-hand batsman, he scored 105 to inspire a one-wicket win over Cheshire in 1979, and took five for 33 with his seamers against Somerset Seconds in 1973, when Shropshire won the Minor Counties Championship (see Eric Marsh). In the NatWest Trophy, he dismissed Ian Botham in 1983, and Geoff Boycott (caught and bowled) the following year as Shropshire embarrassed Yorkshire at Telford. But Perry was better known in football circles: he was Shrewsbury Town's groundsman for 26 years, often battling rising floodwater from the River Severn on their old ground at Gay Meadow.

PHILLIPS, JOHN BURTON, who died on October 18, aged 83, was a fast bowler who won an Oxford Blue in 1955, when he took 38 wickets at 26, with a best of five for 62 against MCC at Lord's. He played four matches for Kent later that season. He had less success for Oxford in 1956, and missed the Varsity Match, although he did collect four for 69 against the Australian tourists, including the wickets of Richie Benaud and Keith Miller. Phillips played for St Lawrence CC in Kent, then for Banbury, after his job as personnel director of Alcan took him to Oxfordshire.

PICHANICK, ALWYN LEONARD ARTHUR, who died on October 9, aged 84, was the president of the Zimbabwe Cricket Union from 1976 to 1990, and did much to prepare the way for their elevation to Test status, which came two years after he stepped down to become chairman of the country's Sports and Recreation Commission. Pichanick was a lawyer and, briefly, an MP. He had been a competent club all-rounder in his youth.

POLLOCK, JOHN STUART, died on February 1, aged 96. For around a decade after the war Stuart Pollock was the best batsman in Ireland, resolute against pace and a sweet cover-driver. He had made his debut in 1939, aged 19, and top-scored with 38 in the annual match with Scotland. A dozen years later he hit his only first-class century, 129, also against the Scots, at Trinity College in Dublin. He had his moments against county opposition too: in 1948, playing for the Northern Cricket Union in Belfast, he made 58 out of 102 in a two-day game against a Derbyshire attack including Bill Copson, Cliff Gladwin and Les Jackson, and the following year cracked 89 against a strong Yorkshire side in Dublin. Pollock also played for MCC at Lord's, while his last first-class match, in 1958, was for the Free Foresters against a Cambridge side captained by Ted Dexter. He was president of the Irish Cricket Union in 1980.

PORTER, DR SIMON ROBERT, who died on February 9, aged 66, was involved with cricket in Oxfordshire almost throughout his adult life, becoming the county club's treasurer in 1974 and holding various administrative posts until stepping down in 2010. Early on, he helped set up the Cherwell League which, after mergers, has grown from an eight-team competition to more than 100. Porter was also a serious player: after gaining a place at Oxford University when only 16, he won a Blue a few years later in 1973, bowling flattish off-spin for a team which also included Tim Lamb and Imran Khan. Lamb remembered "a very steady bowler, with good control. He was particularly effective in limited-overs matches." Porter secured his place in the Varsity Match with four wickets in each innings against Warwickshire.

He played only seven first-class games, but turned out in the Minor Counties Championship for Oxfordshire for nearly 20 years, taking 356 wickets, including seven for 38 against Buckinghamshire in 1977. Mike Nurton, a long-time team-mate, occasionally had to keep wicket to him, and had painful memories of Porter's faster ball: "He seemed more interested in watching me jump out of the way or go to ground than creating problems for the batsman. 'Let me know when you are going to let that Exocet go,' I would plead. 'Just stay down and watch the ball,' he'd say."

Porter was also the treasurer (and later chairman) of Oxford University CC, and was invariably to be found in the Parks on match days. It helped that he was based nearby as bursar at St Cross College, and later Nuffield, before concentrating on his coin business. His two daughters, Genevieve and Eloise, played for the Oxfordshire women's side.

PREEN, ALAN THOMAS, died on November 27, 2016, aged 81. "Punga" Preen bowled left-arm seamers in 13 matches for Western Australia in the mid-1950s. He took six for 97 against Victoria in 1955-56, his victims including Colin McDonald and Neil Harvey, both bowled. In 1960 Preen was Walsden's professional in the Central Lancashire League, finishing with 100 wickets at 14 (at nearby Radcliffe, Garry Sobers took 100 at ten, to add to 1,133 runs), and later spent five seasons with Perthshire in Scotland. He was also an outstanding Australian Rules footballer with East Fremantle in the other Perth.

PRITCHARD, THOMAS LESLIE, died on August 22, five months after his 100th birthday. Probably the fastest bowler to emerge from New Zealand – at least until Shane Bond more than 60 years later – Tom Pritchard sent down rapid outswingers that often cut back in: Gubby Allen once described facing him as "bloody impossible". He narrowly missed selection for the 1937 tour of England, and never played Test cricket. During the war, he served in Egypt and, when New Zealand next visited, in 1949, Pritchard was in the middle of a five-year deal with Warwickshire. He was, according to M. J. K. Smith, "until Brian Statham and Fred Trueman came along, consistently the only genuine fast bowler in the country". He took 172 wickets for Warwickshire in 1948 at 18 apiece, and reached three figures for the next three seasons as well, with 103 at 22 in their title-winning summer of 1951.

That off-cut, imparted from huge Bedser-like hands, meant Pritchard bowled many of his victims. His triumphant 1948 summer included eight for 43 – and 13 in the match – at Northampton. It rounded off a purple patch of 59 wickets in seven games, with a hat-trick – the first of three – against Leicestershire at Edgbaston. Later Pritchard took 12 (eight bowled) against Gloucestershire. He also appeared for the Players against the Gentlemen at Lord's: his five victims were all Test cricketers, all bowled. His best figures, eight for 20, came against Worcestershire at Dudley in 1950. The Warwickshire historian Leslie Duckworth observed: "If only he had been able to get a little more back into his action and less arm he would, despite his comparatively slight build, have been a great fast bowler instead of a very good one. John Snow reminded me of Pritchard – their builds and actions were very similar."

PA Photos

Slick and fast: Tom Pritchard, one of post-war cricket's fastest bowlers, in 1949.

An enthusiastic tailender, Pritchard scored 81 against Nottinghamshire in 1947 – although his best-remembered innings had come a few days previously, a break-neck 50 against Essex on a turning pitch at Brentwood. Promoted to open with his new-ball partner Charlie Grove, and given licence to cane the seamers before the spinners came on, they smacked 105 in 45 minutes.

Pritchard had started as a 20-year-old tearaway for Wellington in 1937-38, taking four for 18 in his first match, against Canterbury. The following season, not long after collecting seven for 32 (six bowled) against Otago, he played for a representative side against Sir

MOST FIRST-CLASS WICKETS BY NEW ZEALAND-BORN BOWLERS

		M	Avge	
1,490	R. J. Hadlee	342	18.11	1971-72 to 1990
1,424	C. V. Grimmett	248	22.28	1911-12 to 1940-41
1,180	A. R. Caddick	275	26.59	1991 to 2009
818	**T. L. Pritchard**	**200**	**23.30**	**1937-38 to 1956**
731	J. S. Patel	254	34.23	1999-2000 to 2017-18
647	C. L. Cairns	217	28.31	1988 to 2005-06
640	S. L. Boock	164	22.36	1973-74 to 1989-90

Grimmett played Test cricket for Australia, and Caddick for England. The New Zealand Test player D. N. Patel (born in Kenya) took 654 first-class wickets at 33.23, while N. Wagner (born in South Africa) had 607 at 26.86 by January 31, 2018.

Julien Cahn's XI, and dismissed Stewie Dempster, one of New Zealand's finest batsmen. Pritchard rated this one appearance for his country as his proudest moment in cricket.

Still, New Zealand's 1949 team were one of their best. Their captain, Walter Hadlee, said he wished he'd had Pritchard opening the bowling with Jack Cowie. Their paths did cross at Edgbaston in August, when Pritchard took six for 96 – although, according to the New Zealand journalist Alan Mitchell, the players felt that "Tom appeared to be anything up to three yards slower than when they knew him in the Dominion".

As his county career wound down, Pritchard captained Warwickshire's Second XI. Still a handful at 37, he took nine for 26 – six bowled – against Staffordshire in 1954. Two years later, he played a few matches for Kent without much success. His last game, by chance, was against Warwickshire at Coventry, when he was part of a Keith Dollery hat-trick. Pritchard remained in England until 1986, when he returned home and became involved in breeding and racing horses. He was only the third first-class cricketer from New Zealand, after Syd Ward and John Wheatley, to reach 100 years of age. His grandson, David Meiring, played for Central Districts.

PUGH, DAWN EDNA, who died on October 17, aged 65, was Worcestershire's first-team scorer from 2012 until falling ill in 2016. She was appointed after ten years with the Second XI, and had been the only woman scorer on the county circuit. Pugh also kept Australia's book for the 2013 Lord's Test. "What a fantastic game to score for," she said. "When you see your name going across the scoreboard and announced on the public address system, it just sets your heart racing."

PYEMONT, CHRISTOPHER PATRICK, died on May 4, aged 69. Chris Pyemont played 14 matches for Cambridge University in 1967, making 61 against Leicestershire and 56 against Nottinghamshire. A fine all-round sportsman, he also represented the university at hockey, rackets and skiing. After a spell in the army, Pyemont turned to teaching, and eventually followed his brother Peter as headmaster of Bede's School in Sussex. His son, James, was also a Cambridge Blue.

RAMCHANDRA RAO, S. R., who died on June 11, aged 85, was an Indian umpire who stood in 20 first-class matches. The last was also his only Test appearance – when Pakistan visited Ahmedabad in March 1987, and Sunil Gavaskar became the first to pass 10,000 runs in Tests. Rao also officiated in three one-day internationals.

RAO, SHARAD GURURAJ, who died on September 1, aged 60, was a hard-working seamer who played ten matches in India's Ranji Trophy, although he never improved on figures of four for 27 on debut for his native Bombay, against Saurashtra in November 1980, before a move to Karnataka. He remained a force in club cricket, once taking six for five and nine for three as the Parsi Cyclists were skittled for ten and 14. In 1988, he came across a precocious 15-year-old, playing his first Kanga League game, who smacked Rao's first ball for six, but was later dismissed by him. "He was a respected name in the cricketing circle," remembered Sachin Tendulkar.

On top of the world: Peter Richardson at Worcester in 1956.

RICHARDSON, PETER EDWARD, who died on February 16, aged 85, made a startlingly successful entry into Test cricket in 1956. Two years later, he seemed to have become England's permanent replacement for Len Hutton but, from this high point, his international career swiftly declined. Not that it appeared to trouble him too much: Richardson was an engaging personality and an inveterate joker, whose target was frequently the *Daily Telegraph's* panjandrum E. W. Swanton.

A stocky, resourceful, left-handed opener, Richardson divided his county career between Worcestershire and Kent, and had the flexibility to adapt: his inclination was to attack, running sharp singles and using his strong forearms to drive and cut, but when he first played for England he was often required to temper his natural aggression. At Johannesburg in 1956-57, he crawled to what was then Test cricket's slowest century, in 488 minutes, driving the crowd to distraction in the first international at the New Wanderers. Swanton observed: "Richardson played like a man who, as some sort of penance, has denied himself the pleasure of playing a stroke."

Perhaps the most crucial – and most overlooked – of his five Test hundreds was his first, against Australia at Old Trafford in 1956. He put on 174 with Colin Cowdrey, and reached three figures with a typically scampered single. The ovation, wrote Alan Ross, "drowned the shunting of a departing engine from Old Trafford station". Then came Jim Laker's 19 wickets. Richardson felt he "batted bloody well", but did not mind being so comprehensively upstaged. "It was a privilege," he wrote, "to be part of one of cricket's most famous matches." He was almost responsible for spoiling the story, when his throw nearly brought a run-out. He apologised to Peter May, his captain, and Laker, but May assured him he was more interested in victory than a Laker ten-for. Richardson made 364 runs in the series at 45, having taken a century off the Australians for Worcestershire in the tour opener. He was named a Wisden Cricketer of the Year.

He was one of three brothers – all first-class cricketers – from a family of farmers. Educated at Hereford Cathedral School, he soon came to the attention of Worcestershire, where he was coached by senior pros Dick Howorth and Syd Buller. He made his first-class debut aged 17 in 1949, but his career did not take off until 1952, when he cemented his place as Don Kenyon's opening partner, passing 1,500 runs and making his first hundred, against Oxford University in the Parks. The following season was even better – 2,294 runs at 39, with three hundreds – and he might have been a candidate for England's tour of the West Indies had it not been for national service. On leaving the Army in 1955, he followed a familiar course for amateurs and became Worcestershire's assistant secretary, succeeding Reg Perks as captain in 1956.

After his performance in the Ashes, he was a natural selection for the winter tour of South Africa, but had to adjust to a new opening partner when, on the outward voyage, Colin Cowdrey decided his technique was not up to facing Neil Adcock and Peter Heine with the new ball. Trevor Bailey was given the job – 15 minutes before the start of the

MOST TEST RUNS IN 1956

		T	*I*	*NO*	*HS*	*100*	*Avge*
491	**P. E. Richardson (England)**	**6**	**10**	**0**	**117**	**2**	**49.10**
473	P. B. H. May (England)	6	9	2	101	1	67.57
468	J. W. Burke (Australia)	9	16	1	161	1	31.20
456	R. N. Harvey (Australia)	9	16	0	140	1	28.50
419	P. Roy (India)	5	8	0	173	2	52.37
418	E. D. Weekes (West Indies)	4	5	0	156	3	83.60
315	J. R. Reid (New Zealand)	6	11	0	84	0	28.63
313	M. H. Mankad (India)	5	7	0	231	1	44.71
313	R. Benaud (Australia)	9	15	1	97	0	22.35
309	M. C. Cowdrey (England)	6	10	0	81	0	30.90

This was Richardson's first year in Test cricket.

Figures for Mankad, Roy and Reid exclude runs scored in 1955 in a Test that began on December 28 and continued to January 2, 1956.

First Test. He recalled: "I said, 'Peter, we are following in the footsteps of Hobbs and Sutcliffe. I've only got three shots and you've got four. You can be Herbert, I'll have the knighthood.'" The pair used "Sir Jack" and "Herbert" for their calling throughout the series. The first day was at Johannesburg on Christmas Eve, and Richardson batted until stumps for 69. "He rarely attempted a scoring stroke unless absolutely safe," said *Wisden*. That night the team attended a party, and Richardson fell into conversation with a woman. "Were you at the cricket today?" she asked. He admitted he had been. "I hope that fellow Richardson is more entertaining socially than he is to watch batting."

Play resumed on Boxing Day, and he was eventually out for 117 in 525 minutes. "Richardson will now be bracketed in *Wisden* with the game's great stonewallers," said *The Times*. But his innings laid the foundations of a 131-run victory, and he was England's leading scorer in the five-match series, with 369 at 36. He was equally impressive at home against West Indies in 1957, scoring more than 400 runs at 58, including hundreds at Trent Bridge and The Oval. At Trent Bridge, his brother Dick won his only Test cap – the first time brothers had appeared for England since Alec and George Hearne in 1891-92; it did not happen again until Adam and Ben Hollioake, also at Nottingham, in 1997.

More runs followed against New Zealand in 1958, but in Australia that winter he was dismissed four times in eight innings by Richie Benaud, passing 50 only once – though he was not the only England batsman to struggle. But his future Test prospects were damaged by his decision to join Kent as a professional. Worcestershire contested the move, and he was forced to spend the 1959 season qualifying by residence. He played for Kent Seconds, and shared driving duties with captain Derek Ufton. "He frightened me to death," said Ufton.

By the time he was available for selection again, Geoff Pullar and Raman Subba Row had proved themselves as Test openers. Richardson returned for the tour of the subcontinent in 1961-62 but, though he performed creditably, was not selected in the home summer of

Taking refuge: Peter Richardson in the New Road dressing-room before going out to bat.

1962, nor for the subsequent Ashes. After one match against West Indies in 1963, his Test career was over. He had won 34 caps, scoring 2,061 runs at 37.

After the delayed start to his Kent career, he was soon into his stride, and passed 2,000 runs in three of his first four seasons. By the early 1960s, he had matured into one of the most attractive batsmen in the game. "He had a tendency to nibble outside off stump, like a lot of left-handers," said Kent batsman Bob Wilson. "But hitting across the line he was as good as anyone since Arthur Fagg."

He led Kent in Cowdrey's frequent absences, but the next prank was seldom far away. At Trent Bridge in 1964, the dressing-room attendant collected the teamsheet and conveyed it to the operators of the ground's impressive new scoreboard. Richardson had included the names of Harold Macmillan, John Profumo, Arnold Palmer and Harold Pinter, who duly appeared on the board. The joke made the papers and – in Richardson's telling – led to his instant removal from the captaincy. In fact, he led Kent five more times. He retired in 1965, after scoring 26,055 runs at nearly 35, with 44 centuries. He fell just short of scoring 10,000 runs for two counties – achieved only by Tom Graveney and Mark Ramprakash.

Richardson loved to prick Swanton's pomposity, and wrote pseudonymous letters to him in the hope that some of his cast of fictitious characters might find their way into the *Telegraph*. At Canterbury in 1963, Richardson and Brian Johnston cooked up a scheme that left Swanton fuming. Richardson was batting, and Johnston waved a handkerchief to signal that Swanton had begun a commentary stint. A few minutes later, Richardson complained to umpire Bill Copson, who was in on the joke, that he couldn't concentrate because of a commotion on the boundary. Copson marched over and shouted towards the box: "Will you please stop that booming noise – it's putting the batsmen off." Swanton, who had assured listeners that the break in play was almost certainly being caused by sun on a windscreen, or unruly boys moving behind the arm, took a few moments to realise he was the butt of the joke. Later, he penned a sharply worded note to Richardson advising him to concentrate on his batting.

RONAYNE, MICHAEL PETER, who died on October 16, 2016, aged 66, was a schoolmaster who, after retiring from the classroom, continued to work for various examination boards and in teacher training in East Anglia. He was also an assiduous cricket statistician, who produced a series of booklets giving intricate details of overseas Test tours and, shortly before his death, a treatise on cricketers' memorials.

ROWAN, LOUIS PATRICK, died on February 3, aged 91. Umpire Lou Rowan was a regular presence in Tests in Australia between 1962-63 and 1970-71. Including his first match, Australia played 29 home Tests in that time, and Rowan stood in 25, with Col Egar at the other end in 19. The former Australian batsman Brian Booth felt they were "by far the two best umpires I ever experienced".

He was authoritative, but had a humorous streak, once telling an optimistic appealer that he'd let him know his decision at the end of the over. However, the England tourists of 1970-71 felt Rowan was officious, particularly when he cautioned John Snow for bowling too many bouncers after a barely short-pitched delivery flew up and cracked Terry Jenner on the head at Sydney. "He's not bowling bouncers," said Ray Illingworth, England's captain. "Well, someone is, and it's not me," countered Rowan. Snow later observed that "some umpires cannot seem to distinguish between a cricket ball bouncer and the dance hall variety". Shortly afterwards Illingworth led his team off after Snow was manhandled on the boundary, and was unamused when Rowan told him he was in danger of forfeiting the match. Illingworth liked to point out that his side won that series without a single lbw decision.

Rowan retired after the 1971-72 season, having stood in 74 first-class matches – and what became the first one-day international, between Australia and England at Melbourne in January 1971, after the Test was washed out. He wrote *The Umpire's Story*, in which he justified his approach to the controversies which had surrounded him; much later, in 2010, he produced *No Shades of Grey*, whose title pointed to a black-and-white view of a world of which he had become fiercely critical. His harsh views on law and order reflected his background as a Queensland policeman, and possibly gave an insight into a capacity for confrontation. Rowan, who had eight children, disappointed historians by directing that his correspondence with Don Bradman be destroyed after his death.

RUSHMERE, COLIN GEORGE, who died on January 20, aged 79, was a stylish opening batsman, mainly for Eastern Province. His highest score, 153, came during a first-wicket stand of 312 with Geoff Dakin against Western Province at Newlands on Boxing Day 1962. Rushmere toured England in 1961 with the South African Fezelas (a precursor of today's A-Team), alongside Eddie Barlow, Colin Bland and Peter Pollock. Latterly he established the Kariega Game Reserve in the Eastern Cape. His brother John played for Western Province – and dismissed him after that career-best 153 – while his son Mark Rushmere had a long domestic career, and opened in South Africa's first Test after readmission, at Bridgetown in April 1992.

SAJID ASGHAR, who died of cancer on April 4, aged 46, played 17 first-class matches in Pakistan from 1985-86, mainly for Hyderabad. His highest first-class score was just 43, but he made an undefeated 201 against Sukkur in January 1994, in the second tier of the Quaid-e-Azam Trophy.

SANGHI, RAKESH, who died on November 10, aged 59, was a long-serving scorer from Chandigarh, and a journalist and writer who produced a book of cricket statistics. He

Varsity velocity: a bespectacled David Sayer steams in against Cambridge at Lord's in 1959.

started scoring in his early teens – contemporaries remembered him keeping a book during Haryana's first Ranji Trophy match, in November 1970 – and covered numerous Tests and one-day internationals.

SATHE, CHANDRA KANT, who died on August 3, aged 69, had a long career as an umpire in India. He stood in 49 first-class matches over 21 years from 1982, and in five one-day internationals, the first of them during England's 1992-93 tour.

SAWANT, RAJESH, died of a heart attack in Mumbai on January 29. He was 45, and had been the fitness trainer of India's Under-19 team for some years, helping them win the World Cup in 2012. They were about to embark on a series against the England Under-19 tourists, and team manager Rahul Dravid sent someone up to Sawant's hotel room when he failed to respond to calls. He had been a fast bowler in Mumbai club cricket in his youth, and also part of the Afghanistan coaching set-up.

SAYER, DAVID MICHAEL, who died on January 23, aged 80, was still at Maidstone Grammar School when he caught a bus to Tunbridge Wells one morning in June 1955 to make his first-class debut for Kent against Sussex. Kent batted first, but before the close the 18-year-old Sayer had launched his career with the wicket of John Langridge. Wicketkeeper Derek Ufton spared him the expense of another bus trip by giving him a lift home. Sayer played one more match that summer, but national service took him away for two years, and it was not until 1958 that he made his next first-class appearance, for Oxford University.

Sayer had one priceless attribute: pace. "He was as fast as anyone around," said Kent batsman Bob Wilson. "He had a short run-up but a quick, strong arm. When we had throwing contests for a bit of fun he always won." During his three years at university, he played for Kent at the end of term, and had his most fruitful season in 1958, with 89 wickets at 13, including seven for 37 against Leicestershire at Grace Road. In the 1959 Varsity Match, Sayer played a significant role in Oxford's first victory for eight years, with eight for 115 in the match. Selection for The Rest against the Champion County in 1960 was followed by an MCC tour of New Zealand – proof he was being considered for higher honours.

Ufton said he was as fast as anyone he kept to: "He was unlucky not to play for England. But at The Oval one day, the umpire warned him about running down the line of leg stump, and I never thought he was quite as fast after that." Kent were blessed with pace bowling, and the presence of John Dye, Alan Brown and Norman Graham meant Sayer was not always selected. "He was very laid back," said Wilson. "He didn't have that fast bowler's nasty streak." Sayer retired in 1968 after 612 wickets in 203 matches, but was summoned back in 1976, aged 39, for one more game and one more wicket. He had already written himself into the record books: he took a hat-trick for Oxford University against Kent in the Parks in 1958, then for Kent against Glamorgan at Maidstone in 1964, becoming the only man to perform the feat both for and against the county. Outside cricket, he ran his own insurance business.

SCHMIDT, KEITH ERNEST, who died on October 4, aged 95, was a useful all-rounder who played 16 matches for Tasmania from 1949-50. An orthodox batsman, his best effort came in his penultimate game, against South Australia at Adelaide in 1960-61, when he made 59. His leg-spin relied more on accuracy and bounce than extravagant turn; at the age of 40, he was persuaded off the golf course and took eight for 93 in a grade match.

SHEPHERD, DONALD JOHN, died on August 18, six days after his 90th birthday. In the winter of 1955-56, concerned about his diminishing powers with the ball, Don Shepherd repaired to an indoor cricket school in Neath, and set about mastering a new style. The space was too cramped for his full run-up, but he laboured tirelessly on a new grip and subtly different ways to confound batsmen. When he emerged for pre-season nets, he had transformed himself into one of the greatest county bowlers of all time. The results were immediate: in the third game of the 1956 season, against mighty Surrey at Cardiff Arms Park, he took 12 wickets, bowling Peter May for a duck. By the end of the season, he was the leading first-class wicket-taker, with 177 at 15. The long winter hours at Neath had not been wasted.

Instead of the regulation seam-up with which he had begun his Glamorgan career in 1950, he now bowled off-spin and cutters at close to medium-pace. His run-up was much the same – around nine bounding strides – but his chief weapons were relentless accuracy and disguised variations of pace and length. "He treasured his action and he looked after it," said team-mate Tony Lewis. "He had a high arm, but occasionally he would drop it slightly and get the batsmen nicking and pushing." Formidably fit and blessed with prodigious stamina, Shepherd usually bowled more than 1,000 overs a season. Glamorgan batsman Allan Watkins recalled that he did not require instructions from captain Wilf Wooller: "Wilf only had to say, 'Right Don, this end,' and then he forgot about him. You just left him."

When he retired aged 45 in 1972, Shepherd had taken 2,218 first-class wickets, the 22nd-highest of all time, and the most by anyone who never won a Test cap: the selectors seemed permanently sceptical of wickets taken on damp or sandy Welsh pitches. But Richie Benaud was among those who believed he would have thrived on the big stage. "Had he been an Australian he would have played for his country many, many times," he said. Lewis added: "I'm sure he would have played Test cricket most successfully." The man who seemed least concerned about the snub was Shepherd: "It never worried me. I was happy enough doing what I did."

"Shep", as he was universally known, was born in the former fishing village of Port Eynon on the Gower Peninsula. He was introduced to cricket by his grandfather, who scored for the village team. When his parents moved to Parkmill, closer to Swansea, to run the family shop, he won a scholarship to the local grammar school. He played cricket with friends on Gower's sandy beaches, and spent hours on his own bowling at a wall, but there were only a handful of matches at school, and no formal coaching. It was not until his national service in the Fleet Air Arm that he took part in a properly organised game. His natural aptitude was such that, after playing for RAF Defford against Worcestershire Seconds and the Gentlemen of Worcestershire in 1947, he was offered a trial at New Road,

"Happy enough doing what I did": Don Shepherd wheels away against Kent at Gravesend in 1966. Bob Wilson is the non-striker, Ossie Wheatley the fielder, and Bert Alderman the umpire.

which led to the chance to join the MCC groundstaff. By the time he took up his place at Lord's in 1948, Worcestershire had allowed him to register with Glamorgan.

After a summer with Glamorgan Seconds, he made his first-class debut against Surrey at The Oval in 1950 and finished the season with 49 at 25. He passed 100 for the first time two years later but, despite career-best figures of nine for 47 against Northamptonshire at Cardiff early in 1954, his performances were less productive. He grew concerned that his contract would not be renewed; during the 1955 season, he decided on a radical rethink.

It was wicketkeeper Haydn Davies who first proposed the change, citing the example of former Glamorgan captain Johnnie Clay, who had switched to off-breaks after starting as a seamer. Wooller initially rejected the idea but, with the county's slow bowling resources thin, he grudgingly let Shepherd give it a try towards the end of the season. In only his second outing since his remodelling, he took ten in the match against Warwickshire – encouragement to complete the transformation in the winter. "I found it an easy changeover," he said. "I had control almost straight away." He developed a grip using the leverage of two fingers and a sharply cocked wrist, which he broke "at the last millisecond" before release. He created pressure by restricting scoring, and *Wisden* called him "perhaps the hardest bowler to get away that the post-war game has produced". Lewis called him "an expert in suffocation".

Shepherd accumulated a vast store of knowledge, and knew exactly how to adjust his length and pace to exploit any batsman's weaknesses. Eifion Jones, one of Glamorgan's wicketkeepers, always stood a few yards back: "He had so much variation – slower balls, quicker balls, straight balls, a variety of things up his sleeve and so accurate at all times." He was aided and abetted by a superb close-catching ring that included the fielding talents of Peter Walker: "If the ball came to me it was usually because the batsman had lost patience and had a slog. He never bowled a bad ball that endangered his fielders." As a tailender, Shepherd was less predictable but, against Derbyshire at Cardiff in 1961, he got to 50 inside 16 minutes, and hit off-spinner Edwin Smith for 26 in an over. Later that summer against the Australians, he reached a half-century in 11 scoring shots.

Matches against the touring teams held huge significance for Glamorgan, and Shepherd enjoyed two memorable victories over the Australians, both at his home ground of

Swansea. In 1964, Bobby Simpson's team were unbeaten when they arrived on the August Bank Holiday weekend, with patriotic fervour stoked up by the National Eisteddfod being held in Swansea. When the teams paid a visit after the first day's play, the Australian innings was wobbling at 63 for six in reply to 197. The Glamorgan players were invited on stage to a thunderous welcome. "We were so full of *hwyl* that there was no way we were going to lose the match," said Shepherd. On a tense final day, he bowled a marathon spell in sweltering heat to take five for 71 as Glamorgan won by 36 runs. "Wales beat Aussies" proclaimed the *Daily Mail*, but Shepherd was too exhausted to answer the crowd's calls for a speech. Then, against the Australians in 1968 in one of his rare matches as captain, he inspired Glamorgan to a 79-run victory with a superbly judged declaration.

The following summer Glamorgan, now led by Lewis and installed at Sophia Gardens, were crowned county champions. The 42-year-old Shepherd was their leading wicket-taker, with 81 at 22, and proved an outstanding lieutenant, using the mathematical skills acquired in winters in the family shop to calculate run-rates and advise on declarations. Against Worcestershire in front of a packed house at Cardiff, he took his 2,000th wicket in the first innings, then clinched the title by having Brian Brain caught at slip in the second. Glamorgan drew their final match, against Surrey, to complete an undefeated season. "The 1969 side were possibly the greatest Glamorgan team of all time," said Shepherd. His efforts were rewarded by being named a Wisden Cricketer of the Year.

Any chance of Test selection had vanished. His best chance may have come and gone in the late 1950s, when the international careers of Jim Laker and Johnny Wardle ended within two years of each other. Yet the selectors turned to the spin of David Allen, John Mortimore and Ray Illingworth. There remained a feeling – confirmed to Shepherd's biographer Douglas Miller by former chairman of selectors Doug Insole in 2004 – that his success owed much to Welsh pitches. He was, though, successful on his few overseas tours, and in Pakistan with a Commonwealth XI in 1967-68 he silenced the Multan crowd by performing the unheard-of feat of dismissing Hanif Mohammad lbw, for 19. Shepherd reached 100 wickets for the season for the 12th time in 1970, and retired two years later. He was allowed to choose his last Championship appearance, and bowed out at The Oval, scene of his first-class debut 22 years earlier. He had made a record 647 appearances for the county.

He returned to running the family business, later finding a niche as a summariser on Glamorgan matches for BBC Radio Wales. In the 1990s, he had a spell as a bowling coach for the club, becoming a mentor to Robert Croft. Lewis believes only Watkins and Gilbert Parkhouse rival Shepherd as the greatest Welsh cricketer. "But he was definitely the most essential," he said. "You had to have him on the field."

SMITH, MARTIN GRAHAM MILNER, who died on March 22, aged 75, was a notable all-round sportsman: he won the British amateur rackets championship twice and the doubles five times, and captained Guildford rugby club when he was 38. As a cricketer, he was a wicketkeeper-batsman who played one first-class match for Cambridge University in 1961, catching Worcestershire's Ron Headley for a duck. Smith later became a distinguished surgeon, specialising in the liver, although he crammed in a lot of club cricket: he led Old Tonbridgians to the Cricketer Cup in 1984, and played for Albury in Surrey for many years, encouraging his team-mates loudly from behind the stumps at a time when this was not quite the done thing. "I'd never known a noisier keeper – he seemed to think it was his job to inflict migraines on the batsmen," remembered David Frith, a frequent on-field adversary. "I assume his work left him with a lot of pressure that he needed to release."

SODHA, NARENDRA SINGH, drowned in the swimming pool of his hotel in Negombo, near Colombo, on September 5, during his Indian club's Under-17 tour of Sri Lanka. He was 13, and "brilliant in studies and sports", according to his family.

SPENCE, LAWRENCE ARTHUR, died on October 10, aged 85. Lol Spence played 20 matches for Leicestershire in the early 1950s, but never surpassed the 44 he made against

Gloucestershire in 1952, his first season. He found far greater fame at Grace Road as the groundsman: after learning the trade at Wyggeston Grammar School and a local golf club, he rejoined the county as assistant groundsman in 1970, and took charge three years later. Spence turned the tennis club next door into an impressive practice area, and oversaw the ground for 24 years, his shed a popular refuge for old players wanting a chat. He shared a benefit with Gordon Parsons in 1994.

SRIDHAR, DR MARUTI VENKAT, died of a heart attack on October 30, aged 51, a month after resigning as the BCCI's general manager of cricket operations. He had failed to inform the board he was also involved with several cricket clubs in his native Hyderabad. Until then, "Doc" Sridhar had seemed a born administrator, having gained plaudits for his calm assurance as media manager during India's fractious tour of Australia in 2007-08, which came close to being called off when Harbhajan Singh was accused of racially abusing Andrew Symonds. He was also tournament director of the World Twenty20 in India in 2016. Sridhar had been a stylish and highly effective batsman for Hyderabad,

HIGHEST FIRST-CLASS SCORES BY NON-TEST PLAYERS

443*	B. B. Nimbalkar	Maharashtra v Kathiawar at Poona	1948-49
383	C. W. Gregory	New South Wales v Queensland at Brisbane	1906-07
366	**M. V. Sridhar**	**Hyderabad v Andhra at Secunderabad**	**1993-94**
359*	S. B. Gohel	Gujarat v Orissa at Jaipur	2016-17
351*	S. M. Gugale	Maharashtra v Delhi at Mumbai	2016-17
350	Rashid Israr	Habib Bank v National Bank at Lahore	1976-77

especially good on turning pitches. He scored 21 first-class centuries, including 366 against Andhra at Secunderabad in 1993-94 – the third-highest individual innings in the Ranji Trophy, as Hyderabad ran up the largest total, 944 for six. It was also the highest score by a medical practitioner, beating W. G. Grace's 344 in 1876. The next man to score a triple for Hyderabad was V. V. S. Laxman, who said: "He was an elder brother to me, who taught me the art of batting long. The entire cricket fraternity will miss him."

SRIRAM, KRISHNARAJ, who died of a heart attack on February 16, aged 43, marked his first-class debut in 1995-96 by scoring 174 for Karnataka (captained by Rahul Dravid) in a total of 716 against Tamil Nadu at Bhadravati. But he fell away, passing 50 only once in 14 further matches. His brother K. Srinath, now a leading umpire, also played for Karnataka, and later Tamil Nadu. They opposed each other in the 1996 Ranji Trophy final, Sriram coming out on top as Karnataka won on first innings.

STANLEY, GRANT LAWRENCE, who died on October 22, aged 65, was a hard-hitting batsman and handy left-arm seamer who missed out on first-class cricket in his native Australia, despite being picked regularly for the Queensland Country XI, and rubbing shoulders with international players for Essendon in Melbourne grade cricket. But he found his niche as a professional for various clubs in Scotland, where he added coaching to his portfolio. "Grant was like a pied piper," said Prestwick president Tommy Halpin. "Youngsters flocked to his coaching sessions." Stanley later lived in Singapore for 22 years, coaching the national side for 11, before returning to the Gold Coast.

STARKIE, SYDNEY, died on September 21, aged 91. A floppy-haired Lancastrian off-spinner, Syd Starkie was an unsung member of the Northamptonshire side in the early 1950s. His best return was six for 33 against Warwickshire at Edgbaston in 1954, which was soon followed by ten wickets in the home game against Somerset, and his county cap. As a batsman, he could hold up an end: against Lancashire at Wantage Road in 1955, he made a career-best 60 during a ninth-wicket stand of 156 with Raman Subba Row, still a county record. Starkie played little in 1956, and left the club at the end of the season to pursue a career in accountancy, which took him to Trinidad for a while; on his return to Britain in the mid-1960s he worked on sponsorships in cricket and football. He had been Northamptonshire's oldest surviving player, a distinction that passed to Peter Arnold.

STEPHENSON, GEORGE, who died of leukaemia on September 29, aged 24, was the grandson of Harold, who captained Somerset in the early 1960s. A good all-round sportsman who also excelled at rugby and squash, George played for Devon's age-group sides, and for Plymouth in the Devon League.

STOKES, RAYMOND GORDON, died on February 26, aged 92. Although he spent most of his life in the small Tasmanian port city of Burnie, left-hander Ray Stokes could match it with big-name bowlers. In the first of his nine first-class games, at Hobart against the 1953 Australian Ashes team en route to England, he drove Ray Lindwall and Doug Ring confidently in a two-hour 83, and shared a fourth-wicket stand of 112 with Rex Davidson (see above). Almost a decade later, against the MCC tourists of 1962-63 – whose attack included Brian Statham, Ray Illingworth and Fred Titmus – he hit 82 and 76 not out at Hobart. "Rarely have I seen a batsman use his feet as Stokes did," wrote the English journalist John Clarke. "He was as neat and quick as a featherweight boxer." A gifted Australian Rules footballer who played for the Richmond club in Melbourne, Stokes was inducted into Tasmania's Sporting Hall of Fame in 1989.

TAYLOR, BRIAN, who died on June 12, aged 84, was known throughout the game by his nickname, "Tonker", in a career that began amid post-war austerity in 1949 and ended in the era of long sideburns and kipper ties in 1973. The name reflected his uncomplicated approach to batting, which could be spectacular and would have made him a prized Twenty20 asset.

But Taylor was a serious cricketer – and a pivotal figure in the history of Essex. He was captain from 1967 until his retirement, taking over from Trevor Bailey and handing on to Keith Fletcher. His reign began in desperate circumstances, with the county broke and the playing staff reduced to 13. "There is only one way Essex can go now," he announced. "Up." With a leadership style that mixed the brusque with the paternal, he turned round their fortunes. Many of the players responsible for the club's 1980s golden era learned under him, and remained forever grateful. "Brian seemed very Victorian," said Fletcher. "We had to put blazers on to go into tea, but he was soft, really. He took over at a time when we needed a father figure."

His leadership and pyrotechnic left-handed batting meant his wicketkeeping skills could go unheralded, but his 1,295 first-class dismissals – 1,084 caught, 211 stumped – put him seventh on the all-time list. He was good enough to be selected as Godfrey Evans's deputy on the 1956-57 tour of South Africa, although he never did play a Test. Taylor was a genuine East Ender, born near West Ham United's Upton Park. He played football for Brentford, though not in the League, as well as Bexley Heath and Dover. He was the first captain of Essex Schools after the war, and benefited from coaching at Alf Gover's indoor school on a scheme run by the *Evening News*.

Taylor first played for Essex in 1949, but had to wait until 1954 for a run of games, and until 1956 before succeeding Paul Gibb as the first-choice keeper. He made 75 dismissals and scored 1,259 runs that summer, and was the Cricket Writers' Club's Young Player of the Year.

His batting was not just reckless slogging: he passed 1,000 runs eight times, and made nine centuries. In a run-chase against Gloucestershire at Clacton in August 1962, Essex were faltering when Bailey sent Taylor in with instructions to redouble the attack. He made an unbeaten 105 in one hour 50 minutes, finishing the match with ten minutes to spare by pulling Tony Brown for his third six. "I suppose it's right to say that if I'd taken more care with my batting I would have got far better results," he admitted. "But I, and perhaps the crowds, have had more enjoyment this way."

His progress to becoming Essex's first professional captain was far from smooth. All-rounder Barry Knight wanted the job, and had Bailey's backing. Knight was not prepared

Tonk! Brian Taylor hits out in the John Player League at Chelmsford in 1971. Eifion Jones is the Glamorgan wicketkeeper.

to serve under Taylor, but the committee would not be browbeaten. Chairman Tom Pearce said: "If a cricketer will only play if he is captain, then perhaps he's not the man to be captain." Knight joined Leicestershire, further depleting Essex's resources, and Taylor took over. They finished 15th in his first season, and *Wisden* reported: "Taylor did not satisfy everybody with his handling of the side." But there were green shoots – the arrival of John Lever and Keith Boyce, and the move into Essex's first proper headquarters at Chelmsford.

The county's financial situation worsened, however, and in 1969 Taylor led a playing staff of 12. Remarkably, they finished sixth in the Championship and reached the quarter-final of the Gillette Cup. In the new 40-over Sunday League they came third, as Taylor's emphasis on fielding and fitness paid dividends. "We run and field like mad," he said. He had identified the importance of marginal gains decades before the expression was coined. The large crowds drawn to the Sunday matches played a major part in turning around the county's finances, and in 1971 they came within a hair's breadth of landing their first trophy, losing the John Player League to Worcestershire on run-rate.

He was a Wisden Cricketer of the Year in 1972, but that July, a month after turning 40, came a sign he could not go on for ever, when his run of consecutive Championship appearances ended after 301 stretching back to May 1961. With his immaculate, bright-white kit and military demeanour he might have been seen as an anachronism, but he remained enormously popular with his young charges, even if they had to employ subterfuge to evade his curfews. On one occasion at Worcester he counted them in at the front door of the hotel, without realising they were promptly leaving again through the back. His philosophy on the game remained unchanged. "Too much theory is out at Essex," he said. "I have always believed cricket, like life itself, to be simple." And he had little time for physios: "The good players don't need them, and the bad players aren't worth it."

He made 539 appearances for the county, second only to Fletcher, and his 18,239 runs put him 11th on their list. In his final report to the committee he was critical of his own lack of adventure and, while praising the ability of his young team, doubted they had the character to become regular winners. He was proved spectacularly wrong when a Championship and Benson and Hedges Cup double in 1979 began a deluge of trophies.

Taylor was a Test selector for two years, and became an inspiring figure to new generations of players as coach of Essex Seconds and Cambridge University. "It is often said that leaders need not be loved, only respected, but with Tonker it was both," said Derek Pringle, who played under him for both teams. When Pringle was unable to bowl after a bad experience with a curry, Taylor barked: "Stay off the exotic food or you'll have to play in nappies."

THAKRE, BHARAT BAPURAO, who died of lung cancer on June 19, aged 53, was a seamer who took 36 wickets in 16 matches for Vidarbha. He claimed five for 44 on debut, against Rajasthan at Jodhpur in 1985-86, and improved his career-best to seven for 129 against Uttar Pradesh in 1990-91. He was a state selector from 2003 until his death.

THOMAS, KENNETH ALWYN, died on May 15, aged 92. Ken Thomas became chairman of the Lancashire and Cheshire Cricket Society in 1968, and was still in office at his death. "He dearly wished to complete 50 years as chair," said a member, "but stalled at 49, still a magnificent achievement."

THORNE, ROBIN KIDGER, who died on April 20, aged 87, was a nippy seamer who played 44 first-class matches in a long career in South Africa, mostly for Border. Making his debut at 18, Thorne claimed a distinguished maiden wicket when he castled Len Hutton during England's 1948-49 tour. He had to wait until 1955-56 for his Currie Cup debut, but then took five for 52 against Orange Free State at Bloemfontein. He remained a consistent wicket-taker for Border, who were in the second division at the time, and claimed a career-best eight for 101 against the 1961-62 New Zealand tourists. Even in 1964-65, his last season, he was accurate enough to return match figures of 63–30–86–10 against Western Province at East London. His only century – a round 100 – came against Orange Free State at Welkom in 1962-63. Thorne also did a lot of coaching, including countless sessions in the black townships, before eventually settling in England.

VAZE, DR PRAKASH, who died in a road accident on December 8, aged 67, was a physiotherapist and well-known sports enthusiast in Mumbai. He was a cricket umpire, and also organised chess tournaments. His sports foundation ran a double-wicket cricket competition and free umpiring courses.

VITTAL RAO, M. B., who died on December 8, aged 92, had the unenviable experience of keeping wicket for Mysore throughout Holkar's total of 912 for eight in the Ranji Trophy semi-final at Indore in 1945-46. After 214.5 overs in almost ten hours, during which six batsmen – including the 50-year-old C. K. Nayudu – made centuries, Vittal Rao went straight back out to open, but was soon dismissed for 14. In the follow-on, he retired hurt (or possibly exhausted) before he had scored. This was the third of his four first-class appearances; he later played for Mysore Gymkhana.

WAJID, MOHAMMED ABDUL, died on May 16, of injuries sustained during a casual game of cricket in Hyderabad, India, two days previously. Wajid, who was 22, ran to field a ball which had been hit into a nearby game. He was struck by the bat of a player in the other match, and hit his head on a pile of stones being used as their wicket. The batsman was charged with "culpable homicide not amounting to murder".

WAKELING, VICTOR NOEL STANLEY, CBE, who died on May 15, aged 73, was a key figure in the history of televised sport in Britain. As head of sport for Rupert Murdoch's Sky TV he was at the forefront of the revolution that led to a string of sports moving to the satellite subscription channel. Wakeling was an old-school print journalist – working for *The Sun*, the *Daily Express* and *The Observer* – and transferred the competitive values of Fleet Street to what was then an entirely new branch of the television industry. Under his guidance, Sky's coverage of the new football Premier League, launched in 1992, was a spectacular success. They immediately brought innovation to coverage of cricket by showing an England overseas series for the first time, when Graham Gooch's side visited the West Indies in 1989-90. And in 2005 Sky secured the exclusive rights to home Tests. "Vic was a passionate supporter of cricket, and instrumental in driving the amount of content on all our platforms," said Bryan Henderson, Sky's head of cricket. "He took a keen interest in the coverage and provided huge support to the production teams."

WATERS, ROBIN HENRY CLOUGH, who died on December 9, three days after his 80th birthday, was a wicketkeeper-batsman who became a well-known figure as player and coach in Ireland, without fulfilling the potential he had shown for Oxford University. He also played a role in a key moment in Indian cricket: at Hove in 1961 he was at the wheel of the car involved in the accident in which Tiger Pataudi suffered the serious eye injury that hampered his career.

Waters was born in Calcutta and educated at Shrewsbury, where his best year was 1954, his first in the XI: 311 runs at 26. He was captain in his last. He made his first-class debut for Colonel L. C. Stevens's XI against Cambridge University at Eastbourne in 1960 – Len Hutton's last first-class appearance in England. At Oxford the following summer, he was the regular wicketkeeper, playing against the Australians, and making 37 against a strong Yorkshire attack. In July, having already been selected for the Varsity Match, he was unbeaten overnight on the first day of the game against Sussex, when he took Pataudi out in his Mini Minor for a meal. As they approached the statue of Queen Victoria on Grand Avenue on their return to the team hotel, they were hit by a car which emerged from a side road. Waters appeared more badly hurt – "pretty badly mangled," he said – but Pataudi's injury was worse: a shard of glass had damaged his right eye. Years later, on a visit to Ireland with a touring Indian team, Pataudi made it clear he had never held Waters responsible.

Waters returned to cricket before the end of the summer, having missed the 1961 Varsity Match; he missed it again in 1962, despite sharing the gloves for Oxford. He kept wicket in six Championship matches for Sussex later in the season, with Jim Parks playing as a batsman. That winter he also made two appearances for Bengal in the Ranji Trophy. In the mid-1960s he was a regular for Sussex Seconds – playing alongside John Snow and Tony Greig – but did not make a first-team breakthrough, and left for Ireland in 1967 to become player-coach at Clontarf. He made three more first-class appearances for Ireland, striking a career-best 70 against Scotland at Glasgow in 1968, and was a member of the team that famously beat the West Indians at Sion Mills in 1969. When the sides began a two-day match at Belfast next morning, Waters top-scored in Ireland's first innings with 41. He later became a coach at Belvedere College in Dublin.

WATSON, ERIC ALEXANDER, who died on March 25, aged 91, had a long if unspectacular career for Otago, making his debut against the touring Fijians in 1948-49, and playing on to 1959-60, occasionally alongside his brother, Leonard. Eric's only century came while opening against Central Districts at Napier in 1951-52; he made 95 in the same fixture the following season. He was also a handy medium-pacer, and took four for 26 – including top-scorer John Reid – against Wellington in 1949-50. Watson became a distinguished rugby coach: despite appearing only once for Otago, he later coached them for several years, before stepping up to the national side in 1979-80. His tenure included All Blacks tours of Australia and Wales.

WIGRAM, LORD (GEORGE NEVILLE CLIVE), MC, DL, died on May 23, aged 101. Neville Wigram survived being shot during the Dunkirk evacuation – he was unaware until he opened his backpack later and found a bullet embedded in his soap dish. A few years earlier, he had played for the North of Scotland in the last match of the Australians' 1934 tour, as he was staying on the Balmoral Estate – his father was private secretary to King George V. Wigram top-scored with 28 not out in the second innings against a team captained by Don Bradman. *The Times* mentioned some "lusty hitting", which included 16 in an over from leg-spinner Arthur Chipperfield, the highlight a six over cover point. He remained in the Army until 1957, becoming the second Lord Wigram in 1960.

WIJESINHA, ROBERT BERTRUM, died on April 9, aged 96. All-rounder Bertie Wijesinha played for Ceylon against visiting teams from Australia, England, India, Pakistan and West Indies, as well as a Commonwealth XI. On tour in March 1950, he scored 57 against Karachi & Sind, then grabbed five for 57 with his medium-pacers against Pakistan Universities, his victims including three Test players. Wijesinha was sports editor of the Colombo *Daily News* from 1953 to 1972, and an occasional radio commentator; he was also a prominent coach, inspiring the three Wettimuny brothers, who all went on to play for their country. "My father built the first indoor nets in Sri Lanka," said Sidath Wettimuny, who scored 190 in the 1984 Lord's Test. "He handed them over to Bertie and told him: 'You can use them for your coaching – but you must also coach my sons!'" When he died, Wijesinha was the oldest Sri Lankan representative cricketer, and had been married for 68 years.

WILKINSON, ROY DONALD, who died on March 1, aged 86, had been Yorkshire's official statistician for 40 years, and also edited their yearbook for a time, introducing written pieces alongside the previously statistical-only content.

WILTSHIRE, GRAHAM GEORGE MORLEY, who died on August 2, aged 86, played occasionally for Gloucestershire in the 1950s as an outswing bowler, before embarking on a long and successful career as a coach, succeeding George Emmett at Bristol in 1962. In his county history, Grahame Parker wrote that Wiltshire "developed a wonderfully perceptive appreciation of an individual cricketer's technical problems". Under his benevolent gaze, Gloucestershire won their first trophies – the Gillette Cup in 1973, and the Benson and Hedges Cup in 1977. He was also a marvellous ambassador. Long-time county team-mate Tony Brown recalled: "It was his willingness to go all over the South-West and overseas – to Malawi, Zambia and Barbados – encouraging and helping clubs, schools and teams, that made him an outstanding coach and person. He just loved helping people play cricket, from basic club standard to county and international."

For all his skills, Wiltshire's greatest single contribution to Gloucestershire cricket probably came in the winter of 1964-65, when he persuaded the parents of two young South Africans to send their sons over to Bristol. Mike Procter and Barry Richards enjoyed their time in England – and when, in 1968, the qualification rules were relaxed and counties allowed to sign an overseas player, Procter returned to Gloucestershire. He became a local legend.

Wiltshire had one great day as a player, claiming seven for 52 against Yorkshire at Headingley in June 1958, finishing the innings with a hat-trick; in 18 other matches, he never took more than two in an innings. In all, he was with Gloucestershire for more than 40 years, enjoying a benefit season in 1973, and a testimonial in 1995.

WINN, CHRISTOPHER ELLIOTT, died on August 27, aged 90. The sporting life of Chris Winn might have appeared in the *Boys' Own Paper*: tall, blond and debonair, he scored a try against South Africa at Twickenham on his international rugby debut, played cricket for Oxford University and Sussex, and married the women's 880 yards world-record holder, Valerie Ball. A winger for Rosslyn Park, "Bruiser" Winn earned eight England rugby caps in all, scoring three tries, including a last-minute winner against Wales in 1954. When it came to cricket, he was an attacking left-hander with a short backlift, and a twinkling fielder who sometimes kept wicket. He won Blues each year from 1948 to 1951, scoring consistently, although his two centuries came in quick succession for Oxford in 1950: an unbeaten 146 against the Free Foresters in the Parks, and a rapid 130 at Lord's against an MCC attack that included Eric Bedser and Fred Titmus. The first of those followed 61 and 31 not out against the West Indian tourists. Winn had less success for Sussex, although he did hit 71 against Leicestershire at Ashby-de-la-Zouch in 1949.

He became a sales manager for Dulux paints, took up real tennis, and in later years would often hold court at Lord's or Twickenham, "never quite losing the slight mischievous glint in his eye", according to a Rosslyn Park team-mate.

ZUBAIR AHMED MOHMAND died on August 14, after being hit on the head twice during a game in Mardan, in northern Pakistan. He was 18. After being struck near the ear, Zubair was hit again on the side of the neck, and died on the way to hospital. His coach confirmed he had been wearing a helmet. Among the other players in the festival match to celebrate Pakistan's independence day was Fakhar Zaman, who two months previously had hit a century in the Champions Trophy final at The Oval.

The obituaries section includes those who died, or whose deaths were notified, in 2017. Wisden always welcomes information about those who might be included: please send details to almanack@wisdenalmanack.com, or to John Wisden & Co, 13 Old Aylesfield, Golden Pot, Alton, Hampshire GU34 4BY.

BRIEFLY NOTED

The following, whose deaths were noted during 2017, played or umpired in a small number of first-class (fc) matches.

	Died	*Age*	*Main team(s)*
AUSTEN, Victor Cecil	29.10.2017	98	South Australia

Medium-pacer: one fc match in 1945-46, against his native Victoria. Australian Rules footballer.

BHATT, Ashutosh Suryaprasad	21.2.2017	77	Gujarat

Batsman: six fc matches from 1959-60, with little success. Prominent local historian and author.

BLENKINSOP, Brian John	21.4.2017	85	Eastern Province

Seamer from Port Elizabeth who played two fc matches in 1954-55; later a leading local golfer.

DESHPANDE, Madhumilind Gajanan	26.11.2017	79	Umpire

Stood in 26 fc matches in India from 1970-71, including the 1987-88 Ranji Trophy final.

GASSTON, Peter Louis	6.3.2017	56	Umpire

Stood in six Plunket Shield matches in New Zealand from 2009-10.

HANUMESH, M. S.	27.9.2017	77	Mysore

One fc match in 1964-65: made a duck and did not bowl.

HARDIKAR, Vidyadhar Yeshwant	12.1.2017	83	Umpire

Stood in three Ranji Trophy matches in India from 1967-68.

HEARN, Trevor Alistair Evans	28.8.2017	65	Orange Free State

Seamer who played two fc matches in 1970-71, after representing South Africa Schools.

HOOPER, Kerry	16.3.2017	74	Tasmania

Left-arm seamer who took 5-106 against the 1965-66 MCC tourists in Hobart.

IQBAL UMAR	18.4.2017	74	Karachi University

Slow left-armer, one fc match in 1964-65: co-founded the Pakistan Veterans Cricket Association.

JOHNSTON, Alan David	29.3.2017	63	Ireland

Opening bowler for Lurgan and Ulster Country: played for Ireland in 1980 NatWest Trophy.

LANGFORD, Ian Frederick	25.2.2017	80	Victoria

One fc match in 1961-62: heavy scorer in Melbourne club cricket, mainly for St Kilda.

MASON, Ian Robert	18.7.2017	75	Wellington

Batsman whose six fc matches in the 1960s included three for New Zealand Under-23s.

SHAW, Dennis George	5.4.2017	86	Warwickshire

Leg-spinner who made one fc appearance, against Combined Services in 1949.

SHAW, Noel Clyde	10.12.2017	80	Victoria

Collingwood seamer: one fc match, v Western Australia in 1957-58; took 3-23 in second innings.

SMYTH, Neil Weston	14.8.2017	89	Victoria

Wicketkeeper: three fc matches in 1950s, all against Tasmania; long club career with Prahran.

VENKATNARYANA, Amruthur Venkatshaiyer	21.10.17	73	Mysore

Left-arm seamer: nine wickets at 20 in four fc matches, with 3-19 against Andhra in 1968-69.

A LIFE IN NUMBERS

	Runs	*Avge*	*Wkts*	*Avge*
Aizazuddin, F. S.	1,872	24.96	19	40.05
Allom, A. T. C.	94	18.80	15	29.26
Amroliwala, H. S.	1,782	44.55	14	24.35
Asher, K. P.	306	38.25	–	–
Banerjee, T. J.	217	15.50	47	19.34
Bartholomew, P. C. S.	1,598	23.85	141	25.56
Becker, D. F.	770	18.78	112	23.10
Bhandari, P. N.	398	39.80	6	33.66
Bore, M. K.	874	8.24	372	30.22
Bradley, R. R. A. F.	–	–	1	31.00
Burke, S. F.	**2,334**	**26.52**	**241**	**21.38**
Chambers, J. L.	1,457	33.11	–	–
Champniss, L. J.	17	–	1	4.00
Chevalier, G. A.	**84**	**4.94**	**154**	**23.72**
Clarke, S. J. S.	99	7.07	–	–
Cosh, S. H.	873	16.16	0	–
Curran, K. P.	234	23.40	–	–
Davidson, T. R.	509	21.20	–	–
Davies, H. D.	247	5.61	115	31.81
Davison, I. J.	1,641	9.06	541	28.81
de Grandhomme, L. L.	428	23.77	26	36.03
Derrick, J.	1,195	22.93	137	38.05
Doggart, S. J. G.	878	22.51	34	65.38
Evans, R. J.	201	25.12	3	32.33
Farr, B. H.	143	14.30	10	53.80
Fenix, P.	2,306	22.38	1	109.00
Ferrant, J. G.	609	11.94	169	23.74
Goldstein, F. S.	4,810	30.25	1	53.00
Gorringe, H. R.	228	7.12	89	34.88
Grant, C. R. W.	125	20.83	–	–
Greetham, C. H. M.	6,723	21.97	195	28.35
Hampshire, J. H.	**28,059**	**34.55**	**30**	**54.56**
Hansell, T. M. G.	319	15.19	0	–
Hector, A.	728	15.82		
Hill, R. G.	105	11.66	–	–
Holland, R. G.	**706**	**9.67**	**316**	**31.19**
Insole, D. J.	**25,241**	**37.61**	**138**	**33.91**
Jichkar, A. M.	101	12.62	7	55.14
Kemp, J. W.	31	10.33	5	27.20
Kippax, P. J.	40	6.66	12	33.00
Krishnamurthy, S.	1,336	27.26	0	–

	Runs	*Avge*	*Wkts*	*Avge*
Latham, H. J.	129	11.72	27	27.81
Laver, J. F. L.	343	14.91	20	42.80
Lewington, P. J.	383	7.36	191	29.86
Mantell, D. N.	150	6.00	–	–
Marjoribanks, H. L.	28	4.66	8	46.75
Marsh, E.	419	24.64	–	–
Mavalwala, S.	93	18.60	8	38.25
Milkha Singh, A. G.	**4,324**	**35.44**	**5**	**49.00**
Morgan, D. C.	18,356	24.94	1,248	25.08
Motley, K. G.	856	22.52	3	34.00
Munilall, C.	461	21.95	1	146.00
Narayanan, P. S.	–	–	0	–
Pathmanathan, G.	1,553	20.98	0	–
Phillips, J. B.	151	5.39	72	35.65
Pollock, J. S.	1,036	25.26	0	–
Porter, S. R.	76	7.60	18	33.33
Preen, A. T.	158	13.16	28	34.96
Pyemont, C. P.	516	22.43	3	27.66
Rao, S. G.	118	19.66	16	33.81
Richardson, P. E.	**26,055**	**34.60**	**11**	**45.36**
Rushmere, C. G.	1,245	23.05	20	28.80
Sajid Asghar	456	16.28	12	53.83
Sayer, D. M.	1,252	8.29	613	23.48
Schmidt, K. E.	551	19.00	19	44.78
Shepherd, D. J.	5,695	9.65	2,218	21.32
Smith, M. G. M.	24	24.00	–	–
Spence, L. A.	326	11.64	0	–
Sridhar, M. V.	6,700	48.90	0	–
Sriram, K.	644	28.00	0	–
Starkie, S.	857	10.71	166	34.24
Stokes, R. G.	323	24.84	0	–
Taylor, B.	19,093	21.79	1	30.00
Thakre, B. B.	82	6.30	36	30.91
Thorne, R. K.	1,751	23.66	164	20.00
Vittal Rao, M. B.	72	10.28	–	–
Waters, R. H. C.	929	18.21	–	–
Watson, E. A.	1,779	21.43	41	30.46
Wijesinha, R. B.	476	21.63	34	36.53
Wiltshire, G. G. M.	218	8.38	25	33.44
Winn, C. E.	2,449	24.98	1	34.0[illegible]

Test players are in bold; their career figures can be found on page 1316.

Asher made ten catches and four stumpings; Cosh 36 and seven; Davidson 12 and four; Hector 4[illegible] and 18; Insole 366 and six; Krishnamurthy 30 and 15; Mantell 28 and two; Smith one and one; Taylor 1,084 and 211; Vittal Rao five and one; Waters 52 and three; Winn 40 and one.

PART THREE

English International Cricket

THE ENGLAND TEAM IN 2017

One night in Bristol

JOHN ETHERIDGE

A flurry of punches, captured by a student's mobile phone, defined England's year. The fallout from the arrest of Ben Stokes on suspicion of causing actual bodily harm in Bristol at 2.35am on September 25 was wide-ranging. It had a profound impact on the Ashes, and it is no exaggeration to say England probably would not have lost 4–0 if he had been tucked up in bed that night – as he should have been in the middle of a one-day series against West Indies.

Stokes spent the rest of 2017 in limbo, awaiting a decision from the Crown Prosecution Service while he played six white-ball games on the other side of the world for his native Canterbury, but in mid-January he was charged with affray. He insisted he would clear his name, and was immediately chosen for

ENGLAND IN 2017

	Played	*Won*	*Lost*	*Drawn/No result*
Tests	11	5	5	1
One-day internationals	20	15	4	1
Twenty20 internationals	7	3	4	–

NOVEMBER / DECEMBER / JANUARY / FEBRUARY	5 Tests, 3 ODIs and 3 T20Is (a) v India	(see *Wisden 2017*, page 342)
MARCH	3 ODIs (a) v West Indies	(page 255)
APRIL		
MAY	2 ODIs (h) v Ireland	(page 260)
JUNE	ICC Champions Trophy (h)	(page 263)
JULY	4 Tests, 3 ODIs and 3 T20Is (h) v South Africa	(page 287)
AUGUST / SEPTEMBER	3 Tests, 5 ODIs and 1 T20I (h) v West Indies	(page 318)
OCTOBER		
NOVEMBER		
DECEMBER / JANUARY	5 Tests and 5 ODIs (a) v Australia	(page 349)

England's tour of New Zealand – only to be summoned to appear at Bristol magistrates' court on February 13, the date of the first Twenty20 international at Wellington. Stokes pleaded not guilty, and so the case moved to the Crown Court. It was chaotic, to say the least. His absence in Australia had upset the balance of the side, in effect robbing them of three players – No. 6 batsman, second-change seamer and athletic fielder, either in the deep or at slip. He had become the team's heartbeat.

Jonny Bairstow's bizarre headbutt of Cameron Bancroft on the opening night of the tour, and England Lions player Ben Duckett's beery dousing of James Anderson – later, but at the same Perth bar – would have been considered little more than fripperies without the shadow cast by Stokes. When he was spotted at Heathrow on his way to play for Canterbury, it provoked all manner of speculation about whether he might appear in the Ashes after all. There were just so many distractions.

Joe Root, who has known Stokes since his teens and canvassed for him to be his deputy, could feel especially let down. His first year as Test skipper was mixed, with home wins over South Africa and West Indies preceding the hammering in Australia. Alastair Cook had waited seven weeks after England's 4–0 defeat in India in 2016-17 before resigning; Root was the only serious candidate, and was confirmed in the position in February. But because of a clump of white-ball cricket, he did not take charge of a match until July. He immediately scored 190 against South Africa at Lord's, but – including the New Year Test at Sydney – converted only one of his next 11 half-centuries into three figures. That frailty left him a notch below Steve Smith and Virat Kohli in the batting pantheon.

Root had quickly discovered the perils of captaincy. He lost his second Test against South Africa at Trent Bridge, and reacted angrily – "I cannot believe he actually said that" – when informed that his old mentor Michael Vaughan had accused England's batsmen of disrespecting Test cricket with their gung-ho approach. Six weeks later, Root's declaration at Headingley challenged West Indies to score 322, which they achieved with five wickets in hand. He then chose to field at Adelaide, but England bowled too short, eventually allowing Australia to declare on a match-winning 442 for eight.

Although he held the respect and admiration of his team-mates, and was a more instinctive tactician than Cook, Root's strategy in Australia erred towards caution. He and the England brains trust produced a variety of plans, but never came close to stopping Smith, who was dismissed just five times in 1,416 balls. Ricky Ponting, the former Australia captain, said Root looked like "a little boy". More pertinently, though, he lacked the bowling armoury at Smith's disposal.

The stars of the home summer had been James Anderson and Moeen Ali. Anderson's 39 wickets at 14, his best haul in an English summer, included his 500th in Tests – when he bowled West Indies opener Kraigg Brathwaite at Lord's – and he added 17 more in Australia. He also ran in from the newly named James Anderson End during the Old Trafford Test and, at 35, remained England's best and most skilful bowler, devastating in friendly conditions at home, and almost unhittable on less helpful surfaces: his 223.3 overs in Australia, the most he had bowled in any series, produced an economy-rate of

Kieran Galvin, NurPhoto/PA Photos

Jason O'Brien, PA Photos

From grovel to granite: Dawid Malan on his knees after being felled by Kagiso Rabada, and an immovable force at Perth in December.

just 2.11. And on the one occasion he found substantial swing with the Kookaburra ball – under lights at Adelaide – he took five for 43, as Australia were bowled out for 138, the lowest total of the series.

Ali harvested 30 wickets at 21 in England, and – surrounded by team-mates – his joy when the DRS confirmed a Test-clinching hat-trick against South Africa at The Oval was one of the images of the year. But what came next embodied England's inconsistency and concerns. Ali took five wickets at 115 in Australia where, hampered first by a side strain, then a cut finger, his confidence evaporated, and he looked utterly lost. His batting disintegrated, too: Nathan Lyon dismissed him seven times in nine innings.

If the lack of a world-class spinner in overseas conditions damaged England, just as it had 12 months earlier in India, there was no sign either of a reliable, injury-free, genuinely fast bowler able to unsettle batsmen on unresponsive pitches. England were producing a phalanx of medium-quick, right-arm bowlers, all possessing fewer tricks than Anderson. The focus settled, as so often, on county cricket – not least the pushing of Championship matches to the beginning and end of the season – and the merits of the ECB Performance Centre at Loughborough. With counties persuaded, reluctantly in some cases, to accept a new city-based Twenty20 event starting in 2020, there appeared little prospect of four-day games returning to high summer. The new tournament formed part of a TV deal that runs from 2020 to 2024, exceeds £1bn for the first time, and will bring some live cricket back to BBC television after more than two decades away.

Stuart Broad went past Ian Botham's total of 383 wickets during England's first home pink-ball Test, against West Indies at Edgbaston, which finished inside three days after the tourists lost 19 wickets on the

Saturday alone. But his irresistible wicket-laden surges were becoming less frequent – in 11 matches he managed just one four-for, in the Boxing Day Test at Melbourne. Chris Woakes laboured in Australia, and never recaptured his best form after returning from a torn rib muscle sustained in England's opening match of the Champions Trophy in June. Toby Roland-Jones, who took 17 wickets in his first four Tests, might have posed a threat with his height in Australia, but did not fly out because of a stress fracture of the back.

England also struggled to find reliable batsmen. Keaton Jennings, Tom Westley and Gary Ballance fell by the wayside, and Haseeb Hameed, so promising in India in late 2016, did not play at all because of a mixture of injury and indifferent form for Lancashire. Mark Stoneman and James Vince, who both averaged in the mid-20s in the Ashes, were retained for the tour of New Zealand. But Stoneman's output dwindled to virtually nothing after he was hit on the head in the Third Test at Perth, while Vince's innings tended towards rinse and repeat – a few stylish strokes before nicking a catch. Cook's numbers were skewed by two double-centuries, and he generally looked below his best on his return to the ranks. In 2017, only he, Root and Stokes averaged above 35 in Tests.

Dawid Malan's Test career started inauspiciously. He was left grovelling on his knees against South Africa at The Oval after being yorked for one by Kagiso Rabada. But he finished as England's find of the year, a left-hander of obduracy and patience whose play against spin and the short delivery improved noticeably during the Ashes. He could whack it, too, scoring 78 from 44 balls on his Twenty20 international debut, against South Africa at Cardiff.

In the shorter formats, England lost a 50-over series 2–1 in India, but then were almost invincible, beating West Indies away, followed by Ireland, South Africa and West Indies again at home. In total, they won 15 ODIs and lost four and built on that success with a series win in Australia in January 2018. The Twenty20 ledger showed a series defeat in India, a home win over South Africa, and defeat in a one-off match against West Indies.

But it was the Champions Trophy semi-final against Pakistan that proved the most significant setback. Trevor Bayliss had been hired, primarily because of his white-ball CV, to win a global limited-overs tournament. Already one opportunity had gone, and only the 2019 World Cup remains before his contract expires that September. England had been the most impressive team in the Champions Trophy group matches, and their three victories included a thumping of Australia at Edgbaston. But they failed to adapt to a slow, tired surface in Cardiff, and Pakistan beat them with more than 12 overs to spare. Bayliss said the experience would help England in the World Cup, but the men's team had a glimpse of what might have been when the women won their World Cup in a memorable final against India a few weeks later.

Liam Plunkett and Adil Rashid, who was overtaken by Hampshire's Mason Crane as the preferred wrist-spinner in Test cricket, were the most successful one-day bowlers, with 36 and 26 wickets respectively. Root was in superb touch, averaging 70, while Bairstow, taking his chance as 50-over opener, finished the summer with two unbeaten centuries against West Indies. He initially replaced the out-of-form Jason Roy, before Alex Hales was omitted from the final two matches for being at the scene of the Stokes fight. Three more players – Plunkett, Bairstow and Jake Ball – were fined around £1,000 each by team director Andrew Strauss for being out late that evening, although they were not present at the fracas. Hales was later cleared by police, and resumed his England career in early 2018.

Two days after Stokes's arrest, *The Sun* acquired a recording of the brawl. The video was shown all over the world, and with particular frequency on Australian TV news channels. The ending, in which a man is knocked to the floor with a single blow, was screened twice in one bulletin of the BBC news.

The ramifications were many. Bayliss had to fly back to the UK from a holiday in Australia because the players' end-of-season assessments were delayed. Jos Buttler's stag weekend in Amsterdam became irresistible to the paparazzi, and players were photographed throwing a black dildo into the air; some were horrified, others thought it harmless high jinks. Another (old) video, in which Stokes apparently mocked the disabled son of the celebrity Katie Price, was dragged up, prompting Stokes to apologise. The American sportswear firm, New Balance, withdrew their sponsorship of him. And so it went on.

Nineteen days after his evening out, Stokes married Clare Ratcliffe, the mother of their two children, in the village of East Brent, 20 miles from Bristol. It will not be the only reason he remembers 2017.

ENGLAND PLAYERS IN 2017

LAWRENCE BOOTH

The following 33 players (there were 32 in 2016, and 33 in 2015) appeared in 2017, when England played 11 Tests, 20 one-day internationals and seven Twenty20 internationals. Statistics refer to the full year, not the 2017 season.

MOEEN ALI — Worcestershire

Not for the first time, it was hard to get a handle on Ali. When everything clicked, as during a spectacular 53-ball hundred against West Indies at Bristol, his insouciance looked class. When nothing clicked, as during the Ashes, it looked crass. He was becoming a man of extremes: 25 wickets at 15 in the Test win over South Africa, including a hat-trick at The Oval, then five at 115 in Australia. Expectation played a part. Ali seemed happier in the shadows than the spotlight, and his ten-for against South Africa at Lord's came when he was billed as the second spinner, behind Dawson. His 50-over form nudged both ends of the spectrum, too: a batting strike-rate of 148 was the best in the world, but his off-breaks were innocuous. And his Test batting disintegrated during the Ashes at the hands of Nathan Lyon. It all added up to a curiosity: integral to England, yet apparently without portfolio – and all the while one of the most watchable of cricketers.

11 Tests: 497 runs @ 27.61; 33 wickets @ 31.63.
17 ODIs: 402 runs @ 44.66, SR 148.88; 6 wickets @ 99.00, ER 5.64.
3 T20Is: 3 runs @ 3.00, SR 60.00; 3 wickets @ 23.66, ER 5.91.

JAMES ANDERSON — Lancashire

A vintage year encouraged analogies with fine wine after concerns about corkage in 2016: even at 35, Anderson kept getting better. In the summer, he was consistently brilliant and brilliantly consistent, averaging exactly 14.10 against both South Africa and West Indies as the ball did his bidding. His performance in a losing cause in Australia was as revealing: 17 wickets at 27, including a masterclass under lights in Adelaide. Among those who claimed ten or more in 2017, Anderson topped the world averages; he finished the year top of the rankings too. Garlands abounded. He passed 500 Test wickets during a career-best seven for 42 against West Indies at Lord's, and overhauled Courtney Walsh at Melbourne to move into fifth on Test cricket's all-time list. Throughout, he was almost unhittable: 2.26 an over was his most economical year yet. The hope was England had enough cotton wool.

11 Tests: 33 runs @ 6.60; 55 wickets @ 17.58.

JONNY BAIRSTOW — Yorkshire

His Test batting fell short of the Olympian standards he had set in 2016, possibly because he spent most of the year either a place too high, or a place too low. When he returned to his natural home at No. 6 for the Third Ashes Test in Perth, he responded with an unequivocal hundred. Bairstow had already forced his way back into the one-day side at the expense of Roy, and it was typical that he made the chance count with a pair of unbeaten centuries against West Indies; his 50-over average and strike-rate both finished in three figures. His keeping maintained its upward curve, and he ended 2017 with a stunning reflex catch to dismiss Shaun Marsh at Melbourne. A couple of years earlier, it might not have stuck. Only the headbutt with which he greeted Cameron Bancroft at the start of the Ashes tour removed any gloss.

11 Tests: 652 runs @ 34.31; 35 catches, 2 stumpings.
10 ODIs: 534 runs @ 106.80, SR 100.18.
3 T20Is: 134 runs @ 67.00, SR 144.08.

JAKE BALL — Nottinghamshire

Progress was slower than hoped from a strapping fast bowler who had been earmarked as a useful weapon in Australia. He was ditched after Brisbane, perhaps unfairly, given that Root used him as a bouncer-bowling workhorse. In one-day internationals he conceded 80 or more four times, suggesting batsmen saw him as the weakest link.

1 Test: 15 runs @ 7.50; 1 wicket @ 115.00.
13 ODIs: 9 runs @ 4.50, SR 60.00; 14 wickets @ 53.85, ER 6.44.

SAM BILLINGS — Kent

Billings's best chance came as a 50-over opener in Antigua in March, but he followed a punchy 52 with a first-ball duck. When Hales returned from injury for the series finale in Barbados, Billings was once more condemned to a year that was more stop than start. England hadn't given up on him, handing him the gloves for the two home games against Ireland, but he gave little in return. Fulfilment looked more likely in the T20 franchise leagues.

7 ODIs: 96 runs @ 19.20, SR 74.41; 2 catches as wicketkeeper.
6 T20Is: 49 runs @ 9.80, SR 140.00.

STUART BROAD — Nottinghamshire

Broad's ingrained optimism – forever believing the next haul was just round the corner – wasn't shaken until an analysis of none for 142 at Perth, the worst of his career. Introspection ensued, though first-innings figures of 28–10–51–4 on a merciless drop-in pitch at Melbourne were the retort of a champion. Luck was not always with him, and catches dropped off his bowling in the summer reached double figures. But the awayswinger to the right-hander remained elusive, and it was hard to dispel the suspicion that his body was starting to rebel. His batting, little more than hit and hope as fast bowlers simply banged it in, produced two entertaining fifties – the second while ushering Cook to a double-hundred at the MCG – but not much else.

11 Tests: 230 runs @ 15.33; 30 wickets @ 36.06.

JOS BUTTLER — Lancashire

Unlike one of Buttler's trademark ramps, his year never really took off. Worse, his red-ball game withered to irrelevance. It was partly his own doing: preferring the IPL to early-season county cricket, he nailed his colours to the white-ball mast. But he couldn't quite fly the flag: 19 international innings produced only two half-centuries and strike-rates below previous years.

If money-spinning Twenty20 tournaments around the world softened the blow of his absence from the Test side, then Buttler was a tale for the times.

18 ODIs: 288 runs @ 28.80, SR 102.49; 26 catches, 4 stumpings.
7 T20Is: 86 runs @ 17.20, SR 124.63; 5 catches.

ALASTAIR COOK — Essex

It wasn't quite a year of two innings, but it was close. The zenith appeared to be a remorseless 243 against West Indies at Edgbaston in England's first day/night Test, only for Cook to carry his bat at Melbourne for 244, after ten innings without a half-century, the longest drought of his career. For those who wondered if his eye or hunger had gone, it was an epic riposte, notable for some uncharacteristic straight-drives. The two doubles made it easy to forget two other contributions, both against South Africa: a second-innings 69 on a turning Lord's track, then a five-hour 88 under Kennington clouds, arguably England's innings of the summer. While his harshest critics bemoaned his contribution to the first three Ashes Tests (83 runs), most simply welcomed the thought that England's leading run-scorer was not done yet. And at Sydney in January 2018, he moved past 12,000 runs in Tests.

11 Tests: 899 runs @ 47.31.

LIAM DAWSON — Hampshire

Through no fault of his own, Dawson's slow left-armers became a tool with which to bash the England management. Since Ali was said not to enjoy the pressure of being the No. 1 Test spinner, Dawson was chosen for the first two games against South Africa and – despite a couple of beauties to Hashim Amla – was utterly outbowled by his supposed inferior. A pair at Lord's did not help. The experiment ended quickly, leaving Dawson to face up to a strictly white-ball future, if that.

2 Tests: 18 runs @ 6.00; 5 wickets @ 33.80.
3 T20Is: 7 runs without being dismissed, SR 140.00; 1 wicket @ 75.00, ER 7.50.

STEVEN FINN — Middlesex

Time was beginning to pass Finn by. Three one-day appearances in the Caribbean suggested all was not lost, but he played just once more for England in 2017, and his call-up for the Ashes squad came to naught when he tore knee cartilage. That was less than two months after an eight-for against Lancashire, though he finished the year lamenting the fast bowler's lot on county cricket's treadmill – a metaphor, perhaps, for the state of his career.

4 ODIs: 5 runs @ 5.00, SR 71.42; 4 wickets @ 39.25, ER 4.61.

ALEX HALES — Nottinghamshire

A summer in which he struck the ball more cleanly than ever ended with Hales playing a walk-on part in Stokes's video nasty in Bristol – a misjudgment that cut short his season with two one-day internationals to go. Until then, he had been talked up as an outsider for the Ashes, though never by the selectors. Instead, the biggest criticism was that he didn't quite make the most of some golden form. To score at more than a run-a-ball in the 50-over game spoke volumes; but only two innings above 61 told a story, too. After Bristol, though, the debate felt less germane, and by the time his suspension was lifted – for the one-day series in Australia in early 2018 – he had lost his place at the top of the order.

15 ODIs: 535 runs @ 38.21, SR 102.49.
3 T20Is: 126 runs @ 63.00, SR 151.80.

KEATON JENNINGS — Durham

His triumphant debut at Mumbai in December 2016 faded from the mind as he spent the South Africa series prodding and poking, often to fatal effect against Vernon Philander. Eight innings produced a best of 48 – even that was scratchy – and a tendency to nibble at the new ball when he should have ignored it. It all meant his stance looked stiff and upright, rather than tall and imposing like Marcus Trescothick. Easier runs might have been available against West Indies, but the selectors had moved on.

4 Tests: 127 runs @ 15.87; no wicket for two runs.

CHRIS JORDAN — Sussex

England reached the conclusion that Jordan's varieties – not all of them deliberate – were better suited to Twenty20 cricket than the 50-over game, and no team-mate claimed more wickets in the shortest format. But he still blew hot and cold: figures of three for 22 at Nagpur were followed three days later by one for 56 at Bangalore.

7 T20Is: 6 runs @ 3.00, SR 60.00; 10 wickets @ 25.10, ER 8.96.

DAWID MALAN — Middlesex

For a while, Malan looked like a white-ball specialist who had won a raffle to play Tests. Four successive failures against South Africa were masked by the struggles of Jennings, and a pair of hard-fought sixties against West Indies barely earned him an Ashes place. But he opened up his left-handed stance, and took Australia on, most memorably at Perth, where his double of 140 and 54 was an English record at the most unEnglish of venues. He finished the series as the tourists' leading scorer. It all felt a world away from his international debut in June: a blistering 78 from 44 balls in a Twenty20 decider against South Africa in Cardiff. To his credit, he refused to be typecast.

9 Tests: 505 runs @ 33.66; no wicket for 61 runs.
1 T20I: 78 runs @ 78.00, SR 177.27.

EOIN MORGAN — Middlesex

A quiet end to the summer belied Morgan's year. Three one-day hundreds – one each in India, Antigua and England – were a reminder of his ability to milk the good times, and he captained the 50-over side to 15 wins out of 19. But one of the four defeats came in the Champions Trophy semi-final against Pakistan, and his runs – internationally and domestically – dried up either side of a fruitless stint at the Caribbean Premier League. Since his previous first-class match had been in July 2015, Morgan was playing less and less cricket, so eyebrows rose when he sat out the Twenty20 decider against South Africa to give Livingstone another chance. His decision to sign up for a ten-over tournament in the UAE in December summed up the sense of a bat for hire.

20 ODIs: 781 runs @ 45.94, SR 98.73.
6 T20Is: 116 runs @ 23.20, SR 124.73.

LIAM PLUNKETT **Yorkshire**

So fundamental did Plunkett become to England's white-ball strategy that many wondered if he could not, once more, do a job at Test level. By the time the international summer finished in late September, no one in the world had more than his 36 ODI wickets in 2017 (next for England was Rashid, ten adrift). His approach was simple and honest: aim back of a length in the middle overs, and induce cross-batted errors. He took at least three wickets in an innings nine times across the limited-overs formats, and was England's meanest seamer in Twenty20. Despite all that, the most common adjective in feature articles was "unsung" – music to England's ears.

18 ODIs: 71 runs @ 14.20, SR 124.56; 36 wickets @ 22.47, ER 5.62.
5 T20Is: 18 runs @ 6.00, SR 128.57; 8 wickets @ 17.37, ER 7.72.

ADIL RASHID **Yorkshire**

In limited-overs internationals, Rashid's scalpel often worked in tandem with Plunkett's sledgehammer. And his googly was never better employed than during a cheap five-for against Ireland at Bristol. But the selectors dispensed with his services at Test level, instead fast-tracking Mason Crane into the Ashes squad. That felt harsh after Rashid's decent 2016-17 Test winter in Bangladesh and India, but it was not entirely perverse: Root, like Cook before him, evidently had doubts. In February came the sting in the tail, when Rashid announced he would not play red-ball cricket for Yorkshire in 2018.

17 ODIs: 76 runs @ 15.20, SR 135.71; 26 wickets @ 25.84, ER 5.44.
4 T20Is: 1 run @ 1.00, SR 50.00; 4 wickets @ 18.00, ER 8.00.

TOBY ROLAND-JONES **Middlesex**

Making the most of Woakes's absence through injury, Roland-Jones instantly looked at home in the Test arena. He took five for 57 on debut against South Africa at The Oval, and eight in the match, using the skills that had helped Middlesex to the Championship in 2016: a bit of wobble and bounce, plus plenty of heart and guts. It was a shame the question of whether his method might succeed in Australia was never answered: he suffered a stress fracture of his lower back towards the end of the domestic season. But in home conditions he ticked so many boxes.

4 Tests: 82 runs @ 20.50; 17 wickets @ 19.64.
1 ODI: 37 runs without being dismissed, SR 100.00; 1 wicket @ 34.00, ER 4.85.

JOE ROOT **Yorkshire**

For the third year running, despair quickly followed delight: Root would invariably reach a sparkling 50 (at Sydney, he did so for the 18th time in 19 Tests), then invariably get out. It left his conversion-rate in Tests since the start of 2015 floundering at 21%. Since no technical flaw was evident, the problem had to be in his head: he wanted to entertain, but was becoming self-conscious about the stat. The Test captaincy made no difference to his output, and his one-day form was more brilliant than ever. But his Test batting reflected a team who won five and lost five in 2017: scintillating one minute, infuriating the next. His leadership veered from the cavalier (defeat by West Indies in Leeds came after his declaration) to the conservative (in Australia, he went too quickly on the defensive). Mainly, though, he owed his team a few hundreds.

11 Tests: 966 runs @ 50.84; 2 wickets @ 37.50.
19 ODIs: 983 runs @ 70.21, SR 92.12; 5 wickets @ 32.80, ER 5.29.
4 T20Is: 143 runs @ 47.66, SR 102.14; no wicket for 11 runs, ER 5.50.

JASON ROY **Surrey**

In an inversion of the normal narrative, Roy's fortunes unravelled after a stint at the IPL. All but ignored by Gujarat Lions, he came home early – minus the rhythm that had brought him four fifties in five one-day innings in India and the Caribbean. A drought kicked in, extending to 68 runs in nine innings; Bairstow replaced him for the Champions Trophy semi-final. But Hales's late-summer suspension offered Roy a way back, and he took it in style, thrashing 180 runs from 136 balls in the final two ODIs against West Indies – then 180 in one innings against Australia at the MCG in January 2018, to break Hales's England record.

16 ODIs: 533 runs @ 33.31, SR 103.89.
7 T20Is: 164 runs @ 23.42, SR 145.13.

BEN STOKES **Durham**

What might have been the time of his life turned into a disaster, for Stokes himself and cricket in general. It all changed when a video of his part in an early-morning street brawl in Bristol – after a one-day game against West Indies in September – was leaked to *The Sun*, effectively ruling him out of the Ashes. Rumours of a comeback followed him all the way to New Zealand, and a white-ball stint with his native Canterbury. In January, he was charged with affray; in February, he pleaded not guilty. His summer feats became a distant memory, not least a blistering one-day hundred at the Rose Bowl, and a Test hundred at The Oval, both against South Africa. Six for 22 with banana-like swing against West Indies at Lord's kept up the other part of the bargain. Then came Bristol.

7 Tests: 527 runs @ 43.91; 16 wickets @ 31.31.
15 ODIs: 616 runs @ 61.60, SR 106.94; 14 wickets @ 39.42, ER 6.48.
3 T20Is: 46 runs @ 23.00, SR 117.94; 2 wickets @ 45.00, ER 8.18.

MARK STONEMAN **Surrey**

His Ashes petered away, but the jury remained out, which was more than could be said for most of Cook's opening partners in the post-Strauss years. Stoneman kept approaching solidity, only to wobble: five scores between 36 and 56 (the 56 coming after three hours of aerial bombardment at the WACA) suggested something was there, even while something was missing. Bowlers enjoyed his left-handed flirtations with gully, and he occasionally looked strokeless against off-spin. But team-mates valued his north-eastern nous and calm grit. They, as much as anyone, were crossing their fingers.

7 Tests: 328 runs @ 29.81.

JAMES VINCE **Hampshire**

When Vince was recalled for the Ashes after averaging 19 during his first Test stint, in 2016, and 32 in the 2017 County Championship, it was widely assumed he must own compromising photos of the selectors. A high-class 83 in Brisbane implied there was more to it, only for old doubts to resurface as he began edging elegant drives once more. A half-century at Perth nudged the pendulum again, but England needed better than tantalising glimpses from their Test No. 3, and he was fortunate to make the trip to New Zealand.

4 Tests: 199 runs @ 28.42.

TOM WESTLEY **Essex**

Promise quickly gave way to confusion. A half-century on Test debut against South Africa at The Oval encouraged hopes that England had found a No. 3, but analysts noted Westley's tendency – well known on the county circuit – to play round his front pad. He aimed straighter after that, but at the expense of his leg-side game, and looked half the batsman, repeatedly falling lbw. An unbeaten 44 to wrap up the series against West Indies at Lord's could not make up for five successive single-figure dismissals, and he missed the Ashes.

5 Tests: 193 runs @ 24.12; no wicket for 12 runs.

DAVID WILLEY **Yorkshire**

Willey struggled for his place in the seam-bowling pecking order, and it didn't help that his role – to swing the new white ball – felt increasingly niche. England appeared not to trust him when the ball got older, and he never managed more than six overs in an ODI. But his left-arm angle meant he could be a useful part of the armoury.

9 ODIs: 43 runs @ 43.00, SR 82.69; 6 wickets @ 43.33, ER 7.05.
4 T20Is: 2 runs @ 1.00, SR 40.00; 2 wickets @ 61.50, ER 8.78.

CHRIS WOAKES **Warwickshire**

After suffering a side injury at the start of the Champions Trophy in June, Woakes was never quite the same, especially with the red ball. He was rushed back into Test cricket against West Indies in Leeds, then – with the exception of Adelaide under floodlights – he laboured on flatter pitches in Australia, which did nothing to quell doubts about his effectiveness overseas. But his white-ball fortunes proved happier: he boasted the figures of a world-class all-rounder, including an unbeaten 68 in Antigua in March to help England to a 3–0 clean sweep.

5 Tests: 198 runs @ 24.75; 12 wickets @ 51.41.
12 ODIs: 169 runs @ 42.25, SR 101.80; 22 wickets @ 20.63, ER 5.15.

MARK WOOD **Durham**

Two 50-over performances encouraged hopes that, this time, Wood's injury saga was over. After salvaging a one-day international against South Africa at the Rose Bowl with clever death bowling – short rather than full – a cheap four-for set up the Champions Trophy win over Australia at Edgbaston. But, as his pace dropped, two Tests against the South Africans yielded next to nothing; it later emerged he had bruised his left heel by putting the wrong insole in his boot. His season never recovered, and whispers that Wood – a Lions tourist – might ride to England's rescue at Perth in December proved wishful thinking. He did, though, make yet another comeback during the one-day series against Australia at the start of 2018.

2 Tests: 34 runs @ 8.50; 1 wicket @ 197.00.
8 ODIs: 3 runs @ 1.50, SR 50.00; 9 wickets @ 35.33, ER 4.73.
1 T20I: did not bat; 2 wickets @ 18.00, ER 9.00.

AND THE REST...

Gary Ballance (Yorkshire; 2 Tests) owed another surprising recall to the advocacy of his county team-mate Root, struggled for runs and was spared the axe after two Tests by a broken finger. For **Craig Overton** (Somerset; 2 Tests), injury intervened after two gutsy Test appearances at Adelaide and Perth included a big maiden wicket (Steve Smith) and a top-scoring 41 from No. 9. **Tom Curran** (Surrey; 1 Test, 1 ODI, 3 T20Is) was up for the craic on his T20I debut, celebrating each of his three South African wickets at Taunton with gusto. Injuries to others meant a Test debut at the MCG, and – like Overton – a treasured first scalp in Smith. Series figures of 12–21–94–3 for **Tymal Mills** (Sussex; 3 T20Is) in India at the start of 2017, when his slower ball repeatedly foxed M. S. Dhoni, earned him a life-changing IPL contract. **Mason Crane** (Hampshire; 2 T20Is) was tidy on his England debut, a T20 against South Africa in Southampton, then held his nerve in the next game at Cardiff under assault from A. B. de Villiers. His reward was an Ashes tour and a debut at Sydney, where he bowled better than one for 193 suggested. **Liam Livingstone** (Lancashire; 2 T20Is) did not live up to the hype in his two 20-over appearances against South Africa, but was a surprise pick in 2018 for the Test trip to New Zealand.

ENGLAND TEST AVERAGES IN CALENDAR YEAR 2017

BATTING AND FIELDING

		T	*I*	*NO*	*R*	*HS*	*100*	*50*	*Avge*	*SR*	*Ct/St*
1	J. E. Root	11	19	0	966	190	2	8	50.84	61.80	11
2	†A. N. Cook	11	20	1	899	244*	2	2	47.31	49.09	15
3	†B. A. Stokes	7	12	0	527	112	2	4	43.91	63.57	16
4	J. M. Bairstow	11	19	0	652	119	1	3	34.31	59.65	35/2
5	†D. J. Malan	9	15	0	505	140	1	4	33.66	42.83	4
6	†M. D. Stoneman	7	12	1	328	56	0	3	29.81	44.50	0
7	J. M. Vince	4	7	0	199	83	0	2	28.42	47.38	2
8	†M. M. Ali	11	19	1	497	87	0	3	27.61	61.28	7
9	C. R. Woakes	5	9	1	198	61*	0	1	24.75	50.25	0
10	T. Westley	5	9	1	193	59	0	1	24.12	42.60	1
11	†G. S. Ballance	2	4	0	85	34	0	0	21.25	49.70	2
12	C. Overton	2	4	1	62	41*	0	0	20.66	43.97	1
13	T. S. Roland-Jones	4	6	2	82	25	0	0	20.50	69.49	0
14	†K. K. Jennings	4	8	0	127	48	0	0	15.87	38.83	1
15	†S. C. J. Broad	11	17	2	230	57*	0	2	15.33	75.65	4
16	M. A. Wood	2	4	0	34	28	0	0	8.50	58.62	1
17	J. T. Ball	1	2	0	15	14	0	0	7.50	93.75	0
18	†J. M. Anderson	11	16	11	33	12	0	0	6.60	32.03	7
19	L. A. Dawson	2	4	1	18	13	0	0	6.00	42.85	2
20	T. K. Curran	1	1	0	4	4	0	0	4.00	26.66	0

BOWLING

		Style	*O*	*M*	*R*	*W*	*BB*	*5I*	*Avge*	*SR*
1	J. M. Anderson	RFM	426	128	967	55	7-42	4	17.58	46.47
2	T. S. Roland-Jones	RFM	89.2	23	334	17	5-57	1	19.64	31.52
3	B. A. Stokes	RFM	156.3	34	501	16	6-22	1	31.31	58.68
4	M. M. Ali	OB	313.2	53	1,044	33	6-53	2	31.63	56.96
5	L. A. Dawson	SLA	44.4	8	169	5	2-34	0	33.80	53.60
6	S. C. J. Broad	RFM	392.1	112	1,082	30	4-51	0	36.06	78.43
7	J. E. Root	OB	25.3	3	75	2	1-1	0	37.50	76.50
8	C. Overton	RFM	59	4	226	6	3-105	0	37.66	59.00
9	C. R. Woakes	RFM	200.2	38	617	12	4-36	0	51.41	100.16
10	J. T. Ball	RFM	26	4	115	1	1-77	0	115.00	156.00
11	T. K. Curran	RFM	41	11	118	1	1-65	0	118.00	246.00
12	M. A. Wood	RFM	56	13	197	1	1-3	0	197.00	336.00
13	K. K. Jennings	RM	1	0	2	0	0-2	0	–	–
14	T. Westley	OB	4	0	12	0	0-12	0	–	–
15	D. J. Malan	LB	22	3	61	0	0-7	0	–	–

ENGLAND ONE-DAY INTERNATIONAL AVERAGES IN CALENDAR YEAR 2017

BATTING AND FIELDING

		M	*I*	*NO*	*R*	*HS*	*100*	*50*	*Avge*	*SR*	*Ct/St*
1	J. M. Bairstow	10	10	5	534	141*	2	3	106.80	100.18	3
2	J. E. Root	19	18	4	983	133*	2	7	70.21	92.12	9
3	†B. A. Stokes	15	13	3	616	102*	2	4	61.60	106.94	6
4	†E. J. G. Morgan	20	18	1	781	107	3	3	45.94	98.73	3
5	†M. M. Ali	17	12	3	402	102	1	2	44.66	148.88	4
6	†D. J. Willey	9	5	4	43	26	0	0	43.00	82.69	5
7	C. R. Woakes	12	8	4	169	68*	0	1	42.25	101.80	4
8	A. D. Hales	15	15	1	535	110	1	4	38.21	102.49	9
9	J. J. Roy	16	16	0	533	96	0	6	33.31	103.89	6
10	J. C. Buttler	18	14	4	288	65*	0	2	28.80	102.49	26/4
11	S. W. Billings	7	5	0	96	52	0	1	19.20	74.41	9
12	A. U. Rashid	17	6	1	76	39	0	0	15.20	135.71	8
13	L. E. Plunkett	18	6	1	71	26*	0	0	14.20	124.56	7
14	S. T. Finn	4	2	1	5	3	0	0	5.00	71.42	2
15	J. T. Ball	13	3	1	9	7	0	0	4.50	60.00	4
16	M. A. Wood	8	2	0	3	3	0	0	1.50	50.00	2
17	T. S. Roland-Jones	1	1	1	37	37*	0	0	–	100.00	0
18	T. K. Curran	1	–	–	–	–	–	–	–	–	0

BOWLING

		Style	*O*	*M*	*R*	*W*	*BB*	*4I*	*Avge*	*SR*	*ER*
1	C. R. Woakes	RFM	88	8	454	22	4-38	3	20.63	24.00	5.15
2	L. E. Plunkett	RFM	143.5	5	809	36	5-52	4	22.47	23.97	5.62
3	A. U. Rashid	LB	123.2	3	672	26	5-27	2	25.84	28.46	5.44
4	J. E. Root	OB	31	0	164	5	3-52	0	32.80	37.20	5.29
5	T. S. Roland-Jones	RFM	7	2	34	1	1-34	0	34.00	42.00	4.85
6	M. A. Wood	RFM	67.1	3	318	9	4-33	1	35.33	44.77	4.73
7	S. T. Finn	RFM	34	3	157	4	2-35	0	39.25	51.00	4.61
8	B. A. Stokes	RFM	85.1	2	552	14	3-43	0	39.42	36.50	6.48
9	D. J. Willey	LFM	36.5	0	260	6	2-47	0	43.33	36.83	7.05
10	J. T. Ball	RFM	117	5	754	14	3-67	0	53.85	50.14	6.44
11	T. K. Curran	RFM	10	1	62	1	1-62	0	62.00	60.00	6.20
12	M. M. Ali	OB	105.1	2	594	6	2-50	0	99.00	105.16	5.64

ENGLAND TWENTY20 INTERNATIONAL AVERAGES IN CALENDAR YEAR 2017

BATTING AND FIELDING

		M	*I*	*NO*	*R*	*HS*	*50*	*Avge*	*SR*	*4*	*6*	*Ct*
1	†D. J. Malan	1	1	0	78	78	1	78.00	**177.27**	12	2	1
2	A. D. Hales	3	3	1	126	47*	0	63.00	**151.80**	13	5	2
3	J. J. Roy	7	7	0	164	67	1	23.42	**145.13**	17	7	1
4	J. M. Bairstow	3	3	1	134	60*	1	67.00	**144.08**	15	4	0
5	S. W. Billings	6	5	0	49	22	0	9.80	**140.00**	3	3	3
6	L. A. Dawson	3	1	1	7	7*	0	–	**140.00**	1	0	1
7	L. E. Plunkett	5	4	1	18	18	0	6.00	**128.57**	2	0	2
8	†E. J. G. Morgan	6	5	0	116	51	1	23.20	**124.73**	5	7	3
9	J. C. Buttler	7	5	0	86	31	0	17.20	**124.63**	5	3	5
10	†B. A. Stokes	3	3	1	46	38	0	23.00	**117.94**	3	2	1
11	J. E. Root	4	4	1	143	46*	0	47.66	**102.14**	12	2	2
12	L. S. Livingstone	2	2	0	16	16	0	8.00	**84.21**	1	0	0
13	C. J. Jordan	7	4	2	6	6	0	3.00	**60.00**	0	0	2
14	†M. M. Ali	3	2	1	3	2	0	3.00	**60.00**	0	0	0
15	A. U. Rashid	4	2	1	1	1	0	1.00	**50.00**	0	0	3
16	T. K. Curran	3	2	2	2	1*	0	–	**50.00**	0	0	1
17	†D. J. Willey	4	2	0	2	1	0	1.00	**40.00**	0	0	2
18	T. S. Mills	3	1	0	0	0	0	0.00	**0.00**	0	0	0
19	M. S. Crane	2	–	–	–	–	–	–	–	–	–	0
20	M. A. Wood	1	–	–	–	–	–	–	–	–	–	0

BOWLING

		Style	*O*	*Dots*	*R*	*W*	*BB*	*4I*	*Avge*	*SR*	*ER*
1	J. E. Root	OB	2	6	11	0	0-11	0	–	–	**5.50**
2	M. M. Ali	OB	12	23	71	3	2-21	0	23.66	24.00	**5.91**
3	L. A. Dawson	SLA	10	17	75	1	1-38	0	75.00	60.00	**7.50**
4	L. E. Plunkett	RFM	18	39	139	8	3-27	0	17.37	13.50	**7.72**
5	M. S. Crane	LB	8	16	62	1	1-38	0	62.00	48.00	**7.75**
6	T. S. Mills	LF	12	21	94	3	1-27	0	31.33	24.00	**7.83**
7	A. U. Rashid	LB	9	18	72	4	3-25	0	18.00	13.50	**8.00**
8	B. A. Stokes	RFM	11	20	90	2	1-32	0	45.00	33.00	**8.18**
9	T. K. Curran	RFM	12	32	101	6	3-33	0	16.83	12.00	**8.41**
10	D. J. Willey	LFM	14	33	123	2	1-29	0	61.50	42.00	**8.78**
11	C. J. Jordan	RFM	28	58	251	10	3-22	0	25.10	16.80	**8.96**
12	M. A. Wood	RFM	4	10	36	2	2-36	0	18.00	12.00	**9.00**

Former England player P. D. Collingwood appeared in one Twenty20 international for the World XI v Pakistan. He did not bat, but bowled 2–2–18–0 and took one catch.

WEST INDIES v ENGLAND IN 2016-17

GEORGE DOBELL

One-day internationals (3): West Indies 0, England 3

If the new West Indies management team were in any doubt about the problems they had inherited, this series would have made things clear. The final game of an underwhelming three-match rubber confirmed a depressing double whammy: their largest defeat by runs in a home one-day international, and their first whitewash by England in the Caribbean. To witness their slide to 45 for six at the Kensington Oval in Barbados, a fortress for so long, was to see a former star reduced to busking outside the theatre. Johnny Grave (WICB chief executive), Jimmy Adams (director of cricket) and Stuart Law (coach) could be forgiven for swallowing hard and wondering if they had made a mistake.

Hampered by an unrealistic selection policy which decreed that players choosing foreign Twenty20 leagues over regional events could not be considered, West Indies put out a second-string team low on experience and box-office allure. Of the side that had so memorably beaten England in the final of the World Twenty20 in Kolkata a year earlier, only Carlos Brathwaite – their hero that night – remained. In the first match, England's captain Eoin Morgan had more one-day caps than the entire West Indies team put together.

But the problems ran deeper. Facilities were poor: the practice area in St Kitts was borderline dangerous, and one member of the England management privately declared the nets in Barbados "the worst in the world". That Rahkeem Cornwall, talented but vastly overweight, came close to selection illustrated how far standards had slipped. Ticket prices aimed at the travelling audience ($US75 and up) further alienated home supporters: for West Indies, all three matches felt like away games.

That is not to detract from England's performances, for they were not at full strength either. They were without injured seamers Mark Wood, David Willey and Reece Topley, while opener Alex Hales joined the squad late after recovering from a broken hand. Tom Curran was also called up, after Jake Ball hurt his knee during the warm-up games. Even Paul Farbrace, the assistant coach, was deputising for the resting Trevor Bayliss.

Arriving with a reputation for relentless aggression, England had the nous to adapt to conditions and judge competitive totals on mediocre surfaces that either started damp or offered variable bounce, and were always two-paced. Morgan, Joe Root (twice) and Hales all showed the temperament to build old-fashioned innings – accumulation followed by acceleration. They also showed resolve and belief in turning an almost hopeless position in the second game in Antigua into a memorable victory. The depth of their batting, epitomised in that match by Chris Woakes, made them tough to kill off.

Throughout, England were helped by West Indies' failure to accept chances in the field, with Morgan and Root benefiting from reprieves early in their match-defining innings. West Indies also won every toss – disproportionately important given the early dampness – but in all three were bowled out inside 50 overs, often falling to outfield catches as they struggled against England's disciplined seamers.

There were some positives for the hosts. For much of the series, their spinners – Ashley Nurse, in particular – outbowled England's, while Jonathan Carter and Jason Mohammed both had encouraging moments with the bat. Shannon Gabriel looked a much-improved pace bowler – his side strain in the second game was a hammer blow to West Indies' hopes – and the young Antiguan Alzarri Joseph caught the eye in Barbados. But England's quicker bowlers, led by the impressive Liam Plunkett (the leading wicket-taker on either side, with ten) and the faultless Woakes, had too much pace, control and skill for a batting line-up in which only Carter and Mohammed totalled more than 63 runs.

It all left West Indies no further forward. Having already failed to reach the Champions Trophy – only the top eight in the rankings made the cut, and they had slipped to ninth – they needed to break back into the top eight by September 30 to avoid going through further qualification games for the 2019 World Cup. England, meanwhile, tested their bench strength and built confidence going into the summer. They knew the opposition would be significantly tougher.

ENGLAND TOURING PARTY

*E. J. G. Morgan (Middlesex), M. M. Ali (Worcestershire), J. M. Bairstow (Yorkshire), J. T. Ball (Nottinghamshire), S. W. Billings (Kent), J. C. Buttler (Lancashire), T. K. Curran (Surrey), L. A. Dawson (Hampshire), S. T. Finn (Middlesex), A. D. Hales (Nottinghamshire), L. E. Plunkett (Yorkshire), A. U. Rashid (Yorkshire), J. E. Root (Yorkshire), J. J. Roy (Surrey), B. A. Stokes (Durham), C. R. Woakes (Warwickshire).

D. J. Willey (Yorkshire) was originally selected, but underwent shoulder surgery and was replaced by Finn. Hales arrived late after recovering from a hand injury. Curran was summoned from the England Lions tour of Sri Lanka after Ball hurt his knee.

Coach: P. Farbrace. *Batting coach:* G. P. Thorpe. *Fast-bowling coach:* O. D. Gibson. *Fielding coach:* P. D. Collingwood. *Operations manager:* A. W. Bentley. *Doctor:* M. G. Wotherspoon. *Physiotherapist:* B. T. Langley. *Masseur:* M. E. S. Saxby. *Strength and conditioning coach:* P. T. Atkinson. *Performance psychologist:* D. J. Young. *Analyst:* G. O. N. Lindsay. *Security manager:* J. A. Shaw. *Head of team communications:* D. M. Reuben.

At Basseterre, St Kitts, February 25, 2017. **England XI won by 117 runs. England XI 379-8** (50 overs) (J. J. Roy 79, J. E. Root 71, E. J. G. Morgan 95, B. A. Stokes 61; J. J. Levy 4-100); **‡University of West Indies Vice-Chancellor's XI 262** (39.5 overs) (C. A. K. Walton 121). *Jason Roy provided a turbocharged start with 79 from 43 balls, before Joe Root and Eoin Morgan added 126. At 239-2 after 30 overs, an eye-watering total looked on the cards. Root went next over as the pace dropped slightly, but Ben Stokes took up the cudgels, and the final score was still an imposing one; in all, England's batsmen hit 18 sixes. Jamaican opening bowler Jermaine Levy leaked 100 runs, though claimed four wickets. Steven Finn grabbed two in the second over of the reply, but the opener and captain Chadwick Walton carved seven sixes of his own – and 12 fours – as he steamed to 121. Stokes's first over cost 23, most of them as Shimron Hetmyer raced to 40, but regular wickets ensured the hosts fell a long way short.*

At Basseterre, St Kitts, February 27, 2017. **England XI won by two wickets. ‡WICB President's XI 233** (48 overs) (J. N. Hamilton 73, R. R. S. Cornwall 59; L. E. Plunkett 3-44, B. A. Stokes 3-35); **England XI 234-8** (48.5 overs) (J. M. Bairstow 86). *When the President's XI declined to 55-5, the tourists sniffed a quick kill – only for skipper Jahmar Hamilton and the giant all-rounder Rahkeem Cornwall to add 123. England started well, a stand of 117 between Jonny Bairstow (dropped at slip* *by Cornwall when 46) and Root (46) taking them to 128-1 in the 26th over. But Cornwall kept things quiet, with 1-39; England subsided to 177-7, before Chris Woakes (47*) guided them home. Jake Ball had limped off with a knee problem after 13 deliveries, and played no further part in the tour.*

WEST INDIES v ENGLAND

First One-Day International

At North Sound, Antigua, March 3, 2017. England won by 45 runs. Toss: West Indies.

An intelligent century from Morgan proved the difference after England were put in on a surface that started damp following a half-hour rain delay. Two wickets fell in the first eight overs, and Morgan – dropped on four in the slips by Kieran Powell, in his first one-day international for three years after briefly flirting with baseball – needed 33 balls to make double figures. But, recognising this was not a pitch for all-out aggression (a sluggish outfield didn't help), he tempered his instincts to ensure a total well above par. Even so, it was the first time in seven games that England had failed to reach 300 batting first. Supported by Billings and Stokes, Morgan brushed off a stumping chance on 69 to accelerate masterfully: in all, 100 runs were plundered from the final ten overs, with Stokes striking three sixes in 12 balls. Morgan's century was his tenth in ODIs (including one for Ireland) and his fifth as captain (an England record, surpassing Andrew Strauss and Alastair Cook). Stokes's 55 was his sixth score above 50 in nine one-day innings. In reply, Mohammed and Carter added 82 for the fifth wicket after the early loss of three for three in 15 balls. But Woakes and Plunkett picked up four apiece as reward for their variation and control, and West Indies were never a serious threat. When Carter was brilliantly caught by Roy, charging in from deep midwicket, and Mohammed run out by some fancy footwork from Finn, playing his first ODI since September 2015, an England victory was assured. Stokes, the IPL's most recent millionaire, wasn't even required to bowl.

Man of the Match: E. J. G. Morgan.

England

J. J. Roy lbw b Gabriel	13	C. R. Woakes not out	0
S. W. Billings c C. R. Brathwaite b Nurse	52		
J. E. Root b Gabriel	4	Lb 7, w 12, nb 1	20
*E. J. G. Morgan run out	107		
†J. C. Buttler c Carter b Nurse	14	1/23 (1) 2/29 (3) (6 wkts, 50 overs)	296
B. A. Stokes c Holder b Bishoo	55	3/96 (2) 4/129 (5)	
M. M. Ali not out	31	5/239 (6) 6/292 (4)	10 overs: 38-2

A. U. Rashid, L. E. Plunkett and S. T. Finn did not bat.

Holder 9–1–46–0; Gabriel 10–0–58–2; C. R. Brathwaite 10–1–54–0; Nurse 10–0–57–2; Bishoo 6–0–49–1; Mohammed 5–0–25–0.

West Indies

K. C. Brathwaite c Rashid b Woakes	14	D. Bishoo not out	12
E. Lewis c Billings b Woakes	21	S. T. Gabriel c Buttler b Plunkett	0
K. O. A. Powell c Roy b Plunkett	1		
†S. D. Hope c Finn b Rashid	31	Lb 4, w 7	11
J. N. Mohammed run out	72		
J. L. Carter c Roy b Plunkett	52	1/36 (2) 2/37 (3) 3/39 (1) (47.2 overs)	251
*J. O. Holder c Buttler b Plunkett	4	4/108 (4) 5/190 (6) 6/201 (7)	
C. R. Brathwaite c Root b Woakes	12	7/210 (5) 8/224 (8) 9/250 (9)	
A. R. Nurse lbw b Woakes	21	10/251 (11)	10 overs: 37-1

Finn 9–0–49–0; Woakes 9–1–47–4; Root 5–0–31–0; Plunkett 8.2–1–40–4; Ali 7–0–37–0; Rashid 9–1–43–1.

Umpires: G. O. Brathwaite and R. S. A. Palliyaguruge. Third umpire: C. B. Gaffaney.
Referee: J. J. Crowe.

WEST INDIES v ENGLAND

Second One-Day International

At North Sound, Antigua, March 5, 2017. England won by four wickets. Toss: West Indies.

A measured unbroken partnership of 102 between Root and Woakes rescued England, and secured the series. When they lost five for 37 against West Indies' spinners, Bishoo and Nurse, they were reeling at 124 for six. But, on another two-paced surface, Root produced a perfectly judged innings containing only three boundaries, while Woakes took a more aggressive approach. England were able to capitalise on a side strain suffered after only three overs by Gabriel, who had removed Billings for a first-ball duck. Carlos Brathwaite proved especially costly, and England got home with ten balls to spare. Roy had given their chase a bright start. He survived a strong appeal for caught behind off Holder on one – Ultra-Edge was not in use because no one could agree who would pay for it – and went on to a 45-ball half-century. It ensured Root and Woakes could take their time as they compiled a seventh-wicket record stand for England against West Indies. But for the second game running the hosts were guilty of spurning chances: Root was missed on 51, Woakes on 42 and 58. Earlier, Mohammed had top-scored again as West Indies failed to adjust to the caprice of the pitch. Plunkett was impressive once more, while Finn became the tenth England bowler to reach 100 one-day international wickets, when he removed Powell.

Man of the Match: J. E. Root.

West Indies

K. C. Brathwaite st Buttler b Ali	42
E. Lewis c Billings b Finn	8
K. O. A. Powell c and b Finn	9
†S. D. Hope c Buttler b Stokes	16
J. N. Mohammed c Rashid b Plunkett	50
J. L. Carter c Rashid b Plunkett	39
*J. O. Holder c and b Rashid	15
C. R. Brathwaite c Billings b Rashid	23
A. R. Nurse b Plunkett	13
D. Bishoo not out	0
S. T. Gabriel run out	1
B 1, lb 2, w 6	9
1/11 (2) 2/21 (3) 3/46 (4) 4/118 (1) 5/159 (5) 6/173 (6) 7/199 (7) 8/219 (8) 9/224 (9) 10/225 (11) (47.5 overs)	225
10 overs: 35-2	

Finn 8–1–38–2; Woakes 8–1–26–0; Plunkett 7.5–1–32–3; Stokes 5–0–29–1; Rashid 9–0–53–2; Ali 10–0–44–1.

England

J. J. Roy c C. R. Brathwaite b Nurse	52
S. W. Billings c Powell b Gabriel	0
J. E. Root not out	90
*E. J. G. Morgan lbw b Nurse	7
B. A. Stokes c Hope b Bishoo	1
†J. C. Buttler c Hope b Bishoo	0
M. M. Ali b Nurse	3
C. R. Woakes not out	68
Lb 1, w 4	5
1/1 (2) 2/87 (1) 3/108 (4) 4/113 (5) 5/117 (6) 6/124 (7) (6 wkts, 48.2 overs)	226
10 overs: 69-1	

A. U. Rashid, L. E. Plunkett and S. T. Finn did not bat.

Gabriel 3–0–17–1; Holder 10–0–46–0; C. R. Brathwaite 4–0–38–0; Bishoo 10–0–43–2; Nurse 10–0–34–3; Mohammed 4–0–15–0; K. C. Brathwaite 5.2–0–22–0; Carter 2–0–10–0.

Umpires: N. Duguid and C. B. Gaffaney. Third umpire: R. S. A. Palliyaguruge.
Referee: J. J. Crowe.

WEST INDIES v ENGLAND

Third One-Day International

At Bridgetown, Barbados, March 9, 2017. England won by 186 runs. Toss: West Indies.

Centuries from Hales and Root helped England to a 3–0 whitewash, their first in the Caribbean in any format. It was West Indies' heaviest home defeat, surpassing their 169-run thumping by Australia in St Kitts in 2008. Hales, fit again after injuring his hand, replaced Sam Billings for only his third

ENGLAND'S BIGGEST ODI WINS BY RUNS

Margin	*Total (overs)*		
210	408-9 (50)	v New Zealand (198) at Birmingham.	2015
202	334-4 (60)	v India (132-3) at Lord's	1975
198	363-7 (55)	v Pakistan (165) at Nottingham	1992
196	290-5 (60)	v East Africa (94) at Birmingham	1975
186	**328 (50)**	**v West Indies (142) at Bridgetown**	**2016-17**
169	444-3 (50)	v Pakistan (275) at Nottingham	2016
168	391-4 (50)	v Bangladesh (223) at Nottingham	2005
161	263-6 (50)	v Zimbabwe (102) at Harare	2004-05
152	299-7 (50)	v Zimbabwe (147) at Birmingham.	2004
144	347-7 (50)	v Bangladesh (203) at Birmingham	2010

international appearance of the winter, and responded with his fifth one-day century in 19 innings. After taking his time, he attacked West Indies' spinners brutally, hitting Bishoo for 22 in six balls, and out of the attack. Root, meanwhile, recorded his ninth ODI century; for England, only Marcus Trescothick (12) had scored more. He was dropped on one and 12, and took 17 balls over his first three runs, but – as conditions eased and the ball softened – ended up adding 192 in 30 overs with Hales, a second-wicket record between these sides. Though England fell away, losing nine for 109, it soon became apparent they had more than enough. Plunkett claimed three for five from a five-over opening spell, and Woakes produced another immaculate performance to help reduce West Indies to 45 for six, amid a string of weak leg-side flaps. To sweeten England's day, Stokes trapped Carlos Braithwaite with his first delivery to him since the climax of the World Twenty20 final almost a year earlier.

Man of the Match: A. D. Hales. *Man of the Series:* C. R. Woakes.

England

J. J. Roy c Holder b Joseph 17
A. D. Hales c Nurse b Joseph 110
J. E. Root c C. R. Brathwaite b Joseph 101
†J. C. Buttler b Holder. 7
*E. J. G. Morgan b Nurse 11
B. A. Stokes c K. C. Brathwaite b Holder. . 34
M. M. Ali c and b Joseph 0
C. R. Woakes c Bishoo b Holder. 13
L. E. Plunkett run out 11
A. U. Rashid run out 9
S. T. Finn not out. 2

B 1, lb 3, w 8, nb 1 13

1/27 (1) 2/219 (2) 3/232 (4) (50 overs) 328
4/249 (5) 5/263 (3) 6/264 (7)
7/304 (8) 8/304 (6) 9/317 (10)
10/328 (9) 10 overs: 39-1

Holder 10–1–41–3; Joseph 10–0–76–4; Bishoo 5–0–44–0; C. R. Brathwaite 10–0–56–0; Nurse 8–0–57–1; Carter 4–0–28–0; K. C. Brathwaite 3–0–22–0.

West Indies

K. O. A. Powell c Hales b Finn. 6
E. Lewis c and b Woakes 0
K. C. Brathwaite c Hales b Woakes 5
†S. D. Hope c Root b Plunkett 16
J. N. Mohammed b Plunkett 10
J. L. Carter c Stokes b Finn. 46
*J. O. Holder c Buttler b Plunkett 0
C. R. Brathwaite lbw b Stokes. 7
A. R. Nurse c Plunkett b Woakes 6
D. Bishoo c Roy b Rashid. 10
A. S. Joseph not out. 22

B 4, lb 1, w 9. 14

1/7 (1) 2/8 (2) 3/13 (3) (39.2 overs) 142
4/32 (5) 5/45 (4) 6/45 (7)
7/75 (8) 8/87 (9) 9/113 (6)
10/142 (10) 10 overs: 27-3

Finn 10–1–35–2; Woakes 8–1–16–3; Stokes 7–2–27–1; Plunkett 8–2–27–3; Ali 5–0–27–0; Rashid 1.2–0–5–1.

Umpires: G. O. Brathwaite and R. S. A. Palliyaguruge. Third umpire: C. B. Gaffaney.
Referee: J. J. Crowe.

ENGLAND v IRELAND IN 2017

TOM COLLOMOSSE

One-day internationals (2): England 2, Ireland 0

"I don't think so," said England's Dublin-born captain Eoin Morgan when asked if Ireland's first one-day international in England was a significant moment in his career. It was typical Morgan, thinking never of the past, only of the next challenge. And this was the start of what he hoped would be ten ODIs in 45 days, culminating – if everything went to plan – with the final of the Champions Trophy on June 18.

Ireland also had one eye on the future. For many years they had aspired to Test status; following an ICC board meeting in June they got it. In the meantime, a repetition of their shock World Cup win over England at Bangalore in 2011 would do them no harm, and in early-season conditions – with Ben Stokes, Jos Buttler and Chris Woakes all at the IPL – the Irish might have sensed an opportunity. But there was to be no repeat. At Bristol, England wrapped up a seven-wicket win before the scheduled interval, as seven Ireland batsmen fell to the spin of Adil Rashid and Joe Root. Then, in Ireland's first official one-day international at Lord's (they had first played MCC there in 1858, and a World Twenty20 game in 2009), the result was closer, but never in doubt.

While England had clearly moved on from Bangalore, Ireland seemed stuck in the past. Seven of their players on show that evening played in this series, whereas England fielded an entirely new XI. The performance of Kevin O'Brien, in particular, did little to quell the suspicion that Ireland had stood still. Having smashed a 50-ball century six years earlier, he fell this time for four and 18.

IRELAND TOURING PARTY

*W. T. S. Porterfield, A. Balbirnie, P. K. D. Chase, G. H. Dockrell, E. C. Joyce, A. R. McBrine, B. J. McCarthy, T. J. Murtagh, K. J. O'Brien, N. J. O'Brien, P. R. Stirling, S. R. Thompson, G. C. Wilson, C. A. Young. *Coach:* J. G. Bracewell.

ENGLAND v IRELAND

First One-Day International

At Bristol, May 5. England won by seven wickets. Toss: Ireland.

Early May is rarely a time to excite spinners but, in England's first match of the summer, Rashid defied the trend. Against an Ireland batting line-up unable to read his googly, he took five for 27, the second-best one-day figures for an England slow bowler. Rashid's success justified the decision to choose him ahead of Moeen Ali, and with Root's off-breaks collecting two for nine, Ireland were hustled out for 126 in 33 overs. Their last eight wickets fell for just 45. England were also encouraged by the form of Wood, who was back after a third ankle operation, and showed venom to bowl the dangerous Stirling. Roy fell to Chase for a five-ball duck at the start of England's reply, and Hales rode his luck en route to a 39-ball 55 containing ten fours, but Root looked in total command. Chase

BEST ODI FIGURES BY AN ENGLAND SPINNER

5-20	V. J. Marks (OB)	v New Zealand at Wellington	1983-84
5-27	**A. U. Rashid (LB)**	**v Ireland at Bristol**	**2017**
5-28	G. P. Swann (OB)	v Australia at Chester-le-Street	2009
5-33	G. A. Hick (OB)	v Zimbabwe at Harare	1999-2000
5-39	V. J. Marks (OB)	v Sri Lanka at Taunton	1983
5-41	S. R. Patel (SLA)	v South Africa at The Oval	2008
5-57	A. F. Giles (SLA)	v India at Delhi	2001-02

had the consolation of career-best figures, but victory came with 30 overs to spare, at 2.45pm, after England had been granted four overs' extra time to complete the job before the break. Embarrassed, Ireland knew they needed to do better at Lord's.

Man of the Match: A. U. Rashid. *Attendance:* 6,411.

Ireland

E. C. Joyce lbw b Willey	23
P. R. Stirling b Wood	20
*W. T. S. Porterfield c Plunkett b Root	13
A. Balbirnie c Billings b Ball	30
†N. J. O'Brien lbw b Rashid	16
G. C. Wilson lbw b Rashid	1
K. J. O'Brien lbw b Rashid	4
S. R. Thompson b Rashid	4
G. H. Dockrell lbw b Root	0
T. J. Murtagh c Hales b Rashid	11
P. K. D. Chase not out	1
Lb 2, w 1	3
1/40 (2) 2/46 (1) 3/81 (4) 4/90 (3) 5/93 (6) 6/104 (7) 7/108 (8) 8/109 (9) 9/121 (5) 10/126 (10) — (33 overs)	126
10 overs: 50-2	

Willey 6–0–34–1; Wood 6–0–24–1; Ball 5–0–16–1; Plunkett 3–0–14–0; Rashid 8–0–27–5; Root 5–0–9–2.

England

J. J. Roy c Dockrell b Chase	0
A. D. Hales c Porterfield b Chase	55
J. E. Root not out	49
*E. J. G. Morgan c K. J. O'Brien b Chase	10
J. M. Bairstow not out	10
Nb 3	3
1/1 (1) 2/78 (2) 3/99 (4) — (3 wkts, 20 overs)	127
10 overs: 69-1	

†S. W. Billings, A. U. Rashid, D. J. Willey, L. E. Plunkett, J. T. Ball and M. A. Wood did not bat.

Chase 8–0–44–3; Murtagh 6–1–33–0; Dockrell 3–0–20–0; Thompson 3–0–30–0.

Umpires: Aleem Dar and R. J. Bailey. Third umpire: P. R. Reiffel.
Referee: R. S. Madugalle.

ENGLAND v IRELAND

Second One-Day International

At Lord's, May 7. England won by 85 runs. Toss: Ireland.

It was hard not to feel sorry for Bairstow – England's fulcrum here, yet for the time being destined to get a game only when others were absent. Soon after he arrived at the crease, England – following seventies from Root and Morgan – were 229 for five with 49 balls to go, and Ireland looking far more accomplished than they had in Bristol. A total of 300 seemed remote. But against a useful attack led by Middlesex's Murtagh on his home ground, Bairstow counter-punched, striking seven fours and three sixes, to finish with 72 not out from 44 deliveries, including 26 from his final seven. With Rashid hitting 39 from 25, England rattled up 328, the total Ireland had chased to win at Bangalore in 2011. Stirling made a rapid 48 from 42 balls, and Porterfield – who had been all at sea two days earlier – a forthright 82. But Plunkett and Root, getting through ten overs in a one-day international for the first time on his way to career-best figures, picked up three apiece; England were always in control. With their IPL contingent returning for the three-match series against South Africa, however, Bairstow knew he had done no more than keep a seat warm.

Man of the Match: J. E. Root. *Attendance:* 24,356.

England

J. J. Roy c Stirling b McCarthy	20	D. J. Willey not out	1
A. D. Hales b Murtagh	32		
J. E. Root c Balbirnie b Chase	73	Lb 4, w 4	8
*E. J. G. Morgan c Joyce b McCarthy	76		
J. M. Bairstow not out	72	1/49 (2) 2/60 (1) (6 wkts, 50 overs)	328
†S. W. Billings c K. J. O'Brien b Dockrell	7	3/200 (3) 4/213 (4)	
A. U. Rashid c N. J. O'Brien b Chase	39	5/229 (6) 6/317 (7)	10 overs: 45-0

L. E. Plunkett, J. T. Ball and M. A. Wood did not bat.

Murtagh 10–0–50–1; Chase 10–0–69–2; K. J. O'Brien 9–0–71–0; McCarthy 10–0–61–2; Dockrell 8–0–52–1; Stirling 3–0–21–0.

Ireland

E. C. Joyce b Root	16	T. J. Murtagh c Ball b Plunkett	2
P. R. Stirling c Billings b Ball	48	P. K. D. Chase not out	6
*W. T. S. Porterfield b Wood	82		
A. Balbirnie lbw b Plunkett	2	Lb 1, w 10	11
†N. J. O'Brien c Willey b Root	15		
G. C. Wilson c Hales b Root	13	1/68 (2) 2/77 (1) 3/87 (4) (46.1 overs)	243
K. J. O'Brien c Ball b Rashid	18	4/113 (5) 5/154 (6) 6/178 (7)	
G. H. Dockrell b Wood	28	7/223 (3) 8/226 (9) 9/231 (10)	
B. J. McCarthy c Ball b Plunkett	2	10/243 (8)	10 overs: 59-0

Wood 8.1–0–38–2; Willey 3–0–23–0; Ball 7–0–38–1; Plunkett 8–0–23–3; Root 10–0–52–3; Rashid 10–0–68–1.

Umpires: P. R. Reiffel and R. T. Robinson. Third umpire: Aleem Dar.
Referee: R. S. Madugalle.

ICC CHAMPIONS TROPHY IN 2017

REVIEW BY LAWRENCE BOOTH

1 Pakistan 2 India 3= Bangladesh, England

A few days into the tournament, it emerged that the Pakistan team were being driven around in a bus made notorious by the previous summer's Brexit campaign. Its giant message, pledging to divert £350m a week from the EU to the NHS, had gone. But the bus carried another notion, apparently just as spurious: the cricketers within were planning to lift the Champions Trophy.

The opening skirmishes had not gone well. Pakistan had been thrashed by India at Edgbaston, looking every inch the competition's bottom-ranked side (they had scraped in ahead of West Indies). And in the tetchy press conference that followed, their coach Mickey Arthur had to fend off suggestions his team were not even trying. Students of Pakistani ebb and flow wondered if this could mean only one thing.

And so, as sure as Eid follows Ramadan, Pakistan set about one of the most stunning transformations since Imran Khan's cornered tigers won the World Cup 25 years earlier. A fortnight after that initial defeat, they were thrashing India, this time in the final. Against the odds, they had provided a competition that had been overshadowed by a general election and terrorist attacks with a punchline to savour. For the second summer in a row, their players cavorted around The Oval. Only partisan Indian fans failed to see the joy in it all.

Pakistan's revival centred on their fast bowling, so often their trump card. After conceding 319 for three in 48 overs during that early mauling by India, they limited South Africa to 219 for eight, Sri Lanka to 236 and – in a semi-final which demanded the world take them seriously – England for 211. Hasan Ali finished with 13 wickets (four more than anyone else), found reverse swing in a tournament notable for an absence of lateral movement, and celebrated with a star-shaped vigour that felt like an heirloom from Shahid Afridi. But the most visceral spell came from Mohammad Amir, whose first five overs in the final took care of Rohit Sharma, Virat Kohli and Shikhar Dhawan. Of the 900 runs those three totalled across five matches, only 26 came on that hazy day in south London. Junaid Khan, Amir's fellow left-arm quick, completed an irresistible trio.

Then there was Fakhar Zaman, 27 and uncapped in the format. He had seemed destined to be known for two things: a stint in the navy, and an unrewarded List A average above 50. But, asked to open in Pakistan's second game, against South Africa, he provided their batting with an adrenaline rush, flailing 31 off 23 balls. Left-handed, fearless and determined to enjoy every minute, he was the Champions Trophy's rabbit from the hat. Next came 50 off 36 deliveries against Sri Lanka, then 57 off 58 against England. In the final, having spent the previous day throwing up, he was caught behind off a Jasprit Bumrah no-ball on three, and went on to 114. Above all, Fakhar allowed steadier colleagues to bat around him. Pakistan's 338 for four that day was the

Many happy returns: Pakistan's victory in the Champions Trophy did not go unnoticed at home, as Sarfraz Ahmed discovers in the streets of Karachi.

tournament's highest total, and ended a sequence of eight games won by the team batting second. It was all so gloriously unexpected, and Arthur could hardly believe his luck. "I've had five semi-finals with South Africa and never got to a final," he chuckled. "Now one final with Pakistan and I've got a medal!"

The progress of Pakistan was not without controversy – especially if you supported **England**. Eoin Morgan's men had emerged from the group stage as the only unbeaten side, confirming their status as favourites with dissections of Bangladesh, New Zealand and Australia. But in the semi-final at Cardiff they encountered their worst nightmare: a worn pitch, used two days earlier for Pakistan's nip-and-tuck win over Sri Lanka, which pivoted on a dreadful drop by Tissara Perera. Batting first, England were spooked; having just blitzed a century against Australia, Ben Stokes prodded 34 off 64 deliveries. The run-a-ball mayhem that had underpinned their renaissance gave way to old-style timidity. Morgan stayed *just* the right side of a whinge, conceding that Pakistan had been the better side, but implying the scheduling had done England no favours. It was odd that they might have had a better chance of reaching the final had they finished second in their group, which would have meant a semi against India on a true surface at Edgbaston. Quite why a major tournament could not produce a fresh pitch for a crucial game was never adequately answered.

England had been the team to beat, despite losing Chris Woakes to a side strain only three overs into the curtain-raiser against Bangladesh. Joe Root's unbeaten 133 turned a chase of 306 into a stroll, and their new-found ability to take wickets in the middle overs – led by Mark Wood and Liam Plunkett, both making liberal use of cross-seam deliveries – meant they were always in the hunt. When they eliminated Australia at Edgbaston, the force seemed with them.

Meanwhile, **India** elbowed their way through. Background tension between captain Kohli and coach Anil Kumble might have derailed lesser sides, but Kohli had the chutzpah to deny the rumours – even if Kumble's resignation two days after the final suggested otherwise – and the players to shrug off the distraction. A surprising defeat by Sri Lanka at The Oval aside, his team looked in good shape to defend their title. Their batting was as Rolls-Royce as ever, even if the success of their top three limited the opportunities of others until the final. But their seam bowling was not far behind, with Bumrah a closing-overs operator par excellence. It felt unjust that his no-ball to Fakhar should have such damaging consequences. Traffic police in Jaipur used a huge side-on image of his transgression to warn drivers: "Don't cross the line. You know it can be costly."

India's passage to the final highlighted both the good and the not-so-good in the tournament's structure. They had reached the semis after winning a group-stage match against South Africa that became sudden death. Since 15 games were scheduled across 18 days, every one counted, and not until New Zealand lost to Bangladesh in the ninth was a team knocked out – a welcome counterpoint to recently bloated World Cups. Yet **Bangladesh**, India's opponents in the last four, had got there thanks to a solitary partnership, between Shakib Al Hasan and Mahmudullah, against New Zealand at Cardiff. The result confirmed Bangladesh were no longer pushovers away from home, but they also knew that, if rain had held off for four more overs against Australia at The Oval, they would already have been out. Tamim Iqbal finished with more runs than anyone bar India's openers but, predictably, the semi-final was a walkover.

Partly because of the weather, **Australia** cut peripheral figures in a competition that took place – as far as their fans at home were concerned – in the middle of the night. If they were unlucky against Bangladesh, the weather had already saved them from probable defeat by New Zealand. Then, presented with the chance to beat England and qualify for the last four, they were swept away by Morgan and Stokes. All the while, captain Steve Smith fielded questions about his players' contractual dispute with the board. For him and his side, it was a tournament to forget.

South Africa, too, ended with little to cherish, and failure came with a familiar kick. Victory over Sri Lanka and a rain-affected defeat by Pakistan had paved the way for a scenario they had hoped to avoid for one more game: a winner-takes-all clash, against India at The Oval. From 140 for two, the South Africans endured a pair of tragicomic run-outs, a collapse – and renewed claims of choking. It was a fair cop, and the post-match insistence of A. B. de Villiers that he remained the man to lead them at the 2019 World Cup sounded faintly deluded.

New Zealand were too reliant on the batting of their captain, Kane Williamson, angelic at the crease and stoic at the mike. He started with a hundred against Australia, but his dismissal in a tough chase against England

Philip Brown, Getty Images

Ups and downs: Ben Stokes was imperious against Australia, imperfect against Pakistan.

signalled the beginning of the end of his side's hopes, and his run-out against Bangladesh encapsulated perhaps his only weakness. Ultimately, the all-rounders who clogged up his team brought to mind the old gag about the former New Zealand seamer Bob Cunis – neither one thing nor the other.

Sri Lanka failed to translate their heady pursuit of 322 against India into a place in the last four. Had Perera caught Pakistan captain Sarfraz Ahmed to end an ultimately match-winning eighth-wicket stand, they would probably have qualified. Graham Ford soon stepped down as coach amid the usual rumours about government interference in selection. And not long after that, following a one-day series defeat at home by Zimbabwe, captain Angelo Mathews followed. Sri Lanka's was not a happy camp.

Yet their fans played their part in an event that underlined why England and to a lesser extent Wales – give or take the odd downpour – were the ideal venues for a global tournament. If some wondered reasonably enough why none of the three grounds was further north than Birmingham, especially when Cardiff failed to sell out its three group matches, then the UK's South Asian diaspora were never less than uplifting. It didn't matter, as it would in almost every other cricket-playing nation, that the hosts played in barely a quarter of the matches. The most vibrant atmospheres came at games involving the four subcontinental teams – proof of the ECB's belated realisation that the future of English cricket will rest largely on Britain's Asian communities. The ICC, as tournament organisers, were alive to the dynamic: two group games – Australia v Bangladesh and Pakistan v South Africa – were day/night affairs, aimed at encouraging Muslim fans to break their Ramadan fast at the cricket after the sun went down. Frustratingly, both were hit by rain.

THE CHAMPIONS TROPHY FINAL

Turning the tables

KAMILA SHAMSIE

I entered The Oval steeling myself for a day on which, as a Pakistan supporter, I would be outnumbered, outvoiced, outplayed. The blue of the Indian team was everywhere, the Pakistani green an occasional interruption. And so, to start with, I was looking for consolations. There was the weather – the sky cloudless, the sun hot. There was the good feeling among the spectators, who stood for each other's national anthem. There was the fact that Pakistan were in the final at all.

Then came the fourth over, and Fakhar Zaman was caught behind. Indian flags flew, blue shirts danced. But the voice in my ear – *TMS* – told me, no, it was a no-ball. I wanted to jump up and cheer, but I'd look as though I were joining the Indian celebrations, so I yelled to my sister: "He's not out!" She stared at me like I might be hallucinating. Then the news spread: the blues slumped, the greens yelped, and suddenly our numbers didn't seem so insignificant. So it went through the morning – the noise from the Pakistan fans growing louder, the jubilation at each boundary more exuberant.

Even so, and despite Fakhar's century, there was still that thought in everyone's head that said with the Pakistan batting line-up you could never rule out a collapse, and with the Indian batting line-up you could never rule out a successful run-chase. When the fourth wicket fell at 267 with seven and a half overs to go, the set of our collective shoulders sagged. That's when Pakistan's unofficial cricket mascot – Chacha, as he's known – started moving through the stand at the Vauxhall End, waving the Pakistan flag, leading the crowd in rousing slogans. When an Indian spectator asked him to sit down and stop obstructing the view, and Chacha responded angrily, I thought we'd see tempers spill over. But others – Indians and Pakistanis – spoke to the old man affectionately, respectfully, and defused the situation. Then a cool breeze blew past and we were united in our sighing gratitude: Indians and Pakistanis brought together in London by their appreciation for respite from the heat. It was that kind of upside-down miracle of a day.

After the break, India came in to bat, and the wickets fell and fell and kept on falling. I was taking it all in, I was WhatsApping friends in other stands and other cities, I was on Twitter, where my timeline was all Pakistan cricket, all disbelief and joy. It felt necessary to be everywhere – on the ground, with friends, and with the wider world of Pakistan supporters, most of whom were unable to know this most magical feeling: to watch your team play live, and win. The only sadness came when I recalled that the last time I had seen such a good-natured Indo–Pak audience had been in Karachi, in 2004, at a time when they played bilateral cricket and the national team played at home. Those were glory days, but so was this. Pakistan won by 180 runs, and all kinds of dreams seemed possible once more.

Kamila Shamsie has been following the fortunes of the Pakistan team most of her life, first in Karachi, then America, and now round the corner from Lord's.

In some ways, this was a strange tournament. The belief that England's win over Bangladesh would presage a string of record-breaking chases proved erroneous. The one-sidedness of every game except Pakistan v Sri Lanka did little to quell the fear that 50-over cricket could not continue to ward off the challenge of Twenty20. And, more than once, hired Scandinavians dressed as Beefeaters held up play as they strolled behind the bowler's arm en route to the drums they banged at key moments.

Then, after the pleasure in Pakistan's win had died down, it transpired that, for the Champions Trophy, the ravens were about to leave the tower. This edition was itself a stay of execution: before the 2013 tournament, the ICC said it would be replaced by a Test championship, only for TV executives to can that idea because it risked excluding India. In the meantime, though, fears over Test cricket's health had intensified, so the championship was back on the table. And since the main chunk of the 2019 World Cup had been reduced to ten teams – only two more than here – the distinction between the two 50-over competitions was becoming meaningless. For the second time, the ICC suggested the Champions Trophy had had its day. If so, it had gone out with a bang.

NATIONAL SQUADS

* *Captain.* ‡ *Did not play.*

Australia *S. P. D. Smith, P. J. Cummins, A. J. Finch, J. W. Hastings, J. R. Hazlewood, T. M. Head, M. C. Henriques, ‡C. A. Lynn, G. J. Maxwell, ‡J. L. Pattinson, M. A. Starc, ‡M. P. Stoinis, M. S. Wade, D. A. Warner, A. Zampa. *Coach:* D. S. Lehmann.

Bangladesh *Mashrafe bin Mortaza, Imrul Kayes, Mahmudullah, Mehedi Hasan, Mosaddek Hossain, Mushfiqur Rahim, Mustafizur Rahman, Rubel Hossain, Sabbir Rahman, ‡Sanjamul Islam, ‡Shafiul Islam, Shakib Al Hasan, Soumya Sarkar, Tamim Iqbal, Taskin Ahmed. *Coach:* U. C. Hathurusinghe.

England *E. J. G. Morgan, M. M. Ali, J. M. Bairstow, J. T. Ball, ‡S. W. Billings, J. C. Buttler, ‡S. T. Finn, A. D. Hales, L. E. Plunkett, A. U. Rashid, J. E. Root, J. J. Roy, B. A. Stokes, ‡D. J. Willey, C. R. Woakes, M. A. Wood. *Coach:* T. H. Bayliss.

Woakes strained his side in the first match, and was replaced by Finn.

India *V. Kohli, R. Ashwin, Bhuvneshwar Kumar, J. J. Bumrah, S. Dhawan, M. S. Dhoni, R. A. Jadeja, K. M. Jadhav, ‡K. D. Karthik, ‡Mohammed Shami, H. H. Pandya, ‡A. M. Rahane, R. G. Sharma, U. T. Yadav, Yuvraj Singh. *Coach:* A. Kumble.

M. K. Pandey was originally selected, but strained his side and was replaced by Karthik.

New Zealand *K. S. Williamson, C. J. Anderson, T. A. Boult, N. T. Broom, ‡C. de Grandhomme, M. J. Guptill, ‡T. W. M. Latham, ‡M. J. McClenaghan, A. F. Milne, J. D. S. Neesham, ‡J. S. Patel, L. Ronchi, M. J. Santner, T. G. Southee, L. R. P. L. Taylor. *Coach:* M. J. Hesson.

Pakistan *Sarfraz Ahmed, Ahmed Shehzad, Azhar Ali, Babar Azam, Fahim Ashraf, Fakhar Zaman, ‡Haris Sohail, Hasan Ali, Imad Wasim, Junaid Khan, Mohammad Amir, Mohammad Hafeez, Rumman Raees, Shadab Khan, Shoaib Malik, Wahab Riaz. *Coach:* J. M. Arthur.

Umar Akmal was originally selected, but failed a fitness test and was replaced by Haris Sohail. Wahab Riaz twisted his right ankle in the first match, and was replaced by Rumman Raees.

South Africa *A. B. de Villiers, H. M. Amla, ‡F. Behardien, Q. de Kock, J-P. Duminy, F. du Plessis, Imran Tahir, ‡K. A. Maharaj, D. A. Miller, M. Morkel, C. H. Morris, W. D. Parnell, A. L. Phehlukwayo, ‡D. Pretorius, K. Rabada. *Coach:* R. C. Domingo.

Sri Lanka *A. D. Mathews, L. D. Chandimal, D. M. de Silva, D. P. D. N. Dickwella, A. N. P. R. Fernando, D. A. S. Gunaratne, M. D. Gunathilleke, C. K. Kapugedera, ‡K. M. D. N. Kulasekara, R. A. S. Lakmal, S. L. Malinga, B. K. G. Mendis, M. D. K. J. Perera, N. L. T. C. Perera, S. Prasanna, ‡P. A. D. L. R. Sandakan, W. U. Tharanga. *Coach:* G. X. Ford.

Kapugedera hurt his knee before their second game, and was replaced by Gunathilleke. M. D. K. J. Perera injured his hamstring during the same match, and was replaced by de Silva.

GROUP A

ENGLAND v BANGLADESH

At The Oval, June 1. England won by eight wickets. Toss: England.

The Champions Trophy started as it hoped to go on, with a full house, two totals above 300 and a pair of sparkling centuries. England prevailed easily enough in the end, with Root hobbling through cramp to a career-best 133 not out from 129 balls. But victory came at a price: Woakes strained his left side after bowling only two overs, and next day was ruled out of the tournament. His departure disturbed the hosts' equilibrium. While Tamim Iqbal – who brushed aside a verbal volley from Stokes – and Mushfiqur Rahim were adding 166 for the third wicket, England missed the variations of Adil Rashid, left out because Morgan felt his opponents would be less comfortable against the pace of Ball. In the event, he went for 82, and it needed Plunkett – who, with successive deliveries in the 45th over, removed Tamim for a regal 128 and Mushfiqur for 79 – to prevent a total of around 330. When Roy continued his slump, ramping Mashrafe bin Mortaza to short fine leg in the third over, Bangladesh's vocal fans began to dream. But Hales and Root put on 159 and, though Hales perished for 95 at deep square leg, aiming for a second successive six, Morgan helped finish things off with a vivacious unbeaten 61-ball 75. Tamim was convinced he had caught him low down at long-on when Morgan had 22, but the soft signal was not out, and the replays were inconclusive. It was Bangladesh's final flicker, and Root's tenth one-day international century ensured England became the first team in the Champions Trophy to chase down more than 300. LAWRENCE BOOTH

Man of the Match: J. E. Root. *Attendance:* 22,243.

Stepping on it: Tamim Iqbal, comfortably Bangladesh's leading scorer in the tournament, hits out.

Bangladesh

Tamim Iqbal c Buttler b Plunkett	128	Mahmudullah not out	6
Soumya Sarkar c sub (J. M. Bairstow) b Stokes	28	Mosaddek Hossain not out	2
Imrul Kayes c Wood b Plunkett	19	B 1, lb 1, w 7	9
†Mushfiqur Rahim c Hales b Plunkett	79	1/56 (2) 2/95 (3) (6 wkts, 50 overs)	305
Shakib Al Hasan c Stokes b Ball	10	3/261 (1) 4/261 (4)	
Sabbir Rahman c Roy b Plunkett	24	5/277 (5) 6/300 (6)	10 overs: 36-0

*Mashrafe bin Mortaza, Rubel Hossain and Mustafizur Rahman did not bat.

Woakes 2–1–4–0; Wood 10–1–58–0; Ball 10–1–82–1; Stokes 7–0–42–1; Plunkett 10–0–59–4; Ali 8–1–40–0; Root 3–0–18–0.

England

J. J. Roy c Mustafizur Rahman b Mashrafe bin Mortaza	1	*E. J. G. Morgan not out	75
A. D. Hales c sub (Sanjamul Islam) b Sabbir Rahman	95	Lb 2, w 2	4
J. E. Root not out	133	1/6 (1) 2/165 (2) (2 wkts, 47.2 overs)	308
			10 overs: 51-1

B. A. Stokes, †J. C. Buttler, M. M. Ali, C. R. Woakes, L. E. Plunkett, M. A. Wood and J. T. Ball did not bat.

Mashrafe bin Mortaza 10–0–56–1; Shakib Al Hasan 8–0–62–0; Mustafizur Rahman 9–0–51–0; Soumya Sarkar 2–0–13–0; Mosaddek Hossain 7.2–0–47–0; Rubel Hossain 10–0–64–0; Sabbir Rahman 1–0–13–1.

Umpires: S. Ravi and R. J. Tucker. Third umpire: B. N. J. Oxenford.
Referee: D. C. Boon.

AUSTRALIA v NEW ZEALAND

At Birmingham, June 2. No result. Toss: New Zealand.

Australia had not enjoyed their recent trips to Birmingham, and heavy showers made it five no-results in six one-day internationals, including the meeting between these sides at the previous Champions Trophy in 2013. Yet if the weather had held, they might have made an even worse start to their tournament. Ronchi, picked ahead of Tom Latham to provide New Zealand with oomph from the off, cracked Cummins for three sixes on his way to a frisky 43-ball 65, his first half-century in 37 ODI innings dating back to January 2015. The assault gave Williamson a chance to bed in with a succession of gentle persuasions to third man. He glided past 50 during a stand of 99 with Taylor then, once set, had the time – even against a high-class pace attack – to pick which balls to force through midwicket as he cantered to 100 in 96 deliveries, his ninth one-day century but his first against Australia. In the field, Smith puffed his cheeks, later criticising the bowlers for their "worst display in a very long time", but after Williamson was run out, they showed their teeth. Hazlewood had conceded 20 from his first two overs (and admitted to Smith's charge), before returning to pick up five for 15 in 18 balls and finish with a career-best six for 52. In an innings reduced to 46 overs by an early shower, New Zealand had collapsed from 254 for three to 291 all out in 45. Rain delayed the resumption, and Australian heads seemed as cloudy as the heavens, losing three quick wickets as they tried and failed to get ahead of the rate – but the end came 11 overs before there could be a result. JAMES GINGELL

Attendance: 18,540.

New Zealand

M. J. Guptill c Maxwell b Hazlewood	26
†L. Ronchi c Maxwell b Hastings	65
*K. S. Williamson run out	100
L. R. P. L. Taylor c Henriques b Hastings	46
N. T. Broom c Maxwell b Hazlewood	14
J. D. S. Neesham c Warner b Hazlewood	6
C. J. Anderson c Henriques b Cummins	8
M. J. Santner c Smith b Hazlewood	8
A. F. Milne c Maxwell b Hazlewood	11
T. G. Southee not out	0
T. A. Boult c Wade b Hazlewood	0
Lb 4, w 3	7
1/40 (1) 2/117 (2) 3/216 (4) 4/254 (3) 5/257 (5) 6/267 (7) 7/270 (6) 8/291 (9) 9/291 (8) 10/291 (11) (45 overs)	291
9.3 overs: 67-1	

Starc 9–0–52–0; Hazlewood 9–0–52–6; Cummins 9–0–67–1; Hastings 9–0–69–2; Head 4–0–22–0; Henriques 5–0–25–0.

Australia

D. A. Warner c Ronchi b Boult	18
A. J. Finch c Taylor b Milne	8
*S. P. D. Smith not out	8
M. C. Henriques c and b Milne	18
Lb 1	1
1/27 (1) 2/35 (2) 3/53 (4) (3 wkts, 9 overs)	53
7 overs: 36-2	

T. M. Head, G. J. Maxwell, †M. S. Wade, J. W. Hastings, M. A. Starc, P. J. Cummins and J. R. Hazlewood did not bat.

Southee 3–0–15–0; Boult 4–0–28–1; Milne 2–0–9–2.

Umpires: R. K. Illingworth and R. A. Kettleborough. Third umpire: N. J. Llong.
Referee: A. J. Pycroft.

AUSTRALIA v BANGLADESH

At The Oval, June 5 (day/night). No result. Toss: Bangladesh.

The weather had probably been kind to Australia three days earlier in the Midlands, but it now cost them certain victory in south London. At 83 for one in pursuit of 183, they needed to see out four more overs for the 20 that constitute a game. Squally showers had stopped play shortly before 6.45, only to relent, encouraging hopes of an 8.30 restart. But the rain returned with a vengeance, leaving a frustrated Smith to question the urgency of the Oval groundstaff, and Bangladesh with an unlikely lifeline. They had done little to deserve it, folding from 122 for three to 182 as Starc – making deadly use of his yorker against a hapless tail – mopped up with four for one in nine balls. Without the talent of Tamim Iqbal, it could have been even more embarrassing. After beginning the competition with 128 against England, he was seventh out for 95, top-edging Starc to long leg; of Bangladesh's 13 boundaries, Tamim managed nine. Only two others made double figures, as leg-spinner Zampa – who had replaced John Hastings – struck twice in his first two overs. Head, meanwhile, conceded 18 from seven overs of gentle off-spin before Tamim tucked in to his eighth. As rain arrived from the south, Rubel Hossain trapped Finch, but Warner – who went past 4,000 one-day international runs – and Smith were doing it with ease. Smith resorted to dead-batting Mashrafe bin Mortaza in a bid to hurry through the overs, but Bangladesh were in no rush, knowing that a point kept their semi-final hopes alive. Australia now needed to beat England. LAWRENCE BOOTH

Attendance: 16,108.

Bangladesh

Tamim Iqbal c Hazlewood b Starc	95	Rubel Hossain b Starc	0
Soumya Sarkar c Wade b Hazlewood	3	Mustafizur Rahman not out	1
Imrul Kayes c Finch b Cummins	6		
†Mushfiqur Rahim lbw b Henriques	9	Lb 6, w 3	9
Shakib Al Hasan lbw b Head	29		
Sabbir Rahman c Smith b Zampa	8	1/22 (2) 2/37 (3) 3/53 (4) (44.3 overs)	182
Mahmudullah b Zampa	8	4/122 (5) 5/141 (6) 6/153 (7)	
Mehedi Hasan b Starc	14	7/181 (1) 8/181 (9) 9/181 (10)	
*Mashrafe bin Mortaza b Starc	0	10/182 (8) 10 overs: 37-1	

Starc 8.3–2–29–4; Hazlewood 10–0–40–1; Cummins 8–1–22–1; Head 8–0–33–1; Henriques 5–0–30–1; Zampa 4–1–13–2; Maxwell 1–0–9–0.

Australia

D. A. Warner not out	40
A. J. Finch lbw b Rubel Hossain	19
*S. P. D. Smith not out	22
Lb 1, w 1	2
1/45 (2) (1 wkt, 16 overs)	83
10 overs: 57-1	

M. C. Henriques, T. M. Head, G. J. Maxwell, †M. S. Wade, M. A. Starc, P. J. Cummins, A. Zampa and J. R. Hazlewood did not bat.

Mustafizur Rahman 5–0–27–0; Mashrafe bin Mortaza 6–0–30–0; Rubel Hossain 4–0–21–1; Mehedi Hasan 1–0–4–0.

Umpires: C. B. Gaffaney and N. J. Llong. Third umpire: I. J. Gould.
Referee: B. C. Broad.

ENGLAND v NEW ZEALAND

At Cardiff, June 6. England won by 87 runs. Toss: New Zealand.

The circus moved to Cardiff, though so ferocious were the westerlies it was a miracle anyone negotiated the Severn Bridge. There were interruptions when gusts swept the boundary rope on to the field, and the illuminated bails – light in both senses – refused to stay put. England's attack had no such problems getting in the groove, and Morgan's side whooshed into the semis. On a slowish pitch that had caused England few problems, New Zealand's target of 311 was gettable. But Ball and Wood promptly hit the perfect length. Ball also hit middle with his fourth delivery to despatch Ronchi for a golden duck, and did not concede a run until his 18th. A key passage came in the 15th over when Plunkett, bowling cross-seamers in search of variable bounce, clonked Williamson and Taylor on the helmet. Doubt seeped into the New Zealand psyche. Williamson blew hot and cold, mixing eye-of-the-needle placement with aerial shots that had fielders jumping like fish in summertime. At 158 for two in the 31st, it was even-steven. Then Wood produced a snorter that kissed Williamson's gloves. He went for 87, looking daggers at the pitch. Rashid, seemingly an odd replacement for the injured Chris Woakes given Sophia Gardens' short straight boundaries, tied down an end, and the fast bowlers cleaned up. Earlier, Roy had failed to pass 20 for the eighth successive one-dayer. Others, however, merrily pulled the overused short ball: England hit ten sixes to New Zealand's one, though a couple came when the twinkle-toed Root lofted Santner over his head. The innings was poised to ignite at any moment, yet regular wickets thwarted acceleration. Ali fell to a spectacular catch by Boult, flying to his left at short fine leg, but that paled beside an extraordinary six from Buttler, whose ramp-cum-back-flick landed on the TV gantry behind the keeper. At 11am, midway through the seventh over, the ground observed a minute's silence for the victims of the London Bridge terror attack three days earlier. HUGH CHEVALLIER

Man of the Match: J. T. Ball. *Attendance:* 13,186.

England

J. J. Roy b Milne	13
A. D. Hales b Milne	56
J. E. Root b Anderson	64
*E. J. G. Morgan c Ronchi b Anderson	13
B. A. Stokes c Milne b Boult	48
†J. C. Buttler not out	61
M. M. Ali c Boult b Anderson	12
A. U. Rashid lbw b Santner	12
L. E. Plunkett c Southee b Milne	15
M. A. Wood c Taylor b Southee	0
J. T. Ball c Boult b Southee	0
Lb 5, w 11	16
1/37 (1) 2/118 (2) 3/134 (4) 4/188 (3) 5/210 (5) 6/230 (7) 7/260 (8) 8/309 (9) 9/310 (10) 10/310 (11) (49.3 overs)	310

10 overs: 50-1

Southee 9.3–0–44–2; Boult 10–0–56–1; Milne 10–0–79–3; Anderson 9–0–55–3; Santner 8–0–54–1; Neesham 3–0–17–0.

New Zealand

M. J. Guptill c Root b Stokes	27
†L. Ronchi b Ball	0
*K. S. Williamson c Buttler b Wood	87
L. R. P. L. Taylor c Root b Ball	39
N. T. Broom lbw b Rashid	11
J. D. S. Neesham c Hales b Plunkett	18
C. J. Anderson c Hales b Plunkett	10
M. J. Santner st Buttler b Rashid	3
A. F. Milne c Rashid b Plunkett	10
T. G. Southee c Roy b Plunkett	2
T. A. Boult not out	0
B 4, lb 8, w 4	16
1/1 (2) 2/63 (1) 3/158 (3) 4/168 (4) 5/191 (6) 6/194 (5) 7/205 (8) 8/211 (7) 9/223 (9) 10/223 (10) (44.3 overs)	223

10 overs: 40-1

Ball 8–2–31–2; Wood 9–0–32–1; Plunkett 9.3–0–55–4; Stokes 8–0–46–1; Rashid 10–0–47–2.

Umpires: B. N. J. Oxenford and P. R. Reiffel. Third umpire: R. J. Tucker.
Referee: A. J. Pycroft.

BANGLADESH v NEW ZEALAND

At Cardiff, June 9. Bangladesh won by five wickets. Toss: New Zealand.

There have been many staging posts in the rise of Bangladesh cricket. A small but raucous crowd in Cardiff witnessed another, as Shakib Al Hasan and Mahmudullah authored a remarkable recovery from 33 for four to eliminate New Zealand, and take their side to the verge of the semi-finals of an ICC global event for the first time. Initially their sweet strokes felt futile, after Southee's alluring late swing had decapitated the reply. But, almost imperceptibly, Bangladesh gained parity, then the ascendancy. As the swing stopped, New Zealand looked bereft of ideas, while the batsmen mixed the sumptuous – Shakib repeatedly charged down the wicket to scythe Southee through the off side – with the sensible. The target of 266 loomed into view, and so did thoughts of previous Bangladesh narrow misses. This, though, was a different team. Shakib moved to his seventh one-day international century by pulling Milne for six and, by the time he fell four balls later, the pair had added 224, Bangladesh's first double-century stand for any wicket. Three balls after that, Mahmudullah brought up his own hundred, his third, with a boundary off Boult, and celebrated with the *sajdah*. New Zealand were left to rue their third successive collapse. They had cleared 150 in the 30th over for the loss of only two wickets, then stumbled – again – after Williamson was run out, for the third time in four one-day innings. But he was not the problem: only 62 came from the final ten overs, which included three wickets for Mosaddek Hossain's auxiliary off-spin. New Zealand's bowling proved equally lop-sided. Bangladesh now just had to sit and wait: a semi-final place would be theirs if Australia failed to beat England at Edgbaston. TIM WIGMORE

Man of the Match: Shakib Al Hasan. *Attendance:* 7,627.

New Zealand

M. J. Guptill lbw b Rubel Hossain	33	C. J. Anderson lbw b Mosaddek Hossain	0
†L. Ronchi c Mustafizur Rahman b Taskin Ahmed	16	M. J. Santner not out	14
*K. S. Williamson run out	57	A. F. Milne b Mustafizur Rahman	7
L. R. P. L. Taylor c Mustafizur Rahman b Taskin Ahmed	63	T. G. Southee not out	10
N. T. Broom c Tamim Iqbal b Mosaddek Hossain	36	W 6	6
J. D. S. Neesham st Mushfiqur Rahim b Mosaddek Hossain	23	1/46 (2) 2/69 (1) 3/152 (3) 4/201 (4) 5/228 (5) 6/229 (7) 7/240 (6) 8/252 (9) (8 wkts, 50 overs)	265
		10 overs: 60-1	

T. A. Boult did not bat.

Mashrafe bin Mortaza 10–1–45–0; Mustafizur Rahman 9–0–52–1; Taskin Ahmed 8–0–43–2; Rubel Hossain 10–0–60–1; Shakib Al Hasan 10–0–52–0; Mosaddek Hossain 3–0–13–3.

Bangladesh

Tamim Iqbal lbw b Southee	0	Mosaddek Hossain not out	7
Soumya Sarkar lbw b Southee	3	Lb 2, w 18	20
Sabbir Rahman c Ronchi b Southee	8		
†Mushfiqur Rahim b Milne	14	1/0 (1) 2/10 (3) 3/12 (2) 4/33 (4) 5/257 (5) (5 wkts, 47.2 overs)	268
Shakib Al Hasan b Boult	114		
Mahmudullah not out	102	10 overs: 24-3	

*Mashrafe bin Mortaza, Taskin Ahmed, Rubel Hossain and Mustafizur Rahman did not bat.

Southee 9–1–45–3; Boult 10–0–48–1; Milne 9.2–0–58–1; Neesham 4–0–30–0; Santner 10–0–47–0; Anderson 3–0–19–0; Williamson 2–0–19–0.

Umpires: I. J. Gould and N. J. Llong. Third umpire: Aleem Dar.
Referee: B. C. Broad.

ENGLAND v AUSTRALIA

At Birmingham, June 10. England won by 40 runs (DLS). Toss: England.

Australia's tournament ended amid familiar scenes, with rain falling and the covers in place. But there were no complaints: a scintillating run-a-ball stand of 159 between Morgan and Stokes spoke for itself. Morgan was eventually run out by Zampa from mid-on for an 81-ball 87 studded with five sixes, but Stokes's third one-day hundred had taken England well ahead on DLS when the rain arrived just before six. The result meant qualification for Bangladesh; one fan tweeted that his country should be renamed "Bengladesh". Australia had two chances to progress. At 136 for one in the 23rd over, they had exploited England's tendency to drop short, only for Morgan to hold on to a swirling monster at cover to see off Finch. Henriques, out of his depth, dragged Rashid to mid-on, and Wood – having already accounted for Warner – persuaded Smith to chip the first ball of his second spell to mid-off. Roy then danced either side of the deep midwicket boundary in catching Maxwell, the first of five to fall for 15 in 26 deliveries. Both Rashid (with his best figures against anyone bar Ireland) and Wood (best bar none) finished with four wickets, and it needed Head's resolve to drag Australia to 277. Roy eased the first ball of the chase through mid-off, then played around the second, using up the review in desperation; Hazlewood accounted for Hales and Root. Had Wade not dropped Morgan down the leg side off Hazlewood on 12, it might have been curtains for England. Instead, after a restorative 40-minute rain break, Morgan and Stokes rattled up the 100 inside 15 overs, ticking off England's best fourth-wicket stand against Australia, beating 139 by Allan Lamb and Derek Randall at Melbourne in 1982-83. Rain confirmed the inevitable: Australia were out and, thanks to the Lions, the Tigers were through. LAWRENCE BOOTH

Man of the Match: B. A. Stokes. *Attendance:* 24,227.

Australia

D. A. Warner c Buttler b Wood	21	A. Zampa b Wood	0
A. J. Finch c Morgan b Stokes	68	J. R. Hazlewood not out	1
*S. P. D. Smith c Plunkett b Wood	56		
M. C. Henriques c Plunkett b Rashid	17	Lb 8, w 8, nb 1	17
T. M. Head not out	71		
G. J. Maxwell c Roy b Wood	20	1/40 (1) 2/136 (2) (9 wkts, 50 overs)	277
†M. S. Wade c and b Rashid	2	3/161 (4) 4/181 (3)	
M. A. Starc c Root b Rashid	0	5/239 (6) 6/245 (7) 7/245 (8)	
P. J. Cummins c and b Rashid	4	8/253 (9) 9/254 (10)	10 overs: 56-1

Ball 9–1–61–0; Wood 10–1–33–4; Plunkett 8–0–49–0; Stokes 8–0–61–1; Rashid 10–1–41–4; Ali 5–0–24–0.

England

J. J. Roy lbw b Starc	4	†J. C. Buttler not out	29
A. D. Hales c Finch b Hazlewood	0	Lb 2, w 1	3
J. E. Root c Wade b Hazlewood	15		
*E. J. G. Morgan run out	87	1/4 (1) 2/6 (2) (4 wkts, 40.2 overs)	240
B. A. Stokes not out	102	3/35 (3) 4/194 (4)	10 overs: 58-3

M. M. Ali, A. U. Rashid, L. E. Plunkett, M. A. Wood and J. T. Ball did not bat.

Starc 10–0–52–1; Hazlewood 9–0–50–2; Cummins 8–1–55–0; Head 2–0–9–0; Henriques 1–0–6–0; Zampa 8.2–0–52–0; Maxwell 2–0–14–0.

Umpires: H. D. P. K. Dharmasena and C. B. Gaffaney. Third umpire: S. Ravi.
Referee: A. J. Pycroft.

GROUP B

SOUTH AFRICA v SRI LANKA

At The Oval, June 3. South Africa won by 96 runs. Toss: Sri Lanka.

South Africa made a slow start on a slow surface, but Amla's century – his 25th in one-day internationals – helped them to an eighth consecutive win over Sri Lanka. The openers managed just 32 off the first ten overs yet, while de Kock muddled and missed, there was a sense Amla was merely selecting the best way to skin the cat. He shelved his favourite checked drives for tucks off the hip and hard running; his first boundary came from his 28th delivery, and he hit only five fours and two sixes in all. Du Plessis adopted a similar approach on his way to 75, after surviving a top edge to fine leg on eight off Pradeep Fernando. Malinga was the culprit, playing his first ODI since November 2015, and looking heavy-legged. Amla and du Plessis added 145 – Sri Lanka were all too biddable in the middle overs – but from 189 for one in the 34th, the final assault never quite arrived. Amla ran out of steam on 103, and the others found hitting out hard, save for Duminy, who blasted the last two balls for four and six in a 20-ball 38. Sri Lanka had taken four hours in the field (earning Tharanga, standing in as captain for the injured Angelo Mathews, a two-match ban), but made a racing start to their reply. Dickwella jigged about his crease and flicked over the infield, while Tharanga waited for short balls from Parnell. They were 94 for one in the 12th, before de Villiers changed the game with a leaping right-handed catch at mid-on to remove Mendis, and a brilliant diving throw – releasing the ball left as his body flew right – to run out Chandimal. Without Mathews to shore up the middle order, the innings decayed against the jubilant Imran Tahir, who picked up four for 27, taking his haul in ten matches against Sri Lanka to 24 wickets at 15, and ran out Lakmal with a direct hit. JAMES GINGELL

Man of the Match: Imran Tahir. *Attendance:* 19,706.

South Africa

H. M. Amla run out	103	W. D. Parnell not out	7
†Q. de Kock c Dickwella b Fernando	23		
F. du Plessis c Chandimal b Fernando	75	Lb 1, w 10	11
*A. B. de Villiers c Kapugedera b Prasanna	4		
D. A. Miller c Prasanna b Lakmal	18	1/44 (2) 2/189 (3) (6 wkts, 50 overs)	299
J-P. Duminy not out	38	3/194 (4) 4/226 (5)	
C. H. Morris run out	20	5/232 (1) 6/277 (7) 10 overs: 32-0	

K. Rabada, M. Morkel and Imran Tahir did not bat.

Malinga 10–0–57–0; Lakmal 10–0–51–1; Fernando 10–0–54–2; Gunaratne 10–0–64–0; Prasanna 10–0–72–1.

Sri Lanka

†D. P. D. N. Dickwella c Parnell b Morkel	41	S. L. Malinga b Rabada	1
*W. U. Tharanga c Miller b Imran Tahir	57	A. N. P. R. Fernando c Duminy b Imran Tahir	5
B. K. G. Mendis c de Villiers b Morris	11		
L. D. Chandimal run out	12	Lb 6, w 8, nb 1	15
C. K. Kapugedera lbw b Imran Tahir	0		
M. D. K. J. Perera not out	44	1/69 (1) 2/94 (3) (41.3 overs)	203
D. A. S. Gunaratne c Parnell b Imran Tahir	4	3/116 (4) 4/117 (5) 5/146 (2)	
S. Prasanna lbw b Morris	13	6/155 (7) 7/191 (8) 8/191 (9)	
R. A. S. Lakmal run out	0	9/192 (10) 10/203 (11) 10 overs: 87-1	

Rabada 8–1–46–1; Parnell 10–0–54–0; Morkel 6–0–31–1; Morris 7–0–32–2; Imran Tahir 8.3–0–27–4; Duminy 2–0–7–0.

Umpires: Aleem Dar and I. J. Gould. Third umpire: P. R. Reiffel.
Referee: D. C. Boon.

INDIA v PAKISTAN

At Birmingham, June 4. India won by 124 runs (DLS). Toss: Pakistan.

The reality fell short of the hype as India romped to their seventh successive victory over Pakistan at ICC tournaments. But a crowd of 24,156 (a record for a one-day international at Edgbaston, for less than a week) had few complaints: Indian fans comfortably outnumbered Pakistanis. With rain in the air, Sharma and Dhawan put on 136 inside 25 overs, Yuvraj Singh smashed a 29-ball half-century, and Kohli finished with a flourish to make 81 not out from 68. Pakistan's fielding was comically bad – Yuvraj was dropped in the deep on eight, Kohli on 43 – and their bowling little better. Towards the end, they disintegrated. Mohammad Amir left the field because of cramp, and Wahab Riaz followed him with a twisted ankle, having bowled 8.4 overs for 87, the most expensive spell in Champions Trophy history; he was soon ruled out of the competition. Pandya supplied the icing with three successive sixes in the final over, from Imad Wasim's left-arm spin, as 72 cascaded from the last four. Persistent showers eventually left a target of 289 from 41 overs – a gargantuan task even for a team with more power than Pakistan. Azhar Ali made a desperately orthodox 50, but his colleagues had no answer to India's accuracy. As the sun came out, the innings wilted: the last seven tumbled for 73, leaving Pakistan's coach Mickey Arthur to scowl: "It was a reality check." That was a generous way of putting it. LAWRENCE BOOTH

Man of the Match: Yuvraj Singh. *Attendance:* 24,156.

India

R. G. Sharma run out	91
S. Dhawan c Azhar Ali b Shadab Khan	68
*V. Kohli not out	81
Yuvraj Singh lbw b Hasan Ali	53
H. H. Pandya not out	20
Lb 2, w 2, nb 2	6
1/136 (2) 2/192 (1) 3/285 (4) (3 wkts, 48 overs)	319
10 overs: 46-0	

†M. S. Dhoni, K. M. Jadhav, R. A. Jadeja, Bhuvneshwar Kumar, U. T. Yadav and J. J. Bumrah did not bat.

Mohammad Amir 8.1–1–32–0; Imad Wasim 9.1–0–66–0; Hasan Ali 10–0–70–1; Wahab Riaz 8.4–0–87–0; Shadab Khan 10–0–52–1; Shoaib Malik 2–0–10–0.

Pakistan

Azhar Ali c Pandya b Jadeja	50
Ahmed Shehzad lbw b Bhuvneshwar Kumar	12
Babar Azam c Jadeja b Yadav	8
Mohammad Hafeez c Bhuvneshwar Kumar b Jadeja	33
Shoaib Malik run out	15
*†Sarfraz Ahmed c Dhoni b Pandya	15
Imad Wasim c Jadhav b Pandya	0
Shadab Khan not out	14
Mohammad Amir c Jadhav b Yadav	9
Hasan Ali c Dhawan b Yadav	0
Wahab Riaz absent hurt	
Lb 2, w 6	8
1/47 (2) 2/61 (3) 3/91 (1) 4/114 (5) 5/131 (4) 6/135 (7) 7/151 (6) 8/164 (9) 9/164 (10) (33.4 overs)	164
10 overs: 38-0	

Bhuvneshwar Kumar 5–1–23–1; Yadav 7.4–1–30–3; Bumrah 5–0–23–0; Pandya 8–0–43–2; Jadeja 8–0–43–2.

Umpires: H. D. P. K. Dharmasena and M. Erasmus. Third umpire: R. A. Kettleborough.
Referee: A. J. Pycroft.

PAKISTAN v SOUTH AFRICA

At Birmingham, June 7 (day/night). Pakistan won by 19 runs (DLS). Toss: South Africa. One-day international debut: Fakhar Zaman.

Written off after a supine performance against India, Pakistan sparked into life – and exposed all South Africa's big-tournament frailties in a rain-shortened match. A buoyant display in the field was the genesis, with slow left-armer Imad Wasim strangling the South Africans, and dismissing de Villiers for the first golden duck of his 221-match career, to make it 61 for three. After du Plessis and Miller briefly steadied the innings, Hasan Ali ripped through the middle order with three wickets – and later held two excellent catches – to whip a largely Pakistani crowd into a frenzy. The energy from the stands flowed on to the field and, although Miller kept his head to give South Africa something to bowl at, the force was with Pakistan. All forecasts pointed to a weather-affected second innings (and therefore DLS), yet de Villiers elected not to open with Morkel, his most threatening bowler. The debutant Fakhar Zaman duly cashed in on an errant Parnell to put Pakistan ahead of the rate. Morkel hauled South Africa back into it with a five-over spell of two for seven but, when he was withdrawn, Pakistan recovered quickly. By the time he returned ten overs later to dismiss Mohammad Hafeez it was too late. The rain arrived as predicted, with Pakistan easily ahead. "If I had known it would only be 27 overs, I would have attacked a lot more," said de Villiers. Given that he had been warned about the weather, it was difficult to have much sympathy. TRISTAN HOLME

Man of the Match: Hasan Ali. *Attendance:* 18,646.

Stu Forster, Getty Images

Charged up: Hasan Ali flies in against South Africa, for the first of four successive three-fors.

South Africa

†Q. de Kock lbw b Mohammad Hafeez	33
H. M. Amla lbw b Imad Wasim	16
F. du Plessis b Hasan Ali	26
*A. B. de Villiers c Mohammad Hafeez b Imad Wasim	0
D. A. Miller not out	75
J-P. Duminy c Babar Azam b Hasan Ali	8
W. D. Parnell b Hasan Ali	0
C. H. Morris c Hasan Ali b Junaid Khan	28
K. Rabada c Hasan Ali b Junaid Khan	26
M. Morkel not out	0
Lb 1, w 5, nb 1	7
1/40 (2) 2/60 (1) (8 wkts, 50 overs)	219

3/61 (4) 4/90 (3) 5/118 (6)
6/118 (7) 7/165 (8) 8/213 (9) 10 overs: 47-1

Imran Tahir did not bat.

Mohammad Amir 10–0–50–0; Junaid Khan 9–0–53–2; Imad Wasim 8–0–20–2; Mohammad Hafeez 10–0–51–1; Hasan Ali 8–1–24–3; Shadab Khan 5–0–20–0.

Pakistan

Azhar Ali c Imran Tahir b Morkel	9
Fakhar Zaman c Amla b Morkel	31
Babar Azam not out	31
Mohammad Hafeez c Imran Tahir b Morkel	26
Shoaib Malik not out	16
Lb 2, w 3, nb 1	6
1/40 (2) 2/41 (1) (3 wkts, 27 overs)	119

3/93 (4) 10 overs: 42-2

*†Sarfraz Ahmed, Imad Wasim, Shadab Khan, Mohammad Amir, Hasan Ali and Junaid Khan did not bat.

Rabada 7–1–36–0; Parnell 4–0–25–0; Morkel 7–1–18–3; Morris 5–1–22–0; Imran Tahir 4–0–16–0.

Umpires: R. K. Illingworth and S. Ravi. Third umpire: H. D. P. K. Dharmasena.
Referee: B. C. Broad.

INDIA v SRI LANKA

At The Oval, June 8. Sri Lanka won by seven wickets. Toss: Sri Lanka.

It was a day when the mighty were humbled. At the ballot box, the Conservatives fell short of an expected majority; at The Oval, an inexperienced Sri Lanka toppled the idols of India for only the fourth time in their last 18 meetings, pulling off the ground's biggest successful chase. It was also the 150th meeting between the teams, a one-day international record. On a cold, breezy morning, India appeared strong and stable: Sharma hit the first ball to the cover boundary and coasted to a frictionless 78, while Dhawan cut and drove with velvety violence. At 138 without loss in the 25th, it was all going to plan. Then, against the most defensive of attacks, Sharma pulled to fine leg, Kohli nibbled behind for a duck, and Yuvraj Singh was bowled for seven. Dhawan kept chopping away to reach a brilliant 125, his third hundred in all Champions Trophy matches, in which he averaged over 90. But India were faltering until Dhoni clubbed a 52-ball 63 to help rack up 103 off the last ten, which included 14 full tosses. Sri Lanka needed 322, and Gunathilleke – added to the squad only the day before – led the way with long-levered power, twice nearly flattening his partner Mendis, who was compact and calm. The pair brought Sri Lanka more than halfway to victory but, with Kohli twitchy enough to try his own awkward wobblers, they both ran themselves out: Gunathilleke for a personal-best 76 in the 28th, and Mendis for 89 five overs later, after an excellent throw from Bhuvneshwar Kumar, following through off his own bowling. Still, Sri Lankan belief held firm: Kusal Perera and Mathews – regal despite a dodgy calf – motored to 271, until Perera popped a hamstring. Gunaratne hauled his fourth ball over backward square for six, then all but sealed it with another, an audacious sweep off Bumrah towards the gas-holder, where the Sri Lankan *papare* band was now drowning out the Indian drummers. All four teams in Group B had two points from two games, turning the last matches into knockouts. JAMES GINGELL

Man of the Match: B. K. G. Mendis. *Attendance:* 22,203.

India

R. G. Sharma c N. L. T. C. Perera b Malinga	78	R. A. Jadeja not out	0
S. Dhawan c Mendis b Malinga	125		
*V. Kohli c Dickwella b Fernando	0	Lb 4, w 10	14
Yuvraj Singh b Gunaratne	7		——
†M. S. Dhoni c Chandimal b N. L. T. C. Perera	63	1/138 (1) 2/139 (3) (6 wkts, 50 overs)	321
H. H. Pandya c M. D. K. J. Perera b Lakmal	9	3/179 (4) 4/261 (2)	
K. M. Jadhav not out	25	5/278 (6) 6/307 (5) 10 overs: 48-0	

Bhuvneshwar Kumar, U. T. Yadav and J. J. Bumrah did not bat.

Malinga 10–0–70–2; Lakmal 10–1–72–1; Fernando 10–0–73–1; N. L. T. C. Perera 9–0–54–1; Gunathilleke 8–0–41–0; Gunaratne 3–0–7–1.

Sri Lanka

†D. P. D. N. Dickwella c Jadeja b Bhuvneshwar Kumar	7	D. A. S. Gunaratne not out	34
M. D. Gunathilleke run out	76	Lb 11, w 5, nb 1	17
B. K. G. Mendis run out	89		——
M. D. K. J. Perera retired hurt	47	1/11 (1) 2/170 (2) (3 wkts, 48.4 overs)	322
*A. D. Mathews not out	52	3/196 (3) 10 overs: 44-1	

L. D. Chandimal, N. L. T. C. Perera, R. A. S. Lakmal, S. L. Malinga and A. N. P. R. Fernando did not bat.

Perera retired hurt at 271-3.

Bhuvneshwar Kumar 10–0–54–1; Yadav 9.4–0–67–0; Bumrah 10–0–52–0; Pandya 7–1–51–0; Jadeja 6–0–52–0; Jadhav 3–0–18–0; Kohli 3–0–17–0.

Umpires: R. A. Kettleborough and R. J. Tucker. Third umpire: M. Erasmus.
Referee: D. C. Boon.

Ian Kington, AFP/Getty Images

Bellyflop: A. B. de Villiers is run out by M. S. Dhoni as the South African batting goes under.

INDIA v SOUTH AFRICA

At The Oval, June 11. India won by eight wickets. Toss: India.

In a quarter-final in all but name, India sauntered to a facile win that booted South Africa out of the tournament. A side ranked No. 1 have rarely played so atrociously – unless it was a previous South Africa buckling under pressure – yet de Villiers said he hoped to remain captain since he was good at running the team. Possibly, though his team were no good at running 22 yards, as three run-outs confirmed. In truth, they weren't good at much. On a Forrest Gump of a pitch – slow but honest – the openers did best, even if a little urgency might not have gone amiss. Both fell looking to up the tempo, which was also du Plessis's aim when, at a steady 140 for two in the 29th, he called his captain for an illusory single. Smart work from Pandya and Dhoni beat de Villiers's headlong lunge. The rest of the side picked up the cue, and nosedived towards oblivion: five balls later, Miller and du Plessis raced to the same end in a comedy classic, and the third umpire had to contain his laughter long enough to determine who was out. Bumrah and Bhuvneshwar Kumar deployed intelligent changes of pace and angle, but a rattled South Africa were happy to do their jobs for them. And the last wicket, which ended a disintegration of eight for 51, brought more slapstick when Duminy and Imran Tahir got themselves in a schoolboy yes–no–maybe mid-pitch pickle. Against India's imperious batting and in such unthreatening conditions, a target of 192 was barely a molehill. Even so, Sharma stumbled, before Dhawan and Kohli collected unflustered fifties. The crushing victory meant India were almost certain to face Bangladesh in the semis rather than England. HUGH CHEVALLIER

Man of the Match: J. J. Bumrah. *Attendance:* 22,828.

"Cricket is always about trying to master the game," she says. "You never do, but it's fun along the way."

Five Cricketers of the Year, page 90

South Africa

†Q. de Kock b Jadeja	53	K. Rabada c Dhoni b Bhuvneshwar Kumar	5
H. M. Amla c Dhoni b Ashwin	35	M. Morkel c Kohli b Bhuvneshwar Kumar	0
F. du Plessis b Pandya	36	Imran Tahir run out	1
*A. B. de Villiers run out	16	Lb 6, w 10	16
D. A. Miller run out	1		—
J-P. Duminy not out	20	1/76 (2) 2/116 (1) (44.3 overs)	191
C. H. Morris c Bhuvneshwar Kumar b Bumrah	4	3/140 (4) 4/142 (5) 5/157 (3) 6/167 (7) 7/178 (8) 8/184 (9)	
A. L. Phehlukwayo lbw b Bumrah	4	9/184 (10) 10/191 (11) 10 overs: 35-0	

Bhuvneshwar Kumar 7.3–0–23–2; Bumrah 8–0–28–2; Ashwin 9–0–43–1; Pandya 10–0–52–1; Jadeja 10–0–39–1.

India

R. G. Sharma c de Kock b Morkel	12
S. Dhawan c du Plessis b Imran Tahir	78
*V. Kohli not out	76
Yuvraj Singh not out	23
Lb 2, w 1, nb 1	4
	—
1/23 (1) 2/151 (2) (2 wkts, 38 overs)	193
10 overs: 37-1	

†M. S. Dhoni, H. H. Pandya, K. M. Jadhav, R. A. Jadeja, R. Ashwin, Bhuvneshwar Kumar and J. J. Bumrah did not bat.

Rabada 9–2–34–0; Morkel 7–1–38–1; Phehlukwayo 5–0–25–0; Morris 8–0–40–0; Imran Tahir 6–0–37–1; Duminy 3–0–17–0.

Umpires: Aleem Dar and P. R. Reiffel. Third umpire: R. K. Illingworth.
Referee: D. C. Boon.

PAKISTAN v SRI LANKA

At Cardiff, June 12. Pakistan won by three wickets. Toss: Pakistan. One-day international debut: Fahim Ashraf.

A thrilling match between Group B's less-fancied sides hinged on two missed chances towards the end of a nerve-ridden chase. With 43 required, and Pakistan seven down, Tissara Perera floored a sitter at mid-on to reprieve Sarfraz Ahmed; four runs later, Sarfraz was dropped again, a tougher chance as the substitute Seekkuge Prasanna careered in from deep square leg. The despairing bowler on both occasions was Malinga, probably taking his final bow on the world stage. Less than five overs later, Pakistan were celebrating a gloriously erratic win, thanks to an unbroken eighth-wicket stand of 75 between Sarfraz and Mohammad Amir. Earlier, Amir had struck equally vital blows with the ball, as he and Junaid Khan claimed four for six between them – including Dickwella for a stylish 73 – to reduce Sri Lanka to 167 for seven. Eventually set 237, Pakistan were given a breezy start by Fakhar Zaman's 34-ball half-century, only for Pradeep Fernando to chip away. When the luckless debutant Fahim Ashraf was run out at the non-striker's end via Perera's fingertips, they had lost seven for 88. Yet Amir proved unflappable, Sarfraz rode his luck, and Sri Lanka degenerated amid a succession of misfields, overthrows and those two drops. As Mathews cursed his side's frailty, Pakistan prepared for a semi-final against England – on the same pitch. RICHARD GIBSON

Man of the Match: Sarfraz Ahmed. *Attendance:* 10,618.

Sri Lanka

†D. P. D. N. Dickwella c Sarfraz Ahmed b Mohammad Amir	73	N. L. T. C. Perera c Babar Azam b Junaid Khan	1
M. D. Gunathilleke c Shoaib Malik b Junaid Khan	13	R. A. S. Lakmal b Hasan Ali	26
B. K. G. Mendis b Hasan Ali	27	S. L. Malinga not out	9
L. D. Chandimal b Fahim Ashraf	0	A. N. P. R. Fernando c and b Fahim Ashraf	1
*A. D. Mathews b Mohammad Amir	39	B 1, lb 5, w 12, nb 1	19
D. M. de Silva c Sarfraz Ahmed b Junaid Khan	1	1/26 (2) 2/82 (3) 3/83 (4) 4/161 (5) 5/162 (6) 6/162 (1) 7/167 (8) 8/213 (9) 9/232 (7) 10/236 (11) (49.2 overs)	236
D. A. S. Gunaratne c Fakhar Zaman b Hasan Ali	27	10 overs: 50-1	

Mohammad Amir 10–0–53–2; Junaid Khan 10–3–40–3; Imad Wasim 8–1–33–0; Fahim Ashraf 6.2–0–37–2; Hasan Ali 10–0–43–3; Mohammad Hafeez 5–0–24–0.

Pakistan

Azhar Ali c Mendis b Lakmal	34	Fahim Ashraf run out	15
Fakhar Zaman c Gunaratne b Fernando	50	Mohammad Amir not out	28
Babar Azam c de Silva b Fernando	10	B 4, lb 6, w 13	23
Mohammad Hafeez c Fernando b Perera	1		
Shoaib Malik c Dickwella b Malinga	11	1/74 (2) 2/92 (3) 3/95 (4) 4/110 (1) 5/131 (5) 6/137 (7) 7/162 (8) (7 wkts, 44.5 overs)	237
*†Sarfraz Ahmed not out	61	10 overs: 65-0	
Imad Wasim c Dickwella b Fernando	4		

Hasan Ali and Junaid Khan did not bat.

Malinga 9.5–2–52–1; Lakmal 10–0–48–1; Fernando 10–0–60–3; Perera 8–0–43–1; Gunaratne 5–0–19–0; Gunathilleke 1–0–2–0; de Silva 1–0–3–0.

Umpires: M. Erasmus and B. N. J. Oxenford. Third umpire: C. B. Gaffaney.
Referee: B. C. Broad.

FINAL GROUP TABLES

Group A	P	W	L	NR	Pts	NRR
ENGLAND	3	3	0	0	6	1.04
BANGLADESH	3	1	1	1	3	0.00
Australia	3	0	1	2	2	–0.99
New Zealand	3	0	2	1	1	–1.05

Group B	P	W	L	NR	Pts	NRR
INDIA	3	2	1	0	4	1.37
PAKISTAN	3	2	1	0	4	–0.68
South Africa	3	1	2	0	2	0.16
Sri Lanka	3	1	2	0	2	–0.79

SEMI-FINALS

ENGLAND v PAKISTAN

At Cardiff, June 14. Pakistan won by eight wickets. Toss: Pakistan. One-day international debut: Rumman Raees.

Of all the days England could have chosen to revert to the tentative cricket that had once been their trademark, they chose the semi-final of the Champions Trophy. Pakistan, it's true, were superb: their bowling made a mockery of the old grumble about the boring middle overs, and their batsmen made a mockery of a target of 212. But England were unsettled by a used pitch – Pakistan had played on it two days earlier, winning a nail-biter against Sri Lanka – and were unable, perhaps even unwilling, to free their arms. A tally of 15 fours was their lowest in a completed innings since the 2015 World Cup; and, despite the beguiling proximity of the River Taff, they failed to hit a single six. So often England's heartbeat, Stokes batted as if he'd undergone a transplant, scoring 34 from

64 balls, and shouldering arms to deliveries he would normally have sent flying over fine leg; a quartet of twos was as extravagant as he got. In fact, the innings had begun reasonably enough. Bairstow, finally replacing the out-of-nick Jason Roy, chanced his arm for 43, and at 128 for two in the 28th all seemed well. But Root was caught behind trying to cut leg-spinner Shadab Khan, and Morgan – having passed 5,000 one-day runs for England – tried to charge Hasan Ali, who was reversing it away from the left-handers from round the wicket. Paralysis struck, and Pakistan were on a roll, confirmed by Fakhar Zaman's leaping catch at deep backward square to intercept Moeen Ali's pull. In total, eight fell for 83, and the last 25 overs produced just 93. A sluggish pitch encouraged England to believe all was not lost, but the freewheeling Fakhar set the tone by top-edging Wood for six in the first over, and the bowlers sacrificed accuracy in search of magic. By the time Fakhar was stumped for 57, heaving at a Rashid googly, Pakistan's opening pair had put on 118. Azhar Ali dragged on against Ball for 76, but it was already game over. Gloriously, Pakistan were in the final. Gallingly, England had not shown up. LAWRENCE BOOTH

Man of the Match: Hasan Ali. *Attendance:* 13,978.

England

J. M. Bairstow c Mohammad Hafeez b Hasan Ali	43
A. D. Hales c Babar Azam b Rumman Raees	13
J. E. Root c Sarfraz Ahmed b Shadab Khan	46
*E. J. G. Morgan c Sarfraz Ahmed b Hasan Ali	33
B. A. Stokes c Mohammad Hafeez b Hasan Ali	34
†J. C. Buttler c Sarfraz Ahmed b Junaid Khan	4
M. M. Ali c Fakhar Zaman b Junaid Khan	11
A. U. Rashid run out	7
L. E. Plunkett c Azhar Ali b Rumman Raees	9
M. A. Wood run out	3
J. T. Ball not out	2
Lb 1, w 3, nb 2	6
1/34 (2) 2/80 (1) 3/128 (3) 4/141 (4) 5/148 (6) 6/162 (7) 7/181 (8) 8/201 (5) 9/206 (9) 10/211 (10) — (49.5 overs)	211
10 overs: 52-1	

Junaid Khan 8.5–0–42–2; Rumman Raees 9–0–44–2; Imad Wasim 5–0–16–0; Shadab Khan 9–0–40–1; Hasan Ali 10–0–35–3; Mohammad Hafeez 8–0–33–0.

Pakistan

Azhar Ali b Ball	76
Fakhar Zaman st Buttler b Rashid	57
Babar Azam not out	38
Mohammad Hafeez not out	31
Lb 1, w 11, nb 1	13
1/118 (2) 2/173 (1) — (2 wkts, 37.1 overs)	215
10 overs: 49-0	

Shoaib Malik, *†Sarfraz Ahmed, Imad Wasim, Shadab Khan, Rumman Raees, Hasan Ali and Junaid Khan did not bat.

Wood 8–1–37–0; Ball 8–0–37–1; Stokes 3.1–0–38–0; Plunkett 6–0–33–0; Rashid 10–0–54–1; Ali 2–0–15–0.

Umpires: M. Erasmus and R. J. Tucker. Third umpire: C. B. Gaffaney.
Referee: A. J. Pycroft.

BANGLADESH v INDIA

At Birmingham, June 15. India won by nine wickets. Toss: India.

An irresistible mix of ruthlessness and flair took India into the final. What the match lacked in tension, it made up for in sumptuous batting. For Bangladesh, there were fifties from Tamim Iqbal and Mushfiqur Rahim that oozed stunning strokes, though anything they could do, India would do better. At the toss – held beneath growling Midland skies but with a forecast of afternoon sun – Kohli's decision was easy. Negotiating the Indian opening bowlers under lights and in occasional drizzle was less so, and Soumya Sarkar's leaden-footed drive second ball downright foolish. Undaunted, Sabbir Rahman crashed four rapid fours until he became Bhuvneshwar Kumar's second victim. That united Tamim and Mushfiqur, who punched and pulled, dabbed and drove their way to 154 for two in the 28th. A score of 330 or more was on. But Jadhav, an innocuous round-arm off-

HIGHEST LIST A TOTALS CONTAINING NO EXTRAS

305-4	Sheikh Jamal Dhanmondi v Prime Doleshwar at Savar	2013-14
271-4	Kerala v Andhra at Chennai	2009-10
265-1	**India v Bangladesh at Birmingham**	**2017**
246	**Sheikh Jamal Dhanmondi v Khelaghar Samaj Kallyan Samity at Savar**	**2017**
233-4	**Galle District v Hambantota District at Maggona**	**2016-17**
229-3	Scotland v United Arab Emirates at Edinburgh	2016
222-5	Karnataka v Andhra at Chennai	2009-10
212-4	Queensland v Tasmania at Hobart	2003-04
208-7	Karachi Blues v Faisalabad at Faisalabad	1993-94
205-6	National Bank v Water and Power Development Authority at Karachi	2015-16

spinner of modest returns, bogged them down, and both fell to risky cross-batted shots. Bumrah hastened the decline, and it needed Mashrafe bin Mortaza – plus keen-eyed umpiring that spotted the ball touching Dhoni's discarded glove for five penalty runs (admittedly in a seven-ball over) – to take Bangladesh past 260. In now ideal conditions and on a reliable strip, India's top-order *galacticos* treated another record Edgbaston crowd to a display of exhilarating batsmanship. Dhawan swashbuckled as ever, and zoomed past 300 runs for the tournament, before Sharma and Kohli vied to outdo each other for elegance and placement during an unbroken stand of 178. Mashrafe held his line, but his colleagues did not, their labours despatched with serenity or contempt, often both. Runs flowed as smoothly as an Astrud Gilberto song on a balmy evening. Sharma's determination to keep scoring after reaching his hundred denied Kohli his own, though he did notch up 8,000 one-day international runs in just 175 innings, seven fewer than A. B. de Villiers, the next-quickest. HUGH CHEVALLIER

Man of the Match: R. G. Sharma. *Attendance:* 24,340.

Bangladesh

Tamim Iqbal b Jadhav	70
Soumya Sarkar b Bhuvneshwar Kumar	0
Sabbir Rahman c Jadeja b Bhuvneshwar Kumar	19
†Mushfiqur Rahim c Kohli b Jadhav	61
Shakib Al Hasan c Dhoni b Jadeja	15
Mahmudullah b Bumrah	21
Mosaddek Hossain c and b Bumrah	15
*Mashrafe bin Mortaza not out	30
Taskin Ahmed not out	10
Lb 9, w 7, nb 2, p 5	23
1/1 (2) 2/31 (3) 3/154 (1) 4/177 (5) 5/179 (4) 6/218 (7) 7/229 (6) (7 wkts, 50 overs)	264
10 overs: 46-2	

Rubel Hossain and Mustafizur Rahman did not bat.

Bhuvneshwar Kumar 10–1–53–2; Bumrah 10–1–39–2; Ashwin 10–0–54–0; Pandya 4–0–34–0; Jadeja 10–0–48–1; Jadhav 6–0–22–2.

India

R. G. Sharma not out	123
S. Dhawan c Mosaddek Hossain b Mashrafe bin Mortaza	46
*V. Kohli not out	96
1/87 (2) (1 wkt, 40.1 overs)	265
10 overs: 63-0	

Yuvraj Singh, †M. S. Dhoni, H. H. Pandya, K. M. Jadhav, R. A. Jadeja, R. Ashwin, Bhuvneshwar Kumar and J. J. Bumrah did not bat.

Mashrafe bin Mortaza 8–0–29–1; Mustafizur Rahman 6–0–53–0; Taskin Ahmed 7–0–49–0; Rubel Hossain 6–0–46–0; Shakib Al Hasan 9–0–54–0; Mosaddek Hossain 2–0–13–0; Mahmudullah 1–0–10–0; Sabbir Rahman 1.1–0–11–0.

Umpires: H. D. P. K. Dharmasena and R. A. Kettleborough. Third umpire: N. J. Llong.
Referee: B. C. Broad.

FINAL

INDIA v PAKISTAN

GIDEON BROOKS

At The Oval, June 18. Pakistan won by 180 runs. Toss: India.

By the time Pakistan captain Sarfraz Ahmed held a skyed top edge from Bumrah to seal a crashing win, The Oval was a sea of green and white. Part of it came from the shirts worn and the flags waved by disbelieving Pakistan supporters, celebrating their country's first 50-over title since 1992. But much of it came from the seats in the OCS Stand left vacant by equally disbelieving Indians, who had comfortably outnumbered their rivals, but could not bear to hang around until the end.

Those who did stay had known their team's fate for some time, despite starting the day – the finest of the tournament, with temperatures nudging 30°C – as overwhelming favourites. Yet from the moment in the fourth over when Fakhar Zaman was caught behind for three but reprieved by a Bumrah no-ball, there was a feeling that the natural order might not last the day. Grabbing his second life, Fakhar ran with it all the way to a rollicking 114 from 106 balls. It was audacious, at times brilliant, and earned him the match award just three months after being plucked from the domestic game – along with 18-year-old leg-spinner Shadab Khan – at a trials day in Lahore.

Fakhar's century was the basis of a total of 338 for four – 101 more than Pakistan had made all tournament, and their second-best in 129 one-day internationals against India, behind 344 for eight in a defeat at Karachi in March 2004. His treatment of spinners Ashwin and Jadeja was brutal, hammering them for 78 from 56 balls, eight of his 12 fours and all his three sixes. He had softened India up nicely for Mohammad Hafeez and Imad Wasim to hit 71 from the innings' last 45 balls. Hafeez was especially carefree, butchering an unbeaten 57 from 37.

India had chased down only three higher totals, and never away from home – yet still fancied their chances. Those hopes were soon left in ruins by a thrilling, searing spell of fast bowling from Mohammad Amir, who blitzed India's top order with three for 16 in six overs. He trapped Sharma with his third ball, then had Kohli dropped at slip by Azhar Ali from his ninth. But Pakistan could

Philip Brown, Getty Images

Shaking it up: Mohammad Amir is congratulated by Virat Kohli after Pakistan's surprise win.

not dwell on the miss: the next ball took Kohli's leading edge and flew high to backward point. When Dhawan dabbed behind in Amir's fifth over, India were 33 for three.

At 18 years and 257 days, Shadab was the youngest to play in an ICC 50-over final, and claimed the wicket of Yuvraj Singh – the previous youngest – when he boldly reviewed an lbw decision: ball had struck pad a fraction before bat. Dhoni pulled Hasan Ali to deep square leg moments later, and it was 72 for six when Jadhav miscued a heave off Shadab.

Pandya provided a flicker, smashing Shadab for 23 in one over, including three of his six sixes, en route to 76 from 43 balls. But his luck, if not his rage, burned out when he and Jadeja botched a quick single and finished at the same end. While Jadeja simply turned his back, Pandya stomped to the pavilion, taking India's last hope with him. Four overs later, Pakistan completed their largest victory by runs over their greatest rivals, and the largest by any side in a global final.

Man of the Match: Fakhar Zaman. *Player of the Tournament:* Hasan Ali.
Attendance: 23,520.

Pakistan

Azhar Ali run out. 59
Fakhar Zaman c Jadeja b Pandya 114
Babar Azam c Yuvraj Singh b Jadhav. 46
Shoaib Malik c Jadhav b Bhuvneshwar Kumar. 12
Mohammad Hafeez not out. 57
Imad Wasim not out 25
Lb 9, w 13, nb 3. 25

1/128 (1) 2/200 (2) 3/247 (4) 4/267 (3) (4 wkts, 50 overs) 338
10 overs: 56-0

*†Sarfraz Ahmed, Shadab Khan, Mohammad Amir, Hasan Ali and Junaid Khan did not bat.

Bhuvneshwar Kumar 10–2–44–1; Bumrah 9–0–68–0; Ashwin 10–0–70–0; Pandya 10–0–53–1; Jadeja 8–0–67–0; Jadhav 3–0–27–1.

India

R. G. Sharma lbw b Mohammad Amir 0
S. Dhawan c Sarfraz Ahmed b Mohammad Amir. 21
*V. Kohli c Shadab Khan b Mohammad Amir 5
Yuvraj Singh lbw b Shadab Khan. 22
†M. S. Dhoni c Imad Wasim b Hasan Ali. . . 4
K. M. Jadhav c Sarfraz Ahmed b Shadab Khan. 9
H. H. Pandya run out. 76
R. A. Jadeja c Babar Azam b Junaid Khan . 15
R. Ashwin c Sarfraz Ahmed b Hasan Ali . . 1
Bhuvneshwar Kumar not out. 1
J. J. Bumrah c Sarfraz Ahmed b Hasan Ali. 1
Lb 2, w 1 3

1/0 (1) 2/6 (3) 3/33 (2) 4/54 (4) 5/54 (5) 6/72 (6) 7/152 (7) 8/156 (8) 9/156 (9) 10/158 (11) (30.3 overs) 158
10 overs: 47-3

Mohammad Amir 6–2–16–3; Junaid Khan 6–1–20–1; Mohammad Hafeez 1–0–13–0; Hasan Ali 6.3–1–19–3; Shadab Khan 7–0–60–2; Imad Wasim 0.3–0–3–0; Fakhar Zaman 3.3–0–25–0.

Umpires: M. Erasmus and R. A. Kettleborough. Third umpire: R. J. Tucker.
Referee: D. C. Boon.

CHAMPIONS TROPHY WINNERS

1998-99†	SOUTH AFRICA (248-6) beat West Indies (245) by four wickets	Dhaka
2000-01‡	NEW ZEALAND (265-6) beat India (264-6) by four wickets	Nairobi (Gymkhana)
2002-03	SRI LANKA v INDIA – no result *(trophy shared)*	Colombo (RPS)
2004	WEST INDIES (218-8) beat England (217) by two wickets.	The Oval
2006-07	AUSTRALIA (116-2) beat West Indies (138) by eight wickets (D/L)	Mumbai (Brabourne)
2009-10	AUSTRALIA (206-4) beat New Zealand (200-9) by six wickets . .	Centurion
2013	INDIA (129-7) beat England (124-8) by five runs	Birmingham
2017	PAKISTAN (338-4) beat India (158) by 180 runs	The Oval

† *Wills International Cup.* ‡ *ICC Knockout Trophy.*

ENGLAND v SOUTH AFRICA IN 2017

REVIEW BY STEVE JAMES

One-day internationals (3): England 2, South Africa 1
Twenty20 internationals (3): England 2, South Africa 1
Test matches (4): England 3, South Africa 1

The end was so swift, and the 3–1 scoreline so clear, that it made you wonder what all the fuss had been about. Two wickets in two balls at Old Trafford for Moeen Ali, who had taken a hat-trick to finish off the Oval Test a week earlier, meant England had beaten South Africa at home for the first time since 1998. Their three previous visits had each seen the resignation of an England captain – Nasser Hussain, Michael Vaughan and Andrew Strauss. And now they arrived on the back of an impressive record, having lost just one away series out of 18 in a decade, and won their most recent four, home and away, under the calmly authoritative Faf du Plessis.

And yet England – whose captain, Joe Root, was in his first series in charge rather than his last – brushed them aside to retain the Basil D'Oliveira Trophy they had won at Johannesburg 18 months earlier. But despite this South African team not being a patch on earlier incarnations, the series was more closely fought than the results suggested.

Both sides had potent bowling attacks, and both had weaknesses in their batting. South Africa could no longer call on the likes of Graeme Smith or Jacques Kallis, while A. B. de Villiers always intended to miss the Tests after captaining in the white-ball formats earlier on the tour. Collapses were too easily initiated – especially South African ones – and often betrayed the tightness of the play preceding them. Nine of the 16 innings failed to pass 252, and none lasted longer than the 108.4 overs England faced in the first at Old Trafford.

While England had more depth, they came no nearer to finalising their Ashes selection, in particular their top five. The stiff, upright opener Keaton Jennings made just 127 runs in eight innings and was dropped for the series against West Indies. Essex's Tom Westley, strong off his legs, shaped up nicely at No. 3 after replacing the injured (and struggling) Gary Ballance, but could not cement his place. And, in two Tests, Dawid Malan of Middlesex failed to make a score.

As if to confirm the complexity of the tale, the leading wicket-taker during a series played largely on seamer-friendly pitches was Ali, who claimed 25. Among England off-spinners, only Jim Laker, Fred Titmus and Graeme Swann had managed more in a series (all from five Tests to Ali's four). He also became the first player to take 25 wickets and score 250 runs in a series of four Tests or fewer. (Ian Botham had done it twice, but in six-match Ashes series, in 1981 and 1985.)

Ali's improved accuracy and more attacking line did not compromise his sharp turn, and – helped by England's spin-bowling consultant Saqlain

Graham Morris

Thinking caps: Joe Root addresses the England huddle in his first series as captain.

Mushtaq – he became more adept at setting his own fields. He dismissed 12 of the 14 South Africans at one time or other, and took a wicket every 29 balls. He was the obvious Man of the Series, yet he had begun it in supposed inferiority. In an attempt to relieve him of pressure, England bizarrely declined to call him their first-choice spinner, selecting Hampshire's Liam Dawson for the first two Tests to bowl slow left-arm and bat at No. 8. The pitch for the First, at Lord's, turned appreciably, and Ali claimed ten wickets to expose the charade. Dawson did take four, including a beauty to dismiss Hashim Amla in the second innings. But his retention for Trent Bridge typified some muddled thinking. He became a passenger as England lost the toss for the only time in the series, and their positive batting lurched towards recklessness.

For this they copped considerable flak, with Vaughan claiming they had failed to respect Test cricket. England were shocked, not least Root, for whom Vaughan – a fellow product of the Sheffield Collegiate club – had been a constant sounding board. But the critique sank in: at The Oval, their batting was much more careful. With Dawson discarded, England now chanced upon a better balance. Malan came in at No. 5, while Jonny Bairstow dropped two places to No. 7, better suited to his counter-attacking game, and the ever-flexible Ali one place to No. 8. A lower-middle order of Stokes, Bairstow and Ali contained too much power for South Africa. There were two other debutants: Westley, and Middlesex's Toby Roland-Jones. Ballance, in his third stab at Test cricket, had been a poor pick at No. 3; he was not even batting that high for Yorkshire. And there was little evidence he had cured his flaw of staying too deep in his crease, his weight back there with him.

Mark Wood, playing because Chris Woakes had not yet recovered from a side injury sustained during the Champions Trophy, was disappointing in the first two Tests. Worse, he revealed he had bruised his left heel at Lord's after inserting the wrong insole into his boot. In came Roland-Jones, a late bloomer at 29. He made an instant impact, taking five wickets in the first innings and three in the second, as well as scoring useful runs. He had a fluid action, and found surprising kick off the pitch, despite lacking express pace.

But with the series now 1–1 it was England's circumspection with the bat at The Oval – first by Alastair Cook, who made a high-class 88, then by Stokes, with a magnificent 112 – that turned the series their way. It was possibly Stokes's finest Test innings to date because of the conditions and circumstances, and his mixture of defence and aggression. He eventually exploded from 91 to 109 with three successive sixes off left-arm spinner Keshav Maharaj, who otherwise proved hard to collar.

This all set Ali up to finish The Oval's 100th men's Test with its first Test hat-trick, but the South Africans were left pondering what might have been. Vernon Philander had been unwell throughout the game, spending the second night in hospital on a drip. He topped his team's bowling averages, with ten wickets at 23 (he topped their batting, too), but dipped in and out too much to shape the series. Had he been able to bowl more on the first morning, when he snared Jennings for a duck, it might have been a different story.

The same could have been said about the First Test at Lord's, where Root was missed twice and stumped off a no-ball in his mainly majestic 190 – not a bad start to a Test captaincy career which, following his appointment in February, had been a long time coming. He grew in confidence as the summer wore on, setting attacking fields and finally getting to grips with DRS, having initially allowed emotion and his bowlers' personalities too much leeway. And his series average of 57 dealt with any concerns that the responsibility might affect his batting. He was head and shoulders above anyone on either side.

It helped England's cause in that opening game that Philander dropped a simple catch off Bairstow at a critical moment in the second innings. Indeed, Philander was a general frustration for the visitors. In addition to his illness at The Oval, he struggled with an ankle injury at Lord's, then missed Old Trafford with back spasms. Afterwards, du Plessis expressed his irritation at Philander's patchy fitness record. In between, he was Man of the Match at Trent Bridge for his five wickets and 96 runs, making up for the absence of Kagiso Rabada, who had been banned after swearing at Stokes in the First Test. Rabada was never quite the force he promised to be, and certainly not the bowler who, before the Tests, had reduced England to 20 for six in the third one-day international at Lord's.

Morne Morkel was South Africa's outstanding player. He took 19 wickets at 26 – including Cook four times, to make it 12 in all, more than any other bowler – and exuded class, especially against the left-handers. Others struggled badly. Heino Kuhn, the 33-year-old opener in his first Test series, averaged 14, while Theunis de Bruyn was little better; J-P. Duminy was released from the tour after the Second Test when the management lost patience with his repeated failures. How they could have done with de Villiers, whose Test future remained in doubt until he announced in late August that he would be available in all formats from mid-October, but was resigning the one-day captaincy.

Opening fire: Keaton Jennings falls to Vernon Philander on the first day of the series, at Lord's.

His absence was felt even more keenly when Test captain du Plessis missed the series opener because of the difficult birth of his first child back in Cape Town; Dean Elgar stepped in. During that game, head coach Russell Domingo left the tour for a second time because his mother's health had deteriorated after a car accident. She died a few hours before he arrived. Domingo had by then reapplied for his job, only for England's fast-bowling coach Ottis Gibson to be chosen instead.

Among the tourists, Amla made most runs, and was part of a magnificent partnership of 123 with du Plessis on the final afternoon in Manchester, after James Anderson and Stuart Broad had bowled like deities in the morning. But in the main Amla was a disappointment, and his unbeaten 311 at The Oval in 2012 seemed an age ago. He was one of those to return home in the nine days between the Second and Third Tests, when – inexplicably – South Africa did not play any cricket. The counties were occupied with the T20 Blast, but the tourists sought no opposition. It was an obvious error.

Their grittiest innings came from Elgar, whose brave 136 at The Oval was their only century. But in technical terms Temba Bavuma was their most competent batsman, staying side-on and playing the moving ball late, though he never grabbed a game by its scruff. He moved from No. 6 to No. 4 for the final Test, as South Africa wrestled with their order. Thanks to a nightwatchman, Quinton de Kock had begun at No. 8, but was soon promoted to No. 4 – too high for a wicketkeeper – and by the end was back at No. 6. Even that did not work. South Africa's batting was just too brittle, and Anderson enjoyed a

FIVE STATS YOU MAY HAVE MISSED

BENEDICT BERMANGE

- Moeen Ali became the second player to score a fifty and take at least ten wickets in a Lord's Test:

D. J. Nash	56	6-76, 5-93	New Zealand v England.	1994
M. M. Ali	**87, 7**	**4-59, 6-53**	**England v South Africa**	**2017**

- When South Africa won by 340 runs at Nottingham, it was the largest Test victory by runs for a team with no centuries. The previous record was England's 338-run win over Australia at Adelaide in January 1933, when their highest score was Wally Hammond's 85.

- Best bowling figures in Tests by double-barrelled players:

6-43	G. H. T. Simpson-Hayward	England v South Africa at Johannesburg. . .	1909-10
6-110	L. O. Fleetwood-Smith . . .	Australia v England at Adelaide	1936-37
5-43	A. Rose-Innes	South Africa v England at Port Elizabeth . .	1888-89
5-57	**T. S. Roland-Jones**	**England v South Africa at The Oval**	**2017**

- Toby Roland-Jones took 5.3 overs to reach four Test wickets, the second-fastest for England. Bob Appleyard needed only 4.3 overs against Pakistan on his debut, at Trent Bridge in 1954.

- At Old Trafford, Jonny Bairstow became the 15th England batsman to be dismissed for 99, and only the second lbw, after Eddie Paynter was trapped by Bill O'Reilly at Lord's in 1938.

magnificent series, picking up 20 wickets at 14, including seven at Old Trafford, five of them from the Pavilion End, which had been renamed after him. Broad chipped in, without finding one of his hot streaks.

The tour was long by modern standards, beginning on May 19 with a one-day match against Sussex, and ending on August 7. Before the Champions Trophy – where they won only once, against Sri Lanka – South Africa had lost the one-day series to England 2–1, when that sole Rabada-inspired victory at Lord's came after they had choked in Southampton. There was further embarrassment at the Rose Bowl in the first Twenty20 international, when they were thrashed by nine wickets after posting a weirdly conservative 142 for three. At Taunton, Chris Morris's aggression (briefly useful in the Trent Bridge Test, too) levelled the series. But England won in Cardiff without their rested captain Eoin Morgan, and gave an international debut to Malan, who thrashed 78 from 44 balls. That followed debuts for Hampshire's Mason Crane, Surrey's Tom Curran and Lancashire's Liam Livingstone. Even while experimenting, England were a step ahead.

SOUTH AFRICAN TOURING PARTY

*F. du Plessis (T/50), H. M. Amla (T/50), T. Bavuma (T), F. Behardien (50/20), T. B. de Bruyn (T), Q. de Kock (T/50), A. B. de Villiers (50/20), J-P. Duminy (T/50), D. Elgar (T), R. R. Hendricks (20), Imran Tahir (50/20), H. G. Kuhn (T), K. A. Maharaj (T/50), A. K. Markram (T), D. A. Miller (50/20), M. Morkel (T/50/20), C. H. Morris (T/50/20), M. Mosehle (20), D. Olivier (T), W. D. Parnell (50/20), D. Paterson (20), A. L. Phehlukwayo (T/50/20), V. D. Philander (T), D. Pretorius (50/20), K. Rabada (T/50), T. Shamsi (20), J. T. Smuts (20).

De Villiers captained in the limited-overs games, and Elgar in the First Test, when du Plessis was on paternity leave. Markram was originally picked to cover for du Plessis but retained when Duminy was sent home after the first two Tests.

Coach: R. C. Domingo. *Team manager:* M. Moosajee. *Assistant coach:* A. V. Birrell. *Batting coach:* N. D. McKenzie. *Bowling coach:* C. K. Langeveldt. *Spin bowling coach:* C. W. Henderson. *Strength and conditioning coach:* G. King. *Physiotherapist:* B. Jackson. *Performance analyst:* P. Agoram. *Psychologist:* M. Aronstam. *Security manager:* Z. Wadee. *Media manager:* L. Malekutu. *Logistics manager:* K. Masubelele.

TEST MATCH AVERAGES

ENGLAND – BATTING AND FIELDING

	T	*I*	*NO*	*R*	*HS*	*100*	*50*	*Avge*	*Ct*
J. E. Root	4	8	0	461	190	1	3	57.62	6
J. M. Bairstow	4	8	0	330	99	0	3	41.25	17
†B. A. Stokes	4	8	0	299	112	1	2	37.37	11
†M. M. Ali	4	8	1	252	87	0	2	36.00	3
†A. N. Cook	4	8	0	268	88	0	2	33.50	6
T. Westley	2	4	0	122	59	0	1	30.50	1
†G. S. Ballance	2	4	0	85	34	0	0	21.25	2
T. S. Roland-Jones	2	4	1	63	25	0	0	21.00	0
†K. K. Jennings	4	8	0	127	48	0	0	15.87	1
†S. C. J. Broad	4	7	1	77	57*	0	1	12.83	1
†D. J. Malan	2	4	0	35	18	0	0	8.75	0
M. A. Wood	2	4	0	34	28	0	0	8.50	1
†J. M. Anderson	4	7	4	19	12	0	0	6.33	3
L. A. Dawson	2	4	1	18	13	0	0	6.00	2

BOWLING

	Style	*O*	*M*	*R*	*W*	*BB*	*5I*	*Avge*
J. M. Anderson	RFM	125.2	39	282	20	5-72	1	14.10
M. M. Ali	OB	121	26	391	25	6-53	2	15.64
T. S. Roland-Jones	RFM	54.4	12	222	10	5-57	1	22.20
S. C. J. Broad	RFM	121.1	32	352	11	3-46	0	32.00
L. A. Dawson	SLA	44.4	8	169	5	2-34	0	33.80
B. A. Stokes	RFM	84	12	301	7	2-34	0	43.00

Also bowled: K. K. Jennings (RM) 1–0–2–0; D. J. Malan (LB) 1–0–7–0; J. E. Root (OB) 4–0–13–0; M. A. Wood (RFM) 56–13–197–1.

SOUTH AFRICA – BATTING AND FIELDING

	T	*I*	*NO*	*R*	*HS*	*100*	*50*	*Avge*	*Ct/St*
V. D. Philander	3	6	2	177	54	0	2	44.25	1
H. M. Amla	4	8	0	329	87	0	3	41.12	3
†D. Elgar	4	8	0	291	136	1	2	36.37	1
T. Bavuma	4	8	0	257	59	0	2	32.12	2
F. du Plessis	3	6	0	171	63	0	2	28.50	7
†Q. de Kock	4	8	0	185	68	0	2	23.12	17/2
C. H. Morris	2	4	0	75	36	0	0	18.75	3
†M. Morkel	4	8	3	78	20*	0	0	15.60	2
T. B. de Bruyn	2	4	0	60	48	0	0	15.00	5
†K. Rabada	3	6	0	85	30	0	0	14.16	3
H. G. Kuhn	4	8	0	113	34	0	0	14.12	1
K. A. Maharaj	4	8	2	83	24*	0	0	13.83	1
D. Olivier	2	3	1	4	4	0	0	2.00	0

Played in one Test: †J-P. Duminy 15, 2.

BOWLING

	Style	*O*	*M*	*R*	*W*	*BB*	*5I*	*Avge*
V. D. Philander	RFM	80	18	234	10	3-24	0	23.40
C. H. Morris	RFM	42.5	5	206	8	3-38	0	25.75
M. Morkel	RF	159	34	501	19	4-41	0	26.36
D. Olivier	RFM	43.2	8	193	7	3-38	0	27.57
K. Rabada	RF	135	28	455	16	4-91	0	28.43
K. A. Maharaj	SLA	162.4	29	516	17	4-85	0	30.35

Also bowled: T. Bavuma (RM) 5–0–14–0; T. B. de Bruyn (RFM) 10–1–48–0; J-P. Duminy (OB) 9–2–21–0; D. Elgar (SLA) 3–0–28–0.

At Hove, May 19 (day/night). **South Africans won by 66 runs. South Africans 289-4** (32 overs) (Q. de Kock 104, W. D. Parnell 61, J-P. Duminy 68); ‡**Sussex 223-9** (32 overs) (H. Z. Finch 62, P. D. Salt 37, D. M. W. Rawlins 41, A. Shahzad 34*). *In a rain-shortened match, the South Africans charged to 289 at nine an over. Quinton de Kock, who shared an opening stand of 121 in 15 overs with Wayne Parnell, hit seven sixes in 78 balls, then retired out, while J-P. Duminy, leading the side as A. B. de Villiers was unwell, lashed out for 68 in 46; Abidine Sakande grabbed two wickets in the penultimate over. Sussex had little hope of catching up after losing both openers for ducks in Kagiso Rabada's first over, but Harry Finch held firm for most of their reply, while Delray Rawlins scored 41 in 30 balls on his one-day debut.*

At Northampton, May 21. **South Africans won by 13 runs.** ‡**South Africans 275-7** (50 overs) (H. M. Amla 59, F. du Plessis 50, D. A. Miller 51, F. Behardien 33); **Northamptonshire 262** (47.1 overs) (M. D. E. Holden 55, C. F. Hughes 31, S. P. Crook 42, T. B. Sole 54; C. H. Morris 3-36). *County debut:* T. B. Sole. *Off-spinner Tom Sole – son of Scotland's 1990 Grand Slam-winning rugby captain David – almost pulled off an astonishing victory in his first senior game, aged 20. Coming in at 185-7, with 91 needed from 17.3 overs, he raced to 54 in 43 balls, striking two of his three sixes off successive balls from Andile Phehlukwayo in the 47th over. The target was down to 14 off three overs when he was last out, to Morne Morkel. Earlier, Sole had dismissed Hashim Amla, who put on a solid 93 with Faf du Plessis after Richard Gleeson trapped de Kock in the game's second over. But the South Africans' progress was more stately than at Hove; only a late surge – 54 in the last 38 balls – from Chris Morris and Duminy put the total just out of Sole's reach.*

LIMITED-OVERS INTERNATIONAL REPORTS BY NEIL MANTHORP

ENGLAND v SOUTH AFRICA

First Royal London One-Day International

At Leeds, May 24 (day/night). England won by 72 runs. Toss: South Africa.

Morgan's 107 from 93 balls could have been a match-winner in itself in the first of three games separated from the rest of South Africa's tour by the Champions Trophy. But it was an assault by Ali, who battered 77 from 51 in the closing overs, that lifted England's total at least 30 above par: 339 for six was the highest in a one-day international at Headingley. Hales had laid the foundations with a relatively conservative run-a-ball 61, but South Africa made a series of tactical blunders in the final ten overs, which yielded 102. They allowed Morgan to accelerate towards his 11th hundred in the format (including one for Ireland), and Ali to clobber boundaries at will in a display of what looked like mind-reading, but was actually cricket-reading: the field, and bowlers' actions, made it obvious what he would receive. Each hit five sixes. Yet with Amla and du Plessis moving to 145 for one just before the halfway point, many had South Africa as favourites. Then Wood, expensive early on, returned to trap Amla, rescinding the not-out decision on review; next over, Plunkett had du Plessis feathering an attempted run to third man. Duminy and Miller, one of Woakes's four victims, soon succumbed to soft dismissals, hoicking short balls to deep midwicket, and the game turned England's way. Before the match, both sides lined up to observe a minute's silence in memory of the victims of the terror attack in Manchester two days earlier.

Man of the Match: M. M. Ali. *Attendance:* 14,505.

England

J. J. Roy c de Kock b Parnell	1
A. D. Hales c de Kock b Phehlukwayo	61
J. E. Root c Amla b Phehlukwayo	37
*E. J. G. Morgan c Duminy b Morris	107
B. A. Stokes c Miller b Rabada	25
†J. C. Buttler c Miller b Morris	7
M. M. Ali not out	77
C. R. Woakes not out	6
B 4, lb 3, w 7, nb 4	18
1/3 (1) 2/101 (2) 3/122 (3) 4/190 (5) 5/198 (6) 6/315 (4) (6 wkts, 50 overs)	339
10 overs: 58-1	

A. U. Rashid, L. E. Plunkett and M. A. Wood did not bat.

Rabada 9–0–63–1; Parnell 7–0–47–1; Morris 10–1–61–2; Imran Tahir 9–0–68–0; Phehlukwayo 9–0–59–2; Duminy 6–0–34–0.

South Africa

H. M. Amla lbw b Wood	73
†Q. de Kock c Buttler b Woakes	5
F. du Plessis c Buttler b Plunkett	67
*A. B. de Villiers c Plunkett b Ali	45
J-P. Duminy c Woakes b Rashid	15
D. A. Miller c Stokes b Woakes	11
C. H. Morris c Buttler b Ali	5
W. D. Parnell c Wood b Woakes	19
A. L. Phehlukwayo b Rashid	4
K. Rabada c Buttler b Woakes	19
Imran Tahir not out	0
Lb 1, w 3	4
1/33 (2) 2/145 (1) 3/149 (3) 4/182 (5) 5/208 (6) 6/216 (7) 7/225 (4) 8/230 (9) 9/267 (8) 10/267 (10) (45 overs)	267
10 overs: 59-1	

Woakes 8–0–38–4; Wood 6–0–49–1; Plunkett 9–0–42–1; Rashid 10–0–69–2; Stokes 2–0–14–0; Ali 9–0–50–2; Root 1–0–4–0.

Umpires: R. T. Robinson and R. J. Tucker. Third umpire: C. B. Gaffaney.
Referee: A. J. Pycroft.

ENGLAND v SOUTH AFRICA

Second Royal London One-Day International

At Southampton, May 27. England won by two runs. Toss: South Africa. One-day international debut: K. A. Maharaj.

South Africa handed the series to England when they failed to score ten from the final ten balls, with five wickets in hand. Morgan played a last, desperate card, instructing Ball and Wood to bowl those ten deliveries short: "No easy runs, make them hit the ball in the air." It worked. Earlier, South Africa's uncharacteristically sloppy fielding reprieved Morgan on 16 and 22, but they paid most heavily for dropping Stokes off his first two deliveries: Amla missed a regulation slip catch and de Kock a thick edge, both off debutant left-arm spinner Keshav Maharaj. Stokes went on to hammer 11 fours and three sixes in an intimidating 79-ball century, before Buttler and Ali plundered 78 off the last 40 deliveries, propelling England to 330. De Villiers's mood had not been improved by a chat with the umpires after 33 overs. Rob Bailey and Chris Gaffaney believed one of the balls was showing more wear and tear than the other; though they didn't change it, de Villiers felt they were implying South Africa had been guilty of tampering. De Kock anchored the chase, adding 96 with de Villiers, but the asking-rate looked excessive when he was caught behind with 120 required from

Stu Forster, Getty Images

Short and sweet: Mark Wood's back-of-a-length final over kept South Africa quiet.

14 overs, and became steeper as Behardien limped to 17 from 25 balls. Then Miller and Morris hauled South Africa back on track with power and precision. They needed 20 off the final two overs; Miller crunched Ball's first two deliveries for six and four, bringing a famous win into sight. But when Ball and Wood kept it short, they continued to swing – and missed, or mistimed, enough to give England the series.

Man of the Match: B. A. Stokes. *Attendance:* 16,111.

England

J. J. Roy b Rabada	8
A. D. Hales c de Kock b Pretorius	24
J. E. Root run out	39
*E. J. G. Morgan c de Kock b Rabada	45
B. A. Stokes c Miller b Maharaj	101
†J. C. Buttler not out	65
M. M. Ali c de Kock b Phehlukwayo	33
B 1, lb 6, w 8	15
1/12 (1) 2/70 (2) 3/80 (3) 4/175 (4) 5/252 (5) 6/330 (7) — (6 wkts, 50 overs)	330
10 overs: 43-1	

A. U. Rashid, L. E. Plunkett, M. A. Wood and J. T. Ball did not bat.

Rabada 10–0–50–2; Morris 10–0–66–0; Pretorius 10–0–61–1; Maharaj 10–0–72–1; Phehlukwayo 10–1–74–1.

South Africa

†Q. de Kock c Buttler b Ali	98
H. M. Amla c Morgan b Stokes	24
F. du Plessis c Buttler b Plunkett	16
*A. B. de Villiers c Buttler b Plunkett	52
D. A. Miller not out	71
F. Behardien c Ali b Plunkett	17
C. H. Morris not out	35
Lb 6, w 9	15
1/56 (2) 2/93 (3) 3/189 (4) 4/211 (1) 5/266 (6) — (5 wkts, 50 overs)	328
10 overs: 56-1	

D. Pretorius, A. L. Phehlukwayo, K. Rabada and K. A. Maharaj did not bat.

Wood 10–0–47–0; Ball 10–0–81–0; Stokes 3–0–12–1; Plunkett 10–0–64–3; Rashid 6–0–41–0; Ali 8–0–59–1; Root 3–0–18–0.

Umpires: R. J. Bailey and C. B. Gaffaney. Third umpire: R. J. Tucker.
Referee: A. J. Pycroft.

ENGLAND v SOUTH AFRICA

Third Royal London One-Day International

At Lord's, May 29. South Africa won by seven wickets. Toss: South Africa. One-day international debut: T. S. Roland-Jones.

England lost their sixth wicket – off the last ball of the fifth over – earlier than any team in one-day internationals. They had only 20 on the board, and that was as good as the match. Canada had owned the record since the Netherlands claimed their sixth wicket in 6.2 overs at King City, Toronto, in 2013. Here, Rabada had both openers caught at first slip with significant seam movement, Parnell accounted for Root and Morgan with disconcerting swing, while Buttler and Rashid drove carelessly at Rabada and were held at second slip. England had been put in on a green pitch under overcast skies, and conditions were awkward in the first hour, but Bairstow proved they were not unplayable,

LOWEST SCORE AT FALL OF SIXTH WICKET IN AN ODI

10-6	(6.2 overs)	Canada (67) v Netherlands at King City, Toronto	2013
12-6	(9.2 overs)	Canada (36) v Sri Lanka at Paarl	2002-03
13-6*	(7.5 overs)	Sri Lanka (43) v South Africa at Paarl	2011-12
14-6	(8 overs)	Pakistan (43) v West Indies at Cape Town	1992-93
17-6	(13.1 overs)	Kenya (84) v Australia at Nairobi	2002
19-6	(9.1 overs)	Pakistan (153) v South Africa at Colombo (SSC)	2000
20-6	**(5 overs)**	**England (153) v South Africa at Lord's**	**2017**
22-6*	(8.4 overs)	Pakistan (75) v Sri Lanka at Lahore	2008-09
25-6	(12.5 overs)	England (81-9) v Pakistan at Birmingham	1974
25-6*	(12.3 overs)	West Indies (91) v Zimbabwe at Sydney	2000-01

* *Batting second.*

All matches were lost by the first-named team.

scoring freely in a chanceless 51 until he charged at Maharaj. Willey and debutant Toby Roland-Jones (England's fifth double-barrelled male player, but the first since Mandy Mitchell-Innes in 1935) calmly helped him add 114 for the next two wickets, to show up the top order's woeful performance. Even so, England were routed in barely 31 overs, and South Africa faced 11 before the interval. Amla and de Kock scored 59 in that time and took an untroubled opening stand to 95 in 15, before three for six in 19 balls gave hope to English optimists. Duminy and de Villiers were in no mood to encourage that, gently but firmly guiding South Africa home with more than 21 overs to spare, and confirming England's first defeat in nine one-day internationals. Morgan later criticised the amount of "live, green grass" on the pitch, adding: "I don't think it was an ODI wicket. It makes it one-sided, which I don't think is good for anybody."

Man of the Match: K. Rabada. *Attendance:* 27,146.

Man of the Series: E. J. G. Morgan.

England

J. J. Roy c Amla b Rabada	4
A. D. Hales c Amla b Rabada	1
J. E. Root lbw b Parnell	2
*E. J. G. Morgan c de Kock b Parnell	8
J. M. Bairstow st de Kock b Maharaj	51
†J. C. Buttler c du Plessis b Rabada	4
A. U. Rashid c du Plessis b Rabada	0
D. J. Willey c Duminy b Parnell	26
T. S. Roland-Jones not out	37
J. T. Ball b Maharaj	7
S. T. Finn c de Villiers b Maharaj	3
Lb 2, w 8	10
1/4 (1) 2/7 (3) 3/15 (4) 4/15 (2) 5/20 (6) 6/20 (7) 7/82 (8) 8/134 (5) 9/143 (10) 10/153 (11) (31.1 overs)	153
10 overs: 40-6	

Rabada 9–1–39–4; Parnell 8–0–43–3; Morkel 4–0–15–0; Maharaj 6.1–0–25–3; Morris 4–0–29–0.

South Africa

H. M. Amla b Roland-Jones	55
†Q. de Kock b Ball	34
J-P. Duminy not out	28
F. du Plessis c Buttler b Ball	5
*A. B. de Villiers not out	27
Lb 1, w 6	7
1/95 (1) 2/95 (2) 3/101 (4) (3 wkts, 28.5 overs)	156
10 overs: 57-0	

D. A. Miller, C. H. Morris, W. D. Parnell, K. A. Maharaj, M. Morkel and K. Rabada did not bat.

Willey 4.5–0–43–0; Ball 10–0–43–2; Finn 7–1–35–0; Roland-Jones 7–2–34–1.

Umpires: M. A. Gough and R. J. Tucker. Third umpire: C. B. Gaffaney.
Referee: A. J. Pycroft.

For South Africa's matches in the Champions Trophy, see pages 273.

ENGLAND v SOUTH AFRICA

First NatWest Twenty20 International

At Southampton, June 21 (floodlit). England won by nine wickets. Toss: South Africa. Twenty20 international debuts: M. S. Crane; D. Pretorius, T. Shamsi.

England romped to victory with 33 balls to spare, hunting down a modest 143 – despite South Africa losing just three wickets, all in the first five overs. Willey and Wood both struck with their opening delivery, and the lively balls that rapped the top order on the gloves persuaded de Villiers and Behardien that caution was required. They batted out the remainder of the innings with care, but England's top three showed they had misread the conditions, playing every stroke without a hint of misbehaviour from the pitch. Though England's new-ball bowlers had made the early inroads, it was the spinners – left-armer Dawson and debutant leggie Mason Crane, on their home ground – who won the game, conceding just 41 (and only two fours) in eight overs. Try as they might to accelerate, neither South African batsman could get under them. The slow men's control and reading of the situation were impeccable, and Crane did not disappoint those with high hopes for his future. Parnell bowled two overs for 26 – Roy cracked 19 in the second – and England were off to a flyer. That allowed Bairstow, who equalled his T20I best, and Hales to treat South Africa's most consistent match-winner, Imran Tahir, with scant respect: his three overs disappeared for 37.

Man of the Match: J. M. Bairstow. *Attendance:* 14,993.

FEWEST WICKETS IN A COMPLETED T20 INTERNATIONAL

4	South Africa (219-4 in 20 overs) v India (71-0 in 7.5) at Johannesburg (D/L)	2011-12
4	**South Africa (142-3 in 20 overs) v England (143-1 in 14.3) at Southampton**	**2017**
5	West Indies (197-4 in 20 overs) v Bangladesh (179-1 in 20) at Mirpur	2012-13
5	India (192-2 in 20 overs) v West Indies (196-3 in 19.4) at Mumbai	2015-16

South Africa

		B	4/6
1 J. T. Smuts *b 8*	0	1	0
2 R. R. Hendricks *c 8 b 11*	3	2	0
3 *A. B. de Villiers *not out*	65	58	4/2
4 D. A. Miller *c 5 b 11*	9	7	0/1
5 F. Behardien *not out*	64	52	4/2
W 1	1		
6 overs: 43-3 (20 overs)	142-3		

1/0 2/7 3/32

6 †M. Mosehle, 7 W. D. Parnell, 8 D. Pretorius, 9 A. L. Phehlukwayo, 10 T. Shamsi and 11 Imran Tahir did not bat.

Willey 4–8–34–1; Wood 4–10–36–2; Jordan 4–6–31–0; Dawson 4–9–17–0; Crane 4–8–24–0.

England

		B	4/6
1 J. J. Roy *lbw b 9*	28	14	3/2
2 A. D. Hales *not out*	47	38	3/2
3 J. M. Bairstow *not out*	60	35	6/2
Lb 6, w 2	8		
6 overs: 59-1 (14.3 overs)	143-1		

1/45

4 *E. J. G. Morgan, 5 †J. C. Buttler, 6 S. W. Billings, 7 L. A. Dawson, 8 D. J. Willey, 9 C. J. Jordan, 10 M. S. Crane and 11 M. A. Wood did not bat.

Smuts 3–7–20–0; Parnell 2–5–26–0; Phehlukwayo 1.3–4–11–1; Imran Tahir 3–4–37–0; Shamsi 3–6–23–0; Pretorius 2–2–20–0.

Umpires: R. J. Bailey and R. T. Robinson. Third umpire: M. A. Gough.
Referee: A. J. Pycroft.

ENGLAND v SOUTH AFRICA

Second NatWest Twenty20 International

At Taunton, June 23. South Africa won by three runs. Toss: England. Twenty20 international debuts: T. K. Curran, L. S. Livingstone.

England were cantering towards a series win when Roy was given out obstructing the field, and the game swung decisively. Chasing 175, they were 133 for two with five overs to go – thanks largely to his first fifty in 11 international innings – when he set off for a single but was sent back by Liam Livingstone. Roy, clearly eyeing Phehlukwayo at mid-on, crossed the pitch as he headed for safety. Although he had his back to the fielder when the throw hit his boot, every South African appealed for an attempt to block the run-out. Third umpire Tim Robinson concurred. It was the opening they needed: Phehlukwayo produced a perfect yorker to bowl Buttler and, when Morgan spliced one in the air, England were underdogs for the first time, with 13 required from seven deliveries. As the debutant Livingstone struggled to get the ball away (and was eventually run out), that became eight from two; Dawson gave England hope with a lofted off-drive only a yard away from being a six, but another yorker from Phehlukwayo concluded an unlikely victory. It would never have come had de Villiers not injected 46 boundary-laden runs following a meaty 45 from Smuts, while Morris slowed down England's charge by conceding just 18, dismissing Bairstow and getting in the ear of Livingstone, who had earlier dropped him badly at deep midwicket. Another England debutant, the Cape Town-born Tom Curran, picked up three wickets, and instantly looked at home. ICC chief executive Dave Richardson later wrote to his ECB counterpart Tom Harrison reminding him of players' responsibilities on social media, after Stokes tweeted that the Roy decision had been an "embarrassment".

Man of the Match: C. H. Morris. *Attendance:* 11,142.

South Africa

		B	4/6
1 J. T. Smuts *c 8 b 7*	45	35	4/3
2 R. R. Hendricks *b 11*	7	8	0
3 †M. Mosehle *c 5 b 8*	15	12	1/1
4 *A. B. de Villiers *c 6 b 9*	46	20	4/3
5 D. A. Miller *c 5 b 8*	8	10	0
6 F. Behardien *lbw b 10*	32	21	2/2
7 C. H. Morris *c 1 b 11*	12	11	1
8 A. L. Phehlukwayo *b 11*	0	1	0
9 M. Morkel *not out*	0	1	0
10 D. Paterson *not out*	4	1	1
W 5	5		
6 overs: 45-1 (20 overs)	174-8		

1/25 2/57 3/96 4/113 5/127 6/157 7/164 8/170

11 T. Shamsi did not bat.

Willey 4–9–29–1; Jordan 4–10–38–1; Curran 4–9–33–3; Plunkett 4–8–36–2; Dawson 4–6–38–1.

England

		B	4/6
1 J. J. Roy *obstructing the field*	67	45	9/1
2 S. W. Billings *c 5 b 7*	3	4	0
3 J. M. Bairstow *c 6 b 7*	47	37	8/1
4 L. S. Livingstone *run out*	16	18	1
5 †J. C. Buttler *b 8*	10	8	1
6 *E. J. G. Morgan *c 4 b 10*	6	4	1
7 L. A. Dawson *not out*	7	5	1
8 L. E. Plunkett *not out*	0	0	0
B 4, lb 5, w 5, nb 1	15		
6 overs: 51-1 (20 overs)	171-6		

1/15 2/125 3/133 4/153 5/162 6/167

9 D. J. Willey, 10 C. J. Jordan and 11 T. K. Curran did not bat.

Morkel 4–9–43–0; Morris 4–16–18–2; Paterson 4–10–32–1; Phehlukwayo 4–7–34–1; Smuts 1–1–11–0; Shamsi 3–4–24–0.

Umpires: R. J. Bailey and M. A. Gough. Third umpire: R. T. Robinson. Referee: A. J. Pycroft.

ENGLAND v SOUTH AFRICA

Third NatWest Twenty20 International

At Cardiff, June 25. England won by 19 runs. Toss: South Africa. Twenty20 international debut: D. J. Malan.

Dawid Malan's 78 from 44 balls on his England debut proved ample to see off South Africa, who slumped to 91 for six in reply. Eoin Morgan had rested himself to give Livingstone another go, and the 29-year-old Malan, England-born but raised in South Africa, made the most of his long-awaited opportunity, complementing powerful off-side cuts and drives with deft tucks and pick-ups off his legs. Arriving in the third over, he offered no shot to his first delivery, from Morris, but mauled the second off a good length over midwicket for six. It was quite a statement. Hales was content to play a secondary role, farming out the strike; he scored 17 in 16 balls as Malan reached his fifty in 31, though he did hit a couple of late sixes. Paterson produced some exemplary death bowling to limit the damage, twice finding himself on a hat-trick as he took four for two from his last ten balls. His yorkers gave South Africa a chance, but that vanished as Jordan and Curran claimed five for 53 in their combined eight overs. De Villiers launched Crane for 16 in three balls before becoming his first international victim, caught at deep backward square attempting a third six in the same over; despite a desperate late surge from Mosehle and Phehlukwayo, England wrapped up the series.

Man of the Match: D. J. Malan. *Attendance:* 14,312.

HIGHEST SCORE ON TWENTY20 INTERNATIONAL DEBUT

98*	R. T. Ponting	Australia v New Zealand at Auckland	2004-05
89	D. A. Warner	Australia v South Africa at Melbourne	2008-09
88*	H. Patel	Canada v Ireland at Colombo (SSC)	2009-10
78	R. R. Rossouw	South Africa v Australia at Adelaide	2014-15
78	**D. J. Malan**	**England v South Africa at Cardiff**	**2017**
71	Junaid Siddique	Bangladesh v Pakistan at Cape Town	2007-08

J. E. Root scored 90 v Australia at Southampton in 2013 after not batting in his first two Twenty20 internationals.*

England

		B	4/6
1 J. J. Roy *c 7 b 9*	8	8	1
2 A. D. Hales *c 5 b 8*	36	28	2/2
3 D. J. Malan *c 10 b 11*	78	44	12/2
4 *†J. C. Buttler *c 1 b 10*	31	22	1/2
5 S. W. Billings *c 4 b 10*	12	11	0/1
6 L. S. Livingstone *b 10*	0	1	0
7 L. E. Plunkett *c 5 b 8*	0	2	0
8 D. J. Willey *b 10*	1	2	0
9 C. J. Jordan *not out*	0	0	0
10 T. K. Curran *not out*	1	2	0
B 5, lb 6, w 3	14		
6 overs: 46-1 (20 overs)	181-8		

1/13 2/118 3/127 4/166 5/166 6/179 7/180 8/180

11 M. S. Crane did not bat.

Morris 4–11–24–0; Morkel 4–12–32–1; Phehlukwayo 4–5–44–2; Paterson 4–11–32–4; Imran Tahir 4–9–38–1.

South Africa

		B	4/6
1 J. T. Smuts *c 3 b 7*	29	30	2/1
2 R. R. Hendricks *c 7 b 10*	0	5	0
3 C. H. Morris *c 2 b 9*	8	9	1
4 *A. B. de Villiers *c 2 b 11*	35	19	2/2
5 D. A. Miller *c 4 b 9*	7	6	0
6 F. Behardien *c 5 b 9*	3	8	0
7 †M. Mosehle *c 5 b 10*	36	22	1/4
8 A. L. Phehlukwayo *not out*	27	20	4
9 M. Morkel *not out*	5	2	1
Lb 9, w 2, nb 1	12		
6 overs: 38-2 (20 overs)	162-7		

1/11 2/22 3/59 4/82 5/86 6/91 7/145

10 D. Paterson and 11 Imran Tahir did not bat.

Willey 4–10–40–0; Curran 4–15–22–2; Jordan 4–9–31–3; Plunkett 4–10–22–1; Crane 4–8–38–1.

Umpires: M. A. Gough and R. T. Robinson. Third umpire: R. J. Bailey.
Referee: A. J. Pycroft.

ENGLAND LIONS v SOUTH AFRICANS

At Worcester, June 29–July 1. Drawn. Toss: England Lions.

Both camps were finalising their Test teams for Lord's. Kuhn, who had scored a century against the Lions for South Africa A the previous week, made sure of his debut by adding 142 with Amla, while Ballance's recall by England was announced on the final day, when he and Westley put on 136. With Kuhn and Amla retiring in sight of centuries, and Bavuma stranded on 85 as Elgar declared on the last morning, the game's only hundred came from Westley – who would replace Ballance later in the series. Garton picked up a couple of wickets with his left-arm pace as the South Africans' first innings spread across two rain-affected days; the tourists dared not risk Philander, still recovering from an ankle injury suffered while playing for Sussex a few weeks earlier. Five of the Lions had been pulled out of their county teams halfway through the day/night Championship round being staged across the country.

Close of play: first day, South Africans 58-1 (Kuhn 30, Amla 16); second day, South Africans 382-6 (Bavuma 85, Morris 25).

South Africans

*D. Elgar c Billings b Garton	5
H. G. Kuhn retired out	80
H. M. Amla retired out	91
J-P. Duminy c Robson b Garton	25
T. Bavuma not out	85
T. B. de Bruyn lbw b Plunkett	0
†Q. de Kock c Clarke b Jennings	51
C. H. Morris not out	25
B 4, lb 10, w 1, nb 5	20
1/12 (1) (6 wkts dec, 97.3 overs)	382

2/154 (2) 3/201 (4)
4/224 (3) 5/232 (6) 6/314 (7)

K. A. Maharaj, K. Rabada and M. Morkel did not bat.

Helm 25–4–77–0; Garton 21–1–90–2; Plunkett 22.3–6–66–1; Jennings 11–2–35–1; Crane 16–0–89–0; Westley 2–0–11–0.

England Lions

S. D. Robson c de Kock b Morris	47	L. S. Livingstone not out	0
K. K. Jennings b Morkel	39	Lb 2, w 1, nb 13	16
T. Westley not out	106		—
*G. S. Ballance lbw b de Bruyn	56	1/71 (2) (4 wkts dec, 80.1 overs)	266
†S. W. Billings lbw b de Bruyn	2	2/126 (1) 3/262 (4) 4/264 (5)	

J. M. Clarke, L. E. Plunkett, T. G. Helm, G. H. S. Garton and M. S. Crane did not bat.

Morkel 16–3–49–1; Rabada 16–2–59–0; Morris 15–5–35–1; de Bruyn 7–2–24–2; Maharaj 18.1–4–46–0; Duminy 8–0–51–0.

Umpires: J. H. Evans and S. C. Gale.

ENGLAND v SOUTH AFRICA

First Investec Test

STEVEN LYNCH

At Lord's, July 6–9. England won by 211 runs. Toss: England. Test debut: H. G. Kuhn.

Joe Root enjoyed a dream start as England's 80th Test captain. He won the toss, shrugged off some early blips to cruise to 190, then stood smiling at slip as a rudderless South Africa capsized twice on an unusually dry pitch, which permitted spin and occasional uneven bounce. It was their first defeat at Lord's since 1960; they had been particularly potent there since readmission, winning four of their five Tests.

As Faf du Plessis was still at home after the birth of his first child, Dean Elgar became the match's second new captain – the first time this had happened in a Test in England since 1968. With Chris Woakes unfit, Dawson retained his place after making his debut at Chennai more than six months earlier, while Bairstow shrugged off a late scare after being hit on the foot in the nets by Sachin Tendulkar's 17-year-old son, Arjun. South Africa gave a first cap to Heino Kuhn, who had made a double-century for the A-team against Hampshire a month earlier, while de Bruyn – an opener in his only Test – moved down the order to replace du Plessis. There was also a first outing for England's new cable-knit sweaters, which received mixed reviews: brilliant white, they looked odd atop cream shirts, giving the players the appearance of a piece of Camembert, according to one press-box wit.

Root took his own £1 coin to the toss, unsure if one would be provided: "I didn't want to look like a tight Yorkshireman." Elgar got the call wrong, and had little luck afterwards; he seemed relieved to hand the armband back for the next Test.

The early exchanges, though, did go South Africa's way. The feisty Philander found Cook's edge in the fourth over, Jennings was lbw in his next, then Morkel pinned Ballance,

HIGHEST SCORE IN FIRST TEST AS CAPTAIN

239	G. T. Dowling	New Zealand v India at Christchurch	1967-68
203*	S. Chanderpaul	West Indies v South Africa at Georgetown	2004-05
191	C. Hill	Australia v South Africa at Sydney	1910-11
190	**J. E. Root**	**England v South Africa at Lord's**	**2017**
173	A. N. Cook	England v Bangladesh at Chittagong	2009-10
164*	V. S. Hazare	India v England at Delhi	1951-52
163	C. H. Lloyd	West Indies v India at Bangalore	1974-75
158	W. W. Armstrong	Australia v England at Sydney	1920-21
153*	W. L. Murdoch	Australia v England at The Oval	1880

The most runs in a player's first Test as captain is 256, by V. Kohli (115 and 141) for India v Australia at Adelaide in 2014-15.

Dan Mullan, Getty Images

Pressure? What pressure? Joe Root scores freely in his first innings as England captain.

back after being dropped in India. Not for the last time, England were rubbish at reviews: Jennings marched straight off, even though the ball was missing leg, and Ballance challenged his, which was not. A score of 49 for three was familiar territory: since the start of 2015, England had lost their third wicket for 55 or fewer in 23 of 61 Test innings (there would be two more instances before the end of the series). And it could have been worse: Root, on five, hooked Rabada to long leg, where Aiden Markram – briefly on as a substitute – had drifted in too far. Then, on 16, he flashed Rabada through Duminy's upstretched hands in the gully.

Root made them pay, with interest. Although Bairstow went shortly before lunch, giving Philander three for 21, no wicket fell in the middle session. The biggest tremor came when Morkel castled Stokes, but it was a no-ball – the 13th time he had been deprived of a Test wicket by overstepping. "World record? Thank you. Somebody needs to hold it!" said Morkel grimly. "But it's not acceptable."

Stokes succumbed to a lazy hook shortly after tea to end a stand of 114; Rabada's verbal send-off was missed by most, but not by the stump mike or the umpires and, when previous offences were taken into account, he copped a one-match ban. He claimed he was swearing at himself.

With Ali his ally, Root scudded through the nineties, and reached his 12th Test hundred with a swept three off slow left-armer Maharaj. Only two of England's first 76 captains (Archie MacLaren and Allan Lamb) had marked their first match in charge with a century, but now the last four had all done it: Andrew Strauss, Kevin Pietersen, Cook and Root. He celebrated with a six into the Pavilion in Maharaj's next over, and Ali followed an uppish waft off Rabada with a Gowerish cover-drive for four: England were rattling along. Another hundred partnership came up in 18 overs before, on 149, Root was stumped – only for replays to show Maharaj had overstepped, a criminal offence for a spinner.

By the close England had romped to 357 for five, Root's unbeaten 184 the best return on a Test skipper's first day since Clem Hill made 191 for Australia against South Africa at Sydney in December 1910. But Root fell in the third over next morning, as did Dawson, and England might have collapsed had South Africa reviewed Philander's lbw shout against Broad, who had only an edged boundary to his name. Instead Broad survived to swish and, with Ali cutting and clipping elegantly, England forged past 400 – which, in the first innings of a Lord's Test, had always insured against defeat (except in 1930, when

MOST WICKETS BY A SPINNER IN A LORD'S TEST

15-104	H. Verity (SLA)	England v Australia	1934
13-71	D. L. Underwood (SLA)	England v Pakistan	1974
12-101	R. Tattersall (OB)	England v South Africa	1951
11-70	D. L. Underwood (SLA)	England v New Zealand	1969
11-74	J. Briggs (SLA)	England v Australia	1886
11-152	S. Ramadhin (OB)	West Indies v England	1950
10-112	**M. M. Ali (OB)**	**England v South Africa**	**2017**
10-141	Yasir Shah (LB)	Pakistan v England	2016
10-175	D. V. P. Wright (LB)	England v South Africa	1947

Don Bradman was about). Ali and Wood departed in the same Rabada over, but the last-wicket pair enjoyed themselves, cracking 45 in 27 balls. Broad completed his first half-century in 66 Test innings since July 2013 by mullering Morkel for successive sixes into the Grand Stand, and inspired Anderson to rasp Rabada into the Mound, his first Test six off a pace bowler.

South Africa's openers survived until lunch, but two overs afterwards Kuhn – stocky rather than sticky at the crease – edged low to first slip. The skies were sunny and the outfield quick, and batting looked simple as Elgar and Amla added 72. But just after Elgar brought up his half-century, Amla faced his first ball from Ali, and missed it. Then, in the second over after tea, Elgar bat-padded into Ballance's chest at short leg. The ball lodged there, giving Ali his 100th wicket in his 38th Test; in the morning, he had scored his 2,000th run. He was the 28th to this double – the seventh from England – but the first to complete it on the same day. Among those who took longer was Garry Sobers (48 Tests), but Ali knew any comparisons were wide of the mark: "In my garden I was better than Sobers…"

Duminy soon fell lbw to Broad, but Bavuma and de Bruyn dug in, putting on 99 before de Bruyn feathered to the keeper near the close. South Africa wobbled next morning when nightwatchman Rabada and Bavuma fell in successive overs just before the new ball. At 248 for seven, England were scenting a big lead, but de Kock – wasted at No. 7, let alone the No. 8 he had become – counter-attacked excitingly, driving Broad for three successive fours en route to a 36-ball half-century. Only Kapil Dev (35 in 1982) had made a quicker Test fifty at Lord's. De Kock flashed his next delivery low to Stokes at square cover, but Philander shrugged off a blow on the hand from Anderson to continue the fightback, before mowing at Ali once too often. An X-ray revealed bruising rather than a break, but he did not reappear until the third evening, and did not bowl until the fourth morning.

Clive Rose, Getty Images

Sworn to silence: Kagiso Rabada, his mouth hastily covered by Dean Elgar's hand, sends Ben Stokes on his way in the second innings, after a verbal farewell in the first.

South Africa had been disciplined in taking the deficit below three figures, but now they lost the plot in helpful conditions, using up both reviews against Cook inside ten overs. There were few frills in England's batting, beyond a reverse-swept boundary by Jennings and a juicy cover-drive from Cook off Duminy, but the opening stand reached the 35th over before Jennings wafted at Morkel. By then, Cook had passed 1,000 Test runs against South Africa – becoming the third batsman, after Sachin Tendulkar and Rahul Dravid, to reach four figures against seven other Test sides (none had done so against Zimbabwe or Bangladesh). Ballance kept him company until the close, by which time the lead was 216, an amount overhauled only three times to win in the fourth innings of a Lord's Test. It had been an unspectacular session, but the next day showed its importance.

Before the fourth morning, the egg-and-bacon-clad experts in the Pavilion were expecting England to build their lead until a declaration around teatime. But a collapse of seven for 43, three to the nagging spin of Maharaj, changed all that. Cook's 192-ball vigil was ended by Morkel – Root reckoned his 69 was "probably worth double on that wicket" – and, after Ballance was caught behind for 34, none of the next five out made double figures, including the unfortunate Dawson, who completed a pair when he lost sight of a big full toss from Rabada.

The collapse could have been terminal: Bairstow lofted to wide long-off, where Philander fumbled a straightforward catch over the boundary. Only seven at the time, Bairstow scurried to 51 after lunch with the help of Wood, and the lead had stretched to 330 when he was finally stumped, leaving Anderson with a 62nd not-out, beating Courtney Walsh's Test record.

South Africa had a day and a half to make the runs – but subsided in less than 37 overs of headless-chickenry. Bairstow started the slide, clinging on one-handed to Kuhn's leg-side tickle, then Elgar drilled a return catch into Ali's beard. And when Ali clasped another screamer – Duminy pulling the last ball before tea to square leg – South Africa were sinking at 25 for three. De Kock was sensibly promoted, but soon lost Amla when he went back to Dawson and was struck on the pad: a despairing review confirmed the ball was hitting off. A quiet period followed, but after ten overs de Kock deflected one from Ali into the stumps via his foot. And, flighting the ball invitingly, Ali conjured a wicket in each of his next four overs, his burst of five for 20 in 25 deliveries giving him ten in a match for the first time.

As the crowd took in the sudden conclusion, which coincided with news of England's women toppling Australia in the World Cup at Bristol, Philander and Morkel coaxed the score past three figures, then swiped three sixes. It couldn't last, and Morkel soon holed out off Dawson – the 19th wicket of a hectic day – to wrap up the perfect present for Root. The honeymoon, however, was to be a short one.

Man of the Match: M. M. Ali. *Attendance:* 112,539.

Close of play: first day, England 357-5 (Root 184, Ali 61); second day, South Africa 214-5 (Bavuma 48, Rabada 9); third day, England 119-1 (Cook 59, Ballance 22).

England

First innings		Second innings	
A. N. Cook c de Kock b Philander	3	c Bavuma b Morkel	69
K. K. Jennings lbw b Philander	8	c de Kock b Morkel	33
G. S. Ballance lbw b Morkel	20	c de Kock b Morkel	34
*J. E. Root c de Kock b Morkel	190	b Maharaj	5
†J. M. Bairstow lbw b Philander	10	st de Kock b Maharaj	51
B. A. Stokes c de Kock b Rabada	56	lbw b Rabada	1
M. M. Ali b Rabada	87	b Maharaj	7
L. A. Dawson lbw b Morkel	0	b Rabada	0
S. C. J. Broad not out	57	c de Bruyn b Maharaj	0
M. A. Wood lbw b Rabada	0	b Rabada	28
J. M. Anderson c de Kock b Morkel	12	not out	0
Lb 2, nb 13	15	Lb 4, nb 1	5
1/14 (1) 2/17 (2) 3/49 (3) 4/76 (5) 5/190 (6) 6/367 (4) 7/367 (8) 8/413 (7) 9/413 (10) 10/458 (11) (105.3 overs)	458	1/80 (2) 2/139 (1) 3/142 (3) 4/146 (4) 5/149 (6) 6/180 (7) 7/181 (8) 8/182 (9) 9/227 (10) 10/233 (5) (87.1 overs)	233

Morkel 25.3–2–115–4; Philander 20–3–67–3; Rabada 28–4–123–3; Maharaj 22–1–107–0; de Bruyn 5–1–30–0; Bavuma 5–0–14–0. *Second innings*—Morkel 21–6–64–3; Rabada 20–5–50–3; Maharaj 32.1–8–85–4; Duminy 9–2–21–0; Philander 5–1–9–0.

South Africa

First innings		Second innings	
*D. Elgar c Ballance b Ali	54	(2) c and b Ali	2
H. G. Kuhn c Cook b Broad	1	(1) c Bairstow b Anderson	9
H. M. Amla lbw b Ali	29	lbw b Dawson	11
J-P. Duminy lbw b Broad	15	c Ali b Wood	2
T. Bavuma c Stokes b Ali	59	(6) b Ali	21
T. B. de Bruyn c Bairstow b Anderson	48	(7) c Stokes b Ali	1
K. Rabada c Bairstow b Dawson	27	(10) c Bairstow b Ali	4
†Q. de Kock c Stokes b Anderson	51	(5) b Ali	18
V. D. Philander b Ali	52	(8) not out	19
K. A. Maharaj lbw b Dawson	9	(9) b Ali	10
M. Morkel not out	2	c Jennings b Dawson	14
B 4, lb 7, nb 3	14	B 7, lb 1	8
1/10 (2) 2/82 (3) 3/98 (1) 4/104 (4) 5/203 (6) 6/244 (7) 7/248 (5) 8/314 (8) 9/337 (10) 10/361 (9) (105 overs)	361	1/12 (1) 2/12 (2) 3/25 (4) 4/28 (3) 5/64 (5) 6/67 (6) 7/72 (7) 8/82 (9) 9/94 (10) 10/119 (11) (36.4 overs)	119

Anderson 19–6–44–2; Broad 18–5–62–2; Wood 20–5–65–0; Dawson 15–2–67–2; Ali 20–7–59–4; Stokes 13–2–53–0. *Second innings*—Anderson 6–2–16–1; Broad 3–1–5–0; Ali 15–4–53–6; Wood 1–0–3–1; Dawson 11.4–4–34–2.

Umpires: S. Ravi and P. R. Reiffel. Third umpire: S. D. Fry.
Referee: J. J. Crowe.

ENGLAND v SOUTH AFRICA

Second Investec Test

TELFORD VICE

At Nottingham, July 14–17. South Africa won by 340 runs. Toss: South Africa.

South Africa had underperformed in consecutive matches about as rarely as England had followed one strong game with another. Only once since early 2009 had the South Africans lost more than one Test in a row. England, meanwhile, had won two in suc-cession only twice since the 2015 Ashes. So there was little surprise when the visitors made up for their supine display at Lord's. Despite all that, England's capitulation – they lasted a delivery fewer in two innings than South Africa did in their first – alarmed many observers.

"They need better batsmen and a better attitude," boomed Geoffrey Boycott on *Test Match Special*. Michael Vaughan agreed: "The England batting has been appalling; maybe it's a lack of respect about what the game is." Coach Trevor Bayliss was even more succinct: "They've had a shocker." Unusually for a Yorkshireman, Root is not given to strong talk, but he made an exception for Vaughan, perhaps because the two have walked a long road together. "I can't believe he's actually said that, to be honest," said Root. Stokes, his deputy, also waded in: "The whole fight and desire thing that's been thrown at us is very, very unfair."

England retained the XI that had won the First Test so handsomely, while for South Africa Duanne Olivier replaced the banned Kagiso Rabada, and J-P. Duminy made way for du Plessis on his return from paternity leave. Perversely, South Africa aimed to fix what was broken – their batting – by bringing in a bowler, Morris, for Theunis de Bruyn. They were also without their coach, Russell Domingo, back home for the funeral of his mother, who had died from injuries sustained in a car accident three weeks earlier.

Yet the infusion of du Plessis's calm and nous more than made up for the absentees. When he decided to bat on a greenish pitch and a steamy morning, he sent a message of confidence to a team who needed it. Individuals benefited, too. Morris is skilful and fierce, but he can be expensive, and when du Plessis saw "his head was spinning" with information after his first few overs on the second morning, he cut through the clutter with winning simplicity: "Bowl as fast as you can." Morris did, and later dismissed Ali and Broad with consecutive deliveries in his return of three for 38. He fared even better in the second innings, removing Root and Cook.

Before all that, though, South Africa had to combat the swinging ball, and Anderson at his favourite venue. They were satisfied with their efforts until tea. But, from 179 for two, they lost four for 56. The slide had begun with the first ball after the break, when de Kock – having made 68 on his elevation to No. 4 in a stand of 113 with Amla – edged Broad to first slip. Amla then top-edged to fine leg to end an accomplished 78; it was the eighth time Broad had claimed his wicket in Tests, more than any other bowler. Bairstow took a superb leg-side catch to see off du Plessis, and it was 235 for six when Stokes had Bavuma caught behind as he tried to leave.

Philander and Morris put on 74 before stumps to stem the bleeding but, unlike the first day when Anderson bent the ball round corners without much luck, there was no escaping him on a muggy second morning which began under lights. He cleaned up with a sniping spell of four for four in 16 balls, including Philander for 54, to finish with his seventh five-for in nine Nottingham Tests; by the end of the game, he had 60 wickets here at under 19 apiece (next was Alec Bedser, with 41, followed by Broad, with 37). Anderson had also become the first fast bowler to take 300 Test wickets in a single country when he removed Elgar on the first morning.

England's fightback did not last long. With the last delivery of the fourth over, Philander had Cook caught behind on review, replays showing the ball had cannoned to de Kock via inside edge and pad as he prodded forward. And from the first delivery of the fifth, Jennings edged Morkel. When Root turned his first ball through midwicket for three, he doubled England's total. Where others floundered, he flourished, hitting Philander for three fours in an over: two through the covers, one off each foot, sandwiching a slash past a diving gully. He went to 50 off 40 balls, equalling Graham Gooch's fastest half-century by an England captain, against Australia at Sydney in 1990-91.

Ballance was bowled in the second over after lunch by Philander, dragging on via his pad, and an hour before tea Root dared once too often, edging Morkel to a low-flying de Kock to turn off a light that had burned brightly in the gloom of a grey afternoon. His 78 had shimmered with a dozen boundaries, and lasted only 76 balls. Stokes was caught behind off Maharaj for a duck and, although Bairstow gutsed out 45, stickability was scarce: the last four fell for six. Morris and Maharaj shared six wickets, and South Africa led by 130.

By the close, they had taken their lead to 205 for the loss of Kuhn, whose hard hands edged Anderson low to second slip. Next day, old-fashioned grind from Elgar, Amla and du Plessis took England out of the match. Elgar in particular found ever uglier ways to

MOST TEST WICKETS IN ONE COUNTRY

Wkts	*Tests*		*Wkts*	*Tests*	
493	73	M. Muralitharan (SL)	265	55	Harbhajan Singh (I)
350	63	A. Kumble (I)	**263**	**46**	**H. M. R. K. B. Herath (SL)**
335*	**76**	**J. M. Anderson (E)**	**252***	**64**	**S. C. J. Broad (E)**
319	69	S. K. Warne (A)	249	53	M. Ntini (SA)
289	66	G. D. McGrath (A)	**243**	**47**	**D. W. Steyn (SA)**

* *Anderson's total includes eight wickets, and Broad's ten, in three Tests in Wales.*

The most by a bowler in a foreign country is Warne's 129 in England.

play, but he and Amla added 135 – though both might have been dismissed by Broad before South Africa reached three figures. Television replays suggested Amla had been caught behind for 25, but England's appeal was anaemic and they did not ask for a review. And, on 55, Elgar hammered a difficult chance to Anderson in the gully.

For England, the rest of the day was about damage limitation. Dawson, whose selection still looked like a luxury, at least denied Amla a century, trapping him on review for 87; earlier, Amla had become only the second player, after Andrew Symonds for Australia against West Indies at Kingston in 2008, to reach both fifties in the same Test with a six. There were also four wickets for Ali as South Africa sought quick runs and a declaration. When it came, with four overs of the third evening to go, England were set 474. Cook was promptly given out first ball, but the inevitable review suggested Morkel's delivery was clearing the stumps. It would prove a temporary reprieve: 40 minutes before tea on the fourth afternoon, on a blameless pitch, England were all out for 133. Scarcely as credible was the regularity with which the sublime Philander moved the ball off the seam, rendering his lack of pace immaterial; Anderson wasn't the only bowler who seemed born to prosper at Trent Bridge.

The first to feel Philander's velvet-gloved punch was Jennings, bowled through a yawning gate early on the fourth morning. He also trapped Ballance, who had already been rattled on the glove by Morkel; it emerged he had broken his left index finger, ruling him out of the series. But the key strikes were delivered by Morris, who bowled Root with a swerving yorker that clattered into the base of off, then produced a bouncer to Cook, on 42, that might have had him locked up for GBH. The ball reared up, prompting one of the best players of short-pitched bowling to react like a vampire confronted by a crucifix. His panicked flap looked as if it would fall safely, but de Kock swooped to his right. In 17 Test innings in Nottingham, Cook had one fifty, and an average of 21.

Graham Morris

Anthony Devlin, AFP/Getty Images

Morris men: Joe Root is yorked, and Alastair Cook caught off a bouncer, as Chris Morris tears England to ribbons.

The rest of the batting was a mess, epitomised by Bairstow's smear off Maharaj to deep mid-on. Olivier knew he would make way for Rabada, but gave himself something to remember when he ended the match by having Wood and Anderson caught off consecutive bouncers. England's first defeat at Trent Bridge for ten years meant a bout of self-flagellation. South Africa, on the other hand, left believing that another series win here was within reach.

Man of the Match: V. D. Philander. *Attendance:* 61,422.

Close of play: first day, South Africa 309-6 (Philander 54, Morris 23); second day, South Africa 75-1 (Elgar 38, Amla 23); third day, England 1-0 (Cook 0, Jennings 0).

South Africa

D. Elgar c Dawson b Anderson	6	– (2) c Anderson b Stokes	80
H. G. Kuhn b Broad	34	– (1) c Root b Anderson	8
H. M. Amla c Wood b Broad	78	– lbw b Dawson	87
†Q. de Kock c Cook b Broad	68	– c Bairstow b Anderson	1
*F. du Plessis c Bairstow b Stokes	19	– lbw b Stokes	63
T. Bavuma c Bairstow b Stokes	20	– c Root b Ali	15
V. D. Philander c Dawson b Anderson	54	– c and b Ali	42
C. H. Morris c and b Anderson	36	– c Ballance b Ali	13
K. A. Maharaj c Root b Anderson	0	– c Broad b Ali	1
M. Morkel c Bairstow b Anderson	8	– not out	17
D. Olivier not out	0		
Lb 12	12	B 8, lb 8	16
1/18 (1) 2/66 (2) 3/179 (4) (96.2 overs)	335	1/18 (1) (9 wkts dec, 104 overs)	343
4/194 (3) 5/220 (5) 6/235 (6)		2/153 (2) 3/154 (4)	
7/309 (7) 8/317 (9) 9/330 (8) 10/335 (10)		4/216 (3) 5/253 (6) 6/275 (5)	
		7/304 (8) 8/307 (9) 9/343 (7)	

Anderson 23.2–6–72–5; Broad 22–4–64–3; Wood 17–3–61–0; Stokes 18–3–77–2; Dawson 7–1–26–0; Ali 8–1–21–0; Jennings 1–0–2–0. *Second innings*—Anderson 20–4–45–2; Broad 19–4–60–0; Wood 18–5–68–0; Ali 16–2–78–4; Stokes 20–4–34–2; Dawson 11–1–42–1.

England

First innings		Second innings	
A. N. Cook c de Kock b Philander	3	c de Kock b Morris	42
K. K. Jennings c de Kock b Morkel	0	b Philander	3
G. S. Ballance b Philander	27	lbw b Philander	4
*J. E. Root c de Kock b Morkel	78	b Morris	8
†J. M. Bairstow b Maharaj	45	c Morris b Maharaj	16
B. A. Stokes c de Kock b Maharaj	0	c and b Philander	18
M. M. Ali c du Plessis b Morris	18	c Kuhn b Maharaj	27
L. A. Dawson c Amla b Maharaj	13	not out	5
S. C. J. Broad lbw b Morris	0	c Morkel b Maharaj	5
M. A. Wood c du Plessis b Morris	6	c Morris b Olivier	0
J. M. Anderson not out	0	c de Kock b Olivier	0
B 4, lb 10, w 1	15	Lb 5	5
1/3 (1) 2/3 (2) 3/86 (3) 4/143 (4) 5/168 (6) 6/177 (5) 7/199 (7) 8/199 (9) 9/199 (8) 10/205 (10) (51.5 overs)	205	1/4 (2) 2/28 (3) 3/55 (4) 4/72 (1) 5/84 (5) 6/122 (7) 7/126 (6) 8/133 (9) 9/133 (10) 10/133 (11) (44.2 overs)	133

Morkel 13–2–45–2; Philander 13–2–48–2; Morris 8.5–1–38–3; Olivier 7–0–39–0; Maharaj 10–1–21–3. *Second innings*—Morkel 13–4–30–0; Philander 10–3–24–3; Olivier 3.2–0–25–2; Morris 6–3–7–2; Maharaj 12–2–42–3.

Umpires: S. D. Fry and P. R. Reiffel. Third umpire: S. Ravi.
Referee: J. J. Crowe.

ENGLAND v SOUTH AFRICA

Third Investec Test

JAMES GINGELL

At The Oval, July 27–31. England won by 239 runs. Toss: England. Test debuts: D. J. Malan, T. S. Roland-Jones, T. Westley.

Along the Harleyford Road, above the bustle of backpacks streaming from Vauxhall station to The Oval's 100th men's Test, there were images of some of the ground's great moments. Hanging from lamp-posts were Bradman playing through leg, Holding hurling a bullet, Pietersen soaring to Ashes glory. Perhaps, for the 150th, Ali will join them. After he completed an emphatic victory with the first Test hat-trick the old place had seen, he was lifted into the air like a prizefighter, face split wide by a mile-long smile. It was a picture of cartoonish rapture.

The graft, though, was done on the first two days. Root chose to bat, despite a lush pitch and pregnant skies. It seemed a brave decision, perhaps designed to show his team did have the grit many questioned after the capitulation at Trent Bridge. If England, and particularly Cook, seemed up for the fight, it helped that Philander was as green as the surface: he struggled with a stomach virus, spent the second evening in hospital, and moped about the field for as little time as he could. Still, if Philander had the runs, he barely conceded any. His first spell counted down 4–3–2–1 as he got the ball to hover and dart like a hummingbird, then peck Jennings's edge in the fourth over. It was the 23rd delivery Jennings had faced from him in the series, the third time he had been out, at a cost of two runs, and his third duck in eight innings. His debut hundred at Mumbai the previous December seemed a long time ago.

Graham Morris

Missing out… An edge evades the England cordon – and a hat-trick evades Toby Roland-Jones in South Africa's second innings.

As for England's latest debutants, Tom Westley confirmed what was known of him at Chelmsford, a man with a leg-side game to drool over; one on-drive against the spin drew sighs. But having left confidently before lunch – he didn't play and miss once – he departed for 25 in the first over after it, to an airy drive. And, after Root was dazzled by another of Vern's jewels, Dawid Malan's own first innings was ruined by Rabada, who sent an inswinging scud scorching towards his toes. The elemental force of it left Malan helpless on all fours, like a drunkard scrabbling in the gutter for his keys.

A couple of overs later, Rabada tried the same trick to Cook, who just about jammed it to safety. There was the odd sweetly timed clip, but in general Cook jiggled about the crease and met all challenges to life like a deep-sea creature – ugly maybe, but perfectly adapted, the master of the murk. With his first smudged four to third man he had gone past Allan Border, another of his like, into ninth on the all-time Test run-scorers list. And when rain finally cut short a day limited to 59 overs, his resolve had helped England to 171 for four.

Morkel, superb throughout, eventually trapped Cook next morning for 88. If that innings was a performance of comforting familiarity, Stokes was a man playing against type, responding to the rhythms of the game rather than drumming his own. When Cook needed an ally, Stokes was stolid. Then, counter-attacking before the new ball, he cracked three fours off an over from Morris, down a little on pace from Trent Bridge, and half the bowler for it. Three overs later, Bairstow repeated the dose off Maharaj, sweeping, driving and dabbing. In a frantic passage, the pair added 50 in 38 balls.

After that, Stokes became watchful again, striking no fours as he used 58 deliveries to move between 52 and 70. But after Rabada rattled the shoulder of Bairstow's bat, and Morkel removed Ali, Stokes uncoiled with the tail, and began slog-sweeping Maharaj with the wind towards the gasholder. The first six got him to 90. Then, in the 102nd over, came a rousing treble: another six was caught by du Plessis, who tumbled into the boundary, the next flew high over long-on to bring up a wonderful hundred, and the last rubbed in the salt. It was the second time an England batsman had scored three consecutive sixes in Tests, after Wally Hammond against New Zealand's Jack Newman at Auckland in 1932-33. When Stokes was last to go, England had 353, which du Plessis said was 100 over par.

Toby Roland-Jones was the third of England's debutants, and the 22nd since James Whitaker took over as chairman of selectors in 2013, seven more than either Australia or South Africa in that time. Few had made an impression, and even fewer as immediate as this. During a jaunty stand with Stokes, he swatted Morris into the stands and was serenaded by the crowd. Then, in 24 balls either side of tea, he had them on their feet, earning four wickets with a high action and just enough wobble.

There was little about a long, slow walk back to his mark to make South African hearts flutter: he bore the sagging shoulders of an accountant returning home from a commute. But after Elgar nicked the thinnest edge – Roland-Jones barely appealed for his maiden wicket – they crumbled in the evening gloom against a both-barrelled onslaught. Kuhn missed a horrible one-legged whirl, then Amla gloved a shorter snorter, and de Kock fell to a leading edge. Each wicket was met with a boyish grin, the county pro enjoying the bright lights and buzz of the Test arena.

South Africa were now giving their wickets away: du Plessis offered no shot to a nip-backer, before Morris and Maharaj meekly offered catches to make it 61 for seven. Bavuma showed steel against a softening ball, sharing 53 with Rabada, then 47 with Morkel, and driving neatly to 52 next day. He guided South Africa past the follow-on, before Roland-Jones became the first England debutant to take five wickets in a maiden Test innings since Graham Onions, against West Indies at Lord's in 2009.

Root would probably have batted again anyway: he wanted his fledglings to flourish, and to exhaust the South Africans. After Morkel bowled Cook with a pearler for seven (leaving him on 999 runs at The Oval), Jennings made 48 but, still prodding with the rigid limbs of a marching cadet, never looked convincing. He needed an overthrow to get off the mark, was dropped on six, had his stumps grazed twice with inside edges, overturned an lbw that pitched a hair outside leg and, after somehow surviving a rain-hit third day, succumbed to Rabada's lifter on the fourth. It was torturous. Westley looked more comfortable at the crease, if a little too happy to stay there, collecting 59 from 141 balls

Shaun Botterill, Getty Images

Arms and the man: Ali appeals for the wicket of Morne Morkel, and the Test ends in a hat-trick.

TEST-ENDING HAT-TRICKS

G. A. Lohmann	England v South Africa at Port Elizabeth	1895-96
H. Trumble	Australia v England at Melbourne	1901-02
L. F. Kline	Australia v South Africa at Cape Town	1957-58
M. M. Ali	**England v South Africa at The Oval**	**2017**

before being stumped trying to up the tempo. And Malan failed again, undone by another inswinger. If Root was happy enough with his own form – barely lifting a finger during another half-century – he must have been uncertain about the recruits.

The crowd grew restless as they waited for his first declaration as captain. But Bairstow was allowed to club 63 on the fourth afternoon, until his dismissal brought an end at 313 for eight. England had made 666 runs in the match and, with 492 to defend, were intent on giving South Africa a beasting.

Elgar did most to resist them, battling to a brilliant hundred. He watched from the other end as Amla was late hoisting his bat for a leave. He watched as a fired-up Stokes squirmed a yorker under de Kock and, next ball, removed du Plessis, again failing to offer a shot. And he watched on the final morning as Roland-Jones trapped Bavuma, then Philander, who followed the captain's example and left his first ball. All the while, Elgar absorbed blows to the bottom hand, exacerbating a tendency for his bat to skew out at ugly acutes. But the odd forthright pull and punchy drive showed his character.

When he finally edged Ali's looper, the resistance snapped, and Rabada immediately followed likewise. After a maiden from Stokes, the drift on Ali's next ball beat Morkel's lunge, the whole crowd went up and, when they were turned down, all called for the review. As the players gathered round Ali, the red lights ran true, and the final perfect picture took shape. It was the first hat-trick by an England spinner since Tom Goddard in 1938-39, the first to comprise only left-handers, and the first time a Test innings had included four golden ducks. In a flash – less a Lambeth walk than a sprint – England had retained the Basil D'Oliveira Trophy.

Man of the Match: B. A. Stokes. *Attendance:* 92,556.

Close of play: first day, England 171-4 (Cook 82, Stokes 21); second day, South Africa 126-8 (Bavuma 34, Morkel 2); third day, England 74-1 (Jennings 34, Westley 28); fourth day, South Africa 117-4 (Elgar 72, Bavuma 16).

England

A. N. Cook lbw b Morkel	88	– b Morkel	7
K. K. Jennings c Elgar b Philander	0	– c Morris b Rabada	48
T. Westley c du Plessis b Morris	25	– st de Kock b Maharaj	59
*J. E. Root c de Kock b Philander	29	– c Morkel b Maharaj	50
D. J. Malan b Rabada	1	– lbw b Morris	10
B. A. Stokes c Rabada b Morkel	112	– b Morris	31
†J. M. Bairstow c du Plessis b Rabada	36	– c Rabada b Maharaj	63
M. M. Ali c de Kock b Morkel	16	– run out	8
T. S. Roland-Jones lbw b Maharaj	25	– not out	23
S. C. J. Broad c Amla b Rabada	3		
J. M. Anderson not out	1		
B 7, lb 7, w 3	17	Lb 11, w 3	14
1/12 (2) 2/64 (3) 3/113 (4) (103.2 overs)	353	1/30 (1) (8 wkts dec, 79.5 overs)	313
4/120 (5) 5/183 (1) 6/258 (7)		2/92 (2) 3/170 (3)	
7/279 (8) 8/316 (9) 9/331 (10) 10/353 (6)		4/180 (4) 5/202 (5)	
		6/251 (6) 7/265 (8) 8/313 (7)	

Morkel 28.2–7–70–3; Philander 17–6–32–2; Rabada 26–4–85–3; Maharaj 15–1–61–1; Morris 17–1–91–1. *Second innings*—Morkel 19–6–44–1; Philander 15–3–54–0; Rabada 18–4–56–1; Morris 11–0–70–2; Maharaj 13.5–2–50–3; Elgar 3–0–28–0.

South Africa

D. Elgar c Bairstow b Roland-Jones	8	– (2) c Stokes b Ali	136
H. G. Kuhn lbw b Roland-Jones	15	– (1) b Broad	11
H. M. Amla c Bairstow b Roland-Jones	6	– c Root b Roland-Jones	5
†Q. de Kock c Stokes b Roland-Jones	17	– b Stokes	5
*F. du Plessis lbw b Anderson	1	– lbw b Stokes	0
T. Bavuma c Bairstow b Roland-Jones	52	– lbw b Roland-Jones	32
C. H. Morris c and b Anderson	2	– (8) c Stokes b Ali	24
K. A. Maharaj c Cook b Stokes	5	– (9) not out	24
K. Rabada b Broad	30	– (10) c Stokes b Ali	0
M. Morkel c Cook b Anderson	17	– (11) lbw b Ali	0
V. D. Philander not out	10	– (7) lbw b Roland-Jones	0
B 4, lb 5, nb 3	12	B 4, lb 7, nb 4	15
1/18 (1) 2/23 (2) 3/30 (3) 4/47 (4) 5/47 (5) 6/51 (7) 7/61 (8) 8/114 (9) 9/161 (10) 10/175 (6) (58.4 overs)	175	1/21 (1) 2/47 (3) 3/52 (4) 4/52 (5) 5/160 (6) 6/160 (7) 7/205 (8) 8/252 (2) 9/252 (10) 10/252 (11) (77.1 overs)	252

Anderson 13–6–25–3; Broad 15–5–44–1; Roland-Jones 16.4–4–57–5; Stokes 7–1–26–1; Root 2–0–5–0; Ali 5–1–9–0. *Second innings*—Anderson 13–3–26–0; Broad 16–4–47–1; Roland-Jones 18–4–72–3; Stokes 14–1–51–2; Ali 16.1–5–45–4.

Umpires: Aleem Dar and J. S. Wilson. Third umpire: H. D. P. K. Dharmasena.
Referee: R. S. Madugalle.

ENGLAND v SOUTH AFRICA

Fourth Investec Test

LAWRENCE BOOTH

At Manchester, August 4–7. England won by 177 runs. Toss: England.

Buoyed by the manner of their victory at The Oval, England strove to repeat it – and, for once, bust did not follow boom. Again, they chose to bat in awkward conditions, and scrapped their way past 350; again, they tore into South Africa's batting, and left the headlines to Moeen Ali. The result, after one last collapse by the tourists, meant Root had achieved what no England captain had since Alec Stewart in 1998, and beaten South Africa at home – the 3–1 margin their most comprehensive against them for 57 years. For a few hours at least, concerns about England's top order, and a winter in Australia, could wait.

England had not lost in Manchester since 2001, and their proprietorial pride swelled when Old Trafford renamed its Pavilion End after James Anderson, canonising him before his time. Burnley's patron saint of swing politely glossed over his preference for the Brian Statham End, and repaid the honour with match figures of 31–12–54–7. There were entire spells in which South Africa could not lay a finger on him.

Anderson would play his part with the bat, too, but until he did, England's first innings had refused to blossom. The absence of Vernon Philander because of back spasms (Chris Morris was missing for the same reason) ought to have eased the pressure, but Morkel – gangly and relentless – gave little away. Unlike the batsmen: before lunch on the first day, the hapless Jennings prodded at Olivier; after it, Cook edged Maharaj, and Westley was superbly snared off Rabada by de Kock, his 100th Test dismissal in his 22nd game as keeper, equalling Adam Gilchrist's record. When Malan thick-edged Morkel to second slip just before tea, England had reached 144 for four at a stately 2.5 an over, a whole run slower than they managed amid the chaos of Trent Bridge. Had this been the Ashes, all they would have needed was sackcloth.

And so the opening day waited for a decisive break. Root, on 40, edged Morkel between the motionless de Kock and first slip Amla, then worked him for three to pass 5,000 Test runs; only Sachin Tendulkar and Cook had got there at a younger age than Root's 26 years 217 days. Soon he was celebrating a half-century for the tenth Test in succession, equalling John Edrich's England record. But this was a day when promise trumped permanence: on 52, Root advanced on Olivier as he aimed through midwicket, missed, and was given leg-before. A wasted review compounded the error.

That decisive break might have arrived had third umpire Joel Wilson agreed with his on-field colleagues' suspicion that Elgar, diving forward from slip, had caught Bairstow off Maharaj on four. Instead, South Africa had to settle for the late wicket of Stokes, his stumps splayed by a Rabada yorker. A close-of-play score of 260 for six told of mutual graft. The early-series frivolity – South Africa's at Lord's, England's at Nottingham – had yielded to something sterner.

The Test continued to bob and weave on the second morning: jab met hook, slug met sidestep. Rabada took care of nightwatchman Roland-Jones – who had not faced a ball the previous evening – and Ali, demoted to No. 9. Morkel then bowled Broad. Anderson emerged to a hero's welcome, with England 312 for nine, and Bairstow 53. Almost instantly, Bairstow was dropped off Rabada by de Kock, diving low to his right. England's response was merciless: seven overs later, the stand was worth 50, of which Anderson's share was four. But Maharaj was less hittable than the seamers and, when Bairstow missed a sweep, umpire Dharmasena ruled the ball had struck him in line with off stump; technology showed it had, by roughly a millimetre. For the first time since Kevin Pietersen at Chittagong in March 2010, an England Test batsman had been dismissed for 99.

The anticlimax was quickly forgotten. With the third ball of South Africa's reply, Anderson – operating from his new favourite end – swung one into Elgar's pads, and Old Trafford roared its approval. After lunch, Roland-Jones strangled Amla down the leg side, his third dismissal of South Africa's most experienced player in three innings, and a 100th in Tests as a keeper for Bairstow. Kuhn's miserable series continued when he edged Ali to slip.

But the occasion challenged Anderson to seize the day, and he met it in style. Ten overs after tea, he bowled Bavuma with one that clipped off stump as the batsman shaped to leave, and du Plessis – once a Lancashire player himself – via the inside edge of a crooked bat. When de Bruyn, dropped on nought off Anderson by Jennings in the gully, steered him to Root at second slip, South Africa were 146 for six; Anderson had three for six in 24 balls. For the tourists, the decline felt terminal. Early on the third morning, Broad curtailed the innings for 226 – a deficit of 136.

Others would have gone on the defensive, but not South Africa's seamers. Cook fell to Morkel for the 12th time in Tests, skewing to backward point, and Westley for the first, slicing to gully. Shortly after lunch, Jennings flashed Rabada high to first slip (he was later dropped for the series against West Indies). Unable to counter the rough outside the left-hander's off stump, Malan lobbed Maharaj to short leg. Olivier bowled Root for 49, then had Stokes caught in the cordon. And when Bairstow's short-arm jab off Olivier picked out fine leg, England were seven down and 289 in front. Could South Africa salvage the game after all?

The answer was provided by the buccaneering Ali. Dropped by Elgar at slip off Maharaj on 15, he flourished to the tune of 75 not out in 66 balls, one of his three sixes – all off Maharaj – finding the hands of Bairstow on the dressing-room balcony; his celebration captured the mood of a raucous hour. Morkel finished with four wickets, though he deserved double that. South Africa needed 380 to draw the series; only two teams had scored as many in the fourth innings of a Manchester Test, and both had lost.

The early exchanges confirmed the apparent hopelessness of their task. In the absence of swing, Anderson and Broad aimed for a wobbly seam and a nagging off-stump line. They could hardly have bowled better and, moments before lunch, South Africa were relieved to have lost only their openers: Elgar caught behind off Broad, Kuhn at slip off

Having a ball: Jonny Bairstow is all smiles after catching one of Moeen Ali's sixes.

Anderson. But Root asked for a review against Bavuma, even though the bowler, Roland-Jones, was unconvinced he had edged through to Bairstow. Root's was a good call: at lunch, it was 40 for three.

Amla and du Plessis, however, were not going down without a fight. Amla unfurled strokes too rarely seen during the summer, while his captain buckled up in the passenger's seat. As if unnerved by the accuracy of their new-ball colleagues, Stokes and Roland-Jones leaked runs. Amla launched Ali for a straight six, and du Plessis pinched two when Anderson let the ball slip through his grasp at mid-off, then ambled to retrieve it. Now, if a team-mate had dared do that to him…

England were losing their bite, but Root continued to attack, granting Ali a silly point and a short leg. Did the gesture get Amla's juices flowing? Who knows, but he went down the track to an off-break and was hit on the pad; England reviewed, and technology confirmed his demise for 83, ending a stand of 123. It released the floodgates. De Kock deflected a flighted delivery low to second slip, and de Bruyn another, low to first; Ali had three for five in 11 balls.

Tea was taken at 182 for six, merely delaying the inevitable. Du Plessis flashed Anderson to the keeper, and Rabada chipped him to cover. The trip home beckoned: Morkel slogged Ali to mid-off, then Olivier prodded his first delivery to Stokes at slip to give Ali five for 69, and 25 in the series at 15 apiece, eight of them caught by Stokes. Only two games earlier, Ali was supposedly the second-choice spinner behind Liam Dawson. How ridiculous that seemed as he collected his fifth match award – with Root the joint-most for England since his debut in 2014.

For only the fourth time since readmission, South Africa had lost three Tests in a series. England, meanwhile, leapfrogged Australia into third place in the rankings – encouraging thoughts that, if they could just sort out their top order, the Ashes might not be such a stretch after all.

Man of the Match: M. M. Ali. *Attendance:* 60,238.

Men of the Series: England – M. M. Ali; South Africa – M. Morkel.

Close of play: first day, England 260-6 (Bairstow 33, Roland-Jones 0); second day, South Africa 220-9 (Morkel 18); third day, England 224-8 (Ali 67, Broad 0).

England

A. N. Cook c de Kock b Maharaj	46	– c de Bruyn b Morkel	10
K. K. Jennings c de Kock b Olivier	17	– c Amla b Rabada	18
T. Westley c de Kock b Rabada	29	– c sub (A. K. Markram) b Morkel	9
*J. E. Root lbw b Olivier	52	– b Olivier	49
D. J. Malan c du Plessis b Morkel	18	– c de Bruyn b Maharaj	6
B. A. Stokes b Rabada	58	– c du Plessis b Olivier	23
†J. M. Bairstow lbw b Maharaj	99	– c Rabada b Olivier	10
T. S. Roland-Jones c Bavuma b Rabada	4	– (9) c Maharaj b Rabada	11
M. M. Ali c du Plessis b Rabada	14	– (8) not out	75
S. C. J. Broad b Morkel	7	– c de Bruyn b Morkel	5
J. M. Anderson not out	4	– c de Bruyn b Morkel	2
B 6, lb 6, nb 2	14	B 9, lb 13, w 2, nb 1	25
1/35 (2) 2/92 (1) 3/92 (3) 4/144 (5) 5/187 (4) 6/252 (6) 7/271 (8) 8/303 (9) 9/312 (10) 10/362 (7) (108.4 overs)	362	1/16 (1) 2/30 (3) 3/55 (2) 4/72 (5) 5/129 (4) 6/134 (6) 7/153 (7) 8/211 (9) 9/237 (10) 10/243 (11) (69.1 overs)	243

Morkel 26–5–92–2; Rabada 26–7–91–4; Olivier 21–3–91–2; Maharaj 30.4–9–58–2; de Bruyn 5–0–18–0. *Second innings*—Morkel 13.1–2–41–4; Rabada 17–4–50–2; Maharaj 27–5–92–1; Olivier 12–5–38–3.

South Africa

D. Elgar lbw b Anderson	0	– (2) c Bairstow b Broad	5
H. G. Kuhn c Stokes b Ali	24	– (1) c Cook b Anderson	11
H. M. Amla c Bairstow b Roland-Jones	30	– lbw b Ali	83
T. Bavuma b Anderson	46	– c Bairstow b Roland-Jones	12
*F. du Plessis b Anderson	27	– c Bairstow b Anderson	61
†Q. de Kock c Bairstow b Broad	24	– c Cook b Ali	1
T. B. de Bruyn c Root b Anderson	11	– c Stokes b Ali	0
K. A. Maharaj lbw b Ali	13	– not out	21
K. Rabada c Stokes b Broad	23	– c Westley b Anderson	1
M. Morkel not out	20	– c Root b Ali	0
D. Olivier c Bairstow b Broad	4	– c Stokes b Ali	0
B 3, nb 1	4	B 4, lb 3	7
1/2 (1) 2/47 (3) 3/84 (2) 4/131 (4) 5/132 (5) 6/146 (7) 7/167 (8) 8/189 (6) 9/220 (9) 10/226 (11) (72.1 overs)	226	1/10 (2) 2/18 (1) 3/40 (4) 4/163 (3) 5/173 (6) 6/173 (7) 7/183 (5) 8/195 (9) 9/202 (10) 10/202 (11) (62.5 overs)	202

Anderson 17–5–38–4; Broad 16.1–4–46–3; Roland-Jones 11–3–41–1; Ali 21–5–57–2; Stokes 6–0–34–0; Malan 1–0–7–0. *Second innings*—Anderson 14–7–16–3; Broad 12–5–24–1; Roland-Jones 9–1–52–1; Ali 19.5–1–69–5; Stokes 6–1–26–0; Root 2–0–8–0.

Umpires: Aleem Dar and H. D. P. K. Dharmasena. Third umpire: J. S. Wilson.
Referee: R. S. Madugalle.

ENGLAND v WEST INDIES IN 2017

REVIEW BY VIC MARKS

Test matches (3): England 2, West Indies 1
Twenty20 international (1): England 0, West Indies 1
One-day internationals (5): England 4, West Indies 0

England's expectation was for a gentle, late-season workout against West Indies, a useful precursor to the Ashes. A few issues of selection and strategy would be fixed, before the team – a sleek, well-oiled machine, coiled for the fray – headed to Australia. Of course, it didn't quite happen like that.

They did win the Test and one-day series (either side of losing the solitary Twenty20 game), but not entirely in the manner anticipated. After thrashing West Indies in the First Test at Edgbaston, they contrived to lose the Second at Headingley, where the tourists confounded everyone by knocking off 322 with remarkable ease. Any thoughts of experimentation for the Third, at Lord's – such as giving an exploratory debut to Hampshire's young leg-spinner, Mason Crane – were immediately shelved.

Yet this setback was infinitesimal compared with the events that followed England's one-day win at Bristol on September 24. The victory was hardly worthy of celebration – Eoin Morgan's team eventually prevailed in all four completed ODIs – but this did not deter Ben Stokes and Alex Hales from staying out late that fateful Sunday night. At 2.35am, Stokes was arrested on suspicion of causing actual bodily harm after a street brawl near the Mbargo nightclub in the Clifton area of the city. Hales, though not arrested, was with him at the time. From this point on, England's winter plans were in disarray.

The incident was bad enough for Stokes and the ECB, though they initially named him in the Ashes squad. But the video footage that soon surfaced in *The Sun* did not look good: it depicted what appeared to be a feral fracas, which left a man in hospital with a fractured eye socket.

Stokes and Hales were withdrawn from the remaining ODIs, though Stokes would not have been fit anyway because of a broken little finger. The ECB went into crisis-management mode. England's director of cricket, Andrew Strauss, announced that neither would be considered for selection "until further notice", and the board waited to see if Stokes would be charged. In the end, he was ruled out of the Ashes.

Trevor Bayliss was desperately disappointed by one of his favourite cricketers. His admiration of Stokes as a player and a character had been transparent since becoming head coach in 2015, and he had been eager to give him responsibility, including the Test vice-captaincy. Yet that trust had been squandered and, at a stroke, England's hopes of retaining the Ashes greatly diminished. Hence their season ended in the most melancholy manner, even though the tally of wins and losses (18–6 across all three formats) was highly encouraging.

Gareth Copley/Getty Images

As sure as night follows day: England relied on the batting of Joe Root and Alastair Cook, especially in the floodlit Test at Edgbaston.

The victory at Edgbaston, in the first day/night Test on British soil, was so emphatic – by an innings and 209 – that West Indies were pilloried from all sides. It was, according to Curtly Ambrose, until recently their bowling coach, "pathetic and embarrassing". Other heavyweights were just as scathing. Before the match there had been much debate about the pink ball's tendency to behave devilishly as darkness approached. That pattern never emerged, but another did. When England bowled, the ball jagged around; when it was the turn of West Indies, minus their quickest bowler, Shannon Gabriel, who was not fully fit (and suffering from a rash of no-balls), it sped on to the middle of the bats of Alastair Cook, who made 243, and Joe Root, 136. Despite several interruptions for rain, the game was all over by the third evening, when Stuart Broad overhauled Ian Botham's tally of 383 Test wickets.

But England's first floodlit Test had its hitches. Warwickshire did everything possible to make it a success. Trading on its novelty value, they marketed the event brilliantly, and enticed punters in great numbers, though it was beyond their powers to keep them there until the close. On the first evening, thousands left early for an amalgam of reasons: the one-sided nature of the game, an eagerness to avoid the late-night snarl-up outside the stadium, and the cold and damp. On the second evening it rained. This all confirmed the suspicion that Birmingham is not quite Adelaide, and never will be.

After that match, no canny Yorkshireman bought tickets for the fourth or fifth days at Headingley, yet a highly entertaining contest, the best of the summer, ended with five overs to go (proponents of four-day Tests, take note), and West Indies triumphant. In Mirpur next day, Bangladesh defeated Australia, so this was an encouraging week for those who opposed two-divisional Test cricket. England had not underestimated their opponents in Birmingham, but they may have done so in Leeds. Toby Roland-Jones, who had made such an impressive start to his Test career, was replaced by Chris Woakes returning from injury and in need of a bowl. And, despite a 169-run deficit on first innings, England should not have lost. Root was able to declare on the fourth evening, leaving West Indies 322 to win from 96 overs. All the experts applauded the move; there again, have the omniscient pundits in the commentary boxes ever chastised a captain for calling a halt too early? It did not work out well for Root, who joined Norman Yardley, David Gower and Kevin Pietersen as England captains who have declared in the third innings of a Test, and lost.

The assumption of Root – and just about everyone else – was that Kraigg Brathwaite and Shai Hope could not possibly emulate their first-innings brilliance, when they added 246. But they could, this time settling for 144. Brathwaite's virtues were familiar, though it was something of a surprise that he could bat so fluently. Hope was a revelation. His talent had long been recognised in the Caribbean, but he had passed 50 just once in 11 Tests. At Headingley, he became the first to score two centuries in a first-class match

COME IN, NO. 3: YOUR TIME IS UP?

The fewest runs by a No. 3 batsman in a Test series (minimum five innings):

Runs	*I*	*Avge*			
15	5	3.00	N. S. Harford	New Zealand v England (in England)	1958
17	6	2.83	S. E. Marsh	Australia v India (in Australia)	2011-12
31	5	6.20	Younis Khan	Pakistan v West Indies (in West Indies)	1999-2000
37	6	6.16	G. H. S. Trott	Australia v England (in England)	1888
38	**5**	**7.60**	**K. A. Hope**	**West Indies v England (in England)**	**2017**
39	5	7.80	G. S. Blewett	Australia v India (in India)	1997-98
40	5	10.00	D. M. Jones	Australia v Pakistan (in Pakistan)	1988-89
40	5	8.00	M. P. Vaughan	England v South Africa (in England)	2008
41	5	8.20	G. Giffen	Australia v England (in Australia)	1891-92
46	5	9.20	J. F. M. Morrison	New Zealand v Australia (in New Zealand)	1981-82

Some of the batsmen scored runs from elsewhere in the order during the series.

there – astonishing, given that it was hosting its 534th. This was surely Hope's landmark Test, the one in which he realised he could prevail at the highest level. Alongside elegant orthodoxy, he seemed to possess that extra millisecond to play his shots. He remained composed even when an epic victory was on the horizon, and in its immediate aftermath. Sky TV's Ian Ward asked him about his new Headingley record. "I didn't know that," Hope said in a deep Bajan drawl. "But thanks for passing on the good news." West Indies had discovered a batsman capable of excelling for the next decade.

The expected order was restored at Lord's, which for the first time hosted a Test starting in September. The sun which had graced Leeds disappeared for two days, and under grey skies the ball darted about. England won by nine

Philip Brown, Getty Images

Bending their backs: Shannon Gabriel and Kemar Roach gave their all, but struggled for fitness.

wickets in a low-scoring match. Jimmy Anderson registered his 500th Test wicket, speeding to career-best figures of seven for 42 in the second innings of his 129th appearance, to cap a superb summer. In the first innings, Stokes had also achieved his best Test figures – six for 22 – as he swung the ball extravagantly. For a few days, English fans could happily ponder: "How can the Aussies possibly cope with this pair if it starts swinging Down Under?"

The batting line-up provoked rather more nervous queries, even after England had retained the Wisden Trophy. Mark Stoneman and Tom Westley guided them to victory at Lord's, but only Stoneman was retained for the Ashes. He had timed his run into the Test team as deftly as Mo Farah in his pomp. Dawid Malan also survived, on the back of two tentative half-centuries at No. 5. By contrast, Westley had been in the team just long enough to reveal his limitations. In his stead, the selectors lurched back to Gary Ballance and James Vince. After Lord's, it was suggested that, if England could take on Australia in an eight-a-side-contest, they would be favourites. After the episode in Bristol, this was amended – to seven-a-side.

For West Indies, the performance of Hope and Brathwaite offered a glimmer for the future, though their only other batsman to score runs of any significance was the skittish Jermaine Blackwood. Kemar Roach and Gabriel – one through guile, the other through brute force – delivered impressive spells, but there was still much rebuilding to do. Jason Holder was dignified, if not tactically astute, in the exacting role of captaining a team whose fragility was obvious, but who at least seemed eager to improve under the no-nonsense guidance of their latest coach, the (very) Australian Stuart Law.

After defeat in the T20 match in Durham, played in conditions so chilly and slippery that at one point captain Carlos Brathwaite wanted to take his players

FIVE STATS YOU MAY HAVE MISSED

BENEDICT BERMANGE

- When Stuart Broad overhauled Ian Botham at Edgbaston, it meant England were fielding their top two wicket-takers in the same Test (Broad and James Anderson) for the first time since Fred Trueman and Brian Statham against West Indies at The Oval in 1963.

- England's 490 for eight at Leeds was their highest in Tests without a century (previously 477 for nine against South Africa at Leeds in 1994). There had been only four higher century-less totals in all Tests:

Total	*HS*		
524-9 dec	70	India v New Zealand at Kanpur	1976-77
520-7 dec	99	Australia v West Indies at Perth	2009-10
517	87*	South Africa v Australia at Adelaide	1997-98
500-8 dec	95	Pakistan v Australia at Melbourne	1981-82
490-8 dec	**84**	**England v West Indies at Leeds**	**2017**

- Shai Hope at Leeds became the 11th batsman to score his first two Test hundreds in the same match, following Warren Bardsley (Australia), Vijay Hazare (India), Jack Moroney (Australia), Lawrence Rowe (West Indies, on debut), Geoff Howarth (New Zealand), Duleep Mendis (Sri Lanka), Wajahatullah Wasti (Pakistan), Yasir Hameed (Pakistan, on debut), Phillip Hughes (Australia) and Peter Fulton (New Zealand).

- Hope's hundreds there meant Weston-super-Mare (191) was now the ground to have staged most first-class matches without anyone making two centuries in the same game (succeeding Headingley's 533).

- In taking seven for 42 in the second innings at Lord's at the age of 35 years 41 days, James Anderson became the second-oldest fast bowler to collect a Test seven-for since the First World War. Only Imran Khan was older, by 88 days, when he claimed seven for 80 for Pakistan against West Indies at Georgetown in 1987-88.

off the field, England emphatically won the ODIs. The only close game came at The Oval, where Moeen Ali and Jos Buttler inched England ahead on DLS before the rain came. Earlier in the day, Evin Lewis, a 25-year-old left-hander from Trinidad, hit a coruscating 176 before retiring hurt. Such was the precision of his strokeplay, one wondered whether he might be effective against a red ball as well.

Lewis partnered Chris Gayle, who played his first ODIs since the 2015 World Cup and delivered one major innings and a couple of cameos, all sprinkled with trademark sixes and the odd quick single to long-on. Even though, at nearly 38, his mobility had diminished, Gayle provided terrific entertainment, and his presence at least hinted that some sort of amnesty was in operation between the West Indian board and their players. The return of Marlon Samuels was less successful: he made a few runs slowly, and was a liability in the field.

Many of England's runs were scored by their openers, although Ali's incandescent 53-ball century at Bristol came from No. 7. Initially, Jonny Bairstow was preferred to Jason Roy, and seized his chance with two centuries notable for fluent strokeplay and swift running. But Roy replaced Hales after Bristol, and showed why he should also be a regular, purring to 84 and 96.

Paul Ellis, AFP/Getty Images

E is for Edgbaston – and experiment. Chilly evenings and occasional rain dogged England's first floodlit Test.

Here was a little headache for the England hierarchy when contemplating their best white-ball side. But, at the end of a long international season (too long, in fact), this conundrum was hardly at the forefront of the minds of the management. Instead, they had to fathom a way to cope with the potential absence of Stokes throughout the winter.

WEST INDIAN TOURING PARTY

*J. O. Holder (T/50), S. W. Ambris (50), R. R. Beaton (20), D. Bishoo (T/50), J. Blackwood (T), C. R. Brathwaite (20), K. C. Brathwaite (T), R. L. Chase (T), M. L. Cummins (T/50), S. O. Dowrich (T), S. T. Gabriel (T), C. H. Gayle (50/20), S. O. Hetmyer (T), K. A. Hope (T/50), S. D. Hope (T/50), A. S. Joseph (T/50), E. Lewis (50/20), J. N. Mohammed (50/20), S. P. Narine (20), A. R. Nurse (50/20), K. A. Pollard (20), K. O. A. Powell (T), R. Powell (50/20), R. A. Reifer (T), K. A. J. Roach (T), M. N. Samuels (50/20), J. E. Taylor (50/20), C. A. K. Walton (20), K. O. K. Williams (50/20).

C. R. Brathwaite captained in the Twenty20 international, when his side included none of the players who had appeared in the Tests.

Coach: S. G. Law. *Batting coach:* T. A. Radford. *Bowling coach:* R. O. Estwick. *Fielding coach:* R. Maron. *Manager:* J. Garner. *Logistics officer:* R. N. Lewis. *Physiotherapist:* C. J. Clark. *Strength and conditioning coach:* R. Rogers. *Massage therapist:* J. Gay. *Psychologist:* S. Sylvester. *Analyst:* D. Augustus. *Media officer:* P. Spooner.

> "Sri Lanka's first innings was a mixture of the sublime (India's bowling) and the ridiculous (their own batting)."
>
> Sri Lanka v India in 2017, Second Test, page 994

TEST MATCH AVERAGES

ENGLAND – BATTING AND FIELDING

	T	*I*	*NO*	*R*	*HS*	*100*	*50*	*Avge*	*Ct/St*
J. E. Root	3	4	0	268	136	1	2	67.00	3
†A. N. Cook	3	5	0	304	243	1	0	60.80	6
†B. A. Stokes	3	4	0	228	100	1	2	57.00	5
†D. J. Malan	3	4	0	154	65	0	2	38.50	0
†M. D. Stoneman	3	5	1	120	52	0	1	30.00	0
†M. M. Ali	3	4	0	109	84	0	1	27.25	1
†S. C. J. Broad	3	3	1	52	38	0	0	26.00	1
T. Westley	3	5	1	71	44*	0	0	17.75	0
J. M. Bairstow	3	4	0	59	21	0	0	14.75	9/2

Played in three Tests: †J. M. Anderson 0*, 8* (2 ct). Played in two Tests: T. S. Roland-Jones 6*, 13. Played in one Test: C. R. Woakes 23, 61*.

BOWLING

	Style	*O*	*M*	*R*	*W*	*BB*	*5I*	*Avge*
J. M. Anderson	RFM	111.1	33	268	19	7-42	2	14.10
T. S. Roland-Jones	RFM	34.4	11	112	7	2-18	0	16.00
B. A. Stokes	RFM	72.3	22	200	9	6-22	1	22.22
S. C. J. Broad	RFM	106	27	326	9	3-34	0	36.22
M. M. Ali	OB	71	10	248	5	2-54	0	49.60

Also bowled: J. E. Root (OB) 1–0–5–0; T. Westley (OB) 4–0–12–0; C. R. Woakes (RFM) 33.2–6–122–2.

WEST INDIES – BATTING AND FIELDING

	T	*I*	*NO*	*R*	*HS*	*100*	*50*	*Avge*	*Ct*
S. D. Hope	3	6	1	375	147	2	1	75.00	2
K. C. Brathwaite	3	6	0	283	134	1	1	47.16	3
J. Blackwood	3	6	1	187	79*	0	1	37.40	3
†K. O. A. Powell	3	6	0	142	45	0	0	23.66	1
J. O. Holder	3	5	0	86	43	0	0	17.20	1
R. L. Chase	3	6	0	80	30	0	0	13.33	1
†D. Bishoo	2	3	1	14	13*	0	0	7.00	0
K. A. Hope	3	6	0	41	25	0	0	6.83	2
K. A. J. Roach	3	5	1	26	12	0	0	6.50	0
S. T. Gabriel	2	3	1	10	10	0	0	5.00	0
S. O. Dowrich	3	6	1	24	14	0	0	4.80	9

Played in one Test: †M. L. Cummins 0, 0*; A. S. Joseph 6, 8.

BOWLING

	Style	*O*	*M*	*R*	*W*	*BB*	*5I*	*Avge*
K. A. J. Roach	RFM	96.5	25	328	11	5-72	1	29.81
S. T. Gabriel	RF	63	8	262	7	4-51	0	37.42
J. O. Holder	RFM	98.2	21	313	8	4-54	0	39.12
R. L. Chase	OB	75.2	9	283	7	4-113	0	40.42
D. Bishoo	LB	42	3	129	3	1-27	0	43.00

Also bowled: K. C. Brathwaite (OB) 7–0–10–0; M. L. Cummins (RFM) 24–3–87–1; A. S. Joseph (RFM) 22–3–109–0.

ESSEX v WEST INDIANS

At Chelmsford, August 1–3. Drawn. Toss: Essex. County debut: S. J. Cook.

Essex went through the first-class season unbeaten, though they might have lost to the tourists but for the rain which prevented any play on the second day after lunch. When the heavens opened, Essex were 47 for four – three to Roach, moving the ball at pace – and were indebted to Walter's maiden fifty next day. That complemented some tidy bowling which brought him four wickets, including the Hope brothers for 22 apiece (and Kyle for a duck in the second innings). The match ended quietly as the West Indians took the chance for batting practice. Chase top-scored in both innings, adding a round 50 to the 81 he had made in front of a sizeable first-day crowd.

Close of play: first day, West Indians 309-8 (Dowrich 28); second day, Essex 47-4 (Browne 16, Taylor 9).

West Indians

First innings		Second innings	
K. C. Brathwaite b Taylor	61	– c Wheater b Walter	2
K. O. A. Powell b Cook	15	– c Wheater b Taylor	27
K. A. Hope b Walter	22	– b Walter	0
S. D. Hope b Walter	22	– c Chopra b Taylor	46
R. L. Chase b Taylor	81	– not out	50
J. Blackwood lbw b ten Doeschate	59	– not out	7
†S. O. Dowrich not out	44		
*J. O. Holder c Chopra b Dixon	6		
D. Bishoo c and b Lawrence	4		
K. A. J. Roach not out	12		
B 1, lb 5, nb 6	12	Lb 1, nb 2	3
1/19 (2) 2/55 (3) 3/106 (4) (8 wkts, 100 overs)	338	1/11 (1) (4 wkts dec, 31 overs)	135
4/150 (1) 5/269 (5) 6/275 (6)		2/15 (3) 3/30 (2)	
7/292 (8) 8/309 (9)		4/112 (4)	

M. L. Cummins did not bat.

Cook 23–6–57–1; Beard 16–0–65–0; Dixon 17–3–56–1; Walter 15–1–54–2; Nijjar 10–2–38–0; Lawrence 4–2–6–1; Taylor 12–2–44–2; ten Doeschate 3–0–12–1. *Second innings*—Cook 6–2–17–0; Walter 3–0–14–2; Taylor 7–2–20–2; Beard 5–0–35–0; Dixon 5–0–30–0; Nijjar 5–0–18–0.

Essex

V. Chopra c K. A. Hope b Roach	0	M. W. Dixon lbw b Bishoo	8
N. L. J. Browne c K. A. Hope b Roach	16	S. J. Cook not out	0
D. W. Lawrence b Roach	8		
†A. J. A. Wheater lbw b Roach	0	B 10, lb 3, nb 13	26
*R. N. ten Doeschate lbw b Cummins	6		
C. J. Taylor c K. A. Hope b Holder	13	1/0 (1) 2/10 (3) (9 wkts dec, 61.5 overs)	185
P. I. Walter not out	68	3/19 (4) 4/33 (5)	
A. S. S. Nijjar c Powell b Cummins	30	5/52 (6) 6/56 (2)	
A. P. Beard b Roach	10	7/106 (8) 8/131 (9) 9/184 (10)	

Roach 18–6–43–5; Cummins 14.5–3–43–2; Holder 15–2–56–1; Chase 5–1–13–0; Bishoo 9–3–17–1.

Umpires: N. G. C. Cowley and T. Lungley.

KENT v WEST INDIANS

At Canterbury, August 6–8. Drawn. Toss: West Indians. First-class debut: Z. Crawley.

By the time lightning drove the players from the field on the third day, a draw was assured – but the West Indian batting had been unconvincing against a second-string attack. The Dartford seamer Charlie Hartley, in his first first-class match for three years (and his only one of 2017), took four wickets as the tourists picked their way to 265 on the first day. Shai Hope made 57, but his brother

Kyle played on for the third innings in a row. When Kent batted, Dickson added 182 for the second wicket with the 19-year-old debutant Zak Crawley, after Bell-Drummond fell in the first over. Dickson went on to 142, and allowed Billings, captaining Kent for the first time, to declare 66 ahead. Three wickets went down before the West Indians cleared the deficit, but there was not enough time for a positive result.

Close of play: first day, Kent 1-1 (Dickson 1, Crawley 0); second day, Kent 331-9 (Haggett 29, Hunn 0).

West Indians

	First innings		Second innings	
*K. C. Brathwaite lbw b Hartley	8	–	c Rouse b Hartley	0
K. O. A. Powell lbw b Hartley	13	–	c Rouse b Ball	23
K. A. Hope b Ball	36	–	c Rouse b Hunn	9
S. D. Hope c Ball b Riley	57	–	c Crawley b Hartley	30
S. O. Hetmyer c Rouse b Ball	0	–	not out	43
J. Blackwood lbw b Hartley	50	–	not out	18
†S. O. Dowrich run out	15			
R. A. Reifer c Hunn b Riley	13			
D. Bishoo c Rouse b Gidman	23			
A. S. Joseph lbw b Hartley	31			
M. L. Cummins not out	8			
Lb 3, w 5, nb 3	11		B 4, lb 5	9
1/9 (1) 2/36 (2) 3/74 (3) 4/78 (5) 5/148 (4) 6/178 (6) 7/183 (7) 8/201 (8) 9/233 (9) 10/265 (10) (83.4 overs)	265		1/1 (1) 2/24 (3) 3/50 (2) 4/88 (4) (4 wkts, 36.4 overs)	132

Hunn 16–4–48–0; Hartley 17.4–4–80–4; Haggett 14–2–46–0; Ball 11–2–27–2; Riley 17–5–37–2; Gidman 8–2–24–1. *Second innings*—Hunn 9–4–14–1; Hartley 11.4–2–44–2; Ball 8–3–27–1; Gidman 4–0–12–0; Riley 4–0–26–0.

Kent

D. J. Bell-Drummond c Dowrich b Joseph	0
S. R. Dickson c Joseph b Bishoo	142
Z. Crawley c Powell b Joseph	62
*S. W. Billings run out	25
W. R. S. Gidman b Reifer	42
A. J. Ball st Dowrich b Brathwaite	3
†A. P. Rouse b Brathwaite	0
C. J. Haggett not out	29
C. F. Hartley c Powell b Joseph	5
A. E. N. Riley b Joseph	0
M. D. Hunn not out	0
Lb 6, w 5, nb 12	23
1/0 (1) 2/182 (3) 3/223 (4) 4/259 (2) 5/291 (6) 6/295 (5) 7/295 (7) 8/328 (9) 9/330 (10) (9 wkts dec, 93.2 overs)	331

Joseph 22–5–72–4; Cummins 22.2–6–58–0; Reifer 24–3–100–1; Bishoo 16–1–74–1; Brathwaite 9–3–21–2.

Umpires: J. D. Middlebrook and A. G. Wharf.

DERBYSHIRE v WEST INDIANS

At Derby, August 11–13 (day/night). Drawn. Toss: West Indians. First-class debuts: C. A. J. Brodrick, M. D. Sonczak, J. P. A. Taylor.

With the first floodlit Test a few days away, several West Indians found their touch against the pink ball under the Derby lights. Kyle Hope reached his side's first hundred of the tour after Powell had narrowly failed, then Shai Hope and Chase added 196, reaching their centuries from consecutive deliveries. When Holder opted for batting practice in the second innings despite a huge lead, Powell made up for his near miss, before discovering a niggle and retiring. These were promising signs for the West Indians, although they were facing a young and inexperienced attack. Their bowlers also adapted well, apart from Gabriel, who bowled only 13 overs in the match and sent down 24 no-balls. Derbyshire gave first-class debuts to three Academy players, including 19-year-old Callum Brodrick, who hit 52 amid the rubble, and seamer James Taylor, just 16, alongside his older brother Tom; they were the first siblings to play together for Derbyshire since Alf and George Pope in 1939.

Close of play: first day, West Indians 340-3 (S. D. Hope 69, Chase 62); second day, West Indians 60-1 (Powell 41, Blackwood 5).

West Indians

First innings		Second innings	
K. C. Brathwaite lbw b Milnes	3	– c Cork b J. P. A. Taylor	11
K. O. A. Powell lbw b Palladino	92	– retired hurt	100
K. A. Hope b Sonczak	105	– (6) c Wood b Macdonell	18
S. D. Hope not out	107	– (7) c T. A. I. Taylor b Macdonell	5
R. L. Chase not out	110	– (8) not out	60
J. Blackwood (did not bat)		– (3) c Slater b T. A. I. Taylor	29
†S. O. Dowrich (did not bat)		– (4) c Wood b Sonczak	37
*J. O. Holder (did not bat)		– (5) c Brodrick b Sonczak	18
K. A. J. Roach (did not bat)		– not out	40
Lb 3, nb 7	10	B 4, lb 3, w 1, nb 1	9
1/6 (1) 2/159 (2) 3/231 (3) (3 wkts, 100 overs)	427	1/45 (1) 2/115 (3) 3/183 (5) 4/212 (4) 5/223 (7) 6/223 (6) (6 wkts dec, 85 overs)	327

A. S. Joseph and S. T. Gabriel did not bat.

In the second innings Powell retired hurt at 158-2.

T. A. I. Taylor 19–3–94–0; Milnes 21–2–94–1; J. P. A. Taylor 14–1–63–0; Palladino 13–1–44–1; Cork 16–2–66–0; Sonczak 16–1–60–1; Macdonell 1–0–3–0. *Second innings*—Milnes 12–4–58–0; T. A. I. Taylor 10–1–46–1; J. P. A. Taylor 3–0–14–1; Palladino 7–1–27–0; Cork 14–2–62–0; Sonczak 19–4–56–2; Macdonell 20–5–57–2.

Derbyshire

First innings		Second innings	
B. T. Slater c Dowrich b Joseph	39	– not out	27
C. M. Macdonell c Dowrich b Roach	9	– not out	17
T. A. Wood c Powell b Gabriel	15		
C. A. J. Brodrick st Dowrich b Chase	52		
†H. R. Hosein c Dowrich b Holder	4		
T. P. Milnes c Dowrich b Holder	0		
G. T. G. Cork c Powell b Holder	0		
T. A. I. Taylor c Dowrich b Gabriel	9		
*A. P. Palladino c Holder b Chase	18		
M. D. Sonczak c Blackwood b Roach	9		
J. P. A. Taylor not out	0		
Lb 1, w 1, nb 24	26	Lb 2, w 1, nb 4	7
1/25 (2) 2/78 (3) 3/78 (1) 4/91 (5) 5/94 (6) 6/100 (7) 7/115 (8) 8/170 (4) 9/177 (9) 10/181 (10) (51.3 overs)	181	(no wkt, 14 overs)	51

Gabriel 9–2–64–2; Roach 13.3–5–31–2; Holder 13–1–48–3; Joseph 12–3–32–1; Chase 4–3–5–2. *Second innings*—Gabriel 4–0–24–0; Holder 2–0–11–0; Chase 5–0–13–0; Brathwaite 3–2–1–0.

Umpires: B. J. Debenham and R. J. Evans.

"The arrival of the Sri Lankans, by contrast, was treated as an obligation – like attending an in-law's wedding to stay on side with the spouse."
Pakistan v Sri Lanka in 2017–18, page 933

ENGLAND v WEST INDIES

First Investec Test

JONATHAN LIEW

At Birmingham, August 17–19 (day/night). England won by an innings and 209 runs. Toss: England. Test debuts: M. D. Stoneman; K. A. Hope.

A little light remained in the Birmingham sky as the last wicket fell, bringing England's first day/night Test to a close. For West Indies, darkness had long since fallen. Bowled out twice in 92.4 overs, losing 19 wickets in a day, suffering their sixth-heaviest defeat: yes, it had been a historic occasion for them too, but not in the manner intended.

As Cook gathered the match award for his superlative 243, as interviews and formalities were dealt with, the Edgbaston crowd shuffled home – their bellies full of drink, their eyes full of wickets, but their souls curiously unsated. It was difficult to know how exactly to classify what had just happened. Was it elite international sport, or ritual sacrifice? A Technicolor window into cricket's future, or a marketing exercise dressed up as innovation?

It was probably a mixture of all four. After three unnerving days in the West Midlands, the only conclusion that could be drawn with any certainty was that it was too early to draw conclusions. The more outlandish warnings about the pink Dukes – that it would swerve alarmingly at twilight and soften into futility, that unsighted fielders would be left rooted to the spot as it sailed past them – came to nothing. So did the more ambitious claims made on behalf of day/night Test cricket: that it would breathe instant life into the format, transforming the demographics of the Test match audience for ever.

By and large, it was the same crowd you would expect at any Edgbaston Test – this was its 50th. But a 2pm start gave an additional three hours of lubrication, which contributed to a marginally livelier atmosphere than normal. Indeed, as the more boisterous elements broke into their evening serenades of "Don't Take Me Home" and "Ali, Ali Cook", the

Stretched to breaking: Jermaine Blackwood is smartly stumped by Jonny Bairstow, and West Indies are 102 for five in the follow-on.

MOST WICKETS LOST BY A TEST TEAM IN A DAY

Wkts	*Runs*		
20	140	India v England at Manchester	1952
20	158	Zimbabwe v New Zealand at Harare	2005-06
20	194	Zimbabwe v New Zealand at Napier	2011-12
19	88	South Africa v England at Cape Town	1888-89
19	**261**	**West Indies v England at Birmingham**	**2017**
19	332	Zimbabwe v England at Lord's	2003
19	344	South Africa v Australia at Manchester	1912

The most wickets lost by both sides on one day is 27, by England (17) and Australia (ten) at Lord's in 1888.

---

most striking parallel was not with Twenty20 or even football, but with darts: a well-oiled, well-voiced crowd paying only the most cursory attention to the game unfolding before them. More regrettably, the stands steadily thinned out after 8pm, as punters hunted down last trains, dinner reservations or simply somewhere warmer. It was hardly the most ringing endorsement of the new schedule. Evening-only tickets, or a Wimbledon-style resale system, must be options for future games.

Did it produce better cricket? Again, hard to say. It certainly produced more visually arresting cricket. As the floodlights blinked into life, and dusk descended in the day's final hour, we were treated to a stunning vista of pink ball on green turf against a sunset of brilliant ochre. Healthy ticket sales – three days of near-sellouts – were at least partly attributable to giddy novelty, with Birmingham city centre plastered in chintzy neon adverts days in advance. But the first and last measure of any cricketing innovation is – or should be – whether it contributes to an even contest between bat and ball. And on this point, all best-laid plans were confounded, as West Indies' attempt to render the contest remotely even failed on every conceivable level.

It had been suggested that the unfamiliarity of the format might balance things out. Within a few hours, that was exposed as a cruel fiction. Cook produced an innings of metronomic mettle, if one fed by a buffet of errant bowling, the West Indians nourishing his cut and leg glance as if they had never seen him play. Unlike during his 294 against India here in 2011, he accelerated as his innings progressed, while still treating each ball on its (limited) merits. Chase admitted afterwards that he gave up on getting him out.

But the star of the first day was Root, who overtook Cook an hour after lunch – or was it tea? – and bullied his way to an assertive hundred, his 13th in Tests. Early movement had accounted for the debutant Stoneman, bowled by one of the deliveries of the summer from Roach, moving the ball away from middle stump to kiss the top of off. Cummins trapped Westley, playing round his front pad once more. But as the pink ball weathered, Root gathered pace, reaching 50 for the 11th Test in succession, breaking John Edrich's England record, and extending his stand with Cook to 248, a record third-wicket partnership on the ground. Cook, who registered his 31st Test century, overhauled Graham Gooch (5,917) to become the leading Test run-scorer in the UK, and David Gower (767) to claim the Edgbaston equivalent.

Root was bowled through the gate by Roach for 136 as night fell, and replaced by Malan, who was never dominant but mainly competent. He had opened up his stance since his debut two Tests earlier and, after being dropped at slip on two, was rewarded with a dependable supply of leg-side nonsense. This was the defining theme of the innings: too often, five tight deliveries were followed by a pressure-reliever. The fielding was little better than club standard; Cook's fourth double-hundred next day arrived as a result of an egregious misfield by Kyle Hope at third man.

West Indian ineptitude stretched to captaincy and selection. With 80 overs bowled on the first evening, the arrival of the second new ball under lights was awaited with eagerness. Instead, Holder withdrew Roach from the attack, and a seething Stuart Law relayed a

Dying fall: Ben Stokes holds an edge from Alzarri Joseph, and West Indies crash to defeat.

message via the twelfth man. Meanwhile, the slow bowlers sent down 32.2 overs in total, occasionally extracting handy turn, which suggested the omission of leg-spinner Devendra Bishoo was a mistake.

England's lower-middle order crumpled like a napkin on the second day. Cook's dismissal not long before tea – or was it dinner? – brought the declaration. West Indies were shaken from their catatonia, and forced to knuckle down to the task in hand, a follow-on target of 315. As it happened, they did not make that many in two innings. Rain truncated the second day by 26 overs, with Powell and Kyle Hope patiently overcoming the early loss of Brathwaite. But both fell within two overs next morning – Hope fending to gully, Powell run out chancing an absurd single to Anderson. When Chase played on for a duck, West Indies had gathered a downward momentum they would never arrest.

Blackwood tried. There was an element of caprice to his unbeaten 79 off 76 balls, but at least he had a plan, cuffing Ali and Broad for clean sixes over long-on, while his team-mates succumbed to a procession of half-strides and half-strokes. Yet when he finally ran out of partners – or rather, ran out his final partner, Cummins, as he tried to keep the strike – Root had little hesitation in enforcing the follow-on, the first time in an Edgbaston Test since 1979.

West Indies needed 346 to make England bat again, and to survive 65 overs to give fourth-day ticket holders something to watch. But not even these mini-battles ever looked like being won. Root rotated his four seamers like a T20 captain, introducing them all in the first ten overs, and refusing to let the batsmen settle. Two early wickets were his reward. After a short period of consolidation, a few turbulent overs from Stokes and Roland-Jones appeared to convince Brathwaite to counter-attack. He collared Ali, but on the stroke of tea took one liberty too many, shuffling across and falling lbw on review.

Broad, sensing there was fun to be had, stormed back with a terrific spell under lights. Once Blackwood had been stumped off Ali, Broad removed Chase and Holder with successive deliveries to draw level with Ian Botham on 383 Test wickets. A few overs later, with his sister and father watching from the stands, he bowled Dowrich off the inside edge. Roland-Jones claimed the final wicket shortly before 9pm, to put the seal on one of the weakest West Indies performances in recent history.

How did it compare with their five heavier defeats? In four of them (The Oval in 1957, Headingley 2007, Centurion 2014-15, Hobart 2015-16), they were a man short in both innings. At Brisbane in 1930-31, they could plead inexperience – it was only their third Test series – and Bradman at his peak.

No such excuses were available this time. "Every player has to look in the mirror and see where they can improve," Holder said. And given what was to follow, it was possible to forget just how abject this was. Perhaps, in retrospect, it was a form of shock therapy, shoving West Indies' backs against the wall and forcing them to fight. Sometimes the darkest hour comes just before the dawn.

Man of the Match: A. N. Cook. *Attendance:* 69,434.

Close of play: first day, England 348-3 (Cook 153, Malan 28); second day, West Indies 44-1 (Powell 18, K. A. Hope 25).

England

A. N. Cook lbw b Chase	243
M. D. Stoneman b Roach	8
T. Westley lbw b Cummins	8
*J. E. Root b Roach	136
D. J. Malan c Blackwood b Chase	65
B. A. Stokes c Blackwood b Chase	10
†J. M. Bairstow b Holder	18
M. M. Ali c Brathwaite b Chase	0
T. S. Roland-Jones not out	6
Lb 10, w 3, nb 7	20
1/14 (2) 2/39 (3) 3/287 (4) 4/449 (5) 5/466 (6) 6/505 (7) 7/506 (8) 8/514 (1) (8 wkts dec, 135.5 overs)	514

S. C. J. Broad and J. M. Anderson did not bat.

Roach 28–8–86–2; Joseph 22–3–109–0; Cummins 24–3–87–1; Holder 29.3–4–103–1; Chase 26.2–2–113–4; Brathwaite 6–0–6–0.

West Indies

K. C. Brathwaite c Bairstow b Anderson	0	– lbw b Ali	40
K. O. A. Powell run out	20	– c Cook b Anderson	10
K. A. Hope c Stokes b Anderson	25	– lbw b Roland-Jones	12
S. D. Hope b Roland-Jones	15	– c Root b Stokes	4
R. L. Chase b Anderson	0	– lbw b Broad	24
J. Blackwood not out	79	– st Bairstow b Ali	12
†S. O. Dowrich lbw b Roland-Jones	4	– b Broad	5
*J. O. Holder c Bairstow b Ali	11	– c Cook b Broad	0
K. A. J. Roach b Broad	5	– b Anderson	12
A. S. Joseph lbw b Broad	6	– c Stokes b Roland-Jones	8
M. L. Cummins run out	0	– not out	0
Lb 1, w 2	3	B 9, lb 1	10
1/0 (1) 2/45 (3) 3/47 (2) 4/47 (5) 5/89 (4) 6/101 (7) 7/129 (8) 8/134 (9) 9/162 (10) 10/168 (11) (47 overs)	168	1/15 (2) 2/41 (3) 3/60 (4) 4/76 (1) 5/102 (6) 6/104 (5) 7/104 (8) 8/115 (7) 9/137 (9) 10/137 (10) (45.4 overs)	137

Anderson 15–6–34–3; Broad 16–3–47–2; Roland-Jones 6–0–31–2; Stokes 7–0–40–0; Ali 3–1–15–1. *Second innings*—Anderson 7–2–12–2; Broad 10–4–34–3; Roland-Jones 6.4–3–18–2; Stokes 9–4–9–1; Ali 13–2–54–2.

Umpires: M. Erasmus and S. Ravi. Third umpire: C. B. Gaffaney.
Referee: D. C. Boon.

"Had Dan Christian hit the last ball of the final for four, the 2018 edition would have been without a defending champion."

The Indian Premier League in 2016-17, page 1105

ENGLAND v WEST INDIES

Second Investec Test

ANDY BULL

At Leeds, August 25–29. West Indies won by five wickets. Toss: England.

Early on the Tuesday morning, the final day of the game, the West Indian players' phones started to ping, flash and buzz. Jason Holder, the captain, had sent a message to his team's chat group: "Just believe". It was a simple order to give, but a hard one to follow. West Indies needed 322 on a fifth-day pitch against an attack versed in the conditions. The only Test side who had made so many in the fourth innings at Headingley were Don Bradman's Australians, in 1948.

But they were one of the great Test teams. West Indies had just lost 19 wickets in a day at Edgbaston and, well as they had played in patches here, they had been horrible on the previous evening, when Root made an aggressive declaration. If Bradman's side were the Invincibles, Holder's were the Inconceivables.

Still, it had been a sinuous match, and one twist remained. At 6.43 on the final day, West Indies completed a famous victory, their first in England in 19 Tests stretching back to Edgbaston 2000. Even old hands tried to remember a more improbable turnaround. In *The Times*, Mike Atherton said he couldn't think of a bigger upset – this from the captain of the England team that had won at Bridgetown in 1993-94 after being bowled out for 46 at Port-of-Spain. In the wild excitement of the moment, fans felt new hope that Test cricket could be rekindled, not just in the Caribbean, but around the world.

MOST RUNS IN A FIRST-CLASS MATCH AT HEADINGLEY

Runs	*Wkts*		
1,723	31	England (496 and 365-8 dec) lost to Australia (458 and 404-3)	1948
1,553	40	England (515 and 345) beat Pakistan (538 and 155)	2006
1,497	**33**	**England (258 and 490-8 dec) lost to West Indies (427 and 322-5)**	**2017**
1,452	30	Australia (601-7 dec and 230-3 dec) beat England (430 and 191)	1989
1,409	38	New Zealand (350 and 454-8 dec) beat England (350 and 266)	2015
1,376	33	Lancashire (373 and 314) lost to Yorkshire (531 and 158-3)	2001
1,376	20	Yorkshire (677-7 dec) drew with Durham (518 and 181-3 dec)	2006

All of which was precious little consolation to Root, who became only the fourth England captain to suffer defeat after declaring in the third innings. "I'm sure it was a great Test match to watch," he said glumly. "But it wasn't great to be on the losing side." After several years of complaints about Cook's caution, few were about to criticise Root for taking a chance now. And after five lopsided home Tests in seven weeks, plus five dispiritingly easy home series victories against West Indies going back over 17 years, a number of English fans seemed to think defeat a fair price to pay for a close, compelling game. Besides, as Root said, England's mistakes had been made earlier in the match.

West Indies were a different side from the one who lost at Edgbaston six days earlier. They recalled Gabriel and Bishoo, their two leading wicket-takers during the previous 12 months, and dropped Miguel Cummins and Alzarri Joseph. Somehow, they retained a belief that they could still compete in the series. It wasn't widely held. In the *Daily Telegraph*, Geoff Boycott described them as "the worst Test match team I have seen in more than 50 years".

England insisted that they, at least, were not taking West Indies lightly. But their focus seemed to have drifted towards the Ashes. They replaced Toby Roland-Jones with Woakes, who had bowled only 20 first-class overs in 2017 because of an intercostal injury. And

First slip: Alastair Cook fluffs a chance to dismiss Kraigg Brathwaite early on the last day, a drop that cost 91 runs.

there was much talk about whether the three greenhorns in their top five – Stoneman, Westley and Malan – could ensure selection for Australia. None did on the first day, all playing shots too ambitious for the circumstances. Since Cook had been caught at third slip early on, responsibility fell, not for the first time, on the middle order.

Gabriel, who bowled with rare speed and accuracy, should have had England 44 for four, but Powell missed Root at first slip on eight. It was the first of a dozen drops, the contagion spreading between the teams like an airborne disease. Roach, slippery quick, also had Stokes put down, by Brathwaite at second slip on nine, allowing England's vice-captain and captain to extend their fifth-wicket stand to 69. Root eventually toe-ended a sweep off Bishoo, though not before he had reached 50 for the 12th consecutive Test, equalling A. B. de Villiers's world record. Stokes, in another of those shrewd and sensible innings that belie his swashbuckling reputation, pressed on towards his hundred. He was dropped again, on 98 by Gabriel at mid-on, after what he called a "brain fart", trying to wallop Roach back over his head. But he was finally caught behind for 100, and the last three wickets fell without addition, leaving Roach and Gabriel with four each, and the total a modest 258. Root later said he thought defeat had stemmed from their failure to realise the trickiness of the conditions.

West Indies, who lost Powell to Anderson on the first evening – a 150th Test catch for Cook – reinforced the point on the second morning. They had been perilously placed at 35 for three, with Anderson irresistible, but Brathwaite was holding his end, and the game turned when he was joined by Shai Hope. If Brathwaite had already established himself as a resilient batsman, Hope had offered little more than his surname suggested since his Test debut two years earlier: one fifty in 21 innings, and an average of 18.

On Saturday afternoon, a new star was born. Hope played with a panache that made spectators sigh: crisp cover-drives, pulls with one leg cocked, and clean, hard cuts past point. Brathwaite played like a man who knew his limitations, and those of the umpires, overturning lbw decisions on 35 and 46. But he did hit out against Ali, despite a couple of deliveries spinning, and raised his fifty by launching him for six over long-on; just before tea, he brought up his sixth Test hundred by doing the same to Westley.

Anderson aside, England struggled. Woakes lacked snap, and Broad never settled on the right length. Hope registered his first Test hundred shortly after tea, and the partnership was worth 246 by the time Broad bowled Brathwaite for 134 late on the second day. For once, this West Indian team lost nothing in comparison with the greats before them: it was their largest partnership at Headingley since Seymour Nurse and Garry Sobers put on 265 back in 1966. Not even the removal of Chase could dent their mood.

MOST RUNS ADDED BY A PAIR IN A TEST AGAINST ENGLAND

480 (451 and 29)	W. H. Ponsford and D. G. Bradman (Australia) at The Oval	1934
405 (405)	S. G. Barnes and D. G. Bradman (Australia) at Sydney	1946-47
399 (399)	G. S. Sobers and F. M. M. Worrell (West Indies) at Bridgetown	1959-60
390 (246 and 144)	**K. C. Brathwaite and S. D. Hope (West Indies) at Leeds**	**2017**
388 (388)	W. H. Ponsford and D. G. Bradman (Australia) at Leeds	1934
379 (363 and 16)	Younis Khan and Mohammad Yousuf (Pakistan) at Leeds	2006

But Hope edged the first ball next morning to depart for 147, and Dowrich his second, giving Anderson his third successive Test five-for at Headingley, after two against Sri Lanka the previous summer. Had Ali not dropped Blackwood at mid-on off Broad – as easy a chance as an international batsman can offer – West Indies would have been eight down and only 75 ahead. Instead, Blackwood and Holder helped extend the lead to 169.

If they had been too carefree in their first innings, England were punctilious second time around. Although Westley drove loosely, and Root was dropped again – by Kyle Hope at gully on ten – Stoneman was sure-footed and steadfast. At stumps, they were three down, and two in front. The match was so finely balanced that Holder said he wanted to restrict the lead to 150; Stoneman wanted it to go past 200. In the end, England went way beyond. Root was out 45 minutes into the fourth day for 72, but Malan batted long into the afternoon for his slowest first-class fifty, in a shade over four hours.

HIGHEST SUCCESSFUL RUN-CHASES AT HEADINGLEY

404-3	Australia (*set 404*) v England	1948
404-5	Hampshire (*set 404*) v Yorkshire	2006
322-5	**West Indies (*set 322*) v England**	**2017**
321-6	**Hampshire (*set 320*) v Yorkshire**	**2017**
315-4	England (*set 315*) v Australia	2001
296-6	Somerset (*set 296*) v Yorkshire	2009

Three quick wickets for Chase lifted West Indian spirits: Stokes lofted the first ball after drinks to long-off, Malan was bowled prodding down the wrong line, and Bairstow dragged on a reverse sweep. England were seven down, and just 158 ahead. But Ali, caught behind off a marginal no-ball from Bishoo on 32, rattled off 117 with Woakes, and Root called his batsmen in so his bowlers could have six overs before the close. It was carnival night for the West Indian community in Leeds, but the cricketers seemed to have no reason for jollity. The only man saying otherwise was bowling coach Roddy Estwick, who cited West Indies' victory at Lord's in 1984, when David Gower set them 342. In truth, it felt optimistic.

Even Stuart Law admitted his first thought had been to save the game. Over the course of the day, though, he and everyone else came round to Estwick's way of thinking. Brathwaite, missed at slip by Cook off Broad on four, and Shai Hope were reunited an

Stand easy: Shai Hope and Kraigg Brathwaite celebrate another landmark in their second epic partnership of the game.

hour in, after Powell skewed to fourth slip, and Brathwaite hit a hard drive back at Broad, who dropped the ball but deflected it on to Kyle Hope's stumps. The pair eased back into their first-innings rhythm. The pitch wasn't as wicked as expected and, with the field up and Ali below his best, England were caught short by the turn of the tide.

Hope's dashing strokes nearly took him past Brathwaite, but he slowed after passing fifty. Then Brathwaite, who was within five runs of becoming the first player to make two hundreds in a first-class game at Headingley, was finally caught at slip, just before tea, off Ali. It meant he and Hope had put on 390 together in the match, becoming the second West Indian pair – after Clyde Walcott and Everton Weekes against Australia at Port-of-Spain in 1954-55 – to register a double- and single-century partnership in the same Test. When Chase was brilliantly held by the substitute fielder Mason Crane at mid-on, West Indies still needed 76.

But, in an update on George Hirst's apocryphal line, Blackwood decided they would get them in boundaries. When England took the new ball, he backed away and clouted Anderson back over his head. Next over, Hope did what Brathwaite couldn't, and registered his second hundred of the game as the celebrations began. There was still time for two more drops – by Cook off Hope at slip, and by Stokes off Blackwood in the deep – and one more twist: determined to end in style, Blackwood removed his helmet, and was stumped two balls later. It meant, appropriately, that Hope hit the winning runs, with 28 deliveries to spare. "Someone had to do it," he said insouciantly. "I just put my hand up." Rarely had a cliché sounded so inadequate.

Man of the Match: S. D. Hope. *Attendance:* 56,005.

Close of play: first day, West Indies 19-1 (Brathwaite 13, Bishoo 1); second day, West Indies 329-5 (S. D. Hope 147, Blackwood 21); third day, England 171-3 (Root 45, Malan 21); fourth day, West Indies 5-0 (Brathwaite 4, Powell 1).

England

A. N. Cook c K. A. Hope b Gabriel	11	– c Dowrich b Holder	23
M. D. Stoneman c Dowrich b Roach	19	– b Gabriel	52
T. Westley lbw b Roach	3	– c Dowrich b Holder	8
*J. E. Root c Blackwood b Bishoo	59	– c S. D. Hope b Gabriel	72
D. J. Malan b Holder	8	– b Chase	61
B. A. Stokes c Dowrich b Gabriel	100	– c Brathwaite b Chase	58
†J. M. Bairstow c Holder b Gabriel	2	– b Chase	18
M. M. Ali c Chase b Roach	22	– c Brathwaite b Bishoo	84
C. R. Woakes c Dowrich b Roach	23	– not out	61
S. C. J. Broad b Gabriel	0	– not out	14
J. M. Anderson not out	0		
B 2, lb 3, w 4, nb 2	11	B 13, lb 5, w 9, nb 12	39
1/19 (1) 2/26 (3) 3/37 (2) 4/71 (5) 5/140 (4) 6/152 (7) 7/220 (8) 8/258 (6) 9/258 (10) 10/258 (9) (70.5 overs)	258	1/58 (1) 2/81 (3) 3/94 (2) 4/212 (4) 5/303 (6) 6/312 (5) 7/327 (7) 8/444 (8) (8 wkts dec, 141 overs)	490

Roach 19.5–1–71–4; Gabriel 17–4–51–4; Holder 16–5–45–1; Chase 12–1–59–0; Bishoo 6–0–27–1. *Second innings*—Gabriel 26–3–125–2; Roach 24–8–95–0; Holder 33–10–95–2; Chase 32–5–86–3; Bishoo 25–1–67–1; Brathwaite 1–0–4–0.

West Indies

K. C. Brathwaite b Broad	134	– c Stokes b Ali	95
K. O. A. Powell c Cook b Anderson	5	– c Stokes b Broad	23
D. Bishoo c Bairstow b Anderson	1		
K. A. Hope c Root b Anderson	3	– (3) run out	0
S. D. Hope c Bairstow b Anderson	147	– (4) not out	118
R. L. Chase c Cook b Stokes	5	– (5) c sub (M. S. Crane) b Woakes	30
J. Blackwood run out	49	– (6) st Bairstow b Ali	41
†S. O. Dowrich c Root b Anderson	0	– (7) not out	0
*J. O. Holder c Ali b Woakes	43		
K. A. J. Roach not out	6		
S. T. Gabriel lbw b Stokes	10		
B 8, lb 11, w 5	24	B 4, lb 9, w 1, nb 1	15
1/11 (2) 2/31 (3) 3/35 (4) 4/281 (1) 5/296 (6) 6/329 (5) 7/329 (8) 8/404 (9) 9/406 (7) 10/427 (11) (127 overs)	427	1/46 (2) 2/53 (3) 3/197 (1) 4/246 (5) 5/320 (6) (5 wkts, 91.2 overs)	322

Anderson 29–7–76–5; Broad 24–2–95–1; Woakes 21–4–78–1; Stokes 25–9–63–2; Ali 24–4–84–0; Westley 4–0–12–0. *Second innings*—Anderson 24–6–73–0; Broad 25–4–91–1; Ali 25–3–76–2; Woakes 12.2–2–44–1; Stokes 5–0–25–0.

Umpires: C. B. Gaffaney and S. Ravi. Third umpire: M. Erasmus.
Referee: D. C. Boon.

At Leicester, September 2–3 (not first-class). **Drawn.** ‡**West Indians 377-7 dec** (88 overs) (K. O. A. Powell 82, S. O. Dowrich 108*, S. O. Hetmyer 128*; D. Klein 3-77); **Leicestershire 70-1** (12.1 overs). *County debuts:* D. N. Butchart, S. T. Evans, M. H. McKiernan, H. J. Swindells. *Leicestershire chose from 13 players, and the West Indians from 15. Only 65 minutes' play was possible on the second day. The tourists had recovered on the first, after wobbling to 64-5: Shane Dowrich and Shimron Hetmyer (who hit five sixes to go with 17 fours) put on 186* for the eighth wicket.*

ENGLAND v WEST INDIES

Third Investec Test

HUGH CHEVALLIER

At Lord's, September 7–9. England won by nine wickets. Toss: West Indies.

At 3.32 on the second afternoon, reality reasserted itself. Twice in three balls, Gabriel bowled Stokes with identical deliveries, and now there was no *deus ex machina*: Gabriel's front foot was safely on the line. Until then, Stokes had swaggered through the Test as though he had slipped a dinner jacket over his whites, finished his dry Martini, checked the magazine of his Walther PPK, and single-handedly set about rescuing his nation from the latest criminal mastermind. Or at least the Wisden Trophy from the clutches of a resurgent West Indies.

The body count had been growing faster than in the opening sequence of a Bond film and, by the end of a violent first day – most of it acted out under lights that seemed right for a day's shooting – Lord's was littered with corpses. Stokes had accounted for six and, with a little help from his friends, West Indies were neutralised for 123. But the fight wasn't over: by nightfall four England batsmen had gone too. Though not Stokes. Next day, he dodged bullets that surely had his name on them. Dropped on 24, he strode to the game's first half-century, before eventually being downed by Gabriel for 60. With the

Cover charge: Ben Stokes off-drives during a combative half-century.

Bristol fracas still a fortnight away, the world was at his feet. An astonishing performance from Anderson then dominated the second half of the Test but, as the credits rolled, there was a colourful cameo by a man called Blofeld.

West Indies' stunning victory at Leeds meant the series was unexpectedly at stake in this, the second-latest Test staged in the UK (after England's Ashes-clinching Oval draw of 2005, which began on September 8). The Headingley success also persuaded West Indies to retain Bishoo's leg-spin, when a swing bowler might have been better. England drafted in Roland-Jones for Chris Woakes, who had cast a thin shadow at Leeds. In a game swirling with subplots and undercurrents, three of their top order were batting for an Ashes place – and Anderson began on 497 Test wickets. West Indies, meanwhile, were distracted by the appalling damage caused in the Caribbean by Hurricane Irma.

Holder won his first toss of the series. Undeterred either by increasing cloud cover or fairy rings – harmless circular marks caused by a fungus on the cut strip – he opted to bat. Anderson quickly found movement and, in the third over, Brathwaite's outside edge. But, just as he had twice at Leeds, Cook fluffed a takeable chance. Others had Teflon fingers, too: not catching was, well, catching, and by some estimates 25 chances went down during the last two games of the series. To Cook's relief, Bairstow clung on soon after, and Anderson, tail up, had 498.

In the right hands it is a wonder of the natural universe: the music of the spheres

Rain stalled England's momentum for 40 minutes; Kyle Hope, another casualty of the Anderson–Bairstow axis, stalled them rather less. The next wicket proved trickier and, if West Indian progress was neither serene nor swift, it was steady. The ball moved a bit, though not outrageously; Powell and Shai Hope middled a few, but not regularly. At 78 for two in the 33rd, both sides could be content. But Roland-Jones got one to hold its own up the hill, Hope nibbled, and Cook took a catch. It didn't matter that it was a doddle: Headingley's first-ever twin centurion had gone for a modest, if neat, 29.

The physics of swing bowling may remain a mystery even to its most skilful practitioners, but in the right hands and the right conditions it is a wonder of the natural universe: the music of the spheres. And so it was for Stokes, who outshone Anderson, a grandmaster of the art. By subtly honing the orientation of the seam, position of the fingers, flick of the wrist and point of delivery, Stokes made the ball sing. (No one heard a snatch of "Chattanooga Choo Choo", but whatever it was, it must have been a swing classic.) In his third over, he gave his colleagues a fielding lesson by grasping a stinging return from Powell, despite being in his follow-through.

There was swing from Blackwood, too, though his wild swish simply presented Roland-Jones with a second, and left West Indies creaking at 87 for five. Now Stokes truly came

A CENTURY AND A FIVE-FOR IN TESTS AT LORD'S

G. O. B. Allen (E). . .	122 v NZ (1931), 5-35 and 5-43 v I (1936)
M. H. Mankad (I) . . .	184 and 5-196 v E (1952)
K. R. Miller (A)	109 v E (1953), 5-72 and 5-80 v E (1956)
R. Illingworth (E) . . .	113 v WI (1969) and 6-29 v I (1967)
I. T. Botham (E)	108 and 8-34 v P (1978), 6-101 and 5-39 v NZ (1978), 5-35 v I (1979), 5-46 v I (1982), 8-103 v WI (1984), 6-90 v SL (1984) and 5-109 v A (1985)
A. Flintoff (E).	142 v SA (2003) and 5-92 v A (2009)
S. C. J. Broad (E) . . .	169 v P (2010), 7-72 v WI (2012) and 7-44 v NZ (2013)
B. A. Stokes (E). . . .	**101 v NZ (2015) and 6-22 v WI (2017)**

G. S. Sobers also appears on both Lord's honours boards: he made 163 in 1966 and 150* in 1973 for West Indies, and in 1970 scored 183 and took 6-21 for the Rest of the World, in a match considered a Test at the time but since ruled unofficial.*

Glyn Kirk AFP/Getty Images

Jimmy Jimmy! Kraigg Brathwaite is victim No. 500 for England's most successful Test bowler.

into his own, his combination of pace, bounce and extravagant movement scaring the living daylights out of anyone unlucky enough to confront him. Swerving the ball away, he hit Chase's off stump and had Dowrich swallowed low down by a newly confident Cook. After tea, taken at 119 for seven, a monstrous inswinger utterly defeated Holder. Anderson then contributed an astounding over to Bishoo – six times he beat him, yet his reward was a streaky four – before Stokes sliced through the tail with dizzying skill. He snatched three for none in six balls, to end with a career-best six for 22 – the cheapest six-for at Lord's – and membership of a small elite whose name appears on both honours boards.

Root would have been cock-a-hoop at dismissing West Indies for 123, less so to be faced with a ticklish hour and a half in conditions so gloomy – despite the floodlights – it felt as if the umpires had forgotten the pink balls. Where England found lavish swing and a little seam, West Indies found lavish seam and a little swing. Roach, having traded in the raw pace of youth for the greater control of maturity, slashed into England's soft underbelly. First he had Stoneman who, in disservice to his name, wafted outside off; then he deceived the grittier Cook with a corker that angled in from round the wicket and straightened. Now Holder joined the party. After squaring up Westley, he made England's sky fall in: Root's back-foot force flew to first slip, and Powell took a smart catch. At 24 for four, the heat was on.

Stokes negotiated a tricky path to stumps, and next morning held on as Roach cut down Malan, only for rain to sweep in after 26 balls. The top five were gone for 64 and yet, after play resumed at 2.15, Holder dispensed with a third slip. Unerringly, the next ball mocked his caution: Kyle Hope at second leapt to his left, but spilled a tough chance. The mockery continued, with the reprieved (Stokes) promptly drilling a boundary past the aggrieved (Gabriel). Well though West Indies juggled their three-man seam attack, England – if not out of the woods – were only four behind when Bairstow was sixth to go.

Stokes had reached an unruffled fifty from 51 balls, and was threatening to make the game his own – until a lightning inducker beat his forward defensive. But Gabriel had overstepped; Stokes would die another day. It turned out that day was close at hand: in a carbon-copy two balls later, he perished, and Gabriel, at last, had his man. Ali completed Roach's quality five-for to leave England 134 for eight, and the Test in the balance. But tail-end flailing, especially from Broad, secured a lead of 71 – untold riches in a low-scoring thriller.

And so the focus of a noisy Lord's shifted back to the quest for No. 500. It came almost immediately, with Andersonian brilliance. At the end of the third over, Brathwaite played round an inswinger, and the ground erupted. As if to prove the capriciousness of fortune, Stokes dropped a regulation chance from Powell three balls later. Instead Broad made do with Kyle Hope, ending a series so wretched that he and his brother – fixtures at Nos 3 and 4 – never batted together.

But the left-handed Powell, a rare shaft of sun in West Indies' saturnine innings, and the compact Shai Hope frustrated England. Deep into the floodlit evening, though, Powell was undone by a delivery of utmost genius from Anderson, coming round the wicket: it pitched on middle, pinged off the seam and pecked the off bail on the cheek. By the close of the second day, West Indies were effectively 22 for three.

WICKET WITH FIRST BALL IN A TEST AT LORD'S

Bowler	*Batsman*		
J. H. Wardle	J. B. Stollmeyer	England v West Indies	1950
C. C. Griffith	J. H. Edrich	West Indies v England	1963
S. D. Anurasiri	C. C. Lewis	Sri Lanka v England	1991
T. J. Friend	N. Hussain	Zimbabwe v England	2003
D. Bishoo	**A. N. Cook**	**West Indies v England**	**2017**

Ball-by-ball data is not available for many early matches, but there are not thought to be any additions to this list.

Research: Charles Davis

Hope, they say, springs eternal, and his team were desperate for runs to flow from their leading scorer. They came, too, though they were not the story. That was the unquenchable desire of the 35-year-old Anderson to take wicket after wicket after wicket. Bowling like this – precise length, seductive swing, exquisite control – he looked good for 600 or more. Sturdier teams than Holder's would have been scattered to the winds. Broad, who was a more dangerous proposition than on day one (when he hurt his heel slipping on the stairs inside the Pavilion), joined in, briefly claiming a third victim. Moments later, however, DRS spared Gabriel the indignity of becoming the first West Indian to suffer a king pair in Tests. It meant Anderson had time to take a seventh, shave a run from his career-best return, and put his feet up.

Thirty wickets had fallen for 494 runs, so a target of 107 was no piece of *Test Match Special* cake. But the sting had gone from the pitch and, with the absence of the injured Roach, from the West Indies attack. Any residual tension involved England batsmen scrabbling for a place on the trip to Australia, though the only failure was an inked-in tourist: Cook fell to Bishoo's first ball. Stoneman and Westley then swept England to the series, clearing the stage for the Test's third conquering hero.

Dressed in a trademark combination of shocking colours, Henry Blofeld called time on 45 years with *TMS*, strolled a lap of honour, and acknowledged the adulation of a full house. Lost in the nostalgia concerning pigeons, seagulls, buses, cranes, helicopters and sundry other dear old things was the identity of the Man of the Match. The name's Stokes. Ben Stokes.

Man of the Match: B. A. Stokes. *Attendance:* 83,603.

Men of the Series: England – J. M. Anderson. West Indies – S. D. Hope.

Close of play: first day, England 46-4 (Malan 13, Stokes 13); second day, West Indies 93-3 (S. D. Hope 35, Chase 3).

West Indies

First innings		Second innings	
K. C. Brathwaite c Bairstow b Anderson	10	b Anderson	4
K. O. A. Powell c and b Stokes	39	b Anderson	45
K. A. Hope c Bairstow b Anderson	0	lbw b Broad	1
S. D. Hope c Cook b Roland-Jones	29	c Bairstow b Anderson	62
R. L. Chase b Stokes	18	c Bairstow b Anderson	3
J. Blackwood b Roland-Jones	1	c Bairstow b Anderson	5
†S. O. Dowrich c Cook b Stokes	1	c Broad b Roland-Jones	14
*J. O. Holder b Stokes	9	c Anderson b Broad	23
D. Bishoo not out	13	b Anderson	0
K. A. J. Roach c Anderson b Stokes	0	b Anderson	3
S. T. Gabriel b Stokes	0	not out	0
Lb 1, nb 2	3	Lb 17	17
(57.3 overs)	123	(65.1 overs)	177

1/18 (1) 2/22 (3) 3/78 (4) 4/78 (2) 5/87 (6) 6/100 (5) 7/101 (7) 8/119 (8) 9/123 (10) 10/123 (11)

1/6 (1) 2/21 (3) 3/69 (2) 4/94 (5) 5/100 (6) 6/123 (7) 7/155 (4) 8/155 (9) 9/177 (8) 10/177 (10)

Anderson 16–7–31–2; Broad 12–5–24–0; Roland-Jones 11–4–32–2; Stokes 14.3–6–22–6; Ali 4–0–13–0. *Second innings*—Anderson 20.1–5–42–7; Broad 19–9–35–2; Roland-Jones 11–4–31–1; Stokes 12–3–41–0; Ali 2–0–6–0; Root 1–0–5–0.

England

First innings		Second innings	
A. N. Cook c Dowrich b Roach	10	lbw b Bishoo	17
M. D. Stoneman c Dowrich b Roach	1	not out	40
T. Westley lbw b Holder	8	not out	44
*J. E. Root c Powell b Holder	1		
D. J. Malan c Dowrich b Roach	20		
B. A. Stokes b Gabriel	60		
†J. M. Bairstow lbw b Roach	21		
M. M. Ali c K. A. Hope b Roach	3		
T. S. Roland-Jones c S. D. Hope b Holder	13		
S. C. J. Broad c Dowrich b Holder	38		
J. M. Anderson not out	8		
Lb 4, nb 7	11	B 4, lb 1, w 1	6
(52.5 overs)	194	(1 wkt, 28 overs)	107

1/1 (2) 2/15 (1) 3/19 (3) 4/24 (4) 5/63 (5) 6/119 (7) 7/128 (6) 8/134 (8) 9/163 (9) 10/194 (10)

1/35 (1)

Roach 24–8–72–5; Gabriel 15–1–64–1; Holder 13.5–1–54–4. *Second innings*—Gabriel 5–0–22–0; Roach 1–0–4–0; Holder 6–1–16–0; Bishoo 11–2–35–1; Chase 5–1–25–0.

Umpires: M. Erasmus and C. B. Gaffaney. Third umpire: S. Ravi.
Referee: D. C. Boon.

At Belfast, September 13. IRELAND v WEST INDIES. Abandoned. (See Overseas Cricket – Ireland).

LIMITED-OVERS INTERNATIONAL REPORTS BY DEAN WILSON

ENGLAND v WEST INDIES

NatWest Twenty20 International

At Chester-le-Street, September 16 (floodlit). West Indies won by 21 runs. Toss: England.

West Indies had rarely enjoyed their trips to chilly Durham, losing their previous four matches – two one-day internationals (including one against Zimbabwe), and two Tests. But Twenty20 was different. Put in to bat, their powerful opening duo of Gayle and Lewis, master and apprentice, delivered on the promise of fireworks. The first of Gayle's four sixes – Lewis hit three – made him the first player to clear the rope 100 times in T20 internationals, and only a typically casual piece of running spared England further damage. The first ten overs brought 106, but the innings slowed once the openers departed, thanks to Plunkett's aggression and the guile of Rashid, who picked up a career-best three for 25. Still, a target of 177 was no formality, and too many of England's own power players went missing. Roy fell first ball, and Hales alone prospered, cracking 43 before he was bowled by Carlos Brathwaite. Denied pace by Narine and Nurse, the batsmen struggled to find the boundary. Buttler and Bairstow added 50 for the fifth wicket but, without Ben Stokes – controversially rested at his home ground – or Moeen Ali, the batting was too light. Three spectators were injured when part of a temporary stand collapsed, leaving one woman with a broken leg; 200 others had to be moved.

Man of the Match: S. P. Narine. *Attendance:* 13,403.

West Indies

		B	4/6
1 C. H. Gayle *run out*	40	21	3/4
2 E. Lewis *c 3 b 9*	51	28	6/3
3 M. N. Samuels *c 3 b 9*	10	13	1
4 †C. A. K. Walton *c 8 b 7*	13	8	0/1
5 K. A. Pollard *c 11 b 9*	6	7	1
6 R. Powell *c 10 b 11*	28	19	1/2
7 *C. R. Brathwaite *b 7*	2	4	0
8 S. P. Narine *lbw b 7*	2	3	0
9 A. R. Nurse *not out*	13	12	0/1
10 J. E. Taylor *lbw b 10*	1	3	0
11 K. O. K. Williams *not out*	2	2	0
Lb 1, w 7	8		
6 overs: 72-0 (20 overs)	176-9		

1/77 2/106 3/115 4/123 5/127 6/138 7/142 8/165 9/167

12th man: J. N. Mohammed.

Willey 2–6–20–0; Root 2–6–11–0; Curran 4–8–46–1; Jordan 4–5–46–1; Plunkett 4–10–27–3; Rashid 4–10–25–3.

England

		B	4/6
1 J. J. Roy *c 2 b 10*	0	1	0
2 A. D. Hales *b 7*	43	17	8/1
3 J. E. Root *c 7 b 9*	17	19	2
4 *E. J. G. Morgan *c 2 b 8*	2	7	0
5 †J. C. Buttler *c 6 b 11*	30	27	2
6 J. M. Bairstow *c 12 b 7*	27	21	1/1
7 A. U. Rashid *c 4 b 11*	1	2	0
8 D. J. Willey *st 4 b 8*	1	3	0
9 L. E. Plunkett *b 7*	18	11	2
10 C. J. Jordan *c 6 b 11*	6	7	0
11 T. K. Curran *not out*	1	2	0
Lb 5, w 4	9		
6 overs: 64-2 (19.3 overs)	155		

1/0 2/64 3/66 4/68 5/118 6/124 7/127 8/129 9/148

Taylor 3–4–40–1; Williams 4–7–35–3; Brathwaite 3.3–11–20–3; Narine 4–13–15–2; Nurse 3–5–23–1; Pollard 2–4–17–0.

Umpires: M. A. Gough and R. T. Robinson. Third umpire: R. J. Bailey. Referee: J. Srinath.

ENGLAND v WEST INDIES

First Royal London One-Day International

At Manchester, September 19 (day/night). England won by seven wickets. Toss: West Indies.

West Indies needed to win the five-match series 4–0 or better to guarantee automatic qualification for the 2019 World Cup, but fell at the first hurdle. Despite the recall of Gayle for his first one-day international since the 2015 edition, they batted for the most part as if from another era. The sight of Samuels failing to find the boundary throughout a 46-ball 17 summed up a listless performance; the fact that he fell to a leg-side delivery from Stokes, his old sparring partner, was the icing on England's cake. Amid consternation from spectators, the game had been reduced to 42 overs because of a wet Old Trafford outfield struggling to cope with the demands of cricket and concerts, but that didn't affect Gayle's approach. He should have gone third ball, only for Root to drop the chance at slip off Woakes, and a trio of sixes followed, including two in an over off Willey. But Root had his redemption when he held a good running catch at cover to end the fun, and change the tempo, as West Indies' middle order took turns to get bogged down, then get out. Only Holder injected any impetus into an innings that ended on 204 for nine. England employed the opening partnership that had ended the Champions Trophy in June, a declaration that this was Bairstow's time for a run in the side. At the ground where he had fallen for 99 in the previous month's Test against South Africa, he responded with a maiden one-day century full of craft and thunder, bringing the contest to a swift conclusion. Root kept him company during a second-wicket stand of 125, and Stokes sealed victory with six over long-on off Nurse.

Man of the Match: J. M. Bairstow. *Attendance:* 13,835.

West Indies

C. H. Gayle c Root b Woakes	37
E. Lewis c Hales b Ali	11
†S. D. Hope c Bairstow b Stokes	35
M. N. Samuels c Buttler b Stokes	17
J. N. Mohammed c Hales b Rashid	18
R. Powell c Willey b Woakes	23
*J. O. Holder not out	41
A. R. Nurse c Root b Rashid	1
D. Bishoo b Willey	5
J. E. Taylor c Buttler b Stokes	2
K. O. K. Williams not out	0
Lb 3, w 9, nb 2	14
1/45 (2) 2/53 (1) 3/103 (3) 4/107 (4) 5/149 (5) 6/150 (6) 7/160 (8) 8/187 (9) 9/202 (10) — (9 wkts, 42 overs)	204
9 overs: 53-2	

Woakes 8–0–41–2; Willey 6–0–39–1; Ali 2–0–5–1; Rashid 9–0–31–2; Plunkett 8–0–42–0; Stokes 9–0–43–3.

England

J. M. Bairstow not out	100
A. D. Hales c Lewis b Taylor	19
J. E. Root b Williams	54
*E. J. G. Morgan c Hope b Williams	10
B. A. Stokes not out	23
W 4	4
1/31 (2) 2/156 (3) 3/175 (4) — (3 wkts, 30.5 overs)	210
9 overs: 63-1	

†J. C. Buttler, M. M. Ali, C. R. Woakes, A. U. Rashid, L. E. Plunkett and D. J. Willey did not bat.

Taylor 7–0–46–1; Holder 3–0–18–0; Williams 6–0–50–2; Nurse 8.5–0–48–0; Bishoo 6–0–48–0.

Umpires: S. D. Fry and R. T. Robinson. Third umpire: R. J. Tucker.
Referee: J. Srinath.

ENGLAND v WEST INDIES

Second Royal London One-Day International

At Nottingham, September 21 (day/night). No result. Toss: West Indies.

Only 14 legal balls were possible before low-lying cloud cover burst open to send the players scurrying off, though not until England had hinted at another run-fest at the venue where they had battered a world-record 444 against Pakistan the previous summer. The game was abandoned at 4.15, though a 20-over match could have begun as late as 5.56. The eventual appearance of the September sun led some to query whether the decision had been premature.

England

J. M. Bairstow not out	9
A. D. Hales not out	10
W 2	2
(no wkt, 2.2 overs)	21

J. E. Root, *E. J. G. Morgan, B. A. Stokes, †J. C. Buttler, M. M. Ali, C. R. Woakes, A. U. Rashid, L. E. Plunkett and D. J. Willey did not bat.

Holder 1.2–0–11–0; Taylor 1–0–10–0.

West Indies

E. Lewis, K. A. Hope, †S. D. Hope, M. N. Samuels, J. N. Mohammed, R. Powell, *J. O. Holder, A. R. Nurse, J. E. Taylor, M. L. Cummins, K. O. K. Williams.

Umpires: R. J. Bailey and R. J. Tucker. Third umpire: S. D. Fry.
Referee: J. Srinath.

ENGLAND v WEST INDIES

Third Royal London One-Day International

At Bristol, September 24. England won by 124 runs. Toss: West Indies.

England's margin of victory suggested a mismatch, but that would be misleading. Twice after they were inserted, Morgan's side were in trouble: at 74 for three in the 12th over, after Morgan himself had fallen first ball; and at 217 for six in the 35th, by which time Root had gone past Graham Gooch's record of most international runs in an English season (1,277 in 1990). With two new batsmen at the crease, an imposing total seemed unlikely. Enter Ali, to provide the Bristol crowd with some wondrous entertainment. Both languid and brutal, he out-hit the hitters, launching eight – mainly leg-side – sixes while moving from 39 to 100 in 14 balls of unmitigated mayhem; in successive overs from Cummins and Holder, the 45th and 46th, he pummelled 48 runs, later

THE LATE LATE SHOW

Latest arrival at the crease for a century-maker in one-day internationals:

Overs			
38.4	A. B. de Villiers (149)	South Africa v West Indies at Johannesburg	2014-15
35.4	J. C. Buttler (116*)	England v Pakistan at Dubai	2015-16
32.6	A. B. de Villiers (102*)	South Africa v India at Ahmedabad	2009-10
32.4	**M. M. Ali (102)**	**England v West Indies at Bristol**	**2017**
31.6	G. J. Maxwell (102)	Australia v Sri Lanka at Sydney	2014-15

describing it all as "a bit of a slog". In 53 balls, Ali had transformed the slog into an art form: it was the quickest one-day international hundred in England, beating Buttler (61 balls) against Sri Lanka at Lord's in 2014, and the second-fastest by an England player anywhere, *behind* Buttler (46) against Pakistan at Dubai in 2015-16. Woakes contributed a run-a-ball 34 to a seventh-wicket stand of 117 in 12 overs, which set West Indies 370. As long as Gayle remained, anything was possible, and his six sixes kept them in the hunt until Rashid's direct hit from midwicket caught him short on 94. Rashid and Plunkett, who picked up a career-best five for 52, ran through the rest. At 2.35am, Stokes was arrested on suspicion of committing actual bodily harm following a fracas outside a nightclub, but was released under investigation; Hales, with him at the time, later returned to Bristol to help Avon and Somerset police with their enquiries. Both were suspended for the rest of the series.

Man of the Match: M. M. Ali. *Attendance:* 12,112.

England

J. M. Bairstow c and b Holder	13	D. J. Willey not out	1
A. D. Hales lbw b Cummins	36	A. U. Rashid not out	9
J. E. Root lbw b Cummins	84		
*E. J. G. Morgan c Hope b Holder	0	Lb 1, w 3, nb 2	6
B. A. Stokes c Lewis b Powell	73		
†J. C. Buttler b Cummins	2	1/27 (1) 2/73 (2) (9 wkts, 50 overs)	369
M. M. Ali c Holder b Nurse	102	3/74 (4) 4/206 (5)	
C. R. Woakes c Powell b Taylor	34	5/210 (6) 6/217 (3) 7/334 (8)	
L. E. Plunkett run out	9	8/354 (7) 9/358 (9)	10 overs: 65-1

Taylor 10–1–75–1; Holder 10–0–81–2; Cummins 9–0–82–3; Bishoo 5–0–33–0; Nurse 8–0–59–1; Powell 8–0–38–1.

West Indies

C. H. Gayle run out	94
E. Lewis c Ali b Willey	13
†S. D. Hope c Buttler b Plunkett	20
M. N. Samuels c Buttler b Plunkett	11
J. N. Mohammed c Bairstow b Plunkett	38
R. Powell c Woakes b Rashid	8
*J. O. Holder c Ali b Plunkett	34
A. R. Nurse lbw b Rashid	1
D. Bishoo c Morgan b Plunkett	12
J. E. Taylor b Rashid	0
M. L. Cummins not out	4
Lb 3, w 7	10
1/15 (2) 2/79 (3) 3/109 (4) 4/176 (1) 5/192 (6) 6/210 (5) 7/212 (8) 8/241 (9) 9/241 (10) 10/245 (7) — (39.1 overs)	245
10 overs: 73-1	

Woakes 7–1–32–0; Willey 4–0–34–1; Plunkett 8.1–0–52–5; Ali 10–0–65–0; Stokes 4–0–25–0; Rashid 6–0–34–3.

Umpires: S. D. Fry and M. A. Gough. Third umpire: R. J. Tucker.
Referee: J. Srinath.

ENGLAND v WEST INDIES

Fourth Royal London One-Day International

At The Oval, September 27 (day/night). England won by six runs (DLS). Toss: England.

Three days after his Bristol heroics, Ali's perfectly timed smash and grab sealed the series, and helped lift spirits after news broke on the eve of the game of Stokes's arrest. Ali had arrived when England, set an imposing 357, were struggling at 181 for five; the 20-year-old Joseph had become the youngest West Indian to take five wickets in a one-day international, all in the space of 28 legal deliveries. With rain imminent, England trailed by 37 on DLS, only for Ali to take 16 from three balls off Nurse, and change the momentum. By the time the downpour arrived, he had 48 from 25, Buttler 43 from 35, and England were narrowly ahead. The late onslaught overshadowed some venomous hitting from Lewis. After Woakes had reduced West Indies to 33 for three, Lewis's 176

IT HURTS SO GOOD

Highest scores in international cricket at which a batsman retired hurt and did not resume:

176*	**E. Lewis**	**West Indies v England (ODI) at The Oval**	**2017**
165*	C. Bannerman	Australia v England (Test) at Melbourne	1876-77
163*	S. R. Tendulkar	India v New Zealand (ODI) at Christchurch	2008-09
138*	Wasim Jaffer	India v Bangladesh (Test) at Mirpur	2007
133*	F. du Plessis	South Africa v India (ODI) at Mumbai	2015-16
129*	Salman Butt	Pakistan v India (ODI) at Mirpur	2008
125*	Shoaib Malik	Pakistan v India (ODI) at Karachi	2008
122*	L. Hutton	England v Australia (Test) at Sydney	1946-47
122*	L. R. P. L. Taylor	New Zealand v Zimbabwe (Test) at Napier	2011-12

In the Test between England and Pakistan at The Oval in 1974, D. L. Amiss retired hurt at 178, but resumed and was out for 183.*

---

from 130 balls, including 17 fours and seven sixes, condemned the boundary-riders to mere spectators. It was the highest ODI score at The Oval (beating Roy's 162 a year earlier against Sri Lanka), and he had his opening partner Gayle's West Indian record 215 in his sights when he jammed a full-length delivery from Ball into his right ankle, forcing him off the field with 3.4 overs to go; an X-ray confirmed a hairline fracture. He had added 168 with Holder, a West Indian record for the fifth wicket, leaving England needing to score more runs to win an ODI batting second than they had ever managed. With Alex Hales unavailable, Roy returned to the top of the order after being dropped for the Champions Trophy semi-final, and creamed 84 in 66 balls during an opening stand of 126 inside 18 overs with Bairstow. Joseph instigated the collapse, but Ali was not to be denied.

Man of the Match: E. Lewis. *Attendance:* 23,936.

Break point: Evin Lewis cracks the ball into his right ankle, ending an astonishing innings.

West Indies

C. H. Gayle c Root b Woakes	2
E. Lewis retired hurt	176
†S. D. Hope c Buttler b Woakes	11
M. N. Samuels lbw b Woakes	1
J. N. Mohammed c Buttler b Rashid	46
*J. O. Holder c Billings b Plunkett	77
R. Powell not out	28
Lb 3, w 12	15
1/2 (1) 2/19 (3) 3/33 (4) 4/150 (5) 5/356 (6) (5 wkts, 50 overs)	356
10 overs: 55-3	

A. R. Nurse, A. S. Joseph, J. E. Taylor and M. L. Cummins did not bat.

Lewis retired hurt at 318-4.

Woakes 10–0–71–3; Ball 10–0–68–0; Plunkett 10–0–67–1; Ali 9–1–70–0; Root 1–0–10–0; Rashid 10–0–67–1.

England

J. J. Roy c Hope b Joseph	84
J. M. Bairstow c Hope b Joseph	39
J. E. Root c Hope b Joseph	14
*E. J. G. Morgan c sub (K. A. Hope) b Joseph	19
†J. C. Buttler not out	43
S. W. Billings c Gayle b Joseph	2
M. M. Ali not out	48
Lb 4, w 3, nb 2	9
1/126 (1) 2/144 (2) 3/157 (3) 4/177 (4) 5/181 (6) (5 wkts, 35.1 overs)	258
10 overs: 57-0	

C. R. Woakes, A. U. Rashid, L. E. Plunkett and J. T. Ball did not bat.

Taylor 7–0–48–0; Holder 9–0–52–0; Joseph 8.1–0–56–5; Cummins 6–0–49–0; Nurse 3–0–39–0; Powell 2–0–10–0.

Umpires: R. J. Bailey and R. J. Tucker. Third umpire: S. D. Fry.
Referee: J. Srinath.

ENGLAND v WEST INDIES

Fifth Royal London One-Day International

At Southampton, September 29 (day/night). England won by nine wickets. Toss: England. One-day international debuts: T. K. Curran; S. W. Ambris.

There was a time, not long ago, when 288 would have been a competitive score in a 50-over game in England. Not any more. The ease with which Bairstow collected his second hundred of the series to wrap up a 4–0 win – and England's 16th victory in 17 completed games in the format against West Indies – made you wonder whether the latest finish to an international summer had really been worth it. England's bowlers had taken a little early punishment from Gayle, who struck Ball for 34 from six deliveries across two overs. But once he fell to a slower ball from Tom Curran, making his one-day international debut, the innings got stuck against England's spinners. At one point, West Indies – led by Jason Mohammed after Jason Holder flew home to attend the funeral of an uncle – did not hit a boundary for nearly 22 overs. It was a bizarre lull which reduced the late hitting from debutant Sunil Ambris and Nurse to window dressing; Ball finished with one for 94, the third-most expensive one-day analysis for England. Bairstow and Roy again suggested they could work well together in the absence of Alex Hales. Roy carted 96 from 70 balls in an opening stand of 156 in 21 overs, and Bairstow carried on unperturbed, with Root for company. Peppering well-judged ones and twos with the odd four, they completed the job with 12 overs to go when Root launched Samuels straight for six, bringing up 4,000 ODI runs. Bairstow finished unbeaten on 141 from 114 balls, England's highest one-day score against West Indies, beating Marcus Trescothick's 130 in St Lucia in May 2004.

Man of the Match: J. M. Bairstow. *Attendance:* 11,687.
Man of the Series: M. M. Ali.

West Indies

C. H. Gayle c Plunkett b Curran	40
K. A. Hope c and b Plunkett	33
†S. D. Hope c Billings b Ball	72
M. N. Samuels st Buttler b Ali	32
*J. N. Mohammed c Root b Rashid	25
S. W. Ambris not out	38
R. Powell b Plunkett	11
A. R. Nurse not out	31
W 6	6
1/52 (1) 2/86 (2) 3/143 (4) 4/195 (5) 5/221 (3) 6/253 (7) — (6 wkts, 50 overs)	288
10 overs: 65-1	

A. S. Joseph, J. E. Taylor and M. L. Cummins did not bat.

Ball 10–1–94–1; Curran 10–1–62–1; Plunkett 10–0–54–2; Rashid 10–1–42–1; Ali 10–0–36–1.

England

J. J. Roy lbw b Cummins	96
J. M. Bairstow not out	141
J. E. Root not out	46
Lb 2, w 9	11
1/156 (1) — (1 wkt, 38 overs)	294
10 overs: 71-0	

*E. J. G. Morgan, †J. C. Buttler, S. W. Billings, M. M. Ali, A. U. Rashid, T. K. Curran, L. E. Plunkett and J. T. Ball did not bat.

Taylor 8–0–52–0; Joseph 7–0–54–0; Cummins 8–0–70–1; Nurse 8–0–56–0; Samuels 4–0–41–0; Powell 3–0–19–0.

Umpires: S. D. Fry and M. A. Gough. Third umpire: R. J. Tucker.
Referee: J. Srinath.

AUSTRALIA v ENGLAND IN 2017-18

REVIEW BY GIDEON HAIGH

Test matches (5): Australia 4, England 0
One-day internationals (5): Australia 1, England 4

During the grim days of one-way Ashes cricket in the nineties and noughties, and the Baggy Green battalions of Allan Border, Mark Taylor and Steve Waugh, Australians would condescendingly plead: "All we want is a contest." Those murmurings were heard again, as Steve Smith's side relieved England of the trophy as readily as contraband at customs.

Ever since the Australians had been knocked from their No. 1 Test perch in August 2009, England had felt a slight but decided edge, winning four Ashes series out of five, and content to downplay the debacle of 2013-14 as the consequence of a freakish winter's work by Mitchell Johnson. This felt rather more like the turning of a page. Only the final day of the Second Test at Adelaide dawned with any mood of impending drama, England needing 178 more with six wickets in hand. That impression lasted the 17 balls it took to dismiss the overnight batsmen.

The rest of the time there was little sense of contest, more of ordeal: how long could a frail England hold out against a competent, consistent, well-drilled Australia, with Smith in the form of his life, three ruthlessly fast bowlers – Mitchell Starc, Josh Hazlewood and Patrick Cummins – not far short of that and Nathan Lyon in complete control with his off-breaks? The answer was never quite long enough.

England were 246 for four before lunch on the second day at Brisbane, 368 for four before lunch on the second at Perth, and 228 for three late on the first at Sydney, whereupon wickets tumbled each time. Nor could they complain about their luck: they were favoured by four tosses and mild temperatures, aside from an inhumanely hot fourth day at the SCG. And they suffered fewer injuries than most visiting teams. The chief blows were to their professional pride.

In fact the signal setback had been self-inflicted – the run-in with the law of Ben Stokes, Joe Root's vice-captain, in Bristol in September. Not only could England never replace his runs or overs, but those who tried – such as Moeen Ali, Jonny Bairstow, Chris Woakes, Craig Overton and Jake Ball – were forced either out of position or into premature responsibility. In this sense, Stokes's arrest did not simply imperil his own career, but those of colleagues. It also made for a tour undershadowed, so to speak, by the issue of off-field behaviour. Storms in tabloid teacups were virtually foreordained and duly swirled, two of them originating in the same hostelry, The Avenue in Perth's Claremont, whose name no journalist will forget in a hurry.

Here, on their first night in Australia, the tourists found themselves in the friendly company of the local state team, and Bairstow gave a jokey headbutt of greeting to Cameron Bancroft – a custom among his northern rugby friends. When Bancroft was chosen for the First Test, and mention of the incident was

Greg Wood, AFP/Getty Images

Leitmotif: the sight of Steve Smith taking off his helmet and waving his bat was a recurring theme.

overheard on the stump microphones, the story ran and ran. England were caught between feeling they needed to look serious about discipline, while considering the incident trivial.

Stung by *l'affaire Stokes*, the management erred on the serious side, imposing a midnight curfew, which made them look silly. They looked still sillier a few weeks later, relaxing the curfew so that players could return to The Avenue with members of the England Lions squad, after which there were reports, apparently originating from the team's own security men, that Ben Duckett had poured a drink over James Anderson. Again, England found

HIGHEST BATTING AVERAGE IN AN ASHES SERIES

		T	*I*	*NO*	*Runs*	*HS*	*100*	
147.33	G. Boycott (E)	3	5	2	442	191	2	1977
139.14	D. G. Bradman (A)	5	7	0	974	334	4	1930
137.40	**S. P. D. Smith (A)**	**5**	**7**	**2**	**687**	**239**	**3**	**2017-18**
127.66	A. N. Cook (E)	5	7	1	766	235*	3	2010-11
126.50	S. R. Waugh (A)	6	8	4	506	177*	2	1989
118.25	L. Hutton (E)	3	4	0	473	364	2	1938
113.12	W. R. Hammond (E)	5	9	1	905	251	4	1928-29
108.50	D. G. Bradman (A)	4	6	2	434	144*	3	1938
107.00	S. R. Waugh (A)	4	5	2	321	157*	2	2001
106.66	**M. R. Marsh (A)**	**3**	**4**	**1**	**320**	**181**	**2**	**2017-18**
102.50	A. E. Trott (A)	3	5	3	205	85*	0	1894-95
101.75	E. Paynter (E)	4	6	2	407	216*	1	1938

Minimum: four innings.

themselves talking out of both corners of their mouth, insisting there was nothing to it, even as they fined Duckett swingeingly, and stood him down.

It all led to an impression of naive players and self-consciously reactive management, not actual disarray. There was no reason to disbelieve Alastair Cook: "I've never seen a team work harder than this side. People are desperate to do well." Had England been only inept and indolent, their defeat might have been easier to stomach, or at least explain. As it was, doing the best they could, they looked ever more inferior. Not a single player could be described as an unqualified success.

IT'S THAT MAN AGAIN

Dismissing the same player seven times in the same Test series:

Bowler	*Batsman*		
C. V. Grimmett	I. J. Siedle	Australia v South Africa	1935-36
J. B. Statham	T. L. Goddard	England v South Africa	1960
G. F. Lawson	D. I. Gower	†Australia v England	1989
G. D. McGrath	M. A. Atherton	†Australia v England	1997
N. M. Lyon	**M. M. Ali**	**Australia v England**	**2017-18**

† *Six-Test series.*

Root topped their batting averages without having a particularly good tour, failing to convert any of his five half-centuries, though the last of them, at Sydney, was interrupted by gastroenteritis. Cook was only two runs behind – after a poor tour for the opposite reason, converting his only score over 40 into an unbeaten double-century at Melbourne. Dawid Malan had moments when he came close to an ideal tempo for Test cricket, although it was his haphazard shots that prompted England's collapses at the Gabba and the WACA. Mark Stoneman and James Vince started encouragingly and ended meekly, while Ali, Woakes and Stuart Broad, treated to predictable short-pitched barrages, sold themselves cheaply. Gary Ballance has now made two tours of Australia for one Test appearance, and was omitted for the trip to New Zealand.

Anderson toiled manfully, and – with an economy rate of 2.11 – was the meanest bowler on either side; almost a third of his overs were maidens. He gave Australia their hardest time under lights at Adelaide, as did Woakes. But in six other innings, Woakes paid 76 for six wickets, while Broad's 11 at 47 continued the slow waning of his powers. Mark Wood, initially absent with an ankle injury, and Steven Finn, who officially replaced Stokes, then returned to England after damaging a knee at the first training session, were missed for their extra speed; Ball, Overton and Tom Curran were seldom better than steady.

The most abject decline was experienced by Ali. Nobody had expected much: 12 wickets at 40 would probably have been judged satisfactory. But five at 115 was an entirely fair reflection of a bowler who could neither penetrate nor restrict; he also batted diffidently, and wandered around outfields as if hoping they would swallow him up. Strangely, one of England's most encouraging performances involved a single wicket taken at the cost of 193 runs. Twenty-year-old Mason Crane could hardly have had a tougher Test

The heat of the battle: Joe Root struggles against illness and dehydration – as well as the Australian bowlers – on the last day of the Sydney Test.

initiation in what was only his 30th first-class match: a flat Sydney pitch, a dominant opponent and a beleaguered captain. But he was undismayed, spun the ball appreciably, survived the brutal heat, and should by rights be back in three years.

On the field, Root cut his coat according to his cloth. He set the tone for an attritional series at Brisbane with a wide range of fortifications, although in doing so also let opportunities slip, and seemed more concerned with preventing happenings than causing them. When England did throw the gauntlet down at Adelaide by sending Australia in, they appeared almost to have forgotten how to attack, the bowlers dropping instinctively on to defensive lengths. One useful change to the order was made, in promoting Bairstow to No. 6, but Root's reluctance to bat at No. 3 yielded the Australians an initiative.

Smith's team took advantage of everything they were offered, the victory more wholesomely satisfying for being lengthily prepared. Australia had decided their first-choice attack – providing a testing variety of air speeds, default lengths and trajectories – almost a year in advance, and managed them carefully between times. Remarkably, they needed reconfiguring only once, a heel injury continuing Starc's odd allergy to the Boxing Day Test (he has played only one). Cummins also demonstrated all-round pretensions, averaging 41, mainly from No. 9, and participating in vital rearguards with Smith at Brisbane and Shaun Marsh at Adelaide.

A formidable combination was completed by Lyon, who had surged back from a lean period to master conditions in the subcontinent on the way to being

2017's leading Test wicket-taker. Eighteen of his 21 victims were left-handers, including his counterpart Ali seven times, and he gave away only 2.36 per over – his tightest performance in a series of three Tests or more. Into the bargain he had become a superbly nimble fielder, throwing his pipe-cleaner physique left and right, taking two sharp return catches, and running out Vince with a direct hit on the first day at the Gabba.

Statistics testified to the attack's cohesion: all four members took between 21 and 23 wickets, at averages between 23 and 29; their ages ranged from 24 to 30. Favoured by fitness and fortune, they could yet form Australia's most potent bowling line-up since the era of McGrath and Warne. And while Australia had completely revamped their pace bowling since their last home Ashes, England were still seeking to make do and mend with Anderson and Broad.

FOUR AND TWENTY

Test series in which four bowlers took 20 or more wickets:

West Indies v England (6 Tests) in England 1995
I. R. Bishop 27, C. A. Walsh 26, K. C. G. Benjamin 23, C. E. L. Ambrose 21.
Australia v England (5 Tests) in Australia 2006-07
S. R. Clark 26, S. K. Warne 23, G. D. McGrath 21, B. Lee 20.
Australia v England (5 Tests) in Australia 2017-18
P. J. Cummins 23, M. A. Starc 22, J. R. Hazlewood 21, N. M. Lyon 21.

In 2017-18, no other bowler took a wicket – unique for a five-Test series.

Elsewhere, Australia's selectors took a bit of a punt, with mixed success. Bancroft, preferred to the young Queenslander Matthew Renshaw, was a failure; he made an unbeaten 82 on debut, but – increasingly intense and introverted – only 97 in another seven hits. His high point came at Brisbane's post-match press conference, where he had the assembled journalists in stitches with a deadpan description of the Bairstow headbutt. Peter Handscomb fell by the wayside after two games, trussed up in an idiosyncratic technique that left him unnaturally deep in his crease, while Usman Khawaja remained his enigmatic self until the Fifth Test, when he took eight and a half hours over a first Ashes hundred. Root's denial-of-service fields slowed David Warner – he hit a single six in the series and struck at just 52 per hundred balls, not much faster than Cook – but didn't stop him. He showed a new resourcefulness by batting more than five hours for 86 to secure Australia from harm at the MCG.

Perhaps the selectors' biggest speculation was wicketkeeper Tim Paine, more than seven years after his previous Test. He had not even been part of his state team, Tasmania, when the season began, and did not keep wicket in his last game before the First Test. A crucial stumping of Ali in Brisbane reminded onlookers of his initial promise and, if his understanding with first slip remained imperfect, he ended up with 26 dismissals and 192 useful runs at 48.

In recalling the Marshes – first Shaun, then Mitchell – the selectors persevered in beliefs rather than came to awakenings, and were rewarded beyond their expectations. (Others expected little too: former Test leg-spinner

The joke of the butt? Cameron Bancroft has his captain, Steve Smith, and everyone at the press conference in stitches when recounting the story of the Bairstow salutation.

Stuart MacGill had damned the selectors before the First Test as "morons masquerading as mentors".) Each Marsh made two hundreds, including in one another's company at Sydney. Shaun had attained these heights before; Mitchell, with a first-class average hovering around 30, was a revelation, piling up 181 in a run-a-minute triple-century partnership with his captain at Perth. The ostensible reason for his inclusion had been to provide Smith with a fifth bowling option. In the event, he sent down 32 wicketless overs in five innings; not that his skipper minded.

Nothing much bothered Smith, the Compton–Miller medallist, at all – certainly no bowler, and no plan. He confessed to doubting his judgment in Adelaide, where he offered England a chink of light by declining to enforce the follow-on. But at the crease he proved remarkably adaptable, compiling his slowest hundred in Brisbane, his briskest in Perth, and possibly his safest in Melbourne; and despite a few drops he snaffled ten catches, twice as many as any other outfielder. The only quibble was that at times it looked too easy. This was another season of bland Australian pitches – so bland in Melbourne's case that it incurred an ICC penalty. The best surface was at the WACA, to

MOST DISMISSALS IN AN ASHES SERIES

29 (29ct)	B. J. Haddin (A)	2013
28 (28ct)	R. W. Marsh (A)	1982-83
27 (25ct, 2st)†	I. A. Healy (A)	1997
26 (21ct, 5st)†	I. A. Healy (A)	1993
26 (24ct, 2st)	A. C. Gilchrist (A)	2001
26 (24ct, 2st)	A. C. Gilchrist (A)	2006-07
26 (25ct, 1st)	**T. D. Paine (A)**	**2017-18**
25 (23ct, 2st)	I. A. Healy (A)	1994-95
25 (23ct, 2st)	A. C. Gilchrist (A)	2002-03
24 (21ct, 3st)†	A. P. E. Knott (E)	1970-71
24 (24ct)	I. A. Healy (A)	1990-91

† *Six-Test series.*

which international cricket was bidding farewell. The series also featured the slowest Ashes run-rate since 1994-95, the last time all five matches reached the fifth day. Four–nil was not unfair, and the 865,451 attendees a testament to the rivalry's brand loyalty. But the aftertaste was of flat champagne.

Vithushan Ehantharajah writes: Games such as the five one-dayers which followed the Tests can be anticlimactic, but England might have felt this victory, their first in a bilateral one-day series in Australia, was instead rather therapeutic. That they were disappointed by their failure to complete a whitewash – they narrowly lost the fourth game, at Adelaide, despite stumbling to eight for five – said much for the ambition of Eoin Morgan's side. This was a big step in the right direction towards the 2019 World Cup.

What Morgan himself lacked with the bat – he scored 99 in five innings – he made up for with his captaincy, and his tactics contributed directly to two of the four wins. At Brisbane, he was quick to turn to spin when the unusual nature of the Gabba surface became clear. And at Sydney, where Jos Buttler hit a remarkable 83-ball hundred to turn a perilous 189 for six into a match-winning 302 for six, Morgan shuffled his bowlers expertly after Liam Plunkett pulled a hamstring in his second over.

Back in the ranks after the Ashes letdown, Root batted with freedom, scoring 226 runs at 75, shepherding England's record chase of 305 at Melbourne with an unbeaten 91 in the series opener, and placing busy industry ahead of big hitting: in all, he limited himself to nine fours. By contrast, Smith and Warner – who had combined for 1,128 runs in the Ashes – managed just 175 in ten innings, without a half-century between them. Some of the slack was picked up by Aaron Finch, who began with two hundreds and a fifty, only to miss the last two games through injury, and Marcus Stoinis. But Australia looked off

Left open-mouthed: at Melbourne, Tim Paine can only look on as Jason Roy powers towards 180, the highest one-day score for England.

the pace as they slipped to their first bilateral one-day defeat at home since Sri Lanka's visit in 2010-11.

England's contributions were spread across the team, typified by Adil Rashid, who was the leading wicket-taker, with ten, but didn't take any of the games by storm. Mark Wood's return had many wondering whether the Ashes might have turned out differently; he managed only four wickets, but his extra zip and bounce provided a welcome antidote to medium-pace. Jason Roy smashed a national record at Melbourne, but Woakes topped the batting averages, scoring 170 runs for once out, with a strike-rate of 117; no one on either team hit more than his eight sixes.

Even those on the sidelines were able to step up, Tom Curran taking the spoils in the last match, the inaugural international at Perth Stadium. And with Stokes hovering on the periphery, there was a sense that England had more talent than they could squeeze into one team. It all left Australia, the 50-over world champions, wondering how they had fallen so far behind.

FIVE STATS YOU MAY HAVE MISSED

BENEDICT BERMANGE

- The England side for the opening Test at Brisbane was the first in which all 11 players were born in England since Galle in December 2003, some 177 matches previously. The Second Test at Adelaide provided the first instance of England playing back-to-back Tests with 11 English-born players since February 1982.

- At Perth, James Anderson, Stuart Broad and Alastair Cook played a Test together for the 100th time. They were only the third trio to achieve this feat:

118 R. Dravid, V. V. S. Laxman, S. R. Tendulkar (India)
103 R. Dravid, S. C. Ganguly and S. R. Tendulkar (India)
102 J. M. Anderson, S. C. J. Broad and A. N. Cook (England)

- Australia's 662 for nine declared at Perth provided the third case of five England bowlers each conceding 100 runs in a Test innings:

v West Indies at Lord's, 1973 (G. G. Arnold 0-111, R. G. D. Willis 4-118, A. W. Greig 3-180, D. L. Underwood 0-105, R. Illingworth 1-114)
v Australia at Cardiff, 2009 (J. M. Anderson 2-110, S. C. J. Broad 1-129, G. P. Swann 0-131, A. Flintoff 1-128, M. S. Panesar 1-115)
v Australia at Perth, 2017-18 (J. M. Anderson 4-116, S. C. J. Broad 0-142, C. R. Woakes 1-128, C. Overton 2-110, M. M. Ali 1-120)

- Only two bowlers have dismissed more left-handers in a series than Nathan Lyon:

22	M. G. Johnson	Australia v England (in Australia)	2013-14
19	R. Ashwin	India v Australia (in India)	2012-13
18	**N. M. Lyon**	**Australia v England** (in Australia)	**2017-18**

- Alastair Cook has now lost more Tests in Australia than any visiting player in one country:

15 A. N. Cook (England) in Australia
14 J. B. Hobbs (England) in Australia
14 S. R. Tendulkar (India) in Australia
13 J. M. Anderson (England) in Australia
13 B. C. Lara (WI/World XI) in Australia
13 S. Chanderpaul (West Indies) in South Africa
12 Rhodes (England) in Australia

ENGLAND TOURING PARTY

*J. E. Root (Yorkshire; T/50), M. M. Ali (Worcestershire; T/50), J. M. Anderson (Lancashire; T), J. M. Bairstow (Yorkshire; T/50), J. T. Ball (Nottinghamshire; T/50), G. S. Ballance (Yorkshire; T), S. W. Billings (Kent; 50), S. C. J. Broad (Nottinghamshire; T), J. C. Buttler (Lancashire; 50), A. N. Cook (Essex; T), M. S. Crane (Hampshire; T), T. K. Curran (Surrey; T/50), S. T. Finn (Middlesex; T), B. T. Foakes (Surrey; T), A. D. Hales (Nottinghamshire; 50), D. J. Malan (Middlesex; T/50), E. J. G. Morgan (Middlesex; 50), C. Overton (Somerset; T), L. E. Plunkett (Yorkshire; 50), A. U. Rashid (Yorkshire; 50), J. J. Roy (Surrey; 50), M. D. Stoneman (Surrey; T), J. M. Vince (Hampshire; T), D. J. Willey (Yorkshire; 50), C. R. Woakes (Warwickshire; T/50), M. A. Wood (Durham; 50).

B. A. Stokes (Durham) was originally selected, but was withdrawn while police enquiries into the incident in Bristol in September continued. His original replacement in the Test party, Finn, hurt his knee before the first tour game: he was replaced by Curran. Malan replaced Stokes in the one-day squad, which was captained by Morgan.

J. M. Clarke (Worcestershire), K. K. Jennings (Durham), D. W. Lawrence (Essex), M. J. Leach (Somerset), L. S. Livingstone (Lancashire) and M. A. Wood (Durham), who were in Australia with the England Lions, played in the two-day game in Perth between the Second and Third Tests.

Coach: T. H. Bayliss (T/50). *Assistant coach:* P. Farbrace (T/50). *Batting coach:* M. R. Ramprakash (T), G. P. Thorpe (50). *Fast-bowling coach:* S. E. Bond (T), C. E. W. Silverwood (50). *Spin-bowling coach:* Saqlain Mushtaq (T). *Fielding coach:* P. D. Collingwood (T/50). *Wicketkeeping coach:* B. N. French (T). *Operations manager:* P. A. Neale (T), A. W. Bentley (50). *Analyst:* G. Lindsay (T), R. J. Lewis (50). *Doctor:* M. G. Wotherspoon (T), G. S. Bhogal (50). *Physiotherapist:* C. A. de Weymarn (T/50). *Masseur:* M. D. Saxby (T), C. N. Clarke-Irons (50). *Strength and conditioning:* P. C. F. Scott (T/50). *Performance psychologist:* D. J. Young (T/50). *Security manager:* R. C. Dickason (T/50). *Head of team communications:* D. M. Reuben (T/50).

TEST MATCH AVERAGES

AUSTRALIA – BATTING AND FIELDING

	T	*I*	*NO*	*R*	*HS*	*100*	*50*	*Avge*	*Ct/St*
S. P. D. Smith	5	7	2	687	239	3	2	137.40	10
M. R. Marsh	3	4	1	320	181	2	0	106.66	1
†S. E. Marsh	5	7	1	445	156	2	2	74.16	2
†D. A. Warner	5	8	1	441	103	1	3	63.00	1
T. D. Paine	5	6	2	192	57	0	1	48.00	25/1
†U. T. Khawaja	5	7	0	333	171	1	2	47.57	3
P. J. Cummins	5	6	2	166	44	0	0	41.50	1
C. T. Bancroft	5	8	1	179	82*	0	1	25.57	5
P. S. P. Handscomb	2	3	0	62	36	0	0	20.66	5
N. M. Lyon	5	5	1	37	14	0	0	9.25	3
†M. A. Starc	4	5	0	44	20	0	0	8.80	3
†J. R. Hazlewood	5	3	1	10	6	0	0	5.00	1

Played in one Test: J. M. Bird 4.

BOWLING

	Style	*O*	*M*	*R*	*W*	*BB*	*5I*	*Avge*
M. A. Starc	LF	162.3	32	518	22	5-88	1	23.54
P. J. Cummins	RF	197.1	43	567	23	4-39	0	24.65
J. R. Hazlewood	RFM	190.5	49	544	21	5-48	1	25.90
N. M. Lyon	OB	260.1	61	614	21	4-60	0	29.23

Also bowled: J. M. Bird (RFM) 30–5–108–0; M. R. Marsh (RFM) 32–4–132–0; S. P. D. Smith (LB) 9–1–33–0.

ENGLAND – BATTING AND FIELDING

	T	*I*	*NO*	*R*	*HS*	*100*	*50*	*Avge*	*Ct/St*
J. E. Root	5	9	1	378	83	0	5	47.25	2
†A. N. Cook	5	9	1	376	244*	1	0	47.00	3
†D. J. Malan	5	9	0	383	140	1	3	42.55	4
J. M. Bairstow	5	9	0	306	119	1	0	34.00	10/1
T. K. Curran	2	3	1	66	39	0	0	33.00	0
J. M. Vince	5	9	0	242	83	0	2	26.88	3
†M. D. Stoneman	5	9	0	232	56	0	2	25.77	0
C. Overton	2	4	1	62	41*	0	0	20.66	1
†M. M. Ali	5	9	0	179	40	0	0	19.88	4
C. R. Woakes	4	7	0	114	36	0	0	16.28	0
†S. C. J. Broad	5	9	0	136	56	0	1	15.11	2
†J. M. Anderson	5	9	6	8	5*	0	0	2.66	2

Played in one Test: J. T. Ball 14, 1; M. S. Crane 4, 2.

BOWLING

	Style	*O*	*M*	*R*	*W*	*BB*	*5I*	*Avge*
J. M. Anderson	RFM	223.3	70	473	17	5-43	1	27.82
C. Overton	RFM	59	4	226	6	3-105	0	37.66
S. C. J. Broad	RFM	195	55	525	11	4-51	0	47.72
C. R. Woakes	RFM	167	32	495	10	4-36	0	49.50
M. M. Ali	OB	169.2	27	575	5	2-74	0	115.00

Also bowled: J. T. Ball (RFM) 26–4–115–1; M. S. Crane (LB) 48–3–193–1; T. K. Curran (RFM) 66–14–200–2; D. J. Malan (LB) 21–3–54–0; J. E. Root (OB) 28.3–6–78–2.

At Perth, November 4–5, 2017. **Drawn.** **†England XI 349-6 dec** (91 overs) (M. D. Stoneman 85, J. M. Vince 82, D. J. Malan 56, G. S. Ballance 51); **Western Australia XI 342** (86 overs) (J. R. Philippe 88, C. D. Hinchliffe 75; J. M. Anderson 4-27). *Western Australia chose from 12 players, and England from 13. Alastair Cook's tour got off to a bad start when he was out for a second-ball duck, caught behind off opposing captain Nathan Coulter-Nile. Later, Joe Root was out for nine. But in between, Mark Stoneman and James Vince (dropped three times) put on 153, before Dawid Malan and Gary Ballance added 104; they retired at the same time. On the second day, the bulk of WA's runs came from two local youngsters with no first-class experience: 20-year-old Josh Philippe hit 16 fours and 21-year-old Clint Hinchliffe, struck a dozen, as the England bowlers reacquainted themselves with the red ball: only James Anderson and Jake Ball (12–5–31–1) had much joy.*

CRICKET AUSTRALIA XI v ENGLAND XI

At Adelaide, November 8–11, 2017 (day/night). England XI won by 192 runs. Toss: Cricket Australia XI. First-class debuts: J. R. Coleman, D. G. Fallins, J. J. S. Sangha.

England's seamers clicked under lights on the third evening, reducing an inexperienced Cricket Australia XI to 70 for seven with the pink ball, then polishing them off inside an hour next day. Anderson, Woakes and Overton finished with combined figures of ten for 44. Until then, honours had been roughly even. After the early departure of Cook, there were half-centuries from Stoneman, Root and Malan. But England's tail looked worryingly fragile: the last five wickets crashed for 22 as debutant leg-spinner Daniel Fallins picked up five for 73. The local team declined to 57 for five, but Tim Paine – soon to be restored to the Test side after seven years – made a gritty half-century, sharing useful stands with Matthew Short and Simon Milenko, who clubbed 19 in one Overton over. There was an early injury scare when Ball twisted an ankle during his fourth over and limped off; fielding coach Paul Collingwood, 41, substituted for a while, on the ground where he scored a Test double-century in 2006-07. England dithered from 121 for three to 124 for seven on the third day – this time it was Milenko's turn for a five-for – before Bairstow thumped a quick half-century to stretch the lead to 267.

Close of play: first day, England XI 278-8 (Crane 0); second day, England XI 5-0 (Cook 1, Stoneman 4); third day, Cricket Australia XI 70-7 (Short 28, Sandhu 17).

England XI

A. N. Cook c Paine b Coleman	15	– c Paine b Milenko	32
M. D. Stoneman c Carder b Fallins	61	– b Coleman	51
J. M. Vince b Fallins	33	– lbw b Sandhu	29
*J. E. Root c Gibson b Fallins	58	– lbw b Sandhu	1
D. J. Malan c Short b Coleman	63	– c Paine b Milenko	5
†J. M. Bairstow c Paine b Fallins	9	– not out	61
C. R. Woakes c Gibson b Coleman	33	– c Paine b Milenko	2
C. Overton c Carder b Sandhu	0	– lbw b Milenko	0
M. S. Crane not out	6	– c Milenko b Fallins	18
J. T. Ball b Sandhu	4	– absent hurt	
J. M. Anderson lbw b Fallins	4	– (10) c Pucovski b Milenko	0
Lb 6, nb 1	7	Lb 8	8
1/24 (1) 2/85 (3) 3/155 (2) 4/178 (4) 5/195 (6) 6/271 (7) 7/278 (8) 8/278 (5) 9/283 (10) 10/293 (11) (95 overs)	293	1/79 (1) 2/93 (2) 3/94 (4) 4/121 (5) 5/121 (3) 6/124 (7) 7/124 (8) 8/194 (9) 9/207 (10) (67.4 overs)	207

Coleman 23–4–72–3; Sandhu 23–3–61–2; Milenko 19–6–49–0; Fallins 22–1–73–5; Short 5–0–19–0; Sangha 3–1–13–0. *Second innings*—Coleman 14–3–55–1; Sandhu 19–5–47–2; Short 5–0–13–0; Milenko 16.4–3–34–5; Fallins 13–1–50–1.

Cricket Australia XI

N. C. R. Larkin lbw b Woakes	6	– c Bairstow b Woakes	2
J. M. Carder c Anderson b Overton	24	– b Woakes	0
R. J. Gibson c Malan b Ball	4	– c Bairstow b Woakes	9
W. J. Pucovski b Crane	4	– c Vince b Woakes	1
*†T. D. Paine lbw b Anderson	52	– b Overton	5
J. J. S. Sangha c Malan b Woakes	3	– c Root b Overton	5
M. W. Short c Bairstow b Anderson	45	– b Overton	28
S. A. Milenko lbw b Crane	50	– c Bairstow b Anderson	1
G. S. Sandhu lbw b Crane	18	– lbw b Anderson	17
D. G. Fallins not out	15	– c Cook b Anderson	1
J. R. Coleman not out	4	– not out	4
B 1, lb 6, nb 1	8	Lb 2	2
1/21 (1) 2/32 (3) 3/41 (2) 4/47 (4) 5/57 (6) 6/143 (7) 7/160 (5) 8/214 (8) 9/217 (9) (9 wkts dec, 76 overs)	233	1/0 (2) 2/3 (1) 3/7 (4) 4/14 (5) 5/18 (3) 6/24 (6) 7/25 (8) 8/70 (7) 9/70 (9) 10/75 (10) (40.2 overs)	75

Anderson 16–7–30–2; Woakes 14–0–48–2; Ball 3.4–2–5–1; Overton 15–6–40–1; Root 4.2–1–11–0; Crane 21–2–78–3; Vince 2–0–14–0. *Second innings*—Anderson 10.2–5–12–3; Woakes 10–4–17–4; Overton 11–6–15–3; Crane 6–0–27–0; Root 3–1–2–0.

Umpires: S. D. Fry and D. J. Shepard. Referee: S. J. A. Taufel.

CRICKET AUSTRALIA XI v ENGLAND XI

At Townsville, November 15–18, 2017. Drawn. Toss: Cricket Australia XI. First-class debut: H. J. Nielsen.

The tourists – and most of their opponents – flew to northern Queensland for the last game before the First Test, and the batsmen enjoyed the trip: after Woakes's six wickets despatched the Cricket Australia XI for 250, England ran up 515, with Cook finding form at last with 70. He shared an opening stand of 172 with Stoneman, who went on to the first century of the tour, before Malan added another, having shared a partnership of 163 with Root. England scented victory when the opposition slipped to 87 for three – but Jason Sangha, who had made his first-class debut in the previous match, and Short showed up the limitations of an Anderson-less attack on a flat surface, both reaching maiden centuries during a stand of 263: England took only one wicket in 75 overs on the final day. Just 18, Sangha was the youngest to score a century against an England team in Australia since Clem Hill in 1894-95. After the match, the tourists' coach Trevor Bayliss renewed calls for the opposition in Ashes warm-ups in both countries to be stronger: "Australia and England should be getting together and having at least one match against the A-team before each series." Bairstow left the field for ten overs on the first day after bruising a finger; substitute Ben Foakes took the gloves, and caught Gibson.

Close of play: first day, Cricket Australia XI 249-9 (Fallins 29, Conway 0); second day, England XI 337-3 (Root 62, Malan 57); third day, Cricket Australia XI 121-3 (Sangha 26, Short 8).

Cricket Australia XI

N. C. R. Larkin c Vince b Woakes	30		
J. M. Carder c Bairstow b Woakes	39	– (1) c Root b Ali	34
R. J. Gibson c sub (†B. T. Foakes) b Woakes	7	– (2) b Ali	49
W. J. Pucovski c Bairstow b Overton	20	– (3) c Root b Crane	1
J. J. S. Sangha lbw b Woakes	0	– (4) c Malan b Crane	133
*M. W. Short c Root b Overton	51	– (5) not out	134
†H. J. Nielsen c Vince b Woakes	20	– (6) not out	2
S. A. Milenko b Woakes	19		
G. S. Sandhu c Vince b Broad	25		
D. G. Fallins not out	29		
H. N. A. Conway c Stoneman b Broad	1		
Lb 4, nb 5	9	B 2, lb 4, w 5	11
1/66 (1) 2/75 (2) 3/91 (3) 4/91 (5) 5/118 (4) 6/162 (7) 7/176 (6) 8/212 (8) 9/230 (9) 10/250 (11) (91.3 overs)	250	1/80 (1) 2/87 (2) 3/87 (3) 4/350 (4) (4 wkts, 110 overs)	364

Broad 16.3–5–33–2; Woakes 19–3–55–6; Ali 16–4–39–0; Overton 18–4–32–2; Crane 22–3–87–0. *Second innings*—Broad 14–1–40–0; Woakes 11–0–50–0; Ali 32–9–88–2; Overton 15–3–65–0; Crane 30–6–97–2; Root 6–1–12–0; Malan 2–0–6–0.

England XI

A. N. Cook c Nielsen b Short	70
M. D. Stoneman c and b Fallins	111
J. M. Vince c Sangha b Fallins	26
*J. E. Root c Nielsen b Milenko	83
D. J. Malan run out	109
†J. M. Bairstow c Gibson b Fallins	19
M. M. Ali b Short	5
C. R. Woakes c Nielsen b Milenko	36
C. Overton c Sangha b Short	0
S. C. J. Broad c Pucovski b Short	10
M. S. Crane not out	25
B 5, lb 4, w 1, nb 11	21
1/172 (1) 2/214 (3) 3/217 (2) 4/380 (4) 5/419 (6) 6/438 (5) 7/439 (7) 8/439 (9) 9/457 (10) 10/515 (8) (142.5 overs)	515

Sandhu 25–7–99–0; Conway 23–5–77–0; Milenko 23.5–3–86–2; Short 32–2–103–4; Fallins 37–2–127–3; Sangha 2–0–14–0.

Umpires: N. R. Johnstone and P. Wilson. Referee: R. L. Parry.

ATTENDANCES IN 1936-37

First Test	Brisbane	72,818
Second Test	Sydney	126,947
Third Test	Melbourne	350,534
Fourth Test	Adelaide	171,135
Fifth Test	Melbourne	236,116
Total		**957,550**

The aggregate attendance of the 2017-18 Ashes was 865,451, second only to 1936-37, when Australia came from 2–0 down to beat England. There were two Tests at the MCG.

AUSTRALIA v ENGLAND

First Test

GREG BAUM

At Brisbane, November 23–27, 2017. Australia won by ten wickets. Toss: England. Test debut: C. T. Bancroft.

The First Test began with a lot of ifs, and finished with a butt. Two iffy teams walked out on day one in a stirred-up atmosphere. The billing was lowly for an Ashes – in a table of ten, England were third in the ICC rankings, Australia fifth – but it was the Ashes, and that was ferment enough. Australia bristled in the prelude. Within the team and without, visions were conjured up of a rerun of England's previous trip to the Gabba, when Mitchell Johnson began his brief but total reign of terror. In an interview with the British media, Lyon – an unlikely agent provocateur – accused former England wicketkeeper Matt Prior of being afraid in that match, and said Australia were out to "end careers" again. Through the approved channels (Twitter), Prior retorted that Lyon's career was in graver peril than any other. Warner had already talked of how Australia were working up their "hatred" for England, leaving some to wonder how genuine was a hatred that had to be cooked up, as if from a recipe. England's position was amused indifference. It seemed Zen-like at the time.

The teamsheets needed explanatory notes. The Australian XI seemed less a selection than an assortment. Opener Cameron Bancroft had banged down the door to his debut, replacing the out-of-form Matt Renshaw, while Shaun Marsh, at 34, was back for his ninth crack at Test cricket, beating off younger pretenders. Most mystifying of all, the 32-year-old Tim Paine was chosen to keep wicket. The week before, Paine had played his first Sheffield Shield game of the season for Tasmania, as a batsman and slip fielder, standing alongside the incumbent Test gloveman, Matthew Wade. The country rubbed its eyes and scratched its head.

MOST TESTS BETWEEN APPEARANCES FOR AUSTRALIA

78	G. B. Hogg	1996-97 to 2002-03	**64**	**P. J. Cummins**	**2011-12 to 2016-17**
78	**T. D. Paine**	**2010-11 to 2017-18**	62	C. J. L. Rogers	2007-08 to 2013
71	R. B. Simpson	1967-68 to 1977-78	59	M. T. G. Elliott	1998-99 to 2004
68	D. R. Martyn	1993-94 to 1999-2000	58	M. R. Whitney	1981 to 1987-88
66	S. J. Rixon	1977-78 to 1984-85	53	A. M. J. Hilditch	1979-80 to 1984-85

If Australia's team were mystifying, England's were a mystery, at least in Australia. One or two might have needed to identify themselves by calling out their names, as park cricketers do to scorers; England included Ball as their fourth seamer ahead of Craig Overton, though few locals would have recognised either. To complete the incompleteness were two missing all-rounders, suspended Ben Stokes and retired Shane Watson, who was no one's idea of a match-winner, but had been such an effective foil for Johnson et al in 2013-14 that Smith remembered him wistfully.

The one apparent certainty about the Gabba – the pitch – also proved confounding. Preparing his last strip before retirement after 27 years, curator Kevin Mitchell was wrong-footed by mild weather. The surface began soft, and was bland throughout, yielding no pace and negligible swing and seam, a far cry from the Johnsonland of four years earlier. It drove the shape and style of the match, deadening the run-rate to around 2.5 an over. Patience and perseverance became key. Gratifyingly, big crowds accepted it for what it was: the stuff – sometimes – of Test cricket. The Big Bash League and its jollies could wait.

Batting first, England lost Cook early, but late on the second morning were 246 for four on the back of disciplined knocks from Stoneman, Vince and Malan – the first instance of three Ashes debutants all making fifty in the same innings. Vince's upright and correct 83 was his first Test half-century, in his eighth match. Australia's vaunted seamers toiled dutifully, but the most threatening bowler was Lyon, who extracted surprising spin that had England's preponderance of left-handers jabbing, as if playing pin the tail on the donkey. He would remain the bowler of the match, though his figures didn't show it, and ran Vince out with a Viv Richards-like swoop and strike from cover. If England had previously thought Lyon and his craft inoffensive, they did so no more.

Malan's wicket, top-edging a pull off Starc just as Smith wondered whether to give up on the short stuff, triggered five more in a rush, leaving them 302 all out. The problem now was not the donkey, but the tail. Between two teams still feeling for each other's soft spots, a point of difference was emerging. Australia's bowlers were faster than England's: on an unhelpful pitch, this did not matter against the top order, but it did against the tail. Apart from deflating the score, this neutered England's plan to exploit Australia's lack of a fourth seamer by detaining the other three in the field.

For Australia's batsmen, England had an intricate blueprint, and at first it worked like the pressing of a button. Bancroft pushed at Broad and was caught behind, Ali laser-lit Khawaja's Achilles heel against off-spin, Warner tried to shovel Ball to leg and was caught at midwicket, and Anderson trapped Handscomb in his back-of-the-crease eyrie. Australia were 76 for four.

But Smith remained, to produce the innings that became the axis of the match. He looks as if he is playing the fiddle, but what emerges is the Vienna Philharmonic in concert, complete with intervals. Can any other batsman have had at once such a disorientating and dominating effect? If England had played tricks, now they missed one, chafing at Smith by denying him boundaries, bowling one side of the wicket to fields constructed like spiderwebs. As far as containment went, it worked: on the third morning, he hit only one four, a leg glance, and 17 runs in all.

England were pleased to have made Smith wait, Smith was pleased that their only tactic was to delay him. It seemed a waste of the penetrative powers of Broad and Anderson in particular. Passive aggression might have worked against him once, but no longer. He could play the same game. It took him seven hours to reach 100 – the slowest of his 21

BRISBANE NOTES AND QUOTES

The Ashes build-up began in peculiar fashion as Nathan Lyon, one of three Australian survivors from the 2013-14 whitewash, launched an attack on all things English to a roomful of British media. He said all England's players in that previous series were scared of Mitchell Johnson: "I was standing at leg slip and I nearly had to push a couple of guys back towards the stumps." Lyon claimed that wicketkeeper Matt Prior had wanted to go home after two Tests, but Prior retorted: "It is wholeheartedly untrue. It is completely ridiculous and all I can do is laugh."

Brisbane's combative newspaper, the *Courier-Mail*, forecast that the Gabba would be "back to its bouncy, green best, despite the attempts of Pommy singer Adele to sabotage Australia's cricket fortress". Adele, not known as a cricket lover, had played a concert on the ground some eight months previously.

Even the local Big Bash franchise, the Brisbane Heat, got in on the tourist-baiting, publishing a video interview with the former Test opener Matthew Hayden, in which he said "the Poms are a rabble", and added that he "looked down the list and didn't know who half these guys were".

The *Courier-Mail* had described Mark Stoneman and James Vince as "a failed Sydney grade cricketer and a bloke averaging 19". The front page labelled England "the Bore-Me Army" and focused on the scoring rate of 2.58 per over. Subsequent days saw Steve Smith's first-innings century being lauded – but no mention of Australia's scoring-rate of 2.51 per over.

All Notes and Quotes compiled by Will Macpherson

Top man: Josh Hazlewood removed three of England's first four in the second innings. Joe Root suffers that sinking feeling.

Test tons, and Australia's slowest for seven years – and eight and a half for his eventual 141 not out. But what mattered was the runs, not the rate.

Marsh, with an assured half-century, muted critics; then, from 209 for seven, Cummins added to his stature with 42. With Smith they propelled Australia into a lead that was never theirs to take. In an awkward last hour on the third day, the Australian quicks gave it everything, and England lost Cook and Vince, before Root – pinged by Starc – lost a chunk of his helmet. Only in this hour could echoes of 2013-14 be heard, doubtless ringing in Root's ears.

From there, England faded out of the Test. On the fourth day, Root was untroubled in making fifty, then fell lbw to Hazlewood next ball, working across the line for the second time in the match. The Australians made a mark in their notebooks. Root had reached 50 more than any of his three big rivals – Smith, Virat Kohli and Kane Williamson – and converted fewest to hundreds.

Ali and Bairstow made forties. Coach Trevor Bayliss had said England needed not sixties, but 160s, so the shortfall was glaring. Paine's snappy stumping of Ali was affirmed by third umpire Chris Gaffaney, only after a granular inspection of replays. A kerfuffle arose about whether it was a fine judgment, or *too* fine; some even pointed to the unevenness of the crease's whitewash. Bairstow, meanwhile, sent an injudicious upper-cut straight to third man, described by Smith as a "pretty ordinary shot"; Bairstow later admitted he hadn't spotted the fielder. It emerged that the Australians had goaded him about an incident in Perth on the day England arrived; he met Bancroft for the first time and, instead of offering his hand, butted his head. Bancroft suffered no ill then, but Bairstow's head spun now. Pitch microphones alerted the media, and even on Mars they know the rest.

England's tail disintegrated again. Over two innings, they lost 11 for 96 in their bottom order, compared with Australia's four for 119 in one. Such are the chinks that in Test cricket form chasms. England were out for 195, leaving Australia 170 to win.

It became an instant article of punditry faith that, if England could only have secured a first-innings lead of, say, 80, they might have set the Australians the sort of target that in the mind is double its face value. But nothing in the pitch bore this out, and a modest Pakistan team had recently come close here to chasing down 490. Airy misses by Warner and Bancroft were well within new-ball norms and, since Ali had cut his spinning finger on the Kookaburra's seam and become ineffectual, the contest was over. A ten-wicket victory came at a canter an hour into the fifth day.

HIGHEST PARTNERSHIPS TO WIN A TEST BY TEN WICKETS

173	**C. T. Bancroft (82)/D. A. Warner (87)**	**Aus v Eng at Brisbane**	**2017-18**
172	W. H. Ponsford (92)/A. A. Jackson (70)	Aus v WI at Adelaide	1930-31
157	M. A. Taylor (67)/G. R. Marsh (72)	Aus v Eng at Brisbane	1990-91
135	K. R. Stackpole (76)/I. R. Redpath (57)	Aus v WI at Georgetown	1972-73
120	M. G. Vandort (40)/W. U. Tharanga (71)	SL v Bang at Bogra	2005-06
106	P. J. Hughes (86)/S. M. Katich (18)	Aus v NZ at Wellington	2009-10
105	J. B. Hobbs (62)/C. B. Fry (35)	Eng v Aus at Birmingham	1909
103	A. F. Rae (46)/J. B. Stollmeyer (52)	WI v Eng at Nottingham	1950

There were no ifs now. For Australia, victory was self-explanatory. England were, as touring teams so often are, wondering where those wheels had gone that had been turning so quietly and efficiently. Still, there was a butt to clear up. For England, injustice added to insult added to injury. Bairstow emerged to say there was nothing in it, Root to say it was "a storm in a teacup", Bayliss to say it had been "dumb" for an England player to put himself in a compromising position so soon after the Stokes incident, and Smith to say Australia would continue to fire at will.

That left only the tyro Bancroft, who had Smith and journalists in hysterics as he reconstructed the night – "weird", "random", but making no mark on him because he had, officially measured, the "heaviest head" in WA cricket. "I don't know Jonny Bairstow," he said, "but he says hello very differently to most others." Smith was beside himself. It was, if not the last laugh, the latest.

Man of the Match: S. P. D. Smith. *Attendance:* 130,665.

Close of play: first day, England 196-4 (Malan 28, Ali 13); second day, Australia 165-4 (Smith 64, Marsh 44); third day, England 33-2 (Stoneman 19, Root 5); fourth day, Australia 114-0 (Bancroft 51, Warner 60).

England

A. N. Cook c Handscomb b Starc	2	– c Starc b Hazlewood	7
M. D. Stoneman b Cummins	53	– c Smith b Lyon	27
J. M. Vince run out	83	– c Smith b Hazlewood	2
*J. E. Root lbw b Cummins	15	– lbw b Hazlewood	51
D. J. Malan c Marsh b Starc	56	– c Smith b Lyon	4
M. M. Ali lbw b Lyon	38	– st Paine b Lyon	40
†J. M. Bairstow c Paine b Cummins	9	– c Handscomb b Starc	42
C. R. Woakes b Lyon	0	– c Smith b Starc	17
S. C. J. Broad c Handscomb b Hazlewood	20	– c Paine b Starc	2
J. T. Ball c Warner b Starc	14	– c Handscomb b Cummins	1
J. M. Anderson not out	5	– not out	0
B 5, w 1, nb 1	7	Nb 2	2
1/2 (1) 2/127 (2) 3/145 (3) (116.4 overs)	302	1/11 (1) 2/17 (3) (71.4 overs)	195
4/163 (4) 5/246 (5) 6/249 (6)		3/62 (2) 4/74 (5)	
7/250 (8) 8/270 (7) 9/286 (10) 10/302 (9)		5/113 (4) 6/155 (6) 7/185 (8)	
		8/194 (7) 9/195 (9) 10/195 (10)	

Starc 28–4–77–3; Hazlewood 22.4–6–57–1; Cummins 30–8–85–3; Lyon 36–12–78–2. *Second innings*—Starc 16–1–51–3; Hazlewood 16–3–46–3; Cummins 12.4–4–23–1; Lyon 24–4–67–3; Smith 3–0–8–0.

Australia

C. T. Bancroft c Bairstow b Broad	5	– not out	82
D. A. Warner c Malan b Ball	26	– not out	87
U. T. Khawaja lbw b Ali	11		
*S. P. D. Smith not out	141		
P. S. P. Handscomb lbw b Anderson	14		
S. E. Marsh c Anderson b Broad	51		
†T. D. Paine c Bairstow b Anderson	13		
M. A. Starc c and b Broad	6		
P. J. Cummins c Cook b Woakes	42		
J. R. Hazlewood b Ali	6		
N. M. Lyon c Cook b Root	9		
Lb 1, w 2, nb 1	4	Lb 2, w 1, nb 1	4
1/7 (1) 2/30 (3) 3/59 (2) 4/76 (5) 5/175 (6) 6/202 (7) 7/209 (8) 8/275 (9) 9/298 (10) 10/328 (11) (130.3 overs)	328	(no wkt, 50 overs)	173

Anderson 29–10–50–2; Broad 25–10–49–3; Ali 30–8–74–2; Woakes 24–5–67–1; Ball 18–3–77–1; Root 4.3–0–10–1. *Second innings*—Anderson 11–2–27–0; Broad 10–2–20–0; Ali 4–0–23–0; Woakes 11–1–46–0; Ball 8–1–38–0; Root 6–1–17–0.

Umpires: Aleem Dar and M. Erasmus. Third umpire: C. B. Gaffaney.
Referee: R. B. Richardson.

AUSTRALIA v ENGLAND

Second Test

LAWRENCE BOOTH

At Adelaide, December 2–6, 2017 (day/night). Australia won by 120 runs. Toss: England. Test debut: C. Overton.

Ashes cricket's first floodlit Test illuminated a familiar tale. For the fourth tour of Australia out of five, England found themselves 2–0 down before reaching Perth, and fending off predictions of another whitewash like bouncers at the WACA. They had their moments, but they came mostly too late, including one at the end of the game: Smith admitted taking a sleeping pill after he declined to enforce the follow-on – a decision that gave England a glimmer of hope, or possibly a stay of execution. Ultimately, Root might have been tempted to reach for something stronger, though his post-match claim that England were still "massively" in the series suggested he had already taken it.

This was a shame, since expectations had been high, wherever you looked. Aficionados of sledging were on red alert after Anderson used a newspaper column to call the Australians "bullies", prompting Smith to call Anderson "one of the biggest sledgers in the game". The niggle continued throughout the match, not least when Anderson chose to position himself provocatively close to the stumps while Smith, unimpressed and fidgety, was at the non-striker's end. It was all rather handbags at dusk.

If the spats looked unedifying, spectators seemed unperturbed: despite a chilly opening day that meant the crowd thinned as darkness fell, 55,317 poured in, an Adelaide record, surpassing 50,962 on the second day during the Bodyline series. In all, 199,147 came through the gates, another ground record. Opponents of pink-ball Test cricket could complain that the discrepancy between conditions before and after dark was too large for comfort, but it felt like a connoisseur's lament: the Big Bash League was gearing up for more razzle-dazzle, and Test cricket should have been grateful for the interest.

English fans exchanged nervous glances when Root became the first captain in seven day/night Tests around the world to win the toss and bowl, and the first at Adelaide since

William West, AFP/Getty Images

Lyon leaps tonight: Moeen Ali fell to Nathan Lyon seven times in the series. Here he is the victim of an outrageous return catch.

Mohammad Azharuddin in 1991-92 (Australia won that one, too). In fact, among visiting teams, only West Indies in 1981-82 had won here after opting to bowl, though the presence of Holding, Roberts, Croft and Garner helped. Root's choice did not quite sit alongside England's two great Brisbane cock-ups (Len Hutton in 1954-55, Nasser Hussain in 2002-03), but his attack did their best to encourage comparisons. Even as clouds loured, Anderson and Broad declined to pitch the ball up, and – after two stoppages for rain – it was from a run-out that the breakthrough came. Ali's misfield at cover ricocheted to mid-off, where Woakes had time to steady himself; with Bancroft scrambling to regain his ground after being sent back by Warner, he threw down the stumps.

Woakes soon had Warner fencing fatally and, the skies now dark, Anderson drew Khawaja into skewing to backward point after a never entirely convincing 53. Craig Overton, preferred to Jake Ball, secured a gold-plated first Test scalp when he jagged one back and bowled Smith, who had taunted him for being too slow. Australia's batsmen were no hares either, but a mutually cagey close-of-play 209 for four from 81 overs suited them fine. England lamented the rain which obstructed a night-time assault with the second new ball but, by bowling like a team who had lost the toss rather than won it, they provided a window into their soul: the floodlights were on, but no one was home.

The second day was their chance to prove the Ben Stokes affair was not – repeat, not – a distraction. Across the Tasman in Rangiora, a peaceful Kiwi town with a population that would have fitted into Adelaide Oval three times over, their all-rounder-in-exile was embarking on a brief career as Canterbury's overseas player, all the while ready to answer an Ashes SOS if the Crown Prosecution Service in the UK chose not to press charges over the Bristol brawl.

The focus on events in New Zealand was fleeting: Stokes had long been dismissed for just two by an Otago left-arm spinner called Anaru Kitchen when, back in Adelaide, Broad trapped Handscomb with the third ball of the second day. And England sensed an opening when Anderson won an lbw shout against Marsh on 29. To general astonishment Virtual Eye claimed it would have gone over the stumps, and England's mood blackened further when, seven balls later, Anderson had another successful leg-before appeal overruled by technology – this time against Paine, though now the naked eye agreed.

Batting with the abandon of the reprieved, Marsh and Paine flayed 85, before Cummins dug in for another forty in an eighth-wicket stand of 99. His caution as the light faded hinted at an addition to cricket's lexicon: the daywatchman, obliged to delay matters until his side got their mitts on the pink ball in the gloaming. Marsh celebrated a gutsy hundred, which meant he and dad Geoff (Brisbane 1986-87 and Nottingham 1989) were the first father-and-son pairing to score Ashes centuries. And, after Marsh belted Broad for 14 in three balls, Smith called a halt: 442 for eight was some riposte to being stuck in.

England's reply was a shambles. Stoneman got a good one from Starc (full and fast), and Malan from Cummins (angling in from round the wicket), but otherwise the lack of conviction recalled the final day of the Test here 11 years earlier, when Andrew Flintoff's team dithered to defeat. At 142 for seven, with Ali and Bairstow having fallen to spectacular return catches by Lyon and Starc, the game felt over. The 66 added by Woakes and Overton – who, after producing England's best figures, became their first No. 9 to top-score on Test debut since the 19th century – merely acted as a reproach for what had gone before. Lyon took care of the tail to secure a lead of 215.

FLYING STARTS

Top-scoring and taking the best bowling figures in the first innings of Test debut:

A. S. Kennedy (41* and 4-37)	England v South Africa at Johannesburg	1922-23
R. C. Blunt (45* and 3-17)	New Zealand v England at Christchurch	1929-30
R. M. Hogg (36 and 6-74)	Australia v England at Brisbane	1978-79
B. S. Sandhu (71 and 2-107)	India v Pakistan at Hyderabad	1982-83
C. Overton (41* and 3-105)	**England v Australia at Adelaide**	**2017-18**

But for that partnership, which put an extra 16 overs into Australia's legs, Smith might have bowled again, not least because twilight beckoned, and the prospect of mischief. Instead, he batted, conjuring up the scenario all England had prayed for in advance: Anderson armed with the new ball under lights. In the event, Australia were relieved to reach stumps at 53 for four, with two apiece for Anderson and Woakes. Not for the first time on the tour, England's cricketers had come to the party after dark, but this time the merriment continued next day: 138 all out, with Anderson collecting his 25th Test five-for, but his first in Australia, at the 30th attempt, and Woakes four for 36, his best figures abroad.

English excitement required perspective, since they needed 354 to square the series, 22 more than they had ever made in the fourth innings to win. They needed luck, too, and for

ADELAIDE NOTES AND QUOTES

Andrew Johns, English-born but long-time Adelaide resident, presented Jonny Bairstow with a pair of wicketkeeping gloves signed by his father David on England's 1978-79 tour. Johns had won them at a local shopping centre, but now wanted to give them back: "I just lost my father – he was 83, but had a great life – and I know if someone gave something to me that belonged to him I'd want it, and that's what I wanted to do for Jonny." The pair chatted for 45 minutes after the presentation.

The increasing number of fans who tune in to earpiece radios at the grounds were deprived of the opportunity to listen to commentary from the ABC or the BBC. "We have five broadcasters and three channels," said a Cricket Australia spokesman. "The Nine Network is allocated one because it engages with the largest audience, and BT provides English fans at the match with the English commentary. This year we are rotating the third slot to be fair to our radio broadcasters."

As the BBC's Jonathan Agnew was returning to his hotel at 12.45am on his last night in Australia before flying home, he was stopped by the police while crossing a road in the city centre, and booked for jaywalking. "Adelaide!" he tweeted. "I used to love you! How sad."

Ryan Pierse, Getty Images

Worth the wait? Jimmy Anderson finally has a five-for in Australia.

a while they got it: had Australia reviewed Hazlewood's lbw shout when Cook had one, DRS would have obliged. And while Cook struggled, especially against Lyon, Stoneman flourished, working three successive deliveries from Starc through midwicket. England couldn't pull it off, could they?

Two quick blows provided the answer. Cook fell to Lyon for the seventh time and a becalmed Stoneman guided Starc low to gully. When, after dinner, Vince edged another millionaire's drive, England were 91 for three. Few could discount a four-day finish, but the twists were not over. Root successfully challenged an lbw decision, playing no shot against Lyon on 32 (the ball was going over), and Smith earned the ridicule of the Barmy Army by wasting both reviews in quick order. When he missed Malan, on eight, at slip off Lyon, you could cut the tension. The stand was worth 78 when, 15 minutes before stumps, Cummins again got Malan from round the wicket, piercing his defence with willpower and pace. Even so, there was a spring in English steps, and the last day dawned bright: 178 runs to go, six wickets to fall.

Rarely has John Cleese's line in *Clockwise* – "I can stand the despair. It's the hope!" – received such an airing. With the second ball, Hazlewood persuaded nightwatchman Woakes to feather behind, and one run later removed Root, the delivery staying low and catching the bottom edge: 177 for six. Lyon did for Ali, swinging across the line, and Starc, armed with the second new ball, immediately trapped Overton. Broad followed, and it was all over when Bairstow chopped on, giving Starc his fifth wicket and Australia victory by 120 runs.

The sobering reality for England was that the margin wasn't as narrow as it felt. Australia had dealt with the scare – and Smith could sleep easily again before the journey to Perth.

Man of the Match: S. E. Marsh. *Attendance:* 199,147.

Close of play: first day, Australia 209-4 (Handscomb 36, Marsh 20); second day, England 29-1 (Cook 11, Vince 0); third day, Australia 53-4 (Handscomb 3, Lyon 3); fourth day, England 176-4 (Root 67, Woakes 5).

Australia

	First innings		Second innings	
C. T. Bancroft run out	10	–	c Bairstow b Anderson	4
D. A. Warner c Bairstow b Woakes	47	–	c Root b Woakes	14
U. T. Khawaja c Vince b Anderson	53	–	lbw b Anderson	20
*S. P. D. Smith b Overton	40	–	lbw b Woakes	6
P. S. P. Handscomb lbw b Broad	36	–	c Malan b Anderson	12
S. E. Marsh not out	126	–	(7) b Woakes	19
†T. D. Paine c Ali b Overton	57	–	(8) c Overton b Woakes	11
M. A. Starc c Anderson b Broad	6	–	(9) c Ali b Anderson	20
P. J. Cummins c Malan b Overton	44	–	(10) not out	11
N. M. Lyon not out	10	–	(6) c Broad b Anderson	14
J. R. Hazlewood (did not bat)		–	c Malan b Overton	3
B 6, lb 6, w 1	13		Lb 2, w 2	4
1/33 (1) 2/86 (2) 3/139 (3) 4/161 (4) 5/209 (5) 6/294 (7) 7/311 (8) 8/410 (9) (8 wkts dec, 149 overs)	442		1/5 (1) 2/39 (3) 3/41 (2) 4/50 (4) 5/71 (6) 6/75 (5) 7/90 (8) 8/122 (7) 9/128 (9) 10/138 (11) (58 overs)	138

Anderson 31–5–74–1; Broad 30–11–72–2; Woakes 27–4–84–1; Overton 33–3–105–3; Ali 24–3–79–0; Root 4–0–16–0. *Second innings*—Anderson 22–7–43–5; Broad 13–6–26–0; Overton 2–0–11–1; Woakes 16–3–36–4; Ali 5–0–20–0.

England

	First innings		Second innings	
A. N. Cook c Smith b Lyon	37	–	lbw b Lyon	16
M. D. Stoneman lbw b Starc	18	–	c Khawaja b Starc	36
J. M. Vince c Paine b Hazlewood	2	–	c Handscomb b Starc	15
*J. E. Root c Bancroft b Cummins	9	–	c Paine b Hazlewood	67
D. J. Malan c Paine b Cummins	19	–	b Cummins	29
M. M. Ali c and b Lyon	25	–	(7) lbw b Lyon	2
†J. M. Bairstow c and b Starc	21	–	(8) b Starc	36
C. R. Woakes c and b Starc	36	–	(6) c Paine b Hazlewood	5
C. Overton not out	41	–	lbw b Starc	7
S. C. J. Broad c Paine b Lyon	3	–	c Paine b Starc	8
J. M. Anderson lbw b Lyon	0	–	not out	0
Lb 15, w 1	16		B 7, lb 5	12
1/29 (2) 2/31 (3) 3/50 (4) 4/80 (1) 5/102 (5) 6/132 (6) 7/142 (7) 8/208 (8) 9/227 (10) 10/227 (11) (76.1 overs)	227		1/53 (1) 2/54 (2) 3/91 (3) 4/169 (5) 5/176 (6) 6/177 (4) 7/188 (7) 8/206 (9) 9/224 (10) 10/233 (8) (84.2 overs)	233

Starc 20–4–49–3; Hazlewood 16–3–56–1; Cummins 16–3–47–2; Lyon 24.1–5–60–4. *Second innings*—Starc 19.2–3–88–5; Hazlewood 20–7–49–2; Cummins 20–6–39–1; Lyon 25–6–45–2.

Umpires: Aleem Dar and C. B. Gaffaney. Third umpire: M. Erasmus.
Referee: R. B. Richardson.

At Perth (Richardson Park), December 9–10, 2017. **Drawn. England XI 314-9 dec** (69.2 overs) (K. K. Jennings 80, T. K. Curran 77*) **and 130-3 dec** (20 overs); †**Cricket Australia XI 151-4 dec** (50 overs) **and 269-8** (36.5 overs) (W. G. Bosisto 50, T. J. Dean 100; T. K. Curran 3-28, M. J. Leach 4-104). *Of England's Adelaide Test team, only the out-of-form Moeen Ali played; six members of the Lions squad made up the numbers (both teams chose from 12 players). After three declarations, the home side were set 294 in 37 overs, and looked on course while openers William Bosisto and skipper Travis Dean (whose hundred took only 68 balls) were adding 152 in 21. But three quick wickets from Tom Curran slowed them down, then Somerset slow left-armer Jack Leach made up for an earlier mauling, finishing with 9.5–0–104–4.*

AUSTRALIA v ENGLAND

Third Test

MALCOLM KNOX

At Perth, December 14–18, 2017. Australia won by an innings and 41 runs. Toss: England.

For the last time, the distinctive qualities of the WACA were seen in the Ashes. England had never beaten a full-strength Australian Test team on this traditionally fast, bouncy wicket in the golden west; their one win in 13 visits had been over Graham Yallop's Packer-depleted side of 1978-79. On the other hand, the pitch had lost some of its pace, and since 2008 Perth had become Australia's unhappiest home ground. They had won just four of the previous nine Tests there, losing to South Africa three times and India once, and drawing with New Zealand.

Brisbane and Adelaide had offered two competing narratives. In one, seesawing encounters broke Australia's way only in the fourth innings. In the other, Australia were again overpowering England, and seemingly en route to a third Ashes whitewash in four home series. Once a cricketing unicorn, that scoreline – or at least talk of it – now felt commonplace.

Root won his third toss and, this time, did not dare bowl. As in the first two matches, England enjoyed a period of dominance, and here it came early. Under sunny skies, Malan and Bairstow joined forces at 131 for four in the middle of the first day after Stoneman had received an old-style WACA working-over. Malan raised a high-class maiden Test century, relieved to have been dropped on 92 by Bancroft at slip from Starc's first offering with the second new ball. By stumps on day one, the fifth-wicket pair had established a stronghold from which England seemed to have put 5–0 out of the question.

The wicket gained pace as the first innings proceeded, and the partnership, which stretched to 237 on the second morning, was a case of skilled adaptation to the bounce, and clean timing that enabled the batsmen to profit from a fast outfield. It was England's highest fifth-wicket stand against Australia (beating 206 between Eddie Paynter and Denis

Robert Cianflone, CA/Getty Images

Point made: Mitchell Starc bowls James Vince with a beauty.

Compton at Trent Bridge in 1938), and their best for any wicket at Perth (beating 223 by openers Chris Broad and Bill Athey in 1986-87).

Batsmen, once set, could go far. Getting set, however, proved the problem and, once Malan fell for 140, miscuing a leg-side loft off Lyon and falling to an excellent diving catch by substitute fielder Peter Handscomb, England subsided. After no wicket had fallen in 69 overs, six fell in 51 deliveries – including Bairstow, bowled by Starc for 119 as he tried to work a full ball to leg. From the heights of 368 for four, England were looking over their shoulder again at 403 all out.

Bancroft and Warner made a careful start for Australia after lunch, but Overton removed both to leave them 55 for two. Out walked Smith. Through partnerships of 124 with Khawaja and 69 with Shaun Marsh, he reasserted the command he had held in Brisbane, but Australia were still a nervous 155 runs adrift when Mitchell Marsh joined him on the third morning.

AUSTRALIA'S HIGHEST PARTNERSHIPS AGAINST ENGLAND

451	for 2nd	W. H. Ponsford (266)/D. G. Bradman (244) at The Oval	1934
405	for 5th	S. G. Barnes (234)/D. G. Bradman (234) at Sydney	1946-47
388	for 4th	W. H. Ponsford (181)/D. G. Bradman (304) at Leeds	1934
346	for 6th	J. H. W. Fingleton (136)/D. G. Bradman (270) at Melbourne	1936-37
332*	for 5th	A. R. Border (200*)/S. R. Waugh (157*) at Leeds	1993
329	for 1st	G. R. Marsh (138)/M. A. Taylor (219) at Nottingham	1989
307	for 6th	M. E. K. Hussey (195)/B. J. Haddin (136) at Brisbane	2010-11
301	for 2nd	A. R. Morris (182)/D. G. Bradman (173*) at Leeds	1948
301	**for 5th**	**S. P. D. Smith (239)/ M. R. Marsh (181) at Perth**	**2017-18**

Recalled at Handscomb's expense, in large part because of the perceived need for a stock bowler to relieve the quicks, Marsh had not enjoyed a happy start to the game, dropping Stoneman at slip and conceding 43 runs from nine overs. But he knew the WACA – he was born 20 minutes away, in Attadale, across the Swan River – and soon found his stride, hitting the ball down the ground with a ringing crack. He dominated a stand of 301 which extended across the third afternoon, raising his maiden Test century to great emotion, and hurtling to 181 from just 236 balls, before Anderson trapped him with the second delivery of the fourth day. It meant the Marshes (Geoff, Shaun, Mitchell) joined India's Amarnaths (Lala, Surinder, Mohinder) in boasting at least one Test century for the father and his two sons.

Smith departed in the same fashion soon after, but by then his highest Test score of 239 – from 399 balls, with 30 fours and one six – had altered the balance of the match. Among Australian captains, only Bobby Simpson and Don Bradman had made more in an Ashes Test. He had been fluent and aggressive from the start, unlike his watchful century in Brisbane, and defied all Root's experimental field placings and bowling changes. For the quality of his shot-making it was as close to a perfect innings as Smith had played in the four years since his first Test century. He now had 22, and had passed 1,000 Test runs for the fourth successive calendar year. Various statistical comparisons with Bradman were inevitable, but most meaningful was his stranglehold on England's bowlers, engendering a frustration and despair they must have had in common with their interwar ancestors.

The fact that his wicket left Anderson and Broad as the most prolific pace-bowling combination in Test history (overhauling 762 wickets by West Indies' Curtly Ambrose and Courtney Walsh) was of little consolation to England. They weren't helped by an injury to Overton. After being hit in the ribs at Adelaide, he aggravated the injury when he dived for a return catch; X-rays revealed a hairline crack.

Paine and Cummins extended Australia's lead, enabling Smith to declare 259 in front on 662 for nine, their highest against England at home (previously 659 for eight at Sydney in 1946-47; they have four higher totals in the UK). It left his bowlers nearly five sessions

Paul Kane, Getty Images

Flying in: Pat Cummins sends down another discomfiting delivery.

to take the Ashes. Stoneman and Cook, in his 150th Test, fell quickly to the in-form Hazlewood, and Smith was on hand again to take a sharp slip catch via Paine's right glove after Root had driven optimistically at Lyon's first ball. When Vince's attractive half-century was cut short by an unplayable delivery from Starc which jagged off a crack like a leg-break, England were facing a battle not only against the bowlers but against rotten luck.

On their side was the satellite, which showed thick storms rolling in from the Southern Ocean. The forecast was for December's entire rainfall to hit Perth that night, and to continue into the fifth day. Malan and Bairstow were batting when rain curtailed the fourth, and England hoped the vagaries of the weather could counterbalance those of the deteriorating pitch.

When the first session on the final morning was washed out, they might have felt themselves saved. A gust of wind had lifted the covers and knocked over Matt Page, the head groundsman, sending him to hospital; it was his final Test before taking a job at the MCG. Either because water had run off the covers or sweated under them, a number of damp patches remained on the wicket, and workers with leaf-blowers set about drying them in the breaks between rain. Players, officials and commentators were on and off the ground, the Australians reacting optimistically to every inspection, the English shaking their heads at the impossibility of a restart. England's prayers were briefly answered: most of Perth's December rain did fall over the period. Trouble was, Perth's December average was a handful of millimetres. When play resumed in the afternoon, Australia needed six wickets in around 60 overs.

With the sixth ball, Hazlewood's first, Bairstow was bowled for 14. The lower order offered some support to Malan, who became only the fourth England batsman to reach 50

PERTH NOTES AND QUOTES

Moeen Ali was asked before the Test if "you blokes will be able to stay out of the pubs?" after Ben Duckett was fined for pouring a pint over James Anderson at The Avenue. Teetotaller Ali responded: "Yeah, I'm not much of a pub guy to be honest with you. It's not my sort of scene." His press conference was followed by Trevor Bayliss, who was in a less relaxed mood.

Tom Harrison, the ECB's chief executive, reminded players that the game's image was being tarnished by their actions. Alastair Cook echoed the message, admitting "the world has changed since September" and the incident involving Ben Stokes.

As the toss approached, Cricket Australia's chief executive James Sutherland was talking to the media about a story in *The Sun* concerning two Indian bookmakers, who were apparently ready to sell advance details of on-field events in Perth, and an Australian match-fixer known as The Silent Man. An ICC spokesman said the allegations were being taken "extremely seriously", but there was no evidence of any spot-fixing.

Whenever Smith raised his bat, it revealed a koala.com sticker. It emerged that Smith, a big investor in start-up companies, was involved with Koala, who make mattresses. For every run he scored, they adopted a real koala, plus 20 for every catch (and 30 for a run-out or 100 for a wicket). By the end of the series he had 687 runs and ten catches, or 887 koalas.

twice in a Perth Test, after Geoff Boycott (1970-71), Derek Randall (1982-83) and Kevin Pietersen (2006-07). But Hazlewood was now in his best rhythm of the series and, with Cummins and Starc supplying the intimidation, and Lyon continuing his personal ascendancy over Ali, England gave way. When another short ball from Cummins removed Woakes, the Ashes were back in Australian hands.

In post-mortems of how England had surrendered to an Australian team neither as talented as their 2006-07 predecessors, nor as openly hostile as in 2013-14, certain factors

CONSECUTIVE WINS OVER ONE COUNTRY AT SAME GROUND

8	**Australia v England at Perth**	**1990-91 to 2017-18**
7	Australia v West Indies at Melbourne	1930-31 to 1975-76
6	Australia v South Africa at Cape Town	1902-03 to 1966-67
6	England v India at Lord's	1932 to 1967
5	England v Australia at The Oval	1886 to 1896
5	England v South Africa at Cape Town	1888-89 to 1905-06
5	Australia v England at Adelaide	1894-95 to 1907-08
5	West Indies v Australia at Perth	1975-76 to 1996-97
5	West Indies v India at Bridgetown	1975-76 to 2001-02
5	Australia v India at Melbourne	1991-92 to 2011-12
5*	New Zealand v Zimbabwe at Bulawayo	2000-01 to 2016

* *New Zealand's sequence at Bulawayo is ongoing. So is Australia's against England at Perth, but it seems unlikely that further Tests will be held at the WACA.*

could be isolated. One was the power and pace of the Australian seam attack. England's newer batsmen had occasionally performed above themselves, but the experienced Root and Cook had repeatedly failed either to convert starts (Root), or make them (Cook). Their lower order had again provided little fight.

Aside from Anderson's spell under lights in Adelaide, the England new-ball pair lacked penetration against the Australian batting line-up, many of whom had been struggling to shore up their places. Broad finished this game with none for 142, his worst Test figures, and his position was called into question. He had, however, done a lot of bowling at the impervious Smith – no enviable job. And that proved to be the theme of the series. It wasn't that England were bad enough or Australia good enough. It was that one batsman had seized the contest and made it his own. These were indeed Smith's Ashes.

Man of the Match: S. P. D. Smith. *Attendance:* 91,955.

Close of play: first day, England 305-4 (Malan 110, Bairstow 75); second day, Australia 203-3 (Smith 92, S. E. Marsh 7); third day, Australia 549-4 (Smith 229, M. R. Marsh 181); fourth day, England 132-4 (Malan 28, Bairstow 14).

England

A. N. Cook lbw b Starc	7	– c and b Hazlewood	14
M. D. Stoneman c Paine b Starc	56	– c Paine b Hazlewood	3
J. M. Vince c Paine b Hazlewood	25	– b Starc	55
*J. E. Root c Paine b Cummins	20	– c Smith b Lyon	14
D. J. Malan c sub (P. S. P. Handscomb) b Lyon	140	– c Paine b Hazlewood	54
†J. M. Bairstow b Starc	119	– b Hazlewood	14
M. M. Ali c Smith b Cummins	0	– lbw b Lyon	11
C. R. Woakes c Cummins b Hazlewood	8	– c Paine b Cummins	22
C. Overton c Bancroft b Hazlewood	2	– c Khawaja b Hazlewood	12
S. C. J. Broad c Bancroft b Starc	12	– c Paine b Cummins	0
J. M. Anderson not out	0	– not out	1
B 10, lb 2, w 1, nb 1	14	B 6, lb 11, nb 1	18
1/26 (1) 2/89 (3) 3/115 (4) 4/131 (2) 5/368 (5) 6/372 (7) 7/389 (8) 8/389 (6) 9/393 (9) 10/403 (10) (115.1 overs)	403	1/4 (2) 2/29 (1) 3/60 (4) 4/100 (3) 5/133 (6) 6/172 (7) 7/196 (5) 8/210 (9) 9/211 (10) 10/218 (8) (72.5 overs)	218

Starc 25.1–5–91–4; Hazlewood 28–9–92–3; Cummins 28–8–84–2; Lyon 22–4–73–1; M. R. Marsh 9–1–43–0; Smith 3–1–8–0. *Second innings*—Starc 17–5–44–1; Hazlewood 18–6–48–5; M. R. Marsh 3–1–14–0; Cummins 19.5–4–53–2; Lyon 15–4–42–2.

Australia

C. T. Bancroft lbw b Overton	25
D. A. Warner c Bairstow b Overton	22
U. T. Khawaja lbw b Woakes	50
*S. P. D. Smith lbw b Anderson	239
S. E. Marsh c Root b Ali	28
M. R. Marsh lbw b Anderson	181
†T. D. Paine not out	49
M. A. Starc run out	1
P. J. Cummins lbw b Anderson	41
N. M. Lyon c Ali b Anderson	4
B 4, lb 16, w 1, nb 1	22
1/44 (2) 2/55 (1) 3/179 (3) 4/248 (5) 5/549 (6) 6/560 (4) 7/561 (8) 8/654 (9) 9/662 (10) (9 wkts dec, 179.3 overs)	662

J. R. Hazlewood did not bat.

Anderson 37.3–9–116–4; Broad 35–3–142–0; Woakes 41–8–128–1; Overton 24–1–110–2; Ali 33–4–120–1; Root 3–0–13–0; Malan 6–1–13–0.

Umpires: M. Erasmus and C. B. Gaffaney. Third umpire: Aleem Dar.
Referee: R. B. Richardson.

"It was only the second Test dismissal – after Rusi Surti of India was caught by Australia's Rex Sellers off Robert (Bob) Simpson at Calcutta in 1964-65 – in which the three participants shared the same initials."

Bangladesh v Australia in 2017–18, page 815

AUSTRALIA v ENGLAND

Fourth Test

STEVEN LYNCH

At Melbourne, December 26–30, 2017. Drawn. Toss: Australia. Test debut: T. K. Curran.

After 83 runs in his first six innings of the series, Alastair Cook went into the Boxing Day Test – the day after his 33rd birthday – fending off questions about his future. He ended it five days later after fending off everything the Australians could hurl at him: on the field for every one of the match's 2,329 deliveries, he climbed three places on the Test-runs list, having carried his bat for 244, the highest by a visiting player at the MCG. Cook's tour de force helped England end record-equalling sequences of seven straight overseas Test defeats, and eight in a row in Australia.

But neither Cook, nor a spirited bowling performance on the second day, could conjure a morale-boosting victory, despite a first-innings lead of 164. The pitch was about as responsive as a Christmas pudding, giving no help to bowlers and little to batsmen, who found scoring quickly a difficult task. To the embarrassment of the Melbourne club, the surface was rated poor by the ICC.

With Craig Overton ruled out by his rib injury, England gave a first cap to Surrey's Tom Curran, the 22-year-old son of the late Zimbabwe all-rounder Kevin. Curran was a feisty addition, but at this level and on this pitch proved short of pace. So did Jackson Bird, brought back for his first Test since the previous Boxing Day, after Mitchell Starc limped into Melbourne on crutches with a bruised heel.

MOST TEST RUNS WITHOUT DISMISSAL ON ONE GROUND

533 (88*, 61*, 280*, 104)	Javed Miandad (Pakistan)	Hyderabad (Pakistan)
512 (365*, 147)	G. S. Sobers (West Indies)	Kingston
467 (241*, 60*, 154*, 12)	S. R. Tendulkar (India)	Sydney
465 (216*, 249)	M. S. Atapattu (Sri Lanka)	Bulawayo
446 (136*, 10*, 204*, 96)	H. P. Tillekeratne (Sri Lanka)	Colombo (SSC)
445 (134*, 70*, 165*, 76)	**S. P. D. Smith (Australia)**	**Melbourne**
431 (112*, 143*, 176*)	V. V. S. Laxman (India)	Kolkata
426 (334*, 92)	M. A. Taylor (Australia)	Peshawar
404 (400*, 4)	B. C. Lara (West Indies)	St John's
403 (235*, 34*, 134)	Zaheer Abbas (Pakistan)	Lahore

On the first day, the one batsman to prosper was Warner, who shot out of the blocks in typical fashion, zooming to 83 (out of 102) in the over before lunch by launching Ali over long-on for six. With the seamers keeping tight lines to dispersed fields, England were – according to the former Test opener Chris Rogers – playing "conservative cricket". Warner certainly wasn't. He had 96 when Bancroft was scuppered by one that kept low and, three runs later, after reaching 6,000 in his 70th Test, spooned a simple catch to Broad at mid-on. It seemed Curran had claimed a notable maiden Test scalp – but replays showed he had overstepped, and Warner returned to the crease, exchanging unpleasantries with several fielders on the way. He brought up his 21st Test hundred next ball, sparking more exhortations, and really was out soon after, when Anderson's pinpoint off-cutter produced his 100th Ashes wicket.

The runs dried up. Australia managed only 1.65 an over during the middle session, and 2.82 in the third: quite a few of the 88,172 crowd – just 3,000 shy of the ground record, set in the previous Ashes series – had gone home before the end. But only one more wicket had fallen, when Khawaja flirted outside off to give Broad his first wicket for 415 balls.

Scott Barbour, Getty Images

One for the purists: Alastair Cook holds his pose after another straight-drive.

With Smith shrugging off a hand injury sustained in the nets, Australia were well placed at 244 for three by the close.

Curran was reasonably upbeat despite, like Ben Stokes and Mark Wood before him, having his maiden wicket chalked off by a no-ball. "Warner would have been nice," he said. "So I'll have to go and get Smith." This looked unlikely as Australia's captain glided to 76 next morning, but then he dragged one into his stumps, and this time there was no unhappy ending for Curran.

Dragging on proved catching. Mitchell Marsh did it four overs later, and Paine bottom-edged a pull off Anderson, taking him past Courtney Walsh's 519 Test wickets. The momentum shifted: Broad insisted on a review that did for Shaun Marsh, then trapped Bird in front, and had Cummins flashing firm-footed to slip, finishing with four wickets after his Perth nightmare. And when Anderson pinned Lyon, seven wickets had gone for 67 – the sort of slide that had characterised England's series rather than Australia's.

Cook almost joined the played-on club, mis-pulling in the second over: the closest Bird would come to a wicket. And, apart from a couple of sharp chances, it was the closest Cook would come to dismissal in what turned into a mountainous innings, notable for crisp straight-drives. He soon lost Stoneman, caught and bowled one-handed by Lyon, extending his right hand like a periscope, while Vince departed to his first ball after tea, adjudged leg-before to Hazlewood. He decided against a review only for the Snickometer to reveal a faint inside edge.

When Cook had 66 he was dropped at slip off Mitchell Marsh by Smith, possibly unsighted by wicketkeeper Paine, who had just gone up to the stumps. And with Cummins feeling unwell, there were few further alarms as Cook and Root finally lived up to pre-series expectations. They raised a century stand shortly before the close, then Smith tried himself for the last over, with Cook contemplating a night in the nineties. He gratefully cracked a full toss for four, tucked two to square leg, then hammered another rank ball to

MELBOURNE NOTES AND QUOTES

A ball-tampering row briefly exercised the tabloids, after Channel Nine showed zoomed-in footage of James Anderson rubbing his thumb against the shiny side. Some websites – including Cricket Australia's – reported that England had been accused of skullduggery. Trevor Bayliss marched to the umpires' room when he saw the footage during a rain delay – and was told there was no case to answer. He said it was a case of "Pommie bashing", and "a beat-up" that started because England were on top.

Alastair Cook's epic innings made the winemakers Hardys look rather silly. Despite being the official wine of both sides, they had run a series of adverts on the big screens throughout the series asking: "Why can't the Poms open a bottle of wine? Because they don't have any openers." The ad – which in any case featured a screw-top bottle – was missing from the final Test at Sydney.

Cook was informed in a press conference after his innings that he had leapt three places to sixth in the overall Test run-list, overtaking Mahela Jayawardene, Shivnarine Chanderpaul and Brian Lara. "I can't really explain that," he replied. "I just feel a bit sorry for Brian Lara."

While guests devoured oysters and prawns in the Melbourne committee room on the fourth day, Linda Dessau, the governor of Victoria, caused some indigestion among visiting MCC bigwigs by telling them they should sell off the Nursery Ground at Lord's, and use the proceeds to build a multi-purpose stadium.

the boundary: a 32nd Test hundred, and a more serene sleep. Cook tried to rationalise his return to form: "There are a lot of moving parts to my batting… I got to 40 and it kind of felt that the old movements were back." He was only the second visiting batsman, after Sunil Gavaskar, to make a hundred on all five of Australia's main Test grounds.

The partnership extended to 138 next day, before a furious Root top-edged a pull off the restored Cummins. But Cook sailed on, crunching another delicious straight-drive off Marsh, before Malan fell to the new ball – another unchallenged lbw, and another inside edge, even thicker this time. For good measure, he was also hit outside the line.

England faltered in indifferent light after lunch. Paine clasped a good catch as Bairstow tried to cut Lyon, then a skittish Ali – who got going with a six that just eluded Cummins at long-off – scythed to cover. "You can see a slightly muddled mind," admitted England's fielding coach Paul Collingwood. Cook survived a difficult chance to Smith at square leg when 153, an hour before tea, and lost Woakes and Curran soon after. But Broad overcame a nervous start to flourish in what turned into England's first hundred partnership for the ninth wicket on the ground. Cook unrolled another superb straight-drive to reach 202 – his fifth double-century – and soon eclipsed Viv Richards's 208, the highest score by a visiting batsman at the MCG (slick work in the members' bar updated the big sign commemorating this feat). The stand was ended by a controversial diving catch: replays showed Broad's pull bobbling out of Khawaja's hands as he tumbled at long leg, but no conclusive evidence that it touched the ground before he held on again. England ended the third day 164 ahead at 491 for nine. The last pair, Cook and Anderson, provided the first instance

TEST DOUBLE-HUNDREDS FOR ENGLAND IN AUSTRALIA

287	R. E. Foster at Sydney	1903-04
251	W. R. Hammond at Sydney	1928-29
244*	**A. N. Cook at Melbourne**	**2017-18**
235*	A. N. Cook at Brisbane	2010-11
231*	W. R. Hammond at Sydney	1936-37
227	K. P. Pietersen at Adelaide	2010-11
206	P. D. Collingwood at Adelaide	2006-07
200	W. R. Hammond at Melbourne	1928-29

Foster was making his Test debut.

TEST DOUBLE-HUNDREDS SCORES AT THE MCG

307	R. M. Cowper	Australia v England	1965-66
270	D. G. Bradman	Australia v England	1936-37
268	G. N. Yallop	Australia v Pakistan	1983-84
257	R. T. Ponting	Australia v India	2003-04
250	J. L. Langer	Australia v England	2002-03
244*	**A. N. Cook**	**England v Australia**	**2017-18**
208	I. V. A. Richards	West Indies v Australia	1984-85
205*	Azhar Ali	Pakistan v Australia	2016-17
205	R. N. Harvey	Australia v South Africa	1952-53
205	W. M. Lawry	Australia v West Indies	1968-69
204	G. A. Faulkner	South Africa v Australia	1910-11
200	W. R. Hammond	England v Australia	1928-29

of England's top run-scorer and wicket-taker batting together in a Test since Arthur Shrewsbury and George Ulyett in 1886.

Next morning, in one of those confounding passages of play, the players trooped off for ten minutes after one delivery, which Anderson poked to short leg. Cook was left undefeated with 244 from 409 balls, 27 of which he hit for four. During his 634-minute stay, he had overtaken Mahela Jayawardene (11,814 runs), Shivnarine Chanderpaul (11,867) and Brian Lara (11,953) to go sixth on the all-time list. It was the highest Test score by someone carrying his bat (previously 223 by Glenn Turner in 1971-72) and, more surprisingly, the first time in 110 Tests anyone had done it at the MCG.

England had two days to bowl Australia out, and removed Bancroft (another played-on victim) and Khawaja by lunch. But the comatose pitch was against them, as was the weather: only 18.5 more overs were possible on the fourth day. Warner and Smith seemed unshakeable on the fifth morning, but the tourists dared to dream when Warner skyed a wild drive into the covers, a 27th-birthday present for Root, bowling a belated first over of the match, and Bairstow latched on to a screamer from Shaun Marsh, from the last ball before lunch.

Australia were 178 for four, just 14 ahead, but there were no further glimmers for England, beyond a sketchy start for the younger Marsh. The new ball thumped into the unchanging surface, the spinners extracted next to nothing, the runs dwindled to less than two an over. When no more wickets had gone down by tea, the game was as dead as the pitch.

Through it all cruised the unflappable Smith, who passed 600 runs in the series during his third century, his 23rd in just 60 matches and his fourth in successive Boxing Day Tests, reached just before the match was euthanised an hour or so early. His homespun technique, with its step across that reveals the stumps between his feet, encourages bowlers… until the bat moves languidly into the right place and persuades the ball into another gap. By the end, Smith's Test average was the best of anyone with more than 15 innings, bar Bradman. In the local shops, Smith's book was piled high – and it would not have been a surprise to discover, in the first chapter, that he had a water tank in the back garden as a kid.

Man of the Match: A. N. Cook. *Attendance:* 261,335.

Close of play: first day, Australia 244-3 (Smith 65, S. E. Marsh 31); second day, England 192-2 (Cook 104, Root 49); third day, England 491-9 (Cook 244, Anderson 0); fourth day, Australia 103-2 (Warner 40, Smith 25).

"At the ground known as the Cake Tin, the hosts failed to rise."

New Zealand v South Africa in 2016–17, Third One-Day International, page 905

Australia

First innings		Second innings	
C. T. Bancroft lbw b Woakes	26	– b Woakes	27
D. A. Warner c Bairstow b Anderson	103	– c Vince b Root	86
U. T. Khawaja c Bairstow b Broad	17	– c Bairstow b Anderson	11
*S. P. D. Smith b Curran	76	– not out	102
S. E. Marsh lbw b Broad	61	– c Bairstow b Broad	4
M. R. Marsh b Woakes	9	– not out	29
†T. D. Paine b Anderson	24		
P. J. Cummins c Cook b Broad	4		
J. M. Bird lbw b Broad	4		
J. R. Hazlewood not out	1		
N. M. Lyon lbw b Anderson	0		
Lb 1, nb 1	2	B 4	4
1/122 (1) 2/135 (2) 3/160 (3) 4/260 (4) 5/278 (6) 6/314 (5) 7/318 (7) 8/325 (9) 9/326 (8) 10/327 (11) (119 overs)	327	1/51 (1) 2/65 (3) 3/172 (2) 4/178 (5) (4 wkts dec, 124.2 overs)	263

Anderson 29–11–61–3; Broad 28–10–51–4; Woakes 22–4–72–2; Ali 12–0–57–0; Curran 21–5–65–1; Malan 7–1–20–0. *Second innings*—Anderson 30–12–46–1; Broad 24–11–44–1; Woakes 26–7–62–1; Curran 20–6–53–0; Ali 13.2–2–32–0; Malan 8–1–21–0; Root 3–2–1–1.

England

A. N. Cook not out	244
M. D. Stoneman c and b Lyon	15
J. M. Vince lbw b Hazlewood	17
*J. E. Root c Lyon b Cummins	61
D. J. Malan lbw b Hazlewood	14
†J. M. Bairstow c Paine b Lyon	22
M. M. Ali c S. E. Marsh b Lyon	20
C. R. Woakes c Paine b Cummins	26
T. K. Curran c Paine b Hazlewood	4
S. C. J. Broad c Khawaja b Cummins	56
J. M. Anderson c Bancroft b Cummins	0
B 4, lb 5, nb 3	12
1/35 (2) 2/80 (3) 3/218 (4) 4/246 (5) 5/279 (6) 6/307 (7) 7/366 (8) 8/373 (9) 9/473 (10) 10/491 (11) (144.1 overs)	491

Hazlewood 30–5–95–3; Bird 30–5–108–0; Lyon 42–9–109–3; Cummins 29.1–1–117–4; M. R. Marsh 12–1–42–0; Smith 1–0–11–0.

Umpires: H. D. P. K. Dharmasena and S. Ravi. Third umpire: J. S. Wilson.
Referee: R. S. Madugalle.

AUSTRALIA v ENGLAND

Fifth Test

PHIL WALKER

At Sydney, January 4–8, 2018. Australia won by an innings and 123 runs. Toss: England. Test debut: M. S. Crane.

When the end finally came, Joe Root was dead to the world. Flat on his back in the dressing-room, poleaxed by a virus that struck after a day spent playing cricket in a kiln, he was briefly, blissfully oblivious to the final unravelling. It may have been the only shut-eye he got in two months.

The boyish vim and energy that marked his early manoeuvres had given way to exhaustion and gastroenteritis. And yet there was a certain magnificence in his refusal to buckle until his legs, literally, gave way. On the fourth day, temperatures peaked at 41°C – the hottest in Sydney since 1939 – pushing the bounds of what sportsmen can reasonably endure; a heat stress tracker, used to record a feels-like temperature, gave a reading out in the middle of 57.6°. Root was in the field for all but six overs of it, and somehow escaped 42 not out.

William West, AFP/Getty Images

Firm ground: Shaun Marsh (left) congratulates brother Mitchell on reaching his hundred.

The final day dawned dramatic, with the news that he had visited hospital, and would initially not be batting. But he made it to the SCG for the start, still wearing his hospital wristband; and it was no great surprise, an hour into play, to see him emerging at the fall of Ali. The hour Root batted until lunch – minimally, in slow motion even against Cummins, the busy persona abandoned to the needs of survival – was mesmerising. He registered his fifth fifty of the series, and drifted through to the break. It was the last we would see of him.

In truth, there hadn't been much to shout about before that. England had avoided the whitewash at Melbourne, and the last rites felt limp. Sydney put on a grand show, especially the pink-drenched splendour of Jane McGrath Day. But, not for the first time in this series, the teams were presented with a pitch cussedly resistant to pace, bounce and, therefore flowing cricket. The SCG must go back to 2009-10 and the visit of Pakistan for the last time it staged a gripping Test. This game did nothing to halt the trend.

Indeed, the result had felt inevitable since the chaotic dying moments of the first day. Root looked set for his first hundred in Australia when, on 83, he tucked a leg-stump half-volley from Starc straight to square leg, and fell to his haunches in disbelief. Then, with what became the final ball of the evening, Bairstow – having spurned a nightwatchman – prodded at Hazlewood. A promising 228 for three had become an inadequate 233 for five, finishing a day on which England's batting problems had been exposed in microcosm. Stoneman had started well, but fell to the first tasty delivery he faced, while Cook – the second player, after Allan Border, to register 150 consecutive Test appearances – was again caught on the crease. Vince's 25 was so exquisitely Vincian, an assortment of aesthetic charm and mental flabbiness, that it felt like a performance piece in its own right.

Next morning, Malan was caught at slip for another hard-fought fifty, and Ali – after Hazlewood somehow dropped him at midwicket – was bounced out. There was some lower-order thrashing in the heat, especially from Broad, who swiped two sixes to bring

SYDNEY NOTES AND QUOTES

The New Year's Test at the SCG is all about tradition. Members queued from 4am on the opening day, and the McGrath Foundation raised more than their target of $A1.3m for breast cancer. As is also customary, the game was a dead rubber, former Australian prime minister Bob Hawke necked a beer live on TV, and one team picked a greenhorn spinner.

The greenhorn, Mason Crane – at 20, England's youngest specialist spinner since 19-year-old Ian Peebles in 1927-28 – revealed himself a bit of a card. How would he bowl to Steve Smith? "Give him a single." Had he faced Pat Cummins during his time with New South Wales the previous season? "No, no. His overs weren't wasted on me." And after Crane's first Test innings was cut short when James Anderson ran him out: "I love my batting, I just wish I was a bit better at it."

The series ended appropriately, for England, in darkness: their dressing-room lights were off, and the players padded up and ate in the dark around their captain, who was sleeping off his viral gastroenteritis bug.

The sides mixed happily after the end: Smith and Anderson – standing in for Root – declared the series had been played in good spirits, while both teams went to the stands to acknowledge the Barmy Army, which at Sydney had included Root's brother, Billy, of Nottinghamshire. Later Smith presented Cook with a bottle of wine in honour of his undefeated 244 at Melbourne, and the feat of scoring a century on all five major Australian grounds.

his tally at the SCG to seven from two Tests (only Adam Gilchrist, with 13, had more). But the overriding impression for England was of the hard yakka to come.

For Australia, Cummins again stood out. Much of the pre-series talk had revolved around whether their pace attack would last the course. It proved a non-issue. While Hazlewood offered potency and parsimony, and Starc shocked and awed and lurked in wait, it was Cummins who emerged as the best of the lot, combining serious pace with nagging lines and an intuitive intelligence. Lyon completed a quartet who would hoover up all England's wickets – barring two run-outs – in the series. Never before had that happened across five Tests. Even on this slowish surface, Cummins was irrepressible. Three of his four first-innings wickets came from catches by the wicketkeeper, and the fourth from the shoulder of Curran's bat. From First Test to Fifth, he extracted life from areas where others had long given up looking, and repaid Australia's faith: six years after first receiving his Baggy Green as a teenager, he had finally made his home Test debut. It was England's fate to face the fully fit version.

That Australia would go way past their score was barely in question, even after Broad removed Bancroft for a duck. The only surprise was that Smith did not do most of the burying. All had seemed in order as he rolled into pink Saturday unbeaten on 44, with Australia 153 behind but only two down. Khawaja, on 91 and ready to salvage his own middling series, was set to carry the robes at the coronation. Then, on 83 – less than three runs past his overall first-innings Test average – Smith smacked a low return catch to Ali. Staggering back to his feet, Ali looked as surprised as anyone. The stand had been worth 188.

Thus, it turned out, Smith's series with the bat was done. His 687 runs at an average of 137 will slip in among other epic one-man Ashes feats, but beyond the final figure was a gargantuan abstinence: he scored at 48 per 100 balls, ten below the strike-rate he had maintained between his first Test hundred, at The Oval in 2013, and the start of this series. From Brisbane onwards, where he had taken such obvious pleasure from barely playing a shot in anger, Smith was redefining long-form batting in the modern game, and others had gone with him: Australia's scoring rate of 2.97 was their lowest in a home series this century. Inevitably, there was a personal landmark: Smith passed 6,000 Test runs in his 111th innings, equal with Garry Sobers and behind only Don Bradman (68).

This, however, was not his Test. Instead, the languorous Khawaja was offered the floor, and he took it, going to his sixth Test century – his first against England – and falling only

MOST RUNS CONCEDED IN AN INNINGS ON TEST DEBUT

73–16–222–2	S. Randiv	Sri Lanka v India at Colombo (SSC)	2010
43.5–1–215–8	J. J. Krejza	Australia v India at Nagpur	2008-09
40–2–204–3	O. A. C. Banks	West Indies v Australia at Bridgetown	2002-03
70–12–195–1	N. M. Kulkarni	India v Sri Lanka at Colombo (RPS)	1997-98
48–3–193–1	**M. S. Crane**	**England v Australia at Sydney**	**2017-18**
47.5–7–179–6	U. D. U. Chandana	Sri Lanka v Pakistan at Dhaka	1998-99
49–10–169–4	R. B. Desai	India v West Indies at Delhi	1958-59
41.2–6–168–6	G. F. Cresswell	New Zealand v England at The Oval	1949
46–8–168–2	Surendranath	India v West Indies at Calcutta	1958-59
44–2–166–1	D. E. Malcolm	England v Australia at Nottingham	1989

three short of his career-best 174. "When I'm scoring runs, I'm elegant," he said, "and when I'm not, I'm lazy." It was the refrain of a stylist.

Even so, through the haze and inertia, his dismissal would rouse England's bedraggled fans – a first Test wicket for the 20-year-old debutant leg-spinner Mason Crane, in for Chris Woakes, who had a side strain. Crane drew the left-handed Khawaja out of his ground, defeated him in the flight, turned the ball sharply through his gate, and handed Bairstow a simple stumping. It was the least Crane deserved; he had already struck Khawaja plumb in front on 132, only for replays to reveal the tightest of no-balls. Crane then passed the bat with four of the first five deliveries he bowled to Mitchell Marsh. It was promising stuff. Many will argue these were mere consolations for a bowler who ended up conceding 193, the fifth-most by any Test debutant. But English leg-break bowlers, reared on unresponsive pitches in a system skewed against them, are no strangers to excavating the positives wherever they can. It was too early to say if England had finally found a Test-class leg-spinner, but Crane appeared to have the tools to give it a go.

Still, for all his pluck, the Marsh brothers made merry with what was left of a threadbare attack, adding 169 at four an over. Good Western Australian boys, they happily scythed their way to hundreds, in each case their second of the series, as England wilted on that furnace of a fourth day. It was only the third time brothers had each reached a Test century with the other at the crease, after Ian and Greg Chappell (Wellington 1973-74) and Steve and Mark Waugh (Kingston 1994-95). It was almost a benevolent call by Smith to pull his men in after 193 overs. Only once before, in 1946-47, when Sid Barnes and Bradman each made 234 in a total of 659 for eight, had Australia scored more against England at Sydney. In the circumstances, Anderson's 34 overs for 56 were heroic.

England's second innings was a write-off, with Ali falling to Lyon for a record-equalling seventh time in the series. When the end arrived on the final afternoon, with the customary sight of Anderson getting bombed by a bunch of quicks, and Cummins collecting another haul of four, England were left staring at two winters of miserable failure in the five-day game. Since Trevor Bayliss took over as head coach in 2015, he had overseen 18 Test defeats. There were mitigating factors around this latest humbling, but the figures remained stark: England had lost all but one of their last nine Tests away from home. In three of them, they had made 400 and lost by an innings. In the sharp white heat of another

BROTHERS SCORING HUNDREDS IN THE SAME TEST INNINGS

I. M. Chappell (118) and G. S. Chappell (113)	A v E at The Oval	1972
I. M. Chappell (145) and G. S. Chappell (247*)	A v NZ at Wellington (*1st inns*)	1973-74
I. M. Chappell (121) and G. S. Chappell (133)	A v NZ at Wellington (*2nd inns*)	1973-74
Sadiq (103*) and Mushtaq Mohammad (101)	P v NZ at Hyderabad (Pakistan)	1976-77
G. W. Flower (201*) and A. Flower (156)	Z v P at Harare	1994-95
M. E. Waugh (126) and S. R. Waugh (200)	A v WI at Kingston	1994-95
M. E. Waugh (120) and S. R. Waugh (157*)	A v E at The Oval	2001
S. E. Marsh (156) and M. R. Marsh (101)	**A v E at Sydney**	**2017-18**

Ryan Pierse, Getty Images

Four-hand smash: Steve Smith's Australians celebrate their resounding victory.

thrashing in Australia, the inevitable clamour for change might have been a simplistic response to a multi-layered problem. But it was also entirely understandable.

Man of the Match: P. J. Cummins. *Attendance:* 182,349.

Man of the Series: S. P. D. Smith. *Compton–Miller medal:* S. P. D. Smith.

Close of play: first day, England 233-5 (Malan 55); second day, Australia 193-2 (Khawaja 91, Smith 44); third day, Australia 479-4 (S. E. Marsh 98, M. R. Marsh 63); fourth day, England 93-4 (Root 42, Bairstow 17).

England

Batsman	First innings		Second innings	
A. N. Cook lbw b Hazlewood		39	b Lyon	10
M. D. Stoneman c Paine b Cummins		24	lbw b Starc	0
J. M. Vince c Paine b Cummins		25	c Smith b Cummins	18
*J. E. Root c M. R. Marsh b Starc		83	retired ill	58
D. J. Malan c Smith b Starc		62	lbw b Lyon	5
†J. M. Bairstow c Paine b Hazlewood		5	lbw b Cummins	38
M. M. Ali c Paine b Cummins		30	lbw b Lyon	13
T. K. Curran c Bancroft b Cummins		39	not out	23
S. C. J. Broad c Smith b Lyon		31	c Paine b Cummins	4
M. S. Crane run out		4	c Paine b Cummins	2
J. M. Anderson not out		0	c Paine b Hazlewood	2
Lb 2, w 2		4	Lb 2, p 5	7
1/28 (2) 2/88 (3) 3/95 (1) 4/228 (4) 5/233 (6) 6/251 (5) 7/294 (7) 8/335 (8) 9/346 (9) 10/346 (10)	(112.3 overs)	346	1/5 (2) 2/15 (1) 3/43 (3) 4/68 (5) 5/121 (7) 6/144 (6) 7/148 (9) 8/156 (10) 9/180 (11) (88.1 overs)	180

In the second innings Root, when 42, retired ill at 93-4 and resumed at 121-5; he retired again at 144-5.

Starc 21–6–80–2; Hazlewood 23–4–65–2; Cummins 24.3–5–80–4; Lyon 37–5–86–1; M. R. Marsh 7–0–33–0. *Second innings*—Starc 16–4–38–1; Hazlewood 17.1–6–36–1; Lyon 35–12–54–3; Cummins 17–4–39–4; Smith 2–0–6–0; M. R. Marsh 1–1–0–0.

Australia

C. T. Bancroft b Broad	0	M. A. Starc c Vince b Ali	11
D. A. Warner c Bairstow b Anderson	56	P. J. Cummins not out	24
U. T. Khawaja st Bairstow b Crane	171	B 2, lb 4, w 1, nb 2	9
*S. P. D. Smith c and b Ali	83		
S. E. Marsh run out	156	1/1 (1) 2/86 (2) (7 wkts dec, 193 overs)	649
M. R. Marsh b Curran	101	3/274 (4) 4/375 (3)	
†T. D. Paine not out	38	5/544 (6) 6/596 (5) 7/613 (8)	

N. M. Lyon and J. R. Hazlewood did not bat.

Anderson 34–14–56–1; Broad 30–2–121–1; Ali 48–10–170–2; Curran 25–3–82–1; Crane 48–3–193–1; Root 8–3–21–0.

Umpires: H. D. P. K. Dharmasena and J. S. Wilson. Third umpire: S. Ravi.
Referee: R. S. Madugalle.

At Sydney (Drummoyne Oval), January 11, 2018 (day/night). **England XI won by five wickets.** **†Cricket Australia XI 258-9** (50 overs) (T. J. Dean 62, M. W. Harvey 59; A. U. Rashid 3-45); **England XI 259-5** (40.5 overs) (A. D. Hales 52, E. J. G. Morgan 81*). *Both teams chose from 12 players. England's newly arrived white-ball specialists took no time to settle, easing to victory with more than nine overs to spare. The CA XI started well, and were 120-2 shortly after halfway, but Moeen Ali (2-28) and Adil Rashid inspired a mid-innings wobble, before 17-year-old Mackenzie Harvey and wicketkeeper Harry Nielsen (son of the former Australian coach Tim) dragged them towards 258. Roy and Bairstow shared an opening stand of 74 in 12.4 overs, then Hales and Morgan scored at better than a run a ball. Hales smacked successive sixes in the home captain Matt Renshaw's only over, which cost 21 while Morgan later took 22 from an over from Ben Pengelley. Joe Root had recovered sufficiently from illness in the Sydney Test to act as twelfth man.*

ONE-DAY INTERNATIONAL REPORTS BY

VITHUSHAN EHANTHARAJAH

AUSTRALIA v ENGLAND

First One-Day International

At Melbourne, January 14, 2018 (day/night). England won by five wickets. Toss: England. One-day international debut: A. J. Tye.

Jason Roy continued England's knack of breaking one-day records with a stunning 180 – beating Hales's national-best 171, set only 18 months earlier against Pakistan at Trent Bridge in August 2016 – as they became the first side to chase over 300 to win an ODI at Melbourne. Five of England's seven successful pursuits of such totals had now taken place since the 2015 World Cup. The exponential development of white-ball cricket, seemingly with each match, meant that even at the halfway stage, after Finch's fourth one-day hundred against England – and his third in his three innings against them at the MCG – the Australians' total of 304 looked light. Finch was unflustered during his 119-ball stay but, despite half-centuries from Mitchell Marsh and the hard-hitting Stoinis, England kept a check on the rate thanks to Ali's one for 39. Their openers then got ahead of the game, flaying 50 in 4.2 overs; even the departures in quick succession of Bairstow and Hales, making his first international appearance since he was suspended for his part in the Bristol night out with Ben Stokes in September, felt like no more than a blip. Then it was the Roy show, with a bit of help from Root. They added 221, an England record for the third wicket (previously 213 between Neil Fairbrother and Graeme Hick against West Indies at Lord's in 1991), and for any wicket against Australia (previously 202 for the second between Graham Gooch and David Gower at Lord's in

HIGHEST SUCCESSFUL CHASES IN ODIs AT MELBOURNE

308-5	**England v Australia**	**2017-18**
297-4	Australia v England	2010-11
296-7	Australia v India	2015-16
291-5	Australia v New Zealand	2006-07
273-6	West Indies v Australia	1984-85
272-7	South Africa v Australia	2008-09
270-4	Australia v England	2013-14
269-6	Australia v India	2014-15
268-7	Australia v South Africa	2014-15
253-6	New Zealand v Australia	1997-98
253-6	England v Australia	2006-07

HIGHEST SCORES FOR ENGLAND IN ODIs

180	**J. J. Roy**	**v Australia at Melbourne**	**2017-18**
171	A. D. Hales	v Pakistan at Nottingham	2016
167*	R. A. Smith	v Australia at Birmingham	1993
162	J. J. Roy	v Sri Lanka at The Oval	2016
158	D. I. Gower	v New Zealand at Brisbane	1982-83
158	A. J. Strauss	v India at Bangalore	2010-11
154	A. J. Strauss	v Bangladesh at Birmingham	2010
152	A. J. Strauss	v Bangladesh at Nottingham	2005

1985). By the time the freewheeling Roy departed in the 43rd over, having faced just 151 balls and blitzed 16 fours and five sixes, the game was up. Morgan and Buttler came and went cheaply, but Root picked off the remainder, and England had their first international win of the tour.

Man of the Match: J. J. Roy. *Attendance:* 37,171.

Australia

A. J. Finch c Bairstow b Ali	107
D. A. Warner c Root b Wood	2
*S. P. D. Smith c Buttler b Rashid	23
T. M. Head b Plunkett	5
M. R. Marsh b Rashid	50
M. P. Stoinis c Root b Woakes	60
†T. D. Paine c Ali b Plunkett	27
P. J. Cummins c Roy b Plunkett	12
M. A. Starc not out	0
A. J. Tye not out	4
Lb 7, w 7	14
1/10 (2) 2/58 (3) 3/78 (4) 4/196 (1) 5/205 (5) 6/285 (6) 7/296 (7) 8/300 (8) (8 wkts, 50 overs)	304
10 overs: 52-1	

A. Zampa did not bat.

Woakes 10–0–65–1; Wood 10–0–49–1; Plunkett 10–0–71–3; Rashid 10–0–73–2; Ali 10–0–39–1.

England

J. J. Roy c sub (J. A. Richardson) b Starc	180
J. M. Bairstow c Paine b Starc	14
A. D. Hales c Stoinis b Cummins	4
J. E. Root not out	91
*E. J. G. Morgan c Smith b Cummins	1
†J. C. Buttler c Starc b Stoinis	4
M. M. Ali not out	5
Lb 5, w 4	9
1/53 (2) 2/60 (3) 3/281 (1) 4/288 (5) 5/302 (6) (5 wkts, 48.5 overs)	308
10 overs: 87-2	

C. R. Woakes, A. U. Rashid, L. E. Plunkett and M. A. Wood did not bat.

Starc 10–0–71–2; Cummins 10–0–63–2; Tye 10–0–43–0; Stoinis 6–0–33–1; Zampa 10–0–72–0; Marsh 2–0–15–0; Head 0.5–0–6–0.

Umpires: S. D. Fry and C. B. Gaffaney. Third umpire: H. D. P. K. Dharmasena.
Referee: R. S. Madugalle.

AUSTRALIA v ENGLAND

Second One-Day International

At Brisbane, January 19, 2018 (day/night). England won by four wickets. Toss: Australia. One-day international debuts: A. T. Carey, J. A. Richardson.

Morgan produced one of his best displays in the field, after a tactical switch to use three spinners at the Gabba helped England restrict Australia to 270. Just when it looked as if the seamers might struggle, and with Australia's openers having put on 68 inside 12 overs, Ali and Root applied the brakes, taking three for 62 in 14 between them. Bowling with a confidence that had eluded him during the Ashes, Ali prised out Warner, while Root trapped Smith, then held a simple return catch from Head. Finch, with his tenth ODI hundred (and fifth against England), fought back with the help of Marsh, but Rashid had Marsh stumped and Stoinis caught behind; in between Plunkett removed Finch. Losing three for seven slowed Australia, so that their last 11 overs produced only 62 – of which 27 were made by debutant wicketkeeper Alex Carey, in for the ill Tim Paine. Roy fell in the first over this time, tucking Starc to short midwicket, but Australia had omitted leg-spinner Adam Zampa, handing a first cap to seamer Jhye Richardson – Josh Hazlewood was missing with a virus – and leaving the spin-bowling duties with part-timer Head. They were powerless as a second-wicket stand of 117 in just 18.4 overs between Bairstow and Hales gave England leeway. Buttler gave them a little more, with 42 in 32 balls, but Australia had a sniff when Starc removed him and Ali in the same over, with England six down and 44 short. Root was still there, however, and a 27-ball cameo from Woakes gave them only their second one-day win against Australia at Brisbane.

Man of the Match: J. E. Root. *Attendance:* 29,685.

Australia

D. A. Warner c Root b Ali	35
A. J. Finch c Roy b Plunkett	106
*S. P. D. Smith lbw b Root	18
T. M. Head c and b Root	7
M. R. Marsh st Buttler b Rashid	36
M. P. Stoinis c Buttler b Rashid	4
C. L. White not out	15
†A. T. Carey run out	27
M. A. Starc c Roy b Woakes	3
A. J. Tye run out	8
Lb 2, w 8, nb 1	11
1/68 (1) 2/110 (3) 3/124 (4) 4/209 (5) 5/213 (2) 6/216 (6) 7/255 (8) 8/261 (9) 9/270 (10) — (9 wkts, 50 overs)	270

10 overs: 56-0

J. A. Richardson did not bat.

Wood 9–0–55–0; Woakes 9–0–37–1; Plunkett 8–0–43–1; Ali 7–0–31–1; Rashid 10–0–71–2; Root 7–0–31–2.

England

J. J. Roy c Finch b Starc	2
J. M. Bairstow c Warner b Richardson	60
A. D. Hales b Richardson	57
J. E. Root not out	46
*E. J. G. Morgan b Starc	21
†J. C. Buttler c Carey b Starc	42
M. M. Ali b Starc	1
C. R. Woakes not out	39
Lb 1, w 5	6
1/2 (1) 2/119 (3) 3/129 (2) 4/157 (5) 5/225 (6) 6/227 (7) — (6 wkts, 44.2 overs)	274

10 overs: 60-1

A. U. Rashid, L. E. Plunkett and M. A. Wood did not bat.

Starc 10–0–59–4; Richardson 10–1–57–2; Head 7–0–55–0; Tye 9–0–47–0; Finch 3–0–17–0; Stoinis 4.2–0–34–0; Marsh 1–0–4–0.

Umpires: H. D. P. K. Dharmasena and S. J. Nogajski. Third umpire: C. B. Gaffaney. Referee: R. S. Madugalle.

"He was the Egon Ronay of fish and chips."

Obituaries, page 187

AUSTRALIA v ENGLAND

Third One-Day International

At Sydney, January 21, 2018 (day/night). England won by 16 runs. Toss: Australia.

England sealed their first bilateral series one-day win in Australia, with Morgan lauding it as the best result of his reign. A combination of his inventive captaincy and a staggering century from Buttler meant that, for the first time, Australia trailed 3–0 at home. The victory was all the more impressive since England were a bowler light, after Plunkett tweaked a hamstring in his second over. Morgan had to call on Root to bowl the balance, while ensuring he didn't overuse Wood and Woakes too early. Chasing 303, Australia were in the game at 181 for three in the 34th over, only to lose Smith to a disputed low catch by Buttler. The on-field umpires' soft signal was out and, when replays proved inconclusive, TV official Kumar Dharmasena upheld their decision. Smith was unimpressed, and later called for the soft signal to be scrapped; Buttler said he had got his fingers under the ball. Marsh and Stoinis hit back with half-centuries, but Australia dropped behind the rate as Wood and Woakes held their nerve. That England had so many to defend was thanks to Buttler who, aided by Woakes, rescued them from 189 for six in the 39th over. His fifty came in 52 balls, after which he pressed the accelerator, reaching his hundred off the last of the innings, his 83rd – the slowest of his five one-day international centuries. With Woakes bashing an unbeaten 53 in 36 balls, the pair added 113 from 71, taking England beyond 300 and, ultimately, Australia.

Man of the Match: J. C. Buttler. *Attendance:* 35,195.

England

J. J. Roy c Finch b Cummins	19
J. M. Bairstow b Zampa	39
A. D. Hales c Zampa b Stoinis	1
J. E. Root b Hazlewood	27
*E. J. G. Morgan c Paine b Hazlewood	41
†J. C. Buttler not out	100
M. M. Ali b Marsh	6
C. R. Woakes not out	53
Lb 2, w 13, nb 1	16
1/38 (1) 2/45 (3) 3/90 (2) 4/107 (4) 5/172 (5) 6/189 (7) (6 wkts, 50 overs)	302
10 overs: 47-2	

A. U. Rashid, L. E. Plunkett and M. A. Wood did not bat.

Starc 10–0–63–0; Hazlewood 10–0–58–2; Cummins 10–1–67–1; Stoinis 8–0–43–1; Zampa 9–0–55–1; Marsh 3–0–14–1.

Australia

A. J. Finch lbw b Rashid	62
D. A. Warner c Hales b Woakes	8
C. L. White c Buttler b Wood	17
*S. P. D. Smith c Buttler b Wood	45
M. R. Marsh c Hales b Rashid	55
M. P. Stoinis c sub (S. W. Billings) b Woakes	56
†T. D. Paine not out	31
P. J. Cummins not out	1
B 4, lb 5, w 2	11
1/24 (2) 2/44 (3) 3/113 (1) 4/181 (4) 5/210 (5) 6/284 (6) (6 wkts, 50 overs)	286
10 overs: 49-2	

M. A. Starc, A. Zampa and J. R. Hazlewood did not bat.

Wood 10–1–46–2; Woakes 10–0–57–2; Plunkett 1.2–0–6–0; Ali 10–0–57–0; Root 8.4–0–60–0; Rashid 10–0–51–2.

Umpires: S. D. Fry and C. B. Gaffaney. Third umpire: H. D. P. K. Dharmasena.
Referee: R. S. Madugalle.

AUSTRALIA v ENGLAND

Fourth One-Day International

At Adelaide, January 26, 2018 (day/night). Australia won by three wickets. Toss: Australia.

England's hopes of becoming the first visiting side to win a one-day series 5–0 in Australia came crashing down inside the first half-hour. Asked to bat in muggy conditions, they were reduced to eight for five in 6.2 overs. It was the third-lowest score at the fall of the fifth wicket in a one-day international. Even with Mitchell Starc resting, Australia's quicks ran amok, Cummins the pick with a career-best four for 24; four of the top six made ducks, including Root, hooking to fine leg. At that point, England's all-time one-day low – 86 against Australia at Old Trafford in 2001 – was under threat, but from the rubble Morgan and Ali did their best to rebuild. Even so, from 120 for eight, it needed a determined 78 from 82 balls from Woakes, including five sixes, and a run-a-ball 35 from

DUCK SOUP

Four of the top six in an ODI innings out for nought:

Sri Lanka (109) v India (292-6) at Johannesburg (World Cup) 2002-03
M. S. Atapattu, J. Mubarak, D. P. M. D. Jayawardene, P. A. de Silva

Pakistan (116) v New Zealand (117-3) at Dambulla 2003
Mohammad Hafeez, Faisal Iqbal, Yousuf Youhanna, Abdul Razzaq

Canada (67) v Netherlands (70-1) at King City 2013
H. Patel, N. R. Kumar, Raza-ur-Rehman, A. S. Hansra

Papua New Guinea (147) v Scotland (148-4) at Dubai **2017-18**
T. P. Ura, D. Bau, S. Bau, M. D. Dai

England (196) v Australia (197-7) at Adelaide **2017-18**
J. J. Roy, J. M. Bairstow, J. E. Root, J. C. Buttler

Tom Curran, in for the injured Liam Plunkett, to give England a sniff. Australia's chase was held together by Head, opening the batting because Aaron Finch had pulled a hamstring. At 136 for five, with Rashid striking three times, Australia were tottering, but nerves were eased by a stand of 44 between Head, who finally fell for 96, and Paine. Eventually, the hosts made it over the line – with plenty of overs, if not many wickets, in hand – to mark Australia Day with only their second ODI win in 12 completed games since their previous Australia Day.

Man of the Match: P. J. Cummins. *Attendance:* 24,329.

England

J. J. Roy c Smith b Hazlewood	0	T. K. Curran c Marsh b Tye	35
J. M. Bairstow c Paine b Hazlewood	0	M. A. Wood not out	2
A. D. Hales b Cummins	3		
J. E. Root c Hazlewood b Cummins	0	B 1, w 4	5
*E. J. G. Morgan c Paine b Cummins	33		
†J. C. Buttler c Paine b Hazlewood	0	1/0 (1) 2/4 (3) 3/4 (2) (44.5 overs)	196
M. M. Ali c Head b Tye	33	4/6 (4) 5/8 (6) 6/61 (5)	
C. R. Woakes c sub (G. J. Maxwell) b Tye	78	7/112 (7) 8/120 (9) 9/180 (8)	
A. U. Rashid c Paine b Cummins	7	10/196 (10)	10 overs: 18-5

Hazlewood 10–0–39–3; Cummins 10–2–24–4; Marsh 5–1–24–0; Tye 7.5–0–33–3; Head 2–0–9–0; Zampa 7–0–42–0; Stoinis 3–0–24–0.

Australia

D. A. Warner c Buttler b Woakes	13	P. J. Cummins run out	3
T. M. Head c Morgan b Wood	96	A. J. Tye not out	3
C. L. White lbw b Curran	3	W 3, nb 1	4
*S. P. D. Smith c Root b Rashid	4		
M. R. Marsh c and b Rashid	32	1/25 (1) 2/48 (3) (7 wkts, 37 overs)	197
M. P. Stoinis c Roy b Rashid	14	3/70 (4) 4/112 (5)	
†T. D. Paine not out	25	5/136 (6) 6/180 (2) 7/185 (8)	10 overs: 61-2

A. Zampa and J. R. Hazlewood did not bat.

Woakes 7–0–36–1; Wood 9–0–58–1; Curran 2–1–10–1; Ali 8–0–41–0; Rashid 10–0–49–3; Root 1–0–3–0.

Umpires: H. D. P. K. Dharmasena and S. J. Nogajski. Third umpire: C. B. Gaffaney.
Referee: R. S. Madugalle.

Will Russell, CA/Getty Images

Electric Curran: Tim Paine is last to go, and England win 4–1.

AUSTRALIA v ENGLAND

Fifth One-Day International

At Perth Stadium, January 28, 2018. England won by 12 runs. Toss: Australia.

A classy display from Curran ensured a triumphant conclusion to the series for England, and a thrilling finish to Perth Stadium's maiden international. With a pinpoint spell of reverse swing, he dragged the game away from Australia to finish with five for 35 in only his third ODI. Western Australia had seemed set to celebrate one of its own, as Perth-born Andrew Tye completed the game's first maiden five-for to knock England over for a below-par 259. Roy had begun well, teeing off on a pitch showing some of the pace familiar from the WACA, just across the Swan River. But, like Bairstow and Hales, he failed to convert a start, and England declined from 151 for two after 26 overs. Pace off the ball did the trick: four of Tye's victims, including Root for 62, were caught as they mistimed slower deliveries. England's bowlers had it all to do, especially with Willey and Ball – brought in for Chris Woakes and Mark Wood – playing their first game of the series. But Curran yorked Warner, Morgan ran out Head, and Ali had Smith stumped, before pulling off an astonishing return catch to dismiss Marsh, the ball lodging between thumb and forefinger as he stretched out his right hand to intercept a rollicking straight-drive. Stoinis biffed 87 from No. 3, but Curran's energy

---

ENGLAND'S BEST ODI BOWLING FIGURES v AUSTRALIA

6-45	C. R. Woakes	Brisbane	2010-11
5-28	G. P. Swann	Chester-le-Street	2009
5-31	M. Hendrick	The Oval	1980
5-33	S. J. Harmison	Bristol	2005
5-35	**T. K. Curran**	**Perth Stadium**	**2017-18**
5-44	D. Gough	Lord's	1997
5-61	B. A. Stokes	Southampton	2013
5-71†	S. T. Finn	Melbourne	2014-15

† *World Cup match; included a hat-trick.*

and skill helped reduce Australia to 203 for eight. Paine and Zampa took advantage of sloppy fielding to add 33, before Curran returned to bowl both, and condemn the Australians to their joint-heaviest one-day defeat at home, after South Africa's 4–1 win in 2008-09.

Man of the Match: T. K. Curran. *Attendance:* 53,781.

Man of the Series: J. E. Root.

England

J. J. Roy c Hazlewood b Tye	49	T. K. Curran not out	11
J. M. Bairstow b Starc	44	J. T. Ball b Tye	0
A. D. Hales c Maxwell b Marsh	35		
J. E. Root c Warner b Tye	62	B 4, lb 2, w 7, nb 1	14
*E. J. G. Morgan c Stoinis b Marsh	3		
†J. C. Buttler c Warner b Tye	21	1/71 (1) 2/117 (2) (47.4 overs)	259
M. M. Ali c Tye b Zampa	6	3/151 (3) 4/157 (5) 5/192 (6)	
A. U. Rashid run out	12	6/214 (7) 7/238 (8) 8/245 (9)	
D. J. Willey c Marsh b Tye	2	9/258 (4) 10/259 (11)	10 overs: 66-0

Starc 9–0–63–1; Hazlewood 9–0–51–0; Marsh 7–0–24–2; Tye 9.4–0–46–5; Zampa 10–0–46–1; Maxwell 3–0–23–0.

Australia

D. A. Warner b Curran	15	A. Zampa b Curran	11
T. M. Head run out	22	J. R. Hazlewood not out	0
M. P. Stoinis c Curran b Rashid	87		
*S. P. D. Smith st Buttler b Ali	12	Lb 7, w 4	11
M. R. Marsh c and b Ali	13		
G. J. Maxwell lbw b Curran	34	1/24 (1) 2/86 (2) (48.2 overs)	247
†T. D. Paine b Curran	34	3/119 (4) 4/133 (5) 5/189 (3)	
M. A. Starc c Buttler b Curran	0	6/192 (6) 7/192 (8) 8/203 (9)	
A. J. Tye c Morgan b Ali	8	9/236 (10) 10/247 (7)	10 overs: 63-1

Willey 9–1–37–0; Curran 9.2–0–35–5; Ali 10–0–55–3; Rashid 10–0–55–1; Ball 10–0–58–0.

Umpires: S. D. Fry and C. B. Gaffaney. Third umpire: H. D. P. K. Dharmasena.
Referee: R. S. Madugalle.

The Trans-Tasman Twenty20 tri-series that followed, involving Australia, England and New Zealand, will be covered in Wisden 2019.

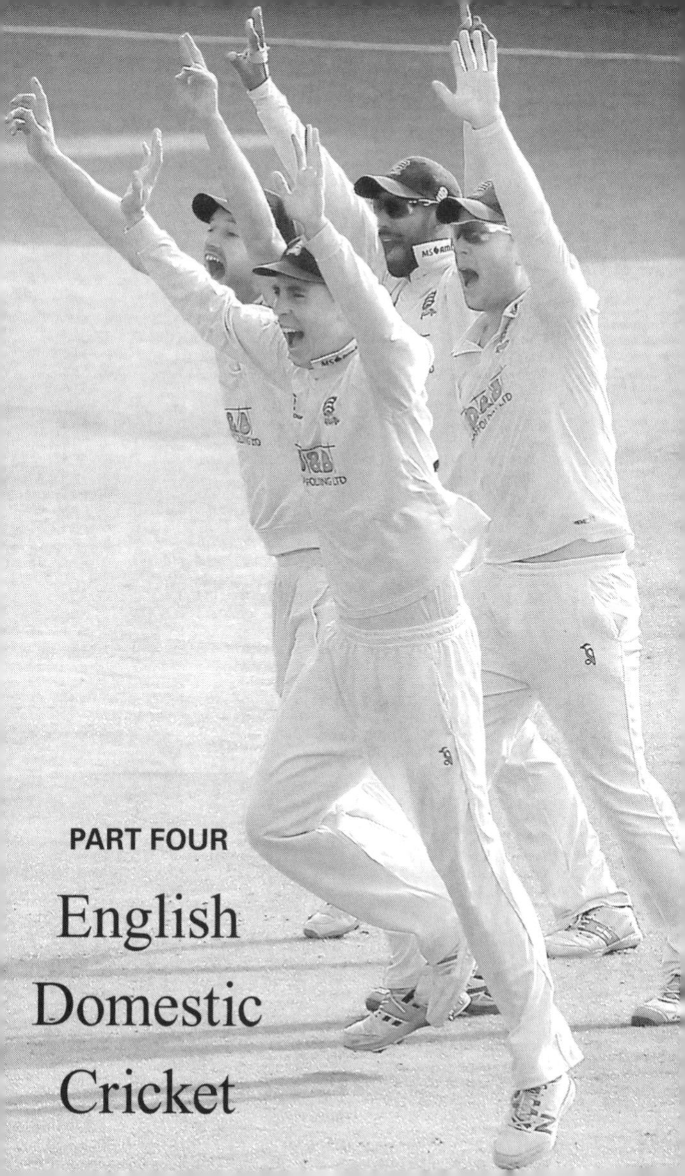

PART FOUR

English Domestic Cricket

FIRST-CLASS AVERAGES IN 2017

These include MCC v Middlesex at Abu Dhabi.

BATTING AND FIELDING (10 innings)

		M	*I*	*NO*	*R*	*HS*	*100*	*50*	*Avge*	*Ct/St*
1	†K. C. Sangakkara (*Surrey*)	10	16	2	1,491	200	8	2	106.50	6
2	†L. W. P. Wells (*Sussex*)	12	22	2	1,292	258	4	4	64.60	4
3	S. D. Hope (*West Indians*)	6	12	2	642	147	3	2	64.20	2
4	†G. S. Ballance (*Yorks, Eng Lions & Eng*)	16	24	4	1,164	203*	3	6	58.20	5
5	J. L. Denly (*Kent*)	14	24	2	1,266	227	5	5	57.54	8
6	D. K. H. Mitchell (*Worcs*)	14	26	3	1,266	161	7	3	55.04	21
7	†M. D. Stoneman (*Surrey, Eng Lions & Eng*)	17	28	1	1,481	197	4	7	54.85	6
8	R. L. Chase (*West Indians*)	5	10	3	381	110*	1	3	54.42	1
9	†A. N. Cook (*Essex & England*)	14	23	0	1,239	243	4	3	53.86	25
10	J. E. Root (*Yorks & England*)	9	15	1	751	190	2	5	53.64	9
11	†S. Chanderpaul (*Lancs*)	13	19	3	831	182	3	1	51.93	3
12	S. A. Northeast (*Kent*)	13	23	3	1,017	173*	3	4	50.85	5
13	M. H. Wessels (*Notts*)	15	20	2	913	202*	3	3	50.72	23
14	B. T. Foakes (*Surrey & England Lions*)	15	22	5	841	127*	2	4	49.47	32/2
15	P. D. Collingwood (*Durham*)	14	24	2	1,087	177	3	5	49.40	23
16	†S. van Zyl (*Sussex*)	13	22	1	1,023	166*	2	4	48.71	6
17	V. D. Philander (*Sussex & South Africans*)	8	13	5	388	73*	0	4	48.50	2
18	†M. J. Cosgrove (*Leics*)	13	25	1	1,161	188	2	6	48.37	1
19	S. R. Patel (*Notts*)	15	21	2	919	257*	2	2	48.36	7
20	M. G. K. Burgess (*Sussex*)	6	10	1	434	146	1	2	48.22	18
21	†R. J. Burns (*Surrey*)	15	24	1	1,106	219*	1	8	48.08	9
22	†N. L. J. Browne (*Essex*)	16	25	0	1,147	221	2	6	45.88	7
23	R. E. Levi (*Northants*)	10	19	3	734	115	2	3	45.87	12
24	D. I. Stevens (*Kent*)	13	21	3	822	115	2	5	45.66	2
25	J. C. Archer (*Sussex*)	13	20	6	638	81*	0	5	45.57	9
26	†C. D. J. Dent (*Glos*)	14	25	3	978	135*	2	8	44.45	13
27	S. J. Mullaney (*Notts*)	12	16	0	709	168	1	5	44.31	15
28	J. M. Clarke (*MCC, Worcs & Eng Lions*)	16	28	5	1,011	142	2	4	43.95	10
29	J. Blackwood (*West Indians*)	6	11	3	350	79*	0	3	43.75	4
30	A. L. Davies (*Lancs*)	15	26	2	1,046	140*	3	5	43.58	46/7
31	H. G. Kuhn (*S Africa A & South Africans*)	7	13	1	513	200*	2	1	42.75	4
32	R. I. Newton (*Northants*)	14	25	0	1,060	166	2	10	42.40	2
33	L. S. Livingstone (*Lancs & England Lions*)	13	22	3	805	224	2	3	42.36	12
34	†M. D. E. Holden (*Northants & Middx*)	11	19	1	758	153	2	3	42.11	5
35	A. D. Hales (*Notts*)	8	11	0	463	218	1	1	42.09	1
36	†B. M. Duckett (*MCC & Northants*)	12	21	0	881	193	3	4	41.95	16
37	A. G. Salter (*Glam*)	13	20	5	623	88	0	5	41.53	6
38	C. B. Cooke (*Glam*)	13	22	5	705	113*	1	4	41.47	40
39	J. M. R. Taylor (*Glos*)	15	21	4	697	143	2	2	41.00	10
40	S. R. Dickson (*Kent*)	14	24	0	982	318	2	4	40.91	9
41	C. T. Steel (*Durham*)	13	24	2	899	224	2	4	40.86	3
42	†D. Elgar (*Somerset & South Africans*)	11	21	1	813	158	3	4	40.65	4
43	I. J. L. Trott (*Warwicks*)	15	27	0	1,097	175	4	5	40.62	10
44	†B. A. Stokes (*Durham & England*)	8	13	0	527	112	2	4	40.53	16
45	C. T. Bancroft (*Glos*)	11	21	4	685	206*	1	4	40.29	14
46	D. W. Lawrence (*Essex & England Lions*)	16	26	4	880	141*	3	3	40.00	11
46	A. L. Hughes (*Derbys*)	13	22	2	800	142	2	3	40.00	15
48	†B. A. Godleman (*Derbys*)	12	22	2	799	156*	3	2	39.95	7
49	R. N. ten Doeschate (*Essex*)	15	20	2	717	168*	1	4	39.83	8
50	†B. T. Slater (*Derbys*)	9	17	3	556	74*	0	2	39.71	4
51	C. M. W. Read (*Notts*)	15	19	2	661	124	1	3	38.88	56/1
52	T. Westley (*Essex, Eng Lions & England*)	18	27	4	894	111	3	3	38.86	9

		M	I	NO	R	HS	100	50	Avge	Ct/St
53	O. J. D. Pope (*Surrey*)	6	10	3	270	100*	1	1	38.57	3
54	D. P. Sibley (*Surrey & Warwicks*)	14	26	5	804	104*	1	8	38.28	7
55	†K. O. A. Powell (*West Indians*)	6	12	1	412	100*	1	1	37.45	6
56	†C. A. Ingram (*Glam*)	12	20	2	672	155*	2	1	37.33	5
	T. Bavuma (*S Africa A & South Africans*)	7	13	1	448	85*	0	4	37.33	3
58	S. D. Robson (*Middx & England Lions*)	13	23	0	858	159	2	4	37.30	11
59	B. C. Brown (*Sussex*)	8	14	1	483	90	0	5	37.15	23
60	L. J. Wright (*Sussex*)	12	21	1	742	118	1	4	37.10	6
61	G. Clark (*Durham*)	12	21	0	769	109	1	6	36.61	10
62	†L. M. Reece (*Derbys*)	12	21	1	732	168	2	5	36.60	4
63	A. C. Voges (*Middx*)	9	14	3	402	92	0	3	36.54	12
64	A. M. Rossington (*Northants*)	9	14	1	475	117	2	2	36.53	19/2
65	P. Coughlin (*Durham*)	8	12	2	364	73*	0	3	36.40	3
66	D. J. Vilas (*Lancs*)	15	24	3	762	244	1	3	36.28	14
67	E. G. Barnard (*Worcs*)	14	20	4	580	75	0	5	36.25	8
68	G. J. Bailey (*Hants*)	11	18	0	651	161	2	3	36.16	5
69	S. W. Billings (*Kent & England Lions*)	8	10	2	289	70*	0	1	36.12	13
70	N. J. Selman (*Glam*)	15	27	2	902	142*	4	3	36.08	16
71	T. Köhler-Cadmore (*Worcs & Yorks*)	7	11	0	393	102	1	2	35.72	5
72	B. L. D'Oliveira (*Worcs*)	14	25	0	891	150	3	3	35.64	10
73	†M. M. Ali (*Worcs & England*)	10	17	1	569	87	0	6	35.56	6
74	A. G. Wakely (*Northants*)	14	26	4	776	112	2	2	35.27	14
75	†S. M. Davies (*Somerset*)	14	24	2	775	142	2	3	35.22	39/7
76	J. M. Vince (*Hants*)	13	21	0	738	147	2	2	35.14	13
77	P. R. Stirling (*Middx*)	8	13	0	454	111	1	3	34.92	4
78	J. A. Leaning (*Yorks*)	11	16	1	518	118	1	3	34.53	6
79	R. S. Bopara (*Essex*)	15	22	2	690	192	1	3	34.50	7
80	D. A. Payne (*Glos*)	11	12	5	238	54*	0	1	34.00	1
81	P. S. P. Handscomb (*Yorks*)	9	14	1	441	101*	1	2	33.92	7
82	J. J. Cobb (*Northants*)	11	19	5	473	96	0	2	33.78	4
83	†J. A. Simpson (*Middx*)	15	24	3	708	90	0	4	33.71	55/1
	D. R. Briggs (*Sussex*)	9	13	6	236	120*	1	0	33.71	5
85	G. H. Roderick (*Glos*)	9	13	1	403	96	0	4	33.58	24/1
86	†L. Wood (*Notts*)	7	10	3	235	44	0	0	33.57	2
87	K. S. Carlson (*Glam*)	9	14	0	469	191	1	1	33.50	4
88	S. S. Eskinazi (*Middx*)	15	27	2	837	179	2	4	33.47	11
89	O. B. Cox (*MCC & Worcs*)	15	23	1	732	124	1	3	33.27	47/1
90	S. J. Thakor (*Derbys*)	6	11	1	328	132	1	0	32.80	1
91	C. N. Ackermann (*Leics*)	12	22	3	618	118	2	1	32.52	2
92	†A. Lyth (*MCC & Yorks*)	15	26	1	805	194	2	2	32.20	22
93	†J. A. Rudolph (*Glam*)	12	21	1	634	142	2	1	31.70	3
94	G. K. Berg (*Hants*)	14	20	2	568	99*	0	2	31.55	2
95	E. J. H. Eckersley (*Leics*)	15	28	3	787	158	1	3	31.48	17
96	†D. J. Malan (*Middx & England*)	14	26	2	752	115	1	5	31.33	4
97	W. A. Tavaré (*Glos*)	11	18	1	532	110	2	2	31.29	7
98	C. J. Jordan (*Sussex*)	11	17	3	438	147	1	2	31.28	13
99	A. P. Rouse (*Kent*)	12	19	2	530	95*	0	3	31.17	35/1
100	G. C. Wilson (*Derbys*)	9	14	1	401	97	0	3	30.84	17
101	L. J. Hill (*Leics*)	12	21	3	554	85*	0	2	30.77	22/2
102	†K. H. D. Barker (*Warwicks*)	13	23	5	552	70*	0	6	30.66	2
	M. J. Richardson (*Durham*)	10	16	1	460	82	0	4	30.66	20
104	†L. A. Procter (*Lancs & Northants*)	6	10	0	306	94	0	3	30.60	3
105	†J. H. K. Adams (*Hants*)	13	19	0	580	166	2	1	30.52	15
106	S. J. Croft (*Lancs*)	10	17	1	487	115	1	1	30.43	7
107	W. L. Madsen (*Derbys*)	13	22	0	667	121	1	5	30.31	14
108	†R. McLaren (*Lancs*)	15	21	1	606	107	1	2	30.30	7
109	J. C. Hildreth (*Somerset*)	14	26	1	756	109	2	2	30.24	12
110	K. J. Abbott (*Hants*)	14	18	4	418	97*	0	2	29.85	1
111	J. S. Foster (*Essex*)	10	12	0	357	121	1	1	29.75	48/1
112	†S. M. Ervine (*Hants*)	15	23	1	653	203	1	3	29.68	14

		M	I	NO	R	HS	100	50	Avge	Ct/St
113	Z. J. Chappell (*Leics*)	7	11	2	267	66	0	1	29.66	0
114	G. H. Rhodes (*Worcs*)	8	15	2	379	52	0	2	29.15	5
115	J. Clark (*Lancs*)	12	16	1	434	140	1	1	28.93	0
116	†P. Mustard (*Glos*)	15	21	0	602	72	0	3	28.66	22
117	†M. E. Trescothick (*Somerset*)	14	27	2	714	119*	2	1	28.56	21
118	J. M. Bairstow (*Yorks & England*)	9	14	0	397	99	0	3	28.35	33/2
119	J. D. Libby (*Notts*)	15	22	2	565	109	1	1	28.25	5
120	C. A. Pujara (*Notts*)	8	12	0	333	112	1	1	27.75	7
121	†N. R. T. Gubbins (*Middx & England Lions*)	9	17	0	471	101	1	4	27.70	2
122	J. S. Patel (*Warwicks*)	13	24	2	608	100	1	2	27.63	9
123	M. L. Pettini (*Leics*)	7	12	1	303	110*	1	2	27.54	1
124	C. D. Nash (*Sussex*)	12	21	0	578	118	1	3	27.52	12
125	A. H. T. Donald (*Glam*)	12	21	1	550	66*	0	5	27.50	12
126	T. K. Curran (*Surrey*)	9	11	2	247	53	0	1	27.44	3
127	†A. Z. Lees (*MCC & Yorks*)	16	28	3	681	102	2	2	27.24	12
128	A. J. A. Wheater (*Essex*)	9	12	0	325	102	1	2	27.08	17/2
129	D. Wiese (*Sussex*)	10	15	0	404	66	0	2	26.93	3
130	N. R. D. Compton (*Middx*)	12	21	2	510	120	1	1	26.84	5
131	S. C. Cook (*Durham*)	7	14	1	348	89*	0	2	26.76	5
132	†E. J. Byrom (*Somerset*)	8	15	0	401	56	0	1	26.73	2
133	†J. C. Tredwell (*Kent*)	7	10	3	184	55	0	1	26.28	7
134	G. T. Hankins (*Glos*)	12	18	1	446	79*	0	4	26.23	20
135	L. Gregory (*MCC & Somerset*)	8	14	0	367	137	1	0	26.21	1
136	I. R. Bell (*Warwicks*)	14	25	1	629	99	0	5	26.20	9
137	†K. K. Jennings (*Durham, Eng Lions & Eng*)	17	32	2	784	102*	1	3	26.13	16
138	V. Chopra (*Essex*)	11	17	1	418	100*	1	1	26.12	18
139	H. Hameed (*Lancs & England Lions*)	14	24	4	522	88	0	3	26.10	8
140	T. B. Abell (*Somerset*)	13	25	3	572	96	0	4	26.00	12
	I. G. Holland (*Hants*)	9	13	4	234	58*	0	2	26.00	1
142	R. D. Pringle (*Durham*)	13	22	4	459	71	0	3	25.50	9
	K. C. Brathwaite (*West Indians & Yorks*)	8	16	0	408	134	1	2	25.50	4
144	P. J. Horton (*Leics*)	11	21	0	534	71	0	2	25.42	9
145	†S. G. Borthwick (*Surrey*)	13	21	1	500	108*	1	1	25.00	21
146	†S. M. Curran (*Surrey & England Lions*)	15	21	2	471	90	0	4	24.78	5
147	C. J. McKay (*Leics*)	11	18	4	347	66	0	1	24.78	2
148	J. T. A. Burnham (*Durham*)	7	11	2	223	93*	0	1	24.77	1
149	†S. C. J. Broad (*Notts & England*)	13	16	3	318	57*	0	4	24.46	7
150	D. J. Bell-Drummond (*Kent*)	14	24	1	561	90	0	3	24.39	10
151	T. D. Groenewald (*Somerset*)	10	14	8	146	41*	0	0	24.33	1
152	A. J. Hodd (*Yorks*)	13	20	2	436	59	0	4	24.22	39/1
153	†N. Wagner (*Essex*)	10	13	3	242	50	0	1	24.20	4
154	H. Z. Finch (*Sussex*)	12	21	2	453	82	0	3	23.84	16
155	†W. T. S. Porterfield (*Warwicks*)	6	11	0	262	89	0	1	23.81	4
156	M. J. Lamb (*Warwicks*)	7	14	0	329	71	0	2	23.50	3
157	A. U. Rashid (*Yorks*)	7	10	1	211	65	0	1	23.44	0
158	A. R. I. Umeed (*Warwicks*)	8	14	0	325	113	1	0	23.21	9
159	†B. A. Raine (*Leics*)	9	17	4	301	57	0	2	23.15	1
160	N. J. Dexter (*Leics*)	8	15	2	300	114	1	0	23.07	2
161	L. D. McManus (*Hants*)	11	16	2	323	41*	0	0	23.07	29/3
162	M. A. Wood (*Durham & England*)	7	12	2	229	72*	0	1	22.90	1
163	T. E. Bailey (*Lancs*)	9	12	2	226	58	0	1	22.60	1
164	T. R. Ambrose (*Warwicks*)	14	26	2	542	104	1	2	22.58	28/3
165	†K. Noema-Barnett (*Glos*)	11	14	1	291	59	0	1	22.38	6
166	G. L. van Buuren (*Glos*)	8	13	1	268	88*	0	2	22.33	3
167	R. K. Kleinveldt (*Northants*)	12	19	1	394	86	0	1	21.88	8
168	†M. T. Coles (*Kent*)	11	16	2	304	56*	0	1	21.71	12
169	†M. A. Carberry (*Hants & Leics*)	12	20	0	431	100	1	2	21.55	3
170	R. I. Keogh (*Northants*)	12	22	3	408	105*	1	1	21.47	5
171	P. D. Trego (*Somerset*)	8	12	0	257	68	0	2	21.41	1
172	†H. E. Dearden (*Leics*)	11	21	0	445	87	0	2	21.19	12

		M	I	NO	R	HS	100	50	Avge	Ct/St
173	O. P. Rayner (*Middx*)	11	15	2	274	52*	0	1	21.07	15
174	T. S. Roland-Jones (*Middx & England*)	13	20	4	334	53	0	1	20.87	2
175	R. Clarke (*Warwicks & Surrey*)	15	22	1	438	83	0	3	20.85	14
176	S. R. Hain (*Warwicks*)	9	16	1	312	81	0	2	20.80	4
177	S. W. Poynter (*Durham*)	9	14	1	269	65	0	1	20.69	30
178	T. T. Bresnan (*Yorks*)	12	16	0	330	61	0	1	20.62	9
179	J. Leach (*Worcs*)	14	19	2	347	57*	0	2	20.41	7
180	N. L. Buck (*Northants*)	9	13	3	201	43	0	0	20.10	6
181	D. M. Bess (*Somerset*)	9	14	4	198	55	0	1	19.80	5
182	J. A. Brooks (*Yorks*)	8	11	2	178	109*	1	0	19.77	2
183	D. Smit (*Derbys*)	8	13	1	237	41	0	0	19.75	18/3
184	†J. E. C. Franklin (*Middx*)	11	16	1	296	112	1	1	19.73	5
185	J. J. Weatherley (*Kent & Hants*)	8	12	0	235	36	0	0	19.58	1
186	†R. R. Rossouw (*Hants*)	8	13	0	253	99	0	1	19.46	7
187	K. A. Hope (*West Indians*)	6	12	0	231	105	1	0	19.25	5
188	L. A. Dawson (*Hants & England*)	13	22	1	404	75	0	2	19.23	7
189	T. A. I. Taylor (*Derbys*)	7	11	1	192	69	0	1	19.20	2
190	†R. J. Sidebottom (*Yorks*)	8	11	8	57	12*	0	0	19.00	2
191	D. L. Lloyd (*Glam*)	9	16	1	282	88	0	1	18.80	4
192	†W. R. S. Gidman (*Kent*)	10	17	0	319	51	0	1	18.76	14
193	J. A. R. Harris (*Middx & Kent*)	11	18	4	260	34	0	0	18.57	3
194	C. J. C. Wright (*Warwicks*)	9	16	3	241	41	0	0	18.53	2
195	S. A. Patterson (*Yorks*)	10	13	4	165	44*	0	0	18.33	5
196	L. J. Carey (*Glam*)	11	14	2	219	54	0	1	18.25	3
197	†T. P. Alsop (*MCC & Hants*)	8	13	0	235	62	0	2	18.07	9
198	S. D. Parry (*Lancs*)	14	18	1	307	44	0	0	18.05	5
199	L. J. Fletcher (*Notts*)	10	11	3	140	92	0	1	17.50	2
200	S. C. Meaker (*Surrey*)	10	14	4	174	49	0	0	17.40	3
201	S. R. Harmer (*Essex*)	15	20	3	281	64	0	2	16.52	12
202	C. Overton (*MCC & Somerset*)	14	23	3	327	44*	0	0	16.35	9
203	H. W. Podmore (*Middx, Glam & Derbys*)	7	12	2	162	66*	0	1	16.20	3
204	B. A. Hutton (*Notts*)	9	13	0	210	61	0	1	16.15	6
205	G. J. Batty (*Surrey*)	13	15	4	176	33	0	0	16.00	0
206	M. de Lange (*Glam*)	11	17	1	254	39	0	0	15.87	5
207	T. C. Fell (*Worcs*)	13	23	1	323	47	0	0	14.68	7
208	Azharullah (*Northants*)	7	10	5	73	23	0	0	14.60	1
209	M. G. Hogan (*Glam*)	13	17	10	100	29*	0	0	14.28	4
210	†M. E. Claydon (*Kent*)	10	13	5	111	21*	0	0	13.87	1
211	†M. J. Leach (*MCC, Somerset & Eng Lions*)	16	24	5	257	52	0	1	13.52	6
212	D. Klein (*Leics*)	9	14	3	138	26	0	0	12.54	5
213	T. G. Helm (*Middx & England Lions*)	8	10	1	112	28	0	0	12.44	4
214	C. Rushworth (*Durham*)	13	17	3	174	57	0	1	12.42	5
215	L. C. Norwell (*Glos*)	12	13	5	99	24	0	0	12.37	4
216	†T. J. Murtagh (*Middx*)	12	17	6	134	27	0	0	12.18	2
217	†B. M. A. J. Mendis (*Derbys*)	7	12	1	132	27	0	0	12.00	3
	†J. M. Anderson (*Lancs & England*)	13	16	11	60	13*	0	0	12.00	8
219	S. T. Finn (*Middx*)	11	14	6	95	31*	0	0	11.87	6
220	B. O. Coad (*Yorks*)	13	16	5	128	28	0	0	11.63	1
221	C. N. Miles (*Glos*)	10	13	1	137	47	0	0	11.41	2
222	K. M. Jarvis (*Lancs*)	10	12	2	106	30	0	0	10.60	3
223	A. P. Palladino (*Derbys*)	11	18	2	161	32	0	0	10.06	3
224	M. S. Crane (*MCC, Hants & Eng Lions*)	10	12	5	69	29	0	0	9.85	3
225	J. C. Tongue (*Worcs*)	14	18	3	138	41	0	0	9.20	2
226	H. F. Gurney (*Notts*)	12	13	5	62	42*	0	0	7.75	1
227	B. W. Sanderson (*Northants*)	10	16	5	72	16*	0	0	6.54	3
228	F. H. Edwards (*Hants*)	10	11	4	43	20	0	0	6.14	0
229	J. A. Porter (*Essex & England Lions*)	15	17	8	53	10*	0	0	5.88	4
230	G. Onions (*Durham*)	8	10	0	58	15	0	0	5.80	1
231	R. N. Sidebottom (*Warwicks*)	6	12	5	26	13	0	0	3.71	0

BOWLING (10 wickets in 5 innings)

		Style	O	M	R	W	BB	5I	Avge
1	J. L. Pattinson (*Notts*)	RFM	139.3	34	386	32	5-29	2	12.06
2	Mohammad Amir (*Essex*)	LF	76.2	19	189	14	5-18	2	13.50
3	J. M. Anderson (*Lancs & England*)	RFM	415	125	938	60	7-42	4	15.63
4	J. A. Porter (*Essex & England Lions*)	RFM	459	108	1,423	85	7-55	5	16.74
5	R. E. van der Merwe (*Somerset*)	SLA	68.4	17	189	11	4-22	0	17.18
6	L. C. Norwell (*Glos*)	RFM	332	70	1,069	59	8-43	5	18.11
7	K. J. Abbott (*Hants*)	RFM	415.3	131	1,092	60	7-41	4	18.20
8	D. I. Stevens (*Kent*)	RM	414.4	109	1,157	63	8-75	7	18.36
9	R. J. Gleeson (*Northants*)	RFM	222.2	44	745	40	5-46	3	18.62
10	K. K. Jennings (*Durham, E Lions & Eng*)	RM	76	11	251	13	3-37	0	19.30
11	S. R. Harmer (*Essex*)	OB	546.3	128	1,429	74	9-95	4	19.31
12	J. Leach (*Worcs*)	RFM	397.5	73	1,338	69	5-32	4	19.39
13	S. J. Mullaney (*Notts*)	RM	177	58	486	25	5-32	1	19.44
14	B. O. Coad (*Yorks*)	RFM	386.4	108	1,081	53	6-25	4	20.39
15	M. G. Hogan (*Glam*)	RFM	383.4	88	1,075	52	6-43	3	20.67
16	R. J. Sidebottom (*Yorks*)	LFM	186.4	43	518	25	5-56	1	20.72
17	R. H. Patel (*Middx*)	SLA	102	8	336	16	7-81	2	21.00
18	O. J. Hannon-Dalby (*Warwicks*)	RFM	108.1	27	316	15	4-29	0	21.06
19	C. Overton (*MCC & Somerset*)	RFM	404.4	114	1,122	53	5-47	2	21.16
20	S. Mahmood (*Lancs*)	RFM	69.3	10	256	12	4-50	0	21.33
21	B. W. Sanderson (*Northants*)	RFM	334.1	93	860	40	5-39	2	21.50
22	G. C. Viljoen (*Derbys*)	RFM	139.5	27	517	24	8-90	3	21.54
23	O. E. Robinson (*Sussex*)	RM/OB	149.3	30	412	19	5-69	1	21.68
24	Azharullah (*Northants*)	RFM	192	36	677	31	5-63	2	21.83
25	L. Gregory (*MCC & Somerset*)	RFM	204.3	56	591	27	5-32	2	21.88
26	I. G. Holland (*Hants*)	RFM	158	45	416	19	4-16	0	21.89
27	M. W. Parkinson (*Lancs*)	LB	76.4	7	308	14	4-68	0	22.00
28	R. N. Sidebottom (*Warwicks*)	RFM	129.5	28	510	23	4-29	0	22.17
29	L. J. Fletcher (*Notts*)	RFM	268.1	51	843	38	4-35	0	22.18
30	K. M. Jarvis (*Lancs*)	RFM	274.3	71	804	36	6-61	2	22.33
	K. A. J. Roach (*West Indians*)	RFM	128.2	36	402	18	5-43	2	22.33
32	N. L. Buck (*Northants*)	RFM	241.4	40	815	36	6-34	3	22.63
33	G. Onions (*Durham*)	RFM	237	48	725	32	6-62	1	22.65
34	T. van der Gugten (*Glam*)	RFM	158.2	43	505	22	5-101	1	22.95
35	J. Overton (*Somerset & England Lions*)	RFM	126	24	391	17	3-30	0	23.00
	A. Sakande (*Sussex*)	RFM	76.4	11	299	13	5-43	1	23.00
37	R. K. Kleinveldt (*Northants*)	RFM	350.1	68	1,153	50	9-65	2	23.06
38	D. M. Bess (*Somerset*)	OB	265.5	62	843	36	7-117	3	23.41
	R. F. Higgins (*Middx*)	OB/RM	98	24	281	12	4-75	0	23.41
40	B. A. Raine (*Leics*)	RFM	256.1	54	777	33	6-66	2	23.54
41	F. H. Edwards (*Hants*)	RFM	221.5	35	794	33	5-49	2	24.06
42	S. J. Cook (*Lough MCCU & Essex*)	RFM	186.4	42	533	22	5-18	2	24.22
43	M. M. Ali (*Worcs & England*)	OB	233	40	805	33	6-53	2	24.39
44	T. E. Bailey (*Lancs*)	RFM	223.2	52	635	26	5-44	2	24.42
45	T. D. Groenewald (*Somerset*)	RFM	243.4	71	646	26	5-58	1	24.84
46	J. A. R. Harris (*Middx & Kent*)	RFM	293.1	61	973	39	4-56	0	24.94
47	R. McLaren (*Lancs*)	RFM	389.1	91	1,150	46	4-37	0	25.00
	J. T. Ball (*Notts*)	RFM	183.2	39	675	27	3-36	0	25.00
49	E. G. Barnard (*Worcs*)	RFM	321.3	48	1,187	47	4-23	0	25.25
50	J. C. Archer (*Sussex*)	RFM	475.1	91	1,543	61	7-67	4	25.29
51	V. D. Philander (*Sussex & South Africans*)	RFM	201.3	47	663	26	4-39	0	25.50
52	J. C. Tongue (*Worcs*)	RFM	333.4	46	1,212	47	6-97	2	25.78
53	C. Rushworth (*Durham*)	RFM	436.3	96	1,217	47	5-52	1	25.89
54	C. McKerr (*Derbys & Surrey*)	RFM	110.5	20	392	15	5-54	2	26.13
55	M. H. A. Footitt (*Surrey & Notts*)	LFM	220.5	33	814	31	6-14	2	26.25
56	Sukhjit Singh (*Warwicks*)	SLA	152.4	30	452	17	6-144	2	26.58
57	G. K. Berg (*Hants*)	RFM	391.5	103	987	37	4-28	0	26.67
58	B. A. Hutton (*Notts*)	RFM	289.2	64	995	37	5-52	2	26.89

		Style	O	M	R	W	BB	5I	Avge
59	T. S. Roland-Jones (*Middx & England*)	RFM	366.4	86	1,214	45	5-57	1	26.97
60	L. A. Dawson (*Hants & England*)	SLA	395	102	1,004	37	4-22	0	27.13
61	M. J. Leach (*MCC, Somerset & Eng Lions*)	SLA	572.1	157	1,494	55	6-78	4	27.16
62	B. J. McCarthy (*Durham*)	RFM	164.2	23	653	24	6-63	1	27.20
63	S. D. Parry (*Lancs*)	SLA	334.1	75	792	29	5-45	1	27.31
64	S. C. J. Broad (*Notts & England*)	RFM	367.2	88	1,038	38	3-34	0	27.31
65	M. Morkel (*South Africans*)	RF	175	37	550	20	4-41	0	27.50
66	T. J. Murtagh (*Middx*)	RFM	372	93	995	36	6-63	1	27.63
67	W. R. S. Gidman (*Kent*)	RFM	78.2	14	279	10	3-0	0	27.90
68	S. R. Patel (*Notts*)	SLA	243	64	732	26	5-43	1	28.15
69	J. D. Shantry (*Worcs*)	LFM	100.3	19	310	11	3-54	0	28.18
70	L. Wood (*Notts*)	LFM	139.2	17	540	19	4-31	0	28.42
71	H. Qadri (*Derbys*)	OB	101.3	22	288	10	5-60	1	28.80
72	R. Clarke (*Warwicks & Surrey*)	RFM	378	96	1,095	38	7-55	1	28.81
73	R. Ashwin (*Worcs*)	OB	184.2	29	583	20	5-68	2	29.15
74	W. S. Davis (*Derbys*)	RFM	103.5	13	410	14	4-60	0	29.28
75	H. F. Gurney (*Notts*)	LFM	307.1	56	1,032	35	4-19	0	29.48
76	J. E. C. Franklin (*Middx*)	LFM	115	22	355	12	4-40	0	29.58
77	P. Coughlin (*Durham*)	RFM	208.1	31	804	27	5-49	2	29.77
78	J. S. Patel (*Warwicks*)	OB	482	149	1,222	41	6-50	1	29.80
79	S. A. Patterson (*Yorks*)	RFM	306.2	78	808	27	4-46	0	29.92
80	J. Clark (*Lancs*)	RM	191.5	26	662	22	4-81	0	30.09
81	D. A. Payne (*Glos*)	LFM	272.1	50	845	28	3-29	0	30.17
82	B. M. A. J. Mendis (*Derbys*)	LB	252	24	908	30	6-204	1	30.26
83	L. J. Carey (*Glam*)	RFM	279.3	54	1,060	35	4-85	0	30.28
84	S. T. Finn (*Middx*)	RFM	287.2	45	1,045	34	8-79	1	30.73
85	T. T. Bresnan (*Yorks*)	RFM	262	56	934	30	4-53	0	31.13
86	Imran Tahir (*Derbys*)	LB	123.1	16	407	13	5-76	2	31.30
87	B. T. J. Wheal (*Hants*)	RFM	120.5	22	476	15	4-98	0	31.73
88	G. J. Batty (*Surrey*)	OB	312.1	67	859	27	3-70	0	31.81
89	K. Noema-Barnett (*Glos*)	RM	254.4	59	737	23	4-31	0	32.04
90	K. Rabada (*South Africans*)	RF	151	30	514	16	4-91	0	32.12
91	N. J. Dexter (*Leics*)	RM	121	23	456	14	5-71	2	32.57
92	T. G. Helm (*Middx & England Lions*)	RFM	234.5	40	815	25	5-59	1	32.60
93	C. F. Parkinson (*Leics*)	SLA	147.2	14	556	17	8-148	1	32.70
94	C. J. Jordan (*Sussex*)	RFM	353.5	57	1,182	36	5-46	1	32.83
95	S. G. Whittingham (*Sussex*)	RFM	105.5	12	494	15	5-80	1	32.93
96	K. A. Maharaj (*South Africans*)	SLA	180.5	33	562	17	4-85	0	33.05
97	M. J. Potts (*Durham*)	RFM	163	37	465	14	3-48	0	33.21
98	D. Olivier (*S Africa A & South Africans*)	RFM	109.2	17	440	13	3-38	0	33.84
99	D. Klein (*Leics*)	LFM	206	21	958	28	6-80	2	34.21
100	K. H. D. Barker (*Warwicks*)	LFM	315	63	994	29	3-21	0	34.27
101	J. W. Hastings (*Worcs*)	RFM	161.1	41	550	16	3-44	0	34.37
102	C. A. J. Meschede (*Glam*)	RM	138	22	482	14	4-61	0	34.42
103	T. K. Curran (*Surrey*)	RFM	256.3	50	832	24	4-69	0	34.66
	M. W. Pillans (*Leics*)	RFM	101.1	9	416	12	3-63	0	34.66
105	G. H. S. Garton (*Sussex & England Lions*)	LFM	98	5	419	12	3-20	0	34.91
106	D. L. Piedt (*South Africa A*)	OB	109.1	20	352	10	3-36	0	35.20
107	W. B. Rankin (*Warwicks*)	RFM	114.2	13	423	12	3-48	0	35.25
108	N. Wagner (*Essex*)	LFM	316.4	54	1,095	31	6-48	1	35.32
109	A. P. Palladino (*Derbys*)	RFM	274.4	58	889	25	4-36	0	35.56
110	J. O. Holder (*West Indians*)	RFM	128.2	24	428	12	4-54	0	35.66
111	H. W. Podmore (*Middx, Glam & Derbys*)	RM	137.4	22	503	14	3-25	0	35.92
112	M. E. Claydon (*Kent*)	RFM	262.5	48	936	26	5-54	1	36.00
113	C. N. Miles (*Glos*)	RFM	245	35	974	27	5-99	1	36.07
114	B. A. Stokes (*Durham & England*)	RFM	176.3	37	582	16	6-22	1	36.37
115	C. J. McKay (*Leics*)	RFM	315.3	97	809	22	4-35	0	36.77
116	S. van Zyl (*Sussex*)	RM	116.1	24	368	10	2-25	0	36.80
117	J. A. Brooks (*Yorks*)	RFM	205	24	865	23	5-113	1	37.60
118	C. J. C. Wright (*Warwicks*)	RFM	221.3	41	757	20	5-113	1	37.85

		Style	O	M	R	W	BB	5I	Avge
119	D. Wiese (*Sussex*)	RFM	248.3	44	834	22	4-63	0	37.90
120	Yasir Shah (*Kent*)	LB	155.5	22	533	14	5-132	1	38.07
121	S. C. Meaker (*Surrey*)	RF	235.3	38	926	24	4-92	0	38.58
122	M. de Lange (*Glam*)	RF	345.5	47	1,315	34	5-95	1	38.67
123	O. P. Rayner (*Middx*)	OB	265.3	62	778	20	4-35	0	38.90
124	J. W. Dernbach (*Surrey*)	RFM	157.3	40	476	12	3-51	0	39.66
125	S. C. Kerrigan (*Lancs & Northants*)	SLA	203.4	38	676	17	4-62	0	39.76
126	W. J. Weighell (*Durham*)	RM	94.5	8	438	11	3-51	0	39.81
127	R. S. Bopara (*Essex*)	RM	145.2	18	525	13	2-10	0	40.38
128	T. A. I. Taylor (*Derbys*)	RFM	173	34	688	17	4-67	0	40.47
129	M. T. Coles (*Kent*)	RFM	335	60	1,313	32	6-84	1	41.03
130	M. A. Wood (*Durham & England*)	RFM	179	30	586	14	5-54	1	41.85
131	S. M. Curran (*Surrey & England Lions*)	LFM	388.5	74	1,312	31	3-74	0	42.32
132	J. Shaw (*Yorks & Glos*)	RFM	143	22	594	14	5-118	1	42.42
133	A. F. Milne (*Kent*)	RF	184	51	572	13	4-68	0	44.00
134	J. M. R. Taylor (*Glos*)	OB	152.2	15	633	14	3-50	0	45.21
135	R. D. Pringle (*Durham*)	OB	197.5	41	688	15	4-73	0	45.86
136	Azeem Rafiq (*Yorks*)	OB	127.4	17	459	10	3-50	0	45.90
137	C. J. Liddle (*Glos*)	LFM	131.1	26	468	10	2-30	0	46.80
138	A. G. Salter (*Glam*)	OB	170.4	13	676	14	3-60	0	48.28
139	M. D. Taylor (*Glos*)	LM	127	19	492	10	3-80	0	49.20
140	D. R. Briggs (*Sussex*)	SLA	264.1	47	788	16	3-40	0	49.25
141	A. U. Rashid (*Yorks*)	LB	108	10	500	10	3-94	0	50.00
142	M. S. Crane (*MCC, Hants & Eng Lions*)	LB	270.1	34	1,058	20	5-40	1	52.90
143	Z. J. Chappell (*Leics*)	RFM	133.5	17	567	10	4-108	0	56.70

The following bowlers took ten wickets in fewer than five innings:

	Style	O	M	R	W	BB	5I	Avge
W. A. T. Beer (*Sussex*)	LB	62.4	5	179	15	6-29	2	11.93
R. J. Crichard (*Cambridge Univ*)	RM	50.4	11	142	11	6-68	2	12.90
B. E. Hendricks (*South Africa A*)	LFM	62.5	13	199	10	5-20	1	19.90

BOWLING STYLES

LB	Leg-breaks (7)	**RF**	Right-arm fast (5)
LF	Left-arm fast (1)	**RFM**	Right-arm fast medium (80)
LFM	Left-arm fast medium (14)	**RM**	Right-arm medium (14)
LM	Left-arm medium (1)	**SLA**	Slow left-arm (11)
OB	Off-breaks (15)		

The total comes to 148 because R. F. Higgins and O. E. Robinson have two styles of bowling.

INDIVIDUAL SCORES OF 100 AND OVER

There were **219** three-figure innings in 153 first-class matches in 2017, 80 fewer than in 2016, when 171 matches were played. Of these, 18 were double-hundreds, compared with 26 in 2016. The list includes 181 in the County Championship, compared with 254 in 2016.

K. C. Sangakkara (8)
136 Surrey v Lancs, The Oval
105 Surrey v Warwicks, Birmingham
114 } Surrey v Middx, Lord's
120 }
200 Surrey v Essex, Chelmsford
180* Surrey v Yorks, Leeds
164 Surrey v Yorks, The Oval
157 Surrey v Somerset, The Oval

D. K. H. Mitchell (7)
120 Worcs v Derbys, Derby
161 Worcs v Northants, Northampton
121 Worcs v Sussex, Hove
142 Worcs v Kent, Worcester
130 Worcs v Glos, Worcester
139* Worcs v Notts, Nottingham
123* Worcs v Durham, Worcester

J. L. Denly (5)
101 Kent v Leeds/Brad MCCU, Canterbury
119 Kent v Sussex, Tunbridge Wells
227 Kent v Worcs, Worcester
182 Kent v Northants, Beckenham
152 Kent v Glam, Canterbury

A. N. Cook (4)
110 Essex v Somerset, Taunton
124 Essex v Hants, Chelmsford
193 Essex v Middx, Chelmsford
243 England v West Indies, Birmingham

N. J. Selman (4)
117 Glam v Leics, Leicester
116* Glam v Durham, Swansea
103 Glam v Durham, Chester-le-Street
142* Glam v Glos, Cardiff

M. D. Stoneman (4)
165 Surrey v Warwicks, The Oval
123 Surrey v Warwicks, Birmingham
197 Surrey v Essex, Guildford
131 Surrey v Yorks, The Oval

I. J. L. Trott (4)
130 Warwicks v Oxford MCCU, Oxford
151 Warwicks v Surrey, The Oval
175 Warwicks v Somerset, Taunton
101 Warwicks v Hants, Southampton

L. W. P. Wells (4)
258 Sussex v Durham, Hove
155 Sussex v Worcs, Hove
122 Sussex v Durham, Chester-le-Street
103 Sussex v Notts, Hove

G. S. Ballance (3)
120 Yorks v Hants, Leeds
108 } Yorks v Hants, Southampton
203* }

S. Chanderpaul (3)
182 Lancs v Surrey, The Oval
106 Lancs v Yorks, Manchester
117* Lancs v Warwicks, Birmingham

P. D. Collingwood (3)
127 Durham v Glam, Swansea
120 Durham v Kent, Canterbury
177 Durham v Derbys, Chester-le-Street

A. L. Davies (3)
140* Lancs v Essex, Chelmsford
130 Lancs v Somerset, Manchester
115 Lancs v Hants, Manchester

B. L. D'Oliveira (3)
150 Worcs v Derbys, Derby
122 Worcs v Durham, Chester-le-Street
138 Worcs v Leics, Worcester

B. M. Duckett (3)
112 Northants v Leics, Northampton
105 Northants v Kent, Beckenham
193 Northants v Sussex, Northampton

D. Elgar (3)
113* Somerset v Lancs, Manchester
158 Somerset v Middx, Lord's
136 South Africa v England, The Oval

B. A. Godleman (3)
156* Derbys v Northants, Derby
141 Derbys v Leics, Derby
121 Derbys v Notts, Nottingham

S. D. Hope (3)
107* West Indians v Derbys, Derby
147 } West Indies v England, Leeds
118* }

D. W. Lawrence (3)
141* Essex v Lancs, Chelmsford
107 Essex v Surrey, Chelmsford
101 Essex v Hants, Southampton

S. A. Northeast (3)
173* Kent v Sussex, Hove
109* Kent v Durham, Canterbury
110 Kent v Durham, Chester-le-Street

M. H. Wessels (3)
202* Notts v Sussex, Nottingham
120 Notts v Glam, Cardiff
116 Notts v Northants, Nottingham

T. Westley (3)
111 Essex v Hants, Chelmsford
108* Essex v Surrey, Guildford
106* England Lions v S. Africans, Worcester

C. N. Ackermann (2)
118 Leics v Derbys, Derby
105 Leics v Northants, Northampton

J. H. K. Adams (2)
166 Hants v Warwicks, Southampton
144 Hants v Surrey, The Oval

G. J. Bailey (2)
127 Hants v Lancs, Manchester
161 Hants v Surrey, The Oval

N. L. J. Browne (2)
113 Essex v Durham MCCU, Chelmsford
221 Essex v Middx, Chelmsford

J. M. Clarke (2)
142 }
110* } Worcs v Kent, Worcester

M. J. Cosgrove (2)
188 Leics v Derbys, Derby
128 Leics v Sussex, Leicester

S. M. Davies (2)
142 Somerset v Surrey, Taunton
111 Somerset v Lancs, Taunton

C. D. J. Dent (2)
101 Glos v Durham, Bristol
135* Glos v Worcs, Cheltenham

S. R. Dickson (2)
318 Kent v Northants, Beckenham
142 Kent v West Indians, Canterbury

S. S. Eskinazi (2)
100 Middx v Essex, Lord's
179 Middx v Warwicks, Birmingham

B. T. Foakes (2)
127* England Lions v S. Africa A, Canterbury
110 Surrey v Yorks, The Oval

J. C. Hildreth (2)
101* Somerset v Yorks, Scarborough
109 Somerset v Middx, Taunton

M. D. E. Holden (2)
124 Northants v Durham, Chester-le-Street
153 Northants v Kent, Beckenham

A. L. Hughes (2)
108 Derbys v Durham, Chesterfield
142 Derbys v Glos, Bristol

C. A. Ingram (2)
137 Glam v Leics, Leicester
155* Glam v Notts, Cardiff

H. G. Kuhn (2)
200* S. Africa A v Hants, Southampton
105 S. Africa A v England Lions, Canterbury

T. W. M. Latham (2)
124 Durham v Leics, Leicester
119 Durham v Kent, Chester-le-Street

A. Z. Lees (2)
100 Yorks v Leeds/Brad MCCU, Leeds
102 Yorks v Surrey, The Oval

R. E. Levi (2)
101 Northants v Glam, Cardiff
115 Northants v Notts, Northampton

L. S. Livingstone (2)
168 Lancs v Somerset, Manchester
224 Lancs v Warwicks, Manchester

A. Lyth (2)
194 Yorks v Leeds/Brad MCCU, Leeds
100 Yorks v Lancs, Leeds

R. I. Newton (2)
166 Northants v Lough MCCU, Northampton
108 Northants v Derbys, Northampton

S. R. Patel (2)
257* Notts v Glos, Bristol
247 Notts v Leics, Nottingham

L. M. Reece (2)
168 Derbys v Northants, Derby
106 Derbys v Durham, Chester-le-Street

S. D. Robson (2)
149 Middx v Essex, Lord's
159 Middx v Yorks, Lord's

J. E. Root (2)
190 England v South Africa, Lord's
136 England v West Indies, Birmingham

A. M. Rossington (2)
117 Northants v Lough MCCU, Northampton
112 Northants v Kent, Beckenham

J. A. Rudolph (2)
142 Glam v Cardiff MCCU, Cardiff
111 Glam v Worcs, Worcester

C. T. Steel (2)
128 Durham v Northants, Chester-le-Street
224 Durham v Leics, Leicester

D. I. Stevens (2)
115 Kent v Leeds/Brad MCCU, Canterbury
100 Kent v Leics, Leicester

B. A. Stokes (2)
112 England v South Africa, The Oval
100 England v West Indies, Leeds

W. A. Tavaré (2)
110 Glos v Durham MCCU, Bristol
101 Glos v Leics, Bristol

J. M. R. Taylor (2)
143 Glos v Worcs, Cheltenham
101* Glos v Worcs, Worcester

M. E. Trescothick (2)
106 Somerset v Warwicks, Taunton
119* Somerset v Warwicks, Birmingham

S. van Zyl (2)
149 Sussex v Durham, Hove
166* Sussex v Leics, Arundel

J. M. Vince (2)
147 Hants v Yorks, Southampton
104 Hants v Surrey, The Oval

A. G. Wakely (2)
104* Northants v Lough MCCU, Northampton
112 Northants v Leics, Northampton

The following each played one three-figure innings:

T. R. Ambrose, 104, Warwicks v Lancs, Manchester.

C. T. Bancroft, 206*, Glos v Kent, Bristol; R. S. Bopara, 192, Essex v Warwicks, Chelmsford; S. G. Borthwick, 108*, Surrey v Lancs, The Oval; J. R. Bracey, 156, Glos v Glam, Cardiff; K. C. Brathwaite, 134, West Indies v England, Leeds; D. R. Briggs, 120*, Sussex v South Africa A, Arundel; J. A. Brooks, 109*, Yorks v Lancs, Manchester; M. G. K. Burgess, 146, Sussex v Notts, Hove; R. J. Burns, 219*, Surrey v Hants, The Oval.

M. A. Carberry, 100, Hants v Cardiff MCCU, Southampton; K. S. Carlson, 191, Glam v Glos, Cardiff; R. L. Chase, 110*, West Indians v Derbys, Derby; V. Chopra, 100*, Essex v Middx, Chelmsford; G. Clark, 109, Durham v Glam, Chester-le-Street; J. Clark, 140, Lancs v Surrey, The Oval; N. R. D. Compton, 120, Middx v Essex, Chelmsford; C. B. Cooke, 113*, Glam v Notts, Cardiff; O. B. Cox, 124, Worcs v Glos, Cheltenham; M. J. J. Critchley, 102, Derbys v Durham, Chesterfield; S. J. Croft, 115, Lancs v Surrey, Manchester.

N. J. Dexter, 114, Leics v Worcs, Worcester.

E. J. H. Eckersley, 158, Leics v Derbys, Derby; S. M. Ervine, 203, Hants v Warwicks, Southampton; S. T. Evans, 114, Loughborough MCCU v Northants, Northampton.

J. S. Foster, 121, Essex v Warwicks, Chelmsford; J. E. C. Franklin, 112, Middx v Surrey, Lord's.

L. Gregory, 137, Somerset v Middx, Lord's; N. R. T. Gubbins, 101, Middx v Essex, Lord's.

A. D. Hales, 218, Notts v Derbys, Derby; P. S. P. Handscomb, 101*, Yorks v Lancs, Manchester; K. A. Hope, 105, West Indians v Derbys, Derby; B. A. C. Howell, 163, Glos v Glam, Cardiff.

K. K. Jennings, 102*, Durham v Notts, Chester-le-Street; C. J. Jordan, 147, Sussex v Notts, Hove.

R. I. Keogh, 105*, Northants v Leics, Northampton; H. Klaasen, 103, South Africa A v Hants, Southampton; T. Köhler-Cadmore, 102, Worcs v Glam, Cardiff; N. R. Kumar, 141, Loughborough MCCU v Northants, Northampton.

J. A. Leaning, 118, Yorks v Lancs, Manchester; J. D. Libby, 109, Notts v Glam, Cardiff; M. J. Lumb, 117, Notts v Glos, Nottingham.

R. McLaren, 107, Lancs v Hants, Manchester; W. L. Madsen, 121, Derbys v Glos, Bristol; D. J. Malan, 115, Middx v Surrey, Lord's; A. K. Markram, 102*, South Africa A v Hants, Southampton; S. E. Marsh, 125*, Yorks v Surrey, The Oval; S. J. Mullaney, 168, Notts v Kent, Nottingham.

C. D. Nash, 118, Sussex v Worcs, Worcester.

J. S. Patel, 100, Warwicks v Yorks, Leeds; M. L. Pettini, 110*, Leics v Glam, Leicester; O. J. D. Pope, 100*, Surrey v Hants, Southampton; K. O. A. Powell, 100*, West Indians v Derbys, Derby; C. A. Pujara, 112, Notts v Glos, Nottingham.

C. M. W. Read, 124, Notts v Sussex, Hove; W. T. Root, 132, Notts v Sussex, Hove.

D. P. Sibley, 104*, Surrey v Oxford MCCU, Oxford; P. R. Stirling, 111, Middx v Yorks, Lord's.

R. N. ten Doeschate, 168*, Essex v Surrey, Guildford; S. J. Thakor, 132, Derbys v Leics, Derby; C. O. Thurston, 126, Loughborough MCCU v Northants, Northampton.

A. R. I. Umeed, 113, Warwicks v Lancs, Birmingham.

D. J. Vilas, 244, Lancs v Hants, Manchester.

I. J. Westwood, 153, Warwicks v Surrey, Birmingham; A. J. A. Wheater, 102, Essex v Durham MCCU, Chelmsford; L. J. Wright, 118, Sussex v Glos, Hove.

FASTEST HUNDREDS BY BALLS...

Balls		
66	A. M. Rossington	Northants v Loughborough MCCU, Northampton.
74	V. Chopra	Essex v Middx, Chelmsford.
76	P. S. P. Handscomb	Yorks v Lancs, Manchester.
77	M. H. Wessels	Notts v Northants, Nottingham.
89	M. H. Wessels	Notts v Sussex, Nottingham.
89	B. M. Duckett	Northants v Leics, Northampton.
91	E. J. H. Eckersley	Leics v Derbys, Derby.
92	R. E. Levi	Northants v Notts, Northampton.
95	R. E. Levi	Northants v Glam, Cardiff.
96	D. I. Stevens	Kent v Leics, Leicester.
97	L. W. P. Wells	Sussex v Notts, Hove.
100	L. J. Wright	Sussex v Glos, Hove.

...AND THE SLOWEST

Balls		
331	A. R. I. Umeed	Warwicks v Lancs, Birmingham.
294	C. A. Ingram	Glam v Notts, Cardiff.
271	W. A. Tavaré	Glos v Leics, Bristol.
261	J. H. K. Adams	Hants v Warwicks, Southampton.
260	J. A. Leaning	Yorks v Lancs, Manchester.
249	N. J. Selman	Glam v Durham, Chester-le-Street.
242	C. T. Steel	Durham v Leics, Leicester.
241	C. D. J. Dent	Glos v Durham, Bristol.
240	N. L. J. Browne	Essex v Middx, Chelmsford.

TEN WICKETS IN A MATCH

There were **22** instances of bowlers taking ten or more wickets in a first-class match in 2017, seven more than in 2016. Nineteen were in the County Championship.

S. R. Harmer (2)
14-128 Essex v Warwicks, Chelmsford
14-172 Essex v Middx, Chelmsford

L. C. Norwell (2)
10-99 Glos v Leics, Bristol
10-95 Glos v Leics, Leicester

The following each took ten wickets in a match on one occasion:

M. M. Ali, 10-112, England v South Africa, Lord's; J. C. Archer, 11-137, Sussex v Leics, Leicester.

T. E. Bailey, 10-98, Lancs v Middx, Lord's; W. A. T. Beer, 11-91, Sussex v South Africa A, Arundel; D. M. Bess, 10-162, Somerset v Hants, Taunton.

B. O. Coad, 10-102, Yorks v Warwicks, Birmingham; P. Coughlin, 10-133, Durham v Northants, Chester-le-Street; R. J. Crichard, 11-142, Cambridge Univ v Oxford Univ, Cambridge.

M. G. Hogan, 10-87, Glam v Kent, Canterbury; B. A. Hutton, 10-126, Notts v Derbys, Derby.

R. K. Kleinveldt, 13-98, Northants v Notts, Northampton.

J. Leach, 10-122, Worcs v Northants, Worcester.

C. McKerr, 10-141, Derbys v Northants, Northampton; Mohammad Amir, 10-72, Essex v Yorks, Scarborough.

C. F. Parkinson, 10-185, Leics v Worcs, Worcester; R. H. Patel, 12-173, Middx v Somerset, Taunton; J. A. Porter, 12-95, Essex v Somerset, Chelmsford.

G. C. Viljoen, 15-170, Derbys v Sussex, Hove.

SPECSAVERS COUNTY CHAMPIONSHIP IN 2017

NEVILLE SCOTT

***Division One** 1 Essex 2 Lancashire*
***Division Two** 1 Worcestershire 2 Nottinghamshire*

Life, it is said (usually by the comfortable), comes down to paths taken or fatefully missed. On June days in both of the last two years, Britons found themselves at the polls, invited by prime ministers who believed their future plans would thus be secured. Each made a massive miscalculation. David Cameron saw the nation opt for Brexit; Theresa May, his successor, found her authority shredded when the people erased her majority. Tricky business, judgment.

COUNTY CHAMPIONSHIP TABLES

Division One	*Matches*	*Won*	*Lost*	*Drawn*	*Bonus points Batting*	*Bonus points Bowling*	*Penalty*	*Points*
1 Essex (*1*)	14	10	0	4	28	40	0	248
2 Lancashire (**7**)	14	5	3	6	29	37	0	176
3 Surrey (**5**)	14	2	2	10	47	34	0	163
4 Yorkshire (**3**)	14	4	5	5	24	35	0	148
5 Hampshire (**8**)	14	3	3	8	24	36	0	148
6 Somerset (**2**)	14	4	6	4	24	39	0	147
7 Middlesex (**1**)	14	3	4	7	28	37	2	146
8 Warwickshire (**6**)	14	1	9	4	19	31	0	86

Division Two	*Matches*	*Won*	*Lost*	*Drawn*	*Bonus points Batting*	*Bonus points Bowling*	*Penalty*	*Points*
1 Worcestershire (*3*)	14	9	3	2	45	39	0	238
2 Nottinghamshire (**9**)	14	7	2	5	44	41	0	222
3 Northamptonshire (*5*)	14	9	3	2	29	39	5	217
4 Sussex (*4*)	14	7	5	2	35	39	0	196
5 Kent (*2*)	14	4	2	7*	35	36	0	175
6 Gloucestershire (*6*)	14	3	4	7	29	35	0	147
7 Glamorgan (*8*)	14	3	7	4	25	40	0	133
8 Derbyshire (*9*)	14	3	7	3*	29	30	0	127
9 Durham (**4**)	14	3	6	5	36	37	48	98
10 Leicestershire (*7*)	14	0	9	5	32	34	16	75

2016 positions are shown in brackets: Division One in bold, Division Two in italic.

* *Plus one match abandoned.*

Win = 16pts; draw = 5pts. *Penalties for slow over-rates, financial or disciplinary reasons.*

Decisions in cricket dictate nothing more than the good cheer or disgruntlement of fans and players but, at some point in the off-season between these momentous errors, **Essex** made their own call, and it determined the 2017 Championship. Simon Harmer, a South African off-spinner of no great repute, was signed as a Kolpak. A lacklustre start brought only 15 wickets at 42. But on June 11, three days after Mrs May's disaster, Harmer embarked on a spree that netted another 32 at just under 12 in five consecutive innings. That day, he took four to help set up a win over Surrey at Guildford that returned Essex to the top of the table with a bare six-point lead; they would never surrender the advantage. By the end of June, with only six games to come, they were 29 points clear after Harmer, on the final day of successive innings wins over Warwickshire and Middlesex, had returned the best figures – eight for 36 and nine for 95 – by a spinner at Chelmsford. Jamie Porter, the 24-year-old opening bowler whose immaculate control of length and late movement brought top-order wickets all summer, ended with 75 scalps to Harmer's 72, but it was this rampant period of 19 days that truly secured Essex's first Championship title for 25 years.

It came only 12 months after they had won the second division, repeating Nottinghamshire's feat of 2005. For their part, defending champions **Middlesex** had lost for the first time in 21 matches, to Lancashire at Southport in June. A fourth defeat on the last day of the season meant they swelled that unhappy list of counties relegated the year after taking the title, joining Lancashire in 2012, Nottinghamshire in 2006 and Yorkshire in 2002. Their earlier fall from grace against Harmer at the end of June, late in the evening of a pink-ball match in the Championship's first day/night round, was little short of astounding. Middlesex surrendered their final five wickets in 64 deliveries, the last four in 27 for one run, to lose under the floodlights with eight balls left. The Essex website declared: "Harmer sends Chelmsford into a frenzy".

It was a little overstated – Chelmsford barely managed frenzy even during those national displays of public euphoria that greeted the end of the Great War – but this was the pivotal moment of the season. Middlesex were far worse hit by weather than Somerset, who escaped relegation by two points – the penalty Middlesex suffered for their slow over-rate at The Oval. They appealed, claiming that the curious (indeed, criminal) incident of the crossbow in the afternoon, when a foreign object fired into the ground caused play to be abandoned 100 minutes early, had denied them time to contrive enough rapid overs to evade the deduction; their fate was sealed in October when the appeal was rejected. Yet shortcomings on the field, in a strangely listless defence, were surely more significant. It was the Chelmsford defeat, and Middlesex's decision not to enforce the follow-on when Essex visited Lord's in April, that told against them.

Lancashire followed their win over Middlesex with another, over Hampshire at Old Trafford, on the same afternoon that Essex beat Warwickshire – the day after the hottest in June since 1976. They went second, and slipped back only once thereafter, when Surrey briefly overtook them in the penultimate round. But Lancashire, whose five wins all came at home while their three defeats were all away, pushed Surrey back into third, beating them in a final match begun with both sides safe.

The real excitement had by then passed to the question of which of four candidates would be demoted with Warwickshire, and whether Northamptonshire could pull off an astonishing late promotion. Any doubts about the title that lingered disappeared in early August when that attention-seeking juvenile, T20, next deigned to let Essex play Championship cricket again. This time

Stephen Pond, Getty Images

Prize pair: Simon Harmer and Jamie Porter shot Essex from newly promoted to new champions.

Mohammad Amir, during a brief spell as overseas player, routed Yorkshire with ten for 72 at Scarborough. Despite 50 wickets from the season's most promising novice, Ben Coad – like Thomas Lord 240 years before, brought up in Thirsk – **Yorkshire** betrayed how much their batting had come to depend on rescues from Jonny Bairstow, now mostly absent with England, and the lower order. In two defeats by Essex, their 40 wickets survived a grand total of 159 overs, the equivalent of being all out four times in five sessions. Not until the final round, when Middlesex failed to take a batting point against Somerset, were Yorkshire secure; they finished fourth by virtue of gaining one more win than Hampshire, yet only two points separated them from seventh.

For all Porter's outstanding consistency, Essex's four consecutive, defining wins thus owed most to imported bowlers; romantic images of home-grown, precocious endeavour are plainly not the full story. It is true, however, and deeply heartening in a game too long denied to the young, that key contributions came from all quarters of a tight squad in which a dozen mostly state-schooled players had learned their cricket in Britain, seven in north-east London. Five drew first breath in the same maternity ward, a mere mile from where Graham Gooch grew up.

Seven times in the last ten seasons the title has gone to Durham, Yorkshire, Lancashire and now Essex, sides encouraging locals brought up together, with bonds of obligation developed in shared dressing-rooms. Someone from afar, knowing nothing of cricket, might conclude that such counties transgress some law: the ECB, falling upon Durham like loan sharks administering punishment beatings in the night, seem happier to grant international fixtures to Glamorgan and Hampshire, counties for whom players raised abroad made over half their Championship appearances last year.

The myth was widespread that, with its reduction to eight sides and 14 games, the top tier was all about winning. In fact, the division's scoring-rate (3.2 per over) was the slowest since the inaugural split Championship in 2000, though essentially on a par with the rate in four of the last six seasons, all subject to those grudging spring or autumn pitches to which so much of the competition is now consigned. No first division season since 2000, save in the miserably wet summer of 2012, has produced a lower average score per wicket than 2017's 29.60, yet slow scoring still dictated a lower percentage of victories – only 57 – than in five of the previous seven campaigns. Far from seeking wins, sides haunted by relegation tried most to avoid defeat: over half the positive results were Essex wins, Warwickshire losses, or both.

In contrast, the scramble for promotion meant 69% of the second-tier games reached a result, a higher percentage than in all but one of the last 15 years. The division achieved its fastest scoring-rate (3.6 per over), yet its fewest balls per wicket (52), a febrile combination. Most sides went for wins and promotion like bats out of hell.

In the cluster of first division teams grappling each other to a standstill, **Surrey** amassed more draws and batting points than any other county, and boasted the only three top-tier players with 1,000 runs, led magnificently by Kumar Sangakkara. He retired, a month short of turning 40, with the highest meaningful average (106) achieved in a county season, bettered in an English summer only by the touring Don Bradman's 115 in 1938. Of home batsmen, Worcestershire opener Daryl Mitchell was first to 1,000, followed the same day by Paul Collingwood, who at 41 was 19 months older than the new French president, Emmanuel Macron. Youth is evidently not all.

Age, though, caught up with **Warwickshire**. With six first-team regulars who would be 35 by the end of the year, they lost five of their first eight games and were past realistic reprieve by July. Yet when the season's final, freezing day dawned, a forlorn trio remained in the dark, desperate to avoid the second relegation slot. **Somerset** escaped at the last gasp after three wins in their final four games, culminating in victory over Middlesex ten minutes before lunch on a lavishly turning pitch at Taunton. The visitors complained bitterly about the surface but, if England are ever to learn how to bat (or bowl) in Bangladesh and India, such pitches seem quite as valid as green April seamers.

The fate of the 2016 champions now rested on events at Edgbaston, where **Hampshire** would be condemned if they failed to avoid defeat. Having covertly signed two of the South African Test party that toured Australia in November, Hampshire had begun with wins in three of their opening six games, thanks largely to Kyle Abbott's pace; their other new Kolpak, Rilee Rossouw, was less of an asset, at one point contributing five ducks in eight Championship innings. But they had not prevailed since, losing their penultimate match to Essex, despite making them follow on. In the first four overs of the final afternoon at Edgbaston, they lost three wickets and slumped to 72 for four, with nearly 62 overs to survive. But with James Vince at one stage adding four in 80 balls, and Liam Dawson scoring nine from 94, they thwarted Warwickshire, drawing with seven wickets down to sink Middlesex.

For most of the season **Nottinghamshire**, more than any first division side, had seemed the second-best team to Essex. The Australian James Pattinson claimed 28 wickets at ten in the first four (all massive wins) of his five matches, and Stuart Broad was also available for five. They and **Worcestershire**, home-grown save for the three players who shared their overseas berth, seemed promotion certainties until **Northamptonshire**, another side nurturing unsung home talent, won each of their last four games. Worcestershire went up minutes into the penultimate day, but Nottinghamshire would be pipped if they lost to Sussex; they seemed disastrously placed at 65 for five, needing another 351 to avoid the follow-on.

Somehow Chris Read, in the final innings of his career, and Billy Root, in only his seventh in the Championship, hit hundreds, saving the match by making Sussex bat again. Northamptonshire, who had missed promotion in both 2009 and 2011 by two points, were now victims of the ten-team division's new, inequable fixture programme: while Nottinghamshire and Worcestershire met only once, Northamptonshire played each key rival twice. The bigger problem, however, was their over-rate when they lost at Trent Bridge: but for an inexcusable five-point penalty there, they would in fact have gone up.

Sussex, squandering a mid-campaign surge, and **Kent**, after beginning so well, faded badly, and the remainder were predictable also-rans. Only Middlesex were more tellingly affected by rain than **Gloucestershire**. The main interest of **Glamorgan** (who twice fielded sides with seven men raised in the southern hemisphere), **Derbyshire** and **Leicestershire** lay in white-ball cricket. In a wonderful first, Derbyshire gave three games to Hamidullah Qadri, an Afghan refugee who arrived in the county as a child. At the professed age of 16 years 206 days, he became the youngest player to claim a five-wicket bag on debut. Meanwhile, vindictively hammered by an ECB whose commercially obsessed management board so notably lacks ex-cricketers, **Durham** had little chance to upstage anyone. Paths are being followed by those who control our game which have come to worry many. There are astute judges, on an increasingly pessimistic circuit, for whom these paths seem likely to conclude in no meaningful Championship to review.

Pre-season betting (best available prices): *Division One* – 5-2 Yorkshire; 7-2 Middlesex; 11-2 Warwickshire; 6-1 Surrey; 17-2 Somerset; 12-1 Hampshire; 16-1 Lancashire; 25-1 ESSEX. *Division Two* – 7-4 Nottinghamshire; 7-2 Sussex; 5-1 Kent; 8-1 WORCESTERSHIRE; 16-1 Northamptonshire and Gloucestershire; 25-1 Glamorgan; 28-1 Durham; 33-1 Derbyshire and Leicestershire.

> “Australia, worthier adversaries than predicted, had encountered in the Himalayas the peak they could not quite conquer.”
>
> India v Australia in 2016–17, Fourth Test, page 844

Prize money

Division One
£532,100 for winners: ESSEX.
£221,020 for runners-up: LANCASHIRE.
£103,022 for third: SURREY.
£27,000 for fourth: YORKSHIRE.
£24,000 for fifth: HAMPSHIRE.

Division Two
£111,050 for winners: WORCESTERSHIRE.
£51,052 for runners-up: NOTTINGHAMSHIRE.

Leaders: *Division One* – from April 10 Surrey; May 21 Essex; May 28 Hampshire; May 29 Essex; June 5 Hampshire; June 12 Essex; Essex became champions on September 15.
Division Two – from April 8 Northamptonshire; April 9 Northamptonshire and Nottinghamshire; April 22 Nottinghamshire; September 15 Worcestershire; Worcestershire became champions on September 28.

Bottom place: *Division One* – from April 17 Warwickshire; April 24 Somerset; June 5 Warwickshire; August 9 Somerset; August 10 Warwickshire.
Division Two – from April 17 Durham; July 6 Leicestershire; July 8 Durham and Leicestershire; August 9 Leicestershire.

Scoring of Points

(*a*) For a win, 16 points plus any points scored in the first innings.
(*b*) In a tie, each side score eight points, plus any points scored in the first innings.
(*c*) In a drawn match, each side score five points, plus any points scored in the first innings.
(*d*) If the scores are equal in a drawn match, the side batting in the fourth innings score eight points, plus any points scored in the first innings, and the opposing side score five points, plus any points scored in the first innings.
(*e*) First-innings points (awarded only for performances in the first 110 overs of each first innings and retained whatever the result of the match):

(i) A maximum of five batting points to be available: 200 to 249 runs – 1 point; 250 to 299 runs – 2 points; 300 to 349 runs – 3 points; 350 to 399 runs – 4 points; 400 runs or over – 5 points. Penalty runs awarded within the first 110 overs of each first innings count towards the award of bonus points.

(ii) A maximum of three bowling points to be available: 3 to 5 wickets taken – 1 point; 6 to 8 wickets taken – 2 points; 9 to 10 wickets taken – 3 points.

(*f*) If a match is abandoned without a ball being bowled, each side score five points.
(*g*) The side who have the highest aggregate of points shall be the champion county of their respective division. Should any sides in the Championship table be equal on points, the following tie-breakers will be applied in the order stated: most wins, fewest losses, team achieving most points in head-to-head contests, most wickets taken, most runs scored.
(*h*) The minimum over-rate to be achieved by counties will be 16 overs per hour. Overs will be calculated at the end of the match, and penalties applied on a match-by-match basis. For each over (ignoring fractions) that a side have bowled short of the target number, one point will be deducted from their Championship total.
(*i*) Penalties for poor and unfit pitches are at the discretion of the Cricket Discipline Commission.

Under ECB playing conditions, two extras were scored for every no-ball bowled, whether scored off or not, and one for every wide. Any runs scored off the bat were credited to the batsman, while byes and leg-byes were counted as no-balls or wides, as appropriate, in accordance with Law 24.13, in addition to the initial penalty.

CONSTITUTION OF COUNTY CHAMPIONSHIP

At least four possible dates have been given for the start of county cricket in England. The first, patchy, references began in 1825. The earliest mention in any cricket publication is in 1864, and eight counties have come to be regarded as first-class from that date, including Cambridgeshire, who dropped out after 1871. For many years, the County Championship was considered to have started in 1873, when regulations governing qualification first applied; indeed, a special commemorative stamp was issued by the Post Office in 1973. However, the Championship was not formally organised until 1890, and before then champions were proclaimed by the press; sometimes publications differed in their views, and no definitive list of champions can start before that date. Eight teams contested the 1890 competition – Gloucestershire, Kent, Lancashire, Middlesex, Nottinghamshire, Surrey, Sussex and Yorkshire. Somerset joined the following year, and in 1895 the Championship began to acquire something of its modern shape, when Derbyshire, Essex, Hampshire, Leicestershire and Warwickshire were added. At that point MCC officially recognised the competition's existence. Worcestershire, Northamptonshire and Glamorgan were admitted in 1899, 1905 and 1921 respectively, and are regarded as first-class from these dates. An invitation in 1921 to Buckinghamshire to enter the Championship was declined, owing to the lack of necessary playing facilities, and an application by Devon in 1948 was unsuccessful. Durham were admitted in 1992 and granted first-class status prior to their pre-season tour of Zimbabwe.

In 2000, the Championship was split for the first time into two divisions, on the basis of counties' standings in the 1999 competition. From 2000 onwards, the bottom three teams in Division One were relegated at the end of the season, and the top three teams in Division Two promoted. From 2006, this was changed to two teams relegated and two promoted. In 2016, two relegated and one promoted, to create divisions of eight and ten teams.

COUNTY CHAMPIONS

The title of champion county is unreliable before 1890. In 1963, *Wisden* formally accepted the list of champions "most generally selected" by contemporaries, as researched by Rowland Bowen (see *Wisden 1959*, page 91). This appears to be the most accurate available list but has no official status. The county champions from 1864 to 1889 were, according to Bowen: 1864 Surrey; 1865 Nottinghamshire; 1866 Middlesex; 1867 Yorkshire; 1868 Nottinghamshire; 1869 Nottinghamshire and Yorkshire; 1870 Yorkshire; 1871 Nottinghamshire; 1872 Nottinghamshire; 1873 Gloucestershire and Nottinghamshire; 1874 Gloucestershire; 1875 Nottinghamshire; 1876 Gloucestershire; 1877 Gloucestershire; 1878 undecided; 1879 Lancashire and Nottinghamshire; 1880 Nottinghamshire; 1881 Lancashire; 1882 Lancashire and Nottinghamshire; 1883 Nottinghamshire; 1884 Nottinghamshire; 1885 Nottinghamshire; 1886 Nottinghamshire; 1887 Surrey; 1888 Surrey; 1889 Lancashire, Nottinghamshire and Surrey.

1890	Surrey
1891	Surrey
1892	Surrey
1893	Yorkshire
1894	Surrey
1895	Surrey
1896	Yorkshire
1897	Lancashire
1898	Yorkshire
1899	Surrey
1900	Yorkshire
1901	Yorkshire
1902	Yorkshire
1903	Middlesex
1904	Lancashire
1905	Yorkshire
1906	Kent
1907	Nottinghamshire
1908	Yorkshire
1909	Kent
1910	Kent
1911	Warwickshire
1912	Yorkshire
1913	Kent
1914	Surrey
1919	Yorkshire
1920	Middlesex
1921	Middlesex
1922	Yorkshire
1923	Yorkshire
1924	Yorkshire
1925	Yorkshire
1926	Lancashire
1927	Lancashire
1928	Lancashire
1929	Nottinghamshire
1930	Lancashire
1931	Yorkshire
1932	Yorkshire
1933	Yorkshire
1934	Lancashire
1935	Yorkshire
1936	Derbyshire
1937	Yorkshire
1938	Yorkshire
1939	Yorkshire
1946	Yorkshire
1947	Middlesex
1948	Glamorgan
1949	Middlesex Yorkshire
1950	Lancashire Surrey
1951	Warwickshire
1952	Surrey
1953	Surrey
1954	Surrey
1955	Surrey
1956	Surrey
1957	Surrey
1958	Surrey
1959	Yorkshire
1960	Yorkshire
1961	Hampshire
1962	Yorkshire
1963	Yorkshire
1964	Worcestershire
1965	Worcestershire
1966	Yorkshire
1967	Yorkshire
1968	Yorkshire
1969	Glamorgan
1970	Kent
1971	Surrey
1972	Warwickshire
1973	Hampshire
1974	Worcestershire
1975	Leicestershire
1976	Middlesex
1977	Middlesex Kent
1978	Kent
1979	Essex
1980	Middlesex
1981	Nottinghamshire
1982	Middlesex
1983	Essex
1984	Essex
1985	Middlesex
1986	Essex
1987	Nottinghamshire
1988	Worcestershire
1989	Worcestershire
1990	Middlesex
1991	Essex
1992	Essex

1993 Middlesex
1994 Warwickshire
1995 Warwickshire
1996 Leicestershire
1997 Glamorgan
1998 Leicestershire
1999 Surrey
2000 Surrey
2001 Yorkshire
2002 Surrey
2003 Sussex
2004 Warwickshire
2005 Nottinghamshire
2006 Sussex
2007 Sussex
2008 Durham
2009 Durham
2010 Nottinghamshire
2011 Lancashire
2012 Warwickshire
2013 Durham
2014 Yorkshire
2015 Yorkshire
2016 Middlesex
2017 Essex

Notes: Since the Championship was constituted in 1890 it has been won outright as follows: Yorkshire 32 times, Surrey 18, Middlesex 11, Lancashire 8, Essex and Warwickshire 7, Kent and Nottinghamshire 6, Worcestershire 5, Durham, Glamorgan, Leicestershire and Sussex 3, Hampshire 2, Derbyshire 1. Gloucestershire, Northamptonshire and Somerset have never won.

The title has been shared three times since 1890, involving Middlesex twice, Kent, Lancashire, Surrey and Yorkshire.

Wooden spoons: Since the major expansion of the Championship from nine teams to 14 in 1895, the counties have finished outright bottom as follows: Derbyshire 16, Leicestershire 13, Somerset 12, Northamptonshire 11, Glamorgan 10, Gloucestershire 9, Nottinghamshire and Sussex 8, Worcestershire 6, Durham and Hampshire 5, Warwickshire 3, Essex and Kent 2, Yorkshire 1. Lancashire, Middlesex and Surrey have never finished bottom. Leicestershire have also shared bottom place twice, once with Hampshire and once with Somerset.

From 1977 to 1983 the Championship was sponsored by Schweppes, from 1984 to 1998 by Britannic Assurance, from 1999 to 2000 by PPP healthcare, in 2001 by Cricinfo, from 2002 to 2005 by Frizzell, from 2006 to 2015 by Liverpool Victoria (LV), and from 2016 by Specsavers.

COUNTY CHAMPIONSHIP – FINAL POSITIONS, 1890–2017

	Derbyshire	Durham	Essex	Glamorgan	Gloucestershire	Hampshire	Kent	Lancashire	Leicestershire	Middlesex	Northamptonshire	Nottinghamshire	Somerset	Surrey	Sussex	Warwickshire	Worcestershire	Yorkshire
1890	–	–	–	–	6	–	3	2	–	7	–	5	–	1	8	–	–	3
1891	–	–	–	–	9	–	5	2	–	3	–	4	5	1	7	–	–	8
1892	–	–	–	–	7	–	7	4	–	5	–	2	3	1	9	–	–	6
1893	–	–	–	–	9	–	4	2	–	3	–	6	8	5	7	–	–	1
1894	–	–	–	–	9	–	4	4	–	3	–	7	6	1	8	–	–	2
1895	5	–	9	–	4	10	14	2	12	6	–	12	8	1	11	6	–	3
1896	7	–	5	–	10	8	9	2	13	3	–	6	11	4	14	12	–	1
1897	14	–	3	–	5	9	12	1	13	8	–	10	11	2	6	7	–	4
1898	9	–	5	–	3	12	7	6	13	2	–	8	13	4	9	9	–	1
1899	15	–	6	–	9	10	8	4	13	2	–	10	13	1	5	7	12	3
1900	13	–	10	–	7	15	3	2	14	7	–	5	11	7	3	6	12	1
1901	15	–	10	–	14	7	7	3	12	2	–	9	12	6	4	5	11	1
1902	10	–	13	–	14	15	7	5	11	12	–	3	7	4	2	6	9	1
1903	12	–	8	–	13	14	8	4	14	1	–	5	10	11	2	7	6	3
1904	10	–	14	–	9	15	3	1	7	4	–	5	12	11	6	7	13	2
1905	14	–	12	–	8	16	6	2	5	11	13	10	15	4	3	7	8	1
1906	16	–	7	–	9	8	1	4	15	11	11	5	11	3	10	6	14	2
1907	16	–	7	–	10	12	8	6	11	5	15	1	14	4	13	9	2	2
1908	14	–	11	–	10	9	2	7	13	4	15	8	16	3	5	12	6	1
1909	15	–	14	–	16	8	1	2	13	6	7	10	11	5	4	12	8	3
1910	15	–	11	–	12	6	1	4	10	3	9	5	16	2	7	14	13	8
1911	14	–	6	–	12	11	2	4	15	3	10	8	16	5	13	1	9	7
1912	12	–	15	–	11	6	3	4	13	5	2	8	14	7	10	9	16	1
1913	13	–	15	–	9	10	1	8	14	6	4	5	16	3	7	11	12	2
1914	12	–	8	–	16	5	3	11	13	2	9	10	15	1	6	7	14	4

	Derbyshire	Durham	Essex	Glamorgan	Gloucestershire	Hampshire	Kent	Lancashire	Leicestershire	Middlesex	Northamptonshire	Nottinghamshire	Somerset	Surrey	Sussex	Warwickshire	Worcestershire	Yorkshire
1919	9	–	14	–	8	7	2	5	9	13	12	3	5	4	11	15	–	1
1920	16	–	9	–	8	11	5	2	13	1	14	7	10	3	6	12	15	4
1921	12	–	15	17	7	6	4	5	11	1	13	8	10	2	9	16	14	3
1922	11	–	8	16	13	6	4	5	14	7	15	2	10	3	9	12	17	1
1923	10	–	13	16	11	7	5	3	14	8	17	2	9	4	6	12	15	1
1924	17	–	15	13	6	12	5	4	11	2	16	6	8	3	10	9	14	1
1925	14	–	7	17	10	9	5	3	12	6	11	4	15	2	13	8	16	1
1926	11	–	9	8	15	7	3	1	13	6	16	4	14	5	10	12	17	2
1927	5	–	8	15	12	13	4	1	7	9	16	2	14	6	10	11	17	3
1928	10	–	16	15	5	12	2	1	9	8	13	3	14	6	7	11	17	4
1929	7	–	12	17	4	11	8	2	9	6	13	1	15	10	4	14	16	2
1930	9	–	6	11	2	13	5	1	12	16	17	4	13	8	7	15	10	3
1931	7	–	10	15	2	12	3	6	16	11	17	5	13	8	4	9	14	1
1932	10	–	14	15	13	8	3	6	12	10	16	4	7	5	2	9	17	1
1933	6	–	4	16	10	14	3	5	17	12	13	8	11	9	2	7	15	1
1934	3	–	8	13	7	14	5	1	12	10	17	9	15	11	2	4	16	5
1935	2	–	9	13	15	16	10	4	6	3	17	5	14	11	7	8	12	1
1936	1	–	9	16	4	10	8	11	15	2	17	5	7	6	14	13	12	3
1937	3	–	6	7	4	14	12	9	16	2	17	10	13	8	5	11	15	1
1938	5	–	6	16	10	14	9	4	15	2	17	12	7	3	8	13	11	1
1939	9	–	4	13	3	15	5	6	17	2	16	12	14	8	10	11	7	1
1946	15	–	8	6	5	10	6	3	11	2	16	13	4	11	17	14	8	1
1947	5	–	11	9	2	16	4	3	14	1	17	11	11	6	9	15	7	7
1948	6	–	13	1	8	9	15	5	11	3	17	14	12	2	16	7	10	4
1949	15	–	9	8	7	16	13	11	17	1	6	11	9	5	13	4	3	1
1950	5	–	17	11	7	12	9	1	16	14	10	15	7	1	13	4	6	3
1951	11	–	8	5	12	9	16	3	15	7	13	17	14	6	10	1	4	2
1952	4	–	10	7	9	12	15	3	6	5	8	16	17	1	13	10	14	2
1953	6	–	12	10	6	14	16	3	3	5	11	8	17	1	2	9	15	12
1954	3	–	15	4	13	14	11	10	16	7	7	5	17	1	9	6	11	2
1955	8	–	14	16	12	3	13	9	6	5	7	11	17	1	4	9	15	2
1956	12	–	11	13	3	6	16	2	17	5	4	8	15	1	9	14	9	7
1957	4	–	5	9	12	13	14	6	17	7	2	15	8	1	9	11	16	3
1958	5	–	6	15	14	2	8	7	12	10	4	17	3	1	13	16	9	11
1959	7	–	9	6	2	8	13	5	16	10	11	17	12	3	15	4	14	1
1960	5	–	6	11	8	12	10	2	17	3	9	16	14	7	4	15	13	1
1961	7	–	6	14	5	1	11	13	9	3	16	17	10	15	8	12	4	2
1962	7	–	9	14	4	10	11	16	17	13	8	15	6	5	12	3	2	1
1963	17	–	12	2	8	10	13	15	16	6	7	9	3	11	4	4	14	1
1964	12	–	10	11	17	12	7	14	16	6	3	15	8	4	9	2	1	5
1965	9	–	15	3	10	12	5	13	14	6	2	17	7	8	16	11	1	4
1966	9	–	16	14	15	11	4	12	8	12	5	17	3	7	10	6	2	1
1967	6	–	15	14	17	12	2	11	2	7	9	15	8	4	13	10	5	1
1968	8	–	14	3	16	5	2	6	9	10	13	4	12	15	17	11	7	1
1969	16	–	6	1	2	5	10	15	14	11	9	8	17	3	7	4	12	13
1970	7	–	12	2	17	10	1	3	15	16	14	11	13	5	9	7	6	4
1971	17	–	10	16	8	9	4	3	5	6	14	12	7	1	11	2	15	13
1972	17	–	5	13	3	9	2	15	6	8	4	14	11	12	16	1	7	10
1973	16	–	8	11	5	1	4	12	9	13	3	17	10	2	15	7	6	14
1974	17	–	12	16	14	2	10	8	4	6	3	15	5	7	13	9	1	11
1975	15	–	7	9	16	3	5	4	1	11	8	13	12	6	17	14	10	2
1976	15	–	6	17	3	12	14	16	4	1	2	13	7	9	10	5	11	8
1977	7	–	6	14	3	11	1	16	5	1	9	17	4	14	8	10	13	12
1978	14	–	2	13	10	8	1	12	6	3	17	7	5	16	9	11	15	4

	Derbyshire	Durham	Essex	Glamorgan	Gloucestershire	Hampshire	Kent	Lancashire	Leicestershire	Middlesex	Northamptonshire	Nottinghamshire	Somerset	Surrey	Sussex	Warwickshire	Worcestershire	Yorkshire
1979	16	–	1	17	10	12	5	13	6	14	11	9	8	3	4	15	2	7
1980	9	–	8	13	7	17	16	15	10	1	12	3	5	2	4	14	11	6
1981	12	–	5	14	13	7	9	16	8	4	15	1	3	6	2	17	11	10
1982	11	–	7	16	15	3	13	12	2	1	9	4	6	5	8	17	14	10
1983	9	–	1	15	12	3	7	12	4	2	6	14	10	8	11	5	16	17
1984	12	–	1	13	17	15	5	16	4	3	11	2	7	8	6	9	10	14
1985	13	–	4	12	3	2	9	14	16	1	10	8	17	6	7	15	5	11
1986	11	–	1	17	2	6	8	15	7	12	9	4	16	3	14	12	5	10
1987	6	–	12	13	10	5	14	2	3	16	7	1	11	4	17	15	9	8
1988	14	–	3	17	10	15	2	9	8	7	12	5	11	4	16	6	1	13
1989	6	–	2	17	9	6	15	4	13	3	5	11	14	12	10	8	1	16
1990	12	–	2	8	13	3	16	6	7	1	11	13	15	9	17	5	4	10
1991	3	–	1	12	13	9	6	8	16	15	10	4	17	5	11	2	6	14
1992	5	18	1	14	10	15	2	12	8	11	3	4	9	13	7	6	17	16
1993	15	18	11	3	17	13	8	13	9	1	4	7	5	6	10	16	2	12
1994	17	16	6	18	12	13	9	10	2	4	5	3	11	7	8	1	15	13
1995	14	17	5	16	6	13	18	4	7	2	3	11	9	12	15	1	10	8
1996	2	18	5	10	13	14	4	15	1	9	16	17	11	3	12	8	7	6
1997	16	17	8	1	7	14	2	11	10	4	15	13	12	8	18	4	3	6
1998	10	14	18	12	4	6	11	2	1	17	15	16	9	5	7	8	13	3
1999	9	8	12	14	18	7	5	2	3	16	13	17	4	1	11	10	15	6
2000	**9**	**8**	*2*	*3*	*4*	**7**	**6**	**2**	**4**	*8*	*1*	*7*	**5**	**1**	*9*	*6*	*5*	**3**
2001	*9*	*8*	**9**	**8**	*4*	*2*	**3**	**6**	**5**	*5*	**7**	*7*	**2**	**4**	*1*	*3*	*6*	**1**
2002	*6*	*9*	*1*	*5*	*8*	**7**	**3**	**4**	**5**	*2*	*7*	*3*	**8**	**1**	**6**	**2**	*4*	**9**
2003	*9*	*6*	**7**	*5*	*3*	*8*	**4**	**2**	**9**	**6**	*2*	**8**	*7*	**3**	**1**	**5**	*1*	*4*
2004	*8*	*9*	*5*	*3*	**6**	*2*	**2**	**8**	*6*	**4**	**9**	*1*	*4*	**3**	**5**	**1**	**7**	*7*
2005	*9*	*2*	*5*	**9**	**8**	**2**	**5**	*1*	*7*	**6**	*4*	**1**	*8*	**7**	**3**	**4**	*6*	*3*
2006	*5*	**7**	*3*	*8*	*7*	**3**	**5**	**2**	*4*	**9**	*6*	**8**	*9*	*1*	**1**	**4**	*2*	**6**
2007	*6*	**2**	*4*	*9*	*7*	**5**	**7**	**3**	*8*	*3*	*5*	*2*	*1*	**4**	**1**	**8**	**9**	**6**
2008	*6*	**1**	*5*	*8*	*9*	**3**	**8**	**5**	*7*	*3*	*4*	**2**	**4**	**9**	**6**	*1*	*2*	**7**
2009	*6*	**1**	*2*	*5*	*4*	**6**	*1*	**4**	*9*	*8*	*3*	**2**	**3**	*7*	**8**	**5**	**9**	**7**
2010	*9*	**5**	**9**	*3*	*5*	**7**	**8**	**4**	*4*	*8*	*6*	**1**	**2**	*7*	*1*	**6**	*2*	**3**
2011	*5*	**3**	*7*	*6*	*4*	**9**	*8*	**1**	*9*	*1*	*3*	**6**	**4**	*2*	**5**	**2**	**7**	**8**
2012	*1*	**6**	*5*	*6*	*9*	*4*	*3*	**8**	*7*	**3**	*8*	**5**	**2**	**7**	**4**	**1**	**9**	*2*
2013	**8**	**1**	*3*	*8*	*6*	*4*	*7*	*1*	*9*	**5**	*2*	**7**	**6**	**9**	**3**	**4**	*5*	**2**
2014	*4*	**5**	*3*	*8*	*7*	*1*	*6*	**8**	*9*	**7**	**9**	**4**	**6**	*5*	**3**	**2**	*2*	**1**
2015	*8*	**4**	*3*	*4*	*6*	**7**	*7*	*2*	*9*	**2**	*5*	**3**	**6**	*1*	**8**	**5**	**9**	**1**
2016	*9*	**4**	*1*	*8*	*6*	**8**	*2*	**7**	*7*	**1**	*5*	**9**	**2**	**5**	*4*	**6**	*3*	**3**
2017	*8*	*9*	**1**	*7*	*6*	**5**	*5*	**2**	*10*	**7**	*3*	*2*	**6**	**3**	*4*	**8**	*1*	**4**

For the 2000–2017 Championships, Division One placings are in bold, Division Two in italic.

MATCH RESULTS, 1864–2017

County	*Years of Play*	*Played*	*Won*	*Lost*	*Drawn*	*Tied*	*% Won*
Derbyshire	1871–87; 1895–2017	2,559	625	944	989	1	24.42
Durham	1992–2017	424	115	175	134	0	27.12
Essex	1895–2017	2,524	741	727	1,050	6	29.35
Glamorgan	1921–2017	2,049	450	708	891	0	21.96
Gloucestershire	1870–2017	2,802	819	1,028	953	2	29.22
Hampshire	1864–85; 1895–2017	2,632	692	881	1,055	4	26.29
Kent	1864–2017	2,917	1,038	871	1,003	5	35.58
Lancashire	1865–2017	2,994	1,103	621	1,267	3	36.84
Leicestershire	1895–2017	2,489	553	910	1,025	1	22.21

County	*Years of Play*	*Played*	*Won*	*Lost*	*Drawn*	*Tied*	*% Won*
Middlesex.	1864–2017	2,699	980	686	1,028	5	36.30
Northamptonshire . . .	1905–2017	2,257	567	768	919	3	25.12
Nottinghamshire.	1864–2017	2,829	858	770	1,200	1	30.32
Somerset.	1882–85; 1891–2017	2,531	612	975	941	3	24.18
Surrey.	1864–2017	3,074	1,195	685	1,190	4	38.87
Sussex	1864–2017	2,968	848	1,006	1,108	6	28.57
Warwickshire.	1895–2017	2,504	697	714	1,091	2	27.83
Worcestershire	1899–2017	2,441	633	848	958	2	25.93
Yorkshire	1864–2017	3,098	1,339	548	1,209	2	43.22
Cambridgeshire	1864–69; 1871	19	8	8	3	0	42.10
		22,905	13,873	13,873	9,007	25	

Matches abandoned without a ball bowled are wholly excluded.

Counties participated in the years shown, except that there were no matches in 1915–1918 and 1940–1945; Hampshire did not play inter-county matches in 1868–1869, 1871–1874 and 1879; Worcestershire did not take part in the Championship in 1919.

COUNTY CHAMPIONSHIP STATISTICS FOR 2017

	For			*Runs scored*	*Against*		
County	*Runs*	*Wickets*	*Avge*	*per 100 balls*	*Runs*	*Wickets*	*Avge*
Derbyshire (*8*).	6,393	211	30.29	58.69	6,612	184	35.93
Durham (*9*)	7,205	217	33.20	59.17	7,211	221	32.62
Essex (**1**).	6,117	175	34.95	51.45	5,883	252	23.34
Glamorgan (*7*)	6,374	225	28.32	55.13	6,331	195	32.46
Gloucestershire (*6*)	6,187	193	32.05	54.71	6,921	199	34.77
Hampshire (**5**).	5,407	194	27.87	54.50	6,320	226	27.96
Kent (*5*).	7,126	203	35.10	62.61	6,656	211	31.54
Lancashire (**2**).	6,403	197	32.50	53.79	5,986	207	28.91
Leicestershire (*10*)	6,707	238	28.18	58.38	6,997	164	42.66
Middlesex (**7**)	6,067	215	28.21	55.41	6,166	204	30.22
Northamptonshire (*3*). .	6,752	225	30.00	64.79	6,840	240	28.50
Nottinghamshire (*2*) . . .	6,460	175	36.91	64.89	6,484	250	25.93
Somerset (**6**)	6,063	231	26.24	55.03	5,757	228	25.25
Surrey (**3**)	7,385	188	39.28	56.71	6,823	172	39.66
Sussex (*4*)	7,882	226	34.87	66.03	7,378	226	32.64
Warwickshire (**8**)	6,178	258	23.94	49.39	6,207	181	34.29
Worcestershire (*1*)	7,069	210	33.66	65.72	6,725	233	28.86
Yorkshire (**4**).	5,649	206	27.42	51.75	6,127	194	31.58
	117,424	3,787	31.00	57.56	117,424	3,787	31.00

2017 Championship positions are shown in brackets; Division One in bold, Division Two in italic.

ECB PITCHES TABLE OF MERIT IN 2017

	First-class	*One-day*		*First-class*	*One-day*
Derbyshire.	5.14	5.50	Surrey	5.25	5.46
Durham	4.88	5.50	Sussex	5.25	5.46
Essex	4.56	5.55	Warwickshire.	5.13	5.69
Glamorgan.	5.25	5.42	Worcestershire.	5.00	5.30
Gloucestershire	4.63	5.08	Yorkshire.	5.11	5.64
Hampshire	5.00	5.67			
Kent.	4.78	4.85			
Lancashire	4.88	5.36	Cambridge MCCU . . .	4.00	
Leicestershire.	4.78	5.91	Cardiff MCCU.	5.50	
Middlesex	4.33	5.40	Durham MCCU	4.67	
Northamptonshire	5.00	5.67	Leeds/Bradford MCCU	5.50	
Nottinghamshire	5.38	5.92	Loughborough MCCU	5.33	
Somerset	4.63	5.85	Oxford MCCU.	3.50	

Each umpire in a match marks the pitch on the following scale: 6 – Very good; 5 – Good; 4 – Above average; 3 – Below average; 2 – Poor; 1 – Unfit.

The tables, provided by the ECB, cover major matches, including Tests, Under-19 internationals, women's internationals and MCCU games, played on grounds under the county's or MCCU's jurisdiction. Middlesex pitches at Lord's are the responsibility of MCC. The "First-class" column includes Under-19 and women's Tests, and inter-MCCU games.

Among the counties, Nottinghamshire had the highest marks for both first-class and one-day cricket, though the ECB point out that the tables of merit are not a direct assessment of the groundsmen's ability. Marks may be affected by many factors, including weather, soil conditions and the resources available.

COUNTY CAPS AWARDED IN 2017

Derbyshire	A. L. Hughes.
Essex	D. W. Lawrence.
Glamorgan*	C. A. Ingram.
Gloucestershire*	O. C. Currill, G. S. Drissell, C. J. Liddle.
Hampshire	K. J. Abbott, G. J. Bailey.
Kent	A. J. Blake.
Lancashire	A. L. Davies, L. S. Livingstone.
Northamptonshire	R. E. Levi, D. Murphy, R. I. Newton.
Nottinghamshire	J. L. Pattinson, C. A. Pujara.
Somerset	S. M. Davies, D. Elgar, M. J. Leach.
Sussex	J. C. Archer.
Worcestershire*	R. Ashwin, P. R. Brown, J. W. Hastings, N. M. Lyon, J. C. Tongue.

* *Glamorgan's capping system is now based on a player's number of appearances. Gloucestershire now award caps to all first-class players. Worcestershire have replaced caps with colours awarded to all Championship players. Durham abolished their capping system after 2005.*

No caps were awarded by Leicestershire, Middlesex, Surrey, Warwickshire or Yorkshire.

COUNTY BENEFITS AWARDED FOR 2018

Derbyshire	A. P. Palladino.
Lancashire	S. J. Croft.
Middlesex	N. R. D. Compton.
Northamptonshire	S. P. Crook.
Somerset	M. E. Trescothick.
Sussex	E. C. Joyce.
Yorkshire	A. U. Rashid.

None of the other 11 counties awarded a benefit for 2018.

DERBYSHIRE

Concerted effort brings mixed rewards

MARK EKLID

Derbyshire could regard 2017 as a season of progress – with the caveat that 2016 set the bar pretty low. Three Championship victories was unquestionably better than none, and they qualified for the Twenty20 quarter-finals for only the second time.

A place in the T20 Blast knockouts was, in fact, the minimum Derbyshire had aimed for: they had committed more resources to the competition, notably by appointing New Zealand's John Wright, their former overseas player, as a specialist coach. Turning around a county with such a wretched 20-over record was a challenge even for Wright, who had coached Mumbai Indians to IPL glory, but his expertise did have a positive effect.

Led by Gary Wilson, a signing from Surrey, the Falcons won eight matches to finish second in the North Group, behind Nottinghamshire; in the quarter-final against Hampshire, they were unfortunate enough to be on the receiving end of the kind of extraordinary innings Shahid Afridi threatens more often than he produces. Though it was the first time they had reached the last eight since 2005, it was for their competitive cricket, rather than the novelty of winning, that the Blast proved the highlight of the summer.

In the Championship, Derbyshire began with three defeats, and went on to lose four more, but they were sounder than in 2016, when they finished bottom of Division Two and never managed 20 wickets in a match. The recruitment of South African fast bowler Hardus Viljoen as a Kolpak was intended to address that problem, but a series of niggling injuries kept him out of four-day cricket until August. He offered a glimpse of his capabilities when he took 15 wickets – the best match figures for Derbyshire since Cliff Gladwin in 1952 – to clinch victory at Hove, but one bowler cannot provide the complete answer. Twelve other seamers, two on loan, were given their chance, but none was consistent enough. In October, Derbyshire went back down the Kolpak route, adding the experienced Trinidadian Ravi Rampaul to their attack on a three-year deal. New Zealand all-rounder Mitchell Santner later signed for the second half of the season.

Director of cricket Kim Barnett, with half an eye on the limited-overs competitions, hired two international leg-spinners to share the overseas position. Sri Lankan Jeewan Mendis proved useful in the first half of the Championship season and in the Royal London Cup, though Derbyshire failed to qualify for the knockouts; Imran Tahir of South Africa, who bowled in only three four-day games, was a big factor in their T20 success. A more exciting development was the emergence of 16-year-old Afghanistan-born off-spinner Hamidullah Qadri, who became the first county cricketer born in the 21st century, as well as Derbyshire's youngest Championship player. He marked his debut with a match-winning five for 60.

Alex Hughes

The form of the batsmen was patchy. Club captain Billy Godleman struck three centuries in the first five Championship games but only two fifties in the next seven, before a broken hand ruled him out of the last two. Wayne Madsen, Derbyshire's best batsman over the previous four seasons, had a lean year in four-day cricket, though he was ranked the Most Valuable Player in the T20 Blast by the Professional Cricketers' Association. Shiv Thakor was suspended in June pending the outcome of a police investigation; in November he was sacked after being convicted for exposing himself to two women, and put on the sex offender register for five years.

Luis Reece, in his first season at Derby following his release by Lancashire, began to fulfil his potential, providing unexpected impact as a T20 big hitter. Another winter recruit, Daryn Smit, was excellent with the gloves – which he shared with Wilson and Harvey Hosein – though less so with the bat. He and Reece both earned contract extensions. Greg Cork, son of Dominic, was released after playing two first-class matches in two years. He was among a group of young players released in the close season, including seamers Ben Cotton, Tom Taylor (who joined Leicestershire) and Tom Milnes.

Alex Hughes was Derbyshire's most reliable performer, and the only one apart from Madsen to appear in every game in all three competitions; the leading first-class run-scorer with 800, he was named Player of the Year. He was maturing nicely from his days at the Academy, but several of his peers needed to follow his example.

Derbyshire have invested heavily in infrastructure in recent years, and were praised for their part in hosting the women's World Cup and an Elton John concert – though they gambled unwisely in moving a Championship fixture to Chesterfield in September so the County Ground could accommodate another concert, by Boyzone. When that match was abandoned without a ball bowled, it led to a warning from the ECB, and ensured Derbyshire would go a third season without a home Championship victory.

Barnett, appointed director of cricket after the 2016 season, had said he would leave after fulfilling his original remit, to implement a new management structure. But he had a change of heart at the end of the summer and agreed to remain, in a new role as "cricket advisor". He understood that, while the season had brought an improvement, Derbyshire remained a work in progress.

Championship attendance: 8,585.

DERBYSHIRE RESULTS

All first-class matches – Played 14: Won 3, Lost 7, Drawn 4.
County Championship matches – Played 13: Won 3, Lost 7, Drawn 3. Abandoned 1.

Specsavers County Championship, 8th in Division 2;
NatWest T20 Blast, quarter-finalists; Royal London One-Day Cup, 7th in North Group.

COUNTY CHAMPIONSHIP AVERAGES, BATTING AND FIELDING

Cap		Birthplace	M	I	NO	R	HS	100	Avge	Ct/St
	B. D. Cotton	*Stoke-on-Trent*	2	4	3	50	32	0	50.00	0
2017	A. L. Hughes	*Wordsley*	13	22	2	800	142	2	40.00	15
2015	†B. A. Godleman	*Islington*	12	22	2	799	156*	3	39.95	7
	M. J. J. Critchley	*Preston*	5	8	1	266	102	1	38.00	2
	†B. T. Slater	*Chesterfield‡*	8	15	2	490	74*	0	37.69	3
	†L. M. Reece	*Taunton*	12	21	1	732	168	2	36.60	4
	H. R. Hosein	*Chesterfield‡*	4	7	2	166	52	0	33.20	7
	S. J. Thakor	*Leicester*	6	11	1	328	132	1	32.80	1
	G. C. Wilson	*Dundonald, N. Ire.*	9	14	1	401	97	0	30.84	17
2011	W. L. Madsen	*Durban, SA*	13	22	0	667	121	1	30.31	14
	H. W. Podmore	*Hammersmith*	4	6	1	133	66*	0	26.60	2
	T. A. I. Taylor	*Stoke-on-Trent*	6	10	1	183	69	0	20.33	1
	D. Smit††	*Durban, SA*	8	13	1	237	41	0	19.75	18/3
	T. P. Milnes	*Stourbridge*	3	5	0	96	53	0	19.20	2
	W. S. Davis	*Stafford*	5	7	2	64	25	0	12.80	2
	B. M. A. J. Mendis¶	*Colombo, SL*	7	12	1	132	27	0	12.00	3
	H. Qadri	*Kandahar, Afg*	3	6	4	20	11*	0	10.00	2
2012	A. P. Palladino	*Tower Hamlets*	10	17	2	143	32	0	9.53	3
	Imran Tahir¶	*Lahore, Pakistan*	4	6	1	41	18*	0	8.20	2
	G. C. Viljoen††	*Witbank, SA*	5	8	1	36	19*	0	5.14	1

Also batted: R. P. Hemmings (*Newcastle-under-Lyme*) (1 match) 19; C. McKerr†† (*Johannesburg, South Africa*) (2 matches) 16*, 0, 17; G. S. Sandhu (*Isleworth*) (1 match) 46*, 9.

‡ *Born in Derbyshire.* ¶ *Official overseas player.* †† *Other non-England-qualified.*

BOWLING

	Style	O	M	R	W	BB	5I	Avge
C. McKerr	RFM	85.5	19	290	14	5-54	2	20.71
G. C. Viljoen	RFM	139.5	27	517	24	8-90	3	21.54
H. Qadri	OB	101.3	22	288	10	5-60	1	28.80
W. S. Davis	RFM	103.5	13	410	14	4-60	0	29.28
B. M. A. J. Mendis	LB	252	24	908	30	6-204	1	30.26
Imran Tahir	LB	123.1	16	407	13	5-76	2	31.30
A. P. Palladino	RFM	254.4	56	818	24	4-36	0	34.08
T. A. I. Taylor	RFM	144	30	548	16	4-67	0	34.25

Also bowled: B. D. Cotton (RFM) 23–2–123–0; M. J. J. Critchley (LB) 10.2–0–66–2; R. P. Hemmings (RM) 24–6–94–0; A. L. Hughes (RM) 33–8–121–0; W. L. Madsen (OB) 60.3–5–260–7; T. P. Milnes (RFM) 64.4–10–306–4; H. W. Podmore (RM) 85.3–12–310–6; L. M. Reece (LM) 127.3–26–473–8; G. S. Sandhu (LFM) 21.3–2–87–3; B. T. Slater (LB) 2–0–6–0; D. Smit (LB) 10.5–0–57–0; S. J. Thakor (RM) 64.3–9–302–6.

LEADING ROYAL LONDON CUP AVERAGES (150 runs/4 wickets)

Batting	Runs	HS	Avge	SR	Ct/St
A. L. Hughes	173	96*	57.66	102.36	6
D. Smit	170	77*	56.66	99.41	6/2
B. T. Slater	312	82	52.00	85.47	0
W. L. Madsen	248	112	49.60	103.33	5
B. A. Godleman	289	95	41.28	78.10	2
S. J. Thakor	280	130	40.00	99.29	2

Bowling	W	BB	Avge	ER
S. J. Thakor	13	3-23	24.53	5.33
B. M. A. J. Mendis	9	2-38	40.00	5.63
G. C. Viljoen	6	3-55	44.66	6.87
B. D. Cotton	5	2-18	71.00	6.01

LEADING NATWEST T20 BLAST AVERAGES (100 runs/15 overs)

Batting	*Runs*	*HS*	*Avge*	*SR*	*Ct*
G. C. Wilson	152	33*	19.00	**152.00**	7
W. L. Madsen	526	86*	47.81	**145.30**	7
B. A. Godleman	270	70	19.28	**144.38**	4
L. M. Reece	433	97*	36.08	**137.89**	6
D. Smit	141	42*	35.25	**136.89**	6/3
M. J. J. Critchley	245	72*	27.22	**133.15**	2
A. L. Hughes	180	36*	18.00	**125.87**	10

Bowling	*W*	*BB*	*Avge*	*ER*
W. L. Madsen	13	2-20	26.61	**7.36**
Imran Tahir	17	4-17	24.47	**7.42**
B. D. Cotton	9	2-14	20.33	**8.44**
G. C. Viljoen	14	3-28	32.85	**9.10**
A. L. Hughes	3	1-19	46.00	**9.39**
M. J. J. Critchley	7	3-32	24.57	**9.55**
M. J. Henry	15	3-18	34.93	**10.37**

FIRST-CLASS COUNTY RECORDS

Highest score for	274	G. A. Davidson v Lancashire at Manchester	1896
Highest score against	343*	P. A. Perrin (Essex) at Chesterfield	1904
Leading run-scorer	23,854	K. J. Barnett (avge 41.12)	1979–98
Best bowling for	10-40	W. Bestwick v Glamorgan at Cardiff	1921
Best bowling against	10-45	R. L. Johnson (Middlesex) at Derby	1994
Leading wicket-taker	1,670	H. L. Jackson (avge 17.11)	1947–63
Highest total for	801-8 dec	v Somerset at Taunton	2007
Highest total against	677-7 dec	by Yorkshire at Leeds	2013
Lowest total for	16	v Nottinghamshire at Nottingham	1879
Lowest total against	23	by Hampshire at Burton-upon-Trent	1958

LIST A COUNTY RECORDS

Highest score for	173*	M. J. Di Venuto v Derbys County Board at Derby	2000
Highest score against	158	R. K. Rao (Sussex) at Derby	1997
Leading run-scorer	12,358	K. J. Barnett (avge 36.67)	1979–98
Best bowling for	8-21	M. A. Holding v Sussex at Hove	1988
Best bowling against	8-66	S. R. G. Francis (Somerset) at Derby	2004
Leading wicket-taker	246	A. E. Warner (avge 27.13)	1985–95
Highest total for	366-4	v Combined Universities at Oxford	1991
Highest total against	369-6	by New Zealanders at Derby	1999
Lowest total for	60	v Kent at Canterbury	2008
Lowest total against	42	by Glamorgan at Swansea	1979

TWENTY20 COUNTY RECORDS

Highest score for	111	W. J. Durston v Nottinghamshire at Nottingham	2010
Highest score against	158*	B. B. McCullum (Warwickshire) at Birmingham	2015
Leading run-scorer	2,114	W. J. Durston (avge 28.95)	2010–16
Best bowling for	5-27	T. Lungley v Leicestershire at Leicester	2009
Best bowling against	5-14	P. D. Collingwood (Durham) at Chester-le-Street	2008
Leading wicket-taker	51	T. D. Groenewald (avge 27.52)	2009–14
Highest total for	222-5	v Yorkshire at Leeds	2010
	222-5	**v Nottinghamshire at Nottingham**	**2017**
Highest total against	**249-8**	**by Hampshire at Derby**	**2017**
Lowest total for	72	v Leicestershire at Derby	2013
Lowest total against	84	by West Indians at Derby	2007

ADDRESS

The 3aa Ground, Nottingham Road, Derby DE21 6DA; 01332 388 101; info@derbyshireccc.com; www.derbyshireccc.com.

OFFICIALS

Captain B. A. Godleman
(Twenty20) G. C. Wilson
Cricket advisor K. J. Barnett
Development coach M. B. Loye
Twenty20 coach J. G. Wright
First XI support coach S. D. Stubbings

President M. A. Holding
Chairman C. I. Grant
Chief executive S. Storey
Head groundsman N. Godrich
Scorer J. M. Brown

At Loughborough, April 7–9. DERBYSHIRE drew with LOUGHBOROUGH MCCU.

DERBYSHIRE v NORTHAMPTONSHIRE

At Derby, April 14–17. Northamptonshire won by three wickets. Northamptonshire 22pts, Derbyshire 5pts. Toss: uncontested. County debut: B. M. A. J. Mendis. Championship debut: D. Smit.

Northamptonshire justified their reputation as a dangerous limited-overs team after they were set 326 off 65 overs: Kleinveldt hit Smit for six to win with a ball to spare. A second successive victory eased the frustration of Newton and Levi, who had narrowly missed centuries. But the result depended on contrivance. The final day saw 539 runs, after Northamptonshire used ten bowlers – including wicketkeeper Rossington – to serve up 209 in 30.2 overs and produce the agreed target. Opener Luis Reece, who like Smit, Wilson and Jeewan Mendis was making his first-class debut for Derbyshire, raised his maiden Championship century to 168, two short of Madsen's 2009 record for a batsman on his first appearance for the county. Reece and Godleman had already shared their second consecutive hundred partnership before the donated runs, following the non-first-class match at Loughborough, but extended it to 333, a Derbyshire first-wicket record (beating 322 by Harry Storer and Joseph Bowden against Essex in 1929) and their third-highest for any wicket. Earlier, Buck had completed career-bests with ball and bat as Northamptonshire – having slipped from 101 without loss to 171 for eight – put on 136 for their last two wickets to claim a small lead.

Close of play: first day, Derbyshire 219-6 (Hughes 1, Mendis 0); second day, Northamptonshire 291-9 (Holden 68, Sanderson 8); third day, Derbyshire 142-0 (Reece 69, Godleman 63).

Derbyshire

L. M. Reece c Kleinveldt b Sanderson	19	– c Buck b Newton	168
*B. A. Godleman lbw b Sanderson	33	– not out	156
S. J. Thakor lbw b Buck	22	– not out	12
W. L. Madsen c Wakely b Kleinveldt	12		
D. Smit c Wakely b Buck	19		
†G. C. Wilson lbw b Buck	72		
A. L. Hughes c Rossington b Kleinveldt	21		
B. M. A. J. Mendis c Duckett b Sanderson	5		
T. P. Milnes c Keogh b Buck	24		
A. P. Palladino not out	6		
W. S. Davis c and b Buck	1		
B 21, lb 16, nb 10	47	B 5, lb 2, w 2, nb 6	15
1/62 (1) 2/77 (2) 3/114 (4) 4/114 (3) 5/206 (5) 6/219 (6) 7/226 (8) 8/268 (7) 9/278 (9) 10/281 (11) (88.1 overs)	281	1/333 (1) (1 wkt dec, 82.2 overs)	351

Kleinveldt 21–4–57–2; Sanderson 23–6–59–3; Buck 24.1–5–68–5; Crook 15–2–47–0; Keogh 5–1–13–0. *Second innings*—Kleinveldt 15–4–51–0; Sanderson 11–3–22–0; Buck 9–3–19–0; Keogh 12–3–39–0; Crook 8–2–17–0; Holden 4–0–12–0; Newton 9–0–82–1; Wakely 9.2–0–75–0; Duckett 2–0–9–0; Rossington 3–0–18–0.

Northamptonshire

B. M. Duckett c Smit b Thakor	53 – c Wilson b Davis	16
R. I. Newton c Madsen b Davis	50 – c Wilson b Mendis	98
*A. G. Wakely c Madsen b Thakor	1 – lbw b Davis	0
R. I. Keogh c Hughes b Davis	7 – c Wilson b Palladino	24
†A. M. Rossington lbw b Davis	17 – c Smit b Palladino	11
R. E. Levi c Wilson b Palladino	11 – c Wilson b Mendis	99
M. D. E. Holden b Milnes	76 – c Godleman b Mendis	44
S. P. Crook c Smit b Mendis	13 – not out	20
R. K. Kleinveldt c Wilson b Davis	1 – not out	16
N. L. Buck lbw b Mendis	43	
B. W. Sanderson not out	8	
B 8, lb 3, w 1, nb 15	27	B 1, w 1 2
1/101 (1) 2/105 (3) 3/123 (2) (82.4 overs)	307	1/56 (1) (7 wkts, 64.5 overs) 330
4/136 (4) 5/153 (6) 6/153 (5)		2/56 (3) 3/112 (4)
7/166 (8) 8/171 (9) 9/260 (10) 10/307 (7)		4/124 (5) 5/214 (2) 6/276 (6) 7/299 (7)

Milnes 15.4–4–58–1; Palladino 12–3–29–1; Reece 3–0–19–0; Davis 17–3–60–4; Mendis 19–4–60–2; Thakor 11.1–2–54–2; Madsen 4.5–0–16–0. *Second innings*—Milnes 11–2–67–0; Palladino 9–2–36–2; Davis 10–1–37–2; Mendis 19–1–84–3; Thakor 3–0–27–0; Reece 2–0–21–0; Smit 10.5–0–57–0.

Umpires: P. K. Baldwin and M. J. Saggers.

At Canterbury, April 21–23. DERBYSHIRE lost to KENT by 169 runs.

DERBYSHIRE v WORCESTERSHIRE

At Derby, May 19–22. Worcestershire won by an innings and 42 runs. Worcestershire 24pts, Derbyshire 5pts. Toss: uncontested. Championship debut: N. M. Lyon.

Bolstered by victories in their opening two Championship games, Worcestershire's batsmen reignited a contest that had lost all but 63 overs to rain in the first two days. The openers put on 243, with Mitchell passing 10,000 first-class runs for the county on the way to his 25th century, and D'Oliveira – given a life on 42 – scoring his fourth. Their reward came when Derbyshire's inept last-day collapse made it three out of three for Leach, Worcestershire's new captain, whose nine wickets in the match gave him 22 for the season at 14 apiece. He declared on the final morning with a first-innings lead of 140, but had only 76 overs to complete what appeared an unlikely victory. It took less than 30. At 34 for six, Derbyshire's lowest total against Worcestershire – 54 at New Road in 1935 – was under threat, but Mendis pulled three fours in an over, and Palladino struck three sixes before the Australian Test off-spinner Nathan Lyon wrapped up Derbyshire's third consecutive defeat, just before 3pm.

Close of play: first day, Derbyshire 111-3 (Reece 53, Godleman 13); second day, Derbyshire 200-6 (Smit 27, Mendis 0); third day, Worcestershire 323-3 (Leach 22).

Derbyshire

B. T. Slater b Leach	2	– c Fell b Barnard	7
L. M. Reece c Köhler-Cadmore b Shantry	54	– run out	8
S. J. Thakor c Mitchell b Shantry	23	– lbw b Barnard	0
W. L. Madsen c Cox b Tongue	11	– c Cox b Leach	12
*B. A. Godleman c Cox b Leach	19	– lbw b Leach	0
A. L. Hughes lbw b Lyon	53	– lbw b Leach	6
†D. Smit c Mitchell b Leach	33	– lbw b Leach	9
B. M. A. J. Mendis c Fell b Leach	19	– c Cox b Leach	16
T. A. I. Taylor c Cox b Barnard	17	– c Cox b Tongue	9
A. P. Palladino lbw b Barnard	32	– c Barnard b Lyon	28
B. D. Cotton not out	0	– not out	1
Lb 8, nb 4	12	Lb 2	2

1/2 (1) 2/57 (3) 3/79 (4) (92.1 overs) 275
4/118 (2) 5/122 (5) 6/200 (6)
7/218 (7) 8/225 (8) 9/270 (9) 10/275 (10)

1/9 (1) 2/15 (3) (29.4 overs) 98
3/18 (2) 4/18 (5)
5/33 (4) 6/34 (6) 7/58 (8)
8/59 (7) 9/78 (9) 10/98 (10)

Leach 23–6–50–4; Barnard 13.1–2–33–2; Shantry 17–3–49–2; Tongue 16–4–62–1; Lyon 23–4–73–1. *Second innings*—Leach 13–2–32–5; Barnard 8–3–34–2; Lyon 6.4–3–27–1; Tongue 2–0–3–1.

Worcestershire

D. K. H. Mitchell lbw b Thakor	120
B. L. D'Oliveira c and b Mendis	150
T. C. Fell b Mendis	13
*J. Leach c Madsen b Mendis	22
J. M. Clarke c Madsen b Taylor	8
T. Köhler-Cadmore b Thakor	42
†O. B. Cox c Reece b Thakor	27
E. G. Barnard st Smit b Thakor	8
J. C. Tongue c Reece b Mendis	2
J. D. Shantry not out	0
B 7, lb 4, nb 12	23

1/243 (1) (9 wkts dec, 89.2 overs) 415
2/282 (3) 3/323 (2)
4/323 (4) 5/341 (5) 6/385 (7)
7/394 (8) 8/413 (9) 9/415 (6)

N. M. Lyon did not bat.

Cotton 13–2–59–0; Palladino 17–0–74–0; Mendis 24–3–98–4; Taylor 12–1–62–1; Thakor 12.2–2–45–4; Reece 5–1–25–0; Madsen 6–0–41–0.

Umpires: S. J. O'Shaughnessy and R. J. Warren.

DERBYSHIRE v LEICESTERSHIRE

At Derby, May 25–28. Drawn. Derbyshire 11pts, Leicestershire 11pts. Toss: Leicestershire.

Derbyshire's losing run came to a halt, but not for many years had a Championship pitch here so overwhelmingly favoured the bat. Both counties plundered their highest totals against each other, both registered a record partnership for this fixture, and only Wilson's dismissal for 97 prevented both having three centurions. Leicestershire took first use of the pitch, and Cosgrove, dropped on eight, passed 13,000 first-class runs en route to the second-highest of his 34 hundreds; six had now come against Derbyshire, including his only double. Ackermann made his first century for Leicestershire, before Eckersley scored the fastest of the match, a career-best 158, adding 239 with Cosgrove, a fourth-wicket record between these teams. The second-wicket record soon followed when Godleman, in his 50th first-class game for Derbyshire, and Thakor, with a Championship-best, put on 236. In a game no bowler will want to recall, Sri Lankan leg-spinner Mendis's first-innings six for 204, and match return of eight for 283, were the most expensive in Derbyshire's history.

Close of play: first day, Leicestershire 415-3 (Cosgrove 137, Eckersley 77); second day, Derbyshire 154-1 (Godleman 60, Thakor 35); third day, Derbyshire 532-8 (Taylor 16, Hemmings 19).

Leicestershire

P. J. Horton c Smit b Palladino	20	– c Smit b Taylor	56
H. E. Dearden c Hughes b Taylor	46	– c Godleman b Mendis	78
C. N. Ackermann c Wilson b Mendis	118	– not out	38
*M. J. Cosgrove c Palladino b Mendis	188	– c Godleman b Mendis	15
E. J. H. Eckersley c Hughes b Taylor	158	– not out	20
M. L. Pettini lbw b Mendis	35		
†L. J. Hill c Smit b Mendis	12		
R. J. Sayer c Hughes b Taylor	0		
Z. J. Chappell not out	9		
C. J. McKay c Palladino b Mendis	7		
D. Klein st Smit b Mendis	7		
Lb 3, nb 16	19	B 1, lb 1, nb 8	10
1/37 (1) 2/101 (2) 3/276 (3) 4/515 (4) 5/581 (5) 6/591 (6) 7/592 (8) 8/596 (7) 9/604 (10) 10/619 (11) — (144.3 overs)	619	1/125 (1) 2/149 (2) 3/166 (4) — (3 wkts dec, 57 overs)	217
110 overs: 488-3			

Taylor 25–2–113–3; Hemmings 19–5–70–0; Thakor 20–3–89–0; Palladino 22–5–97–1; Mendis 52.3–3–204–6; Hughes 3–0–22–0; Madsen 3–1–21–0. *Second innings*—Taylor 11–1–45–1; Hemmings 5–1–24–0; Mendis 22–5–79–2; Palladino 6–1–25–0; Madsen 5–0–10–0; Thakor 6–1–26–0; Slater 2–0–6–0.

Derbyshire

B. T. Slater c Eckersley b Chappell	42	– not out	28
*B. A. Godleman b Chappell	141	– not out	6
S. J. Thakor c Hill b McKay	132		
W. L. Madsen c Eckersley b McKay	2		
A. L. Hughes c Dearden b Klein	4		
G. C. Wilson b Chappell	97		
†D. Smit c Dearden b Klein	40		
B. M. A. J. Mendis c McKay b Ackermann	0		
T. A. I. Taylor not out	17		
R. P. Hemmings c Hill b McKay	19		
A. P. Palladino c Hill b Chappell	0		
B 9, lb 11, nb 14, p 5	39	B 4, nb 4	8
1/85 (1) 2/321 (3) 3/329 (4) 4/334 (5) 5/384 (2) 6/465 (7) 7/472 (8) 8/506 (6) 9/532 (10) 10/533 (11) — (142.5 overs)	533	(no wkt, 10 overs)	42
110 overs: 425-5			

Klein 25–2–108–2; McKay 33–12–78–3; Sayer 38–5–142–0; Chappell 23.5–4–108–4; Ackermann 18–6–48–1; Cosgrove 1–0–5–0; Dearden 4–0–19–0. *Second innings*—Klein 3–0–14–0; McKay 3–1–3–0; Chappell 2–0–16–0; Sayer 2–0–5–0.

Umpires: D. J. Millns and B. V. Taylor.

At Derby, May 29. DERBYSHIRE v SOUTH AFRICA A. No result (see South Africa A tour section).

At Nottingham, June 2–5. DERBYSHIRE drew with NOTTINGHAMSHIRE.

At Northampton, June 9–11. DERBYSHIRE lost to NORTHAMPTONSHIRE by 128 runs.

At Cardiff, June 26–29. DERBYSHIRE beat GLAMORGAN by 39 runs. *Afghan off-spinner Hamidullah Qadri, aged 16, becomes the youngest to take five in an innings in the Championship; it was Derbyshire's first win in two years.*

DERBYSHIRE v DURHAM

At Chesterfield, July 3–6. Durham won by six wickets. Durham 22pts, Derbyshire 7pts. Toss: Derbyshire. County debuts: Imran Tahir, G. S. Sandhu.

Burnham and Pringle stood up to a trial by spin on a deteriorating Queen's Park pitch to win a compelling match for Durham with an unbroken stand of 127. Derbyshire looked to 16-year-old off-spinner Hamidullah Qadri, who had taken five wickets on debut the previous week, and 38-year-old leg-spinner Imran Tahir, who had picked up five on the second day of his debut for his sixth first-class county. But Durham met the challenge positively, and Pringle clinched it with a driven six. Derbyshire had held the advantage, thanks to a century from Critchley in his first Championship game of the season and a tenth-wicket stand of 102 between Godleman and former Middlesex seamer Gurjit Sandhu, who had never reached double figures before. Durham trailed by 163 when Tahir reduced them to 205 for eight. But Coughlin and McCarthy added 90 and, though Hughes made a measured second-innings hundred, Durham's bowlers kept the target down to 282. Two wins in three games lifted them off the bottom of the division, despite their 48-point handicap.

Close of play: first day, Derbyshire 332-9 (Godleman 79, Sandhu 36); second day, Durham 274-8 (Coughlin 62, McCarthy 32); third day, Durham 36-0 (Steel 7, Richardson 29).

Derbyshire

B. T. Slater c Clark b Potts	27	– c Collingwood b Rushworth	2
L. M. Reece lbw b Rushworth	0	– (3) lbw b Coughlin	37
W. L. Madsen c Pringle b Coughlin	54	– (4) c Poynter b Rushworth	4
A. L. Hughes b McCarthy	2	– (5) lbw b Pringle	108
M. J. J. Critchley lbw b Potts	102	– (6) c Poynter b McCarthy	28
*B. A. Godleman c Poynter b Coughlin	98	– (2) b Coughlin	8
†D. Smit c Rushworth b McCarthy	1	– c Collingwood b McCarthy	4
A. P. Palladino c Collingwood b Potts	7	– c Poynter b Pringle	0
H. Qadri c and b McCarthy	0	– (11) not out	0
Imran Tahir c Poynter b Steel	4	– b Potts	5
G. S. Sandhu not out	46	– (9) b Potts	9
B 7, lb 18, w 2	27	Lb 7, w 2	9
1/5 (2) 2/59 (1) 3/74 (4) 4/139 (3) 5/238 (5) 6/241 (7) 7/254 (8) 8/261 (9) 9/266 (10) 10/368 (6) (110.3 overs)	368	1/2 (1) 2/22 (2) 3/31 (4) 4/90 (3) 5/142 (6) 6/146 (7) 7/147 (8) 8/194 (9) 9/214 (10) 10/214 (5) (65.1 overs)	214
110 overs: 364-9			

Rushworth 29–6–69–1; Coughlin 19.3–2–90–2; Potts 27–7–75–3; McCarthy 18–0–87–3; Collingwood 6–4–6–0; Pringle 6–3–7–0; Steel 5–0–9–1. *Second innings*—Rushworth 10–0–29–2; Coughlin 13–2–57–2; Potts 14–4–31–2; McCarthy 9–1–38–2; Pringle 18.1–5–47–2; Steel 1–0–5–0.

Durham

C. T. Steel run out	21	– c Smit b Qadri	25
M. J. Richardson b Qadri	64	– c Madsen b Imran Tahir	62
J. T. A. Burnham b Imran Tahir	35	– not out	93
G. Clark lbw b Imran Tahir	18	– c Madsen b Imran Tahir	23
*P. D. Collingwood b Imran Tahir	4	– c Madsen b Qadri	6
R. D. Pringle lbw b Sandhu	1	– not out	62
P. Coughlin not out	73		
†S. W. Poynter c Palladino b Imran Tahir	20		
M. J. Potts b Imran Tahir	0		
B. J. McCarthy lbw b Sandhu	39		
C. Rushworth lbw b Sandhu	5		
B 4, lb 3, nb 14	21	B 8, lb 6	14
1/52 (1) 2/119 (3) 3/127 (2) 4/134 (5) 5/137 (6) 6/163 (4) 7/205 (8) 8/205 (9) 9/295 (10) 10/301 (11) (87.3 overs)	301	1/91 (1) 2/95 (2) 3/147 (4) 4/158 (5) (4 wkts, 80.2 overs)	285

Palladino 14–4–40–0; Sandhu 14.3–2–60–3; Reece 10–2–42–0; Imran Tahir 33–3–110–5; Qadri 16–3–42–1. *Second innings*—Palladino 10–4–23–0; Sandhu 7–0–27–0; Reece 4–3–5–0; Imran Tahir 31–6–89–2; Qadri 24–2–91–2; Madsen 2–0–12–0; Critchley 2.2–0–24–0.

Umpires: J. W. Lloyds and P. R. Pollard.

DERBYSHIRE v NOTTINGHAMSHIRE

At Derby, August 6–9. Nottinghamshire won by an innings and 61 runs. Nottinghamshire 24pts, Derbyshire 4pts. Toss: uncontested.

An imperious double-century from Hales, ten wickets for Hutton and a county record for Read added up to an utterly dominant performance from division leaders Nottinghamshire. Hales scored a run a ball in a contest previously controlled by the seamers, and fell only two short of matching Derbyshire's first innings on his own. Read joined him in a sixth-wicket stand of 204, then took centre stage on the final day when, on the eve of his 39th birthday, he held a nick off Wilson. It was his 968th first-class dismissal for Nottinghamshire, overhauling Tom Oates's 92-year-old record. The bowler was Footitt, rejoining his native county on a ground where he spent six seasons, though he was overshadowed by Hutton's two five-wicket hauls. South African fast bowler Hardus Viljoen made a long-awaited Championship debut for Derbyshire, following a series of injuries. But even the washout of four sessions could not save his side from a heavy defeat. Needing to survive 75 overs on the last day with nine wickets in hand, they were bowled out with 12 to spare.

Close of play: first day, Nottinghamshire 93-2 (Mullaney 35, Patel 21); second day, Derbyshire 45-1 (Slater 23, Godleman 3); third day, no play.

Derbyshire

B. T. Slater c Wessels b Hutton	23	– c Wessels b Hutton	44
L. M. Reece lbw b Footitt	45	– c Read b Footitt	2
*B. A. Godleman b Ball	11	– c Hutton b Patel	47
W. L. Madsen c Read b Ball	12	– (7) b Hutton	14
A. L. Hughes not out	55	– (4) lbw b Hutton	24
†G. C. Wilson lbw b Hutton	13	– (5) c Read b Footitt	0
H. R. Hosein c Read b Hutton	0	– (6) c Read b Ball	11
T. A. I. Taylor c Read b Hutton	7	– lbw b Hutton	15
G. C. Viljoen lbw b Hutton	0	– b Ball	2
A. P. Palladino c Taylor b Ball	1	– b Hutton	6
B. D. Cotton b Footitt	32	– not out	17
B 1, lb 10, nb 10	21	B 4, lb 22, w 1, nb 18	45
1/34 (1) 2/63 (3) 3/89 (4) 4/108 (2) 5/133 (6) 6/133 (7) 7/157 (8) 8/157 (9) 9/172 (10) 10/220 (11) (59.2 overs)	220	1/14 (2) 2/110 (1) 3/130 (3) 4/137 (5) 5/154 (4) 6/166 (6) 7/172 (7) 8/175 (9) 9/206 (8) 10/227 (10) (74.5 overs)	227

Ball 19–6–63–3; Footitt 14.2–2–49–2; Hutton 16–4–52–5; Mullaney 1–0–4–0; Wood 6–0–25–0; Patel 3–0–16–0. *Second innings*—Ball 19–8–33–2; Footitt 13–2–46–2; Hutton 18.5–1–74–5; Patel 18–9–22–1; Wood 6–1–26–0.

Nottinghamshire

S. J. Mullaney c Slater b Taylor	50	L. Wood not out	12
J. D. Libby c Wilson b Viljoen	7	J. T. Ball c Wilson b Reece	43
B. R. M. Taylor lbw b Palladino	4	B 11, lb 5, w 10, nb 24	50
S. R. Patel run out	25		
A. D. Hales c Viljoen b Madsen	218	1/39 (2) (9 wkts dec, 103.3 overs)	508
M. H. Wessels c Wilson b Viljoen	13	2/56 (3) 3/103 (4)	
*†C. M. W. Read c Wilson b Taylor	75	4/151 (1) 5/231 (6) 6/435 (7)	
B. A. Hutton c Hosein b Madsen	11	7/443 (5) 8/455 (8) 9/508 (10)	

M. H. A. Footitt did not bat.

Viljoen 26–6–103–2; Taylor 16–3–75–2; Palladino 18–2–67–1; Cotton 10–0–64–0; Reece 9.3–0–69–1; Hughes 9–2–36–0; Madsen 15–0–78–2.

Umpires: T. Lungley and N. A. Mallender.

At Derby, August 11–13. DERBYSHIRE drew with WEST INDIANS (see West Indian tour section).

At Chester-le-Street, August 28–31. DERBYSHIRE lost to DURHAM by nine wickets.

DERBYSHIRE v GLAMORGAN

At Derby, September 5–8. Drawn. Derbyshire 6pts, Glamorgan 8pts. Toss: uncontested.

Rain limited play to 72 overs, all on day three, leaving two of the second division's struggling counties little chance to improve their positions. Glamorgan might have restricted Derbyshire's efforts further in helpful bowling conditions, but their lines were inconsistent and they dropped a large number of catches, three off Carey.

Close of play: first day, no play; second day, no play; third day, Derbyshire 236-9 (Critchley 24, Davis 0).

Derbyshire

B. T. Slater lbw b Carey	17	Imran Tahir b Hogan	4
L. M. Reece b de Lange	53	W. S. Davis not out	0
*B. A. Godleman c Cooke b Meschede	10		
W. L. Madsen c Carlson b de Lange	20	B 1, lb 4, nb 6	11
A. L. Hughes c Cooke b Carey	44		
†G. C. Wilson lbw b Carey	45	1/27 (1) 2/54 (3) (9 wkts, 72 overs)	236
M. J. J. Critchley not out	24	3/100 (4) 4/109 (2)	
H. W. Podmore b Hogan	8	5/187 (5) 6/208 (6)	
G. C. Viljoen lbw b Meschede	0	7/228 (8) 8/229 (9) 9/236 (10)	

De Lange 17–4–78–2; Carey 17–2–49–3; Meschede 17–2–60–2; Hogan 19–7–31–2; Salter 2–0–13–0.

Glamorgan

N. J. Selman, J. A. Rudolph, J. R. Murphy, C. A. Ingram, K. S. Carlson, †C. B. Cooke, C. A. J. Meschede, A. G. Salter, M. de Lange, L. J. Carey, *M. G. Hogan.

Umpires: G. D. Lloyd and B. V. Taylor.

At Hove, September 12–15. DERBYSHIRE beat SUSSEX by 45 runs.

DERBYSHIRE v KENT

At Chesterfield, September 19–22. Abandoned. Derbyshire 5pts, Kent 5pts.

A mid-season decision to switch this fixture to Chesterfield, in case a Boyzone pop concert at Derby three days earlier damaged the County Ground, backfired spectacularly. Heavy rain before the scheduled first day soaked the outfield, which never recovered. It was the second time in successive seasons that a four-day match at Queen's Park had been abandoned without a ball bowled, though one was successfully staged in July; Derbyshire said they had learned they should use Chesterfield only in the "core summer months". After a complaint from Kent, the Cricket Discipline Commission cautioned Derbyshire in November. They advised all first-class counties to avoid outgrounds before mid-May or in September, warning that future cases could result in fines or penalty points.

At Bristol, September 25–28. DERBYSHIRE beat GLOUCESTERSHIRE by 157 runs.

DURHAM

Way down in the hole

TIM WELLOCK

Durham began and ended the season under a cloud, largely because of the ECB sanctions imposed in October 2016. After losing four of the first five Championship games, they enjoyed a seven-match unbeaten run, only to lose the last two, as news of three departures emerged. Pre-season talk from new chairman Sir Ian Botham, dismissing the 48-point deduction as "only two wins", was forgotten; their eventual three victories left them next to bottom of Division Two. Even without the penalty, they would have been seventh of ten.

Once they had shrugged off the poor start, Durham performed creditably in the Royal London Cup and would have qualified for a quarter-final on net run-rate had they not begun with a two-point deficit. A handicap of four in the NatWest T20 Blast was too great a hurdle for a squad lacking big hitters; they finished as far adrift as they began. Keaton Jennings was captain in the one-day competition, and Paul Coughlin in the T20; but, as with the last limited-overs captain, Mark Stoneman, a taste of leadership could not dissuade them from leaving. Having resisted the chance to move a year earlier, both took up an option to go if Durham failed to earn promotion: Jennings headed for Lancashire, Coughlin for Nottinghamshire.

Graham Onions's departure at the age of 35 was more surprising. After missing six matches through injury, he broke Simon Brown's county record of 518 first-class wickets in early September, but told the media he had not been offered a new contract. "Leaving Durham is the last thing I want to do," he said, while stressing he wanted coaching opportunities; when a two-year deal did emerge it was conditional on him getting through the first uninjured, and made no promises on coaching. He accepted a two-year offer from Lancashire "with a heavy heart".

Initially continuing his prolific form of 2016, Jennings scored more runs in his first four Championship innings (followed by a couple of one-day centuries) than in the remaining 17; he totalled 97 in his last ten, starting with a duck at Canterbury just before he went on international duty. His loss of form was extraordinary. With his first opening partner, the South African Stephen Cook, failing to shine, Durham rarely got a good start. And when New Zealander Tom Latham took over, he was ruled out for several weeks by a stress fracture in his foot. It left them without an overseas man for much of the T20 Blast, but Latham was invited back after averaging 63 in the Championship games he did play. He was seen as a potential captain in case Paul Collingwood, who signed for a fourth season beyond his intended retirement, decided five and a half years at the first-class helm was enough. Not that his form showed any sign of slipping, even at the age of 41: he was the leading scorer with 1,087 Championship runs, and hit Durham's first T20 century.

Graham Clark

The signing of Cameron Steel was a success, and Graham Clark's consistent scoring finally repaid the faith shown in him. But hopes that others would prosper in the second division were disappointed. Jack Burnham was hampered by a broken thumb, and in October he was suspended for a year for taking cocaine. Michael Richardson began well, especially in the one-day games, but faded after a hamstring strain. He resumed keeping wicket after Stuart Poynter's failure to build on cameos cost him his place. Former captain Will Smith returned after four years at Hampshire, and his fellow 35-year-old Nathan Rimmington, an Australian seam bowler with a British passport, joined on a two-year deal.

Discounting Ben Stokes, whose only (unsuccessful) appearance came in a pink-ball Championship match against Worcestershire, all the seamers were injured at some stage, although Chris Rushworth was almost ever-present. Usman Arshad missed two months through injury, played only T20 cricket, and was released.

For the second successive year, Mark Wood was pressed into service late on, only for it to transpire that decisions at Lord's meant he was risking further injury to no avail. In 2016, he needed ankle surgery after helping Durham stay in Division One, not realising that the ECB had already decided relegation would be part of the financial rescue package. This time, after recovering from a bruised heel, he played the final game to prove his fitness for the winter's Ashes; when the squad was announced mid-match, he wasn't in it, and he lost his Test contract.

Of the three Academy players who made first-class debuts, seamer Matty Potts, from Sunderland, had the biggest impact. Slow left-armers George Harding and Liam Trevaskis played one Championship game each, but off-spinner Adam Hickey, the spinner expected to provide the greatest competition for Ryan Pringle, missed two months through injury.

Chief executive David Harker – the only survivor from the old board apart from Bob Jackson, a director since Minor Counties days – felt that, following the ECB bailout, the club's financial position was more secure than at any time in their first-class history. But the excess borrowing to fund the required ground development appeared futile when the sanctions included the loss of Test status. A Twenty20 international against West Indies in late September attracted a full house, but was overshadowed by an accident when a hole appeared in the flooring of a stand built for the Ashes Test four years earlier. Three spectators were injured, and one broke her leg. It was the last thing Durham needed.

Championship attendance: 23,179.

DURHAM RESULTS

All first-class matches – Played 14: Won 3, Lost 6, Drawn 5.
County Championship matches – Played 14: Won 3, Lost 6, Drawn 5.

Specsavers County Championship, 9th in Division 2;
NatWest T20 Blast, 9th in North Group; Royal London One-Day Cup, 5th in North Group.

COUNTY CHAMPIONSHIP AVERAGES, BATTING AND FIELDING

Cap		Birthplace	M	I	NO	R	HS	100	Avge	Ct
	T. W. M. Latham¶	*Christchurch, NZ*	4	7	1	382	124	2	63.66	5
1998	P. D. Collingwood	*Shotley Bridge‡*	14	24	2	1,087	177	3	49.40	23
	C. T. Steel	*Greenbrae, USA*	13	24	2	899	224	2	40.86	3
	W. J. Weighell	*Middlesbrough*	4	7	3	162	58	0	40.50	0
	G. Clark	*Whitehaven*	12	21	0	769	109	1	36.61	10
	P. Coughlin	*Sunderland‡*	8	12	2	364	73*	0	36.40	3
	M. A. Wood§	*Ashington*	5	8	2	195	72*	0	32.50	0
	B. J. McCarthy	*Dublin, Ireland*	5	6	2	129	39	0	32.25	3
	M. J. Richardson	*Port Elizabeth, SA*	10	16	1	460	82	0	30.66	20
	S. C. Cook¶	*Johannesburg, SA*	7	14	1	348	89*	0	26.76	5
	†K. K. Jennings	*Johannesburg, SA*	11	21	2	490	102*	1	25.78	13
	R. D. Pringle	*Sunderland‡*	13	22	4	459	71	0	25.50	9
	J. T. A. Burnham	*Durham‡*	7	11	2	223	93*	0	24.77	1
	S. W. Poynter	*Hammersmith*	9	14	1	269	65	0	20.69	30
	M. J. Potts	*Sunderland‡*	5	6	2	69	53*	0	17.25	0
	C. Rushworth	*Sunderland‡*	13	17	3	174	57	0	12.42	5
	G. Onions	*Gateshead‡*	8	10	0	58	15	0	5.80	1

Also batted: B. A. Carse†† (*Port Elizabeth, SA*) (2 matches) 7, 61*, 23*; G. H. I. Harding (*Poole*) (1 match) 0; G. T. Main (*Lanark*) (2 matches) 13, 0, 0*; †B. A. Stokes§ (*Christchurch, NZ*) (1 match) 0; †L. Trevaskis (*Carlisle*) (1 match) 5, 9.

‡ *Born in Durham.* § *ECB contract.* ¶ *Official overseas player.* †† *Other non-England-qualified.*

BOWLING

	Style	O	M	R	W	BB	5I	Avge
K. K. Jennings	RM	64	9	214	12	3-37	0	17.83
G. Onions	RFM	237	48	725	32	6-62	1	22.65
C. Rushworth	RFM	436.3	96	1,217	47	5-52	1	25.89
B. J. McCarthy	RFM	164.2	23	653	24	6-63	1	27.20
P. Coughlin	RFM	208.1	31	804	27	5-49	2	29.77
M. A. Wood	RFM	123	17	389	13	5-54	1	29.92
M. J. Potts	RFM	163	37	465	14	3-48	0	33.21
W. J. Weighell	RM	94.5	8	438	11	3-51	0	39.81
R. D. Pringle	OB	197.5	41	688	15	4-73	0	45.86

Also bowled: B. A. Carse (RF) 58–4–191–3; P. D. Collingwood (RM) 77.2–21–199–4; S. C. Cook (RM) 1–0–16–0; G. H. I. Harding (SLA) 36–2–186–4; G. T. Main (RFM) 43–3–219–3; C. T. Steel (LB) 65.2–3–275–8; B. A. Stokes (RFM) 20–3–81–0; L. Trevaskis (SLA) 26–3–126–1.

LEADING ROYAL LONDON CUP AVERAGES (100 runs/4 wickets)

Batting	Runs	HS	Avge	SR	Ct
P. D. Collingwood	224	73*	74.66	111.44	5
M. J. Richardson	424	100*	70.66	89.07	4
K. K. Jennings	460	139	57.50	102.44	6
S. C. Cook	274	106	45.66	87.53	1
G. Clark	275	114	39.28	87.85	6
C. T. Steel	132	77	26.40	72.92	0

Bowling	W	BB	Avge	ER
M. A. Wood	5	3-62	19.20	5.38
W. J. Weighell	18	5-57	23.11	6.30
P. Coughlin	12	3-36	31.00	5.92
P. D. Collingwood	8	3-42	38.00	4.90
C. Rushworth	8	2-50	43.25	5.16
G. H. I. Harding	4	2-52	62.75	5.34

LEADING NATWEST T20 BLAST AVERAGES (100 runs/18 overs)

Batting	Runs	HS	Avge	SR	Ct/St
P. D. Collingwood	346	108*	38.44	**140.08**	3
P. Coughlin	333	53	41.62	**139.91**	2
T. W. M. Latham	139	62	27.80	**139.00**	3
G. Clark	272	71	19.42	**134.65**	5
S. W. Poynter	188	61*	37.60	**134.28**	6/3
M. J. Richardson	261	53	32.62	**122.53**	5
R. D. Pringle	106	25	11.77	**117.77**	5
J. T. A. Burnham	123	53*	15.37	**89.13**	3

Bowling	W	BB	Avge	ER
P. D. Collingwood	8	4-24	35.12	**7.80**
U. Arshad	31	1-28	59.00	**8.10**
R. D. Pringle	11	3-30	24.36	**8.37**
B. J. McCarthy	6	3-33	23.16	**8.68**
C. Rushworth	3	1-14	79.33	**9.15**
W. J. Weighell	9	3-28	38.88	**9.33**
P. Coughlin	13	4-22	24.84	**9.98**

FIRST-CLASS COUNTY RECORDS

Highest score for	273	M. L. Love v Hampshire at Chester-le-Street	2003
Highest score against	501*	B. C. Lara (Warwickshire) at Birmingham	1994
Leading run-scorer	**11,731**	**P. D. Collingwood (avge 35.12)**	**1996–2017**
Best bowling for	10-47	O. D. Gibson v Hampshire at Chester-le-Street	2007
Best bowling against	9-34	J. A. R. Harris (Middlesex) at Lord's	2015
Leading wicket-taker	**527**	**G. Onions (avge 25.58)**	**2004–2017**
Highest total for	648-5 dec	v Nottinghamshire at Chester-le-Street	2009
Highest total against	810-4 dec	by Warwickshire at Birmingham	1994
Lowest total for	67	v Middlesex at Lord's	1996
Lowest total against	18	by Durham MCCU at Chester-le-Street	2012

LIST A COUNTY RECORDS

Highest score for	164	B. A. Stokes v Nottinghamshire at Chester-le-St.	2014
Highest score against	**174**	**J. M. Bairstow (Yorkshire) at Leeds**	**2017**
Leading run-scorer	**5,988**	**P. D. Collingwood (avge 33.45)**	**1995–2017**
Best bowling for	7-32	S. P. Davis v Lancashire at Chester-le-Street	1983
Best bowling against	6-22	A. Dale (Glamorgan) at Colwyn Bay	1993
Leading wicket-taker	298	N. Killeen (avge 23.96)	1995–2010
Highest total for	353-8	v Nottinghamshire at Chester-le-Street	2014
Highest total against	361-7	by Essex at Chelmsford	1996
Lowest total for	72	v Warwickshire at Birmingham	2002
Lowest total against	63	by Hertfordshire at Darlington	1964

TWENTY20 COUNTY RECORDS

Highest score for	**108***	**P. D. Collingwood v Worcestershire at Worcester**	**2017**
Highest score against	127	T. Köhler-Cadmore (Worcs) at Worcester	2016
Leading run-scorer	3,207	P. Mustard (avge 25.05)	2003–16
Best bowling for	5-6	P. D. Collingwood v Northants at Chester-le-St.	2011
Best bowling against	5-16	R. M. Pyrah (Yorkshire) at Scarborough	2011
Leading wicket-taker	93	G. R. Breese (avge 21.56)	2004–14
Highest total for	225-2	v Leicestershire at Chester-le-Street	2010
Highest total against	225-6	by Worcestershire at Worcester	2016
Lowest total for	93	v Kent at Canterbury	2009
Lowest total against	47	by Northamptonshire at Chester-le-Street	2011

ADDRESS

Emirates Durham International Cricket Ground, Riverside, Chester-le-Street, County Durham DH3 3QR; 0191 387 1717; reception@durhamccc.co.uk; www.durhamccc.co.uk.

OFFICIALS

Captain P. D. Collingwood
(50-overs) **2017** K. K. Jennings
(Twenty20) **2017** P. Coughlin
Director of cricket G. Cook
First-team coach J. J. B. Lewis
Academy coach J. B. Windows

Chairman Sir Ian Botham
Chief operating officer R. Dowson
Chief executive D. Harker
Head groundsman V. Demain
Scorer W. R. Dobson

At Chester-le-Street, April 7–9 (not first-class). **Durham won by 459 runs. ‡Durham 404-5 dec** (84.2 overs) (J. T. A. Burnham 150, M. J. Richardson 116, G. Clark 57) **and 270-6 dec** (53 overs) (K. K. Jennings 71, C. T. Steel 82; B. W. M. Graves 3-35); **Durham MCCU 152** (58.3 overs) (G. Onions 4-21, R. D. Pringle 4-37) **and 63** (33.2 overs) (G. Onions 4-3, M. A. Wood 4-6). *County debut:* C. T. Steel. *The 16th encounter between Durham and their university neighbours since 2001 was the first without first-class status, as the students had already played their two allotted first-class games. The county won in seven sessions. Jack Burnham and Michael Richardson shared a third-wicket stand of 209 on the opening day, and Keaton Jennings declared on the final morning with a lead of 522. At 2-5, it seemed the university might fall short of their 18 all out five years earlier, but they held on for a couple more hours. Graham Onions finished with match figures of 8-24.*

DURHAM v NOTTINGHAMSHIRE

At Chester-le-Street, April 14–17. Nottinghamshire won by nine wickets. Nottinghamshire 22pts, Durham 3pts. Toss: uncontested. County debut: S. C. Cook.

With both relegated sides boasting strong seam attacks, the visitors' right to bowl proved a big advantage. The floodlights were on for most of a cloudy opening day – when 13 wickets fell in the first 51 overs – and the pitch was flattest on the last, when Greg Smith and Libby, chasing 108, opened with 93. The decisive contribution had been Fletcher's 92 as nightwatchman, equalling his career-best at Southampton in 2009. He was run out after slipping and dropping his bat as he tried to regain his ground at the non-striker's end, but helped Nottinghamshire to a 143-run lead. South Africa's Stephen Cook made two and nought on debut for Durham, but Jennings was untroubled carrying his bat – for the second successive home game, following his 201 against Surrey the previous September. Collingwood joined him in reviving them from 24 for three, making 40 before falling to a leaping left-handed catch, high above his head, by Wessels at first slip during one of several fiery bursts from Pattinson. Nottinghamshire's second Championship win was Durham's first home defeat since 2015.

Close of play: first day, Nottinghamshire 96-4 (Patel 43, Fletcher 3); second day, Durham 162-5 (Jennings 62, Pringle 2); third day, Durham 201-7 (Jennings 82, Wood 0).

Durham

	First innings		Second innings	
S. C. Cook c Read b Ball	2	–	c Wessels b Ball	0
K. K. Jennings b Pattinson	28	–	not out	102
J. T. A. Burnham b Fletcher	15	–	c Read b Ball	4
M. J. Richardson c Smith b Fletcher	5	–	lbw b Fletcher	8
*P. D. Collingwood lbw b Ball	8	–	c Wessels b Pattinson	40
P. Coughlin c Read b Gurney	3	–	lbw b Pattinson	36
R. D. Pringle c Read b Ball	0	–	b Ball	2
†S. W. Poynter b Fletcher	65	–	b Gurney	17
M. A. Wood lbw b Pattinson	11	–	c Libby b Fletcher	21
G. Onions b Pattinson	2	–	b Gurney	2
C. Rushworth not out	9	–	run out	1
B 5, lb 5, nb 4	14		B 5, lb 6, nb 6	17
1/6 (1) 2/47 (3) 3/55 (2) 4/55 (4) 5/69 (5) 6/69 (7) 7/71 (6) 8/104 (9) 9/110 (10) 10/162 (8) (45.4 overs)	162		1/0 (1) 2/8 (3) 3/24 (4) 4/95 (5) 5/147 (6) 6/162 (7) 7/199 (8) 8/244 (9) 9/249 (10) 10/250 (11) (73.5 overs)	250

Ball 12–3–36–3; Pattinson 13–2–43–3; Gurney 13–3–50–1; Fletcher 7.4–2–23–3. *Second innings*—Ball 22–5–80–3; Pattinson 19–4–41–2; Fletcher 14–4–45–2; Gurney 13.5–2–54–2; Patel 5–1–19–0.

Nottinghamshire

G. P. Smith c Collingwood b Onions	4	– not out	60
J. D. Libby b Rushworth	3	– b Coughlin	39
S. R. Patel c Collingwood b Rushworth	45	– not out	10
A. D. Hales lbw b Rushworth	0		
M. J. Lumb lbw b Wood	33		
L. J. Fletcher run out	92		
M. H. Wessels lbw b Wood	8		
*†C. M. W. Read b Coughlin	17		
J. L. Pattinson c Poynter b Onions	59		
J. T. Ball not out	21		
H. F. Gurney b Rushworth	0		
B 4, lb 13, nb 6	23	Lb 1	1
1/7 (1) 2/7 (2) 3/7 (4) 4/92 (5) 5/98 (3) 6/128 (7) 7/156 (8) 8/264 (6) 9/301 (9) 10/305 (11) (84.3 overs)	305	1/93 (2) (1 wkt, 26.2 overs)	110

Rushworth 23.3–6–54–4; Onions 16–3–58–2; Wood 21–5–63–2; Coughlin 15–1–68–1; Pringle 7–0–30–0; Collingwood 2–0–15–0. *Second innings*—Rushworth 9–2–17–0; Onions 3–1–11–0; Wood 6–0–31–0; Coughlin 4.2–0–26–1; Pringle 4–0–24–0.

Umpires: P. J. Hartley and A. G. Wharf.

At Bristol, April 21–24. DURHAM drew with GLOUCESTERSHIRE.

At Hove, May 21–24. DURHAM lost to SUSSEX by an innings and 177 runs.

At Swansea, May 26–29. DURHAM lost to GLAMORGAN by three wickets.

DURHAM v NORTHAMPTONSHIRE

At Chester-le-Street, June 2–5. Northamptonshire won by two wickets. Northamptonshire 22pts, Durham 3pts. Toss: uncontested.

For the second week running, Durham lost in the final over. Barely 30 spectators remained when play resumed at 5pm on a rain-ravaged fourth day, with Northamptonshire – nine wickets in hand – needing 100 from 17 overs. Wakely's 84 kept them on target, and it came down to three off eight balls. In steady rain, they chaotically lost three wickets, before scampering a bye to win with one delivery to go. With five seamers unavailable, Durham called up Scotsman Gavin Main, three years after his previous Championship appearance, but Coughlin led the attack superbly, converting a first five-wicket haul into match figures of ten for 133. Buck had continued his excellent start at Northamptonshire with a career-best six for 34, though Durham had the worst of the damp conditions. There were maiden centuries for Holden and Steel, team-mates in the Middlesex Second XI the previous year. Holden, on loan to Northamptonshire, was unflappable after being dropped twice early on the second day; Steel showed similar fortitude for Durham after being caught off a no-ball, completing his hundred by hitting Hughes's first delivery, a full toss, over long-on for six.

Close of play: first day, Northamptonshire 59-3 (Holden 19, Hughes 16); second day, Durham 78-1 (Cook 39, McCarthy 3); third day, Northamptonshire 44-1 (Newton 25, Wakely 18).

Durham

S. C. Cook c Wakely b Kleinveldt	16	– b Sanderson	42
K. K. Jennings c Rossington b Buck	20	– st Rossington b Keogh	27
C. T. Steel c Rossington b Sanderson	20	– (4) lbw b Azharullah	128
G. Clark lbw b Buck	20	– (5) b Kleinveldt	6
*P. D. Collingwood c Hughes b Buck	3	– (6) c Rossington b Azharullah	54
M. J. Richardson c Rossington b Buck	27	– (7) c Rossington b Buck	14
R. D. Pringle lbw b Azharullah	0	– (8) not out	47
P. Coughlin c Keogh b Kleinveldt	13	– (9) c sub (R. J. Gleeson) b Azharullah	20
†S. W. Poynter not out	12	– (10) c Wakely b Azharullah	5
B. J. McCarthy c Sanderson b Buck	4	– (3) b Kleinveldt	3
G. T. Main lbw b Buck	13	– lbw b Azharullah	0
Lb 2, w 2, nb 14	18	B 3, lb 2, w 7, nb 18	30
1/30 (1) 2/40 (2) 3/71 (4) 4/77 (5) 5/96 (3) 6/105 (7) 7/125 (6) 8/131 (8) 9/146 (10) 10/166 (11) (45.2 overs)	166	1/69 (2) 2/79 (3) 3/81 (1) 4/98 (5) 5/241 (6) 6/285 (7) 7/325 (4) 8/370 (9) 9/376 (10) 10/376 (11) (112 overs)	376

Kleinveldt 15–3–47–2; Sanderson 11–1–51–1; Buck 11.2–2–34–6; Azharullah 8–1–32–1. *Second innings*—Kleinveldt 25–4–103–2; Sanderson 27–8–67–1; Buck 24–5–57–1; Azharullah 21–5–72–5; Keogh 13–2–56–1; Hughes 2–0–16–0.

Northamptonshire

M. D. E. Holden c Poynter b Collingwood	124	– c Jennings b Coughlin	0
R. I. Newton c Collingwood b Coughlin	2	– c McCarthy b Coughlin	54
*A. G. Wakely c Poynter b McCarthy	0	– run out	84
R. I. Keogh c Poynter b McCarthy	2	– c and b Coughlin	13
C. F. Hughes c Poynter b Coughlin	21	– (7) c Cook b McCarthy	8
†A. M. Rossington c Jennings b McCarthy	65	– (8) c Poynter b Coughlin	0
J. J. Cobb c Collingwood b Coughlin	96	– (5) c Pringle b Coughlin	21
R. K. Kleinveldt c Richardson b Coughlin	0	– (6) c Collingwood b McCarthy	9
N. L. Buck c Jennings b Coughlin	1	– not out	1
B. W. Sanderson b Collingwood	0	– not out	0
Azharullah not out	0		
B 6, lb 13, w 2, nb 6	27	B 5, lb 4, w 2, nb 4	15
1/9 (2) 2/12 (3) 3/28 (4) 4/67 (5) 5/165 (6) 6/327 (7) 7/327 (8) 8/338 (1) 9/338 (9) 10/338 (10) (95.2 overs)	338	1/0 (1) 2/123 (2) 3/159 (3) 4/165 (4) 5/179 (6) 6/202 (7) 7/203 (8) 8/204 (5) (8 wkts, 38.5 overs)	205

Coughlin 27–10–49–5; McCarthy 26–5–128–3; Main 13–0–63–0; Collingwood 12.2–1–32–2; Jennings 9–1–20–0; Pringle 8–2–27–0. *Second innings*—Coughlin 19.5–1–84–5; McCarthy 9–1–61–2; Main 10–1–51–0.

Umpires: M. Burns and S. J. O'Shaughnessy.

At Canterbury, June 8–11. DURHAM drew with KENT.

DURHAM v GLAMORGAN

At Chester-le-Street, June 19–22. Durham won by nine wickets. Durham 23pts, Glamorgan 5pts. Toss: Glamorgan. County debut: T. N. Cullen.

Durham's first win, in their seventh game, took them into credit after starting the season on minus 48 points. Needing 157 in 43 overs, they got home inside 25. In his final innings for Durham – though he did not join South Africa as expected – Cook made an unbeaten 89 in 78 balls, while

Steel, opening because Jennings was with England Lions, contributed 51 off 58. Their tempo was in stark contrast with Glamorgan's 221 for seven in 96 overs on a baking first day, when the dot balls totalled more than 80 overs, and Selman's century occupied 249 deliveries. On the second, Clark's maiden hundred took just 129; he pulled a six and eight of his 17 fours in front of midwicket, sharing a pivotal stand of 185 with Collingwood, whose fifty was his sixth in seven innings. Both fell to de Lange, Glamorgan's biggest threat. Durham were 334 for nine after losing five for six, but McCarthy and Rushworth added 68 to achieve maximum batting points with two balls to spare. Matty Potts, swinging it both ways on home debut, dismissed Glamorgan's top three, while Irish international McCarthy, pressed into lengthy service after Coughlin injured his knee, collected four on the day his country gained Test status.

Close of play: first day, Glamorgan 221-7 (Wagg 6, de Lange 4); second day, Durham 281-4 (Collingwood 71, Pringle 5); third day, Glamorgan 92-2 (Salter 25, Carey 0).

Glamorgan

J. A. Rudolph b Rushworth	13	– c Poynter b Potts	43
N. J. Selman lbw b Rushworth	103	– lbw b Potts	16
A. G. Salter c Poynter b Rushworth	25	– c McCarthy b Potts	26
C. A. Ingram c Poynter b Potts	33	– (5) not out	70
A. H. T. Donald b Rushworth	12	– (6) lbw b McCarthy	0
D. L. Lloyd lbw b Rushworth	7	– (7) c Pringle b McCarthy	0
G. G. Wagg not out	33	– (8) b McCarthy	5
†T. N. Cullen c Pringle b Potts	7	– (9) b Rushworth	13
M. de Lange c Collingwood b McCarthy	37	– (10) c and b Rushworth	20
L. J. Carey c Cook b McCarthy	10	– (4) b Rushworth	49
*M. G. Hogan c Poynter b McCarthy	0	– b McCarthy	4
B 4, lb 11	15	B 9, lb 8	17
1/18 (1) 2/84 (3) 3/166 (4) 4/182 (5) 5/199 (2) 6/202 (6) 7/213 (8) 8/279 (9) 9/295 (10) 10/295 (11) (115.5 overs) 110 overs: 274-7	295	1/49 (2) 2/88 (1) 3/109 (3) 4/165 (4) 5/168 (6) 6/170 (7) 7/183 (8) 8/212 (9) 9/252 (10) 10/263 (11) (95 overs)	263

Rushworth 25–9–52–5; Coughlin 21–1–78–0; Potts 23–4–59–2; McCarthy 19.5–3–55–3; Pringle 19–13–23–0; Collingwood 8–3–13–0. *Second innings*—Rushworth 23–5–59–3; Coughlin 14–3–46–0; McCarthy 25–5–65–4; Potts 20–6–48–3; Collingwood 3–1–4–0; Pringle 10–2–24–0.

Durham

S. C. Cook c Cullen b de Lange	14	– not out	89
C. T. Steel c Cullen b de Lange	32	– c Carey b Salter	51
J. T. A. Burnham c Ingram b Carey	25	– not out	14
G. Clark c Cullen b de Lange	109		
*P. D. Collingwood c Donald b de Lange	92		
R. D. Pringle lbw b Hogan	28		
P. Coughlin c Cullen b Wagg	0		
†S. W. Poynter lbw b Wagg	4		
M. J. Potts c Lloyd b de Lange	0		
B. J. McCarthy not out	30		
C. Rushworth c de Lange b Hogan	38		
B 12, lb 9, w 1, nb 8	30	B 4	4
1/22 (1) 2/63 (3) 3/87 (2) 4/272 (4) 5/328 (6) 6/330 (7) 7/330 (5) 8/334 (8) 9/334 (9) 10/402 (11) (110.1 overs) 110 overs: 402-9	402	1/129 (2) (1 wkt, 24.3 overs)	158

De Lange 31–5–95–5; Carey 17–3–84–1; Wagg 23–5–76–2; Hogan 28.1–8–68–2; Salter 7–0–43–0; Ingram 4–0–15–0. *Second innings*—de Lange 9–0–36–0; Carey 3–0–19–0; Hogan 4–0–27–0; Salter 5.3–0–49–1; Wagg 3–0–23–0.

Umpires: S. C. Gale and M. J. Saggers.

DURHAM v WORCESTERSHIRE

At Chester-le-Street, June 26–29 (day/night). Drawn. Durham 8pts, Worcestershire 12pts. Toss: uncontested.

Rain washed out the last two days of this match, intended to provide pink-ball practice ahead of England's inaugural day/night Test in August. Play started at 2pm, in front of a crowd of around 900; a further 260 took up a reduced rate of £5 after 5pm on the first day, which yielded 410 runs and 14 wickets. Of the England players on show, Jennings made six and Stokes a seven-ball duck as Durham slumped to 18 for five; later, Stokes took nought for 81, though Wood picked up five, topping and tailing Worcestershire with the new ball, while Ali scored 58. Worcestershire had sent in Hastings and Leach early, hoping to soften the ball through big hitting: each struck one six then got out, but the consensus was that it went too soft too quickly anyway. While others slogged, D'Oliveira progressed serenely to 91 by stumps, and completed his century next day before lifting Pringle for two sixes, then hitting a full toss to cover in the same over. With no play possible beyond the second afternoon, two substitutes for England Lions players never took the field. New Zealand's Tom Latham missed his Durham debut because of a foot injury.

Close of play: first day, Worcestershire 213-4 (D'Oliveira 91, Ali 36); second day, Worcestershire 367; third day, no play.

Durham

K. K. Jennings b Leach	6
C. T. Steel c Mitchell b Hastings	5
J. T. A. Burnham c Cox b Hastings	3
G. Clark lbw b Leach	1
B. A. Stokes c Cox b Hastings	0
*P. D. Collingwood c Ali b Tongue	25
R. D. Pringle lbw b Barnard	11
†S. W. Poynter b Tongue	43
M. A. Wood c Whiteley b Tongue	21
B. J. McCarthy not out	29
C. Rushworth c D'Oliveira b Tongue	30
Lb 9, nb 14	23
1/12 (2) 2/14 (1) 3/18 (3) 4/18 (4) 5/18 (5) 6/64 (7) 7/64 (6) 8/118 (9) 9/147 (8) 10/197 (11) (52.2 overs)	197

M. J. Richardson replaced Jennings, who left to join the England Lions squad.

Leach 11–2–45–2; Hastings 17–6–44–3; Tongue 12.2–2–41–4; Barnard 9–3–44–1; Ali 3–1–14–0.

Worcestershire

D. K. H. Mitchell c Poynter b Wood	3
B. L. D'Oliveira c Clark b Pringle	122
J. W. Hastings c Poynter b Wood	12
*J. Leach c Clark b Rushworth	15
J. M. Clarke b Wood	45
M. M. Ali lbw b Pringle	58
G. H. Rhodes c Poynter b Pringle	3
†O. B. Cox not out	32
R. A. Whiteley b Pringle	43
E. G. Barnard b Wood	9
J. C. Tongue c Steel b Wood	6
B 4, lb 11, nb 4	19
1/6 (1) 2/24 (3) 3/59 (4) 4/136 (5) 5/266 (2) 6/269 (6) 7/272 (7) 8/345 (9) 9/359 (10) 10/367 (11) (86.4 overs)	367

T. C. Fell replaced Clarke, who left to join the England Lions squad.

Wood 18.4–2–54–5; Rushworth 20–4–80–1; Stokes 20–3–81–0; McCarthy 12–1–51–0; Pringle 12–3–73–4; Steel 4–0–13–0.

Umpires: N. G. C. Cowley and B. V. Taylor.

At Chesterfield, July 3–6. DURHAM beat DERBYSHIRE by six wickets.

At Leicester, August 6–9. DURHAM drew with LEICESTERSHIRE.

DURHAM v DERBYSHIRE

At Chester-le-Street, August 28–31. Durham won by nine wickets. Durham 24pts, Derbyshire 2pts. Toss: uncontested. County debut: H. W. Podmore.

Durham leapfrogged Derbyshire into eighth place – their highest position of the season – with their third victory in five games. Jennings's poor form continued when he edged the first ball, from Viljoen, though for Derbyshire that was as good as it got. Viljoen posed some threat on his way to five wickets, and Harry Podmore, on loan from Middlesex, was accurate, but Collingwood made his highest Championship score at Riverside, while Steel followed a double-hundred at Leicester with 72; down the order, Coughlin hit a powerful 68 and Potts a maiden fifty, after 16 runs in his first five innings. With the lights on for most of the second day, Derbyshire found batting tough, and followed on 316 behind, after Onions's four wickets took his first-class total to 600. In much better conditions next day, when the home attack was robbed of Coughlin by a side strain, Reece led the resistance with 106, despite being struck on the helmet during a hostile spell from Potts; he shared an opening stand of 99 with Slater, whose attractive 57 was his first half-century of the season. But Durham won before lunch on the final day.

Close of play: first day, Durham 376-7 (Collingwood 127, Potts 13); second day, Derbyshire 164; third day, Derbyshire 305-6 (Hosein 7, Palladino 4).

Durham

K. K. Jennings c Hosein b Viljoen	0	– (2) c Slater b Viljoen	16
T. W. M. Latham b Palladino	27	– (1) not out	23
C. T. Steel c Madsen b Reece	72	– not out	0
J. T. A. Burnham b Viljoen	9		
*P. D. Collingwood c Imran Tahir b Viljoen	177		
†M. J. Richardson c Hosein b Viljoen	20		
R. D. Pringle c Podmore b Palladino	19		
P. Coughlin lbw b Viljoen	68		
M. J. Potts not out	53		
C. Rushworth b Imran Tahir	0		
B 8, lb 26, w 1	35		
1/0 (1) 2/68 (2) 3/94 (4) 4/147 (3) 5/195 (6) 6/217 (7) 7/347 (8) 8/479 (5) 9/480 (10) (9 wkts dec, 120.4 overs)	480	1/31 (2) (1 wkt, 9.2 overs)	39
110 overs: 434-7			

G. Onions did not bat.

Viljoen 33–7–130–5; Podmore 24–4–85–0; Palladino 20–1–92–2; Reece 14–3–42–1; Imran Tahir 27.4–4–87–1; Hughes 2–0–10–0. *Second innings*—Viljoen 5–0–24–1; Podmore 4.2–3–15–0.

Derbyshire

B. T. Slater c Latham b Onions	29	– b Pringle	57
L. M. Reece c Richardson b Onions	6	– c Burnham b Jennings	106
*B. A. Godleman b Rushworth	2	– b Rushworth	0
W. L. Madsen b Coughlin	5	– c Richardson b Steel	48
A. L. Hughes lbw b Jennings	47	– lbw b Potts	39
M. J. J. Critchley lbw b Rushworth	12	– lbw b Onions	19
†H. R. Hosein c Richardson b Jennings	12	– lbw b Onions	16
A. P. Palladino c Latham b Onions	4	– c Richardson b Onions	4
H. W. Podmore c Collingwood b Rushworth	5	– c Pringle b Rushworth	10
G. C. Viljoen c Richardson b Onions	2	– not out	19
Imran Tahir not out	18	– lbw b Steel	10
B 9, lb 8, w 1, nb 4	22	B 8, lb 13, nb 5	26
1/28 (2) 2/32 (3) 3/41 (4) 4/74 (1) 5/97 (6) 6/118 (5) 7/129 (8) 8/129 (7) 9/140 (10) 10/164 (9) (64.3 overs)	164	1/99 (1) 2/100 (3) 3/206 (4) 4/257 (2) 5/288 (6) 6/298 (5) 7/310 (8) 8/325 (9) 9/325 (7) 10/354 (11) (109.2 overs)	354

Rushworth 17.3–5–35–3; Onions 21–5–44–4; Coughlin 4–1–14–1; Potts 13–4–41–0; Jennings 9–3–13–2. *Second innings*—Rushworth 24–4–60–2; Onions 28–6–88–3; Potts 20–2–78–1; Pringle 20–7–37–1; Jennings 11–0–46–1; Steel 6.2–0–24–2.

Umpires: R. J. Bailey and N. L. Bainton.

DURHAM v KENT

At Chester-le-Street, September 5–8. Drawn. Durham 9pts, Kent 9pts. Toss: uncontested.

Onions became Durham's leading wicket-taker but, for the second time in three months, Kent scraped a draw against them with one wicket standing. The hero was Billings, who had been laid low by a migraine for two days, but came in at 74 for five, with 28 overs left, and made an unbeaten 70. With six overs to go, Onions had trapped Milne, his 519th first-class wicket for the club, breaking left-arm seamer Simon Brown's record. That was eight down, and Weighell made it nine, with 11 balls remaining – but once again last man Claydon kept his old county out. Play had begun at 4pm on the first day – poor weather eventually cost four sessions – and Durham slipped to 77 for seven on the second before Wood, returning from a seven-week lay-off, scored a career-best 72 not out and added 106 with Weighell. Claydon hit the pitch hard and deserved his five wickets. Onions was at his best in Kent's first innings, claiming six for 62, while Wood had three (but managed only five overs on the final day, when his sore heel took him off the field). Northeast was Kent's star, with 110 out of 206, followed by 67 of the first 112 in the second innings. Durham built on a slim lead of 11, with Latham's diligence earning his second century in three games, and Collingwood passing 1,000 for the season; they were 308 ahead at lunch but batted on for 7.3 overs to set 371 in 56, believing Kent would have to go for it to retain any hope of promotion. But the chase was off once both openers fell without a run on the board. While Billings was ill, Bell-Drummond and Denly deputised as keeper before Adam Rouse arrived.

Close of play: first day, Durham 61-4 (Clark 6, Richardson 5); second day, Durham 57-2 (Latham 27, Clark 8); third day, Durham 145-2 (Latham 64, Clark 49).

Durham

K. K. Jennings c Dickson b Claydon	17	– (2) c †Bell-Drummond b Haggett	13
T. W. M. Latham lbw b Milne	8	– (1) c Crawley b Haggett	119
C. T. Steel c Dickson b Claydon	10	– b Haggett	0
G. Clark b Stevens	6	– c Northeast b Claydon	86
*P. D. Collingwood c Billings b Milne	11	– b Qayyum	35
†M. J. Richardson c Stevens b Milne	5	– c Dickson b Claydon	5
R. D. Pringle b Milne	8	– not out	30
M. A. Wood not out	72	– b Denly	24
W. J. Weighell c Qayyum b Claydon	55		
C. Rushworth b Claydon	4		
G. Onions c Billings b Claydon	8		
B 5, lb 2, nb 6	13	B 15, lb 13, w 1, nb 18	47
1/19 (2) 2/35 (1) 3/38 (3) 4/53 (5) 5/61 (6) 6/69 (7) 7/77 (4) 8/183 (9) 9/195 (10) 10/217 (11) (67.2 overs)	217	1/35 (2) 2/39 (3) 3/219 (4) 4/282 (5) 5/297 (6) 6/318 (1) 7/359 (8) (7 wkts dec, 88.3 overs)	359

Milne 21–5–68–4; Stevens 13–3–35–1; Haggett 13–4–37–0; Claydon 16.2–3–54–5; Qayyum 4–0–16–0. *Second innings*—Milne 20–6–65–0; Stevens 10–2–27–0; Haggett 24–7–82–3; Claydon 20–3–75–2; Qayyum 14–0–79–1; Denly 0.3–0–3–1.

Kent

Batsman	First innings		Second innings	
D. J. Bell-Drummond	c Rushworth b Wood	26	c Richardson b Rushworth	0
S. R. Dickson	lbw b Onions	7	c Richardson b Onions	0
J. L. Denly	b Onions	4	c Jennings b Weighell	10
*S. A. Northeast	c Richardson b Weighell	110	b Jennings	67
Z. Crawley	lbw b Wood	26	c Richardson b Wood	0
D. I. Stevens	c Richardson b Wood	0	c Latham b Weighell	9
C. J. Haggett	b Onions	2	(8) lbw b Rushworth	4
A. F. Milne	c Richardson b Onions	1	(9) lbw b Onions	8
†S. W. Billings	b Onions	0	(7) not out	70
M. E. Claydon	c Clark b Onions	16	(11) not out	0
I. Qayyum	not out	0	(10) c Collingwood b Weighell	1
	B 2, lb 6, nb 6	14	B 5, lb 8, nb 2	15
	(43.5 overs)	206	(9 wkts, 56 overs)	184

1/10 (2) 2/14 (3) 3/78 (1) 4/134 (5) 5/134 (6) 6/143 (7) 7/147 (8) 8/147 (9) 9/175 (10) 10/206 (4)

1/0 (2) 2/0 (1) 3/47 (3) 4/48 (5) 5/74 (6) 6/112 (4) 7/120 (8) 8/155 (9) 9/176 (10)

Rushworth 11–1–31–0; Onions 14–2–62–6; Wood 11–1–48–3; Weighell 5.5–0–40–1; Jennings 2–0–17–0. *Second innings*—Rushworth 17–5–58–2; Onions 17–5–45–2; Weighell 12–3–51–3; Wood 5–0–9–1; Jennings 5–2–8–1.

Umpires: S. C. Gale and M. A. Gough.

DURHAM v SUSSEX

At Chester-le-Street, September 19–22. Sussex won by 132 runs. Sussex 22pts, Durham 7pts. Toss: Durham.

Luke Wells achieved a personal double first by captaining Sussex and reaching 1,000 Championship runs on his way to 122. When he added 58 on the third day, it took his season's aggregate against Durham to 438 in three knocks. And he capped it all with a win. Van Zyl supported him well, also passing 1,000 in the second innings, when Salt made a flying start before knuckling down for a classy career-best 72. It meant Durham needed 264, which they believed was gettable. But Sussex's young left-arm quick Garton, profligate in the first innings, helped reduce them to 61 for seven. Weighell and Carse, whose first-innings maiden fifty had proved the benefit of working on his batting while recovering from a stress fracture of the back, shared a half-century stand, but Whittingham and Jordan, who ran in strongly throughout, finished them off. For Durham, Jennings had returned his best bowling figures on the opening day before his nightmare run with the bat continued, as one of five victims for Robinson – who collected four with seam, and trapped Pringle with off-spin.

Close of play: first day, Durham 8-1 (Latham 2); second day, Durham 321-6 (Clark 73, Carse 21); third day, Durham 5-0 (Latham 2, Jennings 1).

Sussex

Batsman	First innings		Second innings	
*L. W. P. Wells	c Richardson b Jennings	122	c Richardson b Rushworth	58
H. Z. Finch	lbw b Rushworth	0	c Collingwood b Weighell	37
S. van Zyl	c Steel b Weighell	92	c Richardson b Onions	45
L. J. Evans	c Richardson b Jennings	19	c Richardson b Weighell	4
L. J. Wright	b Onions	43	lbw b Pringle	9
P. D. Salt	lbw b Jennings	11	b Jennings	72
†M. G. K. Burgess	b Rushworth	27	c Onions b Rushworth	20
O. E. Robinson	c Latham b Rushworth	1	lbw b Weighell	20
C. J. Jordan	not out	8	not out	24
G. H. S. Garton	c Clark b Onions	9	b Steel	4
S. G. Whittingham	c Richardson b Rushworth	0	run out	0
	B 3, lb 7, nb 4	14	B 1, lb 2, nb 6	9
	(90.3 overs)	346	(72.1 overs)	302

1/5 (2) 2/191 (3) 3/242 (4) 4/251 (1) 5/275 (6) 6/328 (7) 7/328 (5) 8/336 (8) 9/345 (10) 10/346 (11)

1/101 (2) 2/109 (1) 3/116 (4) 4/137 (5) 5/177 (3) 6/218 (7) 7/255 (8) 8/291 (6) 9/301 (10) 10/302 (11)

Rushworth 20.3–1–64–4; Onions 20–3–58–2; Weighell 15–0–71–1; Carse 12–1–58–0; Pringle 7–2–18–0; Collingwood 4–1–25–0; Jennings 8–0–37–3; Steel 4–1–5–0. *Second innings*—Rushworth 15–4–43–2; Onions 18–1–87–1; Pringle 7.1–0–36–1; Carse 8–3–21–0; Weighell 13–0–68–3; Steel 7–0–33–1; Jennings 4–0–11–1.

Durham

K. K. Jennings lbw b Robinson	6	– (2) b Jordan	10
T. W. M. Latham c Evans b Robinson	77	– (1) lbw b Whittingham	4
C. T. Steel c Garton b Robinson	73	– c Burgess b Garton	5
G. Clark lbw b Jordan	88	– lbw b Jordan	12
*P. D. Collingwood lbw b Garton	4	– run out	9
†M. J. Richardson c Burgess b Jordan	15	– c Finch b Garton	8
R. D. Pringle lbw b Robinson	19	– lbw b Garton	2
B. A. Carse not out	61	– not out	23
W. J. Weighell lbw b Garton	0	– b Whittingham	38
C. Rushworth c van Zyl b Robinson	3	– b Whittingham	0
G. Onions c Evans b Whittingham	4	– c Wright b Jordan	4
B 3, lb 13, w 1, nb 18	35	B 2, lb 10, w 2, nb 2	16
1/8 (1) 2/173 (3) 3/181 (2) 4/193 (5) 5/222 (6) 6/279 (7) 7/363 (4) 8/364 (9) 9/377 (10) 10/385 (11) (106.5 overs)	385	1/19 (1) 2/24 (2) 3/38 (3) 4/42 (4) 5/56 (5) 6/58 (6) 7/61 (7) 8/111 (9) 9/111 (10) 10/131 (11) (42.2 overs)	131

Robinson 26–4–69–5; Jordan 31–9–77–2; Garton 17–0–89–2; Whittingham 18.5–2–96–1; van Zyl 14–1–38–0. *Second innings*—Jordan 16.2–2–50–3; Robinson 6–2–17–0; Whittingham 13–4–26–3; Garton 6–0–20–3; van Zyl 1–0–6–0.

Umpires: J. H. Evans and R. J. Evans.

At Worcester, September 25–28. DURHAM lost to WORCESTERSHIRE by 137 runs.

ESSEX

Not so little now

PAUL HISCOCK

In carrying off their first Championship title since 1992, Essex won ten of their 14 matches, five inside three days. They remained unbeaten for the first time in their history, and took county cricket's top prize by a crushing 72 points, the year after winning the second division.

It was a remarkable performance. Many had predicted Essex would struggle to avoid relegation, particularly as seamers David Masters and Graham Napier had retired after sharing 103 wickets in 2016. But under the shrewd leadership of Ryan ten Doeschate they silenced the doubters with immense resolve and flair – and a team spirit that was a tribute to the man-management skills of coach Chris Silverwood and his support staff. Never was this more evident than against Hampshire at the Rose Bowl, when – with the title already in the bag – they won after following on. Ten Doeschate admitted Essex had been seen as a little club, but added: "We have set very high standards for ourselves, and I'm confident we will continue to punch above our weight."

Everyone played a part, but it was the bowling of seamer Jamie Porter and off-spinner Simon Harmer that did most to send the Championship trophy hurtling towards Chelmsford. They shared 147 wickets, with Porter taking 75, more than anyone in the country. His accuracy and movement always posed problems, especially when conditions were favourable, and it was unfortunate that he missed the winter Lions tour with a stress fracture of the back. The Pretoria-born Harmer, signed as a Kolpak after winning five Test caps for South Africa, varied his flight cleverly, and was able to turn the ball on almost any surface. He claimed 14 wickets in successive matches at Chelmsford in June, against Warwickshire and Middlesex.

The combative New Zealand left-arm seamer Neil Wagner was originally signed for the first half of the season, but returned after a combination of injury and Pakistan commitments restricted Mohammad Amir to three Championship matches. In one, however, his pace and hostility overwhelmed Yorkshire in two days. Chelmsford-born seamer Sam Cook, who turned 20 in August, also made an impression. Given a chance in the last few games, he picked up five-fors against Hampshire and Yorkshire to advertise Essex's successful youth policy.

In the batting, the launch pad was often provided by Alastair Cook. He missed the first Championship match, but in the next seven hit 667 runs. His fellow left-handed opener Nick Browne ended up as the county's leading scorer in the tournament, with 952. Dan Lawrence, who also turned 20, showed relish for a backs-to-the-wall battle with an unbeaten 141 in the season's opening match to deny Lancashire, while in September another defiant hundred set up that come-from-behind victory against Hampshire.

Steve Bardens, Getty Images

Simon Harmer

The 37-year-old James Foster was left out of the first four matches but, once he had reclaimed the gloves from Adam Wheater, showed he was still one of the finest wicketkeepers around. Essex were delighted when Foster signed another contract for 2018. Ravi Bopara, another thirtysomething, had a mixed season, although he did extend his only century, against Warwickshire, to 192. His fellow middle-order scrapper ten Doeschate also scored a big hundred, and averaged 41. Tom Westley, who made his Test debut, scored two centuries, and averaged 43.

Westley was one of several on the England radar, so Essex may need to recruit some experienced players to cover for international calls. Amir indicated he would like to return, while Wagner was due to be back from mid-May until the end of July; he will replace Australian Test seamer Peter Siddle. Australian leg-spinner Adam Zampa also signed, for the T20 Blast. There is exciting home-grown talent in the wings, though former England Under-19 batsman Kishan Velani was released. Arriving from Kent was the lively seamer Matt Coles.

In the Royal London Cup, Essex won seven of their eight qualifying games to top the South Group, but narrowly lost a high-scoring semi-final. There were 743 runs on a hectic day at Chelmsford, with Nottinghamshire (the eventual winners) clinching victory with three balls to spare. Alastair Cook, whose 636 runs included three centuries, was the competition's leading scorer. The wickets were shared around: Wagner collected 14, while Harmer and Porter both had ten.

The T20 Blast provided the season's major disappointment, and only five wins in 12 matches: Varun Chopra scored 427 runs, but both his centuries came in defeat. There was a further setback when Tamim Iqbal, signed to provide fireworks at the top of the order, returned home to Bangladesh after only one match for personal reasons.

Much of the credit for the Championship success was down to Silverwood, so there were mixed feelings when, at the end of October, he was recruited to the England set-up as bowling coach. He had taken over at the end of 2015, after the departure of Paul Grayson, and left with an impressive record. Essex promoted Anthony McGrath, another Yorkshireman, whose credentials as batting coach had been ably demonstrated during 2017. Dimitri Mascarenhas, the former Hampshire and England all-rounder, was later named as his assistant.

Championship attendance: 36,018.

ESSEX RESULTS

All first-class matches – Played 16: Won 10, Drawn 6.
County Championship matches – Played 14: Won 10, Drawn 4.

Specsavers County Championship, winners of Division 1;
NatWest T20 Blast, 8th in South Group; Royal London One-Day Cup, semi-finalists.

COUNTY CHAMPIONSHIP AVERAGES, BATTING AND FIELDING

Cap		*Birthplace*	*M*	*I*	*NO*	*R*	*HS*	*100*	*Avge*	*Ct/St*
2005	†A. N. Cook§	*Gloucester*	7	10	0	667	193	3	66.70	13
2017	D. W. Lawrence	*Leytonstone‡*	13	21	4	761	141*	3	44.76	10
2015	†N. L. J. Browne	*Leytonstone‡*	14	22	0	952	221	1	43.27	6
2013	T. Westley	*Cambridge*	11	15	2	561	111	2	43.15	5
2006	R. N. ten Doeschate††	*Port Elizabeth, SA*	13	17	1	659	168*	1	41.18	8
2005	R. S. Bopara	*Forest Gate‡*	14	20	2	576	192	1	32.00	7
2001	J. S. Foster	*Leytonstone‡*	10	12	0	357	121	1	29.75	48/1
	V. Chopra	*Barking‡*	9	14	1	372	100*	1	28.61	15
	†P. I. Walter	*Basildon‡*	5	5	2	76	32*	0	25.33	0
	†N. Wagner¶	*Pretoria, SA*	10	13	3	242	50	0	24.20	4
	A. J. A. Wheater	*Leytonstone‡*	7	10	0	223	88	0	22.30	14/2
	S. R. Harmer††	*Pretoria, SA*	14	18	2	260	64	0	16.25	11
	†A. P. Beard	*Chelmsford‡*	3	4	3	11	4*	0	11.00	0
2015	J. A. Porter	*Leytonstone‡*	13	15	8	52	10*	0	7.42	1
	S. J. Cook	*Chelmsford‡*	4	4	3	0	0*	0	0.00	0

Also batted: †Ashar Zaidi (*Karachi, Pakistan*) (2 matches) 23, 6 (2 ct); †Mohammad Amir§ (*Gujar Khan, Pakistan*) (3 matches) 22, 22* (1 ct); M. R. Quinn†† (*Auckland, NZ*) (3 matches) 15, 4, 0 (1 ct).

‡ *Born in Essex.* § *ECB contract.* ¶ *Official overseas player.* †† *Other non-England-qualified.*

BOWLING

	Style	*O*	*M*	*R*	*W*	*BB*	*5I*	*Avge*
Mohammad Amir	LF	76.2	19	189	14	5-18	2	13.50
S. J. Cook	RFM	99.4	24	286	18	5-18	2	15.88
J. A. Porter	RFM	399	89	1,262	75	7-55	5	16.82
S. R. Harmer	OB	521.3	121	1,382	72	9-95	4	19.19
N. Wagner	LFM	316.4	54	1,095	31	6-48	1	35.32
R. S. Bopara	RM	127.1	12	489	12	2-10	0	40.75

Also bowled: Ashar Zaidi (LM/SLA) 25–5–43–3; A. P. Beard (RFM) 67–10–241–6; D. W. Lawrence (OB/LB) 23–6–71–1; M. R. Quinn (RFM) 61.5–13–221–6; R. N. ten Doeschate (RM) 13.1–0–60–3; P. I. Walter (LM) 75–19–219–3; T. Westley (OB) 21.3–5–72–3.

LEADING ROYAL LONDON CUP AVERAGES (100 runs/4 wickets)

Batting	*Runs*	*HS*	*Avge*	*SR*	*Ct*
A. N. Cook	636	133	79.50	88.45	3
R. S. Bopara	329	92*	54.83	106.81	4
R. N. ten Doeschate	298	102*	49.66	115.95	3
V. Chopra	334	124	37.11	76.95	3
T. Westley	315	100	35.00	89.48	4
Ashar Zaidi	195	72*	24.37	126.62	3

Bowling	*W*	*BB*	*Avge*	*ER*
J. A. Porter	10	4-40	19.60	5.02
P. I. Walter	7	4-37	22.14	5.81
N. Wagner	14	4-41	25.21	6.15
R. S. Bopara	9	3-34	32.00	5.23
M. R. Quinn	8	3-34	35.25	5.35
R. N. ten Doeschate	4	2-29	36.00	6.26
Ashar Zaidi	7	2-10	41.71	5.09
S. R. Harmer	10	3-56	41.80	5.62

LEADING NATWEST T20 BLAST AVERAGES (100 runs/15 overs)

Batting	*Runs*	*HS*	*Avge*	*SR*	*Ct/St*
V. Chopra	427	116	38.81	**159.32**	2
A. J. A. Wheater	139	50	27.80	**156.17**	2
D. W. Lawrence	235	47	21.36	**141.56**	1
R. S. Bopara	301	75	27.36	**138.70**	3
J. S. Foster	108	50	18.00	**136.70**	10/2
R. N. ten Doeschate	246	56	24.60	**129.47**	4
Ashar Zaidi	140	35	12.72	**113.82**	4

Bowling	*W*	*BB*	*Avge*	*ER*
Mohammad Amir	14	2-13	23.00	**6.77**
R. S. Bopara	13	4-19	25.76	**7.44**
S. R. Harmer	8	3-39	41.00	**9.11**
P. I. Walter	15	3-24	27.06	**9.22**
Ashar Zaidi	7	2-24	31.85	**9.29**
J. A. Porter	6	4-20	30.50	**9.63**

FIRST-CLASS COUNTY RECORDS

Highest score for	343*	P. A. Perrin v Derbyshire at Chesterfield	1904
Highest score against	332	W. H. Ashdown (Kent) at Brentwood	1934
Leading run-scorer	30,701	G. A. Gooch (avge 51.77)	1973–97
Best bowling for	10-32	H. Pickett v Leicestershire at Leyton	1895
Best bowling against	10-40	E. G. Dennett (Gloucestershire) at Bristol	1906
Leading wicket-taker	1,610	T. P. B. Smith (avge 26.68)	1929–51
Highest total for	761-6 dec	v Leicestershire at Chelmsford	1990
Highest total against	803-4 dec	by Kent at Brentwood	1934
Lowest total for	20	v Lancashire at Chelmsford	2013
Lowest total against	14	by Surrey at Chelmsford	1983

LIST A COUNTY RECORDS

Highest score for	201*	R. S. Bopara v Leicestershire at Leicester	2008
Highest score against	158*	M. W. Goodwin (Sussex) at Chelmsford	2006
Leading run-scorer	16,536	G. A. Gooch (avge 40.93)	1973–97
Best bowling for	8-26	K. D. Boyce v Lancashire at Manchester	1971
Best bowling against	7-29	D. A. Payne (Gloucestershire) at Chelmsford	2010
Leading wicket-taker	616	J. K. Lever (avge 19.04)	1968–89
Highest total for	391-5	v Surrey at The Oval	2008
Highest total against	**373-5**	**by Nottinghamshire at Chelmsford**	**2017**
Lowest total for	57	v Lancashire at Lord's	1996
Lowest total against	41	by Middlesex at Westcliff-on-Sea	1972
	41	by Shropshire at Wellington	1974

TWENTY20 COUNTY RECORDS

Highest score for	152*	G. R. Napier v Sussex at Chelmsford	2008
Highest score against	153*	L. J. Wright (Sussex) at Chelmsford	2014
Leading run-scorer	**2,874**	**R. S. Bopara (avge 27.90)**	**2003–17**
Best bowling for	6-16	T. G. Southee v Glamorgan at Chelmsford	2011
Best bowling against	5-11	Mushtaq Ahmed (Sussex) at Hove	2005
	5-11	**T. G. Helm (Middlesex) at Lord's**	**2017**
Leading wicket-taker	123	G. R. Napier (avge 24.74)	2003–16
Highest total for	242-3	v Sussex at Chelmsford	2008
Highest total against	226-3	by Sussex at Chelmsford	2014
Lowest total for	74	v Middlesex at Chelmsford	2013
Lowest total against	82	by Gloucestershire at Chelmsford	2011

ADDRESS

The Cloudfm County Ground, New Writtle Street, Chelmsford CM2 0PG; 01245 252420; administration@essexcricket.co.uk; www.essexcricket.org.uk.

OFFICIALS

Captain R. N. ten Doeschate
Head coach 2017 C. E. W. Silverwood
2018 A. McGrath
President D. L. Acfield
Chairman J. F. Faragher
Chief executive D. W. Bowden
Chairman, cricket committee R. C. Irani
Head groundsman S. G. Kerrison
Scorer A. E. Choat

ESSEX v DURHAM MCCU

At Chelmsford, April 2–4. Drawn. Toss: Essex. First-class debuts: F. P. A. Simon, S. K. Stewart-Taylor. County debut: S. R. Harmer.

An easy-paced pitch allowed the students to escape with a draw – and most of the professionals to polish their averages, although Westley collected a third-ball duck, the second of two quick wickets for 19-year-old Xavier Owen. Browne cracked a dozen fours in his 66 before Wheater hit a forceful century, and there was a maiden fifty for Aaron Beard, his first runs in first-class cricket. Porter made early inroads in the reply, but Darrel Williams and Abhiraj Singh reduced the deficit with an eighth-wicket stand of 84. Browne was soon back in the groove, driving well and striking 20 fours before retiring at 113, then Bopara and ten Doeschate piled on 95 in 14 overs. Facing a notional target of 503, Durham lost both openers after a decent start in six balls from Matt Dixon, but Ed Pollock and Jason Marshall dug in, and there were handshakes all round after 51 overs.

Close of play: first day, Durham MCCU 66-3 (Pollock 25, McCollum 6); second day, Essex 203-2 (Browne 113, Lawrence 25).

Essex

V. Chopra c Cooke b Owen	16	– lbw b Simon	30
N. L. J. Browne c Marshall b Singh	66	– retired out	113
T. Westley lbw b Owen	0	– c Singh b Williams	34
D. W. Lawrence c Singh b Cooke	16	– c Cooke b Singh	43
R. S. Bopara st Stewart-Taylor b Singh	39	– c Cooke b Williams	75
†A. J. A. Wheater c Cooke b Simon	102		
*R. N. ten Doeschate c Williams b Simon	5	– (6) not out	47
S. R. Harmer c Pollock b Williams	14	– (7) not out	7
A. P. Beard not out	58		
J. A. Porter lbw b Singh	1		
M. W. Dixon c Cooke b Owen	4		
B 4, lb 5, w 1, nb 2	12	B 6, lb 1	7
1/21 (1) 2/21 (3) 3/60 (4) 4/126 (2) 5/167 (5) 6/184 (7) 7/238 (8) 8/293 (6) 9/316 (10) 10/333 (11) (85.4 overs)	333	1/61 (1) 2/131 (3) 3/203 (2) 4/247 (4) 5/342 (5) (5 wkts dec, 74 overs)	356

Owen 17.4–3–55–3; Simon 16–3–68–2; Cooke 14–1–61–1; Singh 23–1–79–3; Williams 15–1–61–1. *Second innings*—Owen 17–0–61–0; Simon 16–4–60–1; Cooke 15–2–79–0; Singh 11–0–67–1; Williams 15–0–82–2.

Durham MCCU

W. A. R. Fraine b Porter	23	– c Browne b Dixon	19
J. Clark c Wheater b Porter	0	– c sub (C. J. Taylor) b Dixon	18
E. J. Pollock c Westley b Porter	38	– not out	33
J. D. Marshall lbw b Dixon	6	– not out	41
J. A. McCollum lbw b Porter	7		
*J. Cooke c Westley b Dixon	7		
D. R. Williams c Chopra b Harmer	32		
†S. K. Stewart-Taylor c Westley b Beard	8		
A. R. Singh c Porter b Harmer	44		
F. P. A. Simon c Harmer b Bopara	1		
X. G. Owen not out	1		
B 8, lb 6, nb 6	20	Lb 13	13
1/1 (2) 2/32 (1) 3/55 (4) 4/78 (5) 5/91 (3) 6/93 (6) 7/101 (8) 8/185 (9) 9/185 (7) 10/187 (10) (76.1 overs)	187	1/44 (1) 2/47 (2) (2 wkts, 51 overs)	124

Porter 17–5–35–4; Beard 13–4–45–1; Dixon 13–5–30–2; Bopara 12.1–5–20–1; Harmer 13–5–19–2; ten Doeschate 8–2–24–0. *Second innings*—Porter 9–4–21–0; Beard 11–3–18–0; Dixon 8–2–22–2; Bopara 6–1–16–0; ten Doeschate 2–2–0–0; Harmer 12–2–28–0; Westley 3–0–6–0.

Umpires: N. L. Bainton and C. M. Watts.

ESSEX v LANCASHIRE

At Chelmsford, April 7–10. Drawn. Essex 8pts, Lancashire 11pts. Toss: Lancashire. County debut: N. Wagner. Championship debuts: S. R. Harmer; D. J. Vilas.

Essex had Lawrence to thank for a draw in their first top-tier match since 2010. Set a distant 478 in just over four sessions, they were still well adrift when Jarvis removed Bopara and Wheater in the space of seven balls to make it 198 for five. But Lawrence hung on, defending stoutly for over seven hours, and putting on 102 with ten Doeschate. First division life had begun more rosily, with Lancashire reduced to 160 for six, before Kolpak signing Dane Vilas and the tail lifted them to 319; Beard, varying his line, and Wagner – against his 2016 colleagues – shared the last five wickets. But Essex started badly against Anderson and Jarvis before Bopara offered some backbone; even so, a deficit of 160 looked ominous. Parry's three for 28 was, surprisingly for an England white-ball international, his best Championship return. Buoyed by his display with the gloves, Davies then made his maiden hundred, although he was dropped twice before reaching 30. However, it took him more than six hours and, while Vilas added a punchy 92, the declaration might have come earlier. Lancashire looked on top after Jarvis's double strike, but were denied by a teenager batting, as Scyld Berry put it in the *Telegraph*, "as if he had been Lawrence of Arabia not Chingford".

Close of play: first day, Essex 39-2 (Chopra 8, Westley 12); second day, Lancashire 114-1 (Davies 50, Livingstone 13); third day, Essex 89-2 (Westley 27, Lawrence 13).

Lancashire

†A. L. Davies c Wheater b Porter	5	– not out	140
H. Hameed b Porter	47	– c Wheater b Beard	45
L. S. Livingstone c Chopra b Beard	28	– c Browne b Beard	28
*S. J. Croft c sub (C. J. Taylor) b Harmer	48		
S. Chanderpaul run out	15		
D. J. Vilas c Wagner b Beard	74	– (4) b Porter	92
R. McLaren c Westley b Wagner	0		
J. Clark lbw b Beard	24		
S. D. Parry c Harmer b Wagner	19		
K. M. Jarvis c Chopra b Wagner	28		
J. M. Anderson not out	13		
B 4, lb 14	18	B 1, lb 3, nb 8	12
1/10 (1) 2/50 (3) 3/118 (2) 4/136 (4) 5/160 (5) 6/160 (7) 7/217 (8) 8/264 (9) 9/268 (6) 10/319 (10) (84.1 overs)	319	1/83 (2) 2/134 (3) 3/317 (4) (3 wkts dec, 94.3 overs)	317

Porter 21–4–64–2; Wagner 23.1–1–100–3; Beard 15–4–47–3; Bopara 5–0–31–0; Harmer 20–4–59–1. *Second innings*—Porter 13.3–1–60–1; Wagner 17–4–54–0; Beard 13–2–45–2; Harmer 31–5–78–0; Bopara 9–0–29–0; ten Doeschate 3–0–16–0; Westley 5–0–21–0; Lawrence 3–0–10–0.

Essex

V. Chopra c Davies b Jarvis	15	– b McLaren	29
N. L. J. Browne c Davies b Jarvis	16	– c Hameed b Parry	18
A. P. Beard c Davies b Anderson	3		
T. Westley c Davies b Anderson	15	– (3) b Parry	61
D. W. Lawrence c Livingstone b Parry	37	– (4) not out	141
R. S. Bopara c Parry b Anderson	46	– (5) c Davies b Jarvis	4
†A. J. A. Wheater lbw b Parry	1	– (6) c Hameed b Jarvis	1
*R. N. ten Doeschate c Davies b McLaren	19	– (7) lbw b Jarvis	41
S. R. Harmer lbw b McLaren	4	– (8) not out	12
N. Wagner not out	2		
J. A. Porter lbw b Parry	1		
		B 1, lb 4, nb 4	9
1/22 (2) 2/25 (3) 3/49 (1) 4/53 (4) 5/91 (5) 6/99 (7) 7/147 (6) 8/155 (9) 9/156 (8) 10/159 (11) (65.4 overs)	159	1/40 (2) 2/52 (1) 3/187 (3) 4/196 (5) 5/198 (6) 6/300 (7) (6 wkts, 133.4 overs)	316

Anderson 18–4–56–3; Jarvis 17–4–49–2; Clark 7–4–7–0; McLaren 9–3–19–2; Parry 14.4–5–28–3. *Second innings*—Anderson 24–7–55–0; Jarvis 27–7–58–3; McLaren 21–6–52–1; Parry 33.4–11–52–2; Livingstone 12–2–29–0; Clark 16–3–65–0.

Umpires: N. G. B. Cook and M. J. Saggers.

At Taunton, April 14–16. ESSEX beat SOMERSET by eight wickets.

At Lord's, April 21–24. ESSEX drew with MIDDLESEX.

ESSEX v HAMPSHIRE

At Chelmsford, May 19–21. Essex won by an innings and 97 runs. Essex 22pts, Hampshire 1pt. Toss: uncontested.

This match was all but decided in 17 balls shortly after tea on the second day, when Hampshire lost five wickets with the score on 18. Soon it was 34 for seven, and – after Essex enforced the follow-on – the game was all over by tea next day on a pitch which, though helpful to the bowlers, was hardly unplayable. The initial damage was done by Porter, who finished with a career-best five for 24. Only McManus, who top-scored in both innings from No. 7, and Bailey held Essex up for long; Rossouw made a pair. Before all this, Cook and Westley had taken charge with a stand of 243 – a second-wicket record for Essex against Hampshire, surpassing 221 by Denys Wilcox and Morris Nichols at Southend in 1936 – after Browne departed in the first over. Cook purred to his fourth century of the season in all formats, and batted for five and three-quarter hours; Westley was out to what became the last ball of the first day. After Edwards went off with a shoulder injury, Abbott was a lone beacon for Hampshire, beating the bat several times early in the big stand. He claimed five for 58 at less than two an over, then hit a stubborn 36, one of only two double-figure scores in their embarrassing first innings.

Close of play: first day, Essex 243-2 (Cook 114); second day, Hampshire 92-7 (McManus 30, Abbott 27).

Essex

N. L. J. Browne c Crane b Edwards	0
A. N. Cook c McManus b Abbott	124
T. Westley b Abbott	111
D. W. Lawrence lbw b Abbott	5
R. S. Bopara b Abbott	23
†A. J. A. Wheater lbw b Berg	7
*R. N. ten Doeschate b Abbott	37
S. R. Harmer lbw b Berg	3
N. Wagner c Rossouw b Crane	13
M. R. Quinn lbw b Dawson	15
J. A. Porter not out	0
B 11, lb 10, w 1	22
1/0 (1) 2/243 (3) (132.4 overs)	360

3/249 (4) 4/260 (2) 5/272 (6) 6/323 (5) 7/328 (7) 8/343 (8) 9/359 (9) 10/360 (10) 110 overs: 314-5

Edwards 10–1–35–1; Abbott 30–11–58–5; Berg 33–6–89–2; Ervine 16–5–36–0; Dawson 20.4–4–49–1; Crane 19–4–61–1; Vince 4–0–11–0.

Hampshire

Batsman	First innings		Second innings	
M. A. Carberry	lbw b Quinn	5	lbw b Harmer	6
L. A. Dawson	c Wheater b Porter	7	lbw b Porter	5
J. M. Vince	b Porter	0	c Browne b Wagner	17
*G. J. Bailey	b Porter	0	c Wheater b Quinn	32
R. R. Rossouw	c Wagner b Quinn	0	lbw b Harmer	0
S. M. Ervine	c Wheater b Bopara	9	b Porter	7
†L. D. McManus	b Porter	39	c Quinn b Wagner	37
G. K. Berg	c Wheater b Bopara	2	b Harmer	24
K. J. Abbott	c Cook b Porter	36	run out	0
M. S. Crane	not out	4	c ten Doeschate b Westley	18
F. H. Edwards	c Westley b Wagner	0	not out	0
	B 2, lb 4, w 5, nb 2	13	Nb 2	2
	(37.3 overs)	115	(47.3 overs)	148

1/18 (2) 2/18 (3) 3/18 (1) 4/18 (5) 5/18 (4) 6/32 (6) 7/34 (8) 8/109 (9) 9/110 (7) 10/115 (11)

1/5 (2) 2/24 (3) 3/40 (1) 4/40 (5) 5/50 (6) 6/93 (4) 7/111 (7) 8/115 (9) 9/142 (8) 10/148 (10)

Porter 14–5–24–5; Quinn 12–4–32–2; Bopara 5–0–27–2; Wagner 6.3–1–26–1. *Second innings*—Porter 10–5–21–2; Quinn 11–2–47–1; Wagner 16–7–39–2; Bopara 5–1–12–0; Harmer 5–2–23–3; Westley 0.3–0–6–1.

Umpires: S. A. Garratt and R. T. Robinson.

ESSEX v SURREY

At Chelmsford, May 26–29. Drawn. Essex 11pts, Surrey 11pts. Toss: Surrey. First-class debut: G. S. Virdi.

The teams entered this match first and second in the table – Essex led by a single point – and they remained bracketed together after a draw, although Surrey were happier after slipping to 31 for five inside the first hour. But the rest of the opening day yielded 303 for two, with Sangakkara in the form of his life. Drilling drives and clipping cuts, he put on 191 with Sam Curran – more than 20 years his junior, at almost 19 – and reached his fifth successive century shortly before tea. Next day he glided to 200, his 13th first-class double, sharing another big stand with Meaker. In reply, Browne dropped anchor, then Lawrence batted more expansively for his second hundred of the season. Finally Wagner added his first half-century for Essex to pinch a small lead. There were 752 runs over the two first innings, but no byes, thanks to the keepers, sorcerer Foster and his one-time apprentice Foakes. The main talking point on the final day was whether Sangakkara could emulate C. B. Fry, Don Bradman and Mike Procter in scoring six first-class hundreds in a row, though Porter caused jitters with five wickets in 27 balls to reduce Surrey to 177 for seven, only 163 in front. Then, with Sangakkara stuck on 79, Wagner clonked Meaker on the helmet, and the players left the field for an early tea; they were off for 75 minutes before returning in indifferent light. With a draw now certain, Sangakkara tried to extend his sequence but, on 84, was caught and bowled by Westley as he drove towards mid-off. Sangakkara smiled ruefully, but captain Burns admitted: "We're all probably more upset than he is."

Close of play: first day, Surrey 334-7 (Sangakkara 177, Meaker 43); second day, Essex 215-3 (Lawrence 78, Bopara 33); third day, Surrey 55-1 (Burns 21, Borthwick 1).

Surrey

*R. J. Burns c Lawrence b Quinn	2	– c and b Harmer	50
M. D. Stoneman c Harmer b Quinn	4	– c Cook b Wagner	28
S. G. Borthwick c Foster b Quinn	3	– c Foster b Porter	36
K. C. Sangakkara c Wagner b Harmer	200	– c and b Westley	84
D. P. Sibley b Porter	1	– c Foster b Porter	0
†B. T. Foakes b Porter	8	– c Bopara b Porter	5
S. M. Curran st Foster b Harmer	90	– lbw b Porter	1
T. K. Curran c Browne b Bopara	4	– c Foster b Porter	8
S. C. Meaker c Foster b Porter	49	– b Harmer	24
G. S. Virdi b Porter	5	– not out	8
R. Rampaul not out	1	– not out	0
Nb 2	2	B 7, lb 7, w 2	16
1/6 (2) 2/9 (1) 3/16 (3) 4/17 (5) 5/31 (6) 6/222 (7) 7/239 (8) 8/349 (9) 9/363 (10) 10/369 (4) (109.2 overs)	369	1/50 (2) 2/113 (1) 3/151 (3) 4/151 (5) 5/159 (6) 6/161 (7) 7/177 (8) 8/248 (9) 9/252 (4) (9 wkts dec, 76 overs)	260

Porter 27–1–89–4; Quinn 19–4–66–3; Wagner 31–6–108–0; Harmer 24.2–3–64–2; Bopara 7–0–40–1; Westley 1–0–2–0. *Second innings*—Porter 18–4–71–5; Quinn 10–2–33–0; Wagner 15–4–43–1; Harmer 29–7–90–2; Westley 3–1–7–1; Bopara 1–0–2–0.

Essex

N. L. J. Browne c T. K. Curran b Meaker	52
A. N. Cook lbw b T. K. Curran	36
T. Westley c Foakes b S. M. Curran	16
D. W. Lawrence lbw b Meaker	107
R. S. Bopara b T. K. Curran	39
*R. N. ten Doeschate lbw b Virdi	53
†J. S. Foster b Virdi	21
S. R. Harmer st Foakes b Virdi	0
N. Wagner c Sangakkara b Rampaul	50
M. R. Quinn b Meaker	4
J. A. Porter not out	0
W 1, nb 4	5
1/61 (2) 2/87 (3) 3/126 (1) 4/232 (5) 5/256 (4) 6/305 (7) 7/305 (8) 8/344 (6) 9/383 (9) 10/383 (10) (132.1 overs)	383

110 overs: 311-7

T. K. Curran 31–7–97–2; S. M. Curran 21–6–58–1; Rampaul 27–8–73–1; Virdi 36–7–82–3; Meaker 17.1–3–73–3.

Umpires: J. W. Lloyds and N. A. Mallender.

At Guildford, June 9–12. ESSEX beat SURREY by eight wickets.

ESSEX v WARWICKSHIRE

At Chelmsford, June 19–22. Essex won by an innings and 164 runs. Essex 22pts, Warwickshire 3pts. Toss: Essex.

Essex stretched their lead thanks to Harmer, their South African Kolpak signing, who took six wickets in the first innings, then captured eight for 36 – briefly a career-best – as Warwickshire capsized for 94 in the follow-on. He was the first Essex bowler to claim 14 in a match for 22 years. The only man to escape his clutches on the final day was Bell, who edged a climber to the keeper off Wagner, in his last match for Essex before giving way to Mohammad Amir (Wagner's team-mates presented him with a magnum of champagne at lunch on the final day). The others fell to Harmer's probing off-spin, after he had warmed up with a 33-over spell in the first innings. Essex had earlier built a solid platform: Browne's 84, which occupied more than five hours, was followed by a sixth-wicket stand of 229 between Bopara – who extended his first Championship century for three

BEST BOWLING IN AN INNINGS BY AN ESSEX SPINNER

9-40	W. Mead (OB)	v Hampshire at Southampton	1900
9-52	W. Mead (OB)	v Hampshire at Southampton	1895
9-75	W. Mead (OB)	v Leicestershire at Leyton	1896
9-77	T. P. B. Smith (LB)	v Middlesex at Colchester	1947
9-93	F. G. Bull (OB)	v Surrey at The Oval	1897
9-95	**S. R. Harmer (OB)**	**v Middlesex at Chelmsford**	**2017**
9-108	T. P. B. Smith (LB)	v Kent at Maidstone	1948
9-117	T. P. B. Smith (LB)	v Nottinghamshire at Southend	1948
8-30	R. E. East (SLA)	v Nottinghamshire at Ilford	1977
8-35	W. Mead (OB)	v Worcestershire at Leyton	1911
8-36	**S. R. Harmer (OB)**	**v Warwickshire at Chelmsford**	**2017**

years to a classy 192 – and Foster. Essex eventually declared at 541. Patel had showed there was something in the pitch for the spinners with four wickets, and later held Harmer up by top-scoring with 71 from 72 balls. Warwickshire's fourth defeat in six matches left them rooted to the bottom of the table.

Close of play: first day, Essex 263-5 (Bopara 84, Foster 13); second day, Warwickshire 60-2 (Trott 15, Bell 8); third day, Warwickshire 27-2 (Umeed 13).

Essex

N. L. J. Browne b Clarke	84
A. N. Cook lbw b Patel	39
T. Westley c Clarke b Patel	4
V. Chopra b Rankin	14
R. S. Bopara b Patel	192
*R. N. ten Doeschate lbw b Clarke	4
†J. S. Foster c Barker b Trott	121
P. I. Walter c Sukhjit Singh b Patel	16
S. R. Harmer lbw b Sukhjit Singh	1
N. Wagner not out	24
A. P. Beard not out	4
B 13, lb 18, w 5, nb 2	38
(9 wkts dec, 164 overs)	541

1/60 (2) 2/68 (3) 3/96 (4) 4/223 (1) 5/227 (6) 6/456 (7) 7/504 (8) 8/506 (9) 9/532 (5) — 110 overs: 305-5

Barker 25–7–71–0; Clarke 29–10–84–2; Rankin 28–4–73–1; Patel 45–10–138–4; Sukhjit Singh 21–3–80–1; Trott 15–2–48–1; Umeed 1–0–16–0.

Warwickshire

A. R. I. Umeed run out	7	– lbw b Harmer 21
I. J. Westwood c Cook b Harmer	22	– c Foster b Walter 0
I. J. L. Trott c Chopra b Wagner	19	– lbw b Harmer 8
*I. R. Bell c Cook b Harmer	32	– c Foster b Wagner 11
S. R. Hain c Foster b Walter	58	– c ten Doeschate b Harmer 2
†T. R. Ambrose c Chopra b Wagner	25	– not out 17
R. Clarke lbw b Harmer	7	– lbw b Harmer 12
K. H. D. Barker lbw b Harmer	24	– c Foster b Harmer 0
J. S. Patel c and b Harmer	71	– lbw b Harmer 8
W. B. Rankin lbw b Harmer	1	– lbw b Harmer 1
Sukhjit Singh not out	1	– c Cook b Harmer 0
B 4, lb 8, nb 4	16	B 4, lb 8, nb 2 14
(108.5 overs)	283	(53.2 overs) 94

1/36 (1) 2/39 (2) 3/65 (3) 4/131 (4) 5/171 (5) 6/178 (6) 7/192 (7) 8/268 (8) 9/276 (10) 10/283 (9)

1/4 (2) 2/27 (3) 3/47 (4) 4/53 (1) 5/54 (5) 6/74 (7) 7/74 (8) 8/82 (9) 9/94 (10) 10/94 (11)

Wagner 29–4–95–2; Beard 13–3–34–0; Harmer 45.5–17–92–6; Walter 13–3–36–1; Bopara 7–2–11–0; Westley 1–0–3–0. *Second innings*—Wagner 13–5–18–1; Walter 13–3–17–1; Harmer 20.2–7–36–8; Westley 5–4–2–0; Beard 2–0–9–0.

Umpires: N. L. Bainton and N. J. Llong.

ESSEX v MIDDLESEX

At Chelmsford, June 26–29 (day/night). Essex won by an innings and 34 runs. Essex 24pts, Middlesex 1pt. Toss: Middlesex. County debut: Mohammad Amir.

Simon Harmer followed his 14 Warwickshire wickets with 14 more against Middlesex, the first time anyone had managed so many in successive matches since 1931. It spirited Essex, in their first floodlit Championship game, to their third innings victory in four home games, despite the loss of the second day to rain, and increased their lead to 29 points. Harmer was soon in action, after Mohammad Amir had taken a wicket in his first over for the club. The main resistance came from Eskinazi and Malan, who added 124 before Harmer separated them, then Stirling crashed 77 from 50 balls, with five sixes. But Essex's openers put the Middlesex total of 246 into perspective, posting a county-record first-wicket stand of 373 to eclipse 316 by Graham Gooch and Paul Prichard against Kent at Chelmsford in 1994. Cook fell just short of his double, but Browne made no mistake, batting for 384 balls in all. The icing was a 75-ball century, including six sixes off Rayner, from Chopra, a replacement on the third day after Westley joined the England Lions. Middlesex were 296 adrift, but a draw was possible while Compton was grinding out his first century of the season. When he departed lbw after 381 minutes, it was 252 for six, all to Harmer, with 11.5 overs left. Higgins and Rayner fell six overs later, before Lawrence ended hopes of the first pink-ball ten-for by removing Roland-Jones. But Harmer dismissed Finn with just eight deliveries to spare, snatching Essex's best figures since Mark Ilott took nine for 19 against Northamptonshire at Luton in 1995.

Close of play: first day, Essex 106-0 (Browne 40, Cook 64); second day, no play; third day, Middlesex 27-0 (Gubbins 16, Compton 6).

FOURTEEN WICKETS IN SUCCESSIVE FIRST-CLASS MATCHES

A. W. Mold (Lancashire)	15-131 v Somerset, 14-95 v Gloucestershire	1891
S. T. Callaway (New South Wales)	14-65 v Wellington, 15-175 v New Zealand XI	1895-96
C. L. Townsend (Gloucestershire)	15-205 v Warwickshire, 15-141 v Essex	1898
J. R. Gunn (Nottinghamshire)	14-132 v Surrey, 14-174 v Essex	1903
J. C. White (Somerset)	14-110 v Glamorgan, 15-175 v Worcestershire	1921
G. Geary (Leicestershire)	14-86 v Hampshire, 14-98 v Lancashire	1926
C. W. L. Parker (Gloucestershire)	14-97 v Warwickshire, 15-91 v Surrey	1930
C. W. L. Parker (Gloucestershire)	14-91 v Derbyshire, 15-113 v Nottinghamshire	1931
S. R. Harmer (Essex)	**14-128 v Warwickshire, 14-172 v Middlesex**	**2017**

Townsend is alone in taking 15 in successive first-class matches: he claimed 13 in the game before, and 12 in the one after, giving him 55 in four. Muttiah Muralitharan took 16-220 (for Sri Lanka v England in 1998) and 14-117 (Lancashire v Warwickshire in 1999) in successive first-class matches in which he bowled, but had a rain-affected game in between in which Lancashire did not take the field.

Middlesex

N. R. D. Compton c Foster b Porter	2	– (2) lbw b Harmer	120
N. R. T. Gubbins lbw b Mohammad Amir	0	– (1) c Cook b Harmer	16
S. S. Eskinazi c Cook b Porter	66	– c Chopra b Harmer	12
*D. J. Malan c Foster b Harmer	60	– b Harmer	1
P. R. Stirling c ten Doeschate b Harmer	77	– c Bopara b Harmer	55
†J. A. Simpson lbw b Mohammad Amir	5	– c Cook b Harmer	21
R. F. Higgins c Westley b Harmer	6	– c Cook b Harmer	16
T. S. Roland-Jones not out	11	– lbw b Lawrence	1
O. P. Rayner c ten Doeschate b Harmer	0	– lbw b Harmer	0
T. J. Murtagh lbw b Harmer	0	– not out	1
S. T. Finn c and b Bopara	1	– lbw b Harmer	0
B 5, lb 12, w 1	18	B 12, lb 5, nb 2	19
1/2 (2) 2/2 (1) 3/126 (4) 4/146 (3) 5/158 (6) 6/219 (7) 7/225 (5) 8/225 (9) 9/231 (10) 10/246 (11) (59.1 overs)	246	1/27 (1) 2/49 (3) 3/51 (4) 4/204 (5) 5/239 (6) 6/252 (2) 7/261 (7) 8/261 (9) 9/261 (8) 10/262 (11) (111.4 overs)	262

Porter 12–2–58–2; Mohammad Amir 16–3–53–2; Walter 6–2–27–0; Bopara 4.1–1–11–1; Harmer 20–4–77–5; Lawrence 1–0–3–0. *Second innings*—Porter 19–6–38–0; Mohammad Amir 20–7–42–0; Harmer 46.4–15–95–9; Walter 7–2–25–0; Lawrence 16–6–39–1; Bopara 2–1–4–0; ten Doeschate 1–0–2–0.

Essex

N. L. J. Browne c Malan b Rayner 221
A. N. Cook c Eskinazi b Rayner 193
V. Chopra not out 100
D. W. Lawrence b Higgins 2
R. S. Bopara not out 10
B 2, lb 6, w 2, nb 6 16

1/373 (2) (3 wkts dec, 125 overs) 542
2/502 (1) 3/508 (4) 110 overs: 411-1

*R. N. ten Doeschate, †J. S. Foster, P. I. Walter, S. R. Harmer, Mohammad Amir and J. A. Porter did not bat.

Chopra replaced T. Westley, who left to join the England Lions squad.

Murtagh 23–5–69–0; Roland-Jones 24–3–91–0; Finn 21–3–85–0; Rayner 29–1–152–2; Higgins 16–1–77–1; Stirling 4–1–10–0; Malan 8–0–50–0.

Umpires: P. J. Hartley and D. J. Millns.

At Chelmsford, August 1–3. ESSEX drew with WEST INDIANS (see West Indian tour section).

At Scarborough, August 6–7. ESSEX beat YORKSHIRE by eight wickets. *Mohammad Amir has match figures of ten for 72 in a two-day win.*

ESSEX v SOMERSET

At Chelmsford, August 28–31. Essex won by 179 runs. Essex 19pts, Somerset 3pts. Toss: Essex. Championship debut: P. A. van Meekeren.

Essex shrugged off the loss of most of the third day and romped to a fifth successive victory, leaving them 36 points clear at the top of the table ahead of a visit to second-placed Lancashire. Porter took advantage of helpful conditions to collect 12 wickets, including a career-best seven for 55 as Somerset were polished off an hour after tea on the final day. Honours had been even after two innings: first Craig Overton and the lively Dutch debutant Paul van Meekeren took four wickets apiece to roll Essex for 159, then Porter hit back to limit the deficit to five, despite an injury to Mohammad Amir, who suffered a back spasm early on the second day. Essex stuttered again, slipping to 39 for three before Browne and Wheater injected some backbone in a stand of 118; ten Doeschate added a forthright 67 to take the target to 289. Porter bowled Trescothick second ball – on his way to 50 Championship wickets for the season – and Somerset were soon 42 for five. Only Overton survived much longer than an hour as Essex stormed home. Umpire Neil Mallender fell ill on the second day, and the ECB's liaison officer Phil Whitticase stood at square leg after tea, though only for 2.3 overs before bad light ended play. Billy Taylor deputised for the last two days.

Close of play: first day, Somerset 118-5 (Davies 7, Leach 8); second day, Essex 117-3 (Browne 66, Wheater 36); third day, Essex 158-4 (Wheater 58, ten Doeschate 0).

Essex

V. Chopra lbw b van Meekeren	9 – lbw b Overton	1
N. L. J. Browne c van Meekeren b Overton	44 – b Groenewald	83
D. W. Lawrence c Hildreth b van Meekeren	0 – lbw b Overton	0
R. S. Bopara lbw b Overton	1 – st Davies b Leach	9
A. J. A. Wheater lbw b Groenewald	3 – c Davies b Overton	88
*R. N. ten Doeschate c Trescothick b Overton	35 – c Trescothick b Leach	67
†J. S. Foster c Hildreth b Groenewald	4 – lbw b Groenewald	22
P. I. Walter b van Meekeren	17 – not out	7
S. R. Harmer c Trescothick b van Meekeren	12 – lbw b Bess	2
Mohammad Amir not out	22 – absent hurt	
J. A. Porter b Overton	10 – (10) c Davies b Bess	0
Lb 1, w 1	2 B 1, lb 9, nb 4	14
1/19 (1) 2/21 (3) 3/36 (4) 4/39 (5) 5/90 (6) 6/97 (2) 7/98 (7) 8/121 (9) 9/140 (8) 10/159 (11) (50.2 overs)	159 1/8 (1) 2/8 (3) 3/39 (4) 4/157 (2) 5/234 (5) 6/284 (7) 7/284 (6) 8/293 (9) 9/293 (10) (100.1 overs)	293

Overton 15.2–4–40–4; van Meekeren 14–2–60–4; Groenewald 13–5–25–2; Abell 5–1–15–0; Leach 3–0–18–0. *Second innings*—Overton 25–8–68–3; van Meekeren 20–7–72–0; Groenewald 21–5–74–2; Leach 25–8–52–2; Bess 9.1–3–17–2.

Somerset

M. E. Trescothick c Foster b Porter	2 – b Porter	0
E. J. Byrom b Porter	5 – c Foster b Porter	10
T. D. Rouse c Harmer b Bopara	4 – c Foster b Porter	9
J. C. Hildreth c Bopara b Porter	51 – c Foster b Porter	22
*T. B. Abell c Chopra b Porter	30 – lbw b Harmer	0
†S. M. Davies c Foster b Porter	15 – c Browne b Porter	19
M. J. Leach c Foster b Mohammad Amir	8 – (9) b Porter	8
C. Overton b Mohammad Amir	0 – (7) b Harmer	36
D. M. Bess not out	22 – (8) lbw b Harmer	0
T. D. Groenewald c Foster b Harmer	11 – b Porter	1
P. A. van Meekeren c Wheater b Harmer	0 – not out	1
Lb 4, w 6, nb 6	16 Lb 3	3
1/2 (1) 2/10 (3) 3/20 (2) 4/98 (5) 5/101 (4) 6/118 (7) 7/118 (8) 8/133 (6) 9/164 (10) 10/164 (11) (64 overs)	164 1/0 (1) 2/10 (3) 3/31 (2) 4/32 (5) 5/42 (4) 6/81 (6) 7/82 (8) 8/99 (9) 9/105 (10) 10/109 (7) (37.5 overs)	109

Porter 17–4–40–5; Mohammad Amir 12–4–22–2; Harmer 22–10–42–2; Bopara 5–0–25–1; Walter 8–1–31–0. *Second innings*—Porter 14–2–55–7; Walter 7–3–22–0; Harmer 15.5–6–29–3; Bopara 1–1–0–0.

Umpires: M. Burns and N. A. Mallender.
P. Whitticase replaced Mallender on the second day and B. V. Taylor on the last two.

At Manchester, September 5–8. ESSEX drew with LANCASHIRE.

At Birmingham, September 12–14. ESSEX beat WARWICKSHIRE by an innings and 56 runs. *Essex are confirmed as champions on September 15, after Lancashire lose to Somerset.*

At Southampton, September 19–22. ESSEX beat HAMPSHIRE by 108 runs. *Essex win after following on.*

ESSEX v YORKSHIRE

At Chelmsford, September 25–27. Essex won by 376 runs. Essex 20pts, Yorkshire 3pts. Toss: uncontested.

Essex rounded off their unbeaten Championship season in style, condemning Yorkshire to the heaviest defeat by runs in their history. Yorkshire's batting was dire, with 18 single-figure scores; the only consolation was that results elsewhere meant they avoided the drop. Harmer had been one of Essex's stars of the summer with the ball, but this time they were indebted to his bat, after a season's-best 64 rescued a limp first innings. Yorkshire were even more insipid: Lyth made 35, but Wagner removed him and two more, and ran out Ballance; Porter and Harmer took care of the rest. Looking to build on an unexpectedly healthy lead of 116, Essex lost two wickets in Brooks's second over, but Browne and Lawrence made up for the absence of Westley – who had been struck on the thumb (and dismissed) by Patterson in the first innings – with twin 83s. Fifties for ten Doeschate and Harmer, his second of the match, meant Yorkshire needed 451. After little more than an hour they were 38 for eight, and Essex soon completed their tenth win of the summer, the fifth inside three days. Twenty-year-old seamer Sam Cook, who had claimed five for 18 against Hampshire in the previous match, picked up five for 20.

Close of play: first day, Essex 227; second day, Essex 134-2 (Browne 53, Lawrence 75).

YORKSHIRE'S HEAVIEST DEFEATS BY RUNS

376	**v Essex at Chelmsford**	**2017**
324	v Gloucestershire at Cheltenham	1994
305	v Cambridge University at Cambridge	1906
300	v Gloucestershire at Gloucester	1998
295	v Durham at Chester-le-Street	2008
279	v Somerset at Leeds	1901
262	v West Indians at Harrogate	1906
262	v Surrey at The Oval	1938
259	v Leicestershire at Leeds	1910
248	v Lancashire at Liverpool	1958

Yorkshire's heaviest overall defeat was by an innings and 272 by Surrey at The Oval in 1898.

Essex

V. Chopra c Lees b Coad	28	– lbw b Brooks	4
N. L. J. Browne b Coad	29	– c Lyth b Patterson	83
T. Westley c Lyth b Patterson	13		
D. W. Lawrence lbw b Brooks	8	– lbw b Coad	83
R. S. Bopara lbw b Brooks	1	– (3) lbw b Brooks	0
*R. N. ten Doeschate c Hodd b Patterson	30	– (5) c Hodd b Fisher	57
†J. S. Foster c Brathwaite b Patterson	25	– (6) lbw b Fisher	10
S. R. Harmer lbw b Carver	64	– (7) not out	58
N. Wagner c Patterson b Brooks	19	– (8) c Lees b Fisher	23
J. A. Porter c Patterson b Carver	6	– (9) not out	10
S. J. Cook not out	0		
B 1, lb 3	4	Lb 3, w 1, nb 2	6
1/39 (1) 2/63 (3) 3/74 (4) 4/80 (2) 5/80 (5) 6/135 (7) 7/142 (6) 8/183 (9) 9/222 (8) 10/227 (10) (71.2 overs)	227	1/6 (1) 2/6 (3) 3/145 (4) 4/188 (2) 5/205 (6) 6/280 (5) 7/322 (8) (7 wkts dec, 95.2 overs)	334

Brooks 17–5–54–3; Coad 16–4–56–2; Patterson 20–4–66–3; Fisher 14–4–37–0; Carver 4.2–1–10–2. *Second innings*—Brooks 20–1–84–2; Coad 17–6–37–1; Fisher 20.2–3–69–3; Patterson 21–3–62–1; Carver 12–0–49–0; Lyth 5–0–30–0.

Yorkshire

A. Lyth c Foster b Wagner	35	– c Foster b Cook	2
K. C. Brathwaite b Porter	4	– lbw b Porter	1
A. Z. Lees c Foster b Harmer	4	– b Cook	8
*G. S. Ballance run out	13	– lbw b Cook	5
J. A. Leaning lbw b Wagner	4	– c Foster b Cook	9
†A. J. Hodd lbw b Wagner	21	– lbw b Harmer	6
M. D. Fisher b Porter	9	– c Foster b Wagner	25
S. A. Patterson lbw b Porter	5	– c Foster b Porter	2
J. A. Brooks c Foster b Harmer	0	– c Chopra b Cook	1
K. Carver c Foster b Harmer	6	– lbw b Harmer	9
B. O. Coad not out	6	– not out	2
Lb 4	4	Lb 4	4
1/23 (2) 2/40 (3) 3/48 (1) 4/54 (5) 5/74 (4) 6/90 (6) 7/98 (8) 8/99 (9) 9/99 (7) 10/111 (10) (45.1 overs)	111	1/3 (1) 2/3 (2) 3/17 (3) 4/20 (4) 5/33 (5) 6/35 (6) 7/37 (8) 8/38 (9) 9/72 (10) 10/74 (7) (28.5 overs)	74

Porter 14–4–29–3; Cook 10–3–21–0; Harmer 12.1–4–36–3; Wagner 9–3–21–3. *Second innings*—Porter 9–2–16–2; Cook 8–0–20–5; Harmer 6–2–7–2; Wagner 5.5–1–27–1.

Umpires: R. J. Evans and G. D. Lloyd.

GLAMORGAN

The young ones

EDWARD BEVAN

The results might not suggest it – Glamorgan finished seventh in the Championship's second division, just one place higher than the previous season – but the emergence of several young players, and a first appearance at Twenty20 finals day since 2004, raised hopes that better times were not far away.

Robert Croft, the head coach, had long believed the latest generation had the talent to make the next step, and also knew he had to integrate them with the more experienced heads. The signs were that the mix was working, which was good news now that Jacques Rudolph has retired, and Colin Ingram has decided to concentrate on limited-overs cricket.

When, to grumbles from the membership, five senior players were rested from the Championship match at Colwyn Bay shortly before T20 finals day, the younger brigade came within one wicket of defeating a full-strength Sussex. When the exercise was repeated for the final game of the season, they beat Kent at Canterbury. This group included 19-year-old Kiran Carlson, who scored 191 and 53 against Gloucestershire, and 20-year-old opening bowler Lukas Carey, who claimed 35 first-class wickets and prompted the ECB to send the former England seamer Geoff Arnold, one of their bowling assessors, to watch him. Opener Nick Selman was their leading scorer in the Championship, while Andrew Salter hit twin eighties against Gloucestershire, although his off-spin made little progress.

The start of the season had been distinctly unpromising. Glamorgan lost their first two matches by a distance and, after drawing with Leicestershire, were in danger of a third thumping when Nottinghamshire forced them to follow on at Cardiff. But Ingram and Chris Cooke showed character to bat through the final day and save the game. Rudolph then decided to relinquish the captaincy in the Championship, and was succeeded by fast bowler Michael Hogan, whose reign began with victories over Durham and Worcestershire.

Hopes of a resurgence were rudely shattered when five of the next six Championship matches ended in defeat, the lowlight coming when Gloucestershire wrapped up victory at Cheltenham College inside two days. It was probably a blessing when the break came for the T20 Blast. They lost their first match, and had four other home games washed out, yet Glamorgan topped their group, earning a home quarter-final, where they thrashed Leicestershire. But the semi against Warwickshire at Edgbaston was lost, despite a valiant late blitz from Salter.

Glamorgan's 25 batting points, the fewest in the second division, showed the need for more top-order solidity. Selman confirmed the promise of his inaugural season, but Rudolph again fell short of expectations, though he continued to score well in one-day games. He averaged only 25 in the Championship, and was left out of the last two matches in favour of 20-year-old Connor Brown, born in Caerphilly and a product of the Glamorgan Academy and Cardiff MCCU. Will Bragg, the club's leading scorer in 2016, played only three four-day matches because of illness, and later announced his retirement at 31, while Aneurin Donald's 487 runs from 20 innings was a poor return for one of his ability. The batting should be boosted by the arrival, on a two-year contract, of the Australian Shaun Marsh, fresh from his Ashes exploits. Former club favourite Matthew Maynard joined as batting coach after three years at Somerset.

Stu Forster, Getty Images

Lukas Carey

Hogan led the attack, his 50 Championship wickets including his 500th in first-class cricket. He is one of only nine Australians – Steve Magoffin is the other contemporary – to have taken as many but never played Test cricket. Timm van der Gugten was restricted to five first-class (and 11 white-ball) appearances by injury, but the rest did well to collect 40 bowling points – only Nottinghamshire, with 41, had more in either division. The South African fast bowler Marchant de Lange, who joined thanks to his wife's British passport, proved a useful signing, particularly in one-day cricket, when he was effective at the death. His Championship wickets were expensive, although not for lack of effort.

The slow bowling remained a concern. Salter's off-breaks were taking a long time to develop – his 14 wickets in 2017 cost 46 apiece – but Glamorgan hoped a winter in New Zealand, under the guidance of Warwickshire's Test off-spinner Jeetan Patel, would help him regain the skills that once made him such an exciting prospect.

Ingram was again the outstanding limited-overs performer, and won Glamorgan's Player of the Year award; he will captain in white-ball matches in 2018. In addition to two Twenty20 hundreds, he amassed 564 runs at 70 in the Royal London Cup, and was named the competition's leading player, as he had been for the 2016 T20 Blast. Glamorgan just missed out on a place in the Royal London knockouts.

The season was clouded by the death of Don Shepherd, six days after his 90th birthday in August. A Glamorgan legend, and their leading wicket-taker with 2,174, he was respected far and wide. Croft described him as "my mentor, idol and friend".

Championship attendance: 12,020.

GLAMORGAN RESULTS

All first-class matches – Played 15: Won 3, Lost 7, Drawn 5.
County Championship matches – Played 14: Won 3, Lost 7, Drawn 4.

Specsavers County Championship, 7th in Division 2;
NatWest T20 Blast, semi-finalists; Royal London One-Day Cup, 4th in South Group.

COUNTY CHAMPIONSHIP AVERAGES, BATTING AND FIELDING

Cap		Birthplace	M	I	NO	R	HS	100	Avge	Ct/St
2016	C. B. Cooke	*Johannesburg, SA*	12	21	5	695	113*	1	43.43	39
	A. G. Salter	*Haverfordwest‡*	12	19	4	619	88	0	41.26	5
2017	C. A. Ingram††	*Port Elizabeth, SA*	12	20	2	672	155*	2	37.33	5
	N. J. Selman	*Brisbane, Australia*	14	26	2	872	142*	4	36.33	15
	C. A. J. Meschede	*Johannesburg, SA*	6	8	0	290	87	0	36.25	2
	K. S. Carlson	*Cardiff‡*	8	13	0	443	191	1	34.07	4
2014	†J. A. Rudolph¶	*Springs, SA*	11	20	1	492	111	1	25.89	3
	A. H. T. Donald	*Swansea‡*	11	20	1	487	66*	0	25.63	12
	R. A. J. Smith	*Glasgow*	3	4	0	89	38	0	22.25	0
	T. N. Cullen	*Perth, Australia*	2	4	0	84	42	0	21.00	8/1
	C. R. Brown	*Caerphilly‡*	2	4	0	83	35	0	20.75	0
2013	G. G. Wagg	*Rugby*	3	6	1	93	33*	0	18.60	2
	L. J. Carey	*Carmarthen‡*	10	14	2	219	54	0	18.25	3
	D. L. Lloyd	*St Asaph‡*	8	15	1	247	88	0	17.64	4
	†J. R. Murphy	*Haverfordwest‡*	4	6	0	97	27	0	16.16	1
	M. de Lange††	*Tzaneen, SA*	11	17	1	254	39	0	15.87	5
2013	M. G. Hogan††	*Newcastle, Aust.*	12	17	10	100	29*	0	14.28	4
2015	†W. D. Bragg	*Newport‡*	3	6	1	65	30	0	13.00	2
	T. van der Gugten††	*Hornsby, Australia*	5	7	0	64	21	0	9.14	0
	H. W. Podmore	*Hammersmith*	2	4	1	21	10	0	7.00	1
	A. O. Morgan	*Swansea‡*	3	6	0	28	17	0	4.66	1

‡ *Born in Wales.* ¶ *Official overseas player.* †† *Other non-England-qualified.*

BOWLING

	Style	O	M	R	W	BB	5I	Avge
M. G. Hogan	RFM	370.4	84	1,044	50	6-43	3	20.88
T. van der Gugten	RFM	158.2	43	505	22	5-101	1	22.95
L. J. Carey	RFM	271.3	49	1,051	35	4-85	0	30.02
C. A. J. Meschede	RM	126	18	450	13	4-61	0	34.61
M. de Lange	RF	345.5	47	1,315	34	5-95	1	38.67
A. G. Salter	OB	155.4	12	646	14	3-60	0	46.14

Also bowled: C. R. Brown (OB) 4–0–14–0; C. A. Ingram (LB) 37.1–0–155–2; D. L. Lloyd (RM) 69–7–320–4; H. W. Podmore (RM) 28.1–3–124–3; R. A. J. Smith (RM) 69.4–6–302–9; G. G. Wagg (SLA/LM) 60–10–206–7.

LEADING ROYAL LONDON CUP AVERAGES (100 runs/4 wickets)

Batting	Runs	HS	Avge	SR	Ct
C. A. Ingram	564	142	70.50	104.44	3
W. D. Bragg	233	94	38.83	74.67	2
J. A. Rudolph	305	121	38.12	79.22	2
C. B. Cooke	253	62	36.14	104.97	11
K. S. Carlson	206	63	25.75	100.00	1
D. L. Lloyd	127	48	15.87	64.14	0

Bowling	W	BB	Avge	ER
M. de Lange	18	5-49	22.50	5.52
D. L. Lloyd	6	5-53	32.50	6.50
C. A. Ingram	7	4-39	38.42	6.25
M. G. Hogan	6	2-42	58.00	5.52
T. van der Gugten	4	1-47	63.25	7.09
C. A. J. Meschede	4	2-53	93.00	5.81

LEADING NATWEST T20 BLAST AVERAGES (100 runs/18 overs)

Batting	Runs	HS	Avge	SR	Ct
C. A. Ingram	462	114	46.20	**166.18**	5
D. A. Miller	117	50	39.00	**146.25**	6
A. H. T. Donald	277	76	21.30	**144.27**	9
G. G. Wagg	163	50	81.50	**141.73**	1
C. B. Cooke	172	49	21.50	**131.29**	7
J. A. Rudolph	443	77*	49.22	**129.15**	2

Bowling	W	BB	Avge	ER
A. G. Salter	2	1-10	69.50	**7.72**
C. A. Ingram	9	2-27	35.00	**7.87**
C. A. J. Meschede	10	3-17	19.70	**7.88**
M. de Lange	18	3-19	21.22	**8.30**
M. G. Hogan	20	5-17	19.50	**8.32**
G. G. Wagg	9	2-12	37.88	**9.13**

FIRST-CLASS COUNTY RECORDS

Highest score for	309*	S. P. James v Sussex at Colwyn Bay	2000
Highest score against	322*	M. B. Loye (Northamptonshire) at Northampton	1998
Leading run-scorer	34,056	A. Jones (avge 33.03)	1957–83
Best bowling for	10-51	J. Mercer v Worcestershire at Worcester	1936
Best bowling against	10-18	G. Geary (Leicestershire) at Pontypridd	1929
Leading wicket-taker	2,174	D. J. Shepherd (avge 20.95)	1950–72
Highest total for	718-3 dec	v Sussex at Colwyn Bay	2000
Highest total against	712	by Northamptonshire at Northampton	1998
Lowest total for	22	v Lancashire at Liverpool	1924
Lowest total against	33	by Leicestershire at Ebbw Vale	1965

LIST A COUNTY RECORDS

Highest score for	169*	J. A. Rudolph v Sussex at Hove	2014
Highest score against	268	A. D. Brown (Surrey) at The Oval	2002
Leading run-scorer	12,278	M. P. Maynard (avge 37.66)	1985–2005
Best bowling for	7-16	S. D. Thomas v Surrey at Swansea	1998
Best bowling against	7-30	M. P. Bicknell (Surrey) at The Oval	1999
Leading wicket-taker	356	R. D. B. Croft (avge 31.96)	1989–2012
Highest total for	429	v Surrey at The Oval	2002
Highest total against	438-5	by Surrey at The Oval	2002
Lowest total for	42	v Derbyshire at Swansea	1979
Lowest total against	59	by Combined Universities at Cambridge	1983
	59	by Sussex at Hove	1996

TWENTY20 COUNTY RECORDS

Highest score for	116*	I. J. Thomas v Somerset at Taunton	2004
Highest score against	117	M. J. Prior (Sussex) at Hove	2010
Leading run-scorer	**1,657**	**J. A. Rudolph (avge 42.48)**	**2014–17**
Best bowling for	5-14	G. G. Wagg v Worcestershire at Worcester	2013
Best bowling against	6-5	A. V. Suppiah (Somerset) at Cardiff	2011
Leading wicket-taker	100	D. A. Cosker (avge 30.32)	2003–16
Highest total for	240-3	v Surrey at The Oval	2015
Highest total against	239-5	by Sussex at Hove	2010
Lowest total for	90	v Yorkshire at Cardiff	2016
Lowest total against	81	by Gloucestershire at Bristol	2011

ADDRESS

The SSE SWALEC, Sophia Gardens, Cardiff CF11 9XR; 029 2040 9380; info@glamorgancricket.co.uk; www.glamorgancricket.com.

OFFICIALS

Captain 2017 J. A. Rudolph
2018 M. G. Hogan
(limited-overs) C. A. Ingram
Head coach R. D. B. Croft
Head of talent development R. V. Almond
President A. Jones

Chairman B. J. O'Brien
Chief executive and director of cricket H. Morris
Head groundsman R. Saxton
Scorer/archivist A. K. Hignell

GLAMORGAN v CARDIFF MCCU

At Cardiff, March 28–30. Drawn. Toss: Cardiff MCCU. First-class debuts: A. D. F. Brewster, C. R. Brown, O. L. Pike, J. A. L. Scriven.

Glamorgan's earliest start to a first-class season was spoiled when half of the first two days was lost to rain. Rudolph grabbed the chance for some practice, scoring his 50th first-class hundred; the rest of the top order settled in, but only Donald passed 35. Ollie Pike, a graduate of Glamorgan's Academy, claimed three wickets in an impressive spell with the second new ball. The students batted sedately on the final day: Jeremy Lawlor's half-century used up 161 minutes, after a promising innings from another Academy product, 19-year-old Connor Brown, whose unbeaten 70 a few days earlier had helped Cardiff beat Nottinghamshire in Barbados in a Twenty20 warm-up. This match began with a two-minute silence for the former Glamorgan player and coach John Derrick, who had died of a brain tumour the previous week, aged 54.

Close of play: first day, Glamorgan 122-1 (Rudolph 63, Lloyd 14); second day, Glamorgan 342-7 (Morgan 5, Salter 4).

Glamorgan

*J. A. Rudolph c Lawlor b Rouse	142
N. J. Selman lbw b Lawlor	30
D. L. Lloyd b Nijjar	35
K. S. Carlson c Scriven b Rouse	26
A. H. T. Donald c Brand b Pike	63
†C. B. Cooke b Pike	10
C. A. J. Meschede b Pike	6
A. O. Morgan not out	5
A. G. Salter not out	4
B 13, lb 4, nb 4	21
1/83 (2) 2/158 (3) 3/223 (4) 4/280 (1) 5/301 (6) 6/325 (7) 7/334 (5) (7 wkts dec, 89.2 overs)	342

M. G. Hogan and L. J. Carey did not bat.

Brewster 18–6–62–0; Pike 19.2–2–82–3; Leverock 13–1–46–0; Lawlor 10–2–26–1; Nijjar 17–2–53–1; Rouse 8–1–31–2; Brand 4–0–25–0.

Cardiff MCCU

M. J. Norris c Selman b Meschede	20
C. R. Brown c Salter b Hogan	33
*N. Brand c Cooke b Lloyd	0
T. D. Rouse lbw b Lloyd	18
J. L. Lawlor not out	50
†T. N. Cullen c Meschede b Hogan	20
J. A. L. Scriven not out	2
B 2, lb 2, nb 2	6
1/45 (1) 2/54 (3) 3/65 (2) 4/88 (4) 5/140 (6) (5 wkts dec, 72 overs)	149

A. S. S. Nijjar, K. S. Leverock, A. D. F. Brewster and O. L. Pike did not bat.

Hogan 13–4–31–2; Carey 8–5–9–0; Meschede 12–4–32–1; Lloyd 10–1–21–2; Morgan 14–4–22–0; Salter 15–1–30–0.

Umpires: J. H. Evans and R. J. Warren.

At Northampton, April 7–8. GLAMORGAN lost to NORTHAMPTONSHIRE by an innings and 22 runs.

GLAMORGAN v WORCESTERSHIRE

At Cardiff, April 14–16. Worcestershire won by eight wickets. Worcestershire 24pts, Glamorgan 4pts. Toss: uncontested. Championship debut: J. C. Tongue.

Worcestershire opened their Championship campaign with a convincing victory, completed inside two and a half days. As they had in their shellacking at Northampton, Glamorgan lost eight wickets on the first morning, although Lloyd and the tail salvaged a batting point. Both Worcestershire's openers fell for ducks – two of five catches for Cooke – but Köhler-Cadmore stopped the rot, reaching a three-hour century with a sumptuous drive off Hogan, before falling to the next delivery. Fifties for Barnard and the Australian all-rounder Hastings (in his first Championship match for Worcestershire) pushed the lead close to 200, which proved almost enough as Glamorgan floundered again after a decent start. Donald counter-attacked for 57, but was dismissed three balls after being clonked on the helmet by the lanky 19-year-old Josh Tongue. He completed a maiden five-for as the last seven wickets clattered for 67 on the third morning.

Close of play: first day, Worcestershire 180-4 (Köhler-Cadmore 52, Cox 41); second day, Glamorgan 141-3 (Ingram 41, Donald 10).

Glamorgan

First innings		Second innings	
N. J. Selman c Cox b Leach	16	– (2) c Cox b Hastings	42
*J. A. Rudolph c Clarke b Hastings	2	– (1) b Tongue	29
D. L. Lloyd c Hastings b Shantry	88	– lbw b Tongue	6
C. A. Ingram c Hastings b Leach	0	– c Cox b Leach	42
A. H. T. Donald b Hastings	3	– c Hastings b Tongue	57
†C. B. Cooke run out	5	– lbw b Hastings	1
K. S. Carlson c D'Oliveira b Barnard	13	– c Cox b Tongue	17
H. W. Podmore c Cox b Shantry	1	– not out	6
M. de Lange b Barnard	11	– c Mitchell b Tongue	0
L. J. Carey b Hastings	39	– c Cox b Shantry	5
M. G. Hogan not out	18	– c Barnard b Shantry	2
B 3, lb 2, nb 6	11	B 1, lb 1, nb 14	16
1/14 (2) 2/28 (1) 3/28 (4) 4/33 (5) 5/46 (6) 6/79 (7) 7/82 (8) 8/105 (9) 9/173 (10) 10/207 (3) (40.4 overs)	207	1/74 (1) 2/80 (3) 3/108 (2) 4/156 (4) 5/165 (6) 6/203 (7) 7/210 (5) 8/210 (9) 9/221 (10) 10/223 (11) (62.5 overs)	223

Leach 11–2–60–2; Hastings 11–2–57–3; Tongue 7–1–41–0; Shantry 5.4–1–12–2; Barnard 6–1–32–2. *Second innings*—Leach 16–3–58–1; Hastings 18–3–67–2; Shantry 11.5–1–32–2; Barnard 7–1–19–0; Tongue 10–1–45–5.

Worcestershire

First innings		Second innings	
D. K. H. Mitchell c Cooke b Carey	0	– c Selman b Carey	1
B. L. D'Oliveira c Cooke b Hogan	0	– c and b Hogan	9
T. C. Fell b Carey	35	– not out	15
J. M. Clarke c Cooke b Lloyd	39	– not out	2
T. Köhler-Cadmore c Cooke b Hogan	102		
†O. B. Cox c Cooke b Hogan	42		
E. G. Barnard lbw b de Lange	59		
*J. Leach c Donald b Carey	10		
J. W. Hastings c Rudolph b de Lange	51		
J. C. Tongue run out	6		
J. D. Shantry not out	16		
B 5, lb 19, w 1, nb 18	43	Lb 1	1
1/1 (1) 2/1 (2) 3/80 (4) 4/80 (3) 5/196 (6) 6/283 (5) 7/302 (8) 8/349 (7) 9/371 (10) 10/403 (9) (94.1 overs)	403	1/9 (1) 2/11 (2) (2 wkts, 5.3 overs)	28

Carey 22–2–85–3; Hogan 25–5–78–3; Podmore 15–1–56–0; de Lange 20.1–0–94–2; Lloyd 8–1–51–1; Ingram 4–0–15–0. *Second innings*—Hogan 3–0–14–1; Carey 2.3–0–13–1.

Umpires: N. L. Bainton and S. J. O'Shaughnessy.

At Leicester, April 21–24. GLAMORGAN drew with LEICESTERSHIRE.

GLAMORGAN v NOTTINGHAMSHIRE

At Cardiff, May 19–22. Drawn. Glamorgan 7pts, Nottinghamshire 12pts. Toss: Nottinghamshire. County debut: C. A. Pujara.

When Glamorgan followed on, 261 adrift with two days left, nothing looked more certain than another demoralising defeat. But after coach Robert Croft gave the team an ear-bashing, Ingram exchanged one-day mode – he had just clubbed three white-ball centuries – for limpet mode. He survived for seven minutes short of ten hours, and hit only 14 of the 427 deliveries he faced to the boundary. Ingram and Cooke batted throughout the final day to ensure the draw, sharing an unbroken sixth-wicket stand of 226, a record in this fixture. Nottinghamshire had made the early running through centuries from Libby, a product of Cardiff MCCU, and Wessels. Later Read (who injured a hip, and did not keep wicket) and Hutton muscled the total past 400, although van der Gugten persevered to take five for 101. This was despite the early departure of the Indian Test batsman Pujara, whose dismissal by de Lange followed a double failure here on his debut for Derbyshire in 2014. Pujara responded by running out Bragg and catching de Lange, although the fielding highlight was substitute Luke Wood's one-handed grab on the midwicket boundary to remove Donald for 53.

Close of play: first day, Nottinghamshire 335-6 (Read 47, Hutton 5); second day, Glamorgan 187; third day, Glamorgan 212-5 (Ingram 72, Cooke 8).

Nottinghamshire

S. J. Mullaney c Cooke b van der Gugten	14
J. D. Libby c Cooke b van der Gugten	109
C. A. Pujara c Donald b de Lange	2
S. R. Patel lbw b van der Gugten	5
M. J. Lumb c Cooke b Carey	23
M. H. Wessels lbw b van der Gugten	120
*†C. M. W. Read c Bragg b Carey	88
B. A. Hutton c de Lange b Carey	61
S. C. J. Broad b Ingram	7
L. J. Fletcher not out	5
H. F. Gurney b van der Gugten	1
B 1, lb 8, nb 4	13
1/30 (1) 2/47 (3) 3/68 (4) 4/108 (5) 5/231 (2) 6/330 (6) 7/427 (7) 8/438 (9) 9/442 (8) 10/448 (11) — (126 overs)	448
110 overs: 388-6	

De Lange 34–2–114–1; Carey 28–7–100–3; van der Gugten 32–5–101–5; Lloyd 12–1–59–0; Salter 15–1–48–0; Ingram 5–0–17–1.

Glamorgan

First innings		Second innings	
N. J. Selman c †Wessels b Fletcher	7	b Fletcher	3
*J. A. Rudolph c †Wessels b Gurney	25	c †Wessels b Hutton	14
W. D. Bragg run out	5	lbw b Gurney	30
C. A. Ingram c Mullaney b Hutton	9	not out	155
A. H. T. Donald c sub (L. Wood) b Fletcher	53	b Patel	36
D. L. Lloyd c Mullaney b Broad	34	c Mullaney b Fletcher	37
†C. B. Cooke b Broad	1	not out	113
A. G. Salter not out	15		
M. de Lange c Pujara b Fletcher	4		
T. van der Gugten c Broad b Patel	2		
L. J. Carey c Fletcher b Hutton	22		
B 1, lb 3, nb 6	10	B 16, lb 5, w 1, nb 10	32
1/11 (1) 2/20 (3) 3/47 (4) 4/51 (2) 5/123 (6) 6/125 (7) 7/152 (5) 8/158 (9) 9/162 (10) 10/187 (11) — (62.3 overs)	187	1/3 (1) 2/54 (3) 3/54 (2) 4/116 (5) 5/194 (6) — (5 wkts dec, 171 overs)	420

Broad 13–3–40–2; Fletcher 16–3–60–3; Hutton 11.3–1–41–2; Gurney 9–3–26–1; Patel 13–5–16–1. *Second innings*—Broad 34–10–55–0; Fletcher 25–3–73–2; Hutton 30–7–92–1; Gurney 27–6–64–1; Patel 41–15–80–1; Mullaney 6–2–12–0; Libby 3–0–11–0; Pujara 3–0–7–0; Lumb 2–0–5–0.

Umpires: R. J. Bailey and I. D. Blackwell.

GLAMORGAN v DURHAM

At Swansea, May 26–29. Glamorgan won by three wickets. Glamorgan 23pts, Durham 6pts. Toss: Durham. First-class debut: G. H. I. Harding.

There were only three balls remaining when Selman sealed Glamorgan's first win of the season. Coughlin had started the last over with 14 wanted, but Selman struck the first two deliveries for six – he had never managed one in the Championship before this innings, though he had broken his duck a few overs earlier. He then clipped the winning runs to midwicket. Collingwood was left to rue his declaration, which left Glamorgan 266 from 51 overs: he had been contemplating a tougher target until rain delayed the restart after lunch by an hour. Collingwood had celebrated his 41st birthday with a fine 127, his 33rd first-class century, but once he went Hogan wrapped up the rest with three wickets in four balls. In contrast, Glamorgan's last four added 192. After an uncertain start on a truncated second day, another bright half-century from Donald was followed by useful knocks from Cooke and Salter. Durham lost Cook cheaply again before wiping off the small deficit, but Clark – whose 72 was a career-best – put on 102 with Collingwood, who selflessly declared during the rain delay, just short of his second hundred of the game. As Glamorgan lost regular wickets in the chase, it looked as if he would be rewarded with a draw, at least. But Selman's last-gasp heroics ensured a happy start for Hogan in his first match in charge after Rudolph resigned the four-day captaincy.

Close of play: first day, Durham 342; second day, Glamorgan 225-6 (Cooke 63, Salter 15); third day, Durham 158-3 (Clark 63, Collingwood 40).

Durham

S. C. Cook lbw b van der Gugten	5	– c Salter b de Lange	2
K. K. Jennings b de Lange	4	– lbw b Lloyd	35
C. T. Steel c Selman b Hogan	59	– b van der Gugten	10
G. Clark c Selman b Hogan	48	– c Cooke b Hogan	72
*P. D. Collingwood lbw b Salter	127	– not out	92
R. D. Pringle c Cooke b de Lange	4	– c de Lange b Hogan	41
P. Coughlin lbw b van der Gugten	31	– c Hogan b Salter	1
†S. W. Poynter c Cooke b Hogan	38	– c Cooke b Salter	2
W. J. Weighell not out	0	– not out	6
G. H. I. Harding b Hogan	0		
C. Rushworth c Cooke b Hogan	0		
B 8, lb 14, nb 4	26	B 4, lb 11	15
1/13 (2) 2/17 (1) 3/103 (4) 4/163 (3) 5/169 (6) 6/260 (7) 7/342 (5) 8/342 (8) 9/342 (10) 10/342 (11) (94 overs)	342	1/6 (1) 2/35 (3) 3/75 (2) 4/177 (4) 5/258 (6) 6/259 (7) 7/264 (8) (7 wkts dec, 76 overs)	276

De Lange 21–6–57–2; van der Gugten 23–10–66–2; Lloyd 15–2–64–0; Hogan 22–6–49–5; Salter 9–1–56–1; Ingram 4–0–28–0. *Second innings*—de Lange 20–3–83–1; van der Gugten 16–4–54–1; Hogan 20–3–54–2; Salter 13–2–46–2; Lloyd 7–2–24–1.

Glamorgan

N. J. Selman c Steel b Rushworth	5	– not out	116
J. A. Rudolph c Collingwood b Rushworth	31	– c Clark b Harding	24
W. D. Bragg c Rushworth b Weighell	22	– (8) c Poynter b Coughlin	1
C. A. Ingram c Collingwood b Coughlin	18	– (6) c Poynter b Harding	42
A. H. T. Donald c Jennings b Weighell	51	– (4) c Cook b Harding	28
D. L. Lloyd c Collingwood b Coughlin	16	– (5) b Harding	3
†C. B. Cooke c and b Coughlin	69	– c Clark b Coughlin	31
A. G. Salter c Jennings b Weighell	75	– (3) lbw b Pringle	15
M. de Lange b Rushworth	30	– not out	3
T. van der Gugten c Jennings b Coughlin	0		
*M. G. Hogan not out	29		
Lb 4, w 1, nb 2	7	Lb 2, w 1	3
1/28 (1) 2/39 (2) 3/76 (4) 4/92 (3) 5/119 (6) 6/161 (5) 7/233 (7) 8/278 (9) 9/279 (10) 10/353 (8) (92 overs)	353	1/37 (2) 2/61 (3) 3/104 (4) 4/108 (5) 5/181 (6) 6/228 (7) 7/241 (8) (7 wkts, 50.3 overs)	266

Rushworth 23–7–75–3; Weighell 20–2–86–3; Coughlin 23–4–87–4; Collingwood 6–0–17–0; Harding 17–0–75–0; Pringle 3–0–9–0. *Second innings*—Rushworth 6–2–15–0; Weighell 5–1–12–0; Harding 19–2–111–4; Coughlin 9.3–1–51–2; Pringle 11–0–75–1.

Umpires: P. K. Baldwin and R. J. Evans.

At Worcester, June 9–11. GLAMORGAN beat WORCESTERSHIRE by nine wickets.

At Chester-le-Street, June 19–22. GLAMORGAN lost to DURHAM by nine wickets.

GLAMORGAN v DERBYSHIRE

At Cardiff, June 26–29 (day/night). Derbyshire won by 39 runs. Derbyshire 21pts, Glamorgan 4pts. Toss: Derbyshire. First-class debut: H. Qadri.

Derbyshire's first Championship victory in 27 matches since July 2015 came with the pink ball – and via an unusual route. Hamidullah Qadri, at 16 the youngest to appear for Derbyshire in the competition, was born in Afghanistan, came to England at 11, and honed his off-breaks by watching YouTube footage of Saeed Ajmal and Saqlain Mushtaq. The first county cricketer born in the 21st century, Qadri vindicated his inclusion with 15–8–16–1 in the first innings, then twirled his side to victory with five for 60 in the second. "There was no fear whatsoever," he said. "I only got nervous as we got closer to winning." Glamorgan had needed just 212 but, after Rudolph fell during six scoreless overs on the third evening, Qadri worked through the rest, helped by Mendis. Before all this, Glamorgan had done well to restrict Derbyshire to 157 for seven, but as the floodlights kicked in on the first evening Smit and Milnes knuckled down, before the hosts fell 51 behind on first innings, despite a gritty 50 in 221 minutes from Selman. Derbyshire opened with two nightwatchmen, Taylor and Palladino, who both fell early on the third morning to de Lange (for Glamorgan van der Gugten opened both innings as nightwatchman). And though Reece made 55, and Mendis slapped 27 from 15 deliveries at the end, the target looked inviting.

YOUNGEST TO TAKE A MAIDEN CHAMPIONSHIP FIVE-FOR

Yrs	*Days*			
16	**206**	**H. Qadri (5-60)**	**Derbyshire v Glamorgan at Cardiff**	**2017**
16	287	C. L. Townsend (6-56)	Gloucestershire v Surrey at Clifton	1893
17	2	J. A. R. Harris (7-66)	Glamorgan v Gloucestershire at Bristol	2007
17	41	S. M. Curran (5-101)	Surrey v Kent at The Oval	2015
17	57	R. J. W. Topley (5-46)	Essex v Kent at Chelmsford	2011
17	90	P. F. Judge (5-77)	Middlesex v Surrey at The Oval	1933
17	116	W. N. Tidy (5-82)	Warwickshire v Somerset at Taunton	1970
17	128	W. E. Jones (5-59)	Glamorgan v Essex at Colchester	1929
17	175	B. A. Langford (8-96)	Somerset v Kent at Bath	1953
17	195	P. I. Bedford (5-53)	Middlesex v Surrey at Lord's	1947

Close of play: first day, Glamorgan 5-0 (van der Gugten 5, Rudolph 0); second day, Derbyshire 2-0 (Taylor 1, Palladino 0); third day, Glamorgan 0-1 (van der Gugten 0).

Derbyshire

L. M. Reece lbw b van der Gugten	1	– (3) c sub (T. N. Cullen) b Salter	55
*B. A. Godleman c Cooke b de Lange	34	– (4) c Salter b de Lange	27
W. L. Madsen c Cooke b van der Gugten	70	– (5) c Donald b Salter	13
A. L. Hughes lbw b Wagg	32	– (6) c Salter b Wagg	17
G. C. Wilson c Cooke b de Lange	1	– (7) lbw b Wagg	4
†D. Smit c Salter b de Lange	41	– (8) lbw b Salter	3
B. M. A. J. Mendis c Selman b Wagg	2	– (10) c Rudolph b van der Gugten	27
T. A. I. Taylor c Cooke b van der Gugten	4	– (1) b de Lange	3
T. P. Milnes c Cooke b Hogan	53	– c Selman b van der Gugten	7
A. P. Palladino c Wagg b Hogan	23	– (2) c Morgan b de Lange	2
H. Qadri not out	11	– not out	0
Lb 6, nb 10	16	Lb 2	2
1/1 (1) 2/99 (3) 3/127 (2) 4/139 (5) 5/141 (4) 6/143 (7) 7/157 (8) 8/223 (6) 9/261 (9) 10/288 (10) (92 overs)	288	1/4 (1) 2/7 (2) 3/39 (4) 4/63 (5) 5/108 (6) 6/112 (7) 7/117 (8) 8/126 (3) 9/155 (9) 10/160 (10) (44.2 overs)	160

De Lange 26–6–82–3; van der Gugten 25–6–88–3; Hogan 22–6–54–2; Wagg 18–2–53–2; Salter 1–0–5–0. *Second innings*—Hogan 9–4–13–0; van der Gugten 6.2–2–18–2; de Lange 11–0–53–3; Salter 14–2–60–3; Wagg 4–1–14–2.

Glamorgan

T. van der Gugten lbw b Palladino	19	– c Reece b Qadri	5
J. A. Rudolph c Madsen b Palladino	32	– lbw b Mendis	0
N. J. Selman lbw b Mendis	50	– st Smit b Madsen	43
A. O. Morgan lbw b Palladino	0	– c Wilson b Mendis	7
C. A. Ingram c Wilson b Mendis	18	– c Godleman b Qadri	9
A. H. T. Donald b Reece	38	– c Hughes b Madsen	31
A. G. Salter c Wilson b Qadri	9	– (8) lbw b Qadri	9
†C. B. Cooke c Qadri b Mendis	14	– (7) not out	39
G. G. Wagg lbw b Palladino	20	– c Smit b Qadri	4
M. de Lange b Taylor	22	– run out	20
*M. G. Hogan not out	0	– c Mendis b Qadri	2
B 8, lb 1, nb 6	15	Lb 3	3
1/49 (1) 2/58 (2) 3/68 (4) 4/87 (5) 5/151 (6) 6/170 (3) 7/188 (8) 8/198 (7) 9/237 (10) 10/237 (9) (93.4 overs)	237	1/0 (2) 2/9 (1) 3/31 (4) 4/42 (5) 5/92 (6) 6/99 (3) 7/119 (8) 8/135 (9) 9/160 (10) 10/172 (11) (69.3 overs)	172

Taylor 15–8–28–1; Milnes 10–0–48–0; Reece 13–6–32–1; Palladino 16.4–5–36–4; Qadri 15–8–16–1; Mendis 24–2–68–3. *Second innings*—Palladino 8–5–8–0; Qadri 26.3–8–60–5; Mendis 26–2–80–2; Reece 4–1–9–0; Madsen 5–2–12–2.

Umpires: P. R. Pollard and A. G. Wharf.

At Cheltenham, July 3–4. GLAMORGAN lost to GLOUCESTERSHIRE by ten wickets. *Twenty-five wickets fall on the first day.*

GLAMORGAN v SUSSEX

At Colwyn Bay, August 28–30. Sussex won by one wicket. Sussex 21pts, Glamorgan 5pts. Toss: uncontested. Championship debut: J. R. Murphy.

Some members were unhappy when Glamorgan rested several senior players ahead of Twenty20 finals day. But the mood changed during an absorbing game in which their young team came within a wicket of upsetting a full-strength Sussex, making their first visit to Colwyn Bay since 2000, when Steve James hit a Glamorgan-record 309 not out in a total of 718 for three. The scoring was more restrained this time on a pitch that helped the seamers: Glamorgan reached 294 thanks to Meschede, who shared a seventh-wicket stand of 108 with wicketkeeper Tom Cullen, fresh from Cardiff MCCU. Sussex lost three wickets before the first-day close, but Brown organised a recovery that left them only 26 adrift. Glamorgan's batsmen then struggled against Robinson (playing his first senior match of the season after injury) and Jordan. Meschede top-scored again, but Sussex needed only 209. At 155 for four, they seemed to be strolling; 20 balls later, they were reeling at 160 for eight. But Robinson backed up his seven wickets with an unbeaten 41 from 37 balls, dominating a last-wicket stand of 32 with Briggs to carry his side to victory. He finished the match by crashing Ruaidhri Smith over long-on for six.

Close of play: first day, Sussex 79-3 (Robson 44, Nash 4); second day, Glamorgan 126-6 (Meschede 19, Cullen 11).

Glamorgan

N. J. Selman b Jordan	58	– b Robinson	15
A. O. Morgan lbw b Archer	1	– c Jordan b Robinson	17
J. R. Murphy c Nash b Archer	0	– c Brown b Jordan	27
A. H. T. Donald c Brown b Robinson	5	– c Robson b Jordan	5
K. S. Carlson lbw b Archer	47	– c Brown b Robinson	5
A. G. Salter c Nash b Robinson	13	– c Brown b Archer	13
C. A. J. Meschede b Robinson	87	– c and b Jordan	41
†T. N. Cullen lbw b Jordan	42	– c Wright b Jordan	22
R. A. J. Smith b Jordan	0	– c Brown b Jordan	15
L. J. Carey c Wells b Robinson	13	– c Briggs b Archer	2
*M. G. Hogan not out	4	– not out	1
B 4, lb 12, nb 8	24	Lb 14, w 1, nb 4	19
1/15 (2) 2/15 (3) 3/24 (4) 4/96 (5) 5/132 (6) 6/148 (1) 7/256 (8) 8/266 (9) 9/283 (10) 10/294 (7) (75.3 overs)	294	1/26 (1) 2/69 (2) 3/71 (3) 4/76 (4) 5/90 (5) 6/104 (6) 7/156 (8) 8/174 (9) 9/181 (10) 10/182 (7) (58.3 overs)	182

Archer 16–4–67–3; Wiese 13–2–49–0; Robinson 18.3–5–46–4; Jordan 20–2–82–3; van Zyl 2–1–5–0; Briggs 6–1–29–0. *Second innings*—Archer 20–1–67–2; Robinson 19–3–48–3; Jordan 16.3–4–46–5; Wiese 3–1–7–0.

Sussex

A. J. Robson b Smith	44	– (2) b Hogan	7
L. W. P. Wells b Carey	21	– (1) c Cullen b Carey	0
S. van Zyl c Cullen b Meschede	7	– lbw b Salter	38
D. R. Briggs lbw b Smith	2	– (11) not out	3
C. D. Nash c Donald b Meschede	42	– (4) c Selman b Smith	68
L. J. Wright b Smith	5	– (5) st Cullen b Salter	0
*†B. C. Brown b Meschede	77	– (6) c sub (Z. M. Ringrose) b Carey	37
C. J. Jordan b Carey	10	– (7) c Cullen b Smith	4
D. Wiese c Cullen b Hogan	12	– (8) c sub (Z. M. Ringrose) b Carey	1
O. E. Robinson c Carey b Meschede	15	– (9) not out	41
J. C. Archer not out	27	– (10) lbw b Hogan	6
Lb 3, w 1, nb 2	6	Lb 6	6
1/50 (2) 2/57 (3) 3/74 (4) 4/81 (1) 5/109 (6) 6/139 (5) 7/158 (8) 8/189 (9) 9/225 (10) 10/268 (7) (59.5 overs)	268	1/0 (1) 2/10 (2) 3/100 (3) 4/100 (5) 5/155 (6) 6/157 (4) 7/160 (8) 8/160 (7) 9/179 (10) (9 wkts, 54.4 overs)	211

Carey 14–1–68–2; Hogan 12–1–72–1; Meschede 17.5–3–61–4; Smith 16–0–64–3. *Second innings*—Carey 14–5–40–3; Hogan 14–2–43–2; Meschede 8–1–35–0; Smith 10.4–2–59–2; Salter 8–1–28–2.

Umpires: G. D. Lloyd and R. T. Robinson.

At Derby, September 5–8. GLAMORGAN drew with DERBYSHIRE.

GLAMORGAN v NORTHAMPTONSHIRE

At Cardiff, September 12–15. Northamptonshire won by seven wickets. Northamptonshire 22pts, Glamorgan 4pts. Toss: Glamorgan.

Northamptonshire stayed in the promotion mix after completing the double over Glamorgan. The result was rarely in doubt once Gleeson, who finished with a five-for, and Azharullah reduced them to 102 for six on the first day. Salter dug in, but a stand of 97 ended when Meschede waltzed down the track to Kerrigan, and missed. A rapid century from Levi, who had once played club cricket in Abergavenny, took Northamptonshire in front on the second day. Hogan and de Lange chipped away at the middle order, but the eventual lead was 103. Glamorgan lost three wickets clearing the arrears, before solid contributions throughout – including 39 from de Lange, who clubbed three sixes – meant the target was a teasing 218. Loose bowling from the home seamers on the final morning allowed Newton to put on 90 with Kerrigan, an adhesive nightwatchman. Although a thunderstorm unloaded when Northamptonshire had victory in sight, play resumed after 80 minutes, and the result was quickly confirmed.

Close of play: first day, Northamptonshire 59-2 (Newton 31, Levi 2); second day, Glamorgan 63-1 (Rudolph 26, Murphy 15); third day, Northamptonshire 42-1 (Newton 15, Kerrigan 0).

Glamorgan

N. J. Selman c Wakely b Azharullah	22	– b Gleeson	13
J. A. Rudolph b Gleeson	0	– c Cobb b Kleinveldt	28
J. R. Murphy lbw b Azharullah	12	– lbw b Kleinveldt	15
C. A. Ingram c Murphy b Kleinveldt	25	– b Azharullah	25
K. S. Carlson lbw b Gleeson	10	– b Azharullah	44
†C. B. Cooke c Murphy b Gleeson	12	– c Murphy b Kerrigan	69
A. G. Salter c Kleinveldt b Gleeson	59	– b Keogh	19
C. A. J. Meschede st Murphy b Kerrigan	49	– lbw b Gleeson	34
M. de Lange b Kerrigan	4	– b Gleeson	39
L. J. Carey b Gleeson	0	– b Kleinveldt	1
*M. G. Hogan not out	0	– not out	9
B 8, lb 6	14	B 5, lb 15, nb 4	24
1/6 (2) 2/35 (1) 3/36 (3) 4/75 (4) 5/75 (5) 6/102 (6) 7/199 (8) 8/205 (9) 9/206 (10) 10/207 (7) (64.1 overs)	207	1/21 (1) 2/63 (3) 3/68 (2) 4/136 (5) 5/137 (4) 6/208 (7) 7/244 (6) 8/301 (9) 9/302 (10) 10/320 (8) (94.1 overs)	320

Kleinveldt 16.2–2–54–1; Gleeson 19.1–6–60–5; Azharullah 11.4–4–44–2; Keogh 3–1–6–0; Kerrigan 14–4–29–2. *Second innings*—Kleinveldt 20–5–77–3; Gleeson 24.1–5–71–3; Kerrigan 21–5–67–1; Keogh 12–2–34–1; Azharullah 17–3–51–2.

Northamptonshire

B. M. Duckett c Murphy b Carey	11	– c Cooke b Hogan	23
R. I. Newton lbw b Hogan	67	– b Meschede	53
†D. Murphy c Carlson b Hogan	9		
R. E. Levi c Cooke b Carey	101	– (5) not out	39
R. I. Keogh lbw b de Lange	45		
J. J. Cobb c Meschede b Hogan	9		
*A. G. Wakely b Hogan	0	– (4) not out	39
R. K. Kleinveldt c Carlson b de Lange	26		
S. C. Kerrigan c Cooke b de Lange	5	– (3) b Hogan	62
R. J. Gleeson b Meschede	9		
Azharullah not out	10		
B 5, lb 9, nb 4	18	W 1, nb 4	5
1/24 (1) 2/49 (3) 3/153 (2) 4/241 (4) 5/250 (5) 6/251 (7) 7/260 (6) 8/275 (9) 9/292 (8) 10/310 (10) (78.1 overs)	310	1/34 (1) 2/124 (2) 3/156 (3) (3 wkts, 58.4 overs)	221

Carey 18–3–76–2; de Lange 22–2–85–3; Hogan 22–4–58–4; Meschede 11.1–1–46–1; Salter 5–0–31–0. *Second innings*—Carey 7–0–34–0; de Lange 16.4–3–67–0; Hogan 14–1–36–2; Salter 5–0–28–0; Meschede 10–1–26–1; Ingram 6–0–30–0.

Umpires: S. C. Gale and D. J. Millns.

GLAMORGAN v GLOUCESTERSHIRE

At Cardiff, September 19–22. Drawn. Glamorgan 11pts, Gloucestershire 11pts. Toss: uncontested. County debut: C. R. Brown.

A combination of a docile pitch and Gloucestershire's reluctance to manufacture a result led to a tame end to the season in Wales, and Sophia Gardens was empty when bad light finally stopped play shortly after tea on the last day. The highlight for Glamorgan was a patient 191 from 19-year-old Carlson, who batted for 443 minutes and shared a sixth-wicket stand of 182 with Salter, whose 84 was also a career-best. Ruaidhri Smith then helped Carlson add 97, and the eventual total was 442. Gloucestershire came close, thanks chiefly to a second-wicket partnership of 240 – their record against Glamorgan – between Howell and James Bracey, the Bristol-born Loughborough MCCU wicketkeeper, who motored past his previous-best of 63. A declaration soon after they were separated might have kept the game alive, but Mustard decided that a hamstring injury to Norwell, his leading wicket-taker, meant he lacked the firepower to bowl Glamorgan out again; instead he batted into the final session of the third day. On the somnolent fourth, Selman – who had fallen second ball on the first morning – took the chance to complete his fourth hundred of the season, Carlson carved 53 from 44 balls, and Salter improved his highest score for the second time in the match.

Close of play: first day, Glamorgan 342-7 (Carlson 137, Smith 1); second day, Gloucestershire 161-1 (Howell 96, Bracey 45); third day, Glamorgan 63-1 (Selman 22, Salter 28).

Glamorgan

First innings		Second innings	
N. J. Selman lbw b Payne	0	– not out	142
C. R. Brown lbw b Noema-Barnett	35	– b Payne	13
C. A. Ingram b Norwell	18		
K. S. Carlson c sub (M. A. H. Hammond) b J. M. R. Taylor	191	– lbw b Dent	53
A. H. T. Donald c Hankins b Payne	1		
†C. B. Cooke b Payne	51	– (5) not out	46
A. G. Salter c Bracey b Shaw	84	– (3) c Hankins b J. M. R. Taylor	88
C. A. J. Meschede c Dent b Noema-Barnett	0		
R. A. J. Smith c Hankins b J. M. R. Taylor	38		
M. de Lange lbw b J. M. R. Taylor	0		
*M. G. Hogan not out	2		
B 5, lb 16, w 1	22	B 4, lb 5, nb 2	11
1/0 (1) 2/33 (3) 3/62 (2) 4/63 (5) 5/151 (6) 6/333 (7) 7/336 (8) 8/433 (9) 9/433 (10) 10/442 (4) (117.2 overs) 110 overs: 392-7	442	1/15 (2) 2/200 (3) 3/289 (4) (3 wkts, 80 overs)	353

Payne 22–7–65–3; Norwell 10–4–32–1; Noema-Barnett 31–8–80–2; M. D. Taylor 17–1–89–0; Shaw 22–4–84–1; J. M. R. Taylor 7.2–1–50–3; Howell 8–2–21–0. *Second innings*—Payne 12–1–40–1; M. D. Taylor 13–4–45–0; Shaw 12–1–50–0; Noema-Barnett 8–3–24–0; J. M. R. Taylor 12–1–53–1; Dent 10–0–61–1; Howell 4–0–27–0; Mustard 9–1–44–0.

Gloucestershire

B. A. C. Howell lbw b Hogan	163
C. D. J. Dent c Cooke b Smith	13
†J. R. Bracey c sub (L. J. Carey) b Meschede	156
G. T. Hankins b Hogan	0
*P. Mustard c Selman b de Lange	33
J. M. R. Taylor c Ingram b Meschede	7
K. Noema-Barnett b de Lange	6
D. A. Payne not out	5
J. Shaw c Carlson b Meschede	1
M. D. Taylor not out	3
B 1, lb 3, nb 8	12
1/53 (2) 2/293 (1) 3/293 (4) 4/352 (5) 5/375 (6) 6/384 (7) 7/390 (3) 8/396 (9) (8 wkts dec, 110 overs)	399

L. C. Norwell did not bat.

De Lange 24–2–116–2; Hogan 26–12–46–2; Smith 16–1–80–1; Meschede 24–3–81–3; Salter 16–2–58–0; Brown 4–0–14–0.

Umpires: N. L. Bainton and P. R. Pollard.

At Canterbury, September 25–27. GLAMORGAN beat KENT by five wickets. *Michael Hogan has match figures of ten for 87.*

GLOUCESTERSHIRE

Conserving home produce

ANDY STOCKHAUSEN

At the end of a disappointing season on and off the field, Gloucestershire turned their efforts to the perennial issue of player retention. Financial restraints have obliged a county destined to a 13th successive season in the Championship's second division – Leicestershire are the only team to have been there longer – to nurture talented young cricketers in the hope of future dividends.

Gloucestershire have pursued the policy with some success for many years – only for players to jump ship for wealthier rivals. Will Gidman, James Fuller and Gemaal Hussain are just three recently tempted away by Division One cricket, and the exodus may not stop there.

In 2017, seamer Liam Norwell took 59 Championship wickets – more than twice as many as any of his colleagues – at 17 apiece, a striking performance bound to stir interest from further afield. And, with his contract expiring in 2018, the task of persuading him to stay has become a priority. Opening batsman Chris Dent and all-rounder Jack Taylor, a match-winner on his day, could also find themselves in demand. (Taylor, though, will play solely as a batsman in 2018 after his action was ruled unlawful for a third time, denying Gloucestershire his off-spin for the whole season.) Keen to stop others benefiting from their development programme, they ordered funds to be put aside, rightly prioritising a new deal for Norwell.

Recruitment was not helped by modest profits from the two one-day internationals staged at Nevil Road – against Ireland in May, and West Indies in September. So Gloucestershire preferred to boost their coaching and development resources rather than splash out on overseas players. The priority for 2018 was for someone to work with the batsmen – and strengthen the current coaching set-up of Richard Dawson and his assistant Ian Harvey.

Soon after the season ended, Gloucestershire swooped for the 22-year-old Ryan Higgins. He had come to Gloucestershire's attention at the Cheltenham Festival in July, when an astonishing, never-say-die 68 from 28 balls salvaged a tie for Middlesex in a Twenty20 game that had seemed beyond them. A versatile all-rounder who bowls off-spin and seam, Higgins was born in Zimbabwe but is England-qualified. At Middlesex, his CV was largely limited to white-ball cricket, though his move to Bristol on a three-year deal should afford him greater opportunities.

Gloucestershire's overseas support continues to come from Australia: fast bowler Andrew Tye is expected to play alongside Michael Klinger in the T20 Blast, but Cameron Bancroft, who found his feet only in his last few games (and went on to make his Test debut in the winter Ashes), was replaced by the South Australian seamer Dan Worrall.

Gareth Copley, Getty Images

Liam Norwell

With the Championship side still feeling the loss of stalwarts Hamish Marshall and Klinger the task of scoring enough runs to win a four-day game was always likely to be a challenge. And so it proved: Gloucestershire managed 29 batting points, while the promoted counties, Worcestershire and Nottinghamshire, claimed 45 and 44. A modest tally of eight hundreds was spread around six players, with Dent and Taylor hitting two each. Dent top-scored with 894 at 42; Bancroft was next, with 685, though his season had been threadbare until he made an undefeated double against Kent in September. Phil Mustard, the red-ball captain, and Taylor – the two Championship ever-presents – were the others to pass 500.

It wasn't all doom and gloom in the batting: Academy products James Bracey and George Hankins provided a silver lining with an unbroken third-wicket stand of 170 against Derbyshire. While Hankins improved gradually over the summer, Bracey – a Bristol-born left-hander – made an immediate impact. In six September innings, he hit 370 runs at 74.

Inevitably, though, a lack of runs hampered the bowlers, and the hard-working Norwell gained only patchy support from his fellow seamers. Craig Miles claimed 27 Championship wickets, down from 52 in 2016, and David Payne 25, down from 43. Miles grabbed one five-for, and the young Yorkshire loanee Josh Shaw another; Norwell enjoyed five. Kieran Noema-Barnett chipped in with 23 victims, but of spin there was barely a sign: Taylor's 13 cost 47 each.

There was, all the same, a resilience to Gloucestershire, especially at home, where they lost only once – a contrived finish against Derbyshire at Bristol. The Cheltenham Festival produced a two-day win over Glamorgan (not so good for the coffers) and a draw, as well as a win, a tie and a no-result in three 20-over matches.

Indeed, after ten games of the Blast they seemed likely to reach the quarter-finals: they were second, two points behind leaders Glamorgan with a game in hand. Then the wheels came off, four consecutive defeats consigning them to bottom place in the ultra-competitive South Group. Scores of 138, 121 for eight, 100 and 130 for nine showed where the failing lay. Unusually, Klinger was at fault, totalling 20 in those last four fixtures. It didn't help that Tye injured his shoulder in the IPL and missed the whole tournament. And at no stage did the county suggest a repeat of their 2015 Royal London Cup triumph was imminent: they finished a tepid seventh, winning three and losing four.

Championship attendance: 21,224.

GLOUCESTERSHIRE RESULTS

All first-class matches – Played 15: Won 3, Lost 4, Drawn 8.
County Championship matches – Played 14: Won 3, Lost 4, Drawn 7.

Specsavers County Championship, 6th in Division 2;
NatWest T20 Blast, 9th in South Group; Royal London One-Day Cup, 7th in South Group.

COUNTY CHAMPIONSHIP AVERAGES, BATTING AND FIELDING

Cap		*Birthplace*	*M*	*I*	*NO*	*R*	*HS*	*100*	*Avge*	*Ct/St*
2016	†J. R. Bracey	*Bristol*‡	4	6	1	370	156	1	74.00	6
2010	†C. D. J. Dent	*Bristol*‡	13	24	3	894	135*	2	42.57	12
2016	C. T. Bancroft¶	*Attadale, Australia*	11	21	4	685	206*	1	40.29	14
2010	J. M. R. Taylor	*Banbury*	14	20	3	665	143	2	39.11	10
2013	G. H. Roderick††	*Durban, SA*	8	12	1	400	96	0	36.36	23/1
2011	D. A. Payne	*Poole, Dorset*	10	11	5	203	54*	0	33.83	1
2016	†P. Mustard	*Sunderland*	14	20	0	573	72	0	28.65	21
2014	W. A. Tavaré	*Bristol*‡	10	17	1	422	101	1	26.37	6
2016	G. T. Hankins	*Bath*	11	17	1	387	79*	0	24.18	20
2015	†K. Noema-Barnett††	*Dunedin, NZ*	11	14	1	291	59	0	22.38	6
2016	G. L. van Buuren††	*Pretoria, SA*	7	12	1	233	88*	0	21.18	3
2013	M. D. Taylor	*Banbury*	5	7	3	55	36	0	13.75	0
2017	C. J. Liddle	*Middlesbrough*	5	7	3	54	21	0	13.50	1
2011	L. C. Norwell	*Bournemouth*	11	13	5	99	24	0	12.37	4
2011	C. N. Miles	*Swindon*	10	13	1	137	47	0	11.41	2
2016	J. Shaw	*Wakefield*	4	5	0	23	13	0	4.60	0

Also batted: I. A. Cockbain (*Liverpool*) (cap 2011) (1 match) 27; G. S. Drissell (*Bristol*‡) (cap 2017) (1 match) 0; B. A. C. Howell (*Bordeaux, France*) (cap 2012) (2 matches) 163, 36, 5; T. M. J. Smith (*Eastbourne*) (cap 2013) (2 matches) 8, 9, 14*.

‡ *Born in Gloucestershire.* ¶ *Official overseas player.* †† *Other non-England-qualified.*

BOWLING

	Style	*O*	*M*	*R*	*W*	*BB*	*5I*	*Avge*
L. C. Norwell	RFM	321	66	1,026	59	8-43	5	17.38
K. Noema-Barnett	RM	254.4	59	737	23	4-31	0	32.04
D. A. Payne	LFM	259.1	49	816	25	3-37	0	32.64
C. N. Miles	RFM	245	35	974	27	5-99	1	36.07
J. Shaw	RFM	101.5	15	443	11	5-118	1	40.27
J. M. R. Taylor	OB	146.2	15	619	13	3-50	0	47.61
M. D. Taylor	LM	127	19	492	10	3-80	0	49.20

Also bowled: C. T. Bancroft (RM) 7–0–67–1; C. D. J. Dent (SLA) 16.4–0–130–1; G. S. Drissell (OB) 12–0–58–0; G. T. Hankins (OB) 2.1–0–13–0; B. A. C. Howell (RM) 21–2–82–1; C. J. Liddle (LFM) 119.1–23–438–8; P. Mustard (LB) 20–2–141–0; T. M. J. Smith (SLA) 70.4–7–263–9; W. A. Tavaré (RM) 8–1–52–0; G. L. van Buuren (SLA) 114.3–23–342–5.

LEADING ROYAL LONDON CUP AVERAGES (100 runs/4 wickets)

Batting	*Runs*	*HS*	*Avge*	*SR*	*Ct/St*
I. A. Cockbain	295	108*	59.00	88.85	1
M. Klinger	369	134	52.71	78.01	7
J. M. R. Taylor	302	68	43.14	131.30	2
B. A. C. Howell	163	86*	40.75	98.78	2
G. T. Hankins	100	67	33.33	65.35	2
P. Mustard	180	90	25.71	67.92	9/1
C. D. J. Dent	113	43	18.83	72.90	4

Bowling	*W*	*BB*	*Avge*	*ER*
C. J. Liddle	18	5-36	15.11	5.33
B. A. C. Howell	13	3-40	27.07	5.30
T. M. J. Smith	5	3-33	41.40	5.04
L. C. Norwell	5	5-36	45.80	4.97
M. D. Taylor	4	3-48	81.50	6.03

LEADING NATWEST T20 BLAST AVERAGES (100 runs/15 overs)

Batting	Runs	HS	Avge	SR	Ct
K. Noema-Barnett	110	33	15.71	**144.73**	4
M. Klinger	281	101*	28.10	**137.07**	8
C. T. Bancroft	149	51	29.80	**134.23**	1
I. A. Cockbain	252	47*	25.20	**127.27**	3
J. M. R. Taylor	140	31	17.50	**116.66**	7
B. A. C. Howell	235	34	23.50	**115.19**	8
P. Mustard	230	57	20.90	**109.00**	8/1

Bowling	W	BB	Avge	ER
B. A. C. Howell	16	4-29	14.75	**5.75**
D. A. Payne	17	3-13	17.52	**7.51**
T. M. J. Smith	10	3-28	25.90	**7.54**
N. L. T. C. Perera	10	3-31	13.80	**7.73**
C. J. Liddle	6	2-27	25.66	**9.33**
M. D. Taylor	6	2-29	43.00	**9.55**

FIRST-CLASS COUNTY RECORDS

Highest score for	341	C. M. Spearman v Middlesex at Gloucester	2004
Highest score against	319	C. J. L. Rogers (Northants) at Northamptonshire	2006
Leading run-scorer	33,664	W. R. Hammond (avge 57.05)	1920–51
Best bowling for	10-40	E. G. Dennett v Essex at Bristol	1906
Best bowling against	10-66	A. A. Mailey (Australians) at Cheltenham	1921
	10-66	K. Smales (Nottinghamshire) at Stroud	1956
Leading wicket-taker	3,170	C. W. L. Parker (avge 19.43)	1903–35
Highest total for	695-9 dec	v Middlesex at Gloucester	2004
Highest total against	774-7 dec	by Australians at Bristol	1948
Lowest total for	17	v Australians at Cheltenham	1896
Lowest total against	12	by Northamptonshire at Gloucester	1907

LIST A COUNTY RECORDS

Highest score for	177	A. J. Wright v Scotland at Bristol	1997
Highest score against	189*	J. G. E. Benning (Surrey) at Bristol	2006
Leading run-scorer	7,825	M. W. Alleyne (avge 26.89)	1986–2005
Best bowling for	7-29	D. A. Payne v Essex at Chelmsford	2010
Best bowling against	6-16	Shoaib Akhtar (Worcestershire) at Worcester	2005
Leading wicket-taker	393	M. W. Alleyne (avge 29.88)	1986–2005
Highest total for	401-7	v Buckinghamshire at Wing	2003
Highest total against	496-4	by Surrey at The Oval	2007
Lowest total for	49	v Middlesex at Bristol	1978
Lowest total against	48	by Middlesex at Lydney	1973

TWENTY20 COUNTY RECORDS

Highest score for	126*	M. Klinger v Essex at Bristol	2015
Highest score against	116*	C. L. White (Somerset) at Taunton	2006
Leading run-scorer	2,633	H. J. H. Marshall (avge 27.71)	2006–2016
Best bowling for	5-24	D. A. Payne v Middlesex at Richmond	2015
Best bowling against	5-16	R. E. Watkins (Glamorgan) at Cardiff	2009
Leading wicket-taker	**82**	**B. A. C. Howell (avge 18.89)**	**2012–17**
Highest total for	254-3	v Middlesex at Uxbridge	2011
Highest total against	250-3	by Somerset at Taunton	2006
Lowest total for	68	v Hampshire at Bristol	2010
Lowest total against	97	by Surrey at The Oval	2010

ADDRESS

County Ground, Nevil Road, Bristol BS7 9EJ; 0117 910 8000; reception@glosccc.co.uk; www.gloscricket.co.uk.

OFFICIALS

Captain (first-class) G. H. Roderick
(limited-overs) M. Klinger
Head coach R. K. J. Dawson
Head of talent pathway T. H. C. Hancock
President M. J. Journeaux

Chairman R. M. Cooke
Chief executive W. G. Brown
Head groundsman S. P. Williams
Scorer A. J. Bull

GLOUCESTERSHIRE v DURHAM MCCU

At Bristol, March 28–30. Drawn. Toss: Durham MCCU. First-class debuts: O. C. Currill; J. Cooke, W. A. R. Fraine, B. W. M. Graves, M. F. Jahanfar, J. A. McCollum, A. H. McGrath, J. D. Marshall, X. G. Owen, A. R. Singh.

Tavaré made the most of an inexperienced attack to carve out his first hundred since 2014. Despite frequent interruptions – in all, rain swallowed more than a day's play – he hit a diligent 110, putting on 128 with the more expansive Dent, whose 84 came from 78 balls, and 92 with Hankins; Tavaré and Hankins both retired out. The most penetrative of the student bowlers was left-arm seamer Alex McGrath, who kept the Gloucestershire batsmen honest with his line and length, and claimed four wickets. In reply to 405 for seven, Durham lost their openers to Payne, before Ed Pollock – one of only two in the side with first-class experience – and Jason Marshall added 88. More resistance came from James McCollum, but van Buuren's nagging slow left-arm brought the innings to a hasty conclusion. He grabbed four for 18, all lbw, as the last four wickets vanished for seven.

Close of play: first day, Gloucestershire 292-3 (Tavaré 110, Hankins 48); second day, Durham MCCU 78-2 (Pollock 35, Marshall 30).

Gloucestershire

W. A. Tavaré retired out	110
C. D. J. Dent c Jahanfar b McGrath	84
*G. H. Roderick b McGrath	3
G. L. van Buuren c Cooke b McGrath	35
G. T. Hankins retired out	59
†P. Mustard c Jahanfar b McGrath	29
J. M. R. Taylor not out	32
D. A. Payne b Singh	35
B 7, lb 9, w 2	18
1/128 (2) 2/134 (3) 3/200 (4) 4/292 (1) 5/324 (5) 6/333 (6) 7/405 (8) (7 wkts dec, 101.4 overs)	405

L. C. Norwell, C. J. Liddle and O. C. Currill did not bat.

McGrath 29–4–108–4; Owen 27–6–81–0; Cooke 23–3–107–0; Singh 18.4–2–79–1; McCollum 3–1–8–0; Graves 1–0–6–0.

Durham MCCU

W. A. R. Fraine lbw b Payne	6
J. Clark c Mustard b Payne	0
E. J. Pollock c Tavaré b Liddle	52
J. D. Marshall c Dent b Payne	38
J. A. McCollum b Liddle	64
*J. Cooke c Roderick b Taylor	21
B. W. M. Graves lbw b van Buuren	0
A. H. McGrath lbw b van Buuren	12
A. R. Singh lbw b van Buuren	0
†M. F. Jahanfar lbw b van Buuren	2
X. G. Owen not out	1
B 5, lb 16, w 2, nb 19	42
1/5 (2) 2/14 (1) 3/102 (4) 4/127 (3) 5/177 (6) 6/181 (7) 7/231 (8) 8/231 (5) 9/231 (9) 10/238 (10) (64.4 overs)	238

Payne 13–1–29–3; Norwell 11–4–43–0; Currill 15–2–83–0; Liddle 12–3–30–2; Taylor 6–0–14–1; van Buuren 7.4–2–18–4.

Umpires: M. Burns and T. Lungley.

At Canterbury, April 7–9. GLOUCESTERSHIRE lost to KENT by 334 runs. *Gloucestershire collapse for 61.*

GLOUCESTERSHIRE v LEICESTERSHIRE

At Bristol, April 14–16. Gloucestershire won by an innings and six runs. Gloucestershire 22pts, Leicestershire 3pts. Toss: uncontested.

Norwell claimed a five-for in both innings to guide Gloucestershire to an innings victory inside three days. Having watched Leicestershire's implosion from behind the stumps, Mustard – captain in place of the ill Gareth Roderick – had no hesitation in asking them to bat again, 207 in arrears. Eckersley twice fought a rearguard from No. 6. His defiant first-innings 88 was at odds with a Leicestershire team who seemed affected by a mauling against Nottinghamshire; by contrast, Gloucestershire brushed aside their crushing defeat at Canterbury. Less than 40 minutes into the follow-on, Eckersley was batting again; although he enjoyed support from Raine and McKay, it was a forlorn task. With Ackermann unable to bat after taking a blow on the hand from Miles on the second day, Eckersley was ninth – and last – out for 85. It was the second time the accurate Norwell had taken ten in a match. Gloucestershire had earlier relied on another Tavaré hundred, his 277-ball innings highlighting the value of patience in swinging conditions. Four others capitalised on the waywardness of the Leicestershire attack and passed 50, allowing Mustard to declare on the second afternoon.

Close of play: first day, Gloucestershire 236-4 (Tavaré 73, Mustard 13); second day, Leicestershire 165-6 (Eckersley 25, McKay 8).

Gloucestershire

C. T. Bancroft b Griffiths	32
C. D. J. Dent b Jones	20
W. A. Tavaré b Griffiths	101
G. L. van Buuren c Eckersley b Raine	79
G. T. Hankins c Dearden b Griffiths	1
*†P. Mustard b Dexter	72
J. M. R. Taylor c Eckersley b Griffiths	60
C. N. Miles c Dearden b Jones	5
D. A. Payne not out	54
L. C. Norwell not out	11
B 13, lb 6, w 6, nb 6	31
1/52 (1) (8 wkts dec, 143 overs)	466
2/74 (2) 3/201 (4) 4/204 (5) 5/293 (3) 6/371 (6) 7/378 (8) 8/433 (7) 110 overs: 302-5	

C. J. Liddle did not bat.

McKay 24–5–69–0; Jones 27–5–86–2; Griffiths 34–7–101–4; Raine 29–7–63–1; Dexter 8–0–40–1; Cosgrove 14–1–59–0; Ackermann 4–0–10–0; Dearden 3–0–19–0.

Leicestershire

P. J. Horton lbw b Payne	6 – c Mustard b Payne	6
H. E. Dearden lbw b Norwell	8 – c Bancroft b Norwell	4
N. J. Dexter c Dent b Payne	0 – c Bancroft b Norwell	4
*M. J. Cosgrove c and b Taylor	48 – b Payne	26
M. L. Pettini c Mustard b Norwell	54 – b Norwell	1
†E. J. H. Eckersley b Norwell	88 – c Taylor b Norwell	85
C. N. Ackermann retired hurt	8 – absent hurt	
B. A. Raine c Mustard b Miles	0 – (7) run out	42
C. J. McKay b Norwell	8 – (8) c Hankins b Norwell	29
R. A. Jones not out	23 – (9) c Mustard b Payne	0
G. T. Griffiths c Dent b Norwell	0 – (10) not out	2
B 1, lb 10, w 1, nb 4	16 Lb 2	2
1/10 (1) 2/14 (2) 3/14 (3) 4/116 (4) 5/127 (5) 6/154 (8) 7/166 (9) 8/255 (6) 9/259 (11) (73.2 overs)	259 1/10 (1) 2/14 (2) 3/21 (3) 4/31 (5) 5/51 (4) 6/137 (7) 7/178 (8) 8/179 (9) 9/201 (6) (43.4 overs)	201

In the first innings Ackermann retired hurt at 146-5.

Payne 16–3–43–2; Norwell 21.2–2–66–5; Miles 15–1–69–1; Liddle 10–2–41–0; Taylor 5–1–9–1; van Buuren 6–2–20–0. *Second innings*—Payne 12–1–50–3; Norwell 11.4–2–33–5; Miles 4–0–25–0; Liddle 10–1–65–0; Taylor 6–1–26–0.

Umpires: S. A. Garratt and N. A. Mallender.

GLOUCESTERSHIRE v DURHAM

At Bristol, April 21–24. Drawn. Gloucestershire 9pts, Durham 12pts. Toss: uncontested. Championship debut: C. T. Steel.

Durham made much of the running in a hard-fought draw against a Gloucestershire side keen to prove they could mix it with a team who, but for ECB sanctions, would have been in the first division. In terms of Test experience, the score was 5–0 to Durham, and they held the upper hand at the halfway stage. Inserted in seam-friendly conditions, Gloucestershire were indebted to Dent and Tavaré, who hit defiant fifties; four others fell between 27 and 47 in a total of 303. Durham sailed past three figures during a chanceless opening stand, a platform built on by Collingwood and Richardson, who added 122 for the fifth. Gloucestershire kept at their task, and Miles – the beneficiary of others' discipline – claimed five for 99. Even so, they trailed by 116. Dent was equal to the challenge, occupying the crease for 258 balls as he made a match-saving hundred. Tavaré once more offered valuable support in the face of a testing examination. Had they not slipped to 15 for three, Durham might have had more of a dash at 205 from 31 overs. The captains called it a day with eight unbowled.

Close of play: first day, Gloucestershire 265-7 (Taylor 41, Payne 9); second day, Durham 270-4 (Collingwood 28, Richardson 25); third day, Gloucestershire 175-3 (Dent 64, Hankins 9).

Gloucestershire

First innings		Second innings	
C. T. Bancroft b Rushworth	5	– lbw b Rushworth	13
C. D. J. Dent c Poynter b Collingwood	59	– c Collingwood b Rushworth	101
W. A. Tavaré c Poynter b Rushworth	61	– b Steel	55
G. L. van Buuren lbw b Collingwood	0	– lbw b Onions	23
G. T. Hankins c Collingwood b Carse	27	– c Cook b Carse	20
*†P. Mustard c Collingwood b Jennings	38	– lbw b Onions	15
J. M. R. Taylor c Collingwood b Rushworth	47	– lbw b Rushworth	2
C. N. Miles c Collingwood b Jennings	0	– c Richardson b Onions	0
D. A. Payne c Jennings b Wood	28	– not out	36
L. C. Norwell not out	7	– c Poynter b Carse	8
C. J. Liddle c Poynter b Onions	5	– b Onions	21
B 5, lb 15, nb 6	26	B 7, lb 11, nb 8	26
1/14 (1) 2/97 (2) 3/97 (4) 4/156 (5) 5/187 (3) 6/251 (6) 7/255 (8) 8/291 (7) 9/291 (9) 10/303 (11) (90.2 overs)	303	1/30 (1) 2/115 (3) 3/159 (4) 4/202 (5) 5/253 (6) 6/253 (2) 7/255 (8) 8/255 (7) 9/275 (10) 10/320 (11) (113.4 overs)	320

Rushworth 23–8–55–3; Onions 17.2–3–45–1; Carse 15–0–51–1; Wood 20–2–69–1; Collingwood 10–4–29–2; Jennings 5–0–34–2. *Second innings*—Rushworth 22–3–75–3; Wood 19–4–43–0; Carse 23–0–61–2; Onions 28.4–7–68–4; Steel 9–2–34–1; Collingwood 12–4–21–0.

Durham

First innings		Second innings	
S. C. Cook c Bancroft b Liddle	64	– lbw b Payne	0
K. K. Jennings c Mustard b Liddle	87	– not out	30
C. T. Steel lbw b Miles	31	– (6) not out	17
G. Clark c Mustard b Miles	16	– (3) c Hankins b Norwell	7
*P. D. Collingwood c Hankins b van Buuren	97	– (4) lbw b Payne	4
M. J. Richardson c Mustard b Miles	57	– (5) c Taylor b van Buuren	26
†S. W. Poynter b Miles	9		
B. A. Carse c Mustard b Norwell	7		
M. A. Wood c Liddle b Payne	13		
G. Onions c Taylor b Miles	10		
C. Rushworth not out	6		
B 9, lb 5, nb 8	22	Lb 1	1
1/114 (1) 2/183 (2) 3/208 (4) 4/213 (3) 5/335 (6) 6/353 (7) 7/369 (8) 8/390 (9) 9/407 (10) 10/419 (5) (132.3 overs)	419	1/0 (1) 2/11 (3) 3/15 (4) 4/53 (5) (4 wkts, 23 overs)	85

110 overs: 352-5

Payne 29–5–82–1; Norwell 33–5–94–1; Miles 28–4–99–5; Liddle 24–4–67–2; van Buuren 12.3–3–38–1; Taylor 6–1–25–0. *Second innings*—Payne 5–0–13–2; Norwell 5–1–12–1; van Buuren 7–1–31–1; Miles 6–0–28–0.

Umpires: S. C. Gale and J. W. Lloyds.

At Nottingham, May 26–28. GLOUCESTERSHIRE lost to NOTTINGHAMSHIRE by an innings and 50 runs.

GLOUCESTERSHIRE v NOTTINGHAMSHIRE

At Bristol, June 9–12. Drawn. Gloucestershire 9pts, Nottinghamshire 11pts. Toss: uncontested.

Man for man inferior, Gloucestershire rose to the challenge, with Roderick making 96 on his first Championship appearance of the season after recovering from illness (Mustard retained the captaincy). But then came Samit Patel, who almost single-handedly matched their 303. He batted eight and a quarter hours and faced 452 balls for a career-best 257 not out, sharing stands of 146 with Pujara for the third wicket, 83 with Read for the seventh and an unbroken 95 with Wood for the ninth. Although he was dropped twice, on 52 and 192, Patel showed immense concentration and batted at a consistent tempo to establish a handsome lead of 232. Gloucestershire lost one wicket before the third-day close, and two next morning. But despite bowling tightly and fielding well, Nottinghamshire struggled to make further inroads on a resolutely unhelpful strip – their assistant coach Paul Franks later criticised it for favouring patience and graft over freedom of expression. Dent made 71 from 147 balls, and van Buuren, putting team interest ahead of personal glory, batted over five hours to finish 12 runs from a century. For Gloucestershire, crushed a fortnight earlier at Trent Bridge, it was mission accomplished.

Close of play: first day, Gloucestershire 256-7 (Roderick 88, Miles 14); second day, Nottinghamshire 221-3 (Patel 78, Fletcher 0); third day, Gloucestershire 30-1 (Dent 18, Tavaré 7).

Gloucestershire

	First innings		Second innings	
C. T. Bancroft c Read b Hutton		37	– lbw b Fletcher	2
C. D. J. Dent lbw b Gurney		27	– lbw b Hutton	71
W. A. Tavaré lbw b Fletcher		7	– lbw b Gurney	7
†G. H. Roderick b Wood		96	– lbw b Gurney	2
G. L. van Buuren b Hutton		0	– not out	88
*P. Mustard c Read b Gurney		37	– c Libby b Fletcher	39
J. M. R. Taylor c Pujara b Wood		5	– not out	26
K. Noema-Barnett b Gurney		35		
C. N. Miles lbw b Patel		47		
D. A. Payne b Wood		0		
C. J. Liddle not out		2		
Lb 6, nb 4		10	Lb 5, w 2, nb 12	19
1/45 (2) 2/67 (3) 3/77 (1)	(111.5 overs)	303	1/2 (1) 2/31 (3) (5 wkts, 96 overs)	254
4/77 (5) 5/160 (6) 6/167 (7) 7/232 (8)			3/35 (4) 4/126 (2)	
8/280 (4) 9/280 (10) 10/303 (9)	110 overs: 300-9		5/218 (6)	

Fletcher 18–6–34–1; Wood 23–4–85–3; Mullaney 13–8–17–0; Gurney 30–5–68–3; Hutton 19–3–60–2; Patel 8.5–1–33–1. *Second innings*—Fletcher 16–2–58–2; Wood 11–3–29–0; Gurney 19–4–62–2; Patel 18–7–31–0; Hutton 16–7–33–1; Mullaney 9–5–11–0; Wessels 5–0–15–0; Pujara 2–0–10–0.

Nottinghamshire

S. J. Mullaney c Payne b van Buuren	38
J. D. Libby c Roderick b Miles	30
C. A. Pujara c Noema-Barnett b Taylor	67
S. R. Patel not out	257
L. J. Fletcher c Dent b Miles	0
M. J. Lumb lbw b Liddle	23
M. H. Wessels lbw b Taylor	18
*†C. M. W. Read b Noema-Barnett	40
B. A. Hutton c Roderick b Liddle	11
L. Wood not out	38
B 4, lb 5, nb 4	13
1/72 (1) (8 wkts dec, 166 overs)	535
2/74 (2) 3/220 (3)	
4/225 (5) 5/279 (6) 6/325 (7)	
7/408 (8) 8/440 (9) 110 overs: 313-5	

H. F. Gurney did not bat.

Payne 24–3–77–0; Noema-Barnett 27–7–82–1; Liddle 21–2–89–2; van Buuren 40–10–91–1; Miles 29–1–88–2; Taylor 25–1–99–2.

Umpires: M. J. Saggers and R. J. Warren.

At Hove, June 26–29. GLOUCESTERSHIRE drew with SUSSEX.

GLOUCESTERSHIRE v GLAMORGAN

At Cheltenham, July 3–4. Gloucestershire won by ten wickets. Gloucestershire 19pts, Glamorgan 3pts. Toss: Gloucestershire.

Hogan clearly misread the conditions when opting for a toss beneath leaden skies: 32 overs later, Glamorgan were filleted for 117. On an extraordinary day, the game proceeded at breakneck speed, with 25 wickets falling by the close, all to seam, though Tim Boon, the ECB's liaison officer did not consider the pitch unsatisfactory. In both the first two innings, just one batsman from either side – Donald for Glamorgan, Noema-Barnett for Gloucestershire – passed 22. Noema-Barnett added 41 for the ninth wicket with Payne, helping the hosts to a modest lead of 24. Glamorgan then nosed 12 ahead before losing a wicket, which opened the floodgates: five fell in eight overs and, when the hectic opening day of the Cheltenham festival finally ended, they were in effect 35 for five. Norwell had taken three, and eventually pocketed six for 38 – his fourth five-for of the summer. Given what had gone before, a target of 135 might have proved tricky, but Bancroft and Dent showed a calmness otherwise absent from the game. They hit its only two fifties, as Gloucestershire eased to their second win of the season.

Close of play: first day, Glamorgan 59-5 (Salter 3, van der Gugten 4).

Glamorgan

First innings		Second innings	
N. J. Selman run out	0	– b Noema-Barnett	19
J. A. Rudolph c Roderick b Payne	1	– c Roderick b Norwell	21
A. O. Morgan c Bancroft b Norwell	2	– c Noema-Barnett b Norwell	1
C. A. Ingram c Roderick b Norwell	15	– c van Buuren b Norwell	0
A. H. T. Donald lbw b Noema-Barnett	39	– b Miles	8
A. G. Salter c Roderick b Miles	13	– c Roderick b Miles	31
†C. B. Cooke b Miles	0	– (8) not out	23
G. G. Wagg lbw b Noema-Barnett	1	– (9) lbw b Norwell	30
M. de Lange c Bancroft b Payne	19	– (10) c Taylor b Norwell	2
T. van der Gugten c Roderick b Payne	21	– (7) lbw b Noema-Barnett	17
*M. G. Hogan not out	0	– c Taylor b Norwell	0
Lb 6	6	Lb 4, nb 2	6
1/0 (1) 2/1 (2) 3/16 (4) 4/21 (3) 5/60 (6) 6/60 (7) 7/61 (8) 8/72 (5) 9/116 (9) 10/117 (10) (32.1 overs)	117	1/36 (2) 2/42 (1) 3/42 (3) 4/42 (4) 5/54 (5) 6/100 (7) 7/104 (6) 8/150 (9) 9/158 (10) 10/158 (11) (55 overs)	158

Payne 9.1–2–37–3; Norwell 9–3–17–2; Miles 7–0–24–2; Noema-Barnett 7–2–33–2. *Second innings*—Payne 13–1–39–0; Norwell 18–4–38–6; Noema-Barnett 11–1–39–2; Miles 12–3–30–2; van Buuren 1–0–8–0.

Gloucestershire

First innings		Second innings	
C. T. Bancroft c Cooke b de Lange	0	– not out	62
C. D. J. Dent b de Lange	1	– not out	68
W. A. Tavaré c Selman b de Lange	19		
†G. H. Roderick lbw b van der Gugten	9		
G. L. van Buuren b Hogan	14		
*P. Mustard c Cooke b Wagg	12		
J. M. R. Taylor lbw b Hogan	4		
K. Noema-Barnett c Cooke b van der Gugten	34		
C. N. Miles c Wagg b van der Gugten	12		
D. A. Payne not out	22		
L. C. Norwell c Cooke b Hogan	0		
B 4, lb 2, nb 8	14	B 1, lb 4, nb 2	7
1/0 (1) 2/13 (2) 3/26 (4) 4/30 (3) 5/56 (5) 6/66 (7) 7/68 (6) 8/91 (9) 9/132 (8) 10/141 (11) (41.2 overs)	141	(no wkt, 31.3 overs)	137

De Lange 13–2–54–3; van der Gugten 14–6–39–3; Hogan 8.2–2–25–3; Wagg 6–2–17–1. *Second innings*—de Lange 7–0–36–0; van der Gugten 8–0–34–0; Hogan 5–2–4–0; Wagg 6–0–23–0; Salter 5.3–0–35–0.

Umpires: N. L. Bainton and R. J. Evans.

GLOUCESTERSHIRE v WORCESTERSHIRE

At Cheltenham, July 9–12. Drawn. Gloucestershire 12pts, Worcestershire 11pts. Toss: uncontested.

Gloucestershire's quest for a second win at Cheltenham was frustrated by rain, which allowed only 15 overs on the third day of a hard-fought contest. Jack Taylor's first hundred of the season, a characteristically robust affair, proved the mainstay of their 383. He came in at 129 for five, survived a chance at third slip on 16, and shared stands of 96 with Mustard for the sixth wicket and 89 with Miles for the eighth. After slipping to 69 for four, Worcestershire were rescued by Cox, who compiled a classy career-best century; he dominated a restorative partnership of 141 with Rhodes and steered his side clear of immediate danger. Gloucestershire led by 83 after Leach called in his last pair on reaching 300, but could add only 42 on the third day. On the fourth, Dent – the game's third centurion – and Roderick accelerated, but a late declaration set an irritated Worcestershire 370 in 51 overs. Payne and Norwell skilfully reduced them to five for three, then 47 for four, only for the measured Clarke to ensure safety.

Close of play: first day, Gloucestershire 343-8 (Taylor 118, Payne 13); second day, Gloucestershire 20-0 (Bancroft 9, Dent 7); third day, Gloucestershire 62-1 (Dent 11, Tavaré 23).

Gloucestershire

First innings		Second innings	
C. T. Bancroft lbw b Leach	0	– c Whiteley b Hastings	22
C. D. J. Dent lbw b Barnard	65	– not out	135
W. A. Tavaré c Cox b Leach	21	– lbw b Barnard	32
†G. H. Roderick c Hastings b Barnard	11	– b Tongue	81
G. L. van Buuren c Cox b Rhodes	1	– c Leach b Mitchell	0
*P. Mustard b Barnard	50		
J. M. R. Taylor c Leach b Tongue	143		
K. Noema-Barnett c Cox b Tongue	0		
C. N. Miles c Cox b Barnard	39		
D. A. Payne b Tongue	15		
L. C. Norwell not out	12		
B 3, lb 3, nb 20	26	Lb 2, nb 14	16
1/0 (1) 2/53 (3) 3/79 (4) 4/85 (5) 5/129 (2) 6/225 (6) 7/234 (8) 8/323 (9) 9/346 (10) 10/383 (7) (102.1 overs)	383	1/33 (1) 2/90 (3) 3/279 (4) 4/286 (5) (4 wkts dec, 66.4 overs)	286

Leach 18–1–67–2; Hastings 20–5–86–0; Tongue 22.1–1–74–3; Barnard 28–3–93–4; Rhodes 8–4–29–1; D'Oliveira 3–0–15–0; Mitchell 3–0–13–0. *Second innings*—Leach 11–5–25–0; Hastings 17–6–42–1; Barnard 9–0–40–1; Tongue 8–2–19–1; D'Oliveira 11–0–67–0; Rhodes 9–1–75–0; Mitchell 1.4–0–16–1.

Worcestershire

D. K. H. Mitchell lbw b Payne	6 – b Norwell	5
B. L. D'Oliveira c Norwell b Miles	25 – lbw b Payne	0
T. C. Fell c Noema-Barnett b Norwell	2 – lbw b Payne	0
J. M. Clarke b Noema-Barnett	23 – not out	93
G. H. Rhodes c Tavaré b Miles	52 – b Norwell	9
†O. B. Cox c Roderick b Noema-Barnett	124 – lbw b Noema-Barnett	21
R. A. Whiteley b Norwell	1 – not out	19
E. G. Barnard c Bancroft b Noema-Barnett	23	
*J. Leach not out	17	
J. W. Hastings c Mustard b Noema-Barnett	0	
J. C. Tongue not out	1	
B 4, lb 16, w 2, nb 4	26	B 4, lb 4 8
1/16 (1) 2/25 (3) 3/61 (2) 4/69 (4) 5/210 (5) 6/229 (7) 7/279 (6) 8/286 (8) 9/286 (10)	(9 wkts dec, 77 overs) 300	1/1 (2) 2/1 (3) 3/5 (1) 4/47 (5) 5/110 (6) (5 wkts, 42 overs) 155

Payne 15–2–51–1; Norwell 18–4–74–2; Miles 15–1–64–2; Noema-Barnett 16–4–31–4; van Buuren 10–1–42–0; Tavaré 3–1–18–0. *Second innings*—Payne 5–1–16–2; Norwell 14–3–54–2; Miles 7–2–34–0; Noema-Barnett 11–4–22–1; Taylor 5–1–21–0.

Umpires: I. D. Blackwell and R. J. Evans.

At Northampton, August 6–9. GLOUCESTERSHIRE drew with NORTHAMPTONSHIRE.

At Worcester, August 28–31. GLOUCESTERSHIRE lost to WORCESTERSHIRE by 189 runs.

At Leicester, September 5–8. GLOUCESTERSHIRE beat LEICESTERSHIRE by ten wickets. *Liam Norwell takes eight for 43.*

GLOUCESTERSHIRE v KENT

At Bristol, September 12–15. Drawn. Gloucestershire 11pts, Kent 12pts. Toss: uncontested.

Roderick risked serious injury to steer Gloucestershire out of trouble – and take the wind from Kent's promotion sails. Despite the club website stating he would miss the final day because of a damaged finger sustained while keeping wicket, he came in at No. 8 with Gloucestershire 197 ahead – and, with Stevens causing problems, enough time for a Kent victory. But Roderick contributed a gritty 78 not out and, bolstered by tail-end resistance – Shaw faced 39 balls – thwarted them. Earlier, Bancroft, whose stint as Gloucestershire's overseas player had been unspectacular, came good in his last match before returning to Perth. He carried his bat for 206, sharing century partnerships for the first wicket with Dent, and the last with Matt Taylor (their 111 was a tenth-wicket record in this fixture). With four fifties, Kent's reply was more of a team effort but, thanks to a five-for from Shaw, they led by just a single on first innings. The Gloucestershire openers prospered again in the second, but a flurry of wickets left them in need of Roderick's bravery.

Close of play: first day, Gloucestershire 242-5 (Bancroft 124, J. M. R. Taylor 12); second day, Kent 60-2 (Bell-Drummond 32, Denly 8); third day, Gloucestershire 67-0 (Bancroft 25, Dent 41).

Gloucestershire

Batsman	First innings		Second innings	
C. T. Bancroft not out		206	lbw b Milne	72
C. D. J. Dent lbw b Denly		59	c Billings b Stevens	41
†G. H. Roderick c Crawley b Claydon		10	(8) not out	78
J. R. Bracey lbw b Denly		12	lbw b Stevens	13
G. T. Hankins lbw b Stevens		16	c Billings b Claydon	30
*P. Mustard c Stevens b Milne		0	(3) lbw b Stevens	0
J. M. R. Taylor lbw b Stevens		17	(6) c Billings b Coles	27
K. Noema-Barnett b Stevens		1	(7) c sub (I. Qayyum) b Stevens	5
J. Shaw c Denly b Milne		13	b Stevens	2
L. C. Norwell c Bell-Drummond b Milne		0	run out	8
M. D. Taylor c Bell-Drummond b Claydon		36	not out	0
Lb 6, w 1, nb 8		15	B 6, lb 1, w 1, nb 10	18
	(131.5 overs)	385	(9 wkts dec, 95 overs)	294

1/141 (2) 2/180 (3) 3/193 (4) 4/225 (5) 5/226 (6) 6/247 (7) 7/253 (8) 8/274 (9) 9/274 (10) 10/385 (11) — 110 overs: 319-9

1/67 (2) 2/67 (3) 3/91 (4) 4/146 (5) 5/186 (1) 6/198 (6) 7/210 (7) 8/249 (9) 9/289 (10)

Milne 30–4–91–3; Stevens 19–3–50–3; Haggett 21–6–46–0; Coles 23–5–78–0; Claydon 18.5–6–45–2; Denly 20–2–69–2. *Second innings*—Milne 24–10–64–1; Stevens 20–6–77–5; Coles 20–5–56–1; Haggett 10–2–29–0; Denly 3–1–2–0; Claydon 18–3–59–1.

Kent

Batsman	Runs
D. J. Bell-Drummond c Roderick b Norwell	58
S. R. Dickson c Roderick b Shaw	20
A. F. Milne c Bancroft b Shaw	0
J. L. Denly c Mustard b M. D. Taylor	57
*S. A. Northeast b Noema-Barnett	66
†S. W. Billings run out	47
Z. Crawley c †Bracey b Shaw	10
D. I. Stevens not out	65
C. J. Haggett c †Bracey b Norwell	8
M. T. Coles b Shaw	12
M. E. Claydon c †Bracey b Shaw	10
B 4, lb 8, nb 21	33
(97 overs)	386

1/46 (2) 2/50 (3) 3/104 (1) 4/210 (5) 5/210 (4) 6/264 (7) 7/283 (6) 8/339 (9) 9/370 (10) 10/386 (11)

M. D. Taylor 26–4–102–1; Norwell 27–4–100–2; Shaw 25–4–118–5; Noema-Barnett 17–2–47–1; J. M. R. Taylor 2–0–7–0.

Umpires: J. H. Evans and R. J. Warren.

At Cardiff, September 19–22. GLOUCESTERSHIRE drew with GLAMORGAN.

GLOUCESTERSHIRE v DERBYSHIRE

At Bristol, September 25–28. Derbyshire won by 157 runs. Derbyshire 21pts, Gloucestershire 3pts. Toss: Gloucestershire.

Derbyshire's much-travelled leg-spinner Imran Tahir sent Gloucestershire spiralling to their only home defeat of the season. Nothing rode on this game and, after 172 overs spread across three days had produced just 12 wickets, it looked as though nothing would come of it. But the captains breathed life into the fourth: Gloucestershire declared on their overnight 224 for two – still 236 behind – before Slater and Reece feasted on a diet of tripe from Mustard and Dent. The pair clonked 144 in 35 minutes, hastening a second declaration, which set Gloucestershire 381 in 80 overs on an apparent featherbed. There had certainly been few alarms while Madsen (who passed 10,000 first-class runs during his first hundred of 2017) and Hughes (a career-best 142) were adding 233 for Derbyshire's third wicket, or while Gloucestershire youngsters Bracey and Hankins put on an unbroken 170. By the fourth day, however, the pitch was taking slow turn, which Tahir was quick to exploit. Late on, there was leg-spin from both ends: Critchley claimed two wickets as the last four tumbled for 11 in seven overs. Tahir's five for 76 meant he now had a five-wicket haul for 15 different first-class sides; only W. G. Grace (20), William Lillywhite (19), Alfred Mynn and Johnny Briggs (both 16) had done so for more teams – all in the 19th century.

Close of play: first day, Derbyshire 104-2 (Madsen 24, Hughes 10); second day, Gloucestershire 47-1 (Howell 33, Bracey 5); third day, Gloucestershire 224-2 (Bracey 82, Hankins 79).

Derbyshire

Batsman	First innings		Second innings	
B. T. Slater b M. D. Taylor	45	– not out	74
L. M. Reece lbw b M. D. Taylor	13	– not out	61
W. L. Madsen c Bracey b Shaw	121		
A. L. Hughes c Dent b Noema-Barnett	142		
M. J. J. Critchley b Howell	19		
*†G. C. Wilson c Noema-Barnett b M. D. Taylor	5		
H. R. Hosein not out	37		
H. W. Podmore c Hankins b Smith	43		
G. C. Viljoen b Smith	5		
W. S. Davis c J. M. R. Taylor b Smith	4		
Imran Tahir c Bracey b Noema-Barnett	0		
B 5, lb 14, w 1, nb 6	26	B 4, lb 2, w 1, nb 2	9
1/65 (2) 2/74 (1) 3/307 (3) 4/342 (5) 5/355 (6) 6/380 (4) 7/450 (8) 8/456 (9) 9/460 (10) 10/460 (11) (115.1 overs)	460	(no wkt dec, 13.4 overs)	144

110 overs: 413-6

Payne 23–7–72–0; Shaw 20–2–83–1; M. D. Taylor 23–4–80–3; Noema-Barnett 20.1–7–64–2; Smith 20–0–108–3; Howell 9–0–34–1. *Second innings*—Mustard 7–0–69–0; Dent 6.4–0–69–0.

Gloucestershire

Batsman	First innings	Second innings	
B. A. C. Howell b Podmore	36	– c †Hosein b Podmore	5
C. D. J. Dent lbw b Viljoen	4	– c †Hosein b Podmore	19
†J. R. Bracey not out	82	– c Davis b Imran Tahir	44
G. T. Hankins not out	79	– c and b Imran Tahir	48
*P. Mustard (did not bat)		– b Critchley	37
J. M. R. Taylor (did not bat)		– lbw b Imran Tahir	3
K. Noema-Barnett (did not bat)		– c Davis b Madsen	30
T. M. J. Smith (did not bat)		– not out	14
D. A. Payne (did not bat)		– c Madsen b Critchley	0
J. Shaw (did not bat)		– b Imran Tahir	1
M. D. Taylor (did not bat)		– lbw b Imran Tahir	7
B 12, lb 6, w 1, nb 4	23	B 5, lb 1, w 1, nb 8	15
1/14 (2) 2/54 (1) (2 wkts dec, 57 overs)	224	1/9 (1) 2/42 (2) 3/112 (3) 4/135 (4) 5/147 (6) 6/180 (7) 7/212 (5) 8/214 (9) 9/215 (10) 10/223 (11) (59.3 overs)	223

Viljoen 19–4–54–1; Podmore 17–3–51–1; Imran Tahir 13–1–45–0; Madsen 2–0–20–0; Davis 6–1–36–0. *Second innings*—Viljoen 14–5–36–0; Podmore 12–1–44–2; Davis 4–0–14–0; Imran Tahir 18.3–2–76–5; Madsen 6–0–26–1; Critchley 5–0–21–2.

Umpires: N. L. Bainton and B. J. Debenham.

HAMPSHIRE

Another year of living dangerously

PAT SYMES

At 12.21 on the last day of the season, Somerset beat Middlesex, and sent Hampshire into the relegation zone for the first time all summer. Three weeks earlier, they had been third in the table and in no apparent danger, but their confidence vanished, and the prospect of dropping into Division Two suddenly became real. Avoiding defeat at Edgbaston would bring safety, but batting through more than two sessions, even against an already relegated Warwickshire, proved a nerve-racking business for a hesitant Hampshire.

Thanks to two partnerships, first from James Vince and Liam Dawson, then Ian Holland and Gareth Berg, they clung on – and sent defending champions Middlesex down instead. Remarkably, the five points for a draw took Hampshire up to fifth, their best position since 2008, underlining the intense competition among the counties scrabbling below a rampant Essex and above a despondent Warwickshire.

It might have been better: in early June, after winning three of their first six matches, they were top; and until the last fortnight they were genuine contenders for the runners-up spot. But a sequence of five draws and two defeats – including a morale-sapping reverse after making Essex follow on – led to that last-afternoon drama at Edgbaston.

Hampshire were lucky to be in Division One at all. Their reprieve from relegation at the end of the 2016 season had come courtesy of Durham's controversial demotion, and was not universally popular. Critics labelled them "Kolpakshire" after they signed Kyle Abbott and Rilee Rossouw, both from South Africa, to go with West Indian Fidel Edwards. There was undeniably an international look to the squad once four-day captain George Bailey was recruited from Australia, and Pakistan's Shahid Afridi for the Twenty20 Blast (in February, it emerged that Bailey would not return for the second year of his contract, because his wife was expecting their second child). Of the 27 who played first-team cricket, 11 came from abroad, six of them from southern Africa. And of the four Hampshire-born players, only Jimmy Adams was a regular.

A 42-ball century in the T20 quarter-finals probably justified Afridi's contract, but otherwise he totalled 50 in eight innings. Rossouw's season was blighted by injury: he missed a month in the spring after hurting his hand, and in August needed surgery on a damaged finger. He did not shine in the Championship, but gave a glimpse of his power with 156 in a one-day game at Taunton. Bailey hit a couple of centuries, and Edwards produced spells of genuine speed, but of Hampshire's overseas contingent the unqualified success was Abbott. In the first division, only Essex's Jamie Porter and Simon Harmer took more than his 60 wickets, and he also made 418 useful runs.

Harry Trump, Getty Images

Kyle Abbott

Almost as productive was Berg, who took 37 wickets and hit 568 runs –invaluable given the unreliability of the upper order. James Vince made 1,743 runs across the formats, including a county one-day record 178 against Glamorgan. But he managed only 626 in the Championship, and his inclusion in the Ashes squad was a surprise. So too were Liam Dawson's Test appearances against South Africa; while his bowling improved, his batting fell below expectations. Leg-spinner Mason Crane joined Vince on the Ashes tour, despite playing just seven Championship games and collecting 16 wickets at 44; during September, he bowled just 13 overs. With the white ball, he managed 33 scalps, including one for England – South Africa's A. B. de Villiers – in a Twenty20 international.

The biggest disappointment of the summer was Reece Topley's continuing struggle with injury. Unable to bowl in 2016, he managed two first-class games (and two costly wickets) in 2017. There was some compensation in the unearthing of all-rounder Holland, an American-born Australian with a British passport, who was spotted in club cricket. But no one averaged 40 with the bat, nor exceeded Vince's Championship tally. The arrival of Kent captain Sam Northeast on a four-year deal should help.

It wasn't as if the batsmen could blame the pitch, which stood up to the busy schedule, including two one-day internationals. In the early season it tended to flatten out, which probably prevented the double over Yorkshire.

In the Royal London Cup, Hampshire lost half their eight fixtures, and were never serious contenders to reach the knockouts, despite those startling individual performances from Rossouw and Vince – and a county-record eighth-wicket stand of 152 between Bailey and Abbott in defeat by Surrey. However, Hampshire again prospered in the shortest format, even if they seemed more fallible than usual. They lost six matches, and squeezed into the quarter-finals where, thanks to the Afridi onslaught, they annihilated Derbyshire to reach their seventh finals day in eight seasons. Having restricted Nottinghamshire to a chaseable 169, Afridi fell first ball. Vince kept alive hopes of reaching the final, but his exit for 56 proved crucial.

In September, experienced batsman Will Smith was allowed to rejoin Durham after spending the summer as Second XI captain, but the saddest move was Michael Carberry's departure for Leicestershire. He had missed the second half of 2016 while being treated for cancer, so his return in April with a century against Cardiff MCCU and 98 against Middlesex was heartening. But that proved the high point of a patchy season, which culminated in a loan spell at Grace Road, soon made permanent. Carberry had joined Hampshire in 2006, and totalled 16,862 runs in all cricket, including 10,277 in first-class matches. How Hampshire could have done with him at his best in 2017.

Championship attendance: 20,035.

HAMPSHIRE RESULTS

All first-class matches – Played 16: Won 3, Lost 4, Drawn 9.
County Championship matches – Played 14: Won 3, Lost 3, Drawn 8.

Specsavers County Championship, 5th in Division 1;
NatWest T20 Blast, semi-finalists; Royal London One-Day Cup, 6th in South Group.

COUNTY CHAMPIONSHIP AVERAGES, BATTING AND FIELDING

Cap		*Birthplace*	*M*	*I*	*NO*	*R*	*HS*	*100*	*Avge*	*Ct/St*
2017	G. J. Bailey¶	*Launceston, Aust.*	10	16	0	610	161	2	38.12	5
	I. G. Holland††	*Stevens Point, USA*	8	11	4	233	58*	0	33.28	1
2013	J. M. Vince	*Cuckfield*	12	19	0	626	147	2	32.94	13
2006	†J. H. K. Adams	*Winchester‡*	12	17	0	558	166	2	32.82	14
2016	G. K. Berg	*Cape Town, SA*	14	20	2	568	99*	0	31.55	2
2017	K. J. Abbott††	*Empangeni, SA*	14	18	4	418	97*	0	29.85	1
2005	†S. M. Ervine	*Harare, Zimbabwe*	14	21	1	572	203	1	28.60	13
2006	†M. A. Carberry	*Croydon*	7	11	0	272	98	0	24.72	2
	L. D. McManus	*Poole*	10	14	2	285	41*	0	23.75	28/3
2013	L. A. Dawson	*Swindon*	10	16	0	334	75	0	20.87	5
	†R. R. Rossouw††	*Bloemfontein, SA*	8	13	0	253	99	0	19.46	7
	†T. P. Alsop	*Wycombe*	5	7	0	118	40	0	16.85	9
	M. S. Crane	*Shoreham-by-Sea*	7	8	3	66	29	0	13.20	3
	J. J. Weatherley	*Winchester‡*	3	4	0	45	35	0	11.25	1
	B. T. J. Wheal††	*Durban, SA*	4	4	1	31	18	0	10.33	0
	F. H. Edwards††	*St Peter, Barbados*	9	10	4	43	20	0	7.16	0

Also batted: C. M. Dickinson (*Durban, SA*) (1 match) 1; F. S. Organ (*Sydney, Australia*) (1 match) 16; M. E. T. Salisbury (*Chelmsford*) (2 matches) 17*, 14, 0; B. J. Taylor (*Winchester‡*) (1 match) 18, 17*; R. J. W. Topley (*Ipswich*) (2 matches) 16, 0*, 7*.

‡ *Born in Hampshire.* ¶ *Official overseas player.* †† *Other non-England-qualified.*

BOWLING

	Style	*O*	*M*	*R*	*W*	*BB*	*5I*	*Avge*
K. J. Abbott	RFM	415.3	131	1,092	60	7-41	4	18.20
I. G. Holland	RFM	133	38	351	19	4-16	0	18.47
F. H. Edwards	RFM	208.1	31	772	30	5-49	2	25.73
L. A. Dawson	SLA	333.2	87	809	31	4-22	0	26.09
G. K. Berg	RFM	391.5	103	987	37	4-28	0	26.67
B. T. J. Wheal	RFM	84.5	11	352	11	4-98	0	32.00
M. S. Crane	LB	193.1	32	715	16	5-40	1	44.68

Also bowled: J. H. K. Adams (LM) 1–1–0–0; G. J. Bailey (RM) 2–0–9–0; M. A. Carberry (OB) 2–1–1–0; S. M. Ervine (RFM) 126.4–29–331–6; M. E. T. Salisbury (RFM) 46.2–7–177–4; B. J. Taylor (OB) 40–1–180–2; R. J. W. Topley (LFM) 44.2–6–178–2; J. M. Vince (RM) 8.5–0–38–1; J. J. Weatherley (OB) 15–3–55–1.

LEADING ROYAL LONDON CUP AVERAGES (100 runs/4 wickets)

Batting	*Runs*	*HS*	*Avge*	*SR*	*Ct*
G. J. Bailey	312	145*	78.00	92.30	3
J. M. Vince	463	178	77.16	113.75	2
R. R. Rossouw	196	156	65.33	130.66	0
T. P. Alsop	203	112*	33.83	66.55	1
L. A. Dawson	160	74	26.66	78.04	4
S. M. Ervine	112	33*	22.40	93.33	4

Bowling	*W*	*BB*	*Avge*	*ER*
M. S. Crane	14	3-53	27.42	6.00
R. J. W. Topley	9	4-68	33.33	6.59
L. A. Dawson	9	3-30	33.66	4.45
G. K. Berg	7	3-44	36.14	5.50
K. J. Abbott	7	2-46	42.85	5.73

LEADING NATWEST T20 BLAST AVERAGES (100 runs/15 overs)

Batting	Runs	HS	Avge	SR	Ct/St
J. M. Vince	542	81	38.71	**158.47**	12
Shahid Afridi	151	101	16.77	**157.29**	5
C. M. Dickinson	102	51	20.40	**152.23**	2/2
M. A. Carberry	224	77	32.00	**150.33**	5
R. R. Rossouw	255	60	28.33	**137.09**	7
L. D. McManus	128	59	21.33	**134.73**	3/3
G. J. Bailey	301	89*	30.10	**125.94**	5
T. P. Alsop	267	64	33.37	**120.27**	2

Bowling	W	BB	Avge	ER
M. S. Crane	18	3-15	17.33	**6.63**
Shahid Afridi	13	4-20	24.38	**7.20**
L. A. Dawson	14	3-28	16.92	**7.40**
R. J. W. Topley	7	3-23	27.57	**8.04**
G. K. Berg	13	3-35	30.23	**8.70**
K. J. Abbott	17	3-22	28.64	**8.93**
C. P. Wood	9	2-17	28.55	**9.17**

FIRST-CLASS COUNTY RECORDS

Highest score for	316	R. H. Moore v Warwickshire at Bournemouth	1937
Highest score against	303*	G. A. Hick (Worcestershire) at Southampton	1997
Leading run-scorer	48,892	C. P. Mead (avge 48.84)	1905–36
Best bowling for	9-25	R. M. H. Cottam v Lancashire at Manchester	1965
Best bowling against	10-46	W. Hickton (Lancashire) at Manchester	1870
Leading wicket-taker	2,669	D. Shackleton (avge 18.23)	1948–69
Highest total for	714-5 dec	v Nottinghamshire at Southampton	2005
Highest total against	742	by Surrey at The Oval	1909
Lowest total for	15	v Warwickshire at Birmingham	1922
Lowest total against	23	by Yorkshire at Middlesbrough	1965

LIST A COUNTY RECORDS

Highest score for	**178**	**J. M. Vince v Glamorgan at Southampton**	**2017**
Highest score against	203	A. D. Brown (Surrey) at Guildford	1997
Leading run-scorer	12,034	R. A. Smith (avge 42.97)	1983–2003
Best bowling for	7-30	P. J. Sainsbury v Norfolk at Southampton	1965
Best bowling against	7-22	J. R. Thomson (Middlesex) at Lord's	1981
Leading wicket-taker	411	C. A. Connor (avge 25.07)	1984–98
Highest total for	371-4	v Glamorgan at Southampton	1975
Highest total against	358-6	by Surrey at The Oval	2005
Lowest total for	43	v Essex at Basingstoke	1972
Lowest total against	61	by Somerset at Bath	1973
	61	by Derbyshire at Portsmouth	1990

TWENTY20 COUNTY RECORDS

Highest score for	124*	M. J. Lumb v Essex v Southampton	2009
Highest score against	116*	L. J. Wright (Sussex) at Southampton	2014
Leading run-scorer	**3,182**	**J. M. Vince (avge 33.14)**	**2010–17**
Best bowling for	5-14	A. D. Mascarenhas v Sussex at Hove	2004
Best bowling against	5-13	R. F. Higgins (Middlesex) at Southampton	2016
Leading wicket-taker	119	D. R. Briggs (avge 19.40)	2010–15
Highest total for	**249-8**	**v Derbyshire at Derby**	**2017**
Highest total against	220-4	by Somerset at Taunton	2010
Lowest total for	85	v Sussex at Southampton	2008
Lowest total against	67	by Sussex at Hove	2004

ADDRESS

The Ageas Bowl, Botley Road, West End, Southampton SO30 3XH; 023 8047 2002; enquiries@ageasbowl.com; www.ageasbowl.com.

OFFICIALS

Captain (club and limited-overs) J. M. Vince
(Championship) G. J. Bailey
Cricket operations manager T. M. Tremlett
Director of cricket G. W. White
First-team coach C. White
Head of player development C. R. M. Freeston

President N. E. J. Pocock
Chairman R. G. Bransgrove
Chief executive D. Mann
Head groundsman K. McDermott
Scorer K. R. Baker

HAMPSHIRE v CARDIFF MCCU

At Southampton, April 2–4. Drawn. Toss: Cardiff MCCU. First-class debuts: A. H. J. A. Hart; D. O'Sullivan.

Michael Carberry, in his first game since revealing a cancer diagnosis in July, received a standing ovation on reaching a century, his 35th in first-class cricket. From 31 for three, he and Ervine added 153, though Cardiff captain Neil Brand later took three for seven from 27 balls of left-arm spin to dismiss Hampshire for 289. The students then struggled against the county's pace attack; there were three wickets for debutant seamer Asher Hart (whose second name, Hale–Bopp, refers to the comet visible at his birth in March 1997). Cardiff trailed by 191, but Vince chose to bat again, and Hampshire ended the second day 462 ahead. Overnight rain forced a declaration and, although bad light limited play to 56 overs, the students made a better fist of their second innings.

Close of play: first day, Cardiff MCCU 59-6 (Scriven 4, Nijjar 0); second day, Hampshire 271-6 (Stevenson 19, Hart 0).

Hampshire

First innings		Second innings	
M. A. Carberry c Norris b O'Sullivan	100		
J. H. K. Adams b Brewster	3	– c Cullen b Brewster	19
*J. M. Vince b O'Sullivan	22	– c Cullen b Lawlor	90
T. P. Alsop lbw b Brewster	0	– (1) c Cullen b O'Sullivan	62
S. M. Ervine c Leverock b Nijjar	58	– (4) lbw b Nijjar	23
L. A. Dawson b Lawlor	45	– (5) c Cullen b Leverock	7
†L. D. McManus lbw b O'Sullivan	7	– (6) lbw b Brand	31
R. A. Stevenson b Brand	20	– (7) not out	19
A. H. J. A. Hart lbw b Brand	8	– (8) not out	0
B. T. J. Wheal not out	9		
F. H. Edwards lbw b Brand	0		
B 4, lb 3, w 6, nb 4	17	B 3, lb 8, w 7, nb 2	20
1/4 (2) 2/27 (3) 3/31 (4) 4/184 (1) 5/196 (5) 6/213 (7) 7/271 (8) 8/277 (6) 9/285 (9) 10/289 (11) (63.3 overs)	289	1/65 (2) 2/104 (1) 3/167 (4) 4/187 (5) 5/229 (3) 6/267 (6) (6 wkts dec, 66 overs)	271

Brewster 15–2–87–2; O'Sullivan 12–2–29–3; Leverock 12–1–57–0; Lawlor 8–1–31–1; Rouse 3–0–15–0; Nijjar 9–0–56–1; Brand 4.3–2–7–3. *Second innings*—O'Sullivan 14–1–63–1; Brewster 13–3–42–1; Lawlor 14–2–48–1; Rouse 3–0–12–0; Leverock 12–0–56–1; Nijjar 7–1–37–1; Brand 3–1–2–1.

Cardiff MCCU

First innings		Second innings	
M. J. Norris b Edwards	5	– c Adams b Ervine	16
C. R. Brown b Hart	8	– lbw b Hart	30
*N. Brand lbw b Edwards	0	– not out	44
T. D. Rouse c sub (R. J. W. Topley) b Wheal	12	– not out	12
J. L. Lawlor c Ervine b Hart	17		
†T. N. Cullen lbw b Dawson	8		
J. A. L. Scriven b Wheal	16		
A. S. S. Nijjar b Wheal	0		
K. S. Leverock c Wheal b Hart	21		
D. O'Sullivan c McManus b Edwards	2		
A. D. F. Brewster not out	1		
Lb 4, nb 4	8	Lb 6, nb 2	8
1/6 (1) 2/6 (3) 3/21 (4) 4/32 (2) 5/55 (6) 6/59 (5) 7/67 (8) 8/72 (7) 9/79 (10) 10/98 (9) (36.3 overs)	98	1/44 (1) 2/65 (2) (2 wkts, 56 overs)	110

Edwards 12–3–22–3; Wheal 11–5–32–3; Stevenson 5–1–18–0; Hart 6.3–1–17–3; Dawson 2–0–5–1. *Second innings*—Edwards 1.4–1–0–0; Wheal 5–1–12–0; Hart 12.2–4–20–1; Stevenson 10–1–37–0; Ervine 9–2–10–1; Dawson 15–7–21–0; Carberry 3–1–4–0.

Umpires: I. D. Blackwell and B. V. Taylor.

At Leeds, April 7–9. HAMPSHIRE beat YORKSHIRE by four wickets.

HAMPSHIRE v MIDDLESEX

At Southampton, April 14–17. Drawn. Hampshire 10pts, Middlesex 10pts. Toss: Middlesex.

Halfway through the last day, Middlesex were eight down, only 133 ahead, and in danger of beginning the defence of their title with defeat. But the champions had already batted doggedly for 85 overs, and Hampshire – who a week earlier had beaten Yorkshire – could not turn a strong position into another victory. Rayner survived almost two hours for 17, last man Murtagh over an hour for his 19, and the captains eventually agreed to call it off at 4.50. It did not help Hampshire that Edwards had limped out of the attack with a hamstring injury on the first morning, though his opening partner Abbott had another outstanding match. Seven wickets here took his tally from two rounds to 16, and he also chipped in with a half-century as nightwatchman. Nineties from Carberry and Rossouw – who batted through the pain of a broken finger and was run out going for his hundred – trumped eighties from Robson and Eskinazi to give Hampshire a lead of 82 on a sound pitch. Voges then set the tone for the rearguard with the third ninety of the game.

Close of play: first day, Middlesex 290-6 (Franklin 17, Roland-Jones 10); second day, Hampshire 209-4 (Carberry 84, Abbott 2); third day, Middlesex 111-4 (Voges 29, Finn 6).

Middlesex

S. D. Robson c Adams b Berg	84	– (2) c McManus b Abbott	8
N. R. T. Gubbins c Rossouw b Edwards	13	– (1) c Adams b Abbott	11
S. S. Eskinazi b Ervine	82	– c McManus b Abbott	45
D. J. Malan c Ervine b Wheal	43	– b Wheal	10
A. C. Voges b Abbott	24	– c McManus b Abbott	92
†J. A. Simpson c sub (M. S. Crane) b Wheal	9	– (7) c McManus b Berg	22
*J. E. C. Franklin c Vince b Abbott	19	– (8) c Adams b Abbott	1
T. S. Roland-Jones c Dawson b Wheal	39	– (9) c Adams b Wheal	25
O. P. Rayner lbw b Dawson	26	– (10) not out	17
T. J. Murtagh not out	5	– (11) not out	19
S. T. Finn lbw b Wheal	2	– (6) c sub (F. S. Hay) b Wheal	16
B 1, lb 3, nb 6	10	B 5, lb 4, w 1, nb 2	12
1/45 (2) 2/150 (1) 3/220 (4) 4/234 (3) 5/258 (5) 6/269 (6) 7/294 (7) 8/349 (8) 9/349 (9) 10/356 (11) (113 overs) 110 overs: 344-7	356	1/17 (2) 2/24 (1) 3/44 (4) 4/103 (3) 5/138 (6) 6/213 (5) 7/215 (8) 8/215 (7) 9/252 (9) (9 wkts dec, 112 overs)	278

Edwards 5.1–1–18–1; Abbott 27.5–9–87–2; Berg 27–7–62–1; Wheal 23–2–98–4; Dawson 22–4–72–1; Ervine 8–4–15–1. *Second innings*—Abbott 25–8–59–5; Berg 22–9–38–1; Ervine 14–3–36–0; Wheal 20–3–73–3; Dawson 28–10–62–0; Carberry 2–1–1–0; Adams 1–1–0–0.

Hampshire

M. A. Carberry c Simpson b Murtagh	98
J. H. K. Adams c Franklin b Rayner	34
*J. M. Vince c Rayner b Franklin	8
L. A. Dawson c Simpson b Rayner	19
S. M. Ervine b Finn	53
K. J. Abbott c Rayner b Roland-Jones	56
R. R. Rossouw run out	99
†L. D. McManus c Voges b Roland-Jones	8
G. K. Berg c and b Malan	43
B. T. J. Wheal c Simpson b Malan	0
F. H. Edwards not out	0
Lb 10, nb 10	20
1/57 (2) 2/70 (3) 3/113 (4) 4/206 (5) 5/246 (1) 6/326 (6) 7/346 (8) 8/432 (9) 9/432 (10) 10/438 (7) (133.4 overs) 110 overs: 332-6	438

Murtagh 27–5–97–1; Roland-Jones 27–6–86–2; Finn 26–4–84–1; Rayner 40–8–107–2; Franklin 10–2–35–1; Malan 3.4–0–19–2.

Umpires: R. J. Bailey and J. W. Lloyds.

HAMPSHIRE v YORKSHIRE

At Southampton, April 21–24. Drawn. Hampshire 11pts, Yorkshire 8pts. Toss: uncontested.

Yorkshire were at full strength – they boasted eight internationals – as they attempted to avenge defeat by Hampshire two weeks earlier. However, Root and Bairstow managed 18 runs in four innings, and their most penetrative bowler was the inexperienced Coad. Instead it fell to Ballance, their captain and (for the moment) Test discard, to secure a draw with a monumental effort that in all lasted 12 hours 52 minutes and 582 balls. He made 108 in the first innings and a match-saving unbeaten 203 in the second to become the first Yorkshire captain to hit twin centuries (and only Younis Khan had scored a century and a double for them in the same game). Ballance was on the field for all but 17.2 overs, and erred only in choosing to bowl, which allowed Hampshire to gain the upper hand: buttressed by Vince's first century of the summer and Berg's unbeaten 99, they ran up a useful 455. Berg then chopped the top off the Yorkshire batting to help reduce them to 19 for four. They limped to 231 all out, and followed on, 224 behind. Again they lost early wickets, though this time Ballance enjoyed more support as Hampshire were hampered by an injury to pace bowler Wheal, and by a familiarly lifeless pitch.

Close of play: first day, Hampshire 281-4 (Vince 143, Dawson 8); second day, Yorkshire 128-6 (Ballance 63, Rashid 16); third day, Yorkshire 178-3 (Ballance 78, Handscomb 5).

Hampshire

M. A. Carberry c Bairstow b Coad	6
J. H. K. Adams lbw b Coad	29
*J. M. Vince c Bairstow b Coad	147
T. P. Alsop lbw b Patterson	40
S. M. Ervine c Bairstow b Coad	48
L. A. Dawson lbw b Willey	24
†L. D. McManus c Bairstow b Willey	1
G. K. Berg not out	99
K. J. Abbott run out	22
R. J. W. Topley lbw b Rashid	16
B. T. J. Wheal c Lyth b Root	13
B 2, lb 7, w 1	10
1/9 (1) 2/75 (2) 3/157 (4) 4/267 (5) 5/300 (3) 6/301 (7) 7/302 (6) 8/346 (9) 9/387 (10) 10/455 (11) (144.4 overs)	455

110 overs: 346-8

Willey 36–10–86–2; Coad 30–8–71–4; Patterson 26–6–63–1; Bresnan 25–3–109–0; Rashid 20–1–95–1; Root 7.4–0–22–1.

Yorkshire

First innings		Second innings	
A. Lyth b Berg	8	c McManus b Berg	6
A. Z. Lees lbw b Berg	0	c McManus b Abbott	70
J. E. Root c McManus b Berg	8	lbw b Abbott	2
*G. S. Ballance c Ervine b Dawson	108	not out	203
P. S. P. Handscomb lbw b Abbott	1	c and b Dawson	40
†J. M. Bairstow lbw b Wheal	7	c Vince b Abbott	1
T. T. Bresnan c McManus b Berg	21	c McManus b Topley	37
A. U. Rashid c Vince b Wheal	34	not out	5
D. J. Willey b Dawson	8		
S. A. Patterson not out	22		
B. O. Coad c Ervine b Topley	5		
Lb 5, nb 4	9	B 26, lb 7, w 2	35
1/4 (2) 2/13 (1) 3/18 (3) 4/19 (5) 5/46 (6) 6/94 (7) 7/154 (8) 8/189 (9) 9/216 (4) 10/231 (11) (77.2 overs)	231	1/11 (1) 2/20 (3) 3/170 (2) 4/258 (5) 5/262 (6) 6/356 (7) (6 wkts dec, 132 overs)	399

Abbott 14–8–20–1; Berg 20–3–62–4; Topley 15.2–2–56–1; Wheal 15–2–63–2; Dawson 13–4–25–2. *Second innings*—Abbott 28–8–65–3; Berg 27–6–43–1; Topley 23–3–87–1; Wheal 3–0–17–0; Dawson 34–8–88–1; Ervine 16–1–62–0; Vince 1–0–4–0.

Umpires: B. V. Taylor and A. G. Wharf.

At Chelmsford, May 19–21. HAMPSHIRE lost to ESSEX by an innings and 97 runs.

At Taunton, May 26–28. HAMPSHIRE beat SOMERSET by 90 runs.

HAMPSHIRE v WARWICKSHIRE

At Southampton, June 2–5. Hampshire won by an innings and 94 runs. Hampshire 22pts, Warwickshire 3pts. Toss: Hampshire. County debut: M. E. T. Salisbury. Championship debut: I. G. Holland.

Hampshire went top with their third win in six. They easily overcame a flimsy Warwickshire, despite slipping to 31 for three after Bailey had chosen to bat. But Adams and Ervine added 367 – a county record for the fourth wicket, eclipsing the 278 Adams had put on with Vince at Scarborough in 2010 – as Hampshire built a daunting 515. It was Adams's first century since 2015, and Ervine's third double in all. The one Warwickshire bowler to emerge with credit was 21-year-old left-arm spinner Sukhjit Singh, who claimed six wickets in his second Championship match. Warwickshire plummeted to 81 for seven, but were partially redeemed by Trott – who hit a diligent 101 from No. 8 after dashing home for a family emergency – and Barker. They added 104, but Warwickshire followed on 261 behind. Trott's early dismissal on the last day, hot on the heels of Bell, triggered a rapid decline, as Abbott finished with four. Warwickshire sank to the foot of the table.

HIGHEST PARTNERSHIPS FOR HAMPSHIRE

523 for 3rd	M. A. Carberry (300*)/N. D. McKenzie (237)	v Yorks at Southampton	2011
411 for 6th	R. M. Poore (304)/E. G. Wynyard (225)	v Somerset at Taunton	1899
387 for 3rd	W. R. Smith (151*)/J. M. Vince (240)	v Essex at Southampton	2014
373 for 2nd	J. H. K. Adams (207)/M. A. Carberry (182)	v Somerset at Taunton	2011
367 for 4th	**J. H. K. Adams (166)/S. M. Ervine (203)**	**v Warwicks at Southampton**	**2017**
347 for 1st	V. P. Terry (122)/C. L. Smith (217)	v Warwicks at Birmingham	1987
344 for 3rd	G. Brown (204)/C. P. Mead (183)	v Yorks at Portsmouth	1927
325 for 7th	G. Brown (165)/C. H. Abercrombie (140*)	v Essex at Leyton	1913
321 for 2nd	G. Brown (120)/E. I. M. Barrett (215)	v Glos at Southampton	1920
321 for 3rd	C. L. Smith (193)/T. E. Jesty (187)	v Derbys at Derby	1983
314 for 2nd	M. A. Carberry (162)/M. J. Lumb (158)	v Durham at Basingstoke	2010

Close of play: first day, Hampshire 294-3 (Adams 104, Ervine 160); second day, Warwickshire 49-6 (Thornton 0); third day, Warwickshire 75-2 (Trott 17, Bell 47).

Hampshire

M. A. Carberry c Bell b Barker	2
J. H. K. Adams c Umeed b Sukhjit Singh	166
R. R. Rossouw lbw b Barker	17
*G. J. Bailey c Bell b Rankin	2
S. M. Ervine b Sukhjit Singh	203
I. G. Holland lbw b Sukhjit Singh	32
†L. D. McManus c Clarke b Sukhjit Singh	38
G. K. Berg c sub (W. T. S. Porterfield) b Sukhjit Singh	15
K. J. Abbott c sub (W. T. S. Porterfield) b Umeed	9
M. S. Crane b Sukhjit Singh	0
M. E. T. Salisbury not out	17
B 1, lb 4, w 1, nb 8	14
1/2 (1) 2/28 (3) 3/31 (4) 4/398 (2) 5/406 (5) 6/467 (6) 7/476 (7) 8/491 (8) 9/491 (10) 10/515 (9) (161.5 overs)	515
110 overs: 333-3	

Barker 30–6–92–2; Clarke 30–6–87–0; Rankin 20–1–60–1; Thornton 23–1–96–0; Sukhjit Singh 50–6–144–6; Umeed 5.5–0–25–1; Trott 3–0–6–0.

Warwickshire

First innings		Second innings	
A. R. I. Umeed c McManus b Crane	14	c McManus b Berg	7
I. J. Westwood run out	3	c Adams b Abbott	2
S. R. Hain c McManus b Salisbury	1	(5) lbw b Abbott	14
*I. R. Bell lbw b Salisbury	4	b Abbott	68
†T. R. Ambrose b Holland	3	(6) lbw b Berg	5
R. Clarke lbw b Crane	20	(7) lbw b Abbott	0
G. T. Thornton c Rossouw b Abbott	10	(9) lbw b Crane	9
I. J. L. Trott lbw b Abbott	101	(3) c Ervine b Crane	23
K. H. D. Barker c Bailey b Ervine	63	(8) not out	27
W. B. Rankin b Crane	4	b Ervine	4
Sukhjit Singh not out	16	lbw b Ervine	0
B 7, lb 4, nb 4	15	B 5, lb 1, nb 2	8
1/14 (2) 2/15 (3) 3/19 (4) 4/22 (5) 5/46 (6) 6/49 (1) 7/81 (7) 8/185 (9) 9/200 (10) 10/254 (8) (102.1 overs)	254	1/5 (2) 2/9 (1) 3/102 (4) 4/104 (3) 5/118 (5) 6/120 (7) 7/131 (6) 8/154 (9) 9/159 (10) 10/167 (11) (64.4 overs)	167

Abbott 17.1–4–41–2; Berg 14–5–26–0; Salisbury 17–5–35–2; Holland 9–4–16–1; Crane 36–7–104–3; Ervine 9–2–21–1. *Second innings*—Abbott 18–7–32–4; Berg 12–2–42–2; Holland 5–1–21–0; Salisbury 3–0–15–0; Crane 21–10–50–2; Ervine 5.4–4–1–2.

Umpires: N. G. C. Cowley and P. J. Hartley.

At Southampton, June 8–11. HAMPSHIRE lost to SOUTH AFRICA A by 251 runs (see South Africa A tour section).

At Manchester, June 19–22. HAMPSHIRE lost to LANCASHIRE by an innings and 30 runs.

HAMPSHIRE v SOMERSET

At Southampton, June 26–29 (day/night). Drawn. Hampshire 9pts, Somerset 8pts. Toss: Hampshire. First-class debut: E. J. Byrom.

In their first floodlit Championship match, Hampshire glimpsed a fourth victory when Somerset were 84 for eight – but Craig Overton and Davey survived the seven remaining balls to ensure a draw. After rain had filched swathes of the last three days, Bailey's second declaration set Somerset, still winless, 161 in 31 overs. They were just about on course at 68 for three in the 15th, but the middle order fell away, prompting the tense conclusion; Abell made his fourth and fifth ducks of the season, and dropped himself for the next game. On a pitch that grew more helpful to the faster bowlers, Hampshire had been indebted first to their openers, then to Ian Holland, whose burst of four wickets in his first four overs reduced Somerset from 102 for one to 110 for five; his three previous first-class games had brought just two scalps. (An Australian medium-pace all-rounder born in Wisconsin to an English father, Holland had in 2012 won *Cricket Superstar*, an Australian reality TV series, though his progress had not immediately been stellar.) From a position of strength – Hampshire led by 64 on first innings – Bailey hoped to give his attack, especially the outstanding Berg, more runs and overs to play with, but the weather forced his hand. Somerset debutant Eddie Byrom, a Zimbabwean educated at King's College, Taunton, opened the batting with Trescothick, more than 21 years his senior. The game attracted small crowds, perhaps put off by the damp.

Close of play: first day, Somerset 18-0 (Trescothick 10, Byrom 1); second day, Somerset 43-1 (Byrom 13, Hose 9); third day, Somerset 135-8 (Davey 5).

Hampshire

J. H. K. Adams c Hildreth b Overton	47	– run out	9
L. A. Dawson lbw b Gregory	53	– b Groenewald	20
R. R. Rossouw c Davies b Overton	0	– c Hildreth b Gregory	22
J. M. Vince c Davies b Leach	47	– c Davies b Gregory	20
*G. J. Bailey c Overton b Groenewald	4	– run out	8
S. M. Ervine c Davies b Leach	16	– not out	11
I. G. Holland b Groenewald	0	– not out	6
†L. D. McManus b Gregory	13		
G. K. Berg lbw b Gregory	11		
K. J. Abbott not out	13		
B. T. J. Wheal not out	0		
Lb 7	7		
1/84 (1) 2/86 (3) 3/112 (2) 4/132 (5) 5/169 (6) 6/172 (4) 7/172 (7) 8/198 (9) 9/199 (8) (9 wkts dec, 88 overs)	211	1/24 (1) 2/31 (2) 3/64 (3) 4/79 (4) 5/79 (5) (5 wkts dec, 39 overs)	96

Gregory 17–6–51–3; Davey 13–4–37–0; Groenewald 16–5–27–2; Overton 18–7–35–2; Leach 24–5–54–2. *Second innings*—Gregory 10–2–34–2; Overton 9–3–18–0; Leach 13–3–27–0; Groenewald 4–3–12–1; Davey 3–0–5–0.

Somerset

M. E. Trescothick b Berg	13	– c Vince b Berg	4
E. J. Byrom c Bailey b Holland	43	– (5) b Holland	15
A. J. Hose lbw b Berg	48	– c McManus b Berg	0
J. C. Hildreth lbw b Holland	2	– b Abbott	10
*T. B. Abell c McManus b Holland	0	– (6) c Rossouw b Dawson	0
†S. M. Davies c McManus b Holland	0	– (2) c Bailey b Holland	47
L. Gregory run out	8	– (8) lbw b Berg	3
C. Overton c Adams b Berg	4	– (9) not out	2
J. H. Davey c McManus b Dawson	5	– (10) not out	4
M. J. Leach c McManus b Berg	2		
T. D. Groenewald not out	10	– (7) c McManus b Abbott	3
B 5, w 1, nb 6	12		
1/25 (1) 2/102 (2) 3/104 (4) 4/110 (5) 5/110 (6) 6/126 (7) 7/126 (3) 8/135 (8) 9/135 (9) 10/147 (10) (52.2 overs)	147	1/4 (1) 2/4 (3) 3/27 (4) 4/68 (5) 5/69 (6) 6/79 (2) 7/82 (8) 8/84 (7) (8 wkts, 31 overs)	88

Berg 16.2–8–28–4; Abbott 15–3–43–0; Wheal 4–1–25–0; Dawson 11–3–30–1; Holland 6–1–16–4. *Second innings*—Berg 9–3–17–3; Abbott 9–1–33–2; Holland 4–0–23–2; Dawson 8–3–15–1; Wheal 1–1–0–0.

Umpires: I. D. Blackwell and M. J. Saggers.

At The Oval, July 3–6. HAMPSHIRE drew with SURREY. *Hampshire make 648 for seven, their fifth-highest total.*

HAMPSHIRE v LANCASHIRE

At Southampton, August 6–9. Drawn. Hampshire 9pts, Lancashire 8pts. Toss: Lancashire.

For the first two days, this contest between second and third was keenly fought. But rain washed out the last two, and a watery draw left them level on points, 41 behind runaway leaders Essex. McLaren, a Hampshire all-rounder in 2016 but now captaining Lancashire after Steven Croft dropped himself, opted to bat on a pitch that offered spin and bounce – and his team struggled to justify the decision. There were three wickets for Crane's leg-spin and, by stumps, Hampshire were well placed: with five wickets standing they trailed by just two. Yet despite Dawson's 75 – his highest score of a lean season – the next day belonged to Lancashire. Jarvis's regular breakthroughs brought a county-best six for 61 and kept the deficit to 75, before determined batting from Davies and Hameed, who put on 129 for the first wicket, thrust Lancashire into the ascendancy. With half the match left they led by 239. Then came the rain.

Close of play: first day, Hampshire 147-5 (Dawson 20, Holland 13); second day, Lancashire 314-5 (Hameed 77, McLaren 8); third day, no play.

Lancashire

	First innings		Second innings	
†A. L. Davies c Ervine b Dawson	36	–	c †Vince b Dawson	97
H. Hameed c Adams b Edwards	6	–	not out	77
L. S. Livingstone lbw b Abbott	16	–	lbw b Abbott	40
D. J. Vilas c McManus b Holland	3	–	b Crane	20
S. Chanderpaul run out	13	–	c Adams b Dawson	35
J. C. Buttler b Edwards	17	–	lbw b Edwards	21
*R. McLaren c and b Crane	16	–	not out	8
J. Clark c McManus b Crane	20			
S. D. Parry c Ervine b Berg	8			
K. M. Jarvis not out	0			
M. W. Parkinson c Ervine b Crane	0			
B 1, lb 13	14		B 6, lb 8, nb 2	16
1/39 (2) 2/49 (1) 3/58 (4) 4/67 (3) 5/88 (5) 6/106 (6) 7/114 (7) 8/141 (9) 9/149 (8) 10/149 (11) (57.5 overs)	149		1/129 (1) 2/190 (3) 3/219 (4) 4/267 (5) 5/302 (6) (5 wkts, 76 overs)	314

Abbott 10–5–23–1; Berg 8–3–12–1; Edwards 12–3–27–2; Dawson 17–2–42–1; Holland 5–3–4–1; Crane 5.5–0–27–3. *Second innings*—Abbott 9–1–47–1; Berg 9–2–29–0; Edwards 12–2–51–1; Dawson 22–7–62–2; Crane 18–0–96–1; Holland 6–2–15–0.

Hampshire

J. H. K. Adams c Davies b McLaren	12
†L. D. McManus c Livingstone b Jarvis	13
S. M. Ervine c Davies b McLaren	21
J. M. Vince c Parry b Jarvis	40
*G. J. Bailey c Livingstone b Parkinson	22
L. A. Dawson b Parkinson	75
I. G. Holland lbw b Jarvis	14
G. K. Berg c Vilas b Jarvis	4
K. J. Abbott c Davies b Jarvis	6
M. S. Crane c Davies b Jarvis	0
F. H. Edwards not out	3
B 8, nb 6	14
1/21 (1) 2/27 (2) 3/86 (3) 4/93 (4) 5/119 (5) 6/149 (7) 7/169 (8) 8/177 (9) 9/179 (10) 10/224 (6) (57.4 overs)	224

Jarvis 18–4–61–6; McLaren 16–4–45–2; Clark 9–0–50–0; Parry 8–1–27–0; Parkinson 6.4–1–33–2.

Umpires: S. C. Gale and J. W. Lloyds.

HAMPSHIRE v SURREY

At Southampton, September 5–8. Drawn. Hampshire 10pts, Surrey 9pts. Toss: Hampshire.

Once again, the weather wreaked havoc, allowing only five overs on the first day, and none on the last morning. It meant there was little significance to the closing stages, although Pope, in just his third first-class match, found time to record a maiden century. The draw was agreed the moment he despatched his 137th ball to the boundary. Earlier, fellow teenager Ryan Patel – on his second appearance – had survived two drops in a diligent 81, after Surrey had been inserted on a slow wicket never quite as awkward as the scores suggested. Responding to 200, Hampshire were in trouble at 60 for six on the second evening, but recovered to gain a lead of 90 thanks to some vigorous tail-wagging, led by Berg. There was a glimmer of a positive outcome when Surrey tumbled to 51 for three, and again at 122 for four, but Foakes and the increasingly free-scoring Pope put on an unbeaten 158 in 40 overs.

Close of play: first day, Surrey 16-0 (Burns 9, Patel 7); second day, Hampshire 129-7 (Holland 34, Berg 0); third day, Surrey 135-4 (Foakes 33, Pope 11).

Surrey

R. J. Burns c Vince b Abbott	12	– lbw b Weatherley	63
R. Patel b Edwards	81	– c Ervine b Dawson	20
S. G. Borthwick lbw b Edwards	0	– c Alsop b Dawson	1
J. J. Roy lbw b Abbott	0	– b Abbott	1
†B. T. Foakes c Vince b Dawson	47	– not out	83
O. J. D. Pope c Bailey b Dawson	13	– not out	100
R. Clarke b Edwards	12		
T. K. Curran b Berg	12		
*G. J. Batty lbw b Dawson	2		
S. C. Meaker not out	3		
J. W. Dernbach c and b Dawson	5		
B 4, lb 7, nb 2	13	B 7, lb 1, nb 4	12
1/25 (1) 2/34 (3) 3/35 (4) 4/109 (5) 5/163 (6) 6/171 (2) 7/180 (7) 8/183 (9) 9/193 (8) 10/200 (11) (65.4 overs)	200	1/44 (2) 2/48 (3) 3/51 (4) 4/122 (1) (4 wkts, 88.5 overs)	280

Edwards 16–1–70–3; Abbott 13–3–31–2; Berg 12–5–34–1; Holland 9–3–32–0; Dawson 15.4–9–22–4. *Second innings*—Edwards 12–1–55–0; Abbott 12–3–55–1; Holland 9–2–22–0; Berg 14–2–49–0; Dawson 27–8–35–2; Weatherley 14–3–46–1; Vince 0.5–0–10–0.

Hampshire

J. J. Weatherley b Dernbach	1
J. H. K. Adams lbw b Curran	14
†T. P. Alsop lbw b Dernbach	0
J. M. Vince lbw b Curran	10
*G. J. Bailey lbw b Batty	51
S. M. Ervine c Foakes b Curran	0
L. A. Dawson c Pope b Clarke	9
I. G. Holland b Meaker	51
G. K. Berg c Foakes b Dernbach	80
K. J. Abbott not out	37
F. H. Edwards b Curran	20
B 4, lb 5, w 2, nb 6	17
1/7 (1) 2/14 (3) 3/20 (2) 4/31 (4) 5/31 (6) 6/60 (7) 7/129 (5) 8/170 (8) 9/263 (9) 10/290 (11) (88.5 overs)	290

Curran 19.5–4–69–4; Dernbach 19–6–51–3; Clarke 15–4–50–1; Meaker 13–3–33–1; Patel 10–0–33–0; Batty 12–2–45–1.

Umpires: M. Burns and D. J. Millns.

At Uxbridge, September 12–15. HAMPSHIRE drew with MIDDLESEX.

HAMPSHIRE v ESSEX

At Southampton, September 19–22. Essex won by 108 runs. Essex 19pts, Hampshire 5pts. Toss: uncontested.

Victory after following on was the most remarkable result of Essex's triumphant season. Trailing by 178, the new champions were languishing at 81 for three in their second innings, seemingly doomed to a first defeat. But Hampshire were thwarted by Lawrence, who put on 147 with Bopara, and then by Foster and Wagner: their ninth-wicket stand added 82. Even so, Hampshire's target was a gettable 185 – and though the pitch was lively throughout, it did not explain their being blown away inside 30 overs, especially after they had batted well in their first innings. Cook, a 20-year-old of genuine pace, snatched his first five-for, while none of Hampshire's top seven passed ten. The result had appeared impossible on the second morning, after valiant bowling from Abbott cut a swathe through the Essex batting. Hampshire, who started the game in fourth, were now vulnerable to relegation: they needed at least a draw in their final match, at Edgbaston, to be sure of staying up. The last time they had lost after enforcing the follow-on was also against Essex, at Bournemouth in 1992 – also the last time Essex were champions.

Close of play: first day, Essex 33-5 (Lawrence 8, ten Doeschate 6); second day, Essex 208-3 (Lawrence 78, Bopara 52); third day, Essex 247-5 (ten Doeschate 5, Porter 1).

Hampshire

J. J. Weatherley lbw b Porter	8	– lbw b Cook	1
J. H. K. Adams lbw b Cook	0	– b Cook	1
†T. P. Alsop b Porter	34	– c Foster b Porter	10
J. M. Vince c Foster b Cook	60	– lbw b Cook	8
*G. J. Bailey c Westley b Wagner	89	– b Cook	0
S. M. Ervine c Chopra b Harmer	11	– lbw b Porter	5
L. A. Dawson b Porter	8	– b Harmer	10
I. G. Holland b Harmer	11	– not out	16
G. K. Berg c Foster b Harmer	14	– c Chopra b Wagner	9
K. J. Abbott c Chopra b Porter	7	– c Browne b Wagner	5
F. H. Edwards not out	0	– c Foster b Cook	11
Lb 8, nb 4	12		
1/0 (2) 2/14 (1) 3/85 (3) 4/121 (4) 5/144 (6) 6/187 (7) 7/214 (8) 8/243 (9) 9/254 (10) 10/254 (5) (67.5 overs)	254	1/1 (1) 2/12 (3) 3/12 (2) 4/12 (5) 5/25 (6) 6/29 (4) 7/37 (7) 8/50 (9) 9/56 (10) 10/76 (11) (29.4 overs)	76

Porter 17–3–53–4; Cook 18–3–84–2; Wagner 12.5–1–37–1; Harmer 12–1–47–3; Bopara 7–1–20–0; Lawrence 1–0–5–0. *Second innings*—Porter 8–2–21–2; Cook 11.4–6–18–5; Wagner 6–0–17–2; Harmer 4–0–20–1.

Essex

V. Chopra b Abbott	5	– c Alsop b Berg	5
N. L. J. Browne b Abbott	0	– lbw b Dawson	24
T. Westley lbw b Edwards	6	– c and b Dawson	36
D. W. Lawrence b Abbott	11	– c Alsop b Edwards	101
R. S. Bopara b Berg	7	– c Vince b Edwards	57
S. J. Cook b Edwards	0	– (11) not out	0
*R. N. ten Doeschate lbw b Abbott	26	– (6) lbw b Edwards	9
†J. S. Foster lbw b Holland	10	– lbw b Abbott	47
S. R. Harmer lbw b Abbott	4	– c Alsop b Holland	8
N. Wagner lbw b Abbott	0	– c Abbott b Dawson	44
J. A. Porter not out	0	– (7) b Abbott	4
Lb 6, w 1	7	B 21, lb 6	27
1/1 (2) 2/12 (1) 3/12 (3) 4/26 (5) 5/26 (6) 6/40 (4) 7/69 (7) 8/75 (9) 9/75 (10) 10/76 (8) (35.2 overs)	76	1/11 (1) 2/54 (2) 3/81 (3) 4/228 (5) 5/243 (4) 6/252 (6) 7/254 (7) 8/272 (9) 9/354 (10) 10/362 (8) (123 overs)	362

Edwards 9–2–16–2; Abbott 11–7–20–6; Holland 8.2–2–20–1; Berg 7–3–14–1. *Second innings*—Edwards 26–5–73–3; Berg 22–8–44–1; Holland 18–6–33–1; Abbott 25–4–88–2; Dawson 31–7–88–3; Weatherley 1–0–9–0.

Umpires: N. J. Llong and A. G. Wharf.

At Birmingham, September 25–28. HAMPSHIRE drew with WARWICKSHIRE. *Hampshire survive in Division One.*

KENT

Summer blues after spring blooms

MARK PENNELL

By the end of the 166th Canterbury Week, Kent supporters might have reached three grim conclusions. Already resigned to an eighth successive season in Division Two, they realised that the integrity of the St Lawrence ground had been severely compromised, and that the new lime tree would never again grace the outfield.

The completion in September of the 54 retirement apartments skirting the Old Dover Road boundary aroused a mixed response: delight that the clatter of building work had stopped, disappointment that the proximity of the flats and their landscaped private gardens would prevent the use of the nearest four pitches, or the placing of the boundary rope beyond the young lime. Freeman House may have been named after Tich, the diminutive Kent leg-spinner, but its size seemed destined to have a lasting impact.

The construction was a noisy backdrop to a season that began so promisingly under new head coach Matt Walker – Jimmy Adams had been appointed West Indies' director of cricket – and ended in a familiar Canterbury tale of underachievement. Four Championship wins in five starts saw Kent do the double over Sussex for the first time since 1983, but they lost momentum and were not helped by an antiquated management structure.

In January, former Kent wicketkeeper and England managing director Paul Downton filled the new post of director of cricket. Then, in February, the unsettled Sam Northeast announced he was joining Hampshire, leaving the captaincy in the hands of Sam Billings – though he was set to miss the first few Championship games because of the IPL.

Kent lost two and drew six of their last nine games. The other fixture, scheduled for Derby in mid-September, was switched to Chesterfield – where drainage is poor – to accommodate a concert by Boyzone. Every day was washed out, prompting the ECB to issue new guidance on the use of outgrounds. After the abandonment came a dispiriting collapse against Glamorgan in the final round; it meant Kent finished fifth, a comedown after their high-flying start.

Batting was their stronger suit: Joe Denly struck 1,165 runs (the fourth-highest in the Championship) and the similarly reliable Northeast 1,017. Sean Dickson was next, with 804, though almost 40% came in one innings: his 318 against Northamptonshire was the second-best for Kent, but could not bring victory on a Beckenham shirtfront.

In the spring, Kent could call on Wayne Parnell and James Harris and, though they played just once together, each lent the attack a balance the county never properly regained once they left – Parnell to team up with South Africa, Harris to rejoin Middlesex. Kent seemed to rely on short stints from overseas stars: as well as Parnell, they tried Yasir Shah, Adam Milne and Jimmy

Sarah Ansell, Getty Images

Joe Denly

Neesham, but with unspectacular results. At least the participation of Milne was largely funded by New Zealand Cricket. The young Hampshire batsman Joe Weatherley also turned up on loan; four times he reached 30, but never 40.

The bowlers mostly underperformed. If Kent had hoped to get the best out of Matt Coles, they were disappointed: he did grab a six-for in defeat at Worcester but, after taking 32 wickets at 41, was deemed unfit for the last two games. Dogged by a poor disciplinary record, Coles was allowed to join Essex with a year left on his contract. Despite their experience, neither Will Gidman nor James Tredwell (who lost his place as first-choice spinner to Imran Qayyum) was used in the second half of the season.

Bucking the disappointing trend was the ageless medium-pacer Darren Stevens who, at 41, bagged 63 first-class wickets – his most productive season yet – at an average of 18. Only three bowlers, all at least 13 years his junior, managed more. Stevens also contributed 822 runs. When he does retire, he will be near impossible to replace.

With Billings often away with England or Delhi Daredevils, Adam Rouse had his busiest summer behind the stumps. He kept well, and showed he could be a useful batsman too. They finished bottom of their group in the Royal London Cup, and sixth in the NatWest T20 Blast, though one more victory would have taken them to the knockouts. As in the Championship, the batting tended to be competitive, the bowling less so. That may change now that South African great Allan Donald has been granted a work permit, and can finally take up his role as assistant coach.

As the refurbishment of the ground neared completion – only the sagging, 90-year-old Frank Woolley Stand needs a facelift – there were calls for new ideas and a revamped management structure. Change had begun at the AGM in March 2017, when Kent's chairman-cum-benefactor, George Kennedy, stepped down after nine years. Without his deep pockets and careful husbandry, Kent's financial plight would have worsened. Instead the annual trading of the club improved by over £1m during his chairmanship. His replacement was Simon Philip, the club's former treasurer; he had been a partner at Deloitte, and his City experience is sure to be tested.

The backroom overhaul gathered pace in November when Jamie Clifford announced his departure after 15 years, the last eight as chief executive. He left to become an assistant secretary for MCC. Affable and softly spoken, he will take pride in having overseen the refurbishment of the Canterbury and Beckenham grounds at a combined cost of around £20m. He will be less happy at the lack of trophies. Ben Green, who joined Kent as operations director in August, takes over.

Championship attendance: 26,092.

KENT RESULTS

All first-class matches – Played 15: Won 5, Lost 2, Drawn 8.
County Championship matches – Played 13: Won 4, Lost 2, Drawn 7. Abandoned 1.

Specsavers County Championship, 5th in Division 2;
NatWest T20 Blast, 6th in South Group; Royal London One-Day Cup, 9th in South Group.

COUNTY CHAMPIONSHIP AVERAGES, BATTING AND FIELDING

Cap		Birthplace	M	I	NO	R	HS	100	Avge	Ct/St
2008	J. L. Denly	*Canterbury‡*	13	23	2	1,165	227	4	55.47	8
2012	S. A. Northeast	*Ashford‡*	13	23	3	1,017	173*	3	50.85	5
2015	S. W. Billings	*Pembury‡*	6	8	2	262	70*	0	43.66	12
	Yasir Shah¶	*Swabi, Pakistan*	3	4	1	131	48	0	43.66	1
2005	D. I. Stevens	*Leicester*	12	20	3	707	100	1	41.58	2
	S. R. Dickson††	*Johannesburg, SA*	12	21	0	804	318	1	38.28	9
	J. A. R. Harris	*Morriston*	4	6	2	146	34	0	36.50	1
	A. P. Rouse	*Harare, Zimbabwe*	10	16	2	491	95*	0	35.07	26/1
2007	†J. C. Tredwell	*Ashford‡*	6	9	2	184	55	0	26.28	5
2015	D. J. Bell-Drummond	*Lewisham‡*	13	23	1	561	90	0	25.50	10
	J. J. Weatherley	*Winchester*	5	8	0	190	36	0	23.75	1
2012	†M. T. Coles	*Maidstone‡*	11	16	2	304	56*	0	21.71	12
	A. F. Milne¶	*Palmerston North, NZ*	5	8	2	121	51	0	20.16	1
	†W. R. S. Gidman	*High Wycombe*	8	14	0	236	51	0	16.85	14
2016	†M. E. Claydon	*Fairfield, Australia*	9	13	5	111	21*	0	13.87	1
	Z. Crawley	*Bromley‡*	4	6	0	75	37	0	12.50	3
	Imran Qayyum	*Ealing*	3	5	1	40	39	0	10.00	2
	†C. J. Haggett	*Taunton*	3	5	0	35	21	0	7.00	0

Also batted: M. D. Hunn (*Colchester*) (2 matches) did not bat; †W. D. Parnell¶ (*Port Elizabeth, SA*) (2 matches) 51*, 41, 8; G. Stewart†† (*Kalgoorlie, Australia*) (1 match) 15*, 0.

‡ *Born in Kent.* ¶ *Official overseas player.* †† *Other non-England-qualified.*

BOWLING

	Style	O	M	R	W	BB	5I	Avge
D. I. Stevens	RM	395.4	102	1,121	62	8-75	7	18.08
J. A. R. Harris	RFM	114.2	25	400	19	4-56	0	21.05
Yasir Shah	LB	155.5	22	533	14	5-132	1	38.07
M. E. Claydon	RFM	241.5	45	884	23	5-54	1	38.43
M. T. Coles	RFM	335	60	1,313	32	6-84	1	41.03
A. F. Milne	RF	184	51	572	13	4-68	0	44.00

Also bowled: D. J. Bell-Drummond (RM) 1–0–10–0; J. L. Denly (LB) 66.3–11–228–7; W. R. S. Gidman (RFM) 56–7–230–5; C. J. Haggett (RM) 96–30–256–7; M. D. Hunn (RFM) 46.5–7–202–7; Imran Qayyum (SLA) 50.5–5–198–6; W. D. Parnell (LFM) 57.1–16–162–7; G. Stewart (RFM) 20–5–89–2; J. C. Tredwell (OB) 66–11–228–3.

LEADING ROYAL LONDON CUP AVERAGES (100 runs/4 wickets)

Batting	Runs	HS	Avge	SR	Ct
D. J. Bell-Drummond	443	138	63.28	87.37	6
D. I. Stevens	260	147	37.14	123.80	5
A. J. Blake	252	116	36.00	158.49	0
S. R. Dickson	179	50	29.83	86.05	1
S. A. Northeast	223	55	27.87	71.24	3
J. L. Denly	163	46	23.28	78.36	5

Bowling	W	BB	Avge	ER
J. A. R. Harris	4	2-28	26.50	7.85
I. A. A. Thomas	5	2-51	34.40	6.61
M. T. Coles	8	4-57	34.75	5.65
J. L. Denly	4	3-20	35.00	5.60
W. D. Parnell	5	3-33	36.80	5.93
C. J. Haggett	5	2-59	40.40	7.76
M. E. Claydon	4	2-51	53.75	6.97
D. I. Stevens	6	2-37	55.16	5.42
J. C. Tredwell	5	3-65	61.80	4.75

LEADING NATWEST T20 BLAST AVERAGES (100 runs/18 overs)

Batting	Runs	HS	Avge	SR	Ct/St
J. L. Denly	567	127	43.61	**150.79**	2
S. W. Billings	361	74	32.81	**148.55**	7/2
S. A. Northeast	345	60	31.36	**137.45**	4
D. J. Bell-Drummond	462	90*	38.50	**135.08**	6
J. D. S. Neesham	203	52	29.00	**127.67**	4
D. I. Stevens	113	19	14.12	**124.17**	1
A. J. Blake	116	27	16.57	**111.53**	11

Bowling	W	BB	Avge	ER
A. F. Milne	15	5-11	12.46	**7.23**
C. J. Haggett	8	2-27	23.00	**7.66**
J. C. Tredwell	4	1-18	54.00	**8.00**
Imran Qayyum	7	2-19	39.14	**8.30**
D. I. Stevens	4	2-25	39.75	**8.67**
M. E. Claydon	11	2-24	35.63	**9.33**
M. T. Coles	8	4-32	44.50	**9.36**
J. D. S. Neesham	14	3-37	33.07	**9.41**

FIRST-CLASS COUNTY RECORDS

Highest score for	332	W. H. Ashdown v Essex at Brentwood	1934
Highest score against	344	W. G. Grace (MCC) at Canterbury	1876
Leading run-scorer	47,868	F. E. Woolley (avge 41.77)	1906–38
Best bowling for	10-30	C. Blythe v Northamptonshire at Northampton	1907
Best bowling against	10-48	C. H. G. Bland (Sussex) at Tonbridge	1899
Leading wicket-taker	3,340	A. P. Freeman (avge 17.64)	1914–36
Highest total for	803-4 dec	v Essex at Brentwood	1934
Highest total against	676	by Australians at Canterbury	1921
Lowest total for	18	v Sussex at Gravesend	1867
Lowest total against	16	by Warwickshire at Tonbridge	1913

LIST A COUNTY RECORDS

Highest score for	**147**	**D. I. Stevens v Glamorgan at Swansea**	**2017**
Highest score against	167*	P. Johnson (Nottinghamshire) at Nottingham	1993
Leading run-scorer	7,814	M. R. Benson (avge 31.89)	1980–95
Best bowling for	8-31	D. L. Underwood v Scotland at Edinburgh	1987
Best bowling against	6-5	A. G. Wharf (Glamorgan) at Cardiff	2004
Leading wicket-taker	530	D. L. Underwood (avge 18.93)	1963–87
Highest total for	384-6	v Berkshire at Finchampstead	1994
Highest total against	371-8	by Somerset at Taunton	2014
Lowest total for	60	v Somerset at Taunton	1979
Lowest total against	60	by Derbyshire at Canterbury	2008

TWENTY20 COUNTY RECORDS

Highest score for	**127**	**J. L. Denly v Essex at Chelmsford**	**2017**
Highest score against	151*	C. H. Gayle (Somerset) at Taunton	2015
Leading run-scorer	**3,128**	**D. I. Stevens (avge 27.92)**	**2005–17**
Best bowling for	**5-11**	**A. F. Milne v Somerset at Taunton**	**2017**
Best bowling against	5-17	G. M. Smith (Essex) at Chelmsford	2012
Leading wicket-taker	**119**	**J. C. Tredwell (avge 28.46)**	**2003–17**
Highest total for	231-7	v Surrey at The Oval	2015
Highest total against	224-7	by Somerset at Taunton	2015
Lowest total for	72	v Hampshire at Southampton	2011
Lowest total against	82	by Somerset at Taunton	2010

ADDRESS

The Spitfire Ground, St Lawrence, Old Dover Road, Canterbury CT1 3NZ; 01227 456886; kent@ecb.co.uk; www.kentcricket.co.uk.

OFFICIALS

Captain 2017 S. A. Northeast
2018 S. W. Billings
Head coach M. J. Walker
Assistant coach 2018 A. A. Donald
High performance director J. R. Weaver
President 2017 C. J. C. Rowe
2018 J. N. H. Rice

Chairman S. R. C. Philip
Chief executive 2018 B. Green
Chairman, cricket committee 2017 G. W. Johnson
Director of cricket 2018 P. R. Downton
Head groundsman S. Williamson
Scorer L. A. R. Hart

KENT v LEEDS/BRADFORD MCCU

At Canterbury, March 28–30. Kent won by 212 runs. Toss: Kent. First-class debuts: M. K. Andersson, O. S. Bocking, W. Cook, S. A. Feszczur-Hatchett, O. J. G. Graham, P. F. McDermott, J. T. Potticary, B. J. Shoare.

A strong Kent side gave the students a tough examination, and ran out comfortable winners. Denly batted over four hours for his 101, Stevens not quite three for his 115. The university bowlers were wayward and, although Oliver Bocking, Seb Feszczur-Hatchett and Oliver Graham all took two wickets, Leeds/Bradford conceded 60 extras, including 45 no-balls – both first-class records in a Kent innings. The reply began promisingly, with openers Steve Bullen and Ben Shoare putting on 58, before Kent's bowlers made regular breakthroughs. Gidman, captain in the absence of Sam Northeast, chose not to enforce the follow-on despite a lead of 166. Four more wickets for Bocking hindered Kent's progress, but a second declaration set a target of 323. The students never came close: Tredwell grabbed three for 33, before Gidman polished things off with three for none in eight balls.

Close of play: first day, Kent 370-6 (Blake 46, Haggett 2); second day, Kent 47-1 (Ball 23, Gidman 17).

EIGHT DIFFERENT WICKET-TAKERS IN A FIRST-CLASS INNINGS

I Zingari* v Gentlemen of the South (226) at Canterbury	1866
Sussex v Hampshire (346) at Portsmouth	1969
Essex† v Glamorgan (340) at Swansea	1974
Maharashtra v Mumbai (381) at Pune	1996-97
Guyana v Windward Islands (467) at Providence	2007-08
Southern Rocks† v Mashonaland Eagles (510) at Masvingo	2010-11
North West† v Namibia (169) at Windhoek	2016-17
Kent v Leeds/Bradford MCCU (204) at Canterbury	**2017**

* *Eleven bowlers used in a 12-a-side game.* † *Nine bowlers used.*

Kent

A. J. Ball b Bocking	2	– (2) c Shoare b Cook	50
S. R. Dickson lbw b Feszczur-Hatchett	32	– (1) b Bocking	4
J. L. Denly b Graham	101		
*W. R. S. Gidman c Andersson b Bocking	8	– (3) c Graham b Bocking	33
D. I. Stevens b Feszczur-Hatchett	115		
A. J. Blake not out	46	– (5) c Andersson b Bocking	19
†A. P. Rouse c Andersson b Graham	4	– (4) b Bocking	35
C. J. Haggett not out	2	– (6) not out	7
J. C. Tredwell (did not bat)		– (7) not out	0
B 8, lb 2, w 5, nb 45	60	Lb 2, w 2, nb 4	8
1/6 (1) 2/75 (2) 3/139 (4) 4/244 (3) 5/328 (5) 6/365 (7) (6 wkts dec, 94 overs)	370	1/5 (1) 2/68 (3) 3/110 (2) 4/138 (5) 5/155 (4) (5 wkts dec, 44 overs)	156

M. E. Claydon and I. A. A. Thomas did not bat.

Bocking 16–1–55–2; Ashraf 16.3–5–50–0; Feszczur-Hatchett 25–5–91–2; Cook 13–0–75–0; Graham 19–1–60–2; Bullen 4.3–0–29–0. *Second innings*—Bocking 15–4–52–4; Feszczur-Hatchett 11–0–31–0; Graham 12–2–38–0; Cook 6–0–33–1.

> "The best of West Indies cricket had little to do with Cricket West Indies."
> Cricket in the West Indies in 2017, page 1016

Leeds/Bradford MCCU

S. F. G. Bullen c Rouse b Claydon	24	– lbw b Claydon	3
B. J. Shoare c Rouse b Thomas	47	– run out	2
M. K. Andersson lbw b Ball	3	– lbw b Haggett	0
P. F. McDermott b Gidman	0	– c Haggett b Tredwell	11
O. J. G. Graham b Stevens	4	– b Thomas	10
C. D. Wallace c Ball b Claydon	19	– c Rouse b Tredwell	23
†J. T. Potticary c Tredwell b Haggett	32	– lbw b Gidman	19
W. Cook b Tredwell	3	– c Ball b Tredwell	0
S. A. Feszczur-Hatchett not out	24	– c Rouse b Gidman	10
O. S. Bocking c Tredwell b Ball	0	– b Gidman	0
*M. A. Ashraf c Blake b Denly	24	– not out	0
B 1, lb 7, w 2, nb 14	24	B 8, lb 5, w 1, nb 18	32
1/58 (1) 2/74 (3) 3/75 (4) 4/92 (5) 5/104 (2) 6/147 (6) 7/153 (7) 8/165 (8) 9/166 (10) 10/204 (11) (77 overs)	204	1/5 (2) 2/6 (3) 3/10 (1) 4/27 (5) 5/58 (4) 6/67 (6) 7/69 (8) 8/109 (9) 9/109 (10) 10/110 (7) (51.2 overs)	110

Thomas 12–1–44–1; Stevens 12–4–28–1; Haggett 12–2–29–1; Claydon 11–2–35–2; Gidman 9–4–13–1; Ball 7–2–10–2; Tredwell 10–6–12–1; Denly 4–0–25–1. *Second innings*—Claydon 10–1–17–1; Haggett 11–5–11–1; Thomas 10–5–28–1; Stevens 7–3–8–0; Tredwell 12–3–33–3; Gidman 1.2–1–0–3.

Umpires: M. Newell and M. J. Saggers.

KENT v GLOUCESTERSHIRE

At Canterbury. April 7–9. Kent won by 334 runs. Kent 21pts, Gloucestershire 3pts. Toss: uncontested. County debuts: J. A. R. Harris, J. J. Weatherley.

A gritty all-round display enabled Kent to start with an emphatic three-day win. On a rare green-tinged Canterbury pitch with good carry, the home batsmen did just enough to quell a promising Gloucestershire attack spearheaded by Norwell who, with eight wickets in the match, was unlucky to finish on the losing side. For the first time since 1962, the entire Kent team made double figures – though only two reached 50 in a total of 298. Dent alone made any headway in the Gloucestershire reply and, once Claydon ended his three-hour innings, they avoided the follow-on only by the skin of their teeth. Claydon and Harris, beginning a loan spell from Middlesex, shared seven wickets. Despite Norwell's five-for, Kent built a commanding lead thanks to useful contributions from Denly (his second half-century of the match), Gidman (against his old county) and Tredwell. Asked to make 396, Gloucestershire fell apart for 61 – something of a recovery from 37 for nine – as Stevens's medium-pace snapped up six.

Close of play: first day, Gloucestershire 9-1 (Dent 2, Norwell 6); second day, Kent 118-4 (Gidman 7, Harris 4).

ALL ELEVEN BATSMEN MAKING DOUBLE FIGURES FOR KENT

Total	*Highest*	*Lowest*		
353	63	12	v Sussex at Hove	1893
303	44	10	v Somerset at Gravesend	1950
551-9 dec	162	11	v Leicestershire at Maidstone	1962
298	**62**	**10**	**v Gloucestershire at Canterbury**	**2017**

In 1876, in a first-class 12-a-side game against the Gentlemen of MCC, 11 Kent batsmen reached double figures (the 12th made a duck).

Kent

First innings		Second innings	
D. J. Bell-Drummond c Hankins b Norwell	11	c Hankins b Norwell	1
J. J. Weatherley c Mustard b Miles	36	c Mustard b Norwell	34
J. L. Denly c Bancroft b Norwell	62	c Mustard b Miles	59
*S. A. Northeast c Dent b Liddle	22	lbw b Miles	8
W. R. S. Gidman c Bancroft b Norwell	10	b Taylor	51
D. I. Stevens c Bancroft b van Buuren	50	(7) b Norwell	0
†A. P. Rouse c Mustard b Miles	13	(8) c Tavaré b Norwell	0
J. C. Tredwell c Mustard b Payne	26	(9) not out	47
M. T. Coles c Norwell b van Buuren	11	(10) lbw b Taylor	0
J. A. R. Harris not out	33	(6) c Mustard b Norwell	13
M. E. Claydon c Hankins b Liddle	17	c Norwell b Liddle	16
B 2, lb 3, nb 2	7	B 11, lb 6	17
1/25 (1) 2/76 (2) 3/134 (3) 4/134 (4) 5/154 (5) 6/205 (6) 7/213 (7) 8/224 (9) 9/262 (8) 10/298 (11) (89 overs)	298	1/3 (1) 2/67 (2) 3/104 (4) 4/109 (3) 5/130 (6) 6/134 (7) 7/134 (8) 8/194 (5) 9/194 (10) 10/246 (11) (75.1 overs)	246

Payne 20–2–80–1; Norwell 18–7–46–3; Liddle 14–3–46–2; Miles 18–7–64–2; van Buuren 14–3–28–2; Taylor 5–0–29–0. *Second innings*—Payne 14–4–27–0; Norwell 16–3–59–5; Liddle 15.1–3–44–1; Miles 16–5–32–2; van Buuren 11–1–43–0; Taylor 3–1–24–2.

Gloucestershire

First innings		Second innings	
C. T. Bancroft b Stevens	1	b Harris	2
C. D. J. Dent b Claydon	67	b Stevens	4
L. C. Norwell lbw b Harris	13	(10) c Rouse b Claydon	24
W. A. Tavaré b Gidman	14	(3) c Rouse b Harris	4
G. L. van Buuren c Tredwell b Claydon	10	(4) b Stevens	3
G. T. Hankins b Claydon	1	(5) c Gidman b Harris	0
*†P. Mustard c Gidman b Stevens	7	(6) c Rouse b Stevens	0
J. M. R. Taylor c Coles b Claydon	0	(7) lbw b Stevens	14
C. N. Miles c Coles b Harris	4	(8) b Stevens	0
D. A. Payne not out	20	(9) c Bell-Drummond b Stevens	6
C. J. Liddle c Rouse b Harris	10	not out	0
Lb 2	2	Lb 4	4
1/1 (1) 2/18 (3) 3/89 (4) 4/104 (5) 5/106 (6) 6/115 (2) 7/115 (7) 8/115 (8) 9/137 (9) 10/149 (11) (59.3 overs)	149	1/2 (1) 2/14 (2) 3/14 (3) 4/14 (5) 5/17 (6) 6/18 (4) 7/24 (8) 8/36 (9) 9/37 (7) 10/61 (10) (20.4 overs)	61

Harris 16.3–3–42–3; Stevens 20–6–42–2; Coles 10–1–28–0; Claydon 12–4–35–4; Gidman 1–1–0–1. *Second innings*—Harris 10–3–26–3; Stevens 9–2–22–6; Coles 1–0–5–0; Claydon 0.4–0–4–1.

Umpires: R. J. Bailey and P. K. Baldwin.

At Hove, April 14–17. KENT beat SUSSEX by 226 runs.

KENT v DERBYSHIRE

At Canterbury, April 21–23. Kent won by 169 runs. Kent 21pts, Derbyshire 3pts.Toss: uncontested.

Kent's third straight victory gave them their best start to a Championship season since 1936. A sporting pitch made for tough batting and dramatic passages of play: 19 wickets fell on the second day, when Derbyshire folded for 159. Before the close, though, Kent had stumbled to 111 for seven, in danger of squandering a first-innings lead of 100. They recovered thanks to nineties from Stevens, scoring at better than a run a ball, and a career-best from Rouse. Kent stretched their advantage above

400 – and well beyond Derbyshire, who did at least have the consolation of taking 20 wickets for the first time since September 2015, with Davis leading the way. Stevens, whose six for 47 had scuppered Derbyshire's first innings, claimed three more, and Harris four, including Wilson, whose 97 was his best since arriving from Surrey in the close season. The first day, which lost 15 overs because of bad light, had ended with honours even: six home batsmen reached 20, but none made it to 42.

Close of play: first day, Kent 238-8 (Rouse 27, Harris 21); second day, Kent 142-7 (Stevens 53, Rouse 24).

Kent

D. J. Bell-Drummond c Smit b Reece	38	– c Hughes b Davis	23
S. R. Dickson c Wilson b Davis	41	– lbw b Palladino	2
J. L. Denly lbw b Davis	0	– c Godleman b Davis	6
*S. A. Northeast c Wilson b Reece	32	– c Smit b Milnes	11
W. R. S. Gidman lbw b Davis	0	– c Wilson b Palladino	3
D. I. Stevens c and b Milnes	17	– lbw b Mendis	90
W. D. Parnell c Hughes b Reece	41	– b Milnes	8
†A. P. Rouse lbw b Palladino	29	– (9) not out	95
J. C. Tredwell lbw b Mendis	7	– (11) c Godleman b Madsen	9
J. A. R. Harris not out	27	– c Reece b Davis	32
M. T. Coles c Milnes b Davis	13	– (8) c Godleman b Reece	7
B 5, lb 3, nb 6	14	B 4, lb 13, w 1, nb 4	22
(84.5 overs)	259	(72.4 overs)	308

1/83 (2) 2/83 (3) 3/87 (1) 4/88 (5) 5/114 (6) 6/162 (4) 7/193 (7) 8/203 (9) 9/240 (8) 10/259 (11)

1/19 (2) 2/31 (1) 3/38 (3) 4/49 (4) 5/51 (5) 6/80 (7) 7/111 (8) 8/201 (6) 9/284 (10) 10/308 (11)

Milnes 17–2–75–1; Davis 20.5–5–75–4; Palladino 21–8–34–1; Reece 13–3–38–3; Thakor 2–0–14–0; Hughes 7–4–4–0; Mendis 4–1–11–1. *Second innings*—Palladino 19–5–68–2; Davis 17–3–48–3; Milnes 11–2–58–2; Reece 8–2–41–1; Hughes 4–1–24–0; Mendis 8–0–38–1; Thakor 1–0–5–0; Madsen 4.4–1–9–1.

Derbyshire

L. M. Reece b Parnell	0	– c Coles b Harris	14
*B. A. Godleman c Gidman b Stevens	0	– c Tredwell b Stevens	4
S. J. Thakor c Coles b Stevens	44	– c Denly b Parnell	6
W. L. Madsen c Gidman b Parnell	56	– lbw b Coles	32
D. Smit lbw b Stevens	11	– b Harris	11
†G. C. Wilson b Stevens	0	– lbw b Harris	97
A. L. Hughes c Rouse b Stevens	12	– c Rouse b Stevens	12
B. M. A. J. Mendis c Rouse b Harris	15	– c Rouse b Stevens	17
T. P. Milnes b Stevens	1	– c Rouse b Harris	11
A. P. Palladino c Bell-Drummond b Coles	5	– not out	14
W. S. Davis not out	8	– c Northeast b Coles	8
Lb 5, nb 2	7	Lb 8, p 5	13
(43.2 overs)	159	(61.2 overs)	239

1/2 (1) 2/4 (2) 3/91 (3) 4/113 (5) 5/113 (6) 6/123 (4) 7/131 (7) 8/133 (9) 9/140 (10) 10/159 (8)

1/8 (2) 2/21 (3) 3/62 (1) 4/76 (4) 5/78 (5) 6/158 (7) 7/188 (8) 8/209 (9) 9/224 (6) 10/239 (11)

Parnell 15–5–46–2; Stevens 17–4–47–6; Harris 5.2–0–38–1; Coles 6–0–23–1. *Second innings*—Parnell 9–3–26–1; Stevens 20–4–63–3; Coles 16.2–4–57–2; Harris 13–3–56–4; Gidman 3–0–24–0.

Umpires: N. L. Bainton and R. T. Robinson.

At Leicester, May 19–22. KENT drew with LEICESTERSHIRE.

KENT v SUSSEX

At Tunbridge Wells, May 26–29. Kent won by 147 runs. Kent 23pts, Sussex 3pts. Toss: Kent.

Doubts over the state of both pitch and outfield at the council-owned Nevill prompted talk of relocation to Canterbury but, thanks to groundstaff from HQ and volunteers from the Tunbridge Wells club, it stayed put. After a closely fought first session, Kent dominated the game, and not even a huge storm that deposited four inches of rain on the region early on the last day could save Sussex. On the first, Denly shrugged off three quick wickets to reach the only century of the match and set up a total of 369. In reply, Sussex were skittled inside 50 overs, Stevens claiming the fourth five-for of a successful spring. Armed with a lead of 205, Northeast chose to bat again and, with the top four all in the runs (Denly faced just 49 balls for his unbeaten 71), asked Sussex to make 504 in almost five sessions. They slumped to eight for three, then 73 for four, before van Zyl, Burgess and Philander showed some mettle. Harris mopped up, ushering Kent to the double over their jaded neighbours.

Close of play: first day, Kent 316-8 (Rouse 32, Tredwell 0); second day, Kent 116-0 (Bell-Drummond 68, Dickson 42); third day, Sussex 182-6 (Burgess 44, Wiese 14).

Kent

D. J. Bell-Drummond c Briggs b Wiese	14	– b van Zyl	90
S. R. Dickson c Burgess b Archer	0	– lbw b Briggs	74
J. L. Denly lbw b Philander	119	– not out	71
*S. A. Northeast c Burgess b Philander	9	– not out	46
J. J. Weatherley c Burgess b Wiese	33		
D. I. Stevens c Nash b Briggs	44		
W. R. S. Gidman lbw b Briggs	42		
†A. P. Rouse lbw b Philander	44		
J. A. R. Harris lbw b Wiese	7		
J. C. Tredwell c Nash b Jordan	18		
M. T. Coles not out	15		
Lb 12, nb 12	24	B 4, lb 1, nb 12	17
1/0 (2) 2/45 (1) 3/58 (4) 4/115 (5) 5/175 (6) 6/260 (7) 7/281 (3) 8/315 (9) 9/330 (8) 10/369 (10) (104.1 overs)	369	1/172 (2) 2/188 (1) (2 wkts dec, 67 overs)	298

Philander 21–7–78–3; Archer 26–9–72–1; Jordan 18.1–1–65–1; Wiese 15–3–54–3; Briggs 18–1–65–2; Nash 3–0–14–0; van Zyl 3–0–9–0. *Second innings*—Philander 8–1–36–0; Archer 8–1–19–0; Jordan 14–1–65–0; Wiese 12–1–63–0; Briggs 16–0–68–1; van Zyl 9–1–42–1.

Sussex

C. D. Nash b Harris	4	– (2) b Stevens	3
H. Z. Finch lbw b Stevens	5	– (1) lbw b Coles	5
L. W. P. Wells c Coles b Stevens	25	– c and b Coles	0
S. van Zyl b Stevens	31	– c Rouse b Denly	78
*L. J. Wright c Tredwell b Coles	12	– c Rouse b Harris	38
†M. G. K. Burgess b Stevens	22	– lbw b Coles	68
C. J. Jordan lbw b Stevens	0	– c and b Denly	0
D. Wiese c Dickson b Harris	36	– b Harris	34
V. D. Philander c Coles b Tredwell	20	– not out	73
J. C. Archer b Harris	0	– lbw b Harris	27
D. R. Briggs not out	0	– lbw b Harris	18
Lb 9	9	Lb 12	12
1/4 (1) 2/37 (3) 3/46 (2) 4/69 (5) 5/100 (6) 6/100 (7) 7/109 (4) 8/164 (9) 9/164 (8) 10/164 (10) (49.5 overs)	164	1/6 (1) 2/8 (3) 3/8 (2) 4/73 (5) 5/158 (4) 6/160 (7) 7/211 (8) 8/263 (6) 9/312 (10) 10/356 (11) (105.4 overs)	356

Harris 8.5–2–37–3; Stevens 17–7–40–5; Coles 17–5–51–1; Gidman 5–1–23–0; Tredwell 2–1–4–1. *Second innings*—Coles 23–2–85–3; Stevens 22–5–72–1; Harris 26.4–2–103–4; Tredwell 17–4–35–0; Denly 17–5–49–2.

Umpires: S. C. Gale and P. J. Hartley.

KENT v DURHAM

At Canterbury, June 8–11. Drawn. Kent 8pts, Durham 12pts. Toss: Durham. First-class debut: M. J. Potts. County debut: Yasir Shah.

Yasir Shah and Claydon frustrated Durham to secure a draw that extended Kent's unbeaten run – and their opponents' winless streak – to six. Outplayed for much of the match, Kent were bailed out by their last pair, who survived 46 deliveries, though by then the dangerous Rushworth had left the field with a sore back. Claydon, once of Durham, told Yasir to take Pringle's looping off-spin, while he saw off McCarthy – who had been buoyed by a career-best six-for in the first innings – with a flurry of nervy cover-drives. Collingwood entrusted the last over to Matty Potts, an 18-year-old seamer making his debut. Yasir defended the first, glanced the second to the fence, defended three more and missed the last, bowled to a field of six slips, two gullies and a short leg. Though unable to force a win, Collingwood enjoyed an excellent game. His 120 underpinned Durham's 448 and, after spurning the follow-on, he hit an unbeaten fifty to help set a target of 484. Northeast followed suit, rescuing Kent from the depths of 123 for eight with an undefeated 109, and then striking a responsible 72; the 41-year-old Stevens claimed his fifth five-wicket haul of the summer.

Close of play: first day, Durham 318-5 (Collingwood 93, Poynter 18); second day, Kent 211-8 (Northeast 97, Yasir Shah 37); third day, Kent 35-0 (Bell-Drummond 17, Dickson 16).

Durham

S. C. Cook lbw b Coles	25	– c Rouse b Claydon	44
K. K. Jennings b Gidman	43	– lbw b Stevens	0
C. T. Steel b Stevens	34	– c Yasir Shah b Coles	43
G. Clark c Rouse b Stevens	13	– b Yasir Shah	83
*P. D. Collingwood c Coles b Stevens	120	– not out	51
R. D. Pringle c Rouse b Coles	71	– st Rouse b Denly	8
†S. W. Poynter b Stevens	35	– c Gidman b Yasir Shah	4
M. J. Potts c Rouse b Stevens	0	– not out	14
B. J. McCarthy b Yasir Shah	24		
C. Rushworth c Bell-Drummond b Coles	57		
G. T. Main not out	0		
B 12, lb 2, nb 12	26	B 10, lb 6, w 2, nb 6	24
1/79 (2) 2/81 (1) 3/123 (4) (136.1 overs)	448	1/0 (2) (6 wkts dec, 70 overs)	271
4/148 (3) 5/289 (6) 6/356 (7)		2/68 (1) 3/161 (3)	
7/356 (8) 8/375 (5) 9/448 (9)		4/213 (4) 5/230 (6) 6/245 (7)	
10/448 (10) 110 overs: 356-7			

Coles 31.1–7–118–3; Stevens 35–8–78–5; Claydon 29–5–112–0; Gidman 14–1–58–1; Yasir Shah 26–6–68–1; Denly 1–1–0–0. *Second innings*—Coles 13–3–51–1; Stevens 14–5–32–1; Claydon 9–3–29–1; Gidman 9–0–22–0; Yasir Shah 19–0–94–2; Denly 6–0–27–1.

Kent

D. J. Bell-Drummond c Jennings b McCarthy	22	– b McCarthy	17
S. R. Dickson lbw b McCarthy	0	– c and b Jennings	46
J. L. Denly c Poynter b McCarthy	4	– c Collingwood b Main	45
*S. A. Northeast not out	109	– lbw b Rushworth	72
J. J. Weatherley b Rushworth	6	– b Main	30
W. R. S. Gidman c Pringle b Rushworth	4	– (7) c Poynter b Rushworth	3
†A. P. Rouse c Pringle b Rushworth	8	– (8) lbw b Rushworth	23
D. I. Stevens c Clark b Main	14	– (6) c Poynter b Pringle	0
M. T. Coles c Jennings b McCarthy	2	– lbw b Potts	30
Yasir Shah c Poynter b McCarthy	48	– not out	39
M. E. Claydon lbw b McCarthy	0	– not out	21
B 4, lb 11, nb 4	19	B 4, lb 11, nb 2	17
1/6 (2) 2/16 (3) 3/29 (1) (64.3 overs)	236	1/37 (1) (9 wkts, 106 overs)	343
4/49 (5) 5/55 (6) 6/63 (7)		2/113 (3) 3/117 (2)	
7/116 (8) 8/123 (9) 9/236 (10) 10/236 (11)		4/180 (5) 5/183 (6) 6/193 (7)	
		7/237 (8) 8/262 (4) 9/309 (9)	

Rushworth 21–3–69–3; McCarthy 19.3–2–63–6; Potts 12–3–33–0; Main 7–0–47–1; Collingwood 5–1–9–0. *Second innings*—Rushworth 25–7–62–3; McCarthy 26–5–105–1; Potts 23–5–70–1; Main 13–2–58–2; Jennings 9–3–18–1; Collingwood 4–1–10–0; Pringle 6–1–5–1.

Umpires: J. H. Evans and S. A. Garratt.

At Worcester, June 19–22. KENT lost to WORCESTERSHIRE by four wickets. *Joe Denly hits a career-best 227 as Kent make a second-innings 474, but they lose their unbeaten record.*

At Nottingham, June 26–29. KENT drew with NOTTINGHAMSHIRE.

KENT v NORTHAMPTONSHIRE

At Beckenham, July 3–6. Drawn. Kent 11pts, Northamptonshire 9pts. Toss: Kent.

In a game awash with runs, Dickson's 318 stood out. A study in concentration, technique and stamina, his 408-ball innings lasted eight hours 40 minutes and included 31 fours and three sixes. It was the highest score on home soil for Kent, and the partnership of 382 he shared with the eye-catching Denly was Kent's best for any wicket. Dickson, South African by birth but the holder of a UK passport thanks to his mother, who comes from Beckenham, had endured a so-so season, with three fifties and four ducks. But now he enabled Kent to declare on 701 for seven; only once, against Essex at Brentwood in 1934, when they amassed 803 for four, had they made more. On the truest of surfaces, Northamptonshire, despite needing 552 to avoid the follow-on, were not cowed. A trio of positive centuries from Duckett (who hit 208 here in 2016), Holden (a career-best) and Rossington helped them pass that target, and consigned the game to meaninglessness. In Kent's second innings, the same trio – who before this game had one first-class wicket from a combined 113 matches – bowled half the overs, with Duckett removing Northeast to collect his maiden first-class wicket. Denly took advantage to become the second player, after Kumar Sangakkara, to reach 1,000 first-class runs for the season. Dickson ended with 378 runs, second only for Kent to Arthur Fagg's 446 (244 and 202 not out) against Essex at Colchester in 1938. All told, there were a dozen centuries in the game, five for contented batsmen and seven for discontented bowlers.

Close of play: first day, Kent 434-1 (Dickson 210, Denly 143); second day, Northamptonshire 180-1 (Duckett 101, Wakely 14); third day, Northamptonshire 528-7 (Cobb 12, White 2).

HIGHEST FIRST-CLASS SCORES FOR KENT

332	W. H. Ashdown	v Essex at Brentwood	1934
318	**S. R. Dickson**	**v Northamptonshire at Beckenham**	**2017**
305*	W. H. Ashdown	v Derbyshire at Dover	1935
295	L. E. G. Ames	v Gloucestershire at Folkestone	1933
275*	M. J. Walker	v Somerset at Canterbury	1996
270*	R. W. T. Key	v Glamorgan at Cardiff	2009
270	F. E. Woolley	v Middlesex at Canterbury	1923
269*	A. E. Fagg	v Nottinghamshire at Nottingham	1953

HIGHEST PARTNERSHIPS FOR KENT

382 for 2nd	**S. R. Dickson (318)/J. L. Denly (182)**	**v Northants at Beckenham**	**2017**
368 for 4th	P. A. de Silva (255)/G. R. Cowdrey (137)	v Derbys at Maidstone	1995
366 for 2nd	S. G. Hinks (234)/N. R. Taylor (152*)	v Middx at Canterbury	1990
352 for 2nd	W. H. Ashdown (332)/F. E. Woolley (172)	v Essex at Brentwood	1934
323 for 3rd	R. W. T. Key (189)/M. van Jaarsveld (168)	v Surrey at Tunbridge Wells	2005
321* for 3rd	A. Hearne (162*)/J. R. Mason (181*)	v Notts at Nottingham	1899
315 for 6th	P. A. de Silva (225)/M. A. Ealham (121)	v Notts at Nottingham	1995
309 for 3rd	G. O. Jones (133)/M. van Jaarsveld (182)	v Glam at Canterbury	2009
307 for 2nd	H. T. W. Hardinge (151)/J. Seymour (170)	v Worcs at Kidderminster	1922
307 for 4th	M. J. Walker (140)/D. I. Stevens (163)	v Warwicks at Birmingham	2005
304 for 3rd	A. H. Phebey (155)/R. C. Wilson (159)	v Glam at Blackheath	1960
300 for 1st	N. R. Taylor (146)/M. R. Benson (160)	v Derbys at Canterbury	1991

Kent

D. J. Bell-Drummond c Rossington b Sanderson	49	– b Sanderson	5
S. R. Dickson c Duckett b Holden	318	– c Duckett b Holden	60
J. L. Denly c Holden b Keogh	182	– not out	78
*S. A. Northeast b Cobb	38	– c Buck b Duckett	27
†S. W. Billings c Wakely b Keogh	42		
A. P. Rouse st Rossington b White	8	– (5) not out	8
M. T. Coles b Holden	24		
J. C. Tredwell not out	6		
B 4, lb 6, w 2, nb 22	34	Nb 6	6
1/129 (1) 2/511 (3) 3/579 (4) 4/645 (2) 5/656 (6) 6/695 (7) 7/701 (5) (7 wkts dec, 143.1 overs) 110 overs: 504-1	701	1/7 (1) 2/108 (2) 3/167 (4) (3 wkts dec, 58 overs)	184

Yasir Shah, M. E. Claydon and M. D. Hunn did not bat.

Sanderson 26–5–80–1; Buck 23–1–110–0; Crook 19–0–103–0; White 35–3–176–1; Keogh 19.1–0–110–2; Cobb 11–0–42–1; Holden 9–0–59–2; Duckett 1–0–11–0. *Second innings*—Buck 4–1–17–0; Sanderson 4–1–7–1; Cobb 19–0–64–0; Crook 2–0–10–0; Holden 14–2–35–1; Rossington 9–1–30–0; Duckett 6–0–21–1.

Northamptonshire

B. M. Duckett c Billings b Coles	105
R. I. Newton c Rouse b Yasir Shah	57
*A. G. Wakely b Hunn	32
M. D. E. Holden c Rouse b Hunn	153
R. I. Keogh b Yasir Shah	19
†A. M. Rossington c Billings b Hunn	112
J. J. Cobb not out	34
S. P. Crook c Tredwell b Coles	12
G. G. White c Denly b Yasir Shah	11
N. L. Buck lbw b Yasir Shah	9
B. W. Sanderson c Claydon b Tredwell	0
B 8, lb 6, nb 10	24
1/113 (2) 2/184 (1) 3/219 (3) 4/255 (5) 5/494 (4) 6/507 (6) 7/525 (8) 8/556 (9) 9/567 (10) 10/568 (11) (156.2 overs) 110 overs: 387-4	568

Coles 31–3–133–2; Claydon 13–3–40–0; Yasir Shah 57–10–165–4; Hunn 21–3–90–3; Tredwell 33.2–6–122–1; Denly 1–0–4–0.

Umpires: P. K. Baldwin and D. J. Millns.

At Canterbury, August 6–8. KENT drew with WEST INDIANS (see West Indian tour section).

KENT v LEICESTERSHIRE

At Canterbury, August 28–31. Drawn. Kent 11pts, Leicestershire 12pts. Toss: Leicestershire. County debut: M. A. Carberry. Championship debut: Z. Crawley.

Stubborn first-innings resistance from Leicestershire's last pair, plus a third-day washout, ensured a draw that dented Kent's promotion hopes. They had dominated the early exchanges, with Leicestershire plummeting to 163 for seven, all to 41-year-old medium-pacer Darren Stevens. But he was denied a tilt at ten when Milnes had Pillans caught behind. Hill added 54 with McKay, then 122 with Parkinson, a tenth-wicket record between the sides. Eventually, Stevens dismissed Leicestershire for a healthy 350; his eight for 75, which included the newly recruited Carberry, his 400th first-class wicket, and Parkinson's 75 were both career-bests. In reply, Northeast batted patiently before falling in sight of a hundred; on a pitch that continued to reward gentle accuracy, Dexter claimed five. A tight finish was on the cards by the second-day close when, with their last pair together, Kent trailed by just 37. But rain stole the next day and much of the last, and winless Leicestershire left with a draw – Kent's fifth in ten.

Close of play: first day, Leicestershire 326-9 (Hill 77, Parkinson 59); second day, Kent 313-9 (Milne 20, Qayyum 22); third day, no play.

Leicestershire

M. A. Carberry lbw b Stevens	18 – lbw b Milne	8
H. E. Dearden lbw b Stevens	11 – lbw b Stevens	4
C. N. Ackermann lbw b Stevens	6 – lbw b Qayyum	34
*M. J. Cosgrove c Northeast b Stevens	40 – c Billings b Coles	34
E. J. H. Eckersley b Stevens	11 – lbw b Claydon	15
N. J. Dexter b Stevens	40 – not out	19
†L. J. Hill not out	85 – c Denly b Qayyum	0
B. A. Raine c Coles b Stevens	6 – not out	11
M. W. Pillans c Billings b Milne	11	
C. J. McKay c Milne b Qayyum	32	
C. F. Parkinson c Coles b Stevens	75	
B 2, lb 1, nb 12	15	Lb 2, w 2, nb 6 — 10
1/24 (2) 2/35 (1) 3/36 (3) 4/83 (4) 5/88 (5) 6/155 (6) 7/163 (8) 8/174 (9) 9/228 (10) 10/350 (11) (101.4 overs)	350	1/14 (2) 2/14 (1) 3/62 (4) 4/94 (5) 5/102 (3) 6/114 (7) (6 wkts, 36 overs) 135

Milne 29–8–103–1; Stevens 25.4–8–75–8; Coles 22–4–79–0; Claydon 16–1–69–0; Qayyum 9–0–21–1. *Second innings*—Milne 6–4–11–1; Stevens 10–1–40–1; Coles 3–0–40–1; Qayyum 10–3–25–2; Claydon 7–3–17–1.

Kent

D. J. Bell-Drummond c Eckersley b Dexter	17
S. R. Dickson c Eckersley b Raine	19
J. L. Denly c Hill b Raine	21
*S. A. Northeast lbw b Dexter	97
†S. W. Billings lbw b Dexter	16
Z. Crawley lbw b Dexter	1
D. I. Stevens lbw b Pillans	46
M. T. Coles c Hill b Parkinson	37
A. F. Milne not out	22
M. E. Claydon c Raine b Dexter	8
I. Qayyum c Hill b McKay	39
B 1, lb 7, nb 2	10
1/34 (2) 2/40 (1) 3/79 (3) 4/109 (5) 5/113 (6) 6/193 (7) 7/242 (8) 8/277 (4) 9/287 (10) 10/333 (11) (93.5 overs)	333

McKay 18.5–3–56–1; Raine 19–2–67–2; Dexter 20–7–76–5; Pillans 18–3–67–1; Parkinson 18–4–59–1.

Umpires: M. J. Saggers and R. J. Warren.

At Chester-le-Street, September 5–8. KENT drew with DURHAM. *Kent's last pair survive 11 balls to earn a draw.*

At Bristol, September 12–15. KENT drew with GLOUCESTERSHIRE.

At Chesterfield, September 19–22. DERBYSHIRE v KENT. Abandoned. *For the second year running, Kent suffer a total washout away from home.*

KENT v GLAMORGAN

At Canterbury, September 25–27. Glamorgan won by five wickets. Glamorgan 20pts, Kent 6pts. Toss: uncontested. First-class debut: G. Stewart.

A young Glamorgan team missing the experience of Jacques Rudolph and Colin Ingram swept aside listless opponents. The three-day defeat brought Kent's season – which began so brightly – to a sombre end. Hogan, whose side included seven Welsh-raised players, took four for 44 as Kent were dismissed for 302; without Denly, who hit his sixth first-class century of the summer and passed 10,000 career runs soon after, they would have been in serious trouble. As it was, they secured a lead of 73. There were three wickets for Haggett, and two for fellow seamer Grant Stewart, a 23-year-old

Australian civil engineer with an Italian mother. On the second afternoon, Billings was unexpectedly required for England's one-day side following the late-night fracas in Bristol involving Ben Stokes and Alex Hales, so Rouse was fetched from a round of golf. He was soon walking out to bat at 24 for four. He made 44, but the honours went to Hogan: nigh unplayable, he broke Denly's left foot with a yorker, and next ball claimed his 500th first-class wicket when Northeast edged behind. Hogan finished with career-best figures of ten for 87 as Kent keeled over for 115. The openers broke the back of a target of 189 and, though Stevens claimed three wickets, victory came soon after tea. It was Glamorgan's first red-ball win in Canterbury for 20 years (though they won the Championship's first pink-ball match in 2011).

Close of play: first day, Glamorgan 18-1 (Brown 1, Murphy 13); second day, Kent 98-6 (Rouse 34, Haggett 0).

Kent

D. J. Bell-Drummond c Cooke b Carey	3	– lbw b Hogan	13
S. R. Dickson c Lloyd b Hogan	11	– c Cooke b Smith	18
J. L. Denly b Lloyd	152	– lbw b Hogan	0
*S. A. Northeast c Lloyd b Carey	6	– c Cooke b Hogan	0
†S. W. Billings c Cooke b Smith	18		
Z. Crawley c Meschede b Hogan	37	– (5) lbw b Smith	1
D. I. Stevens lbw b Hogan	3	– b Hogan	31
C. J. Haggett lbw b Lloyd	21	– b Hogan	0
A. F. Milne c Lloyd b Meschede	33	– not out	6
G. Stewart not out	15	– c Selman b Carey	0
I. Qayyum c Selman b Hogan	0	– c Cooke b Hogan	0
A. P. Rouse (did not bat)		– (6) c Hogan b Carey	44
Lb 1, nb 2	3	Lb 2	2
1/14 (2) 2/14 (1) 3/20 (4) 4/39 (5) 5/107 (6) 6/127 (7) 7/214 (8) 8/271 (9) 9/302 (3) 10/302 (11) (81.2 overs)	302	1/23 (1) 2/23 (3) 3/23 (4) 4/24 (5) 5/37 (2) 6/98 (7) 7/106 (8) 8/114 (6) 9/114 (10) 10/115 (11) (43.2 overs)	115

Rouse replaced Billings, who left to join England's one-day squad.

Carey 17–5–65–2; Hogan 18.2–5–44–4; Smith 20–1–82–1; Meschede 20–5–73–1; Lloyd 6–0–37–2. *Second innings*—Carey 15–7–29–2; Hogan 15.2–3–43–6; Smith 7–2–17–2; Meschede 6–1–24–0.

Glamorgan

N. J. Selman c Billings b Milne	0	– c †Rouse b Stevens	70
C. R. Brown lbw b Stevens	2	– c sub (O. G. Robinson) b Haggett	33
J. R. Murphy c Bell-Drummond b Milne	22	– c Crawley b Stevens	21
K. S. Carlson b Haggett	9	– b Stevens	0
D. L. Lloyd c Billings b Haggett	14	– not out	35
†C. B. Cooke c Dickson b Haggett	49	– c and b Qayyum	8
A. G. Salter c Bell-Drummond b Stevens	20	– not out	17
C. A. J. Meschede c Billings b Stewart	44		
R. A. J. Smith c Dickson b Qayyum	36		
L. J. Carey c Dickson b Stewart	4		
*M. G. Hogan not out	6		
B 2, lb 7, nb 14	23	B 5, lb 1, nb 2	8
1/0 (1) 2/20 (2) 3/32 (3) 4/52 (5) 5/65 (4) 6/130 (7) 7/146 (6) 8/203 (8) 9/213 (10) 10/229 (9) (71.3 overs)	229	1/96 (2) 2/119 (1) 3/119 (4) 4/138 (3) 5/153 (6) (5 wkts, 62.2 overs)	192

Milne 21–6–58–2; Stevens 21–6–42–2; Stewart 11–3–52–2; Haggett 15–7–40–3; Qayyum 3.3–0–28–1. *Second innings*—Stevens 19–5–53–3; Milne 10–1–35–0; Haggett 13–4–22–1; Stewart 9–2–37–0; Qayyum 10.2–2–29–1; Bell-Drummond 1–0–10–0.

Umpires: N. G. C. Cowley and J. W. Lloyds.

LANCASHIRE

Strong and stable – and second

PAUL EDWARDS

There was an air of stability around Old Trafford last September. For the first time in the six years since they won the County Championship, Lancashire had entered the final month of the season neither chasing promotion nor fighting relegation. Only Essex could share their confidence in remaining in Division One and, although Lancashire eventually completed only five wins to the champions' ten, they would probably have accepted the runners-up spot had it been offered in April.

Steven Croft's players secured second place with a fine win over Surrey in the last match, but frequently needed resilience to get out of trouble. They were under pressure in three of the first four Championship games, but resolute batting earned them draws against Surrey and Yorkshire, while victory over Somerset after conceding a lead of 169 was justly celebrated. They relied on a combination of home-grown youth and imported experience. Promoted to open, Alex Davies followed his maiden century, against Essex in the first game, with a hundred against Somerset a fortnight later. The combative Davies, whose career had been threatened by a knee injury only a year earlier, became the first wicketkeeper to score 1,000 first-class runs in a season for Lancashire. National selector James Whitaker watched him make a brilliant 92-ball 97 at Southampton, and he was named in the England Lions squad to tour Australia.

Davies's top-order colleagues had contrasting fortunes. At No. 3, Liam Livingstone consolidated his reputation as one of the most intriguing cricketers in England by making big hundreds in four-day cricket, batting explosively in the Twenty20 Blast, catching most things that came his way at slip, and even taking vital wickets with his part-time spin against Surrey. He didn't do himself justice in two T20 internationals against South Africa. But Haseeb Hameed had a poor season following his much-praised Test debut in India, which had been ended by a broken finger. A few useful one-day innings did not make up for some irresponsible first-class dismissals; instead of resuming his place in the Test side, he had to wait until August for his first Championship fifty. He then looked to be regaining his composure, only to suffer another finger fracture in the penultimate game.

Lancashire's success could also be attributed to the impact of three close-season signings, Ryan McLaren, Dane Vilas and Shivnarine Chanderpaul. All were mature cricketers of pedigree, and all from overseas, which led to some trenchant disapproval. However, if the critics were not calmed by Chanderpaul's vigil against Surrey, or quietened by Vilas's double-hundred against Hampshire, they should have been silenced by McLaren's all-round impact on and off the field. It became clear that the trio's influence extended beyond runs and wickets. In the summer when he celebrated his 43rd birthday, Chanderpaul

Liam Livingstone

scored 831 Championship runs; he agreed to return in 2018. Vilas had another year on his contract, though his fellow South African McLaren went home with the Player of the Year award. Australian seamer Joe Mennie joined as overseas player.

Head coach Glen Chapple and assistant Mark Chilton were trying to strike a difficult balance. While they were committed to fielding at least seven or eight players who had learned their cricket in the North-West, they were also intent on building a side to compete in an eight-team division. The recruitment of former internationals helped, but raised the bar for local cricketers. The most notable casualty was the blameless Luke Procter, who had scored 822 Championship runs in 2016, but played only six first-team games and eventually moved to Northamptonshire. In the short term, though, Chapple showed no sign of wavering. The departure of McLaren and Kyle Jarvis – who decided to resume his international career with Zimbabwe – was offset in the autumn by the arrival of Keaton Jennings and Graham Onions from Durham. Pragmatism seemed to be the watchword.

Jarvis claimed 33 wickets in nine Championship games in his final season at Old Trafford, and played an important role in an attack greatly strengthened by the availability of James Anderson for five matches. Slow left-armer Stephen Parry at last got a chance to take on the main spinner's role, and profited from a season in which his cricket was not confined to the limited-overs formats. Matt Parkinson, a leg-spinner who controlled his length and line while still achieving turn, would benefit from comparable opportunities. Pace bowler Saqib Mahmood's three Championship games revealed sufficient promise for him to join Davies and Livingstone in the Lions squad. It did him no harm to dismiss Kumar Sangakkara the week before the tour party was named.

Lancashire's white-ball campaigns were disappointing. Fourth place in the North Group was not enough to qualify for the later stages of the Royal London Cup, and they finished seventh out of nine in their T20 Blast division, after a melodramatic last evening in which a quarter-final was fleetingly within reach. Hoping to regain their title-winning form of 2015, they announced the return of Australian James Faulkner on a two-year T20 contract at the start of December. A day earlier, the 24-year-old Livingstone had replaced the loyal and uncomplaining Croft as first-team captain.

Championship attendance: 29,250.

LANCASHIRE RESULTS

All first-class matches – Played 15: Won 6, Lost 3, Drawn 6.
County Championship matches – Played 14: Won 5, Lost 3, Drawn 6.

Specsavers County Championship, 2nd in Division 1;
NatWest T20 Blast, 7th in North Group; Royal London One-Day Cup, 4th in North Group.

COUNTY CHAMPIONSHIP AVERAGES, BATTING AND FIELDING

Cap		*Birthplace*	*M*	*I*	*NO*	*R*	*HS*	*100*	*Avge*	*Ct/St*
2010	†S. Chanderpaul††	*Unity Village, Guy*	13	19	3	831	182	3	51.93	3
2017	L. S. Livingstone	*Barrow-in-Furness*	11	19	2	803	224	2	47.23	12
2017	A. L. Davies	*Darwen‡*	14	24	1	916	140*	3	39.82	42/6
	†R. McLaren¶	*Kimberley, SA*	14	19	1	602	107	1	33.44	6
	D. J. Vilas††	*Johannesburg, SA*	14	22	2	662	244	1	33.10	13
2010	S. J. Croft	*Blackpool‡*	9	15	1	409	115	1	29.21	6
2016	H. Hameed	*Bolton‡*	12	21	3	513	88	0	28.50	6
	J. Clark	*Whitehaven*	11	14	1	364	140	1	28.00	0
2003	†J. M. Anderson§	*Burnley‡*	5	6	5	23	13*	0	23.00	3
	T. E. Bailey	*Preston‡*	8	11	1	216	58	0	21.60	1
2015	S. D. Parry	*Manchester‡*	13	16	0	293	44	0	18.31	5
	R. P. Jones	*Warrington*	3	5	0	87	35	0	17.40	3
	J. C. Buttler§	*Taunton*	4	6	0	103	49	0	17.16	3
	†L. A. Procter	*Oldham‡*	4	6	0	71	24	0	11.83	1
2015	K. M. Jarvis	*Harare, Zimbabwe*	9	11	2	106	30	0	11.77	3
	M. W. Parkinson	*Bolton‡*	5	6	3	20	13	0	6.66	1
	S. Mahmood	*Birmingham*	3	4	3	5	4*	0	5.00	1

Also batted: S. C. Kerrigan (cap 2013) (*Preston*) (2 matches) 20*, 59 (2 ct).

‡ *Born in Lancashire.* § *ECB contract.* ¶ *Official overseas player.* †† *Other non-England-qualified.*

BOWLING

	Style	*O*	*M*	*R*	*W*	*BB*	*5I*	*Avge*
S. Mahmood	RFM	69.3	10	256	12	4-50	0	21.33
M. W. Parkinson	LB	76.4	7	308	14	4-68	0	22.00
K. M. Jarvis	RFM	255.3	62	779	33	6-61	2	23.60
J. M. Anderson	RFM	162.3	46	373	15	4-20	0	24.86
R. McLaren	RFM	379.1	87	1,130	45	4-37	0	25.11
T. E. Bailey	RFM	217.2	48	629	25	5-44	2	25.16
S. D. Parry	SLA	322.3	68	777	25	5-45	1	31.08
J. Clark	RM	179.5	23	643	19	4-81	0	33.84

Also bowled: S. J. Croft (RFM/OB) 24.5–2–58–0; H. Hameed (LB) 4–1–9–0; S. C. Kerrigan (SLA) 83–14–287–5; L. S. Livingstone (LB) 109–16–345–7; L. A. Procter (RFM) 46–6–160–6.

LEADING ROYAL LONDON CUP AVERAGES (100 runs/4 wickets)

Batting	*Runs*	*HS*	*Avge*	*SR*	*Ct/St*
J. Clark	270	79*	90.00	143.61	0
D. J. Vilas	408	108	58.28	113.64	3
S. J. Croft	219	127	43.80	106.31	1
K. R. Brown	315	63	39.37	89.48	2
H. Hameed	275	88	39.28	80.40	1
R. McLaren	189	79	31.50	95.93	2
A. L. Davies	211	50	26.37	88.28	8/2
L. S. Livingstone	168	39	21.00	84.42	5

Bowling	*W*	*BB*	*Avge*	*ER*
S. C. Kerrigan	5	3-60	19.00	6.62
J. Clark	10	4-34	25.10	6.66
D. J. Lamb	4	2-51	27.00	5.40
K. M. Jarvis	7	3-42	28.85	5.05
J. M. Anderson	9	2-45	38.44	4.94
R. McLaren	4	3-43	61.75	6.86
S. D. Parry	5	3-55	78.20	5.66

LEADING NATWEST T20 BLAST AVERAGES (100 runs/15 overs)

Batting	Runs	HS	Avge	SR	Ct/St
A. M. Lilley	177	38	19.66	**158.03**	6
R. McLaren	228	77	45.60	**149.01**	2
J. C. Buttler	451	80*	50.11	**144.55**	6/5
L. S. Livingstone	345	61	28.75	**136.36**	9
K. R. Brown	221	61	22.10	**126.28**	0
D. J. Vilas	209	40	19.00	**120.80**	2
S. J. Croft	145	62	20.71	**113.28**	8

Bowling	W	BB	Avge	ER
M. W. Parkinson	14	4-23	13.85	**6.06**
S. J. Croft	2	1-12	56.50	**7.45**
S. D. Parry	6	2-27	48.50	**7.46**
A. M. Lilley	5	2-14	27.40	**8.05**
Junaid Khan	13	3-28	24.30	**8.31**
J. Clark	7	3-26	25.28	**8.85**
R. McLaren	11	2-14	33.45	**9.76**

FIRST-CLASS COUNTY RECORDS

Highest score for	424	A. C. MacLaren v Somerset at Taunton	1895
Highest score against	315*	T. W. Hayward (Surrey) at The Oval	1898
Leading run-scorer	34,222	E. Tyldesley (avge 45.20)	1909–36
Best bowling for	10-46	W. Hickton v Hampshire at Manchester	1870
Best bowling against	10-40	G. O. B. Allen (Middlesex) at Lord's	1929
Leading wicket-taker	1,816	J. B. Statham (avge 15.12)	1950–68
Highest total for	863	v Surrey at The Oval	1990
Highest total against	707-9 dec	by Surrey at The Oval	1990
Lowest total for	25	v Derbyshire at Manchester	1871
Lowest total against	20	by Essex at Chelmsford	2013

LIST A COUNTY RECORDS

Highest score for	162*	A. R. Crook v Buckinghamshire at Wormsley	2005
Highest score against	186*	C. G. Greenidge (West Indians) at Liverpool	1984
Leading run-scorer	11,969	N. H. Fairbrother (avge 41.84)	1982–2002
Best bowling for	6-10	C. E. H. Croft v Scotland at Manchester	1982
Best bowling against	8-26	K. D. Boyce (Essex) at Manchester	1971
Leading wicket-taker	480	J. Simmons (avge 25.75)	1969–89
Highest total for	381-3	v Hertfordshire at Radlett	1999
Highest total against	360-9	by Hampshire at Manchester	2014
Lowest total for	59	v Worcestershire at Worcester	1963
Lowest total against	52	by Minor Counties at Lakenham	1998

TWENTY20 COUNTY RECORDS

Highest score for	103*	A. N. Petersen v Leicestershire at Leicester	2016
Highest score against	108*	I. J. Harvey (Yorkshire) at Leeds	2004
Leading run-scorer	**3,053**	**S. J. Croft (avge 30.22)**	**2006–17**
Best bowling for	5-13	S. D. Parry v Worcestershire at Manchester	2016
Best bowling against	**6-19**	**T. T. Bresnan (Yorkshire) at Leeds**	**2017**
Leading wicket-taker	**114**	**S. D. Parry (avge 24.76)**	**2009–17**
Highest total for	231-4	v Yorkshire at Manchester	2015
Highest total against	**211-5**	**by Derbyshire at Derby**	**2017**
Lowest total for	91	v Derbyshire at Manchester	2003
Lowest total against	53	by Worcestershire at Manchester	2016

ADDRESS

Emirates Old Trafford, Talbot Road, Manchester M16 0PX; 0161 282 4000; enquiries@lccc.co.uk; www.lccc.co.uk.

OFFICIALS

Captain 2017 S. J. Croft
2018 L. S. Livingstone
Director of cricket P. J. W. Allott
Head coach G. Chapple
Assistant head coach M. J. Chilton
Academy director G. Yates

President Sir Howard Bernstein
Chairman D. M. W. Hodgkiss
Chief executive D. Gidney
Head groundsman M. Merchant
Scorer C. Rimmer

At Cambridge, April 2–3. LANCASHIRE beat CAMBRIDGE MCCU by 340 runs.

At Chelmsford, April 7–10. LANCASHIRE drew with ESSEX.

At The Oval, April 14–17. LANCASHIRE drew with SURREY.

LANCASHIRE v SOMERSET

At Manchester, April 21–24. Lancashire won by 164 runs. Lancashire 19pts, Somerset 5pts. Toss: uncontested.

Lancashire's first Championship win in 14 matches followed one of their greatest fightbacks. Eighteen wickets fell on the opening day, when nine Lancastrians scored 16 between them. But on the second, Elgar carried his bat for a patient century for Somerset, adding 96 for the ninth wicket with Leach, who hit a maiden fifty, and establishing a lead of 169. When Gregory reduced Lancashire to 23 for two, Somerset were eyeing an innings victory. But the third wicket put on 245, with a career-best 168 for Livingstone, the stand-in captain, and Alex Davies's second century in four innings. Both mixed application with an unfettered willingness to attack. A total of 463 left Somerset needing 295 from 77 overs. After Jarvis trapped Elgar, and Anderson removed Trescothick and Steven Davies in an exacting post-lunch spell, the remainder offered little resistance to the accurate seam of Clark and McLaren. It was all over by 4.30. By then, Craig Overton's five wickets on the first day, when Livingstone's 68 rescued Lancashire from a disastrous 42 for six, were a distant memory. Livingstone was awarded his county cap at the AGM shortly after completing victory.

Close of play: first day, Somerset 153-8 (Elgar 66, Leach 1); second day, Lancashire 152-2 (Davies 78, Livingstone 57); third day, Lancashire 423-7 (McLaren 34, Parry 22).

Lancashire

First innings		Second innings	
†A. L. Davies c Trescothick b Davey	0	– lbw b Gregory	130
H. Hameed c Davies b Davey	0	– c Trego b Gregory	7
L. A. Procter c Davies b Overton	24	– b Gregory	4
*L. S. Livingstone c Leach b Groenewald	68	– c Elgar b Leach	168
R. P. Jones lbw b Overton	0	– lbw b Overton	35
D. J. Vilas lbw b Overton	4	– lbw b Overton	0
R. McLaren c Elgar b Groenewald	2	– c Elgar b Gregory	45
J. Clark c Abell b Overton	9	– st Davies b Leach	5
S. D. Parry c and b Overton	0	– c Davies b Gregory	44
K. M. Jarvis c Trescothick b Groenewald	1	– c Davey b Groenewald	0
J. M. Anderson not out	0	– not out	2
Lb 1	1	Lb 10, w 1, nb 12	23
1/0 (2) 2/1 (1) 3/35 (3) 4/35 (5) 5/39 (6) 6/42 (7) 7/75 (8) 8/83 (9) 9/84 (10) 10/109 (4) (41.4 overs)	109	1/17 (2) 2/23 (3) 3/268 (1) 4/354 (5) 5/354 (6) 6/360 (4) 7/379 (8) 8/456 (7) 9/461 (10) 10/463 (9) (161 overs)	463

Gregory 8–5–20–0; Davey 12–2–33–2; Overton 13–5–47–5; Groenewald 8.4–6–8–3. *Second innings*—Gregory 32–7–74–5; Davey 20–5–40–0; Groenewald 28–6–87–1; Overton 31–5–98–2; Trego 16–3–66–0; Leach 34–7–88–2.

Somerset

M. E. Trescothick c Davies b McLaren	20	– (2) c McLaren b Anderson	36
D. Elgar not out	113	– (1) lbw b Jarvis	8
*T. B. Abell lbw b McLaren	1	– c Davies b McLaren	0
J. C. Hildreth b Procter	12	– lbw b McLaren	43
†S. M. Davies c Davies b Anderson	1	– b Anderson	3
P. D. Trego lbw b McLaren	19	– c Livingstone b Clark	7
L. Gregory lbw b Procter	9	– c Livingstone b Clark	4
J. H. Davey c McLaren b Procter	0	– lbw b McLaren	2
C. Overton lbw b McLaren	8	– not out	17
M. J. Leach c Davies b Clark	52	– c Hameed b Clark	0
T. D. Groenewald b Jarvis	20	– b McLaren	0
B 5, lb 14, nb 4	23	B 9, lb 1	10
1/42 (1) 2/44 (3) 3/63 (4) 4/67 (5) 5/119 (6) 6/134 (7) 7/134 (8) 8/145 (9) 9/241 (10) 10/278 (11) (93 overs)	278	1/29 (1) 2/38 (3) 3/78 (2) 4/86 (5) 5/99 (6) 6/103 (4) 7/107 (8) 8/117 (7) 9/129 (10) 10/130 (11) (47.5 overs)	130

Anderson 26–5–54–1; Jarvis 19–4–60–1; Clark 4–0–16–1; McLaren 25–5–76–4; Procter 13–0–43–3; Livingstone 2–0–7–0; Parry 4–3–3–0. *Second innings*—Anderson 14–7–30–2; Jarvis 10–5–28–1; McLaren 11.5–0–37–4; Parry 4–0–13–0; Clark 8–3–12–3.

Umpires: R. J. Bailey and M. Burns.

LANCASHIRE v YORKSHIRE

At Manchester, May 19–22. Drawn. Lancashire 10pts, Yorkshire 9pts. Toss: Yorkshire.

The Roses match never threatened to achieve a result, but it was still memorable for four contrasting centuries, three of them by Yorkshire. The Lancashire attack could be pleased with their early efforts, especially after Anderson tore a groin muscle (Kyle Jarvis was already out with a bad thumb). But from 178 for six, Leaning and Hodd fought back. Leaning reached his first hundred since June 2015 on a rain-shortened second day which ended with Brooks unbeaten on 94; their 167-run partnership was easily a Roses record for the eighth wicket. Brooks brought up his maiden century next morning, and celebrated with a fifth six, before bowling Hameed for his third duck in four innings. Lancashire were 68 for four straight after lunch on the third day – but their own recovery was led by Chanderpaul, in the tough tradition of these games. He completed his 75th first-class century shortly before being bowled round his legs by Coad, but McLaren and Parry saved the follow-on on the fourth morning, and Handscomb hit a sublime 76-ball hundred on the final afternoon.

Close of play: first day, Yorkshire 251-6 (Leaning 54, Hodd 41); second day, Yorkshire 421-7 (Leaning 118, Brooks 94); third day, Lancashire 264-6 (McLaren 63, Parry 8).

Yorkshire

A. Lyth c Anderson b Bailey	0	– b Kerrigan	9
A. Z. Lees b Anderson	9	– not out	62
P. S. P. Handscomb lbw b McLaren	29	– not out	101
*G. S. Ballance c Parry b Bailey	74		
J. A. Leaning c McLaren b Bailey	118		
T. T. Bresnan b McLaren	13		
Azeem Rafiq c Croft b Parry	16		
†A. J. Hodd b Bailey	44		
J. A. Brooks not out	109		
B. O. Coad not out	10		
B 10, lb 14, nb 2	26	B 2, lb 2, w 1	5
1/9 (1) 2/9 (2) 3/90 (3) 4/138 (4) 5/159 (6) 6/178 (7) 7/256 (8) 8/423 (5) (8 wkts dec, 147 overs) 110 overs: 293-7	448	1/24 (1) (1 wkt dec, 36 overs)	177

R. J. Sidebottom did not bat.

Anderson 5.3–4–5–1; Bailey 35–5–116–4; McLaren 30.3–11–60–2; Parry 43–8–112–1; Kerrigan 22–1–86–0; Livingstone 6–0–31–0; Croft 5–0–14–0. *Second innings*—McLaren 3–0–11–0; Bailey 6–2–13–0; Kerrigan 8–1–65–1; Parry 9–0–33–0; Livingstone 7–0–37–0; Croft 3–0–14–0.

Lancashire

†A. L. Davies c Hodd b Sidebottom	39	S. C. Kerrigan b Bresnan	59
H. Hameed b Brooks	0	J. M. Anderson not out	8
L. S. Livingstone c Lyth b Sidebottom	4		
*S. J. Croft c Handscomb b Bresnan	13	Lb 8, w 1, nb 2	11
S. Chanderpaul b Coad	106		
D. J. Vilas c Hodd b Azeem Rafiq	29	1/10 (2) 2/15 (3) 3/39 (4) (129.4 overs)	432
R. McLaren c Hodd b Azeem Rafiq	84	4/68 (1) 5/135 (6) 6/247 (5)	
S. D. Parry c Leaning b Azeem Rafiq	39	7/317 (8) 8/344 (7) 9/401 (9)	
T. E. Bailey lbw b Bresnan	40	10/432 (10) 110 overs: 328-7	

Sidebottom 22–4–60–2; Brooks 19–3–71–1; Bresnan 18.4–3–69–3; Coad 22–3–70–1; Azeem Rafiq 38–4–128–3; Lyth 8–0–16–0; Leaning 2–0–10–0.

Umpires: N. G. B. Cook and J. W. Lloyds.

At Leeds, June 2–4. LANCASHIRE lost to YORKSHIRE by ten wickets.

LANCASHIRE v MIDDLESEX

At Southport, June 9–12. Lancashire won by eight wickets. Lancashire 22pts, Middlesex 3pts. Toss: Middlesex.

Middlesex could have few complaints after their first defeat in 21 Championship matches since the end of 2015: Lancashire batted more tenaciously and bowled more tightly on a testing pitch at Trafalgar Road. Fourteen wickets fell on the opening day, with three Middlesex players caught down the leg side, but Simpson made a resolute unbeaten 53, and their first-innings 180 looked competitive when Murtagh struck with the second and third balls of Lancashire's reply. The other batsmen worked hard, however, and ground out a 129-run lead after the loss of the second day's play. They were grateful for a ninth-wicket stand of 87 between McLaren and Bailey, who beat his previous career-best with successive sixes, but was last out next ball. The 31-year-old Parry took five wickets in a Championship innings for the first time in his career, while Davies, who had caught six in Middlesex's first innings, finished with ten dismissals in the match, both one shy of Lancashire records. Despite Malan's obdurate 52, Lancashire needed only 108 to win; Hameed seized the opportunity to make a few runs after a difficult start to the season. Chanderpaul equalled a world record in this game when he played on his 115th first-class ground.

Close of play: first day, Lancashire 123-4 (Chanderpaul 32, Vilas 24); second day, no play; third day, Middlesex 156-6 (Malan 45, Harris 15).

PLAYERS APPEARING ON MOST FIRST-CLASS GROUNDS

115	T. W. Graveney	1948 to 1971-72	113	P. E. Richardson	1949 to 1965
115	Mushtaq Mohammad	1956-57 to 1985	112	S. R. Tendulkar	1988-89 to 2013-14
115	**S. Chanderpaul**	**1991-92 to 2017**	112	R. Dravid	1990-91 to 2011-12
114	M. J. K. Smith	1951 to 1975	111	F. J. Titmus	1949 to 1982
113	J. M. Parks	1949 to 1976	110	R. W. Taylor	1960 to 1988

The player who appeared on most UK grounds was G. L. Berry of Leicestershire, who played on 82.

Middlesex

S. D. Robson c Davies b Bailey	15	– (2) c Croft b McLaren	42
N. R. T. Gubbins c Davies b Mahmood	1	– (1) c Davies b Mahmood	1
S. S. Eskinazi c Davies b McLaren	30	– b Parry	34
D. J. Malan c Chanderpaul b Bailey	2	– c Davies b McLaren	52
P. R. Stirling c Davies b Mahmood	49	– lbw b Parry	12
†J. A. Simpson not out	53	– c Vilas b Parry	0
*J. E. C. Franklin b Mahmood	1	– b Mahmood	0
J. A. R. Harris c Davies b Clark	6	– c Davies b McLaren	19
T. S. Roland-Jones c Davies b Clark	4	– lbw b Parry	31
T. J. Murtagh c Croft b McLaren	0	– st Davies b Parry	27
R. H. Patel c Parry b Clark	5	– not out	0
B 2, lb 6, nb 6	14	Lb 13, w 3, nb 2	18
1/18 (2) 2/30 (1) 3/38 (4) 4/72 (3) 5/143 (5) 6/151 (7) 7/166 (8) 8/170 (9) 9/171 (10) 10/180 (11) (51 overs)	180	1/5 (1) 2/64 (3) 3/80 (2) 4/99 (5) 5/99 (6) 6/110 (7) 7/169 (8) 8/180 (4) 9/229 (10) 10/236 (9) (71.3 overs)	236

Bailey 16–3–47–2; Mahmood 14–2–63–3; McLaren 11–2–26–2; Clark 10–0–36–3. *Second innings*—Bailey 16–1–61–0; Mahmood 13–0–57–2; Parry 21.3–2–45–5; McLaren 17–4–48–3; Croft 2–0–5–0; Livingstone 2–0–7–0.

Lancashire

†A. L. Davies c Simpson b Murtagh	0	– c Simpson b Roland-Jones	13
H. Hameed c Simpson b Harris	18	– not out	38
L. S. Livingstone c Simpson b Murtagh	0	– c Simpson b Roland-Jones	22
*S. J. Croft c Patel b Murtagh	31	– not out	34
S. Chanderpaul c Robson b Murtagh	32		
D. J. Vilas c Franklin b Murtagh	27		
R. McLaren b Murtagh	75		
J. Clark lbw b Harris	38		
S. D. Parry c Malan b Harris	4		
T. E. Bailey c Eskinazi b Harris	58		
S. Mahmood not out	1		
B 4, lb 15, nb 6	25	Lb 1, w 1, nb 2	4
1/0 (1) 2/0 (3) 3/50 (2) 4/74 (4) 5/125 (5) 6/136 (6) 7/198 (8) 8/204 (9) 9/291 (7) 10/309 (10) (95.3 overs)	309	1/13 (1) 2/49 (3) (2 wkts, 30.2 overs)	111

Murtagh 28–7–63–6; Roland-Jones 29–9–84–0; Harris 30.3–2–119–4; Patel 7–0–20–0; Stirling 1–0–4–0. *Second innings*—Murtagh 5–2–16–0; Roland-Jones 8–0–34–2; Harris 5–1–19–0; Patel 7.2–1–28–0; Stirling 5–0–13–0.

Umpires: P. J. Hartley and S. J. O'Shaughnessy.

LANCASHIRE v HAMPSHIRE

At Manchester, June 19–22. Lancashire won by an innings and 30 runs. Lancashire 24pts, Hampshire 5pts. Toss: Hampshire.

Hampshire's position looked healthy on the second afternoon. A fine century from Bailey and 97 from Abbott, who ran out of partners in sight of a maiden hundred, had set up a respectable 395, and Lancashire were 69 for three. Two days later, however, an innings victory lifted the home side to second place in the Championship. Hampshire's total had begun to look inadequate as three Lancashire batsmen made centuries in an innings for the first time since 2004. Davies reached his third of the summer before holing out at deep square leg; Vilas survived straightforward chances to slip and mid-off early on the third morning, and went on to a career-best 244, the highest score by a Lancashire No. 6 (previously Graham Lloyd's 225 at Headingley in 1997), and added 231 with McLaren, a sixth-wicket record between these sides. Anderson, like Jarvis returning from injury, bowled magnificently for three wickets as Hampshire collapsed to 50 for five on a steamy evening.

An hour's rain, plus stubborn resistance from McManus and Berg, delayed Lancashire until mid-afternoon on the final day, by which time McLaren, who had spent the previous two seasons at Southampton, had added match figures of five for 99 to his century.

Close of play: first day, Hampshire 351-8 (Abbott 76, Taylor 18); second day, Lancashire 278-5 (Vilas 76, McLaren 23); third day, Hampshire 50-5 (Ervine 1, Salisbury 0).

Hampshire

M. A. Carberry c Davies b McLaren	14	– b Jarvis	10
J. H. K. Adams c Jones b Jarvis	16	– lbw b Anderson	0
R. R. Rossouw c and b Jarvis	4	– c Croft b Anderson	0
J. M. Vince lbw b Procter	22	– c Jones b McLaren	29
*G. J. Bailey b Anderson	127	– lbw b Anderson	10
S. M. Ervine c Davies b Procter	7	– b Jarvis	13
†L. D. McManus c Anderson b Clark	15	– (8) lbw b McLaren	24
G. K. Berg lbw b Parry	27	– (9) c Davies b Jarvis	49
K. J. Abbott not out	97	– (10) c Davies b McLaren	11
B. J. Taylor c McLaren b Anderson	18	– (11) not out	17
M. E. T. Salisbury c Chanderpaul b McLaren	14	– (7) c Vilas b Anderson	0
B 5, lb 6, w 15, nb 8	34	Lb 5	5

1/30 (2) 2/36 (3) 3/38 (1)	(114.1 overs) 395	1/3 (2) 2/3 (3)	(56.5 overs) 168
4/107 (4) 5/125 (6) 6/177 (7)		3/15 (1) 4/26 (5)	
7/232 (8) 8/314 (5) 9/352 (10)		5/50 (4) 6/51 (7) 7/69 (6)	
10/395 (11)	110 overs: 386-9	8/108 (8) 9/120 (10) 10/168 (9)	

Anderson 28–7–89–2; Jarvis 23–5–70–2; McLaren 21.1–2–58–2; Parry 8–0–45–1; Clark 20–3–73–1; Procter 14–3–49–2. *Second innings*—Anderson 15–5–20–4; Jarvis 14.5–2–49–3; McLaren 13–5–41–3; Parry 8–2–30–0; Clark 6–1–23–0.

Lancashire

†A. L. Davies c Carberry b Vince	115
R. P. Jones lbw b Berg	2
L. A. Procter b Berg	8
*S. J. Croft lbw b Abbott	1
S. Chanderpaul st McManus b Taylor	33
D. J. Vilas c Ervine b Salisbury	244
R. McLaren lbw b Berg	107
J. Clark lbw b Salisbury	24
S. D. Parry c Adams b Taylor	4
K. M. Jarvis c Carberry b Berg	30
J. M. Anderson not out	0
B 11, lb 9, w 1, nb 4	25

1/5 (2) 2/31 (3) 3/69 (4) 4/143 (5) 5/223 (1) 6/454 (7) 7/495 (8) 8/506 (9) 9/564 (10) 10/593 (6) (146.2 overs) 593

110 overs: 418-5

Berg 38–9–111–4; Abbott 27–7–75–1; Taylor 40–1–180–2; Salisbury 26.2–2–127–2; Ervine 12–0–67–0; Vince 3–0–13–1.

Umpires: P. K. Baldwin and N. A. Mallender.

At Birmingham, June 26–29. LANCASHIRE drew with WARWICKSHIRE.

At Southampton, August 6–9. LANCASHIRE drew with HAMPSHIRE.

LANCASHIRE v WARWICKSHIRE

At Manchester, August 28–31. Lancashire won by eight wickets. Lancashire 24pts, Warwickshire 2pts. Toss: Warwickshire.

Lancashire's maximum-points win closed the gap on leaders Essex, though they still trailed by 36 once their rivals beat Somerset. But a heavy loss left bottom-placed Warwickshire little hope of escape. It seemed likely after they managed a mediocre 200 batting first, which would have been worse but for Patel's 76-run stand with No. 10 Stone, playing his first Championship game for 15 months. Acting-captain McLaren took three wickets in the opening session, and Jarvis six out of seven in the next (his second successive six-for). By contrast, only three fell next day, as Lancashire confirmed their dominance. Livingstone carefully compiled a career-best 224 over 438 minutes, yet also hit four sixes; he and Chanderpaul added 211. Facing a deficit of 304, Warwickshire made a better fist of their second innings, though McLaren again removed Trott and Bell cheaply. But the home side could wait, and Parkinson's leg-spin made the outcome all but certain. Ambrose delayed it with a determined century, his first of the season, but neither he nor the rain which wiped out the fourth morning could deny Lancashire.

Close of play: first day, Lancashire 112-3 (Livingstone 41, Parry 15); second day, Lancashire 484-6 (Livingstone 215, McLaren 13); third day, Warwickshire 275-6 (Ambrose 76, Patel 18).

Warwickshire

First innings		Second innings	
A. R. I. Umeed c Davies b Jarvis	44	c Davies b Clark	19
D. P. Sibley lbw b McLaren	1	c Hameed b Livingstone	57
*I. J. L. Trott c Buttler b McLaren	4	lbw b McLaren	16
I. R. Bell c Buttler b McLaren	14	lbw b McLaren	15
M. J. Lamb b Jarvis	23	c Livingstone b Parkinson	26
†T. R. Ambrose c Davies b Jarvis	8	lbw b Parkinson	104
K. H. D. Barker lbw b Jarvis	0	lbw b Parkinson	22
J. S. Patel b Jarvis	47	lbw b McLaren	30
C. J. C. Wright lbw b McLaren	0	b Jarvis	11
O. P. Stone c Davies b Jarvis	32	not out	7
R. N. Sidebottom not out	0	b Jarvis	0
Lb 9, nb 18	27	B 7, lb 6, w 1, nb 18, p 5	37
1/3 (2) 2/15 (3) 3/41 (4) 4/92 (1) 5/106 (6) 6/106 (7) 7/115 (5) 8/119 (9) 9/195 (10) 10/200 (8) (62.2 overs)	200	1/52 (1) 2/91 (3) 3/111 (4) 4/117 (2) 5/183 (5) 6/229 (7) 7/315 (8) 8/326 (9) 9/339 (6) 10/344 (11) (104 overs)	344

McLaren 18–5–45–4; Jarvis 18.2–4–67–6; Clark 8–1–25–0; Parry 14–5–27–0; Parkinson 4–0–27–0. *Second innings*—McLaren 25–6–80–3; Jarvis 25–7–77–2; Livingstone 21–5–59–1; Clark 11–0–46–1; Parry 7–0–20–0; Parkinson 15–0–44–3.

Lancashire

First innings		Second innings	
†A. L. Davies c Umeed b Sidebottom	20	lbw b Barker	11
H. Hameed c Umeed b Wright	15	lbw b Barker	21
L. S. Livingstone c Lamb b Sidebottom	224	not out	3
D. J. Vilas b Stone	6	not out	2
S. D. Parry c Lamb b Patel	43		
S. Chanderpaul c Patel b Wright	95		
J. C. Buttler c Sibley b Umeed	49		
*R. McLaren c Patel b Sidebottom	21		
J. Clark not out	3		
B 12, lb 12, nb 4	28	B 5	5
1/32 (2) 2/44 (1) 3/80 (4) 4/165 (5) 5/376 (6) 6/458 (7) 7/501 (3) 8/504 (8) (8 wkts dec, 125 overs) 110 overs: 428-5	504	1/22 (1) 2/35 (2) (2 wkts, 7.2 overs)	42

K. M. Jarvis and M. W. Parkinson did not bat.

Barker 27–5–80–0; Stone 17–3–70–1; Sidebottom 18–4–71–3; Wright 24–2–83–2; Patel 32–2–140–1; Sibley 2–0–17–0; Umeed 5–0–19–1. *Second innings*—Barker 4–0–18–2; Patel 3.2–0–19–0.

Umpires: R. J. Evans and D. J. Millns.

LANCASHIRE v ESSEX

At Manchester, September 5–8. Drawn. Lancashire 9pts, Essex 9pts. Toss: uncontested. Championship debut: S. J. Cook.

Rain ruined a match billed as a Championship decider, with half the playing time lost. The first day was a washout and, under cloudy skies and on a pitch covered for 48 hours, Lancashire were unsurprisingly asked to bat next morning. They didn't do badly in the circumstances, and Hameed's unbeaten 85 by stumps reflected well on his composure and technique. Having spent 108 balls over his first 11 runs, he batted more freely in the evening, hitting 55 from 87, and adding 77 for the eighth wicket with Parry. Though Hameed was Porter's fifth victim early next day, a 57-run stand between Bailey and Jarvis meant the last four wickets had more than tripled the score. McLaren's removal of Browne and Lawrence encouraged hopes of embarrassing the leaders, but these were stifled first by the patience of Chopra and Bopara, then by the rain's return: there were only 32 overs on the final day. Essex declared to avoid conceding a third bowling point; with nothing to gain, Lancashire reciprocated without facing another ball, and a merciful draw was agreed.

Close of play: first day, no play; second day, Lancashire 222-8 (Hameed 85, Bailey 0); third day, Essex 115-4 (Wheater 15).

Lancashire

A. L. Davies c Harmer b Porter	0		
H. Hameed lbw b Porter	88		
L. S. Livingstone b Cook	7		
D. J. Vilas lbw b Porter	7		
S. Chanderpaul c Foster b Walter	23		
†J. C. Buttler c Lawrence b Porter	13		
*R. McLaren b Harmer	22		
J. Clark c Lawrence b Cook	20		
S. D. Parry c Foster b Porter	35		
T. E. Bailey not out	34		
K. M. Jarvis b Harmer	26		
B 7, lb 6, nb 2	15		
1/0 (1) 2/9 (3) 3/22 (4) 4/46 (5) 5/65 (6) 6/92 (7) 7/145 (8) 8/222 (9) 9/233 (2) 10/290 (11) (95.2 overs)	290	(no wkt dec, 0 overs)	0

Porter 24–2–73–5; Cook 26–8–59–2; Harmer 23.2–3–81–2; Walter 12–4–28–1; Bopara 8–1–29–0; Ashar Zaidi 2–0–7–0.

Essex

*V. Chopra lbw b Bailey	40
N. L. J. Browne b McLaren	6
D. W. Lawrence c Vilas b McLaren	12
R. S. Bopara c Livingstone b Parry	34
A. J. A. Wheater c Vilas b McLaren	21
†J. S. Foster b Bailey	17
Ashar Zaidi c Buttler b McLaren	6
P. I. Walter not out	32
S. R. Harmer lbw b Clark	11
J. A. Porter not out	7
B 4, lb 7, w 1, nb 4	16
1/9 (2) 2/23 (3) 3/81 (1) 4/115 (4) 5/141 (5) 6/147 (7) 7/151 (6) 8/172 (9) (8 wkts dec, 80 overs)	202

S. J. Cook did not bat.

McLaren 20–8–45–4; Bailey 22–6–54–2; Jarvis 15–5–36–0; Clark 13–1–34–1; Livingstone 4–1–10–0; Parry 6–1–12–1.

Umpires: S. J. O'Shaughnessy and A. G. Wharf.

At Taunton, September 12–15. LANCASHIRE lost to SOMERSET by seven wickets.

At Lord's, September 19–21. LANCASHIRE lost to MIDDLESEX by 36 runs.

LANCASHIRE v SURREY

At Manchester, September 25–28. Lancashire won by seven wickets. Lancashire 20pts, Surrey 4pts. Toss: Lancashire.

Lancashire's players gave Sangakkara a guard of honour on his final first-class appearance, but they won the battle for second place, despite starting three points behind their opponents. On the opening day, Mahmood returned a career-best four for 50 in his fourth first-class match, though he could not make it five as Surrey declared to deny Lancashire a final bowling point. Next day, Davies became the first keeper to score 1,000 in a season for Lancashire, but was one of three wickets for Clarke as the home side slid to 84 for five by lunch. Then Croft's first first-class hundred for 15 months, and his half-century stands – with McLaren, Bailey and Parry – helped carve out a 67-run lead, which Surrey's openers cancelled out by the close. Burns and Stoneman reached 154 on the third morning before the spin of Livingstone and Parry knocked down all ten for 88. Livingstone followed his career-best six wickets with an unbeaten fifty, which seemed likely to secure a three-day win until bad light intervened. It took only six overs on the last morning, when Chanderpaul concluded by hitting Borthwick for successive sixes and a four. End of term, indeed.

Close of play: first day, Lancashire 17-0 (Jones 7, Davies 10); second day, Surrey 79-0 (Burns 27, Stoneman 44); third day, Lancashire 132-3 (Livingstone 51, Chanderpaul 14).

Surrey

R. J. Burns c Chanderpaul b Mahmood	18	– lbw b Parry	45
M. D. Stoneman b Parkinson	24	– c Vilas b Livingstone	98
S. G. Borthwick lbw b Mahmood	30	– c Vilas b Livingstone	4
K. C. Sangakkara c Jones b Mahmood	14	– not out	35
†B. T. Foakes b Parry	10	– c Parry b Livingstone	0
O. J. D. Pope st Davies b Parkinson	22	– c Mahmood b Livingstone	3
S. M. Curran not out	56	– b Parry	0
R. Clarke lbw b Mahmood	7	– lbw b Livingstone	13
*G. J. Batty c Parkinson b Parry	0	– c and b Livingstone	33
S. C. Meaker not out	7	– b Parry	0
J. W. Dernbach (did not bat)		– lbw b Parry	0
B 3, lb 8, nb 2	13	Lb 3, nb 8	11
1/47 (1) 2/51 (2) 3/80 (4) 4/105 (3) 5/112 (5) 6/166 (6) 7/183 (8) 8/184 (9) (8 wkts dec, 73.3 overs)	201	1/154 (2) 2/156 (1) 3/160 (3) 4/160 (5) 5/174 (6) 6/174 (7) 7/197 (8) 8/241 (9) 9/242 (10) 10/242 (11) (64.5 overs)	242

Bailey 13–6–30–0; McLaren 12–4–26–0; Mahmood 17.3–4–50–4; Parry 14–1–42–2; Parkinson 17–4–42–2. *Second innings*—Bailey 9–0–34–0; McLaren 9–0–51–0; Mahmood 2–0–18–0; Parkinson 4–0–22–0; Parry 20.5–3–59–4; Croft 2–0–3–0; Livingstone 18–1–52–6.

Lancashire

R. P. Jones c Borthwick b Clarke	15	– c Meaker b Batty	35
†A. L. Davies c Stoneman b Clarke	54	– lbw b Clarke	30
L. S. Livingstone lbw b Batty	1	– not out	69
*S. J. Croft c Foakes b Curran	115	– b Clarke	0
S. Chanderpaul lbw b Clarke	1	– not out	43
D. J. Vilas lbw b Batty	2		
R. McLaren lbw b Batty	16		
T. E. Bailey c Pope b Borthwick	31		
S. D. Parry c Borthwick b Dernbach	20		
M. W. Parkinson not out	5		
S. Mahmood c Burns b Dernbach	0		
Lb 6, nb 2	8	Nb 2	2
1/69 (1) 2/72 (3) 3/74 (2) 4/75 (5) 5/84 (6) 6/140 (7) 7/203 (8) 8/262 (4) 9/264 (9) 10/268 (11) (92.3 overs)	268	1/40 (2) 2/88 (1) 3/92 (4) (3 wkts, 38.5 overs)	179

Dernbach 18.3–7–47–2; Curran 14–2–45–1; Clarke 16–7–29–3; Batty 28–6–70–3; Meaker 6–0–42–0; Borthwick 10–0–29–1. *Second innings*—Dernbach 5–2–14–0; Curran 4–0–21–0; Clarke 13–3–50–2; Batty 14–1–57–1; Borthwick 1.5–0–35–0; Meaker 1–0–2–0.

Umpires: P. J. Hartley and N. A. Mallender.

LEICESTERSHIRE

De Bruyn fade

RICHARD RAE

Leicestershire's season was negative from the beginning. On the eve of the opening Championship match, they were hit with a 16-point deficit. A familiar sense of deflation set in, and hung around all summer.

Veteran seam bowler Charlie Shreck had been reported for verbally abusing a student batsman in the fixture against Loughborough MCCU, the club's fifth disciplinary breach over 12 months. They also collected a £5,000 fine, a further eight-point penalty suspended for a year, and a one-match ban for captain Mark Cosgrove. The latest sanctions came just 20 months after another 16-point penalty, also for repeated dissent. Disgruntled supporters could readily list similar unreported incidents by opposing players. But they could not deny the folly of their own.

Managing the rest of the season without a further offence was one of the few positives. Leicestershire failed to win a single Championship match – though they did come close, losing to Northamptonshire by two runs under floodlights on a bitterly cold June evening – nor took 20 wickets in a game.

It was hard to stomach after the optimism of 2016, when they briefly threatened promotion. But, points deduction aside, it was apparent early on that things were going wrong. New head coach Pierre de Bruyn, promoted from Second XI duty, proved a very different character to his predecessor, the popular Australian Andrew McDonald. Opening batsman Angus Robson decided he would not be able to work with him, and moved to Sussex in April. In June, chief executive Wasim Khan denied the players were unhappy, describing the rumours as "100% nonsense". But before the end of the season, de Bruyn had gone, with assistants John Sadler and Graeme Welch stepping in for the last three games; soon after, Welch rejoined Warwickshire.

Matters came to a head at Canterbury in August when, in a rain-affected match, de Bruyn refused to consider setting up a final-day run-chase with declaration bowling. His stubbornness frustrated the players, especially Cosgrove. In fact, the captain had reason to be frustrated for much of the summer. He was consistently magnificent, racking up 1,112 Championship runs. But that was nearly 400 more than any other player. Colin Ackermann and Ned Eckersley were below their best, while former England opener Michael Carberry totalled just 59 in eight innings after arriving on loan from Hampshire. It was a surprise when he signed a permanent contract – even more so when he was given the captaincy.

Absences hurt the club badly, particularly in the bowling. All-rounders Neil Dexter and Ben Raine, so important to the balance of the side in 2016, missed large parts of the summer through injury. Australian seamer Clint McKay struggled for fitness in the four-day game, and left the club at the end of his

David Rogers, Getty Images

Mark Cosgrove

third season after collecting 199 wickets across all formats. Zak Chappell, the young fast-bowling all-rounder, and seamer Richard Jones were also injured for much of the year. And Shreck, who was suspended by the club for two games, played just one Championship match before calling time on a fine career that brought 577 first-class wickets.

Leicestershire looked to the loan market, but the search lacked focus and had mixed results. Carberry was not an immediate success, though South African seamer Mathew Pillans, who joined from Surrey, picked up 12 wickets in four games. The signings of Arun Harinath for two matches, and former England seamer Ajmal Shahzad for a single – wicketless – game, were hard to understand.

More encouragingly, younger players were given opportunities. Wicketkeeper Lewis Hill had been known more for his batting, but his glovework improved steadily, while the considerable promise shown by left-arm spinner Callum Parkinson was exciting. He took ten wickets on a turning pitch at Worcester in September, out-bowling Indian Test star Ravichandran Ashwin. Off-spinning all-rounder Ateeq Javid was signed from Warwickshire to provide support for 2018. The club's overseas role will be shared by Pakistan seamers Mohammad Abbas and Sohail Khan.

At the end of the season, former Leicestershire wicketkeeper Paul Nixon was appointed de Bruyn's full-time replacement. He was a popular choice, having won the Championship twice and the T20 competition three times during two stints at Grace Road. "It's been tough for the players," he said. "They have had a few different managers and coaches. I think a lot of the guys just need a little bit of love."

If the task ahead of him was daunting, he could take hope from some of the performances in white-ball cricket. The form of New Zealand keeper-batsman Luke Ronchi and McKay led them to their first T20 quarter-final since they won the competition in 2011, but they were well beaten by Glamorgan at Cardiff. They should also have reached the knockout stages of the Royal London Cup, though failed to drive home a winning position against Yorkshire at Headingley in their last match.

Khan, under whose guidance Leicestershire's finances have improved, finished the summer with some harsh words. "If you look back on the four-day season, which in many ways is your health check as a club, it has been riddled with disappointment," he said. He added that mediocrity would no longer be accepted. After 2017, the unkind might have said mediocrity was just the start.

Championship attendance: 9,090.

LEICESTERSHIRE RESULTS

All first-class matches – Played 15: Lost 9, Drawn 6.
County Championship matches – Played 14: Lost 9, Drawn 5.

Specsavers County Championship, 10th in Division 2;
NatWest T20 Blast, quarter-finalists; Royal London One-Day Cup, 6th in North Group.

COUNTY CHAMPIONSHIP AVERAGES, BATTING AND FIELDING

Cap		*Birthplace*	*M*	*I*	*NO*	*R*	*HS*	*100*	*Avge*	*Ct/St*
	C. F. Parkinson	*Bolton*	5	6	4	103	75	0	51.50	3
2015	†M. J. Cosgrove††	*Elizabeth, Aust*	12	23	0	1,112	188	2	48.34	1
	L. J. Hill	*Leicester‡*	11	19	3	527	85*	0	32.93	22/2
	C. N. Ackermann††	*George, SA*	12	22	3	618	118	2	32.52	2
	Z. J. Chappell	*Grantham*	6	10	2	258	66	0	32.25	0
2013	E. J. H. Eckersley	*Oxford*	14	26	2	716	158	1	29.83	16
	M. L. Pettini	*Brighton*	7	12	1	303	110*	1	27.54	1
	P. J. Horton	*Sydney, Australia*	10	19	0	504	71	0	26.52	8
2015	C. J. McKay¶	*Melbourne, Aust*	11	18	4	347	66	0	24.78	2
	†B. A. Raine	*Sunderland*	9	17	4	301	57	0	23.15	1
	N. J. Dexter	*Johannesburg, SA*	8	15	2	300	114	1	23.07	2
	R. A. Jones	*Stourbridge*	2	4	2	45	23*	0	22.50	1
	A. M. Ali	*Leicester‡*	3	5	0	110	40	0	22.00	2
	†H. E. Dearden	*Bury*	10	19	0	401	87	0	21.10	11
	†A. Harinath	*Sutton*	2	4	0	68	26	0	17.00	0
	M. W. Pillans††	*Durban, SA*	4	7	0	107	56	0	15.28	1
	D. Klein††	*Lichtenburg, SA*	9	14	3	138	26	0	12.54	5
	R. J. Sayer	*Huntingdon*	3	5	0	39	31	0	7.80	2
	†M. A. Carberry	*Croydon*	4	8	0	59	18	0	7.37	1
	G. T. Griffiths	*Ormskirk*	5	7	2	28	14*	0	5.60	0

Also batted: †C. S. Delport†† (*Durban, SA*) (1 match) 20, 1; S. T. Evans (*Leicester‡*) (1 match) 8, 29 (1 ct); W. N. Fazakerley (*Guernsey*) (1 match) 0, 0; A. Shahzad (*Huddersfield*) (1 match) did not bat (1 ct); C. E. Shreck (*Truro*) (1 match) 26; T. J. Wells (*Grantham*) (2 matches) 46, 16, 24 (1 ct).

‡ *Born in Leicestershire.* ¶ *Official overseas player.* †† *Other non-England-qualified.*

BOWLING

	Style	*O*	*M*	*R*	*W*	*BB*	*5I*	*Avge*
B. A. Raine	RFM	256.1	54	777	33	6-66	2	23.54
N. J. Dexter	RM	121	23	456	14	5-71	2	32.57
C. F. Parkinson	SLA	147.2	14	556	17	8-148	1	32.70
D. Klein	LFM	206	21	958	28	6-80	2	34.21
M. W. Pillans	RFM	101.1	9	416	12	3-63	0	34.66
C. J. McKay	RFM	315.3	97	809	22	4-35	0	36.77

Also bowled: C. N. Ackermann (OB) 104–9–394–6; A. M. Ali (OB) 6–0–46–1; Z. J. Chappell (RFM) 114.5–13–514–9; M. J. Cosgrove (RM) 39–1–163–2; H. E. Dearden (OB) 18.4–0–95–2; C. S. Delport (RM) 7–1–30–0; E. J. H. Eckersley (OB) 1–0–2–0; W. N. Fazakerley (RFM) 12–2–83–1; G. T. Griffiths (RFM) 124–20–403–5; A. Harinath (OB) 1–0–5–0; P. J. Horton (RM) 0.4–0–6–0; R. A. Jones (RFM) 58–5–228–5; R. J. Sayer (OB) 102–9–379–2; A. Shahzad (RFM) 25–1–104–0; C. E. Shreck (RFM) 42–7–141–1; T. J. Wells (RFM) 15–1–120–2.

LEADING ROYAL LONDON CUP AVERAGES (100 runs/4 wickets)

Batting	*Runs*	*HS*	*Avge*	*SR*	*Ct/St*
M. L. Pettini	294	159	42.00	101.73	3
M. J. Cosgrove	277	80	39.57	107.78	3
E. J. H. Eckersley	216	80	36.00	98.18	3
C. S. Delport	243	68	34.71	100.82	1
T. J. Wells	157	67	31.40	96.31	2
L. J. Hill	188	68*	31.33	92.15	7/1
A. M. Ali	153	88	30.60	78.46	3

Bowling	*W*	*BB*	*Avge*	*ER*
G. T. Griffiths	10	3-35	27.40	5.48
D. Klein	8	3-46	30.50	5.20
J. S. Sykes	6	4-57	30.50	6.31
T. J. Wells	10	3-44	40.10	6.20
R. J. Sayer	4	2-65	53.75	5.65
Z. J. Chappell	4	2-44	78.50	6.40

LEADING NATWEST T20 BLAST AVERAGES (100 runs/15 overs)

Batting	Runs	HS	Avge	SR	Ct/St
L. Ronchi	429	63*	33.00	**180.25**	8/4
M. J. Cosgrove	414	79	37.63	**138.92**	2
C. S. Delport	339	109*	26.07	**137.24**	4
C. N. Ackermann	255	62*	28.33	**115.90**	7
M. W. Pillans	107	34*	35.66	**111.45**	2
T. J. Wells	139	31*	12.63	**111.20**	12

Bowling	W	BB	Avge	ER
C. S. Delport	10	3-19	26.60	**7.00**
C. J. McKay	23	5-11	14.26	**7.62**
C. F. Parkinson	15	3-20	25.13	**8.02**
C. N. Ackermann	6	3-21	27.33	**8.20**
D. Klein	7	2-23	20.57	**8.47**
M. W. Pillans	17	3-24	27.64	**8.73**
G. T. Griffiths	8	2-29	44.37	**9.14**

FIRST-CLASS COUNTY RECORDS

Highest score for	309*	H. D. Ackerman v Glamorgan at Cardiff	2006
Highest score against	355*	K. P. Pietersen (Surrey) at The Oval	2015
Leading run-scorer	30,143	L. G. Berry (avge 30.32)	1924–51
Best bowling for	10-18	G. Geary v Glamorgan at Pontypridd	1929
Best bowling against	10-32	H. Pickett (Essex) at Leyton	1895
Leading wicket-taker	2,131	W. E. Astill (avge 23.18)	1906–39
Highest total for	701-4 dec	v Worcestershire at Worcester	1906
Highest total against	761-6 dec	by Essex at Chelmsford	1990
Lowest total for	25	v Kent at Leicester	1912
Lowest total against	24	by Glamorgan at Leicester	1971
	24	by Oxford University at Oxford	1985

LIST A COUNTY RECORDS

Highest score for	201	V. J. Wells v Berkshire at Leicester	1996
Highest score against	201*	R. S. Bopara (Essex) at Leicester	2008
Leading run-scorer	8,216	N. E. Briers (avge 27.66)	1975–95
Best bowling for	6-16	C. M. Willoughby v Somerset at Leicester	2005
Best bowling against	6-21	S. M. Pollock (Warwickshire) at Birmingham	1996
Leading wicket-taker	308	K. Higgs (avge 18.80)	1972–82
Highest total for	406-5	v Berkshire at Leicester	1996
Highest total against	376-3	by Yorkshire at Leicester	2016
Lowest total for	36	v Sussex at Leicester	1973
Lowest total against	62	by Northamptonshire at Leicester	1974
	62	by Middlesex at Leicester	1998

TWENTY20 COUNTY RECORDS

Highest score for	111	D. L. Maddy v Yorkshire at Leeds	2004
Highest score against	103*	A. N. Petersen (Lancashire) at Leicester	2016
Leading run-scorer	1,455	P. A. Nixon (avge 21.71)	2003–*11*
Best bowling for	**5-11**	**C. J. McKay v Worcestershire at Worcester**	**2017**
Best bowling against	5-21	J. A. Brooks (Yorkshire) at Leeds	2013
Leading wicket-taker	69	C. W. Henderson (avge 26.95)	2004–12
Highest total for	221-3	v Yorkshire at Leeds	2004
Highest total against	225-2	by Durham at Chester-le-Street	2010
Lowest total for	90	v Nottinghamshire at Nottingham	2014
Lowest total against	72	by Derbyshire at Derby	2013

ADDRESS

Fischer County Ground, Grace Road, Leicester LE2 8EB; 0116 283 2128; enquiries@leicestershireccc.co.uk; www.leicestershireccc.co.uk.

OFFICIALS

Captain 2017 M. J. Cosgrove
2017 (limited-overs) C. J. McKay
2018 M. A. Carberry
Head coach 2017 P. de Bruyn
2018 P. A. Nixon
Assistant coach J. L. Sadler

Academy director A. P. Siddall
President D. W. Wilson
Chairman P. R. Haywood
Chief executive W. G. Khan
Head groundsman A. Ward
Scorer P. J. Rogers

LEICESTERSHIRE v LOUGHBOROUGH MCCU

At Leicester, March 28–30. Drawn. Toss: Leicestershire. First-class debuts: G. T. Griffiths; S. T. Evans, B. I. W. Ladd-Gibbon, A. D. Tillcock. County debut: J. E. Burke.

Cosgrove, who had picked up a cold on the flight from Australia, opted to bat, only for his side to slip to 194. They struggled against a lively swing attack – Basil Akram was the pick, collecting a maiden first-class five-for – and four were bowled without playing a shot including debutant James Burke. Loughborough opener Hassan Azad led the reply, putting on 87 with James Bracey and batting through an interrupted second day, before falling for 80. That sparked a slide from 240 for four to 278, but the students had a lead. After they reduced Leicestershire to 65 for three, they had a sniff of victory too. Cosgrove and Eckersley batted to safety, but there was trouble to come: Shreck was reported for using "obscene, offensive or insulting language". It was the club's fifth disciplinary breach in a year, earning a £5,000 fine and a 16-point penalty in the Championship, as well as a one-match ban for Cosgrove, captain on each occasion.

Close of play: first day, Loughborough MCCU 20-0 (Hassan Azad 7, Evans 12); second day, Loughborough MCCU 175-4 (Hassan Azad 59).

Leicestershire

P. J. Horton b Cook	20	– c White b Gamble	10
H. E. Dearden b Akram	14	– c White b Cook	30
†L. J. Hill b Ladd-Gibbon	23	– c White b Gamble	4
*M. J. Cosgrove b Akram	9	– not out	40
E. J. H. Eckersley lbw b Akram	49	– not out	22
J. E. Burke b Ladd-Gibbon	0		
T. J. Wells c Akram b Cook	24		
Z. J. Chappell c Tillcock b Ladd-Gibbon	9		
R. J. Sayer c Tillcock b Akram	19		
G. T. Griffiths not out	9		
C. E. Shreck b Akram	0		
B 8, lb 6, nb 4	18	Lb 5, nb 2	7
1/35 (1) 2/39 (2) 3/53 (4) 4/97 (3) 5/101 (6) 6/136 (7) 7/157 (8) 8/173 (5) 9/194 (9) 10/194 (11) (57 overs)	194	1/18 (1) 2/22 (3) 3/65 (2) (3 wkts, 30 overs)	113

Gamble 13–1–36–0; Cook 17–3–38–2; Akram 14–2–54–5; Ladd-Gibbon 11–2–47–3; Tillcock 2–0–5–0. *Second innings*—Gamble 6–2–16–2; Cook 11–2–28–1; Akram 4–1–16–0; Ladd-Gibbon 3–0–13–0; Tillcock 5–0–33–0; Kumar 1–0–2–0.

Loughborough MCCU

Hassan Azad c Eckersley b Griffiths	80
S. T. Evans lbw b Griffiths	12
J. R. Bracey c Horton b Sayer	56
N. R. Kumar lbw b Griffiths	34
†R. G. White lbw b Shreck	7
B. M. R. Akram c Dearden b Wells	44
C. O. Thurston lbw b Chappell	2
A. D. Tillcock not out	16
*R. N. Gamble b Wells	0
S. J. Cook lbw b Wells	3
B. I. W. Ladd-Gibbon lbw b Wells	4
B 3, lb 7, w 6, nb 4	20
1/24 (2) 2/111 (3) 3/162 (4) 4/175 (5) 5/240 (1) 6/252 (7) 7/252 (6) 8/254 (9) 9/270 (10) 10/278 (11) (95.4 overs)	278

Chappell 19–4–53–1; Griffiths 15–4–31–3; Sayer 18–7–31–1; Shreck 21–8–42–1; Burke 10–0–57–0; Horton 1–0–8–0; Wells 11.4–1–46–4.

Umpires: J. D. Middlebrook and S. J. O'Shaughnessy.

LEICESTERSHIRE v NOTTINGHAMSHIRE

At Leicester, April 7–9. Nottinghamshire won by ten wickets. Nottinghamshire 22pts, Leicestershire 5pts. Toss: uncontested. County debuts: C. N. Ackermann; J. L. Pattinson. Championship debut: G. T. Griffiths.

In 2016, Nottinghamshire had won their first Championship match, and failed to win again. But the manner of victory here – a mixture of resolute and ruthless – suggested there would be no repeat in 2017. On the second afternoon, they were struggling at 167 for seven in reply to Leicestershire's hard-fought 251. From there, though, the square-shouldered Australian James Pattinson seized control. First, he put on 122 with Broad, and hit 89 not out to give Nottinghamshire a healthy lead. Then, once Raine – who had already made 55 not out from No. 9 – had wrapped up the innings to finish with a career-best six for 66, Pattinson got to work with the ball. With the help of Fletcher, he blew away Leicestershire's top order before returning on the third morning to complete a first Championship five-for, and all but seal the rout. On the opening day, Read collected his 1,000th first-class catch, a brilliant one-handed scoop after Cosgrove had bottom-edged Broad.

Close of play: first day, Nottinghamshire 52-1 (Libby 10, Lumb 20); second day, Leicestershire 51-6 (Cosgrove 17, Griffiths 3).

Leicestershire

P. J. Horton b Broad	6	– lbw b Broad	2
H. E. Dearden c Read b Gurney	12	– c Read b Pattinson	0
C. N. Ackermann lbw b Pattinson	7	– lbw b Pattinson	14
*M. J. Cosgrove c Read b Broad	57	– c Lumb b Fletcher	21
M. L. Pettini b Gurney	2	– c Patel b Fletcher	1
L. J. Hill c Libby b Pattinson	24	– lbw b Fletcher	3
†E. J. H. Eckersley lbw b Broad	13	– b Fletcher	4
Z. J. Chappell c Patel b Fletcher	30	– (9) c Read b Pattinson	0
B. A. Raine not out	55	– (10) not out	17
C. J. McKay c Wessels b Pattinson	33	– (11) b Pattinson	8
G. T. Griffiths c Read b Patel	1	– (8) c Smith b Pattinson	3
B 4, lb 5, nb 2	11	B 4, lb 4	8
1/6 (1) 2/21 (3) 3/50 (2) (74.1 overs)	251	1/2 (2) 2/2 (1) (31.3 overs)	81
4/70 (5) 5/101 (6) 6/116 (7)		3/18 (3) 4/19 (5)	
7/135 (4) 8/169 (8) 9/250 (10) 10/251 (11)		5/31 (6) 6/39 (7) 7/52 (8)	
		8/54 (9) 9/60 (4) 10/81 (11)	

Broad 15–2–45–3; Pattinson 16–5–55–3; Fletcher 14–2–42–1; Gurney 16–2–53–2; Patel 12.1–0–43–1; Libby 1–0–4–0. *Second innings*—Broad 6–2–9–1; Pattinson 12.3–2–29–5; Fletcher 11–4–35–4; Patel 2–2–0–0.

Nottinghamshire

G. P. Smith lbw b Chappell	11	– not out	8
J. D. Libby c Ackermann b McKay	31	– not out	1
M. J. Lumb c Eckersley b Raine	30		
A. D. Hales b Raine	7		
M. H. Wessels c Dearden b Raine	24		
S. R. Patel lbw b McKay	34		
*†C. M. W. Read c Eckersley b Raine	3		
J. L. Pattinson not out	89		
S. C. J. Broad lbw b Cosgrove	52		
L. J. Fletcher lbw b Raine	12		
H. F. Gurney c Dearden b Raine	4		
B 12, lb 7, w 7, nb 6	32		
1/15 (1) 2/79 (3) 3/87 (2) (89.3 overs)	329	(no wkt, 1.4 overs)	9
4/91 (4) 5/150 (5) 6/150 (6)			
7/167 (7) 8/289 (9) 9/319 (10) 10/329 (11)			

Chappell 19–3–78–1; McKay 22–8–59–2; Griffiths 17–6–44–0; Raine 21.3–9–66–6; Ackermann 6–0–35–0; Cosgrove 4–0–28–1. *Second innings*—Ackermann 1–0–3–0; Horton 0.4–0–6–0.

Umpires: N. G. C. Cowley and S. C. Gale.

At Bristol, April 14–16. LEICESTERSHIRE lost to GLOUCESTERSHIRE by an innings and six runs.

LEICESTERSHIRE v GLAMORGAN

At Leicester, April 21–24. Drawn. Leicestershire 12pts, Glamorgan 13pts. Toss: uncontested. Championship debut: C. S. Delport.

After acting-captain Eckersley's distinctly cautious declaration, Glamorgan needed to survive 57 overs, and had struggled to 65 for four when Donald spliced Shreck's bouncer high towards point. Cameron Delport got both hands to the ball but could not hang on, and Donald's subsequent half-century extinguished any notion of a result. On the first day, Leicestershire had been inserted under heavy cloud and, after 20-year-old opener Harry Dearden's maiden half-century, and Pettini's first in the Championship for Leicestershire at Grace Road (at the 17th attempt), some vigorous tail-wagging on the second morning hauled them to 420. With the home attack deprived of Chappell – hit on the shoulder in the nets before play – Glamorgan responded strongly: Selman and Ingram both struck hundreds, though from 258 for two, the lead they established on the third day might have been bigger than six. Pettini, now enjoying home comforts, batted Leicestershire to an impregnable position, putting on 94 with Eckersley and 86 with Hill, and reaching a century before the declaration an hour after lunch on the final afternoon. Chappell had recovered but, following early breakthroughs, Leicestershire's attack lost teeth when McKay and Raine were forced off by injury. Floodlights were used for the first time in the Championship at Grace Road.

Close of play: first day, Leicestershire 275-5 (Pettini 63, Hill 32); second day, Glamorgan 281-4 (Ingram 84, Cooke 8); third day, Leicestershire 200-3 (Eckersley 70, Pettini 33).

Leicestershire

First innings		Second innings	
P. J. Horton b Carey	41	– lbw b de Lange	42
H. E. Dearden b Salter	87	– c Selman b Hogan	2
N. J. Dexter c Cooke b Carey	0	– run out	32
*E. J. H. Eckersley b Hogan	1	– c Selman b de Lange	73
M. L. Pettini c Donald b de Lange	69	– not out	110
C. S. Delport b Salter	20	– c Carey b de Lange	1
†L. J. Hill c Donald b Carey	32	– c de Lange b Salter	42
B. A. Raine c Cooke b de Lange	45	– not out	29
Z. J. Chappell c Donald b Carey	12		
C. J. McKay not out	41		
C. E. Shreck b Ingram	26		
B 19, lb 5, w 6, nb 16	46	Lb 12, nb 17	29
1/85 (1) 2/85 (3) 3/86 (4) (115.1 overs)	420	1/10 (2) (6 wkts dec, 88 overs)	360
4/176 (2) 5/202 (6) 6/281 (7) 7/281 (5)		2/75 (3) 3/109 (1)	
8/310 (9) 9/359 (8) 10/420 (11) 110 overs: 383-9		4/203 (4) 5/205 (6) 6/291 (7)	

Hogan 30–6–99–1; Carey 31–4–127–4; de Lange 31–6–103–2; Lloyd 11–1–35–0; Salter 10–0–26–2; Ingram 2.1–0–6–1. *Second innings*—Carey 13–0–74–0; Hogan 22–5–69–1; de Lange 19–3–77–3; Lloyd 6–0–31–0; Salter 22–1–72–1; Ingram 6–0–25–0.

Glamorgan

First innings		Second innings	
N. J. Selman lbw b Shreck	117	– (2) lbw b McKay	4
*J. A. Rudolph b Dearden	58	– (1) c Hill b Chappell	19
D. L. Lloyd lbw b Raine	1	– c Dearden b Raine	4
C. A. Ingram b McKay	137	– lbw b Raine	1
A. H. T. Donald b Dexter	5	– not out	66
†C. B. Cooke lbw b Raine	27	– not out	24
K. S. Carlson c Dearden b McKay	24		
A. G. Salter not out	8		
M. de Lange c Dearden b McKay	14		
L. J. Carey c Dexter b Raine	1		
M. G. Hogan c Dexter b Raine	10		
B 11, lb 8, nb 5	24	B 11, w 1, nb 14	26
1/83 (2) 2/97 (3) 3/258 (1) (108.5 overs)	426	1/11 (2) (4 wkts, 46 overs)	144
4/263 (5) 5/321 (6) 6/384 (4)		2/20 (3) 3/24 (4)	
7/391 (7) 8/409 (9) 9/416 (10) 10/426 (11)		4/57 (1)	

McKay 27–5–95–3; Raine 30.5–5–105–4; Shreck 29–5–110–1; Dearden 7–0–33–1; Dexter 12–1–49–1; Delport 3–0–15–0. *Second innings*—Chappell 12–4–28–1; McKay 3–2–4–1; Raine 7–3–23–2; Shreck 13–2–31–0; Dexter 5–1–21–0; Dearden 2–0–11–0; Delport 4–1–15–0.

Umpires: N. G. B. Cook and G. D. Lloyd.

LEICESTERSHIRE v KENT

At Leicester, May 19–22. Drawn. Leicestershire 13pts, Kent 13pts. Toss: uncontested.

Rain washed out the first day, and allowed only 47 overs on the second, but there was plenty of action on the third: 484 runs, 13 wickets, and a counter-attacking innings of rare brutality from Stevens. After Ackermann's measured 89, Leicestershire had slipped to 278 for seven, and needed McKay's rapid 66 – his first-class best – to reach 420 for the second game in a row. In the evening, Klein swung the ball sharply, picking up four as Kent fell to 144 for five. But Stevens was unconcerned, and bludgeoned a fifty in just 30 balls, including a sequence of eight fours in 11 from Wells and left-arm spinner Callum Parkinson, making his first-class debut for Leicestershire. Next day, Stevens reached his first hundred against his former county. There was no chance of a result, but three more half-centuries from the lower order, as well as a second first-class wicket for the off-spin of Dearden (with his only ball), ensured maximum bonus points for both sides.

Close of play: first day, no play; second day, Leicestershire 129-2 (Ackermann 32, Cosgrove 10); third day, Kent 193-5 (Stevens 54, Rouse 9).

Leicestershire

First innings		Second innings	
P. J. Horton lbw b Stevens	48	c †sub (O. G. Robinson) b Gidman	40
H. E. Dearden b Coles	34	c Gidman b Hunn	17
C. N. Ackermann c †Bell-Drummond b Coles	89	not out	4
*M. J. Cosgrove lbw b Stevens	39		
†E. J. H. Eckersley b Tredwell	33		
M. L. Pettini lbw b Harris	8		
T. J. Wells c Harris b Hunn	46		
C. F. Parkinson c sub (A. J. Blake) b Hunn	2		
C. J. McKay run out	66		
D. Klein c sub (A. J. Blake) b Hunn	23		
G. T. Griffiths not out	14		
B 4, lb 14	18		
1/58 (1) 2/113 (2) 3/189 (4) 4/244 (5) 5/265 (3) 6/271 (6) 7/278 (8) 8/335 (7) 9/358 (10) 10/420 (9) — (112.4 overs)	420	1/57 (1) 2/61 (2) — (2 wkts dec, 18.5 overs)	61

110 overs: 409-9

Coles 27–7–114–2; Stevens 21–8–44–2; Harris 28–12–72–1; Gidman 5–1–17–0; Hunn 22–2–110–3; Tredwell 8.4–0–43–1; Denly 1–0–2–0. *Second innings*—Harris 6–0–26–0; Coles 3–0–8–0; Stevens 3–0–13–0; Hunn 3.5–2–2–1; Gidman 3–1–12–1.

Kent

D. J. Bell-Drummond lbw b Wells	35
S. R. Dickson lbw b Klein	0
J. L. Denly b Klein	10
*S. A. Northeast c Cosgrove b Klein	40
W. R. S. Gidman c Eckersley b Klein	24
D. I. Stevens c Klein b Wells	100
†A. P. Rouse b Parkinson	60
J. A. R. Harris lbw b Cosgrove	34
J. C. Tredwell b Dearden	55
M. T. Coles not out	56
B 19, lb 12, nb 12, p 5	48
1/5 (2) 2/25 (3) 3/82 (1) 4/101 (4) 5/144 (5) 6/296 (7) 7/306 (6) 8/373 (8) 9/462 (9) — (9 wkts dec, 96.1 overs)	462

M. D. Hunn did not bat.

Klein 21–4–108–4; McKay 21–8–49–0; Griffiths 19–2–59–0; Wells 11–1–98–2; Parkinson 19–3–102–1; Cosgrove 5–0–10–1; Dearden 0.1–0–0–1.

Umpires: J. H. Evans and R. J. Evans.

At Derby, May 25–28. LEICESTERSHIRE drew with DERBYSHIRE.

LEICESTERSHIRE v SUSSEX

At Leicester, June 9–12. Sussex won by five wickets. Sussex 21pts, Leicestershire 6pts. Toss: uncontested.

Sussex overcame the loss of two of their four seamers to complete an impressive win. By the second afternoon, it looked unlikely: Cosgrove's century had lifted Leicestershire to 340, before McKay's four wickets reduced Sussex to 201 for nine. But Philander – in his last game before joining the South Africa squad – and Briggs began the comeback with a stand of 83 that extended into the third day. Then, after Philander rolled an ankle in the field, and Wiese strained a stomach muscle, Archer shouldered the burden. He combined sharp pace with exemplary control, and found movement beyond everyone else to finish with six for 70, and 11 for 137 in the match. Leicestershire were bowled out for 175 but, with the odd delivery keeping low, a target of 232 was no given, even after Sussex reached 100 for two at the close. Wells was immovable, though, and his patient unbeaten 90, which coach Mark Davis said might have been a better innings than his 258 against Durham in May, brought them home early in the afternoon.

Close of play: first day, Leicestershire 322-7 (Cosgrove 122, Chappell 40); second day, Sussex 276-9 (Philander 69, Briggs 23); third day, Sussex 100-2 (Wells 27, Briggs 10).

Leicestershire

First innings		Second innings	
P. J. Horton b Archer	71	– c Burgess b Archer	16
H. E. Dearden c Jordan b Archer	8	– c Burgess b Archer	36
C. N. Ackermann c van Zyl b Archer	13	– c Burgess b Jordan	3
*M. J. Cosgrove c Philander b Jordan	128	– lbw b Briggs	16
†E. J. H. Eckersley c Archer b Briggs	14	– lbw b Archer	1
M. L. Pettini lbw b Archer	3	– b Archer	4
T. J. Wells lbw b Archer	16	– c Archer b Briggs	24
B. A. Raine c Burgess b Philander	0	– c Jordan b Briggs	9
Z. J. Chappell c Nash b Jordan	44	– not out	27
C. J. McKay c Burgess b Jordan	2	– c Finch b Archer	10
D. Klein not out	5	– b Archer	21
B 6, lb 12, nb 18	36	Lb 7, w 1	8
1/37 (2) 2/59 (3) 3/178 (1) 4/195 (5) 5/212 (6) 6/264 (7) 7/271 (8) 8/329 (9) 9/331 (10) 10/340 (4) (101.5 overs)	340	1/30 (1) 2/46 (3) 3/69 (4) 4/72 (5) 5/78 (6) 6/87 (2) 7/107 (7) 8/130 (8) 9/147 (10) 10/175 (11) (59.4 overs)	175

Philander 16–3–57–1; Jordan 22.5–3–91–3; Archer 30–11–67–5; Wiese 9–5–17–0; van Zyl 5–1–26–0; Briggs 19–3–64–1. *Second innings*—Jordan 14–4–29–1; Archer 19.4–3–70–6; Wiese 6–0–29–0; Briggs 20–3–40–3.

Sussex

First innings		Second innings	
C. D. Nash b Chappell	5	– (2) c Eckersley b Raine	23
H. Z. Finch b Raine	61	– (1) b Raine	14
L. W. P. Wells lbw b McKay	12	– not out	90
S. van Zyl lbw b McKay	0	– (5) b Raine	24
L. J. Wright b Raine	36	– (6) c Horton b Chappell	17
M. G. K. Burgess lbw b McKay	1	– (7) not out	9
C. J. Jordan c Wells b McKay	36		
D. Wiese c Eckersley b Chappell	7		
V. D. Philander not out	73		
J. C. Archer c Pettini b Klein	1		
D. R. Briggs lbw b Raine	27	– (4) c Horton b McKay	14
B 1, lb 16, nb 8	25	B 16, lb 19, nb 8	43
1/7 (1) 2/53 (3) 3/53 (4) 4/118 (5) 5/121 (6) 6/131 (2) 7/156 (8) 8/195 (7) 9/201 (10) 10/284 (11) (84.5 overs)	284	1/25 (1) 2/79 (2) 3/105 (4) 4/175 (5) 5/201 (6) (5 wkts, 68.3 overs)	234

Klein 13–1–72–1; Chappell 13–0–61–2; McKay 22–11–35–4; Raine 20.5–4–49–3; Wells 4–0–22–0; Ackermann 12–1–28–0. *Second innings*—Chappell 10–0–49–1; Raine 19–3–50–3; McKay 20–7–31–1; Klein 10–0–36–0; Ackermann 6–1–19–0; Cosgrove 2–0–3–0; Dearden 1.3–0–11–0.

Umpires: N. N. Menon and A. G. Wharf.

At Nottingham, June 19–21. LEICESTERSHIRE lost to NOTTINGHAMSHIRE by an innings and 280 runs.

At Northampton, June 26–29. LEICESTERSHIRE lost to NORTHAMPTONSHIRE by two runs.

At Arundel, July 5–8. LEICESTERSHIRE lost to SUSSEX by 231 runs.

LEICESTERSHIRE v DURHAM

At Leicester, August 6–9. Drawn. Leicestershire 6pts, Durham 10pts. Toss: Durham. County debut: A. Shahzad.

At 21, California-born opener Cameron Steel became the youngest of Durham's 12 double-centurions, and the seventh born outside the UK. Along the way, he helped establish another record: his stand of 234 with New Zealand opener Latham – making a delayed Championship debut for the club after a stress fracture of the right foot – was the highest for the first wicket between these sides. Leicestershire were without five injured seamers, so gave a trial to the former England bowler Shahzad, who finished with none for 104 in Durham's highest total against them. He did manage to take Steel's edge when he had 165, but Horton dropped the chance at slip, one of four reprieves for him; he cracked the next two balls for four. As Durham pressed for quick runs, Dexter's persistence earned him five wickets, before Potts showed off his aggression and seam movement. The visitors established a dominant position, but rain wiped out the final two days.

Close of play: first day, Durham 324-4 (Steel 145, Richardson 7); second day, Leicestershire 124-4 (Eckersley 16, Dexter 9); third day, no play.

Durham

C. T. Steel c Ali b Dexter 224
T. W. M. Latham c Hill b Dexter 124
J. T. A. Burnham st Hill b Parkinson 10
G. Clark c Shahzad b Klein 0
*P. D. Collingwood lbw b Klein 25
†M. J. Richardson c Horton b Dexter 82
R. D. Pringle c Eckersley b Dexter 0
P. Coughlin not out 31
M. J. Potts c Dearden b Dexter 2
C. Rushworth not out 9
B 6, lb 2, nb 10 18

1/234 (2) 2/252 (3) 3/253 (4) 4/309 (5) 5/467 (1) 6/473 (7) 7/488 (6) 8/492 (9) (8 wkts dec, 142 overs) 525

110 overs: 373-4

G. Onions did not bat.

Klein 25–3–108–2; Shahzad 25–1–104–0; Griffiths 27–3–86–0; Dexter 25–3–71–5; Parkinson 35–4–120–1; Ackermann 5–0–28–0.

Leicestershire

P. J. Horton b Rushworth 38
H. E. Dearden c Latham b Potts 30
C. N. Ackermann lbw b Potts 3
*E. J. H. Eckersley not out 16
A. M. Ali c Richardson b Coughlin. 9
N. J. Dexter not out 9
B 7, lb 4, w 6, nb 2 19

1/62 (1) 2/78 (3) 3/92 (2) 4/111 (5) (4 wkts, 48 overs) 124

†L. J. Hill, A. Shahzad, C. F. Parkinson, D. Klein and G. T. Griffiths did not bat.

Rushworth 15–5–36–1; Onions 12–4–20–0; Potts 11–2–30–2; Coughlin 10–3–27–1.

Umpires: N. L. Bainton and M. Burns.

At Canterbury, August 28–31. LEICESTERSHIRE drew with KENT.

At Leicester, September 2–3. LEICESTERSHIRE drew with WEST INDIANS (see West Indian tour section).

LEICESTERSHIRE v GLOUCESTERSHIRE

At Leicester, September 5–8. Gloucestershire won by ten wickets. Gloucestershire 23pts, Leicestershire 4pts. Toss: uncontested.

Soon after Leicestershire's grimly familiar third-innings collapse had confirmed the result, Gloucestershire head coach Richard Dawson suggested Norwell was as good as any seamer in county cricket. It did not seem misplaced: he had found consistent movement and bounce to complete a career-best eight for 43, the best return for Gloucestershire since Javagal Srinath took nine for 76 against Glamorgan at Abergavenny in 1995. That topped up his match figures to ten for 95 – and 20 for 194 against Leicestershire for the season. After a delayed start in autumnal conditions, the hosts had been inserted, and Cosgrove provided the only meaningful resistance with the first of two half-centuries; no one else passed 31, and 13 innings ended in single figures. In between, Gloucestershire's top seven each made a solid contribution, and built a series of meaty partnerships on their way to a lead of 146. It set up a crushing victory.

Close of play: first day, Leicestershire 90-4 (Cosgrove 38, Dexter 6); second day, Gloucestershire 218-3 (Bracey 17, Hankins 17); third day, Leicestershire 154-7 (Hill 8, Pillans 0).

Leicestershire

First innings		Second innings	
M. A. Carberry c Noema-Barnett b Norwell	2	– c Bancroft b Norwell	8
H. E. Dearden c Dent b Norwell	1	– c Dent b Norwell	17
C. N. Ackermann c Roderick b M. D. Taylor	22	– lbw b Norwell	13
M. J. Cosgrove lbw b M. D. Taylor	92	– c Roderick b Norwell	68
E. J. H. Eckersley c Roderick b Shaw	6	– b Noema-Barnett	30
N. J. Dexter c Roderick b Shaw	8	– b Norwell	0
L. J. Hill c J. M. R. Taylor b Shaw	31	– not out	9
B. A. Raine lbw b Noema-Barnett	6	– b M. D. Taylor	2
M. W. Pillans c J. M. R. Taylor b Noema-Barnett	5	– c Hankins b Norwell	0
C. J. McKay c Hankins b Shaw	7	– c Roderick b Norwell	3
D. Klein not out	15	– c Dent b Norwell	0
B 16, lb 8, w 1, nb 2	27	B 4, nb 6	10
1/11 (2) 2/20 (1) 3/53 (3) 4/74 (5) 5/103 (6) 6/171 (4) 7/180 (8) 8/194 (9) 9/205 (7) 10/222 (10) (59.5 overs)	222	1/8 (1) 2/40 (3) 3/51 (2) 4/130 (5) 5/135 (6) 6/140 (4) 7/152 (8) 8/154 (9) 9/160 (10) 10/160 (11) (49 overs)	160

Norwell 18–5–52–2; M. D. Taylor 15–3–54–2; Shaw 13.5–4–54–4; Noema-Barnett 13–3–38–2. *Second innings*—Norwell 17–5–43–8; M. D. Taylor 10–2–34–1; Shaw 9–0–54–0; Noema-Barnett 13–4–25–1.

Gloucestershire

C. T. Bancroft c Hill b Dexter	42	– not out	4
C. D. J. Dent lbw b Raine	57	– not out	11
†G. H. Roderick c Dearden b Dexter	57		
J. R. Bracey run out	63		
G. T. Hankins b Klein	22		
*P. Mustard b Pillans	26		
J. M. R. Taylor b Klein	36		
K. Noema-Barnett b Pillans	3		
J. Shaw lbw b Raine	6		
L. C. Norwell not out	16		
M. D. Taylor c Klein b Raine	3		
B 8, lb 12, w 5, nb 12	37		
1/96 (1) 2/149 (2) 3/194 (3) 4/227 (5) 5/301 (6) 6/315 (4) 7/318 (8) 8/341 (9) 9/355 (7) 10/368 (11) (93.1 overs)	368	(no wkt, 3.3 overs)	15

Klein 20–2–89–2; McKay 18–6–39–0; Raine 25.1–4–92–3; Dexter 13–4–53–2; Pillans 14–2–63–2; Dearden 1–0–2–0; Ackermann 2–0–10–0. *Second innings*—McKay 2–1–4–0; Raine 1.3–0–11–0.

Umpires: N. G. C. Cowley and J. H. Evans.

At Worcester, September 12–15. LEICESTERSHIRE lost to WORCESTERSHIRE by six wickets.

LEICESTERSHIRE v NORTHAMPTONSHIRE

At Leicester, September 25–28. Northamptonshire won by six wickets. Northamptonshire 20pts, Leicestershire 3pts. Toss: uncontested. Championship debut: S. T. Evans.

After the first day was lost to rain, Sanderson and Gleeson made the most of ideal seaming conditions, reducing Leicestershire to 26 for seven, and finishing with five each. They more than compensated for the absence of Northamptonshire's leading wicket-taker Kleinveldt, who pulled up with a side strain after bowling just 11 deliveries. Raine dragged Leicestershire into three figures with a defiant fifty then – as the clouds closed in and the floodlights came on – proved similarly effective with the ball: he hoovered up five for 54 as Northamptonshire collapsed from 168 for two to 202 all out. From a deficit of 74, Cosgrove's belligerent half-century helped set a target of 197, though it could have been much more: Leicestershire's last five wickets fell for just 39 runs on the third evening. A wet outfield delayed the final day but, in blazing afternoon sunshine Procter – one of two Lancashire loanees, along with Kerrigan – added 94 to a hard-fought first-innings 82. It helped Northamptonshire wrap up a ninth Championship win of the season, but not quite promotion: Nottinghamshire (who had only seven) pipped them with a draw at Sussex. Leicestershire, meanwhile, finished the season winless and bottom.

Close of play: first day, no play; second day, Northamptonshire 199-8 (Cobb 14, Sanderson 0); third day, Northamptonshire 17-0 (Procter 6, Newton 10).

Leicestershire

First innings		Second innings	
M. A. Carberry lbw b Sanderson	1	– lbw b Gleeson	16
S. T. Evans c Murphy b Gleeson	8	– lbw b Keogh	29
E. J. H. Eckersley lbw b Sanderson	5	– lbw b Sanderson	19
*M. J. Cosgrove b Gleeson	1	– lbw b Sanderson	80
A. M. Ali lbw b Sanderson	0	– st Murphy b Kerrigan	37
N. J. Dexter b Gleeson	8	– c Levi b Kerrigan	2
†L. J. Hill lbw b Gleeson	1	– lbw b Gleeson	27
B. A. Raine c Procter b Sanderson	57	– c Keogh b Sanderson	8
Z. J. Chappell c Levi b Sanderson	21	– st Murphy b Kerrigan	1
D. Klein c Procter b Gleeson	14	– b Kerrigan	13
C. F. Parkinson not out	1	– not out	3
B 1, lb 2, nb 8	11	B 25, lb 6, nb 4	35
1/5 (1) 2/15 (3) 3/15 (2) 4/16 (4) 5/16 (5) 6/21 (7) 7/26 (6) 8/94 (9) 9/124 (10) 10/128 (8) (37.2 overs)	128	1/27 (1) 2/65 (3) 3/83 (2) 4/165 (5) 5/171 (6) 6/231 (4) 7/245 (8) 8/248 (9) 9/260 (7) 10/270 (10) (74.4 overs)	270

Kleinveldt 1.5–0–4–0; Sanderson 15.2–4–39–5; Gleeson 14.1–4–49–5; Procter 4–0–27–0; Kerrigan 2–0–6–0. *Second innings*—Sanderson 19–5–60–3; Gleeson 21–2–59–2; Procter 7–0–25–0; Keogh 9–2–29–1; Kerrigan 17.4–2–62–4; Cobb 1–0–4–0.

Northamptonshire

First innings		Second innings	
L. A. Procter b Raine	82	– lbw b Raine	94
R. I. Newton c Hill b Raine	44	– c Hill b Klein	14
*A. G. Wakely c Ali b Klein	4	– c Evans b Klein	38
R. E. Levi lbw b Parkinson	38	– lbw b Parkinson	9
R. I. Keogh c and b Parkinson	2	– not out	15
J. J. Cobb c Hill b Raine	17	– not out	8
†D. Murphy lbw b Parkinson	1		
S. C. Kerrigan lbw b Raine	0		
R. K. Kleinveldt b Raine	4		
B. W. Sanderson b Klein	0		
R. J. Gleeson not out	0		
Lb 2, nb 8	10	B 5, lb 6, nb 8	19
1/90 (2) 2/105 (3) 3/168 (1) 4/171 (5) 5/186 (4) 6/188 (7) 7/189 (8) 8/199 (9) 9/202 (6) 10/202 (10) (59.1 overs)	202	1/31 (2) 2/152 (3) 3/168 (4) 4/174 (1) (4 wkts, 49.2 overs)	197

Klein 11.1–2–38–2; Raine 20–6–54–5; Chappell 9–2–28–0; Dexter 10–2–39–0; Parkinson 9–1–41–3. *Second innings*—Klein 9–2–32–2; Raine 16–2–59–1; Parkinson 10.2–0–49–1; Chappell 7–0–22–0; Dexter 4–2–7–0; Ali 2–0–15–0; Eckersley 1–0–2–0.

Umpires: P. K. Baldwin and N. G. B. Cook.

MIDDLESEX

Prize comes before a fall

KEVIN HAND

The end of the 2017 season could not have been a greater contrast to the one before, when the Championship was secured on a pulsating final evening. Defeat at Taunton meant Middlesex finished one point behind Somerset, whom they had pipped to the title in 2016, and one point short of survival. Relegation, though, was not confirmed until a few weeks later, when the ECB upheld a two-point penalty for a slow over-rate.

The deduction came after their match at The Oval was called off when a crossbow bolt was fired on to the field during the fourth afternoon. Middlesex were contemplating a declaration at the time, to boost their over-rate – and never had the chance. The umpires apparently told the players not to worry about a penalty – but one was imposed anyway. Middlesex left it until after the season to appeal, though it was never likely the sanction would be overturned: the ECB panel concluded the umpires were not in a position to waive the penalty. County officials, privately seething, said the decision was unjust, but declined to pursue the matter, as it was "not in the interests of Middlesex or the wider game".

The sense of injustice was not helped by the last match, when the Taunton pitch had been raked to help Somerset's slow bowlers, Jack Leach and Dom Bess (Middlesex's own leading spinner, Ollie Rayner, was injured and couldn't play). Stand-in captain Adam Voges reported criss-cross marks on the surface near the batting creases. The ECB's pitch inspector Wayne Noon eventually decided the surface was "below average", but that the bounce was not so uneven as to merit a "poor" rating, which would have meant a points deduction. Even so, Angus Fraser, Middlesex's managing director of cricket, called Somerset's actions "disgraceful".

Such controversies, though, could not hide the fact that Middlesex rarely reached the heights of 2016. Things started well enough, with an exciting one-wicket win over MCC in Abu Dhabi, but began to unravel in the first match back at Lord's. With only four sessions remaining, James Franklin chose not to make Essex follow on – and was stymied next day as they hung on, eight down.

A Championship victory did not come until the sixth match, when Yorkshire were despatched inside three days. All systems were firing well, but from then on there were only occasional signs of brilliance. In the first 14-match Championship season, no one made 800 runs – Stevie Eskinazi led the way with 793 – while the leading wicket-taker was the evergreen Tim Murtagh, with 36. Toby Roland-Jones, a star in 2016, missed several matches on England duty, then picked up a stress fracture, while Dawid Malan also cracked the Test side.

A limp defeat in Lancashire summed up the malaise, and by the time Middlesex won the return fixture – the last home game, with only the visit to Taunton to come – the clock was ticking on a six-year stay in the first division. Just before this, the extended international season (which meant a Test at Lord's starting in September for the first time) had forced the match against fellow strugglers Hampshire out to Uxbridge, which has rarely been kind to Middlesex. Rain overwhelmed the out-ground's covers, and the most interesting action over the first three days involved players, coaches and management staff trying to dry the pitch.

Stevie Eskinazi

Away from the Championship, Daniel Vettori's arrival as Twenty20 coach produced a more dynamic approach in the field. But sloppy mistakes remained a problem, and were punished by opponents who generally appeared more confident: in the shortest format, Middlesex remained serial underachievers. The final evening of the group stage typified the old failings: victory might still have brought qualification, but they crumpled in Cardiff. Still, Vettori's efforts did seem to improve the squad, inspiring hopes for his second season. The Royal London Cup campaign began with a no-result and finished with an abadonment, with little to cheer in between: two wins left Middlesex second-bottom in the South Group.

Franklin left himself out of some of the later matches, and in 2018 Malan replaced him as captain; opening bat Sam Robson became his deputy in the four-day game. Voges was not retained, while Ryan Higgins, a former England Under-19 player, joined Gloucestershire. He was an important cog in the T20 side, but rarely featured in the Championship. "Ryan has shown glimpses of the cricketer he could become," said Fraser, "but we couldn't guarantee him the batting positions he wanted." In an unexpected twist, however, England limited-overs captain Eoin Morgan made himself available for the start of the Championship season after failing to win an IPL contract; he had not played a red-ball game since July 2015.

Middlesex conducted a full inquest into the problems that beset them, although Fraser remained convinced only minor tweaks were required to return to winning ways. By the start of 2018 no new signings had been announced, as the county came to terms with the drop. But the priority was clear: another piece of silverware, in the form of the second division title.

Championship attendance: 52,737.

MIDDLESEX RESULTS

All first-class matches – Played 15: Won 4, Lost 4, Drawn 7.
County Championship matches – Played 14: Won 3, Lost 4, Drawn 7.

Specsavers County Championship, 7th in Division 1;
NatWest T20 Blast, 7th in South Group; Royal London One-Day Cup, 8th in South Group.

COUNTY CHAMPIONSHIP AVERAGES, BATTING AND FIELDING

Cap		*Birthplace*	*M*	*I*	*NO*	*R*	*HS*	*100*	*Avge*	*Ct/St*
2013	S. D. Robson	*Paddington, Aust.*	11	20	0	785	159	2	39.25	10
2016	A. C. Voges¶	*Perth, Australia*	9	14	3	402	92	0	36.54	12
2010	†D. J. Malan	*Roehampton*	8	16	2	493	115	1	35.21	4
2016	P. R. Stirling	*Belfast, N. Ireland*	8	13	0	454	111	1	34.92	4
	S. S. Eskinazi††	*Johannesburg, SA*	14	25	2	793	179	2	34.47	11
2011	†J. A. Simpson	*Bury*	14	22	2	570	90	0	28.50	53/1
2006	N. R. D. Compton	*Durban, SA*	11	19	2	446	120	1	26.23	5
2016	†N. R. T. Gubbins	*Richmond*	7	13	0	314	101	1	24.15	0
2015	†J. E. C. Franklin††	*Wellington, NZ*	10	14	1	296	112	1	22.76	4
2015	O. P. Rayner	*Fallingbostel, Ger*	11	15	2	274	52*	0	21.07	15
2012	T. S. Roland-Jones	*Ashford‡*	9	14	2	252	53	0	21.00	2
	R. F. Higgins	*Harare, Zimbabwe*	4	7	0	129	45	0	18.42	0
2015	J. A. R. Harris	*Morriston*	6	10	1	110	19	0	12.22	1
2008	†T. J. Murtagh	*Lambeth*	12	17	6	134	27	0	12.18	2
2009	S. T. Finn§	*Watford*	11	14	6	95	31*	0	11.87	6
	T. G. Helm	*Stoke Mandeville*	5	7	1	65	28	0	10.83	2
	R. H. Patel	*Harrow‡*	2	4	2	12	7*	0	6.00	1

Also batted: †M. D. E. Holden (*Cambridge*) (1 match) 35 (4 ct); N. A. Sowter†† (*Penrith, Australia*) (1 match) 0, 37.

‡ *Born in Middlesex.* § *ECB contract.* ¶ *Official overseas player.* †† *Other non-England-qualified.*

BOWLING

	Style	*O*	*M*	*R*	*W*	*BB*	*5I*	*Avge*
R. H. Patel	SLA	70	7	221	12	7-81	2	18.41
J. E. C. Franklin	LFM	102	21	280	12	4-40	0	23.33
R. F. Higgins	OB/RM	98	24	281	12	4-75	0	23.41
T. J. Murtagh	RFM	372	93	995	36	6-63	1	27.63
S. T. Finn	RFM	287.2	45	1,045	34	8-79	1	30.73
T. S. Roland-Jones	RFM	277.2	63	880	28	4-66	0	31.42
T. G. Helm	RFM	167.5	30	602	19	5-59	1	31.68
J. A. R. Harris	RFM	154.5	32	490	15	4-119	0	32.66
O. P. Rayner	OB	265.3	62	778	20	4-35	0	38.90

Also bowled: N. R. D. Compton (OB) 1–0–2–0; N. R. T. Gubbins (LB) 1–0–4–0; D. J. Malan (LB) 38–4–125–7; J. A. Simpson (OB) 2–0–21–0; N. A. Sowter (LB) 10.1–1–25–1; P. R. Stirling (OB) 57–8–165–4; A. C. Voges (SLA) 17–0–80–1.

LEADING ROYAL LONDON CUP AVERAGES (100 runs/4 wickets)

Batting	*Runs*	*HS*	*Avge*	*SR*	*Ct/St*
J. A. Simpson	224	82*	37.33	92.94	11/1
A. C. Voges	247	81	35.28	76.94	6
N. R. T. Gubbins	225	114	32.14	78.94	2
J. E. C. Franklin	220	69	31.42	82.08	1
D. J. Malan	155	50	22.14	78.68	1
T. S. Roland-Jones	116	65	19.33	70.30	1

Bowling	*W*	*BB*	*Avge*	*ER*
T. S. Roland-Jones	11	4-10	18.27	3.94
R. F. Higgins	5	3-32	20.00	5.08
R. H. Patel	6	2-39	28.83	3.93
T. G. Helm	7	2-42	37.71	4.98
S. T. Finn	4	4-39	40.00	5.51

LEADING NATWEST T20 BLAST AVERAGES (100 runs/15 overs)

Batting	Runs	HS	Avge	SR	Ct
R. F. Higgins	251	68*	25.10	**160.89**	6
A. C. Voges	110	58*	55.00	**152.77**	1
B. B. McCullum	220	88	24.44	**149.65**	5
P. R. Stirling	184	44	18.40	**133.33**	3
S. S. Eskinazi	165	57*	41.25	**133.06**	1
D. J. Malan	132	41	22.00	**132.00**	6
E. J. G. Morgan	319	59	22.78	**129.67**	9
J. A. Simpson	268	51	20.61	**127.61**	8
J. E. C. Franklin	155	38	14.09	**118.32**	5
G. F. B. Scott	121	38*	30.25	**103.41**	2

Bowling	W	BB	Avge	ER
T. G. Southee	15	3-9	22.46	**7.48**
T. G. Helm	19	5-11	15.89	**7.71**
N. A. Sowter	14	4-23	25.07	**7.97**
S. T. Finn	16	4-24	17.37	**8.17**
R. F. Higgins	6	2-13	30.33	**8.27**
T. S. Roland-Jones	7	4-39	24.14	**10.56**

FIRST-CLASS COUNTY RECORDS

Highest score for	331*	J. D. B. Robertson v Worcestershire at Worcester	1949
Highest score against	341	C. M. Spearman (Gloucestershire) at Gloucester	2004
Leading run-scorer	40,302	E. H. Hendren (avge 48.81)	1907–37
Best bowling for	10-40	G. O. B. Allen v Lancashire at Lord's	1929
Best bowling against	9-38	R. C. Robertson-Glasgow (Somerset) at Lord's	1924
Leading wicket-taker	2,361	F. J. Titmus (avge 21.27)	1949–82
Highest total for	642-3 dec	v Hampshire at Southampton	1923
Highest total against	850-7 dec	by Somerset at Taunton	2007
Lowest total for	20	v MCC at Lord's	1864
Lowest total against	31	by Gloucestershire at Bristol	1924
	31	by Glamorgan at Cardiff	1997

LIST A COUNTY RECORDS

Highest score for	163	A. J. Strauss v Surrey at The Oval	2008
Highest score against	163	C. J. Adams (Sussex) at Arundel	1999
Leading run-scorer	12,029	M. W. Gatting (avge 34.96)	1975–98
Best bowling for	7-12	W. W. Daniel v Minor Counties East at Ipswich	1978
Best bowling against	6-27	J. C. Tredwell (Kent) at Southgate	2009
Leading wicket-taker	491	J. E. Emburey (avge 24.68)	1975–95
Highest total for	367-6	v Sussex v Hove	2015
Highest total against	368-2	by Nottinghamshire at Lord's	2014
Lowest total for	23	v Yorkshire at Leeds	1974
Lowest total against	41	by Northamptonshire at Northampton	1972

TWENTY20 COUNTY RECORDS

Highest score for	129	D. T. Christian v Kent at Canterbury	2014
Highest score against	119	K. J. O'Brien (Gloucestershire) at Uxbridge	2011
Leading run-scorer	**2,760**	**D. J. Malan (avge 33.25)**	**2006–17**
Best bowling for	**5-11**	**T. G. Helm v Essex at Lord's**	**2017**
Best bowling against	6-24	T. J. Murtagh (Surrey) at Lord's	2005
Leading wicket-taker	**55**	**S. T. Finn (avge 22.40)**	**2008–17**
Highest total for	221-2	v Sussex at Hove	2015
Highest total against	254-3	by Gloucestershire at Uxbridge	2011
Lowest total for	92	v Surrey at Lord's	2013
Lowest total against	74	by Essex at Chelmsford	2013

ADDRESS

Lord's Cricket Ground, London NW8 8QN; 020 7289 1300; enquiries@middlesexccc.com; www.middlesexccc.com.

OFFICIALS

Captain 2017 J. E. C. Franklin; **2018** D. J. Malan
Managing director of cricket A. R. C. Fraser
Head coach R. J. Scott
Twenty20 coach D. L. Vettori
Academy director A. J. Coleman
President J. E. Emburey
Chairman M. O'Farrell
Secretary/chief executive R. J. Goatley
Head groundsman M. J. Hunt
Scorer D. K. Shelley

At Abu Dhabi, March 26–28 (day/night). MIDDLESEX beat MCC by one wicket (see MCC section).
Middlesex overcome a first-innings deficit of 153.

At Cambridge, April 7–9 (not first-class). MIDDLESEX beat CAMBRIDGE MCCU by 333 runs.

At Southampton, April 14–17. MIDDLESEX drew with HAMPSHIRE.

MIDDLESEX v ESSEX

At Lord's, April 21–24. Drawn. Middlesex 12pts, Essex 8pts. Toss: uncontested.

Middlesex looked set for victory after a first-innings lead of 212. But, on a pitch livelier than most at Lord's, Franklin waived the follow-on – to the surprise of many who had seen the final-day forecast. Finn, who had just taken four wickets, admitted it had been a tight decision, swung by the bowlers' desire for a rest. In the event, rain and bad light accounted for 28 overs – and Essex ended

TOP HEAVY

The first three (or more) in the order scoring centuries in the same first-class innings at Lord's:

MCC (P. F. Warner 107, C. J. Burnup 161, J. R. Mason 107) v Cambridge University	1902
Surrey (T. W. Hayward 116, J. B. Hobbs 202, E. G. Hayes 134) v Yorkshire†	1914
Middlesex (P. F. Warner 139, H. W. Lee 119, J. W. Hearne 116*, N. E. Haig 131) v Sussex	1920
England (J. B. Hobbs 211, H. Sutcliffe 122, F. E. Woolley 134*) v South Africa	1924
Players (J. B. Hobbs 163, H. Sutcliffe 107, E. Tyldesley 131) v Gentlemen	1926
Kent (L. J. Todd 162, J. G. W. Davies 128, L. E. G. Ames 114*) v Middlesex	1946
Australia (M. A. Taylor 111, M. J. Slater 152, D. C. Boon 164*) v England‡	1993
South Africa (G. C. Smith 107, N. D. McKenzie 138, H. M. Amla 104*) v England	2008
Middlesex (S. D. Robson 149, N. R. T. Gubbins 101, S. S. Eskinazi 100) v Essex	**2017**

† *The Oval was being used for military purposes.* ‡ *M. E. Waugh, at No. 4, made 99.*

eight down, nearly 300 adrift. Despite cloudy first-day skies and a greenish surface, Robson and Gubbins opened with a stand of 241, before Eskinazi – helped by the aggressive Simpson – hit the innings' third century. In the reply, Roland-Jones soon accounted for Cook, and only Lawrence and Wheater, who doubled the score from 126 for five, passed 50. Middlesex ramped up the lead at better than a run a ball: it was only the second time, after Somerset against Cambridge University in 1960, that the top three had all scored a hundred and a half-century in the same first-class match. But Essex survived six overs on the third evening and, although Finn and Roland-Jones worked their way through the middle order in between the weather interruptions next day, Harmer and Wagner both survived for more than an hour to force a draw.

Close of play: first day, Middlesex 255-1 (Robson 144, Eskinazi 1); second day, Essex 120-4 (Lawrence 10, Bopara 0); third day, Essex 19-0 (Browne 17, Cook 2).

Middlesex

S. D. Robson c Wheater b Porter	149	– (2) c Lawrence b Harmer	77
N. R. T. Gubbins c Wheater b Beard	101	– (1) c Bopara b Harmer	64
S. S. Eskinazi b Westley	100	– c Wagner b Harmer	62
D. J. Malan b Bopara	14	– not out	20
A. C. Voges lbw b Porter	13	– not out	6
†J. A. Simpson st Wheater b Harmer	90		
*J. E. C. Franklin c Lawrence b ten Doeschate	3		
T. S. Roland-Jones not out	10		
B 10, lb 13, w 2, nb 2	27	B 4, lb 4, nb 2	10
1/241 (2) 2/277 (1) 3/305 (4) 4/331 (5) 5/480 (3) 6/492 (7) 7/507 (6) (7 wkts dec, 131 overs) 110 overs: 391-4	507	1/146 (2) 2/150 (1) 3/225 (3) (3 wkts dec, 36 overs)	239

O. P. Rayner, T. J. Murtagh and S. T. Finn did not bat.

Porter 28–9–90–2; Wagner 27–5–74–0; Harmer 25–1–112–1; Beard 19–1–73–1; Bopara 20–0–81–1; ten Doeschate 6–0–26–1; Lawrence 1–0–2–0; Westley 5–0–26–1. *Second innings*—Porter 7–1–39–0; Wagner 10–0–62–0; Beard 5–0–33–0; Bopara 3–0–25–0; Harmer 11–0–72–3.

Essex

N. L. J. Browne lbw b Rayner	47	– b Murtagh	19
A. N. Cook c Simpson b Roland-Jones	14	– c Robson b Rayner	37
T. Westley b Finn	31	– lbw b Roland-Jones	13
D. W. Lawrence lbw b Finn	75	– c Voges b Finn	15
J. A. Porter b Roland-Jones	4		
R. S. Bopara c Robson b Roland-Jones	6	– (5) b Finn	32
†A. J. A. Wheater c Eskinazi b Rayner	64	– (6) c Malan b Roland-Jones	0
*R. N. ten Doeschate lbw b Murtagh	20	– (7) c Franklin b Roland-Jones	1
S. R. Harmer c Eskinazi b Finn	1	– (8) lbw b Malan	20
N. Wagner b Finn	3	– (9) not out	16
A. P. Beard not out	4	– (10) not out	0
B 5, lb 5, nb 16	26	B 1, lb 6	7
1/34 (2) 2/86 (3) 3/115 (1) 4/120 (5) 5/126 (6) 6/253 (7) 7/282 (8) 8/285 (9) 9/288 (4) 10/295 (10) (95.1 overs)	295	1/38 (1) 2/74 (3) 3/74 (2) 4/104 (4) 5/104 (6) 6/116 (7) 7/130 (5) 8/160 (8) (8 wkts, 74 overs)	160

Murtagh 23–6–58–1; Roland-Jones 23–4–81–3; Franklin 16–3–58–0; Finn 22.1–6–51–4; Rayner 11–3–37–2. *Second innings*—Murtagh 14–4–44–1; Roland-Jones 21–8–42–3; Finn 16–2–39–2; Rayner 21–11–25–1; Malan 2–1–3–1.

Umpires: P. K. Baldwin and I. J. Gould.

MIDDLESEX v SURREY

At Lord's, May 19–22. Drawn. Middlesex 13pts, Surrey 11pts. Toss: Middlesex.

Two chanceless centuries from Sangakkara enabled Surrey to draw a match which started with the Middlesex attack licking their lips after being given the chance to bowl in overcast conditions. But the openers held firm, then Sangakkara – who walked out to bat past his new portrait in the Pavilion – took control in a stand of 114 with Sibley, before reaching his third hundred in three first-class innings. His departure next morning, to one of several fine catches by Rayner, continued a collapse in which the last six tumbled for 49. Middlesex's reply leaned on contrasting centuries from Malan, who batted for more than five hours, and Franklin, who needed only three, and strong-armed four sixes. Roland-Jones soon removed Surrey's openers, but that only restored Sangakkara to the crease, and he enlivened the third day with yet another hundred – the 31st instance of twin centuries at Lord's – before passing 20,000 first-class runs. He nibbled to the keeper early on the final morning, but Foakes and Sam Curran prevented a slide with a stand of 83. By the time Malan's rusty leg-breaks ended the innings, the stalemate was assured.

Close of play: first day, Surrey 265-5 (Sangakkara 113, S. M. Curran 0); second day, Middlesex 296-5 (Malan 103, Franklin 63); third day, Surrey 194-4 (Sangakkara 116, Foakes 6).

Surrey

R. J. Burns c Rayner b Franklin	33	– lbw b Roland-Jones 10
M. D. Stoneman c Simpson b Finn	33	– c Voges b Roland-Jones 0
S. G. Borthwick lbw b Franklin	8	– lbw b Rayner 49
K. C. Sangakkara c Rayner b Franklin	114	– c Simpson b Franklin 120
D. P. Sibley c Voges b Helm	54	– b Roland-Jones 9
†B. T. Foakes c Simpson b Finn	19	– not out 67
S. M. Curran c Rayner b Franklin	2	– c Simpson b Rayner 51
T. K. Curran c Rayner b Roland-Jones	16	– b Rayner 22
*G. J. Batty c Finn b Helm	12	– lbw b Roland-Jones 6
S. C. Meaker c Eskinazi b Helm	17	– b Malan 0
M. H. A. Footitt not out	0	– c Compton b Malan 0
Lb 5	5	Lb 4, w 1 5

1/55 (2) 2/74 (3) 3/83 (1) 4/197 (5) 5/264 (6) 6/268 (4) 7/269 (7) 8/285 (8) 9/309 (9) 10/313 (10) (89.1 overs) 313

1/5 (2) 2/16 (1) 3/139 (3) 4/171 (5) 5/210 (4) 6/293 (7) 7/317 (8) 8/330 (9) 9/331 (10) 10/339 (11) (126.2 overs) 339

Roland-Jones 23–4–70–1; Helm 23.1–2–81–3; Finn 21–3–80–2; Franklin 15–3–40–4; Rayner 7–1–37–0. *Second innings*—Roland-Jones 27–5–76–4; Helm 18–5–54–0; Finn 23–1–94–0; Franklin 11–3–16–1; Rayner 45–11–94–3; Malan 2.2–1–1–2.

Middlesex

N. R. D. Compton c Foakes b Footitt	19	– c S. M. Curran b Footitt 18
N. R. T. Gubbins lbw b S. M. Curran	17	– c Foakes b S. M. Curran 5
S. S. Eskinazi c Foakes b Footitt	67	– not out 31
D. J. Malan c Foakes b Meaker	115	– not out 37
A. C. Voges c Borthwick b Meaker	9	
†J. A. Simpson lbw b Footitt	11	
*J. E. C. Franklin c Burns b Meaker	112	
T. S. Roland-Jones c Footitt b T. K. Curran	30	
O. P. Rayner c Sibley b T. K. Curran	8	
T. G. Helm c S. M. Curran b Meaker	2	
S. T. Finn not out	0	
B 1, lb 10, w 2, nb 8	21	B 1 1

1/20 (2) 2/50 (1) 3/150 (3) 4/172 (5) 5/204 (6) 6/334 (4) 7/387 (8) 8/399 (7) 9/410 (10) 10/411 (9) (107.4 overs) 411

1/6 (2) 2/31 (1) (2 wkts, 28 overs) 92

T. K. Curran 26.4–5–72–2; S. M. Curran 20–4–81–1; Footitt 22–3–105–3; Meaker 23–5–92–4; Batty 14–2–31–0; Borthwick 2–0–19–0. *Second innings*—T. K. Curran 8–1–20–0; S. M. Curran 5–1–19–1; Batty 6–2–13–0; Footitt 2–1–10–1; Meaker 4–0–16–0; Borthwick 3–0–13–0.

Umpires: M. Burns and P. J. Hartley.

MIDDLESEX v SOMERSET

At Lord's, June 2–5. Drawn. Middlesex 10pts, Somerset 11pts. Toss: Somerset.

Middlesex's third consecutive home draw – their eighth in ten matches at Lord's – left the previous season's top two languishing sixth and seventh in the table, without a Championship victory between them. On a well-grassed pitch, Somerset declined to 80 for five during a rain-affected first day, before Elgar and Gregory, who hit his maiden first-class hundred, combined in a stand that reached 249 (a sixth-wicket record for this fixture) on the second as conditions eased. Davey, a former Middlesex player, and Jamie Overton stretched the total to 443. From a comfortable 217 for three, Middlesex's reply hit problems around the time of the second new ball: Stirling departed after a century partnership with Voges, who then hobbled off with a torn calf muscle that would keep him out for two months. At 248 for six, the follow-on seemed a possibility, but Franklin and the tail reduced the deficit to under 100. By the final morning, with Middlesex still batting, a result looked remote, and the draw was confirmed when more rain hit. There was time for Abell to recover some form, latterly against some undistinguished bowling.

Close of play: first day, Somerset 161-5 (Elgar 77, Gregory 27); second day, Middlesex 42-0 (Compton 19, Gubbins 21); third day, Middlesex 311-7 (Franklin 38, Helm 3).

Somerset

First innings		Second innings	
M. E. Trescothick c Eskinazi b Roland-Jones	8	– (2) c Simpson b Roland-Jones	0
D. Elgar c Simpson b Franklin	158	– (1) c Rayner b Helm	33
*T. B. Abell c Simpson b Murtagh	6	– not out	71
J. C. Hildreth c Rayner b Franklin	25	– c Simpson b Stirling	26
†S. M. Davies c Simpson b Helm	6	– not out	23
P. D. Trego c Simpson b Murtagh	2		
L. Gregory c Helm b Roland-Jones	137		
J. H. Davey c Stirling b Helm	47		
J. Overton c sub (J. A. R. Harris) b Rayner	37		
M. J. Leach not out	3		
B 2, lb 10, nb 2	14	Lb 1, w 1, nb 6	8
1/13 (1) 2/20 (3) 3/66 (4) 4/77 (5) 5/80 (6) 6/329 (2) 7/376 (7) 8/432 (8) 9/443 (9) (9 wkts dec, 128.1 overs)	443	1/1 (2) 2/59 (1) 3/101 (4) (3 wkts dec, 45 overs)	161
110 overs: 361-6			

T. D. Groenewald did not bat.

Murtagh 32–4–105–2; Roland-Jones 27–6–98–2; Helm 29–7–105–2; Franklin 16–4–34–2; Rayner 20.1–2–70–1; Voges 4–0–19–0. *Second innings*—Roland-Jones 8–1–30–1; Helm 9–1–48–1; Murtagh 7–4–8–0; Rayner 11–2–22–0; Stirling 6–0–25–1; Simpson 2–0–21–0; Compton 1–0–2–0; Gubbins 1–0–4–0.

Middlesex

N. R. D. Compton lbw b Groenewald	22
N. R. T. Gubbins lbw b Trego	56
S. S. Eskinazi b Gregory	6
A. C. Voges retired hurt	86
P. R. Stirling c Davies b Overton	52
†J. A. Simpson c Davies b Davey	2
*J. E. C. Franklin not out	49
T. S. Roland-Jones c Davies b Groenewald	1
O. P. Rayner b Overton	29
T. G. Helm b Gregory	28
T. J. Murtagh c Davey b Gregory	2
B 2, lb 9, nb 14	25
1/46 (1) 2/64 (3) 3/116 (2) 4/217 (5) 5/222 (6) 6/248 (8) 7/290 (9) 8/352 (10) 9/358 (11) (124.5 overs)	358
110 overs: 315-7	

Voges retired hurt at 245-5.

Gregory 16.5–4–59–3; Davey 27–6–71–1; Groenewald 27–11–46–2; Overton 23–6–59–2; Leach 21–4–77–0; Trego 10–2–35–1.

Umpires: J. W. Lloyds and B. V. Taylor.

At Southport, June 9–12. MIDDLESEX lost to LANCASHIRE by eight wickets. *Middlesex's first Championship defeat since September 2015.*

MIDDLESEX v YORKSHIRE

At Lord's, June 19–21. Middlesex won by an innings and 64 runs. Middlesex 23pts, Yorkshire 3pts. Toss: Middlesex. First-class debut: R. F. Higgins. Championship debut: H. C. Brook.

Middlesex finally broke their duck for the season, completing a fourth successive Championship victory over Yorkshire. It was not the last-gasp classic that had rounded off the 2016 season: a Yorkshire side lacking most of their Test players crashed to defeat inside three days. The first had established Middlesex's superiority. Robson made the most of surviving a return catch to Brooks when 31 by batting all day, putting on 187 with Stirling, whose three-hour 111 was his first Championship century. The innings lost impetus after Robson fell for 159 early on the second morning, but Simpson helped propel the score towards 450. Yorkshire made a decent start through Lyth and the 18-year-old Harry Brook, but once they were separated – a maiden wicket for off-spinning all-rounder Ryan Higgins – only Ballance lasted longer than an hour. Franklin enforced the follow-on this time, and Murtagh soon removed Lyth and Brook. The slide continued: Handscomb survived 100 minutes for 21, and Rashid made 35, but Rayner found turn to claim four of the last five.

Close of play: first day, Middlesex 337-4 (Robson 152, Simpson 13); second day, Yorkshire 186-9 (Ballance 53, Sidebottom 3).

Middlesex

S. D. Robson c Hodd b Coad	159
N. R. D. Compton c Hodd b Patterson	22
S. S. Eskinazi b Brooks	4
P. R. Stirling lbw b Rashid	111
*J. E. C. Franklin b Sidebottom	17
†J. A. Simpson b Sidebottom	49
R. F. Higgins b Coad	13
T. S. Roland-Jones c Handscomb b Rashid	33
O. P. Rayner c Patterson b Sidebottom	2
T. J. Murtagh not out	11
S. T. Finn lbw b Rashid	4
B 2, lb 12, w 1, nb 6	21
1/64 (2) 2/75 (3) 3/262 (4) (132 overs)	446
4/302 (5) 5/364 (1) 6/380 (7)	
7/414 (6) 8/420 (9) 9/440 (8)	
10/446 (11) 110 overs: 385-6	

Sidebottom 26–8–69–3; Brooks 22–3–98–1; Coad 30–8–80–2; Patterson 27–7–80–1; Rashid 26–2–94–3; Lyth 1–0–11–0.

Yorkshire

A. Lyth c Simpson b Higgins	37	– c Simpson b Murtagh	2
A. Z. Lees lbw b Roland-Jones	4	– c Rayner b Roland-Jones	14
H. C. Brook c Eskinazi b Rayner	38	– c Simpson b Murtagh	0
*G. S. Ballance not out	69	– c Simpson b Roland-Jones	19
P. S. P. Handscomb c Robson b Roland-Jones	15	– c Compton b Finn	21
A. U. Rashid b Finn	0	– c Simpson b Franklin	35
†A. J. Hodd b Murtagh	0	– b Rayner	15
S. A. Patterson b Higgins	1	– not out	30
J. A. Brooks b Higgins	0	– c Roland-Jones b Rayner	12
B. O. Coad c Simpson b Finn	14	– c Stirling b Rayner	8
R. J. Sidebottom c Simpson b Finn	9	– c Robson b Rayner	9
Lb 11, nb 10	21	Lb 5, nb 4	9
1/18 (2) 2/82 (1) 3/88 (3) (63.2 overs)	208	1/16 (1) 2/16 (3) (62.3 overs)	174
4/119 (5) 5/120 (6) 6/135 (7)		3/16 (2) 4/52 (4)	
7/140 (8) 8/146 (9) 9/178 (10) 10/208 (11)		5/73 (5) 6/107 (7) 7/111 (6)	
		8/130 (9) 9/154 (10) 10/174 (11)	

Murtagh 12–3–31–1; Roland-Jones 13–5–46–2; Higgins 16–5–35–3; Finn 14.2–4–58–3; Rayner 8–2–27–1. *Second innings*—Murtagh 11–7–13–2; Roland-Jones 14–2–46–2; Finn 7–0–30–1; Higgins 10–3–26–0; Rayner 13.3–5–35–4; Franklin 5–0–12–1; Stirling 2–0–7–0.

Umpires: N. G. B. Cook and J. H. Evans.

At Chelmsford, June 26–29. MIDDLESEX lost to ESSEX by an innings and 34 runs.

At Birmingham, July 3–6. MIDDLESEX beat WARWICKSHIRE by one wicket.

MIDDLESEX v WARWICKSHIRE

At Lord's, August 6–8. Warwickshire won by 190 runs. Warwickshire 19pts, Middlesex 3pts. Toss: Warwickshire. First-class debut: N. A. Sowter. County debut: R. N. Sidebottom.

Middlesex's plea for more helpful pitches at Lord's came home to roost when they slumped to a three-day defeat by the bottom club, failing to total 300 runs over their two innings. Set 327, they disintegrated to 88 for nine inside 25 overs on the third day, with opener Gubbins going in at No. 8 after tweaking a hamstring in the field. Warwickshire's only Championship victory of the season had been set up by a disciplined batting performance on the second day, when 21-year-old Matt Lamb made a stubborn 71 in only his third match; Barker and Wright added 97 for the ninth wicket. This followed a frenetic opening day, when 20 wickets tumbled, all bar three to seam. Finn took four as Warwickshire struggled to 126, then Franklin and Higgins – who had briefly retired hurt after being hit on the head first ball – rescued Middlesex from 59 for six, in the face of a testing spell from the Australian Ryan Sidebottom, playing his second first-class game more than four years after his first, for Victoria. (His first victim, Simpson, had been dismissed by the English Ryan Sidebottom a few weeks earlier against Yorkshire.) Simpson also collected nine catches in the match, including an outstanding one standing up to Higgins to send back Trott for 54.

MOST DISMISSALS IN A MATCH FOR MIDDLESEX

9 (6ct, 3st)	M. Turner	v Nottinghamshire at Prince's, Chelsea	1875
9 (8ct, 1st)	J. T. Murray	v Hampshire at Lord's	1965
9 (9ct)	D. C. Nash	v Yorkshire at Leeds	1999
9 (9ct)	J. A. Simpson	v Gloucestershire at Bristol	2011
9 (9ct)	J. A. Simpson	v Somerset at Taunton	2016
9 (9ct)	**J. A. Simpson**	**v Warwickshire at Lord's**	**2017**

Close of play: first day, Warwickshire 12-0 (Umeed 6, Sibley 6); second day, Warwickshire 293-8 (Barker 30, Wright 11).

Warwickshire

A. R. I. Umeed c Franklin b Helm	1	– b Higgins	30
D. P. Sibley c Eskinazi b Finn	20	– c Simpson b Murtagh	17
I. J. L. Trott c Simpson b Helm	18	– c Simpson b Higgins	54
I. R. Bell c Simpson b Murtagh	14	– lbw b Higgins	0
M. J. Lamb b Higgins	3	– c Simpson b Helm	71
T. R. Ambrose c Robson b Finn	4	– c Simpson b Murtagh	16
C. R. Woakes c Eskinazi b Finn	12	– c Murtagh b Higgins	53
K. H. D. Barker c Simpson b Finn	12	– not out	62
J. S. Patel c Simpson b Murtagh	24	– b Murtagh	0
C. J. C. Wright not out	7	– c Simpson b Finn	41
R. N. Sidebottom b Murtagh	4	– b Sowter	1
B 1, lb 4, nb 2	7	B 9, lb 5, nb 2	16
1/5 (1) 2/34 (2) 3/42 (3) 4/61 (4) 5/61 (5) 6/68 (6) 7/81 (7) 8/98 (8) 9/120 (9) 10/126 (11) (47 overs)	126	1/27 (2) 2/100 (1) 3/100 (4) 4/109 (3) 5/139 (6) 6/241 (7) 7/261 (5) 8/262 (9) 9/359 (10) 10/361 (11) (112.1 overs)	361

Murtagh 16–8–20–3; Helm 14–4–42–2; Finn 12–2–53–4; Higgins 4–2–4–1; Sowter 1–0–2–0. *Second innings*—Murtagh 25–4–63–3; Helm 23–5–89–1; Higgins 24–5–75–4; Finn 23–3–81–1; Franklin 8–2–16–0; Sowter 9.1–1–23–1.

Middlesex

S. D. Robson c Umeed b Woakes	3	– lbw b Barker	19
N. R. T. Gubbins lbw b Woakes	14	– (8) lbw b Sidebottom	15
N. R. D. Compton c and b Wright	22	– (2) c Ambrose b Barker	3
S. S. Eskinazi run out	7	– (3) c Sibley b Barker	2
†J. A. Simpson lbw b Sidebottom	2	– (4) lbw b Woakes	4
*J. E. C. Franklin c Trott b Patel	55	– (5) b Woakes	1
R. F. Higgins lbw b Patel	38	– (6) lbw b Woakes	5
N. A. Sowter b Sidebottom	0	– (7) c Umeed b Sidebottom	37
T. G. Helm b Sidebottom	2	– c Trott b Patel	15
T. J. Murtagh b Sidebottom	4	– b Patel	0
S. T. Finn not out	0	– not out	31
B 4, lb 8, nb 2	14	B 4	4
1/4 (1) 2/31 (2) 3/44 (4) 4/46 (5) 5/56 (3) 6/59 (8) 7/152 (7) 8/155 (9) 9/159 (10) 10/161 (6) (40.2 overs)	161	1/21 (1) 2/23 (3) 3/28 (2) 4/28 (4) 5/34 (6) 6/45 (5) 7/71 (7) 8/88 (9) 9/88 (10) 10/136 (8) (29.5 overs)	136

In the first innings Higgins, when 0, retired hurt at 56-5 and resumed at 59-6.

Woakes 11–0–57–2; Barker 9–2–31–0; Sidebottom 10–2–29–4; Patel 4.2–2–3–2; Wright 6–1–29–1. *Second innings*—Woakes 9–2–38–3; Barker 8–4–21–3; Patel 5–2–19–2; Sidebottom 6.5–1–41–2; Wright 1–0–13–0.

Umpires: P. K. Baldwin and R. T. Robinson.

At The Oval, August 28–31. MIDDLESEX drew with SURREY. *The match is abandoned after a crossbow bolt lands on the square.*

At Leeds, September 5–8. MIDDLESEX drew with YORKSHIRE.

MIDDLESEX v HAMPSHIRE

At Uxbridge, September 12–15. Drawn. Middlesex 9pts, Hampshire 8pts. Toss: uncontested. First-class debut: F. S. Organ. County debut: M. D. E. Holden. Championship debut: C. M. Dickinson.

Rain on each of the 14 days before this match – staged here, since Lord's had just held the late-season West Indies Test – put play in doubt even before it was discovered that water had seeped under one of the covers. Heaters and additional covering were brought in, and several players (plus director of cricket Angus Fraser, armed with a pitchfork) tried to help the groundstaff. But, with the rain returning, only 59 overs were possible over the first three days. The fourth became a scramble for bonus points: Middlesex's last pair scraped the game's only batting point, before Hampshire groped their way to 146. The conditions made the tired Uxbridge square livelier than it had been for a decade or more, but the interruptions meant Middlesex had still not won a first-class match in 17 attempts there since beating Leicestershire by one run in 1995.

Close of play: first day, no play; second day, Middlesex 76-3 (Voges 10, Holden 1); third day, Middlesex 162-7 (Simpson 15, Rayner 4).

Middlesex

S. D. Robson c Adams b Holland	28	– (2) c Adams b Berg	0
N. R. D. Compton b Edwards	16	– (1) not out	11
S. S. Eskinazi c Alsop b Edwards	13	– not out	3
A. C. Voges c Adams b Edwards	27		
M. D. E. Holden c Adams b Holland	35		
†J. A. Simpson b Edwards	36		
*J. E. C. Franklin b Abbott	0		
J. A. R. Harris lbw b Abbott	0		
O. P. Rayner c Crane b Abbott	9		
T. G. Helm lbw b Edwards	1		
S. T. Finn not out	9		
B 4, lb 11, w 1, nb 14	30		
1/40 (2) 2/58 (1) 3/62 (3) 4/120 (4) 5/138 (5) 6/148 (7) 7/154 (8) 8/168 (9) 9/169 (10) 10/204 (6) (72 overs)	204	1/9 (2) (1 wkt, 9 overs)	14

Edwards 26–5–79–5; Abbott 18–8–25–3; Berg 12–2–36–0; Holland 14–6–31–2; Crane 2–0–18–0. *Second innings*—Berg 5–3–9–1; Abbott 4–2–5–0.

Hampshire

J. J. Weatherley c Voges b Helm	35
*J. H. K. Adams c Simpson b Helm	2
†T. P. Alsop c Simpson b Rayner	9
S. M. Ervine c Simpson b Finn	0
F. S. Organ b Harris	16
I. G. Holland b Harris	23
C. M. Dickinson c Simpson b Finn	1
G. K. Berg b Helm	22
K. J. Abbott run out	13
M. S. Crane not out	9
F. H. Edwards b Finn	3
B 4, lb 5, nb 4	13
1/15 (2) 2/46 (1) 3/46 (3) 4/46 (4) 5/89 (6) 6/92 (7) 7/96 (5) 8/127 (9) 9/132 (8) 10/146 (11) (36.1 overs)	146

Helm 11–1–43–3; Finn 10.1–1–41–3; Harris 10–3–27–2; Rayner 5–1–26–1.

Umpires: R. J. Evans and G. D. Lloyd.

MIDDLESEX v LANCASHIRE

At Lord's, September 19–21. Middlesex won by 36 runs. Middlesex 20pts, Lancashire 3pts. Toss: Middlesex.

Adam Voges, captaining after James Franklin dropped himself, caused a shock by opting to bat on the greenest surface seen at Lord's for years. He reasoned that, underneath the grass, the pitch was dry and cracked, so batting last would be problematic – but admitted he was worried when Middlesex lurched to 28 for four inside the first hour. However, Voges and Simpson calmed a few demons, before an eighth-wicket stand of 102 between Roland-Jones and Rayner. Murtagh took four wickets as Lancashire struggled to 165 – a deficit of 68 – but survival remained a trial: only Robson hung around when Middlesex batted again, and shortly after he was out the last five wickets crashed for 22. Bailey finished with ten in a match for the first time, while Jarvis, in his last county game before returning to Zimbabwe, polished the innings off with three in 18 balls. Lancashire needed 221, but were already four down when a delivery from Harris broke a finger on Hameed's right hand, ending any lingering hopes of a Test recall for the Ashes tour (Roland-Jones faced similar heartbreak after suffering a stress fracture of the back). Finn, though, did his own Ashes aspirations no harm, temporarily easing relegation fears with eight for 79, his best figures for seven years. With 38 still wanted, Hameed pluckily returned when the ninth wicket fell, but Finn soon removed No. 11 Parkinson. Middlesex climbed to fifth, 16 points in front of seventh-placed Somerset, but with a trip to Taunton to come.

Close of play: first day, Lancashire 113-5 (Croft 33, McLaren 5); second day, Lancashire 46-1 (Hameed 22, Livingstone 13).

Middlesex

S. D. Robson c Davies b McLaren	6	– (2) c Jarvis b Bailey	58
N. R. D. Compton lbw b McLaren	0	– (1) c Davies b Bailey	9
S. S. Eskinazi c Vilas b Bailey	7	– b Bailey	2
D. J. Malan c Davies b Bailey	12	– lbw b McLaren	18
*A. C. Voges lbw b Bailey	18	– c McLaren b Clark	5
†J. A. Simpson c Davies b Bailey	29	– c Jarvis b Bailey	33
J. A. R. Harris b McLaren	1	– lbw b Jarvis	1
T. S. Roland-Jones lbw b Jarvis	53	– c Croft b Jarvis	9
O. P. Rayner not out	52	– lbw b Bailey	5
S. T. Finn lbw b Bailey	8	– not out	0
T. J. Murtagh c Bailey b McLaren	18	– b Jarvis	5
B 4, lb 11, w 10, nb 4	29	Lb 7	7
1/0 (2) 2/11 (1) 3/25 (3) 4/28 (4) 5/80 (5) 6/81 (7) 7/89 (6) 8/191 (8) 9/208 (10) 10/233 (11) (61.4 overs)	233	1/12 (1) 2/16 (3) 3/54 (4) 4/79 (5) 5/115 (2) 6/130 (6) 7/130 (7) 8/147 (8) 9/147 (9) 10/152 (11) (45.2 overs)	152

Bailey 18–4–54–5; McLaren 15.4–4–63–4; Jarvis 15–4–43–1; Clark 5–1–23–0; Parkinson 8–1–35–0. *Second innings*—Bailey 16–6–44–5; McLaren 12–3–25–1; Jarvis 7.2–1–30–3; Clark 10–1–46–1.

Lancashire

†A. L. Davies lbw b Murtagh	19	– lbw b Finn	1
H. Hameed lbw b Roland-Jones	3	– not out	23
L. S. Livingstone c Compton b Finn	16	– b Finn	15
D. J. Vilas b Murtagh	5	– (6) c Simpson b Finn	37
S. Chanderpaul c Voges b Roland-Jones	29	– lbw b Murtagh	7
*S. J. Croft c Simpson b Murtagh	37	– (4) lbw b Finn	4
R. McLaren c Finn b Rayner	27	– c Rayner b Finn	37
J. Clark c Simpson b Murtagh	6	– c Simpson b Finn	31
T. E. Bailey c Rayner b Harris	9	– lbw b Harris	3
K. M. Jarvis not out	8	– c Voges b Finn	0
M. W. Parkinson lbw b Rayner	0	– c Voges b Finn	13
B 3, lb 1, nb 2	6	B 4, lb 2, w 5, nb 2	13
1/22 (2) 2/22 (1) 3/40 (4) 4/56 (3) 5/95 (5) 6/117 (6) 7/123 (8) 8/149 (9) 9/161 (7) 10/165 (11) (55.3 overs)	165	1/17 (1) 2/48 (3) 3/52 (4) 4/59 (5) 5/116 (6) 6/150 (8) 7/157 (9) 8/158 (10) 9/183 (7) 10/184 (11) (65.4 overs)	184

In the second innings Hameed, when 23, retired hurt at 75-4 and resumed at 183-9.

Murtagh 18–5–49–4; Roland-Jones 10.4–4–30–2; Finn 12–4–40–1; Harris 10–3–40–1; Rayner 4.5–2–2–2. *Second innings*—Murtagh 20–7–44–1; Finn 22.4–4–79–8; Harris 14–3–28–1; Rayner 2–0–15–0; Malan 7–2–12–0.

Umpires: N. A. Mallender and M. J. Saggers.

At Taunton, September 25–28. MIDDLESEX lost to SOMERSET by 231 runs. *Middlesex are relegated.*

NORTHAMPTONSHIRE

Another fine miss

ANDREW RADD

Northamptonshire confirmed their endearing capacity to cause surprise last year. A squad widely expected to enjoy white-ball success failed to reach the knockout stages of either competition, and instead reserved their best performances for the Championship. A total of nine victories from 14 – a winning percentage of 64, their second-highest, behind 70 in 1995, when they won 12 from 17 – sustained their promotion challenge until the final day. But Nottinghamshire, who won seven, pipped them by five points.

The significance of that margin, and those opponents, escaped no one. At Trent Bridge in late August, with captain Alex Wakely nursing a damaged finger, and Rory Kleinveldt in charge, Northamptonshire's painfully slow over-rate earned a five-point deduction. "It's disappointing, but we deserved to lose them," said head coach David Ripley. "It's just a shame that a poor bit of play blemished a fantastic season." It was the latest addition to Northamptonshire's hefty back catalogue of if-onlys.

In truth, other factors weighed more heavily, not least securing maximum batting bonus points only once. There was a lack of ruthlessness: Rob Newton, the team's leading run-scorer in the Championship, converted only one of his 11 fifties into a century. The club appointed former captain David Sales as full-time batting coach at the end of the season: with eight first-class scores of 200 or more – including a triple – he was well placed to underline the importance of exploiting promising starts.

Northamptonshire's main strength in four-day cricket lay in their seam bowling: Kleinveldt, Azharullah, Richard Gleeson, Ben Sanderson and newcomer Nathan Buck shared 197 Championship wickets. Kleinveldt's nine for 65 in the home win over Nottinghamshire was the best return of the competition, and the best by a Northamptonshire seamer since Albert Thomas against Yorkshire at Bradford in 1920. He will play white-ball cricket only in 2018. Sanderson agreed a new three-year contract, and seam-bowling all-rounder Brett Hutton was signed from Nottinghamshire. New Zealand seamer Doug Bracewell was set to appear just in the first four Championship matches.

But Azharullah left Wantage Road after five seasons in which he had played a key role in two Twenty20 triumphs. Plucking him out of the Huddersfield League in 2013 had proved one of Northamptonshire's shrewdest moves in recent years. Another of the team that won the 2013 T20 competition hung up his gloves: David Murphy, the 28-year-old Scotland keeper, opted for a law career in London.

The attack lacked balance, though, with Graeme White's left-arm spin sorely missed. Injury restricted him to three Championship appearances and, more

David Rogers, Getty Images

Rory Kleinveldt

significantly, only four in the Blast; he underwent shoulder surgery at the end of the summer. His absence prompted the loan signing of Lancashire's one-time Test slow left-armer Simon Kerrigan, who picked up 12 wickets over the last four Championship matches.

Sri Lankan leg-spinner Seekkuge Prasanna had been due to rejoin the county for the defence of their T20 crown, but was ruled out by a hamstring injury (he will be back in 2018). Tabraiz Shamsi, the South African left-arm wrist-spinner, deputised for five games and proved comfortably Northamptonshire's most economical bowler, going at less than 6.5 an over. But after his departure Ripley decided he would trust his own. Hindsight suggested that was a mistake. With three matches left, a quarter-final place was on the cards, but heavy defeats by Leicestershire and Yorkshire were followed by a washout against Durham.

The Royal London Cup was something of a dud. Northamptonshire began with a ten-wicket shellacking at home against Warwickshire, won only once, and finished with two washouts. The best that could be said was that it allowed them to focus elsewhere.

Ben Duckett, who hit 2,706 runs in all cricket in 2016, returned to the county game after a chastening experience with England on the subcontinent, and found consistency elusive. He showed glimpses of his best, particularly towards the end of the year, with an unbeaten 92 off 54 balls in the Blast at Worcester, and 193 in the Championship victory over Sussex. He earned selection for the England Lions winter tour of Australia, but was suspended after pouring a beer over James Anderson. If the incident was described as "trivial" by England coach Trevor Bayliss, it was more bad news for Duckett, after he had admitted to drink-driving in 2015. He was given a final written warning, and left out of the Lions' tour of the Caribbean in early 2018.

The most eye-catching batsman was South African Richard Levi. He was out of the first team for nearly eight weeks with concussion after being hit by a bouncer from Worcestershire's Josh Tongue, but still claimed four club awards. His most memorable innings, though, came in the Championship win over Nottinghamshire. Levi's counter-attacking century on a seaming pitch demonstrated he is much more than a T20 short-boundary bully.

Less spectacular but still highly effective was Max Holden, the England Under-19 captain on loan from Middlesex. A mature and diligent cricketer, he scored hundreds against Durham and Kent, and earned Northamptonshire's Young Player of the Year award. Another loan signing, Luke Procter, joined from Lancashire in September and hit three half-centuries in four Championship innings; weeks later, he signed a three-year contract. He seemed an excellent addition to help the club's push for promotion.

Championship attendance: 14,009.

NORTHAMPTONSHIRE RESULTS

All first-class matches – Played 15: Won 9, Lost 3, Drawn 3.
County Championship matches – Played 14: Won 9, Lost 3, Drawn 2.

Specsavers County Championship, 3rd in Division 2;
NatWest T20 Blast, 6th in North Group; Royal London One-Day Cup, 8th in North Group.

COUNTY CHAMPIONSHIP AVERAGES, BATTING AND FIELDING

Cap		*Birthplace*	*M*	*I*	*NO*	*R*	*HS*	*100*	*Avge*	*Ct/St*
	†L. A. Procter	*Oldham*	2	4	0	235	94	0	58.75	2
2017	R. E. Levi††	*Johannesburg, SA*	10	19	3	734	115	2	45.87	12
2016	†B. M. Duckett	*Farnborough, Kent*	11	19	0	799	193	3	42.05	16
	†M. D. E. Holden	*Cambridge*	9	16	0	629	153	2	39.31	4
2017	R. I. Newton	*Taunton*	13	24	0	894	108	1	37.25	1
2012	A. G. Wakely	*Hammersmith*	13	24	3	658	112	1	31.33	14
	A. M. Rossington	*Edgware*	8	13	1	358	112	1	29.83	19/2
	J. J. Cobb	*Leicester*	10	18	4	410	96	0	29.28	3
	S. C. Kerrigan	*Preston*	4	5	1	98	62	0	24.50	2
	G. G. White	*Milton Keynes*	3	4	0	88	47	0	22.00	0
2016	R. K. Kleinveldt¶	*Cape Town, SA*	12	19	1	394	86	0	21.88	8
	R. I. Keogh	*Dunstable*	12	22	3	408	105*	1	21.47	5
	N. L. Buck	*Leicester*	8	13	3	201	43	0	20.10	4
2013	S. P. Crook	*Modbury, Australia*	5	8	1	128	30	0	18.28	2
2015	Azharullah	*Burewala, Pakistan*	7	10	5	73	23	0	14.60	1
	R. J. Gleeson	*Blackpool*	7	9	4	63	25	0	12.60	1
	†C. F. Hughes	*Anguilla*	3	6	0	60	21	0	10.00	3
2017	D. Murphy	*Welwyn Garden City*	5	7	0	67	30	0	9.57	12/3
	B. W. Sanderson	*Sheffield*	10	16	5	72	16*	0	6.54	3

Also batted: A. Carter (*Lincoln*) (1 match) 3, 8; A. Sheikh (*Nottingham*) (1 match) 7.

§ *ECB contract.* ¶ *Official overseas player.* †† *Other non-England-qualified.*

BOWLING

	Style	*O*	*M*	*R*	*W*	*BB*	*5I*	*Avge*
R. J. Gleeson	RFM	222.2	44	745	40	5-46	3	18.62
N. L. Buck	RFM	222.4	37	770	36	6-34	3	21.38
B. W. Sanderson	RFM	334.1	93	860	40	5-39	2	21.50
Azharullah	RFM	192	36	677	31	5-63	2	21.83
R. K. Kleinveldt	RFM	350.1	68	1,153	50	9-65	2	23.06
S. C. Kerrigan	SLA	120.4	24	389	12	4-62	0	32.41

Also bowled: A. Carter (RFM) 22–5–90–5; J. J. Cobb (OB) 32–0–113–1; S. P. Crook (RFM) 74.4–6–333–4; B. M. Duckett (OB) 9–0–41–1; M. D. E. Holden (OB) 33–2–159–3; C. F. Hughes (SLA) 2–0–16–0; R. I. Keogh (OB) 112.1–17–461–9; R. I. Newton (LB) 9–0–82–1; L. A. Procter (RFM) 31–3–138–1; A. M. Rossington (RM) 12–1–48–0; A. Sheikh (LFM) 8–1–36–1; A. G. Wakely (OB/RM) 9.2–0–75–0; G. G. White (SLA) 72–9–305–3.

LEADING ROYAL LONDON CUP AVERAGES (100 runs/4 wickets)

Batting	*Runs*	*HS*	*Avge*	*SR*	*Ct*
R. E. Levi	305	109	61.00	108.15	0
A. M. Rossington	213	69	53.25	129.87	4
A. G. Wakely	247	109*	49.40	86.66	4
R. I. Newton	226	107	45.20	88.97	1
R. I. Keogh	177	69*	44.25	86.34	1
J. J. Cobb	129	56	21.50	87.16	1

Bowling	*W*	*BB*	*Avge*	*ER*
B. W. Sanderson	8	3-36	25.12	5.02
Azharullah	7	3-55	43.28	5.75
R. J. Gleeson	4	2-56	53.25	6.87
G. G. White	5	2-37	56.00	5.09

LEADING NATWEST T20 BLAST AVERAGES (100 runs/15 overs)

Batting	Runs	HS	Avge	SR	Ct/St
R. E. Levi	375	88	46.87	**166.66**	1
A. M. Rossington	308	67	28.00	**161.25**	9/1
S. P. Crook	129	34*	25.80	**150.00**	5
B. M. Duckett	297	92*	29.70	**129.69**	3
A. G. Wakely	258	52	28.66	**121.69**	5
R. I. Keogh	178	41*	25.42	**117.88**	2
J. J. Cobb	113	48	22.60	**111.88**	4

Bowling	W	BB	Avge	ER
R. J. Gleeson	10	3-12	33.10	**7.78**
R. K. Kleinveldt	14	3-16	24.35	**7.93**
Azharullah	7	2-36	25.85	**9.05**
R. I. Keogh	6	2-27	34.33	**9.36**
B. W. Sanderson	7	2-26	43.28	**10.04**

FIRST-CLASS COUNTY RECORDS

Highest score for	331*	M. E. K. Hussey v Somerset at Taunton	2003
Highest score against	333	K. S. Duleepsinhji (Sussex) at Hove	1930
Leading run-scorer	28,980	D. Brookes (avge 36.13)	1934–59
Best bowling for	10-127	V. W. C. Jupp v Kent at Tunbridge Wells	1932
Best bowling against	10-30	C. Blythe (Kent) at Northampton	1907
Leading wicket-taker	1,102	E. W. Clark (avge 21.26)	1922–47
Highest total for	781-7 dec	v Nottinghamshire at Northampton	1995
Highest total against	673-8 dec	by Yorkshire at Leeds	2003
Lowest total for	12	v Gloucestershire at Gloucester	1907
Lowest total against	33	by Lancashire at Northampton	1977

LIST A COUNTY RECORDS

Highest score for	172*	W. Larkins v Warwickshire at Luton	1983
Highest score against	184	M. J. Lumb (Nottinghamshire) at Nottingham	2016
Leading run-scorer	11,010	R. J. Bailey (avge 39.46)	1983–99
Best bowling for	7-10	C. Pietersen v Denmark at Brøndby	2005
Best bowling against	7-35	D. E. Malcolm (Derbyshire) at Derby	1997
Leading wicket-taker	251	A. L. Penberthy (avge 30.45)	1989–2003
Highest total for	425	v Nottinghamshire at Nottingham	2016
Highest total against	445-8	by Nottinghamshire at Nottingham	2016
Lowest total for	41	v Middlesex at Northampton	1972
Lowest total against	56	by Leicestershire at Leicester	1964
	56	by Denmark at Brøndby	2005

TWENTY20 COUNTY RECORDS

Highest score for	111*	L. Klusener v Worcestershire at Kidderminster	2007
Highest score against	**161**	**A. Lyth (Yorkshire) at Leeds**	**2017**
Leading run-scorer	**2,026**	**A. G. Wakely (avge 27.37)**	**2009–17**
Best bowling for	6-21	A. J. Hall v Worcestershire at Northampton	2008
Best bowling against	5-6	P. D. Collingwood (Durham) at Chester-le-Street	2011
Leading wicket-taker	73	D. J. Willey (avge 19.45)	2009–15
Highest total for	224-5	v Gloucestershire at Milton Keynes	2005
Highest total against	**260-4**	**by Yorkshire at Leeds**	**2017**
Lowest total for	47	v Durham at Chester-le-Street	2011
Lowest total against	86	by Worcestershire at Worcester	2006

ADDRESS

County Ground, Abington Avenue, Northampton NN1 4PR; 01604 514455; reception@nccc.co.uk; www.northantscricket.com.

OFFICIALS

Captain A. G. Wakely
Head coach D. Ripley
Academy director K. J. Innes
President Lord Naseby

Chairman G. G. Warren
Chief executive R. Payne
Head groundsman C. Harvey
Scorer A. C. Kingston

NORTHAMPTONSHIRE v LOUGHBOROUGH MCCU

At Northampton, April 2–4. Drawn. Toss: Loughborough MCCU. First-class debuts: M. D. E. Holden, M. A. Richardson, G. Wade. County debut: N. L. Buck.

Loughborough endured a difficult first day: Newton and Rossington hit centuries, and drove Northamptonshire to 435 for six at more than five an over. But they responded brilliantly, amassing 553, the highest total by a university side against a first-class county since 1930. There were hundreds for Charlie Thurston – who had appeared for Northamptonshire's Second XI in the two previous seasons – Nitish Kumar and Sam Evans, while 18-year-old left-arm spinner Saif Zaib claimed a career-best six for 115. But on a pitch that gave no help to the bowlers, Wakely became the sixth century-maker of the match.

Close of play: first day, Loughborough MCCU 37-1 (Thurston 28, Bracey 2); second day, Loughborough MCCU 468-7 (Evans 69, Gamble 1).

FIRST-CLASS HONOURS

Highest scores by universities against first-class counties:

703-9 dec	Cambridge v Sussex at Hove	1890
651	Oxford v Sussex at Hove	1895
612	Oxford v Middlesex at Chelsea	1876
611	Cambridge v Sussex at Hove	1919
577	Oxford v Surrey at Reigate	1909
572	Cambridge v Surrey at The Oval	1930
555	Oxford v Middlesex at Chiswick	1887
554	Oxford v Hampshire at Southampton	1913
553	**Loughborough v Northamptonshire at Northampton**	**2017**
543	Cambridge v Sussex at Hove	1925

Northamptonshire

M. D. E. Holden b Akram	19	– (2) not out	75
R. I. Newton retired out	166		
*A. G. Wakely b Akram	14	– (1) not out	104
A. M. Rossington c Akram b Gamble	117		
J. J. Cobb not out	63		
S. P. Crook c Tillcock b Kumar	3		
†D. Murphy c Hassan Azad b Ladd-Gibbon	14		
S. A. Zaib not out	20		
B 5, nb 14	19	B 1, lb 1, w 4	6
1/46 (1) 2/78 (3) 3/268 (4) 4/355 (2) 5/360 (6) 6/401 (7) — (6 wkts dec, 83 overs)	435	(no wkt dec, 46 overs)	185

N. L. Buck, M. A. Richardson and G. Wade did not bat.

Gamble 16–4–75–1; Cook 19–3–81–0; Akram 15–1–106–2; Ladd-Gibbon 14–1–74–1; Tillcock 12–0–72–0; Kumar 7–0–22–1. *Second innings*—Gamble 7–2–29–0; Cook 11–2–26–0; Akram 6–1–18–0; Tillcock 12–4–41–0; Ladd-Gibbon 5–0–48–0; Evans 5–0–21–0.

> "While the rest of the world gave off heady and exotic scents, county grounds smelled of mildew and wintergreen ointment."
>
> Fifty Years of Overseas Players, page 38

Loughborough MCCU

C. O. Thurston c Buck b Zaib	126
Hassan Azad c Holden b Wade	5
J. R. Bracey b Zaib	23
N. R. Kumar c Cobb b Zaib	141
†R. G. White c Newton b Zaib	69
B. M. R. Akram c and b Holden	7
S. T. Evans b Cobb	114
A. D. Tillcock b Cobb	16
*R. N. Gamble c Buck b Zaib	32
S. J. Cook lbw b Zaib	1
B. I. W. Ladd-Gibbon not out	6
B 6, lb 1, nb 6	13
1/35 (2) 2/88 (3) 3/292 (1) 4/305 (4) 5/325 (6) 6/406 (5) 7/450 (8) 8/545 (7) 9/546 (10) 10/553 (9) (144.3 overs)	553

Buck 19–3–45–0; Richardson 28–3–101–0; Wade 18–0–100–1; Crook 19–0–97–0; Zaib 36.3–6–115–6; Cobb 14–2–44–2; Holden 10–1–44–1.

Umpires: R. J. Bailey and D. J. Millns.

NORTHAMPTONSHIRE v GLAMORGAN

At Northampton, April 7–8. Northamptonshire won by an innings and 22 runs. Northamptonshire 22pts, Glamorgan 3pts. Toss: Glamorgan. County debut: M. de Lange. Championship debut: M. D. E. Holden.

Northamptonshire began a Championship season with a victory for the first time since 1995 – and did it inside two days. After electing to bat, Glamorgan collapsed to 26 for six, as Buck marked his Northamptonshire debut in the competition by removing Ingram, Cooke and Carlson with his second, eighth and ninth balls. But the day belonged to Kleinveldt: he took three wickets of his own to help dismiss Glamorgan for 101, before bringing up a spectacular half-century in just 23 balls. He was finally removed for 86 next morning by Carey, who claimed a career-best four for 85, but Northamptonshire raced to a 209-run lead. Though Ingram dug in, few others did, and Kleinveldt and Sanderson shared seven wickets to help complete the rout.

Close of play: first day, Northamptonshire 268-6 (Crook 29, Kleinveldt 71).

Glamorgan

*J. A. Rudolph c Wakely b Sanderson	9	– c Rossington b Sanderson	21
N. J. Selman lbw b Kleinveldt	0	– b Kleinveldt	4
D. L. Lloyd lbw b Kleinveldt	0	– c Duckett b Sanderson	0
C. A. Ingram c Rossington b Buck	6	– b White	47
A. H. T. Donald c Rossington b Crook	34	– lbw b Sanderson	15
†C. B. Cooke lbw b Buck	0	– c Crook b Sanderson	20
K. S. Carlson c Wakely b Buck	0	– c Buck b Kleinveldt	30
C. A. J. Meschede c and b Kleinveldt	19	– b White	16
H. W. Podmore c Levi b Sanderson	10	– c Rossington b Kleinveldt	4
M. de Lange b Sanderson	18	– c Sanderson b Buck	11
L. J. Carey not out	0	– not out	19
B 4, lb 1	5		
1/3 (2) 2/9 (3) 3/9 (1) 4/22 (4) 5/26 (6) 6/26 (7) 7/67 (8) 8/79 (5) 9/88 (9) 10/101 (10) (31.3 overs)	101	1/21 (1) 2/25 (2) 3/25 (3) 4/49 (5) 5/99 (6) 6/117 (4) 7/139 (8) 8/154 (9) 9/157 (7) 10/187 (10) (65.3 overs)	187

Kleinveldt 12–2–35–3; Sanderson 11.3–4–20–3; Buck 6–1–35–3; Crook 2–0–6–1. *Second innings*—Kleinveldt 16–3–54–3; Sanderson 19–9–31–4; Buck 11.3–1–46–1; Crook 5–1–16–0; White 14–4–40–2.

Northamptonshire

R. I. Newton c de Lange b Carey	10	G. G. White c Selman b de Lange	11
B. M. Duckett lbw b de Lange	12	N. L. Buck not out	0
*A. G. Wakely c and b Podmore	36	B. W. Sanderson c Selman b Podmore	12
M. D. E. Holden c Cooke b Podmore	0	B 4, lb 5, nb 8	17
†A. M. Rossington c Selman b Carey	58		
R. E. Levi b Meschede	38	1/25 (1) 2/25 (2) 3/27 (4) (78.1 overs)	310
S. P. Crook lbw b Carey	30	4/92 (3) 5/156 (6) 6/170 (5)	
R. K. Kleinveldt c Donald b Carey	86	7/270 (7) 8/291 (9) 9/295 (8) 10/310 (11)	

De Lange 24–3–85–2; Carey 23–5–85–4; Podmore 13.1–2–68–3; Meschede 12–1–44–1; Ingram 6–0–19–0.

Umpires: S. A. Garratt and R. T. Robinson.

At Derby, April 14–17. NORTHAMPTONSHIRE beat DERBYSHIRE by three wickets.

At Worcester, April 21–22. NORTHAMPTONSHIRE lost to WORCESTERSHIRE by 20 runs.

At Northampton, May 21. NORTHAMPTONSHIRE lost to SOUTH AFRICANS by 13 runs (see South African tour section).

NORTHAMPTONSHIRE v WORCESTERSHIRE

At Northampton, May 26–28. Worcestershire won by eight wickets. Worcestershire 24pts, Northamptonshire 4pts. Toss: uncontested.

Worcestershire's fourth consecutive victory, and their second over Northamptonshire in little more than a month, owed much to the resilience of Mitchell. He hit 161 in six hours to help establish a 196-run lead on the second day, then calmly completed victory on the third with an unbeaten half-century. His modest accumulation – particularly during a 169-run stand with Köhler-Cadmore – showed up Northamptonshire's slipshod batting: on a sunny first day, several made starts before getting themselves out, and it took a ninth-wicket stand of 69 between White and Buck to secure a batting point. The carelessness continued, as Wakely hooked to long leg on the second evening. Duckett thrashed 67, including 12 fours, and Keogh batted nearly four hours for an unbeaten 88, but a target of 148 proved straightforward on a flat pitch. Levi was taken to hospital after being struck on the head by Tongue, and didn't play again until July.

Close of play: first day, Worcestershire 108-2 (Mitchell 52, Clarke 13); second day, Northamptonshire 53-2 (Duckett 25, Buck 6).

Northamptonshire

Batsman	First innings		Second innings	
M. D. E. Holden c D'Oliveira b Leach	0	–	b Leach	6
B. M. Duckett c Cox b Tongue	24	–	lbw b Lyon	67
*A. G. Wakely lbw b Leach	49	–	c Shantry b Tongue	16
R. I. Keogh c Mitchell b Barnard	3	–	(5) not out	88
R. E. Levi c Köhler-Cadmore b Shantry	10	–	(6) retired hurt	28
†A. M. Rossington c Lyon b Shantry	36	–	(7) st Cox b Lyon	23
S. P. Crook lbw b Barnard	19	–	(8) c Leach b Shantry	18
R. K. Kleinveldt c Fell b Shantry	9	–	(9) c Shantry b Lyon	43
G. G. White c Shantry b Tongue	47	–	(10) b Barnard	19
N. L. Buck c Köhler-Cadmore b Leach	29	–	(4) c Barnard b Shantry	14
B. W. Sanderson not out	1	–	c and b Barnard	4
B 5, lb 6	11		B 4, lb 6, nb 2, p 5	17
1/6 (1) 2/47 (2) 3/63 (4) 4/92 (5) 5/102 (3) 6/150 (7) 7/160 (6) 8/161 (8) 9/230 (10) 10/238 (9) (64.1 overs)	238		1/10 (1) 2/42 (3) 3/76 (4) 4/124 (2) 5/212 (7) 6/243 (8) 7/294 (9) 8/333 (10) 9/343 (11) (87.1 overs)	343

In the second innings Levi retired hurt at 181-4.

Leach 15–5–36–3; Barnard 15–4–50–2; Lyon 8–1–25–0; Tongue 14.1–1–62–2; Shantry 12–1–54–3. *Second innings*—Leach 17–4–59–1; Barnard 9.1–0–38–2; Lyon 29–4–94–3; Tongue 18–1–77–1; Shantry 10–3–50–2; D'Oliveira 4–0–10–0.

Worcestershire

Batsman	First innings		Second innings	
D. K. H. Mitchell lbw b Buck	161	–	not out	78
B. L. D'Oliveira b Buck	35	–	c and b Kleinveldt	13
T. C. Fell lbw b Kleinveldt	0	–	c Crook b Kleinveldt	11
J. M. Clarke b Kleinveldt	24	–	not out	34
T. Köhler-Cadmore b Sanderson	76			
†O. B. Cox c Duckett b Buck	24			
E. G. Barnard lbw b Buck	9			
*J. Leach b Sanderson	50			
J. C. Tongue b Buck	1			
J. D. Shantry not out	30			
N. M. Lyon lbw b Sanderson	0			
B 6, lb 7, w 1, nb 10	24		B 9, lb 4, nb 2	15
1/77 (2) 2/78 (3) 3/130 (4) 4/299 (5) 5/317 (1) 6/352 (6) 7/359 (7) 8/365 (9) 9/434 (8) 10/434 (11) (106.3 overs)	434		1/38 (2) 2/54 (3) (2 wkts, 27.4 overs)	151

Kleinveldt 26–4–95–2; Sanderson 23.3–7–74–3; Crook 10–1–57–0; Buck 23–3–90–5; White 22–2–83–0; Holden 2–0–22–0. *Second innings*—Sanderson 7–2–27–0; Kleinveldt 9–1–28–2; Buck 5–0–20–0; White 1–0–6–0; Holden 4–0–31–0; Crook 1.4–0–26–0.

Umpires: P. A. Gustard and M. J. Saggers.

At Chester-le-Street, June 2–5. NORTHAMPTONSHIRE beat DURHAM by two wickets.

NORTHAMPTONSHIRE v DERBYSHIRE

At Northampton, June 9–11. Northamptonshire won by 128 runs. Northamptonshire 20pts, Derbyshire 3pts. Toss: uncontested.

Northamptonshire wrapped up their fourth Championship victory of 2017 thanks largely to Sanderson and Newton. After Newton's half-century had helped set up a lead of 42, his careful 108 in the second innings – and partnership of 133 with Wakely – gave them a position of dominance. When he was finally trapped by Palladino, Northamptonshire slid from 225 for one to 277 all out, setting Derbyshire 320. But Sanderson had confidence from his first-innings five-for, and reduced them to 38 for four with skilful seam movement; though Taylor countered boldly, they fell well short. On the first morning, Derbyshire's Reece complained of breathlessness while bowling. He went to hospital, where he stayed for two days, suffering from a viral infection, and inflammation around his heart. It placed a bigger burden on 19-year-old Johannesburg-born seamer Conor McKerr – on loan from Surrey – but he bore it well. After taking a maiden five-for in the first innings, he claimed another in the second, and became the youngest Derbyshire bowler to take ten in a match.

Close of play: first day, Derbyshire 153-6 (Hughes 50, Taylor 7); second day, Northamptonshire 247-4 (Buck 3, Duckett 0).

Northamptonshire

First innings		Second innings	
M. D. E. Holden lbw b Taylor	10	– lbw b McKerr	31
R. I. Newton c Smit b Palladino	67	– lbw b Palladino	108
*A. G. Wakely lbw b McKerr	11	– c Smit b Palladino	79
R. I. Keogh c Madsen b McKerr	0	– b McKerr	5
†B. M. Duckett b Palladino	36	– (6) lbw b McKerr	8
C. F. Hughes c Mendis b Madsen	20	– (7) lbw b Palladino	8
J. J. Cobb c Hughes b McKerr	0	– (8) b McKerr	0
R. K. Kleinveldt c Smit b McKerr	40	– (9) b McKerr	9
N. L. Buck b Palladino	9	– (5) b Taylor	8
B. W. Sanderson c sub (R. P. Hemmings) b McKerr	1	– c Hughes b Mendis	0
Azharullah not out	5	– not out	0
B 8, lb 3, w 2, nb 6	19	B 4, lb 9, nb 8	21
1/30 (1) 2/56 (3) 3/56 (4) 4/134 (5) 5/145 (2) 6/157 (7) 7/161 (6) 8/185 (9) 9/200 (10) 10/218 (8) (53.2 overs)	218	1/92 (1) 2/225 (2) 3/244 (3) 4/244 (4) 5/260 (5) 6/260 (6) 7/260 (8) 8/276 (7) 9/277 (10) 10/277 (9) (97.3 overs)	277

Taylor 13–5–37–1; McKerr 16.2–3–87–5; Reece 4–1–12–0; Palladino 14–3–45–3; Hughes 3–0–17–0; Madsen 2–1–4–1; Mendis 1–0–5–0. *Second innings*—Taylor 18–2–63–1; McKerr 24.3–7–54–5; Palladino 24–4–60–3; Mendis 24–1–75–1; Hughes 5–1–8–0; Madsen 2–0–4–0.

Derbyshire

First innings		Second innings	
B. M. A. J. Mendis lbw b Sanderson	0	– lbw b Sanderson	5
*B. A. Godleman c Wakely b Kleinveldt	7	– c sub (T. B. Sole) b Sanderson	2
S. J. Thakor c Duckett b Buck	45	– c Cobb b Sanderson	6
W. L. Madsen lbw b Buck	4	– b Sanderson	4
A. L. Hughes not out	62	– lbw b Buck	23
G. C. Wilson c Duckett b Sanderson	17	– run out	7
†D. Smit lbw b Sanderson	4	– not out	29
T. A. I. Taylor b Sanderson	10	– c Duckett b Buck	69
A. P. Palladino c Duckett b Sanderson	4	– c Wakely b Buck	2
C. McKerr run out	0	– b Keogh	17
L. M. Reece absent hurt		– absent hurt	
B 4, lb 9, nb 10	23	B 6, lb 8, w 7, nb 6	27
1/0 (1) 2/28 (2) 3/41 (4) 4/66 (3) 5/90 (6) 6/108 (7) 7/167 (8) 8/175 (9) 9/176 (10) (52.2 overs)	176	1/11 (2) 2/14 (1) 3/21 (3) 4/38 (4) 5/53 (6) 6/58 (5) 7/164 (8) 8/168 (9) 9/191 (10) (53 overs)	191

Sanderson 17–3–52–5; Kleinveldt 10–1–40–1; Buck 15.2–1–48–2; Azharullah 7–3–16–0; Keogh 3–1–7–0. *Second innings*—Kleinveldt 13–4–39–0; Sanderson 17–4–31–4; Azharullah 8–1–37–0; Buck 10–2–38–3; Keogh 5–1–32–1.

Umpires: N. G. C. Cowley and G. D. Lloyd.

NORTHAMPTONSHIRE v LEICESTERSHIRE

At Northampton, June 26–29 (day/night). Northamptonshire won by two runs. Northamptonshire 21pts, Leicestershire 3pts. Toss: Northamptonshire. County debuts: A. Harinath, M. W. Pillans.

The first day/night Championship fixture at Wantage Road proved a classic. After centuries from Wakely and Keogh helped Northamptonshire declare at 289 for seven on the third evening,

Leicestershire needed 394 for victory. Few gave them a chance, especially after they had crumbled for 157 in the first innings. Ackermann had other ideas, though. In a thrilling final session, he led Leicestershire, five down, to within 95. Then Gleeson struck twice in two balls. But Ackermann cracked 58 with Pillans in nine overs before finally edging behind for 105. When McKay fell the same way next over, the last pair needed 26. Duckett dropped Klein behind the stumps – one of five chances spilled by Northamptonshire on the last day – but Kleinveldt found the splice of Pillans's bat, and Cobb dived forward at point for the winning catch. Despite the prevailing chill, there had been plenty of good cricket: in the first session, Duckett zoomed to the second pink-ball Championship century (after Glamorgan's Stewart Walters at Canterbury in September 2011) and Klein claimed six scalps with some devilish swing. But the breathless denouement capped everything.

Close of play: first day, Leicestershire 65-4 (Ackermann 24, McKay 4); second day, Northamptonshire 60-3 (Wakely 34, Keogh 5); third day, Leicestershire 44-0 (Horton 20, Harinath 20).

Northamptonshire

First innings		Second innings	
R. I. Newton lbw b Klein	1	lbw b Klein	8
†B. M. Duckett c McKay b Sayer	112	c Eckersley b McKay	0
*A. G. Wakely lbw b Klein	2	c Horton b Ackermann	112
M. D. E. Holden lbw b Klein	92	c Horton b Pillans	13
R. I. Keogh b Klein	25	not out	105
C. F. Hughes c Horton b Pillans	0	c Pillans b Ackermann	3
J. J. Cobb run out	0	c Hill b Pillans	18
R. K. Kleinveldt c Hill b Klein	0	c Eckersley b Ackermann	12
B. W. Sanderson c Hill b Pillans	8	not out	2
Azharullah b Klein	10		
R. J. Gleeson not out	0		
B 1, lb 5, nb 5	11	B 11, w 1, nb 4	16
1/8 (1) 2/24 (3) 3/160 (2) 4/211 (5) 5/212 (6) 6/212 (7) 7/212 (8) 8/229 (9) 9/254 (10) 10/261 (4) (68.3 overs)	261	1/8 (1) 2/12 (2) 3/43 (4) 4/214 (3) 5/220 (6) 6/260 (7) 7/283 (8) (7 wkts dec, 61 overs)	289

Klein 15.3–2–80–6; McKay 15–5–44–0; Sayer 20–1–48–1; Pillans 12–0–61–2; Dexter 6–1–22–0. *Second innings*—Klein 7–0–44–1; McKay 15–4–44–1; Dexter 7–0–38–0; Pillans 18–0–85–2; Sayer 2–0–22–0; Ackermann 12–0–45–3.

Leicestershire

First innings		Second innings	
P. J. Horton c Wakely b Sanderson	5	c Duckett b Gleeson	26
A. Harinath c Duckett b Kleinveldt	5	b Sanderson	26
C. N. Ackermann b Sanderson	24	c Duckett b Gleeson	105
*M. J. Cosgrove lbw b Gleeson	17	c Gleeson b Sanderson	76
R. J. Sayer b Azharullah	0	(8) lbw b Gleeson	0
C. J. McKay c Hughes b Gleeson	4	(10) c Duckett b Kleinveldt	5
E. J. H. Eckersley c Holden b Gleeson	0	(5) c sub (H. R. D. Adair) b Azharullah	42
N. J. Dexter lbw b Azharullah	11	(6) c and b Kleinveldt	5
†L. J. Hill not out	38	(7) c Hughes b Gleeson	21
M. W. Pillans b Sanderson	35	(9) c Cobb b Kleinveldt	56
D. Klein b Azharullah	5	not out	7
B 5, lb 4, nb 4	13	B 9, lb 12, w 1	22
1/10 (1) 2/14 (2) 3/51 (4) 4/56 (5) 5/65 (6) 6/65 (3) 7/65 (7) 8/86 (8) 9/146 (10) 10/157 (11) (59.5 overs)	157	1/57 (2) 2/61 (1) 3/188 (4) 4/246 (5) 5/254 (6) 6/299 (7) 7/299 (8) 8/357 (3) 9/368 (10) 10/391 (9) (102.2 overs)	391

Sanderson 20–7–36–3; Kleinveldt 6.3–1–18–1; Azharullah 14.2–2–52–3; Gleeson 15–4–33–3; Keogh 4–1–9–0. *Second innings*—Sanderson 24–7–75–2; Gleeson 29–6–109–4; Azharullah 17–0–72–1; Kleinveldt 22.2–3–65–3; Keogh 10–1–49–0.

Umpires: B. J. Debenham and R. J. Evans.

At Beckenham, July 3–6. NORTHAMPTONSHIRE drew with KENT.

NORTHAMPTONSHIRE v GLOUCESTERSHIRE

At Northampton, August 6–9. Drawn. Northamptonshire 11pts, Gloucestershire 10pts. Toss: Northamptonshire. First-class debut: G. S. Drissell. County debuts: S. C. Kerrigan, A. Sheikh.

Rain prevented any play on the last two days, ruining an intriguingly poised contest. On the second evening, Northamptonshire had resumed 78 ahead, and lost five wickets within six overs against Norwell and Payne. It was not their first display of questionable shot selection: on the opening day, they could have scored more than 343 after reaching 153 for one at lunch. Duckett set the tone, bringing up a run-a-ball half-century, before driving loosely to extra cover. All the top six reached 25; none passed Newton's 70. Still, Northamptonshire's attack – which included one-time Test spinner Simon Kerrigan, on loan from Lancashire – earned them their advantage, mainly thanks to the pacy Gleeson's maiden first-class five-for. Hankins kept Gloucestershire in touch, though, and took an excellent slip catch as they roared back into the match.

Close of play: first day, Northamptonshire 343; second day, Northamptonshire 50-5 (Wakely 23, Rossington 7); third day, no play.

Northamptonshire

B. M. Duckett c Hankins b Miles	52	– c Tavaré b Norwell	5
R. I. Newton c Hankins b Miles	70	– c Hankins b Payne	1
*A. G. Wakely c Roderick b Payne	49	– not out	23
M. D. E. Holden c Hankins b Noema-Barnett	25	– b Payne	5
R. I. Keogh c Tavaré b Taylor	30	– lbw b Norwell	1
R. E. Levi c Tavaré b Payne	56	– b Norwell	2
†A. M. Rossington c Miles b Norwell	5	– not out	7
R. K. Kleinveldt c Roderick b Norwell	21		
S. C. Kerrigan not out	26		
R. J. Gleeson c Roderick b Norwell	0		
A. Sheikh c Mustard b Noema-Barnett	7		
B 2	2	B 4, lb 2	6
1/84 (1) 2/153 (2) 3/182 (3) 4/201 (4) 5/269 (5) 6/283 (7) 7/299 (6) 8/311 (8) 9/315 (10) 10/343 (11) (93.1 overs)	343	1/7 (2) 2/11 (1) 3/16 (4) 4/17 (5) 5/19 (6) (5 wkts, 16 overs)	50

Payne 18–4–75–2; Norwell 23–7–70–3; Miles 16–3–51–2; Drissell 12–0–58–0; Noema-Barnett 19.1–5–54–2; Taylor 5–0–33–1. *Second innings*—Payne 5–0–14–2; Norwell 8–0–25–3; Miles 3–1–5–0.

Gloucestershire

W. A. Tavaré c Wakely b Gleeson	13
*G. H. Roderick c Rossington b Gleeson	0
†P. Mustard b Kerrigan	26
G. T. Hankins c Kerrigan b Keogh	73
I. A. Cockbain c Holden b Keogh	27
J. M. R. Taylor c Levi b Gleeson	28
K. Noema-Barnett lbw b Keogh	59
C. N. Miles b Gleeson	0
D. A. Payne b Sheikh	17
G. S. Drissell b Gleeson	0
L. C. Norwell not out	0
B 5, lb 13, nb 4	22
1/2 (2) 2/19 (1) 3/85 (3) 4/154 (4) 5/165 (5) 6/219 (6) 7/219 (8) 8/265 (9) 9/265 (7) 10/265 (10) (77.3 overs)	265

Kleinveldt 12–0–48–0; Gleeson 19.3–7–46–5; Sheikh 8–1–36–1; Kerrigan 25–5–73–1; Keogh 13–2–44–3.

Umpires: B. J. Debenham and M. A. Gough.

At Nottingham, August 28–31. NORTHAMPTONSHIRE lost to NOTTINGHAMSHIRE by 163 runs.

NORTHAMPTONSHIRE v SUSSEX

At Northampton, September 5–8. Northamptonshire won by six wickets. Northamptonshire 24pts, Sussex 3pts. Toss: uncontested. County debut: L. A. Procter.

Duckett's brilliance gave Northamptonshire the edge in an entertaining match between two sides chasing promotion. Despite rain – no play was possible before lunch – he pummelled 193 from 200 balls on the opening day, propelling his side towards maximum batting points for the only time in 2017. After he had reached his century, a swat back over Archer's head prompted an exchange of words. Any Sussex bowler would have been forgiven bitterness: Duckett finished the match averaging 110 against them, from five games. On a frantic second day, 16 wickets fell – six to Kleinveldt – and Sussex appeared to be heading to a swift defeat on the third when, following on, they slipped to 246 for eight. But Archer, who survived a chance to deep square leg with his side still five in arrears, added a rapid 127 with Wiese, a ninth-wicket record in this fixture, and finished unbeaten on a career-best 81. It frustrated Northamptonshire, who had their victory hopes further jeopardised by rain on the final morning. But, once play resumed, a target of 140 did not stretch them on a pitch showing few signs of deterioration.

Close of play: first day, Northamptonshire 329-5 (Procter 30); second day, Sussex 34-1 (Robson 10, van Zyl 11); third day, Sussex 382-9 (Archer 74, Briggs 3).

Northamptonshire

R. I. Newton b Wiese	32	– c Jordan b Wiese	13
B. M. Duckett c and b Briggs	193	– c Brown b Archer	28
*A. G. Wakely c Wright b Robinson	10	– c Robson b Robinson	14
R. E. Levi c Robson b Archer	44	– not out	54
L. A. Procter c Nash b Robinson	57	– c Brown b Robinson	2
S. C. Kerrigan lbw b Briggs	5		
J. J. Cobb c Robinson b Wiese	41	– (6) not out	22
†D. Murphy c Brown b Robinson	2		
R. K. Kleinveldt b Robinson	13		
R. J. Gleeson not out	6		
Azharullah b Wiese	0		
B 4, lb 18, w 1	23	Lb 2, w 1, nb 4	7
1/91 (1) 2/119 (3) 3/215 (4) 4/317 (2) 5/329 (6) 6/401 (5) 7/407 (8) 8/407 (7) 9/421 (9) 10/426 (11) (101.4 overs)	426	1/28 (1) 2/46 (2) 3/90 (3) 4/93 (5) (4 wkts, 34 overs)	140

Archer 22–0–82–1; Robinson 22–2–81–4; Jordan 21–0–97–0; Wiese 18.4–3–66–3; Briggs 14–2–58–2; van Zyl 4–0–20–0. *Second innings*—Robinson 9–0–47–2; Archer 11–0–36–1; Wiese 7–1–19–1; Briggs 7–0–36–0.

Sussex

A. J. Robson b Kleinveldt	33	– (2) c Levi b Kerrigan	72
L. W. P. Wells c Newton b Azharullah	14	– (1) c Murphy b Kleinveldt	11
S. van Zyl b Kerrigan	32	– c Murphy b Gleeson	35
C. D. Nash c Murphy b Azharullah	30	– b Azharullah	66
L. J. Wright b Gleeson	22	– b Kleinveldt	10
*†B. C. Brown c Murphy b Kleinveldt	9	– lbw b Kleinveldt	0
C. J. Jordan c Levi b Kerrigan	0	– lbw b Kerrigan	1
O. E. Robinson c and b Kleinveldt	4	– lbw b Gleeson	20
J. C. Archer not out	16	– not out	81
D. Wiese b Kleinveldt	8	– lbw b Procter	61
D. R. Briggs b Kleinveldt	1	– c Kerrigan b Azharullah	6
B 1, lb 2	3	B 6, lb 16, w 4, nb 4	30
1/46 (1) 2/48 (2) 3/101 (4) 4/123 (3) 5/139 (5) 6/142 (6) 7/142 (7) 8/146 (8) 9/170 (10) 10/172 (11) (56.4 overs)	172	1/12 (1) 2/89 (3) 3/173 (2) 4/186 (5) 5/186 (6) 6/193 (7) 7/221 (8) 8/246 (4) 9/373 (10) 10/393 (11) (105.4 overs)	393

Kleinveldt 15.4–4–50–5; Gleeson 14–5–41–1; Azharullah 10–3–25–2; Procter 5–2–19–0; Kerrigan 12–3–34–2. *Second innings*—Kleinveldt 19–5–48–3; Azharullah 17.4–3–55–2; Kerrigan 29–5–118–2; Cobb 1–0–3–0; Procter 15–1–67–1; Gleeson 24–3–80–2.

Umpires: I. D. Blackwell and R. A. Kettleborough.

At Cardiff, September 12–15. NORTHAMPTONSHIRE beat GLAMORGAN by seven wickets.

NORTHAMPTONSHIRE v NOTTINGHAMSHIRE

At Northampton, September 19–22. Northamptonshire won by 124 runs. Northamptonshire 19pts, Nottinghamshire 3pts. Toss: uncontested.

Northamptonshire's first Championship win over Nottinghamshire since 2002 kept alive their promotion hopes. Their South African contingent proved irresistible: Kleinveldt claimed 13 for 98, and Levi drove to a buccaneering hundred. On a pitch that helped the seamers throughout, Wood and Hutton had dismantled Northamptonshire's top order, before Kleinveldt returned the favour with interest, recording a personal-best nine for 65 (beating eight for 47 for Cape Cobras against Warriors in 2005-06). Without Duckett, who came into the match with a fractured finger and aggravated it in the slips, and with Wakely coming in at No. 8 because of a facial injury sustained while attempting a catch, Northamptonshire swung the bat boldly to build on a precious 43-run lead. Five were dismissed in single figures, but Levi's luck was in, and his 104-ball 115 helped swell the target to 314, which would have been the biggest total of the match. After a rain-hit third day, Nottinghamshire reached 107 for three but, once Kleinveldt had removed Libby to reach 50 wickets for the season, the remainder offered little resistance.

BEST BOWLING FOR NORTHAMPTONSHIRE

10-127	V. W. C. Jupp	v Kent at Tunbridge Wells	1932
9-30	A. E. Thomas	v Yorkshire at Bradford	1920
9-35	V. Broderick	v Sussex at Horsham	1948
9-43	G. E. Tribe	v Worcestershire at Northampton	1958
9-45	G. E. Tribe	v Yorkshire at Bradford	1955
9-52	R. I. Keogh	v Glamorgan at Northampton	2016
9-64	G. J. Thompson	v Derbyshire at Northampton	1906
9-65	**R. K. Kleinveldt**	**v Nottinghamshire at Northampton**	**2017**
9-66	R. J. Partridge	v Warwickshire at Kettering	1934

Close of play: first day, Nottinghamshire 80-5 (Root 11, Wood 1); second day, Nottinghamshire 33-2 (Libby 6, Wood 13); third day, Nottinghamshire 107-3 (Libby 30, Pujara 7).

Northamptonshire

First innings		Second innings	
R. I. Newton lbw b Wood	1	c Mullaney b Hutton	53
B. M. Duckett c and b Wood	2	absent hurt	
*A. G. Wakely c Wessels b Hutton	13	(8) not out	5
R. E. Levi lbw b Wood	35	(3) b Hutton	115
R. I. Keogh c Mullaney b Hutton	15	(4) c Wessels b Hutton	0
J. J. Cobb c Wessels b Gurney	36	(5) c Mullaney b Patel	8
†D. Murphy c Mullaney b Hutton	0	(2) c and b Wood	2
R. K. Kleinveldt b Patel	43	(6) c sub (M. E. Milnes) b Gurney	48
N. L. Buck b Wood	32	(7) b Wood	26
B. W. Sanderson c Mullaney b Patel	10	(9) c Pujara b Wood	1
R. J. Gleeson not out	2	(10) b Wood	0
B 1, lb 4	5	Lb 11, w 1	12
(63.1 overs)	194	(52.2 overs)	270

1/1 (1) 2/12 (2) 3/34 (3) 4/60 (4) 5/86 (5) 6/94 (7) 7/120 (6) 8/164 (8) 9/182 (10) 10/194 (9)

1/4 (2) 2/151 (1) 3/151 (4) 4/162 (5) 5/206 (3) 6/260 (7) 7/260 (6) 8/270 (9) 9/270 (10)

Hutton 16–4–52–3; Wood 15.1–3–52–4; Mullaney 13–5–30–0; Gurney 13–0–35–1; Patel 6–1–20–2. *Second innings*—Hutton 15–2–74–3; Wood 8.2–1–31–4; Mullaney 3–0–27–0; Gurney 12–2–54–1; Patel 14–1–73–1.

Nottinghamshire

First innings		Second innings	
S. J. Mullaney b Kleinveldt	15	b Kleinveldt	2
J. D. Libby lbw b Kleinveldt	13	c Murphy b Kleinveldt	42
C. A. Pujara c Levi b Kleinveldt	0	(5) c Levi b Kleinveldt	14
S. R. Patel lbw b Buck	13	(6) c sub (S. A. Zaib) b Gleeson	25
M. H. Wessels c Murphy b Kleinveldt	19	(7) lbw b Sanderson	4
W. T. Root c Duckett b Kleinveldt	11	(3) c Keogh b Kleinveldt	7
L. Wood c and b Kleinveldt	44	(4) c Wakely b Buck	44
T. J. Moores lbw b Kleinveldt	1	lbw b Gleeson	0
*†C. M. W. Read c Murphy b Kleinveldt	17	c Levi b Buck	17
B. A. Hutton b Kleinveldt	1	b Gleeson	12
H. F. Gurney not out	0	not out	2
B 4, lb 7, nb 6	17	B 5, lb 11, nb 4	20
(56.2 overs)	151	(66.1 overs)	189

1/22 (1) 2/22 (3) 3/49 (2) 4/56 (4) 5/79 (5) 6/80 (6) 7/86 (8) 8/128 (9) 9/130 (10) 10/151 (7)

1/4 (1) 2/16 (3) 3/91 (4) 4/119 (5) 5/128 (2) 6/139 (7) 7/152 (8) 8/175 (6) 9/187 (9) 10/189 (10)

Kleinveldt 24.2–6–65–9; Sanderson 18–9–23–0; Buck 14–4–52–1. *Second innings*—Kleinveldt 15–3–33–4; Sanderson 22–4–47–1; Buck 14–3–41–2; Gleeson 15.1–0–52–3.

Umpires: J. W. Lloyds and D. J. Millns.

At Leicester, September 25–28. NORTHAMPTONSHIRE beat LEICESTERSHIRE by six wickets. *Northamptonshire miss out on promotion despite their ninth win.*

NOTTINGHAMSHIRE

Up with the cups

JON CULLEY

A year after Mick Newell stepped aside as head coach, manfully taking the rap for Championship relegation, Peter Moores's start in the job could hardly have gone better. After emphatically winning both white-ball competitions, and leading Division Two until September, Nottinghamshire were promoted – but as runners-up. Faltering just as Worcestershire soared, they secured second place only on the last day of the season, with a rampant Northamptonshire snapping at their heels. But two trophies and promotion weren't bad.

For Moores, who had won the County Championship with Sussex and Lancashire, it was another resounding comeback from his frustrations as England coach. Hurt by the way he was portrayed as obsessed by data after his second sacking by the national side, he felt revitalised at Trent Bridge, where his ability to empathise with, and coax improvement from, cricketers of all ages went down a storm.

Nottinghamshire began slowly in both limited-overs competitions but, once they found momentum, did not let up. They lost their first two matches in the Royal London Cup and only just qualified for the knockouts, but then produced one record-breaking performance after another. In the quarter-final at Taunton, Brendan Taylor scored 154 as Nottinghamshire amassed 429 for nine, a ground record. In the semi-final at Chelmsford, Samit Patel and Steven Mullaney added 185 as they overhauled a target of 371, the highest successful run-chase in the UK.

Then came Lord's, where Alex Hales powered them to victory over Surrey with a stunning 187, the highest score in an English one-day final. He accounted for nearly 63% of Nottinghamshire's runs as they chased down 298, backed up by captain Chris Read's diligent 58.

Showing off a trophy at Lord's was not unprecedented for Nottinghamshire, but despite three previous appearances, silverware on Twenty20 finals day was. Their NatWest T20 Blast campaign also began with two defeats, the second notable for an awful injury to Luke Fletcher, whose season ended when Warwickshire's Sam Hain drove the ball straight back at him, smashing into his head. But the third match, against Derbyshire, produced Nottinghamshire's highest T20 total – 227 for three – built around a brilliant 54-ball 110 by Riki Wessels, the county's first century in the format (Hales soon added another). It began a run of eight wins in nine completed games; they headed the North Group and beat Somerset in the quarter-final. In the semi at Edgbaston, Patel dismissed Shahid Afridi with the first ball of Hampshire's innings, and later hit an unbeaten 64 against Warwickshire. Left-arm seamer Harry Gurney was at his best in the tournament; seven wickets was a record for finals day. He took 21 in all, and Jake Ball 22.

Nick Wood, Getty Images

Samit Patel

In the aftermath of the celebrations, their first defeat in the 2017 Championship – by promotion rivals Worcestershire – was perhaps excusable. But when they lost their next match, at Northampton, it seemed that a season which had yielded seven huge victories might end by missing the prime objective: promotion. On the other hand, the wobble allowed Read's career a heroic ending. He signed off with his 26th century in his final innings, followed by his 1,104th dismissal in first-class cricket, helping to secure a draw at Hove that ensured Northamptonshire's ninth win was not enough to pip Nottinghamshire for second place.

Read, who had served his county with distinction for 20 seasons, had agreed a post at Uppingham School, though he would be a part-time coach for Nottinghamshire too. Meanwhile, Michael Lumb was forced to retire by an ankle injury; Greg Smith decided to pursue opportunities outside cricket; Taylor resumed his international career in Zimbabwe; and Brett Hutton, left out of the white-ball side despite being the county's leading Championship wicket-taker with 37, joined Northamptonshire. All-rounder Paul Coughlin moved from Durham, while batsman Chris Nash signed from Sussex.

James Pattinson was the pick of the overseas players, with 32 wickets in five Championship matches, four of them won. Twenty20 captain, and fellow Australian, Dan Christian ran him close. More was expected of Ish Sodhi, the New Zealand leg-spinner hired for the Blast, while Indian Test batsman Cheteshwar Pujara managed one century in eight Championship games, only two of which ended in victory.

In a campaign notable for moments of brilliance rather than the sustained accumulation of runs or wickets, Patel was Player of the Season. More than half his 906 Championship runs came in back-to-back double-hundreds in June, but across all three competitions he scored 1,850 and took 44 wickets with his left-arm spin. All-rounder Mullaney enjoyed his best season to date (1,171 runs and 41 wickets), despite missing a month through injury; in November, he succeeded Read as captain. Billy Root scored maiden centuries in Championship and List A cricket.

Hales made his limited county opportunities count, supplementing his Lord's masterpiece with a T20 century against Yorkshire and a match-winning first-class 218 against Derbyshire. At the end of the season, however, his batting feats were overshadowed by the fracas outside a Bristol nightclub after a one-day victory over West Indies; though Hales was not arrested, as Ben Stokes was, both were suspended by England. It was a low point in a summer of highs.

Championship attendance: 37,333.

NOTTINGHAMSHIRE RESULTS

All first-class matches – Played 15: Won 8, Lost 2, Drawn 5.
County Championship matches – Played 14: Won 7, Lost 2, Drawn 5.

Specsavers County Championship, 2nd in Division 2;
NatWest T20 Blast, winners; Royal London One-Day Cup, winners.

COUNTY CHAMPIONSHIP AVERAGES, BATTING AND FIELDING

Cap		*Birthplace*	*M*	*I*	*NO*	*R*	*HS*	*100*	*Avge*	*Ct*
2008	S. R. Patel	*Leicester*	14	19	2	906	257*	2	53.29	6
2017	†J. L. Pattinson¶	*Melbourne, Aust.*	5	5	1	197	89*	0	49.25	0
2014	M. H. Wessels	*Maroochydore, Aust.*	14	18	1	823	202*	3	48.41	21
2011	A. D. Hales§	*Hillingdon*	7	9	0	424	218	1	47.11	0
2008	†S. C. J. Broad§	*Nottingham‡*	5	5	1	171	57	0	42.75	4
2013	S. J. Mullaney	*Warrington*	11	15	0	620	168	1	41.33	15
1999	C. M. W. Read	*Paignton*	14	18	2	622	124	1	38.87	53
2016	J. T. Ball	*Mansfield‡*	7	9	4	174	43	0	34.80	1
	†L. Wood	*Sheffield*	6	9	3	199	44	0	33.16	2
2012	†M. J. Lumb	*Johannesburg, SA*	8	9	0	292	117	1	32.44	2
	G. P. Smith	*Leicester*	3	5	2	91	60*	0	30.33	5
2017	C. A. Pujara¶	*Rajkot, India*	8	12	0	333	112	1	27.75	7
2015	B. R. M. Taylor††	*Harare, Zimbabwe*	4	5	0	123	61	0	24.60	6
	J. D. Libby	*Plymouth*	14	20	1	464	109	1	24.42	4
2014	L. J. Fletcher	*Nottingham‡*	9	10	2	139	92	0	17.37	2
	B. A. Hutton	*Doncaster*	9	13	0	210	61	0	16.15	6
2014	H. F. Gurney	*Nottingham†*	11	12	5	60	42*	0	8.57	1

Also batted: M. Carter (*Lincoln*) (1 match) 33 (1 ct); M. H. A. Footitt (*Nottingham‡*) (1 match) did not bat (2 ct); †T. J. Moores (*Brighton*) (1 match) 1, 0; †W. T. Root (*Sheffield*) (2 matches) 11, 7, 132.

‡ *Born in Nottinghamshire.* § *ECB contract.* ¶ *Official overseas player.* †† *Other non-England-qualified.*

BOWLING

	Style	*O*	*M*	*R*	*W*	*BB*	*5I*	*Avge*
J. L. Pattinson	RFM	139.3	34	386	32	5-29	2	12.06
S. J. Mullaney	RM	177	58	486	25	5-32	1	19.44
S. C. J. Broad	RFM	122.1	23	334	16	3-40	0	20.87
L. J. Fletcher	RFM	252.3	48	808	36	4-35	0	22.44
J. T. Ball	RFM	183.2	39	675	27	3-36	0	25.00
B. A. Hutton	RFM	289.2	64	995	37	5-52	2	26.89
L. Wood	LFM	130.2	15	512	18	4-31	0	28.44
S. R. Patel	SLA	223	55	682	19	3-17	0	35.89
H. F. Gurney	LFM	288	48	985	27	3-55	0	36.48

Also bowled: M. Carter (OB) 25–3–161–4; M. H. A. Footitt (LFM) 27.2–4–95–4; J. D. Libby (OB) 10–0–41–0; M. J. Lumb (RM) 2–0–5–0; C. A. Pujara (LB) 5–0–17–0; W. T. Root (OB) 7.2–1–29–3; M. H. Wessels (OB) 5–0–15–0.

LEADING ROYAL LONDON CUP AVERAGES (100 runs/4 wickets)

Batting	*Runs*	*HS*	*Avge*	*SR*	*Ct*
A. D. Hales	434	187*	72.33	105.85	0
S. R. Patel	539	122*	67.37	94.23	5
W. T. Root	259	107*	64.75	92.17	1
S. J. Mullaney	378	111	63.00	113.17	4
B. R. M. Taylor	376	154	53.71	106.81	2
M. J. Lumb	311	104	31.10	91.47	2
M. H. Wessels	302	81	30.20	90.96	5
C. M. W. Read	143	61	23.83	111.71	12

Bowling	*W*	*BB*	*Avge*	*ER*
J. L. Pattinson	13	4-42	36.53	5.72
S. J. Mullaney	8	3-66	39.12	6.56
H. F. Gurney	13	3-29	41.15	6.67
S. C. J. Broad	10	2-48	47.00	5.47
L. J. Fletcher	4	1-17	47.00	6.48
S. R. Patel	9	3-51	55.22	6.45
J. T. Ball	5	2-42	59.00	6.55

LEADING NATWEST T20 BLAST AVERAGES (100 runs/15 overs)

Batting	Runs	HS	Avge	SR	Ct
A. D. Hales	507	101	33.80	**204.43**	7
S. J. Mullaney	173	46	24.71	**158.71**	4
D. T. Christian	356	73	35.60	**153.44**	9
M. H. Wessels	559	110	43.00	**151.49**	8
S. R. Patel	405	77*	40.50	**146.20**	8
T. J. Moores	191	57	19.10	**144.69**	12/1
B. R. M. Taylor	351	67*	35.10	**124.46**	5

Bowling	W	BB	Avge	ER
S. R. Patel	16	3-26	27.31	**7.28**
S. J. Mullaney	8	3-22	43.75	**8.75**
J. T. Ball	22	3-27	19.45	**8.79**
H. F. Gurney	21	4-17	23.80	**8.90**
D. T. Christian	11	3-18	23.54	**9.65**
I. S. Sodhi	15	3-39	30.86	**9.85**

FIRST-CLASS COUNTY RECORDS

Highest score for	312*	W. W. Keeton v Middlesex at The Oval	1939
Highest score against	345	C. G. Macartney (Australians) at Nottingham	1921
Leading run-scorer	31,592	G. Gunn (avge 35.69)	1902–32
Best bowling for	10-66	K. Smales v Gloucestershire at Stroud	1956
Best bowling against	10-10	H. Verity (Yorkshire) at Leeds	1932
Leading wicket-taker	1,653	T. G. Wass (avge 20.34)	1896–1920
Highest total for	791	v Essex at Chelmsford	2007
Highest total against	781-7 dec	by Northamptonshire at Northampton	1995
Lowest total for	13	v Yorkshire at Nottingham	1901
Lowest total against	16	by Derbyshire at Nottingham	1879
	16	by Surrey at The Oval	1880

LIST A COUNTY RECORDS

Highest score for	**187***	**A. D. Hales v Surrey at Lord's**	**2017**
Highest score against	191	D. S. Lehmann (Yorkshire) at Scarborough	2001
Leading run-scorer	11,237	R. T. Robinson (avge 35.33)	1978–99
Best bowling for	6-10	K. P. Evans v Northumberland at Jesmond	1994
Best bowling against	7-41	A. N. Jones (Sussex) at Nottingham	1986
Leading wicket-taker	291	C. E. B. Rice (avge 22.60)	1975–87
Highest total for	445-8	v Northamptonshire at Nottingham	2017
Highest total against	425	by Northamptonshire at Nottingham	2016
Lowest total for	57	v Gloucestershire at Nottingham	2009
Lowest total against	43	by Northamptonshire at Northampton	1977

TWENTY20 COUNTY RECORDS

Highest score for	**110**	**M. H. Wessels v Derbyshire at Nottingham**	**2017**
Highest score against	111	W. J. Durston (Derbyshire) at Nottingham	2010
Leading run-scorer	**3,237**	**S. R. Patel (avge 28.39)**	**2003–17**
Best bowling for	5-22	G. G. White v Lancashire at Nottingham	2013
Best bowling against	5-13	A. B. McDonald (Leicestershire) at Nottingham	2010
Leading wicket-taker	**140**	**S. R. Patel (avge 24.81)**	**2003–17**
Highest total for	**227-3**	**v Derbyshire at Nottingham**	**2017**
Highest total against	**227-5**	**by Yorkshire at Leeds**	**2017**
Lowest total for	91	v Lancashire at Manchester	2006
Lowest total against	90	by Leicestershire at Nottingham	2014

ADDRESS

County Cricket Ground, Trent Bridge, Nottingham NG2 6AG; 0115 982 3000; administration@nottsccc.co.uk; www.nottsccc.co.uk.

OFFICIALS

Captain 2017 (Ch'ship/one-day) C. M. W. Read
2018 (Ch'ship/one-day) S. J. Mullaney
(Twenty20) D. T. Christian
Director of cricket M. Newell
Head coach P. Moores
President P. Wynne-Thomas
Chairman R. Tennant
Chief executive L. J. Pursehouse
Chairman, cricket committee W. Taylor
Head groundsman S. Birks
Scorer R. Marshall

At Cambridge, March 28–30. NOTTINGHAMSHIRE beat CAMBRIDGE MCCU by 344 runs.

At Leicester, April 7–9. NOTTINGHAMSHIRE beat LEICESTERSHIRE by ten wickets.

At Chester-le-Street, April 14–17. NOTTINGHAMSHIRE beat DURHAM by nine wickets.

NOTTINGHAMSHIRE v SUSSEX

At Nottingham, April 21–22. Nottinghamshire won by an innings and 88 runs. Nottinghamshire 24pts, Sussex 3pts. Toss: uncontested. County debut: A. P. Barton.

Nottinghamshire pulled clear at the top of the division after clinching a third win, in just two days. Hit by injuries, Sussex fielded five players with a total of 34 first-class appearances, three of them seamers, but they chose to bowl and had Nottinghamshire in trouble at 88 for five. The balance shifted decisively on the first afternoon, however, when Magoffin – their one experienced seamer – left the field with knee trouble, having taken five of the first seven wickets. Wessels, who had been dropped for the final four games of 2016, came into his own. Gathering runs by means both classical and unconventional, he made the most of an escape in the slips on 47 to reach a maiden double-century in 170 balls, with seven sixes. With lower-order support – Broad helped him add 132 in 16 overs – he transformed a crisis into a position of strength, from which Nottinghamshire seized 20 wickets inside 90 overs, seven of them through Pattinson. The most eye-catching Sussex performance came from Jofra Archer, who bowled with pace and batted with an entertaining disrespect for his opponents.

Close of play: first day, Sussex 11-3 (Rawlins 0, van Zyl 2).

Nottinghamshire

G. P. Smith c Evans b Magoffin	8
J. D. Libby lbw b Archer	21
S. R. Patel c Brown b Magoffin	4
A. D. Hales c Brown b Archer	45
M. J. Lumb c Evans b Magoffin	1
M. H. Wessels not out	202
*†C. M. W. Read b Magoffin	30
J. L. Pattinson c Brown b Magoffin	12
S. C. J. Broad b Whittingham	57
L. J. Fletcher lbw b van Zyl	25
J. T. Ball b Archer	18
B 5, lb 7, nb 12	24
1/14 (1) 2/22 (3) 3/83 (4) 4/84 (2) 5/88 (5) 6/152 (7) 7/180 (8) 8/312 (9) 9/382 (10) 10/447 (11) (77.5 overs)	447

Magoffin 18–7–51–5; Archer 27.5–3–155–3; Whittingham 10–0–88–1; Barton 11–0–81–0; van Zyl 7–1–48–1; Rawlins 3–0–7–0; Nash 1–0–5–0.

Sussex

C. D. Nash lbw b Pattinson	1	– (2) lbw b Pattinson 53
H. Z. Finch lbw b Broad	4	– (1) lbw b Broad 0
S. G. Whittingham b Pattinson	0	– (9) c Read b Fletcher 6
D. M. W. Rawlins c Read b Pattinson	4	– (3) c Smith b Broad 0
S. van Zyl c Read b Ball	28	– (4) c Read b Pattinson 21
L. J. Evans c Patel b Pattinson	9	– (5) lbw b Pattinson 0
*L. J. Wright b Ball	34	– (6) c Broad b Fletcher 34
†B. C. Brown lbw b Fletcher	10	– (7) c Smith b Fletcher 20
J. C. Archer c Smith b Broad	40	– (8) c Ball b Patel 47
A. P. Barton not out	13	– b Broad 5
S. J. Magoffin c Wessels b Patel	5	– not out 0
Lb 2, w 1, nb 4	7	Lb 10, nb 8 18
1/7 (1) 2/7 (2) 3/7 (3) 4/19 (4) 5/35 (6) 6/64 (5) 7/93 (7) 8/103 (8) 9/146 (9) 10/155 (11) (37.5 overs)	155	1/0 (1) 2/10 (3) 3/72 (4) 4/78 (5) 5/83 (2) 6/142 (7) 7/147 (6) 8/171 (9) 9/192 (10) 10/204 (8) (51.5 overs) 204

Broad 10–1–38–2; Pattinson 8–2–22–4; Fletcher 9–1–43–1; Ball 7–1–44–2; Patel 3.5–1–6–1. *Second innings*—Broad 12–2–40–3; Pattinson 12–2–33–3; Fletcher 14–4–43–3; Ball 12–0–65–0; Patel 1.5–0–13–1.

Umpires: P. J. Hartley and D. J. Millns.

At Cardiff, May 19–22. NOTTINGHAMSHIRE drew with GLAMORGAN.

NOTTINGHAMSHIRE v GLOUCESTERSHIRE

At Nottingham, May 26–28. Nottinghamshire won by an innings and 50 runs. Nottinghamshire 24pts, Gloucestershire 2pts. Toss: uncontested.

Nottinghamshire's fourth win in five matches, and the second by an innings, was set up by centuries from Pujara and Lumb, and completed by Mullaney's gentle but canny medium-pace. Gloucestershire were without their leading first-class wicket-takers – Liam Norwell and David Payne were both injured – yet felt there was enough in their favour to bowl first. Pujara, making his home debut as Nottinghamshire's overseas player while James Pattinson was with Australia's Champions Trophy squad, survived two confident appeals for caught behind before he got going, and Lumb was woefully dropped by Tavaré on 12. But, having ridden their luck, they added 185 for the fourth wicket, the basis for a total of 430. Jake Ball sat out at England's behest, but Broad was allowed to play, and he combined with Fletcher to reduce Gloucestershire to 43 for four; they never really recovered. Dismissed inside 45 overs, they were asked to follow on, whereupon opening bat Mullaney emerged as an unexpected match-winner with the ball, taking five in an innings for the first time.

Close of play: first day, Nottinghamshire 357-5 (Wessels 12, Read 10); second day, Gloucestershire 37-1 (Bancroft 22, Tavaré 0).

Nottinghamshire

S. J. Mullaney c J. M. R. Taylor b Miles	35
J. D. Libby lbw b M. D. Taylor	32
C. A. Pujara c Mustard b Miles	112
S. R. Patel c Bancroft b Liddle	15
M. J. Lumb c van Buuren b Miles	117
M. H. Wessels c Noema-Barnett b M. D. Taylor	37
*†C. M. W. Read c Mustard b M. D. Taylor	36
B. A. Hutton c and b Miles	9
S. C. J. Broad c van Buuren b Noema-Barnett	5
L. J. Fletcher not out	1
B 5, lb 8, w 2, nb 16	31
1/53 (1) 2/100 (2) 3/122 (4) 4/307 (3) 5/342 (5) 6/412 (6) 7/419 (7) 8/425 (8) 9/430 (9) — (9 wkts dec, 116.4 overs)	430

110 overs: 417-6

H. F. Gurney did not bat.

M. D. Taylor 23–1–88–3; Miles 25–3–123–4; Noema-Barnett 21.4–2–57–1; Liddle 25–8–86–1; van Buuren 13–2–41–0; J. M. R. Taylor 9–0–22–0.

Gloucestershire

	First innings		Second innings	
C. T. Bancroft	c Read b Fletcher	3	lbw b Mullaney	53
C. D. J. Dent	c Read b Fletcher	1	c Hutton b Fletcher	2
W. A. Tavaré	lbw b Broad	6	lbw b Broad	20
G. L. van Buuren	b Fletcher	15	c Wessels b Mullaney	0
G. T. Hankins	c Read b Gurney	15	b Broad	0
*†P. Mustard	c Fletcher b Broad	53	c Wessels b Mullaney	49
J. M. R. Taylor	c Mullaney b Hutton	24	lbw b Gurney	9
K. Noema-Barnett	b Mullaney	14	c Broad b Hutton	30
C. N. Miles	c Read b Mullaney	3	c Broad b Mullaney	16
C. J. Liddle	c Pujara b Broad	4	not out	12
M. D. Taylor	not out	0	lbw b Mullaney	6
	Lb 1, nb 10	11	Lb 12, w 10, nb 12	34
	1/3 (1) 2/12 (3) 3/18 (2) 4/43 (4) 5/59 (5) 6/104 (7) 7/136 (6) 8/144 (8) 9/149 (9) 10/149 (10) — (44.1 overs)	149	1/20 (2) 2/98 (1) 3/98 (4) 4/99 (5) 5/104 (3) 6/117 (7) 7/170 (8) 8/208 (6) 9/215 (9) 10/231 (11) — (60.1 overs)	231

Broad 12.1–1–40–3; Fletcher 10–2–32–3; Gurney 7–0–27–1; Hutton 10–3–35–1; Mullaney 5–3–14–2. *Second innings*—Broad 10–2–39–2; Fletcher 14–2–52–1; Gurney 12–3–59–1; Mullaney 14.1–6–32–5; Hutton 10–3–37–1.

Umpires: M. Burns and J. H. Evans.

NOTTINGHAMSHIRE v DERBYSHIRE

At Nottingham, June 2–5. Drawn. Nottinghamshire 9pts, Derbyshire 12pts. Toss: uncontested. First-class debut: C. McKerr.

Derbyshire were unlucky not to end a run of nearly two years without a first-class win. The final morning was washed out and, by the time division leaders Nottinghamshire were dismissed, the target was 216 from 49 overs. It looked well within Derbyshire's scope against an attack lacking Jake Ball and James Pattinson, both on Champions Trophy duty, plus the rested Stuart Broad. Madsen and Wilson scored at more than a run a ball to put them in touching distance, but bad light drove the players off with 36 needed from 14; they returned for a single over, scored ten and lost Hughes, but heavy rain ended play with 26 required from eight, and five wickets in hand. Derbyshire had given a first-class debut to 19-year-old Conor McKerr, a 6ft 6in South African fast bowler with a British passport on loan from Surrey. He took a wicket with his fourth delivery, before Godleman's third century of the season helped them build a 134-run lead. Nottinghamshire were effectively 99 for five on the third afternoon, but Read supervised a recovery, and the rain helped preserve their unbeaten record.

Close of play: first day, Derbyshire 52-2 (Godleman 18); second day, Nottinghamshire 67-2 (Mullaney 20, Patel 17); third day, Nottinghamshire 313-6 (Read 46, Hutton 6).

Nottinghamshire

First innings		Second innings	
S. J. Mullaney b Palladino	76	– c Taylor b Mendis	62
J. D. Libby c Madsen b McKerr	4	– c Smit b McKerr	15
C. A. Pujara c Smit b Palladino	29	– c Smit b Taylor	13
S. R. Patel b Palladino	28	– lbw b McKerr	82
M. J. Lumb c Madsen b Reece	8	– c Hughes b Mendis	21
M. H. Wessels c Smit b Taylor	39	– b Mendis	46
*†C. M. W. Read c Smit b McKerr	0	– not out	74
B. A. Hutton b Taylor	9	– b Taylor	11
L. Wood not out	21	– c Hughes b Taylor	0
L. J. Fletcher lbw b Palladino	3	– lbw b Taylor	1
H. F. Gurney b Mendis	2	– c Thakor b Mendis	0
Lb 2, nb 8	10	B 5, lb 7, w 2, nb 10	24
1/4 (2) 2/60 (3) 3/132 (4) 4/141 (1) 5/159 (5) 6/168 (7) 7/200 (6) 8/209 (8) 9/216 (10) 10/229 (11) (67 overs)	229	1/20 (2) 2/35 (3) 3/172 (1) 4/185 (4) 5/233 (5) 6/282 (6) 7/321 (8) 8/325 (9) 9/326 (10) 10/349 (11) (93.3 overs)	349

Taylor 16–6–58–2; McKerr 18–4–53–2; Palladino 14–2–44–4; Thakor 6–1–28–0; Reece 10–1–34–1; Mendis 3–0–10–1. *Second innings*—Taylor 18–2–67–4; McKerr 27–5–96–2; Mendis 25.3–2–96–4; Palladino 10–2–40–0; Reece 9–1–22–0; Thakor 3–0–14–0; Madsen 1–0–2–0.

Derbyshire

First innings		Second innings	
L. M. Reece c Wessels b Wood	17	– c Lumb b Fletcher	14
*B. A. Godleman c Read b Wood	121	– c Read b Wood	22
S. J. Thakor c Patel b Hutton	13	– c Read b Gurney	25
W. L. Madsen lbw b Hutton	56	– c Hutton b Patel	61
A. L. Hughes lbw b Gurney	13	– lbw b Fletcher	24
G. C. Wilson c Read b Gurney	12	– not out	31
†D. Smit lbw b Patel	32		
B. M. A. J. Mendis c Gurney b Hutton	20	– (7) not out	6
T. A. I. Taylor c Patel b Gurney	32		
A. P. Palladino lbw b Patel	5		
C. McKerr not out	16		
B 4, lb 14, nb 8	26	Lb 1, nb 6	7
1/25 (1) 2/52 (3) 3/164 (4) 4/197 (5) 5/217 (6) 6/275 (7) 7/296 (2) 8/324 (8) 9/329 (10) 10/363 (9) (106.1 overs)	363	1/16 (1) 2/36 (2) 3/103 (3) 4/141 (4) 5/182 (5) (5 wkts, 36 overs)	190

Fletcher 23–3–64–0; Wood 18–2–68–2; Gurney 18.1–1–55–3; Hutton 19–1–65–3; Mullaney 10–1–32–0; Libby 3–0–14–0; Patel 15–3–47–2. *Second innings*—Fletcher 13–4–46–2; Wood 7–1–35–1; Gurney 6–1–39–1; Hutton 3–0–25–0; Patel 6–0–36–1; Mullaney 1–0–8–0.

Umpires: P. A. Gustard and G. D. Lloyd.

At Bristol, June 9–12. NOTTINGHAMSHIRE drew with GLOUCESTERSHIRE. *Samit Patel scores a career-best 257 not out.*

NOTTINGHAMSHIRE v LEICESTERSHIRE

At Nottingham, June 19–21. Nottinghamshire won by an innings and 280 runs. Nottinghamshire 24pts, Leicestershire 2pts. Toss: uncontested.

A magnificent 247 from Patel and eight wickets from Pattinson ensured another thumping win over Leicestershire, after Nottinghamshire's ten-wicket victory in the opening Championship game. Patel became the first player to score back-to-back double-centuries for the county. He batted more than seven hours, and passed three milestones: 11,000 first-class runs, 10,000 for Nottinghamshire and 9,000 in the Championship. Leicestershire were not helped by losing Raine to a side strain on the first morning, though Klein managed six wickets, his best return in England. Nottinghamshire's attack was at full strength with the return of Pattinson, Ball and Broad, and Leicestershire succumbed for 134 inside 50 overs on the second evening. Next day, following on 414 behind, they crumbled for the same total in just 31. Pattinson finished with eight for 71 in the match, having taken eight for 84 at Grace Road in April, and four for 42 when Nottinghamshire beat Leicestershire in the Royal London One-Day Cup in May. In the Championship, he now had 28 at 10.50 from four games.

Close of play: first day, Nottinghamshire 345-4 (Patel 157, Wessels 28); second day, Leicestershire 134.

Nottinghamshire

Batsman	Runs
S. J. Mullaney b Griffiths	40
J. D. Libby c Hill b Klein	7
B. R. M. Taylor c Hill b Klein	61
S. R. Patel c Klein b Ackermann	247
M. J. Lumb b Klein	36
M. H. Wessels c Horton b Klein	30
*†C. M. W. Read c Hill b Klein	7
J. L. Pattinson c Horton b Ackermann	33
S. C. J. Broad not out	50
L. J. Fletcher c Hill b Klein	0
J. T. Ball not out	6
Lb 17, nb 14	31
(9 wkts dec, 134 overs)	548

1/21 (2) 2/76 (1) 3/156 (3) 4/239 (5) 5/352 (6) 6/370 (7) 7/452 (8) 8/503 (4) 9/504 (10)

110 overs: 402-6

Klein 31–1–142–6; McKay 28.4–8–78–0; Raine 3.2–1–5–0; Griffiths 27–2–113–1; Cosgrove 13–0–58–0; Ackermann 31–1–135–2.

Leicestershire

First innings	Runs	Second innings	Runs
P. J. Horton c Taylor b Ball	31	c Read b Pattinson	6
H. E. Dearden c Read b Pattinson	6	c Taylor b Ball	0
C. N. Ackermann c Read b Fletcher	8	lbw b Fletcher	18
*M. J. Cosgrove c Read b Pattinson	9	lbw b Fletcher	22
E. J. H. Eckersley c Read b Ball	3	lbw b Mullaney	20
M. L. Pettini c Taylor b Pattinson	14	c Mullaney b Fletcher	2
†L. J. Hill b Pattinson	10	c Taylor b Pattinson	15
C. J. McKay not out	18	not out	41
D. Klein b Mullaney	1	b Pattinson	1
G. T. Griffiths b Pattinson	8	c Mullaney b Ball	0
B. A. Raine c Taylor b Mullaney	1	absent hurt	
B 2, lb 11, w 2, nb 10	25	Lb 2, w 1, nb 6	9
(49.5 overs)	134	(31.1 overs)	134

1/9 (2) 2/22 (3) 3/35 (4) 4/51 (5) 5/75 (1) 6/98 (7) 7/103 (6) 8/104 (9) 9/113 (10) 10/134 (11)

1/6 (1) 2/6 (2) 3/49 (4) 4/51 (3) 5/61 (6) 6/91 (5) 7/119 (7) 8/125 (9) 9/134 (10)

Pattinson 12–3–33–5; Broad 9–0–20–0; Fletcher 7–1–32–1; Ball 9–3–18–2; Mullaney 8.5–5–16–2; Patel 4–2–2–0. *Second innings*—Pattinson 10–3–38–3; Ball 8.1–2–29–2; Fletcher 6–1–16–3; Broad 1–0–8–0; Mullaney 6–0–41–1.

Umpires: S. J. O'Shaughnessy and P. R. Pollard.

NOTTINGHAMSHIRE v KENT

At Nottingham, June 26–29 (day/night). Drawn. Nottinghamshire 12pts, Kent 8pts. Toss: Kent. County debut: A. F. Milne.

After escaping defeat by Derbyshire thanks to the weather, Nottinghamshire were denied victory by rain in the first pink-ball first-class match at Trent Bridge: only 58.2 overs were possible across the final two days. The last was delayed by two and a half hours and, after bowling out Kent for 265, Nottinghamshire needed 75 from 46 overs, but the umpires called off play as Mullaney and Hales were walking out. The weather was not the only factor. Although they secured a first-innings lead of 191, they had surrendered their last six for 45 once Mullaney was dismissed for a career-best 168. Despite losing Ball to a knee injury early in Kent's second innings, they reduced them to 167 for seven (effectively eight, with Stevens retired hurt), still 24 behind. But they conceded a further 98, with New Zealand seamer Adam Milne scoring 51 on county debut. Stevens, who had gone to hospital after a ball from Gurney hit the back of his helmet on the third evening, was given the all-clear but, under new ECB guidelines, prevented from playing the next match. It had been a busy time for Kent's batsmen – all 12 of them. Billings, 39 not out at stumps on the second day, was required next morning by England Lions, so Weatherley batted in his place; it meant that last man Claydon was the 12th player to contribute to Kent's second innings. On the first day, Bell-Drummond had shown composure to carry his bat, no mean feat after Pattinson's opening spell had reduced Kent to six for three.

Close of play: first day, Nottinghamshire 135-3 (Mullaney 63, Hales 28); second day, Kent 105-4 (Billings 39, Gidman 12); third day, Kent 214-7 (Rouse 18, Milne 27).

Kent

D. J. Bell-Drummond not out	84	– b Ball	6
S. R. Dickson lbw b Pattinson	0	– c Mullaney b Gurney	12
J. L. Denly lbw b Pattinson	0	– c Read b Fletcher	19
*S. A. Northeast c Mullaney b Pattinson	0	– c Read b Gurney	5
S. W. Billings b Fletcher	30	– retired not out	39
D. I. Stevens c Read b Fletcher	10	– (8) retired hurt	31
W. R. S. Gidman b Gurney	25	– (6) b Mullaney	26
†A. P. Rouse c Wessels b Mullaney	22	– (9) c Patel b Mullaney	35
M. T. Coles c Wessels b Mullaney	4	– (10) c Read b Gurney	0
A. F. Milne b Mullaney	0	– (11) c Read b Fletcher	51
M. E. Claydon b Ball	0	– (12) not out	7
J. J. Weatherley (did not bat)		– (7) b Pattinson	16
Lb 3, nb 2	5	B 4, lb 3, w 1, nb 10	18
1/6 (2) 2/6 (3) 3/6 (4) 4/52 (5) 5/70 (6) 6/125 (7) 7/163 (8) 8/173 (9) 9/173 (10) 10/180 (11) (54 overs)	180	1/9 (1) 2/41 (3) 3/46 (4) 4/63 (2) 5/130 (6) 6/167 (7) 7/167 (10) 8/246 (11) 9/265 (9) (92.2 overs)	265

Weatherley replaced Billings, who left to join the England Lions squad.

In the second innings Billings retired not out at 105-4 and Stevens retired hurt at 167-6.

Ball 12–3–52–1; Pattinson 12–4–30–3; Fletcher 13–0–46–2; Gurney 13–3–42–1; Patel 1–0–5–0; Mullaney 3–1–2–3. *Second innings*—Ball 2.1–0–13–1; Pattinson 25–7–62–1; Fletcher 21.5–4–64–2; Gurney 21–6–63–3; Mullaney 18.2–6–44–2; Patel 4–0–12–0.

Nottinghamshire

S. J. Mullaney c Rouse b Coles	168
J. D. Libby c Dickson b Stevens	16
B. R. M. Taylor c Rouse b Milne	6
S. R. Patel b Coles	4
A. D. Hales c Dickson b Denly	85
M. H. Wessels c Rouse b Gidman	17
*†C. M. W. Read not out	20
J. L. Pattinson b Coles	4
L. J. Fletcher c sub (J. C. Tredwell) b Gidman	0
J. T. Ball c Gidman b Claydon	19
H. F. Gurney run out	0
B 1, lb 13, w 6, nb 12	32
(104 overs)	371

1/36 (2) 2/45 (3) 3/52 (4) 4/274 (5) 5/326 (1) 6/336 (6) 7/345 (8) 8/346 (9) 9/366 (10) 10/371 (11)

Coles 23–2–99–3; Stevens 20–7–46–1; Milne 23–7–77–1; Claydon 21–4–68–1; Gidman 10–1–48–2; Denly 7–1–19–1.

Umpires: N. L. Bainton and G. D. Lloyd.

At Derby, August 6–9. NOTTINGHAMSHIRE beat DERBYSHIRE by an innings and 61 runs.

NOTTINGHAMSHIRE v NORTHAMPTONSHIRE

At Nottingham, August 28–31. Nottinghamshire won by 163 runs. Nottinghamshire 20pts, Northamptonshire –2pts (after 5pt penalty). Toss: Nottinghamshire.

A seventh win seemed to put Nottinghamshire in an impregnable position, 51 points ahead of third place, in their bid for an immediate return to Division One. Twenty wickets fell on an opening day of marked seam movement and more than two sessions were lost over the next couple. But a 77-ball hundred by Wessels took him past 10,000 career runs and allowed Nottinghamshire to build handsomely on their 72-run lead. Meanwhile, Wakely and Rossington had suffered hand injuries in the field – Murphy took over the wicketkeeping duties – and Sanderson limped off with a hamstring strain. Wessels and Ball added 117, a ninth-wicket record between these sides, before Read's declaration set a target of 417; no county had scored so many in the fourth innings at Trent Bridge since 1926. Four down overnight and still 249 behind, Northamptonshire folded in an hour on the last morning, with Rossington unable to bat and Sanderson needing a runner. They were fined five points for a slow over-rate, which ultimately denied them promotion.

Close of play: first day, Nottinghamshire 19-0 (Mullaney 2, Libby 1); second day, Nottinghamshire 317-8 (Wessels 107, Ball 10); third day, Northamptonshire 167-4 (Wakely 31, Cobb 36).

Nottinghamshire

S. J. Mullaney b Kleinveldt	58	– b Kleinveldt	28
J. D. Libby c Levi b Gleeson	14	– c Kleinveldt b Azharullah	2
C. A. Pujara b Azharullah	18	– lbw b Azharullah	34
S. R. Patel b Azharullah	4	– b Kleinveldt	64
A. D. Hales c Wakely b Azharullah	4	– b Kleinveldt	25
M. H. Wessels c Rossington b Gleeson	69	– c Keogh b Azharullah	116
*†C. M. W. Read c Sanderson b Azharullah	8	– c Levi b Gleeson	2
B. A. Hutton b Azharullah	5	– c †Murphy b Gleeson	13
L. Wood lbw b Gleeson	7	– b Gleeson	1
J. T. Ball c Rossington b Gleeson	0	– not out	28
H. F. Gurney not out	4		
B 12, lb 8, nb 2	22	B 15, lb 7, w 1, nb 8	31
(50.1 overs)	213	(9 wkts dec, 67.2 overs)	344

1/35 (2) 2/70 (3) 3/76 (4) 4/88 (5) 5/124 (1) 6/141 (7) 7/167 (8) 8/174 (9) 9/182 (10) 10/213 (6)

1/26 (2) 2/62 (1) 3/144 (4) 4/176 (5) 5/176 (3) 6/195 (7) 7/221 (8) 8/227 (9) 9/344 (6)

Kleinveldt 16–5–61–1; Sanderson 11–3–31–0; Gleeson 9.1–1–38–4; Azharullah 14–2–63–5. *Second innings*—Gleeson 18–1–107–3; Sanderson 7.5–1–28–0; Azharullah 18.2–2–73–3; Kleinveldt 19.1–4–81–3; Keogh 4–0–33–0.

Northamptonshire

R. I. Newton c Read b Ball	16	– c Hutton b Ball	53
D. Murphy c Read b Wood	23	– lbw b Patel	30
*A. G. Wakely b Ball	4	– c Read b Hutton	37
R. E. Levi b Wood	5	– c Read b Ball	4
R. I. Keogh lbw b Hutton	5	– c Hutton b Gurney	0
†A. M. Rossington lbw b Mullaney	2	– absent hurt	
J. J. Cobb not out	46	– (6) c Read b Ball	38
R. K. Kleinveldt c Read b Mullaney	2	– (7) c Read b Hutton	12
B. W. Sanderson lbw b Hutton	9	– (10) not out	16
R. J. Gleeson lbw b Hutton	25	– (8) c Wessels b Patel	21
Azharullah c Read b Wood	0	– (9) c Pujara b Patel	23
Lb 4	4	B 4, lb 9, nb 6	19
1/28 (1) 2/36 (3) 3/44 (2) (37.5 overs)	141	1/69 (2) 2/113 (1) (66.5 overs)	253
4/49 (4) 5/57 (5) 6/57 (6)		3/117 (4) 4/122 (5)	
7/59 (8) 8/84 (9) 9/132 (10) 10/141 (11)		5/174 (3) 6/192 (7)	
		7/192 (6) 8/224 (9) 9/253 (8)	

Ball 10–2–32–2; Wood 8.5–0–35–3; Hutton 9–3–25–3; Mullaney 6–2–29–2; Gurney 4–0–16–0. *Second innings*—Ball 20–1–86–3; Wood 8–0–44–0; Hutton 21–6–69–2; Mullaney 7–2–8–0; Patel 4.5–1–17–3; Gurney 6–1–16–1.

Umpires: J. W. Lloyds and S. J. O'Shaughnessy.

NOTTINGHAMSHIRE v WORCESTERSHIRE

At Nottingham, September 5–8. Worcestershire won by eight wickets. Worcestershire 20pts, Nottinghamshire 3pts. Toss: uncontested.

Three days after completing the white-ball double by winning the T20 Blast, Nottinghamshire surrendered their unbeaten Championship record to second-placed Worcestershire, who had also beaten them in both limited-overs competitions. The visitors' first first-class win at Trent Bridge since 2000 cast a damper on Read's final appearance there, after he had served Nottinghamshire with grace, dignity and skill for two decades. All-rounder Barnard's lively seam had claimed four wickets in 25 balls on a truncated first day, while on the second he arrived with Worcestershire 89 for six, scored the game's first half-century and propelled them towards a 50-run lead. Their fielders formed a guard of honour as Read emerged from the pavilion, bat in hand; his last innings on the ground did at least keep his side in the match, as he supervised two useful late-order stands to leave a target of 226. It caused Worcestershire few problems. Mitchell completed his sixth century of the summer to pull level with Kumar Sangakkara, and became the second player (after Sangakkara) to reach 1,000 Championship runs.

Close of play: first day, Nottinghamshire 188-9 (Ball 0, Gurney 0); second day, Nottinghamshire 138-5 (Libby 42, Hutton 2); third day, Worcestershire 123-2 (Mitchell 63, Clarke 0).

Nottinghamshire

S. J. Mullaney b Leach	7	–	c Cox b Leach	5
J. D. Libby c Mitchell b Barnard	34	–	b Barnard	44
C. A. Pujara c Cox b Barnard	28	–	lbw b Leach	4
S. R. Patel c Cox b Barnard	14	–	c Ashwin b Tongue	9
A. D. Hales c Mitchell b Tongue	28	–	c Clarke b Leach	12
M. H. Wessels b Barnard	0	–	c Rhodes b Tongue	60
B. R. M. Taylor lbw b Leach	33	–	(8) c Cox b Leach	19
*†C. M. W. Read c and b Tongue	26	–	(9) lbw b Barnard	38
B. A. Hutton run out	4	–	(7) lbw b Leach	32
J. T. Ball c Rhodes b Leach	5	–	not out	34
H. F. Gurney not out	0	–	c Cox b Barnard	5
B 8, lb 4, nb 2	14		Lb 9, nb 4	13
1/10 (1) 2/79 (2) 3/82 (3) 4/117 (4) 5/121 (6) 6/127 (5) 7/171 (8) 8/188 (7) 9/188 (9) 10/193 (10) (49.2 overs)	193		1/12 (1) 2/16 (3) 3/25 (4) 4/43 (5) 5/135 (6) 6/145 (2) 7/186 (8) 8/209 (7) 9/265 (9) 10/275 (11) (76.4 overs)	275

Leach 13.2–2–47–3; Tongue 14–3–41–2; Barnard 16–1–71–4; Shantry 6–1–22–0. *Second innings*—Leach 19–2–69–5; Tongue 20–2–65–2; Barnard 21.4–1–78–3; Ashwin 12–3–47–0; Shantry 4–1–7–0.

Worcestershire

D. K. H. Mitchell c Read b Hutton	23	–	not out	139
G. H. Rhodes c Read b Ball	32	–	b Hutton	21
T. C. Fell c Read b Mullaney	5	–	b Mullaney	30
J. M. Clarke b Mullaney	0	–	not out	28
B. L. D'Oliveira c Pujara b Hutton	1			
R. Ashwin c Wessels b Ball	19			
†O. B. Cox c Wessels b Hutton	47			
E. G. Barnard lbw b Mullaney	55			
*J. Leach c Mullaney b Ball	28			
J. D. Shantry b Mullaney	20			
J. C. Tongue not out	1			
B 4, lb 6, nb 2	12		B 6, lb 3, nb 2	11
1/38 (1) 2/51 (3) 3/55 (4) 4/56 (5) 5/84 (2) 6/89 (6) 7/164 (7) 8/221 (8) 9/223 (9) 10/243 (10) (57.4 overs)	243		1/57 (2) 2/123 (3) (2 wkts, 61.3 overs)	229

Ball 18–5–75–3; Hutton 17–2–69–3; Mullaney 12.4–4–31–4; Gurney 7–2–44–0; Patel 3–0–14–0. *Second innings*—Ball 13–0–49–0; Hutton 20–5–56–1; Patel 7.3–2–40–0; Mullaney 12–2–43–1; Gurney 8–1–27–0; Libby 1–0–5–0.

Umpires: N. G. B. Cook and M. J. Saggers.

At Northampton, September 19–22. NOTTINGHAMSHIRE lost to NORTHAMPTONSHIRE by 124 runs.

At Hove, September 25–28. NOTTINGHAMSHIRE drew with SUSSEX. *A century in Chris Read's final first-class innings helps Nottinghamshire clinch promotion.*

SOMERSET

Slow season ends with a Hurry

RICHARD LATHAM

After the excitement of 2016, when a late charge nearly brought them a first Championship, Somerset endured a largely disappointing year. But, as they scrapped to avoid the drop, there was tension until the last day of the season – and beyond. Even after they had beaten Middlesex on a raging turner at Taunton, gaining enough bonus points to leapfrog their opponents out of the relegation zone, Somerset's survival was in the hands of the administrators.

First, they had to wait four agonising days before the ECB decided there would be no punishment for the pitch, rated "below average". Middlesex then appealed against a two-point penalty they had received for a slow over-rate during their match against Surrey in August, which ended abruptly when a crossbow bolt was fired on to the outfield. Somerset threatened legal action if the decision was overturned, but finally – by the middle of October – they were safe.

For Tom Abell, handed the captaincy at the age of 22, it was a turbulent year. He had admitted to sobbing on the team coach after a pair against Hampshire in June, at which point he had just 171 runs from seven games at an average of 14, and dropped himself for the following fixture, against Yorkshire at Scarborough. Director of cricket Matthew Maynard gave his full support, praising Abell as a "genuine leader of men" but, under the guidance of Lewis Gregory, Somerset romped to their first Championship victory of the season. Then, after batsman Adam Hose left for Warwickshire, Abell was brought back for the run-in. He averaged 40 from then on, starting with 96 against Surrey, and skippered with great maturity.

Even so, survival seemed unlikely with four games left. Somerset had just been hammered by Essex, and were 23 points adrift. But by the time Jack Leach claimed his 51st wicket of the season to complete a third victory in four and send Middlesex down, Abell's season had come full circle. He wept again, this time from "total elation".

Somerset's bowlers were to thank for the rescue act: time and again, they atoned for the failings of the batsmen, none of whom reached 800 Championship runs. Marcus Trescothick observed that never in his long career had he been in a team where so many were out of form for so long. Dean Elgar was the exception, averaging 47 in six matches at the beginning of the summer before joining the South African touring squad. Somerset chose not to replace him, instead promoting Zimbabwe-born opener Eddie Byrom, who displayed plenty of promise but managed a single fifty. Australian Test opener Cameron Bancroft was signed for 2018.

With two seamers, Jamie Overton and Gregory, forced to miss the second half of the season through injury, Craig Overton put in a mighty effort: apart

Harry Trump, Getty Images

Craig Overton

from one Championship match, which he missed because of England Lions duty, he was ever-present. He took 46 Championship wickets, and earned first a place in the Ashes squad for the winter, which he said he could only have dreamed of at the start of the season, and then a Test debut in December. The nature of the Taunton pitches – far more conducive to spin – made Overton's achievements all the more impressive. Leach, who came back strongly after remodelling his action over the winter, and the rapidly improving Dom Bess enjoyed the turn on offer, reeling in 63 victims between them over the seven home fixtures.

The Royal London Cup campaign began with four victories, inspired by four different centurions. White-ball captain Jim Allenby – who left at the end of the summer – registered his only hundred in three years at the club, against Glamorgan, after Roelof van der Merwe smashed an unbeaten 165 against Surrey. But Somerset's form dipped and, though they scraped into the quarter-finals, they lost to eventual champions Nottinghamshire in a thrilling game containing 834 runs. Elgar, who hit 91 that day, finished the competition averaging 103.

The T20 Blast proved unpredictable. Just one point came from the opening three games, but a thumping win in the final round edged Somerset into the knockouts on net run-rate. History repeated itself: they lost in the quarter-finals to Nottinghamshire, who went on to lift the trophy. While Australian Dan Christian backed up two wickets with a rapid 36, Somerset struggled without an overseas star, as they had for most of the season. New Zealand all-rounder Corey Anderson averaged 71 over four games, before a stress fracture of the back forced him to return home. Fakhar Zaman, the Pakistan opener who cracked a hundred in the Champions Trophy final, was due to join as a replacement. But the day before his flight, the Pakistan Cricket Board recalled their players: they had rescheduled their fixtures to accommodate the visit of the World XI. James Hildreth, in his benefit season, finished as the leading run-scorer with 293, but it was the explosive Johann Myburgh who caught the eye: he hit three half-centuries, and earned himself a new white-ball contract.

After the end of the season, chief executive Guy Lavender left to become secretary of MCC; Lee Cooper, a former Second XI player, took over. If that change was known in advance, another was more of a surprise: Maynard moved back to Glamorgan after three polished years in charge, in which Somerset matched their highest Championship finish. He was replaced as director of cricket by Andy Hurry, a former first-team coach returning after leading the England Development Programme since 2014.

Championship attendance: 41,664.

SOMERSET RESULTS

All first-class matches – Played 14: Won 4, Lost 6, Drawn 4.
County Championship matches – Played 14: Won 4, Lost 6, Drawn 4.

Specsavers County Championship, 6th in Division 1;
NatWest T20 Blast, quarter-finalists; Royal London One-Day Cup, quarter-finalists.

COUNTY CHAMPIONSHIP AVERAGES, BATTING AND FIELDING

Cap		*Birthplace*	*M*	*I*	*NO*	*R*	*HS*	*100*	*Avge*	*Ct/St*
2017	†D. Elgar¶	*Welkom, SA*	6	12	1	517	158	2	47.00	3
2017	†S. M. Davies	*Bromsgrove*	14	24	2	775	142	2	35.22	39/7
	A. J. Hose	*Newport, IoW*	3	6	0	194	68	0	32.33	1
2007	J. C. Hildreth	*Milton Keynes*	14	26	1	756	109	2	30.24	12
1999	†M. E. Trescothick	*Keynsham‡*	14	27	2	714	119*	2	28.56	21
	†E. J. Byrom††	*Harare, Zimbabwe*	8	15	0	401	56	0	26.73	2
	T. B. Abell	*Taunton‡*	13	25	3	572	96	0	26.00	12
2015	L. Gregory	*Plymouth*	7	12	0	299	137	1	24.91	1
2016	T. D. Groenewald	*Pietermaritzburg, SA*	10	14	8	146	41*	0	24.33	1
2007	P. D. Trego	*Weston-super-Mare‡*	8	12	0	257	68	0	21.41	1
	D. M. Bess	*Exeter*	9	14	4	198	55	0	19.80	5
	T. D. Rouse	*Sheffield*	3	5	0	83	69	0	16.60	1
2016	C. Overton	*Barnstaple*	13	21	3	287	44*	0	15.94	9
2017	†M. J. Leach	*Taunton‡*	14	21	5	237	52	0	14.81	4
	J. H. Davey††	*Aberdeen*	3	5	1	58	47	0	14.50	2
	G. A. Bartlett	*Frimley*	4	8	1	100	28	0	14.28	3
	J. Overton	*Barnstaple*	5	8	1	92	37	0	13.14	1
	R. E. van der Merwe††	*Johannesburg, SA*	3	5	0	33	24	0	6.60	2

Also batted: J. Allenby (*Perth, Australia*) (2 matches) 19, 9 (5 ct); P. A. van Meekeren†† (*Amsterdam, Netherlands*) (1 match) 0, 1* (1 ct).

‡ *Born in Somerset.* ¶ *Official overseas player.* †† *Other non-England-qualified.*

BOWLING

	Style	*O*	*M*	*R*	*W*	*BB*	*5I*	*Avge*
R. E. van der Merwe	SLA	68.4	17	189	11	4-22	0	17.18
C. Overton	RFM	373.5	106	1,030	46	5-47	2	22.39
L. Gregory	RFM	176.3	49	484	21	5-74	1	23.04
D. M. Bess	OB	265.5	62	843	36	7-117	3	23.41
T. D. Groenewald	RFM	243.4	71	646	26	5-58	1	24.84
M. J. Leach	SLA	520.1	150	1,315	51	6-78	4	25.78
J. Overton	RFM	103	22	312	12	3-30	0	26.00

Also bowled: T. B. Abell (RM) 27–6–96–2; J. Allenby (RM) 14–6–25–0; J. H. Davey (RFM) 75–17–186–3; D. Elgar (SLA) 1–0–4–1; T. D. Rouse (OB) 1–0–1–0; P. D. Trego (RFM) 79.5–13–265–7; P. A. van Meekeren (RFM) 34–9–132–4.

LEADING ROYAL LONDON CUP AVERAGES (100 runs/4 wickets)

Batting	*Runs*	*HS*	*Avge*	*SR*	*Ct*
D. Elgar	519	131*	103.80	98.85	3
R. E. van der Merwe	280	165*	70.00	133.97	6
A. J. Hose	330	101*	55.00	105.76	5
J. Allenby	377	144*	53.85	87.26	3
J. G. Myburgh	120	57	40.00	193.54	0
P. D. Trego	313	135	39.12	110.60	2
J. C. Hildreth	175	64	29.16	106.06	5
J. Overton	100	40	25.00	142.85	3

Bowling	*W*	*BB*	*Avge*	*ER*
C. Overton	16	3-21	24.06	6.11
J. Overton	9	4-64	25.11	7.29
M. T. C. Waller	4	3-37	30.25	5.29
L. Gregory	8	4-60	30.62	7.90
J. H. Davey	7	2-26	32.85	6.57
R. E. van der Merwe	11	3-21	35.00	6.01
T. D. Groenewald	5	2-48	67.20	6.00

LEADING T20 BLAST AVERAGES (100 runs, SR 150/15 overs)

Batting	*Runs*	*HS*	*Avge*	*SR*	*Ct*
C. J. Anderson	142	81	71.00	**184.41**	0
J. G. Myburgh	290	87	36.25	**171.59**	1
L. Gregory	203	43	16.91	**158.59**	5
S. M. Davies	214	62	19.45	**156.20**	2/4

Bowling	*W*	*BB*	*Avge*	*ER*
R. E. van der Merwe	15	3-13	26.13	**7.39**
M. T. C. Waller	16	2-13	23.68	**7.73**
C. Overton	15	3-17	27.33	**8.54**
T. D. Groenewald	11	2-26	25.54	**8.96**
L. Gregory	12	2-42	34.08	**9.89**

FIRST-CLASS COUNTY RECORDS

Highest score for	342	J. L. Langer v Surrey at Guildford	2006
Highest score against	424	A. C. MacLaren (Lancashire) at Taunton	1895
Leading run-scorer	21,142	H. Gimblett (avge 36.96)	1935–54
Best bowling for	10-49	E. J. Tyler v Surrey at Taunton	1895
Best bowling against	10-35	A. Drake (Yorkshire) at Weston-super-Mare	1914
Leading wicket-taker	2,165	J. C. White (avge 18.03)	1909–37
Highest total for	850-7 dec	v Middlesex at Taunton	2007
Highest total against	811	by Surrey at The Oval	1899
Lowest total for	25	v Gloucestershire at Bristol	1947
Lowest total against	22	by Gloucestershire at Bristol	1920

LIST A COUNTY RECORDS

Highest score for	184	M. E. Trescothick v Gloucestershire at Taunton	2008
Highest score against	167*	A. J. Stewart (Surrey) at The Oval	1994
Leading run-scorer	7,374	M. E. Trescothick (avge 36.87)	1993–2014
Best bowling for	8-66	S. R. G. Francis v Derbyshire at Derby	2004
Best bowling against	7-39	A. Hodgson (Northamptonshire) at Northampton	1976
Leading wicket-taker	309	H. R. Moseley (avge 20.03)	1971–82
Highest total for	413-4	v Devon at Torquay	1990
Highest total against	**429-9**	**by Nottinghamshire at Taunton**	**2017**
Lowest total for	58	v Essex at Chelmsford	1977
	58	v Middlesex at Southgate	2000
Lowest total against	60	by Kent at Taunton	1979

TWENTY20 COUNTY RECORDS

Highest score for	151*	C. H. Gayle v Kent at Taunton	2015
Highest score against	122*	J. J. Roy (Surrey) at The Oval	2015
Leading run-scorer	**2,956**	**J. C. Hildreth (avge 24.03)**	**2004–17**
Best bowling for	6-5	A. V. Suppiah v Glamorgan at Cardiff	2011
Best bowling against	**5-11**	**A. F. Milne (Kent) at Taunton**	**2017**
Leading wicket-taker	137	A. C. Thomas (avge 20.17)	2008–15
Highest total for	250-3	v Gloucestershire at Taunton	2006
Highest total against	227-4	by Gloucestershire at Bristol	2006
	227-7	by Kent at Taunton	2015
Lowest total for	82	v Kent at Taunton	2010
Lowest total against	73	by Warwickshire at Taunton	2013

ADDRESS

Cooper Associates County Ground, St James's Street, Taunton TA1 1JT; 0845 337 1875; enquiries@somersetcountycc.co.uk; www.somersetcountycc.co.uk.

OFFICIALS

Captain T. B. Abell
(limited-overs) **2017** J. Allenby
(Twenty20) **2018** L. Gregory
Director of cricket 2017 M. P. Maynard
2018 A. Hurry
Head coach J. I. D. Kerr
Academy director S. D. Snell
President R. Parsons

Chairman 2017 A. J. Nash
2018 C. F. B. Clark
Chief executive 2017 G. W. Lavender
2018 L. A. Cooper
Chairman, cricket committee V. J. Marks
Head groundsman S. Lee
Scorer G. A. Stickley and L. M. Rhodes

At Taunton, April 7–8 (not first-class). **Somerset won by 506 runs.** ‡**Somerset 452-8 dec** (73.4 overs) (R. E. van der Merwe 209, L. Gregory 60*; J. N. McIver 3-108, S. R. Green 3-79) **and 277-6 dec** (53.2 overs) (P. D. Trego 161, M. J. Leach 65); **Oxford MCCU 72** (26.2 overs) (L. Gregory 3-32, C. Overton 3-18) **and 151** (30.5 overs) (M. B. Lake 65; C. Overton 3-14, J. Overton 3-32). *Roelof van der Merwe opened the batting for Somerset and smashed 209 off 166 balls. Then, after their seamers had skittled Oxford MCCU for 72 by the second morning, Peter Trego added to a 380-run lead with a swashbuckling 161. Somerset declared for a second time to set a target of 658. Zimbabwean Malcolm Lake hit a 37-ball 65, but no one else passed 20 in either innings, the Overton twins shared six wickets, and it was all over in two days. Oxford batted just 57.1 overs in total.*

SOMERSET v ESSEX

At Taunton, April 14–16. Essex won by eight wickets. Essex 19pts, Somerset 4pts. Toss: Somerset. County debut: S. M. Davies.

Relinquishing the Test captaincy had clearly not diminished Cook's appetite for runs. He kept Essex afloat with a first-innings 52, then shepherded the chase for a comeback victory with a brilliant 110. After Somerset had stumbled from 108 for two to 209 on the opening day, the match broke open on the second, when 18 wickets fell on a two-paced pitch. Essex began it at 60 for two, but were all out early in the afternoon, leaving a deficit of 80. Then Wagner began a short-pitched assault, and Somerset collapsed again. He had gone at five an over in the first innings, but his rib-tickling accuracy in the second earned him the last six wickets, all caught, as the batsmen tried to take him on with cramped pulls and cuts. Defending 255, Somerset hoped the third-day pitch would begin turning, as at the end of the previous season. Left-arm spinners Leach and van der Merwe had taken five between them in the first innings, but were wicketless now, and Westley's classy 86 not out helped Cook see Essex home.

Close of play: first day, Essex 60-2 (Cook 39); second day, Essex 10-0 (Browne 6, Cook 4).

Somerset

M. E. Trescothick c Cook b Bopara	26	– (2) lbw b Porter	5
D. Elgar st Wheater b Ashar Zaidi	34	– (1) lbw b Harmer	27
*T. B. Abell c Cook b Bopara	1	– c Wheater b Porter	0
J. C. Hildreth c Bopara b Porter	36	– c Harmer b Bopara	35
†S. M. Davies b Harmer	12	– c Porter b Wagner	11
P. D. Trego c Ashar Zaidi b Harmer	48	– c Wheater b Wagner	17
L. Gregory c Harmer b Wagner	3	– c Browne b Wagner	16
R. E. van der Merwe lbw b Ashar Zaidi	7	– c ten Doeschate b Wagner	2
C. Overton c Wheater b Wagner	10	– c Ashar Zaidi b Wagner	22
J. Overton b Ashar Zaidi	3	– c Wheater b Wagner	2
M. J. Leach not out	4	– not out	27
B 10, lb 9, nb 6	25	B 4, lb 4, nb 2	10
1/52 (1) 2/54 (3) 3/108 (2) 4/112 (4) 5/130 (5) 6/143 (7) 7/176 (8) 8/188 (6) 9/197 (10) 10/209 (9) (72.2 overs)	209	1/11 (2) 2/25 (3) 3/69 (1) 4/71 (4) 5/100 (5) 6/109 (6) 7/111 (8) 8/122 (7) 9/124 (10) 10/174 (9) (50.2 overs)	174

Porter 17–7–34–1; Wagner 15.2–2–78–2; Harmer 23–10–51–2; Bopara 5–1–10–2; Ashar Zaidi 12–2–17–3. *Second innings*—Porter 8–1–43–2; Wagner 12.2–0–48–6; Harmer 14–4–26–1; Bopara 5–0–30–1; Ashar Zaidi 11–3–19–0.

Essex

	First innings		Second innings	
N. L. J. Browne b C. Overton	11	– c Davies b J. Overton	35
A. N. Cook b Gregory	52	– c Hildreth b Elgar	110
T. Westley b van der Merwe	10	– not out	86
D. W. Lawrence lbw b C. Overton	0	– not out	11
R. S. Bopara b Leach	8		
†A. J. A. Wheater b van der Merwe	4		
*R. N. ten Doeschate c Hildreth b Gregory	4		
Ashar Zaidi c Davies b Leach	23		
S. R. Harmer c Davies b van der Merwe	9		
N. Wagner c Davies b J. Overton	5		
J. A. Porter not out	0		
Lb 3	3	B 8, w 5, nb 2	15
1/21 (1) 2/60 (3) 3/64 (4) 4/81 (5) 5/81 (2) 6/91 (7) 7/91 (6) 8/119 (9) 9/129 (10) 10/129 (8) (54.5 overs)	129	1/82 (1) 2/216 (2) (2 wkts, 84.1 overs)	257

Gregory 12–4–28–2; C. Overton 12–6–17–2; J. Overton 6–0–30–1; Leach 16.5–5–25–2; van der Merwe 8–1–26–3. *Second innings*—Gregory 9.1–2–28–0; C. Overton 11–2–54–0; Leach 27–4–69–0; J. Overton 11–5–30–1; van der Merwe 22–6–45–0; Trego 3–0–19–0; Elgar 1–0–4–1.

Umpires: M. A. Gough and G. D. Lloyd.

At Manchester, April 21–24. SOMERSET lost to LANCASHIRE by 164 runs.

SOMERSET v WARWICKSHIRE

At Taunton, May 19–22. Drawn. Somerset 8pts, Warwickshire 12pts. Toss: Warwickshire. First-class debut: G. T. Thornton. Championship debut: Sukhjit Singh.

It was a good match for the veterans, if not the weather. The first two days allowed just 39 overs, mainly because of rain, but also an arcane ECB directive, which had the umpires vacating the field on the first afternoon: the gap between lightning and thunder suggested an electrical storm was close enough to endanger the players (though not, it seemed, the spectators, who were left bemused in the stands). It meant 36-year-old Trott, batting by the 12th over, took until the third day to reach 175, his 20th first-class score of 150. He put on 146 with Ambrose – who was caught superbly by Trescothick, running from slip to leg slip after anticipating a sweep – then 95 with Clarke as Warwickshire racked up 413. Debutant seamer Grant Thornton accounted for two as Somerset slipped to 94 for four by the close, and added two more on the last day. The 41-year-old Trescothick reached 25,000 first-class runs, and became the first to 50 first-class centuries for Somerset, passing Harold Gimblett. He couldn't prevent Somerset from following on, but did prevent a late disaster with an unbeaten 46 after Elgar had gone for a duck. Trott was lost in admiration. Asked if he would continue as long as Trescothick, he replied: "No chance. That's just silly!"

Close of play: first day, Warwickshire 93-3 (Trott 30, Hain 8); second day, Warwickshire 124-3 (Trott 50, Hain 19); third day, Somerset 94-4 (Trescothick 41, Leach 7).

Warwickshire

A. R. I. Umeed b J. Overton	24
I. J. Westwood b J. Overton	21
I. J. L. Trott c van der Merwe b J. Overton	175
*I. R. Bell c Trescothick b C. Overton	8
S. R. Hain b Leach	39
†T. R. Ambrose c Trescothick b Leach	63
R. Clarke c Davies b van der Merwe	57
K. H. D. Barker c Bess b van der Merwe	2
J. S. Patel b van der Merwe	14
G. T. Thornton not out	0
Sukhjit Singh run out	0
Lb 10	10
1/46 (2) 2/51 (1) 3/81 (4) 4/150 (5) 5/296 (6) 6/391 (3) 7/394 (8) 8/410 (9) 9/413 (7) 10/413 (11) (113.4 overs)	413

110 overs: 395-7

Trego 13–2–50–0; C. Overton 24–4–75–1; J. Overton 21–2–76–3; Leach 28–12–70–2; Bess 10–1–54–0; van der Merwe 17.4–3–78–3.

Somerset

M. E. Trescothick c Ambrose b Thornton	106	– (2) not out	46
D. Elgar lbw b Barker	11	– (1) c Bell b Sukhjit Singh	0
*T. B. Abell b Patel	8	– not out	35
J. C. Hildreth lbw b Thornton	14		
†S. M. Davies c Hain b Thornton	7		
M. J. Leach lbw b Clarke	16		
P. D. Trego lbw b Patel	52		
R. E. van der Merwe b Thornton	0		
C. Overton b Clarke	8		
J. Overton c Westwood b Clarke	0		
D. M. Bess not out	0		
Lb 3, p 5	8	B 4, lb 1	5
1/21 (2) 2/46 (3) 3/78 (4) 4/86 (5) 5/127 (6) 6/208 (1) 7/208 (8) 8/224 (9) 9/226 (10) 10/230 (7) (78.3 overs)	230	1/1 (1) (1 wkt, 25.1 overs)	86

Barker 12–3–31–1; Clarke 11–1–29–3; Sukhjit Singh 15.4–1–35–0; Patel 27.3–3–93–2; Thornton 12.2–3–34–4. *Second innings*—Barker 5–2–25–0; Sukhjit Singh 8–1–29–1; Thornton 1–0–8–0; Patel 8–3–11–0; Clarke 3–0–5–0; Umeed 0.1–0–3–0.

Umpires: P. K. Baldwin and A. G. Wharf.

SOMERSET v HAMPSHIRE

At Taunton, May 26–28. Hampshire won by 90 runs. Hampshire 19pts, Somerset 3pts. Toss: Hampshire.

For the third time in four matches, Somerset lost a game they seemed to have under control. On a dry pitch, the ball turned from the first day, and Leach – with six for 78 – and Bess shared nine victims as Hampshire rolled over for 162. Somerset reached 90 for one in reply but, once Elgar was caught at short leg for 60, familiar frailties resurfaced, and they crashed to 197 all out. Spin continued to cause havoc, and Bess – mixing his angles, while flighting the ball bravely – collected seven for 117, and ten for 162 in all, both career-bests; his last wicket meant 15 had fallen on the second day, as on the first. Hampshire batted aggressively, though, and while Carberry was the only half-centurion, vital runs came down the order. Berg hit a 39-ball 49 from No. 8 – Hampshire's third 49 of the match – and the last four wickets more than doubled the score, leaving a challenging 259 to win. After a decent start, Somerset surrendered on the third day to Dawson and Crane, who took nine wickets between them and made it 30 in the match for spinners. Elgar made another 60, only to be yorked on the second bounce by a mildly embarrassed Crane. Play was briefly held up on the last day when Brian, a ginger cat who is a regular at Taunton, walked in front of the sightscreen.

Close of play: first day, Somerset 157-5 (Davies 16, Gregory 4); second day, Somerset 39-0 (Elgar 17, Trescothick 22).

Hampshire

M. A. Carberry c Davies b Bess	17	– c Abell b Bess	51
L. A. Dawson c Bess b Leach	13	– c Davies b Bess	33
J. M. Vince b Leach	11	– b Bess	19
*G. J. Bailey b Leach	49	– c Abell b Bess	0
R. R. Rossouw c Hildreth b Leach	0	– lbw b Bess	13
S. M. Ervine b Bess	8	– c Bess b J. Overton	27
†L. D. McManus c Hildreth b Bess	0	– b Leach	13
G. K. Berg st Davies b Leach	10	– b Bess	49
K. J. Abbott lbw b Leach	49	– c Davies b J. Overton	33
M. S. Crane c Davies b C. Overton	1	– c J. Overton b Bess	29
R. J. W. Topley not out	0	– not out	7
Lb 4	4	B 4, lb 4, nb 6, p 5	19
1/34 (2) 2/34 (1) 3/62 (3) 4/62 (5) 5/81 (6) 6/81 (7) 7/100 (8) 8/137 (4) 9/154 (10) 10/162 (9) (49.1 overs)	162	1/84 (1) 2/85 (2) 3/85 (4) 4/116 (5) 5/125 (3) 6/140 (7) 7/206 (8) 8/246 (6) 9/257 (9) 10/293 (10) (67.3 overs)	293

Gregory 6–2–12–0; C. Overton 8–3–16–1; Leach 20.1–5–78–6; Bess 11–2–45–3; J. Overton 4–1–7–0. *Second innings*—Gregory 8–1–16–0; C. Overton 9–3–26–0; Leach 15–2–78–1; Bess 23.3–2–117–7; J. Overton 12–2–43–2.

Somerset

First innings		Second innings	
M. E. Trescothick c Berg b Abbott	6	– (2) c McManus b Dawson	34
D. Elgar c Bailey b Dawson	60	– (1) b Crane	60
*T. B. Abell c McManus b Dawson	40	– b Dawson	5
J. C. Hildreth lbw b Abbott	7	– b Crane	2
†S. M. Davies lbw b Dawson	22	– lbw b Dawson	5
P. D. Trego c Ervine b Dawson	14	– run out	5
L. Gregory c Vince b Abbott	4	– lbw b Dawson	25
C. Overton b Berg	12	– c Vince b Crane	10
M. J. Leach c Ervine b Abbott	0	– lbw b Crane	7
D. M. Bess b Berg	12	– (11) not out	0
J. Overton not out	9	– (10) st McManus b Crane	2
B 5, lb 4, nb 2	11	B 8, lb 1, nb 4	13
1/15 (1) 2/90 (3) 3/119 (4) 4/121 (2) 5/141 (6) 6/162 (7) 7/164 (5) 8/169 (9) 9/184 (8) 10/197 (10) (57.3 overs)	197	1/58 (2) 2/70 (3) 3/73 (4) 4/100 (5) 5/111 (6) 6/118 (1) 7/146 (8) 8/166 (9) 9/168 (7) 10/168 (10) (54.2 overs)	168

Topley 4–0–23–0; Abbott 14–2–49–4; Dawson 25–3–63–4; Crane 10–0–45–0; Ervine 2–2–0–0; Berg 2.3–0–8–2. *Second innings*—Abbott 5–1–24–0; Topley 2–1–12–0; Dawson 25–8–66–4; Berg 1–1–0–0; Ervine 8–2–17–0; Crane 13.2–2–40–5.

Umpires: N. G. B. Cook and G. D. Lloyd.

At Lord's, June 2–5. SOMERSET drew with MIDDLESEX.

SOMERSET v YORKSHIRE

At Taunton, June 9–12. Yorkshire won by three runs. Yorkshire 20pts, Somerset 4pts. Toss: Yorkshire. First-class debut: M. J. Waite. Championship debut: A. J. Hose.

On the last day, Somerset seemed on course for their first win of the season. Adam Hose and Davies were maintaining their good work from the previous evening, hitting fifties and raising a century stand. Then Gregory and Craig Overton settled in and brought the score to 231 for six, just 31 short of victory. But Sidebottom got the ball to reverse, and picked up three quick scalps before Jamie Overton chipped Lyth's part-time off-spin to midwicket with four needed. It was a triumph for Yorkshire captain Ballance. His unbeaten 98 – together with 70 from Handscomb – had given them a chance. And his brave decisions in the field – he declined the second new ball at the end – paid off. Afterwards, Ballance said he was in the form of his life. His Somerset counterpart, Abell, continued to struggle, making nought and four. Again, his bowlers had given him a grasp on the game, dismissing Yorkshire for 202 on the first day. And, again, the batsmen failed to press home the advantage, slipping to 114 for six. They managed to scrape 224 as Sidebottom claimed five but, for the fourth time in six matches, Somerset lost after earning a first-innings lead.

Close of play: first day, Somerset 41-3 (Hildreth 21, Davies 6); second day, Yorkshire 127-2 (Handscomb 57, Ballance 15); third day, Somerset 101-4 (Hose 27, Davies 26).

Yorkshire

A. Lyth c Gregory b J. Overton	24	– lbw b Bess	10
A. Z. Lees c Abell b Bess	6	– b C. Overton	38
P. S. P. Handscomb lbw b J. Overton	25	– c Trescothick b Bess	70
*G. S. Ballance b Leach	19	– not out	98
J. A. Leaning c C. Overton b J. Overton	3	– c Trescothick b Bess	3
M. J. Waite c Trescothick b Leach	4	– c Hildreth b Leach	18
†A. J. Hodd c Abell b Gregory	59	– lbw b Bess	1
Azeem Rafiq b C. Overton	6	– lbw b Leach	7
S. A. Patterson b Gregory	1	– c Davies b Leach	0
K. Carver lbw b Bess	20	– run out	13
R. J. Sidebottom not out	12	– lbw b Bess	0
B 4, lb 19	23	B 8, lb 3, w 3, nb 6, p 5	25
1/34 (1) 2/34 (2) 3/82 (4) 4/86 (3) 5/95 (5) 6/95 (6) 7/134 (8) 8/152 (9) 9/171 (7) 10/202 (10) (75 overs)	202	1/35 (1) 2/93 (2) 3/158 (3) 4/180 (5) 5/213 (6) 6/214 (7) 7/223 (8) 8/223 (9) 9/274 (10) 10/283 (11) (109.2 overs)	283

Gregory 13–7–31–2; C. Overton 16–10–21–1; Bess 12–3–35–2; J. Overton 15–4–30–3; Leach 15–5–53–2; Abell 4–2–9–0. *Second innings*—Gregory 10–2–36–0; C. Overton 16–3–60–1; Bess 36.2–13–80–5; Leach 35–12–53–3; J. Overton 11–2–37–0; Abell 1–0–1–0.

Somerset

M. E. Trescothick b Sidebottom	6	– (2) c Hodd b Patterson	7
D. Elgar c Lees b Sidebottom	6	– (1) c Hodd b Patterson	7
*T. B. Abell c Hodd b Sidebottom	0	– lbw b Patterson	4
J. C. Hildreth lbw b Patterson	23	– lbw b Waite	27
†S. M. Davies c Hodd b Azeem Rafiq	35	– (6) lbw b Lyth	59
L. Gregory lbw b Sidebottom	43	– (7) c Carver b Sidebottom	26
A. J. Hose lbw b Waite	0	– (5) c Handscomb b Carver	68
C. Overton not out	44	– c Hodd b Sidebottom	34
J. Overton lbw b Sidebottom	19	– c Carver b Lyth	20
M. J. Leach c Hodd b Waite	17	– lbw b Sidebottom	1
D. M. Bess c Lyth b Carver	20	– not out	0
B 4, lb 5, nb 2	11	Lb 3, nb 2	5
1/7 (2) 2/7 (3) 3/18 (1) 4/48 (4) 5/113 (5) 6/114 (7) 7/149 (6) 8/173 (9) 9/199 (10) 10/224 (11) (64 overs)	224	1/7 (1) 2/17 (3) 3/38 (2) 4/49 (4) 5/167 (5) 6/189 (6) 7/231 (7) 8/242 (8) 9/250 (10) 10/258 (9) (85.3 overs)	258

Sidebottom 17–2–56–5; Patterson 20–7–50–1; Azeem Rafiq 15–2–66–1; Waite 10–0–41–2; Carver 2–1–2–1. *Second innings*—Sidebottom 19–3–59–3; Patterson 14–5–28–3; Waite 6–0–29–1; Carver 17–2–57–1; Azeem Rafiq 12–2–37–0; Lyth 17.3–2–45–2.

Umpires: N. L. Bainton and D. J. Millns.

At Southampton, June 26–29. SOMERSET drew with HAMPSHIRE.

At Scarborough, July 3–6. SOMERSET beat YORKSHIRE by 179 runs.

SOMERSET v SURREY

At Taunton, August 7–10. Drawn. Somerset 13pts, Surrey 11pts. Toss: uncontested.

Influenced by overcast skies, Surrey captain Batty chose to bowl, which surprised those who expected a dry pitch – used for the teams' T20 match the day before – and help for the spinners later on. But persistent rain made the call irrelevant. Somerset recovered from 96 for four thanks to a gritty century partnership between two players who had been struggling. Abell, who had dropped himself for Somerset's victory at Scarborough, showed application and artistry while making 96, and

Davies hit a first hundred for his new team, against his old one. Bess added a maiden first-class fifty to help Somerset secure maximum batting points for the only time in the season. After the weather shortened the first two days and stole the third, Surrey's reply had reached only 69 for one at the start of the fourth. There was just time for Stoneman to mark his Test call-up with a half-century, before he became one of Bess's five victims; it was the fifth time he had claimed five or more wickets, in only six Championship matches.

Close of play: first day, Somerset 234-4 (Abell 88, Davies 68); second day, Surrey 69-1 (Stoneman 34, Borthwick 0); third day, no play.

Somerset

M. E. Trescothick c Borthwick b Meaker	26	M. J. Leach not out	17
E. J. Byrom b Batty	42	T. D. Groenewald c and b Borthwick	31
T. D. Rouse c Foakes b Clarke	0		
J. C. Hildreth lbw b Clarke	0	B 7, lb 4, w 1, nb 6	18
*T. B. Abell c Foakes b Clarke	96		——
†S. M. Davies c Borthwick b S. M. Curran	142	1/43 (1) 2/46 (3) (112.1 overs)	436
J. Allenby c Foakes b Meaker	9	3/46 (4) 4/96 (2) 5/251 (5)	
C. Overton lbw b Meaker	0	6/270 (7) 7/270 (8) 8/380 (9)	
D. M. Bess b Batty	55	9/388 (6) 10/436 (11) 110 overs: 429-9	

T. K. Curran 17–3–79–0; S. M. Curran 20–3–99–1; Clarke 24–5–83–3; Meaker 28–8–87–3; Batty 19–4–55–2; Borthwick 4.1–0–22–1.

Surrey

R. J. Burns run out	30	*G. J. Batty not out	20
M. D. Stoneman c Abell b Bess	67	S. C. Meaker st Davies b Bess	18
S. G. Borthwick c Abell b Bess	7		
J. J. Roy c Abell b Leach	26	B 5, lb 13	18
A. J. Finch c Trescothick b Bess	39		——
†B. T. Foakes c Davies b Overton	20	1/58 (1) 2/99 (3) (108.4 overs)	345
S. M. Curran c and b Bess	32	3/136 (4) 4/138 (2)	
R. Clarke c Davies b Groenewald	33	5/178 (6) 6/208 (5) 7/243 (7)	
T. K. Curran run out	35	8/291 (8) 9/306 (9) 10/345 (11)	

Overton 22–7–49–1; Groenewald 18–4–61–1; Allenby 5–1–13–0; Leach 33–6–102–1; Bess 29.4–7–101–5; Rouse 1–0–1–0.

Umpires: N. G. B. Cook and N. G. C. Cowley.

At Chelmsford, August 28–31. SOMERSET lost to ESSEX by 179 runs.

At Birmingham, September 5–8. SOMERSET beat WARWICKSHIRE by 169 runs.

SOMERSET v LANCASHIRE

At Taunton, September 12–15. Somerset won by seven wickets. Somerset 22pts, Lancashire 3pts. Toss: uncontested.

Lancashire began with faint hopes of catching leaders Essex, but were duffed up on a worn Taunton pitch. After being inserted, Somerset spluttered again – four of the top five failed to convert starts – and were indebted to another determined hundred from Steven Davies. Lancashire's main weapon was young leg-spinner Parkinson, who overcame nerves to claim four for 68. But the turn he extracted augured well for Somerset's own spinners: after the openers went cheaply on the second day, Leach ripped through Lancashire as they folded for 133. They made a better fist of things following on, with half-centuries from Hameed and Livingstone. But from 144 for one, they lost their last nine for 125; Leach and Bess shared seven victims, taking their combined tally to 68 from the last nine Championship matches. Somerset gobbled up the 68 needed for victory, stoking their survival hopes, and confirming Essex's coronation.

Close of play: first day, Somerset 330-9 (Leach 25, Groenewald 4); second day, Lancashire 28-0 (Davies 15, Hameed 9); third day, Lancashire 247-8 (Bailey 7, Jarvis 2).

Somerset

M. E. Trescothick lbw b Bailey	25	– c Livingstone b Parkinson	21
E. J. Byrom b McLaren	38	– b Parkinson	10
G. A. Bartlett lbw b Jarvis	3	– not out	27
J. C. Hildreth b McLaren	25	– c Hameed b Parkinson	0
*T. B. Abell c Livingstone b Parkinson	46	– not out	8
†S. M. Davies b Bailey	111		
P. D. Trego st Davies b Parkinson	17		
C. Overton c Livingstone b Parkinson	4		
D. M. Bess st Davies b Parkinson	17		
M. J. Leach c Vilas b Bailey	29		
T. D. Groenewald not out	5		
Lb 5, nb 10	15	Lb 1, nb 2	3
1/39 (1) 2/44 (3) 3/90 (4) (97.2 overs)	335	1/19 (2) (3 wkts, 13.3 overs)	69
4/105 (2) 5/224 (5) 6/252 (7)		2/46 (1) 3/46 (4)	
7/264 (8) 8/288 (9) 9/322 (6) 10/335 (10)			

McLaren 18–2–74–2; Bailey 17.2–6–40–3; Jarvis 12–3–47–1; Parry 25–3–74–0; Parkinson 17–1–68–4; Livingstone 8–0–27–0. *Second innings*—McLaren 2–0–10–0; Jarvis 2–1–8–0; Parkinson 5–0–37–3; Parry 4.3–1–13–0.

Lancashire

†A. L. Davies c Trescothick b Overton	2	– c and b Leach	49
H. Hameed c Bartlett b Trego	4	– c Abell b Leach	62
L. S. Livingstone c Overton b Leach	21	– c Davies b Leach	57
*S. J. Croft c Davies b Overton	41	– lbw b Bess	5
S. Chanderpaul c Trescothick b Leach	17	– b Bess	9
D. J. Vilas c Davies b Groenewald	8	– c Davies b Overton	14
R. McLaren lbw b Leach	30	– c Trescothick b Leach	15
S. D. Parry b Leach	1	– c Hildreth b Bess	12
T. E. Bailey st Davies b Bess	2	– lbw b Overton	17
K. M. Jarvis c Davies b Leach	1	– b Overton	12
M. W. Parkinson not out	0	– not out	2
B 5, lb 1	6	B 8, lb 5, nb 2	15
1/6 (1) 2/22 (2) 3/39 (3) (57.3 overs)	133	1/82 (1) 2/144 (2) (127 overs)	269
4/82 (5) 5/86 (4) 6/99 (6)		3/151 (4) 4/171 (5)	
7/108 (8) 8/111 (9) 9/112 (10) 10/133 (7)		5/189 (6) 6/215 (3) 7/234 (7)	
		8/238 (8) 9/258 (10) 10/269 (9)	

Overton 11–4–26–2; Groenewald 10–4–17–1; Leach 22.3–10–47–5; Trego 5–0–13–1; Bess 9–3–24–1. *Second innings*—Overton 22–7–39–3; Groenewald 14–2–28–0; Leach 51–17–94–4; Bess 38–10–85–3; Trego 2–0–10–0.

Umpires: N. G. B. Cook and B. V. Taylor.

At The Oval, September 19–22. SOMERSET lost to SURREY by six wickets.

SOMERSET v MIDDLESEX

At Taunton, September 25–28. Somerset won by 231 runs. Somerset 20pts, Middlesex 3pts. Toss: Somerset.

In 2016, these two scrapped to win Division One; a year later, they scrapped to stay in it. Somerset, needing to win – and match Middlesex's bonus points – to escape relegation, asked groundsman Simon Lee for a turning pitch. Middlesex captain Voges described the surface as having rake marks at both ends. It hardly helped their mood that senior spinner Ollie Rayner was missing through injury. Slow left-armer Patel had been wicketless in his only other Championship appearance of 2017, but picked up seven wickets on the first day – as Somerset subsided to 236 – and 12 in the match, both career-bests. Somerset fielded three specialist spinners: Leach, Bess and van der Merwe, well supported by the seam of Craig Overton, routed Middlesex for 142 and 113. In between, Hildreth was a man apart, and notched a decisive century. Leach finished it off with a five-for, taking his season's haul past 50. Van der Merwe chipped in with four, including Eskinazi, caught by Trescothick fielding on his knees in the gully; he had adopted the tactic (first tested by Gregory in the game against Hampshire at Southampton) earlier in the summer to account for low pitches, but this was the first time it had paid off. Afterwards, ECB cricket liaison officer Wayne Noon rated the pitch "below average" for excessive turn on days one and two – but crucially not "poor". That spared Somerset a penalty, and meant they pipped Middlesex by a point.

Close of play: first day, Middlesex 18-3 (Malan 9, Voges 4); second day, Somerset 159-3 (Hildreth 82, Abell 34); third day, Middlesex 40-3 (Eskinazi 16, Voges 1).

Somerset

First innings		Second innings	
M. E. Trescothick lbw b Patel	37	– lbw b Harris	31
E. J. Byrom c Voges b Stirling	56	– c Harris b Stirling	5
G. A. Bartlett b Patel	25	– lbw b Patel	5
J. C. Hildreth lbw b Patel	41	– b Harris	109
*T. B. Abell run out	25	– c Voges b Patel	45
†S. M. Davies c Voges b Patel	27	– lbw b Patel	8
R. E. van der Merwe c Voges b Patel	0	– c Finn b Patel	24
C. Overton c Compton b Patel	1	– st Simpson b Patel	1
D. M. Bess c Finn b Stirling	0	– lbw b Murtagh	8
M. J. Leach c Finn b Patel	14	– not out	10
T. D. Groenewald not out	0	– not out	1
B 6, lb 4	10	Lb 3	3
1/93 (2) 2/114 (1) 3/139 (3) (84.4 overs)	236	1/20 (2) (9 wkts dec, 78 overs)	250
4/176 (5) 5/206 (4) 6/206 (7)		2/26 (3) 3/59 (1)	
7/214 (8) 8/214 (9) 9/230 (10) 10/236 (6)		4/185 (5) 5/199 (6) 6/223 (4)	
		7/226 (8) 8/237 (9) 9/239 (7)	

Murtagh 7–4–10–0; Finn 12–4–36–0; Harris 12–7–15–0; Patel 29.4–3–81–7; Stirling 20–3–70–2; Malan 3–0–9–0; Voges 1–0–5–0. *Second innings*—Murtagh 9–3–34–1; Stirling 18–4–31–1; Finn 8–0–37–0; Patel 26–3–92–5; Harris 13–1–33–2; Malan 1–0–5–0; Voges 3–0–15–0.

Middlesex

First innings		Second innings	
S. D. Robson c Trescothick b Leach	4	– (2) c Overton b Leach	8
N. R. D. Compton c Davies b Overton	0	– (1) lbw b Leach	10
S. S. Eskinazi c Trescothick b Leach	1	– c Trescothick b van der Merwe	16
D. J. Malan lbw b Leach	38	– c Davies b Bess	0
*A. C. Voges c Abell b Bess	4	– c Overton b Leach	13
†J. A. Simpson run out	0	– lbw b Leach	19
P. R. Stirling st Davies b Leach	41	– c Overton b van der Merwe	5
J. A. R. Harris b Overton	19	– c Bartlett b van der Merwe	13
S. T. Finn lbw b van der Merwe	1	– lbw b Leach	5
T. J. Murtagh not out	14	– b van der Merwe	8
R. H. Patel c van der Merwe b Overton	0	– not out	7
B 16, lb 4	20	B 4, lb 5	9
1/1 (2) 2/4 (3) 3/5 (1) (50.3 overs)	142	1/20 (2) 2/27 (1) (53.5 overs)	113
4/18 (5) 5/22 (6) 6/95 (4)		3/28 (4) 4/43 (3)	
7/100 (7) 8/117 (9) 9/128 (8) 10/142 (11)		5/71 (5) 6/80 (6) 7/80 (7)	
		8/93 (8) 9/101 (10) 10/113 (9)	

Overton 5.3–1–7–3; Leach 25–12–54–4; Bess 12–3–43–1; van der Merwe 8–1–18–1. *Second innings*—Overton 3–1–6–0; Leach 26.5–12–57–5; van der Merwe 13–6–22–4; Bess 11–3–19–1.

Umpires: M. Burns and A. G. Wharf.

SURREY

The long goodbye

RICHARD SPILLER

Kumar Sangakkara's spectacular finale dominated a season in which Surrey finished third in the Championship, their highest position since 2004. He had been determined to close his first-class career in style, and did so with eight centuries in 11 innings, including five in a row, before falling 16 short of a record-equalling sixth. He was the country's leading scorer, with 1,491 runs in ten matches at 106, a higher average than anyone had ever managed in an English season – bar Don Bradman.

Yet when the cheers died down, there was a feeling Surrey might have done even better. They reached the Royal London Cup final for the third year running, but again left empty-handed, outdone by a phenomenal innings from Nottinghamshire's Alex Hales. And a stuttering Twenty20 campaign was ended by Warwickshire in the quarter-final, after Surrey failed to defend 204.

Michael Di Venuto, the head coach, described the Championship placing as flattering: they were 85 points behind champions Essex, and only 17 above the relegation zone. But if they had drawn their last game at Old Trafford, Surrey would have been runners-up, despite winning only twice. Survival was cemented by victory over Somerset in the penultimate match – a long wait from the first win, on April 10 – and ensured a third season in the top flight, a feat beyond them in their two previous visits.

A bulging bag of 47 batting bonuses – 18 more than any of their rivals – owed much to Sangakkara, but also to the only other players to pass 1,000 in Division One, openers Mark Stoneman and Rory Burns. Stoneman enjoyed the pitches at his new home after moving from Durham, earned a Test debut, and finished with four Championship centuries (plus one in the Royal London final). Burns reached four figures for the fourth successive summer, but was still ignored by the selectors. It was Sangakkara, though, who spectators came to watch, and the authority and precision of his strokeplay were much admired, not least by fellow players. The only surprise about his two centuries on a farewell first-class trip to Lord's was that he needed a bridge to cross the river.

Support for this trio of left-handers proved patchy. Scott Borthwick, another Durham exile, fell away after an early century and briefly lost his place, although his catching had few peers, while Jason Roy made just five Championship appearances between international commitments.

Before the season, Surrey's director of cricket Alec Stewart had raised eyebrows by saying Ben Foakes was the equal of any wicketkeeper in the world, but few who saw him disagreed. He secured an Ashes tour with several elegant one-day innings, and runs in the later stages of the Championship.

The bowling was more of a problem: only Warwickshire collected fewer bonus points. To begin with, left-arm speedster Mark Footitt maintained his

016 form, but he was released in July on personal grounds, and subsequently re-signed for Nottinghamshire. Footitt's departure was the second major blow: a month into the season, Zafar Ansari, the 25-year-old all-rounder who had won three England caps the previous winter, decided to retire, saying he had lost his appetite for the game. Not long after, Dominic Sibley stunned Surrey by agreeing a move to Warwickshire, who had promised him more opportunities in the top order. Rikki Clarke had already agreed a switch in the opposite direction, so a swap was arranged. Clarke returned to The Oval after ten years, and his bowling was crucial in the win over Somerset. Worryingly, though, his career-best seven for 55 meant he was the only man apart from Footitt to claim a five-for in the Championship.

Charlie Crowhurst, Getty Images

Kumar Sangakkara

While the lower order rarely flourished, they found their opponents more stubborn. The loss of Ansari's left-arm spin affected the balance of the attack, and Gareth Batty ended up as the joint leading wicket-taker with just 25, the lowest for Surrey since 1855. His captaincy was more attritional than enterprising, and he stood down at the end of the year to be replaced by Burns, with Jade Dernbach taking charge for T20.

Sam Curran also managed 25, but at great cost and, like older brother Tom, looked weary long before the end. Tom's growing prowess and competitive nature swung several tight limited-overs games and later earned him an Ashes call-up, while Sam's 20 wickets spearheaded the Royal London run. Dernbach excelled with the white ball, and made a few Championship appearances. Stuart Meaker offered express pace, but was wayward at times. Kolpak signing Ravi Rampaul's 18 victims smoothed the path to Lord's, but after two unremarkable seasons he accepted a three-year deal with Derbyshire.

In the T20 Blast, Surrey proved too dependent on Aaron Finch, who made 489 runs at a strike-rate of 166. On their day, he and Roy could destroy any attack. Moises Henriques, another Australian, had a limited impact, while Kevin Pietersen's much-hyped comeback lasted two injury-affected games.

Batsman Ryan Patel, wicketkeeper-batsman Ollie Pope and off-spinner Amar Virdi (who was selected for the Lions tour) all enjoyed promising starts. The club's Academy could also be proud of Will Jacks and Gus Atkinson, who signed professional contracts. Meanwhile, the task of replacing Sangakkara in 2018 was handed to the Australian all-rounder Mitchell Marsh.

Off the field, Surrey continued to thrive. They made a pre-tax profit of £1.6m, and unveiled plans to extend capacity at The Oval from around 25,000 to 40,000, through developments on each side of the pavilion. It was renamed in honour of Micky Stewart, their former captain, manager and president.

Championship attendance: 40,901.

SURREY RESULTS

All first-class matches – Played 15: Won 2, Lost 2, Drawn 11.
County Championship matches – Played 14: Won 2, Lost 2, Drawn 10.

Specsavers County Championship, 3rd in Division 1;
NatWest T20 Blast, quarter-finalists; Royal London One-Day Cup, finalists.

COUNTY CHAMPIONSHIP AVERAGES, BATTING AND FIELDING

Cap		Birthplace	M	I	NO	R	HS	100	Avge	Ct/St
2015	†K. C. Sangakkara¶	Matale, SL	10	16	2	1,491	200	8	106.50	6
	†M. D. Stoneman	Newcastle-u-Tyne	12	19	0	1,156	197	4	60.84	4
2014	†R. J. Burns	Epsom‡	14	22	1	1,041	219*	1	49.57	7
2014	J. J. Roy§	Durban, SA	5	7	1	257	87	0	42.83	0
2016	B. T. Foakes	Colchester	14	20	4	680	110	1	42.50	29/2
	O. J. D. Pope	Chelsea	5	8	2	226	100*	1	37.66	2
	D. P. Sibley	Epsom‡	7	12	2	330	69	0	33.00	3
	†R. Patel	Sutton‡	4	6	0	170	81	0	28.33	2
2016	T. K. Curran	Cape Town, SA	9	11	2	247	53	0	27.44	3
	†S. M. Curran	Northampton	13	17	1	423	90	0	26.43	4
	†S. G. Borthwick	Sunderland	12	19	1	446	108*	1	24.77	21
2005	R. Clarke	Orsett	6	7	0	157	50	0	22.42	7
2011	G. J. Batty	Bradford	12	14	4	175	33	0	17.50	0
2012	S. C. Meaker	Pietermaritzburg, SA	9	13	3	174	49	0	17.40	3
	G. S. Virdi	Chiswick	3	4	1	18	8*	0	6.00	0
2011	J. W. Dernbach	Johannesburg, SA	5	5	1	17	8*	0	4.25	0
	†R. Rampaul††	Preysal, Trinidad	2	4	2	4	3	0	2.00	0
	M. H. A. Footitt	Nottingham	7	8	1	7	4	0	1.00	2

Also batted: †Z. S. Ansari (*Ascot*) (cap 2014) (1 match) 3; A. J. Finch¶ (*Colac, Australia*) (1 match) 39; C. McKerr†† (*Johannesburg, SA*) (2 matches) 1; F. O. E. van den Bergh (*Bickley*) (1 match) 5.

‡ *Born in Surrey.* § *ECB contract.* ¶ *Official overseas player.* †† *Other non-England-qualified.*

BOWLING

	Style	O	M	R	W	BB	5I	Avge
R. Clarke	RFM	166.2	52	436	22	7-55	1	19.81
M. H. A. Footitt	LFM	178.3	25	686	23	6-14	2	29.82
G. J. Batty	OB	308.1	64	857	25	3-70	0	34.28
T. K. Curran	RFM	256.3	50	832	24	4-69	0	34.66
S. C. Meaker	RF	215.3	33	869	21	4-92	0	41.38
J. W. Dernbach	RFM	140.3	32	433	10	3-51	0	43.30
S. M. Curran	LFM	339.5	60	1,179	25	3-74	0	47.16

Also bowled: Z. S. Ansari (SLA) 27–5–88–0; S. G. Borthwick (LB) 77.1–1–347–4; C. McKerr (RFM) 25–1–102–1; R. Patel (RM) 42–8–128–2; R. Rampaul (RFM) 62–15–193–3; D. P. Sibley (LB) 6.4–0–50–1; F. O. E. van den Bergh (SLA) 57–13–145–4; G. S. Virdi (OB) 88–13–271–6.

LEADING ROYAL LONDON CUP AVERAGES (100 runs/4 wickets)

Batting	Runs	HS	Avge	SR	Ct
B. T. Foakes	482	92	96.40	105.47	19
K. C. Sangakkara	545	124*	77.85	96.97	4
M. D. Stoneman	456	144*	50.66	102.01	3
J. J. Roy	160	92	40.00	102.56	0
R. J. Burns	192	67*	32.00	72.72	9
O. J. D. Pope	118	55	29.50	106.30	2
S. G. Borthwick	171	45	24.42	70.37	0
S. M. Curran	124	39	17.71	95.38	4

Bowling	W	BB	Avge	ER
J. W. Dernbach	15	4-31	18.46	4.96
R. Rampaul	18	4-40	24.66	5.62
S. M. Curran	20	3-43	24.90	5.56
S. C. Meaker	6	4-37	37.00	5.45
G. J. Batty	9	5-40	40.22	4.82
T. K. Curran	9	2-45	53.55	5.91

LEADING NATWEST T20 BLAST AVERAGES (100 runs/15 overs)

Batting	Runs	HS	Avge	SR	Ct/St
A. J. Finch	489	114*	40.75	**166.89**	7
J. J. Roy	350	78	29.16	**159.09**	4
K. C. Sangakkara	120	70	30.00	**146.34**	2/1
T. K. Curran	119	51*	29.75	**132.22**	4
O. J. D. Pope	253	46	25.30	**124.63**	3
D. P. Sibley	141	61	23.50	**121.55**	3
S. M. Curran	122	39	10.16	**112.96**	2
M. C. Henriques	187	48*	31.16	**109.35**	3

Bowling	W	BB	Avge	ER
G. J. Batty	14	4-14	17.78	**7.11**
T. K. Curran	12	3-28	23.41	**7.80**
R. Clarke	10	4-16	17.90	**8.01**
S. M. Curran	13	4-13	28.76	**8.31**
S. C. Meaker	6	2-27	29.16	**8.33**
J. W. Dernbach	16	3-29	25.93	**8.58**
R. Rampaul	4	2-41	40.25	**10.61**

FIRST-CLASS COUNTY RECORDS

Highest score for	357*	R. Abel v Somerset at The Oval	1899
Highest score against	366	N. H. Fairbrother (Lancashire) at The Oval	1990
Leading run-scorer	43,554	J. B. Hobbs (avge 49.72)	1905–34
Best bowling for	10-43	T. Rushby v Somerset at Taunton	1921
Best bowling against	10-28	W. P. Howell (Australians) at The Oval	1899
Leading wicket-taker	1,775	T. Richardson (avge 17.87)	1892–1904
Highest total for	811	v Somerset at The Oval	1899
Highest total against	863	by Lancashire at The Oval	1990
Lowest total for	14	v Essex at Chelmsford	1983
Lowest total against	16	by MCC at Lord's	1872

LIST A COUNTY RECORDS

Highest score for	268	A. D. Brown v Glamorgan at The Oval	2002
Highest score against	**187***	**A. D. Hales (Nottinghamshire) at Lord's**	**2017**
Leading run-scorer	10,358	A. D. Brown (avge 32.16)	1990–2008
Best bowling for	7-30	M. P. Bicknell v Glamorgan at The Oval	1999
Best bowling against	7-15	A. L. Dixon (Kent) at The Oval	1967
Leading wicket-taker	409	M. P. Bicknell (avge 25.21)	1986–2005
Highest total for	496-4	v Gloucestershire at The Oval	2007
Highest total against	429	by Glamorgan at The Oval	2002
Lowest total for	64	v Worcestershire at Worcester	1978
Lowest total against	44	by Glamorgan at The Oval	1999

TWENTY20 COUNTY RECORDS

Highest score for	122*	J. J. Roy v Somerset at The Oval	2015
Highest score against	**116***	**J. L. Denly (Kent) at The Oval**	**2017**
Leading run-scorer	**2,814**	**J. J. Roy (avge 30.92)**	**2008–17**
Best bowling for	6-24	T. J. Murtagh v Middlesex at Lord's	2005
Best bowling against	4-9	D. J. Willey (Northamptonshire) at Birmingham	2013
Leading wicket-taker	**91**	**J. W. Dernbach (avge 25.53)**	**2005–17**
Highest total for	224-5	v Gloucestershire at Bristol	2006
Highest total against	240-3	by Glamorgan at The Oval	2015
Lowest total for	88	v Kent at The Oval	2012
Lowest total against	68	by Sussex at Hove	2007

ADDRESS

The Kia Oval, Kennington, London SE11 5SS; 0844 375 1845; enquiries@surreycricket.com; www.surreycricket.com.

OFFICIALS

Captain 2017 G. J. Batty
2018 R. J. Burns
(Twenty20) J. W. Dernbach
Director of cricket A. J. Stewart
Head coach M. J. Di Venuto
Assistant head coach V. S. Solanki
Academy director G. T. J. Townsend
President D. P. Stewart
Chairman R. W. Thompson
Chief executive R. A. Gould
Head groundsman L. E. Fortis
Scorer P. J. Makepeace

At Oxford, March 28–30. SURREY drew with OXFORD MCCU.

SURREY v WARWICKSHIRE

At The Oval, April 7–10. Surrey won by an innings and one run. Surrey 23pts, Warwickshire 1pt. Toss: uncontested.

Bell's decision to bowl first rebounded spectacularly on a quick pitch offering erratic bounce. Surrey's openers put on 154, and the former Durham left-hander Stoneman batted almost all day for 165, becoming the 12th overall – but the third in three years, after Sangakkara and Aaron Finch – to score a century on Championship debut for Surrey. Wright helped bottle things up on the second day, when the last seven wickets fell for 76, but Warwickshire were soon in desperate straits. Swinging the ball at pace, Footitt swept away six for three in 32 balls either side of tea, inflicting five ducks: Borthwick held on to some fizzers in the slips as Warwickshire crashed to 48 for eight. The follow-on proved harder work, thanks to unseasonally warm temperatures and a superb rearguard from Trott, ninth out after 404 minutes. He put on 103 with Bell, who compiled his first half-century in 15 first-class innings since the previous July, also against Surrey. It might still have been all over on the third day if Burns at slip had held an edge from Barker: 13 at the time, he lasted two and a half hours for 57. In the event, Tom Curran wrapped things up early on the final morning, with Warwickshire one short of making Surrey bat again.

Close of play: first day, Surrey 327-3 (Sangakkara 47, Sibley 7); second day, Warwickshire 29-0 (Porterfield 17, Mellor 8); third day, Warwickshire 322-7 (Trott 141, Patel 11).

Surrey

Batsman	Runs
R. J. Burns c Ambrose b Barker	71
M. D. Stoneman c Ambrose b Wright	165
S. G. Borthwick c Clarke b Hannon-Dalby	23
K. C. Sangakkara lbw b Hannon-Dalby	71
D. P. Sibley c Patel b Wright	34
†B. T. Foakes c Ambrose b Wright	34
S. M. Curran c Mellor b Wright	18
T. K. Curran st Ambrose b Patel	2
*G. J. Batty not out	14
J. W. Dernbach lbw b Patel	0
M. H. A. Footitt b Wright	1
B 4, lb 14, w 1, nb 2	21
(140.1 overs)	454

1/154 (1) 2/230 (3) 3/314 (2) 4/378 (4) 5/405 (5) 6/429 (6) 7/437 (7) 8/445 (8) 9/445 (10) 10/454 (11)

110 overs: 362-3

Barker 25–6–81–1; Wright 29.1–4–113–5; Clarke 16–3–52–0; Hannon-Dalby 26–4–90–2; Patel 40–14–92–2; Trott 4–0–8–0.

Warwickshire

Batsman	First innings		Second innings	
W. T. S. Porterfield c Foakes b Footitt	18	–	lbw b S. M. Curran	19
A. J. Mellor c Sibley b S. M. Curran	18	–	c Sangakkara b Dernbach	14
I. J. L. Trott lbw b Footitt	0	–	c Sibley b Footitt	151
*I. R. Bell c Borthwick b Footitt	0	–	c Borthwick b Footitt	64
S. R. Hain c Borthwick b Footitt	0	–	lbw b Dernbach	3
†T. R. Ambrose c Borthwick b Dernbach	6	–	lbw b T. K. Curran	0
R. Clarke lbw b Footitt	0	–	c Foakes b T. K. Curran	6
K. H. D. Barker b Footitt	0	–	lbw b Batty	57
J. S. Patel c Borthwick b S. M. Curran	8	–	lbw b T. K. Curran	29
C. J. C. Wright not out	28	–	b T. K. Curran	8
O. J. Hannon-Dalby c S. M. Curran b T. K. Curran	2	–	not out	1
B 4, lb 6, w 1	11		B 5, w 1, nb 4	10
(36.2 overs)	91		(118.2 overs)	362

First innings: 1/30 (2) 2/35 (3) 3/35 (4) 4/39 (5) 5/42 (1) 6/42 (7) 7/42 (8) 8/48 (6) 9/61 (9) 10/91 (11)

Second innings: 1/35 (1) 2/37 (2) 3/140 (4) 4/154 (5) 5/169 (6) 6/181 (7) 7/305 (8) 8/345 (9) 9/356 (3) 10/362 (10)

T. K. Curran 10.2–5–14–1; S. M. Curran 11–2–30–2; Footitt 9–2–14–6; Dernbach 6–1–23–1. *Second innings*—T. K. Curran 28.2–6–88–4; S. M. Curran 21–5–68–1; Footitt 24–1–104–2; Dernbach 20–6–48–2; Borthwick 5–0–16–0; Batty 20–3–33–1.

Umpires: R. K. Illingworth and B. V. Taylor.

SURREY v LANCASHIRE

At The Oval, April 14–17. Drawn. Surrey 9pts, Lancashire 11pts. Toss: Lancashire.

Grinding down the bowlers has been a life's work for 42-year-old Chanderpaul, who rescued Lancashire on a blameless surface after they had been hobbled by Footitt, on his way to a fifth five-for in five matches. Almost strokeless at first, then dropped by Borthwick at slip on 47, Chanderpaul extended his 74th first-class century to a monumental 182, the last 59 with a runner after damaging a hamstring. His eight-hour masterpiece was complemented by Clark, who reached his maiden hundred by pulling Footitt out of the ground and made all but 30 of his runs in boundaries. Their stand of 243 was a seventh-wicket record for the fixture. The reply almost juddered to a halt after Jarvis stymied Burns's hopes of a century: at one stage left-arm spinners Parry and Kerrigan twirled through 14 overs for four runs. Surrey just failed to avoid the follow-on, after Parry took two wickets in two balls, but the track remained docile, and the match was saved with ease, thanks to centuries from Borthwick – his first for Surrey – and Sangakkara.

Close of play: first day, Lancashire 294-6 (Chanderpaul 85, Clark 108); second day, Surrey 112-2 (Burns 48); third day, Surrey 55-1 (Stoneman 22, Borthwick 4).

Lancashire

Batsman	Runs
†A. L. Davies lbw b Footitt	26
H. Hameed c Foakes b S. M. Curran	0
L. A. Procter c Borthwick b T. K. Curran	12
*L. S. Livingstone c Stoneman b Footitt	16
S. Chanderpaul c Borthwick b Batty	182
D. J. Vilas lbw b Footitt	4
R. McLaren lbw b Batty	28
J. Clark c Burns b Batty	140
S. D. Parry c Foakes b Footitt	21
K. M. Jarvis c Foakes b Footitt	0
S. C. Kerrigan not out	20
B 4, lb 13, w 2, nb 2	21
(138.5 overs)	470

1/0 (2) 2/31 (3) 3/44 (1) 4/63 (4) 5/67 (6) 6/122 (7) 7/365 (8) 8/407 (9) 9/407 (10) 10/470 (5)   110 overs: 388-7

T. K. Curran 30–8–79–1; S. M. Curran 24–2–71–1; Footitt 32–7–118–5; Ansari 27–5–88–0; Batty 21.5–3–72–3; Borthwick 4–0–25–0.

Surrey

Batsman	First innings		Second innings	
R. J. Burns c Davies b Jarvis	91	–	c Davies b Kerrigan	20
M. D. Stoneman lbw b Clark	40	–	st Davies b Parry	27
S. G. Borthwick c Davies b Jarvis	19	–	not out	108
K. C. Sangakkara c Livingstone b Parry	46	–	b Kerrigan	136
D. P. Sibley run out	10	–	not out	0
†B. T. Foakes b Kerrigan	9			
Z. S. Ansari b Kerrigan	3			
S. M. Curran c Kerrigan b McLaren	14			
T. K. Curran not out	33			
*G. J. Batty c Procter b Parry	33			
M. H. A. Footitt lbw b Parry	0			
B 6, lb 1, nb 14	21		B 13, lb 5, w 7, nb 2, p 5	32
(125.2 overs)	319		(3 wkts dec, 92 overs)	323

1/67 (2) 2/112 (3) 3/211 (1) 4/216 (4) 5/229 (6) 6/230 (5) 7/245 (7) 8/262 (8) 9/319 (10) 10/319 (11)   110 overs: 270-8

1/43 (1) 2/66 (2) 3/322 (4)

Jarvis 21–4–72–2; McLaren 16–0–76–1; Livingstone 13–5–32–0; Procter 9–2–25–0; Clark 13–2–41–1; Parry 24.2–10–31–3; Kerrigan 29–12–35–2. *Second innings*—Jarvis 11–2–24–0; McLaren 10–0–29–0; Parry 25–4–71–1; Kerrigan 24–0–101–2; Livingstone 16–2–54–0; Clark 5–0–21–0; Hameed 1–1–0–0.

Umpires: J. H. Evans and D. J. Millns.

At Birmingham, April 21–24. SURREY drew with WARWICKSHIRE.

At Lord's, May 19–22. SURREY drew with MIDDLESEX.

At Chelmsford, May 26–29. SURREY drew with ESSEX. *Kumar Sangakkara hits 200 (his fifth successive century) and 84.*

SURREY v ESSEX

At Guildford, June 9–12. Essex won by eight wickets. Essex 24pts, Surrey 7pts. Toss: uncontested.

Surrey looked in charge while Stoneman was dominating a rain-shortened first day, peppering the short square boundaries during a stand of 186 with Sibley. Sam Curran then spanked a forthright 65 against an attack lacking Quinn, out with back spasms. But things changed once Stoneman tickled the persistent Wagner to the keeper next morning, as the last four wickets evaporated for seven. When Essex batted, Bopara put on 120 with ten Doeschate, who made his highest Championship score, beating an undefeated 159, also at Woodbridge Road, in 2009. Surrey had lost their way with the ball – only Rampaul offered much control – and now did so with the bat. Off-spinner Harmer applied the brakes during a marathon spell from the Railway End, while seamers Porter and Wagner pounded away in front of the building site of the pavilion. Foakes ran out of partners before he could inflict too much damage on his former Essex colleagues, who were left requiring 253 in 83 overs. Browne kick-started the pursuit, then Westley and Lawrence completed the job shortly after tea.

Close of play: first day, Surrey 353-5 (Stoneman 181, Curran 54); second day, Essex 367-7 (ten Doeschate 120, Wagner 20); third day, Surrey 253-7 (Foakes 46, Meaker 4).

Surrey

First innings		Second innings	
R. J. Burns c Foster b Porter	14	– c Foster b Porter	57
M. D. Stoneman c Foster b Wagner	197	– c Cook b Porter	10
S. G. Borthwick c Foster b Wagner	14	– c Lawrence b Harmer	36
K. C. Sangakkara c Cook b Porter	4	– c Foster b Harmer	26
D. P. Sibley c Foster b ten Doeschate	69	– lbw b Porter	28
†B. T. Foakes lbw b ten Doeschate	4	– not out	65
S. M. Curran lbw b Wagner	65	– c sub (C. J. Taylor) b Harmer	4
*G. J. Batty c sub (C. J. Taylor) b Bopara	13	– c Lawrence b Harmer	19
S. C. Meaker not out	0	– c Harmer b Wagner	14
R. Rampaul c Foster b Porter	3	– c ten Doeschate b Wagner	0
M. H. A. Footitt c ten Doeschate b Porter	0	– run out	0
Lb 11, w 3, nb 2	16	B 7, lb 18, nb 4	29
1/32 (1) 2/75 (3) 3/88 (4) 4/274 (5) 5/280 (6) 6/368 (7) 7/392 (8) 8/396 (2) 9/399 (10) 10/399 (11) (96 overs)	399	1/15 (2) 2/108 (3) 3/128 (1) 4/158 (4) 5/182 (5) 6/199 (7) 7/241 (8) 8/286 (9) 9/286 (10) 10/288 (11) (92.4 overs)	288

Porter 24–3–102–4; Quinn 9.5–1–43–0; Bopara 10–1–43–1; Wagner 26–3–110–3; Harmer 22–1–69–0; ten Doeschate 3.1–0–16–2; Westley 1–0–5–0. *Second innings*—Porter 21–4–58–3; Wagner 25.4–3–96–2; Harmer 39–5–83–4; Bopara 6–0–14–0; Lawrence 1–0–12–0.

Essex

First innings		Second innings	
N. L. J. Browne lbw b Batty	43	– c Burns b Batty	77
A. N. Cook lbw b Curran	31	– c Borthwick b Rampaul	31
T. Westley c Foakes b Footitt	23	– not out	108
D. W. Lawrence c Curran b Batty	21	– not out	32
R. S. Bopara lbw b Meaker	64		
*R. N. ten Doeschate not out	168		
†J. S. Foster c Foakes b Footitt	12		
S. R. Harmer c Foakes b Footitt	20		
N. Wagner c Foakes b Curran	34		
J. A. Porter b Meaker	6		
M. R. Quinn b Rampaul	0		
B 4, lb 1, w 2, nb 6	13	Lb 2, w 3	5
1/55 (2) 2/91 (3) 3/121 (1) 4/134 (4) 5/254 (5) 6/279 (7) 7/326 (8) 8/398 (9) 9/423 (10) 10/435 (11) (106 overs)	435	1/53 (2) 2/148 (1) (2 wkts, 64.2 overs)	253

Curran 24–2–94–2; Footitt 22–0–96–3; Rampaul 22–4–73–1; Batty 14–1–64–2; Meaker 24–3–103–2. *Second innings*—Curran 6–1–15–0; Footitt 7–0–28–0; Batty 22–2–80–1; Rampaul 13–3–47–1; Meaker 6.2–0–43–0; Borthwick 10–0–38–0.

Umpires: R. J. Bailey and N. G. B. Cook.

At Leeds, June 26–29. SURREY drew with YORKSHIRE. *Kumar Sangakkara scores 180*, and becomes the first to 1,000 first-class runs in the season.*

SURREY v HAMPSHIRE

At The Oval, July 3–6. Drawn. Surrey 10pts, Hampshire 12pts. Toss: Hampshire.

Rory Burns, on the field for all but the last half hour of the match, dealt with everything Hampshire could throw at him – plus soaring temperatures and the demands of captaincy, which he inherited when Gareth Batty reported an injured calf muscle before play started. Perhaps it was just as well for Batty: on a pancake-flat pitch, Hampshire proceeded to amass their highest total against Surrey, taking advantage of a youthful attack which faded after a lively start. Adams played sedately for 144, but Vince made a free-flowing ton, then Bailey weighed in with 161. After fielding for 161.4 overs, Burns began the reply and was still there after ten hours, having survived a sharp chance in the slips on 98. He piloted a side also lacking Sangakkara (hand injury) to 483, despite some thunderbolts from Edwards and three late wickets for Holland, the Australian seamer. Burns was only the third to carry his bat during a double-century for Surrey, after Bobby Abel (1899) and Jack Hobbs (1919) – but the follow-on was not quite avoided, and out he came again. Stoneman helped him put on 109 for the first wicket and, although Burns was finally dismissed for 68 – the ball rebounding off the keeper's pads into the stumps after he missed a leg-side flick – a draw was agreed ten overs later. In all, he batted for 756 minutes, faced 535 balls, and hit 37 fours and a six.

Close of play: first day, Hampshire 361-4 (Bailey 61); second day, Surrey 113-1 (Burns 45, McKerr 0); third day, Surrey 410-7 (Burns 174, T. K. Curran 35).

Hampshire

J. H. K. Adams b Virdi	144
†L. D. McManus b S. M. Curran	13
R. R. Rossouw c Borthwick b T. K. Curran	28
J. M. Vince c Foakes b T. K. Curran	104
*G. J. Bailey c Footitt b Borthwick	161
S. M. Ervine b McKerr	83
I. G. Holland not out	58
G. K. Berg c T. K. Curran b Sibley	35
B 4, lb 5, w 5, nb 8	22
1/24 (2) 2/71 (3) 3/232 (4) 4/361 (1) 5/528 (6) 6/600 (5) 7/648 (8) — 110 overs: 429-4 — (7 wkts dec, 161.4 overs)	648

K. J. Abbott, M. S. Crane and F. H. Edwards did not bat.

T. K. Curran 25–5–85–2; S. M. Curran 26–6–82–1; Footitt 24–5–89–0; McKerr 25–1–102–1; Virdi 32–3–135–1; Borthwick 23–0–96–1; Sibley 6.4–0–50–1.

Surrey

*R. J. Burns not out	219	– st McManus b Ervine	68
M. D. Stoneman c Rossouw b Ervine	57	– lbw b Holland	47
C. McKerr lbw b Crane	1		
S. G. Borthwick c McManus b Abbott	3	– (3) b Holland	0
J. J. Roy lbw b Berg	27	– (4) not out	37
D. P. Sibley lbw b Abbott	57	– (5) not out	12
†B. T. Foakes c Rossouw b Edwards	14		
S. M. Curran c McManus b Edwards	12		
T. K. Curran b Holland	53		
G. S. Virdi b Holland	4		
M. H. A. Footitt c Berg b Holland	4		
B 10, lb 7, w 1, nb 14	32	B 1, lb 1	2
1/103 (2) 2/128 (3) 3/137 (4) 4/193 (5) 5/297 (6) 6/332 (7) 7/348 (8) 8/447 (9) 9/453 (10) 10/483 (11) — 110 overs: 375-7 — (147.5 overs)	483	1/109 (2) 2/109 (3) 3/127 (1) — (3 wkts dec, 52 overs)	166

Abbott 27–14–45–2; Berg 19–3–58–1; Edwards 23–2–120–2; Crane 45–8–161–1; Holland 16.5–4–37–3; Ervine 17–2–45–1. *Second innings*—Berg 7–0–19–0; Abbott 4–1–12–0; Edwards 4–1–23–0; Crane 12–1–61–0; Ervine 16–3–24–1; Holland 7–2–16–2; Bailey 2–0–9–0.

Umpires: N. G. B. Cook and A. G. Wharf.

At Taunton, August 7–10. SURREY drew with SOMERSET.

SURREY v MIDDLESEX

At The Oval, August 28–31. Drawn. Surrey 10pts, Middlesex 7pts (after 2pt penalty). Toss: Middlesex. First-class debut: R. Patel. Championship debut: O. J. D. Pope.

A match heading for a draw after a third-day washout was propelled on to the front pages when a foot-long crossbow bolt – apparently fired from outside the ground – landed about ten metres from close fielder Rory Burns. The umpires hurried the players off the field, and spectators were warned to take cover while police, some armed, investigated. "It could very easily have killed someone," said Surrey's chief executive Richard Gould. The match was soon called off. Earlier in the day, Sam Curran struck three times in ten balls, and Middlesex were in even deeper trouble at 94 for six, only 61 in front. But the obstinate Simpson shared half-century stands with Rayner and Compton, who returned after retiring overnight with back trouble. It had been a good effort by an injury-hit Surrey, who included four teenagers (the first instance in the Championship since 1939), although they might have fashioned a bigger lead: nightwatchman Meaker survived past lunch on the second day, then Roy and Foakes cashed in on some wayward bowling by Finn to add 125, the only time bat dominated ball in the match. At the time of the abandonment Middlesex were contemplating a declaration, to allow them to improve a tardy over-rate – but were prevented from doing so, and penalised two points. This proved crucial at the end of the season, when they were relegated by one. An appeal about the exceptional circumstances was turned down in mid-October.

Close of play: first day, Surrey 26-2 (Meaker 1, Borthwick 0); second day, Middlesex 15-0 (Compton 6, Robson 9); third day, no play.

FOUR TEENAGERS IN A COUNTY CHAMPIONSHIP TEAM

Northamptonshire v Glamorgan at Northampton
H. F. Bagnall, E. W. Clark, W. W. Timms, P. A. Wright 1922
Glamorgan v Warwickshire at Swansea
J. T. Morgan, A. L. B. Perkins, M. J. L. Turnbull, C. F. Walters* 1925
Northamptonshire v Worcestershire at Northampton
W. W. Coverdale, H. Nunley, R. J. Partridge, A. W. Snowden 1931
Leicestershire v Hampshire at Southampton and v Sussex at Hastings
G. O. Dawkes, C. H. Drake, G. F. Knew, A. R. West 1939
Surrey v Middlesex at The Oval
S. M. Curran, R. Patel, O. J. D. Pope, G. S. Virdi 2017

* *Walters's 20th birthday was on the last day of the match.* *Research: Philip Bailey*

Middlesex

S. D. Robson b Meaker	57 – (2) c Foakes b Curran	21
N. R. D. Compton c Borthwick b Meaker	20 – (1) not out	28
S. S. Eskinazi lbw b Virdi	13 – lbw b Curran	6
A. C. Voges lbw b Clarke	40 – c Clarke b Curran	0
P. R. Stirling b Meaker	0 – b Patel	12
†J. A. Simpson lbw b Batty	31 – not out	88
*J. E. C. Franklin c Borthwick b Clarke	7 – c Foakes b Clarke	15
T. S. Roland-Jones lbw b Batty	5 – c and b Clarke	0
O. P. Rayner lbw b Virdi	38 – lbw b Meaker	30
S. T. Finn not out	18	
T. J. Murtagh c Clarke b Curran	5	
B 4, lb 7, nb 2	13	B 8, lb 2, nb 4 14

1/34 (2) 2/68 (3) 3/131 (1) (84.2 overs) 247
4/131 (5) 5/150 (4) 6/158 (7)
7/163 (8) 8/210 (6) 9/224 (9) 10/247 (11)

1/33 (2) (7 wkts, 68.1 overs) 214
2/33 (4) 3/38 (3)
4/60 (5) 5/86 (7) 6/94 (8) 7/158 (9)

In the second innings Compton, when 6, retired hurt at 15-0 and resumed at 158-7.

Curran 15.2–3–50–1; Clarke 16–5–31–2; Meaker 14–1–55–3; Batty 14–3–40–2; Patel 11–5–22–0; Virdi 14–3–38–2. *Second innings*—Curran 18–2–76–3; Clarke 16–8–31–2; Patel 8–3–18–1; Meaker 14–3–51–1; Batty 6–3–8–0; Virdi 6–0–16–0; Borthwick 0.1–0–4–0.

Surrey

R. J. Burns c Simpson b Roland-Jones	11
R. Patel c Robson b Roland-Jones	11
S. C. Meaker c Simpson b Finn	42
S. G. Borthwick c Simpson b Finn	24
J. J. Roy c Roland-Jones b Voges	79
†B. T. Foakes lbw b Franklin	73
O. J. D. Pope lbw b Murtagh	25
S. M. Curran c Rayner b Murtagh	4
R. Clarke c Finn b Roland-Jones	1
*G. J. Batty not out	0
G. S. Virdi b Roland-Jones	1
Lb 2, w 1, nb 6	9

1/21 (2) 2/26 (1) 3/89 (4) (87.4 overs) 280
4/106 (3) 5/231 (5) 6/257 (6)
7/266 (8) 8/279 (9) 9/279 (7) 10/280 (11)

Murtagh 20–3–51–2; Roland-Jones 22.4–6–66–4; Rayner 20–8–41–0; Finn 15–0–82–2; Franklin 7–1–23–1; Voges 3–0–15–1.

Umpires: P. K. Baldwin and M. A. Gough.

At Southampton, September 5–8. SURREY drew with HAMPSHIRE.

SURREY v YORKSHIRE

At The Oval, September 12–15. Drawn. Surrey 12pts, Yorkshire 10pts. Toss: Surrey. Championship debut: F. O. E. van den Bergh.

Batsmen bossed this game, so Surrey's bowlers – after 210 overs in harness – were relieved when the final 31 were lost to bad light. By then Yorkshire were safe, thanks to Marsh and Lees, who made his only Championship century of the season in a stand of 215, a county second-wicket record against Surrey. On the opening day, Stoneman (with an Ashes place to secure) and Burns (unwanted even by England Lions despite another productive summer) were rarely troubled by a lacklustre attack, then Sangakkara showed his appetite for runs had not been sated by a spell in the Caribbean Premier League. His sublime 164 took less than four hours, and he put on 258 with the wristy Foakes. Surrey did not quite reach 600, with Brooks proving that pace and vim could conquer the docile surface. Köhler-Cadmore and Marsh began with a partnership of 162, but Yorkshire were still forced to follow on. There was an encouraging debut for slow left-armer Freddie van den Bergh, after seven years on The Oval staff. He removed both openers, bowled 32 overs unchanged, and athletically ran out Ballance. But doing it a second time was beyond Surrey. The game turned out to be Sidebottom's last; the wicket of Patel was his 762nd in first-class cricket.

Close of play: first day, Surrey 398-3 (Sangakkara 85, Foakes 64); second day, Yorkshire 171-1 (Marsh 77, Lees 7); third day, Yorkshire 59-1 (Marsh 27, Lees 19).

Surrey

R. J. Burns c Hodd b Brooks	75
M. D. Stoneman c Marsh b Bresnan	131
R. Patel c Hodd b Sidebottom	27
K. C. Sangakkara c sub (B. O. Coad) b Brooks	164
†B. T. Foakes c Hodd b Brooks	110
O. J. D. Pope c Köhler-Cadmore b Brooks	0
S. M. Curran b Brooks	5
R. Clarke c Bresnan b Patterson	41
F. O. E. van den Bergh lbw b Patterson	5
S. C. Meaker lbw b Patterson	0
*G. J. Batty not out	12
B 1, lb 17, nb 4	22
1/178 (1) 2/233 (2) 3/255 (3) 4/513 (4) 5/513 (6) 6/531 (7) 7/540 (5) 8/555 (9) 9/555 (10) 10/592 (8) (137.2 overs)	592
110 overs: 465-3	

Sidebottom 21–4–67–1; Brooks 28–3–113–5; Patterson 30.2–5–120–3; Bresnan 25–1–136–1; Azeem Rafiq 29–3–122–0; Leaning 4–0–16–0.

Yorkshire

T. Köhler-Cadmore c Patel b van den Bergh	78	– lbw b Curran	12
S. E. Marsh st Foakes b van den Bergh	78	– not out	125
A. Z. Lees c Patel b van den Bergh	46	– b van den Bergh	102
*G. S. Ballance run out	29	– not out	28
J. A. Leaning c Foakes b Curran	32		
†A. J. Hodd c Meaker b Batty	57		
T. T. Bresnan c Clarke b Batty	25		
Azeem Rafiq lbw b Batty	0		
S. A. Patterson b Meaker	7		
J. A. Brooks c Foakes b Curran	8		
R. J. Sidebottom not out	0		
B 9, lb 20, w 1, nb 4	34	B 4, lb 8, nb 2	14
1/162 (1) 2/181 (2) 3/234 (3) 4/243 (4) 5/302 (5) 6/343 (7) 7/343 (8) 8/362 (9) 9/394 (10) 10/394 (6) (122.2 overs)	394	1/24 (1) 2/239 (3) (2 wkts, 88 overs)	281
110 overs: 354-7			

Curran 17–3–64–2; Clarke 19–9–48–0; Meaker 21–2–92–1; Batty 28.2–8–77–3; van den Bergh 37–10–84–3. *Second innings*—Curran 16–2–57–1; Clarke 13–5–31–0; Meaker 12–1–65–0; Batty 21–11–28–0; van den Bergh 20–3–61–1; Patel 6–0–27–0.

Umpires: M. Burns and N. A. Mallender.

SURREY v SOMERSET

At The Oval, September 19–22. Surrey won by six wickets. Surrey 23pts, Somerset 4pts. Toss: Somerset.

A tense encounter was settled in Surrey's favour with 8.2 overs to spare, which guaranteed them safety from relegation but left Somerset in trouble. Trescothick's vintage form on the opening morning preceded Clarke's devastating postprandial burst: he hit the perfect length on a well-grassed pitch to take five for 17 in 34 balls, and finished with seven for 55, the best figures of his 15-year career. Somerset owed much to Davies, who reminded his previous club of his strokeplay, and rescued his new one from 138 for six. But a total of 269 was soon exposed by the inevitable Sangakkara, who marked his last appearance at The Oval with 157, the eighth century of his memorable summer. Only Trego, given a rare extended bowl and constantly finding movement, contained the lead. The loss of 37 overs on the third day boosted Somerset's hopes of a draw, before Davies and Trego again led the resistance on the fourth. But Meaker bowled fast and straight, and Batty also took three wickets as the target was limited to 143. There were only 41 overs remaining when Surrey started their chase, but Sangakkara – given an emotional farewell by players and crowd – and Foakes made sure they won comfortably enough. They moved into second, ahead of Lancashire.

Close of play: first day, Surrey 42-0 (Burns 16, Stoneman 21); second day, Surrey 328-6 (Sangakkara 119, Clarke 1); third day, Somerset 113-4 (Abell 11, Davies 15).

Somerset

M. E. Trescothick lbw b Batty	65	– c Burns b Curran	1
E. J. Byrom c Meaker b Clarke	42	– b Batty	39
G. A. Bartlett c Sangakkara b Clarke	4	– lbw b Meaker	28
J. C. Hildreth lbw b Clarke	1	– lbw b Meaker	11
*T. B. Abell b Clarke	0	– c Burns b Clarke	18
†S. M. Davies c Stoneman b Clarke	86	– c Clarke b Batty	52
P. D. Trego b Clarke	2	– b Patel	68
C. Overton b Curran	24	– lbw b Meaker	10
D. M. Bess c and b Clarke	27	– c Foakes b Clarke	35
M. J. Leach lbw b Batty	2	– c Clarke b Batty	15
T. D. Groenewald not out	8	– not out	5
Lb 8	8	B 4, lb 10, w 1, nb 4, p 5	24
1/96 (1) 2/103 (3) 3/105 (4) (80 overs)	269	1/5 (1) 2/58 (3) (91.2 overs)	306
4/105 (5) 5/122 (2) 6/138 (7)		3/74 (4) 4/98 (2)	
7/191 (8) 8/252 (9) 9/257 (10) 10/269 (6)		5/132 (5) 6/198 (6) 7/234 (8)	
		8/242 (7) 9/290 (10) 10/306 (9)	

Dernbach 13–2–41–0; Curran 16–4–58–1; Clarke 18–2–55–7; Meaker 14–0–50–0; Batty 15–2–40–2; Patel 4–0–17–0. *Second innings*—Dernbach 14–4–40–0; Curran 15–1–59–1; Clarke 16.2–4–28–2; Meaker 18–4–65–3; Batty 25–4–84–3; Patel 3–0–11–1.

Surrey

R. J. Burns b Trego	43	– c Groenewald b Overton	13
M. D. Stoneman c Davies b Trego	51	– c Davies b Groenewald	24
R. Patel c Davies b Groenewald	14	– b Bess	17
K. C. Sangakkara c Leach b Abell	157	– c and b Bess	35
†B. T. Foakes c Davies b Trego	26	– not out	42
O. J. D. Pope c Davies b Groenewald	50	– not out	13
S. M. Curran c Overton b Trego	17		
R. Clarke run out	50		
*G. J. Batty lbw b Abell	5		
S. C. Meaker b Trego	0		
J. W. Dernbach not out	8		
B 1, lb 11	12	Lb 2	2
1/97 (2) 2/114 (1) 3/114 (3) (129.4 overs)	433	1/38 (1) (4 wkts, 32.4 overs)	146
4/169 (5) 5/278 (6) 6/317 (7)		2/39 (2) 3/73 (3)	
7/416 (4) 8/425 (8) 9/425 (9)		4/128 (4)	
10/433 (10) 110 overs: 357-6			

Overton 28–4–86–0; Groenewald 34–7–107–2; Trego 28.4–5–67–5; Bess 13–0–65–0; Abell 17–3–71–2; Leach 9–0–25–0. *Second innings*—Overton 6–0–29–1; Groenewald 6–0–25–1; Bess 10.4–2–47–2; Trego 0.1–0–1–0; Leach 9.5–0–42–0.

Umpires: I. J. Gould and S. J. O'Shaughnessy.

At Manchester, September 25–28. SURREY lost to LANCASHIRE by seven wickets. *Defeat means Surrey slip behind runners-up Lancashire.*

SUSSEX

Summer of six captains

BRUCE TALBOT

Not for the first time in Sussex's recent history, events off the field created the bigger stir. If it wasn't quite 1996, when the exodus of five capped players led to the overthrow of the committee, two departures left supporters wondering what had gone wrong at Hove, which had been a standard-bearer for the smaller counties. On successive days in October, Chris Nash – involved with Sussex since the age of eight – and head coach Mark Davis both left the club.

Davis had been part of the set-up as player or coach for 17 years and, though his exit was sad, it was no surprise. Once again Sussex had underachieved, even if the margin between a good and a middling season was slim: in each competition, one slip proved costly. In the Championship, an unexpected home defeat by lowly Derbyshire put paid to a promotion challenge that was taking shape after a poor start. Against Middlesex in the T20 Blast, they failed to make five in the final over, and so missed the knockouts on net run-rate. And in the Royal London Cup, they lost to Gloucestershire from a strong position in their first game at Eastbourne for 17 years; victory would have brought progress.

There were injuries too. After five outstanding years, the 37-year-old Steve Magoffin suffered knee and Achilles problems, restricting him to two Championship games. His Sussex record – 334 first-class wickets at under 21 – was magnificent, but at the end of the season he joined Worcestershire. Ben Brown, Luke Wells and Luke Wright were all sidelined as well.

It was difficult for Davis to forge a strong relationship with his captain. Wright stepped down in June because he felt leadership was affecting his batting, and Nash took over (Harry Finch was in charge for the first-class game against South Africa A). But rather than give Nash the reins permanently, Sussex preferred Brown, once he had recovered from a broken finger. Former New Zealand skipper Ross Taylor led the side in the Blast and, when Brown was injured again, Wells became the sixth captain of the summer.

Although Sussex's last trophy came in 2010, a generation of supporters have become accustomed to their being competitive on most fronts. But 2018 is the third successive season in Division Two, and they have qualified for the knockout stages of either limited-overs competition only once in five years. With that in mind, Afghanistan's teenage leg-spinning sensation Rashid Khan joined for the first half of the 2018 T20 Blast. Chief executive Rob Andrew had taken tough decisions during his time with the Rugby Football Union and, after conducting a review of the club's entire operation, he concluded Davis had to go. In November, Sussex announced his replacement would be former Australia Test bowler Jason Gillespie, who signed a three-year deal. In five

Jofra Archer

seasons at Headingley, he had turned Yorkshire into a dominant red-ball force: they were champions in 2014 and 2015, and lost only seven games during his tenure.

In many ways, the departure of Nash was the greater shock. He was a member of the team who won Championships in 2006 and 2007, and helped secure four one-day trophies. It seemed unthinkable he wouldn't finish his career in his native Sussex, and the curt statement announcing his departure mentioned neither his 17,776 runs in all formats, nor his 27 centuries since his debut in 2002. Nash was being lined up for a role in the commercial department when he eventually retired but, miffed at not being made captain, he opted for a three-year deal with Nottinghamshire. Sussex will struggle to replace his tenacity in the first-class game and his belligerence in limited-overs cricket: in the 2017 Blast he scored 520 runs at a strike-rate of 141.

With Nash and Magoffin gone, Gillespie inherited a young squad, if one of considerable promise. Jofra Archer, who turns 23 in April, was the undoubted player of the season, and Sussex were delighted he agreed to commit until the end of 2020. One of just two in the Championship to combine 50 wickets with 500 runs (Kent's Darren Stevens was the other), he can touch 90mph with little apparent effort, and is capable of batting at No. 6 or 7. Mentored by his fellow Barbadian Chris Jordan, he hoped to qualify for England by 2022. After he produced a double-wicket maiden for Hobart Hurricanes in Australia's Big Bash League in December, many were left wishing he could qualify sooner.

Archer and Jordan, who took 36 wickets, were the only Sussex bowlers to manage 25 in the Championship, but it was a flaky top order that ultimately scuppered a promotion push fuelled by a run of five victories and a draw. Several times, lower-order runs bailed them out, especially at Colwyn Bay, where Ollie Robinson guided them to a one-wicket win over Glamorgan. Stiaan van Zyl outperformed his fellow Kolpak David Wiese by passing 1,000 runs, but the pre-eminent batsman was Wells, who hit 1,292 at 64, including a career-best 258 against Durham. He was Division Two's leading scorer, and some wondered whether he might be of use to England.

George Garton played only two Championship games, but is a highly regarded member of a young seam attack with real potential and, with Wells, was part of the Lions' tour of Australia. Gillespie's priority will be to recruit experienced players who can help ensure the emerging talent is not wasted. The signing of Indian Test seamer Ishant Sharma for the first two months of the season was a start.

Championship attendance: 28,888.

SUSSEX RESULTS

All first-class matches – Played 16: Won 8, Lost 5, Drawn 3.
County Championship matches – Played 14: Won 7, Lost 5, Drawn 2.

Specsavers County Championship, 4th in Division 2;
NatWest T20 Blast, 5th in South Group; Royal London One-Day Cup, 5th in South Group.

COUNTY CHAMPIONSHIP AVERAGES, BATTING AND FIELDING

Cap		*Birthplace*	*M*	*I*	*NO*	*R*	*HS*	*100*	*Avge*	*Ct*
2016	†L. W. P. Wells	*Eastbourne‡*	12	22	2	1,292	258	4	64.60	4
	V. D. Philander¶	*Bellville, SA*	5	7	3	211	73*	0	52.75	1
	†S. van Zyl††	*Cape Town, SA*	13	22	1	1,023	166*	2	48.71	6
	M. G. K. Burgess	*Epsom*	6	10	1	434	146	1	48.22	18
2017	J. C. Archer††	*Bridgetown, Barb.*	13	20	6	638	81*	0	45.57	9
2014	B. C. Brown	*Crawley‡*	8	14	1	483	90	0	37.15	23
2007	L. J. Wright	*Grantham*	12	21	1	742	118	1	37.10	6
2014	C. J. Jordan	*Lowlands, Barbados*	11	17	3	438	147	1	31.28	13
2008	C. D. Nash	*Cuckfield‡*	12	21	0	578	118	1	27.52	12
	D. Wiese††	*Roodepoort, SA*	10	15	0	404	66	0	26.93	3
	P. D. Salt	*Bodelwyddan*	2	4	0	100	72	0	25.00	1
	A. J. Robson	*Darlinghurst, Aust.*	4	8	1	169	72	0	24.14	3
	H. Z. Finch	*Hastings‡*	11	20	2	405	82	0	22.50	14
	O. E. Robinson	*Margate*	4	8	1	116	41*	0	16.57	2
	D. R. Briggs	*Newport, IoW*	8	12	5	116	27	0	16.57	5
	†D. M. W. Rawlins	*Bermuda*	4	8	0	121	55	0	15.12	0
	†G. H. S. Garton	*Brighton‡*	2	4	0	43	18	0	10.75	2
	S. G. Whittingham	*Derby*	5	8	2	43	22	0	7.16	1
	L. J. Evans	*Lambeth*	4	8	0	48	19	0	6.00	4

Also batted: A. P. Barton (*Epsom*) (1 match) 13*, 5; W. A. T. Beer (*Crawley‡*) (1 match) 25; †S. J. Magoffin†† (*Corinda, Australia*) (2 matches) 5, 0*; A. Sakande (*Chester*) (3 matches) 7*, 6, 1*; A. Shahzad (*Huddersfield*) (1 match) 1, 5 (1 ct).

‡ *Born in Sussex.* ¶ *Official overseas player.* †† *Other non-England-qualified.*

BOWLING

	Style	*O*	*M*	*R*	*W*	*BB*	*5I*	*Avge*
O. E. Robinson	RM/OB	149.3	30	412	19	5-69	1	21.68
J. C. Archer	RFM	475.1	91	1,543	61	7-67	4	25.29
V. D. Philander	RFM	121.3	29	429	16	4-39	0	26.81
C. J. Jordan	RFM	353.5	57	1,182	36	5-46	1	32.83
S. G. Whittingham	RFM	105.5	12	494	15	5-80	1	32.93
S. van Zyl	RM	116.1	24	368	10	2-25	0	36.80
D. Wiese	RFM	248.3	44	834	22	4-63	0	37.90
D. R. Briggs	SLA	218.1	36	677	14	3-40	0	48.35

Also bowled: A. P. Barton (LFM) 11–0–81–0; W. A. T. Beer (LB) 27.3–1–88–4; H. Z. Finch (RFM) 1–0–2–0; G. H. S. Garton (LFM) 56–0–262–9; S. J. Magoffin (RFM) 27–10–69–5; C. D. Nash (OB) 24–6–66–0; D. M. W. Rawlins (SLA) 39–1–154–1; A. Sakande (RFM) 51.4–8–212–7; A. Shahzad (RFM) 48–6–187–6.

LEADING NATWEST T20 BLAST AVERAGES (100 runs/15 overs)

Batting	*Runs*	*HS*	*Avge*	*SR*	*Ct*
S. van Zyl	170	52	24.28	**161.90**	3
L. J. Wright	235	101	23.50	**153.59**	2
C. D. Nash	520	73*	47.27	**141.68**	5
L. J. Evans	214	47*	26.75	**121.59**	5
B. C. Brown	185	49	20.55	**119.35**	13
L. R. P. L. Taylor	177	47*	19.66	**112.73**	1

Bowling	*W*	*BB*	*Avge*	*ER*
T. S. Mills	5	3-20	19.20	**6.40**
D. R. Briggs	13	2-12	23.69	**7.00**
C. J. Jordan	16	3-17	20.43	**7.81**
J. C. Archer	14	4-18	26.14	**8.34**
D. Wiese	9	2-16	29.66	**9.00**
W. A. T. Beer	7	3-36	25.85	**9.05**
G. H. S. Garton	7	3-35	32.42	**9.08**

LEADING ROYAL LONDON CUP AVERAGES (100 runs/4 wickets)

Batting	*Runs*	*HS*	*Avge*	*SR*	*Ct*
L. J. Evans	289	134*	57.80	120.41	2
C. D. Nash	278	82	46.33	91.44	0
H. Z. Finch	217	80	36.16	77.50	0
L. J. Wright	245	84	35.00	81.12	3
S. van Zyl	203	96	33.83	90.22	1

Bowling	*W*	*BB*	*Avge*	*ER*
D. Wiese	11	4-29	30.54	5.49
D. R. Briggs	9	3-53	35.88	5.38
J. C. Archer	9	3-54	37.88	5.35
J. E. Taylor	6	3-65	46.33	6.46
G. H. S. Garton	4	2-34	50.25	6.28

FIRST-CLASS COUNTY RECORDS

Highest score for	344*	M. W. Goodwin v Somerset at Taunton	2009
Highest score against	322	E. Paynter (Lancashire) at Hove	1937
Leading run-scorer	34,150	J. G. Langridge (avge 37.69)	1928–55
Best bowling for	10-48	C. H. G. Bland v Kent at Tonbridge	1899
Best bowling against	9-11	A. P. Freeman (Kent) at Hove	1922
Leading wicket-taker	2,211	M. W. Tate (avge 17.41)	1912–37
Highest total for	742-5 dec	v Somerset at Taunton	2009
Highest total against	726	by Nottinghamshire at Nottingham	1895
Lowest total for	19	v Surrey at Godalming	1830
	19	v Nottinghamshire at Hove	1873
Lowest total against	18	by Kent at Gravesend	1867

LIST A COUNTY RECORDS

Highest score for	163	C. J. Adams v Middlesex at Arundel	1999
Highest score against	198*	G. A. Gooch (Essex) at Hove	1982
Leading run-scorer	7,969	A. P. Wells (avge 31.62)	1981–96
Best bowling for	7-41	A. N. Jones v Nottinghamshire at Nottingham	1986
Best bowling against	8-21	M. A. Holding (Derbyshire) at Hove	1988
Leading wicket-taker	370	R. J. Kirtley (avge 22.35)	1995–2010
Highest total for	399-4	v Worcestershire at Horsham	2011
Highest total against	377-9	by Somerset at Hove	2003
Lowest total for	49	v Derbyshire at Chesterfield	1969
Lowest total against	36	by Leicestershire at Leicester	1973

TWENTY20 COUNTY RECORDS

Highest score for	153*	L. J. Wright v Essex at Chelmsford	2014
Highest score against	152*	G. R. Napier (Essex) at Chelmsford	2008
Leading run-scorer	**3,277**	**C. D. Nash (avge 28.25)**	**2006–17**
Best bowling for	5-11	Mushtaq Ahmed v Essex at Hove	2005
Best bowling against	5-14	A. D. Mascarenhas (Hampshire) at Hove	2004
	5-14	K. J. Abbott (Middlesex) at Hove	2015
Leading wicket-taker	77	C. J. Liddle (avge 22.68)	2008–15
	77	M. H. Yardy (avge 28.02)	2004–15
	77	**W. A. T. Beer (avge 28.07)**	**2008–17**
Highest total for	242-5	v Gloucestershire at Bristol	2016
Highest total against	242-3	by Essex at Chelmsford	2008
Lowest total for	67	v Hampshire at Hove	2004
Lowest total against	85	by Hampshire at Southampton	2008

ADDRESS

The 1st Central County Ground, Eaton Road, Hove BN3 3AN; 0844 264 0202; info@sussexcricket.co.uk; www.sussexcricket.co.uk.

OFFICIALS

Captain 2017 L. J. Wright
Director of cricket K. Greenfield
Head coach 2017 M. J. G. Davis
2018 J. N. Gillespie
Academy director C. D. Hopkinson
President J. M. Abbott

Chairman R. Warren
Chief executive C. R. Andrew
Chairman, cricket committee J. R. T. Barclay
Head groundsman A. Mackay
Scorer M. J. Charman

At Hove, April 7–9 (not first-class). **Drawn.** ‡**Sussex 317-8 dec** (86 overs) (L. J. Evans 84; K. S. Leverock 3-57) **and 414** (95.1 overs) (C. D. Nash 103*, M. G. K. Burgess 61, D. R. Briggs 103; A. S. S. Nijjar 3-113); **Cardiff MCCU 141** (50.4 overs) (J. C. Archer 5-35, A. Shahzad 3-18) **and 86-3** (30 overs). *County debuts:* M. G. K. Burgess, L. J. Evans, D. M. W. Rawlins, S. van Zyl. *Sussex gave debuts to four players, including Michael Burgess, deputising for Ben Brown, who had been hit on the head in a pre-season friendly against Surrey. Burgess batted well and kept neatly. For the students, Kamau Leverock, nephew of Bermuda's 2007 World Cup cult hero Dwayne, bowled at good pace and broke through three times. Sussex declared on 317-8 and, thanks to Archer and Shahzad, soon led by 176. But they opted for batting practice rather than push for victory. Both Nash and Briggs, who scored his maiden hundred in senior cricket, retired on 103 – though Nash did so after injury. Slow left-armer Aron Nijjar also took three wickets.*

SUSSEX v KENT

At Hove, April 14–17. Kent won by 226 runs. Kent 22pts, Sussex 5pts. Toss: Kent. First-class debut: D. M. W. Rawlins. County debut: V. D. Philander. Championship debut: S. van Zyl.

Sussex's offer of free last-day admission to supporters of Brighton & Hove Albion heading to the Falmer Stadium was widely taken up. And with their side clinching a place in football's Premier League, they – at least – had something to celebrate. Not that Sussex began badly: in only his seventh Championship match, Archer took seven wickets, including four clean bowled. Footage of the outrageous delivery that sent Bell-Drummond's middle stump for a walk went viral. Kent's 304 did not seem daunting, until Sussex slipped to 58 for five. They were rescued by the punchy Brown and the combative Archer, who added 99 for the last wicket, and kept the deficit to 13. But with Philander nursing a groin injury, Sussex could not prevent Northeast from leading Kent into an impregnable position. His 17th first-class hundred – and sixth over 150 within a year – allowed him to declare, 426 ahead, before the last day started. Stevens, who had already contributed two perky fifties, exploited ideal conditions for swing to dismiss the top five, and Sussex capitulated well before Brighton had sealed promotion. The Bermuda-born Delray Rawlins, who had starred on England Under-19's tour of India earlier in the year, had a quiet debut.

Close of play: first day, Sussex 11-1 (Finch 2, Shahzad 0); second day, Kent 82-2 (Dickson 34, Tredwell 1); third day, Kent 413-5 (Northeast 173, Stevens 71).

Kent

First innings		Second innings	
D. J. Bell-Drummond b Archer	13	– lbw b Shahzad	35
S. R. Dickson c Brown b Archer	68	– lbw b Shahzad	89
J. L. Denly b Shahzad	24	– b Shahzad	3
*S. A. Northeast c Wiese b Shahzad	23	– (5) not out	173
W. R. S. Gidman c Wright b Archer	11	– (6) c Archer b Rawlins	6
D. I. Stevens c Brown b Shahzad	68	– (7) not out	71
†A. P. Rouse b Archer	0		
W. D. Parnell not out	51		
J. C. Tredwell c Nash b Archer	1	– (4) b Wiese	15
M. T. Coles b Archer	7		
M. E. Claydon b Archer	0		
B 8, lb 3, w 15, nb 12	38	B 4, lb 4, w 1, nb 12	21
1/27 (1) 2/62 (3) 3/116 (4) 4/141 (5) 5/152 (2) 6/152 (7) 7/275 (6) 8/276 (9) 9/304 (10) 10/304 (11) (87.3 overs)	304	1/60 (1) 2/78 (3) 3/112 (4) 4/235 (2) 5/252 (6) (5 wkts dec, 97 overs)	413

Philander 17–6–57–0; Archer 23.3–8–67–7; Wiese 16–4–48–0; Shahzad 21–3–91–3; van Zyl 8–0–25–0; Nash 2–0–5–0. *Second innings*—Archer 23–5–95–0; Wiese 19–2–108–1; Shahzad 27–3–96–3; van Zyl 13–2–37–0; Nash 6–1–23–0; Rawlins 9–0–46–1.

Sussex

C. D. Nash lbw b Coles	5	– (2) c Rouse b Stevens	31
H. Z. Finch b Parnell	15	– (1) c Tredwell b Stevens	24
A. Shahzad c Gidman b Parnell	1	– (11) c Denly b Parnell	5
D. M. W. Rawlins c Gidman b Parnell	22	– (3) c Rouse b Stevens	9
S. van Zyl c Gidman b Claydon	13	– (4) c sub (A. J. Ball) b Stevens	0
L. J. Evans c Rouse b Claydon	0	– (5) lbw b Stevens	2
*L. J. Wright c Rouse b Coles	29	– (6) lbw b Claydon	7
†B. C. Brown lbw b Coles	90	– (7) not out	69
D. Wiese c sub (C. F. Hartley) b Claydon	22	– (8) c Bell-Drummond b Coles	25
V. D. Philander c Northeast b Claydon	13	– (9) c Denly b Coles	8
J. C. Archer not out	60	– (10) c sub (A. J. Ball) b Coles	6
B 4, lb 10, w 1, nb 6	21	Lb 5, w 1, nb 8	14
1/10 (1) 2/24 (2) 3/25 (3) 4/58 (5) 5/58 (6) 6/97 (7) 7/121 (4) 8/174 (9) 9/192 (10) 10/291 (8) (76.5 overs)	291	1/59 (1) 2/66 (2) 3/68 (4) 4/74 (5) 5/83 (6) 6/83 (3) 7/137 (8) 8/174 (9) 9/188 (10) 10/200 (11) (50.1 overs)	200

Coles 21.5–5–81–3; Parnell 21–7–48–3; Claydon 16–2–87–4; Stevens 10–4–28–0; Gidman 3–0–9–0; Tredwell 5–0–24–0. *Second innings*—Parnell 12.1–1–42–1; Coles 10–0–44–3; Stevens 15–4–51–5; Claydon 13–2–58–1.

Umpires: M. Burns and R. J. Evans.

At Nottingham, April 21–22. SUSSEX lost to NOTTINGHAMSHIRE by an innings and 88 runs.

At Hove, May 19. SUSSEX lost to SOUTH AFRICANS by 66 runs (see South African tour section).

SUSSEX v DURHAM

At Hove, May 21–24. Sussex won by an innings and 177 runs. Sussex 24pts, Durham 3pts. Toss: Sussex. Championship debut: M. G. K. Burgess.

In his first Championship appearance after knee surgery in the winter, Wells hit a career-best 258 to set up an emphatic win over a depleted Durham. The highlight of his second double-hundred was an assault on Pringle: Wells walloped four sixes and two fours in an over which, with a no-ball, cost 34, as he roared to 250. Not noted for big hitting, he cleared the ropes seven times, attributing it to work with batting coach Mike Yardy. Wells and van Zyl, who made his first hundred for Sussex, added 376, the highest by any county for any wicket against Durham. The Sussex quicks did their bit, too. On the first day, Archer bolstered his burgeoning reputation with another five-wicket haul, again losing little in comparison with Philander. Throughout the game they moved the ball both ways off the seam, and shared seven in both innings. Pringle had earlier made himself unpopular with the crowd after standing his ground when Wiese claimed a catch at fine leg. The umpires gave Pringle the benefit of the doubt, but Sussex supporters booed as he walked off shortly afterwards – and cheered when Wells despatched his off-spin to all parts.

HIGHEST FIRST-CLASS TOTALS BY SUSSEX

742-5 dec	v Somerset at Taunton	2009
705-8 dec	v Surrey at Hastings	1902
686-8	v Leicestershire at Leicester	1900
670-9 dec	v Northamptonshire at Hove	1921
668	**v Durham at Hove**	**2017**
644	v Somerset at Taunton	2002
631-4 dec	v Northamptonshire at Northampton	1938
631-6 dec	v Hampshire at Hove	2002
620-9 dec	v Worcestershire at Worcester	2009
619-7 dec	v Nottinghamshire at Horsham	2003

Close of play: first day, Sussex 43-1 (Nash 22, Wells 16); second day, Sussex 452-4 (van Zyl 141, Burgess 15); third day, Durham 97-4 (Collingwood 31, Pringle 18).

Durham

	First innings		Second innings	
S. C. Cook lbw b Philander	45	–	c Jordan b Philander	0
K. K. Jennings b Archer	12	–	b Philander	5
C. T. Steel c Wells b Philander	10	–	c Nash b Jordan	14
G. Clark lbw b Briggs	23	–	lbw b Jordan	16
*P. D. Collingwood lbw b Archer	9	–	lbw b Wiese	31
R. D. Pringle c Burgess b Jordan	60	–	not out	38
P. Coughlin c Briggs b Archer	73	–	b Archer	15
†S. W. Poynter lbw b van Zyl	15	–	c Burgess b Archer	0
W. J. Weighell not out	5	–	b Archer	58
G. Onions c Burgess b Archer	0	–	(11) b Philander	0
C. Rushworth c Jordan b Archer	2	–	(10) c Finch b Philander	1
Lb 8, nb 25	33		B 2, lb 14, nb 10	26
1/32 (2) 2/72 (3) 3/79 (1) 4/90 (5) 5/129 (4) 6/239 (6) 7/269 (8) 8/279 (7) 9/279 (10) 10/287 (11) (82.4 overs)	287		1/0 (1) 2/11 (2) 3/32 (3) 4/41 (4) 5/97 (5) 6/118 (7) 7/126 (8) 8/195 (9) 9/204 (10) 10/204 (11) (86.2 overs)	204

Philander 13–1–60–2; Archer 19.4–3–76–5; Wiese 18–5–45–0; Jordan 16–3–38–1; Briggs 13–1–56–1; van Zyl 3–0–4–1. *Second innings*—Philander 15.2–5–39–4; Archer 24–8–49–3; Jordan 10–3–41–2; Briggs 18–8–29–0; Wiese 10–4–15–1; Nash 9–3–15–0.

Sussex

C. D. Nash c Poynter b Onions	22
H. Z. Finch c Pringle b Onions	0
L. W. P. Wells c Jennings b Coughlin	258
S. van Zyl b Rushworth	149
*L. J. Wright c Poynter b Coughlin	2
†M. G. K. Burgess b Pringle	76
C. J. Jordan c and b Coughlin	1
D. Wiese c Pringle b Steel	30
V. D. Philander c Cook b Steel	17
J. C. Archer c Rushworth b Pringle	70
D. R. Briggs not out	18
B 8, lb 9, nb 8	25
1/0 (2) 2/43 (1) 3/419 (3) 4/422 (5) 5/469 (4) 6/492 (7) 7/550 (8) 8/566 (6) 9/588 (9) 10/668 (10) (150.3 overs)	668
110 overs: 469-4	

Rushworth 28–3–106–1; Onions 10–1–38–2; Coughlin 28–2–127–3; Pringle 36.3–2–148–2; Weighell 24–2–110–0; Steel 18–0–88–2; Collingwood 5–1–18–0; Cook 1–0–16–0.

Umpires: B. J. Debenham and G. D. Lloyd.

At Tunbridge Wells, May 26–29. SUSSEX lost to KENT by 147 runs.

SUSSEX v WORCESTERSHIRE

At Hove, June 2–5. Sussex won by an innings and seven runs. Sussex 23pts, Worcestershire 4pts. Toss: uncontested.

Such an emphatic Sussex win looked unlikely on the third morning. They had made a healthy 579 for eight, though Worcestershire, having won all four Championship matches so far, were 215 for none – a first-wicket record in this fixture – with Mitchell making his third century in three games. But the pitch became unreliable, ten wickets fell in 30 overs (including Philander's 500th in first-class cricket when he dismissed Tongue) and Worcestershire followed on. Only Mitchell and Whiteley offered much resistance second time round as the Sussex seamers, enjoying sharp bounce, wrapped up victory not long before rain arrived. Worcestershire's blunder had been choosing to bowl. Sussex saw off the new ball, and flourished. Wells followed his career-best 258 in the previous home game with a well-crafted 155, Finch compiled a Championship-best, and Wright, after passing the captaincy to Nash, attacked with the freedom of old. There was a moment of controversy when

D'Oliveira was reprieved: Steve Garratt gave him out lbw on 70 but, after consulting Neil Mallender, the umpires agreed he had hit the ball first.

Close of play: first day, Sussex 339-3 (Wells 139, Wright 27); second day, Worcestershire 139-0 (Mitchell 85, D'Oliveira 43); third day, Worcestershire 124-4 (Cox 3, Tongue 7).

Sussex

*C. D. Nash c Lyon b Leach	22
H. Z. Finch c Mitchell b Tongue	82
L. W. P. Wells b Lyon	155
S. van Zyl b Barnard	54
L. J. Wright c D'Oliveira b Barnard	87
†M. G. K. Burgess b Barnard	46
C. J. Jordan c Clarke b Leach	37
D. Wiese c Whiteley b Leach	66
V. D. Philander not out	7
B 2, lb 10, w 1, nb 10	23
1/40 (1) (8 wkts dec, 145.1 overs)	579

2/165 (2) 3/302 (4)
4/376 (3) 5/462 (5) 6/466 (6)
7/557 (7) 8/579 (8) 110 overs: 379-4

J. C. Archer and S. J. Magoffin did not bat.

Leach 27.1–2–101–3; Barnard 21–1–120–3; Shantry 23–5–53–0; Tongue 22–2–97–1; Lyon 40–6–123–1; Whiteley 2–0–20–0; D'Oliveira 9–0–51–0; Mitchell 1–0–2–0.

Worcestershire

First innings		Second innings	
D. K. H. Mitchell c van Zyl b Wiese	121	lbw b van Zyl	54
B. L. D'Oliveira c van Zyl b Wiese	80	c Jordan b Wiese	12
T. C. Fell c Jordan b van Zyl	6	c Archer b Jordan	22
J. M. Clarke c van Zyl b Archer	22	b Jordan	10
†O. B. Cox c Jordan b Philander	12	c Nash b Philander	3
R. A. Whiteley b Archer	3	(7) c Burgess b Wiese	53
E. G. Barnard lbw b Philander	22	(8) c Burgess b van Zyl	21
*J. Leach lbw b Archer	6	(9) c Wells b Philander	23
J. C. Tongue c sub (W. A. T. Beer) b Philander	0	(6) b Archer	11
J. D. Shantry c Burgess b Archer	16	c Finch b Philander	5
N. M. Lyon not out	0	not out	5
B 6, lb 11, w 1, nb 6	24	B 10, lb 10, w 5, nb 16	41
1/215 (1) 2/220 (2) 3/224 (3) (96.2 overs)	312	1/26 (2) 2/90 (3) (86.1 overs)	260
4/260 (4) 5/260 (5) 6/276 (6)		3/109 (4) 4/115 (1)	
7/294 (7) 8/296 (8) 9/308 (9) 10/312 (10)		5/126 (5) 6/128 (6) 7/207 (8)	
		8/237 (7) 9/253 (9) 10/260 (10)	

Magoffin 9–3–18–0; Philander 19–4–72–3; Archer 24.2–5–91–4; Jordan 15–4–37–0; Wiese 18–1–62–2; Nash 1–1–0–0; van Zyl 10–6–15–1. *Second innings*—Jordan 21–2–70–2; Archer 16–2–45–1; van Zyl 18–9–44–2; Wiese 19–2–51–2; Philander 12.1–2–30–3.

Umpires: S. A. Garratt and N. A. Mallender.

At Leicester, June 9–12. SUSSEX beat LEICESTERSHIRE by five wickets.

At Arundel, June 14–16. SUSSEX beat SOUTH AFRICA A by an innings and 50 runs (see South Africa A tour section).

SUSSEX v GLOUCESTERSHIRE

At Hove, June 26–29 (day/night). Drawn. Sussex 9pts, Gloucestershire 8pts. Toss: Sussex. Championship debut: A. Sakande.

Hove's first taste of pink-ball, floodlit Championship cricket was a modest success. Warm sunshine – and around 600 schoolchildren – ensured a crowd more typical of a Sunday than a two o'clock start on a Monday. But numbers thinned slightly after five, with some of Sussex's elderly members reluctant to take public transport in the evening. On a sluggish pitch, the ball became soft after about 40 overs, making life exasperating for bowlers – even spinners – despite a dry surface. At least the children saw a sparkling opening-day run-a-ball hundred by Wright; he hit his first delivery, from Taylor, for six, and reached his first century since 2015 from his 100th. With all the second day and half the third lost to rain, the captains conjured a potentially exciting finish over a late-night pint in the Sussex Cricketer pub. Two declarations and some joke bowling set Gloucestershire 351 in 75 overs, but they were six down with a session to go, Archer picking up two stunning boundary catches. With the ball, though, he and his team-mates could make no more inroads, and Taylor and Noema-Barnett had little trouble picking their way to safety.

Close of play: first day, Gloucestershire 31-0 (Bancroft 18, Dent 7); second day, no play; third day, Gloucestershire 150-1 (Bancroft 69, Tavaré 43).

Sussex

D. M. W. Rawlins c Roderick b Norwell	7	– c Roderick b Bancroft	24
H. Z. Finch c Dent b Payne	11	– not out	74
L. W. P. Wells c Hankins b Taylor	35	– not out	44
S. van Zyl c Bancroft b Taylor	35		
L. J. Wright c Mustard b Taylor	118		
*†B. C. Brown c Hankins b Noema-Barnett	52		
C. J. Jordan lbw b Payne	50		
D. Wiese lbw b Miles	25		
J. C. Archer c Mustard b Miles	0		
D. R. Briggs not out	5		
A. Sakande not out	7		
B 1, lb 2, nb 10	13		
1/19 (1) 2/23 (2) 3/66 (3) 4/165 (4) 5/257 (6) 6/283 (5) 7/340 (8) 8/340 (9) 9/350 (7) (9 wkts dec, 87 overs)	358	1/36 (1) (1 wkt dec, 18.1 overs)	142

Payne 17–6–35–2; Norwell 19–3–84–1; Noema-Barnett 14–2–51–1; Miles 16–2–92–2; Taylor 21–2–93–3. *Second innings*—Bancroft 7–0–67–1; Tavaré 5–0–34–0; Mustard 4–1–28–0; Hankins 2.1–0–13–0.

Gloucestershire

C. T. Bancroft not out	69	– b Sakande	13
C. D. J. Dent c van Zyl b Sakande	21	– c Brown b Archer	10
W. A. Tavaré not out	43	– lbw b Sakande	10
†G. H. Roderick (did not bat)		– b Archer	0
G. T. Hankins (did not bat)		– c Archer b Jordan	51
*P. Mustard (did not bat)		– c Archer b Jordan	10
J. M. R. Taylor (did not bat)		– not out	69
K. Noema-Barnett (did not bat)		– not out	37
Lb 1, nb 16	17	B 6, lb 2, nb 4	12
1/68 (2) (1 wkt dec, 51 overs)	150	1/26 (1) 2/30 (2) 3/30 (4) 4/46 (3) 5/84 (6) 6/117 (5) (6 wkts, 72.1 overs)	212

C. N. Miles, D. A. Payne and L. C. Norwell did not bat.

Jordan 9–2–33–0; Archer 12–2–29–0; Sakande 12–2–38–1; Wiese 8–0–21–0; Briggs 9–1–26–0; Rawlins 1–0–2–0. *Second innings*—Jordan 16–1–47–2; Archer 18–6–31–2; Sakande 16–5–53–2; Wiese 4–1–6–0; Briggs 13.1–1–40–0; Rawlins 5–0–27–0.

Umpires: P. K. Baldwin and S. J. O'Shaughnessy.

SUSSEX v LEICESTERSHIRE

At Arundel, July 5–8. Sussex won by 231 runs. Sussex 21pts, Leicestershire 5pts. Toss: Sussex. First-class debut: W. N. Fazakerley.

The game was evenly balanced until the third day, when van Zyl's big century swung the match Sussex's way. McKay apart, Leicestershire's attack had little bite, and their spin resources were especially threadbare. Although the pitch did not deteriorate markedly on the last day, Sussex's bowlers sped them to victory with a session to spare. Neither team made the most of their first innings: all told, 13 batsmen reached 20, but none went on to a half-century. Leicestershire led by 19. Under a baking sun, the pitch eased, and van Zyl, strong on the cut and pull, cashed in. Wright and Brown provided good support, before Archer thrashed 42 off 14 balls. He then claimed four wickets, taking his total in Sussex's three successive victories against Leicestershire (starting the previous September) to 25 at an average of 11. However, it was Jordan's hostile spell after lunch that broke their resistance. Will Fazakerley, born in Guernsey, educated at nearby Lancing College and once on Sussex's books, endured a pair on debut, though he did take a wicket. There was embarrassment for Martin Saggers, who failed to turn up on the opening morning after muddling the start date; Martin Bodenham came out of retirement to stand at square leg for the first session.

Close of play: first day, Leicestershire 77-2 (Ackermann 21, Cosgrove 21); second day, Sussex 74-1 (Wells 39, Finch 13); third day, Leicestershire 36-0 (Horton 15, Harinath 17).

Sussex

First innings		Second innings	
C. D. Nash b McKay	15	– (2) lbw b McKay	21
L. W. P. Wells c Hill b Pillans	42	– (1) lbw b Pillans	43
H. Z. Finch lbw b Jones	0	– lbw b McKay	18
S. van Zyl lbw b McKay	49	– not out	166
L. J. Wright b Jones	29	– c Sayer b Pillans	60
*†B. C. Brown c Sayer b McKay	18	– lbw b Jones	67
C. J. Jordan lbw b Fazakerley	34	– b Sayer	9
W. A. T. Beer c Ackermann b Pillans	25		
J. C. Archer c Jones b McKay	20	– (8) not out	42
D. R. Briggs not out	6		
A. Sakande c Hill b Pillans	6		
B 4, lb 4, nb 10	18	B 4, lb 2, nb 6, p 5	17
1/32 (1) 2/33 (3) 3/74 (2) 4/138 (5) 5/160 (4) 6/165 (6) 7/219 (7) 8/248 (9) 9/256 (8) 10/262 (11) (69.1 overs)	262	1/35 (2) 2/83 (1) 3/87 (3) 4/222 (5) 5/368 (6) 6/386 (7) (6 wkts dec, 104 overs)	443

McKay 20–4–59–4; Jones 14–0–50–2; Pillans 16.1–2–63–3; Fazakerley 6–1–32–1; Sayer 12–1–43–0; Ackermann 1–0–7–0. *Second innings*—McKay 23–7–62–2; Jones 17–0–92–1; Pillans 23–2–77–2; Sayer 28–2–119–1; Fazackerley 6–1–51–0; Ackermann 6–0–26–0; Harinath 1–0–5–0.

Leicestershire

First innings		Second innings	
P. J. Horton lbw b Jordan	9	– lbw b Archer	35
A. Harinath c Finch b Archer	20	– c Finch b Briggs	17
C. N. Ackermann c Brown b Archer	40	– c Brown b Archer	43
*M. J. Cosgrove c Jordan b Briggs	41	– c Brown b Jordan	20
E. J. H. Eckersley b Archer	35	– b Jordan	12
†L. J. Hill c Wright b Jordan	49	– lbw b Sakande	35
W. N. Fazakerley lbw b Beer	0	– c Nash b Beer	0
R. J. Sayer b Sakande	31	– lbw b Archer	8
M. W. Pillans c Finch b Jordan	0	– c Brown b Archer	0
C. J. McKay not out	32	– c Briggs b Beer	1
R. A. Jones b Beer	6	– not out	16
Lb 8, nb 10	18	Nb 6	6
1/28 (1) 2/34 (2) 3/104 (3) 4/138 (4) 5/188 (5) 6/189 (7) 7/226 (6) 8/226 (9) 9/262 (8) 10/281 (11) (97.3 overs)	281	1/41 (2) 2/93 (1) 3/106 (3) 4/123 (4) 5/136 (5) 6/149 (7) 7/164 (8) 8/166 (9) 9/167 (10) 10/193 (6) (69.1 overs)	193

Jordan 24–5–66–3; Archer 24–7–51–3; Sakande 10–0–54–1; Briggs 24–7–49–1; Beer 15.3–0–53–2. *Second innings*—Jordan 16–3–56–2; Archer 19–8–30–4; Briggs 21–3–65–1; Beer 12–1–35–2; Sakande 1.1–0–7–1.

Umpires: M. J. Saggers and B. V. Taylor. M. J. D. Bodenham deputised for Saggers on the first day.

At Worcester, August 6–8. SUSSEX beat WORCESTERSHIRE by nine wickets.

At Colwyn Bay, August 28–30. SUSSEX beat GLAMORGAN by one wicket. *Sussex's last pair add 32 to secure victory.*

At Northampton, September 5–8. SUSSEX lost to NORTHAMPTONSHIRE by six wickets.

SUSSEX v DERBYSHIRE

At Hove, September 12–15. Derbyshire won by 45 runs. Derbyshire 22pts, Sussex 5pts. Toss: Sussex.

Superb fast bowling by Hardus Viljoen wrecked Sussex's hopes of promotion. His match figures of 15 for 170 were the best for Derbyshire since 1952. On a flat pitch, Sussex were well placed at 267 for three in pursuit of 390 with 30 overs left, but Viljoen had van Zyl caught at third man, and seven wickets tumbled for 77; until Podmore claimed the ninth, it looked as if Viljoen might manage all ten. Derbyshire's runs had been spread around, with seven men hitting between 45 and 66, Slater doing so twice. Viljoen's hostility – he bowled four in the first innings and would add another two in the second – ensured a lead of 67. Godleman was unable to bat after Whittingham broke his hand with a beamer, but his declaration gave Derbyshire a day to dismiss Sussex. (Derby-born Whittingham had been wicketless on the first day, but claimed a maiden five-for on the third.) Wright and Wells fought hard in both innings, and van Zyl in the second, but otherwise Sussex were poor.

BEST MATCH FIGURES AT HOVE

17-67	A. P. Freeman	Kent v Sussex	1922
16-100	J. E. B. B. P. Q. C. Dwyer	Sussex v Middlesex	1906
15-77	A. E. Relf	Sussex v Leicestershire	1912
15-87	A. W. Mold	Lancashire v Sussex	1894
15-98	G. A. Lohmann	Surrey v Sussex	1889
15-100	J. E. Walsh	Leicestershire v Sussex	1948
15-119	R. G. Marlar	Sussex v Lancashire	1955
15-142	H. Baldwin	Hampshire v Sussex	1898
15-170	**G. C. Viljoen**	**Derbyshire v Sussex**	**2017**

Close of play: first day, Derbyshire 338-9 (Hosein 38, Qadri 9); second day, Derbyshire 31-1 (Slater 13, Madsen 10); third day, Derbyshire 322-8 (Podmore 66, Qadri 0).

Derbyshire

First innings		Second innings	
B. T. Slater c Archer b Garton	48	– b Whittingham	45
L. M. Reece lbw b Garton	51	– c Nash b Archer	8
*B. A. Godleman c Brown b Garton	51		
W. L. Madsen lbw b Wiese	25	– (3) lbw b Robinson	31
A. L. Hughes c Wells b van Zyl	46	– (4) lbw b Garton	14
M. J. J. Critchley c and b Wiese	11	– (5) c Garton b Whittingham	51
†H. R. Hosein not out	38	– (6) c Wright b Whittingham	52
H. W. Podmore c Brown b Wiese	1	– (7) not out	66
G. C. Viljoen lbw b van Zyl	7	– (8) b Whittingham	1
W. S. Davis c and b Wiese	18	– (9) c Robinson b Whittingham	25
H. Qadri b Archer	9	– (10) not out	0
B 5, lb 12, nb 16	33	B 12, lb 11, nb 6	29
1/101 (2) 2/106 (1) 3/145 (4) (96.1 overs)	338	1/9 (2) (8 wkts dec, 101 overs)	322
4/232 (3) 5/249 (6) 6/263 (5)		2/85 (3) 3/95 (1)	
7/264 (8) 8/287 (9) 9/317 (10) 10/338 (11)		4/127 (4) 5/187 (5)	
		6/252 (6) 7/262 (8) 8/314 (9)	

Archer 17.1–0–69–1; Robinson 23–8–47–0; Wiese 21–6–63–4; Garton 14–0–79–3; Whittingham 12–3–38–0; van Zyl 9–0–25–2. *Second innings*—Archer 17–3–46–1; Robinson 26–6–57–1; Wiese 9–0–33–0; Whittingham 24–2–80–5; Garton 19–0–74–1; van Zyl 6–2–9–0.

Sussex

A. J. Robson c Hughes b Podmore	1	– (2) c Critchley b Viljoen	8
L. W. P. Wells b Viljoen	46	– (1) lbw b Viljoen	77
S. van Zyl b Viljoen	17	– c Critchley b Viljoen	85
C. D. Nash b Viljoen	20	– c Hughes b Viljoen	9
L. J. Wright not out	70	– b Viljoen	80
*†B. C. Brown c Hughes b Viljoen	23	– c Hughes b Viljoen	0
O. E. Robinson lbw b Davis	0	– b Viljoen	15
J. C. Archer c Podmore b Viljoen	10	– c Madsen b Viljoen	25
D. Wiese c Hosein b Qadri	47	– c Slater b Podmore	8
G. H. S. Garton c Hosein b Viljoen	18	– c Qadri b Podmore	12
S. G. Whittingham b Viljoen	0	– not out	4
B 1, lb 9, w 1, nb 8	19	B 5, lb 8, w 4, nb 4	21
1/3 (1) 2/62 (3) 3/90 (4) 4/95 (2) 5/125 (6) 6/126 (7) 7/149 (8) 8/229 (9) 9/271 (10) 10/271 (11) (63.5 overs)	271	1/9 (2) 2/137 (1) 3/147 (4) 4/267 (3) 5/271 (6) 6/272 (5) 7/303 (7) 8/318 (8) 9/332 (10) 10/344 (9) (80.1 overs)	344

Viljoen 17.5–2–80–7; Podmore 12–0–41–1; Davis 16–0–82–1; Qadri 9–1–31–1; Reece 9–1–27–0. *Second innings*—Viljoen 25–3–90–8; Podmore 16.1–1–74–2; Davis 13–0–58–0; Reece 10–1–35–0; Qadri 11–0–48–0; Critchley 3–0–21–0; Madsen 2–0–5–0.

Umpires: I. D. Blackwell and J. W. Lloyds.

At Chester-le-Street, September 19–22. SUSSEX beat DURHAM by 132 runs.

SUSSEX v NOTTINGHAMSHIRE

At Hove, September 25–28. Drawn. Sussex 13pts, Nottinghamshire 12pts. Toss: uncontested.

Nottinghamshire captain Chris Read ended his 20-season career a fulfilled man. His county had wrapped up a white-ball double, and 12 points here would confirm an immediate return to the top flight – even if it was not as winners, which for most of the summer had seemed a certainty. Without him, promotion might have evaporated. After a delayed start, Nottinghamshire soon had Sussex 107 for five. But while the new ball made batting tricky, life was easier when it grew soft and the attack tired. Burgess and Jordan made career-best 140s and added 189 for the seventh wicket, before Archer contributed a swift 72. Sussex had 565 and, for the only time all season, Nottinghamshire just two bowling points. Their reply followed a familiar course. Whittingham and Archer reduced them to 65 for five, but again the older ball offered little. Now Root and Read performed the rescue act, putting on 242; Read went to his 26th hundred with a top-edged six. The tail then banked full batting points, ensuring Northamptonshire's late challenge would come to naught if Nottinghamshire avoided defeat. And with nearly a day's play lost, a positive result was not on the cards. Sussex chose to bat on into the last evening, allowing Wells to become the second division's leading scorer. Read left the field through a guard of honour from both teams, having declined the offer of trying to take a maiden first-class wicket, instead making his 1,104th dismissal: "I've been a keeper for 20 years, so I wanted to walk off with my pads and gloves on."

Close of play: first day, Sussex 230-5 (Rawlins 55, Burgess 67); second day, Nottinghamshire 108-5 (Root 31, Read 13); third day, Nottinghamshire 477.

Sussex

Batsman	1st inns		2nd inns	
*L. W. P. Wells lbw b Mullaney	46	–	b Patel	103
H. Z. Finch c Read b Wood	10	–	c sub (T. J. Moores) b Patel	43
P. D. Salt c Pujara b Hutton	16	–	b Carter	1
L. J. Evans lbw b Mullaney	1	–	b Carter	13
C. D. Nash c Hutton b Mullaney	19	–	c Libby b Carter	1
D. M. W. Rawlins c Read b Gurney	55	–	c Mullaney b Carter	0
†M. G. K. Burgess b Gurney	146	–	c Read b Patel	19
C. J. Jordan c Wessels b Root	147	–	not out	19
J. C. Archer c Carter b Root	72	–	not out	29
S. G. Whittingham b Root	22			
A. Sakande not out	1			
B 7, lb 18, w 1, nb 4	30		Lb 1	1

1/20 (2) 2/51 (3) 3/52 (4) 4/100 (5) 5/107 (1) 6/232 (6) 7/421 (7) 8/517 (8) 9/551 (9) 10/565 (10) (133.2 overs) 565

110 overs: 457-7

1/123 (2) 2/126 (3) 3/156 (1) 4/157 (5) 5/161 (6) 6/180 (4) 7/180 (7) (7 wkts dec, 50 overs) 229

Hutton 30–10–111–1; Wood 19–0–82–1; Mullaney 23–5–60–3; Gurney 27–2–97–2; Patel 19–0–106–0; Carter 8–1–55–0; Root 7.2–1–29–3. *Second innings*—Hutton 8–2–25–0; Gurney 6–1–34–0; Mullaney 5–1–25–0; Carter 17–2–106–4; Patel 12–4–31–3; Libby 2–0–7–0.

Nottinghamshire

Batsman	Runs
S. J. Mullaney b Whittingham	22
J. D. Libby c Finch b Archer	0
C. A. Pujara lbw b Whittingham	12
S. R. Patel lbw b Whittingham	21
M. H. Wessels c Burgess b Archer	1
W. T. Root lbw b Sakande	132
*†C. M. W. Read c Salt b Archer	124
B. A. Hutton c and b Jordan	31
L. Wood c Nash b Jordan	32
M. Carter c Burgess b Sakande	33
H. F. Gurney not out	42
Lb 14, w 6, nb 7	27

1/2 (2) 2/33 (3) 3/44 (1) 4/54 (5) 5/65 (4) 6/307 (7) 7/345 (6) 8/380 (8) 9/404 (9) 10/477 (10) (102.3 overs) 477

Jordan 22–2–90–2; Archer 28–0–129–3; Whittingham 16–1–106–3; Sakande 12.3–1–60–2; Rawlins 21–1–72–0; Nash 2–1–4–0; Finch 1–0–2–0.

Umpires: M. J. Saggers and B. V. Taylor.

WARWICKSHIRE

Toothless Bears given pause

PAUL BOLTON

When Warwickshire brought Ashley Giles back from Lancashire as director of cricket in January 2017, they hoped he would transport them to another era. The preferred destination was the glory years of the mid-1990s. But his comeback season was more reminiscent of the grim days of the 1980s.

Relegation in the Championship, which appeared probable from the moment Warwickshire were twice thumped by an innings in April, was matched by a feeble defence of the one-day trophy. The Twenty20 Blast, in which they lost to Nottinghamshire in the final at Edgbaston, proved a welcome distraction but failed to mask inadequacies elsewhere.

It was too easy to blame Giles's close friend and predecessor, Dougie Brown, who had ignored warning signs: an ageing squad in decline and a dearth of talent coming through the Academy. But Giles was also complicit. He used 26 players in a Championship season that brought just one victory – a selection policy that suggested panic, not planning. And he himself had appointed Brown as Academy director and second-team coach, during his first stint in charge of the club, between 2007 and 2012. Despite Brown's boundless enthusiasm, Warwickshire had failed to produce a home-grown capped player since Chris Woakes.

The cricket committee, chaired by the aptly named John Dodge, ducked criticism, despite several years of inertia. Instead Alan Richardson, the bowling coach, and Chris Armstrong, in charge of strength and conditioning, became the fall guys. Richardson could count himself particularly unfortunate: Warwickshire's problems stemmed from the failures of their batsmen, whose 19 bonus points were the lowest in the country. Five of their nine defeats were by an innings.

The bowlers in his charge were also creaking with age. Keith Barker, Rikki Clarke, Boyd Rankin and Chris Wright, who during the 2012 title-winning campaign had shared 154 wickets in 52 appearances, now collected just 69 in 33. Clarke returned to Surrey in mid-season (and promptly produced career-best bowling of seven for 55), while injuries to Rankin and Wright left Barker, a willing workhorse, leading a thin attack. They drafted in a seamer called Ryan Sidebottom, but he had rather less experience than his namesake: just one first-class match for his native Victoria, back in 2013. And though he took 23 wickets in six matches and topped the averages, he couldn't stop the rot.

Only Jeetan Patel, the durable New Zealand off-spinner who was given the captaincy for 2018, reached 30 wickets. But a succession of inadequate first-innings totals meant he was used mostly in a holding role. The emergence of left-arm spinner Sunny Singh, born in India, raised in Birmingham and the first product of the Chance to Shine scheme to play county cricket, lifted some of

Ed Pollock

the gloom – but not much. The new bowling coach Graeme Welch, returning from Leicestershire to the role he held between 2010 and 2014, will not have it easy.

Among the batsmen only Jonathan Trott, helped by an early-season century at Oxford, made 1,000 first-class runs. He also stood in as Championship captain after Ian Bell resigned in August. The burden of leading a side lacking spirit and confidence had taken its toll, and Bell's form deserted him: for the first time since 2002, he went through an English season without a first-class century. And there was little comfort in white-ball cricket. He was dropped for the closing stages of the T20, and replaced as captain by the former New Zealand all-rounder Grant Elliott. But a late reminder of his best, a glorious counter-attack in the final match of the season against Hampshire, gave hope for 2018.

Former captain Ian Westwood, who had played alongside Bell in Warwickshire's youth system, retired in June. The injuries, particularly to his hands, had mounted, and his absence from the white-ball teams had left him struggling for motivation. But his fighting qualities were much admired by Giles, and he was made development coach in the winter. Warwickshire hoped Westwood would fill the hole in their talent identification system, which has gaped since Neal Abberley's death in 2011.

William Porterfield was released after an unfulfilled seven-year career at the club, which produced just one Championship century, while all-rounders Mark Adair and Ateeq Javid also moved on. Javid, Birmingham born and bred, made two centuries in 2013, then lost his place when Trott dropped out of the England reckoning: he made just 11 Championship appearances in his last four seasons at Edgbaston, with a single game in 2017. He signed for Leicestershire.

Giles started the rebuilding process by signing Will Rhodes from Yorkshire, plus two who joined in mid-season: Adam Hose from Somerset and – in a swap deal for Clarke – Dom Sibley from Surrey. Together with 22-year-old left-hander Ed Pollock, a former Worcestershire Academy off-spinner, they transformed the club's approach to T20 cricket, adding power to the top order. Pollock announced himself with a belligerent half-century on debut against Derbyshire, and bludgeoned 50 from 23 balls against Glamorgan in the semi-final.

His refreshingly uncomplicated approach helped Warwickshire stumble on a winning formula in T20 cricket. Regaining their place in the top flight of the County Championship may prove more challenging.

Championship attendance: 17,956.

WARWICKSHIRE RESULTS

All first-class matches – Played 15: Won 1, Lost 9, Drawn 5.
County Championship matches – Played 14: Won 1, Lost 9, Drawn 4.

Specsavers County Championship, 8th in Division 1;
NatWest T20 Blast, finalists; Royal London One-Day Cup, 9th in North Group.

COUNTY CHAMPIONSHIP AVERAGES, BATTING AND FIELDING

Cap		*Birthplace*	*M*	*I*	*NO*	*R*	*HS*	*100*	*Avge*	*Ct/St*
2005	I. J. L. Trott	*Cape Town, SA*	14	26	0	967	175	3	37.19	10
2008	†I. J. Westwood	*Birmingham‡*	4	7	0	253	153	1	36.14	1
2013	†K. H. D. Barker	*Manchester*	12	22	4	536	70*	0	29.77	2
	D. P. Sibley	*Epsom*	6	12	1	310	92*	0	28.18	4
2012	J. S. Patel¶	*Wellington*	13	24	2	608	100	1	27.63	9
2001	I. R. Bell	*Walsgrave‡*	13	24	1	596	99	0	25.91	9
2009	C. R. Woakes§	*Birmingham‡*	2	4	0	100	53	0	25.00	0
	M. J. Lamb	*Wolverhampton*	7	14	0	329	71	0	23.50	3
	A. R. I. Umeed	*Glasgow*	8	14	0	325	113	1	23.21	9
2007	T. R. Ambrose	*Newcastle, Aust.*	13	24	1	513	104	1	22.30	25/3
2011	R. Clarke	*Orsett*	8	14	0	265	83	0	18.92	6
2013	C. J. C. Wright	*Chipping Norton*	8	16	3	241	41	0	18.53	2
	A. T. Thomson	*Macclesfield*	2	4	0	70	26	0	17.50	1
	S. R. Hain	*Hong Kong*	8	14	0	216	58	0	15.42	4
2014	†W. T. S. Porterfield††	*Londonderry*	5	9	0	137	45	0	15.22	3
	L. Banks	*Newcastle-u-Lyme*	2	4	0	57	29	0	14.25	1
2013	†W. B. Rankin††	*Londonderry*	5	9	4	61	21*	0	12.20	1
	†A. J. Mellor	*Stoke-on-Trent*	3	6	0	59	18	0	9.83	3
	†O. J. Hannon-Dalby	*Halifax*	4	7	2	44	12	0	8.80	0
	R. N. Sidebottom††	*Shepparton, Aust.*	6	12	5	26	13	0	3.71	0
	†Sukhjit Singh	*Manolian, India*	4	7	2	18	16*	0	3.60	1

Also batted: H. J. H. Brookes (*Solihull‡*) (1 match) 4, 11; A. Javid (*Birmingham‡*) (1 match) 14, 8; G. D. Panayi (*Enfield*) (2 matches) 16, 1, 0; O. P. Stone (*Norwich*) (1 match) 32, 7*; †G. T. Thornton (*Coventry*) (2 matches) 0*, 10, 9.

‡ *Born in Warwickshire.* § *ECB contract.* ¶ *Official overseas player.* †† *Other non-England-qualified.*

BOWLING

	Style	*O*	*M*	*R*	*W*	*BB*	*5I*	*Avge*
R. N. Sidebottom	RFM	129.5	28	510	23	4-29	0	22.17
O. J. Hannon-Dalby	RFM	89.1	22	269	11	4-29	0	24.45
J. S. Patel	OB	482	149	1,222	41	6-50	1	29.80
Sukhjit Singh	SLA	122.4	13	400	13	6-144	2	30.76
W. B. Rankin	RFM	114.2	13	423	12	3-48	0	35.25
K. H. D. Barker	LFM	301	59	950	26	3-21	0	36.53
R. Clarke	RFM	199	41	615	15	3-29	0	41.00
C. J. C. Wright	RFM	199.3	37	694	16	5-113	1	43.37

Also bowled: H. J. H. Brookes (RFM) 11–1–43–0; A. Javid (OB) 4–0–15–0; M. J. Lamb (RFM) 20–4–66–3; G. D. Panayi (RFM) 38.3–7–141–4; D. P. Sibley (LB) 2–0–17–0; O. P. Stone (RFM) 17–3–70–1; A. T. Thomson (OB) 3–2–1–0; G. T. Thornton (RFM) 36.2–4–138–4; I. J. L. Trott (RM) 36–4–111–1; A. R. I. Umeed (LB) 14–0–73–2; C. R. Woakes (RFM) 44–7–159–7.

LEADING ROYAL LONDON CUP AVERAGES (100 runs/4 wickets)

Batting	*Runs*	*HS*	*Avge*	*SR*	*Ct*
S. R. Hain	456	109	65.14	94.60	7
I. R. Bell	410	104	58.57	94.90	1
R. Clarke	257	84*	51.40	135.97	2
I. J. L. Trott	308	104	44.00	93.90	1
T. R. Ambrose	297	83	42.42	97.69	8
A. D. Thomason	105	28	21.00	92.92	4

Bowling	*W*	*BB*	*Avge*	*ER*
G. T. Thornton	8	4-42	23.12	7.11
K. H. D. Barker	10	3-63	35.30	6.57
J. S. Patel	10	3-48	35.30	5.12
A. D. Thomason	4	4-64	36.75	9.18
O. J. Hannon-Dalby	7	3-24	45.14	8.38
R. Clarke	8	2-18	51.62	5.73

LEADING NATWEST T20 BLAST AVERAGES (200 runs/25 overs)

Batting	Runs	HS	Avge	SR	Ct
E. J. Pollock	283	66	31.44	**174.69**	3
C. de Grandhomme	322	65*	26.83	**170.37**	9
A. J. Hose	200	76	25.00	**158.73**	1
A. D. Thomason	200	42	25.00	**149.25**	5
S. R. Hain	458	82*	32.71	**134.70**	13
G. D. Elliott	332	59*	33.20	**134.41**	8
I. R. Bell	251	75*	25.10	**117.28**	7

Bowling	W	BB	Avge	ER
J. S. Patel	20	4-22	21.85	**6.82**
G. D. Elliott	12	4-37	28.66	**8.19**
W. B. Rankin	10	3-26	26.50	**8.54**
O. J. Hannon-Dalby	14	3-33	17.21	**8.60**
O. P. Stone	9	3-29	29.11	**9.35**
A. D. Thomason	10	3-33	25.20	**9.69**
C. de Grandhomme	5	2-29	69.60	**9.89**

FIRST-CLASS COUNTY RECORDS

Highest score for	501*	B. C. Lara v Durham at Birmingham	1994
Highest score against	322	I. V. A. Richards (Somerset) at Taunton	1985
Leading run-scorer	35,146	D. L. Amiss (avge 41.64)	1960–87
Best bowling for	10-41	J. D. Bannister v Comb. Services at Birmingham	1959
Best bowling against	10-36	H. Verity (Yorkshire) at Leeds	1931
Leading wicket-taker	2,201	W. E. Hollies (avge 20.45)	1932–57
Highest total for	810-4 dec	v Durham at Birmingham	1994
Highest total against	887	by Yorkshire at Birmingham	1896
Lowest total for	16	v Kent at Tonbridge	1913
Lowest total against	15	by Hampshire at Birmingham	1922

LIST A COUNTY RECORDS

Highest score for	206	A. I. Kallicharran v Oxfordshire at Birmingham	1984
Highest score against	172*	W. Larkins (Northamptonshire) at Luton	1983
Leading run-scorer	11,254	D. L. Amiss (avge 33.79)	1963–87
Best bowling for	7-32	R. G. D. Willis v Yorkshire at Birmingham	1981
Best bowling against	6-27	M. H. Yardy (Sussex) at Birmingham	2005
Leading wicket-taker	396	G. C. Small (avge 25.48)	1980–99
Highest total for	392-5	v Oxfordshire at Birmingham	1984
Highest total against	415-5	by Nottinghamshire at Nottingham	2016
Lowest total for	59	v Yorkshire at Leeds	2001
Lowest total against	56	by Yorkshire at Birmingham	1995

TWENTY20 COUNTY RECORDS

Highest score for	158*	B. B. McCullum v Derbyshire at Birmingham	2015
Highest score against	100*	I. J. Harvey (Gloucestershire) at Birmingham	2003
Leading run-scorer	1,911	I. J. L. Trott (avge 39.81)	2003–14
Best bowling for	5-19	N. M. Carter v Worcestershire at Birmingham	2005
Best bowling against	5-25	D. J. Pattinson (Nottinghamshire) at Birmingham	2011
Leading wicket-taker	**113**	**J. S. Patel (avge 21.80)**	**2009–17**
Highest total for	242-2	v Derbyshire at Birmingham	2015
Highest total against	215-6	by Durham at Birmingham	2010
Lowest total for	73	v Somerset at Taunton	2013
Lowest total against	96	by Northamptonshire at Northampton	2011
	96	by Gloucestershire at Cheltenham	2013

ADDRESS

County Ground, Edgbaston, Birmingham B5 7QU; 0844 635 1902; info@edgbaston.com; www.edgbaston.com.

OFFICIALS

Captain 2017 I. R. Bell
2018 J. S. Patel
(Twenty20) G. D. Elliott
Sport director A. F. Giles
First-team coach J. O. Troughton
Elite development manager P. Greetham

President Earl of Aylesford
Chairman N. Gascoigne
Chief executive N. Snowball
Chairman, cricket committee J. H. Dodge
Head groundsman G. Barwell
Scorer M. D. Smith

At Oxford, April 2–4. WARWICKSHIRE drew with OXFORD MCCU.

At The Oval, April 7–10. WARWICKSHIRE lost to SURREY by an innings and one run.

WARWICKSHIRE v YORKSHIRE

At Birmingham, April 14–17. Yorkshire won by an innings and 88 runs. Yorkshire 23pts, Warwickshire 2pts. Toss: uncontested.

Yorkshire romped to their fourth win in five visits to Edgbaston, and their third by an innings. They preyed on feeble batting: Warwickshire slid to 77 for seven on a rain-hit first day, and seven for five to all but seal defeat on the third. They had the worst of the conditions, but it was never as difficult as they made it appear: none of the top seven passed 20, and only Barker and Patel put up any fight. Coad, meanwhile, hit a consistent length at decent pace, and picked up a pair of five-fors for a maiden ten-wicket haul, more than making up for the absence of injured senior bowlers Jack Brooks, Liam Plunkett and Ryan Sidebottom. In between those collapses, Yorkshire proved what could be achieved with a little application, and three half-centuries helped them to 381. Warwickshire limped into the fourth day on 85 for nine, before slumping to a second consecutive innings defeat. "Our goals may have to change," said Ashley Giles, their coach. "We came into the season with high hopes, but now we want to stay in Division One."

Close of play: first day, Warwickshire 152-8 (Barker 33, Wright 8); second day, Yorkshire 295-6 (Rashid 35, Hodd 8); third day, Warwickshire 85-9 (Patel 30, Hannon-Dalby 1).

Warwickshire

W. T. S. Porterfield c Ballance b Coad	16	– c Bresnan b Coad	20
A. J. Mellor c Hodd b Coad	13	– c Bresnan b Willey	0
I. J. L. Trott lbw b Coad	13	– lbw b Willey	0
*I. R. Bell c Hodd b Patterson	11	– c Bresnan b Coad	1
S. R. Hain lbw b Bresnan	1	– b Coad	1
†T. R. Ambrose c Hodd b Patterson	1	– lbw b Coad	0
R. Clarke lbw b Coad	6	– c Lyth b Coad	12
K. H. D. Barker c Hodd b Bresnan	50	– c Hodd b Patterson	10
J. S. Patel b Rashid	36	– not out	49
C. J. C. Wright b Coad	9	– b Rashid	6
O. J. Hannon-Dalby not out	7	– b Rashid	12
B 6, lb 8, w 1	15	Lb 4	4
1/21 (1) 2/47 (2) 3/52 (3) (61.1 overs)	178	1/4 (2) 2/4 (3) 3/5 (4) (42 overs)	115
4/55 (5) 5/65 (4) 6/73 (6)		4/7 (5) 5/7 (6) 6/29 (7)	
7/77 (7) 8/130 (9) 9/165 (10) 10/178 (8)		7/40 (8) 8/54 (1) 9/79 (10) 10/115 (11)	

Willey 14–1–42–0; Coad 22–7–52–5; Bresnan 7.1–1–16–2; Patterson 11–3–30–2; Rashid 7–0–24–1. *Second innings*—Coad 18–7–50–5; Willey 10–4–20–2; Patterson 5–2–17–1; Bresnan 2–0–11–0; Rashid 6–4–7–2; Lyth 1–0–6–0.

Yorkshire

A. Lyth c Ambrose b Wright	8
A. Z. Lees c Clarke b Barker	36
P. S. P. Handscomb b Wright	75
*G. S. Ballance c Ambrose b Hannon-Dalby	22
J. A. Leaning c Hain b Patel	40
T. T. Bresnan lbw b Barker	61
A. U. Rashid c Trott b Clarke	65
†A. J. Hodd b Barker	28
D. J. Willey c Ambrose b Hannon-Dalby	19
S. A. Patterson c Trott b Clarke	13
B. O. Coad not out	3
B 2, lb 9	11
1/9 (1) 2/97 (2) (114.3 overs)	381
3/132 (3) 4/165 (4) 5/225 (5)	
6/279 (6) 7/331 (8) 8/357 (7)	
9/377 (10) 10/381 (9) 110 overs: 368-8	

Barker 27–7–74–3; Wright 22–4–77–2; Hannon-Dalby 21.3–4–63–2; Patel 22–9–51–1; Clarke 18–0–87–2; Trott 4–0–18–0.

Umpires: N. G. C. Cowley and R. T. Robinson.

WARWICKSHIRE v SURREY

At Birmingham, April 21–24. Drawn. Warwickshire 10pts, Surrey 13pts. Toss: uncontested.

After suffering a broken foot in pre-season nets, Westwood returned to help Warwickshire earn their first batting points of the summer, and a draw. He had played with rare fluency on the first day, reaching a century in 130 balls, the fastest of his 13 Championship hundreds. And he put on 126 for the first wicket with Porterfield, Warwickshire's best start in three years. Still, they retained some flakiness, crumbling from 263 for three to 332 all out, as the Curran brothers cut through with the second new ball. Stoneman led a strong reply with a second century of the season against Warwickshire, and Sangakkara stroked a majestic hundred against one of his former counties. But, having been 306 for three, Surrey had to settle for a lead of 105 – handy rather than match-winning. Westwood saw Warwickshire back into the black with another fifty, passing 8,000 first-class runs. And Bell eased fears of a collapse on the last day, though he just missed a first hundred in over a year, before Ambrose and Barker hit half-centuries of their own.

Close of play: first day, Warwickshire 292-6 (Clarke 0, Barker 0); second day, Surrey 299-3 (Sangakkara 98, Sibley 12); third day, Warwickshire 162-4 (Bell 68, Ambrose 8).

Warwickshire

W. T. S. Porterfield c Sangakkara b T. K. Curran	45	– c Foakes b Dernbach	15
I. J. Westwood c Borthwick b Footitt	153	– c Foakes b T. K. Curran	52
I. J. L. Trott c Borthwick b T. K. Curran	14	– c Sangakkara b Dernbach	0
*I. R. Bell c Borthwick b Footitt	33	– c Foakes b Batty	99
A. Javid c Burns b T. K. Curran	14	– b Borthwick	8
†T. R. Ambrose lbw b S. M. Curran	23	– c Sangakkara b T. K. Curran	85
R. Clarke lbw b Footitt	3	– c Borthwick b T. K. Curran	27
K. H. D. Barker not out	23	– not out	70
J. S. Patel c T. K. Curran b S. M. Curran	0	– lbw b T. K. Curran	20
C. J. C. Wright b S. M. Curran	4	– not out	36
O. J. Hannon-Dalby c Stoneman b T. K. Curran	9		
Lb 11	11	B 14, lb 5, nb 4	23
1/126 (1) 2/144 (3) 3/223 (4) (96.3 overs)	332	1/43 (1) (8 wkts dec, 123 overs)	435
4/263 (5) 5/290 (6) 6/292 (2)		2/45 (3) 3/113 (2)	
7/295 (7) 8/296 (9) 9/304 (10) 10/332 (11)		4/147 (5) 5/222 (4)	
		6/302 (7) 7/303 (6) 8/344 (9)	

T. K. Curran 21.3–1–98–4; S. M. Curran 27–7–74–3; Dernbach 20–1–71–0; Footitt 26–6–66–3; Batty 2–0–12–0. *Second innings*—T. K. Curran 33–4–112–4; S. M. Curran 14.3–2–52–0; Footitt 10.3–0–56–0; Batty 26–7–48–1; Dernbach 25–3–98–2; Borthwick 14–1–50–1.

Surrey

R. J. Burns c Trott b Wright	6
M. D. Stoneman lbw b Barker	123
S. G. Borthwick c Trott b Clarke	50
K. C. Sangakkara c Clarke b Barker	105
D. P. Sibley lbw b Clarke	56
†B. T. Foakes c Patel b Hannon-Dalby	21
S. M. Curran lbw b Patel	32
T. K. Curran not out	18
*G. J. Batty lbw b Patel	6
J. W. Dernbach c Bell b Wright	4
M. H. A. Footitt c Porterfield b Patel	2
B 4, lb 6, nb 4	14
1/11 (1) 2/127 (3) (119.3 overs)	437
3/267 (2) 4/306 (4) 5/354 (6)	
6/394 (5) 7/419 (7) 8/429 (9)	
9/434 (10) 10/437 (11) 110 overs: 410-6	

Barker 25–3–92–2; Wright 27–3–102–2; Patel 30.3–6–74–3; Clarke 19–2–90–2; Hannon-Dalby 14–1–54–1; Javid 4–0–15–0.

Umpires: R. J. Evans and M. A. Gough.

At Taunton, May 19–22. WARWICKSHIRE drew with SOMERSET.

At Southampton, June 2–5. WARWICKSHIRE lost to HAMPSHIRE by an innings and 94 runs.

At Chelmsford, June 19–22. WARWICKSHIRE lost to ESSEX by an innings and 164 runs.

WARWICKSHIRE v LANCASHIRE

At Birmingham, June 26–29 (day/night). Drawn. Warwickshire 10pts, Lancashire 9pts. Toss: Lancashire. First-class debut: G. D. Panayi.

A combination of the pink ball, which went soft quickly, and a pitch used for a Champions Trophy semi-final, produced a turgid contest. Even Anderson struggled for movement or bounce. He released some of his frustration at Umeed, who had been called up by Warwickshire after Ian Westwood announced his retirement. Grinding his way through the second day, Umeed reached a half-century in 291 minutes, the slowest for the club, and a century in 429, the second-slowest in Championship history; it took him 331 balls. In 96 overs, he scored 95 runs and, with Trott and Patel chipping in with fifties, Warwickshire crawled to 321, a lead of 48. On the opening day, Lancashire's Chanderpaul had completed a more fluent hundred, but found little support against a persistent attack in which George Panayi, a tall seamer from Shrewsbury School, caught the eye. In their second innings, Lancashire pushed Buttler up to open in search of quick runs but, after that failed, they buckled down. By stumps on the third day the game looked to be fizzling out, even before the final-day washout.

SLOWEST FIRST-CLASS HUNDREDS IN ENGLAND

Mins			
458	K. W. R. Fletcher	England v Pakistan at The Oval	1974
453	J. E. R. Gallian	Lancashire v Derbyshire at Blackpool	1994
434	M. C. Cowdrey	England v West Indies at Birmingham	1957
429	**A. R. I. Umeed**	**Warwickshire v Lancashire at Birmingham**	**2017**
420	W. H. Denton	Northamptonshire v Derbyshire at Derby	1914
416	M. A. Atherton	England v West Indies at The Oval	2000
402	M. H. Richardson	New Zealand v England at Lord's	2004

Close of play: first day, Warwickshire 23-1 (Umeed 8, Trott 14); second day, Warwickshire 259-7 (Umeed 103, Patel 36); third day, Lancashire 178-4 (Chanderpaul 24, Vilas 14).

Lancashire

†A. L. Davies run out	31	– c Barker b Rankin	79
H. Hameed c Bell b Panayi	17	– (3) lbw b Clarke	23
J. C. Buttler lbw b Patel	2	– (2) c Porterfield b Barker	1
*S. J. Croft c Clarke b Rankin	3	– c Umeed b Rankin	34
S. Chanderpaul not out	117	– not out	24
D. J. Vilas c Ambrose b Rankin	44	– not out	14
R. McLaren c Ambrose b Barker	24		
J. Clark lbw b Barker	0		
S. D. Parry lbw b Barker	5		
T. E. Bailey b Panayi	17		
J. M. Anderson lbw b Panayi	0		
Lb 9, w 2, nb 2	13	Lb 2, w 1	3
1/43 (2) 2/49 (1) 3/53 (3) (80.3 overs)	273	1/2 (2) 2/55 (3) (4 wkts, 70 overs)	178
4/55 (4) 5/151 (6) 6/219 (7)		3/135 (1) 4/144 (4)	
7/219 (8) 8/233 (9) 9/273 (10) 10/273 (11)			

Barker 18–3–59–3; Clarke 16–3–42–0; Panayi 14.3–3–41–3; Patel 16–5–56–1; Rankin 12–3–54–2; Trott 3–1–6–0; Umeed 1–0–6–0. *Second innings*—Panayi 9–3–34–0; Barker 13–2–35–1; Rankin 13–3–35–2; Clarke 14–7–20–1; Patel 21–8–52–0.

Warwickshire

A. R. I. Umeed lbw b Parry	113	G. D. Panayi b Clark	16
W. T. S. Porterfield lbw b Anderson	1	W. B. Rankin not out	20
I. J. L. Trott lbw b Clark	56		
*I. R. Bell c Davies b Clark	0	Lb 2, nb 8	10
S. R. Hain c and b Anderson	10		
†T. R. Ambrose c Vilas b Clark	19	1/3 (2) 2/77 (3) 3/77 (4) (132.5 overs)	321
R. Clarke b Bailey	26	4/103 (5) 5/135 (6) 6/184 (7)	
K. H. D. Barker lbw b Bailey	0	7/184 (8) 8/284 (9) 9/285 (1)	
J. S. Patel st Davies b Parry	50	10/321 (10) 110 overs: 259-7	

Anderson 32–7–64–2; Bailey 30–7–75–2; McLaren 23–7–68–0; Clark 22.5–2–81–4; Parry 22–7–28–2; Croft 3–1–3–0.

Umpires: N. G. B. Cook and J. W. Lloyds.

WARWICKSHIRE v MIDDLESEX

At Birmingham, July 3–6. Middlesex won by one wicket. Middlesex 22pts, Warwickshire 6pts. Toss: uncontested.

There was nothing between the teams after the first innings, and little for the remainder, until last man Murtagh punched a three to condemn Warwickshire to their fifth defeat. Trott, standing in for the injured Ian Bell as Warwickshire captain for the first time, did his best to arrest the decline. His 49 in the first innings, together with half-centuries from Matthew Lamb – in his first home Championship match – and Clarke, who was about to rejoin Surrey, helped Warwickshire make 334. And Trott's 99 held them together in the second, when they suffered a familiar collapse: from 179 for four, their last six went down for 54, as Helm claimed a maiden five-wicket haul. In between, Eskinazi frustrated Warwickshire. They thought he had gone for none, caught at gully off his pads, but he rode more luck – he was dropped by Ambrose, and nearly run out – to make a career-best 179. Later, after Middlesex began their pursuit of 234 by losing Robson without a run on the board for the second time, Eskinazi arrived to a volley from Clarke. Umpire Neil Mallender stepped in, and again when Eskinazi departed for a duck to wild celebrations – this time addressing the entire fielding side. Wickets tumbled throughout the final day, but forties from Compton, Simpson and Higgins were enough, leaving Warwickshire quiet at the end, and glued to the bottom.

Close of play: first day, Warwickshire 302-7 (Barker 40); second day, Middlesex 302-6 (Eskinazi 178, Harris 8); third day, Middlesex 36-2 (Compton 17, Malan 19).

Warwickshire

A. R. I. Umeed c Eskinazi b Harris	14	– lbw b Helm	10
W. T. S. Porterfield c Simpson b Murtagh	3	– c Rayner b Helm	0
*I. J. L. Trott c and b Helm	49	– c Compton b Helm	99
S. R. Hain c Simpson b Higgins	35	– c Rayner b Higgins	37
M. J. Lamb c Robson b Rayner	51	– c Simpson b Harris	4
†T. R. Ambrose lbw b Higgins	4	– lbw b Malan	44
R. Clarke lbw b Harris	83	– c Eskinazi b Murtagh	6
K. H. D. Barker c and b Murtagh	49	– c Rayner b Malan	13
J. S. Patel not out	19	– c Stirling b Helm	14
G. D. Panayi c Simpson b Helm	1	– c Robson b Helm	0
W. B. Rankin lbw b Murtagh	0	– not out	1
Lb 10, w 6, nb 10	26	Lb 2, w 1, nb 2	5
1/15 (2) 2/19 (1) 3/86 (4) (105 overs)	334	1/4 (2) 2/17 (1) (69.4 overs)	233
4/119 (3) 5/141 (6) 6/219 (5)		3/80 (4) 4/85 (5)	
7/302 (7) 8/330 (8) 9/333 (10) 10/334 (11)		5/179 (6) 6/196 (7) 7/211 (8)	
		8/231 (3) 9/232 (9) 10/233 (10)	

Murtagh 28–3–85–3; Helm 25–3–81–2; Harris 22–1–86–2; Higgins 19–6–38–2; Rayner 10–2–33–1; Malan 1–0–1–0. *Second innings*—Murtagh 18–3–58–1; Helm 15.4–2–59–5; Harris 10–0–46–1; Higgins 9–2–26–1; Rayner 7–1–17–0; Malan 10–0–25–2.

Middlesex

S. D. Robson lbw b Barker	0 – (2) lbw b Clarke	0
N. R. D. Compton c Ambrose b Clarke	33 – (1) st Ambrose b Patel	49
S. S. Eskinazi b Barker	179 – c Ambrose b Barker	0
*D. J. Malan c Ambrose b Patel	39 – lbw b Barker	32
P. R. Stirling c Lamb b Rankin	1 – lbw b Panayi	15
†J. A. Simpson c Hain b Patel	24 – c Porterfield b Clarke	40
R. F. Higgins c Ambrose b Patel	6 – c Hain b Patel	45
J. A. R. Harris not out	18 – c Ambrose b Rankin	14
O. P. Rayner b Barker	6 – lbw b Rankin	15
T. G. Helm c Umeed b Clarke	5 – not out	12
T. J. Murtagh c Ambrose b Clarke	10 – not out	5
B 5, lb 5, w 1, nb 2	13 Lb 4, w 1, nb 2	7
1/0 (1) 2/114 (4) 3/195 (2) (94 overs)	334 1/0 (2) (9 wkts, 71.1 overs)	234
4/196 (5) 5/253 (6) 6/273 (7)	2/1 (3) 3/54 (4)	
7/303 (3) 8/309 (9) 9/316 (10) 10/334 (11)	4/79 (5) 5/122 (1) 6/170 (6)	
	7/193 (8) 8/210 (7) 9/227 (9)	

In the first innings Compton, when 12, retired hurt at 25-1 and resumed at 114-2.

Barker 26–2–89–3; Clarke 23–5–61–3; Panayi 7–0–39–0; Rankin 14–2–77–1; Patel 16–4–29–3; Trott 7–1–25–0; Umeed 1–0–4–0. *Second innings*—Barker 16–4–39–2; Clarke 20–4–58–2; Patel 16–6–45–2; Rankin 11.1–0–61–2; Panayi 8–1–27–1.

Umpires: G. D. Lloyd and N. A. Mallender.

At Lord's, August 6–8. WARWICKSHIRE beat MIDDLESEX by 190 runs. *Warwickshire win their only match of the season.*

At Manchester, August 28–31. WARWICKSHIRE lost to LANCASHIRE by eight wickets.

WARWICKSHIRE v SOMERSET

At Birmingham, September 5–8. Somerset won by 169 runs. Somerset 21pts, Warwickshire 3pts. Toss: Somerset. First-class debut: G. A. Bartlett.

In this relegation tussle, neither side wanted to bat last: a worn surface used for Twenty20 finals day three days earlier turned from the beginning. Somerset enjoyed the luck of the toss and, led by Abell, reached 216 for four, before Patel and Sukhjit Singh destroyed the tail to finish with nine wickets between them. In reply, Warwickshire folded to the pace of Craig Overton and the intelligence of Leach, who picked up five; it meant spinners had claimed 15 first-innings wickets, the most at Edgbaston since Northamptonshire visited in 2000. The follow-on was saved by an eighth-wicket partnership of 49 between Barker and Wright. With Somerset leading by 136, Trescothick played himself back into form with a gritty unbeaten century, his sixth at Edgbaston (including three for England), which allowed them to declare, and set Warwickshire a notional 402. Rain on the final morning briefly threatened to frustrate the visitors, but Groenewald mopped up with five, to keep their survival hopes alive, and all but extinguish those of his former county.

Close of play: first day, Somerset 203-4 (Abell 38, Davies 39); second day, Somerset 75-2 (Trescothick 36, Hildreth 24); third day, Warwickshire 172-6 (Ambrose 17, Patel 8).

Somerset

M. E. Trescothick c Ambrose b Patel	28	– not out	119
E. J. Byrom c Trott b Sukhjit Singh	43	– b Sidebottom	4
G. A. Bartlett b Sidebottom	8	– lbw b Sidebottom	0
J. C. Hildreth c Trott b Sukhjit Singh	33	– c Umeed b Lamb	68
*T. B. Abell b Sukhjit Singh	82	– b Sidebottom	51
†S. M. Davies c Umeed b Patel	46		
P. D. Trego c Sibley b Patel	6		
C. Overton b Sukhjit Singh	5		
D. M. Bess c Ambrose b Sukhjit Singh	2		
M. J. Leach c Trott b Patel	2		
T. D. Groenewald not out	10		
B 4, lb 4, w 5, nb 4	17	B 14, lb 5, nb 4	23
1/51 (1) 2/72 (3) 3/114 (2) 4/131 (4) 5/216 (6) 6/242 (7) 7/249 (8) 8/253 (9) 9/256 (10) 10/282 (5) (81 overs)	282	1/17 (2) 2/17 (3) 3/165 (4) 4/265 (5) (4 wkts dec, 63 overs)	265

Barker 9–1–41–0; Wright 10–1–43–0; Patel 37–9–90–4; Sidebottom 6–0–28–1; Sukhjit Singh 19–1–72–5. *Second innings*—Sidebottom 16–3–69–3; Patel 24–2–81–0; Wright 9–0–37–0; Sukhjit Singh 9–1–40–0; Lamb 5–0–19–1.

Warwickshire

A. R. I. Umeed c Hildreth b Overton	9	– c Hildreth b Groenewald	12
D. P. Sibley c Leach b Overton	4	– c Davies b Groenewald	6
*I. J. L. Trott c Abell b Leach	4	– lbw b Bess	74
I. R. Bell c Trescothick b Leach	14	– b Leach	24
M. J. Lamb c Abell b Leach	26	– c Davies b Groenewald	23
†T. R. Ambrose c Byrom b Leach	4	– lbw b Overton	21
K. H. D. Barker lbw b Overton	52	– lbw b Bess	0
J. S. Patel b Bess	2	– c Bartlett b Groenewald	42
C. J. C. Wright b Overton	25	– b Groenewald	13
Sukhjit Singh st Davies b Leach	0	– b Bess	1
R. N. Sidebottom not out	0	– not out	4
B 2, lb 4	6	B 12	12
1/12 (1) 2/17 (2) 3/21 (3) 4/36 (4) 5/40 (6) 6/93 (5) 7/96 (8) 8/145 (7) 9/146 (9) 10/146 (10) (61.3 overs)	146	1/18 (2) 2/21 (1) 3/51 (4) 4/117 (5) 5/163 (3) 6/163 (7) 7/184 (6) 8/219 (9) 9/228 (8) 10/232 (10) (88.3 overs)	232

Overton 14–7–33–4; Groenewald 3–1–7–0; Leach 27.3–8–50–5; Bess 17–4–50–1. *Second innings*—Overton 17–5–46–1; Leach 28–9–51–1; Groenewald 18–6–58–5; Trego 2–1–4–0; Bess 23.3–6–61–3.

Umpires: R. J. Bailey and P. J. Hartley.

WARWICKSHIRE v ESSEX

At Birmingham, September 12–14. Essex won by an innings and 56 runs. Essex 23pts, Warwickshire 3pts. Toss: uncontested. First-class debut: H. J. H. Brookes.

This match decided matters at both ends of the table. After a three-day drubbing, Warwickshire knew their fate, while Essex had only to wait until the morning – when Lancashire were beaten at Taunton – before they were confirmed champions. To add insult to injury, it was Warwickshire's former captain Chopra who played a leading role in their fifth innings defeat of the season, and Essex's fourth innings win. He had left Edgbaston 12 months earlier after falling out with then director of cricket Dougie Brown, but enjoyed his return, hitting 98 as Essex racked up a big lead. Their solid batting down the order contrasted with two panic-stricken efforts by Warwickshire. In the first, they lost their last five wickets in 32 balls against disciplined bowling from Porter and Harmer; only Sibley emerged with any credit, stroking 76 before he was last out. In the second,

Lamb was alone in passing 20. The news from the West Country meant Essex had become just the second side – after Nottinghamshire in 2005 – to follow promotion with the Championship.

Close of play: first day, Essex 69-0 (Chopra 42, Browne 23); second day, Warwickshire 7-0 (Hain 6, Sibley 1).

Warwickshire

	First innings		Second innings	
S. R. Hain lbw b Porter	4	–	lbw b Porter	11
D. P. Sibley c Foster b Porter	76	–	c Chopra b Porter	3
*I. J. L. Trott lbw b Porter	3	–	b Cook	6
I. R. Bell lbw b Wagner	37	–	c Foster b Cook	5
M. J. Lamb c Foster b Cook	32	–	c Lawrence b Harmer	35
C. R. Woakes lbw b Harmer	22	–	c Bopara b Harmer	13
†A. J. Mellor lbw b Harmer	10	–	c Chopra b Harmer	4
K. H. D. Barker lbw b Porter	0	–	c Foster b Porter	0
J. S. Patel lbw b Harmer	1	–	c Lawrence b Cook	19
H. J. H. Brookes b Harmer	4	–	c Chopra b Harmer	11
R. N. Sidebottom not out	0	–	not out	1
B 4, lb 8	12		B 1, lb 3	4
1/8 (1) 2/12 (3) 3/58 (4) 4/110 (5) 5/153 (6) 6/181 (7) 7/184 (8) 8/187 (9) 9/193 (10) 10/201 (2) (66.5 overs)	201		1/9 (2) 2/14 (1) 3/20 (3) 4/25 (4) 5/47 (6) 6/55 (7) 7/64 (8) 8/82 (5) 9/105 (9) 10/112 (10) (46 overs)	112

Porter 18.5–6–62–4; Cook 14–1–42–1; Wagner 12–3–38–1; Harmer 22–2–47–4. *Second innings*—Porter 14–5–37–3; Harmer 16–6–25–4; Cook 12–3–42–3; Wagner 4–1–4–0.

Essex

V. Chopra lbw b Lamb	98
N. L. J. Browne c Patel b Barker	24
T. Westley c Mellor b Woakes	28
D. W. Lawrence c Bell b Sidebottom	78
R. S. Bopara lbw b Barker	20
*R. N. ten Doeschate b Sidebottom	0
†J. S. Foster lbw b Patel	68
S. R. Harmer lbw b Woakes	24
N. Wagner c Mellor b Barker	9
J. A. Porter not out	2
S. J. Cook not out	0
B 8, lb 8, nb 2	18
1/72 (2) 2/128 (3) 3/220 (1) 4/252 (4) 5/256 (6) 6/271 (5) 7/347 (8) 8/367 (9) 9/369 (7) (9 wkts dec, 115 overs)	369

110 overs: 363-7

Woakes 24–5–64–2; Barker 22–2–71–3; Patel 33–15–69–1; Sidebottom 18–4–84–2; Brookes 11–1–43–0; Lamb 7–2–22–1.

Umpires: S. J. O'Shaughnessy and M. J. Saggers.

At Leeds, September 19–22. WARWICKSHIRE lost to YORKSHIRE by two wickets.

WARWICKSHIRE v HAMPSHIRE

At Birmingham, September 25–28. Drawn. Warwickshire 8pts, Hampshire 8pts. Toss: uncontested.

A year after Hampshire were reprieved in an ECB committee room – Durham were relegated instead because of their financial difficulties – they just about managed to escape through their efforts on the pitch. Middlesex's defeat at Taunton meant a draw would be sufficient, though Hampshire made even that a struggle. After an hour of the final morning was lost to rain, they hardly seemed interested in chasing 259. Yet they lost three wickets in four overs after lunch, and two more soon after tea, including Vince, selected in England's Ashes squad for his strokeplay, but almost strokeless while chewing through 124 balls. Holland finally settled nerves. Warwickshire finished the season without a home Championship win for only the seventh time, and the first since 2000. Heavy weather had wiped out the first day, before Sibley carried his bat for 92, and Hampshire capitulated for 116, of which Bailey made 55. Bell blazed away to put Hampshire under pressure, but ended a disappointing summer without a first-class hundred for the first time since 2002.

Close of play: first day, no play; second day, Warwickshire 0-0 (Banks 0, Sibley 0); t. Hampshire 20-1 (Alsop 6, Ervine 2).

Warwickshire

L. Banks run out	1	– c Alsop b Edwards	14
D. P. Sibley not out	92	– c Alsop b Holland	13
*I. J. L. Trott c Vince b Abbott	0	– c Alsop b Berg	20
I. R. Bell b Abbott	0	– not out	77
M. J. Lamb b Edwards	6	– lbw b Berg	0
†T. R. Ambrose b Edwards	6	– c Adams b Berg	0
A. T. Thomson c Vince b Berg	26	– b Abbott	24
J. S. Patel c Holland b Dawson	14	– b Abbott	0
C. J. C. Wright c Alsop b Edwards	26	– run out	11
O. J. Hannon-Dalby b Edwards	4	– b Edwards	9
R. N. Sidebottom b Edwards	2	– lbw b Holland	13
Lb 1, nb 10	11	Lb 5	5
1/1 (1) 2/1 (3) 3/5 (4) 4/12 (5) 5/28 (6) 6/108 (7) 7/127 (8) 8/166 (9) 9/186 (10) 10/188 (11) (61 overs)	188	1/15 (1) 2/41 (2) 3/51 (3) 4/65 (5) 5/65 (6) 6/95 (7) 7/95 (8) 8/114 (9) 9/127 (10) 10/186 (11) (49.5 overs)	186

Edwards 14–1–49–5; Abbott 6.3–4–5–2; Berg 13.3–5–30–1; Holland 9–2–44–0; Dawson 10–2–20–1; Crane 8–0–39–0. *Second innings*—Abbott 12–2–45–2; Edwards 18–5–62–2; Holland 6.5–0–21–2; Berg 9–2–40–3; Crane 3–0–13–0; Dawson 1–1–0–0.

Hampshire

†T. P. Alsop lbw b Sidebottom	3	– c Trott b Patel	22
J. H. K. Adams b Sidebottom	3	– c Sibley b Hannon-Dalby	4
S. M. Ervine lbw b Hannon-Dalby	16	– c Ambrose b Sidebottom	26
J. M. Vince lbw b Wright	4	– c Ambrose b Sidebottom	30
*G. J. Bailey c Ambrose b Hannon-Dalby	55	– lbw b Patel	0
L. A. Dawson c Wright b Patel	3	– c Ambrose b Sidebottom	9
I. G. Holland lbw b Hannon-Dalby	1	– not out	21
G. K. Berg lbw b Hannon-Dalby	8	– b Hannon-Dalby	34
K. J. Abbott st Ambrose b Patel	9	– not out	6
M. S. Crane not out	5		
F. H. Edwards lbw b Patel	0		
B 4, lb 5	9	B 21, lb 9, w 1, nb 12	43
1/5 (1) 2/8 (2) 3/13 (4) 4/51 (3) 5/64 (6) 6/81 (7) 7/93 (8) 8/102 (5) 9/112 (9) 10/116 (11) (34.2 overs)	116	1/18 (2) 2/68 (3) 3/68 (1) 4/72 (5) 5/113 (6) 6/124 (4) 7/185 (8) (7 wkts, 87.4 overs)	195

Wright 7–1–26–1; Sidebottom 8–1–33–2; Hannon-Dalby 12–6–29–4; Patel 7.2–3–19–3. *Second innings*—Wright 18–8–46–0; Sidebottom 19–5–55–3; Hannon-Dalby 15.4–7–33–2; Patel 31–19–30–2; Lamb 2–1–1–0; Thomson 2–2–0–0.

Umpires: J. H. Evans and R. J. Warren.

WORCESTERSHIRE

Academy graduates gain first-class honours

JOHN CURTIS

With a late-season surge, Worcestershire overhauled long-time leaders Nottinghamshire to finish top of Division Two for the first time since 2003. They won their last four matches, including a crucial success at Trent Bridge, and secured a fifth promotion in 12 years since Steve Rhodes became director of cricket. The challenge ahead was to end the club's yo-yo existence: only once, in 2011, had Worcestershire avoided instant relegation. It would be even more difficult now that a quarter of teams go down.

No one was predicting Worcestershire could emulate Essex, and follow promotion with the Championship. But there was a growing belief that a rapidly maturing squad would at least be competitive among the elite. In 2015, they had failed to survive only by a dozen points; the nucleus of that squad remains, older, wiser, and better prepared.

Worcestershire were rewarded for a strong emphasis on home-grown talent. If the policy was forced upon them, after the financially ruinous flood of 2007 and the exodus of half a dozen senior players in 2009, they had shown its worth. In the last game of the season, they fielded ten Academy products, and picked up their ninth victory.

In recognition, Rhodes was asked to coach the England Under-19 team for their trip to South Africa and the World Cup in New Zealand over the winter. But things soon turned sour. In November, Worcestershire's 21-year-old all-rounder Alex Hepburn was charged with rape. It was alleged that Rhodes had known soon after the original incident had occurred in April, but did not inform the board; he also picked Hepburn in the first team for five T20 matches, and awarded him a one-year contract extension in October. Rhodes was replaced as England Under-19 coach and sacked by Worcestershire, ending an association which stretched back three decades. In January, Second XI batting coach Kevin Sharp was appointed his successor.

Tom Köhler-Cadmore left for Yorkshire midway through the summer. He had arranged to leave at the end, but was dropped as soon as news of his plans emerged. The bulk of the squad signed long-term deals, however, including England all-rounder Moeen Ali, scotching speculation of a return to Warwickshire. Worcestershire also recognised the importance of a top-notch overseas player. After they lost Australian John Hastings to a foot injury in August – he subsequently retired from all but T20 cricket – they pulled off a masterstroke in signing Indian off-spinner Ravichandran Ashwin. A disappointing T20 Blast campaign had derailed the early-season momentum, but Ashwin's arrival reignited belief, and spurred Worcestershire to their final four victories. For 2018, the main overseas player across all formats will be the Australian batsman Travis Head.

Joe Leach

Their top-order batting was not their strongest suit, and they were reliant on long-serving opener Daryl Mitchell. Sacked as captain at the end of the 2016season, he responded with seven centuries and 1,266 runs at 55, the second-highest aggregate in Division Two, behind Luke Wells of Sussex. Mitchell, who had become chairman of the PCA before the summer, rated his match-winning century at Trent Bridge in testing conditions the best of his career. It was no surprise when he was voted Players' Player of the Year.

Joe Clarke and Brett D'Oliveira provided support, but Tom Fell had a season to forget, failing to reach fifty once. Worcestershire hoped he could recapture the form that brought him over 1,000 Division One runs in 2015. The middle and lower order often rode to the rescue: keeper Ben Cox hit 675, while seam-bowling all-rounder Ed Barnard added 580 to his 47 wickets, and earned the supporters' award.

Joe Leach stepped into the captaincy at the end of Mitchell's six-year reign, and led from the front. Since Alan Richardson left, Leach has been magnificent, collecting 226 Championship wickets in four seasons. His haul of 69 was the highest in Division Two, and he had a habit of getting the good players out.

He had excellent back-up: Josh Tongue, like Barnard, finished with 47 wickets. Despite struggling with back problems in previous years, he played in all 14 matches and earned a call-up to the England Lions squad over the winter, along with Clarke, as a replacement for the injured Jamie Porter of Essex. A seam attack of Leach, Tongue and Barnard, plus the returning Steve Magoffin – if he can put injury problems at Sussex behind him – should have the potency to take wickets in Division One.

Worcestershire also looked formidable in the Royal London Cup, topping the North Group. It secured a lucrative home semi-final, but Surrey overpowered them to end hopes of a first Lord's showpiece for 13 years.

The major disappointment was the T20 Blast campaign, which was all but over after they failed to win any of the first five games. Worcestershire struggled for runs, despite Clarke's successful conversion to opener, and lacked control with the ball, with the exception of D'Oliveira and New Zealand spinner Mitchell Santner.

Chief executive Tom Scott unexpectedly stood down in September. Since assuming the role in February 2016 he had overseen a restructuring of the club's business model in an attempt to eradicate substantial debts. But he had fallen out with Rhodes over the handling of Köhler-Cadmore's departure, and was frustrated with the structure of the club, which placed the chief executive and the director of cricket on the same footing. In January 2018, the former Worcestershire left-arm spinner Matt Rawnsley was named as Scott's successor.

Championship attendance: 30,797.

WORCESTERSHIRE RESULTS

All first-class matches – Played 15: Won 10, Lost 3, Drawn 2.
County Championship matches – Played 14: Won 9, Lost 3, Drawn 2.

Specsavers County Championship, winners of Division 2;
NatWest T20 Blast, 8th in North Group; Royal London One-Day Cup, semi-finalists.

COUNTY CHAMPIONSHIP AVERAGES, BATTING AND FIELDING

Cap		*Birthplace*	*M*	*I*	*NO*	*R*	*HS*	*100*	*Avge*	*Ct/St*
2005	D. K. H. Mitchell	*Badsey‡*	14	26	3	1,266	161	7	55.04	21
2014	T. Köhler-Cadmore	*Chatham*	4	5	0	242	102	1	48.40	4
2015	J. M. Clarke	*Shrewsbury*	14	26	5	920	142	2	43.80	9
2017	R. Ashwin¶	*Madras, India*	4	6	1	214	82	0	42.80	2
2007	†M. M. Ali§	*Birmingham*	3	5	0	208	63	0	41.60	2
2015	E. G. Barnard	*Shrewsbury*	14	20	4	580	75	0	36.25	8
2012	B. L. D'Oliveira	*Worcester‡*	14	25	0	891	150	3	35.64	10
2009	O. B. Cox	*Wordsley‡*	14	21	1	675	124	1	33.75	42/1
2016	G. H. Rhodes	*Birmingham*	8	15	2	379	52	0	29.15	5
2009	†J. D. Shantry	*Shrewsbury*	6	8	4	94	30*	0	23.50	3
2013	†R. A. Whiteley	*Sheffield*	5	9	1	170	53	0	21.25	6
2012	J. Leach	*Stafford*	14	19	2	347	57*	0	20.41	7
2017	J. W. Hastings¶	*Penrith, Australia*	6	8	1	139	51	0	19.85	5
2013	T. C. Fell	*Hillingdon*	13	23	1	323	47	0	14.68	7
2017	J. C. Tongue	*Redditch‡*	14	18	3	138	41	0	9.20	2
2017	N. M. Lyon¶	*Young, Australia*	4	5	3	15	6*	0	7.50	2
2017	P. R. Brown	*Peterborough*	4	5	3	12	5*	0	6.00	1

‡ *Born in Worcestershire.* § *ECB contract.* ¶ *Official overseas player.*

BOWLING

	Style	*O*	*M*	*R*	*W*	*BB*	*5I*	*Avge*
J. Leach	RFM	397.5	73	1,338	69	5-32	4	19.39
E. G. Barnard	RFM	321.3	48	1,187	47	4-23	0	25.25
J. C. Tongue	RFM	333.4	46	1,212	47	6-97	2	25.78
J. D. Shantry	LFM	100.3	19	310	11	3-54	0	28.18
R. Ashwin	OB	184.2	29	583	20	5-68	2	29.15
J. W. Hastings	RFM	161.1	41	550	16	3-44	0	34.37

Also bowled: M. M. Ali (OB) 41–4–166–3; P. R. Brown (RM) 42.4–4–199–6; B. L. D'Oliveira (LB) 60–0–271–0; N. M. Lyon (OB) 131.4–21–403–6; D. K. H. Mitchell (RM) 7.4–0–37–1; G. H. Rhodes (OB) 38–7–202–3; R. A. Whiteley (LM) 2–0–20–0.

LEADING ROYAL LONDON CUP AVERAGES (100 runs/4 wickets)

Batting

	Runs	*HS*	*Avge*	*SR*	*Ct/St*
E. G. Barnard	112	42*	37.33	134.93	6
T. Köhler-Cadmore	290	118	36.25	100.34	6
D. K. H. Mitchell	250	75	35.71	93.63	3
R. A. Whiteley	210	55	35.00	122.80	5
M. M. Ali	186	90	31.00	102.19	1
O. B. Cox	277	82	30.77	96.85	9/2
J. M. Clarke	245	56	30.62	90.07	1
B. L. D'Oliveira	222	73*	27.75	94.06	4
J. W. Hastings	133	36	26.60	138.54	2
J. Leach	102	41	17.00	102.00	1

Bowling

	W	*BB*	*Avge*	*ER*
D. K. H. Mitchell	8	3-38	25.12	5.58
J. C. Tongue	4	2-46	40.50	6.89
J. Leach	12	4-66	41.41	6.71
J. W. Hastings	11	3-50	43.00	6.45
B. L. D'Oliveira	7	2-34	43.57	4.84
E. G. Barnard	7	3-37	44.85	6.40
J. D. Shantry	6	3-64	45.16	5.53
M. M. Ali	5	2-49	62.60	5.58

LEADING NATWEST T20 BLAST AVERAGES (100 runs/15 overs)

Batting	Runs	HS	Avge	SR	Ct/St
J. M. Clarke	381	124*	31.75	**183.17**	4
J. W. Hastings	179	51	25.57	**179.00**	0
E. G. Barnard	122	34*	20.33	**152.50**	3
R. A. Whiteley	276	65	23.00	**137.31**	3
M. J. Santner	239	38	19.91	**120.10**	9
O. B. Cox	297	51	24.75	**116.47**	4/7
D. K. H. Mitchell	208	36*	26.00	**114.91**	3
B. L. D'Oliveira	201	52	20.10	**108.06**	3

Bowling	W	BB	Avge	ER
M. J. Santner	13	3-16	26.07	**6.64**
B. L. D'Oliveira	11	2-19	21.09	**6.82**
D. K. H. Mitchell	5	1-10	45.60	**7.60**
J. W. Hastings	8	3-31	41.62	**10.46**
J. D. Shantry	2	1-29	86.50	**10.48**
J. Leach	6	2-33	54.00	**11.36**

FIRST-CLASS COUNTY RECORDS

Highest score for	405*	G. A. Hick v Somerset at Taunton	1988
Highest score against	331*	J. D. B. Robertson (Middlesex) at Worcester	1949
Leading run-scorer	34,490	D. Kenyon (avge 34.18)	1946–67
Best bowling for	9-23	C. F. Root v Lancashire at Worcester	1931
Best bowling against	10-51	J. Mercer (Glamorgan) at Worcester	1936
Leading wicket-taker	2,143	R. T. D. Perks (avge 23.73)	1930–55
Highest total for	701-6 dec	v Surrey at Worcester	2007
Highest total against	701-4 dec	by Leicestershire at Worcester	1906
Lowest total for	24	v Yorkshire at Huddersfield	1903
Lowest total against	30	by Hampshire at Worcester	1903

LIST A COUNTY RECORDS

Highest score for	180*	T. M. Moody v Surrey at The Oval	1994
Highest score against	158	W. Larkins (Northamptonshire) at Luton	1982
	158	R. A. Smith (Hampshire) at Worcester	1996
Leading run-scorer	16,416	G. A. Hick (avge 44.60)	1985–2008
Best bowling for	7-19	N. V. Radford v Bedfordshire at Bedford	1991
Best bowling against	7-15	R. A. Hutton (Yorkshire) at Leeds	1969
Leading wicket-taker	370	S. R. Lampitt (avge 24.52)	1987–2002
Highest total for	404-3	v Devon at Worcester	1987
Highest total against	399-4	by Sussex at Horsham	2011
Lowest total for	58	v Ireland v Worcester	2009
Lowest total against	45	by Hampshire at Worcester	1988

TWENTY20 COUNTY RECORDS

Highest score for	127	T. Köhler-Cadmore v Durham at Worcester	2016
Highest score against	141*	C. L. White (Somerset) at Worcester	2006
Leading run-scorer	**2,080**	**D. K. H. Mitchell (avge 24.47)**	**2005–17**
Best bowling for	**5-24**	**A. Hepburn v Nottinghamshire at Worcester**	**2017**
Best bowling against	6-21	A. J. Hall (Northamptonshire) at Northampton	2008
Leading wicket-taker	**92**	**J. D. Shantry (avge 28.21)**	**2010–17**
Highest total for	227-6	v Northamptonshire at Kidderminster	2007
Highest total against	**233-6**	**by Yorkshire at Leeds**	**2017**
Lowest total for	53	v Lancashire at Manchester	2016
Lowest total against	93	by Gloucestershire at Bristol	2008

ADDRESS

Blackfinch New Road, Worcester WR2 4QQ; 01905 748474; info@wccc.co.uk; www.wccc.co.uk.

OFFICIALS

Captain J. Leach
Director of cricket 2017 S. J. Rhodes
Head coach 2018 K. Sharp
Academy coach E. J. Wilson
President N. Gifford

Chairman S. Taylor
Chief executive 2017 T. Scott
2018 M. J. Rawnsley
Head groundsman T. R. Packwood
Scorer S. M. Drinkwater and P. M. Mellish

At Weetwood, Leeds, April 7–9. WORCESTERSHIRE beat LEEDS/BRADFORD MCCU by an innings and 42 runs.

At Cardiff, April 14–16. WORCESTERSHIRE beat GLAMORGAN by eight wickets.

WORCESTERSHIRE v NORTHAMPTONSHIRE

At Worcester, April 21–22. Worcestershire won by 20 runs. Worcestershire 19pts, Northamptonshire 3pts. Toss: uncontested. County debut: A. Carter.

There wasn't much wrong with the pitch, yet it took just two days for Worcestershire to edge home by 20 runs. On the first, Ali showed some application, scoring the only half-century of the game, and putting on a handy 62 with Mitchell. He showed flair, too, smashing Andy Carter's first ball for six over midwicket. But once Carter – coaxed out of retirement to address an injury crisis at Northamptonshire, his sixth county – got Ali shortly after lunch, the ball held sway. Too few batsmen had confidence in their technique against good swing bowling, and several perished chancing their arm: Worcestershire collapsed to 188 all out, then Northamptonshire to 102 for six by the close, Duckett alone resisting. Next morning, Worcestershire earned a slender lead, before sliding to three for three. Leach promoted Hastings and himself up the order, but the ploy failed, and only a last-wicket partnership of 45 between Barnard and Tongue dragged the target to 185. Northamptonshire seemed well placed for a sixth consecutive Championship victory at 85 for three but, once Leach removed Rossington and Holden, the pattern resumed. Tongue destroyed the middle order, and Leach trapped last man Carter, completing a five-for for the second time in the day, and career-best figures of ten for 122.

Close of play: first day, Northamptonshire 102-6 (Duckett 45, Crook 2).

Worcestershire

D. K. H. Mitchell lbw b Crook	30	– c Rossington b Buck	0
B. L. D'Oliveira c Rossington b Azharullah	5	– lbw b Azharullah	1
M. M. Ali b Carter	50	– c Duckett b Azharullah	0
T. C. Fell lbw b Azharullah	5	– (6) b Buck	23
J. M. Clarke lbw b Crook	33	– (7) c Duckett b Buck	4
T. Köhler-Cadmore b Carter	0	– (8) c Levi b Crook	22
†O. B. Cox c Rossington b Carter	4	– (9) c Rossington b Carter	11
E. G. Barnard c Rossington b Buck	1	– (10) not out	26
*J. Leach c Holden b Buck	20	– (5) b Carter	16
J. W. Hastings not out	20	– (4) b Azharullah	22
J. C. Tongue c Azharullah b Buck	4	– b Buck	15
Lb 14, nb 2	16	Lb 6, w 1, nb 6	13
1/8 (2) 2/70 (1) 3/75 (4) 4/117 (3) 5/117 (6) 6/135 (7) 7/144 (8) 8/150 (5) 9/174 (9) 10/188 (11) (49.4 overs)	188	1/0 (1) 2/2 (3) 3/3 (2) 4/24 (5) 5/56 (4) 6/67 (7) 7/82 (6) 8/102 (9) 9/108 (8) 10/153 (11) (40.4 overs)	153

Buck 14.4–2–53–3; Azharullah 15–5–35–2; Carter 13–3–51–3; Crook 7–0–35–2. *Second innings*—Buck 13.4–3–42–4; Azharullah 13–2–50–3; Carter 9–2–39–2; Crook 5–0–16–1.

Northamptonshire

R. I. Newton lbw b Leach	1	– b Tongue	21
B. M. Duckett c Cox b Hastings	47	– b Leach	5
M. D. E. Holden c D'Oliveira b Barnard	13	– b Leach	37
R. I. Keogh c Mitchell b Leach	1	– b Barnard	3
†A. M. Rossington c D'Oliveira b Leach	0	– c Fell b Leach	22
R. E. Levi lbw b Leach	24	– lbw b Tongue	22
*J. J. Cobb lbw b Barnard	7	– c and b Tongue	9
S. P. Crook b Hastings	16	– b Tongue	0
N. L. Buck not out	24	– c Hastings b Leach	5
Azharullah c Köhler-Cadmore b Leach	8	– not out	17
A. Carter b Hastings	3	– lbw b Leach	8
B 2, lb 2, w 1, nb 8	13	B 1, lb 8, nb 6	15
1/2 (1) 2/55 (3) 3/56 (4) 4/56 (5) 5/90 (6) 6/100 (7) 7/120 (2) 8/125 (8) 9/154 (10) 10/157 (11) (35 overs)	157	1/8 (2) 2/42 (1) 3/45 (4) 4/85 (5) 5/98 (3) 6/122 (6) 7/122 (8) 8/127 (9) 9/149 (7) 10/164 (11) (43.4 overs)	164

Hastings 11–2–60–3; Leach 16–0–60–5; Barnard 5–0–23–2; Tongue 3–1–10–0. *Second innings*—Hastings 11–2–28–0; Leach 15.4–2–62–5; Tongue 11–1–45–4; Barnard 6–2–20–1.

Umpires: J. H. Evans and N. A. Mallender.

At Derby, May 19–22. WORCESTERSHIRE beat DERBYSHIRE by an innings and 42 runs.

At Northampton, May 26–28. WORCESTERSHIRE beat NORTHAMPTONSHIRE by eight wickets.

At Hove, June 2–5. WORCESTERSHIRE lost to SUSSEX by an innings and seven runs. *Daryl Mitchell scores a century for the third consecutive match.*

WORCESTERSHIRE v GLAMORGAN

At Worcester, June 9–11. Glamorgan won by nine wickets. Glamorgan 23pts, Worcestershire 5pts. Toss: uncontested.

Glamorgan completed back-to-back Championship wins for the first time in nearly two years thanks to a stirring second-day fightback. On the first morning, Worcestershire had slipped to 14 for three before Cox hit 93, his best since May 2015, and Barnard contributed 60 to help cobble together 267. That looked considerably above par when Tongue's explosive burst of five wickets in four overs reduced Glamorgan to 58 for six before stumps. But Rudolph survived the wreckage and next day led the recovery with his first Championship hundred in over two years (he had recently given up the captaincy to focus on his batting). He shared a seventh-wicket stand of 168 with Cooke, a record for the fixture. Leach dismissed both in the same over, with Glamorgan still 40 in arrears, but Salter and Carey hit career-bests in a ninth-wicket partnership of 124, and they finished with a lead of 114; Tongue's six for 97 was another best. Dizzied by the turnaround, Worcestershire capitulated on the third morning against fine bowling from Hogan, who picked up five for 38 as the last nine wickets went down for 75, leaving just 16 for victory.

Close of play: first day, Glamorgan 76-6 (Rudolph 49, Cooke 10); second day, Worcestershire 34-1 (D'Oliveira 12, Fell 4).

Worcestershire

	First innings		Second innings	
D. K. H. Mitchell b Carey		0	c Ingram b Hogan	18
B. L. D'Oliveira c Donald b van der Gugten		7	lbw b Hogan	22
T. C. Fell lbw b van der Gugten		7	c Ingram b van der Gugten	33
J. M. Clarke b Hogan		25	c Bragg b Hogan	17
†O. B. Cox c Salter b van der Gugten		93	c Ingram b Carey	3
R. A. Whiteley c Donald b van der Gugten		6	c Donald b Carey	16
E. G. Barnard c Hogan b Salter		60	c Cooke b van der Gugten	2
*J. Leach lbw b Hogan		13	b Hogan	7
J. D. Shantry c Cooke b Carey		3	not out	4
J. C. Tongue c Rudolph b Salter		41	c Cooke b Carey	1
N. M. Lyon not out		6	b Hogan	4
Lb 2, nb 4		6	Lb 2	2
1/0 (1) 2/13 (3) 3/14 (2) 4/83 (4) 5/109 (6) 6/168 (5) 7/190 (8) 8/204 (9) 9/246 (7) 10/267 (10)	(70.4 overs)	267	1/22 (1) 2/54 (2) 3/75 (4) 4/82 (5) 5/107 (3) 6/113 (7) 7/120 (8) 8/120 (6) 9/124 (10) 10/129 (11) (46.3 overs)	129

Carey 18–4–69–2; van der Gugten 19–4–66–4; Hogan 17–0–79–2; Lloyd 4–0–19–0; Salter 12.4–1–32–2. *Second innings*—Carey 12–1–34–3; van der Gugten 15–6–39–2; Hogan 14.3–2–38–5; Salter 5–1–16–0.

Glamorgan

	First innings		Second innings	
J. A. Rudolph b Leach		111	not out	11
N. J. Selman b Leach		4	b Barnard	3
W. D. Bragg b Tongue		7	not out	0
C. A. Ingram c Whiteley b Tongue		2		
A. H. T. Donald c Mitchell b Tongue		0		
D. L. Lloyd c Clarke b Tongue		2		
T. van der Gugten c Cox b Tongue		0		
†C. B. Cooke c Clarke b Leach		93		
A. G. Salter not out		80		
L. J. Carey c D'Oliveira b Tongue		54		
*M. G. Hogan b Leach		13		
B 5, lb 4, nb 6		15	Nb 4	4
1/39 (2) 2/46 (3) 3/52 (4) 4/56 (5) 5/58 (6) 6/58 (7) 7/226 (8) 8/227 (1) 9/351 (10) 10/381 (11)	(101.5 overs)	381	1/14 (2) (1 wkt, 8.5 overs)	18

Leach 22.5–4–85–4; Barnard 13–2–77–0; Tongue 25–4–97–6; Shantry 11–3–31–0; Lyon 25–3–61–0; D'Oliveira 5–0–21–0. *Second innings*—Leach 4.5–1–12–0; Barnard 4–1–6–1.

Umpires: M. Burns and M. A. Gough.

WORCESTERSHIRE v KENT

At Worcester, June 19–22. Worcestershire won by four wickets. Worcestershire 22pts, Kent 5pts. Toss: Kent.

Hundreds from Mitchell and Clarke helped Worcestershire complete their third-highest successful chase, and climb above Kent – previously unbeaten – into the promotion spots. Clarke had already made a century in the first innings, having begun the game without a Championship fifty in 2017. His classy 142 had held Worcestershire together on the second day, and meaty partnerships with Rhodes and Leach helped them to a lead of 76, despite Coles's six-wicket haul. Kent, who had been guilty of poor shot selection in their first innings, looked in danger of a three-day defeat when they lost their sixth wicket before lunch just 129 in front. But Denly demonstrated immense concentration in sapping heat to score a career-best 227 spanning nearly eight hours. After a seventh-wicket stand of 149 with Rouse – a county record against Worcestershire – he put on another 120 for the last three to leave a target of 399. With Pakistan leg-spinner Yasir Shah part of their armoury on a baked pitch,

Kent looked favourites, but Mitchell's rich form – he hit a fourth hundred in five Championship games – laid ideal foundations, and Clarke saw the job home. By the time Yasir completed his five-for, the game was all but over. After Worcestershire had lost Tom Köhler-Cadmore to Yorkshire, two successive Championship matches, and a Royal London Cup semi-final to Surrey, it was a sorely needed victory.

Close of play: first day, Worcestershire 95-3 (Clarke 34, Rhodes 16); second day, Kent 120-3 (Denly 67, Weatherley 24); third day, Worcestershire 16-0 (Mitchell 6, D'Oliveira 10).

Kent

First innings		Second innings	
D. J. Bell-Drummond c Mitchell b Leach	1	– c Cox b Leach	0
S. R. Dickson b Leach	7	– c Cox b Tongue	12
J. L. Denly c D'Oliveira b Barnard	12	– c Barnard b Leach	227
*S. A. Northeast c Mitchell b Tongue	42	– b Tongue	14
J. J. Weatherley c Cox b Leach	11	– c Mitchell b Leach	24
D. I. Stevens c Barnard b Hastings	39	– lbw b Leach	19
W. R. S. Gidman c Cox b Tongue	12	– c Whiteley b Hastings	19
†A. P. Rouse c Mitchell b Tongue	34	– c Whiteley b Ali	68
M. T. Coles lbw b Ali	47	– c Cox b Ali	39
Yasir Shah c Leach b Hastings	17	– c Ali b Hastings	27
M. E. Claydon not out	16	– not out	0
B 12, lb 6, nb 4	22	Lb 17, nb 8	25
1/6 (1) 2/17 (2) 3/46 (3) 4/76 (4) 5/88 (5) 6/131 (7) 7/139 (6) 8/218 (8) 9/230 (9) 10/260 (10) (73.1 overs)	260	1/0 (1) 2/44 (2) 3/64 (4) 4/125 (5) 5/169 (6) 6/205 (7) 7/354 (8) 8/408 (9) 9/449 (10) 10/474 (3) (116.4 overs)	474

Leach 14–3–42–3; Hastings 16.1–5–44–2; Tongue 19–3–56–3; Barnard 11–0–52–1; Ali 13–1–48–1. *Second innings*—Leach 20.4–3–79–4; Hastings 21–2–80–2; Tongue 22–2–92–2; Ali 25–2–104–2; Barnard 16–3–57–0; Rhodes 1–0–4–0; D'Oliveira 9–0–35–0; Mitchell 2–0–6–0.

Worcestershire

First innings		Second innings	
D. K. H. Mitchell c Gidman b Coles	6	– c Coles b Yasir Shah	142
B. L. D'Oliveira c Coles b Stevens	0	– b Stevens	27
M. M. Ali c Weatherley b Coles	37	– lbw b Yasir Shah	63
J. M. Clarke c Rouse b Coles	142	– not out	110
G. H. Rhodes c Gidman b Coles	45	– c Denly b Yasir Shah	2
†O. B. Cox lbw b Yasir Shah	19	– c Northeast b Yasir Shah	2
R. A. Whiteley lbw b Yasir Shah	0	– b Yasir Shah	29
E. G. Barnard run out	16	– not out	4
*J. Leach not out	57		
J. W. Hastings c Gidman b Coles	0		
J. C. Tongue c Gidman b Coles	4		
Lb 4, nb 6	10	B 12, lb 6, nb 4	22
1/2 (2) 2/45 (3) 3/48 (1) 4/179 (5) 5/208 (6) 6/220 (7) 7/240 (8) 8/330 (4) 9/330 (10) 10/336 (11) (85.4 overs)	336	1/52 (2) 2/164 (3) 3/339 (1) 4/345 (5) 5/355 (6) 6/397 (7) (6 wkts, 81.5 overs)	401

Coles 18.4–5–84–6; Stevens 20–4–84–1; Claydon 15–1–54–0; Yasir Shah 26–5–74–2; Gidman 3–1–17–0; Denly 3–0–19–0. *Second innings*—Coles 15–2–79–0; Stevens 15–0–60–1; Yasir Shah 27.5–1–132–5; Claydon 17–2–78–0; Denly 7–1–34–0.

Umpires: R. K. Illingworth and N. N. Menon.

At Chester-le-Street, June 26–29. WORCESTERSHIRE drew with DURHAM.

At Cheltenham, July 9–12. WORCESTERSHIRE drew with GLOUCESTERSHIRE.

WORCESTERSHIRE v SUSSEX

At Worcester, August 6–8. Sussex won by nine wickets. Sussex 23pts, Worcestershire 4pts. Toss: Sussex. First-class debut: P. R. Brown. County debut: A. J. Robson.

Nash ended a dismal run of form with his first century of the season, and inspired Sussex to a convincing three-day victory. Dropping down from opener – where he had been averaging 17 in the Championship – to No. 5, he rescued his side from 49 for three on the first morning with signature stout defence and forthright pulls. Worcestershire's haplessness was summed up when all-rounder Barnard, twice bowled Archer with no-balls; the second came in the 110th over – the last in which bonuses can be earned – and would have sealed maximum bowling points. Archer lifted Sussex over 400 with 59, then helped the excellent Jordan, who had also struck a fifty, force Worcestershire to follow on with probing accuracy. Finch's razor-sharp work in the slips made him the seventh Sussex fielder to pick up five catches in an innings, and the first since Javed Miandad against Oxford at Pagham in 1976. When Worcestershire went in again, Wiese's three-wicket burst with the new ball effectively sealed a fourth Sussex win in five.

Close of play: first day, Sussex 342-7 (Jordan 57, Archer 6); second day, Worcestershire 231-8 (Barnard 30, Tongue 9).

Sussex

First innings		Second innings	
A. J. Robson c Cox b Leach	0	(2) not out	4
L. W. P. Wells c Mitchell b Rhodes	85	(1) c Leach b Barnard	5
H. Z. Finch c Cox b Tongue	0	not out	2
S. van Zyl c Rhodes b Barnard	24		
C. D. Nash lbw b Leach	118		
*†B. C. Brown c Cox b Barnard	11		
C. J. Jordan b Tongue	58		
D. Wiese c Cox b Barnard	22		
J. C. Archer c Fell b Brown	59		
D. R. Briggs c Fell b Leach	16		
S. G. Whittingham not out	11		
B 2, lb 10, nb 14	26		
1/0 (1) 2/7 (3) 3/49 (4) 4/146 (2) 5/180 (6) 6/298 (5) 7/335 (8) 8/353 (7) 9/391 (10) 10/430 (9) — (120.1 overs)	430	1/5 (1) — (1 wkt, 2.5 overs)	11
110 overs: 391-8			

Leach 22–4–94–3; Tongue 25–6–64–2; Hastings 19–8–42–0; Barnard 26–3–93–3; Brown 12.1–0–73–1; Rhodes 4–0–12–1; D'Oliveira 12–0–40–0. *Second innings*—Brown 1.5–0–10–0; Barnard 1–0–1–1.

Worcestershire

First innings		Second innings	
D. K. H. Mitchell c Finch b Archer	7	b Wiese	6
B. L. D'Oliveira c Finch b Wiese	27	lbw b Whittingham	28
T. C. Fell c Archer b Jordan	12	c Finch b Wiese	0
J. M. Clarke c Finch b Jordan	77	b Wiese	14
G. H. Rhodes b Briggs	13	c Brown b Whittingham	9
†O. B. Cox c Finch b Archer	0	lbw b Archer	28
E. G. Barnard not out	65	c Whittingham b van Zyl	46
*J. Leach lbw b Jordan	1	c Jordan b Archer	0
J. W. Hastings c Finch b van Zyl	34	c and b Archer	0
J. C. Tongue c Brown b Jordan	9	lbw b Briggs	16
P. R. Brown c Brown b Wiese	2	not out	5
B 4, lb 15, nb 2	21	B 4, lb 8, nb 6	18
1/39 (1) 2/58 (2) 3/60 (3) 4/137 (5) 5/138 (6) 6/165 (4) 7/167 (8) 8/215 (9) 9/234 (10) 10/268 (11) — (73.5 overs)	268	1/15 (1) 2/19 (3) 3/41 (4) 4/65 (5) 5/66 (2) 6/110 (6) 7/110 (8) 8/110 (9) 9/154 (10) 10/170 (7) — (45.1 overs)	170

Jordan 21–5–77–4; Archer 20–1–61–2; Wiese 10.5–1–43–2; Whittingham 5–0–30–0; Briggs 16–4–37–1; van Zyl 1–0–1–1. *Second innings*—Jordan 10–1–25–0; Wiese 12–2–35–3; Archer 9–1–39–3; Whittingham 7–0–30–2; Briggs 4–1–15–1; van Zyl 3.1–0–14–1.

Umpires: J. H. Evans and R. J. Evans.

WORCESTERSHIRE v GLOUCESTERSHIRE

At Worcester, August 28–31. Worcestershire won by 189 runs. Worcestershire 23pts, Gloucestershire 5pts. Toss: Worcestershire. County debut: R. Ashwin.

A used pitch held together well, but there was enough turn towards the end for Indian off-spinner Ravichandran Ashwin to seal a Worcestershire win with a five-for on debut; he left the field to a standing ovation. Earlier, D'Oliveira's 93 was the cornerstone of Worcestershire's first innings, which contained useful contributions throughout. Norwell picked up four wickets and was easily the biggest threat, but Gloucestershire had to struggle without him for much of the opening day after he dislocated a finger fielding a return drive. After lunch on the second, they were struggling even more: Barnard's superb burst of three for nought in 14 balls helped reduce them to 93 for five. Jack Taylor prevented the follow-on with a century, his fourth in four Championship matches against Worcestershire. But it hardly mattered. Mitchell hit his fifth first-class hundred of the summer, before a declaration on the third evening. It left Gloucestershire pursuing a notional 401, but they subsided to Ashwin and Leach, who claimed his 50th first-class scalp of 2017.

Close of play: first day, Worcestershire 338-7 (Cox 56, Leach 0); second day, Worcestershire 10-0 (Mitchell 5, D'Oliveira 4); third day, Gloucestershire 55-3 (Roderick 17, Smith 2).

Worcestershire

First innings		Second innings	
D. K. H. Mitchell c Bancroft b Norwell	6	– run out	130
B. L. D'Oliveira c Tavaré b Smith	93	– b Norwell	55
T. C. Fell lbw b Smith	38	– c Roderick b Norwell	0
J. M. Clarke c Dent b Noema-Barnett	32	– c Norwell b Smith	5
G. H. Rhodes c Hankins b Smith	19	– lbw b Smith	45
R. Ashwin c Dent b Norwell	36	– c Hankins b Norwell	28
†O. B. Cox b Norwell	61	– run out	15
E. G. Barnard run out	46	– not out	3
*J. Leach b Miles	17	– st Roderick b Smith	7
J. C. Tongue not out	0		
P. R. Brown c Roderick b Norwell	3		
B 2, lb 6, w 2, nb 2	12	Lb 4, w 1, nb 2	7
1/10 (1) 2/82 (3) 3/143 (4) (102.4 overs)	363	1/76 (2) (8 wkts dec, 71.4 overs)	295
4/186 (5) 5/206 (2) 6/252 (6)		2/76 (3) 3/95 (4)	
7/338 (8) 8/360 (7) 9/360 (9) 10/363 (11)		4/209 (5) 5/264 (6)	
		6/284 (1) 7/286 (7) 8/295 (9)	

Norwell 15–2–54–4; Noema-Barnett 20.4–5–80–1; Miles 16–1–81–1; Smith 31–6–82–3; Taylor 20–3–58–0. *Second innings*—Norwell 20–2–73–3; Miles 12–1–65–0; Smith 19.4–1–73–3; Noema-Barnett 5–0–10–0; Taylor 15–2–70–0.

Gloucestershire

C. T. Bancroft b Barnard	33	– c Cox b Leach	14
C. D. J. Dent c Clarke b Tongue	22	– c Rhodes b Ashwin	16
W. A. Tavaré c and b Barnard	9	– b Ashwin	0
†G. H. Roderick c and b Ashwin	9	– b Leach	47
G. T. Hankins b Barnard	4	– (6) lbw b Ashwin	0
*P. Mustard run out	29	– (7) c Leach b Brown	40
J. M. R. Taylor not out	101	– (8) lbw b Ashwin	43
K. Noema-Barnett lbw b Ashwin	15	– (9) c Brown b Ashwin	22
T. M. J. Smith lbw b Rhodes	8	– (5) lbw b Barnard	9
C. N. Miles c Barnard b Ashwin	7	– not out	4
L. C. Norwell b Barnard	0	– b Leach	0
B 11, lb 8, nb 2	21	B 12, lb 1, nb 3	16
1/38 (2) 2/70 (3) 3/73 (1) 4/79 (5) 5/93 (4) 6/171 (6) 7/206 (8) 8/225 (9) 9/255 (10) 10/258 (11) (75.3 overs)	258	1/25 (1) 2/26 (3) 3/51 (2) 4/72 (5) 5/75 (6) 6/105 (4) 7/176 (7) 8/202 (8) 9/211 (9) 10/211 (11) (77.2 overs)	211

Leach 9–1–36–0; Tongue 7–1–22–1; Ashwin 29–1–94–3; Barnard 13.3–4–23–4; D'Oliveira 5–0–27–0; Rhodes 12–2–37–1. *Second innings*—Leach 16.2–5–50–3; Tongue 6–1–20–0; Ashwin 34–8–68–5; Rhodes 2–0–9–0; Barnard 9–1–17–1; D'Oliveira 2–0–5–0; Brown 8–2–29–1.

Umpires: P. J. Hartley and A. G. Wharf.

At Nottingham, September 5–8. WORCESTERSHIRE beat NOTTINGHAMSHIRE by eight wickets.

WORCESTERSHIRE v LEICESTERSHIRE

At Worcester, September 12–15. Worcestershire won by six wickets. Worcestershire 24pts, Leicestershire 6pts. Toss: Leicestershire.

Worcestershire went top for the first time, overtaking Nottinghamshire with a third straight win, despite an outstanding performance from 20-year-old left-arm spinner Callum Parkinson. He took eight for 148 in their first innings – doubling his previous best haul – then added two more in the second. But Parkinson didn't get enough support as Worcestershire, replying to 404, fought back impressively. D'Oliveira defied a persistent shoulder problem with a nuggety 138, before the lower order, so often a strength, helped establish a lead of 89. A three-day finish looked likely when Leach and Tongue reduced Leicestershire to ten for four. But an eighth-wicket stand of 103 between Hill and Chappell kept Worcestershire waiting until the final afternoon when, with rain imminent, they hurried to a modest target. On the first day, Cosgrove completed 1,000 Championship runs for a third successive season, before Dexter hustled to a century in 120 balls.

Close of play: first day, Leicestershire 325-7 (Dexter 102, Chappell 32); second day, Worcestershire 270-4 (D'Oliveira 121, Tongue 0); third day, Leicestershire 111-7 (Hill 18).

Leicestershire

Batsman	First innings		Second innings	
M. A. Carberry c Cox b Tongue	5	–	b Leach	1
E. J. H. Eckersley c Mitchell b Leach	12	–	c Cox b Tongue	0
C. N. Ackermann b Barnard	4	–	c Cox b Tongue	4
*M. J. Cosgrove c Clarke b Barnard	74	–	lbw b Leach	0
A. M. Ali lbw b Leach	40	–	lbw b Barnard	24
N. J. Dexter lbw b Ashwin	114	–	lbw b Ashwin	48
†L. J. Hill lbw b Tongue	33	–	c D'Oliveira b Ashwin	60
B. A. Raine b Leach	3	–	c Mitchell b Ashwin	10
Z. J. Chappell c Fell b Brown	48	–	c D'Oliveira b Brown	66
D. Klein b Ashwin	26	–	c Clarke b Brown	0
C. F. Parkinson not out	22	–	not out	0
B 5, lb 14, nb 4	23		B 1, lb 6	7
1/19 (1) 2/21 (2) 3/25 (3) 4/129 (5) 5/172 (4) 6/272 (7) 7/285 (8) 8/354 (6) 9/360 (9) 10/404 (10) — (114.4 overs); 110 overs: 379-9	404		1/0 (2) 2/4 (3) 3/5 (4) 4/10 (1) 5/59 (5) 6/97 (6) 7/111 (8) 8/214 (9) 9/216 (10) 10/220 (7) — (63.2 overs)	220

Leach 25–4–80–3; Tongue 19–3–60–2; Barnard 20–6–58–2; Ashwin 36.4–5–132–2; Brown 14–1–55–1. *Second innings*—Leach 10–3–27–2; Tongue 10–1–36–2; Ashwin 25.2–2–94–3; Barnard 14–2–41–1; Brown 4–1–15–2.

Worcestershire

Batsman	First innings		Second innings	
D. K. H. Mitchell c Klein b Parkinson	58	–	b Parkinson	24
B. L. D'Oliveira c and b Parkinson	138	–	b Parkinson	15
T. C. Fell b Parkinson	0	–	b Raine	18
J. M. Clarke c Eckersley b Raine	28	–	lbw b Ali	35
G. H. Rhodes c Carberry b Parkinson	47	–	not out	22
J. C. Tongue st Hill b Parkinson	10			
R. Ashwin c Eckersley b Parkinson	44	–	(6) not out	5
†O. B. Cox c Klein b Parkinson	77			
E. G. Barnard c Hill b Raine	30			
*J. Leach c and b Parkinson	28			
P. R. Brown not out	2			
B 10, lb 9, nb 12	31		B 2, lb 4, w 1, nb 6	13
1/119 (1) 2/120 (3) 3/161 (4) 4/270 (5) 5/294 (6) 6/313 (2) 7/380 (7) 8/443 (9) 9/486 (10) 10/493 (8) — (118 overs); 110 overs: 453-8	493		1/40 (2) 2/51 (1) 3/69 (3) 4/124 (4) — (4 wkts, 30.2 overs)	132

Klein 12–2–67–0; Raine 31–7–90–2; Chappell 16–0–108–0; Parkinson 45–1–148–8; Dexter 11–2–40–0; Ali 3–0–21–0. *Second innings*—Raine 12–1–43–1; Chappell 3–0–16–0; Parkinson 11–1–37–2; Klein 3.2–0–20–0; Ali 1–0–10–1.

Umpires: N. L. Bainton and P. J. Hartley.

WORCESTERSHIRE v DURHAM

At Worcester, September 25–28. Worcestershire won by 137 runs. Worcestershire 22pts, Durham 4pts. Toss: Worcestershire. First-class debut: L. Trevaskis.

Worcestershire secured a fifth promotion in 12 seasons under director of cricket Steve Rhodes, and finished top of Division Two for the first time since 2003. Their first objective was achieved on the third morning, when rivals Northamptonshire failed to gather maximum batting points at Leicester. Victory a day later – their 15th in 25 Championship matches since May 2016 – ensured Worcestershire finished top, ahead of Nottinghamshire, who had led for most of the season. After a shortened first day (when Onions announced this game would be his last for Durham) a classy 82 from Ashwin and a career-best 75 from Barnard lifted Worcestershire to 335. The home bowlers then whistled through Durham before lunch on the third – the last six fell for 68 – then Mitchell's golden summer continued with a seventh hundred. The declaration set Durham 370 in 76 overs, but they were plunging to defeat after Leach's early double strike; one more took him to 69 wickets for the season, the most in Division Two. Clark and Collingwood held up the victory parade but, after they departed in quick succession, Ashwin soon completed another five-for, and his fourth victory in four games.

Close of play: first day, Worcestershire 90-3 (Clarke 46, Rhodes 5); second day, Durham 142-5 (Richardson 12, Pringle 1); third day, Worcestershire 157-3 (Mitchell 68, Rhodes 21).

Worcestershire

First innings		Second innings	
D. K. H. Mitchell c Jennings b Rushworth	5	– not out	123
B. L. D'Oliveira c Collingwood b Jennings	22	– lbw b Onions	4
T. C. Fell b Onions	1	– lbw b Pringle	47
J. M. Clarke c Collingwood b Onions	65	– c Clark b Pringle	5
G. H. Rhodes lbw b Pringle	9	– not out	51
R. Ashwin lbw b Trevaskis	82		
†O. B. Cox b Steel	30		
E. G. Barnard b Wood	75		
*J. Leach c Clark b Onions	10		
J. C. Tongue b Onions	10		
P. R. Brown not out	0		
B 8, lb 12, nb 6	26	B 4, lb 2, nb 6	12
1/10 (1) 2/13 (3) 3/69 (2) (90.2 overs)	335	1/10 (2) (3 wkts dec, 55 overs)	242
4/113 (4) 5/132 (5) 6/198 (7)		2/123 (3) 3/131 (4)	
7/284 (6) 8/307 (9) 9/319 (10) 10/335 (8)			

Rushworth 17–4–36–1; Onions 22–5–68–4; Wood 14.2–2–46–1; Trevaskis 16–2–69–1; Jennings 2–0–10–1; Pringle 11–1–54–1; Steel 8–0–32–1. *Second innings*—Rushworth 12–2–37–0; Onions 10–2–33–1; Wood 8–1–26–0; Trevaskis 10–1–57–0; Steel 3–0–32–0; Pringle 12–0–51–2.

Durham

First innings		Second innings	
C. T. Steel c Cox b Leach	10	– lbw b Leach	5
K. K. Jennings c Cox b Tongue	9	– c Mitchell b Ashwin	20
J. T. A. Burnham b Tongue	4	– lbw b Leach	11
G. Clark c and b Leach	60	– lbw b Barnard	62
*P. D. Collingwood b Ashwin	27	– lbw b Barnard	36
†M. J. Richardson not out	45	– b Leach	17
R. D. Pringle c Cox b Leach	2	– c Rhodes b Ashwin	6
L. Trevaskis lbw b Ashwin	5	– c Mitchell b Ashwin	9
M. A. Wood b Barnard	0	– not out	33
C. Rushworth c Mitchell b Barnard	9	– b Ashwin	0
G. Onions c Mitchell b Brown	13	– c Clarke b Ashwin	15
B 6, lb 10, nb 8	24	B 10, lb 1, w 1, nb 6	18
1/12 (2) 2/24 (3) 3/30 (1) (63.4 overs)	208	1/6 (1) 2/34 (3) (56.2 overs)	232
4/106 (5) 5/140 (4) 6/144 (7)		3/48 (2) 4/136 (5)	
7/165 (8) 8/166 (9) 9/178 (10) 10/208 (11)		5/145 (4) 6/160 (7) 7/173 (6)	
		8/201 (8) 9/201 (10) 10/232 (11)	

Leach 15–3–30–3; Tongue 10–3–25–2; Ashwin 24–9–53–2; Barnard 11–2–39–2; Rhodes 2–0–36–0; Brown 1.4–0–9–1. *Second innings*—Leach 12–4–32–3; Tongue 11–0–58–0; Ashwin 23.2–1–95–5; Barnard 9–2–28–2; Brown 1–0–8–0.

Umpires: S. C. Gale and S. J. O'Shaughnessy.

YORKSHIRE

Pair of aces lift ordinary hand

DAVID WARNER

All that glistered early on was not gold. Yorkshire led both the Royal London Cup and the NatWest T20 Blast tables for a while, and were briefly second in the County Championship, but lost their shine: they failed to make the semi-finals in either limited-overs competition, and flirted with relegation. Fourth place in the Championship sounded respectable, but it was just two points above Middlesex, who went down. Only a narrow win against bottom side Warwickshire in the penultimate match, and the squandering of bonus points by other teams, saved them.

Yorkshire had expected to expand on five strong years under Jason Gillespie. But his successor as coach, former captain Andrew Gale, was unable to continue a sequence which started with promotion and brought top-three finishes, including two titles, over the next four seasons. Gale needed to rebuild if his side were to claim their first Championship without an Australian coach since 1968 (Wayne Clark had been in charge in 2001). They were weakened by pre-season injuries and international duty, but the call-ups were not unexpected and there was ample cover.

There were, though, two encouraging early developments. It was soon evident that Gary Ballance's first summer as captain would not weigh heavily on his shoulders. He made a blazing start – with a fifty, two hundreds and a double in four innings against Hampshire in April – and won back his Test place after 815 runs gushed from the first half of the Championship. But time out with a broken finger disturbed his rhythm.

Then there was the dramatic impact of Ben Coad, a 23-year-old from Harrogate, who had gained a yard of pace over the winter. Called in when five senior seamers were unavailable, he was straight out of the blocks with 18 wickets in two games; his place cemented, he remained Yorkshire's most successful bowler, with 50 Championship wickets at 20 apiece.

The problem was that nobody else came close to matching either his wickets or Ballance's 951 Championship runs at 67. Adam Lyth was the second-leading run-scorer with 555 at 25, though he was more effective in the white-ball arena; Tim Bresnan, no longer an all-round force, was Coad's nearest rival, with 27 wickets at 32. Ryan Sidebottom, in his farewell season – his debut had been in 1997 – was his usual in-your-face self when available, but injuries kept him out of the first three matches and the last two, and he was briefly rested in June because of fatigue. Sidebottom was not fit enough for a last hurrah against Warwickshire, making do with a guard of honour and a standing ovation in recognition of his 450 first-class wickets for Yorkshire.

Peter Handscomb, the main overseas player, gave satisfactory service, with 1,042 runs in 25 matches across the three formats, and his fellow Australian

Stephen Pond, Getty Images

Ben Coad

Shaun Marsh was a steadying influence in the Blast. But Sarfraz Ahmed and Kraigg Brathwaite, who was brought on board after shining for West Indies in the Headingley Test, had no impact. Brathwaite's presence in the last two Championship matches served only to squeeze out the talented Tom Köhler-Cadmore, signed from Worcestershire mid-season to return to the county where he played age-group cricket. In December, it was announced that New Zealand captain Kane Williamson would return for his fourth stint at the club. Indian Test batsman Cheteshwar Pujara signed for the early part of 2018.

Shortly before his death in March, Yorkshire president John Hampshire had said he hoped the team could be as successful in limited-overs cricket as in the Championship, and felt a trophy was imperative. Things looked promising when they romped home in their first three 50-over games; Jonny Bairstow's 174 against Durham was Yorkshire's third-highest one-day score, and their best by a home-grown player. Positive batting and shrewd bowling, especially from off-spinner Azeem Rafiq, saw them breeze into the quarter-finals, with six wins out of eight; then they came up against Kumar Sangakkara, and his 100th century in all formats. He made the White Rose wilt again with a pink-ball hundred in Headingley's first day/night Championship game, and another in the return (red-ball) match at The Oval.

After starting off the T20 Blast with a win, a defeat, an abandonment and a Roses tie, Yorkshire went top with a hat-trick of victories in which David Willey was in destructive form. His 118 against Worcestershire was briefly the county's best in T20 cricket, yet he was upstaged when Sheffield-born Ross Whiteley plundered six sixes in an over off slow left-armer Karl Carver. From a position of strength, Yorkshire lost out in three tight finishes and were unable to claw it back, despite Lyth's thunderous 161 – an English T20 record – against Northamptonshire.

The season ended on a dismal note, with Yorkshire suffering their heaviest defeat by runs against the unbeatable new champions, Essex. But not all was gloom and doom. Coad claimed at least one wicket in every Championship innings in which he bowled, while Matthew Fisher returned from injury setbacks towards the end of the season to prove he was still one of the most promising all-rounders in the country. Most crucially, Yorkshire remained a top-tier county.

Championship attendance: 46,394.

YORKSHIRE RESULTS

All first-class matches – Played 15: Won 5, Lost 5, Drawn 5.
County Championship matches – Played 14: Won 4, Lost 5, Drawn 5.

Specsavers County Championship, 4th in Division 1;
NatWest T20 Blast, 5th in North Group; Royal London One-Day Cup, quarter-finalists.

COUNTY CHAMPIONSHIP AVERAGES, BATTING AND FIELDING

Cap		Birthplace	M	I	NO	R	HS	100	Avge	Ct
2012	†G. S. Ballance§	*Harare, Zimbabwe*	12	18	4	951	203*	3	67.92	3
	P. S. P. Handscomb¶	*Box Hill, Australia*	9	14	1	441	101*	1	33.92	7
2016	J. A. Leaning	*Bristol*	10	15	0	454	118	1	30.26	5
2010	†A. Lyth	*Whitby‡*	13	23	1	555	100	1	25.22	19
	T. Köhler-Cadmore	*Chatham*	3	6	0	151	78	0	25.16	1
2014	†A. Z. Lees	*Halifax‡*	14	25	3	531	102	1	24.13	7
2016	A. J. Hodd	*Chichester*	12	19	1	428	59	0	23.77	39
2008	A. U. Rashid§	*Bradford‡*	7	10	1	211	65	0	23.44	0
	M. D. Fisher	*York‡*	2	4	0	86	37	0	21.50	0
2013	J. A. Brooks	*Oxford*	8	11	2	178	109*	1	19.77	2
2000	†R. J. Sidebottom	*Huddersfield‡*	8	11	8	57	12*	0	19.00	2
2006	T. T. Bresnan	*Pontefract‡*	11	15	0	284	61	0	18.93	8
2012	S. A. Patterson	*Beverley‡*	9	13	4	165	44*	0	18.33	5
	H. C. Brook	*Keighley‡*	4	6	0	82	38	0	13.66	1
	†K. Carver	*Northallerton‡*	2	4	0	48	20	0	12.00	2
	B. O. Coad	*Harrogate‡*	12	16	5	128	28	0	11.63	1
	K. C. Brathwaite¶	*Belfield, Barbados*	2	4	0	40	18	0	10.00	1
2016	Azeem Rafiq	*Karachi, Pakistan*	5	7	0	54	17	0	7.71	0

Also batted: J. M. Bairstow§ (*Bradford‡*) (cap 2011) (2 matches) 7, 1 (7 ct); †S. E. Marsh¶ (*Narrogin, Australia*) (2 matches) 22, 78, 125* (1 ct); L. E. Plunkett§ (*Middlesbrough‡*) (cap 2013) (2 matches) 19, 39, 34; J. E. Root§ (*Sheffield‡*) (cap 2012) (2 matches) 8, 2, 12*; J. Shaw (*Wakefield‡*) (1 match) 3, 0; M. J. Waite (*Leeds*) (1 match) 4, 18; †D. J. Willey§ (*Northampton*) (cap 2016) (2 matches) 19, 8.

‡ *Born in Yorkshire.* § *ECB contract.* ¶ *Official overseas player.*

BOWLING

	Style	O	M	R	W	BB	5I	Avge
R. J. Sidebottom	LFM	186.4	43	518	25	5-56	1	20.72
B. O. Coad	RFM	356.4	93	1,043	50	6-25	4	20.86
S. A. Patterson	RFM	280.2	72	754	23	4-46	0	32.78
T. T. Bresnan	RFM	240	49	887	27	4-53	0	32.85
J. A. Brooks	RFM	205	24	865	23	5-113	1	37.60
A. U. Rashid	LB	108	10	500	10	3-94	0	50.00

Also bowled: Azeem Rafiq (OB) 107–13–393–5; H. C. Brook (RM) 19–4–65–1; K. Carver (SLA) 35.2–4–118–4; M. D. Fisher (RFM) 60.3–11–195–8; J. A. Leaning (RFM) 6–0–26–0; A. Lyth (OB) 39.3–2–127–2; L. E. Plunkett (RFM) 43–11–136–6; J. E. Root (OB) 13.4–0–53–1; J. Shaw (RFM) 16–3–59–0; M. J. Waite (RFM) 16–0–70–3; D. J. Willey (LFM) 60–15–148–4.

LEADING ROYAL LONDON CUP AVERAGES (100 runs/4 wickets)

Batting	Runs	HS	Avge	SR	Ct
G. S. Ballance	483	152*	69.00	105.00	2
P. S. P. Handscomb	504	140	63.00	109.56	9/1
J. E. Root	241	83	60.25	84.56	1
J. M. Bairstow	268	174	53.60	115.51	5/1
M. J. Waite	185	71	37.00	97.88	0
A. Lyth	304	75	33.77	95.89	10
T. T. Bresnan	138	65	23.00	80.70	4

Bowling	W	BB	Avge	ER
K. Carver	5	3-24	22.60	4.70
Azeem Rafiq	18	4-47	22.66	5.78
B. O. Coad	8	4-63	24.37	6.50
D. J. Willey	6	2-22	25.83	6.24
M. J. Waite	10	4-65	28.40	6.68
A. U. Rashid	6	2-34	35.66	4.86
T. T. Bresnan	9	3-22	39.55	5.65
M. D. Fisher	6	2-73	52.83	6.74

LEADING NATWEST T20 BLAST AVERAGES (100 runs/15 overs)

Batting	*Runs*	*HS*	*Avge*	*SR*	*Ct*
D. J. Willey	446	118	40.54	**168.30**	6
A. Lyth	535	161	44.58	**164.61**	7
T. Köhler-Cadmore	286	75	26.00	**156.28**	8
J. A. Leaning	161	32*	26.83	**150.46**	8
T. T. Bresnan	105	24	21.00	**140.00**	3
S. E. Marsh	289	60*	41.28	**127.31**	1

Bowling	*W*	*BB*	*Avge*	*ER*
A. U. Rashid	15	4-19	22.73	**7.10**
S. A. Patterson	14	3-37	24.21	**8.10**
Azeem Rafiq	17	5-19	21.64	**8.36**
T. T. Bresnan	17	6-19	19.88	**8.55**
D. J. Willey	11	2-23	31.72	**9.43**

FIRST-CLASS COUNTY RECORDS

Highest score for	341	G. H. Hirst v Leicestershire at Leicester	1905
Highest score against	318*	W. G. Grace (Gloucestershire) at Cheltenham	1876
Leading run-scorer	38,558	H. Sutcliffe (avge 50.20)	1919–45
Best bowling for	10-10	H. Verity v Nottinghamshire at Leeds	1932
Best bowling against	10-37	C. V. Grimmett (Australians) at Sheffield	1930
Leading wicket-taker	3,597	W. Rhodes (avge 16.02)	1898–1930
Highest total for	887	v Warwickshire at Birmingham	1896
Highest total against	681-7 dec	by Leicestershire at Bradford	1996
Lowest total for	23	v Hampshire at Middlesbrough	1965
Lowest total against	13	by Nottinghamshire at Nottingham	1901

LIST A COUNTY RECORDS

Highest score for	191	D. S. Lehmann v Nottinghamshire at Scarborough	2001
Highest score against	177	S. A. Newman (Surrey) at The Oval	2009
Leading run-scorer	8,699	G. Boycott (avge 40.08)	1963–86
Best bowling for	7-15	R. A. Hutton v Worcestershire at Leeds	1969
Best bowling against	7-32	R. G. D. Willis (Warwickshire) at Birmingham	1981
Leading wicket-taker	308	C. M. Old (avge 18.96)	1967–82
Highest total for	411-6	v Devon at Exmouth	2004
Highest total against	375-4	by Surrey at Scarborough	1994
Lowest total for	54	v Essex at Leeds	2003
Lowest total against	23	by Middlesex at Leeds	1974

TWENTY20 COUNTY RECORDS

Highest score for	**161**	**A. Lyth v Northamptonshire at Leeds**	**2017**
Highest score against	111	D. L. Maddy (Leicestershire) at Leeds	2004
Leading run-scorer	2,260	A. W. Gale (avge 25.39)	2004–15
Best bowling for	**6-19**	**T. T. Bresnan v Lancashire at Leeds**	**2017**
Best bowling against	4-9	C. K. Langeveldt (Derbyshire) at Leeds	2008
Leading wicket-taker	108	R. M. Pyrah (avge 21.43)	2005–15
Highest total for	**260-4**	**v Northamptonshire at Leeds**	**2017**
Highest total against	231-4	by Lancashire at Manchester	2015
Lowest total for	90-9	v Durham at Chester-le-Street	2009
Lowest total against	90	by Glamorgan at Cardiff	2016

ADDRESS

Emerald Headingley, Leeds LS6 3BU; 0843 504 3099; cricket@yorkshireccc.com; www.yorkshireccc.com.

OFFICIALS

Captain G. S. Ballance
Director of cricket M. D. Moxon
First-team coach A. W. Gale
2nd XI coach and academy director I. M. Dews
President R. A. Hutton
Chairman S. J. Denison
Chief executive M. A. Arthur
Head groundsman A. Fogarty
Scorer J. T. Potter

YORKSHIRE v LEEDS/BRADFORD MCCU

At Leeds, April 2–4. Yorkshire won by an innings and 224 runs. Toss: Yorkshire. First-class debut: D. Houghton.

Ben Coad, who appeared to have added pace and accuracy during the winter, stood out in a Yorkshire attack depleted by pre-season injuries, with match figures of 30–15–38–3. The students could not muster a half-century in either innings, and their bowlers generally provided easy pickings. Lees rushed to a century in 103 balls, while Lyth enjoyed six hours in the middle, hitting four sixes, though he just missed a double-hundred. Although weary and footsore by the time Ballance declared, Leeds/Bradford kept their spirits up, holding out until 3pm on the final day.

Close of play: first day, Yorkshire 179-1 (Lyth 61, Callis 2); second day, Leeds/Bradford MCCU 40-0 (Bullen 28, Shoare 9).

Leeds/Bradford MCCU

*S. F. G. Bullen c Lyth b Coad	5 – lbw b Bresnan	29
B. J. Shoare lbw b Coad	0 – lbw b Bresnan	9
M. K. Andersson c Bresnan b Patterson	12 – c Lees b Coad	1
P. F. McDermott lbw b Patterson	20 – lbw b Patterson	15
O. J. G. Graham run out	41 – b Bresnan	1
C. D. Wallace c Leaning b Patterson	35 – lbw b Shaw	32
†J. T. Potticary lbw b Shaw	9 – lbw b Lyth	12
W. Cook b Azeem Rafiq	0 – st Hodd b Azeem Rafiq	42
S. A. Feszczur-Hatchett lbw b Azeem Rafiq	0 – b Azeem Rafiq	1
D. Houghton not out	6 – c Lyth b Azeem Rafiq	29
O. S. Bocking c Lyth b Shaw	0 – not out	1
B 2, lb 7	9 B 4, lb 6	10
1/4 (2) 2/13 (1) 3/24 (3) 4/57 (4) 5/122 (6) 6/123 (5) 7/123 (8) 8/123 (9) 9/137 (7) 10/137 (11) (64.1 overs)	137 1/41 (1) 2/42 (2) 3/42 (3) 4/45 (5) 5/81 (4) 6/95 (6) 7/106 (7) 8/111 (9) 9/177 (10) 10/182 (8) (60.4 overs)	182

Bresnan 14–4–35–0; Coad 15–9–17–2; Shaw 13.1–4–35–2; Patterson 15–4–25–3; Azeem Rafiq 7–2–16–2. *Second innings*—Coad 15–6–21–1; Shaw 12–0–57–1; Bresnan 8–3–12–3; Patterson 11–2–29–1; Azeem Rafiq 13.4–2–50–3; Lyth 1–0–3–1.

Yorkshire

A. Lyth b Cook	194
A. Z. Lees b Graham	100
E. Callis lbw b Bocking	17
*G. S. Ballance c Andersson b Shoare	72
J. A. Leaning not out	64
T. T. Bresnan lbw b Graham	46
†A. J. Hodd not out	8
B 1, lb 8, w 2, nb 31	42
1/174 (2) 2/222 (3) 3/376 (4) 4/439 (1) 5/519 (6) (5 wkts dec, 120 overs)	543

Azeem Rafiq, S. A. Patterson, J. Shaw and B. O. Coad did not bat.

Bocking 27–2–116–1; Feszczur-Hatchett 22–3–98–0; Graham 22–3–90–2; Houghton 25–2–108–0; Cook 16–1–94–1; Shoare 8–0–28–1.

Umpires: S. C. Gale and S. A. Garratt.

YORKSHIRE v HAMPSHIRE

At Leeds, April 7–9. Hampshire won by four wickets. Hampshire 19pts, Yorkshire 5pts. Toss: uncontested. County debuts: P. S. P. Handscomb; R. R. Rossouw.

Hampshire turned the tables by chasing down 320 for a three-day win. Yorkshire had led by 247 when they reached 115 for three in their second innings. Then they hit the rocks, while Hampshire found the grit they had lacked. The sun had been slow to appear on the first day; with the ball nipping around off a good length, Ballance batted resolutely while team-mates struggled, then shared an eighth-wicket stand of 106 with Patterson. By the close, Hampshire were 58 for five, all to the unerring Coad, playing his second Championship match because five seamers were injured. Next morning, he added a sixth, before Bresnan took the last four. Abbott responded in kind with Yorkshire's first five, and finished with seven. Ballance again stood alone until Hodd hit a spate of boundaries. Thirty wickets had fallen in two days, but Hampshire were unfazed, despite both openers being dropped early on the third; Adams made 72, six others reached 30, and Berg hit a six to win in the first over of the extra half-hour. Their coach Craig White rated this win against his old county among the best he had seen.

Close of play: first day, Hampshire 58-5 (Abbott 2, Dawson 0); second day, Hampshire 10-0 (Carberry 5, Adams 5).

Yorkshire

First innings		Second innings	
A. Lyth c McManus b Berg	30	c McManus b Abbott	29
A. Z. Lees b Edwards	20	lbw b Abbott	21
P. S. P. Handscomb b Edwards	25	c Ervine b Abbott	4
*G. S. Ballance b Dawson	120	c McManus b Wheal	55
J. A. Leaning lbw b Berg	7	lbw b Abbott	15
T. T. Bresnan b Edwards	0	c Dawson b Abbott	0
†A. J. Hodd c Rossouw b Abbott	0	not out	54
Azeem Rafiq b Abbott	6	c Ervine b Dawson	2
S. A. Patterson not out	37	lbw b Abbott	2
J. Shaw lbw b Dawson	3	b Abbott	0
B. O. Coad c Vince b Wheal	4	b Berg	0
B 8, lb 8, w 1, nb 4	21	Lb 5	5
1/41 (2) 2/59 (1) 3/110 (3) 4/125 (5) 5/132 (6) 6/132 (7) 7/152 (8) 8/258 (4) 9/266 (10) 10/273 (11) (76.5 overs)	273	1/40 (1) 2/44 (3) 3/59 (2) 4/115 (5) 5/115 (6) 6/156 (4) 7/165 (8) 8/186 (9) 9/186 (10) 10/187 (11) (55.3 overs)	187

Edwards 14–1–58–3; Abbott 20–5–64–2; Berg 19–4–50–2; Wheal 9.5–1–54–1; Ervine 3–1–7–0; Dawson 11–4–24–2. *Second innings*—Edwards 7–0–36–0; Abbott 14–3–41–7; Berg 13.3–2–37–1; Dawson 12–0–46–1; Wheal 9–1–22–1.

Hampshire

First innings		Second innings	
M. A. Carberry c Leaning b Coad	22	c Patterson b Coad	41
J. H. K. Adams lbw b Coad	5	lbw b Azeem Rafiq	72
*J. M. Vince c Lees b Coad	6	c and b Coad	44
R. R. Rossouw lbw b Coad	23	c Hodd b Bresnan	47
S. M. Ervine c Ballance b Coad	0	c Hodd b Bresnan	8
K. J. Abbott c Leaning b Coad	9		
L. A. Dawson lbw b Bresnan	9	(6) c and b Bresnan	37
†L. D. McManus not out	41	(7) not out	30
G. K. Berg c Lyth b Bresnan	0	(8) not out	33
B. T. J. Wheal b Bresnan	18		
F. H. Edwards b Bresnan	6		
Lb 2	2	B 6, lb 3	9
1/6 (2) 2/18 (3) 3/49 (1) 4/55 (5) 5/58 (4) 6/71 (6) 7/75 (7) 8/75 (9) 9/127 (10) 10/141 (11) (48.5 overs)	141	1/91 (1) 2/160 (2) 3/176 (3) 4/195 (5) 5/252 (4) 6/263 (6) (6 wkts, 101 overs)	321

Bresnan 13.5–3–53–4; Coad 17–5–37–6; Patterson 12–4–30–0; Shaw 6–1–19–0. *Second innings*—Bresnan 25–8–73–3; Coad 25–4–96–2; Patterson 27–9–62–0; Shaw 10–2–40–0; Azeem Rafiq 12–2–35–1; Lyth 2–0–6–0.

Umpires: R. A. Kettleborough and S. J. O'Shaughnessy.

At Birmingham, April 14–17. YORKSHIRE beat WARWICKSHIRE by an innings and 88 runs.

At Southampton, April 21–24. YORKSHIRE drew with HAMPSHIRE.

At Manchester, May 19–22. YORKSHIRE drew with LANCASHIRE.

At Leeds, May 27. YORKSHIRE v SOUTH AFRICA A. No result.

YORKSHIRE v LANCASHIRE

At Leeds, June 2–4. Yorkshire won by ten wickets. Yorkshire 21pts, Lancashire 3pts. Toss: Lancashire.

Ballance became the first Yorkshire captain born outside the county to secure a Roses victory since Lord Hawke in 1908, while Coad enhanced his claim to be the country's best young bowler, and Lyth made his first Championship hundred of the season. Lancashire were outclassed from the moment Croft chose to bat on a warm, damp first day, when play began at 1.10. No one mastered the pace and movement of Coad, whose career-best six for 25 was his fourth haul of five or more in five games. Yorkshire would have faltered too but for a masterly hundred from Lyth. His first seven Championship innings in 2017 had totalled 90; here, he batted for five hours 16 minutes, starting at a cracking pace against the new ball, then adopting caution as partners came and went. A 150-run lead was less than Yorkshire had wanted, but more than adequate. Coad removed Hameed and Chanderpaul for a second time, Sidebottom excelled and Bresnan wrapped up the innings with three in 16 balls. Lyth and Lees knocked off a target of 60 in 21 overs, all but two bowled by spinners as Lancashire staved off an over-rate penalty.

Close of play: first day, Yorkshire 93-2 (Lyth 40, Ballance 8); second day, Lancashire 141-4 (Chanderpaul 43, Vilas 22).

Lancashire

Batsman	1st inns		2nd inns	
†A. L. Davies c Lees b Sidebottom	9	–	lbw b Brooks	10
H. Hameed c Hodd b Coad	9	–	lbw b Coad	10
L. A. Procter c Hodd b Sidebottom	0	–	c Bresnan b Brooks	23
*S. J. Croft lbw b Coad	16	–	c Lyth b Sidebottom	27
S. Chanderpaul c Handscomb b Coad	3	–	c Hodd b Coad	47
D. J. Vilas c Hodd b Coad	4	–	c Lyth b Sidebottom	22
R. McLaren lbw b Sidebottom	30	–	c Leaning b Bresnan	15
J. Clark lbw b Brooks	7	–	c Hodd b Bresnan	37
S. D. Parry c Lyth b Coad	30	–	c Hodd b Bresnan	8
T. E. Bailey c Lees b Coad	2	–	c Handscomb b Sidebottom	3
S. Mahmood not out	4	–	not out	0
Lb 9	9		B 2, lb 5	7
1/18 (1) 2/18 (3) 3/33 (2) 4/44 (4) 5/47 (5) 6/48 (6) 7/75 (8) 8/89 (7) 9/112 (10) 10/123 (9) (43.4 overs)	123		1/23 (1) 2/33 (2) 3/61 (3) 4/81 (4) 5/145 (6) 6/149 (5) 7/197 (7) 8/198 (8) 9/205 (10) 10/209 (9) (69 overs)	209

Sidebottom 14–5–30–3; Brooks 12–2–40–1; Bresnan 6–0–19–0; Coad 11.4–4–25–6. *Second innings*—Sidebottom 19–7–38–3; Brooks 19–3–75–2; Coad 17–7–34–2; Bresnan 13–3–50–3; Azeem Rafiq 1–0–5–0.

Yorkshire

A. Lyth c Davies b Clark	100	– not out	28
A. Z. Lees c Croft b Bailey	5	– not out	25
P. S. P. Handscomb c Davies b Procter	33		
*G. S. Ballance c Vilas b McLaren	28		
J. A. Leaning c McLaren b Mahmood	15		
T. T. Bresnan c Vilas b Mahmood	0		
†A. J. Hodd c Vilas b Mahmood	23		
Azeem Rafiq c sub (R. P. Jones) b Clark	17		
J. A. Brooks c Hameed b Bailey	18		
B. O. Coad c Davies b Clark	4		
R. J. Sidebottom not out	8		
B 4, lb 3, w 3, nb 12	22	B 4, lb 2, nb 2	8
1/21 (2) 2/85 (3) 3/120 (4) (82 overs)	273	(no wkt, 20.5 overs)	61
4/178 (5) 5/178 (6) 6/214 (7)			
7/236 (8) 8/245 (1) 9/249 (10) 10/273 (9)			

Bailey 18–2–52–2; McLaren 20–6–65–1; Procter 10–1–43–1; Mahmood 22–4–62–3; Clark 12–1–44–3. *Second innings*—Bailey 1–0–9–0; Mahmood 1–0–6–0; Croft 9.5–1–19–0; Parry 6–1–12–0; Hameed 3–0–9–0.

Umpires: R. J. Bailey and M. A. Gough.

At Taunton, June 9–12. YORKSHIRE beat SOMERSET by three runs.

At Lord's, June 19–21. YORKSHIRE lost to MIDDLESEX by an innings and 64 runs.

YORKSHIRE v SURREY

At Leeds, June 26–29 (day/night). Drawn. Yorkshire 7pts, Surrey 10pts. Toss: Surrey. County debut: C. McKerr.

Four times Sangakkara cued the pink for six in a dazzling masterclass which proved that, whatever colour the ball, whatever the conditions, he remained – in his 40th year – one of the world's best. If spectators found it difficult to follow the ball, Sangakkara had no difficulty despatching it to all pockets of the ground. On a rain-hit second day, he advanced from 82 to 180 in a mere 75 minutes and 59 deliveries, the first batsman of the summer to reach 1,000 first-class runs (all in the Championship), in 11 innings. Batty declared when Tom Curran departed after adding 158 with Sangakkara, a seventh-wicket record between these sides which took Surrey to their highest total in Yorkshire; the first day had witnessed authoritative half-centuries from Burns, who gave Bresnan his 500th first-class wicket, and Roy. Ballance was available for two days before leaving to lead England Lions, but never discovered if his colour blindness would impair his batting against the pink ball. Test captain Root managed 15 minutes at the crease before the last two days were washed out.

Close of play: first day, Surrey 374-6 (Sangakkara 82, T. K. Curran 4); second day, Yorkshire 27-1 (Lees 5, Root 12); third day, no play.

Surrey

R. J. Burns c Bairstow b Bresnan	90
M. D. Stoneman c Bairstow b Coad	30
S. G. Borthwick c Brooks b Patterson	31
J. J. Roy lbw b Brooks	87
K. C. Sangakkara not out	180
†B. T. Foakes c Handscomb b Coad	23
S. M. Curran c Bairstow b Patterson	20
T. K. Curran c Patterson b Bresnan	44
B 4, lb 2, w 1, nb 4	11
1/39 (2) (7 wkts dec, 115.1 overs)	516
2/75 (3) 3/222 (4)	
4/271 (1) 5/320 (6)	
6/358 (7) 7/516 (8) 110 overs: 474-6	

*G. J. Batty, C. McKerr and M. H. A. Footitt did not bat.

Coad 24–3–99–2; Brooks 18–1–109–1; Patterson 26–5–73–2; Bresnan 25.1–7–91–2; Rashid 16–0–107–0; Root 6–0–31–0.

Yorkshire

A. Lyth lbw b S. M. Curran	8
A. Z. Lees not out	5
J. E. Root not out	12
Lb 2	2
1/11 (1) (1 wkt, 10.5 overs)	27

H. C. Brook, P. S. P. Handscomb, †J. M. Bairstow, T. T. Bresnan, A. U. Rashid, S. A. Patterson, J. A. Brooks and B. O. Coad.

*Brook replaced *G. S. Ballance, who left to join the England Lions squad.*

T. K. Curran 5.5–1–19–0; S. M. Curran 5–2–6–1.

Umpires: R. A. Kettleborough and N. A. Mallender.

YORKSHIRE v SOMERSET

At Scarborough, July 3–6. Somerset won by 179 runs. Somerset 21pts, Yorkshire 4pts. Toss: Somerset. County debut: T. Köhler-Cadmore. Championship debut: T. D. Rouse.

Yorkshire's title hopes nosedived as they were comprehensively outplayed by Somerset, who registered their first Championship win at the eighth attempt. Even though they lost Sidebottom to a back injury in his fifth over of the match – and Plunkett limped off with a groin strain after bowling six on the third day – Yorkshire could hardly complain. In his first Championship outing of the summer, Plunkett had rattled Somerset with his best figures in nearly two years, but the last pair, Craig Overton and Groenewald, thrashed 61 in eight overs, Groenewald heaving Rashid for three sixes and two fours in six balls. From that point, Somerset never looked back. Overton bowled with pace and hostility for match figures of nine for 134, a career-best; in between, Hildreth hurried to his first century of the season. Somerset promptly declared, setting Yorkshire 337 in 90 overs. Within four, chaos reigned: Lees, Brook and Handscomb all made ducks, undone by Gregory and Overton, who quickly added Köhler-Cadmore, a recent recruit from Worcestershire. The collapse was completed inside 39 overs, delighting Gregory, who was leading Somerset for the first time.

Close of play: first day, Yorkshire 42-3 (Brook 16, Köhler-Cadmore 6); second day, Yorkshire 159-7 (Rashid 30, Plunkett 5); third day, Somerset 234-3 (Hildreth 85, Hose 7).

Somerset

First innings		Second innings	
M. E. Trescothick c Handscomb b Bresnan	15	– c Lyth b Coad	27
E. J. Byrom b Plunkett	9	– b Brook	40
T. D. Rouse c Bresnan b Plunkett	1	– b Coad	69
J. C. Hildreth c Hodd b Bresnan	32	– not out	101
A. J. Hose b Rashid	62	– c Lyth b Bresnan	16
†S. M. Davies lbw b Plunkett	16	– not out	22
J. Allenby b Coad	19		
*L. Gregory b Plunkett	21		
C. Overton b Coad	35		
M. J. Leach c Bresnan b Rashid	3		
T. D. Groenewald not out	41		
B 5, lb 5, nb 4	14	Lb 6	6
1/20 (1) 2/25 (3) 3/30 (2) 4/67 (4) 5/110 (6) 6/141 (7) 7/180 (5) 8/200 (8) 9/207 (10) 10/268 (9) (75.2 overs)	268	1/53 (1) 2/80 (2) 3/224 (3) 4/243 (5) (4 wkts dec, 73 overs)	281

Sidebottom 4.4–2–5–0; Coad 16.2–8–52–2; Bresnan 15.2–4–43–2; Plunkett 21–5–73–4; Rashid 13–2–74–2; Brook 5–2–11–0. *Second innings*—Coad 20–5–62–2; Bresnan 21–4–97–1; Plunkett 6–2–10–0; Brook 14–2–54–1; Rashid 10–0–47–0; Lyth 2–0–5–0.

Yorkshire

Batsman	First innings		Second innings	
A. Lyth	c Allenby b Overton	4	b Gregory	37
A. Z. Lees	c Trescothick b Overton	12	b Gregory	0
H. C. Brook	c Trescothick b Overton	31	c Davies b Overton	0
P. S. P. Handscomb	c Trescothick b Groenewald	2	lbw b Overton	0
T. Köhler-Cadmore	b Groenewald	31	c Rouse b Overton	13
*T. T. Bresnan	c Allenby b Overton	11	b Leach	25
A. U. Rashid	c Overton b Gregory	49	c Allenby b Leach	11
†A. J. Hodd	lbw b Overton	28	c Byrom b Overton	5
L. E. Plunkett	b Gregory	19	c Allenby b Leach	39
B. O. Coad	c Allenby b Groenewald	15	c Hose b Leach	17
R. J. Sidebottom	not out	2	not out	0
	B 4, lb 5	9	B 4, lb 1, w 5	10
	(76.3 overs)	213	(38.3 overs)	157

First innings: 1/13 (1) 2/18 (2) 3/21 (4) 4/71 (3) 5/88 (5) 6/105 (6) 7/153 (8) 8/180 (9) 9/203 (10) 10/213 (7)

Second innings: 1/3 (2) 2/12 (3) 3/12 (4) 4/36 (5) 5/67 (1) 6/91 (6) 7/92 (7) 8/96 (8) 9/133 (10) 10/157 (9)

Gregory 25.3–6–62–2; Overton 24–3–87–5; Groenewald 18–6–43–3; Allenby 9–5–12–0. *Second innings*—Gregory 9–1–33–2; Overton 14–4–47–4; Groenewald 5–0–21–0; Leach 10.3–4–51–4.

Umpires: S. J. O'Shaughnessy and R. T. Robinson.

YORKSHIRE v ESSEX

At Scarborough, August 6–7. Essex won by eight wickets. Essex 20pts, Yorkshire 3pts. Toss: uncontested.

The only happy Yorkshiremen leaving North Marine Road on the second evening were Essex coaches Chris Silverwood and Anthony McGrath, whose side strengthened their position as Championship leaders while virtually ending Yorkshire's ambitions. Apart from Lyth in the first innings and Leaning in the second, the hosts were ripped apart by Mohammad Amir, whose 28.2 overs of mayhem yielded career-best figures of ten for 72. Hesitant batsmen were no match for his skills on a blameless pitch. He had support from Porter, the second bowler to take 50 first-class wickets in the season, an hour after Harmer had become the first. Yorkshire also bowled well, but ten Doeschate added 52 for the ninth wicket with Amir, helping Essex to a lead of 118 and setting up Yorkshire's third defeat in four games. More than 10,700 attended the two days, but it was the shortest of Scarborough's 131 festivals, as the previous home game was not part of it, and the local club and shops were counting the cost of the early finish. With Yorkshire nine down on the first morning, the umpires had delayed lunch for half an hour, but came off after only seven of the statutory eight overs. Informed of the error, they had to recall the players while spectators were cleared off the outfield.

Close of play: first day, Essex 188-8 (ten Doeschate 61, Mohammad Amir 11).

Yorkshire

Batsman	First innings		Second innings	
A. Lyth	c Chopra b Mohammad Amir	68	lbw b Porter	0
A. Z. Lees	c Lawrence b Mohammad Amir	0	c Foster b Mohammad Amir	0
H. C. Brook	c Foster b Porter	4	c Chopra b Porter	9
T. Köhler-Cadmore	b Mohammad Amir	4	lbw b Mohammad Amir	13
J. A. Leaning	c Foster b Porter	1	c Mohammad Amir b Porter	70
*T. T. Bresnan	lbw b Porter	0	c Harmer b Mohammad Amir	0
A. U. Rashid	lbw b Bopara	12	c Foster b Mohammad Amir	0
†A. J. Hodd	c Foster b Bopara	5	lbw b Porter	6
J. A. Brooks	c ten Doeschate b Mohammad Amir	5	c Wheater b Harmer	17
B. O. Coad	b Mohammad Amir	0	c Harmer b Mohammad Amir	28
R. J. Sidebottom	not out	8	not out	0
	Nb 6	6	B 4, lb 3	7
	(35.2 overs)	113	(49.4 overs)	150

First innings: 1/12 (2) 2/19 (3) 3/24 (4) 4/25 (5) 5/25 (6) 6/49 (7) 7/63 (8) 8/74 (9) 9/74 (10) 10/113 (1)

Second innings: 1/0 (1) 2/0 (2) 3/14 (4) 4/31 (3) 5/33 (6) 6/37 (7) 7/56 (8) 8/86 (9) 9/131 (10) 10/150 (5)

Porter 10–1–44–3; Mohammad Amir 11.2–4–18–5; Bopara 5–1–25–2; Walter 6–1–20–0; Harmer 3–1–6–0. *Second innings*—Porter 13.4–5–41–4; Mohammad Amir 17–1–54–5; Bopara 7–1–20–0; Walter 3–0–13–0; Harmer 9–1–15–1.

Essex

V. Chopra lbw b Brooks	11	– run out	13
N. L. J. Browne c Hodd b Coad	23	– c Sidebottom b Brooks	13
D. W. Lawrence lbw b Bresnan	14	– not out	8
R. S. Bopara c Brook b Brooks	23	– not out	0
A. J. A. Wheater c Hodd b Coad	34		
*R. N. ten Doeschate c Brooks b Bresnan	88		
†J. S. Foster c Lyth b Coad	0		
P. I. Walter lbw b Sidebottom	4		
S. R. Harmer c Lyth b Brooks	7		
Mohammad Amir c Hodd b Sidebottom	22		
J. A. Porter not out	2		
Lb 1, nb 2	3		
1/13 (1) 2/46 (2) 3/48 (3) 4/81 (4) 5/139 (5) 6/139 (7) 7/144 (8) 8/164 (9) 9/216 (10) 10/231 (6) (69 overs)	231	1/26 (1) 2/28 (2) (2 wkts, 10 overs)	34

Sidebottom 19–4–64–2; Brooks 17–0–89–3; Coad 15–2–36–3; Bresnan 13–5–27–2; Rashid 5–1–14–0. *Second innings*—Sidebottom 5–2–8–0; Brooks 5–0–26–1.

Umpires: R. J. Bailey and B. V. Taylor.

YORKSHIRE v MIDDLESEX

At Leeds, September 5–8. Drawn. Yorkshire 11pts, Middlesex 10pts. Toss: uncontested. Championship debut: S. E. Marsh.

The two most recent county champions found themselves scrapping for bonus points on the last day of a rain-ruined encounter; they ended the game joint-fifth in the table, 13 points above the relegation zone with three rounds to go. The match lost 200 overs in all, including the whole of the first day, and the fourth did not begin until 3.10, when Middlesex resumed on 108 for three with 38 overs available. The unflappable Voges ensured two batting points, while Yorkshire chipped away to collect a second for bowling. Both were looking for a third but, when Rayner was eighth out at 272, with Middlesex needing 28 runs and Yorkshire one wicket from 3.1 overs, Franklin declared to deny the bowlers. Earlier, Yorkshire's Australian opener Shaun Marsh managed 22 on Championship debut, before Leaning and Hodd provided some spine in a fifth-wicket stand of 114, helping them to four batting points for the first time since April; Harris began with six maidens, and Murtagh persevered for four wickets. Robson and Compton gave Middlesex a solid start before Sidebottom removed the top three, and although Voges was rarely troubled in a three-hour stay, Plunkett's pace worried his colleagues.

Close of play: first day, no play; second day, Yorkshire 317-7 (Bresnan 26, Plunkett 34); third day, Middlesex 108-3 (Voges 5, Stirling 4).

Yorkshire

A. Lyth c Simpson b Harris	40
S. E. Marsh lbw b Finn	22
A. Z. Lees lbw b Franklin	27
*G. S. Ballance c Simpson b Finn	12
J. A. Leaning b Murtagh	85
†A. J. Hodd c Simpson b Franklin	51
T. T. Bresnan c Stirling b Harris	44
A. U. Rashid lbw b Murtagh	0
L. E. Plunkett lbw b Murtagh	34
B. O. Coad c Robson b Murtagh	10
R. J. Sidebottom not out	9
B 5, lb 9, nb 10	24
1/39 (2) 2/79 (1) 3/100 (4) 4/116 (3) 5/230 (6) 6/270 (5) 7/270 (8) 8/318 (9) 9/336 (10) 10/358 (7) (111.2 overs) 110 overs: 353-9	358

Murtagh 29–6–77–4; Finn 22–4–75–2; Harris 28.2–11–77–2; Franklin 14–3–46–2; Rayner 11–2–38–0; Voges 6–0–26–0; Stirling 1–0–5–0.

Middlesex

S. D. Robson c Hodd b Sidebottom	47
N. R. D. Compton b Sidebottom	42
S. S. Eskinazi c Leaning b Sidebottom	5
A. C. Voges not out	65
P. R. Stirling b Plunkett	24
†J. A. Simpson c Lyth b Plunkett	2
*J. E. C. Franklin c Lyth b Coad	16
J. A. R. Harris c Sidebottom b Rashid	19
O. P. Rayner b Bresnan	37
B 4, lb 10, w 1	15
1/73 (2) 2/83 (3) 3/104 (1) 4/137 (5) 5/143 (6) 6/184 (7) 7/206 (8) 8/272 (9) (8 wkts dec, 66.5 overs)	272

S. T. Finn and T. J. Murtagh did not bat.

Sidebottom 20–2–62–3; Coad 17–3–65–1; Plunkett 16–4–53–2; Bresnan 8.5–2–40–1; Rashid 5–0–38–1.

Umpires: R. K. Illingworth and J. W. Lloyds.

At The Oval, September 12–15. YORKSHIRE drew with SURREY.

YORKSHIRE v WARWICKSHIRE

At Leeds, September 19–22. Yorkshire won by two wickets. Yorkshire 21pts, Warwickshire 4pts. Toss: Warwickshire. First-class debut: L. Banks. County debuts: K. C. Brathwaite; A. T. Thomson.

This should have been Ryan Sidebottom's final home game, but the only Ryan Sidebottom on the field was his Warwickshire namesake, as Yorkshire's version had strained his thigh. In his absence, Fisher made his first Championship appearance for two years – a torn hamstring had kept him out in 2016 – and responded with a career-best five wickets on the opening day, and a match-winning partnership on the last. Set 175, Yorkshire struggled against Patel, bowling unchanged from the tenth over, and seemed doomed at 96 for seven. But Patterson followed four second-innings wickets by joining Fisher in a pugnacious stand of 78. The scores were level when Fisher became Patel's sixth victim; Patterson hit his ninth four to ease Yorkshire's relegation fears, earning a standing ovation, and the retiring Sidebottom walked on through a guard of honour. Already down, Warwickshire had fought hard after dipping to 49 for six: Patel hit his third century (and second against Yorkshire), while Bell contributed only his fourth fifty of the season. Patel became the second player to score a hundred and take eight or more wickets in this fixture, after Frank Foster at Edgbaston in 1911.

Close of play: first day, Yorkshire 62-1 (Lyth 35, Patterson 1); second day, Warwickshire 49-1 (Banks 22, Trott 9); third day, Yorkshire 56-3 (Ballance 16).

Warwickshire

D. P. Sibley c Hodd b Brooks	3	– (2) lbw b Coad	18
L. Banks c Hodd b Fisher	13	– (1) c Hodd b Brooks	29
*I. J. L. Trott c Lyth b Brooks	1	– lbw b Patterson	59
I. R. Bell lbw b Fisher	51	– c Hodd b Patterson	14
M. J. Lamb c Hodd b Patterson	4	– lbw b Patterson	25
†T. R. Ambrose c Lyth b Coad	6	– c Lees b Bresnan	49
A. T. Thomson b Coad	0	– b Bresnan	20
J. S. Patel lbw b Fisher	100	– b Patterson	11
C. J. C. Wright lbw b Fisher	6	– c Ballance b Bresnan	10
W. B. Rankin not out	21	– not out	9
R. N. Sidebottom b Fisher	0	– c Lyth b Coad	1
B 4, lb 10	14	B 2, lb 4	6
1/6 (1) 2/10 (3) 3/29 (2) 4/34 (5) 5/47 (6) 6/49 (7) 7/145 (4) 8/151 (9) 9/217 (8) 10/219 (11) (70.1 overs)	219	1/35 (2) 2/86 (1) 3/109 (4) 4/138 (3) 5/161 (5) 6/209 (7) 7/216 (6) 8/230 (9) 9/244 (8) 10/251 (11) (87.4 overs)	251

Brooks 13–2–48–2; Coad 17–5–54–2; Patterson 15–5–27–1; Fisher 15.1–3–54–5; Bresnan 9–2–17–0; Lyth 1–0–5–0. *Second innings*—Brooks 15–1–58–1; Coad 21.4–4–67–2; Patterson 26–7–46–4; Fisher 11–1–35–0; Bresnan 12–3–36–3; Lyth 2–0–3–0.

Yorkshire

A. Lyth b Rankin	62	– lbw b Sidebottom	8
K. C. Brathwaite c Patel b Wright	18	– c Banks b Patel	17
S. A. Patterson c Patel b Sidebottom	1	– (9) not out	44
A. Z. Lees b Wright	11	– (3) c Ambrose b Patel	6
*G. S. Ballance c Ambrose b Patel	28	– (4) lbw b Patel	21
J. A. Leaning c Bell b Lamb	36	– (5) c Bell b Patel	16
†A. J. Hodd c Ambrose b Wright	14	– (6) c Patel b Sidebottom	11
T. T. Bresnan b Patel	47	– (7) c Thomson b Patel	0
M. D. Fisher c and b Rankin	37	– (8) c Bell b Patel	15
J. A. Brooks c Patel b Rankin	8	– not out	0
B. O. Coad not out	2		
B 15, lb 5, nb 12	32	B 15, lb 15, nb 10	40
1/61 (2) 2/62 (3) 3/98 (4) 4/115 (1) 5/158 (5) 6/179 (7) 7/228 (6) 8/264 (8) 9/289 (10) 10/296 (9) (96.1 overs)	296	1/13 (1) 2/25 (3) 3/56 (2) 4/71 (4) 5/86 (5) 6/86 (7) 7/96 (6) 8/174 (8) (8 wkts, 64.2 overs)	178

Wright 25–7–73–3; Sidebottom 17–3–70–1; Rankin 13.1–0–48–3; Lamb 6–1–24–1; Patel 35–10–61–2. *Second innings*—Wright 21.2–6–52–0; Sidebottom 11–5–30–2; Patel 28–17–50–6; Thomson 1–0–1–0; Rankin 3–0–15–0.

Umpires: M. Burns and R. A. Kettleborough.

At Chelmsford, September 25–27. YORKSHIRE lost to ESSEX by 376 runs. *Despite a heavy defeat, three points saved Yorkshire from relegation – and secured fourth-place prize money.*

NATWEST T20 BLAST IN 2017

REVIEW BY ALAN GARDNER

1 Nottinghamshire 2 Warwickshire 3= Glamorgan, Hampshire

The phrase "disruptive innovation" has become common business jargon, describing technological advances such as the smartphone that radically alter established markets. Twenty20 was not dreamed up by a San Francisco tech giant, but cricket fans may instinctively feel they understand the concept. In 2017, the NatWest Blast claimed eight weeks of prime real estate from July to early September, as the tournament returned to a single block for the first time in four years, and celebrated with record attendances and a surge in run-rates. Had it been the promotional reel for a pioneering start-up, plenty would have been tempted to invest.

In truth, though, the Blast already felt like the past. The growth of T20 elsewhere, and the limits imposed by the 18-county structure, had been of increasing concern to the ECB. In response, they planned a new competition that Tom Harrison, the chief executive, said would "future-proof" the English game (at least, presumably, until the rise of Ten10). It would kick off in 2020 – when the existing broadcast deal ends – and involve eight freshly created teams, a move with little precedent in the history of professional sport in England and Wales. The Blast, meanwhile, would continue as a sort of warm-up act. "Our clear ambition is that this new competition will sit alongside the IPL and Big Bash League as one of the world's major cricket tournaments," said the ECB chairman, Colin Graves, after it was voted through in April. Two months later, the board agreed a new broadcast deal worth £1.1bn over five years, including the return of live cricket to free-to-air TV, with ten out of 36 games in the proposed T20 competition to be shown on the BBC. It was as well they moved quickly: in October, South Africa's proposed T20 Global League was postponed for a year after failing to secure a lucrative television agreement.

If there were mutterings of discontent among the old guard – fearing an end to clubs outside the big cities – those at finals day didn't seem to care. A record crowd of 24,400 charged and recharged their glasses as Nottinghamshire completed the white-ball double on a cool September evening in Birmingham. In 2016, they fell in the semis to eventual winners Northamptonshire, who had less star quality but were closer-knit. This time, Dan Christian's team were supremely balanced, focused and drilled – worthy winners of Nottinghamshire's first T20 title. "They've worked really hard and probably hit more balls than anybody else," said head coach Peter Moores. His comment underplayed the growing sophistication of T20 tactics, while also summing up the format's thrumming baseline appeal.

Nottinghamshire used only 14 players throughout, including two who were unavailable for the final. In July, opening batsman Michael Lumb was forced into early retirement by an ankle injury. Earlier that month, Luke Fletcher had been struck on the head in his follow-through by a shot from Warwickshire's Sam Hain; it was so horrifying as to suggest protective headgear for bowlers should be considered. By the end of the match, Nottinghamshire's form (they had lost their first two games) was secondary to Fletcher's health. He was ruled out for the rest of the season, but well enough to join in his side's celebrations. "Today is going to be a long one!" he tweeted the morning after the final. "For the second time this season I've left Birmingham with a sore head."

At the heart of their triumph was another broad-beamed club favourite. Samit Patel could rarely be accused of undervaluing himself, but there was no arguing with his worth in the final, as Warwickshire were rumbled on their home patch. After Nottinghamshire had been inserted, Patel and Brendan Taylor resurrected the innings from 30 for three with a finals day-record partnership of 132. The Bears were soon lost in the woods, and Patel's direct-hit run-out of dashing young opener Ed Pollock – whose 23-ball fifty had helped see off Glamorgan in the semi-final – was another pivotal contribution.

Glamorgan were making their first finals day appearance since 2004, having topped the South Group despite four washouts. Hampshire, meanwhile, had made it this far seven times in eight seasons. In their quarter-final at Derby, they raised some eyebrows when they promoted Shahid Afridi to open: he had 50 runs from seven innings in the competition. As he had done throughout his quixotic career, he confounded expectations, thrashing a maiden T20 hundred. But consistency was never his strength, and in the semi-final, after Nottinghamshire had made a laboured 169 for seven, he holed out off the first ball of the Hampshire reply, bowled by that man Patel. It was regression to the mean, Afridi style.

Even without a contribution from Afridi, the Edgbaston scorers were kept busy. The three games produced 1,012 runs – the first four-figure aggregate in the 15-year history of finals day – although none featured a particularly close finish, despite a valiant attempt by Glamorgan's Andrew Salter to hit Chris Woakes for 26. The same could be said for the quarter-finals, which were largely predictable, one-sided, or both. The exception was Warwickshire's victory over Surrey on a febrile night at The Oval, dubbed the "Dom Sibley derby" because of an acrimonious transfer in which he left Surrey, and Rikki Clarke headed in the other direction. Regardless, the visitors pulled off the highest successful chase in a T20 knockout match in England.

Qualification from the group stage was more tense: by the final round, Nottinghamshire, Glamorgan and Hampshire were through, but almost everyone else had a chance of progressing. After some of those matches went down to the last over, six points separated top from bottom in the South Group, while net run-rate was the difference between second (guaranteeing a home quarter-final) and fourth in the North. Three of the four teams who contested finals day in 2016 faltered, with Yorkshire and Northamptonshire eventually squeezed out, and Durham unable to recover from starting with a four-point handicap, imposed by the ECB because of financial mismanagement.

When it came to scoring, the Blast underwent a spurt. The overall run-rate of 8.61 – up from 8.30 in 2016 – was the second-highest in any domestic T20 tournament comprising at least ten matches, behind 8.63 in New Zealand's

Nigel Roddis, Getty Images

Boom Boom and bust: Shahid Afridi scored a hundred in the quarter-final, a duck in the semi.

HRV Cup in 2012-13. It was the summer of the six: 1,292 to be precise, another competition record. Nottinghamshire channelled the zeitgeist, whacking more (110) than anyone, aided by a flat pitch and short boundaries at Trent Bridge. It was, to adapt Neville Cardus, a "lotus land for batsmen, where it was always evening under lights and runs came at 10.12 to the over". Nottinghamshire also claimed the world-record powerplay score when they bulldozed 106 off Durham in six overs at Trent Bridge. Alex Hales reached 95 off 30 balls, and was dismissed trying to hit the six that would have tied Chris Gayle's record for the fastest T20 hundred.

They were not alone in pushing (or clearing) the boundaries. Glamorgan's Colin Ingram hit 30 sixes, the most in a Blast season. And Adam Lyth smashed 161 as Yorkshire racked up 260 for four against Northamptonshire, both competition bests. In all, there were 17 hundreds, and 27 totals of 200 or more, both records. Five came in successful chases, which included two of the three highest in English domestic T20 matches. Somehow, amid the carnage, Ross Whiteley's six sixes in an over for Worcestershire against Yorkshire – the first Englishman to achieve the feat – was relegated to a footnote.

Understandably, bowlers enjoyed themselves a little less, but some still stood out. Leg-spinners in particular used guile to combat gung-ho batting, and Imran Tahir played a key role in Derbyshire reaching the quarter-finals for only the second time, with 17 wickets and an economy-rate of 7.42. Fellow wrist-spinners Mason Crane, Matt Parkinson, Adil Rashid, Max Waller and Ish Sodhi all had impressive tournaments, though offie Jeetan Patel, wily as ever, remained the most prolific of the slow brigade. Among the seamers, the

Nottinghamshire pair of Jake Ball and Harry Gurney were dangerous, if expensive: only Leicestershire's Clint McKay took more wickets. The most frugal was Gloucestershire's Benny Howell, the only player to cost less than a run a ball. Surrey's Sam Curran conjured a triple-wicket maiden against Gloucestershire, while Tim Bresnan's six for 19 sealed the Roses match for Yorkshire at Headingley.

The turnaround at Derbyshire, who had finished seventh, ninth and ninth in the North Group over the three previous seasons, highlighted another trend – the specialist T20 coach. John Wright, the sagacious New Zealander who spent 12 summers as Derbyshire's overseas player, became the first such appointment in English cricket in October 2016, and masterminded their best season since 2005. Middlesex also headhunted a Kiwi to oversee their tournament, though Daniel Vettori got less out of a more talented squad.

Whether handing the best months of the season to T20 – the Blast was interrupted by a single round of Championship matches – was good for the game as a whole, it was hard to be sure. But it was also hard to argue against the contention of players and coaches that the move had improved standards, certainly when it came to batting. Britain's weather remains outside the ECB's control but, apart from a nine-day period in late July which included 11 of the 16 no-results, the sun smiled and the crowds thronged. Overall attendances of 902,000 were a 10.6% increase on 2015, the previous best; and an average of 7,500 at every match continued an upward trend that began when the competition was rebranded in 2014.

All very impressive, but the ECB had already commissioned an upgrade. The future was on its way, disruptions expected.

Prize Money

£256,060 for winners: NOTTINGHAMSHIRE.
£123,934 for runners-up: WARWICKSHIRE.
£30,212 for losing semi-finalists: GLAMORGAN, HAMPSHIRE.
£4,500 for losing quarter-finalists: DERBYSHIRE, LEICESTERSHIRE, SOMERSET, SURREY.
Match-award winners received £2,500 in the final, £1,000 in the semi-finals, £500 in the quarter-finals and £225 in the group games.

FINAL GROUP TABLES

North Group

	North Group	*Played*	*Won*	*Lost*	*Tied*	*No-result*	*Points*	*NRR*
1	NOTTINGHAMSHIRE	14	8	4	0	2	18	0.48
2	DERBYSHIRE	14	8	5	0	1	17	0.45
3	WARWICKSHIRE	14	8	5	0	1	17	0.23
4	LEICESTERSHIRE	14	8	5	0	1	17	0.13
5	Yorkshire	14	6	5	1	2	15	1.12
6	Northamptonshire	14	6	5	0	3	15	–0.63
7	Lancashire	14	5	6	1	2	13	0.17
8	Worcestershire	14	3	10	0	1	7	–0.71
9	Durham	14	3	10	0	1	3*	–1.20

* *Durham were docked four points as part of an ECB punishment for accruing excessive debts.*

South Group

		Played	*Won*	*Lost*	*Tied*	*No-result*	*Points*	*NRR*
1	GLAMORGAN	14	7	3	0	4	18	0.04
2	SURREY	14	7	5	0	2	16	–0.13
3	HAMPSHIRE	14	7	6	0	1	15	–0.02
4	SOMERSET	14	6	6	0	2	14	0.49
5	Sussex	14	5	5	1	3	14	0.42
6	Kent	14	6	7	1	0	13	–0.15
7	Middlesex	14	5	7	1	1	12	0.22
8	Essex	14	5	7	0	2	12	–0.20
9	Gloucestershire	14	4	6	1	3	12	–0.64

Where counties finished tied on points, positions were decided by (a) most wins, (b) net run-rate.

NATWEST T20 BLAST AVERAGES

BATTING (300 runs, strike-rate 140)

		M	*I*	*NO*	*R*	*HS*	*100*	*50*	*Avge*	*SR*	*4*	*6*
1	A. D. Hales (*Notts*)	16	16	1	507	101	1	3	33.80	**204.43**	78	20
2	J. M. Clarke (*Worcs*)	13	13	1	381	124*	1	2	31.75	**183.17**	45	19
3	L. Ronchi (*Leics*)	15	14	1	429	63*	0	3	33.00	**180.25**	52	18
4	C. de Grandhomme (*Warwicks*)	16	15	3	322	65*	0	1	26.83	**170.37**	27	17
5	†D. J. Willey (*Yorks*)	12	12	1	446	118	1	1	40.54	**168.30**	34	26
6	A. J. Finch (*Surrey*)	13	13	1	489	114*	1	2	40.75	**166.89**	49	25
7	R. E. Levi (*Northants*)	9	8	0	375	88	0	3	46.87	**166.66**	40	21
8	†C. A. Ingram (*Glam*)	14	13	3	462	114	2	1	46.20	**166.18**	37	30
9	†A. Lyth (*Yorks*)	12	12	0	535	161	1	4	44.58	**164.61**	56	22
10	A. M. Rossington (*Northants*)	12	11	0	308	67	0	1	28.00	**161.25**	46	9
11	V. Chopra (*Essex*)	13	12	1	427	116	2	0	38.81	**159.32**	31	26
12	J. J. Roy (*Surrey*)	12	12	0	350	78	0	4	29.16	**159.09**	41	13
13	J. M. Vince (*Hants*)	15	15	1	542	81	0	5	38.71	**158.47**	68	18
14	D. T. Christian (*Notts*)	16	14	4	356	73	0	1	35.60	**153.44**	25	20
15	M. H. Wessels (*Notts*)	16	16	3	559	110	1	1	43.00	**151.49**	53	28
16	J. L. Denly (*Kent*)	14	14	1	567	127	2	1	43.61	**150.79**	53	25
17	S. W. Billings (*Kent*)	14	14	3	361	74	0	3	32.81	**148.55**	30	14
18	S. R. Patel (*Notts*)	16	14	4	405	77*	0	3	40.50	**146.20**	39	15
19	W. L. Madsen (*Derbys*)	14	14	3	526	86*	0	4	47.81	**145.30**	61	8
20	J. C. Buttler (*Lancs*)	12	12	3	451	80*	0	5	50.11	**144.55**	33	15
21	C. D. Nash (*Sussex*)	14	13	2	520	73*	0	6	47.27	**141.68**	55	19
22	P. D. Collingwood (*Durham*)	11	11	2	346	108*	1	1	38.44	**140.08**	25	13

BOWLING (10 wickets, economy-rate 7.70)

		Style	*O*	*Dots*	*R*	*W*	*BB*	*4I*	*Avge*	*SR*	***ER***
1	B. A. C. Howell (*Glos*)	RM	41	97	236	16	4-29	1	14.75	15.37	**5.75**
2	M. W. Parkinson (*Lancs*)	LB	32	73	194	14	4-23	1	13.85	13.71	**6.06**
3	M. S. Crane (*Hants*)	LB	47	98	312	18	3-15	0	17.33	15.66	**6.63**
4	M. J. Santner (*Worcs*)	LB	51	123	339	13	3-16	0	26.07	23.53	**6.64**
5	Mohammad Amir (*Essex*)	LFM	47.3	135	322	14	2-13	0	23.00	20.35	**6.77**
6	J. S. Patel (*Warwicks*)	OB	64	153	437	20	4-22	1	21.85	19.20	**6.82**
7	B. L. D'Oliveira (*Worcs*)	LB	34	58	232	11	2-19	0	21.09	18.54	**6.82**
8	D. R. Briggs (*Sussex*)	SLA	44	94	308	13	2-12	0	23.69	20.30	**7.00**
9	C. S. Delport (*Leics*)	RM	38	70	266	10	3-19	0	26.60	22.80	**7.00**
10	A. U. Rashid (*Yorks*)	LB	48	96	341	15	4-19	1	22.73	19.20	**7.10**
11	G. J. Batty (*Surrey*)	OB	35	76	249	14	4-14	2	17.78	15.00	**7.11**
12	Shahid Afridi (*Hants*)	LB	44	89	317	13	4-20	2	24.38	20.30	**7.20**
13	A. F. Milne (*Kent*)	RF	25.5	72	187	15	5-11	1	12.46	10.33	**7.23**
14	S. R. Patel (*Notts*)	SLA	60	106	437	16	3-26	0	27.31	22.50	**7.28**
15	W. L. Madsen (*Derbys*)	OB	47	110	346	13	2-20	0	26.61	21.69	**7.36**
16	R. E. van der Merwe (*Som*)	SLA	53	99	392	15	3-13	0	26.13	21.20	**7.39**
17	L. A. Dawson (*Hants*)	SLA	32	78	237	14	3-28	0	16.92	13.71	**7.40**

		Style	O	Dots	R	W	BB	4I	Avge	SR	ER
18	Imran Tahir (*Derbys*)	LB	56	105	416	17	4-17	1	24.47	19.76	**7.42**
19	R. S. Bopara (*Essex*)	RM	45	79	335	13	4-19	1	25.76	20.76	**7.44**
20	T. G. Southee (*Middx*)	RFM	45	90	337	15	3-9	0	22.46	18.00	**7.48**
21	D. A. Payne (*Glos*)	LFM	39.4	105	298	17	3-13	0	17.52	14.00	**7.51**
22	T. M. J. Smith (*Glos*)	SLA	34.2	59	259	10	3-28	0	25.90	20.60	**7.54**
23	C. J. McKay (*Leics*)	RFM	43	105	328	23	5-11	1	14.26	11.21	**7.62**
24	R. Clarke (*Warwicks, Surrey*)	RFM	30.2	76	232	13	4-16	1	17.84	14.00	**7.64**

LEADING WICKETKEEPERS

Dismissals	*M*	
13 (13 ct)	14	B. C. Brown (*Sussex*)
13 (12 ct, 1 st)	16	T. J. Moores (*Notts*)
12 (10 ct, 2 st)	13	J. S. Foster (*Essex*)
12 (8 ct, 4 st)	15	L. Ronchi (*Leics*)
11 (6ct, 5 st)	12	J. C. Buttler (*Lancs*)
11 (4 ct, 7 st)	13	O. B. Cox (*Worcs*)
10 (9 ct, 1 st)	12	A. M. Rossington (*Northants*)

LEADING FIELDERS

Ct	*M*	
13	16	S. R. Hain (*Warwicks*)
12	14	M. T. C. Waller (*Somerset*)
12	15	J. M. Vince (*Hants*)
12	15	T. J. Wells (*Leics*)
11	14	A. J. Blake (*Kent*)
10	14	A. L. Hughes (*Derbys*)
9	12	L. S. Livingstone (*Lancs*)
9	13	M. J. Santner (*Worcs*)
9	14	A. H. T. Donald (*Glam*)
9	14	E. J. G. Morgan (*Middx*)
9	16	D. T. Christian (*Notts*)
9	16	C. de Grandhomme (*Warwicks*)

NORTH GROUP

DERBYSHIRE

At Chesterfield, July 8. **Derbyshire won by three runs.** ‡**Derbyshire 165-8** (20 overs) (W. L. Madsen 42, D. Smit 30*); **Yorkshire 162-7** (20 overs) (A. Lyth 68, D. J. Willey 42; Imran Tahir 3-18). *MoM:* W. L. Madsen. *Attendance:* 4,500. *From 48-4 in the ninth over, Derbyshire hustled a useful 165-8, thanks to effective hitting from Wayne Madsen, Matt Henry (28*) and Daryn Smit. Adam Lyth's 68 kept Yorkshire in the hunt, but his exit in the 19th left 18 required from the last, which proved just beyond Tim Bresnan.*

At Derby, July 25 (floodlit). **Derbyshire won by 35 runs. Derbyshire 211-5** (20 overs) (L. M. Reece 97*, D. Smit 42*); ‡**Lancashire 176-9** (20 overs) (K. R. Brown 41, L. S. Livingstone 44, A. M. Lilley 38; M. J. Henry 3-37). *MoM:* L. M. Reece. *Attendance:* 4,155. *Luis Reece earned a sweet victory. Released by Lancashire at the end of 2016, he made 97* off 55 balls, and propelled Derbyshire to 211-5, their highest T20 score at home. Lancashire looked like challenging it at 93-2, but fell away after Matt Critchley (2-16) removed Karl Brown and Jos Buttler in consecutive overs.*

At Derby, July 28 (floodlit). **Derbyshire v Northamptonshire. Abandoned.**

At Derby, July 30. **Derbyshire won by seven wickets. Leicestershire 104-9** (20 overs) (M. J. Henry 3-18); ‡**Derbyshire 107-3** (13.5 overs) (W. L. Madsen 49*, A. L. Hughes 36*). *MoM:* W. L. Madsen. *Attendance:* 2,339. *At no stage did Leicestershire appear likely to set Derbyshire a testing target; Henry's 3-18 was the pick of a suffocating performance. After a top-order stutter, a fourth-wicket partnership of 86* between Madsen and Alex Hughes eased the hosts to victory.*

At Derby, August 4 (floodlit). **Nottinghamshire won by eight runs. Nottinghamshire 189-4** (20 overs) (M. H. Wessels 37, T. J. Moores 57, D. T. Christian 30*); ‡**Derbyshire 181-7** (20 overs) (L. M. Reece 53, W. L. Madsen 31; J. T. Ball 3-33). *MoM:* T. J. Moores. *Attendance:* 3,924. *After Tom Moores's 57, Dan Christian hit sixes off the last two balls to lift Nottinghamshire to 189-4. Derbyshire's Reece was not cowed: dropped on 14, he celebrated his 27th birthday with a 32-ball 53. But the quality of Jake Ball and Harry Gurney, who conceded just seven from the last over, proved decisive.*

At Derby, August 15 (floodlit). **Derbyshire won by three wickets.** ‡**Durham 161-7** (20 overs) (J. T. A. Burnham 34, S. W. Poynter 61*; M. J. Henry 3-42); **Derbyshire 164-7** (19.3 overs) (L. M. Reece 66; P. Coughlin 4-22). *MoM:* L. M. Reece. *Attendance:* 2,634. *Thanks to a flurry from Stuart Poynter, who hit a personal-best 61* from 32 balls, Durham racked up 46 from the last three overs. Despite Paul Coughlin's 4-22, their bowlers couldn't back it up, and Reece led Derbyshire to another victory.*

At Derby, August 18 (floodlit). **Derbyshire won by 48 runs. Derbyshire 146-8** (20 overs) (W. L. Madsen 55); ‡**Worcestershire 98** (15.4 overs) (Imran Tahir 4-17). *MoM:* Imran Tahir. *Attendance:* 2,911. *Derbyshire's batsmen underperformed, apart from Madsen, with his fourth half-century of the tournament. But their bowlers had far too much for struggling Worcestershire, who were bowled out for under 100 for only the third time. Imran Tahir took 4-17, to lead Derbyshire to their first quarter-final since 2005.*

Derbyshire away matches

July 7: beat Northamptonshire by seven wickets.
July 16: lost to Lancashire by five wickets.
July 19: beat Worcestershire by seven wickets.
July 21: lost to Nottinghamshire by five runs.
July 23: lost to Warwickshire by 20 runs.
August 3: beat Yorkshire by five wickets.
August 17: lost to Leicestershire by four wickets.

DURHAM

At Chester-le-Street, July 7 (floodlit). **Lancashire won by 52 runs. Lancashire 192-6** (20 overs) (K. R. Brown 35, A. M. Lilley 30, J. C. Buttler 59, D. J. Vilas 35; W. J. Weighell 3-28); ‡**Durham 140-7** (20 overs) (P. D. Collingwood 48; J. Clark 3-26). *MoM:* J. C. Buttler. *Attendance:* 5,115. *Durham's new T20 captain, Paul Coughlin, went for 22 in his first over, which set the tone for a one-sided match. Jos Buttler tucked in, cracking 59 off 39 balls, while James Weighell did most to keep Lancashire in check with 3-28 on T20 debut. The chase was limp, Paul Collingwood's 48 aside.*

At Chester-le-Street, July 9. **Northamptonshire won by six wickets. Durham 161-7** (20 overs) (J. T. A. Burnham 53*, P. D. Collingwood 38; R. K. Kleinveldt 3-28); ‡**Northamptonshire 162-4** (19.2 overs) (B. M. Duckett 72). *MoM:* B. M. Duckett. *Attendance:* 3,657. *In a rerun of the 2016 final, Durham batted first against Northamptonshire, and didn't quite make enough. Jack Burnham completed his maiden T20 half-century but, after he put on 57 with Collingwood, Rory Kleinveldt picked up three quick wickets, and only 35 came from the last five overs. Ben Duckett led the reply with 72 from 56 balls, and Rob Keogh (20*) calmly finished it with a lofted drive in the last over.*

At Chester-le-Street, July 20 (floodlit). **Leicestershire won by 27 runs. Leicestershire 144-8** (20 overs) (L. Ronchi 32, M. J. Cosgrove 33; P. D. Collingwood 4-24); ‡**Durham 117-8** (20 overs) (P. Coughlin 42*; C. F. Parkinson 3-20). *MoM:* C. F. Parkinson. *Attendance:* 3,345. *Durham looked set for their first victory of the campaign after Collingwood and off-spinner Adam Hickey (1-11) restricted Leicestershire to 144-8. But they slumped to 39-5, as spin proved more effective than usual at Riverside; Colin Ackermann and Callum Parkinson took a combined 5-42.*

At Chester-le-Street, July 25 (floodlit). **Nottinghamshire won by nine wickets.** ‡**Durham 123** (18.1 overs) (G. Clark 41; S. R. Patel 3-26); **Nottinghamshire 129-1** (16 overs) (M. H. Wessels 49*, A. D. Hales 44, B. R. M. Taylor 33*). *MoM:* S. R. Patel. *Attendance:* 3,483. County debut: L. Trevaskis (Durham). *Durham's inexperience was all too obvious: despite a pugnacious 41 from Graham Clark, they were all out for 123. Samit Patel caused most trouble, taking 3-26. Alex Hales launched the reply with 44 off 22 balls, leaving Riki Wessels and Brendan Taylor to cruise home.*

At Chester-le-Street, August 4 (floodlit). **Durham won by one run.** ‡**Durham 157-3** (20 overs) (P. D. Collingwood 88*, M. J. Richardson 32*); **Yorkshire 156-7** (20 overs) (D. J. Willey 40; B. J. McCarthy 3-33, P. Coughlin 3-34). *MoM:* P. D. Collingwood. *Attendance:* 6,230. *County debut:* T. W. M. Latham (Durham). *Collingwood continued his remarkable form, following his maiden Twenty20 century at Worcester five days earlier with 88* off 54 balls. Still, Yorkshire's target of 158 seemed manageable, and they were favourites until David Willey hoisted to deep midwicket. It came down to three off the last ball, but Azeem Rafiq missed, and they could manage only a bye.*

At Chester-le-Street, August 11 (floodlit). **Durham won by 13 runs.** ‡**Durham 165-5** (20 overs) (T. W. M. Latham 62, M. J. Richardson 49*); **Worcestershire 152-5** (20 overs) (O. B. Cox 34, E. G. Barnard 34*). *MoM:* T. W. M. Latham. *Attendance:* 3,520. *The day after being dropped from the*

Test team, Keaton Jennings returned to Durham duty and scored four from ten balls. But, after Worcestershire's chase began strongly, his gentle medium-pace earned 2-21 to turn the tide. Earlier, Tom Latham's classy 62 had laid the platform for Durham, and Mark Richardson's 49 lifted them to a defendable total. Having begun the tournament with a four-point penalty, they were finally in the black.*

At Chester-le-Street, August 13. **Warwickshire won by eight wickets.** ‡**Durham 145-8** (20 overs) (P. Coughlin 53, S. W. Poynter 36*); **Warwickshire 148-2** (14.5 overs) (E. J. Pollock 52, D. P. Sibley 51*, C. de Grandhomme 34). *MoM:* D. P. Sibley. *Attendance:* 4,607. *Ed Pollock surprised Durham with 52 off 25 balls, including four sixes, and allowed Dom Sibley to amble through the rest of Warwickshire's chase. Durham had never looked like setting an intimidating score; they plunged to 30-4 after six overs, before Coughlin hit his first T20 fifty. But 145 was not enough.*

Durham away matches

July 23: lost to Lancashire by 31 runs.
July 26: lost to Yorkshire by 24 runs.
July 28: beat Leicestershire by six wickets.
July 30: lost to Worcestershire by eight wickets.
August 5: lost to Nottinghamshire by five wickets.
August 15: lost to Derbyshire by three wickets.
August 18: no result v Northamptonshire.

LANCASHIRE

At Liverpool, July 9. **Leicestershire won by three wickets. Lancashire 173-9** (20 overs) (L. S. Livingstone 48, A. M. Lilley 30, J. C. Buttler 39; C. J. McKay 3-29); ‡**Leicestershire 178-7** (20 overs) (M. J. Cosgrove 34, C. N. Ackermann 62*; D. J. Lamb 3-30). *MoM:* C. N. Ackermann. *Attendance*: 4,332. *County debut:* L. Ronchi (Leicestershire). *Colin Ackermann paced Leicestershire's chase superbly: needing two off the final ball, he managed six. Earlier, Liam Livingstone and Jos Buttler put on 72 in six overs, but Lancashire added only 61 from their last nine.*

At Manchester, July 14 (floodlit). **Tied** (DLS). ‡**Lancashire 176-4** (20 overs) (K. R. Brown 61, L. S. Livingstone 34, R. McLaren 34*); **Yorkshire 64-2** (8.1 overs). *MoM:* K. R. Brown. *Attendance*: 18,987. *The largest crowd for a T20 Blast match outside London was denied a proper climax when a downpour forced abandonment – and a tie on DLS. Earlier, Karl Brown rattled off 61 off 47 balls for Lancashire.*

At Manchester, July 16. **Lancashire won by five wickets.** ‡**Derbyshire 152-8** (20 overs) (M. J. J. Critchley 40, L. M. Reece 37, W. L. Madsen 52; M. W. Parkinson 3-17, Junaid Khan 3-28); **Lancashire 155-5** (18.3 overs) (K. R. Brown 30, J. C. Buttler 42*). *MoM:* M. W. Parkinson. *Attendance*: 6,500. *On his limited-overs debut, Matt Parkinson's 3-17 restricted Lancashire's target to a modest 153, before Buttler's measured 42* completed victory. Derbyshire's batting at the death was fatal: in the last six overs, they made 41-6. Sixteen bowlers were used, one behind the record: Mashonaland Eagles v Matabeleland Tuskers at Harare in 2009-10.*

At Manchester, July 23. **Lancashire won by 31 runs.** ‡**Lancashire 174-5** (20 overs) (L. S. Livingstone 61, S. J. Croft 35*, R. McLaren 32*; R. D. Pringle 3-30); **Durham 143-8** (20 overs) (C. T. Steel 37; J. Clark 3-36). *MoM:* L. S. Livingstone. *Attendance*: 6,589. *County debut:* G. J. Harte (Durham). *Livingstone's career-best 61 gave Lancashire a racing start, before Steven Croft and Ryan McLaren plundered 64 from the final six overs. A total of 174-5 proved ample. Graham Clark flayed a couple of boundaries off younger brother Jordan, who nonetheless finished with bragging rights, picking up three of the top five.*

At Manchester, July 28 (floodlit). **Lancashire v Nottinghamshire. Abandoned.**

At Manchester, August 16 (floodlit). **Lancashire won by seven wickets. Worcestershire 127-8** (20 overs) (B. L. D'Oliveira 30); ‡**Lancashire 128-3** (17.3 overs) (L. S. Livingstone 36, A. M. Lilley 33, J. C. Buttler 52*). *MoM:* A. M. Lilley. *Attendance*: 6,061. *Lancashire kept their qualifying hopes alive with an easy win. Arron Lilley took 2-18, then hit 33 to earn the match award. A third-wicket stand of 76 between Buttler and Livingstone – who went boundaryless in a 37-ball 36 – did the rest.*

At Manchester, August 18 (floodlit). **Warwickshire won by two wickets. Lancashire 163-4** (20 overs) (L. S. Livingstone 39, J. C. Buttler 58, D. J. Vilas 30); ‡**Warwickshire 169-8** (19.3 overs) (E. J. Pollock 49, D. P. Sibley 53, A. J. Hose 49). *MoM:* E. J. Pollock. *Attendance*: 7,269. *In a dramatic conclusion to the group stage, Olly Stone's straight six off Livingstone in the last over* *ensured Warwickshire's qualification. Lancashire's 163-4 had seemed competitive, before Ed Pollock blitzed a 24-ball 49, and Dom Sibley and Adam Hose added 84 in ten overs. That left only 19 required off 29 balls, but Warwickshire – captained by Grant Elliott after Ian Bell was dropped – lost seven for 15, and needed Stone to stay calm.*

Lancashire away matches

July 7: beat Durham by 52 runs.
July 21: no result v Worcestershire.
July 25: lost to Derbyshire by 35 runs.
July 30: lost to Warwickshire by five wickets.
August 3: lost to Northamptonshire by 11 runs.
August 4: beat Leicestershire by four runs.
August 11: lost to Yorkshire by 19 runs.

LEICESTERSHIRE

At Leicester, July 21 (floodlit). **Northamptonshire won by two runs** (DLS). **Northamptonshire 165-8** (20 overs) (R. E. Levi 41, A. G. Wakely 34, R. I. Keogh 37; M. W. Pillans 3-33); **‡Leicestershire 107-3** (14.3 overs) (C. S. Delport 30, M. J. Cosgrove 41). *MoM:* R. I. Keogh. *Attendance:* 3,512. *In their fifth match – but first at home – Leicestershire lost their 100% record. Richard Levi's zippy 41 had given Northamptonshire a strong start, and Rob Keogh's 37 kept up the tempo, though 3-33 from Mathew Pillans – who bowled with impressive pace – pegged them back to 165-8. Leicestershire were ahead on DLS for most of the reply, mainly thanks to Mark Cosgrove, but they fell behind after he missed a heave in the 13th, and rain ended things two overs later.*

At Leicester, July 25 (floodlit). **Warwickshire won by 30 runs. Warwickshire 187-7** (20 overs) (S. R. Hain 57, W. T. S. Porterfield 35); **‡Leicestershire 157-8** (20 overs) (M. W. Pillans 34*; W. B. Rankin 3-26, A. D. Thomason 3-33). *MoM:* S. R. Hain. *Attendance:* 2,945. *After Warwickshire slipped to 13-2, Sam Hain led a recovery, and Keith Barker's 11-ball 23* lifted the total to 187-7. Leicestershire's chase never gained momentum: seamers Aaron Thomason and Boyd Rankin shared six wickets, while Jeetan Patel conceded just 17 from his four overs.*

At Leicester, July 28 (floodlit). **Durham won by six wickets. ‡Leicestershire 88-2** (7 overs) (L. Ronchi 63*); **Durham 90-4** (6.5 overs) (P. D. Collingwood 34, P. Coughlin 38*). *MoM:* P. D. Collingwood. *Attendance:* 1,826. *In a match shortened by rain to seven overs, Luke Ronchi smashed a 16-ball half-century, equalling the third-fastest in T20 cricket in England and Wales; he finished with 63* out of 88, including 26 off James Weighell's only over. But Barry McCarthy helped turn the tide, conceding just one, then rapid thirties from Paul Collingwood and Paul Coughlin spirited Durham to their first T20 victory of the season.*

FASTEST T20 FIFTIES IN ENGLAND AND WALES

Balls			
13	M. E. Trescothick	Somerset v Hampshire at Taunton	2010
14	G. L. Brophy	Yorkshire v Derbyshire at Derby	2006
16	A. D. Hales	Nottinghamshire v Derbyshire at Nottingham	2010
16	D. T. Christian	Nottinghamshire v Leicestershire at Nottingham	2016
16	**L. Ronchi**	**Leicestershire v Durham at Leicester**	**2017**
17	M. H. Wessels	Nottinghamshire v Worcestershire at Nottingham	2016
17	M. J. Lumb	Nottinghamshire v Leicestershire at Nottingham	2016
18	B. B. McCullum	Glamorgan v Worcestershire at Cardiff	2006
18	J. E. C. Franklin	Glamorgan v Warwickshire at Birmingham	2006
18	A. Lyth	Yorkshire v Worcestershire at Leeds	2010
18	C. Kieswetter	Somerset v Middlesex at Taunton	2011
18	T. M. Dilshan	Sri Lankans v Sussex at Hove	2014
18	M. T. Coles	Hampshire v Essex at Chelmsford	2014
18	**A. D. Hales**	**Nottinghamshire v Yorkshire at Nottingham**	**2017**

At Leicester, August 2 (floodlit). **No result** (DLS). **Nottinghamshire 210-8** (20 overs) (M. H. Wessels 63, A. D. Hales 51, D. T. Christian 33) **v ‡Leicestershire.** *Attendance:* 2,244. *Nottinghamshire openers Riki Wessels and Alex Hales set up an intimidating total with a century stand, but rain prevented a Leicestershire reply.*

At Leicester, August 4 (floodlit). **Lancashire won by four runs. Lancashire 173-5** (20 overs) (L. S. Livingstone 30, J. C. Buttler 57, D. J. Vilas 32); ‡**Leicestershire 169-3** (20 overs) (M. J. Cosgrove 77*, A. M. Ali 35*). *MoM:* S. D. Parry. *Attendance:* 3,239. *A rapid half-century from Jos Buttler, and 18 extras, helped Lancashire to 173 – the score they had made in the reverse fixture at Liverpool. This time, though, Leicestershire failed in pursuit. Cosgrove, who required a runner after being hit early in his innings by Aadil Ali's drive, cracked 77* off 58 deliveries, but couldn't muster a last-ball six. Stephen Parry's economy won him the match award: he conceded 18 from three overs.*

At Leicester, August 12. **Leicestershire won by four wickets. Yorkshire 182-5** (20 overs) (T. Köhler-Cadmore 75, S. E. Marsh 60); ‡**Leicestershire 183-6** (19.4 overs) (L. Ronchi 57, C. N. Ackermann 58*; L. E. Plunkett 3-42). *MoM:* C. N. Ackermann. *Attendance:* 3,108. *After Yorkshire opener Tom Köhler-Cadmore crunched 75 off 40 balls, they should have made over 200, but only Shaun Marsh built on the foundation. Leicestershire needed 183, and another remarkable Luke Ronchi half-century – this time from 19 balls – together with a more patient one from Colin Ackermann steered them to their first home win, having won five away.*

At Leicester, August 17 (floodlit). **Leicestershire won by four wickets. Derbyshire 139-7** (20 overs) (M. J. J. Critchley 72*); ‡**Leicestershire 143-6** (18.3 overs) (L. Ronchi 32, M. J. Cosgrove 57*). *MoM:* M. J. Cosgrove. *Attendance:* 3,049. *Derbyshire struggled on a slow pitch: opener Matt Critchley batted through for 72*, but the next highest score was 13. The familiar figures of Ronchi (32 off 15) and Cosgrove, with an unbeaten 57*, saw Leicestershire to a comfortable victory. It meant they could progress to the quarter-finals if they won at Nottingham.*

Leicestershire away matches

July 9: beat Lancashire by three wickets.
July 14: beat Worcestershire by five wickets.
July 16: beat Warwickshire by nine runs.
July 20: beat Durham by 27 runs.
July 30: lost to Derbyshire by seven wickets.
August 11: beat Northamptonshire by 48 runs.
August 18: beat Nottinghamshire by two runs.

NORTHAMPTONSHIRE

At Northampton, July 7 (floodlit). **Derbyshire won by seven wickets. Northamptonshire 179-6** (20 overs) (B. M. Duckett 69, J. J. Cobb 38, S. P. Crook 34*; G. C. Viljoen 3-28); ‡**Derbyshire 180-3** (19.1 overs) (L. M. Reece 75*, W. L. Madsen 37). *MoM:* L. M. Reece. *Attendance:* 6,169. *County debuts:* T. Shamsi (Northamptonshire); M. J. Henry (Derbyshire). *Northamptonshire's title defence began inauspiciously: Luis Reece's maiden Twenty20 half-century helped Derbyshire chase 180 for their first victory at Wantage Road in the format since 2010. Earlier, Ben Duckett's 69 off 52 laid firm foundations, but four wickets in five overs, and 3-28 for Hardus Viljoen, meant Northamptonshire finished below par.*

At Northampton, July 11 (floodlit). **Northamptonshire v Yorkshire. Abandoned.**

At Northampton, July 27 (floodlit). **Northamptonshire won by seven wickets. Worcestershire 158** (20 overs) (D. K. H. Mitchell 33, M. J. Santner 37, B. L. D'Oliveira 52; R. K. Kleinveldt 3-25, R. J. Gleeson 3-12); ‡**Northamptonshire 160-3** (17.4 overs) (R. E. Levi 47, A. M. Rossington 42, A. G. Wakely 46*). *MoM:* R. J. Gleeson. *Attendance:* 2,888. *Worcestershire slumped to their fifth defeat after Northamptonshire openers Richard Levi and Adam Rossington blasted 83 – more than half the requirement – in seven overs. But Richard Gleeson had done most to decide the match: he bowled Joe Clarke, Ben Cox and John Hastings in the space of nine balls. Mitchell Santner and Brett D'Oliveira ensured respectability, but 158 was never enough.*

At Northampton, August 1 (floodlit). **Warwickshire won by two runs. Warwickshire 172-9** (20 overs) (C. de Grandhomme 37); ‡**Northamptonshire 170-7** (20 overs) (R. E. Levi 33, A. M. Rossington 43, A. G. Wakely 52). *MoM:* A. D. Thomason. *Attendance:* 3,327. *At 85-1, requiring 88 from 68 deliveries and with Rossington going well, Northamptonshire looked favourites. But Jeetan Patel (2-27) took two in two balls and, despite Alex Wakely's battling half-century, 20-year-old seamer Aaron Thomason defended 13 off the final over. Warwickshire's batsmen had struggled for momentum, only Colin de Grandhomme cutting loose in a 16-ball 37.*

At Northampton, August 3 (floodlit). **Northamptonshire won by 11 runs. Northamptonshire 158-4** (20 overs) (R. E. Levi 71, A. G. Wakely 35*); ‡**Lancashire 147-9** (20 overs) (D. J. Vilas 40, R. McLaren 77; R. J. Gleeson 3-29, R. K. Kleinveldt 3-16). *MoM:* R. K. Kleinveldt. *Attendance:* 4,801. *After Gleeson and Rory Kleinveldt reduced Lancashire to 25-5, they looked in for a hiding. But Ryan McLaren added 91 with Dane Vilas, then belted the first two balls of the final over for six. With 14 still needed, an extraordinary victory looked possible, but he holed out for a career-best 77. Northamptonshire had built their score around a third-wicket stand of 98 between Levi and Wakely.*

At Northampton, August 11 (floodlit). **Leicestershire won by 48 runs. Leicestershire 193-5** (20 overs) (L. Ronchi 59, M. J. Cosgrove 79); ‡**Northamptonshire 145-7** (20 overs) (A. M. Rossington 67; C. S. Delport 3-19). *MoM:* M. J. Cosgrove. *Attendance:* 3,595. *Leicestershire's emphatic victory left Northamptonshire needing to win one of their last two games. After Luke Ronchi provided early momentum, Mark Cosgrove cracked 79 from 48 balls to swell the total to 193-5, a Leicestershire record in this fixture. Levi and Duckett fell early in the reply, and Cameron Delport hoovered up 3-19, including Rossington for 67, to kill off any hope of a recovery.*

At Northampton, August 18 (floodlit). **No result. Durham 208-3** (20 overs) (T. W. M. Latham 37, G. Clark 71, M. J. Richardson 47*, P. Coughlin 36*) **v** ‡**Northamptonshire.** *Attendance:* 3,221. *Northamptonshire's competition was ended by rain at the halfway stage – though by then victory looked unlikely anyway. Graham Clark shared a century stand with Tom Latham on his way to 71 from 37 balls, then Michael Richardson and Paul Coughlin hoisted Durham to their fourth-best total.*

Northamptonshire away matches

July 9: beat Durham by six wickets.
July 14: beat Warwickshire by five wickets.
July 21: beat Leicestershire by two runs (DLS).
July 22: lost to Nottinghamshire by 12 runs (DLS).
July 28: no result v Derbyshire.
August 5: beat Worcestershire by 24 runs.
August 17: lost to Yorkshire by 124 runs.

NOTTINGHAMSHIRE

At Nottingham, July 21 (floodlit). **Nottinghamshire won by five runs. Nottinghamshire 227-3** (20 overs) (M. H. Wessels 110, B. R. M. Taylor 67*, D. T. Christian 32*); ‡**Derbyshire 222-5** (20 overs) (B. A. Godleman 43, W. L. Madsen 86*). *MoM:* M. H. Wessels. *Attendance:* 14,123. *After two away defeats, Nottinghamshire's batsmen enjoyed home comforts: Riki Wessels hit their first T20 century, and shared a county-record 153 with Brendan Taylor as they reached their format-best total. Wayne Madsen responded with a brutal 86*, but couldn't manage six off the last for a tie.*

At Nottingham, July 22. **Nottinghamshire won by 12 runs** (DLS). **Northamptonshire 195-8** (20 overs) (R. E. Levi 88; H. F. Gurney 3-46, I. S. Sodhi 3-39); ‡**Nottinghamshire 52-0** (5.1 overs) (A. D. Hales 30*). *MoM:* R. E. Levi. *Attendance:* 7,638. *Richard Levi hit eight sixes as Northamptonshire set a challenging 196, but rain limited Nottinghamshire's reply to 5.1 overs, at which point DLS had them in front.*

At Nottingham, July 26 (floodlit). **Worcestershire won by 13 runs. Worcestershire 208-8** (20 overs) (J. M. Clarke 60, M. J. Santner 35, R. A. Whiteley 42; J. T. Ball 3-34); ‡**Nottinghamshire 195-5** (20 overs) (M. H. Wessels 49, A. D. Hales 63; J. W. Hastings 3-31). *MoM:* J. M. Clarke. *Attendance:* 8,502. *County debut:* P. R. Brown (Worcestershire). *After a 27-ball 63 from Alex Hales – including six fours in seven deliveries – Nottinghamshire's middle order misfired. Joe Clarke's 27-ball 60 had set Worcestershire fair, and Ross Whiteley kept them motoring, taking 24 off one Harry Gurney over; his 0-57 were the most expensive figures in Nottinghamshire history.*

At Nottingham, July 30. **Nottinghamshire won by five wickets. Yorkshire 223-5** (20 overs) (A. Lyth 59, T. Köhler-Cadmore 37, S. E. Marsh 47, P. S. P. Handscomb 31; S. R. Patel 3-29); ‡**Nottinghamshire 225-5** (19.1 overs) (M. H. Wessels 34, A. D. Hales 101, B. R. M. Taylor 41). *MoM:* A. D. Hales. *Attendance:* 8,363. *Hales scored his first domestic T20 century, in 45 balls, to help Nottinghamshire to their best chase, beating 210-7 against the same opponents on the same ground in 2004. In the UK, only Sussex had made more batting second: 226-3 against Essex at Chelmsford in 2014. Five Yorkshire players reached 28, but Hales trumped them all.*

At Nottingham, August 5. **Nottinghamshire won by five wickets. Durham 183-7** (20 overs) (C. T. Steel 35, M. J. Richardson 53, P. Coughlin 42*); ‡**Nottinghamshire 184-5** (13.5 overs) (M. H.

Wessels 41*, A. D. Hales 95). *MoM:* A. D. Hales. *Attendance:* 8,393. *Hales made 95 from 29 balls before he was out attempting a tenth six; had he been successful, he would have equalled Chris Gayle's record for the fastest T20 hundred. Wessels helped Nottinghamshire crack a record 106 from the powerplay, and helped finish off a humiliating defeat for Durham.*

At Nottingham, August 11 (floodlit). **Nottinghamshire won by five wickets. Warwickshire 180-7** (20 overs) (S. R. Hain 82*, A. D. Thomason 42; J. T. Ball 3-27); ‡**Nottinghamshire 183-5** (18.1 overs) (B. R. M. Taylor 36, S. R. Patel 77*). *MoM:* S. R. Patel. *Attendance:* 12,881. *Warwickshire made 180-7 – respectable at most grounds, but not Trent Bridge. Sam Hain thrashed 82* from 50 balls, and Aaron Thomason 42 from 23, before Nottinghamshire lost Hales for a duck. But they still cruised to victory, led by Samit Patel's unbeaten half-century.*

At Nottingham, August 18 (floodlit). **Leicestershire won by two runs. Leicestershire 203-5** (20 overs) (C. S. Delport 109*, M. J. Cosgrove 37, E. J. H. Eckersley 30); ‡**Nottinghamshire 201-8** (20 overs) (S. R. Patel 39, D. T. Christian 73; M. W. Pillans 3-24). *MoM:* C. S. Delport. *Attendance:* 10,776. *Nottinghamshire were already through, and Leicestershire joined them with a hard-fought victory. Cameron Delport hit six sixes while becoming the fifth player – and the fourth from Leicestershire – to score a T20 century against Nottinghamshire. In reply, Dan Christian hit five more sixes in a 32-ball 73. But he was out in the penultimate over, and the nerveless Mat Pillans defended eight from the last.*

Nottinghamshire away matches

July 7: lost to Yorkshire by 48 runs.
July 8: lost to Warwickshire by six wickets.
July 25: beat Durham by nine wickets.
July 28: no result v Lancashire.
August 2: no result v Leicestershire.
August 4: beat Derbyshire by eight runs.
August 13: beat Worcestershire by 11 runs.

WARWICKSHIRE

At Birmingham, July 8 (floodlit). **Warwickshire won by six wickets. Nottinghamshire 158-6** (20 overs) (S. R. Patel 55, S. J. Mullaney 46; J. S. Patel 4-22); ‡**Warwickshire 159-4** (20 overs) (I. R. Bell 47, G. D. Elliott 38). *MoM:* J. S. Patel. *Attendance:* 9,218. *The match was overshadowed by a serious head injury to Nottinghamshire seamer Luke Fletcher who, delivering his first ball, was struck by Sam Hain's fierce drive. Fletcher managed to walk off, but was kept in hospital overnight, and was not cleared to play until January. Play stopped for 25 minutes while his distressed team-mates considered abandonment; Samit Patel, who had earlier top-scored with 55 out of 158, was in tears. After resumption, Nottinghamshire should have managed a tie, but Michael Lumb fluffed a run-out, and Rikki Clarke scrambled the winning single. Earlier, Jeetan Patel had taken 4-22, a Warwickshire record against Nottinghamshire in Twenty20 cricket.*

At Birmingham, July 14 (floodlit). **Northamptonshire won by five wickets. Warwickshire 156-4** (20 overs) (S. R. Hain 30, I. R. Bell 50); ‡**Northamptonshire 160-5** (20 overs) (A. M. Rossington 34, J. J. Cobb 48, R. I. Keogh 41*). *MoM:* R. I. Keogh. *Attendance:* 9,784. *Rob Keogh cover-drove the last ball for four to end Warwickshire's unbeaten start. Earlier, they had been 103-1 but, after Tabraiz Shamsi took two wickets in the 13th over, including Ian Bell for 50, managed only 156-4. Clarke was hit on the thumb, retired hurt, and was unable to bowl in what proved to be his final first-team game before returning to Surrey. Josh Cobb and Keogh took advantage with forties.*

At Birmingham, July 16. **Leicestershire won by nine runs. Leicestershire 147-9** (20 overs) (L. Ronchi 46, C. S. Delport 37; W. B. Rankin 3-26); ‡**Warwickshire 138-8** (20 overs) (W. T. S. Porterfield 30; C. N. Ackermann 3-21). *MoM:* C. N. Ackermann. *Attendance:* 8,708. *Leicestershire's 147-9 appeared modest, but their slow bowlers strangled Warwickshire on a used pitch; off-spinner Colin Ackermann returned 3-21, his T20 best. Earlier, Luke Ronchi, a Warwickshire player in 2016, had top-scored with a 23-ball 46, in an opening stand of 59.*

At Birmingham, July 23. **Warwickshire won by 20 runs. Warwickshire 197-4** (20 overs) (E. J. Pollock 66, S. R. Hain 34, C. de Grandhomme 65*); ‡**Derbyshire 177-9** (20 overs) (L. M. Reece 33; K. H. D. Barker 3-33, G. D. Elliott 4-37). *MoM:* G. D. Elliott. *Attendance:* 9,902. *County debut:* E. J. Pollock. *Ed Pollock, a 22-year-old left-hander who had been rejected by Worcestershire, pummelled 66 from 44 balls on his Warwickshire debut. That softened the bowling for Colin* *de Grandhomme, who smashed five sixes in a 28-ball 65. Chasing 198, Derbyshire floundered, particularly against the canny Grant Elliott, who picked up 4-37.*

At Birmingham, July 28 (floodlit). **Warwickshire v Yorkshire. Abandoned.**

At Birmingham, July 30. **Warwickshire won by five wickets. Lancashire 174-8** (20 overs) (J. C. Buttler 80*); ‡**Warwickshire 176-5** (19.4 overs) (A. J. Hose 76, G. D. Elliott 45*). *MoM:* A. J. Hose. *Attendance:* 8,891. *County debut:* A. J. Hose (Warwickshire). *Adam Hose, recruited from Somerset just days before, guided a brilliant chase on his Warwickshire debut. He hit 76, launched five sixes – including one on top of the pavilion – and shared 69 with Elliott, whose 45* saw them home with two balls to spare. It was hard on Jos Buttler: his audacious strokeplay in a 43-ball 80* had seemingly put Lancashire in command.*

At Birmingham, August 4 (floodlit). **Worcestershire won by five runs. Worcestershire 190-7** (20 overs) (J. W. Hastings 51, J. M. Clarke 34, B. L. D'Oliveira 35*); ‡**Warwickshire 185-7** (20 overs) (D. P. Sibley 49, G. D. Elliott 38, A. D. Thomason 33*; M. J. Santner 3-16). *MoM:* J. W. Hastings. *MoM:* J. W. Hastings. *Attendance:* 15,113. *County debut:* D. P. Sibley. *In the 18th over of the match, Warwickshire wicketkeeper Alex Mellor fumbled the ball back on to his helmet, incurring five penalty runs. It proved the exact margin. Dom Sibley, signed from Surrey the day before, led Warwickshire's pursuit of 191 with an impressive 49, but it wasn't enough, as Mitchell Santner picked up 3-16. Earlier, John Hastings and Joe Clarke had got Worcestershire off to a flyer, hammering 75 off the first five overs.*

Warwickshire away matches

July 7: beat Worcestershire by eight wickets.
July 21: lost to Yorkshire by 29 runs.
July 25: beat Leicestershire by 30 runs.
August 1: beat Northamptonshire by two runs.
August 11: lost to Nottinghamshire by five wickets.
August 13: beat Durham by five wickets.
August 18: beat Lancashire by two wickets.

WORCESTERSHIRE

At Worcester, July 7 (day/night). **Warwickshire won by eight wickets. Worcestershire 152-9** (20 overs) (O. B. Cox 43, R. A. Whiteley 40; R. Clarke 3-20, O. J. Hannon-Dalby 3-33); ‡**Warwickshire 153-2** (19 overs) (S. R. Hain 47, I. R. Bell 75*). *MoM:* I. R. Bell. *Attendance:* 4,848. *County debuts:* C. de Grandhomme, G. D. Elliott, O. P. Stone (Warwickshire). *After being inserted, Worcestershire were shackled by Rikki Clarke and Jeetan Patel (2-18), who reduced them to 66-5; only a sixth-wicket stand of 78 between Ben Cox and Ross Whiteley lifted the total to respectability. Still, Warwickshire cantered to their target of 153, led by Ian Bell's 55-ball 75*.*

At Worcester, July 14 (day/night). **Leicestershire won by five wickets.** ‡**Worcestershire 148-8** (20 overs) (D. K. H. Mitchell 31, O. B. Cox 51; C. J. McKay 5-11); **Leicestershire 149-5** (18.3 overs) (C. N. Ackermann 47*, T. J. Wells 31*). *MoM:* C. J. McKay. *Attendance:* 3,440. *Worcestershire floundered batting first again, as Clint McKay took 5-11, despite feeling sick earlier in the day. They were the best T20 figures by a Leicestershire bowler, beating Andrew McDonald's 5-13 against Nottinghamshire at Trent Bridge in 2010. Three Worcestershire bowlers – Mitchell Santner, Daryl Mitchell and Brett D'Oliveira – took a wicket with their first ball, but Colin Ackermann's 47* ensured a comfortable Leicestershire victory.*

At Worcester, July 19 (day/night). **Derbyshire won by seven wickets. Worcestershire 186-5** (20 overs) (J. M. Clarke 42, O. B. Cox 40*, R. A. Whiteley 39); ‡**Derbyshire 189-3** (18.2 overs) (B. A. Godleman 70, M. J. J. Critchley 31, W. L. Madsen 58*). *MoM:* W. L. Madsen. *Attendance:* 2,245. *County debut:* C. A. J. Brodrick (Derbyshire). *This time Worcestershire finally set a challenging target, though it was still easily overhauled. Joe Clarke improvised his way to 42 off 18 balls, while Cox and Whiteley chipped in to swell the target to 187. But Billy Godleman's 70 – his highest T20 score, and his first half-century for Derbyshire – broke the back of the chase, and Wayne Madsen completed the job with an unbeaten 58*, to go with 2-20 for his off-spin.*

At Worcester, July 21 (day/night). **Worcestershire v Lancashire. Abandoned.**

At Worcester, July 30. **Worcestershire won by eight wickets. Durham 201-2** (20 overs) (G. Clark 52, P. D. Collingwood 108*); ‡**Worcestershire 204-2** (18.1 overs) (J. M. Clarke 124*, O. B. Cox 43). *MoM:* J. M. Clarke. *Attendance:* 2,315. *Worcestershire secured their first home win of 2017, at* *the fifth attempt. Paul Collingwood smashed his, and Durham's, first T20 century, and shared 106 for the second wicket with Graham Clark, then 92 for the third with Paul Coughlin, both county records against Worcestershire. But Joe Clarke, exactly 20 years younger than Collingwood, trumped him with his own maiden T20 century, finishing unbeaten on 124* off 53 balls. In a 405-run match, D'Oliveira had done well to take 1-16.*

OLDEST TWENTY20 CENTURIONS

Yrs	*Days*			
41	**65**	**P. D. Collingwood (108*)**	**Durham v Worcs at Worcester**	**2017**
41	37	G. A. Hick (110)	Worcs v Northants at Kidderminster	2007
39	**208**	**D. P. M. D. Jayawardene (116)**	**CD v Otago at New Plymouth**	**2016-17**
39	184	A. C. Gilchrist (106)	Kings XI Punjab v RCB at Dharamsala	2011
38	319	S. T. Jayasuriya (114*)	Mumbai v CSK at Mumbai	2007-08
38	216	M. W. Goodwin (100*)	Sussex v Surrey at Hove	2011
38	209	A. C. Gilchrist (106)	Middx v Kent at Canterbury	2010
38	43	G. A. Hick (116*)	Worcs v Northants at Luton	2004
38	**30**	**Shaiman Anwar (117*)**	**UAE v PNG at Abu Dhabi**	**2016-17**
37	356	S. R. Tendulkar (100*)	Mumbai v Kochi at Mumbai	2011

At Worcester, August 5. **Northamptonshire won by 24 runs. Northamptonshire 195-4** (20 overs) (B. M. Duckett 92*, S. P. Crook 34*); ‡**Worcestershire 171-6** (20 overs) (J. W. Hastings 35, M. J. Santner 38, D. K. H. Mitchell 36*). *MoM:* B. M. Duckett. *Attendance:* 2,110. *County debut:* G. L. S. Scrimshaw (Worcestershire). *Ben Duckett and Steven Crook plundered 90 off the final six overs to lift Northamptonshire to 195; Duckett finished on 92* off 54 balls, including consecutive sixes in the last over. Only when John Hastings was in full swing did Worcestershire threaten victory; with his departure, for 35 off 19, went their faint qualification hopes.*

At Worcester, August 13. **Nottinghamshire won by 11 runs. Nottinghamshire 145** (19.3 overs) (M. H. Wessels 32, W. T. Root 37; A. Hepburn 5-24); ‡**Worcestershire 134-8** (20 overs) (D. K. H. Mitchell 32; D. T. Christian 3-18). *MoM:* A. Hepburn. *Attendance:* 2,457. *In a low-scoring game, Nottinghamshire clinched a quarter-final spot, despite medium-pacer Alex Hepburn returning 5-24, Worcestershire's best T20 figures (surpassing Daryl Mitchell's 5-28 at Northampton in 2014). His efforts left Nottinghamshire defending just 146, but Dan Christian took 3-18, and Harry Gurney conceded only three from a superb final over.*

Worcestershire away matches

July 23: lost Yorkshire by 37 runs.
July 26: beat Nottinghamshire by 13 runs.
July 27: beat Northamptonshire by seven wickets.
August 4: beat Warwickshire by five runs.
August 11: lost to Durham by 13 runs.
August 16: lost to Lancashire by seven wickets.
August 18: lost to Derbyshire by 48 runs.

YORKSHIRE

At Leeds, July 7 (floodlit). **Yorkshire won by 48 runs.** ‡**Yorkshire 227-5** (20 overs) (A. Lyth 82, S. E. Marsh 60*; H. F. Gurney 3-49); **Nottinghamshire 179-8** (20 overs) (A. D. Hales 47, S. J. Mullaney 39). *MoM:* A. Lyth. *Attendance:* 10,037. *County debuts:* S. E. Marsh (Yorkshire); I. S. Sodhi (Nottinghamshire). *Yorkshire put their indifferent Championship form behind them with a rollicking start to their T20 campaign. Adam Lyth's 50-ball 82, backed up by Shaun Marsh's fluent 60*, rushed them to an intimidating 227-5. While Alex Hales was plundering boundaries, Nottinghamshire had a chance, but he fell to Azeem Rafiq's first ball.*

At Leeds, July 21 (floodlit). **Yorkshire won by 29 runs. Yorkshire 179-5** (20 overs) (D. J. Willey 70, S. E. Marsh 30, J. A. Leaning 32*; W. B. Rankin 3-39); ‡**Warwickshire 150** (18 overs) (A. D. Thomason 31, K. H. D. Barker 35; T. T. Bresnan 3-21, Azeem Rafiq 3-37). *MoM:* D. J. Willey. *Attendance:* 8,110. *David Willey blazed six sixes in a 38-ball 70 before being run out off a free hit. Without him, Yorkshire struggled for fluency in the last seven overs, but 179-5 proved adequate.*

Tim Bresnan dismissed Warwickshire's openers in quick succession, and they slid to 58-6. There was no way back.

At Leeds, July 23. **Yorkshire won by 37 runs. Yorkshire 233-6** (20 overs) (A. Lyth 31, D. J. Willey 118); ‡**Worcestershire 196-7** (20 overs) (J. M. Clarke 51, R. A. Whiteley 65). *MoM:* D. J. Willey. *Attendance:* 6,628. *Sheffield-born Ross Whiteley became the fifth to hit six sixes in an over in senior cricket, with Karl Carver, Yorkshire's 21-year-old slow left-armer conceding 37 – he bowled a wide – and 47 in all, the joint-most expensive two-over spell in T20 history. Even so, Worcestershire still fell well short. They were up against it thanks to Willey's personal-best 118 from 55 balls, including eight sixes, which boosted Yorkshire to 233-6, beating the county record they had set earlier in the month. It meant the required run-rate was never in hand – even after Whiteley's heroics.*

SIX SIXES IN AN OVER

Batsman	*Bowler*		
G. S. Sobers	M. A. Nash	Glam v Notts (FC) at Swansea	1968
R. J. Shastri	Tilak Raj	Bombay v Baroda (FC) at Bombay.	1984-85
H. H. Gibbs	D. L. S. van Bunge	SA v Netherlands (ODI) at Basseterre. . . .	2006-07
Yuvraj Singh	S. C. J. Broad	India v England (T20I) at Durban	2007-08
R. A. Whiteley	* **K. Carver**	**Worcs v Yorks (T20) at Leeds**	**2017**

* *Over also contained a wide.*

At Leeds, July 26 (floodlit). **Yorkshire won by 24 runs.** ‡**Yorkshire 152-8** (20 overs) (D. J. Willey 44, S. E. Marsh 36; P. D. Collingwood 3-32); **Durham 128-7** (20 overs) (S. W. Poynter 35*; A. U. Rashid 4-19). *MoM:* A. U. Rashid. *Attendance:* 9,046. *After a middling Yorkshire batting display, Durham seemed capable of their first victory of the season. But they dawdled to 51-3 at the halfway point, and crumbled to a sixth defeat. Adil Rashid was magnificent, earning a personal-best 4-19.*

At Leeds, August 3 (floodlit). **Derbyshire won by five wickets.** ‡**Yorkshire 180-5** (20 overs) (A. Lyth 34, S. E. Marsh 31*, Sarfraz Ahmed 42); **Derbyshire 184-5** (19.4 overs) (B. A. Godleman 67, W. L. Madsen 47, G. C. Wilson 33*; S. A. Patterson 3-37). *MoM:* B. A. Godleman. *Attendance:* 7,902. *County debut:* Sarfraz Ahmed (Yorkshire). *After Billy Godleman's 67 had put Derbyshire on course for the double over Yorkshire, they lost two wickets in the penultimate over to make things interesting. But, needing 18 from nine balls, Gary Wilson and Alex Hughes raced there in seven. After nine consecutive home victories, Yorkshire – without Marsh in the field after he was struck on the helmet by Matt Henry – had finally lost.*

At Leeds, August 11 (floodlit). **Yorkshire won by 19 runs.** ‡**Yorkshire 182-7** (20 overs) (T. Köhler-Cadmore 45, A. Lyth 50; M. W. Parkinson 4-23); **Lancashire 163** (20 overs) (S. J. Croft 62; T. T. Bresnan 6-19). *MoM:* T. T. Bresnan. *Attendance:* 15,735. *In front of a capacity crowd, Bresnan returned the best figures of the 2017 competition, and helped Yorkshire end a sequence of three defeats. He took three in a raucous final over, and added a run-out for good measure. Earlier, leg-spinner Matt Parkinson's four wickets checked Yorkshire after their openers had put on 95 in eight overs. One of those was a stunning catch from Lancashire captain Steven Croft. But, on a night of excellent fielding, Jack Leaning's one-handed effort at deep cover was even better.*

T20 SIX-FORS IN ENGLAND AND WALES

6-5	A. V. Suppiah	Somerset v Glamorgan at Cardiff	2011
6-16	T. G. Southee	Essex v Glamorgan at Chelmsford	2011
6-19	**T. T. Bresnan**	**Yorkshire v Lancashire at Leeds**.	**2017**
6-21	A. J. Hall	Northamptonshire v Worcestershire at Northampton	2008
6-24	T. J. Murtagh	Surrey v Middlesex at Lord's	2005

At Leeds, August 17 (floodlit). **Yorkshire won by 124 runs.** ‡**Yorkshire 260-4** (20 overs) (A. Lyth 161, T. Köhler-Cadmore 41, D. J. Willey 40); **Northamptonshire 136** (14.5 overs) (R. E. Levi 65; Azeem Rafiq 5-19, A. U. Rashid 3-31). *MoM:* A. Lyth. *Attendance:* 7,680. *Lyth's extraordinary* *hundred drove Yorkshire to 260, a total bettered only twice, by Royal Challengers Bangalore v Pune Warriors in 2012-13, and Australia v Sri Lanka in 2016-17 – both made 263. It was also the third time Yorkshire had broken their county record score in 2017. Lyths's 161 came off 73 balls, and included 20 fours and seven sixes. Another Yorkshireman fared less well: Sheffield-born Ben Sanderson recorded 0-77, the second-most expensive figures in T20s, behind Sarmad Anwar's 0-81 for Sialkot Stallions against Lahore Lions in 2011. Northamptonshire launched a rapid reply, reaching 73-1 after five overs, before crumbling to spin; Rafiq collected a career-best 5-19. Yorkshire rose to second in the group, and buffed their net run-rate, but needed results elsewhere to go their way to progress.*

Yorkshire away matches

July 8: lost to Derbyshire by three runs.
July 11: no result v Northamptonshire.
July 14: tied with Lancashire (DLS).
July 28: no result v Warwickshire.
July 30: lost to Nottinghamshire by five wickets.
August 4: lost to Durham by one run.
August 12: lost to Leicestershire by four wickets.

SOUTH GROUP

ESSEX

At Chelmsford, July 7 (floodlit). **Surrey won by two runs. Surrey 188-8** (20 overs) (A. J. Finch 56, D. P. Sibley 61); ‡**Essex 186-6** (20 overs) (R. S. Bopara 75; T. K. Curran 3-28). *MoM:* T. K. Curran. *Attendance:* 5,012. *With Essex needing ten from the final over, Tom Curran conceded seven, and dismissed Ravi Bopara (who had hit five sixes) and Ashar Zaidi. Earlier, Aaron Finch zoomed to 50 from 23 balls, then Dom Sibley and Scott Borthwick (11*) boosted Surrey's total by muscling 37 from the last 17.*

At Chelmsford, July 13 (floodlit). **Essex won by 22 runs. Essex 170-6** (20 overs) (R. N. ten Doeschate 56, Ashar Zaidi 35); ‡**Somerset 148-9** (20 overs) (S. R. Harmer 3-39, P. I. Walter 3-28). *MoM:* R. N. ten Doeschate. *Attendance:* 4,709. *Ryan ten Doeschate's stands of 65 with Zaidi and 50 with Bopara proved the difference. Essex were without Tamim Iqbal, who had returned to Bangladesh for personal reasons after only one T20 appearance.*

At Chelmsford, July 16. **Glamorgan won by five wickets.** ‡**Essex 219-4** (20 overs) (V. Chopra 103*, R. S. Bopara 63); **Glamorgan 224-5** (20 overs) (C. A. Ingram 114, C. B. Cooke 49). *MoM:* C. A. Ingram. *Attendance:* 4,778. *Colin Ingram, who slammed nine sixes and eight fours, made his fifth limited-overs century against Essex to help Glamorgan ace an imposing chase. But it was close: they needed nine from the last over, and managed only three from Paul Walter's first four balls, before Craig Meschede (12*) carved a four and cut a six. Earlier, Varun Chopra (who hit eight sixes) and Bopara (five) put on 122 for Essex's third wicket in 11 overs.*

NOT HIM AGAIN!

Colin Ingram's scores in white-ball cricket for Glamorgan against Essex:

24	(T20 at Cardiff)	2015	107	(RLODC at Chelmsford)	2016
70	(T20 at Chelmsford)	2015	101	(T20 at Chelmsford)	2016
130	(RLODC at Cardiff)	2015	**142**	**(T20 at Cardiff)**	**2017**
26	(T20 at Cardiff)	2016	**114**	**(T20 at Chelmsford)**	**2017**

At Chelmsford, July 21 (floodlit). **Essex won by seven wickets. Hampshire 124-9** (20 overs) (M. A. Carberry 30; R. S. Bopara 4-19); ‡**Essex 129-3** (14 overs) (A. J. A. Wheater 44*, D. W. Lawrence 47). *MoM:* R. S. Bopara. *Attendance:* 4,891. *Hampshire paid for some woeful batting, and did not hit a boundary after the sixth over. Bopara, cleverly varying his pace, took three of his four wickets with the first ball of an over; later he polished off the chase with six overs to spare by clubbing Gareth Berg for six. Essex moved off the bottom of the table.*

At Chelmsford, July 29 (floodlit). **Essex v ‡Gloucestershire. Abandoned.**

At Chelmsford, August 11 (floodlit). **Essex won by nine runs. Essex 172-9** (20 overs) (A. J. A. Wheater 43; N. A. Sowter 4-23); **‡Middlesex 163-7** (20 overs) (J. A. Simpson 30, E. J. G. Morgan 37, G. F. B. Scott 34). *MoM:* N. A. Sowter. *Attendance:* 5,049. *Middlesex looked on course at 120-4 after 14 overs, but the next four produced only 15 runs, and a late blitz still left them short. Essex's win was hard on leg-spinner Nathan Sowter, who took four wickets in a T20 innings for the first time.*

At Chelmsford, August 17 (floodlit). **Kent won by 11 runs. Kent 221-2** (20 overs) (J. L. Denly 127, D. J. Bell-Drummond 80*); **‡Essex 210-5** (20 overs) (D. W. Lawrence 41, V. Chopra 116). *MoM:* J. L. Denly. *Attendance:* 5,006. *Joe Denly (66 balls, 11 fours and seven sixes) and Daniel Bell-Drummond kicked off the match with 207, a record Twenty20 opening partnership. Dan Lawrence and Chopra, who hit nine sixes, replied with a first-wicket stand of 118 in 8.2 overs, but others could not sustain the rate, leaving Essex unlikely to qualify for the quarter-finals. The start was delayed after a steward fell ill, and an air ambulance landed on the outfield.*

HIGHEST PARTNERSHIPS IN TWENTY20 MATCHES

229	for 2nd	V. Kohli/A. B. de Villiers, RC Bangalore v Gujarat Lions at Bangalore .	2016
215*	for 2nd	V. Kohli/A. B. de Villiers RC Bangalore v Mumbai Indians at Mumbai .	2015
207	**for 1st**	**J. L. Denly/D. J. Bell-Drummond, Kent v Essex at Chelmsford**	**2017**
206	for 2nd	A. C. Gilchrist/S. E. Marsh, K XI Punjab v RC Bangalore at Dharamsala	2011
204*	for 2nd	C. H. Gayle/V. Kohli, RC Bangalore v Delhi Daredevils at Delhi	2012
202*	for 2nd	M. C. Juneja/A. Malik, Gujarat v Kerala at Indore	2012-13
201	for 1st	P. J. Ingram/J. M. How, C Districts v Wellington at New Plymouth	2011-12

Essex away matches

July 9: lost to Kent by seven wickets.
July 19: lost to Surrey by ten runs.
July 23: no result v Glamorgan.
July 27: lost to Middlesex by 72 runs.
August 4: beat Hampshire by four wickets.
August 13: beat Gloucestershire by three wickets.
August 18: lost to Sussex by 55 runs.

GLAMORGAN

At Cardiff, July 7 (floodlit). **Hampshire won by 22 runs. Hampshire 167-5** (20 overs) (J. M. Vince 31, G. J. Bailey 37*, L. D. McManus 59); **‡Glamorgan 145-9** (20 overs) (G. G. Wagg 50; R. J. W. Topley 3-23, Shahid Afridi 4-20). *MoM:* L. D. McManus. *Attendance:* 6,720. *Hampshire slipped from 52-0 to 70-4, but a stand of 95 between George Bailey and Lewis McManus, who hit five sixes, took them to a score that proved beyond Glamorgan. The hosts lost two wickets in the first over, from Reece Topley, and never really recovered.*

At Cardiff, July 15 (floodlit). **No result. Glamorgan 171-5** (17.2 overs) (C. A. Ingram 39, J. A. Rudolph 65*) **v ‡Somerset.** *Attendance:* 4,248. *Glamorgan were in sight of a big total when rain ended play in the 18th over. Jacques Rudolph's 65* included a reverse-swept six off seamer Tim Groenewald which sailed 20 yards over the point boundary.*

At Cardiff, July 21 (floodlit). **No result. Sussex 87-2** (8 overs) (L. R. P. L. Taylor 40*) **v ‡Glamorgan.** *After a two-hour delay, a nine-over match began – but only eight were possible before the rain returned.*

At Cardiff, July 23. **Glamorgan v Essex. Abandoned.**

At Cardiff, July 28 (floodlit). **Glamorgan v Surrey. Abandoned.** *Heavy rain meant another washout, the fourth in a row at Sophia Gardens. However, Glamorgan's fine away form left them level with Surrey in first place.*

At Cardiff, August 3 (floodlit). **Gloucestershire won by five runs** (DLS). **Gloucestershire 150-9** (20 overs) (P. Mustard 57; M. G. Hogan 5-17); **‡Glamorgan 32-2** (5 overs). *MoM:* M. G. Hogan.

Attendance: 4,201. With rain falling, Rudolph faced the last ball of the fifth over – the minimum required for a result – from Tissara Perera. A run would have left Glamorgan one ahead on DLS; a dot would have put the teams level. But Rudolph was dismissed and, when that turned out to be the final exchange, Gloucestershire had won. It was tough on Michael Hogan, after his maiden T20 five-for, the wickets coming in nine balls.

At Cardiff, August 18 (floodlit). **Glamorgan won by seven wickets. Middlesex 99-8** (14 overs) (A. C. Voges 58*; M. de Lange 3-19, M. G. Hogan 3-14); ‡**Glamorgan 100-3** (13 overs) (A. H. T. Donald 33). *MoM:* M. de Lange. *Attendance:* 5,126. *Middlesex crashed to 24-5 in the fifth over of a contest reduced to 14 a side – Glamorgan's sixth rain-affected game in a row. Adam Voges saved some face, but Glamorgan won easily, to earn a third home quarter-final in four years. Middlesex slipped from third to sixth and missed the knockouts.*

Glamorgan away matches

July 9: beat Sussex by 18 runs.
July 16: beat Essex by five wickets.
July 25: beat Gloucestershire by 25 runs.
July 30: beat Kent by 25 runs.
August 4: beat Surrey by six runs.
August 10: lost to Hampshire by eight wickets.
August 13: beat Somerset by one run.

GLOUCESTERSHIRE

At Cheltenham, July 7. **Tied. Gloucestershire 182-5** (20 overs) (C. T. Bancroft 51, B. A. C. Howell 33); ‡**Middlesex 182-9** (20 overs) (D. J. Malan 36, R. F. Higgins 68*). *MoM:* R. F. Higgins. *Attendance:* 4,999. *County debut:* T. G. Southee (Middlesex). *Nathan Sowter smashed the final ball of the game, bowled by Benny Howell, straight to cover, and a riveting contest ended in a tie. After Gloucestershire's top five all made at least 20, a target of 183 looked far too many for Middlesex, who slipped to 91-5 in the 12th over. But No. 7 Ryan Higgins was unfazed: he struck six sixes and four fours, and had roared to 68* from just 28 deliveries when – to the delight of a sell-out festival crowd – his partner was smartly caught by Tom Smith.*

At Cheltenham, July 13. **Gloucestershire won by six wickets. Kent 152-8** (20 overs) (J. L. Denly 39, S. W. Billings 36; B. A. C. Howell 4-29); ‡**Gloucestershire 156-4** (19.1 overs) (P. Mustard 42, I. A. Cockbain 31, C. T. Bancroft 34*). *MoM:* B. A. C. Howell. *Attendance:* 4,318. *After a bright start, Kent were restricted to a disappointing 152-8, thanks in part to one-day specialist Howell, who claimed 4-29 in an impressive performance in the field by Gloucestershire. The usually dependable Michael Klinger fell for 13, but contributions from the rest of the top order brought victory.*

At Cheltenham, July 16. **No result.** ‡**Sussex 156-8** (20 overs) (C. D. Nash 33, B. C. Brown 30, L. R. P. L. Taylor 47*; D. A. Payne 3-13) **v Gloucestershire.** *Attendance:* 4,999. *County debut:* N. L. T. C. Perera (Gloucestershire). *Dropped on three by Gloucestershire's new overseas player Tissara Perera, Ross Taylor capitalised to hit 47*. David Payne took 3-13 from three overs, but Chris Liddle was removed from the attack for two high full tosses. On a sluggish pitch a target of 157 might have proved challenging, but rain ended proceedings at the innings break.*

At Bristol, July 25 (floodlit). **Glamorgan won by 25 runs. Glamorgan 176-5** (20 overs) (J. A. Rudolph 51, D. A. Miller 50); ‡**Gloucestershire 151-7** (20 overs) (M. Klinger 52). *MoM:* D. A. Miller. *Attendance:* 4,532. *County debut:* D. A. Miller (Glamorgan). *Fifties from Jacques Rudolph and David Miller (on his debut) paved the way for Glamorgan to inflict a first T20 defeat of the season on Gloucestershire, who had seemed set for victory while Klinger remained at large. But once he fell for 52, they faltered in the face of Glamorgan's accuracy: all six of their bowlers claimed at least one wicket.*

At Bristol, July 28 (floodlit). **Hampshire won by 24 runs** (DLS). **Gloucestershire 174-5** (19 overs) (M. Klinger 101*); ‡**Hampshire 121-3** (11.4 overs) (J. M. Vince 42, R. R. Rossouw 45*). *MoM:* M. Klinger. *Attendance:* 3,565. *Klinger reached 50 from 38 balls, then raced to a brilliant century from the next 18. It was his seventh in Twenty20 cricket; only Chris Gayle, with 18, had more. One over from Chris Wood cost 31 as Klinger, with three successive sixes, guided Gloucestershire to 174-5. But rain, which had meant a 19-over game, eventually ended play with Hampshire 121-3, comfortably ahead on DLS. Their openers, James Vince and Rilee Rossouw, had given them a flying start, with 85 in eight overs.*

At Bristol, August 4 (floodlit). **Gloucestershire won by seven wickets. Somerset 146** (19.4 overs) (J. G. Myburgh 42, C. Overton 33*; D. A. Payne 3-29); ‡**Gloucestershire 152-3** (18.2 overs) (M. Klinger 35, I. A. Cockbain 47*, K. Noema-Barnett 33; R. E. van der Merwe 3-34). *MoM:* K. Noema-Barnett. *Attendance:* 8,385. *The game started 45 minutes late after the Somerset team coach was stuck in traffic for around four hours. A patient sell-out crowd got their money's worth, though: Kieran Noema-Barnett smashed 33 from 12 balls to propel Gloucestershire towards a convincing win. Somerset's batting had displayed less patience, with wickets falling to a series of poor strokes. David Payne took 3-29, and Howell, who did not concede a boundary in his four overs, 2-15. Gloucestershire moved second in the table.*

At Bristol, August 13. **Essex won by three wickets. Gloucestershire 121-8** (20 overs) (I. A. Cockbain 32; J. A. Porter 4-20); ‡**Essex 122-7** (16.2 overs) (V. Chopra 44; T. M. J. Smith 3-29). *MoM:* J. A. Porter. *Attendance:* 4,364. *Jamie Porter, dropped by Essex a fortnight earlier after disappointing Twenty20 form, stormed back with a career-best 4-20. Together with Mohammad Amir (2-18) and Paul Walter (2-17), he dismantled the Gloucestershire batting. Left-arm spinner Tom Smith later took three wickets in ten balls to give the hosts hope, but they had too few runs to cause Essex serious problems.*

Gloucestershire away matches

July 18: beat Kent by eight runs.
July 21: no result v Somerset.
July 29: no result v Essex.
August 3: beat Glamorgan by five runs (DLS).
August 11: lost to Sussex by five wickets.
August 15: lost to Middlesex by 61 runs.
August 17: lost to Surrey by two wickets.

HAMPSHIRE

At Southampton, July 14 (floodlit). **Hampshire won by 29 runs.** ‡**Hampshire 189-8** (20 overs) (J. M. Vince 34, R. R. Rossouw 30, M. A. Carberry 77; T. S. Roland-Jones 4-39, J. E. C. Franklin 3-19); **Middlesex 160-7** (20 overs) (J. A. Simpson 37*, T. G. Southee 64*; M. S. Crane 3-15). *MoM:* M. A. Carberry. *Attendance:* 8,621. *Michael Carberry hit a 45-ball 77, his best T20 score for Hampshire since 2014. Toby Roland-Jones spearheaded the Middlesex attack, and James Franklin, with three wickets from the last four balls, ensured they finished on a high. It did not last: leg-spinner Mason Crane helped reduce them to 74-7 in the 13th over, before a boisterous stand of 86* between John Simpson and Tim Southee.*

At Southampton, July 20 (floodlit). **Sussex won by six wickets.** ‡**Hampshire 126-9** (20 overs) (T. P. Alsop 64; J. C. Archer 4-18); **Sussex 127-4** (17.2 overs) (C. D. Nash 32, B. C. Brown 42). *MoM:* J. C. Archer. *Attendance:* 5,128. *A competition-best 4-18 by Jofra Archer helped winless Sussex defeat unbeaten Hampshire. Danny Briggs, on his first return to his old county, picked up 2-17 and did not concede a boundary in his four overs. Hampshire, who had relied heavily on Tom Alsop, were doomed once Chris Nash and Ben Brown put on 82 for the second wicket.*

At Southampton, July 23. **Hampshire v Surrey. Abandoned.**

At Southampton, August 1 (floodlit). **Kent won by five runs.** ‡**Kent 159-6** (20 overs) (J. L. Denly 31, D. J. Bell-Drummond 62; Shahid Afridi 4-26); **Hampshire 154-4** (20 overs) (J. M. Vince 39, T. P. Alsop 43*, G. J. Bailey 41). *MoM:* D. J. Bell-Drummond. *Attendance:* 5,438. *Four wickets for Shahid Afridi kept Kent in check after Daniel Bell-Drummond underpinned a bright start. Despite the slowness of the pitch, Hampshire were well placed after 15 overs: 39 more needed with eight wickets in hand. However, the departure of Bailey scuppered any acceleration, and Matt Claydon defended 16 from the final over.*

At Southampton, August 4 (floodlit). **Essex won by four wickets. Hampshire 168-6** (20 overs) (R. R. Rossouw 36, G. J. Bailey 89*); ‡**Essex 169-6** (19.4 overs) (A. J. A. Wheater 50, V. Chopra 30, J. S. Foster 33*; L. A. Dawson 3-41). *MoM:* A. J. A. Wheater. *Attendance:* 6,617. *Adam Wheater gave Essex an ideal start to their chase by walloping 50 from 26 balls. He and Varun Chopra clonked 23 from Liam Dawson's first over and, although the scoring slowed – Dawson finished with 3-41 – Essex never looked likely to squander the advantage. The cornerstone of the Hampshire innings had been Bailey's 89*, his Twenty20 highest, in his 150th innings.*

At Southampton, August 10 (floodlit). **Hampshire won by eight wickets.** ‡**Glamorgan 118-6** (20 overs) (A. G. Salter 37*; M. S. Crane 3-21); **Hampshire 119-2** (13.5 overs) (J. M. Vince 60*).

MoM: M. S. Crane. *Attendance:* 7,830. *Leaders Glamorgan came a cropper on a slow strip that took spin. Crane (named in the squad for the West Indies Tests), Dawson (unwanted by England) and Afridi had combined figures of 12–34–52–6. A rally by Graham Wagg (16*) and Andrew Salter guided Glamorgan from the depths of 65-6, but James Vince steered Hampshire to a straightforward victory.*

At Southampton, August 18 (floodlit). **Somerset won by 98 runs.** ‡**Somerset 189-3** (20 overs) (J. G. Myburgh 58, P. D. Trego 84*, J. C. Hildreth 39*); **Hampshire 91** (18.3 overs) (T. P. Alsop 36; C. Overton 3-17, R. E. van der Merwe 3-13). *MoM:* P. D. Trego. *Attendance:* 8,281. *County debut:* J. B. Lintott (Hampshire). *The scale of Somerset's victory – their third-largest win was Hampshire's heaviest defeat – allowed them to slip into the quarter-finals on net run-rate. They had begun hesitantly, with Dawson claiming a wicket in the first over for the third match running, but the middle order sped away. Hampshire, whose progress was guaranteed, seemed distracted, and crashed to 10-3 after two overs. Nine batsmen fell in single figures as Craig Overton and Roelof van der Merwe both claimed career-bests.*

Hampshire away matches

July 7: beat Glamorgan by 22 runs.
July 12: beat Sussex by 19 runs.
July 21: lost to Essex by seven wickets.
July 26: lost to Somerset by 14 runs.
July 28: beat Gloucestershire by 24 runs (DLS).
August 3: beat Middlesex by six wickets.
August 11: beat Kent by six wickets.

KENT

At Beckenham, July 9. **Kent won by seven wickets.** ‡**Essex 166-8** (20 overs) (V. Chopra 47, R. S. Bopara 45, R. N. ten Doeschate 38; J. D. S. Neesham 3-37); **Kent 169-3** (18.3 overs) (D. J. Bell-Drummond 90*, J. L. Denly 32, S. A. Northeast 33). *MoM:* D. J. Bell-Drummond. *Attendance:* 4,395. *County debuts:* J. D. S. Neesham (Kent); Tamim Iqbal (Essex). *In Essex's final over, New Zealand all-rounder Jimmy Neesham dismissed James Foster and Ashar Zaidi, then brilliantly ran out Paul Walter to make it three wickets in three balls. It left Kent needing 169, which opener Daniel Bell-Drummond overhauled with his fourth six; he finished with 90* from 55 deliveries.*

At Canterbury, July 18 (floodlit). **Gloucestershire won by eight runs. Gloucestershire 138-9** (20 overs) (I. A. Cockbain 40); ‡**Kent 130** (20 overs) (N. L. T. C. Perera 3-31, T. M. J. Smith 3-28). *MoM:* B. A. C. Howell. *Attendance:* 3,863. *Chasing 139, Kent seemed to have tamed a two-paced pitch when they reached 68-2 at halfway. But the crafty Benny Howell put the skids on with 2-12, while Tissara Perera and Tom Smith chipped in with three scalps each. Earlier, left-arm spinner Imran Qayyum took 2-19, including Ian Cockbain, whose low-key 40 proved the top score.*

At Canterbury, July 27 (floodlit). **Kent won by seven wickets** (DLS). ‡**Somerset 197-6** (20 overs) (S. M. Davies 62, J. G. Myburgh 64); **Kent 181-3** (16.3 overs) (J. L. Denly 46, D. J. Bell-Drummond 39, S. A. Northeast 54*). *MoM:* S. A. Northeast. *Attendance:* 3,808. *Kent roared to a seventh successive T20 win over Somerset. Openers Joe Denly and Bell-Drummond put on 82 before rain reduced the target to 181 in 18 overs; Sam Northeast held his nerve with a fantastic 27-ball 54*. Somerset had taken advantage of some poor bowling, but sixties from Steven Davies and Johann Myburgh weren't enough to end the losing streak.*

At Canterbury, July 30. **Glamorgan won by 25 runs. Glamorgan 199-2** (20 overs) (J. A. Rudolph 77*, A. H. T. Donald 50, D. A. Miller 43*); ‡**Kent 174-4** (20 overs) (J. L. Denly 68, S. A. Northeast 60). *MoM:* J. A. Rudolph. *Attendance:* 4,583. *On a good pitch, Glamorgan made a testing 199, underpinned by fifties from Aneurin Donald and Jacques Rudolph. Kent were coasting at 110-1 in the 12th, with Denly and Northeast zipping along. But after they were separated, fluency deserted them.*

At Canterbury, August 4 (floodlit). **Sussex won by five wickets.** ‡**Kent 163-9** (20 overs) (S. W. Billings 74; C. J. Jordan 3-38); **Sussex 167-5** (19 overs) (C. D. Nash 73*, B. C. Brown 49). *MoM:* C. D. Nash. *Attendance:* 5,229. *A noisy Canterbury Week crowd were buoyed by Sam Billings's 74, then silenced by Sussex opener Chris Nash's sublime 73*. After choosing to bat, Kent lost wickets with jarring frequency against David Wiese (2-27) and Chris Jordan. By contrast, Nash and Ben Brown stuck together for a stand of 88, which set the platform for victory.*

At Canterbury, August 11 (floodlit). **Hampshire won by six wickets. Kent 167-7** (20 overs) (S. A. Northeast 59, S. W. Billings 40); **‡Hampshire 171-4** (17.2 overs) (C. M. Dickinson 51, J. M. Vince 57, T. P. Alsop 32). *MoM:* C. M. Dickinson. *Attendance:* 4,503. *In only his second T20, Calvin Dickinson upstaged the stars with a 24-ball 51 that drove Hampshire to an emphatic victory. Kent's workmanlike total was built around Northeast's fourth half-century of the competition; only he and Billings found rhythm against a disciplined Hampshire attack, with Liam Dawson (2-25) the pick. Dickinson kickstarted the chase, leaving James Vince to coast home with a classy fifty.*

At Canterbury, August 18 (floodlit). **Surrey won by ten runs. ‡Surrey 154-9** (20 overs) (J. J. Roy 78; A. F. Milne 3-26); **Kent 144-8** (20 overs) (J. L. Denly 40; R. Clarke 4-16). *MoM:* J. J. Roy. *Attendance:* 6,024. *Surrey edged a low-scoring thriller to secure a quarter-final. Despite Jason Roy's 78, their total was modest, and Kent had sight of the knockouts when they reached 94-2. But they grew timid and left themselves 15 from the last over; Rikki Clarke, guileful throughout, conceded just four, and picked up three wickets to finish with 4-16.*

Kent away matches

July 13: lost to Gloucestershire by six wickets.
July 12: beat Surrey by eight wickets.
July 20: lost to Middlesex by 16 runs.
July 23: tied with Sussex (DLS).
August 1: beat Hampshire by five runs.
August 12: beat Somerset by six wickets.
August 17: beat Essex by 11 runs.

MIDDLESEX

At Lord's, July 13 (floodlit). **Middlesex won by one wicket. ‡Surrey 158-9** (20 overs) (K. C. Sangakkara 70; T. G. Helm 3-29); **Middlesex 161-9** (18.4 overs) (D. J. Malan 41, E. J. G. Morgan 31; G. J. Batty 4-14). *MoM:* T. G. Helm. *Attendance:* 27,302. *Middlesex were gliding towards a target of 159 at 133-3 in the 16th over in front of a capacity crowd. But panic set in after Eoin Morgan and Tim Southee fell to successive balls from Gareth Batty – who finished with 4–13–14–4 – and it was left to last man Steven Finn to drag the winning four through midwicket.*

At Uxbridge, July 16. **Somerset won by 21 runs. ‡Somerset 207-9** (20 overs) (L. Gregory 37, A. J. Hose 59, J. C. Hildreth 38; N. A. Sowter 3-43); **Middlesex 186-7** (20 overs) (P. R. Stirling 39, E. J. G. Morgan 33, R. F. Higgins 35*; C. Overton 3-24). *MoM:* A. J. Hose. *Attendance:* 3,296. *County debut:* T. Banton (Somerset). *A rapid 59 from Adam Hose, who sent ten of the 28 balls he faced to the boundary, set up a Somerset total that Middlesex never really threatened, despite collecting 26 from the 15th over, bowled by their former player Josh Davey. It was Somerset's first win in 11 T20 Blast matches, following nine defeats and a no-result.*

At Richmond, July 20 (floodlit). **Middlesex won by 16 runs. Middlesex 179-8** (20 overs) (B. B. McCullum 88, D. J. Malan 33; M. T. Coles 4-32); **‡Kent 163-8** (20 overs) (S. A. Northeast 59, J. D. S. Neesham 52). *MoM:* B. B. McCullum. *Attendance:* 4,092. *Middlesex's T20 captain Brendon McCullum had managed only 36 runs in four matches before this, but now – after surviving a chance to his opposite number, Sam Northeast, in the covers on 17 – sprinted to 88 from 51 balls, with nine sixes. Matt Coles grabbed three wickets in the final over, but Kent – who were 2-2 after the openers fell to successive balls – were always adrift, despite sprightly fifties for Northeast and Jimmy Neesham.*

At Lord's, July 27 (floodlit). **Middlesex won by 72 runs. Middlesex 203-6** (20 overs) (B. B. McCullum 63, J. A. Simpson 51, E. J. G. Morgan 39; D. W. Lawrence 3-21); **‡Essex 131** (16.2 overs) (J. S. Foster 50; T. G. Helm 5-11). *MoM:* B. B. McCullum. *Attendance:* 27,277. *Middlesex reserved their best performance for another sell-out crowd. McCullum smashed 63 from 28 balls, with 54 in boundaries, then John Simpson and Morgan put on 69 in seven overs. Chasing 204, Essex lost opener Adam Wheater for a duck, before Tom Helm claimed Middlesex's best T20 figures.*

At Lord's, August 3 (floodlit). **Hampshire won by six wickets. ‡Middlesex 136** (19.1 overs) (S. S. Eskinazi 43; K. J. Abbott 3-26); **Hampshire 137-4** (17.3 overs) (R. R. Rossouw 60). *MoM:* R. R. Rossouw. *Attendance:* 22,822. *County debut:* T. E. Barber (Middlesex). *Middlesex, lacking three men on England duty and their New Zealand pair of McCullum (at the Caribbean Premier League) and Southee (injured), failed to adapt to a slow pitch, and couldn't capitalise on a very short boundary on the Tavern side. Stevie Eskinazi was the only man to pass 22 and, despite two sloppy* *run-outs, Hampshire strolled home, led by Rilee Rossouw, who shrugged off a blow on the head from the lively debutant Tom Barber.*

At Lord's, August 10 (floodlit). **Middlesex won by two runs. Middlesex 147-6** (20 overs) (P. R. Stirling 40, S. S. Eskinazi 57*); ‡**Sussex 145-8** (20 overs) (C. D. Nash 69, S. van Zyl 34). *MoM:* T. G. Helm. *Attendance:* 22,664. *A slow pitch produced a low-scoring thriller, which Middlesex edged thanks to Helm, who conceded two from the final over when five were required. Sussex had looked in control at 77-1 in the tenth, with Chris Nash and Stiaan van Zyl going well, but no one else managed double figures. Earlier, Eskinazi hit his maiden T20 half-century.*

At Uxbridge, August 15 (floodlit). **Middlesex won by 61 runs. Middlesex 161-5** (20 overs) (P. R. Stirling 44, S. S. Eskinazi 47, A. C. Voges 38); ‡**Gloucestershire 100** (15.5 overs) (B. A. C. Howell 34, J. M. R. Taylor 31; T. G. Southee 3-9, S. T. Finn 4-24, T. G. Helm 3-14). *MoM:* S. T. Finn. *Attendance:* 2,437. *Middlesex had never beaten Gloucestershire in 11 previous T20 matches – nine defeats, a no-result and a tie – but now they administered a thrashing. Eskinazi and Adam Voges batted well on a slow track, then Finn knocked the stuffing out of the reply with his best T20 figures. Southee and Helm helped polish off the tail as the last five wickets tumbled for 11.*

Middlesex away matches

July 7: tied with Gloucestershire.
July 14: lost to Hampshire by 29 runs.
July 21: lost to Surrey by 15 runs.
July 23: lost to Somerset by five wickets.
July 28: no result v Sussex.
August 11: lost to Essex by nine runs.
August 18: lost to Glamorgan by seven wickets.

SOMERSET

At Taunton, July 21 (day/night). **Somerset v Gloucestershire. Abandoned.**

At Taunton, July 23. **Somerset won by five wickets. Middlesex 162-6** (16 overs) (E. J. G. Morgan 59); ‡**Somerset 166-5** (15.5 overs) (J. C. Hildreth 63). *MoM:* J. C. Hildreth. Attendance: 6,826. *Middlesex captain Brendon McCullum was unhappy at playing in wet conditions and fell cheaply, before Eoin Morgan improved his mood with seven sixes (and no fours) in a 28-ball 59. In a 16-over game, 163 was a challenging target, but James Hildreth's 63 gave Somerset hope and, with 13 required off the last, they got there with a delivery to spare.*

At Taunton, July 26 (day/night). **Somerset won by 14 runs.** ‡**Somerset 204-9** (20 overs) (L. Gregory 43, S. M. Davies 32, J. Allenby 37; G. K. Berg 3-35); **Hampshire 190** (19.3 overs) (J. M. Vince 33, M. A. Carberry 30, L. D. McManus 34, G. K. Berg 31). *MoM:* L. Gregory. *Attendance:* 7,298. *Relishing his recent promotion to opener, Lewis Gregory propelled Somerset over 200 with a lightning start: he and Steven Davies racked up 61 off four overs. Hampshire made a good fist of the chase but, while four batsmen reached 30, none passed 34.*

At Taunton, July 30. **Somerset won by 32 runs** (DLS). **Somerset 102-3** (8 overs) (C. J. Anderson 41*); ‡**Sussex 71-4** (8 overs) (S. van Zyl 42*). *MoM:* C. J. Anderson. *Attendance:* 6,648. *New Zealander Corey Anderson blasted 41* off 17 balls to lift Somerset to 102 – an intimidating score in a game reduced to eight overs. It proved to be his last appearance for them after succumbing to a stress fracture of the back. With Sussex chasing a revised 104, Stiaan van Zyl batted through heavy rain for 42* off 22 balls, but he alone made double figures.*

At Taunton, August 6. **Somerset won by four wickets.** ‡**Surrey 157-6** (20 overs) (O. J. D. Pope 46); **Somerset 158-6** (18.2 overs) (J. C. Hildreth 45*, R. E. van der Merwe 36, C. Overton 35*; J. W. Dernbach 3-29). *MoM:* C. Overton. *Attendance:* 7,529. *At 47-5 in the ninth over, requiring another 111, Somerset seemed out of it. But Hildreth guided them to a fourth successive home win with 45*, helped by thirties from Roelof van der Merwe and Craig Overton. Earlier, Ollie Pope had top-scored for Surrey with a perky 46.*

At Taunton, August 12. **Kent won by six wickets. Somerset 149** (18.5 overs) (J. C. Hildreth 36; A. F. Milne 5-11); ‡**Kent 151-4** (18.2 overs) (J. L. Denly 33, S. W. Billings 56*). *MoM:* A. F. Milne. *Attendance:* 7,529. *New Zealand fast bowler Adam Milne took the game by the throat with 5-11, including Somerset's top-scorer Hildreth. It left Kent needing 150, and Sam Billings did most of the work. Somerset had lost to Kent for the eighth T20 game in a row – and their unbeaten home record.*

At Taunton, August 13. **Glamorgan won by one run. Glamorgan 183-6** (20 overs) (A. H. T. Donald 33, N. J. Selman 66, C. A. Ingram 35); ‡**Somerset 182-6** (20 overs) (J. G. Myburgh 87). *MoM:* J. G. Myburgh. *Attendance:* 7,529. *With three overs left, Somerset were in the box seat: Johann Myburgh was on 87, and just 22 were needed. Even after Myburgh fell to Marchant de Lange in the 18th, they plundered 12 from the next and needed eight from the last. But de Lange conceded six in a spell of 2–9–7–1, and left Somerset's quarter-final hopes hanging by a thread.*

Somerset away matches

July 9: lost to Surrey by four runs.
July 13: lost to Essex by 22 runs.
July 15: no result v Glamorgan.
July 16: beat Middlesex by 21 runs.
July 27: lost to Kent by seven wickets.
August 4: lost to Gloucestershire by seven wickets.
August 18: beat Hampshire by 98 runs.

SURREY

At The Oval, July 9. **Surrey won by four runs. Surrey 181-7** (20 overs) (A. J. Finch 61, S. M. Curran 39; R. E. van der Merwe 3-27); ‡**Somerset 177-9** (20 overs) (C. J. Anderson 81). *MoM:* T. K. Curran. *Attendance:* 15,293. *County debut:* C. J. Anderson (Somerset). *Somerset looked sunk at 49-6 in the ninth over, but got close thanks to explosive hitting from their debutant, the New Zealander Corey Anderson – who crunched seven sixes in 81 from 45 balls – and a 12-run penalty for Surrey's slow over-rate. It was left to Tom Curran to defend 12 from the last over: he conceded seven, helped when Anderson was run out by Aaron Finch from the third ball.*

At The Oval, July 14 (floodlit). **Kent won by eight wickets. Surrey 205-5** (20 overs) (J. J. Roy 55, A. J. Finch 49, D. P. Sibley 33); ‡**Kent 207-2** (19.3 overs) (D. J. Bell-Drummond 64, J. L. Denly 116*). *MoM:* J. L. Denly. *Attendance:* 21,626. *Boosted by a first-wicket stand of 108 in nine overs between Jason Roy and Finch, Surrey reached a total they had exceeded only once before at The Oval – but it wasn't enough. Kent's openers put on 163, and Joe Denly was still there at the end with 116* from 63 balls.*

At The Oval, July 19 (floodlit). **Surrey won by ten runs. Surrey 150-9** (20 overs) (K. P. Pietersen 52; P. I. Walter 3-24); ‡**Essex 140-7** (20 overs). *MoM:* K. P. Pietersen. *Attendance:* 23,989. *Kevin Pietersen's first appearance in English cricket for two years was key to Surrey's narrow victory. He made the most of a let-off on 12, when Dan Lawrence at deep midwicket grassed a slog-sweep off Ashar Zaidi, and went on to his first T20 half-century for Surrey. It included four sixes in one over from Simon Harmer, and five in all. Essex made a decent start in reply, but were squeezed in the middle overs, skipper Gareth Batty returning 4–7–19–2.*

At The Oval, July 21 (floodlit). **Surrey won by 15 runs.** ‡**Surrey 156-7** (20 overs) (A. J. Finch 40, O. J. D. Pope 31); **Middlesex 141-7** (20 overs) (E. J. G. Morgan 32, J. E. C. Franklin 38; S. M. Curran 3-28). *MoM:* S. M. Curran. *Attendance:* 24,231. *After a 22-ball 40, Finch was run out when he was sent back by Pietersen. It was the first delivery Pietersen faced, but he aggravated the calf injury which had stopped him fielding in the previous match. Play was held up for ten minutes while he received attention – and a runner. Middlesex dipped to 39-3 in the seventh over and, hard as Eoin Morgan and James Franklin fought, they fell short in the face of disciplined Surrey bowling.*

At The Oval, August 4 (floodlit). **Glamorgan won by six runs.** ‡**Glamorgan 181-6** (20 overs) (A. H. T. Donald 76, C. A. Ingram 42); **Surrey 175-7** (20 overs) (A. J. Finch 33, M. D. Stoneman 34, T. K. Curran 51*; M. de Lange 3-29). *MoM:* A. H. T. Donald. *Attendance:* 22,764. *Glamorgan were always in charge once Aneurin Donald had slapped 76 from 40 balls, dominating a second-wicket stand of 95 with Colin Ingram. Roy fell first ball of the reply, and Surrey looked out of it at 134-7, needing 48 from three overs. Tom Curran carved 51* from 27 balls, but nine off the last four proved beyond him.*

At The Oval, August 13. **Surrey won by 17 runs.** ‡**Surrey 193-2** (20 overs) (J. J. Roy 50, A. J. Finch 114*); **Sussex 176-7** (20 overs) (C. D. Nash 53; G. J. Batty 4-24). *MoM:* A. J. Finch. *Attendance:* 12,672. *Finch's withering assault set up Surrey's comfortable victory. He launched seven sixes – four in a David Wiese over costing 30 – and put on 102 in 11 overs with Roy, and 59* in 25 balls with Ollie Pope, whose contribution was seven. Chris Nash kicked off the reply with a 31-ball half-century, before becoming one of four victims for Batty.*

At The Oval, August 17 (floodlit). **Surrey won by two wickets.** ‡**Gloucestershire 130-9** (20 overs) (S. M. Curran 4-13); **Surrey 134-8** (19.2 overs) (M. C. Henriques 45; C. N. Miles 3-25). *MoM:*

S. M. Curran. *Attendance:* 16,859. *Surrey fans were anticipating an easy victory after Sam Curran took four for none in nine balls – including a triple-wicket maiden – to reduce Gloucestershire to 37-4. A total of 130 hardly looked imposing, but Surrey's batsmen also struggled, apart from Moises Henriques, who made 45 before his run-out in the 16th over set nerves jangling. Three more wickets went down, making it 123-8, before Batty clipped Kieran Noema-Barnett for the winning boundary.*

Surrey away matches

July 7: beat Essex by two runs.
July 13: lost to Middlesex by one wicket.
July 23: no result v Hampshire.
July 28: no result v Glamorgan.
August 3: lost to Sussex by eight wickets.
August 6: lost to Somerset by four wickets.
August 18: beat Kent by ten runs.

SUSSEX

At Arundel, July 9. **Glamorgan won by 18 runs. Glamorgan 198-3** (20 overs) (C. A. Ingram 101*, J. A. Rudolph 49, C. B. Cooke 37*); ‡**Sussex 180-6** (20 overs) (L. J. Wright 101). *MoM:* C. A. Ingram. *Attendance:* 5,098. *Thanks to Colin Ingram, Glamorgan won their first Twenty20 game on Sussex soil, at the sixth attempt. His 46-ball hundred was their quickest, while his stand of 130 with Jacques Rudolph was a county third-wicket record. Luke Wright responded by striking his seventh T20 century – it took him 52 deliveries – but had scant support: Sussex's next highest contribution was 17 from Ross Taylor, the first of two victims for Ingram.*

At Hove, July 12 (floodlit). **Hampshire won by 19 runs. Hampshire 188-3** (20 overs) (J. M. Vince 81, R. R. Rossouw 46, M. A. Carberry 41*); ‡**Sussex 169-7** (20 overs) (L. J. Wright 50; K. J. Abbott 3-22). *MoM:* K. J. Abbott. *Attendance:* 4,517. *Two Hampshire players with Sussex connections stole the show. First Cuckfield-born James Vince hit 81 – including four successive boundaries off Jofra Archer – to engineer an imposing total on a slow pitch. Then Mason Crane, from Shoreham-by-Sea and once part of Sussex's youth system, removed Wright and Taylor when the home side were thriving. Kyle Abbott, bowling with accuracy and varying his pace, ensured there was no way back.*

At Hove, July 23. **Tied** (DLS). **Kent 176-4** (20 overs) (S. W. Billings 64, J. D. S. Neesham 51*); ‡**Sussex 87-3** (8 overs) (C. D. Nash 50*). *MoM:* J. D. S. Neesham. *Attendance:* 5,035. *When Alex Blake's direct hit from long-on beat Laurie Evans's dive, Kent celebrated as if they had won – and not tied – a compelling game. Set a revised 88 from eight overs after rain delayed their reply, Sussex needed eight off the last, with Evans, who made 23, and Chris Nash well set. But Matt Claydon kept his cool, and Sussex could not scramble a second off the final ball. Earlier, Sam Billings and Jimmy Neesham had plundered 112 from Kent's last ten overs.*

At Hove, July 28 (floodlit). **No result.** ‡**Middlesex 136-6** (17.4 overs) (G. F. B. Scott 38*, R. F. Higgins 31) **v Sussex.** *Attendance:* 5,666. *Sussex bowled tightly – left-arm spinner Danny Briggs took the new ball and claimed 1-20 from his four overs – but their efforts counted for naught when rain swept in, producing their third no-result in seven games.*

At Hove, August 3 (floodlit). **Sussex won by eight wickets.** ‡**Surrey 148-8** (20 overs) (M. C. Henriques 41, O. J. D. Pope 34; T. S. Mills 3-20); **Sussex 150-2** (13.3 overs) (C. D. Nash 64, S. van Zyl 52). *MoM:* C. D. Nash. *Attendance:* 5,296. *Surrey were on the receiving end of a mauling, after Tymal Mills's thunderbolts blasted away their illustrious openers, Aaron Finch and Jason Roy. The middle order did little more than tick over, and on an excellent pitch their total felt 30 or 40 short. Sussex tore into the bowling and, by the time the first wicket fell, in the ninth over, Nash and Stiaan van Zyl had put on 120.*

At Hove, August 11 (floodlit). **Sussex won by five wickets. Gloucestershire 138** (18.5 overs) (P. Mustard 43, C. T. Bancroft 37; C. J. Jordan 3-17, G. H. S. Garton 3-35); ‡**Sussex 139-5** (17.4 overs) (L. J. Evans 45*). *MoM:* C. J. Jordan. *Attendance:* 4,702. *From the word go, Sussex were in control: Michael Klinger edged to slip from the first ball, and Ian Cockbain was run out by Archer's direct hit from the sixth. Although Cameron Bancroft and Phil Mustard orchestrated resistance, the Gloucestershire lower order were blitzed by Chris Jordan and George Garton. Sussex had a wobble themselves – lurching from 42-0 to 58-4 in four overs – but David Wiese steadied the ship. Evans, dropped by Mustard on 30, sealed victory with a six on to the pavilion.*

At Hove, August 18 (floodlit). **Sussex won by 55 runs. Sussex 172-4** (20 overs) (C. D. Nash 73, L. J. Wright 37, L. J. Evans 47*); ‡**Essex 117** (15.5 overs) (W. A. T. Beer 3-36). *MoM:* C. D. Nash.

Attendance: 5,528. *In a fiercely competitive group, both teams had a chance of progressing, though in the end neither did, once Somerset had thrashed Hampshire to oust Sussex on net run-rate. Despite suffering a hamstring injury that forced him to use a runner, Nash made his sixth half-century of the tournament; no other Sussex player managed more than one, though Evans did provide impetus at the end. Essex had no option but to go for a big win – and lost regular wickets.*

Sussex away matches

July 16: no result v Gloucestershire.
July 20: beat Hampshire by six wickets.
July 21: no result v Glamorgan.
July 30: lost to Somerset by 32 runs (DLS).
August 4: beat Kent by five wickets.
August 10: lost to Middlesex by two runs.
August 13: lost to Surrey by 17 runs.

QUARTER-FINALS

At Derby, August 22. **Hampshire won by 101 runs. Hampshire 249-8** (20 overs) (Shahid Afridi 101, J. M. Vince 55; M. J. J. Critchley 3-32); **‡Derbyshire 148** (19.5 overs) (B. D. Cotton 30*; L. A. Dawson 3-28, K. J. Abbott 3-25). *MoM:* Shahid Afridi. *Attendance:* 3,949. *Shahid Afridi smashed an extraordinary maiden T20 century, in his 256th match, to power Hampshire to finals day for the seventh year in eight. Opening for the first time in the tournament, he blasted seven sixes and ten fours – with a mixture of placement, power and luck – and led his side to 249-8, the fourth-highest total in the competition's history. Matt Critchley took three wickets in the penultimate over, but by then the damage was done. At 102-9, Derbyshire were in danger of the biggest defeat by runs in English T20, though the last pair spared them that ignominy.*

FASTEST TWENTY20 HUNDREDS IN ENGLAND

Balls			
34	A. Symonds	Kent v Middlesex at Maidstone	2004
37	S. B. Styris	Sussex v Gloucestershire at Hove	2012
40	D. J. Willey	Northamptonshire v Sussex at Hove	2015
42	B. B. McCullum	Warwickshire v Derbyshire at Birmingham	2015
42	**Shahid Afridi**	**Hampshire v Derbyshire at Derby**	**2017**
43	T. Köhler-Cadmore	Worcestershire v Durham at Worcester	2016

At Cardiff, August 23. **Glamorgan won by nine wickets. ‡Leicestershire 123** (19.2 overs) (C. A. J. Meschede 3-17); **Glamorgan 126-1** (13.4 overs) (J. A. Rudolph 46*, C. A. Ingram 70*). *MoM:* C. A. Ingram. *Attendance:* 5,829. *Leicestershire made a spirited start, reaching 57-2 in the powerplay, then slipped to 102-9 in the 16th against accurate seam bowling. Glamorgan lost Aneurin Donald in the first over, but Jacques Rudolph and Colin Ingram steered them to T20 finals day for the first time since 2004 with a stand of 121*. The next man in, David Miller, had been playing for South Africa A the previous day against India A in Potchefstroom. After a helicopter to Johannesburg, a plane to London, and a car to Cardiff, he was not required to bat.*

At Nottingham, August 24. **Nottinghamshire won by five wickets. Somerset 151-6** (20 overs) (S. M. Davies 59, P. D. Trego 40); **‡Nottinghamshire 152-5** (18.3 overs) (S. R. Patel 45, D. T. Christian 36*). *MoM:* S. R. Patel. *Attendance:* 12,171. *On a pitch slower than most at Trent Bridge, Nottinghamshire bowled with discipline to restrict Somerset to 151-6, the lowest total batting first here in 2017. The hosts lost Riki Wessels in the first over of the chase, and Alex Hales soon after to a disputed catch, which Peter Trego was roundly booed for claiming. But Samit Patel, who had collected a tidy 2-26, righted the ship with a 28-ball 45, and Nottinghamshire sailed through.*

At The Oval, August 25. **Warwickshire won by six wickets. Surrey 204-5** (20 overs) (J. J. Roy 74, A. J. Finch 39, M. C. Henriques 48*); **‡Warwickshire 207-4** (19.2 overs) (A. J. Hose 36, G. D. Elliott 59*, C. de Grandhomme 39*). *MoM:* G. D. Elliott. *Attendance:* 11,184. *Surrey threatened a huge total as Jason Roy and Aaron Finch piled on 98 in the first nine overs, but they were contained after that. Warwickshire still needed a record chase to win a Twenty20 knockout match in England – and got there thanks to New Zealand internationals Grant Elliott and Colin de Grandhomme, who* *put on 64* for the fifth wicket in 38 balls. But tempers flared after the substitute Rory Burns claimed a diving catch at deep cover when Elliott – a former Surrey player – had 46. He stood his ground, and was reprieved after several TV replays.*

FINALS DAY REPORTS BY RICHARD GIBSON

SEMI-FINALS

WARWICKSHIRE v GLAMORGAN

At Birmingham, September 2. Warwickshire won by 11 runs. Toss: Glamorgan.

On his return to Warwickshire at the start of 2017, coach Ashley Giles had found outmoded Twenty20 tactics, so opted for revolution: of the team who won the trophy in 2014, only three remained. Among the newcomers was 22-year-old Ed Pollock. He cast aside the stodginess that had been his hallmark at Shewsbury School and – using a bat borrowed from Woakes after breaking three in practice the day before – smote four sixes, surging to 39 before opening partner Sibley had scored. Pollock's 50 provided impetus, and thirties from Elliott and de Grandhomme maintained it. By contrast, Glamorgan lost four wickets in the powerplay, including Ingram to a superb overhead catch by Elliott. Rudolph, one of three South African left-handers in the Glamorgan side, put together a classy 65 before Thomason ran him out with a reverse flick in his follow-through. By the final over, they were nine down, with 26 required. Salter belted Woakes for two fours and a six but Hose, despite being barged by Sibley, clung on to a skyer to condemn Glamorgan to only their fourth defeat of the tournament. No team lost fewer.

Man of the Match: E. J. Pollock. *Attendance* (for all three matches on finals day): 24,400.

Warwickshire

		B	*4/6*
1 E. J. Pollock *c 5 b 10*	50	27	5/4
2 D. P. Sibley *c 4 b 3*	27	23	3
3 A. J. Hose *c 2 b 8*	1	4	0
4 S. R. Hain *lbw b 8*	9	7	1
5 *G. D. Elliott *c 8 b 11*	32	26	5
6 C. de Grandhomme *c 2 b 10*	30	18	4
7 A. D. Thomason *run out*	17	14	1
8 C. R. Woakes *run out*	2	2	0
9 J. S. Patel *c 4 b 11*	0	1	0
10 O. P. Stone *not out*	0	0	0
W 3, nb 4	7		
6 overs: 65-1 (20 overs)	175-9		

1/65 2/68 3/83 4/93 5/139 6/164 7/174 8/174 9/175

11 †T. R. Ambrose did not bat.

Ingram 4–7–30–1; Hogan 4–7–38–2; de Lange 4–10–36–2; Wagg 3–3–41–0; Meschede 4–7–24–2; Salter 1–3–6–0.

Glamorgan

		B	*4/6*
1 *J. A. Rudolph *run out*	65	39	9/1
2 A. H. T. Donald *c 4 b 8*	4	2	1
3 C. A. Ingram *c 5 b 10*	11	8	2
4 D. A. Miller *c 11 b 7*	0	2	0
5 K. S. Carlson *c 11 b 10*	3	6	0
6 †C. B. Cooke *c 2 b 5*	10	12	2
7 G. G. Wagg *c 5 b 8*	25	22	1/1
8 C. A. J. Meschede *c 4 b 7*	1	3	0
9 A. G. Salter *c 3 b 8*	27	14	3/1
10 M. de Lange *b 10*	16	10	1/1
11 M. G. Hogan *not out*	0	0	0
W 2	2		
6 overs: 48-4 (19.4 overs)	164		

1/5 2/31 3/39 4/48 5/67 6/117 7/120 8/127 9/150

Woakes 3.4–8–40–3; Patel 4–11–27–0; Stone 4–10–29–3; Thomason 4–8–32–2; Elliott 3–2–25–1; de Grandhomme 1–1–11–0.

Umpires: R. T. Robinson and A. G. Wharf. Third umpire: R. J. Bailey.

HAMPSHIRE v NOTTINGHAMSHIRE

At Birmingham, September 2. Nottinghamshire won by 23 runs. Toss: Hampshire.

This was Hampshire's seventh visit to finals day – and their fifth semi-final exit. Yet at the halfway stage of their chase they had been in the pound seats. Vince deposited Patel for six over midwicket to bring up a 25-ball 50, leaving 79 required with eight wickets in hand, and Nottinghamshire – whose depth meant they could omit Stuart Broad – in need of inspiration. It came from an unlikely source. Gentle dobber Mullaney, victim of Trent Bridge's postage-stamp boundaries throughout the summer, proved deadly on a larger ground: Alsop, Bailey and Vince departed during a spell of

4–9–22–3. Patel hurried Hampshire's demise with a direct hit to get rid of Carberry and, with vaseline smeared over his eyebrows, looked game for hard work, proving influential in all aspects. He had compiled 35 in the middle overs while Hampshire's spinners applied the squeeze, and laid the platform for Christian to launch a counter that included three sixes in one Abbott over. Patel then made an immediate impact with the ball: Afridi, who had marmalised Derbyshire with a 42-ball hundred in the quarters, shovelled a drag-down to deep midwicket for the 12th golden duck of his T20 career. The contrast summed up Hampshire's day.

Man of the Match: S. J. Mullaney.

Nottinghamshire

		B	*4/6*
1 M. H. Wessels *c 3 b 11*	48	27	5/2
2 A. D. Hales *c 1 b 10*	15	7	1/1
3 †T. J. Moores *c 9 b 10*	0	4	0
4 B. R. M. Taylor *c 10 b 1*	19	20	1
5 S. R. Patel *c 5 b 7*	35	31	3/1
6 *D. T. Christian *c 6 b 9*	24	12	0/3
7 S. J. Mullaney *c 1 b 7*	0	2	0
8 W. T. Root *not out*	11	8	0
9 I. S. Sodhi *not out*	15	9	0/1
B 1, lb 1	2		
6 overs: 56-2 (20 overs)	169-7		

1/23 2/49 3/71 4/99 5/122 6/143 7/148

10 J. T. Ball and 11 H. F. Gurney did not bat.

Dawson 4–9–36–2; Berg 3–4–29–0; Wood 2–5–17–2; Abbott 3–6–41–1; Crane 4–10–22–1; Shahid Afridi 4–8–22–1.

Hampshire

		B	*4/6*
1 Shahid Afridi *c 2 b 5*	0	1	0
2 †C. M. Dickinson *c 6 b 10*	27	21	4
3 *J. M. Vince *c 4 b 7*	56	32	5/3
4 T. P. Alsop *c and b 7*	20	17	2
5 G. J. Bailey *b 7*	4	6	0
6 M. A. Carberry *run out*	13	9	1/1
7 L. A. Dawson *c 1 b 11*	4	7	0
8 G. K. Berg *c 1 b 11*	15	12	2
9 K. J. Abbott *c 6 b 11*	0	1	0
10 C. P. Wood *b 10*	2	4	0
11 M. S. Crane *not out*	3	2	0
Lb 1, w 1	2		
6 overs: 55-2 (18.4 overs)	146		

1/0 2/55 3/97 4/105 5/120 6/120 7/140 8/140 9/140

Patel 4–9–32–1; Gurney 3–9–19–3; Ball 3.4–7–32–2; Christian 1–1–16–0; Sodhi 3–2–24–0; Mullaney 4–9–22–3.

Umpires: R. J. Bailey and M. A. Gough. Third umpire: A. G. Wharf.

FINAL

WARWICKSHIRE v NOTTINGHAMSHIRE

At Birmingham, September 2 (floodlit). Nottinghamshire won by 22 runs. Toss: Warwickshire.

Another poised performance from Samit Patel helped Nottinghamshire to a maiden Twenty20 title, and the first domestic cup double since Hampshire's five years earlier. Ostensibly, the contest followed the template of the day: the team that won the toss chose to bowl, only for scoreboard pressure to derail the chase. But there was more drama this time.

Unperturbed by his treatment against Glamorgan, Woakes had left Nottinghamshire in the mire at 30 for three. After Patel joined Taylor, though, the innings changed. Their placement was precise, their timing true. They played wily off-spinner Jeetan Patel with care, but were full throttle against the others, particularly after Samit Patel launched Elliott into the third tier in the tenth over. Each hit 40 or so in boundaries, as the ball glided into gaps.

After the underused New Zealander de Grandhomme (his one over cost four) ended the fourth-wicket alliance at 132, a finals-day record to go with a record attendance, there came another Christian uprising. He turned Stone's impressive speed against him and, in a final over that cost 23, a couple of forearm smashes carried ten rows deep. In all, the last 11 overs leaked 132, swelling the total to 190.

In the build-up, Giles said he fancied his new-look side to go toe-to-toe with Nottinghamshire in a slugfest. But they lost too many expressionists in the early stages, most gallingly the pocket rocket Pollock. He became Samit Patel's second direct-hit run-out of the day, after driving to mid-off and ambling the first ten paces. From 36 for three, Hain rallied with a half-century and – despite cramp – helped reduce the requirement to 80 off seven. Hope remained while de Grandhomme, with a career strike-rate of 169, the world's best, was at the other end. But Gurney deceived him with a slower one, and added two more wickets in the penultimate over to become the first to take seven across finals day.

Philip Brown, Getty Images

Off the hook: Nottinghamshire began poorly, but Samit Patel rescued them with an unbeaten 64.

For Nottinghamshire, the lyrics of "Sweet Caroline" – "Good times never seemed so good" – belted out by Lancastrian duo David Lloyd and Andrew Flintoff during the interval, took on real significance. For Samit Patel, Gurney, and the coach Peter Moores, there was a sense of accomplishment after rejection by England. For Taylor, it was a fitting farewell before returning to international cricket with Zimbabwe, and for Luke Fletcher, a spectator here, an emotional experience at the ground where a blow to the head had ended his season two months earlier. This time, the only damage to a player was relatively superficial: Christian received a shiner at the presentation when the trophy caught him in the eye.

Man of the Match: S. R. Patel.

Nottinghamshire

		B	*4/6*
1 M. H. Wessels *c 10 b 8*	19	12	4
2 A. D. Hales *b 8*	7	6	0/1
3 †T. J. Moores *c 2 b 8*	0	3	0
4 B. R. M. Taylor *c 2 b 6*	65	49	9/1
5 S. R. Patel *not out*	64	42	4/4
6 *D. T. Christian *not out*	24	8	2/2
B 1, lb 7, w 3	11		
6 overs: 44-3 (20 overs)	190-4		

1/21 2/21 3/30 4/162

7 S. J. Mullaney, 8 W. T. Root, 9 I. S. Sodhi, 10 J. T. Ball and 11 H. F. Gurney did not bat.

Patel 4–13–24–0; Stone 4–6–50–0; Woakes 4–12–29–3; Thomason 2–2–26–0; Elliott 2–1–20–0; Sibley 3–5–29–0; de Grandhomme 1–3–4–1.

Warwickshire

		B	*4/6*
1 E. J. Pollock *run out*	14	11	1
2 D. P. Sibley *b 11*	2	5	0
3 S. R. Hain *c 6 b 11*	72	44	5/3
4 A. J. Hose *b 10*	7	8	1
5 *G. D. Elliott *lbw b 6*	9	11	0
6 C. de Grandhomme *b 11*	27	19	0/2
7 A. D. Thomason *c 3 b 11*	26	13	0/2
8 C. R. Woakes *not out*	4	4	0
9 J. S. Patel *b 10*	4	3	0
10 †T. R. Ambrose *not out*	1	2	0
Lb 1, w 1	2		
6 overs: 38-3 (20 overs)	168-8		

1/12 2/16 3/36 4/63 5/118 6/157 7/160 8/166

11 O. P. Stone did not bat.

Patel 4–3–42–0; Gurney 4–9–17–4; Ball 4–8–26–2; Christian 4–4–43–1; Mullaney 3–1–28–0; Sodhi 1–1–11–0.

Umpires: M. A. Gough and A. G. Wharf. Third umpire: R. T. Robinson.

WINNERS

Year	Result	*Man of the Match*
2003	SURREY beat Warwickshire by nine wickets at Nottingham.	J. Ormond
2004	LEICESTERSHIRE beat Surrey by seven wickets at Birmingham.	B. J. Hodge
2005	SOMERSET beat Lancashire by seven wickets at The Oval.	G. C. Smith
2006	LEICESTERSHIRE beat Nottinghamshire by four runs at Nottingham.	D. L. Maddy
2007	KENT beat Gloucestershire by four wickets at Birmingham.	R. McLaren
2008	MIDDLESEX beat Kent by three runs at Southampton.	O. A. Shah
2009	SUSSEX beat Somerset by 63 runs at Birmingham.	D. R. Smith
2010	HAMPSHIRE beat Somerset by virtue of losing fewer wickets at Soton.	N. D. McKenzie
2011	LEICESTERSHIRE beat Somerset by 18 runs at Birmingham.	J. J. Cobb
2012	HAMPSHIRE beat Yorkshire by ten runs at Cardiff.	D. A. Miller
2013	NORTHAMPTONSHIRE beat Surrey by 102 runs (D/L) at Birmingham.	D. J. Willey
2014	WARWICKSHIRE beat Lancashire by four runs at Birmingham.	L. J. Evans
2015	LANCASHIRE beat Northamptonshire by 13 runs at Birmingham.	A. L. Davies
2016	NORTHAMPTONSHIRE beat Durham by four wickets at Birmingham.	J. J. Cobb
2017	NOTTINGHAMSHIRE beat Warwickshire by 22 runs at Birmingham.	S. R. Patel

ROYAL LONDON ONE-DAY CUP IN 2017

REVIEW BY VITHUSHAN EHANTHARAJAH

1 Nottinghamshire 2 Surrey 3= Essex, Worcestershire

"It was like a switch went on and I started middling everything, so thanks, Deano, for that 156." Of the abuse Rilee Rossouw received for going Kolpak, a sledge from South African compatriot Dean Elgar in a Royal London Cup group match stirred him most. "I'm not going to say what was said, but it was something to do with the pound." Elgar's own 78 had helped Somerset to a total of 249. Rossouw responded with a career-best 156 from 113 balls, driving Hampshire to a comprehensive victory. And he typified a curious trend: if you had a score to settle, this was the competition for you.

Alastair Cook, the Test captaincy off his shoulders, enjoyed a white-ball fling at Essex, striking three hundreds and three fifties to finish as the competition's highest run-scorer, with 636 at 79. While he was making hay, the England ODI team – who had jettisoned Cook long before – were making poor starts in the Champions Trophy, returning opening partnerships of six, 37, four and 34. #BringBackCook?

Jason Roy carried the can for those figures, and was dropped before Pakistan knocked England out at Cardiff. But Surrey made him feel loved once more: he returned for their semi-final at Worcestershire and thrashed 92 to set up victory. "It showed it could have been a different story at Cardiff," said Surrey captain Gareth Batty. "He is a wonderful talent. We will have him back every day of the week."

But it was another England opener who stole the show a few weeks later. Alex Hales has endured occasional calls to be dropped, despite regular match-winning displays. In the final, he produced another, single-handedly out-muscling Surrey with an unbeaten 187. It was an innings that, in its capacity to prove a point, summed up this Royal London Cup.

With the NatWest T20 Blast jammed into a prime-summer block, the one-day competition had to make do with an earlier start. Three rounds of Championship games and – in late April – 50-over cricket was upon us. For many sides, that meant a pre-season with equal exposure to red ball and white; not many were sure how it would play out.

Haseeb Hameed made his List A debut, and registered two half-centuries in eight matches for Lancashire. If that was so-so, his Championship form became a concern. Had the white-ball game impaired his judgment? Who knows. But, having burst on to the Test scene at the end of 2016 with assured performances in India, he was dropped for the home series with South Africa.

It was a story the domestic 50-over game, still battling to justify its importance, could have done without. The format already had to contend with the ECB's plans for Twenty20 cricket: given a packed schedule, a city-based T20 competition launched in 2020 was set to run concurrently with the one-day tournament, and deprive it of the best white-ball players. It would be one

Kevin Galvin, NurPhoto/Getty Images

Flat-bat bully: Nottinghamshire's Alex Hales dominates Surrey in the final.

thing for them to miss a domestic competition because of the IPL; deliberately engineering a clash on home soil would be another matter.

Star quality was still in evidence in 2017, at least. While many thought an early start would mean greener, seaming pitches, batsmen across the country cashed in. If Hales produced the knock of the tournament, Roelof van der Merwe pushed him close with one of the most remarkable displays of hitting seen at Taunton. Again, Surrey were on the receiving end, though Somerset were swimming against the tide when they fell to 22 for five chasing 291. But van der Merwe led the comeback, hitting an unbeaten 165 off 122 balls as they roared home.

James Vince made 178 for Hampshire against Glamorgan – a personal and county best, beating Gordon Greenidge by a run – but his team still lost, thanks chiefly to Colin Ingram's own whirlwind century. Prior to the Champions Trophy, Jonny Bairstow's place in the England squad was still in doubt because of their preference for Sam Billings as the back-up keeper. Yorkshire allowed Bairstow to open against Durham at the start of May and, a target of 336 in his sights, he smashed 174 off 113 balls, an innings that helped him secure a squad number. Darren Stevens, 41 and in his 21st season, slaughtered 147 off 67 balls – including ten fours and 14 sixes – at Swansea, only for Kent to finish short of another huge Ingram-inspired Glamorgan total. It was one of three times in the competition Kent passed 300 and lost. All the big hitting made the performance of Middlesex's Toby Roland-Jones more special: he topped the bowling averages and gave away less than four an over.

New rules for the play-offs meant only the top three progressed to the knockouts: topping the group brought passage to the semi-finals, while second and third met in two quarter-finals. Had Durham not been docked two points by the ECB for running up substantial debts, they, and not eventual winners Nottinghamshire, would have progressed along with Worcestershire and Yorkshire in the North Group. Surrey also scraped into the knockouts, some way off the pace set by Essex. Somerset completed the set of qualifiers.

The Nottinghamshire–Surrey final was a mouth-watering match-up. Surrey had the best attack, but were up against the best batting line-up, and needed plenty of runs. Opener Mark Stoneman gritted his teeth through a middle-order collapse, remained unbeaten, and scored nearly half their 297. It appeared defendable, but Hales had history in his sights, trumping Stoneman's 144, then Geoffrey Boycott's record of 146 in a Lord's final. "In a one-day game?" asked Hales, when informed of the identity of the previous record holder. "That's surprising."

The agony of Surrey's third straight final defeat was embodied by 19-year-old Ollie Pope, who missed an easy chance to catch Hales on nine, off Sam Curran, the competition's leading wicket-taker. As Hales exploited Pope's clemency, it allowed Chris Read – who had already announced he would retire at the season's end – to sign off in style. Not that Read was a passenger: just as Surrey were clawing back into the match, reducing Nottinghamshire to 150 for five, his arrival calmed nerves. He took them to within 11 runs of victory with a perky 58, before enjoying a standing ovation that spoke as much of Read's distinguished career as his contribution on the day.

"I've had some great times here," he said. "Winning in 2013, the MCC bicentenary game, playing with the legends of my era, and then today." It felt fitting that Read had the last word on a competition that continues to find its voice, despite others doing most of the shouting. "Good pitches, nice weather, high-scoring games… I think 50-over cricket has definitely got a future."

Prize Money

£154,000 for winners: NOTTINGHAMSHIRE.
£72,000 for runners-up: SURREY.
£23,150 for losing semi-finalists: ESSEX, WORCESTERSHIRE.
There was no financial reward for winning individual matches.

FINAL GROUP TABLES

North Group

	North Group	*Played*	*Won*	*Lost*	*Tied*	*No result*	*Points*	*NRR*
1	WORCESTERSHIRE	8	6	1	1	0	13	0.02
2	YORKSHIRE	8	6	2	0	0	12	0.86
3	NOTTINGHAMSHIRE	8	4	3	0	1	9	−0.05
4	Lancashire	8	4	4	0	0	8	0.19
5	Durham	8	4	3	0	1	7*	0.24
6	Leicestershire	8	3	4	0	1	7	0.00
7	Derbyshire	8	2	5	0	1	5	−0.33
8	Northamptonshire	8	1	4	1	2	5	−0.72
9	Warwickshire	8	2	6	0	0	4	−0.52

* *Durham were docked two points as part of an ECB punishment for accruing excessive debts.*

	South Group	*Played*	*Won*	*Lost*	*Tied*	*No result*	*Points*	*NRR*
1	ESSEX	8	7	1	0	0	14	0.88
2	SOMERSET	8	5	2	0	1	11	0.54
3	SURREY	8	4	3	0	1	9	0.10
4	Glamorgan	8	4	4	0	0	8	−0.66
5	Sussex	8	3	3	0	2	8	0.53
6	Hampshire	8	3	4	0	1	7	−0.10
7	Gloucestershire	8	3	4	0	1	7	−0.43
8	Middlesex	8	2	4	0	2	6	−0.24
9	Kent	8	1	7	0	0	2	−0.40

Where two or more counties finished with an equal number of points, the positions were decided by (a) most wins, (b) net run-rate.

ROYAL LONDON ONE-DAY CUP AVERAGES

BATTING (300 runs at 50.00)

		M	*I*	*NO*	*R*	*HS*	*100*	*50*	*Avge*	*SR*	*4*	*6*
1	†D. Elgar (*Somerset*)	6	6	1	519	131*	1	5	103.80	98.85	40	12
2	B. T. Foakes (*Surrey*)	10	8	3	482	92	0	6	96.40	105.47	44	3
3	†A. N. Cook (*Essex*)	9	9	1	636	133	3	3	79.50	88.45	74	0
4	G. J. Bailey (*Hants*)	6	6	2	312	145*	1	2	78.00	92.30	25	4
5	†K. C. Sangakkara (*Surrey*)	9	9	2	545	124*	2	3	77.85	96.97	52	8
6	J. M. Vince (*Hants*)	7	7	1	463	178	1	3	77.16	113.75	50	8
7	A. D. Hales (*Notts*)	7	7	1	434	187*	2	1	72.33	105.85	50	9
8	M. J. Richardson (*Durham*)	8	8	2	424	100*	1	4	70.66	89.07	32	7
9	†C. A. Ingram (*Glam*)	8	8	0	564	142	3	2	70.50	104.44	31	29
10	†G. S. Ballance (*Yorks*)	9	9	2	483	152*	1	3	69.00	105.00	45	7
11	S. R. Patel (*Notts*)	11	10	2	539	122*	2	3	67.37	94.23	56	7
12	S. R. Hain (*Warwicks*)	8	8	1	456	109	2	2	65.14	94.60	53	0
13	D. J. Bell-Drummond (*Kent*)	8	8	1	443	138	2	2	63.28	87.37	35	3
14	P. S. P. Handscomb (*Yorks*)	9	9	1	504	140	1	3	63.00	109.56	43	10
15	S. J. Mullaney (*Notts*)	8	7	1	378	111	1	3	63.00	113.17	33	14
16	R. E. Levi (*Northants*)	7	6	1	305	109	1	3	61.00	108.15	37	4
17	I. R. Bell (*Warwicks*)	8	7	0	410	104	1	3	58.57	94.90	40	6
18	D. J. Vilas (*Lancs*)	8	8	1	408	108	2	2	58.28	113.64	46	2
19	†K. K. Jennings (*Durham*)	8	8	0	460	139	2	2	57.50	102.44	58	4
20	A. J. Hose (*Somerset*)	8	7	1	330	101*	1	2	55.00	105.76	28	7
21	R. S. Bopara (*Essex*)	8	8	2	329	92*	0	2	54.83	106.81	29	6
22	J. Allenby (*Somerset*)	8	8	1	377	144*	1	2	53.85	87.26	38	7
23	B. R. M. Taylor (*Notts*)	9	8	1	376	154	1	3	53.71	106.81	43	6
24	M. Klinger (*Glos*)	7	7	0	369	134	1	2	52.71	78.01	38	8
25	†B. T. Slater (*Derbys*)	8	7	1	312	82	0	3	52.00	85.47	39	2
26	†M. D. Stoneman (*Surrey*)	10	10	1	456	144*	1	4	50.66	102.01	55	2

BOWLING (10 wickets)

		Style	*O*	*M*	*R*	*W*	*BB*	*4I*	*Avge*	*SR*	*ER*
1	T. S. Roland-Jones (*Middx*)	RFM	51	7	201	11	4-10	1	18.27	27.81	3.94
2	J. W. Dernbach (*Surrey*)	RFM	55.5	1	277	15	4-31	1	18.46	22.33	4.96
3	J. A. Porter (*Essex*)	RFM	39	4	196	10	4-40	1	19.60	23.40	5.02
4	M. de Lange (*Glam*)	RF	73.2	4	405	18	5-49	1	22.50	24.44	5.52
5	Azeem Rafiq (*Yorks*)	OB	70.3	0	408	18	4-47	1	22.66	23.50	5.78
6	W. J. Weighell (*Durham*)	RM	66	4	416	18	5-57	2	23.11	22.00	6.30
7	C. Overton (*Somerset*)	RFM	63	7	385	16	3-21	0	24.06	23.62	6.11
8	S. J. Thakor (*Derbys*)	RM	59.5	1	319	13	3-23	0	24.53	27.61	5.33
9	R. Rampaul (*Surrey*)	RFM	79	2	444	18	4-40	2	24.66	26.33	5.62
10	S. M. Curran (*Surrey*)	LFM	89.3	0	498	20	3-43	0	24.90	26.85	5.56
11	J. Clark (*Lancs*)	RM	37.4	0	251	10	4-34	1	25.10	22.60	6.66
12	N. Wagner (*Essex*)	LFM	57.2	7	353	14	4-41	2	25.21	24.57	6.15

		Style	O	M	R	W	BB	4I	Avge	SR	ER
13	B. A. C. Howell (*Glos*)	RM	66.2	1	352	13	3-40	0	27.07	30.61	5.30
14	G. T. Griffiths (*Leics*)	RFM	50	1	274	10	3-35	0	27.40	30.00	5.48
15	M. S. Crane (*Hants*)	LB	64	1	384	14	3-53	0	27.42	27.42	6.00
16	M. J. Waite (*Yorks*)	RFM	42.3	1	284	10	4-65	1	28.40	25.50	6.68
17	D. Wiese (*Sussex*)	RFM	61.1	2	336	11	4-29	1	30.54	33.36	5.49
18	P. Coughlin (*Durham*)	RFM	62.5	2	372	12	3-36	0	31.00	31.41	5.92
19	R. E. van der Merwe (*Somerset*)	SLA	64	1	385	11	3-21	0	35.00	34.90	6.01
20	K. H. D. Barker (*Warwicks*)	LFM	53.4	1	353	10	3-63	0	35.30	32.20	6.57
21	J. S. Patel (*Warwicks*)	OB	68.5	1	353	10	3-48	0	35.30	41.30	5.12
22	J. L. Pattinson (*Notts*)	RFM	83	0	475	13	4-42	1	36.53	38.30	5.72
23	T. J. Wells (*Leics*)	RFM	64.4	0	401	10	3-44	0	40.10	38.80	6.20
24	H. F. Gurney (*Notts*)	LFM	80.1	3	535	13	3-29	0	41.15	37.00	6.67
25	J. Leach (*Worcs*)	RFM	74	2	497	12	4-66	1	41.41	37.00	6.71
26	S. R. Harmer (*Essex*)	OB	74.2	2	418	10	3-56	0	41.80	44.60	5.62
27	J. W. Hastings (*Worcs*)	RFM	73.2	3	473	11	3-50	0	43.00	40.00	6.45
28	S. C. J. Broad (*Notts*)	RFM	85.5	0	470	10	2-48	0	47.00	51.50	5.47

NORTH GROUP

DERBYSHIRE

At Derby, April 30. **Derbyshire won by six wickets. Northamptonshire 307-7** (50 overs) (J. J. Cobb 56, R. E. Levi 109); ‡**Derbyshire 309-4** (48.4 overs) (B. A. Godleman 95, S. J. Thakor 130). *Attendance: 318. Derbyshire pulled off their highest successful one-day chase – beating 296 against Worcestershire in 2016 – after second-wicket pair Billy Godleman and Shiv Thakor put on 168 at a run a ball. Godleman fell for 95, but Thakor completed his first limited-overs hundred, having earlier kept Northamptonshire in check with three wickets, including fellow centurion Richard Levi.*

At Derby, May 2. **Nottinghamshire won by four wickets** (DLS). ‡**Derbyshire 303-4** (50 overs) (B. T. Slater 72, B. A. Godleman 90, W. L. Madsen 66*); **Nottinghamshire 286-6** (46.2 overs) (A. D. Hales 77, M. H. Wessels 67, S. R. Patel 59). *Attendance: 859. On the pitch he had enjoyed two days previously, Godleman hit another ninety to help Derbyshire to their highest List A score against Nottinghamshire, beating 275 at Sookholme in 2016. It was the first time they had topped 300 in consecutive 50-over matches. But half-centuries from Alex Hales, Riki Wessels and Samit Patel gave Nottinghamshire a racing start and, though a rain break precipitated a flurry of wickets, they reached the revised target of 286 in 47 overs with relative ease.*

At Derby, May 10. **Derbyshire won by four wickets. Warwickshire 292-7** (50 overs) (S. R. Hain 109, I. R. Bell 93); ‡**Derbyshire 296-6** (49.4 overs) (B. T. Slater 82). *Attendance: 661. Derbyshire knocked out holders Warwickshire with more superb batting: four of their top 19 List A totals had come in a fortnight. Ben Slater began their chase with a patient 82, and Jeewan Mendis finished it in the nick of time with his seventh boundary in a 23-ball 44*. Earlier, Sam Hain hit 109, his highest one-day score, and shared a second-wicket stand of 182 with Ian Bell. But a limp finish – only 44 runs came off Warwickshire's last seven overs – proved costly.*

At Derby, May 16 (day/night). **Worcestershire won by five wickets** (DLS). **Derbyshire 209-8** (36 overs) (S. J. Thakor 60); ‡**Worcestershire 218-5** (32 overs) (D. K. H. Mitchell 67, T. Köhler-Cadmore 63). *County debut:* N. M. Lyon (Worcestershire). *Attendance: 350. Worcestershire sealed first place in the North Group thanks to a rollicking opening stand of 90 in ten overs between Daryl Mitchell and Tom Köhler-Cadmore, who larruped a 34-ball 63. That made overhauling a tricky revised target of 218 in 36 overs a doddle. Worcestershire had been sloppy in the field: they dropped five catches, including top-scorer Thakor. But Ed Barnard's incisiveness (3-37), and Jack Shantry's accuracy – he conceded just 28 from seven overs – meant Derbyshire's total was always in reach.*

Derbyshire away matches

April 27: no result v Durham.
May 7: lost to Yorkshire by 15 runs.
May 12: lost to Lancashire by three wickets (DLS).
May 14: lost to Leicestershire by five wickets.

DURHAM

At Chester-le-Street, April 27. **No result. Durham 194-2** (34 overs) (K. K. Jennings 79, M. J. Richardson 83*) **v ‡Derbyshire.** *Attendance: 729. Michael Richardson hit a career-best 83*, but persistent showers scotched a conclusion.*

At Gosforth, May 5. **Durham won by five wickets. Leicestershire 211** (49.5 overs) (Z. J. Chappell 59*; W. J. Weighell 4-34); **‡Durham 215-5** (43.2 overs) (S. C. Cook 67, M. J. Richardson 51, P. D. Collingwood 65*). *Attendance: 1,673. Three weeks before his 41st birthday, Paul Collingwood provided a reminder of his class. After taking 3-42 to help restrict Durham's target to 212, he shepherded them home with a composed 65*. Earlier, Leicestershire had subsided to 13-4 in a blur of poor strokes, then 68-6, before Zak Chappell salvaged some respectability with his maiden one-day half-century. James Weighell finished with 4-34, taking his haul in three games to 12 wickets.*

At Chester-le-Street, May 7. **Durham won by 19 runs. Durham 291-7** (50 overs) (K. K. Jennings 101, M. J. Richardson 68, P. D. Collingwood 53*); **‡Northamptonshire 272-8** (50 overs) (R. E. Levi 66, A. M. Rossington 69). *Attendance: 1,288. With excellent placement and running, Keaton Jennings hit his second century of the tournament, and put on 158 with Richardson. Collingwood weighed in with 53* to lift Durham's total to 291, then produced an athletic stop, swivel, and direct hit to run out Richard Levi for 66. Still, the match was in the balance during Northamptonshire's sixth-wicket stand of 99, until Adam Rossington missed a scoop and lost his middle stump.*

At Chester-le-Street, May 16 (day/night). **Lancashire won by 28 runs. Lancashire 304-8** (50 overs) (A. L. Davies 50, D. J. Vilas 108); **‡Durham 276-9** (50 overs) (M. J. Richardson 58). *Attendance: 1,513. After Dane Vilas smashed his way from 53 to 100 in just 26 balls, Durham needed 305 to progress. But that never looked likely, particularly after Collingwood (20) was run out while Richardson was using a runner. Neither team made the knockouts.*

Durham away matches

May 1: beat Warwickshire by 72 runs.
May 3: lost to Yorkshire by six wickets.
May 11: beat Nottinghamshire by four wickets.
May 14: lost to Worcestershire by 15 runs.

LANCASHIRE

At Manchester, April 28 (day/night). **Leicestershire won by three wickets** (DLS). **‡Lancashire 314-8** (50 overs) (H. Hameed 88; J. S. Sykes 4-57); **Leicestershire 311-7** (48.2 overs) (M. L. Pettini 59, C. S. Delport 62, M. J. Cosgrove 67). *Attendance: 1,479. Haseeb Hameed made an impressive 88 on his white-ball debut, but Leicestershire responded with a superb chase. Three half-centuries set them up – the pick an excellent 67 from Mark Cosgrove – and Tom Wells's 27-ball 32* saw them past their revised target of 309 in 49 overs. Left-arm spinner Jamie Sykes had done most to keep Lancashire quiet with 4-57, his best return in all cricket.*

At Liverpool, May 5. **Northamptonshire won by six wickets. Lancashire 324-8** (50 overs) (K. R. Brown 58, D. J. Vilas 61, R. McLaren 79, J. Clark 76*); **‡Northamptonshire 326-4** (46.4 overs) (R. E. Levi 63, R. I. Keogh 69, A. G. Wakely 109*). *Attendance: 2,185. Lancashire slipped to 94-5 in the 19th over, before Ryan McLaren hit 79, and helped set record partnerships for the sixth and seventh wickets in this fixture: 82 with Dane Vilas and 108 with Jordan Clark, who blasted a 51-ball 76*. It left Northamptonshire needing 325 but, on the truest of Aigburth pitches, they gobbled it up. Alex Wakely put on 152 for the fourth wicket with Rob Keogh, and finished on 109*. Both sides made their highest total against each other.*

At Manchester, May 10. **Lancashire won by 152 runs. ‡Lancashire 313-5** (50 overs) (K. R. Brown 63, D. J. Vilas 100*, J. Clark 79*); **Worcestershire 161** (34.5 overs) (J. Clark 4-34). *Attendance: 1,936. A powerful all-round display from Jordan Clark ended Worcestershire's unbeaten run, and boosted Lancashire's hopes of qualification. He crashed a 58-ball 79*, and added 160* with centurion Vilas – a sixth-wicket record in this fixture – before claiming 4-34 as six Worcestershire players fell in single figures.*

At Blackpool, May 12. **Lancashire won by three wickets** (DLS). **Derbyshire 132-2** (21.3 overs) (B. T. Slater 60*); **‡Lancashire 162-7** (17.5 overs). *Attendance: 1,572. Lancashire were challenged by DLS to score 161 in 18 overs, and got there with a ball to spare. Karl Brown led the chase with*

39 off 30, despite Shiv Thakor (3-23) keeping things tight. It came down to 24 off the last two overs, but Stephen Parry (22 off nine) stayed calm and wellied Hardus Viljoen for three consecutive fours; he finished it with another in the last. Earlier, Ben Slater's 60* had held Derbyshire together before a two-and-a-half-hour rain break set up a damp but dramatic conclusion.*

Lancashire away matches

May 1: lost to Yorkshire by 79 runs.
May 7: beat Warwickshire by 26 runs.
May 14: lost to Nottinghamshire by seven wickets.
May 16: beat Durham by 28 runs.

LEICESTERSHIRE

At Leicester, April 30. **Worcestershire won by 42 runs. Worcestershire 361-8** (50 overs) (M. M. Ali 90); ‡**Leicestershire 319** (47.2 overs) (M. J. Cosgrove 67, A. M. Ali 88; J. Leach 4-66). *Attendance: 789. Eight Worcestershire batsmen passed 20 as they racked up a match-winning 361; Moeen Ali's 87-ball 90 gave them initial momentum, before John Hastings and Ed Barnard smashed 42 from the last three overs. Half-centuries from Mark Cosgrove and Aadil Ali kept Leicestershire in the hunt, but scoreboard pressure brought regular wickets – Joe Leach picked up 4-66 – and Ali was last out trying to steal the strike.*

At Leicester, May 2 (day/night). **Leicestershire won by 103 runs.** ‡**Leicestershire 363-7** (50 overs) (M. L. Pettini 159, A. M. Ali 52, T. J. Wells 67); **Warwickshire 260** (44 overs) (S. R. Hain 103, T. R. Ambrose 83). *Attendance: 1,091. Leicestershire reached 363, their highest one-day score against a first-class county (beating 344 v Durham at Chester-le-Street in 1996), to set up a thumping victory. Mark Pettini held everything together with a career-best 159, and Ali and Tom Wells – who hit four sixes – backed him up. Sam Hain led Warwickshire's reply with a century, and put on 118 with Tim Ambrose, but his dismissal began a collapse of seven for 31.*

At Leicester, May 12 (day/night). **No result. Northamptonshire 121-1** (16.5 overs) (R. I. Newton 55*, R. E. Levi 59*) **v** ‡**Leicestershire.**

At Leicester, May 14. **Leicestershire won by five wickets. Derbyshire 219** (47.4 overs) (A. L. Hughes 96*); ‡**Leicestershire 222-5** (39.5 overs) (C. S. Delport 53, E. J. H. Eckersley 80, L. J. Hill 68*). *Attendance: 1,042. After Derbyshire slipped to 47-4 on a flat pitch, Alex Hughes's 96* – a List A best – gave their bowlers a chance. But Leicestershire chased 220 with ten overs to spare, thanks to half-centuries from Cameron Delport, Ned Eckersley and Lewis Hill. The result kept alive their slim hopes of qualification.*

Leicestershire away matches

April 28: beat Lancashire by three wickets (DLS).
May 5: lost to Durham by five wickets.
May 7: lost to Nottinghamshire by six wickets.
May 16: lost to Yorkshire by 20 runs.

NORTHAMPTONSHIRE

At Northampton, April 27. **Warwickshire won by ten wickets** (DLS). **Northamptonshire 151** (29.4 overs) (R. I. Keogh 69*); ‡**Warwickshire 162-0** (26 overs) (W. T. S. Porterfield 63*, S. R. Hain 89*). *County debut:* G. T. Thornton (Warwickshire). *Attendance: 842. In cold and bleak conditions, Warwickshire's trophy defence began in emphatic style: their openers reached a revised target of 159 from 30 overs at a canter. Earlier, Rob Keogh hit 69*, but a combination of three rain interruptions and Rikki Clarke, who finished with 7–1–18–2, prevented Northamptonshire gaining momentum. By the time Hain passed 50 off 30 balls, the issue was settled.*

At Northampton, May 3 (day/night). **Tied. Worcestershire 277-9** (50 overs) (D. K. H. Mitchell 75, O. B. Cox 82); ‡**Northamptonshire 277-7** (50 overs) (R. I. Newton 107, A. G. Wakely 52, A. M. Rossington 63*). *Attendance: 851. With Northamptonshire requiring 14 off the final over, Adam Rossington struck three fours, then scrambled a bye off the last for a tie. Rob Newton's maiden one-day hundred, and a century partnership with Alex Wakely (52), had helped them to 198-3 in the 39th, but they lost three for 21 and were grateful to Rossington's 45-ball 63*. Earlier, Ben Sanderson's 1-34 had kept Worcestershire in check, but Daryl Mitchell and Ben Cox ensured a solid total.*

At Northampton, May 10 (day/night). **Yorkshire won by 164 runs. Yorkshire 300-6** (50 overs) (G. S. Ballance 152*); ‡**Northamptonshire 136** (28.1 overs). *Attendance: 930. After being inserted, Yorkshire looked in trouble at 73-4. But captain Gary Ballance guided them to 300, sharing century stands with Matthew Waite (43) and Adil Rashid (41), and finishing with 152*, his fourth century of the season in all cricket. Northamptonshire capitulated, losing their first four for 11, before Azeem Rafiq ended their chances of progressing with three wickets in three overs.*

At Northampton, May 16 (day/night). **No result. Northamptonshire 79-0** (14.4 overs) (B. M. Duckett 56*) v ‡**Nottinghamshire.** *A point sent Nottinghamshire into the quarter-finals.*

Northamptonshire away matches

April 30: lost to Derbyshire by six wickets.
May 5: beat Lancashire by six wickets.
May 7: lost to Durham by 19 runs.
May 12: no result v Leicestershire.

NOTTINGHAMSHIRE

At Nottingham, April 29. **Yorkshire won by seven wickets. Nottinghamshire 185** (40.5 overs) (B. R. M. Taylor 60); ‡**Yorkshire 191-3** (32.4 overs) (J. E. Root 75*). *Attendance: 3,948. Joe Root led Yorkshire's chase with aplomb, and finished it with a pulled six off brother Billy's off-spin; it was their first senior match in opposition. "Don't bowl half-trackers at me," he said later. Nottinghamshire had little hope after losing their last seven for 49, even with five international bowlers.*

At Sookholme, May 7. **Nottinghamshire won by six wickets. Leicestershire 217** (43.5 overs) (M. J. Cosgrove 80; J. L. Pattinson 4-42); ‡**Nottinghamshire 218-4** (38.2 overs) (S. R. Patel 79, B. R. M. Taylor 51*, S. J. Mullaney 50). *Attendance: 2,075. Mark Cosgrove hit a run-a-ball 80 at the Welbeck Colliery ground, but his departure started a collapse from 179-4 to 217 all out; James Pattinson and Harry Gurney picked up five wickets in five overs. Michael Lumb fell to the first ball of the reply, but a trio of half-centurions breezed Nottinghamshire home with 12 overs to spare.*

At Nottingham, May 11 (day/night). **Durham won by four wickets. Nottinghamshire 297** (49.5 overs) (A. D. Hales 104, W. T. Root 66, C. M. W. Read 61); ‡**Durham 299-6** (49.1 overs) (G. Clark 92, C. T. Steel 77, P. D. Collingwood 73*). *Attendance: 2,771. Graham Clark and Cameron Steel, who was dropped twice, broke the back of Durham's chase with a third-wicket stand of 160 (a record in this fixture), before Paul Collingwood completed it with a superb 73* off 47 balls. Earlier, Alex Hales – dropped three times himself – rattled off a 15th one-day hundred, and passed 5,000 List A runs. Billy Root and Chris Read chipped in with sixties, but six others were stuck in single figures, and the innings fizzled rather than flared at the end.*

At Nottingham, May 14. **Nottinghamshire won by seven wickets.** ‡**Lancashire 260-6** (50 overs) (K. R. Brown 52, H. Hameed 75*); **Nottinghamshire 265-3** (46 overs) (S. R. Patel 103*, S. J. Mullaney 77*). *Attendance: 9,518. County debut:* D. J. Lamb (Lancashire). *Chasing 261, Nottinghamshire romped to a fourth win in five. Samit Patel hit a brilliant hundred, and shared an unbroken fourth-wicket stand of 181* (a county record against Lancashire) with Steven Mullaney, who had earlier picked up a miserly 2-31. Lancashire's innings had stalled after their openers put on 98 and, despite Haseeb Hameed showing his improvisational side with 75*, their total proved below par.*

Nottinghamshire away matches

April 27: lost to Worcestershire by five wickets (DLS).
May 2: beat Derbyshire by four wickets (DLS).
May 5: beat Warwickshire by ten runs.
May 16: no result v Northamptonshire.

WARWICKSHIRE

At Birmingham, May 1. **Durham won by 72 runs. Durham 313-5** (39 overs) (S. C. Cook 60, K. K. Jennings 139; A. D. Thomason 4-64); ‡**Warwickshire 241** (38.2 overs) (I. J. L. Trott 92; W. J. Weighell 5-57). *Attendance: 1,572. Rain reduced the contest to 39 overs, but Durham still piled up 313. Keaton Jennings hit a one-day best 139 off 101 balls, and shared century partnerships with Stephen Cook and Michael Richardson (49) for the first two wickets. Amid the runs, 19-year-old* *seamer Aaron Thomason picked up his own career-best (4-64). Mark Wood softened up Warwickshire's reply with a rapid opening spell, then James Weighell floored them. Playing only his second List A match, he collected five scalps including Jonathan Trott for 92, his sixth half-century in eight innings in the competition.*

At Birmingham, May 5. **Nottinghamshire won by ten runs.** ‡**Nottinghamshire 303-6** (50 overs) (M. J. Lumb 56, S. J. Mullaney 89, W. T. Root 107*); **Warwickshire 293-9** (50 overs) (I. J. L. Trott 104, I. R. Bell 51). *Attendance: 1,452. While elder brother Joe was helping England trounce Ireland at Bristol, Billy Root pummelled a maiden one-day century from 91 balls to inspire Nottinghamshire to a narrow win. Coming in at 92-4, he put on 159 with Steven Mullaney – a Nottinghamshire record for the fifth wicket – and reached his hundred in the final over, in which he cracked two sixes and a four. Trott's 21st one-day century provided a solid platform – Warwickshire were 181-1 after 33 overs – but the middle order sputtered.*

At Birmingham, May 7. **Lancashire won by 26 runs. Lancashire 351-8** (50 overs) (D. J. Vilas 55, S. J. Croft 127); ‡**Warwickshire 325** (48.3 overs) (T. R. Ambrose 68, R. Clarke 76). *Attendance: 1,845. One over from Warwickshire seamer Oliver Hannon-Dalby proved the difference: it cost 35. It included four sixes – three from Steven Croft, who hit a one-day best 127 off 83 balls – and three wides, as a short boundary towards the Eric Hollies Stand was exploited mercilessly. Warwickshire needed 352, and were well placed at 212-4 after 31, but lost steam when Rikki Clarke was out the ball after his sixth six; it was the fourth successive game they had fallen short of a target above 300.*

At Birmingham, May 14. **Warwickshire won by five wickets.** ‡**Yorkshire 281-8** (50 overs) (J. E. Root 83, T. T. Bresnan 65, M. J. Waite 71); **Warwickshire 284-5** (47.3 overs) (I. J. L. Trott 70, S. R. Hain 55, I. R. Bell 98). *Attendance: 1,675. Warwickshire ended a run of six defeats thanks to a third consecutive 90-plus from Ian Bell. Yorkshire had thought their 281 – which included a maiden one-day half-century from Matthew Waite – would be competitive, but a used pitch improved. Warwickshire wobbled from 124-0 to 167-4, before Bell and Clarke (44*) steadied things with a stand of 111. The result dislodged Yorkshire from the top of the group, forcing them to play a quarter-final.*

Warwickshire away matches

April 27: beat Northants by ten wickets (DLS).
May 2: lost to Leicestershire by 103 runs.
May 10: lost to Derbyshire by four wickets.
May 12: lost to Worcs by three wickets (DLS).

WORCESTERSHIRE

At Worcester, April 27. **Worcestershire won by five wickets** (DLS). **Nottinghamshire 273-6** (50 overs) (M. J. Lumb 104); ‡**Worcestershire 169-5** (20 overs). *Attendance: 1,094. After Nottinghamshire were inserted, opener Michael Lumb batted until the 47th over for an eighth one-day century, sharing 84 for the fifth wicket with List A debutant Billy Root. Several rain interruptions reduced Worcestershire's target to 168 in 22 overs and, after Joe Clarke's classy 40 off 26 balls, Ross Whiteley's 41* off 19 ensured they got there. Captain Joe Leach hit the winning runs in terrible light, having earlier restrained Nottinghamshire with 3-50.*

At Worcester, May 5. **Worcestershire won by 51 runs. Worcestershire 342** (48.5 overs) (D. K. H. Mitchell 69, T. Köhler-Cadmore 118; M. J. Waite 4-65); ‡**Yorkshire 291** (46.3 overs) (A. Lyth 59, P. S. P. Handscomb 88). *Attendance: 1,911. A few weeks before joining Yorkshire, Tom Köhler-Cadmore biffed them for 118 off 119 balls, with five sixes, and put on 135 for the first wicket with Daryl Mitchell. Yorkshire needed 343, and fifties from Adam Lyth and Peter Handscomb gave them hope, before Mitchell – who had been left out of the first two games – sapped momentum with three wickets.*

At Worcester, May 12. **Worcestershire won by three wickets** (DLS). Reduced to 49 overs a side. **Warwickshire 304-5** (49 overs) (I. R. Bell 104, R. Clarke 84*); ‡**Worcestershire 241-7** (31.5 overs) (J. M. Clarke 56; G. T. Thornton 4-42). *Attendance: 1,458. After rain in the interval, Worcestershire overhauled a revised 241 from 34 overs. They were in trouble at 57-4, but Clarke's 56 stabilised them, Ben Cox's 41-ball 49 changed the mood, and Whiteley sealed victory with a 22-ball 35*. It meant Ian Bell's first hundred for 13 months came in vain, so too Rikki Clarke's power hitting: he struck 84* off 52 balls, including six sixes.*

At Worcester, May 14. **Worcestershire won by 15 runs. Worcestershire 270-8** (50 overs) (B. L. D'Oliveira 73*); ‡**Durham 255-9** (50 overs) (G. Clark 114). *Attendance: 1,896. At 122-0 in the 24th, Durham were cruising towards 271, before tight spells from Moeen Ali and Brett D'Oliveira – who had earlier hit 73* – applied pressure. Graham Clark completed a maiden List A century but, as the asking-rate increased, no one below the openers made more than 17; John Hastings and Mitchell picked up three apiece. Victory ensured Worcestershire would progress.*

Worcestershire away matches

April 30: beat Leicestershire by 42 runs.
May 3: tied with Northamptonshire.
May 10: lost to Lancashire by 152 runs.
May 16: beat Derbyshire by five wickets (DLS).

YORKSHIRE

At Leeds, May 1. **Yorkshire won by 79 runs. Yorkshire 296-9** (50 overs) (P. S. P. Handscomb 86, G. S. Ballance 85); ‡**Lancashire 217** (43.2 overs) (Azeem Rafiq 4-47). *Attendance:* 4,867. *In a commanding Yorkshire display, Peter Handscomb hit 86, and Gary Ballance 85, while Azeem Rafiq picked up four wickets. But it was Adil Rashid (2-34) who really caught the eye. His control was suffocating, and two wicked googlies snuffed out the threat of Alex Davies and Liam Livingstone. Lancashire were outplayed, and only their death bowling looked in order, keeping Yorkshire below 300 after they reached 230-3 in the 38th over.*

At Leeds, May 3. **Yorkshire won by six wickets.** ‡**Durham 335-5** (50 overs) (S. C. Cook 106, K. K. Jennings 72, M. J. Richardson 100*); **Yorkshire 339-4** (47.4 overs) (J. M. Bairstow 174, J. E. Root 55). *County debut:* G. H. I. Harding (Durham). *Attendance:* 2,624. *Durham's monster total, built on centuries from Stephen Cook and Michael Richardson, did not scare Jonny Bairstow. He cut loose with a stunning 113-ball 174, the highest List A score for Yorkshire by an Englishman, and the best at Headingley, beating Stephen Fleming's 139* against Warwickshire in 2003. Bairstow was dropped at long-off by Cook on 71, but was otherwise in total control, dominating a stand of 189 with Joe Root, and smashing 16 fours and seven sixes.*

HIGHEST ONE-DAY SCORES FOR YORKSHIRE

191	D. S. Lehmann	v Nottinghamshire at Scarborough	2001
175	T. M. Head	v Leicestershire at Leicester	2016
174	**J. M. Bairstow**	**v Durham at Headingley**	**2017**
160	M. J. Wood	v Devon at Exmouth	2004
152*	**G. S. Ballance**	**v Northamptonshire at Northampton**	**2017**
148	C. White	v Leicestershire at Leicester	1997
148	A. McGrath	v Somerset at Taunton	2006
†146	G. Boycott	v Surrey at Lord's	1965
142	G. Boycott	v Worcestershire at Worcester	1980
141*	M. D. Moxon	v Glamorgan at Cardiff	1991

† *Gillette Cup final.*

At Leeds, May 7. **Yorkshire won by 15 runs. Yorkshire 349-7** (50 overs) (P. S. P. Handscomb 140, G. S. Ballance 63); ‡**Derbyshire 334-8** (50 overs) (W. L. Madsen 112, D. Smit 77*; B. O. Coad 4-63). *County debut:* G. C. Viljoen (Derbyshire). *Attendance:* 2,125. *Handscomb's century drove Yorkshire to 349-7, the highest List A score at Headingley, beating their 345-5 against Nottinghamshire in 1996. Still, had Derbyshire pressed the accelerator a little earlier, they might have taken the record for themselves. Wayne Madsen's resolute hundred laid the platform for a late assault from Daryn Smit and Matt Critchley (49), who together plundered 88 in seven overs. Critchley needed 29 from the last, and managed two sixes, before becoming one of Ben Coad's four victims. If Yorkshire had suffered a scare, they had also shown off their strength: they won with five players on England duty.*

At Leeds, May 16 (day/night). **Yorkshire won by 20 runs. Yorkshire 258-7** (45 overs) (A. Lyth 52, G. S. Ballance 71, Azeem Rafiq 52*); ‡**Leicestershire 238** (42.4 overs) (C. S. Delport 68). *County debut:* C. F. Parkinson (Leicestershire). *Attendance:* 2,025. *In a match reduced to 45 overs a side, Ballance helped Yorkshire, who had already qualified for the knockouts, to 258. Leicestershire might have joined them, but their batting malfunctioned. The target seemed within reach, particularly after Cameron Delport and Ned Eckersley put on a hundred in quick time. But Azeem Rafiq – who had earlier cracked a 30-ball 52* – started a collapse with two wickets in an over, and the controlled left-arm spin of Karl Carver (3-24) kept it in motion.*

Yorkshire away matches

April 29: beat Nottinghamshire by seven wickets.
May 5: lost to Worcestershire by 51 runs.
May 10: beat Northamptonshire by 164 runs.
May 14: lost to Warwickshire by five wickets.

SOUTH GROUP

ESSEX

At Chelmsford, April 30. **Essex won by 25 runs. Essex 304-7** (50 overs) (T. Westley 93, Ashar Zaidi 72*); ‡**Hampshire 279** (48.2 overs) (J. M. Vince 68, G. J. Bailey 63; N. Wagner 4-41). *Attendance:* 1,844. *Ashar Zaidi's 40-ball burst – he smacked six fours and four sixes – helped Essex plunder 109 from their last ten overs. Hampshire were in contention at 242-5 after 43, but the last five wickets could muster only 37. Both teams lost their first wicket without a run on the board: Nick Browne was bowled by his former Essex team-mate Reece Topley, while Michael Carberry was the first of four scalps for Neil Wagner.*

At Chelmsford, May 4. **Essex won by 29 runs. Essex 315-8** (50 overs) (A. N. Cook 127; C. J. Liddle 4-54); ‡**Gloucestershire 286-8** (50 overs) (P. Mustard 90, I. A. Cockbain 79). *Attendance:* 1,563. *Alastair Cook's fifth List A century ensured Essex passed 300 again, then Ravi Bopara – on his 32nd birthday – set Gloucestershire back with three middle-order wickets.*

At Chelmsford, May 10 (day/night). **Essex won by ten runs. Essex 295-7** (50 overs) (A. N. Cook 109, R. N. ten Doeschate 102); ‡**Sussex 285** (48.1 overs) (C. D. Nash 66, S. van Zyl 61). *Attendance:* 1,857. *Cook's second successive century at Chelmsford helped Essex recover after Jerome Taylor's hat-trick reduced them to 19-3. Ryan ten Doeschate then pushed the score close to 300 with a hundred of his own, from 90 balls. Sussex looked out of it at 208-6 in the 42nd, but Jofra Archer's 45 from 22 got them close, before left-arm seamer Paul Walter, in his first List A match, took the last three wickets in seven deliveries.*

At Chelmsford, May 12. **Essex won by seven wickets. Middlesex 148** (40.2 overs) (J. A. Porter 4-40, P. I. Walter 4-37); ‡**Essex 149-3** (29.4 overs) (A. N. Cook 67*). *Attendance:* 1,875. *Four wickets from Jamie Porter and four from Walter – including former Test players Adam Voges and James Franklin with successive balls – condemned Middlesex to a poor total. Essex strolled past it, anchored by the consistent Cook. This was the only one of the eight group games in which ten Doeschate won the toss, although it didn't matter: Essex won seven, to top the group and claim an automatic semi-final place.*

Essex away matches

May 2: beat Surrey by one wicket.
May 7: lost to Glamorgan by one run.
May 14: beat Somerset by 72 runs.
May 17: beat Kent by 57 runs (DLS).

GLAMORGAN

At Cardiff, April 30. **Surrey won by eight wickets** (DLS). **Glamorgan 239** (48.3 overs) (J. A. Rudolph 57, C. A. Ingram 72); ‡**Surrey 183-2** (24 overs) (M. D. Stoneman 74, K. C. Sangakkara 81*). *Attendance:* 416. *The South African pair of Jacques Rudolph and Colin Ingram rescued Glamorgan from 7-2 with a stand of 113; Ingram, capped before the game, struck three sixes,* *including one that carried around 150 yards over deep backward square. The eventual total was not huge, although rain meant Surrey's target was amended to 182 off 29 overs; a second-wicket partnership of 125 between Mark Stoneman, who cuffed 14 fours from 48 balls, and Kumar Sangakkara eased them home.*

At Cardiff, May 5. **Somerset won by 170 runs. Somerset 338-3** (50 overs) (J. Allenby 144*, D. Elgar 96, J. C. Hildreth 58*); ‡**Glamorgan 168** (36.4 overs) (K. S. Carlson 63). *Attendance:* 855. *The former Glamorgan player Jim Allenby, now captaining Somerset, smacked six sixes as he extended his maiden List A century to 144*. He shared stands of 187 with Dean Elgar and 109* with James Hildreth (58* from 28 balls), and 134 runs cascaded from the last ten overs. Glamorgan were soon floundering at 27-3, and only Kiran Carlson emerged with much credit.*

At Cardiff, May 7. **Glamorgan won by one run.** ‡**Glamorgan 281-7** (50 overs) (W. D. Bragg 59, C. A. Ingram 142; N. Wagner 4-58); **Essex 280-9** (50 overs) (V. Chopra 124, R. S. Bopara 56). *Attendance:* 840. *After Neil Wagner removed both openers, Ingram clubbed eight sixes – two on to the pavilion roof – in his highest one-day score, as Glamorgan reached 281. Despite losing Nick Browne and Tom Westley for ducks, Essex seemed on course to maintain their 100% record at 214-3 after 41 overs. But Ravi Bopara was run out, Varun Chopra followed not long afterwards for a fine 124 and the lower order panicked: seven were needed from the final over, but the canny Michael Hogan kept them to five.*

At Swansea, May 14. **Glamorgan won by 15 runs. Glamorgan 356-7** (50 overs) (W. D. Bragg 94, C. A. Ingram 114); ‡**Kent 341** (47.2 overs) (D. I. Stevens 147; D. L. Lloyd 5-53). *Attendance:* 724. *This high-scoring game included 35 sixes, equalling the record for a List A match, set by Nottinghamshire and Northamptonshire in 2016. Fourteen came from 41-year-old Darren Stevens as he scorched to a career-best 147 from just 67 balls. But Kent still fell short of Glamorgan's total, which had owed much to a third-wicket stand of 212 between Will Bragg and Ingram, who collected eight sixes himself, taking his tally for this season's competition to 29.*

Glamorgan away matches

April 27: beat Gloucestershire by 18 runs (DLS).
May 2: lost to Sussex by 59 runs (DLS).
May 10: lost to Middlesex by 16 runs.
May 12: beat Hampshire by three wickets.

GLOUCESTERSHIRE

At Bristol, April 27. **Glamorgan won by 18 runs** (DLS). **Glamorgan 277-7** (50 overs) (J. A. Rudolph 121); ‡**Gloucestershire 232-8** (44 overs) (M. Klinger 78, G. L. van Buuren 51, J. M. R. Taylor 51). *Attendance:* 1,168. *A superbly paced 121 by Jacques Rudolph – he batted 49 overs and ran 63 singles – carried Glamorgan to victory. On a reliable track, he and Colin Ingram added 89 in 17 overs for the third wicket, providing the backbone of their 277. Gloucestershire's reply suffered three interruptions. Soon after the second, they were 146-3, but the dismissals of Michael Klinger and Graeme van Buuren in the same Ingram over holed them beneath the waterline and, despite some Jack Taylor heroics, they fell short of a revised target of 251 from 44.*

At Bristol, May 10. **Gloucestershire won by 11 runs. Gloucestershire 275-8** (50 overs) (M. Klinger 134; M. T. Coles 4-57); ‡**Kent 264-9** (50 overs) (D. J. Bell-Drummond 90, S. R. Dickson 50; C. J. Liddle 5-36). *Attendance:* 1,072. *A burst of 4-11 in 21 balls from Chris Liddle, who varied his pace intelligently, helped Gloucestershire turn the tables on a Kent side apparently sailing to success. Needing 276, they were 200-2 with almost 12 overs remaining when Liddle dismissed Daniel Bell-Drummond for 90, and instigated a collapse. Gloucestershire's total had been founded on a measured 145-ball 134 from Klinger, who passed 7,000 runs in List A cricket.*

At Bristol, May 12. **Somerset won by 81 runs** (DLS). ‡**Somerset 294-6** (46 overs) (J. Allenby 90, A. J. Hose 101*); **Gloucestershire 215** (41.5 overs) (J. M. R. Taylor 68). *Attendance:* 1,382. *Adam Hose reached his first hundred in county cricket from his 93rd ball, the last of the shortened Somerset innings. With Jim Allenby making 90 – together they added 123 for the fourth wicket – they totalled 294, comfortably enough to defeat Gloucestershire, who could no longer reach the knockouts. Jack*

Taylor and George Hankins did take the score from 62-4 to 165-5, but they never threatened a revised target of 297 from 46 overs. Somerset remained top.

At Bristol, May 17 (day/night). **Gloucestershire v Surrey. Abandoned.**

Gloucestershire away matches

April 30: beat Middlesex by five wickets.
May 4: lost to Essex by 29 runs.
May 7: lost to Hampshire by seven wickets.
May 14: beat Sussex by six wickets.

HAMPSHIRE

At Southampton, May 3 (day/night). **Middlesex won by 89 runs** (DLS). **Middlesex 295** (50 overs) (N. R. T. Gubbins 114; R. J. W. Topley 4-68); ‡**Hampshire 146-7** (30.3 overs) (G. J. Bailey 52*; T. S. Roland-Jones 4-10). *Attendance:* 1,387. *A devastating burst from Toby Roland-Jones, who took 4-10 from seven overs, left Hampshire reeling at 34-4. George Bailey and Sean Ervine added 70 but, when rain ended play in the 30th over, they were 146-7, and far behind. Nick Gubbins had glued the Middlesex innings together with his second one-day century, though from 180-1 in the 32nd they should have passed 300; Reece Topley claimed his first four-for since joining Hampshire.*

At Southampton, May 7. **Hampshire won by seven wickets.** ‡**Gloucestershire 237** (49.2 overs) (J. M. R. Taylor 63); **Hampshire 239-3** (42.3 overs) (T. P. Alsop 53, J. M. Vince 89*). *Attendance:* 1,838. *After Topley's opening spell had started with three maidens, Hampshire spinners Mason Crane and Liam Dawson enjoyed combined figures of 20–2–83–6 as Gloucestershire, who lost their last five for 32, were dismissed for 237. Hampshire coasted to victory on the back of their top four – and some poor fielding.*

At Southampton, May 12. **Glamorgan won by three wickets.** Reduced to 49 overs a side. **Hampshire 332-6** (49 overs) (J. M. Vince 178, L. A. Dawson 74; M. de Lange 5-49); ‡**Glamorgan 334-7** (48.5 overs) (C. A. Ingram 115, C. B. Cooke 59*). *Attendance:* 1,429. *In a thrilling game, James Vince hit Hampshire's highest one-day score, yet could not prevent defeat. Vince, who faced 138 balls and put on 221 for the fourth wicket with Dawson, eventually became the fourth victim of a career-best 5-49 by Marchant de Lange (later removed from the attack at the start of his last over for a second high full toss). Colin Ingram walloped seven sixes in his 115, but Glamorgan relied on a brutal 27-ball 59* from Chris Cooke to see them home from the penultimate delivery. All three of Crane's wickets were stumpings by Lewis McManus.*

HIGHEST ONE-DAY SCORES FOR HAMPSHIRE

178	**J. M. Vince**	**v Glamorgan at Southampton**	**2017**
177	C. G. Greenidge	v Glamorgan at Southampton (Northlands Road)	1975
173*	C. G. Greenidge	v Minor Counties South at Amersham	1973
172	C. G. Greenidge	v Surrey at Southampton (Northlands Road)	1987
167*	S. M. Ervine	v Ireland at Southampton	2009
166*	T. E. Jesty	v Surrey at Portsmouth	1983
165*	V. P. Terry	v Berkshire at Southampton (Northlands Road)	1985
163*	C. G. Greenidge	v Warwickshire at Birmingham	1979
162*	C. G. Greenidge	v Lancashire at Manchester	1983
159	C. L. Smith	v Cheshire at Chester	1989

At Southampton, May 17 (day/night). **Hampshire v Sussex. Abandoned.**

Hampshire away matches

April 27: beat Kent by six wickets.
April 30: lost to Essex by 25 runs.
May 10: beat Somerset by four wickets.
May 14: lost to Surrey by 66 runs (DLS).

KENT

At Canterbury, April 27. **Hampshire won by six wickets. Kent 258** (49.4 overs) (D. J. Bell-Drummond 56, D. I. Stevens 60); ‡**Hampshire 260-4** (45.1 overs) (T. P. Alsop 112*, J. M. Vince 69). *Attendance:* 2,509. *County debut:* I. G. Holland (Hampshire). *Kent's opening pair, Daniel Bell-Drummond and Joe Denly (46), put on a classy 94 in 15 overs, but Darren Stevens was the only other batsman to pass 20. The most successful – and most expensive – bowler was left-arm seamer Reece Topley, who took 3-65. Facing a target of 259 on a two-paced pitch, Hampshire were unfazed by the loss of Michael Carberry second ball. His fellow opener Tom Alsop hit an unbeaten hundred, sharing a second-wicket stand of 112 with the hard-hitting James Vince.*

At Canterbury, May 5. **Sussex won by six wickets. Kent 331-7** (50 overs) (D. J. Bell-Drummond 138, A. J. Blake 76); ‡**Sussex 332-4** (47.5 overs) (L. J. Wright 64, H. Z. Finch 80, L. J. Evans 134*). *Attendance:* 1,403. *For the second time in three days, Bell-Drummond hit a century, steered Kent past 330 – and ended on the losing side. His 138 came at a run a ball, and Alex Blake's murderous 76 from just 43, yet Laurie Evans, whose previous best was 70*, stole the game with a coruscating 134* from 86. Sussex's chase had been given firm foundations by Chris Nash (39) and Luke Wright, though when Harry Finch joined Evans at 123-3, the required rate was nearing eight. Together they tore into some feeble Kent bowling, and had put on 207 – a record partnership in this fixture – when they were separated two from victory.*

At Canterbury, May 7. **Kent won by 46 runs. Kent 200** (46 overs) (S. A. Northeast 55); ‡**Middlesex 154** (46 overs). *Attendance:* 1,571. *Batting was never easy in overcast conditions. After Toby Roland-Jones dismissed Bell-Drummond with the game's first delivery, Sam Northeast made the day's only half-century as Kent stuttered to 200. Even with the ball holding sway, Middlesex should have had few problems overhauling that, but Wayne Parnell removed their openers in single figures, then Nick Compton hung around for 85 balls in making 37. And when Denly's occasional leg-spin accounted for three middle-order wickets – the last a spectacular return catch to see off the dangerous James Franklin – Kent were in sight of their first win.*

At Canterbury, May 17 (day/night). **Essex won by 57 runs** (DLS). **Essex 307-6** (50 overs) (V. Chopra 83, A. N. Cook 54); ‡**Kent 50-3** (11 overs). *Attendance:* 1,135. *County debut:* Z. Crawley (Kent). *A seventh win for Essex was a seventh defeat for Kent, confirming one team at the top of the table, and the other at the foot. With progress impossible, Kent fielded a weakened team, including inexperienced slow left-armer Imran Qayyum and Tonbridge School prodigy Zak Crawley. Qayyum removed Alastair Cook and fellow opener Varun Chopra for half-centuries, as Essex sailed past 300. Crawley, however, had gone for two when rain ended Kent's uncertain reply after 11 overs.*

Kent away matches

May 2: lost to Somerset by four wickets.
May 10: lost to Gloucestershire by 11 runs.
May 12: lost to Surrey by 44 runs (DLS).
May 14: lost to Glamorgan by 15 runs.

MIDDLESEX

At Lord's, April 27. **No result. Middlesex 341-5** (50 overs) (P. R. Stirling 71, J. A. Simpson 82*, J. E. C. Franklin 69); ‡**Sussex 26-1** (4 overs). *Attendance:* 1,700. *Paul Stirling led off with a 60-ball 71, then John Simpson (who hit his best List A score) and James Franklin put on 117 for the fifth wicket as Middlesex reached what remained their highest one-day total of the summer. Things looked even better when Tom Helm's first ball accounted for Luke Wright – but then the rain descended.*

At Lord's, April 30. **Gloucestershire won by five wickets.** ‡**Middlesex 256-9** (50 overs) (A. C. Voges 81, T. S. Roland-Jones 65; L. C. Norwell 5-36); **Gloucestershire 257-5** (49.1 overs) (I. A. Cockbain 108*, B. A. C. Howell 86*). *Attendance:* 2,248. *The pacy Liam Norwell bowled his ten overs off the reel, and took the first five wickets as Middlesex staggered to 114-6. Toby Roland-Jones, with his maiden List A half-century, helped Adam Voges add 111, then snaffled two wickets as Gloucestershire declined to 65-5 in the 23rd over. But Ian Cockbain, who reached his first one-day hundred, and Benny Howell fought back in a stand of 192*, crowned when Howell thumped the first ball of the final over, from Ryan Higgins, over cover for the winning six.*

At Radlett, May 10. **Middlesex won by 16 runs.** ‡**Middlesex 243** (48.4 overs) (D. J. Malan 50, J. E. C. Franklin 54; C. A. Ingram 4-39); **Glamorgan 227** (48.3 overs) (C. A. Ingram 53; S. T. Finn 4-39). *Attendance:* 871. *Colin Ingram's leg-breaks claimed four scalps in a List A innings for the first time, to restrict Middlesex on a sluggish outground pitch. But Steven Finn hit back with what proved his only four wickets of the competition, and Glamorgan fell short despite Ingram's 53.*

At Lord's, May 17 (day/night). **Middlesex v Somerset. Abandoned.** *Somerset's point ensured they finished second in the group behind Essex, and progressed to the quarter-finals.*

Middlesex away matches

May 3: beat Hampshire by 89 runs (DLS).
May 5: lost to Surrey by seven wickets.
May 7: lost to Kent by 46 runs.
May 12: lost to Essex by seven wickets.

SOMERSET

At Taunton, April 28. **Somerset won by four wickets. Surrey 290-8** (50 overs) (M. D. Stoneman 56, B. T. Foakes 92); ‡**Somerset 291-6** (43.5 overs) (D. Elgar 68, R. E. van der Merwe 165*). *Attendance: 2,694. After Ben Foakes's 92 had lifted Surrey to 290, Somerset looked doomed when Jade Dernbach and Sam Curran reduced them to 22-5. Enter Roelof van der Merwe to turn an extraordinary game on its head. He dominated a partnership of 230 with Dean Elgar – who was badly dropped on five – and smashed 24 fours and a six in 165*, his maiden List A hundred.*

At Taunton, May 2. **Somerset won by four wickets.** ‡**Kent 352-6** (50 overs) (D. J. Bell-Drummond 106, S. A. Northeast 51, A. J. Blake 116); **Somerset 354-6** (47.3 overs) (P. D. Trego 135, D. Elgar 55, J. C. Hildreth 64). *Attendance: 2,909. Daniel Bell-Drummond's century had put Kent in a strong position, which Alex Blake made stronger still with a breathtaking 58-ball 116. But Peter Trego led a brilliant reply: he smashed six sixes in 135 against his former county, and shared century stands with Elgar and James Hildreth. Somerset raced to their first one-day victory over Kent since 2009.*

At Taunton, May 10. **Hampshire won by four wickets. Somerset 249** (44.2 overs) (P. D. Trego 55, D. Elgar 78, A. J. Hose 50); ‡**Hampshire 250-6** (37.2 overs) (R. R. Rossouw 156; J. Overton 4-64). *Attendance: 3,823. After four successive group wins, Somerset's batting underperformed: three hit half-centuries, but six were dismissed in single figures. Hampshire needed 250, and Rilee Rossouw – sledged by compatriot Elgar for abandoning the South African team and becoming a Kolpak – got most of them, middling everything in a 113-ball 156. "The way Rilee played," said Somerset's director of cricket Matthew Maynard, "400 would not have been enough."*

At Taunton, May 14. **Essex won by 72 runs. Essex 334-6** (50 overs) (A. N. Cook 65, T. Westley 100, R. S. Bopara 92*); ‡**Somerset 262** (43.2 overs) (J. G. Myburgh 57, J. Allenby 77). *Attendance: 4,101. Tom Westley and Ravi Bopara made hay on a plum track to propel Essex to 334. Johann Myburgh got Somerset's chase off to a flyer, hitting 57 in an opening stand of 64 inside seven overs. But after Jim Allenby departed for 77, the last five fell for 50; Neil Wagner and Simon Harmer (like Myburgh born in Pretoria) picked up three apiece to give Essex top spot.*

Somerset away matches

April 30: beat Sussex by nine runs (DLS).
May 5: beat Glamorgan by 170 runs.
May 12: beat Gloucestershire by 81 runs (DLS).
May 17: no result v Middlesex.

SURREY

At The Oval, May 2. **Essex won by one wicket.** ‡**Surrey 210** (47.4 overs) (B. T. Foakes 77*); **Essex 212-9** (49.2 overs) (J. W. Dernbach 4-31). *Attendance:* 2,023. *Essex came out on top – just – in a tale of two recoveries. Ben Foakes's 77* against his former team-mates rescued Surrey from 119-6, then Essex slid to 128-7, in the face of an exacting spell from Jade Dernbach. But Ryan ten Doeschate steadied the ship with 45, and No. 9 Simon Harmer (44*) steered her home in the final over.*

At The Oval, May 5. **Surrey won by seven wickets. Middlesex 243-9** (50 overs) (N. R. T. Gubbins 65, J. A. Simpson 75; R. Rampaul 4-40); ‡**Surrey 244-3** (45.2 overs) (K. C. Sangakkara 59, R. J. Burns 67*, B. T. Foakes 55*). *Attendance:* 2,619. *Middlesex wasted a decent start with some ill-disciplined batting, then Foakes starred again. He helped Rory Burns put on 117* for the fourth wicket, both batsmen running aggressively and picking the gaps.*

At The Oval, May 12. **Surrey won by 44 runs** (DLS). **Surrey 251-7** (41 overs) (B. T. Foakes 82*); ‡**Kent 204** (35.4 overs) (S. W. Billings 69; S. C. Meaker 4-37). *Attendance:* 6,627. *Foakes took his tally for three home games to 214 runs without being dismissed. Sam Curran (39) helped him add 79 for the sixth wicket in 11 overs, which proved vital in a match reduced to 41 a side by a late start and two further rain interruptions. Kent's target was revised slightly to 249, and things looked ominous for Surrey while Sam Billings was in. But from 170-5 Kent lost four for 14, including a double-wicket maiden from Stuart Meaker.*

At The Oval, May 14. **Surrey won by 66 runs** (DLS). ‡**Hampshire 271-8** (50 overs) (G. J. Bailey 145*, K. J. Abbott 56; R. Rampaul 4-61); **Surrey 238-2** (38 overs) (M. D. Stoneman 53, K. C. Sangakkara 124*). *Attendance:* 3,767. *Hampshire creaked to 89-7 before George Bailey took charge with a magnificent century. He put on 152 for the eighth wicket with Kyle Abbott, a Hampshire record, to ensure a reasonable target. But Kumar Sangakkara made it look simple, sharing stands of 93 with Mark Stoneman and 128* with Burns (39*), before rain arrived with Surrey comfortably ahead.*

Surrey away matches

April 28: lost to Somerset by four wickets.
April 30: beat Glamorgan by eight wickets (DLS).
May 7: lost to Sussex by 95 runs.
May 17: no result v Gloucestershire.

SUSSEX

At Hove, April 30. **Somerset won by nine runs** (DLS). **Somerset 303-5** (49 overs) (D. Elgar 131*, A. J. Hose 76); ‡**Sussex 155-9** (20 overs). *Attendance:* 1,129. *A high-class career-best 131* by Dean Elgar – he put on 151 in 20 overs with Adam Hose – helped propel Somerset to a total their captain, Jim Allenby, felt was 40 or so better than expected on a slow pitch. One over was lost at the end of the Somerset innings and, after more rain, Sussex were set 165 in 20. Laurie Evans took advantage of a short boundary and plundered five sixes, but Sussex's hopes vanished when, on 40, he hit his 20th ball to deep point.*

At Hove, May 2. **Sussex won by 59 runs** (DLS). ‡**Sussex 292-6** (50 overs) (S. van Zyl 96, B. C. Brown 60); **Glamorgan 221** (40 overs) (J. A. Rudolph 51, C. B. Cooke 62). *Attendance:* 1,049. *County debut:* J. E. Taylor (Sussex). *Sussex won a one-day game for only the second time in 21 scheduled fixtures, dating back to August 2014. They were largely indebted to Stiaan van Zyl, whose chanceless 96 from 88 balls belied another slow Hove pitch, and to wicketkeeper Ben Brown, whose typically perky contribution to a stand of 115 helped set up a demanding score. Rain interrupted the Glamorgan reply at 138-6 and, although Chris Cooke got into his stride, a target of 281 in 43 overs was always beyond their grasp.*

At Hove, May 7. **Sussex won by 95 runs. Sussex 300-8** (50 overs) (C. D. Nash 82, H. Z. Finch 61); ‡**Surrey 205** (41.1 overs) (M. D. Stoneman 60, O. J. D. Pope 55; D. Wiese 4-29). *Attendance:* 1,254. *A third successive win for Sussex was not in doubt once David Wiese – whose 4-29 were his best one-day figures since joining the county – removed Mark Stoneman for an assured 60. Ollie Pope, aged 19, made a defiant half-century, but Surrey's innings dribbled to a halt well short of their target which, thanks to Chris Nash, the improving Harry Finch and the in-form Laurie Evans, nipped past 300. Michael Burgess, keeping in place of the injured Ben Brown, held a brilliant one-handed catch to remove Ben Foakes.*

At Eastbourne, May 14. **Gloucestershire won by six wickets. Sussex 240** (49.5 overs) (L. J. Wright 84; C. J. Liddle 5-52); ‡**Gloucestershire 241-4** (48.4 overs) (M. Klinger 53, G. T. Hankins 67, J. M. R. Taylor 64). *Attendance:* 3,249. *County cricket returned to The Saffrons after 17 years, and drew a crowd of over 3,000. Well placed at 169-3 in the 35th over, Sussex were pegged back by* *former players Chris Liddle and Tom Smith, who shared eight wickets. Michael Klinger and George Hankins led the chase with half-centuries, before Jack Taylor (dropped twice) produced the best hitting of the day. His fourth fifty of the tournament came from just 36 balls. Sussex retained a chance of making the quarters, but not Gloucestershire.*

Sussex away matches

April 27: no result v Middlesex.
May 5: beat Kent by six wickets.
May 10: lost to Essex by ten runs.
May 17: no result v Hampshire.

QUARTER-FINALS

At Taunton, June 13. **Nottinghamshire won by 24 runs. Nottinghamshire 429-9** (50 overs) (M. H. Wessels 81, S. R. Patel 66, B. R. M. Taylor 154; L. Gregory 4-60); ‡**Somerset 405** (48 overs) (D. Elgar 91, P. D. Trego 66). *Attendance:* 4,332. *Taunton groundsman Simon Lee received praise for the pitch, though probably not from the bowlers: there were 110 boundaries. Brendan Taylor thrashed 22 of them in a 97-ball 154, propelling Nottinghamshire to a ground-record 429-9. Dean Elgar gave Somerset hope with 93 – his sixth 50-plus score in six innings in the competition – and a stand of 154 with Peter Trego in 16 overs. After they departed, the others biffed Somerset to a county-best 405 (beating 371-8 from 48 overs against Kent at Taunton in 2014), but not quite into the semi-finals.*

HIGHEST LIST A MATCH AGGREGATES

872	Australia (434-4) v South Africa (438-9)	at Johannesburg	2005-06
870	Nottinghamshire (445-8) v Northamptonshire (425)	at Nottingham	2016
867	Surrey (438-5) v Glamorgan (429)	at The Oval	2002
834	**Nottinghamshire (429-9) v Somerset (405)**	**at Taunton**	**2017**
827	South Africa A (433-3) v India A (394)	at Pretoria	2013
825	India (414-7) v Sri Lanka (411-8)	at Rajkot	2009-10
815	Central Districts (417-6) v Northern Districts (398)	at Hamilton	2012-13
800	Tasmania (398-1) v Queensland (402-3)	at Sydney	2014-15

At Leeds, June 13 (day/night). **Surrey won by 24 runs.** ‡**Surrey 313-7** (50 overs) (K. C. Sangakkara 121, B. T. Foakes 86); **Yorkshire 289-9** (50 overs) (A. Lyth 75, P. S. P. Handscomb 60). *Attendance:* 2,870. *The Headingley crowd might have been aware that Kumar Sangakkara's 100th century in all formats would probably cost Yorkshire a semi-final place, but they still gave his latest masterpiece a standing ovation. After his partnership of 180 with Ben Foakes, Surrey were lifted over 300 by a lively 37 from Ollie Pope. Yorkshire were never able to break free against tight bowling; Adam Lyth and Peter Handscomb hit half-centuries, but neither could play a dominant hand.*

SEMI-FINALS

ESSEX v NOTTINGHAMSHIRE

At Chelmsford, June 16 (day/night). Nottinghamshire won by five wickets. Toss: Essex.

Steven Mullaney's maiden one-day century powered Nottinghamshire into the final, after a record chase for a limited-overs match in England. Entering at 180 for four when Taylor was run out by Porter, Mullaney spanked six sixes and eight fours from just 75 balls, before falling with victory in sight. He shared a stand of 185 with Patel – who contributed the match's fourth century, and completed an unlikely pursuit with two meaty edges in Walter's final over. Essex, who had won seven of their eight group games, looked impregnable after they ran up 370, a total they had exceeded against county opposition only once. Cook, the leading run-scorer in the competition, led the way with his third century of the summer, and was followed by a more rumbustious knock from ten

HIGHEST WINNING CHASES IN ENGLISH ONE-DAY CRICKET

373-5	**Nottinghamshire beat Essex (370-5) at Chelmsford**	**2017**
359-8	Hampshire beat Surrey (358-6) at The Oval	2005
354-6	**Somerset beat Kent (352-6) at Taunton**	**2017**
350-3	England beat New Zealand (349-7) at Nottingham	2015
345-6	Somerset beat Australians (342-5) at Taunton	2005
340-5	Kent beat Nottinghamshire (335) at Nottingham	2015
339-4	**Yorkshire beat Durham (335-5) at Leeds**	**2017**
337-7	Kent beat Sussex (336-5) at Canterbury†	2013
335-6	Gloucestershire beat Middlesex (333-4) at Southgate‡	2005
334-7	**Glamorgan beat Hampshire (332-6) at Southampton§**	**2017**
332-4	**Sussex beat Kent (331-7) at Canterbury**	**2017**

† *40 overs.* ‡ *45 overs.* § *49 overs.* *All the others were 50-over games.*

Doeschate, who clouted five sixes – three off Gurney in the penultimate over – in reaching his hundred from 64 balls. After a match that produced 743 runs, a rueful ten Doeschate said he wanted to turn the clock back to the end of his side's innings: "At that point you'd think there was no way we could lose."

Man of the Match: S. J. Mullaney. *Attendance:* 4,401.

Essex

V. Chopra c Read b Mullaney	23
A. N. Cook c Read b Patel	133
T. Westley c Taylor b Patel	33
R. S. Bopara c Read b Broad	16
*R. N. ten Doeschate not out	102
Ashar Zaidi c Taylor b Broad	16
†J. S. Foster not out	27
B 2, lb 7, w 7, nb 4	20
1/87 (1) 2/136 (3) 3/173 (4) 4/271 (2) 5/295 (6) (5 wkts, 50 overs)	370
10 overs: 67-0	

P. I. Walter, S. R. Harmer, N. Wagner and J. A. Porter did not bat.

Gurney 7–0–75–0; Ball 10–0–68–0; Patel 9–0–51–2; Pattinson 8–0–61–0; Mullaney 6–0–50–1; Broad 10–0–56–2.

Nottinghamshire

M. J. Lumb c Harmer b Porter	11
A. D. Hales b Porter	39
M. H. Wessels b Porter	23
S. R. Patel not out	122
B. R. M. Taylor run out	62
S. J. Mullaney c Foster b Wagner	111
*†C. M. W. Read not out	0
Lb 2, w 3	5
1/21 (1) 2/73 (2) 3/80 (3) 4/180 (5) 5/365 (6) (5 wkts, 49.3 overs)	373
10 overs: 80-3	

J. L. Pattinson, S. C. J. Broad, J. T. Ball and H. F. Gurney did not bat.

Wagner 8–0–71–1; Porter 8–1–56–3; Ashar Zaidi 10–0–67–0; Bopara 10–0–59–0; Walter 6.3–0–51–0; Harmer 6–0–58–0; ten Doeschate 1–0–9–0.

Umpires: N. G. B. Cook and J. W. Lloyds. Third umpire: D. J. Millns.

WORCESTERSHIRE v SURREY

At Worcester, June 17. Surrey won by 153 runs. Toss: Surrey.

Enduring a torrent of taunts from the home crowd, Batty destroyed the Worcestershire chase with five for 40. Afterwards, he was asked what he thought of the supporters of the club he had left eight years earlier. "We are playing in a Lord's final," he said, "which they will never do." His batsmen had set up victory. Roy, dropped by England for the Champions Trophy semi-final, returned to form with 92, and Sangakkara and Foakes continued theirs, helping Surrey rack up 363 in glorious sunshine. Hastings's battle was bloodiest: he spilled 97 from his ten. Ali came out firing, smashing two sixes off Dernbach in the fifth over, before miscuing a slower one in the seventh. That made it 42 for three, before Batty picked away at the middle order, celebrating each scalp with a primal scream. D'Oliveira resisted with a sparky 53, and Whiteley clubbed 55, but the end came 17 overs early.

Man of the Match: G. J. Batty. *Attendance:* 4,122.

Surrey

J. J. Roy lbw b Mitchell	92	T. K. Curran not out	9
M. D. Stoneman b Ali	41	*G. J. Batty not out	1
K. C. Sangakkara c Cox b Hastings	73	B 1, lb 4, w 6, nb 2	13
R. J. Burns b D'Oliveira	5		
†B. T. Foakes run out	86	1/114 (2) 2/179 (1) (7 wkts, 50 overs)	363
O. J. D. Pope c and b Leach	22	3/186 (4) 4/259 (3)	
S. M. Curran hit wkt b Leach	21	5/310 (6) 6/353 (5) 7/354 (7) 10 overs: 90-0	

R. Rampaul and J. W. Dernbach did not bat.

Hastings 10–0–97–1; Leach 8–0–66–2; Tongue 4–0–25–0; Mitchell 10–0–59–1; Ali 10–0–55–1; D'Oliveira 7–0–39–1; Barnard 1–0–17–0.

Worcestershire

M. M. Ali c T. K. Curran b Dernbach	36	E. G. Barnard c Batty b Dernbach	9
D. K. H. Mitchell c Foakes b S. M. Curran	0	J. C. Tongue not out	11
T. C. Fell run out	2		
J. M. Clarke c Foakes b Batty	15	W 4, nb 2	6
B. L. D'Oliveira lbw b Batty	53		
J. W. Hastings c Burns b Batty	3	1/8 (2) 2/33 (3) (33.2 overs)	210
†O. B. Cox c Dernbach b Batty	13	3/42 (1) 4/90 (4) 5/104 (6)	
R. A. Whiteley c Burns b S. M. Curran	55	6/115 (5) 7/131 (7) 8/160 (9)	
*J. Leach c Pope b Batty	7	9/187 (10) 10/210 (8) 10 overs: 63-3	

Dernbach 8–0–64–2; S. M. Curran 5.2–0–19–2; Batty 9–0–40–5; T. K. Curran 6–0–48–0; Rampaul 5–0–39–0.

Umpires: R. J. Bailey and A. G. Wharf. Third umpire: M. J. Saggers.

FINAL

NOTTINGHAMSHIRE v SURREY

JAMES GINGELL

At Lord's, July 1. Nottinghamshire won by four wickets. Toss: Surrey.

Not many would cast Nottinghamshire's cavalier opener Alex Hales as the heir to Geoffrey Boycott. Yet here he inherited Boycott's 52-year record for the best score in a Lord's final, charging to 187 not out. Both innings condemned Surrey to a runners-up medal, and this one was their third in succession.

Hales dominated not just Surrey, but Nottinghamshire too: when they reached 100 in pursuit of 298, he had 82. He hit 24 of the match's 58 boundaries and all four sixes, and finished with a string of List A bests: his own, the ground's, and Nottinghamshire's. Yet nothing was loose, nothing frantic; all drives were merited, all pulls were just. In an England shirt, Hales has sometimes appeared too eager to prove his masculinity with a flex of a tattooed biceps. Now, he was a zen master-blaster, calm until the last hurried single, when he leapt into the air with delight.

Still, he needed luck. On nine, he leaned back to drive Sam Curran, and 19-year-old Pope dropped a straightforward catch at cover. In Curran's next over, Hales pumped his first six over midwicket. Pope wore sunglasses, but behind the blue lenses, you could tell the eyes burned red.

Hales needed a partner, too. At 150 for five, he was on 114, while no one else had made more than 11. Sam Curran had just picked up his second lbw, and the middle order of meaty middles – Patel,

Taylor and Mullaney, who had between them made 452 runs in the two knockout games – had departed. Surrey sensed that while they might not be able to prise Hales out, they might not need to.

But out came Read for his last Lord's final before retirement, drove his fourth delivery for four, and stroked a run-a-ball 58 while putting on 137 with Hales. On 49, Read ducked a bouncer, leaving his bat periscopically raised. The ball hit the edge, but dropped to square leg for a single. Afterwards, he remembered another duck with a less fortunate result, when in 1999 he had misread a slower one from New Zealand's Chris Cairns, and lost his stumps, as well as his standing as a Test player. As he acknowledged the Nottinghamshire fans singing his name in the Compton Stand, greyer but with the same elfin blue eyes, that all felt like a lifetime ago.

Nottinghamshire had begun in slovenly fashion. On a sticky morning, their fingers were anything but: Wessels put down Roy off the first ball of the match, then Mullaney reprieved Stoneman on 32. The bowling was not much better, too full or too wide. Without forcing a shot, Surrey had raced to 83 without loss after 11 overs and were bearing down on a huge total. But Roy, who never settled, pushed tentatively at Patel's first ball, which gripped down the slope and took a leading edge. Sangakkara glided to 30 before nibbling into Read's gloves. Borthwick prodded to midwicket, Foakes – averaging over 120 in the competition – missed a straight one, and Pope nicked to slip. All had gone to Patel or Mullaney, who also held three catches.

Amid it all stood Stoneman, driving in the same gear throughout. Unwanted by England, who announced their Test squad without him earlier that day, he was essential for Surrey, and reached a controlled hundred with an edged four off Patel, about the first to miss the middle of his bat. But he struggled for boundaries towards the end, and couldn't drag Surrey to 300; after Nottinghamshire had totalled 802 in their knockouts, it never looked enough.

Later, Stoneman caught Read in the deep just as the sun remembered it was midsummer – this was the first July Lord's final – and cast its shadows; Hales's was longest, while all around him those in black hitched hands on hips, waiting to complete an unwelcome hat-trick.

Man of the Match: A. D. Hales. *Attendance:* 17,059

Surrey

J. J. Roy c Mullaney b Patel	23	J. W. Dernbach c Wessels b Gurney	5
M. D. Stoneman not out	144	R. Rampaul not out	0
K. C. Sangakkara c Read b Mullaney	30		
S. G. Borthwick c Mullaney b Patel	14	B 1, lb 12, w 10, nb 2	25
†B. T. Foakes b Mullaney	1		
O. J. D. Pope c Mullaney b Patel	4	1/83 (1) 2/141 (3) (9 wkts, 50 overs)	297
S. M. Curran b Pattinson	24	3/172 (4) 4/175 (5)	
T. K. Curran run out	16	5/180 (6) 6/228 (7) 7/255 (8)	
*G. J. Batty b Fletcher	11	8/282 (9) 9/296 (10)	10 overs: 74-0

Fletcher 5–0–37–1; Gurney 7–0–47–1; Pattinson 10–0–48–1; Patel 10–0–51–3; Broad 9–0–51–0; Mullaney 9–0–50–2.

Nottinghamshire

M. J. Lumb lbw b S. M. Curran	4	J. L. Pattinson not out	9
A. D. Hales not out	187		
M. H. Wessels lbw b Rampaul	6	Lb 3, w 4, nb 4	11
S. R. Patel c S. M. Curran b Rampaul	7		
B. R. M. Taylor c Foakes b Dernbach	11	1/25 (1) 2/60 (3) (6 wkts, 47.5 overs)	298
S. J. Mullaney lbw b S. M. Curran	5	3/104 (4) 4/128 (5)	
*†C. M. W. Read c Stoneman b S. M. Curran	58	5/150 (6) 6/287 (7)	10 overs: 66-2

S. C. J. Broad, L. J. Fletcher and H. F. Gurney did not bat.

Dernbach 10–0–53–1; S. M. Curran 9.5–0–68–3; T. K. Curran 6–0–52–0; Rampaul 10–0–52–2; Borthwick 3–0–29–0; Batty 9–0–41–0.

Umpires: R. T. Robinson and A. G. Wharf. Third umpire: D. J. Millns.

SOUTH AFRICA A IN ENGLAND IN 2017

JAMES GINGELL

England's search for a worthy Test opener to join Alastair Cook had become a saga, and here was its latest stanza. At Canterbury, four Lions were pitted against each other for the role. With a Test series against South Africa's seniors coming up, the situation might have lent a little more bite to the glove taps.

Haseeb Hameed and Keaton Jennings – the captain here against the South African A side – had already lined up with Cook in India the previous winter, with some success. But neither had enjoyed their return to county cricket, so they were back on trial. Hameed, in particular, was in a terrible trot: struggling outside off, he was averaging under 20 for Lancashire. Mark Stoneman, meanwhile, had earned his chance with three early hundreds for his new county, Surrey. Nick Gubbins of Middlesex was in the mix, too, even if he felt the least likely.

In the event, Stoneman hit two fifties, but Jennings matched him, and won the spot. Others shone more brightly, though. Ben Foakes, the keeper, stroked a brilliant century, while the two Jamies – Overton and Porter – proved an excellent opening attack. Dawid Malan and Liam Livingstone, alphas of previous Lions squads, savaged the tourists in the 50-over games.

Still, any insights gained might have been illusory, so weak were the South Africans. They did have Test players in their ranks, including Temba Bavuma, Duanne Olivier and Theunis de Bruyn, sent to acclimatise before the series with England. And they were led by Aiden Markram, who had captained South Africa to the Under-19 World Cup in 2014, and was considered by many back home to be the next Graeme Smith. But, with a collapse never far away, they were hammered in the one-dayers, and hammered in the A-team Test. There was little respite against the counties either: after two no-results, they were trounced at Arundel by an inexperienced Sussex.

Heino Kuhn was perhaps their only success, hitting a double-century in the sole victory, against Hampshire, and averaging over 100 for the tour. It earned him a Test place; if he struggled after stepping up, it wasn't as if anyone else had made a stronger case.

SOUTH AFRICA A TOURING PARTY

*A. K. Markram (FC/50), T. Bavuma (FC/50), C. J. Dala (FC/50), T. B. de Bruyn (FC/50), B. E. Hendricks (FC), R. R. Hendricks (50), H. Klaasen (FC), H. G. Kuhn (FC/50), S. S. B. Magala (50), M. Mosehle (50), P. W. A. Mulder (FC), L. T. Ngidi (FC/50), D. Olivier (FC/50), D. Paterson (FC/50), D. L. Piedt (FC), R. S. Second (FC), T. Shamsi (50), J. F. Smith (FC/50), J. T. Smuts (50), K. Zondo (FC/50). *Coach:* S. Conrad.

Zondo captained in the one-day matches. D. Pretorius and D. W. Steyn were originally included, but Pretorius joined South Africa's Champions Trophy squad and Steyn withdrew with a shoulder injury. Smith was added to the 50-over squad, and Mulder to the first-class squad.

At Leeds, May 27. **No result. ‡South Africa A 129-4** (35.3 overs) (K. Zondo 56*) **v Yorkshire.**

At Derby, May 29. **No result. South Africa A 145-1** (20.1 overs) (R. R. Hendricks 68*, T. B. de Bruyn 65*) **v ‡Derbyshire.** *County debuts:* A. F. Gleadall, H. Qadri.

First A-team one-day international At Nottingham, June 1. **England Lions won by nine wickets. South Africa A 268** (49 overs) (R. R. Hendricks 79, H. G. Kuhn 81*; S. T. Finn 3-54); ‡**England Lions 269-1** (40.3 overs) (B. M. Duckett 69, D. J. Malan 125*, D. J. Bell-Drummond 62*). *At 194-4, with 15 overs left, South Africa A were ready for lift-off. But three wickets for Steven Finn in eight balls kept them grounded, and the last five fell in single figures; Heino Kuhn was stranded on 81*. Dawid Malan made chasing 269 look simple. He put on 134 with Ben Duckett – who had earlier pulled off a stunning catch at short cover to remove Khaya Zondo – then scorched to a third one-day hundred for the Lions.*

Second A-team one-day international At Northampton, June 3. **England Lions won by 144 runs. England Lions 349-7** (50 overs) (D. J. Malan 84, L. S. Livingstone 129; A. K. Markram 4-45); ‡**South Africa A 205** (41.3 overs) (A. K. Markram 50; L. A. Dawson 4-41). *After another smooth half-century from Malan – taking his List A average from ten innings for the Lions to 80 – Liam Livingstone dished out some rough stuff. He launched eight sixes, including one into a neighbouring garden, and finished with 129 off 83 balls, his first one-day hundred. Amid the wreckage, Aiden Markram managed 4-45 with his off-spin, his best figures, then led the reply with a run-a-ball 50. But the rest of the top order crumbled meekly, Liam Dawson swept up 4-41, and the Lions eased to a series win.*

Third A-team one-day international At Northampton, June 5. **No result. England Lions 28-0** (5 overs) v ‡**South Africa A.**

HAMPSHIRE v SOUTH AFRICA A

At Southampton, June 8–11 (day/night). South Africa A won by 251 runs. Toss: Hampshire. County debut: C. M. Dickinson.

When South Africa A slipped to 126 for five on the second day – the first had nearly all been lost to rain – they looked miles away from a first tour win. But Kuhn led a determined fightback: he put on 209 with Heinrich Klaasen, and ground out a fourth first-class double-century. After the declaration at 370 for seven, skiddy seamer Dane Paterson completed the turnaround with seven for 27, as Hampshire could only halve the deficit. It might have been worse: they had been 56 for seven, before Durban-born wicketkeeper Calvin Dickinson prevented total embarrassment with a career-best 99. The match – played with a pink ball at Hampshire's request, ahead of the round of day/night Championship games a fortnight later – flowed to its inevitable conclusion. Aiden Markram hit a hundred, then declared overnight, before left-armer Beuran Hendricks blew Hampshire away on the last day with five for 20.

Close of play: first day, South Africa A 18-2 (Kuhn 9, Second 0); second day, Hampshire 18-2 (Smith 9, Holland 0); third day, South Africa A 185-1 (Markram 102, de Bruyn 72).

South Africa A

*A. K. Markram c and b Wheal	3	– not out	102
H. G. Kuhn not out	200	– lbw b Salisbury	10
T. B. de Bruyn c Dickinson b Salisbury	6	– not out	72
R. S. Second c Dickinson b Salisbury	8		
J. F. Smith c Hart b Taylor	14		
K. Zondo b Taylor	6		
†H. Klaasen c Dickinson b Hart	103		
D. L. Piedt c Dickinson b Salisbury	6		
B. E. Hendricks not out	3		
B 9, lb 11, w 1	21	Nb 1	1
1/4 (1) 2/18 (3) 3/62 (4) 4/103 (5) 5/126 (6) 6/335 (7) 7/359 (8) — (7 wkts dec, 104.1 overs)	370	1/32 (2) — (1 wkt dec, 51 overs)	185

D. Paterson and C. J. Dala did not bat.

Wheal 13–4–36–1; Salisbury 19.1–3–65–3; Holland 20–6–48–0; Crane 21–1–90–0; Hart 16–0–53–1; Taylor 14–1–57–2; Wood 1–0–1–0. *Second innings*—Wheal 7–1–44–0; Salisbury 9–1–29–1; Hart 9–3–21–0; Wood 2–0–11–0; Taylor 10–1–38–0; Holland 5–1–17–0; Crane 9–1–25–0.

Hampshire

T. P. Alsop lbw b Paterson	4 – b Hendricks	51
W. R. Smith b Paterson	18 – c Kuhn b Hendricks	2
M. S. Crane c Kuhn b Paterson	0 – (9) c Markram b Hendricks	0
I. G. Holland c Klaasen b Hendricks	1 – (3) c Markram b Paterson	0
*G. J. Bailey c Piedt b Paterson	8 – (4) c de Bruyn b Dala	33
C. P. Wood c Klaasen b Dala	5 – (5) b Piedt	0
†C. M. Dickinson c Smith b de Bruyn	99 – (6) b Piedt	13
B. J. Taylor b Paterson	7 – (7) not out	13
A. H. J. A. Hart c Klaasen b Paterson	36 – (8) c Klaasen b Hendricks	0
M. E. T. Salisbury not out	0 – c Klaasen b Piedt	2
B. T. J. Wheal b Paterson	0 – c Klaasen b Hendricks	0
B 4, lb 2, nb 1	7 B 2, lb 1, w 1, nb 1	5
1/13 (1) 2/13 (3) 3/24 (4) 4/32 (2) 5/41 (5) 6/41 (6) 7/56 (8) 8/185 (7) 9/185 (9) 10/185 (11) (51.4 overs)	185 1/10 (2) 2/11 (3) 3/65 (4) 4/66 (5) 5/84 (6) 6/102 (1) 7/104 (8) 8/107 (9) 9/110 (10) 10/119 (11) (45.5 overs)	119

Paterson 13.4–6–27–7; Hendricks 12–2–43–1; Dala 10–0–53–1; Smith 4–1–9–0; Piedt 7–3–25–0; Markram 1–0–6–0; de Bruyn 4–2–16–1. *Second innings*—Paterson 9–3–35–1; Hendricks 13.5–5–20–5; Dala 6–1–25–1; Piedt 17–5–36–3.

Umpires: R. J. Evans and S. C. Gale.

SUSSEX v SOUTH AFRICA A

At Arundel, June 14–16. Sussex won by an innings and 50 runs. Toss: Sussex. First-class debuts: J. W. Hutson, J. W. Jenner, L. P. Smith.

It wasn't so much the scale of the South African defeat that should have worried them, as its architects. First, Delray Rawlins hit 96 – beating his previous best by 74 – and added 172 for the fifth wicket with fellow teenager Jonty Jenner, a Guernsey-born Jersey player, who struck 68 on first-class debut. Then, on the second day, Briggs – with only one first-class fifty to his name – reached a maiden century. Paterson, unplayable the week before, went wicketless, while all-rounder Wiaan Mulder bowled nine no-balls, and Olivier five. The South African batsmen were little better, and only Bavuma and Zondo emerged with credit from two spectacular collapses against unspectacular bowling: the last six fell for 53 in the first innings, then for 26 in the second. Leg-spinner Will Beer – a white-ball specialist – picked up the first two five-fors of his first-class career, while seamer Abidine Sakande collected his first, too.

Close of play: first day, Sussex 325-7 (Briggs 39, Sakande 0); second day, South Africa A 151-6 (Second 21, Piedt 2).

Sussex

W. A. T. Beer lbw b Mulder	27	A. Sakande b Piedt	17
*H. Z. Finch b Mulder	48	†J. W. Hutson c Markram b Olivier	25
P. D. Salt c Smith b Olivier	5	A. P. Barton c Mulder b Piedt	2
D. M. W. Rawlins b Dala	96	B 15, lb 12, w 1, nb 22	50
L. P. Smith c Second b Olivier	0		
J. W. Jenner c Paterson b Mulder	68	1/83 (1) 2/90 (2) 3/90 (3) (126.3 overs)	458
D. R. Briggs not out	120	4/90 (5) 5/262 (6) 6/289 (4)	
G. H. S. Garton c Second b Piedt	0	7/290 (8) 8/369 (9) 9/439 (10) 10/458 (11)	

Olivier 30–3–108–3; Paterson 19–4–66–0; Dala 18–2–72–1; Piedt 36.3–7–99–3; Mulder 18–3–71–3; Smith 5–1–15–0.

South Africa A

*A. K. Markram lbw b Garton	0 – b Sakande	33
T. Bavuma lbw b Briggs	63 – c and b Sakande	0
J. F. Smith c Finch b Beer	18 – c Salt b Sakande	3
K. Zondo b Sakande	24 – c Hutson b Beer	95
†R. S. Second lbw b Briggs	31 – c Finch b Beer	21
P. W. A. Mulder b Beer	7 – lbw b Sakande	42
H. Klaasen lbw b Beer	5 – lbw b Beer	1
D. L. Piedt b Beer	17 – lbw b Sakande	2
D. Olivier not out	2 – b Beer	0
D. Paterson lbw b Beer	0 – not out	18
C. J. Dala c Hutson b Beer	3 – b Beer	4
B 7, w 5, nb 3	15 Lb 4	4
1/5 (1) 2/61 (3) 3/108 (2) (76.1 overs)	185 1/8 (2) 2/18 (3) (65 overs)	223
4/118 (4) 5/132 (6) 6/142 (7)	3/55 (1) 4/89 (5)	
7/173 (5) 8/181 (8) 9/181 (10) 10/185 (11)	5/197 (6) 6/199 (4) 7/200 (7)	
	8/200 (9) 9/212 (8) 10/223 (11)	

Garton 13–3–48–1; Sakande 12–0–44–1; Barton 7–1–15–0; Briggs 27–8–42–2; Beer 17.1–2–29–6. *Second innings*—Garton 8–1–19–0; Sakande 13–3–43–5; Briggs 19–3–69–0; Beer 18–2–62–5; Barton 6–2–19–0; Rawlins 1–0–7–0.

Umpires: N. G. C. Cowley and J. H. Evans.

ENGLAND LIONS v SOUTH AFRICA A

A-Team Test

At Canterbury, June 21–24. England Lions won by 257 runs. Toss: England Lions.

The England selectors had come to see the top order – and Stoneman, with the help of a couple of drops, and Jennings made their case with twin half-centuries. But those nearer the other end swung the contest. It was Foakes who firmed up a wobbly first innings with an unbeaten 127 out of 386. Then, after the South Africans began with 164 for their first wicket, Jamie Overton cracked open the game with a rapid spell on the second evening. He bounced out Markram and trapped Kuhn with a rapid yorker after he had made a fluent century. That sparked panic, and all ten went down for 119. Hameed added two to his first-innings duck, but his rivals for the Test opening spot prospered, including Gubbins, who raced to 63 off 65 balls. That helped the Lions to a third-evening declaration, setting 412, and Overton did the damage again, blasting out three by the close, while Porter claimed three as the tourists wilted. "We had a proper international-class attack," said Jennings. "It made it easy for me as captain."

Close of play: first day, England Lions 302-7 (Foakes 77, Helm 9); second day, South Africa A 227-7 (Mulder 13, Hendricks 0); third day, South Africa A 29-4 (Bavuma 16, Klaasen 2).

England Lions

M. D. Stoneman c Bavuma b Hendricks	58 – b Olivier	86
H. Hameed c Markram b Olivier	0 – c Klaasen b Hendricks	2
*K. K. Jennings c Mulder b Dala	57 – c de Bruyn b Piedt	71
N. R. T. Gubbins b Piedt	4 – c Markram b Piedt	63
D. W. Lawrence c Kuhn b Dala	34 – c Klaasen b Hendricks	18
†B. T. Foakes not out	127 – c de Bruyn b Piedt	34
S. M. Curran lbw b de Bruyn	18 – not out	7
J. Overton c Klaasen b Hendricks	15	
T. G. Helm b Olivier	20	
M. J. Leach b Mulder	16	
J. A. Porter b Dala	0	
B 5, lb 8, w 4, nb 20	37 B 1, lb 22, nb 4	27
1/12 (2) 2/117 (1) 3/131 (4) (109.4 overs)	386 1/19 (2) (6 wkts dec, 62.4 overs)	308
4/144 (3) 5/218 (5) 6/267 (7)	2/164 (1) 3/192 (3)	
7/288 (8) 8/332 (9) 9/385 (10) 10/386 (11)	4/214 (5) 5/283 (6) 6/308 (4)	

Hendricks 24–4–75–2; Olivier 22–4–79–2; Dala 17.4–1–63–3; Piedt 30–5–98–1; Mulder 9–0–48–1; de Bruyn 7–1–10–1. *Second innings*—Olivier 14–2–60–1; Hendricks 13–2–61–2; Dala 10–1–52–0; Piedt 18.4–0–94–3; Mulder 7–0–18–0.

South Africa A

*A. K. Markram c Helm b Overton	71	– lbw b Porter	3
H. G. Kuhn lbw b Overton	105	– c Foakes b Overton	5
T. B. de Bruyn c Hameed b Porter	11	– c Hameed b Overton	2
T. Bavuma b Helm	10	– lbw b Curran	33
K. Zondo c Jennings b Porter	1	– c Foakes b Overton	1
†H. Klaasen c Jennings b Porter	0	– lbw b Porter	43
P. W. A. Mulder c Foakes b Curran	18	– b Porter	1
D. L. Piedt lbw b Curran	7	– c Porter b Leach	31
B. E. Hendricks b Leach	20	– c Porter b Curran	12
D. Olivier not out	15	– lbw b Lawrence	8
C. J. Dala c Overton b Lawrence	14	– not out	4
B 1, lb 2, w 1, nb 7	11	B 4, lb 5, w 1, nb 1	11
1/164 (1) 2/194 (2) 3/196 (3) 4/200 (5) 5/200 (6) 6/210 (4) 7/225 (8) 8/238 (7) 9/264 (9) 10/283 (11) (81 overs)	283	1/8 (1) 2/8 (2) 3/19 (3) 4/25 (5) 5/92 (4) 6/99 (7) 7/100 (6) 8/125 (9) 9/143 (8) 10/154 (10) (46 overs)	154

Porter 21–8–58–3; Curran 21–7–64–2; Overton 14–2–43–2; Helm 11–1–36–1; Leach 13–1–71–1; Lawrence 1–0–8–1. *Second innings*—Porter 13–2–47–3; Overton 9–0–36–3; Helm 8–2–24–0; Curran 8–1–21–2; Leach 7–3–17–1; Lawrence 1–1–0–1.

Umpires: M. Burns and T. Lungley.

THE UNIVERSITIES IN 2017

CAMBRIDGE MCCU v NOTTINGHAMSHIRE

At Cambridge, March 28–30. Nottinghamshire won by 344 runs. Toss: Nottinghamshire. First-class debuts: L. J. Chapman, A. D. Greenidge, C. J. Guest, T. H. Moses, S. E. Rippington, M. S. Zaidi.

In 2016, Nottinghamshire won this fixture by 517 runs, with centuries from Mullaney and Wessels, and they returned to plague a largely new cast of undergraduates. Both ended just short of three figures this time, Wessels thanks to a second-innings declaration that left a target of 424. Cambridge managed just 79, with more than half the runs coming from skipper Joe Tetley; Akil Greenidge, son of the former West Indian opener Alvin, made 22, but seven others failed to score more than a single. On the first day, Nottinghamshire had been kept in check by six wickets from 18-year-old off-spinner Luke Chapman, including Wessels and Patel for ducks in successive balls. Patel retaliated in Cambridge's first innings, sharing nine wickets with Gurney, who finished with match figures of eight for 47.

Close of play: first day, Cambridge MCCU 8-0 (Colverd 1, Palmer 4); second day, Nottinghamshire 46-2 (Libby 16, Wessels 11).

Nottinghamshire

First innings		Second innings	
S. J. Mullaney c Greenidge b Chapman	89		
J. D. Libby b Chapman	22	– (1) not out	79
G. P. Smith b Chapman	73		
A. D. Hales c Palmer b Barton	35	– (3) c Palmer b Moses	4
M. H. Wessels c and b Chapman	0	– (4) not out	90
S. R. Patel c Barton b Chapman	0	– (2) b Rippington	13
*†C. M. W. Read b Rippington	39		
L. Wood c Guest b Chapman	36		
S. C. J. Broad b Rippington	18		
L. J. Fletcher not out	1		
H. F. Gurney b Rippington	2		
B 10, lb 10, nb 4	24	B 8, lb 3, w 6, nb 4	21
1/87 (2) 2/140 (1) 3/212 (4) 4/213 (5) 5/217 (6) 6/246 (3) 7/287 (7) 8/335 (8) 9/337 (9) 10/339 (11) (101.3 overs)	339	1/20 (2) 2/27 (3) (2 wkts dec, 56 overs)	207

Moses 9–0–51–0; Rippington 19.3–4–51–3; Barton 15–3–37–1; Guest 18–2–65–0; Chapman 32–11–78–6; Zaidi 6–0–22–0; Arif 2–0–15–0. *Second innings*—Moses 8–1–19–1; Rippington 12–4–45–1; Chapman 7–0–40–0; Barton 8–3–22–0; Guest 12–1–34–0; Zaidi 9–0–36–0.

Cambridge MCCU

First innings		Second innings	
T. G. L. Colverd c Smith b Gurney	12	– c Smith b Broad	0
H. J. Palmer b Fletcher	19	– c Smith b Broad	1
A. D. Greenidge c Patel b Gurney	12	– c Broad b Gurney	22
C. J. Guest c Wessels b Patel	9	– lbw b Wood	5
*†J. W. Tetley c sub (C. R. Marshall) b Patel	8	– c Read b Gurney	42
A. T. Arif c Libby b Patel	9	– st Read b Patel	0
T. H. Moses c Read b Patel	25	– c Read b Gurney	3
M. S. Zaidi lbw b Gurney	3	– lbw b Patel	1
L. J. Chapman c sub (C. R. Marshall) b Patel	13	– c Hales b Gurney	0
S. E. Rippington not out	0	– c Wessels b Fletcher	0
A. P. Barton lbw b Gurney	0	– not out	0
B 4, lb 7, nb 2	13	Lb 5	5
1/37 (2) 2/51 (1) 3/54 (3) 4/62 (4) 5/69 (5) 6/80 (6) 7/109 (7) 8/121 (8) 9/123 (9) 10/123 (11) (49.1 overs)	123	1/1 (2) 2/2 (1) 3/19 (4) 4/35 (3) 5/38 (6) 6/51 (7) 7/70 (8) 8/74 (9) 9/75 (5) 10/79 (10) (32.4 overs)	79

Broad 12–2–21–0; Wood 7–2–17–0; Fletcher 6–1–12–1; Gurney 11.1–5–19–4; Patel 13–4–43–5. *Second innings*—Broad 6–4–5–2; Fletcher 9.4–2–23–1; Wood 2–0–11–1; Gurney 8–3–28–4; Patel 7–5–7–2.

Umpires: B. J. Debenham and S. A. Garratt.

At Cardiff, March 28–30. CARDIFF MCCU drew with GLAMORGAN.

At Bristol, March 28–30. DURHAM MCCU drew with GLOUCESTERSHIRE.

At Canterbury, March 28–30. LEEDS/BRADFORD MCCU lost to KENT by 212 runs.

At Leicester, March 28–30. LOUGHBOROUGH MCCU drew with LEICESTERSHIRE.

OXFORD MCCU v SURREY

At Oxford, March 28–30. Drawn. Toss: Surrey. First-class debuts: T. D. Heathfield, R. Hussain, D. N. C. Scott, D. A. C. Wells, A. R. Wilkinson; O. J. D. Pope. County debuts: S. G. Borthwick, M. D. Stoneman.

The loss of nearly half the second day to rain compromised Surrey's chances of victory, although Oxford's callow side – their five debutants included Nasser Hussain's nephew Reece – stuck to their task. Surrey's batsmen never quite cut loose on the first day, despite Sibley's century, only his second in first-class cricket after 242 against Yorkshire as an 18-year-old in 2013. Batty's declaration left the student openers seven overs to survive, which they did, and next day the batsmen applied themselves well against a strong attack, with Footitt looking sharp. Another attractive innings from Sibley preceded another Surrey declaration, but Oxford held on, despite early strikes by Meaker and Sam Curran.

Close of play: first day, Oxford MCCU 17-0 (Wells 5, Scott 8); second day, Surrey 29-0 (Burns 14, Stoneman 13).

Surrey

R. J. Burns lbw b Wilkinson	37	– c Ellis b Grundy	28
M. D. Stoneman lbw b Heathfield	47	– c Grundy b Heathfield	14
S. G. Borthwick c Ellis b McIver	49	– c Ellis b Wilkinson	5
D. P. Sibley not out	104	– not out	60
Z. S. Ansari b McIver	37	– c Ellis b Wilkinson	12
S. M. Curran c Hussain b Grundy	13	– b Wilkinson	10
†O. J. D. Pope c Ellis b Lake	38	– not out	6
*G. J. Batty c Broughton b Grundy	1		
S. C. Meaker not out	0		
Lb 2, w 1, nb 6	9	B 5, nb 2	7
1/51 (1) 2/94 (2) (7 wkts dec, 91 overs)	335	1/33 (2) (5 wkts dec, 49 overs)	142
3/147 (3) 4/229 (5)		2/44 (3) 3/53 (1)	
5/254 (6) 6/330 (7) 7/333 (8)		4/91 (5) 5/121 (6)	

J. W. Dernbach and M. H. A. Footitt did not bat.

Lake 12–0–59–1; Wilkinson 18–2–82–1; Grundy 21–3–86–2; Heathfield 15–4–46–1; McIver 25–7–60–2. *Second innings*—Lake 3–1–16–0; Wilkinson 15–6–35–3; Heathfield 9–1–26–1; Grundy 8–2–20–1; McIver 14–3–40–0.

Oxford MCCU

D. A. C. Wells b Dernbach	33	– c Pope b Curran	5
D. N. C. Scott b Dernbach	8	– c Stoneman b Meaker	18
J. N. McIver lbw b Meaker	7	– lbw b Meaker	5
R. Hussain b Footitt	12	– c Stoneman b Batty	15
A. T. A. Martin b Ansari	5	– lbw b Batty	11
M. B. Lake lbw b Footitt	48	– not out	4
B. M. Broughton c and b Curran	25	– not out	1
*J. O. Grundy c Burns b Footitt	8		
†E. J. Ellis lbw b Borthwick	4		
T. D. Heathfield not out	0		
A. R. Wilkinson c Burns b Footitt	0		
B 8, lb 10, w 2, nb 2	22	B 4, lb 1	5
1/25 (2) 2/47 (3) 3/66 (4) 4/79 (5) 5/79 (1) 6/141 (7) 7/167 (8) 8/172 (9) 9/172 (6) 10/172 (11) (60 overs)	172	1/17 (1) 2/27 (2) 3/42 (3) 4/58 (5) 5/61 (4) (5 wkts, 28 overs)	64

Dernbach 14–6–40–2; Curran 14–3–37–1; Meaker 13–3–35–1; Footitt 10–4–15–4; Ansari 8–3–22–1; Borthwick 1–0–5–1. *Second innings*—Dernbach 3–2–3–0; Curran 6–3–11–1; Meaker 7–2–22–2; Footitt 5–0–18–0; Batty 4–3–2–2; Ansari 3–2–3–0.

Umpires: N. G. C. Cowley and C. M. Watts.

CAMBRIDGE MCCU v LANCASHIRE

At Cambridge, April 2–3. Lancashire won by 340 runs. Toss: Cambridge MCCU. County debuts: R. McLaren, D. J. Vilas.

Faced by an international-class attack, Cambridge were predictably clueless, and were skittled for 62 and 56 to sink to another heavy defeat, this time inside two days. Lancashire batted competently if unspectacularly on the first day, when Hameed retired hurt after being hit on the left hand by Tim Moses (though there was no serious damage). Davies top-scored with 80 from 165 balls, then Anderson shook off any early-season cobwebs with five cheap wickets, three of them as the last six tumbled for six runs. Croft tinkered with his batting order in the second innings, when left-arm seamer Adam Barton – later to play for Sussex – claimed five wickets, including four in 11 balls with the score on 28. Dane Vilas, Lancashire's Kolpak signing from South Africa, and Davies stopped the rot, and the eventual target of 397 was always fanciful.

Close of play: first day, Cambridge MCCU 15-2 (Senaratne 6, Greenidge 0).

Lancashire

†A. L. Davies c Palmer b Barton	80	– (9) not out	50
H. Hameed retired hurt	7		
L. S. Livingstone lbw b Rippington	1	– (8) b Moses	1
*S. J. Croft c Senaratne b Barton	78	– (6) b Barton	0
D. J. Vilas c Guest b Barton	58	– (2) not out	42
R. McLaren b Chapman	0	– (1) lbw b Rippington	4
J. Clark b Chapman	64	– (3) lbw b Barton	6
S. D. Parry not out	14	– (4) lbw b Barton	0
T. E. Bailey not out	10		
K. M. Jarvis (did not bat)		– (5) c and b Barton	0
J. M. Anderson (did not bat)		– (7) c Tice b Barton	10
B 13, lb 3, nb 10	26	B 4, lb 3	7
1/18 (3) 2/173 (4) 3/182 (1) 4/183 (6) 5/282 (5) 6/324 (7) (6 wkts dec, 88 overs)	338	1/9 (1) 2/28 (3) 3/28 (4) 4/28 (5) 5/28 (6) 6/44 (7) 7/45 (8) (7 wkts dec, 32 overs)	120

In the first innings Hameed retired hurt at 17-0.

Moses 12–1–40–0; Rippington 20–7–52–1; Barton 24–3–75–3; Chapman 25–3–111–2; Guest 7–0–44–0. *Second innings*—Barton 12–3–31–5; Rippington 12–3–29–1; Moses 5–1–24–1; Chapman 3–0–29–0.

Cambridge MCCU

T. G. L. Colverd c McLaren b Anderson	1	– c Croft b McLaren	4
H. J. Palmer lbw b Anderson	8	– b Anderson	1
N. V. S. Senaratne b Anderson	31	– b Clark	4
A. D. Greenidge c Davies b Bailey	0	– c Vilas b Clark	1
*J. W. Tetley lbw b Jarvis	4	– (7) b Livingstone	11
C. J. Guest b Jarvis	7	– (5) c Davies b Clark	0
T. H. Moses lbw b Parry	0	– (8) c Davies b Livingstone	18
†P. J. A. Tice not out	1	– (6) b Jarvis	4
L. J. Chapman st Davies b Parry	3	– b Parry	2
S. E. Rippington c Davies b Anderson	0	– not out	2
A. P. Barton b Anderson	2	– lbw b Parry	0
Lb 5	5	Lb 5, nb 4	9
1/8 (1) 2/13 (2) 3/17 (4) (43 overs)	62	1/5 (2) 2/14 (1) (37.4 overs)	56
4/34 (5) 5/56 (6) 6/56 (7)		3/14 (3) 4/14 (5)	
7/56 (3) 8/59 (9) 9/60 (10) 10/62 (11)		5/17 (4) 6/29 (6) 7/34 (7)	
		8/47 (9) 9/55 (8) 10/56 (11)	

Anderson 11–5–10–5; Jarvis 11–4–15–2; Bailey 6–4–6–1; Clark 6–2–8–0; McLaren 5–1–18–0; Parry 4–4–0–2. *Second innings*—Anderson 5–2–5–1; Jarvis 8–5–10–1; McLaren 5–3–2–1; Clark 6–1–11–3; Parry 7.4–3–15–2; Livingstone 6–3–8–2.

Umpires: P. K. Baldwin and R. T. Robinson.

At Chelmsford, April 2–4. DURHAM MCCU drew with ESSEX.

At Southampton, April 2–4. CARDIFF MCCU drew with HAMPSHIRE.

At Northampton, April 2–4. LOUGHBOROUGH MCCU drew with NORTHAMPTONSHIRE.
Loughborough make 553, the highest total by a university against a first-class county since 1930.

OXFORD MCCU v WARWICKSHIRE

At Oxford, April 2–4. Drawn. Toss: Warwickshire. First-class debut: Sukhjit Singh.

Oxford followed their draw against Surrey with another tenacious performance, hanging on despite slipping from 27 for one to 38 for six late in the match. Their star on the opening day was seamer Tom Heathfield, who conceded just 21 runs from 17 overs as Warwickshire made otherwise serene progress: Porterfield and Trott put on 187, but it took them three and a half hours. Oxford then batted capably enough, nine men reaching double figures, although the highest score was Bruno Broughton's 46 from No. 8. Warwickshire concentrated on practice, Mellor atoning for his first-innings duck with a maiden fifty, and Hain hitting 81. Heathfield again made a mark, forcing Barker to retire hurt with an injured hand and giving Clarke a painful crack on the arm. Bell's declaration halfway through the final day left his bowlers little time to force a win, and Broughton blocked the way again. Warwickshire's Indian-born left-arm spinner Sukhjit "Sunny" Singh completed a promising debut with match figures of 30–17–52–4.

Close of play: first day, Oxford MCCU 42-2 (McIver 12, Ellis 8); second day, Warwickshire 109-1 (Mellor 43, Hain 24).

Warwickshire

W. T. S. Porterfield lbw b McIver	89	– retired out	36
A. J. Mellor c Scott b Wilkinson	0	– c Broughton b Wilkinson	59
I. J. L. Trott retired out	130		
*I. R. Bell c Broughton b Wilkinson	33		
S. R. Hain not out	15	– (3) b Heathfield	81
†T. R. Ambrose not out	13	– (4) run out	16
R. Clarke (did not bat)		– (5) not out	16
K. H. D. Barker (did not bat)		– (6) retired hurt	16
Sukhjit Singh (did not bat)		– (7) lbw b Lake	0
O. J. Hannon-Dalby (did not bat)		– (8) not out	3
Lb 1, nb 4	5	B 4, lb 9, w 1	14
1/9 (2) 2/196 (1) (4 wkts dec, 86 overs) 3/244 (3) 4/262 (4)	285	1/75 (1) (5 wkts dec, 78 overs) 2/151 (2) 3/193 (4) 4/203 (3) 5/225 (7)	241

C. J. C. Wright did not bat.

In the second innings Barker retired hurt at 225-4.

Wilkinson 17–2–89–2; Heathfield 17–10–21–0; Grundy 16–5–54–0; Lake 16–4–48–0; McIver 20–4–72–1. *Second innings*—Heathfield 13–5–34–1; Wilkinson 12–2–53–1; McIver 30–5–82–0; Lake 14–4–33–1; Grundy 9–0–26–0.

Oxford MCCU

D. A. C. Wells lbw b Barker	4	– b Sukhjit Singh	0
D. N. C. Scott c Ambrose b Wright	11	– c Ambrose b Wright	8
J. N. McIver lbw b Wright	19	– c Mellor b Hannon-Dalby	22
†E. J. Ellis b Barker	18	– (8) not out	5
R. Hussain b Wright	6	– (4) b Sukhjit Singh	1
A. T. A. Martin lbw b Sukhjit Singh	28	– (5) lbw b Hannon-Dalby	4
M. B. Lake c Porterfield b Hannon-Dalby	11	– (6) c Clarke b Hannon-Dalby	0
B. M. Broughton c Ambrose b Barker	46	– (7) not out	14
*J. O. Grundy b Sukhjit Singh	24		
T. D. Heathfield not out	12		
A. R. Wilkinson b Clarke	12		
B 8, lb 6, nb 10	24	Lb 6, nb 2	8
1/4 (1) 2/24 (2) 3/57 (3) (67.4 overs) 4/59 (4) 5/73 (5) 6/88 (7) 7/141 (6) 8/170 (8) 9/202 (9) 10/215 (11)	215	1/7 (1) 2/27 (2) (6 wkts, 31 overs) 3/28 (4) 4/33 (5) 5/35 (6) 6/38 (3)	62

Barker 14–4–44–3; Wright 17–1–56–3; Sukhjit Singh 15–10–21–2; Hannon-Dalby 11–1–39–1; Clarke 10.4–3–41–1. *Second innings*—Wright 5–3–7–1; Sukhjit Singh 15–7–31–2; Hannon-Dalby 8–4–8–3; Clarke 2–0–3–0; Hain 1–0–7–0.

Umpires: N. G. B. Cook and P. R. Pollard.

At Leeds, April 2–4. LEEDS/BRADFORD MCCU lost to YORKSHIRE by an innings and 224 runs.

At Cambridge, April 7–9 (not first-class). **Middlesex won by 333 runs.** ‡**Middlesex 392** (105 overs) (D. J. Malan 116, J. A. Simpson 57, T. S. Roland-Jones 51*; S. E. Rippington 5-91, L. J. Chapman 3-101) **and 175-4 dec** (35 overs) (S. S. Eskinazi 64, O. P. Rayner 91); **Cambridge MCCU 123** (39.5 overs) (A. D. Greenidge 65) **and 111** (39 overs) (A. D. Greenidge 52; O. P. Rayner 4-9). *Dawid Malan led the way as Middlesex scored freely on an opening day that eventually included 109 overs. Left-arm seamer Sam Rippington took the last four wickets to finish with 5-91. But that was the end of the good news for the students: they were 0-2 in both innings, the openers bagging a pair apiece, and staggered to three figures twice thanks to defiant half-centuries from Akil Greenidge,* *who hit precisely half Cambridge's combined total of 234. Ollie Rayner followed up a 90-ball 91 with 7–2–9–4 as the match was completed before lunch on the third day. Cambridge lost their three county games in 2017 by 344, 340 and 333 runs.*

At Chester-le-Street, April 7–9 (not first-class). DURHAM MCCU lost to DURHAM by 459 runs.

At Weetwood, Leeds, April 7–9 (not first-class). **Worcestershire won by an innings and 42 runs. Leeds/Bradford MCCU 162** (58.2 overs) (J. D. Shantry 3-36) **and 249** (80.4 overs) (C. D. Wallace 75*; B. L. D'Oliveira 3-70, C. A. J. Morris 3-36); ‡**Worcestershire 453-4 dec** (95.5 overs) (B. L. D'Oliveira 82, T. C. Fell 64, J. M. Clarke 109, T. Köhler-Cadmore 101*, O. B. Cox 66*). *County debut:* J. W. Hastings. *Centuries for young guns Joe Clarke and Tom Köhler-Cadmore propelled Worcestershire to a total that proved way beyond the students. The county's bowlers had grabbed the upper hand on the first day, when Martin Andersson's 33 was the top score of an underwhelming effort. Leeds/Bradford batted better in the second innings, but a deficit of 291 proved too much, despite 75* from the Scotland international Craig Wallace; he shared a long stand with wicketkeeper Jack Potticary, who used up 102 minutes for 16.*

At Loughborough, April 7–9 (not first-class). **Drawn. Derbyshire 363-8 dec** (79 overs) (B. A. Godleman 76, G. C Wilson 106; S. J. Cook 3-51) **and 255-2 dec** (58 overs) (L. M. Reece 58, B. A. Godleman 65*, W. L. Madsen 80*); ‡**Loughborough MCCU 388** (111.4 overs) (J. R. Bracey 104, N. R. Kumar 57, R. G. White 62; L. M. Reece 3-22). *County debuts:* L. M. Reece, D. Smit, G. C. Wilson. *Loughborough made it three draws out of three against county opposition in 2017 – with a first-innings lead each time. Gary Wilson's century had lifted Derbyshire to 363 after being inserted on the first day, before James Bracey followed suit for Loughborough. Bracey, who played for Gloucestershire in 2016, put on 94 with Nitish Kumar and 109 with Robbie White. The last pair, Sam Cook and Ben Ladd-Gibbon, had the satisfaction of pinching a lead on the final morning in a stand of 47, before Derbyshire settled for batting practice.*

At Taunton, April 7–8 (not first-class). OXFORD MCCU lost to SOMERSET by 506 runs.

At Hove, April 7–9 (not first-class). CARDIFF MCCU drew with SUSSEX.

THE UNIVERSITY MATCHES IN 2017

At Cambridge, June 16. **Cambridge University won by ten runs.** ‡**Cambridge University 133-7** (20 overs) (T. H. Moses 43; T. H. S. Pettman 3-17); **Oxford University 123-7** (20 overs) (M. S. T. Hughes 59). *Cambridge hardly looked likely winners as they wobbled to 45-5 in the tenth over, but Tim Moses struck 43 from 34 balls to ensure a competitive total. Moses then removed Dan Escott in the second over of the chase, and two wickets for Ruari Crichard made it 20-3, all to catches by keeper-captain Patrick Tice. His opposite number Matt Hughes collected 59 from 52 balls, but the defeat was confirmed when he fell to the penultimate delivery. Cambridge made the score in the Varsity T20 match 4–3 since the first in 2008 (two were no-results and one abandoned).*

At Lord's, June 23. **Oxford University won by nine runs.** ‡**Oxford University 264-8** (50 overs) (M. S. T. Hughes 32, M. A. Naylor 52, J. S. D. Gnodde 76, N. P. Taylor 32*; T. H. Moses 4-56); **Cambridge University 255** (49.5 overs) (A. D. Dalgleish 68, T. H. Moses 45; J. Marsden 4-33, B. Swanson 4-58). *Moses was again the star for Cambridge, following four wickets with a 35-ball 45 – but it wasn't quite enough, as Oxford made up for the previous week's T20 defeat with their fifth consecutive victory in the one-day Varsity match, giving them a 14–9 lead. Their total owed much to James Gnodde's forthright 76 from 60 balls. Angus Dalgleish seemed to be anchoring Cambridge to victory, but his departure in the 42nd over, which made it 206-6, proved crucial.*

CAMBRIDGE UNIVERSITY v OXFORD UNIVERSITY

At Cambridge, July 4–7. Cambridge University won by 216 runs. Toss: Cambridge University. First-class debuts: A. C. H. Dewhurst, R. A. Sale, N. J. Winder; T. M. J. Brock, J. Harrison, M. A. Naylor, T. H. S. Pettman, A. J. W. Rackow, B. Swanson, N. P. Taylor.

Cambridge avenged their 2016 defeat with a convincing victory at Fenner's, set up by a consistent batting performance in the third innings after the teams had been on level terms. Tim Moses, a thorn in Oxford flesh in all three formats, hit five sixes in a brisk undefeated 80, which backed up Alistair Dewhurst's dogged 91, as Cambridge declared 430 ahead. Dewhurst narrowly missed out on a century on first-class debut, as did Oxford's Alex Rackow, who had rescued their first innings from 38 for five. Patrick Tice's declaration left Oxford around 110 overs to survive, and it looked as if they might manage it at 130 for two. But Ruari Crichard broke through, finishing with six wickets, and 11 for 142 overall. He was the first to take ten or more in the Varsity Match since the Oxford leg-spinner Michael Munday claimed 11 for 143 in 2006. "It's the last first-class game I'll play," he said. "It will stay with me for the rest of my life."

Close of play: first day, Oxford University 51-5 (Rackow 15, Harrison 7); second day, Cambridge University 118-2 (Colverd 47, Dewhurst 15); third day, Oxford University 49-0 (Escott 21, Hughes 28).

Cambridge University

T. G. L. Colverd lbw b Pettman	22	– c Harrison b Marsden	64
D. Chohan lbw b Pettman	4	– c Harrison b Brock	26
N. V. S. Senaratne b Marsden	33	– c Escott b Swanson	11
A. C. H. Dewhurst c Rackow b Marsden	3	– b Brock	91
A. D. Dalgleish c Harrison b Brock	19	– lbw b Pettman	25
*†P. J. A. Tice c Harrison b Marsden	54	– c Harrison b Brock	36
T. H. Moses c Escott b Pettman	19	– not out	80
R. A. Sale c Swanson b Brock	14	– st Harrison b Hughes	28
R. J. Crichard c Escott b Brock	17		
J. E. Poulson not out	16	– (9) not out	5
N. J. Winder b Marsden	1		
B 7, lb 6, nb 10	23	B 21, lb 7, w 7, nb 16	51
1/10 (2) 2/54 (1) 3/65 (4) (71.4 overs)	225	1/52 (2) (7 wkts dec, 116 overs)	417
4/93 (5) 5/111 (3) 6/156 (7)		2/75 (3) 3/154 (1)	
7/182 (6) 8/203 (9) 9/220 (8) 10/225 (11)		4/211 (5) 5/271 (6) 6/314 (4) 7/379 (8)	

Marsden 21.4–10–47–4; Pettman 22–6–82–3; Brock 20–2–61–3; Swanson 8–2–22–0. *Second innings*—Marsden 22–8–56–1; Pettman 24–3–102–1; Brock 18–1–76–3; Swanson 23–11–40–1; Gnodde 2–0–15–0; Escott 14–1–34–0; Hughes 13–0–66–1.

Oxford University

D. A. Escott c Tice b Crichard	14	– c and b Crichard	22
*M. S. T. Hughes c Tice b Crichard	1	– c Tice b Moses	41
M. A. Naylor c Tice b Crichard	0	– c Tice b Crichard	19
J. S. D. Gnodde b Moses	4	– run out	54
N. P. Taylor c Tice b Crichard	2	– c Sale b Crichard	4
A. J. W. Rackow c Moses b Poulson	95	– c Dewhurst b Moses	23
†J. Harrison c Sale b Poulson	38	– c Senaratne b Crichard	14
T. M. J. Brock c Tice b Crichard	2	– b Moses	0
T. H. S. Pettman run out	25	– b Crichard	9
J. Marsden not out	8	– c Dalgleish b Crichard	0
B. Swanson lbw b Poulson	0	– not out	0
B 6, lb 11, nb 6	23	Lb 11, w 1, nb 16	28
1/7 (2) 2/17 (3) 3/20 (1) (75.5 overs)	212	1/70 (1) 2/70 (2) (88.4 overs)	214
4/22 (5) 5/38 (4) 6/144 (7)		3/130 (3) 4/146 (5)	
7/151 (8) 8/197 (6) 9/199 (9) 10/212 (11)		5/167 (4) 6/180 (6) 7/180 (8)	
		8/201 (9) 9/201 (10) 10/214 (7)	

Crichard 29–5–74–5; Moses 20–5–42–1; Poulson 16.5–6–30–3; Winder 8–0–41–0; Sale 2–0–8–0. *Second innings*—Crichard 21.4–6–68–6; Moses 26–7–62–3; Winder 20–11–30–0; Sale 7–3–13–0; Poulson 9–5–22–0; Dalgleish 3–1–6–0; Colverd 2–1–2–0.

Umpires: B. J. Debenham and C. M. Watts.

Cambridge University *P. J. A. Tice (*St Columba's, Dublin, and Fitzwilliam*), D. Chohan (*Dulwich College and St Catharine's*), T. G. L. Colverd (*Haberdashers' Aske's Boys' School and Robinson*), R. J. Crichard (*King's College School, Wimbledon, and St John's*), A. D. Dalgleish (*St Olave's*

Grammar School, Orpington, and Trinity Hall), A. C. H. Dewhurst (*St Paul's School and Robinson*), T. H. Moses (*Hurstpierpoint College and Hughes Hall*), J. E. Poulson (*King Edward VI School, Bury St Edmunds, and Homerton*), R. A. Sale (*Uppingham School and Fitzwilliam*), N. V. S. Senaratne (*Eton College and Jesus*), N. J. Winder (*Tonbridge School and Robinson*).

C. M. Webster (*Trinity School, Croydon, and Girton*) replaced Dewhurst in the 50- and 20-over matches, and J. J. Das (*Forest School and Darwin*) replaced Chohan in the T20 game.

Oxford University *M. S. T. Hughes (*Stockport Grammar School and Hertford*), T. M. J. Brock (*Millfield School and St Hilda's*), D. A. Escott (*Winchester College and Lincoln*), J. S. D. Gnodde (*Eton College and Pembroke*), J. Harrison (*The Grammar School, Leeds, and Pembroke*), J. Marsden (*King's School, Macclesfield, and Christ Church*), M. A. Naylor (*Finham Park School, Coventry, and Merton*), T. H. S. Pettman (*Tonbridge School and Jesus*), A. J. W. Rackow (*Dulwich College and St Hilda's*), B. Swanson (*Alleyn's School and St Peter's*), N. P. Taylor (*The Perse School and St Catherine's*).

M. J. Dawes (*City of London Freemen's School and St Hugh's*) replaced Taylor in the Twenty20 match.

This was the 172nd University Match, a first-class fixture dating back to 1827. Cambridge have won 60 and Oxford 56, with 56 drawn. It was played at Lord's until 2000.

MCC UNIVERSITIES CHAMPIONSHIP

	Played	*Won*	*Lost*	*1st-inns wins*	*1st-inns losses*	*Drawn*	*Bonus points*	*Points*
Loughborough (1)	5	0	0	3	1	1	45	80
Cardiff (5)	5	0	0	3	0	2	37	77
Durham (4)	5	0	0	2	2	1	37	62
Leeds/Bradford (3)	5	0	0	2	3	0	41	61
Cambridge (6)	5	0	0	2	3	0	37	57
Oxford (2)	5	0	0	1	4	0	38	48

Outright win = 17pts; first-innings win in a drawn match = 10pts; no result on first innings = 5pts.

WINNERS

2001 Loughborough
2002 Loughborough
2003 Loughborough
2004 Oxford
2005 Loughborough
2006 Oxford
2007 Cardiff/Glamorgan
2008 Loughborough
2009 Leeds/Bradford
2010 Durham
2011 Cardiff
2012 Cambridge
2013 Leeds/Bradford
2014 Loughborough
2015 Cardiff
2016 Loughborough
2017 Loughborough

MCC UNIVERSITIES CHALLENGE FINAL

At Lord's, June 15. **Cardiff MCCU won by 25 runs. Cardiff MCCU 291** (50 overs) (N. Brand 42, A. G. Milton 63, J. A. L. Scriven 73, T. N. Cullen 45*; A. D. Tillcock 3-46); **‡Loughborough MCCU 266** (49.2 overs) (Hassan Azad 40, N. R. Kumar 70, R. G. White 81; A. T. Thomson 5-41). *Cardiff set a stiff target, largely thanks to a fourth-wicket stand of 121 between Alex Milton and Jack Scriven, who faced only 61 balls and belted four sixes. Loughborough looked on course while the Canadian international Nitish Kumar and wicketkeeper Robbie White were adding 118, also for the fourth wicket, but after they were separated off-spinner Alex Thomson mopped up to complete Cardiff's victory.*

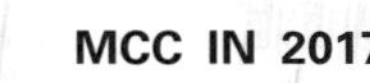

MCC IN 2017

STEVEN LYNCH

Once again the question of how best to continue the redevelopment of Lord's kept the committee-room busy. The choice was between an elaborate scheme, drawn up by the Rifkind Levy Partnership, which included residential flats behind the Nursery Ground, and a less ambitious plan funded by MCC. Consultations were arranged around the country, so members could consider the plans in detail. Eventually, the committee recommended using the club's own resources, and that was accepted by the required majority.

Feelings ran high on both sides, and the constant churn of meetings may have contributed to the decision of Derek Brewer, the secretary and chief executive, to step down six months ahead of his 60th birthday in April 2018, after six years in the role. His deputy, Colin Maynard, also retired, after more than 42 years at Lord's, which meant a new team at the top. Guy Lavender was recruited from Somerset as chief executive, while Jamie Clifford joined from Kent to take over most of Maynard's duties. One of the first items on the new administration's agenda was to facilitate the rebuilding of the Compton and Edrich Stands, with more seating and new entertaining areas, for which £38m has been budgeted. They will be helped by the business nous of the new president, the former Tesco (and ECB) chairman Lord MacLaurin.

A new Code of Laws came into force on October 1. It included provision for umpires to send players from the field in extreme circumstances, and also introduced new limits on the thickness of bats. This stemmed from a recommendation from MCC's influential world cricket committee, now chaired by Mike Gatting, who succeeded his old Middlesex captain Mike Brearley.

Notable deaths during the year included Rachael Heyhoe Flint, the former England women's captain and one of MCC's first female members, and Doug Insole, whose bulging portfolio of administrative appointments included the MCC presidency in 2006-07.

In all, MCC teams played more than 500 matches in 2017, including Afghanistan's first visit to Lord's, which was ruined by the weather. The year was rounded off with a defeat by Melbourne CC on the same MCG pitch enjoyed by Alastair Cook during his undefeated 244 in the fourth Ashes Test. At home, MCC played 486 matches, of which 224 were won, 84 drawn, two tied, 102 lost, and 74 abandoned or cancelled. The women's team had 22 games, winning ten, drawing three and losing four, with five abandoned. Club teams toured Belize and Mexico, Germany, Hong Kong and China, and Tanzania.

MCC v MIDDLESEX

At Abu Dhabi, March 26–28, 2017 (day/night). Middlesex won by one wicket. Toss: MCC.

With England's first day/night Tests on the horizon, this was an opportunity to stake a specialist's claim, particularly for MCC's team, picked with significant input from the ECB. The incentive helped produce a thriller. The pink Dukes ball – reinstated after a red one had been used a year earlier – swung handsomely, but batting was not impossible. Facing a second-string attack, MCC racked up

332 on the opening day, with Duckett bullish and Clarke impish. Gregory had Robson nicking to the slips before stumps, then took four more next day as Somerset bowlers, perhaps still smarting from the near-miss of the previous summer, took all ten. Middlesex conceded a deficit of 153, but from there showed all the grit that had defined their title win. With Plunkett unable to bowl – he had been hit on the calf by a ball during practice, then felt the muscle tighten running a two on the first evening – MCC declined the follow-on and slipped to 145 for seven by the second-day close. Next morning, they were all out for 151, leaving 305 for victory. Gubbins and Compton began with half-centuries and, after a brief wobble, Eskinazi and Simpson added 84. Middlesex needed just 63 with six wickets left, when Overton, rounding off a superb performance, took a hat-trick, including Franklin for a pair. Crane's leg-breaks winkled out two more, but Simpson, so often the guiding hand in tricky chases, saw Middlesex home. WILL MACPHERSON

Close of play: first day, Middlesex 9-1 (Gubbins 2, Helm 1); second day, MCC 145-7 (Overton 25, Crane 0).

MCC

First innings		Second innings	
A. Lyth lbw b Helm	14	– c Helm b Patel	42
*A. Z. Lees c Simpson b Patel	41	– lbw b Podmore	9
T. P. Alsop lbw b Harris	0	– lbw b Podmore	0
B. M. Duckett lbw b Patel	69	– c and b Harris	13
J. M. Clarke lbw b Harris	89	– b Harris	2
†O. B. Cox lbw b Podmore	40	– lbw b Podmore	17
L. Gregory c Franklin b Patel	36	– b Helm	32
L. E. Plunkett c Gubbins b Harris	15	– absent hurt	
C. Overton lbw b Helm	12	– (8) b Helm	28
M. J. Leach c Simpson b Podmore	4	– c Gubbins b Helm	0
M. S. Crane not out	0	– (9) not out	3
B 4, lb 8	12	B 1, lb 4	5
1/15 (1) 2/16 (3) 3/125 (2) 4/140 (4) 5/221 (6) 6/290 (7) 7/301 (5) 8/320 (8) 9/327 (10) 10/332 (9) (89.1 overs)	332	1/23 (2) 2/23 (3) 3/47 (4) 4/49 (5) 5/76 (6) 6/100 (1) 7/140 (7) 8/151 (8) 9/151 (10) (41.5 overs)	151

Podmore 15–4–44–2; Helm 11.1–0–46–2; Harris 14–2–49–3; Patel 25–1–83–3; Franklin 9–1–50–0; Malan 12–1–36–0; Robson 3–0–12–0. *Second innings*—Podmore 9–3–25–3; Helm 11.5–3–30–3; Harris 10–2–34–2; Franklin 4–0–25–0; Patel 7–0–32–1.

Middlesex

First innings		Second innings	
S. D. Robson c Lees b Gregory	6	– (2) c Lees b Leach	20
N. R. T. Gubbins c Lees b Gregory	38	– (1) lbw b Crane	52
T. G. Helm b Leach	15	– (10) c Leach b Crane	12
N. R. D. Compton b Gregory	5	– (3) c Lees b Crane	59
D. J. Malan lbw b Overton	56	– (4) b Gregory	14
S. S. Eskinazi c Cox b Gregory	0	– (5) lbw b Overton	44
†J. A. Simpson c Cox b Gregory	49	– (6) not out	89
*J. E. C. Franklin c Cox b Overton	0	– (7) c Cox b Overton	0
J. A. R. Harris not out	4	– (8) lbw b Overton	0
H. W. Podmore c Leach b Overton	1	– (9) c Cox b Crane	7
R. H. Patel b Overton	0	– not out	0
B 1, lb 4	5	B 5, lb 1, w 1, nb 2	9
1/6 (1) 2/44 (3) 3/65 (4) 4/68 (2) 5/68 (6) 6/164 (5) 7/164 (8) 8/174 (7) 9/179 (10) 10/179 (11) (62.4 overs)	179	1/43 (2) 2/107 (1) 3/144 (4) 4/158 (3) 5/242 (5) 6/242 (7) 7/242 (8) 8/278 (9) 9/300 (10) (9 wkts, 71.1 overs)	306

Gregory 13–6–32–5; Overton 15.4–6–37–4; Leach 17–1–39–1; Crane 10–0–44–0; Lyth 7–1–22–0. *Second innings*—Gregory 15–1–75–1; Overton 15.1–2–55–3; Leach 15–2–52–1; Crane 21–0–95–4; Lyth 5–0–23–0.

Umpires: R. J. Evans and A. G. Wharf.

At Lord's, July 11. **No result.** ‡**MCC 217-6** (40 overs) (S. R. Hain 76, S. R. Patel 53; Shapoor Zadran 3-28); **Afghanistan 31-1** (5 overs). *The weather spoiled Afghanistan's first appearance at Lord's, to the disappointment of an enthusiastic crowd. Rain meant a late start – and an early finish, after only five overs of the chase. MCC were captained by Brendon McCullum, and included Shivnarine Chanderpaul, Misbah-ul-Haq and Yasir Shah. But on the pitch used for the South Africa Test which finished two days before, it was the unheralded Warwickshire batsman Sam Hain who glued the innings together with 76 from 101 balls after opening with McCullum. Later Samit Patel smacked 53 from 47. The official scorers were the unrelated Mulhollands, Brian and Connor.*

ECB NORTH–SOUTH SERIES IN 2017

WILL MACPHERSON

50-over matches (3): North 0, South 3

Andrew Strauss, the ECB's director of England cricket, had revived the old North–South rivalry to help remedy a World Cup record he described as "awful". The regions had last clashed in 1971, in a 50-over exhibition match at the John Player Ground in Nottingham. Now, though, the emphasis was on unearthing new talent, and little heed was paid to capturing public imagination: the series was staged in the UAE amid minimal local interest and, because of the Dubai Stadium's rights demands, only the third game was broadcast on radio.

Still, it was a worthwhile exercise. The watching Trevor Bayliss, possessing only a rudimentary knowledge of the domestic ranks, saw a diverse range of players, from Steven Finn and his 102 one-day international wickets to Graeme White, a 29-year-old left-arm spinner subsisting on a limited-overs contract at Northamptonshire. White was one of eight selected using the PCA's Most Valuable Player rankings. And, with a full complement of ECB staff – including an anti-corruption officer – the more sheltered players got a taste of the elite-level experience. Not all got the message: Kent captain Sam Northeast missed the flight out, and some came out of hibernation with a touch more lagging.

On offer was £50,000 – comprising £10,000 for each game, plus £20,000 for the series – and the South won the lot. Mason Crane, Liam Dawson and Dawid Malan all left with reputations enhanced, and the concept, scheduled to run at least until 2019 (though not necessarily in the UAE), will only gain credence if they are picked for higher honours.

SQUADS

North *K. K. Jennings (Durham), †T. T. Bresnan (Yorkshire), J. M. Clarke (Worcestershire), P. Coughlin (Durham), †B. M. Duckett (Northamptonshire), †H. F. Gurney (Nottinghamshire), S. R. Hain (Warwickshire), J. A. Leaning (Yorkshire), L. S. Livingstone (Lancashire), S. Mahmood (Lancashire), J. E. Poysden (Warwickshire), †G. G. White (Northamptonshire), M. A. Wood (Durham). *Coach:* O. D. Gibson.

R. J. Gleeson (Northamptonshire) was originally selected, but withdrew with a knee injury and was replaced by Coughlin.

South *J. M. Vince (Hampshire), T. P. Alsop (Hampshire), D. J. Bell-Drummond (Kent), M. S. Crane (Hampshire), T. K. Curran (Surrey), †L. A. Dawson (Hampshire), S. T. Finn (Middlesex), B. T. Foakes (Surrey), †L. Gregory (Somerset), †T. D. Groenewald (Somerset), D. J. Malan (Middlesex), S. A. Northeast (Kent), T. S. Roland-Jones (Middlesex). *Coach:* P. Farbrace.

†M. T. Coles (Kent) was originally selected in the squad, but injured a toe and was replaced by Roland-Jones.

† *Selected on PCA MVP rankings for the 2016 Royal London One-Day Cup.*

First match At Dubai, March 17. **South won by ten wickets.** ‡**North 202** (43.3 overs) (J. M. Clarke 57; T. K. Curran 3-19); **South 205-0** (33.3 overs) (D. J. Bell-Drummond 92*, D. J. Malan 109*). *Things looked grim for the North when captain Keaton Jennings, Ben Duckett and Liam Livingstone were seen off cheaply by the seamers. Joe Clarke, one of the brightest talents in the land, rallied with a zesty fifty, before being bowled attempting to ramp Tom Curran. He should have focused on guiding his team through the final overs: 202 was never adequate. Mason Crane cost 72 runs, but Curran (3-19) and Liam Dawson (2-29), who bagged Tim Bresnan (40) just as he was looking dangerous, were miserly. The South's openers, mixing deft deflections with authoritative smites, raced home with 99 balls to spare. Daniel Bell-Drummond didn't have time to reach his century, but Dawid Malan did. Looking wonderful throughout, he pulled hard from square leg to mid-on, and cut with power, before eventually plonking Jack Leaning down the ground to put the North out of their misery.*

Second match At Dubai, March 19 (day/night). **South won by 47 runs. South 346-6** (50 overs) (D. J. Malan 78, S. A. Northeast 118*, L. A. Dawson 83); ‡**North 299-9** (50 overs) (B. M. Duckett 64, T. T. Bresnan 74). *The South's innings began with a wicket-maiden from Bresnan, but Malan, again in fine touch, and captain James Vince (46) recovered with a century stand. When they departed, Sam Northeast took responsibility, hitting a superb unbeaten hundred in his only knock on tour: a hamstring injury ruled him out of the third match, and of captaining MCC against county champions Middlesex. Dawson's 83 was a gem, too; he shared 170 with Northeast, before being caught trying to hit Harry Gurney for a third consecutive six. Briefly, with Duckett and Livingstone purring, it seemed the North could haul in 347. But after some stunning shots – Livingstone smacked Curran on the up over extra cover for six – their stand ended on 74 from 40 balls. It was Dawson (2-46), excellent once more, who did for Duckett, and with him went the game. From there, only Bresnan, ninth out for 74, showed any spine.*

Third match At Abu Dhabi, March 21. **South won by 20 runs. South 228-8** (40 overs) (D. J. Bell-Drummond 81; J. E. Poysden 3-55); ‡**North 208** (39.2 overs) (L. S. Livingstone 50; T. K. Curran 3-51, M. S. Crane 4-39). *MoS:* Liam Dawson (South). *Given the money on offer, and the team spirit fostered by Paul Farbrace, the South were desperate to inflict a whitewash, and achieved it with the hardest fought of their victories. On a tougher pitch, and with the game reduced to 40 overs by rain, their batting – Bell-Drummond aside – lacked oomph, until Roland-Jones biffed 43 off 24 balls to lift them to 228. Mark Wood bowled with fire to dismiss Malan cheaply, while the specialist spinners, Graeme White (2-30) and Josh Poysden (3-55), gave control. Duckett tore after the target, cracking 37 off 17, before taking one risk too many, but Sam Hain and Livingstone picked up the mantle, and with 13 overs and eight wickets remaining they needed 84. Then Crane wrenched the match from them with his leg-spin. In the space of 12 balls, he bowled Hain and Clarke with consecutive deliveries – the latter a flighted beauty – added Leaning in the same fashion, then had Livingstone stumped. Bresnan (35 from 27 balls) again raged against the dying of the light, but the support was not there, and Curran returned to finish the job.*

THE MINOR COUNTIES IN 2017

PHILIP AUGUST

Berkshire went one better than in 2016, adding the one-day trophy to the Championship title they were defending – but they were pushed all the way by Lincolnshire, runners-up in both competitions. And in the 36-year-old slow left-armer Chris Peploe, formerly of Middlesex, Berkshire had the player of the season. He took 50 wickets at 16 while conceding just 2.2 an over, and averaged 46 with the bat, providing invaluable support for Richard Morris, Andy Rishton and Euan Woods. Coach Tom Lambert produced a sharp fielding unit in both formats.

Lee Dixon led a youthful **Cheshire** side, in which Calum Rowe hit five fifties in 11 innings, and a strong bowling unit of Jack White, Wayne White and Jack Williams shared 67 wickets. Thanks to former Leicestershire off-spinner Jigar Naik, who topped the bowling averages with 47 wickets at ten, **Dorset** finished in their highest position since they were divisional champions in 2010.

Shropshire captain Steve Leach enjoyed a consistent season with the bat, but a fourth-place finish in the Championship disguised a generally disappointing summer. Three rain-affected games harmed **Devon's** prospects, though good wins against Cheshire and Wiltshire confirmed continued progress under Josh Bess. The Nottinghamshire captain Chris Read, Devon born and bred, played his first Minor Counties Championship games since 1997.

Oxfordshire's policy of playing youngsters who have progressed through their system saw them exceed expectations, with wins against Devon and Dorset, and a mid-table finish. Matt Pardoe scored fourth-innings centuries to ensure **Herefordshire** won their final two games against Cornwall and Wales. Peter Burgoyne enjoyed a steady all-round season, averaging 42 with the bat and taking 22 wickets at 25. **Cornwall** returned after a 16-year absence to play at Penzance, but a fine 188 by Tom Rowe could not save them in a close game against Herefordshire. Failing to enforce the follow-on against Shropshire cost them victory when rain intervened on the last day.

A young **Wiltshire** side had just one Championship victory, against Dorset, which was built on Steve Bullen's first-innings 201. Once again, the bowling leaned heavily on the left-arm medium of Tahir Afridi, who took his 200th Championship wicket in just seven seasons. **Wales** finished without a win but, like many other teams, relied on youth. Callum Taylor's 28 wickets equalled their best haul in a season, and included seven for 16 (and 11 for 34 in the match) in their opening game against Shropshire, only for the weather to deny them victory.

After drawing their first two matches, **Lincolnshire** steamrollered their next four opponents in the Eastern Division, and over the season collected 45 bonus points out of a possible 48. Led by Andy Carter (31 wickets) and Alex Willerton (30), their pace attack was potent, and Willerton in particular caused discomfort to a number of good players, often on docile pitches. The unexpected return from Australia of Matt Lineker was a considerable bonus; his 813 runs included three hundreds.

Suffolk went through the season undefeated under new captain Adam Mansfield, but they could win only twice. Jaik Mickleburgh, once of Essex, was the leading batsman in the country, with 815 runs at 116, including 218 not out against Northumberland. A lack of penetration with the new ball prevented **Staffordshire** from mounting a challenge, although they too remained unbeaten. Kadeer Ali again scored heavily – eight of his 11 innings passed 50 – while Tim Maxfield and Peter Wilshaw scored just under 500 runs each.

Toby Bulcock of **Cumberland** achieved two milestones. Against Buckinghamshire at Sedbergh, he took eight for 39, the best Championship figures in the county's history. Earlier in the season, his six for 14 against Northumberland at Gosforth had been their best one-day figures. Gary Pratt and Mattie McKiernan were in the runs, but rain hampered the team's chances. **Norfolk** finished in mid-table, with Rob Taylor enjoying a good season: 450 runs and 16 wickets. With the return from injury of Paul McMahon and an early victory against Bedfordshire, **Cambridgeshire** had high hopes – but they faded, as McMahon was able to play in only three games.

The highlights for **Hertfordshire** came in one-day cricket, with two teenage spinners, Ben Waring and Luke Chapman, performing superbly. Waring, Wisden Schools Cricketer of the Year in 2015, took seven for 41 in a losing cause against Lincolnshire in the Trophy semi-final, including a hat-trick. In the Championship, Steve Gale was the outstanding player: he hit four hundreds, including 227 against Norfolk.

The bottom three sides were all winless. For **Buckinghamshire**, it was a repeat of 2016. Garry Park scored 163 against Staffordshire, and the batting was steady, but the bowling lacked penetration. **Bedfordshire** have won just one Championship game in six seasons, but some narrow defeats – they lost in the last over to Lincolnshire – showed progress. Slow left-armers Monty Panesar and Tom Brett sent down almost 550 overs between them. Panesar, the former Test spinner, produced a match analysis of 72.4–21–146–10 against Staffordshire, although he was outbowled by Brett in nearly every other innings. In one of the most memorable innings of the season, George Thurstance scored 200 not out against Hertfordshire, the first double-century in the 35-year history of the Trophy. But **Northumberland** had a summer to forget. The unavailability of four key players meant a young side. They lost all four Trophy games and, with just two batting bonus points in the Championship, were never in a winning position.

The Minor Counties season is poised to take on a new look with the introduction of a Twenty20 competition, following a trial in 2015. T20 and 50-over cricket will now be played in coloured clothing and with a white ball. The Trophy will revert to a knockout format, and the T20 will comprise four groups of five, with the group winners progressing to a finals day. The first Championship games, meanwhile, will be moved to the last week of June in an effort to boost the availability of young players.

MINOR COUNTIES CHAMPIONSHIP IN 2017

	Eastern Division	P	W	L	D	Bonus points Batting	Bonus points Bowling	Points	NRPW
1	LINCOLNSHIRE (1)	6	4	0	2	21	24	117	14.88
2	Suffolk (8)	6	2	0	4	20	24	92	9.53
3	Staffordshire (3)	6	2	0	4	21	16	85	4.93
4	Cumberland (6)	6	2	0	4	13	22	83	7.78
5	Norfolk (4)	6	2	1	3	15	23	82	0.62
6	Cambridgeshire (5)	6	1	1	4	15	22	69	–5.93
7	Hertfordshire (7)	6	1	2	3	18	20	66	–3.93
8	Buckinghamshire (10)	6	0	2	4	9	20	45	–10.99
9	Bedfordshire (9)	6	0	4	2	11	22	33*	–3.21
10	Northumberland (2)	6	0	4	2	2	19	29	–16.49

	Western Division	P	W	L	D	Bonus points Batting	Bonus points Bowling	Points	NRPW
1	BERKSHIRE (1)	6	4	0	2	18	24	114	14.05
2	Cheshire (7)	6	3	1	2	14	23	93	1.17
3	Dorset(8)	6	3	2	1	15	22	89	8.83
4	Shropshire (4)	6	2	0	4	13	20	81	–11.27
5	Devon (5)	6	2	1	3	8	22	74	0.18
6	Oxfordshire (9)	6	2	2	2	9	22	71	–4.29
7	Herefordshire (3)	6	2	2	2	12	18	70	–0.80
8	Cornwall (2)	6	1	3	2	11	24	59	–0.05
9	Wiltshire (6)	6	1	4	1	9	24	53	–0.64
10	Wales Minor Counties (10)	6	0	5	1	9	21	34	–8.63

Win = 16pts; Draw = 4pts. NRPW is net runs per wicket (runs per wicket for, less runs per wicket against).

* *Deducted 8pts for fielding an ineligible player.*

LEADING AVERAGES IN 2017

BATTING (350 runs at 45.00)

		M	I	NO	R	HS	100	50	Avge	Ct
1	J. C. Mickleburgh (*Suffolk*)	6	11	4	815	218*	3	4	116.42	3
2	J. M. Kettleborough (*Bedfordshire*)	3	6	1	463	144	3	1	92.60	3
3	J. D. Williams (*Cambridgeshire*)	4	7	2	380	86*	0	5	76.00	2
4	K. Ali (*Staffordshire*)	6	11	0	772	148	3	5	70.18	2
5	S. R. W. Gale (*Hertfordshire*)	6	11	0	758	227	4	1	68.90	9
6	M. S. Lineker (*Lincolnshire*)	7	13	1	813	148	3	3	67.75	4
7	M. H. McKiernan (*Cumberland*)	6	11	4	449	100	1	4	64.14	9
8	T. C. Rowe (*Cornwall*)	4	8	1	409	188	1	2	58.42	5
9	R. K. Morris (*Berkshire*)	4	7	0	406	205	1	2	58.00	0
10	G. J. Pratt (*Cumberland*)	6	10	2	447	143*	1	3	55.87	5
11	C. Rowe (*Cheshire*)	6	11	2	495	95	0	5	55.00	2
12	C. J. Guest (*Cambridgeshire*)	4	7	0	376	101	1	2	53.71	4
13	S. F. G. Bullen (*Wiltshire*)	4	8	0	428	201	1	3	53.50	4
14	J. A. J. Rishton (*Berkshire*)	5	9	2	371	93	0	4	53.00	7
15	M. G. Cull (*Suffolk*)	6	11	1	520	100	1	4	52.00	2
16	M. G. Pardoe (*Herefordshire*)	5	10	0	518	127	2	1	51.80	6
17	C. T. Peploe (*Berkshire*)	7	11	3	374	103	1	2	46.75	9
18	R. P. Zelem (*Cumberland*)	6	11	2	418	92	0	4	46.44	6
19	S. S. Arthurton (*Norfolk*)	6	12	3	414	104*	2	1	46.00	5
20	T. Maxfield (*Staffordshire*)	6	11	0	498	130	2	2	45.27	5
21	R. M. L. Taylor (*Norfolk*)	6	10	0	450	100	1	3	45.00	5

BOWLING (20 wickets at 30.00)

		Style	O	M	R	W	BB	5I	Avge
1	J. K. H. Naik (*Dorset*)	OB	207.3	69	479	47	7-22	5	10.19
2	T. Bulcock (*Cumberland*)	SLA	261.3	82	601	45	8-39	5	13.35
3	C. Z. Taylor (*Wales*)	OB	153.5	48	443	28	7-16	1	15.82
4	C. T. Peploe (*Berkshire*)	SLA	354.1	122	793	50	8-15	5	15.86
5	A. J. Willerton (*Lincolnshire*)	RFM	212.4	58	509	30	6-15	2	16.96
6	J. J. Bess (*Devon*)	RFM	135	31	379	21	5-38	1	18.04
7	C. Brown (*Norfolk*)	OB	185	41	489	26	5-47	2	18.08
8	Tahir Afridi (*Wiltshire*)	LFM	155.3	43	491	26	6-93	2	18.88
9	A. Carter (*Lincolnshire*)	RFM	198.4	37	623	31	4-54	0	20.09
10	H. Douglas (*Suffolk*)	RFM	124	20	421	20	6-39	1	21.05
11	W. A. White (*Cheshire*)	RFM	194.4	41	549	26	5-90	1	21.11
12	T. M. Nugent (*Berkshire*)	RFM	198.1	39	644	30	6-61	2	21.46
13	A. C. Libby (*Cornwall*)	SLA	169.4	36	547	25	7-17	2	21.88
14	J. J. Williams (*Cheshire*)	LB	160.4	32	574	25	7-47	2	22.96
15	B. J. France (*Norfolk*)	RFM	215.4	43	652	28	7-90	2	23.28
16	P. A. Byrne (*Staffordshire*)	SLA	245.4	62	663	28	5-35	1	23.67
17	H. E. Eltham (*Oxfordshire*)	OB	175.1	25	590	24	7-151	2	24.58
18	B. A. Waring (*Hertfordshire*)	SLA	301.3	79	921	37	6-107	2	24.89
19	P. I. Burgoyne (*Herefordshire*)	OB	181.5	40	551	22	4-42	0	25.04
20	M. S. Panesar (*Bedfordshire*)	SLA	251	67	646	25	6-78	2	25.84
21	T. Brett (*Bedfordshire*)	SLA	295.2	45	1055	39	8-87	3	27.05

CHAMPIONSHIP FINAL

At Banbury, August 27–30. **Berkshire won by six wickets.** ‡**Lincolnshire 182** (57 overs) (M. S. Lineker 40, A. J. Willerton 39; C. T. Peploe 5-71) **and 319** (139.4 overs) (M. S. Lineker 148, C. Wilson 42; J. A. J. Rishton 3-54, C. T. Peploe 6-113); **Berkshire 215** (69.4 overs) (J. Davies 30, E. D. Woods 97, S. R. Davison 34*; M. Carter 3-46, A. Carter 4-58) **and 291-4** (72 overs) (J. Davies 127*, J. A. J. Rishton 76*). *Lincolnshire collapsed from 99-4 to 107-8 on the first day, and not even a last-wicket partnership of 61 was sufficient to post a respectable total. Chris Peploe took his fourth five-for of the season. Berkshire fared little better, with the exception of 18-year-old Euan Woods, star of the 2016 final, who resisted a hostile Lincolnshire pace attack to take his team to a lead of 33. Matt Lineker then hit 148 in 332 balls, restricting himself to 11 boundaries. With help down the order from Adam Tillcock (18 in 123) and captain Carl Wilson (42 in 151), they were able to set a challenging target of 287; Peploe's marathon stint brought him 6-113 from 60 overs. Berkshire were 120-3 when rain brought a halt on the third afternoon, but when play resumed on the fourth, 16-year-old Jack Davies showed wonderful composure for 127*. After Andy Rishton joined him on 135-4, they raced to victory in less than two hours, Rishton hitting a run-a-ball 76*.*

TROPHY FINAL

At Wormsley, August 23. **Berkshire won by four wickets. Lincolnshire 245-5** (50 overs) (M. S. Lineker 49, C. J. Louth 94*, A. D. Tillcock 51); ‡**Berkshire 248-6** (40.3 overs) (Waqas Hussain 49, R. K. Morris 56*, D. J. Lincoln 42, C. T. Peploe 35*). *After being asked to bat, Lincolnshire made heavy weather of it: 245-5 felt like old-school 50-over cricket. Only Conrad Louth, with 94* from 102 balls, prospered on a sluggish pitch, but his acceleration came late. In reply, Berkshire seemed to have the same problem, and a tense climax beckoned until Chris Peploe smashed 35* from 14 balls at No. 8.*

SECOND ELEVEN CHAMPIONSHIP IN 2017

	North Division	P	W	L	D	A	Bonus points Bat	Bowl	Pen	Total points
1	Lancashire (2)	9	4	1	4	0	32	27	0	143
2	Warwickshire (6)	9	3	1	5	0	28	24	0	125
3	Worcestershire (4)	9	3	2	3	1	26	28	0	122
4	Yorkshire (5)	9	2	0	6	1	28	25	0	120
5	Derbyshire (8)	9	2	1	6	0	29	21	0	112
6	Nottinghamshire (7)	9	3	2	3	1	14	26	0	108
7	Leicestershire (9)	9	2	4	3	0	28	33	0	108
8	Durham (1)	9	2	2	4	1	19	27	0	103
9	MCCYC (3)	9	0	4	5	0	26	21	–1	71
10	Northamptonshire (10)	9	0	4	5	0	10	23	0	58

	South Division	P	W	L	D	A	Bonus points Bat	Bowl	Pen	Total points
1	Hampshire (8)	9	4	1	4	0	20	36	0	140
2	Middlesex (1)	9	3	0	5	1	22	26	0	126
3	Surrey (7)	9	3	2	4	0	24	33	0	125
4	Kent (4)	9	3	2	4	0	24	24	0	116
5	Somerset (9)	9	2	1	6	0	17	29	0	108
6	Sussex (2)	9	2	3	4	0	23	32	0	107
7	Gloucestershire (10)	9	3	2	3	1	14	17	0	99
8	Glamorgan (5)	9	0	3	6	0	24	29	0	83
9	MCC Universities (3)	9	0	2	7	0	21	26	0	82
10	Essex (6)	9	1	5	3	0	17	29	0	77

Win = 16pts; draw/abandoned = 5pts. Penalties were for slow over-rates. In 2016, MCC Young Cricketers played in the South Division, and MCC Universities in the North.

LEADING AVERAGES IN 2017

BATTING (450 runs)

		M	I	NO	R	HS	100	50	Avge	Ct/St
1	P. J. Horton (*Leics*)	4	6	1	521	277*	2	1	104.20	3
2	†A. Z. Lees (*Yorks*)	4	6	0	610	202	3	2	101.66	4
3	R. P. Jones (*Lancs*)	9	13	3	775	138	3	4	77.50	9
4	G. J. Harte (*Durham, MCCYC*)	7	11	3	613	183	2	2	76.62	2
5	T. C. Fell (*Worcs*)	6	9	0	626	223	3	1	69.55	6
6	M. J. Lamb (*Warwicks*)	8	9	1	542	164	2	3	67.75	2
7	H. R. Hosein (*Derbys*)	9	14	4	615	115*	2	3	61.50	22
8	L. Banks (*Warwicks*)	7	11	1	570	181	1	4	57.00	3
9	W. R. Smith (*Hants*)	8	12	1	616	136	3	1	56.00	12
10	A. J. Robson (*Sussex*)	9	17	2	775	137	2	4	51.66	0
11	I. G. Holland (*Hants*)	6	10	0	506	192	2	1	50.60	2
12	A. Hepburn (*Worcs*)	8	13	2	556	98	0	6	50.54	4
13	†W. M. H. Rhodes (*Yorks*)	7	11	0	551	147	1	3	50.09	2
14	†R. Patel (*Surrey*)	8	12	0	598	226	1	5	49.83	3
15	A. R. I. Umeed (*Warwicks*)	7	11	0	535	203	1	3	48.63	5
16	J. J. Bohannon (*Lancs*)	8	11	1	471	99*	0	5	47.10	6
17	M. A. Jones (*Durham, Derbys, Leics*)	9	13	0	595	172	2	1	45.76	5
18	J. A. Tattersall (*Yorks*)	8	14	2	501	117	2	0	41.75	5
19	Z. Crawley (*Kent*)	7	12	0	467	134	1	3	38.91	6
20	†B. J. Curran (*Leics, MCCYC, Warwicks*)	11	19	1	601	192	1	0	33.38	2
21	O. C. Soames (*Hants, MCCU*)	10	17	2	483	106*	1	1	32.20	4
22	S. M. Imtiaz (*Durham, Kent, MCCYC, Surrey*)	12	20	0	560	118	1	3	28.00	20/1

BOWLING (18 wickets)

		Style	*O*	*M*	*R*	*W*	*BB*	*5I*	*Avge*
1	R. N. Sidebottom (*Nhants, Notts, Warks*)	RFM	110.3	25	356	27	8-33	2	13.18
2	G. S. Virdi (*Surrey*)	OB	202.3	60	533	26	6-77	2	20.50
3	T. E. Barber (*MCCYC, Middx*)	LFM	124.1	21	497	24	5-27	1	20.70
4	L. A. Procter (*Lancs*)	RM	125.1	18	381	18	3-49	0	21.16
5	B. J. Taylor (*Hants*)	OB	136.4	25	466	22	3-6	0	21.18
6	A. Hepburn (*Worcs*)	RM	170.4	30	595	28	5-43	2	21.25
7	M. E. Milnes (*Northants*)	RFM	140	34	425	20	4-41	0	21.25
8	G. Stewart (*Kent*)	RFM	137	33	406	19	4-54	0	21.36
9	S. G. Whittingham (*Sussex*)	RFM	177.3	34	668	30	6-66	2	22.26
10	F. O. E. van den Bergh (*Surrey*)	SLA	171.2	18	525	23	5-57	1	22.82
11	A. S. S. Nijjar (*Essex*)	SLA	166.3	36	553	24	6-113	1	23.04
12	A. T. Thomson (*MCCU, Warwicks*)	OB	119.2	13	468	19	7-148	2	24.63
13	M. E. T. Salisbury (*Essex, Hants*)	RFM	178.5	40	592	24	5-82	1	24.66
14	A. P. Beard (*Essex*)	RFM	147.4	28	520	21	4-58	0	24.76
15	S. C. Kerrigan (*Lancs, Northants*)	SLA	153.2	33	446	18	6-26	2	24.77
16	I. G. Holland (*Hants*)	RFM	148.2	32	481	19	5-46	1	25.31
17	L. J. Hurt (*Durham, Lancs, MCCYC*)	RFM	183.4	34	576	22	3-21	0	26.18
18	A. Sakande (*Sussex*)	RFM	148.1	21	577	22	6-96	2	26.22
19	D. Manthorpe (*Leics*)	LFM	167	31	626	22	3-36	0	28.45
20	M. Carter (*Notts*)	OB	211.5	59	524	18	4-47	0	29.11
21	T. J. Lester (*Lancs*)	LFM	172	28	644	22	5-79	1	29.27
22	K. A. Bull (*Glam*)	OB	198	28	603	20	5-30	1	30.15
23	B. J. Twohig (*Worcs*)	SLA	196.3	18	698	22	5-87	1	31.72
24	X. G. Owen (*MCCU*)	RM	173	39	582	18	4-56	0	32.33
25	J. C. Wainman (*Yorks*)	LM	146.5	30	596	18	5-79	1	33.11
26	O. W. Smithson (*Durham, MCCYC, Nhants*)	LFM	188.3	27	755	18	3-53	0	41.94

SECOND ELEVEN CHAMPIONSHIP FINAL

At Newport, Isle of Wight, September 5–8. **Drawn. Hampshire 248** (67.5 overs) (F. S. Hay 59, C. M. Dickinson 34, C. P. Wood 76*; S. Mahmood 4-76) **and 66-6** (28 overs) (J. J. Bohannon 3-8); **‡Lancashire 352** (104.4 overs) (R. P. Jones 38, T. J. Lester 47, A. M. Lilley 72, M. H. McKiernan 34, L. J. Hurt 42, Extras 42; C. P. Wood 3-61, B. Mugochi 3-46).

SECOND ELEVEN TROPHY FINAL

At Leeds, June 8. **Yorkshire won by 99 runs** (DLS). **Yorkshire 265-5** (38.4 overs) (H. C. Brook 112, R. Gibson 58, W. M. H. Rhodes 50*); **‡Middlesex 179** (27.3 overs) (N. R. D. Compton 57, D. S. Manuwelege 40; J. W. Shutt 4-19).

SECOND ELEVEN TWENTY20 FINAL

At Arundel, August 10. **Sussex won by 24 runs. ‡Sussex 171-6** (20 overs) (H. Z. Finch 54, D. M. W. Rawlins 40); **Hampshire 147** (19.3 overs) (W. R. Smith 31; A. Sakande 3-26, A. P. Barton 3-9).

LEAGUE CRICKET IN 2017

Trebles all round – in Yorkshire!

GEOFFREY DEAN

While Durham's county side had a season they will want to forget, one of their feeder clubs not only regained the North East Premier League title but also won the National Club T20 trophy. South Northumberland, who are based in Gosforth, beat Wimbledon in the final at the County Ground in Derby.

Hanging Heaton went one better, clinching a treble in dramatic circumstances. They won the Bradford League for the first time in 18 years, lifted the league's Twenty20 competition, then triumphed in the play-offs of the four Yorkshire Premier League winners in a seesaw final at Headingley. After beating York in the semi, they overcame Wakefield Thornes by just three runs. Thornes, the inaugural play-off champions in 2016, would probably have defended their crown but for a five-run penalty for a slow over-rate, which raised their 50-over target to 232. Callum Geldart made 90 not out for Hanging Heaton in the semi, and 85 in the final.

Wanstead and Snaresbrook just missed a double of their own; they were pipped by Chelmsford in the Essex League but won the Royal London Club Championship, when they overcame the Liverpool & District Competition winners Ormskirk on familiar turf in Chelmsford.

In the Birmingham League, Knowle & Dorridge, who were fourth in 2016, were crowned champions after finishing level on points with Shrewsbury, who won more matches, but – crucially – collected five fewer bonus points. "This has been a real team effort," said Knowle and Dorridge captain Jack Grundy. "We've had the brilliance of George Worker, 900 runs from Alex Phillips, and Henry Brookes breaking into the Warwickshire team, but other guys coming in have made a real impact."

There was euphoria for the J&G Meakin club, who won the North Staffs & South Cheshire League, the first top-flight title for a team who started as the works side for a pottery company. Porthill Park led before the final round but, needing 136 to beat Hem Heath at home, collapsed for 121. Meakins had to beat already relegated Betley, and skittled them for 138 to win by 93.

Ealing, fifth in 2016, ran away with the Middlesex League, finishing with 149 points, a competition record. "Last year was a wake-up call for the first team," admitted Tom Morton, their wicketkeeper and director of cricket. "We had a young side, and it was quite a challenge."

In the same league, Stanmore's Steven Reingold, just 18, produced one of the all-round performances of the season. An off-spinner, he took six for 60 in 19 overs against Shepherds Bush, then struck 128 off 123 balls to steer his side to a target of 292 with two wickets remaining. With a word in the right place from his club-mate Mark Ramprakash, Reingold bowled in the England nets at Lord's and The Oval.

In the South Wales League, Alex Milton amassed 1,103 runs at 84, with five hundreds, as Cardiff – pipped by Newport on the final day in 2016 – edged past their old rivals, winning fewer games but picking up 21 more bonus points.

Lower down the Welsh league pyramid, Carew caused controversy – and national headlines – in their attempts to secure the Pembroke county title. Their last match was against their closest rivals, Cresselly. Carew led by 21 points and, with 20 available for a win, they channelled their inner Brian Rose and declared at 18 for one, to prevent Cresselly gaining any bonus points. Uproar followed. "It's against the spirit of the game," thundered the former Glamorgan captain Steve James in *The Times*. "Unfortunately it's within the rules." Even *The Sun* reported the "back-handed tactics". The captain, Brian Hall, was fined and banned, and his club were relegated to the second division for 2018. Bizarrely, they were allowed to keep the title.

Chris Aspin writes: The 2017 Lancashire League season also ended in disarray when two clubs and some individuals alleged that Clitheroe had paid three amateurs, a charge they denied. In their first season in the league, Clitheroe had topped the table, losing only three matches, and also won the Second and Third XI competitions. A league rule says disputes must be addressed within 21 days but, when Clitheroe engaged a lawyer, the presentation dinner was cancelled and a disciplinary panel set up, headed by retired judge Edward Slinger, who played for Enfield between 1954 and 1975, and represented Lancashire's Second XI. The panel heard evidence in December and January, but made no judgment, amid suggestions that Clitheroe were prepared to go to the High Court. A resolution was still awaited when *Wisden* went to press.

On the field, the season was one for the record books. It began with the South African Kelly Smuts hammering 211 from 139 balls for Todmorden against Enfield. It was only the second double-century in the league's 125 years, after Australia's Michael Clarke hit 200 not out for Ramsbottom in 2002, also against Enfield. A fortnight later Nelson's Devon Conway – another South African – broke the record again, with an unbeaten 231 against Rishton in the Worsley Cup. But the trophy eventually went to newcomers Darwen, who skittled Church for 67 in the final, John Cordingley taking six for 11, including a hat-trick.

Darwen also finished second in the Championship, which had a new format: all 17 teams played each other during the first half of the season, then the top nine formed Division A, and the remaining eight Division B. The clubs in each section then played one another again.

Ockert Erasmus, the Lowerhouse pro, scored 985 runs at nearly 60, and his team-mate Ben Heap was the leading amateur with 739 at 35. He hit 175 against Great Harwood in a total of 333 for five, both club records. Chris Bleazard, who has been piling up runs for Lowerhouse since 1983, took his total to 16,333, not far short of Michael Ingham's 17,118 for Haslingden, whose opener Graham Knowles became the league's most prolific amateur century-maker with 15.

For the first time since the Lancashire League was formed in 1892, no bowler took 50 wickets. David Bowden, Darwen's left-arm spinner, claimed 49 at 10.95 to join the select group of amateurs who have topped the list. Nick Benton (Haslingden) and Chris Holt (Burnley) led the pros with 46 apiece.

Fourteen-year-old J-J. Fielding made an unbeaten 55 for Ramsbottom against Burnley, sharing a match-winning stand of 107 with his father Jon, who scored 61. He is thought to be the youngest to hit a league half-century.

Alex Davies, the Lancashire wicketkeeper, made 117 against East Lancashire as Darwen ran up 336 for six, the highest league total of the season. On the same day, Enfield dismissed Accrington for 38; Fergus Bailey took seven for 11, with keeper Tiarnan Hamill accounting for six of his victims. Church fared even worse when they met Clitheroe – dismissed for 34, with six batsmen failing to score. The openers knocked off the runs in 7.1 overs, and spectators were on their way home after 90 minutes. Colne could muster only 30 against Burnley, whose slow left-armer Holt took four for two after hitting 82. Sachithra Serasinghe, standing in as Accrington's pro, cracked 171 not out against Colne – several of his ten sixes flew out of the ground – and shared a record second-wicket partnership of 225 with Simon Hanson (60).

David Ormerod hung up his boots after 27 seasons with Bacup and Accrington, having taken 1,383 wickets in the league, plus 72 in the cup. He was the leading amateur bowler eight times.

Emma Pickup achieved a notable first when she captained Rawtenstall Seconds against Haslingden, while Jasmine Ashraf became the first woman to umpire in the league, when she and her husband Naeem took charge of Burnley's game at Rawtenstall. Mo Basharat, son Faheem and daughter Saira all played for Enfield's Third XI against Rishton, while Alex Hartley, a member of England's World Cup-winning women's side, made one appearance for Clitheroe's Second XI, taking two for 11 against Todmorden.

Lowerhouse shared the LCB Cup with Ormskirk, the Liverpool & District Competition champions, after rain washed out two attempts to stage the final.

The Pennine League, formed in 2016 by the merger of the Central Lancashire and Saddleworth Leagues, is no more. Former CLL clubs Crompton, Littleborough, Middleton, Milnrow, Norden, Rochdale and Walsden have joined the Lancashire League, and the other 17 were accepted into the Greater Manchester League, though they will still compete for their traditional cups.

Walsden won the Premiership for the second year running, and Rochdale took the Lees Wood Cup. Middleton topped the Championship. Walsden's pro, Umesh Karunaratne, scored 713 runs at 101 and took 47 wickets at 12, while Josh Tolley of Norden made 729 at 66. Stayley's Hamza Nadeem was the leading wicket-taker, with 56 at 7.73.

In the Championship, Royton's Indian amateur Chairag Khurana smashed an unbeaten 227 – another club record – out of 329 for five against Friarmere, then took six for 34. He topped the averages with 1,113 runs at 92, and collected 46 wickets at 10.80. Michael Pritchard of Middleton took seven for seven to shoot out Ashton for 23, the season's lowest total. He finished with 45 wickets at 10.73. Norden sacked their professional, Naveed Zamurad, for allegedly tripping an opponent in a game against Walsden.

The indestructible Mel Whittle, now 70, joined Shaw in mid-season, and took six for 22 to beat Friarmere. Tom White, just 13, made 107 not out – 82 in boundaries – to help Micklehurst's Second XI to a nine-wicket win over Uppermill, whose 254 for five had included 119 from 70-year-old Jim Bradbury. White faced 36 overs, six of which were sent down by Cec Wright, aged 83. Wright, who played for Jamaica, then spent many seasons as a pro in the northern leagues, claimed 25 second-team wickets at 20, including seven for 27 in an 11-over spell against Shaw. He has taken more than 7,000 wickets in a career which shows no sign of ending.

A PATHWAY... BACK HOME

A appeal tribunal of the Two Counties Championship, which covers Essex and Suffolk, dismissed an appeal in 2017 by Frinton-on-Sea CC against a 36-point deduction for fielding an ineligible player.

The case, seemingly as obscure as the one involving a Slovak handball player called Maroš Kolpak, could yet have equally wide ramifications for cricketers who want to play outside their home country. But this time it means fewer opportunities, not more.

It concerned a 22-year-old Australian called Blake Reed, who was in the UK on a youth mobility visa, which apparently allowed him to play league cricket as an amateur. However, the ECB – acting on guidance from the Home Office – had told leagues that in this context amateurism was not defined by whether a cricketer was paid for playing.

Reed had made six appearances for Western Australia Under-19s in 2013. And though he was not paid for those matches, he was deemed to have been on a "player pathway" towards the professional game. That in turn meant – despite never receiving a penny for his cricket – he was ineligible to play in the UK. This appeared to rule out all ex-professionals, and even those to have featured in Australian grade matches.

Cricketers who have played at least five first-class matches can apply for temporary work visas, but those at a lower level – including aspiring professionals such as Reed – seemed to be barred by the new rules.

Something similar was happening in reverse. After the 2016 season, Ben Cox of Worcestershire and Chris Rushworth of Durham both landed in Australia with the wrong visas. They were held, interrogated, deported – and banned from returning for three years.

These decisions seemed to reflect a general tightening of immigration rules, caused by political pressures in both countries. There was also a sense that good – but perhaps not very good – cricketers were getting undeclared benefits akin to old-fashioned boot money.

When they were penalised for playing Reed, Frinton had initially sought a county court injunction against the Two Counties Championship. But the costs and risks of the legal system persuaded them to drop the case and take the matter to a tribunal instead.

Chaired by barrister David Lamming, this accepted a QC's opinion that the immigration rules were being interpreted too rigidly. But it found against Frinton because, "on the balance of probabilities", it believed Reed was in fact being paid.

In December 2017, however, the Home Office amended the regulations, making them stricter still. In years to come, Aussie accents may be heard less on England's green fields of summer.

ECB PREMIER LEAGUE TABLES IN 2017

Birmingham & District League

		P	W	L	Pts
1	**Knowle & Dorridge**	**22**	**15**	**4**	**375**
2	Shrewsbury	22	16	5	369
3	Berkswell	22	11	3	338
4	Ombersley	22	13	5	321
5	Barnt Green	22	11	7	280
6	West Bromwich Dartmouth	22	9	9	262
7	Dorridge	22	9	10	261
8	Wolverhampton	22	5	9	216
9	Kenilworth Wardens	22	5	9	196
10	Walsall	22	5	13	166
11	Kidderminster Victoria	22	2	16	149
12	Brockhampton	22	3	14	118

Bradford Premier League

		P	W	L	Pts
1	**Hanging Heaton**	**22**	**16***	**2**	**340**
2	Woodlands	22	15	5	302
3	Farsley	22	14	4	301
4	Pudsey St Lawrence	22	12	7	282
5	New Farnley	22	12	9	270
6	Townville	22	11*	7	270
7	Bradford & Bingley	22	8	11	214
8	Lightcliffe	22	7	13	203
9	Cleckheaton	22	5*	13	181
10	East Bierley	22	4*	14	166
11	Batley	22	5	15	164
12	Pudsey Congs	22	5	14	161

* *Plus one tie.*

Cheshire County League Premier Division

		P	W	L	Pts
1	**Chester Boughton Hall**	**22**	**14**	**4**	**411**
2	Nantwich	22	12	3	398
3	Alderley Edge	22	12	6	352
4	Toft	22	9	8	322
5	Neston	22	8*	5	317
6	Timperley	22	8	7	309
7	Didsbury	22	7	9	278
8	Bramhall	22	6	8	275
9	Grappenhall	22	7	9	261
10	Cheadle	22	6†	13	261
11	Hyde	22	3*	8	226
12	Bowdon	22	4	16	186

* *Plus one tie.*
† *Plus two ties.*

Cornwall Premier Division

		P	W	L	Pts
1	**Truro**	**18**	**13***	**2**	**297**
2	St Just	18	14	2	291
3	Penzance	18	14	2	290
4	Werrington	18	9	7	236
5	St Austell	18	6*	8	207
6	Redruth	18	7	9	190
7	Falmouth	18	6	10	187
8	Hayle	18	4	12	142
9	Grampound Road	18	2	13	121
10	Helston	18	3	13	115

* *Plus one tie.*

Derbyshire Premier League

		P	W	L	Pts
1	**Sandiacre Town**	**22**	**15**	**3**	**429**
2	Spondon	22	10	6	366
3	Eckington	22	11	6	358
4	Chesterfield	22	9	5	347
5	Swarkeston	22	8	8	323
6	Ticknall	22	6*	5	319
7	Denby	22	6	6	293
8	Alvaston & Boulton	22	8	6	292
9	Ockbrook & Borrowash	22	6	10	271
10	Rolleston	22	7	8	239
11	Marehay	22	3	13	171
12	Cutthorpe	22	1*	14	169

* *Plus one tie.*

Devon League Premier Division

		P	W	L	Pts
1	**Bovey Tracey**	**18**	**14**	**3**	**291**
2	Bradninch	18	11	5	246
3	Sidmouth	18	9	7	215
4	Exmouth	18	9	6	212
5	North Devon	18	7	9	198
6	Exeter	18	7	9	189
7	Heathcoat	18	5	11	183
8	Plymouth	18	6	10	179
9	Torquay	18	7	9	177
10	Paignton	18	5	11	176

East Anglian Premier League

		P	W	L	Pts
1	**Sudbury**	**22**	**16**	**4**	**445**
2	Swardeston	22	14	3	424
3	Great Witchingham	22	12	5	394
4	Cambridge Granta	22	10	5	343
5	Copdock & Old Ipswichian	22	10	8	333
6	Frinton-on-Sea	22	8	8	327
7	Vauxhall Mallards	22	8	10	296
8	Burwell	22	5	13	244
9	Mildenhall	22	9	11	240
10	Norwich	22	5	13	226
11	Bury St Edmunds	22	7	12	207
12	Horsford	22	5	10	186

Essex League Premier Division

		P	W	L	Pts
1	**Chelmsford**	**18**	**12**	**3**	**287**
2	Wanstead & Snaresbrook	18	11	5	280
3	Brentwood	18	10	3	271
4	Shenfield	18	8	6	239
5	Hornchurch	18	8	7	226
6	Chingford	18	8	6	224
7	Ilford	18	5	9	186
8	Southend-on-Sea	18	3	10	154
9	Colchester & East Essex	18	3	11	153
10	Upminster	18	3	11	118

Hertfordshire League Premier Division

		P	W	L	Pts
1	**Welwyn Garden City**	**18**	**11**	**3**	**390**
2	Totteridge Millhillians	18	10	3	372
3	North Mymms	18	9	2	353
4	Radlett	18	9	5	317
5	Harpenden	18	7	6	309
6	Potters Bar	18	6	8	268
7	Bishop's Stortford	18	5	5	262
8	Letchworth Garden City	18	5	8	244
9	Hertford	18	2	13	149
10	Luton Town & Indians	18	2	13	133

Home Counties Premier League Division One

		P	W	L	Pts
1	**Henley**	**18**	**11***	**2**	**306**
2	Oxford	18	8	6	248
3	Finchampstead	18	7*	6	244
4	Banbury	18	7†	6	240
5	High Wycombe	18	7	7	235
6	Tring Park	18	7	8	224
7	Slough	18	6	5	223
8	Horspath	18	6	8	204
9	Great & Little Tew	18	6	9	201
10	Burnham	18	3	11	98

* *Plus one tie.*
† *Plus two ties.*

Kent League Premier Division

		P	W	L	Pts
1	**Beckenham**	**18**	**14**	**2**	**274**
2	Bexley	18	13	4	260
3	Sandwich Town	18	10	5	230
4	Lordswood	18	9	7	208
5	Blackheath	18	8	7	203
6	Tenterden	18	8	8	196
7	Tunbridge Wells	18	7	9	180
8	Sevenoaks Vine	18	7	11	168
9	Hartley Country Club	18	4	12	164
10	Holmesdale	18	1	16	84

Leics & Rutland League Premier Division

		P	W	L	Pts
1	**Sileby Town**	**22**	**13**	**2**	**466**
2	Kibworth	22	6	5	393
3	Kegworth Town	22	10	8	375
4	Loughborough Town	22	9	7	358
5	Leicester Ivanhoe	22	9	5	353
6	Market Harborough	22	9	7	348
7	Syston Town	22	10	9	337
8	Barrow Town	22	7	11	324
9	Barkby United	22	5	9	306
10	Lutterworth	22	7	8	214
11	Enderby	22	2	15	190
12	Rothley Park	22	7	8	45*

* *Penalised 264 points for fielding ineligible players.*

Lincolnshire Cricket Board Premier League

		P	W	L	Pts
1	**Bracebridge Heath**	**22**	**17**	**2**	**370**
2	Grantham	22	15	3	331
3	Bourne	22	13	5	299
4	Woodhall Spa	22	10*	7	271
5	Sleaford	22	11	9	270
6	Lindum	22	10	9	246
7	Boston	22	10	10	243
8	Market Deeping	22	8*	11	229
9	Louth	22	5†	11	189
10	Alford & District	22	5	16	178
11	Grimsby Town	22	5	14	163
12	Spalding	22	4	16	126

* *Plus one tie.*
† *Plus two ties.*

Liverpool & District Competition

		P	W	L	Pts
1	**Ormskirk**	**22**	**13**	**3**	**386**
2	Bootle	22	13	2	343
3	Rainhill	22	12	4	330
4	Colwyn Bay	22	12*	4	322
5	Northern	22	11	7	316
6	New Brighton	22	11	7	314
7	Leigh	22	8	9	244
8	Wallasey	22	7*	11	232
9	Lytham	22	5	12	199
10	Formby	22	5	13	192
11	Southport & Birkdale	22	3	15	160
12	Ainsdale	22	3	16	147

* *Plus one tie.*

Middlesex County League Division One

		P	W	L	Pts
1	**Ealing**	**18**	**13**	**1**	**149**
2	Teddington	18	12	4	125
3	North Middlesex	18	10	5	109
4	Richmond	18	8	6	94
5	Hampstead	18	8	7	89
6	Shepherds Bush	18	6	9	75
7	Finchley	18	5	9	63
8	Brondesbury	18	4	9	52
9	Southgate	18	4	11	51
10	Stanmore	18	3	12	43

Northamptonshire League Premier Division

		P	W	L	Pts
1	**Old Northamptonians**	**22**	**12**	**3**	**345**
2	Rushton	22	12	3	324
3	Peterborough Town	22	11	3	324
4	Finedon Dolben	22	12	4	316
5	Oundle Town	22	11	7	274
6	Brixworth	22	8	8	254
7	Northampton Saints	22	5	9	219
8	Horton House	22	5	9	215
9	Geddington	22	5	7	208
10	Rushden Town	22	6	11	194
11	Wollaston	22	4	14	154
12	Stony Stratford	22	3	16	133

North East Premier Division – 2016

Last year's Wisden *erroneously included the first division of the NEPL, not the Premier. Here, with apologies, is the correct table:*

		P	W	L	Pts
1	**Chester-le-Street**	**22**	**11**	**3**	**384**
2	Newcastle	22	8	2	351
3	Tynemouth	22	10	3	340
4	South Northumberland	22	8	4	327
5	Durham Cricket Academy	22	7*	7	287
6	South Shields	22	8	6	286
7	Hetton Lyons	22	7	5	285
8	Whitburn	22	7	7	255
9	Stockton	22	5	9	235
10	Benwell Hill	22	1	8	201
11	Eppleton	22	2	10	178
12	Gateshead Fell	22	2*	12	156

* *Plus one tie.*

North East Premier Division – 2017

		P	W	L	Pts
1	**South Northumberland**	**22**	**14**	**2**	**444**
2	Benwell Hill	22	8*	5	309
3	Newcastle	22	13	5	305†
4	Durham Cricket Academy	22	7	5	294
5	Hetton Lyons	22	6	6	271
6	Eppleton	22	6*	7	271
7	Tynemouth	22	7	7	269
8	Chester-le-Street	22	8	5	226†
9	Whitburn	22	4	8	205
10	Felling	22	4	11	191
11	Stockton	22	5	12	152†
12	South Shields	22	4	13	143†

* *Plus one tie.* † *Penalised points for fielding ineligible overseas players.*

Northern Premier League

		P	W	L	Pts
1	**Netherfield**	**22**	**17**	**1**	**284**
2	St Annes	22	12	7	215
3	Leyland	22	12	5	211
4	Blackpool	22	9	7	199
5	Chorley	22	10	6	192
6	Penrith	22	8	9	165
7	Fleetwood	22	7	9	164
8	Preston	22	7	13	153
9	Morecambe	22	6	9	143
10	Barrow	22	6	12	132
11	Kendal	22	5	12	130
12	Lancaster	22	5	14	129

N Staffs & S Cheshire League Premier Division

		P	W	L	Pts
1	**J & G Meakin**	**22**	**14**	**3**	**398**
2	Porthill Park	22	15	3	390
3	Leek	22	13	4	357
4	Stone	22	10	8	310
5	Whitmore	22	10	10	304
6	Burslem	22	9	9	277
7	Checkley	22	9	8	259
8	Longton	22	7	9	258
9	Hem Heath	22	8	10	253
10	Ashcombe Park	22	5	12	225
11	Audley	22	5	14	207
12	Betley	22	2	17	146

North Wales League Premier Division

		P	W	L	Pts
1	**Bangor**	**22**	**16***	**3**	**234**
2	Menai Bridge	22	14*	6	211
3	St Asaph	22	15	7	206
4	Denbigh	22	13	8	192
5	Llandudno	22	14	8	187
6	Brymbo	22	12	7	177
7	Connah's Quay	22	10*	10	160
8	Hawarden Park	22	9	12	139
9	Gresford	22	7	14	133
10	Chirk	22	6	14	99
11	Mochdre	22	2*	17	80
12	Llanrwst	22	3	15	74

* *Plus one tie.*

N York & S Durham League Premier Division

		P	W	L	Pts
1	**Great Ayton**	**22**	**12**	**2**	**375**
2	Richmondshire	22	14	2	360
3	Barnard Castle	22	12	7	332
4	Marton	22	11	6	309
5	Stokesley	22	12	5	308
6	Middlesbrough	22	5	6	263
7	Marske	22	6	5	259
8	Darlington	22	5	7	234
9	Seaton Carew	22	6	11	223
10	Hartlepool	22	5	9	219
11	Guisborough	22	3	11	165
12	Norton	22	0	20	44

Nottinghamshire Cricket Board Premier League

		P	W	L	Pts
1	**Cuckney**	**22**	**13**	**1**	**346**
2	Plumtree	22	12	3	342
3	Kimberley Institute	22	12	4	311
4	West Indian Cavaliers	22	9	6	286
5	Hucknall	22	7	7	264
6	Mansfield Hosiery Mills	22	8	6	253
7	Radcliffe-on-Trent	22	8	8	249
8	Notts CCC Academy	22	4	9	243
9	Caythorpe	22	5	10	190
10	Farnsfield	22	4	10	186
11	Attenborough	22	2	12	154
12	Welbeck	22	2	10	144

Southern Premier League

		P	W	L	Pts
1	**Havant**	**18**	**10**	**3**	**283**
2	Bashley (Rydal)	18	11	5	271
3	South Wilts	18	10	5	248
4	Lymington	18	9	6	244
5	St Cross Symondians	18	8	6	223
6	Burridge	18	6	9	189
7	New Milton	18	6	9	179
8	Hants CCC Academy	18	5	9	174
9	Alton	18	5	10	158
10	Andover	18	4	12	133

South Wales Premier League Division One

		P	W	L	Pts
1	**Cardiff**	**18**	**8**	**3**	**268**
2	Newport	18	9	1	263
3	Neath	18	8	3	229
4	Pontarddulais	18	8	5	223
5	Port Talbot Town	18	6	4	205
6	Bridgend Town	18	4	5	203
7	Mumbles	18	6	6	194
8	Ammanford	18	3	5	167
9	Ynysygerwn	18	2	9	152
10	Penarth	18	0	13	111

Surrey Championship Premier Division

		P	W	L	Pts
1	**Normandy**	**18**	**12**	**2**	**299**
2	Sunbury	18	10	4	253
3	Reigate Priory	18	10	7	245
4	Wimbledon	18	9*	5	228
5	Weybridge	18	8	6	227
6	Cranleigh	18	8	6	213
7	Ashtead	18	7	10	207
8	East Molesey	18	6*	8	180
9	Guildford	18	3	12	127
10	Valley End	18	1	14	59

* *Plus one tie.*

Sussex League Premier Division

		P	W	L	Pts
1	**East Grinstead**	**18**	**13**	**2**	**432**
2	Roffey	18	12	2	419
3	Cuckfield	18	10	4	367
4	Horsham	18	10	3	362
5	Hastings & St Leonards	18	8	7	314
6	Preston Nomads	18	6	8	281
7	Middleton	18	5	10	273
8	Brighton & Hove	18	6	9	250
9	Ansty	18	2	12	186
10	Bexhill	18	1	16	155

West of England Premier League

		P	W	L	Pts
1	**Bath**	**18**	**14**	**3**	**301**
2	Clevedon	18	12	5	252
3	Frocester	18	9	8	230
4	Bristol	18	9	9	227
5	Downend	18	8	10	220
6	Potterne	18	7	9	218
7	Bedminster	18	8*	9	216
8	Bridgwater	18	8*	9	214
9	Lechlade	18	7	9	201
10	Corsham	18	3	14	142

* *Plus one tie.*

Yorkshire Premier League North

		P	W	L	Pts
1	**York**	**22**	**15**	**2**	**176**
2	Stamford Bridge	22	12	3	172
3	Yorkshire Academy	22	14	2	163
4	Harrogate	22	9	4	154
5	Sheriff Hutton Bridge	22	10	7	126
6	Woodhouse Grange	22	9	3	112
7	Driffield Town	22	7	9	106
8	Scarborough	22	7	8	105
9	Acomb	22	3	13	64
10	Clifton Alliance	22	1	13	54
11	Hull	22	3	10	53
12	Easingwold	22	0	16	5

Yorkshire Premier League South

		P	W	L	Pts
1	**Wakefield Thornes**	**22**	**17**	**3**	**216**
2	Sheffield Collegiate	22	15	3	196
3	Whitley Hall	21	10*	8	154
4	Treeton	21	9	7	150
5	Appleby Frodingham	22	10*	9	146
6	Wickersley Old Village	22	10	9	140
7	Hallam	22	9	9	138
8	Barnsley	22	9	11	128
9	Cleethorpes	22	8	10	128
10	Aston Hall	22	7	11	120
11	Tickhill	21	5	14	90
12	Sheffield & Phoenix	19	1	16	20

* *Plus one tie.*
Sheffield & Phoenix did not complete the season.

The following leagues do not have ECB Premier League status:

LANCASHIRE LEAGUE TABLES IN 2017

Lancashire League A Division

		P	W	L	Pts
1	**Clitheroe**	**24**	**18***	**3**	**220**
2	Darwen	24	16	2	201
3	Todmorden	24	14	6	183
4	Burnley	24	12	6	170
5	Lowerhouse	24	11	8	156
6	Nelson	24	11	8	151
7	Ramsbottom	24	9	7	133
8	Haslingden	24	8	10	130
9	East Lancashire	24	8	12	121

* *Plus one tie.*

Lancashire League B Division

		P	W	L	Pts
1	**Enfield**	**23**	**10**	**8**	**144**
2	Church	23	9	8	125
2	Accrington	23	8*	9	124
3	Bacup	23	7*	12	116
4	Great Harwood	23	5*	12	97
5	Rishton	23	4	15	90
6	Colne	23	4	15	69
7	Rawtenstall	23	2	15	48

* *Plus one tie.*

Pennine Cricket League Premiership

		P	W	L	Pts
1	**Walsden**	**22**	**15***	**1**	**86**
2	Norden	22	13	2	79
3	Monton & Weaste	22	11*	5	70
4	Rochdale	22	11	5	62
5	Greenfield	22	9	8	59
6	Crompton	22	8	7	53
7	Littleborough	22	6*	9	48
8	Stayley	22	5	8	45
9	Glodwick	22	6	11	41
10	Heyside	22	5	13	37
11	Austerlands	22	4	13	31
12	Saddleworth	22	2*	13	27

* *Plus one tie.*

OTHER LEAGUE WINNERS IN 2017

Airedale & Wharfedale	Beckwithshaw
Bolton	Farnworth
Cambs & Hunts	Ketton
Greater Manchester	Denton St Lawrence
Huddersfield	Hoylandswaine
Norfolk Alliance	Downham Town
North Essex	Wivenhoe
North Lancs & Cumbria	Workington
Northumberland & Tyneside Senior	Swalwell
Pembrokeshire	Carew
Quaid-e-Azam	Bhalot Strikers
Ribblesdale	Settle
Shropshire	Whitchurch
South Wales Association	Llanelli
Thames Valley	Wokingham
Two Counties	Elmstead
Warwickshire	Rugby
Worcestershire	Redditch

ECB CITY CUP IN 2017

JAMES GINGELL

The Chance to Shine programme, established in 2005 to revive cricket in primary schools, was beginning to make its mark. Many of its beneficiaries were now playing in the ECB City Cup, which in 2017 expanded to include Sheffield and Leeds. Some struggled with their first experience of a hard ball, but others flourished. In the final at Leicester, 18-year-old all-rounder Asad Ali Rizvi – who began with Chance to Shine – helped Manchester beat South London in glorious September sun. Later, he was named the team's Player of the Year at the Lancashire awards evening.

It was the third time in five seasons Manchester had won the title, but this side were very different from those before: since 2016, six of the 11 have had to be under 18, so there was a natural evolution. They did not have the individual ability of previous years but, according to team manager Farouk Hussain, they possessed mental toughness. South London had arguably the best player – George Jackson, who opened the bowling and hit a sparkling half-century – but the collective effort of Manchester won the day.

The tournament was increasingly being seen by the cricket establishment as an important scouting ground. David Graveney, the ECB's national performance manager, was on the look out at the semi-finals at Dunstable, and spoke to the players about what it takes to be a professional. He emphasised that success is not just about talent and technique; preparation and tactics are essential ingredients, too. In partnership with the National Asian Cricket Council, MCC's head coach Steve Kirby also invited two from each team to a two-day camp at Lord's. Through a series of drills, the players measured themselves against first-class standards, and met Kabir Ali, Gemaal Hussain and Ajmal Shahzad. Kirby intends to keep a few of the most promising in the development squad for MCC's Young Cricketers programme.

One star from the previous year's competition made a few tentative steps into higher-level cricket. Shan Ahmadzai, a 20-year-old left-arm spinner who came to England from Afghanistan in 2011, played for Northamptonshire Second XI in May, returning a tidy two for 33 against Durham. Later in the summer, he was twelfth man for MCC as they took on Afghanistan at Lord's. As his countrymen revelled in the stands, he soaked up all he could from those around him in the dressing-room – including former Test stars Misbah-ul-Haq and Brendon McCullum – and hoped he could one day play there.

FINAL

At Leicester, September 17. **Manchester won by 36 runs. Manchester 142-7** (20 overs) (Hashir Khan 57); ‡**South London 106** (18.5 overs) (G. Jackson 55). *South London looked capable of avenging their 2016 final defeat, after George Jackson and Nick Wilson – both from Sanderstead CC in Croydon – reduced Manchester to 10-3. But Hashir Khan fought back, putting on 47 with Asad Ali Rizvi, and finishing with 57*. South London needed 143, and endured a nightmare start themselves, plunging to 11-3, then 33-5. Jackson summoned a defiant fifty, but there was little support.*

ROYAL LONDON CLUB CHAMPIONSHIP AND NATWEST CLUB T20 IN 2017

PAUL EDWARDS

The summer of 2017 was challenging for those organising the national club competitions. One problem was familiar: the weather in the second half of the season caused a number of postponements. But other difficulties stemmed from elite clubs bending the rules. When South Northumberland went too far, fielding Scotland's Calum MacLeod in victories over Sheriff Hutton Bridge and York, the ECB had to decide who should play Ormskirk in the last 16. After the prospect of a court case was raised, York got the nod. "The reality is that winning these competitions are massive things for clubs and they put sizeable investment into that," said the ECB's Aaron Campbell. "But when the phrase 'we're taking legal advice' comes our way, we have to get our own lawyers involved."

Ormskirk, who eventually lost to Wanstead & Snaresbrook in a low-scoring final, were most affected by the weather. Already forced into sharing the Lancashire Cup after consecutive rain-hit Sundays, they saw their league cup final put back to April 2018; had there been less hoo-ha, they might have squeezed it all in. Meanwhile, South Northumberland picked themselves up to win the NatWest Club T20, their fourth national trophy in a decade, having earlier secured the North East Premier League. Finals day at Derby was particularly memorable for Simon Birtwisle, who scored runs in both matches and took three wickets in victory over two-time champions Wimbledon. The occasion was also significant for C&R Hawks of the Birmingham League, and Clifton from the Greater Manchester Cricket League, both making their first appearance in the semi-finals of a national competition.

In 2018, the one-day cup will be reduced from 45 to 40 overs, with entry still limited to 256 clubs. It remains a concern, though, that only a handful from some areas enter. The difficulty of getting cricketers to commit to both Saturday league games and Sunday cup matches remains formidable.

ROYAL LONDON CLUB CHAMPIONSHIP FINAL

ORMSKIRK v WANSTEAD & SNARESBROOK

At Chelmsford, September 17. Wanstead & Snaresbrook won by 12 runs. Toss: Ormskirk.

Wanstead & Snaresbrook, playing just a 45-minute drive from their ground, edged an absorbing final contested by two overwhelmingly home-grown teams. Leading the revels was 19-year-old seamer Jack Lord, whose four early wickets did most to scupper Ormskirk's chase of 160. Mikey Jones and Matt Glayzer helped repair the damage, but Wanstead's four spinners contained the batsmen on a day when only one six was hit. With 14 needed off 17 balls and two wickets in hand, Scott Lees was run out, before 50-year-old slow left-armer Mohammad Fayyaz finished it off. Ormskirk were left to regret their wayward start, when Wanstead openers Arfan Akram and Hassan Chowdhury plundered 46 off eight overs. Once the seamers realised a tight line and length was all that was needed on a greenish pitch, they gained their rewards. But Wanstead skipper Joe Ellis-Grewal guided them to a defendable total and, two days after Essex celebrated winning the Championship, the locals were toasting further triumph.

Man of the Match: J. Lord.

Wanstead & Snaresbrook

Arfan Akram c Glayzer b Barnes 38
H. M. Chowdhury c Hartley b Lees 25
F. I. N. Khushi lbw b Caunce 4
K. S. Velani c Hartley b Bohannon 14
Adnan Akram c Lavelle b Bohannon 0
T. G. Cummins lbw b Hartley 7
*J. S. E. Ellis-Grewal run out 25
A. S. S. Nijjar c Knight b Lees 11
†J. J. Das run out 10
J. Lord c Lees b Hartley 10
Mohammad Fayyaz not out 0
B 1, lb 8, w 6 15

1/46 (2) 2/59 (3) 3/81 (1) (41.4 overs) 159
4/91 (4) 5/93 (5) 6/109 (6)
7/130 (8) 8/142 (7) 9/158 (10) 10/159 (9)

Lees 7–2–34–2; Caunce 7.4–2–32–1; Bohannon 9–1–32–2; Barnes 9–1–27–1; Hartley 9–1–25–2.

Ormskirk

A. J. Baybutt lbw b Lord 4
M. Jones c Das b Nijjar 40
J. J. Bohannon b Lord 1
G. Lavelle lbw b Lord 18
†G. Knight b Lord 0
I. R. Robinson c sub (J. Rising) b Nijjar . . . 15
*M. S. Glayzer b Mohammad Fayyaz 34
T. Hartley c Lord b Ellis-Grewal 8
N. T. Caunce c Arfan Akram
b Mohammad Fayyaz . 16
S. Lees run out 0
J. Barnes not out 0

B 1, lb 2, w 6, nb 2 11

1/7 (1) 2/16 (3) (44.2 overs) 147
3/43 (4) 4/43 (5)
5/68 (6) 6/104 (2)
7/121 (8) 8/146 (7)
9/146 (10) 10/147 (9)

Mohammad Fayyaz 8.2–0–22–2; Lord 9–1–33–4; Ellis-Grewal 9–1–26–1; Nijjar 9–1–24–2; Velani 9–0–39–0.

Umpires: H. Davies and J. Marshall.

WINNERS 2005–2017

2005 Horsham
2006 South Northumberland
2007 Bromley
2008 Kibworth
2009 Chester-le-Street
2010 South Northumberland
2011 Shrewsbury
2012 York
2013 West Indian Cavaliers
2014 Sandiacre Town
2015 Blackheath
2016 South Northumberland
2017 Wanstead & Snaresbrook

A full list of winners from 1969 to 2004 appears in Wisden 2005, *page 941.*

NATWEST CLUB T20

First semi-final At Derby, September 11. **South Northumberland won by 17 runs. South Northumberland 139-4** (16 overs) (S. J. Birtwisle 43, J. A. Graham 56*); **‡C&R Hawks 122-9** (16 overs) (Omar Ali 47).

Second semi-final At Derby, September 11. **Wimbledon won by eight wickets. Clifton 94-7** (16 overs); **‡Wimbledon 98-2** (13.1 overs) (N. R. Welch 60).

Final At Derby, September 11. **South Northumberland won by seven wickets. ‡Wimbledon 117** (18.1 overs) (J. R. Wightman 3-18, S. J. Birtwisle 3-23); **South Northumberland 123-3** (19.2 overs) (S. J. Birtwisle 47, R. Peyton 37*).

WINNERS

2008 South Northumberland
2009 Bournemouth
2010 Swardeston
2011 Ealing
2012 Wimbledon
2013 Wimbledon
2014 Chester Boughton Hall
2015 Ealing
2016 Swardeston
2017 South Northumberland

WATSONS VILLAGE CUP IN 2017

BENJ MOOREHEAD

This competition was founded on romantic ideals but, come the final at Lord's, it is a cut-throat business. Those that get there are not carefree amateurs grinning at their good fortune; they are slick, young athletes (mostly), raised on a diet of tough league cricket. Thus Reed, the Hertfordshire club who won in 2012, deposed Sessay, the defending champions from Yorkshire, with probably the most clinical fielding performance in a Village Cup final. Certainly the short boundary by the Tavern Stand has never been defended with such ferocity, and it must be doubtful that a wicketkeeper has put in a more assured display than Richard Wharton, a 25-year-old special constable who also made 86 not out in a seven-wicket win.

Reed are the only southern club to have won the cup this decade. Eight of the XI at Lord's had come through their colts system, and they were indebted to the Tidey brothers. In the quarter-final against Bledlow Village from Buckinghamshire, all-rounder Sean made 75 from 44 balls, and seamer Jack collected five for 21. Notable contributions also came from Tom Greaves – captain, teasing off-spinner (12 wickets at 11), and counter-punching batsman. Coming in at 88 for five in the semi-final against Aston Rowant (Oxfordshire), he hit five sixes in a rapid 48.

Promotion to the ECB Yorkshire Premier League North means Sessay's first team can no longer play in the Village Cup; they may enter their second team. Falkland, winners of the Scottish section, treated them to pipers for their last-16 match at Scroggie Park in Fife, and had planned to land paragliders on the ground, only for rain to spoil the fun. After an abandonment, Sessay won the rearranged fixture at Thirsk by 96 runs, but were distant runners-up in the bar afterwards.

Further back in the field were names to stir the imagination, such as Ballinger Waggoners (Buckinghamshire), Spencer Bruerne (Northamptonshire) and SinjunGrammarians (Surrey). In the Herefordshire section there was the tantalising prospect of a meeting between Brampton Bryan & Leintwardine, and Bartestree & Lugwardine. Alas, it did not come to pass. Bartestree & Lugwardine were one of more than 50 clubs – around a fifth of all entrants – who exited because they could not raise a side. This, though, was a lesser concern for *The Cricketer*, the competition organisers, who announced milk suppliers Watsons as the headline sponsor at the 11th hour.

Despite the no-shows, there was plenty of cricket. In Derbyshire, Shipley Hall seamer James Parkin took the best figures of the competition (seven for 28) to dismiss Elvaston for 84. In Essex Belhus and Horndon on the Hill racked up a competition-record match aggregate of 648. In Pembrokeshire, Cresselly beat Carew by eight wickets in the Dyfed regional final. Ten weeks later this same fixture would invoke the wrath of Mother Cricket herself (see page 725).

FINAL

SESSAY v REED

At Lord's, September 17. Reed won by seven wickets. Toss: Reed.

Reed's Richard Wharton was on the field for every ball, following up some high-class wicketkeeping (including a leg-side stumping) with an unbeaten 86. He was the catalyst for an inspired performance in the field. Toby Fynn and Jack Tidey bowled full and straight with the new ball, while Stuart Smith, Reed's player-chairman, clung on to a steepler which knocked him to the ground and forced him off for treatment. That initiated a collapse of five for 26, off-spinner Tom Greaves taking three for 19 with a mixture of flight and accuracy. Reed's control induced soft dismissals: Nick Thorne, Sessay's leading run-scorer, drove to mid-off in frustration, immediately after a sharp stop had denied him four. Only Chris Till was able to break through. Sessay had the worst of the conditions: overcast when they batted, unbroken sunshine when they bowled. Wharton was dropped on four and 21, but he and James Heslam – dancing and driving after a cautious start – put on 107, before Greaves walloped the winning six towards the Pavilion.

Man of the Match: R. J. T. Wharton.

Sessay

*M. Wilkie c Smith b Fynn	15
M. O. Jackson c Cooper b Greaves	28
J. P. Watson c Smith b Greaves	11
N. J. Thorne c Fynn b Greaves	2
J. K. Spencer lbw b Ward	10
T. A. Hall st Wharton b Cooper	22
L. Carver st Wharton b Ward	0
†C. J. Till c Ward b S. W. Tidey	46
S. M. Peirse b Cooper	4
B. R. Scaling not out	5
Lb 5, w 15, nb 1	21
1/31 (1) 2/55 (3) 3/64 (4) 4/70 (2) 5/78 (5) 6/81 (7) 7/131 (6) 8/152 (9) 9/164 (8) (9 wkts, 40 overs)	164

S. J. Langstaff did not bat.

Fynn 6–2–17–1; J. P. Tidey 8–1–28–0; Greaves 8–0–19–3; Ward 8–0–35–2; Cooper 6–0–36–2; S. W. Tidey 4–0–24–1.

Reed

W. J. Heslam c Till b Hall	6
†R. J. T. Wharton not out	86
R. A. Lankester lbw b Peirse	0
J. A. Heslam st Till b Scaling	54
*T. D. Greaves not out	8
Lb 3, w 13	16
1/23 (1) 2/46 (3) 3/153 (4) (3 wkts, 35.5 overs)	170

S. G. Smith, S. W. Tidey, M. D. Cooper, K. J. Ward, J. P. Tidey and T. G. Fynn did not bat.

Peirse 8–2–24–1; Hall 6–0–39–1; Wilkie 6–1–21–0; Watson 2–0–17–0; Langstaff 7–0–30–0; Carver 3–0–20–0; Scaling 3.5–0–16–1.

Umpires: S. C. Chilmaid and A. J. Wheeler.

DISABILITY CRICKET IN 2017

PAUL EDWARDS

The progress made by disabled cricketers in 2017 can be measured by success in tournaments or by the employment of coaches. It can also be gauged by the respect in which the disabled game is now held, or by the ECB's outstanding efforts to promote it. But its value was perhaps best expressed by Peter Blueitt, England's Player of the Tournament in the Blind Cricket T20 World Cup in India in January and February. "I had a tumour," said Blueitt. "I have no sight at all in my right eye and only light perception in my left. I thought it was the end of my world, but after ten years you just get used to it and carry on. Another life came along. Thank you, England, for letting me wear this shirt."

Blueitt scored 509 runs at 127 in the group stages, but his efforts could not disguise the fact that England still lag behind subcontinental teams in the visually impaired game. This was shown in defeats by India and Pakistan in the group stages, and reinforced by the 147-run loss to Pakistan in the semi-final.

Immediately after the World Cup, Ian Martin, the ECB's head of disability cricket, decided the squad would concentrate solely on T20 cricket, with the aim of closing the gap. Accordingly, England chose not to take part in the longer-form World Cup in January 2018. Yet even this suggests change. Until recently, there were few competitions for disabled cricketers; now there is a choice.

Nathan Stirk, ECB/Getty Images

Widening appeal: Chris Edwards in action against South Africa.

The term "disability cricket" may also foster the misconception that the England teams progress at roughly the same rate. This has never been the case. While the Visually Impaired side were given a clear indication of the ground they needed to make up, England's Learning Disability team again asserted their dominance by not losing a match in the INAS Learning Disability Tri-Series, which was hosted by the ECB in Cheshire and supported by NatWest.

Australia and South Africa were defeated in the one-day international and T20 formats, and England have now lost only one match since 2009. Their leading batsman was Dan Bowser, whose 464 runs at 77 included a 56-ball 108 against South Africa at Bramhall. However, the Player of the Series was all-rounder Chris Edwards, who averaged 58 with the bat and took nine wickets. Edwards was presented with the Lord's Taverners Disability Cricketer of the Year award at Cricket Writers' Club lunch in October.

The disabled game also made important strides off the field. In March, former England leg-spinner Ian Salisbury (Physical Disability) and Ross Hunter (Visually Impaired) became the world's first full-time head coaches of disabled teams. "This is an important step change in disabled cricket," said Martin. "It will increase the capacity of our coaches to work with the performance squads, and is further evidence of the culture shift within our national teams. I'm proud of the fact that we are able to support our players as they pursue both their sporting aspirations and their professional careers." Sports scientist Emma Foden was also brought in, as the pathway support manager for disability cricket, with responsibility for players beneath the national squads in all impairment groups.

Disabled cricket also had its share of photo opportunities. In May, the team captains and players stood alongside Joe Root and Heather Knight at the launch of the ECB's new commercial partnerships with NatWest and New Balance. The presence of Root and Knight was another indication of the remarkable recent progress the game has taken.

SENIOR CRICKET IN 2017

JAMES GINGELL

At least one of the England sides won their Ashes in 2017: while the men's and women's teams returned from Australia empty-handed, the Over-60s had been victorious on home soil in three one-dayers. Since the first official series in 2011, the England seniors had now won four times out of five.

The core of the squad were veterans of the successful tour to Australia in 2016-17, including the three outstanding players. Murphy Walwyn was the top-scorer, with 154 at over a run a ball. His feats were no surprise to those who knew him well. After coming to England from the Leeward Island of Nevis as a 14-year-old in 1970, he had cut his teeth in the Bradford League, playing for East Bierley alongside Roy Gilchrist. He once hit a fifty in 14 minutes – the fastest in the league's history – and twice took ten wickets in an innings.

John Foster, the captain, was the only other to pass 100 runs, and provided calm assurance from the top of the order. He also came with a fine pedigree. Early in his career, he had played in the Lancashire Leagues against Joel Garner and Garry Sobers, and been part of the Shropshire side that beat Yorkshire in the 1984 NatWest Trophy. Rupert Staple, the fastest bowler in English senior cricket, was the pick of the attack; though he was not the top wicket-taker – he took three to John Punchard's five – he cost only a shade above two an over. He had learned his economy by bowling to the best: Barry Richards and Gordon Greenidge were among his net-mates at Alf Gover's cricket school in south London.

In the first match at Blackpool in July, Mark Gaskell's 80 had helped Australia to 191, which seemed a strong total on a difficult pitch. But after a stodgy start England squeaked home by two wickets with three balls to spare thanks to Walwyn's swift 37. With a long boundary on one side, there were some weary legs after the game.

Walwyn starred again to clinch the series at Kidderminster, ushering another tricky chase home with a series of powerful drives to finish with an unbeaten 56 off 39 balls, including 27 off his last seven. And in the final, rain-affected, match at Salisbury, Staple took three for 20 to hold Australia off by nine runs, and complete the whitewash. Amid the speeches and presentations, the stumps and bails were auctioned and, combined with money raised from fines throughout the tour, £830 was handed over to the Andy Payne Fund a Nurse charity.

ENGLAND UNDER-19 v INDIA UNDER-19 IN 2017

Under-19 Tests (2): England 0, India 2
Under-19 one-day internationals (5): England 0, India 5

The optimism engendered by the drawn Test series on the subcontinent earlier in the year was demolished, as England Under-19 were comprehensively beaten at home. India won seven out of seven in two formats, and England were left seeking scraps of consolation in individual performances.

Just one player who had appeared for India in the Tests in February – Anukul Roy – made the trip, and he appeared only in the one-day series. Nevertheless, the team of 11 debutants laid down a marker in the First Test at Chesterfield by reaching 519, a record between these sides, after being asked to bat. Manjot Kalra hit a rapid 122, and 17-year-old pace bowler Kamlesh Nagarkoti took ten for 112 to set up a thumping 334-run win.

But England regained some pride in the Second Test at Worcester. Ryan Patel led an excellent bowling effort, before Shivam Mavi helped India recover from 106 for seven to 292. An aggressive century from Will Jacks guided England close to first-innings parity, before India took control.

James Taylor and Darren Gough joined England's coaching team before the one-day series, but their knowhow could not prevent a rampant India completing a clean sweep. Shubman Gill's 147 in the third match at Hove provided the highlight of the series. England were more competitive in the final two games, but India showed composure to win the fourth on DLS. The best finish came in the final match, at Taunton, where India completed a one-wicket victory with four balls to spare, as Nagarkoti calmly got them over the line.

Gill scored 452 at 64 in six games and Prithvi Shaw 410 in seven, whereas England's best aggregate was 235 from Jacks. Seamers Nagarkoti and Mavi dominated the Tests, with 24 wickets between them, while spinners Roy and Rahul Chahar collected ten each in the one-day series.

SQUADS

England *M. D. E. Holden (Middlesex; T/50), B. M. J. Allison (Essex; 50), L. Banks (Warwickshire; T/50), T. Banton (Somerset; 50), G. A. Bartlett (Somerset; T), J. M. Blatherwick (Nottinghamshire; T/50), H. C. Brook (Yorkshire; T/50), H. J. H. Brookes (Warwickshire; T/50), A. W. Finch (Worcestershire; 50), A. F. Gleadall (Derbyshire; 50), B. G. F. Green (Somerset; T), W. G. Jacks (Surrey; T/50), T. A. Lammonby (Somerset; 50), F. S. Organ (Hampshire; 50), G. D. Panayi (Warwickshire; T), R. Patel (Surrey; T), L. A. Patterson-White (Nottinghamshire; T/50), J. H. Plom (Essex; 50), M. J. Potts (Durham; T/50), H. Qadri (Derbyshire; 50), O. G. Robinson (Kent; T/50), H. J. Swindells (Leicestershire; T), J. C. Tongue (Worcestershire; T), L. Trevaskis (Durham; 50), G. S. Virdi (Surrey; T). *Coach:* A. Hurry.

For the one-day games that followed the Tests, Brook took over as captain, except for the first, when he was playing for Yorkshire, and Jacks led the team.

India *H. J. Rana (T/50), R. D. Chahar (T/50), R. P. Das (T), H. M. Desai (T/50), S. Gill (T/50), M. Kalra (T), S. F. Khan (50), S. P. Mavi (T/50), K. L. Nagarkoti (T/50), D. G. Nalkande (T), H. J. Patel (T/50), I. C. Porel (50), S. Radhakrishnan (T/50), A. S. Roy (50), A. Sandhu (T), A. Sharma (50), P. P. Shaw (T/50), Shiva Singh (50), Y. S. Thakur (50), V. A. Tiwari (T), H. Tyagi (T). *Coach:* W. V. Raman.

Shaw captained in the one-day series.

ENGLAND v INDIA

First Under-19 Test

At Chesterfield, July 23–26. India won by 334 runs. Toss: England.

India outclassed their hosts almost from the moment they were put in. Their captain, Himanshu Rana, fell early, but after that it was a stroll. Prithvi Shaw, the former Mumbai schoolboy prodigy, hit a run-a-ball 86, before Manjot Kalra cracked 122 off 117, adding 138 for the fourth wicket with 15-year-old Riyan Parag Das. A patient 89 from keeper Harvik Desai helped India to their highest score in a youth Test against England, beating 492 for four at Chennai in 2000-01. England reached 136 for three, but didn't get much further: seven tumbled for 59, the new-ball pair of Kamlesh Nagarkoti and Shivam Mavi finishing with nine between them. Despite a lead of 324, India batted again. Shaw thrashed 69 and Das a 34-ball 50, setting England 498. More realistically, they needed to survive 130 overs – and never came close. By stumps on the third day, they were in tatters, with only Max Holden showing any fight. Next morning, Nagarkoti wrapped up the largest win by runs in Under-19 Tests; his figures of ten for 112 were India's best at this level in England, surpassing Iqbal Siddiqui's nine for 163 at Taunton in 1994.

Close of play: first day, India Under-19 389-6 (Desai 34, Nagarkoti 14); second day, England Under-19 164-4 (Jacks 46, Green 6); third day, England Under-19 132-7 (Potts 3, Tongue 0).

India Under-19

P. P. Shaw c Holden b Virdi	86	– c sub (L. Banks) b Virdi	69
*H. J. Rana c Green b Tongue	0	– c Robinson b Tongue	3
S. Gill c Robinson b Potts	29	– lbw b Potts	25
M. Kalra c Green b Virdi	122	– b Potts	1
R. P. Das c Patel b Virdi	68	– (6) c Brook b Virdi	50
S. Radhakrishnan c Robinson b Brookes	6	– (5) c Robinson b Potts	7
†H. M. Desai lbw b Tongue	89	– not out	12
K. L. Nagarkoti b Tongue	19		
D. G. Nalkande c Patel b Brookes	10		
S. P. Mavi not out	41		
A. Sandhu lbw b Brookes	1		
B 25, lb 11, w 6, nb 6	48	Lb 1, w 1, nb 4	6
1/6 (2) 2/83 (3) 3/137 (1) 4/275 (4) 5/292 (6) 6/336 (5) 7/401 (8) 8/429 (9) 9/499 (7) 10/519 (11) (133.4 overs)	519	1/19 (2) 2/70 (3) 3/72 (4) 4/99 (5) 5/118 (1) 6/173 (6) (6 wkts dec, 32 overs)	173

Tongue 27–6–69–3; Brookes 19.4–0–85–3; Green 22–2–98–0; Potts 23–4–81–1; Virdi 37–3–134–3; Holden 5–0–16–0. *Second innings*—Tongue 4–1–19–1; Brookes 8–0–61–0; Potts 8–2–20–3; Green 1–0–9–0; Virdi 11–0–63–2.

England Under-19

H. C. Brook b Mavi	17	– c Desai b Nagarkoti	9
*M. D. E. Holden c Sandhu b Rana	32	– lbw b Sandhu	60
R. Patel b Mavi	38	– c Mavi b Rana	14
G. A. Bartlett b Nagarkoti	2	– lbw b Sandhu	18
W. G. Jacks c Rana b Nagarkoti	46	– b Nagarkoti	4
B. G. F. Green b Nagarkoti	6	– c Desai b Nagarkoti	6
†O. G. Robinson b Mavi	1	– b Nagarkoti	0
M. J. Potts lbw b Mavi	0	– not out	20
J. C. Tongue c Desai b Nagarkoti	6	– b Mavi	3
H. J. H. Brookes b Nagarkoti	7	– lbw b Mavi	5
G. S. Virdi not out	5	– b Nagarkoti	5
B 3, lb 19, w 1, nb 12	35	B 1, nb 18	19
1/56 (1) 2/78 (2) 3/86 (4) 4/136 (3) 5/165 (5) 6/171 (6) 7/171 (7) 8/178 (8) 9/184 (9) 10/195 (10) (54.2 overs)	195	1/16 (1) 2/58 (3) 3/94 (4) 4/99 (5) 5/115 (6) 6/115 (7) 7/128 (2) 8/135 (9) 9/153 (10) 10/163 (11) (46.1 overs)	163

Nagarkoti 16.2–2–49–5; Mavi 18–5–51–4; Nalkande 6–1–20–0; Rana 4–1–11–1; Sandhu 10–0–42–0. *Second innings*—Nagarkoti 14.1–1–63–5; Mavi 12–2–47–2; Nalkande 6–0–30–0; Rana 4–1–8–1; Sandhu 10–3–14–2.

Umpires: G. D. Lloyd and J. W. Lloyds.

ENGLAND v INDIA

Second Under-19 Test

At Worcester, July 31–August 3. India won by 97 runs. Toss: India.

England gave a better account of themselves, but were left to regret their inability to polish off India's lower order on the opening day. From the depths of 106 for seven, the tourists rallied to 292, supervised by an unbeaten 86 from Mavi, who put on 97 for the ninth wicket with Ashok Sandhu. England, at one point 242 for five, should have secured a lead; instead, they trailed by eight, after losing their last five for 42, including Jacks for a lively 102 bolstered by six sixes. In India's second innings, Shubman Gill also hit 102, before becoming one of four wickets for Surrey off-spinner Amar Virdi. It all meant England needed 339 to square the series. They were in contention at 164 for two, but Ryan Patel fell for 47, George Bartlett was run out for 73, and the last eight tumbled for 77 to hand India a 2–0 victory.

Close of play: first day, England Under-19 19-1 (Holden 8, Patel 7); second day, India Under-19 24-0 (Shaw 20, Rana 4); third day, India Under-19 169-3 (Gill 55, Das 25).

India Under-19

P. P. Shaw c Swindells b Patel	51	– c Bartlett b Patel	44
*H. J. Rana c Holden b Panayi	4	– c Swindells b Patel	28
S. Gill c Brook b Brookes	18	– b Virdi	102
M. Kalra b Patel	18	– c and b Panayi	9
R. P. Das c Brook b Patel	8	– c Swindells b Patel	52
†H. M. Desai c Patel b Virdi	3	– lbw b Virdi	32
K. L. Nagarkoti b Patel	0	– c Holden b Panayi	9
S. P. Mavi not out	86	– b Virdi	9
R. D. Chahar lbw b Blatherwick	25	– c Banks b Holden	17
A. Sandhu c Swindells b Panayi	50	– lbw b Virdi	13
V. A. Tiwari c Holden b Brookes	12	– not out	0
B 3, lb 10, nb 4	17	B 2, lb 7, w 1, nb 5	15
1/21 (2) 2/68 (3) 3/87 (1) 4/98 (5) 5/106 (4) 6/106 (7) 7/106 (6) 8/169 (9) 9/266 (10) 10/292 (11) (80.4 overs)	292	1/72 (1) 2/77 (2) 3/101 (4) 4/232 (5) 5/249 (3) 6/285 (7) 7/297 (6) 8/300 (8) 9/330 (10) 10/330 (9) (75.2 overs)	330

Panayi 14–1–75–2; Blatherwick 15–1–64–1; Brookes 17.4–2–34–2; Patel 6–1–21–4; Virdi 22–3–67–1; Brook 3–0–11–0; Holden 3–0–7–0. *Second innings*—Brookes 16–2–71–0; Blatherwick 15–0–80–0; Patel 8–0–29–3; Panayi 11–1–52–2; Virdi 24–2–82–4; Brook 1–0–7–0; Holden 0.2–0–0–1.

England Under-19

First innings		Second innings	
H. C. Brook run out	2	– b Tiwari	28
*M. D. E. Holden lbw b Sandhu	71	– c Desai b Tiwari	19
R. Patel lbw b Rana	24	– c Gill b Nagarkoti	47
G. A. Bartlett lbw b Nagarkoti	56	– run out	73
L. Banks lbw b Tiwari	1	– st Desai b Sandhu	21
W. G. Jacks b Mavi	102	– lbw b Mavi	26
†H. J. Swindells lbw b Sandhu	16	– c Nagarkoti b Chahar	2
H. J. H. Brookes c Mavi b Chahar	0	– b Sandhu	5
G. D. Panayi c Desai b Nagarkoti	0	– not out	1
G. S. Virdi b Nagarkoti	0	– b Mavi	0
J. M. Blatherwick not out	0	– lbw b Mavi	0
B 7, lb 3, w 1, nb 1	12	B 8, lb 6, nb 5	19
1/4 (1) 2/45 (3) 3/138 (2) 4/141 (5) 5/170 (4) 6/242 (7) 7/243 (8) 8/272 (9) 9/272 (10) 10/284 (6) (85.4 overs)	284	1/49 (1) 2/61 (2) 3/164 (3) 4/197 (4) 5/220 (5) 6/225 (7) 7/236 (8) 8/241 (6) 9/241 (10) 10/241 (11) (53.4 overs)	241

Mavi 17.4–3–57–1; Nagarkoti 18–5–40–3; Rana 8–4–19–1; Tiwari 12–2–36–1; Chahar 14–1–56–1; Sandhu 16–5–66–2. *Second innings*—Mavi 11.4–3–40–3; Nagarkoti 14–4–60–1; Tiwari 4–0–21–2; Rana 5–0–21–0; Chahar 10–0–51–1; Sandhu 9–0–34–2.

Umpires: M. J. Saggers and A. G. Wharf.

First Under-19 one-day international At Cardiff, August 7. **India won by five wickets.** ‡**England 181** (46.4 overs) (S. P. Mavi 3-30, R. D. Chahar 3-30, A. S. Roy 4-30); **India 185-5** (34.3 overs) (S. F. Khan 69*). *MoM:* A. S. Roy. *England's openers, the Liams Trevaskis (33) and Banks (43), made a good start – but the rest struggled against leg-spinner Rahul Chahar, who had played for Pune in the IPL, and slow left-armer Anukul Roy. India were in trouble themselves at 70-5 in the 14th over, before Roy helped Salman Khan put on 115*. Will Jacks led England as Harry Brook, the appointed captain, was playing for Yorkshire in the County Championship.*

Second Under-19 one-day international At Canterbury, August 9 (day/night). **India won by eight wickets.** ‡**England 175** (44.4 overs) (R. D. Chahar 3-26, A. S. Roy 4-27); **India 177-2** (33.2 overs) (H. J. Rana 74). *MoM:* H. J. Rana. *This match, live on TV, followed a similar course to the first: England's openers laid a platform – 48 this time – then India's spinners got to work. Chahar and Roy again shared seven wickets. Brook, back as captain, started with a six, but was out for 21. India's skipper Prithvi Shaw (48) shared an opening stand of 110 with Himanshu Rana as his side eased to victory.*

Third Under-19 one-day international At Hove, August 12. **India won by 169 runs.** ‡**India 327-7** (50 overs) (S. Gill 147; M. J. Potts 4-61); **England 158** (40.5 overs) (T. Banton 59; K. L. Nagarkoti 3-20). *MoM:* S. Gill. *India clinched the series at the earliest opportunity, turning on the power after winning the toss. Shubman Gill, still only 17, hammered 147; he had hit 160 against England in Mumbai earlier in the year. Four wickets for Durham quick Matty Potts, in his first youth ODI, kept the rest in check, but England were done for once both openers fell for ducks to Kamlesh Nagarkoti.*

Fourth Under-19 one-day international At Bristol, August 14. **India won by one run** (DLS). **England 276-8** (50 overs) (L. Trevaskis 50, F. S. Organ 61, T. A. Lammonby 50; Shiva Singh 5-38); ‡**India 151-4** (28 overs) (S. Gill 66). *An improved batting performance from England led to a much closer match. Sydney-born Felix Organ shared a fourth-wicket stand of 107 with Tom Lammonby, although slow left-armer Shiva Singh, in his first game of the series, put the brakes on. With rain forecast, India kept an eye on the DLS equation, and were one ahead when the weather closed in.*

Fifth Under-19 one-day international At Taunton, August 16. **India won by one wicket.** ‡**England 222-9** (50 overs) (L. Banks 51; R. D. Chahar 4-63, A. Sharma 3-33); **India 226-9** (49.2 overs) (P. P. Shaw 52; H. J. H. Brookes 3-57). *MoS:* S. Gill. *England looked set for a consolation win when India dipped from 216-6 to 217-9. With one run needed, the 49th over was a maiden, bowled by Trevaskis to last man Ishan Porel. But Nagarkoti (26*) kept his head, and struck the winning four in Henry Brookes's last over to seal a 5–0 whitewash. England's bowlers conceded 16 in wides. Earlier, Banks had put on 87 with Brook (49), before Chahar took three wickets in four balls to reduce England to 128-5.*

YOUTH CRICKET IN 2017

JAMES GINGELL

In 2014, the ECB discovered that, among children aged seven to 12, only 2% nominated cricket their favourite sport. Something had to be done. In October 2017, they doubled investment in Chance to Shine to £2.5m a year to help bring the sport into schools. That came after the ECB launched the All Stars Cricket programme in March, for children aged five to eight. For £40, every child received bright blue playing gear and a plastic bat and ball to use during eight one-hour sessions. They learned the rudiments of the game, but the emphasis was squarely on enjoyment; a high elbow could come later.

Tom Harrison, the ECB's chief executive, said he was keen to get away from a culture of children learning cricket by "turning up at a men's game and sitting at third man for an hour". The strategy meant those running the sessions, called activators, did not have to be qualified coaches – in fact, three-quarters were new to the game themselves.

The programme was heavily marketed to local clubs, who were not charged to get involved, and were given £5 for every child enlisted. That helped drum up interest, but the ECB wanted to attract new audiences – families without any connection to local clubs – and worked with the parenting website Mumsnet to spread the word.

By the end of summer, 37,000 children had taken part in 1,500 locations across the country, with the majority of feedback positive. If the overall attendance was slightly lower than hoped for, one statistic was encouraging: seven in ten were new to their club.

The counties pitched in, promoting the scheme with varying degrees of enthusiasm. Lancashire and Leicestershire recruited for an All Stars Cricket "champion", Warwickshire brought children into Edgbaston's indoor school, and Somerset gave free T20 Blast tickets to those who signed up from Somerset, Devon and Cornwall. Many professionals also came along to sessions to lend a hand, while the blue of the All Stars kit became a familiar sight during intervals at international matches.

With the foundations in place, the ECB's aim for 2018 was to almost treble participation, to 100,000. To achieve that, some issues would need addressing: certain clubs were concerned about how All Stars would mesh with successful colts sections, while others struggled to find a suitable activator.

Regardless, there were plans for the programme to expand through the age brackets, and guide older children into something resembling cricket proper. When the ECB announced their shiny new city-based T20 competition, earmarked for 2020, they said the tournament would "dovetail with the All Stars programme", with a particular emphasis on eight to 12s. Quite how that would work in practice was hard to divine, though it was undeniable that the return of a dozen matches to free-to-air TV would certainly help. In the management speak so beloved of the ECB, there seemed at last to be some joined-up thinking.

THE 2017 BUNBURY FESTIVAL

After stepping up a level, many cricketers are tempted to play safe: risks can lead to humiliation. But some are different. At the 31st Bunbury Festival, held at Stowe School in July, Rishi Wijeratne of London & the East (and Middlesex) was one such. If his aggregate of 189 runs was good, his strike-rate of 150 was extraordinary. In two games against the Midlands, he cracked an unbeaten 80 off 47 balls, then 66 off 38. Almost as reliable as he was flamboyant, he was an easy choice for Batsman of the Tournament.

London & the East, captained by Josh de Caires, the son of former England captain Michael Atherton, also had the tournament's best bowler and all-rounder, both from Kent. Left-arm seamer Ben Mills did not take most wickets, nor top the averages, but still impressed those watching with zippy pace, while wicketkeeper Harry Houillon showed a classy touch, particularly with a run-a-ball 80 against South & West. Though they slipped up against the North, when Wijeratne endured his only failure, London & East deserved the 50-over title.

South & West had a dreary time in the longer format, losing all three games, but enjoyed success in the Twenty20s. They edged a low-scoring thriller against the North thanks to some late dash from Hampshire's Fletcha Middleton, then denied London & the East the double in the final. The captain, Will Smeed of Somerset, who finished the week third in the run-charts, led his team home with an unbeaten half-century.

After the festival, the four regions were condensed into two, and the best of the best invited to Loughborough for four matches over three sunny days in August. In the first game, Luke Doneathy of Durham scored a hundred for the combined Midlands & the North, who racked up a match-winning 319. But the South hit back, easing to wins in the back-to-back T20s, before Smeed's sparkling century inspired them to an eight-wicket victory in the final game. The hard pitch was unforgiving for most bowlers, but Harry Sullivan – a left-arm spinner named the outstanding player in the Yorkshire youth system – was a cut above.

Earlier in the year, a Bunbury XI managed by David Graveney, the ECB's national performance manager, toured Sri Lanka to celebrate the 30th anniversary of the festival. They struggled in alien conditions, winning just once, on the back of captain Jack Haynes's 93. But one of their number excelled when he came home: Derbyshire's 16-year-old off-spinner Hamidullah Qadri picked up a five-for on his first-class debut, and was later called into the England Under-19 squad. Many had trodden the same path, but few had done so quite as quickly.

SCHOOLS CRICKET IN 2017

REVIEW BY DOUGLAS HENDERSON

For the first time, *Wisden's* schools averages include Twenty20 matches. Some see this as a step too far, as though equating a song from a musical with a three-act opera. Others welcome an acceptance of what, especially for smaller schools, is the reality: that many fixtures are 20-over games. Even in some larger schools with a strong cricket pedigree, the pressure to perform in academic league tables – whatever happened to the idea of a rounded liberal education? – has endangered all-day games. Saturdays used to offer a bastion, but more and more have become 35-over affairs. It remains possible to fit two 40-over innings into an afternoon, yet young players see so much faffing about from the professionals that 20 an hour (built into the regulations for the last 60 minutes of a declaration game) seems almost laughable. Another consequence of the relentless drive for examination success is that schools can struggle to field their strongest XI; some masters are forced to resort to complex spreadsheets of player availability, even for weekend matches.

If exams remain the biggest headache for those in charge of schools cricket, there are signs of an analgesic. A-level grades are now determined by one set of final exams, rather than two. The fact that papers taken in Year 12 no longer count towards the final mark should, in theory, allow greater participation. No one pretends organising schools cricket is ever painless, but this might reduce the discomfort a little.

Last October, a fundamental redrafting of the Laws came into effect, and one change gave umpires greater powers to deal with poor behaviour. Previously, they were unable to apply any on-field sanctions – a quirk apparently shared only with Aussie Rules football. Conduct has become an issue in recent years, and the old saw "it's not cricket" has lost much of its relevance. The claim that the new penalties smack of sledgehammers and nuts is misguided: while it's true the umpires can, in the last resort, send a player from the field, such powers should rarely be applied. But the sanctions need to be there to act as a deterrent.

Unusually for a British summer, the part of it shared with the schools cricket season (April–June) was distinctly better than what followed, which allowed some striking performances. It was remarkable that eight players passed 1,000 runs, and six took 40 wickets or more. Several batsmen broke school records. While the inclusion of Twenty20 may have swollen both aggregates a little, its effect on the averages is to bring them down, the batting slightly more than the bowling. Even so, five managed over 100 with the bat; there were 17 under ten with the ball.

Of those five, however, only Will Jacks, from St George's, Weybridge, did so from at least five completed innings. Haaris Sohoye of Bancroft's School proved almost impossible to dislodge, remaining unbeaten in seven of his eight innings, and averaging exactly 150. At Llandaff Cathedral School, bravely playing their first season of competitive cricket, Richard Sen was not far

Ben Berryman

Teddie Casterton of RGS, High Wycombe: the 11th Wisden Schools Cricketer of the Year.

behind: undefeated in two of his three knocks, he managed 142. There were similar achievements from John Oliver (The Glasgow Academy), who averaged 122 from three completed innings, and Ben Sidwell (City of London Freemen's School), who averaged 107 from four.

St Edward's, Oxford, benefited from two heavy-scoring batsmen: their skipper, Brandon Allen, and Ben Charlesworth both passed 1,200 runs. Billy Mead reached four figures for Marlborough, just like his great-uncle, the former Sussex captain Mike Griffith, back in 1961. Four others to reach 1,000 were Jack Davies (Wellington College), Sam Perry (The Manchester Grammar School), Charlie Scott (St Albans) and Joshua Smith (Kimbolton).

The highest innings of the summer came from Will Jacks, as St George's ran up a scarcely believable 531 in 50 overs against Reading Blue Coat. Jacks's monumental 279 eclipsed 263 by Solihull's Chris Williamson in 2010 as the best score recorded in a one-day schools match in the UK. Blue Coat answered with a respectable 330, yet lost by 201. That same day, Teddie Casterton of RGS High Wycombe struck an unbeaten 267 from 153 balls in a declaration game against John Hampden Grammar School. It was the high-water mark of his astonishingly productive summer that brought 1,423 runs from 21 innings, and an average of almost 90.

Around the country, there were some talented wicketkeepers. Leading the field, perhaps, was George Lavelle, though his appearances for Merchant Taylors' School, Crosby, were limited by call-ups to Lancashire Seconds. At Arundel, on finals day of the National Schools Twenty20, Millfield's Fin Trenouth made two brilliant stumpings, one standing up to the brisk Brad Currie. Meanwhile, Brandon Allen (St Edward's) added 43 dismissals to his 1,234 runs, and Bryanston captain Ollie Thomas completed more stumpings than catches – often the sign of skilful glovework. Will Thomson from St Albans took 17 catches and made five stumpings, and is another keeper of great flair.

WISDEN SCHOOLS CRICKETERS OF THE YEAR

2007	Jonathan Bairstow	St Peter's School, York
2008	James Taylor	Shrewsbury School
2009	Jos Buttler	King's College, Taunton
2010	Will Vanderspar	Eton College
2011	Daniel Bell-Drummond	Millfield School
2012	Thomas Abell	Taunton School
2013	Tom Köhler-Cadmore	Malvern College
2014	Dylan Budge	Woodhouse Grove
2015	Ben Waring	Felsted School
2016	A. J. Woodland	St Edward's School, Oxford
2017	**Teddie Casterton**	**RGS, High Wycombe**

All-rounders' performances can be trickier to gauge, but two who achieved the feat of appearing in the tables of highest run-scorers *and* wicket-takers were off-spinner Harrison Ward of St Edward's (964 runs and 45 wickets) and Clifton's slow left-armer Prem Sisodya (918 and 39). Seamer Ben Charlesworth (St Edward's) combined 1,263 runs at 54 with 22 wickets at 11.

Sedbergh were the deserving winners of the National Schools Twenty20. Even though they had to negotiate finals day without their captain and outstanding player, Harry Brook – he was playing for Yorkshire in the County Championship – they rattled up 221 for five against a robust Merchant Taylors', Northwood, and 200 for five against Millfield's strong attack. Max Silvester struck 111 from 61 balls in that game, the first century on finals day. Sedbergh's triumph was overdue: in five of the competition's eight years they had reached the last four, but this was their first appearance in the final.

A major plank of Sedbergh's success – they won 23 of their 26 games – was the leg-spin of Kyme Tahirkheli, whose 58 victims made him comfortably the country's leading wicket-taker. Cranleigh managed a better win-rate, prevailing in 16 of their 18 matches, but there was precious little in it. Five other schools finished with a success rate above 80%. Now that *Wisden's* results include the National Schools T20 (the knockout competition entered by the majority of establishments in this section), it is exceptionally difficult for a team to go through a season unbeaten. None did in 2017, though the table on page 754 lists six schools who were beaten just once.

Tahirkheli, Allen, Jacks, Mead, Ward and a few others made a compelling case for being named the Wisden Schools Cricketer of the Year, but the 2017 winner is Teddie Casterton of RGS High Wycombe. His main strength was an ability to score off nearly every delivery: good balls were guided into gaps for ones and twos, and bad ones tended to disappear. His unbeaten 109 in a chase of 161 against Radley in the National T20 competition also demonstrated his calmness at the crease and ability to manipulate the field. According to his school coach Ben Berryman, "Teddie always seemed to find the boundary when it was required." If those traits hinted at a mature cricket brain, his selfless captaincy confirmed it; the high standards of RGS High Wycombe were a point of pride. Casterton – whose father Peter won *Wisden's* writing competition in 2014 – carried his form into club cricket, notching his maiden Home Counties Premier League century for High Wycombe CC, where Adam Dobb is the coach. Dobb's advice and chivvying have played a key role in his development, and left him well placed for a push into the professional game.

Douglas Henderson is editor of Schools Cricket Online, where all the schools reports from past Wisdens *can be browsed and searched.*

MCC Schools v ESCA

At Lord's, August 30. Abandoned.

MCC *E. A. Brookes (*Solihull School*), R. M. Yates (*Warwick School*), C. F. B. Scott (*St Albans School*), N. J. Tilley (*Reed's School*), E. B. Fluck (*Cheadle Hulme School*), I. V. A. Dilkes (*St Lawrence College*), †S. J. W. Hall (*Reigate GS*), P. Sisodiya (*Clifton College*), G. C. H. Barlow (*Charterhouse*), F. Hand (*Queen's College, Taunton*), J. S. Subramanyan (*Wellington College*).

ESCA *J. A. Haynes (*Malvern College*), B. G. Charlesworth (*St Edward's School, Oxford*), †J. M. Cox (*Felsted School*), R. H. Sheemar (*Bedford School*), S. C. Dorsey (*The Swinton HS*), L. P. Goldsworthy (*Millfield*), S. C. Sullivan (*New Hall School*), T. E. Davis (*Simon Langton GS*), J. P. Morley (*Siddal Moor Sports College*), K. B. Szymanski (*King's College, Taunton*), L. C. Botes (*Wirral GS*).

The following tables cover only those schools listed in the Schools A–Z section.

SCHOOLS AVERAGES

BEST BATTING AVERAGES (5 completed innings)

		I	*NO*	*Runs*	*HS*	*100*	*Avge*
1	W. G. Jacks (*St George's College, Weybridge*)	6	1	626	279	3	125.20
2	A. N. N. Hinton (*Merchiston Castle School*)	10	4	593	128*	2	98.83
3	R. M. Yates (*Warwick School*)	8	3	447	144*	2	89.40
4	E. T. D. Casterton (*RGS High Wycombe*)	21	5	1,423	267*	6	88.93
5	C. F. Gibson (*Trent College*)	16	7	784	116	2	87.11
6	H. C. Brook (*Sedbergh School*)	12	1	950	163	5	86.36
7	W. J. Thomas (*Dauntsey's School*)	18	6	993	129	2	82.75
8	J. Smith (*Whitgift School*)	9	3	491	103	2	81.83
9	F. Hand (*Queen's College, Taunton*)	9	3	485	135*	2	80.83

		I	NO	Runs	HS	100	Avge
10	C. F. B. Scott (*St Albans School*)	16	3	1,025	136*	4	78.84
11	J. J. Smith (*Kimbolton School*)	17	4	1,020	135*	4	78.46
12	I. V. A. Dilkes (*St Lawrence College*)	12	3	700	163	3	77.77
13	L. W. James (*Oakham School*)	17	6	845	106	1	76.81
14	S. J. Perry (*Manchester GS*)	17	3	1,052	159*	5	75.14
15	J. S. Rymell (*Ipswich School*)	14	4	750	154*	2	75.00
16	A. S. Bramley (*The Leys School*)	15	4	803	104	3	73.00
17	J. L. H. MacGregor (*Ipswich School*)	14	5	656	111*	4	72.88
18	C. R. Campbell (*Hampton School*)	17	4	935	151*	3	71.92
19	N. J. Tilley (*Reed's School*)	15	3	857	153*	5	71.41
20	G. G. Conner (*Fettes College*)	10	4	423	130*	1	70.50
21	B. W. Aitchison (*Merchant Taylors', Crosby*)	13	5	535	113	1	66.87
22	T. Banton (*King's College, Taunton*)	7	0	462	155	2	66.00
23	W. E. Rigg (*Solihull School*)	11	3	523	116*	1	65.37
24	A. E. J. Cole (*Dr Challoner's GS*)	10	2	515	129	1	64.37
25	S. W. Mead (*Marlborough College*)	19	3	1,009	214*	2	63.06
26	E. B. Litvin (*The Grammar School at Leeds*)	9	2	440	142	1	62.85
27	J. D. M. Evison (*Stamford School*)	11	2	560	135	1	62.22

Four other batsmen averaged over 100, but from fewer than five completed innings: H. Sohoye (Bancroft's School) 150.00; R. Sen (Llandaff Cathedral School) 142.00; J. L. Oliver (Glasgow Academy) 122.33; and B. D. Sidwell (City of London Freemen's School) 107.25.

MOST RUNS

		I	NO	Runs	HS	100	Avge
1	E. T. D. Casterton (*RGS High Wycombe*)	21	5	1,423	267*	6	88.93
2	B. G. Charlesworth (*St Edward's School, Oxford*)	26	3	1,263	112*	4	54.91
3	B. L. Allen (*St Edward's School, Oxford*)	27	1	1,234	100	1	47.46
4	J. L. B. Davies (*Wellington College*)	24	1	1,071	126	4	46.56
5	S. J. Perry (*Manchester GS*)	17	3	1,052	159*	5	75.14
6	C. F. B. Scott (*St Albans School*)	16	3	1,025	136*	4	78.84
7	J. J. Smith (*Kimbolton School*)	17	4	1,020	135*	4	78.46
8	S. W. Mead (*Marlborough College*)	19	3	1,009	214*	2	63.06
9	W. J. Thomas (*Dauntsey's School*)	18	6	993	129	2	82.75
10	N. J. Lee (*Monmouth School*)	16	0	974	130	3	60.87
11	H. D. Ward (*St Edward's School, Oxford*)	26	2	964	101*	1	40.16
12	H. C. Brook (*Sedbergh School*)	12	1	950	163	5	86.36
13	C. R. Campbell (*Hampton School*)	17	4	935	151*	3	71.92
14	J. J. O'Riordan (*Tonbridge School*)	22	3	931	121	2	49.00
15	P. Sisodiya (*Clifton College*)	20	4	918	165*	2	57.37
	J. A. Haynes (*Malvern College*)	23	1	918	137*	4	41.72
17	A. W. Shoff (*Wellington College*)	21	1	895	150	2	44.75
18	S. H. Patel (*KCS, Wimbledon*)	19	1	864	128	1	48.00
19	T. J. Haines (*Hurstpierpoint College*)	18	2	860	141	2	53.75
20	N. J. Tilley (*Reed's School*)	15	3	857	153*	5	71.41
21	L. W. James (*Oakham School*)	17	6	845	106	1	76.81
	T. M. Ryan	19	1	845	206*	2	46.94
23	E. I. Samuel (*Marlborough College*)	18	2	828	161*	1	51.75
24	A. S. Bramley (*The Leys School*)	15	4	803	104	3	73.00
25	T. R. W. Gnodde (*Eton College*)	20	0	797	121	2	39.85
26	F. D. W. McCreath (*Rugby School*)	16	3	793	111*	2	61.00
27	R. Patel (*Brentwood School*)	15	2	789	103	2	60.69
28	S. J. Mulvey (*Wellingborough School*)	23	2	788	84	0	37.52
29	C. F. Gibson (*Trent College*)	16	7	784	116	2	87.11
30	T. J. Price (*Magdalen College School*)	16	3	774	99*	0	59.53
	A. E. King (*Stowe School*)	23	6	774	91*	0	45.52

		I	NO	Runs	HS	100	Avge
32	C. O. Gwynn (*Bradfield College*)	24	5	759	110*	1	39.94
33	M. D. Barker (*King's School, Canterbury*)	19	0	753	122	1	39.63
	J. G. T. Crawley (*Shrewsbury School*)	24	2	753	118*	1	34.22
35	J. S. Rymell (*Ipswich School*)	14	4	750	154*	2	75.00

BEST BOWLING AVERAGE (10 wickets)

		O	M	Runs	W	BB	Avge
1	B. C. Mills (*St Edmund's School, Canterbury*)	28	5	84	14	4-6	6.00
2	C. J. Byrne (*Shrewsbury School*)	16	0	60	10	3-11	6.00
3	E. Bamber (*Mill Hill School*)	91	29	194	31	6-18	6.25
4	E. Solomon (*Shebbear College*)	25	1	104	16	5-17	6.50
5	E. C. R. O'Mahoney (*Birkenhead School*)	43.5	9	132	17	3-13	7.76
6	N. L. Ward (*Harvey GS*)	33	5	102	13	4-17	7.84
7	J. T. M. Weale (*Shebbear College*)	34	7	96	12	3-9	8.00
8	F. Hand (*Queen's College, Taunton*)	43	6	140	17	4-8	8.23
9	J. P. Woodward (*Harvey GS*)	23	4	96	11	3-21	8.72
10	A. Cruickshank (*Culford School*)	40	7	114	13	8-38	8.76
11	J. Lambton (*St Edmund's School, Canterbury*)	20.1	1	90	10	5-12	9.00
12	H. Wren (*Harvey GS*)	21	4	93	10	3-16	9.30
13	B. J. Currie (*Millfield School*)	94	15	291	31	4-28	9.38
14	N. Aslam (*Dr Challoner's GS*)	62	11	208	22	4-19	9.45
15	J. R. Percival (*Glasgow Academy*)	32	2	153	16	5-14	9.56
16	A. V. Joshi (*Tiffin School*)	30.3	5	119	12	5-42	9.91
17	J. Pistorius (*Wrekin College*)	48	7	219	22	4-22	9.95
18	L. C. A. Vanaesebroeck (*Mill Hill School*)	52	7	161	16	4-8	10.06
19	L. A. Head (*Epsom College*)	126	17	394	39	6-29	10.10
20	C. J. Searle (*Hampton School*)	46	5	123	12	3-23	10.25
21	M. W. Mills (*Wellingborough School*)	24.5	0	115	11	2-8	10.45
22	S. Harle (*King Edward's School, Birmingham*)	30	2	136	13	5-34	10.46
23	O. G. F. Pooler (*Manchester GS*)	30	1	126	12	6-26	10.50
24	H. Pounds (*Leicester GS*)	25	2	132	12	3-27	11.00
25	V. Patel (*Aldenham School*)	27	4	121	11	4-7	11.00
26	B. G. Charlesworth (*St Edward's School, Oxford*)	67	8	244	22	4-23	11.09
27	K. Krishnakumar (*The Leys School*)	31	1	145	13	4-9	11.15
28	G. J. West (*Fettes College*)	45	9	134	12	3-5	11.16
29	G. S. Ealham (*Cranleigh School*)	25	2	123	11	3-6	11.18
30	S. J. R. Browne (*Charterhouse*)	57.2	9	168	15	3-18	11.20

Two other bowlers averaged under 11.20, but took fewer than ten wickets: G. Drissell (South Gloucestershire and Stroud College) 10.14; and T. B. Barnes (Judd School) 11.12.

MOST WICKETS

		O	M	R	W	BB	Avge
1	K. K. Tahirkheli (*Sedbergh School*)	177.5	18	711	58	6-82	12.25
2	H. D. Ward (*St Edward's School, Oxford*)	200	23	752	45	6-65	16.71
3	P. J. H. Clark (*Shrewsbury School*)	151.3	16	518	43	6-19	12.04
4	G. B. S. Pearson (*Eton College*)	206	14	943	42	4-44	22.45
5	J. T. Hazelgrove (*Bristol GS*)	109.1	13	490	40	5-32	12.25
	H. J. M. Millett (*Dulwich College*)	192	18	704	40	6-32	17.60
7	L. A. Head (*Epsom College*)	126	17	394	39	6-29	10.10
	P. Sisodiya (*Clifton College*)	168.1	33	530	39	5-15	13.58
	B. J. Thompson (*Clayesmore School*)	122.2	10	536	39	8-57	13.74
10	J. A. Curtis (*St Edward's School, Oxford*)	177	8	818	38	3-23	21.52
11	B. R. Sutton (*RGS, Worcester*)	154.3	17	573	37	4-36	15.48

		O	M	R	W	BB	Avge
	B. S. Twine (*Eastbourne College*)	129.4	22	404	35	4-10	11.54
	N. M. A. Lubbock (*Cranleigh School*)	109.2	13	437	35	5-17	12.48
12	A. H. Cook (*RGS, Worcester*)	126.4	6	533	35	4-25	15.22
	J. J. Henry (*Wellington College*)	141.4	10	726	35	4-33	20.74
	J. H. R. I. Hardman (*Eton College*)	204	21	755	35	4-28	21.57
	K. Nayee (*Worth School*)	125	12	450	34	4-60	13.23
17	J. S. Subramanyan (*Wellington College*)	122.1	12	460	34	6-26	13.52
	P. Singh (*Charterhouse*)	149	22	490	34	5-34	14.41
	G. S. Cook (*RGS, Worcester*)	146	18	601	34	5-35	17.67
	J. L. S. Clark (*King's College, Taunton*)	114	19	379	33	5-10	11.48
	G. Freeman (*Christ's Hospital*)	120.1	18	432	33	6-57	13.09
	G. C. H. Hill (*Sedbergh School*)	135.3	17	447	33	5-35	13.54
21	O. D. Clarke (*Stowe School*)	180.2	41	490	33	8-44	14.84
	T. Z. Meher (*Whitgift School*)	145.3	21	527	33	6-15	15.96
	A. Mahtani (*Charterhouse*)	173.3	22	542	33	4-15	16.42
	M. R. Chalcraft (*Wellingborough School*)	139	14	560	33	3-20	16.96
	J. O. King (*Felsted School*)	171	28	668	33	4-25	20.24
	J. A. Pocklington (*Eastbourne College*)	126.3	14	421	32	6-14	13.15
	O. D. Jackson (*Dauntsey's School*)	125.5	14	426	32	4-21	13.31
	J. J. Smith (*Kimbolton School*)	122	22	439	32	5-25	13.71
29	C. W. G. Sanders (*Sedbergh School*)	109	16	445	32	5-13	13.90
	T. Olsen (*Stowe School*)	136.5	33	479	32	3-8	14.96
	J. R. Clarke (*Wellingborough School*)	120.4	9	555	32	4-25	17.34
	W. C. H. P. Collard (*Hurstpierpoint College*)	113.5	6	585	32	4-41	18.28

OUTSTANDING SEASONS (minimum 7 matches)

	P	W	L	T	D	A	%W
Cranleigh School	18	16	1	0	1	0	88.88
Sedbergh School	26	23	3	0	0	3	88.46
Glasgow Academy	8	7	1	0	0	3	87.50
The Leys School	15	13	2	0	0	3	86.66
Harvey Grammar School	7	6	1	0	0	0	85.71
Dr Challoner's Grammar School	12	10	1	0	1	2	83.33
Mill Hill School	11	9	1	1	1	0	81.81
Bromsgrove School	14	11	3	0	0	3	78.57
Trent College	18	14	1	1	2	0	77.77
Eastbourne College	26	20	6	0	0	1	76.92
Manchester Grammar School	17	13	4	0	0	1	76.47
King's College, Taunton	16	12	4	0	0	4	75.00
Mount Kelly School	16	12	4	0	0	3	75.00
Wilson's School	16	12	4	0	0	0	75.00
Bryanston School	12	9	3	0	0	0	75.00
Merchant Taylors' School, Crosby	19	14	5	0	0	5	73.68
Reed's School	15	11	2	0	2	0	73.33
Cheadle Hulme School	15	11	4	0	0	4	73.33
St Peter's School, York	21	15	5	0	1	3	71.42
Radley College	14	10	2	0	2	0	71.42
Oakham School	17	12	3	0	2	1	70.58
Hampton School	20	14	4	0	2	2	70.00
Merchant Taylors' School, Northwood	20	14	4	0	2	1	70.00

SCHOOLS A–Z

In the results line, A = abandoned without a ball bowled. An asterisk indicates captain. The qualification for the averages (which now include Twenty20 games, but not overseas tour games) is 150 runs or ten wickets. Counties have been included for all schools. Since cricket does not follow the current complex system of administrative division, *Wisden* adheres to the county boundaries in existence before the dissolution of Middlesex in 1965. Those schools affected by the boundary changes of the last five decades – such as Eton College, which was removed from Buckinghamshire and handed to Berkshire – are listed under their former county.

Abingdon School *Berkshire* P14 W3 L11 A1

Master i/c J. M. Golding **Coach** Dr C. J. Burnand

Abingdon's U14 and U15 teams won their county cups, but the senior sides endured a more difficult season, hampered by shortages of players and runs. Jamie Lawson showed his talents, though, and 14-year-old Freddie Smith made his First XI debut in the latter part of the summer, having already scored over 800 runs in 2017.

Batting J. A. T. Lawson 240 at 30.00; A. P. Ling 234 at 23.40; O. J. Fountain 250 at 20.83; M. E. M. Owen 186 at 18.60.

Bowling *M. J. Mortimer 14 at 26.28; S. H. C. Warren 11 at 40.18.

Aldenham School *Hertfordshire* P16 W7 L7 T1 D1

Master i/c L. J. Kirsten **Coach** D. J. Goodchild

In an excellent season, highlights included Hemanshu Hirani's 110 not out, Sam Harvey's brilliant new-ball bowling, and Umer Zeeshan-Lohya's consistent all-round class.

Batting H. Hirani 495 at 49.50; D. Travers 301 at 37.62; U. Zeeshan-Lohya 255 at 23.18.

Bowling V. Patel 11 at 11.00; S. A. Harvey 26 at 11.61; U. Zeeshan-Lohya 20 at 15.20; R. D. Selliah 11 at 15.72; H. Hirani 17 at 19.52; J. S. Michelin 16 at 22.62.

Alleyn's School *Surrey* P10 W4 L6 A1

Master i/c R. N. Ody **Coach** P. E. Edwards

The team were well captained by Robbie Matthews and, as the averages were led by two Year 12s – Oliver Mawdsley and Daniel Smith – there was much hope for a bright 2018.

Batting O. J. E. Mawdsley 167 at 23.85; Z. B. Wood 164 at 23.42.

Bowling D. W. Smith 12 at 14.50; *R. C. Matthews 10 at 15.70; M. Swanson 10 at 16.10.

Ampleforth College *Yorkshire* P9 W4 L4 D1 A1

Masters i/c C. M. Booth and G. D. Thurman **Coach** J. D. Love

Friendly victories in early summer were followed by competitive defeats. But encouragement came from the development of a number of younger players, who supported senior figures such as Michael Blakiston-Houston, Arthur Campion and Charlie Buchanan.

Batting A. G. Campion 309 at 44.14; *B. M. B. Fawcett 240 at 34.28; L. P. MacLellan 179 at 29.83.

Bowling M. P. Blakiston-Houston 10 at 16.20.

Bancroft's School *Essex* P17 W10 L6 D1

Master i/c C. G. Greenidge

Bancroft's batting relied on the consistency of captain Angad Nijjar and Alex Agedah, while Deven Solanki's bowling showed promise for 2018.

Batting H. Sohoye 150 at 150.00; A. K. Agedah 604 at 54.90; *A. S. Nijjar 426 at 38.72; M. W. Sydenham 298 at 37.25; W. F. T. Hopkins 351 at 31.90; L. Oliver 178 at 29.66; N. H. A. Jani 311 at 25.91; Z. A. Piracha 255 at 23.18; S. C. Handa 207 at 23.00; T. N. Oliver 314 at 20.93.

Bowling D. V. Solanki 26 at 16.50; H. Vallance 12 at 17.58; S. C. Handa 27 at 17.77; H. Sohoye 12 at 31.25.

Bede's School *Sussex* P13 W6 L7 A1

Master i/c A. P. Wells

A talented team improved as the season went on, and recaptured the Sussex T20 Cup after narrow defeats in 2015 and 2016. Three members of the First XI – Sussex Academy players Henry Crocombe, Scott Lenham and Felix Sheppard – also helped the school win the Under-15 ESCA National Cup, beating Merchant Taylors' School, Crosby, in the final.

Batting *J. Billings 545 at 45.41; S. H. Lenham 223 at 27.87; A. G. H. Orr 298 at 27.09.

Bowling S. H. Lenham 20 at 21.05; D. A. K. Heater 12 at 23.33.

Bedford Modern School *Bedfordshire* P15 W8 L6 D1

Master i/c P. J. Woodroffe

Matt Taylor led the team superbly, and hit a century against Akeley Wood, while there were fine all-round performances from Robert Bassin, Sam Pitkin and Advait Vaidya. With the whole bowling attack returning, the future looked promising.

Charlie Nicholls, Berkhamsted's captain, hit 727 runs, including two hundreds.

Batting R. G. S. Bassin 350 at 35.00; *M. J. Taylor 381 at 34.63; M. S. Rodgers 296 at 26.90; S. A. Pitkin 183 at 26.14; E. J. Else 239 at 15.93; A. Vaidya 158 at 13.16.
Bowling J. H. Taylor 21 at 14.38; A. Vaidya 16 at 16.00; R. G. S. Bassin 16 at 16.43; S. A. Pitkin 22 at 17.27.

Bedford School *Bedfordshire* P14 W7 L5 D2 A1

Master i/c I. G. S. Steer
This was a very successful season: Bedford School teams won over 70% of their games and reached the latter stages of county and national competitions. The First XI enjoyed excellent wins against Felsted, St Albans and Rugby in Saturday fixtures, and reached the regional final of the National Schools T20 competition.
Batting E. N. Gay 212 at 42.40; A. Hassan 565 at 40.35; J. M. George 159 at 31.80; *S. Tomlinson-Patel 347 at 28.91; R. H. Sheemar 396 at 28.28; H. O. Gouldstone 297 at 27.00; A. H. Miller 162 at 23.14.
Bowling A. I. Rennie 26 at 23.19; R. H. Sheemar 20 at 23.85; A. Hassan 11 at 34.45.

Berkhamsted School *Hertfordshire* P16 W11 L4 D1

Master i/c G. R. A. Campbell **Coaches** D. J. Gibson and B. R. Mahoney
Berkhamsted exceeded expectations, winning 11 of 16 games. Captain Charlie Nicholls excelled, scoring 727 runs, while Freddie Thompson hit 436, and picked up 21 wickets to boot.
Batting *C. A. Nicholls 727 at 51.92; L. A. K. Golding 191 at 31.83; S. J. T. Rolfe 283 at 31.44; R. M. Skelton 178 at 29.66; F. A. Thompson 436 at 29.06; S. A. J. Quinn 271 at 22.58.
Bowling F. M. Gates 14 at 14.42; D. J. H. Young 15 at 17.86; J. C. Dunkley 17 at 18.82; F. A. Thompson 21 at 20.00; J. J. Woodley 14 at 22.42.

Birkenhead School *Cheshire* P16 W11 L5 A2

Master i/c R. E. Lytollis **Coach** G. J. Rickman
The highlight was the National T20 competition, in which Armand Rabot hit two hundreds in one day at Wilmslow to take Birkenhead to the North-West final; they lost to eventual winners Sedbergh. Six bowlers took ten wickets or more, ensuring another successful season.
Batting A. J. N. Rabot 728 at 60.66; D. P. Shillinglaw 366 at 28.15; T. A. Brown 322 at 26.83; *A. T. Watkins 308 at 22.00; D. R. Cooke 240 at 21.81.

Bowling E. C. R. O'Mahoney 17 at 7.76; C. M. Andrews 17 at 11.41; G. V. Johnson-Aley 14 at 11.85; G. J. T. Wild 10 at 15.30; T. A. Brown 10 at 23.30; T. M. Corran 13 at 24.23.

Bishop's Stortford College *Hertfordshire* P11 W3 L7 T1 A1

Master i/c M. Drury **Coach** N. D. Hughes

The highlight of the season was an excellent win against MCC, based around an outstanding 84 from Joseph Hawkins, the leading run-scorer for the year. The side was captained superbly by Alex Portas.

Batting J. S. Hawkins 488 at 61.00; *A. J. Portas 417 at 46.33; H. J. Harnack 159 at 31.80; T. H. Snelling 160 at 17.77.

Bowling J. R. Tasker 15 at 16.66.

Blundell's School *Devon* P14 W5 L9 A2

Master i/c L. J. Lewis

In a tough season, an excellent win over MCC stood out. They were ably led by Christian Cabburn, who topped the batting and bowling averages.

Batting *C. Cabburn 338 at 33.80; S. Maunder 199 at 28.42; J. Lockwood 390 at 27.85; H. Hamilton-Green 186 at 23.25; T. Mortiboys 202 at 18.36; C. Fanous 184 at 15.33.

Bowling C. Cabburn 16 at 31.68; T. Mortiboys 11 at 36.00.

Bradfield College *Berkshire* P23 W14 L9 A2

Master i/c M. S. Hill **Coach** J. R. Wood

The season started well, but as the weather dried out, the runs dried up, particularly in the longer games. Charlie Gwynn was the outstanding player, and captained with confidence and maturity.

Batting *C. O. Gwynn 759 at 39.94; R. Patel 326 at 32.60; I. A. Malik 588 at 29.40; F. J. Brabham 447 at 27.93; E. J. S. Bray 222 at 22.20; J. R. Thompson 301 at 20.06; P. Khanna 310 at 16.31.

Bowling C. O. Gwynn 29 at 18.96; I. A. Malik 23 at 20.43; S. D. Waddington 22 at 22.90; T. J. Watson 11 at 27.81; E. J. S. Bray 11 at 30.45; F. J. Brabham 11 at 31.45; O. C. Waddington 19 at 33.89.

Bradford Grammar School *Yorkshire* P18 W3 L13 D2 A2

Master i/c A. G. Smith **Coach** S. A. Kellett

The batting, led by captain Robbie Williams and opener Will Smith, rarely failed. But a lack of depth in the bowling – particularly in the spin department – made it hard to win games.

Batting W. F. Smith 438 at 33.69; O. J. Croudson 308 at 30.80; *R. G. Williams 460 at 28.75; W. A. Luxton 338 at 22.53; B. M. Merchant 176 at 19.55; C. R. Andrews 228 at 13.41.

Bowling T. Zamir 19 at 25.89; D. J. Brennan 14 at 28.21.

Brentwood School *Essex* P17 W7 L8 D2 A1

Master i/c S. Salisbury **Coach** G. O. Jones

In a mixed season, captain Rishi Patel was dominant. His attacking batting stunned several opponents, but he lacked support. Spinners Tom Wingrove and Jack Levy – a Year 9 – shone with the ball.

Batting *R. Patel 789 at 60.69; M. A. Fox 336 at 33.60; R. Das 470 at 27.64; R. J. Wantling 387 at 25.80.

Bowling M. A. Fox 15 at 12.66; W. Steinberg 19 at 13.15; T. Wingrove 18 at 13.33; R. Patel 17 at 13.41; J. S. Levy 16 at 14.62.

Brighton College *Sussex* P19 W2 L17 A2

Master i/c M. P. Smethurst **Coach** N. J. Buoy

Runs were hard to come by, and victories even more so. Still, a promising group of young players emerged, and James D'Orsaneo won Best Bowler at the BOWS Festival.

Batting *A. J. Bone 368 at 21.64; H. M. E. Moorat 324 at 21.60; W. S. Longley 262 at 16.37; M. M. Burrows 211 at 14.06; M. J. Clark 194 at 12.93; W. S. Crombie 168 at 11.20.

Bowling J. A. D'Orsaneo 21 at 25.28; W. S. Longley 23 at 26.04; G. E. Cook 15 at 28.93; I. R. G. Christie 10 at 29.30; J. Z. Montfort Bebb 17 at 36.29.

Bristol Grammar School *Gloucestershire* P18 W8 L10

Master i/c K. R. Blackburn

Jude Hazelgrove's haul of 40 wickets gave Bristol Grammar School a competitive edge all season, while the batting was led by Under-16 Matty Brewer, who scored 111 against King Edward's School, Bath. Joe Cuthbert and Tom Quinlan, both Under-15, also excelled, suggesting a bright future for the school.

Batting M. J. M. Brewer 334 at 47.71; J. J. Marks 234 at 21.27; S. G. Maskell 221 at 20.09; H. S. Canagarajah 170 at 17.00; T. H. J. Quinlan 264 at 15.52.
Bowling *J. T. Hazelgrove 40 at 12.25; J. W. C. Cuthbert 16 at 18.25; T. H. J. Quinlan 18 at 27.22; S. Gandhi 11 at 37.54.

Bromsgrove School *Worcestershire* P14 W11 L3 A3

Master i/c D. J. Fallows

Among the 11 victories, those against Millfield and Wellington stood out, as did Fahd Janjua's T20 century, the first for Bromsgrove. George Marshall gave strong performances with the ball, and earned valuable experience for 2018.
Batting J. Banton 201 at 67.00; F. K. Janjua 354 at 50.57; J. S. Johal 269 at 33.62; G. T. Hatfield 275 at 30.55; *J. P. Kinder 251 at 25.10; B. P. Herridge 179 at 17.90.
Bowling G. O. Marshall 13 at 16.23; J. S. Johal 11 at 26.09; J. M. Smith 10 at 35.80.

Bryanston School *Dorset* P12 W9 L3

Master i/c S. J. Turrill **Coach** P. J. Norton

Outstanding captain and keeper Ollie Thomas, batsman Owen Morris and bowler Frank Turrill all finished strongly after a combined 14 years of service in the First XI. There were victories over Sherborne, Portsmouth, MCC, Dorset Under-17 and Clayesmore.
Batting O. A. Morris 304 at 43.42; M. A. Trueman 340 at 37.77; H. G. Clarke 260 at 37.14; J. L. R. Plimmer 178 at 29.66; A. Dijkhuizen-Sands 168 at 28.00.
Bowling F. J. Turrill 21 at 11.42; H. J. C. Maclean 14 at 14.92; H. G. Clarke 11 at 15.45; A. Dijkhuizen-Sands 10 at 17.70; A. F. Chetwood 14 at 21.07.

Caterham School *Surrey* P18 W3 L14 D1

Master i/c J. N. Batty

Caterham had a tough season, though victories over Eltham College, Judd and Wallington were sweet. Joe Foggin captained the side strongly, and was leading run-scorer with 370 runs, while his deputy, Sam Thorpe, lent support with 24 wickets.
Batting *J. A. Foggin 370 at 23.12; J. S. Ireland 222 at 14.80; L. F. Brown 191 at 12.73; M. J. Terry 201 at 12.56.
Bowling J. W. Parkin 10 at 15.50; S. D. J. Thorpe 24 at 20.70; M. J. Terry 19 at 26.21; I. A. Haywood 19 at 30.47.

Charterhouse *Surrey* P20 W13 L6 D1

Master i/c M. P. Bicknell

Led by George Barlow, superb with bat and ball, Charterhouse racked up 13 victories, the best season of recent years. William Melhuish was also central to success – he averaged over 50 – as were prolific bowlers Aman Mahtani and Prince Singh.
Batting W. G. B. Melhuish 505 at 50.50; *G. C. H. Barlow 539 at 35.93; A. Mahtani 380 at 19.00; A. R. R. Wilman 223 at 15.92; H. N. Gilbey 287 at 15.10; T. C. P. Rawlings 192 at 12.80; P. Singh 205 at 10.78.
Bowling S. J. R. Browne 15 at 11.20; P. Singh 34 at 14.41; A. Mahtani 33 at 16.42; O. B. G. Sheen 14 at 18.07; A. R. R. Wilman 12 at 18.75; G. C. H. Barlow 25 at 20.04; J. A. E. Hawkings 17 at 24.41.

Cheadle Hulme School *Cheshire* P15 W11 L4 A4

Master i/c G. J. Clinton **Coach** R. C. Kitzinger

The season's highlight came during the tour of India, when Ed Fluck struck a school-record 215 off 110 balls. James Scott, who captained with distinction, also a hit a century.
Batting E. B. Fluck 651 at 59.18; *J. S. A. Scott 393 at 49.12; A. E. Hunt 257 at 32.12; B. S. Haspell 301 at 23.15; B. J. Staniforth 200 at 22.22.
Bowling J. S. A. Scott 15 at 12.13; H. M. Collins 12 at 17.50; B. S. Haspell 11 at 21.18; A. J. Tittle 12 at 23.50; J. P. Fullwood 10 at 24.10; E. B. Fluck 10 at 26.50.

Cheltenham College *Gloucestershire* P19 W9 L9 D1 A1

Master i/c M. K. Coley **Coach** M. P. Briers

The results – nine wins and nine defeats – summed up a mixed season. Jono Jamieson-Black led from the front, with 715 runs and 20 wickets for his off-spin. But excellent bowling was often let down by an absence of significant partnerships.

Batting *J. W. Jamieson-Black 715 at 51.07; D. J. Ward 491 at 35.07; J. C. Soames 460 at 28.75; O. Hill 188 at 26.85; M. H. Dymoke 256 at 23.27; J. K. Palmer 380 at 21.11; B. Frisby 246 at 18.92; G. M. Wells 164 at 13.66.
Bowling B. Frisby 26 at 19.80; J. Clement 11 at 25.72; A. Sharam 18 at 26.16; J. W. Jamieson-Black 20 at 26.45; J. C. Soames 13 at 27.30; M. H. Dymoke 15 at 29.93.

Chigwell School *Essex* P15 W6 L6 D3

Master i/c F. A. Griffith **Coach** V. Chopra
Aryan Gupta ran a tight ship, and senior players Reevo Chahal, Arun Kudhail, Fergal McArdle, Owen McCausland, Charles Peck and Charlie Redhead were all outstanding during their last school season. Portia Blogg also had a successful year, with 13 wickets at 16.
Batting *A. Gupta 369 at 46.12; A. R. Kudhail 186 at 23.25; F. J. J. McArdle 160 at 17.77; B. H. P. Kearin 157 at 17.44.
Bowling R. Chahal 16 at 14.56; P. E. M. Blogg 13 at 16.15; M. T. Choudhry 12 at 17.50; A. R. Kudhail 11 at 19.00; M. Z. Chaudhary 10 at 19.90; O. R. McCausland 10 at 22.00.

Chislehurst & Sidcup Grammar School *Kent* P6 W2 L4 A5

Master i/c R. A. Wallbridge **Coach** D. L. Pask
With all but one player available in 2018, the results were encouraging: MCC were pushed to the last over, while the school finished runners-up in the Kent Under-19 League for the first time.
Batting N. L. Harris 166 at 27.66.
Bowling The leading bowler was M. R. E. Leeves, who took seven wickets at 12.00.

Christ College, Brecon *Breconshire* P11 W2 L8 T1

Master i/c T. J. Trumper **Coach** R. F. Evans
Harry Roberts did well to rally his troops across a tough summer. The team finished on a high with some stirring performances in Christ College's annual T20 Festival, which included special guests Geelong College from Australia.
Batting The leading batsman was *H. J. Roberts, who hit 128 runs at 12.80.
Bowling H. F. Morgan-Gervis 14 at 13.71.

Christ's Hospital *Sussex* P18 W9 L8 D1

Masters i/c H. P. Holdsworth and D. H. Messenger **Coach** T. E. Jesty
The team lacked consistency, but there were moments to cherish, particularly from the Freeman brothers: Will hit an excellent century during victory over MCC, and 14-year-old brother Gus took six wickets with his leg-spin in a narrow defeat by Sussex Martlets. The season finished with the festival at King's Bruton, where keeper-batsman Eric Swinn-Ward caught the eye.
Batting *W. E. Freeman 454 at 28.37; E. J. R. Swinn-Ward 327 at 27.25; A. P. Burgess 338 at 22.53; B. Kinnear 206 at 20.60; G. Freeman 185 at 20.55.
Bowling G. Freeman 33 at 13.09; O. H. Williams 11 at 17.72; W. E. Freeman 25 at 20.04; H. Condron 12 at 25.66; A. P. Burgess 13 at 29.61; W. A. Thwaites 13 at 32.53.

Churcher's College *Hampshire* P9 W5 L4 A4

Master i/c R. Maier
Five victories from nine was a good haul, particularly with so many returning in 2018.
Batting J. Paul 187 at 37.40; B. I. Crane 210 at 35.00; J. McMillan 240 at 26.66.
Bowling The leading bowler was C. Tuffin, who took seven wickets at 16.00.

City of London Freemen's School *Surrey* P13 W7 L5 D1 A2

Master i/c A. E. Buhagiar **Coach** N. M. Stewart
A successful year included a 72-run victory over Lord Wandsworth College, a nine-wicket win over Emanuel, and first place in the Martin Berrill League. Oli Graham, Jack Symonds, Oli Williams and Ben Sidwell – who averaged over 100 – depart, having contributed significantly.
Batting *B. D. Sidwell 429 at 107.25; J. Symonds 260 at 43.33; T. C. Youngman 272 at 34.00; F. G. Rose 332 at 27.66; L. J. Butcher 231 at 21.00.
Bowling J. W. Hamilton 15 at 17.06; L. Hunter 16 at 20.25.

Clifton's Prem Sisodiya struck 918 runs and took 39 wickets, while Angus Dahl, from Cranleigh, collected 618 and 30.

Clayesmore School *Dorset* P17 W8 L9

Master i/c D. O. Conway

After a memorable tour to Sri Lanka, Clayesmore played fantastic cricket throughout the year. Outstanding performers included batsman Matthew Meredith and bowler Ben Thompson.

Batting J. J. Gordon 205 at 29.28; M. K. Meredith 404 at 28.85; M. W. Tipping 275 at 21.15; *B. J. Thompson 249 at 14.64; J. E. Miles 170 at 11.33.

Bowling B. J. Thompson 39 at 13.74; J. E. Miles 16 at 20.06; O. L. J. Betts 17 at 21.17; M. W. Tipping 15 at 21.60.

Clifton College *Gloucestershire* P19 W11 L7 D1 A1

Master i/c J. C. Bobby **Coach** J. R. A. Williams

Clifton's results tailed off as exam pressure took hold, but there were good wins against Marlborough, Blundell's and Cheltenham. The outstanding all-round performer was Glamorgan Academy player Prem Sisodiya, who hit 918 runs and took 39 wickets with his slow left-armers.

Batting P. Sisodiya 918 at 57.37; *L. J. P. Shaw 601 at 40.06; C. P. C. Griffith 320 at 22.85; C. J. S. Argent 243 at 22.09; R. E. Clarke 323 at 21.53; J. J. Hughes 171 at 17.10.

Bowling P. Sisodiya 39 at 13.58; L. J. P. Shaw 17 at 20.41; C. P. C. Griffith 26 at 21.03; F. A. P. Cole 24 at 21.08; R. E. Clarke 10 at 43.00.

Colchester Royal Grammar School *Essex* P6 W3 L3

Master i/c M. S. A. McEvoy **Coach** D. W. Hardy

The season started with promising performances, including victory over Woodbridge, and finished with a win on the last day against Newcastle RGS.

Batting C. E. Everett 228 at 45.60; J. P. Patient 179 at 44.75; J. A. Smith 202 at 40.40.

Bowling I. S. Thomas 10 at 14.60.

Cranleigh School *Surrey* P18 W16 L1 D1

Master i/c A. P. Forsdike **Coach** S. D. Welch

Cranleigh were superb again, winning every major fixture. Lewis Bedford hit 172 against RGS Guildford, a school record, and brought his First XI aggregate to 2,088 runs over three years. Angus Dahl, the captain, also ended his time at Cranleigh; in four years, he collected 1,434 runs and 113 wickets.

Batting L. Bedford 682 at 52.46; F. D. C. Austin 638 at 49.07; *A. E. C. Dahl 618 at 47.53; E. J. Tristem 391 at 32.58; S. J. A. Dickson 209 at 29.85; E. W. Cooper 384 at 27.42.

Bowling G. S. Ealham 11 at 11.18; N. M. A. Lubbock 35 at 12.48; A. E. C. Dahl 30 at 12.86; S. J. A. Dickson 28 at 14.53; J. Turner 21 at 16.85; M. A. Bell 18 at 19.66.

Culford School *Suffolk* P9 W3 L4 D2 A2

Master i/c A. M. Northcote

The First XI were handicapped by unavailability, but a solid middle order played positive cricket, and gave enjoyment to all who watched them.

Batting M. Whittaker 285 at 40.71; A. Packer 184 at 36.80; M. Mitchum 283 at 35.37; A. Oxley 246 at 35.14.

Bowling A. Cruickshank 13 at 8.76; *F. Allum 12 at 16.33; A. Dhesi 12 at 19.33.

Dauntsey's School *Wiltshire* P18 W12 L5 D1 A2

Master i/c A. J. Palmer **Coach** J. R. Ayling

Oliver Jackson, skippering for a second year, led the team to the Monkhouse Intersport League title. Key performers included Will Thomas, who scored his maiden century and fell just short of 1,000 runs, and leg-spinner Jack Grant, who built on his promising debut season in 2016.

Batting W. J. Thomas 993 at 82.75; *O. D. Jackson 312 at 34.66; H. E. Baker 382 at 31.83; R. N. Patel 364 at 28.00.

Bowling O. D. Jackson 32 at 13.31; T. J. Swanton 18 at 20.72; J. B. Grant 28 at 21.07; H. M. J. Cox 10 at 24.30; N. M. Cannon 16 at 24.81.

Dean Close School *Gloucestershire* P15 W9 L6

Master i/c A. G. A. Milne **Coach** M. J. Powell

Dean Close enjoyed a strong season, reaching the final of the Chesterton Cup, and recording wins over Wrekin, RGS Worcester, King's Gloucester and, in a two-day game, Sir Thomas Rich's. Danielle Gibson, who turned 16 in May, represented Gloucestershire and won a contract with Western Storm for the Kia Super League.

Batting H. Sleeman 251 at 35.85; J. H. Richards 244 at 27.11; J. Gray 206 at 17.16; O. Horne 251 at 16.73; *S. W. P. Norwood 214 at 15.28.

Bowling B. Tarrant 26 at 15.57; A. Cook 13 at 21.38; M. S. Court 12 at 26.08; O. Horne 12 at 31.75.

Denstone College *Staffordshire* P14 W7 L5 D2 A1

Master i/c T. A. H. Williams **Coach** S. M. Guy

Denstone's improvement was reflected in their results, with three more victories than 2016, and four fewer defeats. Their spinners were always a threat, with Andrew Billington and Jack Motley taking 47 wickets between them.

Batting E. M. R. Barlow 355 at 35.50; A. I. Cooper 323 at 32.30; D. M. Afford 387 at 32.25; *J. J. Russell 348 at 23.20; M. A. Webber 280 at 21.53.

Bowling A. R. Cawley 21 at 11.95; J. J. Russell 15 at 19.00; B. E. S. Wakefield 19 at 20.84; A. D. Billington 22 at 24.95; J. A. Motley 25 at 29.56.

Dr Challoner's Grammar School *Buckinghamshire* P12 W10 L1 D1 A2

Master i/c N. J. S. Buchanan

It was a triumphant season for Dr Challoner's, with just one defeat. Alex Cole (515 runs) and Nouman Aslam (22 wickets) stood out, but there were strong performances throughout the team; three players scored centuries.

Batting A. E. J. Cole 515 at 64.37; S. G. Walsh 206 at 51.50; D. C. Goodman 230 at 46.00; N. Aslam 163 at 40.75; *F. A. Mason 216 at 30.85; H. J. Moore 313 at 28.45.

Bowling N. Aslam 22 at 9.45; W. J. Arnold 17 at 12.76; H. Alam 11 at 17.27.

Dollar Academy *Clackmannanshire* P10 W6 L3 D1 A3

Master i/c J. G. A. Frost

Dollar Academy won more games than they lost in a season affected by poor weather. Victory over Strathallan early in the summer was a highlight, as was the inclusive approach adopted by the captain Lachlan Peterson: he regularly used six bowlers.

Batting T. B. Douglas 232 at 46.40; *L. J. L. Peterson 166 at 33.20.

Bowling L. McLaren 11 at 11.81.

Will Shepherd was the mainstay of the John Hampden Grammar School batting, while Will Thomas, from Dauntsey's, hit 993 runs.

Dover College *Kent* — P8 W2 L6 A3

Master i/c G. R. Hill

Despite infrequent victories, Dover's captain, Rupesh Punone, fostered an enthusiastic spirit in a team containing only a few sixth-formers.

Batting The leading batsman was T. L. Douglas, who hit 111 runs at 18.50.

Bowling R. P. Sewell 10 at 16.60.

Dulwich College *Surrey* — P20 W10 L8 T1 D1

Master i/c D. C. Shirazi — **Coach** C. W. J. Athey

Results were mixed – crushing defeats by St Paul's and Whitgift were followed by a tie against MCC and a thumping victory over Taunton School – but the overall picture was positive. Jake Scarisbrick led the batting, while Harry Millett and Joshua Simpson were incisive with the ball.

Batting *J. H. Scarisbrick 640 at 33.68; O. G. A. Sofolarin 320 at 29.09; M. H. L. Tidmarsh 245 at 27.22; M. B. P. Faulkner 288 at 22.15; S. G. A. Fetherston 418 at 22.00; L. B. Wilson 394 at 20.73.

Bowling J. T. Stone 10 at 16.80; H. J. M. Millett 40 at 17.60; J. W. H. Simpson 26 at 17.61; H. D. B. Loynes 22 at 23.63; O. G. A. Sofolarin 14 at 25.85; H. J. M. Pearce 16 at 29.31.

Durham School *County Durham* — P17 W11 L6 A4

Master i/c M. B. Fishwick

Outstanding teamwork delivered 11 victories, before an enjoyable tour of Sri Lanka. In a side defined by their electric fielding, Sol Bell's dynamism stood out.

Batting S. J. D. Bell 353 at 39.22; *J. A. O'Brien 361 at 32.81; C. M. Fyfe 358 at 27.53; J. Bushnell 175 at 25.00; W. D. Jewitt 189 at 21.00; D. T. Scott 204 at 20.40.

Bowling C. M. Fyfe 23 at 11.65; L. R. Dinsdale 14 at 12.71; D. T. Scott 19 at 13.15; S. M. E. North 17 at 15.76; J. S. Megginson 17 at 17.29.

Eastbourne College *Sussex* — P26 W20 L6 A1

Master i/c R. S. Ferley — **Coach** A. C. Waller

An exceptional bowling unit delivered a school-record 20 wins for the season. They dismissed ten teams for under 100, with six bowlers taking 23 wickets or more.

Batting B. S. Twine 713 at 37.52; *W. T. Huchu 580 at 32.22; C. Edwards 308 at 30.80; B. C. M. McIntosh 561 at 29.52; O. J. Carter 559 at 29.42; J. A. Pocklington 416 at 26.00; J. W. Casebourne 238 at 18.30; G. H. P. Skinner 181 at 10.64.

Bowling B. S. Twine 35 at 11.54; J. A. Pocklington 32 at 13.15; L. J. Barron 25 at 13.40; J. W. Casebourne 25 at 15.04; W. T. Huchu 23 at 15.13; B. C. M. McIntosh 25 at 16.48; O. J. Carter 10 at 17.70; G. H. P. Skinner 11 at 18.09.

Edinburgh Academy *Midlothian* P11 W2 L8 D1 A5

Master i/c R. W. Sales

Edinburgh flattered to deceive. Their bowling was strong but, without enough support from the batsmen, they lost numerous matches they had in their grasp.

Batting H. J. O'Brien 163 at 18.11.

Bowling *F. D. N. Carmichael 14 at 18.00; J. Mann 17 at 20.11; S. H. I. Bell 12 at 24.50; C. D. Woodward 10 at 24.90.

Elizabeth College, Guernsey *Channel Islands* P16 W6 L10 A2

Master i/c T. Eisenhuth

From the final ball of the season, Elizabeth College needed two runs to beat Melbourne Grammar School, with one wicket in hand. The batsman missed and was run out at the non-striker's end, handing the tourists a thrilling victory. Still, a 200-strong crowd of parents and pupils had never been prouder.

Batting N. C. Guilbert 558 at 34.87; D. N. Le Messurier 346 at 24.71; *A. C. Stokes 336 at 24.00; N. M. Hutchinson 214 at 19.45.

Bowling D. N. Le Messurier 11 at 19.00; R. J. Guilbert 18 at 19.22; N. M. Le Tissier 18 at 20.77.

Ellesmere College *Shropshire* P12 W6 L4 D2

Master i/c G. Owen **Coach** R. Jones

Strength in depth enabled Ellesmere to remain competitive throughout a substantial friendly programme, the cup competitions and the examination period. With the majority returning, the future looks promising.

Batting I. Gangwani 212 at 53.00; C. A. Davies 309 at 51.50; *S. J. C. Ellis 273 at 39.00.

Bowling C. A. Davies 17 at 13.76; H. J. Newton 15 at 13.80.

Eltham College *Kent* P17 W8 L8 D1 A2

Master i/c J. L. Baldwin **Coach** Yasir Arafat

The First XI were almost unchanged from 2016, and won all but one of their Saturday fixtures. Sam Smith captained the side impressively and scored 455 runs, while Dom Lester, Nico Murlowski and Irvine Turner were key all-rounders.

Batting I. Turner 333 at 47.57; N. C. Murlowski 372 at 41.33; *S. Smith 455 at 28.43; D. J. Lester 225 at 22.50; J. O. M. Williams 224 at 20.36; A. J. L. Khanna 240 at 18.46.

Bowling J. A. Smith 21 at 15.00; D. J. Lester 26 at 15.19; I. Turner 19 at 18.15; N. C. Murlowski 14 at 21.28; T. Gallo 11 at 24.00.

Emanuel School *Surrey* P12 W6 L6

Master i/c T. Gwynne **Coach** M. G. Stear

A young team were quick to meet the demands of First XI cricket, and recorded notable victories over Alleyn's and Kingston Grammar School. Callum and Nancy Hughes, brother and sister, played in the same side.

Batting S. K. Mahmud 305 at 27.72; I. P. Barker 255 at 23.18; *T. P. S. Lelean 197 at 17.90.

Bowling C. W. Hughes 10 at 14.70; I. P. Barker 15 at 19.33; R. C. Hawken 10 at 21.40; B. S. Emery-Dickinson 11 at 25.63.

Epsom College *Surrey* P19 W13 L6

Master i/c N. R. Taylor

After a difficult start, Epsom won ten of their last 12. Andrew McCallum hit a century, and Ed Hughes struck two, while captain Liam Head was outstanding: he took 39 wickets with his slow left-arm, including three five-fors.

Batting E. D. Hughes 725 at 55.76; A. W. McCallum 577 at 36.06; *L. A. Head 440 at 33.84; B. R. J. Mitchell 286 at 23.83; B. E. Holder 220 at 20.00; A. M. Koep 189 at 13.50; F. B. Savill 174 at 13.38.

Bowling L. A. Head 39 at 10.10; E. Rumble 18 at 17.77; A. J. Lawrence 20 at 18.05; C. E. Lansdown 19 at 18.73; A. W. McCallum 15 at 20.40; B. E. Holder 13 at 30.92.

Eton College *Buckinghamshire* P20 W8 L8 D4

Master i/c T. M. Roberts **Coach** R. D. Oliphant-Callum

Tom Gnodde and Hector Hardman stood out with two centuries each, while Hardman, James Gammell and George Pearson led the bowling.

Batting T. R. W. Gnodde 797 at 39.85; *J. H. R. I. Hardman 681 at 35.84; T. C. Prentis 578 at 34.00; B. M. Elias 448 at 32.00; T. W. T. Loup 231 at 25.66; W. D. G. Lowther 204 at 25.50; O. C. B. Bradley 351 at 21.93.

Bowling J. H. R. I. Hardman 35 at 21.57; G. B. S. Pearson 42 at 22.45; J. W. Gammell 20 at 25.30; C. D. G. Penny 10 at 29.80; O. C. B. Bradley 14 at 38.21.

Felsted School *Essex* P18 W9 L6 D3

Master i/c J. E. R. Gallian **Coaches** C. S. Knightley, A. Mohindru and N. J. Lockhart

Felsted improved as the summer progressed, winning nine of their 18 games. Sam Holland captained adroitly, and chipped in with useful runs and wickets.

Batting J. M. Cox 734 at 61.16; J. H. Burslem 486 at 30.37; *S. R. Holland 395 at 26.33; W. E. L. Buttleman 181 at 22.62; C. S. Latham 202 at 22.44; O. W. S. Hills 169 at 21.12; J. O. King 153 at 13.90.

Bowling J. O. King 33 at 20.24; S. R. Holland 13 at 22.00; O. W. S. Hills 23 at 27.34; J. P. A. V. Hoile 14 at 27.78.

Fettes College *Midlothian* P13 W9 L2 D2 A3

Master i/c A. B. Russell

It was another rewarding season for Fettes: they retained the Scottish Schools T20 Cup in some style, and lost only two matches. George West and George Conner provided the bulk of the runs, while a varied and skilful attack were too strong for most sides.

Batting G. G. Conner 423 at 70.50; *G. J. West 483 at 60.37; H. S. Paterson 150 at 25.00; R. A. Edwards 187 at 23.37; N. J. Miller 160 at 16.00.

Bowling G. J. West 12 at 11.16; B. J. Thompson 14 at 12.28; B. G. Sperling 19 at 14.05; B. M. Macleod 10 at 25.20.

Forest School *Essex* P15 W5 L10

Master i/c S. J. Foulds **Coach** J. S. Foster

Without any Year 13s, there was a shortage of runs, but Forest School had a love of the game and a strong team ethic. Three of their defeats were by four runs or fewer.

Batting D. Leung 201 at 25.12; E. J. Risby 279 at 23.25; J. J. Coghlan 300 at 23.07; *T. H. Kelsey 209 at 19.00.

Bowling J. B. O'Callaghan 13 at 16.76; T. H. Kelsey 15 at 19.46; O. Ashraf 22 at 19.54; E. J. Risby 16 at 24.37; A. Ragutharan 11 at 26.81.

Framlingham College *Suffolk* P18 W9 L7 T1 D1

Master i/c M. J. Marvell **Coach** S. D. Greenall

Ben Boyden's side proved the most competitive in years, winning seven more games than in 2016. Harrison Stiles and the Heldreich brothers provided the cutting edge, while Rob Taylor and Josh Lecompte scored runs with panache. But it was a team effort: nine hit fifties.

Batting R. M. Taylor 508 at 36.28; J. Lecompte 431 at 35.91; J. L. Hobbs 463 at 28.93; *B. A. M. Boyden 413 at 24.29; H. O. J. Finbow 334 at 23.85; H. Bureau 160 at 22.85; O. H. Ellis 231 at 19.25; W. J. H. Donsworth 255 at 17.00.

Bowling F. Heldreich 23 at 19.82; H. Stiles 28 at 20.50; G. W. Heldreich 20 at 26.40; H. Bureau 14 at 34.57.

George Heriot's School *Midlothian* P8 W2 L6

Master i/c E. L. Harrison

An inexperienced team led by Priyanshu Agarwal fought hard, but recorded only two victories.

Batting The leading batsman was *P. Agarwal, who hit 128 runs at 18.28.

Bowling D. D. Blood 11 at 13.45.

George Watson's College *Midlothian* P16 W9 L7 A2

Master i/c M. J. Leonard **Coach** A. D. W. Patterson

Among some mixed performances, there were memorable one-run victories over Loretto School and Merchiston Castle. Tom Counsell captained with aplomb, Callum Martin's new-ball bowling was exceptional, and Sarah Bryce showed class behind the stumps.

Batting *T. D. Counsell 355 at 25.35; M. A. Brian 314 at 20.93; C. J. Macdonald 264 at 18.85; M. K. Whitaker 173 at 15.72; C. J. Martin 182 at 13.00.
Bowling P. M. Brown 18 at 15.77; J. L. Milligan 16 at 16.56; C. J. Martin 21 at 23.19; O. J. Snodgrass 13 at 23.84; M. A. Brian 10 at 29.80.

Giggleswick School *Yorkshire* P11 W4 L6 D1 A3

Master i/c R. T. F. Bunday
Giggleswick bowled and fielded well throughout the summer, but results might have been better had the batsmen converted starts into significant scores.
Batting E. A. Leech 260 at 32.50; *A. C. E. Hancock 217 at 31.00; H. G. Milton 217 at 19.72.
Bowling T. W. Lothian 13 at 18.15.

The Glasgow Academy *Lanarkshire* P8 W7 L1 A3

Master i/c P. J. W. Smith **Coach** V Hariharan
The First Xl enjoyed their best season in recent history, with just a single defeat. Excellent teamwork was the bedrock, but the pre-season tour to South Africa, Ruairidh Russell's leadership and John Oliver's outstanding batting – he averaged 122 – were all important factors.
Batting J. L. Oliver 367 at 122.33; *R. G. Russell 206 at 51.50; R. S. Heginbottom 241 at 48.20.
Bowling J. R. Percival 16 at 9.56; J. L. Oliver 10 at 16.50.

The High School of Glasgow *Lanarkshire* P9 W1 L7 D1 A3

Master i/c D. N. Barrett **Coach** K. J. A. Robertson
The High School of Glasgow never quite managed to realise their evident potential, and won just once. But there were encouraging signs for the future, with Year 9 pupil John Greene acquitting himself well in his debut season.
Batting The leading batsman was *A. M. FitzGerald, who hit 143 runs at 15.88.
Bowling The leading bowler was J. A. Greene, who took nine wickets at 27.11.

Gordonstoun School *Morayshire* P7 W2 L4 D1

Master i/c R. Denyer
Gordonstoun looked to Ishaq Raheel for inspiration – he led the batting and bowling – but there were strong performances elsewhere, including the keeping of 13-year-old Gabriel Gallmann-Findlay.
Batting *M. I. S. Raheel 209 at 29.85.
Bowling M. I. S. Raheel 13 at 19.53.

Gresham's School *Norfolk* P18 W6 L8 D4 A1

Master i/c D. J. Atkinson **Coaches** A. Horsley and C. Brown
Six victories represented a 50% improvement on 2016. Hudson de Lucchi hit two hundreds, while Tatenda Chiradza, Davis Murwendo and Kieran Peters took the lion's share of the wickets.
Batting W. G. Buckingham 367 at 30.58; H. A. de Lucchi 474 at 27.88; M. N. W. Skerritt 193 at 27.57; *T. Chiradza 412 at 27.46; D. Murwendo 209 at 20.90; K. T. Peters 267 at 20.53; A. Taylor 296 at 17.41.
Bowling T. Chiradza 23 at 14.91; W. G. Buckingham 10 at 18.80; K. T. Peters 26 at 20.30; D. Murwendo 22 at 22.54; H. A. de Lucchi 12 at 23.75; C. A. G. Douds 16 at 29.00.

Haberdashers' Aske's Boys' School *Hertfordshire* P20 W10 L8 D2 A3

Master i/c S. D. Charlwood **Coaches** D. H. Kerry and J. P. Hewitt
Haberdashers' batting was frail at times, but ended on a high note when captain Jordan Urban's undefeated century led a successful chase against Devon Under-16. His deputy, Naresh Rasakulasuriar, bowled with hostility to finish as leading wicket-taker, and now has 80 for the First XI.
Batting *J. H. Urban 590 at 42.14; S. W. Kaye 381 at 25.40; F. J. Wright 416 at 24.47; V. Jegatheesan 280 at 23.33; N. Rasakulasuriar 358 at 22.37; A. S. Lakhani 375 at 20.83.
Bowling N. Rasakulasuriar 29 at 14.72; A. S. Lakhani 17 at 21.52; N. N. Chavda 20 at 22.45; S. D. Shah 22 at 28.36; F. J. Wright 11 at 32.90; G. N. Lawrence 10 at 38.00.

Haileybury *Hertfordshire* P13 W4 L7 D2 A1

Master i/c D. L. S. van Bunge **Coach** C. E. Igolen-Robinson
Victories over Bishop's Stortford and Berkhamsted were highlights, as was the two-day game against Cheltenham College, where Andrew Neal and Ben Morris batted four hours to secure a draw. That fighting spirit was evident throughout the season.

Batting A. J. Neal 375 at 41.66; J. C. Stibbs 412 at 29.42; B. W. Morris 274 at 22.83; *O. M. Heazel 267 at 22.25; K. O. Roomans 190 at 19.00.
Bowling A. J. Neal 21 at 15.76; J. E. Bridge 13 at 16.15; A. J. Kenton 10 at 19.00; I. K. Shah 10 at 34.90.

Hampton School *Middlesex* P20 W14 L4 D2 A2

Master i/c A. M. Banerjee **Coach** C. P. Harrison

It was a season to remember, with star performers everywhere. Cole Campbell hit 935 runs, with three hundreds, and Todd Ryan smashed a school-record 206*. Joe Wheeler also shone, collecting two five-wicket hauls in his first season.
Batting C. R. Campbell 935 at 71.92; T. M. Ryan 845 at 46.94; G. P. A. Gregory 202 at 40.40; M. H. Starling 186 at 31.00; B. C. Cullen 254 at 28.22; A. J. Lee 330 at 25.38; *C. J. Searle 325 at 25.00; J. F. D. Wheeler 243 at 20.25; O. T. George 211 at 17.58.
Bowling C. J. Searle 12 at 10.25; J. F. D. Wheeler 30 at 13.66; L. O. Minshull 27 at 14.33; B. C. Cullen 20 at 15.60; W. J. Christophers 23 at 18.91; M. H. Starling 27 at 19.51.

Harrow School *Middlesex* P21 W13 L7 D1

Master i/c R. S. C. Martin-Jenkins **Coach** S. A. Jones

After three early-season defeats, Harrow won 11 all-day games on the trot, including a six-wicket victory over Eton at Lord's. Rahul Wijeratne's batting was imperious at times, while George Reid was leading wicket-taker, despite not switching to left-arm seam until the winter.
Batting *R. S. Wijeratne 713 at 41.94; G. F. Reid 424 at 35.33; J. M. C. Bowie 192 at 24.00; F. G. Hall 258 at 23.45; M. W. Ayliffe 187 at 23.37; H. H. Dicketts 392 at 23.05; A. P. Ferreira 369 at 21.70.
Bowling G. F. Reid 20 at 20.00; R. Shah 17 at 20.05; H. J. S. Maxwell 19 at 21.36; A. E. W. Maxwell 10 at 26.40; R. S. Wijeratne 20 at 27.00; W. A. Falcon 15 at 29.33; C. S. Boland 11 at 41.54.

The Harvey Grammar School *Kent* P7 W6 L1

Master i/c P. M. Castle

Captained by Harry Wren, son of former Kent seamer Tim, the team played attacking cricket, and lost just once.
Batting J. McVittie 153 at 51.00; N. L. Ward 232 at 38.66; *H. Wren 189 at 31.50.
Bowling N. L. Ward 13 at 7.84; J. P. Woodward 11 at 8.72; H. Wren 10 at 9.30.

Highgate School *Middlesex* P10 W5 L5

Master i/c A. G. Tapp **Coach** A. Igaa

Under the astute captaincy of Dan Marshall, Highgate won the Under-19 Middlesex Cup Final.
Batting *D. P. Marshall 252 at 31.50.
Bowling O. G. H. Everitt 11 at 18.00.

Hurstpierpoint College *Sussex* P23 W14 L9

Master i/c N. J. K. Creed **Coaches** J. P. Anyon and P. G. Hudson

Hurstpierpoint reached the final of the Sussex T20 Cup, where they were overpowered by Bede's. Tom Haines, who had made his first-class debut for Sussex in September 2016, topped the averages in both suits, while Will Collard played for the county's Second XI.
Batting *T. J. Haines 860 at 53.75; J. A. J. Wood 734 at 36.70; R. J. M. Whyte 379 at 29.15; T. L. Heath 243 at 27.00; M. L. Robinson 241 at 26.77; J. S. Gilligan 434 at 25.52; V. A. Lawson 221 at 22.10.
Bowling T. J. Haines 24 at 17.33; W. C. H. P. Collard 32 at 18.28; J. A. J. Wood 21 at 23.80; H. N. Grayston 10 at 36.20; J. W. Brehaut 11 at 43.36.

Hymers College *Yorkshire* P15 W6 L8 D1 A2

Master i/c G. Tipping

Hymers had no outstanding player, but lots of effort and the skilful leadership of Alfie Juckes helped them to six victories.
Batting S. J. Elstone 427 at 35.58; A. R. F. Brocklesby 268 at 19.14; B. L. Renwick 210 at 17.50; H. T. F. Marsden 227 at 17.46.
Bowling S. J. Elstone 19 at 20.15; W. J. Atkinson 12 at 20.91; *A. J. Juckes 17 at 21.11; B. L. Renwick 15 at 23.53.

Ibstock Place School *Surrey* P10 W2 L4 T2 D2 A1

Master i/c R. S. Brown **Coach** M. W. Costin

Olivia Daniels, who became the first girl to play for the First XI, and Emma Tyson were selected by the Surrey Emerging Players Programme. They led Ibstock Place's strong performances in the county cup competitions.

Batting C. Rattigan 215 at 35.83; O. Welton 231 at 25.66.

Bowling *D. Jago 10 at 16.20.

Ipswich School *Suffolk* P16 W10 L5 D1 A1

Master i/c A. K. Golding

Ten victories and success at the Brentwood School festival constituted a good summer. Josh Rymell and Joe MacGregor provided reliable runs and wickets, backed up by useful contributions from Luke Froggatt and Finn O'Reilly.

Batting G. A. Frettingham 166 at 83.00; *J. S. Rymell 750 at 75.00; J. L. H. MacGregor 656 at 72.88; W. A. J. Froggatt 175 at 21.87; L. R. C. Froggatt 235 at 21.36.

Bowling F. T. O'Reilly 19 at 15.73; J. S. Rymell 22 at 21.81; J. L. H. MacGregor 16 at 25.62; L. R. C. Froggatt 13 at 34.38.

John Hampden Grammar School *Buckinghamshire* P13 W3 L9 D1 A3

Master i/c S. K. Parbery

The highlight of the season was a high-scoring draw against local rivals RGS High Wycombe. Opening batsman Will Shepherd scored consistently, including three half-centuries.

Batting W. M. Shepherd 292 at 36.50; *W. A. Kidd 176 at 16.00; N. A. Dearsley 154 at 15.40.

Bowling F. R. B. Harmen 10 at 15.10.

The John Lyon School *Middlesex* P16 W6 L7 T1 D2

Master i/c A. S. Ling **Coach** C. T. Peploe

The results were mixed, but there were glimpses of excellence – including a well-deserved draw against MCC, and Jash Gandhi's century. Abhay Hirani led the batting, with 436 runs, while Owen Marshall reached 50 First XI wickets.

Batting A. Hirani 436 at 39.63; J. V. Gandhi 303 at 27.54; A. Mirzai 267 at 24.27; R. V. Luthra 169 at 18.77.

Bowling J. C. R. Francis 18 at 15.61; *O. J. Marshall 21 at 22.33; Z. Mahmood 15 at 27.80; C. A. O. Rashid 11 at 30.81.

The Judd School *Kent* P11 W2 L9 A1

Master i/c R. M. Richardson

The team were led superbly by Owen Tucker and his vice-captain Callum Gallagher, but struggled for victories. Over 30 students represented the First XI.

Batting D. B. A. Howel 151 at 18.87.

Bowling The leading bowler was T. B. Barnes, who took eight wickets at 11.12.

Kimbolton School *Huntingdonshire* P17 W7 L9 D1

Master i/c M. S. Gilbert **Coach** A. J. Tudor

There were a host of excellent Kimbolton School performers in 2017: Alec Bryden hit two centuries, fast bowler David Adesida took 23 wickets, and spinner Chris Oliver 22. But Joshua Smith eclipsed them all with 1,020 runs – including four centuries – and 32 wickets for his off-spin.

Batting J. J. Smith 1,020 at 78.46; A. M. Bryden 383 at 23.93; J. P. Wilkins 246 at 17.57; C. W. Jennings 170 at 14.16; A. C. Kenyon 220 at 13.75; *H. W. B. Peak 181 at 12.06.

Bowling J. J. Smith 32 at 13.71; D. O. Adesida 23 at 16.17; C. M. Oliver 22 at 22.22; A. R. Carroll 10 at 25.60; J. E. Oliver 12 at 26.00.

King Edward VI School, Southampton *Hampshire* P15 W10 L4 D1

Master i/c D. Kent **Coach** A. D. Penn

An excellent team ethic helped earn ten victories – seven more than in 2016. The best came against Portsmouth GS and Lancing, both bowled out cheaply, and Bryanston, in a cracking game.

Batting G. W. V. McKenzie 564 at 56.40; J. Dhariwal 240 at 34.28; J. Z. Khan 159 at 22.71; T. J. Smart 235 at 19.58; F. H. M. Davies 192 at 19.20; B. M. D. Millar 191 at 17.36; E. X. Sharpe 191 at 17.36; J. L. Fay 156 at 17.33.

Bowling *A. S. M. Damley-Jones 18 at 14.00; J. L. Fay 19 at 16.31; G. W. V. McKenzie 26 at 17.84; A. A. P. Millar 15 at 22.26.

Elijah Samuel in full flow for Marlborough; Joshua Smith topped both averages at Kimbolton.

King Edward's School, Birmingham *Warwickshire* P19 W10 L8 D1 A1

Master i/c L. M. Roll **Coach** N. W. Round

In their final game for the school, Tarush Gupta and Josh Ray hit their maiden First XI hundreds, and put on 255 for the second wicket, a school record. Eleven players from Year 11 played for the seniors, hinting at a bright future.

Batting J. S. Ray 543 at 54.30; *T. Gupta 396 at 39.60; A. Hussain 484 at 34.57; T. R. Kulkarni 285 at 25.90; S. S. Mangat 247 at 24.70.

Bowling S. Harle 13 at 10.46; T. R. Kulkarni 19 at 21.10; S. C. Johnstone 18 at 22.83; V. A. Sriram 14 at 28.71; F. A. R. Abbott Black 14 at 29.57.

King's College School, Wimbledon *Surrey* P25 W12 L10 D3 A2

Master i/c J. S. Gibson **Coach** P. J. Scott

From a large squad, two players stood out: Under-16 Sanjay Patel scored 864 runs, while Alex Spencer took 29 wickets and was named Player of the Season. Jake Hennessey, the captain, finished with over 70 First XI appearances, and more than 1,500 runs.

Batting S. H. Patel 864 at 48.00; *J. J. S. Hennessey 585 at 30.78; A. Hughes 208 at 26.00; A. R. Pillai 229 at 22.90; O. C. D. Little 469 at 22.33; A. J. R. Kinsella 241 at 21.90; A. S. Bond 342 at 20.11; A. G. Spencer 180 at 18.00; F. M. Bennett 187 at 14.38.

Bowling M. S. Chelvam 16 at 16.68; A. R. Pillai 16 at 18.68; D. Harish 11 at 19.27; A. G. Spencer 29 at 19.68; P. W. Barton 17 at 24.35; S. H. Patel 12 at 25.50; R. E. Woodcock 21 at 25.80; G. A. V. Betts 17 at 26.58.

King's College, Taunton *Somerset* P16 W12 L4 A4

Master i/c P. D. Lewis **Coach** R. J. Woodman

Nearly 20 players got a taste of First XI cricket during another successful summer. Tom Banton was outstanding again and appeared for Somerset, James Clark picked up his 100th wicket, and William Smeed, a 15-year-old batsman, was prolific.

Batting *T. Banton 462 at 66.00; W. Smeed 449 at 56.12; J. T. H. Scrivens 395 at 39.50; L. Machado 289 at 36.12; S. G. Wyatt 323 at 29.36.

Bowling J. L. S. Clark 33 at 11.48; J. H. Gibbs 26 at 11.61; K. B. Szymanski 23 at 15.60; E. W. O. Middleton 16 at 24.81.

King's School, Bruton *Somerset* P11 W6 L4 D1 A1

Master i/c R. S. Hamilton **Coach** M. Davies

Despite scant experience, King's Bruton won more than they lost, and finished the season with four victories on the bounce.

Batting A. L. Harman 317 at 31.70; T. S. D. Woods 251 at 27.88; T. A. G. Rogers 186 at 18.60; *B. J. Latham 200 at 18.18; T. Williams 176 at 17.60.

Bowling A. L. Harman 22 at 17.77; S. Houldsworth 13 at 17.92; I. J. Elms 11 at 22.36; B. J. Latham 13 at 22.76.

The King's School, Canterbury *Kent* P19 W5 L13 D1 A1

Master i/c R. A. L. Singfield **Coach** M. A. Ealham

After many of the successful 2016 vintage left, this was a difficult season. Matthew Barker led the side well, and topped the averages with bat and ball.

Batting *M. D. Barker 753 at 39.63; R. P. Heywood 372 at 19.57; G. W. R. Meddings 162 at 16.20; S. Ravishankar 243 at 15.18; W. J. Oates 272 at 15.11; I. A. Rahman 204 at 14.57.

Bowling M. D. Barker 22 at 16.45; G. Howard Smith 12 at 17.16; R. Heywood 16 at 26.00; T. Edgar 10 at 29.60.

The King's School, Chester *Cheshire* P12 W5 L6 D1

Master i/c S. Neal **Coach** J. Potts

At either end of the season, captain Matthew Thompson and his opening partner Sheil Sethi hit magnificent unbeaten hundreds. Frazer Marsden's five for 48 against Gentlemen of Cheshire was the best of the bowling.

Batting *M. J. Thompson 412 at 51.50; S. Sethi 459 at 51.00; S. E. Thompson 203 at 22.55.

Bowling F. W. Marsden 11 at 19.00; S. E. Thompson 12 at 19.33; O. F. Jones 11 at 25.00.

The King's School in Macclesfield *Cheshire* P15 W6 L9 A5

Master i/c S. Moores **Coach** A. Kennedy

Statistically, it wasn't the best season, as flimsy batting left the team struggling. But Oliver Quinn's side enjoyed themselves, particularly Harry Elms, who claimed 30 wickets.

Batting A. J. Thomson 183 at 20.33; H. H. S. Elms 218 at 19.81; *O. J. Quinn 255 at 19.61; S. S. Crosby 182 at 16.54; S. J. Buckingham 192 at 16.00; O. R. Jones 207 at 14.78.

Bowling H. H. S. Elms 30 at 14.10; J. B. Bryning 23 at 16.91; F. J. B. Calder 14 at 21.42.

King's School, Rochester *Kent* P13 W2 L11 A3

Master i/c C. H. Page **Coaches** J. Waite and D. A. Saunders

Just two victories, the same as 2016, might have suggested a lack of progress, but the bigger picture was brighter: King's Rochester scored far more runs, and competed much more fiercely. James Carslaw bowled well all season and topped the averages, while Tom Miles and Tobey Castle – neither of whom were in sixth form – provided the bulk of the runs.

Batting T. J. Miles 445 at 44.50; T. D. J. Castle 310 at 34.44; *J. W. Carslaw 235 at 23.50; T. D. Hafeez 150 at 15.00.

Bowling J. W. Carslaw 20 at 13.25; T. J. Miles 16 at 24.31.

Kingswood School, Bath *Somerset* P16 W9 L7 A1

Master i/c J. O. Brown

The team exceeded expectations, proving themselves a resilient unit. The opening pair of Tommy Phillips, who made five fifties, and Joe Han-Hauser were integral, as were the all-round contributions of Al Mackenzie and Henry Brearey.

Batting *T. A. Phillips 393 at 30.23; H. R. Brearey 316 at 28.72; H. J. Walker 288 at 20.57; J. Han-Hauser 281 at 20.07; O. B. Parry 257 at 19.76; J. Taylor 155 at 19.37.

Bowling C. Patterson 16 at 12.56; A. F. G. Mackenzie 22 at 13.54; T. A. Phillips 16 at 15.37; H. R. Brearey 21 at 16.09; H. E. Hodges 14 at 22.57.

Kirkham Grammar School *Lancashire* P12 W2 L8 D2

Master i/c J. R. Lyon

Kirkham were led with maturity by Edward Bailey, the only leaver, and there were consistent performances from Nathan Pope with bat and ball.

Batting J. Thomson 195 at 39.00; *E. J. Bailey 239 at 29.87; N. Pope 160 at 22.85.

Bowling The leading bowler was C. Partington, who took nine wickets at 14.66.

Lancaster Royal Grammar School *Lancashire* P15 W6 L9 A3

Master i/c I. W. Ledward **Coaches** G. A. J. Mason and I. Perryman

Captain Laurie Atkinson gave the younger players opportunity to develop. An impressive win over MCC in April was followed by victories over QEGS Wakefield and Woodhouse Grove; two more came in the RGS Festival. Rohan Parekh was the leading bowler, while Callum Robinson-Brooks and Ruairidh Barker hit centuries.

Batting R. N. Barker 407 at 31.30; *L. J. Atkinson 401 at 28.64; A. N. Grunshaw 212 at 21.20; C. J. Robinson-Brooks 262 at 18.71; J. A. Wills 202 at 15.53.

Bowling R. V. Parekh 24 at 17.75; L. J. Atkinson 17 at 19.94; G. J. Marshall 12 at 31.66; R. N. Barker 12 at 39.83.

Lancing College *Sussex* P12 W6 L5 D1 A2

Master i/c R. J. Maru

Oliver John led from the front with bat and ball. Though results were mixed, the majority of this side will be back in 2018, and better for the experience.

Batting J. L. Dawling 181 at 60.33; *O. J. John 431 at 39.18; F. Desjarlais 154 at 22.00.

Bowling W. H. Edgeler 14 at 12.64; M. G. E. Lee 22 at 14.86; A. Symonds 14 at 17.00; O. J. John 18 at 17.16.

The Grammar School at Leeds *Yorkshire* P11 W4 L4 D3 A5

Master i/c S. H. Dunn **Coach** A. Dobson

A season that promised so much was handicapped by exam pressure and poor weather. Openers Eitan Litvin and Ollie Robinson had another solid season, but there was not enough consistency in the middle order, nor bite with the ball.

Batting E. B. Litvin 440 at 62.85; *O. F. J. Robinson 243 at 34.71; J. C. M. Dracup 194 at 27.71.

Bowling B. Wyard 12 at 13.66; T. B. Burton 13 at 20.76.

Leicester Grammar School *Leicestershire* P12 W6 L5 D1

Master i/c L. Potter

Leicester Grammar School recorded fine wins over Stowe and Oundle, and captain James Hunt left on a high.

Batting *J. A. Hunt 206 at 34.33; J. A. Scudamore 211 at 23.44; H. Pounds 152 at 21.71; R. Spencer 150 at 21.42; D. R. Scudamore 154 at 19.25.

Bowling H. Pounds 12 at 11.00; J. A. Hunt 11 at 18.27; D. R. Scudamore 13 at 19.23; J. A. Scudamore 10 at 28.10.

The Leys School *Cambridgeshire* P15 W13 L2 A3

Master i/c R. I. Kaufman **Coach** W. J. Earl

The Leys had an outstanding season, winning 13 out of 15, and missing out on the last four of the National T20 competition by only one run, to Shrewsbury. Andrew Bramley, the captain, was the outstanding performer, with 803 runs and 25 wickets.

Batting *A. S. Bramley 803 at 73.00; W. A. Latham 257 at 36.71; M. J. I. Aubrey 315 at 26.25; T. S. Waldock 153 at 25.50; D. R. Hoole 157 at 17.44.

Bowling K. Krishnakumar 13 at 11.15; W. A. Latham 14 at 12.14; A. S. Bramley 25 at 12.24; T. S. Waldock 17 at 16.70; M. J. I. Aubrey 16 at 18.56; J. A. Gunn-Roberts 16 at 18.62; F. J. C. Tucker 12 at 19.33.

The Cathedral School, Llandaff *Glamorgan* P4 L3 D1

Master i/c M. G. Barrington **Coach** A. P. Thomas

The school's inaugural First XI season included a fixture against MCC, and entry into the National T20 competition. Richard Sen's leadership and two half-centuries deserved much credit.

Batting The leading batsman was *R. Sen, who hit 142 runs at 142.00.

Bowling The leading bowler was W. Youngs, who took five wickets at 23.60.

Lord Wandsworth College *Hampshire* P11 W6 L4 D1

Master i/c D. M. Beven

Charlie Young scored his maiden century in his final innings, and captained the team to more victories than defeats.

Batting *C. J. Young 373 at 46.62; W. W. Wyatt 174 at 34.80; J. A. Young 174 at 21.75; G. R. Walker 169 at 21.12.

Bowling S. M. Gilley 10 at 28.90.

Loughborough Grammar School *Leicestershire* P12 W6 L6

Master i/c M. I. Gidley

James O'Kelly and Ashish Trusz helped earn six victories, but unavailability scuppered greater success. Harry Bates was outstanding with the new ball.

Batting A. N. Trusz 450 at 56.25; J. W. O'Kelly 565 at 47.08; F. J. Towne 327 at 27.25; H. Bates 200 at 22.22.

Bowling H. Bates 18 at 14.88; C. G. Crowson 16 at 19.18; A. Bates 16 at 20.87.

Magdalen College School *Oxfordshire* P18 W11 L5 D2

Master i/c D. Bebbington **Coaches** A. J. Scriven and A. A. Duncan

Despite a challenging fixture list, Magdalen College School achieved a record number of victories. There were other records, too: against Stowe, they made 381 for nine declared, their highest total, and Ollie Price hit an unbeaten 167, an individual best.

Batting *T. J. Price 774 at 59.53; T. R. A. Scriven 339 at 56.50; O. J. Price 505 at 42.08; A. T. C. Higgins 214 at 23.77; A. T. Spittles 362 at 20.11; J. S. Moorman 197 at 14.07.

Bowling T. J. Price 28 at 14.03; A. P. S. Chapman 10 at 15.30; T. J. Brine 17 at 19.58; O. J. Price 20 at 20.00; T. N. S. Chesser 20 at 20.20.

Malvern College *Worcestershire* P22 W15 L5 D2

Master i/c M. A. Hardinges **Coach** N. A. Brett

Jack Haynes racked up four centuries, while brother Josh hit one in the final of the Chesterton Cup to lead Malvern to victory – just as he had done in 2016. Mahaaz Ahmed took most wickets, including seven for 38 against Bradfield.

Batting D. N. Holland 526 at 52.60; C. E. Lea 724 at 42.58; *J. A. Haynes 918 at 41.72; M. Ahmed 637 at 39.81; J. L. Haynes 257 at 36.71; W. D. Annetts 361 at 32.81; J. J. White 383 at 23.93; O. G. Garnett 317 at 22.64; A. Manur 172 at 21.50.

Bowling J. A. Haynes 14 at 17.71; J. P. O'Gorman 27 at 22.18; C. E. Lea 10 at 22.40; M. Ahmed 30 at 24.06; G. R. M. Amphlett 22 at 26.95; W. A. J. Sharp 21 at 32.28.

The Manchester Grammar School *Lancashire* P17 W13 L4 A1

Master i/c M. Watkinson

Following a five-match tour to South Africa, the school enjoyed success under the captaincy of Sam Perry, who scored over 1,000 runs, including five centuries. He drew support from all-rounders Ollie Pooler and Alec Makin. Leading bowlers George Poyser, Tom Robinson and George Valentine will return in 2018.

Batting *S. J. Perry 1,052 at 75.14; A. H. Makin 474 at 33.85; O. G. F. Pooler 307 at 30.70.

Bowling O. G. F. Pooler 12 at 10.50; S. J. Perry 15 at 15.66; G. J. Valentine 23 at 17.73; A. H. Makin 18 at 20.11; G. W. Poyser 22 at 21.31; T. N. Robinson 16 at 24.75.

Marlborough College *Wiltshire* P19 W11 L6 D2

Master i/c M. P. L. Bush **Coaches** M. W. Alleyne and J. P. Carroll

In a summer of ups and downs, captain Billy Mead became the first Marlburian to pass 1,000 runs since his great-uncle, former Sussex captain Mike Griffith, in 1961. Mead's 214* against Sherborne also broke the College's record. Fellow Hampshire youth player Elijah Samuel amassed 828 runs. Against Rugby at Lord's, Max Read stroked 141*, and David West took six for 57 in a 25-run victory.

Batting *S. W. Mead 1,009 at 63.06; E. I. Samuel 828 at 51.75; M. P. K. Read 603 at 46.38; D. A. West 195 at 27.85; J. A. R. Thistlethwayte 270 at 16.87; D. H. Coulson 212 at 16.30; J. M. Hodgskin 189 at 11.81.

Ollie Price made 167 not out, Magdalen College School's highest score; Brad Currie took 31 wickets for Millfield at under ten apiece.

Bowling S. W. Mead 18 at 19.27; W. P. Davies 19 at 23.31; J. G. Crossland 16 at 24.12; D. A. West 18 at 28.88; D. H. Coulson 15 at 31.53.

Merchant Taylors' School, Crosby *Lancashire* P19 W14 L5 A5

Master i/c S. P. Sutcliffe **Coach** J. Cole

The 2017 team equalled the school record for victories in a season; they were unbeaten in the inaugural North-West Merit Table, and hammered MCC by seven wickets. That was despite keeper-batsman George Lavelle's limited availability: he was regularly called up to Lancashire's Second XI.

Batting B. W. Aitchison 535 at 66.87; A. D. J. Rankin 539 at 59.88; I. Lea 475 at 36.53; *T. W. Hartley 235 at 33.57; K. T. Mahambrey 252 at 31.50; J. E. C. Hodkinson 177 at 16.09.

Bowling T. W. Hartley 17 at 14.17; A. Bassi 12 at 18.66; T. E. Barker-Weinberg 10 at 21.10; B. W. Aitchison 11 at 22.09; I. Lea 15 at 22.20; A. B. S. Soin 10 at 24.80; J. E. C. Hodkinson 11 at 27.00; E. L. Brown 11 at 32.81.

Merchant Taylors' School, Northwood *Hertfordshire* P20 W14 L4 D2 A1

Master i/c T. Webley

Merchant Taylors' reached finals day of the National T20 competition for the first time, and recorded superb victories over Whitgift and Tonbridge.

Batting A. L. Wijesuriya 502 at 55.77; D. J. Burnell 635 at 52.91; O. A. Karim 536 at 44.66; A. R. Amin 486 at 44.18; M. John 387 at 38.70; A. Palmer 480 at 36.92; *J. Regan 385 at 32.08.

Bowling A. R. Amin 29 at 13.31; A. K. Randev 20 at 14.85; A. L. Wijesuriya 26 at 15.23; M. John 24 at 15.50; S. Shah 18 at 15.83; J. Regan 22 at 16.18.

Merchiston Castle School *Midlothian* P13 W8 L5 A2

Master i/c R. D. McCann

After an exhilarating run to the final of the Scottish T20 Cup, Merchiston Castle slipped to 17 for seven batting first against Fettes, and never recovered.

Batting *A. N. N. Hinton 593 at 98.83.

Bowling C. T. Fullarton 14 at 14.64; H. A. Fisher 10 at 15.80; M. A. Currie 14 at 17.42.

Mill Hill School *Middlesex* P12 W9 L1 T1 D1

Master i/c S. Patel

A record nine victories included the first against MCC for 17 years. Ethan Bamber and Josh Drage were the obvious players of the season, but they couldn't have done it alone.

Batting J. Drage 409 at 58.42; *E. R. Bamber 285 at 35.62; W. Kilbourn 203 at 25.37; R. Hart-Badger 187 at 20.77.

Bowling E. R. Bamber 31 at 6.25; L. C. A. Vanaesebroeck 16 at 10.06; J. Lewis 11 at 13.72; M. G. Thal 13 at 17.92.

Millfield School *Somerset* P23 W16 L7

Master i/c M. Garaway **Coach** C. D. Gange

Millfield reached the final of the National T20 competition, where they lost to Sedbergh. Brad Currie led the attack magnificently with 31 wickets, Danny Chesham was an inspirational leader and Tom Bevan scored 749 runs in aggressive fashion.

Batting T. R. Bevan 749 at 46.81; M. E. W. Critchley 452 at 32.28; F. R. Trenouth 469 at 31.26; K. L. Aldridge 213 at 30.42; *D. Chesham 326 at 27.16; J. T. S. S. Sumerauer 186 at 20.66; A. J. Eckland 262 at 18.71; C. Clist 354 at 16.85; E. V. H. Dunning 237 at 15.80.

Bowling B. J. Currie 31 at 9.38; J. T. S. S. Sumerauer 24 at 20.25; E. V. H. Dunning 27 at 20.70; T. R. Bevan 19 at 31.57.

Monkton School *Somerset* P19 W6 L11 D2 A3

Master i/c S. P. J. Palmer **Coaches** M. C. Parfitt and J. C. A. Leggett

The side were well led by William Bishop, the sole Year 13, but brittle batting held them back. Only keeper Ben Wells scored heavily. The highlight was winning the inaugural Bath Schools T20 Cup.

Batting B. J. J. Wells 698 at 58.16; W. G. K. Arney 410 at 21.57; L. J. Walker 193 at 14.84; D. R. Call 235 at 14.68; *W. F. A. Bishop 230 at 12.10.

Bowling D. R. Call 21 at 19.71; L. J. Hunnisett 20 at 20.65; A. W. Parashar 22 at 22.04; O. A. A. Adeleye 18 at 25.94; L. J. Walker 10 at 27.20.

Monmouth School *Monmouthshire* P19 W11 L8 A1

Master i/c A. J. Jones **Coach** G. I. Burgess

Captain Ben Lander was excellent with bat and ball, but two younger players shone brightest. Nathan Lee, an Under-16, fell just short of 1,000 runs, while Under-14 leg-spinner Sam Swingwood topped the bowling averages.

Batting N. J. Lee 974 at 60.87; A. D. Mcintyre 488 at 28.70; *B. R. Lander 500 at 27.77; C. J. Mcintosh 369 at 21.70.

Bowling S. Swingwood 13 at 20.46; B. R. Lander 28 at 24.21; J. Bowden 14 at 25.85; I. M. Hodgson 11 at 26.72; L. O. Harrell 18 at 29.00; H. C. Badcock-Scruton 11 at 32.45.

Mount Kelly School *Devon* P16 W12 L4 A3

Master i/c G. D. James **Coach** T. Honey

Among several emphatic victories, back-to-back wins against Plymouth College were two to savour. Ben Grove captained valiantly, while Leon Horn scored 577 runs and took 20 wickets.

Batting L. Horn 577 at 57.70; A. S. Kopparambil 405 at 31.15; *B. G. Grove 360 at 30.00; M. J. Brady 165 at 20.62; E. C. Clarke 205 at 20.50; A. Creasey 168 at 14.00.

Bowling A. S. Kopparambil 14 at 11.85; L. Horn 20 at 15.30; T. J. Rogers 15 at 17.80; J. Staig 16 at 20.00.

New Hall School *Essex* P16 W7 L7 T1 D1

Master i/c P. M. Davidge

There were as many defeats as victories, but 2017 had much to recommend it: wins against Felsted, Kimbolton, The Perse and Haileybury, and school-record totals for T20 (227), 40-over (238), and 50-over matches (289). Nathan Khelawon shared double-century partnerships with Sean Sullivan and James Berry.

Batting *S. C. Sullivan 406 at 58.00; N. Khelawon 683 at 52.53; A. D. Berry 121 at 27.00; J. H. J. Berry 313 at 24.07; V. A. Gandhi 174 at 14.50.

Bowling A. D. Berry 14 at 18.85; N. Khelawon 11 at 27.54; V. A. Gandhi 19 at 27.63; J. P. Aggarwal 18 at 30.50.

Newcastle under Lyme School *Staffordshire* P17 W6 L10 D1 A1

Master i/c G. M. Breen **Coach** J. Dawson

Newcastle under Lyme reached the regional final of the National T20 Cup, but their form suffered in Saturday matches – they won just once. Leg-spinner Rhys Owens took 26 wickets, while keeper Joe Wagg averaged over 50, including 119 against The King's School in Macclesfield.

Batting J. H. Wagg 267 at 53.40; P. J. Vickers 313 at 39.12; R. G. Hesketh 162 at 23.14; J. M. Pokora 160 at 17.77.

Bowling R. C. Owens 26 at 16.23; O. J. Tinsley 22 at 18.68; P. J. Vickers 15 at 20.46; H. Ojha 11 at 29.54.

Norwich School *Norfolk* P17 W9 L5 D3

Master i/c J. L. O. Cawkwell **Coaches** D. R. Thomas, J. S. Gatting and R. W. Sims

Norwich had a strong summer, but for a few below-par performances. The outstanding trio of Oscar Binny, Thomas Harris and Charlie Rogers led the way.

Batting O. R. Binny 614 at 43.85; T. A. Harris 470 at 31.33; *A. J. H. Cooper 344 at 28.66; C. W. Rogers 219 at 24.33; W. P. Kidner 351 at 21.93; T. J. J. Murphy 181 at 18.10.

Bowling C. W. Rogers 30 at 16.36; A. B. Woodrow 11 at 24.81; A. J. H. Cooper 10 at 25.20; T. A. W. Hipper 13 at 29.23; O. R. Binny 11 at 33.81.

Nottingham High School *Nottinghamshire* P12 W3 L7 D2 A2

Master i/c M. Baker **Coach** P. M. Borrington

Nottingham High School experienced much frustration in 2017. But the batting of Hassan Chaudry, the new-ball dynamism of Jack Peirce and Haris Khalil, and the glovework of Deep Desai helped deliver three victories. Year 9 Ben Martindale, an exciting all-rounder, was a revelation.

Batting H. Chaudry 355 at 39.44; B. J. R. Martindale 233 at 29.12; D. D. Desai 197 at 21.88; *M. I. Ratchev 161 at 16.10.

Bowling J. W. Peirce 15 at 23.93; H. U. Khalil 15 at 28.06.

Oakham School *Rutland* P17 W12 L3 D2 A1

Master i/c N. C. Johnson **Coaches** F. C. Hayes, D. J. Bicknell and J. R. Tratt

A powerful side, captained for the third year running by Lyndon James, triumphed over Uppingham, Bedford, Felsted, Stowe, Oundle, Brighton and Sedbergh, with rain denying them probable victory over Stamford. Defeat by Wellington in the final match failed to colour a superb summer.

Batting *L. W. James 845 at 76.81; S. J. Wolstenholme 511 at 39.30; D. N. Butchart 392 at 30.15; A. W. Grieve 221 at 24.55; H. Merriman 207 at 18.81.

Bowling A. W. G. Jones 25 at 15.20; E. M. F. Tattersall 21 at 18.09; D. N. Butchart 26 at 19.69; L. W. James 15 at 21.00; W. Means 11 at 25.54.

The Oratory School *Oxfordshire* P14 W7 L5 D2

Master i/c S. C. B. Tomlinson

After a tough start, The Oratory gained momentum as the summer progressed. Craig Rintoul deserved credit for his mature leadership of a young team: over half came from Year 11.

Batting M. R. Williams 520 at 52.00; *C. Rintoul 420 at 38.18; J. K. Wallace 210 at 26.25; J. Winterbottom 170 at 18.88.

Bowling J. K. Wallace 19 at 12.00; J. M. Gallagher 17 at 14.11; J. Winterbottom 11 at 17.09.

Oswestry School *Shropshire* P15 W5 L9 D1 A3

Master i/c T. L. N. Root **Coach** D. P. Bradburne

After a single victory in 2016, five wins represented a dramatic improvement. James Wigley's captaincy helped the side beat Dover College and Rydal Penrhos, but they often lacked the confidence to close out tight games.

Batting T. Sithole 250 at 22.72; *J. Wigley 221 at 17.00; J. Thorpe 165 at 13.75; O. Woodward 151 at 13.72.

Bowling T. Sithole 15 at 15.06; J. Wigley 18 at 17.22; J. Thorpe 12 at 17.58; A. O. Edwards 11 at 19.90.

Oundle School *Northamptonshire* P16 W6 L7 D3

Master i/c J. P. Crawley **Coach** M. Genis

Against some excellent opposition, batsmen Simon Fernandes and Hugh Stanton shone, while wickets were shared around.

Batting S. M. L. Fernandes 628 at 44.85; W. H. D. Stanton 627 at 41.80; *C. L. Fernandes 324 at 23.14; O. P. T. Lawes 266 at 22.16; J. I. Esler 240 at 18.46.

Bowling T. J. Reyner 16 at 15.93; B. G. B. Stocks 15 at 19.93; F. E. D. Turner 18 at 23.66; J. I. Esler 22 at 24.50; S. M. L. Fernandes 12 at 30.08.

The Perse School *Cambridgeshire* P12 W2 L10 A2

Master i/c S. M. Park **Coach** J. Coleman

In a season containing just two victories, The Perse concentrated on development, blooding a host of promising individuals from the lower years. Sacha Abbasi and Zaman Akhter once again performed with distinction.

Batting N. V. Gorantla 197 at 49.25; Z. Akhter 387 at 43.00; *S. J. Abbasi 348 at 31.63; A. W. C. Lockie 244 at 24.40; J. O. V. Meakin 219 at 21.90.

Bowling Z. Akhter 14 at 22.92.

Pocklington School *Yorkshire* P19 W11 L7 D1 A3

Master i/c D. Byas

Pocklington's summer was a success, but better performances against Ampleforth and St Peter's would have made it a triumph. Jonty Atkinson shepherded the team astutely, and received excellent support from Lewis Medley and Adam Harrison.

Batting L. J. Medley 494 at 30.87; J. J. Atkinson 348 at 26.76; C. B. Foster 349 at 20.52.

Bowling L. J. Medley 14 at 16.00; H. E. Bayston 10 at 16.80; J. A. Wraith 19 at 18.10; R. Stephenson 12 at 27.08.

The Portsmouth Grammar School *Hampshire* P13 W7 L6

Master i/c S. J. Curwood **Coach** S. D. Lavery

Portsmouth Grammar's increasing depth allowed players to be rotated, without compromising performance in a competitive fixture list.

Batting O. T. Wright 366 at 40.66; C. E. Dean 151 at 37.75; S. G. Caldera 257 at 36.71; J. F. Kooner-Evans 195 at 27.85; D. T. Wallis 271 at 27.10; *D. J. Mugford 161 at 26.83; J. J. McBride 156 at 26.00; A. V. Willoughby 211 at 23.44.

Bowling J. F. Kooner-Evans 17 at 11.82; C. E. Dean 10 at 12.70; M. Beckett 11 at 14.63; D. T. Wallis 14 at 14.85; H. W. J. Hoolahan 12 at 16.33; G. Littlehales 10 at 16.60; D. J. Mugford 10 at 17.00.

Prior Park College *Somerset* P14 W5 L5 T1 D3 A1

Master i/c M. D. Bond **Coach** M. K. Knights

Alex Carruthers led the team and topped the run-scoring charts. His enthusiasm also spurred several younger players to flourish, giving encouragement for future years.

Batting *A. Carruthers 289 at 28.90; J. T. Cahill 189 at 27.00; W. A. South 197 at 19.70.

Bowling G. C. Harden 17 at 16.00; J. E. Willson 10 at 18.90; W. A. South 10 at 21.00.

Queen Elizabeth Grammar School, Wakefield *Yorks* P9 W4 L4 D1 A2

Master i/c S. A. Wood and S. E. Davies **Coach** C. Lawson

Adarsh Vani, the captain and leading bowler, took QEGS Wakefield to victories over Silcoates, Woodhouse Grove, Barnard Castle, and – in the National T20 – Birkdale. Keeper-batsman Harry Duke averaged over 50 and was the team's outstanding performer.

Batting H. G. Duke 217 at 54.25; H. D. Thompson 196 at 32.66.

Bowling *A. D. Vani 10 at 13.10; V. Patel 13 at 14.53.

Queen Elizabeth's Hospital, Bristol *Gloucestershire* P8 W3 L5 A1

Master i/c P. E. Joslin **Coach** D. C. Forder

After a winless 2016, three victories were an achievement. With all but one of the side returning in 2018, things should get better.

Batting *E. W. T. Wilson 206 at 29.42; D. J. Ahmed 182 at 22.75.

Bowling E. W. T. Wilson 11 at 11.54.

Queen Mary's Grammar School, Walsall *Staffordshire* P12 W5 L7

Master i/c B. T. Gibbons **Coaches** T. E. Hodgson and M. Hingley

The exam period depleted the team of senior players, but the recruits competed manfully. Joe Millerchip and Rohit Suglani were comfortably the best batsmen, while Matthew Curtiss (Year 10) and Hashim Iqbal (Year 9) showed great promise.

Batting J. J. Millerchip 233 at 33.28; *R. R. Suglani 251 at 27.88; U. B. J. Iqbal 166 at 15.09.

Bowling The leading bowler was H. J. Iqbal, who took six wickets at 15.66.

Queen's College, Taunton *Somerset* P12 W8 L2 D2 A1

Master i/c A. V. Suppiah **Coach** A. G. Hamilton

Aggressive and disciplined bowling made Queen's competitive throughout the summer. The highlight was a second-wicket partnership of 298 between Kieran Rust and Fionn Hand against Blundell's.

Batting F. Hand 485 at 80.83; K. Rust 635 at 57.72; *E. P. Trotman 180 at 36.00; T. Hazell Evans 341 at 31.00; S. G. Wansbrough 169 at 18.77.

Bowling F. Hand 17 at 8.23; J. Gore 13 at 14.61; F. M. Caddick 13 at 22.76; O. J. Carlson 12 at 24.91.

Radley College *Berkshire* P14 W10 L2 D2

Master i/c S. H. Dalrymple **Coach** A. R. Wagner

Thrilling victories against Bradfield, Charterhouse, Eton, Tonbridge and Wellington made it a memorable year. The statistical highlight came when Radley claimed six wickets in six balls against Marlborough, who crashed from 220-4 to 221. There was a hat-trick from Jonty Robinson and a run-out at the end of one over, and two wickets at the beginning of the next.

Batting *R. A. Betley 470 at 52.22; O. F. R. Martyn Hemphill 304 at 50.66; S. D. Hoddinott 423 at 42.30; D. V. Brooke 418 at 34.83; W. C. K. Carr 187 at 15.58.

Bowling J. Folkestone 26 at 17.38; J. A. Robinson 25 at 20.16; W. C. K. Carr 11 at 21.09; M. C. Martin-Zakheim 18 at 21.33; H. W. Purton 10 at 30.00.

Ratcliffe College *Leicestershire* P13 W8 L2 D3 A3

Master i/c E. O. Woodcock

After defeats in their first two games, Ratcliffe went unbeaten, making it the best season in years. Teamwork and mutual trust were the ingredients for success.

Batting T. Snell 381 at 38.10; J. E. Nightingale 263 at 37.57; *R. N. Senavirathna-Yapa 308 at 25.66.

Bowling G. W. A. Morgan-Jones 15 at 21.33; T. Snell 10 at 35.10.

Reading Blue Coat School *Berkshire* P19 W8 L9 D2

Master i/c P. J. B. Davies **Coach** P. D. Wise

A stiffer fixture list was a good challenge for a young Blue Coat side. After a record-breaking match against St George's, Weybridge – 861 runs were scored in a day – notable victories came against Oratory and Shiplake. Year 10 Toby Greatwood averaged over 50, while Ben Cole's bowling turned heads.

Batting T. L. Greatwood 359 at 51.28; J. P. Rogers 247 at 35.28; E. W. Lee 194 at 24.25; B. F. Cole 191 at 21.22; W. J. Perkin 227 at 20.63.

Bowling J. L. O. Harris 10 at 16.90; B. F. Cole 18 at 22.38; J. L. Etherington 11 at 27.09; T. L. Greatwood 13 at 29.07; R. S. Palihawadana 12 at 30.66; K. Shah 12 at 40.58.

Reed's School *Surrey* P15 W11 L2 D2

Master i/c M. R. Dunn **Coach** K. T. Medlycott

Nathan Tilley hit five centuries, and his inventive leadership made for exciting cricket. He drew support from Harry Alderson and Sam Moldon, who scored consistently, and Harry Williams and Jack Kenningham, who bowled with control. George Griffiths was the leading all-rounder.

Batting *N. J. Tilley 857 at 71.41; H. G. D. Alderson 524 at 47.63; S. G. Moldon 403 at 44.77; M. J. Males 181 at 30.16; G. W. Griffiths 336 at 25.84; N. J. L. Morgan 188 at 23.50; N. Gigani 195 at 15.00.

Bowling H. P. R. Williams 12 at 17.66; W. K. Stephen 15 at 17.93; G. W. Griffiths 29 at 18.03; J. D. Kenningham 23 at 21.34; T. R. Clough 12 at 26.41.

Reigate's captain, George Elliston, steams in; he collected 20 wickets, 539 runs and 15 catches.

Reigate Grammar School *Surrey* P22 W14 L8

Master i/c J. M. C. Leck **Coach** J. E. Benjamin

A strong all-round squad, superbly led by George Elliston, romped to 14 victories, the most successful summer since records began.

Batting S. J. W. Hall 539 at 38.50; *G. A. Elliston 539 at 35.93; A. Bhat 499 at 31.18; T. H. T. Guise 330 at 23.57; W. J. Elliston 298 at 21.28; J. J. M. Noblett 178 at 16.18.

Bowling G. A. Elliston 20 at 15.05; O. A. Simms 18 at 21.94; H. J. C. Elliss 27 at 22.62; T. D. P. Allen 16 at 24.06; T. H. T. Guise 10 at 27.70; J. A. Bennett 11 at 27.90; J. J. M. Noblett 11 at 32.54; J. M. V. Flanders 11 at 32.90.

Repton School *Derbyshire* P21 W10 L9 T1 D1 A1

Master i/c I. M. Pollock **Coaches** H. B. Dytham and J. A. Afford

Repton's form was fickle, but there were moments of brilliance, including the opening stand of 311 between Ben Chapman-Lilley and Will Hobson against Derbyshire Under-17.

Batting B. J. Chapman-Lilley 707 at 50.50; C. T. Harvey 509 at 31.81; W. A. Hobson 429 at 28.60; *J. H. Sookias 399 at 24.93; K. Marcelle 258 at 21.50; A. S. Chima 334 at 20.87.

Bowling W. A. Hobson 15 at 15.93; B. J. Chapman-Lilley 19 at 24.47; J. F. Cheshire 23 at 24.69; J. W. Bull 21 at 30.00; C. T. Harvey 17 at 30.35; T. A. Buffin 10 at 47.60.

Rossall School *Lancashire* P14 W3 L6 T1 D4 A2

Master i/c M. J. Kelly

The leadership of captain Bradley Gosling and deputy James Amor helped Rossall improve throughout the year. Though they lost more than they won, they were always competitive.

Batting *B. N. Gosling 183 at 26.14; J. S. Amor 203 at 25.37; J. Hamnett 175 at 25.00; C. Ardron 221 at 18.41.

Bowling J. S. Amor 15 at 16.66.

Royal Grammar School, Guildford *Surrey* P15 W7 L6 D2

Master i/c C. J. L. Sandbach **Coach** G. D. G. Cover

Harrison Green scored runs reliably, while Abhay Gonella's all-round excellence lent the team balance. RGS Guildford will miss captain Ali Curran, opening bowler Ben Shaw and destructive hitter Max James, who all gave stellar performances for three years.

Batting H. S. M. Green 590 at 53.63; A. Gonella 487 at 37.46; M. H. James 368 at 28.30; *A. J. P. Curran 304 at 23.38; B. E. Thomas 269 at 20.69; N. W. Lindsay 193 at 16.08; Y. S. Hafiz 154 at 15.40.

Bowling A. Bose 13 at 11.38; A. Gonella 28 at 15.32; B. M. Shaw 20 at 23.35; A. J. P. Curran 21 at 24.42; Y. S. Hafiz 14 at 36.57; T. J. Eves 11 at 41.90.

Royal Grammar School, High Wycombe *Bucks* P22 W11 L9 D2

Master i/c B. T. R. Berryman

Teddie Casterton had an extraordinary season, scoring 1,423 runs, including six hundreds, one of them a double. Rousing wins against Radley and Oratory were highlights, as were the games against Bradfield and Merchant Taylors', Northwood, which went to the wire.

Batting *E. T. D. Casterton 1,423 at 88.93; Y. Rastogi 657 at 46.92; A. A. King 345 at 24.64; M. Umar 171 at 14.25; B. E. J. Ward 194 at 12.93.

Bowling R. Perera 14 at 17.14; S. J. Parry 21 at 20.80; A. A. King 21 at 22.80; H. M. E. Cameron 20 at 22.85; Y. Rastogi 19 at 23.63; J. C. Dennis 16 at 26.75; E. T. D. Casterton 14 at 27.64.

Royal Grammar School, Newcastle *Northumberland* P17 W6 L11 A2

Master i/c M. J. Smalley

There were highs – including a win against Durham School under lights at Chester-le-Street – and lows, but this young side will be better for the experience. The season finished with the annual RGS Festival, which included victory over Worcester.

Batting G. J. H. Halliday 160 at 26.66; L. N. Hudson 196 at 24.50; N. W. Gough 179 at 22.37; R. J. N. Hanley 234 at 19.50; A. J. Elder 216 at 16.61.

Bowling *P. E. Davison 12 at 21.41; G. J. Pearce 14 at 22.28; R. J. N. Hanley 12 at 22.50; J. V. Boaden 11 at 24.90.

The Royal Grammar School, Worcester *Worcs* P22 W14 L7 D1 A2

Master i/c M. D. Wilkinson **Coach** P. J. Newport

A superb Easter tour to Sri Lanka heralded an excellent summer. Victories over Malvern College and King's, Worcester, stood out, but winning the RGS Festival was the season's souvenir. The Cooks – Alfie and George – combined for a strong attack with Ben Sutton and Rhodri Williams, while Cal Turner, Sam Hughes, James Allen and Alex Wheeler scored the bulk of the runs.

Batting C. D. Turner 643 at 30.61; S. M. Hughes 484 at 28.47; A. C. Wheeler 369 at 26.35; R. H. S. Williams 379 at 22.29; W. A. Reading 284 at 21.84; *J. J. Allen 455 at 21.66; B. O. Selby 250 at 16.66; G. S. Cook 255 at 13.42.

Bowling A. H. Cook 35 at 15.22; B. R. Sutton 37 at 15.48; G. S. Cook 34 at 17.67; W. A. Reading 15 at 23.00; B. M. Hawkes 14 at 23.42; R. H. S. Williams 20 at 25.05.

Rugby School *Warwickshire* P16 W6 L6 D4 A1

Master i/c A. E. L. Thomson **Coach** M. J. Powell

As part of their 450th anniversary celebrations, Rugby took on Marlborough College at Lord's for the first time since 1972 and, despite the best efforts of Scotland Under-19 Finlay McCreath, lost a wonderful game. Excellent two-day performances against Clifton and Marlborough rounded off a cracking season.

Batting F. D. W. McCreath 793 at 61.00; *E. W. Beard 723 at 42.52; W. J. Hardman 232 at 38.66; W. J. Hatton 382 at 34.72; T. N. Astley-Jones 200 at 25.00; H. J. R. Anton 327 at 21.80; E. J. J. Robinson 209 at 19.00.

Bowling E. W. Beard 12 at 19.41; F. D. W. McCreath 26 at 19.61; S. F. Choudhary 26 at 20.53; E. J. J. Robinson 21 at 24.33; J. P. Fagan 16 at 26.75.

Rydal Penrhos *Denbighshire* P8 W3 L5 A3

Master i/c M. T. Leach

In their final year, the Sissons brothers, Jack and William, were the standout players once again. Both gave much to Rydal Penrhos cricket, not just with their own performances, but with their encouragement of others.

Batting *J. R. E. Sissons 358 at 89.50; W. B. S. Sissons 239 at 39.83.

Bowling The leading bowler was J. R. E. Sissons, who took nine wickets at 17.77.

St Albans School *Hertfordshire* P17 W9 L7 D1 A1

Master i/c M. C. Ilott

It was the year for stunning batting: Charlie Scott hit 1,025 runs, a school record, Gus Laws-Mather smashed his maiden hundred off 37 balls, and Josh de Caires, just 15, scored four half-centuries. Will Thomson was sensational behind the stumps.

Batting *C. F. B. Scott 1,025 at 78.84; J. M. de Caires 439 at 39.90; W. E. Thomson 361 at 25.78; A. Laws-Mather 414 at 24.35; C. V. Townsend 166 at 20.75.
Bowling C. V. Townsend 14 at 17.85; W. J. Stewart 12 at 25.33; A. Laws-Mather 17 at 30.35; R. J. Thapar 10 at 31.80.

St Benedict's School, Ealing *Middlesex* P21 W6 L13 T2

Master i/c K. Newell

Two spectacular centuries from Sam Allen stood out from a mixed summer, but him team-mates kept plugging away. Spin twins George Johnson and Stefan Tsang had productive final seasons, while all-rounder Tomek Tsang showed great promise.
Batting S. J. L. Allen 498 at 41.50; T. J. L. Tsang 355 at 23.66; *F. G. Greenwood 255 at 19.61; T. J. Knight 228 at 19.00; L. E. L. Campbell 284 at 18.93; J. M. L. Chippendale 201 at 18.27.
Bowling G. D. Johnson 25 at 13.20; T. J. L. Tsang 10 at 15.30; S. J. F. Tsang 19 at 16.73; T. O. A. Morris 14 at 26.21.

St Edmund's School, Canterbury *Kent* P7 W4 L3 A1

Master i/c A. R. Jones **Coach** H. L. Alleyne

It was a short and frustrating season: too many games were lost from positions of strength. Still, the impressive form of two young Kent age-group players – bowler Ben Mills and batsman Joe Gordon – suggested a bright 2018.
Batting *H. C. Rutherford-Roberts 217 at 54.25.
Bowling B. C. Mills 14 at 6.00; J. Lambton 10 at 9.00.

St Edward's School, Oxford *Oxfordshire* P27 W18 L6 D3 A1

Master i/c R. W. J. Howitt **Coach** D. P. Simpkins

A triumphant summer included 1,263 runs for Year 11 Ben Charlesworth, a school record. Brandon Allen was also excellent: he captained shrewdly, passed 1,000 runs, and made 43 dismissals behind the stumps. England Under-19 Harrison Ward was another all-round star, with 964 runs and 45 wickets. And, with eight players returning, there is genuine optimism for 2018.
Batting B. G. Charlesworth 1,263 at 54.91; *B. L. Allen 1,234 at 47.46; H. D. Ward 964 at 40.16; J. A. Curtis 153 at 30.60; T. E. R. Powell 349 at 23.26; W. N. Deasy 321 at 21.40; W. J. Pickford 237 at 14.81.
Bowling B. G. Charlesworth 22 at 11.09; K. Barman 12 at 11.91; H. D. Ward 45 at 16.71; J. A. Curtis 38 at 21.52; T. E. R. Powell 24 at 22.91; L. A. Charlesworth 16 at 23.06.

St George's College, Weybridge *Surrey* P13 W7 L5 D1 A1

Master i/c O. J. Clayson **Coach** R. Hall

The game against Reading Blue Coat will live long in the memory: Will Jacks scored 279 in a 50-over total of 531, and averaged 125 for the summer.
Batting W. G. Jacks 626 at 125.20; W. Arkell 523 at 40.23; A. Behl 338 at 28.16.
Bowling W. G. Jacks 12 at 16.66; W. Arkell 12 at 30.75.

St John's School, Leatherhead *Surrey* P14 W3 L9 D2

Master i/c D. J. Hammond

There were only three victories, but plenty of rays of sunshine. Ben Geddes, just 15, scored three magnificent hundreds, while Sam Hunt led the bowling with 22 wickets at 20.
Batting B. B. A. Geddes 526 at 43.83; L. C. Trimming 347 at 26.69; J. Bond 238 at 26.44.
Bowling S. A. Hunt 22 at 20.00; *O. J. Hunt 20 at 25.00; A. P. Tubman 12 at 28.75; M. A. Simpson 10 at 40.00.

St Lawrence College *Kent* P15 W7 L5 D3 A1

Master i/c S. M. Simmons **Coach** T. Moulton

Kent Academy player Isaac Dilkes was excellent, and hit three centuries. The performance of the season, though, went to Year 10 Lewis Wain, with six for four against King's, Rochester.
Batting I. V. A. Dilkes 700 at 77.77; H. C. Smith 449 at 34.53; *J. Valentine 178 at 13.69.
Bowling L. P. Wain 14 at 19.35; A. E. Ralph-Harding 12 at 20.00; I. V. A. Dilkes 14 at 25.50; S. J. Smith 12 at 30.75; H. C. Smith 11 at 34.90.

St Alban's captain, Charlie Scott, scored a school-record 1,025 runs; Ben Geddes hit three hundreds for St John's, Leatherhead.

St Paul's School *Surrey* P14 W7 L7

Master i/c N. E. Briers

After eight stalwarts left in 2016, this was a new start, but there were impressive wins against Dulwich, MCC, KCS Wimbledon, St John's, RGS Guildford, Tiffin and Fettes College. Left-arm spinner Abdullah Nazir, who played for Sussex Second XI, offered control and penetration.

Batting F. P. Eltringham 479 at 39.91; F. R. Walter 264 at 26.40; O. X. F. Simpson 215 at 23.88; A. Nazir 209 at 23.22; I. A. Macdonald 162 at 20.25; R. P. N. Tegner 207 at 17.25.

Bowling A. Nazir 27 at 13.40; D. J. Leon 11 at 15.72; A. Jenkyn-Jones 23 at 17.60; F. R. Walter 13 at 32.07.

St Peter's School, York *Yorkshire* P21 W15 L5 D1 A3

Master i/c G. J. Sharp

St Peter's gained a wealth of experience from some exhilarating games and reached the regional final of the National T20 competition, where they lost to eventual champions Sedbergh. Chris Wood was selected in the North of England Under-15 squad.

Batting *E. J. Patmore 692 at 40.70; H. R. Contreras 455 at 25.27; A. Liley 340 at 24.28; C. D. S. Wood 470 at 23.50; C. J. Burdass 344 at 21.50; M. T. Roberts 350 at 19.44; J. J. Amsden 160 at 17.77; S. R. Elliot 177 at 13.61.

Bowling E. J. Patmore 31 at 13.38; J. J. Amsden 11 at 13.54; C. D. S. Wood 30 at 15.06; C. J. Burdass 19 at 17.05; M. T. Roberts 18 at 18.88; J. Black 11 at 24.18; S. R. Elliot 13 at 26.84.

Sedbergh School *Yorkshire* P26 W23 L3 A3

Master i/c C. P. Mahon **Coach** M. P. Speight

In an outstanding season, Sedbergh beat Lancashire and Durham Academies, MCC and Shrewsbury. The highlight, though, was overcoming Millfield to win the National T20 competition for the first time. Captain and leading batsman Harry Brook was in such fine form he was called up to Yorkshire's Championship side, while leg-spinner Kyme Tahirkheli took 58 wickets, a school record.

Batting *H. C. Brook 950 at 86.36; G. C. H. Hill 269 at 33.62; M. B. Silvester 720 at 31.30; S. M. Barrett 539 at 29.94; G. R. Cameron 535 at 29.72; C. W. G. Sanders 372 at 28.61; M. G. Stables 438 at 25.76; K. K. Tahirkheli 188 at 23.50; C. Park-Johnson 171 at 21.37; J. C. H. Park-Johnson 192 at 14.76.

Bowling K. K. Tahirkheli 58 at 12.25; G. C. H. Hill 33 at 13.54; C. W. G. Sanders 32 at 13.90; J. C. H. Park-Johnson 31 at 17.96; H. C. Brook 10 at 19.20; S. M. Barrett 29 at 21.10.

Sevenoaks School *Kent* P15 W7 L7 D1 A1

Master i/c C. J. Tavaré **Coach** P. J. Hulston

Captain Nick Bett led from the front with fiery pace and powerful batting, while the averages were led by Year 10 Harry Houillon, who scored his first century, and Rhys Joseph, who recorded two five-fors. The outstanding victory was a seven-wicket thrashing of King's, Canterbury.

Batting H. F. Houillon 426 at 60.85; *N. M. Bett 282 at 31.33; R. L. Joseph 373 at 28.69; P. D. Nickols 282 at 20.14; T. V. H. Allen 242 at 18.61.

Bowling R. L. Joseph 28 at 13.28; N. M. Bett 12 at 21.33; S. S. Brar 10 at 27.30; O. Nasser 10 at 28.40; A. G. Sackville-West 11 at 31.27.

Shebbear College *Devon* P6 W5 L1 A4

Master i/c A. B. Bryan **Coach** N. Law

The weather stole four of the ten scheduled games but, when Shebbear got on the field, they were dominant. Captain Jabez Weale spearheaded the bowling attack, while opener Eddie Jones provided solid bases to most innings. Overseas players Justin Gilliland, Tim Ngcizela, Mitch Proffit and Ethan Solomon all contributed.

Batting The leading batsman was E. Jones, who hit 144 runs at 36.00.

Bowling E. Solomon 16 at 6.50; *J. T. M. Weale 12 at 8.00.

Sherborne School *Dorset* P15 W8 L7

Master i/c A. D. Nurton **Coach** M. I. Jamieson

Away wins at Cheltenham and Clifton, where Sherborne's bowlers demonstrated excellent discipline and variety, were the keepsakes of the summer. There were eight victories but, with more robustness in the batting, there could have been more.

Batting *B. E. G. J. Heber 194 at 32.33; H. S. Fisher 300 at 27.27; P. J. R. Reynolds 175 at 25.00; S. D. F. Hambro 170 at 24.28; C. G. B. Fish 166 at 16.60.

Bowling C. G. B. Fish 22 at 14.13; T. C. Perkins 21 at 21.47; B. E. G. J. Heber 15 at 22.26; J. A. M. Pyman 17 at 24.52.

Shiplake College *Oxfordshire* P15 W8 L7 A2

Master i/c J. H. Howorth **Coach** C. Ellison

Three last-over run-chases were the most satisfying of eight victories for Shiplake. Captain Miles Bridgman and keeper Oliver Brown scored the bulk of the runs, while Year 10 Callum Creighton topped the averages with bat and ball.

Batting C. J. Creighton 260 at 37.14; B. Monson 173 at 24.71; O. H. N. Brown 311 at 23.92; *M. A. Bridgman 307 at 23.61; J. W. Tucker 237 at 19.75; J. Howard 184 at 18.40; S. W. K. Neil 151 at 15.10.

Bowling C. J. Creighton 23 at 15.56; J. W. Tucker 17 at 17.76; L. G. Bishop 15 at 27.80; F. G. T. Bowcock 13 at 34.84.

Shrewsbury School *Shropshire* P24 W15 L8 D1

Master i/c A. S. Barnard **Coach** A. J. Shantry

George Garrett's superb captaincy led Shrewsbury to victories over Millfield and Eton, and a trip to Arundel Castle for the National T20 finals day. Jamie Crawley was top run-scorer with 753, while Peter Clark took 43 wickets at 12. The Under-17 side reached their national final.

Batting *G. A. Garrett 532 at 38.00; J. G. T. Crawley 753 at 34.22; G. T. Hargrave 395 at 32.91; G. W. Newton 521 at 24.80; J. S. Zaza 290 at 20.71; D. J. Humes 326 at 20.37; C. J. Byrne 241 at 15.06.

Bowling C. J. Byrne 10 at 6.00; P. J. H. Clark 43 at 12.04; A. W. Garrett 23 at 17.73; P. J. Jacob 26 at 21.57; G. A. Garrett 18 at 21.77; G. W. Newton 14 at 40.00.

Silcoates School *Yorkshire* P19 W7 L12 A1

Master i/c G. M. Roberts

Silcoates suffered from inexperience, but the team will have learned much along the way. The highlight was a memorable pre-season tour to South Africa.

Batting M. A. Nawaz 264 at 18.85; T. G. Wilby 195 at 17.72; L. J. Webb 186 at 12.40.

Bowling M. A. Nawaz 10 at 32.10.

Sir Thomas Rich's School *Gloucestershire* P12 W4 L6 D2 A3

Master i/c N. D. O'Neil **Coach** S. M. Rideout

Joel Price couldn't quite hit the heights of 2016 – when he scored three centuries – but he captained with distinction, and led the side to notable victories over QEH Bristol and Hereford Cathedral.

Batting S. R. J. Campbell 242 at 60.50; M. A. Cox 269 at 33.62; S. J. Price 175 at 19.44; J. A. Tayler 176 at 17.60; *J. A. Price 210 at 17.50.

Bowling C. T. Holland 17 at 17.70; J. A. Price 13 at 20.23; S. J. Price 15 at 20.80; M. A. Cox 10 at 23.00.

Solihull School *Warwickshire* P15 W9 L5 D1 A4

Master i/c D. L. Maddy **Coach** D. Smith

There were five more victories than in 2016, demonstrating the growth of the team. Ethan Brookes had another outstanding all-round season, while Will Rigg destroyed many an attack.

Batting W. E. Rigg 523 at 65.37; *E. A. Brookes 621 at 51.75; F. A. H. Roll 223 at 24.77; T. E. Serle 165 at 16.50.

Bowling E. A. Brookes 25 at 12.92; A. J. S. Townend 12 at 23.25.

South Gloucestershire and Stroud College *Glos* P12 W6 L6 A3

Master i/c S. G. Hinks

George Drissell's all-round contributions helped him earn a contract with Gloucestershire, while Vishal Mamgai, Mahin Omar, Ben Parker and Kieran Slade made great strides.

Batting V. Mamgai 405 at 36.81; M. Omar 182 at 30.33; *G. Drissell 174 at 29.00; B. Parker 208 at 23.11; K. Slade 158 at 17.55.

Bowling B. Parker 13 at 12.53; M. Omar 12 at 14.66.

Stamford School *Lincolnshire* P18 W9 L6 T1 D2

Master i/c C. A. R. Esson **Coach** D. W. Headley

Jacob Turp captained superbly, and fostered a cohesion that helped the team win a number of tight games. There were five centuries, but no five-fors.

Batting J. D. M. Evison 560 at 62.22; *J. M. Turp 565 at 37.66; N. J. Green 437 at 36.41; B. M. Woodward 349 at 26.84; J. R. Martin 313 at 19.56; S. Saleem 202 at 18.36.

Bowling C. K. Headley 15 at 20.60; N. J. Green 14 at 22.64; S. Saleem 19 at 26.78; E. J. Cox 11 at 31.90; H. C. P. Carter 12 at 41.58.

Stewart's Melville College, Edinburgh *Midlothian* P16 W7 L8 D1 A4

Master i/c A. Ranson.

Despite the rain, Stewart's Melville managed 16 games. Star performers Andrew Appleton, Ben Davidson, Patrick Ritchie, and Charlie and Freddie Peet were called up by Cricket Scotland for their age groups.

Batting F. T. Peet 152 at 21.71; P. G. F. Ritchie 234 at 19.50; *A. L. Appleton 268 at 19.14; B. J. Davidson 172 at 19.11; M. I. C. Hay-Smith 294 at 18.37.

Bowling C. D. Peet 19 at 11.36; C. C. Phipps 11 at 16.36; F. T. Peet 12 at 19.83; A. L. Appleton 14 at 21.14.

Stonyhurst College *Lancashire* P5 W2 L2 D1 A3

Master i/c G. Thomas **Coach** D. F. Haasbroek

Of the eight scheduled fixtures, only four produced results, with three abandoned completely. The outstanding performance came from Christian Butschok-Brain against Rossall. He came in at eight for three and hit 107*, before collecting five for 24 to seal victory.

Batting C. A. Butschok-Brain 175 at 87.50.

Bowling The leading bowler was C. A. Butschok-Brain, who took seven wickets at 13.28.

Stowe School *Buckinghamshire* P23 W16 L4 D3 A1

Master i/c J. A. Knott **Coach** P. R. Arnold

A successful tour to Dubai, where Stowe won the Schools Arch Trophy, set the platform for a strong season. The captain, Brandon Lee, was superb throughout, while Adam King – who appeared for Northamptonshire in a warm-up game – scored most runs. Olly Clarke led the bowling, and turned in mature performances for Oxfordshire.

Batting T. H. Worrall 205 at 51.25; T. Olsen 355 at 50.71; A. E. King 774 at 45.52; *B. J. Lee 601 at 40.06; C. L. Renshaw 411 at 25.68; O. D. Clarke 311 at 23.92; J. F. Jackman 153 at 17.00.

Bowling O. D. Clarke 33 at 14.84; T. Olsen 32 at 14.96; C. V. Leefe 24 at 17.66; A. S. A. Johnson 17 at 19.00; T. H. Worrall 15 at 21.53; J. F. Jackman 10 at 26.40; W. J. Garrett 15 at 28.73; R. E. A. Easdale 10 at 43.20.

Sutton Valence School *Kent* P14 W9 L4 D1 A2

Master i/c V. J. Wells

Opening batsman and leg-spinner Rishi Roy-Mukajee was top run-scorer and joint-top wicket-taker, along with left-armer Will Edwards. The Aiken brothers – Tom and Elliot – provided thrust, while James Bevan-Thomas was a sure-handed captain.

Batting R. Roy-Mukajee 507 at 50.70; T. E. Lazarides 192 at 32.00; *J. R. Bevan-Thomas 276 at 30.66; J. J. Aucamp 224 at 24.88; J. W. Drewe 213 at 23.66.

Bowling W. M. Edwards 22 at 13.50; E. P. Aiken 16 at 14.87; M. R. Webb 12 at 15.00; T. F. Aiken 21 at 19.28; R. Roy-Mukajee 22 at 23.68.

Taunton School *Somerset* P16 W6 L10

Master i/c P. N. Sanderson

Before half-term, things looked bright, with victories over Blundell's, Clifton and Colston's. But poor results followed. Dominic Court and Ed Eminson both scored centuries, and notched over 300 runs, while Travis Green took most wickets, and Max Fiske claimed a five-for.

Batting E. F. Eminson 323 at 26.91; D. S. Court 371 at 26.50; *S. P. Whitefield 263 at 18.78; M. E. Cave 206 at 14.71.

Bowling T. E. Green 20 at 20.55; E. F. Eminson 15 at 24.06; M. A. Fiske 11 at 28.18; S. P. Whitefield 15 at 29.66; P. J. Lee 10 at 32.70.

Tiffin School *Surrey* P15 W5 L7 D3 A1

Master i/c M. J. Williams

With the exam season encroaching ever more, Tiffin struggled. Nevertheless, three centuries, two from the highly talented Sami Shori, led to three fine victories. Krishan Sachdeva captained the side brilliantly and was the leading all-rounder.

Batting S. Shori 513 at 36.64; *K. K. Sachdeva 409 at 27.26; K. Khaira 270 at 20.76.

Bowling A. V. Joshi 12 at 9.91; K. K. Sachdeva 27 at 20.22; Y. I. M. Jackson 22 at 21.72; J. N. Parker 10 at 32.30.

Tonbridge School *Kent* P23 W10 L10 D3

Masters i/c J. P. Arscott and P. T. Sadler **Coach** I. Baldock

Tonbridge were excellent before half-term, but fell away. Reaching the quarter-finals of the National T20 competition was a highlight, as was the T20 victory against Cranleigh the day after losing to them in a 50-over match.

Batting J. J. O'Riordan 931 at 49.00; *A. J. Moen 546 at 26.00; O. E. Carr-Hill 254 at 25.40; C. A. Winder 186 at 23.25; D. A. Heggie 396 at 22.00; B. J. E. Robinson 430 at 21.50; J. O. A. Prideaux 327 at 19.23; D. O. Edwards 245 at 16.33.

Bowling J. O. A. Prideaux 27 at 15.07; A. J. Moen 23 at 19.69; J. J. O'Riordan 28 at 20.50; H. N. Forster 22 at 22.50; C. A. L. Spawforth 19 at 28.42; J. N. Maddison 11 at 29.63; C. V. Oster 14 at 30.85.

Trent College *Derbyshire* P18 W14 L1 T1 D2

Master i/c S. A. J. Boswell **Coach** P. Johnson

Fourteen victories and a single defeat added up to a highly successful season for Trent College. Chris Gibson's 784 runs played a big part, as did the varied bowling attack, which had the depth to keep sides under pressure at all times.

Batting C. F. Gibson 784 at 87.11; M. J. Kimmitt 448 at 44.80; *T. R. Wyatt 537 at 38.35; S. J. Riordan 164 at 32.80; C. R. Livesey 302 at 30.20; A. D. Moore 247 at 27.44.

Bowling D. L. Blatherwick 19 at 18.94; S. G. Westbrook 18 at 19.05; S. J. Riordan 13 at 23.61; C. F. Gibson 13 at 24.69.

Trinity School *Surrey* P23 W14 L8 D1

Master i/c R. J. Risebro **Coaches** S. D. Schofield and A. D. Brown

Selfless teamwork and dedication – off the pitch and on – paid dividends. They reached the regional final of the National T20 competition for the first time, and picked up strong wins against King's, Canterbury and against KCS Wimbledon.

Batting *D. J. Johnsen 561 at 40.07; H. S. Neale-Smith 663 at 33.15; P. Peethamber 473 at 27.82; A. W. E. Roberts 538 at 26.90; J. W. Blake 203 at 25.37; R. Hari 383 at 22.52; A. Sabesan 194 at 19.40; F. G. Baker 152 at 19.00.
Bowling F. G. Baker 24 at 17.58; P. Peethamber 28 at 18.71; N. M. Johnsen 11 at 19.54; M. L. Cadiz 21 at 19.76; H. S. Neale-Smith 22 at 20.09; E. J. Lilley 23 at 25.17.

University College School, Hampstead *Middlesex* P13 W2 L10 D1

Master i/c L. J. Greany **Coaches** M. Lane and A. Wilkes
Although these were largely the same group of players, and they had an exemplary attitude, the team couldn't repeat the successes of 2016: they won five fewer matches.
Batting *J. F. Raschke 199 at 24.87; L. H. Rehman 184 at 23.00; H. L. Raschke 192 at 19.20; D. A. S. Grabinar 184 at 18.40.
Bowling J. A. Grabinar 12 at 17.91; N. R. Bor 12 at 35.25.

Uppingham School *Rutland* P12 W8 L1 D3 A1

Master i/c T. R. Ward **Coach** J. C. J. Sharrock
An experienced Uppingham team captained by Sam Charlton recorded an impressive eight wins, their most successful season for some time. Harry Funnell racked up three centuries, while George Loyd took 21 wickets at a stingy 13 each.
Batting H. Funnell 611 at 61.10; W. Rogers 483 at 48.30; G. Loyd 319 at 39.87; *S. R. Charlton 278 at 34.75.
Bowling G. Loyd 21 at 13.61; S. R. Charlton 16 at 18.75; H. Funnell 11 at 25.36; W. Rogers 10 at 34.70.

Victoria College, Jersey *Channel Islands* P16 W8 L8 A2

Master i/c M. D. Smith **Coach** M. Dixon
David Bourne excelled with 22 wickets and 677 runs, including a brilliant 143 against Monmouth at the Castles Festival, where Victoria College were joint winners. They were also runners-up in the Jersey T20 competition.
Batting D. A. Bourne 677 at 52.07; *B. P. Tait 230 at 28.75; J. A. Heward 396 at 26.40; E. J. W. Giles 252 at 25.20; M. G. Donaldson 301 at 21.50; G. E. G. Moore 304 at 20.26; J. A. D. Lawrenson 182 at 15.16.
Bowling D. A. Bourne 22 at 18.45; M. G. Donaldson 22 at 19.18; B. P. Tait 22 at 25.27; J. A. D. Lawrenson 10 at 28.90; E. J. Giles 12 at 37.41.

Warwick School *Warwickshire* P17 W6 L11 A2

Master i/c S. R. G. Francis
When not playing for Warwickshire Seconds, Rob Yates showed his class with two centuries. But, other than outstanding wins against MCC and King's, Worcester, it was a tough season. There was a silver lining, though, as three Under-14 players became integral to the squad.
Batting R. M. Yates 447 at 89.40; T. C. Hornby 222 at 31.71; F. P. Lowe 301 at 23.15; *S. J. P. Forster 209 at 19.00; M. Leatherdale 201 at 16.75; E. J. W. Briggs 176 at 14.66; H. W. Mortimer 154 at 14.00.
Bowling R. M. Yates 11 at 13.45; C. R. Curtis 16 at 17.12; R. S. Mohan 15 at 21.66; H. R. Miles 11 at 24.63; W. J. Kelley 16 at 24.93.

Wellingborough School *Northamptonshire* P23 W15 L6 D2

Master i/c G. E. Houghton **Coach** D. J. Sales
Wellingborough managed more cricket than ever before, largely due to the dry weather. They beat Haberdashers' Aske's and The Perse, and retained the Bablake T20 festival title, while captain Sean Mulvey passed 2,000 First XI runs in the penultimate match.
Batting J. W. Saxby 603 at 43.07; *S. J. Mulvey 788 at 37.52; M. W. Mills 189 at 27.00; A. J. Mills 447 at 24.83; M. G. Clarke 443 at 23.31; J. T. Stockdale 169 at 21.12; B. Dhaliwal 222 at 15.85; N. J. Piper 173 at 15.72.
Bowling M. W. Mills 11 at 10.45; C. T. Blake 14 at 16.35; M. R. Chalcraft 33 at 16.96; J. R. Clarke 32 at 17.34; J. W. Saxby 13 at 17.53; M. G. Clarke 25 at 20.80; T. R. S. Pope 14 at 21.78; J. T. Stockdale 11 at 38.27.

Wellington College *Berkshire* P24 W12 L10 D2

Master i/c D. M. Pratt **Coach** G. D. Franklin

When the team played well they were excellent, with victories over Harrow, Tonbridge and Marlborough, and their triumph in the BOWS festival. But there was some dross, too. Jack Davies and the captain Alex Shoff dominated the batting, while the bowling attack was led by Joe Henry and leg-spinner Jhatha Subramanyan.

Batting J. L. B. Davies 1,071 at 46.56; *A. W. Shoff 895 at 44.75; W. J. Sinfield 417 at 29.78; J. S. Subramanyan 321 at 24.69; K. Sodhi 409 at 24.05; S. J. Sweetland 283 at 21.76; J. J. Henry 243 at 17.35; T. J. Petrie 255 at 17.00; B. Z. Barnard 181 at 15.08.

Bowling J. S. Subramanyan 34 at 13.52; J. J. Henry 35 at 20.74; M. P. O'Donoghue 11 at 30.81; T. J. Petrie 11 at 40.54; A. S. Dale 12 at 40.58.

Wells Cathedral School *Somerset* P12 W3 L7 D2

Master i/c J. A. Boot **Coach** C. Vickery

Considering the strong opposition, three victories constituted a successful summer. Rhodri Moss scored 96* in his last match, while Alistair Padgett took five wickets on debut versus Sexey's.

Batting *R. E. Moss 355 at 32.27; P. T. G. Tully 217 at 19.72; S. H. Pritchard 159 at 15.90.

Bowling T. D. Sturdy 11 at 27.45; A. J. Padgett 11 at 31.72.

Westminster School *Middlesex* P11 W5 L4 D2 A2

Master i/c J. D. Kershen **Coach** S. K. Ranasinghe

It wasn't a vintage season, but Westminster played some excellent cricket, including Alex Benson's century and Lucas McConnell's hat-trick. And the future is bright, after victory in the ESCA London Under-14 Cup.

Batting A. C. Benson 263 at 32.87; A. McConnell 253 at 31.62; *S. R. Amin 228 at 28.50; A. S. Vinen 246 at 24.60; D. F. Thomas du Toit 153 at 15.30.

Bowling A. C. Benson 10 at 18.30; L. F. McConnell 17 at 24.41; A. S. Vinen 11 at 33.36.

Whitgift School *Surrey* P23 W13 L10

Master i/c S. Litchfield **Coach** P. Hindmarch

A lack of batting phlegm held Whitgift back in 2017. But the team were young – half were 16 – and will have learned from the challenges.

Batting J. Smith 491 at 81.83; N. M. J. Riefer 698 at 43.62; R. Jafri 287 at 26.09; S. Nathan 414 at 21.78; J. E. Culff 206 at 18.72; B. P. M. Sewell 241 at 18.53; *T. Z. Meher 215 at 16.53; J. A. Cleaver 198 at 15.23; J. A. G. Rodnight 152 at 10.13.

Bowling R. Jafri 15 at 14.60; T. Z. Meher 33 at 15.96; W. G. Heaver 22 at 17.27; N. M. J. Reifer 16 at 24.06; B. P. M. Sewell 17 at 24.35; J. E. Culff 13 at 35.38.

Wilson's School *Surrey* P16 W12 L4

Master i/c A. Parkinson **Coach** C. K. Bullen

Wilson's had their best year of recent times, with 12 wins out of 16. Alex Lane anchored the batting with 379 runs, while the bowling unit brimmed with menace. George Kellingley was the spearhead, with support from Dan Moore, Janaken Prabhakaran, 14-year-old Pranav Madan and spinner Riley Jarrold.

Batting A. E. Lane 379 at 42.11; *D. S. Moore 192 at 17.45.

Bowling R. D. Jarrold 16 at 13.12; D. S. Moore 19 at 15.31; P. Madan 14 at 17.14; G. P. C. Kellingley 16 at 18.62; J. Prabhakaran 13 at 19.69.

Winchester College *Hampshire* P21 W7 L10 D4

Master i/c G. J. Watson **Coach** P. N. Gover

Yet again, combative bowling failed to compensate for a lack of runs. Henry Adams and Kehan Shirvani were always a threat, and spinners Angus Dodd and 15-year-old James Flatt gave quality back-up. But they seldom had enough to defend.

Batting S. D. Rooney 545 at 38.92; S. A. F. Lee 285 at 28.50; S. G. Byers 408 at 24.00; A. G. Younger 377 at 23.56; F. J. Egleston 193 at 17.54; K. D. Shirvani 180 at 15.00.

Bowling H. L. Adams 31 at 18.38; K. D. Shirvani 23 at 19.86; J. S. Scull 12 at 22.75; *A. F. J. Dodd 20 at 23.85; J. T. F. Flatt 17 at 26.35.

Wolverhampton Grammar School *Staffordshire* P16 W10 L5 D1

Master i/c T. King

Kieron Patel's excellent captaincy led a strong all-round Wolverhampton Grammar team to their best summer in a long time. His wicket-taking ability, and Archie O'Hara's 520 runs (which included two outstanding centuries), were a winning formula.

Batting C. Singh 318 at 39.75; A. O'Hara 520 at 37.14; O. Singh 393 at 35.72; L. Pickin 215 at 30.71.

Bowling *K. Patel 22 at 12.36; A. O'Hara 15 at 19.60; O. Singh 12 at 21.83; A. Uppal 11 at 23.72; J. Timmins 12 at 24.16.

Woodbridge School *Suffolk* P13 W4 L5 D4

Master i/c I. J. Simpson **Coaches** D. Brous and S. Manthorpe

With only three sixth-form students, the eye was on the future rather than the results column. Many of the team developed rapidly, with Daniel Davies and Daniel Norman shining most brightly.

Batting D. I. S. Norman 295 at 36.87; J. P. G. Ashken 151 at 21.57; B. E. Harper 221 at 20.09.

Bowling D. R. Davies 16 at 13.81.

Woodhouse Grove School *Yorkshire* P12 W4 L6 T1 D1 A3

Master i/c R. I. Frost **Coach** A. Sidebottom

In a modest season, captain Joel Godfrey's excellent 96 against MCC stood out, as did victory against Bradford Grammar School. Adbi Ahmed and Josh Stephenson represented Yorkshire at Under-19 and Under-14 levels.

Batting *J. B. Godfrey 460 at 38.33; Ali H. Ahmed 169 at 15.36; L. Fairbank 161 at 13.41.

Bowling Ali H. Ahmed 20 at 16.15; G. E. Butler 11 at 19.90; Adbi H. Ahmed 13 at 23.46; T. Kaznowski 10 at 25.20; J. B. Godfrey 13 at 26.46.

Worksop College *Nottinghamshire* P14 W9 L4 D1 A2

Master i/c N. J. Longhurst **Coaches** I. C. Parkin

Worksop went unbeaten against schools in 40- and 50-over cricket, but a disappointing exit to St Peter's, York, in the National T20 competition took off some of the sheen. Nic Keast was outstanding in his first year: he hit two centuries and two fifties, and collected a five-wicket haul.

Batting N. Keast 422 at 46.88; S. G. Routledge 321 at 35.66; P. K. Delahunty 202 at 25.25; *R. A. Parker-Cole 199 at 22.11; N. A. Lowe 249 at 20.75.

Bowling J. C. Holden 14 at 11.71; N. Keast 24 at 12.37; R. A. Parker-Cole 18 at 13.72; S. G. Routledge 12 at 13.75; A. S. Boyd 12 at 18.08; D. Harris 11 at 23.09; A. R. Shannon 11 at 23.18.

Worth School *Sussex* P16 W3 L8 D5

Master i/c R. Chaudhuri

Without many of the seniors from the previous year, 2017 was expected to be a challenge, but the new recruits stepped up brilliantly. Krishan Nayee was inspirational with bat and ball.

Batting K. Nayee 600 at 60.00; A. Padalkar 283 at 23.58; L. W. Wills 219 at 19.90.

Bowling K. Nayee 34 at 13.23; V. Kohli 14 at 15.71; W. G. F. Seibert 16 at 25.25.

Wrekin College *Shropshire* P18 W8 L10 A1

Master i/c J. R. Mather **Coach** G. A. Davies

After a disappointing T20-focused May, Wrekin enjoyed a marvellous June. Charlie Home proved a fine leader, and joined Dillon Pennington in the Shropshire team.

Batting *C. E. Home 321 at 53.50; M. R. Batkin 193 at 16.08; J. Pistorius 167 at 15.18.

Bowling J. Pistorius 22 at 9.95; C. E. Home 11 at 15.36; O. G. Davies 14 at 16.28; M. R. Batkin 13 at 21.07; H. J. Davies 12 at 28.16.

Wycliffe College *Gloucestershire* P13 W2 L9 D2 A2

Master i/c M. J. Kimber **Coach** B. Gannon

Among an inexperienced squad, Year 9 pupil Will Naish was superb, with two centuries.

Batting W. L. Naish 442 at 40.18; H. Rapley 263 at 29.22; J. G. Ealey 259 at 23.54; M. C. Cole 158 at 14.36.

Bowling The leading bowler was O. Wood, who took nine wickets at 33.33.

PART FIVE
Overseas Cricket

AFGHANISTAN CRICKET IN 2017

Look out, here they come!

SHAHID HASHMI

The biggest news of the year came in June: Afghanistan, along with long-time rivals Ireland, were granted Test status by the ICC. It was testimony to the hard work of the players and officials, as well as the support of the ardent fans. In July, their first match at Lord's, against MCC, felt like a celebration; if rain prevented a conclusion, it could not dampen the spirit in the stands.

The year ended with more big news: Afghanistan's maiden Test would be against India in Bangalore in June 2018. There was already a connection between the countries, as Greater Noida – around 25 miles from Delhi – had been their base for international matches since April 2016. As a first assignment, it could not have been more difficult. But such was their rapid progress, no one was betting against Afghanistan making a fist of it. In 2008, they were in Division Five of the World Cricket League, edging Jersey by two wickets in the final. A year later, they won one-day international status. Since their first four-day Intercontinental Cup match in 2009, they have played 22 times in the competition, winning 17 and losing just once, to Ireland.

AFGHANISTAN IN 2017

	Played	*Won*	*Lost*	*Drawn/No result*
Tests	–	–	–	–
One-day internationals	15	8	7	–
Twenty20 internationals	10	7	3	–

JANUARY	Desert T20 Challenge (in the UAE)	(page 1081)
FEBRUARY	5 ODIs (a) v Zimbabwe	(page 1043)
MARCH	5 ODIs and 3 T20Is (h) v Ireland (in India)	(page 790)
APRIL		
MAY		
JUNE	3 ODIs and 3 T20Is (a) v West Indies	(page 1033)
JULY		
AUGUST		
SEPTEMBER		
OCTOBER		
NOVEMBER		
DECEMBER	3 ODIs (h) v Ireland (in the UAE)	(page 793)

Their results remained encouraging, particularly in first-class cricket, where they proved they were ready to move up. Wins over Ireland and Hong Kong extended their run of innings victories in the Intercontinental Cup to four, and Afghanistan then secured the trophy with a ten-wicket mauling of the UAE. Captain Asghar Stanikzai hit hundreds in all three matches, while leg-spinner Rashid Khan picked up 25 wickets at 16, including three five-fors. And after they clinched one-day series wins over Zimbabwe (away) and Ireland (in Greater Noida), they visited the Caribbean for the first time, and earned a maiden ODI victory over West Indies, with Rashid picking up seven for 18; a washout in the final game meant they left with a 1–1 draw.

Fighting spirit had helped them get this far, but the 17 academies in Afghanistan needed to instil perseverance in the players to ready them for Test cricket. The role models were already in place. Alongside all-rounder Mohammad Nabi and fiery opening bowler Hamid Hassan, Rashid – who turned 19 in September – became an icon. Either side of that seven-for in St Lucia, he starred in the IPL and the Big Bash League. Following in his footsteps was 16-year-old mystery spinner Mujeeb Zadran, who in November took 21 wickets to help Afghanistan win the Under-19 Asia Cup in Kuala Lumpur. He made his ODI debut against Ireland at Sharjah a few weeks later and, in his first spell, recorded 7–2–12–4 to set up a convincing victory. While Afghanistan went on to lose the series, they now had a formidable slow-bowling attack.

The only real downer of 2017 came when wicket-keeper batsman Mohammad Shahzad was banned for a year after testing positive for clenbuterol. It was part of a weight-loss product he was taking and his admission meant the ICC backdated the suspension to January 17, 2017 – the date of the sample.

AFGHANISTAN v IRELAND IN 2016-17

IAN CALLENDER

Twenty20 internationals (3): Afghanistan 3, Ireland 0
One-day internationals (5): Afghanistan 3, Ireland 2
First-class match (1): Afghanistan 1, Ireland 0

Afghanistan and Ireland, the two Associate Members who would in June win full Test status, met in northern India in March 2017, playing each other across three formats over nearly four weeks. Ireland arrived fresh from beating the UAE 2–0 in a one-day series in Dubai, but found their main rivals a much tougher proposition. In their new home from home in Uttar Pradesh, Afghanistan consolidated their status as No. 1 Associate, winning seven of the nine games. Three Twenty20 wins gave them 11 in succession, a world record in the format, while an innings victory in the last fixture, a first-class match, meant they leapfrogged Ireland to the top of the Intercontinental Cup table. Ireland's only successes came in the one-day internationals: they won the third and fourth games to set up a decider, but lost that by seven wickets.

In 18-year-old leg-spinner Rashid Khan, Afghanistan had the player of the series. He finished with 33 wickets at 12 in all three formats, including one six-wicket haul and two five-fors. A week later, he became the first Afghan to play in the IPL. In only one match did Ireland keep him out – the first of their two victories – while in the other Kevin O'Brien hit him for successive boundaries in a match-turning over which cost 18. But a hamstring injury meant it would be O'Brien's last game of the tour. Combined with the loss of Boyd Rankin to a back injury – he failed to start a single match – this was a body blow to the Ireland squad, but it was not the difference between the teams.

Afghanistan were undoubtedly helped by playing in familiar conditions, and by Asghar Stanikzai winning six of the nine tosses. But their lower-order batting was vastly superior and, in Dawlat Zadran and Mohammad Nabi, Rashid had support which the Irish could not match. Ireland's leading wicket-taker was O'Brien, with 12 from his five games. Paul Stirling, who scored 341 in the one-day series, also took six in the second one-day international, when he filled in for the injured leg-spinner Jacob Mulder. But Ireland still lost after Afghanistan piled up 338, their highest one-day total.

Predictably, Ireland lost the Twenty20 series 3–0 – they had won just three of their previous 11 in the format. But the Intercontinental Cup defeat was only their third in the competition, and the crushing margin – an innings and 172 – was their biggest first-class thrashing, beating an innings and 169 by the touring South Africans in 1912.

Relations between the teams were not improved in the four-day game, when Nabi was reprimanded for claiming a catch that replays showed had hit the ground. It came eight months after he was involved in a run-out controversy against Ireland at Stormont (see *Wisden 2017*, page 786).

IRELAND TOURING PARTY

*W. T. S. Porterfield (FC/50/20), J. Anderson (FC), A. Balbirnie (FC/50), P. K. D. Chase (FC/50/20), G. H. Dockrell (FC/50/20), E. C. Joyce (FC/50), A. R. McBrine (FC/50/20), B. J. McCarthy (FC/50/20), J. Mulder (FC/50/20), T. J. Murtagh (FC/50), K. J. O'Brien (FC/50/20), N. J. O'Brien (FC/50), W. B. Rankin (FC/50/20), P. R. Stirling (FC/50/20), G. J. Thompson (20), S. R. Thompson (50/20), L. J. Tucker (20), G. C. Wilson (FC/50/20), C. A. Young (FC/50/20). *Coach:* J. G. Bracewell.

Rankin accompanied the party but never started a match and went home during the 50-over series, as did K. J. O'Brien. J. Little was originally selected for the Twenty20 matches but pulled out to concentrate on his studies and was replaced by Chase.

First Twenty20 international At Greater Noida, March 8, 2017. **Afghanistan won by six wickets.** ‡**Ireland 165-5** (20 overs) (S. R. Thompson 56, W. T. S. Porterfield 39, G. C. Wilson 41*); **Afghanistan 171-4** (18 overs) (Mohammad Shahzad 47, Samiullah Shenwari 56). *MoM:* Samiullah Shenwari. *Ireland reached 100-2 in 12 overs, after Stuart Thompson's maiden international fifty, but William Porterfield was run out going for a third at the start of the 13th. Only 24 came off the next 29 balls as Rashid Khan tied up one end, and Ireland finished on 165. Like Afghanistan, Ireland opened their bowling with two overs of spin. But, while they had scored 12-1, the Afghans made 23-0 and never relinquished control. Mohammad Shahzad, dropped on 27, was run out for 47; Samiullah Shenwari hit his first three balls for four, then added three more, plus three of Afghanistan's eight sixes (Ireland had three) as they eased home. Afghanistan's ninth successive T20I win since they beat West Indies in the World Twenty20 nearly 12 months earlier broke the record shared by England (from May 2010 to January 2011) and Ireland (February to March 2012).*

Second Twenty20 international At Greater Noida, March 10, 2017. **Afghanistan won by 17 runs** (DLS). ‡**Afghanistan 184-8** (20 overs) (Najeeb Tarakai 90, Mohammad Nabi 34; B. J. McCarthy 4-33); **Ireland 93-9** (11 overs) (P. R. Stirling 34; Karim Janat 3-24, Rashid Khan 5-3). *MoM:* Najeeb Tarakai and Rashid Khan. *T20I debut:* B. J. McCarthy. *In the 600th Twenty20 international, Rashid equalled the fourth-best figures in the format and hurried Afghanistan to a series victory. He was allowed only two overs, as Ireland's run-chase was reduced to 111 in 11, but finished with 5-3 as they lost seven for 14. Before the rain they were going well, reaching 65-2 at the start of the seventh over in reply to Afghanistan's 184-8; Paul Stirling thumped four sixes in ten deliveries. On resuming, Ireland needed 46 from 29, but Rashid caught Porterfield to start the collapse. Najeeb Tarakai had dominated Afghanistan's batting with 90 from 58 balls (including five sixes) before becoming the third of debutant Barry McCarthy's four wickets. Mohammad Nabi was dismissed by McCarthy's next delivery – for a 15-ball 34.*

Third Twenty20 international At Greater Noida, March 12, 2017. **Afghanistan won by 28 runs. Afghanistan 233-8** (20 overs) (Mohammad Shahzad 72, Mohammad Nabi 89; K. J. O'Brien 4-45); ‡**Ireland 205** (19.2 overs) (P. R. Stirling 49, S. R. Thompson 43, G. C. Wilson 59; Rashid Khan 3-28). *MoM:* Mohammad Nabi. *MoS:* Rashid Khan. *Shahzad was the launch pad for Afghanistan's clean sweep, with five sixes in his 72 from 43 balls, but Nabi hoisted them to their highest T20 total with an astonishing 30-ball 89 and nine sixes; he was run out off the innings' final delivery, after Afghanistan crashed 104 from the last six overs. McCarthy bowled two of those, conceded 43 and finished with 0-69, the most expensive bowling in a T20 international. Ireland needed a daunting 234 – yet, thanks to a powerplay score of 91-1, a joint record in all T20Is, were still ahead midway through the penultimate over. Openers Stirling and Thompson had smashed eight sixes and 92 runs in 38 balls between them, while Gary Wilson's defiant 59 took Ireland past 200, but their last five fell for four in seven deliveries.*

First one-day international At Greater Noida, March 15, 2017. **Afghanistan won by 30 runs.** ‡**Afghanistan 292-7** (50 overs) (Noor Ali Zadran 51, Rahmat Shah 78); **Ireland 262** (46.5 overs) (P. R. Stirling 68, W. T. S. Porterfield 119; Dawlat Zadran 4-53, Rashid Khan 4-48). *MoM:* W. T. S. Porterfield. *A change of format failed to change Ireland's fortunes. Needing 79 from 80 balls with seven wickets left, they added just 48 and were bowled out with three overs to spare after Dawlat Zadran and Rashid sparked another collapse. Porterfield's highest one-day score had led Ireland to a commanding position. He put on 157 at a run a ball with Stirling, who reached his first ODI fifty since 2015, but Dawlat dismissed Porterfield and Wilson with consecutive legal deliveries, and Ireland's next 41 balls produced a wide, 22 singles and three wickets. Batting first, Afghanistan were disappointed to miss 300. They passed 100 in the 16th over and, although Stirling and Stuart Thompson conceded just 34 from their combined eight, fifties from Rahmat Shah and Noor Ali*

Zadran steered them to 150-1 in 29 overs. Still, Nabi's power hitting brought 32 off the last three, which proved more than enough.

Second one-day international At Greater Noida, March 17, 2017. **Afghanistan won by 34 runs.** ‡**Afghanistan 338** (50 overs) (Mohammad Shahzad 63, Rahmat Shah 68, Asghar Stanikzai 101; P. R. Stirling 6-55); **Ireland 304** (47.3 overs) (E. C. Joyce 55, P. R. Stirling 95; Rashid Khan 6-43). *MoM:* P. R. Stirling. *This was the third time Ireland had played an international on St Patrick's Day: memorably, they had beaten Pakistan at the 2007 World Cup, and Zimbabwe at the 2014 World T20, but their luck ran out here, despite a stunning all-round performance from Stirling. In his 200th game for Ireland, he became their first player to take six wickets in an ODI, and was one hit away from following up with a century – a double achieved only by England's Paul Collingwood. He had sent down just six overs in his previous 13 internationals but, bowling predominantly leg-spin, collected 6-34 in his second five-over spell. Next, chasing 339, Stirling put on 113 with Ed Joyce, Ireland's first century opening partnership for six years. He had hit five sixes in 80 balls when he was given lbw, a verdict undermined by TV replays. The dismissal seriously affected the run-chase, and was the first of six wickets for Rashid, an Afghan record; it was also the first time in 3,851 ODIs that two bowlers had taken six. Captain Asghar Stanikzai had struck a maiden one-day century, including six sixes in 90 balls, to provide the backbone of Afghanistan's highest ODI total.*

Third one-day international At Greater Noida, March 19, 2017. **Ireland won by six wickets.** ‡**Afghanistan 264-8** (50 overs) (Gulbadeen Naib 51, Rashid Khan 56, Shafiqullah Shinwari 50*); **Ireland 265-4** (48.3 overs) (P. R. Stirling 99, A. Balbirnie 85*). *MoM:* P. R. Stirling. *On the day Boyd Rankin left the tour with a back injury, Ireland won for the first time. Stirling was again denied a century – only the second Ireland batsman dismissed for 99 in an ODI, after Eoin Morgan (on debut) against Scotland in 2006 – but Andrew Balbirnie saw them home with 85* from 74 balls. Significantly, Rashid finished wicketless. Peter Chase's first over lasted ten deliveries, before he removed the openers in his next two, and Afghanistan slumped to 67-5 at the start of the 18th. But fifties for Nos 7, 8 and 9 – a first in 3,852 ODIs – meant they batted out the 50 overs and scored another 197 for the loss of only three more wickets. Shafiqullah was especially brutal in his 28-ball 50 from No. 9. Ireland still needed 86 from 12.2 when Stirling was bowled by Nabi, but Balbirnie averted fears of another collapse.*

Fourth one-day international At Greater Noida, March 22, 2017. **Ireland won by three wickets.** ‡**Afghanistan 220** (49.5 overs) (K. J. O'Brien 4-26); **Ireland 224-7** (46.5 overs) (K. J. O'Brien 72*; Mohammad Nabi 4-30). *MoM:* K. J. O'Brien. *Kevin O'Brien levelled the series with 72* in the country where he made his name in the 2011 World Cup. Afghanistan were favourites when he retired hurt on nine in the 20th over, with the hamstring injury which was to end his tour; that left Ireland on 73-3, with Joyce, Stirling and Porterfield back in the pavilion. But O'Brien returned at 130-6, and soon hit consecutive balls from Rashid for six and four; under pressure, Rashid bowled a wide which went for five, and 18 came off the over. O'Brien won the game with successive fours off Dawlat. Earlier, opening the bowling in place of the dropped Chase, he had taken four wickets, including Afghanistan's top three in his first three overs. Spinners Jacob Mulder and Andy McBrine reduced them to 83-7, before three of their last five batsmen passed 40, and they looked capable of settling the series. This time, however, Ireland finished the job.*

Fifth one-day international At Greater Noida, March 24, 2017. **Afghanistan won by seven wickets.** ‡**Ireland 229** (48.1 overs) (P. R. Stirling 51; Rashid Khan 4-29); **Afghanistan 231-3** (48.4 overs) (Rahmat Shah 108*, Samiullah Shenwari 62*). *MoM:* Rahmat Shah. *MoS:* P. R. Stirling. *ODI debut:* Najeeb Tarakai (Afghanistan). *The one-day series ended with another Irish collapse, which handed Afghanistan a straightforward target. Rahmat Shah completed his second ODI century just before winning the game with his only six, to ensure a 3–2 victory; he shared a fourth-wicket stand of 133* with the entertaining Samiullah. Afghanistan should have had more than 230 to chase after Porterfield won his first toss since the T20Is. Though Rashid became the youngest player (18 years 185 days) to take 50 ODI wickets when he removed Joyce, Stirling scored his fourth half-century in five innings. And when Porterfield hit successive fours off Fareed Ahmad in the 32nd over, Ireland were 156-2. But Porterfield was caught behind next ball. Rashid and Dawlat then stepped in to make it 193-7; McBrine and George Dockrell put on 34 for the eighth wicket before Fareed dismissed both in the 48th over.*

For the match between Afghanistan and Ireland in the Intercontinental Cup (March 28–30), see page 1069.

AFGHANISTAN v IRELAND IN THE UAE IN 2017-18

IAN CALLENDER

One-day internationals (3): Afghanistan 1, Ireland 2

Since Afghanistan and Ireland first faced each other in 2009, they have squabbled over who was the pre-eminent Associate Member. At Greater Noida earlier in the year, Afghanistan won across all three formats. But Ireland snapped back here. It was a triumphant, if somewhat illusory, send-off for John Bracewell, who handed the reins to Graham Ford after an unremarkable two and a half years in charge. Leg-spinner Rashid Khan proved dangerous throughout. But they were caught on the hop by another teenager. Mujeeb Zadran, a genre-busting slow bowler who had bowled Afghanistan to victory in the Under-19 Asia Cup a month before, took four wickets in the first game. But Ireland developed plans, inspired by opener Paul Stirling, easily the best batsman on either side. He started the comeback with 82, and lit up the decider with a brilliant century.

IRISH TOURING PARTY

*W. T. S. Porterfield, J. Anderson, A. Balbirnie, P. K. D. Chase, G. H. Dockrell, B. J. McCarthy, J. I. Mulder, T. J. Murtagh, K. J. O'Brien, N. J. O'Brien, S. W. Poynter, W. B. Rankin, S. Singh, P. R. Stirling, G. C. Wilson. *Coach:* J. G. Bracewell.

First one-day international At Sharjah, December 5, 2017. **Afghanistan won by 138 runs. Afghanistan 238-9** (50 overs) (Rahmat Shah 50, Nasir Ahmadzai 53; T. J. Murtagh 3-28, W. B. Rankin 4-44); **‡Ireland 100** (31.4 overs) (Mujeeb Zadran 4-24, Rashid Khan 3-28). *MoM:* Mujeeb Zadran. *ODI debut:* Mujeeb Zadran. *Sixteen-year-old mystery spinner Mujeeb Zadran, the first male international born this century, claimed four wickets in his first seven overs in ODIs. He took the new ball, pinned Paul Stirling and hit the stumps three times. Rashid Khan was initially outshone, but removed the last two batsmen to dismiss Ireland for 100, their fifth-lowest total in ODIs. By contrast, Ireland's three slow bowlers had returned 0-110 from 20 overs as Afghanistan scored 238-9, set up by a century partnership for the third wicket between Rahmat Shah and Nasir Ahmadzai. They lost four for five, but the tail wagged: Shafiqullah hit 36 off 23 balls, while Rashid made 48, before gifting Kevin O'Brien his 100th ODI wicket – the first Irishman to the mark.*

Second one-day international At Sharjah, December 7, 2017. **Ireland won by 51 runs. ‡Ireland 271-9** (50 overs) (P. R. Stirling 82, G. H. Dockrell 62*); **Afghanistan 220** (45.2 overs) (B. J. McCarthy 5-46). *MoM:* B. J. McCarthy. *Mujeeb and Rashid managed four wickets between them, but Ireland racked up a match-winning total. William Porterfield and Stirling put on 115 for the first wicket and, though they lost three on 160 after Stirling was lbw to Rashid for 82, George Dockrell's career-best 62* provided late impetus. Even so, Afghanistan needed 90 with six wickets in hand and 13 overs to go. But Peter Chase bowled Mohammad Nabi, then had Gulbadeen Naib caught low by Stuart Poynter. Barry McCarthy killed off any hope with three wickets in eight balls for his maiden ODI five-for.*

Third one-day international At Sharjah, December 10, 2017. **Ireland won by five wickets. ‡Afghanistan 177** (48.2 overs) (G. H. Dockrell 4-28, B. J. McCarthy 3-32); **Ireland 180-5** (38 overs) (P. R. Stirling 101). *MoM:* P. R. Stirling. *Stirling's century helped Ireland complete a comeback series win. The bowlers had set it up, dismantling Afghanistan for 177, with Dockrell finally getting some turn to finish with four wickets. Rahmat and Rashid hit 44 each. Though Mujeeb bowled Porterfield with a beauty, Andy Balbirnie and Gary Wilson stuck around with Stirling, who went from 81 to 101 in four balls off Shapoor Zadran. It was his tenth century for Ireland, two and a half years after his ninth, bookending John Bracewell's reign as coach.*

AUSTRALIAN CRICKET IN 2017

Crowning glory

DANIEL BRETTIG

The Ashes Crown the Year was the title of a book by Jack Fingleton about Australia's 1953 tour of England, amid celebrations of the coronation. It might also describe Australia's fortunes in 2017, which was punctuated by overseas (mis)adventures, commercial uncertainties, and an ugly pay dispute that led to the cancellation of an A tour of South Africa. But the year was deemed ultimately successful when the Ashes were reclaimed in emphatic style.

That result was a triumph for Australia's prolific captain Steve Smith, his leading spin bowler Nathan Lyon, and the support staff who guided the big

AUSTRALIA IN 2017

	Played	*Won*	*Lost*	*Drawn/No result*
Tests	11	6	3	2
One-day internationals	15	5	8	2
Twenty20 internationals	5	2	3	–

DECEMBER / JANUARY	3 Tests and 5 ODIs (h) v Pakistan	(see *Wisden 2017*, page 865)
JANUARY	3 ODIs (a) v New Zealand	(page 896)
FEBRUARY	3 T20Is (h) v Sri Lanka	(page 798)
FEBRUARY / MARCH	4 Tests (a) v India	(page 831)
APRIL		
MAY		
JUNE	ICC Champions Trophy (in England)	(page 263)
JULY		
AUGUST / SEPTEMBER	2 Tests (a) v Bangladesh	(page 811)
SEPTEMBER / OCTOBER	5 ODIs and 3 T20Is (a) v India	(page 846)
NOVEMBER		
DECEMBER / JANUARY / FEBRUARY	5 Tests and 5 ODIs (h) v England	(page 349)

For a review of Australian domestic cricket from the 2016-17 season, see page 801.

Matt King, Getty Images

Broad appeal: off-spinner Nathan Lyon pleads for another Ashes wicket.

three pacemen – Mitchell Starc, Josh Hazlewood and Pat Cummins – to a physical and technical peak in front of the second-biggest aggregate attendance in Ashes history. But it arrived at the end of 12 months that fluctuated wildly, whether on the pitch, on the physio's bench, or in the boardroom.

A willingness to learn had informed Australia's preparation for the Test tour of India in February and March, after they had twice been thrashed in Asian conditions by Pakistan (in 2014) and Sri Lanka (2016). Smith's rallying call – "To succeed in India, you've got to forget what you do in Australia" – was taken on board by a squad granted the luxury of a training camp in carefully curated conditions at Dubai Sports City, as opposed to the usual pantomime of tour games in India on pitches a world apart from the Test strips.

The preparation paid dividends in Pune, where the ball was spitting and turning inside the first hour. Australia's batsmen, playing rigidly down the line of the stumps instead of fencing at deliveries that spun expansively, put up a reasonable total. Then, after a session with spin coach Sridharan Sriram, Steve O'Keefe tore down India's batting. Smith's masterful century ensured the chase was beyond India, leaving O'Keefe to clean up again.

The result shook up the world, and it was to India's credit that they bounced back with victories in Bangalore and Dharamsala. Australia made their mark by fighting to the end, even if, on the final afternoon in Bangalore, Smith erred by looking for dressing-room assistance on whether to review an lbw. Virat Kohli claimed this was a systematic tactic – an accusation that said more about the harried state of India's out-of-form captain than Australian skulduggery. He missed the decider through injury – Ajinkya Rahane led calmly in his absence – and had to hoist the Border–Gavaskar Trophy in the home side's viewing area. Smith, who described the incident as a "brain fade", led allcomers with the bat. Lyon took over from O'Keefe as the main weapon, and was similarly effective with the ball, having grown immeasurably in Asian conditions since looking lost in Sri Lanka.

Drained by the tour and frustrated by the result, the players were treated to a rare public show of support by Cricket Australia's chairman David Peever. But they discovered that the board were keen to renegotiate the basis of player remuneration. Relations between CA and the Australian Cricketers' Association had deteriorated for some years. Now, as the end of the existing agreement crept closer, they fell apart completely.

James Sutherland, CA's chief executive, fired a warning shot in May by telling Alistair Nicholson, his opposite number, that the players would be out of contract after June 30 should the ACA not accept the thrust of the board's offer, which replaced revenue-sharing with fixed wages and a capped bonus system for elite players only. The Test vice-captain David Warner, over at the IPL, pointed out that if CA remained stubborn "they might not have a team for the Ashes".

As the saga rolled on, the Champions Trophy campaign was brief, the women took part in their World Cup under short-term deals, and an A tour of South Africa in July fell by the wayside. CA's lead negotiator, Kevin Roberts, announced that money due to out-of-contract players after June 30 would be redirected to the game's lower levels. It did not work, and pre-season training continued without payment. Ultimately, CA blinked, under pressure from commercial partners and state associations to deal more constructively with the union.

Roberts, considered a successor to Sutherland, was sidelined at the ACA's request, leaving Sutherland, Nicholson and their lieutenants to thrash out an agreement in order to save the tour of Bangladesh. When in August the two chief executives announced a peace deal, which included women for the first time and also enhanced the players' voice in issues such as scheduling, they looked exhausted. But there was little doubt CA's bluff had been called. "Neither side have got everything they wanted," said Sutherland. "These negotiations shouldn't be approached with a winner-takes-all mindset." His pragmatism contrasted with the views of Peever and Roberts, both steeped in business knowledge but with little appreciation of how player power had grown over a 20-year period in which Australia's corporate sector had seen the erosion of unions.

When Smith's team lost the First Test in Bangladesh, they were immediately branded overpaid prima donnas by sections of the media. A dominant performance at Chittagong squared the Test series and silenced most of the critics, but a side injury to Hazlewood emphasised the careful work ahead to get the pace bowlers right. Only Cummins was in Bangladesh and for part of the limited-overs series that followed in India, where Australia meandered to defeats overshadowed by the events in Bristol that ultimately ruled Ben Stokes out of the Ashes. His absence was a decided advantage for Smith's team, and set England on a more conservative tactical path.

Questions remained about the composition of the Australian squad for the First Ashes Test at the Gabba, where the selectors' choices caused a major stir. Shaun Marsh was recalled a few months after losing his central contract, while Tim Paine won the wicketkeeping spot, despite being Tasmania's No. 2, behind the national incumbent Matthew Wade. In the event, both Marsh and Paine contributed well in a series defined by Smith's crease occupation and the fast bowlers' collaboration with a Lyon rampant. Starc was fit and fast for the first three Tests, Hazlewood bowled the most important spell of the series on a tense final day at Adelaide, and Cummins surprised even himself by maturing from years on the injury sidelines to playing nine Tests in a row.

Smith, who paced his hotel suite nervously after not enforcing the follow-on under the Adelaide floodlights, so granting England a glimmer of hope via the hooping pink ball, batted endlessly and relentlessly. He and his team were rewarded for finding a true Test match tempo to outlast England's depleted attack, even if a moribund Melbourne pitch, rated poor by the ICC, ensured a draw and no 5–0 whitewash to follow those of 2006-07 and 2013-14. The narcotic quality of much of the cricket did not dissuade the crowds which, when combined with those for the flourishing Big Bash, threatened to pass two million mark for the first time in an Australian summer. All this was a good sign, given the looming broadcast deals, and it looked as if an ever-so-slightly more convivial partnership between the players and their board might have more revenue to share.

AUSTRALIA v SRI LANKA IN 2016-17

DANIEL BRETTIG

Twenty20 internationals (3): Australia 1, Sri Lanka 2

This series provided one of the starkest examples of international cricket's madness: the concluding game at Adelaide ended just 15 hours before an entirely separate Australian squad embarked on a Test match against India at Pune. Cricket Australia's chief executive, James Sutherland, defended the scheduling and the enforced absence of many senior players, insisting the Twenty20s offered opportunities to the likes of Michael Klinger – making his international debut at the age of 36 – and wicketkeeper Tim Paine, nearly six years after he last appeared for Australia. But there was an evident lack of cohesion, despite the efforts of the high-profile interim coaching trio of Justin Langer, Jason Gillespie and Ricky Ponting.

Sri Lanka themselves made a raft of changes from the side that had defeated South Africa in the same format a month earlier, but still appeared the more settled, and wrapped things up in the first two matches. Upul Tharanga captained adroitly, even if he barely scored a run, while the return of Lasith Malinga lent skill and leadership to the attack. A sense of calm and game-awareness permeated through the Sri Lankans, exemplified by the Man of the Series, Asela Gunaratne, during his two match-winning innings; even with 48 runs to collect from the final three overs at Geelong, there was no panic. The contrast with the Australian batting line-up, which habitually started well before subsiding, was obvious.

SRI LANKAN TOURING PARTY

*W. U. Tharanga, J. R. M. V. S. Bandara, D. P. D. N. Dickwella, D. A. S. Gunaratne, C. K. Kapugedera, K. M. D. N. Kulasekara, S. L. Malinga, B. K. G. Mendis, E. M. D. Y. Munaweera, S. S. Pathirana, S. Prasanna, P. A. D. L. R. Sandakan, M. D. Shanaka, T. A. M. Siriwardene, I. Udana. *Coach:* G. X. Ford.

AUSTRALIA v SRI LANKA

First Twenty20 International

At Melbourne, February 17, 2017 (floodlit). Sri Lanka won by five wickets. Toss: Sri Lanka. Twenty20 international debuts: M. Klinger, B. Stanlake, A. J. Turner; J. R. M. V. S. Bandara.

Sri Lanka's greater experience and composure won the night, though not until the last ball. After Australia were inserted, acting-captain Finch and Michael Klinger – comfortably the oldest of their three debutants – laid a sound foundation, but the innings never quite accelerated. In his first international appearance since February 2016, Malinga's slingy speed and slower balls were as difficult to hit as ever, while Prasanna's skiddy leg-breaks went at less than a run a ball. Still, Sri Lanka needed 169 to win, and lost Tharanga in the first over to a fierce Cummins awayswinger. Dickwella and Munaweera took 24 off the fourth – bowled by 6ft 8in Queenslander Billy Stanlake, in his first match – and kept the chase within sight, before Gunaratne made Sri Lanka favourites, finding the gaps with panache en route to a 37-ball 52. Australia's other debutant, off-spinning all-rounder Ashton Turner, took two wickets in three balls, but only six were needed from the last over. With the scores level, Kapugedera calmly drove Tye's final ball through cover.

Man of the Match: D. A. S. Gunaratne.

Australia

		B	4/6
1 *A. J. Finch *c 9 b 4*	43	34	2/2
2 M. Klinger *c 9 b 10*	38	32	4
3 T. M. Head *c 7 b 9*	31	25	0/1
4 M. C. Henriques *c 6 b 11*	17	10	0/1
5 A. J. Turner *c 7 b 9*	18	13	1
6 J. P. Faulkner *not out*	14	7	2
7 †T. D. Paine *run out*	0	0	0
8 P. J. Cummins *not out*	0	0	0
B 1, lb 1, w 4, nb 1	7		
6 overs: 47-0 (20 overs)	168-6		

1/76 2/86 3/116 4/153 5/153 6/162

9 A. Zampa, 10 A. J. Tye and 11 B. Stanlake did not bat.

Malinga 4–6–29–2; Kulasekara 4–5–38–0; Bandara 3–4–35–1; Prasanna 4–10–23–0; Sandakan 4–8–30–1; Gunaratne 1–1–11–1.

Sri Lanka

		B	4/6
1 †D. P. D. N. Dickwella *c 2 b 9*	30	25	4/1
2 *W. U. Tharanga *c 7 b 8*	0	2	0
3 E. M. D. Y. Munaweera *c 1 b 9*	44	29	6
4 D. A. S. Gunaratne *st 7 b 5*	52	37	7
5 T. A. M. Siriwardene *lbw b 5*	15	11	1
6 C. K. Kapugedera *not out*	10	7	1
7 S. Prasanna *not out*	8	9	1
B 1, lb 3, w 9	13		
6 overs: 62-1 (20 overs)	172-5		

1/5 2/79 3/91 4/151 5/152

8 K. M. D. N. Kulasekara, 9 S. L. Malinga, 10 P. A. D. L. R. Sandakan and 11 J. R. M. V. S. Bandara did not bat.

Cummins 4–11–29–1; Stanlake 3–6–42–0; Faulkner 4–9–27–0; Tye 3–6–32–0; Zampa 4–6–26–2; Turner 2–4–12–2.

Umpires: M. D. Martell and P. Wilson. Third umpire: S. J. Nogajski.
Referee: J. J. Crowe.

AUSTRALIA v SRI LANKA

Second Twenty20 International

At Geelong, February 19, 2017 (floodlit). Sri Lanka won by two wickets. Toss: Sri Lanka. Twenty20 international debut: J. A. Richardson.

In the first senior men's international at Kardinia Park, south-west of Melbourne, Gunaratne pulled off a series-sealing heist. Australia seemed certain to have the better of a chilly night when Sri Lanka needed a distant 48 runs from the final three overs, and remained comfortable when that became 36 off two. But Gunaratne climbed into Henriques's military medium, clouting three consecutive sixes, then a four, to leave 14 from the last. Tye's knuckle ball induced Kulasekara to sky the first delivery, but Gunaratne managed to cross and, in an exhilarating sequence, hammered three more boundaries, to the delight of a sizeable Sri Lankan expatriate contingent. Australia were left to lament their earlier collapse from 113 for two in the 14th over to 173 all out; No. 4 Henriques made an unbeaten fifty, but no one after him reached double figures. Kulasekara's four-for deserved much of the credit: even when Sri Lanka slid to 40 for five, the chase was never out of reach.

Man of the Match: D. A. S. Gunaratne.

Australia

		B	4/6
1 M. Klinger *c 1 b 11*	43	37	2/1
2 *A. J. Finch *c and b 11*	12	10	2
3 B. R. Dunk *b 5*	32	14	3/3
4 M. C. Henriques *not out*	56	37	2/2
5 T. M. Head *c 1 b 9*	4	4	0
6 A. J. Turner *c 6 b 8*	7	6	0
7 J. P. Faulkner *lbw b 10*	1	2	0
8 †T. D. Paine *lbw b 10*	7	4	1
9 P. J. Cummins *b 9*	3	3	0
10 A. J. Tye *lbw b 9*	0	2	0
11 J. A. Richardson *b 9*	0	1	0
Lb 5, w 3	8		
6 overs: 60-1 (20 overs)	173		

1/18 2/63 3/113 4/121 5/134 6/144 7/162 8/169 9/173

Sri Lanka

		B	4/6
1 †D. P. D. N. Dickwella *c 8 b 7*	14	8	3
2 *W. U. Tharanga *c 11 b 6*	4	4	1
3 E. M. D. Y. Munaweera *c 8 b 10*	10	4	1/1
4 B. K. G. Mendis *c 8 b 11*	5	7	0
5 D. A. S. Gunaratne *not out*	84	46	6/5
6 T. A. M. Siriwardene *c 6 b 10*	0	1	0
7 C. K. Kapugedera *c 3 b 9*	32	32	4
8 S. Prasanna *c 5 b 7*	7	9	1
9 K. M. D. N. Kulasekara *c 1 b 10*	12	8	2
10 S. L. Malinga *not out*	1	1	0
Lb 2, w 5	7		
6 overs: 45-5 (20 overs)	176-8		

1/5 2/22 3/27 4/40 5/40 6/92 7/119 8/160

11 J. R. M. V. S. Bandara did not bat.

Malinga 4–6–31–2; Kulasekara 4–9–31–4; Bandara 4–8–32–2; Munaweera 1–2–22–0; Gunaratne 3–3–26–1; Prasanna 4–8–26–1.

Turner 2–6–15–1; Cummins 3–6–28–1; Faulkner 4–6–32–2; Richardson 3–7–24–1; Tye 4–10–37–3; Henriques 4–9–38–0.

Umpires: S. D. Fry and S. J. Nogajski. Third umpire: P. Wilson.
Referee: J. J. Crowe.

AUSTRALIA v SRI LANKA

Third Twenty20 International

At Adelaide, February 22, 2017 (floodlit). Australia won by 41 runs. Toss: Sri Lanka.

Australia hit their highest total of the series to set up victory in the dead rubber. The recall of Zampa also proved crucial: Sri Lanka's chase began better than in the first two matches, but foundered once he had skidded one into the pads of the previously supreme Gunaratne. Zampa met his three wickets – all balls that zipped through the batsman's defence – with the air of a man who knew he should have played in Geelong. Faulkner lent excellent support, picking up three with his combination of seamers and over-the-wrist slower balls. It helped that there were plenty of runs to defend; Finch had been badly dropped on nought by Munaweera, and zoomed to a 32-ball 53, while opening partner Klinger hit his maiden international fifty. The innings petered out once again, as the pitch offered a little more variation to the bowlers, but Australia turned that to their advantage to end their home international season with a cheering win. Mendis kept wicket in the absence of Niroshan Dickwella, who was beginning a two-match ban for dissent.

Man of the Match: A. Zampa. *Man of the Series:* D. A. S. Gunaratne.

Australia

		B	4/6
1 *A. J. Finch *c 5 b 8*	53	32	5/3
2 M. Klinger *run out*	62	43	6/1
3 B. R. Dunk *c 8 b 7*	28	21	2/2
4 T. M. Head *c 6 b 10*	30	16	1/2
5 M. C. Henriques *not out*	2	3	0
6 A. J. Turner *c 6 b 10*	1	2	0
7 J. P. Faulkner *c 6 b 7*	2	2	0
8 †T. D. Paine *not out*	1	2	0
Lb 2, w 5, nb 1	8		
6 overs: 62-0 (20 overs)	187-6		

1/79 2/128 3/179 4/180 5/182 6/184

9 P. J. Cummins, 10 A. Zampa and 11 J. A. Richardson did not bat.

Malinga 4–10–35–2; Kulasekara 4–5–40–0; Bandara 3–7–34–0; Prasanna 3–5–25–1; Siriwardene 1–1–12–0; Gunaratne 1–1–12–0; Shanaka 4–9–27–2.

Sri Lanka

		B	4/6
1 E. M. D. Y. Munaweera *c 6 b 4*	37	25	3/2
2 *W. U. Tharanga *c 11 b 7*	14	12	1/1
3 †B. K. G. Mendis *c 9 b 11*	14	10	2
4 D. A. S. Gunaratne *lbw b 10*	4	5	0
5 T. A. M. Siriwardene *c and b 7*	35	27	1/2
6 C. K. Kapugedera *b 10*	7	6	1
7 M. D. Shanaka *lbw b 10*	0	2	0
8 S. Prasanna *c 11 b 7*	12	8	2
9 K. M. D. N. Kulasekara *not out*	8	7	1
10 S. L. Malinga *run out*	1	3	0
11 J. R. M. V. S. Bandara *run out*	5	3	1
Lb 2, w 7	9		
6 overs: 60-1 (18 overs)	146		

1/41 2/68 3/69 4/76 5/91 6/91 7/120 8/138 9/140

Turner 2–6–15–0; Richardson 3–4–38–1; Cummins 3–9–20–0; Faulkner 3–8–20–3; Henriques 1–2–10–0; Zampa 4–11–25–3; Head 2–2–16–1.

Umpires: M. D. Martell and P. Wilson. Third umpire: S. D. Fry.
Referee: J. J. Crowe.

DOMESTIC CRICKET IN AUSTRALIA IN 2016-17

PETER ENGLISH

Cricket has always been at the heart of Australia's summer, but it was a first in March 2017 when the domestic campaign wound up in the nation's Red Centre. With the MCG unavailable because of the perennial autumn clash with Australian Rules football, Alice Springs was briefly painted the dark blue of **Victoria** after they completed their first hat-trick of Sheffield Shield titles, in a competition they first won in 1892-93. The use of outgrounds has expanded in recent years, and Victoria have become the most accustomed at coping with a scattered itinerary: their nearest final venue in the past three years had been in Hobart, 370 miles from Melbourne.

Nor were Victoria fazed by another change of coach: Andrew McDonald replaced David Saker, who had moved on to the national side one season after Greg Shipperd started the winning run. Such was their dominance, they finished the regular Shield fixtures 13 points ahead of the field, set up by 50 wickets from slow left-armer Jon Holland (including eight in the drawn final), 42 from the tall seamer Chris Tremain, and Marcus Harris's 808 runs. The campaign was also brightened by the return of Test bowler James Pattinson, who headed the averages with 24 wickets at 17 after a long lay-off with back and leg injuries. Cameron White led the Matador BBQs One-Day Cup run-scorers with 457 at 76 but, despite his scene-stealing form, Victoria were knocked out in the play-off.

At the start of the Shield's last round, four teams with four wins apiece were competing to meet Victoria at Alice Springs. Fourth-placed **South Australia** leapfrogged New South Wales and Queensland to secure a replay of the previous final – but could not force the win needed to steal the title. Their chief causes for celebration were 25-year-old wicketkeeper Alex Carey, who combined 59 dismissals – a Shield record – with 594 runs, and Chadd Sayers, the season's leading wicket-taker with 62, including a career-best 11 for 76 against Tasmania; he was unlucky to miss a Test debut. South Australia had found the one-day competition harder work; only the development side **Cricket Australia XI**, who lost all six matches, kept them off the bottom of the table.

Western Australia finished third in the Shield and waved goodbye to Adam Voges after 15 seasons and 7,522 runs in the competition. But the future appeared bright, thanks to Hilton Cartwright, who was second on the tournament's run-list with 861 at 53, and gained a first Test cap in January 2017. The bowling revolved around Jason Behrendorff, who took 37 wickets in seven games, and Simon Mackin, with 35, while slow left-armer Ashton Agar renewed his promise. Life was upbeat, too, in the Twenty20 arena, where **Perth Scorchers** won the Big Bash for the third time in four years, sweeping past Sydney Sixers in the final.

Ed Cowan led the Shield's run-list with 959 at 73, showing a particular liking for the Dukes ball trialled in the second half of the season, but **New South Wales** missed the final when they slipped seven short of victory in their last match. They did retain the one-day title on the back of some suffocating off-spin from Nathan Lyon, whose four for ten from ten overs in the final ended Queensland's hopes.

Queensland had harboured hopes of a place in the Shield final, too, until they collapsed for 61 on the penultimate day of the group stage, and finished fifth. Captain and wicket-keeper Chris Hartley retired with a record 550 Shield dismissals. Joe Burns scored 724, but a poor run in November cost him his Test place.

Tasmania had a summer of turmoil. Coach Dan Marsh, who as captain had guided the state to their first Shield a decade earlier, was sacked in February as they headed towards a second successive wooden spoon. Amid the ruins, George Bailey managed 839 runs; he and Alex Doolan both reached maiden double-centuries, and Doolan's batting – in whites and coloured clothes – made him Tasmania's Player of the Year.

FIRST-CLASS AVERAGES IN 2016-17

BATTING (525 runs)

		M	*I*	*NO*	*R*	*HS*	*100*	*Avge*	*Ct/St*
1	P. S. P. Handscomb (*Victoria/Australia*)	8	13	3	809	215	3	80.90	5
2	†C. D. Hartley (*Queensland*)	8	15	8	535	102*	1	76.42	24/1
3	†E. J. M. Cowan (*New South Wales*)	9	16	3	959	212	3	73.76	1
4	M. C. Henriques (*New South Wales*)	9	13	1	775	265	2	64.58	5
5	S. P. D. Smith (*NSW/Australia*)	8	15	2	836	165*	3	64.30	16
6	†U. T. Khawaja (*Queensland/Australia*)	9	17	1	1,013	157	3	63.31	7
7	G. J. Bailey (*Tasmania*)	9	17	3	839	200*	2	59.92	3
8	A. J. Turner (*Western Australia*)	9	15	1	742	110	2	53.00	15
9	H. W. R. Cartwright (*W Aust/Australia*)	11	19	2	898	170*	2	52.82	2
10	A. J. Finch (*Victoria*)	7	13	2	581	102	1	52.81	6
11	†D. A. Warner (*NSW/Australia*)	8	15	0	769	144	3	51.26	4
12	P. M. Nevill (*NSW/Australia*)	11	17	3	717	179*	3	51.21	33/3
13	†K. R. Patterson (*New South Wales*)	10	17	2	668	111	1	44.53	4
14	†T. M. Head (*South Australia*)	9	16	1	645	137*	2	43.00	4
15	†M. S. Harris (*Victoria*)	11	20	1	808	120	2	42.52	4
16	†J. S. Lehmann (*South Australia*)	11	20	3	692	129*	1	40.70	12
17	T. L. W. Cooper (*South Australia*)	11	20	1	736	138	2	38.73	22
18	J. W. Wells (*Western Australia*)	9	17	2	578	120	2	38.53	5
19	M. Labuschagne (*Queensland*)	10	19	2	626	96	0	36.82	10
20	J. A. Burns (*Queensland/Australia*)	11	21	1	725	129	2	36.25	14
21	†D. P. Hughes (*New South Wales*)	9	16	1	543	110	1	36.20	9
22	T. J. Dean (*Victoria*)	11	20	1	664	134	1	34.94	10
23	†A. T. Carey (*South Australia*)	11	19	1	594	79	0	33.00	57/2
24	†J. B. Weatherald (*South Australia*)	11	21	1	634	135	1	31.70	9
25	C. T. Bancroft (*Western Australia*)	10	19	0	536	104	2	28.21	13

BOWLING (20 wickets)

		Style	*O*	*M*	*R*	*W*	*BB*	*5I*	*Avge*
1	J. L. Pattinson (*Victoria*)	RFM	121.5	24	418	24	5-7	2	17.41
2	J. P. Behrendorff (*Western Australia*)	LFM	212.4	44	651	37	9-37	3	17.59
3	C. P. Tremain (*Victoria*)	RFM	296.1	78	797	42	4-22	0	18.97
4	C. J. Sayers (*South Australia*)	RFM	446.2	133	1,178	62	7-84	5	19.00
5	J. R. Hazlewood (*NSW/Australia*)	RFM	309.1	88	768	38	6-89	1	20.21
6	J. M. Holland (*Victoria*)	SLA	361	66	1,039	50	7-82	2	20.78
7	J. M. Mennie (*S Australia/Australia*)	RFM	240.4	59	645	28	5-67	1	23.03
8	W. E. R. Somerville (*New South Wales*)	OB	324	84	810	35	8-136	3	23.14
9	L. W. Feldman (*Queensland*)	RFM	157	37	534	23	5-68	1	23.21
10	S. P. Mackin (*Western Australia*)	RFM	289.4	73	885	35	7-81	4	25.28
11	K. W. Richardson (*South Australia*)	RFM	270	57	830	32	5-69	1	25.93
12	S. M. Boland (*Victoria*)	RFM	261.3	55	801	29	3-39	0	27.62
13	D. J. Worrall (*South Australia*)	RFM	213.4	40	722	26	5-85	1	27.76
14	J. M. Bird (*Tasmania/Australia*)	RFM	286.2	59	872	31	3-23	0	28.12
15	P. R. George (*Queensland*)	RFM	279.2	69	822	28	3-11	0	29.35
16	J. D. Wildermuth (*Queensland*)	RFM	187.4	36	627	20	5-40	1	31.35
17	D. J. M. Moody (*Western Australia*)	RFM	256.4	53	882	28	5-59	1	31.50
18	M. A. Starc (*NSW/Australia*)	LF	284.2	56	961	29	4-36	0	33.13
19	S. L. Rainbird (*Tasmania*)	LFM	243.3	66	706	20	4-25	0	35.30
20	S. A. Milenko (*Tasmania*)	RFM	289.4	68	953	25	4-60	0	38.12
21	T. A. Copeland (*New South Wales*)	RFM	351.2	91	992	26	6-54	1	38.15
22	A. Zampa (*South Australia*)	LB	303.2	25	1,149	30	6-62	1	38.30
23	C. A. H. Stevenson (*Tasmania*)	RFM	218.2	28	845	22	4-110	0	38.40
24	N. M. Lyon (*NSW/Australia*)	OB	355.3	52	1,232	24	3-33	0	51.33

SHEFFIELD SHIELD IN 2016-17

	Played	*Won*	*Lost*	*Drawn*	*Bonus points Batting*	*Bonus points Bowling*	*Points*
VICTORIA	10	7	2	1	8.31	9	60.31
SOUTH AUSTRALIA	10	5	5	0	8.34	8.9	47.24
Western Australia	10	5	5	0	6.88	8.6	45.48
New South Wales	10	4	3	3	10.20	7.4	44.60
Queensland	10	4	5	1	8.33	8.2	41.53
Tasmania	10	1	6	3	3.64	7	19.64

Outright win = 6pts; draw = 1pt. Bonus points awarded for the first 100 overs of each team's first innings: 0.01 batting points for every run over the first 200; 0.1 bowling points for each wicket taken.

At Brisbane, October 25–28, 2016 (day/night). **New South Wales won by 225 runs. New South Wales 327-7 dec** (S. P. D. Smith 117, K. R. Patterson 111; L. W. Feldman 5-68) **and 367-7 dec** (D. A. Warner 134); **‡Queensland 330-6 dec** (J. A. Burns 129) **and 139.** *New South Wales 7.87pts, Queensland 2pts. In the first of two day/night rounds, both NSW innings featured a double-century stand. First time round, Steve Smith and Kurtis Patterson added 228 for the third wicket; later, David Warner and Ed Cowan (95) opened with 230. After three declarations, Doug Bollinger – a full sub for Mitchell Starc, withdrawn by Cricket Australia – bowled out Queensland with 4-32.*

At Melbourne, October 25–28, 2016 (day/night). **Victoria won by 113 runs. Victoria 415** (M. S. Harris 115) **and 204-9 dec; ‡Tasmania 255 and 251.** *Victoria 8.73pts, Tasmania 0.95pts. Marcus Harris scored 115 and 77 on his Shield debut for Victoria after leaving Western Australia. In his first first-class match since February, Victoria's Peter Siddle bowled 26 overs to earn a brief Test recall.*

At Perth, October 25–28, 2016 (day/night). **South Australia won by ten wickets. Western Australia 271-9 dec and 302** (S. E. Marsh 110); **‡South Australia 505-9 dec** (C. J. Ferguson 101, T. L. W. Cooper 138) **and 69-0.** *South Australia 9.61pts, Western Australia 1.51pts. Tom Cooper and Alex Carey (79) added 198 for South Australia's seventh wicket to set up a comfortable win.*

At Sydney, November 4–7, 2016. **New South Wales won by three wickets. ‡Western Australia 216** (S. N. J. O'Keefe 5-65) **and 177** (W. E. R. Somerville 5-65); **New South Wales 298** (N. J. Maddinson 116; A. C. Agar 6-110) **and 96-7.** *New South Wales 7.98pts, Western Australia 1.16pts. Spinners took 28 of the 37 wickets, with eight for Steve O'Keefe and nine for Will Somerville, before Ashton Agar, on his way to 10-141, gave NSW a scare, grabbing four as they chased 96.*

At Adelaide, November 4–6, 2016. **South Australia won by an innings and 94 runs. ‡Tasmania 98** (C. J. Sayers 6-32) **and 289** (G. J. Bailey 142*; C. J. Sayers 5-44); **South Australia 481** (J. B. Weatherald 135, J. S. Lehmann 129*). *South Australia 8.98pts, Tasmania 0.8pts. No one reached 20 as Tasmania folded for 98. After Jake Weatherald completed a maiden century on his 22nd birthday, Tasmania slumped again, to 18-4; George Bailey fought back with 142*, but Sayers's 11-76 gave him 21 wickets in his last two games against them.*

At Melbourne, November 4–6, 2016. **Victoria won by an innings and 81 runs. ‡Queensland 137 and 199; Victoria 417** (C. L. White 104*). *Victoria 8.61pts, Queensland 0.7pts. Queensland collapsed to 11-4 in their first innings, and 23-4 – after a triple-wicket maiden from left-arm spinner Jon Holland – in their second. Victoria won with more than four sessions in hand. Their captain Matthew Wade completed five catches and a stumping in the first innings.*

At Sydney, November 17–20, 2016. **Victoria won by 198 runs. ‡Victoria 510-6 dec** (T. J. Dean 134, P. S. P. Handscomb 215) **and 105-2 dec; New South Wales 225 and 192.** *Victoria 7.94pts, New South Wales 0.55pts. Peter Handscomb earned a Test debut after his maiden double-hundred, putting on 225 with Travis Dean for Victoria's third wicket as they coasted to a third win.*

At Brisbane, November 17–20, 2016. **Queensland won by 128 runs. Queensland 475-7 dec** (M. T. Renshaw 108, U. T. Khawaja 106) **and 228-7 dec; ‡South Australia 258 and 317.** *Queensland 8.43pts, South Australia 1.08pts. A week after 20-year-old Matt Renshaw added 184 for Queensland's second wicket with Usman Khawaja, they were batting together in the Adelaide Test. South Australia came close to surviving the final day, before being bowled out with two overs to spare.*

At Perth, November 17–20, 2016. **Tasmania won by nine wickets. Western Australia 262** (A. J. Turner 110) **and 345** (J. W. Wells 120, S. M. Whiteman 104); **‡Tasmania 402** (A. J. Doolan 202*;

J. P. Behrendorff 5-80) **and 209-1.** *Tasmania 7.9pts, Western Australia 1.22pts. Two batsmen retired with concussion: Western Australia's captain Adam Voges was struck by a bouncer from Cameron Stevenson, while Alex Doolan retired hurt after completing a maiden double-hundred. Jonathan Wells made the most of a reprieve on 13 – the umpire changed his mind about a slip catch – to reach his first century, but Tasmania cruised past a target of 206.*

At Townsville, November 26–29, 2016. **Queensland won by 97 runs. ‡Queensland 422 and 252-6 dec; Western Australia 340-6 dec** (C. T. Bancroft 103) **and 237.** *Queensland 7.96pts, Western Australia 1.45pts. Western Australia's strike bowler Jason Behrendorff injured his left calf after bowling 12 overs, and took no further part in his side's defeat.*

At Hobart, November 26–29, 2016. **Drawn. New South Wales 495-5 dec** (M. C. Henriques 115, P. M. Nevill 179*) **and 128-1 dec; ‡Tasmania 209** (T. A. Copeland 6-54) **and 266-4** (J. P. Faulkner 100*). *Tasmania 1.37pts, New South Wales 2.86pts. Dropped by Australia, NSW keeper Peter Nevill scored 179* and added 221 for the fourth wicket with Moises Henriques. Set 415 to win, or more than a day to survive, Tasmania saved the game thanks to a fifth-wicket stand of 185* between Beau Webster (80*) and James Faulkner, whose century was his first in the Shield.*

At Melbourne, November 26–29, 2016. **Victoria won by five wickets. South Australia 405** (T. M. Head 130) **and 162; ‡Victoria 367** (A. J. Finch 102) **and 201-5.** *Victoria 8.11pts, South Australia 2.6pts. Victoria's 19-year-old keeper Sam Cooper – called up because Matthew Wade was on international duty – made six catches in South Australia's first innings, when Travis Head and Cooper added 188 for the fifth wicket. Aaron Finch raised his first Shield century since March 2010, before a South Australian collapse cleared the way for Victoria's fourth win in four.*

At Adelaide, December 5–7, 2016 (day/night). **South Australia won by two wickets. New South Wales 269 and 87** (C. J. Sayers 5-27); **‡South Australia 236 and 121-8.** *South Australia 7.36pts, New South Wales 1.69pts. The second round of day/night matches produced a low-scoring thriller. On the third day, NSW collapsed for 87 – almost all of it from Cowan (45) and Ryan Carters (25*). South Australia needed only 121. But debutant Charles Stobo seized their first three wickets for the second time in the match; they slumped to 49-5 before Jake Lehmann's 47* got them across the line.*

At Hobart, December 5–8, 2016 (day/night). **Drawn. Tasmania 203** (J. M. Holland 5-49) **and 387-9 dec** (B. J. Webster 122*); **‡Victoria 230 and 319-8.** *Tasmania 2.03pts, Victoria 2.3pts. Tasmania lost their chance of victory when rain arrived with 4.5 overs to go; set 361, Victoria were eight down, with John Hastings unlikely to bat after a knee injury. Victoria retained their unbeaten record, and went into the Christmas break leading the table by six points.*

At Perth, December 5–8, 2016 (day/night). **Western Australia won by eight wickets. ‡Queensland 353** (U. T. Khawaja 157; S. P. Mackin 5-68) **and 138** (S. P. Mackin 6-33); **Western Australia 265** (A. J. Turner 100) **and 227-2** (J. W. Wells 113*). *Western Australia 7.35pts, Queensland 2.39pts. Western Australia completed their first victory of the season early on the final day. Simon Mackin had improved his career-best figures twice to finish with 11-101, but their prospects seemed bleak at 93-6 in their first innings, replying to 353. Ashton Turner and the tail reduced the deficit to 88, Mackin ripped through Queensland's second innings, and Wells steered his side home.*

At Brisbane, February 1–4, 2017. **Queensland won by 133 runs. ‡Queensland 405-9 dec** (C. D. Hartley 102*) **and 146-6 dec; Tasmania 200 and 218.** *Queensland 7.71pts, Tasmania 0.6pts. The Sheffield Shield resumed after the Big Bash, with the teams switching from Kookaburra to Dukes balls. Queensland's Chris Hartley followed a century by becoming the leading wicketkeeper in Shield history, overtaking Darren Berry's 546 dismissals, and led his team to victory.*

At Adelaide (Glenelg Oval), February 1–3, 2017. **Western Australia won by seven runs. Western Australia 201** (C. J. Sayers 5-68) **and 245** (K. W. Richardson 5-69); **‡South Australia 247** (S. P. Mackin 7-81) **and 192** (S. P. Mackin 5-82). *Western Australia 7.01pts, South Australia 1.47pts. Mackin improved his best figures for the third successive innings, and finished with 12-163 – giving him 23 in two Shield matches – as South Australia fell just short of a target of 200.*

At Melbourne, February 1–4, 2017. **New South Wales won by an innings and 77 runs. Victoria 258 and 188; ‡New South Wales 523** (E. J. M. Cowan 212, P. M. Nevill 118). *New South Wales 8.08pts, Victoria 0.98pts. Victoria suffered their first defeat of the season, as New South Wales adjusted far better to the Dukes ball. Cowan scored his second double-hundred – though his first century since October 2015 – and added 202 for NSW's fifth wicket with Nevill. But only Dean, who carried his bat through Victoria's second innings for 79*, stood firm against Sean Abbott and Somerville. Debutant Will Pucovski could not bat after suffering concussion in the field.*

Sayers 34.2–13–84–7; Worrall 32–10–86–1; Mennie 26–10–53–1; Zampa 44–5–175–1; Head 27–6–62–0; Dalton 1–0–1–0; Lehmann 2–0–10–0. *Second innings*—Sayers 27–9–57–1; Worrall 15–2–46–2; Mennie 23–6–41–2; Zampa 30.5–8–86–2; Dalton 5–1–12–0; Head 7–2–31–2; Weatherald 4–0–14–1; Cooper 5–3–4–0; Lehmann 6–2–19–0.

South Australia

J. D. Dalton b Pattinson	0	– b Fawad Ahmed	32
J. B. Weatherald b Holland	60	– c White b Pattinson	2
C. J. Ferguson c White b Holland	26	– c Fawad Ahmed b Pattinson	2
*T. M. Head lbw b Holland	0	– not out	137
J. S. Lehmann c Quiney b Holland	14	– st Gotch b Fawad Ahmed	1
T. L. W. Cooper b Pattinson	6	– c White b Fawad Ahmed	10
†A. T. Carey c White b Holland	57	– b Holland	45
J. M. Mennie c Gotch b Holland	36	– not out	5
A. Zampa c Finch b Christian	31		
C. J. Sayers not out	23		
D. J. Worrall c White b Holland	17		
B 3, lb 12, w 2	17	Lb 2	2
1/0 (1) 2/76 (3) 3/76 (4) (84.3 overs)	287	1/3 (2) (6 wkts, 65 overs)	236
4/106 (5) 5/115 (6) 6/121 (2)		2/11 (3) 3/108 (1)	
7/189 (8) 8/232 (7) 9/256 (9) 10/287 (11)		4/112 (5) 5/140 (6) 6/226 (7)	

Pattinson 17–5–47–2; Tremain 17–5–41–0; Holland 26.3–5–82–7; Fawad Ahmed 10–0–55–0; Christian 14–3–47–1. *Second innings*—Pattinson 12–1–45–2; Tremain 7–3–20–0; Holland 18–2–70–1; Fawad Ahmed 21–2–81–3; Christian 5–1–12–0; Quiney 2–0–6–0.

Umpires: S. D. Fry and P. Wilson. Third umpire: S. J. Nogajski.
Referee: R. W. Stratford.

SHEFFIELD SHIELD WINNERS

1892-93	Victoria	1923-24	Victoria	1956-57	New South Wales
1893-94	South Australia	1924-25	Victoria	1957-58	New South Wales
1894-95	Victoria	1925-26	New South Wales	1958-59	New South Wales
1895-96	New South Wales	1926-27	South Australia	1959-60	New South Wales
1896-97	New South Wales	1927-28	Victoria	1960-61	New South Wales
1897-98	Victoria	1928-29	New South Wales	1961-62	New South Wales
1898-99	Victoria	1929-30	Victoria	1962-63	Victoria
1899-1900	New South Wales	1930-31	Victoria	1963-64	South Australia
1900-01	Victoria	1931-32	New South Wales	1964-65	New South Wales
1901-02	New South Wales	1932-33	New South Wales	1965-66	New South Wales
1902-03	New South Wales	1933-34	Victoria	1966-67	Victoria
1903-04	New South Wales	1934-35	Victoria	1967-68	Western Australia
1904-05	New South Wales	1935-36	South Australia	1968-69	South Australia
1905-06	New South Wales	1936-37	Victoria	1969-70	Victoria
1906-07	New South Wales	1937-38	New South Wales	1970-71	South Australia
1907-08	Victoria	1938-39	South Australia	1971-72	Western Australia
1908-09	New South Wales	1939-40	New South Wales	1972-73	Western Australia
1909-10	South Australia	1940–46	*No competition*	1973-74	Victoria
1910-11	New South Wales	1946-47	Victoria	1974-75	Western Australia
1911-12	New South Wales	1947-48	Western Australia	1975-76	South Australia
1912-13	South Australia	1948-49	New South Wales	1976-77	Western Australia
1913-14	New South Wales	1949-50	New South Wales	1977-78	Western Australia
1914-15	Victoria	1950-51	Victoria	1978-79	Victoria
1915–19	*No competition*	1951-52	New South Wales	1979-80	Victoria
1919-20	New South Wales	1952-53	South Australia	1980-81	Western Australia
1920-21	New South Wales	1953-54	New South Wales	1981-82	South Australia
1921-22	Victoria	1954-55	New South Wales	1982-83	New South Wales*
1922-23	New South Wales	1955-56	New South Wales	1983-84	Western Australia

1984-85	New South Wales	1995-96	South Australia	2006-07	Tasmania
1985-86	New South Wales	1996-97	Queensland*	2007-08	New South Wales
1986-87	Western Australia	1997-98	Western Australia	2008-09	Victoria
1987-88	Western Australia	1998-99	Western Australia*	2009-10	Victoria
1988-89	Western Australia	1999-2000	Queensland	2010-11	Tasmania
1989-90	New South Wales	2000-01	Queensland	2011-12	Queensland
1990-91	Victoria	2001-02	Queensland	2012-13	Tasmania
1991-92	Western Australia	2002-03	New South Wales*	2013-14	New South Wales
1992-93	New South Wales	2003-04	Victoria	2014-15	Victoria
1993-94	New South Wales	2004-05	New South Wales*	2015-16	Victoria*
1994-95	Queensland	2005-06	Queensland	2016-17	Victoria

New South Wales have won the title 46 times, Victoria 31, Western Australia 15, South Australia 13, Queensland 7, Tasmania 3.

The tournament was known as the Pura Milk Cup in 1999-2000, and the Pura Cup from 2000-01 to 2007-08.

* *Second in table but won final. Finals were introduced in 1982-83.*

MATADOR BBQs ONE-DAY CUP IN 2016-17

50-over league plus play-off and final

	Played	*Won*	*Lost*	*Tied*	*Bonus pts*	*Points*	*NRR*
QUEENSLAND	6	5	1	0	1	21	0.33
NEW SOUTH WALES	6	4	2	0	1	17	0.20
VICTORIA	6	3	3	0	4	16	1.22
Western Australia	6	3	2	1	1	15	0.02
Tasmania	6	3	3	0	1	13	0.03
South Australia	6	2	3	1	2	12	–0.33
Cricket Australia XI	6	0	6	0	0	0	–1.60

Win = 4 points; tie= 2 points; 1 bonus point awarded for achieving victory with a run-rate 1.25 times that of the opposition, and 2 bonus points for victory with a run-rate twice that of the opposition.

Play-off At Sydney (Drummoyne Oval), October 21, 2016 (day/night). **New South Wales won by 31 runs** (DLS). **Victoria 242** (49.3 overs); **‡New South Wales 238-5** (46 overs). *Rain ended play as Nick Larkin, the first "concussion substitute" under Cricket Australia's new rule, was walking out to bat. He was a replacement for New South Wales opener Daniel Hughes, who had been hit on the helmet by Peter Siddle. NSW's retrospective target was 208.*

Final At North Sydney, October 23, 2016. **New South Wales won by six wickets. Queensland 186** (46.5 overs); **‡New South Wales 188-4** (43.1 overs). *New South Wales retained the title in their fourth successive final. Nathan Lyon tied Queensland down with 10–3–10–4 (the most economical completed one-day spell by any NSW bowler) but Michael Neser reduced NSW to 19-3, before Moises Henriques (85) and Kurtis Patterson (77*) put on 131.*

The KFC T20 Big Bash League has its own section (page 1100).

BANGLADESH CRICKET IN 2017

Triumphs and tribulations

UTPAL SHUVRO

There was much for Bangladesh to savour in 2017, including the glory of maiden Test victories over Sri Lanka and Australia, and a first Champions Trophy semi-final. They also finally ticked off playing a Test in every nation. India, who had been instrumental in Bangladesh's elevation to Full Membership in 2000, had been happy to play them, but never at home. After much rescheduling, the teams met in Hyderabad in February and, though India won comfortably, it was no embarrassment.

But Bangladesh had their fair share of lows, too. During two tours at either end of the year, they lost every match, though in contrasting fashion. In New Zealand, they played brilliantly in patches and, with more assurance, might have picked up a couple of victories. Defeat in the First Test at Wellington after they declared their first innings on 595 for eight was especially harrowing.

BANGLADESH IN 2017

	Played	*Won*	*Lost*	*Drawn/No result*
Tests	9	2	7	–
One-day internationals	14	4	7	3
Twenty20 internationals	7	1	6	–

DECEMBER / JANUARY	2 Tests, 3 ODIs and 3 T20Is (a) v New Zealand	(see *Wisden 2017*, page 966)
FEBRUARY	1 Test (a) v India	(page 828)
MARCH / APRIL	2 Tests, 3 ODIs and 2 T20Is (a) v Sri Lanka	(page 978)
MAY	Triangular ODI tournament (in Ireland) v Ireland and New Zealand	(page 887)
JUNE / JULY	ICC Champions Trophy (in England)	(page 263)
AUGUST / SEPTEMBER	2 Tests (h) v Australia	(page 811)
SEPTEMBER / OCTOBER	2 Tests, 3 ODIs and 2 T20Is (a) v South Africa	(page 952)
NOVEMBER		
DECEMBER		

For a review of Bangladeshi domestic cricket from the 2016-17 season, see page 818.

But a first tour to South Africa in nine years was an outright disaster, with seven insipid defeats out of seven across the formats.

It led to the sacking of Mushfiqur Rahim, who had been Bangladesh's most successful Test captain, and in 2017 scored more Test runs, at a higher average – 766 at 54 – than any of his team-mates. But he had fallen out with the top brass and, more than six years after being sacked himself, Shakib Al Hasan was given the role, having already assumed the T20 captaincy. Mashrafe bin Mortaza, whose inspirational limited-overs leadership had taken Bangladesh to new heights, retired unexpectedly from Twenty20 internationals after the series against Sri Lanka in April. Though Mashrafe kept mum, it was widely believed there had been pressure from the board to step down. He continued to lead the ODI team, but a unified captaincy seemed likely in the near future.

Shakib had earned his promotion. His double-hundred against New Zealand at Wellington in January had ended in that heartbreaking defeat, but his century against Sri Lanka in Colombo in March helped Bangladesh to victory in their 100th Test. And he was instrumental in the historic win against Australia at Mirpur, scoring 84 on the first day and picking up two five-fors. Though he withdrew from the Test series in South Africa, citing the need for a break, his 29 Test wickets in 2017 were five more than Bangladesh's next best, Mehedi Hasan. He averaged 54 and was unable to build on his stellar debut series against England the previous year. Of the other regular bowlers, only left-arm quick Mustafizur Rahman (16 wickets at 36) averaged under 50, which revealed the team's general lack of penetration with the ball.

Shakib was also one of the heroes of the Champions Trophy run. After Bangladesh had slipped to 33 for four chasing 266 against New Zealand, he and Mahmudullah led them into the semi-finals with superb centuries. They ended up being thumped by India, but had surprised all with their skill in English conditions – not least opening batsman Tamim Iqbal, who followed 128 against England with 95 against Australia, then 70 against the Indians.

In January 2018, Sabbir Rahman, who had begun 2017 with a pair of fifties at Wellington but managed only one half-century in 14 Test innings after that, was stripped of his central contract – though not for his iffy form with the bat. During Rajshahi's game against Dhaka Metropolis in the National Cricket League, he took exception to abuse from the stands, and left the field to assault a young fan behind the sightscreen. He was fined 2m taka (£18,000), and banned from domestic cricket for six months.

The most shocking news of the year, though, was the departure of Sri Lankan head coach Chandika Hathurusinghe. In 2016, he renewed his contract up to the 2019 World Cup. But in November, it emerged that he had tendered his resignation midway through the South Africa tour. There was confusion as to the reason, with some pointing to his authoritarian style: though he watched hardly any domestic matches, he had the final say in selection. All became clear when he was named Sri Lanka's head coach in December. Intriguingly, his first assignment would be a return in early 2018 to Bangladesh, who under his watch had become intimidating at home, winning six consecutive ODI series before England beat them in late 2016, and earning a clutch of historic Test victories.

BANGLADESH v AUSTRALIA IN 2017-18

ADAM COLLINS

Test matches (2): Bangladesh 1, Australia 1

A tour which looked as if it might never happen turned into quite the show. After a classic scrap at Mirpur, where Bangladesh won their first Test against Australia at the fifth attempt, there was enough individual brilliance from the tourists at Chittagong to ensure a drawn series. Both teams were left feeling content. Bangladesh did not fold after they had carved out an opportunity to claim another scalp, following maiden victories over England in late 2016, and Sri Lanka in early 2017. Australia, meanwhile, managed to settle pre-Ashes nerves.

For some time, the series seemed likely to be a casualty of the long-running contracts dispute between the Australian board and their players. That would have meant two cancellations in succession, after Steve Smith's side pulled out of their trip here in October 2015 because of security concerns, and cynics suggested the row would be resolved only in time for the Ashes, starting in November 2017. In the end, a deal was agreed for the tour to go ahead, although Bangladesh rejected a suggestion of replacing the Tests with limited-overs matches.

MOST WICKETS IN A TWO-TEST SERIES

Wkts	*Avge*			
23	15.13	H. M. R. K. B. Herath. . .	Sri Lanka v Pakistan (in Sri Lanka)	2014
22	**14.31**	**N. M. Lyon**.	**Australia v Bangladesh (in Bangladesh)** . . .	**2017-18**
22	18.04	M. Muralitharan	Sri Lanka v South Africa (in Sri Lanka)	2006
21	4.80	J. Briggs	England v South Africa (in South Africa). . . .	1888-89
21	11.28	I. K. Pathan.	India v Zimbabwe (in Zimbabwe).	2005-06
21	14.85	A. Kumble	India v Pakistan (in India).	1998-99
20	9.20	D. W. Steyn	South Africa v New Zealand (in South Africa)	2007-08
20	11.20	D. L. Vettori	New Zealand v Bangladesh (in Bangladesh) .	2004-05
20	13.90	H. M. R. K. B. Herath. . .	Sri Lanka v New Zealand (Sri Lanka).	2012-13
20	20.15	Saqlain Mushtaq	Pakistan v India (in India).	1998-99

The First Test was defined by collapses, starting with Bangladesh losing three wickets in the first four overs. They recovered thanks to Shakib Al Hasan, who then led the way with the ball. He finished with ten wickets to add to his first-day 84, the value of which swelled as the game developed.

The Australians were thought to have improved their technique against spin after they battled biting turn in India earlier in the year, but stumbles in both Tests – including a fatal one in the Mirpur chase – told a different story. This middle order didn't do consolidation. But by winning the Second Test in punishing heat, they did show resilience. It was best demonstrated by David Warner, whose Test average in Asia had been barely 30, and Nathan Lyon, who had also struggled on the subcontinent. Warner's turnaround was founded on what he later described as an aggressive form of defence. Whether he was storming forward or bouncing back, his assertive movements were designed to prevent him being trapped on the crease. It worked, bringing back-to-back hundreds of differing tempos but consistent footwork.

As for Lyon, his 22 wickets were one short of the record for a two-match series. Full of confidence and cunning, his 13 for 154 at Chittagong was the second-best return by an Australian spinner. He received durable support from Pat Cummins – so long his side's most injury-prone player, but now the man for all seasons, which was doubly important after Josh Hazlewood broke down with a side strain. Ashton Agar's return to Test cricket after four years proved how far he had come, while fellow slow left-armer Steve O'Keefe did enough to justify the cost of flying him out mid-series to replace Hazlewood, even if his call-up raised eyebrows: he was serving a ban in domestic cricket for making "highly inappropriate comments" while drunk to a female cricketer at an awards evening.

Down the order, Peter Handscomb showed guts by combatting extreme humidity during the defining partnership of the Second Test, which helped compensate for Steve Smith's single half-century. Glenn Maxwell's starts were reliable enough, but so were his departures. Matt Renshaw's first innings of the series was necessarily stoic as wickets tumbled, but it was the only shot he fired. Matthew Wade's glovework went from negligent to excellent after he was nearly dropped, but his batting was poor. And Usman Khawaja was left out after a frazzled double failure at Mirpur.

For Bangladesh, Tamim Iqbal's twin seventies were vital in the First Test, but he failed at Chittagong. Soumya Sarkar and Imrul Kayes were walking wickets, which added to the pressure on the experienced pair of Shakib and Mushfiqur Rahim. Like Tamim, Shakib had a quiet Second Test, when Sabbir Rahman looked ready to take on more heavy lifting. Their three main slow bowlers also failed to maintain their early standards, most notably off-spinner Mehedi Hasan, who had tormented England the previous year. Taijul Islam's importance on the final day at Mirpur alongside fellow slow left-armer Shakib shouldn't be underestimated, but neither was as dangerous in the Second Test.

Mustafizur Rahman shouldered a big workload as his side's sole seamer in Chittagong, and discharged his duties with venom. He should be a handful in Australian in 2018, if the tour is confirmed. It should be: Bangladesh showed they belong at the top table.

AUSTRALIAN TOURING PARTY

*S. P. D. Smith, A. C. Agar, J. M. Bird, H. W. R. Cartwright, P. J. Cummins, P. S. P. Handscomb, J. R. Hazlewood, U. T. Khawaja, N. M. Lyon, G. J. Maxwell, S. N. J. O'Keefe, M. T. Renshaw, M. J. Swepson, M. S. Wade, D. A. Warner. *Coach:* D. S. Lehmann.

Swepson was a late addition to the team after M. A. Starc failed to recover from a foot injury. J. L. Pattinson was originally selected, but pulled out with back trouble and was replaced by Bird. O'Keefe was called up before the Second Test after Hazlewood injured his side.

BANGLADESH v AUSTRALIA

First Test

7–30, 2017. Bangladesh won by 20 runs. Toss: Bangladesh.
ians would have been happy not to tour. And, yes, their administrators
educe the trip to limited-overs fare. But none of this detracted from a
h victory, their first over Australia in Tests. The narrow margin reflected
sh and pull across four captivating days. Shakib Al Hasan, in his 50th
difference, with ten wickets. Australia's hunt for 265 was an improvement
ings, thanks to a superb century from Warner, but a late collapse of six for
minal.

that Bangladesh were primed for something special after an accomplished
Test level looked shaky when Cummins found the edges of Soumya Sarkar, Imrul
Kayes and Sabbir Rahman inside the opening 20 minutes. Tamim Iqbal, also winning his 50th cap, watched the mess unfold, but he and Shakib batted with purpose, and Tamim paraded his defiance by dancing down to Lyon and slaying him over the rope.

Maxwell had not originally been in Smith's bowling plans, yet he was in action by the first afternoon in an effort to end a partnership that was threatening to shape the day. It worked, the stand broken at 155 when Maxwell jagged one away from Tamim. Shakib had prospered by swinging hard when given width, but he soon followed, tickling a catch off Lyon. Agar sent a ball sliding into Mushfiqur Rahim's pads for his first Test wicket since the 2013 Ashes, but Nasir Hossain and Mehedi Hasan rallied, putting on 42 before Lyon clipped Mehedi's inside edge to move past Richie Benaud's Test tally of 248; among Australian spinners, only Shane Warne lay (miles) ahead. But Australia's good day – they had dismissed Bangladesh for 260 – was undone before the close. Warner was caught on the crease by Mehedi, and Khawaja inexplicably set off for a single after not offering a shot. Nightwatchman Lyon came and went, leaving the innings tottering at 14 for three.

When Smith frolicked down the pitch to Mehedi in the third over next morning, that became 33 for four. Renshaw and Handscomb scrapped well, but both fell near lunch to deliveries that didn't demand strokes. The collapse was on again when Wade was lbw, and Maxwell aped Smith in charging and missing. Agar and Cummins batted maturely to conjure 49 for the ninth wicket, before Shakib became the fourth bowler with a Test five-for against nine different teams, matching Muttiah Muralitharan, Dale Steyn and Rangana Herath. The eventual deficit was 43, which Bangladesh had doubled before Soumya skyed Agar to a juggling Khawaja.

Australia's comeback started in earnest on the third morning. Lyon was too good for Taijul Islam, the nightwatchman, and produced a beauty to snare Imrul. Tamim again looked unfazed, with support from Mushfiqur, before he copped a brute from Cummins on 78. Cummins was in the action again, holding on at cover as Shakib miscued Lyon, who then ran out Mushfiqur with a fingertip deflection. It was something from nothing, and provoked two more wickets in the next eight balls, with Wade – in an otherwise scrappy display – taking an excellent low chance off Agar, before Lyon had Sabbir prodding to short leg. Another bat–pad snaffle from Handscomb secured Lyon's five-for, and Mehedi holed out to give him nine in the match.

With a lead of 264, Bangladesh had failed to bat Australia out of the game, but they soon grabbed back the initiative: Renshaw was pinned by Mehedi, and Khawaja made it two poor dismissals with a loose sweep at Shakib. Smith thought he had been stumped first ball, only to be saved by replays. It would have been 28 for three, but instead captain and deputy knuckled down. Smith inched to 25 from 20 overs, while Warner took on the spinners with pronounced footwork. By stumps, Australia were 156 short of victory, with eight wickets in hand. Even so, one more seemed likely to open the door.

Next morning, Warner continued to a drought-breaking subcontinental century he described as the best of his 19 Test hundreds, but when Shakib trapped him in front to end a stand of 130 – Australia's highest in a fourth innings in Asia – And when Smith edged Shakib four overs later, the stadium erupted. accomplice. He winkled out Handscomb – his 50th Test wicket – and to Shakib, who didn't miss out. It completed a miserable game for Wade 30 byes and contributed just nine runs. Agar provided a return catch and bowled Maxwell first ball after lunch, it looked all over at 199 for eight.

Nobody told Cummins. He put on 29 with Lyon and, after being joined Hazlewood with 37 still needed, smacked Mehedi twice over the square-leg boun he couldn't keep the strike, and Hazlewood was exposed to Taijul for a full over. lbw to the fifth ball, sparking wild celebrations. When things got tight, Banglades their nerve, and proved themselves worthy of more frequent contact with Australia, had now lost 12 of their last 14 Tests in Asia.

Man of the Match: Shakib Al Hasan.

Close of play: first day, Australia 18-3 (Renshaw 6, Smith 3); second day, Bangladesh 45-1 (Tamim Iqbal 30, Taijul Islam 0); third day, Australia 109-2 (Warner 75, Smith 25).

Bangladesh

First innings		Second innings	
Tamim Iqbal c Warner b Maxwell	71	– c Wade b Cummins	78
Soumya Sarkar c Handscomb b Cummins	8	– c Khawaja b Agar	15
Imrul Kayes c Wade b Cummins	0	– (4) c Warner b Lyon	2
Sabbir Rahman c Wade b Cummins	0	– (7) c Handscomb b Lyon	22
Shakib Al Hasan c Smith b Lyon	84	– (6) c Cummins b Lyon	5
*†Mushfiqur Rahim lbw b Agar	18	– (5) run out	41
Nasir Hossain lbw b Agar	23	– (8) c Wade b Agar	0
Mehedi Hasan c Handscomb b Lyon	18	– (9) c Khawaja b Lyon	26
Taijul Islam lbw b Lyon	4	– (3) lbw b Lyon	4
Shafiul Islam c Hazlewood b Agar	13	– c Handscomb b Lyon	9
Mustafizur Rahman not out	0	– not out	0
B 15, lb 3, w 1, nb 2	21	B 15, lb 3, w 1	19
1/10 (2) 2/10 (3) 3/10 (4) 4/165 (1) 5/188 (5) 6/198 (6) 7/240 (8) 8/246 (7) 9/246 (9) 10/260 (10) (78.5 overs)	260	1/43 (2) 2/61 (3) 3/67 (4) 4/135 (1) 5/143 (6) 6/186 (5) 7/186 (8) 8/186 (7) 9/214 (10) 10/221 (9) (79.3 overs)	221

Hazlewood 15–5–39–0; Cummins 16–1–63–3; Lyon 30–6–79–3; Agar 12.5–2–46–3; Maxwell 5–0–15–1. *Second innings*—Hazlewood 4.1–2–3–0; Cummins 14–3–38–1; Lyon 34.3–10–82–6; Maxwell 5–0–24–0; Agar 20.5–2–55–2; Khawaja 1–0–1–0.

Australia

First innings		Second innings	
D. A. Warner lbw b Mehedi Hasan	8	– lbw b Shakib Al Hasan	112
M. T. Renshaw c Soumya Sarkar b Shakib Al Hasan	45	– lbw b Mehedi Hasan	5
U. T. Khawaja run out	1	– c Taijul Islam b Shakib Al Hasan	1
N. M. Lyon lbw b Shakib Al Hasan	0	– (10) c Soumya Sarkar b Mehedi Hasan	12
*S. P. D. Smith b Mehedi Hasan	8	– (4) c Mushfiqur Rahim b Shakib Al Hasan	37
P. S. P. Handscomb lbw b Taijul Islam	33	– (5) c Soumya Sarkar b Taijul Islam	15
G. J. Maxwell st Mushfiqur Rahim b Shakib Al Hasan	23	– (6) b Shakib Al Hasan	14
†M. S. Wade lbw b Mehedi Hasan	5	– (7) lbw b Shakib Al Hasan	4
A. C. Agar not out	41	– (8) c and b Taijul Islam	2
P. J. Cummins b Shakib Al Hasan	25	– (9) not out	33
J. R. Hazlewood c Imrul Kayes b Shakib Al Hasan	5	– lbw b Taijul Islam	0
B 15, lb 3, w 5	23	B 7, lb 2	9
1/9 (1) 2/14 (3) 3/14 (4) 4/33 (5) 5/102 (6) 6/117 (2) 7/124 (8) 8/144 (7) 9/193 (10) 10/217 (11) (74.5 overs)	217	1/27 (2) 2/28 (3) 3/158 (1) 4/171 (4) 5/187 (5) 6/192 (7) 7/195 (8) 8/199 (6) 9/228 (10) 10/244 (11) (70.5 overs)	244

, Mehedi Hasan 26–6–62–3; Shakib Al Hasan 25.5–7–68–5; Taijul Islam ahman 8–3–13–0; Nasir Hossain 1–0–3–0. *Second innings*—Mehedi Hasan sain 3–2–2–0; Shakib Al Hasan 28–7–85–5; Taijul Islam 19.5–2–60–3; 0–8–0.

ires: Aleem Dar and N. J. Llong. Third umpire: I. J. Gould.
Referee: J. J. Crowe.

BANGLADESH v AUSTRALIA

Second Test

g, September 4–7, 2017. Australia won by seven wickets. Toss: Bangladesh.

trast to the capricious weather, the consistency of Australia's two most seasoned ers saved the series. Lyon's 13 wickets were the stuff of dreams, while Warner's second successive century suggested he had finally adapted to Asian conditions. The question for Bangladesh shifted from whether they could win a Test to whether they could close a series. Replacing a bowler (Shafiul Islam) with a batsman (Mominul Haque) probably wise, yet runs were ultimately what they lacked.

For Australia, the defeat at Mirpur demanded change. Steve O'Keefe was flown from his sofa at home straight into the team, while all-rounder Hilton Cartwright replaced Usman Khawaja to support the sole seamer, Cummins. But he was barely needed: Lyon took the new ball on a steamy opening day and pinned left-handers Tamim Iqbal, Imrul

BEST MATCH FIGURES FOR AUSTRALIA IN TESTS

16-137	R. A. L. Massie (8-84, 8-53)	v England at Lord's (*on debut*)	1972
14-90	F. R. Spofforth (7-46, 7-44)........	v England at The Oval..............	1882
14-199	C. V. Grimmett (7-116, 7-83)	v South Africa at Adelaide	1931-32
13-77	M. A. Noble (7-17, 6-60)..........	v England at Melbourne	1901-02
13-110	F. R. Spofforth (6-48, 7-62)........	v England at Melbourne	1878-79
13-148	B. A. Reid (6-97, 7-51)	v England at Melbourne	1990-91
13-154	**N. M. Lyon (7-94, 6-60)**	**v Bangladesh at Chittagong**	**2017-18**
13-173	C. V. Grimmett (7-100, 6-73)	v South Africa at Durban (*his last Test*)	1935-36
13-217	M. G. Hughes (5-130, 8-87)	v West Indies at Perth	1988-89
13-236	A. A. Mailey (4-115, 9-121)	v England at Melbourne	1920-21

Kayes and Soumya Sarkar before lunch with deliveries going straight on with the arm. Mominul went the same way after the interval, the first time the first four wickets of a Test had fallen lbw.

Wade had narrowly retained his spot after a nightmarish First Test, but reminded onlookers that specialist wicketkeepers are not for nothing with a sharp take off Agar to remove Shakib Al Hasan. At 117 for five, Bangladesh seemed to have misfired – but Mushfiqur Rahim reloaded the cannons with Sabbir Rahman, adding 105 either side of tea. Sabbir eventually became Wade's second victim, via a sharp back-handed stumping, to give Lyon his second successive five-for. He was back for more next morning, turning one through the gate to cut short Mushfiqur's stay at 68. Nasir Hossain made a useful 45 before Agar struck again and, after Warner ran out Mehedi Hasan, Lyon finished the job with seven for 94. Bangladesh were all out for 305.

Mustafizur Rahman made the first incision in the reply, when Mushfiqur pulled in a superb diving leg-side catch off Renshaw. It was only the second Test dismissal – after Rusi Surti of India was caught by Australia's Rex Sellers off Robert (Bob) Simpson at Calcutta in 1964-65 – in which the three participants shared the same initials. Smith joined

Warner for a 93-run stand founded on patience, the field spread from t… Islam's introduction finished Smith, bowled between bat and pad.

Bangladesh had never previously staged a Test in September, the mons… was never far off, but on the second afternoon it was humidity that drenc… Handscomb nearly collapsed after passing 50, but hung on until the cl… Warner. The third morning was washed away, so Warner's wait to complete… hundred mirrored an innings in which he had to keep his cool throughout. … harder than he struck, with only five boundaries in his century (at 209 balls, his s… 55), although his first go at bringing up three figures resulted in the run-out of Hand… Their brave stand of 152 proved defining.

When Warner was finally caught via his hip, Australia were only seven beh… but Bangladesh's spinners got going and restricted the deficit to 72. Cartwright po… Mehedi to slip when looking sound, then Wade and Maxwell both blew reviews. … the close loomed, Cummins was trapped in front, befo… Shakib sneaked one through… Agar's defence.

The innings was over early on the fourth day, Bangladesh se…mingly back in the hunt after taking seven for 79. But their hopes were quickly dashed. Sou…ya nicked Cummins in the fifth over, then four wickets crashed for 11, leaving them still 29 …he red: Lyon drew Tamim from the crease and Imrul gave catching practice to cover. Lyon's b… of the series followed, drifting in to left-hander Shakib, then ragging away to have him pouc… at gully.

A brief recovery ended when Wade's glovework accounted for Sabbir, who became the first Bangladeshi to be stumped twice in a Test, and the 20th in all. Cummins blasted out Mushfiqur and held on to Mominul's top-edged sweep after a dive at backward square. Lyon bowled Taijul to become the first Australian spinner since Clarrie Grimmett in 1935-36 to bank three successive six-fors, and only the second from outside Asia to take 13 there, after Ian Botham at Bombay in February 1980. By the time O'Keefe ended Bangladesh's limp resistance, Australia needed only 86.

Conscious of ominous weather forecasts, they avoided a fifth day by smacking the runs inside 16 overs. Maxwell finished things off with a bang, launching Nasir for six over midwicket – an abrupt conclusion that did not reflect an engaging series.

Man of the Match: N. M. Lyon. *Men of the Series:* N. M. Lyon and D. A. Warner.

Close of play: first day, Bangladesh 253-6 (Mushfiqur Rahim 62, Nasir Hossain 19); second day, Australia 225-2 (Warner 88, Handscomb 69); third day, Australia 377-9 (O'Keefe 8, Lyon 0).

Bangladesh

Tamim Iqbal lbw b Lyon	9	– st Wade b Lyon	12
Soumya Sarkar lbw b Lyon	33	– c Renshaw b Cummins	9
Imrul Kayes lbw b Lyon	4	– c Maxwell b Lyon	15
Mominul Haque lbw b Lyon	31	– (8) c Cummins b Lyon	29
Shakib Al Hasan c Wade b Agar	24	– c Warner b Lyon	2
*†Mushfiqur Rahim b Lyon	68	– c Wade b Cummins	31
Sabbir Rahman st Wade b Lyon	66	– st Wade b Lyon	24
Nasir Hossain c Wade b Agar	45	– (4) c Smith b O'Keefe	5
Mehedi Hasan run out	11	– not out	14
Taijul Islam c Smith b Lyon	9	– b Lyon	4
Mustafizur Rahman not out	0	– b O'Keefe	0
B 5	5	B 12	12
(113.2 overs)	305	(71.2 overs)	157

1/13 (1) 2/21 (3) 3/70 (2) 4/85 (4) 5/117 (5) 6/222 (7) 7/265 (6) 8/293 (8) 9/296 (9) 10/305 (10)

1/11 (2) 2/32 (1) 3/37 (3) 4/39 (5) 5/43 (4) 6/97 (7) 7/129 (6) 8/149 (8) 9/156 (10) 10/157 (11)

Cummins 22–5–46–0; Lyon 36.2–7–94–7; O'Keefe 23–0–79–0; Agar 23–9–52–2; Maxwell 4–0–13–0; Cartwright 5–1–16–0. *Second innings*—Cummins 11–3–27–2; Lyon 33–11–60–6; O'Keefe 22.2–6–49–2; Agar 5–1–9–0.

alia

. Renshaw c Mushfiqur Rahim b Mustafizur Rahman	4	– c Mushfiqur Rahim b Shakib Al Hasan	22
D. A. Warner c Imrul Kayes b Mustafizur Rahman	123	– c Soumya Sarkar b Mustafizur Rahman	8
*S. P. D. Smith b Taijul Islam	58	– c Mushfiqur Rahim b Taijul Islam	16
P. S. P. Handscomb run out	82	– not out	16
G. J. Maxwell c Mushfiqur Rahim b Mehedi Hasan	38	– not out	25
H. W. R. Cartwright c Soumya Sarkar b Mehedi Hasan	18		
†M. S. Wade lbw b Mustafizur Rahman	8		
A. C. Agar b Shakib Al Hasan	22		
P. J. Cummins lbw b Mehedi Hasan	4		
S. N. J. O'Keefe not out	8		
N. M. Lyon c Imrul Kayes b Mustafizur Rahman	0		
B 8, lb 3, w 1	12		
1/5 (1) 2/98 (3) 3/250 (4) 4/298 (2) 5/321 (6) 6/342 (7) 7/346 (5) 8/364 (9) 9/376 (8) 10/377 (11) (119.5 overs)	377	1/13 (2) 2/44 (3) 3/48 (1) (3 wkts, 15.3 overs)	87

Mehedi Hasan 38–6–93–3; Mustafizur Rahman 20.5–2–84–4; Shakib Al Hasan 31–3–82–1; Taijul Islam 21–1–78–1; Nasir Hossain 6–2–14–0; Mominul Haque 2–0–6–0; Sabbir Rahman 1–0–9–0. *Second innings*—Mustafizur Rahman 5–1–16–1; Shakib Al Hasan 6–1–35–1; Taijul Islam 4–0–26–1; Nasir Hossain 0.3–0–10–0.

Umpires: I. J. Gould and N. J. Llong. Third umpire: Aleem Dar.
Referee: J. J. Crowe.

DOMESTIC CRICKET IN BANGLADESH IN 2016-17

UTPAL SHUVRO

Khulna established themselves as the dominant force in Bangladesh's domestic cricket by winning their third National Cricket League in five seasons. It was their fifth in all, equalling the record of Rajshahi and Dhaka Division. **Dhaka** were hot on their heels in the final stages, but could not quite close the gap, and Khulna took the title with a day to spare. In a powerful batting line-up, their brightest star was Tushar Imran, with strong support from Anamul Haque; seamer Al-Amin Hossain collected 23 wickets, and all-rounder Abdur Razzak contributed usefully while leading the side.

Rajshahi had won four consecutive titles from 2008-09 to 2011-12, but declined after the retirement of their charismatic leader Khaled Mashud, and found themselves in the second tier when the Bangladesh Cricket Board split the league in 2015-16. They had high hopes of promotion this time, until **Rangpur** overtook them in the last two rounds – a swift return to the top level for a team who had suffered the ignominy of relegation only one season after their first title in 2014-15. Dhaka Metropolis were demoted.

With the leading players on international duty for most of the season, there was an opportunity for those discarded from the national team to put themselves forward. Alok Kapali was the NCL's highest run-scorer, with 598 at 66 for Sylhet, but Tushar – who last played for Bangladesh in December 2007 – stole the limelight with three centuries in successive games for Khulna. The first was his 19th, beating the record for a Bangladeshi batsman he had shared with Kapali and Mohammad Ashraful. He celebrated by scoring two more in the two remaining rounds, then followed up with two double-hundreds for South Zone in the other first-class tournament, the Bangladesh Cricket League. Tushar finished the season with 1,249 runs, another national record. He was 11 behind the 1,232 scored by Liton Das in 2014-15 after hitting 217 in the first innings of his last game, but with two overs remaining on the final evening he was sent out to open, and raced to 28 in 12 balls. Another Test outcast, Junaid Siddique, also passed 1,000 runs, while the season's leading wicket-taker was the consistent seamer Abu Jayed, whose 44 put him just ahead of Razzak.

Poor weather resulted in the second half of the NCL being postponed until December and January. In the final round, a match between Dhaka and Barisal was halted for eight minutes by an earthquake near Sylhet. "We never experienced anything like this before," said umpire Masudur Rahman. "Everyone was panicked, so I gave them a break." Barisal's captain, Fazle Mahmud, told the media that "the dressing-room and gallery were shaking". Dhaka's batsmen evidently recovered from the shock: Saif Hasan and Taibur Rahman both reached double-hundreds after they resumed.

In the fifth edition of the Bangladesh Cricket League, **North Zone** became champions for the first time, boosted by the batting of Naeem Islam, who scored four hundreds, and Junaid. The only one of the four teams in this franchise-based tournament without a commercial sponsor, North Zone were supported by the BCB.

The BCL produced some new entries for the record books. Left-arm spinner Sanjamul Islam returned the best innings figures by a Bangladeshi, nine for 80 for North Zone against Central Zone; the only batsman he failed to dismiss in the second innings was opener Abdul Majid, who was run out. Central's Shuvagata Hom became the second Bangladeshi to score a century and take ten wickets in a match, against South Zone, following Shakib Al Hasan, who did it in a Test against Zimbabwe. But a few weeks later Shuvagata conceded 202 in an innings, as Tushar and Shahriar Nafees guided South Zone to 749 for eight, the second-highest total scored in Bangladesh.

In the Dhaka Premier League, **Gazi Group Cricketers** became champions after a fierce three-way title fight. Gazi, Prime Doleshwar and Abahani all finished with 24 points from 16 matches, but Gazi emerged victorious on head-to-head results, leaving Prime Doleshwar as runners-up for the third year running.

FIRST-CLASS AVERAGES IN 2016-17

BATTING (400 runs, average 35.00)

		M	*I*	*NO*	*R*	*HS*	*100*	*Avge*	*Ct/St*
1	Tushar Imran (*Khulna/South Zone*)	12	16	2	1,249	220	5	89.21	3
2	†Junaid Siddique (*Rajshahi/North Zone*)	12	19	2	1,024	181	3	60.23	8
3	Liton Das (*Rangpur/East Zone*)	6	10	2	464	219	1	58.00	9
4	†Taibur Rahman (*Dhaka/Central Zone*)	12	17	3	811	242	2	57.92	3
5	†Shahriar Nafees (*Barisal/South Zone*)	12	18	2	894	207*	2	55.87	3
6	Yasir Ali (*Chittagong/East Zone*)	12	21	5	873	110*	2	54.56	9
7	Nasir Hossain (*Rangpur/North Zone*)	9	12	1	575	201	1	52.27	9
8	Anamul Haque (*Khulna/South Zone*)	11	15	1	725	136	2	51.78	13/2
9	Farhad Hossain (*Rajshahi/North Zone*)	10	17	1	807	132	4	50.43	8
10	Saif Hasan (*Dhaka/Central Zone*)	11	15	0	755	204	2	50.33	4
11	Nurul Hasan (*Khulna/Central Zone*)	7	10	1	445	113	2	49.44	16/6
12	Dhiman Ghosh (*Rangpur/North Zone*)	11	15	1	688	113	1	49.14	21/3
13	Alok Kapali (*Sylhet/East Zone*)	12	19	2	825	200*	2	48.52	15
14	Naeem Islam (*Rangpur/North Zone*)	11	16	2	672	185	4	48.00	5
15	Suhrawadi Shuvo (*Rangpur/North Zone*)	10	14	2	557	121	1	46.41	5
16	Jahurul Islam (*Rajshahi/North Zone*)	11	15	1	556	131	1	39.71	8
17	Mithun Ali (*Khulna/South Zone*)	12	14	2	472	131	1	39.33	17/2
18	†Fazle Mahmud (*Barisal/South Zone*)	11	17	1	624	147	1	39.00	6
18	Tasamul Haque (*Chittagong/East Zone*)	11	19	3	624	104	2	39.00	10
20	†Abul Hasan (*Sylhet/East Zone*)	9	13	1	430	64	0	35.83	6

BOWLING (15 wickets, average 35.00)

		Style	*O*	*M*	*R*	*W*	*BB*	*5I*	*Avge*
1	Ashiquzzaman (*Khulna*)	RM	67.2	8	232	16	6-57	1	14.50
2	Mehedi Hasan (*Khulna/Bangladesh*)	OB	157.2	27	433	23	6-77	3	18.82
3	Mohammad Saddam (*Rangpur/N Zone*)	RM	126.4	19	405	21	5-57	1	19.28
4	Mamun Hossain (*Rajshahi*)	RFM	130.4	24	420	21	5-81	1	20.00
5	Abu Jayed (*Sylhet/East Zone*)	RFM	301.4	50	965	44	6-48	6	21.93
6	Farhad Reza (*Rajshahi/North Zone*)	RFM	265.5	68	775	35	5-91	1	22.14
7	Al-Amin Hossain (*Khulna/South Zone*)	RFM	234.2	48	699	28	6-41	1	24.96
8	Saqlain Sajib (*Rajshahi/East Zone*)	SLA	278.2	72	707	28	5-54	1	25.25
9	Mohammad Sharif (*Dhaka/C Zone*)	RFM	156.3	32	598	23	4-35	0	26.00
10	Monir Hossain (*Barisal*)	SLA	216.1	39	634	24	6-66	3	26.41
11	Alauddin Babu (*Rangpur/North Zone*)	RFM	152.4	27	535	20	4-67	0	26.75
12	Taibur Rahman (*Dhaka/Central Zone*)	SLA	150.3	21	518	19	4-52	0	27.26
13	Shahanur Rahman (*Sylhet/East Zone*)	OB	206	32	574	20	5-66	1	28.70
14	Rahatul Ferdous (*Sylhet/East Zone*)	SLA	187.5	31	575	20	5-48	1	28.75
15	Shuvagata Hom (*Dhaka/C Zone/Bang*)	OB	219.3	32	739	25	6-91	2	29.56
16	Suhrawadi Shuvo (*Rangpur/North Zone*)	SLA	275	36	872	29	7-45	2	30.06
17	Mohammad Saifuddin (*Chittagong/EZ*)	RM	203.5	31	662	22	4-55	0	30.09
18	Sanjamul Islam (*Rajshahi/North Zone*)	SLA	320.3	68	1,002	33	9-80	2	30.36
19	Abu Haider (*Dhaka Metropolis/C Zone*)	LFM	171.3	20	613	20	4-42	0	30.65
20	Alok Kapali (*Sylhet/East Zone*)	LB	154.4	17	484	15	3-43	0	32.26
21	Abdur Razzak (*Khulna/South Zone*)	SLA	476.4	93	1,391	42	6-44	3	33.11

WALTON LED TV NATIONAL CRICKET LEAGUE IN 2016-17

Tier One	*P*	*W*	*L*	*D*	*Pts*
Khulna	6	2	0	4	58
Dhaka	6	2	0	4	54
Barisal	6	0	2	4	32
Dhaka Metropolis	6	0	2	4	28

Tier Two	*P*	*W*	*L*	*D*	*Pts*
Rangpur	6	3	0	3	72
Rajshahi	6	3	0	3	65
Sylhet	6	0	3	3	36
Chittagong	6	0	3	3	33

Outright win = 10pts; draw = 3pts; first-innings lead = 1pt. Bonus points were awarded for the first 110 overs of each team's first innings: one batting point for the first 250 runs and then for 300, 350, 400 and 450; one bowling point for the third wicket taken and then for the sixth and ninth.

Rangpur were promoted to Tier One, and Dhaka Metropolis relegated.

Tier One

At Bogra, September 25–28, 2016. **Drawn. ‡Dhaka Metropolis 47-2 v Dhaka.** *Dhaka Metropolis 3pts, Dhaka 3pts. Rain spared only 15 overs, all on the first day.*

At Khulna, September 25–28, 2016. **Drawn. ‡Barisal 261 and 248-8; Khulna 424.** *Khulna 11pts, Barisal 7pts. Defending champions Khulna could not complete a win, but nineties from Tushar Imran and Abdur Razzak got them off to a solid start.*

At Khulna, October 2–5, 2016. **Drawn. ‡Barisal 419** (Sohag Gazi 142); **Dhaka Metropolis 245 and 353-7.** *Barisal 10pts, Dhaka Metropolis 5pts.*

At Bogra, October 2–5, 2016. **Drawn. Khulna 172-1 v ‡Dhaka.** *Dhaka 3pts, Khulna 3pts. The last three days were washed out, with Dhaka still waiting for their first bat in the tournament.*

At Cox's Bazar, October 8–11, 2016. **Drawn. ‡Dhaka 523** (Taibur Rahman 147; Monir Hossain 5-152); **Barisal 103-1 dec**. *Dhaka 7pts, Barisal 5pts. Dhaka's batsmen finally reached the crease in the NCL's third round. But, when the last two days were washed out, they had lost eight days of a potential 12. Hoping for better weather, the BCB postponed the fourth round until after the BPL.*

At Cox's Bazar (No 2), October 8–11, 2016. **Drawn. ‡Khulna 293** (Nurul Hasan 103*); **Dhaka Metropolis 59-0 dec**. *Khulna 5pts, Dhaka Metropolis 6pts. Nurul Hasan rescued Khulna from 67-5 before rain wiped out the last two days.*

At Savar (BKSP No. 3), December 20–22, 2016. **Khulna won by ten wickets. ‡Barisal 171 and 211** (Ashiquzzaman 6-57); **Khulna 371** (Anamul Haque 136, Tushar Imran 108; Monir Hossain 6-66) **and 15-0.** *Khulna 17pts, Barisal 3pts. Resuming the tournament in better weather, Khulna romped home in three days to replace Barisal at the top of Tier One. Tushar's 19th first-class hundred was a record for a Bangladeshi batsman. He and Anamul Haque, who hit six sixes, put on 217 for Khulna's third wicket. Medium-pacer Ashiquzzaman took 9-90 in the match on first-class debut.*

At Fatullah (KSOA), December 20–22, 2016. **Dhaka won by five wickets. Dhaka Metropolis 166 and 125**; **‡Dhaka 187 and 106-5.** *Dhaka 14pts, Dhaka Metropolis 3pts. No one reached 50 as Dhaka completed a three-day win.*

At Savar (BKSP No. 3), December 27–30, 2016. **Drawn. Dhaka Metropolis 292** (Monir Hossain 5-51) **and 223; ‡Barisal 280 and 171-6.** *Barisal 6pts, Dhaka Metropolis 8pts.*

At Fatullah (KSOA), December 27–30, 2016. **Drawn. Dhaka 366** (Saif Hasan 109, Raqibul Hasan 111; Abdur Razzak 5-103) **and 278-8 dec; ‡Khulna 342** (Tushar Imran 141; Dewan Sabbir 5-58) **and 92-3.** *Dhaka 10pts, Khulna 8pts. In this draw between the top teams, Dhaka narrowed the gap with leaders Khulna, but still trailed by seven points entering the final round. Tushar notched his 20th first-class century.*

At Sylhet, January 3–6, 2017. **Dhaka won by an innings and 78 runs. Dhaka 588-6 dec** (Saif Hasan 204, Taibur Rahman 242; Towhidul Islam 5-87); **‡Barisal 189 and 321** (Shahriar Nafees 104). *Dhaka 17pts, Barisal 1pt. Play was briefly interrupted on the first afternoon by an earthquake of magnitude 5.5 on the Bangladesh–India border. Undaunted, Saif Hasan – at 18 the youngest Bangladeshi to score a double-century – and Taibur Rahman, with his second double, went on to add 304, a fourth-wicket record for Dhaka. But an innings win was still not enough to overtake Khulna.*

At Fatullah (KSOA), January 3–5, 2017. **Khulna won by 398 runs. Khulna 207** (Dolar Mahmud 5-53) **and 423-5 dec** (Anamul Haque 122, Tushar Imran 138); **‡Dhaka Metropolis 122 and 110** (Al-Amin Hossain 6-41). *Khulna 14pts, Dhaka Metropolis 3pts. Khulna made sure of the title with a three-day victory – their biggest by runs – over Dhaka Metropolis, whose relegation was confirmed. Tushar scored his third century of the competition and shared successive stands of 160 with Anamul (whose five sixes took him to 19 in the tournament) and 104 with Mithun Ali (50), while Al-Amin Hossain claimed 9-80 as Dhaka Metropolis collapsed twice.*

Tier Two

At Sylhet, September 25–28, 2016. **Drawn. Chittagong 368 and 251** (Suhrawadi Shuvo 5-50); **‡Rangpur 355** (Yasir Arafat Mishu 5-65) **and 224-5.** *Chittagong 10pts, Rangpur 9pts.*

At Rajshahi, September 25–28, 2016. **Drawn. Rajshahi 199** (Abu Jayed 5-59) **and 120-4; ‡Sylhet 175.** *Rajshahi 7pts, Sylhet 6pts.*

At Rajshahi, October 2–4, 2016. **Rajshahi won by an innings and 242 runs. ‡Chittagong 141 and 175**; **Rajshahi 558-9 dec** (Mizanur Rahman 144, Jahurul Islam 131). *Rajshahi 18pts, Chittagong 1pt. Jahurul Islam and Hamidul Islam (92) added 206 for Rajshahi's fifth wicket to set up their biggest win.*

At Sylhet, October 2–5, 2016. **Rangpur won by 56 runs. ‡Rangpur 217 and 183**; **Sylhet 247** (Zakir Hasan 112) **and 97** (Suhrawadi Shuvo 7-45). *Rangpur 13pts, Sylhet 4pts. Suhrawadi Shuvo's career-best seven for 45 ensured Sylhet's collapse as they chased 154.*

At Savar (BKSP No. 3), October 8–11, 2016. **Drawn. Rangpur 234 and 233-7; ‡Rajshahi 268** (Junaid Siddique 126). *Rangpur 6pts, Rajshahi 8pts. Rajshahi wicketkeeper Hamidul made five dismissals in Rangpur's first innings.*

At Fatullah (KSOA), October 8–11, 2016. **Drawn. Sylhet 444** (Alok Kapali 137, Shahanur Rahman 102) **and 243-5 dec; ‡Chittagong 315** (Shahanur Rahman 5-66) **and 146-9** (Rahatul Ferdous 5-48). *Sylhet 9pts, Chittagong 7pts. Set 373, Chittagong fought back from 26-4, but were nine down when bad light thwarted Sylhet with eight overs left.*

At Sylhet, December 20–23, 2016. **Rangpur won by ten wickets. Rangpur 450** (Suhrawadi Shuvo 121) **and 33-0; ‡Chittagong 182 and 297.** *Rangpur 18pts, Chittagong 3pts. With Rangpur 190-6, Shuvo added 112 with Ariful Haque (52) and 130 with Alauddin Babu (64) for the next two wickets; he then took 3-48 to help make Chittagong follow on.*

At Bogra, December 20–23, 2016. **Rajshahi won by 151 runs. Rajshahi 204** (Abu Jayed 6-48) **and 344** (Farhad Hossain 132); **‡Sylhet 219** (Farhad Reza 5-91) **and 178.** *Rajshahi 13pts, Sylhet 4pts. Sylhet wicketkeeper Zakir Hasan took eight catches in the match, and his Rajshahi opposite number Hamidul five in Sylhet's first innings.*

At Chittagong (ZAC), December 27–30, 2016. **Rajshahi won by eight wickets. Chittagong 315** (Tasamul Haque 104; Saqlain Sajib 5-54) **and 299-3 dec** (Tasamul Haque 100*, Yasir Ali 105*); **‡Rajshahi 230 and 387-2** (Junaid Siddique 104*, Farhad Hossain 113*). *Rajshahi 13pts, Chittagong 6pts. Tasamul Haque scored twin hundreds, and shared a fourth-wicket stand of 203* with Yasir Ali in Chittagong's second innings. But the match was won by a stand of 199* in 25 overs between Junaid Siddique (104* in 97 balls) and Farhad Hossain (113* in 77) which carried them past a target of 385, the third-highest successful chase in Bangladeshi first-class cricket.*

At Sylhet, December 27–30, 2016. **Rangpur won by ten wickets. ‡Sylhet 272 and 150**; **Rangpur 398-9 dec** (Nasir Hossain 201; Abu Jayed 5-112) **and 27-0.** *Rangpur 16pts, Sylhet 3pts. Nasir Hossain scored a maiden double-century to rescue Rangpur from 29-4 and set them on the way to their second successive ten-wicket victory, lifting them above Rajshahi in the table; he added 146 for the seventh wicket with Shuvo, and was last out, a fourth catch for fielder Jaker Ali.*

At Chittagong (ZAC), January 3–6, 2017. **Drawn. ‡Sylhet 555-7 dec** (Imtiaz Hossain 134, Alok Kapali 200*) **and 165-7 dec; Chittagong 320** (Abu Jayed 5-63) **and 261-7.** *Chittagong 6pts, Sylhet 10pts. Alok Kapali hit ten sixes in his third double-hundred, which occupied 266 balls; it was his 19th first-class century overall, second only to Tushar Imran among Bangladeshi batsmen.*

At Bogra, January 3–6, 2017. **Drawn. Rajshahi 191** (Mohammad Saddam 5-57) **and 403-7 dec** (Maisuqur Rahman 160); **‡Rangpur 351** (Mamun Hossain 5-81) **and 196-2.** *Rajshahi 6pts, Rangpur 10pts. This match was a battle for promotion; Rangpur started three points ahead and increased that to seven, with Rajshahi's second-innings fightback coming too late.*

NATIONAL CRICKET LEAGUE WINNERS

†1999-2000	Chittagong	2005-06	Rajshahi	2012-13	Khulna
2000-01	Biman Bangladesh Airlines	2006-07	Dhaka	2013-14	Dhaka
2001-02	Dhaka	2007-08	Khulna	2014-15	Rangpur
2002-03	Khulna	2008-09	Rajshahi	2015-16	Khulna
2003-04	Dhaka	2009-10	Rajshahi	2016-17	Khulna
2004-05	Dhaka	2010-11	Rajshahi		
		2011-12	Rajshahi		

† *The National Cricket League was not first-class in 1999-2000.*

Dhaka, Khulna and Rajshahi have won the title 5 times, Biman Bangladesh Airlines, Chittagong and Rangpur 1.

BANGLADESH CRICKET LEAGUE IN 2016-17

	Played	*Won*	*Lost*	*Drawn*	*Innings win pts*	*1st-inns pts*	*Pts*
North Zone	6	2	0	4	2	4	22
South Zone	6	1	0	5	1	4	16
East Zone	6	1	2	3	0	4	13
Central Zone	6	1	3	2	0	2	10

Outright win = 6pts; bonus for innings win = 1pt; draw = 1pt; first-innings lead in draw = 2pts.

At Bogra, January 28–30, 2017. **East Zone won by nine wickets. Central Zone 224** (Abu Jayed 5-37) **and 198; ‡East Zone 367** (Liton Das 219; Shuvagata Hom 5-101) **and 57-1.** *East Zone 6pts. Liton Das scored 219, his maiden double-century, in 241 balls – 128 of his runs came in boundaries.*

At Sylhet, January 28–31, 2017. **Drawn. ‡North Zone 492-9 dec** (Naeem Islam 185; Abdur Razzak 5-185) **and 69-2; South Zone 448** (Fazle Mahmud 147; Taijul Islam 5-136). *North Zone 3pts, South Zone 1pt. Abdur Razzak became the first Bangladeshi to take 450 first-class wickets.*

At Chittagong (ZAC), February 4–6, 2017. **North Zone won by an innings and 50 runs. North Zone 502** (Junaid Siddique 181); **‡Central Zone 233 and 219** (Nurul Hasan 113; Sanjamul Islam 9-80). *North Zone 7pts. Slow left-armer Sanjamul Islam's 9-80 was the best innings return in first-class cricket in Bangladesh, beating 9-82 by Saqlain Sajib against Zimbabwe A in 2014-15. Sanjamul finished with 12-144, the best match return of the season. Central Zone wicketkeeper Nurul Hasan hit 113 in 111 balls, but his side went down to an innings defeat.*

At Sylhet, February 4–6, 2017. **South Zone won by an innings and 44 runs. South Zone 403; ‡East Zone 144** (Rubel Hossain 5-22) **and 215** (Abdur Razzak 6-44). *South Zone 7pts. Rubel Hossain took five wickets in ten overs, and Razzak completed the innings win.*

At Fatullah (KSOA), February 11–14, 2017. **Drawn. South Zone 260** (Shuvagata Hom 6-91) **and 317; ‡Central Zone 299** (Shuvagata Hom 100) **and 190-5.** *Central Zone 3pts, South Zone 1pt. Shuvagata Hom collected 10-168 in addition to a century and a second-innings 52.*

At Chittagong (ZAC), February 11–14, 2017. **Drawn. ‡East Zone 490** (Afif Hossain 105, Yasir Ali 110*) **and 92-1; North Zone 404** (Naeem Islam 100). *East Zone 3pts, North Zone 1pt. Seventeen-year-old Afif Hossain hit 105 on debut – in an opening stand of 197 with Imtiaz Hossain.*

At Fatullah (KSOA), February 19–22, 2017. **Central Zone won by 227 runs. Central Zone 328** (Abu Jayed 5-77) **and 282-7 dec; ‡East Zone 211 and 172.** *Central Zone 6pts. Abu Jayed took five or more in an innings for the sixth time in the season.*

At Savar (BKSP No. 4), February 19–22, 2017. **Drawn. ‡South Zone 501** (Tushar Imran 220); **North Zone 242** (Nahidul Islam 5-104) **and 403-8** (Farhad Hossain 119, Naeem Islam 129*; Nahidul Islam 5-130). *North Zone 1pt, South Zone 3pts. Tushar Imran scored his second double-hundred, a career-best 220, and added 215 with Shahriar Nafees (74) for South Zone's fourth wicket. In the same innings, Mosaddek Hossain hit 57 in 65 balls, with five sixes. Off-spinner Nahidul Islam took 10-234 in the match, which ended with North and South tied on 12 points at the top of the table.*

At Sylhet, February 26–March 1, 2017. **North Zone won by an innings and 85 runs. Central Zone 181** (Sanjamul Islam 5-45) **and 271; ‡North Zone 537** (Naeem Islam 142, Nazmul Hossain 123,

Dhiman Ghosh 113). *North Zone 7pts. Naeem Islam, with his fourth century of this tournament, put on 197 for North Zone's fifth wicket with Nazmul Hossain and 126 for the seventh with Dhiman Ghosh. Victory put North six points ahead of South.*

At Chittagong (ZAC), February 26–March 1, 2017. **Drawn. ‡South Zone 296** (Imrul Kayes 136) **and 198-5; East Zone 523-7 dec** (Afif Hossain 137). *East Zone 3pts, South Zone 1pt. Afif, with his second century in the first three matches of his career, and Tasamul Haque (98) added 222 for East Zone's second wicket; in the same innings, Mohammad Saifuddin (50*) and Rahatul Ferdous (60*) shared an eighth-wicket stand of 104*. Tushar reached 1,000 first-class runs for the season.*

At Savar (BKSP No. 3), March 5–8, 2017. **Drawn. ‡South Zone 749-8 dec** (Mithun Ali 131, Tushar Imran 217, Shahriar Nafees 207*) **and 33-0; Central Zone 415** (Shadman Islam 113). *Central Zone 1pt, South Zone 3pts. South Zone's 749-8 was the second-highest first-class total in Bangladesh; all 11 Central players had a bowl. Tushar's third double-hundred – and second in three matches – gave him five centuries in the season, and 23 in all; he shared partnerships of 230 for the third wicket with Mithun Ali and 215 for the fourth with Shahriar, who scored a second double-century. There was a third double-hundred in the innings – 202 runs conceded by Shuvagata. With two overs left in the match, Tushar opened South Zone's second innings so he could break the national record for runs in a first-class season; his 28* took him to 1,249.*

At Fatullah (KSOA), March 5–8, 2017. **Drawn. North Zone 374** (Farhad Hossain 108) **and 295-8 dec** (Nazmul Hossain 122*); **‡East Zone 216** (Shafiul Islam 6-70) **and 128-3.** *East Zone 1pt, North Zone 3pts. Bad light on the final day forced a draw, which confirmed North Zone's first BCL title. Farhad Hossain scored his fourth century of the season in their first innings, adding 204 for the second wicket with Junaid Siddique, who later completed 1,000 first-class runs for the season.*

DHAKA PREMIER LEAGUE IN 2016-17

50-over league plus Super League and Relegation League

Preliminary League	*Played*	*Won*	*Lost*	*Points*	*NRR*
GAZI GROUP CRICKETERS	11	9	2	18	0.40
PRIME DOLESHWAR	11	8	3	16	0.58
ABAHANI	11	8	3	16	1.01
PRIME BANK	11	8	3	16	0.52
SHEIKH JAMAL DHANMONDI	11	7	4	14	0.05
MOHAMMEDAN	11	6	5	12	–0.12
Legends of Rupganj	11	6	5	12	–0.19
Brothers Union	11	5	6	10	0.42
Kala Bagan Krira Chakra	11	4	7	8	–0.12
Khelaghar Samaj Kallyan Samity	11	3	8	6	–0.33
Victoria	11	1	10	2	–1.30
Partex	11	1	10	2	–0.81

Super League	*Played*	*Won*	*Lost*	*Points*	*NRR*
Gazi Group Cricketers	16	12	4	24	0.60
Prime Doleshwar	16	12	4	24	0.53
Abahani	16	12	4	24	1.11
Prime Bank	16	10	6	20	0.29
Mohammedan	16	8	8	16	–0.35
Sheikh Jamal Dhanmondi	16	7	9	14	–0.46

Relegation League	*Played*	*Won*	*Lost*	*Points*	*NRR*
Khelaghar Samaj Kallyan Samity	13	5	8	10	0.31
Victoria	13	2	11	4	–1.45
Partex	13	1	12	2	–1.09

The top six teams advanced to the Super League, carrying forward all their results from the Preliminary League and then playing the other five qualifiers again. Teams tied on points were separated on head-to-head results.

The Bangladesh Premier League has its own section (page 1103).

INDIAN CRICKET IN 2017

The more things change…

DILEEP PREMACHANDRAN

The Indian Test juggernaut rolled along, bar one eventful detour into a Pune ditch. The white-ball sides dominated most opposition, but not the game that mattered. The team parted ways with a coach who had barely lost a match, and were reunited with an old mentor. The women beat England, New Zealand and Australia on their way to a World Cup final, but lost their nerve with one hand on the trophy. The IPL rights were sold for a figure so obscene it taxed your imagination. And Virat Kohli, after nearly provoking a diplomatic crisis, continued to pile on the runs. Yes, it was another humdrum year for Indian cricket.

The game's administration remained a rudderless ship, with the Lodha Committee recommendations yet to be implemented, a full 18 months after the Supreme Court's edict. The panel, headed by a former chief justice of the court, had asked – among other things – for age limits for office-bearers,

INDIA IN 2017

	Played	*Won*	*Lost*	*Drawn/No result*
Tests	11	7	1	3
One-day internationals	29	21	7	1
Twenty20 internationals	13	9	4	–

NOVEMBER / DECEMBER / JANUARY	5 Tests, 3 ODIs and 3 T20Is (h) v England	(see *Wisden 2017*, page 342)
FEBRUARY	1 Test (h) v Bangladesh	(page 828)
FEBRUARY / MARCH	4 Tests (h) v Australia	(page 831)
APRIL		
MAY		
JUNE / JULY	ICC Champions Trophy (in England)	(page 263)
JUNE / JULY	5 ODIs and 1 T20I (a) v West Indies	(page 1027)
AUGUST / SEPTEMBER	3 Tests, 5 ODIs and 1 T20I (a) v Sri Lanka	(page 990)
SEPTEMBER / OCTOBER	5 ODIs and 3 T20Is (h) v Australia	(page 846)
OCTOBER / NOVEMBER	3 ODIs and 3 T20Is (h) v New Zealand	(page 853)
NOVEMBER / DECEMBER	3 Tests, 3 ODIs and 3 T20Is (h) v Sri Lanka	(page 859)

For a review of Indian domestic cricket from the 2016-17 season, see page 872.

Ishara S. Kodikara, AFP/Getty Images

Smiles better: new coach Ravi Shastri enjoys an easier relationship with captain Virat Kohli than did Anil Kumble, his predecessor.

restrictions on the number of terms they could serve, and only one vote for states that housed more than one team. But the enfeebled Indian board dragged their feet on the implementation, and were then backed into a corner at an ICC meeting in February, where their share of cricket's global revenue was reduced from their hoped-for $570m to $293m, before they settled on $405m.

Even as confusion reigned in the courtrooms and boardrooms, with the power brokers of old reduced to wheeling and dealing, the national side provided plenty of distractions. After the straightforward romps over New Zealand and England in late 2016, Indian cricket badly needed a heavyweight arm-wrestle to get the crowds enthused about the five-day game. It was provided by Australia, who had lost their previous nine Tests in Asia, and had sent a team many considered their weakest to tour India.

A draw on a comatose surface in Ranchi did little more than showcase Cheteshwar Pujara's incredible powers of concentration. But Pune, Bangalore and Dharamsala were another matter, and fortunes fluctuated before India crashed over the line. Their 333-run defeat on a worn Pune pitch expected to play into their hands had been a cold-water wake-up call, with slow left-armer Steve O'Keefe taking 12 for 70. When India were skittled for 189 on the opening day at Bangalore, with Nathan Lyon collecting eight for 50, the series looked to be slipping away. But the bowlers dug deep, as did batsmen Pujara and Ajinkya Rahane, and Ravichandran Ashwin completed a stunning turnaround with a six-for on the final afternoon.

A powder-keg atmosphere on the field spilled into the press conference, where Kohli suggested Smith and the Australians had been guilty of seeking dressing-room advice about DRS. Smith called his transgression a "brain fade", but Kohli was convinced there was more to it. In the days before the BCCI's wings were clipped, a president such as Jagmohan Dalmiya or N. Srinivasan might have stood by their captain. But the irate Australians demanded proof, and the board quietly backed down. Kohli missed the final Test with a shoulder injury, but India pulled off a famous victory without him. It proved Anil Kumble's last Test as coach.

The Supreme Court had already appointed a Committee of Administrators in January 2017 to run the BCCI until board elections could be held. Vinod Rai, a bureaucrat, had been India's comptroller and auditor-general. Vikram Limaye came from the world of finance, but left in July to take over the National Stock Exchange. Diana Edulji was a pioneer of women's cricket, and Ramachandra Guha, a historian of the sport and of modern India. But Guha quit in June, protesting at what he called the "superstar culture" permeating the national side, after a month-long saga involving Kohli and Kumble either side of the Champions Trophy in England. By then, their working relationship had broken down, and the BCCI were already eyeing successors when Pakistan upset India in the final at The Oval. Kumble exited after making clear his dismay at how things had played out, and Ravi Shastri, not even on the original shortlist of potential replacements, was appointed to help the captain implement his vision.

Shastri was no stranger to Kohli, having already been team director for 18 months, and temperamentally seemed a better fit; Kumble was especially hurt when his style was described as "schoolmasterish". In India's first assignment after Shastri's return, they won 3–0 in Sri Lanka, twice by an innings. The Sri Lankans were then seen off 1–0 back in India, a series notable for smog stopping play in Delhi.

By the end of the year, four Test players stood out: Pujara (1,140 runs at 67) and Kohli (1,059 at 75) made nine of India's 19 hundreds, while spinners Ashwin (56 wickets at 27) and Ravindra Jadeja (54 at 23) took 110 of the 200 wickets claimed by bowlers. In all formats, though, Kohli was supreme, his total of 2,818 runs more than 1,000 ahead of Rohit Sharma in second place. And with India imperious in home conditions over the past half-decade, the consensus was that only the overseas trips to come – South Africa, England and Australia – would reveal whether their plans were more robust than their predecessors'. Defeat in South Africa in January 2018 was not a good start.

Long-term progress depended on the Supreme Court, and whether it would finally see some of its suggested reforms put in place. Elements of overreach in the original recommendations had the potential to keep a generation of judges busy for years, and there was little appetite on either side for a compromise. As long as India kept winning – and in 2017 they had a win–loss record of 7–1 in Tests, 21–7 in ODIs and 9–4 in T20Is – the common man wasn't unduly bothered by the messes at administrative level. Both the BCCI strongmen and the judges who kept delaying decisions seemed well aware of that.

INDIA v BANGLADESH IN 2016-17

SHAMYA DASGUPTA

Test match (1): India 1, Bangladesh 0

After Bangladesh gained Full Member status at the turn of the century, India took more than 16 years to invite them for a Test match. Fans in Dhaka blamed the BCCI, but the truth was a little more complex. Bangladesh's board had always been keen, for commercial reasons, to host India, who had played eight Tests there (winning six and drawing two) across five trips, including Bangladesh's first. It was also true that, for many years, fears of a mismatch – and a financial deficit – fuelled the BCCI's reluctance to return the favour. Still, it was an embarrassment that this was the first bilateral meeting between the sides in India, and even then there was time only for a solitary Test, squeezed in between the visits of England and Australia.

But the timing was good in one respect: Bangladesh were no longer pushovers, having beaten England in Mirpur in October 2016, and performed creditably in New Zealand soon after. And they were not overwhelmed in Hyderabad, although India's victory was comfortable enough after they cantered past 600 for the third match running, powered by Virat Kohli's 204. Afterwards, Kohli joined the chorus calling for Bangladesh to be given more opportunities in the Test arena. It's a fair bet it won't be another 16 years before they play in India again.

BANGLADESH TOURING PARTY

*Mushfiqur Rahim, Imrul Kayes, Kamrul Islam, Liton Das, Mahmudullah, Mehedi Hasan, Mominul Haque, Mosaddek Hossain, Sabbir Rahman, Shafiul Islam, Shakib Al Hasan, Soumya Sarkar, Subashis Roy, Taijul Islam, Tamim Iqbal, Taskin Ahmed. *Coach:* U. C. Hathurusinghe.

Imrul Kayes injured his left thigh in a two-day warm-up game against India A, and was replaced by Mosaddek Hossain.

INDIA v BANGLADESH

Test Match

At Hyderabad, February 9–13, 2017. India won by 208 runs. Toss: India.

Mushfiqur Rahim knew he was up against it the moment he lost the toss: the pitch was as flat as a roti, and his team were facing the world's top-ranked side, fresh from their triumph against England. And, although Taskin Ahmed struck in the first over, India's batsmen were soon making hay once more. Kohli became the first to score double-centuries in four successive Test series, and declared late on the second day – but Bangladesh did not roll over, and batted for more than 100 overs in both innings, pushing the match into the fifth afternoon. In the end, though, spinners Ashwin and Jadeja proved too effective, as India took their unbeaten run to a national record 19 Tests, 15 of which had been won.

They had taken charge early on, with a second-wicket stand of 178 between Vijay – who went on to his ninth Test century – and Pujara, whose 83 took him past the record for most first-class runs in a season in India (1,604 by Chandu Borde in 1964-65). And when Mehedi Hasan removed Pujara, Mushfiqur gratefully grabbing a big outside edge that had bounced up off his own pad, it brought in Kohli. His resplendent form continued, and by the close he had already reached his fourth hundred in 11 Test innings, which he extended next day to 204. His stand with the fit-again Rahane – back in place of Karun Nair, dropped despite his triple-century against England in the previous Test – reached 222,

BOTH WICKETKEEPERS SCORING A HUNDRED IN SAME TEST

India (A. Ratra 115*) v West Indies (R. D. Jacobs 118) at St John's	2001-02
India (M. S. Dhoni 110) v Sri Lanka (H. A. P. W. Jayawardene 154*) at Ahmedabad	2009-10
Sri Lanka (L. D. Chandimal 116*) v Bangladesh (Mushfiqur Rahim 200) at Galle	2012-13
India (W. P. Saha 106*) v Bangladesh (Mushfiqur Rahim 127) at Hyderabad	**2016-17**

then Saha chimed in as the total spiralled towards 700. Bangladesh's fielding was patchy – Mushfiqur had a torrid time behind the stumps – but a raw attack stuck to their task: apart from Shakib Al Hasan, the frontline bowlers had only 21 Test caps between them.

All too often, Bangladesh had crumbled in such circumstances, but now they dug in bravely, helped by a pitch that refused to collapse. There was some poor running, and a couple of loose shots. But the most experienced pair showed the way in a stand of 107: Shakib hit 14 fours in his 82, and Mushfiqur went on to a characterful century, his fifth in

FEWEST TESTS TO REACH 250 WICKETS

45	**R. Ashwin (India)**	**2011-12 to 2016-17**
48	D. K. Lillee (Australia)	1970-71 to 1980-81
49	D. W. Steyn (South Africa)	2004-05 to 2011-12
50	A. A. Donald (South Africa)	1991-92 to 1998-99
51	Waqar Younis (Pakistan)	1989-90 to 1997-98
51	M. Muralitharan (Sri Lanka)	1992-93 to 1999-2000
53	R. J. Hadlee (New Zealand)	1972-73 to 1984-85
53	M. D. Marshall (West Indies)	1978-79 to 1987-88

52 Tests, and passed 3,000 runs during a 381-minute stay. He was last out, providing Ashwin with his 250th Test wicket. But the Indian slow men, so dominant against England, had been forced to toil; the bowler who caught the eye was Yadav, who made the batsmen hop around during several fiery spells.

A sprightly maiden fifty from Mehedi limited the deficit to 299, but Kohli ignored the follow-on. Pujara cracked an unbeaten 54 from 58 balls as India cantered along at five and a half an over, and the declaration, at tea on the fourth day, left a target of 459. Another of Bangladesh's seniors, Mahmudullah, took the lead this time, his 64 using up 200 minutes, while Soumya Sarkar made a pleasant 42. But the spinners worked their way inexorably through the line-up, with Shakib and Mushfiqur two of five batsmen to fall in the twenties. Despite four wickets apiece for Ashwin and Jadeja, Mushfiqur knew where the crucial difference lay: "Unfortunately, our team doesn't have a Virat Kohli."

Man of the Match: V. Kohli.

Close of play: first day, India 356-3 (Kohli 111, Rahane 45); second day, Bangladesh 41-1 (Tamim Iqbal 24, Mominul Haque 1); third day, Bangladesh 322-6 (Mushfiqur Rahim 81, Mehedi Hasan 51); fourth day, Bangladesh 103-3 (Mahmudullah 9, Shakib Al Hasan 21).

India

First innings		Second innings	
K. L. Rahul b Taskin Ahmed	2	(2) c Mushfiqur Rahim b Taskin Ahmed	10
M. Vijay b Taijul Islam	108	(1) c Mushfiqur Rahim b Taskin Ahmed	7
C. A. Pujara c Mushfiqur Rahim b Mehedi Hasan	83	not out	54
*V. Kohli lbw b Taijul Islam	204	c Mahmudullah b Shakib Al Hasan	38
A. M. Rahane c Mehedi Hasan b Taijul Islam	82	b Shakib Al Hasan	28
†W. P. Saha not out	106		
R. Ashwin c Soumya Sarkar b Mehedi Hasan	34		
R. A. Jadeja not out	60	(6) not out	16
Lb 5, w 1, nb 2	8	Lb 5, w 1	6
1/2 (1) 2/180 (3) 3/234 (2) 4/456 (5) 5/495 (4) 6/569 (7) (6 wkts dec, 166 overs)	687	1/12 (1) 2/23 (2) 3/90 (4) 4/128 (5) (4 wkts dec, 29 overs)	159

Bhuvneshwar Kumar, U. T. Yadav and I. Sharma did not bat.

Taskin Ahmed 25–2–127–1; Kamrul Islam 19–1–100–0; Soumya Sarkar 1–0–4–0; Mehedi Hasan 42–0–165–2; Shakib Al Hasan 24–4–104–0; Taijul Islam 47–6–156–3; Sabbir Rahman 3–0–10–0; Mahmudullah 5–0–16–0. *Second innings*—Taijul Islam 6–1–29–0; Taskin Ahmed 7–0–43–2; Shakib Al Hasan 9–0–50–2; Mehedi Hasan 7–0–32–0.

Bangladesh

First innings		Second innings	
Tamim Iqbal run out	24	c Kohli b Ashwin	3
Soumya Sarkar c Saha b Yadav	15	c Rahane b Jadeja	42
Mominul Haque lbw b Yadav	12	c Rahane b Ashwin	27
Mahmudullah lbw b Sharma	28	c Bhuvneshwar Kumar b Sharma	64
Shakib Al Hasan c Yadav b Ashwin	82	c Pujara b Jadeja	22
*†Mushfiqur Rahim c Saha b Ashwin	127	c Jadeja b Ashwin	23
Sabbir Rahman lbw b Jadeja	16	lbw b Sharma	22
Mehedi Hasan b Bhuvneshwar Kumar	51	c Saha b Jadeja	23
Taijul Islam c Saha b Yadav	10	(10) c Rahul b Jadeja	6
Taskin Ahmed c Rahane b Jadeja	8	(11) lbw b Ashwin	1
Kamrul Islam not out	0	(9) not out	3
Lb 15	15	B 4, lb 7, nb 3	14
1/38 (2) 2/44 (1) 3/64 (3) 4/109 (4) 5/216 (5) 6/235 (7) 7/322 (8) 8/339 (9) 9/378 (10) 10/388 (6) (127.5 overs)	388	1/11 (1) 2/71 (2) 3/75 (3) 4/106 (5) 5/162 (6) 6/213 (7) 7/225 (4) 8/242 (8) 9/249 (10) 10/250 (11) (100.3 overs)	250

Bhuvneshwar Kumar 21–7–52–1; Sharma 20–5–69–1; Ashwin 28.5–7–98–2; Yadav 25–6–84–3; Jadeja 33–8–70–2. *Second innings*—Bhuvneshwar Kumar 8–4–15–0; Ashwin 30.3–10–73–4; Sharma 13–3–40–2; Yadav 12–2–33–0; Jadeja 37–15–78–4.

Umpires: M. Erasmus and J. S. Wilson. Third umpire: C. B. Gaffaney.
Referee: A. J. Pycroft.

INDIA v AUSTRALIA IN 2016-17

ADAM COLLINS

Test matches (4): India 2, Australia 1

Few imagined this series would be a minor classic. Fewer still imagined the young Australians, fresh from rebuilding their team – and with nine consecutive Test defeats in Asia behind them – would overcome India, unbeaten in 20 home Tests and sitting on top of the rankings. Not even Australia's captain said they could triumph. Ultimately, they didn't. But Steve Smith's underdogs scrapped their way into the lead, and stayed in contention until halfway through the last Test. The margins of victory – 333 runs by Australia, 75 runs and eight wickets by India – belied oscillating fortunes across four pulsating contests.

A tinder-dry surface at Pune, one of three grounds making its Test debut during the series, was designed to expose Australian vulnerability to spin. It proved an epic miscalculation: after preparing for just this eventuality in a Dubai training camp, the touring slow bowlers caused chaos instead. Left-arm spinner Steve O'Keefe's career-defining 12 wickets inspired two spectacular Indian collapses, and Australia were one up inside three days.

The Australians, who had arrived as holders of the Border–Gavaskar Trophy, increased the pressure when Smith pointed out that one more stumble might see them leaving with it too. And when Nathan Lyon's off-breaks induced another Indian collapse on the opening day at Bangalore, that seemed distinctly possible. But the hosts rediscovered their batting backbone and match-winning steel, and showed why they had lost just one series at home to Australia since 1969-70.

Ranchi's flat track brought the only draw. Both sides boasted two centurions, and both sides created chances; neither capitalised. Stoicism had not been a feature of the batting, but Australia found enough. The final chapter in Dharamsala gave Smith's men a tilt at victory, but debutant left-arm wrist-spinner Kuldeep Yadav derailed them after they were well placed at 144 for one. Australia kept the deficit to a modest 32, but a second-innings slump handed the series to India.

Almost as common as collapses were controversies, ranging from consequential to cringeworthy. After Bangalore, India's captain Virat Kohli accused Smith of systematically trying to cheat DRS. Smith did admit to what he called a "brain fade" when – pondering a review of an lbw decision – he looked to his dressing-room for advice. He apologised, and said it was a one-off. The ICC took the matter no further, but Kohli would not let it lie, and the BCCI briefly threatened to pursue Smith and his batting partner, Peter Handscomb. The affair rolled on, involving varied scraps and subplots extending to broadcasters and journalists. Kohli declared his friendship with some Australians was over; the sentiment was shared. Fortunately, the cricket was gripping enough for the fracas never to become more than a sideshow, and none of the protagonists brought charges.

After their sputtering start, most of India's batsmen regained their self-assurance, though not Kohli. Magnificent against England a couple of months earlier, he was not even mediocre now. His fight was limited to verbal jousts, and he hit just 46 runs in five innings, before a shoulder injury sidelined him for the Fourth Test. Cheteshwar Pujara made up for the captain's failure, his double-hundred in Ranchi following a second-innings 92 at Bangalore that was more valuable than many a century. Patience was his weapon: in all, he faced 1,049 balls.

K. L. Rahul – Pujara's near-equal for runs, if not quite endurance – built reliable platforms at the top of the innings, reaching 50 six times out of seven. Ajinkya Rahane was at the heart of the turnaround in Bangalore, adding 118 for the fifth wicket with Pujara, and led India to the series win as stand-in captain in Dharamsala.

BEST TEST AVERAGE AGAINST INDIA

		T	*I*	*NO*	*R*	*HS*	*100*	
106.78	E. D. Weekes (WI)	10	15	1	1,495	207	7	1948-49 to 1952-53
94.83	A. Flower (Z)	9	18	6	1,138	232*	3	1992-93 to 2001-02
88.06	Younis Khan (P)	9	17	2	1,321	267	5	2004-05 to 2007-08
87.00	Zaheer Abbas (P)	19	25	5	1,740	235*	6	1978-79 to 1984-85
84.05	**S. P. D. Smith (A)**	**10**	**20**	**3**	**1,429**	**192**	**7**	**2012-13 to 2016-17**
83.47	G. S. Sobers (WI)	18	30	7	1,920	198	8	1958-59 to 1970-71
75.27	K. F. Barrington (E)	14	21	3	1,355	172	3	1959 to 1967
72.57	M. P. Vaughan (E)	9	16	2	1,016	197	4	2001-02 to 2007
70.82	D. C. Boon (A)	11	20	3	1,204	135	6	1985-86 to 1991-92
70.64	I. T. Botham (E)	14	17	0	1,201	208	5	1979 to 1982

Minimum 1,000 runs.

Wriddhaman Saha came into his own down the order. His century from No. 8 helped bat Australia out of the Ranchi Test, and at Dharamsala he shared a vital 96 with Man of the Series Ravindra Jadeja. Seemingly at the peak of his powers, Jadeja took 25 wickets at under 19 (and hit two spirited half-centuries) to leapfrog his fellow spinner, Ravichandran Ashwin, to the top of the Test rankings. Ashwin managed 21, including the six that routed Australia's chase at Bangalore. Umesh Yadav was the outstanding seamer, generating pace and swing with new ball and old, and claimed 17 victims.

For Australia, one batsman outshone the rest. Smith hit 499 runs, including three centuries, and averaged 71 – more than 31 ahead of any of his colleagues. Despite the varied conditions, he thrived, strengthening his claim as the world No. 1. He was let down by his team-mates, though numbers didn't tell everything. Matt Renshaw, who turned 21 on the last day of the series, was the only other to make 200 runs; he showed courage when he resumed after illness in Pune, and patience for his half-century in Bangalore.

Neither Handscomb nor Shaun Marsh made huge contributions, yet by battling through 62 pressure-cooker overs on the last day at Ranchi they saved the match. By then, Glenn Maxwell had reached a maiden Test century on the second morning, proving he was no one-trick T20 pony, while wicketkeeper

Danish Siddiqui, Reuters

KO'd by O'K: Virat Kohli is bowled by Steve O'Keefe, and India slide towards defeat at Pune.

Matthew Wade, his glovework much improved, also landed several counter-punches. However, vice-captain David Warner did not burnish his reputation, and the gap widened between his home and away averages to 59 versus 36. He made one fifty, after being dropped first ball; his 16 Test innings in India had produced 388 runs at 24.

All Australia's bowlers left a dent. O'Keefe and Lyon wreaked early havoc, and finished with 19 victims each. Josh Hazlewood was fierce in the second innings at Bangalore, and steady throughout. After a vital half-century, Mitchell Starc dismissed Pujara and Kohli to spur the initial Pune collapse, but he returned home halfway through the series with a broken foot. Pat Cummins stepped in, playing his first Tests since his 2011-12 debut, and regularly bothered India.

For all that, Smith's men were still not ready to conquer what Steve Waugh had called Australia's final frontier – largely because India were remarkable in turning around seemingly dire situations. It was proof, yet again, of the endless fascination of Test cricket.

AUSTRALIA TOURING PARTY

*S. P. D. Smith, A. C. Agar, J. M. Bird, P. J. Cummins, P. S. P. Handscomb, J. R. Hazlewood, U. T. Khawaja, N. M. Lyon, M. R. Marsh, S. E. Marsh, G. J. Maxwell, S. N. J. O'Keefe, M. T. Renshaw, M. A. Starc, M. P. Stoinis, M. J. Swepson, M. S. Wade, D. A. Warner. *Coach:* D. S. Lehmann.

Stoinis and Cummins were called into the squad when M. R. Marsh (shoulder) and Starc (foot) returned home.

TEST AVERAGES

INDIA – BATTING AND FIELDING

	T	*I*	*NO*	*R*	*HS*	*100*	*50*	*Avge*	*Ct/St*
K. L. Rahul	4	7	1	393	90	0	6	65.50	2
C. A. Pujara	4	7	0	405	202	1	2	57.85	4
W. P. Saha	4	6	1	174	117	1	0	34.80	13/1
A. M. Rahane	4	7	1	198	52	0	1	33.00	4
†R. A. Jadeja	4	6	1	127	63	0	2	25.40	3
M. Vijay	3	5	0	113	82	0	1	22.60	6
K. K. Nair	3	4	0	54	26	0	0	13.50	3
V. Kohli	3	5	0	46	15	0	0	9.20	3
R. Ashwin	4	6	0	53	30	0	0	8.83	2
U. T. Yadav	4	6	3	23	16	0	0	7.66	0
I. Sharma	3	5	2	8	6	0	0	2.66	1

Played in one Test: Bhuvneshwar Kumar 0; †A. Mukund 0, 16; J. Yadav 2, 5; †K. Yadav 7 (1 ct).

BOWLING

	Style	*O*	*M*	*R*	*W*	*BB*	*5I*	*Avge*
R. A. Jadeja	SLA	213.1	54	464	25	6-63	2	18.56
K. Yadav	SLW	28	3	91	4	4-68	0	22.75
U. T. Yadav	RF	129	22	398	17	4-32	0	23.41
R. Ashwin	OB	225.2	51	575	21	6-41	1	27.38
I. Sharma	RFM	78	11	209	3	1-28	0	69.66

Also bowled: Bhuvneshwar Kumar (RFM) 19.3–3–68–2; K. K. Nair (OB) 1–0–7–0; M. Vijay (OB) 3–0–17–0; J. Yadav (OB) 23–2–101–2.

AUSTRALIA – BATTING AND FIELDING

	T	*I*	*NO*	*R*	*HS*	*100*	*50*	*Avge*	*Ct/St*
S. P. D. Smith	4	8	1	499	178*	3	0	71.28	9
G. J. Maxwell	2	4	0	159	104	1	0	39.75	2
†M. S. Wade	4	8	2	196	57	0	1	32.66	9/4
†M. A. Starc	2	4	0	118	61	0	1	29.50	1
†M. T. Renshaw	4	8	0	232	68	0	2	29.00	1
P. S. P. Handscomb	4	8	1	198	72*	0	1	28.28	6
†D. A. Warner	4	8	0	193	56	0	1	24.12	6
†S. E. Marsh	4	8	0	151	66	0	2	18.87	1
M. R. Marsh	2	4	0	48	31	0	0	12.00	1
P. J. Cummins	2	3	0	33	21	0	0	11.00	0
S. N. J. O'Keefe	4	7	1	45	25	0	0	7.50	0
N. M. Lyon	4	8	0	31	13	0	0	3.87	1
†J. R. Hazlewood	4	7	4	6	2*	0	0	2.00	1

BOWLING

	Style	*O*	*M*	*R*	*W*	*BB*	*5I*	*Avge*
S. N. J. O'Keefe	SLA	179.1	36	442	19	6-35	2	23.26
N. M. Lyon	OB	166.2	19	480	19	8-50	2	25.26
M. A. Starc	LF	42	10	151	5	2-38	0	30.20
P. J. Cummins	RF	77	20	242	8	4-106	0	30.25
J. R. Hazlewood	RFM	119	30	295	9	6-67	1	32.77

Also bowled: M. R. Marsh (RFM) 5–0–6–0; G. J. Maxwell (OB) 6–0–18–0.

At Mumbai (Brabourne), February 17–19, 2017. **Drawn. Australians 469-7 dec** (127 overs) (S. P. D. Smith 107, S. E. Marsh 104, M. R. Marsh 75, M. S. Wade 64) **and 110-4** (36 overs); ‡**India A 403** (91.5 overs) (S. S. Iyer 202*, K. J. Gowtham 74; N. M. Lyon 4-162, S. N. J. O'Keefe 3-101). *Steve Smith and Shaun Marsh retired out soon after reaching three figures, and there were seven wickets for the Australian spinners, though at a cost. On a flat pitch, Steve O'Keefe went for more than four an over, and Nathan Lyon not far short of six. Chief run-scorer was Shreyas Iyer, whose career-best 202* included 150 in boundaries.*

INDIA v AUSTRALIA

First Test

At Pune, February 23–25, 2017. Australia won by 333 runs. Toss: Australia.

What? How? Such expressions of incredulity were uttered by players and spectators alike after Steve Smith's team converted a hesitant 256 for nine on the first evening into victory by 333 runs two days later. It was India's first defeat in a home Test since England won at Kolkata in 2012. Suddenly Smith looked like he might become the second Australian captain to win a series in India since the Beatles' last LP.

To pull off such a thumping win, he required a cast of match-winners. That he could fill one role himself was no surprise: his second-innings hundred was a study in concentration on a pitch that turned so crudely it was rated "poor" by the ICC. But O'Keefe's contributions were less expected. He was the real star, his twin hauls of six for 35 defined by unstinting accuracy. Starc also displayed his all-round class to set the show in motion.

The idea was to win the toss in Pune's first Test, and bat. All went to plan until, at 82 for none and lunch approaching, Warner chopped on Umesh Yadav, and the innings went pear-shaped. Renshaw was forced to trail his partner off the ground because of stomach trouble, a move that did not impress former Test captain Allan Border. "I hope he's lying on a table half-dead, because otherwise I wouldn't be happy as captain," he said. Then Shaun Marsh, included for his supposed subcontinental skills, got in a muddle trying to sweep Jayant Yadav and was caught off the back of the bat. Handscomb burned a start, duped by Jadeja's slider, which – after Smith had miscued to midwicket off Ashwin – also did for Mitchell Marsh. At 166 for five, the morning's gains had been undone.

Wade fell lbw during a spell of quality reverse swing from Umesh and, although the unwell Renshaw had returned to make a steely half-century, Australia were a precarious 205 for nine once Ashwin found his edge, and Umesh despatched O'Keefe and Lyon with consecutive deliveries. Starc, however, hit through the line at will and clobbered 61 from 63 balls; Hazlewood, who faced 31, was the perfect foil. By the time Starc went next morning Australia were in the game.

The upturn with the bat didn't immediately translate to the bowling, with Starc and O'Keefe – perhaps unused to the new ball – struggling at first. A long day loomed, but in the seventh over Hazlewood claimed Vijay's edge. Sensing an opening, Smith brought back Starc. A flinching Pujara gloved a snorter behind; two balls later, Kohli played one

---

DOUBLE FIGURES

Bowlers with the same return in both innings of a Test (minimum three wickets):

R. S. Cunis (3-12)	New Zealand v India at Hyderabad (Lal Bahadur)	1969-70
Intikhab Alam (5-91)	Pakistan v New Zealand at Dacca	1969-70
B. S. Chandrasekhar (6-52)	India v Australia at Melbourne	1977-78
C. E. L. Stuart (3-45)	West Indies v Zimbabwe at Bulawayo	2001
B. Lee (3-57)	Australia v South Africa at Johannesburg	2005-06
Abdur Rehman (4-105)	Pakistan v South Africa at Karachi	2007-08
M. Muralitharan (3-112)	Sri Lanka v West Indies at Providence	2007-08
R. A. Jadeja (3-33)	India v Australia at Hyderabad (Uppal)	2012-13
S. N. J. O'Keefe (6-35)	**Australia v India at Pune**	**2016-17**

he should have left, and the world's in-form batsman had gone for a duck. Either side of lunch, Rahul drove fluently, putting on 50 with Rahane.

During the break, O'Keefe – ineffectual all morning – had returned to the middle for some fine-tuning. It did the trick: he struck with the second, fourth and sixth balls of his third over after lunch. Rahul holed out to long-off for reasons understood only by him, Rahane was skilfully taken by Handscomb at second slip, and Saha departed to another edge. Ashwin then became the fourth in eight chaotic balls, when Lyon's delivery ricocheted off his boot into the right hand of Handscomb, swooping forward at short leg to complete another beauty. O'Keefe wasn't done yet, deceiving Jayant, before Jadeja and Umesh both hit out and got out. In 48 balls, India had plummeted from 94 for three to a humiliating 105.

That collapse of seven for 11 was the worst handed out by Australia since 1950. Yet despite a lead of 155, Smith knew a stumble of their own might reopen the game, especially when Warner and the promoted Shaun Marsh were trapped early by Ashwin. Smith counter-attacked and, although he lacked a long-term partner, several gave useful support. Renshaw, at No. 5, slapped five boundaries between bouts of vomiting, while Mitchell Marsh accompanied Smith to the second-day close, when Australia led by 298 with six

BEST MATCH FIGURES IN A TEST IN INDIA

16-136	N. D. Hirwani	India v West Indies at Madras	1987-88
15-217	Harbhajan Singh	India v Australia at Chennai	2000-01
14-124	J. M. Patel	India v Australia at Kanpur	1959-60
14-149	A. Kumble	India v Pakistan at Delhi	1998-99
13-106	I. T. Botham	England v India at Bombay	1979-80
13-131	V. Mankad	India v Pakistan at Delhi	1952-53
13-132	J. Srinath	India v Pakistan at Calcutta	1998-99
13-140	R. Ashwin	India v New Zealand at Indore	2016-17
13-181	A. Kumble	India v Australia at Chennai	2004-05
13-196	Harbhajan Singh	India v Australia at Kolkata	2000-01
12-70	**S. N. J. O'Keefe**	**Australia v India at Pune**	**2016-17**

wickets left. Even so, the pressure rarely diminished: Jadeja beat the bat at will, and Smith was dropped four times.

Next day, Smith shrugged off the loss of Marsh to bring up his 18th Test century, and first in India. Never had he reacted more emotionally to reaching three figures – he later said it was his best innings yet. By the time Jadeja ended his stupendous effort, the lead had swollen past 400. Ultimately, India were set a mammoth 441.

The first incision didn't take long, O'Keefe trapping Vijay in the fifth over. Worse, Vijay challenged the decision, as did Rahul moments later when Lyon turned one sharply. Two wickets and both reviews gone; all that stood between India and disaster was Kohli. And when he inexplicably watched O'Keefe hit his off stump without offering a shot, disaster it undoubtedly was. Rahane chipped to cover, before Ashwin, Saha and Pujara formed an orderly queue to miss straight ones. O'Keefe had six of the seven wickets, though Lyon grabbed the remainder. When Jayant was wrongly deemed to have edged behind, the entire innings was done and dusted inside 34 overs.

Australia's first Test victory in India for 4,502 days was also India's fourth-heaviest defeat by runs. No one had taken 12 wickets in a Test for fewer than O'Keefe's 70 (though four bowlers had taken more at a lower cost). His figures were the best by an Australian in India, and the second-best by any visiting bowler, behind Ian Botham. The statistics aside, it was a daunting show of strength by the visitors, and a shambles from the hosts. Expectations utterly confounded, we had ourselves a series.

Man of the Match: S. N. J. O'Keefe.

Close of play: first day, Australia 256-9 (Starc 57, Hazlewood 1); second day, Australia 143-4 (Smith 59, M. R. Marsh 21).

Australia

M. T. Renshaw c Vijay b Ashwin	68	– (5) c Sharma b J. Yadav	31
D. A. Warner b U. T. Yadav	38	– (1) lbw b Ashwin	10
*S. P. D. Smith c Kohli b Ashwin	27	– lbw b Jadeja	109
S. E. Marsh c Kohli b J. Yadav	16	– (2) lbw b Ashwin	0
P. S. P. Handscomb lbw b Jadeja	22	– (4) c Vijay b Ashwin	19
M. R. Marsh lbw b Jadeja	4	– c Saha b Jadeja	31
†M. S. Wade lbw b U. T. Yadav	8	– c Saha b U. T. Yadav	20
M. A. Starc c Jadeja b Ashwin	61	– c Rahul b Ashwin	30
S. N. J. O'Keefe c Saha b U. T. Yadav	0	– c Saha b Jadeja	6
N. M. Lyon lbw b U. T. Yadav	0	– lbw b U. T. Yadav	13
J. R. Hazlewood not out	1	– not out	2
Lb 6, nb 9	15	B 4, lb 9, nb 1	14
1/82 (2) 2/119 (4) 3/149 (5) 4/149 (3) 5/166 (6) 6/190 (7) 7/196 (1) 8/205 (9) 9/205 (10) 10/260 (8) (94.5 overs)	260	1/10 (1) 2/23 (2) 3/61 (4) 4/113 (5) 5/169 (6) 6/204 (7) 7/246 (3) 8/258 (8) 9/279 (10) 10/285 (9) (87 overs)	285

In the first innings Renshaw, when 36, retired ill at 82-1 and resumed at 149-3.

Sharma 11–0–27–0; Ashwin 34.5–10–63–3; J. Yadav 13–1–58–1; Jadeja 24–4–74–2; U. T. Yadav 12–3–32–4. *Second innings*—Ashwin 28–3–119–4; Jadeja 33–10–65–3; U. T. Yadav 13–1–39–2; J. Yadav 10–1–43–1; Sharma 3–0–6–0.

India

M. Vijay c Wade b Hazlewood	10	– lbw b O'Keefe	2
K. L. Rahul c Warner b O'Keefe	64	– lbw b Lyon	10
C. A. Pujara c Wade b Starc	6	– lbw b O'Keefe	31
*V. Kohli c Handscomb b Starc	0	– b O'Keefe	13
A. M. Rahane c Handscomb b O'Keefe	13	– c Lyon b O'Keefe	18
R. Ashwin c Handscomb b Lyon	1	– lbw b O'Keefe	8
†W. P. Saha c Smith b O'Keefe	0	– lbw b O'Keefe	5
R. A. Jadeja c Starc b O'Keefe	2	– b Lyon	3
J. Yadav st Wade b O'Keefe	2	– c Wade b Lyon	5
U. T. Yadav c Smith b O'Keefe	4	– (11) not out	0
I. Sharma not out	2	– (10) c Warner b Lyon	0
Nb 1	1	B 8, lb 4	12
1/26 (1) 2/44 (3) 3/44 (4) 4/94 (2) 5/95 (5) 6/95 (7) 7/95 (6) 8/98 (9) 9/101 (8) 10/105 (10) (40.1 overs)	105	1/10 (1) 2/16 (2) 3/47 (4) 4/77 (5) 5/89 (6) 6/99 (7) 7/100 (3) 8/102 (8) 9/102 (10) 10/107 (9) (33.5 overs)	107

Starc 9–2–38–2; O'Keefe 13.1–2–35–6; Hazlewood 7–3–11–1; Lyon 11–2–21–1. *Second innings*—Starc 2–2–0–0; Lyon 14.5–2–53–4; O'Keefe 15–4–35–6; Hazlewood 2–0–7–0.

Umpires: R. A. Kettleborough and N. J. Llong. Third umpire: R. K. Illingworth.
Referee: B. C. Broad.

INDIA v AUSTRALIA

Second Test

At Bangalore, March 4–7, 2017. India won by 75 runs. Toss: India.

If the First Test was a reminder never to write off Australia, the Second made it clear this India team would not surrender meekly: from the brink of defeat, they rallied to level the series. In a gripping fixture, with runs at a premium, a third-innings stand of 118 between Pujara and Rahane proved as vital as Ashwin's six wickets in the fourth.

Australia had begun by running through India for 189, thanks to Lyon's faultless eight-for. Then, armed with a lead of 87, they reduced them to 120 for four, and seemed on course to retain the Border–Gavaskar Trophy in straight sets. But India would not buckle and, although they never managed a position of dominance, shifted the pressure back on to Smith's young side, who crumpled for 112.

Despite the widespread expectation of a flat pitch, the surface had cracks from the outset. Kohli still chose to bat. Mukund, deputising for the injured Murali Vijay, went first, Starc's full toss proving too fast. Rahul batted as he had in Pune, driving the largely unpenetrative quicks. But the day altered when Lyon came on. He had played second fiddle to O'Keefe at Pune, but snared Pujara at forward short leg before lunch.

With Kohli striding out, the crowd grew. But again he went without playing a stroke: DRS confirmed Lyon's lbw shout, and silenced the Chinnaswamy. Rahane ran past Lyon's top-spinner, while Nair, brought in to bolster the batting after a triple-century against England, was purposeful but short-lived. O'Keefe had him stumped as India went five down. The capitulation felt familiar, even if this time it was Lyon cashing in: Ashwin

BEST TEST FIGURES BY VISITING BOWLERS IN INDIA

8-50	**N. M. Lyon (Australia) at Bangalore**	**2016-17**
8-64	†L. Klusener (South Africa) at Calcutta	1996-97
8-69	Sikander Bakht (Pakistan) at Delhi	1979-80
8-215	†J. J. Krejza (Australia) at Nagpur	2008-09
7-42	Fazal Mahmood (Pakistan) at Lucknow	1952-53
7-43	R. R. Lindwall (Australia) at Madras	1956-57
7-46	†J. K. Lever (England) at Delhi	1976-77
7-48	I. T. Botham (England) at Bombay	1979-80
7-49	H. Verity (England) at Madras	1933-34
7-51	D. W. Steyn (South Africa) at Nagpur	2009-10

† *On debut.*

gloved, Saha and Jadeja edged. Rahul fell for 90, as if acknowledging that his time for a ton had expired. He was probably right: Sharma pushed to short leg next ball. From 88 for two, India had lost eight for 101. CricViz analysis revealed Lyon never once missed a good length. His eight for 50 were the best figures by a visiting bowler in India, and second-best for an Australian spinner anywhere, after Arthur Mailey's nine for 121 at the MCG in the 1920-21 Ashes.

Australia reached 40 without loss by the close, and India looked spent. But a new day brought new energy. Hard-nosed action followed. Ashwin turned one past the bat and into Warner's stumps, while Smith was worked over by Sharma and Yadav, floored by bouncers, beaten by length balls and badgered by appeals and relentless chat. India got him at last when an inside edge off Jadeja went to hand. The session had added 47 runs, but no one ate lunch unsatisfied.

For much of the afternoon Renshaw showed discipline – until he charged Jadeja, who later persuaded Handscomb to chip to midwicket. Mitchell Marsh was the unlucky recipient of a Sharma grubber, but his brother Shaun hung around for 66 – quite an achievement in this scrap. He had added 57 with Wade before he too was caught at midwicket. India's fightback was stirring. Next day, Wade and Starc stretched their stand to 49 when Jadeja intervened. First he held the catch that dismissed Starc, then he wrapped up the last three to complete a superb six-wicket shift. The last four fell for seven, and the lead, which had threatened to be significant, was 87.

Australia's attack seemed unsettled by the batsmen's failure to stamp their authority on the game. India jumped to 38 without loss by lunch and, while Hazlewood hit Mukund's

Danish Siddiqui, Reuters

Llong stop? Umpire Nigel Llong tries to pacify India captain Virat Kohli after Steve Smith (far right) was seen looking to his dressing-room for DRS guidance.

stumps on resumption, Pujara was twice dropped in single figures, by Wade and Smith, who partly atoned with a spectacular slip catch to despatch Rahul for 51. Kohli led India into the black, though little further, undone by a Hazlewood delivery that kept low. He referred, but DRS could not determine whether the ball had hit pad or bat first, and a fuming Kohli had to go.

Jadeja's elevation backfired when – trying to drive Hazlewood – he lost middle stump. Four down, India led by 33. But Rahane and Pujara played immaculately through the final session to extend the lead to a healthier 126. With the wicket deteriorating, Australia's chances were starting to dwindle. Eventually they broke through – Starc did just enough to trap Rahane lbw – and the floodgates opened. Next ball, a 95mph bomb, snapped Nair's leg stump in half. Then Pujara edged just short of a ton, and Ashwin was bowled. It was five in 19 when Umesh became Hazlewood's sixth. Saha swung away, but the target was a manageable 188.

Now it was India's turn to strike. Sharma had Renshaw nicking behind, before Warner, sweeping messily, fell to Ashwin for the third time in a row. DRS didn't save him, and the lost review dissuaded Shaun Marsh from referring one that was missing. Australia teetered, the crowd roared and, when Smith was trapped by a shooter from Umesh to make it 74 for four, the stadium erupted.

It heralded the most controversial moment of the tour. Smith looked to his partner for guidance about a review and – after Handscomb suggested advice from the dressing-room – turned towards his team-mates with an enquiring shrug. Umpire Llong immediately intervened, making it clear the decision belonged solely on the field, and there could now be no referral. Smith later apologised, while – extraordinarily – Handscomb pleaded ignorance of the regulations. Kohli was less happy to put the incident to one side, claiming the Australians had been seeking external assistance throughout the Test, and that he had already alerted the match officials. When a journalist asked if he would describe the incident as cheating, Kohli answered: "I didn't say that; you did." The business soured relations for some time, and the BCCI considered formal charges, though none materialised.

Accumulating with growing ease, Handscomb and Mitchell Marsh took the score past 100, and India looked concerned. Just before tea, though, Ashwin persuaded Marsh to pop to short leg and then – after Jadeja raced through his over to squeeze in another for his colleague – he found Wade's inside edge.

Starc and O'Keefe did not resist for long, Handscomb mistimed a huge shot as the pressure became too much and, when Lyon hit a return catch two balls later, the last six had gone for 11. Ashwin became the fourth different bowler in the Test to claim a six-for, a unique occurrence. The 75-run margin flattered India – a game this good deserved to go to the wire – but it was still a classic.

Man of the Match: K. L. Rahul.

Close of play: first day, Australia 40-0 (Warner 23, Renshaw 15); second day, Australia 237-6 (Wade 25, Starc 14); third day, India 213-4 (Pujara 79, Rahane 40).

India

K. L. Rahul c Renshaw b Lyon	90	– c Smith b O'Keefe	51
A. Mukund lbw b Starc	0	– b Hazlewood	16
C. A. Pujara c Handscomb b Lyon	17	– c M. R. Marsh b Hazlewood	92
*V. Kohli lbw b Lyon	12	– lbw b Hazlewood	15
A. M. Rahane st Wade b Lyon	17	– (6) lbw b Starc	52
K. K. Nair st Wade b O'Keefe	26	– (7) b Starc	0
R. Ashwin c Warner b Lyon	7	– (9) b Hazlewood	4
†W. P. Saha c Smith b Lyon	1	– not out	20
R. A. Jadeja c Smith b Lyon	3	– (5) b Hazlewood	2
U. T. Yadav not out	0	– c Warner b Hazlewood	1
I. Sharma c Handscomb b Lyon	0	– c S. E. Marsh b O'Keefe	6
B 12, lb 4	16	B 11, w 4	15
1/11 (2) 2/72 (3) 3/88 (4) 4/118 (5) 5/156 (6) 6/174 (7) 7/178 (8) 8/188 (9) 9/189 (1) 10/189 (11) (71.2 overs)	189	1/39 (2) 2/84 (1) 3/112 (4) 4/120 (5) 5/238 (6) 6/238 (7) 7/242 (3) 8/246 (9) 9/258 (10) 10/274 (11) (97.1 overs)	274

Starc 15–5–39–1; Hazlewood 11–2–42–0; O'Keefe 21–5–40–1; M. R. Marsh 2–0–2–0; Lyon 22.2–4–50–8. *Second innings*—Starc 16–1–74–2; Hazlewood 24–5–67–6; Lyon 33–4–82–0; O'Keefe 21.1–3–36–2; M. R. Marsh 3–0–4–0.

Australia

D. A. Warner b Ashwin	33	– lbw b Ashwin	17
M. T. Renshaw st Saha b Jadeja	60	– c Saha b Sharma	5
*S. P. D. Smith c Saha b Jadeja	8	– lbw b Yadav	28
S. E. Marsh c Nair b Yadav	66	– lbw b Yadav	9
P. S. P. Handscomb c Ashwin b Jadeja	16	– c Saha b Ashwin	24
M. R. Marsh lbw b Sharma	0	– c Nair b Ashwin	13
†M. S. Wade lbw b Jadeja	40	– c Saha b Ashwin	0
M. A. Starc c Jadeja b Ashwin	26	– b Ashwin	1
S. N. J. O'Keefe not out	4	– b Jadeja	2
N. M. Lyon lbw b Jadeja	0	– c and b Ashwin	2
J. R. Hazlewood c Rahul b Jadeja	1	– not out	0
B 14, lb 3, nb 5	22	B 8, lb 2, w 1	11
1/52 (1) 2/82 (3) 3/134 (2) 4/160 (5) 5/163 (6) 6/220 (4) 7/269 (8) 8/274 (7) 9/274 (10) 10/276 (11) (122.4 overs)	276	1/22 (2) 2/42 (1) 3/67 (4) 4/74 (3) 5/101 (6) 6/101 (7) 7/103 (8) 8/110 (9) 9/110 (5) 10/112 (10) (35.4 overs)	112

Sharma 27–8–48–1; Yadav 24–7–57–1; Ashwin 49–13–84–2; Jadeja 21.4–1–63–6; Nair 1–0–7–0. *Second innings*—Sharma 6–1–28–1; Ashwin 12.4–4–41–6; Yadav 9–2–30–2; Jadeja 8–5–3–1.

Umpires: R. K. Illingworth and N. J. Llong. Third umpire: R. A. Kettleborough.
Referee: B. C. Broad.

INDIA v AUSTRALIA

Third Test

At Ranchi, March 16–20, 2017. Drawn. Toss: Australia.

By defying the home spinners on a dusty last afternoon, the Australians earned the right to contest a winner-takes-all encounter five days later. India conceded 451 in the first innings, but from then on could hardly have fared better – until the penultimate session. They kept Australia in the field for 210 overs, built a lead of 152, and had nabbed four wickets by lunch on the fifth day. But Shaun Marsh and Handscomb knuckled down for 62 overs to see Australia to safety. Given the strength of India's position, it felt like an opportunity lost.

Ranchi, the birthplace of former Indian captain M. S. Dhoni, was staging its first Test, and the look of the pitch was a cause of concern. It shouldn't have been: the apparent mud pit was in fact a road. Smith gained first use, and Australia had flown to 50 before India drew first blood, Warner hitting a full toss back to Jadeja. Renshaw, picked primarily for conservatism, clipped and drove boundaries with his first six scoring shots, but blew his promising start by steering to slip. Marsh pushed to bat–pad, and lunch, taken at 109 for three, arrived with a familiar balance.

Also familiar was Kohli's commitment while chasing into the deep. He landed awkwardly on his right shoulder, and played no further part in the innings; Rahane took charge. Umesh sneaked a yorker into Handscomb's pad, and out walked Maxwell, playing his first Test for two and a half years because Mitchell Marsh was injured. Maxwell, the white-ball maestro, was admirably circumspect, mindful of the demands of the occasion. There was no sweeping, conventional or otherwise, and his first boundary came from his 57th delivery. Higher gears were not employed until the attack tired, largely thanks to Smith, whose 19th Test century arrived before the close. Busy at the start, he was chanceless thereafter, impossible to remove. Having carefully negotiated the afternoon and evening, Maxwell reached stumps on 82.

Next morning he inched towards a precious maiden hundred. His emotion on unleashing the final cut shot was palpable, and he leapt into Smith's arms. Not long after, he was caught behind off Jadeja, to end a stand of 191. Wade smacked 37, and O'Keefe dug in to raise another fifty partnership, before Lyon gave Jadeja his eighth five-for in 29 Tests. Smith saw it all, unbeaten on 178 after 361 balls. He had done it again.

Losing Mitchell Starc to a broken foot had been a hefty blow for Australia, who risked playing Pat Cummins in a Test for the first time since his sensational debut aged 18 in November 2011. Rahul struck his fourth half-century in five starts before edging a short ball; if the Australians were frustrated to have achieved one breakthrough all day, there was happiness Cummins had made it. The real grind began on the third morning. Vijay dug foundations with Pujara, but threw it away on the stroke of lunch when he charged O'Keefe. After much speculation, the injured Kohli came out after the break, but edged a full delivery from Cummins, armed with the new ball. Within an hour, he had a third, when Rahane parried another short one to Wade.

Notions of an Australian lead took shape when Hazlewood slipped a gem through Nair. And when Ashwin became the third victim of the Cummins bouncer, India were 123 adrift with four wickets left. The final piece of the puzzle was Pujara, but he was glued to the table. He had reached his 11th Test century earlier in the day, and had no intention of going anywhere. By stumps, he and Saha had closed the gap to 91. Next day, Cummins had Saha lbw with his first ball, only for DRS to show it was missing leg. Soon after lunch, India moved into the lead.

Saha's third Test hundred, via a flick off the underused Maxwell, came from the first ball after tea. And in the 192nd over, Pujara – who had arrived in the 32nd – reached his third double. Two overs later, with the seventh-wicket stand worth 199, he at last made an error as he tried to up the tempo; his innings had occupied more deliveries than any either

LONGEST TEST INNINGS IN INDIA (BY BALLS FACED)

525	**C. A. Pujara (202)**	**India v Australia at Ranchi**	**2016-17**
504	Younis Khan (267)	Pakistan v India at Bangalore	2004-05
473	H. M. Amla (253*)	South Africa v India at Nagpur	2009-10
472	S. M. Gavaskar (172)	India v England at Bangalore	1981-82
454	A. J. Hall (163)	South Africa v India at Kanpur	2004-05
452	V. V. S. Laxman (281)	India v Australia at Kolkata	2000-01
444	A. Flower (232*)	Zimbabwe v India at Nagpur	2000-01
436	A. D. Gaekwad (201)	India v Pakistan at Jullundur	1983-84
435	D. P. M. D. Jayawardene (275)	Sri Lanka v India at Ahmedabad	2009-10
425	S. M. Gavaskar (236*)	India v West Indies at Madras	1983-84

Information unavailable for some earlier innings.

in, or for, India. Saha fell with the same intention, but a fresh Jadeja swung 54 in 55, allowing Kohli to declare 152 ahead.

O'Keefe had bowled 77 overs by the time the ordeal ended, the most by an Australian in a Test innings since off-spinner Tom Veivers sent down 95.1 at Old Trafford in 1964 (though leg-spinner Jim Higgs did get through 59.6 eight-ball overs against England at Sydney in 1978-79). India made the most of the eight overs available on day four, when Jadeja bowled Warner through the gate, then nightwatchman Lyon past the outside edge.

India had eight wickets to take, Australia a day to survive – a little less if they could inch into the lead. Renshaw and Smith blunted the attack by playing the ball later and later. But seam did for Renshaw when Sharma pinned him in front; soon after, Smith watched helpless as a ripper from Jadeja pitched outside leg and clattered into off. The path to safety had grown steeper.

Few would have nominated Marsh or Handscomb to play the most important hand of their careers. The left-handed Marsh had to contend with a giant patch of rough in Jadeja's bowling zone, while Handscomb grew in confidence, hitting a trio of boundaries in one Ashwin over. The hardest work was done by tea, yet India retained a chance if the pair could be quickly parted. They couldn't, and each made a half-century as diligent and disciplined as any in the series. When Marsh fell, caught at short leg off Jadeja, Australia led by 35, and the match was safe. Handscomb was still there when the teams shook hands. The circus moved to Dharamsala, over 1,000 miles north-west, with all to play for.

Man of the Match: C. A. Pujara.

Close of play: first day, Australia 299-4 (Smith 117, Maxwell 82); second day, India 120-1 (Vijay 42, Pujara 10); third day, India 360-6 (Pujara 130, Saha 18); fourth day, Australia 23-2 (Renshaw 7).

Australia

M. T. Renshaw c Kohli b Yadav	44	– (2) lbw b Sharma	15
D. A. Warner c and b Jadeja	19	– (1) b Jadeja	14
*S. P. D. Smith not out	178	– (4) b Jadeja	21
S. E. Marsh c Pujara b Ashwin	2	– (5) c Vijay b Jadeja	53
P. S. P. Handscomb lbw b Yadav	19	– (6) not out	72
G. J. Maxwell c Saha b Jadeja	104	– (7) c Vijay b Ashwin	2
†M. S. Wade c Saha b Jadeja	37	– (8) not out	9
P. J. Cummins b Jadeja	0		
S. N. J. O'Keefe c Vijay b Yadav	25		
N. M. Lyon c Nair b Jadeja	1	– (3) b Jadeja	2
J. R. Hazlewood run out	0		
B 9, lb 11, nb 2	22	B 9, lb 4, nb 3	16
1/50 (2) 2/80 (1) 3/89 (4) 4/140 (5) 5/331 (6) 6/395 (7) 7/395 (8) 8/446 (9) 9/449 (10) 10/451 (11) (137.3 overs)	451	1/17 (1) 2/23 (3) 3/59 (2) 4/63 (4) 5/187 (5) 6/190 (7) (6 wkts, 100 overs)	204

Sharma 20–2–70–0; Yadav 31–3–106–3; Ashwin 34–2–114–1; Jadeja 49.3–8–124–5; Vijay 3–0–17–0. *Second innings*—Ashwin 30–10–71–1; Jadeja 44–18–54–4; Yadav 15–2–36–0; Sharma 11–0–30–1.

India

K. L. Rahul c Wade b Cummins	67	U. T. Yadav c Warner b O'Keefe	16
M. Vijay st Wade b O'Keefe	82	I. Sharma not out	0
C. A. Pujara c Maxwell b Lyon	202		
*V. Kohli c Smith b Cummins	6	B 14, lb 5	19
A. M. Rahane c Wade b Cummins	14		
K. K. Nair b Hazlewood	23	1/91 (1) (9 wkts dec, 210 overs)	603
R. Ashwin c Wade b Cummins	3	2/193 (2) 3/225 (4)	
†W. P. Saha c Maxwell b O'Keefe	117	4/276 (5) 5/320 (6) 6/328 (7)	
R. A. Jadeja not out	54	7/527 (3) 8/541 (8) 9/595 (10)	

Hazlewood 44–10–103–1; Cummins 39–10–106–4; O'Keefe 77–17–199–3; Lyon 46–2–163–1; Maxwell 4–0–13–0.

Umpires: C. B. Gaffaney and I. J. Gould. Third umpire: N. J. Llong.
Referee: R. B. Richardson.

INDIA v AUSTRALIA

Fourth Test

At Dharamsala, March 25–28, 2017. India won by eight wickets. Toss: Australia. Test debut: K. Yadav.

Picking the moment to flex their muscles, India secured a come-from-behind triumph in a blockbuster decider. It meant they had not lost a series at home since England prevailed in December 2012, and reinforced their status as the world's leading Test team.

Smith said visiting the Dalai Lama – based a few miles away at McLeod Ganj – on the eve of the Test had given his team perspective. But it's unlikely supporters of either side would have appreciated the sentiment. Anticipation was high, helped by the stunning Himalayan backdrop. Also on view was debutant left-arm wrist-spinner Kuldeep Yadav; he had enjoyed a successful Ranji season with Uttar Pradesh and now teamed up with Jadeja and Ashwin. The pitch for Dharamsala's inaugural Test was expected to aid the seamers, but those three secured the bulk of the wickets.

With Virat Kohli sidelined by his shoulder injury – Rahane led in his absence – some saw Australia as favourites. The toss went their way, though Smith's decision to bat almost backfired first ball, only for Nair to shell Warner at third slip. Renshaw was less fortunate, his stumps clonked by an Umesh Yadav special. Warner played himself into form, while Smith raced from the blocks. A flurry of boundaries took the score to 131 for one by lunch.

It looked as if Warner had settled, but his dismissal soon after the break – caught at slip off the top of the bat – heralded a day-changing spell from Kuldeep and his delightfully bouncy spin. Marsh quickly fell to the other Yadav, Umesh, before Handscomb became Kuldeep's second victim: tempted into driving, he was undone by drift, and bowled through the gate. Kuldeep then delved into his bag of tricks to produce a wrong'un that hit Maxwell's off stump: 178 for five.

All the while Smith was progressing assiduously to his seventh hundred in ten Tests against India, and 20th in all. Masterful from the outset, he broke the attack early. But, minutes before tea, Ashwin's straighter ball took the edge of his bat, and Rahane completed a stunning reflex slip catch; it was Smith's first false move. India had bossed the session, and Australia, in stumbling to 208 for six, had lost any control gleaned in the morning. The lower order scrapped hard for 300, Wade especially, but there was no meaningful revival. Kuldeep had a fourth when Cummins gave him a return catch, and Jadeja bowled Wade aiming a sweep.

Embodying Australia's fight during the series, the seamers hit back on the second day. Vijay fell quickly, edging Hazlewood, and Rahul should have joined him, but Renshaw dropped a slip chance off Cummins. Rahul again reached 50, later saying this was the most penetrative bowling he had faced. After lunch, though, in response to protracted confrontation with Cummins, he hooked, miscued and departed. Pujara and Rahane ensured safe passage to tea and, at 153 for two, the Australians' push felt in vain.

Until then, Lyon had been flat in trajectory, as he had since his eight wickets in Bangalore. But by varying his pace, he shifted the game – just like Kuldeep the previous day. First Pujara, on 57, edged a flighted off-break to bat–pad. The same method accounted for Nair, and then Rahane, after steadying the ship, nicked a faster ball to Smith, meaning each captain had caught the other. Ashwin was Lyon's fourth in the session, and India – 79 adrift and six down – had ceded the ascendancy. Australia should have strengthened their position, but a second bad drop off Cummins (Renshaw again the culprit) wasted Saha's nick as the shadows lengthened. He stuck around on the third morning, while Jadeja rode his luck in a half-century that took India into the lead.

But the rhythm of a compelling series demanded more swings in momentum. Jadeja played on to Cummins, whose short ball was too much for Saha. Australia trailed by a modest 32. Yet their resistance was about to crumble. Both openers were caught behind off Umesh: if there was little Warner could do, Renshaw was loose. In between came the killer blow. Smith dragged a nondescript delivery from Bhuvneshwar Kumar – preferred to Ishant Sharma – into his stumps one short of 500 runs for the series, and Australia one short of scoreboard parity.

Unperturbed, Maxwell made scoring look easy through cover, and set about a rebuild. But Handscomb was never comfortable, Marsh came and went, and not long after tea Maxwell padded up to Ashwin. India had reduced Australia to 106 for six. The lower order offered little, though there was time for a final flashpoint when Vijay claimed a catch cameras showed had not carried. Lip-readers saw Smith forcefully questioning his integrity from beyond the boundary. It hardly mattered: Hazlewood fell two balls later.

A total of 137 set India just 106. They lost two wickets on 46, but Rahane blazed a pair of sixes off Cummins to head off a late twist. Rahul hit the winning runs, reaching his fifth successive half-century and sixth in seven innings. Kohli joined Rahane to collect the Border–Gavaskar Trophy. It wasn't always pretty, but India had shown immense resolve to triumph after losing the First Test – only the fourth time they had done so. Australia, worthier adversaries than predicted, had encountered in the Himalayas the peak they could not quite conquer. But a young team hinted that they may yet scale the heights.

Man of the Match: R. A. Jadeja. *Man of the Series:* R. A. Jadeja.

Close of play: first day, India 0-0 (Rahul 0, Vijay 0); second day, India 248-6 (Saha 10, Jadeja 16); third day, India 19-0 (Rahul 13, Vijay 6).

Australia

First innings		Second innings	
D. A. Warner c Rahane b K. Yadav	56	– (2) c Saha b U. T. Yadav	6
M. T. Renshaw b U. T. Yadav	1	– (1) c Saha b U. T. Yadav	8
*S. P. D. Smith c Rahane b Ashwin	111	– b Bhuvneshwar Kumar	17
S. E. Marsh c Saha b U. T. Yadav	4	– (6) c Pujara b Jadeja	1
P. S. P. Handscomb b K. Yadav	8	– (4) c Rahane b Ashwin	18
G. J. Maxwell b K. Yadav	8	– (5) lbw b Ashwin	45
†M. S. Wade b Jadeja	57	– not out	25
P. J. Cummins c and b K. Yadav	21	– c Rahane b Jadeja	12
S. N. J. O'Keefe run out	8	– c Pujara b Jadeja	0
N. M. Lyon c Pujara b Bhuvneshwar Kumar	13	– c Vijay b U. T. Yadav	0
J. R. Hazlewood not out	2	– lbw b Ashwin	0
B 1, lb 10	11	B 4, lb 1	5
1/10 (2) 2/144 (1) 3/153 (4) 4/168 (5) 5/178 (6) 6/208 (3) 7/245 (8) 8/269 (9) 9/298 (7) 10/300 (10) (88.3 overs)	300	1/10 (2) 2/31 (3) 3/31 (1) 4/87 (4) 5/92 (6) 6/106 (5) 7/121 (8) 8/121 (9) 9/122 (10) 10/137 (11) (53.5 overs)	137

Bhuvneshwar Kumar 12.3–2–41–1; U. T. Yadav 15–1–69–2; Ashwin 23–5–54–1; Jadeja 15–1–57–1; K. Yadav 23–3–68–4. *Second innings*—Bhuvneshwar Kumar 7–1–27–1; U. T. Yadav 10–3–29–3; K. Yadav 5–0–23–0; Jadeja 18–7–24–3; Ashwin 13.5–4–29–3.

India

K. L. Rahul c Warner b Cummins	60	– not out	51
M. Vijay c Wade b Hazlewood	11	– c Wade b Cummins	8
C. A. Pujara c Handscomb b Lyon	57	– run out	0
*A. M. Rahane c Smith b Lyon	46	– not out	38
K. K. Nair c Wade b Lyon	5		
R. Ashwin lbw b Lyon	30		
†W. P. Saha c Smith b Cummins	31		
R. A. Jadeja b Cummins	63		
Bhuvneshwar Kumar c Smith b O'Keefe	0		
K. Yadav c Hazlewood b Lyon	7		
U. T. Yadav not out	2		
B 4, lb 11, w 5	20	B 4, lb 5	9
1/21 (2) 2/108 (1) 3/157 (3) 4/167 (5) 5/216 (4) 6/221 (6) 7/317 (8) 8/318 (9) 9/318 (7) 10/332 (10) (118.1 overs)	332	1/46 (2) 2/46 (3) (2 wkts, 23.5 overs)	106

Hazlewood 25–8–51–1; Cummins 30–8–94–3; Lyon 34.1–5–92–5; O'Keefe 27–4–75–1; Maxwell 2–0–5–0. *Second innings*—Cummins 8–2–42–1; Hazlewood 6–2–14–0; O'Keefe 4.5–1–22–0; Lyon 5–0–19–0.

Umpires: M. Erasmus and I. J. Gould. Third umpire: C. B. Gaffaney.
Referee: R. B. Richardson.

INDIA v AUSTRALIA IN 2017-18

R. KAUSHIK

One-day internationals (5): India 4, Australia 1
Twenty20 internationals (3): India 1, Australia 1

Australia arrived in India fresh from a Test series in Bangladesh, boosted by a series-levelling victory in Chittagong. But old failings resurfaced against a revamped Indian attack. In the one-day series, Australia's inadequacies against the turning ball were exposed by leg-spinner Yuzvendra Chahal and Kuldeep Yadav, a left-arm wrist-spinner who had taken them by surprise on his Test debut at Dharamsala six months earlier.

In search of the right balance before the 2019 World Cup, India had dispensed with senior finger-spinners Ravichandran Ashwin and Ravindra Jadeja, and were rewarded with greater penetration in the middle overs. While Bhuvneshwar Kumar and Jasprit Bumrah were exceptional with the new ball and at the death, that extra incisiveness drove the Indians to a 4–1 triumph, and back to No. 1 in the 50-over rankings.

Australia had opportunities, but failed to seize them: fast-bowling coach David Saker, temporarily promoted while Darren Lehmann took a breather, described his batsmen's performance as "a little bit scared". In the first game, Nathan Coulter-Nile had India on the mat at 11 for three, before Hardik Pandya set up victory with the first of a string of superb displays. And though Australia had a run of fast starts, particularly after Aaron Finch returned from a calf injury, their middle-order struggles hurt them.

Before the Twenty20s, Steve Smith injured a shoulder, and Pat Cummins was sent home to rest. Without them, Australia were spanked in a truncated game at Ranchi, then bounced back strongly in favourable conditions at Guwahati. In only his second international, left-arm seamer Jason Behrendorff worked his way through India's top order, and laid the base for a commanding victory. There was no finale, though: the decider at Hyderabad was abandoned, and Australia were left wondering if a white-ball tour of India was really the ideal preparation for a home Ashes.

AUSTRALIAN TOURING PARTY

*S. P. D. Smith (50), A. C. Agar (50), J. P. Behrendorff (20), H. W. R. Cartwright (50), D. T. Christian (20), N. M. Coulter-Nile (50/20), P. J. Cummins (50), J. P. Faulkner (50), A. J. Finch (50/20), P. S. P. Handscomb (50), T. M. Head (50/20), M. C. Henriques (20), G. J. Maxwell (50/20), T. D. Paine (20), K. W. Richardson (50/20), M. P. Stoinis (50/20), A. J. Tye (20), M. S. Wade (50), D. A. Warner (50/20), A. Zampa (50/20). *Coach:* D. J. Saker.

Smith was originally due to lead in the Twenty20s, but injured his shoulder and returned home. Warner captained instead, and Stoinis retained in the party.

INDIA v AUSTRALIA

First One-Day International

At Chennai, September 17, 2017 (day/night). India won by 26 runs (DLS). Toss: India. One-day international debut: H. W. R. Cartwright.

Swinging the ball away from the right-handers, Coulter-Nile destroyed India's top order, including Kohli for a duck. From 11 for three, Sharma and Jadhav briefly steadied the ship but, after both fell to short ones from Stoinis, India's depth was tested. They answered any concerns. With Dhoni's calming influence, Pandya burnished his all-round reputation, starting cautiously before exploding with five sixes, four off leg-spinner Zampa. The pair put on 118, helping India to 281 for seven, before sharp showers at the break revised Australia's target to 164 in 21 overs. India's seamers made three quick breakthroughs, then their wrist-spinners took control, Yadav and Chahal weaving wicked webs on their way to combined figures of five for 63. Maxwell flickered briefly, smashing Yadav for a four and three sixes off consecutive deliveries. But, when Chahal gobbled him up in the next over, the fight drained from the Australians.

Man of the Match: H. H. Pandya.

India

A. M. Rahane c Wade b Coulter-Nile	5	Bhuvneshwar Kumar not out	32
R. G. Sharma c Coulter-Nile b Stoinis	28	K. Yadav not out	0
*V. Kohli c Maxwell b Coulter-Nile	0	B 4, lb 2, w 5, nb 3	14
M. K. Pandey c Wade b Coulter-Nile	0		——
K. M. Jadhav c Cartwright b Stoinis	40	1/11 (1) 2/11 (3) (7 wkts, 50 overs)	281
†M. S. Dhoni c Warner b Faulkner	79	3/11 (4) 4/64 (2)	
H. H. Pandya c Faulkner b Zampa	83	5/87 (5) 6/205 (7) 7/277 (6)	10 overs: 34-3

J. J. Bumrah and Y. S. Chahal did not bat.

Cummins 10–1–44–0; Coulter-Nile 10–0–44–3; Faulkner 10–1–67–1; Stoinis 10–0–54–2; Zampa 10–0–66–1.

Australia

D. A. Warner c Dhoni b Yadav	25	N. M. Coulter-Nile c Jadhav	
H. W. R. Cartwright b Bumrah	1	b Bhuvneshwar Kumar	2
*S. P. D. Smith c Bumrah b Pandya	1	A. Zampa not out	5
T. M. Head c Dhoni b Pandya	5	Lb 1, w 5	6
G. J. Maxwell c Pandey b Chahal	39		——
M. P. Stoinis c sub (R. A. Jadeja) b Yadav	3	1/15 (2) 2/20 (3) (9 wkts, 21 overs)	137
†M. S. Wade st Dhoni b Chahal	9	3/29 (4) 4/35 (1)	
J. P. Faulkner not out	32	5/76 (5) 6/76 (6) 7/93 (7)	
P. J. Cummins c Bumrah b Chahal	9	8/109 (9) 9/127 (10)	4 overs: 15-1

Bhuvneshwar Kumar 4–0–25–1; Bumrah 4–0–20–1; Pandya 4–0–28–2; Yadav 4–0–33–2; Chahal 5–0–30–3.

Umpires: A. K. Chaudhary and M. Erasmus. Third umpire: R. K. Illingworth.
Referee: J. J. Crowe.

INDIA v AUSTRALIA

Second One-Day International

At Kolkata, September 21, 2017 (day/night). India won by 50 runs. Toss: India.

Smith called wrong again, and paid the price: his side were forced to field in enervating humidity, and subsided to another defeat. Kohli shrugged off a lean trot against Australia – 46 runs in six innings, starting with the Test series earlier in the year – with a well-crafted 92 that seemed to have set India up for a commanding total. But Australia didn't throw in the towel (they needed it for the sweat), and kept chipping away through Coulter-Nile and Richardson. From 186 for three in the 36th over, India were bowled out for 252 off the last delivery. Still, on a two-paced surface, covered for long periods before the game because of showers, it proved plenty. Bhuvneshwar Kumar's swing was mesmeric, nipping out Cartwright and Warner in the first five overs. Smith, in his 100th one-day international, added 76 with Head, but the introduction of the wrist-spinners was again decisive. Chahal dismissed Head with a full toss, then settled into a beautiful rhythm, while Yadav recovered from an ordinary start to become the third Indian to take an ODI hat-trick, after Chetan Sharma against New Zealand at Nagpur in the 1987 World Cup, and Kapil Dev against Sri Lanka at Calcutta in 1990-91. Stoinis hit out boldly, but too late.

Man of the Match: V. Kohli.

India

A. M. Rahane run out	55
R. G. Sharma c and b Coulter-Nile	7
*V. Kohli b Coulter-Nile	92
M. K. Pandey b Agar	3
K. M. Jadhav c Maxwell b Coulter-Nile	24
†M. S. Dhoni c Smith b Richardson	5
H. H. Pandya c Warner b Richardson	20
Bhuvneshwar Kumar c Maxwell b Richardson	20
K. Yadav c Wade b Cummins	0
J. J. Bumrah not out	10
Y. S. Chahal run out	1
B 1, w 13, nb 1	15
(50 overs)	252

1/19 (2) 2/121 (1) 3/131 (4) 4/186 (5) 5/197 (3) 6/204 (6) 7/239 (8) 8/239 (9) 9/246 (7) 10/252 (11) — 10 overs: 44-1

Cummins 10–1–34–1; Coulter-Nile 10–0–51–3; Richardson 10–0–55–3; Stoinis 9–0–46–0; Agar 9–0–54–1; Head 2–0–11–0.

Australia

H. W. R. Cartwright b Bhuvneshwar Kumar	1
D. A. Warner c Rahane b Bhuvneshwar Kumar	1
*S. P. D. Smith c sub (R. A. Jadeja) b Pandya	59
T. M. Head c Pandey b Chahal	39
G. J. Maxwell st Dhoni b Chahal	14
M. P. Stoinis not out	62
†M. S. Wade b Yadav	2
A. C. Agar lbw b Yadav	0
P. J. Cummins c Dhoni b Yadav	0
N. M. Coulter-Nile c and b Pandya	8
K. W. Richardson lbw b Bhuvneshwar Kumar	0
B 4, lb 6, w 6	16
(43.1 overs)	202

1/2 (1) 2/9 (2) 3/85 (4) 4/106 (5) 5/138 (3) 6/148 (7) 7/148 (8) 8/148 (9) 9/182 (10) 10/202 (11) — 10 overs: 47-2

Bhuvneshwar Kumar 6.1–2–9–3; Bumrah 7–1–39–0; Pandya 10–0–56–2; Chahal 10–1–34–2; Yadav 10–1–54–3.

Umpires: A. K. Chaudhary and R. K. Illingworth. Third umpire: M. Erasmus.
Referee: J. J. Crowe.

INDIA v AUSTRALIA

Third One-Day International

At Indore, September 24, 2017 (day/night). India won by five wickets. Toss: Australia.

Elevated to No. 4, Pandya launched an assault that drove India to a series-clinching victory, and returned them to the top of the ICC one-day rankings. Earlier, he had broken a threatening opening stand of 70, before Finch – back after injury – and Smith negated India's spinners in the middle overs. For once, Australia looked like calling the shots, but Finch's dismissal in the 38th over for a run-a-ball 124 altered the tempo. They added just 69 from the final 74 deliveries to finish on 293 for six – their highest total of the series, yet still below par on an excellent surface surrounded by short boundaries. The Indian openers began with typical gusto, Sharma clearing the ropes with ridiculous ease, and Rahane sailing in his slipstream. After they fell for seventies, India pushed Pandya up to take on Agar's left-arm spin. Striking the ball clean and long, he hit him for four sixes on his way to 78 off 72 deliveries, while Australia's fielding crumbled. When Pandey edged the winning run, India had equalled two national records: a ninth straight ODI victory, and a sixth straight bilateral series triumph.

Man of the Match: H. H. Pandya.

Australia

D. A. Warner b Pandya	42	A. C. Agar not out	9
A. J. Finch c Jadhav b Yadav	124		
*S. P. D. Smith c Bumrah b Yadav	63	Lb 2, w 14	16
G. J. Maxwell st Dhoni b Chahal	5		—
T. M. Head b Bumrah	4	1/70 (1) 2/224 (2) (6 wkts, 50 overs)	293
M. P. Stoinis not out	27	3/243 (3) 4/243 (4)	
†P. S. P. Handscomb c Pandey b Bumrah	3	5/260 (5) 6/275 (7)	10 overs: 49-0

P. J. Cummins, N. M. Coulter-Nile and K. W. Richardson did not bat.

Bhuvneshwar Kumar 10–0–52–0; Bumrah 10–0–52–2; Chahal 10–0–54–1; Pandya 10–0–58–1; Yadav 10–0–75–2.

India

A. M. Rahane lbw b Cummins	70	†M. S. Dhoni not out	3
R. G. Sharma c sub (H. W. R. Cartwright) b Coulter-Nile	71	Lb 3, w 3	6
*V. Kohli c Finch b Agar	28		—
H. H. Pandya c Richardson b Cummins	78	1/139 (2) 2/147 (1) (5 wkts, 47.5 overs)	294
K. M. Jadhav c Handscomb b Richardson	2	3/203 (3) 4/206 (5)	
M. K. Pandey not out	36	5/284 (4)	10 overs: 68-0

Bhuvneshwar Kumar, K. Yadav, J. J. Bumrah and Y. S. Chahal did not bat.

Cummins 10–0–54–2; Coulter-Nile 10–0–58–1; Richardson 8.5–0–45–1; Stoinis 8–0–61–0; Agar 10–0–71–1; Maxwell 1–0–2–0.

Umpires: M. Erasmus and C. Shamshuddin. Third umpire: R. K. Illingworth.
Referee: J. J. Crowe.

INDIA v AUSTRALIA

Fourth One-Day International

At Bangalore, September 28, 2017 (day/night). Australia won by 21 runs. Toss: Australia.

In his 100th one-day international, Warner blazed a brilliant 124 to help Australia to their first victory of the tour. After he shared an opening stand of 231 with Finch, the middle order finally kicked on, and set an intimidating 334. Even for an in-form India, it was a bridge too far. The surface at the M. Chinnaswamy Stadium played true to its reputation, allowing batsmen to hit through the line without fear. That, as well as a lightning outfield and short boundaries, helped Warner and Finch impose themselves against an Indian attack lacking the rested Bhuvneshwar Kumar and Jasprit Bumrah. Handscomb then provided a flourish with a 30-ball 43. India's reply began brightly with half-centuries from Rahane and Sharma. But while their top seven all made double figures, they lost wickets at inopportune moments, and Australia at last had reason to smile.

Man of the Match: D. A. Warner.

CELEBRATING IN STYLE

Batsmen who hit hundreds in their 100th one-day international:

C. G. Greenidge (102*)	West Indies v Pakistan at Sharjah	1988-89
C. L. Cairns (115)	New Zealand v India at Christchurch	1998-99
Yousuf Youhana (129)	Pakistan v Sri Lanka at Sharjah	2001-02
K. C. Sangakkara (101)	Sri Lanka v Australia at Colombo (RPS)	2003-04
C. H. Gayle (132*)	West Indies v England at Lord's	2004
M. E. Trescothick (100*)	England v Bangladesh at The Oval	2005
R. R. Sarwan (115*)	West Indies v India at Basseterre	2005-06
D. A. Warner (124)	**Australia v India at Bangalore**	**2017-18**

Australia

A. J. Finch c Pandya b Yadav	94	†M. S. Wade not out	3
D. A. Warner c Patel b Jadhav	124	B 4, lb 7, w 12	23
T. M. Head c Rahane b Yadav	29		
*S. P. D. Smith c Kohli b Yadav	3	1/231 (2) 2/231 (1) (5 wkts, 50 overs)	334
P. S. P. Handscomb b Yadav	43	3/236 (4) 4/299 (3)	
M. P. Stoinis not out	15	5/319 (5) 10 overs: 63-0	

P. J. Cummins, N. M. Coulter-Nile, A. Zampa and K. W. Richardson did not bat.

Mohammed Shami 10–1–62–0; Yadav 10–0–71–4; Patel 10–0–66–0; Pandya 5–0–32–0; Chahal 8–0–54–0; Jadhav 7–0–38–1.

India

A. M. Rahane c Finch b Richardson	53	Mohammed Shami not out	6
R. G. Sharma run out	65	U. T. Yadav not out	2
*V. Kohli b Coulter-Nile	21		
H. H. Pandya c Warner b Zampa	41	Lb 4, w 3	7
K. M. Jadhav c Finch b Richardson	67		
M. K. Pandey b Cummins	33	1/106 (1) 2/135 (2) (8 wkts, 50 overs)	313
†M. S. Dhoni b Richardson	13	3/147 (3) 4/225 (4)	
A. R. Patel c sub (G. J. Maxwell) b Coulter-Nile	5	5/286 (5) 6/289 (6) 7/301 (7)	
		8/306 (8) 10 overs: 65-0	

Y. S. Chahal did not bat.

Cummins 10–0–59–1; Coulter-Nile 10–0–56–2; Richardson 10–0–58–3; Stoinis 4.5–0–34–0; Finch 0.1–0–1–0; Zampa 9–0–63–1; Head 6–0–38–0.

Umpires: R. K. Illingworth and C. Shamshuddin. Third umpire: M. Erasmus.
Referee: J. J. Crowe.

INDIA v AUSTRALIA

Fifth One-Day International

At Nagpur, October 1, 2017 (day/night). India won by seven wickets. Toss: Australia.

Sharma produced the big one he had been threatening all series, conjuring 125 off 109 deliveries to make a tricky chase appear straightforward on a sluggish track. The tourists again rued their inability to cash in on a position of promise. Warner and Finch had put on 66 but, as the ball got softer and the spinners came on, Australia tied themselves in knots. Kohli used his resources judiciously, giving Jadhav a full ten overs as the ball held up and turned, if slowly. It was left-arm spinner Patel, though, who did most damage, with three for 38 in the middle overs, before expert death bowling from Bhuvneshwar Kumar and Bumrah restricted Australia to 242 for nine. Sharma took his time – he was scoreless after 14 deliveries – but then unleashed a flurry of sixes. He targeted the straight boundaries, and dominated a third consecutive hundred stand with Rahane, who made a fourth successive fifty. Sharma added 99 with Kohli to all but seal the rout. Smith injured his shoulder in the field and was later ruled out of the Twenty20 series.

Man of the Match: R. G. Sharma. *Man of the Series:* H. H. Pandya.

Australia

D. A. Warner c Pandey b Patel	53	P. J. Cummins not out	2
A. J. Finch c Bumrah b Pandya	32	N. M. Coulter-Nile b Bhuvneshwar Kumar	0
*S. P. D. Smith lbw b Jadhav	16	B 1, lb 2, w 3	6
P. S. P. Handscomb c Rahane b Patel	13		
T. M. Head b Patel	42	1/66 (2) 2/100 (3) (9 wkts, 50 overs)	242
M. P. Stoinis lbw b Bumrah	46	3/112 (1) 4/118 (4)	
†M. S. Wade c Rahane b Bumrah	20	5/205 (5) 6/210 (6) 7/237 (7)	
J. P. Faulkner run out	12	8/242 (8) 9/242 (10) 10 overs: 60-0	

A. Zampa did not bat.

Bhuvneshwar Kumar 8–0–40–1; Bumrah 10–2–51–2; Pandya 2–0–14–1; Yadav 10–1–48–0; Jadhav 10–0–48–1; Patel 10–0–38–3.

India

A. M. Rahane lbw b Coulter-Nile	61
R. G. Sharma c Coulter-Nile b Zampa	125
*V. Kohli c Stoinis b Zampa	39
K. M. Jadhav not out	5
M. K. Pandey not out	11
Lb 1, w 1	2
1/124 (1) 2/223 (2) 3/227 (3) (3 wkts, 42.5 overs)	243
10 overs: 43-0	

H. H. Pandya, †M. S. Dhoni, A. R. Patel, Bhuvneshwar Kumar, K. Yadav and J. J. Bumrah did not bat.

Cummins 7–1–29–0; Coulter-Nile 9–0–42–1; Stoinis 4–0–20–0; Faulkner 5.5–0–37–0; Zampa 8–0–59–2; Head 6–0–38–0; Finch 3–0–17–0.

Umpires: M. Erasmus and C. K. Nandan. Third umpire: R. K. Illingworth.
Referee: J. J. Crowe.

INDIA v AUSTRALIA

First Twenty20 International

At Ranchi, October 7, 2017 (floodlit). India won by nine wickets (DLS). Toss: India. Twenty20 international debut: J. P. Behrendorff.

Just as they had at Chennai at the beginning of the one-day series, India lorded a truncated game. Another tidy bowling performance had stunted Australia's progress, Finch alone showing intent on his way to a 30-ball 42; the rest floundered against an accurate pace attack and the sustained pressure of Chahal and Yadav, who finished with a combined three for 39. With only two others reaching double figures, Australia stuttered to 118 for eight in 18.4 overs when the rain arrived, leaving India a revised target of 48 from six. Sharma fell quickly, but Kohli and Dhawan hurried home with bustling efficiency.

Man of the Match: K. Yadav.

Australia

		B	4/6
1 *D. A. Warner *b 8*	8	5	2
2 A. J. Finch *b 9*	42	30	4/1
3 G. J. Maxwell *c 10 b 11*	17	16	2
4 T. M. Head *b 7*	9	16	0
5 M. C. Henriques *b 9*	8	9	1
6 D. T. Christian *run out*	9	13	0
7 †T. D. Paine *b 10*	17	16	1/1
8 N. M. Coulter-Nile *b 10*	1	2	0
9 A. J. Tye *not out*	0	2	0
10 A. Zampa *not out*	4	3	1
Lb 1, w 2	3		
6 overs: 49-1 (18.4 overs)	118-8		

1/8 2/55 3/76 4/87 5/89 6/111 7/113 8/114

11 J. P. Behrendorff did not bat.

Bhuvneshwar Kumar 3.4–11–28–1; Bumrah 3–7–17–2; Pandya 4–8–33–1; Chahal 4–11–23–1; Yadav 4–9–16–2.

India

		B	4/6
1 R. G. Sharma *b 8*	11	7	1/1
2 S. Dhawan *not out*	15	12	3
3 *V. Kohli *not out*	22	14	3
Lb 1	1		
2 overs: 16-1 (5.3 overs)	49-1		

1/11

4 M. K. Pandey, 5 K. M. Jadhav, 6 †M. S. Dhoni, 7 H. H. Pandya, 8 Bhuvneshwar Kumar, 9 K. Yadav, 10 J. J. Bumrah and 11 Y. S. Chahal did not bat.

Behrendorff 1–4–5–0; Coulter-Nile 2–4–20–1; Tye 1–2–10–0; Zampa 1–3–6–0; Christian 0.3–0–7–0.

Umpires: N. N. Menon and C. Shamshuddin. Third umpire: A. K. Chaudhary.
Referee: R. B. Richardson.

INDIA v AUSTRALIA

Second Twenty20 International

At Guwahati, October 10, 2017 (floodlit). Australia won by eight wickets. Toss: Australia.

Jason Behrendorff, a tall left-arm seamer from Western Australia, ripped the heart out of India, and fashioned a series-levelling win. In the first men's international at the Barsapara Cricket Stadium, Behrendorff got the ball to swing and nip off the deck, removing Sharma, Kohli and Pandey with his first eight deliveries. When he added Dhawan – superbly caught by Warner, back-pedalling at mid-off – it was 27 for four, and India never recovered. Behrendorff finished with four for 21, the fifth-best figures for Australia in T20Is. Zampa provided the middle-overs penetration his side had sorely lacked in the one-dayers, seeing off Dhoni and Jadhav, and helping restrict the target to 119. Having relied heavily on Finch and Warner all tour, Australia lost both early. But India were a seamer light, and Henriques and Head lapped up wayward offerings from Yadav, who struggled with a wet ball. They charged home with a partnership of 109 in just 76 deliveries. As the Australians left the ground, a rock was thrown at their bus, smashing a window. Next day, Indian fans gathered outside their hotel and at the airport to hold signs expressing apology.

Man of the Match: J. P. Behrendorff.

India

		B	4/6
1 R. G. Sharma *lbw b 11*	8	4	2
2 S. Dhawan *c 2 b 11*	2	6	0
3 *V. Kohli *c and b 11*	0	2	0
4 M. K. Pandey *c 7 b 11*	6	7	1
5 K. M. Jadhav *b 10*	27	27	3/1
6 †M. S. Dhoni *st 7 b 10*	13	16	1
7 H. H. Pandya *c 12 b 6*	25	23	0/1
8 Bhuvneshwar Kumar *c 3 b 8*	1	6	0
9 K. Yadav *c 7 b 9*	16	19	1
10 J. J. Bumrah *run out*	7	9	1
11 Y. S. Chahal *not out*	3	2	0
Lb 5, w 4, nb 1	10		
6 overs: 38-4 (20 overs)	118		

1/8 2/8 3/16 4/27 5/60 6/67 7/70 8/103 9/115

Behrendorff 4–17–21–4; Coulter-Nile 4–12–23–1; Tye 4–9–30–1; Zampa 4–11–19–2; Stoinis 4–10–20–1.

Australia

		B	4/6
1 A. J. Finch *c 3 b 8*	8	8	1
2 *D. A. Warner *c 3 b 10*	2	5	0
3 M. C. Henriques *not out*	62	46	4/4
4 T. M. Head *not out*	48	34	5/1
W 2	2		
6 overs: 34-2 (15.3 overs)	122-2		

1/11 2/13

5 G. J. Maxwell, 6 M. P. Stoinis, 7 †T. D. Paine, 8 N. M. Coulter-Nile, 9 A. J. Tye, 10 A. Zampa and 11 J. P. Behrendorff did not bat.

12th man: D. T. Christian.

Bhuvneshwar Kumar 3–13–9–1; Bumrah 3–8–25–1; Pandya 2–6–13–0; Yadav 4–5–46–0; Chahal 3.3–7–29–0.

Umpires: N. N. Menon and C. K. Nandan. Third umpire: C. Shamshuddin.
Referee: R. B. Richardson.

INDIA v AUSTRALIA

Third Twenty20 International

At Hyderabad, October 13, 2017 (floodlit). Abandoned.

Though there was none on the day, continuous rain for the three weeks before had left the outfield sodden – to the disappointment of a 30,000-strong crowd.

INDIA v NEW ZEALAND IN 2017-18

DEBASHISH DATTA

One-day internationals (3): India 2, New Zealand 1
Twenty20 internationals (3): India 2, New Zealand 1

India came close to losing a first bilateral home series in two years, as New Zealand took them to a decider in both white-ball formats. The outcomes were a reflection of the captains. India followed Virat Kohli's lead: hungry and intense. The tourists, meanwhile, were quiet and humble, like Kane Williamson, and eventually conceded narrow defeats.

New Zealand asked questions in every department, with their slow bowlers a particular mischief. Left-armer Mitchell Santner and leg-spinner Ish Sodhi showed an excellent understanding of the conditions, and dovetailed with a potent new-ball attack. Their batsmen also had the nous to succeed on Indian pitches. Colin Munro scored runs he could cash at the IPL, Tom Latham enhanced his reputation, and Ross Taylor underlined his class.

But two of their guns were spiked: Williamson came good just once, while opener Martin Guptill was unable to unfurl his big shots. Their failings, and India's excellent bowling, tipped the balance. With Jasprit Bumrah and Bhuvneshwar Kumar doing damage at either end of the innings, and leg-spinner Yuzvendra Chahal causing doubts in the middle, there was threat throughout.

The team management deserved credit for making the attack a weapon. In July, when Ravi Shastri was brought back as head coach, former opening bowler Zaheer Khan was named bowling consultant. But Shastri recommended the BCCI appoint Bharat Arun, who had assisted him during his first stint in charge. They agreed – though Zaheer was maintained in an advisory capacity – and the improvement of the bowlers seemed an endorsement of the switch.

Kohli, too, was superb: in the first match, he stroked his 31st one-day international century, to pull clear of Ricky Ponting into second on the all-time list (behind only Sachin Tendulkar). He added another in the decider. If the composition of the middle order remained uncertain, his skill and desire to win were anything but.

NEW ZEALAND TOURING PARTY

*K. S. Williamson (50/20), T. A. Boult (50/20), T. C. Bruce (20), C. de Grandhomme (50/20), M. J. Guptill (50/20), M. J. Henry (50/20), T. W. M. Latham (50/20), A. F. Milne (50/20), C. Munro (50/20), H. M. Nicholls (50/20), G. D. Phillips (50/20), M. J. Santner (50/20), I. S. Sodhi (50/20), T. G. Southee (50/20), L. R. P. L. Taylor (50/20), G. H. Worker (50). *Coach:* M. J. Hesson.

T. D. Astle was originally named in both squads, but injured his groin and was replaced by Sodhi for the ODIs, and Taylor for the T20Is.

INDIA v NEW ZEALAND

First One-Day International

At Mumbai, October 22, 2017 (day/night). New Zealand won by six wickets. Toss: India.

Kohli became the second batsman, after A. B. de Villiers, to score a hundred in his 200th one-day international – only for a double-century stand between Latham and Taylor to condemn his side to defeat. India made 280 for eight, the sort of total which had not been safe on the subcontinent for some time. On a slow pitch, though, they were confident, particularly as New Zealand had never topped 250 batting second in India. After Williamson fell to Yadav, and Guptill skyed Pandya to make it 80 for three, a successful chase looked distant. But Latham, who swept the spinners to distraction, and Taylor were superb, putting on exactly 200 in 31 overs – a record partnership for any wicket by New Zealand against India, beating 190, also for the fourth, between Taylor and Scott Styris at Dambulla in 2010. Despite Kohli's century, India's innings had failed to hit top gear, with the middle order stuck in the mud. Boult was their major source of discomfort, accounting for the openers, and coming back to finish with four for 35.

Man of the Match: T. W. M. Latham.

THE FOUR PHASES OF KOHLI

Matches	*Runs*	*Avge*	*SR*	*100*
0–50	1,827	45.67	83.04	5
50–100	2,280	51.81	88.54	8
100–150	2,125	57.83	99.48	8
150–200	2,656	68.10	94.42	10

India

R. G. Sharma b Boult	20
S. Dhawan c Latham b Boult	9
*V. Kohli c Boult b Southee	121
K. M. Jadhav c and b Santner	12
K. D. Karthik c Munro b Southee	37
†M. S. Dhoni c Guptill b Boult	25
H. H. Pandya c Williamson b Boult	16
Bhuvneshwar Kumar c Nicholls b Southee	26
K. Yadav not out	0
Lb 4, w 10	14
1/16 (2) 2/29 (1) 3/71 (4) 4/144 (5) 5/201 (6) 6/238 (7) 7/270 (3) 8/280 (8) — (8 wkts, 50 overs)	280
10 overs: 37-2	

J. J. Bumrah and Y. S. Chahal did not bat.

Southee 10–0–73–3; Boult 10–1–35–4; Milne 9–0–62–0; Santner 10–0–41–1; de Grandhomme 4–0–27–0; Munro 7–0–38–0.

New Zealand

M. J. Guptill c Karthik b Pandya	32
C. Munro c Karthik b Bumrah	28
*K. S. Williamson c Jadhav b Yadav	6
L. R. P. L. Taylor c Chahal b Bhuvneshwar Kumar	95
†T. W. M. Latham not out	103
H. M. Nicholls not out	4
Lb 11, w 5	16
1/48 (2) 2/62 (3) 3/80 (1) 4/280 (4) — (4 wkts, 49 overs)	284
10 overs: 52-1	

C. de Grandhomme, M. J. Santner, T. G. Southee, A. F. Milne and T. A. Boult did not bat.

Bhuvneshwar Kumar 10–0–56–1; Bumrah 9–0–56–1; Yadav 10–0–64–1; Pandya 10–0–46–1; Chahal 10–0–51–0.

Umpires: M. A. Gough and C. K. Nandan. Third umpire: R. J. Tucker.
Referee: B. C. Broad.

INDIA v NEW ZEALAND

Second One-Day International

At Pune, October 25, 2017 (day/night). India won by six wickets. Toss: New Zealand.

The match began amid news that groundsman Pandurang Salgaoncar had been suspended after a sting operation. He gave journalists posing as bookmakers an unauthorised tour of the pitch, which he suggested would turn out to be a "340-run wicket". New Zealand, who chose to bat, did not bear this out. India's bowlers, led by the craft of Bhuvneshwar Kumar, probed with the new ball and were persistent with the old. After Williamson failed again, and Latham was knocked over by Patel – whose flat trajectory proved harder to sweep – they were on the rack at 118 for five. New Zealand hauled themselves to 230 for nine, but it was never enough to secure the series. Dhawan got the chase going with a half-century full of crisp cuts and pulls, and Karthik – the latest to be tried in India's problem No. 4 position – ensured there would be a decider, with an unbeaten 64. This was the 100th one-day international between the sides, and India now led 50–44.

Man of the Match: Bhuvneshwar Kumar.

New Zealand

M. J. Guptill c Dhoni b Bhuvneshwar Kumar 11
C. Munro b Bhuvneshwar Kumar 10
*K. S. Williamson lbw b Bumrah 3
L. R. P. L. Taylor c Dhoni b Pandya 21
†T. W. M. Latham b Patel 38
H. M. Nicholls b Bhuvneshwar Kumar 42
C. de Grandhomme c Bumrah b Chahal 41
M. J. Santner c Kohli b Bumrah 29
A. F. Milne lbw b Chahal 0
T. G. Southee not out 25
T. A. Boult not out 2

Lb 3, w 5 8

1/20 (1) 2/25 (3) 3/27 (2) 4/58 (4) 5/118 (5) 6/165 (6) 7/188 (7) 8/188 (9) 9/220 (8) (9 wkts, 50 overs) 230

10 overs: 35-3

Bhuvneshwar Kumar 10–0–45–3; Bumrah 10–2–38–2; Jadhav 8–0–31–0; Pandya 4–0–23–1; Patel 10–1–54–1; Chahal 8–1–36–2.

India

R. G. Sharma c Munro b Southee 7
S. Dhawan c Taylor b Milne 68
*V. Kohli c Latham b de Grandhomme 29
K. D. Karthik not out 64
H. H. Pandya c Milne b Santner 30
†M. S. Dhoni not out 18

Lb 7, w 9 16

1/22 (1) 2/79 (3) 3/145 (2) 4/204 (5) (4 wkts, 46 overs) 232

10 overs: 64-1

K. M. Jadhav, A. R. Patel, Bhuvneshwar Kumar, J. J. Bumrah and Y. S. Chahal did not bat.

Southee 9–1–60–1; Boult 10–0–54–0; Milne 8–1–21–1; Santner 10–0–38–1; de Grandhomme 7–0–40–1; Munro 2–0–12–0.

Umpires: C. Shamshuddin and R. J. Tucker. Third umpire: M. A. Gough.
Referee: B. C. Broad.

INDIA v NEW ZEALAND

Third One-Day International

At Kanpur, October 29, 2017 (day/night). India won by six runs. Toss: New Zealand.

In a game dominated by the bat – the 668 scored here was a ground record – Bumrah had the last laugh. After Munro's early hits, Williamson's only half-century of the tour, and Latham's middle-order resourcefulness, New Zealand were well placed for their first ODI series win in India. Nicholls paddled a six over the keeper's head at the end of the 46th, leaving 35 needed with six wickets in hand. But Bhuvneshwar Kumar bowled Nicholls next over, his only good one of the day, Latham was run out for a 52-ball 65, and Bumrah was unhittable. With the series on the line, and dew on the ball, the precision of his laser-guided yorkers was all the more impressive. India's innings had been more of a two-man effort. Sharma and Kohli hit gorgeous hundreds, and became the first pair in ODIs to share four 200-plus stands. Kohli passed 9,000 ODI runs, in his 194th innings – beating A. B. de Villiers's record of 205 – and 2,000 in all formats in 2017 alone. It gave India just enough for a seventh bilateral series win in a row, their longest streak.

Man of the Match: R. G. Sharma. *Man of the Series:* V. Kohli.

India

R. G. Sharma c Southee b Santner	147	K. D. Karthik not out	4
S. Dhawan c Williamson b Southee	14	Lb 1, w 7	8
*V. Kohli c Williamson b Southee	113		—
H. H. Pandya c Southee b Santner	8	1/29 (2) 2/259 (1) (6 wkts, 50 overs)	337
†M. S. Dhoni c Munro b Milne	25	3/273 (4) 4/302 (3)	
K. M. Jadhav c Guptill b Milne	18	5/331 (5) 6/337 (6)	10 overs: 53-1

A. R. Patel, Bhuvneshwar Kumar, J. J. Bumrah and Y. S. Chahal did not bat.

Southee 10–0–66–2; Boult 10–0–81–0; Milne 10–0–64–2; de Grandhomme 8–0–57–0; Santner 10–0–58–2; Munro 2–0–10–0.

New Zealand

M. J. Guptill c Karthik b Bumrah	10	M. J. Santner c Dhawan b Bumrah	9
C. Munro b Chahal	75	T. G. Southee not out	4
*K. S. Williamson c Dhoni b Chahal	64	Lb 4, w 16	20
L. R. P. L. Taylor c Jadhav b Bumrah	39		—
†T. W. M. Latham run out	65	1/44 (1) 2/153 (2) (7 wkts, 50 overs)	331
H. M. Nicholls b Bhuvneshwar Kumar	37	3/168 (3) 4/247 (4)	
C. de Grandhomme not out	8	5/306 (6) 6/312 (5) 7/326 (8)	10 overs: 74-1

A. F. Milne and T. A. Boult did not bat.

Bhuvneshwar Kumar 10–0–92–1; Bumrah 10–0–47–3; Pandya 5–0–47–0; Patel 7–0–40–0; Jadhav 8–0–54–0; Chahal 10–0–47–2.

Umpires: A. K. Chaudhary and M. A. Gough. Third umpire: R. J. Tucker.
Referee: B. C. Broad.

INDIA v NEW ZEALAND

First Twenty20 International

At Delhi, November 1, 2017 (floodlit). India won by 53 runs. Toss: New Zealand. Twenty20 international debut: S. S. Iyer.

At the seventh attempt (including one abandonment), India earned their first T20 win against New Zealand, thanks to an opening stand of 158. It was their record partnership for any wicket, beating 138 for the second between Sharma and Kohli against South Africa at Dharamsala in October 2015. But sloppy fielding helped their cause. Santner dropped Dhawan on eight, and Southee put down Sharma on 16. Even after Sodhi – who alone staunched the flow – took two wickets in the 17th over, they dropped Kohli, who hammered 26 off 11. That took India to 202, way above par on a damp pitch. New Zealand needed their own openers to fire, but neither reached double figures, with Guptill falling to a brilliant catch by Pandya at long-off; at 65 for three from ten overs, the game was up. They lost their No. 1 ranking, while India lost Ashish Nehra who, on his home ground, retired from the game after 18 years as an international. "I could not have asked for anything more," he said. "I have no regrets. I am always happy, retired or otherwise."

Man of the Match: S. Dhawan.

India

		B	4/6
1 R. G. Sharma *c 4 b 11*	80	55	6/4
2 S. Dhawan *c 4 b 10*	80	52	10/2
3 H. H. Pandya *c 4 b 10*	0	2	0
4 *V. Kohli *not out*	26	11	0/3
5 †M. S. Dhoni *not out*	7	2	0/1
B 5, lb 1, w 1, nb 2	9		
6 overs: 46-0 (20 overs)	202-3		

1/158 2/158 3/185

6 S. S. Iyer, 7 A. R. Patel, 8 Bhuvneshwar Kumar, 9 A. Nehra, 10 J. J. Bumrah and 11 Y. S. Chahal did not bat.

Santner 4–9–30–0; Boult 4–8–49–1; Southee 4–5–44–0; de Grandhomme 3–3–34–0; Sodhi 4–8–25–2; Munro 1–0–14–0.

New Zealand

		B	4/6
1 M. J. Guptill *c 3 b 11*	4	8	1
2 C. Munro *b 8*	7	8	0
3 *K. S. Williamson *c 5 b 3*	28	24	1/1
4 †T. W. M. Latham *st 5 b 11*	39	36	3/1
5 T. C. Bruce *c 1 b 7*	10	10	1
6 C. de Grandhomme *c 2 b 7*	0	1	0
7 H. M. Nicholls *run out*	6	7	1
8 M. J. Santner *not out*	27	14	2/2
9 T. G. Southee *c 5 b 10*	8	4	2
10 I. S. Sodhi *not out*	11	9	2
Lb 3, w 5, nb 1	9		
6 overs: 33-2 (20 overs)	149-8		

1/6 2/18 3/54 4/83 5/84 6/94 7/99 8/111

11 T. A. Boult did not bat.

Nehra 4–11–29–0; Chahal 4–10–26–2; Bhuvneshwar Kumar 3–10–23–1; Bumrah 4–12–37–1; Patel 4–6–20–2; Pandya 1–1–11–1.

Umpires: N. N. Menon and C. Shamshuddin. Third umpire: A. K. Chaudhary.
Referee: B. C. Broad.

INDIA v NEW ZEALAND

Second Twenty20 International

At Rajkot, November 4, 2017 (floodlit). New Zealand won by 40 runs. Toss: New Zealand. Twenty20 international debut: M. Siraj.

The pattern was the same as the first game, though the victor was not. New Zealand batted first and, helped by iffy fielding, racked up a big score, then stifled India's chase to set up a decider. Munro, who was dropped on 36 and 79, stroked his way to a second T20I century, joining Chris Gayle, Brendon McCullum and Evin Lewis in an elite club. He bunted three of his seven sixes off the Hyderabad seamer Mohammed Siraj, who had a torrid debut, returning one for 53. India dragged it back a little in the closing stages, but 196 for two was still New Zealand's highest against them. Boult made the chase tougher by removing the openers with bounce and movement and, although Kohli looked in superb touch, he had little support. Dhoni held up an end, but could not force the pace, and the result was obvious long before he fell in the final over.

Man of the Match: C. Munro.

New Zealand

		B	4/6
1 M. J. Guptill *c 5 b 11*	45	41	3/3
2 C. Munro *not out*	109	58	7/7
3 *K. S. Williamson *c 1 b 10*	12	9	2
4 T. C. Bruce *not out*	18	12	2
Lb 2, w 10	12		
6 overs: 48-0 (20 overs)	196-2		

1/105 2/140

5 †G. D. Phillips, 6 C. de Grandhomme, 7 H. M. Nicholls, 8 M. J. Santner, 9 A. F. Milne, 10 I. S. Sodhi and 11 T. A. Boult did not bat.

India

		B	4/6
1 R. G. Sharma *c 5 b 11*	5	6	1
2 S. Dhawan *b 11*	1	4	0
3 S. S. Iyer *c and b 2*	23	21	4
4 *V. Kohli *c 5 b 8*	65	42	8/1
5 H. H. Pandya *b 10*	1	2	0
6 †M. S. Dhoni *c 8 b 11*	49	37	2/3
7 A. R. Patel *c 3 b 11*	5	3	1
8 Bhuvneshwar Kumar *not out*	2	3	0
9 J. J. Bumrah *not out*	1	2	0
B 2, lb 1, w 1	4		
6 overs: 40-2 (20 overs)	156-7		

1/6 2/11 3/65 4/67 5/123 6/130 7/154

10 M. Siraj and 11 Y. S. Chahal did not bat.

Bhuvneshwar Kumar 4–11–29–0; Siraj 4–4–53–1; Bumrah 4–9–23–0; Chahal 4–9–36–1; Patel 3–3–39–0; Pandya 1–1–14–0.

Milne 4–10–30–0; Boult 4–10–34–4; de Grandhomme 1–2–10–0; Santner 4–7–31–1; Sodhi 4–9–25–1; Munro 3–3–23–1.

Umpires: A. K. Chaudhary and C. K. Nandan. Third umpire: C. Shamshuddin.
Referee: B. C. Broad.

INDIA v NEW ZEALAND

Third Twenty20 International

At Thiruvananthapuram, November 7, 2017 (floodlit). India won by six runs. Toss: New Zealand.

Rain shortened the first senior match at Greenfield Stadium to an eight-over thrash, and India just about clung on. The claggy pitch restricted strokemaking, and they struggled for momentum against the square turn of Santner – who was also exceptional in the field – and canny changes of pace from Southee and Boult. There were just four fours and three sixes in the innings, and 67 for five didn't look enough. But, thanks to Bumrah, who wins matches even when conditions favour batting, India squeezed out another series victory. He choked batsmen for space when they were desperate for big shots, removed the dangerous Munro, and finished with 2–8–9–2. Chahal, who kept the ball away from the hitting zone, backed him up with 2–6–8–0. New Zealand threw the bat at the others, but left themselves 19 from the last, which proved out of reach.

Man of the Match: J. J. Bumrah. *Man of the Series:* J. J. Bumrah.

India

		B	*4/6*
1 R. G. Sharma *c 8 b 9*	8	9	1
2 S. Dhawan *c 8 b 9*	6	6	1
3 *V. Kohli *c 11 b 10*	13	6	1/1
4 S. S. Iyer *c 1 b 10*	6	6	0
5 M. K. Pandey *c 5 b 11*	17	11	1/1
6 H. H. Pandya *not out*	14	10	0/1
7 †M. S. Dhoni *not out*	0	0	0
Lb 2, w 1	3		
2 overs: 14-0 (8 overs)	67-5		

1/15 2/15 3/30 4/48 5/62

8 Bhuvneshwar Kumar, 9 K. Yadav, 10 J. J. Bumrah and 11 Y. S. Chahal did not bat.

Boult 2–5–13–1; Santner 2–6–16–0; Southee 2–4–13–2; Sodhi 2–3–23–2.

New Zealand

		B	*4/6*
1 M. J. Guptill *b 8*	1	3	0
2 C. Munro *c 1 b 10*	7	6	0/1
3 *K. S. Williamson *run out*	8	10	0
4 †G. D. Phillips *c 2 b 9*	11	9	2
5 C. de Grandhomme *not out*	17	10	0/2
6 H. M. Nicholls *c 4 b 10*	2	4	0
7 T. C. Bruce *run out*	4	2	1
8 M. J. Santner *not out*	3	4	0
B 4, lb 1, w 3	8		
2 overs: 11-2 (8 overs)	61-6		

1/8 2/8 3/28 4/28 5/39 6/48

9 T. G. Southee, 10 I. S. Sodhi and 11 T. A. Boult did not bat.

Bhuvneshwar Kumar 2–5–18–1; Bumrah 2–8–9–2; Chahal 2–6–8–0; Yadav 1–2–10–1; Pandya 1–2–11–0.

Umpires: A. K. Chaudhary and N. N. Menon. Third umpire: C. K. Nandan.
Referee: B. C. Broad.

INDIA v SRI LANKA IN 2017-18

R. KAUSHIK

Test matches (3): India 1, Sri Lanka 0
One-day internationals (3): India 2, Sri Lanka 1
Twenty20 internationals (3): India 3, Sri Lanka 0

Hammered out of sight at home just three months previously, when India ran up a perfect 9–0 scoreline across the formats, Sri Lanka offered greater resistance after making the short hop across the Palk Strait. India won all three series again, but faced more of a fight, particularly in the Tests and the one-day internationals. Prompted by Virat Kohli, they tried to create the conditions they expected to encounter in South Africa early in 2018, but the tactic backfired: batting meltdowns on seam-friendly pitches in the First Test at Kolkata and the first one-dayer at Dharamsala – both orchestrated by Suranga Lakmal – sent out warning signals.

But the biggest talking point was the toxic level of smog in Delhi during the Third Test. On the second day, Sri Lanka had to field despite air-pollution readings well above the recommended World Health Organisation limits. After gasping for breath and in some cases throwing up, they emerged after lunch sporting masks, which drew some ill-advised condemnation. Play stopped for more than 20 minutes while the umpires consulted with doctors. Eventually, Sri Lanka ran out of fit fielders: interim coach Nic Pothas and another member of the support staff were slipping into whites to come on as substitutes when Kohli declared. "It's not normal for players to suffer like that while playing the game," said Pothas.

It wasn't just Lakmal and his new-ball partner Lahiru Gamage who needed oxygen in the dressing-room. The Indian trio of Murali Vijay, Ravichandran Ashwin and local boy Ishant Sharma had their problems too, raising questions about the wisdom of scheduling sporting events in the Indian capital at a time when pollution levels have often been dangerously high.

Despite their discomfort, the tourists battled hard and came away with a draw on a surface that, even late on the fifth day, offered nothing to the bowlers. Their second-innings fightback was orchestrated by the inexperienced pair of Dhananjaya de Silva and Roshen Silva, an encouraging sign for Sri Lanka after the abject surrender earlier in the year.

India rested Kohli for the white-ball internationals, with Rohit Sharma taking charge for the first time. Sri Lanka also had a new leader in Tissara Perera, after jettisoning Upul Tharanga. Sharma's reign got off to the worst possible start in Dharamsala, where Lakmal harnessed seam and swing beautifully. But in the second game, in Mohali, Sharma flogged a spectacular double-century, his third in ODIs. A few days later, at Indore, he galloped to another hundred, his 35-ball blitz equalling David Miller's record as the fastest in Twenty20 internationals. That ensured a tough baptism for Chandika Hathurusinghe, who had taken over as Sri Lanka's new full-time coach for the 20-over games.

SRI LANKA TOURING PARTY

*L. D. Chandimal (T), P. V. D. Chameera (50/20), A. Dananjaya (50/20), D. M. de Silva (T/50/20), P. C. de Silva (50/20), D. P. D. N. Dickwella (T/50/20), A. N. P. R. Fernando (50/20), M. V. T. Fernando (T/20), P. L. S. Gamage (T), D. A. S. Gunaratne (50/20), M. D. Gunathilleke (50/20), H. M. R. K. B. Herath (T), F. D. M. Karunaratne (T), R. A. S. Lakmal (T/50/20), A. D. Mathews (T/ 50/20), S. S. Pathirana (50/20), M. D. K. Perera (T), M. D. K. J. Perera (50/20), N. L. T. C. Perera (50/20), W. S. R. Samarawickrama (T/50/20), P. A. D. L. R. Sandakan (T), M. D. Shanaka (T/20), A. R. S. Silva (T), W. U. Tharanga (50/20), H. D. R. L. Thirimanne (T/50/20). *Coach:* N. Pothas (T/ 50), U. C. Hathurusinghe (20).

N. L. T. C. Perera captained in the limited-overs matches.

TEST MATCH AVERAGES

INDIA – BATTING AND FIELDING

	T	*I*	*NO*	*R*	*HS*	*100*	*50*	*Avge*	*Ct*
R. G. Sharma	2	3	2	217	102*	1	2	217.00	1
V. Kohli	3	5	1	610	243	3	1	152.50	3
M. Vijay	2	3	0	292	155	2	0	97.33	1
C. A. Pujara	3	5	0	289	143	1	1	57.80	1
†S. Dhawan	2	4	0	192	94	0	2	48.00	2
K. L. Rahul	2	3	0	86	79	0	1	28.66	2
W. P. Saha	3	4	2	44	29	0	0	22.00	9
†R. A. Jadeja	3	4	2	40	22	0	0	20.00	1
R. Ashwin	3	4	0	20	7	0	0	5.00	1
A. M. Rahane	3	5	0	17	10	0	0	3.40	5

Played in two Tests: Mohammed Shami 24, 12* (1 ct); U. T. Yadav 6*; I. Sharma did not bat (1 ct). Played in one Test: Bhuvneshwar Kumar 13, 8.

BOWLING

	Style	*O*	*M*	*R*	*W*	*BB*	*5I*	*Avge*
Bhuvneshwar Kumar	RFM	38	13	96	8	4-8	0	12.00
R. A. Jadeja	SLA	117	35	259	10	3-56	0	25.90
I. Sharma	RFM	68.3	16	210	8	3-37	0	26.25
Mohammed Shami	RFM	77	21	269	9	4-100	0	29.88
R. Ashwin	OB	123.4	24	359	12	4-63	0	29.91
U. T. Yadav	RF	50	7	177	5	2-30	0	35.40

Also bowled: V. Kohli (RM) 2.1–0–6–0; M. Vijay (OB) 1–0–3–0.

SRI LANKA – BATTING AND FIELDING

	T	*I*	*NO*	*R*	*HS*	*100*	*50*	*Avge*	*Ct/St*
L. D. Chandimal	3	6	0	366	164	1	2	61.00	0
A. D. Mathews	3	6	0	196	111	1	1	32.66	2
†D. P. D. N. Dickwella	3	6	1	134	44*	0	0	26.80	6/3
†H. M. R. K. B. Herath	2	4	1	71	67	0	1	23.66	0
†H. D. R. L. Thirimanne	2	4	0	90	51	0	1	22.50	2
R. A. S. Lakmal	3	5	1	69	31*	0	0	17.25	2
†F. D. M. Karunaratne	3	6	0	91	51	0	1	15.16	2
M. D. K. Perera	3	5	0	62	42	0	0	12.40	4
W. S. R. Samarawickrama	3	6	0	74	33	0	0	12.33	2
M. D. Shanaka	2	4	1	25	17	0	0	8.33	1
P. L. S. Gamage	3	4	2	1	1	0	0	0.50	0

Played in one Test: D. M. de Silva 1, 119*; P. A. D. L. R. Sandakan 0* (1 ct); A. R. S. Silva 0, 74*.

BOWLING

	Style	*O*	*M*	*R*	*W*	*BB*	*5I*	*Avge*
M. D. Shanaka	RFM	60.1	9	215	6	3-76	0	35.83
P. A. D. L. R. Sandakan	SLW	43.5	1	217	5	4-167	0	43.40
R. A. S. Lakmal	RFM	108	23	370	8	4-26	0	46.25
P. L. S. Gamage	RFM	113.2	23	396	7	2-59	0	56.57
M. D. K. Perera	OB	107.1	5	469	8	3-202	0	58.62

Also bowled: D. M. de Silva (OB) 21–0–79–1; H. M. R. K. B. Herath (SLA) 47–12–115–1; F. D. M. Karunaratne (RM) 4–0–25–0.

INDIA v SRI LANKA

First Test

At Kolkata, November 16–20, 2017. Drawn. Toss: Sri Lanka.

Lakmal gave Sri Lanka a flying start, but despite rain limiting the first three days to 105 overs, they were hanging on for dear life by the end. The build-up had been unusual. With only 11 days between the end of this tour and a Test in Cape Town, Kohli wanted the groundsmen to replicate the conditions he expected India to face in South Africa. Through a combination of accident and design, Eden Gardens provided precisely that: overcast skies and a liberal covering of grass. It all helped Lakmal's spectacular opening salvo, which underlined the fallibility of India's top order against the moving ball.

Only Pujara, playing close to the body in textbook style, had an answer to Lakmal's seam and swing: at the end of a first day restricted to 11.5 overs, India were tottering at 17 for three. Rahul fell to the first ball of the match, Dhawan paid the price for not respecting seam movement, and Kohli was trapped in front. Lakmal's first seven overs were maidens, and his first spell – spread over two days – was 11–9–5–3. When Rahane edged Shanaka, it was 30 for four, but Pujara's three-hour resistance, and a lower order willing to take their chances, lifted the total to 172. Even though they had the worst batting conditions of the match, it was a poor effort by a line-up which had recently been piling up huge totals.

MOST INTERNATIONAL CENTURIES

		T	*100*	*ODI*	*100*	*T20I*	*100*
100	S. R. Tendulkar (India)	200	51	463	49	1	0
71	R. T. Ponting (Australia/World)	168	41	375	30	17	0
63	K. C. Sangakkara (Sri Lanka/Asia/World)	134	38	404	25	56	0
62	J. H. Kallis (South Africa/World/Africa)	166	45	328	17	25	0
55	**V. Kohli (India)**	**66**	**21**	**205**	**34**	**55**	**0**
54	**H. M. Amla (South Africa/World)**	**113**	**28**	**162**	**26**	**43**	**0**
54	D. P. M. D. Jayawardene (Sri Lanka/Asia)	149	34	448	19	55	1
53	B. C. Lara (West Indies/World)	131	34	299	19	–	–
48	R. Dravid (India/World/Asia)	164	36	344	12	1	0
46	**A. B. de Villiers (South Africa/Africa)**	**110**	**21**	**225**	**25**	**78**	**0**

As at January 31, 2018.

As the pitch dried out, Sri Lanka stitched together several useful partnerships, none better than 99 for the third wicket between Thirimanne and Mathews. Bhuvneshwar Kumar and Mohammed Shami toiled hard, reducing them to 201 for seven, before Herath slapped ten fours in an entertaining innings which helped swell the lead to 122. Ashwin and Jadeja bowled ten overs between them in the match, but failed to strike – the first time no Indian spinner had taken a wicket in 262 home Tests.

With less than a day and a half to go, Kohli might have settled for batting practice. But he wanted to make a statement, and led a beefy reply with a superb unbeaten 104, his 50th international century, after an opening stand of 166 from Rahul and Dhawan.

Still, when India declared 45 minutes before tea on the final day with a lead of 230, few envisaged the thrilling finale. Kumar and Shami produced fast bowling of the highest quality, and both openers fell in the seven overs before the interval; soon, it was 22 for four. The feisty Dickwella kept his wits about him, and tried to rile the Indians by wasting time: Kohli told his players not to get involved. But with the floodlights taking over from the natural light, the umpires called a halt. Lakmal's first-innings heroics were a distant memory as the Sri Lankans celebrated getting out of jail. Just.

Man of the Match: Bhuvneshwar Kumar.

Close of play: first day, India 17-3 (Pujara 8, Rahane 0); second day, India 74-5 (Pujara 47, Saha 6); third day, Sri Lanka 165-4 (Chandimal 13, Dickwella 14); fourth day, India 171-1 (Rahul 73, Pujara 2).

India

First innings		Second innings	
K. L. Rahul c Dickwella b Lakmal	0	– b Lakmal	79
S. Dhawan b Lakmal	8	– c Dickwella b Shanaka	94
C. A. Pujara b Gamage	52	– c Perera b Lakmal	22
*V. Kohli lbw b Lakmal	0	– not out	104
A. M. Rahane c Dickwella b Shanaka	4	– lbw b Lakmal	0
R. Ashwin c Karunaratne b Shanaka	4	– (7) b Shanaka	7
†W. P. Saha c Mathews b Perera	29	– (8) c Samarawickrama b Shanaka	5
R. A. Jadeja lbw b Perera	22	– (6) c Thirimanne b Perera	9
Bhuvneshwar Kumar c Dickwella b Lakmal	13	– c Perera b Gamage	8
Mohammed Shami c Shanaka b Gamage	24	– not out	12
U. T. Yadav not out	6		
B 6, lb 4	10	B 7, lb 1, w 3, nb 1	12
1/0 (1) 2/13 (2) 3/17 (4) 4/30 (5) 5/50 (6) 6/79 (3) 7/127 (8) 8/128 (7) 9/146 (9) 10/172 (10) (59.3 overs)	172	1/166 (2) 2/192 (1) 3/213 (3) 4/213 (5) 5/249 (6) 6/269 (7) 7/281 (8) 8/321 (9) (8 wkts dec, 88.4 overs)	352

Lakmal 19–12–26–4; Gamage 17.3–5–59–2; Shanaka 12–4–36–2; Karunaratne 2–0–17–0; Herath 2–0–5–0; Perera 7–1–19–2. *Second innings*—Lakmal 24.4–4–93–3; Gamage 23–2–97–1; Shanaka 22–1–76–3; Perera 13–2–49–1; Herath 6–1–29–0.

Sri Lanka

First innings		Second innings	
W. S. R. Samarawickrama c Saha b Bhuvneshwar Kumar	23	– b Bhuvneshwar Kumar	0
F. D. M. Karunaratne lbw b Bhuvneshwar Kumar	8	– b Mohammed Shami	1
H. D. R. L. Thirimanne c Kohli b Yadav	51	– c Rahane b Bhuvneshwar Kumar	7
A. D. Mathews c Rahul b Yadav	52	– lbw b Yadav	12
*L. D. Chandimal c Saha b Mohammed Shami	28	– b Mohammed Shami	20
†D. P. D. N. Dickwella c Kohli b Mohammed Shami	35	– lbw b Bhuvneshwar Kumar	27
M. D. Shanaka lbw b Bhuvneshwar Kumar	0	– not out	6
M. D. K. Perera c Saha b Mohammed Shami	5	– b Bhuvneshwar Kumar	0
H. M. R. K. B. Herath c Mohammed Shami b Bhuvneshwar Kumar	67	– not out	0
R. A. S. Lakmal b Mohammed Shami	16		
P. L. S. Gamage not out	0		
B 4, lb 4, w 1	9	Lb 1, nb 1	2
1/29 (2) 2/34 (1) 3/133 (3) 4/138 (4) 5/200 (6) 6/201 (7) 7/201 (5) 8/244 (8) 9/290 (9) 10/294 (10) (83.4 overs)	294	1/0 (1) 2/2 (2) 3/14 (3) 4/22 (4) 5/69 (5) 6/69 (6) 7/75 (8) (7 wkts, 26.3 overs)	75

Bhuvneshwar Kumar 27–5–88–4; Mohammed Shami 26.3–5–100–4; Yadav 20–1–79–2; Ashwin 8–2–13–0; Kohli 1.1–0–5–0; Jadeja 1–0–1–0. *Second innings*—Bhuvneshwar Kumar 11–8–8–4; Mohammed Shami 9.3–4–34–2; Yadav 5–0–25–1; Jadeja 1–0–7–0.

Umpires: R. A. Kettleborough and N. J. Llong. Third umpire: J. S. Wilson.
Wilson replaced Kettleborough (ill) after two days; A. K. Chaudhary took over as third umpire.
Referee: D. C. Boon.

INDIA v SRI LANKA

Second Test

At Nagpur, November 24–27, 2017. India won by an innings and 239 runs. Toss: Sri Lanka.

The seam and swing of Kolkata gave way to a typical subcontinental surface at Nagpur – slow and dry, with a touch of crumble. India's hopes of hitting Sri Lanka with pace, and of their batsmen getting another workout in unfamiliar conditions, were dashed. But they played the hand they were dealt with aplomb, equalling their biggest margin of victory in Tests, while Sri Lanka slumped to their heaviest defeat.

Wicketless at Eden Gardens, India's spinners came into their own. Ashwin claimed his 300th wicket in his 54th Test, undercutting Dennis Lillee's world record 56. He finished with eight in the match, while Jadeja collected five. The Sri Lankans' tendency to crack at the first hint of pressure was evident again, and India jumped all over them. They didn't even need Bhuvneshwar Kumar, Man of the Match in the previous Test, but now busy with his wedding.

It had been a good toss for Chandimal to win, but his side made a hash of it, slipping from a half-decent 160 for four to 205 all out. Karunaratne, who completed 1,000 runs for the calendar year, and Chandimal flickered briefly, but the rest barely turned up, leading India to think Christmas had come a month early.

Their batsmen then feasted on an attack that was as toothless here as it had been threatening in Kolkata. Rahul and Rahane missed out, but the rest of the top six all helped themselves to centuries, only the third time India had had four in an innings. Vijay and Pujara added 209 for the second wicket, their fourth consecutive century stand and their tenth in all: they had now put on 2,740 runs in 38 innings, at 72. After them came Kohli and Rohit Sharma. In his first Test innings for more than 13 months, Sharma brought up his first ton since November 2013; Kohli rattled along to 213 in just 267 deliveries in another exhibition of attacking batting against defensive-minded opposition. It was his fifth double-century, all since July 2016, which equalled Brian Lara's record for the most by a captain. And it was his 12th three-figure score as skipper, another Indian record. He eventually declared, late on the third day, with the lead past 400.

Dispirited and drained after fielding for more than 12 hours – and with Shanaka losing 75% of his match fee for ball-tampering – Sri Lanka keeled over again. India could probably have knocked them down with a feather, but instead used heavy artillery. Ashwin feasted on some easy prey, and the other bowlers pitched in to pack Sri Lanka off inside 50 overs, with a day and a half to spare. Chandimal made his second fifty of the match, but there was not much resistance from the rest.

Man of the Match: V. Kohli.

Close of play: first day, India 11-1 (Vijay 2, Pujara 2); second day, India 312-2 (Pujara 121, Kohli 54); third day, Sri Lanka 21-1 (Karunaratne 11, Thirimanne 9).

Sri Lanka

W. S. R. Samarawickrama c Pujara b I. Sharma	13	– b I. Sharma	0
F. D. M. Karunaratne lbw b I. Sharma	51	– c Vijay b Jadeja	18
H. D. R. L. Thirimanne b Ashwin	9	– c Jadeja b Yadav	23
A. D. Mathews lbw b Jadeja	10	– c R. G. Sharma b Jadeja	10
*L. D. Chandimal lbw b Ashwin	57	– c Ashwin b Yadav	61
†D. P. D. N. Dickwella c I. Sharma b Jadeja	24	– c Kohli b I. Sharma	4
M. D. Shanaka b Ashwin	2	– c Rahul b Ashwin	17
M. D. K. Perera lbw b Jadeja	15	– lbw b Ashwin	0
H. M. R. K. B. Herath c Rahane b Ashwin	4	– c Rahane b Ashwin	0
R. A. S. Lakmal c Saha b I. Sharma	17	– not out	31
P. L. S. Gamage not out	0	– b Ashwin	0
Lb 2, nb 1	3	Lb 2	2
1/20 (1) 2/44 (3) 3/60 (4) 4/122 (2) 5/160 (6) 6/165 (7) 7/184 (8) 8/184 (5) 9/205 (10) 10/205 (9) (79.1 overs)	205	1/0 (1) 2/34 (2) 3/48 (3) 4/68 (4) 5/75 (6) 6/102 (7) 7/107 (8) 8/107 (9) 9/165 (5) 10/166 (11) (49.3 overs)	166

I. Sharma 14–3–37–3; Yadav 16–4–43–0; Ashwin 28.1–7–67–4; Jadeja 21–4–56–3. *Second innings*—I. Sharma 12–4–43–2; Ashwin 17.3–4–63–4; Jadeja 11–5–28–2; Yadav 9–2–30–2.

India

K. L. Rahul b Gamage	7
M. Vijay c Perera b Herath	128
C. A. Pujara b Shanaka	143
*V. Kohli c Thirimanne b Perera	213
A. M. Rahane c Karunaratne b Perera	2
R. G. Sharma not out	102
R. Ashwin b Perera	5
†W. P. Saha not out	1
B 4, lb 4, w 1	9
1/7 (1) 2/216 (2) 3/399 (3) 4/410 (5) 5/583 (4) 6/597 (7) (6 wkts dec, 176.1 overs)	610

R. A. Jadeja, U. T. Yadav and I. Sharma did not bat.

Lakmal 29–2–111–0; Gamage 35–8–97–1; Herath 39–11–81–1; Shanaka 26.1–4–103–1; Perera 45–2–202–3; Karunaratne 2–0–8–0.

Umpires: R. A. Kettleborough and J. S. Wilson. Third umpire: N. J. Llong.
Referee: D. C. Boon.

INDIA v SRI LANKA

Third Test

At Delhi, December 2–6, 2017. Drawn. Toss: India. Test debut: A. R. S. Silva.

The Test will always be remembered for the debilitating effects of toxic air, which led to a 20-minute hold-up on the second afternoon. Sri Lanka's new-ball pair of Lakmal and Gamage were worst affected – they threw up on the field and were given oxygen in the dressing-room – but most of the other players sported face masks in a vague attempt at safety. It didn't make for pretty viewing. New Delhi is at its most polluted in the winter, and the scheduling reflected poorly on the BCCI. The Sri Lankans were unfairly castigated for their concerns, which gained credence when some of India's players also had problems.

It was easy to forget there was a Test series at stake and, when the final day began at the Feroz Shah Kotla, still hazy and thick with pollution, the chances of Sri Lanka escaping

FEWEST INNINGS TO REACH 20 TEST CENTURIES

55	D. G. Bradman (Australia)	116	R. T. Ponting (Australia)
93	S. M. Gavaskar (India)	117	W. R. Hammond (England)
95	M. L. Hayden (Australia)	118	G. S. Sobers (West Indies)
99	S. P. D. Smith (Australia)	118	Mohammad Yousuf (Pakistan)
105	**V. Kohli (India)**	120	R. N. Harvey (Australia)
107	S. R. Tendulkar (India)	121	K. F. Barrington (England)

with their heads held high ranged from bleak to none. In the previous four and a half months they had been overpowered by India in four of five Tests, escaping with one draw thanks to bad light in Kolkata. And, needing an unlikely 410 to square the series, they had suffered a familiar top-order collapse, ending the fourth day at 31 for three. When Mathews, one of two first-innings centurions, fell inside the first half-hour on the last morning, it looked like a case of when rather than whether. But in an encouraging display of pluck and resilience on an admittedly docile surface, Sri Lanka were hauled to safety by their young guns.

Dhananjaya de Silva conjured a memorable third Test century, despite battling severe cramps which eventually forced him to retire after a four-and-a-quarter-hour vigil. And Roshen Silva, the 29-year-old debutant who had made a third-ball duck in the first innings, ground it out for three hours for an unbeaten 74. He put team before self, ignoring Dickwella's exhortations to go for a century. Sri Lanka probably surprised even themselves by losing just two wickets in 87 overs on the final day.

DOUBLE-CENTURIES IN SUCCESSIVE TEST INNINGS

W. R. Hammond (England)	251 (Sydney), 200 (Melbourne) v Australia	1928-29
W. R. Hammond (England)	227 (Christchurch), 336* (Auckland) v New Zealand	1932-33
D. G. Bradman (Australia)	304 (Leeds), 244 (The Oval) v England	1934
V. Kambli (India)	224 (Bombay) v England, 227 (Delhi) v Zimbabwe	1992-93
K. C. Sangakkara (Sri Lanka)	200* (Colombo, PSS), 222* (Kandy) v Bangladesh	2007
M. J. Clarke (Australia)	259* (Brisbane), 230 (Adelaide) v South Africa	2012-13
V. Kohli (India)	**213 (Nagpur), 243 (Delhi) v Sri Lanka**	**2017-18**

Earlier, Kohli had become only the sixth batsman to score double-hundreds in consecutive Test innings. He brought up 5,000 Test runs during his uninhibited 243, which included 25 fours from 287 balls, and was his highest score in all cricket. He piled on 283 for the third wicket with Vijay, whose 155 was his second successive hundred. As the game slowed – Sri Lanka's interim coach Nic Pothas was preparing to come on and field as a substitute – Kohli declared earlier than he would have liked, to prevent further loss of time.

Sri Lanka started poorly – Karunaratne fell to the first ball, and de Silva soon followed – but were bailed out by Chandimal, the captain, and Mathews, his predecessor. They used up nearly 80 overs in adding 181 for the fourth wicket. In all, Sri Lanka batted for 135.3 overs – 7.4 more than India – despite conceding a deficit of 163.

Looking for quick runs, India zipped along before Kohli declared again, leaving his attack about seven hours to bowl Sri Lanka out. At 35 for four, an Indian victory looked certain, before de Silva and Silva salvaged a draw. They could not, though, prevent a ninth successive Test series win for Kohli's India.

Man of the Match: V. Kohli. *Man of the Series:* V. Kohli.

Close of play: first day, India 371-4 (Kohli 156, R. G. Sharma 6); second day, Sri Lanka 131-3 (Mathews 57, Chandimal 25); third day, Sri Lanka 356-9 (Chandimal 147, Sandakan 0); fourth day, Sri Lanka 31-3 (de Silva 13, Mathews 0).

India

M. Vijay st Dickwella b Sandakan	155	– c Dickwella b Lakmal	9
S. Dhawan c Lakmal b Perera	23	– st Dickwella b Sandakan	67
C. A. Pujara c Samarawickrama b Gamage	23	– (4) c Mathews b de Silva	49
*V. Kohli lbw b Sandakan	243	– (5) c Lakmal b Gamage	50
A. M. Rahane st Dickwella b Sandakan	1	– (3) c Sandakan b Perera	10
R. G. Sharma c Dickwella b Sandakan	65	– not out	50
R. Ashwin c Perera b Gamage	4		
†W. P. Saha not out	9		
R. A. Jadeja not out	5	– (7) not out	4
Lb 1, nb 7	8	B 1, lb 2, w 1, nb 3	7
1/42 (2) 2/78 (3) 3/361 (1) 4/365 (5) 5/500 (6) 6/519 (7) 7/523 (4) (7 wkts dec, 127.5 overs)	536	1/10 (1) 2/29 (3) 3/106 (4) 4/144 (2) 5/234 (5) (5 wkts dec, 52.2 overs)	246

I. Sharma and Mohammed Shami did not bat.

Lakmal 21.2–2–80–0; Gamage 25.3–7–95–2; Perera 31.1–0–145–1; Sandakan 33.5–1–167–4; de Silva 16–0–48–0. *Second innings*—Lakmal 14–3–60–1; Gamage 12.2–1–48–1; Perera 11–0–54–1; de Silva 5–0–31–1; Sandakan 10–0–50–1.

Sri Lanka

F. D. M. Karunaratne c Saha b Mohammed Shami	0	– c Saha b Jadeja	13
M. D. K. Perera lbw b Jadeja	42		
D. M. de Silva lbw b I. Sharma	1	– retired hurt	119
A. D. Mathews c Saha b Ashwin	111	– (5) c Rahane b Jadeja	1
*L. D. Chandimal c Dhawan b I. Sharma	164	– (6) b Ashwin	36
W. S. R. Samarawickrama c Saha b I. Sharma	33	– (2) c Rahane b Mohammed Shami	5
A. R. S. Silva c Dhawan b Ashwin	0	– not out	74
†D. P. D. N. Dickwella b Ashwin	0	– not out	44
R. A. S. Lakmal c Saha b Mohammed Shami	5	– (4) b Jadeja	0
P. L. S. Gamage lbw b Jadeja	1		
P. A. D. L. R. Sandakan not out	0		
B 4, lb 5, nb 2, p 5	16	B 5, lb 1, nb 1	7
1/0 (1) 2/14 (3) 3/75 (2) 4/256 (4) 5/317 (6) 6/318 (7) 7/322 (8) 8/331 (9) 9/343 (10) 10/373 (5) (135.3 overs)	373	1/14 (2) 2/31 (1) 3/31 (4) 4/35 (5) 5/147 (6) (5 wkts, 103 overs)	299

In the second innings de Silva retired hurt at 205-5.

Mohammed Shami 26–6–85–2; I. Sharma 29.3–7–98–3; Jadeja 45–13–86–2; Ashwin 35–8–90–3. *Second innings*—I. Sharma 13–2–32–0; Mohammed Shami 15–6–50–1; Ashwin 35–3–126–1; Jadeja 38–13–81–3; Vijay 1–0–3–0; Kohli 1–0–1–0.

Umpires: N. J. Llong and J. S. Wilson. Third umpire: A. K. Chaudhary.
Referee: D. C. Boon.

> "The only surprise about his two centuries on a farewell trip to Lord's was that he needed a bridge to cross the river."
> Surrey in 2017, page 587

First one-day international At Dharamsala, December 10, 2017 (day/night). **Sri Lanka won by seven wickets. India 112** (38.2 overs) (M. S. Dhoni 65; R. A. S. Lakmal 4-13); ‡**Sri Lanka 114-3** (20.4 overs) (W. U. Tharanga 49). *MoM:* R. A. S. Lakmal. *ODI debut:* S. S. Iyer (India). *The freshness of the Dharamsala air – a welcome relief after Delhi's suffocating smog – and generous movement off the pitch enabled Sri Lanka to end a 12-match losing streak in ODIs, dating back to their home series against Zimbabwe in July. Suranga Lakmal again ripped the heart out of the Indian batting, taking four wickets as they crashed to 29-7, and finishing with 10–4–13–4. M. S. Dhoni, who hit 52 in boundaries, made sure India passed their lowest ODI total (54 v Sri Lanka in Sharjah in October 2000), but 112 was never enough. Upul Tharanga, recently replaced as Sri Lanka's ODI skipper by Tissara Perera, ignited the chase with a rapid 49. With Virat Kohli given a rest before the South African tour, India were captained by Rohit Sharma.*

Second one-day international At Mohali, December 13, 2017 (day/night). **India won by 141 runs. India 392-4** (50 overs) (R. G. Sharma 208*, S. Dhawan 68, S. S. Iyer 88; N. L. T. C. Perera 3-80); ‡**Sri Lanka 251-8** (50 overs) (A. D. Mathews 111*, D. A. S. Gunaratne 34; Y. S. Chahal 3-60). *MoM:* R. G. Sharma. *ODI debut:* M. S. Washington Sundar (India). *Sharma atoned for India's batting woes in the first match in spectacular style, cracking 13 fours and a dozen sixes in his third ODI double-century (no one else has more than one). He and Shikhar Dhawan had started circumspectly, scoring 33 in the first ten overs, before taking their stand to 115 in 21; Sharma then added 213 in 24 overs with Shreyas Iyer, playing only his second ODI. In all, Sharma faced just 153 balls. Sri Lanka lost both openers inside eight overs and were never in touch; Angelo Mathews was a lone beacon, reaching his second ODI hundred.*

Third one-day international At Visakhapatnam, December 17, 2017 (day/night). **India won by eight wickets. Sri Lanka 215** (44.5 overs) (W. U. Tharanga 95, W. S. R. Samarawickrama 42; K. Yadav 3-42, Y. S. Chahal 3-46); ‡**India 219-2** (32.1 overs) (S. Dhawan 100*, S. S. Iyer 65). *MoM:* K. Yadav. *MoS:* S. Dhawan. *Tharanga made a sublime 95 from 82 balls, but the game changed when he was lured from his crease by Kuldeep Yadav and stumped by Dhoni. From 160-2 after 27 overs, Sri Lanka declined to 215 all out, as wrist-spinners Yadav and Yuzvendra Chahal shared six scalps. A second-wicket stand of 135 between Dhawan and Iyer ensured India took the series 2–1.*

First Twenty20 international At Cuttack, December 20, 2017 (floodlit). **India won by 93 runs. India 180-3** (20 overs) (K. L. Rahul 61, M. S. Dhoni 39*, M. K. Pandey 32*); ‡**Sri Lanka 87** (16 overs) (H. H. Pandya 3-29, Y. S. Chahal 4-23). *MoM:* Y. S. Chahal. *T20I debut:* M. V. T. Fernando (Sri Lanka). *Dhoni and Manish Pandey slammed 61 from the last four overs as Sri Lanka's bowlers struggled with a ball soaked by heavy dew. Their batsmen then collapsed against wrist-spin again: 55-3 in the ninth over became 87 all out, with left-armer Yadav (2-18) backing up the leg-breaks of Chahal as India raced to their biggest win by runs in T20 internationals.*

Second Twenty20 international At Indore, December 22, 2017 (floodlit). **India won by 88 runs. India 260-5** (20 overs) (R. G. Sharma 118, K. L. Rahul 89); ‡**Sri Lanka 172** (17.2 overs) (W. U. Tharanga 47, M. D. K. J. Perera 77; K. Yadav 3-52, Y. S. Chahal 4-52). *MoM:* R. G. Sharma. *India's stand-in captain dominated the match, scorching to his hundred in just 35 balls to equal the T20 international record set less than two months earlier by South Africa's David Miller. Sharma crashed ten sixes and 12 fours, and was the first out after an opening stand of 165 with K. L. Rahul, who went on to hit eight sixes himself. Needing 13 an over, Sri Lanka never had much hope, despite Kusal Perera's 37-ball 77, and a familiar submission to spin saw 145-1 turn into 172 all out.*

Third Twenty20 international At Mumbai, December 24, 2017 (floodlit). **India won by five wickets. Sri Lanka 135-7** (20 overs) (D. A. S. Gunaratne 36); ‡**India 139-5** (19.2 overs) (S. S. Iyer 30, M. K. Pandey 32). *MoM:* J. D. Unadkat. *MoS:* J. D. Unadkat. *T20I debut:* M. S. Washington Sundar (India). *A grassy pitch, with significant bounce, produced the closest match of the series. Sri Lanka dipped to 18-3, stifled by left-arm seamer Jaydev Unadkat, who bowled 15 dot balls; he later picked up the series award for overall figures of 9–28–44–4. Asela Gunaratne ensured a reasonable target, and India were 108-5 when the pacy Dushmantha Chameera (2-22) removed top-scorer Pandey. But Dinesh Karthik and Dhoni sealed the T20 whitewash, which meant India had not lost a series of any kind at home since losing the ODIs to South Africa in October 2015.*

INDIA UNDER-19 v ENGLAND UNDER-19 IN 2016-17

Under-19 one-day internationals (5): India 3, England 1
Under-19 Tests (2): India 0, England 0

As the England seniors' disastrous tour of India dribbled to a close, their Under-19s arrived. And as if trying to cheer Trevor Bayliss & Co before their flight home, Bermuda-born Delray Rawlins pummelled a majestic unbeaten hundred in the first one-dayer, igniting a glorious run of form. While the Under-19s failed to win either series – though, unlike Alastair Cook's side, they did avoid defeat in the Tests – the sustained excellence of Rawlins was a worthy souvenir.

If his accent now bears little of a Bermudian burr after three years at Bede's School in Sussex, Rawlins's batting – all latent power, tap-dancer feet and extravagant follow-throughs – has retained an unquestionably exotic flavour. Most striking was his ability to clear the ropes. Before the series, white-ball captain Matt Fisher played down suggestions that his team could match the seniors' raw power. Rawlins ignored him, crunching five sixes during that debut century – three with brutal pulls reminiscent of fellow left-hander Brian Lara – and added 12 more across the tour as he topped England's batting charts with 549 runs at 78. He had been playing for Bermuda's senior team since he was 15, and had even appeared in their World Cricket League Division 4 tournament as recently as November. Here he was more like a man.

Fisher, too, began on a higher plane. Unsettling the Indians with pace and bounce, he took four wickets in each of the first two matches, but a groin strain meant he played only once more. After hamstring trouble had kept him out of the Yorkshire side throughout 2016, it was hard for him to take.

By the end of the one-dayers, Rawlins had moved from No. 6 to No. 4; he stayed there for the Tests and continued to prosper. In the first, after a marathon partnership between four-day captain Max Holden and George Bartlett, he pushed along the scoring to speed a first-innings declaration that might have brought a win had it not been for Suresh Lokeshwar's rearguard. In the second, he rescued England from deep trouble on the first morning with another sparkling hundred.

India prevailed in the one-day series thanks to greater strength in batting. Their top three made four centuries – including two for Shubman Gill, an impressive opener – to England's one, while the lower order bailed them out when needed. Their spinners were also far superior: slow left-armer Anukul Roy and leg-spinner Rahul Chahar smothered the tourists. Rawlins's left-arm darts took eight wickets, but lacked the reliability of his batting. If he can improve his bowling, he may be the first of this crop to progress to higher honours.

ENGLAND UNDER-19 TOURING SQUAD

*M. D. E. Holden (Middlesex), T. Banton (Somerset), G. A. Bartlett (Somerset), A. P. Beard (Essex), J. M. Blatherwick (Nottinghamshire), H. C. Brook (Yorkshire), H. Brookes (Warwickshire), M. D. Fisher (Yorkshire), A. Godsal (Middlesex), D. Houghton (Lancashire), W. G. Jacks (Surrey),

L. A. Patterson-White (Nottinghamshire), O. J. D. Pope (Surrey), D. M. W. Rawlins (Sussex), L. J. P. Shaw (Somerset), E. D. Woods (Surrey). *Coach:* A. Hurry.

Fisher led the one-day team until his injury, leaving Holden, the four-day captain, in charge. J. Bruce (Middlesex) was originally selected, but withdrew with injury and was replaced by Godsal. Houghton, who was in Mumbai with the Lancashire Academy, was added as cover for Blatherwick.

First Under-19 one-day international At Mumbai (Wankhede), January 30, 2017. **England won by 23 runs. England 256-7** (50 overs) (H. C. Brook 51, D. M. W. Rawlins 107*); ‡**India 233** (42.5 overs) (H. J. Rana 101; M. D. Fisher 4-41). *England were tottering at 98-4, then 126-6, but Delray Rawlins countered with an 88-ball 107*, displaying power beyond his peers. Matt Fisher contributed 26 to a seventh-wicket partnership of 116, then took four wickets as India came up short, despite Himanshu Rana's 101. Earlier, opener Harry Brook had made 51, watched by his father, David, who had applied to Bradford Magistrates Court to have a curfew – handed down because of damage to a caravan – lifted for two weeks.*

Second Under-19 one-day international At Mumbai (Brabourne), February 1, 2017. **India won by 129 runs. India 287-8** (50 overs) (H. J. Rana 58, H. M. Desai 75; M. D. Fisher 4-44, H. Brookes 3-60); ‡**England 158** (33.4 overs) (A. S. Roy 3-34). *On a slower pitch, Fisher still hurried the Indians, but Rana's fourth consecutive score above 50 for India Under-19, and Harvik Desai's 62-ball 75, set up a crushing victory. England's chase seemed buried at 101-6 in the 24th and, though Rawlins (46) again looked fluent, there was no miracle.*

Third Under-19 one-day international At Mumbai (Brabourne), February 3, 2017. **India won by seven wickets.** ‡**England 215** (49 overs) (G. A. Bartlett 55, D. M. W. Rawlins 96; R. D. Chahar 4-33, A. S. Roy 3-39). **India 216-3** (44.1 overs) (S. Gill 138*). *Shubman Gill hit three fours in the first over of the Indian chase and made the rest look easy with a brilliant unbeaten hundred. The spinners had set up victory: Rahul Chahar and Anukul Roy shackled England with a combined 7-72. Only Rawlins scored freely against them, but he reverse-swept to short third man on 96, part of a collapse in which the last seven fell for 44.*

Fourth Under-19 one-day international At Mumbai (Wankhede), February 6, 2017. **India won by 230 runs. India 382-9** (50 overs) (S. Gill 160, P. P. Shaw 105); ‡**England 152** (37.4 overs) (O. J. D. Pope 59; K. L. Nagarkoti 4-31, V. A. Tiwari 3-20). *Gill hit the joint seventh-highest individual innings in Under-19 one-dayers, and Prithvi Shaw his first hundred at this level as India racked up their second-highest total. England waved the series goodbye when the top four departed within nine overs of the reply. Ollie Pope and Will Jacks resisted, but the task was far beyond them, and England slumped to their second-biggest defeat by runs (India beat them by 234 at Colombo in the 2006 Under-19 World Cup). Seamer Kamlesh Nagarkoti took 4-31 to finish his series with an average of 13.*

Fifth Under-19 one-day international At Mumbai (Wankhede), February 8, 2017. **Tied. England 226-9** (50 overs) (A. S. Jamwal 3-40); ‡**India 226** (50 overs) (S. Radhakrishnan 65; H. Brookes 3-30). *India made nine changes, yet still scraped a tie. Chasing 227, they appeared out of it at 137-7, before Ayush Jamwal – who had earlier taken 3-40 with his off-breaks – put on 65 with Yash Thakur. Disciplined seamer Henry Brookes removed them both and, by the time it got down to the last over, bowled by left-arm spinner Liam Patterson-White, India needed six. Last man Heramb Parab hit a four and a single, but Ishan Porel chipped to short cover off the final delivery. England's bowlers had saved their batsmen: six of the top seven made double figures, but none reached 50.*

INDIA v ENGLAND

First Under-19 Test

At Nagpur, February 13–16, 2017. Drawn. Toss: England Under-19.

When off-spinner Sijomon Joseph took six for 62 on the last day to leave a target of 238, India scented victory. But Henry Brookes and Aaron Beard reduced them to 48 for five, and they had to block out instead; wicketkeeper Suresh Lokeshwar shepherded the tail expertly and finished on 92.

The match ended as it had begun, with England on top. From 57 for one, Max Holden and George Bartlett had hit huge hundreds, batting well into the second day for a stand of 321, the joint second-biggest in youth Tests (Gautam Gambhir and Vinayak Mane had put on 391 against England at Chennai in 2000-01). When they were finally separated, Delray Rawlins upped the rate, crashing four sixes in a swift 70 and allowing Holden to declare on 501 for five. Led by a hundred from all-rounder Daryl Ferrario, India kept in touch, before their own declaration on the third evening seemed to change the tenor of the match. The bowlers were now in charge, and England collapsed against spin from 151 for four to 167 all out to set up the tense finale.

Close of play: first day, England Under-19 311-1 (Holden 135, Bartlett 132); second day, India Under-19 156-2 (Saurabh Singh 53, Sidhu 23); third day, England Under-19 23-1 (Brook 15, Brookes 0).

England Under-19

First innings		Second innings	
H. C. Brook c Lokeshwar b Seth	21	– b Bhagat	29
*M. D. E. Holden b Ferrario	170	– lbw b Seth	8
G. A. Bartlett st Lokeshwar b Joseph	179	– (4) c Bhagat b Joseph	68
D. M. W. Rawlins not out	70	– (5) lbw b Joseph	15
†O. J. D. Pope c Joseph b Seth	18	– (6) c Joseph b Ferrario	26
W. G. Jacks c Ferrario b Sidhu	9	– (8) b Joseph	0
E. D. Woods not out	1	– not out	5
H. Brookes (did not bat)		– (3) c Saurabh Singh b Joseph	3
A. P. Beard (did not bat)		– c Goswami b Joseph	1
L. A. Patterson-White (did not bat)		– c Goswami b Joseph	3
A. Godsal (did not bat)		– st Lokeshwar b Ferrario	0
B 10, lb 6, w 10, nb 7	33	B 2, lb 6, nb 1	9
1/57 (1) 2/378 (3) 3/418 (2) 4/479 (5) 5/490 (6) (5 wkts dec, 131.1 overs)	501	1/23 (2) 2/28 (3) 3/48 (1) 4/78 (5) 5/151 (4) 6/157 (6) 7/158 (8) 8/162 (9) 9/166 (10) 10/167 (11) (53 overs)	167

Seth 26–6–85–2; Bhagat 24–2–75–0; Panwar 14–0–71–0; Joseph 22–3–84–1; Ferrario 25–7–87–1; Saurabh Singh 9–1–41–0; Sidhu 11.1–0–42–1. *Second innings*—Seth 9–5–17–1; Bhagat 9–4–29–1; Ferrario 8–3–17–2; Panwar 7–1–34–0; Joseph 20–5–62–6.

India Under-19

First innings		Second innings	
A. Goswami c Bartlett b Patterson-White	66	– c Brook b Brookes	4
R. S. Kunnummal c Woods b Beard	13	– b Beard	4
Saurabh Singh lbw b Brookes	62	– (5) b Brookes	5
*J. Sidhu lbw b Patterson-White	33	– c Pope b Beard	1
R. Thakur lbw b Woods	31	– (3) st Pope b Brookes	8
D. S. Ferrario b Brookes	117	– c Pope b Godsal	37
†S. Lokeshwar b Woods	22	– not out	92
K. K. Seth lbw b Rawlins	4	– (9) c Godsal b Holden	18
S. Joseph not out	62	– (8) lbw b Patterson-White	12
V. Panwar not out	4	– not out	0
B 8, lb 9	17	B 7, w 1	8
1/23 (2) 2/120 (1) 3/176 (4) 4/176 (3) 5/263 (5) 6/323 (7) 7/334 (8) 8/386 (6) (8 wkts dec, 122 overs)	431	1/4 (1) 2/16 (3) 3/16 (2) 4/20 (4) 5/48 (5) 6/61 (6) 7/100 (8) 8/161 (9) (8 wkts, 49 overs)	189

R. Bhagat did not bat.

Beard 12–1–65–1; Brookes 24–9–75–2; Godsal 13–2–46–0; Patterson-White 37–4–104–2; Rawlins 14–4–48–1; Holden 8–0–21–0; Woods 14–2–55–2. *Second innings*—Brookes 14–3–56–3; Beard 6–2–24–2; Patterson-White 17–4–53–1; Godsal 4–0–16–1; Woods 2–1–9–0; Rawlins 2–0–7–0; Holden 4–1–17–1.

Umpires: U. V. Gandhe and N. Pandit.
Referee: N. R. Goel.

INDIA v ENGLAND

Second Under-19 Test

At Nagpur, February 21–24, 2017. Drawn. Toss: England Under-19.

Rawlins showed he could dig in as well as dash, rescuing England from one for three with a 280-ball 140. By the time he was dismissed on the second morning, the tourists had reached 273 for six, and half-centuries from Will Jacks and Henry Brookes hauled them to a competitive 375. In reply, Saurabh Singh dropped anchor, facing 292 balls for 109, while others chipped in to scrape a lead. With memories of a second-innings collapse still fresh, England were wobbling on 34 for two by the third-day close, before Bartlett, who hit another fifty to finish the Test series as highest run-scorer, and Rawlins eased concerns with a stand of 121. Left-arm spinner Harsh Tyagi prised out four, and was accurate throughout – he bowled 57 overs in the match for only 127 runs – but couldn't engineer a tilt at victory.

Close of play: first day, England Under-19 243-5 (Rawlins 124, Jacks 66); second day, India Under-19 153-3 (Saurabh Singh 43, Seth 0); third day, England Under-19 34-2 (Houghton 0, Bartlett 0).

England Under-19

First innings		Second innings	
H. C. Brook lbw b Bhagat	1	– c Tyagi b Ferrario	16
*M. D. E. Holden c Akre b Seth	0	– b Tyagi	13
G. A. Bartlett b Bhagat	0	– (4) b Tyagi	76
D. M. W. Rawlins b Roy	140	– (5) c Akre b Roy	49
†O. J. D. Pope c Ferrario b Tyagi	42	– (6) c Akre b Tyagi	0
E. D. Woods c Lokeshwar b Ferrario	6	– (7) c Akre b Tyagi	16
W. G. Jacks b Ferrario	77	– (8) c Goswami b Saurabh Singh	19
A. P. Beard lbw b Roy	27	– (9) not out	34
L. A. Patterson-White c Lokeshwar b Ferrario	0	– (10) run out	8
H. Brookes not out	60	– (11) c Lokeshwar b Akre	0
D. Houghton c Lokeshwar b Bhagat	12	– (3) retired ill	0
B 5, lb 5	10	B 12, lb 10, w 1, nb 1	24
1/1 (1) 2/1 (3) 3/1 (2) 4/99 (5) 5/112 (6) 6/273 (4) 7/279 (7) 8/279 (9) 9/330 (8) 10/375 (11) (135.5 overs)	375	1/30 (2) 2/30 (1) 3/155 (5) 4/162 (6) 5/193 (4) 6/194 (7) 7/244 (8) 8/253 (10) 9/255 (11) (82 overs)	255

In the second innings Houghton retired ill at 34-2.

Seth 26–4–80–1; Bhagat 19.5–6–58–3; Tyagi 32–11–60–1; Ferrario 26–1–90–3; Roy 27–4–67–2; U. R. Singh 1–0–5–0; Sidhu 3–2–3–0; Saurabh Singh 1–0–2–0. *Second innings*—Seth 11–2–29–0; Bhagat 5–0–19–0; Ferrario 8–0–41–1; Tyagi 25–7–67–4; Roy 20–9–42–1; Sidhu 3–1–8–0; Saurabh Singh 5–0–9–1; U. R. Singh 3–0–15–0; Goswami 1–0–2–0; Akre 1–0–1–1.

India Under-19

Batsman	Runs
A. Goswami b Beard	58
U. R. Singh c Brook b Patterson-White	19
Saurabh Singh c Brookes b Woods	109
*J. Sidhu c Holden b Woods	17
K. K. Seth lbw b Brookes	12
D. S. Ferrario b Beard	55
S. N. Akre b Holden	54
†S. Lokeshwar c Holden b Patterson-White	4
A. S. Roy not out	17
R. Bhagat c Bartlett b Holden	13
B 7, lb 18, nb 5	30
1/68 (2) 2/104 (1) 3/146 (4) 4/166 (5) 5/263 (6) 6/337 (3) 7/355 (7) 8/363 (8) 9/388 (10) (9 wkts dec, 120.1 overs)	388

H. Tyagi did not bat.

Beard 21–5–56–2; Brookes 20–5–53–1; Houghton 7–0–41–0; Patterson-White 25–0–83–2; Woods 27–9–61–2; Rawlins 2–0–6–0; Holden 18.1–2–63–2.

Umpires: A. D. Deshmukh and U. V. Gandhe.
Referee: S. Verma.

DOMESTIC CRICKET IN INDIA IN 2016-17

R. MOHAN

Gujarat won their first Ranji Trophy, a year after lifting the 50-over competition, and two years after the state T20 title. After reaching the final for only the second time – and the first since 1950-51 – they took a first-innings lead of 100 over defending champions Mumbai. That would have been enough to secure the title had they drawn but, after Mumbai's strong second innings, captain Parthiv Patel propelled Gujarat to the highest successful chase in a Ranji final, scoring 143 out of 313. Mumbai had won 41 of their 46 finals, and claimed 11 titles since their last defeat, by Kapil Dev's Haryana in 1990-91.

Controversially, the entire tournament was staged at neutral venues, to avoid pitches prepared to suit the hosts. With no home games, most matches were played in front of empty stands with little atmosphere, and the experiment was dropped for 2017-18. Players were also riled by poor standards of umpiring. And there was a fierce argument about whether to reschedule two games abandoned because of Delhi's smog.

But batsmen thrived. There were 24 double-hundreds in the Ranji season, equalling the previous two combined (there were nine extra matches, with a new team, Chhattisgarh, joining the competition). Five players went on to triple-centuries, two of them – Maharashtra's Swapnil Gugale and Delhi's Rishabh Pant – in a single game (the only previous instance of two in one first-class match had been in the same innings). Gugale and Ankit Bawne shared an undefeated stand of 594 in that fixture, the second-highest in all first-class cricket; they might have beaten the 624 added by Sri Lanka's Kumar Sangakkara and Mahela Jayawardene against South Africa in a 2006 Test, but stand-in captain Gugale, unaware they were 30 short of the world record, called a halt on the second evening to give his bowlers five overs before the close. He realised the situation only on returning to the dressing-room to find 100 missed calls and 200 messages.

Both Gujarat openers, Samit Gohel and Priyank Panchal, also scored triple-centuries, and Panchal finished with 1,310 runs, the third-highest total in any Ranji tournament. Cheteshwar Pujara became the first man to score 2,000 first-class runs in an Indian season – with a purple patch running from the Duleep Trophy in September to the Tests against Australia in March.

In the Duleep final, Pujara made 256 not out to help **India Blue** to a 355-run win over India Red. Citing the need to try out the pink ball in day/night cricket, the BCCI had dropped the five zonal teams from the Duleep Trophy, replacing them with three combined teams chosen by the national selectors. It was unclear why the zonal teams could not have carried out the same task. There were mixed reviews of the pink ball: batsmen said they were comfortable enough sighting it, even if they thought it moved more, while bowlers claimed it stayed in shape, precluding reverse swing.

After missing most of the Ranji Trophy while on international duty, Pujara clocked up another century for **Rest of India** against champions Gujarat in the Irani Cup match; his studious 116 anchored the fourth innings while Wriddhaman Saha was making a lively 203 in a match-winning stand of 313.

Tamil Nadu won the Vijay Hazare Trophy and completed a 50-over double by adding the Deodhar Trophy nine days later. The Deodhar had also been an interzonal competition until the previous season, when it was revamped as a mini-tournament for two combined teams plus the Vijay Hazare winners. The zonal sides appeared only in the Twenty20 Syed Mushtaq Ali Trophy, whose old format – a series of leagues for state teams leading to a final – was replaced by five preliminary interstate groups followed by an interzonal league, with five zonal teams selected after the state games. **East Zone** were the eventual winners. The Indian board said the new format would leave space for franchise competitions within states, like the widely televised Tamil Nadu Premier League, which threw the spotlight on unseen talents.

FIRST-CLASS AVERAGES IN 2016-17

BATTING (700 runs, average 40.00)

		M	*I*	*NO*	*R*	*HS*	*100*	*Avge*	*Ct/St*
1	C. A. Pujara (*Ind Bl/Saur'tra/Rest/Ind*)	17	29	4	2,064	256*	7	82.56	12
2	P. K. Panchal (*Gujarat/India A*)	12	20	2	1,449	314*	5	80.50	6
3	†R. R. Pant (*Delhi/India A*)	9	13	0	993	308	4	76.38	25/1
4	†G. Rahul Singh (*Services*)	9	15	2	945	182	2	72.69	4
5	D. Hooda (*Baroda*)	8	13	2	789	293*	3	71.72	10
6	V. Kohli (*India*)	12	21	2	1,252	235	4	65.89	12
7	N. Saini (*Haryana*)	10	18	2	989	227	4	61.81	29/1
8	K. M. Gandhi (*Tamil Nadu*)	10	15	2	785	202	3	60.38	5
9	†Yuvraj Singh (*India Red/Punjab*)	8	12	0	724	260	2	60.33	6
10	I. R. Jaggi (*Jharkhand*)	10	16	1	890	173	4	59.33	16
11	K. K. Nair (*Karnataka/Rest/India*)	11	15	2	761	303*	2	58.53	10
12	P. Chopra (*Himachal Pradesh*)	9	17	0	978	237	3	57.52	7
13	†A. Mukund (*Ind Red/Tamil N/Rest/Ind*)	15	22	2	1,140	169	5	57.00	7
14	A. R. Bawne (*Maharashtra/India A*)	9	14	1	712	258*	2	54.76	3
15	†S. K. Kamat (*Goa*)	9	17	1	876	304*	3	54.75	11
16	S. S. Iyer (*Mumbai/India A*)	11	19	2	927	202*	3	54.52	5
17	K. L. Rahul (*Karnataka/India*)	11	19	1	971	199	2	53.94	7
18	S. B. Gohel (*Gujarat*)	11	19	2	915	359*	2	53.82	15
	K. D. Karthik (*Tamil Nadu*)	13	19	2	915	163	1	53.82	34/1
20	†I. P. Kishan (*Jharkhand/India A*)	11	17	2	803	273	3	53.53	18/3
21	S. Khajuria (*Jammu & Kashmir*)	9	17	2	777	111	2	51.80	3
22	†P. A. Patel (*India Green/Gujarat/India*)	14	24	2	1,110	143	2	50.45	48/4
23	S. P. Jackson (*India Blue/Saurashtra*)	11	19	2	837	134	4	49.23	6/1
24	M. C. Juneja (*Gujarat*)	11	18	1	818	201*	1	48.11	6
25	A. N. Khare (*Chhattisgarh*)	9	17	2	703	143	3	46.86	9
26	I. Dev Singh (*Jammu & Kashmir*)	9	16	1	702	129*	2	46.80	12/1
	R. Samarth (*Karnataka*)	9	17	2	702	235	1	46.80	14
28	†S. S. Tiwary (*India Green/Jharkhand*)	12	20	3	720	91	0	42.35	15
29	M. A. Agarwal (*India Blue/Karnataka*)	10	18	1	704	161	1	41.41	6

BOWLING (33 wickets)

		Style	*O*	*M*	*R*	*W*	*BB*	*5I*	*Avge*
1	A. A. Sanklecha (*Maharashtra*)	RFM	259	65	696	43	8-73	5	16.18
2	M. Siraj (*Hyderabad/Rest*)	RFM	301.3	84	864	43	5-52	1	20.09
3	M. Ravi Kiran (*Hyderabad*)	RM	275.1	89	703	34	4-32	0	20.67
4	K. Vignesh (*Tamil Nadu*)	RFM	295	71	818	37	5-23	2	22.10
5	R. A. Jadeja (*India Blue/India*)	SLA	769.3	194	1,792	81	7-48	6	22.12
6	C. V. Milind (*Hyderabad*)	LFM	271.4	70	776	35	5-28	2	22.17
7	P. K. Rao (*Chhattisgarh*)	RM	304.4	70	823	37	5-44	3	22.24
8	R. R. Singh (*Goa*)	RM	233.3	51	758	34	7-42	2	22.29
9	Y. S. Chahal (*Haryana*)	LB	285	78	746	33	6-44	2	22.60
10	Pankaj Singh (*Ind Bl/Raj'than/Rest*)	RFM	354.3	85	1,189	51	5-39	2	23.31
11	S. Kaul (*Punjab/Rest*)	RM	337.4	55	1,018	43	6-27	4	23.67
12	K. V. Sharma (*India Blue/Railways*)	LB	282.1	43	1,001	41	5-71	2	24.41
13	A. B. Dinda (*Ind Gr/Bengal/India A*)	RFM	338	66	1,103	45	6-45	5	24.51
14	S. B. Jakati (*Goa*)	SLA	344	68	1,031	41	8-53	2	25.14
15	R. Ashwin (*India*)	OB	738.2	141	2,073	82	7-59	7	25.28
16	R. Shreyas Gopal (*Ind Gr/Karnataka*)	LB	228.2	23	937	37	5-75	3	25.32
17	I. C. Pandey (*Ind Red/Madhya Prad*)	RFM	309.2	79	857	33	8-102	2	25.96
18	Parvez Rasool (*Ind Blue/Jammu & K*)	OB	406.2	98	1,097	41	5-89	2	26.75
19	B. A. Bhatt (*Andhra*)	SLA	415.1	92	1,030	38	6-36	2	27.10
20	A. A. Crist (*Tamil Nadu*)	RM	326.3	79	966	35	6-31	1	27.60
21	S. Nadeem (*Jharkhand/Rest/India A*)	SLA	584	110	1,688	61	7-74	4	27.67
22	K. Yadav (*Ind Red/Uttar P/Rest/Ind*)	SLW	436	50	1,609	56	6-79	3	28.73

DULEEP TROPHY IN 2016-17

At Greater Noida, August 23–26, 2016 (day/night). **India Red won by 219 runs. ‡India Red 161 and 486** (A. Mukund 169, S. D. Chatterjee 114; R. Shreyas Gopal 5-123); **India Green 151** (N. B. Singh 6-53) **and 277** (K. Yadav 6-88). *India Red 6pts. This was the first first-class match in India with the pink ball under floodlights. Only Abhinav Mukund (77) held firm on the opening day, after India Red slid to 60-6; in the second innings, he built on a ten-run lead by adding 240 for the second wicket with Sudip Chatterjee. Left-arm wrist-spinner Kuldeep Yadav took 9-120 in all.*

At Greater Noida, August 29–September 1, 2016 (day/night). **Drawn. India Blue 285-5 v ‡India Red.** *India Blue 1pt, India Red 1pt. Rain meant a draw, which guaranteed Red's place in the final.*

At Greater Noida, September 4–7, 2016 (day/night). **Drawn. ‡India Blue 707** (M. A. Agarwal 161, C. A. Pujara 166, S. P. Jackson 105; R. Shreyas Gopal 5-173) **and 298; India Green 237 and 179-4.** *India Blue 3pts, India Green 1pt. Blue openers Mayank Agarwal and Gautam Gambhir (90) put on 212; later, No. 7 Sheldon Jackson lifted the total past 700, hitting five sixes in his 114-ball 105. Agarwal and Gambhir completed a second century opening stand on the final day, when Green's Pragyan Ojha was stretchered off after being struck on the head fielding at mid-on.*

Final At Greater Noida, September 10–14, 2016 (day/night). **India Blue won by 355 runs. ‡India Blue 693-6 dec** (C. A. Pujara 256*, S. P. Jackson 134) **and 179-5 dec; India Red 356** (R. A. Jadeja 5-95) **and 161** (R. A. Jadeja 5-76). *Blue captain Gambhir scored 94, his fourth successive fifty. Cheteshwar Pujara passed 10,000 first-class runs on the way to his tenth double-century, adding 243 with Jackson for the fifth wicket. Ravindra Jadeja grabbed 10-171 to secure a massive win.*

RANJI TROPHY IN 2016-17

Group A	Played	Won	Lost	Drawn	1st-inns points	Bonus points	Points	NRR
MUMBAI	8	3	0	5	11	1	30	0.02
GUJARAT	8	2	0	6*	14	0	26	0.36
TAMIL NADU	8	2	1	5	13	1	26	0.16
Punjab	8	2	1	5	9	0	21	0.10
Bengal	8	2	1	5*	9	0	21	–0.23
Madhya Pradesh	8	2	1	5	7	1	20	0.02
Uttar Pradesh	8	1	4	3	7	0	13	–0.12
Baroda	8	1	3	4	4	0	10	–0.00
Railways	8	1	5	2	4	0	10	–0.36

Group B	Played	Won	Lost	Drawn	1st-inns points	Bonus points	Points	NRR
JHARKHAND	8	5	0	3	7	2	39	0.39
KARNATAKA	8	5	1	2	4	3	37	0.27
ODISHA	8	2	1	5	9	1	22	–0.05
Delhi	8	2	2	4	8	1	21	0.57
Maharashtra	8	2	3	3	7	2	21	–0.05
Vidarbha	8	2	2	4	8	0	20	–0.02
Saurashtra	8	2	4	2	6	0	18	0.10
Rajasthan	8	1	4	3	5	1	12	–0.63
Assam	8	1	5	2	2	0	8	–0.62

Group C	Played	Won	Lost	Drawn	1st-inns points	Bonus points	Points	NRR
HYDERABAD	9	4	1	4*	6	1	31	–0.11
HARYANA	9	3	1	5	13	0	31	0.21
Andhra	9	3	1	5	9	1	28	0.11
Himachal Pradesh	9	3	0	6	8	0	26	0.66
Kerala	9	1	1	7	19	0	25	0.20
Goa	9	2	3	4	6	0	18	–0.33
Services	9	1	2	6	10	0	16	–0.17
Jammu & Kashmir	9	1	3	5	9	0	15	–0.38
Chhattisgarh	9	1	4	4	8	0	14	–0.01
Tripura	9	1	4	4*	8	0	14	–0.19

* *Includes one abandoned match.*

Outright win = 6pts; bonus for winning by an innings or ten wickets = 1pt; lead on first innings in a drawn match = 3pts; deficit on first innings in a drawn match = 1pt; no decision on first innings = 1pt; abandoned = 1pt. Teams tied on points were ranked on most wins, and then on net run-rate. The top three from Groups A and B, and the top two from Group C, advanced to the quarter-finals.

In 2017-18, the format was changed to four groups of seven, with two from each group entering the quarter-finals.

Group A

At Jaipur (Sawai Mansingh), October 6–9, 2016. **Drawn. Baroda 544-8 dec** (A. A. Waghmode 142, D. Hooda 118); **‡Gujarat 555-4** (M. C. Juneja 201*, A. R. Patel 110*). *Baroda 1pt, Gujarat 3pts. Gujarat's fifth wicket put on 378* in all; Manprit Juneja, who equalled his previous best score, added 140* with Rujul Bhatt (58*) before he retired hurt, and 238* with Akshar Patel.*

At Hyderabad (Uppal), October 6–9, 2016. **Madhya Pradesh won by an innings and 64 runs. ‡Madhya Pradesh 465** (H. S. Bhatia 216*); **Uttar Pradesh 176 and 225** (C. R. Sakure 6-40). *Madhya Pradesh 7pts. Harpreet Bhatia scored his first double-hundred.*

At Rohtak, October 6–8, 2016. **Mumbai won by two wickets. Tamil Nadu 87 and 185** (D. S. Kulkarni 6-47); **‡Mumbai 176** (K. Vignesh 5-41) **and 97-8.** *Mumbai 6pts. Mumbai began their title defence by winning in two and a half days, with Dhawal Kulkarni collecting 10-78. Tamil Nadu's debutant seamer Krishnamoorthy Vignesh claimed 9-70, reducing Mumbai to 35-5 chasing 97.*

At Delhi (Palam), October 6–9, 2016. **Drawn. Railways 331** (S. S. Shukla 128; S. Kaul 5-68) **and 245-7 dec; ‡Punjab 215 and 170-3.** *Punjab 1pt, Railways 3pts.*

At Delhi (Palam), October 13–16, 2016. **Drawn. ‡Baroda 305 and 383-5 dec** (K. H. Devdhar 145, D. Hooda 100*); **Mumbai 323** (A. A. Herwadkar 106) **and 224-5.** *Baroda 1pt, Mumbai 3pts.*

At Jaipur (Sawai Mansingh), October 13–16, 2016. **Drawn. ‡Bengal 466** (A. R. Easwaran 142, M. K. Tiwary 110; K. Yadav 5-115) **and 274-6 dec** (A. R. Easwaran 110*, S. P. Goswami 100); **Uttar Pradesh 410** (U. A. Sharma 136) **and 70-0.** *Bengal 3pts, Uttar Pradesh 1pt. Bengal opener Abhimanyu Easwaran scored a century in each innings.*

At Rohtak, October 13–16, 2016. **Punjab won by 126 runs. Punjab 378** (Yuvraj Singh 177, Gurkeerat Singh 103; I. C. Pandey 8-102) **and 175-9 dec; ‡Madhya Pradesh 247** (M. S. Gony 6-36) **and 180.** *Punjab 6pts. The first day brought 347-3, the next 215-12. Seamers Ishwar Pandey (11-127) and Manpreet Gony (10-77) enjoyed themselves.*

At Bilaspur, October 13–16, 2016. **Tamil Nadu won by 174 runs. Tamil Nadu 121 and 452-8 dec** (A. Mukund 100, K. D. Karthik 163); **‡Railways 173 and 226** (S. P. Wakaskar 120). *Tamil Nadu 6pts. Dinesh Karthik hit 163 in 145 balls.*

At Bilaspur, October 20–23, 2016. **Bengal won by 115 runs. Bengal 404** (S. S. Mondal 135) **and 226** (S. Kaul 6-57); **‡Punjab 271** (A. B. Dinda 5-58, A. S. Kuila 5-76) **and 244.** *Bengal 6pts.*

At Rohtak, October 20–23, 2016. **Gujarat won by 294 runs. Gujarat 187** (D. Bansal 6-46) **and 437-7 dec** (P. K. Panchal 101); **‡Railways 124** (M. B. Patel 5-35) **and 206.** *Gujarat 6pts.*

At Naya Raipur, October 20–23, 2016. **Drawn. ‡Madhya Pradesh 445** (R. M. Patidar 106); **Mumbai 568-7 dec** (A. A. Herwadkar 153, S. D. Lad 100*, A. M. Nayar 103*). *Madhya Pradesh 1pt, Mumbai 3pts. The first match at the Shaheed Veer Narayan Singh Stadium, in the new Ranji state of Chhattisgarh (formerly part of Madhya Pradesh); Chhattisgarh were not themselves playing because of the neutral venue policy. Siddhesh Lad and Abhishek Nayar added 200* for Mumbai's eighth wicket.*

At Dharamsala, October 20–23, 2016. **Drawn. ‡Uttar Pradesh 524** (Samarth Singh 187) **and 114-1 dec; Tamil Nadu 480** (A. Mukund 154, R. N. B. Indrajith 127*). *Tamil Nadu 1pt, Uttar Pradesh 3pts.*

At Delhi (Feroz Shah Kotla), October 27–30, 2016. **Drawn. ‡Baroda 529** (D. Hooda 293*) **and 37-0; Punjab 670** (M. Vohra 224, Yuvraj Singh 260). *Baroda 1pt, Punjab 3pts. Deepak Hooda, who advanced from his third century in successive games to a maiden double, was stranded seven short of 300 after batting two minutes short of ten hours. Manan Vohra also scored his first double-hundred, and Yuvraj Singh his fourth and highest; they added 343 for Punjab's third wicket.*

At Dharamsala, October 27–30, 2016. **Bengal won by 43 runs. Bengal 205 and 214**; **‡Railways 105** (A. B. Dinda 5-45) **and 271** (A. B. Dinda 5-67). *Bengal 6pts. Railways wicketkeeper Mahesh Rawat held nine catches in the match.*

At Delhi (Palam), October 27–30, 2016. **Gujarat won by 132 runs. ‡Gujarat 347** (Imtiyaz Ahmed 5-73) **and 201** (K. Yadav 6-79); **Uttar Pradesh 241 and 175** (H. P. Patel 7-72). *Gujarat 6pts.*

At Cuttack (Dhaneswar Rath), October 27–30, 2016. **Drawn. Tamil Nadu 555-7 dec** (K. M. Gandhi 157, N. Jagadeesan 123*); **‡Madhya Pradesh 273 and 222-5.** *Madhya Pradesh 1pt, Tamil Nadu 3pts. Tamil Nadu lost both openers for ducks, but were rescued by maiden centuries from Kaushik Gandhi and Narayan Jagadeesan (on debut).*

At Naya Raipur, November 5–7, 2016. **Tamil Nadu won by an innings and 44 runs. Baroda 93** (K. Vignesh 5-23) **and 200**; **‡Tamil Nadu 337** (A. Mukund 100). *Tamil Nadu 7pts.*

At Delhi (Feroz Shah Kotla), November 5–8, 2016. **Bengal v Gujarat. Abandoned.** *Bengal 1pt, Gujarat 1pt. The game was finally abandoned after two days because of poor visibility caused by air pollution; Bengal players left the ground wearing masks. Two matches the following week were moved to other cities. The games were initially rescheduled for mid-December, after the rest of the group matches, but cancelled after Mumbai and Tamil Nadu argued smog should not be treated differently from rain, and playing after rival teams had completed the programme was an unfair advantage.*

At Mysore (Srikantdatta Narasimha Rao Wadeyar), November 5–8, 2016. **Mumbai won by ten wickets. ‡Mumbai 345** (S. A. Yadav 110; K. V. Sharma 5-81) **and 24-0; Railways 160** (V. D. Gohil 5-64) **and 208** (T. U. Deshpande 5-35). *Mumbai 7pts.*

At Hyderabad (Uppal), November 5–8, 2016. **Punjab won by seven wickets. ‡Uttar Pradesh 335** (S. Sharma 5-85) **and 95** (S. Kaul 6-27); **Punjab 319 and 112-3.** *Punjab 6pts.*

At Nagpur (VCA Academy), November 13–16, 2016. **Railways won by seven wickets. ‡Baroda 183** (A. B. Yadav 5-50) **and 239**; **Railways 310** (S. P. Wakaskar 104) **and 113-3.** *Railways 6pts.*

At Rajkot (Madhavrao Scindia), November 13–16, 2016. **Drawn. ‡Bengal 337** (S. D. Chatterjee 100) **and 196-9; Tamil Nadu 354** (S. S. Ghosh 5-123). *Bengal 1pt, Tamil Nadu 3pts.*

At Nagothane, November 13–16, 2016. **Drawn. ‡Gujarat 302 and 324-6 dec** (S. B. Gohel 104, P. A. Patel 139*); **Madhya Pradesh 252 and 176-5** (H. S. Bhatia 103*). *Gujarat 3pts, Madhya Pradesh 1pt.*

At Mysore (Srikantdatta Narasimha Rao Wadeyar), November 13–16, 2016. **Mumbai won by 121 runs. ‡Mumbai 233 and 286**; **Uttar Pradesh 225 and 173** (A. S. Dhumal 5-53). *Mumbai 6pts. Umpire Virender Sharma stood at both ends on the second day because Sam Nogajski, an Australian officiating in his first match in India, had food poisoning. The reserve umpire was not on the BCCI panel, so stood at square leg; a fully authorised umpire, P. Jaipla, arrived for the final two days.*

At Rohtak, November 21–22, 2016. **Baroda won by 21 runs. Baroda 97** (A. B. Dinda 6-45) **and 133** (Mukesh Kumar 5-45); **‡Bengal 76** (A. A. Sheth 7-36) **and 133.** *Baroda 6pts. Baroda's only win of the season came in two days; 23 wickets fell on the first, 17 on the second, all to seamers. Atit Sheth (10-94) was the fourth to take ten or more at Rohtak in four matches. Bengal captain Manoj Tiwary, the top-scorer with 39, complained about green patches and inconsistent bounce.*

At Hubli, November 21–24, 2016. **Drawn. ‡Gujarat 437** (P. K. Panchal 232; V. V. Dabholkar 6-118) **and 82-0; Mumbai 422** (S. S. Iyer 194; J. J. Bumrah 6-71). *Gujarat 3pts, Mumbai 1pt. Priyank Panchal scored a maiden double-hundred.*

At Delhi (Feroz Shah Kotla), November 21–24, 2016. **Drawn. ‡Railways 371** (N. S. Bhille 102; A. N. Sharma 6-108) **and 150-1; Madhya Pradesh 510-8 dec** (D. Bundela 188, S. S. Sharma 119). *Madhya Pradesh 3pts, Railways 1pt. Devendra Bundela and Shubham Sharma put on 242 for Madhya Pradesh's sixth wicket.*

At Nagpur (VCA Academy), November 21–24, 2016. **Drawn. ‡Punjab 284 and 375-5 dec** (Mandeep Singh 128); **Tamil Nadu 354** (K. M. Gandhi 164) **and 103-1.** *Punjab 1pt, Tamil Nadu 3pts.*

At Dharamsala, November 29–December 2, 2016. **Madhya Pradesh won by 232 runs. Madhya Pradesh 217** (B. A. Pathan 5-48) **and 293**; **‡Baroda 164** (I. C. Pandey 5-29) **and 114** (C. R. Sakure 5-17). *Madhya Pradesh 6pts. This was Madhya Pradesh captain Bundela's 137th Ranji match, beating the competition record of Amol Muzumdar.*

At Nagpur (VCA Academy), November 29–December 2, 2016. **Drawn. Bengal 99** (S. N. Thakur 6-31) **and 437** (S. D. Chatterjee 130, M. K. Tiwary 169; D. S. Kulkarni 5-110); **‡Mumbai 229** (A. B. Dinda 5-88) **and 203-6.** *Bengal 1pt, Mumbai 3pts. Chatterjee and Tiwary added 271 for Bengal's fourth wicket, and Ashok Dinda took five for the fifth time in this tournament, but first-innings points saw Mumbai into the knockout stage with a round to spare.*

At Belagavi, November 29–December 2, 2016. **Drawn. Gujarat 624-6 dec** (P. K. Panchal 314*); **‡Punjab 247 and 241-2** (Jiwanjot Singh 101*). *Gujarat 3pts, Punjab 1pt. This was the first match played at the Karnataka SCA Stadium in Belagavi. Eight days after his 232 against Mumbai, Panchal reached Gujarat's first triple-hundred, batting for four minutes short of 13 hours.*

At Rajkot (Khandheri), November 29–December 2, 2016. **Uttar Pradesh won by 220 runs. Uttar Pradesh 259 and 330** (S. Chaudhary 124; K. V. Sharma 5-71); **‡Railways 214** (Imtiyaz Ahmed 5-34) **and 155.** *Uttar Pradesh 6pts.*

At Nasik, December 7–10, 2016. **Drawn. Uttar Pradesh 481** (K. Yadav 117, Saurabh Kumar 105) **and 417-3** (S. Chaudhary 124, A. D. Nath 107*); **‡Baroda 458** (K. H. Devdhar 157). *Baroda 1pt, Uttar Pradesh 3pts. All three innings passed 400, with a total 1,356 for 23 wickets. Kuldeep Yadav and Saurabh Kumar scored maiden centuries, adding 192 for Uttar Pradesh's eighth wicket.*

At Delhi (Palam), December 7–10, 2016. **Drawn. ‡Bengal 475-9 dec** (S. P. Goswami 225*) **and 261-2; Madhya Pradesh 370** (S. S. Ghosh 5-94). *Bengal 3pts, Madhya Pradesh 1pt. Shreevats Goswami, with a maiden double-century, and Sayan Ghosh (20*) put on 119* for the last wicket.*

At Belagavi, December 7–10, 2016. **Drawn. ‡Gujarat 307** (P. K. Panchal 113); **Tamil Nadu 580-6 dec** (K. M. Gandhi 202, V. Shankar 102*). *Gujarat 1pt, Tamil Nadu 3pts. Panchal became the first Gujarat batsman to reach 1,000 runs in a Ranji season, in his seventh match (11 innings). Gandhi batted 12 hours 50 minutes for a maiden double-hundred in an innings where Vijay Shankar, still having trouble with his leg after knee surgery, retired hurt twice – once on 68, and again after completing his century. The draw was enough for both teams to qualify for the knockouts.*

At Rajkot (Khandheri), December 7–10, 2016. **Drawn. ‡Punjab 468** (M. Sidana 115); **Mumbai 185 and 227-4** (S. S. Iyer 123). *Mumbai 1pt, Punjab 3pts. Pursuing their faint hope of reaching the quarter-finals, Punjab took a 283-run lead, but could not bowl out Mumbai a second time.*

Group B

At Vadodara (Reliance), October 6–9, 2016. **Delhi won by an innings and 83 runs. Assam 193 and 313** (M. Sharma 5-108); **‡Delhi 589-8 dec** (N. Rana 146, R. R. Pant 146, P. Sangwan 100*; A. N. Ahmed 5-106). *Delhi 7pts. Rishabh Pant, who had just turned 19, added 220 for Delhi's fourth wicket with Nitish Rana. He and Pradeep Sangwan hit maiden centuries; Pant's 146 came off 124 balls, with eight sixes, while No. 9 Sangwan scored 100* in 125, with four.*

At Delhi (Karnail Singh), October 6–9, 2016. **Jharkhand won by six wickets. Maharashtra 210 and 188**; **‡Jharkhand 306** (Kaushal Singh 130; A. A. Sanklecha 5-71) **and 93-4.** *Jharkhand 6pts.*

At Visakhapatnam (Rajasekhara Reddy), October 6–9, 2016. **Drawn. ‡Odisha 150 and 274-9 dec; Vidarbha 272-6 dec.** *Odisha 1pt, Vidarbha 3pts.*

At Vizianagram (Dr P. V. G. Raju), October 6–9, 2016. **Drawn. Saurashtra 430** (J. N. Shah 193); **‡Rajasthan 105** (S. M. Sanandiya 6-14) **and 30-4.** *Rajasthan 1pt, Saurashtra 3pts. Saurya Sanandiya rolled over Rajasthan's first innings with 9.4–4–14–6, but rain left too little time to force a win.*

At Visakhapatnam (Rajasekhara Reddy), October 13–15, 2016. **Rajasthan won by an innings and eight runs. Assam 195** (Pankaj Singh 5-39) **and 69** (A. V. Choudhary 5-35); **‡Rajasthan 272.** *Rajasthan 7pts. Pankaj Singh (4-26) and Aniket Choudhary bowled unchanged as Assam crumbled.*

At Mumbai (Wankhede), October 13–16, 2016. **Drawn. ‡Maharashtra 635-2 dec** (S. M. Gugale 351*, A. R. Bawne 258*) **and 58-0; Delhi 590** (R. R. Pant 308). *Delhi 1pt, Maharashtra 3pts. This match produced 1,283 runs for only 12 wickets. Nearly half the runs came from Swapnil Gugale and Ankit Bawne, who added 594* for Maharashtra's third wicket – the second-highest partnership in all first-class cricket, after 624 by Kumar Sangakkara and Mahela Jayawardene for Sri Lanka v South Africa in Colombo in 2006. Both reached maiden double-hundreds, and Gugale advanced to a triple. In reply, Pant became the fourth-youngest player to score a triple-century, at 19 years 12 days; he totalled 222 in boundaries (42 fours, nine sixes), in eight and a half hours. This was only* *the second first-class match to feature two triple-hundreds, and the first with one on each side; Woorkeri Raman and Arjan Kripal Singh both reached 300 for Tamil Nadu v Goa in 1988-89.*

At Greater Noida, October 13–16, 2016. **Drawn. ‡Karnataka 577-6 dec** (R. Samarth 235) **and 162-3; Jharkhand 374** (I. P. Kishan 159*). *Jharkhand 1pt, Karnataka 3pts. Ravikumar Samarth scored a maiden double-hundred, while their slow left-armer Shahbaz Nadeem conceded 199 in 57 overs.*

At Hyderabad (Uppal), October 13–16, 2016. **Odisha won by 32 runs. Odisha 228** (S. P. Pattnaik 123) **and 169** (D. Punia 5-39); **‡Saurashtra 186 and 179** (S. B. Pradhan 5-69). *Odisha 6pts.*

At Thumba, October 20–23, 2016. **Drawn. ‡Vidarbha 416** (G. Satish 105; S. P. Purkayastha 5-133); **Assam 227** (A. A. Sarwate 5-72) **and 73-2.** *Assam 1pt, Vidarbha 3pts. This was the first first-class match at St Xavier's College.*

At Kolkata (Eden Gardens), October 20–22, 2016. **Karnataka won by an innings and 160 runs. Delhi 90 and 164** (K. J. Gowtham 5-35); **‡Karnataka 414.** *Karnataka 7pts.*

At Vadodara (Reliance), October 20–23, 2016. **Jharkhand won by 42 runs. ‡Jharkhand 209** (Pankaj Singh 5-60) **and 277** (I. R. Jaggi 100; M. K. Lomror 5-51); **Rajasthan 207** (S. Nadeem 7-74) **and 237** (S. Nadeem 5-94). *Jharkhand 6pts. Nadeem collected 12-168 in Jharkhand's victory; earlier, another slow left-armer, 16-year-old Mahipal Lomror, had taken five.*

At Vizianagram (Dr P. V. G. Raju), October 20–23, 2016. **Drawn. Saurashtra 657-8 dec** (S. P. Jackson 105, J. N. Shah 217, C. S. Jani 100*); **‡Maharashtra 182** (K. D. Patel 5-43, D. A. Jadeja 5-41) **and 345-8** (M. S. Trunkwala 117). *Maharashtra 1pt, Saurashtra 3pts. Jaydev Shah scored a maiden double-hundred, and Dharmendrasinh Jadeja collected 9-105. But Murtuza Trunkwala made a debut century, and Maharashtra's ninth-wicket pair saw out the last 13 balls, still 130 behind.*

At Mumbai (Bandra Kurla), October 27–30, 2016. **Karnataka won by ten wickets. ‡Assam 325** (A. A. Verma 166*; S. Aravind 5-70) **and 264** (K. J. Gowtham 7-108); **Karnataka 570-9 dec** (R. V. Uthappa 128, K. K. Nair 145, S. T. R. Binny 156) **and 21-0.** *Karnataka 7pts. Robin Uthappa and Karun Nair added 265 for Karnataka's third wicket after both openers had gone for ducks.*

At Mohali, October 27–30, 2016. **Drawn. Odisha 237 and 274-8; ‡Delhi 495-8 dec** (G. Gambhir 147, Milind Kumar 106*). *Delhi 3pts, Odisha 1pt.*

At Wayanad, October 27–30, 2016. **Drawn. Vidarbha 105 and 444** (S. R. Ramaswamy 102); **‡Jharkhand 362-8 dec** (I. R. Jaggi 112*) **and 75-4.** *Jharkhand 3pts, Vidarbha 1pt.*

At Hyderabad (Uppal), October 27–30, 2016. **Drawn. ‡Maharashtra 461** (N. S. Shaikh 143) **and 145**; **Rajasthan 330 and 4-0.** *Maharashtra 3pts, Rajasthan 1pt.*

At Kolkata (Eden Gardens), November 5–8, 2016. **Assam won by nine wickets. Saurashtra 153** (A. K. Das 7-49) **and 81** (A. K. Das 5-21); **‡Assam 171** (J. D. Unadkat 6-48) **and 66-1.** *Assam 6pts. Arup Das took 12-70 – six of them ducks.*

At Thumba, November 5–8, 2016. **Drawn. Jharkhand 493** (I. P. Kishan 273); **‡Delhi 334** (U. Chand 109, R. R. Pant 117) **and 480-6** (R. R. Pant 135). *Delhi 1pt, Jharkhand 3pts. Coming in at 80-4, Ishan Kishan hit 14 sixes in a maiden double-century. Pant's 82-ball hundred could not save Delhi from following on, but turned out to be a warm-up for a 48-ball century second time round; in all, he scored 252 from 173 deliveries and hit 21 sixes (13 in the second innings). Only Colin Munro had hit more sixes in a first-class match: 23 for Auckland v Central Districts in 2014-15.*

At Vadodara (Moti Bagh), November 5–7, 2016. **Karnataka won by 189 runs. Karnataka 267** (L. M. Yadav 5-67) **and 209**; **‡Vidarbha 176 and 111** (R. Vinay Kumar 5-28). *Karnataka 6pts.*

At Patiala (Dhruve Pandove), November 5–8, 2016. **Drawn. Rajasthan 323** (S. F. Khan 110); **‡Odisha 172 and 508-6 dec** (Ranjit Singh 116, S. P. Senapati 137, A. S. Yadav 115*). *Odisha 1pt, Rajasthan 3pts. Salman Khan and Abhishek Yadav both scored centuries on first-class debut. Ranjit Singh and Subhranshu Senapati added 233 for Odisha's third wicket as they followed on..*

At Hyderabad (Uppal), November 13–16, 2016. **Drawn. ‡Assam 301** (K. N. Saikia 135) **and 166-4; Odisha 459-7 dec** (G. B. Poddar 225, B. B. Samantray 103). *Assam 1pt, Odisha 3pts. This game was moved out of Delhi because of air pollution. Govinda Poddar scored a maiden double-century.*

At Agartala (Maharaja Bir Bikram), November 13–15, 2016. **Jharkhand won by an innings and 46 runs. Saurashtra 277 and 144**; **‡Jharkhand 467** (I. R. Jaggi 173, I. P. Kishan 136; K. D. Patel 5-95). *Jharkhand 7pts. Kishan hit 136 in 120 balls.*

At Vizianagram (Dr P. V. G. Raju), November 13–16, 2016. **Karnataka won by 393 runs. ‡Karnataka 374** (Tanveer-ul-Hak 5-82) **and 298-6 dec** (K. L. Rahul 106); **Rajasthan 148 and 131** (R. Vinay Kumar 5-54). *Karnataka 6pts. K. L. Rahul's century helped Karnataka to their fourth consecutive victory – and he forced his way back into the Indian Test side against England.*

At Kolkata (Eden Gardens), November 13–15, 2016. **Maharashtra won by an innings and three runs. Vidarbha 59** (A. A. Sanklecha 7-25) **and 270** (A. A. Sanklecha 7-69); **‡Maharashtra 332** (N. S. Shaikh 127, A. R. Bawne 111; L. M. Yadav 5-81). *Maharashtra 7pts. Anupam Sanklecha took seven in each innings, with his career-best 7-25 sweeping Vidarbha aside on the opening day to set up an innings victory. His 14-94 was the best return of the season. Naushad Shaikh and Bawne put on 201 for Maharashtra's fourth wicket.*

At Chennai (IIT), November 21–24, 2016. **Maharashtra won by an innings and 52 runs. ‡Maharashtra 542** (K. M. Jadhav 115, C. G. Khurana 112*); **Assam 256** (A. A. Sanklecha 8-73) **and 234.** *Maharashtra 7pts. Sanklecha made it 22 in three innings with another career-best, on his way to completing another innings win; he finished with 12-144.*

At Wayanad, November 21–24, 2016. **Delhi won by two wickets. Rajasthan 238** (A. V. Gautam 106) **and 221**; **‡Delhi 307 and 156-8.** *Delhi 6pts. Pant's flashing blade brought him a 59-ball 75 out of 93 while he was at the wicket in Delhi's first innings.*

At Delhi (Palam), November 21–24, 2016. **Drawn. Karnataka 179 and 393** (Dhiraj Kumar 5-98); **‡Odisha 342** (R. Shreyas Gopal 5-75) **and 63-0.** *Karnataka 1pt, Odisha 3pts.*

At Delhi (Karnail Singh), November 21–24, 2016. **Vidarbha won by eight wickets. Saurashtra 301** (S. P. Jackson 116) **and 189**; **‡Vidarbha 347 and 146-2.** *Vidarbha 6pts.*

At Vizianagram (Dr P. V. G. Raju), November 29–December 2, 2016. **Jharkhand won by five wickets. Jharkhand 316 and 111-5; ‡Assam 126 and 299** (R. K. Das 113). *Jharkhand 6pts. Jharkhand secured a place in the quarter-finals.*

At Chennai (SSNC), November 29–December 2, 2016. **Drawn. Vidarbha 183 and 37-3; ‡Delhi 250-8 dec.** *Delhi 3pts, Vidarbha 1pt. The first first-class match at the Sri Sivasubramaniya Nadar College of Engineering.*

At Patiala (Dhruve Pandove), November 29–December 2, 2016. **Saurashtra won by four wickets. ‡Karnataka 200 and 216**; **Saurashtra 359** (P. N. Mankad 126) **and 58-6.** *Saurashtra 6pts. Saurashtra pulled off the bottom of the table by inflicting the first defeat of the season on the group leaders – but results elsewhere ensured Karnataka were through to the knockouts.*

At Wayanad, November 29–30, 2016. **Odisha won by an innings and 118 runs. Odisha 319** (A. A. Sanklecha 5-75); **‡Maharashtra 94 and 107.** *Odisha 7pts. Sanklecha took five for the fifth time in this tournament, but Odisha won in two days, dismissing Maharashtra twice in a total of 62.4 overs.*

At Vadodara (Reliance), December 7–10, 2016. **Saurashtra won by four runs. Saurashtra 92 and 420** (K. M. Parmar 149); **‡Delhi 237** (K. D. Patel 5-72) **and 271** (S. M. Sanandiya 5-93). *Saurashtra 6pts. Saurashtra crashed for 92, but a strong second-innings performance – including 80 from No. 9 Jaydev Unadkat – left a target of 276; Delhi reached 256-7 before Kushang Patel claimed three in four overs, dashing their hopes of reaching the quarter-finals. Pant hit his 49th six of the season – but failed to manage a 50th here or in his final match, for India A against the Australians.*

At Mohali, December 7–9, 2016. **Karnataka won by ten wickets. Maharashtra 163** (R. Vinay Kumar 5-46) **and 218**; **‡Karnataka 345 and 39-0.** *Karnataka 7pts. Ranganath Vinay Kumar became the Ranji's leading seamer, overtaking Madan Lal's 351 wickets (but a long way behind 637, the spinners' record). Maharashtra initially denied Karnataka's request for a full substitute when Manish Pandey was called up by India on the first day, but gave way on the second.*

At Greater Noida, December 7–10, 2016. **Vidarbha won by six wickets. Rajasthan 140 and 163** (L. M. Yadav 6-60); **‡Vidarbha 116** (Tanveer-ul-Hak 6-21) **and 191-4.** *Vidarbha 6pts.*

At Thumba, December 15–17, 2016. **Jharkhand won by an innings and 93 runs. Odisha 152 and 103**; **‡Jharkhand 348.** *Jharkhand 7pts. The match was postponed and moved from Natham in Tamil Nadu, in mourning for the state's first minister. Jharkhand overtook Karnataka to head the group.*

Group C

At Bhubaneswar (Kalinga), October 6–9, 2016. **Drawn. ‡Himachal Pradesh 357** (P. Chopra 117, S. Verma 142); **Andhra 167-1.** *Andhra 1pt, Himachal Pradesh 1pt.*

At Ranchi (Jharkhand SCA Oval), October 6–8, 2016. **Chhattisgarh won by nine wickets. ‡Tripura 118 and 149; Chhattisgarh 255** (Ashutosh Singh 140) **and 13-1.** *Chhattisgarh 6pts. Led by former Test player Mohammad Kaif, Chhattisgarh won their first first-class match in three days. Ashutosh Singh, one of eight debutants, scored 140 and Kaif passed 10,000. It was their only victory.*

At Nagpur (VCA Academy), October 6–9, 2016. **Hyderabad won by nine wickets. ‡Goa 164 and 258; Hyderabad 388** (P. Akshath Reddy 128, B. P. Sandeep 108) **and 35-1.** *Hyderabad 6pts. This was the first match at the Academy.*

At Mumbai (Brabourne), October 6–9, 2016. **Drawn. Services 197 and 329-6 dec; ‡Haryana 248 and 136-1** (N. Saini 101*). *Haryana 3pts, Services 1pt.*

At Kalyani, October 6–9, 2016. **Drawn. Kerala 304** (S. V. Samson 154; S. Beigh 6-80); **‡Jammu & Kashmir 121 and 91-4.** *Jammu & Kashmir 1pt, Kerala 3pts.*

At Kalyani, October 13–16, 2016. **Drawn. Chhattisgarh 394** (A. N. Khare 143, A. R. Chauhan 123); **‡Andhra 199 and 282-8.** *Andhra 1pt, Chhattisgarh 3pts.*

At Surat, October 13–15, 2016. **Jammu & Kashmir won by 116 runs. ‡Jammu & Kashmir 227 and 261; Goa 77 and 295** (Parvez Rasool 5-89). *Jammu & Kashmir 6pts.*

At Jamshedpur, October 13–16, 2016. **Haryana won by eight wickets. ‡Hyderabad 191** (Y. S. Chahal 6-44) **and 224** (M. Sharma 5-26); **Haryana 331** (Mehdi Hasan 6-93) **and 85-2.** *Haryana 6pts.*

At Kolkata (Eden Gardens), October 13–15, 2016. **Himachal Pradesh won by six wickets. Kerala 248 and 115** (Gurvinder Singh 5-37); **‡Himachal Pradesh 261** (J. S. Saxena 5-76) **and 103-4.** *Himachal Pradesh 6pts.*

At Guwahati (Barsapara), October 13–16, 2016. **Tripura won by 219 runs. Tripura 275 and 340-3 dec** (U. U. Bose 165, S. K. Patel 127*); **‡Services 233** (S. Yadav 101*) **and 163.** *Tripura 6pts. Udiyan Bose and Smit Patel added 292 for Tripura's second wicket, paving the way for their first win in 30 matches since December 2012 – and only their eighth in 32 seasons as a first-class side.*

At Mumbai (Brabourne), October 20–23, 2016. **Andhra won by four wickets. Jammu & Kashmir 334 and 111** (B. A. Bhatt 5-60); **‡Andhra 255** (Aamir Aziz 5-62) **and 194-6.** *Andhra 6pts.*

At Guwahati (Barsapara), October 20–23, 2016. **Haryana won by 161 runs. ‡Haryana 178 and 289** (P. K. Rao 5-74); **Chhattisgarh 189** (J. Sharma 5-32) **and 117** (M. Sharma 5-27). *Haryana 6pts.*

At Cuttack (Dhaneswar Rath), October 20–23, 2016. **Drawn. Goa 606-6 dec** (S. P. Amonkar 101, S. K. Kamat 304*); **‡Services 279 and 188-4.** *Goa 3pts, Services 1pt. Sumiran Amonkar scored 101 on first-class debut and added 237 for the second wicket with Sagun Kamat, who advanced from a maiden double-century to Goa's first triple-hundred, and guided them to 600 for the first time.*

At Kalyani, October 20–23, 2016. **Drawn. Tripura 549** (B. B. Ghosh 146, S. K. Patel 111; M. Dagar 5-138); **‡Himachal Pradesh 311** (R. K. Datta 6-58) **and 349-5** (A. Bains 113). *Himachal Pradesh 1pt, Tripura 3pts. Rana Bishal Ghosh and Smit Patel added 230 for Tripura's second wicket. Rana Datta helped ensure Himachal Pradesh followed on, with a career-best 6-58, including a hat-trick.*

At Bhubaneswar (Kalinga), October 20–23, 2016. **Drawn. ‡Kerala 517-9 dec** (Iqbal Abdulla 159*); **Hyderabad 281 and 220-3** (B. Anirudh 120*). *Hyderabad 1pt, Kerala 3pts.*

At Mumbai (Wankhede), October 27–30, 2016. **Andhra won by 77 runs. Andhra 253** (Y. S. Chahal 5-81) **and 220; ‡Haryana 103** (D. Sivakumar 5-25) **and 293** (S. Rohilla 118). *Andhra 6pts.*

At Jamshedpur, October 27–30, 2016. **Drawn. ‡Kerala 207** (S. S. Ruikar 5-50) **and 307-2 dec** (P. Rohan Prem 123*); **Chhattisgarh 187 and 249-6** (S. S. Gupta 123*). *Chhattisgarh 1pt, Kerala 3pts.*

At Bhubaneswar (Kalinga), October 27–30, 2016. **Drawn. Tripura 283 and 328-9 dec** (Gurender Singh 103*; S. B. Jakati 5-86); **‡Goa 269 and 328-8.** *Goa 1pt, Tripura 3pts.*

At Guwahati (Barsapara), October 27–30, 2016. **Drawn. Himachal Pradesh 36 and 301; ‡Hyderabad 126** (R. Dhawan 7-50) **and 200-6.** *Himachal Pradesh 1pt, Hyderabad 3pts. Himachal*

Pradesh were dismissed for 36, their lowest total, with five ducks; leg-spinner Akash Bhandari took 3–3–0–4. But they drew when bad light halted Hyderabad 12 short of victory.

At Jaipur (Sawai Mansingh), October 27–30, 2016. **Drawn. ‡Services 477** (G. Rahul Singh 182; Parvez Rasool 5-117); **Jammu & Kashmir 612-8** (S. Khajuria 111, I. Dev Singh 120, S. Beigh 109*). *Jammu & Kashmir 3pts, Services 1pt. Shamsher Yadav (72) and Rahul Singh added 216 for Services' fourth wicket. J&K No. 9 Samiullah Beigh came in at 418-7 and steered them to three first-innings points by scoring a maiden century and adding 163* with No. 10 Aamir Aziz (59*).*

At Indore (Holkar), November 5–8, 2016. **Drawn. ‡Services 446** (S. Yadav 136, G. Rahul Singh 127*) **and 27-0; Andhra 341** (D. B. Prasanth Kumar 110; A. M. Bloch 5-92). *Andhra 1pt, Services 3pts.*

At Cuttack (Barabati), November 5–8, 2016. **Goa won by eight wickets. Chhattisgarh 198** (R. R. Singh 6-60) **and 162**; **‡Goa 270 and 94-2.** *Goa 6pts. Goa recovered from 70-6 on the second day when Samar Dubhashi (97) and Shadab Jakati (92) added 160. Chhattisgarh's second innings included seven ducks, one short of the world record.*

At Jaipur (Sawai Mansingh), November 5–8, 2016. **Drawn. Haryana 303** (S. Sandeep Warrier 5-79) **and 315-3** (N. Saini 152*); **‡Kerala 404-9 dec**. *Haryana 1pt, Kerala 3pts.*

At Ranchi (Jharkhand SCA Oval), November 5–8, 2016. **Himachal Pradesh won by five wickets. ‡Jammu & Kashmir 162 and 417**; **Himachal Pradesh 370 and 210-5.** *Himachal Pradesh 6pts.*

At Delhi (Karnail Singh), November 5–8, 2016. **Hyderabad v Tripura. Abandoned.** *Hyderabad 1pt, Tripura 1pt. Like the Gujarat v Bengal fixture in Delhi on the same dates, this game was called off because of air pollution, and initial plans to reschedule it in mid-December were dropped.*

At Valsad, November 13–16, 2016. **Andhra won by an innings and 38 runs. Tripura 171 and 315**; **‡Andhra 524-6 dec** (D. B. Prasanth Kumar 129, G. H. Vihari 233*). *Andhra 7pts. Prasanth Kumar and Hanuma Vihari, who made his fourth double-century, put on 240 for the second wicket.*

At Kanpur (Modi), November 13–16, 2016. **Drawn. ‡Chhattisgarh 238 and 311-9 dec** (A. R. Chauhan 110); **Himachal Pradesh 314** (S. S. Ruikar 7-112) **and 139-7.** *Chhattisgarh 1pt, Himachal Pradesh 3pts.*

At Mumbai (Brabourne), November 13–16, 2016. **Drawn. Kerala 342** (B. J. Thakkar 117, P. Rohan Prem 130; R. R. Singh 7-42) **and 268-8 dec** (S. S. Bandekar 5-70); **‡Goa 286 and 279-5** (S. K. Kamat 151). *Goa 1pt, Kerala 3pts. Bhavin Thakkar and Rohan Prem added 234 for Kerala's second wicket; the last eight fell for 41 as Riturah Singh collected a career-best 7-42.*

At Cuttack (Barabati), November 13–16, 2016. **Drawn. Haryana 502** (R. Paliwal 194); **‡Jammu & Kashmir 262 and 249-3** (S. Khajuria 110*). *Haryana 3pts, Jammu & Kashmir 1pt.*

At Mumbai (Bandra Kurla), November 13–16, 2016. **Hyderabad won by ten wickets. Hyderabad 580-9 dec** (B. P. Sandeep 203*, C. V. Milind 136; R. R. Raj 5-73) **and 20-0; ‡Services 360** (S. Yadav 104) **and 239.** *Hyderabad 7pts. This was moved from Delhi due to smog. Bavanaka Sandeep, with a first double-hundred, and Chama Milind added 267, a Hyderabad eighth-wicket record.*

At Guwahati (Barsapara), November 21–24, 2016. **Drawn. Kerala 219** (P. D. Vijaykumar 6-47) **and 302-6 dec; ‡Andhra 226 and 193-4.** *Andhra 3pts, Kerala 1pt.*

At Valsad, November 21–24, 2016. **Hyderabad won by 44 runs. Hyderabad 351** (S. Badrinath 134; P. K. Rao 5-89) **and 122** (P. K. Rao 5-44); **‡Chhattisgarh 188 and 241.** *Hyderabad 6pts. Subramaniam Badrinath passed 10,000 runs. His team-mate Tanmay Agarwal went to hospital after being hit on the head fielding at short leg, but batted in the second innings (for a duck).*

At Ghaziabad, November 21–24, 2016. **Drawn. Goa 413** (S. S. Kauthankar 225) **and 152-5; ‡Haryana 568** (N. Saini 227). *Goa 1pt, Haryana 3pts. Snehal Kauthankar rescued Goa from 74-4 with a maiden double-hundred; Nitin Saini responded with another, adding 227 with Chaitanya Bishnoi (90), and had secured first-innings lead before he was out at 443-5.*

At Surat, November 21–24, 2016. **Drawn. ‡Services 401** (N. Verma 117, R. Chauhan 149; R. Dhawan 5-82) **and 295-9 dec; Himachal Pradesh 296 and 145-2.** *Himachal Pradesh 1pt, Services 3pts. Nakul Verma and Ravi Chauhan added 264 for Services' second wicket; the rest of the top six totalled 15.*

At Mumbai (Bandra Kurla), November 21–24, 2016. **Drawn. Jammu & Kashmir 315 and 318-4 dec** (I. Dev Singh 129*); **‡Tripura 297 and 168-8.** *Jammu & Kashmir 3pts, Tripura 1pt.*

At Dhanbad (Railway), November 29–December 1, 2016. **Goa won by 34 runs. Goa 115** (B. A. Bhatt 6-36) **and 276**; ‡**Andhra 159** (S. B. Jakati 8-53) **and 198.** *Goa 6pts. Twenty wickets fell on the first day, 19 to spinners; slow left-armer Jakati's 8-53 was the domestic season's best return.*

At Mumbai (Bandra Kurla), November 29–December 2, 2016. **Services won by 18 runs.** ‡**Services 225** (S. S. Ruikar 5-73) **and 340-7 dec** (N. Verma 156*); **Chhattisgarh 281** (D. Pathania 6-78) **and 266.** *Services 6pts.*

At Valsad, November 29–December 2, 2016. **Drawn. Haryana 402** (Guntashveer Singh 120; K. Abhinay 6-84) **and 162-3** (S. Rohilla 100*); ‡**Himachal Pradesh 233** (S. Pahal 5-71) **and 432-5 dec** (P. Chopra 237). *Haryana 3pts, Himachal Pradesh 1pt. Guntashveer Singh scored 120 on debut, while in Himachal Pradesh's follow-on Prashant Chopra hit 237, his maiden double-century, in 241 balls with seven sixes.*

At Vadodara (Moti Bagh), November 29–December 2, 2016. **Hyderabad won by 286 runs. Hyderabad 328** (T. D. Agarwal 119) **and 244-2 dec** (T. D. Agarwal 103*); ‡**Jammu & Kashmir 169 and 117.** *Hyderabad 6pts. Hyderabad opener Agarwal scored twin centuries, helping them pull ahead of group leaders Andhra with one round to go.*

At Cuttack (Barabati), November 29–December 2, 2016. **Kerala won by seven wickets.** ‡**Tripura 213 and 162**; **Kerala 193 and 183-3.** *Kerala 6pts.*

At Lucknow (Ekana), December 7–10, 2016. **Drawn. Andhra 190** (C. V. Milind 5-28) **and 171-6 dec;** ‡**Hyderabad 143 and 56-5.** *Andhra 3pts, Hyderabad 1pt. The first match at Ekana was a battle between two teams seeking a place in the knockouts – but Andhra were denied the win they needed after fog allowed only 40 overs on the final day, and Hyderabad went through.*

At Gwalior, December 7–10, 2016. **Drawn. Chhattisgarh 370** (A. N. Khare 106; S. Beigh 5-94) **and 264-3 dec** (A. N. Khare 117*); ‡**Jammu & Kashmir 242** (S. S. Ruikar 5-59) **and 243-7.** *Chhattisgarh 3pts, Jammu & Kashmir 1pt. Chhattisgarh could not round off their first first-class season with a win, but 19-year-old Amandeep Khare scored two centuries, the second in 79 balls.*

At Mumbai (Bandra Kurla), December 7–10, 2016. **Himachal Pradesh won by seven wickets.** ‡**Goa 380** (S. K. Kamat 104, D. W. Misal 106) **and 286** (D. W. Misal 119); **Himachal Pradesh 528** (P. Chopra 194, S. Verma 160) **and 139-3.** *Himachal Pradesh 6pts. Darshan Misal scored a century in each innings. In between, Chopra reached three figures in 70 balls, and finished with 194 from 170, with seven sixes; he added 241 for Himachal Pradesh's third wicket with Sumeet Verma.*

At Kolkata (Eden Gardens), December 7–9, 2016. **Haryana won by 119 runs. Haryana 231 and 261-9 dec** (N. Saini 104); ‡**Tripura 178** (S. K. Patel 102; H. V. Patel 5-27) **and 195.** *Haryana 6pts. Haryana's victory secured entry to the quarter-finals.*

At Delhi (Karnail Singh), December 7–10, 2016. **Drawn. Services 322** (A. H. Gupta 105); ‡**Kerala 518-5 dec** (S. Baby 250*, A. R. Chandran 102*). *Kerala 3pts, Services 1pt. Sachin Baby, who made his second double-hundred, put on 257* for Kerala's sixth wicket with Akshay Chandran.*

Knockouts

Quarter-final At Jaipur (Sawai Mansingh), December 23–27, 2016. **Drawn.** Gujarat qualified for the semi-final by virtue of their first-innings lead. **Gujarat 263** (B. C. Mohanty 5-68) **and 641** (S. B. Gohel 359*; Dhiraj Kumar 6-147); ‡**Odisha 199** (J. J. Bumrah 5-41) **and 81-1.** *Gujarat's second-innings 641 was their highest total, and opener Samit Gohel's 359* their highest score. Gohel batted for 16 hours four minutes, facing 723 balls, and hit 45 fours but only one six. It was the fifth and highest triple-hundred of this tournament, and the highest score by any player carrying his bat, beating 357* by Bobby Abel for Surrey against Somerset at The Oval in 1899.*

Quarter-final At Vadodara (Moti Bagh), December 23–26, 2016. **Jharkhand won by five wickets.** ‡**Haryana 258** (S. Nadeem 7-79) **and 262**; **Jharkhand 345** (Virat Singh 107) **and 178-5.** *Nadeem took 11-157 to reach 50 wickets in the season and steer Jharkhand towards the semi-final.*

Quarter-final At Naya Raipur, December 23–27, 2016. **Mumbai won by 30 runs.** ‡**Mumbai 294** (S. D. Lad 110; C. V. Milind 5-80) **and 217** (M. Siraj 5-52); **Hyderabad 280 and 201** (A. M. Nayar 5-40, V. D. Gohil 5-64). *Chasing 232, Hyderabad were lifted to 185-7 by Balchander Anirudh (84) and Milind (29), but Nayar claimed the last three wickets.*

Quarter-final At Visakhapatnam (Rajasekhara Reddy), December 23–24, 2016. **Tamil Nadu won by seven wickets. Karnataka 88** (A. A. Crist 6-31) **and 150; ‡Tamil Nadu 152 and 87-3.** *Tamil Nadu completed victory on the second day, when 19 wickets fell. Aswin Crist claimed a career-best 6-31, and Karthik hit the winning six in his 100th Ranji match.*

Semi-final At Nagpur (VCA Academy), January 1–4, 2017. **Gujarat won by 123 runs. ‡Gujarat 390** (P. K. Panchal 149) **and 252** (S. Nadeem 5-69); **Jharkhand 408** (I. R. Jaggi 129; R. P. Singh 6-90) **and 111** (J. J. Bumrah 6-29). *Panchal scored his fifth century of the tournament but, when Jharkhand claimed first-innings lead, Gujarat had to win to reach their first Ranji final in 66 years; they achieved their goal when Jharkhand collapsed against Jasprit Bumrah's career-best 6-29.*

Semi-final At Rajkot (Khandheri), January 1–5, 2017. **Mumbai won by six wickets. ‡Tamil Nadu 305 and 356-6 dec** (A. Mukund 122, R. N. B. Indrajith 138); **Mumbai 411 and 251-4** (P. P. Shaw 120). *Seventeen-year-old Prithvi Shaw, already famous for scoring 546 in a school game in 2013-14, made 120 on first-class debut. He was the second-youngest player to reach a century for Mumbai – after a 15-year-old Sachin Tendulkar.*

Final At Indore (Holkar), January 10–14, 2017. **Gujarat won by five wickets. Mumbai 228 and 411** (C. T. Gaja 6-121); **‡Gujarat 328 and 313-5** (P. A. Patel 143). *Gujarat claimed their first Ranji Trophy, against 41-time winners Mumbai. Parthiv Patel and Juneja shared fourth-wicket century stands in both innings, and seamer Chintan Gaya took 6-121 in his third first-class match. But Nayar (last out for 91 in Mumbai's second innings) ensured Gujarat had to survive the final day, to take the trophy on first-innings lead, or score 312, the highest successful chase in a Ranji final. Patel rose to the challenge; he was out only 13 short of victory. Panchal ended the tournament with 1,310 runs; only V. V. S. Laxman (1,415 in 1999-2000) and Shreyas Iyer (1,321 in 2015-16) had scored more in a Ranji season. Patel passed 1,000 for the whole first-class season. Mumbai captain/wicketkeeper Aditya Tare made six catches, giving him 53 dismissals in the tournament.*

RANJI TROPHY WINNERS

1934-35	Bombay	1962-63	Bombay	1990-91	Haryana
1935-36	Bombay	1963-64	Bombay	1991-92	Delhi
1936-37	Nawanagar	1964-65	Bombay	1992-93	Punjab
1937-38	Hyderabad	1965-66	Bombay	1993-94	Bombay
1938-39	Bengal	1966-67	Bombay	1994-95	Bombay
1939-40	Maharashtra	1967-68	Bombay	1995-96	Karnataka
1940-41	Maharashtra	1968-69	Bombay	1996-97	Mumbai
1941-42	Bombay	1969-70	Bombay	1997-98	Karnataka
1942-43	Baroda	1970-71	Bombay	1998-99	Karnataka
1943-44	Western India	1971-72	Bombay	1999-2000	Mumbai
1944-45	Bombay	1972-73	Bombay	2000-01	Baroda
1945-46	Holkar	1973-74	Karnataka	2001-02	Railways
1946-47	Baroda	1974-75	Bombay	2002-03	Mumbai
1947-48	Holkar	1975-76	Bombay	2003-04	Mumbai
1948-49	Bombay	1976-77	Bombay	2004-05	Railways
1949-50	Baroda	1977-78	Karnataka	2005-06	Uttar Pradesh
1950-51	Holkar	1978-79	Delhi	2006-07	Mumbai
1951-52	Bombay	1979-80	Delhi	2007-08	Delhi
1952-53	Holkar	1980-81	Bombay	2008-09	Mumbai
1953-54	Bombay	1981-82	Delhi	2009-10	Mumbai
1954-55	Madras	1982-83	Karnataka	2010-11	Rajasthan
1955-56	Bombay	1983-84	Bombay	2011-12	Rajasthan
1956-57	Bombay	1984-85	Bombay	2012-13	Mumbai
1957-58	Baroda	1985-86	Delhi	2013-14	Karnataka
1958-59	Bombay	1986-87	Hyderabad	2014-15	Karnataka
1959-60	Bombay	1987-88	Tamil Nadu	2015-16	Mumbai
1960-61	Bombay	1988-89	Delhi	2016-17	Gujarat
1961-62	Bombay	1989-90	Bengal		

Bombay/Mumbai have won the Ranji Trophy 41 times, Karnataka 8, Delhi 7, Baroda 5, Holkar 4, Bengal, Hyderabad, Madras/Tamil Nadu, Maharashtra, Railways and Rajasthan 2, Gujarat, Haryana, Nawanagar, Punjab, Uttar Pradesh and Western India 1.

IRANI CUP IN 2016-17

Ranji Trophy Champions (Gujarat) v Rest of India

At Mumbai (Brabourne), January 20–24, 2017. **Rest of India won by six wickets.** ‡**Gujarat 358** (C. J. Gandhi 169; S. Kaul 5-86) **and 246**; **Rest of India 226 and 379-4** (C. A. Pujara 116*, W. P. Saha 203*). *Gujarat took a 132-run lead on the back of Chirag Gandhi's first century, and he later extended the advantage to 378 before being last out for 70. The Rest of India were 63-4 before Cheteshwar Pujara, with his sixth hundred of the season, and Wriddhaman Saha, who hit six sixes in a maiden double-century, added 316* for the fifth wicket – the third-highest partnership to win a game (after two instances in 1998-99: 345* for the second wicket by Greg Blewett and Corey Richards, for Australian XI v England XI at Hobart, and 332* for the first by Abdul Basit and Naved Latif, for Sargodha v Lahore City). Gujarat captain Parthiv Patel's four catches took him to 52 dismissals in the season, but a disputed umpiring decision left him five short of 10,000 career runs.*

VIJAY HAZARE TROPHY IN 2016-17

Four 50-over leagues plus knockout

Quarter-final At Delhi (Feroz Shah Kotla), March 12, 2017. **Baroda won by seven wickets. Karnataka 233** (48.5 overs); ‡**Baroda 234-3** (45.5 overs).

Quarter-final At Delhi (Palam), March 12, 2017. **Tamil Nadu won by five wickets.** ‡**Gujarat 211** (49.4 overs); **Tamil Nadu 217-5** (42.2 overs).

Quarter-final At Delhi (Feroz Shah Kotla), March 15, 2017. **Bengal won by four wickets.** ‡**Maharashtra 318-6** (50 overs); **Bengal 320-6** (49.5 overs).

Quarter-final At Delhi (Palam), March 15, 2017. **Jharkhand won by six wickets.** ‡**Vidarbha 159-9** (50 overs); **Jharkhand 165-4** (45.1 overs).

Semi-final At Delhi (Feroz Shah Kotla), March 16, 2017. **Tamil Nadu won by six wickets.** ‡**Baroda 219** (49.3 overs); **Tamil Nadu 220-4** (47.3 overs). *MoM:* K. D. Karthik.

Semi-final At Delhi (Palam), March 18, 2017. **Bengal won by 41 runs. Bengal 329-4** (50 overs) (S. P. Goswami 101, A. R. Easwaran 101); ‡**Jharkhand 288** (50 overs) (P. P. Ojha 5-71). *MoM:* S. P. Goswami. *The second semi was delayed a day after a fire at the Jharkhand team's hotel.*

Final At Delhi (Feroz Shah Kotla), March 20, 2017. **Tamil Nadu won by 37 runs.** ‡**Tamil Nadu 217** (47.2 overs) (K. D. Karthik 112); **Bengal 180** (45.5 overs). *Dinesh Karthik rescued Tamil Nadu from 49-4 with his tenth one-day hundred, and finished the tournament with 607 runs, a record for the Vijay Hazare Trophy.*

DEODHAR TROPHY IN 2016-17

50-over knockout for India A, India B and the winner of the Vijay Hazare Trophy

Final At Visakhapatnam (Rajasekhara Reddy), March 29, 2017. **Tamil Nadu won by 42 runs.** ‡**Tamil Nadu 303-9** (50 overs) (K. D. Karthik 126; D. S. Kulkarni 5-39); **India B 261** (46.1 overs). *Following a similar course to the Vijay Hazare final nine days earlier, Karthik came in at 39-3 to score a decisive century – 126 from 91 balls. He ended the season with 854 one-day runs at 85.*

SYED MUSHTAQ ALI TROPHY IN 2016-17

Five interstate 20-over leagues, followed by a further league for five zonal teams

In the first stage, **Madhya Pradesh** won the Central Zone league, **Bengal** won the East Zone, **Delhi** the North Zone, **Karnataka** the South Zone and **Mumbai** the West Zone. Each zone then selected their team for an interzone league, which was won by **East Zone**.

The Indian Premier League has its own section (page 1105).

CRICKET IN IRELAND IN 2017

Young actors needed for big stage

IAN CALLENDER

The undoubted highlight of 2017 came on June 22, the day Ireland were granted Test status. Three months later, the date of their first match was confirmed, against Pakistan at Malahide starting on May 11, 2018.

The worry was that Ireland were joining the elite at the wrong time. Since first announcing themselves at the 2007 World Cup – when Pakistan were among their victims – they had slipped back. But there were signs of an upturn in fortunes at the end of the year. They beat Scotland by 203 runs in their final Intercontinental Cup match, then clinched a comeback win at Sharjah in three one-day internationals against Afghanistan.

It was the last series overseen by head coach John Bracewell. After two and a half years he had a win percentage of 38, and his contract was not renewed; Graham Ford, the former South Africa and Sri Lanka coach, who had been

IRELAND IN 2017

	Played	*Won*	*Lost*	*Drawn/No result*
Tests	–	–	–	–
One-day internationals	16	6	9	1
Twenty20 internationals	7	2	5	–

JANUARY	Desert T20 Challenge (in the UAE)	(page 1082)
FEBRUARY		
MARCH	2 ODIs (a) v UAE 5 ODIs and 3 T20Is (a) v Afghanistan (in India)	(page 1084) (page 790)
APRIL		
MAY	2 ODIs (a) v England Triangular ODI tournament (h) v Bangladesh and New Zealand	(page 260) (page 887)
JUNE		
JULY		
AUGUST		
SEPTEMBER	1 ODI (h) v West Indies	(page 889)
OCTOBER		
NOVEMBER		
DECEMBER	3 ODIs (a) v Afghanistan (in the UAE)	(page 793)

For a review of Irish domestic cricket from the 2017 season, see page 890.

part of the support staff in Sharjah, was given the reins. His first task was to identify fresh blood. Ed Joyce remained Ireland's best batsman, even at the age of 39, and was determined to play Test cricket, having missed out with England. Niall O'Brien and Tim Murtagh were also the wrong side of 35. A failure to develop the team was the main criticism levelled at Bracewell: he gave new caps to eight players, but there was still a reliance on the old guard.

Ireland's year had begun in the doldrums. In the final of the Desert T20 at Dubai, they were bowled out for 71 by Afghanistan, who raced to victory inside eight overs. Then, after two comfortable wins against the UAE, they travelled to Greater Noida in India for nine matches across the formats against Afghanistan.

Predictably, after slumping to the bottom of the ICC's Twenty20 rankings, Ireland crashed in the opening 20-over games. In the second, they needed 46 off 29 balls with eight wickets in hand, but lost seven for 22. They finished the series with a collapse of five for four to confirm the whitewash.

Despite Man of the Match performances from William Porterfield (119) and Paul Stirling (95 and six for 55), Afghanistan won the first two one-day internationals. Ireland drew level, though: Stirling hit 99 in a chase of 265 then, three days later, a limping Kevin O'Brien backed up four wickets with 72 not out. But leg-spinner Rashid Khan took four cheap wickets in the decider to take his tally to 25 across eight games, and set up a stroll for Afghanistan.

The final fixture of the tour was a top-of-the-table Intercontinental Cup clash, with the winners almost certain to claim the trophy. It turned into the low point of the year: Afghanistan piled up 537 for eight, then skittled Ireland, the holders, for 261 and 104. The Afghans, who were also made Full Members in June, went on to win their remaining two matches, while Ireland were held by the Netherlands at Malahide in August.

The glamour match was Ireland's first ODI at Lord's, against England. Two days after a seven-wicket defeat at Bristol, where the end came before the scheduled break, there was much to prove. They conceded 328, but Stirling's fast start and Porterfield's 82 kept them in the hunt. Only after Kevin O'Brien perished going for his third six did hopes vanish of a repeat of Bangalore 2011.

A tri-series followed against Bangladesh and New Zealand, both warming up for the Champions Trophy in England. Ireland were competitive only in the first completed game, against the New Zealanders: Niall O'Brien scored 109 before another collapse, the last six falling for 50.

The women's side had a quiet year. They were squeezed out of the World Cup qualifying tournament in Sri Lanka in February, and managed just one victory – against Zimbabwe – in a quadrangular series in South Africa. India gave them their worst beatings: by ten wickets in one game, 249 runs in another.

IRELAND TRI-NATION SERIES IN 2017

IAN CALLENDER

1 New Zealand 2 Bangladesh 3 Ireland

The first tri-series in Ireland involving two Full Member nations was won by New Zealand, though Bangladesh probably had more to celebrate. Despite the rain, they improved with every game, culminating in their first victory over New Zealand away from home. It took them up to sixth in the ODI rankings, and greatly improved their chances of an automatic place at the 2019 World Cup.

Tamim Iqbal was their leading scorer with 199 runs, as well as being involved in three of the tournament's four highest stands. He received excellent support from opening partner Soumya Sarkar and Mahmudullah, who totalled 140 for only once out. Their batting made up for their bowling, which lacked penetration; seamers Mustafizur Rahman and Mashrafe bin Mortaza were comfortably the best.

As the series began, New Zealand had ten players still at the IPL, including captain Kane Williamson. That allowed them to show off their strength in depth – they fielded 16 in all – and they won their first three games with ease. Tom Latham stood in as captain, and thrived under the extra responsibility. He made 257 runs, hitting one of only two centuries across the six games, played on slow but good pitches at Malahide and Clontarf. Scott Kuggeleijn, a 25-year-old seam-bowling all-rounder (whose Test-playing father Chris had turned out for Dublin University), made his debut against Ireland and claimed three for 41. In the same game, slow left-armer Mitchell Santner snatched five for 50; he finished the tournament with eight.

It was a desperately disappointing series for Ireland, who in two one-day internationals earlier in May had offered England little competition. The nadir came in their last game, when they lost to New Zealand by 190 runs. It didn't help that the experienced Ed Joyce missed the first two matches with a back injury. Niall O'Brien hit more in one innings – his first ODI century in his 85th match – than any of his team-mates could manage in total. They failed to bat 47 overs in any game and took only 19 wickets. The coach, John Bracewell, had plenty to ponder, especially after their elevation to Test status was confirmed in June.

NATIONAL SQUADS

Ireland *W. T. S. Porterfield, A. Balbirnie, P. K. D. Chase, G. H. Dockrell, E. C. Joyce, B. J. McCarthy, T. J. Murtagh, K. J. O'Brien, N. J. O'Brien, S. Singh, P. R. Stirling, S. R. Thompson, G. C. Wilson, C. A. Young. *Coach:* J. G. Bracewell.

Bangladesh *Mashrafe bin Mortaza, Imrul Kayes, Mahmudullah, Mehedi Hasan, Mosaddek Hossain, Mushfiqur Rahim, Mustafizur Rahman, Nasir Hossain, Nurul Hasan, Rubel Hossain, Sabbir Rahman, Sanjamul Islam, Shafiul Islam, Shakib Al Hasan, Soumya Sarkar, Subashis Roy, Tamim Iqbal, Taskin Ahmed. *Coach:* U. C. Hathurusinghe.

New Zealand *T. W. M. Latham, C. J. Anderson, H. K. Bennett, N. T. Broom, M. J. Henry, S. C. Kuggeleijn, A. F. Milne, C. Munro, J. D. S. Neesham, H. M. Nicholls, J. S. Patel, S. H. A. Rance, L. Ronchi, M. J. Santner, I. S. Sodhi, L. R. P. L. Taylor, N. Wagner, G. H. Worker. *Coach:* M. J. Hesson.

Anderson, Henry and Milne arrived midway through the tour, after leaving the IPL. Patel joined in time for the last match.

At Malahide, May 12. **No result. Bangladesh 157-4** (31.1 overs) (Tamim Iqbal 64*, Mahmudullah 43*; P. K. D. Chase 3-33) **v ‡Ireland.** *Rain allowed just over two hours' play. Thanks to some lively pace bowling from Peter Chase, Ireland reduced Bangladesh to 70-4 after William Porterfield inserted them on a green pitch – including the wicket of Shakib Al Hasan, standing in as captain while Mashrafe bin Mortaza served a one-match ban for slow over-rates. But a stand of 87* between Tamim Iqbal and Mahmudullah seemed to have put them in control.*

At Malahide, May 14. **New Zealand won by 54 runs. New Zealand 289-7** (50 overs) (L. Ronchi 37, G. H. Worker 50, L. R. P. L. Taylor 52, N. T. Broom 79, J. D. S. Neesham 30); **‡Ireland 238** (45.3 overs) (N. J. O'Brien 109, A. Balbirnie 36, G. C. Wilson 30; S. C. Kuggeleijn 3-41, M. J. Santner 5-50). *MoM:* M. J. Santner. *ODI debuts:* S. Singh (Ireland); S. C. Kuggeleijn, S. H. A. Rance (New Zealand). *Left-arm spinner Mitchell Santner's best one-day return ensured a winning start for New Zealand, though as long as Niall O'Brien was batting Ireland were in contention. He hit five sixes and reached his first ODI century, off 124 balls, before becoming Santner's fourth victim at 235-8; the end soon followed. New Zealand's top six had all enjoyed starts, Neil Broom leading the way with 79 from 63 balls, and George Worker hitting his maiden ODI fifty. Oddly, Simi Singh, a 30-year-old off-spinning all-rounder from Punjab granted Irish citizenship in April, did not bowl on his ODI debut. Ireland, still without the injured Ed Joyce, needed a solid start to have a chance of reaching 290, though they did have the advantage of facing an inexperienced attack – New Zealand's opening pair of Seth Rance and Scott Kuggeleijn were also making debuts. They slipped to 26-2, before recovering to a healthier 188-4 after 35 overs. Then the rot set in, and six wickets fell for 50.*

At Clontarf, May 17. **New Zealand won by four wickets. Bangladesh 257-9** (50 overs) (Soumya Sarkar 61, Mushfiqur Rahim 55, Mahmudullah 51, Mosaddek Hossain 41; H. K. Bennett 3-31); **‡New Zealand 258-6** (47.3 overs) (T. W. M. Latham 54, N. T. Broom 48, J. D. S. Neesham 52). *MoM:* J. D. S. Neesham. *An 80-run fifth-wicket stand between Broom and Jimmy Neesham helped New Zealand ease home. Broom fell just short of another fifty, and Neesham departed soon after reaching his, but there were no late scares. With Mortaza back as captain, Bangladesh had begun promisingly, Soumya Sarkar striking a crisp 61. Few of the Bangladeshis made the most of the short boundaries – Mahmudullah hit six fours, and Mushfiqur Rahim the only six of the innings – while Hamish Bennett's reward for an economical spell was two wickets in his tenth over. Luke Ronchi struck a run-a-ball 27 to give New Zealand a fast start to their chase and, on a pitch offering bowlers plenty of assistance, they shrugged off the loss of regular wickets.*

At Malahide, May 19. **Bangladesh won by eight wickets. Ireland 181** (46.3 overs) (E. C. Joyce 46, N. J. O'Brien 30; Mustafizur Rahman 4-23); **‡Bangladesh 182-2** (27.1 overs) (Tamim Iqbal 47, Soumya Sarkar 87*, Sabbir Rahman 35). *MoM:* Mustafizur Rahman. *ODI debut:* Sanjamul Islam (Bangladesh). *This was a day for Ireland to forget. In front of an expectant home crowd they batted and bowled poorly, and Bangladesh cruised to victory. Only Joyce, who hit 46 on his return from injury, prevented a complete collapse after Ireland were put in. He was fifth out at 126 in the 29th over, the first wicket for Sanjamul Islam, the latest in a long line of Bangladeshi left-arm spinners. Kevin O'Brien and Gary Wilson followed quickly to give Mustafizur Rahman four wickets and leave Ireland in tatters at 136-7. A stand of 35 between George Dockrell (25) and Barry McCarthy (12) provided some resistance, but the Bangladesh batsmen were even more dominant than their bowlers. Openers Tamim and Soumya put on 95 in 14 overs, before Kevin O'Brien's 99th ODI wicket prised them apart. Soumya sailed on to 87* from 68 balls.*

At Malahide, May 21. **New Zealand won by 190 runs. New Zealand 344-6** (50 overs) (L. Ronchi 35, T. W. M. Latham 104, N. T. Broom 38, L. R. P. L. Taylor 57, C. Munro 44); **‡Ireland 154** (39.3 overs) (W. T. S. Porterfield 48, G. C. Wilson 30; M. J. Henry 3-36). *MoM:* T. W. M. Latham. *Before the tournament, Ireland coach (and former New Zealand coach) John Bracewell said he would love nothing more than for his current team to beat his old one, but he had to watch his players suffer another hammering. The decision to drop experienced seamers Kevin O'Brien and Tim Murtagh backfired when Tom Latham hit a century, setting up a commanding total. He enjoyed a life on 89 when he holed out to long leg and turned for the pavilion before completing a run, only for the third umpire to rule that Craig Young had overstepped. Since the batsmen had crossed, New*

Zealand were credited with the uncompleted run, in line with Law 18.10.b.ii. When Latham was eventually dismissed, at 212-3 in the 36th over, it led to a period of consolidation. Colin Munro made up for that by smashing 44 off 15 balls (as well as a spectator's chair with one of his four sixes); in all, 72 cascaded from the last four overs. New Zealand had drafted in Corey Anderson, Matt Henry and Adam Milne – all back from the IPL – and they shared six wickets. Porterfield top-scored with 48 from 50, but once he went the innings headed downhill fast. Victory meant New Zealand had won the tournament with a game to spare.

At Clontarf, May 24. **Bangladesh won by five wickets. New Zealand 270-8** (50 overs) (T. W. M. Latham 84, N. T. Broom 63, L. R. P. L. Taylor 60*); ‡**Bangladesh 271-5** (48.2 overs) (Tamim Iqbal 65, Sabbir Rahman 65, Mushfiqur Rahim 45*, Mahmudullah 46*). *MoM:* Mushfiqur Rahim. *MoS:* T. W. M. Latham. *New Zealand had won the series, but a Bangladesh victory gave them an edge before their Champions Trophy rematch in Cardiff a couple of weeks later. Their batting and bowling were sound, though not their fielding: four catches were put down, including Latham twice, on nought and 50. He shared a century stand with Broom but, from the prosperity of 167-2 at the end of the 30th, New Zealand dribbled away, and the last ten produced just 53. Tamim hit the first ball of the reply for six, though Jeetan Patel exacted some revenge two deliveries later when he removed Soumya for a golden duck. Tamim and Sabbir Rahman added 136 for the second wicket, but Bangladesh briefly lost their footing and slid to 160-4, before Mushfiqur and Mahmudullah (who passed 3,000 ODI runs) shored things up. They added 72* in ten overs to complete a convincing win that lifted Bangladesh to sixth in the ODI rankings for the first time – above Sri Lanka, Pakistan and West Indies.*

New Zealand 12pts, Bangladesh 10pts, Ireland 2pts.

IRELAND v WEST INDIES IN 2017

IRELAND v WEST INDIES

At Belfast, September 13. Only one-day international. **Abandoned.** *Ireland's first international since being given Test status was an embarrassment, as inadequate covering meant no play was possible at Stormont after several days of rain, even though the sun was shining from 8am on the morning of the match.*

DOMESTIC CRICKET IN IRELAND IN 2017

IAN CALLENDER

Leinster Lightning dominated Ireland's inaugural season of first-class cricket, winning all three tournaments. It was the fifth year of the current interprovincial competitions in Ireland, but the first in which the three-day championship enjoyed first-class status, with equivalent upgrades for the one-day and Twenty20 formats. As before, they were contested by three of Ireland's five cricket unions, with a fourth, Munster, joining the T20 Trophy for the first time; Connacht were not yet ready to step up.

Leinster had won all four previous three-day championships, and their class once again showed. Ed Joyce, who hit two of the competition's four centuries, headed its averages with 363 runs at 90, and slow left-armer George Dockrell was easily the leading wicket-taker with 22 at 13. John Anderson stepped down as captain in September after two all-conquering years, but was expected to remain a key player. Such was Leinster's strength in depth – most of their squad were internationals – that Dubliner Niall O'Brien, Ireland's first-choice wicketkeeper, was asked to play for **North West Warriors**.

The Belfast-based **Northern Knights** finished second, and their captain, James Shannon, was the leading first-class run-scorer with 446. In a season badly affected by the weather, Northern and North West (who straddle the border between Northern Ireland and the Republic) had the honour of playing the historic opening first-class fixture, at Eglinton. North West were well placed to win a low-scoring game, but rain prevented play on the final day. In the return match, the second day was wiped out; both times, the teams benefited from the extra three points awarded for a draw with more than eight hours' play lost. Leinster's first two fixtures were fully played out, but still drawn. They completed innings victories in both the remaining games, however, to retain the title; Dockrell clinched the final match with his second six-wicket haul.

Leinster comfortably won three of their games in the one-day Interprovincial Cup – the other was washed out after they scored 299 for eight – and claimed the title with one to spare, after North West beat Northern by a single wicket in a thriller at Waringstown. Ireland captain William Porterfield made his first appearance for North West in 14 years in that match and, now that he had left Warwickshire, they could look forward to him being available in 2018. Joyce was the leading scorer and made the only century, in that rained-off game – in the same innings, Northern seamer Shane Getkate produced the competition's only five-for – and Dockrell was again the leading bowler, with ten wickets at nine apiece. Both sets of averages were topped by Andrew Balbirnie, who hit an unbeaten double-hundred against the Netherlands in the Intercontinental Cup.

FIRST-CLASS AVERAGES IN 2017

BATTING (125 runs)

		M	*I*	*NO*	*R*	*HS*	*100*	*Avge*	*Ct*
1	A. Balbirnie (*Leinster/Ireland*)	5	4	1	311	205*	1	103.66	6
2	†W. T. S. Porterfield (*Ireland*)	1	2	0	168	108	1	84.00	0
3	J. N. K. Shannon (*Northern*)	4	7	1	446	140*	1	74.33	1
4	†E. C. Joyce (*Leinster/Ireland*)	5	7	1	415	167*	2	69.16	6
5	J. B. Tector (*Leinster*)	4	5	1	182	75	0	45.50	4
6	J. A. McCollum (*Northern*)	4	7	1	232	119*	1	38.66	0
7	E. J. Richardson (*Leinster*)	4	4	0	137	81	0	34.25	4
8	K. J. O'Brien (*Leinster/Ireland*)	4	5	0	163	74	0	32.60	1
9	†R. Allen (*North West*)	4	7	1	193	81	0	32.16	1
10	†S. R. Thompson (*North West*)	4	6	0	179	46	0	29.83	2
11	J. Anderson (*Leinster/Ireland*)	5	7	1	141	74	0	23.50	3
12	†A. R. McBrine (*North West*)	4	6	0	133	67	0	22.16	5

BOWLING (7 wickets)

		Style	O	M	R	W	BB	5I	Avge
1	A. Balbirnie (*Leinster/Ireland*)	OB	45.3	13	84	8	4-23	0	10.50
2	G. H. Dockrell (*Leinster*)	SLA	130	47	288	22	6-29	2	13.09
3	G. E. Kidd (*Northern*)	SLA	51	8	140	9	3-36	0	15.55
4	C. A. Young (*North West*)	RM	66.3	10	206	13	5-37	1	15.84
5	T. E. Kane (*Leinster*)	RFM	46	13	115	7	3-45	0	16.42
6	N. L. Smith (*Northern*)	RM	50.5	12	121	7	2-25	0	17.28
7	S. C. Getkate (*Northern*)	RFM	37	3	148	8	4-62	0	18.50
8	E. J. Richardson (*Leinster*)	RM	78	24	208	10	4-33	0	20.80
9	D. Scanlon (*North West*)	RM	70.1	10	288	12	5-29	1	24.00
10	S. R. Thompson (*North West*)	RM	62.4	10	226	7	3-32	0	32.28
11	P. K. D. Chase (*Leinster/Ireland*)	RFM	108.4	19	412	12	3-30	0	34.33

HANLEY ENERGY INTERPROVINCIAL CHAMPIONSHIP IN 2017

	Played	Won	Lost	Drawn	Bonus points Batting	Bonus points Bowling	Rain points	Points
Leinster	4	2	0	2	14	16	0	68
Northern	4	0	1	3	3	15	6	33
North West	4	0	1	3	5	11	6	31

Win = 16pts; draw = 3pts; more than eight hours lost in draw = 3pts. Bonus points awarded for the first 100 overs of each team's first innings: one batting point for the first 150 runs and then for 200, 250 and 300; one bowling point for the third wicket taken and for every subsequent two.

At Eglinton, May 30–June 1. **Drawn. Northern 130** (C. A. Young 5-37) **and 161** (D. Scanlon 5-29); **‡North West 167 and 48-2.** *North West 11pts, Northern 10pts. There were 12 debutants in the inaugural first-class interprovincial match; two of them shone for North West in Northern's second innings, when David Scanlon emulated his international team-mate Craig Young by taking five wickets, and wicketkeeper Rickie-Lee Dougherty made five catches. North West needed only 125 to win, but the last day was washed out.*

At Belfast, June 5–7. **Drawn. Northern 233** (J. A. McCollum 119*) **and 328-6 dec** (J. N. K. Shannon 140*); **‡Leinster 288.** *Northern 9pts, Leinster 10pts. James McCollum, aged 21, completed the tournament's first century, batting for all but three overs of Northern's first innings; the next highest score was 29, by Rob McKinley, who helped him add 77 for the eighth wicket. Leinster took the lead, but Northern batted out the final day: James Shannon scored 140* off 161 balls, with three sixes, and put on 162* for the seventh wicket with Graeme McCarter (62*).*

At Oak Hill, June 20–22. **Drawn. ‡North West 235 and 296** (G. H. Dockrell 6-67); **Leinster 365-9 dec** (E. C. Joyce 156) **and 123-3.** *Leinster 11pts, North West 8pts. Ed Joyce steered Leinster into the lead with 156, his 46th first-class century, hitting three sixes. When North West batted again, Niall O'Brien (87) and Steve Lazars (62) added 132 for the fourth wicket before left-arm spinner George Dockrell separated them on his way to 6-67. On the final day, the players heard that Ireland had been granted Test status.*

At Comber, August 1–3. **Drawn. ‡North West 208-9 dec and 84-1 dec; Northern forfeited first innings and 264-8.** *Northern 10pts, North West 8pts. After the second day was washed out, North West declared twice and Northern forfeited an innings to set up a target of 293; both sides were in with a chance, but the game ended with one needing 29 runs and the other two wickets.*

At Bready, August 30–31. **Leinster won by an innings and four runs. North West 122 and 148; ‡Leinster 274.** *Leinster 23pts, North West 4pts. Leinster's Kevin O'Brien came in at 36-4 and hit 74 in 87 balls, before Eddie Richardson (81) and Tyrone Kane (38) added 70 for the ninth wicket. Dockrell and Andrew Balbirnie bowled out North West for a two-day victory.*

At Dublin, September 5–7. **Leinster won by an innings and 12 runs. Northern 195 and 176** (G. H. Dockrell 6-29); **‡Leinster 383-8 dec** (E. C. Joyce 167*). *Leinster 24pts, Northern 4pts. On the first day, Northern lost their last four for three runs, with David Delany claiming three in five balls. Joyce* *batted throughout Leinster's innings, more than six hours, for the tournament's highest score, in its highest total; he put on 144 for the third wicket with Sean Terry (73) and 138 for the eighth with Tyrone Kane (75). With the title already secured on points, Dockrell collected another six wickets to seal victory. Two fifties for Shannon gave him five in seven innings, in which he also hit ten sixes.*

INTERPROVINCIAL CHAMPIONS

2013	Leinster	2015	Leinster	2017	Leinster
2014	Leinster	2016	Leinster		

The Interprovinical Championship was not first-class for 2013 to 2016.

HANLEY ENERGY INTERPROVINCIAL CUP IN 2017

50-over league

	Played	*Won*	*Lost*	*No result*	*Bonus points*	*Points*	*NRR*
Leinster	4	3	0	1	2	16	1.49
North West	4	1	2	1	0	6	–1.00
Northern	4	0	2	2	0	4	–1.01

The Hanley Energy Interprovincial Trophy appears on page 1116.

Winners of Irish Leagues and Cups
Irish Senior Cup Waringstown. **Leinster League** Leinster. **Leinster Senior Cup** The Hills. **Munster League and Senior Cup** Cork County. **Northern League** Waringstown. **Northern Challenge Cup** CIYMS. **North West League and Senior Cup** Donemana.

NEW ZEALAND CRICKET IN 2017

The dizzy heights

ANDREW ALDERSON

New Zealand's men and women enjoyed spells of brilliance in 2017, but struggled on the biggest stage. They clambered over teams ranked below them, but vertigo often struck against those further up the ladder.

The men's team played seven Tests during the year, all at home, defeating Bangladesh and West Indies 2–0, but losing 1–0 to South Africa. Victory hardly looked likely in the first match, when Bangladesh amassed 595 for eight at Wellington – no side had lost a Test after making as many in the first innings – but after Tom Latham's 177 the visitors collapsed for 160, and New Zealand knocked off the runs with an hour to spare.

It was a different story in the rain-affected series against South Africa. Even without the injured trio of Ross Taylor, Trent Boult and Tim Southee, New Zealand would probably have won the Third Test – and squared the series –

NEW ZEALAND IN 2017

	Played	*Won*	*Lost*	*Drawn/No result*
Tests	7	4	1	2
One-day internationals	20	11	8	1
Twenty20 internationals	8	5	3	–

DECEMBER / JANUARY	2 Tests, 3 ODIs and 2 T20Is (h) v Bangladesh	(see *Wisden 2017*, page 966)
JANUARY / FEBRUARY	3 ODIs (h) v Australia	(page 896)
FEBRUARY / MARCH	3 Tests, 5 ODIs and 1 T20I (h) v South Africa	(page 900)
APRIL		
MAY	Triangular ODI tournament (in Ireland) v Bangladesh and Ireland	(page 887)
JUNE	ICC Champions Trophy (in England)	(page 263)
JULY		
AUGUST		
SEPTEMBER		
OCTOBER / NOVEMBER	3 ODIs and 3 T20Is (a) v India	(page 853)
DECEMBER / JANUARY	2 Tests, 3 ODIs and 3 T20Is (h) v West Indies	(page 914)

For a review of New Zealand domestic cricket from the 2016-17 season, see page 920.

Martin Hunter, Getty Images

Sideways movement: swing bowler Trent Boult throws himself into the fray.

but for the weather. The final day of the season, at Hamilton, was washed out with South Africa, 175 behind on first innings, struggling at 80 for five. Still, it represented a welcome turnaround after a three-day trouncing at Wellington.

All the top five averaged more than 40, led by Taylor (408 runs at 81) and Kane Williamson (566 at 62). The combative Neil Wagner took most wickets – 36 at 25 – and his short-of-a-length bowling often proved incisive, notably when he took seven for 39 in the First Test against West Indies, the fourth-best figures in New Zealand's history. Boult led the way in all formats with 69, well clear of Southee (40).

Several other significant milestones illustrated why this Test side ranked among the country's finest. Southee and Boult became the fifth and sixth New Zealanders to reach 200 Test wickets. Boult got there in his 52nd match, behind only Richard Hadlee (44), but in front of Southee (56), Chris Cairns (58), Chris Martin (62) and Daniel Vettori (63).

Martin Crowe's national record of 17 Test centuries was equalled twice. Williamson got there first, as he grabbed back the initiative against South Africa at Hamilton in March, and Taylor followed him at the same venue in December with the defining knock of the Second Test against West Indies. Taylor then paid tribute to his late mentor: "There was one moment out there. He always said when there's a butterfly, that's him. So I saw a butterfly when I was on about 70… That was pretty good."

The one-day highlight was regaining the Chappell–Hadlee Trophy, even if it was against a depleted Australian side. The first match at Auckland was a cracker: chasing 287, Australia had limped to 54 for five after 13 overs, before Marcus Stoinis exploded with 146 not out from 117 balls. When he reached his century, he received a standing ovation from patrons more accustomed to jeering the opposition after a thirsty day in the sun. But Williamson secured a six-run win when he ran out non-striker Josh Hazlewood from silly mid-on.

There were setbacks in the deciding matches of 50-over series against South Africa and India, but the biggest disappointment came in the Champions Trophy, where defeat by Bangladesh in Cardiff ended New Zealand's interest in the group stages. They had started the year on top of the Twenty20 rankings, but relinquished the No. 1 spot after losing to South Africa before also losing to India, who had never beaten them before in the format.

The women's team stumbled at vital moments, too. Hopes of a first Rose Bowl triumph over Australia in 18 years ended when they lost the decider with four balls to spare. The first match had been notable for Amy Satterthwaite – later named the ICC women's ODI Player of the Year – following Kumar Sangakkara in scoring four consecutive centuries in 50-over internationals. But the women's World Cup was a letdown, with the White Ferns finishing outside the top four for the first time. Their fate was sealed when India skittled them for 79, New Zealand's lowest in all 11 editions of the tournament.

The Champions Trophy was New Zealand's only cricket during the northern summer, so several contracted players took the chance to perform overseas: Wagner had a big part in Essex's County Championship victory. Another left-arm seamer, Mitchell McClenaghan, caused a stir by opting out of his NZC contract in favour of a freelance life. His decision to pursue the T20 dollar ignited a debate over whether national selection still represented the pinnacle of a New Zealand playing career.

Grant Elliott, Peter Fulton, Jeetan Patel and Luke Ronchi retired from international cricket, although all except Fulton continued at domestic level worldwide. Elliott bowed out in September by helping take the international game back to Pakistan, when he played for the World XI at Lahore.

Tom Blundell provided a highlight when he replaced the injured B-J. Watling as wicketkeeper in the First Test against West Indies. He demonstrated assured glovework before becoming the 11th New Zealander to score a century on debut. As a Wellington College old boy, Blundell spent his adolescent years commuting past the Basin Reserve. And he walked home after the Test carrying his gear – plus a souvenir stump.

NZC's budgeted NZ$5.7m operating loss blew out to $9.3m for the 2016-17 financial year, mainly because of a revamped ICC funding model and the strong New Zealand dollar, which reduced revenues calculated in US dollars. However, those financial losses came with social gains. A total of 175,000 played cricket in the 12 months to July 2017, up 11% on the previous year; that included a 12% growth among women. For the first time, modified games – with teams of fewer than 11 a side – outnumbered traditional fixtures, which now embraced the once-radical Twenty20 format. The days of New Zealand's parents and children spending their summer Saturdays engaged in the sport are dwindling. Flexibility has become a fundamental thread in the nation's cricket fabric, something the governing body are more conscious of than ever.

NEW ZEALAND v AUSTRALIA IN 2016-17

ANDREW ALDERSON

One-day internationals (3): New Zealand 2, Australia 0

In the build-up to this series, neither country seemed bursting with enthusiasm for 50-over cricket. Their last meeting, in Australia in December, had been a one-sided affair, New Zealand yielding the Chappell–Hadlee Trophy 3–0. Soon after, it was announced that one of the scheduled rematches would morph into a Twenty20 triangular tournament in 2017-18 also involving England. Meanwhile the lustrous Big Bash League, which finished two days before the first match, in Auckland, continued to distract from the international stage.

The sense of apathy was compounded by selection: Australia had a Test tour to India on their minds, and rested David Warner and Usman Khawaja. Steve Smith was also left out, after spraining an ankle. His replacement was not Cameron White, recently named domestic one-day Player of the Year, but Sam Heazlett, a 21-year-old left-hander who had not even appeared in a 50-over game for his native Queensland.

White suggested the national side had come to resemble a development team, and questioned whether weight of runs in state cricket was being ignored in favour of form in the BBL. His comments drew support from former players, but the chairman of selectors, Trevor Hohns, who had worked with Heazlett in his previous role as Queensland talent manager, defended the decision: he said White had been picked as a young man himself and given plenty of opportunities, but performed "OK without being earth-shattering". There was more shuffling when Matthew Wade, captain in place of Smith, pulled out with a back injury on the morning of the first game; Aaron Finch led the side.

Yet the series had its moments, particularly the epic denouement in Auckland, where Australian all-rounder Marcus Stoinis won the favour of a partisan crowd, if not quite the match. Napier's squelching turf meant things sagged in the middle, but New Zealand held their nerve at Hamilton, where Ross Taylor and Trent Boult swung a tense encounter, as New Zealand regained the trophy at the first opportunity.

"There was little about a long, slow walk back to his mark to make South African hearts flutter: he bore the sagging shoulders of an accountant returning home from a commute."

England v South Africa in 2017, Third Test, page 312

AUSTRALIAN TOURING PARTY

*M. S. Wade, P. J. Cummins, J. P. Faulkner, A. J. Finch, P. S. P. Handscomb, J. R. Hazlewood, T. M. Head, S. D. Heazlett, S. E. Marsh, G. J. Maxwell, B. Stanlake, M. A. Starc, M. P. Stoinis, A. Zampa. *Coach:* D. S. Lehmann.

S. P. D. Smith withdrew unfit and was replaced by Heazlett, with Wade taking over as captain. Wade injured his back before the first game, and went home; Finch took charge for all three games.

NEW ZEALAND v AUSTRALIA

First One-Day International

At Auckland, January 30, 2017. New Zealand won by six runs. Toss: Australia. One-day international debut: S. D. Heazlett.

In his second one-day international, Marcus Stoinis walked to the crease with little hope of victory: chasing 287, Australia had slipped to 54 for five, soon to become 67 for six. But he staged a remarkable comeback, unleashing 11 sixes on his way to a 117-ball 146 not out, 90 more than the top six combined, and a List A ground record. Even the locals, notorious for their boozy barracking, stood to applaud. Having earlier shown his worth as a heavy-set, chest-on bowler, Stoinis became the first Australian to collect three wickets and score a hundred in the same ODI. After the ninth wicket fell with his side still 61 short, he faced every ball, and hit two consecutive sixes off Southee to bring up the most unequal of fifty partnerships. One more blow would have tied the scores, but Stoinis drove to short mid-on, where Williamson gathered smartly and underarmed at the stumps. Hazlewood, trying to regain his ground, was out for the first time in his 34th ODI, having not faced a ball in 26 minutes at the crease. As the fielders engulfed Williamson, so did relief: he had dropped Stoinis at mid-off on 91. New Zealand had relied on a more collective approach, as Neesham's breezy 48 complemented half-centuries from Guptill and Broom. Latham scored just seven but, keeping for only the fourth time in his 50th ODI, equalled the national record with five dismissals, including two stumpings off the calm and accurate Santner.

Man of the Match: M. P. Stoinis.

HIGHEST SCORE FROM NO. 7 IN ONE-DAY INTERNATIONALS

170*	L. Ronchi	New Zealand v Sri Lanka at Dunedin	2014-15
146*	**M. P. Stoinis**	**Australia v New Zealand at Auckland**	**2016-17**
139*	M. S. Dhoni	Asia v Africa at Chennai	2007
130	S. M. Pollock	Africa v Asia at Bangalore	2007
121	J. C. Buttler	England v Sri Lanka at Lord's	2014
116	J. P. Faulkner	Australia v India at Bangalore	2013-14
113*	M. S. Dhoni	India v Pakistan at Chennai	2012-13
111*	M. Kaif	India v Zimbabwe at Colombo (RPS)	2002-03
111*	T. M. Odoyo	Kenya v Canada at Nairobi (Gymkhana)	2007-08
109*	Abdul Razzaq	Pakistan v South Africa at Abu Dhabi	2010-11

New Zealand

M. J. Guptill b Stoinis	61
†T. W. M. Latham c Handscomb b Starc	7
*K. S. Williamson c Maxwell b Stoinis	24
L. R. P. L. Taylor b Head	16
N. T. Broom c Starc b Faulkner	73
C. Munro c Finch b Stoinis	2
J. D. S. Neesham c Head b Hazlewood	48
M. J. Santner c Maxwell b Cummins	7
T. G. Southee c Faulkner b Cummins	0
L. H. Ferguson not out	3
T. A. Boult not out	16
B 8, lb 5, w 16	29
1/13 (2) 2/87 (3) 3/128 (4) 4/130 (1) 5/134 (6) 6/210 (7) 7/246 (8) 8/251 (9) 9/269 (5) — 10 overs: 62-1 (9 wkts, 50 overs)	286

Starc 10–0–59–1; Hazlewood 10–0–48–1; Cummins 9–0–67–2; Faulkner 6–0–29–1; Stoinis 10–0–49–3; Head 5–0–21–1.

Australia

*A. J. Finch c Neesham b Boult	4	M. A. Starc c Neesham b Santner	3
T. M. Head c Munro b Boult	5	J. R. Hazlewood run out	0
S. E. Marsh st Latham b Santner	16		
†P. S. P. Handscomb c Latham b Southee	7	Lb 2, w 12	14
G. J. Maxwell c Latham b Ferguson	20		—
S. D. Heazlett c Latham b Ferguson	4	1/9 (1) 2/10 (2) 3/18 (4) (47 overs)	280
M. P. Stoinis not out	146	4/48 (3) 5/54 (5) 6/67 (6)	
J. P. Faulkner b Munro	25	7/148 (8) 8/196 (9) 9/226 (10)	
P. J. Cummins st Latham b Santner	36	10/280 (11)	10 overs: 45-3

Southee 10–0–63–1; Boult 9–0–58–2; Ferguson 10–0–44–2; Santner 10–1–44–3; Neesham 5–0–49–0; Munro 3–0–20–1.

Umpires: W. R. Knights and R. S. A. Palliyaguruge. Third umpire: H. D. P. K. Dharmasena. Referee: R. S. Madugalle.

NEW ZEALAND v AUSTRALIA

Second One-Day International

At Napier, February 2, 2017 (day/night). Abandoned.

After the region's driest January on record, the drought broke on the morning of the game. The weather cleared before 2pm, but appalling drainage prevented play. It was Napier's second successive one-day international abandonment, and an inquiry began next day, led by the local council, who own the ground, and New Zealand Cricket. Within a fortnight, the ODI against South Africa scheduled for March 1 was moved to Hamilton to avoid the risk of a repeat.

NEW ZEALAND v AUSTRALIA

Third One-Day International

At Hamilton, February 5, 2017. New Zealand won by 24 runs. Toss: New Zealand.

Leading New Zealand's defence of 281, Boult claimed six for 33, his best return, to underline his No. 1 one-day ranking and secure New Zealand's eighth successive win in home bilateral 50-over series. Australia lost wickets in bunches: Marsh and Handscomb fell with the total on 44 in the eighth over, Finch and Maxwell six balls apart in the 21st and 22nd, and Head and Faulkner in the 33rd, to make it 174 for six. Santner, on his 25th birthday, lured Stoinis into a slapped drive to long-on for his second scalp, and had conceded only 19 at the end of his eighth over. Starc and Cummins belted 31 off his last two to rekindle Australian hopes but, when Boult beat Cummins for pace, the contest was finished. Earlier, Taylor had cruised to his 16th ODI century, equalling Nathan Astle's New Zealand record. He was savage early on – beating Brownlie to 50 despite conceding a 36-run head start – then consolidated after four wickets fell for 33, including Brownlie for a personal-best 63. Taylor went from 68 to 97 in singles, expertly guiding New Zealand into a winning position.

Man of the Match: T. A. Boult.

BEST BOWLING FOR NEW ZEALAND IN AN ODI

7-33	T. G. Southee	v England at Wellington	2014-15
6-19	S. E. Bond	v India at Bulawayo	2005-06
6-23	S. E. Bond	v Australia at Port Elizabeth	2002-03
6-25	S. B. Styris	v West Indies at Port-of-Spain	2002
6-33	**T. A. Boult**	**v Australia at Hamilton**	**2016-17**

New Zealand

D. G. Brownlie c Handscomb b Faulkner . . 63
†T. W. M. Latham c Hazlewood b Starc 0
*K. S. Williamson c Handscomb b Cummins 36
L. R. P. L. Taylor c Stoinis b Faulkner 107
N. T. Broom c Handscomb b Faulkner 8
C. Munro c Starc b Hazlewood 3
J. D. S. Neesham b Hazlewood 1
M. J. Santner not out 38
T. G. Southee b Starc. 10
L. H. Ferguson b Starc. 0
T. A. Boult not out 1

Lb 6, w 7, nb 1. 14

1/6 (2) 2/76 (3) (9 wkts, 50 overs) 281
3/176 (1) 4/198 (5)
5/205 (6) 6/209 (7) 7/246 (4)
8/265 (9) 9/265 (10) 10 overs: 59-1

Starc 10–1–62–3; Hazlewood 10–0–44–2; Stoinis 4–0–22–0; Cummins 10–0–47–1; Zampa 7–0–41–0; Faulkner 9–0–59–3.

Australia

*A. J. Finch c Boult b Williamson 56
S. E. Marsh run out 22
†P. S. P. Handscomb b Boult 0
T. M. Head c Brownlie b Boult. 53
G. J. Maxwell c Latham b Santner 0
M. P. Stoinis c Neesham b Santner 42
J. P. Faulkner c Taylor b Boult 0
P. J. Cummins c Santner b Boult. 27
M. A. Starc not out 29
A. Zampa c Taylor b Boult 1
J. R. Hazlewood b Boult 4

Lb 12, w 11 23

1/44 (2) 2/44 (3) 3/119 (1) (47 overs) 257
4/120 (5) 5/173 (4) 6/174 (7)
7/198 (6) 8/249 (8) 9/253 (10)
10/257 (11) 10 overs: 52-2

Southee 8–0–39–0; Boult 10–1–33–6; Ferguson 9–1–62–0; Neesham 3–0–17–0; Santner 10–0–50–2; Williamson 7–0–44–1.

Umpires: C. M. Brown and R. S. A. Palliyaguruge. Third umpire: H. D. P. K. Dharmasena.
Referee: R. S. Madugalle.

NEW ZEALAND v SOUTH AFRICA IN 2016-17

MARK GEENTY

Twenty20 international (1): New Zealand 0, South Africa 1
One-day internationals (5): New Zealand 2, South Africa 3
Test matches (3): New Zealand 0, South Africa 1

The chattering teeth of Faf du Plessis finally eased into a smile on the last day of South Africa's six-week tour. Having previously cursed New Zealand's fickle weather, he now welcomed one final downpour, which sealed another series win, and left the New Zealanders kicking the saturated Hamilton turf. Du Plessis had won his three previous Test series as captain, and that record was under serious threat. But after going to sleep with his team on the brink of defeat in the Third Test, he woke to the sound of pouring rain. A few hours later, he was shaking hands with Kane Williamson. As they had five years earlier, South Africa emerged from New Zealand celebrating victory in all three formats.

This tour followed quickly on the heels of South Africa's home series against Sri Lanka, and they set the tone with a big win in the Twenty20 international on a bouncy drop-in pitch at Eden Park. They then clinched the five-match one-day series in a decider on the same ground. The genius of A. B. de Villiers shone throughout, and New Zealand were grateful he opted out of the Test series, citing a desire to be fit and fresh for the 2019 World Cup. But his absence did not cost South Africa.

The hosts fought hard but, when South Africa won, they did so emphatically, aided by four alarming New Zealand collapses at Auckland and Wellington across the formats. These followed a similar pattern: softened up by South African pace, then finished off by spin – Imran Tahir with the white ball, Keshav Maharaj with the red.

Slow and steady couldn't win the race for New Zealand, even if the groundsmen tried to help out, going against the recent trend of grassy, seaming pitches in an attempt to nullify South Africa's pace attack. It partially worked: Vernon Philander was far less effective than in 2011-12, when he took 21 wickets at 15; and on dry, sluggish surfaces at Dunedin and Hamilton, New Zealand chose two spinners – Jeetan Patel and Mitchell Santner – in a home Test for the first time since March 2010. But South Africa's slow bowlers also enjoyed the conditions.

The Tests were decided by the only result of the series, over three days at Wellington, where New Zealand subsided softly against Maharaj's left-arm spin on a Basin Reserve pitch better suited to fast bowling. Equally crucial was a counter-attack from Quinton de Kock after New Zealand had taken control, while Morne Morkel returned in impressive style after a Test absence of more than a year. The other two Tests left New Zealand ruing their climate. Dunedin gave the South Africans a frigid welcome, and the umpires donned gloves before rain intervened, with New Zealand holding a slight advantage. Then, at

Hamilton, the home bowlers required only five more wickets, with South Africa still 95 behind, to level the series.

A mammoth season, which had begun in Zimbabwe in July, took its toll, and New Zealand limped into that game without Ross Taylor, Trent Boult or Tim Southee, all injured. Taylor and Boult had also been absent in Wellington. It made New Zealand's comeback all the more impressive, inspired by Williamson's epic 176, which at the age of 26 drew him level with Martin Crowe's national record of 17 Test centuries.

By the end, Williamson must have wondered what he had done to upset the cricketing gods. He had led strongly, and helped his side into good positions at Dunedin and Hamilton – but lost eight tosses out of nine. For New Zealand, it made an already daunting task even harder.

SOUTH AFRICAN TOURING PARTY

*F. du Plessis (T/50/20), H. M. Amla (T/50/20), T. Bavuma (T), F. Behardien (50/20), S. C. Cook (T), T. B. de Bruyn (T), Q. de Kock (T/50/20), A. B. de Villiers (50/20), J-P. Duminy (T/50/20), D. Elgar (T), Imran Tahir (50/20), H. Klaasen (T), K. A. Maharaj (T), D. A. Miller (50/20), M. Morkel (T), C. H. Morris (T/50/20), D. Olivier (T), W. D. Parnell (T/50/20), D. Paterson (50/20), A. L. Phehlukwayo (50/20), V. D. Philander (T), D. L. Piedt (T), D. Pretorius (50/20), K. Rabada (T/50/20), T. Shamsi (50/20). *Coach:* R. C. Domingo.

De Villiers captained in the limited-overs matches. Pretorius joined the tour late after the birth of his first child, after which Paterson went home. Piedt joined the squad before the Third Test, and Morris left the tour.

TEST AVERAGES

NEW ZEALAND – BATTING AND FIELDING

	T	*I*	*NO*	*R*	*HS*	*100*	*50*	*Avge*	*Ct*
K. S. Williamson	3	4	0	309	176	2	0	77.25	2
†J. A. Raval	3	4	0	256	88	0	3	64.00	1
†H. M. Nicholls	3	4	0	137	118	1	0	34.25	2
B-J. Watling	3	4	0	137	50	0	1	34.25	10
C. de Grandhomme	2	3	0	61	57	0	1	20.33	1
†N. Wagner	3	4	2	38	32	0	0	19.00	1
†T. W. M. Latham	3	4	0	74	50	0	1	18.50	3
J. S. Patel	3	4	1	38	17*	0	0	12.66	1
N. T. Broom	2	3	0	32	20	0	0	10.66	0
†J. D. S. Neesham	2	3	0	26	15	0	0	8.66	5

Played in two Tests: †M. J. Santner 4, 41. Played in one Test: T. A. Boult 2 (1 ct); M. J. Henry 12; T. G. Southee 27, 4; L. R. P. L. Taylor 15* (1 ct).

BOWLING

	Style	*O*	*M*	*R*	*W*	*BB*	*5I*	*Avge*
T. A. Boult	LFM	47.4	16	98	5	4-64	0	19.60
M. J. Henry	RFM	35	6	113	5	4-93	0	22.60
C. de Grandhomme	RFM	63	17	149	6	3-52	0	24.83
N. Wagner	LFM	118.2	20	385	12	3-88	0	32.08
J. S. Patel	OB	102	30	266	7	2-22	0	38.00
T. G. Southee	RFM	33	9	115	3	2-98	0	38.33

Also bowled: J. D. S. Neesham (RFM) 27.3–4–123–2; M. J. Santner (SLA) 49–14–100–2.

SOUTH AFRICA – BATTING AND FIELDING

	T	*I*	*NO*	*R*	*HS*	*100*	*50*	*Avge*	*Ct/St*
F. du Plessis	3	5	2	198	56*	0	3	66.00	2
†Q. de Kock	3	5	1	210	91	0	2	52.50	13/2
†M. Morkel	3	3	2	49	40	0	0	49.00	0
†D. Elgar	3	6	0	265	140	1	1	44.16	3
T. Bavuma	3	5	0	189	89	0	2	37.80	0
V. D. Philander	3	4	2	70	37*	0	0	35.00	2
H. M. Amla	3	6	1	153	50	0	1	30.60	3
†J-P. Duminy	3	6	1	104	39	0	0	20.80	5
†K. Rabada	3	3	0	47	34	0	0	15.66	0
K. A. Maharaj	3	3	0	15	9	0	0	5.00	1
S. C. Cook	2	4	0	17	11	0	0	4.25	0

Played in one Test: T. B. de Bruyn 0, 12.

BOWLING

	Style	*O*	*M*	*R*	*W*	*BB*	*5I*	*Avge*
K. A. Maharaj	SLA	114.5	26	299	15	6-40	2	19.93
M. Morkel	RF	89.1	16	294	11	4-100	0	26.72
J-P. Duminy	OB	25.3	3	107	4	4-47	0	26.75
K. Rabada	RF	100	21	311	8	4-122	0	38.87

Also bowled: T. Bavuma (RM) 2–0–7–0; D. Elgar (SLA) 1–0–13–0; V. D. Philander (RFM) 87–28–203–2.

NEW ZEALAND v SOUTH AFRICA

Twenty20 International

At Auckland, February 17, 2017 (floodlit). South Africa won by 78 runs. Toss: New Zealand. Twenty20 international debut: G. D. Phillips.

South Africa's previous trip to Eden Park had ended in tears. But, nearly two years on from their gripping World Cup semi-final defeat by New Zealand, it was the exuberant celebrations of Imran Tahir that provided the indelible image. This was some statement from South Africa. After Amla had come through a testing new-ball spell from Boult to set up what seemed a par total, their bowlers overpowered a jittery batting line-up for 107 inside 15 overs. New Zealand had introduced the 20-year-old South African-born opener Glenn Phillips – the star of the domestic T20 competition, and yet to make his first-class debut for Auckland – and were without Martin Guptill and Ross Taylor. Guptill was nursing a hamstring injury, but Taylor's absence dominated the build-up, as he spoke of his frustration at a lack of communication from the selectors. With bigger assignments ahead, South Africa rested Kagiso Rabada, and it proved wise. The hostile Morris extracted enough bounce to unnerve an inexperienced New Zealand top order – his second over was a double-wicket maiden – and Tahir also relished the springy surface, his googly too hot to handle. He became the third South African bowler to take five wickets in a Twenty20 international, racing across the turf to rejoice in each dismissal as if it were his first.

Man of the Match: Imran Tahir.

South Africa

		B	4/6
1 H. M. Amla *c 4 b 9*	62	43	9/1
2 †Q. de Kock *c 8 b 11*	0	4	0
3 *F. du Plessis *lbw b 6*	36	25	1/3
4 A. B. de Villiers *c 9 b 6*	26	17	3/1
5 J-P. Duminy *run out*	29	16	2/2
6 F. Behardien *c 5 b 11*	8	7	0/1
7 C. H. Morris *not out*	9	7	0/1
8 W. D. Parnell *not out*	4	1	1
B 4, lb 4, w 3	11		
6 overs: 56-1 (20 overs)	185-6		

1/15 2/102 3/123 4/145 5/171 6/181

9 A. L. Phehlukwayo, 10 Imran Tahir and 11 D. Paterson did not bat.

Boult 4–16–8–2; Wheeler 4–9–49–1; Southee 4–8–47–0; Santner 4–3–40–0; de Grandhomme 3–5–22–2; Munro 1–3–11–0.

New Zealand

		B	4/6
1 G. D. Phillips *c 2 b 7*	5	11	0
2 *K. S. Williamson *c 8 b 9*	13	13	2
3 C. Munro *b 7*	0	1	0
4 T. C. Bruce *b 10*	33	27	3/2
5 C. J. Anderson *c 2 b 9*	6	10	0
6 C. de Grandhomme *c 5 b 10*	15	7	0/2
7 †L. Ronchi *c 2 b 10*	0	1	0
8 M. J. Santner *c 1 b 9*	5	6	1
9 B. M. Wheeler *b 10*	6	6	1
10 T. G. Southee *b 10*	20	6	0/3
11 T. A. Boult *not out*	1	1	0
Lb 1, w 2	3		
6 overs: 34-2 (14.5 overs)	107		

1/10 2/10 3/38 4/55 5/60 6/60 7/68 8/80 9/106

Morris 3–14–10–2; Paterson 2–5–13–0; Parnell 3–4–40–0; Phehlukwayo 3–9–19–3; Imran Tahir 3.5–12–24–5.

Umpires: C. M. Brown and W. R. Knights. Third umpire: S. B. Haig.
Referee: J. Srinath.

NEW ZEALAND v SOUTH AFRICA

First One-Day International

At Hamilton, February 19, 2017 (day/night). South Africa won by four wickets. Toss: South Africa.

De Villiers guided South Africa home once again, with a ball to spare, hitting the winning runs after Phehlukwayo had struck a six apiece off Boult and Southee to wrest back a match that was slipping away. It also extended South Africa's winning streak in one-day internationals to 12, the previous 11 all at home. De Villiers described the conditions as some of the toughest he had experienced, as both sets of batsmen grappled with sharp turn on a crusty pitch that had spent hours under cover. Requiring a tick above a run a ball in a game reduced to 34 overs by rain, he nudged it around and negotiated some snorters from spinners Santner and Sodhi on their home track. A rapid opening stand of 88 between de Kock and Amla had set up the chase, then de Villiers showed enough faith in Phehlukwayo against New Zealand's senior pace bowlers. Earlier, their batsmen looked to have scored enough after de Grandhomme and Southee plundered 51 off 23 balls at the death. That included 25 off the last over, from Morris, who had snared four of the top five in another lively display. Williamson fought back with 59 off 53, while Rabada bowled impressively in his first international in New Zealand.

Man of the Match: Q. de Kock.

New Zealand

D. G. Brownlie c Behardien b Morris	31
†T. W. M. Latham lbw b Morris	0
*K. S. Williamson b Shamsi	59
L. R. P. L. Taylor c and b Morris	1
N. T. Broom c Behardien b Morris	2
J. D. S. Neesham c de Kock b Rabada	29
M. J. Santner c de Kock b Rabada	17
C. de Grandhomme not out	34
T. G. Southee not out	24
B 1, w 9	10
1/19 (2) 2/69 (1) 3/72 (4) 4/82 (5) 5/108 (3) 6/136 (7) 7/156 (6) (7 wkts, 34 overs)	207
7 overs: 31-1	

I. S. Sodhi and T. A. Boult did not bat.

Rabada 7–1–31–2; Morris 7–0–62–4; Phehlukwayo 5–0–28–0; Imran Tahir 7–0–42–0; Shamsi 7–1–39–1; Duminy 1–0–4–0.

South Africa

†Q. de Kock c Taylor b Boult	69	A. L. Phehlukwayo not out	29
H. M. Amla c and b Williamson	35		
F. du Plessis lbw b Sodhi	14	B 2, lb 3, w 4	9
*A. B. de Villiers not out	37		—
J-P. Duminy c and b Southee	1	1/88 (2) 2/117 (3) (6 wkts, 33.5 overs)	210
F. Behardien b Southee	0	3/125 (1) 4/126 (5)	
C. H. Morris c Boult b Santner	16	5/126 (6) 6/156 (7)	7 overs: 37-0

K. Rabada, Imran Tahir and T. Shamsi did not bat.

Santner 7–0–33–1; Boult 7–0–45–1; Southee 6.5–0–47–2; de Grandhomme 4–0–27–0; Sodhi 7–0–36–1; Williamson 2–0–17–1.

Umpires: W. R. Knights and J. S. Wilson. Third umpire: P. R. Reiffel.
Referee: J. Srinath.

NEW ZEALAND v SOUTH AFRICA

Second One-Day International

At Christchurch (Hagley Oval), February 22, 2017. New Zealand won by six runs. Toss: South Africa.

Off the final ball of New Zealand's innings, Taylor crashed Parnell to the cover boundary, and brought the Christchurch crowd to their feet. A few hours later, they rose again for a nail-biting victory, and an end to South Africa's winning streak. But this was Taylor's day. Paced to perfection, his unbeaten 110-ball century was his 17th in one-day internationals, taking him past Nathan Astle's national record, and beyond 6,000 runs in the format, in his 166th innings, the fastest of the four New Zealanders to reach the mark. He and Williamson had set up the match with a third-wicket stand of 104, though Taylor was not at his free-flowing best. Neesham's blistering 71 not out off 57 balls added impetus, before Taylor hit out to lift his team to a defendable, if not unbeatable, total. Again, de Villiers and Boult were the key combatants – and this time Boult won, having de Villiers caught behind for 45. Then, after a late onslaught from Pretorius took the game to the wire, Boult – who had dropped him at long-off on 15 – held his nerve, bowling Pretorius for a 27-ball 50, and leaving Southee to defend 15 off the last over. Phehlukwayo failed to score from the first four balls, all pinpoint yorkers, rendering irrelevant his boundaries off the last two. On the sixth anniversary of the earthquake that had destroyed much of the city, the locals had something to cheer.

Man of the Match: L. R. P. L. Taylor.

New Zealand

D. G. Brownlie lbw b Pretorius	34	J. D. S. Neesham not out	71
†T. W. M. Latham c Phehlukwayo b Parnell	2		
*K. S. Williamson c Phehlukwayo b Imran Tahir	69	Lb 2, w 7	9
			—
L. R. P. L. Taylor not out	102	1/13 (2) 2/53 (1) (4 wkts, 50 overs)	289
N. T. Broom c Duminy b Pretorius	2	3/157 (3) 4/166 (5)	10 overs: 39-1

M. J. Santner, C. de Grandhomme, T. G. Southee, I. S. Sodhi and T. A. Boult did not bat.

Morris 10–0–58–0; Parnell 8–0–49–1; Pretorius 10–0–40–2; Imran Tahir 10–0–61–1; Phehlukwayo 9–0–62–0; Duminy 3–0–17–0.

South Africa

H. M. Amla lbw b Southee	10
†Q. de Kock c Neesham b Boult	57
F. du Plessis b de Grandhomme	11
J-P. Duminy st Latham b Santner	34
*A. B. de Villiers c Latham b Boult	45
D. A. Miller c Latham b Sodhi	28
D. Pretorius b Boult	50
C. H. Morris run out	7
W. D. Parnell lbw b Santner	0
A. L. Phehlukwayo not out	29
Imran Tahir not out	0
Lb 5, w 7	12
(9 wkts, 50 overs)	283

1/22 (1) 2/51 (3) 3/108 (4) 4/124 (2) 5/192 (6) 6/199 (5) 7/214 (8) 8/214 (9) 9/275 (7)

10 overs: 48-1

Southee 10–0–60–1; Boult 10–0–63–3; Neesham 3–0–20–0; de Grandhomme 4–1–10–1; Williamson 3–0–16–0; Sodhi 10–0–63–1; Santner 10–0–46–2.

Umpires: C. M. Brown and P. R. Reiffel. Third umpire: J. S. Wilson.
Referee: J. Srinath.

NEW ZEALAND v SOUTH AFRICA

Third One-Day International

At Wellington (Westpac Stadium), February 25, 2017 (day/night). South Africa won by 159 runs. Toss: South Africa.

Another batting masterclass from de Villiers was made to look superhuman when New Zealand succumbed meekly to give South Africa the upper hand once more. At the ground known as the Cake Tin, the hosts failed to rise, and their collapse for 112 ensured their heaviest defeat by South Africa, surpassing the 143-run margin at Auckland in March 1999. De Villiers's 85 off 80 balls took him past 9,000 one-day international runs, in his 205th innings, breaking the record of 228 held by India's Sourav Ganguly; he finished with 9,080 runs from precisely 9,080 balls. De Villiers was so good he masked the demons in the surface which later tormented New Zealand. His solid defence and deft placement were occasionally interrupted by a bullet-like blur to the concrete surrounds, after de Kock had set things up with his fifth successive ODI score of 50-plus, equalling Jonty Rhodes's national record. A late flurry from Parnell lifted South Africa to 271, which was handy enough, but still offered New Zealand hope. It looked a different game after the break, however, as the ball seamed just enough to cause headaches. Latham fell for his third duck in four innings, and South Africa's pace quartet dismantled the chase, which properly unravelled after Phehlukwayo nipped one back to rattle Williamson's stumps. That was the first of eight wickets to fall for 64, Pretorius ending with a career-best three for five.

Man of the Match: A. B. de Villiers.

South Africa

†Q. de Kock c Neesham b de Grandhomme	68
H. M. Amla c Williamson b Southee	7
F. du Plessis c Southee b de Grandhomme	36
*A. B. de Villiers c Neesham b Boult	85
J-P. Duminy run out	16
D. A. Miller c Broom b Santner	3
D. Pretorius b Ferguson	11
W. D. Parnell run out	35
A. L. Phehlukwayo not out	1
Lb 2, w 7	9
(8 wkts, 50 overs)	271

1/41 (2) 2/114 (3) 3/115 (1) 4/157 (5) 5/164 (6) 6/180 (7) 7/264 (4) 8/271 (8)

10 overs: 48-1

K. Rabada and Imran Tahir did not bat.

Southee 10–0–66–1; Boult 10–0–47–1; Ferguson 10–0–71–1; de Grandhomme 10–0–40–2; Santner 10–0–45–1.

New Zealand

D. G. Brownlie c de Kock b Rabada	2	L. H. Ferguson b Imran Tahir	4
†T. W. M. Latham c Duminy b Parnell	0	T. A. Boult c de Villiers b Pretorius	4
*K. S. Williamson b Phehlukwayo	23		
L. R. P. L. Taylor lbw b Pretorius	18	W 8	8
N. T. Broom c Amla b Phehlukwayo	0		—
J. D. S. Neesham c and b Parnell	13	1/2 (2) 2/11 (1) 3/48 (3) (32.2 overs)	112
M. J. Santner b Pretorius	1	4/48 (4) 5/51 (5) 6/58 (7)	
C. de Grandhomme not out	34	7/77 (6) 8/82 (9) 9/95 (10)	
T. G. Southee c de Kock b Rabada	5	10/112 (11)	10 overs: 38-2

Rabada 10–0–39–2; Parnell 8–0–33–2; Phehlukwayo 5–0–12–2; Pretorius 5.2–1–5–3; Imran Tahir 4–1–23–1.

Umpires: C. M. Brown and J. S. Wilson. Third umpire: P. R. Reiffel.
Referee: J. Srinath.

NEW ZEALAND v SOUTH AFRICA

Fourth One-Day International

At Hamilton, March 1, 2017 (day/night). New Zealand won by seven wickets. Toss: South Africa.

As each ball disappeared further into the Hamilton night off Guptill's blade, even the man himself looked disbelieving. His file of great ODI hits was already bulging, including a World Cup quarter-final double-century, and this one left him with New Zealand's highest three scores in the format. In his first game back after a month out with a hamstring injury, Guptill – who overturned an lbw

HIGHEST SCORES IN ODI RUN-CHASES

185*	S. R. Watson	Australia v Bangladesh at Mirpur	2010-11
183*	M. S. Dhoni	India v Sri Lanka at Jaipur	2005-06
183	V. Kohli	India v Pakistan at Mirpur	2011-12
180*	**M. J. Guptill**	**New Zealand v South Africa at Hamilton**	**2016-17**
178	Q. de Kock	South Africa v Australia at Centurion	2016-17
175	H. H. Gibbs	South Africa v Australia at Johannesburg	2005-06
175	S. R. Tendulkar	India v Australia at Hyderabad	2009-10
173	D. A. Warner	Australia v South Africa at Cape Town	2016-17
162	J. J. Roy	England v Sri Lanka at The Oval	2016
161*	S. R. Watson	Australia v England at Melbourne	2010-11

All led to victory, except for Tendulkar and Warner.

decision off Pretorius when 62 – swung freely and rapidly, to help his side cruise to a target of 280, and square the series with five overs to spare. His 180 not out required just 138 deliveries; 15 of them disappeared for four, while 11 soared over Seddon Park's white picket fence and, in some cases, on to nearby streets. No one could quell him, not even South Africa's trump card, Imran Tahir: of the 56 runs he conceded on another turning pitch, Guptill made 43, including 30 in sixes. Tahir did remove Taylor for a measured 66, but not before he and his best mate had added 180 for the third wicket, the highest for any New Zealand wicket against South Africa. New Zealand had ordered a spin-friendly pitch, and gave the new balls to Patel and Santner – the first time two slow bowlers had opened in the first innings of a one-day international. Patel removed the in-form de Kock first ball, but South Africa were boosted to a competitive total by a blistering 72 not out from 59 balls by de Villiers, as 100 came from the last eight overs. For once, however, his success did not lead his side to victory.

Man of the Match: M. J. Guptill.

South Africa

H. M. Amla b Patel	40	W. D. Parnell run out	29
†Q. de Kock c Ronchi b Patel	0		
F. du Plessis c Santner b Neesham	67	W 7	7
J-P. Duminy b Southee	25		—
*A. B. de Villiers not out	72	1/1 (2) 2/66 (1) (8 wkts, 50 overs)	279
D. A. Miller c Brownlie b Santner	1	3/128 (4) 4/140 (3)	
D. Pretorius run out	10	5/143 (6) 6/158 (7)	
C. H. Morris b Boult	28	7/216 (8) 8/279 (9)	10 overs: 51-1

K. Rabada and Imran Tahir did not bat.

Patel 10–0–57–2; Santner 10–0–40–1; Boult 10–0–70–1; Southee 10–0–70–1; de Grandhomme 2–0–10–0; Williamson 3–0–17–0; Neesham 5–0–15–1.

New Zealand

M. J. Guptill not out	180
D. G. Brownlie c de Kock b Rabada	4
*K. S. Williamson lbw b Imran Tahir	21
L. R. P. L. Taylor c Amla b Imran Tahir	66
†L. Ronchi not out	1
Lb 4, w 4	8
	—
1/5 (2) 2/77 (3) (3 wkts, 45 overs)	280
3/257 (4)	10 overs: 57-1

J. D. S. Neesham, M. J. Santner, C. de Grandhomme, T. G. Southee, J. S. Patel and T. A. Boult did not bat.

Rabada 8–0–41–1; Parnell 7–1–44–0; Morris 9–0–54–0; Duminy 3–0–26–0; Pretorius 8–0–55–0; Imran Tahir 10–2–56–2.

Umpires: W. R. Knights and P. R. Reiffel. Third umpire: J. S. Wilson.
Referee: J. Srinath.

NEW ZEALAND v SOUTH AFRICA

Fifth One-Day International

At Auckland, March 4, 2017 (day/night). South Africa won by six wickets. Toss: South Africa.

The bouncy Eden Park drop-in pitch again offered South Africa a reminder of home, and they enjoyed it hugely, storming to victory in an anticlimactic decider. From as early as the first five overs – when Rabada gave Guptill, the hero of Hamilton, a working-over, then shattered his stumps – there was only one side in it. South Africa's bowlers never let up, and New Zealand's innings barely got

---

MOST ECONOMICAL FIGURES BY LEG-SPINNERS IN ODIs

ER			
0.90	Abdul Qadir (10–4–9–4)	Pakistan v New Zealand at Sharjah	1985-86
0.91	D. S. de Silva (12–5–11–2)	Sri Lanka v New Zealand at Derby	1983
1.10	S. K. Warne (10–4–11–3)	Australia v West Indies at Manchester	1999
1.22	A. Kumble (9–3–11–1)	India v Sri Lanka at Sharjah	1998-99
1.30	P. A. Strang (10–1–13–1)	Zimbabwe v New Zealand at Harare	1997-98
1.33	Shahid Afridi (9–3–12–7)	Pakistan v West Indies at Providence	2013
1.40	A. Kumble (10–4–14–3)	India v Kenya at Bloemfontein	2001-02
1.40	**Imran Tahir (10–0–14–2)**	**South Africa v New Zealand at Auckland**	**2016-17**
1.50	**A. G. Cremer (8–1–12–2)**	**Zimbabwe v Afghanistan at Harare**	**2016-17**

Minimum eight overs.

out of first gear. After Rabada's venom, Imran Tahir spun a web, taking two for 14 at the scene of his Twenty20 heroics a couple of weeks earlier. For New Zealand, it all snowballed. Some quick thinking from de Villiers at midwicket accounted for Williamson, whose bat jammed in the turf as he tried to make his ground, and Phehlukwayo trapped Taylor to leave them 51 for four. De Grandhomme resisted briefly and, when South Africa found themselves three down for 48, there were slim hopes that Auckland might be set for another low-scoring thriller. De Villiers followed to make it 88 for four, but du Plessis and Miller averted further trouble, completing the chase with almost 18 overs to spare and the lights barely taking effect. While New Zealand slipped to their first one-day bilateral series defeat at home out of eight, South Africa's victory was their seventh in succession (including a one-off win against Ireland), and took them back to the top of the rankings – a position they had briefly ceded to Australia after defeat at Hamilton. Few could argue.

Man of the Match: K. Rabada.

New Zealand

M. J. Guptill b Rabada	4	J. S. Patel lbw b Imran Tahir	0
D. G. Brownlie lbw b Phehlukwayo	24	T. A. Boult not out	0
*K. S. Williamson run out	9		
L. R. P. L. Taylor lbw b Phehlukwayo	8	Lb 5, w 5	10
†L. Ronchi c de Kock b Morris	8		—
J. D. S. Neesham c Duminy b Rabada	24	1/17 (1) 2/42 (3) 3/42 (2) (41.1 overs)	149
M. J. Santner run out	24	4/51 (4) 5/72 (5) 6/87 (6)	
C. de Grandhomme c de Kock b Rabada	32	7/132 (7) 8/140 (9) 9/147 (10)	
T. G. Southee c and b Imran Tahir	6	10/149 (8) 10 overs: 41-1	

Rabada 7.1–1–25–3; Morris 9–0–34–1; Imran Tahir 10–0–14–2; Phehlukwayo 7–1–35–2; Pretorius 8–0–36–0.

South Africa

†Q. de Kock c Williamson b Patel	6	D. A. Miller not out	45
H. M. Amla c Santner b de Grandhomme	8	Lb 5, w 9	14
F. du Plessis not out	51		—
J-P. Duminy c Santner b Patel	3	1/6 (1) 2/35 (2) (4 wkts, 32.2 overs)	150
*A. B. de Villiers c Ronchi b Neesham	23	3/48 (4) 4/88 (5) 10 overs: 32-1	

D. Pretorius, C. H. Morris, A. L. Phehlukwayo, K. Rabada and Imran Tahir did not bat.

Patel 5–0–26–2; Boult 9.2–0–44–0; Southee 10–1–40–0; de Grandhomme 4–0–16–1; Santner 2–0–9–0; Neesham 2–0–10–1.

Umpires: C. M. Brown and J. S. Wilson. Third umpire: P. R. Reiffel.
Referee: J. Srinath.

NEW ZEALAND v SOUTH AFRICA

First Test

At Dunedin (University Oval), March 8–12, 2017. Drawn. Toss: South Africa.

Destination Dunedin is a familiar first Test stop for touring sides, and the world's southernmost venue gave South Africa a predictably uncomfortable stay. Had it not rained on the last day – just as it did during the corresponding Test five years earlier – New Zealand might have won. They had to settle for maintaining their unbeaten record at University Oval (although this was their fifth draw out of eight).

It was cold. Both teams used hand warmers in the field, and umpires Bruce Oxenford and Kumar Dharmasena wore gloves. On the third day, it briefly threatened to get hot: a smoke alarm blared in the main stand, spectators were evacuated, and the players and officials stood bemused on the field during a 20-minute delay.

Elgar was the game's dominant figure, with Williamson not far behind, and each held his side's innings together on a dry, low, sluggish pitch. Fast scoring was difficult – the rate throughout was just 2.57 an over, making it the slowest Test in New Zealand for nearly two decades – and the bowlers toiled. But Elgar was outstanding, lasting 772 minutes in all, facing 548 deliveries (the most, where information is available, by an overseas player in a Test in New Zealand), and winning the battle with his former schoolboy rival, the Pretoria-born Neil Wagner, who had returned for New Zealand after a month out with a fractured finger.

On a brilliantly fine first morning there was intrigue and uncertainty. So keen were New Zealand to play two spinners that they dropped their senior seamer, Tim Southee, enabling Patel to play his first home Test for seven years. South Africa welcomed Morkel, their towering fast bowler, for his first Test in 13 months after a back injury. Du Plessis decided to bat – the first time a captain had done so in 23 Tests in New Zealand stretching back to January 2011.

SLOWLY DOES IT

South African spinners taking five wickets in a Test innings against New Zealand:

Q. McMillan (LB)	5-66 at Christchurch	1931-32
Q. McMillan (LB)	5-125 at Wellington	1931-32
H. J. Tayfield (OB)	5-62 at Auckland	1952-53
H. J. Tayfield (OB)	6-62 at Durban	1953-54
H. J. Tayfield (OB)	6-13 at Johannesburg (Ellis Park)	1953-54
D. B. Pithey (OB)	6-58 at Dunedin (Carisbrook)	1963-64
K. A. Maharaj (SLA)	**5-94 at Dunedin (University)**	**2016-17**
K. A. Maharaj (SLA)	**6-40 at Wellington**	**2016-17**

As South Africa slumped to 22 for three against the swinging ball, du Plessis might have rued his choice. But Watling dropped Elgar off Boult down the leg side on 36, and he and the captain set about repairing the damage, adding 126. Elgar fell next morning for a patient 140, and a half-century from Bavuma helped them to a passable 308.

In reply, Williamson batted 380 minutes for 130, his 16th Test century. He received back-up from Raval and Watling, which was just as well: Taylor had to be helped from the field after tearing a calf muscle when he had eight, eventually limping back on after the fall of the ninth wicket to add seven. It was his final contribution of the series. Meanwhile, Maharaj's accurate left-arm spin collected a maiden Test five-for, limiting the lead to 33. It was the first five-wicket haul by a South African spinner against New Zealand since David Pithey, across town at Carisbrook, in 1963-64.

Once more, Elgar dug in after the struggling Cook and Amla had fallen cheaply, but Boult failed to return after tea because of a groin injury; like Taylor, he played no further part in the series. Williamson used Patel as his go-to spinner, and three wickets fell for 25 to him and slow left-armer Santner. That included Elgar for 89 (though not before he had taken his tally of dot balls in the Test to 433) and de Kock, bowled by a gem from Patel. Du Plessis stood firm, but South Africa – just 191 ahead with only four wickets in hand – were wobbling a touch at stumps on the fourth day. A gripping finale loomed, only for the rain to arrive on cue.

Man of the Match: D. Elgar.

Close of play: first day, South Africa 229-4 (Elgar 128, Bavuma 38); second day, New Zealand 177-3 (Williamson 78, Patel 9); third day, South Africa 38-1 (Elgar 12, Amla 23); fourth day, South Africa 224-6 (du Plessis 56, Philander 1).

South Africa

S. C. Cook lbw b Boult	3	– c Watling b Boult	0
D. Elgar c Watling b Wagner	140	– c Williamson b Patel	89
H. M. Amla b Wagner	1	– c sub (T. G. Southee) b Wagner	24
J-P. Duminy c Taylor b Wagner	1	– lbw b Wagner	39
*F. du Plessis c Boult b Neesham	52	– not out	56
T. Bavuma c Watling b Boult	64	– b Santner	6
†Q. de Kock c Wagner b Patel	10	– b Patel	4
V. D. Philander b Boult	21	– not out	1
K. A. Maharaj c Neesham b Boult	5		
K. Rabada b Patel	4		
M. Morkel not out	0		
B 4, lb 1, w 2	7	B 1, lb 3, w 1	5
1/10 (1) 2/20 (3) 3/22 (4) 4/148 (5) 5/252 (2) 6/265 (7) 7/279 (6) 8/298 (9) 9/308 (10) 10/308 (8) (122.4 overs)	308	1/0 (1) 2/39 (3) 3/113 (4) 4/193 (2) 5/206 (6) 6/218 (7) (6 wkts, 102 overs)	224

Boult 32.4–12–64–4; Wagner 31–8–88–3; Patel 33–12–85–2; Santner 18–5–32–0; Neesham 8–2–34–1. *Second innings*—Boult 15–4–34–1; Wagner 27–7–57–2; Santner 19–6–37–1; Patel 36–15–72–2; Neesham 5–0–20–0.

New Zealand

T. W. M. Latham c de Kock b Philander	10
J. A. Raval c Elgar b Maharaj	52
*K. S. Williamson c de Kock b Rabada	130
L. R. P. L. Taylor not out	15
H. M. Nicholls c Amla b Maharaj	12
J. S. Patel c du Plessis b Philander	16
J. D. S. Neesham c de Kock b Morkel	7
†B-J. Watling b Maharaj	50
M. J. Santner c Maharaj b Morkel	4
N. Wagner c Duminy b Maharaj	32
T. A. Boult b Maharaj	2
Lb 8, w 1, nb 2	11
1/15 (1) 2/117 (2) 3/165 (5) 4/184 (6) 5/193 (7) 6/277 (3) 7/297 (9) 8/304 (8) 9/324 (11) 10/341 (10) (114.3 overs)	341

Taylor, when 8, retired hurt at 148-2 and resumed at 324-9.

Rabada 30–7–92–1; Philander 27–11–67–2; Morkel 24–6–62–2; Maharaj 28.3–7–94–5; Duminy 5–0–18–0.

Umpires: H. D. P. K. Dharmasena and B. N. J. Oxenford. Third umpire: R. J. Tucker.
Referee: D. C. Boon.

NEW ZEALAND v SOUTH AFRICA

Second Test

At Wellington (Basin Reserve), March 16–18, 2017. South Africa won by eight wickets. Toss: South Africa. Test debut: N. T. Broom.

Without Ross Taylor and Trent Boult, New Zealand's depth was under scrutiny – and they failed, caving in spectacularly inside three days. South Africa were presented with the quickest pitch of the series and, while their seamers relished it, the match award went to left-arm spinner Maharaj, whose six for 40 was his second Test-best in a week.

An unchanged South Africa got what they wanted, which was to bowl first on a damp pitch that had been sweating under covers. The movement and bounce of Rabada made early inroads, including the wicket of Williamson, whose eventual match tally of three was his lowest in a Test in which he had batted twice. He had called for DRS after being

...re, ut the ball-tracking system was scuppered by mud flying off given out leg. The umpire's call stood, though New Zealand did not lose a review.
...est innings of 33-year-old Neil Broom, Ross Taylor's replacement, lasted Rabada's ...iveries – he was brilliantly caught by de Kock off Rabada – and it needed a The attacking maiden century by left-hander Nicholls to salvage the innings from 101 ...e. Nicholls had yet to nail the No. 5 spot, but in his 13th Test he dispelled any doubt, ...wing poise and purpose, using his feet to spin, and taking on anything short.

Slow bowling rarely plays a role on the fifth day at the Basin Reserve, let alone the first, but something changed. Duminy found drift with his part-time off-breaks, occasionally looking unplayable; he snared four of the last five, which fell for 51.

But, by lunch on the second, New Zealand had dramatically taken control. With the recalled new-ball duo of Southee and de Grandhomme generating swing, South Africa had slipped to 94 for six. One more quick wicket, and it might have been game over. Instead, de Kock played the only way he knows; in a flash, Williamson scattered the field, and tried to bounce him out. The ploy failed, and the Test turned. De Kock found a resolute ally in Bavuma, and they put on 160 in 39 overs, draining the energy from New Zealand legs, and proving the pitch harboured few demons. Last man Morkel equalled his Test-best 40, and South Africa led by 91, having added 265 for their final four wickets.

On a cold, grey Saturday, their bowlers went in for the kill. Morkel gave the New Zealand top order a fearsome examination of their back-foot defence, persuading the out-of-touch Latham to chase a wider one, and ending a forgettable Test for Williamson with a beauty that straightened and bounced. Then Maharaj ran through a spooked line-up with minimal fuss – and minimal turn. Raval batted over four hours for his brave 80, but finally charged Maharaj and got in a tangle against one that drifted a fraction; Nicholls and Neesham played reckless shots and, of the rest, only Broom and Watling reached double figures.

The third day at the Basin is usually a run-fest, yet New Zealand were bundled out for 171. Set 81 to take a 1–0 lead to Hamilton and preserve their unbeaten series record against the New Zealanders, South Africa claimed the extra half-hour. Duminy's pull off Neesham provided a decisive conclusion to the decisive day of the series.

Man of the Match: K. A. Maharaj.

Close of play: first day, South Africa 24-2 (Rabada 8, Amla 0); second day, South Africa 349-9 (Philander 36, Morkel 31).

New Zealand

First innings		Second innings	
J. A. Raval c Amla b Maharaj	36	– (2) st de Kock b Maharaj	80
T. W. M. Latham c Elgar b Morkel	8	– (1) c Duminy b Morkel	6
*K. S. Williamson lbw b Rabada	2	– c de Kock b Morkel	1
N. T. Broom c de Kock b Rabada	0	– c de Kock b Morkel	20
H. M. Nicholls b Duminy	118	– b Maharaj	7
J. D. S. Neesham st de Kock b Maharaj	15	– c du Plessis b Maharaj	4
†B-J. Watling c de Kock b Duminy	34	– c Duminy b Maharaj	29
C. de Grandhomme c Amla b Duminy	4	– b Maharaj	0
T. G. Southee c Philander b Morkel	27	– c Duminy b Maharaj	4
J. S. Patel not out	17	– c de Kock b Rabada	0
N. Wagner lbw b Duminy	2	– not out	4
Lb 4, w 1	5	B 10, lb 1, w 5	16
1/11 (2) 2/13 (3) 3/21 (4) 4/73 (1) 5/101 (6) 6/217 (5) 7/221 (8) 8/222 (7) 9/266 (9) 10/268 (11) (79.3 overs)	268	1/16 (1) 2/26 (3) 3/64 (4) 4/86 (5) 5/90 (6) 6/155 (2) 7/161 (8) 8/167 (9) 9/167 (10) 10/171 (7) (63.2 overs)	171

Morkel 18–3–82–2; Philander 15–7–29–0; Rabada 19–6–59–2; Duminy 11.3–2–47–4; Maharaj 16–4–47–2. *Second innings*—Morkel 11–0–50–3; Philander 12–3–28–0; Rabada 17–5–38–1; Maharaj 20.2–7–40–6; Duminy 3–1–4–0.

South Africa

S. C. Cook c Neesham b Southee	3	– c Neesham b Southee	[illegible]
D. Elgar c Neesham b de Grandhomme	9	– c Watling b Wagner	[illegible]
K. Rabada b Southee	9		
H. M. Amla c Nicholls b de Grandhomme	21	– (3) not out	[illegible]
J-P. Duminy c Nicholls b Wagner	16	– (4) not out	1[illegible]
*F. du Plessis c Watling b de Grandhomme	22		
T. Bavuma c Neesham b Wagner	89		
†Q. de Kock c Watling b Neesham	91		
V. D. Philander not out	37		
K. A. Maharaj c Williamson b Wagner	1		
M. Morkel b Patel	40		
B 4, lb 5, w 12	21	W 2	2
1/12 (1) 2/12 (2) 3/26 (3) 4/59 (5) 5/79 (4) 6/94 (6) 7/254 (8) 8/290 (7) 9/302 (10) 10/359 (11) (98 overs)	359	1/18 (1) 2/48 (2) (2 wkts, 24.3 overs)	83

Southee 27–7–98–2; de Grandhomme 23–7–52–3; Wagner 22–1–102–3; Patel 14–1–57–1; Neesham 12–2–41–1. *Second innings*—Southee 6–2–17–1; de Grandhomme 8–1–20–0; Wagner 8–2–18–1; Neesham 2.3–0–28–0.

Umpires: H. D. P. K. Dharmasena and R. J. Tucker. Third umpire: B. N. J. Oxenford.
Referee: D. C. Boon.

NEW ZEALAND v SOUTH AFRICA

Third Test

At Hamilton, March 25–29, 2017. Drawn. Toss: South Africa. Test debut: T. B. de Bruyn.

South Africa needed only a draw to close out the series – and, thanks in no small part to Hamilton's weather, they got it. Last-day rain ruined New Zealand's hopes of forcing a result, as it had at Dunedin, and maintained South Africa's stranglehold on the fixture: of 45 Tests between the sides stretching back to 1931-32, they had won 25 and lost four.

New Zealand had entered the game without the injured Tim Southee, leaving the new ball in the hands of Henry and de Grandhomme, and they were immediately in the action after du Plessis chose to bat first on a dark, grassy surface, having won South Africa's eighth toss in succession. By now, Williamson wore a wry grin every time the coin went up, but his bowlers exploited swing and seam movement. On the second morning, after rain had limited the first day to 41 overs, South Africa – who had given a debut to Theunis de Bruyn in place of Stephen Cook – found themselves 190 for six. Once more, de Kock produced a Gilchristian response, hammering 90 off 118 balls, and lifting the total to a workable 314.

New Zealand set about giving themselves a chance. Latham finally ended his slump (33 runs in eight international innings), leaving well and enjoying some welcome luck in his first half-century of the series, while Raval was in determined mood, batting more than six and a half hours for 88. It felt as if they had found the two dogged openers they had searched for since the retirement of Mark Richardson more than a decade earlier.

But the innings belonged to Williamson. On the third day, he equalled Martin Crowe's New Zealand record of 17 Test centuries, but – typically – played down the achievement with a shrug of the shoulders. Victory was all that mattered. He finished with a vintage 176, New Zealand's highest score at home against South Africa (previously 170 by Scott Styris at Auckland in 2003-04), and had given the bowlers little to aim at, obliging them to come to him in a watertight display of concentration. Philander went wicketless at the venue where he had destroyed New Zealand five years earlier and, although Morkel and Rabada shared eight victims, they sent down 70 overs between them; Maharaj managed two wickets in 50.

With rain forecast, de Grandhomme stepped up the pace, scoring 57 – his maiden Test half-century – from 70 balls, and by the time South Africa bowled New Zealand out, the lead was 175; four sessions remained. The hosts had waited all series for Patel and Santner to bowl them to victory. South Africa, meanwhile, wearied by a long tour and 162 overs in the field, looked to be nearing the end of their run. Sure enough, on the fourth evening, they were soon 59 for five, jolting the handful of spectators at Seddon Park to attention.

De Grandhomme found the edge of Elgar's broad bat, and de Bruyn completed an unhappy debut when he was run out after a mid-pitch collision with Amla. Patel, used to ushering in victories for Warwickshire, sensed a chance to do the same for his country: Amla nicked one that drifted away, Duminy left one that went straight on. Du Plessis and de Kock clung on until stumps, with South Africa trailing by 95 and New Zealand dreaming of their first win against them since 2003-04. Instead, rain left their comeback unfulfilled.

Man of the Match: K. S. Williamson.

Close of play: first day, South Africa 123-4 (du Plessis 33, Bavuma 13); second day, New Zealand 67-0 (Latham 42, Raval 25); third day, New Zealand 321-4 (Williamson 148, Santner 13); fourth day, South Africa 80-5 (du Plessis 15, de Kock 15).

South Africa

D. Elgar b de Grandhomme	5	– c Watling b de Grandhomme	5
T. B. de Bruyn c Latham b Henry	0	– run out	12
H. M. Amla b de Grandhomme	50	– c de Grandhomme b Patel	19
J-P. Duminy c Patel b Henry	20	– b Patel	13
*F. du Plessis c Latham b Santner	53	– not out	15
T. Bavuma c Raval b Henry	29	– c Watling b Henry	1
†Q. de Kock lbw b Wagner	90	– not out	15
V. D. Philander c Latham b Henry	11		
K. A. Maharaj c Watling b Wagner	9		
K. Rabada c Watling b Wagner	34		
M. Morkel not out	9		
Lb 1, w 3	4		
1/5 (2) 2/5 (1) 3/64 (4) 4/97 (3) 5/148 (6) 6/190 (5) 7/219 (8) 8/249 (9) 9/295 (7) 10/314 (10) (89.2 overs)	314	1/13 (1) 2/25 (2) 3/49 (3) 4/50 (4) 5/59 (6) (5 wkts, 39 overs)	80

Henry 24–2–93–4; de Grandhomme 24–4–62–2; Wagner 25.2–2–104–3; Patel 7–0–30–0; Santner 9–3–24–1. *Second innings*—Henry 11–4–20–1; de Grandhomme 8–5–15–1; Wagner 5–0–16–0; Patel 12–2–22–2; Santner 3–0–7–0.

New Zealand

T. W. M. Latham c de Kock b Morkel	50
J. A. Raval c de Kock b Morkel	88
*K. S. Williamson c Philander b Morkel	176
N. T. Broom lbw b Rabada	12
H. M. Nicholls c de Kock b Rabada	0
M. J. Santner c Duminy b Rabada	41
†B-J. Watling b Maharaj	24
C. de Grandhomme c de Kock b Morkel	57
M. J. Henry c Elgar b Maharaj	12
J. S. Patel c de Kock b Rabada	5
N. Wagner not out	0
Lb 12, w 5, nb 7	24
1/83 (1) 2/273 (2) 3/293 (4) 4/293 (5) 5/381 (3) 6/397 (6) 7/443 (7) 8/477 (9) 9/489 (10) 10/489 (8) (162.1 overs)	489

Philander 33–7–79–0; Morkel 36.1–7–100–4; Rabada 34–3–122–4; Maharaj 50–8–118–2; Duminy 6–0–38–0; Elgar 1–0–13–0; Bavuma 2–0–7–0.

Umpires: B. N. J. Oxenford and R. J. Tucker. Third umpire: H. D. P. K. Dharmasena.
Referee: D. C. Boon.

NEW ZEALAND v WEST INDIES IN 2017-18

MARK GEENTY

Test matches (2): New Zealand 2, West Indies 0
One-day internationals (3): New Zealand 3, West Indies 0
Twenty20 internationals (3): New Zealand 2, West Indies 0

West Indies arrived without a Test win in New Zealand for nearly 23 years, but with reason for optimism. A stable line-up under coach Stuart Law and captain Jason Holder had won a match in England, then – less surprisingly – a series in Zimbabwe, and looked battle-hardened; New Zealand hadn't played a Test in eight months. But the tourists' confidence evaporated during a first-day collapse at Wellington. Five weeks later they were on the plane home after defeats in every completed game of the tour.

With the exception of opener Kraigg Brathwaite, the ill discipline of West Indies' batting was alarming; they could not handle the steep New Zealand bounce, nor the skill and variety of the home pace attack. Neil Wagner's prolonged short-pitched assaults, and Trent Boult's swing and speed, overwhelmed batsmen itching for the million dollar shot. Meanwhile the hitting power of the Colins – de Grandhomme in the Tests, Munro elsewhere – was too much for any West Indian to match, or quell. Ross Taylor was another in superb touch.

After an innings defeat in the First Test, Holder was banned at Hamilton for a slow over-rate. Brathwaite took the reins, but couldn't inspire others to follow his lead: the 444 balls he faced across the series was more than double any of his team-mates. In the bowling they were barely steady, with Miguel Cummins and Shannon Gabriel the brightest of a drab bunch.

Sunil Ambris made one of the more unfortunate starts to a Test career, after scoring 153 in a warm-up match. At Wellington, he created history when, facing his first ball in Test cricket, he trod on his stumps. Then, after his first scoring shot in the second innings was a top-edged six, he was again dismissed hit wicket at Hamilton. To cap it all, his tour was ended abruptly by a Wagner bouncer, which broke his left forearm.

Chris Gayle's arrival for the white-ball matches, in what looked likely to be his final tour of New Zealand, was cause for renewed hope, particularly after two whirlwind centuries in the Bangladesh Premier League. But he was anonymous: with sound plans, the New Zealand bowlers kept him to 38 runs from four innings. He also missed a one-day international because of illness.

"I'm anonymous in the Mumbles," said Richard Madley, a proud South Walian. "But famous in Mumbai."
Cricket People, page 163

Fielding a full-strength side remained a challenge for West Indies, despite a recent thawing in relations between the players and board. The all-rounder Dwayne Bravo, who had captained them in limited-overs matches on their previous tour in 2013-14, was at Australia's Big Bash League, and said he was unlikely to play international cricket again. Two others, Sunil Narine and Kieron Pollard, withdrew late, while Evin Lewis missed the T20s, all for personal reasons.

WEST INDIES TOURING PARTY

*J. O. Holder (T/50), S. W. Ambris (T), S. Badree (20), R. R. Beaton (50/20), D. Bishoo (T), J. Blackwood (T), C. R. Brathwaite (20), K. C. Brathwaite (T), R. L. Chase (T), S. S. Cotterell (50/20), M. L. Cummins (T), S. O. Dowrich (T), R. R. Emrit (20), A. D. S. Fletcher (20), S. T. Gabriel (T/50), C. H. Gayle (50/20), S. O. Hetmyer (T/50/20), K. A. Hope (50), S. D. Hope (T/50/20), A. S. Joseph (T/50), E. Lewis (50), N. O. Miller (50), J. N. Mohammed (50/20), A. R. Nurse (50/20), K. O. A. Powell (T), R. Powell (50/20), R. A. Reifer (T), K. A. J. Roach (T), J. E. Taylor (20), C. A. K. Walton (50/20), K. O. K. Williams (50/20). *Coach:* S. G. Law.

C. R. Brathwaite captained in the Twenty20s. Ambris and Joseph were originally named in the ODI squad but, after injuries, were replaced by Hetmyer and Cotterell. M. N. Samuels was originally named in both limited-overs squads, but hurt his hand; Walton, already present for the T20s, filled the ODI spot. S. P. Narine and K. A. Pollard were originally in the Twenty20 squad, but withdrew for personal reasons.

NEW ZEALAND v WEST INDIES

First Test

At Wellington, December 1–4, 2017. New Zealand won by an innings and 67 runs. Toss: New Zealand. Test debuts: T. A. Blundell; S. W. Ambris.

Wagner had begun 2017 in ferocious form, peppering the Bangladeshis at the Basin Reserve. In December, he returned – and gave West Indies the same treatment. His figures of seven for 39 on the opening day were the fourth-best for New Zealand, and jolted the tourists into meek submission.

Wellington's now customary emerald green pitch cause the West Indian batsmen angst, but it was bounce and questionable technique, not swing and seam movement, that did for them. After being inserted, openers Brathwaite and Powell appeared comfortable against Boult and Henry, who deputised for expectant father Tim Southee, and they reached 59 without loss. But Wagner was a highly effective plan B. Either side of lunch, he demonstrated his knack for an intense, concerted attack, and felled six victims with short stuff, while Holder was stunned by a first-ball yorker. All ten fell for 75, and by the close, New Zealand had reached 85 for two, just 49 behind.

Next day, Taylor eased them into the lead, before two newcomers took control in the evening session. De Grandhomme's highest score in six previous Tests was 57. But with West Indies flagging, and Chase and Brathwaite serving up inviting spin, he unleashed 11 fours and three sixes to reach a century in 71 deliveries. It was the second-fastest for New Zealand in Tests, behind Brendon McCullum's 54 balls against Australia at Christchurch in 2015-16, and the joint ninth-fastest overall.

Amid the fireworks, wicketkeeper Tom Blundell chugged along, putting on 148 for the seventh wicket with de Grandhomme, and reaching stumps on 57. He had been summoned for a Test debut after a hip injury ruled out B-J. Watling, and appeared at home – or near to it. The ground was within walking distance of his house, and across the road from his old school, Wellington College. At the end of the match, he was spotted strolling home in

FASTEST MAIDEN TEST HUNDREDS

Balls			
71	**C. de Grandhomme**	**New Zealand v West Indies at Wellington**	**2017-18**
76	G. L. Jessop	England v Australia at The Oval	1902
85	†S. Dhawan	India v Australia at Mohali	2012-13
86	C. L. Cairns	New Zealand v Zimbabwe at Auckland	1995-96
86	M. G. Johnson	Australia v South Africa at Cape Town	2008-09
86	**H. H. Pandya**	**India v Sri Lanka at Pallekele**	**2017**
88	R. J. Hadlee	New Zealand v West Indies at Christchurch	1979-80
89	R. R. Lindwall	Australia v England at Melbourne	1946-47
93	†D. R. Smith	West Indies v South Africa at Cape Town	2003-04
93	M. S. Dhoni	India v Pakistan at Faisalabad	2005-06

† *On debut.*

---

his whites. But when he resumed on the third day, with New Zealand nine down, he seemed unlikely to reach three figures. Instead, he found a willing ally in Boult, one of world cricket's better No. 11s. The pair added an unbroken 78, with Blundell earning a rousing ovation for a polished century. Soon after, captain Williamson called time, and West Indies faced a deficit of 386.

They fared much better, with Brathwaite defying the bowling for over five hours, and Hetmyer showing off breathtaking strokeplay in an entertaining 66. But after they departed, there wasn't much resolve. Debutant Sunil Ambris, who had trodden on his stumps first ball on the opening day, didn't hang around, top-edging a six to get off the mark before poking to slip first ball after lunch. Wagner, who had clanged the helmets of Powell and Hetmyer in consecutive overs, was not as dangerous on the whole but, when he removed Dowrich and Holder in quick succession, the end was nigh. To crown a miserable match, Holder was fined 60% of his fee for a slow over-rate, and banned for a Test. The result meant New Zealand led West Indies for the first time in overall Test wins between the sides: 14–13.

Man of the Match: N. Wagner.

Close of play: first day, New Zealand 85-2 (Raval 29, Taylor 12); second day, New Zealand 447-9 (Blundell 57, Boult 2); third day, West Indies 214-2 (Brathwaite 79, Hope 21).

West Indies

K. C. Brathwaite c Nicholls b Wagner	24	– lbw b Santner	91
K. O. A. Powell c Raval b Boult	42	– c and b Henry	40
S. O. Hetmyer c Latham b Wagner	13	– c Raval b Henry	66
S. D. Hope c Blundell b Wagner	0	– c Williamson b Boult	37
R. L. Chase c Raval b Wagner	5	– b Henry	18
S. W. Ambris hit wkt b Wagner	0	– c Taylor b de Grandhomme	18
†S. O. Dowrich run out	18	– c Santner b Wagner	3
*J. O. Holder b Wagner	0	– c Boult b Wagner	7
K. A. J. Roach not out	14	– lbw b de Grandhomme	7
M. L. Cummins b Boult	1	– b Boult	14
S. T. Gabriel c Latham b Wagner	10	– not out	4
B 2, lb 5	7	B 4, lb 4, w 6	14
(45.4 overs)	134	(106 overs)	319

1/59 (1) 2/75 (2) 3/79 (3) 4/80 (4) 5/80 (6) 6/97 (5) 7/97 (8) 8/104 (7) 9/105 (10) 10/134 (11)

1/72 (2) 2/166 (3) 3/231 (1) 4/257 (4) 5/273 (5) 6/286 (6) 7/288 (7) 8/301 (9) 9/301 (8) 10/319 (10)

Boult 16–8–36–2; Henry 11–1–39–0; de Grandhomme 4–1–13–0; Wagner 14.4–2–39–7. *Second innings*—Boult 23–5–87–2; Henry 24–6–57–3; de Grandhomme 19–3–40–2; Wagner 22–3–102–2; Santner 17–7–25–1; Williamson 1–1–0–0.

New Zealand

T. W. M. Latham c Roach b Holder	37
J. A. Raval c Dowrich b Roach	42
*K. S. Williamson c Hope b Roach	1
L. R. P. L. Taylor lbw b Roach	93
H. M. Nicholls c Gabriel b Cummins	67
M. J. Santner b Cummins	17
C. de Grandhomme c Powell b Chase	105
†T. A. Blundell not out	107
N. Wagner b Chase	3
M. J. Henry c Dowrich b Gabriel	4
T. A. Boult not out	18
B 4, lb 6, w 1, nb 15	26
1/65 (1) (9 wkts dec, 148.4 overs)	520

2/68 (3) 3/109 (2) 4/236 (4) 5/272 (5) 6/281 (6) 7/429 (7) 8/437 (9) 9/442 (10)

Gabriel 29–4–90–1; Roach 22–6–85–3; Cummins 27–7–92–2; Holder 34–8–102–1; Chase 28–4–95–2; Brathwaite 8.4–0–46–0.

Umpires: I. J. Gould and R. J. Tucker. Third umpire: B. N. J. Oxenford.
Referee: B. C. Broad.

NEW ZEALAND v WEST INDIES

Second Test

At Hamilton, December 9–12, 2017. New Zealand won by 240 runs. Toss: West Indies. Test debut: R. A. Reifer.

This was Taylor's Test. His late mentor Martin Crowe had challenged him to better his own tally of 17 Test centuries and, eight months after Williamson reached the mark on the same ground against South Africa, Taylor also drew level. Interviewed afterwards, he had a tear in his eye. "I'm sure he'd be happy," he said.

He did it in style, too, with a straight-drive off debutant Raymon Reifer on the third day, before removing his helmet and poking out his tongue, a traditional celebration for his daughter Mackenzie. Soon after, Williamson declared, setting West Indies 444 to level the series. Again, they weren't up to a fierce attack led by Wagner, who took three wickets and sent the hapless Ambris to hospital with a broken arm. The tourists were dismissed for 203 on the fourth afternoon.

As at Wellington, the pitch looked as if it would offer more for the seamers than it did and, after being sent in, New Zealand were away and racing thanks to opener Raval's 84. A few unconverted starts stalled momentum, before de Grandhomme again freed the arms and blasted four sixes. When the last pair added 61 on the second day, it left New Zealand happy, with 373. West Indies spearhead Gabriel was expensive and overstepped seven times, but eventually hit his stride to collect four wickets.

Brathwaite knuckled down again, but his 66 was by far the best effort in reply. Boult was the pick of the bowlers, helping New Zealand earn a lead of 152. His typically athletic return catch removed Hetmyer and he forced Ambris to tread on his stumps once more, before mopping up the tail on the third morning. Cummins had looked handy in Wellington and, after he removed Raval, Williamson and Nicholls, West Indies had a glimmer. But Taylor stood firm, cutting and driving exquisitely as the lead soared past 400.

Boult made early inroads once more and, when Brathwaite played loosely, and Williamson held a fine gully catch, he became the sixth New Zealander to 200 wickets, in his 52nd Test. Wagner gritted his teeth and charged towards victory, enjoying the Seddon Park bounce. After he struck Ambris, he ended any serious resistance with a short ball to Chase. To add to the West Indian gloom, stand-in captain Brathwaite was fined 40% of his match fee, again for a slow over-rate.

Man of the Match: L. R. P. L. Taylor.

Close of play: first day, New Zealand 286-7 (Blundell 12, Wagner 1); second day, West Indies 215-8 (Reifer 22, Cummins 10); third day, West Indies 30-2 (Brathwaite 13, Hope 1).

New Zealand

J. A. Raval c Dowrich b Gabriel	84 – c and b Cummins	4
T. W. M. Latham c Dowrich b Cummins	22 – lbw b Reifer	22
*K. S. Williamson c Dowrich b Cummins	43 – b Cummins	54
L. R. P. L. Taylor c Dowrich b Roach	16 – not out	107
H. M. Nicholls lbw b Reifer	13 – c Dowrich b Cummins	5
M. J. Santner b Gabriel	24 – c Ambris b Chase	26
C. de Grandhomme b Gabriel	58 – lbw b Gabriel	22
†T. A. Blundell b Gabriel	28 – c Powell b Gabriel	1
N. Wagner c Hope b Roach	1 – c Hope b Chase	8
T. G. Southee c and b Roach	31 – not out	22
T. A. Boult not out	37	
Lb 1, w 3, nb 12	16	B 4, lb 2, w 2, nb 12 20
1/65 (2) 2/154 (3) 3/159 (1) 4/186 (4) 5/189 (5) 6/265 (6) 7/275 (7) 8/286 (9) 9/312 (8) 10/373 (10) (102.2 overs)	373	1/11 (1) 2/42 (2) 3/100 (3) 4/111 (5) 5/161 (6) 6/212 (7) 7/235 (8) 8/257 (9) (8 wkts dec, 77.4 overs) 291

Gabriel 25–4–119–4; Roach 23.2–8–58–3; Cummins 20–4–57–2; Chase 13–1–90–0; Reifer 17–8–36–1; Brathwaite 4–0–12–0. *Second innings*—Gabriel 15–0–52–2; Roach 6–1–28–0; Cummins 17–1–69–3; Reifer 13–1–52–1; Brathwaite 9–0–33–0; Chase 17.4–1–51–2.

West Indies

*K. C. Brathwaite c Southee b de Grandhomme	66 – c Williamson b Boult	20
K. O. A. Powell c Blundell b Southee	0 – c Southee b Boult	0
S. O. Hetmyer c and b Boult	28 – c Wagner b Southee	15
S. D. Hope c Taylor b Southee	15 – c de Grandhomme b Wagner	23
R. L. Chase b de Grandhomme	12 – c de Grandhomme b Wagner	64
S. W. Ambris hit wkt b Boult	2 – retired hurt	5
†S. O. Dowrich c and b Wagner	35 – c Nicholls b Wagner	0
R. A. Reifer not out	23 – c Williamson b Southee	29
K. A. J. Roach c Boult b Wagner	17 – b Santner	32
M. L. Cummins b Boult	15 – c Boult b Santner	9
S. T. Gabriel b Boult	0 – not out	0
B 1, w 7	8	Lb 5, w 1 6
1/5 (2) 2/46 (3) 3/90 (4) 4/112 (5) 5/117 (6) 6/135 (1) 7/169 (7) 8/204 (9) 9/221 (10) 10/221 (11) (66.5 overs)	221	1/4 (2) 2/27 (3) 3/43 (1) 4/68 (4) 5/80 (7) 6/158 (5) 7/166 (8) 8/203 (10) 9/203 (9) (63.5 overs) 203

In the second innings Ambris retired hurt at 80-4.

Southee 19–9–34–2; Boult 20.5–5–73–4; de Grandhomme 12–1–40–2; Wagner 15–2–73–2. *Second innings*—Southee 19–3–71–2; Boult 16–1–52–2; Wagner 15–5–42–3; de Grandhomme 9–5–20–0; Santner 4.5–0–13–2.

Umpires: B. N. J. Oxenford and R. J. Tucker. Third umpire: I. J. Gould.
Referee: B. C. Broad.

First one-day international At Whangarei, December 20, 2017. **New Zealand won by five wickets. West Indies 248-9** (50 overs) (E. Lewis 76, R. Powell 59; D. A. J. Bracewell 4-55, T. D. Astle 3-33); ‡**New Zealand 249-5** (46 overs) (G. H. Worker 57, C. Munro 49, K. S. Williamson 38, L. R. P. L. Taylor 49*). *MoM:* D. A. J. Bracewell. *ODI debuts:* T. D. Astle (New Zealand); R. R. Beaton, S. O. Hetmyer (West Indies). *Doug Bracewell was a surprise replacement for Colin de Grandhomme, who had returned to Zimbabwe following the death of his father. After time out with a serious knee injury, during which he was convicted for drink-driving, Bracewell hadn't played an international in over a year. But he made an immediate impact, dismissing Chris Gayle and Shai Hope with his first two legitimate deliveries, and ending with 4-55. As in the Tests, West Indies' batting never got going. Evin Lewis managed a composed 76 but, when they needed him to kick on, he missed a googly from debutant Todd Astle and was hit on the pad without recourse to review; it* *was probably missing off stump. Four sixes from Rovman Powell gave late impetus, though 248-9 appeared light. Opener George Worker, standing in for the injured Martin Guptill, looked the part, adding 108 with a charging Colin Munro, before Ross Taylor confirmed another clinical victory.*

Second one-day international At Christchurch, December 23, 2017. **New Zealand won by 204 runs. New Zealand 325-6** (50 overs) (G. H. Worker 58, C. Munro 30, L. R. P. L. Taylor 57, H. M. Nicholls 83*, T. D. Astle 49; S. S. Cotterell 3-62); ‡**West Indies 121** (28 overs) (T. A. Boult 7-34, L. H. Ferguson 3-17). *MoM:* T. A. Boult. *New Zealand gave Kane Williamson and Tim Southee a Christmas break, but there was no respite for West Indies. Trent Boult found the swing that had been largely elusive with the red ball and, deploying the occasional short one, destroyed them with the second-best ODI figures for New Zealand, one run worse than Southee's 7-33 against England at the 2015 World Cup. Opener Kyle Hope, in for the ill Chris Gayle, got the best of the lot, the ball hooping between bat and pad, while a lifter to Ashley Nurse took Boult to 100 ODI wickets. It was all done in 28 overs, handing New Zealand their sixth victory of 200 runs or more. Earlier, Worker registered a second successive half-century and, though stand-in captain Tom Latham stuttered (20 off 34 balls), Taylor continued his form. Two Canterbury boys – Henry Nicholls and Astle – then powered New Zealand past 300 with a stand of 130 in 98 balls. After the game, West Indies spirits flagged even more when seamer Ronsford Beaton was reported for a suspect action.*

Third one-day international At Christchurch, December 26, 2017. **New Zealand won by 66 runs** (DLS). ‡**New Zealand 131-4** (23 overs) (L. R. P. L. Taylor 47*, T. W. M. Latham 37); **West Indies 99-9** (23 overs) (J. O. Holder 34; T. A. Boult 3-18, M. J. Santner 3-15). *MoM:* L. R. P. L. Taylor. *MoS:* T. A. Boult. *West Indies began with festive cheer, as left-armer Sheldon Cotterell (2-19) snared two early wickets and showed off a dramatic celebratory salute. But there was no collapse. Either side of a rain break, Taylor and Latham helped New Zealand set a tricky target, revised to 166 off 23 overs, before West Indies slumped to 9-5. Gayle toed a Matt Henry delivery, Jason Mohammed played one of the worst shots of the tour, and a brilliant Boult yorker shattered Chadwick Walton's stumps. The captain, Jason Holder, hit out valiantly, but Mitchell Santner's left-arm spin squeezed any remaining life out of the chase.*

First Twenty20 international At Nelson, December 29, 2017. **New Zealand won by 47 runs. New Zealand 187-7** (20 overs) (C. Munro 53, G. D. Phillips 56); ‡**West Indies 140** (19 overs) (S. H. A. Rance 3-30, T. G. Southee 3-36). *MoM:* G. D. Phillips. *T20I debuts:* A. K. Kitchen, S. H. A. Rance (New Zealand); S. D. Hope (West Indies). *Twenty20 captain Carlos Brathwaite provided West Indies with welcome all-round ability, but he could not work miracles. After an accurate spell from Samuel Badree (1-22), Brathwaite took a brilliant grab at long-on to remove the dangerous Munro, then added a slick caught and bowled. New Zealand were finally under some pressure, but Kesrick Williams (1-52) conceded 25 from the final over, including three no-balls. Defending an above-par 187, New Zealand's swing bowlers, Southee and debutant Seth Rance, took three wickets each, while Santner (1-21) was miserly. Wicketkeeper Glenn Phillips, just 21, who earlier hit 56 off 40 balls, took a stunning catch to dismiss Gayle, sprinting back to take a top-edged pull.*

Second Twenty20 international At Mount Maunganui, January 1, 2018 (floodlit). **No result. New Zealand 102-4** (9 overs) (C. Munro 66) **v** ‡**West Indies.** *T20I debut:* S. O. Hetmyer (West Indies). *Munro's fireworks were as good as any seen the previous night: he helped take 21 off one Brathwaite over, and reached 50 in 18 deliveries, the second-fastest for New Zealand, behind his own 14-ball effort against Sri Lanka at Auckland in 2016-17. But rain spared West Indies further torment.*

Third Twenty20 international At Mount Maunganui, January 3, 2018 (floodlit). **New Zealand won by 119 runs.** ‡**New Zealand 243-5** (20 overs) (M. J. Guptill 63, C. Munro 104); **West Indies 124** (16.3 overs) (A. D. S. Fletcher 46; T. G. Southee 3-21). *MoM:* C. Munro. *MoS:* C. Munro. *T20I debut:* R. R. Emrit (West Indies). *After an appetiser two days before, Munro provided a sumptuous main course, becoming the first to score three T20 international centuries. He took just 47 balls, and hit ten sixes, mostly monstrous swats over wide long-on. There was chaos on the grass hill as spectators scrambled over each other: a brewer had offered $NZ50,000 for a one-handed catch. But much like West Indies' fielders, few got close; two days later, NZC said they would provide special enclosures at most grounds for those keen to take part in the stunt. Opening partner Guptill helped bludgeon 136 for the first wicket, en route to a New Zealand record total of 243-5, beating 214-6 against Australia at Christchurch in 2009-10; Jerome Taylor, Brathwaite and Badree all conceded half-centuries. West Indies' openers both fell for ducks in Southee's first over, Gayle to another short one, and the accuracy of Boult (2-29) and Ish Sodhi (2-25) ensured New Zealand picked up their biggest win in the format, beating 95 runs against Pakistan at Wellington in 2015-16. In his first game for West Indies for 11 years, Rayad Emrit removed Guptill and scored five.*

DOMESTIC CRICKET IN NEW ZEALAND IN 2016-17

MARK GEENTY

The champagne had barely dried on the Plunket Shield when Peter Fulton announced his retirement. In his 17th season, the popular Fulton – nicknamed Two-Metre Peter, as his boot spikes topped up his 1.98m frame – helped **Canterbury** win two of the three domestic trophies. His 10,569 first-class runs at 39 made him Canterbury's leading run-scorer, and he was one of only four batsmen to hit a Plunket Shield triple-century. Fulton also played 23 Tests, the most notable against England in 2012-13, when he scored twin hundreds at Auckland.

His most significant contribution in his farewell season came in the final of the one-day Ford Trophy against Wellington, reduced by rain to 20 overs. Though rarely known as a dasher, he unleashed a 50-ball century, beating Brendon McCullum's tournament record of 52, and hammering anything short or straight into the on side. Fulton's 19th and last first-class hundred came in the first-class Plunket Shield's penultimate round – but the prize almost slipped from Canterbury's grasp as they lost that match, and their last. Trying to force the victory that would keep them ahead of defending champions Auckland, they twice declared to set targets, only to see Central Districts and Wellington meet the challenge. But Auckland also lost their final game, slipping to third, while Northern Districts won their last two, but finished two points short of the title.

Experience counted as Canterbury secured the Shield for the third time in four years. All-rounder Andrew Ellis, who took over the captaincy in all three formats, was in the top ten for both runs scored (652 at 40) and wickets taken (27). Leg-spinner Todd Astle was their most successful bowler, collecting 31; overall, four of the top five wicket-takers were spinners.

Wellington, fourth in the Plunket Shield, had a remarkable white-ball season, though they could not quite follow up the Twenty20 title with the Ford Trophy. As table leaders, they should have had home advantage in the first play-off, but the Basin Reserve was booked for a concert, and Westpac Stadium was also unavailable, so they agreed to play in Christchurch; Canterbury duly won, securing home advantage for the final, when they won again. Wellington had stepped up a level with two key signings: Hamish Marshall, who had spent a decade with Gloucestershire, returned to New Zealand as he planned a career in insurance, and fast bowler Hamish Bennett arrived from Canterbury.

Northern Districts went empty-handed for the third year running, though they had as many Shield wins as Canterbury and fewer defeats. Ish Sodhi and Scott Kuggeleijn collected 74 wickets between them, and Kuggeleijn was also leading wicket-taker in the Ford Trophy, though Northern Districts were bundled out in the play-offs.

Auckland were in contention to retain their first-class title until their last-round stumble, when Central Districts chased down 301. They missed the punch of fast bowler Lockie Ferguson, who was injured after taking eight wickets in the preceding win. Tarun Nethula's leg-breaks claimed 43 victims, while Colin Munro did his usual demolition job with the bat, averaging 85 from nine Shield innings with a strike-rate of 135, though his disciplinary issues continued as he was banned for one game.

Central Districts' season ended with George Worker's 130 guiding them to victory over Auckland, but it was only their second win and they finished fifth. Slow left-armer Ajaz Patel was the Plunket Shield's leading wicket-taker, with 44. **Otago** had another difficult season, bottom in all three competitions despite a new coach, South African Rob Walter. Though they boasted the Shield's two leading run-scorers, Brad Wilson (730) and Anaru Kitchen (695), they managed only one victory and lacked depth late in the season.

The pink Kookaburra ball got its first airing in New Zealand first-class cricket in March, a trial run for the country's first day/night Test, scheduled against England in March 2018. Rain dominated all three games, though when the sun did shine batsmen prospered, before the pink ball played tricks under lights.

FIRST-CLASS AVERAGES IN 2016-17

BATTING (500 runs)

		M	*I*	*NO*	*R*	*HS*	*100*	*Avge*	*Ct/St*
1	†C. Munro (*Auckland*)	6	9	1	685	146	4	85.62	0
2	A. K. Kitchen (*Otago*)	6	12	1	695	207	4	63.18	2
3	K. S. Williamson (*New Zealand*)	7	11	1	588	176	3	58.80	6
4	T. A. Blundell (*Wellington/NZ A*)	10	15	3	656	113	1	54.66	18/1
5	D. G. Brownlie (*N Districts/NZ A*)	8	13	2	512	143	2	46.54	6
6	C. J. Bowes (*Canterbury*)	8	13	1	548	155	3	45.66	7
7	B. S. Wilson (*Otago*)	10	17	1	730	117*	2	45.62	6
8	M. H. W. Papps (*Wellington*)	9	15	0	676	160	3	45.06	10
9	W. A. Young (*Central Districts/NZ A*)	10	16	2	591	128*	2	42.21	5
10	T. C. Bruce (*Central Districts*)	9	15	2	540	127*	2	41.53	8
11	†J. A. Raval (*Auckland/NZ A/NZ*)	12	20	1	784	88	0	41.26	13
12	†L. J. Woodcock (*Wellington/NZ A*)	10	15	1	571	203*	2	40.78	10
13	A. M. Ellis (*Canterbury*)	10	16	0	652	196	3	40.75	6
14	D. Cleaver (*Central Districts*)	9	15	2	513	108*	2	39.46	24/3
15	R. J. Nicol (*Auckland*)	10	18	1	663	89	0	39.00	3
15	†H. M. Nicholls (*Canterbury/NZ A/NZ*)	12	19	3	624	118	1	39.00	5
17	H. J. H. Marshall (*Wellington*)	9	15	1	534	105*	1	38.14	4
18	T. D. Astle (*Canterbury/New Zealand*)	9	14	0	522	195	1	37.28	10
19	T. L. Seifert (*Northern Districts*)	10	18	1	624	151	1	36.70	22
20	G. R. Hay (*Central Districts*)	9	16	1	550	136	1	36.66	7
21	M. L. Guptill-Bunce (*Auckland*)	10	18	1	542	109	1	31.88	15
22	P. G. Fulton (*Canterbury*)	10	17	0	513	110	1	30.17	18

BOWLING (15 wickets)

		Style	*O*	*M*	*R*	*W*	*BB*	*5I*	*Avge*
1	K. A. Jamieson (*Canterbury/NZ A*)	RFM	123.1	27	432	24	8-74	1	18.00
2	K. A. Maharaj (*South Africa*)	SLA	114.5	26	299	15	6-40	2	19.93
3	S. H. A. Rance (*Central Districts*)	RFM	136	31	401	20	6-31	1	20.05
4	B. J. Arnel (*Wellington*)	RFM	288	89	642	30	4-35	0	21.40
5	T. G. Southee (*N Districts/NZ*)	RFM	240	67	745	34	6-80	3	21.91
6	L. H. Ferguson (*Auckland/NZ A*)	RFM	229.4	59	661	30	5-44	2	22.03
7	N. Wagner (*Otago/New Zealand*)	LFM	339.3	66	1,007	45	5-55	1	22.37
8	T. A. Boult (*New Zealand*)	LFM	169.3	41	497	22	4-64	0	22.59
9	A. M. Ellis (*Canterbury*)	RFM	273.1	72	664	27	6-35	1	24.59
10	M. J. Henry (*Canterbury/NZ*)	RFM	154.2	42	404	16	5-62	1	25.25
11	I. S. Sodhi (*Northern Districts*)	LB	299	48	1,037	40	7-59	2	25.92
12	M. B. McEwan (*Wellington*)	RFM	161.4	35	508	19	6-81	1	26.73
13	T. D. Astle (*Canterbury/NZ*)	LB	261.3	34	833	31	5-36	2	26.87
14	S. C. Kuggeleijn (*N Districts*)	RFM	280.3	56	928	34	6-60	2	27.29
15	C. de Grandhomme (*Auckland/NZ*)	RFM	235.5	64	577	21	6-41	1	27.47
16	T. S. Nethula (*Auckland*)	LB	396.3	51	1,293	43	6-36	4	30.06
17	D. J. Mitchell (*Northern Districts*)	RM	149.1	21	547	18	4-39	0	30.38
18	M. D. Rae (*Otago*)	RFM	171.3	18	739	24	4-82	0	30.79
19	A. Y. Patel (*Central Districts*)	SLA	441.4	92	1,356	44	5-22	4	30.81
20	J. S. Patel (*Wellington/NZ*)	OB	313.2	103	804	26	6-55	1	30.92
21	H. K. Bennett (*Wellington*)	RFM	230.1	45	810	25	4-19	0	32.40
22	N. A. Patel (*Central Districts*)	RM	149	27	542	16	5-71	1	33.87
23	E. J. Nuttall (*Canterbury/NZ A*)	LFM	152.1	19	678	19	5-67	1	35.68
24	D. J. Grobbelaar (*Auckland*)	LM	183.5	30	584	16	2-23	0	36.50
25	I. G. McPeake (*Wellington*)	RFM	212.2	27	886	24	3-24	0	36.91
26	J. D. Baker (*Northern Districts*)	RFM	224.1	52	649	17	3-90	0	38.17
27	C. Viljoen (*Otago*)	RM	225.1	49	701	18	5-101	1	38.94
28	B. M. Tickner (*Central Districts*)	RFM	269.3	41	908	21	3-54	0	43.23

PLUNKET SHIELD IN 2016-17

	Played	Won	Lost	Drawn	Bonus points Batting	Bonus points Bowling	Points	Net avge runs/wkt
Canterbury	10	4	4	2	22	35	105	4.95
Northern Districts	10	4	2	4	18	37	103	–2.96
Auckland	10	3	3	4	26	36	98	1.99
Wellington	10	2	2	6†	22	35	86	4.17
Central Districts	10	2	1	7†	20	30	79	–1.34
Otago	10	1	4	5	16	32	60	–7.58

† *Includes one abandoned match.*

Outright win = 12pts; abandoned = 2pts (but NZC awarded Wellington and Central Districts an extra 3pts each after their match was abandoned because of an earthquake). Bonus points were awarded as follows for the first 110 overs of each team's first innings: one batting point for the first 200 runs and then for 250, 300 and 350; one bowling point for the third wicket taken and then for the fifth, seventh and ninth. Net average runs per wicket is calculated by subtracting average runs conceded per wicket from average runs scored per wicket.

At Mount Maunganui, October 22–25, 2016. **Wellington won by six wickets. Auckland 269 and 278; ‡Wellington 273** (S. J. Murdoch 109; L. H. Ferguson 5-44) **and 275-4.** *Wellington 18pts, Auckland 6pts. Wellington captain Michael Papps became the first player to complete 10,000 runs in the Plunket Shield, in his 19th season, during their successful chase.*

At Christchurch, October 22–25, 2016. **Northern Districts won by five wickets. Canterbury 445** (T. D. Astle 195) **and 165** (S. C. Kuggeleijn 6-60); **‡Northern Districts 415** (D. G. Brownlie 104) **and 198-5.** *Northern Districts 19pts, Canterbury 7pts. Todd Astle came in at 60-4 in Canterbury's first innings and struck 195 in 189 balls. In their second, Scott Kuggeleijn took a career-best 6-60, leaving a target of 196. Kuggeleijn also hit opener Chad Bowes on the head with a bouncer; concussion kept him out of the next two matches, and in December he was sidelined again in the T20 Super Smash after top-edging a delivery from Otago's Nathan Smith on to his helmet.*

At Nelson, October 22–25, 2016. **Drawn. ‡Otago 479-5 dec** (H. D. Rutherford 143, B. S. Wilson 111) **and 238-2** (B. S. Wilson 117*); **Central Districts 365-5 dec** (G. R. Hay 136). *Central Districts 5pts, Otago 5pts. Hamish Rutherford and Brad Wilson opened with 227 in Otago's first innings and 133 in the second, when Wilson completed twin centuries.*

At Auckland (Eden Park Outer Oval), October 29–November 1, 2016. **Auckland won by two wickets. Otago 164** (T. S. Nethula 6-36) **and 353** (N. T. Broom 161); **‡Auckland 145** (N. Wagner 5-55) **and 376-8** (C. de Grandhomme 144*; C. Viljoen 5-101). *Auckland 16pts, Otago 4pts. Leg-spinner Tarun Nethula collected 10-124, but Auckland faced a target of 373; Colin de Grandhomme's career-best 144* got them over the line with two wickets left.*

At Christchurch, October 29–November 1, 2016. **Canterbury won by 71 runs. Canterbury 202** (A. Y. Patel 5-41) **and 354** (A. Y. Patel 5-118); **‡Central Districts 399** (D. Cleaver 104) **and 86** (T. D. Astle 5-36). *Canterbury 17pts, Central Districts 8pts. After slow left-armer Ajaz Patel claimed 10-159, Central Districts needed only 158, with one man absent; leg-spinner Astle bowled them out for 86.*

At Wellington (Basin Reserve), October 29–November 1, 2016. **Drawn. Northern Districts 285** (S. C. Kuggeleijn 112) **and 156-6; ‡Wellington 376-8 dec** (L. J. Woodcock 120). *Wellington 8pts, Northern Districts 5pts.*

At Auckland (Eden Park Outer Oval), November 5–8, 2016. **Drawn. Wellington 475-8 dec** (L. J. Woodcock 203*) **and 240-9 dec** (T. S. Nethula 5-71); **‡Auckland 374** (M. L. Guptill-Bunce 109) **and 276-6** (M. J. Guptill 128*). *Auckland 7pts, Wellington 8pts. Luke Woodcock batted throughout Wellington's first innings for his second double-hundred, then succumbed first ball in the second.*

At Hamilton, November 5–8, 2016. **Northern Districts won by 21 runs. Northern Districts 138 and 181; ‡Canterbury 112** (T. G. Southee 5-39) **and 186.** *Northern Districts 16pts, Canterbury 4pts. Northern Districts completed the double over Canterbury in a low-scoring game.*

At Dunedin, November 5–8, 2016. **Drawn. ‡Otago 402** (A. K. Kitchen 133) **and 213-7 dec** (H. D. Rutherford 110); **Central Districts 216 and 266-7.** *Otago 8pts, Central Districts 5pts. Otago recovered from 101-5 when 19-year-old Josh Finnie (98) and Anaru Kitchen added 182.*

At Mount Maunganui, November 14–17, 2016. **Drawn. Northern Districts 417-7 dec** (D. G. Brownlie 143, C. J. Anderson 103) **and 110-5; ‡Auckland 348** (M. J. Guptill 151). *Northern Districts 8pts, Auckland 6pts.*

At Invercargill, November 14–17, 2016. **Drawn. Canterbury 446-6 dec** (C. E. McConchie 103, A. M. Ellis 196) **v ‡Otago.** *Otago 2pts, Canterbury 4pts. Cole McConchie and Andrew Ellis added 258 for Canterbury's fifth wicket; Ellis struck eight sixes before missing a maiden double-hundred. Canterbury scored 405 on the first day, but only 8.1 overs were bowled during the last three.*

At Wellington (Basin Reserve), November 15–18, 2016. **Wellington v Central Districts. Abandoned.** *Wellington 5pts, Central Districts 5pts. The match was postponed for a day, then cancelled, after an earthquake (7.8 on the Richter scale) hit the South Island. Structural engineers found no damage to the Basin Reserve, but New Zealand Cricket declared that "frequent aftershocks have left players sleep-deprived and anxious, and in no fit state to start the game". They awarded the teams five points each, the average scored by the other four sides during this round.*

At Rangiora, November 22–25, 2016. **Canterbury won by ten runs. Canterbury 245 and 400-7 dec** (C. J. Bowes 155; T. S. Nethula 5-128); **‡Auckland 285** (C. Munro 108*; K. A. Jamieson 8-74) **and 350** (E. J. Nuttall 5-67). *Canterbury 17pts, Auckland 6pts. Colin Munro hit an 81-ball century, with five sixes, despite Kyle Jamieson recording this tournament's best return. But Bowes, back after concussion with a career-best 155, helped set a target of 361; Auckland reached 341-6, but Jamieson, who finished with 11-160, and Ed Nuttall grabbed the last four in five overs.*

At Napier (Nelson Park), November 22–25, 2016. **Drawn. ‡Central Districts 225 and 377-5 dec** (T. C. Bruce 115, D. Cleaver 108*); **Northern Districts 153** (A. Y. Patel 5-22) **and 295-7.** *Central Districts 5pts, Northern Districts 4pts. Patel had first-innings figures of 17.2–6–22–5. Northern Districts needed 450 to win, but instead batted out 129 overs to secure the draw, which kept them top of the table at the tournament's midsummer break.*

At Dunedin, November 22–25, 2016. **Drawn. ‡Otago 208** (J. S. Patel 6-55); **Wellington 350-7 dec** (L. Ronchi 119*). *Otago 4pts, Wellington 8pts.*

At Auckland (Colin Maiden Park), February 25–28, 2017. **Drawn. ‡Auckland 385-5 dec** (C. Munro 146) **and 260-6 dec** (C. Munro 142); **Central Districts 256-7 dec** (T. C. Bruce 127*) **and 115-1.** *Auckland 7pts, Central Districts 4pts. After a first-day washout, Munro scored twin centuries, reaching three figures in 84 balls on the second day, when he added 210 for the fourth wicket with Rob Nicol (86), and in just 60 on the fourth, when he made 121* before lunch; he hit 12 sixes in all.*

At Whangarei, February 25–28, 2017. **Otago won by five wickets. Northern Districts 278** (N. G. Smith 5-56) **and 286; ‡Otago 276** (S. C. Kuggeleijn 5-68) **and 289-5** (A. K. Kitchen 120*). *Otago 18pts, Northern Districts 6pts. Otago reduced leaders Northern Districts to 0-3, then 61-5, in their second innings, and Kitchen steered them to their only win of the tournament.*

At Wellington (Basin Reserve), February 26–March 1, 2017. **Canterbury won by seven wickets. Wellington 297** (M. J. Henry 5-62) **and 269; ‡Canterbury 243 and 325-3** (C. J. Bowes 149). *Canterbury 17pts, Wellington 6pts. Canterbury's third victory put them on top of the table.*

At Auckland (Eden Park), March 6–9, 2017 (day/night). **Drawn. ‡Canterbury 305-8 dec** (A. M. Ellis 103); **Auckland 333** (T. D. Astle 5-75). *Auckland 6pts, Canterbury 7pts. This round featured New Zealand's first day/night first-class fixtures, played with a pink ball. Domestic cricket returned to Eden Park's main ground – scheduled to host a day/night Test against England in 2017-18 – but the second and third days were washed out. Munro was found guilty of "inappropriate language", his third breach of the Code of Conduct in three years, and banned for the next round.*

At Hamilton, March 6–9, 2017 (day/night). **Drawn. ‡Central Districts 274-9 dec** (I. S. Sodhi 7-107); **Northern Districts 119-9** (S. H. A. Rance 6-31). *Northern Districts 4pts, Central Districts 6pts. Rain allowed only 41 overs across the last three days.*

At Wellington (Westpac), March 6–9, 2017 (day/night). **Drawn. Wellington 302-8 dec** (M. H. W. Papps 105); **‡Otago 98 and 304** (S. R. Wells 118). *Wellington 7pts, Otago 3pts. This was the first first-class match at Westpac Stadium, as the Basin Reserve lacked floodlights. Otago were 135-7 following on, still 69 behind, but Sam Wells and Nathan Smith (59) put on 141 to draw.*

At Auckland (Eden Park Outer Oval), March 14–17, 2017. **Auckland won by 71 runs. ‡Auckland 461 and 202-4 dec** (G. D. Phillips 109); **Northern Districts 334** (H. R. Cooper 101) **and 258** (T. S. Nethula 5-84). *Auckland 20pts, Northern Districts 7pts. Mitchell McClenaghan (73*) and Raja Sandhu (82) both scored maiden fifties as they added 139 for Auckland's last wicket. Northern*

Districts' first innings was boosted by 51 extras. Glenn Phillips, a 20-year-old who had made his T20I debut against South Africa in February before playing a first-class match, became the first player to score hundreds in all three formats in the same New Zealand domestic season.

At Christchurch, March 14–16, 2017. **Canterbury won by an innings and 119 runs. Otago 140** (A. M. Ellis 6-35) **and 173** (L. V. van Beek 5-43); **‡Canterbury 432-9 dec** (C. J. Bowes 137). *Canterbury 20pts, Otago 2pts. Canterbury's fourth win earned maximum points, which meant they led by 19 entering the penultimate round.*

At Napier (McLean Park), March 14–17, 2017. **Drawn. Wellington 245 and 336** (M. H. W. Papps 116; A. Y. Patel 5-106); **‡Central Districts 382** (W. A. Young 124; M. B. McEwan 6-81) **and 191-9.** *Central Districts 7pts, Wellington 4pts. Chasing 200, Central Districts were 158-2 with eight overs to go, then lost seven wickets (three each to Iain McPeake and Brent Arnel); their last pair survived four balls, but were nine short of victory.*

At Nelson, March 21–24, 2017. **Central Districts won by four wickets. Canterbury 388** (P. G. Fulton 110) **and 273-8 dec** (C. E. McConchie 131); **‡Central Districts 315** (W. A. Young 128*) **and 349-6** (J. D. Ryder 109*). *Central Districts 18pts, Canterbury 8pts. Peter Fulton scored his 19th (and, it turned out, final) first-class hundred. Hoping to make sure of the title with a round to go, Ellis declared and set Central Districts 347 – but Jesse Ryder guided them to victory, cutting Canterbury's lead over Auckland to eight points.*

At Mount Maunganui, March 21–24, 2017. **Northern Districts won by nine wickets. ‡Wellington 151** (J. G. Walker 5-46) **and 269** (M. H. W. Papps 160); **Northern Districts 262** (P. F. Younghusband 5-89) **and 162-1.** *Northern Districts 18pts, Wellington 4pts. A convincing victory kept Northern Districts in the title race, 14 points behind Canterbury, six behind Auckland.*

At Dunedin, March 21–23, 2017. **Auckland won by eight wickets. Otago 282** (L. H. Ferguson 5-53) **and 205** (A. K. Kitchen 108); **‡Auckland 304** (C. Munro 102) **and 185-2.** *Auckland 19pts, Otago 6pts. Munro scored his fourth hundred of the season, this time off 80 balls, as Auckland hurried to a three-day win that raised their hopes of retaining the Shield.*

At Christchurch, March 29–April 1, 2017. **Wellington won by seven wickets. Canterbury 197 and 293-8 dec** (A. M. Ellis 110); **‡Wellington 264** (T. A. Blundell 113) **and 230-3** (H. J. H. Marshall 105*). *Wellington 18pts, Canterbury 4pts. Canterbury collapsed to 40-5 in their first innings and 55-5 in their second, and Wellington to 74-5 first time round; Tom Blundell and Peter Younghusband (97) put Wellington ahead with 184 for the sixth wicket, while their team-mate, Test wicketkeeper Luke Ronchi, held nine catches in all. Anxious to complete victory in case Auckland won at Napier, Ellis declared again, setting Wellington 227. Hamish Marshall saw them home with his 31st first-class century – and first since joining Wellington. But, once Auckland lost too, Canterbury's four bowling points were just enough to secure the Plunket Shield.*

At Napier (McLean Park), March 29–April 1, 2017. **Central Districts won by three wickets. Auckland 200-9 dec** (N. A. Patel 5-71) **and 281-7 dec; ‡Central Districts 181 and 301-7** (G. H. Worker 130). *Central Districts 16pts, Auckland 5pts. Munro rounded off his season with two whirlwind fifties – the second in 26 balls – and seven sixes, which took him to 35 in the season; of his 685 runs, 462 had come from boundaries. But Auckland had to win to overtake Canterbury, so they set Central Districts a target of 301. Led by George Worker, the home side thwarted their ambitions.*

At Dunedin, March 29–April 1, 2017. **Northern Districts won by three wickets. Otago 432-8 dec** (A. K. Kitchen 207) **and 189-8 dec** (I. S. Sodhi 7-59); **‡Northern Districts 275 and 350-7** (D. J. Mitchell 106, T. L. Seifert 151). *Northern Districts 16pts, Otago 8pts. Kitchen converted his fourth century of the season into a maiden double, with nine sixes, and added 213 for Otago's fifth wicket with Derek de Boorder, but became the third batsman in this tournament to score 160-plus against Northern Districts in a losing cause. Challenged to score 347, Northern slid to 56-4 before Daryl Mitchell and Tim Seifert added 226; Seifert was out for a career-best 151 only 26 short of victory. Ish Sodhi took seven in an innings for the second time in four matches, and 11-189 in all. But Northern would have needed another three bonus points to overtake Canterbury, and finished runners-up.*

PLUNKET SHIELD WINNERS

1921-22	Auckland
1922-23	Canterbury
1923-24	Wellington
1924-25	Otago
1925-26	Wellington
1926-27	Auckland
1927-28	Wellington
1928-29	Auckland
1929-30	Wellington
1930-31	Canterbury
1931-32	Wellington
1932-33	Otago
1933-34	Auckland
1934-35	Canterbury
1935-36	Wellington
1936-37	Auckland
1937-38	Auckland
1938-39	Auckland
1939-40	Auckland
1940–45	*No competition*
1945-46	Canterbury
1946-47	Auckland
1947-48	Otago
1948-49	Canterbury
1949-50	Wellington
1950-51	Otago
1951-52	Canterbury
1952-53	Otago
1953-54	Central Districts
1954-55	Wellington
1955-56	Canterbury
1956-57	Wellington
1957-58	Otago
1958-59	Auckland
1959-60	Canterbury
1960-61	Wellington
1961-62	Wellington
1962-63	Northern Districts
1963-64	Auckland
1964-65	Canterbury
1965-66	Wellington
1966-67	Central Districts
1967-68	Central Districts
1968-69	Auckland
1969-70	Otago
1970-71	Central Districts
1971-72	Otago
1972-73	Wellington
1973-74	Wellington
1974-75	Otago
1975-76	Canterbury
1976-77	Otago
1977-78	Auckland
1978-79	Otago
1979-80	Northern Districts
1980-81	Auckland
1981-82	Wellington
1982-83	Wellington
1983-84	Canterbury
1984-85	Wellington
1985-86	Otago
1986-87	Central Districts
1987-88	Otago
1988-89	Auckland
1989-90	Wellington
1990-91	Auckland
1991-92	Central Districts Northern Districts
1992-93	Northern Districts
1993-94	Canterbury
1994-95	Auckland
1995-96	Auckland
1996-97	Canterbury
1997-98	Canterbury
1998-99	Central Districts
1999-2000	Northern Districts
2000-01	Wellington
2001-02	Auckland
2002-03	Auckland
2003-04	Wellington
2004-05	Auckland
2005-06	Central Districts
2006-07	Northern Districts
2007-08	Canterbury
2008-09	Auckland
2009-10	Northern Districts
2010-11	Canterbury
2011-12	Northern Districts
2012-13	Central Districts
2013-14	Canterbury
2014-15	Canterbury
2015-16	Auckland
2016-17	Canterbury

Auckland have won the title outright 23 times, Wellington 20, Canterbury 19, Otago 13, Central Districts 8, Northern Districts 7. Central Districts and Northern Districts also shared the title once.

The tournament was known as the Shell Trophy from 1975-76 to 2000-01, and the State Championship from 2001-02 to 2008-09.

THE FORD TROPHY IN 2016-17

50-over league plus knockout

	Played	*Won*	*Lost*	*NR/A*	*Bonus points*	*Points*	*NRR*
WELLINGTON	8	5	1	2	1	25	0.11
CANTERBURY	8	4	3	1	1	19	–0.11
CENTRAL DISTRICTS	8	3	4	1	2	16	0.82
NORTHERN DISTRICTS	8	3	5	0	3	15	–0.30
Auckland	8	3	4	1	1	15	0.00
Otago	8	3	4	1	1	15	–0.44

Northern Districts qualified ahead of Auckland because they had earned more bonus points.

Preliminary finals 1st v 2nd: Canterbury beat Wellington by 27 runs. **3rd v 4th:** Central Districts beat Northern Districts by 48 runs. **Final play-off:** Wellington beat Central Districts by five wickets.

Final At Rangiora, February 18, 2017. **Canterbury won by 28 runs. Canterbury 199-3** (20 overs) (P. G. Fulton 116*); ‡**Wellington 171** (19.3 overs). *Reduced by rain to 20 overs a side. Peter Fulton smashed a 50-ball hundred, beating Brendon McCullum's tournament record of 52 for Otago v Auckland in 2007-08; in all, Fulton hit 116* in 58, with 11 fours and seven sixes.*

The McDonald's Super Smash has its own section (page 1108).

PAKISTAN CRICKET IN 2017

Predictably unpredictable

MAZHER ARSHAD

Pakistan may one day hark back to 2017 and consider it a watershed. The year brought a refreshing change to their limited-overs approach, and with it a global one-day trophy for the first time since Imran Khan's cornered tigers of 1992. It also witnessed landmark matches returning to Lahore, and produced players with the potential to serve the team for a long time to come.

As well as lifting the Champions Trophy in England, where they began a streak of nine successive one-day wins – their best for nearly a decade – Pakistan finished the year top of the T20 rankings, having won eight out of ten matches in 2017. They extended that to ten out of 13 with a 2–1 victory in New Zealand in January 2018. But the thrill of a maiden Test series win in the Caribbean was offset by losing to Sri Lanka – Pakistan's first defeat in the UAE since making it their home in 2010. Only Bangladesh and Zimbabwe finished the year with a worse win/loss ratio in Tests.

PAKISTAN IN 2017

	Played	*Won*	*Lost*	*Drawn/No result*
Tests	6	2	4	–
One-day internationals	18	12	6	–
Twenty20 internationals	10	8	2	–

Month	Fixtures	Page
DECEMBER / JANUARY	3 Tests and 5 ODIs (a) v Australia	(see *Wisden 2017*, page 865)
FEBRUARY		
MARCH / APRIL	3 Tests, 3 ODIs and 4 T20Is (a) v West Indies	(page 1017)
MAY		
JUNE	ICC Champions Trophy (in England)	(page 263)
JULY		
AUGUST		
SEPTEMBER / OCTOBER	3 T20Is (h) v World XI	(page 929)
	2 Tests, 5 ODIs and 3 T20Is (h) v Sri Lanka (in UAE and Pakistan)	(page 933)
NOVEMBER		
DECEMBER		

For a review of Pakistan domestic cricket from the 2016-17 season, see page 940.

Aamir Quereshi, AFP/Getty Images

Taking guard: fans are well protected as they queue outside the Gaddafi Stadium in Lahore before the first ODI against a World XI.

The team bade farewell to Younis Khan, who became the first Pakistan batsman to score 10,000 Test runs, and Misbah-ul-Haq, their most successful captain, with 26 wins out of 56. Both retired from Tests at the end of a dramatic and historic victory in Dominica, where West Indies came within a few balls of saving the series. The win was sealed by the leg-spin of Yasir Shah, whose 43 Test wickets in 2017 were 20 more than Pakistan's next best, the promising seamer Mohammad Abbas. Yasir also took five of their seven five-wicket hauls.

The year had begun inauspiciously, with the bowlers conceding a century before lunch to David Warner at the SCG, and Australia soon completing a 3–0 sweep in the Tests. Pakistan then lost the ODIs 4–1. At that point, direct qualification for the World Cup in 2019 was in doubt, amid concerns that their one-day cricket had fallen alarmingly behind the rest of the world. But a 2–1 win in the Caribbean, followed by four victories in the Champions Trophy, eased those fears.

Indeed, their success in that competition was arguably the story of the year, confirming Pakistan's status as the most unpredictable side in the game. Their 50-over cricket had appeared to be at its lowest ebb when they were crushed by India in the opening match, and recovery was largely down to their rookies. Three players – Fakhar Zaman, Fahim Ashraf and Rumman Raees – made their debuts during the Champions Trophy, and opening batsman Fakhar starred with a century in the final against India at The Oval. Leg-spinner Shadab Khan had already proved his worth in the West Indies, while seamer Hasan Ali – whose 13 wickets, each greeted by a Shahid Afridi-style star-shaped celebration, made him the Player of the Tournament – had barely been in the side a year. Hasan then added 14 wickets in the 5–0 one-day whitewash of Sri Lanka in the UAE, elevating himself to No. 1 in the ODI rankings – only the second Pakistan fast bowler to get there, after Wasim Akram.

He also played a match-winning role in the final of the second Pakistan Super League, with two wickets for Peshawar Zalmi against Quetta Gladiators in Lahore. The efforts to bring top level cricket back to Pakistan began to produce results when the likes of Darren Sammy, Dawid Malan, Marlon Samuels and Chris Jordan flew in for the final. That was first of the three high-octane events hosted by the city in 2017. The next was the arrival of a World XI for three T20 internationals, which Pakistan won 2–1. Perhaps most significantly, Sri Lanka – victims of the Lahore terrorist attack in 2009 – visited for a T20 game in October.

A few players, such as Quetta Gladiators' Kevin Pietersen and Sri Lanka's Upul Tharanga, decided against travelling to Pakistan because of security fears, but these events were an encouraging sign. The 2018 PSL was scheduled to have three matches in Pakistan, including the final in Karachi, while West Indies had agreed to send a team for three Twenty20 matches in March.

Then there were the controversies. The PSL was hit by a spot-fixing scandal which forced the Pakistan Cricket Board to suspend Sharjeel Khan and Khalid Latif on the second day of the tournament, eventually banning both for five years; for Sharjeel, half the punishment was suspended. Meanwhile, Mohammad Irfan and Mohammad Nawaz were fined and suspended for six and two months respectively for failing to report suspect approaches. Nasir Jamshed didn't play in the PSL, but was handed a one-year ban for failing to cooperate with the PCB's anti-corruption unit.

Despite that, 2017 was a memorable year for Pakistan. The challenge now is to make sure it does not turn out to be a false dawn.

PAKISTAN v WORLD XI IN 2017-18

MIKE SELVEY

Twenty20 internationals (3): Pakistan 2, World XI 1

The inevitable aftermath of the atrocity perpetrated in March 2009 on the Sri Lankan cricket team, as well as Pakistan police and civilians, was sporting isolation. No international cricket had been staged in Pakistan since then, apart from a fleeting visit by Zimbabwe in 2015, with so-called home matches played in neutral venues – usually the UAE. It meant a generation of Pakistan cricketers had been deprived of the intimate relationship that comes from performing in front of a home crowd, while countless youngsters were unable to gain inspiration from watching their heroes in the flesh. The Lahore attack changed the sporting dynamic of the country: Shoaib Malik, who was playing in that Test, said he could now walk the city streets without being recognised.

The ICC initially tried to help maintain bilateral agreements, and set up the Pakistan Task Team, headed by Giles Clarke, then the ECB chairman. Once neutral venues became established, the focus gradually shifted to the return of international cricket to Pakistan itself. Clearly there would need to be an extremely high level of security before any team agreed to visit.

In 2013, the Punjab province drew up a new template. The Safe Cities Authority was an integrated system incorporating policing and intelligence, while a nationwide initiative diverted massive resources to eradicating terrorist cells. Eventually, the Pakistan Cricket Board decided to hold the final of their Twenty20 Super League in Lahore in March 2017 (the earlier stages were in the UAE). It was a success, with four overseas players – Chris Jordan, Dawid Malan, Darren Sammy and Marlon Samuels – appearing for the eventual winners, Peshawar Zalmi. Their attendance was crucial, given that other overseas players pulled out. Reports from a host of international security experts also proved positive.

Now came the next stage: a visit by a World XI to three official Twenty20 internationals against the full Pakistan team. The former England coach Andy Flower was asked to assemble a global squad. Despite the hectic international schedule, he managed to recruit a high-profile captain in South Africa's Faf du Plessis, and other world-class performers such as Hashim Amla, Morne Morkel and Tamim Iqbal. There was even a Sri Lankan, Tissara Perera, though he had not been part of the 2009 team.

The squad arrived in Lahore early on September 11 and, under the protection of probably the most stringent and expensive security ever laid on for a sports team, played three matches over four days before flying out again on the morning of September 16. The expense of the trip was incalculable: it involved not just thousands of police and troops, but losses to shops and businesses forced to shut because of road closures. Ticket applications were cross-checked with biometric identity data, and spectators had to negotiate four security checkpoints before they could enter the ground.

And yet the Gaddafi Stadium was full for the Independence Cup, the crowd overwhelmingly joyful. They accepted the inconveniences, and witnessed three fine matches, culminating in a win for Pakistan in the decider.

The trip showed that, with investment, it was possible to bring international cricket back to Pakistan, if only in Lahore to start with. The cost would be set against the advantage to the local economy, and the return of a national obsession. The World XI's visit was a small, but important, step. Further matches were mooted. And Shoaib Malik found himself mobbed once more.

WORLD XI SQUAD

*F. du Plessis (South Africa), H. M. Amla (South Africa), S. Badree (West Indies), G. J. Bailey (Australia), P. D. Collingwood (England), B. C. J. Cutting (Australia), G. D. Elliott (New Zealand), Imran Tahir (South Africa), D. A. Miller (South Africa), M. Morkel (South Africa), T. D. Paine (Australia), N. L. T. C. Perera (Sri Lanka), D. J. G. Sammy (West Indies), Tamim Iqbal (Bangladesh). *Coach:* A. Flower.

PAKISTAN v WORLD XI

First Twenty20 International

At Lahore, September 12, 2017 (floodlit). Pakistan won by 20 runs. Toss: World XI. Twenty20 international debut: Fahim Ashraf.

Pakistan's first home international for more than two years carried an understandable sense of occasion, which overshadowed the match itself. Their home win was no surprise, given that they had been training for several weeks, while the World XI had managed only a couple of practice sessions in Dubai before arriving in Lahore the day before the game. Some of their players looked rusty, judging from lacklustre fielding and one-dimensional bowling. Babar Azam took advantage, creaming 86 from 52 balls, then Shoaib Malik hit out, and Imad Wasim clouted two sixes from the four balls he faced as 36 came from the last two overs. Local wisdom had it that a total of 197 was about 20 over par, and that proved the exact margin of victory. Defying strong winds and a nearby electrical storm, Pakistan's attack proved too skilful: a number of the World XI's batsmen made starts, but none reached 30. A flourish from Sammy, who hit three sixes, was too little, too late.

Man of the Match: Babar Azam.

Pakistan

		B	*4/6*
1 Fakhar Zaman *c 2 b 10*	8	4	2
2 Ahmed Shehzad *c 8 b 9*	39	34	3
3 Babar Azam *c 5 b 11*	86	52	10/2
4 Shoaib Malik *b 7*	38	20	4/2
5 *†Sarfraz Ahmed *c 3 b 7*	4	5	0
6 Imad Wasim *not out*	15	4	0/2
7 Fahim Ashraf *not out*	0	1	0
Lb 1, w 6	7		
6 overs: 49-1 (20 overs)	197-5		

1/8 2/130 3/142 4/161 5/182

8 Sohail Khan, 9 Shadab Khan, 10 Hasan Ali and 11 Rumman Raees did not bat.

12th man: Umar Amin.

Morkel 4–7–32–1; Perera 4–9–51–2; Cutting 4–4–38–1; Imran Tahir 4–5–34–1; Elliott 2–1–17–0; Sammy 2–1–24–0.

World XI

		B	*4/6*
1 Tamim Iqbal *b 11*	18	18	3
2 H. M. Amla *c 6 b 11*	26	17	4/1
3 †T. D. Paine *c 11 b 8*	25	25	2/1
4 *F. du Plessis *c 12 b 9*	29	18	4/1
5 D. A. Miller *st 5 b 9*	9	7	0/1
6 G. D. Elliott *c 6 b 8*	14	8	2
7 N. L. T. C. Perera *run out*	17	11	3
8 D. J. G. Sammy *not out*	29	16	1/3
9 B. C. J. Cutting *not out*	0	0	0
Lb 6, w 4	10		
6 overs: 48-2 (20 overs)	177-7		

1/43 2/48 3/101 4/108 5/123 6/145 7/173

10 M. Morkel and 11 Imran Tahir did not bat.

Imad Wasim 4–11–22–0; Sohail Khan 4–10–28–2; Hasan Ali 4–8–44–0; Rumman Raees 3–7–37–2; Fahim Ashraf 1–2–7–0; Shadab Khan 4–9–33–2.

Umpires: Ahsan Raza and Aleem Dar. Third umpire: Shozab Raza.
Referee: R. B. Richardson.

PAKISTAN v WORLD XI

Second Twenty20 International

At Lahore, September 13, 2017 (floodlit). World XI won by seven wickets. Toss: Pakistan.

The World XI rang the changes, and a more cohesive team levelled the series in a match that went down to the penultimate delivery, from Rumman Raees, which Perera thumped back over the sightscreen for his fifth six. The crucial moment had come with 22 needed from nine balls: Perera lashed Sohail Khan high to long-on, where Shoaib Malik made good ground but fumbled the catch.

OLDEST PLAYERS IN TWENTY20 INTERNATIONALS

Yrs	*Days*			
44	34	R. J. Campbell	Hong Kong v Scotland at Nagpur	2015-16
43	179	Mohammad Tauqir	United Arab Emirates v Netherlands at Edinburgh	2015
43	45	G. B. Hogg	Australia v Pakistan at Mirpur	2013-14
42	273	Khurram Khan	United Arab Emirates v Zimbabwe at Sylhet	2013-14
42	172	Najeeb Amar	Hong Kong v Nepal at Chittagong	2013-14
42	154	S. O. Tikolo	Kenya v Canada at Sharjah	2013-14
41	360	S. T. Jayasuriya	Sri Lanka v England at Bristol	2011
41	115	S. Dhaniram	Canada v Kenya at Dubai	2009-10
41	**110**	**P. D. Collingwood**	**World XI v Pakistan at Lahore**	**2017-18**
40	16	Munir Dar	Hong Kong v Bangladesh at Chittagong	2013-14

The oldest man to play a T20 international for England is P. A. Nixon (36 years 80 days against Australia at Sydney in 2006-07).

Perera finished with 47 from 19, dominating his unbroken partnership of 69 with Amla, who was exhausted by the sweltering conditions. Earlier, an improved display in the field kept Pakistan to 174, in which Babar Azam top-scored again. Paul Collingwood, now 41 and the only Englishman in the World XI squad, made his first international appearance since 2010-11, and pulled off a fine diving catch off Shoaib from the last ball of the innings.

Man of the Match: N. L. T. C. Perera.

Pakistan

		B	*4/6*
1 Fakhar Zaman *lbw b 10*	21	13	4
2 Ahmed Shehzad *c 6 b 11*	43	34	5/1
3 Babar Azam *c 6 b 10*	45	38	5
4 Shoaib Malik *c 7 b 8*	39	23	1/3
5 Imad Wasim *c 11 b 5*	15	11	2
6 *†Sarfraz Ahmed *c 11 b 5*	0	1	0
7 Sohail Khan *not out*	1	1	0
Lb 1, w 8, nb 1	10		
6 overs: 43-1 (20 overs)	174-6		

1/41 2/100 3/135 4/156 5/157 6/174

8 Mohammad Nawaz, 9 Shadab Khan, 10 Usman Shinwari and 11 Rumman Raees did not bat.

Morkel 4–14–20–0; Cutting 4–3–52–1; Badree 4–6–31–2; Collingwood 2–2–18–0; Perera 3–4–23–2; Imran Tahir 3–4–29–1.

World XI

		B	*4/6*
1 Tamim Iqbal *c 4 b 7*	23	19	2/1
2 H. M. Amla *not out*	72	55	5/2
3 †T. D. Paine *b 5*	10	12	1
4 *F. du Plessis *c 9 b 8*	20	14	0/2
5 N. L. T. C. Perera *not out*	47	19	0/5
Lb 1, w 2	3		
6 overs: 49-1 (19.5 overs)	175-3		

1/47 2/71 3/106

6 D. A. Miller, 7 P. D. Collingwood, 8 B. C. J. Cutting, 9 M. Morkel, 10 S. Badree and 11 Imran Tahir did not bat.

Imad Wasim 4–10–27–1; Sohail Khan 4–4–44–1; Usman Shinwari 1–2–10–0; Rumman Raees 3.5–7–36–0; Mohammad Nawaz 3–6–25–1; Shadab Khan 4–2–32–0.

Umpires: Ahmed Shahab and Shozab Raza. Third umpire: Ahsan Raza.
Referee: R. B. Richardson.

PAKISTAN v WORLD XI

Third Twenty20 International

At Lahore, September 15, 2017 (floodlit). Pakistan won by 33 runs. Toss: World XI.

To the delight of a packed, noisy crowd, Pakistan won the final match comprehensively to take the Independence Cup 2–1. Du Plessis won the toss and, after seemingly changing his mind at the last moment, decided to bowl. His plans were undone by Ahmed Shehzad and Babar Azam, who added 102 for the second wicket in less than ten overs of vibrant batting. Shehzad's 89 from 53 balls included three successive sixes off Cutting's seamers, before he was run out in the same over, slipping while backing up and unable to regain his ground. Shoaib Malik's late hitting powered Pakistan to 183, which always looked beyond them. The World XI had juggled their team to ensure every member of the squad had appeared – Bailey, new to the art, kept wicket – and lost three wickets in the powerplay. Du Plessis was run out in the tenth over, to make it 67 for five. Although Miller and Perera had a go, there was always too much to do, especially as Pakistan's death bowling, led by Hasan Ali and Rumman Raees, was vastly improved from the previous matches.

Man of the Match: Ahmed Shehzad. *Man of the Series:* Babar Azam.

Pakistan

		B	*4/6*
1 Fakhar Zaman *run out*	27	25	2/1
2 Ahmed Shehzad *run out*	89	55	8/3
3 Babar Azam *c 4 b 7*	48	31	5
4 Shoaib Malik *not out*	17	7	0/2
5 Imad Wasim *c 4 b 7*	0	2	0
6 *†Sarfraz Ahmed *not out*	0	0	0
W 2	2		
6 overs: 51-0 (20 overs)	183-4		

1/61 2/163 3/175 4/182

7 Mohammad Nawaz, 8 Shadab Khan, 9 Hasan Ali, 10 Usman Shinwari and 11 Rumman Raees did not bat.

Badree 3–4–28–0; Morkel 4–7–42–0; Cutting 2–3–26–0; Perera 4–5–37–2; Sammy 4–5–24–0; Imran Tahir 3–2–26–0.

World XI

		B	*4/6*
1 Tamim Iqbal *b 10*	14	10	3
2 H. M. Amla *run out*	21	12	4
3 B. C. J. Cutting *b 9*	5	4	1
4 *F. du Plessis *run out*	13	13	1
5 †G. J. Bailey *b 5*	3	12	0
6 D. A. Miller *c 3 b 9*	32	29	2/1
7 N. L. T. C. Perera *c 3 b 11*	32	13	2/3
8 D. J. G. Sammy *not out*	24	23	2/1
9 M. Morkel *run out*	1	2	0
10 S. Badree *not out*	0	2	0
Lb 1, w 4	5		
6 overs: 43-3 (20 overs)	150-8		

1/15 2/41 3/41 4/53 5/67 6/112 7/137 8/139

11 Imran Tahir did not bat.

Imad Wasim 4–10–34–1; Usman Shinwari 4–10–26–1; Hasan Ali 4–10–28–2; Rumman Raees 4–14–20–1; Mohammad Nawaz 1–2–7–0; Shadab Khan 3–2–34–0.

Umpires: Ahsan Raza and Shozab Raza. Third umpire: Ahmed Shahab.
Referee: R. B. Richardson.

PAKISTAN v SRI LANKA IN 2017-18

OSMAN SAMIUDDIN

Test matches (2): Pakistan 0, Sri Lanka 2
One-day internationals (5): Pakistan 5, Sri Lanka 0
Twenty20 internationals (3): Pakistan 3, Sri Lanka 0

This was Sri Lanka's third tour of the UAE since 2011 – the most by any opponent. Pakistan have also toured Sri Lanka three times since then, so there was a distinct feeling that, had this series not happened, no one would have minded. The Pakistan Cricket Board had spent much of their time and energy on the series before, the World XI's visit to Lahore. The arrival of the Sri Lankans, by contrast, was treated as an obligation – like attending an in-law's wedding to stay onside with the spouse.

The scheduling was careless throughout. This was the first time a Test had begun in the UAE in September, when daytime temperatures can top 40°C. And the second match was day/night, despite there being no real justification: crowds don't turn up for Test cricket here, regardless of the time of day. It was appropriate that, during the tour, the ICC finalised plans for a new Test championship, to give more meaning to contests such as this.

Still, in their own Emirati way – where matters tend to drift aimlessly, then hurtle towards a taut conclusion – the Tests were compelling. Neither side were high on quality, though Pakistan's decline since going top of the rankings in August 2016 was startling; by the end of the series, they had slumped to seventh. This was their first Test foray after the Misbah-ul-Haq/Younis Khan era, and it was frightening, with batting failures commonplace. Losing a first Test series in the UAE since 2002-03, to beleaguered opponents, drove home the impact of their exits.

For Sri Lanka, it was brief respite from a turbulent year in which they had burned through captain after captain and lurched from one embarrassing defeat to the next. There were signs they had some of the personnel to see them back to health, but a wipeout in the limited-overs leg only restored the doom and gloom.

There were mitigating circumstances, though, for the Twenty20 defeats. As Sri Lanka Cricket had agreed to play the last match in Lahore – where their team had been attacked by terrorists in March 2009 – only those willing to travel to Pakistan were picked for the overall squad.

A demoralised side – already missing the injured Angelo Mathews – were thus deprived of Dinesh Chandimal, Akila Dananjaya, Niroshan Dickwella and Upul Tharanga; Tissara Perera, who had been part of the World XI side in September, now took over as captain. Sections of the city close to the stadium were locked down, as part of a huge security operation comparable to a state visit. But none of that mattered to a packed Gaddafi Stadium crowd, who revelled in the first contest between top-eight countries in Pakistan since that tragic day.

SRI LANKAN TOURING PARTY

*L. D. Chandimal (T/50), J. R. M. W. S. Bandara (20), P. V. D. Chameera (50), A. Dananjaya (50), P. C. de Silva (20), D. P. D. N. Dickwella (T/50), A. N. P. R. Fernando (T/50), M. V. T. Fernando (T/50), P. L. S. Gamage (T/50/20), M. D. Gunathilleke (20), H. M. R. K. B. Herath (T), C. K. Kapugedera (50), F. D. M. Karunaratne (T), R. A. S. Lakmal (T/50), B. K. G. Mendis (T/50/20), E. M. D. Y. Munaweera (20), S. S. Pathirana (20), M. D. K. Perera (T), N. L. T. C. Perera (50/20), S. Prasanna (50/20), S. M. A. Priyanjan (20), M. B. Ranasinghe (20), W. S. R. Samarawickrama (T/50/20), P. A. D. L. R. Sandakan (T), M. D. Shanaka (20), A. R. S. Silva (T), J. K. Silva (T), T. A. M. Siriwardene (50), W. U. Tharanga (50), H. D. R. L. Thirimanne (T/50), I. Udana (20), M. L. Udawatte (20), J. D. F. Vandersay (50/20). *Coach:* N. Pothas.

Tharanga captained in the ODIs, and Tissara Perera in the T20Is.

PAKISTAN v SRI LANKA

First Test

At Abu Dhabi, September 28–October 2, 2017. Sri Lanka won by 21 runs. Toss: Sri Lanka. Test debut: Haris Sohail.

Somehow, after four meandering days, the match arrived at a dead-eyed shootout: Herath versus Pakistan. The last time they had met in Tests, in 2015, Pakistan devised a strategy. They used their feet and they swept, restricting Herath to two wickets across two matches; he was dropped for the decider.

They figured it would work again. After all, Herath was older, and had endured a poor series against India earlier in the year. But he had a plan of his own: he did for them when they used their feet, he did for them when they swept. He did for them every which way, in fact, and led Sri Lanka's defence of 136, the lowest target they had protected in Tests, beating 168 against the same opposition at Galle in 2009 – and the lowest Pakistan had failed to chase, beating 146 against South Africa at Faisalabad in 1997-98. The result was unexpected: Pakistan had never tasted Test defeat in Abu Dhabi, while Sri Lanka had lost nine out of nine in all formats at home to India, and had been without an away Test victory against top-eight opposition since beating England at Leeds in 2014.

Herath's second-innings six-for, to go with five in the first, included his 100th against Pakistan, making him their biggest destroyer (Kapil Dev had 99). Humble to his very last molecule, he said he had got there simply because he had played them 20 times. He also became, at the age of 39, the first left-arm spinner to reach 400 Test scalps, with half coming after turning 35. His has been a fabulous, late-blooming career.

It would not slight Herath or Sri Lanka to suggest Pakistan's blowout had been foretold: this was the eighth time they had lost ten wickets in a day since July 2016. And they had

MOST TEST WICKETS BY LEFT-ARM SPINNERS

W		*M*	*BB*	*5I*	*Avge*	
406	**H. M. R. K. B. Herath (SL)**	**87**	**9-127**	**33**	**28.03**	**1999-2000 to 2017-18**
362	D. L. Vettori (NZ/World)	113	7-87	20	34.36	1996-97 to 2014-15
297	D. L. Underwood (E)	86	8-51	17	25.83	1966 to 1981-82
266	B. S. Bedi (I)	67	7-98	14	28.71	1966-67 to 1979
188	**Shakib Al Hasan (B)**	**51**	**7-36**	**17**	**32.37**	**2007 to 2017-18**
174	G. A. R. Lock (E)	49	7-35	9	25.58	1952 to 1967-68
171	Iqbal Qasim (P)	50	7-49	8	28.11	1976-77 to 1988-89
167	M. S. Panesar (E)	50	6-37	12	34.71	2005-06 to 2013-14
165	**R. A. Jadeja (I)**	**35**	**7-48**	**9**	**23.73**	**2012-13 to 2017-18**
162	M. H. Mankad (I)	44	8-52	8	32.32	1946 to 1958-59

As at January 30, 2018.

done it in five different countries. Each Test had been on the watch of Mickey Arthur, who wasn't sure what could be done. He pointed to the youth of the batting line-up, but the average age of the top seven was 27.

The first four and a half days had been less dramatic. Chandimal, a captain setting the tone for the series, hit a nine-hour 155 not out, and was well supported by Karunaratne and Dickwella. But Pakistan grabbed a three-run lead, with Azhar Ali passing 5,000 Test runs, and Haris Sohail making an attractive 76 on debut. If he was a controversial selection – this was his first first-class game in three and a half years – he delivered a fine riposte. When yet another Yasir Shah five-for scuttled Sri Lanka on the fifth morning, the stage was set for a Pakistan victory. Apparently.

Man of the Match: H. M. R. K. B. Herath.

Close of play: first day, Sri Lanka 227-4 (Chandimal 60, Dickwella 42); second day, Pakistan 64-0 (Shan Masood 30, Sami Aslam 31); third day, Pakistan 266-4 (Azhar Ali 74); fourth day, Sri Lanka 69-4 (Mendis 16, Lakmal 2).

Sri Lanka

First innings		Second innings	
F. D. M. Karunaratne run out	93	c Shan Masood b Yasir Shah	10
J. K. Silva b Hasan Ali	12	lbw b Haris Sohail	25
H. D. R. L. Thirimanne lbw b Yasir Shah	0	c Sarfraz Ahmed b Asad Shafiq	7
B. K. G. Mendis c Sarfraz Ahmed b Yasir Shah	10	lbw b Mohammad Abbas	18
*L. D. Chandimal not out	155	c Asad Shafiq b Yasir Shah	7
†D. P. D. N. Dickwella b Hasan Ali	83	(7) not out	40
M. D. K. Perera lbw b Haris Sohail	33	(8) lbw b Yasir Shah	6
H. M. R. K. B. Herath c Babar Azam b Yasir Shah	4	(9) c Shan Masood b Yasir Shah	0
R. A. S. Lakmal lbw b Mohammad Abbas	7	(6) c Babar Azam b Mohammad Abbas	13
P. A. D. L. R. Sandakan lbw b Mohammad Abbas	8	c Mohammad Amir b Yasir Shah	8
A. N. P. R. Fernando b Mohammad Abbas	0	b Hasan Ali	0
Lb 11, nb 3	14	Lb 3, nb 1	4
1/34 (2) 2/35 (3) 3/61 (4) 4/161 (1) 5/295 (6) 6/387 (7) 7/396 (8) 8/408 (9) 9/419 (10) 10/419 (11) (154.5 overs)	419	1/20 (1) 2/33 (3) 3/51 (2) 4/65 (5) 5/73 (4) 6/86 (6) 7/101 (8) 8/101 (9) 9/135 (10) 10/138 (11) (66.5 overs)	138

Mohammad Amir 27–5–63–0; Mohammad Abbas 26.5–0–75–3; Yasir Shah 57–11–120–3; Hasan Ali 27–6–88–2; Shan Masood 1–1–0–0; Haris Sohail 13–0–51–1; Asad Shafiq 3–0–11–0. *Second innings*—Mohammad Amir 12–4–27–0; Mohammad Abbas 12–3–22–2; Yasir Shah 27–5–51–5; Hasan Ali 7.1–0–21–1; Asad Shafiq 3.4–0–7–1; Haris Sohail 5–2–7–1.

Pakistan

First innings		Second innings	
Shan Masood b Herath	59	c Silva b Perera	7
Sami Aslam lbw b Perera	51	c Karunaratne b Herath	2
Azhar Ali c sub (W. S. R. Samarawickrama) b Herath	85	c Dickwella b Lakmal	0
Asad Shafiq c Thirimanne b Herath	39	c Karunaratne b Herath	20
Babar Azam c Dickwella b Fernando	28	c Dickwella b Perera	3
Haris Sohail c Lakmal b Fernando	76	lbw b Perera	34
*†Sarfraz Ahmed b Lakmal	18	st Dickwella b Herath	19
Mohammad Amir lbw b Lakmal	4	(9) b Herath	9
Yasir Shah c Thirimanne b Herath	8	(10) not out	6
Hasan Ali st Dickwella b Herath	29	(8) b Herath	8
Mohammad Abbas not out	1	lbw b Herath	0
B 5, lb 9, w 2, nb 8	24	B 1, lb 4, nb 1	6
1/114 (2) 2/116 (1) 3/195 (4) 4/266 (5) 5/294 (3) 6/316 (7) 7/326 (8) 8/340 (9) 9/390 (10) 10/422 (6) (162.3 overs)	422	1/4 (2) 2/7 (3) 3/16 (1) 4/32 (5) 5/36 (4) 6/78 (7) 7/98 (6) 8/100 (8) 9/111 (9) 10/114 (11) (47.4 overs)	114

Lakmal 22–5–42–2; Fernando 25.3–1–77–2; Perera 37–10–92–1; Sandakan 35–7–98–0; Herath 40–12–93–5; Karunaratne 3–1–6–0. *Second innings*—Lakmal 5–1–12–1; Herath 21.4–4–43–6; Perera 18–4–46–3; Fernando 2–1–4–0; Sandakan 1–0–4–0.

Umpires: R. A. Kettleborough and N. J. Llong. Third umpire: Ahsan Raza.
Referee: A. J. Pycroft.

PAKISTAN v SRI LANKA

Second Test

At Dubai, October 6–10, 2017 (day/night). Sri Lanka won by 68 runs. Toss: Sri Lanka. Test debuts: P. L. S. Gamage, W. S. R. Samarawickrama.

Since moving their base to the UAE in 2010, Pakistan had not lost a Test series here. But the fortress now fell. There was no more emphatic way to illustrate the loss of Misbah-ul-Haq and Younis Khan.

On the final afternoon of Dubai's second day/night Test – but Sri Lanka's first – Pakistan could still have saved their proud record. Asad Shafiq and Sarfraz Ahmed were at the crease, and a target of 317 was less than a hundred away. But after another collapse, Sarfraz was left to acknowledge that Test captaincy was tough.

In many ways, the match was like the previous day/night Test here, a year earlier against West Indies, when Pakistan had won rather than lost: a big first innings followed by a weak reply, then a collapse and a valiant but futile chase. Karunaratne's career-best 196 in nine and a quarter hours was the kind of knock he had played often in 2017: barely noticeable, never vulnerable. The middle order gave strong support, while Yasir Shah picked up another six, to become the first spinner to collect a five-for or better in five successive Tests (and the fourth in all, after Charlie Turner, S. F. Barnes and Alec Bedser).

Pakistan's response was inadequate. Younis had been a master converter, with 34 hundreds to 33 fifties. Without him, an inability to capitalise on starts was crippling. Their best batsman, Azhar Ali, hit another half-century, so too Haris Sohail. But neither went on, and Sri Lanka's bowlers did enough to secure a 220-run lead.

That should have been that. With about an hour left of the third night, Sri Lanka needed to bat another day, on a benign surface, to secure the series. But they were unused to winning positions, and by stumps were 34 for five. Wahab Riaz was the instigator. He returned to the side because of an injury to Hasan Ali and proceeded, as he sometimes does, to turn a game around. He hurtled in and discomfited Sri Lanka with pace and hostility, claiming three wickets that evening, and another next day, when Sohail picked up three in an over to wrap things up at 96. The 386-run gap between their two innings was a Sri Lankan record (beating 383 against Australia in Colombo in 1992-93). Despite losing Mohammad Amir, unable to bowl in the second innings because of a shin injury, Pakistan had forced their way back into the game.

Then they went nowhere for 33 overs, scoring just 52 for the loss of five wickets. Shan Masood played one of the horror hands of the year, finally nicking behind after crawling to 21 in 101 balls. It was difficult to remember one he middled. Shafiq, who crafted a majestic hundred, and Sarfraz injected life into the innings. But once Dilruwan Perera had induced a sweep from Sarfraz to deep square leg, ending a 173-run stand, Pakistan imploded from 225 for five to 248. Perera finished with five to complete an incisive all-round performance, as Sri Lanka raced to a series victory that surprised everyone.

Man of the Match: F. D. M. Karunaratne. *Man of the Series:* F. D. M. Karunaratne.

Close of play: first day, Sri Lanka 254-3 (Karunaratne 133, Chandimal 49); second day, Pakistan 51-0 (Shan Masood 15, Sami Aslam 30); third day, Sri Lanka 34-5 (Mendis 8); fourth day, Pakistan 198-5 (Asad Shafiq 86, Sarfraz Ahmed 57).

Sri Lanka

First innings		Second innings	
F. D. M. Karunaratne b Wahab Riaz	196	b Wahab Riaz	7
J. K. Silva c Sarfraz Ahmed b Yasir Shah	27	c Sarfraz Ahmed b Mohammad Abbas	3
W. S. R. Samarawickrama c and b Mohammad Amir	38	c Sarfraz Ahmed b Wahab Riaz	13
B. K. G. Mendis c Asad Shafiq b Yasir Shah	1	c Sarfraz Ahmed b Haris Sohail	29
*L. D. Chandimal lbw b Yasir Shah	62	(6) lbw b Wahab Riaz	0
†D. P. D. N. Dickwella c Sarfraz Ahmed b Mohammad Abbas	52	(7) c Sarfraz Ahmed b Wahab Riaz	21
M. D. K. Perera b Yasir Shah	58	(8) lbw b Yasir Shah	0
H. M. R. K. B. Herath not out	27	(9) c Babar Azam b Haris Sohail	17
R. A. S. Lakmal lbw b Mohammad Abbas	8	(5) lbw b Yasir Shah	1
P. L. S. Gamage st Sarfraz Ahmed b Yasir Shah	1	not out	1
A. N. P. R. Fernando c Asad Shafiq b Yasir Shah	0	lbw b Haris Sohail	0
B 1, lb 3, w 3, nb 5	12	Lb 1, nb 3	4
1/63 (2) 2/131 (3) 3/136 (4) 4/282 (5) 5/370 (6) 6/429 (1) 7/454 (7) 8/469 (9) 9/474 (10) 10/482 (11) (159.2 overs)	482	1/3 (2) 2/22 (1) 3/26 (3) 4/33 (5) 5/34 (6) 6/59 (7) 7/60 (8) 8/95 (9) 9/96 (4) 10/96 (11) (26 overs)	96

Mohammad Amir 19.3–5–74–1; Mohammad Abbas 33–9–100–2; Wahab Riaz 26–6–62–1; Yasir Shah 55.5–9–184–6; Asad Shafiq 11–1–24–0; Haris Sohail 14–3–34–0. *Second innings*—Mohammad Abbas 4–2–6–1; Yasir Shah 12–2–47–2; Wahab Riaz 9–0–41–4; Haris Sohail 1–0–1–3.

Pakistan

First innings		Second innings	
Shan Masood b Gamage	16	c Dickwella b Perera	21
Sami Aslam lbw b Perera	39	c Mendis b Gamage	1
Azhar Ali lbw b Herath	59	c Silva b Fernando	17
Asad Shafiq c Mendis b Lakmal	12	(5) c Mendis b Lakmal	112
Babar Azam c Samarawickrama b Herath	8	(6) c Silva b Perera	0
Haris Sohail lbw b Perera	56	(4) c Dickwella b Perera	10
*†Sarfraz Ahmed c Mendis b Perera	14	c Fernando b Perera	68
Mohammad Amir lbw b Herath	7	lbw b Perera	4
Yasir Shah b Lakmal	24	st Dickwella b Herath	5
Wahab Riaz c Samarawickrama b Gamage	16	c Chandimal b Herath	1
Mohammad Abbas not out	1	not out	3
B 4, lb 2, nb 4	10	Lb 1, nb 5	6
1/61 (1) 2/65 (2) 3/92 (4) 4/109 (5) 5/180 (3) 6/199 (7) 7/214 (8) 8/220 (6) 9/250 (10) 10/262 (9) (90.3 overs)	262	1/5 (2) 2/36 (3) 3/49 (4) 4/52 (1) 5/52 (6) 6/225 (7) 7/230 (8) 8/244 (9) 9/244 (5) 10/248 (10) (90.2 overs)	248

Lakmal 17.3–5–41–2; Fernando 9–2–21–0; Gamage 15–2–38–2; Perera 26–3–72–3; Herath 23–3–84–3. *Second innings*—Lakmal 14–4–35–1; Gamage 16–5–29–1; Herath 22.2–3–57–2; Fernando 11–3–21–1; Perera 26–1–98–5; Mendis 1–0–7–0.

Umpires: R. A. Kettleborough and N. J. Llong. Third umpire: S. Ravi.
Referee: A. J. Pycroft.

First one-day international At Dubai, October 13, 2017 (day/night). **Pakistan won by 83 runs. Pakistan 292-6** (50 overs) (Fakhar Zaman 43, Babar Azam 103, Mohammad Hafeez 32, Shoaib Malik 81); ‡**Sri Lanka 209-8** (50 overs) (H. D. R. L. Thirimanne 53, A. Dananjaya 50*; Rumman Raees 3-49, Hasan Ali 3-36). *MoM:* Shoaib Malik. *If Babar Azam's Test career was yet to take off, he continued to be imperious in colours, the young prince of Pakistani batting. A sixth ODI hundred – from just 32 innings – provided the platform for a comfortable victory. Upul Tharanga had surprisingly chosen to bowl, and Babar initially looked out of sorts, carrying over his red-ball hesitancy. But as the surface settled, so did he. As usual, there was no blistering 360-degree batting; he took his time, building his innings on elegant strokeplay and good running. Shoaib Malik brought* *the ammunition in a 61-ball 81 that drove Pakistan close to 300. And after Niroshan Dickwella and Dinesh Chandimal fell in successive Rumman Raees overs, Hasan Ali grabbed two wickets in the 16th over, leaving Sri Lanka 67-5. Akila Dananjaya hit a maiden one-day half-century, but it was academic.*

Second one-day international At Abu Dhabi, October 16, 2017 (day/night). **Pakistan won by 32 runs.** ‡**Pakistan 219-9** (50 overs) (Babar Azam 101, Shadab Khan 52*; P. L. S. Gamage 4-57); **Sri Lanka 187** (48 overs) (W. U. Tharanga 112*; Shadab Khan 3-47). *MoM:* Shadab Khan. *Another Babar hundred – his fifth in a row in the UAE – set up another home victory. But his was not the critical performance. That came from Shadab Khan, an electric talent. First, he showed sense beyond his 19 years with the bat. After an early collapse, he put on 109 with Babar for the seventh wicket, and kept him company from the 28th over until the last. There was no flashiness, just a steady supply of ones and twos – smart on a slow surface. Then, after Junaid Khan and Hasan struck top-order blows, Shadab took three wickets in three overs to send Sri Lanka into a tailspin. The first two were treats, Chandimal and Milinda Siriwardene undone by googlies. At 93-7, complacency crept in, and Tharanga and Jeffrey Vandersay bedded down for a stand of 76. Pakistan missed chances from Tharanga, who eventually reached a classy hundred but, just as they started to panic, Rumman dismissed Vandersay for 22, and the game was up.*

Third one-day international At Abu Dhabi, October 18, 2017 (day/night). **Pakistan won by seven wickets.** ‡**Sri Lanka 208** (48.2 overs) (W. U. Tharanga 61, N. L. T. C. Perera 38; Hasan Ali 5-34); **Pakistan 209-3** (42.3 overs) (Imam-ul-Haq 100, Babar Azam 30, Mohammad Hafeez 34*). *MoM:* Imam-ul-Haq. *ODI debut:* Imam-ul-Haq. *There were charges of nepotism when bespectacled opener Imam-ul-Haq was picked – uncle Inzamam was the chief selector – but his performance silenced them. He became only the second Pakistani to hit a century on ODI debut, after Salim Elahi against Sri Lanka at Gujranwala in 1995-96, and the 13th overall. Imam's style bore no similarity to Inzamam's: left-handed and unafraid to go aerial, even on the off side. When he fell a ball after reaching three figures, Pakistan were only six runs away from securing the series. After a swift start, Sri Lanka had been tied down by the spinners and taken apart by Hasan. Aiming at the stumps with the pace – and changes in it – that has marked him out as Pakistan's star limited-overs bowler, he became the ninth to pick up three five-fors in a year. Sri Lanka were rumbled for 208, leaving Imam to begin his international career in ideal circumstances: a no-pressure target against deflated opponents.*

MOST ODI FIVE-FORS IN A CALENDAR YEAR

5W		*M*	*W*	*BB*	*Avge*	
5	Waqar Younis (Pakistan)	19	47	6-26	12.63	1990
4	Shahid Afridi (Pakistan)	27	45	5-16	20.82	2011
3	Mustafizur Rahman (Bangladesh)	9	26	6-43	12.34	2015
3	R. J. Harris (Australia)	16	40	5-19	15.17	2010
3	B. A. W. Mendis (Sri Lanka)	18	48	6-13	10.12	2008
3	**Hasan Ali (Pakistan)**	**18**	**45**	**5-34**	**17.04**	**2017**
3	L. Klusener (South Africa)	19	34	6-49	22.58	1997
3	S. L. Malinga (Sri Lanka)	24	48	6-38	19.25	2011
3	Azhar Mahmood (Pakistan)	27	46	6-18	18.82	1999

Fourth one-day international At Sharjah, October 20, 2017 (day/night). **Pakistan won by seven wickets.** ‡**Sri Lanka 173** (43.4 overs) (H. D. R. L. Thirimanne 62; Hasan Ali 3-37); **Pakistan 177-3** (39 overs) (Babar Azam 69*, Shoaib Malik 69*). *MoM:* Babar Azam. *ODI debuts:* Usman Shinwari (Pakistan); W. S. R. Samarawickrama (Sri Lanka). *After the latest crushing victory, Sarfraz Ahmed said Pakistan had the best attack in the world. Here they showed their depth, drafting in Usman Shinwari – yet another left-arm seamer – and Imad Wasim, in place of Rumman Raees and Fahim Ashraf, with no discernible dip in performance. Shinwari took a wicket with his second ball in ODIs, a ripper that skidded through Tharanga's gate, while Imad took 2-13 off seven. The only bowler not to take a wicket, Mohammad Hafeez, was at least miserly, conceding just three an over. Lahiru Thirimanne apart, Sri Lanka were hapless. Pakistan's task was simple and, after they slipped to 58-3, Babar saw them home with 69*. If he was a strange choice for the match award, it might have been unfair to choose between the bowlers.*

Fifth one-day international At Sharjah, October 23, 2017 (day/night). **Pakistan won by nine wickets. ‡Sri Lanka 103** (26.2 overs) (Usman Shinwari 5-34); **Pakistan 105-1** (20.2 overs) (Imam-ul-Haq 45*, Fakhar Zaman 48). *MoM:* Usman Shinwari. *MoS:* Hasan Ali. *Shinwari secured a five-for in his first 21 balls, the third-quickest after Sri Lanka's Chaminda Vaas (16) against Bangladesh at Pietermaritzburg in the 2003 World Cup, and the Netherlands' Timm van der Gugten (20) against Canada at King City in 2013. It was a very Pakistani spectacle: extravagant early swing, energetic pace, and smashed stumps. Sri Lanka were blown out of the game, even if 103 all out represented a recovery from 20-5. It was their shortest innings after choosing to bat, undercutting 27.4 overs against New Zealand at Christchurch in 2015-16. This was their 12th ODI defeat in a row, and third 5–0 whitewash in 2017, after losing to South Africa and India.*

First Twenty20 international At Abu Dhabi, October 26, 2017 (floodlit). **Pakistan won by seven wickets. Sri Lanka 102** (18.3 overs) (Hasan Ali 3-23); **‡Pakistan 103-3** (17.2 overs) (Shoaib Malik 42*). *MoM:* Usman Shinwari. *T20I debut:* W. S. R. Samarawickrama (Sri Lanka). *Sri Lanka were a different side from the ODIs, but the result was the same. Pakistan's attack, with every angle and genre covered, were once again too much. Shinwari received the match award for his 2-20, but it could easily have been Hasan. They stuttered in reply, but once Mohammad Hafeez (25*) and Shoaib settled, it was over quickly.*

Second Twenty20 international At Abu Dhabi, October 27, 2017 (floodlit). **Pakistan won by two wickets. Sri Lanka 124-9** (20 overs) (M. D. Gunathilleke 51, W. S. R. Samarawickrama 32; Fahim Ashraf 3-16); **‡Pakistan 125-8** (19.5 overs) (N. L. T. C. Perera 3-24). *MoM:* Shadab Khan. *Finally, a contest: Sri Lanka slugged it out to the end, but it was settled in Pakistan's favour by the nerveless boy wonder Shadab. Off the fourth ball of the final over, he punched a six down the ground, then pushed two more in the same direction to clinch the series. The game had walked through a jalebi to reach that point. Sri Lanka had been well placed at 106-1, with four overs left and two batsmen set. Then they lost eight for 18, including a hat-trick for Fahim Ashraf, the first for Pakistan in the format, and the sixth overall. Sri Lanka defended gamely, Tissara Perera leading the way with 3-24. And they might have won had Dhanushka Gunathilleke held on to a difficult chance from Hasan in the last over. But his drop allowed three runs and, crucially, Shadab to regain the strike.*

Third Twenty20 international At Lahore, October 29, 2017 (floodlit). **Pakistan won by 36 runs. Pakistan 180-3** (20 overs) (Fakhar Zaman 31, Umar Amin 45, Babar Azam 34*, Shoaib Malik 51); **‡Sri Lanka 144-9** (20 overs) (M. D. Shanaka 54; Mohammad Amir 4-13). *MoM:* Shoaib Malik. *MoS:* Shoaib Malik. *T20I debut:* P. C. de Silva (Sri Lanka). *Those who attended Gaddafi Stadium had memories of a grand occasion to take back with them, if not a competitive one. The packed crowd were in good spirits, welcoming back the team who in 2009 had been attacked barely a kilometre from the ground. Shoaib's 24-ball 51 gave a strong Pakistan batting performance a final flourish, before a familiar collapse shattered any hopes of a Sri Lankan consolation. Mohammad Amir did most damage, with a T20-best 4-13 in his first international game on home turf after 97 elsewhere: he had made his debut three months after the terrorist attack, had been serving a ban for spot-fixing when Zimbabwe visited in 2015, and was in England attending the birth of his first child when the World XI came in September.*

DOMESTIC CRICKET IN PAKISTAN IN 2016-17

ABID ALI KAZI

While the authorities attempted to prepare the way for the return of international cricket to Pakistan, another kind of rehabilitation was in progress at domestic level. Salman Butt, the former Test captain, and fast bowler Mohammad Asif, who had both been jailed in 2011 for conspiracy to cheat and accept corrupt payments during Pakistan's tour of England the previous year, and banned from cricket by the ICC, made their return to the first-class game. Now in their early thirties, they played for the Water and Power Development Authority's team in the Quaid-e-Azam Trophy.

Butt's ICC ban had originally been for ten years and Asif's for seven, but with five and two years suspended respectively, allowing for their return after five; the Pakistan Cricket Board also insisted they should go through a rehabilitation programme. Their younger colleague Mohammad Amir, who had been given a shorter sentence, had resumed his career in 2015, and represented Pakistan again from January 2016. Butt and Asif were allowed to play one-day cricket for WAPDA in the same month, but did not make their first-class comeback until October – seven years after their last appearances in the Quaid-e-Azam Trophy. Their impact, especially Butt's, was immediate. Appointed captain, he led **WAPDA** to a maiden first-class title, scoring twin hundreds in the final, against Habib Bank, and finishing the season with four centuries (including another against Habib Bank) and 741 runs.

The final, a day/night game, ended in a draw. After WAPDA took a first-innings lead of 42, Habib Bank replied with 485 for one across the third and fourth days: Imam-ul-Haq, nephew of Inzamam, put on 303 with Fakhar Zaman and an unbroken 182 with Ahmed Shehzad. They gave themselves four sessions to bowl out WAPDA, and picked up two wickets on the fourth evening, but only one fell on the final day, when Butt's painstaking second century – an unbeaten 105 stretching across 111 overs – denied them the outright victory they needed; WAPDA were crowned national champions on the basis of that first-innings advantage.

Unusually, the format for the Quaid-e-Azam Trophy had not changed since 2015-16, with a mix of eight regional and eight departmental sides competing in two parallel leagues, and the top four from each league advancing to two Super Eight groups before the final. Since the previous year, Pakistan International Airlines and Karachi Blues had replaced Port Qasim Authority and Hyderabad, the lowest-ranked departmental and regional teams; both went straight down again. WAPDA were easily the most consistent side, with seven wins in their ten qualifying games. As usual, the departmental teams (which can pay better) dominated the competition, supplying seven of the Super Eight.

Their wicketkeeper, Kamran Akmal, was the only batsman to reach four figures, with 1,035 at 79, including five hundreds. The next highest aggregate was Asif Zakir of Sui Southern Gas, who topped the averages with 853 at 85. Mohammad Abbas of Khan Research Labs led the bowlers for the second season running, with 71 wickets at 12. Karachi Whites keeper Mohammad Hasan pulled off seven catches in succession against Sui Northern Gas, but missed his chance to make it eight because one man was absent hurt.

The regional and departmental teams were separated in the 50-over tournaments. The regional table was headed by the two Karachi teams, Blues and Whites, but fourth-placed **Peshawar** beat them both in the knockout to take the title. In the departmental competition, Sui Northern Gas, WAPDA and Habib Bank were tied on points, but in the knockout **Habib Bank** found consolation for their Quaid-e-Azam disappointment. In September, **Karachi Blues** had beaten their sister team, Karachi Whites, in the National T20 Cup.

Domestic cricket concluded with a one-day competition for five provincial teams; **Federal Areas** beat table-leaders Baluchistan off the last ball of the final to claim their first trophy.

FIRST-CLASS AVERAGES IN 2016-17

BATTING (450 runs, average 35.00)

		M	*I*	*NO*	*R*	*HS*	*100*	*Avge*	*Ct/St*
1	Asif Zakir (*Sui Southern Gas*)	9	11	1	853	200*	4	85.30	13
2	Kamran Akmal (*WAPDA*)	9	14	1	1,035	162	5	79.61	36/1
3	Usman Salahuddin (*National Bank*)	10	17	5	843	113*	3	70.25	7
4	†Fawad Alam (*Sui Southern Gas*)	9	11	2	499	108	1	55.44	2
5	Sohaib Maqsood (*United Bank*)	7	10	1	466	222*	1	51.77	7
6	†Fakhar Zaman (*Habib Bank*)	8	14	1	663	170	2	51.00	3
7	Adil Amin (*Sui Southern Gas*)	8	10	1	452	90	0	50.22	3
8	†Imam-ul-Haq (*Habib Bank*)	11	20	3	848	200*	3	49.88	4
9	†Salman Butt (*WAPDA*)	10	16	1	741	125	4	49.40	6
10	Abdul Rehman Muzammil (*KRL*)	10	20	4	749	170	2	46.81	9
11	Ashfaq Ahmed (*Peshawar*)	7	12	1	503	119	1	45.72	4
12	†Awais Zia (*Sui Southern Gas*)	9	10	0	454	158	1	45.40	4
13	Iftikhar Ahmed (*Sui Northern Gas*)	9	17	1	713	181	3	44.56	17
14	Hammad Azam (*United Bank*)	10	12	0	530	102	1	44.16	6
15	Behram Khan (*Karachi Whites*)	10	18	2	701	155	2	43.81	7
16	Adnan Akmal (*Sui Northern Gas*)	7	13	2	467	114*	2	42.45	23/2
17	†Mohammad Naeem (*FATA*)	7	14	0	592	105	1	42.28	5
18	†Saeed Anwar (*KRL*)	9	17	1	670	157	2	41.87	5
19	Fazal Subhan (*Karachi Blues*)	7	14	0	584	149	1	41.71	2
20	Sahibzada Farhan (*Peshawar*)	7	12	0	497	97	0	41.41	6
21	†Imran Farhat (*Habib Bank*)	10	15	1	562	133	3	40.14	7
22	Khurram Manzoor (*Karachi Blues*)	7	14	0	557	250	1	39.78	5
23	Agha Salman (*Lahore Blues*)	7	13	1	473	155	2	39.41	12
24	†Hamza Ghanchi (*Karachi Whites*)	10	19	1	700	300*	1	38.88	7
25	Fahad Iqbal (*PIA*)	7	14	1	493	106	1	37.92	6
26	†Rameez Aziz (*Habib Bank*)	10	15	1	528	119*	1	37.71	14
27	Anas Mahmood (*Lahore Whites*)	7	14	1	486	147	1	37.38	7
28	†Faraz Ali (*Karachi Whites*)	10	19	1	661	128	2	36.72	7

BOWLING (25 wickets, average 25.00)

		Style	*O*	*M*	*R*	*W*	*BB*	*5I*	*Avge*
1	Mohammad Abbas (*KRL*)	RFM	355.1	97	905	71	8-46	8	12.74
2	Sameen Gul (*United Bank*)	RM	164	44	459	34	8-44	3	13.50
3	Tabish Khan (*Karachi Whites*)	RFM	315.3	79	840	62	7-56	7	13.54
4	Mir Hamza (*United Bank*)	LFM	276.4	81	694	48	7-59	6	14.45
5	Ahmed Bashir (*KRL*)	RFM	175	30	569	32	6-35	1	17.78
6	Irfanullah Shah (*FATA*)	RFM	175.2	28	592	32	7-29	3	18.50
7	Tahir Khan (*PIA*)	OB	143	26	514	26	8-102	2	19.76
8	Khalid Usman (*WAPDA*)	SLA	286.1	65	682	34	8-63	1	20.05
9	Adeel Malik (*Karachi Blues*)	RFM	217.4	61	630	31	7-55	3	20.32
10	Abid Hasan (*Rawalpindi*)	RFM	242.3	67	716	34	5-31	3	21.05
11	Shehzad Azam (*Islamabad*)	RFM	168.2	30	612	29	7-49	3	21.10
12	Ataullah (*Rawalpindi*)	RFM	265.2	64	709	33	5-53	1	21.48
13	Abdur Rehman (*Habib Bank*)	SLA	297.2	67	685	31	4-52	0	22.09
14	Mohammad Irfan (*Sui Southern Gas*)	SLA	299.1	67	671	30	5-27	1	22.36
15	Atif Jabbar (*National Bank*)	RFM	360.2	65	1,140	50	7-74	4	22.80
16	Sadaf Hussain (*KRL*)	LFM	209.5	48	646	28	4-26	0	23.07
17	Waqas Maqsood (*WAPDA*)	LFM	242.3	54	740	32	5-35	2	23.12
18	Fahim Ashraf (*Habib Bank*)	RFM	213.1	49	651	28	6-65	2	23.25
19	Ahmed Jamal (*Sui Southern Gas*)	RFM	192.2	45	583	25	6-64	2	23.32
20	Bilawal Bhatti (*Sui Northern Gas*)	RFM	211.3	32	735	31	5-40	1	23.70
21	Bilawal Iqbal (*Lahore Blues*)	RFM	209.5	33	713	30	5-54	1	23.76
22	Ghulam Mudassar (*Karachi Whites*)	LFM	175	27	605	25	7-52	1	24.20
23	Usman Shinwari (*Habib Bank*)	LFM	297.3	73	926	38	4-40	0	24.36

QUAID-E-AZAM TROPHY IN 2016-17

PRELIMINARY GROUPS

Pool A	P	W	L	D	Pts
WAPDA	7	5	1	1	46
UNITED BANK	7	3	1	3	36
SUI SOUTHERN GAS	7	2	0	5	26
HABIB BANK	7	2	2	3	21
Islamabad	7	2	3	2	21
Lahore Blues	7	2	3	2	19
Peshawar	7	1	2	4	9
Karachi Blues	7	0	5	2	0

Pool B	P	W	L	D	Pts
KRL	7	4	0	3	45
SUI NORTHERN GAS	7	4	2	1	36
NATIONAL BANK	7	3	0	4	29
KARACHI WHITES	7	3	2	2	27
FATA	7	3	2	2	24
Rawalpindi	7	1	4	2	15
Lahore Whites	7	1	4	2	9
PIA	7	1	6	0	9

SUPER EIGHT

Group A	P	W	L	D	Pts
WAPDA	3	2	0	1	22
Sui Southern Gas	3	2	0	1	19
Sui Northern Gas	3	1	2	0	9
Karachi Whites	3	0	3	0	0

Group B	P	W	L	D	Pts
HABIB BANK	3	2	0	1	16
United Bank	3	1	0	2	10
KRL	3	1	1	1	9
National Bank	3	0	3	0	0

FATA = Federally Administered Tribal Areas; KRL = Khan Research Laboratories; PIA = Pakistan International Airlines; WAPDA = Water and Power Development Authority.

Outright win = 6pts; win by an innings = 1pt extra; lead on first innings in a won or drawn game = 3pts; draw after following on = 1pt; no result on first innings = 1pt. Teams tied on points were ranked on most wins, then fewest losses, then net run-rate.

The top four teams from the preliminary groups advanced to the Super Eight groups, but did not carry forward their earlier results. Karachi Blues and PIA were relegated for 2017-18, with Faisalabad and Pakistan Television promoted.

Pool A

At Quetta, October 1–4, 2016. **Drawn. Habib Bank 462-9 dec** (Imran Farhat 112) **and 147-7 dec** (Shahzaib Ahmed 5-57); **‡Peshawar 239 and 307-5** (Ashfaq Ahmed 119). *Habib Bank 3pts.*

At Islamabad (Diamond), October 1–4, 2016. **Drawn. Islamabad 417** (Abid Ali 101, Shahid Yousuf 102; Ahmed Jamal 6-86) **and 275-2** (Afaq Raheem 121*, Ali Sarfraz 109*); **‡Sui Southern Gas 382** (Shehzad Azam 5-93). *Islamabad 3pts. Afaq Raheem and Ali Sarfraz added 226* for the third wicket in Islamabad's second innings.*

At Karachi (National), October 1–4, 2016 (day/night). **Drawn. ‡Karachi Blues 111 and 702-7** (Khurram Manzoor 250, Khalid Latif 148; Yasim Murtaza 5-213); **United Bank 285** (Umair Khan 101*). *United Bank 3pts. This was the first of 11 day/night games, played with pink balls. On the first day, Karachi Blues lost their last seven for 21, but hit back with the highest second-innings total in first-class cricket in Pakistan. Khurram Manzoor scored his fourth double-hundred and shared three successive century stands, starting with 202 for the first wicket with Haris Ali (92). Even so, United Bank took first-innings points, thanks to Umair Khan, who carried his bat.*

At Lahore (LCCA), October 1–4, 2016. **WAPDA won by ten wickets. ‡WAPDA 330** (Kamran Akmal 115) **and 28-0; Lahore Blues 140** (Mohammad Irfan 5-38) **and 217** (Khalid Usman 8-63). *WAPDA 9pts. Salman Butt returned to first-class cricket, as captain of WAPDA, after being jailed for corruption in the 2010 Lord's Test v England. He scored 31 and led his new team to a ten-wicket victory. Slow left-armer Khalid Usman took a career-best 8-63, and 10-106 in the match.*

At Islamabad (Diamond), October 7–9, 2016. **Habib Bank won by five wickets. ‡Islamabad 180 and 145; Habib Bank 168** (Shehzad Azam 7-49) **and 160-5.** *Habib Bank 6pts. Islamabad batsman Umar Abid Kiyani was suspended for aiming a punch at bowler Amad Butt, and abusive language.*

At Karachi (National), October 7–10, 2016. **WAPDA won by 46 runs. WAPDA 342** (Mohammad Saad 106; Abdul Ameer 6-79) **and 223** (Ayaz Tasawwar 113; Adeel Malik 7-55); **‡Karachi Blues**

192 and 327 (Waqas Maqsood 5-91). *WAPDA 9pts. WAPDA's first-innings 342 contained 50 extras, but Karachi Blues wicketkeeper Mohammad Waqas held six catches (and ten in the match).*

At Lahore (Gaddafi), October 7–10, 2016. **Drawn. United Bank 448** (Umar Siddiq 185); **‡Lahore Blues 277** (Waqas Saleem 106) **and 294-3** (Zain-ul-Hasan 113*). *Lahore Blues 1pt, United Bank 3pts.*

At Peshawar (Arbab Niaz), October 7–10, 2016. **Drawn. ‡Peshawar 333 and 247-6; Sui Southern Gas 462** (Awais Zia 158; Asif Fawad 6-106). *Sui Southern Gas 3pts. Ali Asad (91) and Awais Zia put on 222 for Sui Southern's first wicket. Both were lbw to Asif Fawad in his career-best 6-106.*

At Rawalpindi (Cricket), October 15–18, 2016 (day/night). **WAPDA won by an innings and 100 runs. ‡WAPDA 504** (Kamran Akmal 103); **Islamabad 156** (Waqas Maqsood 5-35) **and 248.** *WAPDA 10pts. Mohammad Asif, who had been jailed with Butt for spot-fixing, joined him in the WAPDA team; he took four wickets on his first-class comeback, delayed by a hamstring strain.*

At Karachi (UBL), October 15–18, 2016. **Habib Bank won by nine wickets. Karachi Blues 157 and 286; ‡Habib Bank 420-9 dec** (Rameez Aziz 119*) **and 24-1.** *Habib Bank 9pts. Rameez Aziz and Yamin Ahmadzai (30*) added 102* for Habib Bank's tenth wicket. Zohaib Khan held five catches in the field in Karachi Blues' second innings.*

At Lahore (LCCA), October 15–18, 2016. **Sui Southern Gas won by an innings and 46 runs. ‡Lahore Blues 266** (Waqas Saleem 122; Zafar Gohar 6-80) **and 111** (Aamer Yamin 6-13); **Sui Southern Gas 423** (Asif Zakir 128). *Sui Southern Gas 10pts. Aamer Yamin claimed 10–5–13–6.*

At Peshawar (Arbab Niaz), October 15–17, 2016. **United Bank won by nine wickets. Peshawar 311 and 109** (Sameen Gul 5-40); **‡United Bank 320 and 103-1.** *United Bank 9pts.*

At Faisalabad (Iqbal), October 22–24, 2016. **Lahore Blues won by six wickets. Habib Bank 170 and 116; ‡Lahore Blues 119** (Umar Gul 5-39) **and 169-4.** *Lahore Blues 6pts.*

At Islamabad (Diamond), October 22–24, 2016. **United Bank won by seven wickets. ‡Islamabad 275** (Shahid Yousuf 105; Mir Hamza 5-55) **and 142** (Mir Hamza 6-49); **United Bank 370 and 50-3.** *United Bank 9pts.*

At Karachi (National), October 22–25, 2016. **Drawn. Karachi Blues 206 and 448-7** (Fazal Subhan 149, Saud Shakil 100*); **‡Sui Southern Gas 424** (Asif Zakir 127, Shoaib Malik 114). *Sui Southern Gas 3pts.*

At Peshawar (Arbab Niaz), October 22–25, 2016. **WAPDA won by six wickets. Peshawar 273 and 129; ‡WAPDA 180** (Sajid Khan 5-50) **and 224-4** (Kamran Akmal 116*). *WAPDA 6pts.*

At Peshawar (Arbab Niaz), October 28–31, 2016. **Drawn. Habib Bank 299** (Fakhar Zaman 100) **and 210** (Mohammad Irfan 5-27); **‡Sui Southern Gas 235 and 166-5.** *Habib Bank 3pts.*

At Karachi (National), October 29–November 1, 2016. **Islamabad won by six wickets. Karachi Blues 254** (Hamza Nadeem 5-67) **and 267; ‡Islamabad 359** (Adeel Malik 5-77) **and 163-4.** *Islamabad 9pts.*

At Lahore (Gaddafi), October 29–November 1, 2016 (day/night). **Drawn. Lahore Blues 533** (Agha Salman 155, Bilawal Iqbal 106*) **and 170-3; ‡Peshawar 380** (Jamaluddin 104). *Lahore Blues 3pts. No. 8 Bilawal Iqbal and Yousuf Ali (65) added 142 for Lahore Blues' eighth wicket.*

At Sialkot (Jinnah), October 29–November 1, 2016. **WAPDA won by 20 runs. WAPDA 227 and 243** (Mir Hamza 5-103); **‡United Bank 145** (Mohammad Irfan 6-66) **and 305** (Azhar Attari 5-101). *WAPDA 9pts. Needing 326 to win, United Bank reached 260-6 before Azhar Attari finished them off. WAPDA's fifth straight win guaranteed their place in the Super Eight with two rounds to go.*

At Multan (Cricket), November 5–8, 2016. **United Bank won by ten wickets. ‡Habib Bank 139** (Sameen Gul 8-44) **and 175; United Bank 295** (Shan Masood 106) **and 20-0.** *United Bank 9pts. Sameen Gul's career-best 8-44 (and 10-83) ensured United Bank's passage to the next stage.*

At Lahore (Gaddafi), November 5–8, 2016 (day/night). **Drawn. ‡Peshawar 472** (Israrullah 107, Sajid Khan 105); **Islamabad 715-8** (Faizan Riaz 103, Sarmad Bhatti 260, Zohaib Ahmed 116). *Islamabad 3pts. Sajid Khan, scoring a maiden century from No. 8, put on 101 for Peshawar's ninth wicket with Taj Wali (26). Sarmad Bhatti's first double-hundred was the highest individual score for Islamabad, and 715-8 their highest total. He batted for 11 hours 32 minutes, adding 209 for the fifth wicket with Faizan Riaz and 258 for the seventh with Zohaib Ahmed.*

At Karachi (National), November 5–8, 2016. **Lahore Blues won by five wickets. Karachi Blues 153 and 286; ‡Lahore Blues 262** (Adeel Malik 5-49) **and 181-5** (Agha Salman 107*). *Lahore Blues 9pts.*

At Sialkot (Jinnah), November 5–8, 2016. **Sui Southern Gas won by an innings and 83 runs. ‡Sui Southern Gas 529-8 dec** (Asif Zakir 200*); **WAPDA 332** (Zahid Mansoor 179*; Ahmed Jamal 6-64) **and 114.** *Sui Southern Gas 10pts. Asif Zakir scored his third double-hundred. Zahid Mansoor carried his bat for 179*, but could not prevent the follow-on and WAPDA's first defeat.*

At Multan (Cricket), November 12–15, 2016. **Drawn. WAPDA 361** (Salman Butt 112, Mohammad Saad 118; Fahim Ashraf 5-123) **and 90-1; ‡Habib Bank 269** (Zulfiqar Babar 6-94). *WAPDA 3pts. Salman Butt and Mohammad Saad added 228 for WAPDA's third wicket. Habib Bank conceded first-innings points, but scraped into the Super Eight as they had lost fewer matches than Islamabad.*

At Islamabad (Diamond), November 12–14, 2016. **Islamabad won by 58 runs. Islamabad 134** (Waqas Ahmed 5-47, Bilawal Iqbal 5-54) **and 227** (Faizan Riaz 122*; Waqas Ahmed 5-96); **‡Lahore Blues 165** (Shehzad Azam 5-63, Hasan Ali 5-67) **and 138** (Hasan Ali 6-27). *Islamabad 6pts. Without the extra points for first-innings lead, Islamabad's win was not enough to qualify.*

At Peshawar (Arbab Niaz), November 12–14, 2016. **Peshawar won by nine wickets. Karachi Blues 181** (Sajjad Hussain 5-67) **and 133** (Sajjad Hussain 7-54); **‡Peshawar 184** (Abdul Ameer 5-47) **and 131-1.** *Peshawar 9pts. Sajjad Hussain laid the ground for victory with 12-121.*

At Sialkot (Jinnah), November 12–15, 2016. **Drawn. Sui Southern Gas 291** (Fawad Alam 108; Mir Hamza 7-59); **‡United Bank 551-3** (Umair Khan 105*, Sohaib Maqsood 222*, Akbar-ur-Rehman 110*). *United Bank 3pts. Mir Hamza took a career-best 7-59. After Umair Khan retired hurt, Sohaib Maqsood scored a maiden double-hundred and put on 325* for United Bank's fourth wicket with Akbar-ur-Rehman. Results elsewhere ensured Sui Southern qualified.*

Pool B

At Sialkot (Jinnah), October 1–4, 2016. **Sui Northern Gas won by 177 runs. Sui Northern Gas 493-7 dec** (Iftikhar Ahmed 127, Adnan Akmal 114*) **and 234-4 dec; ‡FATA 359 and 191.** *Sui Northern Gas 9pts.*

At Karachi (UBL), October 1–3, 2016. **Karachi Whites won by five wickets. PIA 167** (Tabish Khan 6-47) **and 177** (Tabish Khan 5-29); **‡Karachi Whites 160** (Ali Imran 7-20) **and 185-5.** *Karachi Whites 6pts.*

At Faisalabad (Iqbal), October 1–4, 2016. **National Bank won by seven wickets. Lahore Whites 258** (Sami Aslam 140) **and 187** (Atif Jabbar 5-56); **‡National Bank 324 and 122-3.** *National Bank 9pts.*

At Rawalpindi (Cricket), October 1–4, 2016. **KRL won by 48 runs. KRL 175 and 181** (Ataullah 5-53); **‡Rawalpindi 114 and 194** (Mohammad Abbas 5-49). *KRL 9pts.*

At Sialkot (Jinnah), October 7–10, 2016. **Drawn. KRL 352** (Saeed Anwar 157; Asif Afridi 5-102) **and 310-8 dec** (Abdul Rehman Muzammil 101*; Asif Afridi 6-102); **‡FATA 298** (Mohammad Abbas 5-79) **and 229-6.** *KRL 3pts.*

At Lahore (LCCA), October 7–10, 2016. **Lahore Whites won by 96 runs. ‡Lahore Whites 365** (Tahir Khan 6-101) **and 224** (Umar Akmal 101); **PIA 175 and 318** (Umaid Asif 5-55). *Lahore Whites 9pts.*

At Karachi (NBP), October 7–10, 2016. **Drawn. ‡Karachi Whites 628-5 dec** (Hamza Ghanchi 300*, Behram Khan 155); **National Bank 318** (Usman Salahuddin 113*; Tabish Khan 5-63) **and 262-3.** *National Bank 1pt, Karachi Whites 3pts. Hamza Ghanchi became only the sixth player to convert a maiden century into a triple, batting six minutes short of 11 hours and adding 343 for the second wicket with Behram Khan. Off-spinner Bilal Asif manfully bowled 58.3–6–210–0.*

At Rawalpindi (Cricket), October 7–10, 2016 (day/night). **Sui Northern Gas won by four wickets. Rawalpindi 173** (Asad Ali 5-40) **and 317; ‡Sui Northern Gas 137** (Abid Hasan 5-40) **and 355-6** (Taufeeq Umar 119). *Sui Northern Gas 6pts.*

At Sialkot (Jinnah), October 15–18, 2016. **FATA won by 157 runs. FATA 237 and 342; ‡PIA 235** (Irfanullah Shah 5-49) **and 187.** *FATA 9pts.*

At Karachi (National), October 15–17, 2016. **KRL won by 149 runs. KRL 145 and 237** (Tabish Khan 5-53); ‡**Karachi Whites 77** (Mohammad Abbas 6-47) **and 156** (Mohammad Abbas 8-46). *KRL 9pts. In a low-scoring match, both pairs of openers made ducks in the first innings. Karachi Whites never recovered, and were dismissed for 77 by Mohammad Abbas and Sadaf Hussain, bowling unchanged for 30.5 overs. Abbas took a career-best 8-46 in the second innings, and 14-93 gave him 29 in his first three games of the season.*

At Lahore (Gaddafi), October 15–18, 2016. **Drawn. Lahore Whites 367** (Anas Mahmood 147) **and 39-0; ‡Sui Northern Gas 545-9 dec** (Mohammad Rizwan 167, Adnan Akmal 107). *Sui Northern Gas 3pts.*

At Islamabad (Diamond), October 15–18, 2016. **Drawn. Rawalpindi 266 and 214** (Altaf Ahmed 5-44, Mohammad Irfan 5-65); ‡**National Bank 253** (Sohail Tanvir 6-58) **and 215-9** (Abid Hasan 5-31). *Rawalpindi 3pts. National Bank were 92-6 chasing 228 – but with the help of 50 from Qaiser Abbas and 40 extras, the last pair almost did it. They added 23*, but had to settle for a draw.*

At Lahore (Gaddafi), October 22–25, 2016 (day/night). **Drawn. FATA 192 and 584-5** (Khushdil Shah 101, Asif Ali 225, Abdul Aziz 109*); ‡**National Bank 527-8 dec** (Ahsan Ali 200, Qaiser Abbas 151*). *National Bank 3pts. Ahsan Ali scored his second double-hundred, at a run a ball, in four and three-quarter hours; Asif Ali converted a maiden century into 225 at a statelier pace, batting almost ten hours, and adding 279 for the fifth wicket with Abdul Aziz. It was the first double-century for FATA, who had not reached 500 before.*

At Karachi (UBL), October 22–24, 2016. **Sui Northern Gas won by 25 runs. Sui Northern Gas 128** (Tabish Khan 5-23) **and 235; ‡Karachi Whites 118** (Azizullah 5-42) **and 220** (Asad Ali 6-60). *Sui Northern Gas 9pts. The opening day saw 21 wickets fall; Karachi Whites were hopeful of victory at 220-8 but lost their last two without addition.*

At Lahore (LCCA), October 22–25, 2016. **Drawn. KRL 352 and 242-6 dec** (Qaiser Ashraf 5-72); ‡**Lahore Whites 259 and 229-5** (Rizwan Hussain 126). *KRL 3pts. Rizwan Hussain, aged 20, scored a century on first-class debut.*

At Rawalpindi (Cricket), October 22–25, 2016. **PIA won by two wickets. Rawalpindi 198 and 337-7 dec** (Sarmad Bhatti 100); ‡**PIA 276** (Mohammad Talha 5-83) **and 261-8.** *PIA 9pts.*

At Karachi (NBP), October 29–November 1, 2016. **Drawn.** ‡**Karachi Whites 198 and 325** (Kashif Bhatti 6-77); **Rawalpindi 350** (Mukhtar Ahmed 107, Umar Waheed 120) **and 35-3.** *Rawalpindi 3pts.*

At Faisalabad (Iqbal), October 29–November 1, 2016. **KRL won by 149 runs. KRL 231 and 182** (Azizullah 6-55); ‡**Sui Northern Gas 128** (Mohammad Abbas 6-36) **and 136.** *KRL 9pts. KRL reached the Super Eight with two rounds to spare.*

At Lahore (LCCA), October 29–31, 2016. **FATA won by 57 runs. FATA 235 and 163** (Saif-ur-Rehman 6-44); ‡**Lahore Whites 204** (Asif Afridi 5-62) **and 137** (Mohammad Irfan 5-66). *FATA 9pts.*

At Multan (Cricket), October 29–November 1, 2016. **National Bank won by an innings and 25 runs. ‡PIA 274 and 176; National Bank 475** (Ahsan Ali 156). *National Bank 10pts.*

At Karachi (UBL), November 5–7, 2016. **Karachi Whites won by 92 runs. Karachi Whites 257 and 134; ‡FATA 179** (Mohammad Naeem 105; Tabish Khan 7-56) **and 120** (Ghulam Mudassar 7-52). *Karachi Whites 9pts.*

At Abbottabad, November 5–8, 2016. **KRL won by six wickets. PIA 121 and 355** (Fahad Iqbal 106, Shoaib Khan 135); ‡**KRL 339** (Tahir Khan 8-102) **and 139-4.** *KRL 9pts.*

At Lahore (LCCA), November 5–8, 2016. **Rawalpindi won by eight wickets. Lahore Whites 190** (Abid Hasan 5-53) **and 141** (Nazar Hussain 6-50); ‡**Rawalpindi 298** (Kashif Bhatti 128*; Asif Raza 6-57) **and 34-2.** *Rawalpindi 9pts. Kashif Bhatti hit 128* from No. 8, then had figures of 18–10–12–3 with his left-arm spin in Lahore Whites' second innings.*

At Faisalabad (Iqbal), November 5–8, 2016. **National Bank won by five wickets. Sui Northern Gas 262 and 161; ‡National Bank 157 and 267-5** (Hamza Paracha 116). *National Bank 6pts. National Bank's third win ensured their place in the Super Eight.*

At Rawalpindi (KRL), November 12–15, 2016. **Drawn. KRL 503-9 dec** (Abdul Rehman Muzammil 170, Saeed Anwar 108) **and 197-4** (Shoaib Ahmed 116*); ‡**National Bank 228** (Usman Salahuddin

108*; Mohammad Abbas 5-30). *KRL 3pts. Abdul Rehman Muzammil and Saeed Anwar put on 232 for KRL's fifth wicket. Mohammad Abbas passed 50 wickets in the season.*

At Lahore (Gaddafi), November 12–15, 2016 (day/night). **Karachi Whites won by eight wickets. Lahore Whites 236 and 317; ‡Karachi Whites 500-8 dec** (Behram Khan 136, Faraz Ali 113) **and 54-2.** *Karachi Whites 9pts. A nine-point win pulled Karachi Whites into the Super Eight.*

At Faisalabad (Iqbal), November 12–15, 2016. **Sui Northern Gas won by six wickets. PIA 280 and 189** (Mohammad Imran 5-62); **‡Sui Northern Gas 313 and 160-4.** *Sui Northern Gas 9pts. A fourth win, over bottom-placed PIA, confirmed the progression of defending champions Sui Northern Gas.*

At Rawalpindi (Cricket), November 12–14, 2016. **FATA won by 16 runs. ‡FATA 120 and 136** (Nazar Hussain 5-44); **Rawalpindi 152** (Irfanullah Shah 6-59) **and 88** (Irfanullah Shah 7-29). *FATA 6pts. Rawalpindi needed 105 to win, but Irfanullah Shah bowled them out for 88; he improved on his career-best twice in the match, finishing with 13-88. Without first-innings points, however, FATA's victory was not enough for them to qualify.*

Super Eight Group I

At Karachi (UBL), November 19–21, 2016. **Sui Southern Gas won by five wickets. Sui Southern Gas 240 and 174-5; ‡Karachi Whites 84 and 329** (Faraz Ali 128). *Sui Southern Gas 9pts. Tabish Khan's 4-23 in Sui Southern's first innings took him to 50 in the season. Karachi Whites were bowled out in double figures for the second time in six matches.*

At Karachi (National), November 19–21, 2016 (day/night). **WAPDA won by 189 runs. WAPDA 273** (Kamran Akmal 162) **and 183** (Bilawal Bhatti 5-40); **‡Sui Northern Gas 115** (Naseer Akram 5-32) **and 152.** *WAPDA 9pts.*

At Karachi (NBP), November 26–28, 2016. **WAPDA won by an innings and 80 runs. ‡Karachi Whites 172** (Zulfiqar Babar 5-75) **and 169; WAPDA 421** (Salman Butt 120, Zahid Mansoor 102). *WAPDA 10pts.*

At Karachi (SBP), November 26–28, 2016. **Sui Southern Gas won by an innings and 45 runs. ‡Sui Southern Gas 355** (Asif Zakir 105); **Sui Northern Gas 85** (Aamer Yamin 6-33) **and 225** (Iftikhar Ahmed 100). *Sui Southern Gas 10pts.*

At Karachi (National), December 3–6, 2016 (day/night). **Sui Northern Gas won by 190 runs. ‡Sui Northern Gas 361** (Iftikhar Ahmed 181; Tabish Khan 7-77) **and 237** (Babar Rehman 5-51); **Karachi Whites 206 and 202.** *Sui Northern Gas 9pts. Tabish Khan took 11-143, his third return of ten or more in 2016-17; his team-mate Mohammad Hasan held seven successive catches in Sui Northern's second innings – when one man was absent hurt – and finished with 11 in all.*

At Hyderabad (Niaz), December 3–6, 2016. **Drawn. WAPDA 353** (Kamran Akmal 144) **and 136-4; ‡Sui Southern Gas 306.** *WAPDA 3pts. The two teams started tied on 19 points, but first-innings advantage took WAPDA into the final. Kamran Akmal scored his fifth hundred of the campaign in their first innings, and reached 1,000 for the season in the second.*

Super Eight Group II

At Karachi (SBP), November 19–22, 2016. **Habib Bank won by ten wickets. National Bank 279** (Usman Salahuddin 112*) **and 184; ‡Habib Bank 439-9 dec** (Imam-ul-Haq 108, Imran Farhat 108) **and 25-0.** *Habib Bank 9pts.*

At Hyderabad (Niaz), November 19–22, 2016. **Drawn. KRL 293** (Mir Hamza 5-49) **and 295; ‡United Bank 240** (Mohammad Abbas 5-62) **and 233-8.** *KRL 3pts.*

At Karachi (National), November 26–29, 2016 (day/night). **Habib Bank won by 197 runs. Habib Bank 151** (Ahmed Bashir 6-35) **and 393-8 dec; ‡KRL 157** (Fahim Ashraf 6-65) **and 190.** *Habib Bank 6pts.*

At Karachi (UBL), November 26–29, 2016. **United Bank won by 228 runs. United Bank 176** (Mohammad Irfan 5-84) **and 301** (Hammad Azam 102; Atif Jabbar 7-74); **‡National Bank 171 and 78** (Sameen Gul 5-20). *United Bank 9pts. Left more than a day to chase 307, National Bank collapsed for 78, losing their last seven for 16.*

At Karachi (NBP), December 3–6, 2016. **Drawn.** **‡Habib Bank 486** (Imam-ul-Haq 129, Imran Farhat 133; Mir Hamza 5-66); **United Bank 20-0.** *Habib Bank 1pt, United Bank 1pt. Imam-ul-Haq and Imran Farhat added 248 for Habib Bank's third wicket. Play was abandoned after a fire broke out at the United Bank team hotel in the early hours of the third day; at least 11 people died, and two players were injured, one breaking his ankle as he jumped from a window. With the points shared, Habib Bank preserved their six-point advantage over United Bank, the only team with a chance of overtaking them, and advanced to the final.*

At Karachi (UBL), December 3–6, 2016. **KRL won by 26 runs.** **‡KRL 244** (Usman Arshad 121; Atif Jabbar 5-43) **and 184** (Atif Jabbar 5-50); **National Bank 287** (Rameez Raja 102) **and 115** (Mohammad Abbas 7-52). *KRL 6pts. Atif Jabbar's 10-93 gave him 21 wickets in two matches, and 50 in the season, while Mohammad Abbas's 10-99 was his third ten-for, which took him to 71.*

Final At Karachi (National), December 10–15, 2016 (day/night). **Drawn.** WAPDA won the Quaid-e-Azam Trophy by virtue of their first-innings lead. **Habib Bank 236 and 485-1 dec** (Imam-ul-Haq 200*, Fakhar Zaman 170, Ahmed Shehzad 104*); **‡WAPDA 278** (Salman Butt 125) **and 198-3** (Salman Butt 105*). *Mohammad Asif and Mohammad Irfan grabbed three wickets each to leave Habib Bank reeling at 21-6 on the first morning. Though they fought back, with Rameez Aziz and captain Abdur Rehman adding 99 for the ninth wicket, a hundred from Butt helped WAPDA take the lead. But, resuming on December 13 after a rest day for the Prophet's birthday, WAPDA's last five fell for nine. In Habib Bank's second innings, Imam-ul-Haq scored a maiden double-century, putting on 303 for the first wicket with Fakhar Zaman and 182 for the second with Ahmed Shehzad. Abdur declared 443 ahead, with four sessions remaining. Butt, however, batted throughout the final day for a second century, completing a triumphant return by claiming the title on first-innings lead.*

QUAID-E-AZAM TROPHY WINNERS

1953-54	Bahawalpur	1978-79	National Bank	1998-99	Peshawar
1954-55	Karachi	1979-80	PIA	1999-2000	PIA
1956-57	Punjab	1980-81	United Bank	2000-01	Lahore City Blues
1957-58	Bahawalpur	1981-82	National Bank	2001-02	Karachi Whites
1958-59	Karachi	1982-83	United Bank	2002-03	PIA
1959-60	Karachi	1983-84	National Bank	2003-04	Faisalabad
1961-62	Karachi Blues	1984-85	United Bank	2004-05	Peshawar
1962-63	Karachi A	1985-86	Karachi	2005-06	Sialkot
1963-64	Karachi Blues	1986-87	National Bank	2006-07	Karachi Urban
1964-65	Karachi Blues	1987-88	PIA	2007-08	Sui Northern Gas
1966-67	Karachi	1988-89	ADBP	2008-09	Sialkot
1968-69	Lahore	1989-90	PIA	2009-10	Karachi Blues
1969-70	PIA	1990-91	Karachi Whites	2010-11	Habib Bank
1970-71	Karachi Blues	1991-92	Karachi Whites	2011-12	PIA
1972-73	Railways	1992-93	Karachi Whites	2012-13	Karachi Blues
1973-74	Railways	1993-94	Lahore City	2013-14	Rawalpindi
1974-75	Punjab A	1994-95	Karachi Blues	2014-15	Sui Northern Gas
1975-76	National Bank	1995-96	Karachi Blues	2015-16	Sui Northern Gas
1976-77	United Bank	1996-97	Lahore City	2016-17	WAPDA
1977-78	Habib Bank	1997-98	Karachi Blues		

The competition has been contested sometimes by regional teams, sometimes by departments, and sometimes by a mixture of the two. Karachi teams have won the Quaid-e-Azam Trophy 20 times, PIA 7, National Bank 5, Lahore teams and United Bank 4, Sui Northern Gas 3, Bahawalpur, Habib Bank, Peshawar, Punjab, Railways and Sialkot 2, ADBP, Faisalabad, Rawalpindi and WAPDA 1.

DEPARTMENTAL ONE-DAY CUP IN 2016-17

50-over league plus knockout

Semi-final At Karachi (National), December 31, 2016. **Habib Bank won by six wickets.** **Sui Northern Gas 284-8** (50 overs) (Imran Khalid 105*); **‡Habib Bank 287-4** (46.1 overs) (Ahmed Shehzad 166). *Habib Bank's captain, Ahmed Shehzad, scored 166 in 133 balls with six sixes.*

Semi-final At Karachi (NBP), December 31, 2016. **Sui Southern Gas won by six wickets. WAPDA 145-9** (45 overs); **‡Sui Southern Gas 148-4** (29.3 overs). *WAPDA's successful season was abruptly halted when they were dismissed cheaply in a match reduced to 45 overs a side, and fourth-placed Sui Southern strolled home with 20 to spare.*

Final At Karachi (National), January 2, 2017. **Habib Bank won by five wickets. Sui Southern Gas 232-7** (50 overs); **‡Habib Bank 235-5** (47.4 overs). *Habib Bank made sure of the trophy in their second final of the season; though opener Fakhar Zaman had to retire hurt twice, Ahmed Shehzad put them back on track with 68 in 51 balls.*

REGIONAL ONE-DAY CUP IN 2016-17

50-over league plus knockout

Semi-final At Karachi (National), January 23, 2017. **Karachi Whites won by 70 runs. Karachi Whites 375-6** (50 overs) (Shahzaib Hasan 171); **‡Islamabad 305** (48.1 overs) (Shan Masood 136; Anwar Ali 5-49). *Shahzaib Hasan hit seven sixes in a 117-ball 171, adding 162 for Karachi Whites' second wicket with Akbar-ur-Rehman (58). Shan Masood struck back with 136 in 116, but after he was out Anwar Ali claimed Islambad's last five in 25 deliveries.*

Semi-final At Karachi (National), January 24, 2017. **Peshawar won by 23 runs. ‡Peshawar 303-5** (50 overs) (Israrullah 153*); **Karachi Blues 280** (47.4 overs). *Israrullah batted throughout Peshawar's innings to set a daunting target; there were four run-outs in Karachi Blues' reply.*

Final At Karachi (National), January 27, 2017. **Peshawar won by 124 runs. Peshawar 321-2** (50 overs) (Gauhar Ali 145*, Iftikhar Ahmed 131*); **‡Karachi Whites 197** (39.5 overs). *Gauhar Ali and Iftikhar Ahmed added 276* in 38 overs to put the final beyond Karachi Whites' reach.*

PAKISTAN CUP IN 2017

50-over league plus final

	Played	*Won*	*Lost*	*NR*	*Points*	*NRR*
BALUCHISTAN	4	3	1	0	6	0.07
FEDERAL AREAS	4	2	1	1	5	0.01
Sind	4	2	2	0	4	0.88
Punjab	4	1	2	1	3	–0.04
Khyber Pakhtunkhwa	4	1	3	0	2	–0.93

Final At Rawalpindi (Cricket), April 29 (day/night). **Federal Areas won by one wicket. Baluchistan 323-9** (50 overs) (Sahibzada Farhan 112); **‡Federal Areas 327-9** (50 overs) (Sami Aslam 109). *Sami Aslam added 158 with Mohammad Hafeez (83), and his run-a-ball 109 took Federal Areas to 239-4, but wickets fell until Sarmad Bhatti hit four to win off the final delivery.*

COOL AND COOL PRESENTS NATIONAL T20 CUP IN 2016-17

20-over league plus knockout

Semi-final At Multan (Cricket), September 15, 2016 (floodlit). **Karachi Whites won by eight wickets. Peshawar 178-7** (20 overs); **‡Karachi Whites 179-2** (18.2 overs). *Peshawar, who had led the table, succumbed in the face of Asad Shafiq's 55-ball 92*.*

Semi-final At Multan (Cricket), September 15, 2016 (floodlit). **Karachi Blues won by nine wickets. ‡Lahore Whites 127-6** (20 overs); **Karachi Blues 133-1** (12 overs). *Shahzaib Hasan and Khalid Latif took Karachi Blues most of the way to the final in an opening stand of 115 in 11 overs.*

Final At Multan (Cricket), September 16, 2016 (floodlit). **Karachi Blues won by three runs. ‡Karachi Blues 182-3** (20 overs); **Karachi Whites 179-8** (20 overs). *Khurram Manzoor (70) and Fawad Alam (67*) added 112 for Blues' third wicket; Whites needed only 11 off the final over with four wickets left, but Mohammad Nawaz took two of those and conceded just seven.*

The HBL Pakistan Super League has its own section (page 1110).

SOUTH AFRICAN CRICKET IN 2017

Clouds blow in from England

COLIN BRYDEN

The departure of Haroon Lorgat as chief executive, and the abandonment of a Twenty20 competition, overshadowed a frustrating year for the South African team. Typically, they were ruthless in despatching inferior opponents, and failed again in their quest to win a global tournament. Less typically, they could not rise to the occasion in a Test series in England.

Sri Lanka were treated brutally at the start of the year and, though a tour of New Zealand provided stiffer competition, South Africa won in all formats. A 1–0 Test victory took them second in the rankings, having been seventh a few months before. Despite their 3–1 setback in England, they were still second, behind India, whom they beat in early 2018.

In the one-day rankings, South Africa were top when they set off for a three-match series in England that preceded the Champions Trophy. They had won 14 of their previous 16 matches, but there were a few disquieting factors. For

SOUTH AFRICA IN 2017

	Played	*Won*	*Lost*	*Drawn/No result*
Tests	12	7	3	2
One-day internationals	19	13	6	–
Twenty20 internationals	9	5	4	–

DECEMBER / JANUARY	3 Tests, 5 ODIs and 3 T20Is (h) v Sri Lanka	(see *Wisden 2017*, page 1024)
FEBRUARY / MARCH	3 Tests, 5 ODIs and 1 T20I (a) v New Zealand	(page 900)
APRIL		
MAY / JUNE / JULY	4 Tests, 3 ODIs and 3 T20Is (a) v England	(page 287)
	ICC Champions Trophy (in England)	(page 263)
AUGUST		
SEPTEMBER / OCTOBER	2 Tests, 3 ODIs and 2 T20Is (h) v Bangladesh	(page 952)
NOVEMBER		
DECEMBER	1 Test (h) v Zimbabwe	(page 959)

For a review of South African domestic cricket from the 2016-17 season, see page 964.

one thing, the commitment of A. B. de Villiers was in doubt. He had stated he wanted to captain South Africa's one-day team through to the 2019 World Cup, but had opted for a break from Test cricket, and was unavailable for the marquee series against England. Yet by year's end de Villiers had relinquished the one-day captaincy and made a renewed commitment to the Test side. There was also uncertainty about the future of the coach: Russell Domingo's contract expired at the end of the England tour, and the hunt for a successor had already begun.

The trip started with a 2–1 defeat in the 50-over games, and never really picked up. In the Champions Trophy itself, South Africa beat Sri Lanka, but failed to reach the knockouts after insipid performances against Pakistan and India. The Tests were another disappointment: the Proteas had won their last two series in England, and drawn the one before. But the absence of captain Faf du Plessis, at home for the birth of his first child, was keenly felt: South Africa lost the First Test at Lord's heavily. With du Plessis back in charge, they won the Second just as convincingly, only to be outplayed in the remaining two. A key difference was the depth of England's batting.

South Africa's fast bowlers, so often a strength, should have enjoyed the conditions. But because of injuries and illness – as well as the suspension of Kagiso Rabada for one Test – the only constant was Morne Morkel, who was deservedly their Man of the Series.

With Ottis Gibson, the former West Indies seamer, now in place as the new coach – having left his job as England's fast-bowling coach – South Africa beat Bangladesh at home with almost embarrassing ease in two Tests and five white-ball matches. A one-off day/night Test against Zimbabwe – scheduled, with the blessing of the ICC, for four 98-over days – was over so quickly that the lights were needed only on the first.

Dean Elgar, South Africa's left-handed opener, was their outstanding Test performer. He hit 1,128 runs at 53 in 2017, and was at his most dogged when conditions were difficult. By contrast, J-P. Duminy lost confidence, and was dropped after the First Test in England; he later announced his retirement from the first-class game. Aiden Markram, captain of South Africa's victorious Under-19 World Cup team in 2014, showed rich promise as Elgar's latest partner. Run out for 97 on Test debut, against Bangladesh, he reeled off a century in the next match, and another against Zimbabwe. After three undemanding Tests he had scored 380 runs at 95; tougher challenges lay ahead.

Rabada, who turned 22 in May, often led the attack in the absence of his fellow fast bowlers – through injury or rotation – and did so manfully. His 57 wickets cost only 20, and came in 11 Tests. South Africa's next-highest wicket-taker was left-arm spinner Keshav Maharaj, who claimed 48 at 23.

While the men fared poorly at the Champions Trophy, South Africa's women exceeded expectations at the World Cup, also held in England. They reached the semi-finals, where they lost narrowly to the hosts (and eventual winners). It was the culmination of steady progress over two years.

For much of 2017, Cricket South Africa trumpeted their proposed T20 Global League, a city-based franchise tournament along the lines of the Indian Premier League and Australia's Big Bash. Several extravagant launches were held. Team owners – seven of the eight were from Asia – and big-name players

Gianluigi Guercia, AFP/Getty Images

Newlands, we have lift-off: Morne Morkel, Dean Elgar and Kagiso Rabada celebrate an Indian wicket in the Cape Town Test of 2018.

were announced. A player draft was staged, and 144 were signed up. Conspicuously missing, though, was a television deal or a major sponsor.

There were whispers about the way Lorgat was negotiating without consulting CSA. Then, in late September, it was announced he was departing with immediate effect because of a breakdown of relations. Initially, the board pledged the league would go ahead regardless but, 12 days after Lorgat left – and less than four weeks before the start – it was agreed that the tournament would be postponed until November 2018 to avoid "potential financial ruin".

After an internal audit, which found "pervasive governance lapses", CSA admitted to losses in the region of R180m (more than £10m), which included compensation to players. Forecasts suggested those losses might have exceeded R300m had the league gone ahead. South African cricketers received 60% of their contracted earnings, while foreigners were paid 50% – on the basis that they still had the opportunity to play in other leagues.

At an end-of-year briefing, there were hints of a frosty relationship between the board and the South African Cricketers' Association. "Ultimately the people that make money for cricket are the CSA – it's not a union," said the board's acting chief executive, Thabang Moroe. SACA countered that such statements were "concerning and go against the spirit of how things have worked in the past". It would be an untypical year in South African cricket without at least one cloud on the horizon.

SOUTH AFRICA v BANGLADESH IN 2017-18

NEIL MANTHORP

Test matches (2): South Africa 2, Bangladesh 0
One-day internationals (3): South Africa 3, Bangladesh 0
Twenty20 internationals (2): South Africa 2, Bangladesh 0

When Bangladesh first toured South Africa in 2002-03, they were given manufactured assurances of respect, but were twice thrashed by an innings. Six years later, the hosts didn't bother with pleasantries: their head coach at the time, Mickey Arthur, admitted Bangladesh were a warm-up for a tour of Australia. There were two more maulings.

This time, though, the respect was genuine. In the preceding 12 months, Bangladesh had won Tests against England, Sri Lanka and Australia, and in 2015 had clinched the most recent one-day international series between these teams. But the result was the same: a South African clean sweep across the formats. The brutal truth was Bangladesh never came close to winning even once.

While the home side were flourishing in a honeymoon period under new coach Ottis Gibson, the tourists were a rabble. Soon after they had gone home, it emerged that their own coach, Chandika Hathurusinghe – the most successful in their history – had handed in his resignation halfway through the trip. Meanwhile, captain Mushfiqur Rahim threw a strop in the Second Test, fielding in the deep for a session. He was upset by low wages, players not pulling their weight, and the enormous criticism levelled at him for twice bowling first on flat pitches. The Bangladesh Cricket Board president, Nazmul Hassan, patronisingly described him as "an emotional personality".

Mushfiqur's strained relationship with the BCB was always likely to harm morale – as was Shakib Al Hasan's request to miss the Tests. Several senior players admitted they were aggrieved he had asked – more so when the board accepted. Many interpreted his wish to spend time with his family as a distaste for Test cricket.

Cricket South Africa rolled back their three-year policy of limiting international matches to the major venues, and staged games at Potchefstroom, Kimberley, Paarl and East London. If the Tests were barely attended, the vibrant atmospheres for the limited-overs games justified the move. Wherever they played, though, the tourists were steamrollered.

BANGLADESH TOURING PARTY

*Mushfiqur Rahim (T/50/20), Imrul Kayes (T/50/20), Liton Das (T/50/20), Mahmudullah (T/50/20), Mashrafe bin Mortaza (50), Mehedi Hasan (T/50/20), Mohammad Saifuddin (50/20), Mominul Haque (T/50/20), Mustafizur Rahman (T/50), Nasir Hossain (50/20), Rubel Hossain (T/50/20), Sabbir Rahman (T/50/20), Shafiul Islam (T/20), Shakib Al Hasan (50/20), Soumya Sarkar (T/50/20), Subashis Roy (T), Taijul Islam (T), Tamim Iqbal (T/50), Taskin Ahmed (T/50/20). *Coach:* U. C. Hathurusinghe.

Mashrafe captained in the ODIs, and Shakib in the T20Is.

SOUTH AFRICA v BANGLADESH

First Test

At Potchefstroom, September 28–October 2, 2017. South Africa won by 333 runs. Toss: Bangladesh. Test debuts: A. K. Markram, A. L. Phehlukwayo.

Bangladesh produced a spirited first innings which lasted almost 90 overs and, aided by thunderstorms, took the game to the fifth morning. But that did not mean it was remotely close. They lost their last seven wickets in an hour to be dismissed for 90 – a fair reflection of the gulf in class. In truth, they had not helped themselves. Mushfiqur Rahim's decision to bowl baffled everybody. Frost had covered the outfield just two days before the start, and the pitch was lifeless after a bitter winter. Du Plessis admitted he was "very surprised… but happily surprised".

The South African openers were watchful against Mustafizur Rahman. But the slowness of the surface rendered Shafiul Islam's medium-pace innocuous and, as with all his colleagues, the slightest errors were ruthlessly punished. Aiden Markram, making his debut six days before his 23rd birthday, lived up to his reputation as an uncomplicated, technically correct player, armed with a pleasing on-drive. At first, he was happy to play second fiddle to Elgar, already his senior partner at franchise level. But he shed his nerves after lunch, and the pair entered the nineties together.

199 IN A TEST

Mudassar Nazar	Pakistan v India at Faisalabad	1984-85
M. Azharuddin	India v Sri Lanka at Kanpur	1986-87
M. T. G. Elliott	Australia v England at Leeds	1997
S. T. Jayasuriya	Sri Lanka v India at Colombo (SSC)	1997-98
S. R. Waugh	Australia v West Indies at Bridgetown	1998-99
*A. Flower	Zimbabwe v South Africa at Harare	2001-02
Younis Khan	Pakistan v India at Lahore	2005-06
I. R. Bell	England v South Africa at Lord's	2008
*K. C. Sangakkara	Sri Lanka v Pakistan at Galle	2012
S. P. D. Smith	Australia v West Indies at Kingston	2015
K. L. Rahul	India v England at Chennai	2016-17
D. Elgar	**South Africa v Bangladesh at Potchefstroom**	**2017-18**

* *Not out.*

Markram was 97 when Elgar, on 99, made a false start for a single. Eager to please, Markram launched himself into a hopeless sprint, and was easily run out. Still, the hosts continued to cruise: a stand of 196 was followed by one of 215, with Amla hitting the ball characteristically late, wherever he wanted.

Elgar kept things simple, accepting the gifts which came regularly, and attacking off-spinner Mehedi Hasan only when he was certain there was no turn. He was eventually dismissed for 199, prompting observations about cricket's version of natural justice. After half a dozen messy pull shots, a well-directed slower bouncer from Mustafizur had Elgar in two minds. The delivery was on its way down by the time he checked the shot: the ball kissed the top edge and looped to midwicket.

Amla's greatest challenge was remaining interested after reaching his 27th Test hundred. In the first over after lunch on the second day he did well to reach a wide half-volley from Shafiul, but could only whack it to backward point. Bavuma improved his average with a ponderous unbeaten 31 from 87 deliveries, while du Plessis was content to snack from the buffet, until he declared at tea. Gamesmanship played its part in the timing, too: Tamim Iqbal had spent nearly an hour off the field in the second session, so was prevented from opening. It was the first time he had not faced the first ball in 99 Test innings.

Mominul Haque made a combative 77, Bangladesh's highest score in 11 Tests against South Africa, beating 75 by Habibul Bashar at Chittagong in 2002-03. He was composed and patient against a predictably short-pitched attack. At 227 for four, including a scrambling 44 from Mushfiqur and an angry-looking 39 from Tamim, there was faint hope of something near parity. But after Mominul was splendidly caught at short leg by Markram, they had to settle for 320.

ALL FOR NAUGHT

Most expensive wicketless match returns in Tests:

37–1–260–0	Imran Tahir	South Africa v Australia at Adelaide	2012-13
54–5–259–0	Khan Mohammad	Pakistan v West Indies at Kingston	1957-58
67–5–247–0	**Mehedi Hasan**	**Bangladesh v South Africa at Potchefstroom**	**2017-18**
65–5–221–0	N. Boje	South Africa v Sri Lanka at Colombo (SSC)	2006
45.2–2–211–0	R. W. Price	Zimbabwe v South Africa at Harare	2001-02
55–8–191–0	R. Dhanraj	West Indies v England at Nottingham	1995
43–6–188–0	D. E. Malcolm	England v West Indies at Bridgetown	1989-90
36–5–187–0	R. W. Price	Zimbabwe v Australia at Perth	2003-04
100–39–184–0	M. W. Tate	England v Australia at Melbourne	1928-29
33–6–184–0	I. D. K. Salisbury	England v Pakistan at Manchester	1992

South Africa resumed with a lead of 176 and, on the fourth day, Bavuma pushed his average a little higher into the 30s with a more fluent 71, while du Plessis bossed his way to 81. When the merciful declaration came – leaving South Africa's bowlers four and a half sessions to win the game, and Bangladesh a notional 424 runs – Mehedi had bowled 67–5–247–0, the third-most expensive none-for in history. Meanwhile, Mominul's slow left-armers earned him three for 27 in six overs, quadrupling his career haul.

Rabada bullied away the middle order, and Maharaj cleaned up the tail. Morkel had begun the rot on the fourth afternoon, taking two wickets in the first over without a run on the board: Tamim bowled, Mominul lbw. He would have had another soon after had he not overstepped when castling Mushfiqur. It was his 251st Test no-ball, and the 14th time one had denied him a wicket. A side strain ruled him out of the final morning – and the Second Test – but South Africa would barely miss him.

Man of the Match: D. Elgar.

Close of play: first day, South Africa 298-1 (Elgar 128, Amla 68); second day, Bangladesh 127-3 (Mominul Haque 28, Tamim Iqbal 22); third day, South Africa 54-2 (Amla 17, Bavuma 3); fourth day, Bangladesh 49-3 (Mushfiqur Rahim 16).

South Africa

D. Elgar c Mominul Haque b Mustafizur Rahman	199	– (2) lbw b Shafiul Islam	18
A. K. Markram run out	97	– (1) c Liton Das b Mustafizur Rahman	15
H. M. Amla c Mehedi Hasan b Shafiul Islam	137	– c Liton Das b Mustafizur Rahman	28
T. Bavuma not out	31	– c Liton Das b Mominul Haque	71
*F. du Plessis not out	26	– lbw b Mominul Haque	81
†Q. de Kock (did not bat)		– st Liton Das b Mominul Haque	8
A. L. Phehlukwayo (did not bat)		– not out	6
K. A. Maharaj (did not bat)		– not out	19
Lb 4, w 2	6	Nb 1	1
1/196 (2) 2/411 (3) 3/445 (1) (3 wkts dec, 146 overs)	496	1/30 (2) 2/38 (1) 3/70 (3) 4/212 (5) 5/217 (4) 6/222 (6) (6 wkts dec, 56 overs)	247

K. Rabada, M. Morkel and D. Olivier did not bat.

Mustafizur Rahman 27–2–98–1; Shafiul Islam 25–5–74–1; Mehedi Hasan 56–4–178–0; Taskin Ahmed 26–5–88–0; Mahmudullah 5–0–24–0; Mominul Haque 2–0–15–0; Sabbir Rahman 5–1–15–0. *Second innings*—Mehedi Hasan 11–1–69–0; Shafiul Islam 13–1–46–1; Mustafizur Rahman 11–2–30–2; Taskin Ahmed 6–0–29–0; Sabbir Rahman 5–0–25–0; Mahmudullah 4–0–21–0; Mominul Haque 6–0–27–3.

Bangladesh

First innings		Second innings	
†Liton Das c Amla b Morkel	25	– (6) lbw b Rabada	4
Imrul Kayes c Markram b Rabada	7	– c de Kock b Maharaj	32
Mominul Haque c Markram b Maharaj	77	– lbw b Morkel	0
*Mushfiqur Rahim c Markram b Maharaj	44	– c Amla b Rabada	16
Tamim Iqbal c de Kock b Phehlukwayo	39	– (1) b Morkel	0
Mahmudullah b Morkel	66	– (5) b Rabada	9
Sabbir Rahman b Olivier	30	– lbw b Maharaj	4
Mehedi Hasan c Elgar b Rabada	8	– not out	15
Taskin Ahmed run out	1	– lbw b Maharaj	4
Shafiul Islam c Amla b Maharaj	2	– run out	2
Mustafizur Rahman not out	10	– c and b Maharaj	1
B 1, lb 9, nb 1	11	B 1, nb 2	3
1/16 (2) 2/36 (1) 3/103 (4) 4/158 (5) 5/227 (3) 6/292 (7) 7/304 (6) 8/305 (9) 9/308 (8) 10/320 (10) (89.1 overs)	320	1/0 (1) 2/0 (3) 3/49 (2) 4/55 (4) 5/62 (5) 6/67 (6) 7/67 (7) 8/71 (9) 9/75 (10) 10/90 (11) (32.4 overs)	90

Morkel 19–7–51–2; Rabada 24–5–84–2; Maharaj 27.1–8–92–3; Olivier 11–1–52–1; Phehlukwayo 6–2–18–1; Markram 2–0–13–0. *Second innings*—Morkel 5.2–2–19–2; Rabada 10–3–33–3; Olivier 5.4–1–12–0; Maharaj 10.4–1–25–4; Phehlukwayo 1–1–0–0.

Umpires: C. B. Gaffaney and B. N. J. Oxenford. Third umpire: H. D. P. K. Dharmasena. Referee: R. S. Madugalle.

SOUTH AFRICA v BANGLADESH

Second Test

At Bloemfontein, October 6–8. South Africa won by an innings and 254 runs. Toss: Bangladesh.

As if to prove his idiotic decision to bowl first at Potchefstroom was not a one-off, Mushfiqur Rahim did it again. This pitch might have had a little more grass, but it was thin and brown: every local knew it would be a batting delight. A bewildered du Plessis shook his head, before his team gorged themselves on what rarely looked anything more than junior net bowling.

It was only the second time South Africa had four centurions in the same innings, after Antigua in 2004-05. Bangladesh made four changes, including three to their bowling attack – they dropped Taskin Ahmed, whose pace might have been helpful on the faster surface, and the rate approached five an over.

Elgar and Markram – who did now manage a maiden hundred – put on 243 before a change in tactics produced the breakthrough. Courtney Walsh, the former West Indies great and now Bangladesh bowling coach, reset the field midway through the afternoon session – while Mushfiqur was sulking in the deep – and encouraged the seamers to change from half-volleys to long hops in the knowledge that Elgar was having trouble pulling. It paid off: soon after, Rubel Hossain yorked Markram, before Subashis Roy found extra bounce to remove Bavuma.

But Amla and du Plessis weren't about to squander such a boot-filling opportunity; they didn't need to do anything more than hit the regular supply of bad balls to the boundary. By stumps, South Africa were 428 for three, their joint-second-best start, equal with the first day against Australia at the old Wanderers in 1902-03, and behind 445 for three against Pakistan at Newlands a century later.

The fourth-wicket partnership reached 247 before Amla – who hit his 28th hundred to move ahead of Graeme Smith and behind only Jacques Kallis in the national list – missed a full one. Du Plessis made certain of a seventh without much fuss, and de Kock just had time for a frustrated whack before the declaration, half an hour after lunch on the second day. Across three innings, South Africa had scored 1,316 runs for the loss of 13 wickets.

Rabada was younger than most of the Bangladesh side, but still appeared a man against boys: he was too quick, too smart and too determined. Olivier, on his home ground, also thrived, claiming one of his three victims thanks to a breathtaking one-handed catch by

THANK YOU KINDLY

Biggest first-innings opening stands after being asked to bat:

301	G. C. Smith/H. H. Gibbs	South Africa v West Indies at Centurion	2003-04
255	J. L. Langer/M. L. Hayden	Australia v Sri Lanka at Cairns	2004
243	**D. Elgar/A. K. Markram**	**South Africa v Bangladesh at Bloemfontein**	**2017-18**
224	J. L. Langer/M. L. Hayden	Australia v New Zealand at Brisbane	2001-02
223	J. L. Langer/M. L. Hayden	Australia v New Zealand at Hobart	2001-02
197	A. F. Rae/J. B. Stollmeyer	West Indies v New Zealand at Auckland	1951-52
196	**D. Elgar/A. K. Markram**	**South Africa v Bangladesh at Potchefstroom**	**2017-18**
179	M. A. Butcher/M. A. Atherton	England v South Africa at Birmingham	1998
177	G. C. Smith/H. H. Gibbs	South Africa v New Zealand at Auckland	2003-04
176	M. A. Taylor/M. J. Slater	Australia v Pakistan at Rawalpindi	1994-95

Bavuma in the gully to dismiss Mushfiqur. Liton Das enjoyed the attacking fields, and fought back with 70, but there was precious little else.

Bangladesh began again on the second evening, and finished on the third afternoon. Rabada had two caught in the cordon, one at deep square leg, and two bowled to finish with ten for 63. Only Dale Steyn, with 11 for 60 against Pakistan at Johannesburg in 2012-13, had taken a cheaper ten-for for South Africa. If Rabada, who scooted past 100 Test wickets, was the obvious Man of the Match, Andile Phehlukwayo quietly eased himself into South Africa's Test picture. After an uneventful debut a week earlier, he produced an expert spell of medium-paced reverse swing to claim three for 36.

Imrul Kayes, Mushfiqur – who was hit hard on the head and later taken to hospital – and Mahmudullah did at least show some heart, but none managed a half-century. It meant South Africa secured their biggest Test victory, topping an innings and 229 against Sri Lanka at Cape Town in 2000-01. Bangladesh, meanwhile, had much to lament. They had made considerable ground in Test cricket over the preceding year, but this match – their heaviest defeat since England walloped them by an innings and 261 at Lord's in 2005 – represented a big step backwards.

Man of the Match: K. Rabada. *Man of the Series:* D. Elgar.

Close of play: first day, South Africa 428-3 (Amla 89, du Plessis 62); second day, Bangladesh 7-0 (Imrul Kayes 6, Soumya Sarkar 1).

South Africa

D. Elgar c Mustafizur Rahman b Subashis Roy	113
A. K. Markram b Rubel Hossain	143
H. M. Amla b Subashis Roy	132
T. Bavuma c Liton Das b Subashis Roy	7
*F. du Plessis not out	135
†Q. de Kock not out	28
B 4, lb 2, w 8, nb 1	15
1/243 (1) 2/276 (2) 3/288 (4) 4/535 (3) (4 wkts dec, 120 overs)	573

A. L. Phehlukwayo, K. A. Maharaj, W. D. Parnell, K. Rabada and D. Olivier did not bat.

Mustafizur Rahman 25–3–113–0; Subashis Roy 29–3–118–3; Rubel Hossain 22–1–113–1; Soumya Sarkar 5–0–21–0; Taijul Islam 27–0–145–0; Mahmudullah 9–2–35–0; Mominul Haque 1–0–6–0; Sabbir Rahman 2–0–16–0.

Bangladesh

First innings		Second innings	
Imrul Kayes c de Kock b Rabada	26	– c de Kock b Olivier	32
Soumya Sarkar b Rabada	9	– c du Plessis b Rabada	3
Mominul Haque c de Kock b Olivier	4	– c Maharaj b Rabada	11
*Mushfiqur Rahim c Bavuma b Olivier	7	– lbw b Parnell	26
Mahmudullah c de Kock b Parnell	4	– c Elgar b Rabada	43
†Liton Das c du Plessis b Rabada	70	– b Phehlukwayo	18
Sabbir Rahman c Parnell b Rabada	0	– c du Plessis b Phehlukwayo	4
Taijul Islam b Olivier	12	– b Rabada	2
Rubel Hossain b Rabada	10	– b Rabada	7
Mustafizur Rahman c Markram b Maharaj	0	– (11) b Phehlukwayo	7
Subashis Roy not out	2	– (10) not out	12
Lb 3	3	Lb 6, nb 1	7
1/13 (2) 2/26 (3) 3/36 (4) 4/49 (5) 5/61 (1) 6/65 (7) 7/115 (8) 8/143 (6) 9/143 (10) 10/147 (9) (42.5 overs)	147	1/13 (2) 2/29 (3) 3/63 (1) 4/92 (4) 5/135 (6) 6/139 (5) 7/145 (7) 8/145 (8) 9/156 (9) 10/172 (11) (42.4 overs)	172

Rabada 13.5–4–33–5; Olivier 12–3–40–3; Parnell 7–1–36–1; Maharaj 5–2–7–1; Phehlukwayo 5–1–28–0. *Second innings*—Rabada 11–1–30–5; Olivier 11–1–39–1; Maharaj 6–1–30–0; Parnell 5–0–31–1; Phehlukwayo 9.4–2–36–3.

Umpires: H. D. P. K. Dharmasena and B. N. J. Oxenford. Third umpire: C. B. Gaffaney. Referee: R. S. Madugalle.

First one-day international At Kimberley, October 15, 2017. **South Africa won by ten wickets.** ‡**Bangladesh 278-7** (50 overs) (Imrul Kayes 31, Mushfiqur Rahim 110*; K. Rabada 4-43); **South Africa 282-0** (42.5 overs) (Q. de Kock 168*, H. M. Amla 110*). *MoM:* Q. de Kock. *ODI debuts:* D. Paterson (South Africa); Mohammad Saifuddin (Bangladesh). *After Mushfiqur Rahim's meticulous century underpinned a respectable total, nobody foresaw how easily South Africa would win. On a perfect batting pitch, Quinton de Kock and Hashim Amla cruised to the third-highest opening partnership in ODIs, and the highest successful chase without losing a wicket, beating England's 256 by Jason Roy and Alex Hales against Sri Lanka at Birmingham in 2016. There was no hint of swing or seam, so they feasted contentedly, while Bangladesh were bereft of ideas, lacking the accuracy to exert even momentary pressure. Their own top order had been too cautious, and Kagiso Rabada – commanding respect through speed and guile – prevented a late flourish. Only Dane Paterson, the debutant seamer and supposed death-overs specialist, provided Bangladesh with a reliable source of runs. Shakib Al Hasan had the minor consolation of becoming the fastest to reach the double of 5,000 runs and 200 wickets, in his 178th ODI, beating Jacques Kallis (221).*

Second one-day international At Paarl, October 18, 2017. **South Africa won by 104 runs. South Africa 353-6** (50 overs) (H. M. Amla 85, Q. de Kock 46, A. B. de Villiers 176, J-P. Duminy 30; Rubel Hossain 4-62); ‡**Bangladesh 249** (47.5 overs) (Imrul Kayes 68, Mushfiqur Rahim 60, Mahmudullah 35; A. L. Phehlukwayo 4-40, Imran Tahir 3-50). *MoM:* A. B. de Villiers. *He didn't get a chance to bat three days earlier, but A. B. de Villiers made up for it with a vintage display of savagery to set up a series-sealing victory. After Shakib took two wickets in four deliveries, de Villiers put on 136 with Amla at more than seven an over. Then, after reaching 100 in 68 balls, he opened his bag of tricks at the end; it was to captain Mashrafe bin Mortaza's credit that he kept himself in the firing line. As de Villiers closed on the national record, he toed another attempted six to deep midwicket, and departed to a standing ovation. In reply, Imrul Kayes and Mushfiqur produced workmanlike half-centuries, but Andile Phehlukwayo used all his variations to take 4-40 and enhance his reputation as a canny wicket-taker.*

Third one-day international At East London, October 22, 2017. **South Africa won by 200 runs.** ‡**South Africa 369-6** (50 overs) (T. Bavuma 48, Q. de Kock 73, F. du Plessis 91*, A. K. Markram 66, F. Behardien 33*); **Bangladesh 169** (40.4 overs) (Shakib Al Hasan 63, Sabbir Rahman 39;

D. Paterson 3-44). *MoM:* F. du Plessis. *MoS:* Q. de Kock. *ODI debuts:* A. K. Markram, P. W. A. Mulder (South Africa). *South Africa experimented with their starting XI, but the game was still one-sided. Bavuma, in for Amla, lashed a run-a-ball 48 in a century opening stand with de Kock who, after cruising to 73 in the 22nd over, was furious with himself when he pushed a leading edge back to Mehedi Hasan. But the foundation was laid. Debutant Aiden Markram, a career opener, looked at ease at No. 4, while du Plessis reached 91* from only 67 balls. He seemed sure to extend the total beyond 400, until he wrenched a back muscle turning for a second, and had to retire; de Villiers took over the captaincy. At the last, Rabada revealed an unsuspected explosiveness with the bat, bludgeoning 23* from 11 balls, including a one-knee flick over fine leg for six. Facing another mountainous target, Bangladesh collapsed to 61-5. Paterson looked comfortable after two shaky performances, and the latest debutant – 19-year-old all-rounder Wiaan Mulder (1-32) – showed impressive control. As the match meandered to its end, even the most partisan among the crowd hoped Bangladesh might find some fight. Shakib and Sabbir Rahman clung on, but there was no pride in a defeat by 200 runs.*

First Twenty20 international At Bloemfontein, October 26, 2017 (floodlit). **South Africa won by 20 runs. ‡South Africa 195-4** (20 overs) (Q. de Kock 59, A. B. de Villiers 49, F. Behardien 36*); **Bangladesh 175-9** (20 overs) (Soumya Sarkar 47, Mohammad Saifuddin 39*). *MoM:* A. B. de Villiers. *T20I debut:* R. Frylinck (South Africa). *The format changed, but Bangladesh's fortunes barely did. De Kock compiled a low-risk half-century, and put on 79 with de Villiers, who cut and pulled his way to 49 from 27 balls. It was Farhaan Behardien, though, who inflated South Africa's total above par, smashing 36* off 17. Bangladesh were either unaware of his strength – heaving to leg – or unable to do anything about it. Still, they maintained a thrilling rate in reply, and it was anyone's game at 92-2 at the start of the tenth. But after Soumya Sarkar was trapped by a Phehlukwayo inswinger for a skilful 47, seven wickets fell in eight overs. All-rounder Mohammad Saifuddin displayed power and a good eye, but had little help.*

Second Twenty20 international At Potchefstroom, October 29, 2017. **South Africa won by 83 runs. South Africa 224-4** (20 overs) (H. M. Amla 85, D. A. Miller 101*); **‡Bangladesh 141** (18.3 overs) (Soumya Sarkar 44). *MoM:* D. A. Miller. *MoS:* D. A. Miller. *David Miller was on 57 with 12 balls remaining; he finished with 101*. He hit the first five deliveries of the penultimate over, bowled by Saifuddin, for six, spraying the ball in an arc between cover and backward square leg. The final delivery was a wide yorker, which Miller could only chunk to long-off for a single. He made no effort to disguise his disappointment at missing a rare moment of history (later, he gave Saifuddin his shirt as a consolation). Two edges past the keeper and a couple more drives brought him a hundred in 35 balls, comfortably the fastest in T20 internationals, beating 45 by compatriot Richard Levi against New Zealand at Hamilton in 2011-12. Once more, Bangladesh had let it happen: Mushfiqur dropped Miller on nought when he gloved Rubel Hossain's bouncer. While Bangladesh went through the motions of a chase – they never had a chance after plummeting to 37-4 – Amla might have reflected on how his superb 51-ball 85 had been forgotten so quickly.*

SOUTH AFRICA v ZIMBABWE IN 2017-18

TELFORD VICE

Test match (1): South Africa 1, Zimbabwe 0

Africa's first day/night Test was also the first anywhere since February 1973 to be scheduled for four days. The venue for this experiment – which had the blessing of the ICC – was Port Elizabeth where, in March 1889, Aubrey Smith's England had played the first Test in South Africa. Like that one, this sped to a conclusion inside two days.

St George's Park is an endearing hotchpotch of architecture, influential wind (bowl if it's east, bat if it's west) and crooked corridors of uncertainty, where you can buy pancakes from the good women of the Westering Methodist Church for the equivalent of 30p apiece. It is, in the best way, venerable, and it deserved better than this gimmick of a game. For that, blame Haroon Lorgat, who had lost his job as Cricket South Africa's chief executive over the mess of the T20 Global League, postponed when it emerged it would bleed £18m in its first year.

However, another of Lorgat's ideas stuck. The notion of lopping a day off Test matches is worthy of consideration, in an era when covering is so much better and most grounds have floodlights. Play them from Thursday to Sunday (and, most importantly, play more of them). But against Zimbabwe, who hardly play under lights at all, much less with a pink ball? Against an attack bristling with some of the best fast bowlers around? And on the most responsive pitch seen at St George's Park since, probably, Aubrey Smith's day? Locals were unenthusiastic: only 4,400 turned up for the first day, more than 2,000 fewer than for the start of the Sri Lanka Test a year earlier.

ZIMBABWE TOURING PARTY

*A. G. Cremer, R. P. Burl, R. W. Chakabva, T. L. Chatara, C. J. Chibhabha, T. S. Chisoro, C. R. Ervine, K. M. Jarvis, H. Masakadza, S. F. Mire, P. J. Moor, C. B. Mpofu, B. Muzarabani, Sikandar Raza, B. R. M. Taylor. *Coach:* H. H. Streak.

SOUTH AFRICA v ZIMBABWE

Only Test

At Port Elizabeth, December 26–27, 2017 (day/night). South Africa won by an innings and 120 runs. Toss: South Africa. Test debuts: R. P. Burl, B. Muzarabani.

Even in ordinary circumstances, this would have been a mismatch. In this pink-ball game – controversially scheduled for four days, but over in two – the chasm between the teams widened to tragicomic proportions. Thirteen wickets fell on the first day (nine in the third session), and 16 on the second. Zimbabwe were put out of their misery for 68, asked to follow on, and bundled out again inside three hours.

Such was the abruptness of the second day that the floodlights, upgraded at a cost of £1.6m, were not needed. The match lasted a total of 907 deliveries – the third-shortest

SHORTEST COMPLETED TEST MATCHES

Balls		
656	Australia (153) beat South Africa (36 and 45) at Melbourne	1931-32
672	England (81-7 dec and 75-6) beat West Indies (102 and 51-6 dec) at Bridgetown	1934-35
788	England (172) beat Australia (81 and 70) at Manchester	1888
792	Australia (116 and 60) beat England (53 and 62) at Lord's	1888
796	England (292) beat South Africa (47 and 43) at Cape Town	1888-89
815	England (176 and 14-0) beat South Africa (95 and 93) at The Oval	1912
872	Australia (199-8 dec) beat New Zealand (42 and 54) at Wellington	1945-46
893	Australia (310) beat Pakistan (59 and 53) at Sharjah	2002-03
907	**South Africa (309-9 dec) beat Zimbabwe (68 and 121) at Port Elizabeth**	**2017-18**
911	Australia (284) beat England (65 and 72) at Sydney	1894-95
940	South Africa (340-3 dec) beat Zimbabwe (54 and 265) at Cape Town	2004-05
941	England (272) beat West Indies (172 and 61) at Leeds	2000

A Test at Centurion in 1999-2000, in which England declared at 0-0 in their first innings, and South Africa forfeited their second, lasted 883 balls.

Test since the Second World War. Never mind four days: it was the first two-day Test anywhere since New Zealand overwhelmed Zimbabwe at Harare in August 2005. "Something started happening when the sun went down and the lights came on," said Cremer, Zimbabwe's captain. "I think that will play a big part in day/night Tests – declaring a bit earlier or a bit later, because every seam attack will want to bowl at night. It's also about not pushing your seamers too hard during the day, and keeping them for that night period."

The portents were ominous from the start, when Zimbabwe's bowlers proved a handful in broad daylight. Unusually for St George's Park, the pitch had been left with a decent covering of grass, and the ball moved appreciably off the seam. But it did not move enough to prevent Markram showing off his rare talent, and making 125. It was his second century, in his third Test, and left him with an unsustainable average of 95. He shared handy partnerships with Elgar and Bavuma, although the highlight, in between, was a stand of 96 with de Villiers, playing his first Test since January 2016, after choosing to sit out 17. He was temporary captain because a virus had hindered Faf du Plessis's recovery from back and shoulder injuries.

Few teams would have found an answer to Markram's unimpeachable orthodoxy and de Villiers's profane innovation, and the Zimbabweans didn't come close. In the end, de Villiers had to help them out: never without several options, whatever the delivery, he shaped to drive but instead bunted a return catch to Mpofu. Markram finally fell, pushing wide of his body at Jarvis, and was well caught one-handed by the diving Taylor, who had previously proved somewhat statuesque during his return to wicketkeeping duties.

De Villiers declared with an hour left of the first evening, a canny nod to the ball's exaggerated dance under lights. Zimbabwe lost Masakadza to the first delivery, and were soon in tatters at 14 for four, three of them to Morkel. "We had four of our tailenders padded up to get them out of the way and give our batsmen a chance next day," said Cremer. It might have been a short game, but it was an eventful one for de Villiers – he also had to keep wicket, after de Kock had strained a hamstring while batting, and held on to eight catches.

The seamers did all the damage in Zimbabwe's brief first innings – Morkel's five for 21 was his first five-for in 36 Tests, spread over more than five years – but the main destroyer in the second was slow left-armer Maharaj, who added to his burgeoning reputation with five for 59. For all the cynicism sparked by these not-quite-two days of not-quite-day/night Test cricket, no one could say they hadn't seen 907 eventful balls. Progress, they call it.

Man of the Match: A. K. Markram.

Close of play: first day, Zimbabwe 30-4 (Burl 15, Jarvis 4).

South Africa

D. Elgar c Moor b Jarvis	31
A. K. Markram c Taylor b Jarvis	125
H. M. Amla c Moor b Mpofu	5
*A. B. de Villiers c and b Mpofu	53
T. Bavuma c Taylor b Jarvis	44
†Q. de Kock lbw b Cremer	24
V. D. Philander lbw b Cremer	10
A. L. Phehlukwayo not out	4
K. Rabada run out	1
K. A. Maharaj c Burl b Mpofu	5
B 2, lb 2, w 1, nb 2	7
1/72 (1) 2/77 (3) 3/173 (4) 4/251 (2) 5/272 (5) 6/298 (7) 7/303 (6) 8/304 (9) 9/309 (10) (9 wkts dec, 78.3 overs)	309

M. Morkel did not bat.

Jarvis 18–2–57–3; Muzarabani 13–2–48–0; Mpofu 13.3–1–58–3; Chibhabha 11–1–51–0; Cremer 18–0–66–2; Sikandar Raza 5–0–25–0.

Zimbabwe

H. Masakadza lbw b Morkel	0	– c †de Villiers b Maharaj	13
C. J. Chibhabha c Bavuma b Morkel	6	– c †de Villiers b Rabada	15
C. R. Ervine lbw b Philander	4	– lbw b Phehlukwayo	23
†B. R. M. Taylor c †de Villiers b Morkel	0	– c Amla b Maharaj	16
R. P. Burl b Morkel	16	– c †de Villiers b Phehlukwayo	0
K. M. Jarvis c †de Villiers b Phehlukwayo	23	– (9) b Philander	5
Sikandar Raza c †de Villiers b Morkel	0	– (6) c Phehlukwayo b Maharaj	5
P. J. Moor b Phehlukwayo	9	– (7) c †de Villiers b Phehlukwayo	1
*A. G. Cremer c †de Villiers b Rabada	2	– (8) not out	18
C. B. Mpofu c Bavuma b Rabada	0	– b Maharaj	0
B. Muzarabani not out	4	– b Maharaj	10
Lb 2, nb 2	4	B 8, lb 7	15
1/0 (1) 2/11 (2) 3/11 (4) 4/14 (3) 5/36 (5) 6/36 (7) 7/55 (6) 8/63 (9) 9/63 (8) 10/68 (10) (30.1 overs)	68	1/54 (2) 2/75 (4) 3/75 (3) 4/80 (6) 5/80 (5) 6/87 (7) 7/91 (1) 8/98 (9) 9/103 (10) 10/121 (11) (42.3 overs)	121

In the second innings Masakadza, when 7, retired hurt at 8-0 and resumed at 80-5.

Morkel 11–5–21–5; Philander 10–4–21–1; Rabada 6.1–2–12–2; Phehlukwayo 3–0–12–2. *Second innings*—Morkel 4–0–12–0; Philander 7–3–10–1; Maharaj 17.3–5–59–5; Rabada 7–3–12–1; Phehlukwayo 7–2–13–3.

Umpires: R. A. Kettleborough and P. R. Reiffel. Third umpire: M. A. Gough.
Referee: B. C. Broad.

SOUTH AFRICA UNDER-19 TRI-SERIES IN 2017-18

1 South Africa 2 England 3 Namibia

In the run-up to the Under-19 World Cup, held in New Zealand in early 2018, South Africa hosted a tri-series of 50-over games in December, and invited fellow World Cup contestants England and Namibia to join their preparations.

England's team, also known as the Young Lions, waltzed through the qualifying round, winning all four games with ease, and dropping only one bonus point, even though half the 18-strong squad had not played Under-19 internationals before. They slipped up for the first time in the final, when South African all-rounder Jason Niemand grabbed three wickets, then steered his side home with two balls to spare.

The captain, Yorkshire's Harry Brook, was England's leading scorer, with 217 runs at 72 across their five matches, ahead of opener Savin Perera's 178. Surrey all-rounder Will Jacks and Middlesex leg-spinner Luke Hollman were the leading wicket-takers with nine apiece; Jacks, who also scored 147 runs, was named the Player of the Tournament. Overall, the most successful batsman was South Africa's Matthew Breetzke, who totalled 243, including the series' only century.

Following the appointment of their previous coach, Andy Hurry, as director of cricket at Somerset, England Under-19s were originally to be supervised by Worcestershire's Steve Rhodes. But he was suspended, then sacked, by his county for his role in failing to pass on allegations of rape against Alex Hepburn, which the player denied. Gloucestershire's Richard Dawson stepped in as interim head coach, assisted by former England batsman James Taylor, pace specialist Neil Killeen and fielding coach Chris Taylor.

ENGLAND UNDER-19 TOURING SQUAD

*H. C. Brook (Yorkshire), E. R. Bamber (Middlesex), L. Banks (Warwickshire), T. Banton (Somerset), J. L. Davies (Middlesex), A. W. Finch (Worcestershire), L. B. K. Hollman (Middlesex), W. G. Jacks (Surrey), T. A. Lammonby (Somerset), F. S. Organ (Hampshire), D. Y. Pennington (Worcestershire), S. D. Perera (Middlesex), J. H. Plom (Essex), H. Qadri (Derbyshire), T. A. R. Scriven (Hampshire), P. Sisodiya (Glamorgan), F. R. Trenouth (Somerset), R. I. Walker (Glamorgan). *Coach:* R. K. J. Dawson.

Namibia also took part, but their games did not count as official Under-19 ODIs. They lost twice to South Africa and twice to England.

At Potchefstroom, December 3, 2017 (day/night). **England won by 112 runs** (DLS). **England 289-5** (49 overs) (S. D. Perera 84, H. C. Brook 91, T. A. Lammonby 62*); ‡**South Africa 166** (37.2 overs) (M. P. Breetzke 52; W. G. Jacks 3-33, L. B. K. Hollman 4-30). *England 5pts. MoM:* H. C. Brook. *Invited to bat, Savin Perera and captain Harry Brook put on 149 in 24 overs for the second wicket to set England on course for a healthy total. Rain cut short their innings by one over, and South Africa's target was revised to 279 in 44. Will Jacks ended an opening stand of 81 between Jiveshen Pillay and Matthew Breetzke, and leg-spinner Luke Hollman took three in four overs as South Africa's last six fell for 23.*

At Potchefstroom, December 7, 2017 (day/night). **England won by eight wickets.** ‡**South Africa 248-9** (50 overs) (M. P. Breetzke 101; J. H. Plom 3-47, W. G. Jacks 3-41); **England 252-2** (41.1 overs) (T. Banton 74, H. C. Brook 63*, W. G. Jacks 71*). *England 4pts. MoM:* W. G. Jacks.

Breetzke scored his third century at this level, but none of his team-mates passed 41, and the South African innings fell away as Breetzke became one of three wickets in three overs for seamer Jack Plom. Two century partnerships – 109 between Tom Banton and Liam Banks, then 117 between Brook and Will Jacks, who scored 71* in 53 balls – ensured England completed the group stage with four convincing wins out of four.*

England 19pts, South Africa 10pts, Namibia 0pts.

Final At Potchefstroom, December 10, 2017 (day/night). **South Africa won by three wickets. England 259** (49.1 overs) (L. Banks 51, T. A. R. Scriven 53; J. Niemand 3-52); ‡**South Africa 260-7** (49.4 overs) (J. Niemand 60*). *MoM:* H. C. Brook. *MoT:* W. G. Jacks. *England finally stumbled, suffering their first defeat in the last match. They were beaten by a storming all-round performance from Jason Niemand, who trapped Perera and Banks with his off-breaks, after their opening stand of 74 in 12.4 overs; by the time he added Tom Lammonby, England were 119-5. Tom Scriven fought back, putting on another 74 for the eighth wicket with Hollman (34), but they were bowled out for the first time on the tour for 259. All South Africa's top six passed 25, and Niemand completed victory in the final over with a 53-ball 60*.*

DOMESTIC CRICKET IN SOUTH AFRICA IN 2016-17

COLIN BRYDEN

Two old international team-mates faced up to each other at the helm of domestic franchises. Nicky Boje, confirmed as the full-time Knights coach after standing in during the previous season, guided them to victory in the first-class Sunfoil Series, their first trophy in any format for six years. Meanwhile, Mark Boucher, the former Test wicketkeeper who took charge of the Titans, enjoyed instant success, winning both limited-overs competitions and finishing a close second in the four-day tournament.

Boje could feel especially proud of his achievement with the Bloemfontein-based **Knights**, as he had fewer resources. He made two important signings – fast bowler Marchant de Lange from the Titans, and batsman David Miller from the Dolphins. The pace pairing of de Lange and Duanne Olivier, who made his Test debut during the season, was the key to their success: Olivier led the competition's wicket-takers with 52, and de Lange was joint-second on 34. Theunis de Bruyn, handed the captaincy shortly before his 24th birthday, scored 751 runs at 57.

Boucher's appointment by the **Titans** was not universally welcomed. As a Test player he already had a Level Two coaching qualification, but his experience was limited to a few days with the South African team and a brief stint as a consultant for the IPL's Kolkata Knight Riders. His commitment was questioned when he missed the start of the season for a pro–am golf tournament in Scotland – especially when the Titans collapsed for 57 to lose at home to the Knights. They lost the next game as well.

But once Boucher settled in, the Titans enjoyed almost uninterrupted success. They could not quite retain the first-class title they won in 2015-16: they were eventually squeezed into second place by 1.78 bonus points, the equivalent of 89 runs or four wickets across the season. But they topped the leagues of the Momentum One-Day Cup and the CSA T20 Challenge, earning home finals (both against Warriors) which they duly won.

Though he inherited a strong playing staff and administrative structure, Boucher was credited with instilling an extra edge of professionalism; he was named South African Coach of the Year, and his contract extended from two years to four. With the likes of A. B. de Villiers, Faf du Plessis and Quinton de Kock seldom available, he was pleased to oversee the development of young players such as Heinrich Klaasen, Aiden Markram and Lungi Ngidi. Wicketkeeper-batsman Klaasen was the Titans' Player of the Year, while opener Markram, who had led South Africa's Under-19 World Cup winners in 2014, had an exceptional debut at franchise level, scoring 565 runs at 51 in the Sunfoil Series and 508 at 56 in the one-day cup. Ngidi's fast bowling, particularly in limited-overs games, earned him a Test debut in January against India.

Another former team-mate of Boje and Boucher, Paul Adams, was forced out as coach of the **Cape Cobras** by a player revolt. The franchise initially refused to respond to complaints, but finally gave way when the Cobras were bottom of the Sunfoil Series at the halfway mark. With a new coach, former Test batsman Ashwell Prince, and a new captain, Dane Piedt, the Cobras won three games and scored more points than any other team during the second half, climbing to third. They could not maintain that momentum in the one-day cup, however, and finished last.

The **Dolphins** briefly led the four-day table, but failed to follow through on some promising performances; both Vaughn van Jaarsveld and Khaya Zondo passed 700 runs. The **Lions** found it difficult to overcome the loss of players to international calls, though they uncovered a new talent in 18-year-old all-rounder Wiaan Mulder. The **Warriors** reached both limited-overs finals, boosted by the all-round form of Jon-Jon Smuts, but struggled in the longer game.

In the provincial competitions, **Northerns** shared the three-day title with Free State and beat Namibia in the 50-over final. **Eastern Province** won the Africa T20 Cup.

FIRST-CLASS AVERAGES IN 2016-17

BATTING (600 runs, average 40.00)

		M	*I*	*NO*	*R*	*HS*	*100*	*Avge*	*Ct/St*
1	P. J. Malan (*W Province/Cape Cobras*)	10	16	6	1,077	211*	5	107.70	7
2	†D. P. Conway (*Gauteng/Lions*)	9	14	5	887	205*	4	98.55	6
3	S. Pillay (*Gauteng*)	10	11	4	682	118	3	97.42	7
4	A. P. Agathangelou (*SW Districts*)	7	13	4	710	199*	4	78.88	6
5	R. S. Second (*Knights/Free State*)	11	17	4	982	151	5	75.53	53/4
6	K. Zondo (*Dolphins*)	10	15	4	740	157	2	67.27	3
7	†P. Botha (*Free State*)	9	14	2	724	145	3	60.33	8
8	T. B. de Bruyn (*Knights*)	9	14	1	751	182	2	57.76	12
9	K. Verreynne (*Western Province*)	10	15	3	690	107*	1	57.50	34/2
10	A. J. Malan (*North West*)	9	16	4	679	177*	4	56.58	3
11	J. L. Ontong (*Boland/Cape Cobras*)	8	13	1	663	225	2	55.25	1
12	†M. J. Ackerman (*North West*)	9	14	2	642	122	2	53.50	5
13	†V. B. van Jaarsveld (*Dolphins*)	10	15	0	799	203	2	53.26	6
14	†Y. Valli (*Gauteng/Lions*)	12	19	2	897	182	4	52.76	8
15	D. Smit (*Dolphins/KwaZulu-Natal*)	9	15	3	625	150*	3	52.08	22/3
16	C. N. Ackermann (*Warriors*)	10	17	0	883	150	3	51.94	17
17	A. K. Markram (*Northerns/Titans*)	8	13	1	612	162	2	51.00	6
18	J. N. Malan (*North West*)	8	14	0	703	174	3	50.21	8
19	†W. Coulentianos (*Easterns*)	10	17	4	636	119	2	48.92	7
20	H. Klaasen (*Titans*)	9	14	1	635	195	1	48.84	33/4
21	†D. J. van Wyk (*KZN Inland/Dolphins*)	11	15	0	725	153	1	48.33	9
22	†S. Muthusamy (*KZN/Dolphins*)	12	21	2	840	181	3	44.21	6
23	†E. H. Kemm (*Easterns*)	10	17	0	741	126	1	43.58	9
24	W. B. Marshall (*Easterns*)	10	17	1	665	152	1	41.56	9
25	†S. van Zyl (*Cape Cobras/W Province*)	12	22	4	748	108	3	41.55	12
26	†E. M. Moore (*Warriors/E Province*)	15	27	3	991	81	0	41.29	11
27	F. D. Adams (*Boland*)	9	15	0	615	146	2	41.00	3

BOWLING (30 wickets)

		Style	*O*	*M*	*R*	*W*	*BB*	*5I*	*Avge*
1	P. Fojela (*Border*)	RFM	207.3	61	562	41	5-21	3	13.70
2	D. Olivier (*Knights/Free State/SA*)	RFM	343.1	75	1,057	64	6-60	6	16.51
3	M. Pretorius (*Northerns*)	RF	245.5	62	747	42	6-38	1	17.78
4	S. C. van Schalkwyk (*Knights/FS*)	RFM	229.4	62	639	33	7-82	1	19.36
5	E. L. Hawken (*Northerns*)	RF	255.1	67	743	38	6-29	2	19.55
6	G. A. Stuurman (*SW Districts*)	RM	280.4	72	819	39	7-12	2	21.00
7	L. M. Zuma (*Free State/Knights*)	RFM	201.2	36	693	33	6-50	3	21.00
8	M. P. Siboto (*Titans*)	RFM	246.5	52	711	33	7-48	1	21.54
9	S. H. Jamison (*Lions/Gauteng*)	RFM	291	68	891	41	5-40	2	21.73
10	T. Bokako (*E Province/Warriors*)	RF	242.4	57	718	32	5-50	2	22.43
11	S. von Berg (*Titans/Northerns*)	LB	271	41	889	39	6-144	3	22.79
12	T. I. Ntuli (*Free State/Knights*)	OB	204	36	772	32	6-45	1	24.12
13	C. J. August (*Easterns*)	LFM	266	64	801	33	4-17	0	24.27
14	M. Arnold (*Easterns*)	RF	267	48	895	36	5-41	2	24.86
15	B. L. Barends (*North West*)	RM	252	54	748	30	5-33	1	24.93
16	S. Muthusamy (*KZN/Dolphins*)	SLA	273.1	36	945	36	5-67	1	26.25
17	K. I. Simmonds (*Boland/C Cobras*)	SLA	376.1	80	1,133	41	6-49	3	27.63
18	M. de Lange (*Knights/Free State*)	RF	302.4	72	991	35	7-23	2	28.31
19	C. J. Alexander (*Dolph/KZNI/KZN*)	RF	258.4	46	909	32	4-43	0	28.40
20	B. D. Walters (*Warriors*)	RF	282.2	56	886	31	4-72	0	28.58
21	A. A. Nortje (*E Province/Warriors*)	RF	331.4	70	1,085	35	6-44	1	31.00
22	S. R. Harmer (*Warriors*)	OB	408.5	87	1,238	34	4-63	0	36.41

Averages include CSA Provincial Three-Day Challenge matches played in Namibia.

SUNFOIL SERIES IN 2016-17

	Played	Won	Lost	Drawn	Bonus points Batting	Bonus points Bowling	Points
Knights	10	4	2	4†	36.94	31	112.94
Titans	10	4	3	3†	33.16	33	111.16
Cape Cobras	10	3	3	4	30.76	33	93.76
Dolphins	10	2	2	6	40.68	32	92.68
Lions	10	3	3	4	24.32	33	87.32
Warriors	10	2	5	3	34.40	30	84.40

† *Includes one abandoned match.*

Outright win = 10pts; abandoned = 5pts. Bonus points awarded for the first 100 overs of each team's first innings: one batting point for the first 150 runs and 0.02 of a point for every subsequent run; one bowling point for the third wicket taken and for every subsequent two.

At Johannesburg, October 5–7, 2016. **Lions won by ten wickets.** ‡**Cape Cobras 102 and 211** (G. C. Viljoen 6-75); **Lions 154 and 160-0.** *Lions 15.08pts, Cape Cobras 4pts. Lions' 18-year-old schoolboy debutant Wiaan Mulder took seven wickets, backing up Hardus Viljoen. In Cape Cobras' second innings, Jason Smith scored 95; the rest of the top eight managed 25 between them.*

At Centurion, October 5–7, 2016. **Knights won by four wickets.** ‡**Titans 287** (D. Olivier 6-60) **and 57** (M. de Lange 7-23); **Knights 174 and 172-6.** *Knights 15.48pts, Titans 7.74pts. On debut for Knights, Marchant de Lange claimed a career-best 7.2–3–23–7, routing Titans in 14.2 overs in their second innings with Duanne Olivier (who had achieved his own career-best on the opening day).*

At East London, October 5–8, 2016. **Dolphins won by an innings and 70 runs.** ‡**Dolphins 478** (D. Smit 121); **Warriors 230** (K. A. Maharaj 7-89) **and 178** (K. A. Maharaj 6-68). *Dolphins 18.14pts, Warriors 4.6pts. Left-arm spinner Keshav Maharaj scored a run-a-ball 72, then collected 13-157.*

At Bloemfontein, October 11–14, 2016. **Knights won by 175 runs.** ‡**Knights 342 and 342** (P. J. van Biljon 123, R. S. Second 106); **Cape Cobras 241 and 268** (J. F. Smith 100*; M. de Lange 6-61). *Knights 18.84pts, Cape Cobras 6.82pts. Pite van Biljon and Rudi Second added 243 for Knights' fourth wicket. In Cobras' first innings, Zubayr Hamza was given out handled the ball, and his captain Omphile Ramela's reaction earned him a one-match ban.*

At Potchefstroom, October 11–13, 2016. **Dolphins won by 77 runs.** ‡**Dolphins 253 and 83** (P. W. A. Mulder 7-25); **Lions 110** (R. Frylinck 8-30) **and 149** (R. Frylinck 6-32). *Dolphins 17.06pts, Lions 4pts. There were three first-ball dismissals in Dolphins' first innings: Viljoen trapped Imraan Khan with the very first delivery, and Sean Jamison later took a hat-trick. In his second first-class match, Mulder claimed 7-25 in the second innings – but Dolphins still won in three days, thanks to Robert Frylinck, whose 8-30 was the best return of the season. His match figures of 14-62 were the best since the franchises took over the first-class competition in 2004.*

At Port Elizabeth, October 11–14, 2016. **Warriors won by six wickets.** ‡**Titans 227 and 235; Warriors 358** (C. N. Ackermann 136) **and 105-4.** *Warriors 17.9pts, Titans 4.54pts. Heinrich Klaasen made six catches and a stumping in Warriors' first innings, then scored 97* in Titans' second, adding 100 for the ninth wicket with Morne Morkel (36) – but Titans lost again.*

At Cape Town, October 20–23, 2016. **Drawn.** ‡**Warriors 525-7 dec** (C. N. Ackermann 146); **Cape Cobras 567-7** (O. A. Ramela 170, A. G. Puttick 124). *Cape Cobras 3.82pts, Warriors 4.98pts. Cobras openers Ramela and Andrew Puttick put on 266. Five bowlers in the match conceded more than 100, with Warriors' off-spinner Simon Harmer yielding 176 from his 69 overs.*

At Kimberley, October 20–23, 2016. **Drawn.** ‡**Lions 483** (N. J. van den Bergh 101, P. W. A. Mulder 104) **and 310-9** (D. Olivier 6-93); **Knights 572** (M. N. Erlank 103, D. A. Miller 177). *Knights 8.88pts, Lions 8.78pts. Mulder scored a maiden century in his third match. In Knights' reply, Theunis de Bruyn hit 91 out of 128 for the second wicket, then Michael Erlank and David Miller added 243 for the third; their eventual 572 remained the highest total of the season.*

At Centurion, October 20–22, 2016. **Titans won by an innings and 38 runs. Dolphins 207** (L. T. Ngidi 5-39) **and 187**; ‡**Titans 432** (A. K. Markram 162). *Titans 19.72pts, Dolphins 4.14pts. With Boucher now in charge, and Lungi Ngidi and Aiden Markram making their first-class franchise* *debuts, there was a sudden change in Titans' fortunes. Ngidi removed Dolphins' top four in five overs, while Markram scored 162, sharing an opening stand of 203 with Heino Kuhn (88).*

At Cape Town, October 27–29, 2016. **Titans won by an innings and 50 runs. Cape Cobras 235** (S. von Berg 5-88) **and 115** (S. von Berg 5-25); **‡Titans 400** (A. K. Markram 139). *Titans 19.92pts, Cape Cobras 5.7pts. Markram made another century, and leg-spinner Shaun von Berg took 10-113.*

At Durban, October 27–30, 2016. **Drawn. Dolphins 311** (R. J. Peterson 6-83) **and 12-1; ‡Knights 221.** *Dolphins 8.22pts, Knights 6.42pts.*

At Johannesburg, October 27–30, 2016. **Lions won by 148 runs. ‡Lions 308 and 335-8 dec; Warriors 356** (D. Pretorius 6-81) **and 139** (G. C. Viljoen 5-29). *Lions 18.16pts, Warriors 9.12pts.*

At Paarl, November 3–6, 2016. **Drawn. Dolphins 478** (K. Zondo 157; D. Paterson 5-79) **and 207-4; ‡Cape Cobras 447** (J. L. Ontong 225). *Cape Cobras 6.52pts, Dolphins 7.02pts. Khaya Zondo and Morne van Wyk (79) added 201 for Dolphins' sixth wicket. Then Justin Ontong, with a maiden double-century, put on 202 with Keegan Petersen (86), and 144 for the eighth with Dane Piedt.*

At Potchefstroom, November 3–6, 2016. **Drawn. ‡Lions 206** (M. P. Siboto 7-48) **and 187-2; Titans 431-6 dec** (H. Davids 150*). *Lions 4.12pts, Titans 7.82pts. Titans led the table at the halfway break.*

At Port Elizabeth, November 3–6, 2016. **Warriors won by 107 runs. Warriors 339** (S. C. van Schalkwyk 7-82) **and 236** (D. Olivier 5-66); **‡Knights 179** (A. A. Nortje 6-44) **and 289** (T. B. de Bruyn 108). *Warriors 18.2pts, Knights 5.58pts. Shadley van Schalkwyk claimed a career-best 7-82 in Warriors' first innings, and wicketkeeper Second seven dismissals – six catches and a stumping – in their second, giving him 11 in the match, but Knights suffered their first defeat.*

At Oudtshoorn, January 5–8, 2017. **Cape Cobras won by six wickets. Lions 126 and 383; ‡Cape Cobras 273 and 239-4** (W. D. Parnell 103*). *Cape Cobras 17.46pts, Lions 4pts. Resuming in the New Year with a new coach (Ashwell Prince) and captain (Piedt), Cobras recorded their first win.*

At Durban, January 5–8, 2017. **Drawn. Warriors 231; ‡Dolphins 361-4** (V. B. van Jaarsveld 154). *Dolphins 9.22pts, Warriors 3.62pts.*

At Bloemfontein, January 5–8, 2017. **Knights v Titans. Abandoned.** *Knights 5pts, Titans 5pts.*

At Kimberley, January 12–15, 2017. **Drawn. Knights 487-7 dec** (T. B. de Bruyn 182, R. S. Second 125); **‡Dolphins 538-7 dec** (S. Muthusamy 181, V. B. van Jaarsveld 203). *Knights 6.78pts, Dolphins 8.08pts. De Bruyn and Second added 258 for Knights' fourth wicket. In Dolphins' reply, Senuran Muthusamy and Vaughn van Jaarsveld, who reached a maiden double-century, added 355 for the second, as Knights used ten bowlers; Second gave up his gloves and took 4-105.*

At Benoni, January 12–15, 2017. **Drawn. Lions 347 and 308-6 dec** (D. A. Hendricks 103*, M. Mosehle 100); **‡Titans 251 and 143-2.** *Titans 6.02pts, Lions 7.46pts.*

At East London, January 12–15, 2017. **Drawn. Cape Cobras 291 and 71-3; ‡Warriors 260.** *Warriors 7.2pts, Cape Cobras 7.82pts.*

At Pietermaritzburg, January 19–22, 2017. **Drawn. ‡Dolphins 339** (K. Zondo 141*; D. Pretorius 5-54) **and 189-6 dec; Lions 267** (K. A. Maharaj 6-86) **and 74-1.** *Dolphins 6.78pts, Lions 5.58pts.*

At Bloemfontein, January 26–29, 2017. **Knights won by 121 runs. ‡Knights 431** (R. S. Second 151) **and 189; Warriors 299** (D. Olivier 6-82) **and 200** (D. Olivier 5-67). *Knights 20.2pts, Warriors 6.98pts. Second scored his third hundred in successive first-class innings, one of them for Free State. A fortnight after his Test debut, Olivier's 11-149 took him past 50 first-class wickets in the season.*

At Centurion, January 26–29, 2017. **Cape Cobras won by nine wickets. ‡Titans 195 and 168** (R. K. Kleinveldt 5-45); **Cape Cobras 326-9 dec** (J. L. Ontong 110; D. Wiese 5-41) **and 41-1.** *Cape Cobras 18.52pts, Titans 5.9pts.*

At Paarl, February 2–4, 2017. **Cape Cobras won by 151 runs. ‡Cape Cobras 154 and 330** (S. van Zyl 106); **Knights 153 and 180** (D. L. Piedt 6-87). *Cape Cobras 15.08pts, Knights 5.06pts. The second day was interrupted by smoke from a bush fire. Cobras completed their third win in four.*

At Pietermaritzburg, February 2–5, 2017. **Titans won by two wickets. ‡Dolphins 301 and 192; Titans 403** (H. Klaasen 195) **and 91-8** (P. Subrayen 5-35). *Titans 17.96pts, Dolphins 6.02pts. Titans were 35-5, then 81-8, chasing 91, but edged home and went back to the top of the table.*

At East London, February 2–5, 2017. **Lions won by 14 runs. Lions 307 and 153-2 dec; ‡Warriors 203-6 dec and 243.** *Lions 16.14pts, Warriors 6.06pts. Two declarations left Warriors needing 258; after Ayavuya Moli reduced them to 42-4, they fought back to 237-8 before losing two in nine balls.*

At Durban, February 9–12, 2017. **Drawn. ‡Cape Cobras 381** (A. G. Puttick 116, S. van Zyl 108; S. Muthusamy 5-67) **and 291-7** (S. van Zyl 101*); **Dolphins 329-8 dec** (D. Smit 150*). *Dolphins 8pts, Cape Cobras 8.02pts. Stiaan van Zyl's two centuries gave him three in successive innings.*

At Johannesburg, February 9–11, 2017. **Knights won by an innings and 121 runs. ‡Knights 443** (P. J. van Biljon 119; B. E. Hendricks 5-89); **Lions 87 and 235** (R. R. Hendricks 112). *Knights 20.7pts, Lions 4pts. Knights made sure of the title on the third morning, completing their fourth victory after making Lions follow on 356 behind. Olivier finished with 52 in the tournament.*

At Benoni, February 9–12, 2017. **Titans won by four wickets. ‡Warriors 187 and 354** (C. N. Ackermann 150; S. von Berg 6-144); **Titans 227** (S. von Berg 103) **and 316-6** (H. G. Kuhn 165*). *Titans 16.54pts, Warriors 5.74pts. Von Berg took ten wickets for the second time, and combined them with a century. Titans matched Knights' four wins, but knew after the first two days – when they did not secure enough bonus points – that they were fighting for second place.*

CHAMPIONS

Season	Champions
1889-90	Transvaal
1890-91	Kimberley
1892-93	Western Province
1893-94	Western Province
1894-95	Transvaal
1896-97	Western Province
1897-98	Western Province
1902-03	Transvaal
1903-04	Transvaal
1904-05	Transvaal
1906-07	Transvaal
1908-09	Western Province
1910-11	Natal
1912-13	Natal
1920-21	Western Province
1921-22	Transvaal / Natal / Western Province
1923-24	Transvaal
1925-26	Transvaal
1926-27	Transvaal
1929-30	Transvaal
1931-32	Western Province
1933-34	Natal
1934-35	Transvaal
1936-37	Natal
1937-38	Natal / Transvaal
1946-47	Natal
1947-48	Natal
1950-51	Transvaal
1951-52	Natal
1952-53	Western Province
1954-55	Natal
1955-56	Western Province
1958-59	Transvaal
1959-60	Natal
1960-61	Natal
1962-63	Natal
1963-64	Natal
1965-66	Natal / Transvaal
1966-67	Natal
1967-68	Natal
1968-69	Transvaal
1969-70	Transvaal / Western Province
1970-71	Transvaal
1971-72	Transvaal
1972-73	Transvaal
1973-74	Natal
1974-75	Western Province
1975-76	Natal
1976-77	Natal
1977-78	Western Province
1978-79	Transvaal
1979-80	Transvaal
1980-81	Natal
1981-82	Western Province
1982-83	Transvaal
1983-84	Transvaal
1984-85	Transvaal
1985-86	Western Province
1986-87	Transvaal
1987-88	Transvaal
1988-89	Eastern Province
1989-90	Eastern Province / Western Province
1990-91	Western Province
1991-92	Eastern Province
1992-93	Orange Free State
1993-94	Orange Free State
1994-95	Natal
1995-96	Western Province
1996-97	Natal
1997-98	Free State
1998-99	Western Province
1999-2000	Gauteng
2000-01	Western Province
2001-02	KwaZulu-Natal

2002-03	Easterns
2003-04	Western Province
2004-05	{ Dolphins Eagles
2005-06	{ Dolphins Titans
2006-07	Titans
2007-08	Eagles
2008-09	Titans
2009-10	Cape Cobras
2010-11	Cape Cobras
2011-12	Titans
2012-13	Cape Cobras
2013-14	Cape Cobras
2014-15	Lions
2015-16	Titans
2016-17	Knights

Transvaal/Gauteng have won the title outright 25 times, Natal/KwaZulu-Natal 21, Western Province 18, Cape Cobras and Titans 4, Orange Free State/Free State 3, Eagles/Knights and Eastern Province 2, Easterns, Kimberley and Lions 1. The title has been shared seven times as follows: Transvaal 4, Natal and Western Province 3, Dolphins 2, Eagles, Eastern Province and Titans 1.

The tournament was the Currie Cup from 1889-90 to 1989-90, the Castle Cup from 1990-91 to 1995-96, the SuperSport Series from 1996-97 to 2011-12, and the Sunfoil Series from 2012-13.

From 1971-72 to 1990-91, the non-white South African Cricket Board of Control (later the South African Cricket Board) organised their own three-day tournaments. These are now recognised as first-class (see *Wisden 2006*, pages 79–80). A list of winners appears in *Wisden 2007*, page 1346.

SUNFOIL THREE-DAY CUP IN 2016-17

Pool A	*P*	*W*	*L*	*D*	*Pts*
NORTHERNS	10	6	0	4	140.06
North West	10	6	0	4	130.48
Western Province	10	5	1	4	126.86
Northern Cape	10	2	5	3	80.56
Border	10	2	3	5	80.50
SW Districts	10	1	8	1	61.98
KwaZulu-Natal	10	1	5	4	61.44

Pool B	*P*	*W*	*L*	*D*	*Pts*
FREE STATE	10	6	2	2	132.78
Gauteng	10	3	1	6	108.44
KZN Inland	10	3	1	6	100.00‡
Easterns	10	3	1	6	98.02
Eastern Province	10	2	4	4	81.76
Boland	10	1	5	4	70.92†
Namibia	10	1	6	3	56.82

† *1pt deducted for slow over-rate.* ‡ *3pts deducted for slow over-rate.*

Outright win = 10pts. Bonus points awarded for the first 100 overs of each team's first innings: one batting point for the first 150 runs and 0.02 of a point for every subsequent run; one bowling point for the third wicket taken and for every subsequent two.

The teams were divided into two pools of seven. Each played the other six in their pool, plus four teams from the other pool; all results counted towards the table. The two pool leaders met in a final.

Pool A

At Potchefstroom, October 6–8, 2016. **Drawn. ‡KwaZulu-Natal 269** (C. S. Delport 147) **and 359-7 dec** (S. Muthusamy 145); **North West 208** (M. J. Ackerman 112; C. P. Savage 5-62) **and 280-3** (I. M. Dikgale 101*). *North West 6.16pts, KwaZulu-Natal 7.38pts.*

At Oudtshoorn, October 13–15, 2016. **Western Province won by 96 runs. Western Province 306-7 dec and 152; ‡South Western Districts 128** (G. F. Linde 5-10) **and 234** (A. D. Galiem 5-60). *Western Province 18.12pts, South Western Districts 3pts.*

At East London, October 20–22, 2016. **Drawn. North West 154** (P. Fojela 5-32) **and 383-9** (B. L. Barends 105*); **‡Border 320-5 dec.** *Border 8.4pts, North West 3.08pts.*

At Chatsworth, October 20–22, 2016. **Northern Cape won by 225 runs. ‡Northern Cape 179 and 293-9 dec; KwaZulu-Natal 145 and 102** (W. L. Coetsee 5-11). *Northern Cape 15.58pts, KwaZulu-Natal 4pts.*

At Centurion, October 28–30, 2016. **Northerns won by ten wickets. KwaZulu-Natal 197 and 160** (E. L. Hawken 6-29); **‡Northerns 340** (J. J. Pienaar 102) **and 19-0.** *Northerns 18.8pts, KwaZulu-Natal 5.94pts. Northerns recorded their second successive ten-wicket victory.*

At Rondebosch, November 3–5, 2016. **Drawn. Northern Cape 370 and 246-2 dec; ‡Western Province 295-5 dec** (K. Verreynne 107*) **and 198-6.** *Western Province 7.9pts, Northern Cape 7.4pts.*

At East London, November 10–12, 2016. **Drawn. Border 120-7 v ‡Northerns.** *Northerns 3pts.*

At Oudtshoorn, November 17–19, 2016. **South Western Districts won by six wickets. KwaZulu-Natal 74** (O. E. G. Baartman 7-27) **and 281** (J. P. Oakes 108, S. Muthusamy 142; O. E. G. Baartman 7-68); **‡South Western Districts 107 and 251-4** (A. P. Agathangelou 125*). *South Western Districts 14pts, KwaZulu-Natal 4pts. Ottniel Baartman took 14-95. Jason Oakes and Muthusamy added 228 for KZN's third wicket. Andrea Agathangelou scored his fourth hundred in five innings.*

At East London, December 1–3, 2016. **Border won by 214 runs. Border 289 and 227; ‡Northern Cape 69** (P. Fojela 5-21, T. Mnyaka 5-17) **and 233.** *Border 17.78pts, Northern Cape 4pts. More than half Northern Cape's 69 came from debutant Jacques Snyman (38).*

At Durban, December 15–17, 2016. **KwaZulu-Natal won by six wickets. Border 216** (M. Calana 106) **and 266-4 dec; ‡KwaZulu-Natal 130 and 357-4.** *KwaZulu-Natal 14pts, Border 6.32pts.*

At Cape Town, December 15–17, 2016. **North West won by seven wickets. Western Province 354-7 dec** (S. A. Engelbrecht 166) **and 215-1 dec** (P. J. Malan 117*); **‡North West 219 and 354-3** (J. N. Malan 135, A. J. Malan 103*). *North West 15.38pts, Western Province 9.08pts.*

At Centurion, January 6–8, 2017. **Drawn. Western Province 372-7** (M. C. Kleinveldt 111*) **v ‡Northerns.** *Northerns 3pts, Western Province 5.44pts. Western Province were boosted by 55 extras.*

At Oudtshoorn, January 12–14, 2017. **Northerns won by nine wickets. South Western Districts 246** (B. I. Louw 106) **and 131; ‡Northerns 303** (T. de Zorzi 103) **and 75-1.** *Northerns 18.06pts, South Western Districts 6.92pts.*

At Durban, January 19–21, 2017. **Drawn. ‡Western Province 279 and 42-5; KwaZulu-Natal 124 and 349** (C. Chetty 141; A. D. Galiem 5-67). *KwaZulu-Natal 4pts, Western Province 7.58pts.*

At Potchefstroom, February 9–11, 2017. **Drawn. Northerns 469-6 dec** (M. Q. Adams 202*, R. Moonsamy 130) **and 275-7 dec; ‡North West 327** (W. J. Lubbe 101; E. L. Hawken 5-72) **and 204-3** (A. J. Malan 100*). *North West 6.54pts, Northerns 10.9pts. Qaasim Adams scored a maiden double-century and added 277 with Rivaldo Moonsamy.*

At Oudtshoorn, February 9–11, 2017. **Northern Cape won by eight wickets. South Western Districts 132 and 251** (C. A. Dry 5-63); **‡Northern Cape 265** (G. J. Snyman 133) **and 119-2.** *Northern Cape 17.3pts, South Western Districts 4pts.*

At Kimberley, March 2–4, 2017. **North West won by six wickets. North West 322** (M. J. Ackerman 122; W. E. Bell 5-61) **and 115-4; ‡Northern Cape 97 and 339.** *North West 18.44pts, Northern Cape 4pts.*

At Cape Town, March 2–4, 2017. **Western Province won by five wickets. Border 220 and 226; ‡Western Province 286 and 161-5.** *Western Province 17.72pts, Border 6.4pts.*

At East London, March 9–11, 2017. **Border won by seven wickets. South Western Districts 111** (P. Fojela 5-31) **and 224; ‡Border 250 and 86-3.** *Border 17pts, South Western Districts 4pts.*

At Potchefstroom, March 23–25, 2017. **North West won by three wickets. South Western Districts 226 and 172; ‡North West 272** (J. N. Malan 106; N. M. Serame 6-73) **and 130-7** (G. A. Stuurman 6-37). *North West 17.44pts, South Western Districts 6.52pts.*

At Pretoria (L. C. de Villiers), March 23–25, 2017. **Northerns won by nine wickets. ‡Northern Cape 134** (M. Pretorius 6-38) **and 195; Northerns 292** (T. de Zorzi 121*; K. Mohale 5-64) **and 39-1.** *Northerns 17.84pts, Northern Cape 4pts.*

Pool B

At Benoni, October 6–8, 2016. **Drawn. ‡Free State 308 and 337-6 dec** (P. Botha 145); **Easterns 344** (E. H. Kemm 126) **and 201-4.** *Easterns 8.88pts, Free State 8.16pts.*

At Johannesburg (Bottom Oval), October 13–15, 2016. **Gauteng won by 109 runs. Gauteng 150** (G. I. Hume 5-31) **and 340-4 dec** (D. P. Conway 129); **‡KwaZulu-Natal Inland 151** (M. K. McGillivray 5-44) **and 230** (L. Mokoena 5-46). *Gauteng 15pts, KwaZulu-Natal Inland 5.02pts.*

At Johannesburg, October 20–22, 2016. **Drawn. Gauteng 372-7 dec** (Y. Valli 150*) **and 71-1; ‡Eastern Province 248** (E. Leie 5-67). *Gauteng 8.92pts, Eastern Province 5.96pts.*

At Pietermaritzburg, October 20–22, 2016. **Drawn. ‡KwaZulu-Natal Inland 208** (K. I. Simmonds 6-55) **and 173-5; Boland 338-7 dec** (A. M. Maposa 5-65). *KwaZulu-Natal Inland 4.16pts, Boland 8.02pts.*

At Port Elizabeth, November 10–12, 2016. **Drawn. ‡Easterns 342-8 dec** (W. Coulentianos 107); **Eastern Province 161 and 42-1.** *Eastern Province 4.22pts, Easterns 8.84pts.*

At Paarl, November 24–25, 2016. **Free State won by an innings and 206 runs. Boland 92** (D. du Preez 6-27) **and 78**; **‡Free State 376-6 dec** (R. S. Second 106*). *Free State 19.52pts, Boland 2pts.*

At Benoni, November 24–26, 2016. **Drawn. ‡Gauteng 394-5 dec** (Y. Valli 182, S. Pillay 115*); **Easterns 159-6 dec**. *Easterns 3.18pts, Gauteng 7.88pts. Yaseen Valli and Shaylen Pillay put on 226 for Gauteng's fifth wicket.*

At Walvis Bay, November 24–26, 2016. **Drawn. ‡Namibia 198 and 439-6** (M. G. Erasmus 192); **KwaZulu-Natal Inland 402-9 dec** (D. J. van Wyk 153). *Namibia 3.96pts, KwaZulu-Natal Inland 8.6pts.*

At Bloemfontein, December 8–9, 2016. **Free State won by an innings and 65 runs. Free State 375-5 dec** (P. J. van Biljon 116, P. Botha 111*); **‡Namibia 114** (T. I. Ntuli 6-45) **and 196** (D. Olivier 5-41). *Free State 19.5pts, Namibia 2pts. Off-spinner Tshepo Ntuli took a hat-trick.*

At Pietermaritzburg, December 8–10, 2016. **Drawn. ‡KwaZulu-Natal Inland 411-9 dec** (I. Khan 110, L. N. Mosena 113); **Easterns 177 and 178-6.** *KwaZulu-Natal Inland 9.62pts, Easterns 4.54pts.*

At Port Elizabeth (Grey HS), December 15–17, 2016. **Eastern Province won by ten wickets. ‡Boland 246 and 249** (T. Bokako 5-50); **Eastern Province 373** (M. L. Price 116) **and 124-0.** *Eastern Province 19.46pts, Boland 6.92pts. Eastern Province openers Edward Moore and Michael Price shared stands of 113 and 124*.*

At Johannesburg, December 15–17, 2016. **Gauteng won by 95 runs. Gauteng 331-2 dec** (Y. Valli 144, D. P. Conway 175*) **and 222-2 dec** (D. P. Conway 122*); **‡Namibia 317 and 141** (L. Mokoena 5-66). *Gauteng 18.62pts, Namibia 4.34pts. Valli and Devon Conway put on 303 for Gauteng's second wicket; Conway added another unbeaten century in the next innings.*

At Paarl, January 12–14, 2017. **Drawn. ‡Boland 238 and 139-1; Gauteng 374** (R. D. Rickelton 139, S. Pillay 118; N. Botha 6-108). *Boland 4.76pts, Gauteng 8.62pts.*

At Windhoek (Wanderers), January 12–14, 2017. **Drawn. ‡Namibia 230 and 165-9; Easterns 334** (W. B. Marshall 152). *Namibia 6.6pts, Easterns 8.68pts. Ernest Kemm (80) and Wesley Marshall opened with 212 for Easterns.*

At Bloemfontein, January 19–21, 2017. **Free State won by eight wickets. ‡Gauteng 270** (J. H. van Dyk 5-81) **and 269** (S. Pillay 108); **Free State 447** (M. N. Erlank 172, P. Botha 132) **and 93-2.** *Free State 20.38pts, Gauteng 5.4pts. Erlank and Patrick Botha added 213 for Free State's fourth wicket.*

At Windhoek (Wanderers), January 19–21, 2017. **Eastern Province won by eight wickets. ‡Namibia 271** (J. Dawood 5-89) **and 163** (J. Dawood 8-70); **Eastern Province 272** (D. van Schoor 6-86) **and 164-2.** *Eastern Province 17.44pts, Namibia 7.28pts. In his fourth first-class match, 20-year-old leg-spinner Junaid Dawood collected 13-159.*

At Bloemfontein, February 9–11, 2017. **Free State won by eight wickets. ‡Eastern Province 169 and 107; Free State 242 and 35-2.** *Free State 16.84pts, Eastern Province 5.38pts.*

At Port Elizabeth, February 23–25, 2017. **KwaZulu-Natal Inland won by 38 runs. KwaZulu-Natal Inland 270** (R. Pretorius 151) **and 206-9 dec** (L. B. Adam 5-68); **‡Eastern Province 196 and 242.** *KwaZulu-Natal Inland 17.4pts, Eastern Province 5.92pts. Craig Alexander ended KwaZulu-Natal Inland's first innings with a hat-trick; Pretorius responded with figures of 10–7–7–3.*

At Pietermaritzburg, March 9–11, 2017. **KwaZulu-Natal Inland won by six wickets. ‡Free State 160 and 138; KwaZulu-Natal Inland 187** (S. F. Mofokeng 5-49) **and 114-4.** *KwaZulu-Natal Inland 15.74pts, Free State 5.2pts.*

At Benoni, March 16–17, 2017. **Easterns won by nine wickets. ‡Boland 24-8 dec and 206; Easterns 196** (F. D. Adams 5-68) **and 38-1.** *Easterns 14.92pts, Boland 4pts.*

At Paarl, March 23–25, 2017. **Drawn. Namibia 279** (L. Louwrens 110; K. I. Simmonds 5-45) **and 326-7 dec** (C. G. Williams 152*; Z. Abrahams 5-98); ‡**Boland 250 and 288-7.** *Boland 7pts, Namibia 7.58pts.*

Cross Pool

At Walvis Bay, October 6–8, 2016. **Western Province won by an innings and 72 runs.** ‡**Western Province 397-6 dec** (P. J. Malan 211*); **Namibia 125 and 200.** *Western Province 18.46pts, Namibia 1pt. Pieter Malan scored a maiden double-hundred, before off-spinner Matthew Kleinveldt ended Namibia's first innings with a hat-trick.*

At Centurion, October 14–16, 2016. **Northerns won by ten wickets. Eastern Province 282** (G. L. Cloete 135; L. T. Ngidi 5-57) **and 73;** ‡**Northerns 336** (T. Bokako 5-75) **and 20-0.** *Northerns 18.72pts, Eastern Province 7.64pts.*

At Paarl, October 27–29, 2016. **Western Province won by an innings and 33 runs.** ‡**Boland 282** (F. D. Adams 132) **and 157; Western Province 472-6 dec** (P. J. Malan 204*, R. E. Levi 144). *Western Province 19.02pts, Boland 5.64pts. Malan made his second double-hundred – in the space of three matches – and added 243 with Richard Levi for the second wicket.*

At Benoni, October 27–29, 2016. **Easterns won by one wicket.** ‡**Easterns 378** (W. Coulentianos 119) **and 237-9; South Western Districts 209** (A. P. Agathangelou 109) **and 405-5 dec** (A. P. Agathangelou 199*). *Easterns 18.9pts, South Western Districts 5.18pts. On debut for South Western Districts, Agathangelou scored twin centuries; in the follow-on, he added 240 with Brendon Louw (95) for the fourth wicket but missed a maiden double when they declared at tea to set a target of 237 in 32 overs. Five Easterns batsmen were run out, but their last pair scraped home.*

At Bloemfontein, October 27–29, 2016. **Drawn. Border 442-7 dec** (G. V. J. Koopman 130, M. D. Walters 128) **and 183-5 dec;** ‡**Free State 363-9 dec** (J. L. du Plooy 103*). *Free State 6.66pts, Border 9.1pts. Gionne Koopman and Martin Walters put on 230 for Border's second wicket.*

At Pietermaritzburg, November 3–5, 2016. **Drawn. KwaZulu-Natal Inland 317-9 dec** (G. M. Dukes 102) **and 67-3;** ‡**South Western Districts 350** (A. P. Agathangelou 115*). *KwaZulu-Natal Inland 7.62pts, South Western Districts 8pts. Agathangelou made it three successive centuries.*

At Kimberley, November 10–12, 2016. **Drawn.** ‡**Boland 272 and 310-3** (D. G. Bedingham 107*); **Northern Cape 375-9 dec** (A. R. Swanepoel 167). *Northern Cape 9.5pts, Boland 7.44pts.*

At Windhoek (Wanderers), November 17–19, 2016. **North West won by an innings and 85 runs.** ‡**North West 421-6 dec** (J. N. Malan 174); **Namibia 167 and 169.** *North West 20.14pts, Namibia 3.34pts. Janneman Malan and Kagiso Rapulana added 259 for North West's second wicket.*

At Paarl, December 1–3, 2016. **Boland won by seven wickets.** ‡**South Western Districts 318** (N. B. Hornbuckle 109) **and 150** (K. I. Simmonds 6-49); **Boland 384** (F. D. Adams 146) **and 85-3.** *Boland 17.88pts, South Western Districts 6.36pts.*

At Kimberley, December 15–16, 2016. **KwaZulu-Natal Inland won by an innings and 33 runs.** ‡**Northern Cape 162 and 117; KwaZulu-Natal Inland 312** (P. E. Kruger 5-35). *KwaZulu-Natal Inland 18.24pts, Northern Cape 5.24pts.*

At Port Elizabeth, January 5–7, 2017. **Drawn. Eastern Province 144** (A. Gqamane 5-21) **and 194-3;** ‡**Border 352-9 dec**. *Eastern Province 4pts, Border 9.04pts.*

At Chatsworth, January 12–14, 2017. **Drawn. KwaZulu-Natal 374-5 dec** (D. Smit 121*, P. Subrayen 134*) **and 66-3;** ‡**Eastern Province 229.** *KwaZulu-Natal 7.74pts, Eastern Province 4.58pts. Daryn Smit and Prenelan Subrayen added 228* for KwaZulu-Natal's sixth wicket.*

At Benoni, January 19–21, 2017. **Drawn.** ‡**Easterns 289 and 184-4; Northerns 409-9 dec** (G. M. Thomson 106, S. von Berg 110*). *Easterns 6.78pts, Northerns 9.28pts.*

At Potchefstroom, January 19–21, 2017. **North West won by 82 runs. North West 298** (Z. C. Qwabe 5-74) **and 290-2 dec** (A. J. Malan 103*); ‡**Boland 313 and 193** (B. L. Barends 5-33). *North West 17.96pts, Boland 8.26pts.*

At Kimberley, January 26–28, 2017. **Free State won by 239 runs. Free State 236 and 277-8 dec;** ‡**Northern Cape 109** (L. M. Zuma 6-50) **and 165** (L. M. Zuma 5-53). *Free State 16.72pts, Northern Cape 4pts. Lwandiswa Zuma routed Northern Cape with 11-103.*

At Pietermaritzburg, February 9–11, 2017. **Drawn. KwaZulu-Natal 269-8 dec; ‡KwaZulu-Natal Inland 373-7** (S. Nhlebela 6-150). *KwaZulu-Natal Inland 8.46pts, KwaZulu-Natal 6.38pts.*

At Cape Town, February 9–11, 2017. **Western Province won by six wickets. ‡Easterns 288** (S. Masondo 107) **and 238** (G. F. Linde 6-101); **Western Province 207** (M. Arnold 5-60) **and 323-4** (P. J. Malan 133*). *Western Province 16.14pts, Easterns 7.76pts.*

At East London, February 16–18, 2017. **Easterns won by 84 runs. Easterns 177 and 183; ‡Border 141** (M. Arnold 5-41) **and 135** (T. L. N. Simelane 5-22). *Easterns 15.54pts, Border 4pts.*

At Chatsworth, February 16–18, 2017. **Free State won by six wickets. KwaZulu-Natal 69** (D. du Preez 5-18) **and 223** (S. F. Mofokeng 5-39); **‡Free State 116** (S. Nhlebela 7-33) **and 180-4.** *Free State 14pts, KwaZulu-Natal 4pts.*

At Potchefstroom, February 23–25, 2017. **Drawn. Gauteng 363-3 dec** (Y. Valli 103, M. Y. Cook 105*); **‡North West 438-6** (A. J. Malan 177*). *North West 7.76pts, Gauteng 7.24pts.*

At Oudtshoorn, March 2–3, 2017. **Namibia won by 70 runs. Namibia 44** (G. A. Stuurman 7-12) **and 212; ‡South Western Districts 88** (S. F. Burger 5-13) **and 98.** *Namibia 14pts, South Western Districts 4pts. Namibia won in two days despite being bowled out inside 17 overs on the first, when 22 wickets fell. Craig Williams scored 32* of their first-innings 44, and followed up with 74.*

At Port Elizabeth, March 9–11, 2017. **North West won by two wickets. Eastern Province 258 and 220** (J. N. Diseko 5-63); **‡North West 279** (R. H. Frenz 141; L. B. Adam 6-87) **and 200-8** (L. L. Sipamla 5-53). *North West 17.58pts, Eastern Province 7.16pts.*

At Johannesburg, March 9–11, 2017. **Gauteng won by an innings and 29 runs. Gauteng 370** (R. D. Rickelton 191); **‡KwaZulu-Natal 147 and 194** (S. H. Jamison 5-59). *Gauteng 19.4pts, KwaZulu-Natal 4pts. Ryan Rickelton and Pillay put on 201 for Gauteng's fourth wicket.*

At Centurion, March 9–11, 2017. **Northerns won by an innings and 83 runs. Namibia 236 and 172; ‡Northerns 491** (G. M. Thomson 221, R. Moonsamy 146). *Northerns 21.82pts, Namibia 6.72pts. Grant Thomson scored a maiden double-hundred and added 232 with Moonsamy for Northerns' third wicket.*

At Bloemfontein, March 16–18, 2017. **Northerns won by an innings and 42 runs. ‡Free State 190 and 100; Northerns 332** (M. Q. Adams 102). *Northerns 18.64pts, Free State 5.8pts.*

At Kimberley, March 16–18, 2017. **Drawn. ‡Northern Cape 550-8 dec** (G. J. Snyman 109, Z. A. Kathrada 103*) **and 124** (N. Burger 5-38); **Gauteng 487-8 dec** (K. Mogotsi 112*) **and 105-2.** *Northern Cape 9.54pts, Gauteng 8.28pts.*

At Johannesburg, March 23–25, 2017. **Drawn. ‡Gauteng 492-3 dec** (D. P. Conway 205*) **and 81-1; Border 223** (S. H. Jamison 5-40). *Gauteng 9.08pts, Border 2.46pts. Coming in at 75-1, Conway scored a maiden double-century and shared successive stands of 174, 107 and 136*.*

At Cape Town, March 23–25, 2017. **Drawn. Western Province 270 and 340-9** (P. J. Malan 164*); **‡KwaZulu-Natal Inland 307.** *Western Province 7.4pts, KwaZulu-Natal Inland 8.14pts. Malan's fifth hundred of the season took him past 1,000 first-class runs.*

Final At Pretoria (L. C. de Villiers), April 6–9, 2017. **Drawn. ‡Free State 285-9 dec** (R. S. Second 118*) **and 241-6 dec; Northerns 170** (L. M. Zuma 5-46) **and 198-5** (J. D. Vandiar 101*). *Second also scored his fifth century of the season, but Free State and Northerns shared the trophy.*

MOMENTUM ONE-DAY CUP IN 2016-17

50-over league plus knockout

	Played	*Won*	*Lost*	*NR*	*Bonus points*	*Points*	*NRR*
TITANS	10	7	3	0	5	33	1.27
KNIGHTS	10	6	4	0	3	27	0.30
WARRIORS	10	5	4	1	4	26	0.19
Dolphins	10	5	4	1	2	24	0.23
Lions	10	3	7	0	1	13	–0.95
Cape Cobras	10	3	7	0	1	12†	–0.93

† *1pt deducted for slow over-rate.*

Play-off At Bloemfontein, March 26, 2017. **No result. ‡Warriors 88-3** (28 overs) **v Knights.** *The match was replayed the following day.*

Play-off At Bloemfontein, March 27, 2017 (day/night). **Warriors won by 18 runs. ‡Warriors 249-7** (50 overs); **Knights 231-6** (50 overs). *Gihahn Cloete and Colin Ingram put on 104 for Warriors' second wicket, while Keegan Petersen and David Miller shared 110 for Knights' third.*

Final At Centurion, March 31, 2017 (day/night). **Titans won by 236 runs. ‡Titans 425-5** (50 overs) (A. K. Markram 161, H. Davids 114); **Warriors 189** (31 overs). *Titans ensured a massive win, and their second trophy of the season, with the highest total in South African domestic one-day cricket. Aiden Markram and Henry Davids – who finished as the tournament's leading scorer, with 673 – opened with 212 in 29.3 overs. Markram hit seven sixes in his 123-ball 161, and later Chris Morris thumped six as he raced to 47* in just 12 deliveries. Warriors barely lasted as long as Titans' opening stand.*

The CSA T20 Challenge has its own section (page 1112).

CSA PROVINCIAL 50-OVER CHALLENGE IN 2016-17

50-over league

Pool A	P	W	L	NR	Pts
NORTHERNS	10	8	1	1	40
KwaZulu-Natal	10	6	3	1	30
North West	10	6	4	0	27
Northern Cape	10	4	4	2	22
Western Province	10	4	5	1	18
South Western Districts	10	3	5	2	17
Border	10	2	7	1	11

Pool B	P	W	L	NR	Pts
NAMIBIA	10	6	4	0	27
Eastern Province	10	5	4	1	24
Easterns	10	4	4	2	21
Boland	10	4	5	1	19
Gauteng	10	4	5	1	18
Free State	10	4	6	0	17
KwaZulu-Natal Inland	10	2	5	3	16

Final At Centurion, April 2, 2017. **Northerns won by seven wickets. Namibia 245** (48.3 overs) (G. M. Thomson 5-50); **‡Northerns 251-3** (43.1 overs). *Grant Thomson bowled out Namibia, before Jonathan Vandiar and Tony de Zorzi put Northerns on their way with 161 for the second wicket. Vandiar was out two short of victory and one short of his century.*

AFRICA T20 CUP IN 2016-17

20-over league plus semi-finals and final

Pool A	P	W	L	NR	Pts
NORTH WEST	3	3	0	0	13
KZN Inland	3	1	2	0	5
Namibia	3	1	2	0	4
Western Province	3	1	2	0	4

Pool B	P	W	L	NR	Pts
N CAPE	3	2	0	1	11
Northerns	3	2	1	0	8
Kenya	3	1	2	0	4
SW Districts	3	0	2	1	2

Pool C	P	W	L	NR	Pts
Border	3	1	0	2	9
Free State	3	1	0	2	8
ZIMBABWE	3	0	1	2	4
Easterns	3	0	1	2	4

Pool D	P	W	L	NR	Pts
E PROVINCE	3	3	0	0	13
Gauteng	3	2	1	0	9
Boland	3	1	2	0	4
KwaZulu-Natal	3	0	3	0	0

After four of the six Pool C matches were washed out, the other two results were declared null and void, and a draw determined which team would play in the semi-finals; Zimbabwe went through.

Semi-final At Oudtshoorn, September 30, 2016. **Eastern Province won by 76 runs. Eastern Province 163-8** (20 overs); **‡Zimbabwe 87** (18.5 overs).

Semi-final At Oudtshoorn, September 30, 2016. **Tied. ‡North West 181-6** (20 overs); **Northern Cape 181-6** (20 overs). *Northern Cape won an eliminator over, scoring 22-0 to North West's 9-0.*

Final At Oudtshoorn, October 1, 2016. **Eastern Province won by 31 runs. ‡Eastern Province 165-6** (20 overs); **Northern Cape 134-9** (20 overs). *Eastern Province won with a 100% record.*

SRI LANKAN CRICKET IN 2017

From bleakness to bravery

SA'ADI THAWFEEQ

Sri Lanka were happy to see the end of a wretched 2017. Their fortunes dipped so low that even their most ardent supporters turned their backs. And at Pallekele in August, the dissatisfaction found violent expression during a one-day international against India, when the crowd hurled plastic objects on to the pitch, stopping play for more than half an hour.

The crunch came in England in June, when Sri Lanka failed to progress from the group stage of the Champions Trophy. Graham Ford, 15 months into a second stint as head coach, stepped down, even though his contract ran until the 2019 World Cup. It emerged that his relationship with Sri Lanka Cricket had been strained by the appointment of Asanka Gurusinha – a member of the 1996 World Cup-winning team – first as cricket manager and then also as a selector. Ford felt he was no longer in control, and resigned.

SRI LANKA IN 2017

	Played	*Won*	*Lost*	*Drawn/No result*
Tests	13	4	7	2
One-day internationals	29	5	23	1
Twenty20 internationals	15	5	10	–

DECEMBER / JANUARY	3 Tests, 5 ODIs and 3 T20Is (a) v South Africa	(see *Wisden 2017*, page 1024)
FEBRUARY	3 T20Is (a) v Australia	(page 798)
MARCH / APRIL	2 Tests, 3 ODIs and 2 T20Is (h) v Bangladesh	(page 978)
MAY		
JUNE / JULY	ICC Champions Trophy (in England)	(page 263)
	1 Test and 5 ODIs (h) v Zimbabwe	(page 985)
AUGUST / SEPTEMBER	3 Tests, 5 ODIs and 1 T20I (h) v India	(page 990)
OCTOBER	2 Tests, 5 ODIs and 3 T20Is (a) v Pakistan (in UAE and Pakistan)	(page 933)
NOVEMBER / DECEMBER	3 Tests, 3 ODIs and 3 T20Is (a) v India	(page 859)

For a review of Sri Lankan domestic cricket from the 2016-17 season, see page 1004.

Ishara S. Kodikara, AFP/Getty Images

Hand on heart: despite the prowess of Rangana Herath and Dinesh Chandimal, Sri Lanka endured a poor 2017.

Sri Lanka did not find it easy to recruit a replacement, and for the next six months they made do with former South Africa and Hampshire wicketkeeper Nic Pothas, who had been in charge of the team's fielding but had no previous experience of handling a national side. There were successes in his tenure – Sri Lanka beat Pakistan 2–0 in a Test series in the UAE, and inflicted a rare ODI defeat on India on a green Dharamsala pitch – yet the overall performance was dreadful.

It was hard to identify the nadir. Losing a one-day series to Zimbabwe soon after the Champions Trophy was a possibility, and for a while it looked as if they might be defeated in the Test that followed; ultimately, though, they overhauled a target of 388. Next came a truly awful sequence at home to India, when they were whitewashed in all formats. Then, after the Test win against Pakistan, they were worsted 5–0 in the 50-over matches, and 3–0 in the Twenty20s. Things didn't improve much: SLC brought forward to December a tour of India that had been scheduled for March 2018. And so, still in the early stages of rebuilding, Sri Lanka faced their tormentors barely three months after they had crushed them at home. Now they lost 1–0 in the three-Test series, then 2–1 in the ODIs and 3–0 in the T20Is.

So many defeats heaped pressure on politician-cum-SLC-president Thilanga Sumathipala to resign. But he was adamant he would see out his two-year term, which ended in January 2018, claiming the administration were blameless for the on-field slump. Many doubted that, and there were reports that interference by high-ranking SLC officials had twice prompted the selection committee of former captain Sanath Jayasuriya to threaten to resign.

SLC were also accused of diluting the first-class tournament by increasing the number of participating teams from 14 to 24; the motive, allegedly, was to gain votes in the May 2018 board elections that would keep them in power for another term. The Jayasuriya-led committee did eventually tender their resignation after the crowd disruption at Pallekele. He was criticised for making too many changes, having no clear vision, and failing to persist with talented players. In the 16 months in which his committee were in place, Sri Lanka fielded 52 cricketers across formats, including 41 in ODIs alone.

Their problems had begun before the Champions Trophy. As 2016 faded into 2017, they were swept aside by South Africa in Tests and one-dayers (restoring a modicum of pride in the Twenty20 games in between). Then came a drawn Test series which included Bangladesh's first victory in Sri Lanka.

A year characterised by defeat had other knock-on effects. Angelo Mathews quit as captain of all three sides in the wake of the humiliation by Zimbabwe, pitching the team into even choppier waters. Because of resignation and injury, the Sri Lankan ship was in the charge of five different skippers, but none could navigate a happy course, especially not in the shorter formats. In 2017, they lost 23 of 28 completed ODIs and ten of 15 T20Is.

Despite the gloom, some optimism remained. Two of the year's captains prospered, at least on an individual level. Dinesh Chandimal hit three hundreds – including 164 in the Delhi smog – and in 2017 totalled 1,003 Test runs at 45 (Dimuth Karunaratne made 1,031, though at 39). Rangana Herath, meanwhile, who took 52 wickets at 27, was the only regular bowler to average under 40; in October, he became the first left-arm spinner to reach 400 Test wickets.

A new selection committee, under former fast bowler Graeme Labrooy, had been appointed in September; three months later, Chandika Hathurusinghe, the Sri Lankan Test all-rounder who had guided Bangladesh to unprecedented success, was made the new head coach. He was promised a role free from external intervention. And in January 2018, Mathews was restored to the limited-overs captaincy.

If there was renewed hope that such changes might see Sri Lanka cricket turn a corner, there was one other story of renewed hope: back in October, they bravely did their bit to help re-establish international cricket in Pakistan by playing a Twenty20 match in Lahore, scene of the 2009 terrorist attack on their team bus.

SRI LANKA v BANGLADESH IN 2016-17

FIDEL FERNANDO

Test matches (2): Sri Lanka 1, Bangladesh 1
One-day internationals (3): Sri Lanka 1, Bangladesh 1
Twenty20 internationals (2): Sri Lanka 1, Bangladesh 1

Muttiah Muralitharan's record is often derided for containing too many Bangladeshi wickets. Kumar Sangakkara occasionally seemed bored while amassing 1,816 Test runs against them at an average of 95. In 16 previous Tests, Sri Lanka had won 14 at a canter, and were unthreatened in two draws. In their inaugural Test encounter in 2001-02, two batsmen had even retired out, in a total of 555 for five, after their attack had dismissed Bangladesh for 90.

But teams rise and dynasties fall. On this tour, the world discovered that the curve of Test cricket's youngest nation had intersected with that of their long-time tormentors. Arriving in Sri Lanka with newly minted confidence, Bangladesh rode the momentum of two excellent years, in which charismatic bowlers, and batsmen with delicious timing. had emerged. A few months earlier, they had beaten England at home; a Test win at the P. Sara Oval was an even greater landmark.

Bangladesh could take immense pleasure from drawing 1–1 in all three formats: on the heels of disappointing tours of New Zealand and India, they had proved they could win away from home. And yet, despite the sense of history, the team greeted their success calmly. Gone were the batsmen's convulsive celebrations on reaching three figures; instead, they raised their bats in dignified manner, and carefully retook their guard. Rarely did the bowlers indulge in hollering or extravagant send-offs. Even the handsome victory in the Second Test prompted measured jubilation.

To underscore their serious intentions, Bangladesh played some serious cricket. In the Test win, left-arm seamer Mustafizur Rahman bowled with exceptional wit and quality on the fourth afternoon. Tamim Iqbal's batting in the run-chase, and his century in the first one-day international, were intelligently paced. Shakib Al Hasan and Mushfiqur Rahim made contributions befitting their seniority, while less experienced men such as Soumya Sarkar and Mehedi Hasan were skilful and vivacious. It was difficult not to feel that Bangladesh's recent upswing would continue, more surely than it did after they defeated a second-string West Indian side in the Caribbean in 2009.

Beset by bumbling administration and a crumbling domestic system, meanwhile, Sri Lanka faced uncertainty. Murali, Sangakkara and Mahela Jayawardene were gone; Angelo Mathews was injured. Standing in for him as Test captain, Rangana Herath tried to save his team embarrassment, but received only fleeting support from his batsmen. There were some moments of joy, thanks to a clutch of their own youngsters. Kusal Mendis, aged 22, hit the highest score in any of the games, 194 in the First Test, and left-arm wrist-spinner Lakshan Sandakan further demonstrated his promise. But the tour brought the Sri Lankan set-up's shortcomings into sharp focus. Abysmal fielding, inconsistency in selection policy, and the decline of the domestic competitions all came in for caustic criticism.

There was one more small consolation. With their former players Chandika Hathurusinghe, Thilan Samaraweera and Mario Villavarayan all coaching the opposition, Sri Lanka had staffed the backroom of what was Bangladesh's finest away tour.

BANGLADESH TOURING PARTY

*Mushfiqur Rahim (T/50/20), Imrul Kayes (T/50/20), Kamrul Islam (T), Liton Das (T), Mahmudullah (T/50/20), Mashrafe bin Mortaza (50/20), Mehedi Hasan (T/50/20), Mohammad Saifuddin (20), Mominul Haque (T), Mosaddek Hossain (T/50/20), Mustafizur Rahman (T/50/20), Nurul Hasan (50/20), Rubel Hossain (T), Sabbir Rahman (T/50/20), Sanjamul Islam (50/20), Shakib Al Hasan (T/50/20), Shuvagata Hom (50), Soumya Sarkar (T/50/20), Subashis Roy (T/50/20), Taijul Islam (T), Tamim Iqbal (T/50/20), Taskin Ahmed (T/50/20). *Coach:* U. C. Hathurusinghe.

Mashrafe bin Mortaza captained in the limited-overs matches. Imrul Kayes arrived for the Second Test after recovering from a thigh injury. Mehedi Hasan was a late addition to the ODI squad.

SRI LANKA v BANGLADESH

First Test

At Galle, March 7–11, 2017. Sri Lanka won by 259 runs. Toss: Sri Lanka.

This Test followed a familiar course, with no hint of the chastening that awaited Sri Lanka in Colombo. Their strategy at Galle has often been simple: bat first, bat big, then let the spinners loose. The execution was clinical.

Kusal Mendis was the primary architect of the victory, though he did have a vital reprieve. Having played extravagantly outside his off stump during Sri Lanka's recent tour of South Africa, he nicked his first delivery, but was saved by a Subashis Roy no-ball. Thus startled into conservatism, Mendis played himself in before venturing his more ambitious strokes; it was only after he had hit an unusually compact fifty that the booming drives, searing cuts, rapid sweeps and merry jaunts down the pitch returned. Batting nearly seven and a half hours and narrowly missing a maiden double-century, Mendis put on 196 with the responsible Gunaratne and 110 with Dickwella, who scored a run a ball. Dilruwan Perera added another half-century to guide Sri Lanka to 494. Only off-spinner Mehedi Hasan, England's nemesis in the October Test series, seemed capable of breaking the big stands, picking up four for 113.

Bangladesh made a promising start, as Tamim Iqbal and Soumya Sarkar put on 118, but Tamim surrendered his wicket heedlessly – looking for a single while wrongly imagining the ball had beaten wicketkeeper Dickwella, who was up to the stumps – and Sri Lanka's spinners worked their way into the batting. Though Mehedi shared a century stand with his captain, Mushfiqur Rahim, which took them to 298 for six, the last four wickets fell for 14 as Perera and Herath claimed three apiece.

MOST FIVE-WICKET HAULS IN FOURTH INNINGS OF A TEST

			Fourth-innings figures		
			W	*BB*	*Avge*
10	**H. M. R. K. B. Herath (SL)**	**SLA**	**94**	**8-63**	**19.09**
7	S. K. Warne (A)	LB	138	8-71	23.14
7	M. Muralitharan (SL)	OB	106	8-46	21.01
6	**R. Ashwin (I)**	**OB**	**56**	**7-59**	**15.71**
5	G. D. McGrath (A)	RFM	103	8-24	19.49
5	A. Kumble (I)	LB	94	10-74	22.39
5	B. S. Bedi (I)	SLA	60	6-42	14.46
5	Wasim Akram (P)	LF	59	5-43	21.66
5	D. W. Steyn (SA)	RF	48	5-33	23.64

Sri Lanka led by 182, and some thought they batted on too long before declaring. Tharanga's attractive hundred – his first in home Tests – helped them extend their advantage to 429 by tea on the fourth day. But, seemingly intent on providing the out-of-sorts Chandimal with a chance to regain form, Herath delayed another five overs until he reached 50, by which time the target was 457.

Sri Lanka could have got away with far fewer, so meekly did Bangladesh succumb. Their openers shared another half-century stand, but resistance grew thin once that was broken: after a 49-ball 53 from Soumya, no one else passed 35. The Galle surface was unusually flat, but Herath squeezed enough life from it to winkle out the middle and lower order. He collected his ninth five-wicket haul on this ground, and his tenth in the fourth innings of a Test. Herath's nine wickets in the match also took him to 366 overall, past Daniel Vettori as the most successful slow left-armer in Test cricket. He bowled out Bangladesh midway through the final afternoon – his third win in three as acting-captain.

Man of the Match: B. K. G. Mendis.

Close of play: first day, Sri Lanka 321-4 (Mendis 166, Dickwella 14); second day, Bangladesh 133-2 (Soumya Sarkar 66, Mushfiqur Rahim 1); third day, Bangladesh 312; fourth day, Bangladesh 67-0 (Tamim Iqbal 13, Soumya Sarkar 53).

Sri Lanka

First innings		Second innings	
F. D. M. Karunaratne b Mehedi Hasan	30	– c Mahmudullah b Taskin Ahmed	32
W. U. Tharanga b Subashis Roy	4	– b Mehedi Hasan	115
B. K. G. Mendis c Tamim Iqbal b Mehedi Hasan	194	– c Taskin Ahmed b Shakib Al Hasan	19
L. D. Chandimal c Mehedi Hasan b Mustafizur Rahman	5	– not out	50
D. A. S. Gunaratne b Taskin Ahmed	85	– b Shakib Al Hasan	0
†D. P. D. N. Dickwella c Mahmudullah b Mehedi Hasan	75	– c Liton Das b Mehedi Hasan	15
M. D. K. Perera lbw b Mehedi Hasan	51	– c Liton Das b Mustafizur Rahman	33
*H. M. R. K. B. Herath c Soumya Sarkar b Mustafizur Rahman	14		
R. A. S. Lakmal run out	8		
P. A. D. L. R. Sandakan c Mehedi Hasan b Shakib Al Hasan	5		
C. B. R. L. S. Kumara not out	0		
B 4, lb 10, w 4, nb 5	23	B 2, lb 1, w 6, nb 1	10
1/15 (2) 2/60 (1) 3/92 (4) 4/288 (5) 5/398 (3) 6/432 (6) 7/457 (8) 8/480 (9) 9/494 (7) 10/494 (10) (129.1 overs)	494	1/69 (1) 2/134 (3) 3/198 (2) 4/199 (5) 5/222 (6) 6/274 (7) (6 wkts dec, 69 overs)	274

Mustafizur Rahman 25–5–68–2; Taskin Ahmed 21–3–77–1; Subashis Roy 24–4–103–1; Mehedi Hasan 22–1–113–4; Shakib Al Hasan 32.1–5–100–1; Soumya Sarkar 3–0–9–0; Mahmudullah 2–0–10–0. *Second innings*—Subashis Roy 7–0–34–0; Mehedi Hasan 20–1–77–2; Mustafizur Rahman 9–4–24–1; Shakib Al Hasan 25–2–104–2; Taskin Ahmed 8–0–32–1.

Bangladesh

Tamim Iqbal run out	57	– c Gunaratne b Perera	19
Soumya Sarkar c Kumara b Lakmal	71	– b Gunaratne	53
Mominul Haque lbw b Perera	7	– lbw b Perera	5
*Mushfiqur Rahim b Herath	85	– c Dickwella b Sandakan	34
Shakib Al Hasan c Dickwella b Sandakan	23	– c Karunaratne b Herath	8
Mahmudullah b Kumara	8	– lbw b Herath	0
†Liton Das c Gunaratne b Herath	5	– c Tharanga b Herath	35
Mehedi Hasan lbw b Perera	41	– c Kumara b Herath	28
Taskin Ahmed lbw b Perera	0	– c Mendis b Herath	5
Subashis Roy not out	0	– (11) not out	0
Mustafizur Rahman c Mendis b Herath	4	– (10) b Herath	0
Lb 6, w 3, nb 2	11	B 1, lb 4, w 1, nb 4	10
1/118 (1) 2/127 (3) 3/142 (2) (97.2 overs)	312	1/67 (2) 2/80 (3) (60.2 overs)	197
4/170 (5) 5/184 (6) 6/192 (7)		3/83 (1) 4/104 (5)	
7/298 (8) 8/298 (9) 9/308 (4) 10/312 (11)		5/104 (6) 6/158 (4) 7/166 (7)	
		8/180 (9) 9/194 (10) 10/197 (8)	

Lakmal 14–0–42–1; Kumara 16–1–70–1; Perera 19–4–53–3; Herath 26.2–4–72–3; Sandakan 22–5–69–1. *Second innings*—Lakmal 7–3–12–0; Perera 15–0–66–2; Herath 20.2–5–59–6; Gunaratne 6–1–16–1; Sandakan 9–0–29–1; Kumara 3–0–10–0.

Umpires: Aleem Dar and M. Erasmus. Third umpire: S. Ravi.
Referee: A. J. Pycroft.

SRI LANKA v BANGLADESH

Second Test

At Colombo (PSO), March 15–19, 2017. Bangladesh won by four wickets. Toss: Sri Lanka. Test debut: Mosaddek Hossain.

Bangladesh's 100th Test produced their ninth win, and their first over Sri Lanka. Two passages of play defined the match. The first was an hour of mutual incompetence at the end of the second day, when Bangladesh sought to collapse in witless fashion, while Sri Lanka's slapstick fielding denied them this self-sabotage. The second was a spell of searing fast bowling on the fourth when, surging in from round the wicket, Mustafizur Rahman broke Sri Lanka's middle order and cracked the game open.

The closing stages of the second day were not without comedic charm. For a couple of years, Sri Lanka had operated as if their fielding coach was Charlie Chaplin, often fist-bumping the ball instead of catching it, sometimes escorting it valiantly to the fence. They were in vintage form here, as fielders repeatedly dived over the ball, palmed it towards the boundary, and spilled two straightforward catches.

Meanwhile, Bangladesh's batsmen seemed determined to get out. At 165 for two, responding to Sri Lanka's 338, Imrul Kayes sent an innocuous short delivery to deep square leg, where Chandimal – whose 138 had helped his side recover from 70 for four – made an awful mess of it. Kayes was soon out regardless, nightwatchman Taijul Islam contributed a golden duck and, in the next over, Sabbir Rahman fell to the short-ball trap, tenderly stroking to de Silva at leg slip, moments after watching him move into position. Shakib Al Hasan was dropped off the fifth delivery he faced, on the square-leg boundary by Tharanga – and it was this miss that would haunt Sri Lanka. Had it been held, Bangladesh would have been 206 for six, but Shakib batted with far greater maturity on the third day, hitting 116 with solid support from Mushfiqur Rahim and Mosaddek Hossain, who steered them to a 129-run lead.

Sri Lanka cleared the deficit by lunch on the fourth, with nine wickets still in hand. Then Mustafizur's magic began. Angling the ball into the right-handers, then nipping it away, he had Mendis nicking behind in his first over of the afternoon, before dismissing

BANGLADESH'S FIRST 100 TESTS

Tests	*W*	*L*	*D*	*Tests*	*W*	*L*	*D*
1–10	0	9	1	51–60	1	8	1
11–20	0	10	0	61–70	1	8	1
21–30	0	8	2	71–80	1	7	2
31–40	1	8	1	81–90	3	4	3
41–50	0	9	1	91–100	2	5	3

The first 100 Tests produced 9 wins, 76 defeats and 15 draws.

Chandimal and de Silva in identical fashion, in a spell of 7–1–24–3. Karunaratne completed a century before becoming one of four victims for Shakib and, an hour into the final day, Bangladesh found themselves needing 191 for victory. With the pitch not yet spitting for the spinners, it looked difficult but gettable.

Briefly, it seemed as if Herath's fourth-innings charms would sink them again: sharing the new ball with Perera, he struck twice in his fourth over to leave Bangladesh 22 for two. At the other end, however, was Tamim Iqbal. He had endured a quiet few months, but chose this moment to produce one of the most measured and valuable innings of his career. He did not hit a boundary until he had faced 36 balls and, for much of his stay, took only chanceless runs into the outfield; in the past, such intense pressure might have panicked him into hitting out. He did attack eventually – a four and six off successive Sandakan deliveries – but only after he had crossed 50. Sri Lanka's hopes rekindled when they dismissed him for 82, still 60 short of victory, but there was too much quality in the middle order to let the match slip. Mushfiqur helped them over the line with four wickets in hand, and teenager Mehedi Hasan hit the winning runs to complete Bangladesh's first away victory in nearly four years – only their fourth overall in 47 Tests – and prompt decorous celebrations.

Man of the Match: Tamim Iqbal. *Man of the Series:* Shakib Al Hasan.

Close of play: first day, Sri Lanka 238-7 (Chandimal 86, Herath 18); second day, Bangladesh 214-5 (Shakib Al Hasan 18, Mushfiqur Rahim 2); third day, Sri Lanka 54-0 (Karunaratne 25, Tharanga 25); fourth day, Sri Lanka 268-8 (Perera 26, Lakmal 16).

Sri Lanka

Batsman	First innings		Second innings	
F. D. M. Karunaratne	c Mehedi Hasan b Mustafizur Rahman	7	c Soumya Sarkar b Shakib Al Hasan	126
W. U. Tharanga	c Soumya Sarkar b Mehedi Hasan	11	b Mehedi Hasan	26
B. K. G. Mendis	st Mushfiqur Rahim b Mehedi Hasan	5	c Mushfiqur Rahim b Mustafizur Rahman	36
L. D. Chandimal	c Mosaddek Hossain b Mehedi Hasan	138	c Mushfiqur Rahim b Mustafizur Rahman	5
D. A. S. Gunaratne	lbw b Subashis Roy	13	lbw b Shakib Al Hasan	7
D. M. de Silva	b Taijul Islam	34	c Mushfiqur Rahim b Mustafizur Rahman	0
†D. P. D. N. Dickwella	b Shakib Al Hasan	34	c Mushfiqur Rahim b Shakib Al Hasan	5
M. D. K. Perera	c Soumya Sarkar b Mustafizur Rahman	9	run out	50
*H. M. R. K. B. Herath	c Soumya Sarkar b Shakib Al Hasan	25	lbw b Taijul Islam	9
R. A. S. Lakmal	c Soumya Sarkar b Subashis Roy	35	c Mosaddek Hossain b Shakib Al Hasan	42
P. A. D. L. R. Sandakan	not out	5	not out	0
	B 1, lb 13, w 6, nb 2	22	B 4, lb 8, w 1	13
	1/13 (1) 2/24 (3) 3/35 (2) 4/70 (5) 5/136 (6) 6/180 (7) 7/195 (8) 8/250 (9) 9/305 (4) 10/338 (10) (113.3 overs)	338	1/57 (2) 2/143 (3) 3/165 (4) 4/176 (5) 5/177 (6) 6/190 (7) 7/217 (1) 8/238 (9) 9/318 (8) 10/319 (10) (113.2 overs)	319

Mustafizur Rahman 21–6–50–2; Subashis Roy 17.3–2–53–2; Mehedi Hasan 21–2–90–3; Taijul Islam 17–2–40–1; Shakib Al Hasan 33–4–80–2; Mosaddek Hossain 4–0–11–0. *Second innings*—Subashis Roy 16–4–36–0; Mehedi Hasan 24–0–71–1; Mustafizur Rahman 23–3–78–3; Shakib Al Hasan 36.2–9–74–4; Mosaddek Hossain 3–0–10–0; Taijul Islam 11–1–38–1.

Bangladesh

Tamim Iqbal lbw b Herath	49	– c Chandimal b Perera	82
Soumya Sarkar b Sandakan	61	– c Tharanga b Herath	10
Imrul Kayes lbw b Sandakan	34	– c Gunaratne b Herath	0
Sabbir Rahman c de Silva b Lakmal	42	– lbw b Perera	41
Taijul Islam lbw b Sandakan	0		
Shakib Al Hasan c Chandimal b Sandakan	116	– (5) b Perera	15
*†Mushfiqur Rahim b Lakmal	52	– (6) not out	22
Mosaddek Hossain st Dickwella b Herath	75	– (7) c Dickwella b Herath	13
Mehedi Hasan lbw b Herath	24	– (8) not out	2
Mustafizur Rahman lbw b Herath	0		
Subashis Roy not out	0		
B 4, lb 8, w 2	14	B 4, lb 1, w 1	6
1/95 (1) 2/130 (2) 3/192 (3) 4/192 (5) 5/198 (4) 6/290 (7) 7/421 (6) 8/454 (9) 9/454 (10) 10/467 (8) (134.1 overs)	467	1/22 (2) 2/22 (3) 3/131 (1) 4/143 (4) 5/162 (5) 6/189 (7) (6 wkts, 57.5 overs)	191

Lakmal 25–3–90–2; Perera 33–5–100–0; Herath 34.1–6–82–4; Gunaratne 7–0–38–0; Sandakan 33–2–140–4; de Silva 2–0–5–0. *Second innings*—Perera 22–1–59–3; Herath 24.5–2–75–3; de Silva 2–0–7–0; Sandakan 6–1–34–0; Lakmal 2–0–7–0; Gunaratne 1–0–4–0.

Umpires: Aleem Dar and S. Ravi. Third umpire: M. Erasmus.
Referee: A. J. Pycroft.

First one-day international At Dambulla, March 25, 2017 (day/night). **Bangladesh won by 90 runs. Bangladesh 324-5** (50 overs) (Tamim Iqbal 127, Sabbir Rahman 54, Shakib Al Hasan 72); **‡Sri Lanka 234** (45.1 overs) (L. D. Chandimal 59, S. S. Pathirana 31, N. L. T. C. Perera 55; Mustafizur Rahman 3-56). *MoM:* Tamim Iqbal. *ODI debut:* Mehedi Hasan (Bangladesh). *Tamim Iqbal crafted a mature 127 off 142 balls. He was efficient in the powerplay, moving smoothly to 25 off 28, then unhurried when the field spread – he struck only two fours in his next 66 deliveries – before gathering momentum with nine, plus a six, in his last 48. Tamim left it to his team-mates to spur on the run-rate, against bowling that sometimes seemed listless: Sabbir Rahman hit 54 off 56 balls, and Shakib Al Hasan 72 off 71, helping plunder 109 from the last ten overs. Bangladesh's 324 was their third-highest ODI total, and best away from home. Sri Lanka lost too many top-order batsmen too quickly; though No. 8 Tissara Perera struck a 35-ball 55, Mustafizur Rahman's third wicket wrapped up the win.*

Second one-day international At Dambulla, March 28, 2017 (day/night). **No result. ‡Sri Lanka 311** (49.5 overs) (W. U. Tharanga 65, B. K. G. Mendis 102, D. A. S. Gunaratne 39, T. A. M. Siriwardene 30; Taskin Ahmed 4-47) **v Bangladesh.** *It was Sri Lanka's turn to bat first and pass 300, but they were denied by rain; no team had won an ODI in Sri Lanka chasing over 300. Given the foundation provided by Kusal Mendis's maiden one-day hundred, they could have managed even more. Mendis shared two big partnerships – 111 for the second wicket with Upul Tharanga, and 83 for the third with Dinesh Chandimal (24) – and departed in the 38th over, at 216-4. But six wickets fell in the last five overs, including two to run-outs, and a hat-trick to Taskin Ahmed, Bangladesh's fifth in ODIs.*

Third one-day international At Colombo (SSC), April 1, 2017. **Sri Lanka won by 70 runs. Sri Lanka 280-9** (50 overs) (M. D. Gunathilleke 34, W. U. Tharanga 35, B. K. G. Mendis 54, D. A. S. Gunaratne 34, N. L. T. C. Perera 52; Mashrafe bin Mortaza 3-65); **‡Bangladesh 210** (44.3 overs) (Soumya Sarkar 38, Shakib Al Hasan 54, Mehedi Hasan 51; K. M. D. N. Kulasekara 4-37). *MoM:* N. L. T. C. Perera. *MoS:* B. K. G. Mendis. *Riding a fast start and a fast finish, Sri Lanka scored a competitive 280-9, then bowled and fielded with spirit to level the series – and snap a losing streak of six ODIs. Tharanga and Dhanushka Gunathilleke smashed 76 in the powerplay, Mendis contributed a half-century, and Perera a closing salvo. Virtually all the frontline bowlers then delivered good spells; Nuwan Kulasekara collected his best figures since November 2013, relying* *on tight lines and nous rather than his once-characteristic inswing. Bangladesh collapsed to 11-3, then 118-6 in the 24th over. They were briefly kept afloat by an energetic maiden ODI fifty from Mehedi Hasan at No. 8, proving the pitch remained a good one.*

First Twenty20 international At Colombo (RPS), April 4, 2017 (floodlit). **Sri Lanka won by six wickets.** ‡**Bangladesh 155-6** (20 overs) (Mosaddek Hossain 34*, Mahmudullah 31); **Sri Lanka 158-4** (18.5 overs) (M. D. K. J. Perera 77). *MoM:* M. D. K. J. Perera. *T20I debut:* Mohammad Saifuddin (Bangladesh). *Dropped in South Africa, Kusal Perera made a roaring return, cracking 77 off 53 balls in Sri Lanka's successful hunt. He hit only five off his first eight deliveries, then smoked four fours and a six off his next seven. Tharanga, who had provided the initial impetus, departed in the next over, but Perera reached 50 in 31 balls and almost saw the chase through: Sri Lanka needed only nine when he fell, which they gathered in the next four deliveries. They could thank their bowlers for leaving only 156 to chase; Bangladesh had raced to 57-1 in five overs, but stumbled as the attack surged back, despite Mosaddek Hossain's 34*.*

Second Twenty20 international At Colombo (RPS), April 6, 2017 (floodlit). **Bangladesh won by 45 runs.** ‡**Bangladesh 176-9** (20 overs) (Imrul Kayes 36, Soumya Sarkar 34, Shakib Al Hasan 38; S. L. Malinga 3-34); **Sri Lanka 131** (18 overs) (C. K. Kapugedera 50; Shakib Al Hasan 3-24, Mustafizur Rahman 4-21). *MoM:* Shakib Al Hasan. *MoS:* S. L. Malinga. *T20I debut:* Mehedi Hasan (Bangladesh). *A thundering start with the bat and incisive turn with the new ball ensured Bangladesh drew all three series 1–1, and provided a happy swansong for their captain, Mashrafe bin Mortaza, who had announced his retirement from Twenty20s at the toss of the previous match. This game was won and lost in the first six overs of each innings: Bangladesh's openers – Imrul Kayes and Soumya Sarkar – were fearless in their powerplay, hustling 68 stylish runs without loss, while Sri Lanka slumped to 47-5. Shakib Al Hasan followed up his side's top score, a 31-ball 38, with three wickets, and Mustafizur Rahman claimed four. Sri Lanka's best moment came when Malinga took a hat-trick in Bangladesh's penultimate over – to go with his three in ODIs. Only Wasim Akram, with two in Tests and two in ODIs, had previously claimed four at international level.*

SRI LANKA v ZIMBABWE IN 2017

SA'ADI THAWFEEQ

One-day internationals (5): Sri Lanka 2, Zimbabwe 3
Test match (1): Sri Lanka 1, Zimbabwe 0

Zimbabwe's first tour of Sri Lanka in more than 15 years was not expected to be a success. In 2016, they had been soundly beaten at home by the Sri Lankans, with red ball and white. And their form in 2017 had been indifferent: they had lost a one-day series against Afghanistan, drawn 1–1 with Scotland, and only edged past the Netherlands.

The first one-day international changed expectations: Zimbabwe pulled off a record chase in Sri Lanka – and did it comfortably. The hosts hit back, winning the next two games. Openers Niroshan Dickwella and Dhanushka Gunathilleke constructed the first of consecutive double-century stands in Hambantota. But the second was not enough to prevent a rain-affected defeat and, when the pair were separated early in the decider, Zimbabwe had the belief to secure their first one-day series win against Sri Lanka. "It's one of the lowest points in my career," said Angelo Mathews. A day later, he resigned the captaincy in all formats. It was all a chastening experience for interim coach, Nic Pothas.

Zimbabwe's slow bowlers, led by leg-spinning captain Graeme Cremer, performed with stifling accuracy. And their own batsmen countered the familiar Sri Lankan spin challenge well, using their feet bravely and sweeping with authority. It all gave the tourists much confidence ahead of the only Test. The match swung back and forth, with Zimbabwe showing doggedness to recover from two early collapses. When Sikandar Raza's maiden Test hundred helped lift Sri Lanka's target to 388, the tourists were on the verge of a historic victory. But Dickwella and Asela Gunaratne spared any more blushes, shepherding an excellent chase. It was a badly needed victory for new Test captain Dinesh Chandimal ahead of a tough series against India.

ZIMBABWE TOURING PARTY

*A. G. Cremer (T/50), R. P. Burl (T/50), R. W. Chakabva (T), T. L. Chatara (T/50), C. J. Chibhabha (50), C. R. Ervine (T/50), H. Masakadza (T/50), W. P. Masakadza (50), S. F. Mire (50), P. J. Moor (T/50), C. B. Mpofu (T/50), N. M'shangwe (T), C. T. Mumba (T/50), T. K. Musakanda (T/50), R. Ngarava (50), Sikandar Raza (T/50), D. T. Tiripano (T/50), M. N. Waller (T/50), N. R. Waller (T), S. C. Williams (T/50). *Coach:* H. H. Streak.

W. P. Masakadza was originally picked in the one-day squad, but sprained an ankle before the first game. He was replaced by Mumba, who had been named in the Test party, but he injured his knee in the third ODI and did not play again on the tour.

First one-day international At Galle, June 30. **Zimbabwe won by six wickets.** ‡**Sri Lanka 316-5** (50 overs) (M. D. Gunathilleke 60, B. K. G. Mendis 86, W. U. Tharanga 79*, A. D. Mathews 43); **Zimbabwe 322-4** (47.4 overs) (S. F. Mire 112, S. C. Williams 65, Sikandar Raza 67*, M. N. Waller 40*). *MoM:* S. F. Mire. *In the first one-day international at Galle since 2000, Zimbabwe became the first ODI team to successfully chase a target over 300 in Sri Lanka. Opener Solomon Mire provided*

HIGHEST SUCCESSFUL ODI CHASES IN SRI LANKA

Total		
322-4	**Zimbabwe** (*set 317*) **v Sri Lanka at Galle**	**2017**
312-2	**Sri Lanka** (*set 311*) **v Zimbabwe at Hambantota**	**2017**
289-4	Sri Lanka (*set 289*) v Pakistan at Dambulla	2009
288-5	India (*set 287*) v Sri Lanka at Colombo (RPS)	2012
288-8	Sri Lanka (*set 288*) v Pakistan at Pallekele	2015
286-6	Sri Lanka (*set 282*) v Zimbabwe at Colombo (SSC)	1997-98
277-6	Pakistan (*set 275*) v Sri Lanka at Hambantota	2014
271-2	India (*set 270*) v England at Colombo (RPS)	2002-03
271-7	India (*set 268*) v Pakistan at Dambulla	2010

the backbone, smashing his maiden international century – 112 in 96 balls, including 87 runs through the leg side – and sharing a third-wicket stand of 161 with Sean Williams, a national all-wicket record against these opponents. They were dismissed 12 balls apart, but Sikandar Raza and Malcolm Waller coolly negotiated the remainder with a partnership of 102 off 80 deliveries. Sri Lanka had only themselves to blame: they spilled three catches, including Mire twice. Niroshan Dickwella, meanwhile, got into trouble trying to stump him. His gloves hovered over the bails as he waited for Mire to leave the crease – a delay that displeased the umpires and earned him two demerit points. Half-centuries from Dhanushka Gunathilleke, Kusal Mendis and Upul Tharanga gave them a competitive total but, from 238-3 after 40 overs, they could have been more ambitious. It was Zimbabwe's eighth win against Sri Lanka in 51 ODIs, and their first away from home.*

Second one-day international At Galle, July 2. **Sri Lanka won by seven wickets. Zimbabwe 155** (33.4 overs) (H. Masakadza 41, M. N. Waller 38; P. A. D. L. R. Sandakan 4-52, P. W. H. de Silva 3-15); ‡**Sri Lanka 158-3** (30.1 overs) (D. P. D. N. Dickwella 35, W. U. Tharanga 75*). *MoM:* P. A. D. L. R. Sandakan. *ODI debut:* P. W. H. de Silva. *After Sri Lanka's slow bowlers were hammered in the first match, two new spinners bowled them back into the series. Lakshan Sandakan destroyed Zimbabwe's middle order with a career-best 4-52, then 19-year-old leg-spinner Wanindu Hasaranga de Silva cleaned up with a hat-trick. He became only the third to achieve the feat on debut, after Taijul Islam for Bangladesh v Zimbabwe in 2014-15, and Kagiso Rabada for South Africa v Bangladesh in 2015. The sweeps and reverse sweeps Zimbabwe had employed so successfully in the first match were their undoing here: Nos 4, 5 and 6 all perished in the attempt. Sri Lanka needed just 156, and Tharanga saw them home with a sensible 75*.*

Third one-day international At Hambantota, July 6. **Sri Lanka won by eight wickets. Zimbabwe 310-8** (50 overs) (H. Masakadza 111, T. K. Musakanda 48, S. C. Williams 43); ‡**Sri Lanka 312-2** (47.2 overs) (D. P. D. N. Dickwella 102, M. D. Gunathilleke 116, W. U. Tharanga 44*). *MoM:* M. D. Gunathilleke. *For the second time in a week, a one-day international in Sri Lanka was settled by a chase above 300 – after no instances in the previous 295 matches. This time it was the hosts who prevailed, after openers Dickwella and Gunathilleke hit maiden ODI centuries and put on 229 in 37 overs. Dickwella skittered about and scored freely behind square, while Gunathilleke stood still and drove powerfully in front. Earlier, Hamilton Masakadza had given Zimbabwe hope of a series lead, reaching three figures off 83 balls, the third-fastest hundred for his country, behind Brendan Taylor (79) and Grant Flower (82). He added 127 with Tarisai Musakanda, which carried Zimbabwe to 166-1. They both fell in a mid-innings stumble, before clean striking by Sikandar (25*) and Peter Moor (24) helped fetch 80 from the last ten overs.*

Fourth one-day international At Hambantota, July 8. **Zimbabwe won by four wickets** (DLS). ‡**Sri Lanka 300-6** (50 overs) (D. P. D. N. Dickwella 116, M. D. Gunathilleke 87, A. D. Mathews 42); **Zimbabwe 219-6** (29.2 overs) (S. F. Mire 43, T. K. Musakanda 30, C. R. Ervine 69*; P. W. H. de Silva 3-40). *MoM:* C. R. Ervine. *ODI debut:* A. M. Fernando (Sri Lanka). *Dickwella and Gunathilleke became the first pair in ODI history to compile back-to-back double-century partnerships, but it wasn't enough to clinch the series. After off-spinner Malcolm Waller dismissed them in successive overs, Sri Lanka slipped from 209-0 to 263-5, and only scraped 300. Zimbabwe began their reply strongly and, as the rain arrived, captain Angelo Mathews – fearing defeat on DLS – attempted delaying tactics to prevent the 20th over being bowled, the minimum for a result. The umpires had none of it, though there was a 90-minute delay after 21 overs, with Zimbabwe 139-3. When the weather cleared, the calculator set them a revised 219 from another ten. Williams was soon stumped, but Craig Ervine's resourceful 69* completed the job with time to spare.*

Fifth one-day international At Hambantota, July 10. **Zimbabwe won by three wickets. Sri Lanka 203-8** (50 overs) (M. D. Gunathilleke 52, D. A. S. Gunaratne 59*; Sikandar Raza 3-21); ‡**Zimbabwe 204-7** (38.1 overs) (H. Masakadza 73, S. F. Mire 43, T. K. Musakanda 37; A. Dananjaya 4-47). *MoM:* Sikandar Raza. *MoS:* H. Masakadza. *Zimbabwe won their first toss, and took control of the decider: their spinners restricted Sri Lanka to 203-8, then Masakadza and Mire rattled off 92 from the first 86 balls of the reply. Nerves jangled when, with fielders crowding the bat, and off-spinner Akila Dananjaya finding vicious turn, they lost five for 27 and slipped to 175-7. But Sikandar, who had earlier bowled magnificently for 3-21, struck 27*, and sealed victory with a straight six, just as he had in the first ODI. It was only Zimbabwe's fourth bilateral series win overseas, after New Zealand in 2000-01, Bangladesh in 2001-02, and Kenya in 2008-09. Sri Lanka had failed to find momentum in their innings. Sikandar opened the bowling and took two wickets as they struggled to 31-3 after nine overs. Gunathilleke ground out 52 to finish the series as top run-scorer, but they were in worse trouble at 126-7; only a ninth-wicket stand of 50* between Asela Gunaratne and Dushmantha Chameera dragged them over 200. On a bruising day for Sri Lankan egos, the groundstaff were humiliated, too: day-workers were ordered to hand back their SLC-branded trousers, or forgo payment, forcing them to leave the stadium in their underpants. The board swiftly suspended the official responsible, and offered the workers new clothes and an extra day's pay.*

SRI LANKA v ZIMBABWE

Only Test

At Colombo (RPS), July 14–18. Sri Lanka won by four wickets. Toss: Zimbabwe. Test debut: T. K. Musakanda.

For a brief moment on the opening day, when Zimbabwe slipped to 70 for four, it looked as if they were going to roll over. But they recovered brilliantly, and in the end were disappointed not to record their first Test victory over Sri Lanka.

Ervine led the resistance, weathering the heat and humidity, as well as the guile of Herath, to make a monumental 160, only his second Test century. It was the third-highest score by a Zimbabwean overseas, after Andy Flower's unbeaten epics in 2000-01 against India (183 at Delhi and 232 at Nagpur). The help Ervine received from the lower order,

ALL FOUR INNINGS OVER 300

South Africa (482 and 360) beat Australia (465 and 339)	Adelaide	1910-11
Australia (354 and 582) beat England (447 and 370)	Adelaide	1920-21
England (417 and 332-7) beat Australia (397 and 351)	Melbourne	1928-29
England (334 and 383) beat Australia (369 and 336)	Adelaide	1928-29
South Africa (530 and 481) drew with England (316 and 654-5)	Durban	1938-39
Australia (365 and 536) drew with England (351 and 310-7)	Melbourne	1946-47
England (427 and 325-6) drew with South Africa (302 and 423-7)	The Oval	1947
Australia (458 and 404-3) beat England (496 and 365-8)	Leeds	1948
West Indies (410 and 317-2) beat Pakistan (408 and 318)	Georgetown	1957-58
Australia (394 and 342-8) beat India (402 and 330-9)	Perth	1977-78
England (519 and 320-4) drew with India (432 and 343-6)	Manchester	1990
South Africa (532 and 335-3) drew with West Indies (427 and 354-5)	Cape Town	2003-04
Sri Lanka (321 and 352-9) beat South Africa (361 and 311)	Colombo (PSO)	2006
Sri Lanka (346 and 391-6) beat Zimbabwe (356 and 377)	**Colombo (RPS)**	**2017**

including a stand of 74 for the ninth wicket with Tiripano, a national record against Sri Lanka, helped Zimbabwe to 356 on the second morning. In reply, seven Sri Lankans passed 20, but only Tharanga and Chandimal, in his first Test as captain, made half-centuries. None could master Cremer, who gained turn and bounce off the flat surface to record his first five-for in a Test, and earn his side a lead of ten.

Early on the third afternoon, though, Zimbabwe were back in trouble; when Herath turned one through Williams's airy drive, they were 59 for five. Once again, they fought back. Sikandar Raza hit his maiden Test century, and shared 86 with Moor, then 144 with Waller. When Sikandar finally fell attempting a reverse sweep, Herath had his second five-for in the match, his 31st in all, and his eighth ten-wicket haul. Still, Zimbabwe were not finished, and Cremer's 48 helped swell the target to 388, six more than had ever been made to win a Test in Sri Lanka.

As play began on the final day, the game was in the balance: having lost three wickets, Sri Lanka needed a further 218, with Mendis and Mathews settled. Within the first hour, Cremer snared both, his dip drawing them into false strokes. Then, when Sikandar floated one up, and Chakabva removed the bails, it seemed Dickwella was gone as well, for 37. Replays showed no scrap of rubber behind the line, but somehow the third umpire, Shamshuddin, ruled not out. Unabashed, Dickwella motored on with Gunaratne, and when Zimbabwe finally turned to seam – they began with 72 overs of spin – he smote a length ball from Mpofu over midwicket to bring up a sparky fifty.

Dickwella was all action, and eventually dismissed reverse-sweeping for 81 to end a stand of 121; Gunaratne kept things simple, after hamstring trouble had prevented him fielding in the second innings. But the Zimbabwean spinners tired, particularly Cremer, whose 87.3 overs in the match beat Ray Price's national record (79, in a single innings, against South Africa at Bulawayo in 2001-02). Gunaratne quietly led Sri Lanka home in an unbroken partnership of 67 with Dilruwan Perera, finishing 80 not out to earn the match award, but bizarrely not the series equivalent: that went to Herath. The relieved Sri Lankans had pulled off the fifth-highest successful chase in Test history.

Man of the Match: D. A. S. Gunaratne.

Man of the Series: H. M. R. K. B. Herath.

Close of play: first day, Zimbabwe 344-8 (Ervine 151, Tiripano 24); second day, Sri Lanka 293-7 (Gunaratne 24, Herath 5); third day, Zimbabwe 252-6 (Sikandar Raza 97, Waller 57); fourth day, Sri Lanka 170-3 (Mendis 60, Mathews 17).

Zimbabwe

First innings		Second innings	
H. Masakadza c Mendis b Herath	19	– lbw b Herath	7
†R. W. Chakabva b Herath	12	– b Herath	6
T. K. Musakanda c Dickwella b Kumara	6	– c Karunaratne b Herath	0
C. R. Ervine c Perera b Kumara	160	– c Karunaratne b Perera	5
S. C. Williams c Gunaratne b Perera	22	– b Herath	22
Sikandar Raza lbw b Herath	36	– b Herath	127
P. J. Moor c Kumara b Gunaratne	19	– c sub (M. D. Gunathilleke) b Kumara	40
M. N. Waller b Herath	36	– c Tharanga b Perera	68
*A. G. Cremer b Gunaratne	13	– c Karunaratne b Herath	48
D. T. Tiripano c Karunaratne b Herath	27	– lbw b Perera	19
C. B. Mpofu not out	0	– not out	9
W 1, nb 5	6	B 4, lb 14, w 7, nb 1	26
1/23 (2) 2/38 (1) 3/38 (3) 4/70 (5) 5/154 (6) 6/195 (7) 7/260 (8) 8/282 (9) 9/356 (10) 10/356 (4) (94.4 overs)	356	1/14 (2) 2/16 (3) 3/17 (1) 4/23 (4) 5/59 (5) 6/145 (7) 7/289 (8) 8/306 (6) 9/361 (10) 10/377 (9) (107.1 overs)	377

Lakmal 14–1–58–0; Kumara 17.4–2–68–2; Herath 32–4–116–5; Perera 24–0–86–1; Gunaratne 7–0–28–2. *Second innings*—Lakmal 14–0–43–0; Herath 39.1–5–133–6; Perera 30–2–95–3; Kumara 20–3–72–1; Mendis 4–0–16–0.

Sri Lanka

F. D. M. Karunaratne c Masakadza b Tiripano	25	– b Williams	49
W. U. Tharanga run out	71	– c Moor b Cremer	27
B. K. G. Mendis c Chakabva b Cremer	11	– c Williams b Cremer	66
*L. D. Chandimal c Chakabva b Cremer	55	– c Masakadza b Cremer	15
A. D. Mathews c Masakadza b Williams	41	– c and b Cremer	25
†D. P. D. N. Dickwella b Cremer	6	– c Chakabva b Williams	81
M. D. K. Perera run out	33	– (8) not out	29
D. A. S. Gunaratne b Cremer	45	– (7) not out	80
H. M. R. K. B. Herath st Chakabva b Williams	22		
R. A. S. Lakmal c and b Cremer	14		
C. B. R. L. S. Kumara not out	1		
B 8, lb 10, w 1, nb 3	22	B 9, lb 8, w 2	19
1/84 (1) 2/107 (3) 3/116 (2) (102.3 overs)	346	1/58 (2) (6 wkts, 114.5 overs)	391
4/212 (4) 5/226 (6) 6/238 (5)		2/108 (1) 3/133 (4)	
7/274 (7) 8/322 (9) 9/343 (10) 10/346 (8)		4/178 (3) 5/203 (5) 6/324 (6)	

Mpofu 11–2–41–0; Tiripano 10–1–38–1; Sikandar Raza 18–2–60–0; Cremer 39.3–4–125–5; Waller 1–0–2–0; Williams 23–3–62–2. *Second innings*—Sikandar Raza 13–1–58–0; Williams 43.5–2–146–2; Cremer 48–6–150–4; Waller 4–0–10–0; Mpofu 6–3–10–0.

Umpires: I. J. Gould and N. J. Llong. Third umpire: C. Shamshuddin.
Referee: B. C. Broad.

SRI LANKA v INDIA IN 2017

R. KAUSHIK

Test matches (3): Sri Lanka 0, India 3
One-day internationals (5): Sri Lanka 0, India 5
Twenty20 international (1): Sri Lanka 0, India 1

Two years previously in Sri Lanka, India had kickstarted their campaign to reclaim top spot in the Test rankings. After defeat to England in 2014 and Australia a few months later, an inexperienced side carved out a come-from-behind 2–1 victory, Virat Kohli's first away win as Test captain.

By the time they returned in July 2017, India had indeed reached No. 1, helped by four successive series victories at home. Ravi Shastri had been reinstalled as coach following Anil Kumble's resignation, and seemed to gel with Kohli. India were expected to win, and did so with ease, recording a maiden 3–0 overseas sweep. Sri Lanka had only once lost as heavily at home, to Australia in 2003-04. India then won all five one-day internationals with something to spare, and rounded things off by claiming the sole Twenty20 international, to finish 9–0 overall.

Sri Lanka, it has to be said, were ripe for the taking. They had just lost a one-day series to Zimbabwe for the first time – at home – following early elimination from the Champions Trophy in England. They also had to cast around for a new coach when Graham Ford resigned after 16 months, with two years left on his contract. Nic Pothas, the former South African wicketkeeper, assumed temporary charge. Angelo Mathews had also stepped down as captain after the Zimbabwe debacle. Dinesh Chandimal took over as Test skipper, while Upul Tharanga was handed the limited-overs reins.

They were also beset by illness and injury. Chandimal missed the First Test with pneumonia, while Asela Gunaratne broke his thumb barely an hour into the series, ruling him out for the rest of the tour. Fast bowler Nuwan Pradeep Fernando recorded his first five-for in the First Test, but lasted just one day of the Second before tearing a hamstring, and Rangana Herath, Sri Lanka's talismanic left-arm spinner, missed the Third with back spasms. Soon after the one-dayers started, Tharanga was suspended for two matches because of a slow over-rate; his deputy, Chamara Kapugedera, immediately injured his shoulder.

India were relentless, and insulated themselves from the goings-on in the rival camp. Just about the only time they were up against it was while Dimuth Karunaratne and Kusal Mendis were making centuries in the Second Test, but that was as Sri Lanka followed on. Essentially, India marched on unchallenged. Led by Shikhar Dhawan, the batsmen piled up big runs, then the spinners, Ravichandran Ashwin and Ravindra Jadeja, chopped down the Sri Lankans mercilessly.

Those two were surprisingly left out for the limited-overs games, with Kohli plumping for the leg-breaks of Yuzvendra Chahal and the wristy variations of slow left-armer Kuldeep Yadav; Ashwin played instead for Worcestershire in the County Championship. But it made little difference: Sri Lanka's batting was fragile and uncertain, and they failed to reach 250 in the 50-over series.

Disgruntled fans turned their ire on the board, and briefly halted the third one-dayer in Pallekele by throwing stones and bottles on to the ground. The outrage led to the resignation of the selection panel, headed by Sanath Jayasuriya.

INDIAN TOURING PARTY

*V. Kohli (T/50/20), R. Ashwin (T), Bhuvneshwar Kumar (T/50/20), J. J. Bumrah (50/20), Y. S. Chahal (50/20), S. Dhawan (T/50/20), M. S. Dhoni (50/20), R. A. Jadeja (T), K. M. Jadhav (50/20), Mohammed Shami (T), A. Mukund (T), M. K. Pandey (50/20), H. H. Pandya (T/50/20), A. R. Patel (T/50/20), C. A. Pujara (T), A. M. Rahane (T/50/20), K. L. Rahul (T/50/20), W. P. Saha (T), I. Sharma (T), R. G. Sharma (T/50/20), S. N. Thakur (50/20), K. Yadav (T/50/20), U. T. Yadav (T). *Coach:* R. J. Shastri.

M. Vijay was originally selected for the Tests, but failed to recover from a wrist injury and was replaced by Dhawan, who flew home after the third ODI to be with his sick mother. Patel joined the squad after Jadeja was suspended from the Third Test.

TEST MATCH AVERAGES

SRI LANKA – BATTING AND FIELDING

	T	*I*	*NO*	*R*	*HS*	*100*	*50*	*Avge*	*Ct/St*
†F. D. M. Karunaratne	3	6	0	285	141	1	1	47.50	3
†D. P. D. N. Dickwella	3	6	0	227	67	0	2	37.83	6/2
M. D. K. Perera	3	6	2	150	92*	0	1	37.50	3
B. K. G. Mendis	3	6	0	200	110	1	0	33.33	1
A. D. Mathews	3	6	0	182	83	0	1	30.33	4
L. D. Chandimal	2	4	0	96	48	0	0	24.00	1
†W. U. Tharanga	3	6	0	88	64	0	1	14.66	2
P. M. Pushpakumara	2	4	1	42	16	0	0	14.00	0
†H. M. R. K. B. Herath	2	3	1	28	17*	0	0	14.00	0
†C. B. R. L. S. Kumara	2	4	1	12	10	0	0	4.00	0
A. N. P. R. Fernando	2	4	0	11	10	0	0	2.75	0

Played in one Test: D. M. de Silva 0, 17; M. V. T. Fernando 0, 4*; †M. D. Gunathilleke 16, 2 (1 ct); P. A. D. L. R. Sandakan 10, 8 (1 ct); D. A. S. Gunaratne did not bat.

BOWLING

	Style	*O*	*M*	*R*	*W*	*BB*	*5I*	*Avge*
P. A. D. L. R. Sandakan	SLW	35.3	4	132	5	5-132	1	26.40
A. N. P. R. Fernando	RFM	60.4	6	258	6	6-132	1	43.00
P. M. Pushpakumara	SLA	61.2	4	238	5	3-82	0	47.60
H. M. R. K. B. Herath	SLA	91	13	347	5	4-154	0	69.40
C. B. R. L. S. Kumara	RFM	60.1	5	294	4	3-131	0	73.50

Also bowled: D. M. de Silva (OB) 12–0–59–0; M. V. T. Fernando (LFM) 26–3–87–2; M. D. Gunathilleke (OB) 12–0–57–1; F. D. M. Karunaratne (RM) 15–0–61–1; M. D. K. Perera (OB) 93–5–380–2.

INDIA – BATTING AND FIELDING

	T	*I*	*NO*	*R*	*HS*	*100*	*50*	*Avge*	*Ct/St*
†S. Dhawan	3	4	0	358	190	2	0	89.50	4
C. A. Pujara	3	4	0	309	153	2	0	77.25	3
A. M. Rahane	3	4	1	229	132	1	1	76.33	8
H. H. Pandya	3	3	0	178	108	1	1	59.33	4
V. Kohli	3	4	1	161	103*	1	0	53.66	3
R. Ashwin	3	3	0	132	54	0	1	44.00	0
W. P. Saha	3	3	0	99	67	0	1	33.00	8/2
Mohammed Shami	3	3	0	57	30	0	0	19.00	1
U. T. Yadav	3	3	3	22	11*	0	0	–	0

Played in two Tests: †R. A. Jadeja 15, 70*; K. L. Rahul 57, 85 (2 ct). Played in one Test: †A. Mukund 12, 81 (1 ct); †K. Yadav 26.

BOWLING

	Style	*O*	*M*	*R*	*W*	*BB*	*5I*	*Avge*
Mohammed Shami	RFM	60.5	13	177	10	3-32	0	17.70
K. Yadav	SLW	30	6	96	5	4-40	0	19.20
H. H. Pandya	RFM	32	3	95	4	2-31	0	23.75
R. Ashwin	OB	145.4	27	440	17	5-69	1	25.88
R. A. Jadeja	SLA	108.2	18	374	13	5-152	1	28.76
U. T. Yadav	RF	57.1	9	215	6	2-21	0	35.83

SRI LANKA v INDIA

First Test

At Galle, July 26–29, 2017. India won by 304 runs. Toss: India. Test debuts: M. D. Gunathilleke; H. H. Pandya.

Shikhar Dhawan was not supposed to be in Sri Lanka at all: he had been left out of the original squad, and called up only because of a wrist injury to Murali Vijay. K. L. Rahul was next in line, but he was down with a fever. Dhawan seized his chance, celebrating his Test return after ten months on the sidelines with a bruising career-best 190, setting the tone for India's commanding victory.

Without their new captain Dinesh Chandimal, who had pneumonia, Sri Lanka endured a horrible first day. India cantered to 399 for three, with Dhawan leading the way. His runs came off just 168 balls, and he smacked 126 between lunch and tea, the most by anyone in the middle session of a Test for 63 years (in 1954, Denis Compton battered an inexperienced Pakistan attack for 173 at Trent Bridge). Dhawan was put down at second slip when he had 31 – a double blow for Sri Lanka, as Gunaratne broke his thumb attempting the catch, and played no further part in the series. Dhawan sailed on, adding 253 – a second-wicket record for India against Sri Lanka – with Pujara, whose unhurried 153 was his 12th Test century (and his sixth of 150 or more). The carnage continued next day: Hardik Pandya marked his Test debut with a run-a-ball 50 as the total reached 600. It might have been even more but for a fine effort from Pradeep Fernando, who persevered for a maiden Test five-for, and finished with six for 132.

Sri Lanka were soon in more trouble. Karunaratne fell in the second over, and Mendis went fourth ball. There were half-centuries for Tharanga, Mathews and Perera, who was stranded just short of a first Test hundred, but there was a desperation to their strokeplay. In less than 79 overs, Sri Lanka were all out, 309 adrift, briefly their record first-innings deficit at home to India. Kohli waived the follow-on, perhaps remembering India's collapse here in 2015 when, after leading by 192, they folded in search of 176 in the final innings. But this Galle pitch was not as spin-friendly as usual, and now their batsmen cantered along at more than four an over. Mukund hit his second Test half-century, six years after the first, and Kohli made up for a poor home series against Australia with a majestic hundred, his 17th in Tests. His declaration left the bowlers almost two days to force a win.

As it turned out, they barely needed five hours. Sri Lanka had knocked off a national-record 388 to overcome a spirited Zimbabwe side just 11 days previously – but 550 against India was several bridges too far, especially with Gunaratne and stand-in skipper Herath (who had injured a finger in the field) unable to bat. Opener Karunaratne bolstered his reputation as a second-innings specialist with 97, but it was all over soon after he was dismissed by the probing Ashwin. Karunaratne had earlier put on 101 with the feisty Dickwella, whose luck ran out when he tried one sweep too many. Ashwin shared six wickets with Jadeja, who claimed the last to earn his side victory, and a day off.

Man of the Match: S. Dhawan.

Close of play: first day, India 399-3 (Pujara 144, Rahane 39); second day, Sri Lanka 154-5 (Mathews 54, Perera 6); third day, India 189-3 (Kohli 76).

India

First innings		Second innings	
S. Dhawan c Mathews b Fernando	190	– c Gunathilleke b Perera	14
A. Mukund c Dickwella b Fernando	12	– lbw b Gunathilleke	81
C. A. Pujara c Dickwella b Fernando	153	– c Mendis b Kumara	15
*V. Kohli c Dickwella b Fernando	3	– not out	103
A. M. Rahane c Karunaratne b Kumara	57	– not out	23
R. Ashwin c Dickwella b Fernando	47		
†W. P. Saha c Perera b Herath	16		
H. H. Pandya c sub (D. M. de Silva) b Kumara	50		
R. A. Jadeja b Fernando	15		
Mohammed Shami c Tharanga b Kumara	30		
U. T. Yadav not out	11		
B 2, lb 5, w 6, nb 3	16	Lb 1, w 2, nb 1	4
1/27 (2) 2/280 (1) 3/286 (4) 4/423 (3) 5/432 (5) 6/491 (7) 7/495 (6) 8/517 (9) 9/579 (10) 10/600 (8) (133.1 overs)	600	1/19 (1) 2/56 (3) 3/189 (2) (3 wkts dec, 53 overs)	240

Fernando 31–2–132–6; Kumara 25.1–3–131–3; Perera 30–1–130–0; Herath 40–6–159–1; Gunathilleke 7–0–41–0. *Second innings*—Fernando 12–2–63–0; Perera 15–0–67–1; Kumara 12–1–59–1; Herath 9–0–34–0; Gunathilleke 5–0–16–1.

Sri Lanka

First innings		Second innings	
F. D. M. Karunaratne lbw b Yadav	2	– b Ashwin	97
W. U. Tharanga run out	64	– b Mohammed Shami	10
M. D. Gunathilleke c Dhawan b Mohammed Shami	16	– c Pujara b Yadav	2
B. K. G. Mendis c Dhawan b Mohammed Shami	0	– c Saha b Jadeja	36
A. D. Mathews c Kohli b Jadeja	83	– c Pandya b Jadeja	2
†D. P. D. N. Dickwella c Mukund b Ashwin	8	– c Saha b Ashwin	67
M. D. K. Perera not out	92	– not out	21
*H. M. R. K. B. Herath c Rahane b Jadeja	9	– absent hurt	
A. N. P. R. Fernando b Pandya	10	– (8) c Kohli b Ashwin	0
C. B. R. L. S. Kumara b Jadeja	2	– (9) c Mohammed Shami b Jadeja	0
D. A. S. Gunaratne absent hurt		– absent hurt	
Lb 4, w 1	5	Lb 3, w 7	10
1/7 (1) 2/68 (3) 3/68 (4) 4/125 (2) 5/143 (6) 6/205 (5) 7/241 (8) 8/280 (9) 9/291 (10) (78.3 overs)	291	1/22 (2) 2/29 (3) 3/108 (4) 4/116 (5) 5/217 (6) 6/240 (1) 7/240 (8) 8/245 (9) (76.5 overs)	245

Mohammed Shami 12–2–45–2; Yadav 14–1–78–1; Ashwin 27–5–84–1; Jadeja 22.3–3–67–3; Pandya 3–0–13–1. *Second innings*—Mohammed Shami 9–0–43–1; Yadav 9–0–42–1; Jadeja 24.5–4–71–3; Ashwin 27–4–65–3; Pandya 7–0–21–0.

Umpires: R. K. Illingworth and B. N. J. Oxenford. Third umpire: R. J. Tucker.
Referee: R. B. Richardson.

SRI LANKA v INDIA

Second Test

At Colombo (SSC), August 3–6, 2017. India won by an innings and 53 runs. Toss: India. Test debut: P. M. Pushpakumara.

With such a gulf between the sides, Sri Lanka's best chance was to come up with a dry, crumbling surface to help the spinners. But the ploy backfired when Kohli won the toss again. It wasn't quite a dustbowl, though there was generous help for Sri Lanka's three slow bowlers as early as the first session. However, they could not make the most of it and, with the pitch growing sluggish, there was no stopping India once they reached 600 for the sixth time in nine Tests. Another four-day victory, this time by an innings, gave them a unassailable 2–0 lead.

As in the First Test, strong batting was followed by incisive bowling, spearheaded by Ashwin and Jadeja, whose all-round talents enabled Kohli to go in with five specialist bowlers. Ashwin, meanwhile, completed the double of 2,000 Test runs and 250 wickets in his 51st game, beating Richard Hadlee's record by three.

But it was the specialist batsmen who made the early running against a Sri Lankan side that welcomed back skipper Chandimal and handed a debut to Malinda Pushpakumara, a 30-year-old slow left-armer with more than 550 first-class wickets to his name. Bolstering the spin department left Sri Lanka with only one fast bowler, Pradeep Fernando – and when he tore a hamstring late on the first day, they were well and truly stuffed.

MASTERS OF BOTH TRADES

Two players from the same team hitting a fifty and taking a five-for in the same Test:

G. Giffen (58; 5-76), A. E. Trott (72*; 8-43)	A v E at Adelaide	1894-95
T. T. Bresnan (90; 5-48), S. C. J. Broad (64; 6-46).	E v I at Nottingham.	2011
R. Ashwin (54; 5-69), R. A. Jadeja (70*; 5-152)	**I v SL at Colombo (SSC)** . . .	**2017**

Rahul marked his return after illness with an attractive half-century, but the real stars were Pujara, who brought up his third hundred in three Tests in Sri Lanka, and Rahane. Their fourth-wicket stand of 217 was the bedrock on which India constructed a mammoth total swelled by fifties from Ashwin, Saha and Jadeja.

Sri Lanka's first innings was a mix of the sublime (India's bowling) and the ridiculous (their own batting). An addiction to sweeps of all kinds, coupled with Ashwin's craft and Jadeja's cunning, lured batsmen to their doom. They were shot out for 183 inside 50 overs, and this time Kohli did enforce the follow-on. The pitch would only flatten out, so it made no sense to add to a stratospheric lead of 439 – the largest against Sri Lanka.

Tharanga fell in the third over, but that brought Karunaratne and Mendis together for Sri Lanka's best period of the series. Put down by Dhawan at mid-on before he had scored, Mendis unfurled some fabulous back-foot strokes, while Karunaratne used his feet beautifully against the slowly turning ball. Perhaps because they had not expected such resistance, the Indians briefly looked bereft of ideas during a second-wicket stand that reached 191. The pair were eventually separated late on the third evening, when Pandya had Mendis caught behind for a classy 110.

Next day Karunaratne moved to 141, in over six hours, before receiving a beast from Jadeja that exploded off a length and flew to slip via handle and glove. That was almost the end: Mathews and Dickwella flickered, until Jadeja doused the fire to finish with a hard-earned five-for. He also earned an unexpected rest: he was suspended from the next Test after picking up three more demerit points for throwing the ball dangerously close to Karunaratne, who had not left his crease.

Man of the Match: R. A. Jadeja.

Close of play: first day, India 344-3 (Pujara 128, Rahane 103); second day, Sri Lanka 50-2 (Mendis 16, Chandimal 8); third day, Sri Lanka 209-2 (Karunaratne 92, Pushpakumara 2).

India

S. Dhawan lbw b Perera	35
K. L. Rahul run out	57
C. A. Pujara lbw b Karunaratne	133
*V. Kohli c Mathews b Herath	13
A. M. Rahane st Dickwella b Pushpakumara	132
R. Ashwin b Herath	54
†W. P. Saha st Dickwella b Herath	67
H. H. Pandya c Mathews b Pushpakumara	20
R. A. Jadeja not out	70
Mohammed Shami c Tharanga b Herath	19
U. T. Yadav not out	8
B 8, lb 4, nb 2	14
1/56 (1) (9 wkts dec, 158 overs)	622
2/109 (2) 3/133 (4)	
4/350 (3) 5/413 (5) 6/451 (6)	
7/496 (8) 8/568 (7) 9/598 (10)	

Fernando 17.4–2–63–0; Herath 42–7–154–4; Karunaratne 8–0–31–1; Perera 40–3–147–1; Pushpakumara 38.2–2–156–2; de Silva 12–0–59–0.

Sri Lanka

F. D. M. Karunaratne c Rahane b Ashwin	25	– c Rahane b Jadeja	141
W. U. Tharanga c Rahul b Ashwin	0	– b Yadav	2
B. K. G. Mendis c Kohli b Yadav	24	– c Saha b Pandya	110
*L. D. Chandimal c Pandya b Jadeja	10	– (5) c Rahane b Jadeja	2
A. D. Mathews c Pujara b Ashwin	26	– (6) c Saha b Jadeja	36
†D. P. D. N. Dickwella b Mohammed Shami	51	– (7) c Rahane b Pandya	31
D. M. de Silva b Jadeja	0	– (9) c Rahane b Jadeja	17
M. D. K. Perera b Ashwin	25	– st Saha b Jadeja	4
H. M. R. K. B. Herath b Mohammed Shami	2	– (10) not out	17
P. M. Pushpakumara not out	15	– (4) b Ashwin	16
A. N. P. R. Fernando b Ashwin	0	– c Dhawan b Ashwin	1
B 4, lb 1	5	Lb 5, w 2, nb 2	9
1/0 (2) 2/33 (1) 3/60 (4) (49.4 overs)	183	1/7 (2) 2/198 (3) (116.5 overs)	386
4/64 (3) 5/117 (5) 6/122 (7)		3/238 (4) 4/241 (5)	
7/150 (6) 8/152 (9) 9/171 (8) 10/183 (11)		5/310 (1) 6/315 (6)	
		7/321 (8) 8/343 (9)	
		9/384 (7) 10/386 (11)	

Mohammed Shami 6–1–13–2; Ashwin 16.4–3–69–5; Jadeja 22–6–84–2; Yadav 5–1–12–1. *Second innings*—Yadav 13–2–39–1; Ashwin 37.5–7–132–2; Mohammed Shami 12–3–27–0; Jadeja 39–5–152–5; Pandya 15–2–31–2.

Umpires: B. N. J. Oxenford and R. J. Tucker. Third umpire: R. K. Illingworth.
Referee: R. B. Richardson.

SRI LANKA v INDIA

Third Test

At Pallekele, August 12–14, 2017. India won by an innings and 171 runs. Toss: India.

Nothing looked more likely than a 3–0 clean sweep, especially once Kohli won his third toss of the series. And so it proved, helped by an inept Sri Lankan performance: India's first-innings 487 was their lowest total of the series, but they still cruised to the heaviest of their victories, this time inside three days. Even without the suspended Ravindra Jadeja, they were just too strong. His replacement, the left-arm wrist-spinner Kuldeep Yadav, befuddled several batsmen in the first innings, while Ashwin shared the spoils with seamer Mohammed Shami in the second.

The most demanding conditions were on the first morning, but Dhawan and Rahul countered some lacklustre bowling by putting on 188, the highest first-wicket stand by a visiting team in Sri Lanka, beating 171 by Manoj Prabhakar and Navjot Sidhu for India at Colombo's SSC in 1993-94. Rahul's 85 was his seventh successive Test score over 50, equalling the record held by five others.

The openers easily negotiated the rejigged pace attack of Vishwa Fernando and Kumara, who both pitched too short on a grassy track. Pushpakumara – operating in the absence of Rangana Herath, who missed the match after back spasms – kept things tight, but it was Sandakan, the left-arm wrist-spinner, who posed the more demanding questions. His working-over of Pujara and Rahane, two of the finest modern players of the turning ball, made for electrifying viewing.

Early on the second day, India were in danger of wasting the openers' start. Then Pandya broke loose, in only his third Test. After making a half-century from 61 balls, and

MOST SIXES IN A TEST INNINGS FOR INDIA

8	N. S. Sidhu (124)	v Sri Lanka at Lucknow	1993-94
7	V. Sehwag (293)	v Sri Lanka at Mumbai (Brabourne)	2009-10
7	Harbhajan Singh (111*)	v New Zealand at Hyderabad	2010-11
7	**H. H. Pandya (108)**	**v Sri Lanka at Pallekele**	**2017**
6	R. J. Shastri (121*)	v Australia at Bombay (Wankhede)	1986-87
6	V. Sehwag (309)	v Pakistan at Multan	2003-04
6	M. S. Dhoni (69)	v West Indies at St John's	2005-06
6	M. S. Dhoni (100*)	v Sri Lanka at Mumbai (Brabourne)	2009-10
6	M. S. Dhoni (224)	v Australia at Chennai	2012-13

with only last man Umesh Yadav for company, he unleashed the cleanest, longest blows of the series, despite all nine fielders on the boundary. He crashed 26 from one Pushpakumara over (446660) – an Indian Test record, beating Kapil Dev's 24 off Eddie Hemmings at Lord's in 1990 – and reached three figures off just 86 deliveries. In all, he hit seven sixes. It was his first century in senior cricket: he was the fifth Indian to score his maiden first-class hundred in a Test, but the first since Harbhajan Singh in 2010-11. He couldn't remember his previous three-figure score: "For the Under-19s, I think." (In fact, it was for Baroda Under-23s.)

Sri Lanka's openers could not match their opponents. Shami removed both in single figures, before Mendis was run out and Mathews pinned by the irrepressible Pandya for a duck. Then Kuldeep got to work, teasing out the middle order to finish with four for 40; only Chandimal put up much resistance. Sri Lanka were hustled out inside three hours for 135, a severe disappointment after their second-innings fight in Colombo.

With a lead of 352 and his bowlers still fresh, Kohli stuck them back in. Umesh extended Tharanga's horror run, Ashwin produced a beauty to evict Karunaratne and, with Shami mixing up his lengths, it was soon 39 for four. Chandimal put his head down again, and for a while found an ally in Mathews, putting on 65 in 28 overs with his predecessor as captain. But after lunch a more skittish Chandimal fell to an adventurous stroke against Kuldeep, which signalled the beginning of the end. Three more wickets for Ashwin, giving him 17 in the series, brought the curtain down on another clinical performance. Nic Pothas, Sri Lanka's interim coach, likened the Indians to rugby's All Blacks. "They are very ruthless in the way they go about their work," he said admiringly.

Man of the Match: H. H. Pandya. *Man of the Series:* S. Dhawan.

Close of play: first day, India 329-6 (Saha 13, Pandya 1); second day, Sri Lanka 19-1 (Karunaratne 12, Pushpakumara 0).

India

S. Dhawan c Chandimal b Pushpakumara	119
K. L. Rahul c Karunaratne b Pushpakumara	85
C. A. Pujara c Mathews b Sandakan	8
*V. Kohli c Karunaratne b Sandakan	42
A. M. Rahane b Pushpakumara	17
R. Ashwin c Dickwella b Fernando	31
†W. P. Saha c Perera b Fernando	16
H. H. Pandya c Perera b Sandakan	108
K. Yadav c Dickwella b Sandakan	26
Mohammed Shami c and b Sandakan	8
U. T. Yadav not out	3
B 10, lb 6, w 6, nb 2	24
1/188 (2) 2/219 (1) 3/229 (3) 4/264 (5) 5/296 (4) 6/322 (6) 7/339 (7) 8/401 (9) 9/421 (10) 10/487 (8) (122.3 overs)	487

Fernando 26–3–87–2; Kumara 23–1–104–0; Karunaratne 7–0–30–0; Perera 8–1–36–0; Sandakan 35.3–4–132–5; Pushpakumara 23–2–82–3.

Sri Lanka

	First innings		Second innings	
F. D. M. Karunaratne c Saha b Mohammed Shami	4	–	c Rahane b Ashwin	16
W. U. Tharanga c Saha b Mohammed Shami	5	–	b U. T. Yadav	7
B. K. G. Mendis run out	18	–	(4) lbw b Mohammed Shami	12
*L. D. Chandimal c Rahul b Ashwin	48	–	(5) c Pujara b K. Yadav	36
A. D. Mathews lbw b Pandya	0	–	(6) lbw b Ashwin	35
†D. P. D. N. Dickwella st Saha b K. Yadav	29	–	(7) c Rahane b U. T. Yadav	41
M. D. K. Perera c Pandya b K. Yadav	0	–	(8) c Pandya b Ashwin	8
P. M. Pushpakumara b K. Yadav	10	–	(3) c Saha b Mohammed Shami	1
P. A. D. L. R. Sandakan c Dhawan b Ashwin	10	–	c Saha b Mohammed Shami	8
M. V. T. Fernando b K. Yadav	0	–	not out	4
C. B. R. L. S. Kumara not out	0	–	b Ashwin	10
B 4, lb 1, w 6	11		B 2, nb 1	3
1/14 (2) 2/23 (1) 3/38 (3) 4/38 (5) 5/101 (6) 6/107 (7) 7/125 (4) 8/125 (8) 9/135 (10) 10/135 (9) (37.4 overs)	135		1/15 (2) 2/26 (1) 3/34 (3) 4/39 (4) 5/104 (5) 6/118 (6) 7/138 (8) 8/166 (9) 9/168 (7) 10/181 (11) (74.3 overs)	181

Mohammed Shami 6.5–1–17–2; U. T. Yadav 3.1–0–23–0; Pandya 6–1–28–1; K. Yadav 13–2–40–4; Ashwin 8.4–2–22–2. *Second innings*—Mohammed Shami 15–6–32–3; Ashwin 28.3–6–68–4; U. T. Yadav 13–5–21–2; K. Yadav 17–4–56–1; Pandya 1–0–2–0.

Umpires: R. K. Illingworth and R. J. Tucker. Third umpire: B. N. J. Oxenford.
Referee: R. B. Richardson.

First one-day international At Dambulla, August 20, 2017 (day/night). **India won by nine wickets. Sri Lanka 216** (43.2 overs) (D. P. D. N. Dickwella 64, M. D. Gunathilleke 35, B. K. G. Mendis 36, A. D. Mathews 36*; A. R. Patel 3-34); ‡**India 220-1** (28.5 overs) (S. Dhawan 132*, V. Kohli 82*). *MoM:* S. Dhawan. *ODI debut:* M. V. T. Fernando (Sri Lanka). *After a good start, Sri Lanka found various ways to self-destruct. They were 139-1 in the 25th over, but then lost nine for 77, as spinners Yuzvendra Chahal (2-60), Kedhar Jadhav (2-26) and Akshar Patel got to work. Rohit Sharma departed for four, run out when he lost control of the bat and had both feet in the air as the stumps were broken – he would have survived later in the year under the new Code of Laws. Shikhar Dhawan, with a 71-ball hundred, and Virat Kohli hurtled home, putting on 197* in less than 24 overs.*

Second one-day international At Pallekele, August 24, 2017 (day/night). **India won by three wickets** (DLS). **Sri Lanka 236-8** (50 overs) (D. P. D. N. Dickwella 31, T. A. M. Siriwardene 58, C. K. Kapugedera 40; J. J. Bumrah 4-43); ‡**India 231-7** (44.2 overs) (R. G. Sharma 54, S. Dhawan 49, M. S. Dhoni 45*, Bhuvneshwar Kumar 53*; A. Dananjaya 6-54). *MoM:* A. Dananjaya. *Sprinkling leg-breaks and googlies among his usual off-spinners, Akila Dananjaya nearly derailed what had seemed a regulation chase for India – at least while the openers, Sharma and Dhawan, were putting on 109 inside 16 overs. Dananjaya took three wickets in five balls on his way to career-best figures as India lurched to 131-7. But Sri Lanka's hopes of squaring the series were denied by the eighth-wicket pair, who put on 100*: M. S. Dhoni dropped anchor for 68 balls, while Bhuvneshwar Kumar's 53* from 80 was his maiden ODI half-century. Sri Lanka's innings had owed much to a sixth-wicket* *stand of 91 between Milinda Siriwardene and Chamara Kapugedera. Rain between innings meant India's target was revised slightly, to 231 from 47 overs.*

Third one-day international At Pallekele, August 27, 2017 (day/night). **India won by six wickets.** ‡**Sri Lanka 217-9** (50 overs) (L. D. Chandimal 36, H. D. R. L. Thirimanne 80; J. J. Bumrah 5-27); **India 218-4** (45.1 overs) (R. G. Sharma 124*, M. S. Dhoni 67*). *MoM:* J. J. Bumrah. *India lost their first toss of the tour, but it made no odds. Sri Lanka, captained by Kapugedera after Upul Tharanga was suspended for two matches for a slow over-rate, struggled against Jasprit Bumrah, who picked up his first ODI five-for. Two quick wickets for Dananjaya reduced India to 61-4, but there were no further alarms: Sharma purred to his 12th ODI century, and put on 157* with the imperturbable Dhoni, undefeated for a record 73rd time in ODIs, to seal the series. For the second time in two years, an international in Sri Lanka was held up by serious crowd trouble: spectators enraged by the home team's perceived lack of fight – and what they felt were questionable selections – threw bottles on to the outfield, causing a 35-minute delay.*

Fourth one-day international At Colombo (RPS), August 31, 2017 (day/night). **India won by 168 runs.** ‡**India 375-5** (50 overs) (R. G. Sharma 104, V. Kohli 131, M. K. Pandey 50*, M. S. Dhoni 49*); **Sri Lanka 207** (42.4 overs) (A. D. Mathews 70, T. A. M. Siriwardene 39). *MoM:* V. Kohli. *ODI debuts:* E. M. D. Y. Munaweera, P. M. Pushpakumara (Sri Lanka); S. N. Thakur (India). *Kohli decided to bat first and spare his bowlers the worst of the Colombo climate. Instead it was the Sri Lankan attack which felt the heat: shrugging off the early loss of Dhawan, India's second-wicket pair piled on 219 in 28 overs. Kohli sprinted to 131 from 96 balls before providing Lasith Malinga (Sri Lanka's third captain in three games after a shoulder injury to Kapugedera) with his 300th ODI wicket, then Sharma fell for 104 from 88 balls. India might have breached 400 were it not for Angelo Mathews, who struck twice with successive deliveries. But late fireworks from Manish Pandey and Dhoni, in his 300th ODI, powered them to 375 by adding 101* in 12.2 overs. It was more than enough. Sri Lanka were soon 68-4 and, although Mathews hit ten fours in a defiant 70, the defeat was their heaviest by runs at home.*

Fifth one-day international At Colombo (RPS), September 3, 2017 (day/night). **India won by six wickets.** ‡**Sri Lanka 238** (49.4 overs) (W. U. Tharanga 48, H. D. R. L. Thirimanne 67, A. D. Mathews 55; Bhuvneshwar Kumar 5-42); **India 239-4** (46.3 overs) (V. Kohli 110*, M. K. Pandey 36, K. M. Jadhav 63). *MoM:* Bhuvneshwar Kumar. *MoS:* J. J. Bumrah. *Once again, Sri Lanka threw away a promising position: after reaching 185-3 in the 39th over, they lost seven for 53. Bhuvneshwar, who had taken the first two wickets, returned to complete his first limited-overs five-for, while Bumrah claimed two, to finish the five games with 15 at 11. It was still Sri Lanka's highest total of the series, and they were heartened when India slipped to 29-2. But Kohli remained in prime form, putting on 99 with Pandey and 109 with Jadhav as he glided to his 30th ODI hundred, taking him level with Ricky Ponting and behind only Sachin Tendulkar (49). Fittingly, Kohli hit the winning run, to complete the 5–0 whitewash.*

Twenty20 international At Colombo (RPS), September 6, 2017 (floodlit). **India won by seven wickets. Sri Lanka 170-7** (20 overs) (E. M. D. Y. Munaweera 53, S. M. A. Priyanjan 40*; Y. S. Chahal 3-43); ‡**India 174-3** (19.2 overs) (V. Kohli 82, M. K. Pandey 51*). *MoM:* V. Kohli. *MoS:* V. Kohli. *T20I debut:* S. M. A. Priyanjan. *Kohli unveiled another masterpiece – 82 off 54 balls – to complete a 9–0 demolition across the three formats. Dilshan Munaweera gave Sri Lanka a flying start with 53 from 29, then debutant Ashan Priyanjan and the lower order collected 52 from the last five overs. A total of 170 looked good when India slipped to 42-2 in the sixth – but by then Kohli was settling in, and he dominated a third-wicket partnership of 119 with Pandey.*

SRI LANKA A v ENGLAND LIONS IN 2016-17

JAMES GINGELL

A-Team Test matches (2): Sri Lanka A 1, England Lions 1
A-Team one-day internationals (5): Sri Lanka A 3, England Lions 2

Lions tours are curious affairs, since results matter less than individual displays: everyone is on the lookout for the next big thing. Before this trip, many expected the Test openers designate – captain Keaton Jennings and Haseeb Hameed – to catch the eye. Both had made their senior debuts before Christmas in India, and were among the scant positives from England's 4–0 drubbing. Others were keeping tabs on Ben Duckett, picked for the one-dayers here and eager to regain the selectors' faith in his technique against slow bowling after a tough start to his Test career. Left-arm spinner Jack Leach, superb during the 2016 Championship with Somerset, also had many backers.

There were flashes of class from each, but none came home with reputation enhanced. Leach had a particularly difficult time. Forced to address a kink in his action after the English summer, he struggled in the warm-up game, was left out of the first A-Team Test at Pallekele – where a strong bowling effort brought the Lions a crushing victory – and was hammered when he returned for the second at Dambulla, which the Sri Lankans won.

So there was a vacancy for a tour star, and Lancashire all-rounder Liam Livingstone filled it. Tall but not lanky, and humming with power, he had something of Kevin Pietersen in his batting, particularly the shimmying sixes over long-on and the tip-toed flails through midwicket. At Dambulla, the similarities went further: Livingstone became the second, after Pietersen, to score twin hundreds in an England A/Lions game. It was not enough to force victory, following a huge partnership between Dimuth Karunaratne and Sadeera Samarawickrama, and the excellence of slow left-armer Malinda Pushpakumara. But Livingstone's application and flexibility against the spinners impressed all. He had made his first-class debut at No. 7 in April 2016, with his coach Ashley Giles unsure of his technique against the red ball; but he topped Lancashire's averages, and now commanded the Lions' middle order. Livingstone nearly added another hundred in the one-dayers, where his all-sorts bowling – leg-spin to right-handers, off-spin to left-handers – brought seven wickets, with an economy-rate of 3.60, easily the best on either side.

But the Sri Lankans' greater white-ball experience won out. They began with only one player uncapped in limited-overs internationals, while the Lions had only Duckett's three one-day appearances between them. Danushka Gunathilleke averaged 93 from four games at a strike-rate over 100, and their spin-heavy attack throttled the tourists. Mark Wood's zip might have helped: he had been due to join the one-day party, but pulled out to continue rehab from ankle surgery. From 3–0 down, the Lions at least narrowed the gap, thanks to a hundred from Kent batsman Daniel Bell-Drummond in the fourth game, and five wickets for Middlesex seamer Tom Helm in the fifth.

ENGLAND LIONS TOURING PARTY

*K. K. Jennings (Durham; FC/50), T. P. Alsop (Hampshire; FC/50), D. J. Bell-Drummond (Kent; 50), J. M. Clarke (Worcestershire; FC/50), S. M. Curran (Surrey; FC/50), T. K. Curran (Surrey; FC), B. M. Duckett (Northamptonshire; 50), B. T. Foakes (Surrey; FC/50), J. K. Fuller (Middlesex; 50), N. R. T. Gubbins (Middlesex; FC), H. Hameed (Lancashire; FC), T. G. Helm (Middlesex; FC/50), M. J. Leach (Somerset; FC), L. S. Livingstone (Lancashire; FC/50), C. Overton (Somerset; FC/50), J. E. Poysden (Warwickshire; 50), O. P. Rayner (Middlesex; FC/50), T. S. Roland-Jones (Middlesex; FC/50), T. Westley (Essex; FC), G. G. White (Northamptonshire; 50). *Coach:* A. Flower.

T. K. Curran was picked for both squads, but called up to the senior team in the West Indies after the Tests. Roland-Jones was retained for the one-dayers. M. A. Wood (Durham) withdrew after ankle surgery.

At Moratuwa, February 12–14, 2017 (not first-class). **Drawn.** ‡**Sri Lanka Board President's XI 153** (53.3 overs) (T. G. Helm 3-18) **and 324** (100.5 overs) (R. K. Chandraguptha 91, L. K. Fransisco 72; O. P. Rayner 3-55); **England Lions 279** (69.1 overs) (T. Westley 95, L. S. Livingstone 84; P. M. Pushpakumara 3-82) **and 171-6** (37.1 overs) (N. R. T. Gubbins 52*; P. M. Pushpakumara 3-35). *Sri Lanka Board President's XI chose from 13, England Lions from 15. A fifth-wicket partnership of 136 between Tom Westley and Liam Livingstone gave the tourists a first-innings advantage, but the President's XI fought back, and left a target of 199, which proved just out of reach.*

SRI LANKA A v ENGLAND LIONS

First A-Team Test

At Pallekele, February 17–20, 2017. England Lions won by 195 runs. Toss: England Lions.

On the recent Test tour of India, Hameed had won comparisons to Ranjitsinhji, while Jennings struck a century in his first innings. Neither seemed a class above here, though, and it was their less heralded team-mates who delivered. After the Lions' top order misfired, Westley put on a fluent 128 with Livingstone, before falling just short of a century and sparking a slide from 189 for three to 210 for eight. Roland-Jones rallied: he hit a forthright 82 while coaxing 106 from the last two wickets, then ripped out two before the close to help reduce Sri Lanka A to 29 for four. He added two more next day, and Middlesex colleague Rayner chipped in with three, ensuring the Lions resumed with a healthy advantage. Even so, the batsmen needed another bailout: the first six fell for 85, the last four 130. Hameed completed a miserable return after a broken finger with a duck, and was the only one to fall to seam; Test off-spinner Perera scooped five, and slow left-armer Pushpakumara the rest. The Sri Lankans needed 365 but, apart from Jayasundera, who carried his bat, none had the appetite; Sam Curran picked off the last wicket just after lunch on the final day, meaning all 20 had been shared by Middlesex and Surrey players, including a run-out by Tom Curran.

Close of play: first day, Sri Lanka A 29-4 (Weerakkody 15); second day, England Lions 112-6 (S. M. Curran 14, T. K. Curran 13); third day, Sri Lanka A 41-2 (Jayasundera 18, Silva 7).

England Lions

Batsman	First innings		Second innings	
*K. K. Jennings	b Perera	23	c de Silva b Pushpakumara	37
H. Hameed	c Weerakkody b Fernando	4	b Gamage	0
N. R. T. Gubbins	lbw b Fernando	0	lbw b Perera	2
T. Westley	c Jayasundera b Rajitha	97	lbw b Perera	15
L. S. Livingstone	c Karunaratne b Pushpakumara	59	lbw b Pushpakumara	16
†B. T. Foakes	c Asalanka b Pushpakumara	7	b Pushpakumara	2
S. M. Curran	b Pushpakumara	0	lbw b Perera	36
T. K. Curran	lbw b Pushpakumara	0	st Weerakkody b Perera	29
T. S. Roland-Jones	lbw b Gamage	82	c de Silva b Perera	7
O. P. Rayner	lbw b Jayasundera	13	not out	32
T. G. Helm	not out	13	b Pushpakumara	26
	B 8, lb 6, nb 4	18	B 6, lb 5, nb 2	13
	1/10 (2) 2/14 (3) 3/61 (1) 4/189 (4) 5/203 (5) 6/203 (7) 7/205 (8) 8/210 (6) 9/248 (10) 10/316 (9) (80.2 overs)	316	1/9 (2) 2/16 (3) 3/46 (4) 4/71 (5) 5/80 (6) 6/85 (1) 7/147 (7) 8/152 (8) 9/165 (9) 10/215 (11) (80.5 overs)	215

Gamage 11.2–0–32–1; Fernando 8–1–31–2; Perera 19–3–66–1; Rajitha 10–0–67–1; Pushpakumara 30–4–97–4; Jayasundera 2–0–9–1. *Second innings*—Perera 33–3–73–5; Gamage 8–2–26–1; Fernando 1–0–8–0; Pushpakumara 32.5–4–77–4; Rajitha 1–0–5–0; de Silva 2–1–5–0; Jayasundera 3–0–10–0.

Sri Lanka A

M. D. U. S. Jayasundera c Livingstone b T. K. Curran	0	– (2) not out	64
F. D. M. Karunaratne lbw b Roland-Jones	6	– (1) lbw b T. K. Curran	0
†D. S. Weerakkody lbw b Rayner	68	– lbw b Roland-Jones	16
K. I. C. Asalanka lbw b Roland-Jones	0	– (5) c Foakes b Helm	10
A. R. S. Silva c Foakes b Helm	4	– (4) c Foakes b T. K. Curran	7
*D. M. de Silva run out	3	– c Livingstone b Rayner	20
M. D. K. Perera c T. K. Curran b Rayner	37	– b Rayner	15
P. M. Pushpakumara b Roland-Jones	26	– b T. K. Curran	5
P. L. S. Gamage not out	8	– c Rayner b S. M. Curran	0
C. A. K. Rajitha lbw b Roland-Jones	5	– b S. M. Curran	0
A. M. Fernando b Rayner	0	– c Gubbins b S. M. Curran	30
Lb 6, nb 4	10	Lb 1, nb 1	2
1/1 (1) 2/12 (2) 3/12 (4) 4/29 (5) 5/58 (6) 6/109 (3) 7/154 (7) 8/154 (8) 9/160 (10) 10/167 (11) (47.4 overs)	167	1/0 (1) 2/19 (3) 3/42 (4) 4/63 (5) 5/84 (6) 6/102 (7) 7/114 (8) 8/115 (9) 9/115 (10) 10/169 (11) (58.1 overs)	169

T. K. Curran 10–0–42–1; Roland-Jones 13–3–51–4; Helm 5–0–18–1; S. M. Curran 6–1–19–0; Rayner 12.4–5–27–3; Livingstone 1–0–4–0. *Second innings*—T. K. Curran 12–2–35–3; Roland-Jones 10–3–25–1; Rayner 19–9–53–2; Westley 5–1–15–0; Helm 4–0–19–1; S. M. Curran 8.1–1–21–3.

Umpires: W. N. de Silva and L. E. Hannibal.
Referee: M. C. Mendis.

SRI LANKA A v ENGLAND LIONS

Second A-Team Test

At Dambulla, February 24–27, 2017. Sri Lanka A won by three wickets. Toss: England Lions.

Livingstone announced himself as a player of thrilling potential, but a lesson in subcontinental grind brought a series-levelling win for Sri Lanka A. First, left-arm spinner Pushpakumara, with a simple wicket-to-wicket style, picked up eight scalps from 41 overs of toil (finishing with 13 in the match, and 21 in the series). Then, from 30 for three on the second morning, Karunaratne and Samarawickrama batted into the third for personal-best scores, split only after piling up a stand of 315; a swift 74 from de Silva, who hit 13 fours, swelled the lead to 195. At 58 for four on the last morning, the Lions were heading for a heavy defeat. But Livingstone resisted for 225 balls, showing steel and skill, tactics and ticker, to repel spin from both ends. He hit a second hundred in the match – taking his first-class tally to four – shared a century stand with Foakes, and ended not out on a career-best 140. It gave the tourists a glimmer, and Sri Lanka A lost wickets regularly chasing 90, including four to Tom Curran; Foakes collected his tenth dismissal of the match, a record for the Lions and all their previous incarnations. But the target was too small to defend, and the series was squared.

Close of play: first day, England Lions 339-9 (Rayner 10, Leach 17); second day, Sri Lanka A 333-3 (Karunaratne 140, Samarawickrama 177); third day, England Lions 32-2 (Jennings 11, Westley 1).

England Lions

*K. K. Jennings c Chandraguptha b Pushpakumara	44	– st Samarawickrama b Pushpakumara	18
H. Hameed c Weerakkody b Fernando	15	– c Samarawickrama b Pushpakumara	14
T. P. Alsop c and b Pushpakumara	13	– lbw b de Silva	4
T. Westley b Pushpakumara	68	– b Vandersay	12
L. S. Livingstone lbw b Pushpakumara	105	– not out	140
†B. T. Foakes c Samarawickrama b Pushpakumara	30	– c de Silva b Pushpakumara	54
S. M. Curran st Samarawickrama b de Silva	14	– c Karunaratne b Vandersay	1
T. K. Curran c de Silva b Pushpakumara	9	– c Weerakkody b Pushpakumara	7
T. S. Roland-Jones lbw b Pushpakumara	7	– lbw b de Silva	12
O. P. Rayner c de Silva b Pushpakumara	19	– c Pushpakumara b Vandersay	10
M. J. Leach not out	22	– b Pushpakumara	1
B 4, w 1, nb 2	7	B 10, lb 1	11
1/49 (2) 2/76 (3) 3/77 (1) 4/187 (4) 5/270 (6) 6/287 (5) 7/299 (7) 8/310 (9) 9/313 (8) 10/353 (10) (97.5 overs)	353	1/26 (2) 2/31 (3) 3/44 (4) 4/58 (1) 5/165 (6) 6/172 (7) 7/193 (8) 8/229 (9) 9/255 (10) 10/284 (11) (92.1 overs)	284

Gamage 10–0–64–0; Fernando 8–0–41–1; Pushpakumara 40.5–3–127–8; de Silva 19–4–44–1; Vandersay 17–1–61–0; Jayasundera 3–0–12–0. *Second innings*—Fernando 2–0–9–0; Pushpakumara 37.1–10–78–5; Gamage 7–0–28–0; de Silva 16–3–47–2; Vandersay 27–0–102–3; Jayasundera 3–1–9–0.

Sri Lanka A

M. D. U. S. Jayasundera c Foakes b T. K. Curran	0	– (2) c Foakes b T. K. Curran	32
F. D. M. Karunaratne c T. K. Curran b Rayner	212	– (6) c Foakes b Rayner	5
R. K. Chandraguptha c Foakes b Roland-Jones	1	– (1) c Foakes b T. K. Curran	8
D. S. Weerakkody lbw b Rayner	14	– (3) c Hameed b T. K. Curran	3
†W. S. R. Samarawickrama lbw b Roland-Jones	185	– (4) lbw b T. K. Curran	8
*D. M. de Silva c Foakes b Rayner	74	– (5) st Foakes b Leach	23
A. R. S. Silva c and b Roland-Jones	2	– st Foakes b Leach	2
J. D. F. Vandersay c Foakes b Leach	26	– not out	3
P. M. Pushpakumara c Foakes b T. K. Curran	20	– not out	5
P. L. S. Gamage not out	8		
A. M. Fernando c Alsop b Rayner	1		
B 4, lb 1	5	Lb 1	1
1/6 (1) 2/11 (3) 3/30 (4) 4/345 (5) 5/476 (6) 6/489 (2) 7/489 (7) 8/527 (9) 9/539 (8) 10/548 (11) (135.2 overs)	548	1/12 (1) 2/18 (3) 3/34 (4) 4/68 (2) 5/78 (5) 6/82 (7) 7/82 (6) (7 wkts, 17.4 overs)	90

T. K. Curran 22–3–74–2; Roland-Jones 20–3–67–3; S. M. Curran 11–0–68–0; Rayner 48.2–8–164–4; Leach 18–1–97–1; Westley 9–0–33–0; Livingstone 3–0–28–0; Jennings 4–0–12–0. *Second innings*—T. K. Curran 7–0–38–4; Roland-Jones 5–0–31–0; Rayner 2.4–0–17–1; Leach 3–1–3–2.

Umpires: I. D. Gunawardene and R. A. Kottahachchi.
Referee: B. C. M. S. Mendis.

First A-Team one-day international At Dambulla, March 2, 2017. **Sri Lanka A won by 47 runs** (DLS). **Sri Lanka A 278-7** (48.1 overs) (M. D. K. J. Perera 59, M. D. Gunathilleke 64, N. L. T. C. Perera 56*); **‡England Lions 230-9** (43 overs) (K. K. Jennings 64, C. Overton 60*; L. D. Madushanka 3-50). *The Sri Lankan openers put on 123 without rush, and Tissara Perera – veteran of 114 ODIs – finished the innings with a 35-ball 56*, including five sixes. Liam Livingstone did most to contain, with 1-28 from his ten overs, while leg-spinner Josh Poysden leaked 38 from four. Despite a tidy 64 from Keaton Jennings, England Lions never looked in it, limping to 133-7. Craig Overton swung hard for his first List A fifty, until bad light forced an early conclusion, but received little help.*

Second A-Team one-day international At Dambulla, March 4, 2017. **Sri Lanka A won by 119 runs** (DLS). ‡**England Lions 217** (42.5 overs) (B. M. Duckett 59, L. S. Livingstone 94; T. A. M. Siriwardene 4-40); **Sri Lanka A 201-0** (28.4 overs) (M. D. K. J. Perera 70*, M. D. Gunathilleke 121*). *Dhanushka Gunathilleke's superb hundred had Sri Lanka A cantering home before rain brought victory by calculator; he hit a 65-ball century, faced 88 in all, and cracked six sixes. Earlier, Duckett had showed signs of a return to form, and Livingstone fell just short of a third century on this ground, but Joe Clarke (26) was the only other to make double figures. Livingstone batted through cramp, and heat exhaustion limited him to bowling just one over; Jennings tried to fill in, but his over cost 21, as the Sri Lankan openers put an unbroken double-century stand.*

Third A-Team one-day international At Kurunegala, March 6, 2017. **Sri Lanka A won by four wickets.** ‡**England Lions 184** (40.2 overs) (D. J. Bell-Drummond 51; G. S. N. F. G. Jayasuriya 5-35); **Sri Lanka A 187-6** (37 overs) (G. S. N. F. G. Jayasuriya 83). *Shehan Jayasuriya dazed England Lions with 5-35 from his gentle off-spinners, then knocked them out with a run-a-ball 83. After the Lions won the toss, Daniel Bell-Drummond helped them to 110-2, before a palsy against slow bowling – which accounted for nine wickets in all – left the Sri Lankans a straightforward chase to seal the series.*

Fourth A-Team one-day international At Colombo (RPS), March 9, 2017. **England Lions won by five wickets.** ‡**Sri Lanka A 242** (46.5 overs) (W. S. R. Samarawickrama 54; T. S. Roland-Jones 3-58, G. G. White 3-53); **England Lions 246-5** (47.2 overs) (D. J. Bell-Drummond 100, T. P. Alsop 96). *After Gunathilleke's latest assault – 44 from 29 balls – England looked set for another tough day when Sri Lanka A reached 172-2 in the 30th over. But Toby Roland-Jones and Graeme White shared six wickets to dismantle the middle order. The tourists stuttered to 12-2, before Bell-Drummond, with his second List A hundred (both for the Lions against Sri Lanka A), and Tom Alsop put on 200 – a Lions third-wicket record – to set up victory. All ten Sri Lankan fielders had a bowl.*

Fifth A-Team one-day international At Colombo (RPS), March 11, 2017. **England Lions won by 12 runs** (DLS). ‡**Sri Lanka A 192** (46.1 overs) (M. D. Gunathilleke 51; T. G. Helm 5-33); **England Lions 124-5** (26.3 overs). *Tom Helm took two wickets in his first over, then added three more as Sri Lanka A were toppled for 192. Livingstone backed him up with another miserly spell, claiming 2-27 from his ten. It looked a simple task but, as the spinners applied the brake, the Lions slid from 81-1 to 122-5, and were grateful when rain came two runs later. DLS found in their favour, limiting the series deficit to 3–2.*

DOMESTIC CRICKET IN SRI LANKA IN 2016-17

SA'ADI THAWFEEQ

With Thilanga Sumathipala back in charge of Sri Lanka Cricket, plans to shift the first-class domestic game towards a provincial structure had been dropped. The board promised greater support for the traditional clubs, with grants of approximately £50,000 for each of the 14 who formed Tier A of the Premier League, and £40,000 for each of the ten in Tier B, which was also given first-class status. So it was unfortunate that the season was overshadowed by legal disputes concerning Tier B.

Indeed, the Tier's winners could not be declared until an inquiry had been held into allegations of match-fixing between Panadura and Kalutara PCC – for mutual benefit, rather than betting purposes, with the teams accused of agreeing that Panadura should win and gain promotion to Tier A, while giving Kalutara enough bonus points to avoid relegation. Attention focused on the final day: Panadura, resuming at 180 for two, added 243 at more than ten an over; Kalutara were bowled out for 197 in 22.5 overs, and Panadura, chasing 165 in 15, got there with eight balls to spare. Ports Authority, who originally finished second to Panadura, claimed they had been cheated of promotion. The inquiry finally found both teams guilty of misconduct, but not of match-fixing. The game was declared void, the points table adjusted (so Ports Authority went up after all) and the clubs fined, while the players and coaches were suspended for a year (and the captains for two). But, after an appeal to the sports minister, the teams were allowed to play in 2017-18 pending a further inquiry.

Meanwhile, an order from the Colombo District Court prevented the launch of a revamped Premier Limited-Overs Tournament, following a legal challenge by Negombo. They had gained promotion to Tier B in place of Sebastianites, who had beaten them in the 2015-16 Sara Trophy final but were ruled to have included six ineligible players. Sebastianites filed a counter-challenge demanding reinstatement and, after Negombo refused to replay the final, Tier B went ahead without either. When they were also excluded from the one-day tournament, Negombo went to court. To sidestep the problem, SLC scrapped the planned competition and replaced it with a tournament for 24 districts; in practice, it was soon clear that this was effectively a rebranding of the same teams who formed the Premier League. They were divided into eight groups of three, with the winners advancing to quarter-finals. **Colombo District** beat Kegalle District in the final, fielding sides indistinguishable from Colombo CC and Colts.

A few weeks later, a rather different Colombo District beat Galle in the final of a one-day tournament staged to prepare for the Champions Trophy. Though the teams were still labelled as districts, there were only four, drawn from the top players.

Back in the premier domestic competition, **Sinhalese** won their eighth first-class title (and their 32nd going back to the pre-first-class era). Chilaw Marians had dominated Tier A of the Premier League for most of the season, thanks to slow left-armer Malinda Pushpakumara, who took 77 wickets in the tournament; they won seven of their first nine games, and entered the final round of the Super Eight in pole position. But, after Pushpakumara was called up to play against England Lions, they lost their last game to Ragama, while Sinhalese romped to a two-day victory over Colombo to clinch the trophy.

With their international stars mostly unavailable – though Dhanushka Gunathilleke scored 420 at 70 in the five games he did play – Sinhalese owed much to the spinners Sachithra Senanayake and Jeffrey Vandersay, who took 83 wickets between them. Pushpakumara, who took a further 21 for Sri Lanka A, finished with 98, a Sri Lankan record, beating Muttiah Muralitharan's 96 in 2003-04 (Gayan Sirisoma, another left-arm spinner, took third place, with 91 in Tier B). Sadeera Samarawickrama, an exciting strokemaker from Colts, was the season's leading batsman, with 1,209 and four centuries in all first-class cricket. Samarawickrama and Pushpakumara later made Test debuts.

FIRST-CLASS AVERAGES IN 2016-17

BATTING (550 runs)

		M	*I*	*NO*	*R*	*HS*	*100*	*Avge*	*Ct/St*
1	†M. M. M. S. Cooray (*Saracens*)	7	12	4	569	189	1	71.12	5
2	W. S. R. Samarawickrama (*Colts/SL A*)	11	21	2	1,209	185	4	63.63	9/4
3	M. H. P. Gunathilake (*Kurunegala Youth*)	8	14	4	619	109*	1	61.90	6
4	†F. D. M. Karunaratne (*Sinhal/SL A/SL*)	10	19	2	971	212	5	57.11	10
5	A. K. Perera (*Nondescripts*)	10	19	3	908	139*	3	56.75	13
6	†K. Y. de Silva (*Ports Authority*)	8	12	1	615	165*	1	55.90	8
7	†K. P. N. M. Karunanayake (*Bloomfield*)	9	17	0	926	183	3	54.47	3
8	†R. K. Chandraguptha (*Colombo/SL A*)	10	18	2	846	157	4	52.87	7
9	†P. C. de Silva (*Nondescripts*)	7	14	1	650	95	0	50.00	2
10	†B. K. E. L. Milantha (*Ragama*)	10	16	2	667	144	1	47.64	7
11	†D. P. D. N. Dickwella (*Nondesc/SL A/SL*)	9	18	1	808	183	1	47.52	14/4
12	D. V. B. Hasaranga (*Navy*)	8	13	1	570	94	0	47.50	15
13	†G. S. N. F. G. Jayasuriya (*Chilaw Mar*)	10	18	0	853	237	2	47.38	15
14	†D. S. Weerakkody (*Nondescripts/SL A*)	9	17	1	758	113	2	47.37	13/1
15	†M. L. R. Buddika (*Burgher*)	9	14	0	612	133	2	43.71	5
16	S. C. Serasinghe (*Chilaw Marians*)	10	18	0	784	207	2	43.55	12
17	†N. T. Paranavitana (*Tamil Union*)	9	15	0	641	109	2	42.73	9
18	J. A. L. H. Jayakody (*Bloomfield*)	9	17	1	676	118*	1	42.25	9
19	D. A. S. Gunaratne (*Army/SL A/SL*)	10	18	1	705	158	1	41.47	17
20	†M. D. U. S. Jayasundera (*Ragama/SL A*)	11	18	3	611	144	3	40.73	8
21	N. M. N. P. Nawela (*Badureliya*)	9	16	2	566	86	0	40.42	11
22	P. W. H. de Silva (*Colombo*)	10	17	2	586	116*	1	39.06	10
23	I. S. S. Samarasooriya (*Saracens*)	9	16	1	583	110	1	38.86	6
24	†M. L. Udawatte (*Chilaw Marians*)	10	18	0	699	89	0	38.83	10
25	†S. G. Liyanage (*Tamil Union*)	10	17	0	616	127	1	36.23	7
26	A. R. S. Silva (*Ragama/Sri Lanka A*)	14	21	0	751	109	1	35.76	5
27	†L. K. Fransisco (*Army*)	9	17	1	556	116*	2	34.75	25/6
28	A. V. L. Madushan (*Army*)	10	19	0	629	152	1	33.10	8

BOWLING (35 wickets)

		Style	*O*	*M*	*R*	*W*	*BB*	*5I*	*Avge*
1	N. C. Komasaru (*Ports Authority*)	SLA	272.3	79	622	52	6-50	7	11.96
2	R. M. G. K. Sirisoma (*Panadura*)	SLA	368.1	71	1,118	91	9-38	12	12.28
3	E. M. C. D. Edirisinghe (*Ports Auth*)	SLA	252.3	52	681	53	6-86	4	12.84
4	P. M. Pushpakumara (*Chilaw M/SL A*)	SLA	485	87	1,441	98	8-127	11	14.70
5	M. A. Aponso (*Ragama*)	SLA	297.1	50	837	51	7-71	3	16.41
6	S. M. S. M. Senanayake (*Sinhalese*)	OB	285.1	50	818	43	4-15	0	19.02
7	N. M. Kavikara (*Lankan*)	SLA	311.1	44	968	49	6-73	4	19.75
8	K. M. M. de Silva (*Bloomfield*)	SLA	324.5	38	1,133	57	6-120	6	19.87
9	D. R. F. Weerasinghe (*Lankan*)	OB	304.4	44	901	45	6-42	3	20.02
10	M. A. Liyanapathiranage (*Chilaw M*)	OB	233.2	47	764	37	6-36	2	20.64
11	P. C. de Silva (*Nondescripts*)	SLA	260	39	856	41	6-67	2	20.87
12	M. D. K. Perera (*Colts/SL A/SL*)	OB	256	29	785	37	6-82	2	21.21
13	J. D. F. Vandersay (*Sinhalese/SL A*)	LB	298.3	32	1,103	51	6-44	6	21.62
14	K. D. V. Wimalasekara (*Army*)	RFM	228	42	788	35	4-37	0	22.51
15	A. A. S. Silva (*Badureliya*)	OB	359.1	48	1,218	51	7-87	3	23.88
16	D. S. Hettiarachchi (*Burgher*)	SLA	415.2	56	1,290	52	7-158	5	24.80
17	S. Randiv (*Saracens*)	OB	327.4	58	1,004	39	6-85	2	25.74
18	P. H. T. Kaushal (*Nondescripts*)	OB	278.3	36	968	36	6-78	4	26.88
19	P. A. D. L. R. Sandakan (*Col/SL A/SL*)	SLW	323	42	1,101	39	4-51	0	28.23
20	C. A. K. Rajitha (*Saracens/SL A*)	RFM	283.2	30	1,130	38	6-59	4	29.73
21	D. K. R. C. Jayatissa (*Galle*)	OB	290	38	1,081	35	5-101	2	30.88
22	P. L. S. Gamage (*Colombo/SL A*)	RFM	322.5	56	1,178	35	5-51	2	33.65

PREMIER LEAGUE TOURNAMENT TIER A IN 2016-17

Group A	P	W	L	D	Pts
CHILAW MARIANS	6	4	1	1	82.520
SINHALESE	6	2	1	3	68.155
TAMIL UNION	6	2	0	4	67.060
NONDESCRIPTS	6	1	1	4	66.170
Badureliya	6	2	3	1	51.365
Bloomfield	6	0	2	4	42.800
Galle	6	0	3	3	32.090

Group B	P	W	L	D	Pts
RAGAMA	6	2	0	4	68.190
COLOMBO	6	1	0	5	62.355
COLTS	6	1	0	5	60.555
ARMY	6	0	0	6	53.420
Burgher	6	0	1	5	42.645
Saracens	6	0	1	5	41.895
Moors	6	0	2	4	34.480

Super Eight	P	W	L	D	Pts
Sinhalese	7	4	1	2	88.885
Chilaw Marians	7	4	2	1	84.580
Nondescripts	7	2	2	3	76.790
Ragama	7	2	1	4	73.985
Colombo	7	2	2	3	71.310
Army	7	1	3	3	54.380
Tamil Union	7	1	3	3	49.395
Colts	7	1	3	3	46.540

Plate	P	W	L	D	Pts
Saracens	5	0	0	5	61.310
Burgher	5	0	0	5	54.100
Badureliya	5	1	0	4	41.725
Bloomfield	5	0	0	5	37.835
Moors	5	0	0	5	29.555
Galle	5	0	1	4	28.080

The top four teams from each group advanced to the Super Eight, carrying forward their results against fellow qualifiers, then played the other four qualifiers. The bottom three from each group entered the Plate competition, run on the same principles. The bottom-placed Plate team, Galle, were relegated and replaced by Ports Authority, the winners of Tier B.

Outright win = 12pts; win by an innings = 2pts extra; lead on first innings in a drawn game = 8pts; tie on first innings in a drawn game = 4pts. Bonus points were awarded as follows: 0.15 of a point for each wicket taken and 0.005 of a point for each run scored, up to 400 runs per innings.

Group A

At Katunayake (FTZ), December 2–4, 2016. **Chilaw Marians won by 291 runs. ‡Chilaw Marians 235** (A. A. S. Silva 5-102) **and 262-7 dec; Badureliya 113** (P. M. Pushpakumara 6-41) **and 93** (M. A. Liyanapathiranage 6-36). *Chilaw Marians 17.485pts, Badureliya 3.58pts. Slow left-armer Malinda Pushpakumara began a record-breaking season with 10-88.*

At Colombo (PSO), December 2–4, 2016. **Drawn. Sinhalese 503** (F. D. M. Karunaratne 149, M. D. Gunathilleke 117) **and 51-1; ‡Tamil Union 460** (K. D. K. Vithanage 125; J. D. F. Vandersay 5-110). *Tamil Union 3.65pts, Sinhalese 11.755pts. Dimuth Karunaratne and Dhanushka Gunathilleke put on 201 for Sinhalese's second wicket.*

At Colombo (NCC), December 3–5, 2016. **Nondescripts won by nine wickets. Nondescripts 443-9 dec** (D. P. D. N. Dickwella 183; K. M. M. de Silva 5-83) **and 104-1; ‡Bloomfield 200 and 346** (K. P. N. M. Karunanayake 124; P. H. T. Kaushal 5-132). *Nondescripts 17.52pts, Bloomfield 4.23pts.*

At Galle, December 8–10, 2016. **Drawn. ‡Galle 352 and 189-5; Tamil Union 338** (S. G. Liyanage 127; D. K. R. C. Jayatissa 5-101). *Galle 12.205pts, Tamil Union 3.94pts.*

At Colombo (Bloomfield), December 9–11, 2016. **Drawn. Badureliya 156** (K. M. M. de Silva 5-41) **and 337-7 dec; ‡Bloomfield 233** (K. P. N. M. Karunanayake 108) **and 248-6.** *Bloomfield 12.955pts, Badureliya 4.865pts.*

At Colombo (NCC), December 9–11, 2016. **Drawn. ‡Nondescripts 385** (D. S. Weerakkody 113; P. M. Pushpakumara 5-74) **and 199; Chilaw Marians 285** (P. H. T. Kaushal 6-78) **and 193-9** (P. H. T. Kaushal 5-53). *Nondescripts 13.77pts, Chilaw Marians 5.39pts.*

At Katunayake (FTZ), December 15–17, 2016. **Tamil Union won by six wickets. ‡Tamil Union 450** (N. T. Paranavitana 100, B. M. A. J. Mendis 115; P. M. Pushpakumara 5-134) **and 69-4; Chilaw Marians 219 and 297.** *Tamil Union 17.345pts, Chilaw Marians 4.68pts.*

At Colombo (SSC), December 15–17, 2016. **Drawn. Nondescripts 393 and 232-4 dec; ‡Sinhalese 219** (M. D. Gunathilleke 112*; P. C. de Silva 6-72) **and 172-4.** *Sinhalese 4.055pts, Nondescripts 13.225pts.*

At Colombo (PSO), December 19–21, 2016. **Tamil Union won by 38 runs. ‡Tamil Union 252 and 239-9 dec** (A. A. S. Silva 7-87); **Badureliya 129** (R. L. B. Rambukwella 5-47) **and 324** (N. M. Subasinghe 126). *Tamil Union 17.455pts, Badureliya 5.115pts.*

At Katunayake (FTZ), December 21–23, 2016. **Chilaw Marians won by an innings and 231 runs. ‡Chilaw Marians 552-8 dec** (G. S. N. F. G. Jayasuriya 168, S. C. Serasinghe 151); **Galle 157** (P. M. Pushpakumara 5-70) **and 164** (P. M. Pushpakumara 6-78). *Chilaw Marians 19pts, Galle 2.805pts. Another 11 wickets for Pushpakumara ensured a massive win.*

At Colombo (SSC), December 21–23, 2016. **Drawn. Sinhalese 490** (S. M. S. M. Senanayake 120); **‡Bloomfield 201** (J. D. F. Vandersay 5-53) **and 296-9** (J. A. L. H. Jayakody 118*). *Sinhalese 12.85pts, Bloomfield 3.985pts. Sachithra Senanayake, with a maiden century, and Kasun Madushanka (50) added 148 for Sinhalese's ninth wicket.*

At Colombo (Bloomfield), December 28–30, 2016. **Drawn. ‡Tamil Union 314** (P. G. C. S. P. Pussegolla 5-102) **and 120-6 dec; Bloomfield 115 and 172-4.** *Bloomfield 3.835pts, Tamil Union 12.27pts.*

At Colombo (NCC), December 28–30, 2016. **Drawn. Nondescripts 370** (D. S. Weerakkody 110, A. K. Perera 139*) **and 330** (D. K. R. C. Jayatissa 5-153); **‡Galle 170** (P. C. de Silva 6-67). *Nondescripts 13pts, Galle 3.85pts.*

At Colombo (SSC), December 28–30, 2016. **Sinhalese won by ten wickets. ‡Sinhalese 347** (A. A. S. Silva 6-126) **and 39-0; Badureliya 143** (J. D. F. Vandersay 6-44) **and 237** (P. A. S. S. Jeewantha 129). *Sinhalese 16.93pts, Badureliya 3.4pts. Badureliya were 66-7, but No. 8 Saliya Saman Jeewantha hit 129 in 119 balls – with 13 sixes – to delay Sinhalese's first victory.*

At Colombo (Bloomfield), January 2–4, 2017. **Drawn. ‡Bloomfield 276 and 343-7 dec** (K. P. N. M. Karunanayake 183); **Galle 185** (K. M. M. de Silva 5-60) **and 220-7.** *Bloomfield 13.645pts, Galle 4.575pts.*

At Maggona, January 6–8, 2017. **Badureliya won by seven wickets. Galle 218 and 233; ‡Badureliya 316** (S. Weerakoon 5-96) **and 139-3.** *Badureliya 17.275pts, Galle 4.205pts.*

At Katunayake (FTZ), January 6–8, 2017. **Chilaw Marians won by 34 runs. ‡Chilaw Marians 193** (J. D. F. Vandersay 5-61) **and 309** (J. D. F. Vandersay 5-94); **Sinhalese 179** (P. M. Pushpakumara 7-52) **and 289.** *Chilaw Marians 17.51pts, Sinhalese 5.34pts. Chilaw Marians' third win ensured their place in the Super Eight. Pushpakumara's 10-144 took him past 500 first-class wickets.*

At Colombo (PSO), January 6–8, 2017. **Drawn. ‡Nondescripts 268 and 349-6; Tamil Union 446** (B. M. A. J. Mendis 151*). *Tamil Union 12.4pts, Nondescripts 4.585pts. Both teams reached the Super Eight.*

At Maggona, January 11–13, 2017. **Badureliya won by seven wickets. Nondescripts 185** (D. S. Tillakaratne 6-78) **and 239** (D. S. Tillakaratne 5-81); **‡Badureliya 330** (P. H. T. Kaushal 5-86) **and 96-3.** *Badureliya 17.13pts, Nondescripts 4.07pts.*

At Colombo (Bloomfield), January 14–16, 2017. **Chilaw Marians won by 378 runs. ‡Chilaw Marians 291** (M. L. S. M. P. Fernando 6-93) **and 437-6 dec** (G. S. N. F. G. Jayasuriya 237); **Bloomfield 136** (P. M. Pushpakumara 5-78) **and 214** (M. A. Liyanapathiranage 5-86). *Chilaw Marians 18.455pts, Bloomfield 4.15pts. Chilaw Marians' fourth win took they to the top of Group A. Arosh Janoda hit eight sixes in a 55-ball 80, out of 105 for the ninth wicket with Maduka Liyanapathiranage. Seven wickets took Pushpakumara to 55 in six games.*

At Galle, January 14–16, 2017. **Sinhalese won by five wickets. ‡Galle 128 and 312** (M. M. Jaleel 144); **Sinhalese 379** (M. B. Ranasinghe 148) **and 66-5.** *Sinhalese 17.225pts, Galle 4.45pts. Sinhalese leapt from fifth place to second in their group to qualify for the Super Eight.*

Group B

At Colombo (Colts), November 29–30, 2016. **Colts won by an innings and 77 runs. Colts 367** (C. K. B. Kulasekara 5-77); **‡Moors 158 and 132.** *Colts 18.835pts, Moors 2.95pts.*

At Colombo (CCC), December 2–4, 2016. **Colombo won by 109 runs. Colombo 195** (C. A. K. Rajitha 6-59) **and 208** (S. K. C. Randunu 5-66); **‡Saracens 173 and 121.** *Colombo 17.015pts, Saracens 4.47pts.*

At Panagoda, December 2–4, 2016. **Drawn. Army 316** (D. A. S. Gunaratne 158; J. R. M. W. S. Bandara 6-73) **and 202-9 dec; ‡Burgher 219 and 192-6.** *Army 12.99pts, Burgher 4.905pts.*

At Colombo (BRC), December 9–11, 2016. **Drawn. ‡Saracens 302** (D. S. Hettiarachchi 5-96) **and 212** (I. S. S. Samarasooriya 110); **Burgher 197** (C. A. K. Rajitha 5-72) **and 183-3** (T. M. N. Sampath 100*). *Burgher 4.9pts, Saracens 12.52pts.*

At Colombo (CCC), December 9–11, 2016. **Drawn. ‡Colombo 218 and 309-7 dec** (R. K. Chandraguptha 116); **Army 216 and 227-7** (S. S. Pathirana 5-78). *Colombo 13.185pts, Army 4.765pts.*

At Colombo (Moors), December 9–11, 2016. **Ragama won by ten wickets. ‡Moors 217 and 181** (S. Nanayakkare 6-55); **Ragama 361** (M. D. U. S. Jayasundera 112; S. S. M. Perera 5-119) **and 40-0.** *Ragama 17.005pts, Moors 3.49pts.*

At Colombo (Thurstan), December 14–16, 2016. **Drawn. ‡Saracens 401** (M. M. M. S. Cooray 189) **and 5-0; Ragama 448** (M. D. U. S. Jayasundera 109). *Ragama 11.5pts, Saracens 3.525pts. Sangeeth Cooray and Kaushalya Gajasinghe (99) added 245 for Saracens' fifth wicket.*

At Colombo (Colts), December 15–17, 2016. **Drawn. Colts 276** (H. Dumindu 105) **and 316-6; ‡Colombo 384** (P. W. H. de Silva 116*). *Colts 4.46pts, Colombo 12.32pts. Wanindu Hasaranga de Silva hit a maiden hundred and added 150 for the ninth wicket with Lahiru Madushanka (59).*

At Colombo (BRC), December 15–17, 2016. **Drawn. ‡Moors 376** (S. D. Withanawasam 181*) **and 219-8 dec; Army 242** (N. S. Pathirana 5-69) **and 169-3.** *Moors 12.925pts, Army 4.755pts.*

At Colombo (BRC), December 21–23, 2016. **Drawn. ‡Burgher 293 and 280; Moors 226 and 325-8** (K. P. A. Perera 104; H. H. Ramanayake 5-88). *Burgher 13.565pts, Moors 5.755pts.*

At Colombo (Colts), December 21–23, 2016. **Drawn. Colts 374** (A. J. A. D. D. L. A. Jayasinghe 109; S. K. C. Randunu 6-94) **and 170-5; ‡Saracens 351.** *Colts 12.22pts, Saracens 4.005pts.*

At Panagoda, December 21–23, 2016. **Drawn. Army 276** (L. K. Fransisco 103; M. A. Aponso 7-71) **and 234**; **Ragama 304** (A. R. S. Silva 109; R. P. N. Priyadarshana 5-52) **and 40-2.** *Army 4.35pts, Ragama 12.72pts.*

At Colombo (BRC), December 28–30, 2016. **Drawn. Colts 360** (W. S. R. Samarawickrama 119; D. S. Hettiarachchi 6-115) **and 150-3; ‡Burgher 249** (N. G. R. P. Jayasuriya 6-74). *Burgher 3.195pts, Colts 12.05pts.*

At Colombo (Moors), December 28–30, 2016. **Drawn. ‡Saracens 292 and 296** (S. S. M. Perera 7-92); **Moors 256.** *Moors 4.28pts, Saracens 12.44pts.*

At Maggona, December 28–30, 2016. **Drawn. Ragama 406-9 dec** (P. L. S. Gamage 5-103); **‡Colombo 232-4.** *Ragama 2.6pts, Colombo 2.51pts.*

At Colombo (BRC), January 6–8, 2017. **Ragama won by eight wickets. ‡Burgher 194** (M. A. Aponso 5-34) **and 152**; **Ragama 254** (T. M. N. Sampath 5-98) **and 93-2.** *Ragama 16.735pts, Burgher 3.53pts. Ragama qualified for the Super Eight.*

At Colombo (Colts), January 6–8, 2017. **Drawn. Army 297** (C. Sudaraka 5-98) **and 288-5 dec** (L. K. Fransisco 116*); **‡Colts 112 and 445-9** (W. S. R. Samarawickrama 130). *Colts 4.81pts, Army 13.775pts. Sadeera Samarawickrama struck 130 in 98 balls as Colts chased 474 in 80 overs; they reached 397-5, but after a frantic finale their last pair had to hold out for 13 balls, 29 runs short.*

At Colombo (Moors), January 6–8, 2017. **Drawn. ‡Colombo 560** (S. M. A. Priyanjan 124, L. Abeyratne 156*) **and 137** (N. S. Pathirana 6-72); **Moors 275 and 141-6.** *Moors 5.08pts, Colombo 13.085pts. Colombo's 560 was the tournament's highest total, and ensured qualification.*

At Colombo (CCC), January 14–16, 2017. **Drawn. ‡Colombo 326** (E. M. D. Y. Munaweera 191; D. S. Hettiarachchi 6-137) **and 222-7** (R. K. Chandraguptha 102*); **Burgher 465** (T. M. N. Sampath 123). *Colombo 4.24pts, Burgher 12.55pts.*

At Colombo (NCC), January 14–16, 2017. **Drawn. ‡Colts 366** (M. A. Aponso 7-85) **and 170-2** (W. S. R. Samarawickrama 112*); **Ragama 366** (M. D. U. S. Jayasundera 144; N. T. Gamage 5-70). *Ragama 7.63pts, Colts 8.18pts. Akila Dananjaya (92) and Prabath Jayasuriya (79) put on 157 for Colts' ninth wicket, helping them into the Super Eight.*

At Colombo (Moors), January 14–16, 2017. **Drawn. ‡Saracens 358** (T. A. M. Siriwardene 121) **and 179-5 dec; Army 361** (A. V. L. Madushan 152; S. Randiv 6-85) **and 146-5.** *Saracens 4.935pts, Army 12.785pts. The Army annexed the final place in the Super Eight.*

Super Eight

At Colombo (PSO), January 20–22, 2017. **Chilaw Marians won by 15 runs. ‡Chilaw Marians 190** (G. D. Bandara 5-36) **and 148** (R. P. N. Priyadarshana 5-68); **Army 183 and 140** (P. M. Pushpakumara 5-59). *Chilaw Marians 16.69pts, Army 4.615pts. Needing 156, the Army were 140-7 before Janoda and Pushpakumara seized their last three wickets in ten deliveries.*

At Colombo (Colts), January 20–23, 2017. **Colombo won by ten wickets. Tamil Union 377** (K. D. K. Vithanage 130) **and 149** (P. L. S. Gamage 5-51); **‡Colombo 497** (R. K. Chandraguptha 157, L. D. Madushanka 164) **and 30-0.** *Colombo 17.15pts, Tamil Union 4.13pts. Ron Chandraguptha and Madushanka put on 240 for Colombo's sixth wicket.*

At Katunayake (FTZ), January 20–22, 2017. **Sinhalese won by 209 runs. ‡Sinhalese 293** (F. D. M. Karunaratne 125) **and 193; Colts 100 and 177.** *Sinhalese 17.43pts, Colts 4.385pts. Colts were 80-7 when Ishan Jayaratne came in and hit seven sixes in a career-best 85 from 40 balls.*

At Colombo (CCC), January 20–23, 2017. **Ragama won by one wicket. Nondescripts 265 and 213; ‡Ragama 127 and 352-9.** *Ragama 17.395pts, Nondescripts 5.24pts.*

At Colombo (Colts), January 28–30, 2017. **Sinhalese won by ten wickets. Army 228 and 106; ‡Sinhalese 323 and 12-0.** *Sinhalese 16.675pts, Army 3.17pts.*

At Colombo (CCC), January 28–29, 2017. **Chilaw Marians won by an innings and seven runs. Colts 150** (J. G. A. Janoda 7-38) **and 39; ‡Chilaw Marians 196.** *Chilaw Marians 17.98pts, Colts 2.445pts. Chilaw Marians won in two days after bowling out Colts for 39 in 13.4 overs; Pushpakumara's figures were 3.4–1–3–4.*

At Colombo (PSO), January 28–31, 2017. **Colombo won by three wickets. Nondescripts 200 and 332** (A. K. Perera 108); **‡Colombo 293** (R. K. Chandraguptha 108) **and 240-7** (L. Ambuldeniya 5-85). *Colombo 17.665pts, Nondescripts 5.21pts.*

At Colombo (RPS), January 28–31, 2017. **Drawn. Tamil Union 318** (D. T. Hewathantri 113, N. T. Paranavitana 109) **and 146-6; ‡Ragama 506-7 dec** (B. K. E. L. Milantha 144, K. L. J. Vimukthi 130). *Ragama 12.4pts, Tamil Union 3.37pts. Dineth Thimodya Hewathantri and Tharanga Paranavitana added 214 for Tamil Union's third wicket before they lost eight for 57. In reply, Lahiru Milantha and Janith Liyanage Vimukthi shared a second-wicket stand of 277.*

At Colombo (SSC), February 5–7, 2017. **Army won by an innings and 30 runs. Tamil Union 174 and 179; ‡Army 383** (B. M. A. J. Mendis 5-97). *Army 18.915pts, Tamil Union 3.265pts.*

At Panagoda, February 5–7, 2017. **Chilaw Marians won by 366 runs. Chilaw Marians 213 and 461-9 dec** (A. K. V. Adikari 101, S. C. Serasinghe 207); **‡Colombo 190 and 118** (P. M. Pushpakumara 7-58). *Chilaw Marians 18.065pts, Colombo 4.39pts. Serasinghe reached a maiden double-century and put on 227 with Vidura Adikari for Chilaw Marians' third wicket. Pushpakumara took ten or more in a match for the fourth time in this tournament to finish with 77 in nine games, ensuring his team's seventh win and an eight-point lead entering the final round.*

At Katunayake (FTZ), February 5–7, 2017. **Nondescripts won by six wickets. ‡Colts 192** (L. Ambuldeniya 6-63) **and 222; Nondescripts 307** (M. D. K. Perera 6-82) **and 111-4.** *Nondescripts 17.09pts, Colts 4.17pts.*

At Colombo (RPS), February 5–7, 2017. **Sinhalese won by eight wickets. ‡Ragama 220** (N. V. R. Perera 5-33) **and 201; Sinhalese 389 and 35-2.** *Sinhalese 17.12pts, Ragama 3.905pts. Slow left-armer Amila Aponso reached 50 wickets in the season.*

At Colombo (SSC), February 14–16, 2017. **Nondescripts won by 176 runs. Nondescripts 268 and 266** (A. K. Perera 106); **‡Army 227 and 131.** *Nondescripts 17.67pts, Army 4.79pts.*

At Colombo (Colts), February 14–17, 2017. **Ragama won by seven wickets. Chilaw Marians 168** (W. G. H. N. Premaratne 5-41) **and 295** (S. Nanayakkare 7-92); **‡Ragama 276** (J. G. A. Janoda 5-45) **and 191-3.** *Ragama 17.335pts, Chilaw Marians 4.265pts. Chilaw Marians' defeat cost them the title.*

At Colombo (BRC), February 14–15, 2017. **Sinhalese won by 84 runs. ‡Sinhalese 147** (P. W. H. de Silva 5-15) **and 155; Colombo 101 and 117.** *Sinhalese 16.51pts, Colombo 4.09pts. Sinhalese's two-day victory meant they leapfrogged Chilaw Marians to win the Premier League.*

At Panagoda, February 14–17, 2017. **Colts won by 182 runs.** ‡**Colts 218** (B. M. D. K. Mendis 5-71) **and 411** (P. M. Liyanagamage 5-112); **Tamil Union 168** (H. I. A. Jayaratne 5-40) **and 279** (A. Dananjaya 5-103). *Colts 18.09pts, Tamil Union 5.235pts. Samarawickrama passed 1,000 runs for the season, during his 93 in Colts' second innings.*

CHAMPIONS

1988-89	Nondescripts / Sinhalese	1997-98	Sinhalese	2008-09	Colts
1989-90	Sinhalese	1998-99	Bloomfield	2009-10	Chilaw Marians
1990-91	Sinhalese	1999-2000	Colts	2010-11	Bloomfield
1991-92	Colts	2000-01	Nondescripts	2011-12	Colts
1992-93	Sinhalese	2001-02	Colts	2012-13	Sinhalese
1993-94	Nondescripts	2002-03	Moors	2013-14	Nondescripts
1994-95	Bloomfield / Sinhalese	2003-04	Bloomfield	2014-15	Ports Authority
1995-96	Colombo	2004-05	Colts	2015-16	Tamil Union
1996-97	Bloomfield	2005-06	Sinhalese	2016-17	Sinhalese
		2006-07	Colombo		
		2007-08	Sinhalese		

Sinhalese have won the title outright 8 times, Colts 6, Bloomfield 4, Nondescripts 3, Colombo 2, Chilaw Marians, Moors, Ports Authority and Tamil Union 1. Sinhalese have shared it twice, Bloomfield and Nondescripts once each.

The tournament was known as the Lakspray Trophy from 1988-89 to 1989-90, the P. Saravanamuttu Trophy from 1990-91 to 1997-98, and the Premier League from 1998-99.

Plate

At Colombo (BRC), January 20–22, 2017. **Drawn. Badureliya 300** (M. S. R. Wijeratne 102; N. S. Pathirana 5-52) **and 259-8 dec** (M. S. R. Wijeratne 100*); ‡**Moors 214 and 76-4.** *Badureliya 12.895pts, Moors 4.15pts. Sahan Wijeratne scored a century in each innings.*

At Panagoda, January 20–22, 2017. **Drawn.** ‡**Bloomfield 317** (D. S. Hettiarachchi 6-103); **Burgher 391-9** (C. G. Wijesinghe 130*; K. M. M. de Silva 5-91). *Bloomfield 2.935pts, Burgher 11.455pts.*

At Colombo (Bloomfield), January 20–22, 2017. **Drawn.** ‡**Galle 301** (C. A. K. Rajitha 5-57) **and 259-5 dec** (P. K. J. R. N. Nonis 108*); **Saracens 315** (T. A. M. Siriwardene 115) **and 84-2.** *Galle 4.6pts, Saracens 12.245pts.*

At Colombo (BRC), January 27–29, 2017. **Drawn. Badureliya 302** (W. A. D. P. Madusanka 110*); ‡**Saracens 321-6** (G. K. Amarasinghe 130). *Badureliya 2.41pts, Saracens 11.105pts. Pathum Madusanka carried his bat for a maiden hundred.*

At Maggona, January 27–29, 2017. **Drawn.** ‡**Bloomfield 152 and 201-4; Moors 371** (K. M. M. de Silva 6-148). *Bloomfield 3.265pts, Moors 11.955pts.*

At Colombo (Bloomfield), January 27–29, 2017. **Drawn.** ‡**Galle 407** (A. K. K. Y. Lanka 167; D. S. Hettiarachchi 7-158); **Burgher 447-6** (M. L. R. Buddika 116). *Burgher 11.5pts, Galle 2.9pts.*

At Moratuwa (Tyronne Fernando), February 5–7, 2017. **Drawn.** ‡**Burgher 358** (M. L. R. Buddika 133) **and 278-7; Badureliya 346** (T. M. N. Sampath 5-81). *Badureliya 4.28pts, Burgher 12.68pts. Badureliya's Alankara Silva and Burgher's Dinuka Hettiarachchi reached 50 wickets in the season.*

At Colombo (Colts), February 5–7, 2017. **Drawn. Bloomfield 207** (S. Randiv 5-65) **and 380** (C. A. K. Rajitha 5-152); ‡**Saracens 351** (K. M. M. de Silva 6-120) **and 49-4.** *Bloomfield 5.035pts, Saracens 13pts. Bloomfield's Malith de Silva passed 50 wickets – but Saracens won the Plate.*

At Colombo (BRC), February 5–7, 2017. **Drawn.** ‡**Moors 175 and 238-5; Galle 310-9 dec.** *Galle 11.8pts, Moors 3.415pts.*

PREMIER LEAGUE TOURNAMENT TIER B IN 2016-17

	Played	*Won*	*Lost*	*Tied*	*Drawn*	*Abandoned*	*Points*
Ports Authority	9	6	0	0	2	1	125.335
Panadura	8*	5	0	0	2	1	116.270
Navy SC	9	3	1	0	4	1	93.490
Lankan CC	9	3	2	0	3	1	88.945
Kalutara Town.	9	1	3	0	4	1	58.510
Police SC.	9	2	3	1	2	1	57.750
Kurunegala Youth	9	1	6	0	1	1	49.755
Air Force SC	9	1	6	0	1	1	49.275
Kalutara PCC	8*	1	2	1	3	1	43.970
Negombo†	9	0	0	0	0	9	0

* *The match between Panadura and Kalutara PCC was expunged after allegations of collusion; Ports Authority were promoted and Kalutara PCC relegated.*

† *Negombo's nine fixtures were cancelled because of a dispute over whether they or Sebastianites should have been promoted into Tier B.*

Outright win = 12pts; win by an innings = 2pts extra; tie = 6pts; lead on first innings in a drawn game = 8pts. Bonus points were awarded as follows: 0.15 of a point for each wicket taken and 0.005 of a point for each run scored, up to 400 runs per innings.

At Welisara, December 2–4, 2016. **Ports Authority won by an innings and three runs. Air Force 172 and 172** (N. C. Komasaru 5-47); **‡Ports Authority 347.** *Ports Authority 18.735pts, Air Force 3.22pts.*

At Maggona, December 2–4, 2016. **Drawn. Kalutara Town 327** (T. D. T. N. Siriwardene 107; W. M. V. Weerakoon 5-94) **and 222-3 dec; ‡Kalutara PCC 237 and 135-4.** *Kalutara PCC 3.81pts, Kalutara Town 12.845pts. Thirteen players made their debuts, and Nawamini Siriwardene began his first-class career with a century.*

At Kurunegala, December 2–4, 2016. **Drawn. Navy 294 and 337-5** (M. M. Madushanka 120, W. S. C. Sadamal 105*); **‡Kurunegala Youth 389** (W. P. D. P. Dharmasiri 134, M. H. P. Gunathilake 109*). *Kurunegala Youth 12.195pts, Navy 4.655pts. Four of the 12 debutants made hundred: for Kurunegala, Dhanushka Dharmasiri and Hashan Prabath Gunathilake, who put on 103 for the tenth wicket with Chirath Mapatuna (25); for the Navy, Madura Madushanka and Sameera Sadamal.*

At Panadura, December 2–3, 2016. **Panadura won by an innings and 15 runs. Panadura 263; ‡Police 97** (R. M. G. K. Sirisoma 9-38) **and 151** (T. C. B. Fernando 5-42). *Panadura 18.315pts, Police 2.74pts. Left-arm spinner Gayan Sirisoma's 13.3–4–38–9 was the best return of the season.*

At Panadura, December 7–9, 2016. **Drawn. ‡Panadura 353 and 153-6; Kalutara Town 166** (R. M. G. K. Sirisoma 7-53) **and 342** (N. Gamage 148*; R. M. G. K. Sirisoma 6-107). *Panadura 13.53pts, Kalutara Town 4.94pts. In Panadura's first innings, debutant Hasitha Nirmal struck with his first delivery; in the second, opener Nisal Randika raced to 80 in 42 balls, with seven sixes.*

At Panagoda, December 9–11, 2016. **Lankan won by an innings and five runs. Air Force 230** (N. M. Kavikara 5-63) **and 80** (N. M. Kavikara 5-30); **‡Lankan 315.** *Lankan 18.575pts, Air Force 3.05pts.*

At Maggona, December 9–11, 2016. **Kalutara PCC won by five wickets. ‡Kurunegala Youth 197** (R. Selvaraj 6-63) **and 151; Kalutara PCC 192** (E. M. K. K. R. Ekanayake 5-40) **and 159-5.** *Kalutara PCC 16.755pts, Kurunegala Youth 3.99pts. Leg-spinner Ruwantha Ekanayake took a wicket with his first ball on debut, and finished with six in the match.*

At Welisara, December 9–11, 2016. **Navy won by an innings and 119 runs. Navy 376** (D. K. L. Edusuriya 145; S. Madanayake 5-108); **‡Police 96 and 161.** *Navy 18.88pts, Police 2.785pts.*

At Welisara, December 15–16, 2016. **Navy won by an innings and 124 runs. ‡Navy 316; Air Force 103 and 89** (A. D. R. Batagoda 5-31). *Navy 18.58pts, Air Force 2.46pts.*

At Panadura, December 15–16, 2016. **Panadura won by nine wickets. Lankan 163 and 176** (R. M. G. K. Sirisoma 5-55); **‡Panadura 294** (M. Silva 105; D. R. F. Weerasinghe 6-81) **and 48-1.** *Panadura 16.71pts, Lankan 3.345pts.*

At Hambantota, December 15–17, 2016. **Ports Authority won by an innings and 14 runs. Police 103** (N. C. Komasaru 5-35) **and 106** (D. M. G. S. Dissanayake 5-29); **‡Ports Authority 223-8 dec.** *Ports Authority 18.115pts, Police 2.245pts.*

At Kurunegala, December 16–18, 2016. **Kalutara Town won by eight wickets. Kurunegala Youth 232** (E. M. K. K. R. Ekanayake 111) **and 213** (V. K. G. Perera 5-58); **‡Kalutara Town 414-9 dec** (M. R. P. U. Dias 130) **and 34-2.** *Kalutara Town 17.17pts, Kurunegala Youth 3.875pts.*

At Panagoda, December 21–23, 2016. **Ports Authority won by an innings and 78 runs. Kalutara PCC 49** (N. C. Komasaru 5-17) **and 273** (P. Nissanka 104; N. C. Komasaru 6-54); **‡Ports Authority 400-7 dec** (W. A. I. Rangana 109). *Ports Authority 19pts, Kalutara PCC 2.66pts. Left-arm spinners Chanaka Komasaru and Chamikara Edirisinghe (6.2–2–8–4) bowled out Kalutara PCC for 49.*

At Kurunegala, December 21–23, 2016. **Lankan won by an innings and 79 runs. Lankan 422** (L. A. C. Ruwansiri 100); **‡Kurunegala Youth 253 and 90** (D. R. F. Weerasinghe 6-42). *Lankan 19pts, Kurunegala Youth 3.215pts.*

At Welisara, December 21–23, 2016. **Panadura won by 99 runs. ‡Panadura 268 and 288-8 dec; Navy 125** (R. M. G. K. Sirisoma 8-46) **and 332** (R. M. G. K. Sirisoma 5-152). *Panadura 17.78pts, Navy 4.985pts.*

At Hambantota, December 21–23, 2016. **Police won by one wicket. ‡Air Force 168 and 142** (H. M. Jayawardene 7-59); **Police 184 and 128-9** (W. S. Rangika 5-42). *Police 16.56pts, Air Force 4.4pts. Needing 127, Police were 73-6, then 119-9, against Shohan Rangika's off-breaks, but inched home.*

At Panagoda, December 26–28, 2016. **Drawn. Lankan 428** (H. S. M. Zoysa 127, G. C. M. Fernando 104); **‡Kalutara PCC 152** (N. M. Kavikara 6-73) **and 102-5.** *Kalutara PCC 2.77pts, Lankan 12.25pts.*

At Maggona, December 28–30, 2016. **Ports Authority won by an innings and 13 runs. ‡Kalutara Town 156 and 166** (E. M. C. D. Edirisinghe 5-34); **Ports Authority 335-7 dec** (K. Y. de Silva 165*; V. K. G. Perera 5-109). *Ports Authority 18.675pts, Kalutara Town 2.66pts.*

At Panadura, December 28–30, 2016. **Panadura won by an innings and 49 runs. Panadura 320; ‡Air Force 137** (R. M. G. K. Sirisoma 7-56) **and 134.** *Panadura 18.6pts, Air Force 2.855pts. Sirisoma passed 50 wickets for the season.*

At Katunayake (FTZ), December 28–30, 2016. **Police won by seven wickets. ‡Kurunegala Youth 109 and 134** (W. W. A. K. R. Fernando 8-36); **Police 148** (H. M. T. I. Herath 8-48) **and 96-3.** *Police 16.22pts, Kurunegala Youth 3.165pts.*

At Panagoda, January 6–8, 2017. **Lankan won by ten wickets. ‡Lankan 446-9 dec** (H. S. M. Zoysa 203, Lal Kumar 107; A. Y. R. de Silva 5-137) **and 24-0; Kalutara Town 289 and 178.** *Lankan 17.12pts, Kalutara Town 3.685pts. Maduranga Zoysa struck nine sixes in a maiden double-century, the only one in Tier B; he added 222 for Lankan's fourth wicket with Pakistani batsman Lal Kumar.*

At Kurunegala, January 6–8, 2017. **Kurunegala Youth won by seven wickets. Air Force 200** (H. M. T. I. Herath 7-66) **and 190; ‡Kurunegala Youth 307 and 84-3.** *Kurunegala Youth 16.955pts, Air Force 3.9pts.*

At Welisara, January 6–8, 2017. **Drawn. ‡Navy 258 and 325-7 dec; Kalutara PCC 224 and 165-4.** *Navy 13.015pts, Kalutara PCC 4.495pts.*

At Panadura, January 6–8, 2017. **Drawn. ‡Panadura 306** (E. M. C. D. Edirisinghe 5-101) **and 202-9 dec** (E. M. C. D. Edirisinghe 6-86); **Ports Authority 210** (R. M. G. K. Sirisoma 7-95) **and 172-5.** *Panadura 12.79pts, Ports Authority 4.76pts.*

At Colombo (BRC), January 14–16, 2017. **Tied. Police 235 and 85** (G. W. R. T. Silva 7-31); **‡Kalutara PCC 139 and 181** (S. Madanayake 7-70). *Kalutara PCC 10.6pts, Police 10.6pts. This was the first tie in Sri Lankan first-class cricket. Suwanji Madanayake, stranded on 96* in Police's first innings, combined 104 runs in the match with 10-107.*

At Maggona, January 14–16, 2017. **Navy won by ten wickets. Kalutara Town 143 and 214; ‡Navy 350** (N. D. Malan 113; K. M. P. Kumara 7-98) **and 10-0.** *Navy 16.8pts, Kalutara Town 3.285pts.*

At Mattegoda, January 14–16, 2017. **Ports Authority won by 252 runs. ‡Ports Authority 248 and 259-6 dec; Lankan 108 and 147.** *Ports Authority 17.535pts, Lankan 3.675pts.*

At Maggona, January 20–22, 2017. **Air Force won by an innings and 120 runs. Air Force 426-9 dec** (M. W. L. S. Lakmal 115, R. P. Thattil 175); **‡Kalutara PCC 160 and 146.** *Air Force 19pts, Kalutara PCC 2.88pts. Lahiru Lakmal and Roscoe Thattil added 226 for Air Force's fourth wicket.*

At Kurunegala, January 20–22, 2017. **Ports Authority won by seven wickets. Kurunegala Youth 143** (N. C. Komasaru 6-50) **and 161** (N. C. Komasaru 5-46, E. M. C. D. Edirisinghe 5-56); **‡Ports Authority 154 and 151-3.** *Ports Authority 16.525pts, Kurunegala Youth 3.47pts.*

At Colombo (Moors), January 20–22, 2017. **Drawn. Lankan 436** (A. B. L. D. Rodrigo 133) **and 69-5; ‡Navy 483** (D. R. F. Weerasinghe 5-146). *Lankan 3.845pts, Navy 12.25pts. Lakshan Rodrigo (133 in 113 balls) and Shasheen Fernando (96) put on 215 for Lankan's second wicket.*

At Hambantota, January 20–22, 2017. **Drawn. Kalutara Town 307** (S. L. Jayawardene 101) **and 127-5; ‡Police 287** (T. D. T. N. Siriwardene 5-55). *Police 3.685pts, Kalutara Town 11.67pts.*

At Maggona, January 23–25, 2017. **Panadura won by three wickets. Kalutara PCC 390** (R. M. G. K. Sirisoma 7-131) **and 197** (R. M. G. K. Sirisoma 6-88); **‡Panadura 423** (W. L. P. Fernando 111; G. W. R. T. Silva 5-102) **and 167-7.** *Panadura 17.835pts, Kalutara PCC 5.485pts: points later annulled. This match was expunged from the competition after an inquiry ruled that the teams had colluded to bring about Panadura's promotion while protecting Kalutara PCC from relegation through bonus points; on the final day, the two teams scored 607 for 23 from 60 overs. Another 13 wickets for Sirisoma took him past 500 in his career.*

At Hambantota, January 26–28, 2017. **Drawn. Lankan 159 and 108-4 dec; ‡Police 118** (N. M. Kavikara 5-41) **and 45-2.** *Police 2.915pts, Lankan 11.135pts.*

At Horana, January 27–29, 2017. **Drawn. Kalutara Town 147 and 4-1; ‡Air Force 148** (A. Y. R. de Silva 6-38). *Kalutara Town 2.255pts, Air Force 10.39pts. The first first-class match at Arons CC.*

At Welisara, January 27–29, 2017. **Drawn. Ports Authority 260 and 148; ‡Navy 232** (N. C. Komasaru 5-59) **and 33-3.** *Navy 4.325pts, Ports Authority 11.99pts. Ports Authority's slow left-armers Komasaru and Edirisinghe both passed 50 wickets for the season. Their team apparently finished second, until their successful protest against Panadura gave them the title and promotion.*

At Panadura, January 27–28, 2017. **Panadura won by an innings and 31 runs. Panadura 309; ‡Kurunegala Youth 131** (R. M. G. K. Sirisoma 7-42) **and 147** (R. M. G. K. Sirisoma 7-24). *Panadura 18.545pts, Kurunegala Youth 2.89pts. Aruna Dharmasena (90*) and Sirisoma (23) added 118 for Panadura's last wicket. Sirisoma's 14-66, the best figures of the season and his seventh ten-for in the tournament, gave him 91 in eight games. Panadura believed they were champions, but the circumstances of their previous win returned to haunt them.*

DISTRICTS ONE-DAY TOURNAMENT IN 2016-17

Eight 50-over mini-leagues plus knockout

Semi-final At Colombo (NCC), March 31, 2017. **Colombo District won by seven wickets. ‡Mannar District 130** (37.1 overs); **Colombo District 136-3** (27 overs).

Semi-final At Colombo (PSO), March 31, 2017. **Kegalle District won by seven wickets. ‡Kandy District 96** (29 overs); **Kegalle District 98-3** (20 overs).

Final At Colombo (PSO), April 2, 2017. **Colombo District won by 72 runs. Colombo District 295-6** (50 overs) (S. M. A. Priyanjan 107); **‡Kegalle District 223** (47.4 overs) (P. A. D. L. R. Sandakan 5-39). *Colombo captain Ashan Priyanjan led from the front with 107 from 98 balls, before left-arm wrist-spinner Lakshan Sandakan wiped out Kegalle's middle order with five in 12 deliveries.*

SUPER PROVINCIAL LIMITED-OVERS TOURNAMENT IN 2016-17

50-over league plus final

Final At Colombo (RPS), April 29, 2017 (day/night). **Colombo District won by 137 runs. ‡Colombo District 307-8** (50 overs) (L. D. Chandimal 113*); **Galle District 170** (30.3 overs). *Colombo captain Dinesh Chandimal steered his side past 300, and Tissara Perera grabbed four wickets in 11 balls as they wiped out Galle with nearly 20 overs in hand.*

WEST INDIES CRICKET IN 2017

New brand, still panned

VANEISA BAKSH

West Indies ended the year on a low, losing seven matches in New Zealand across the formats, and winning none. The Test and one-day failures were no longer a surprise, but West Indies relinquished any remaining esteem with a poor showing in the Twenty20s, the one arena in which they could usually be relied upon.

Not even the presence of Chris Gayle – joining the squad after blitzing 146 in the final of the Bangladesh Premier League – could turn things round: he totalled 38 runs across four innings. Earlier in the year, he had rejoined the one-day side thanks to a rapprochement with the board. Previously, players would be considered for international selection only if they were available for the corresponding format in domestic cricket. But a new management team headed by new chief executive Johnny Grave introduced a more pragmatic approach and, on the tour of England in September, Gayle was picked for the

WEST INDIES IN 2017

	Played	*Won*	*Lost*	*Drawn/No result*
Tests	10	3	6	1
One-day internationals	21	3	16	2
Twenty20 internationals	10	6	4	–

JANUARY		
FEBRUARY		
MARCH / APRIL	3 ODIs (h) v England	(page 255)
	3 Tests, 3 ODIs and 4 T20Is (h) v Pakistan	(page 1017)
MAY		
JUNE / JULY	2 ODIs and 3 T20Is (h) v Afghanistan	(page 1027)
	5 ODIs and 1 T20I (h) v India	(page 1029)
AUGUST / SEPTEMBER	3 Tests, 5 ODIs and 1 T20I (a) v England	(page 318)
	1 ODI (a) v Ireland	(page 889)
OCTOBER / NOVEMBER	2 Tests (a) v Zimbabwe	(page 1045)
DECEMBER / JANUARY	2 Tests, 3 ODIs and 3 T20Is (a) v New Zealand	(page 914)

For a review of West Indian domestic cricket from the 2016-17 season, see page 1035.

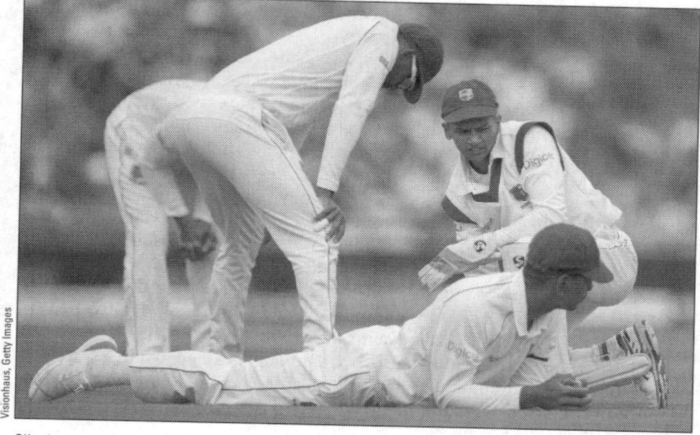

Slipping away: West Indies' cordon reflect on another missed opportunity.

first time since 2015. By then, though, it seemed too late to rescue automatic World Cup qualification. They needed to hammer England to squeeze into the top eight of the ICC's rankings, but lost 4–0, and were left having to navigate the ten-team qualification tournament in Zimbabwe in March 2018.

The inclusion of Gayle was designed to add experience as much as explosiveness: without him, and the other exiles including the Bravos and Kieron Pollard, West Indies looked so young that the team led by baby-faced Test captain Jason Holder appeared to have recently emerged from school. But that was no excuse. They had been around long enough; they just did not seem to have the instincts of professionals.

Somewhere between the youth teams and seniors, there was a gap, something essential left out of the education. The system produced players with poor judgment and an inability to adapt to conditions: wasteful batsmen and wayward bowlers. Those in charge of the high-performance academies needed to address the cricketing illiteracy.

But that would have required a coherent approach from the cricket administrators. In May, the WICB rebranded themselves as Cricket West Indies – and the team as "the Windies" – but it made little difference. The president, Dave Cameron, was still there, as was the board's characteristic obduracy, and the row over who owned cricket in the region grew toxic. In July, Keith Rowley, the prime minister of Trinidad and Tobago, said: "They are handling large sums of money from the ICC, unearned money, used to strengthen people who are in office."

The Caribbean Community – a bloc that aim to promote co-operation between their 15 members – had called for the dissolution of the board. But Gaston Browne, the prime minister of Antigua and Barbuda, broke ranks, insisting they should not interfere. After a tense summit, Rowley aired concerns that the issue had the potential to "destroy" the Caribbean Community.

A host of different players were tried, but results remained poor. West Indies lost their first Test series at home to Pakistan, after No. 11 Shannon Gabriel's ill-advised swipe in the decider at Roseau. They then lost a one-day international against Afghanistan at Gros Islet, with leg-spinner Rashid Khan running riot, and were battered by the touring Indians until a consolation in the sole T20. West Indies travelled to England in August and were on course for total embarrassment after the First Test. But they salvaged pride at Headingley, edging a thriller thanks to Kraigg Brathwaite and Shai Hope, who hit 494 runs between them. They scrapped hard in the low-scoring decider at Lord's, before finally succumbing to the skill of James Anderson and Ben Stokes.

After winning comfortably in Zimbabwe, it was on to New Zealand to ice the miserable cake of 2017. At the turn of the year, they had only two players in the top-ten lists, both in T20s: Evin Lewis, who blasted 176 in a one-dayer at The Oval before retiring hurt, was second among batsmen, while leg-spinner Samuel Badree was sixth among bowlers. The women had a tough time, too. At the World Cup in England, they lost five of seven matches and failed to reach the knockouts. Hammering Sri Lanka in October was little comfort.

Despite it all, the people found some cricket that was drenched in the spirit of the region. The Caribbean Premier League filled stadiums with patriotic posses and blaring music, casting aside – at least for a while – the woes of the international game. Amid the cacophony, an irony was not lost: in 2017, the best moments in West Indies cricket had little to do with Cricket West Indies.

WEST INDIES v PAKISTAN IN 2016-17

MAZHER ARSHAD

Twenty20 internationals (4): West Indies 1, Pakistan 3
One-day internationals (3): West Indies 1, Pakistan 2
Test matches (3): West Indies 1, Pakistan 2

West Indies needed to block seven balls to draw the Test decider in Dominica, with No. 11 Shannon Gabriel on strike. To general astonishment, he swiped at an innocuous Yasir Shah delivery – and was bowled, gifting Pakistan their first Test series win in the Caribbean at the eighth attempt, and a clean sweep across all formats. Amid wild Pakistani celebrations, the Trinidadian TV commentator Fazeer Mohammed summed up the mood, his cry of "Why did he do that?" becoming a social media hit. Misbah-ul-Haq was kinder, suggesting Gabriel might not have been confident blocking with so many close fielders, though he had appeared comfortable until then. Misbah's charity was understandable. Before the Test series, he and Younis Khan had announced their intention to retire at the end of it; Gabriel gave them the perfect swansong.

After Pakistan had easily won in Jamaica, where Younis became the first Pakistani to reach 10,000 Test runs, and Yasir picked up eight of his 25 wickets, few predicted a thrilling finale. But West Indies bounced back in Barbados, defending a small target on the final day. Gabriel was the hero then, his brimstone bowling claiming five for 11; ten days later, he was to play the villain, leaving Roston Chase, who was 101 not out, crestfallen: his 403 runs in the series at over 100 had done most to keep West Indies competitive.

Another Test had been in the original schedule, but two extra Twenty20 internationals were slotted in earlier in the tour; the WICB abandoned the idea of staging them in Florida. It was only the second time – after Bangladesh v Zimbabwe in 2015-16 – that two Full Members had played a four-match 20-over series. In none did West Indies look like the team that had lifted the World T20 a year earlier. Pakistan won the first two – making Sarfraz Ahmed the third, after Kumar Sangakkara and Misbah, to win his first six T20Is as captain – and took the series 3–1. Shadab Khan, a teenage leg-spinner who had starred in the Pakistan Super League, finished with ten wickets at 7.50.

The one-dayers were more significant than usual: the teams were desperate for rankings points to help them squeeze into the ICC's top eight by September 30, and qualify automatically for the 2019 World Cup (in the event, neither team budged: Pakistan stayed eighth, and West Indies ninth). All three matches were played at the Providence Stadium in Guyana, which had been relaid after gaining a reputation for low scoring. West Indies pulled off their record chase to take the first, before Pakistan won the series convincingly. Sarfraz had passed his first test since becoming permanent one-day captain. Yet his leadership style was criticised for being too demonstrative, and often shouted at his fielders during crunch moments. After that dramatic finale in Dominica, however, he and his team-mates could make as much noise as he wanted.

PAKISTAN TOURING PARTY

*Misbah-ul-Haq (T), Ahmed Shehzad (T/50/20), Asad Shafiq (T), Asif Zakir (50), Azhar Ali (T), Babar Azam (T/50/20), Faheem Ashraf (50), Fakhar Zaman (50/20), Hasan Ali (T/50/20), Imad Wasim (50/20), Junaid Khan (50), Kamran Akmal (50/20), Mohammad Abbas (T), Mohammad Amir (T/50), Mohammad Asghar (T/50), Mohammad Hafeez (50/20), Mohammad Nawaz (20), Rumman Raees (20), Sarfraz Ahmed (T/50/20), Shadab Khan (T/50/20), Shan Masood (T), Shoaib Malik (50/20), Sohail Tanvir (20), Usman Khan (20), Usman Salahuddin (T), Wahab Riaz (T/50/20), Yasir Shah (T), Younis Khan (T). *Coach:* J. M. Arthur.

Sarfraz Ahmed captained in the limited-overs matches.

TEST AVERAGES

WEST INDIES – BATTING AND FIELDING

	T	*I*	*NO*	*R*	*HS*	*100*	*50*	*Avge*	*Ct/St*
R. L. Chase	3	6	2	403	131	2	2	100.75	2
J. O. Holder	3	6	2	182	58	0	2	45.50	1
†K. O. A. Powell	3	6	0	161	49	0	0	26.83	5
S. D. Hope	3	6	0	149	90	0	1	24.83	5
S. O. Dowrich	3	6	0	109	56	0	1	18.16	11/1
K. C. Brathwaite	3	6	0	101	43	0	0	16.83	1
†S. O. Hetmyer	3	6	0	96	25	0	0	16.00	2
†D. Bishoo	3	6	0	83	28	0	0	13.83	1
†V. A. Singh	3	6	0	63	32	0	0	10.50	2
A. S. Joseph	3	6	0	21	8	0	0	3.50	1
S. T. Gabriel	3	6	2	9	5	0	0	2.25	2

BOWLING

	Style	*O*	*M*	*R*	*W*	*BB*	*5I*	*Avge*
S. T. Gabriel	RFM	117	27	282	15	5-11	1	18.80
J. O. Holder	RFM	113.4	35	210	10	3-23	0	21.00
A. S. Joseph	RFM	107	27	284	10	3-53	0	28.40
D. Bishoo	LB	114.2	18	356	9	3-116	0	39.55
R. L. Chase	OB	68.4	8	245	6	4-103	0	40.83

Also bowled: K. C. Brathwaite (OB) 7–1–22–0.

PAKISTAN – BATTING AND FIELDING

	T	*I*	*NO*	*R*	*HS*	*100*	*50*	*Avge*	*Ct*
Misbah-ul-Haq	3	6	2	271	99*	0	3	67.75	1
Azhar Ali	3	6	0	261	127	2	0	43.50	5
Ahmed Shehzad	2	4	0	121	70	0	1	30.25	0
Sarfraz Ahmed	3	5	0	141	54	0	2	28.20	9
Babar Azam	3	6	1	136	72	0	2	27.20	3
Younis Khan	3	6	0	122	58	0	1	20.33	10
Yasir Shah	3	5	1	70	38*	0	0	17.50	2
†Mohammad Amir	3	5	0	75	27	0	0	15.00	1
Asad Shafiq	3	5	0	67	22	0	0	13.40	1
Mohammad Abbas	3	4	2	6	4	0	0	3.00	1

Played in one Test: Hasan Ali 8*, 15* (1 ct); Shadab Khan 16, 1; †Shan Masood 9, 21 (2 ct); Wahab Riaz 9 (1 ct).

BOWLING

	Style	*O*	*M*	*R*	*W*	*BB*	*5I*	*Avge*
Mohammad Amir	LFM	129	48	227	13	6-44	1	17.46
Hasan Ali	RFM	37	11	55	3	3-33	0	18.33
Mohammad Abbas	RFM	126	33	288	15	5-46	1	19.20
Yasir Shah	LB	188.2	40	549	25	7-94	3	21.96

Also bowled: Asad Shafiq (LB) 2–0–15–0; Azhar Ali (LB) 9–1–22–1; Shadab Khan (LB) 40–3–145–1; Wahab Riaz (LF) 29–6–95–2.

First Twenty20 international At Bridgetown, Barbados, March 26, 2017. **Pakistan won by six wickets. West Indies 111-8** (20 overs) (C. R. Brathwaite 34*; Shadab Khan 3-7); ‡**Pakistan 115-4** (17.1 overs) (Shoaib Malik 38*). *MoM:* Shadab Khan. *T20I debuts:* R. Powell (West Indies); Shadab Khan. *Teenage leg-spinner Shadab Khan bamboozled West Indies on his senior debut to set up a straightforward Pakistan victory. He picked up three wickets from his first eight balls, two with googlies, and would have had a fourth if Kamran Akmal – returning as a specialist batsman after almost three years out of the national side – had not grassed Kieron Pollard at backward point. Shadab conceded just seven runs in all, the cheapest four-over return by a debutant in Twenty20 internationals. Captain Carlos Brathwaite's 34* dragged West Indies from 49-6 to 111, but it was never enough. Babar Azam (29) and Shoaib Malik came together at 49-3, and added a leisurely 46.*

Second Twenty20 international At Port-of-Spain, Trinidad, March 30, 2017. **Pakistan won by three runs. Pakistan 132** (20 overs) (S. P. Narine 3-22, C. R. Brathwaite 3-37); ‡**West Indies 129-8** (20 overs) (M. N. Samuels 44; Shadab Khan 4-14). *MoM:* Shadab Khan. *T20I debut:* Fakhar Zaman (Pakistan). *Pakistan defended a mediocre 132 thanks to another stirring performance from Shadab. After Marlon Samuels struck Imad Wasim for consecutive sixes, West Indies needed 73 with 12 overs and nine wickets left. But Shadab punctured the chase, and his last delivery – a googly that took Samuels's edge – gave him a fourth wicket, reducing West Indies to 81-6. Jason Holder (26*) didn't give up, though, and Sunil Narine hit boundaries off the first two balls of the last over, reducing the requirement to six. Hasan Ali bowled a wide, but the rest were on the mark and, after Narine ran himself out, Pakistan escaped. Earlier in the chase, there was a spate of collisions while batsmen scampered for singles. In the second over, Evin Lewis bumped into Shadab and was run out. In the fourth, Chadwick Walton was involved in two tangles: a brush with Sohail Tanvir, followed by a hard crash with Ahmed Shehzad. An ambulance arrived, and paramedics strapped Shehzad into a neck brace, but a few overs later he was back on the field, merrily swearing at Samuels. After being inserted, Pakistan had been struggling at 95-8, but a 36-run partnership between Shadab and Wahab Riaz set up a total they could just about protect.*

Third Twenty20 international At Port-of-Spain, Trinidad, April 1, 2017. **West Indies won by seven wickets.** ‡**Pakistan 137-8** (20 overs) (Kamran Akmal 48, Babar Azam 43); **West Indies 138-3** (14.5 overs) (E. Lewis 91). *MoM:* E. Lewis. *T20I debut:* J. N. Mohammed (West Indies). *Lewis's brutal 51-ball 91, including nine sixes – both Twenty20 records against Pakistan – propelled West Indies to an emphatic win and kept the series alive. He pulled and slog-swept at will, even hitting Shadab over the ropes three times, before falling to him at long-off with the line in sight. Lendl Simmons hit the next ball for four, meaning West Indies had romped home with 31 deliveries to spare, their most in an uninterrupted T20I. It also ended Pakistan's six-match winning streak since Sarfraz Ahmed had become captain in the format. In previous games, his plan had been to field first and restrict the runs with spinners; here he decided to bat. Sarfraz's experimentation extended to the line-up: Imad went in at No. 3 after two balls (and came back after four) while Fakhar Zaman, usually an opener, batted at No. 6. Kamran and Babar made forties, but of the others only Fakhar reached double figures in a below-par total.*

Fourth Twenty20 international At Port-of-Spain, Trinidad, April 2, 2017. **Pakistan won by seven wickets. West Indies 124-8** (20 overs) (C. A. K. Walton 40, C. R. Brathwaite 37*); ‡**Pakistan 127-3** (19 overs) (Ahmed Shehzad 53, Babar Azam 38). *MoM:* Hasan Ali. *MoS:* Shadab Khan.

Pakistan's miserly bowlers sent down 66 dot balls, and restricted West Indies to 124, which their batsmen easily trumped to take the series. Hasan Ali was the pick, his mixture of inswingers and cunning slower deliveries picking up 2-12. He also bowled two maidens, and another from left-arm seamer Rumman Raees – replacing Sohail Tanvir, whom Lewis had destroyed in the previous game – made it a Pakistan record in T20Is. Walton hit some meaty blows, and Brathwaite a career-best 37, but six West Indians were dismissed in single figures. In reply, Shehzad and Babar took Pakistan past 100 for the loss of one wicket, making the result a formality.*

First one-day international At Providence, Guyana, April 7, 2017. **West Indies won by four wickets. Pakistan 308-5** (50 overs) (Ahmed Shehzad 67, Kamran Akmal 47, Mohammad Hafeez 88, Shoaib Malik 53; A. R. Nurse 4-62); ‡**West Indies 309-6** (49 overs) (E. Lewis 47, K. O. A. Powell 61, J. N. Mohammed 91*, A. R. Nurse 34*). *MoM:* J. N. Mohammed. *ODI debut:* Shadab Khan (Pakistan). *With 150 needed from 16 overs, West Indies looked unlikely winners, even with six wickets in hand. They had never successfully chased a target over 300, and had just 176 one-day international caps between them, 69 fewer than Pakistan's Shoaib Malik alone. Pakistan's 308 was also a ground record. But Jason Mohammed blasted 91* off 58 balls – his best in ODIs – and rattled off the last 50 with Ashley Nurse, whose 15-ball 34* helped West Indies home with an over to spare. Pakistan were lacklustre in the field. Shadab took two wickets on his one-day debut, yet was far less threatening than in the Twenty20 series. They lacked intensity with the bat, too. Mohammad Hafeez – for some reason coming in at No. 3 instead of Babar, who had hit four hundreds in his last seven innings in that position – top-scored with 88, and shared half-century stands with Shehzad and Shoaib. But Hafeez dithered in the middle overs, taking 14 balls to move from 27 to 30, and couldn't build up enough steam at the end.*

Second one-day international At Providence, Guyana, April 9, 2017. **Pakistan won by 74 runs. Pakistan 282-5** (50 overs) (Babar Azam 125*, Mohammad Hafeez 32, Imad Wasim 43*); ‡**West Indies 208** (44.5 overs) (J. O. Holder 68, A. R. Nurse 44; Hasan Ali 5-38). *MoM:* Babar Azam. *Babar moved back to No. 3, scored a career-best 125* from 132 balls, and helped Pakistan reach 282. On a pitch that looked tired after 99 overs in the first match, it was more than enough to square the series. When Hafeez was stumped off a wide in the 26th over, the score was 113-3, and 250 looked a struggle. But a rapid 99-run partnership between Babar and Imad – including 62 off the last five overs – provided match-winning impetus. Hasan then crippled the reply with five wickets. Jason Mohammed, so violent just two days before, faced 16 balls for one, and only Holder and Nurse put up much resistance, making personal-bests and hitting over half the team's runs.*

Third one-day international At Providence, Guyana, April 11, 2017. **Pakistan won by six wickets.** ‡**West Indies 233-9** (50 overs) (S. D. Hope 71, J. N. Mohammed 59); **Pakistan 236-4** (43.1 overs) (Mohammad Hafeez 81, Shoaib Malik 101*). *MoM:* Shoaib Malik. *MoS:* Shoaib Malik. *After Shannon Gabriel dismissed Kamran with the first ball of the chase, and two more quickly followed, Pakistan were stumbling in pursuit of 234. They established command over the series decider, though, thanks to Hafeez and Shoaib, who stitched together a 113-run partnership. Hafeez top-edged a sweep on 81, but Shoaib stayed the course. He knocked off the remaining runs with Sarfraz, and finished with a six to bring up his ninth century in one-day internationals, and second outside Asia. It was Pakistan's 460th ODI victory, taking them past India, and behind only Australia (554). West Indies dropped catches and declined a review against Hafeez when he was trapped in front on 39. Their batting had been hesitant, too, particularly against left-arm spinner Imad, who conceded 24 from his ten overs. Shai Hope and Jason Mohammed put on 101, but Hope took 97 balls to reach 50, the slowest by a West Indian in ODIs since Darren Bravo needed 102 against Bangladesh at Mirpur in 2012-13.*

> "The ball reared up, prompting one of the best players of short-pitched bowling in the modern game to react like a vampire confronted by a crucifix."
>
> England v South Africa in 2017, Second Test, page 308

At Trelawny Greenfields, Jamaica, April 15–17, 2017. **Drawn.** ‡**West Indies Board President's XI 419** (126.1 overs) (K. O. A. Powell 58, S. O. Hetmyer 97, V. A. Singh 135*; Mohammad Amir 3-66) **and 152-2** (42 overs) (K. O. A. Powell 84*); **Pakistanis 192** (68 overs) (Ahmed Shehzad 55, Sarfraz Ahmed 50; D. K. Jacobs 4-45). *Shimron Hetmyer, Kieran Powell and Vishaul Singh all forced their way into West Indies' Test squad, as the Pakistanis struggled. Hasan Ali strained his groin in the field, delaying his Test debut.*

WEST INDIES v PAKISTAN

First Test

At Kingston, Jamaica, April 21–25, 2017. Pakistan won by seven wickets. Toss: Pakistan. Test debuts: S. O. Hetmyer, V. A. Singh; Mohammad Abbas.

Younis Khan had last played a Test in Jamaica in June 2005, when he scored a hundred in a Pakistan victory. In between, he had amassed 7,212 runs and was now within 23 of 10,000. It was a goal that staved off his retirement, and brought him back to Sabina Park, hosting its 50th Test.

At tea on the third day, Younis walked off on 9,999. Two balls after the break, he swept Chase fine, ran towards the dressing-room, punched the air, and pointed to the emblem on his breast. He had become the first from Pakistan to reach the landmark, the 13th in all and, at 39 years and 145 days, the oldest. It took him 116 matches, making him third-fastest, behind Brian Lara (111) and Kumar Sangakkara (115).

While the focus was on batting milestones (Misbah-ul-Haq also became the seventh Pakistani to 5,000 runs), it was their bowling that won the match. Mohammad Abbas, making his debut because of Hasan Ali's injury in the warm-up game, impressed many with his movement, and had Kraigg Brathwaite poking to slip with the eighth ball of the series. Mohammad Amir was the pick, though, claiming three of the top four – including Kieran Powell, playing his first Test in almost three years after a dalliance with baseball – and cleaning up the tail to finish with a career-best six for 44. He added another in the second innings for match figures of 40–15–64–7, another best.

Powell's dismissal early on the first afternoon left West Indies 71 for five, and their prospects looked as gloomy as the skies. But the last five wickets quadrupled the score, and Holder was stranded on 57 when they were all out for 286 on the third morning (only 11 overs had been possible on the second day because of rain and a leaking cover). Chase had begun the resistance with 63, and put on 118 with Dowrich, before he was caught in stunning fashion by Wahab Riaz, who ran back from mid-off and dived near the boundary. Wahab also surprised everyone by not overstepping in a Test for the first time, at the 25th attempt.

In reply, Pakistan had four half-centurions, but none made three figures. Misbah came closest, running out of partners on 99 when last man Abbas unsuccessfully reviewed an lbw. Misbah smiled, comfortable with a 121-run lead on a wearing surface. West Indies were less enthused, and Gabriel was fined 50% of his match fee for barging into Sarfraz Ahmed at the end of an over.

The hosts reached 72 for one on the fourth evening, but by stumps Yasir Shah had knocked over the top four, and the rest crumbled on the last day; he collected six for 63, as West Indies lost their last nine for 80. Three quick wickets meant Misbah had to finish the paltry chase, hitting successive sixes off Bishoo; it was the fourth time he had secured victory with a six, extending his own world record.

Man of the Match: Yasir Shah.

Close of play: first day, West Indies 244-7 (Holder 30, Bishoo 23); second day, West Indies 278-9 (Holder 55, Gabriel 4); third day, Pakistan 201-4 (Misbah-ul-Haq 5, Asad Shafiq 5); fourth day, West Indies 93-4 (Bishoo 0, Singh 0).

West Indies

First innings		Second innings	
K. C. Brathwaite c Younis Khan b Mohammad Abbas	0	– b Yasir Shah	14
K. O. A. Powell c Younis Khan b Mohammad Amir	33	– c Younis Khan b Yasir Shah	49
S. O. Hetmyer b Mohammad Amir	11	– b Yasir Shah	20
S. D. Hope b Mohammad Amir	2	– lbw b Yasir Shah	6
V. A. Singh c Azhar Ali b Wahab Riaz	9	– (6) b Mohammad Amir	9
R. L. Chase c Wahab Riaz b Yasir Shah	63	– (7) not out	16
†S. O. Dowrich b Yasir Shah	56	– (8) lbw b Mohammad Abbas	0
*J. O. Holder not out	57	– (9) c Sarfraz Ahmed b Wahab Riaz	14
D. Bishoo c Sarfraz Ahmed b Mohammad Amir	28	– (5) c Younis Khan b Mohammad Abbas	18
A. S. Joseph b Mohammad Amir	0	– lbw b Yasir Shah	1
S. T. Gabriel b Mohammad Amir	5	– c Mohammad Abbas b Yasir Shah	0
B 4, lb 18	22	Lb 5	5
1/1 (1) 2/24 (3) 3/32 (4) 4/53 (5) 5/71 (2) 6/189 (6) 7/189 (7) 8/264 (9) 9/274 (10) 10/286 (11) (95 overs)	286	1/22 (1) 2/72 (3) 3/84 (4) 4/89 (2) 5/110 (6) 6/129 (5) 7/129 (8) 8/151 (9) 9/152 (10) 10/152 (11) (52.4 overs)	152

Mohammad Amir 26–11–44–6; Mohammad Abbas 22–4–63–1; Wahab Riaz 23–6–66–1; Yasir Shah 24–5–91–2. *Second innings*—Mohammad Amir 14–4–20–1; Mohammad Abbas 11–1–35–2; Yasir Shah 21.4–4–63–6; Wahab Riaz 6–0–29–1.

Pakistan

First innings		Second innings	
Azhar Ali c Dowrich b Joseph	15	– b Joseph	1
Ahmed Shehzad lbw b Holder	31	– c Dowrich b Gabriel	6
Babar Azam b Gabriel	72	– not out	9
Younis Khan c Brathwaite b Gabriel	58	– lbw b Bishoo	6
*Misbah-ul-Haq not out	99	– not out	12
Asad Shafiq c Dowrich b Gabriel	22		
†Sarfraz Ahmed b Bishoo	54		
Mohammad Amir c Dowrich b Joseph	11		
Wahab Riaz b Joseph	9		
Yasir Shah run out	8		
Mohammad Abbas lbw b Chase	1		
B 4, lb 10, w 1, nb 12	27	Lb 2	2
1/23 (1) 2/54 (2) 3/185 (4) 4/186 (3) 5/236 (6) 6/324 (7) 7/341 (8) 8/355 (9) 9/373 (10) 10/407 (11) (138.4 overs)	407	1/7 (2) 2/7 (1) 3/24 (4) (3 wkts, 10.5 overs)	36

Gabriel 29–6–92–3; Joseph 31–8–71–3; Holder 30–6–65–1; Bishoo 33–2–106–1; Chase 8.4–1–37–1; Brathwaite 7–1–22–0. *Second innings*—Gabriel 3–1–7–1; Joseph 3–1–6–1; Bishoo 2.5–0–19–1; Holder 2–1–2–0.

Umpires: R. K. Illingworth and R. A. Kettleborough. Third umpire: B. N. J. Oxenford.
Referee: B. C. Broad.

WEST INDIES v PAKISTAN

Second Test

At Bridgetown, Barbados, April 30–May 4, 2017. West Indies won by 106 runs. Toss: West Indies. Test debut: Shadab Khan.

This match brought back memories of West Indies' fiery prime. Gabriel's pace and menace earned him nine wickets, including five on the last day, when Pakistan – attempting to become the first Asian team to win in Barbados – were blown away for 81 in pursuit of 188. It was the fourth-lowest target successfully defended by West Indies.

When they slipped to 41 for two on the fourth morning, still 40 behind, West Indies had relied on Hope. He enjoyed home comfort – each of his five first-class centuries had come at Kensington Oval – and batted 209 balls for a Test-best 90, sharing half-century partnerships with Brathwaite, Chase and Singh.

PAKISTAN'S LOWEST TEST TOTALS

49	v South Africa at Johannesburg	2012-13
53	v Australia at Sharjah (*second innings*)	2002-03
59	v Australia at Sharjah (*first innings*)	2002-03
62	v Australia at Perth	1981-82
72	v Australia at Perth	2004-05
72	v England at Birmingham	2010
74	v England at Lord's	2010
77	v West Indies at Lahore	1986-87
80	v England at Nottingham	2010
81	**v West Indies at Bridgetown**	**2016-17**

With Yasir Shah turning the ball sharply from the rough, it was a superb effort to reach 235 for four but, once Hope picked out cover, the last six fell for 33. Yasir finished with seven for 94, the second-best figures for Pakistan against West Indies, after Imran Khan's seven for 80 in Guyana in 1987-88. It was also his tenth five-for in just 25 Tests.

Yet when, on the last afternoon, he became the last of Gabriel's five – his stumps flattened by one that kept low – Yasir's feats were relegated to a footnote. Among West Indians, only Jermaine Lawson, with six for three against Bangladesh at Dhaka in 2002-03, had collected a cheaper Test five-for than Gabriel's five for 11 (though Jerome Taylor also took five for 11 against England at Kingston in 2008-09).

West Indies' first innings had also relied on Bajan ballast. From 107 for five, Chase's second Test century ensured they batted into the second day, and made it to 312. Pakistan's selection had also helped relieve the pressure. Misreading the conditions, they swapped Wahab Riaz for 18-year-old leg-spinner Shadab Khan, Pakistan's youngest debutant since Mohammad Amir in 2009. Shadab struggled with fitness, and took just one wicket from 40 overs. With more grunt, they might have been able to press home their advantage.

The go-slow approach of Pakistan's batsmen on the second day drew severe criticism, with former coach Waqar Younis accusing the openers of playing selfishly. Ahmed

TWO OR MORE SCORES OF 99 IN TESTS

Misbah-ul-Haq (P)	**v NZ at Wellington, 2010-11; v WI at Kingston, 2016-17*; v WI at Bridgetown, 2016-17**
M. A. Atherton (E)	v A at Lord's, 1993; v SA at Leeds, 1994
G. S. Blewett (A)	v WI at Adelaide, 1996-97; v NZ at Hobart, 1997-98
G. Boycott (E)	v WI at Port-of-Spain, 1973-74; v A at Perth, 1979-80*
S. C. Ganguly (I)	v SL at Nagpur, 1997-98; v E at Nottingham, 2002
S. M. Katich (A)	v I at Nagpur, 2004-05; v WI at Perth, 2009-10
R. B. Richardson (WI)	v I at Port-of-Spain, 1988-89; v A at Bridgetown, 1990-91
Salim Malik (P)	v E at Leeds, 1987; v SA at Johannesburg, 1994-95
M. J. K. Smith (E)	v SA at Lord's, 1960; v P at Lahore, 1961-62
J. G. Wright (NZ)	v A at Melbourne, 1987-88; v E at Christchurch, 1991-92

* *Not out.* *A further 69 batsmen have scored 99 once in a Test.*

Shehzad scored just 23 runs from his first 104 deliveries on his way to 70 off 191. He was dropped on three, and twice dismissed off no-balls, by Gabriel and Chase (his first in Test cricket). Azhar Ali, meanwhile, took 268 balls to score his 13th Test hundred.

From 155 for none, Pakistan lost three for six, including Babar Azam for the first half of a pair, before Misbah-ul-Haq prevented a collapse and guided them into the lead. He calmly reached 99 (for the second match running), survived an lbw shout off Holder, then tried to leave the next delivery. But he hid his hands too late, and the ball ballooned off his glove to gully. He became the only Test batsman to collect three scores of 99, a stat as unwanted as a seventh defeat in eight matches since October 2016 after Pakistan's last-day collapse.

Man of the Match: S. T. Gabriel.

Close of play: first day, West Indies 286-6 (Chase 131, Holder 58); second day, Pakistan 172-3 (Azhar Ali 81, Misbah-ul-Haq 7); third day, West Indies 40-1 (Brathwaite 8, Hetmyer 22); fourth day, West Indies 264-9 (Bishoo 16, Gabriel 0).

West Indies

K. C. Brathwaite c Sarfraz Ahmed b Mohammad Amir	9	– c Younis Khan b Yasir Shah	43
K. O. A. Powell lbw b Mohammad Amir	38	– c Sarfraz Ahmed b Mohammad Abbas	6
S. O. Hetmyer c Azhar Ali b Mohammad Abbas	1	– b Mohammad Amir	22
S. D. Hope c Sarfraz Ahmed b Yasir Shah	5	– c Azhar Ali b Yasir Shah	90
R. L. Chase c Younis Khan b Mohammad Amir	131	– c and b Yasir Shah	23
V. A. Singh c Younis Khan b Mohammad Abbas	3	– b Mohammad Abbas	32
†S. O. Dowrich c Younis Khan b Shadab Khan	29	– c Asad Shafiq b Yasir Shah	2
*J. O. Holder c Sarfraz Ahmed b Mohammad Abbas	58	– c Younis Khan b Yasir Shah	1
D. Bishoo c Yasir Shah b Mohammad Abbas	14	– c Azhar Ali b Yasir Shah	20
A. S. Joseph b Yasir Shah	8	– c Mohammad Amir b Yasir Shah	7
S. T. Gabriel not out	0	– not out	0
B 4, lb 10, w 2	16	B 16, lb 2, w 3, nb 1	22
1/12 (1) 2/13 (3) 3/37 (4) 4/102 (2) 5/107 (6) 6/154 (7) 7/286 (8) 8/286 (5) 9/312 (9) 10/312 (10) (98.5 overs)	312	1/8 (2) 2/41 (3) 3/97 (1) 4/155 (5) 5/235 (4) 6/235 (6) 7/236 (8) 8/252 (7) 9/261 (10) 10/268 (9) (102.5 overs)	268

Mohammad Amir 26–5–65–3; Mohammad Abbas 23–6–56–4; Yasir Shah 25.5–2–83–2; Shadab Khan 23–3–90–1; Azhar Ali 1–0–4–0. *Second innings*—Mohammad Amir 21–8–44–1; Mohammad Abbas 25–6–57–2; Yasir Shah 39.5–12–94–7; Shadab Khan 17–0–55–0.

Pakistan

Azhar Ali c Dowrich b Bishoo	105	– c Hetmyer b Gabriel	10
Ahmed Shehzad c Hope b Bishoo	70	– lbw b Joseph	14
Babar Azam c and b Gabriel	0	– c Dowrich b Joseph	0
Younis Khan c Gabriel b Bishoo	0	– lbw b Holder	5
*Misbah-ul-Haq c Hope b Holder	99	– c Hope b Gabriel	0
Asad Shafiq lbw b Holder	15	– c Powell b Gabriel	0
†Sarfraz Ahmed c Powell b Gabriel	9	– c Chase b Holder	23
Shadab Khan c Chase b Gabriel	16	– c Dowrich b Holder	1
Mohammad Amir c Hope b Holder	10	– c Singh b Gabriel	20
Yasir Shah c Dowrich b Gabriel	24	– b Gabriel	0
Mohammad Abbas not out	1	– not out	0
B 16, lb 16, nb 12	44	B 4, lb 1, nb 3	8
1/155 (2) 2/156 (3) 3/161 (4) 4/259 (1) 5/316 (5) 6/325 (7) 7/329 (6) 8/354 (9) 9/384 (8) 10/393 (10) (140 overs)	393	1/10 (1) 2/11 (3) 3/27 (4) 4/30 (5) 5/30 (6) 6/35 (2) 7/36 (8) 8/78 (9) 9/81 (10) 10/81 (7) (34.4 overs)	81

Gabriel 32–6–81–4; Joseph 19–5–48–0; Chase 19–2–74–0; Holder 29–11–42–3; Bishoo 41–11–116–3. *Second innings*—Gabriel 11–4–11–5; Joseph 12–1–42–2; Holder 11.4–4–23–3.

Umpires: R. A. Kettleborough and B. N. J. Oxenford. Third umpire: R. K. Illingworth. Referee: B. C. Broad.

WEST INDIES v PAKISTAN

Third Test

At Roseau, Dominica, May 10–14, 2017. Pakistan won by 101 runs. Toss: West Indies. Test debut: Hasan Ali.

With two overs left and drizzle falling, the prospect of Misbah-ul-Haq and Younis Khan enjoying a victorious final bow was receding. Yasir Shah was bowling to last man Gabriel, who was defending stoutly. Even when the finger went up after the fourth ball – a bat–pad to silly point – Gabriel survived on review. Chase leant on his bat at the other end, ready to add one more over's defiance to his six-hour stay.

But when Yasir floated his last delivery of the tour outside off stump, Gabriel swung heedlessly, the ball clipped the inside edge, and flew on to the stumps. So Misbah, Pakistan's most successful captain, and Younis, their most prolific batsman, who had begun their illustrious Test careers over 15 years earlier, ended them as part of the first Pakistan team to win a Test series in the Caribbean. Yasir, meanwhile, sprinted towards long-off and leapt into a full-length dive. It was his third five-for of a series in which he had claimed a personal-best 25 victims, beating 24 in Sri Lanka in 2015.

The first three days had given no hint of the gripping climax. West Indies, unchanged for a third successive Test for the first time since England toured in 2008-09, won the toss and elected to bowl on a slow surface. The outfield proved sluggish, as did the scoring: Pakistan needed until late on the second evening to reach 376 (although nearly an hour was lost to rain on the first day). Azhar Ali stayed in first gear while making another careful century – this time reaching three figures in 266 balls, two quicker than at Bridgetown – and others chipped in.

Mohammad Abbas got a good idea of the pitch while batting – facing 43 balls for his four – and took a maiden Test five-for, including Chase for 69. Abbas also removed the last three for ducks, as West Indies lost five for 29; Younis collected his tenth catch of the series, a record for a Pakistan outfielder.

Pakistan resumed with a 129-run lead on the fourth day. After a third duck of the series for Babar Azam – following a pair in Bridgetown – Misbah top-edged a slog-sweep, and Younis did the same with a more conventional one. Soon it was 90 for seven; somewhere between the hugs, handshakes, guards of honour and the hashtag #MisYou, Pakistan had apparently forgotten they were in a match. It needed a partnership of 61 between Mohammad Amir and Yasir to reassert authority.

After Amir was dismissed, Misbah gave his bowlers 30 minutes and a day to bowl out West Indies. Chase's staunch defence held Pakistan up after his side had plunged to 93 for six with more than 53 overs to go. But the lower order all knuckled down: Holder made 22 in 85 minutes, Bishoo three in 71, Joseph five in 59, and Gabriel four in 32. Another few minutes, and West Indies would have saved the series.

Man of the Match: R. L. Chase. *Man of the Series:* Yasir Shah.

Close of play: first day, Pakistan 169-2 (Azhar Ali 85, Younis Khan 10); second day, West Indies 14-0 (Brathwaite 5, Powell 9); third day, West Indies 218-5 (Dowrich 20, Holder 11); fourth day, West Indies 7-1 (Brathwaite 3).

Pakistan

First innings		Second innings	
Azhar Ali b Chase	127	c sub (J. Blackwood) b Gabriel	3
Shan Masood c Holder b Chase	9	lbw b Gabriel	21
Babar Azam c Powell b Joseph	55	c Hetmyer b Chase	0
Younis Khan lbw b Holder	18	c Powell b Bishoo	35
*Misbah-ul-Haq c Dowrich b Chase	59	c Dowrich b Bishoo	2
Asad Shafiq c Singh b Chase	17	c and b Joseph	13
†Sarfraz Ahmed c Hope b Bishoo	51	c Dowrich b Joseph	4
Mohammad Amir b Holder	7	c Bishoo b Joseph	27
Yasir Shah c Powell b Holder	0	not out	38
Mohammad Abbas st Dowrich b Bishoo	4		
Hasan Ali not out	8	(10) not out	15
B 4, lb 6, w 3, nb 8	21	Lb 5, w 7, nb 4	16
1/19 (2) 2/139 (3) 3/177 (4) 4/241 (1) 5/274 (6) 6/311 (5) 7/322 (8) 8/322 (9) 9/367 (7) 10/376 (10) (146.3 overs)	376	1/6 (1) 2/8 (3) 3/57 (2) 4/65 (5) 5/72 (4) 6/82 (7) 7/90 (6) 8/151 (8) (8 wkts dec, 57 overs)	174

Gabriel 32–9–67–0; Joseph 27–9–64–1; Chase 32–5–103–4; Holder 32–9–71–3; Bishoo 23.3–3–61–2. *Second innings*—Gabriel 10–1–24–2; Joseph 15–3–53–3; Chase 9–0–31–1; Holder 9–4–7–0; Bishoo 14–2–54–2.

West Indies

First innings		Second innings	
K. C. Brathwaite c Sarfraz Ahmed b Yasir Shah	29	c Hasan Ali b Yasir Shah	6
K. O. A. Powell c Azhar Ali b Yasir Shah	31	c Shan Masood b Yasir Shah	4
S. O. Hetmyer c Sarfraz Ahmed b Yasir Shah	17	b Mohammad Amir	25
S. D. Hope c Misbah-ul-Haq b Azhar Ali	29	lbw b Hasan Ali	17
R. L. Chase b Mohammad Abbas	69	not out	101
V. A. Singh lbw b Mohammad Abbas	8	c Babar Azam b Yasir Shah	2
†S. O. Dowrich b Mohammad Amir	20	c Babar Azam b Yasir Shah	2
*J. O. Holder not out	30	lbw b Hasan Ali	22
D. Bishoo c Younis Khan b Mohammad Abbas	0	c Shan Masood b Mohammad Abbas	3
A. S. Joseph b Mohammad Abbas	0	c Sarfraz Ahmed b Hasan Ali	5
S. T. Gabriel c Babar Azam b Mohammad Abbas	0	b Yasir Shah	4
B 4, lb 2, w 5, nb 3	14	B 6, w 2, nb 3	11
1/43 (2) 2/69 (3) 3/97 (1) 4/152 (4) 5/189 (6) 6/218 (7) 7/239 (5) 8/239 (9) 9/241 (10) 10/247 (11) (115 overs)	247	1/7 (2) 2/22 (1) 3/47 (3) 4/66 (4) 5/76 (6) 6/93 (7) 7/151 (8) 8/181 (9) 9/197 (10) 10/202 (11) (96 overs)	202

In the first innings Chase, when 60, retired hurt at 183-4 and resumed at 218-6.

Mohammad Amir 27–12–32–1; Mohammad Abbas 25–7–46–5; Yasir Shah 40–4–126–3; Hasan Ali 17–4–22–0; Azhar Ali 6–1–15–1. *Second innings*—Mohammad Amir 15–8–22–1; Mohammad Abbas 20–9–31–1; Yasir Shah 37–13–92–5; Hasan Ali 20–7–33–3; Azhar Ali 2–0–3–0; Asad Shafiq 2–0–15–0.

Umpires: R. K. Illingworth and B. N. J. Oxenford. Third umpire: R. A. Kettleborough.
Referee: B. C. Broad.

WEST INDIES v AFGHANISTAN IN 2017

Twenty20 internationals (3): West Indies 3, Afghanistan 0
One-day internationals (3): West Indies 1, Afghanistan 1

West Indies were not invited to their old pals' party – they had failed to qualify for the Champions Trophy – so they stayed in and had a new friend round instead. Upwardly mobile Afghanistan, on their first bilateral Caribbean tour, secured a precious memento: a share of the 50-over series after leg-spinner Rashid Khan's seven for 18 in the first one-day international in St Lucia. Things had gone less well in the Twenty20 games, despite their victory over West Indies at the 2016 World T20 in India, the first of a record 11 consecutive wins in the format. West Indies were without seven of their world champions but refused to sulk and romped to a whitewash thanks to greater bowling depth – Afghanistan took just ten wickets to West Indies' 26 – and the nous needed for low-scoring games.

Marlon Samuels won the series award for his 146 runs, more than double anyone else, including 89 not out in the third match. But it could easily have been zippy Vincentian seamer Kesrick Williams: he showed off a fierce yorker, took eight wickets, and was the pick of a balanced attack that exploited Afghanistan's soft spot for the slog. West Indies handled Rashid Khan's leg-spin with caution in the Twenty20s, saving their aggression for the others. And it worked: though he was the only bowler to concede less than five an over, Rashid took just two wickets. But the same tactic failed in the one-day series. With a scuttling approach and whipcrack arm, he hurried the batsmen and, as few could read his variations, beat both edges with thrilling regularity. After combined figures of 29.4–2–94–12 over five matches, Rashid had given them every reason to be anxious. In the end, though, the home side squared the series, and rain spared them any more torment in the decider.

It all left West Indies unsure of regaining their place in high society. They desperately needed to gain ground in the ODI rankings to be sure of an invitation to the 2019 World Cup; if they did not break into the top eight by September 2017, they would have to enter a gruelling ten-team qualifying tournament. But even if they had won the final game, their defeat had cost them crucial points.

AFGHANISTAN TOURING PARTY

*Asghar Stanikzai (50/20), Afsar Zazai (50/20), Dawlat Zadran (50/20), Fareed Ahmad (50/20), Gulbadeen Naib (50/20), Hamza Hotak (50/20), Javed Ahmadi (50/20), Karim Janat (50/20), Mohammad Nabi (50/20), Najibullah Zadran (50/20), Nasir Ahmadzai (50), Naveen-ul-Haq (20), Noor Ali Zadran (50/20), Rahmat Shah (50), Rashid Khan (50/20), Samiullah Shenwari (50/20), Shafiqullah Shinwari (50/20), Shapoor Zadran (50/20), Sharafuddin Ashraf (20), Usman Ghani (50/20). *Coach:* L. S. Rajput.

First Twenty20 international At Basseterre, St Kitts, June 2 (floodlit). **West Indies won by six wickets.** ‡**Afghanistan 110** (20 overs) (Rashid Khan 33; S. P. Narine 3-11); **West Indies 114-4** (16.3 overs) (M. N. Samuels 35). *MoM:* S. P. Narine. *Afghanistan got their tempo all wrong: they faced 65 dot balls and, when they went for the big shot, mostly failed. Gulbadeen Naib cracked three* *fours, then missed a straight one, Asghar Stanikzai was involved in a run-out before being late on a pull, and Karim Janat got a tiny edge on a massive swipe. By the 14th over, Sunil Narine had bamboozled three more, and Afghanistan were 58-8. Only late-order hitting from Rashid Khan, who nailed two consecutive sixes off the expensive Jerome Taylor, spared them more humiliation. West Indies hared after their target of 111 as if it were twice that amount: Chadwick Walton crunched four fours in the first two overs, and Evin Lewis three sixes in a rapid 26. It left Marlon Samuels able to coast towards victory, even if he fell with the line in sight. Before the game, the players observed a minute's silence after a bomb outside the German Embassy in Kabul killed over 150 people.*

Second Twenty20 international At Basseterre, St Kitts, June 3 (floodlit). **West Indies won by 29 runs** (DLS). ‡**West Indies 112-3** (15 overs); **Afghanistan 93** (13.3 overs) (K. O. K. Williams 3-11). *MoM:* K. O. K. Williams. *After rain, Afghanistan were chasing a manageable 123 from 15 overs, but fluffed their lines. As on the previous day, eight batsmen failed to reach double figures, and there was a familiarity to their dismissals: Gulbadeen missed a straight one, and Asghar was involved in a run-out, before being late on a pull. Samuel Badree (1-11) was hardest to hit, while Kesrick Williams was most dangerous, adroitly mixing yorkers, slower balls and bat-jarring bouncers to pick up a format-best 3-11. Earlier, Walton had got West Indies off to a flyer, hammering 29 off 17 as Afghanistan strayed too short. The change bowlers, and heavy showers, slowed momentum, but twenties from Lewis and Samuels still gave them enough to clinch the series.*

Third Twenty20 international At Basseterre, St Kitts, June 5 (floodlit). **West Indies won by seven wickets.** ‡**Afghanistan 146-6** (20 overs) (Noor Ali Zadran 35, Mohammad Nabi 38; K. O. K. Williams 3-34); **West Indies 147-3** (19.2 overs) (M. N. Samuels 89*). *MoM:* M. N. Samuels. *MoS:* M. N. Samuels. *After Afghanistan managed a competitive 146, they got rid of Walton second ball, and might have had Samuels in the tenth over. But Mohammad Nabi couldn't hold on to a sharp return catch and, while Lewis fell two balls later, to end a stand of 61, Samuels calmly shepherded the rest of the chase. Striking cleanly between mid-off and midwicket, he cracked 15 off Nabi in the 16th over, and finished with 89*, his highest score in T20Is. Earlier, Afghanistan's innings was a three-act play: 40-1 off four, 66-3 off 12, and 146-6 all told. Noor Ali Zadran had given them the fast start, racing to a 19-ball 35, before his dismissal led to a period of introspection. Nabi and Shafiqullah Shinwari – who hit Williams out of the stadium in a 15-ball 25 – added late oomph, but it wasn't enough to prevent the whitewash.*

First one-day international At Gros Islet, St Lucia, June 9 (day/night). **Afghanistan won by 63 runs.** ‡**Afghanistan 212-6** (50 overs) (Javed Ahmadi 81, Gulbadeen Naib 41); **West Indies 149** (44.4 overs) (S. D. Hope 35; Rashid Khan 7-18). *MoM:* Rashid Khan. *ODI debut:* R. L. Chase (West Indies). *When Rashid came on in the 23rd over of the chase, the first one-day international between these sides was in the balance. West Indies were 68-2, needing a little more than five an over. By the 29th, he had dizzied the batsmen with an inscrutable googly, and picked up a rapid five-for. Even Roston Chase, making his debut after averaging 100 in the Test series against Pakistan (and Yasir Shah) had no clue, trapped on the crease for a golden duck. At times, Rashid employed three catchers round the bat, a Test field for a Test-calibre bowler. He returned to end the torture with another two, finishing with 7-18 – all bowled, lbw, or caught by Nabi at slip – the fourth-best figures in ODIs. Earlier, Afghanistan seemed to have paced their innings poorly again. Rahmat Shah chewed through 51 balls for 17 before poking the miserly Shannon Gabriel (1-21) to point, and they had only 87 at the halfway mark. But opener Javed Ahmadi held things together, equalling his personal-best 81, and Gulbadeen muscled five boundaries in a rapid 41 at the end.*

Second one-day international At Gros Islet, St Lucia, June 11 (day/night). **West Indies won by four wickets.** ‡**Afghanistan 135** (37.3 overs) (Gulbadeen Naib 51); **West Indies 138-6** (39.2 overs) (E. Lewis 33, S. D. Hope 48; Rashid Khan 3-26). *MoM:* S. D. Hope. *Once again, eight Afghans failed to reach double figures. And, again, the short delivery did the damage, as the three West Indian fast bowlers dug the ball into the ribs. There was little plan, other than a succession of Panglossian flails. Even the experienced Asghar and Nabi had no answer to bouncers from Alzarri Joseph (2-15), and by the 17th over Afghanistan were 51-6. That brought in Gulbadeen, who resisted with a half-century; the next best was 13 as they crumbled for 135. West Indies rattled off 37 in the six overs before the break, but Rashid soon picked up both left-handed openers with googlies. When he added a third wicket – Chase stumped after groping for a leg-break – West Indies had slipped to 98-5, and there was anxiety in the air. By then, though, Rashid had used up eight overs, and Shai Hope ground out 48* off 77 balls to square the series.*

Third one-day international At Gros Islet, St Lucia, June 14 (day/night). **West Indies v** ‡**Afghanistan. Abandoned.**

WEST INDIES v INDIA IN 2017

BHARAT SUNDARESAN

One-day internationals (5): West Indies 1, India 3
Twenty20 international (1): West Indies 1, India 0

This three-week, three-island tour of the Caribbean was one the Indians could happily have done without: it started five days after their bruising defeat by Pakistan in the Champions Trophy final in England. But by the end they were refreshed – in more ways than one.

They sent an almost full-strength squad (only Rohit Sharma and Jasprit Bumrah were rested), but no head coach. Anil Kumble had been scheduled to join the tour after an ICC committee meeting in London, but when the players arrived in St Lucia to change planes, they learned he had resigned. In a letter to the BCCI, he shed some light on his relationship with Virat Kohli, the captain, which had been the subject of intense speculation. "It was apparent the partnership was untenable," he wrote. "I therefore believe it is best for me to move on." M. V. Sridhar, the BCCI's general manager and a former Hyderabad batsman, took on the management role on an interim basis. The Indian cricket community was stunned when, later in the year, he died aged 51.

While rumours ran wild back home – about what had gone sour, and about the identity of Kumble's long-term replacement – the Indian team enjoyed time with sand beneath their feet, and indulged in bonding sessions on jet skis. On the field, they seemed almost as relaxed, at least until the solitary Twenty20, when they were beasted by Evin Lewis. With the World Cup still two years away, veterans Yuvraj Singh and M. S. Dhoni were under the spotlight. Dhoni responded with a match-winning performance in the third one-day international, but Yuvraj tweaked a hamstring in the second game and limped out of the third. Meanwhile, opening batsman Ajinkya Rahane and the debutant left-arm wrist-spinner Kuldeep Yadav enhanced their prospects of making the squad for 2019.

For West Indies, languishing outside the top eight in the rankings, the chances of qualifying directly for that World Cup were running out. They made no ground here. Let down by their batting – Shai Hope struck their only two half-centuries – they won just a single one-dayer, defending a small total in Antigua. The stars returned for the T20, which West Indies won with ease. But that merely served as a reminder of the squabbling between players and administrators.

INDIAN TOURING PARTY

*V. Kohli, R. Ashwin, Bhuvneshwar Kumar, S. Dhawan, M. S. Dhoni, R. A. Jadeja, K. M. Jadhav, K. D. Karthik, Mohammed Shami, H. H. Pandya, R. R. Pant, A. M. Rahane, K. Yadav, U. T. Yadav, Yuvraj Singh. *Coach:* M. V. Sridhar.

WEST INDIES v INDIA

First One-Day International

At Port-of-Spain, Trinidad, June 23. No result. Toss: West Indies. One-day international debut: K. Yadav.

Less than a week after Pakistan stunned them in the final of the Champions Trophy, India were denied the chance to atone by the weather. On a sticky pitch, half-centuries from Dhawan and Rahane had put them on course for 300, but the innings was cut short after 39 overs.

India

A. M. Rahane c Holder b Joseph	62
S. Dhawan lbw b Bishoo	87
*V. Kohli not out	32
Yuvraj Singh c Lewis b Holder	4
†M. S. Dhoni not out	9
W 5	5
1/132 (1) 2/168 (2) 3/185 (4) (3 wkts, 39.2 overs)	199
10 overs: 47-0	

K. M. Jadhav, H. H. Pandya, R. Ashwin, K. Yadav, Bhuvneshwar Kumar and U. T. Yadav did not bat.

Holder 8–0–34–1; Joseph 8–0–53–1; Nurse 4–1–22–0; Cummins 8–0–46–0; Bishoo 10–0–39–1; Carter 1.2–0–5–0.

West Indies

E. Lewis, K. O. A. Powell, †S. D. Hope, J. N. Mohammed, R. L. Chase, J. L. Carter, *J. O. Holder, A. R. Nurse, D. Bishoo, A. S. Joseph, M. L. Cummins.

Umpires: H. D. P. K. Dharmasena and J. S. Wilson. Third umpire: C. B. Gaffaney.
Referee: D. C. Boon.

WEST INDIES v INDIA

Second One-Day International

At Port-of-Spain, Trinidad, June 25. India won by 105 runs. Toss: West Indies.

After morning rain, few expected to see any action, and the Indian team contemplated returning to their hotel. But somehow the pitch dried up fast enough for a 43-over game. Rahane was pleased it did. He had struggled to convert starts in one-day internationals, but he took his chance as Rohit Sharma's deputy with a decisive hundred. Dhawan continued his good form with another half-century, before Kohli took over, peppering the crowd in a 66-ball 87. West Indies lost the plot, with Holder removed from the attack after one high full toss too many. Their batting was even more clueless, and they seemed content to use up their allocation rather than pursue a target of 311. Hope alone showed intent during his 88-ball 81, but he was one of three bamboozled by Kuldeep Yadav, a left-arm wrist-spinner playing on the ground where Ellis Achong had once honed the art.

Man of the Match: A. M. Rahane.

India

A. M. Rahane b Cummins	103
S. Dhawan st Hope b Nurse	63
*V. Kohli c Nurse b Joseph	87
H. H. Pandya c Cummins b Joseph	4
Yuvraj Singh c Hope b Holder	14
†M. S. Dhoni not out	13
K. M. Jadhav not out	13
Lb 4, w 4, nb 5	13
1/114 (2) 2/211 (1) 3/223 (4) 4/254 (5) 5/285 (3) (5 wkts, 43 overs)	310
9 overs: 57-0	

R. Ashwin, K. Yadav, Bhuvneshwar Kumar and U. T. Yadav did not bat.

Joseph 8–0–73–2; Holder 8.5–0–76–1; Nurse 9–0–38–1; Bishoo 9–0–60–0; Cummins 8–0–57–1; Carter 0.1–0–2–0.

West Indies

K. O. A. Powell c Dhoni b Bhuvneshwar Kumar	0	R. L. Chase not out	33
†S. D. Hope lbw b K. Yadav	81	A. R. Nurse not out	19
J. N. Mohammed c Pandya b Bhuvneshwar Kumar	0	Lb 6, w 3	9
E. Lewis st Dhoni b K. Yadav	21	1/0 (1) 2/4 (3) (6 wkts, 43 overs)	205
J. L. Carter lbw b Ashwin	13	3/93 (4) 4/112 (2)	
*J. O. Holder st Dhoni b K. Yadav	29	5/132 (5) 6/174 (6) 9 overs: 28-2	

D. Bishoo, A. S. Joseph and M. L. Cummins did not bat.

Bhuvneshwar Kumar 5–1–9–2; U. T. Yadav 6–0–36–0; Pandya 9–0–32–0; Ashwin 9–0–47–1; K. Yadav 9–0–50–3; Yuvraj Singh 5–0–25–0.

Umpires: N. Duguid and C. B. Gaffaney. Third umpire: H. D. P. K. Dharmasena. Referee: D. C. Boon.

WEST INDIES v INDIA

Third One-Day International

At North Sound, Antigua, June 30. India won by 93 runs. Toss: West Indies. One-day international debuts: K. A. Hope, K. O. K. Williams.

"It is what it is." A phrase you hear often in the Caribbean when something hasn't quite gone to plan was fast becoming the mantra of West Indies' one-day team. They were in this game for the first 40 overs, as their bowlers strangled the mighty Indians on an up-and-down pitch. The run-rate hovered around four while Rahane completed a responsible fifty but, after he was caught acrobatically by Bishoo, the tenor of the innings changed. Dhoni had started sluggishly, struggling to rotate the strike with his usual skill, and twice nearly holed out. But Jadhav's tapeball innovations – including a swept four off the pace of Cummins – inspired Dhoni to a couple of meaty sixes, as the pair added 81 from 46 balls and lifted the target to 252. West Indies had more Hope than before, with Kyle joining brother Shai in the top order. But both fell to Pandya, before the spinners wreaked havoc, claiming seven for 69. Holder could do little but draw the inevitable conclusion: "It is what it is."

Man of the Match: M. S. Dhoni.

India

A. M. Rahane c Bishoo b Cummins	72	K. M. Jadhav not out	40
S. Dhawan c Chase b Cummins	2	Lb 1, w 8	9
*V. Kohli c K. A. Hope b Holder	11		
Yuvraj Singh lbw b Bishoo	39	1/11 (2) 2/34 (3) (4 wkts, 50 overs)	251
†M. S. Dhoni not out	78	3/100 (4) 4/170 (1) 10 overs: 34-2	

H. H. Pandya, R. Ashwin, K. Yadav, Bhuvneshwar Kumar and U. T. Yadav did not bat.

Cummins 10–0–56–2; Holder 10–1–53–1; Williams 10–0–69–0; Nurse 10–0–34–0; Bishoo 10–0–38–1.

West Indies

E. Lewis b U. T. Yadav	2	M. L. Cummins lbw b Ashwin	1
K. A. Hope c Jadhav b Pandya	19	K. O. K. Williams b Jadhav	1
†S. D. Hope c and b Pandya	24		
R. L. Chase b K. Yadav	2	Lb 6, w 17	23
J. N. Mohammed lbw b K. Yadav	40		
*J. O. Holder st Dhoni b Ashwin	6	1/9 (1) 2/54 (2) (38.1 overs)	158
R. Powell c Pandya b K. Yadav	30	3/58 (4) 4/69 (3) 5/87 (6)	
A. R. Nurse c U. T. Yadav b Ashwin	6	6/141 (7) 7/148 (8) 8/156 (5)	
D. Bishoo not out	4	9/157 (10) 10/158 (11) 10 overs: 40-1	

Bhuvneshwar Kumar 5–0–19–0; U. T. Yadav 7–0–32–1; Pandya 6–0–32–2; K. Yadav 10–1–41–3; Ashwin 10–1–28–3; Jadhav 0.1–0–0–1.

Umpires: H. D. P. K. Dharmasena and N. Duguid. Third umpire: C. B. Gaffaney. Referee: D. C. Boon.

WEST INDIES v INDIA

Fourth One-Day International

At North Sound, Antigua, July 2. West Indies won by 11 runs. Toss: West Indies.

Dhoni, once beyond reproach in India, now had his critics. Here was more evidence he was no longer the finisher *nonpareil*: against an inexperienced attack he muddled to a half-century in 108 balls – his slowest, and the slowest by an Indian since Sadagoppan Ramesh took 116 against Kenya in 1999-2000. He hit just one boundary, as India fell short of their target of 190, the tenth-smallest chase they had failed to achieve in ODIs. On a stodgy pitch, they had lost early wickets, before Rahane and Dhoni put on a defiant 54. But another flurry of dismissals left Dhoni with a familiar scenario: a chase to manage, with no real company at the other end. In the 49th over, he was up against Kesrick Williams, playing just his second ODI, with 16 required for victory. After a few excellent slower balls, Dhoni smeared to long-on. Holder, whose grandmother was operating the manual scoreboard, cleaned up with two wickets to finish with a maiden five-for. Earlier, West Indies had hardly looked as if they would keep the series alive: their top five all reached 20, but none passed 35. Yet, after Dhoni's dithering, they had a chance of levelling the series.

Man of the Match: J. O. Holder.

West Indies

E. Lewis c Kohli b K. Yadav	35
K. A. Hope c Jadhav b Pandya	35
†S. D. Hope c Dhoni b Pandya	25
R. L. Chase b K. Yadav	24
J. N. Mohammed c Jadeja b Pandya	20
*J. O. Holder c Dhoni b U. T. Yadav	11
R. Powell c Jadeja b U. T. Yadav	2
A. R. Nurse c and b U. T. Yadav	4
D. Bishoo run out	15
A. S. Joseph not out	5
K. O. K. Williams not out	2
Lb 1, w 10	11
1/57 (2) 2/80 (1) 3/121 (4) 4/136 (3) 5/154 (6) 6/161 (7) 7/162 (5) 8/179 (8) 9/184 (9) (9 wkts, 50 overs)	189
10 overs: 31-0	

Mohammed Shami 10–2–33–0; U. T. Yadav 10–1–36–3; Jadeja 10–0–48–0; Pandya 10–0–40–3; K. Yadav 10–1–31–2.

India

A. M. Rahane c S. D. Hope b Bishoo	60
S. Dhawan c Holder b Joseph	5
*V. Kohli c S. D. Hope b Holder	3
K. D. Karthik c S. D. Hope b Joseph	2
†M. S. Dhoni c Joseph b Williams	54
K. M. Jadhav c S. D. Hope b Nurse	10
H. H. Pandya b Holder	20
R. A. Jadeja c Powell b Holder	11
K. Yadav not out	2
U. T. Yadav b Holder	0
Mohammed Shami c Chase b Holder	1
W 10	10
1/10 (2) 2/25 (3) 3/47 (4) 4/101 (1) 5/116 (6) 6/159 (7) 7/173 (8) 8/176 (5) 9/176 (10) 10/178 (11) (49.4 overs)	178
10 overs: 33-2	

Joseph 9–2–46–2; Holder 9.4–2–27–5; Williams 10–0–29–1; Bishoo 10–1–31–1; Nurse 10–0–29–1; Chase 1–0–16–0.

Umpires: C. B. Gaffaney and J. S. Wilson. Third umpire: H. D. P. K. Dharmasena.
Referee: D. C. Boon.

WEST INDIES v INDIA

Fifth One-Day International

At Kingston, Jamaica, July 6. India won by eight wickets. Toss: West Indies.

Kohli had been overshadowed by his team-mates on this trip, and twice bounced out cheaply in Antigua. But he saved his best until last, sealing the series with a chanceless hundred, his 28th in one-day internationals, and his 18th in a chase, a world record. He withstood the inevitable short-pitched assault and stroked the ball to every corner of Sabina Park before celebrating with a leap, a clenched fist, and some barked expletives. Karthik, playing his first ODI since 2014, chipped in with an unbeaten half-century as the target of 206 – tiny on such an excellent pitch – was overhauled with 13 overs to spare. The West Indian innings had looked promising at 76 for one. But it stalled after Umesh Yadav took two in two balls and, though Shai Hope resisted with 51, he used up 98 balls. "I sympathise with the batsmen," said Holder. "But they need to learn quickly."

Man of the Match: V. Kohli. *Man of the Series:* A. M. Rahane.

West Indies

E. Lewis c Kohli b Pandya	9
K. A. Hope c Dhawan b U. T. Yadav	46
†S. D. Hope c Rahane b Mohammed Shami	51
R. L. Chase lbw b U. T. Yadav	0
J. N. Mohammed c and b Jadhav	16
*J. O. Holder c Dhawan b Mohammed Shami	36
R. Powell c Dhoni b U. T. Yadav	31
A. R. Nurse c K. Yadav b Mohammed Shami	0
D. Bishoo c Dhoni b Mohammed Shami	6
A. S. Joseph not out	3
K. O. K. Williams not out	0
Lb 1, w 6	7
1/39 (1) 2/76 (2) 3/76 (4) 4/115 (5) 5/163 (6) 6/168 (3) 7/171 (8) 8/182 (9) 9/205 (7) — (9 wkts, 50 overs)	205
10 overs: 49-1	

Mohammed Shami 10–0–48–4; U. T. Yadav 10–1–53–3; Pandya 6–0–27–1; Jadeja 10–1–27–0; K. Yadav 10–0–36–0; Jadhav 4–0–13–1.

India

A. M. Rahane lbw b Bishoo	39
S. Dhawan c Lewis b Joseph	4
*V. Kohli not out	111
K. D. Karthik not out	50
Lb 1, w 1	2
1/5 (2) 2/84 (1) — (2 wkts, 36.5 overs)	206
10 overs: 50-1	

†M. S. Dhoni, K. M. Jadhav, H. H. Pandya, R. A. Jadeja, K. Yadav, U. T. Yadav and Mohammed Shami did not bat.

Joseph 7–0–39–1; Holder 8–1–35–0; Bishoo 8–0–42–1; Williams 8–0–40–0; Nurse 4–0–34–0; Powell 1–0–6–0; Chase 0.5–0–9–0.

Umpires: H. D. P. K. Dharmasena and L. S. Reifer. Third umpire: C. B. Gaffaney.
Referee: D. C. Boon.

WEST INDIES v INDIA

Twenty20 International

At Kingston, Jamaica, July 9. West Indies won by nine wickets. Toss: West Indies. Twenty20 international debut: K. Yadav.

Local interest shot up after the West Indies team were announced. Among the returning heroes was Gayle, the Kingston king playing his first international since the World Twenty20 final in April 2016. But it was an emerging star who stole the show: Lewis smashed his second hundred in three T20 innings against India with a blitz that was sure to spark interest at the next IPL auction. Sabina Park was a carnival – despite the 10am start – and Kohli began with a flurry of fours before he spooned a slower ball from Williams, who celebrated the catch in trademark style, writing his victim's name in an imaginary notebook. Karthik top-scored with 48 in his first T20 international for seven years, lifting the target to 191. Gayle went cheaply, but not before he and Lewis had put on 82 at ten an over. Lewis went on to blast 12 monstrous sixes – the most for West Indies – including one into the car park behind the dressing-rooms, and his unbeaten 125 from just 62 balls meant he became the third player, after Gayle and Brendon McCullum, to score more than one T20 international century. Samuels's contribution to an unbeaten stand of 112 was a steady 36.

Man of the Match: E. Lewis.

India

		B	4/6
1 *V. Kohli *c 8 b 11*	39	22	7/1
2 S. Dhawan *run out*	23	12	5
3 R. R. Pant *c 5 b 9*	38	35	2/1
4 K. D. Karthik *b 3*	48	29	5/3
5 †M. S. Dhoni *c 3 b 9*	2	3	0
6 K. M. Jadhav *c 8 b 11*	4	4	0
7 R. A. Jadeja *not out*	13	8	0/1
8 R. Ashwin *not out*	11	7	1
Lb 6, w 6	12		
6 overs: 66-2 (20 overs)	190-6		

1/64 2/65 3/151 4/156 5/156 6/164

9 K. Yadav, 10 Bhuvneshwar Kumar and 11 Mohammed Shami did not bat.

Badree 4–9–31–0; Taylor 4–5–31–2; Williams 4–6–42–2; Brathwaite 2–5–26–0; Narine 3–6–22–0; Samuels 3–5–32–1.

West Indies

		B	4/6
1 C. H. Gayle *c 5 b 9*	18	20	1/1
2 E. Lewis *not out*	125	62	6/12
3 M. N. Samuels *not out*	36	29	5/1
B 1, lb 6, w 8	15		
6 overs: 66-0 (18.3 overs)	194-1		

1/82

4 K. A. Pollard, 5 †C. A. K. Walton, 6 R. Powell, 7 *C. R. Brathwaite, 8 S. P. Narine, 9 J. E. Taylor, 10 S. Badree and 11 K. O. K. Williams did not bat.

Bhuvneshwar Kumar 4–10–27–0; Ashwin 4–11–39–0; Mohammed Shami 3–3–46–0; Yadav 4–10–34–1; Jadeja 3.3–10–41–0.

Umpires: N. Duguid and L. S. Reifer. Third umpire: J. S. Wilson.
Referee: D. C. Boon.

DOMESTIC CRICKET IN THE WEST INDIES IN 2016-17

HAYDN GILL

The West Indian Cricket Board renamed themselves Cricket West Indies in June 2017, but more drastic action was needed to raise the modest standards of the Caribbean's restructured franchise set-up. One problem – spin's stranglehold on the domestic game – was acknowledged by a change to the points system to reward pace bowling, but the reform had little immediate impact, and batting statistics in the first-class competition remained an embarrassment.

In spite of the mediocrity dogging the four-day regional tournament, **Guyana** deserved to complete a hat-trick of titles, though they won only five matches, compared with eight the previous two seasons. They owed much to the 42-year-old Shivnarine Chanderpaul, who scored 622 runs at 62, and seasoned left-arm spinner Veerasammy Permaul, who took 41 wickets at 17. They nailed the championship with a game to spare, though they concluded by losing a rescheduled fixture against **Leeward Islands**, who finished bottom for the third consecutive year. Adding to the sense of a familiar script, **Barbados** were runners-up again, with four wins – the same as **Trinidad & Tobago** and **Jamaica**, who were separated by a fraction of a point. But while the top two teams were usually hard to beat, losing only three games between them, the other four each lost five out of ten.

The distressing patterns of recent seasons were repeated. The 30 first-class matches had 23 outright results (down from 25), including 11 three-day finishes. In 2015-16, the competition produced eight totals over 400, though none of 500; in 2016-17, there were only four, though three of those (all against Leewards at the small Warner Park ground) reached 540 or more. By contrast, there were 32 totals under 200, compared with 33 the previous season. There was an almost laughable fixture between Jamaica – contenders for most of the season – and Leeward Islands, in which neither side could manage more than 133. In that game, Jamaica were bowled out for 56, their lowest total since the domestic tournament began, but they repeated it three weeks later, against **Windward Islands**. There were 21 centuries in all, down from 26.

Despite the gloomy picture, there was some satisfaction that the list of leading run-scorers featured new names. In addition to Chanderpaul and Devon Smith, five players who had not yet appeared for West Indies topped 600 runs at an average of 40-plus – Trinidad & Tobago's Yannic Cariah and Kyle Hope, Leeward Islands' Jahmar Hamilton and Montcin Hodge, and Windward Islands' Sunil Ambris.

But there were few surprises among the leading wicket-takers. Once more, not a single pace bowler made the top five, despite the introduction of a rule awarding 0.2 of a point for every wicket taken by seam. Jamaica's captain, slow left-armer Nikita Miller, headed the list for the second successive season, with 58, but as he turned 35 in May he was not expecting an international recall. No one else managed 50, though Trinidad & Tobago leg-spinner Imran Khan took 44, as he had done in 2015-16.

Two seamers did quietly enhance their credentials – both Barbadian-born all-rounders representing other franchises. Raymon Reifer, playing his third season for Guyana (he had initially appeared for the now defunct Combined Campuses & Colleges), was a vital cog in the champions' wheel, combining 445 runs with his handy medium-pace, which produced 36 wickets. Roshon Primus won admirers in his first season by scoring 352 and capturing 21 wickets, including six on first-class debut.

In February, Trinidad & Tobago were denied a third successive Super50 title when Barbados supplanted them. Both teams had won seven of their eight preliminary matches, but Trinidad made the fatal error of inviting Jamaica to bat in their semi-final; they responded with 434, the highest total in West Indian one-day cricket. Meanwhile, Barbados had crushed Leeward Islands in their own semi, when Shai Hope hit a century and made seven dismissals behind the stumps – another national record. He scored a second hundred to set up victory against Jamaica in the final.

FIRST-CLASS AVERAGES IN 2016-17

BATTING (350 runs, average 25.00)

		M	*I*	*NO*	*R*	*HS*	*100*	*Avge*	*Ct/St*
1	†S. Chanderpaul (*Guyana*)	7	11	1	622	143	2	62.20	2
2	R. L. Chase (*Barbados/West Indies*)	12	19	6	776	131	2	59.69	4
3	B. A. King (*Jamaica*)	4	7	0	361	194	1	51.57	2
4	S. D. Hope (*Barbados/West Indies*)	7	13	2	526	215*	1	47.81	7
5	S. S. J. Brooks (*Barbados/Bd Pres XI*)	9	14	4	464	76*	0	46.40	9
6 {	J. N. Hamilton (*Leeward Is/Bd Pres XI*)	10	16	1	674	125	2	44.93	27/3
	K. A. Hope (*Trinidad & Tobago/BP XI*)	9	17	2	674	105*	1	44.93	8
8	S. W. Ambris (*Windward Islands*)	10	16	2	608	231	1	43.42	17/2
9	†Y. Cariah (*Trinidad & Tobago*)	10	18	2	691	196	2	43.18	6
10	M. V. Hodge (*Leeward Islands*)	10	18	3	616	114	1	41.06	7
11	†D. S. Smith (*Windward Islands*)	10	19	4	611	103	2	40.73	10
12	R. S. Primus (*Trinidad & Tobago*)	7	11	2	352	65	0	39.11	9
13	†R. A. Reifer (*Guyana/Board Pres XI*)	10	16	3	490	55	0	37.69	1
14	K. A. Stoute (*Barbados*)	10	13	2	391	81*	0	35.54	7
15	†A. T. Alleyne (*Barbados*)	10	17	0	587	186	1	34.52	7
16	†K. O. A. Powell (*Leeward Is/BP XI/WI*)	12	20	1	645	84*	0	33.94	12
17	†S. O. Hetmyer (*Guyana/Bd Pres XI/WI*)	12	23	2	711	97	0	33.85	10
18	†C. F. Hughes (*Leeward Islands*)	7	12	1	363	71	0	33.00	4
19	R. Chandrika (*Guyana*)	8	14	3	360	86	0	32.72	7
20	J. Blackwood (*Jamaica*)	10	19	1	578	96	0	32.11	18
21	K. U. Carty (*Leeward Islands*)	7	13	0	386	103	1	29.69	4
22	†J. D. Campbell (*Jamaica*)	9	17	0	495	88	0	29.11	9
23	D. C. Thomas (*Jamaica*)	10	19	2	493	114*	1	29.00	13
24	†I. Rajah (*Trinidad & Tobago*)	8	14	0	404	69	0	28.85	4
25	†V. A. Singh (*Guyana/West Indies*)	12	20	2	515	135*	1	28.61	5
26	N. E. Bonner (*Leeward Islands*)	8	13	0	370	94	0	28.46	6
27	R. R. S. Cornwall (*Leeward Is/Bd Pres XI*)	10	16	1	416	84	0	27.73	10

BOWLING (17 wickets, average 30.00)

		Style	*O*	*M*	*R*	*W*	*BB*	*5I*	*Avge*
1	N. O. Miller (*Jamaica*)	SLA	402.5	105	829	58	9-41	4	14.29
2	R. S. Primus (*Trinidad & Tobago*)	RFM	98	19	356	21	6-30	2	16.95
3	V. Permaul (*Guyana*)	SLA	343.2	120	718	41	7-48	3	17.51
4	K. A. J. Roach (*Barbados/Bd Pres XI*)	RFM	164	37	443	25	4-18	0	17.72
5	K. R. Mayers (*Windward Islands*)	RM	179.2	41	500	27	6-29	1	18.51
6	K. A. Joseph (*Guyana/Bd Pres XI*)	RFM	150	30	465	25	7-53	1	18.60
7	D. K. Jacobs (*Jamaica/Bd Pres XI*)	LB	246.5	36	772	38	5-64	2	20.31
8	J. A. Warrican (*Barbados*)	SLA	259.4	72	651	32	5-87	1	20.34
9	S. S. Cotterell (*Trinidad & Tobago*)	LFM	129.5	27	409	20	3-27	0	20.45
10	I. Khan (*Trinidad & Tobago*)	LB	304.1	54	913	44	6-74	5	20.75
11	R. A. Reifer (*Guyana/Bd Pres XI*)	LFM	239.5	57	798	38	6-74	3	21.00
12	D. E. Johnson (*Windward Islands*)	LF	183	43	510	24	5-46	1	21.25
13	J. S. Louis (*Leeward Islands*)	RFM	128.1	35	382	17	4-4	0	22.47
14	J. P. Greaves (*Barbados*)	RM	141.1	37	440	19	5-63	1	23.15
15	R. L. Chase (*Barbados/West Indies*)	OB	242.1	56	705	30	7-22	1	23.50
16	G. C. Tonge (*Leeward Islands*)	RFM	204	44	659	28	5-56	1	23.53
17	S. Shillingford (*Windward Islands*)	OB	328.3	66	948	39	7-91	5	24.30
18	B. N. L. Charles (*Trinidad & Tobago*)	OB	186	45	520	20	4-79	0	26.00
19	Yasir Shah (*Pakistan*)	LB	241.2	43	738	28	7-94	3	26.35
20	A. S. Joseph (*Leeward Is/West Indies*)	RFM	228.1	53	716	26	5-42	2	27.53
21	R. R. S. Cornwall (*Leeward Is/BP XI*)	OB	365.4	68	1,132	41	6-68	3	27.60
22	K. A. Stoute (*Barbados*)	RFM	185	62	529	19	4-51	0	27.84
23	G. Motie (*Guyana*)	SLA	218.3	57	611	21	4-35	0	29.09

DIGICEL REGIONAL FOUR-DAY TOURNAMENT IN 2016-17

	Played	*Won*	*Lost*	*Drawn*	*Bonus points* *Batting*	*Bowling*	*Pace*	*Points*
Guyana	10	5	2	3	22	26	17.8	134.8
Barbados	10	4	1	5	20	25	16.0	124.0
Trinidad & Tobago	10	4	5	1	12	27	12.8	102.8
Jamaica	10	4	5	1	14	29	8.6	102.6
Windward Islands	10	3	5	2	11	29	15.6	97.6
Leeward Islands	10	3	5	2	9	25	13.2	89.2

Win = 12pts; draw = 3pts. Bonus points were awarded as follows for the first 110 overs of each team's first innings: one batting point for the first 200 runs and then for 250, 300, 350 and 400; one bowling point for the third wicket taken and then for the sixth and ninth. In addition, 0.2 of a point awarded for every wicket taken by a pace bowler across both innings.

At Providence, Guyana, November 11–14, 2016. **Guyana won by 181 runs. ‡Guyana 298 and 238-4 dec; Jamaica 208** (V. Permaul 5-60) **and 147.** *Guyana 17.8pts, Jamaica 4.8pts. Guyana made a winning start to their title defence, though 16 wickets for their left-arm spinners Veerasammy Permaul and Gudakesh Motie meant they derived little benefit from the new pace-bowling bonus point system.*

At Basseterre, St Kitts, November 11–14, 2016. **Drawn. ‡Leeward Islands 377 and 164-6 dec; Barbados 237** (R. R. S. Cornwall 5-117) **and 235-5.** *Leeward Islands 8.8pts, Barbados 6pts. Off-spinner Rahkeem Cornwall scored a pair of fifties and took nine wickets in the match.*

At Port-of-Spain, November 11–13, 2016 (day/night). **Trinidad & Tobago won by nine wickets. Windward Islands 142** (R. S. Primus 6-30) **and 254** (I. Khan 5-84); **‡Trinidad & Tobago 242 and 157-1.** *Trinidad & Tobago 18pts, Windward Islands 4pts. This was one of six day/night games, the first in the West Indian first-class tournament since 2013-14. On the opening day, debutant seamer Roshon Primus took 6–1–30–6. Devon Smith carried his bat for 86*, and more than half Windwards' total came from his ninth-wicket stand of 73 with Delorn Johnson (38); no one else passed five, and there were six ducks.*

At Kingston, November 18–21, 2016. **Jamaica won by 41 runs. Jamaica 151** (S. Shillingford 5-32) **and 159** (L. M. Edwards 6-20); **‡Windward Islands 205 and 64** (N. O. Miller 5-22). *Jamaica 16.2pts, Windward Islands 5.6pts. Oshane Thomas dismissed Devon Smith with his first delivery on first-class debut. Chasing 106, Windwards collapsed for 64 against Nikita Miller's left-arm spin, with Sunil Ambris absent hurt.*

At Basseterre, St Kitts, November 18–21, 2016. **Leeward Islands won by four wickets. Guyana 293** (R. R. S. Cornwall 6-87) **and 233-8 dec; ‡Leeward Islands 158 and 372-6** (M. V. Hodge 114). *Leeward Islands 15.4pts, Guyana 6.2pts. Montcin Hodge's century helped Leeward Islands overcome a 135-run deficit and chase down 369.*

At Port-of-Spain, November 18–21, 2016. **Barbados won by 292 runs. Barbados 242 and 317-2 dec** (A. T. Alleyne 186); **‡Trinidad & Tobago 168 and 99.** *Barbados 18.4pts, Trinidad & Tobago 4pts. Anthony Alleyne scored a maiden century, putting on 101 with Omar Phillips (40) for Barbados's first wicket and 216 with Sharmarh Brooks (76*) for the second. Set 392, Trinidad & Tobago subsided from 50-1 to 99.*

At Kingston, November 25–28, 2016. **Drawn. Jamaica 224 and 112-2; ‡Barbados 273.** *Jamaica 7.6pts, Barbados 9pts.*

At Port-of-Spain, November 25–28, 2016. **Drawn. Trinidad & Tobago 287-8 v ‡Leeward Islands.** *Trinidad & Tobago 5pts, Leeward Islands 5.2pts. Only 92 overs escaped the weather; they were dominated by a 162-run opening partnership between Kyle Hope (86) and debutant Isaiah Rajah (69).*

At Greenfields, Jamaica, November 26–29, 2016 (day/night). **Drawn. Windward Islands 192** (R. A. Reifer 6-82) **and 90-4; ‡Guyana 219.** *Windward Islands 8pts, Guyana 9.6pts.*

At Kingston, December 8–10, 2016. **Jamaica won by 132 runs. ‡Jamaica 314 and 229** (I. Khan 5-50); **Trinidad & Tobago 206 and 205** (N. O. Miller 9-41). *Jamaica 18.2pts, Trinidad & Tobago 5.4pts. Jamaica went top of the table after Miller took 9-41, the best return in the history of the West*

Indian domestic competition, and the 25th time he had taken five or more in an innings. He might have made it all ten, but Damion Jacobs claimed the final wicket.

NINE WICKETS IN WEST INDIAN FIRST-CLASS COMPETITION

9-41	**N. O. Miller**	**Jamaica v Trinidad & Tobago at Kingston**	**2016-17**
9-68	R. O. Hinds	Barbados v Leeward Islands at Charlestown	2000-01
9-76	D. R. Parry	Combined Islands v Jamaica at Kingston	1979-80
9-78	D. Bishoo	Guyana v Trinidad & Tobago at Providence	2013-14
9-97	B. D. Julien	Trinidad & Tobago v Jamaica at Port-of-Spain	1981-82
9-97	R. Dhanraj	Trinidad & Tobago v Leeward Islands at Charlestown	1995-96

At Providence, Guyana, December 9–12, 2016 (day/night). **Drawn.** ‡**Guyana 311** (S. Chanderpaul 100) **and 137**; **Barbados 288 and 25-3.** *Guyana 10.4pts, Barbados 9.8pts. Shivnarine Chanderpaul scored his 72nd century – but in the second innings was one of Jonathan Carter's five catches.*

At Roseau, Dominica, December 9–12, 2016. **Windward Islands won by 94 runs. Windward Islands 293** (G. C. Tonge 5-56) **and 333-8 dec**; ‡**Leeward Islands 259** (S. Shillingford 5-96) **and 273** (J. N. Hamilton 125). *Windward Islands 17.6pts, Leeward Islands 7.2pts. Windwards' first innings was rescued from 48-7 by Liam Sebastien (82*), who helped put on 245 for the last three wickets, including 97 for the tenth with Mervin Matthew (73). He also claimed four in each innings.*

At Basseterre, St Kitts, December 15–17, 2016 (day/night). **Jamaica won by an innings and 73 runs.** ‡**Leeward Islands 243** (J. N. Hamilton 103; D. K. Jacobs 5-103) **and 234** (D. K. Jacobs 5-64); **Jamaica 550-7 dec** (B. A. King 194, D. C. Thomas 114*). *Jamaica 20.8pts, Leeward Islands 2.8pts. Brandon King, who almost converted his maiden century into a double, hit 13 sixes and added 309 with Devon Thomas, a Jamaican fifth-wicket record. Jacobs's leg-spin claimed ten wickets.*

At Providence, Guyana, December 16–19, 2016. **Guyana won by ten wickets.** ‡**Trinidad & Tobago 162 and 235** (V. Permaul 5-53); **Guyana 378** (S. Chanderpaul 143) **and 21-0.** *Guyana 20.6pts, Trinidad & Tobago 3.2pts. Another Chanderpaul century and nine more wickets for Permaul (including his 20th five-for) set up a straightforward win.*

At Roseau, Dominica, December 16–19, 2016. **Drawn. Barbados 200-8 dec;** ‡**Windward Islands 42-0.** *Windward Islands 6.4pts, Barbados 4pts.*

At Kingston, March 10–13, 2017. **Guyana won by seven wickets. Jamaica 255** (C. A. K. Walton 101; K. A. Joseph 7-53) **and 188** (R. A. Reifer 5-60); ‡**Guyana 262 and 184-3.** *Guyana 20.2pts, Jamaica 5.4pts. Resuming after the winter break, Guyana beat Jamaica to replace them as table leaders, thanks to seamers Keon Joseph and Raymon Reifer. It was the fifth time the Chanderpauls (Shivnarine, aged 42, and his son Tagenarine, 20) had played in the same first-class team, but the first time they batted together; they put on 38.*

At St George's, Grenada, March 10–13, 2017. **Trinidad & Tobago won by 172 runs. Trinidad & Tobago 275** (Y. Cariah 102*) **and 203-5 dec** (K. A. Hope 105*); ‡**Windward Islands 104 and 202** (I. Khan 5-67). *Trinidad & Tobago 18pts, Windward Islands 5.6pts. Maiden centuries from Yannic Cariah (who retired hurt briefly on 92) and Kyle Hope set up Trinidad's win.*

At Bridgetown, March 11–13, 2017. **Barbados won by an innings and 26 runs.** ‡**Barbados 313** (A. S. Joseph 5-42); **Leeward Islands 163 and 124.** *Barbados 20.8pts, Leeward Islands 4.6pts. The match was postponed 24 hours in order to fit in a one-day international against England at Kensington Oval. Leewards slumped to 37-6 in their first innings and 38-6 following on.*

At Bridgetown, March 17–19, 2017. **Barbados won by nine wickets.** ‡**Windward Islands 293** (D. S. Smith 103) **and 71** (R. L. Chase 7-22); **Barbados 324 and 41-1.** *Barbados 19.4pts, Windward Islands 6.2pts. Roston Chase claimed a career-best 12.1–4–22–7 as Windwards folded for 71.*

At Kingston, March 17–19, 2017 (day/night). **Leeward Islands won by 34 runs. Leeward Islands 71** (J. E. Taylor 5-31) **and 133**; ‡**Jamaica 56 and 114** (A. S. Joseph 5-43). *Leeward Islands 19pts, Jamaica 5.6pts. After a washout on the first day, 25 wickets fell on the second. Leewards had suffered only one worse innings than their 71 here – 39 against Campuses & Colleges in 2011-12 – while a total of 56 was Jamaica's lowest since 33 against R. A. Bennett's XI in 1901-02, before the West*

Indian first-class tournament had begun. Seamer Jeremiah Louis took 10–7–4–4, and Leewards became the first team to win maximum bonus points for claiming all 20 wickets with pace.

At Port-of-Spain, March 17–20, 2017. **Guyana won by ten wickets. ‡Trinidad & Tobago 202 and 183** (V. Permaul 7-48); **Guyana 330 and 56-0.** *Guyana 18.4pts, Trinidad & Tobago 4.8pts. Guyana's third successive win was their second by ten wickets against Trinidad & Tobago in 2016-17. Permaul took nine wickets in each game – following 17 in their two encounters the previous season.*

At Bridgetown, March 23–27, 2017. **Drawn. ‡Barbados 480-3 dec** (K. C. Brathwaite 143, S. D. Hope 215*) **and 75-5; Guyana 250** (M. L. Cummins 5-41) **and 322.** *Barbados 11.8pts, Guyana 6.6pts. Kraigg Brathwaite and Shai Hope, who scored his second double-century, added 205 for the second wicket, and Miguel Cummins made Guyana follow on. But Barbados lost their chance to overtake them at the top of the table when they failed to score 93 in 12 overs. There was a rest day on March 26 to accommodate a Twenty20 international against Pakistan on the same ground.*

At Basseterre, St Kitts, March 24–27, 2017. **Windward Islands won by seven wickets. Windward Islands 540** (S. W. Ambris 231) **and 52-3; ‡Leeward Islands 240** (S. Shillingford 6-78) **and 351** (K. U. Carty 103; S. Shillingford 6-114). *Windward Islands 20.8pts, Leeward Islands 3.4pts. Ambris hit 231 in 256 balls, a maiden double-century and the highest score of the season, and added 173 for Windwards' seventh wicket with Kyle Mayers (76). Off-spinner Shane Shillingford's 12-192 took him past 500 first-class wickets.*

At Port-of-Spain, March 24–26, 2017. **Jamaica won by 87 runs. Jamaica 201 and 201; ‡Trinidad & Tobago 174 and 141** (N. O. Miller 5-45). *Jamaica 16.6pts, Trinidad & Tobago 5.4pts. Another nine wickets from Miller ensured Jamaica's fourth win, keeping them in touch with the top.*

At Bridgetown, April 7–9, 2017 (day/night). **Trinidad & Tobago won by 130 runs. ‡Trinidad & Tobago 196 and 211** (J. P. Greaves 5-63); **Barbados 168 and 109** (R. S. Primus 5-21). *Trinidad & Tobago 18.2pts, Barbados 6pts. A couple of fifties and nine wickets from Primus helped T&T inflict Barbados's only defeat of the tournament, inside three days.*

At Arnos Vale, St Vincent, April 7–9, 2017. **Windward Islands won by eight wickets. ‡Jamaica 56** (K. R. Mayers 6-29) **and 262** (S. Shillingford 7-91); **Windward Islands 223-9 dec** (D. S. Smith 100*; N. O. Miller 5-58) **and 96-2.** *Windward Islands 18.6pts, Jamaica 3.4pts. Jamaica were bundled out for 56 for the second time in three matches, with Johnson (4-26) and Mayers bowling 19.4 overs unchanged. Devon Smith then batted throughout Windwards' reply, when Miller passed 50 first-class wickets for the season.*

At Bridgetown, April 15–18, 2017. **Barbados won by 26 runs. Barbados 377** (J. P. Greaves 114) **and 187; ‡Jamaica 224 and 314** (J. A. Warrican 5-87). *Barbados 18.8pts, Jamaica 4pts. In a closely fought battle for the runners-up spot, Jamaica need 341 to win, and reached 242-4 before slow left-armers Sulieman Benn and Jomel Warrican removed four for ten in five overs. Fabian Allen revived their hopes with six sixes in a 35-ball 60, only to be last out, still 27 short.*

At Providence, Guyana, April 15–17, 2017. **Guyana won by an innings and 122 runs. ‡Windward Islands 95** (K. M. A. Paul 6-28) **and 162; Guyana 379** (A. B. Fudadin 125; D. E. Johnson 5-46). *Guyana 21.6pts, Windward Islands 4.8pts. Guyana claimed their third successive title early on the third day. On the first, 19-year-old seamer Keemo Paul's career-best 6-28 dismissed Windwards for 95, and a century from Assad Fudadin helped establish a match-winning lead of 284.*

At Basseterre, St Kitts, April 15–18, 2017. **Trinidad & Tobago won by an innings and 17 runs. Trinidad & Tobago 553** (Y. Cariah 196, T. Webster 109); **‡Leeward Islands 299** (I. Khan 5-66) **and 237** (I. Khan 6-74). *Trinidad & Tobago 20.8pts, Leeward Islands 5pts. A fourth victory gave Trinidad & Tobago third place, 0.2pts (or one pace bowler's wicket) ahead of Jamaica. Tion Webster scored 109 out of 158 in his seventh-wicket stand with Cariah, and opener Imran Khan made up for a duck by collecting 11-140 with his leg-spin. Hodge carried his bat for 96* when Leewards followed on.*

At Providence, Guyana, April 21–23, 2017. **Leeward Islands won by ten wickets. ‡Guyana 187** (R. R. S. Cornwall 6-68) **and 143; Leeward Islands 306** (R. A. Reifer 6-74) **and 25-0.** *Leeward Islands 17.8pts, Guyana 3.4pts. Bottom-placed Leewards ended the season with a consolation win over the champions, in a game postponed while the ground hosted a one-day series against Pakistan.*

REGIONAL CHAMPIONS

1965-66	Barbados	1982-83	Guyana	1999-2000	Jamaica
1966-67	Barbados	1983-84	Barbados	2000-01	Barbados
1967-68	No competition	1984-85	Trinidad & Tobago	2001-02	Jamaica
1968-69	Jamaica	1985-86	Barbados	2002-03	Barbados
1969-70	Trinidad	1986-87	Guyana	2003-04	Barbados
1970-71	Trinidad	1987-88	Jamaica	2004-05	Jamaica
1971-72	Barbados	1988-89	Jamaica	2005-06	Trinidad & Tobago
1972-73	Guyana	1989-90	Leeward Islands	2006-07	Barbados
1973-74	Barbados	1990-91	Barbados	2007-08	Jamaica
1974-75	Guyana	1991-92	Jamaica	2008-09	Jamaica
1975-76	Trinidad	1992-93	Guyana	2009-10	Jamaica
	Barbados	1993-94	Leeward Islands	2010-11	Jamaica
1976-77	Barbados	1994-95	Barbados	2011-12	Jamaica
1977-78	Barbados	1995-96	Leeward Islands	2012-13	Barbados
1978-79	Barbados	1996-97	Barbados	2013-14	Barbados
1979-80	Barbados	1997-98	Leeward Islands	2014-15	Guyana
1980-81	Combined Islands		Guyana	2015-16	Guyana
1981-82	Barbados	1998-99	Barbados	2016-17	Guyana

Barbados have won the title outright 21 times, Jamaica 12, Guyana 8, Trinidad/Trinidad & Tobago 4, Leeward Islands 3, Combined Islands 1. Barbados, Guyana, Leeward Islands and Trinidad have also shared the title.

The tournament was known as the Shell Shield from 1965-66 to 1986-87, the Red Stripe Cup from 1987-88 to 1996-97, the President's Cup in 1997-98, the Busta Cup from 1998-99 to 2001-02, the Carib Beer Cup from 2002-03 to 2007-08, the Headley–Weekes Trophy from 2008-09 to 2012-13, the President's Trophy in 2013-14, the WICB Professional Cricket League from 2014-15, and the Digicel Regional Four-Day Tournament from 2016-17.

NAGICO REGIONAL SUPER50 IN 2016-17

50-over league plus knockout

Zone A	P	W	L	BP	Pts
TRINIDAD & TOBAGO	8	7	1	3	31
LEEWARD ISLANDS	8	6	2	4	28
Kent	8	3	5	1	13
Windward Islands	8	3	5	0	12
West Indies Under-19	8	1	7	0	4

Zone B	P	W	L	BP	Pts
BARBADOS	8	7	1	5	33
JAMAICA	8	6	2	4	28
Guyana	8	4	4	2	18
Campuses/Colleges	8	2	6	1	9
ICC Americas	8	1	7	1	5

Semi-final At Coolidge, Antigua, February 15, 2017 (day/night). **Jamaica won by 292 runs. Jamaica 434-4** (50 overs) (C. A. K. Walton 117, J. Blackwood 108*); **‡Trinidad & Tobago 142** (26.3 overs) (R. Powell 5-36). *Put in, Jamaica amassed the highest total in West Indian List A cricket. Chadwick Walton added 174 with Steven Taylor (88), and Jermaine Blackwood 163 in 14 overs with Rovman Powell (95 in 45 balls); the top four hit 27 sixes in all. Powell followed up with a career-best 5-36 as defending champions Trinidad & Tobago were swept away.*

Semi-final At Coolidge, Antigua, February 16, 2017 (day/night). **Barbados won by 110 runs. ‡Barbados 314-7** (50 overs) (S. D. Hope 125); **Leeward Islands 204** (47.3 overs). *Shai Hope hit 125 in 108 balls before making seven dismissals (five catches and two stumpings), a West Indian record.*

Final At Coolidge, Antigua, February 18, 2017 (day/night). **Barbados won by 59 runs. ‡Barbados 271-9** (50 overs) (S. D. Hope 101); **Jamaica 212** (44.3 overs). *Hope scored another century, adding 127 with Jason Holder (69 in 47 balls) for Barbados's sixth wicket. Kemar Roach and Sulieman Benn reduced Jamaica to 78-5, and despite a late fightback they were all out in the 45th over.*

The Caribbean Premier League has its own section (page 1114).

ZIMBABWE CRICKET IN 2017

Gap year

LIAM BRICKHILL

Zimbabwe doesn't produce many good-news stories, and a military coup in a failing state doesn't sound like a tale with a happy ending. But, in November, the country moved peacefully into the post-Mugabe era. Rarely can a people have deposed a dictator with such joy and dignity. Harare Sports Club is just across the road from State House, the president's official residence, but a first-class match overlapping the coup was completely unaffected. The players were so close to the action that a six could have been pinged on to one of the armoured personnel carriers outside. Perhaps fortunately, no one did.

Quite how the country will change in the new era remains to be seen, but there seems more opportunity now, and that is just as true of the cricket. Even so, the international year was stop–start, with long gaps between matches. It began with a disappointment: a 3–2 defeat in a home one-day series by Afghanistan. It was their third straight victory over Zimbabwe, whom they will soon be taking on in Test matches as well.

ZIMBABWE IN 2017

	Played	*Won*	*Lost*	*Drawn/No result*
Tests	4	–	3	1
One-day internationals	12	6	6	–
Twenty20 internationals	–	–	–	–

JANUARY		
FEBRUARY	5 ODIs (h) v Afghanistan	(page 1043)
MARCH		
APRIL		
MAY		
JUNE / JULY	2 ODIs (a) v Scotland	(page 1080)
	1 Test and 5 ODIs (a) v Sri Lanka	(page 985)
AUGUST		
SEPTEMBER		
OCTOBER / NOVEMBER	2 Tests (h) v West Indies	(page 1045)
DECEMBER	1 Test (a) v South Africa	(page 959)

For a review of Zimbabwean domestic cricket from the 2016-17 season, see page 1050.

A couple of months later, in June, Graeme Cremer's team visited Europe, where they drew 1–1 with a spirited Scotland, then eased past the Netherlands 2–1. Those games might have felt low-key, but ahead of a tour of Sri Lanka, they proved an effective warm-up. In the first match, at Galle, Zimbabwe became the first team to successfully chase over 300 in a one-day international in Sri Lanka. Then they recovered from 175 for seven in the decider at Hambantota to win their first series there, a result that persuaded Angelo Mathews to resign as Sri Lanka's captain. Zimbabwe also forced the hosts to dig deep in the one-off Test in Colombo: Sri Lanka chased down 388 – the highest fourth-innings target to win a Test in Asia – and might not have got there had Niroshan Dickwella been given out stumped, as he should have, when he had 37 of his eventual 81.

That one-day success was Zimbabwe's first overseas series victory since visiting Kenya in 2008-09 but, with no more cricket for three months, they couldn't maintain the momentum. In October, after bowling West Indies out for 219 on the opening day of the First Test at Bulawayo, they conceded a first-innings lead, then collapsed on the fifth afternoon. Shedding the rust, Zimbabwe made a better fist of the Second Test, and battled to a draw.

Then came another gap of almost two months, and the Zimbabweans were hopelessly out of their depth in the experimental four-day floodlit Boxing Day Test against South Africa at Port Elizabeth. It lasted only two: Zimbabwe's 68 was the lowest Test total of 2017, and the match was one of the shortest in history, at only 907 balls. St George's Park seemed a long way from Hambantota. As ever, Zimbabwe were able to make different sorts of history – good, bad and ugly.

The administration of Zimbabwe Cricket deserved credit for keeping the game afloat. Former ICC chief financial officer Faisal Hasnain joined in April, officially taking over from Wilfred Mukondiwa as managing director in June. He formed a workable partnership with board chairman Tavengwa Mukuhlani, and under their tenure ZC tightened their belt and achieved stability, though a worrying debt of $US19m remains.

Their efforts complemented those of coach Heath Streak and convenor of selectors Tatenda Taibu, who were able to give Brendan Taylor and Kyle Jarvis such confidence that they left county cricket behind and returned to the national fold.

It wasn't all good news. The domestic season was postponed yet again in December: ZC were scrambling to get four grounds ready for the World Cup Qualifiers in March 2018, and were unable to pay November and December salaries in full, until the first disbursement of ICC cash arrived in January. But both on and off the field, the peaks generally outshone the troughs, which added up to a modest renaissance. And not a moment too soon: Zimbabwe had a relatively busy 2018 on the horizon, starting with the litmus test of those World Cup qualifying matches. Should they make it to the big event, all the hard yakka in 2017 will have been worth it.

ZIMBABWE v AFGHANISTAN IN 2016-17

JOHN WARD

One-day internationals (5): Zimbabwe 2, Afghanistan 3

Afghanistan continued their seemingly inexorable progress towards Test status, though Zimbabwe could claim to have had the worst of the luck: they lost four tosses, and wet weather prevented them from preparing the fast, bouncy pitches they would have preferred. But Afghanistan, who won the first two matches, might have done better still had it not been for over-confidence. After bowling Zimbabwe out for 129 in the third game, they collapsed recklessly with victory in sight, and did not regain their composure until the decider – when they skittled Zimbabwe for 54.

It was a bowlers' series. The biggest total was Afghanistan's 253 for nine in the final game, and no batsman averaged 30; the highest individual score was 64, by Mohammad Shahzad. The tourists' slow bowlers were especially impressive: leg-spinner Rashid Khan took ten wickets at ten apiece, many with the quick, sharp-turning googly that soon made him a star in the IPL, while Mohammad Nabi's off-breaks claimed ten at 11, and went for just 3.57 an over. Zimbabwe's strong pace attack, led by Christopher Mpofu (12 wickets at 15) and Tendai Chatara (ten at 18), generally restrained the aggressive Afghan batting, while the captain Graeme Cremer commanded respect with his leg-breaks. In fact, Zimbabwe had the better-balanced attack; it was their poor batting that let them down. They also began under a self-imposed handicap, omitting five players who had failed stringent fitness tests, although Hamilton Masakadza and Sean Williams later passed.

Afghanistan's success was marred by their behaviour. The Zimbabweans deserved much credit for their composure in the face of excessive appealing, sledging, triumphalism and verbal send-offs, with Shahzad the leading culprit. ICC officials were also to blame for their failure to clamp down.

AFGHANISTAN TOURING PARTY

*Asghar Stanikzai, Aftab Alam, Dawlat Zadran, Fareed Ahmad, Gulbadeen Naib, Hamza Hotak, Hashmatullah Shahidi, Ihsanullah Janat, Karim Janat, Mohammad Nabi, Mohammad Shahzad, Najibullah Zadran, Noor Ali Zadran, Rahmat Shah, Rashid Khan, Samiullah Shenwari. *Coach:* L. S. Rajput.

First one-day international At Harare, February 16, 2017. **Afghanistan won by 12 runs** (DLS). ‡**Afghanistan 215** (49.2 overs) (Noor Ali Zadran 39, Rahmat Shah 31, Asghar Stanikzai 50, Rashid Khan 32; A. G. Cremer 3-46); **Zimbabwe 99-4** (27.2 overs) (C. R. Ervine 38*). *MoM:* Asghar Stanikzai. *ODI debuts:* R. P. Burl, R. Ngarava (Zimbabwe). *With rain falling, and Zimbabwe one run ahead on DLS, Rashid Khan trapped Ryan Burl to nudge Afghanistan in front. Only one more delivery – a dot ball – was possible before the players left the field. After the visitors complained about a wet area at the edge of the square, the game was abandoned in their favour. Unsettled weather had made conditions tricky for batting and, from 156-3 in the 39th over, several Afghans fell to miscues; captain Asghar Stanikzai's 57-ball 50 stood out, although No. 9 Rashid bashed 32 from 18. Zimbabwe's batsmen also struggled with their timing, stumbling to 44-3 in the 15th. But*

Craig Ervine and Burl – one of two debutants, along with left-arm seamer Richard Ngarava, 19 and yet to play a first-class match – added 55 to inch them into the lead. Rashid ended their ascendancy in the nick of time.

Second one-day international At Harare, February 19, 2017. **Afghanistan won by 54 runs.** ‡**Afghanistan 238-9** (50 overs) (Mohammad Shahzad 64, Rahmat Shah 53, Mohammad Nabi 33, Najibullah Zadran 45; T. L. Chatara 3-36); **Zimbabwe 184** (42.1 overs) (S. F. Mire 54, C. R. Ervine 34; Mohammad Nabi 3-38, Rashid Khan 3-25). *MoM:* Rashid Khan. *Afghanistan went 2–0 up after Zimbabwe's batsmen succumbed to the spin of Rashid and Mohammad Nabi, who shared six wickets. At 139-3 in the 32nd over, the Zimbabweans were on course to chase down 239, but Ervine became the first of seven wickets to fall for just 45. Afghanistan had faltered too, only doubling the score after reaching 118-1. A second-wicket stand of 84 between an unusually restrained Mohammad Shahzad and the more fluent Rahmat Shah had suggested greater riches, and Najibullah Zadran clouted three sixes. In reply, Solomon Mire batted with panache in his first international series since the 2015 World Cup, making a career-best 54 out of 69 for the first wicket before falling to Rashid's googly. Rain threatened, but they were well ahead on DLS as Ervine and Burl added 55 for the second game in a row – but Ervine fell to Gulbadeen Naib, and the rest crumbled.*

Third one-day international At Harare, February 21, 2017. **Zimbabwe won by three runs.** ‡**Zimbabwe 129** (32.4 overs) (T. K. Musakanda 60, M. N. Waller 36*; Gulbadeen Naib 4-27, Rashid Khan 3-29); **Afghanistan 126** (29.3 overs) (Asghar Stanikzai 31; T. L. Chatara 3-30, S. C. Williams 3-15, C. B. Mpofu 3-24). *MoM:* T. L. Chatara and S. C. Williams. *Chasing 130 to maintain their unbeaten one-day series record against Zimbabwe, Afghanistan folded from 121-5 to 126 all out against Christopher Mpofu and Sean Williams, who collected a career-best 3-15 in his first game of the series. Zimbabwe bowled and fielded well, but the Afghans had been over-confident from the moment Shahzad miscued the second ball of the reply high over mid-on. Wickets fell steadily, with Tendai Chatara removing three of the top four en route to a career-best of his own, and a share of the match award. But it could easily have gone to Tarisai Musakanda: in only his fourth ODI, he stood firm as Zimbabwe slipped to 40-5 on a blameless pitch against bowling that was good but hardly lethal (Gulbadeen helped himself to another career-best). Musakanda finally found a resolute partner in Malcolm Waller, who helped add 81. But when Musakanda went for 60, it was the first of five wickets to fall for eight. Fortunately for Zimbabwe, an even more careless collapse was still to come, leaving Mpofu to declare: "I actually had tears in my eyes." The previous-lowest they had defended was 134, against England during the 1992 World Cup in Australia, shortly before they won Test status.*

Fourth one-day international At Harare, February 24, 2017. **Zimbabwe won by seven wickets** (DLS). ‡**Afghanistan 111** (38.5 overs) (C. B. Mpofu 3-25); **Zimbabwe 107-3** (22.2 overs) (S. F. Mire 46, P. J. Moor 36*). *MoM:* C. B. Mpofu. *ODI debuts:* Ihsanullah Janat, Karim Janat (Afghanistan). *The Afghans appeared to be still in shock after the previous match. So timidly did they bat that, by the time the debutant opener Ihsanullah Janat fell for a 20-ball duck in the seventh over, only three runs had been scored – and one of those from a misfield. Only Stanikzai tried to break the shackles, hitting three of his team's seven boundaries, but no one bettered his 19, and Afghanistan were fortunate to pass 100; Graeme Cremer's leg-spin brought him 8–1–12–2. Zimbabwe, set 105 in 42 overs because of rain interruptions, made certain of victory with an opening stand of 79 between the aggressive Mire and the steady Peter Moor.*

Fifth one-day international At Harare, February 26, 2017. **Afghanistan won by 106 runs** (DLS). ‡**Afghanistan 253-9** (50 overs) (Noor Ali Zadran 46, Rahmat Shah 50, Mohammad Nabi 48; C. B. Mpofu 3-46); **Zimbabwe 54** (13.5 overs) (Hamza Hotak 3-20, Mohammad Nabi 3-14). *MoM:* Rahmat Shah. *Zimbabwe plunged to their fourth-lowest ODI total after rain left them a testing DLS target of 161 in 22 overs. They never got close: batting conditions had deteriorated, the outfield was damp and heavy, and the strokeplay desperate. After staggering to 13-4 against the left-arm spin of Hamza Hotak, there was no way back; only skipper Cremer played with any judgment, top-scoring with 14*. Zimbabwe's 54 was the lowest all-out total against Afghanistan, undercutting their own 82 at Sharjah in December 2015. By contrast, the Afghans treated the series decider as if their meltdowns in the previous two matches had never happened, producing the fearless cricket that normally characterises their game. Zimbabwe's seamers put in their poorest performance yet, with the exception of Ngarava's opening spell. Rahmat played a finely controlled innings, while Nabi's timely late hitting enabled his team to reach the highest total of the series.*

ZIMBABWE v WEST INDIES IN 2017-18

LIAM BRICKHILL

Test matches (2): Zimbabwe 0, West Indies 1

West Indies bested Zimbabwe in a short series in Bulawayo, where lifeless pitches meant hard graft for bowlers and batsmen alike. Yet there were bright moments in both matches, and the teams looked evenly matched.

Zimbabwe had the two leading run-scorers: Hamilton Masakadza added a second century against West Indies, 16 years after making one on debut at Harare aged 17, while Sikandar Raza contributed a pair of eighties, as well as a maiden five-for with his off-breaks. For West Indies, Devendra Bishoo shone after a nondescript tour of England, and was named Man of the Series for his 13 wickets. Not far behind was Zimbabwe's captain Graeme Cremer. In conditions heavily weighted towards the slow men, the two leggies took 22 of the 64 wickets to fall to bowlers, while spin accounted for 43 overall.

Even so, a reinvigorated Kemar Roach unfurled slower balls, cutters and reverse swing, and dealt menace with new ball and old. He gave Bishoo and the other spinners the freedom to attack, and ensured West Indies usually kept control, even when wickets were not falling.

Kyle Jarvis, returning for Zimbabwe after a four-year Kolpak stint with Lancashire, offered similar control in the First Test, only for an early batting meltdown to set up a comfortable West Indies victory. But he missed the Second with an ankle injury, and the home spinners were unable to force a win. The series also marked the return of the former Zimbabwe captain Brendan Taylor, who had cut short his stay with Nottinghamshire for family reasons, but was unable to build on a fighting 73 in the first match.

West Indies had arrived with the same Test squad they had taken to England, and made consistency – in both performance and selection – their watchword for the tour. A settled group performed well, and they registered their first series win under Jason Holder. Importantly, they also gained experience in conditions some of them would encounter again at the World Cup qualifying tournament, due to be hosted here in March 2018.

It might have been a low-key series, but it was still touched by a hint of corruption: Cremer reported an illegal approach to him before the First Test, leading to an investigation by the ICC.

These were West Indies' first Tests in Zimbabwe since 2003-04, when Brian Lara's 191 in Bulawayo set up another overall win. It is unclear when, if ever, they will be back for more: soon after, the impecunious Zimbabwean board announced they would scale back on home Tests.

> "To witness their slide to 45 for six at the Kensington Oval in Barbados, a fortress for so long, was to see a former star reduced to busking outside the theatre."
> West Indies v England in 2016–17, page 255

WEST INDIAN TOURING PARTY

*J. O. Holder, D. Bishoo, J. Blackwood, K. C. Brathwaite, R. L. Chase, M. L. Cummins, S. O. Dowrich, S. T. Gabriel, S. O. Hetmyer, K. A. Hope, S. D. Hope, A. S. Joseph, K. O. A. Powell, R. A. Reifer, K. A. J. Roach. *Coach:* S. G. Law.

ZIMBABWE v WEST INDIES

First Test

At Bulawayo, October 21–24, 2017. West Indies won by 117 runs. Toss: West Indies. Test debut: S. F. Mire.

A Test that started in fast-forward, slowed to a glacial crawl and giddied up to a comedic finish ended with a day to spare. Bishoo turned things West Indies' way on the second and, once they had grabbed the initiative, they stayed ahead. Zimbabwe were almost halfway to West Indies' modest first-innings 219 when he took his first two wickets, and three more on the second afternoon completed the collapse. Zimbabwe lost nine for 68 and trailed by 60.

The pitch turned markedly on the first morning, but otherwise had a stultifying effect. West Indies' batsmen were more than happy to play their part in slowing things down: Shai Hope's unbeaten 90 on the first day, over nearly four and a half hours, showed the virtue of temperance, while Brathwaite batted even longer for his 86 on the second and third. Only Chase bucked the trend, with an adventurous 95 in the second innings, but by then Zimbabwe's bowlers had been ground down.

Their batsmen clearly didn't get the message. Instead of following Hope's example, they went too hard at the ball, and this short-format approach backfired in the first innings after they had reached 91 for one. The turnaround was engineered by Bishoo, whose first ball of the second morning had been thundered imperiously over long-on by Masakadza. He collected his fourth five-for in Tests, and added four more in the second innings – though, with the pitch flattening out, he had to work a little harder.

Zimbabwe, set a distant 434, batted more responsibly: Masakadza and Taylor both made half-centuries, and at 219 for four an hour after tea on the fourth day, they had half an eye on a record chase. But Sikandar Raza cuffed a loose one from Bishoo straight to short extra cover, and the spell was broken. Taylor was complicit in the run-out of Waller (Shai Hope scored a direct hit from midwicket), and shortly afterwards was run out himself, trying an optimistic second to Brathwaite at deep square. Suddenly it was 263 for nine. Jarvis and Mpofu laid about the bowling entertainingly – they put on 53 in nine overs, which at least took Zimbabwe past 300 – but it couldn't last.

If Bishoo finished with match figures of nine for 184, his fellow leg-spinner Cremer, Zimbabwe's captain, had bowled with more vim and variation. But he was let down by his team-mates' catching, and ought to have improved his own haul of eight for 178. Both made excellent use of the conditions, and more pace in the pitch might have rendered their extravagant turn almost unplayable. A measure of the sluggishness of the surface was that not a single catch was taken in the slips off a quick bowler. In the end, though, it was West Indies who adapted better.

Man of the Match: D. Bishoo.

Close of play: first day, Zimbabwe 19-0 (Masakadza 0, Mire 17); second day, West Indies 88-1 (Brathwaite 38, K. A. Hope 32); third day, West Indies 369-8 (Chase 91).

West Indies

Batsman	First innings		Second innings	
K. C. Brathwaite	c Chakabva b Jarvis	3	lbw b Sikandar Raza	86
K. O. A. Powell	c Ervine b Cremer	56	b Cremer	17
K. A. Hope	c Chakabva b Mire	16	lbw b Jarvis	43
S. D. Hope	not out	90	lbw b Jarvis	44
R. L. Chase	c Ervine b Sikandar Raza	31	b Williams	95
J. Blackwood	st Chakabva b Cremer	1	st Chakabva b Williams	3
†S. O. Dowrich	c Masakadza b Williams	11	c Masakadza b Williams	12
*J. O. Holder	lbw b Williams	8	c Mpofu b Cremer	24
D. Bishoo	c Ervine b Williams	0	c Williams b Cremer	44
K. A. J. Roach	lbw b Cremer	0	b Cremer	0
S. T. Gabriel	c Ervine b Cremer	0	not out	0
	B 3	3	B 3, lb 2	5
	(82.5 overs)	219	(126 overs)	373

1/14 (1) 2/35 (3) 3/110 (2) 4/174 (5) 5/179 (6) 6/202 (7) 7/212 (8) 8/218 (9) 9/219 (10) 10/219 (11)

1/25 (2) 2/107 (3) 3/174 (1) 4/211 (4) 5/224 (6) 6/244 (7) 7/277 (8) 8/369 (9) 9/369 (10) 10/373 (5)

Jarvis 14–2–40–1; Mpofu 14–4–28–0; Mire 7–0–22–1; Cremer 23.5–3–64–4; Sikandar Raza 11–1–42–1; Williams 13–4–20–3. *Second innings*—Jarvis 24–1–66–2; Mpofu 10–3–30–0; Williams 35–8–91–3; Cremer 34–5–114–4; Sikandar Raza 19–4–53–1; Mire 2–0–5–0; Waller 2–0–9–0.

Zimbabwe

Batsman	First innings		Second innings	
H. Masakadza	c Dowrich b Bishoo	42	c S. D. Hope b Brathwaite	57
S. F. Mire	c Brathwaite b Roach	27	b Roach	47
C. R. Ervine	lbw b Bishoo	39	lbw b Bishoo	18
B. R. M. Taylor	c Blackwood b Bishoo	1	run out	73
S. C. Williams	c Dowrich b Roach	7	st Dowrich b Bishoo	6
Sikandar Raza	c Gabriel b Bishoo	6	c Chase b Bishoo	30
M. N. Waller	b Holder	11	run out	11
†R. W. Chakabva	c Chase b Bishoo	12	c and b Chase	1
*A. G. Cremer	b Holder	0	c and b Bishoo	9
K. M. Jarvis	not out	2	not out	23
C. B. Mpofu	c Dowrich b Gabriel	10	c Powell b Chase	33
	Lb 2	2	B 5, lb 1, nb 2	8
	(61.3 overs)	159	(90.4 overs)	316

1/44 (2) 2/91 (1) 3/93 (4) 4/110 (5) 5/123 (6) 6/133 (3) 7/139 (7) 8/147 (8) 9/147 (9) 10/159 (11)

1/99 (1) 2/109 (2) 3/141 (3) 4/155 (5) 5/219 (6) 6/246 (7) 7/249 (8) 8/253 (4) 9/263 (9) 10/316 (11)

Gabriel 11.3–4–24–1; Holder 14–5–25–2; Bishoo 24–4–79–5; Chase 1–0–6–0; Roach 11–5–23–2. *Second innings*—Roach 13–3–34–1; Gabriel 10–2–50–0; Holder 12–4–30–0; Bishoo 32–8–105–4; Chase 13.4–2–61–2; Brathwaite 10–1–30–1.

Umpires: H. D. P. K. Dharmasena and P. R. Reiffel. Third umpire: S. D. Fry.
Referee: J. Srinath.

ZIMBABWE v WEST INDIES

Second Test

At Bulawayo, October 29–November 2, 2017. Drawn. Toss: Zimbabwe. Test debut: T. S. Chisoro.

Zimbabwe's batsmen put right many of their mistakes from the previous match, but another placid pitch made the prospect of either side taking 20 wickets wholly fanciful. October is usually Zimbabwe's hottest month, and three days before the game Bulawayo was a 38°C oven. But it plummeted to 14 on the eve of the match, forcing the West Indians to unpack the thick sweaters and hand-warmers still in their kitbags from the England tour. Shai Hope thought the first day was one of the coldest he had experienced, and tweeted: "Am I back in the UK? #numbfingers".

The thermometer shot back up to the mid-thirties for the remainder of the match. But the result of the cold snap was that the pitch, which had been expected to break up, firmed up instead. It helped neither seamers nor spinners, and in effect ruled out any chance of a comeback win for Zimbabwe.

Dowrich and Holder made particularly good use of the conditions to stitch together an eighth-wicket partnership of 212, a West Indian record (previously 148 by Jimmy Adams and Franklyn Rose, also against Zimbabwe, at Kingston in 1999-2000). Dowrich completed a maiden Test hundred, after a lean time in England, while Holder's was his second. Only once before had Nos 8 and 9 scored centuries in the same Test innings, after Roger Hartigan and Clem Hill (batting down the order after illness) for Australia against England at Adelaide in 1907-08.

Their resistance allowed West Indies to recover from a perilous 230 for seven and take a handy lead of 122, overshadowing what had been a superb century by Masakadza. Zimbabwe had been in trouble themselves at 14 for three on the Arctic first day, but Masakadza reshaped their fortunes with stands of 142 with Moor – who found out he was playing only that morning, when Sean Williams was taken ill – and then 90 with Sikandar Raza.

Masakadza's hundred was only the second by a Zimbabwean opener since 2001 (Tino Mawoyo made one in 2011), his first in three years, and his second against West Indies, 16 years after his first. Masakadza also became the fifth Zimbabwean to pass 2,000 Test runs, after the Flower brothers, Alistair Campbell and Guy Whittall.

Chakabva resisted for almost four hours on the last day and – against some increasingly friendly bowling – shared an unbroken partnership of 91 with Cremer that spanned more than 48 overs. As the prospects of a result receded, attention turned to individual milestones. Bishoo had become the first West Indian leg-spinner to collect 100 Test wickets, and Sikandar was the second player to reach 80 in both innings and take a five-for in the same Test, after South Africa's Jacques Kallis, also against West Indies, at Cape Town in 1998-99.

Man of the Match: Sikandar Raza. *Man of the Series:* D. Bishoo.

Close of play: first day, Zimbabwe 169-4 (Masakadza 101, Sikandar Raza 9); second day, West Indies 78-1 (Powell 43, Bishoo 0); third day, West Indies 374-7 (Dowrich 75, Holder 71); fourth day, Zimbabwe 140-4 (Moor 39, Sikandar Raza 58).

Zimbabwe

First innings		Second innings	
H. Masakadza c Dowrich b Bishoo	147	– b Roach	5
S. F. Mire c Dowrich b Roach	4	– lbw b Roach	0
C. R. Ervine b Gabriel	0	– b Bishoo	22
B. R. M. Taylor b Roach	1	– lbw b Gabriel	10
P. J. Moor b Chase	52	– c S. D. Hope b Gabriel	42
Sikandar Raza c K. A. Hope b Gabriel	80	– b Holder	89
M. N. Waller b Brathwaite	0	– c Blackwood b Bishoo	15
†R. W. Chakabva b Bishoo	10	– not out	71
*A. G. Cremer run out	11	– not out	28
T. S. Chisoro lbw b Roach	9		
C. B. Mpofu not out	4		
Lb 6, nb 2	8	B 10, lb 8, nb 1	19
1/4 (2) 2/11 (3) 3/14 (4) 4/156 (5) 5/246 (1) 6/248 (7) 7/267 (8) 8/310 (6) 9/319 (9) 10/326 (10) (109.1 overs)	326	1/5 (1) 2/8 (2) 3/23 (4) 4/46 (3) 5/144 (5) 6/172 (7) 7/210 (6) (7 wkts, 144 overs)	301

Gabriel 22–4–64–2; Roach 18.1–5–44–3; Blackwood 4–1–8–0; Holder 16–2–49–0; Bishoo 25–2–82–2; Chase 14–1–50–1; Brathwaite 10–0–23–1. *Second innings*—Gabriel 21–7–34–2; Roach 22–10–37–2; Brathwaite 17–2–44–0; Holder 22–7–42–1; Bishoo 34–7–74–2; Chase 17–3–31–0; Blackwood 10–4–21–0; Powell 1–1–0–0.

West Indies

K. C. Brathwaite c Masakadza b Cremer	32
K. O. A. Powell c Ervine b Mpofu	90
D. Bishoo c and b Sikandar Raza	23
K. A. Hope lbw b Sikandar Raza	1
S. D. Hope b Sikandar Raza	40
R. L. Chase lbw b Sikandar Raza	32
J. Blackwood c Cremer b Sikandar Raza	5
†S. O. Dowrich lbw b Chisoro	103
*J. O. Holder b Chisoro	110
K. A. J. Roach lbw b Chisoro	0
S. T. Gabriel not out	5
B 3, lb 3, nb 1	7
1/76 (1) 2/131 (3) 3/135 (4) 4/163 (2) 5/219 (6) 6/225 (7) 7/230 (5) 8/442 (8) 9/443 (9) 10/448 (10) (178.2 overs)	448

Mpofu 28–10–55–1; Mire 5–2–5–0; Cremer 52–8–161–1; Sikandar Raza 48–12–99–5; Chisoro 41.2–9–113–3; Masakadza 4–1–9–0.

Umpires: H. D. P. K. Dharmasena and S. D. Fry. Third umpire: P. R. Reiffel. Referee: J. Srinath.

DOMESTIC CRICKET IN ZIMBABWE IN 2016-17

JOHN WARD

It was another season of erratic scheduling and poor standards – and a new pay row, after Zimbabwe Cricket had got through 2015-16 without one.

Again, the Logan Cup programme was arranged to avoid tours, so national players could take part; the first matches were delayed until December, after a tri-series with Sri Lanka and West Indies. But the New Year brought further rescheduling, which meant the domestic programme stretched into May, with the Twenty20 competition postponed until the next season. The teams were undermined and, by the final two rounds, the Harare-based side were missing eight first-choice players. The new ZC board had scrapped the franchise system introduced in 2009, which paired weak provinces with stronger ones, who were responsible for nurturing them; the weak now played club cricket, while the strong stood by themselves under revised names. As far as the actual cricket was concerned, they played at the same venues with the same squads.

On the positive side, the number of first-class matches played by each team reverted to nine rather than six, but a wet spell between December and February wiped out most of the first three rounds, the only result coming in controversial circumstances.

The ever-changing fixture list, the apparent lack of importance attached to the Logan Cup, unstable teams and erratic payments – a result of ZC's financial constraints – caused much dissatisfaction. When the domestic season started a month later than planned, poor communication led the players who lacked national contracts to believe they would not be paid for training in November. On the third day of the opening round, the players agreed that Bulawayo Metropolitan Tuskers would concede to Midlands Rhinos, who were already well ahead. ZC later penalised both teams five points for refusing to take the field.

The frequent international calls favoured **Manicaland Mountaineers**, whose Mutare-based squad had the most depth. They played more professionally than in the previous season and headed the table by 17 points. But the lack of celebration when they confirmed the title in their penultimate match, against Eagles in Harare, demonstrated the indifference prevalent in domestic cricket. They were steady rather than dominant: eight batsmen averaged over 30, with Kevin Kasuza beginning to realise his promise, hitting 446 in 11 innings. The experienced seamer Shingi Masakadza and leg-spinner Natsai M'shangwe carried the bowling, with 47 wickets between them.

Harare Metropolitan Eagles, who had won all three trophies as Mashonaland Eagles in 2015-16, could not reproduce that form. Despite being the only team with overseas professionals – Pakistanis Jalat Khan and Rizwan Haider – they rarely rose to the occasion, and lost the chance to beat Tuskers in Bulawayo after delaying a declaration far too long. The development of three younger players – Ryan Burl, Kudzai Maunze and Nathan Waller – offered some comfort. **Midlands Rhinos** punched above their weight. When Graeme Cremer, Malcolm Waller and Prince Masvaure were available, they could hold the team together in tight situations. Neville Madziva was disappointing, but Mike Chinouya and Carl Mumba formed a good opening attack.

Matabeleland Tuskers had been a powerhouse in recent years; now the **Bulawayo Metropolitan Tuskers**, they were dismal in first-class cricket, clinching their only victory in the final match. Most of their top batsmen failed to deliver. Brian Vitori, suspended from international cricket for an illegal action, could have spearheaded their attack, but was unfit for most of the Logan Cup. They greatly missed Tawanda Mupariwa, who moved to Australia, and Keith Dabengwa, who retired to coach in the Netherlands. Batsman Charles Kunje and slow left-armer Ainsley Ndlovu made most progress.

The Tuskers did enjoy a superb one-day season, winning the Pro50 by seven points, with five victories out of six. Brian Chari, Sean Williams and Craig Ervine were prolific with the bat; Vitori was devastating with the ball, taking 20 wickets at ten.

FIRST-CLASS AVERAGES IN 2016-17

BATTING (250 runs)

		M	*I*	*NO*	*R*	*HS*	*100*	*Avge*	*Ct/St*
1	†Zain Abbas (*Pakistan A*)	2	4	1	268	137	1	89.33	6
2	†F. D. M. Karunaratne (*Sri Lanka*)	2	4	0	280	110	1	70.00	3
3	K. O. Maunze (*Harare Met Eagles*)	3	6	1	280	150*	1	56.00	3
4	A. G. Cremer (*Z A/Zim/Midlands Rhinos*)	6	8	1	357	144	2	51.00	5
5	C. T. Mutombodzi (*Harare Met Eagles*)	5	7	1	291	87	0	48.50	1
6	T. Maruma (*Manicaland Mountaineers*)	5	7	1	270	87	0	45.00	1
7	K. T. Kasuza (*Manicaland Mountaineers*)	7	11	1	446	104	1	44.60	5
8	†S. C. Williams (*Z A/Zim/Bul Met Tuskers*)	6	12	1	471	112	2	42.81	7
9	P. J. Moor (*Zim A/Zim/Midlands Rhinos*)	7	13	1	508	157	1	42.33	18/1
10	C. Kunje (*Bulawayo Metropolitan Tuskers*)	7	11	1	415	100	1	41.50	4
11	R. Mutumbami (*Zim A/Bul Met Tuskers*)	8	12	2	367	97	0	36.70	15
12	†P. S. Masvaure (*Zim A/Midlands Rhinos*)	8	15	3	427	123*	1	35.58	2
13	T. M. K. Mawoyo (*Z A/Zim/Mountaineers*)	6	12	0	371	122	1	30.91	5
14	M. N. Waller (*Zim A/ZimMidlands Rhinos*)	7	12	0	370	112	1	30.83	8
15	F. Mutizwa (*Manicaland Mountaineers*)	7	11	2	275	79	0	30.55	13
16	B. B. Chari (*Zim A/Zim/Bul Met Tuskers*)	9	15	1	420	118	1	30.00	3
17	H. Masakadza (*Zim A/Zim/Mountaineers*)	6	12	0	346	95	0	28.83	7
18	D. T. Tiripano (*Zim A/Zim/Mountaineers*)	7	10	1	257	70	0	28.55	5
19	T. P. Maruma (*Midlands Rhinos*)	5	9	0	251	86	0	27.88	1
20	†B. M. Chapungu (*Midlands Rhinos*)	8	15	1	319	63	0	22.78	4

BOWLING (10 wickets, average 35.00)

		Style	*O*	*M*	*R*	*W*	*BB*	*5I*	*Avge*
1	N. R. Waller (*Harare Met Eagles*)	RFM	44	7	131	13	5-21	2	10.07
2	T. P. Kamungozi (*Mountaineers*)	LB	64	25	125	12	6-43	1	10.41
3	T. M. Mboyi (*Bulawayo Met Tuskers*)	RM	59.2	13	144	10	5-36	1	14.40
4	H. M. R. K. B. Herath (*Sri Lanka*)	SLA	116	28	287	19	8-63	2	15.10
5	M. T. Chinouya (*Zim A/Mid Rhinos*)	RFM	135.4	37	359	20	5-25	1	17.95
6	T. Muzarabani (*Harare Met Eagles*)	RFM	83.3	21	217	12	4-31	0	18.08
7	S. W. Masakadza (*Mountaineers*)	RFM	169.4	42	424	23	5-52	1	18.43
8	A. Ndlovu (*Bulawayo Met Tuskers*)	SLA	105	30	301	14	6-47	1	21.50
9	N. M'shangwe (*Mountaineers*)	LB	147.1	19	518	24	8-91	1	21.58
10	A. G. Cremer (*Zim A/Zim/Mid Rhinos*)	LB	232	34	729	33	4-16	0	22.09
11	B. V. Vitori (*Zim A/Bul Met Tuskers*)	LFM	85.1	9	361	16	4-66	0	22.56
12	W. T. Mashinge (*Mountaineers*)	RFM	76.2	16	251	11	5-23	1	22.81
13	Jalat Khan (*Harare Met Eagles*)	SLA	135.2	49	372	16	4-64	0	23.25
14	L. M. Jongwe (*Bulawayo Met Tuskers*)	RFM	136.1	24	466	20	5-44	1	23.30
15	Shadab Khan (*Pakistan A*)	LB	90.2	10	328	14	5-82	1	23.42
16	Mohammad Asghar (*Pakistan A*)	SLA	129.4	28	385	13	4-81	0	29.61
17	C. T. Mumba (*Zim A/Zim/Mid Rhinos*)	RFM	248.5	58	801	26	4-50	0	30.80
18	S. D. Chimhamhiwa (*Bul Met Tuskers*)	RFM	92.4	16	316	10	3-39	0	31.60

LOGAN CUP IN 2016-17

	P	*W*	*L*	*D*	*A*	*1st-inns*	*Pts*
Manicaland Mountaineers	9	4	0	3	2	5	39
Midlands Rhinos	9	3	3	2	1	3	22†
Harare Metropolitan Eagles	9	1	2	4	2	2	20
Bulawayo Metropolitan Tuskers	9	1	3	3	1	3	12†

† *5pts deducted for failing to take the field on the final day of their opening match.*

Win = 6pts; draw = 2pts; lead on first innings = 1pt; abandoned = 2pts.

At Bulawayo (Queens), December 18–20, 2016. **Midlands Rhinos won by a concession. Midlands Rhinos 323** (A. G. Cremer 144) **and 64-4 dec; ‡Bulawayo Metropolitan Tuskers 112 and 68-1.** *Midlands Rhinos 2pts, Bulawayo Metropolitan Tuskers –5pts. Rhinos were 49-5 on the opening day, but were rescued by a century from Graeme Cremer, who went on to take 4-16, rolling over Tuskers for 112. On the third day, the provincial players refused to take the field because of a pay row, and agreed that Rhinos should be awarded victory. Both teams later had five points deducted.*

At Mutare, December 18–21, 2016. **Manicaland Mountaineers v Harare Metropolitan Eagles. Abandoned.** *Manicaland Mountaineers 2pts, Harare Metropolitan Eagles 2pts. Rain prevented any play in this match, or the next two.*

At Harare (Sports Club), January 17–20, 2017. **Harare Metropolitan Eagles v Midlands Rhinos. Abandoned.** *Harare Metropolitan Eagles 2pts, Midlands Rhinos 2pts.*

At Mutare, January 17–20, 2017. **Manicaland Mountaineers v Bulawayo Metropolitan Tuskers. Abandoned.** *Manicaland Mountaineers 2pts, Bulawayo Metropolitan Tuskers 2pts.*

At Bulawayo (Queens), February 21–24, 2017. **Drawn. Bulawayo Metropolitan Tuskers 148** (W. T. Mashinge 5-23); **‡Manicaland Mountaineers 13-1.** *Bulawayo Metropolitan Tuskers 2pts, Manicaland Mountaineers 2pts. Rain permitted only 62.2 overs across the first two days and none after that. William Mashinge's 5-23 doubled his previous first-class haul.*

At Kwekwe, February 21–24, 2017. **Drawn. ‡Midlands Rhinos 224 and 51-3; Harare Metropolitan Eagles 272** (M. T. Chinouya 5-25). *Midlands Rhinos 2pts, Harare Metropolitan Eagles 3pts. The last two days were washed out. Mike Chinouya took a career-best 5-25, only to be dropped.*

At Harare (Country Club), March 4–7, 2017. **Drawn. ‡Harare Metropolitan Eagles 299-8 v Bulawayo Metropolitan Tuskers.** *Harare Metropolitan Eagles 2pts, Bulawayo Metropolitan Tuskers 2pts. The only cricket was on the second day, when Tuskers wicketkeeper Richmond Mutumbani held five catches. The umpires called the game off on a damp fourth day, although both teams were keen to play.*

At Kwekwe, March 4–7, 2017. **Drawn. Manicaland Mountaineers 370** (T. S. Chisoro 6-145) **and 238-5 dec; ‡Midlands Rhinos 302 and 1-0.** *Midlands Rhinos 2pts, Manicaland Mountaineers 3pts. Kevin Kasuza (97) and Hamilton Masakadza (95) put on 176 for Mountaineers' second wicket, in the first innings, when Tendai Chisoro claimed an expensive career-best.*

At Harare (Sports Club), March 22–25, 2017. **Harare Metropolitan Eagles won by an innings and 85 runs. ‡Harare Metropolitan Eagles 379; Bulawayo Metropolitan Tuskers 103** (N. R. Waller 5-29) **and 191.** *Harare Metropolitan Eagles 7pts. Taurai Muzarabani (4-31) and Nathan Waller shattered the fragile Tuskers batting, and Eagles' innings win would have been even bigger but for last man Chris Mpofu, who scored 41 off 36 balls in the follow-on.*

At Kwekwe, March 22–24, 2017. **Manicaland Mountaineers won by seven wickets. ‡Midlands Rhinos 123 and 268** (M. N. Waller 112); **Manicaland Mountaineers 317 and 78-3.** *Manicaland Mountaineers 7pts. A second-wicket stand of 148 between Kasuza (61) and Hamilton Masakadza (94) outscored Rhinos' entire first innings; Shingi Masakadza and Victor Nyauchi then reduced Rhinos to 1-3, before Remembrance Nyathi (57) and Malcolm Waller added 179. But Mountaineers needed only 75 to win; Timycen Maruma hit 51* in 23 balls.*

At Bulawayo (Queens), April 4–7, 2017. **Manicaland Mountaineers won by 82 runs. ‡Manicaland Mountaineers 206** (A. Ndlovu 6-47) **and 264; Bulawayo Metropolitan Tuskers 228** (C. Kunje 100) **and 160.** *Manicaland Mountaineers 6pts, Metropolitan Tuskers 1pt. Charles Kunje's century gave Tuskers first-innings lead – the only time in the season Mountaineers conceded a deficit. At 55-5 in their second innings, Mountaineers were still only 33 ahead, but Foster Mutizwa (79) and Donald Tiripano (70) put on 130, enabling them to set a target of 243.*

At Kwekwe, April 4–5, 2017. **Midlands Rhinos won by nine wickets. ‡Harare Metropolitan Eagles 92 and 111; Midlands Rhinos 195** (N. R. Waller 5-21) **and 9-1.** *Midlands Rhinos 7pts. Hopeless batting resulted in a two-day finish. Bothwell Chapungu's 63 for Rhinos was the only innings over 34, but a lead of 103 was quite enough.*

At Bulawayo (Queens), April 19–22, 2017. **Drawn. ‡Harare Metropolitan Eagles 187** (L. M. Jongwe 5-44) **and 532-4 dec** (C. J. Chibhabha 127, R. P. Burl 151); **Bulawayo Metropolitan Tuskers 282** (S. C. Williams 106) **and 153-3.** *Bulawayo Metropolitan Tuskers 3pts, Harare Metropolitan Eagles 2pts. Luke Jongwe reduced Eagles' first innings to 29-5, but their second was the biggest of this tournament – no other team managed even 400 – and included the largest stand,*

186 by openers Regis Chakabva (99) and Chamu Chibhabha; Ryan Burl's maiden century was the highest individual score. But Eagles made no attempt to declare and force a victory until the last afternoon, when Tuskers gratefully accepted the draw.

At Mutare, April 19–21, 2017. **Manicaland Mountaineers won by nine wickets. ‡Midlands Rhinos 131** (S. W. Masakadza 5-52) **and 283** (N. M'shangwe 8-91); **Manicaland Mountaineers 327 and 92-1.** *Manicaland Mountaineers 7pts. Shingi Masakadza reduced Rhinos to 7-3, and followed up with 61* in 51 balls to establish a lead of 196. Natsai M'shangwe worked through Rhinos' second innings for 8-91, and 11-100 in all – both returns the best of this tournament. Vusi Sibanda steered Mountaineers to a third successive win with 52* in 36 balls in fading light.*

At Bulawayo (Queens), May 6–9, 2017. **Midlands Rhinos won by 220 runs. Midlands Rhinos 282** (C. B. Mpofu 5-81) **and 338-4 dec** (P. S. Masvaure 123*); **‡Bulawayo Metropolitan Tuskers 204 and 196.** *Midlands Rhinos 7pts. Prince Masvaure and Malcolm Waller (72) added 151 for Rhinos' fourth wicket; Cremer took four in each innings to complete a big win.*

At Harare (Old Hararians), May 6–9, 2017. **Drawn. ‡Harare Metropolitan Eagles 231 and 312-8 dec** (K. O. Maunze 150*); **Manicaland Mountaineers 281 and 168-3.** *Harare Metropolitan Eagles 2pts, Manicaland Mountaineers 3pts. Mountaineers recovered from 69-5 in their first innings, with No. 10 M'shangwe hitting 66* off 55 balls. Kudzai Maunze batted almost six hours for 150*, a maiden century, to save Eagles from defeat, but the draw gave Mountaineers the Logan Cup.*

At Harare (Takashinga), May 17–20, 2017. **Manicaland Mountaineers won by 153 runs. Manicaland Mountaineers 319** (T. M. K. Mawoyo 122) **and 258** (K. T. Kasuza 104); **‡Harare Metropolitan Eagles 211 and 213** (T. P. Kamungozi 6-43). *Manicaland Mountaineers 7pts. This match was moved from Mutare to Takashinga, a new Logan Cup venue, though it had staged two first-class tour games in 2003-04. Tino Mawoyo scored his first century for four and a half years, despite not being fully fit; in the second innings his fellow opener Kasuza made his first in five and a half, to help set a target of 367. Eagles fell well short, despite Cephas Zhuwao's seven sixes in a 52-ball 62. Tafadzwa Kamungozi outshone fellow leg-spinner M'shangwe with 10-73.*

At Kwekwe, May 17–20, 2017. **Bulawayo Metropolitan Tuskers won by 103 runs. Bulawayo Metropolitan Tuskers 256 and 189; ‡Midlands Rhinos 207 and 135** (T. M. Mboyi 5-36). *Bulawayo Metropolitan Tuskers 7pts. Tuskers completed their only win of the season, thanks to a pair of determined fifties from captain Mutumbami and Thabo Mboyi's career-best 5-36.*

LOGAN CUP WINNERS

1993-94	Mashonaland U24	2001-02	Mashonaland	2009-10	Mashonaland Eagles
1994-95	Mashonaland	2002-03	Mashonaland	2010-11	Matabeleland Tuskers
1995-96	Mashonaland	2003-04	Mashonaland	2011-12	Matabeleland Tuskers
1996-97	Mashonaland	2004-05	Mashonaland	2012-13	Matabeleland Tuskers
1997-98	Mashonaland	2005-06	*No competition*	2013-14	Mountaineers
1998-99	Mashonaland	2006-07	Easterns	2014-15	Matabeleland Tuskers
1999-2000	Mashonaland	2007-08	Northerns	2015-16	Mashonaland Eagles
2000-01	Mashonaland	2008-09	Easterns	2016-17	Manicaland Mountaineers

Mashonaland/Northerns/Mashonaland Eagles have won the title 12 times, Matabeleland/Matabeleland Tuskers 6, Easterns/Mountaineers 4, Mashonaland Under-24 1.

PRO50 CHAMPIONSHIP IN 2016-17

50-over league

	Played	*Won*	*Lost*	*No result*	*Bonus points*	*Points*	*NRR*
Bulawayo Metropolitan Tuskers.	6	5	1	0	3	23	1.01
Midlands Rhinos.	6	3	2	1	2	16	0.79
Manicaland Mountaineers.	6	2	4	0	0	8	–0.60
Harare Metropolitan Eagles	6	1	4	1	0	6	–1.41

The Twenty20 competition was postponed until 2017-18.

INTERNATIONAL RESULTS IN 2017

TEST MATCHES

	Tests	*Won*	*Lost*	*Drawn*	*% won*	*% lost*	*% drawn*
India	11	7	1	3	**63.63**	9.09	27.27
South Africa	12	7	3	2	**58.33**	25.00	16.66
New Zealand	7	4	1	2	**57.14**	14.28	28.57
Australia	11	6	3	2	**54.54**	27.27	18.18
England	11	5	5	1	**45.45**	45.45	9.09
Pakistan	6	2	4	0	**33.33**	66.66	0.00
Sri Lanka	13	4	7	2	**30.76**	53.84	15.38
West Indies	10	3	6	1	**30.00**	60.00	10.00
Bangladesh	9	2	7	0	**22.22**	77.77	0.00
Zimbabwe	4	0	3	1	**0.00**	75.00	25.00
Totals	47	40	40	7	**85.10**	85.10	14.89

ONE-DAY INTERNATIONALS

	ODIs	*Won*	*Lost*	*NR*	*% won*	*% lost*
England	20	15	4	1	**78.94**	21.05
India	29	21	7	1	**75.00**	25.00
South Africa	19	13	6	0	**68.42**	31.57
Pakistan	18	12	6	0	**66.66**	33.33
New Zealand	20	11	8	1	**57.89**	42.10
Afghanistan	16	8	7	1	**53.33**	46.66
Zimbabwe	10	5	5	0	**50.00**	50.00
Australia	15	5	8	2	**38.46**	61.53
Bangladesh	14	4	7	3	**36.36**	63.63
Ireland	14	4	9	1	**30.76**	69.23
Sri Lanka	29	5	23	1	**17.85**	82.14
West Indies	22	3	16	3	**15.78**	84.21
Totals	113	106	106	7		

Matches between Full Members only. The % won and lost excludes no-results.

The following teams also played official one-day internationals in 2017, some against Full Members (not included above): Hong Kong (P4 W3 L1); United Arab Emirates (P7 W4 L3); Scotland (P8 W4 L4); Papua New Guinea (P9 W2 L7).

TWENTY20 INTERNATIONALS

	T20Is	*Won*	*Lost*	*% won*	*% lost*
Pakistan	10	8	2	**80.00**	20.00
India	13	9	4	**69.23**	30.76
Afghanistan	8	5	3	**62.50**	37.50
New Zealand	8	5	3	**62.50**	37.50
West Indies	10	6	4	**60.00**	40.00
South Africa	9	5	4	**55.55**	44.44
England	7	3	4	**42.85**	57.14
Australia	5	2	3	**40.00**	60.00
Sri Lanka	15	5	10	**33.33**	66.66
World XI	3	1	2	**33.33**	66.66
Bangladesh	7	1	6	**14.28**	85.71
Ireland	5	0	5	**0.00**	100.00
Totals	50	50	50		

Matches between Full Members only. Zimbabwe did not play any T20 internationals in 2017. The following teams also played official T20 internationals in 2017, some against Full Members (not included above): Scotland (P4 W3 L1); United Arab Emirates (P5 W3 L2); Hong Kong (P3 W1 L2); Netherlands (P3 W1 L2); World XI (P3 W1 L2); Oman (P4 W1 L3); Papua New Guinea (P3 L3).

MRF TYRES ICC TEAM RANKINGS

TEST CHAMPIONSHIP (as at January 27, 2018)

		Matches	*Points*	*Rating*
1	India	44	5,313	121
2	South Africa	39	4,484	115
3	Australia	40	4,174	104
4	New Zealand	35	3,489	100
5	England	49	4,829	99
6	Sri Lanka	43	4,058	94
7	Pakistan	34	2,988	88
8	West Indies	36	2,606	72
9	Bangladesh	23	1,651	72
10	Zimbabwe	14	12	1

ONE-DAY CHAMPIONSHIP (as at December 31, 2017)

		Matches	*Points*	*Rating*
1	South Africa	53	6,387	121
2	India	56	6,680	119
3	Australia	52	5,948	114
4	England	54	6,156	114
5	New Zealand	52	5,812	112
6	Pakistan	46	4,562	99
7	Bangladesh	34	3,114	92
8	Sri Lanka	67	5,630	84
9	West Indies	43	3,260	76
10	Zimbabwe	41	2,129	52
11	Afghanistan	33	1,691	51
12	Ireland	28	1,240	44

TWENTY20 CHAMPIONSHIP (as at January 3, 2018)

		Matches	*Points*	*Rating*
1	New Zealand	18	2,262	126
2	Pakistan	23	2,843	124
3	India	28	3,385	121
4	England	17	2,029	119
5	West Indies	22	2,538	115
6	South Africa	20	2,238	112
7	Australia	15	1,665	111
8	Sri Lanka	27	2,385	88
9	Afghanistan	25	2,157	86
10	Bangladesh	17	1,289	76
11	Scotland	11	737	67
12	Zimbabwe	13	842	65
13	United Arab Emirates	16	827	52
14	Netherlands	9	441	49
15	Hong Kong	13	599	46
16	Papua New Guinea	6	235	39
17	Oman	9	345	38
18	Ireland	15	534	36

The ratings are based on all Test series, one-day and T20 internationals completed since May 1, 2014.

MRF TYRES ICC PLAYER RANKINGS

Introduced in 1987, the rankings have been backed by various sponsors, but were taken over by the ICC in January 2005. They rank cricketers on a scale up to 1,000 on their performances in Tests. The rankings take into account playing conditions, the quality of the opposition and the result of the matches. In August 1998, a similar set of rankings for one-day internationals was launched, and Twenty20 rankings were added in October 2011.

The leading players in the Test rankings on January 27, 2018, were:

	Batsmen	*Points*		*Bowlers*	*Points*
1	S. P. D. Smith (A)	947	1	J. M. Anderson (E)	887
2	V. Kohli (I)	912	2	K. Rabada (SA)	875
3	J. E. Root (E)	881	3	R. A. Jadeja (I)	844
4	K. S. Williamson (NZ)	855	4	J. R. Hazlewood (A)	814
5	D. A. Warner (A)	827	5	R. Ashwin (I)	803
6	C. A. Pujara (I)	810	6	H. M. R. K. B. Herath (SL)	799
7	H. M. Amla (SA)	771	7	V. D. Philander (SA)	791
8	Azhar Ali (P)	755	8	N. Wagner (NZ)	784
9	L. D. Chandimal (SL)	743	9	M. Morkel (SA)	773
10	A. N. Cook (E)	742	10	M. A. Starc (A)	769
				N. M. Lyon (A)	769

The leading players in the one-day international rankings on December 31, 2017, were:

	Batsmen	*Points*		*Bowlers*	*Points*
1	V. Kohli (I)	876	1	Hasan Ali (P)	759
2	A. B. de Villiers (SA)	872	2	Imran Tahir (SA)	743
3	D. A. Warner (A)	865	3	J. J. Bumrah (I)	729
4	Babar Azam (P)	846	4	T. A. Boult (NZ)	723
5	R. G. Sharma (I)	816	5	J. R. Hazlewood (A)	714
6	Q. de Kock (SA)	808	6	K. Rabada (SA)	708
7	J. E. Root (E)	802	7	M. A. Starc (A)	684
8	F. du Plessis (SA)	773	8	Rashid Khan (Afg)	649
9	H. M. Amla (SA)	766	9	L. E. Plunkett (E)	646
10	K. S. Williamson (NZ)	750	10	M. J. Santner (NZ)	644

The leading players in the Twenty20 international rankings on January 3, 2018, were:

	Batsmen	*Points*		*Bowlers*	*Points*
1	C. Munro (NZ)	793	1	I. S. Sodhi (NZ)	726
2	A. J. Finch (A)	784	2	Imad Wasim (P)	719
3	V. Kohli (I)	776	3	Rashid Khan (Afg)	717
4	E. Lewis (WI)	734	4	J. J. Bumrah (I)	702
5	K. L. Rahul (I)	726	5	M. J. Santner (NZ)	695
6	G. J. Maxwell (A)	700	6	S. Badree (WI)	691
7	K. S. Williamson (NZ)	695	7	Imran Tahir (SA)	691
8	A. D. Hales (E)	690	8	Mustafizur Rahman (B)	667
9	J. E. Root (E)	683	9	J. P. Faulkner (A)	661
	H. M. Amla (SA)	683		Shakib Al Hasan (B)	661

TEST AVERAGES IN CALENDAR YEAR 2017

BATTING (400 runs)

		T	I	NO	R	HS	100	50	Avge	SR	Ct/St
1	L. R. P. L. Taylor (NZ)	5	7	2	408	107*	1	3	81.60	63.15	3
2	S. P. D. Smith (A)	11	20	3	1,305	239	6	3	76.76	50.71	21
3	V. Kohli (I)	10	16	2	1,059	243	5	1	75.64	76.24	10
4	†S. Dhawan (I)	5	8	0	550	190	2	2	68.75	92.43	6
5	C. A. Pujara (I)	11	18	1	1,140	202	4	5	67.05	45.89	9
6	K. S. Williamson (NZ)	7	10	1	566	176	3	2	62.88	65.89	7
7	Mushfiqur Rahim (B)	8	16	2	766	159	2	3	54.71	47.81	12/2
8	F. du Plessis (SA)	10	17	4	706	135*	1	6	54.30	55.81	16
9	†D. Elgar (SA)	12	21	0	1,128	199	5	4	53.71	50.85	8
10	M. Vijay (I)	6	10	0	520	155	3	1	52.00	53.60	7
11	J. E. Root (E)	11	19	0	966	190	2	8	50.84	61.80	11
12	†D. A. Warner (A)	11	21	1	997	123	4	4	49.85	63.66	12
13	K. L. Rahul (I)	9	14	1	633	90	0	9	48.69	58.88	7
14	†Shakib Al Hasan (B)	7	14	0	665	217	2	3	47.50	69.56	0
15	H. M. Amla (SA)	12	21	1	947	137	3	4	47.35	54.30	12
16	†A. N. Cook (E)	11	20	1	899	244*	2	2	47.31	49.09	15
17	†T. W. M. Latham (NZ)	7	11	1	457	177	1	2	45.70	52.22	6
18	L. D. Chandimal (SL)	12	24	2	1,003	164	3	5	45.59	44.87	14
19	S. D. Hope (WI)	10	19	2	773	147	2	3	45.47	42.89	12
20	†B. A. Stokes (E)	7	12	0	527	112	2	4	43.91	63.57	16
21	R. L. Chase (WI)	10	19	2	740	131	2	4	43.52	49.30	6
22	†J. A. Raval (NZ)	7	11	0	475	88	0	4	43.18	44.30	6
23	W. P. Saha (I)	11	14	4	423	117	2	1	42.30	47.26	34/3
24	Azhar Ali (P)	6	12	0	504	127	2	3	42.00	38.94	5
25	P. S. P. Handscomb (A)	9	17	3	556	110	1	2	39.71	49.77	15
26	†F. D. M. Karunaratne (SL)	13	26	0	1,031	196	3	4	39.65	44.74	14
27	†D. P. D. N. Dickwella (SL)	11	22	2	773	83	0	6	38.65	74.97	21/9
28	†M. T. Renshaw (A)	7	13	0	492	184	1	2	37.84	46.41	3
29	K. C. Brathwaite (WI)	10	19	0	706	134	1	4	37.15	40.71	5
30	†Q. de Kock (SA)	12	19	2	619	101	1	4	36.41	73.25	45/5
31	A. M. Rahane (I)	11	18	2	554	132	1	3	34.62	51.10	20
32	J. M. Bairstow (E)	11	19	0	652	119	1	3	34.31	59.65	35/2
33	†S. E. Marsh (A)	8	14	1	440	126*	1	4	33.84	36.85	3
34	†D. J. Malan (E)	9	15	0	505	140	1	4	33.66	42.83	4
35	†Tamim Iqbal (B)	8	16	0	537	82	0	5	33.56	52.69	1
36	B. K. G. Mendis (SL)	10	20	0	669	194	2	1	33.45	57.62	13
37	†Soumya Sarkar (B)	7	14	0	451	86	0	4	32.21	57.23	12
38	T. Bavuma (SA)	12	20	1	609	89	0	5	32.05	47.13	8
39	J. O. Holder (WI)	9	16	2	417	110	1	2	29.78	52.05	2
40	A. D. Mathews (SL)	9	18	0	524	111	1	2	29.11	46.57	8
41	†K. O. A. Powell (WI)	10	19	0	548	90	0	2	28.84	46.28	9
42	†W. U. Tharanga (SL)	8	16	1	430	115	1	2	28.66	60.05	7
43	M. D. K. Perera (SL)	11	21	3	514	92*	0	4	28.55	51.29	8
44	†M. M. Ali (E)	11	19	1	497	87	0	3	27.61	61.28	7

BOWLING (10 wickets)

		Style	O	M	R	W	BB	5I	Avge	SR
1	J. M. Anderson (E)	RFM	426	128	967	55	7-42	4	17.58	46.47
2	T. S. Roland-Jones (E)	RFM	89.2	23	334	17	5-57	1	19.64	31.52
3	K. Rabada (SA)	RF	360	78	1,156	57	6-55	3	20.28	37.89
4	Bhuvneshwar Kumar (I)	RFM	86.3	27	231	11	4-8	0	21.00	47.18
5	Mohammad Abbas (P)	RFM	201.5	47	491	23	5-46	1	21.34	52.65

		Style	*O*	*M*	*R*	*W*	*BB*	*5I*	*Avge*	*SR*
6	M. Morkel (SA)	RF	287.3	64	898	39	5-21	1	23.02	44.23
7	R. A. Jadeja (I)	SLA	508.3	130	1,245	54	6-63	3	23.05	56.50
8	D. Olivier (SA)	RFM	101	19	393	17	3-38	0	23.11	35.64
9	K. A. Maharaj (SA)	SLA	370.5	76	1,124	48	6-40	3	23.41	46.35
10	Mohammed Shami (I)	RFM	137.5	34	446	19	4-100	0	23.47	43.52
11	N. M. Lyon (A)	OB	548.2	106	1,484	63	8-50	5	23.55	52.22
12	V. D. Philander (SA)	RFM	234	64	606	25	4-27	0	24.24	56.16
13	T. A. Boult (NZ)	LFM	212.2	50	669	27	4-64	0	24.77	47.18
14	J. R. Hazlewood (A)	RFM	334.4	90	864	34	6-67	2	25.41	59.05
15	N. Wagner (NZ)	LFM	274	47	917	36	7-39	1	25.47	45.66
16	K. A. J. Roach (WI)	RFM	212.2	63	637	25	5-72	1	25.48	50.96
17	M. A. Starc (A)	LF	210.3	41	685	26	5-88	1	26.34	48.57
18	S. N. J. O'Keefe (A)	SLA	261.3	49	673	25	6-35	2	26.92	62.76
19	H. M. R. K. B. Herath (SL)	SLA	465.1	77	1,432	52	6-43	5	27.53	53.67
20	R. Ashwin (I)	OB	554	119	1,545	56	6-41	2	27.58	59.35
21	Wahab Riaz (P)	LF	99	16	315	11	4-41	0	28.63	54.00
22	S. T. Gabriel (WI)	RF	313.3	60	977	34	5-11	1	28.73	55.32
23	Yasir Shah (P)	LB	394.1	69	1,242	43	7-94	5	28.88	55.00
24	U. T. Yadav (I)	RF	273.1	46	907	31	4-32	0	29.25	52.87
25	P. J. Cummins (A)	RF	295.4	66	864	29	4-106	0	29.79	61.17
26	T. G. Southee (NZ)	RFM	159.2	40	554	18	5-94	1	30.77	53.11
27	B. A. Stokes (E)	RFM	156.3	34	501	16	6-22	1	31.31	58.68
28	M. M. Ali (E)	OB	313.2	53	1,044	33	6-53	2	31.63	56.96
29	S. C. Williams (Z)	SLA	114.5	17	319	10	3-20	0	31.90	68.90
30	D. Bishoo (WI)	LB	271.2	42	825	25	5-79	1	33.00	65.12
31	Shakib Al Hasan (B)	SLA	304	45	968	29	5-68	2	33.37	62.89
32	Mohammad Amir (P)	LF	211.3	64	474	14	6-44	1	33.85	90.64
33	A. G. Cremer (Z)	LB	215.2	26	680	20	5-125	1	34.00	64.60
34	J. O. Holder (WI)	RFM	310	82	771	22	4-54	0	35.04	84.54
35	S. C. J. Broad (E)	RFM	392.1	112	1,082	30	4-51	0	36.06	78.43
36	Mustafizur Rahman (B)	LFM	175.5	31	582	16	4-84	0	36.37	65.93
37	C. de Grandhomme (NZ)	RFM	152	36	412	11	3-52	0	37.45	82.90
38	I. Sharma (I)	RFM	179.3	35	528	14	3-37	0	37.71	76.92
39	A. S. Joseph (WI)	RFM	129	30	393	10	3-53	0	39.30	77.40
40	C. B. R. L. S. Kumara (SL)	RFM	179	14	805	19	6-122	1	42.36	56.52
41	A. N. P. R. Fernando (SL)	RFM	161.5	24	551	13	6-132	1	42.38	74.69
42	R. A. S. Lakmal (SL)	RFM	319.2	59	995	23	4-26	0	43.26	83.30
43	P. A. D. L. R. Sandakan (SL)	SLW	185.2	20	723	16	5-132	1	45.18	69.50
44	R. L. Chase (WI)	OB	248.2	29	912	20	4-103	0	45.60	74.50
45	P. L. S. Gamage (SL)	RFM	144.2	30	463	10	2-38	0	46.30	86.60
46	M. D. K. Perera (SL)	OB	450.1	40	1,616	34	5-98	1	47.52	79.44
47	C. R. Woakes (E)	RFM	200.2	38	617	12	4-36	0	51.41	100.16
48	Mehedi Hasan (B)	OB	359.4	32	1,298	24	4-113	0	54.08	89.91
49	Taijul Islam (B)	SLA	160.5	14	604	11	3-60	0	54.90	87.72

MOST DISMISSALS BY A WICKETKEEPER

Dis		*T*	
50	(45ct, 5st)	12	Q. de Kock (SA)
37	(35ct, 2st)	11	J. M. Bairstow (E)
37	(34ct, 3st)	11	W. P. Saha (I)
34	(32ct, 2st)	10	S. O. Dowrich (WI)
30	(21ct, 9st)	11	D. P. D. N. Dickwella (SL)
24	(17ct, 7st)	7	M. S. Wade (A)

MOST CATCHES IN THE FIELD

Ct	*T*	
21	11	S. P. D. Smith (A)
20	11	A. M. Rahane (I)
16	7	B. A. Stokes (E)
16	10	F. du Plessis (SA)
15	9	P. S. P. Handscomb (A)
15	11	A. N. Cook (E)

ONE-DAY INTERNATIONAL AVERAGES IN CALENDAR YEAR 2017

BATTING (500 runs)

		M	I	NO	R	HS	100	50	Avge	SR	4	6
1	J. M. Bairstow (E)	10	10	5	534	141*	2	3	106.80	100.18	57	5
2	V. Kohli (I)	26	26	7	1,460	131	6	7	76.84	99.11	136	22
3	R. G. Sharma (I)	21	21	3	1,293	208*	6	5	71.83	99.46	116	46
4	J. E. Root (E)	19	18	4	983	133*	2	7	70.21	92.12	82	7
5	Babar Azam (P)	18	17	4	872	125*	4	2	67.07	79.27	62	6
6	†Tamim Iqbal (B)	12	11	1	646	128	2	4	64.60	83.14	67	9
7	A. D. Mathews (SL)	15	14	5	573	111*	1	3	63.66	76.91	56	8
8	†B. A. Stokes (E)	15	13	3	616	102*	2	4	61.60	106.94	44	24
9	M. S. Dhoni (I)	29	22	9	788	134	1	6	60.61	84.73	60	19
10	L. R. P. L. Taylor (NZ)	20	20	4	968	107	2	7	60.50	81.89	91	1
11	F. du Plessis (SA)	19	18	3	905	185	2	6	60.33	92.34	78	8
12	A. B. de Villiers (SA)	19	18	5	773	176	1	5	59.46	116.94	67	15
13	†D. A. Warner (A)	13	13	1	691	179	3	1	57.58	102.82	67	13
14	Shoaib Malik (P)	17	15	6	516	101*	1	3	57.33	93.98	39	15
15	†Q. de Kock (SA)	19	19	1	956	168*	2	7	53.11	94.84	106	8
16	H. M. Amla (SA)	18	18	1	862	154	3	4	50.70	88.41	84	10
17	A. M. Rahane (I)	12	12	0	586	103	1	7	48.83	77.71	63	4
18	†W. U. Tharanga (SL)	25	25	4	1,011	119	2	6	48.14	91.65	123	15
19	†S. Dhawan (I)	22	22	2	960	132*	3	6	48.00	101.37	124	14
20	†T. M. Head (A)	15	13	2	518	128	1	3	47.09	91.35	46	10
21	†E. J. G. Morgan (E)	20	18	1	781	107	3	3	45.94	98.73	66	26
22	P. R. Stirling (Ire)	16	15	0	656	101	1	5	43.73	88.76	70	18
23	†W. T. S. Porterfield (Ire)	16	15	0	644	119	2	2	42.93	81.31	70	4
24	K. S. Williamson (NZ)	14	14	0	596	100	1	5	42.57	85.26	55	6
25	K. M. Jadhav (I)	25	18	4	561	120	1	3	40.07	111.08	62	11
26	Mohammad Hafeez (P)	18	17	3	555	88	0	4	39.64	82.10	46	14
27	Rahmat Shah (Afg)	16	15	1	551	108*	1	5	39.35	70.10	36	8
28	†T. W. M. Latham (NZ)	15	15	1	546	104	2	3	39.00	84.78	51	7
29	A. D. Hales (E)	15	15	1	535	110	1	4	38.21	102.49	66	11
30	†M. D. Gunathilleke (SL)	15	15	0	539	116	1	4	35.93	83.05	55	5
31	H. H. Pandya (I)	28	19	3	557	83	0	4	34.81	120.56	35	30
32	S. D. Hope (WI)	22	19	1	600	81	0	4	33.33	67.26	43	8
33	J. J. Roy (E)	16	16	0	533	96	0	6	33.31	103.89	72	7
34	†D. P. D. N. Dickwella (SL)	26	26	1	826	116	2	4	33.04	96.04	95	6
35	†E. Lewis (WI)	20	17	1	512	176*	1	1	32.00	82.84	46	14
36	J. N. Mohammed (WI)	22	19	1	523	91*	0	4	29.05	71.93	44	10
37	B. K. G. Mendis (SL)	22	22	1	587	102	1	4	27.95	78.79	64	3

BOWLING (18 wickets)

		Style	O	M	R	W	BB	4I	Avge	SR	ER
1	Rashid Khan (Afg)	LB	118	6	449	43	7-18	4	10.44	16.46	3.80
2	Hasan Ali (P)	RFM	152.2	7	767	45	5-34	3	17.04	20.31	5.03
3	C. R. Woakes (E)	RFM	88	8	454	22	4-38	3	20.63	24.00	5.15
4	J. R. Hazlewood (A)	RFM	86.5	2	426	19	6-52	1	22.42	27.42	4.90
5	L. E. Plunkett (E)	RFM	143.5	5	809	36	5-52	4	22.47	23.97	5.62
6	M. A. Starc (A)	LF	81.4	5	417	18	4-29	2	23.16	27.22	5.10
7	T. A. Boult (NZ)	LFM	144.2	7	762	31	7-34	3	24.58	27.93	5.27
8	K. Yadav (I)	SLW	111.4	5	545	22	3-41	0	24.77	30.45	4.88
9	Imran Tahir (SA)	LB	145.2	7	672	27	4-27	1	24.88	32.29	4.62
10	Dawlat Zadran (Afg)	RFM	89.4	9	453	18	4-53	1	25.16	29.88	5.05
11	A. G. Cremer (Z)	LB	107.1	3	454	18	5-29	1	25.22	35.72	4.23
12	Mohammad Nabi (Afg)	OB	122.1	2	532	21	4-30	1	25.33	34.90	4.35

		Style	*O*	*M*	*R*	*W*	*BB*	*4I*	*Avge*	*SR*	*ER*
13	Shadab Khan (P)	LB	97	3	484	19	3-47	0	25.47	30.63	4.98
14	A. U. Rashid (E)	LB	123.2	3	672	26	5-27	2	25.84	28.46	5.44
15	J. J. Bumrah (I)	RFM	199.2	13	1,024	39	5-27	2	26.25	30.66	5.13
16	M. J. Santner (NZ)	SLA	149	2	686	26	5-50	1	26.38	34.38	4.60
17	W. D. Parnell (SA)	LFM	84.1	2	486	18	4-58	1	27.00	28.05	5.77
18	K. Rabada (SA)	RF	155.1	12	746	27	4-39	2	27.62	34.48	4.80
19	Y. S. Chahal (I)	LB	121	6	600	21	3-30	0	28.57	34.57	4.95
20	A. S. Joseph (WI)	RFM	92.1	3	582	19	5-56	2	30.63	29.10	6.31
21	Junaid Khan (P)	LFM	110.5	4	600	19	3-40	0	31.57	35.00	5.41
22	Mohammad Amir (P)	LF	108.3	4	570	18	3-16	0	31.66	36.16	5.25
23	A. Dananjaya (SL)	OB	117.1	4	595	18	6-54	2	33.05	39.05	5.07
24	Bhuvneshwar Kumar (I)	RFM	187.5	11	949	28	5-42	1	33.89	40.25	5.05
25	R. A. S. Lakmal (SL)	RFM	125	9	649	19	4-13	1	34.15	39.47	5.19
26	P. K. D. Chase (Ire)	RFM	94.2	0	653	19	3-33	0	34.36	29.78	6.92
27	H. H. Pandya (I)	RFM	197.2	3	1,101	31	3-40	0	35.51	38.19	5.57
28	J. O. Holder (WI)	RFM	168	11	891	23	5-27	1	38.73	43.82	5.30
29	A. R. Nurse (WI)	OB	164.2	2	853	21	4-62	1	40.61	46.95	5.19

MOST DISMISSALS BY A WICKETKEEPER

Dis		*M*	
39	(26ct, 13st)	29	M. S. Dhoni (I)
30	(26ct, 4st)	18	J. C. Buttler (E)
26	(23ct, 3st)	22	S. D. Hope (WI)
25	(23ct, 2st)	19	Q. de Kock (SA)
23	(21ct, 2st)	13	Sarfraz Ahmed (P)
22	(17ct, 5st)	23	D. P. D. N. Dickwella (SL)

Dickwella played three further one-day internationals when not keeping wicket but took no catches.

MOST CATCHES IN THE FIELD

Ct	*M*	
12	13	G. J. Maxwell (A)
12	18	H. M. Amla (SA)
12	18	Babar Azam (P)
12	22	B. K. G. Mendis (SL)
12	25	K. M. Jadhav (I)

TWENTY20 INTERNATIONAL AVERAGES IN CALENDAR YEAR 2017

BATTING (200 runs)

		M	*I*	*NO*	*R*	*HS*	*100*	*50*	*Avge*	*SR*	*4*	*6*
1	Mohammad Nabi (Afg)	10	8	1	209	89	0	1	29.85	**175.63**	15	15
2	R. G. Sharma (I)	9	9	0	283	118	1	1	31.44	**171.51**	30	16
3	†C. Munro (NZ)	8	8	1	277	109*	2	1	39.57	**163.90**	20	17
4	G. C. Wilson (Ire)	7	7	2	218	65*	0	2	43.60	**162.68**	20	8
5	†D. A. Miller (SA/World)	11	10	2	243	101*	1	0	30.37	**162.00**	14	15
6	†Soumya Sarkar (B)	7	7	0	235	47	0	0	33.57	**156.66**	27	8
7	†E. Lewis (WI)	9	9	1	357	125*	1	2	44.62	**154.54**	20	31
8	P. R. Stirling (Ire)	7	7	0	224	60	0	1	32.00	**154.48**	22	12
9	V. Kohli (I)	10	10	2	299	82	0	2	37.37	**152.55**	32	8
10	A. B. de Villiers (SA)	7	7	1	304	65*	0	2	50.66	**152.00**	24	12
11	H. M. Amla (SA/World)	6	6	1	269	85	0	3	53.80	**147.80**	33	5
12	Shoaib Malik (P)	10	10	4	273	51	0	1	45.50	**144.44**	21	11
13	†D. P. D. N. Dickwella (SL)	9	9	0	233	68	0	1	25.88	**141.21**	34	5
14	K. L. Rahul (I)	7	7	0	279	89	0	3	39.85	**140.90**	24	12
15	Shaiman Anwar (UAE)	5	5	1	214	117*	1	1	53.50	**139.86**	22	7
16	M. S. Dhoni (I)	13	12	6	252	56	0	1	42.00	**138.46**	19	9
17	F. Behardien (SA)	9	9	4	213	64*	0	1	42.60	**136.53**	13	8

		M	I	NO	R	HS	100	50	Avge	SR	4	6
18	D. A. S. Gunaratne (SL) . .	11	11	3	221	84*	0	2	27.62	**133.13**	19	6
19	Mohammad Shahzad (Afg)	7	7	1	299	80	0	3	49.83	**131.71**	38	10
20	Babar Azam (P)	10	10	1	352	86	0	1	39.11	**119.72**	33	4
21	Ahmed Shehzad (P)	9	9	0	304	89	0	2	33.77	**119.68**	29	5
22	K. S. Williamson (NZ) . . .	7	7	1	206	73*	0	2	34.33	**113.81**	18	4
23	M. N. Samuels (WI)	9	9	2	283	89*	0	1	40.42	**109.26**	27	12

BOWLING (10 wickets)

		Style	O	D	R	W	BB	4I	Avge	SR	ER
1	Rashid Khan (Afg)	LB	35	110	160	17	5-3	1	9.41	12.35	**4.57**
2	S. P. Narine (WI)	OB	33	89	196	10	3-11	0	19.60	19.80	**5.93**
3	S. Badree (WI/World)	LB	42	120	266	11	2-14	0	24.18	22.90	**6.33**
4	Shadab Khan (P)	LB	35.5	91	233	14	4-14	1	16.64	15.35	**6.50**
5	J. I. Mulder (Ire)	LB	25	62	167	11	4-16	1	15.18	13.63	**6.68**
6	J. J. Bumrah (I)	RFM	34.4	96	240	12	3-14	0	20.00	17.33	**6.92**
7	C. R. Brathwaite (WI)	RFM	29.3	69	212	14	3-20	0	15.14	12.64	**7.18**
8	I. S. Sodhi (NZ)	LB	22	44	161	11	3-36	0	14.63	12.00	**7.31**
9	K. O. K. Williams (WI) . . .	RFM	35.3	91	271	18	3-11	0	15.05	11.83	**7.63**
10	K. Yadav (I)	SLW	29	59	222	12	3-52	0	18.50	14.50	**7.65**
11	Hasan Ali (P)	RFM	33.3	86	257	12	3-23	0	21.41	16.75	**7.67**
12	Y. S. Chahal (I)	LB	41.3	106	325	23	6-25	3	14.13	10.82	**7.83**
13	Imran Tahir (SA/World) . . .	LB	30.5	62	243	14	5-24	1	17.35	13.21	**7.88**
14	S. L. Malinga (SL)	RFM	24	48	198	12	3-34	0	16.50	12.00	**8.25**
15	A. L. Phehlukwayo (SA) . .	RFM	27.3	58	231	10	3-19	0	23.10	16.50	**8.40**
16	T. A. Boult (NZ)	LFM	21	52	180	11	4-34	1	16.36	11.45	**8.57**
17	K. M. D. N. Kulasekara (SL) .	RFM	29	53	250	10	4-31	1	25.00	17.40	**8.62**
18	C. J. Jordan (E)	RFM	28	58	251	10	3-22	0	25.10	16.80	**8.96**
19	N. L. T. C. Perera (SL/Wld)	RFM	36.4	58	329	13	3-24	0	25.30	16.92	**8.97**

MOST DISMISSALS BY A WICKETKEEPER

Dis		M	
13	(6ct, 7st)	13	M. S. Dhoni (I)
10	(4ct, 6st)	7	Mohammad Shahzad (Afg)
10	(8ct, 2st)	10	C. A. K. Walton (WI)
9	(7ct, 2st)	7	T. D. Paine (A/World)
8	(6ct, 2st)	7	M. Mosehle (SA)
7	(4ct, 3st)	10	Sarfraz Ahmed (P)

MOST CATCHES IN THE FIELD

Ct	M	
10	7	G. H. Dockrell (Ire)
9	11	D. A. Miller (SA/World)
9	11	H. H. Pandya (I)
7	10	C. R. Brathwaite (WI)
7	10	Imad Wasim (P)

OTHER FIRST-CLASS TOURS IN 2017

AFGHANISTAN A IN ZIMBABWE IN 2016-17

The first full tour by an Afghanistan A side was a success, the team led by Shafiqullah Shinwari winning the one-day series 4–1. Shafiqullah made the most runs (156, from 104 balls), but two 21-year-olds made a mark: Younas Ahmadzai hit their only century, in the third match, while seamer Nawaz Khan took 11 wickets. Zimbabwe fielded a largely inexperienced side, captained by wicketkeeper Peter Moor.

At Harare (Sports Club), January 27, 2017. **Afghanistan A won by five wickets. Zimbabwe A 120** (26.5 overs) (Abdullah Adil 4-22, Zia-ur-Rehman 3-24); **‡Afghanistan A 121-5** (23.3 overs) (N. R. Waller 3-36). *A late start meant a reduction to 28 overs a side. Zimbabwe A's innings ended with three wickets in successive balls – a run-out, then two for seamer Abdullah Adil.*

At Harare (Sports Club), January 29, 2017. **Afghanistan A won by 55 runs** (DLS). **Afghanistan A 208** (47.3 overs) (Shafiqullah Shinwari 50; C. T. Mumba 5-54); **‡Zimbabwe A 126** (27.5 overs) (R. P. Burl 55; Fazal Niazai 3-20). *Rain stopped play early in Zimbabwe A's reply – but by then they were 9-3. That became 10-4 (and 45-7) when they resumed, chasing a revised 182 in 31 overs. Seamer Carl Mumba had earlier taken his first List A five-for.*

At Harare (Sports Club), January 31, 2017. **Afghanistan A won by 20 runs. Afghanistan A 279-4** (50 overs) (Younas Ahmadzai 104, Khaibar Omar 54*, Shafiqullah Shinwari 70*); **‡Zimbabwe A 259-9** (50 overs) (I. Kaia 100, R. P. Burl 70; Nawaz Khan 5-51). *Afghanistan were 3-2 after Tendai Chatara struck twice in four balls, but were rescued by Younas Ahmadzai, who shared stands of 92 and 99 with Waheedullah Shafaq (42) and Khaibar Omar. Shafiqullah Shinwari then blasted 70* from 23 balls, with eight sixes. It proved too much for Zimbabwe A, despite a recovery led by Innocent Kaia (who was run out after completing his hundred from 154 balls) and Ryan Burl, who put on 157. The Zimbabweans needed 23 from the last over, but Nawaz Khan conceded just two, and took three wickets as the tourists clinched the series.*

At Harare (Sports Club), February 3, 2017. **Afghanistan A won by six wickets** (DLS). **Zimbabwe A 212-8** (50 overs) (C. T. Mutombodzi 62; Nawaz Khan 5-51); **‡Afghanistan A 162-4** (36.3 overs) (Waheedullah Shafaq 51*). *Nawaz's second successive five-for restricted Zimbabwe A to 212, then the Afghans' target was revised to 162 in 40 overs.*

At Harare (Sports Club), February 5, 2017. **Zimbabwe A won by 215 runs. ‡Zimbabwe A 288-8** (50 overs) (R. P. Burl 105, M. N. Waller 68; Abdullah Adil 3-67); **Afghanistan A 73** (25.4 overs) (T. L. Chatara 3-13, R. Ngarava 3-24, B. A. Mavuta 3-20). Ryan Burl's maiden List A century set up the highest total of the series, then seamers Chatara and Richard Ngarava, and 19-year-old leg-spinner Brandon Mavuta, then ran through Afghanistan A for a thumping consolation victory; the highest score was Noor-ul-Haq's 12.

ZIMBABWE A IN NAMIBIA IN 2016-17

A strong Zimbabwe A side, captained by Sikandar Raza, won all four 50-over matches, two by large margins. The batting star was Chamu Chibhabha, who amassed 250 runs, although Peter Moor was not far behind, with 212, and Innocent Kaia scored a century the only time he batted. Craig Williams was a lone beacon for Namibia, passing 50 in all four games.

At Windhoek (Wanderers), April 30, 2017. **Zimbabwe A won by 31 runs. ‡Zimbabwe A 236-6** (50 overs) (P. J. Moor 79*, T. Maruma 58; S. F. Burger 3-28); **Namibia 205** (49.3 overs) (S. J. Baard 61, C. G. Williams 51; T. L. Chatara 3-33, N. R. Waller 3-38). *Zimbabwe A were in some trouble at 120-5 in the 35th over, before Peter Moor, who faced 67 balls and hit six sixes, and Timycen Maruma put on 115.*

At Windhoek (Wanderers), May 2, 2017. **Zimbabwe A won by 135 runs.** Reduced to 45 overs a side. **Zimbabwe A 240-6** (45 overs) (C. J. Chibhabha 76, R. W. Chakabva 58); **‡Namibia 105** (29.1 overs) (C. G. Williams 67; N. R. Waller 4-37). *Craig Williams hit five sixes in his run-a-ball 67, but the only other man to reach double figures in Namibia's disappointing chase was No. 9 Zhivago Groenewald, who made 14 before becoming seamer Nathan Waller's fourth victim.*

At Windhoek (Wanderers), May 4, 2017. **Zimbabwe A won by 112 runs. Zimbabwe A 276-6** (50 overs) (C. J. Chibhabha 110, P. J. Moor 70*); ‡**Namibia 164** (38.4 overs) (C. G. Williams 51, J. N. Frylinck 60; Sikandar Raza 4-46). *Zimbabwe A's total, which owed much to a fourth-wicket stand of 130 between Chamu Chibhabha and Moor, proved well beyond Namibia.*

At Windhoek (Wanderers), May 5, 2017. **Zimbabwe A won by 26 runs.** ‡**Zimbabwe A 280-9** (50 overs) (I. Kaia 101; J. N. Frylinck 3-55); **Namibia 254** (48.4 overs) (J. Fourie 51, C. G. Williams 86, J. N. Frylinck 55; D. T. Tiripano 4-42, W. P. Masakadza 3-43). *Williams's fourth successive half-century took Namibia close but, after Jan Frylinck fell, Donald Tiripano closed out the innings with three wickets in seven balls.*

A-TEAM TRI-SERIES IN SOUTH AFRICA IN 2017

India A, captained by Manish Pandey, came out on top in this tri-series in Pretoria, which also included teams from South Africa (led by Khaya Zondo) and Afghanistan (Shafiqullah Shinwari), who lost all four of their matches. Afghanistan were a late replacement for Australia A, whose South African tour was cancelled as a contracts dispute rumbled on at home. Pandey led the way with the bat, too, scoring 307 runs for once out, while his team-mate Shreyas Iyer settled the final with an undefeated 140. South Africa's Reeza Hendricks totalled 266, most of them during a memorable undefeated 173 against Afghanistan. The leading bowler was South Africa's slow left-armer Aaron Phangiso, with ten wickets; Indian seamer Shardul Thakur had nine.

At Pretoria (Groenkloof Oval), July 26, 2017. **South Africa A won by two wickets. India A 152** (41.5 overs) (M. K. Pandey 55; D. Pretorius 3-24, A. M. Phangiso 4-30); ‡**South Africa A 153-8** (37.4 overs) (Y. S. Chahal 3-41). *MoM:* D. Pretorius. *India A's imposing batting line-up, which boasted the recent Test triple-centurion Karun Nair, made a poor start, slipping to 89-6; only skipper Manish Pandey made more than 25. South Africa A were also rocking, at 71-5, but Farhaan Behardien (37* from 62 balls) and Dwaine Pretorius (38 from 54) saved them in a stand of 62.*

At Pretoria (L. C. de Villiers Oval), July 28, 2017. **India A won by seven wickets. Afghanistan A 149** (40.5 overs) (A. R. Patel 3-33, V. Shankar 3-24); ‡**India A 150-3** (30.4 overs) (K. K. Nair 57). *MoM:* K. K. Nair. *The varied spin of Akshar Patel (left-arm), Vijay Shankar (off-breaks) and Yuzvendra Chahal (whose leggies brought him 2-42) dismantled Afghanistan A, who lurched from 93-3 to 106-8.*

At Pretoria (L. C. de Villiers Oval), July 30, 2017. **South Africa A won by 164 runs. South Africa A 336-5** (50 overs) (R. R. Hendricks 173*, K. Zondo 62); ‡**Afghanistan A 172** (32.2 overs) (Rahmat Shah 55; D. Paterson 3-29, T. Shamsi 4-19). *MoM:* R. R. Hendricks. *Afghanistan were overwhelmed by Reeza Hendricks, who batted through the innings for 173*, from 145 balls with 14 fours and five sixes. Rahmat Shah later managed 55 before becoming one of four victims for left-arm wrist-spinner Tabraiz Shamsi.*

At Pretoria (L. C. de Villiers Oval), August 1, 2017. **India A won by 113 runs. India A 322-5** (50 overs) (R. R. Pant 60, M. K. Pandey 86*); ‡**Afghanistan A 209-9** (50 overs) (Najibullah Zadran 62; M. Siraj 3-49). *MoM:* M. K. Pandey.

At Pretoria (L. C. de Villiers Oval), August 3, 2017. **India A won by one wicket. South Africa A 266** (48.2 overs) (H. Klaasen 127, P. W. A. Mulder 66; S. N. Thakur 4-35, S. Kaul 3-41); ‡**India A 267-9** (49.4 overs) (S. V. Samson 68, M. K. Pandey 93*; C. J. Dala 3-56, T. Shamsi 3-55). *MoM:* H. Klaasen. *India A came out on top – just – in the only close match of the tournament. Pandey guided the chase with 93* from 85 balls, but the last over – bowled by the Zambian-born Junior Dala – started with one run needed and the No. 11 Mohammed Siraj on strike. After three dot balls, Siraj spirited the fourth away for the winning single. Earlier, wicketkeeper Heinrich Klaasen's 127 from 108 deliveries had rescued South Africa A from 20-3.*

At Pretoria (L. C. de Villiers Oval), August 5, 2017. **South Africa A won by seven wickets. Afghanistan A 202-9** (50 overs) (Usman Ghani 54; A. M. Phangiso 3-39); ‡**South Africa A 203-3** (36.4 overs) (R. R. Hendricks 76). *MoM:* A. M. Phangiso. *South Africa A made sure of the bonus-point victory that left them top of the qualifying table with 15 points: India A had 14, Afghanistan A none.*

Final At Pretoria (L. C. de Villiers Oval), August 8, 2017. **India A won by seven wickets. South Africa A 267-7** (50 overs) (F. Behardien 101*, D. Pretorius 58; S. N. Thakur 3-52); ‡**India A 270-3** (46.5 overs) (S. S. Iyer 140*, V. Shankar 72). *MoM:* S. S. Iyer. *Shreyas Iyer, who had not reached 50 in the previous four matches, settled the final with a superb 140*, sharing stands of 141 with Shankar and 109* with Pandey, who took his tournament average to 307. South Africa A had recovered from 115-5 thanks to Behardien, who reached his first representative hundred in the final over. He put on 101 with Pretorius, before Dane Paterson hit the last two balls of the innings, from seamer Siddharth Kaul, for six.*

INDIA A IN SOUTH AFRICA IN 2017

After winning the one-day tri-series, India A – now captained by Karun Nair – stayed on in South Africa for two four-day games, winning one and losing the other. The tourists' stand-out performer was slow left-armer Shahbaz Nadeem, who took 11 wickets. For the home side, Stephen Cook hit 120 in the first match, then 98 and 70 not out in the second, but it was the other opener – the South Africa A captain Aiden Markram – who booked a Test place, with innings of 79 and 74.

At Pretoria (L. C. de Villiers Oval), August 12–15, 2017. **South Africa A won by 235 runs.** ‡**South Africa A 346** (117.3 overs) (S. C. Cook 120, D. A. Miller 78; M. Siraj 4-61, S. Nadeem 4-117) **and 220-5 dec** (56.3 overs) (A. K. Markram 79, R. S. Second 74; N. Saini 3-20); **India A 120** (39 overs) (B. E. Hendricks 3-23, D. L. Piedt 3-32) **and 211** (52.1 overs) (C. J. Dala 5-36). *After Stephen Cook batted more than seven hours for 120, India A made a disastrous start: both openers fell first ball, and soon it was 42-5. There was no way back. Aiden Markram declared 446 in front, and his bowlers worked their way through the Indian batting again.*

At Potchefstroom, August 19–22, 2017. **India A won by six wickets.** ‡**South Africa A 322** (124.4 overs) (S. C. Cook 98, A. K. Markram 74, O. A. Ramela 51; N. Saini 3-66, S. Nadeem 4-118) **and 177** (65.2 overs) (S. C. Cook 70*; A. Rajpoot 3-15, S. Nadeem 3-47); **India A 276** (89.4 overs) (R. Samarth 77, S. S. Iyer 65; D. Paterson 3-48, D. L. Piedt 4-70) **and 226-4** (62.3 overs) (R. Samarth 55, K. K. Nair 90). *India A gained revenge, making light of a target of 224 thanks to Karun Nair.*

NEW ZEALAND A IN INDIA IN 2017-18

New Zealand A, captained by the Test left-hander Henry Nicholls, had a chastening tour of India. After innings defeats in both four-day matches, they lost three of the four completed one-dayers. The only shaft of light came with a tie in the second game, in which Glenn Phillips hit a sparkling undefeated 140.

At Mulapadu, September 23–25, 2017. **India A won by an innings and 31 runs.** ‡**New Zealand A 147** (63 overs) (K. V. Sharma 4-58, S. Nadeem 4-39) **and 142** (63.1 overs) (S. Nadeem 4-51, K. V. Sharma 4-62); **India A 320** (67.2 overs) (R. Samarth 54, S. S. Iyer 108, R. R. Pant 67; I. S. Sodhi 5-94). *New Zealand's batsmen laboured against the spin of Karn Sharma and Shahbaz Nadeem: no one managed more than wicketkeeper Tim Seifert's 35 in the first innings, although George Worker matched that in the second.*

At Mulapadu, September 30–October 3, 2017. **India A won by an innings and 26 runs.** ‡**New Zealand A 211** (69.5 overs) (C. Munro 65; S. N. Thakur 3-34, K. V. Sharma 3-49) **and 210** (79.3 overs) (H. M. Nicholls 94; S. Nadeem 4-41, K. V. Sharma 5-78); **India A 447** (110 overs) (S. S. Iyer 82, A. R. Bawne 162*, P. A. Patel 65; I. S. Sodhi 3-120). *Leg-spinner Sharma took his haul for the two first-class matches to 16, as New Zealand's batsmen struggled again, although Jeet Raval (47) and skipper Henry Nicholls did share a 41-over stand of 105 in the second innings. But their efforts were dwarfed by Ankit Bawne, who hit 21 fours and five sixes in nearly six hours, and put on 166 for the fifth wicket with Parthiv Patel.*

At Visakhapatnam, October 6, 2017. **India A v New Zealand A. Abandoned.**

At Visakhapatnam, October 10, 2017 (day/night). **Tied.** ‡**New Zealand A 269-6** (42 overs) (G. D. Phillips 140*; S. Kaul 3-65); **India A 269-9** (42 overs) (S. S. Iyer 90, A. R. Bawne 83*; S. C. Kuggeleijn 3-56, T. D. Astle 4-22). *A superb century from 20-year-old Glenn Phillips looked to have given New Zealand A enough to play with in a match reduced to 42 overs a side, especially when India A crashed to 84-5 after two wickets in three balls for leg-spinner Todd Astle. But captain Shreyas Iyer hauled his side back into it, smacking five sixes in a 73-ball 90, then Bawne took over.*

A clatter of wickets meant 11 were needed from the final over with last man Siddharth Kaul at the crease, but he had to face only one ball as Bawne levelled the scores.

At Visakhapatnam, October 11, 2017 (day/night). **India A won by six wickets. ‡New Zealand A 143** (37.1 overs) (K. V. Sharma 5-22); **India A 144-4** (24.4 overs). *New Zealand A reached 134-4 in the 30th over, but then lost six for nine as Sharma cast his web.*

At Visakhapatnam, October 13, 2017. **India A won by 64 runs. ‡India A 289-6** (50 overs) (A. R. Easwaran 83, D. Hooda 59, V. Shankar 61); **New Zealand A 225** (45.1 overs) (G. H. Worker 108; S. Kaul 3-25, S. Nadeem 4-33). *Bengal's Abhimanyu Easwaran made 83 in his first match for India A, and later Vijay Shankar clouted five sixes in 61 from 33 balls. New Zealand A never threatened, despite Worker's workmanlike century.*

At Visakhapatnam, October 15, 2017. **India A won by three wickets. ‡New Zealand A 173** (44.2 overs) (B. Thampi 3-19); **India A 174-7** (32.1 overs) (L. H. Ferguson 3-24). *India A took the series 3–0.*

IRELAND WOLVES IN BANGLADESH IN 2017-18

Andy Balbirnie captained Ireland's A team – rebranded as the Wolves – in Bangladesh in October. Bangladesh A won the four-day game, and all the completed one-day matches, but there were promising signs for Ireland in the form of Simranjit "Simi" Singh: he made a forthright maiden century in the first-class fixture, although he was less successful in the one-dayers. Bangladesh's spinners did much of the damage – slow left-armer Sanjamul Islam took nine wickets at 15 – but the leading wicket-taker was the left-arm seamer, Abu Haider, with ten.

At Sylhet, October 11–14, 2017. **Bangladesh A won by five wickets. ‡Ireland Wolves 255** (74.5 overs) (S. Singh 121, A. R. McBrine 57; Mehedi Hasan 3-47) **and 213** (60.2 overs) (J. N. K. Shannon 90; Sanjamul Islam 5-90, Mehedi Hasan 3-48); **Bangladesh A 337** (116.4 overs) (Shadman Islam 108, Nazmul Hossain 69, Nurul Hasan 54; A. R. McBrine 3-64, G. H. Dockrell 3-90) **and 132-5** (39.3 overs) (A. R. McBrine 4-63). *A maiden century from Simi Singh, who hit 19 fours and four sixes, and a late burst from No. 10 Andy McBrine took Ireland Wolves to a respectable total, but the home batsmen chiselled out a lead of 82. James Shannon was the only Wolf to exceed 26 in the second innings and, although McBrine reduced Bangladesh A to 60-4, they reached their target with little fuss.*

At Cox's Bazar, October 17, 2017. **No result. ‡Ireland Wolves 229** (49.1 overs) (S. P. Terry 65); **Bangladesh A 75-3** (14 overs). *Sean Terry rescued Ireland Wolves from 14-4, but rain ended the match shortly before DLS could be applied.*

At Cox's Bazar (No. 2), October 19, 2017. **Bangladesh A won by three wickets. ‡Ireland Wolves 195** (48.1 overs) (Sanjamul Islam 4-33, Abul Hasan 3-25); **Bangladesh A 196-7** (46.3 overs) (Tanveer Haider 61*; J. Mulder 3-42). *MoM:* Tanveer Haider. *Singh top-scored with 33 in Ireland Wolves' underwhelming total. Bangladesh A were in trouble at 114-6, but Tanveer Haider took them home with 61* from 91 balls.*

At Cox's Bazar, October 21, 2017. **Bangladesh A v Ireland Wolves. Abandoned.**

At Cox's Bazar (No. 2), October 24, 2017. **Bangladesh A won by eight wickets. ‡Ireland Wolves 103** (35.4 overs) (A. Balbirnie 52; Abu Haider 3-29); **Bangladesh A 106-2** (23 overs). *MoM:* Abu Haider. *Apart from skipper Andy Balbirnie, only Shane Getkate (23) made it into double figures as Ireland Wolves limped past 100.*

At Cox's Bazar (No. 2), October 25, 2017. **Bangladesh A won by four wickets. Ireland Wolves 170-7** (20 overs) (A. Balbirnie 83; Imran Ali 3-33); **‡Bangladesh A 172-6** (19.4 overs) (Al-Amin 67). *MoM:* A. Balbirnie. *After rain reduced this to a Twenty20 match in all but name, Balbirnie thrashed 83 in 51 balls to give his side a chance. When McBrine bowled Al-Amin for a 40-ball 67, the hosts needed nine from the last seven deliveries – and got there with two to spare.*

At Cox's Bazar, October 26, 2017. **Bangladesh A won by 76 runs. Bangladesh A 286-6** (50 overs) (Shadman Islam 68, Yasir Ali 102*); **‡Ireland Wolves 210** (43.4 overs) (J. B. Tector 66; Abu Haider 3-38). *MoM:* Yasir Ali. *Bangladesh A ran out 4–0 winners in the one-day series, with Yasir Ali's run-a-ball century underpinning a big total. Jack Tector hit ten fours in his 66, but wickets fell regularly.*

SRI LANKA A IN THE WEST INDIES IN 2017-18

Dhananjaya de Silva led a strong Sri Lanka A team to the Caribbean, where they had three four-day matches and three one-day games against West Indies A, all in Jamaica. Slow left-armer Malinda Pushpakumara, who had made his Test debut two months previously against India, took 23 wickets in the first-class fixtures, including 12 in the second, which Sri Lanka A won by an innings. Sunil Ambris, who would soon win his own first Test cap, scored two centuries for the West Indians.

At Trelawny Greenfields, Jamaica, October 11–14, 2017. **West Indies A won by an innings and 13 runs.** ‡**West Indies A 364-8 dec** (120 overs) (J. D. Campbell 56, V. A. Singh 81, S. W. Ambris 106; P. M. Pushpakumara 3-104); **Sri Lanka A 212** (56.4 overs) (D. M. de Silva 104; K. A. Joseph 3-33, R. R. S. Cornwall 3-69) **and 139** (44.2 overs) (D. S. Weerakkody 56; R. R. S. Cornwall 3-53, D. K. Jacobs 6-27). *Sunil Ambris's four-hour century lifted West Indies A to 364 before Sharmarh Brooks declared at the end of a rain-shortened second day. The third was also weather-affected, but Sri Lanka A surrendered 13 wickets on the fourth, with Rakheem Cornwall (off-spin) and Damion Jacobs (leg-breaks) sharing 14 in the match.*

At Trelawny Greenfields, Jamaica, October 19–21, 2017. **Sri Lanka A won by 280 runs.** ‡**Sri Lanka A 294** (73.3 overs) (D. M. de Silva 73, M. D. Shanaka 102*; K. A. Joseph 3-32) **and 267-9 dec** (67.5 overs) (A. R. S. Silva 86, M. D. Shanaka 60, P. W. H. de Silva 50*; R. R. S. Cornwall 5-107); **West Indies A 137** (44.3 overs) (P. M. Pushpakumara 6-52) **and 144** (54 overs) (P. M. Pushpakumara 6-46). *Dasun Shanaka came in at No. 7 and pummelled eight sixes in 102*, to boost Sri Lanka A to 294, more than West Indies A managed in two attempts. Slow left-armer Malinda Pushpakumara took six wickets in each innings as his side squared the series.*

At Kingston, Jamaica, October 26–28, 2017 (day/night). **Sri Lanka A won by ten wickets.** ‡**West Indies A 181** (60.3 overs) (S. W. Ambris 101; P. M. Pushpakumara 4-67) **and 118** (37.3 overs) (S. S. J. Brooks 52; G. S. N. F. G. Jayasuriya 6-60, P. M. Pushpakumara 4-19); **Sri Lanka A 273** (76.2 overs) (D. M. de Silva 64, A. R. S. Silva 52*) **and 27-0** (5.5 overs). *Changing to the pink ball under the Sabina Park floodlights made little difference to Pushpakumara, who took eight wickets in the match. Off-spinner Shehan Jayasuriya claimed a career-best 6-60 as Sri Lanka A surged to another convincing victory.*

At Kingston, Jamaica, November 1, 2017 (day/night). **Sri Lanka A won by two wickets.** ‡**West Indies A 176** (48.4 overs) (M. V. Hodge 54; C. B. R. L. S. Kumara 3-26, M. A. Aponso 3-34); **Sri Lanka A 181-8** (48 overs) (S. S. Cotterell 4-44). *MoM:* M. A. Aponso. *West Indies A conceded 23 in wides, which probably made the difference in a low-scoring match.*

At Kingston, Jamaica, November 3, 2017 (day/night). **West Indies A v Sri Lanka A. Abandoned.**

At Trelawny Greenfields, Jamaica, November 5, 2017. **West Indies A won by 45 runs.** ‡**West Indies A 152** (44.1 overs) (N. V. R. Perera 4-25); **Sri Lanka A 107** (38.3 overs) (S. S. Cotterell 4-19, K. R. Mayers 3-24). *MoM:* S. S. Cotterell. *Sheldon Cotterell, the slippery local left-armer, took four more wickets as West Indies A squared the one-day series.*

ZIMBABWE A IN THE UNITED ARAB EMIRATES IN 2017-18

There was an upset in November, when Zimbabwe A – captained now by Chamu Chibhabha – lost all five matches on a brief trip to the United Arab Emirates. The locals continued their good form under new coach Dougie Brown, despite rotating their personnel (three different men captained the side). The hard-hitting Prince Masvaure was the tourists' leading run-scorer with 182, while leg-spinner Brendon Mavuta took 11 wickets.

At Dubai (ICC Academy), November 9, 2017. **United Arab Emirates won by four wickets.** ‡**Zimbabwe A 224-9** (50 overs) (R. P. Burl 85; Rohan Mustafa 3-46); **United Arab Emirates 228-6** (45.2 overs) (Ghulam Shabbir 71; B. A. Mavuta 4-53).

At Dubai (ICC Academy), November 11, 2017. **United Arab Emirates won by five wickets. Zimbabwe A 244** (50 overs) (P. S. Masvaure 86, T. S. Chisoro 59; Amjad Javed 3-59); ‡**United Arab Emirates 245-5** (46 overs) (Ashfaq Ahmed 51, Mohammad Boota 71, Mohammad Usman

76*). *MoM:* Mohammad Usman. *Zimbabwe A recovered from 68-5 thanks to Prince Masvaure, who put on 71 with Timycen Maruma (33) and 82 with Tendai Chisoro – but 244 wasn't enough to ruffle the UAE. Mohammad Boota struck 71 on his List A debut, and Mohammad Usman made his highest score.*

At Dubai (Sports City), November 13, 2017 (day/night). **United Arab Emirates won by 25 runs.** ‡**United Arab Emirates 214-8** (50 overs); **Zimbabwe A 189** (46.2 overs) (Zahoor Khan 3-40). *MoM:* Amjad Javed. *The UAE clinched the series under the lights, defending a modest total: their captain/opener Rohan Mustafa made 46, which turned out to be the highest score of the match.*

At Dubai (ICC Academy), November 16, 2017 (day/night). **United Arab Emirates won by 77 runs.** ‡**United Arab Emirates 283-5** (50 overs) (Ashfaq Ahmed 65, Chirag Suri 58, Ghulam Shabbir 65*, Mohammad Boota 51; N. Madziva 3-38); **Zimbabwe A 206** (43.4 overs) (B. B. Chari 60; Zahoor Khan 5-45). *MoM:* Zahoor Khan. *Seamer Zahoor Khan took 5-45 as Zimbabwe A slipped to another defeat.*

At Dubai (ICC Academy), November 18, 2017. **United Arab Emirates won by four wickets. Zimbabwe A 312-9** (50 overs) (C. J. Chibhabha 60, P. S. Masvaure 53, T. K. Musakanda 70, P. J. Moor 75; Rohan Mustafa 3-69, Zahoor Khan 3-50); ‡**United Arab Emirates 316-6** (48.1 overs) (Rameez Shahzad 61, L. Sreekumar 54; B. A. Mavuta 3-69). *The Zimbabwean batting finally clicked – Tarisai Musakanda and Peter Moor put on 114 in 11 overs, after fifties from Chibhabha and Masvaure – but 312 still wasn't enough. The UAE strolled to a 5–0 victory with something to spare.*

THE ICC INTERCONTINENTAL CUP IN 2017

STEVEN LYNCH

Much of the sting was taken out of the Intercontinental Cup with the announcement in June that Afghanistan and Ireland had been elevated to full membership of the ICC. Previously the winners alone had expected a shot at Test cricket – and then only if they defeated the lowest-ranked Full Member in a play-off. Afghanistan had, in any case, all but clinched the title with a thumping win over holders Ireland in March – their third in succession by an innings in the tournament. They soon added a fourth, against Hong Kong, and missed a fifth by a whisker in their final match, when the UAE narrowly forced them to bat again. Overall, it was an impressive show of strength, and suggested Afghanistan were rather more ready for Test cricket than an ageing Ireland side. The Netherlands took third place, finishing with a victory over Namibia that owed a lot to the all-round talents of Roelof van der Merwe, who followed an innings of 175 by sending down 50 overs across the two innings, and taking five wickets. Babar Hayat of Hong Kong ended up as the three-year tournament's leading run-scorer, with 712, while Asad Vala of Papua New Guinea and Ireland's Ed Joyce both made 700. Slow left-armer Ahmed Raza of the UAE was the leading wicket-taker with 32, one ahead of Afghanistan's teenage left-arm wrist-spinner Zahir Khan.

INTERCONTINENTAL CUP TABLE

	P	*W*	*L*	*D*	*A*	*1st-inns lead*	*Pts*
Afghanistan	7	6	0	1	0	5	121
Ireland	7	5	1	1	0	6	109
Netherlands	7	3	2	2	0	4	72
Hong Kong	7	2	3	1	1	3	59
United Arab Emirates	7	2	4	1	0	2	47
Scotland	7	0	2	4	1	2	46
Papua New Guinea	7	2	4	1	0	2	43
Namibia	7	1	5	1	0	1	27

Win = 14pts. Tie = 7pts. Draw with more than ten hours lost = 7pts. Draw with less than ten hours lost = 3pts. First-innings lead = 6pts. Tie on first innings = 3pts. Abandoned = 10pts.

At Mong Kok, February 10–13, 2017. **Drawn. Hong Kong 527-9 dec** (142.2 overs) (C. J. Carter 84, Babar Hayat 173, Nizakat Khan 55, A. Rath 98*; V. J. Kingma 4-125) **and 263-6 dec** (53 overs) (A. Rath 88); ‡**Netherlands 284** (65.2 overs) (B. N. Cooper 52, R. E. van der Merwe 135) **and 393-5** (111 overs) (B. N. Cooper 173*, P. M. Seelaar 138*; Ehsan Nawaz 3-85). Hong Kong 9pts, Netherlands 3pts. *First-class debuts:* M. Stiller (Hong Kong); Sikander Zulfiqar (Netherlands). *Babar Hayat's five-hour 173, and century stands with Chris Carter, Nizakat Khan and Anshuman Rath, underpinned Hong Kong's huge total. The Netherlands looked sunk at 105-5 in the follow-on, but Ben Cooper and Pieter Seelaar dropped anchor for more than four hours, adding 288*, to force the draw, both making maiden centuries. The Dutch debutant, Sikander Zulfiqar, is one of a set of triplets born on March 28, 1997; the other two, Asad and Saqib, also played for the Netherlands before the year was out.*

At Greater Noida, India, March 28–30, 2017. **Afghanistan won by an innings and 172 runs.** ‡**Afghanistan 537-8 dec** (138.5 overs) (Mohammad Shahzad 85, Asghar Stanikzai 145, Nasir Ahmadzai 73, Afsar Zazai 103*; G. H. Dockrell 3-160); **Ireland 261** (91.4 overs) (A. Balbirnie 62, J. Anderson 61*; Rashid Khan 5-99) **and 104** (40 overs) (Mohammad Nabi 6-40, Rashid Khan

3-44). *Afghanistan 20pts. This match had always been expected to settle the title, and so it proved: Afghanistan overwhelmed the holders with more than a day to spare. Asghar Stanikzai smacked seven sixes in his career-best 145, and later wicketkeeper Afsar Zazai reached a maiden century during a ninth-wicket stand of 109* with Dawlat Zadran (32*). Ireland offered little resistance once Andy Balbirnie and Ed Joyce (45) were separated after a second-wicket partnership of 117; Afghanistan's spinners took 17 wickets between them. Two Afghans were reprimanded by the referee: Dawlat hit Peter Chase with a return when he was not attempting a run, while Mohammad Nabi claimed a catch which had hit the ground.*

At Abu Dhabi, April 7–10, 2017. **United Arab Emirates won by nine wickets. ‡Papua New Guinea 194** (85.3 overs) (Qadeer Ahmed 3-43, Ahmed Raza 3-38) **and 286** (86.4 overs) (L. Siaka 142*; Mohammad Naveed 4-78, Imran Haider 4-93); **United Arab Emirates 441-8 dec** (150.3 overs) (Rameez Shahzad 63, Mohammad Usman 103, Saqlain Haider 102*; M. D. Dai 4-126) **and 42-1** (5.5 overs). *United Arab Emirates 20pts. First-class debuts:* Imran Haider (UAE); N. Pokana (PNG). *Maiden centuries from Mohammad Usman and wicketkeeper Saqlain Haider gave the UAE the initiative, which they pressed home despite the efforts of Lega Siaka, who hit 23 fours in 142*, his own maiden ton. It was the UAE's first first-class victory since beating Namibia in September 2013.*

At Ayr, June 6–9. **Drawn. ‡Namibia 403-7 dec** (104 overs) (S. J. Baard 88, J. N. Frylinck 158, C. Viljoen 77; S. M. Sharif 3-63); **Scotland 223-2** (57.5 overs) (H. G. Munsey 100*, C. S. MacLeod 79). *Scotland 7pts, Namibia 7pts. There was no play on the first or third days because of rain. Jan Frylinck, who came in after Safyaan Sharif took three wickets in an over, and George Munsey both recorded their maiden first-class centuries.*

At Malahide, August 15–18. **Drawn. Ireland 477-6 dec** (131 overs) (W. T. S. Porterfield 60, A. Balbirnie 205*, J. Anderson 74; S. Snater 5-116) **and 240-7 dec** (52 overs) (W. T. S. Porterfield 108, A. Balbirnie 50, K. J. O'Brien 58; W. Barresi 3-42); **‡Netherlands 375** (113.5 overs) (B. N. Cooper 82, M. P. O'Dowd 105, L. V. van Beek 76; W. B. Rankin 5-49) **and 186-4** (76 overs) (S. J. Myburgh 85). *Ireland 9pts, Netherlands 3pts. First-class debuts:* D. J. ter Braak, Saqib Zulfiqar, T. P. Visee (Netherlands). *Ireland looked to have resumed normal service after their pasting by Afghanistan, as Balbirnie batted more than seven hours for his first double-century. But the Netherlands recovered from 149-6 thanks to a stand of 160 between the New Zealand-born pair of Max O'Dowd and Logan van Beek. William Porterfield's fifth first-class century for Ireland set up a target of 343 and, although Wesley Barresi fell in the first over, the Dutch held on with ease.*

At Windhoek (Wanderers), September 16–18, 2017. **United Arab Emirates won by 34 runs. ‡United Arab Emirates 269** (85.3 overs) (Adnan Mufti 110; J. J. Smit 4-37, P. Burger 3-44) **and 157** (48.5 overs) (C. G. Williams 5-22); **Namibia 212** (67.5 overs) (M. G. Erasmus 78*; Ahmed Raza 6-61) **and 180** (66.2 overs) (Rohan Mustafa 3-38). *United Arab Emirates 20pts. First-class debuts:* P. Burger (Namibia); Chirag Suri (UAE). *After no wins for four years, the UAE made it two out of two in 2017. Adnan Mufti's maiden century, in his 48th first-class match (the first 46 of them in domestic cricket in Pakistan), and slow left-armer Ahmed Raza's six wickets forged a lead of 57, and a target of 215 proved tantalisingly out of reach for Namibia.*

At Port Moresby, October 1–4, 2017. **Drawn. ‡Papua New Guinea 404** (116.3 overs) (V. V. Morea 53, S. Bau 51, C. A. Soper 60, N. Vanua 64; S. M. Sharif 4-94) **and 263-3** (68 overs) (T. P. Ura 75, L. Siaka 83, A. Vala 61*); **Scotland 514** (168.2 overs) (H. G. Munsey 53, R. D. Berrington 129, M. A. Leask 58, M. R. J. Watt 81*; M. D. Dai 3-91). *Papua New Guinea 3pts, Scotland 9pts. First-class debuts:* D. Ravu (PNG); M. A. Leask (Scotland). *Batsmen enjoyed the pitch for only the second first-class match at Amini Park, with a match aggregate of 1,181 runs for 23 wickets. There was little chance of a result once Scotland – for whom Richie Berrington faced 297 balls for his career-best 129 – made a solid start in reply to PNG's 404, in which Norman Vanua top-scored from No. 9.*

At Mong Kok, October 20–21, 2017. **Afghanistan won by an innings and 173 runs. ‡Hong Kong 142** (47 overs) (Dawlat Zadran 3-15, Rashid Khan 5-65) **and 150** (39.4 overs) (A. Rath 59*; Zahir Khan 4-16); **Afghanistan 465-5 dec** (88 overs) (Javed Ahmadi 108, Ihsanullah Janat 63, Rahmat Shah 57, Asghar Stanikzai 125, Mohammad Nabi 63). *Afghanistan 20pts. First-class debuts:* K. Christie, Haroon Arshed (Hong Kong). *Afghanistan romped to their fourth successive innings victory, this one inside two days. Their spinners led the demolition as 13 Hong Kong batsmen fell in single figures. Stanikzai hit seven sixes, and Nabi six in his 44-ball 63.*

At Sharjah, November 29–December 1, 2017. **Hong Kong won by an innings and 29 runs. ‡Papua New Guinea 237** (77.3 overs) (T. P. Ura 62; Nadeem Ahmed 5-72, Ehsan Khan 3-66) **and 82** (33.5 overs) (Nadeem Ahmed 4-43, Ehsan Khan 5-13); **Hong Kong 348** (139.3 overs) (Babar

Hayat 214*; C. A. Soper 4-33). *Hong Kong 20pts. First-class debuts:* C. L. McAuslan (Hong Kong); K. Doriga (PNG). *A maiden double-century from Hayat, who hit 27 fours and six sixes from 421 balls, set up a huge Hong Kong victory. Off-spinners Nadeem Ahmed and Ehsan Khan shared 17 wickets.*

At Dubai (Sports City), November 29–December 1, 2017. **Ireland won by 203 runs. Ireland 251** (81 overs) (K. J. O'Brien 78*; C. B. Sole 3-79, S. G. Whittingham 3-23, M. R. J. Watt 3-60) **and 271** (68.4 overs) (G. C. Wilson 56, Simranjit Singh 59; S. G. Whittingham 5-70); ‡**Scotland 141** (52.2 overs) (W. B. Rankin 4-45, K. J. O'Brien 3-14) **and 178** (57.3 overs) (T. J. Murtagh 3-35, P. K. D. Chase 4-52). *Ireland 20pts. First-class debut:* M. D. Rao (Scotland). *Four-time winners Ireland ended their involvement in the Intercontinental Cup with a crushing win over familiar rivals Scotland in the unfamiliar surroundings of Dubai. The Irish seamers claimed all but one of the wickets as the Scots collapsed twice. Ireland's long-serving all-rounder Kevin O'Brien rescued their first innings from 124-6 with 78*, then took three wickets in successive overs.*

At Dubai (ICC Academy), November 29–December 2, 2017. **Netherlands won by 231 runs. Netherlands 501-8 dec** (117.4 overs) (B. N. Cooper 65, R. E. van der Merwe 175, M. P. O'Dowd 126, S. Snater 50*; C. G. Williams 4-71) **and 223-5 dec** (52.3 overs) (P. W. Borren 85, B. F. W. de Leede 56*); ‡**Namibia 203** (72 overs) (S. J. Baard 111; V. J. Kingma 3-22, R. E. van der Merwe 3-50) **and 290** (88.4 overs) (L. P. van der Westhuizen 52, S. F. Burger 70; S. Snater 5-88). *Netherlands 20pts. First-class debuts:* Ali Ahmed, B. F. W. de Leede, S. Edwards (Netherlands). *The Netherlands cemented third place – and sentenced Namibia to the wooden spoon – with a powerful performance. After slipping to 147-5, they took control thanks to a partnership of 285, at nearly five an over, between Roelof van der Merwe and O'Dowd; later Shane Snater biffed a 39-ball half-century to whisk the total past 500.*

At Abu Dhabi, November 29–December 2, 2017. **Afghanistan won by ten wickets. Afghanistan 510-9 dec** (147 overs) (Ihsanullah Janat 124, Rahmat Shah 103, Asghar Stanikzai 114, Afsar Zazai 50*; Mohammad Naveed 3-112, Ahmed Raza 5-148) **and 21-0** (5.3 overs); ‡**United Arab Emirates 197** (64.5 overs) (Shaiman Anwar 85*; Rashid Khan 3-69, Zahir Khan 3-30) **and 331** (100.3 overs) (Rohan Mustafa 68, Chirag Suri 81; Rashid Khan 5-83). *Afghanistan 20pts. First-class debut:* Amir Hayat (UAE). *Afghanistan rounded off a triumphant tournament with another thumping win, their sixth out of seven (four by an innings); their other match, in 2015, was a rain-affected draw in Scotland. Leg-spinner Rashid Khan whirled to 35 wickets in four first-class matches, with a five-for in each.*

INTERCONTINENTAL CUP CHAMPIONS

2004	Scotland
2005	Ireland
2006–07	Ireland
2007–08	Ireland
2009–10	Afghanistan
2011–13	Ireland
2015–17	Afghanistan

"In 1970–71, it was sort of 'Oh, we won the Ashes.' It wasn't hyped up as tremendous. In fact, it *was* tremendous to win the Ashes out there. If we'd have done it now, we'd have been heroes and gone up to the Palace and got OBEs."

England 1,000 not out, page 50

ICC WORLD CRICKET LEAGUE CHAMPIONSHIP IN 2017

The Netherlands clinched the prize of the 13th and final place in the ICC's new One-Day League by finishing top of the World Cricket League, and also reclaimed the official ODI status they lost in 2014. They won ten of 12 completed matches, and welcomed back the Essex captain Ryan ten Doeschate for their last two games – his first internationals since the 2011 World Cup. Scotland, Hong Kong and Papua New Guinea, the next three in the table, secured automatic entry to the World Cup Qualifier in Zimbabwe in March 2018; the other teams faced a further elimination competition for the last two spots. PNG had headed the table at the start of the year but, facing tougher opposition in 2017, slipped to fourth. The tournament came to a climax in December, with all eight teams assembled in the UAE for the last two rounds of matches. The leading scorer overall was Hong Kong's Anshuman Rath, with 678 at 75, while his captain Babar Hayat (543) and Scotland's Kyle Coetzer (574) also passed 500. Scotland seamer Alasdair Evans and Hong Kong off-spinner Nadeem Ahmed both took 24 wickets.

WORLD CRICKET LEAGUE CHAMPIONSHIP TABLE

	P	*W*	*L*	*T*	*NR*	*Pts*	*NRR*
Netherlands	14	10	2	0	2	22	0.97
Scotland	14	8	3	0	3	19	0.84
Hong Kong	14	8	4	0	2	18	1.08
Papua New Guinea	14	8	6	0	0	16	–0.37
Kenya	14	6	8	0	0	12	–0.55
United Arab Emirates	14	5	9	0	0	10	–0.37
Nepal	14	4	9	0	1	9	–0.45
Namibia	14	3	11	0	0	6	–0.60

Win = 2pts. Tie/no result = 1pt. Only Papua New Guinea's matches against Hong Kong, Scotland and the United Arab Emirates in 2017 were official one-day internationals.

At Mong Kok, February 16, 2017. **Netherlands won by five runs.** ‡**Netherlands 330-7** (50 overs) (S. J. Myburgh 88, R. E. van der Merwe 62, P. M. Seelaar 50*); **Hong Kong 325-9** (50 overs) (A. Rath 134, Babar Hayat 83; M. J. G. Rippon 4-67). *MoM:* M. J. G. Rippon. *Hong Kong seemed to be cruising to their lofty target while Anshuman Rath and Babar Hayat were adding 197 for the third wicket. Although Hayat was superbly stumped by Wesley Barresi in the 41st over, it was 285-3 at the start of the 45th – but Rath was caught on the boundary next ball, and the rest could not conjure the runs. The Netherlands went top of the table – and stayed there.*

At Mong Kok, February 18, 2017. **Netherlands won by 13 runs.** ‡**Netherlands 314-9** (50 overs) (M. J. G. Rippon 53, B. N. Cooper 78; Ehsan Khan 3-59); **Hong Kong 301-8** (50 overs) (A. Rath 85, Babar Hayat 86). *MoM:* M. J. G. Rippon. *Another run-fest at the compact Mission Road ground again found Hong Kong coming up just short. Rath and Hayat once more scored most of their runs.*

At Kirtipur, March 11, 2017. **Kenya won by five wickets** (DLS). **Nepal 112-8** (36 overs) (S. O. Ngoche 3-18); ‡**Kenya 98-5** (24.1 overs). *Rain led to a late start and a 38-over match, then more showers meant Kenya's target was revised to 94 in 26. They slipped to 21-3 and 71-5, but skipper Rakep Patel (34*) and Gurdeep Singh (12*) got them over the line. Earlier, slow left-armer Shem Ngoche had kept Nepal in check with 6–1–18–3. There was no match award in this game (or several others).*

At Kirtipur, March 13, 2017. **Nepal won by seven wickets. Kenya 155** (46.1 overs) (S. Vesawkar 4-28); ‡**Nepal 160-3** (30.2 overs) (G. Malla 64*, D. S. Airee 62). *A full game – and a total embarrassment for Kenya, who lost six batsmen in single figures. Nepal romped home with nearly 20 overs to spare, captain Gyanendra Malla and Dipendra Airee putting on 111 for the third wicket.*

At Abu Dhabi, March 31, 2017. **United Arab Emirates won by 82 runs. United Arab Emirates 292-5** (50 overs) (Ghulam Shabbir 50, Rameez Shahzad 87, Mohammad Usman 58*); ‡**Papua New Guinea 210** (47.3 overs) (T. P. Ura 61; Ahmed Raza 3-30, Imran Haider 4-49). *ODI debuts:* A. Nao, N. Pokana (PNG). *After Rameez Shahzad's career-best 87, Mohammad Usman and Mohammad Naveed (34*) plundered 52* from the last four overs. PNG started well, openers Tony Ura and Vani Morea (32) putting on 82, but never recovered after leg-spinner Imran Haider took four wickets in 20 balls.*

At Abu Dhabi, April 2, 2017. **Papua New Guinea won by 26 runs.** ‡**Papua New Guinea 232-8** (50 overs) (V. V. Morea 52); **United Arab Emirates 206** (47.4 overs) (Ghulam Shabbir 70; A. Vala 3-20). *UAE seemed set for another victory when they reached 148-2 in the 34th over, but lost eight for 58. PNG's captain Asad Vala snared top-scorer Ghulam Shabbir with his off-spin, and finished with miserly figures of 10–1–20–3.*

At Edinburgh, June 11–12. **Scotland won by 51 runs** (DLS). **Scotland 268-5** (43 overs) (R. D. Berrington 110); ‡**Namibia 217** (39.4 overs) (S. M. Sharif 3-40). *Richie Berrington's 90-ball 110 proved the difference in a match that spilled into the reserve day because of rain. He added 101 for the fifth wicket with former captain Preston Mommsen, who made 49* from 35 balls on his comeback, having announced his international retirement in November 2016. Further rain delays meant DLS was called into play, although Namibia's target remained the same. They were never in touch, slipping to 133-7 in the 29th over, before No. 10 Zhivago Groenewald top-scored with 42 from 20 balls.*

At Edinburgh, June 13. **Namibia won by 50 runs.** ‡**Namibia 324-5** (50 overs) (S. J. Baard 78, Z. E. Green 61, C. G. Williams 69*); **Scotland 274-9** (50 overs) (K. J. Coetzer 112, R. D. Berrington 61; C. Viljoen 3-58, J. N. Frylinck 3-45). *An improved display set up a victory for bottom-of-the-table Namibia: their bowlers worked their way through, after Kyle Coetzer and Berrington added 117 for the third wicket. Defeat left Scotland three points adrift of the Netherlands, with four matches remaining.*

At Windhoek (Wanderers), September 21, 2017. **United Arab Emirates won by six wickets. Namibia 89** (28.3 overs) (Ahmed Raza 3-18, Imran Haider 3-27); ‡**United Arab Emirates 92-4** (25.1 overs). *Opener Stephan Baard fell in the first over for a duck – and things just got worse for Namibia, who were bundled out for 89; only Louis van der Westhuizen (41) and Craig Williams (25) made it into double figures. The UAE bustled to victory shortly after the scheduled halfway mark.*

At Windhoek (Wanderers), September 23, 2017. **Namibia won by four wickets.** ‡**United Arab Emirates 272-7** (50 overs) (Rohan Mustafa 96, Ghulam Shabbir 71, Shaiman Anwar 50; J. N. Frylinck 3-37); **Namibia 274-6** (48.5 overs) (M. G. Erasmus 77, S. F. Burger 57*). *Given Namibia's collapse in the previous match, the UAE looked safe when skipper Rohan Mustafa's 96 set up the prospect of a big total. But from 256-2 in the 46th over, the UAE managed just 16 more, and Namibia seized the initiative with five wickets, two in Jan Frylinck's final over, which cost only a single. They dipped to 130-5 after 26, but Gerhard Erasmus and captain Sarel Burger put on 96, then Erasmus and Johannes Smit (22*) finished things off.*

At Port Moresby, October 6, 2017. **Scotland won by 101 runs.** ‡**Scotland 278-9** (50 overs) (C. S. MacLeod 154, R. D. Berrington 54; N. Vanua 3-57, A. Nao 3-40); **Papua New Guinea 177** (43.3 overs). *ODI debut:* S. G. Whittingham (Scotland). *Calum MacLeod's 154, his fifth ODI century, took Scotland beyond the reach of PNG, although they might have expected even more runs after being 240-2 in the 45th over. The hosts were never on terms after dipping to 30-3.*

At East London, October 6, 2017. **Netherlands won by six wickets. Kenya 226-7** (50 overs) (D. M. Gondaria 53, C. O. Obuya 72; M. J. G. Rippon 3-30); ‡**Netherlands 227-4** (48.5 overs) (P. W. Borren 86*, M. J. G. Rippon 56*). *Scoring proved difficult in a match moved to South Africa because of security concerns about playing in Nairobi. Kenya reached 226 thanks to a sixth-wicket stand of 95 between Collins Obuya and Nelson Odhiambo (39). The Netherlands in turn subsided to 98-4 in the 26th over, before captain Peter Borren and Michael Rippon – who had earlier taken three wickets with his left-arm wrist-spin – put on 127*.*

At Port Moresby, October 8, 2017. **Papua New Guinea won by five wickets.** ‡**Scotland 203** (49.2 overs) (M. H. Cross 91); **Papua New Guinea 204-5** (48 overs) (M. D. Dai 63*). *Scotland would only have been a point behind the Netherlands if they had won – but their batting misfired, failing to support opener Matthew Cross's 91. Mahuru Dai made sure of victory, and PNG replaced the Scots in second place.*

At East London, October 8, 2017. **Kenya won by two wickets. Netherlands 224-9** (50 overs) (S. J. Myburgh 50, W. Barresi 69, M. J. G. Rippon 51; S. O. Ngoche 4-33); ‡**Kenya 225-8** (49.3 overs) (D. M. Gondaria 63, C. O. Obuya 56*). *It looked like business as usual for the Dutch while openers Stephan Myburgh and Barresi were putting on 120 – but when they were separated only Rippon made more than 11. After Dhiren Gondaria's 61-ball 63, Kenya needed just 51 from the last ten overs – and Obuya inched them over the line with three balls to spare. It left the Netherlands needing one victory from their last two matches to win the tournament.*

At Mong Kok, October 13, 2017. **Hong Kong won by 83 runs. Hong Kong 194** (50 overs) (J. J. Atkinson 76; S. Lamichhane 3-48); ‡**Nepal 111** (34.5 overs) (Aizaz Khan 3-14, Ehsan Khan 5-17). *MoM:* J. J. Atkinson. *Hong Kong maintained their challenge with a comfortable victory over Nepal on a testing pitch, with Aizaz and Ehsan Khan taking a combined eight for 31.*

At Mong Kok, October 15–16, 2017. **Hong Kong v Nepal. Abandoned.** *The after-effects of Typhoon Khanun meant no play was possible. Hong Kong remained fourth.*

At Dubai (ICC Academy), December 6, 2017. **Hong Kong won by 23 runs. Hong Kong 230-8** (50 overs) (Babar Hayat 77); ‡**Papua New Guinea 207** (47 overs) (S. Bau 59, M. D. Dai 60). *MoM:* Babar Hayat. *ODI debut:* S. S. McKechnie (Hong Kong). *All eight teams came together in the UAE, with three places in the World Cup Qualifier up for grabs (the Netherlands were already through). After Hayat's 77 led Hong Kong to a middling 230, PNG recovered from 29-4 to 127-4 after 29 overs – but Dai fell for 60, and the others could not coax the necessary runs. Hong Kong's victory meant they reached the Qualifier – and Scotland's defeat of Kenya meant PNG had got there too.*

At Dubai (Sports City), December 6, 2017. **Scotland won by eight wickets. Kenya 140** (46.2 overs) (S. M. Sharif 3-33); ‡**Scotland 145-2** (28 overs) (K. J. Coetzer 52, C. S. MacLeod 56*). *MoM:* K. J. Coetzer. *Scotland ensured their place at the World Cup Qualifier with a comfortable victory. Seamer Chris Sole had figures of 9–0–20–2, and slow left-armer Mark Watt 10–2–17–1.*

At Dubai (ICC Academy No. 2), December 6, 2017. **Netherlands won by eight wickets. Namibia 269-8** (50 overs) (L. P. van der Westhuizen 54, M. G. Erasmus 52; R. E. van der Merwe 3-54); ‡**Netherlands 270-2** (41.1 overs) (W. Barresi 120, B. N. Cooper 109*). *MoM:* B. N. Cooper. *A target of 270 posed few problems for Barresi and Cooper, who put on 236 for the second wicket in 36 overs. Fittingly, skipper Borren (16*) was in at the end as the Netherlands sealed the victory that ensured they topped the table and claimed the final spot in the ICC's new One-Day League. Essex's captain Ryan ten Doeschate, now 37, returned for his first international since the 2011 World Cup, but did not bat or bowl.*

At Abu Dhabi, December 6, 2017. **United Arab Emirates won by seven wickets. Nepal 221-6** (50 overs) (G. Malla 54, S. Vesawkar 81*); ‡**United Arab Emirates 225-3** (45.5 overs) (Rohan Mustafa 62, Ghulam Shabbir 81*). *MoM:* Ghulam Shabbir. *A patient innings from Ghulam Shabbir ensured a home win, despite Sharad Vesawkar's career-best 81*.*

At Dubai (ICC Academy), December 8, 2017. **Hong Kong won by 93 runs. Hong Kong 323-4** (50 overs) (A. Rath 143*, Babar Hayat 89); ‡**Papua New Guinea 230** (42.2 overs) (K. Doriga 89*; Ehsan Nawaz 4-54). *MoM:* A. Rath. *Hong Kong secured third place with this victory over PNG, who finished fourth. It was set up by a second-wicket stand of 142 between their big-scoring pair of Rath – who batted through the innings for his first ODI century – and Hayat.*

At Dubai (Sports City), December 8, 2017. **Scotland won by 161 runs. Scotland 266-8** (50 overs) (K. J. Coetzer 121; E. R. Bundi 3-60); ‡**Kenya 105** (33.2 overs) (C. B. Sole 4-24). *MoM:* K. J. Coetzer. *Scotland rounded off their campaign with another comprehensive victory. After Coetzer's century set up a big total, Sole derailed the chase with three wickets in seven balls as Kenya plummeted to 47-6.*

At Dubai (ICC Academy No. 2), December 8, 2017. **Netherlands won by five wickets. Namibia 181** (36.4 overs) (M. G. Erasmus 81; V. J. Kingma 6-39); ‡**Netherlands 182-5** (41.1 overs) (R. N. ten Doeschate 65*). *MoM:* V. J. Kingma. *Dutch seamer Vivian Kingma's maiden List A five-for – which he rounded off with a hat-trick – ensured a modest target. The Netherlands tumbled to 105-5, but that only brought in ten Doeschate, whose 58-ball 65* secured a comfortable victory.*

At Abu Dhabi, December 8, 2017. **United Arab Emirates won by 63 runs. United Arab Emirates 195** (49.2 overs) (Adnan Mufti 104; S. Kami 5-27); ‡**Nepal 132** (42.2 overs) (Amjad Javed 3-23). *MoM:* Adnan Mufti. *The UAE owed almost everything to Mufti, who slammed 104 from 89 balls after entering at 39-5. With Sompal Kami claiming his first List A five-for, Nepal still needed only 196, but lost their way.*

CRICKET IN HONG KONG IN 2017

Cricket to go

NAZVI CAREEM

Cricket officials in Hong Kong have long recognised the need to cater for a population in a hurry. In 1987, they hosted the Silk Cut Challenge, a gimmicky competition between the great all-rounders of the time, in which Imran Khan prevailed over Richard Hadlee and Clive Rice. In 1992, they came up with the Hong Kong Sixes, pitching countries against each other across two days in a series of 45-minute, five-over thrashes. But sponsorship dried up after 2012, and the Hong Kong Cricket Association were forced to shelve the competition.

The governing body re-entered the market in 2016 with the T20 Blitz. Only three matches of the inaugural edition survived the weather – it was scheduled during the wet season – but the follow-up in March 2017 was an undoubted success, with Misbah-ul-Haq and Kumar Sangakkara adding stardust to a thrilling tournament won by Kowloon Cantons.

However, the man behind it, Australian Tim Cutler, left his post as chief executive of the board – renamed Cricket Hong Kong – a few months later. No reason was given, and he was bound by a non-disclosure agreement. Even so, the success of the Blitz emboldened CHK to revive the Sixes in October. There were financial losses, but the move felt justified after an exciting final in which South Africa's Aubrey Swanepoel hit a last-ball four to pip Pakistan. A strong online following was an essential ingredient – as it was with the Blitz – with millions tuning in to live streams available on Facebook and YouTube. CHK were hoping it had laid the foundation for future tournaments to turn a profit.

The national side finished third in the one-day World Cricket League, earning an invitation to the ten-team World Cup qualifying tournament in Zimbabwe in 2018. In the last game of the year, old Harrovian Anshuman Rath hit a career-best 143 not out to set up victory over Nepal, and finished top run-scorer in the competition, with 678. Captain Babar Hayat also had an excellent time, particularly in the Intercontinental Cup where Hong Kong came fourth. He began with 173 in a draw against the Netherlands, and ended with a maiden first-class double-century against Papua New Guinea.

CRICKET IN THE NETHERLANDS IN 2017

Orange glow

DAVE HARDY

The Netherlands made notable progress on two fronts in 2017. They secured the World Cricket League title, and with it the huge bonus prize of qualification for the ICC's new 13-team One-Day League. And they finished third, their best position, in the first-class Intercontinental Cup, behind Afghanistan and Ireland. There was much to feel encouraged about.

A competition-record partnership of 236 for the second wicket between Wesley Barresi (120) and Ben Cooper (109 not out) earned the win over Namibia in Dubai that – once Hong Kong had beaten Papua New Guinea on an adjoining ground an hour later – clinched the WCL with a match to go. Captain Peter Borren reflected on "three years of hard work", and was delighted by the squad's new-found strength in depth: "We probably have 22 or 23 guys who could play now." Borren's point was underlined during that Namibia game by the return of Ryan ten Doeschate, who made himself available for the first time since the 2011 World Cup. The Netherlands can look forward to regular matches against elite opposition when the new league begins in 2020.

The year began with two close victories – by five runs and seven runs – away to Hong Kong, followed by a win and a defeat against Kenya. A highly satisfactory campaign concluded with a pair of wins over Namibia. Interim coach Chris Adams took charge in Hong Kong, but in April Ryan Campbell, the former Western Australia wicketkeeper-batsman, began a two-year contract as permanent successor to Anton Roux. Allan Donald and Trevor Penney were later added to the coaching team.

The Netherlands were also unbeaten in three Intercontinental Cup matches. There were draws away to Hong Kong – where Cooper and Pieter Seelaar scored centuries during the follow-on – and Ireland, and a win over Namibia in Dubai. During the home summer, however, they lost one-day series 2–1 to Zimbabwe and the UAE. Against the UAE at Amstelveen, the 20-year-old Zulfiqar triplets – Sikander, Saqib and Asad – played together for the Netherlands for the first time. Campbell is keen to integrate young home-grown players into the national squad: soon after his 18th birthday, Bas de Leede, son of former captain Tim, made 56 not out against Namibia on his first-class debut.

Excelsior '20, of Schiedam, retained their title in a *Topklasse* expanded to ten teams and not featuring play-offs for the first time since 2006. They won 16 of 18 matches, at one point establishing a run of 14 victories stretching over two seasons. ACC, of Amstelveen, completed a hat-trick of Twenty20 Cup wins. For only the third time in the top tier, three batsmen passed 1,000 runs: Jonathan Vandiar of HCC (1,139), Borren of VRA Amstelveen (1,009) and Jaron Morgan of HBS (1,002). Borren became the first batsman to average over 100 in a *Topklasse* season since Australian Peter Cantrell in 1988.

CRICKET IN OMAN IN 2017

Growing pains

PAUL BIRD

Oman consolidated the gains of 2016 with another year of rapid progress. There may have been nothing to match the profile built and publicity generated by the win over Ireland in the World T20 the previous year, but there was still much cause for satisfaction. Oman moved swiftly through the divisions of the ICC World Cricket League, from fifth to second, and earned a top 20 ranking in both short formats.

But how to maintain the momentum? The official line from Pankaj Khimji, director of the Oman Cricket Club, is that the future is at grassroots level, spreading the word outside of the capital, Muscat, and introducing young people to the game. In conjunction with MCC, the club are casting their net across the regions and targeting children as young as five. A new pavilion is taking shape at the national ground, where the UAE have already played. There were plans for games against Afghanistan and Zimbabwe as warm-ups for the next WCL tournament in early 2018 after a thumping 3-0 win over the USA in December.

Sultan Ahmed returned to the captaincy at the age of 40, while Zeeshan Maqsood, the player of the year, is now 30. There was a need to identify new talent, but Oman's youth development team are still dominated by South Asians, and it will be years before any of the local Arab children being introduced to the game will be ready for international cricket.

One short cut may lie in Mabella, an outer suburb of Muscat, where the Al Hail Cricket Club, a privately financed ground, has the country's third grass pitch. Omanis of all ages train, coach and play here with OCC approval. The club aims to "oversee and ensure the development and growth of all Omani cricket players", and advertisements in glorious colour promote their activities across the capital. Native Omanis have taken and passed ICC level coaching and umpiring awards, and are now knocking on the club's doors asking to be recognised and involved at professional level.

Mohammad Azharuddin, Mohammad Wasim and Rumesh Ratnayake have visited, and pictures of the owner, Moula Bakhsh Al Balushi, with government officials adorn the clubhouse walls. His ten-year plan is to see other Omanis follow Sufyan Mehmood, the one regular currently in the national side. Al Hail work with the OCC, who operate as a kind of cricket agency for the government. They also work around them if necessary, promoting their agenda for home-grown talent. It may be the only way to promote Omani cricket.

For Oman's matches in the Desert T20 Challenge, see page 1082.

CRICKET IN PAPUA NEW GUINEA IN 2017

Wrong direction

ANDREW NIXON

Anyone seeking proof of the value of stability in sport should look no further than Papua New Guinea in 2017. Having ended the previous year first in the ICC World Cricket League and fourth in the Intercontinental Cup, they went backwards, while changing coach with alarming frequency.

Dipak Patel, the former New Zealand off-spinner, had taken over in 2014 and led PNG successfully. But at the end of his contract in July, there was surprise when he was not re-engaged. His departure caused rancour, with Patel claiming an extension had been agreed before the offer was withdrawn. The manner of his exit, he said, left a "sour taste". He had been in charge for the tour of the UAE in March and April, when results were poor: PNG lost the Intercontinental Cup game, the T20 series 3–0, and the ODIs 2–1.

Jason Gillespie took charge on an interim basis for a home series against Scotland. A high-scoring draw in the Intercontinental Cup was followed by a shared two-match ODI series, which at least secured PNG's place at the 2018 World Cup Qualifier – the year's main aim.

To conclude 2017, Joe Dawes – the former Queensland player and India fast-bowling coach – stepped in, again on an interim basis, for another trip to the UAE. Two ODIs against Scotland were both lost, before an innings defeat by Hong Kong meant PNG ended their Intercontinental Cup campaign languishing in seventh. Yet they were still well placed to win the World Cricket League and secure a place in the ICC's new 13-team One-Day League – assuming they achieved better results than the Netherlands in the final two rounds. As it was, they lost the key games and slumped to fourth.

Even before Patel's three-year stint, a succession of part-time coaches had been customary for PNG. That lack of consistency was reflected in results, and the board would do well to follow the example of other Associates and appoint a permanent coach.

The women's team played in the World Cup Qualifier in Sri Lanka in February, when they were narrowly beaten by Scotland, but heavily so by Bangladesh, Pakistan and South Africa. Soon after, they travelled to Japan for a regional World Twenty20 qualifier, which they won, edging out Samoa on net run-rate. The Under-19 team also won their regional tournament, beating Vanuatu, Fiji and hosts Samoa to return to their World Cup, after losing in qualifying to Fiji in 2015.

For Papua New Guinea's matches in the Intercontinental Cup and the World Cricket League, see page 1069; and for their matches against the UAE and Scotland, see page 1081.

CRICKET IN SCOTLAND IN 2017

Short shrift

WILLIAM DICK

With a place in the World Cup Qualifier secured in the last month of the year, 2017 could be considered a partial success for Scotland. Two victories over Kenya in Dubai meant they finished second in the ICC World Cricket League Championship, and kept alive hopes of reaching the World Cup, to be staged in England next year. Kyle Coetzer's side also made history with a first win over a Full Member. In fact, they achieved two. In May, Scotland beat Sri Lanka by seven wickets at Beckenham in a Champions Trophy warm-up match that was not granted official ODI status. Undaunted, they defeated Zimbabwe at Edinburgh a few weeks later to make the landmark official.

However, other highlights proved elusive, and that second-place finish in the WCL will prove costly in the years to come. Only the winners, the Netherlands, were given a place in the ICC's new One-Day League. While the Dutch contemplate the benefits of regular competition against the world's best, Scotland were left to rue earlier defeats by Namibia and Papua New Guinea.

England are to visit Edinburgh for an ODI this summer, and Pakistan for two T20s, but where they will find regular meaningful competition in the immediate future remains uncertain. It may not be the last time Grant Bradburn, the national coach, delivers his end-of-season report before the height of summer, as was the case in 2017. Astonishingly – and alarmingly – Scotland played their final match of the season on home soil on June 17, completing a meagre programme of eight days' cricket, two fewer than the previous year.

Of those eight, two were lost to the weather, which hit the drawn Intercontinental Cup match against Namibia at Ayr. The occasion was at least memorable for George Munsey, who scored his maiden first-class century. Scotland were forced to share their WCL series with the Namibians. And that was that for the Scottish cricketing public, who had to follow from afar as the team headed to Port Moresby in the autumn, and drew an Intercontinental Cup match with PNG. In the WCL double header, they again won the first game before coming up short in the second.

The year ended in the UAE, with two one-day wins against PNG in Dubai, followed by a heavy Intercontinental Cup defeat by Ireland. Finally, however, came those crucial wins against Kenya, the second of which saw Coetzer score his fourth international century of 2017.

There was a high-profile departure from the National Cricket Academy: John Blain's absence will deprive cricketers at all levels of his coaching talents. He left for undisclosed personal reasons, though a cryptic tweet suggested some disenchantment: "Just sometimes you have to step away and care for something from afar."

There was disappointment for the Under-19s, who appeared to have a place at the World Cup in New Zealand in their grasp until they failed to chase 108 against Ireland. The women's game continued to make steady progress, with a healthy programme of fixtures including participation in ECB competitions in the 50-over and T20 formats. A highlight of the year saw Abbi Aitken's team win the ICC Women's World T20 Qualifier for the Europe–Americas Region. Aitken, though, will not lead the side to the main event, having chosen to stand down after an outstanding eight years in charge.

Domestically, the Eastern Knights retained the Regional Pro50 Cup in a campaign badly affected by rain. But they lost their T20 Blitz title to a resurgent Western Warriors. Prestwick, having punched above their weight to win the Western Premier Division, then went on to become the first team from the west to win the Grand Final, outplaying Heriot's in a low-scoring thriller.

Winners of Scottish Leagues and Cups
Eastern Premier Division Heriot's. **Western Premier Division** Prestwick. **National Champions** Prestwick. **Citylets Scottish Cup** Carlton. **Regional T20 Blitz** Western Warriors. **Regional Pro50 Cup** Eastern Knights. **CDD Women's Premier League** Carlton. **Beyond Boundaries Women's T20 Scottish Cup** George Watson's College.

SCOTLAND v ZIMBABWE

Scotland recorded their first victory over a Test-playing nation in an official one-day international – after 23 defeats – when Zimbabwe visited The Grange in June. The heroes were Kyle Coetzer, the captain, who made a century, and left-arm spinner Con de Lange, with a maiden five-wicket haul. The Zimbabweans were unhappy about the boundary catch that accounted for their top-scorer, Malcolm Waller, and – grimly determined – won the second match comfortably to square the first series between the sides.

First one-day international At Edinburgh, June 15. **Scotland won by 26 runs** (DLS). ‡**Scotland 317-6** (50 overs) (K. J. Coetzer 109, C. D. Wallace 58, M. A. Leask 59*); **Zimbabwe 272** (41.4 overs) (S. C. Williams 70, M. N. Waller 92; C. D. de Lange 5-60). *Kyle Coetzer's fifth ODI century set up a big total, which was pushed past 300 by fifties from Craig Wallace and Michael Leask. Solomon Mire and Hamilton Masakadza started the chase with an opening stand of 55, but Con de Lange removed Masakadza in his first over, then Chris Sole nabbed Craig Ervine for a duck. Rain caused a 100-minute delay with Zimbabwe 107-4, and left a revised target of 299 from 43 overs. Sean Williams zoomed to 79 in 59 balls, and Malcolm Waller thrashed 92 from 62, with 70 in boundaries – one of his five sixes flew 30 yards beyond deep point. But de Lange worked his way through, claiming his fifth wicket when, with eight balls remaining and 30 still wanted, Waller was caught by Sole at deep square leg. Waller complained but, with no TV coverage, he had to go; video footage suggested Sole's heel had touched the rope. Scotland's first victory over a Test-playing nation in an official ODI was completed in the next over, when Sole held a more straightforward catch.*

Second one-day international At Edinburgh, June 17. **Zimbabwe won by six wickets.** ‡**Scotland 169** (42 overs) (K. J. Coetzer 61, C. S. MacLeod 58; A. G. Cremer 5-29); **Zimbabwe 171-4** (37 overs) (Sikandar Raza 58*; C. B. Sole 3-36). *Zimbabwe squared the series with an emphatic victory. Apart from Coetzer and Calum MacLeod, only Leask (11*) reached double figures in a disappointing Scotland batting display. Zimbabwe were in a spot of bother at 99-4, but Sikandar Raza and Ryan Burl (30*) saw them home.*

For Scotland's matches in the Intercontinental Cup and the World Cricket League, see page 1069; for the Desert T20 Challenge, their tri-series in the UAE, and their matches against Papua New Guinea in the UAE, see page 1081.

CRICKET IN THE UNITED ARAB EMIRATES IN 2017

Signs of life in the desert

PAUL RADLEY

The fortunes of UAE cricket were transformed by an appointment that happened almost by accident. In February, Dougie Brown became the third former England player – after Paul Franks and Owais Shah – to become interim coach of the national side while they awaited a permanent successor to Aqib Javed, who had returned to Pakistan in 2016.

Former India all-rounder Sridharan Sriram had been earmarked to take the role on a full-time basis after he finished a stint with Delhi Daredevils at the IPL, but he pulled out when his family expressed reservations about moving to Dubai. Brown was the obvious solution: he had overseen the UAE's best run of results in a long time. Twenty years after his England debut at Sharjah (part of Adam Hollioake's Champions Trophy-winning team), and ten years after his last first-class match for Scotland, also at Sharjah, Brown was making the desert his home.

The effect of both his arrival and the promotion of Rohan Mustafa to the captaincy was startling. After finishing 2016 bottom of the World Cricket League and Intercontinental Cup tables, the UAE began a hot streak. They beat Papua New Guinea in all three formats, overcame the Netherlands away in a 50-over series, beat Nepal, and whitewashed Zimbabwe A.

The players registered a variety of national records. Seamer Zahoor Khan's six for 34 against Ireland was the best return by a UAE bowler in ODIs, while Shaiman Anwar hit their first T20 international century, against PNG. And Mustafa's year reached its zenith when he became the third to score a century and take five wickets in a one day international (also against PNG), after Viv Richards and Paul Collingwood.

The players registered a variety of national records

Despite improved performances, a lack of exposure – particularly on television – meant the players were still largely overlooked by the major T20 teams around the world. But Chirag Suri, a Delhi-born, Dubai-raised batsman, landed a shock deal for Gujarat Lions, making him the first from the UAE to earn an IPL contract. He enjoyed the experience of netting with Brendon McCullum and Suresh Raina, though did not get a game.

Local involvement in the first T10 League was guaranteed by the creator of the competition, Dubai-based businessman Shaji Ul Mulk. Two places in each squad, apart from Team Sri Lanka, were reserved for Emirati players; each was given a $10,000 deal, and one was guaranteed to play. In front of impressive crowds at Sharjah in December, Ghulam Shabbir of Punjabi Legends faced Mustafa's Kerala Kings in the final. Neither batted or bowled, though, as Kerala romped to victory.

DESERT T20 CHALLENGE IN 2016-17

1 Afghanistan 2 Ireland

Group A

At Abu Dhabi, January 14, 2017 (floodlit). **Afghanistan won by five wickets.** ‡**Ireland 125-6** (20 overs); **Afghanistan 126-5** (18.4 overs) (Najeeb Tarakai 31). *MoM:* Mohammad Nabi. *No one could exceed Paul Stirling's 25 in Ireland's below-par innings, and Afghanistan were rarely troubled in the chase.*

At Abu Dhabi, January 15, 2017 (floodlit). **United Arab Emirates won by six wickets.** ‡**Namibia 152-7** (20 overs) (J. P. Kotze 50, S. F. Burger 32; Mohammad Naveed 3-35); **United Arab Emirates 153-4** (20 overs) (Rohan Mustafa 56, Shaiman Anwar 53). *MoM:* Mohammad Naveed. *After Shaiman Anwar was run out with the scores level, Mohammad Usman hit the winning single off the last ball, from Jan Frylinck. Unlike all the others, Namibia's matches in this tournament were not official Twenty20 internationals, as they did not have the requisite status.*

At Abu Dhabi, January 16, 2017 (floodlit). **Afghanistan won by five wickets. United Arab Emirates 146-7** (20 overs) (Shaiman Anwar 52; Dawlat Zadran 4-44); ‡**Afghanistan 147-5** (18.5 overs) (Asghar Stanikzai 30, Samiullah Shenwari 42). *MoM:* Dawlat Zadran. *T20I debut:* Zahoor Khan (UAE).

At Abu Dhabi, January 17, 2017. **Ireland won by five wickets.** ‡**Namibia 146-9** (20 overs) (S. J. Baard 32, L. P. van der Westhuizen 50); **Ireland 149-5** (19.4 overs) (S. W. Poynter 38, G. C. Wilson 38*). *MoM:* K. J. O'Brien. *Like Namibia's previous match, this one went down to the last over, which started with Ireland needing eight: Andy McBrine hit Frylinck for four then, after two singles, smacked another boundary. Kevin O'Brien followed 2-21 with 22.*

At Dubai (Sports City), January 18, 2017. **Ireland won by 24 runs.** ‡**Ireland 160-6** (20 overs) (P. R. Stirling 39, K. J. O'Brien 40); **United Arab Emirates 136-7** (20 overs) (Amjad Javed 47*; W. B. Rankin 3-16). *MoM:* W. B. Rankin. *The UAE crashed to 21-5 in the fourth over, and never recovered.*

At Dubai (Sports City), January 19, 2017. **Afghanistan won by 64 runs.** ‡**Afghanistan 167-6** (20 overs) (Mohammad Shahzad 31, Nawroz Mangal 32, Asghar Stanikzai 31, Samiullah Shenwari 35; B. M. Scholtz 3-17); **Namibia 103** (19.2 overs) (Rashid Khan 3-4). *MoM:* Rashid Khan. *Two days after testing positive for the banned drug clenbuterol, Mohammad Shahzad hit 31, though he was not charged with violating the ICC's anti-doping code until April. Chasing eight an over, Namibia were 7-4 after three.*

AFGHANISTAN 6pts, IRELAND 4pts, United Arab Emirates 2pts, Namibia 0pts.

Group B

At Abu Dhabi, January 14, 2017. **Scotland won by 24 runs.** ‡**Scotland 189-3** (20 overs) (K. J. Coetzer 31, C. S. MacLeod 60, R. D. Berrington 60*); **Hong Kong 165-6** (20 overs) (Shahid Wasif 40, Ehsan Khan 42*). *MoM:* C. S. MacLeod. *Calum MacLeod and Richie Berrington added 127 for the third wicket in 12 overs, then MacLeod ran out Aizaz Khan before he had faced a ball in the first over of the chase.*

At Abu Dhabi, January 15, 2017. **Netherlands won by five wickets.** ‡**Oman 146-7** (20 overs) (Zeeshan Maqsood 34); **Netherlands 148-5** (19.2 overs) (M. J. G. Rippon 40, W. Barresi 48, R. E. van der Merwe 35*). *MoM:* M. J. G. Rippon. *T20I debut:* A. Poulose (Oman). *After Michael Rippon followed 1-15 with 40, Roelof van der Merwe carried the Netherlands to victory with 35* from 15 balls.*

At Abu Dhabi, January 16, 2017. **Oman won by seven wickets. Hong Kong 87** (18.3 overs) (Bilal Khan 3-18); ‡**Oman 89-3** (11 overs) (Aaqib Ilyas 56*). *MoM:* Bilal Khan. *Aaqib Ilyas blasted 56* from 30 balls, with 46 in boundaries, as Oman hurried to victory.*

At Abu Dhabi, January 17, 2017 (floodlit). **Scotland won by seven runs. Scotland 148-7** (20 overs) (R. D. Berrington 38); ‡**Netherlands 141** (19.2 overs) (M. J. G. Rippon 42; J. H. Davey 4-34). *MoM:* J. H. Davey.

At Dubai (Sports City), January 18, 2017 (floodlit). **Hong Kong won by 91 runs. ‡Hong Kong 183-4** (20 overs) (Nizakat Khan 59, A. Rath 44, Waqas Khan 33*); **Netherlands 92** (15.3 overs) (A. Rath 3-6). *MoM:* A. Rath. *Hong Kong's total was their highest in T20 internationals, beating 175-7 against Oman at Fatullah in February 2016.*

At Dubai (Sports City), January 19, 2017 (floodlit). **Scotland won by seven wickets. ‡Oman 133** (20 overs) (S. M. Sharif 3-33); **Scotland 134-3** (19 overs) (M. H. Cross 47, C. S. MacLeod 35*). *MoM:* M. H. Cross. *T20I debut:* C. B. Sole (Scotland). *Scotland maintained their 100% record, but Oman qualified as well on net run-rate.*

SCOTLAND 6pts, OMAN 2pts (NRR 0.89), Hong Kong 2pts (–0.005), Netherlands 2pts (–1.52).

Semi-final At Dubai (Sports City), January 20, 2017. **Afghanistan won by eight wickets. Oman 149-8** (20 overs) (Zeeshan Maqsood 33; Fareed Ahmad 3-35); **‡Afghanistan 150-2** (18.3 overs) (Mohammad Shahzad 80, Nawroz Mangal 34). *MoM:* Mohammad Shahzad. *Afghanistan always looked likely winners once Shahzad got going: he made 80 from 60 balls, and was out with 14 needed.*

Semi-final At Dubai (Sports City), January 20, 2017. **Ireland won by 98 runs. Ireland 211-6** (20 overs) (P. R. Stirling 60, S. W. Poynter 39, K. J. O'Brien 30, G. C. Wilson 65*); **‡Scotland 113** (15.1 overs) (K. J. Coetzer 40, M. H. Cross 35; G. H. Dockrell 3-28, J. Mulder 4-16). *MoM:* G. C. Wilson. *Stirling cracked 60 from 36 balls, and Gary Wilson 65* from 29, as Ireland amassed their second-highest total in T20 internationals, after 225-7 against Afghanistan in November 2013. Scotland's openers made a reasonable start, but from 72-1 nine wickets tumbled for 41, seven of them to slow left-armer George Dockrell and leg-spinner Jacob Mulder.*

Final At Dubai (Sports City), January 20, 2017 (floodlit). **Afghanistan won by ten wickets. ‡Ireland 71** (13.2 overs) (Mohammad Nabi 4-10); **Afghanistan 75-0** (7.5 overs) (Mohammad Shahzad 52*). *MoM:* Mohammad Nabi. *The final was a disappointment, as Afghanistan cruised to a ten-wicket victory after skittling Ireland for a paltry 71. Only Stirling (17) and Greg Thompson (10*) reached double figures. Afghanistan's former captain Nawroz Mangal, in his 81st and last official international before retiring, was in at the end, finishing with 17* as Shahzad sprinted to another half-century. "It's a very proud stage for me to retire," said Mangal, who had been allowed to carry out the toss in his last match.*

ONE-DAY TRI-SERIES IN 2016-17

At Abu Dhabi, January 22, 2017. **Hong Kong won by seven wickets. Scotland 205** (48.4 overs) (C. D. Wallace 53; Nadeem Ahmed 4-33); **‡Hong Kong 206-3** (44.2 overs) (Babar Hayat 79*). *MoM:* Babar Hayat. *ODI debuts:* C. L. McAuslan (Hong Kong); H. G. Munsey (Scotland). *Hong Kong won comfortably, thanks to Babar Hayat's 110-ball innings and his stand of 97* with Waqas Khan (35*).*

At Dubai (Sports City), January 24, 2017. **United Arab Emirates won by four wickets. ‡Scotland 173** (45.2 overs) (R. D. Berrington 50; Imran Haider 3-36, Zahoor Khan 3-17); **United Arab Emirates 174-6** (41.5 overs). *ODI debuts:* Adnan Mufti, Ghulam Shabbir, Imran Haider, Mohammad Qasim, Zahoor Khan (UAE). *A UAE side containing five format debutants looked in trouble at 39-4, chasing a modest 174, but regrouped well: Mohammad Usman (45) put on 62 with Adnan Mufti, who was still there with 43* when victory was secured.*

At Dubai (Sports City), January 26, 2017. **United Arab Emirates won by six wickets. Hong Kong 174** (48.5 overs) (Nizakat Khan 93; Imran Haider 4-25, Zahoor Khan 3-29); **‡United Arab Emirates 175-4** (38.1 overs) (Shaiman Anwar 50; Ehsan Khan 3-30). *MoM:* Imran Haider. *The UAE won their own tri-series, overhauling another middling target with ease. Nizakat Khan made 93 from 111 balls for Hong Kong, but no one else reached 30.*

UNITED ARAB EMIRATES v IRELAND IN 2016-17

First one-day international At Dubai (ICC Academy), March 2, 2017. **Ireland won by 85 runs. Ireland 270** (49.3 overs) (W. T. S. Porterfield 100, K. J. O'Brien 69; Mohammad Naveed 3-40, Zahoor Khan 6-34); **‡United Arab Emirates 185** (41.4 overs) (G. H. Dockrell 3-27). *MoM:* W. T. S. Porterfield. *William Porterfield's eighth ODI century, and a 53-ball burst from Kevin O'Brien, took Ireland to a lofty total. The UAE slipped from 93-2 to 112-7, and that was that.*

Second one-day international At Dubai (ICC Academy), March 4, 2017. **Ireland won by eight wickets. ‡United Arab Emirates 202** (47.5 overs) (C. A. Young 3-48, A. R. McBrine 3-42); **Ireland 203-2** (41.5 overs) (W. T. S. Porterfield 76, A. Balbirnie 58*). *MoM:* W. T. S. Porterfield. *Ireland won the series 2–0, with Porterfield again leading the way: he outscored the usually aggressive Paul Stirling (41) in an opening stand of 94.*

UNITED ARAB EMIRATES v PAPUA NEW GUINEA IN 2016-17

Papua New Guinea stayed on after their two World Cricket League matches against the UAE, and played a third ODI, which the home side won to take the series 2–1. After the Intercontinental Cup match between the sides, they then contested three Twenty20 internationals. For details of the Intercontinental Cup and WCL matches, see page 1069.

Third one-day international At Abu Dhabi, April 4, 2017. **United Arab Emirates won by 103 runs. ‡United Arab Emirates 251-9** (50 overs) (Rohan Mustafa 109; A. Vala 3-30); **Papua New Guinea 148** (35.2 overs) (Rohan Mustafa 5-25). *This match was a triumph for the UAE's captain Rohan Mustafa, who became only the third player – after Viv Richards and Paul Collingwood – to score a century and take a five-for in the same ODI. He had never previously taken more than three in an innings, or scored more than 43.*

First Twenty20 international At Abu Dhabi, April 12, 2017. **United Arab Emirates won by five wickets. Papua New Guinea 102** (18.2 overs) (M. D. Dai 31; Amjad Javed 3-12, Mohammad Naveed 3-24); **‡United Arab Emirates 108-5** (15.1 overs) (Shaiman Anwar 39). *T20I debut:* Sultan Ahmed (UAE). *PNG slumped to 23-4 in the eight over, and limped to 102, a total the UAE surpassed with ease.*

Second Twenty20 international At Abu Dhabi, April 14, 2017. **United Arab Emirates won by 30 runs. United Arab Emirates 180-3** (20 overs) (Shaiman Anwar 117*); **‡Papua New Guinea 150** (20 overs) (S. Bau 30, J. N. T. Vare 38; Amjad Javed 3-38, Mohammad Naveed 3-18). *Shaiman Anwar, who faced 68 balls and thumped ten fours and six sixes, hit the UAE's first century in Twenty20 internationals. Their total was also a national record, beating 179-4 against Afghanistan in Dubai in December 2016.*

Third Twenty20 international At Abu Dhabi, April 14, 2017. **United Arab Emirates won by five wickets. ‡Papua New Guinea 128-5** (20 overs) (L. Siaka 31); **United Arab Emirates 130-5** (19.1 overs) (Mohammad Usman 58, Rameez Shahzad 47; N. Vanua 3-35). *T20I debuts:* L. Sreekumar (UAE); D. Bau (PNG). *The UAE completed a clean sweep despite being 6-3 after seven deliveries: opener Laxman Sreekumar was lbw first ball on debut. Mohammad Usman and Rameez Shahzad righted the ship with a stand of 100.*

SCOTLAND v PAPUA NEW GUINEA IN THE UAE IN 2017-18

First one-day international At Dubai (Sports City), November 24, 2017. **Scotland won by six wickets. Papua New Guinea 147** (44.2 overs) (A. C. Evans 3-23, S. M. Sharif 4-38); **‡Scotland 148-4** (38.1 overs) (C. S. MacLeod 60*). *MoM:* C. S. MacLeod. *ODI debut:* K. Doriga (PNG). *Alasdair Evans and Safyaan Sharif reduced PNG to 10-5 after six overs. Captain Asad Vala (40) and the debutant Kiplin Doriga (34) put on 69, and PNG did well to reach 147 – but that caused Scotland few headaches.*

Second one-day international At Dubai (Sports City), November 25, 2017. **Scotland won by four wickets. Papua New Guinea 192-8** (50 overs) (M. R. J. Watt 3-21); **‡Scotland 196-6** (46.2 overs) (K. J. Coetzer 66; J. B. Reva 3-40). *MoM:* K. J. Coetzer. *ODI debut:* D. Ravu (PNG). *Another poor start – 51-4 in the 22nd over – sentenced PNG to another defeat.*

For the UAE's matches in the Intercontinental Cup and the World Cricket League, see page 1069.

CRICKET ROUND THE WORLD IN 2017

COMPILED BY JAMES COYNE AND TIMOTHY ABRAHAM

ICC WORLD CRICKET LEAGUE

Oman's third successive World Cricket League promotion left them one away from matching the feat of Afghanistan a decade earlier. A growing cricket infrastructure had helped them achieve back-to-back second-place finishes in Divisions Five and Four, and they finally got their hands on a trophy by winning Division Three in Uganda in May. They were proclaimed champions on countback, after the final against Canada was halted by rain. In 2014, USA and Bermuda players had threatened to pull out of a WCL tournament in Uganda, citing concerns about terror cells in Kampala, and forcing the event to be moved. This time, the only problem was the weather. The WCL needed success stories such as Oman if it was going to survive below two or three tiers.

It also came as a relief to ICC officials when the USA – given substantial backing by ICC Americas, despite the impending expulsion of the USA Cricket Association – clung on to Division Three status by defending 145 against Uganda. Fifteen of the 20 WCL tournaments had ended with a host nation promoted, so Uganda's relegation prompted soul-searching in the local press. The top two teams in Division Two in February 2018 would reach the World Cup Qualifier in Zimbabwe in March.

By the time eight teams (including five regional qualifiers) convened in South Africa for Division Five in September, they were all officially Associate nations, following the ICC's scrapping of Affiliate status in June. As expected, Jersey secured an immediate return to Division Four, as champions. Germany, probably the world's fastest-growing Associate nation (following Afghanistan's promotion to Full Membership), looked favourites to join Jersey from their group when they racked up 227 against Vanuatu, then reduced them to 58 for four.

That was the cue for an astonishing 139 from Patrick Matautaava, featuring eight sixes, which carried Vanuatu to victory and through on net run-rate, despite defeats in their first two games. They then chased down 184 to beat Italy in the semi-final, sealing their promotion. Italy, in the WCL since the start, face regional qualification.

The most eye-catching scores came in the WCL Asia Qualifier. China, who pick passport holders only, received predictable hammerings from Saudi Arabia (by 390 runs), Kuwait (293) and Qatar (265) – all sides full with South Asian immigrants. China even lost by ten wickets to Bhutan, another home-grown team. With the women's side also stagnating, it presented a dilemma for the ICC and MCC, who had both staked much on China's development. MCC, led by their World Cricket Committee chairman Mike Gatting, toured Shanghai and Hong Kong later in the year, and he sent his recommendations to the ICC's new head of global development, William Glenwright, who was putting together a renewed China strategy. JAMES COYNE

BRITISH VIRGIN ISLANDS

Incredibly – for anyone who saw pictures from the British Virgin Islands last autumn – cricket is still standing. Hurricane Irma tore through the territory on September 7, wrecking towns and killing four people. British foreign secretary Boris Johnson said the devastation reminded him of Hiroshima. Two weeks after Irma, Hurricane Maria brought more damage. The main cricket ground, on the biggest island, Tortola, was badly affected. The bleachers, fencing, and food and drink area have gone. The artificial wicket survived, but will need replacing. As of January 2018, "a lot of work" was needed to make the ground playable, according to Charlie Jackson, president of the BVI Cricket Association. "The future of the game here is totally dependent on a self-help process," he says. Even so, Jackson was hopeful the season would start in February, with a Ten10 tournament, then the regular T20 league.

Daniel Singh is a 45-year-old umpire who represented the BVI as wicketkeeper in two Stanford T20 tournaments (he was run out by future West Indies captain Darren Sammy in 2006). He lost his apartment and his furnishings, and his family had to move to the USA for two months. "The area was basically unlivable," he says. Although some people left the BVI after the hurricanes, Singh thinks most cricketers will return: "Quite a few work in construction, which is obviously booming now."

The BVI are part of the Leeward Islands Cricket Association, and in 2002 hosted a first-class game, against the Windwards, at the A. O. Shirley Recreation Ground on Tortola. This is the islands' main sports stadium and, like the cricket ground, was badly damaged. Hard-ball cricket hasn't been played there recently – a corporate tape-ball league has used it – but Singh hopes the repaired stadium may open its doors to T20 matches in future. Jackson is also optimistic: "Together, we can make sure cricket continues – stronger and more successfully than before." OWEN AMOS

CANADA

Pepper spray stopped play in the Toronto & District Cricket Association final at the end of September. Police were called after a skirmish broke out between supporters of Vikings and Centurions and, though no cricketers were involved, the spray wafted on to the pitch; curiously, it affected the players of one team only. Rather than waiting for the air to clear – it was a bright and pleasant day – the umpires declared a no-result and ordered a rematch the following week. That game ended even more bizarrely. With short autumnal days, a late start – caused by dew – was always likely to be problematic in a 50-over contest. It remains disputed by umpires and captains whether a reduction of overs was offered by the officials at the outset. As the match wound down, and DLS entered the frame, there were accusations of time-wasting. Inevitably, bad light had the final say and, with matters becoming heated, the umpires abdicated responsibility and turned the matter over to the TDCA. Such is the degree of politicking in Canadian cricket that they in turn reached out to ICC Americas for guidance. The TDCA were advised to look within for the answer, and the sorry matter eventually came to an end more than a week after the match, with the Championship shared – a result that pleased none and embarrassed all. Otherwise, Canada's national side put the brakes on years of decline by climbing out of WCL Division Three, following the return of Rizwan Cheema and the appointment of Henry Osinde as coach. And Cricket Canada kept the creative juices flowing with a proposal to pay people $C500 for identifying cricketing talent. A counter-proposal suggested by some fans to pay $500 for identifying new board members also proved popular. FARAZ SARWAT

CHILE

In late January 2017, wicketkeeper and volunteer firefighter José Tomás Andreu returned from Chile's extreme south in time for a match at Cencosud Oval, in the foothills of the Andes. Exhausted from fighting some of the worst forest fires in the country's recent history, Andreu was still able to take a smart leg-side catch. Unfortunately, he wasn't at the ground on July 23, when the pavilion went up in flames. A fire, cause unknown, raged overnight, reducing most of the country's cricket equipment to ashes. With the Junior South American Championships set to be held in Santiago three months later, Cricket Chile were left without stumps, bats or balls. The ground's only mower was destroyed too, while the windows, doors and walls were blackened by soot. In a country where cricket relies on a handful of volunteers, the inferno threatened to derail the season before it had started. But the crisis galvanised the cricket community, with players of all ages and nationalities coming together. Since then, there has been a resurgence in the sport, with the founding of a women's team, *Las Loicas*, who came third in the 2017 South American Championships in Buenos Aires. There was also a return to cricket's spiritual home at the Prince of Wales Country Club (which earned its name when the future Edward VIII visited Santiago with his brother George in 1925). A new ground will be inaugurated in the south of the country at Molina, which miraculously escaped the forest fires, though the scars of the July flames can still be seen on the charred helmets and blackened pads that survived. There is work to be done to the Cencosud Oval pavilion but, as cricket in Chile celebrates its bicentennial year, there are hopes it can return to its former glory. JOSEPH WILLIAMS

If you would like to contribute towards Cricket Chile's rebuilding effort, please email info@cricketchile.cl.

EASTER ISLAND

The *Tangata manu* – birdman – competition was well known on Easter Island. Entrants had to obtain the first sooty-tern egg of the season from the islet of Motu Nui, swim back to Easter Island and climb the dangerous cliff of Rano Kau to the village of Orongo. Competitors ran the risk of being eaten by sharks, slain by rivals or killed by a fall, but the winner would enjoy a lavish life for a year. So when Patricio Caamaño pitched up on Easter Island and invited some of the indigenous Rapu Nui to give cricket a whirl, the sport did not seem quite so bizarre. Caamaño, a Chilean cricketer, was visiting for an environmental study, and brought his bat and ball along to this remote outpost 2,000 miles from mainland Chile. As far back as 1825, sailors from HMS *Blossom* had played cricket in Valparaiso, near Caamaño's home in Viña del Mar. The famous Moai headstones, carved by the Rapu Nui, provided an unusual backdrop to the ad hoc games played during Caamaño's stay. He ensured the island's novice cricketers did not venture too close: in 2008, Finnish tourist Marko Kulju broke an earlobe off as a souvenir, prompting Easter Island's mayor to threaten to chop off Kulju's ear. A court later fined him $17,000. TIMOTHY ABRAHAM

ICELAND

"I think mainly about sex, death and cricket, probably in that order," said Sebastian Faulks on the evening news on RUV, Iceland's national television station. It was September, and he was being interviewed as a member of the Authors XI, captained by Charlie Campbell, who were about to take on the national team. The tale of the three-match series for the Halldór Laxness Trophy, named in honour of the great Icelandic writer, had three stark chapters: a slaying in the first; a bout of moderate bodily harm in the second; and a consolation win for the visitors in the third. Cricket in Iceland is, in truth, a faltering saga. The historian and Authors player Tom Holland told RUV he found a possible reference to a forerunner of cricket in the 13th-century *Egil's Saga*, which mentions *knattleikr*. It involved hitting a hard ball with a stick, and could be played for days.

In 1944, the RAF had beaten a Royal Navy side in two matches in Reykjavik. Modern Icelandic cricket, though, was founded in 2000 by Ragnar Kristinsson and Kari Olafsson, who formed the Kylfan and Glaumur teams. Glaumur, from Stykkisholmer, over 100 miles north of Reykjavik, claimed to be the most northerly club in the world. They combined to form Iceland's first national side, beating a team brought by English barrister Jonathan Rule. A third domestic side, from the Tryggingamidstodin insurance company, were created in 2001. Two years later, a team of bankers known as the Effigies toured Iceland, with Henry Blofeld in the party, arriving on an aeroplane piloted by Iron Maiden lead singer Bruce Dickinson. They played a game under the midnight sun, and another on a glacier which could be reached only by snowmobile. A fallow period followed, though the Fellowship of Fairly Odd Places CC did arrive from the Netherlands in 2011. It was another four years before the current group of players breathed new life into Icelandic cricket, among them Lee Nelson, Iceland's only professional circus clown. In 2017, Iceland toured England, and as well as the Authors – whose players sampled Icelandic delicacies of seal and puffin during a visit that coincided with the Reykjavik Literary Festival – there were visits by three other English clubs. KIT HARRIS

ISRAEL

Naomi Eytan, a 14-year-old Israeli girl, found herself at the centre of a storm during the 2017 Maccabiah Games. A Tel Aviv District Court ruling backed the decision of the Games' organising committee preventing Eytan, the only female in Israel's Under-19 team, from taking her place in the squad for the junior cricket competition at the Maccabiah – where Jewish athletes compete for international sides. The Maccabiah had concerns over her safety. "Just a couple of years ago an Israeli umpire [Hillel Awasker] was killed when he was hit by a ball," Games chairman Amir Peled told the *Jewish Chronicle*. "We have our regulations and we cannot allow mixed teams." Eytan's attorney, Gali Etzion, was concerned that the court had reached its decision partly due to cricket terminology: the court cited the terms "12th and 13th man" – routinely used in both men's and women's cricket. The Maccabiah Games committee quoted a passage from the ICC's own Gender Recognition Policy: "Because of the significant advantages in size, strength and power enjoyed (on average) by males over females from puberty onwards… it is necessary to have separate competition categories for males and females in order to preserve the safety, fairness and integrity of the sport." However, ICC Europe development manager Ed Shuttleworth backed Eytan's selection: "If there is no female team it would seem logical to have a meritocratic system where if a player is good enough – irrespective of gender – they can participate." Separate men's and women's tournaments would appear to be desirable if ICC development officers are to achieve their aim of a 50/50 gender split in newcomers to cricket by 2023. Israel Cricket Association chairman Steve Leigh contributed an affidavit to Eytan's petition, and said he had no fears over her ability to handle the boys' game. As for Eytan, she declared: "I'm an athlete and I'll always be one. My way of proving I am equal to the boys is to continue training and participate in the European Championships. No judge's decision can break me." JAMES COYNE

ITALY

In Parco Mignone, on the banks of the Adige river in sleepy Bolzano, the signs have gone up: "No Cricket". Mayor Renzo Caramaschi banned the sport in the city's parks after a two-year-old child was left concussed from being struck on the head by a ball. He was on the family's balcony which overlooked the park. The game has been played in the city, a gateway to the Dolomites with a substantial German-speaking population, for a decade, with the initially small number of immigrants having founded Südtirol Alto Adige CC. However, with around 1,000 cricket-crazy Pakistani and Afghan immigrants now in Bolzano, there are more impromptu games. Tennis courts and a baseball diamond are now the only permitted places for cricket. SONJA REITERER

MONGOLIA

Mongolia welcomed their first two touring teams to the new Friendship Cricket Ground, when Craigengower and Lamma Island visited from Hong Kong in July. The tourists won all their matches, which included the ground's first century – and its first hat-trick, gratifyingly taken by a Mongolian. A much-improved outfield meant it was finally possible to score runs along the ground.

The venue is a work in progress, and the Mongolian Amateur Cricket Association are hoping to buy a small tractor, rollers and a chain harrow. An embryonic league was introduced, with the teams all inspired by local fauna – Marmot Union (the 2017 champions), Tiger Union, Bogd Khan Wolves, and Eagles, who are made up of Mongolian students at the Law and Order University. The Australian embassy generously provided funding and a coach, Rob Moran, with G. Anand and J. Davaa recruited as his Mongolian assistants. Anand had a sporting (but not cricketing) background, and your correspondent was given the task of teaching him the game from scratch – as rewarding as it was challenging. Moran took sessions at schools, orphanages and the International Children's camp at Nairamdal, a former Soviet-style retreat still popular in Ulan Bator. In all, Moran coached more than 1,400 kids, as well as seven sports teachers. There was valuable support from donors old and new – most crucially, Oyu Tolgoi, Mongolia's largest copper- and gold-mining company. It will help fund a pavilion to provide dressing-rooms and first-aid facilities. An application for second-hand kit was approved by the Lord's Taverners, and manufacturer John Surridge – the creator of Graham Gooch's famous SS Turbo and Clive Rice's SS Jumbo – donated prototypes used to develop their top-of-the-range Swannack bats. ADAM HOQUE

Adam Hoque is the secretary of the Mongolian Amateur Cricket Association. Contact him on adamulhoque@yahoo.com to enquire about possible fixtures.

RWANDA

A heavy shower almost put paid to the biggest event in Rwanda's short cricket history. The storm broke on October 28, just after president Paul Kagame had arrived to formally open the new ground at Gahanga, overlooking the Kigali hills. Miraculously, Marshallah Dube, the 37-year-old Zimbabwean groundsman, got the pitch playable for the official opening match. "We worked like Trojans," he said, looking out across what a few hours earlier had been a flooded field. "The pitch played beautifully, and I am glad of that."

The £1m ground has a dramatic backdrop and a unique cone-shaped pavilion devised by Earth Light Designs. Perhaps just as important is Dube's grass square, which provides Rwanda with strips of international standard, and the best cricket facility in Africa north of the Limpopo. Herschelle Gibbs rated it the third-most beautiful venue he had played at, after Dharamsala in the Himalayas and his home ground of Newlands.

In front of scores of cricket lovers, and an equal number of mystified locals, Michael Vaughan's XI ran up 184 for six, with England batsman Sam Billings treating the crowd to 49. Their total was overhauled by Gibbs's XI, with a crucial 56 from Kenya's Steve Tikolo. It ended a week of celebratory cricket involving five British and three African teams, with a Uganda Select XI beating Christopher Shale's XI in the final by six wickets; Roger Mukasa's 51 not out earned him the match award, presented by the Duchess of York.

But the real point was to promote cricket as a vehicle for co-operation and social cohesion between people who, as recently as 1994, were at war. As

Rwanda has risen from genocide, so has cricket. This former Belgian colony has joined the Commonwealth and adopted English as an official language – and the economy is opening up. It was Christopher Shale, the chairman of the West Oxfordshire Conservative Association, and a close friend of David Cameron, who saw the potential for cricket in Rwanda, and set the wheels in motion. He died in 2011. His son Alby, 27, is now project director of the Rwanda Cricket Stadium Foundation and its offshoot, Cricket Builds Hope, which he hopes to turn into a development arm in other countries, aiming to succeed where the ICC have faltered. COLIN MACBETH

SERBIA

Migrants using the Balkan route through Serbia to try to reach the EU face intimidating borders at Croatia and Hungary. Most are doomed to stay in the 17 asylum centres scattered throughout Serbia. Since the majority of those in the centres (10,000 in May 2017, falling to 4,000 by September) are from Afghanistan or Pakistan, the Serbian Commissariat for Refugees and Migrations approached the Serbian Cricket Federation to provide relief from the tedium. The SCF started twice-weekly tape-ball sessions in three asylum centres, Krnjača and Obrenovac (both near Belgrade) and Sombor – cities with established cricket clubs and coaches. The Belgrade camps have up to 1,000 people, and Obrenovac, a former Yugoslav Army barracks, has sports facilities. One curiosity is that Bodrog Deers CC, based in the village of Bački Monoštor, seven miles from Sombor, are made up of local Roma, and their chairman Ivan Civric coaches in the centre. Only a tiny percentage of the migrant cricketers wished to apply for asylum in Serbia, so were ineligible to participate in the domestic leagues. But the Obrenovac tape-ball tournament was a massive event, with Afghan Champions beating Kabul Kings by five wickets in the final. Krnjača, a slightly smaller camp, fielded two teams at the home ground of Serbian cricket, Lisičji Jarak Oval, where Prince's XI beat Hasrat's XI in the first match many of the Afghans had played using a leather ball and full equipment. Prince, an all-rounder from Kabul, is now playing for Dunav CC. Basic equipment was provided to all camps by the Lord's Taverners, though later in the season than had been hoped, after the administrative delays that abound in the Balkans. VLADIMIR NINKOVIĆ

Vladimir Ninković is the general secretary of the Serbian Cricket Federation.

SWEDEN

Bradford League club New Farnley paid for the Sweden captain Mitchell O'Connor to fly in from Stockholm for most weekends of the 2017 season. A 33-year-old Australian with an EU passport, O'Connor did not need a visa to enter at Leeds Bradford Airport, so came and went for ten games. He had been approached by New Farnley's cricket manager, Paul Hutchison, the former England A seamer who doubles as Sweden's national coach and kit supplier.

VIETNAM

The Test cricketer who served in Vietnam

CHARLES FELLOWS-SMITH

More than 50 years ago, Australian involvement in the Vietnam War was at its peak. In 1967, at Phan Rang airbase, Ninh Thuan province, a squadron of the Royal Australian Air Force were attached to one from the US Air Force, and conducting operations against Communist forces in the Central Highlands. Vietnam was a part of French Indochina, and there was no cricket – until the Australians arrived.

The two sets of airmen organised a cricket challenge to compete, not for the Ashes but the Cinders – a trophy fashioned from the starting cartridge of a Canberra bomber and a 20mm cannon shell. Predictably, the Australians prevailed. Photographs show more organised cricket (and Aussie Rules football) played at an ordnance depot in the port of Vung Tau, 75 miles south-east of Saigon. The depot is now known as the Lam Son Stadium, and hosts weekly greyhound races.

The draft had been introduced in 1964, and over the next eight years more than 60,000 national servicemen were called up. Among these "nashos" was Doug Walters, who as a teenager made 155 on Test debut against England at the Gabba in December 1965. Although he missed the 1966-67 South Africa tour for military training, Walters was exempted from Vietnam service in order to pursue his cricket career.

Tony Dell was one of over 15,000 Australians who did serve in Vietnam, and is believed to be the only surviving Test cricketer to have seen active service. He was born in Hampshire, but moved to Queensland with his family and, aged 19, was called up. From May 1967 to the following March, he served with an infantry battalion in southern Vietnam. On return to Brisbane, Dell established himself as a tall left-arm fast bowler in the Queensland side and, by February 1971, made his Test debut. At the SCG, he opened the bowling with Dennis Lillee in the decisive Seventh Test of the 1970-71 Ashes (when Ray Illingworth led his team off the field to avoid being hit by bottles and cans thrown from the crowd). Dell claimed five wickets in the match, but England regained the urn. He also played in New Zealand's first official Test in Australia, in 1973-74, dismissing Glenn Turner.

But that proved the end of Dell's international career, and dark moods later cost him a job at a Brisbane advertising agency. In 2008, he was finally diagnosed with post-traumatic stress disorder. He remembers only fragments of his military service: "My PTS has wiped out most of my memory of Vietnam and my cricket career. I have visions of playing games in among the tents at Nui Dat, but that's all." Ruefully, he says: "Twelve months in Vietnam was good training to be in Ian Chappell's dressing-room."

Dell now devotes his time to Stand Tall for PTS, a charity providing support for those affected, and to raising awareness – and reducing the stigma – of the condition. In January 2015, Stand Tall were the official charity partners of the Prime Minister's XI in the traditional fixture against England at Canberra.

These days, cricket in Vietnam has a little more infrastructure. The Vietnam Cricket Association, based in Ho Chi Minh City (formerly Saigon), run a T20 competition for clubs organised by national background. In the 2017 final, Sri Lanka Sports Club defeated Indian Cricket Club Saigon by two wickets. A new ground is being developed in District Nine of the city, a little distance from the Royal Melbourne Institute of Technology.

O'Connor had been out of the game for four years before being cajoled into a return with Stockholm's Akademiska Cricketällskap in 2016, and went on to average 98 on Sweden's artificial tracks, including a Twenty20 double-hundred. In West Yorkshire, he hit an unbeaten 168 against East Bierley on debut in the Priestley Cup. Hutchison saw the experience as good grass-wicket practice for the ICC European Championship that took place in the Netherlands in June. And, though O'Connor bagged two ducks and a four, his unbeaten 70 against Germany helped Sweden finish second to them overall. EVAN DAHLIN

USA

For most of their modern existence, the USA Cricket Association have been memorable for inactivity – often through their own choice. However, inactivity became a virtual mandate in 2017, when the ICC finally decided to pull the plug, ending 52 years as the official governing body. After two years in limbo – serving their third suspension since the millennium – USACA could not find a way back, primarily because they refused to ratify an ICC-approved constitution.

A major sticking point was the requirement for officials to have a limit on how long they could spend in post. Such a reform would have ended Gladstone Dainty's chequered reign as USACA president, a position he has held since 2003. Eventually, the ICC got their wish, courtesy of a unanimous vote at June's annual conference in London. Dainty had hinted at legal action if USACA were expelled, but nothing had happened by the start of 2018. It looked like the end of the road.

More quietly, the rival American Cricket Federation's website shut down late in the year, perhaps signalling the culmination of their brief but significant existence. The ACF were formed by a group of leagues which felt disenfranchised by USACA. ACF figureheads gained key positions on ICC advisory committees as a new governing body, USA Cricket, prepared for elections that would allow them to take over from ICC caretaker staff in the spring of 2018. And before 2017 was out, USA Cricket's constitution was agreed.

One of the final acts before USACA's expulsion had been the national side's underwhelming performance in WCL Division Three, despite specialist coaching input from Trevor Penney and Beau Casson: their slim chances of reaching the 2019 World Cup had gone. The revived women's team were given special dispensation to play in the European event of the Women's World T20 Qualifier, but Scotland and the Netherlands proved too strong.

Steven Taylor's acceptance of a first-class contract with Jamaica meant he was replaced as captain by Ibrahim Khaleel, a 35-year-old wicketkeeper who had played for Hyderabad in the Ranji Trophy. He began his tenure in style, leading his adopted homeland to a series victory over Canada in the three-match Auty Cup held in King City, Ontario – USA's first victory since 1991.

The Caribbean Premier League returned to south Florida. But after sell-out crowds for the weekend double-header in 2016, local support was dreadful in year two. Central Broward Regional Park, Lauderhill, was well under half-full for the opening weekend in August, and just a few hundred turned up for the first ball on the second day, as fans baulked at a 50% increase in the ticket price of most seats. It led to another hefty financial loss in Florida for the CPL, casting into doubt the viability of a US-based franchise.

West Indies matches, on the other hand, have been a success in Florida. Following a sold-out weekend of Twenty20 internationals against India back in 2016, an agreement was announced for a West Indies–Pakistan series in 2018. Peter Della Penna

GLOBAL TOURNAMENTS

ICC WORLD CRICKET LEAGUE

Tournament	*Date*	*Winner*	*Runner-up*	*Others (in finishing order)*
Division Three	May	Oman	Canada	Singapore, USA, Uganda, Malaysia
Division Five	Sep	Jersey	Vanuatu	Qatar, Italy, Germany, Guernsey, Ghana, Cayman Islands

REGIONAL MEN'S TOURNAMENTS

Tournament	*Date*	*Winner*	*Runner-up*	*Others (in finishing order)*
WCL Africa Qualifier	Apr	Ghana	Botswana	Tanzania, Nigeria, Zambia, Sierra Leone
WCL Americas Qualifier	Mar	Cayman Islands	Argentina	
WCL Asia Qualifier	Apr/May	Qatar	Saudi Arabia	Bahrain, Kuwait, Thailand, Bhutan, China
WCL East Asia–Pacific Qualifier	Feb	Vanuatu	Fiji	Samoa, Philippines, Indonesia, Japan
WCL Europe Qualifier	Jun	Germany	Sweden	Norway, Austria, Belgium, France
Southeast Asian Games 50-over	Aug	Malaysia	Singapore	Thailand, Myanmar, Indonesia
Southeast Asian Games T20	Aug	Singapore	Malaysia	Indonesia, Thailand, Myanmar, Vietnam

WOMEN'S TOURNAMENTS

Tournament	*Date*	*Winner*	*Runner-up*	*Others (in finishing order)*
World T20 Africa Qualifier	Sep	Uganda	Zimbabwe	Kenya, Namibia, Tanzania
World T20 Asia Qualifier	Nov	Thailand	UAE	Nepal, Hong Kong, Malaysia, China
World T20 East Asia–Pacific Qualifier	Apr/May	PNG	Samoa	Vanuatu, Japan
World T20 Europe–Americas Qualifier	Aug	Scotland	Netherlands	USA
East Asia Cup T20	Sep	Hong Kong	Japan	China, South Korea
Southeast Asian Games T20	Aug	Thailand	Indonesia	Malaysia, Singapore

PART SIX

Overseas Domestic Twenty20 Cricket

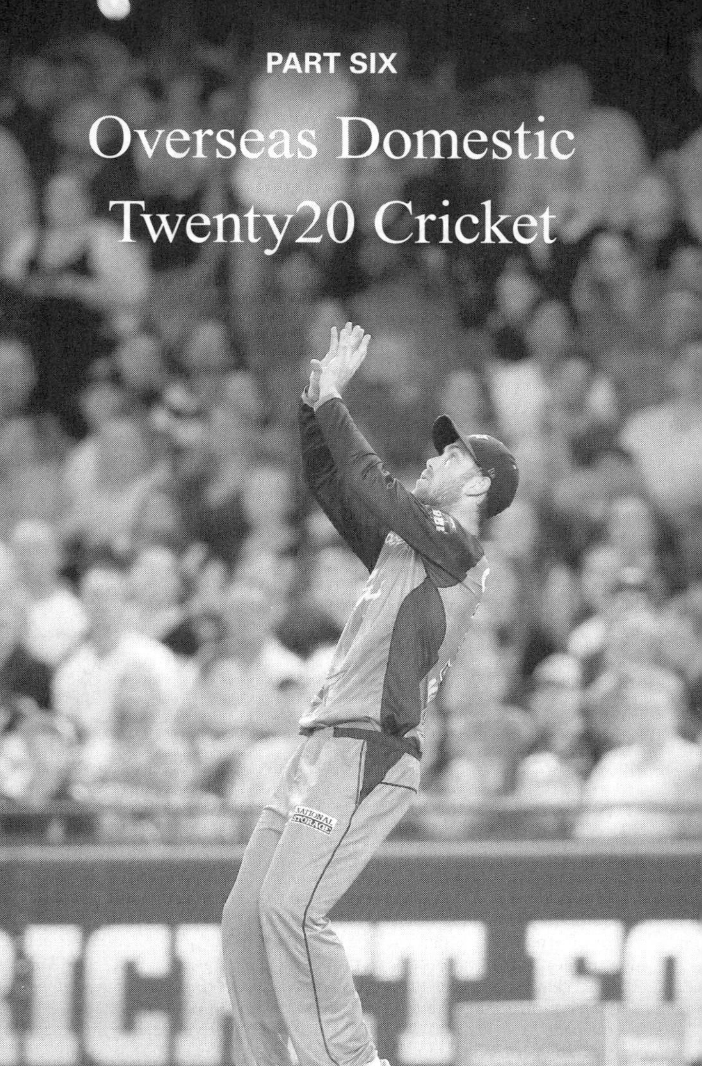

OVERSEAS DOMESTIC T20 CRICKET IN 2016-17

FREDDIE WILDE

This was a landmark year for domestic T20 cricket. The sale of the Indian Premier League broadcasting rights to Star India for £1.97bn over five years confirmed just how stratospheric the tournament had become. Each IPL match was now worth £6.56m, more than an Indian home international, and comparable to market leaders across all domestic sports events.

The T20 calendar was packed. Despite the postponement of two tournaments in 2017 – one in South Africa because it lacked a television deal, one in Zimbabwe because it lacked players – only June and October did not feature a major competition. And the schedule was only going to get tighter: England announced plans to launch their city-based tournament in 2020. But if there was a familiar group of players and coaches funnelling around the circuit, each league managed to retain a unique flavour.

Run-rates have risen steadily since T20 cricket began, and in 2017 broke eight an over around the world for the first time. Improvements in technique and physical strength were enhanced by tactical shifts: teams recognised that

ROLL OF HONOUR

	Winner	
Bangladesh Premier League	Dhaka Dynamites	Nov–Dec 2016
CSA T20 Challenge (South Africa)	Titans	Nov–Dec 2016
Super Smash (New Zealand)	Wellington Firebirds	Dec 2016–Jan 2017
Big Bash League (Australia)	Perth Scorchers	Dec 2016–Jan 2017
Pakistan Super League (UAE/Pakistan)	Peshawar Zalmi	Feb–Mar 2017
Indian Premier League	Mumbai Indians	Apr–May 2017
Caribbean Premier League (West Indies)	Trinbago Knight Riders	Jul–Aug 2017
T20 Blast (England)	Notts Outlaws	Jul–Sep 2017

maximising the powerplay mattered more than whether they lost wickets. It led to the resurgence of the pinch-hitter, typified by off-spinner Sunil Narine. Having faced less than two balls per match before 2017, he was employed successfully as an opener in the Big Bash League, the Caribbean Premier League and the IPL, where he hit a fifty in 15 balls, the fastest in the tournament's history.

New Zealand's Super Smash (with a run-rate of 8.59) and England's T20 Blast (8.61), were the fastest-scoring tournaments. But nowhere was the powerplay more important than the CPL, where sluggish pitches and heavy dew meant runs became scarcer through the innings. The Trinbago Knight Riders, with Narine and the New Zealand duo of Brendon McCullum and Colin Munro forming the top three, were deserving winners. The star of the tournament, however, was St Kitts & Nevis Patriots' Evin Lewis, who outshone his opening partner and idol Chris Gayle for brutal power-hitting, including 97 not out off 32 balls against Barbados Tridents.

The BBL confirmed the talent of Chris Lynn, who blitzed 309 runs off 174 balls in five matches, before injury brought a premature end to the media-stoked "Lynnsanity". He was perhaps the purest hitter in the game, with a lean frame that seems to produce greater oopmh than more muscular players. Later in the year, he opened the batting with Narine for Kolkata Knight Riders in the IPL, and together they cracked a record 105 from the powerplay against Royal Challengers Bangalore. It stood for less than two months, before Nottinghamshire's Alex Hales and Riki Wessels bettered it by a run.

This put a premium on effective bowlers, with leg-spin sensation Rashid Khan soaring to prominence. He became the first of two Afghans (along with Mohammad Nabi) to play in the IPL, and lit up the tournament with a quick arm and a deadly googly. Later, he took the CPL's first hat-trick, all with wrong'uns. In all, he claimed 80 T20 wickets in 2017.

Mumbai Indians were the best bowling side in the IPL, and claimed their third trophy, after defending just 129 in the final. At their core were the Pandya brothers, seamer Hardik and left-arm spinner Krunal. Their batting was also brilliant and, in the absence of Andre Russell – given a one-year suspension in January 2017 after failing to file his whereabouts to an anti-doping commission – they laid claim to being T20's premier all-rounders.

The Perth Scorchers' low-key squad flew under the radar for most of the BBL, but swept to the title thanks to pace-bowling strength. This was their third title in the competition's six years, making them one of the T20 era's first great teams.

The UAE-based PSL was nearly derailed by a match-fixing scandal on the opening day of its second season. The Pakistan board acted swiftly, banning two players for five years and punishing four others for failing to report corrupt approaches, and an entertaining tournament provided a much-needed antidote. Once more, some wonderful young talent was unearthed, with fast bowler Hasan Ali and leg-spinning all-rounder Shadab Khan the best. The final, held in Lahore, was a joyous occasion, though Quetta Gladiators' overseas contingent refused to play because of security concerns. If it detracted from the spectacle, Peshawar Zalmi were not bothered, romping to a convincing victory thanks to another strong and balanced attack.

Player safety threatened the Bangladesh Premier League, after a terrorist attack in Dhaka in July 2016. The Professional Cricketers' Association warned English players against participating, while the Federation of International Cricketers' Association were similarly inclined. But, in the age of freelance cricketers, the advice was largely unheeded, and the tournament went ahead without incident. Well-used pitches produced intriguing, if low-scoring matches, with Dhaka Dynamites finishing convincing winners.

Perhaps the most heart-warming moment of the year came in the final of South Africa's T20 Challenge. Warriors had left themselves seven off the last ball, but Titans' Malusi Siboto, tearful with emotion, delivered a wide. A torturous wait ensued as he composed himself, before he closed out the match with a dot. He screamed with joy, shed more tears and later embraced his mother in the crowd. There might be soul in this game after all.

Coverage of the 2017 T20 Blast can be found on page 651.

THE LEADING TWENTY20 CRICKETER IN 2017

Rashid Khan

TIM WIGMORE

When the first professional game of Twenty20 took place in 2003, Rashid Khan was a four-year-old in Afghanistan. His ascent speaks of the extraordinary changes brought about by the format. In short, he embodies the democratisation of cricket. It has always been besotted with hierarchies – from the Gentlemen against the Players to the distinction between Full and Associate Members of the ICC. Yet the T20 ecosystem revolves around domestic leagues, so it doesn't care where cricketers are from – only their quality.

Rashid also reflects the importance of his trade in the 20-over game. During T20's first forays, it was blithely assumed that, with short boundaries, and batsmen on the attack, leg-spinners would become as defunct as cassettes. Instead, they have proved more sought-after than any other type of bowler. And those who are thriving are not purveyors of dour, wicket-to-wicket, risk-free fare. They are the ones with the best variations, able to prevent batsmen lining them up.

Most of all, there is Rashid's skill. He is both shaped by leg-spin's traditions – as a boy, he looked up to Mushtaq Ahmed and Anil Kumble – and in sync with its new age. He has many traits of the classical leggie. He can beat batsmen in the air and off the pitch. And while he has a fine stock ball, his most potent delivery is a sharp-turning googly, disguised as well as a poker player concealing a royal flush. As with Pakistan's Shadab Khan and West Indies' Samuel Badree, Rashid bowls quickly for one of his kind, regularly passing 60mph, which means batsmen are reluctant to use their feet. He is brilliantly flexible – equally at home in the powerplay, the middle overs or at the death – and adroit in shielding a short boundary. He is also shrewd, relying not just on his natural talent, but on footage and data analysis.

Rashid is imbued with a chutzpah that enables him to thrive in new environments. Last year, he made the transition from Associate into a $600,000 bowler in the IPL. He performed marvellously in India, then excelled in leagues in the Caribbean – where he took a hat-trick exclusively with those googlies – Bangladesh and Australia. The analysts demystified him, but they could not stop him bamboozling opponents.

T20 bowlers tend to divide into those who seek to contain and those who pursue wickets. In 2017, Rashid was a world leader in both. He took 80 wickets in the format at 14 apiece, with an economy-rate of just 5.53. The next best, Sunil Narine, managed 62; only Dwayne Bravo – 87 in 2016 – had taken more in a calendar year. And Rashid is still a teenager. He is shaping up as the Muttiah Muralitharan of T20, setting records that may never be surpassed.

As a young Afghan leg-spinner who has become the most coveted bowler in the format, Rashid encapsulates T20's new possibilities. More than anyone, he is a beneficiary of the new landscape – and a harbinger of its future.

Mark Brake, Getty Images

The Leading Twenty20 Cricketer in the World in 2017: Rashid Khan.

KFC T20 BIG BASH LEAGUE IN 2016-17

WILL MACPHERSON

1 Perth Scorchers   2 Sydney Sixers

Perth Scorchers' triumph – their third in the competition's six seasons – marked the end of the first era of the Big Bash League. The day before the final, Cricket Australia announced the BBL would grow from 35 games to 43, taking in more venues. But, for now, there would be no new teams, and the tournament would not stretch beyond the successful confines of the six-week school holiday period. The Scorchers' dominance of that first era was borne out by a one-sided triumph over **Sydney Sixers**. It was their fifth final – their fourth at home – and a repeat of the first (when the Sixers prevailed). And in victory the Scorchers overturned an odd jinx: no team had previously won the BBL after topping the table.

They were by some distance the strongest squad, and coach Justin Langer seemed intent on building a dynasty. This was illustrated by the central roles played in the final by Michael Klinger – the league's all-time top run-scorer who, at 36, enjoyed his most prolific season yet – and Jhye Richardson. They were 16 years apart in age, but within three weeks both had gained maiden international call-ups. The success of the Scorchers was all the more remarkable given that Jason Behrendorff, Nathan Coulter-Nile and Joel Paris did not bowl a single ball, while the Marsh brothers missed games on Australia duty.

The 2017 final might have been the last BBL game at the WACA since the hulking Perth Stadium was planned to stage future matches; the Scorchers will hope they can take their daunting spirit with them. It felt appropriate that Mitchell Johnson, a fearsome practitioner at the old ground, should give such a menacing performance as they bade farewell: his final three games of the season brought combined figures of six for 31 from 12 overs, including an inspired spell in the semi-final to scatter Melbourne Stars' top three.

Meanwhile **Brisbane Heat**, reborn under the leadership of Brendon McCullum, lost a cracking semi-final against the Sixers – but only after a super over. Brisbane fielded their talisman Chris Lynn for just five games because of injury, although that was enough for him to be named Player of the Tournament for 309 runs, including 26 sixes, seven more than anyone else. Eleven came in a brilliant unbeaten 98 that sped Brisbane to victory at the WACA. Lynn and McCullum (who totalled 323) drew record crowds to the Gabba, which sold out for the first time in ten years.

Overall, 20 of the 35 games attracted full houses; the average crowd topped 30,000 for the first time; a million fans flocked to the BBL for the second successive summer; and average TV viewing figures also scaled one million. The competition's march to the heart of the southern summer continued, so the announcement of expansion came as no surprise.

The standard of cricket, however, was not always vintage. It did not help that teams were weakened by Australian call-ups at inopportune moments –

the January ODIs and the BBL appear on a collision course – and the catching was poor. But the teams were evenly matched: in the pool stages, none won more than five matches, or fewer than three. It took 27 of the 32 group fixtures for the first side to be knocked out, and 28 for one to make the semis. Anyone really could beat anyone.

Sydney Thunder, the defending champions, lost their opening four matches and finished bottom. They had to settle for providing memorable vignettes. Against the Stars, Eoin Morgan smote the last ball of the game – and his last before joining England in India – for a sweet straight six. Then, having easily beaten the Hurricanes, they limited the Sixers to 99 at the SCG to win with ten overs to spare. It was a crushing defeat for the Sixers, who were either excellent or excruciating, though the bowling of Sean Abbott, whose bag of variations made him top wicket-taker with 20, was central to their victories.

Adelaide Strikers, yet to reach a final, were disappointing, though not Ben Dunk: after joining from **Hobart Hurricanes** (in a horribly lopsided trade for Hamish Kingston), he walloped 364 runs. The Hurricanes themselves again failed to make the semis, but a champagne moment came when Ben McDermott – son of Craig – scored 114 from 52 balls to help accomplish a target of 223 against **Melbourne Renegades**.

That was one of several near-misses for the Renegades, a team that will just not quite click, though they beat their rivals **Melbourne Stars** for the first time in four years. The Stars made the semis before being razed by Johnson, but theirs was a frustrating season, with their top-heavy batting badly hampered by international call-ups. As the tournament's opening era came to an end, so did the career of one of its finest servants, the Stars' captain David Hussey.

KFC T20 BIG BASH LEAGUE

	Played	*Won*	*Lost*	*Points*	*Net run-rate*
PERTH SCORCHERS	8	5	3	10	0.61
BRISBANE HEAT	8	5	3	10	0.51
SYDNEY SIXERS	8	5	3	10	–0.84
MELBOURNE STARS	8	4	4	8	0.39
Melbourne Renegades	8	4	4	8	0.04
Adelaide Strikers	8	3	5	6	0.33
Hobart Hurricanes	8	3	5	6	–0.53
Sydney Thunder	8	3	5	6	–0.60

Teams tied on points were separated on net run-rate.

First semi-final At Perth, January 24, 2017 (floodlit). **Perth Scorchers won by seven wickets. Melbourne Stars 136-8** (20 overs) (S. E. Gotch 48; M. G. Johnson 3-3); ‡**Perth Scorchers 139-3** (16.5 overs) (S. M. Whiteman 31, S. E. Marsh 56*). *Mitchell Johnson, who conceded only three singles in his four-over spell, reduced the Stars to 0-2, then 21-3. The Stars' Kevin Pietersen, who was miked up in the field, was fined $A5,000 for his on-air description of an umpiring decision as "an absolute shocker".*

Second semi-final At Brisbane, January 25, 2017 (floodlit). **Sydney Sixers won an eliminator over, following a tie. Brisbane Heat 167-9** (20 overs) (B. B. McCullum 46; S. A. Abbott 4-40, N. M. Lyon 4-23); ‡**Sydney Sixers 167-8** (20 overs) (D. P. Hughes 46, M. C. Henriques 64). *Chasing 168, the Sixers looked in control at 133-2 in the 15th over, but Brisbane fought back to force an eliminator over: the Sixers made 22-0 (Henriques 18* in 5 balls), and Brisbane 15-0.*

CHEAPEST FOUR-OVER RETURNS IN TWENTY20 CRICKET

4–22–2–4	U. W. M. B. C. A. Welagedara	Tamil Union v Sinhalese at Colombo (CCC)	2014-15
4–23–2–2	C. H. Morris	Lions v Cape Cobras at Johannesburg	2014-15
4–21–3–3	**M. G. Johnson**	**Perth Scorchers v Melbourne Stars at Perth**	**2016-17**
4–21–3–2	Zulfiqar Babar	Multan Tigers v Quetta Bears at Lahore	2012-13
4–22–3–1	Shoaib Malik	Barbados v Antigua at North Sound	2013
4–21–3–0	S. P. Narine	Guyana v Antigua at St George's	2014

FINAL

PERTH SCORCHERS v SYDNEY SIXERS

At Perth, January 28, 2017 (floodlit). Perth Scorchers won by nine wickets. Toss: Perth Scorchers.

As in their previous two outings – a demolition of Hobart Hurricanes in the group stage and the Johnson-led rout of Melbourne Stars in the semi – the Scorchers put in a near perfect performance. Electing to bowl first, as they preferred, they could again thank Johnson for setting an aggressive tone: he sent down 16 dot balls en route to miserly figures of one for 13. He was well supported by the 20-year-old Richardson and the more experienced Bresnan, who claimed three wickets each. Haddin and Botha offered some resistance, but 141 was light and, after Whiteman's 41 from 21 balls, the class of Klinger and Bell sped the Scorchers to the most emphatic victory of the competition's six finals. Klinger delivered the *coup de grâce* with the sweetest of sixes over long-on.

Man of the Match: J. A. Richardson. *Attendance:* 21,832.

Man of the Tournament: C. A. Lynn (Brisbane Heat).

Sydney Sixers

		B	*4/6*
1 D. P. Hughes *c 8 b 5*	8	10	0/1
2 M. J. Lumb *c 1 b 10*	5	5	1
3 N. J. Maddinson *run out*	1	2	0
4 *M. C. Henriques *c 2 b 11*	21	22	1/1
5 †B. J. Haddin *c 2 b 11*	38	25	4/2
6 J. C. Silk *c 10 b 11*	3	5	0
7 J. Botha *c 11 b 8*	32	25	3/1
8 S. A. Abbott *c 7 b 8*	5	10	0
9 B. J. Dwarshuis *b 8*	9	7	1
10 N. M. Lyon *not out*	9	7	1
11 J. M. Bird *not out*	2	2	0
Lb 3, w 5	8		
6 overs: 33-3 (20 overs)	141-9		

1/9 2/15 3/17 4/74 5/79 6/80 7/105 8/122 9/129

Johnson 4–16–13–1; Turner 1–3–8–1; Richardson 4–11–30–3; Tye 4–7–25–0; Bresnan 4–7–40–3; Agar 3–8–22–0.

Perth Scorchers

		B	*4/6*
1 †S. M. Whiteman *st 5 b 10*	41	21	5/3
2 M. Klinger *not out*	71	49	5/5
3 I. R. Bell *not out*	31	25	2/1
Lb 1	1		
6 overs: 61-0 (15.5 overs)	144-1		

1/75

4 *A. C. Voges, 5 A. J. Turner, 6 H. W. R. Cartwright, 7 A. C. Agar, 8 T. T. Bresnan, 9 A. J. Tye, 10 M. G. Johnson and 11 J. A. Richardson did not bat.

Dwarshuis 4–13–30–0; Bird 2–2–28–0; Lyon 4–14–28–1; Abbott 3–5–33–0; Botha 1.5–4–19–0; Henriques 1–1–5–0.

Umpires: M. D. Martell and P. Wilson. Third umpire: S. J. Nogajski.
Referee: R. W. Stratford.

BIG BASH FINALS

2011-12	SYDNEY SIXERS beat Perth Scorchers by seven wickets at Perth.
2012-13	BRISBANE HEAT beat Perth Scorchers by 34 runs at Perth.
2013-14	PERTH SCORCHERS beat Hobart Hurricanes by 39 runs at Perth.
2014-15	PERTH SCORCHERS beat Sydney Sixers by four wickets at Canberra.
2015-16	SYDNEY THUNDER beat Melbourne Stars by three wickets at Melbourne.
2016-17	PERTH SCORCHERS beat Sydney Sixers by nine wickets at Perth.

THE AKL BANGLADESH PREMIER LEAGUE IN 2016-17

MOHAMMAD ISAM

1 Dhaka Dynamites   2 Rajshahi Kings

Dhaka Dynamites chalked up the third win for a Dhaka franchise in the Bangladesh Premier League, but the first since their rebranding, after the owners of Dhaka Gladiators were forced out in a match-fixing scandal four years earlier. The new franchise seemed to raise a conflict of interest – their owner, Beximco, employed Nazmul Hassan and Ismail Haider Mallick, the president and director of the Bangladesh Cricket Board. But such practices are so commonplace in Bangladesh that the authorities barely acknowledged it.

The BPL expanded to seven teams, with the Khulna and Rajshahi franchises returning, while Sylhet dropped out for one year for disciplinary reasons. As in 2015-16, there were few high scores. Players cited the overuse of the Mirpur ground: logistical problems meant three-quarters of the 46 matches were played there, with the rest in Chittagong. Meanwhile, unseasonal rain delayed the start by four days; the first six games had to be rescheduled.

Dhaka Dynamites were always favourites. They built a formidable team around the top-order stability provided by Kumar Sangakkara, and headed the group table with eight wins out of 12. The only teams to beat them were Khulna and Rajshahi, but they crushed both in the knockouts.

Khulna Titans, who won seven group games, began with a thriller against Rajshahi. With seven required off the final over, Mahmudullah took three wickets and gave away just three runs with his sly off-spin. Three days later, he did even better: **Chittagong Vikings** required six off the last, but Mahmudullah again dismissed three batsmen, and this time conceded a single. **Rajshahi Kings** featured in another tight finish, against **Barisal Bulls**. Chasing 193, Sabbir Rahman smashed 122 in 61 balls – the tournament's only century – but his dismissal in the 16th over threw Rajshahi into a spiral, and they lost by four runs. Halfway through the league, Rajshahi were sixth. But a run of four wins – culminating in victory over **Rangpur Riders**, when they recovered from 43 for seven to 128, before bowling out Rangpur for 79 – helped them squeeze into the knockouts on net run-rate, and they went on to the final. Defending champions **Comilla Victorians** finished sixth.

Tamim Iqbal was easily the top run-scorer, with 476 for Chittagong, including six fifties. Mahmudullah, Sabbir, Sangakkara and Rangpur's Afghan batsman Mohammad Shahzad all made 350. Barisal's Shahriar Nafees looked a much-improved hitter of the ball, while Mehdi Hasan Maruf, who scored 347 for Dhaka at a strike-rate of 135, stood out among the less familiar home-grown faces. The top three wicket-takers were all foreigners – West Indian Dwayne Bravo took 21 for Dhaka, with 20 for Pakistan's Junaid Khan at Khulna, and 19 for another Afghan, Mohammad Nabi, at Chittagong. Khulna's Shafiul Islam was the leading Bangladeshi, with 18.

The BPL still required many improvements, not least an expansion to smaller venues such as Khulna, Cox's Bazar and Sylhet. The BCB also needed to promote more local talent by giving the franchises long-term goals, while the five-week jamboree was not profitable for the team owners, who craved a swift move to a better business model.

BANGLADESH PREMIER LEAGUE IN 2016-17

	Played	*Won*	*Lost*	*Points*	*NRR*
DHAKA DYNAMITES	12	8	4	16	0.91
KHULNA TITANS	12	7	5	14	–0.21
CHITTAGONG VIKINGS	12	6	6	12	0.23
RAJSHAHI KINGS	12	6	6	12	0.20
Rangpur Riders	12	6	6	12	–0.10
Comilla Victorians	12	5	7	10	–0.34
Barisal Bulls	12	4	8	8	–0.68

Teams tied on points were separated on net run-rate.

3rd v 4th At Mirpur, December 6, 2016. **Rajshahi Kings won by three wickets. Chittagong Vikings 142-8** (20 overs) (Tamim Iqbal 51, C. H. Gayle 44; K. O. K. Williams 4-11); ‡**Rajshahi Kings 143-7** (18.3 overs) (Nurul Hasan 34, D. J. G. Sammy 55*). *MoM:* D. J. G. Sammy. *Rajshahi's Windward Islanders kept their hopes alive, despite Chittagong enjoying runs from fellow West Indian Chris Gayle and local hero Tamim Iqbal. Tamim scored his sixth fifty of the tournament before becoming one of four victims for Kesrick Williams (the other three made ducks). But Rajshahi seemed to be sliding out of contention at 57-6 – until captain Darren Sammy pulled them through with 55* in 27 balls.*

1st v 2nd At Mirpur, December 6, 2016 (floodlit). **Dhaka Dynamites won by 54 runs. Dhaka Dynamites 140-8** (20 overs) (A. D. Russell 46; Junaid Khan 4-24); ‡**Khulna Titans 86** (16.2 overs) (A. D. Russell 3-16, D. J. Bravo 3-10). *MoM:* A. D. Russell. *West Indians held sway again as Dhaka made sure of their place in the final. Though they slipped to 89-6 after Junaid Khan removed their top three – including Kumar Sangakkara – Andre Russell hit back with 46 from 25 balls, then shared six wickets with Dwayne Bravo as Khulna folded for 86. Dhaka captain Shakib Al Hasan was fined and given two demerit points for his reaction to a rejected lbw appeal.*

Final play-off At Mirpur, December 7, 2016 (floodlit). **Rajshahi Kings won by seven wickets.** ‡**Khulna Titans 125-9** (20 overs) (Ariful Haque 32*; S. R. Patel 3-19); **Rajshahi Kings 129-3** (19.2 overs) (Sabbir Rahman 43*, J. E. C. Franklin 30*). *MoM:* S. R. Patel. *Rajshahi clinched their berth in the final with an efficient win. Both Khulna openers were run out in the third over, and tight bowling, especially by Williams and Nottinghamshire's Samit Patel, kept Rajshahi's target down to little more than a run a ball. Sabbir Rahman, with a controlled 43* from 52, and New Zealander James Franklin steered them home with four deliveries to spare.*

Final At Mirpur, December 9, 2016 (floodlit). **Dhaka Dynamites won by 56 runs. Dhaka Dynamites 159-9** (20 overs) (E. Lewis 45, K. C. Sangakkara 36; Farhad Reza 3-28); ‡**Rajshahi Kings 103** (17.4 overs). *MoM:* K. C. Sangakkara. *MoS:* Mahmudullah (Khulna Titans). *Dhaka's 159, which leaned heavily on Evin Lewis and Sangakkara, was the highest total of the knockouts but, at 62-1 in the tenth over, Rajshahi still had a chance of beating them for the third time in a row. Then Sabbir was run out for 26, and the chase collapsed. There was a curious ending after Bravo tried to run out Williams: the throw bounced off his right elbow for a boundary, Williams retired hurt, and last man Nazmul Islam was caught behind next over to give Dhaka an emphatic victory.*

BPL FINALS

2011-12 DHAKA GLADIATORS beat Barisal Burners by eight wickets.
2012-13 DHAKA GLADIATORS beat Chittagong Kings by 43 runs.
2015-16 COMILLA VICTORIANS beat Barisal Bulls by three wickets.
2016-17 DHAKA DYNAMITES beat Rajshahi Kings by 56 runs.

There was no tournament in 2013-14 or 2014-15, following a match-fixing scandal and pay disputes.

THE VIVO INDIAN PREMIER LEAGUE IN 2016-17

ANAND VASU

1 Mumbai Indians 2 Rising Pune Supergiant

For the second season running, the Indian Premier League passed without the focus shifting from cricket to corruption. The lack of incident was almost disconcerting. But the tenth edition of the IPL, the last of the originally conceived cycle, had enough action to keep the public gripped.

Mumbai Indians won for the third time in five years, after a thrilling last-ball finish against **Rising Pune Supergiant**. Mumbai had a familiar squad, with five players each boasting 100 appearances: Harbhajan Singh, Lasith Malinga, Kieron Pollard, Ambati Rayudu and Rohit Sharma. For Rohit, the captain, it was a record fourth title – he had also won with the now defunct Deccan Chargers in 2009.

In contrast, Pune had not even existed until 2016, one of two teams – along with Gujarat Lions – who replaced Chennai Super Kings and Rajasthan Royals while they served a two-year ban for betting offences. Had Pune's Australian all-rounder Dan Christian hit the last ball of the final for four, the 2018 edition might have been without a defending champion.

Royal Challengers Bangalore floundered, despite retaining perhaps the strongest Twenty20 top order ever assembled. The *galacticos* – led by Virat Kohli and including Chris Gayle and A. B. de Villiers – finished last, with only three wins. They were hamstrung by pitch repairs at the M. Chinnaswamy Stadium: seven inches of clay had been shaved off the square to correct a slope, and what was once the truest surface in the country became a sluggish turner.

Gujarat Lions, who had topped the table the previous year, matched RCB's ten defeats, while **Delhi Daredevils** also endured a miserable tournament. They followed a ten-wicket drubbing by **Kings XI Punjab** with a 146-run defeat by Mumbai, the heaviest in IPL history. Hashim Amla was in sublime touch for Punjab, striking two centuries and averaging 60, the best in the competition. But he was needed by South Africa ahead of the last game, a virtual knockout against Pune. Punjab were skittled for 73, their lowest total.

A new cast, meanwhile, shot themselves into the IPL firmament. Pune's Rahul Tripathi looked the real deal, whether coming down the pitch to the world's fastest bowlers, or sweeping with assurance against spin. He made 250 runs fewer than Sunrisers Hyderabad captain David Warner, who headed the charts with 641, but Tripathi's strike-rate of 146 was second only to Kolkata's Robin Uthappa among the top ten run-scorers.

Washington Sundar, a 17-year-old off-spinning all-rounder, was called up by Pune after Ravichandran Ashwin suffered a hernia, and proved an inspired choice, ending with an economy-rate of six. He also had the highest dot-ball percentage – 47 – of any bowler who delivered more than 30 overs.

A host of other spinners enjoyed themselves, too. Imran Tahir, unsold in the auction despite being ranked the world's No. 1 Twenty20 bowler, was picked up by Pune when Mitchell Marsh injured his shoulder before the tournament, and claimed 18 wickets. Fellow leg-spinner Rashid Khan – the first Afghan to play in the IPL – finished with 17, repaying the Sunrisers' faith.

Among the seamers, Bhuvneshwar Kumar – another Sunriser – was one of only a few to enhance his reputation. He acquired an extra yard of pace, and developed a yorker, which added miserly death bowling to his repertoire; he seized the purple cap for the leading wicket-taker early in the tournament, and clung on to it, finishing with 26. **Sunrisers Hyderabad's** potent attack counted for little in the knockouts, where they were trumped by **Kolkata Knight Riders** in a rain-affected game. West Indian spinner Sunil Narine had been a hit for Kolkata, though more with bat than ball: employed as a clean-striking opener, he smashed fifty in 15 deliveries against Bangalore, the fastest in IPL history. But he failed to spark in the second qualifying final, where his side were destroyed by Mumbai.

There were more England players than ever before. Kevin Pietersen and Eoin Morgan had long been part of the furniture, but seven others were available for an extended period. Ben Stokes, who hogged the headlines when he was bought by Pune for £1.7m – a record for an overseas player – was superb in all facets and named Man of the Tournament. But both he and Mumbai's Jos Buttler missed the knockouts: they had a long-scheduled training camp in Spain. Tymal Mills, whose left-arm pace attracted a price tag of £1.4m, was hampered by the slow Bangalore pitch, but Sam Billings and Chris Woakes had their moments. Chris Jordan and Jason Roy had few opportunities.

And so the initial ten-year cycle came to a close. The BCCI may have been in a state of flux, but the IPL juggernaut rumbled on: a new TV deal, with Star India (a subsidiary of 21st Century Fox), was worth a staggering £1.97bn, a 150% increase on the previous contract. The competition has a new – or rather old – look for 2018, with the return of the Chennai and Rajasthan franchises. That meant more player movement, some of it ahead of the high-profile annual auction. Not for the last time, the IPL was rarely out of the news.

INDIAN PREMIER LEAGUE IN 2016-17

	Played	*Won*	*Lost*	*No result*	*Points*	*NRR*
MUMBAI INDIANS	14	10	4	0	20	0.78
RISING PUNE SUPERGIANT	14	9	5	0	18	0.17
SUNRISERS HYDERABAD	14	8	5	1	17	0.59
KOLKATA KNIGHT RIDERS	14	8	6	0	16	0.64
Kings XI Punjab	14	7	7	0	14	0.00
Delhi Daredevils	14	6	8	0	12	–0.51
Gujarat Lions	14	4	10	0	8	–0.41
Royal Challengers Bangalore	14	3	10	1	7	–1.29

First qualifying final At Mumbai, May 16, 2017 (floodlit). **Rising Pune Supergiant won by 20 runs. Rising Pune Supergiant 162-4** (20 overs) (A. M. Rahane 56, M. K. Tiwary 58, M. S. Dhoni 40*); ‡**Mumbai Indians 142-9** (20 overs) (P. A. Patel 52; Washington Sundar 3-16, S. N. Thakur 3-37). *MoM:* Washington Sundar. *Mumbai were foxed by Washington Sundar's stump-to-stump wiles: he took three wickets in two overs to reduce them to 51-4 on a slow pitch, and they never recovered. Earlier, Ajinkya Rahane and Manoj Tiwary struck patient fifties, before M. S. Dhoni battered four sixes in the last two overs, which leaked 41.*

Elimination final At Bangalore, May 17, 2017 (floodlit). **Kolkata Knight Riders won by seven wickets** (DLS). **Sunrisers Hyderabad 128-7** (20 overs) (D. A. Warner 37; N. M. Coulter-Nile 3-20); ‡**Kolkata Knight Riders 48-3** (5.2 overs) (G. Gambhir 32*). *MoM:* N. M. Coulter-Nile. *Kolkata bowled superbly to limit defending champions Hyderabad to 128-7. Then the rain came. Had the playing conditions been the same as in the earlier rounds, the delay would have been enough for an abandonment, and Kolkata would have been knocked out by virtue of a lower league placing. But play resumed more than three hours later, with the target revised to 48 in six overs. Gautam Gambhir gritted his teeth and led Kolkata to victory, at 1.27am.*

Second qualifying final At Bangalore, May 19, 2017 (floodlit). **Mumbai Indians won by six wickets. Kolkata Knight Riders 107** (18.5 overs) (S. A. Yadav 31; J. J. Bumrah 3-7, K. V. Sharma 4-16); ‡**Mumbai Indians 111-4** (14.3 overs) (K. H. Pandya 45*). *MoM:* Karn Sharma. *Jasprit Bumrah and Karn Sharma took a combined 7-23 to lead Mumbai into a fourth IPL final. After seven overs, they had reduced Kolkata to 31-5. Ishank Jaggi and Suryakumar Yadav put on 56, but 107 was never going to be enough: Krunal Pandya waltzed home with a 30-ball 45*.*

FINAL

MUMBAI INDIANS v RISING PUNE SUPERGIANT

At Hyderabad, May 21, 2017 (floodlit). Mumbai Indians won by one run. Toss: Mumbai Indians.

Pune had won three out of three against Mumbai in the 2017 IPL. At the halfway stage of the final, they looked like making it four. Mean bowling from their balanced attack had limited Mumbai to 129 for eight, the second-lowest total in IPL finals, behind Chennai's 125 in 2012-13. Only Krunal Pandya, who put on 50 for the ninth wicket with Johnson, achieved any fluency. Still, Pune made a cautious start: with five overs left, they were only two down, needing 47. Smith relieved some pressure with an outrageous reverse-swept six, but Bumrah snared Dhoni, and helped build the tension until 11 were needed from the last. Tiwary clipped Johnson's first ball to the boundary, before he and Smith holed out. Three deliveries later, Christian needed four to win. He could only squirt to square leg, where the ball was fumbled and – amid frantic screaming – finally returned to prevent a tie. Mumbai's players revelled in a record third IPL title; Pune, in probably their last ever game, had run out of puff.

Man of the Match: K. H. Pandya. *Man of the Tournament:* B. A. Stokes.

Mumbai Indians

		B	4/6
1 L. M. P. Simmons *c and b 9*	3	8	0
2 †P. A. Patel *c 8 b 9*	4	6	0
3 A. T. Rayudu *run out*	12	15	1
4 *R. G. Sharma *c 8 b 11*	24	22	4
5 K. H. Pandya *c 1 b 6*	47	38	3/2
6 K. A. Pollard *c 5 b 11*	7	3	0/1
7 H. H. Pandya *lbw b 6*	10	9	0/1
8 K. V. Sharma *run out*	1	5	0
9 M. G. Johnson *not out*	13	14	0/1
B 1, lb 2, w 5	8		
6 overs: 32-2 (20 overs)	129-8		

1/7 2/8 3/41 4/56 5/65 6/78 7/79 8/129

10 J. J. Bumrah and 11 S. L. Malinga did not bat.

Unadkat 4–11–19–2; Washington Sundar 4–15–13–0; Thakur 2–6–7–0; Ferguson 2–5–21–0; Zampa 4–7–32–2; Christian 4–10–34–2.

Rising Pune Supergiant

		B	4/6
1 A. M. Rahane *c 6 b 9*	44	38	5
2 R. A. Tripathi *lbw b 10*	3	8	0
3 *S. P. D. Smith *c 3 b 9*	51	50	2/2
4 †M. S. Dhoni *c 2 b 10*	10	13	1
5 M. K. Tiwary *c 6 b 9*	7	8	1
6 D. T. Christian *not out*	4	2	0
7 M. S. Washington Sundar *run out*	0	1	0
B 1, lb 5, w 3	9		
6 overs: 38-1 (20 overs)	128-6		

1/17 2/71 3/98 4/123 5/123 6/128

8 S. N. Thakur, 9 J. D. Unadkat, 10 L. H. Ferguson and 11 A. Zampa did not bat.

K. H. Pandya 4–8–31–0; Johnson 4–10–26–3; Bumrah 4–8–26–2; Malinga 4–11–21–0; K. V. Sharma 4–12–18–0.

Umpires: N. J. Llong and S. Ravi. Third umpire: A. K. Chaudhary.
Referee: J. Srinath.

McDONALD'S SUPER SMASH IN 2016-17

MARK GEENTY

1 Wellington Firebirds   2 Central Stags

A fortnight into the tournament, **Wellington Firebirds** had four defeats from four. But new captain Hamish Marshall and his fellow veterans had learned over their long careers not to panic. They won five of their remaining six group games, edged past **Canterbury Kings** in the semi, and sealed the title with a 14-run win over **Central Stags**. In such an evenly matched competition, it was a remarkable streak. Marshall's relaxed, inclusive leadership was a hit, and helped extract strong performances from Wellington's core of internationals.

The Firebirds' fortunes changed when they parted with their two imports, England's Jade Dernbach and Australian Evan Gulbis. Neither set the competition alight and, after a night out on the eve of a match at Nelson, they were dropped for the next game, against Auckland. They didn't play again: Gulbis had come to the end of his short-term contract, while Dernbach was released.

After that, senior players cemented the team ethic, and the Firebirds flew. They recorded back-to-back wins over defending champions Auckland Aces, the second by two runs thanks to a cool final over from off-spinner Jeetan Patel. By the last round, they knew they had to defeat **Otago Volts**, the tournament's weakest side, to make the play-offs. Rain threatened a washout before the umpires agreed to a five-over match, which ended in a tie – 48 each. But Wellington squeezed through in the one-over eliminator after Michael Pollard clubbed two sixes and a four off Neil Wagner, and Hamish Bennett recorded two for eight.

Bennett, a bustling seamer lured from Canterbury by Wellington coach Bruce Edgar, proved a quality signing. He was hostile early on, and deceptive at the death, taking three for 18 against his old team in the semi, then two for 34 in the final as the Firebirds defended 172 for seven on the tiny Pukekura Park. Veteran seamer Brent Arnel – also the team's bowling coach – took two himself in the final to finish as the competition's equal top wicket-taker with 15, alongside the Stags' Seth Rance.

The Stags were chasing a first T20 title since 2009-10, and were dominant for much of the competition. Sri Lankan import Mahela Jayawardene was their driving force, with 367 runs at a strike-rate of 176, behind only Auckland youngster Glenn Phillips (369 at 143). But Jayawardene fell for a golden duck in the final, and his team couldn't compensate.

Phillips's unbeaten 116 from 57 balls in **Auckland Aces'** last match was one of the innings of the tournment, but it wasn't enough for his side to make the knockouts. After they amassed 212 for four, rain revised the Stags' target to 72 off eight. It proved elementary on Eden Park's outer oval, even with

England's Tymal Mills in the Auckland ranks, the most economical bowler in the competition to have played more than five matches.

The **Knights** (who dropped Northern from their name) were most affected by inbound Pakistan and Bangladesh tours: Kane Williamson, Corey Anderson, Trent Boult and Tim Southee spent most of the tournament either resting or on international duty. Still, they had a chance of making the play-offs until the final round, when they narrowly lost to Canterbury.

New Zealand Cricket had previously staged the competition in November, when the weather – and the attendance – was poor. The shift to a December start was welcome, with the business end played in the holiday period. The only downside was the overlap with Australia's Big Bash, which meant high-profile imports were rare.

McDONALD'S SUPER SMASH IN 2016-17

	Played	*Won*	*Lost*	*No result*	*Points*	*NRR*
CENTRAL STAGS	10	7	2	1	30	0.93
WELLINGTON FIREBIRDS	10	5	5	0	20	0.11
CANTERBURY KINGS	10	5	5	0	20	−0.21
Auckland Aces	10	5	5	0	20	−0.22
Knights	10	4	5	1	18	−0.04
Otago Volts	10	3	7	0	12	−0.41

2nd v 3rd At Wellington, January 5, 2017. **Wellington Firebirds won by three wickets.** ‡**Canterbury Kings 151-7** (20 overs) (C. J. Bowes 56, H. M. Nicholls 34, P. G. Fulton 33; H. K. Bennett 3-18); **Wellington Firebirds 155-7** (19.2 overs) (M. H. W. Papps 45, H. J. H. Marshall 36; T. D. Astle 3-18). *After stifling bowling from Hamish Bennett and Jeetan Patel (2-22) kept Canterbury to 151-7, Michael Papps and Hamish Marshall put Wellington in command with a rapid 73 for the first wicket. It meant that, even after they collapsed from 103-1 to 110-5, they had time to hobble into the final.*

Final At New Plymouth (Pukekura Park), January 7, 2017 (floodlit). **Wellington Firebirds won by 14 runs. Wellington Firebirds 172-7** (20 overs) (M. A. Pollard 32, M. J. Taylor 48*; B. M. Tickner 4-34); ‡**Central Stags 158-8** (20 overs) (J. A. Clarkson 53*). *Wellington appeared to be choking when rangy seamer Blair Tickner picked up his fourth wicket to reduce them to 114-7, with four overs left. But a rollicking stand of 58* between Matt Taylor and Patel (28*) was an effective Heimlich, and they were full of life when Central Districts slid to 6-3 in reply; Brent Arnel (2-16) picked up Mahela Jayawardene first ball, then added Jesse Ryder for another duck. As wickets tumbled, Josh Clarkson raged against the light with a 31-ball 53*, but it was too much to do alone, and Wellington clinched the cup.*

SUPER SMASH FINALS

2005-06 CANTERBURY WIZARDS beat Auckland Aces by six wickets.
2006-07 AUCKLAND ACES beat Otago Volts by 60 runs.
2007-08 CENTRAL STAGS beat Northern Knights by five wickets.
2008-09 OTAGO VOLTS headed the table; the final against Canterbury Wizards was washed out.
2009-10 CENTRAL STAGS beat Auckland Aces by 78 runs.
2010-11 AUCKLAND ACES beat Central Stags by four runs.
2011-12 AUCKLAND ACES beat Canterbury Wizards by 44 runs.
2012-13 OTAGO VOLTS beat Wellington Firebirds by four wickets.
2013-14 NORTHERN KNIGHTS beat Otago Volts by five wickets.
2014-15 WELLINGTON FIREBIRDS beat Auckland Aces by six runs.
2015-16 AUCKLAND ACES beat Otago Volts by 20 runs.
2016-17 WELLINGTON FIREBIRDS beat Central Stags by 14 runs.

HBL PAKISTAN SUPER LEAGUE IN 2016-17

CHARLES REYNOLDS

1 Peshawar Zalmi   2 Quetta Gladiators

In the crowded world of Twenty20 franchise tournaments, it looked as if the Pakistan Super League might struggle to find a niche. It was never going to outdo the IPL for glamour, or the Big Bash League for family-friendliness. But, as time goes on, the PSL may prove the most important.

After various aborted attempts, the inaugural competition in 2015-16 had been notable only for taking place. The second edition was more significant. Since terrorists attacked the Sri Lankans in 2009, only Zimbabwe had come to Pakistan, playing five limited-overs games in 2014-15. This tournament brought high-profile cricket back from exile. After the preliminary rounds in Dubai and Sharjah, the final, where **Peshawar Zalmi** thrashed **Quetta Gladiators** by 58 runs, was played at Lahore. Quetta's overseas corps – Nathan McCullum, Tymal Mills, Kevin Pietersen, Rilee Rossouw and Luke Wright – pulled out citing safety concerns. But replacements were reportedly offered up to $US50,000 to step in, and Anamul Haque, Elton Chigumbura, Rayad Emrit, Sean Ervine and Morné van Wyk accepted. Meanwhile, Peshawar's own overseas players, including captain Darren Sammy, chose to remain, and were rewarded with the trophy.

But if the event ended on a joyous note, it began under a depressingly familiar cloud. Another corruption scandal threatened to engulf Pakistan cricket when two Islamabad United batsmen, Sharjeel Khan and Khalid Latif, were suspended on the tournament's second day for involvement in spot-fixing. They were later banned for five years, while Mohammad Irfan (six months) and Mohammad Nawaz (two months) were later suspended for not reporting approaches from bookmakers.

Still, the cloud passed, and a closely fought competition broke out, even if its structure remained a sticking point: the five franchises played 20 games just to eliminate one of them. The much-improved **Lahore Qalandars** missed out again, despite finishing only three points from the top. The inclusion of a new Multan franchise for 2017-18 should help stir things up.

As usual for a T20 tournament, overseas stars – including a healthy contingent of English players – gave some stellar performances. But the PSL is different. In a country forced to play international fixtures abroad, and with an archaic, disorganised domestic set-up, it can be hard for young cricketers to gain experience and worldwide recognition. This competition gives them that opportunity.

Pakistan's shock triumph in the 2017 Champions Trophy in England felt like a vindication. Fakhar Zaman, Hasan Ali, Rumman Raees and Shadab Khan – key components of the victorious squad – all rose to prominence during the PSL. Rumman finished equal third in the wickets table, showing off nerveless death bowling to snatch some unlikely victories. However, it was leg-spinner Shadab, just 18, who was the star, taking nine wickets, with an economy-rate under seven. Together, they helped **Islamabad United** reach the knockouts, where **Karachi Kings** routed them for 82. Neither made the final, though: Peshawar's Kamran Akmal hit the only century of the tournament to down Karachi.

The sparse crowds in the league stages, and the relatively bowler-friendly pitches, meant the PSL did not hit the excitement level of other global competitions. But that misses the point: for a country in need of it, the tournament provides genuine optimism that one day things will be better.

PAKISTAN SUPER LEAGUE IN 2016-17

	Played	*Won*	*Lost*	*No result*	*Points*	*NRR*
PESHAWAR ZALMI	8	4	3	1	9	0.30
QUETTA GLADIATORS	8	4	3	1	9	0.16
KARACHI KINGS	8	4	4	0	8	−0.09
ISLAMABAD UNITED	8	4	4	0	8	−0.13
Lahore Qalandars	8	3	5	0	6	−0.22

1st v 2nd At Sharjah, February 28, 2017. **Quetta Gladiators won by one run. Quetta Gladiators 200-7** (20 overs) (Ahmed Shehzad 71, K. P. Pietersen 40; Wahab Riaz 3-39); ‡**Peshawar Zalmi 199-9** (20 overs) (D. J. Malan 56, Mohammad Hafeez 77, Shahid Afridi 34; Mohammad Nawaz 3-51). *MoM:* Ahmed Shehzad. *It was déjà vu for Peshawar. At this stage in 2016, they needed eight off the last to beat Quetta, but managed only six. A year later, left-arm spinner Mohammad Nawaz had seven to protect and, though Darren Sammy struck four off the second ball, they fell short: the last three deliveries produced wickets, including two run-outs. Ahmed Shehzad's 38-ball 71 seemed to have given Quetta a strong grip, before Peshawar's Dawid Malan and Mohammad Hafeez responded with a rapid century partnership. Four sixes from Shahid Afridi made them favourites, but his dismissal in the penultimate over sparked panic.*

3rd v 4th At Sharjah, March 1, 2017. **Karachi Kings won by 44 runs. Karachi Kings 126** (19.4 overs) (Rumman Raees 4-25); ‡**Islamabad United 82** (15.2 overs) (Asif Ali 39; Mohammad Amir 3-7, Imad Wasim 3-18, Usama Mir 3-24). *MoM:* Imad Wasim. *Karachi began their innings with 13 dots and, after struggling to 126, looked like bowing out. But an inspired bowling performance destroyed defending champions Islamabad: Mohammad Amir started the fightback with two wickets in the third over, before spinners Imad Wasim and Usama Mir filleted the middle order with three apiece.*

Final play-off At Dubai (Sports City), March 3, 2017. **Peshawar Zalmi won by 24 runs. Peshawar Zalmi 181-3** (20 overs) (Kamran Akmal 104, D. J. Malan 36, M. N. Samuels 37*); ‡**Karachi Kings 157-7** (20 overs) (C. H. Gayle 40, K. A. Pollard 47; C. J. Jordan 3-26, Wahab Riaz 3-24). *MoM:* Kamran Akmal. *Kamran Akmal hit the first two balls for four and raced to a magnificent hundred, which helped Peshawar rack up 181-3. On an excellent surface, it was not unreachable, and forties from Chris Gayle and Kieron Pollard gave Karachi a fighting chance. But Wahab Riaz removed both, and finished with an excellent 3-24 as Peshawar eased into the final. They would be without Afridi, who sustained a deep cut in his finger attempting a catch.*

Final At Lahore (Gaddafi), March 7, 2017. **Peshawar Zalmi won by 58 runs. Peshawar Zalmi 148-6** (20 overs) (Kamran Akmal 40; R. R. Emrit 3-30); ‡**Quetta Gladiators 90** (16.3 overs) (Mohammad Asghar 3-16). *MoM:* D. J. G. Sammy. *A superb collective bowling display secured Peshawar the title. Hasan Ali and Wahab each took 2-13, while left-arm spinner Mohammad Asghar was the pick with 3-16. Only Mohammad Hafeez conceded more than 20, but he chipped in with the key wicket of Sarfraz Ahmed. Peshawar had been struggling themselves at 112-6 in the 17th over, in danger of losing steam. But Sammy – who had shown courage and charm in leading his side back to Pakistan – clubbed three sixes, and zoomed to 28 off 11 to lift them to a defendable total.*

CSA T20 CHALLENGE IN 2016-17

TRISTAN HOLME

1 Titans 2 Warriors

This tournament was caught between two eras. A year earlier, the Ram Slam T20 had been the stage for South Africa's biggest match-fixing scandal in a generation, resulting in long bans for seven players. And Cricket South Africa's glitzy Global League was supposed to be only a year away. The result was something that lacked the confidence of a premier T20 show.

There were few big stars and no headline sponsor: Ram had decided to step away after the blighted 2015-16 edition. Attendances were poor, at least until a capacity crowd saw the **Titans** clinch the title at Centurion, and give former South Africa Test wicketkeeper Mark Boucher a first trophy as head coach.

In previous years, each franchise had made efforts to sign an overseas player, but this time budgets were limited. The Cape Cobras retained the services of West Indian all-rounder Kieron Pollard, and Kevin Pietersen returned to the Dolphins once he had completed his commentary stint with Channel Nine in Australia.

That series kept the national team players away for the first half of the league phase. CSA tried to encourage them to take part in the later stages, by reworking their fixtures against Sri Lanka. But most players used the time to rest. It was no great surprise the fans decided to stay at home as well.

While the Titans were the best team – continuing a dominant run after winning the T20 and four-day competitions the previous season – the bigger story was the resurgence of the **Warriors**. They did not end a trophy drought stretching back to the 2009-10 season, but finished second in the table, and easily despatched the **Lions** in the play-off. The Warriors' Jon-Jon Smuts hit most runs, with 371, and backed it up with 35 overs of left-arm spin at an economy-rate of 6.17. Christiaan Jonker's late-innings blitzes were also important: he hit 263 runs at a strike-rate of 156.

But with Albie Morkel, Farhaan Behardien and David Wiese in their side, the Titans had too much nous and depth. They even coped after Morkel pulled up with a hamstring strain during his first over in the final, when they were defending a low total. Wiese took over the captaincy and marshalled the bowlers well: Malusi Siboto just about held his nerve at the death.

A close final gave the competition a stirring finish, but the rest had lacked appeal. It didn't help that the bottom three – the **Cobras**, the **Dolphins** and the **Knights** – were all awful, winning just three games each.

It was clear South African cricket still needed a jazzed-up Twenty20 tournament. Many hoped the Global League would inject funds into the game, and attract new audiences. But less than a month before the competition was due to begin, in November 2017, there was no agreed television rights deal, nor central sponsor, so CSA postponed the inaugural edition until 2018. It seemed the revolution would need to wait another year.

CSA T20 CHALLENGE IN 2016-17

	Played	*Won*	*Lost*	*No result*	*Bonus points*	*Points*	*NNR*
TITANS	10	7	2	1	3	33	0.96
WARRIORS	10	6	4	0	3	27	1.04
LIONS	10	5	5	0	0	20	–0.56
Cape Cobras	10	3	5	2	1	17	0.01
Dolphins	10	3	6	1	1	15	–0.48
Knights	10	3	7	0	2	13	–0.81

2nd v 3rd At Port Elizabeth, December 13, 2016 (floodlit). **Warriors won by seven wickets.** ‡**Lions 136-7** (20 overs) (R. R. Hendricks 32); **Warriors 138-3** (18.2 overs) (C. A. Ingram 56*). *Batsman of the Match:* C. A. Ingram. *Bowler of the Match:* J. T. Smuts. *On a slow pitch, Lions reached 77-2 by the halfway point, and looked primed for a challenging total. But they struggled to hit the slow bowlers – particularly Jon-Jon Smuts, who conceded just 17 from his four overs – and tumbled from 110-3 to 120-7. Colin Ingram led the stroll to the final with a leisurely 56*, backing up a tidy 2-24 with his leg-spin.*

Final At Centurion, December 16, 2016 (floodlit). **Titans won by six runs. Titans 155-6** (20 overs) (A. K. Markram 33); ‡**Warriors 149-6** (20 overs) (C. N. Ackermann 34, C. Jonker 33). *Batsman of the Match:* D. Wiese. *Bowler of the Match:* L. T. Ngidi. *Titans' 155 seemed vulnerable on a slick surface, particularly when captain Albie Morkel pulled a hamstring bowling the first over of the Warriors' chase. But after Smuts and Ingram failed, they turned timid and, though Colin Ackermann and Christiaan Jonker cobbled together a stand of 48, Warriors left themselves 12 off the last. A nervy Malusi Siboto delivered a wide that meant they could tie with a six. But stand-in captain David Wiese – who had earlier belted an important 15-ball 24* – offered calm assurance, and Siboto eventually bowled the dot that retained the trophy for Titans.*

THE HERO CARIBBEAN PREMIER LEAGUE IN 2017

PETER MILLER

1 Trinbago Knight Riders *2 St Kitts & Nevis Patriots*

The fifth edition of the CPL was won by **Trinbago Knight Riders**, the season's most consistent team. After finishing top of the group, they defeated St Kitts & Nevis Patriots in a home final, of sorts: the play-offs were staged at the Brian Lara Cricket Academy in Tarouba, the first professional games at the new facility in south Trinidad.

The final was a thriller to entertain a sell-out crowd. The Patriots seemed to have done enough, reducing the Knight Riders to 90 for seven before a counter-attacking partnership between Denesh Ramdin and Kevon Cooper hustled them home. The Patriots had actually beaten them in the first play-off match but, as they had topped the qualifying table, the Knight Riders had another chance, and walloped Guyana Amazon Warriors to reach the final.

The success of **St Kitts & Nevis Patriots** was down to their opening pair, the big-hitting left-handers Chris Gayle and Evin Lewis. Unusually, it was often Gayle who played the supporting role while Lewis went on the rampage, targeting the leg side. He hammered 31 sixes, and finished with 371 runs at a dizzying strike-rate of 184; Gayle scored 376 at 127.

The 2016 champions, **Jamaica Tallawahs**, were led by the evergreen Kumar Sangakkara. Taking a few weeks off from his prolific county season with Surrey, he added 379 more runs here, at a strike-rate of 135. He was well supported by Andre McCarthy, who had a breakthrough year with the bat (292 runs at 127), and Kesrick Williams, whose 15 wickets were embellished by outlandish celebrations. There was a change of ownership for the Tallawahs, who were bought by the Florida-based businessman Kris Persaud. He also owned the staging rights for international cricket at the Central Broward Regional Park in Lauderhill, which put on four matches in this tournament, and was pushing for more.

Guyana Amazon Warriors sneaked into the knockout stages, despite fielding the tournament's leading run-getter and highest wicket-taker. Chadwick Walton's 458 runs at 145 won him the Player of the Tournament award. Meanwhile, Pakistan seamer Sohail Tanvir claimed 17 wickets, with an astonishing return of five for three – including Kane Williamson, Eoin Morgan and Kieron Pollard for ducks – as the Barbados Tridents were skittled for 59 at Kensington Oval. The Warriors' Afghan leg-spinner, Rashid Khan, grabbed the first CPL hat-trick, in the play-off against the Tallawahs. All three victims were bowled by his googly, fast becoming one of the most dangerous deliveries in world cricket.

Barbados Tridents' tournament ended in controversial fashion. They needed a massive win over the Patriots to improve their net run-rate, but were effectively eliminated once they had stumbled to 128 for nine. Gayle and Lewis then blasted their way to 128 in seven overs, with Lewis on 97 from

31 balls. One more boundary would have brought him the second-fastest T20 hundred – but Pollard, the Tridents' captain, sent down a looping no-ball that bounced high over Lewis's head. Pollard denied he had done it to deprive him of his ton.

Bringing up the rear were **St Lucia Stars**, who did not win a single match; their only point came from a rain-ruined game. It was an unhappy team, and the captain, St Lucia's own Darren Sammy, was fired during the tournament and replaced by Shane Watson.

CARIBBEAN PREMIER LEAGUE IN 2017

	Played	*Won*	*Lost*	*NR/A*	*Points*	*NNR*
TRINBAGO KNIGHT RIDERS	10	8	2	0	16	1.16
ST KITTS & NEVIS PATRIOTS	10	6	3	1	13	1.02
JAMAICA TALLAWAHS	10	6	4	0	12	–0.41
GUYANA AMAZON WARRIORS	10	5	5	0	10	0.83
Barbados Tridents	10	4	6	0	8	–0.94
St Lucia Stars	10	0	9	1	1	–1.64

1st v 2nd At Tarouba, Trinidad, September 5 (floodlit). **St Kitts & Nevis Patriots won by 38 runs. St Kitts and Nevis Patriots 149-7** (20 overs) (C. H. Gayle 54*, B. A. King 30; D. J. Bravo 4-38); ‡**Trinbago Knight Riders 111** (19.3 overs) (S. S. Cottrell 3-17). *MoM:* C. H. Gayle. *The Patriots upset the table-toppers to reach the final, thanks to Chris Gayle, who batted throughout the innings, and left-arm seamer Sheldon Cottrell (4–15–17–3). The Knight Riders' innings had a bad start when pinch-hitting opener Sunil Narine was run out without facing, and things got little better: only the Bravo brothers, Darren (29) and Dwayne (24), reached 20.*

3rd v 4th At Tarouba, Trinidad, September 6 (floodlit). **Guyana Amazon Warriors won by five wickets. Jamaica Tallawahs 168-8** (20 overs) (L. M. P. Simmons 34, K. C. Sangakkara 57*; Rashid Khan 3-32); ‡**Guyana Amazon Warriors 169-5** (17.5 overs) (C. A. K. Walton 39, L. Ronchi 70; Mahmudullah 3-25). *MoM:* L. Ronchi. *The Tallawahs were set back by Rashid Khan's hat-trick – the first in a CPL match – all bowled by googlies, from the first three balls of the 15th over. Then Luke Ronchi biffed 70 from 33 deliveries, with five sixes, as the Warriors reached the final play-off.*

Final play-off At Tarouba, Trinidad, September 7 (floodlit). **Trinbago Knight Riders won by six wickets. Guyana Amazon Warriors 159-6** (20 overs) (C. A. K. Walton 37, G. Singh 39, R. S. Primus 35*); ‡**Trinbago Knight Riders 160-4** (18 overs) (C. Munro 57*, D. M. Bravo 43). *MoM:* C. Munro. *The Knight Riders made sure of a final spot at the second attempt, overhauling a target of 160 with two overs to spare, despite losing Narine first ball. New Zealander Colin Munro anchored the chase with 57* from 51 deliveries, while Darren Bravo smacked four sixes in his 27-ball innings.*

Final At Tarouba, Trinidad, September 9 (floodlit). **Trinbago Knight Riders won by three wickets. St Kitts & Nevis Patriots 135-6** (20 overs) (C. R. Brathwaite 30*); ‡**Trinbago Knight Riders 136-7** (19 overs). *MoM:* K. K. Cooper. *MoS:* C. A. K. Walton (Guyana Amazon Warriors). *After losing Gayle for a single, the Patriots managed only 28-2 in the six-over powerplay, and found it difficult to accelerate on a sluggish pitch. But the Knight Riders also had trouble, and looked sunk at 90-7 in the 15th over, before Denesh Ramdin (26* from 31 balls) and Kevon Cooper (29* from 14) biffed them to the title.*

CPL FINALS

2013 JAMAICA TALLAWAHS beat Guyana Amazon Warriors by seven wickets.
2014 BARBADOS TRIDENTS beat Guyana Amazon Warriors by eight runs (DLS).
2015 TRINIDAD & TOBAGO RED STEEL beat Barbados Tridents by 20 runs.
2016 JAMAICA TALLAWAHS beat Guyana Amazon Warriors by nine wickets.
2017 TRINBAGO KNIGHT RIDERS beat St Kitts & Nevis Patriots by three wickets.

OTHER DOMESTIC T20 COMPETITIONS

JAMES GINGELL

In Ireland, Leinster Lightning won the **Interprovincial Trophy** for the fourth time in five years. The competition was expanded to four teams, with Munster Reds taking part for the first time. Leinster's outstanding performer was Punjab-born Simi Singh, once voted the best Under-14 all-rounder in India. A month after he made his debut for Ireland, he hit 109 off 53 balls against Munster, the only century of the tournament, and helped Leinster to a total of 247 for four, the competition's highest total. His off-spin was also handy, earning seven wickets with an economy rate of less than seven, including two in a second victory over Munster to clinch the title.The most potent bowler was North West Warriors' seamer Craig Young, who took 11 wickets at under seven. Against Leinster he claimed five for 22, the best bowling of the season, to inflict their only defeat and ensure the outcome of the championship was not settled until the final round. James Shannon, of Northern Knights, was the highest run–scorer with 251 at 42.

The **Hong Kong T20 Blitz** in March had star power, but some horrible mismatches (and no official T20 status). Former Pakistan captain Misbah-ul-Haq led the Hong Kong Island United team, and hit six consecutive sixes across two overs against Hung Hom Jaguars: two off former Worcestershire and Sussex seamer Imran Arif, and four off Ashley Caddy, a left-arm trundler who used to play for Uplyme & Lyme Regis in the E Division of the Devon League. Kowloon Cantons had to share the trophy in 2016, when only three matches escaped the weather. But they were sole victors in 2017, comfortably beating City Kaitak thanks to an opening stand of 149 between the Barbadian Dwayne Smith, the tournament's top-scorer, and Hong Kong captain Babar Hayat.

HANLEY ENERGY INTERPROVINCIAL TROPHY IN 2017

20-over league

	Played	*Won*	*Lost*	*Abandoned*	*Bonus points*	*Points*	*NRR*
Leinster Lightning	6	5	1	0	3	23	1.63
North West Warriors	6	3	2	1	0	14	−0.22
Northern Knights	6	3	3	0	1	13	0.27
Munster Reds	6	0	5	1	0	2	−2.24

PART SEVEN

Women's Cricket

WOMEN'S INTERNATIONAL CRICKET IN 2017

MELINDA FARRELL

For some time now, annual reviews of the women's game have had a familiar theme – and 2017 was no different. It was a stellar year, and the sport has taken massive strides in professionalism, media coverage and the growth of viewers. And while repetition is often regarded as boring, in the case of women's cricket it is more than welcome.

The World Cup was an unprecedented hit, in terms of both crowds and TV audiences, while the domestic Twenty20 competitions in Australia and England built on their earlier successes. It was also, just possibly, the year the Indian board finally woke up to the potential of the women's game. A contingent from the BCCI attended the final at Lord's between England and India, and awarded their players bonuses of Rs 50 lakh (£55,000), three times a yearly contract. Whether or not the sight of a packed house, and the fact that seven television stations broadcast the game back in India, will inspire the BCCI to launch a women's IPL remains to be seen. But, if it does happen, the seeds were surely sown that day in July. The profile of players such as captain Mithali Raj and Harmanpreet Kaur increased enormously, through TV appearances and public support from India's male stars.

Other countries benefited too. Chamari Atapattu's astonishing 178 against Australia meant she became the first Sri Lankan player to land a contract in the Kia Super League and the Women's Big Bash League, an example of how increased coverage can lead to life-changing opportunities for players from countries with less wealthy boards.

And the performance of South Africa, beaten in dramatic fashion by England in the semi-final, cemented them as a force in world cricket. With Cricket Australia, the ECB and the BCCI increasing wages significantly, there is a growing danger other teams could be left behind. South Africa's success was therefore important in a wider context; in progressing beyond New Zealand and a disappointing West Indies, they emerged as serious rivals to the traditional powers of the women's game.

England's first challenge after winning the World Cup came in the multi-format Ashes in Australia. They lost the first two one-day internationals, but pulled back by winning the third. The four-day game was a historic event: the first women's floodlit Test. It was held at North Sydney Oval, a ground where a men's one-day domestic match had been abandoned earlier in the season because of an unsafe pitch – but the only danger this time was that it might bore the players and spectators to death. One of Australia's smaller grounds should have been the ideal venue for a women's match, with naturally short boundaries that keep the crowds close and allow a few sixes. Instead, a flat, grassless track gave little help to bowlers or batsmen, and a draw seemed a foregone conclusion from the start. Still, Ellyse Perry's outstanding double-century – the highest score in a women's Ashes Test – was one of the memories of the summer.

It was no surprise the surface was rated below average by the ICC, but it is astonishing that boards continue to allow the preparation of substandard pitches. If decent wickets are important for the men – especially in Test cricket – they are vital for the women, who have less raw power to generate pace out of the hand or off the bat. Poor pitches remain arguably the biggest impediment to improving the quality of women's cricket worldwide.

This was the third consecutive women's Ashes Test played on a slow and lifeless surface, following similar pitches at Wormsley and Canterbury, so it seems the administrators are not getting the message. Cricket Australia's chief executive James Sutherland highlighted the slow scoring of the Test as one reason why there may be few longer-format matches in the future – possibly none outside the Ashes – but the point seemed moot after the men's Ashes Tests produced comparable run-rates.

After the Test was drawn, England won two of the three Twenty20 internationals to level the series at eight points each, but Australia retained the Ashes they had won in 2015. The result was a disappointment for England's captain Heather Knight and her team-mates, but many of them stayed on in Australia to play in the third instalment of the highly successful WBBL. It capped eight months of almost continuous high-level cricket, something that would have been impossible just a few years ago.

LEADING WOMAN CRICKETER IN THE WORLD IN 2017

Mithali Raj

RAF NICHOLSON

"Don't be satisfied with stories, how things have gone with others," wrote the 13th-century Persian poet Rumi. "Unfold your own myth." In 2017, Mithali Raj, who in June at Derby was spotted calmly perusing some of Rumi's work as she waited to bat in the opening game of the World Cup between India and England, seemed to have taken heed. She soon broke two records. Her 71 off 73 balls that day was her seventh consecutive half-century, the longest sequence in women's one-day internationals. Two and a half weeks later, during India's group match against Australia, she passed Charlotte Edwards's one-day tally of 5,992 – another world record.

India had begun the year still needing to qualify for the World Cup, with few championing the cause of a team who were not just unsung, but under-resourced. But a triumphant campaign at the qualifying event in Colombo – where Raj was dismissed only once in making 207 runs – was followed in England by an against-the-odds rampage to their first World Cup final in 12 years. Along the way, the apple cart was well and truly upset. First, India knocked out the highly rated New Zealanders, with Raj scoring 109; then they sent reigning champions Australia packing in a semi-final memorable for the big hitting of Harmanpreet Kaur. Only a sensational late spell from England's Anya Shrubsole at Lord's prevented Raj from becoming a World Cup-winning captain.

Born in 1982 in Jodhpur, Raj has been playing international cricket since 1999, when she made an unbeaten 114 against Ireland at Milton Keynes. Three years later, aged 19, she became only the fifth woman to hit a Test double-century, against England at Taunton. By 2004, she was captaining her country. But for most of her time at the top, she has played under a board who have barely invested in the women's game. The last time she led India to a World Cup final, in South Africa in 2005, many back home barely knew who she was. Not any more. Despite throwing away their chance of winning the 2017 trophy, India's women now know what it feels like to be heroes. Raj had led them out of the shadows.

Rumi, she says, has taught her "how you deal with criticism, how you deal with pressure, how you deal with failure". One way to overcome losing a World Cup final, for instance, was to understand that even reaching that final had transformed the standing of the women's game. "Very few people were aware of women's cricket in our country before the World Cup," says Raj. "But young girls now see a career in women's cricket. Today, when we walk on the street, even young kids recognise the players in the squad." Perhaps they will even unfold their own myth. And with thoughts of retirement banished for the time being, Raj will be there to show them the way.

WOMEN'S WORLD CUP IN 2017

REVIEW BY RAF NICHOLSON

1 England 2 India 3= Australia, South Africa

The women's game had made great strides in recent years, but this tournament was a watershed. It helped that the cricket was often edge-of-the-seat quality, culminating in a sell-out final at Lord's and a trophy-stealing spell from Anya Shrubsole as England pipped India. But the media coverage and levels of public interest were unprecedented, and – unheard of for a women's game – ticket touts lined the streets of St John's Wood on the day of the final.

At the previous World Cup, in India in 2013, only ten of the 25 matches had been broadcast. This time, all 31 were either televised or live-streamed by the ICC, with coverage available in almost 200 countries. The investment paid dividends, and the group stage reached a global TV audience of over 50m (80% up on 2013), which had stretched to 180m by the end. Of those, 156m were in India, a country previously lukewarm towards the women's game. In the UK, 1.1m tuned in for the final, three times as many as had watched the most recent day of men's Test cricket at Lord's.

Billboards in the host towns and cities – Bristol, Taunton, Derby and Leicester – ensured awareness was high, and crowds gathered in their thousands. Ticket sales for the group matches averaged almost 1,700, with two sell-outs at Derby: England v India, the tournament opener, and India v Pakistan. Encouragingly for the ECB, 50% of ticket holders were female, and 31% under 16 – audiences English cricket has struggled to reach.

There were further moves towards parity with the men's game. All teams flew business class to England, a first for a women's global tournament, while prize money increased tenfold on the 2013 edition, to $2m. Hawk-Eye's cameras were used and, in the final, so was Spidercam. The fact that DRS was available for only ten matches led to some criticism, but England captain Heather Knight labelled it a "brilliant addition". Certainly, it added to the sense that women's cricket was being watched more closely than ever.

The buzz at Lord's before the final was electric, and fans queued round the block. They got a humdinger, as India – aiming to secure their maiden World Cup title – fell apart under the pressure of a chase. Their last seven wickets fell for 28 as a magical spell from Shrubsole, who finished with six for 46, the best figures in a World Cup final, took England home by nine runs. Their triumph hogged the front and back pages; in *The Times*, Michael Atherton called it "one of the great Lord's finals".

England's achievement was all the more powerful for coming just 16 months after their humiliating semi-final defeat by Australia in the World Twenty20 in Delhi. This was a team transformed, and not just because Charlotte Edwards – following her controversial axing by coach Mark Robinson – was in the commentary box. Afterwards, Knight spoke of Robinson's tough love: "Mark has challenged us, made us a lot smarter, made

Spice of life: England's Nat Sciver pulls off the "Natmeg" against New Zealand.

us get away with a lot less." Credit also went to Ian Durrant, the team's strength and conditioning coach, and Ali Maiden, who had worked with England's batsmen since his appointment as assistant coach in 2016.

This was a tougher side, physically and mentally, and almost everyone chipped in. Four top-order batsmen – Knight, Nat Sciver, Sarah Taylor and Tammy Beaumont – made hundreds. There were crucial runs from lower down, especially Jenny Gunn; in the semi-final, a boundary from No. 10 Shrubsole completed an emotional victory over South Africa with two balls to spare. At last, England's long-cherished dream of winning a final on home territory and singing their team song on the Lord's balcony – Depeche Mode's "I just can't get enough" – became a reality. To avoid tempting fate, England had kept the song secret: not until the words rang around the ground was its identity clear.

A new format added to the sense of a more meaningful competition: each team played the other seven in a round-robin group, with the top four progressing to the semi-finals. And the group stage was not without surprises, beginning with India's defeat of England. **Sri Lanka's** Chamari Atapattu then dismantled the Australian attack with 178 not out, the third-highest score in women's ODIs, only for Meg Lanning to reply with a match-winning unbeaten 152. While Sri Lanka finished with just one win – against wooden-spoonists Pakistan – Atapattu's innings was their greatest moment yet, and earned her selection in the 2017 Kia Super League. But the performance of **West Indies** was a rude awakening after their triumph at the 2016 World T20: they lost five out of seven, including an annihilation by South Africa, who bowled them out for 48.

South Africa took the chance to showcase the vast improvement they had made since the previous World Cup. Dane van Niekerk marshalled them to

THE WOMEN'S WORLD CUP FINAL

A day like no other

ISABELLE WESTBURY

Lord's was barely a seventh full when it last hosted a women's World Cup final, in 1993. In 2017, it was brimming, the 25,000 seats on offer sold out in the week before the game. Touts loitered at the gates, and corporate packages fetched generous sums. There was another difference: a third of tickets were bought by women, and more than a quarter went to children. If alcohol takings were on the low side, there was a run on coffee and cake. Female spectators were no longer docile accompaniments.

"We arrived to a jam-packed ground," says Emily Clark, who plays for Worcestershire Under-15 girls, and made the trip to London with her younger brother and parents. "There was excitement everywhere – people were just happy. The men's matches are incredibly serious and they're aware of that expectation on them. The women's matches tend to be more free, as they are all so excited to be there.

"Other times we have watched the women, it has been a bit of a downer, as not many turned up. But the World Cup was brilliant. We went to England versus Sri Lanka in Taunton with a group of girls from school, and Fran Wilson took an amazing catch right in front of us. We've got some loud girls, so she heard us cheering and waved at us. At the end we met her, and all got pictures. I don't think the men would have felt able to do that, not that they don't want to – it's just different."

As Emily's father, Richard, puts it: "The World Cup has done more to raise my daughter's interest in the game than any coaching session or televised match." The Clarks' experience was no anomaly, and it wasn't just the big names who piqued interest: widespread coverage of the World Cup, which coincided with the launch of the ECB's All Stars Cricket programme, meant the ensuing Kia Super League saw healthy crowds and media coverage.

Emma Whiteman, a police officer who also volunteers as the Middlesex women's team manager, has a five-year-old son and three-year-old daughter. "Eliza, my daughter, had been exposed to cricket before, but she wasn't a fan as such," she says. "It has all been down to All Stars and watching live cricket." Eliza watched every Surrey Stars home match and the final, decked out in a replica shirt adorned with the name of all-rounder Sophia Dunkley. "She's adamant she will play for them when she grows up!"

For many parents, the World Cup was the first clear proof that cricket was not just for boys. Rob McGregor has a five-year-old daughter in Cambridgeshire: "All the evidence she had seen up to the World Cup had backed up her boys-only perception of the sport. The tournament gave her the opportunity to break that view."

Even Paul Collingwood – England's only male captain to have lifted a global trophy – felt the event was a turning point. "I've been trying for years and today finally my daughters want to play cricket!" he tweeted, watching the final with his three girls, aged 11, eight and six, from their home in Northumberland. "Thank you England women, inspirational!"

It was a tournament noticeable not just for the numbers it attracted, but for a culture shift: girls can't merely see their heroes, they now know how to be their heroes. And they're already eyeing up the competition they will have to face to get there.

Isabelle Westbury is a sports broadcaster and former captain of Middlesex.

Stu Forster, Getty Images

Sweeping statement: India's Harmanpreet Kaur hits 171 not out against Australia in the semi-final.

their first semi-final in 17 years, claiming three four-fors with her leg-spin. She finished as the tournament's leading wicket-taker, with 15 at an average of ten – including four for none during the rout of West Indies – and conceded just 3.46 an over, the best economy-rate of anyone who bowled at least 20. The South Africans took England to the wire in the semi at Bristol, and the emotion on show after Shrubsole's winning hit was contagious. The image of her placing a consoling hand on van Niekerk's shoulder earned comparisons with Andrew Flintoff commiserating with Brett Lee at Edgbaston in 2005, a gesture that later won her the Christopher Martin-Jenkins Spirit of Cricket award.

England's route to the final, then, was not straightforward: a loss to India, a three-run victory against Australia – their first in a World Cup since 1993 – and that tightest of semi-finals. But what finished as an eight-match winning streak highlighted their dominance with the bat (they managed 377 against Pakistan and 373 against South Africa), and Beaumont came of age to be named Player of the Tournament for her 410 runs. Sciver's between-the-legs stroke against New Zealand, meanwhile, was instantly termed the "Natmeg", and went viral. England were also happy to see the return of Taylor after more than a year out because of anxiety. She averaged almost 50, and her stumping of South Africa's Trisha Chetty in the semi-final off a leg-side wide was among the tournament's most memorable moments.

For **India's** captain Mithali Raj, a place in the final was not such a bad way to sign off her international career. In the group match against Australia, she had overhauled Edwards's aggregate of 5,992 to become the leading run-scorer in women's ODI cricket. She also hit her sixth century to set up victory in what was effectively a quarter-final against New Zealand, who were sent packing for 79. **New Zealand** had been among the favourites, and their pool of talent included

Sophie Devine, who crashed a record-breaking nine sixes against Pakistan. But their group-stage exit left question marks over their temperament. Not long after **Pakistan** got home, a report by the coach Sabih Azhar was leaked to the media, blaming captain Sana Mir for her team's struggles, and calling her "self-obsessed"; in August, Mir – who denied the accusation – resigned.

fy410,1,7.75,8.5 The last shock came in the second semi-final, at Derby, where **Australia** missed their first global final since 2009. The match belonged to Harmanpreet Kaur, who hit an unbeaten 171 in a display of outrageous skill and placement, as Australia's bowlers were torn to pieces for the second time in the tournament. It confirmed suspicions that their pace attack were distinctly under par. Five successive half-centuries from Ellyse Perry were left unrewarded.

Overall, the tournament screamed progress: there were 15 totals above 250 (compared with eight in 2013); 111 sixes (67); and 14 hundreds (11). The importance for the world game of India reaching the final – their first since 2005 – could not be overstated, as a nation of cricket lovers woke up to the fact that women, too, could be heroes. They met with a frenzied reception on their return to Mumbai airport, and the BCCI awarded each squad member Rs 50 lakh (approximately £60,000).

For the ECB, too, there were hopes that success would inspire a new generation of girls. World Cups, though, always present a unique opportunity for women's cricket to reach a new audience; as ever the challenge will be not to squander it. It remained to be seen whether calls for renewed investment in domestic women's cricket by both the BCCI and the ECB, including a women's IPL and an extension of England's Super League, would be answered. What could not be denied was that those calls were louder than ever.

WOMEN'S WORLD CUP STATISTICS

Leading run-scorers

	M	*I*	*NO*	*R*	*HS*	*100*	*50*	*Avge*	*SR*	*4*	*6*
T. T. Beaumont (E)	9	9	0	410	148	1	1	45.55	76.92	54	3
M. D. Raj (I)	9	9	0	409	109	1	3	45.44	70.15	36	1
E. A. Perry (A)	8	8	3	404	71	0	5	80.80	77.54	34	3
S. J. Taylor (E)	9	9	1	396	147	1	2	49.50	99.00	54	0
P. G. Raut (I)	9	9	0	381	106	1	2	42.33	67.43	35	3
N. R. Sciver (E)	9	9	1	369	137	2	1	46.12	107.58	35	4
H. C. Knight (E)	9	9	1	364	106	1	2	45.50	80.53	34	5
H. Kaur (I)	9	8	2	359	171*	1	2	59.83	95.47	33	11
†N. E. Bolton (A)	8	8	1	351	107*	1	2	50.14	77.82	45	0
M. M. Lanning (A)	6	6	2	328	152*	1	1	82.00	92.13	38	3
L. Wolvaardt (SA)	7	7	2	324	71	0	4	64.80	68.21	39	0
†A. M. C. Jayangani (SL)	7	7	1	311	178*	1	1	51.83	88.85	40	6

> "So often England's heartbeat, Stokes batted as if he'd undergone a transplant, scoring 34 from 64 balls."
>
> Champions Trophy in 2017, England v India, page 282

Best strike-rates

	SR	Runs
S. F. M. Devine (NZ)	117.75	126
E. J. Villani (A)	112.97	148
V. Krishnamurthy (I)	112.50	153
A. J. Blackwell (A)	109.72	203
N. R. Sciver (E)	107.58	369
L. Lee (SA)	103.46	269
F. C. Wilson (E)	102.58	159
R. H. Priest (NZ)	101.62	125

Minimum 125 runs.

Leading wicket-takers

	Style	O	M	R	W	BB	4I	Avge	SR	ER
D. van Niekerk (SA)	LB	43.2	6	150	15	4-0	3	10.00	17.33	3.46
M. Kapp (SA)	RFM	56.3	6	252	13	4-14	1	19.38	26.07	4.46
K. M. Beams (A)	LB	65	3	266	12	3-23	0	22.16	32.50	4.09
A. Shrubsole (E)	RFM	65.4	6	304	12	6-46	1	25.33	32.83	4.62
D. B. Sharma (I)	OB	78.4	8	370	12	3-47	0	30.83	39.33	4.70
P. Yadav (I)	LB	74	5	286	11	2-19	0	26.00	40.36	3.86
L. M. Kasperek (NZ)	OB	40	9	146	10	3-17	0	14.60	24.00	3.65
S. E. Luus (SA)	LB	36	1	174	10	5-67	1	17.40	21.60	4.83
A. C. Kerr (NZ)	LB	50	2	224	10	4-51	1	22.40	30.00	4.48
S. Ismail (SA)	RFM	56.1	3	264	10	3-14	0	26.40	33.70	4.70
J. N. Goswami (I)	RFM	64.1	7	266	10	3-23	0	26.60	38.50	4.14
A. Hartley (E)	SLA	72	6	302	10	3-44	0	30.20	43.20	4.19
M. L. Schutt (A)	RFM	63.5	7	306	10	3-40	0	30.60	38.30	4.79

Most economical bowlers

	ER	Overs
D. van Niekerk (SA)	3.46	43.2
L. M. Kasperek (NZ)	3.65	40
K. H. Brunt (E)	3.77	67
A. Khaka (SA)	3.85	57
P. Yadav (I)	3.86	74
H. R. Huddleston (NZ)	3.89	28
S. R. Taylor (WI)	3.94	49.1
L. A. Marsh (E)	4.00	49
A. K. Gardner (A)	4.01	74
K. M. Beams (A)	4.09	65
S. F. M. Devine (NZ)	4.09	26.5
J. N. Goswami (I)	4.14	64.1
J. L. Jonassen (A)	4.18	66
A. Hartley (E)	4.19	72

Minimum 25 overs.

Leading wicketkeepers

	Dis	M
S. Verma (I)	15 (7ct, 8st)	9
A. J. Healy (A)	8 (5ct, 3st)	8
R. H. Priest (NZ)	7 (5ct, 2st)	6
M. R. Aguilleira (WI)	7 (4ct, 3st)	7
T. Chetty (SA)	7 (4ct, 3st)	7
Sidra Nawaz (P)	7 (7ct)	7
S. J. Taylor (E)	6 (4ct, 2 st)	9

Leading fielders

	Ct	M
A. E. Satterthwaite (NZ)	8	6
M. Kapp (SA)	7	7
J. N. Goswami (I)	7	9
Sana Mir (P)	6	7
N. R. Sciver (E)	6	9
A. M. C. Jayangani (SL)	5	7
E. J. Villani (A)	5	8
S. S. Mandhana (I)	5	9

NATIONAL SQUADS

* *Captain.* ‡ *Did not play.*

Australia *M. M. Lanning, S. E. Aley, K. M. Beams, A. J. Blackwell, N. E. Bolton, A. K. Gardner, R. L. Haynes, A. J. Healy, J. L. Jonassen, B. L. Mooney, E. A. Perry, M. L. Schutt, B. W. Vakarewa, E. J. Villani, A-J. Wellington. *Coach:* M. P. Mott.

England *H. C. Knight, T. T. Beaumont, K. H. Brunt, ‡G. A. Elwiss, J. L. Gunn, A. Hartley, D. Hazell, ‡B. A. Langston, L. A. Marsh, N. R. Sciver, A. Shrubsole, S. J. Taylor, F. C. Wilson, L. Winfield, D. N. Wyatt. *Coach:* M. A. Robinson.

India *M. D. Raj, E. K. Bisht, R. S. Gayakwad, J. N. Goswami, M. Joshi, H. Kaur, V. Krishnamurthy, S. S. Mandhana, M. R. Meshram, S. S. Pandey, ‡N. M. Parween, P. G. Raut, D. B. Sharma, S. Verma, P. Yadav. *Coach:* T. B. Arothe.

New Zealand *S. W. Bates, E. M. Bermingham, S. F. M. Devine, M. L. Green, H. R. Huddleston, L. M. Kasperek, A. C. Kerr, K. J. Martin, ‡T. M. M. Newton, K. T. Perkins, A. M. Peterson, R. H. Priest, H. M. Rowe, A. E. Satterthwaite, L-M. M. Tahuhu. *Coach:* H. M. Tiffen.

Pakistan *Sana Mir, Asmavia Iqbal, Ayesha Zafar, Bismah Maroof, Diana Baig, ‡Ghulam Fatima, Iram Javed, Javeria Khan, Kainat Imtiaz, Marina Iqbal, Nahida Khan, Nain Abidi, Nashra Sandhu, Sadia Yousuf, Sidra Nawaz, ‡Waheeda Akhtar. *Coach:* Sabih Azhar.

Iram Javed replaced Bismah Maroof, who injured her hand against England.

South Africa *D. van Niekerk, T. Chetty, M. R. Daniels, ‡N. de Klerk, M. du Preez, S. Ismail, M. Kapp, A. Khaka, ‡O. Kirsten, M. M. Klaas, L. Lee, S. E. Luus, ‡R. Ntozakhe, ‡A. Steyn, C. L. Tryon, L. Wolvaardt. *Coach:* H. K. Moreeng.

Kirsten replaced Steyn, who injured her ankle while training.

Sri Lanka *I. Ranaweera, H. H. C. Gunaratne, M. D. N. Hansika, A. M. C. Jayangani, K. A. D. A. Kanchana, L. E. Kaushalya, P. R. C. S. Kumarihami, G. W. H. M. Perera, K. D. U. Prabodhani, O. U. Ranasinghe, H. M. D. Samarawickrama, H. A. S. D. Siriwardene, M. A. D. D. Surangika, W. P. M. Weerakkodi, S. S. Weerakkody. *Coach:* H. H. Devapriya.

West Indies *S. R. Taylor, M. R. Aguilleira, R. Boyce, S. S. Connell, S. F. Daley, D. J. S. Dottin, A. S. S. Fletcher, Q. Joseph, Kycia A. Knight, Kyshona A. Knight, H. K. Matthews, A. Mohammed, ‡S. L. Munroe, C. N. Nation, A. K. Peters, S. C. Selman, F. Walters. *Coach:* V. C. Drakes.

Selman was hit on the head against Australia, and Connell injured her hip against India. Kycia Knight and Subrina Munroe replaced them.

GROUP STAGE

At Derby, June 24. **India won by 35 runs. India 281-3** (50 overs) (P. G. Raut 86, S. S. Mandhana 90, M. D. Raj 71); **‡England 246** (47.3 overs) (H. C. Knight 46, F. C. Wilson 81; D. B. Sharma 3-47). *PoM:* S. S. Mandhana. *Attendance:* 2,343. *The excellence of India's batting and fielding – helped by the ordinariness of England's bowling – proved too much for the hosts. Heather Knight inserted India beneath heavy cloud, but the openers were not parted until they had put on 144 in 26 overs. Punam Raut was dropped twice in the twenties, while her faster-scoring partner, 20-year-old Smriti Mandhana, made 90 from 72 balls. Mithali Raj maintained the pace, and her majestic form, becoming the second player, male or female, to hit seven successive ODI fifties (Pakistan's Javed Miandad made nine). A target of 282 looked tricky, but not impossible. England welcomed back Sarah Taylor, playing her first international for 15 months after suffering from anxiety; she made 22. Despite losing regular wickets, they remained in contention at 134-3 and 216-5. Ultimately, though, four run-outs by India's live-wire fielders confirmed their downfall. One of those casualties was top-scorer Fran Wilson, who hit a career-best 81 from 75 balls.*

At Bristol, June 24. **New Zealand won by nine wickets. Sri Lanka 188-9** (50 overs) (M. D. N. Hansika 31, P. R. C. S. Kumarihami 49, A. M. C. Jayangani 53; H. R. Huddleston 5-35); **‡New Zealand 189-1** (37.4 overs) (S. W. Bates 106*, A. E. Satterthwaite 78*). *PoM:* H. R. Huddleston. *Attendance:* 579. *New Zealand eased to their tenth win in ten ODIs against Sri Lanka after Suzie Bates (106* from 109 balls, her eighth century in the format) and Amy Satterthwaite put on 170* in 32 overs for the second wicket. Earlier, Bates had pulled off a superb catch to dismiss Chamari Atapattu Jayangani for 53, kick-starting a horrible collapse of eight for 47. That included five wickets for seamer Holly Huddleston on her World Cup debut, and left New Zealand a modest 189. Despite the early loss of Rachel Priest, they scooted home with more than 12 overs to spare.*

At Leicester, June 25. **South Africa won by three wickets. Pakistan 206-8** (50 overs) (Nahida Khan 79); ‡**South Africa 207-7** (49 overs) (L. Wolvaardt 52, L. Lee 60, M. du Preez 30). *PoM:* S. Ismail. *Attendance:* 346. *South Africa were cruising while openers Laura Wolvaardt and Lizelle Lee were adding 113, but panic set in soon after they were separated. There were three run-outs as the score lurched to 177-7, before Suné Luus (15*) and Shabnim Ismail (22*) spirited their side across the line with six balls in hand, adding 30* in four overs. Ismail had earlier taken 2-52 and run out top-scorer Nahida Khan, while her fellow seamer Moseline Daniels returned 10–4–21–2.*

At Taunton, June 26. **Australia won by eight wickets.** ‡**West Indies 204** (47.5 overs) (H. K. Matthews 46, C. N. Nation 39, S. R. Taylor 45; E. A. Perry 3-47); **Australia 205-2** (38.1 overs) (B. L. Mooney 70, N. E. Bolton 107*). *PoM:* N. E. Bolton. *ODI debut:* F. Walters (West Indies). *Attendance:* 1,374. *Australia, who had crushed West Indies in the 2013 World Cup final, did it again – after a strange start. West Indies captain Stafanie Taylor told Meg Lanning she wanted to bat, then changed her mind while being interviewed on TV; when Lanning protested, referee David Jukes said the first call had to stand. Taylor played steadily for 45, and later claimed both Australian wickets, but West Indies lost their last seven for 47 once Deandra Dottin, trying to lift the rate, was bowled by Ellyse Perry. Beth Mooney and Nicole Bolton ran up 171 for Australia's first wicket, and Bolton reached her hundred before completing a straightforward victory.*

At Leicester, June 27. **England won by 107 runs** (DLS). **England 377-7** (50 overs) (H. C. Knight 106, N. R. Sciver 137, D. N. Wyatt 42*, F. C. Wilson 33; Asmavia Iqbal 3-62); ‡**Pakistan 107-3** (29.2 overs) (Ayesha Zafar 56*). *PoM:* N. R. Sciver. *Attendance:* 2,169. *Ferocious hitting from Nat Sciver helped England to a thumping win, and persuaded Knight, her captain, to compare her to Ben Stokes. Sciver thrashed 137 in 92 balls, hit 14 fours and four sixes – three in succession off Asmavia Iqbal – and added 213 in 30 punishing overs for the third wicket with Knight. Both scored their maiden ODI hundred. With Danielle Wyatt adding 42* in 27, and Wilson 33 in 19, England finished only one short of their previous best, against Pakistan at Worcester in 2016. Their total was the fifth-highest in all women's ODIs. Katherine Brunt made two early incisions, and Pakistan were 67-3 when Alex Hartley's left-arm spin prised out Asmavia. Ayesha Zafar gritted it out for a half-century but, when rain engulfed Grace Road, they were well off the pace.*

At Derby, June 28. **New Zealand v South Africa. Abandoned.**

At Bristol, June 29. **Australia won by eight wickets. Sri Lanka 257-9** (50 overs) (A. M. C. Jayangani 178*); ‡**Australia 262-2** (43.5 overs) (N. E. Bolton 60, M. M. Lanning 152*, E. A. Perry 39*). *PoM:* A. M. C. Jayangani. *ODI debut:* B. W. Vakarewa (Australia). *Attendance:* 703. *On a benign pitch Australia were pushed harder than expected, thanks almost entirely to Atapattu. Her 178* from just 143 balls was Sri Lanka's highest score in ODIs (she had now hit all three of their hundreds) and the third-highest overall, after Belinda Clark's 229* for Australia v Denmark in the 1997-98 World Cup, and Deepti Sharma's 188 for India v Ireland earlier in 2017. Atapattu hit an ODI-record 124 in boundaries – 22 fours and six sixes – but her team-mates managed only 60 runs between them: she made 69.2% of the total, beating the ODI record of England's Lynne Thomas, who scored 70* out of 113 (61.9%) while captaining an International XI against India in the 1981-82 World Cup in New Zealand. Only England (279-3 at Birmingham in the inaugural tournament in 1973) had made a higher World Cup total against Australia. Bolton, bowling for the first time in her 32nd ODI, took 2-18 in three overs of off-spin as regular wickets went down at the other end. But Atapattu was trumped by Lanning, who entered when Mooney was out for a duck in the second over and zoomed to her 11th ODI hundred, dominating stands of 133 with Bolton and 124* with Perry. Her career-best 152* needed only 135 balls.*

At Taunton, June 29. **India won by seven wickets. West Indies 183-8** (50 overs) (H. K. Matthews 43, S. F. Daley 33, A. S. S. Fletcher 36*); ‡**India 186-3** (42.3 overs) (S. S. Mandhana 106*, M. D. Raj 46). *PoM:* S. S. Mandhana. *Attendance:* 591. *This game followed form: India collected another convincing win, West Indies another heavy defeat. Mandhana took up where she left off against England and, though she was dropped at deep midwicket on 94, reached a hundred of great authority (and some beauty) to steer India to their unchallenging target. She and Raj, who narrowly failed to hit an eighth successive fifty, added 108 for the third wicket. Earlier, West Indies had batted in treacle during 37 overs of stifling spin: Poonam Yadav's leg-breaks took 2-19 from ten. For Taylor and Dottin, both playing their 100th ODI, it was otherwise a day to forget.*

At Bristol, July 2. **Australia won by five wickets.** ‡**New Zealand 219-9** (50 overs) (S. W. Bates 51, K. T. Perkins 52, E. M. Bermingham 35; M. L. Schutt 3-40, J. L. Jonassen 3-33); **Australia 220-5** (48.4 overs) (B. L. Mooney 32, M. M. Lanning 48, E. A. Perry 71, A. J. Blackwell 36*). *PoM:* E. A. Perry. *Attendance:* 1,036. *While New Zealand were compiling a middling 219, Perry couldn't take a*

Hit parade: Sri Lanka's Chamari Atapattu launches one of her 28 boundaries against Australia.

wicket. But she later proved her worth, hitting a powerful 71, passing 2,000 ODI runs, and leading Australia to a third win from three. The only wobble came when 16-year-old leg-spinner Amelia Kerr picked up two in two balls – the second a googly that ripped through Elyse Villani's defences – to make it 143-4. Earlier, left-arm spinner Jess Jonassen had been the pick of the Australian bowlers, enjoying the slow surface and collecting 3-33, including Bates the ball after she had brought up her 23rd half-century, in her 100th ODI.

At Taunton, July 2. **England won by seven wickets.** ‡**Sri Lanka 204-8** (50 overs) (G. W. H. M. Perera 46, H. A. S. D. Siriwardene 33, K. A. D. A. Kanchana 34*; L. A. Marsh 4-45); **England 206-3** (30.2 overs) (S. J. Taylor 74*, H. C. Knight 82). *PoM:* L. A. Marsh. *Attendance:* 3,426. *England cantered to a second victory with nearly 20 overs in hand. In her first game of the tournament, off-spinner Laura Marsh reduced Sri Lanka to 145-7 as she bowled ten overs off the reel. Then Taylor, now in her preferred position at No. 3 after the return from a wrist injury of opener Lauren Winfield, moved fluently to the first fifty of her comeback. She added 148 for England's third wicket with Knight, who was caught at the end of the 30th over, with seven required; Taylor got them by striking the next two deliveries for four to finish with a 67-ball 74*.*

At Derby, July 2. **India won by 95 runs.** ‡**India 169-9** (50 overs) (P. G. Raut 47, S. Verma 33; Nashra Sandhu 4-26); **Pakistan 74** (38.1 overs) (E. K. Bisht 5-18). *PoM:* E. K. Bisht. *Attendance:* 2,649. *For the second time in the year, Ekta Bisht routed Pakistan with her accurate slow left-armers. At a World Cup qualifier in Colombo in February, she had returned figures 10–7–8–5 as Pakistan were skittled for 67. This time, she managed 5-18 – the first three lbw – in a total of 74, taking the overall score in ODIs between the sides to 10–0. Only Nahida Khan (23 from 62 balls) and captain Sana Mir (29 from 73, batting at No. 8) reached double figures. India's own innings had come unstuck against left-arm spin too, as 19-year-old Nashra Sandhu picked up a career-best 4-26. But 169-9 proved plenty.*

At Leicester, July 2. **South Africa won by ten wickets. West Indies 48** (25.2 overs) (M. Kapp 4-14, D. van Niekerk 4-0); ‡**South Africa 51-0** (6.2 overs). *PoM:* M. Kapp. *ODI debuts:* R. Boyce, Q. Joseph (West Indies). *Attendance:* 486. *Even on the village green, few matches are so one-sided. Bowling with pace and swing, Ismail (2-16) and Marizanne Kapp cut a swathe through the West Indian batting. The eighth over – a triple-wicket maiden for Kapp – sent them spiralling to 16-5, and matters scarcely improved. Such fight as there was came from Chedean Nation, whose 26 included 11 of West Indies' 21 scoring strokes, and Merissa Aguilleira, who survived 38 balls for three. The loopy leg-breaks of Dane van Niekerk foxed them both, and she became the first bowler in all one-day internationals to hoover up four wickets at no cost. South Africa zipped to their target in 27 minutes, and the entire contest lasted less than 32 overs.*

CHEAPEST FOUR-FORS IN A WOMEN'S ODI

4-0	**D. van Niekerk**	**South Africa v West Indies at Leicester**	**2017**
4-1	D. M. Marathe	India v South Africa at Pretoria	2004-05
5-2	S. Sivanantham	Sri Lanka v Pakistan at Colombo (Moors)	2001-02
4-2	A. L. Mason	New Zealand v South Africa at Bowral	2008-09
4-3	C. A. Hodges	England v Denmark at Banstead	1993
4-3	W. R. P. Fernando	Sri Lanka v Pakistan at Colombo (PSS)	2001-02
4-3	A. D. Janakanthymala	Sri Lanka v Pakistan at Colombo (Moors)	2001-02
7-4	Sajjida Shah	Pakistan v Japan at Amsterdam	2003
4-4	K. M. Brown	Australia v Netherlands at Perth	1988-89
4-4	B. L. Calver	Australia v West Indies at Tunbridge Wells	1993
4-4	C. E. Eksteen	South Africa v Ireland at Belfast	1997
4-4	G. Sultana	India v Sri Lanka at Visakhapatnam	2013-14

At Leicester, July 5. **Australia won by 159 runs.** ‡**Australia 290-8** (50 overs) (E. A. Perry 66, E. J. Villani 59, A. J. Healy 63*; Sana Mir 3-49); **Pakistan 131** (50 overs) (Sana Mir 45; K. M. Beams 3-23, A. K. Gardner 3-28). *PoM:* E. J. Villani. *ODI debut:* S. E. Aley (Australia). *Attendance:* 545. *Australia's captain Meg Lanning was out with a shoulder niggle, but they still had the might to trounce Pakistan. Rachael Haynes – leading in her first appearance of the tournament, despite the presence of Lanning's official deputy, Alex Blackwell – chose to bat, and saw her team limp to 18-2 after ten. Then they started motoring: Perry stroked 66, Villani clubbed 59 from 40 balls (including four sixes, equalling the most in an innings by an Australian), and Alyssa Healy added 63* from 40. Pakistan needed 291, but lacked any belief in an upset. At halfway, they were 62-5, and dribbled to 131 all out, unable to answer the spinners, who managed 28–10–63–7 between them. Only Sana Mir resisted, her 45 backing up figures of 3-49.*

At Bristol, July 5. **England won by 68 runs.** ‡**England 373-5** (50 overs) (T. T. Beaumont 148, S. J. Taylor 147; M. Kapp 3-77); **South Africa 305-9** (50 overs) (L. Wolvaardt 67, L. Lee 72, M. du Preez 43, C. L. Tryon 54; D. Hazell 3-70). *PoM:* S. J. Taylor. *Attendance:* 1,966. *Only three days after skittling West Indies for 48, South Africa's bowlers were battered by Tammy Beaumont, who clobbered 22 fours and a six, and Taylor, whose 147 – studded with 24 fours, five in succession in one Ismail over – was the highest of her six ODI centuries. They piled on 275, a World Cup record for any wicket, exceeded in women's ODIs only by the 320 of Deepti Sharma and Raut for India v Ireland earlier in 2017. The huge stand ensured a comfortable victory for England, despite a spirited reply by South Africa, for whom Chloe Tryon spanked 54 from 26 balls after the openers put on 128. The match aggregate of 678 was easily a record for any women's ODI, beating 577 by New Zealand (288-6) and Australia (289-6) in Sydney in 2012-13.*

At Derby, July 5. **India won by 16 runs.** ‡**India 232-8** (50 overs) (D. B. Sharma 78, M. D. Raj 53; S. S. Weerakkody 3-28); **Sri Lanka 216-7** (50 overs) (H. A. S. D. Siriwardene 37, M. A. D. D. Surangika 61). *PoM:* D. B. Sharma. *Attendance:* 423. *India's win was their fourth in four matches, but their narrowest so far. Their total depended heavily on a third-wicket stand of 118 between 19-year-old left-hander Sharma and Raj, who had made her international debut before Sharma's second birthday. But Sripali Weerakkody was on a hat-trick in the penultimate over, checking the final charge. Yadav conceded just 23 in a single ten-over spell and picked up two top-order wickets. Dilani Manodara Surangika batted on into the 48th over for a career-best 61 before being stumped off Sharma's off-spin, and the tail could not quite close the gap.*

At Taunton, July 6. **New Zealand won by eight wickets. West Indies 150** (43 overs) (Kyshona A. Knight 41; L-M. M. Tahuhu 3-39, L. M. Kasperek 3-17); ‡**New Zealand 151-2** (18.2 overs) (S. W. Bates 40*, R. H. Priest 90). *PoM:* L. M. Kasperek. *ODI debut:* A. K. Peters (West Indies). *Attendance:* 1,178. *Four days after they rolled over for 48 against South Africa, West Indies all but surrendered once more. From 53-2, they lost three for none in eight balls – two to off-spinner Leigh Kasperek, in her first ODI since February 2016 – and never properly recovered, despite 41 from Kyshona Knight; Kasperek finished with 10–6–17–3. Priest took care of the chase almost by herself, powering a 55-ball 90, of which 80 came in boundaries during an opening stand of 120 inside 15 overs with Bates. The one-way traffic condemned West Indies to their fourth defeat out of four.*

At Leicester, July 8. **South Africa won by 115 runs. South Africa 273-9** (50 overs) (L. Lee 92, D. van Niekerk 57; S. S. Pandey 3-40); ‡**India 158** (46 overs) (D. B. Sharma 60, J. N. Goswami 43*; D. van Niekerk 4-22). *PoM:* D. van Niekerk. *Attendance:* 1,442. *India slumped to their first* *defeat of the tournament, scuppered by a collapse from 47-1 to 65-7. Van Niekerk's leg-spin accounted for Raj and Harmanpreet Kaur for ducks in the space of three balls (Raj's nought was her first in 49 ODIs since March 2012), and she returned to remove top-scorer Sharma, whose 60 occupied 111 deliveries. Ismail, pummelled by England to the tune of 1-89, now returned 9–1–18–1. Earlier, Lee had spanked seven sixes and ten fours in a 65-ball 92, then van Niekerk steered her side to a competitive total.*

At Taunton, July 8. **New Zealand won by eight wickets.** ‡**Pakistan 144** (46.5 overs) (Sana Mir 50; H. M. Rowe 3-22); **New Zealand 147-2** (15 overs) (A. E. Satterthwaite 38*, S. F. M. Devine 93). *PoM:* H. M. Rowe. *Attendance:* 899. *The brutal Sophie Devine reached her fifty from 27 balls, and had roared to 93 when she skied a return catch to Nashra Sandhu off her 41st. Her innings included nine sixes – a record for women's one-day internationals – eight sailing over the arc from midwicket to long-on. Nobody else on either side managed one. Watching calmly from the other end was Satterthwaite, who struck 38 from 42. Earlier, Hannah Rowe, a tall seamer making her World Cup debut, had figures of 9–2–22–3 as Pakistan failed to build on a promising opening stand of 35. Sana Mir, their captain, hit her third fifty in her 100th game, but no one else escaped the teens. A fifth successive defeat meant Pakistan could not progress.*

At Bristol, July 9. **England won by three runs.** ‡**England 259-8** (50 overs) (T. T. Beaumont 49, S. J. Taylor 35, K. H. Brunt 45*, J. L. Gunn 39, Extras 32; E. J. Villani 3-42); **Australia 256-8** (50 overs) (B. L. Mooney 31, E. A. Perry 70, M. M. Lanning 40). *PoM:* K. H. Brunt. *Attendance:* 4,316. *Needing six off the final delivery, Jonassen managed two; England beat Australia in a World Cup game for the first time since 1993, to go top of the table. Beaumont had anchored them while team-mates hit out, but England prospects looked uncertain at 174-6, until Katherine Brunt and Jenny Gunn battered 85 in 12 overs to set a target of 260. Australia whittled that down to 45 off 24 balls before Brunt removed Blackwell and Perry in five deliveries, and 16 when Gunn began the final over; Jonassen hit two fours, but Brunt caught Ashleigh Gardner at long-on, and England closed in. Their victory arrived three minutes before the men's team won the Lord's Test against South Africa, with fans frantically switching channels to keep up.*

At Derby, July 9. **West Indies won by 47 runs. West Indies 229-9** (50 overs) (D. J. S. Dottin 38, M. R. Aguilleira 46*; S. S. Weerakkody 3-38); ‡**Sri Lanka 182** (48 overs) (H. A. S. D. Siriwardene 33, W. P. M. Weerakkodi 30; A. Mohammed 3-39). *PoM:* A. Mohammed. *Attendance:* 368. *After another muddled batting display, West Indies relied on spin to defend 229 and earn their first win of the tournament. Anisa Mohammed – the pick of their five slow bowlers – took 3-1 in nine balls, and added a direct-hit run-out, to hobble the Sri Lankan chase. Dottin, the lone seamer, bowled two wicketless overs. Earlier, her knock had been typical of the West Indian innings: she hit seven fours in zooming to 38, before yielding her wicket carelessly by missing a reverse dab. It needed the nous of Aguilleira, who top-scored with 46* and hit just two fours, to haul them to a defendable score.*

At Leicester, July 11. **West Indies won by 19 runs** (DLS). **West Indies 285-4** (50 overs) (S. R. Taylor 90, C. N. Nation 35, D. J. S. Dottin 104*); ‡**Pakistan 117-3** (24 overs) (Nahida Khan 40, Javeria Khan 58*). *PoM:* D. J. S. Dottin. *Attendance:* 253. *A maiden one-day international hundred from Dottin, in her 99th innings, powered West Indies to a total that proved beyond Pakistan when the rain that had hung around all day intervened one last time. Dottin, who celebrated her 71-ball century – the fastest by a West Indian – by hurling her bat towards square leg, had added 91 with Taylor and 81* with Aguilleira. In all, 74 came from the last seven overs, during which Dottin thrashed 52 from 21 balls. The weather meant Pakistan needed 245 in 38 overs, but allowed them only 24; not even a second-wicket stand of 80 between Nahida Khan and Javeria Khan could drag them ahead on DLS.*

At Bristol, July 12. **Australia won by eight wickets. India 226-7** (50 overs) (P. G. Raut 106, M. D. Raj 69); ‡**Australia 227-2** (45.1 overs) (N. E. Bolton 36, B. L. Mooney 45, M. M. Lanning 76*, E. A. Perry 60*). *PoM:* M. M. Lanning. *Attendance:* 947. *Australia sealed a semi-final place despite a century from Raut. She put on 157 for the second wicket with Raj, who passed England's Charlotte Edwards (5,992) as the leading scorer in women's ODIs when she reached 34*. But it took her 82 balls to get there, and in all the stand lasted 37 overs against some disciplined bowling, meaning the target was not a frightening one. After Australia's openers put on 62, Lanning and Perry had few alarms in sealing victory with a stand of 124*.*

At Derby, July 12. **England won by 75 runs.** ‡**England 284-9** (50 overs) (T. T. Beaumont 93, N. R. Sciver 129; A. C. Kerr 4-51); **New Zealand 209** (46.4 overs) (S. W. Bates 44, A. E. Satterthwaite 35, K. T. Perkins 43*; A. Hartley 3-44). *PoM:* N. R. Sciver. *Attendance:* 2,273. *England were indebted to*

Beaumont and Sciver, who added 170 for the fourth wicket, while none of their team-mates passed 11. Both were pursuing their second century of the tournament until Beaumont became the first of four victims for Kerr. Sciver advanced to 129 in 111 balls – improvising a shot christened the Natmeg when she tapped Huddleston's yorker between her legs. Bates and Satterthwaite, in her 100th ODI, took New Zealand to 89-1, only for the innings to crumble around Katie Perkins's 43. When Hartley wrapped up victory, England waltzed into the semi-finals; New Zealand now had to fight India for a place.*

At Taunton, July 12. **South Africa won by eight wickets.** ‡**Sri Lanka 101** (40.3 overs) (S. Ismail 3-14, D. van Niekerk 4-24); **South Africa 104-2** (23.1 overs) (L. Wolvaardt 48*, M. du Preez 38*). *PoM:* D. van Niekerk. *Attendance:* 1,056. *South Africa reached the semis – ensuring a top-four finish for the first time since 2000 – with a resounding win. After Inoka Ranaweera chose to bat on a cloudy morning, Sri Lanka lost the influential Atapattu for a single. Progress was never quick, though at 48-2 in the 20th there was some hope of a competitive total. Instead, van Niekerk dismantled the middle order. Her third four-for of the tournament included a catch by Trisha Chetty – her 134th ODI dismissal as a keeper, one clear of New Zealand's Rebecca Rolls, the previous record holder. A target of 102 looked a little steeper at 26-2, but Wolvaardt and Mignon du Preez added 78*.*

At Taunton, July 15. **Australia won by 59 runs.** ‡**Australia 269** (48.3 overs) (B. L. Mooney 53, N. E. Bolton 79, E. A. Perry 55, A. J. Blackwell 33; S. E. Luus 5-67); **South Africa 210** (50 overs) (L. Wolvaardt 71, T. Chetty 37). *PoM:* E. A. Perry. *Attendance:* 1,584. *At 99-1 in pursuit of 270, South Africa looked capable of a maiden victory over Australia. But once Perry ran out Chetty with a rocket from the boundary, the rot set in. Haynes, again captain in place of the rested Meg Lanning, took a wicket with her first ball in one-day internationals for over four years, a rank full toss. Next over, she added Wolvaardt – who had cover-driven beautifully to 71 – and the last nine went down for 111. Earlier, Mooney and Bolton had set Australia fair with a century opening stand. Perry then hit her fifth consecutive half-century – and her 21st in her last 29 ODI innings – to advance them to a winning score, despite five wickets for the leg-spin of Luus. Perry finished the group stage averaging 91.*

At Bristol, July 15. **England won by 92 runs. England 220-7** (50 overs) (T. T. Beaumont 42, H. C. Knight 67, L. A. Marsh 31*; A. S. S. Fletcher 3-33); ‡**West Indies 128-9** (50 overs) (N. R. Sciver 3-3). *PoM:* H. C. Knight. *Attendance:* 2,318. *England finished top after West Indies failed hopelessly to get to grips with a slow Bristol track. Seven players fell lbw, beating the women's record – England's six against India at Bangalore in February 2010 – as they chugged along at barely 2.5 an over. They managed only ten fours and a six. Sciver returned career-best figures of 4–1–3–3, having earlier made a duck as England slipped to 105-5 against the leg-breaks of Afy Fletcher. But Heather Knight dragged things round, and a late flurry from Marsh (31* in 19 balls) gave England something to bowl at. West Indies began with an opening stand of 34, but no one passed Hayley Matthews's 29.*

At Derby, July 15. **India won by 186 runs. India 265-7** (50 overs) (M. D. Raj 109, H. Kaur 60, V. Krishnamurthy 70; L. M. Kasperek 3-45); ‡**New Zealand 79** (25.3 overs) (R. S. Gayakwad 5-15). *PoM:* M. D. Raj. *Attendance:* 841. *The one-sided scorecard read like many in the tournament, but unlike any involving New Zealand in the history of the women's World Cup. Defeat in what was effectively a quarter-final meant that for the first time they would not finish in the top four. After Bates opted to bowl, all initially went to plan, New Zealand removing the openers by the eighth over. Then Raj, who went to her sixth ODI century, shared stands of 132 with Harmanpreet and 108 with the hard-hitting Veda Krishnamurthy to set a demanding target; 57 cascaded from the last five overs. Now the wheels properly came off the New Zealand wagon. Only three players made more than seven as Rajeshwari Gayakwad, in her first game of the competition, bamboozled them with intelligent left-arm spin. It was New Zealand's heaviest ODI defeat by runs, beating 131 by Australia at Wellington in 1998-99.*

At Leicester, July 15. **Sri Lanka won by 15 runs.** ‡**Sri Lanka 221-7** (50 overs) (M. A. D. D. Surangika 84; Diana Baig 3-41); **Pakistan 206** (46.4 overs) (Nain Abidi 57, Asmavia Iqbal 38*; H. H. C. Gunaratne 4-41). *PoM:* H. H. C. Gunaratne. *Attendance:* 383. *Sri Lanka emerged victorious in the battle between the tournament's two winless teams. But it was close: they slipped to 98-5 before Surangika put on 76 in 16 overs with Eshani Kaushalya (28). Pakistan stuttered early on, but passed 100 only three down. Left-arm spinner Chandima Gunaratne, who had removed both openers, returned to trap captain Sana Mir shortly after top-scorer Nain Abidi was run out. That made it 135-6 and, although Asmavia Iqbal kept Pakistan in touch, wickets continued to tumble – the last to Sri Lanka's skipper Ranaweera, another slow left-armer, who finished with 9.4–2–17–1.*

GROUP TABLE

	P	*W*	*L*	*A*	*Pts*	*NRR*
ENGLAND	7	6	1	0	12	1.29
AUSTRALIA	7	6	1	0	12	1.00
INDIA	7	5	2	0	10	0.66
SOUTH AFRICA	7	4	2	1	9	1.18
New Zealand	7	3	3	1	7	0.30
West Indies	7	2	5	0	4	–1.52
Sri Lanka	7	1	6	0	2	–1.09
Pakistan	7	0	7	0	0	–1.93

SEMI-FINALS

ENGLAND v SOUTH AFRICA

At Bristol, July 18. England won by two wickets. Toss: South Africa.

England scraped into the final with two balls to spare when No. 10 Shrubsole hit her first delivery through point for four to spark emotional scenes in both camps. They had needed three from the last over, bowled by Ismail: Gunn was dropped off the first ball and ran a single off the second, before Marsh was bowled by the third. South Africa had elected to bat, and – after a sensational stumping by Taylor to dismiss Chetty off a leg-side wide – their hopes were boosted by fifties from Wolvaardt and du Preez, but they could not force the pace; a target of 219 seemed modest, even after Khaka dismissed both England openers. Taylor and Knight progressed smoothly to 139 for two – and then the innings was rocked by three wickets in 12 deliveries. Taylor was run out by van Niekerk's direct hit from cover, Knight caught by a leaping Wolvaardt at square leg as she swept a Luus full toss, and Sciver bowled by Luus round her legs. Brunt followed to make it 173 for six, though the match looked safe when Wilson and Gunn steered England to 213, with six needed from 13 balls. But, once Wilson was caught behind, the runs dried up, until Shrubsole hit the winning boundary – and paused to console the distraught van Niekerk. "If you were in our changing-room right now," van Niekerk said later, "you'd probably start crying too."

Player of the Match: S. J. Taylor. *Attendance:* 2,206.

South Africa

L. Wolvaardt b Knight	66
L. Lee b Shrubsole	7
†T. Chetty st Taylor b Sciver	15
M. du Preez not out	76
M. Kapp run out	1
*D. van Niekerk run out	27
C. L. Tryon c and b Gunn	1
S. E. Luus not out	21
W 4	4
1/21 (2) 2/48 (3) 3/125 (1) 4/126 (5) 5/168 (6) 6/170 (7) — (6 wkts, 50 overs)	218
10 overs: 41-1	

S. Ismail, A. Khaka and M. R. Daniels did not bat.

Brunt 10–1–40–0; Shrubsole 10–1–33–1; Sciver 4–0–25–1; Marsh 9–0–37–0; Hartley 9–0–40–0; Gunn 6–0–35–1; Knight 2–0–8–1.

England

L. Winfield c du Preez b Khaka	20
T. T. Beaumont b Khaka	15
†S. J. Taylor run out	54
*H. C. Knight c Wolvaardt b Luus	30
N. R. Sciver b Luus	3
F. C. Wilson c Chetty b Kapp	30
K. H. Brunt b Daniels	12
J. L. Gunn not out	27
L. A. Marsh b Ismail	1
A. Shrubsole not out	4
B 5, w 17, nb 3	25
1/42 (1) 2/61 (2) 3/139 (3) 4/142 (4) 5/145 (5) 6/173 (7) 7/213 (6) 8/217 (9) — (8 wkts, 49.4 overs)	221
10 overs: 52-1	

A. Hartley did not bat.

Ismail 9.4–1–49–1; Kapp 10–1–43–1; Khaka 10–2–28–2; Daniels 10–0–47–1; van Niekerk 5–0–25–0; Luus 5–0–24–2.

Umpires: G. O. Brathwaite and C. M. Brown. Third umpire: P. Wilson.
Referee: S. R. Bernard.

AUSTRALIA v INDIA

At Derby, July 20. India won by 36 runs. Toss: India.

After 26 overs of their allotted 42, with India on 102 for three, and Harmanpreet Kaur 40 off 59 balls, there was little to suggest the carnage to come. Then, the wildest of full tosses from Beams, landing around fifth slip, triggered an astonishing assault. Harmanpreet smashed the free hit for six over long-on, and crunched a pull through midwicket to bring up a half-century; her next fifty took 26 balls, the one after just 17. Without thuggery, she laced seven sixes and 20 fours to all corners, ending on 171 not out from 115, the highest score in the knockout stages of a women's World Cup, and the fifth-highest in all one-day internationals. Gardner's figures told the story: her first five overs went for nine, her last three for 34. By the 39th over, Australia had lost control, and tried Villani as the sixth bowler: her over cost 19. The only time *Harmanpreet* lost control was with a team-mate, screaming and throwing her bat on the ground after Sharma was slow to return for a century-sealing second and was nearly caught short. The total of 281 was the most conceded by Australia in one-day internationals, and left them needing the highest successful chase in World Cups. When Goswami bowled Lanning with a beautiful leg-cutter for her first ODI duck since August 2014, their totem was toppled. Run-rate pressure told and, though Villani released some with a 58-ball 75, wickets tumbled. After the ninth went down, Blackwell refused to go quietly, biffing 65 in a partnership of 76, but when she was bowled for 90, India were through to their second final.

Player of the Match: H. Kaur. *Attendance:* 1,823.

India

S. S. Mandhana c Villani b Schutt	6	V. Krishnamurthy not out	16
P. G. Raut c Mooney b Gardner	14	Lb 3, w 9, nb 1	13
*M. D. Raj b Beams	36		
H. Kaur not out	171	1/6 (1) 2/35 (2) (4 wkts, 42 overs)	281
D. B. Sharma b Villani	25	3/101 (3) 4/238 (5)	9 overs: 35-1

†S. Verma, J. N. Goswami, S. S. Pandey, P. Yadav and R. S. Gayakwad did not bat.

Schutt 9–0–64–1; Perry 9–1–40–0; Jonassen 7–0–63–0; Gardner 8–0–43–1; Beams 8–0–49–1; Villani 1–0–19–1.

Australia

N. E. Bolton c and b Sharma	14	M. L. Schutt c Goswami b Sharma	2
B. L. Mooney b Pandey	1	K. M. Beams not out	11
*M. M. Lanning b Goswami	0		
E. A. Perry c Verma b Pandey	38	Lb 1, w 6	7
E. J. Villani c Mandhana b Gayakwad	75		
A. J. Blackwell b Sharma	90	1/4 (2) 2/9 (3) (40.1 overs)	245
†A. J. Healy c Pandey b Goswami	5	3/21 (1) 4/126 (5) 5/140 (4)	
A. K. Gardner c Raj b Yadav	1	6/148 (7) 7/152 (8) 8/154 (9)	
J. L. Jonassen run out	1	9/169 (10) 10/245 (6)	9 overs: 29-3

Goswami 8–0–35–2; Pandey 6–1–17–2; Sharma 7.1–0–59–3; Gayakwad 9–0–62–1; Yadav 9–0–60–1; Krishnamurthy 1–0–11–0.

Umpires: Ahsan Raza and S. George. Third umpire: A. T. Holdstock.
Referee: D. T. Jukes.

FINAL

ENGLAND v INDIA

LAWRENCE BOOTH

At Lord's, July 23. England won by nine runs. Toss: England.

Anya Shrubsole had endured a quiet World Cup, a modest haul of six wickets overshadowed by her nerveless boundary to seal the semi-final against South Africa. Now, as India threatened to canter home, she gathered her strength for one last thrust. And what a thrust it was: five for 11 in 19 balls, six for 46 in total, a World Cup winner's medal and a place in folklore – all in front of a packed house. It might just have been the best 20 minutes a cricketer at Lord's had ever experienced.

At 191 for three in the 43rd over chasing 229, India had been on course for their first World Cup. All day, looming clouds promised rain (though it fell only briefly). But the Indians had DLS under control, and were ahead entering the final straight. The return of Shrubsole had not initially been a success, as Krishnamurthy carted her first two balls for four. But with her fifth she pinned Raut for 86 – the score she had made during the victory over England in the tournament's opening match, at Derby, almost a month earlier.

Her departure felt like more than one wicket. Four deliveries later, Hartley bowled Verma round her legs for a second-ball duck, then in the next over Shrubsole struck twice: the dangerous Krishnamurthy lofted a slower one to midwicket, and Goswami was yorked first ball for a record 17th one-day international duck, one clear of former England captain Charlotte Edwards, who was chewing her fingernails up in the media centre. While Sharma remained, India had hope: she survived a lightning-fast stumping attempt by Taylor, and the equation was soon 11 from 16 balls with three wickets left.

But Shrubsole hurled herself to her right at point to intercept Pandey's cut, then hurled the ball back to Taylor before Pandey could regain her ground. Moments later, Sharma skewed Shrubsole to midwicket and, when Yadav gently lobbed to Gunn at mid-off, England began to celebrate. Perhaps Gunn had too much time to think: somehow, she grassed the catch. Knight later said, half-jokingly, that she feared Gunn had dropped the trophy; it might have gone down as an all-time blooper. Instead, Shrubsole bowled Gayakwad next ball to complete the best figures in a World Cup final, by man or woman. India's last seven had fallen for 28 in 36 deliveries. Their lower order, said captain Raj, "could not handle the pressure".

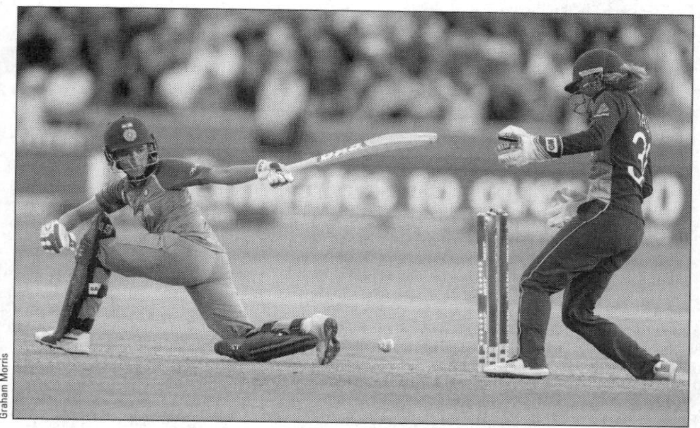

Graham Morris

Big swing: Sushma Verma is bowled by Alex Hartley as the momentum shifts.

England's innings had been patchy, too. Six women got to 23 on a pitch that did not encourage strokeplay, but none more than Sciver's 51. The centrepiece was a fourth-wicket stand of 83 in 16 overs between Taylor and Sciver, though England needed Brunt's belligerence and Gunn's experience to drag them up to 228. Goswami was combative and rangy, taking three for 23.

Shrubsole bowled Mandhana – who had made 90 in that game at Derby – in the second over of the chase, but England landed an even more telling blow when Raj seemed to give up her pursuit of a single, and was run out by smart work from Sciver and Taylor. A few days later, she said her spikes had got stuck in the turf – a metaphor for India's late collapse. While Raut and Harmanpreet, slayer of Australia three days earlier, were adding 95 for the third wicket, and Raut and Krishnamurthy 53 for the fourth, they were in charge. Enter Shrubsole, and a spell for the ages.

Player of the Match: A. Shrubsole. *Attendance:* 26,500.

Player of the Tournament: T. T. Beaumont.

England

L. Winfield b Gayakwad	24
T. T. Beaumont c Goswami b Yadav	23
†S. J. Taylor c Verma b Goswami	45
*H. C. Knight lbw b Yadav	1
N. R. Sciver lbw b Goswami	51
F. C. Wilson lbw b Goswami	0
K. H. Brunt run out	34
J. L. Gunn not out	25
L. A. Marsh not out	14
Lb 3, w 7, nb 1	11
1/47 (1) 2/60 (2) 3/63 (4) 4/146 (3) 5/146 (6) 6/164 (5) 7/196 (7) — (7 wkts, 50 overs) — 10 overs: 43-0	228

A. Shrubsole and A. Hartley did not bat.

Goswami 10–3–23–3; Pandey 7–0–53–0; Gayakwad 10–1–49–1; Sharma 9–0–39–0; Yadav 10–0–36–2; Kaur 4–0–25–0.

India

P. G. Raut lbw b Shrubsole	86
S. S. Mandhana b Shrubsole	0
*M. D. Raj run out	17
H. Kaur c Beaumont b Hartley	51
V. Krishnamurthy c Sciver b Shrubsole	35
†S. Verma b Hartley	0
D. B. Sharma c Sciver b Shrubsole	14
J. N. Goswami b Shrubsole	0
S. S. Pandey run out	4
P. Yadav not out	1
R. S. Gayakwad b Shrubsole	0
Lb 3, w 7, nb 1	11
1/5 (2) 2/43 (3) 3/138 (4) 4/191 (1) 5/196 (6) 6/200 (5) 7/201 (8) 8/218 (9) 9/218 (7) 10/219 (11) — (48.4 overs) — 10 overs: 31-1	219

Brunt 6–0–22–0; Shrubsole 9.4–0–46–6; Sciver 5–1–26–0; Gunn 7–2–17–0; Marsh 10–1–40–0; Hartley 10–0–58–2; Knight 1–0–7–0.

Umpires: G. O. Brathwaite and S. George. Third umpire: P. Wilson.
Referee: S. R. Bernard.

WOMEN'S WORLD CUP WINNERS

1973	*ENGLAND (279-3) beat Australia (187-9) by 92 runs	Birmingham
1978	*AUSTRALIA (100-2) beat England (96-8) by eight wickets	Hyderabad
1982	AUSTRALIA (152-7) beat England (151-5) by three wickets	Christchurch
1988	AUSTRALIA (129-2) beat England (127-7) by eight wickets	Melbourne
1993	ENGLAND (195-5) beat New Zealand (128) by 67 runs	Lord's
1997	AUSTRALIA (165-5) beat New Zealand (164) by five wickets	Calcutta
2000	NEW ZEALAND (184) beat Australia (180) by four runs	Lincoln
2005	AUSTRALIA (215-4) beat India (117) by 98 runs	Centurion
2009	ENGLAND (167-6) beat New Zealand (166) by four wickets	North Sydney
2013	AUSTRALIA (259-7) beat West Indies (145) by 114 runs	Mumbai
2017	**ENGLAND (228-7) beat India (219) by nine runs**	**Lord's**

* *The first two World Cups were played solely as a round-robin league, but in both the last scheduled match was between England and Australia, and decided the title.*

WOMEN'S INTERNATIONAL SERIES IN 2017

BANGLADESH v SOUTH AFRICA IN 2016-17

One-day internationals (5): Bangladesh 1, South Africa 4

South Africa eventually overwhelmed Bangladesh, after the series looked as if it might develop into a close contest. The stand-out performer was the tourists' Lizelle Lee, who made 268 runs at 53, and twice shared century stands with her opening partner, Andrie Steyn. Bangladesh often struggled to score quickly enough, but were cheered by a ten-run victory in the third match, in which off-spinner Khadija Tul Kobra took a career-best four for 33. All told, her 11 wickets in the series cost just 17 apiece. This was not part of the ICC Women's Championship, as Bangladesh were not one of the top eight teams.

First one-day international At Cox's Bazar, January 12, 2017. **South Africa won by 86 runs. South Africa 251-3** (50 overs) (L. Lee 87, A. Steyn 68, M. du Preez 62*); ‡**Bangladesh 165-6** (50 overs) (Rumana Ahmed 37, Nigar Sultana 59*; S. E. Luus 3-52). *PoM:* L. Lee. *Bangladesh gambled by putting South Africa in, but it backfired spectacularly as openers Lizelle Lee and Andrie Steyn raced to 122. Lee hit six fours and seven sixes in her 71-ball 87, while Steyn eased to her first ODI fifty in more measured fashion. Bangladesh's reply was stuck in first gear: captain Rumana Ahmed took 80 balls for her 37, although wicketkeeper Nigar Sultana made a fighting 59*.*

Second one-day international At Cox's Bazar, January 14, 2017. **South Africa won by 17 runs.** ‡**South Africa 223** (49 overs) (L. Lee 70, A. Steyn 66; Khadija Tul Kobra 4-56); **Bangladesh 206-8** (50 overs) (Sharmin Akter 74, Rumana Ahmed 68). *PoM:* L. Lee. *Lee and Steyn again gave South Africa a flying start, but Khadija Tul Kobra took four wickets as the visitors collapsed from 115-0 to 223 all out; for the second time in three days, Steyn was stumped in the sixties. Bangladesh sniffed an opportunity, especially when Sharmin Akter and Rumana were sharing a third-wicket stand of 127. But, with 54 needed from 47 balls, Bangladesh crumbled, adding only 36 more for the loss of six wickets, to give South Africa a 2–0 lead.*

Third one-day international At Cox's Bazar, January 16, 2017. **Bangladesh won by ten runs.** ‡**Bangladesh 136** (49 overs); **South Africa 126** (31.2 overs) (L. Lee 46, D. van Niekerk 42*; Khadija Tul Kobra 4-33). *PoM:* Khadija Tul Kobra. *ODI debut:* Sharmin Sultana (Bangladesh). *Tul Kobra's off-breaks kept Bangladesh in the series. Batting first, they managed 136 – the last seven falling for 32 – which hardly looked defendable. But she removed Lee for a hard-hit 46, and South Africa slumped to 96-9. While captain Dane van Niekerk hung on there was hope but, when Salma Khatun bowled No. 11 Marcia Letsoalo, Bangladesh could celebrate only their second ODI win over South Africa, more than four years after the first.*

Fourth one-day international At Cox's Bazar, January 18, 2017. **South Africa won by 94 runs.** ‡**South Africa 251-7** (50 overs) (M. du Preez 79, C. L. Tryon 47; Khadija Tul Kobra 3-48); **Bangladesh 157** (50 overs) (Farzana Haque 67, Salma Khatun 30; A. Khaka 3-34). *PoM:* M. du Preez. *Stung into action, South Africa sealed the series with a crushing victory. Mignon du Preez held their innings together with 79, adding 74 for the third wicket with Chloe Tryon; 32 came off the last three overs. In contrast, the first ten of the Bangladesh reply yielded just 28, for the loss of three wickets, and they were never up with the rate.*

Fifth one-day international At Cox's Bazar, January 20, 2017. **South Africa won by eight wickets.** ‡**Bangladesh 68** (36.3 overs) (O. Kirsten 4-10, M. M. Letsoalo 3-13); **South Africa 69-2** (10 overs) (L. Lee 37). *PoM:* O. Kirsten. *PoS:* L. Lee. *The teams headed for the World Cup qualifiers in Sri Lanka in differing moods after Bangladesh were hurried out for 68. Seamers Odine Kirsten and Letsoalo both claimed career-bests, and only two batsmen got into double figures. Lee hit seven fours in 19 balls as South Africa knocked off the target in ten overs.*

WOMEN'S WORLD CUP QUALIFIER IN 2016-17

1 India 2 South Africa 3 Sri Lanka 4 Pakistan

The ten teams who met in Sri Lanka had much to play for: the top four would join Australia, England, New Zealand and West Indies at the World Cup in England, as well as in the second ICC Women's Championship, in 2017–2020. Qualification for the Super Six stage, meanwhile, would secure one-day international status for the next cycle. But by the end it seemed a waste of time and energy: the pecking order was undisturbed. Ireland and Bangladesh did enough to retain their status, but seemed no closer to storming the citadel. The four teams who did not have ODI status were completely outclassed.

On lifeless pitches, the cricket proceeded at a plodding pace. The average first-innings total across all 30 games was 175, while in the 16 ODIs five regular bowlers had an economy-rate of less than three, and a further 21 less than four. For the non-ODI nations, the highest score was Zimbabwe's 191 for eight against Thailand; the lowest was 40 by Papua New Guinea in response to Pakistan's 276 for five, the tournament's biggest total, in one of many one-sided games.

India rose above the mire, winning every match and tested only in the final against South Africa, when they squeaked home off the last ball with a wicket to spare. All-rounder Deepti Sharma, just 19, showed class, averaging over 50 at the top of the order, and contributed wily off-spin to a suffocating attack. With captain Mithali Raj maintaining her excellent standards – she passed fifty in all three of her innings, and was out just once – India looked in fine fettle for the World Cup. The other qualifiers, Sri Lanka and Pakistan, did not scare any of the major sides.

Despite the stodgy batting and the mismatches, there was a large online audience, with live streaming attracting 1.7m views, and highlights reels a further 17.8m on the ICC's website and social media channels. Interest seemed to be growing, even if the number of quality teams did not.

Group A

Thailand and Zimbabwe also played in this group but their matches do not count as ODIs. Zimbabwe beat Thailand, but lost all their other games.

At Colombo (PSO), February 7, 2017. **India won by 114 runs.** ‡**India 259-4** (50 overs) (D. B. Sharma 54, D. P. Vaidya 89, M. D. Raj 70*); **Sri Lanka 145-8** (50 overs) (A. M. C. Jayangani 30, G. W. H. M. Perera 34). *PoM:* D. P. Vaidya. *ODI debuts:* K. G. M. Shehani (Sri Lanka); S. K. Yadav (India). *India maintained their stranglehold over Sri Lanka – this was their 23rd win in 24 completed ODIs against them – thanks to powerful batting and parsimonious bowling. Devika Vaidya made a career-best 89, and Mithali Raj a lively 70* from 62 balls, as India racked up 259-4. Sri Lanka reached 42-0 in 11.2 overs, but could manage only 103 more from 38.4. Deepti Sharma, who had earlier made a patient half-century, was unhittable, finishing with 10–3–12–1.*

At Colombo (NCC), February 8, 2017. **Sri Lanka won by 146 runs.** ‡**Sri Lanka 239-8** (50 overs) (M. D. N. Hansika 30, W. P. M. Weerakkodi 61, M. A. D. D. Surangika 53*; I. M. H. C. Joyce 4-39); **Ireland 93** (36.1 overs) (C. M. A. Shillington 36*; S. I. P. Fernando 3-21). *PoM:* S. I. P. Fernando. *ODI debut:* R. A. Lewis (Ireland). *Ireland's pursuit of 240 never recovered after Inoshi Priyadharshani Fernando's career-best burst reduced them to 27-4. The Sri Lankan innings had hinged on half-centuries from Prasadini Weerakkodi and Dilani Manodara Surangika, though Isobel*

Joyce – sister of Ed – limited the damage with 4-39. She and Cecelia – her twin – were not the only siblings in the Irish team: Gaby and Robyn Lewis managed three wickets between them.

At Colombo (PSO), February 10, 2017. **India won by 125 runs.** ‡**India 250-2** (50 overs) (D. B. Sharma 89, M. D. Thirush Kamini 113*); **Ireland 125** (49.1 overs) (I. M. H. C. Joyce 31, G. H. Lewis 33; P. Yadav 3-30). *PoM:* M. D. Thirush Kamini. *ODI debut:* M. Joshi (India). *India flexed their muscles again to produce another dominant victory and ensure they topped the group. Opener Thirush Kamini hit 113* with 11 fours and four sixes, and had an opening stand of 174 with Sharma – they were not parted until the 40th over. Ireland were soon 15-3 and, although Isobel Joyce and Gaby Lewis passed 30, the result was never in doubt.*

India 8pts, Sri Lanka 6pts, Ireland 4pts, Zimbabwe 2pts, Thailand 0pts. Points gained against other qualifiers were carried through to the Super Six.

Group B

Papua New Guinea and Scotland also played in this group but their matches do not count as ODIs. Scotland beat Papua New Guinea, but lost all their other games.

At Colombo (NCC), February 7, 2017. **South Africa won by 63 runs.** ‡**South Africa 258-9** (50 overs) (M. du Preez 40, M. Kapp 38, C. L. Tryon 79, D. van Niekerk 30; Nashra Sandhu 3-51); **Pakistan 195-6** (50 overs) (Nahida Khan 35, Nain Abidi 62, Sana Mir 38*). *PoM:* C. L. Tryon. *ODI debuts:* Ghulam Fatima, Nashra Sandhu (Pakistan). *A punishing 69-ball 79 from Chloe Tryon took South Africa out of reach in a game which ultimately meant they, not Pakistan, topped Group B. The Pakistanis batted out their overs, but never came close – their approach typified by Nain Abidi's careful 62 from 105 deliveries. Seamer Marcia Letsoalo (9–2–22–1) proved hardest to get away.*

At Colombo (PSO), February 8, 2017. **Pakistan won by 67 runs.** ‡**Pakistan 227** (50 overs) (Ayesha Zafar 34, Bismah Maroof 35, Rabiya Shah 34, Aliya Riaz 31, Extras 31; Rumana Ahmed 3-40); **Bangladesh 160** (49.3 overs) (Sanjida Islam 34, Nigar Sultana 41; Ghulam Fatima 3-28). *PoM:* Ghulam Fatima. *ODI debut:* Aimen Anwar (Pakistan). *A steady batting display from Pakistan was enough to see off Bangladesh, after six of their top seven made between 27 and 35 – though only Rabiya Shah (34 off 33 balls) and Aliya Riaz (31 off 32) found any fluency. The Bangladeshis lost regular wickets, including three to leg-spinner Ghulam Fatima in just her second ODI.*

At Colombo (PSO), February 11, 2017. **South Africa won by six wickets.** ‡**Bangladesh 100** (46.5 overs) (Rumana Ahmed 39; S. Ismail 3-14, S. E. Luus 3-17); **South Africa 101-4** (25.2 overs) (L. Lee 34, L. Wolvaardt 30). *PoM:* S. Ismail. *ODI debut:* Suraiya Azmin (Bangladesh). *The outcome was set in stone by the fifth over, with Bangladesh reeling at 8-3. South Africa showed no mercy. Seamer Shabnim Ismail and leg-spinner Sune Luus both took three cheap wickets, and only Rumana Ahmed's 39 disturbed their progress. Openers Lizelle Lee and 17-year-old Laura Wolvaardt knocked off half the runs, though South Africa carelessly surrendered four wickets before wrapping it up.*

South Africa 8pts, Pakistan 6pts, Bangladesh 4pts, Scotland 2pts, Papua New Guinea 0pts. Points gained against other qualifiers were carried through to the Super Six.

Super Six

At Colombo (CCC), February 15, 2017. **Bangladesh won by seven wickets. Ireland 144** (47.1 overs) (C. M. A. Shillington 37, L. K. Delany 37; Jahanara Alam 3-21); ‡**Bangladesh 145-3** (39.1 overs) (Sharmin Akter 52, Farzana Haque 34*). *PoM:* Jahanara Alam. *Bangladesh began their Super Six campaign with a comfortable victory. Put in, a disappointing Ireland were soon 15-2 – both to Jahanara Alam – and Bangladesh were in no mood to let them off the hook. Sharmin Akter and Farzana Haque made sure the target was reached without alarm.*

At Colombo (PSO), February 15, 2017. **India won by 49 runs. India 205-8** (50 overs) (M. R. Meshram 55, M. D. Raj 64); ‡**South Africa 156** (46.4 overs) (T. Chetty 52; S. S. Pandey 4-34, E. K. Bisht 3-22). *PoM:* M. D. Raj. *India continued their impressive form, thanks in part to a second-wicket stand of 96 between Mona Meshram and Raj after they were asked to bat. South Africa lost both openers cheaply, and only a half-century from wicketkeeper Trisha Chetty held India up after that, as Shikha Pandey took a career-best 4-34.*

At Colombo (NCC), February 15, 2017. **Sri Lanka won by five wickets. Pakistan 212-7** (50 overs) (Nahida Khan 64, Javeria Khan 63); ‡**Sri Lanka 216-5** (47.4 overs) (M. D. N. Hansika 37, A. M. C.

Jayangani 35, W. P. M. Weerakkodi 45, L. E. Kaushalya 65*). *PoM:* L. E. Kaushalya. *The match turned on a fourth-wicket partnership of 88 between Weerakkodi and Eshani Kaushalya, whose 65* was a career-best. Pakistan's challenging total owed most to Nahida Khan and Javeria Khan, who put on 119 for the second wicket.*

At Colombo (NCC), February 17, 2017. **India won by nine wickets. Bangladesh 155-8** (50 overs) (Sharmin Akter 35, Farzana Haque 50; M. Joshi 3-25); ‡**India 158-1** (33.3 overs) (M. R. Meshram 78*, M. D. Raj 73*). *PoM:* M. R. Meshram. *India qualified for the World Cup with another victory that highlighted the power of their top order as Meshram (with a career-best 78*) and Raj (with her third half-century of the tournament) took them past their target with a stand of 136*, India's highest for any wicket against Bangladesh. Earlier, the Bangladeshis struggled against tight bowling, with seamer Mansi Joshi's 3-25 the highlight.*

At Colombo (CCC), February 17, 2017. **Pakistan won by 86 runs.** ‡**Pakistan 271-5** (50 overs) (Nahida Khan 72, Javeria Khan 90*, Nain Abidi 44); **Ireland 185** (48.5 overs) (C. N. I. M. Joyce 41, K. J. Garth 33, I. M. H. C. Joyce 33). *PoM:* Javeria Khan. *Pakistan's 271-5 was the highest total between ODI teams in this tournament, and Ireland only fleetingly looked like making a match of it. Javeria made 90* off 104 balls, despite briefly retiring hurt after adding 133* with Nahida, who was in dominant mood with 72 off 76. Ireland's reply at least showed grit: Cecelia Joyce and Kim Garth put on 74 for the second wicket, but only Isobel Joyce offered support down the order.*

At Colombo (PSO), February 17, 2017. **South Africa won by nine wickets.** ‡**Sri Lanka 142-9** (50 overs) (M. D. N. Hansika 48; S. E. Luus 3-40); **South Africa 145-1** (36.1 overs) (L. Lee 35, L. Wolvaardt 50*, S. E. Luus 50*). *PoM:* S. E. Luus. *South Africa booked their World Cup place with a thumping victory inspired by Luus. First, she took 3-40 with her leg-spin, then hit 50*, adding 99* with Wolvaardt as South Africa made short work of their target. Sri Lanka had reached 70-1 in the 21st over, but eight wickets fell for 72.*

At Colombo (PSO), February 19, 2017. **India won by seven wickets. Pakistan 67** (43.4 overs) (E. K. Bisht 5-8); ‡**India 70-3** (22.3 overs). *PoM:* E. K. Bisht. *India's slow bowlers hypnotised Pakistan's batters: their highest contribution was 24 from Extras, and only opener Ayesha Zafar (19) and Bismah Maroof (13) got past three. Slow left-armer Ekta Bisht returned dream figures of 10–7–8–5, while Deepti Sharma's off-spin was even more economical – 10–5–6–1, including three wides – and leg-spinner Poonam Yadav had 7–3–7–0. It wasn't all bad news for Pakistan: Bangladesh's defeat by Sri Lanka meant they qualified for the World Cup.*

At Colombo (CCC), February 19, 2017. **South Africa won by 36 runs** (DLS). ‡**Ireland 166** (49.5 overs) (I. M. H. C. Joyce 30, M. V. Waldron 33*); **South Africa 82-1** (21 overs) (L. Wolvaardt 32*). *Ireland lost all their Super Six games after collapsing to 166, in which wicketkeeper Mary Waldron top-scored from No. 8. Seven South African bowlers took at least one wicket, and – when the rain came – they were well ahead of a retrospective target of 47 in 21 overs.*

At Colombo (NCC), February 19, 2017. **Sri Lanka won by 42 runs** (DLS). **Sri Lanka 197-9** (50 overs) (G. W. H. M. Perera 32, A. M. C. Jayangani 84; Salma Khatun 3-18); ‡**Bangladesh 68-5** (21 overs). *PoM:* A. M. C. Jayangani. *Sri Lanka made sure of a World Cup place after Chamari Atapattu Jayangani anchored their innings with 84 from 114 balls. Sharmin Sultana fell to the first delivery of the reply, and Bangladesh struggled to 62-5 at the drinks break – only one more over was possible before rain set in, and they would have needed 111.*

India 10 pts, South Africa 8pts, Sri Lanka 6pts, Pakistan 4pts, Bangladesh 2pts, Ireland 0pts.

Final At Colombo (PSO), February 21, 2017. **India won by one wicket.** ‡**South Africa 244** (49.4 overs) (L. Lee 37, M. du Preez 40, D. van Niekerk 37, S. E. Luus 35; R. S. Gayakwad 3-51); **India 245-9** (50 overs) (M. R. Meshram 59, D. B. Sharma 71, V. Krishnamurthy 31, H. Kaur 41*). *PoM:* D. B. Sharma. *PoT:* S. E. Luus. *The final produced the most exciting match of the tournament. India were coasting at 186-3 in the 41st, but a collapse set in: when Yadav was run out off the first ball of the last over, it was 237-9. After three dot balls, eight were still needed from two: Harmanpreet Kaur hoisted Letsoalo over midwicket for six, then scampered two from the last. "I was waiting for that ball because that is my strong area," said Harmanpreet, leading India in place of Raj, who had tweaked a hamstring. Earlier, South Africa had batted consistently, with eight scores between 14 and 40.*

AUSTRALIA v NEW ZEALAND IN 2016-17

Twenty20 internationals (3): Australia 1, New Zealand 2

Australia, missing Ellyse Perry because of a hamstring injury, began the three-match Twenty20 series with a sturdy 151. Although New Zealand's response of 111 proved inadequate in that game, similar totals were enough to bring them consecutive victories. And while Australia could point to the success of young leg-spinner Amanda-Jade Wellington, who burst on to the scene with nine wickets at under six apiece (and an economy-rate of 4.41), it was the all-round excellence of the visitors' attack that won out. Seamer Lea Tahuhu took only three wickets, but her 12 overs cost just 46. Suzie Bates, the New Zealand captain, passed 25 in all three games – invaluable consistency in a low-scoring series.

First Twenty20 international At Melbourne, February 17, 2017. **Australia won by 40 runs. Australia 151-4** (20 overs) (M. M. Lanning 60, E. J. Villani 73*); ‡**New Zealand 111-8** (20 overs) (A. E. Satterthwaite 40*; A. Wellington 3-15). *PoM:* E. J. Villani. *T20I debuts:* A. K. Gardner, M. R. Strano, A. Wellington (Australia). *Meg Lanning and Elyse Villani, who added 110 in 13 overs for the third wicket, powered Australia to a demanding 151. New Zealand's reply also depended on two contributors – Suzie Bates made 26 and Amy Satterthwaite 40* – but no pair could manage a stand of 30, as 19-year-old leg-spinner Amanda-Jade Wellington dismantled the middle order.*

Second Twenty20 international At Geelong, February 19, 2017. **New Zealand won by eight runs** (DLS). **New Zealand 101-9** (20 overs) (S. W. Bates 30; M. R. Strano 5-10); ‡**Australia 61-9** (13 overs) (A. M. Peterson 3-2). *PoM:* A. M. Peterson. *After Molly Strano's off-breaks had cut a swathe through New Zealand – only two bowlers in women's T20 internationals had better figures than her 5-10 – Australia seemed to be heading for a series win. But rain interrupted their assault on a target of 102, and the target was revised to 70 in 13 overs. When another off-spinner, Anna Peterson, was introduced for the final over, they needed 11 with five wickets left. Three slogs later, she had a hat-trick, and the game was as good as up.*

HAT-TRICKS IN WOMEN'S TWENTY20 INTERNATIONALS

Asmavia Iqbal	Pakistan v England at Loughborough	2012
E. K. Bisht	India v Sri Lanka at Colombo (NCC)	2012-13
M. Kapp	South Africa v Bangladesh at Potchefstroom	2013-14
N. R. Sciver	England v New Zealand at Bridgetown	2013-14
Sana Mir	Pakistan v Sri Lanka at Sharjah	2014-15
A. M. Peterson	**New Zealand v Australia at Geelong**	**2016-17**

Third Twenty20 international At Adelaide, February 22, 2017. **New Zealand won by 47 runs.** ‡**New Zealand 113-8** (20 overs) (S. W. Bates 31; A. Wellington 4-16); **Australia 66** (16 overs) (A. J. Blackwell 30*). *PoM:* S. W. Bates. *PoS:* S. W. Bates. *The decider proved very decisive. Despite Wellington taking four more cheap wickets to help limit New Zealand to 113, with Bates top-scoring again, Australia were thrashed: 66 was their lowest 20-over total (New Zealand had dismissed them for 73 at Wellington in 2009-10). Alex Blackwell made 30*, but nine fell in single figures.*

NEW ZEALAND v AUSTRALIA IN 2016-17

One-day internationals (3): New Zealand 1, Australia 2

The teams who had just contested a Twenty20 series in Australia switched country and format. New Zealand were without off-spinner Leigh Kasperek and all-rounder Sophie Devine, but won the first one-day international on the back of Amy Satterthwaite's fourth successive ODI century. "We were in this position last year," she said, "and Australia ended up winning the series, so we have a lot of hard work to do." Her warning was not heeded. In a high-scoring series, the Australian batting proved more resilient. Beth Mooney was consistency itself, hitting 100, 57 and 69, while in the decider Meg Lanning scored a world-record tenth hundred – in her 57th ODI – to maintain Australia's 17-year hold on the Rose Bowl (the equivalent of the men's Chappell–Hadlee Trophy).

First one-day international At Auckland (Eden Park Outer Oval), February 26, 2017. **New Zealand won by five wickets.** ‡**Australia 275** (48.4 overs) (B. L. Mooney 100, R. L. Haynes 50, E. J. Villani 50; L. M. Tahuhu 4-59, H. R. Huddleston 3-46); **New Zealand 276-5** (49.1 overs) (S. W. Bates 55, A. E. Satterthwaite 102*, K. J. Martin 43). *PoM:* A. E. Satterthwaite. *ODI debut:* L. R. Cheatle (Australia). *After 41 overs, Australia were whizzing along at 232-3. But concentration lapsed, and both established batsmen fell just after celebrating landmarks: Beth Mooney her maiden hundred and Elyse Villani her first half-century. (Earlier, Rachael Haynes had reached her seventh fifty, only to be caught off her next delivery.) The innings dribbled away, as New Zealand's opening pair Lea Tahuhu and Holly Huddleston shared seven wickets. Amy Satterthwaite then hit her fourth hundred in successive ODI innings – no other woman had managed even three in a row – as New Zealand timed the chase with precision.*

Second one-day international At Mount Maunganui, March 2, 2017. **Australia won by four wickets. New Zealand 253-8** (50 overs) (S. W. Bates 35, A. E. Satterthwaite 85, K. J. Martin 43, K. T. Perkins 38; A. Wellington 3-52); ‡**Australia 256-6** (47.2 overs) (B. L. Mooney 57, M. M. Lanning 44, A. J. Blackwell 65, A. J. Healy 36; A. C. Kerr 4-54). *PoM:* A. J. Blackwell. *ODI debut:* A. K. Gardner (Australia). *Australia drew level thanks to the cool head of Alex Blackwell. She came in at 109-3, survived a hat-trick ball from 16-year-old leg-spinner Amelia Kerr, and had steered her side to within 17 of victory when she went for 65. Earlier, it looked as though Satterthwaite would march on to a fifth consecutive century, but she was dismissed 15 short. Her last five innings – three against Pakistan, two in this series – had brought 562 runs for twice out. On a true pitch, though, New Zealand's 253 proved a fraction light.*

Third one-day international At Mount Maunganui, March 5, 2017. **Australia won by five wickets. New Zealand 270-9** (50 overs) (R. H. Priest 77, K. J. Martin 77, K. T. Perkins 34; J. L. Jonassen 3-47, A. K. Gardner 3-56); ‡**Australia 273-5** (49.2 overs) (B. L. Mooney 69, M. M. Lanning 104*, E. J. Villani 37, A. J. Blackwell 32; H. R. Huddleston 3-44). *PoM:* M. M. Lanning. *Meg Lanning's unparalleled tenth ODI hundred – she had shared the record with England's Charlotte Edwards – was the beating heart of the victory that retained the Rose Bowl for Australia. Mooney dominated a second-wicket partnership of 93 with Lanning, who could have been stumped by Rachel Priest in the 30s. Priest had done her bit in the New Zealand innings, though: she and Katey Martin both made 77 to help set a target of 271.*

Women's Championship: Australia 4pts, New Zealand 2pts.

WOMEN'S QUADRANGULAR SERIES IN 2017

1 India 2 South Africa 3 Ireland 4 Zimbabwe

India warmed up for the World Cup by winning this 14-match quadrangular, held in Potchefstroom. It was the second time in three months they had won a one-day final against South Africa, though this was more decisive than the thriller which concluded the World Cup Qualifier in Colombo. Victory came at a canter, with Mithali Raj celebrating her 100th one-day international in charge – a landmark shared with Australia's Belinda Clark and England's Charlotte Edwards – with a record-equalling sixth successive half-century. But the batting feat of the tournament was Deepti Sharma's 188 during a destruction of Ireland; of the 16 successive games India had won before South Africa pipped them towards the end of the group stage, She had been Player of the Match in five. Zimbabwe also took part, but their games did not count as official ODIs. They beat Ireland twice, only to lose to them in the third-place play-off.

At Potchefstroom (University), May 7. **India won by ten wickets. Ireland 96** (44.4 overs) (E. K. Bisht 3-24, D. B. Sharma 3-20); ‡**India 99-0** (18.4 overs) (D. B. Sharma 51*, P. G. Raut 46*). *PoM:* D. B. Sharma. *ODI debuts:* A. Beggs, R. Delany, L. Maritz, L. Paul (Ireland). *Ireland were brushed aside, after Deepti Sharma followed 3-20 with an unbeaten half-century. The Irish lost their last eight for 52 en route to their first ten-wicket defeat since July 2008, and India's first such victory since March 2009.*

At Potchefstroom (University), May 9. **India won by seven wickets. South Africa 119** (39.3 overs) (M. du Preez 31; J. N. Goswami 3-20, S. S. Pandey 3-22); ‡**India 121-3** (41.2 overs) (M. R. Meshram 38, M. D. Raj 51*). *PoM:* S. S. Pandey. *ODI debuts:* N. de Klerk, R. Ntozakhe (South Africa). *India's attack leader Jhulan Goswami became the leading wicket-taker in women's one-day internationals when she dismissed South Africa No. 11 Raisibe Ntozakhe, moving one clear of Australian fast bowler Cathryn Fitzpatrick's haul of 180. That was the last of seven South African wickets to tumble for 19 runs in 12.3 overs. Sharma fell in the first over of the chase, but Indian captain Mithali Raj's unbeaten half-century settled the issue.*

At Potchefstroom, May 11. **South Africa won by 178 runs.** ‡**South Africa 337-5** (50 overs) (L. Lee 40, L. Wolvaardt 149, T. Chetty 70, M. du Preez 32; A. Beggs 3-64); **Ireland 159-8** (50 overs) (M. V. Waldron 35). *PoM:* L. Wolvaardt. *ODI debuts:* L. Little, R. Stokell (Ireland). *Teenager Laura Wolvaardt's run-a-ball 149 powered South Africa to their first 300-plus total (they would achieve two more before the end of July), and – for four days – the highest conceded by Ireland. She finally departed in the 46th over, only four short of Johmari Logtenberg's national-record 153* against the Netherlands at Deventer in 2007. Ireland reached 66-1, but it had taken them until the 22nd over, and a heavy defeat was always inevitable. At 13 years 360 days, their medium-pacer Louise Little became the fifth-youngest ODI cricketer (but only the third-youngest for Ireland, behind Lucy O'Reilly and Elena Tice), and had Trisha Chetty stumped for 70.*

At Potchefstroom, May 15. **India won by 249 runs.** ‡**India 358-2** (50 overs) (D. B. Sharma 188, P. G. Raut 109*); **Ireland 109** (40 overs) (M. V. Waldron 35; S. S. Pandey 3-16, R. S. Gayakwad 4-18). *PoM:* D. B. Sharma. *ODI debuts:* N. M. Parween (India); S. MacMahon (Ireland). *Records cascaded as India smote their largest total (previously 298-2 v West Indies at Dhanbad in 2003-04), and their biggest win by runs (previously 207 v Pakistan at Dambulla in 2008). Sharma's 188 from 160 balls, her maiden ODI century, was easily their highest score, beating Jaya Sharma's 138* v Pakistan at Karachi in 2005-06, and behind only Belinda Clark's 229* for Australia v Denmark in 1997-98. And her opening stand of 320 with Punam Raut, who also made her first hundred in the format, was the biggest for any wicket in women's ODIs, beating 268 between England openers Sarah Taylor and Caroline Atkins against South Africa at Lord's in 2008. Sharma's haul of 27 fours was yet another women's record. In reply, Ireland slipped from 42-0 to 109 all out, with slow left-armer Rajeshwari Gayakwad collecting a career-best 4-18.*

At Potchefstroom, May 17. **South Africa won by eight runs. South Africa 269-5** (50 overs) (A. Steyn 83, T. Chetty 76, C. L. Tryon 77*); ‡**India 261-9** (50 overs) (D. B. Sharma 71, P. G. Raut 35, M. D. Raj 54, S. S. Pandey 36*; S. Ismail 3-54). *PoM:* C. L. Tryon. *India were on course for victory at 151-1 after 26 overs. Then leg-spinner Sune Luus removed Sharma for a run-a-ball 71, Raj went for 54, and Shabnim Ismail made short work of the tail to give South Africa a tense win. Their own innings had begun with the first-ball dismissal of Lizelle Lee, but Andrie Steyn and Chetty added 151, before Chloe Tryon provided late fireworks with 77* from 39, including six sixes. The* *result meant India failed to equal the world record for most successive ODI victories, held by Australia, who won 17 between December 1997 and February 1999.*

At Potchefstroom (University), May 19. **South Africa won by 120 runs.** ‡**South Africa 323-8** (50 overs) (A. Steyn 117, S. E. Luus 83, T. Chetty 33; R. Delaney 3-70); **Ireland 203-6** (50 overs) (M. V. Waldron 41; A. Khaka 3-15). *PoM:* A. Steyn. *Ireland slumped to their sixth defeat in six after Steyn, with her maiden ODI hundred, and Luus, whose 83 was also a career-best, began with 209 – a South African record for the first wicket, beating 192 between Chetty and Wolvaardt, also against Ireland, at Dublin in 2016. All eight Irish players who batted reached double figures, but none made more than Mary Waldron's 41.*

India 24pts, South Africa 24pts, Zimbabwe 8pts, Ireland 0pts.

Final At Potchefstroom, May 21. **India won by eight wickets. South Africa 156** (40.2 overs) (S. E. Luus 55, M. du Preez 30; J. N. Goswami 3-22, P. Yadav 3-32); ‡**India 160-2** (33 overs) (P. G. Raut 70*, M. D. Raj 62*). *PoM:* P. G. Raut. *PoT:* D. B. Sharma. *The teams had been separated only by net run-rate during the group stage, but India romped home in the final after a clinical bowling display. A half-century from Luus had helped lift South Africa to 131-4, but six fell for 25, and victory was secured with 17 overs to spare thanks to a third-wicket stand of 127* between Raut and Raj. For Raj, it was a sixth successive ODI half-century, equalling the world record held jointly by Lindsay Reeler and Ellyse Perry of Australia and England's Charlotte Edwards; she would break the record at the World Cup the following month.*

WEST INDIES v SRI LANKA IN 2017-18

One-day internationals (3): West Indies 3, Sri Lanka 0
Twenty20 internationals (3): West Indies 3, Sri Lanka 0

After a disappointing World Cup in which they failed to make the knockouts, West Indies dished out a pair of whitewashes to Sri Lanka. But so limp were the tourists against a spin-heavy attack, it was hard to know what to make of it. In the three one-day internationals – the first rubber in the 2017–2020 Women's Championship – Sri Lanka's top score was 162. And they were an embarrassment in the first Twenty20, crawling to 69 for seven. It meant the West Indies batsmen hardly needed to break sweat. Stafanie Taylor hit the only two half-centuries of the one-day series, while Deandra Dottin blazed a brilliant hundred in the final T20, the brightest moment of six drab matches.

First one-day international At Tarouba, Trinidad, October 11, 2017. **West Indies won by six wickets.** ‡**Sri Lanka 136** (49.4 overs) (B. Y. A. Mendis 34; A. S. S. Fletcher 3-42, H. K. Matthews 3-18, S. R. Taylor 3-24); **West Indies 138-4** (39 overs) (M. R. Aguilleira 32*). *PoM:* H. K. Matthews. *Sri Lanka were clueless against West Indies' quartet of spinners, 136 all out in the last over. Hayley Matthews – the pick of the bowlers, with 3-18 for her off-spin – was stretchered off with thigh cramp in the 20th over of the reply, but there was otherwise little trouble for West Indies.*

Second one-day international At Tarouba, Trinidad, October 13, 2017 (day/night). **West Indies won by seven wickets.** Reduced to 47 overs a side. **Sri Lanka 162** (46.3 overs) (B. Y. A. Mendis 34, A. M. C. Jayangani 31; A. S. S. Fletcher 3-26); ‡**West Indies 163-3** (39.4 overs) (S. R. Taylor 62*, D. J. S. Dottin 37*). *PoM:* S. R. Taylor. *It was more of the same: though Sri Lanka began more positively, driven by Yashoda Mendis's sprightly 34, they had no idea against the slow bowlers. West Indies captain Stafanie Taylor collected 2-31, then clinched the series in a stand of 77* with Deandra Dottin.*

Third one-day international At Tarouba, Trinidad, October 15, 2017. **West Indies won by 40 runs.** Reduced to 45 overs a side. **West Indies 182-8** (45 overs) (H. K. Matthews 41, S. R. Taylor 55, M. R. Aguilleira 37*; H. A. S. D. Siriwardene 3-26); ‡**Sri Lanka 142** (40.4 overs) (M. A. D. D. Surangika 42, R. S. Vandort 34; S. C. Selman 3-30, S. R. Taylor 3-29). *PoM:* S. R. Taylor. *PoS:* S. R. Taylor. *West Indies showed their own deficiencies against spin, but still did enough to claim a whitewash. After Shashikala Siriwardene took three wickets in three overs, including Taylor for 55,* *they could muster only 182-8. But Sri Lanka's batting had not improved: Nipuni Hansika was trapped first ball by Shakera Selman, who finished with three victims, as did the insatiable Taylor.*

Women's Championship: West Indies 6pts, Sri Lanka 0pts.

First Twenty20 international At Coolidge, Antigua, October 19, 2017 (floodlit). **West Indies won by 71 runs. West Indies 140-4** (20 overs) (H. K. Matthews 37, S. R. Taylor 31); **‡Sri Lanka 69-7** (20 overs). *T20I debut:* A. K. Peters (West Indies). *Chasing a gettable 141, Sri Lanka crawled to 69-7. Ama Kanchana (17) hit their solitary four, in the second over; only she (and Extras) made double figures, while Selman (2-6) and Dottin (1-6) applied the noose.*

Second Twenty20 international At Coolidge, Antigua, October 21, 2017 (floodlit). **West Indies won by 47 runs. ‡West Indies 154-6** (20 overs) (S. R. Taylor 49); **Sri Lanka 107** (19.4 overs) (A. M. C. Jayangani 30; A. S. S. Fletcher 5-13). *PoM:* A. S. S. Fletcher. *Leg-spinner Afy Fletcher had been excellent throughout the tour, and now sealed the series with 5-13, the third-best T20 figures for West Indies (Anisa Mohammed had twice done better). Sri Lanka had seemed ready to challenge, when they reached 85-3 in pursuit of 155 – but, after Fletcher took her first wicket, they fell apart. Earlier, Taylor top-scored once more, with 49.*

Third Twenty20 international At Coolidge, Antigua, October 22, 2017 (floodlit). **West Indies won by 31 runs. ‡West Indies 159-6** (20 overs) (H. K. Matthews 34, D. J. S. Dottin 112); **Sri Lanka 128-5** (20 overs) (H. A. S. D. Siriwardene 50, R. S. Vandort 50; H. K. Matthews 4-18). *PoM:* D. J. S. Dottin. *PoS:* D. J. S. Dottin. *Dottin became the first woman to hit two T20I centuries, with a barnstorming 112 off 67 balls, including five sixes. She had little support – Matthews was the only other to reach double figures – and they lost four wickets in the final over, including two run-outs. But it hardly mattered. Siriwardene and Rebeca Vandort replied with the only fifties of Sri Lanka's tour, but could not match Dottin's dynamism. Needing 36 off the last over, both fell to Matthews, who finished with 4-18.*

AUSTRALIA v ENGLAND IN 2017-18

ADAM COLLINS

One-day internationals (3): Australia 2, England 1
Test match (1): Australia 0, England 0
Twenty20 internationals (3): Australia 1, England 2
Overall Ashes points: Australia 8, England 8

In 2013-14, the last time the women's Ashes were held in Australia, it was largely a family and friends affair. The sport was yet to turn professional, and even its premier bilateral event had meagre coverage. There was at best a vague awareness, and mostly because it was tacked on to the men's series.

This time, there was a dedicated window: crowd numbers and viewing figures soared. After the success of the World Cup earlier in the year, it felt like another reference point in the development of the women's game. The standard of play certainly warranted attention. Unlike four years previously, both sides had full-time contracts: cricket was no longer a passion to balance against a job. It made for an absorbing, seesaw series, which finished all square. The current points system – four for the Test, two for each white-ball match – was in use for the second time. With many of the same players competing across the formats, the rivalries and storylines persisted throughout.

Australia came into the series bruised after failing to make the World Cup final. England, meanwhile, had triumphed with a young team, and subsequently edged past them to the top of the ICC rankings. Their preparations were disrupted by poor weather, though, and they were rusty when the one-dayers

Mark Evans, Getty Images

Driving force: Ellyse Perry hits a double-hundred at North Sydney.

began, surrendering a low-scoring game. Then, in Coffs Harbour four days later, they were badly beaten. As the Australians held the trophy – and needed only to draw on points to retain it – England's situation looked dire.

But Heather Knight's charges bounced back in the final one-dayer, and carried momentum through to the early stages of the first women's day/night Test. Then, after Ellyse Perry's wonderful double-century, they had to battle to a draw on a compliant North Sydney Oval pitch. On the same ground for the first of the T20s, a masterclass from Beth Mooney gave Australia the two points they required to keep the Ashes. Once more, England picked themselves up, and levelled the series in a scintillating floodlit finale, when a hundred from Mooney was trumped by one from Danni Wyatt.

Still, England had rarely looked capable of regaining the trophy. The new-ball pair Katherine Brunt and Anya Shrubsole were off-colour, claiming just ten wickets between them. And their batting was unreliable, except for Knight, who hit four half-centuries and was named Player of the Series.

Australia's success was built around Megan Schutt's outstanding seam and swing, which earned her 18 wickets at an average of 15, and was backed up by ten each for Perry and left-arm spinner Jess Jonassen. And, in contrast to

> "A year in Vietnam was good training to be in Ian Chappell's dressing-room."
> Cricket Round the World in 2017, page 1092

England, their batting was dependable, with six averaging 34 or more; Mooney, Perry and Alyssa Healy were relentlessly excellent.

In the absence of full-time skipper Meg Lanning, nursing a shoulder problem, they did what was needed under the captaincy of Rachael Haynes, even if they couldn't win outright. As for England, they clung on to their No. 1 ranking, and now had a better idea of what was required to stay there.

ENGLAND TOURING PARTY

*H. C. Knight (Berkshire), T. T. Beaumont (Kent), K. H. Brunt (Yorkshire), S. Ecclestone (Lancashire), G. A. Elwiss (Sussex), J. L. Gunn (Warwickshire), A. Hartley (Lancashire), D. Hazell (Yorkshire), L. A. Marsh (Kent), N. R. Sciver (Surrey), A. Shrubsole (Somerset), S. J. Taylor (Sussex), F. C. Wilson (Middlesex), L. Winfield (Yorkshire), D. N. Wyatt (Sussex). *Coach:* M. A. Robinson.

First one-day international At Brisbane (Allan Border Field), October 22, 2017. **Australia won by two wickets. England 228-9** (50 overs) (L. Winfield 48, S. J. Taylor 34, N. R. Sciver 36; A. K. Gardner 3-47); ‡**Australia 231-8** (49.1 overs) (E. J. Villani 38, R. L. Haynes 30, A. J. Blackwell 67*). Australia 2pts. *PoM:* A. J. Blackwell. *It was not a game to turn into a commemorative DVD, but Australia did just enough to claim first blood. After Ellyse Perry was stumped and Elyse Villani run out in quick succession, they were 87-4, and England's modest total looked defendable. But Alex Blackwell showed poise, and steered the chase with 67*. She put on 63 with captain Rachael Haynes, before Ashleigh Gardner smacked 27 in 18 balls to make sure. It could have tipped the other way had Alex Hartley taken a return chance off Blackwell on 35; the drop reflected a scrappy English performance. Opener Lauren Winfield had success using the long handle, twice clearing the rope, but the innings spluttered and the last ten overs yielded just 56 runs for five wickets. Australia's trio of spinners proved hardest to hit, Gardner the pick with 3-47.*

Second one-day international At Coffs Harbour, October 26, 2017 (day/night). **Australia won by 75 runs** (DLS). **Australia 296-6** (50 overs) (N. E. Bolton 66, A. J. Healy 56, E. A. Perry 67, R. L. Haynes 89*; J. L. Gunn 4-55); ‡**England 209** (42.2 overs) (H. C. Knight 36, F. C. Wilson 37, K. H. Brunt 52; M. L. Schutt 4-26). Australia 2pts. *PoM:* R. L. Haynes. *Haynes's selection as Australia captain in place of the injured Meg Lanning had been controversial: during the World Cup she was not even a regular first-teamer. But she repaid the faith with a punishing 89* in 56 balls to drive a second home victory. Her opposite number, Heather Knight, had raised eyebrows when she elected to field, and Australia racked up 296, their second-best score against England in ODIs, behind 299-2 at Newcastle (New South Wales) in 1999-2000. Nicole Bolton and Alyssa Healy started with 98, before Perry hit the third half-century. But the main action came in the final ten overs, when Australia added 94 and England's fielding splintered; Haynes unleashed fury, smashing 21 off one Katherine Brunt over. After a short shower, the target was revised to 285 from 46, though England almost gave up hope when they slumped to 91-5. Brunt fought back, recording her maiden ODI fifty but, after she became the fourth of Megan Schutt's victims, the series was in danger of fizzling out.*

Third one-day international At Coffs Harbour, October 29, 2017. **England won by 20 runs** (DLS). ‡**England 284-8** (50 overs) (T. T. Beaumont 74, S. J. Taylor 69, H. C. Knight 88*; M. L. Schutt 4-44); **Australia 257-9** (48 overs) (A. J. Healy 71, N. E. Bolton 62, A. J. Blackwell 37; A. L. Hartley 3-45). England 2pts. *PoM:* H. C. Knight. *England's batting finally clicked, and the Ashes came alive. Tammy Beaumont and Sarah Taylor swept liberally, and put on 122 for the second wicket. Then, after Schutt induced a mid-innings wobble, Knight batted with panache, finishing with 88* from 80 balls. England ended with 284-8, their best ODI total against Australia, beating 279-3 (in 60 overs) to secure the 1973 World Cup. A heavy shower reduced Australia's target to 278 off 48, and Healy cracked a run-a-ball 71 before holing out off Hartley. It was a sign of what was to come. From 159-1, Australia lost six for 57, with five falling to miscues. Blackwell, in her 250th international, kept England waiting, but they held their nerve to claim their first points in the series.*

Women's Championship: Australia 4pts, England 2pts.

AUSTRALIA v ENGLAND

Only Test

At North Sydney, November 9–12 (day/night). Drawn. Australia 2pts, England 2pts. Toss: England. Test debuts: T. M. McGrath, B. L. Mooney, A. Wellington; S. Ecclestone, F. C. Wilson.

This was the first Ashes contest played with a pink ball but, in an otherwise sedate affair, it was Ellyse Perry's superlative unbeaten 213 that made it truly special. She batted nearly eight hours, faced 374 deliveries, and finished with the third-highest score in women's Tests, behind Kiran Baluch's 242 for Pakistan against West Indies at Karachi in 2003-04 and Mithali Raj's 214 for India against England at Taunton in 2002.

In an instant it became clear that demands for a lively surface had been ignored: the first delivery of the match didn't carry to the keeper. It made for slow going, before England captain Knight lifted the tempo in a stand of 104 with Beaumont. Australia's spinners plugged away for three wickets: Amanda-Jade Wellington's beautiful flight found Beaumont's edge, before Knight and Sciver were trapped by flatter ones from Jonassen. Then, under lights, and with the second new ball, the seamers found joy. From 214 for four, England lost three for 13, including Taylor, caught reflexively by Perry in her follow-through. Next day, they were all out for 280.

Australia were also careful at first, before the openers scooped catches to midwicket. The dismissal of Mooney gave a maiden scalp to 18-year-old slow left-armer Sophie

HIGHEST SCORES IN WOMEN'S ASHES

213*	**E. A. Perry (Australia)**	**North Sydney**	**2017-18**
209*	K. L. Rolton (Australia)	Leeds	2001
204	M. A. J. Goszko (Australia)	Shenley	2001
200	J. Broadbent (Australia)	Guildford	1998
193	D. A. Annetts (Australia)	Collingham	1987
179	R. Heyhoe Flint (England)	The Oval	1976
176*	K. L. Rolton (Australia)	Worcester	1998
167	J. A. Brittin (England)	Harrogate	1998
157	H. C. Knight (England)	Wormsley	2013

Ecclestone, who soon added another: Blackwell fell lbw to a crafty arm-ball. When Villani was brilliantly caught by Taylor, standing up to the seam of Shrubsole, they were limping at 95 for four.

But Perry, 70 overnight, was immovable on the third day. With a clip to fine leg, she finally made it to a first international hundred – after 28 fifties. And she anchored consecutive century partnerships with Healy and debutant Tahlia McGrath that firmly shut the door on England. Healy helped the scoring tick over, twice depositing the ball over long-on, before trying one whack too many. At that point, England were still ten in front, and could have seized the initiative had Knight caught McGrath first ball.

Instead, McGrath made them pay with a gutsy 47, while Perry pressed on with clinical cuts and drives. She modified her approach only when, in touching distance of a double-century, the ninth wicket fell. A hoist over midwicket brought celebrations, only for replays to show it was four, not six; a straight-drive next over completed the job, and the celebrations. When the declaration came after a punishing 166 overs, Australia had a lead of 168.

Still, with the pitch dead, England gritted their teeth for a draw. Wellington bowled Beaumont with a perfect leg-break, but Knight dug in with Elwiss, facing a combined 410 balls. If the points were split, the honours were all Perry's.

Close of play: first day, England 235-7 (Wilson 11, Shrubsole 0); second day, Australia 177-5 (Perry 70, Healy 1); third day, England 40-0 (Winfield 12, Beaumont 25).

England

L. Winfield c Bolton b McGrath	4	– lbw b McGrath	34
T. T. Beaumont c Blackwell b Wellington	70	– b Wellington	37
*H. C. Knight lbw b Jonassen	62	– not out	79
G. A. Elwiss c Schutt b Perry	27	– not out	41
N. R. Sciver lbw b Jonassen	18		
†S. J. Taylor c and b Perry	29		
F. C. Wilson c Perry b Schutt	13		
K. H. Brunt c Jonassen b McGrath	1		
A. Shrubsole c Villani b Schutt	20		
L. A. Marsh c Healy b Perry	13		
S. Ecclestone not out	8		
B 3, lb 8, nb 4	15	B 7, lb 2, nb 6	15
1/25 (1) 2/129 (2) 3/145 (3) 4/177 (5) 5/214 (4) 6/226 (6) 7/227 (8) 8/249 (7) 9/262 (9) 10/280 (10) (116 overs)	280	1/71 (2) 2/89 (1) (2 wkts, 105 overs)	206

Schutt 24–7–52–2; Perry 21–2–59–3; McGrath 19–8–45–2; Jonassen 31–7–52–2; Wellington 21–1–61–1. *Second innings*—Schutt 13–4–28–0; Jonassen 23–10–40–0; McGrath 11–4–12–1; Perry 14–3–26–0; Wellington 36–8–69–1; Bolton 5–1–10–0; Haynes 2–0–8–0; Villani 1–0–4–0.

Australia

N. E. Bolton c Shrubsole b Marsh	24
B. L. Mooney c Sciver b Ecclestone	27
A. J. Blackwell lbw b Ecclestone	6
E. A. Perry not out	213
E. J. Villani c Taylor b Shrubsole	14
*R. L. Haynes lbw b Brunt	33
†A. J. Healy c Shrubsole b Marsh	45
T. M. McGrath c Sciver b Elwiss	47
J. L. Jonassen c Winfield b Marsh	24
A. Wellington lbw b Ecclestone	2
M. L. Schutt not out	1
B 1, lb 10, w 1	12
1/48 (1) 2/54 (2) 3/61 (3) 4/95 (5) 5/168 (6) 6/270 (7) 7/373 (8) 8/420 (9) 9/427 (10) (9 wkts dec, 166 overs)	448

Brunt 22–8–44–1; Shrubsole 22–7–57–1; Marsh 44–11–109–3; Ecclestone 37–7–107–3; Sciver 20–2–59–0; Knight 8–1–21–0; Elwiss 13–2–40–1.

Umpires: G. A. Abood and G. C. Joshua. Third umpire: G. J. Davidson.
Referee: S. R. Bernard.

First Twenty20 international At North Sydney, November 17, 2017 (floodlit). **Australia won by six wickets. England 132-9** (20 overs) (D. N. Wyatt 50; M. L. Schutt 4-22); **‡Australia 134-4** (15.5 overs) (B. L. Mooney 86*). Australia 2pts. *PoM:* B. L. Mooney. T20I debut: S. E. Aley (Australia). *Beth Mooney led Australia to a comfortable victory that ensured they would retain the Ashes. After being left out of the one-day series, she made mincemeat of a modest target, crunching 86* off 56 deliveries. Twice she cleared the rope at backward square, but more impressive were the cover-drives, the last of which had her team-mates flooding the field. England had started atrociously, losing four wickets inside five overs, with Perry removing Beaumont and Brunt in two balls. Danni Wyatt saved embarrassment, putting on 64 with Sciver, and reached a maiden international half-century. But Schutt was lethal at the death, and finished with her third four-for of the series.*

Second Twenty20 international At Canberra, November 19, 2017. **England won by 40 runs. ‡England 152-6** (20 overs) (S. J. Taylor 30, N. R. Sciver 40, K. H. Brunt 32*); **Australia 112** (18 overs) (J. L. Gunn 4-13). England 2pts. *PoM:* K. H. Brunt. *England's veterans steered them to a win that gave hope of tying the series on points. After their top order flickered, Brunt turbocharged the innings with 32 from 24 balls, then took two key wickets as Australia slipped from 45-0 to 65-5: Villani stumped by Taylor's magic gloves, Perry bowled for five. Jenny Gunn, playing her 250th match for England, had started the collapse, running out Mooney with a direct hit, before fooling the dangerous Healy (24) with a slower one. She proved a nuisance throughout, and snipped off the tail to finish with 4-13.*

Third Twenty20 international At Canberra, November 21, 2017 (floodlit). **England won by four wickets.** ‡**Australia 178-2** (20 overs) (B. L. Mooney 117*); **England 181-6** (19 overs) (D. N. Wyatt 100, H. C. Knight 51). England 2pts. *PoM:* D. N. Wyatt. *PoS:* H. C. Knight. *This was an instant classic. Mooney's 117* off 70 balls was perhaps the finest women's 20-over innings ever played, but Wyatt struck back with a wonderful hundred of her own to square the series for England. After they subsided to 30-3, a target of 179 looked a mile away. But Wyatt was undaunted and, with brilliant inside-out driving, scorched to England's first T20 century, in 56 deliveries. Along the way, she shared a decisive stand of 139 in 75 balls with Knight, the fifth-highest in women's T20Is, and the second-best by England. The Australians contributed to their downfall, shelling four straightforward chances, with Healy twice the culprit. After a flurry of wickets, Fran Wilson's scoop completed a record chase in the format, beating England's own 165-2 against Australia at The Oval in the 2009 World Twenty20 semi-final. It was also England's second-biggest total, behind 187-5 against Pakistan at Bristol in 2016. Earlier, Mooney was joyous. She struck a classic square-drive off the first ball, and was still going 20 overs later, finishing with four consecutive boundaries off Anya Shrubsole. But Wyatt had the last word.*

HIGHEST AGGREGATES IN WOMEN'S T20Is

Runs		
359	**Australia (178-2) v England (181-6) at Canberra**	**2017-18**
333	West Indies (175-5) v South Africa (158-4) at Basseterre	2010
329	Australia (166-9) v New Zealand (163-7) at Invercargill	2010-11
328	Australia (163-5) v England (165-2) at The Oval	2009
324	England (172-2) v New Zealand (152-6) at Bath	2007
316	Ireland (179-5) v Netherlands (137-4) at Potchefstroom (Witrand)	2010-11

PAKISTAN v NEW ZEALAND IN THE UAE IN 2017-18

One-day internationals (3): Pakistan 1, New Zealand 2
Twenty20 internationals (4): Pakistan 0, New Zealand 4

New Zealand had endured a poor World Cup, failing to reach the semi-finals for the first time, and their fluctuating form continued in their first internationals afterwards. Pakistan had lost all ten previous ODIs against them – but nearly broke their duck in the first match, and finally did so in the third, thanks to a third solid innings from Bismah Maroof, who had taken over as captain from Sana Mir. The usual order was restored in the four Twenty20 internationals, all of which New Zealand won comfortably. Sophie Devine was the star of the tour, scoring 167 runs in the ODIs, and 158 in the T20s.

First one-day international At Sharjah, October 31, 2017. **New Zealand won by eight runs.** ‡**New Zealand 240-9** (50 overs) (S. F. M. Devine 103, S. W. Bates 36, A. C. Kerr 30; Sana Mir 3-33); **Pakistan 232** (48.3 overs) (Nahida Khan 51, Javeria Khan 55, Bismah Maroof 41, Sidra Ameen 33). *PoM:* S. F. M. Devine. *Sophie Devine's second ODI century seemed to have set New Zealand up for a big total but, after she fell to the first ball of the 45th over, they scraped together only 25 more runs. Pakistan batted solidly in reply, Nahida Khan and Javeria Khan putting on 77 after Ayesha Zafar made a 12-ball duck. Bismah Maroof then took over, and Pakistan were favourites at 217-5 in the 46th – but panic set in, two run-outs contributing to the loss of five for 15.*

Second one-day international At Sharjah, November 2, 2017. **New Zealand won by seven wickets.** ‡**Pakistan 147** (49.1 overs) (Nahida Khan 39, Bismah Maroof 36, Sana Mir 31; A. C. Kerr 3-35); **New Zealand 148-3** (24 overs) (S. W. Bates 33, S. F. M. Devine 62). *PoM:* S. F. M. Devine. *Pakistan underperformed with the bat, losing their last three wickets without addition, and New Zealand knocked off the target with ease, Devine making 62 from 48 balls.*

Third one-day international At Sharjah, November 5, 2017. **Pakistan won by five wickets.** ‡**New Zealand 155** (43.4 overs) (S. R. H. Curtis 50; Sana Mir 4-25); **Pakistan 156-5** (48.5 overs) (Sidra Ameen 32, Bismah Maroof 36*). *PoM:* Sana Mir. *Pakistan had never beaten New Zealand in 12 previous ODIs stretching back to January 1997 – but overhauled a modest total with seven balls to spare. The dangerous Devine was run out in the second over, and only Sam Curtis, who hung around for 77 balls, did much after that. Nahida and Sidra Ameen made a patient start – 40 in 13.3 overs – then Bismah (36* in 69 balls) and Sana Mir (12* in 34, after four wickets for her off-breaks) calmly guided their side home.*

Women's Championship: New Zealand 4pts, Pakistan 2pts.

First Twenty20 international At Sharjah, November 8, 2017. **New Zealand won by 15 runs.** **New Zealand 147-8** (20 overs) (S. F. M. Devine 41, K. J. Martin 46; Sadia Yousuf 3-30); ‡**Pakistan 132-7** (20 overs) (Nahida Khan 34). *PoM:* K. J. Martin. *Katey Martin's late burst of 46 from 27 ensured New Zealand's total was just beyond Pakistan, who were in with a shout until Bismah (25) fell at the end of the 15th over, which made it 94-3.*

Second Twenty20 international At Sharjah, November 9, 2017. **New Zealand won by 39 runs.** ‡**New Zealand 150-8** (20 overs) (S. F. M. Devine 70, S. W. Bates 52); **Pakistan 111-7** (20 overs). *PoM:* S. F. M. Devine. *T20I debuts:* Nashra Sandhu, Natalia Pervaiz (Pakistan). *The experienced pair of Devine (who clobbered five sixes) and Suzie Bates led off with an opening stand of 116 in 13.4 overs, but New Zealand capsized from 136-2 to 139-8 in the space of ten balls – including three run-outs in the 18th over. Pakistan, however, were soon behind the rate, and never recovered; their highest score was 23 from Aliya Riaz.*

Third Twenty20 international At Sharjah, November 12, 2017. **New Zealand won by 42 runs.** ‡**New Zealand 126-4** (20 overs) (S. W. Bates 65*); **Pakistan 84** (19 overs) (H. M. Rowe 3-18). *PoM:* S. W. Bates. *Bates batted through the innings, but New Zealand's total was not imposing. Pakistan reached 39-0 in reply, then lost all ten for 45. The 17-year-old leg-spinner Amelia Kerr finished with 2-8 from her four overs, and seamer Hannah Rowe 3-18.*

Fourth Twenty20 international At Sharjah, November 14, 2017. **New Zealand won by seven wickets.** ‡**Pakistan 89-8** (20 overs) (Javeria Khan 36; H. M. Rowe 3-22); **New Zealand 93-3** (11 overs) (S. F. M. Devine 41, A. E. Satterthwaite 35). *PoM:* S. F. M. Devine. *PoS:* S. F. M. Devine. *New Zealand completed a T20 clean sweep with the easiest win of the four, after Devine (who hit seven fours and a six) and Amy Satterthwaite ignited the chase by taking 56 from the first 27 balls.*

ICC WOMEN'S CHAMPIONSHIP IN 2017–2020

In 2014, the ICC introduced a Women's Championship as a qualifying tournament for the World Cup, and to create a more meaningful programme for the leading teams. Each of the eight sides from the previous World Cup played one another in three one-day internationals over two and a half years (they could arrange more games if they chose, but only the designated three carried points). The top four advanced directly to the next World Cup, while the bottom four had to go through a further qualifying tournament with six other teams. The inaugural Championship, won by Australia, ended in November 2016; after the bottom four made it safely through the World Cup Qualifier in February, the same eight teams were reunited in the 2017 World Cup, staged in England, and then restarted the cycle in October, when West Indies hosted Sri Lanka in the first round of the second Championship.

QUALIFYING TABLE

	Played	*Won*	*Lost*	*Points*	*NRR*
West Indies	3	3	0	6	0.80
New Zealand	3	2	1	4	0.78
Australia	3	2	1	4	0.43
England	3	1	2	2	–0.43
Pakistan	3	1	2	2	–0.78
Sri Lanka	3	0	3	0	–0.80

As at December 31, 2017, by which time India and South Africa had not played. Win = 2pts; no result = 1pt. Where teams are tied on points, their position is determined on net run-rate.

MRF TYRES ICC WOMEN'S RANKINGS

TEAM RANKINGS (as at December 31, 2017)

		Matches	*Points*	*Rating*
1	England	41	5,274	129
2	Australia	47	6,025	128
3	New Zealand	50	5,842	117
4	India	45	5,216	116
5	West Indies	41	4,243	103
6	South Africa	55	5,112	93
7	Pakistan	46	3,338	73
8	Sri Lanka	46	3,010	65
9	Bangladesh	19	704	37
10	Ireland	17	504	30

The ratings are based on all women's Tests, one-day and Twenty20 internationals played since October 1, 2014.

PLAYER RANKINGS

In October 2008, the ICC launched a set of rankings for women cricketers, on the same principles as those for men, based on one-day international performances. Twenty20 rankings were added in September 2012. There are no Test rankings.

The leading players in the one-day international rankings on December 31, 2017, were:

	Batsmen	*Points*
1	M. D. Raj (I)	753
2	E. A. Perry (A)	725
3	M. M. Lanning (A)	718
4	A. E. Satterthwaite (NZ)	683
5	H. Kaur (I)	677
6	A. J. Blackwell (A)	672
7	S. W. Bates (NZ)	668
8	L. Lee (SA)	625
9	N. R. Sciver (E)	609
10	S. J. Taylor (E)	604

	Bowlers	*Points*
1	M. Kapp (SA)	656
2	J. N. Goswami (I)	652
3	S. R. Taylor (WI)	626
4	M. L. Schutt (A)	619
5	J. L. Jonassen (A)	616
6	A. Shrubsole (E)	595
7	Sana Mir (P)	593
8	A. Khaka (SA)	578
9	D. van Niekerk (SA)	573
10	S. Ismail (SA)	565

The leading players in the Twenty20 international rankings on December 31, 2017, were:

	Batsmen	*Points*
1	S. R. Taylor (WI)	678
2	S. W. Bates (NZ)	661
3	D. J. S. Dottin (WI)	623
4	M. M. Lanning (A)	618
5	M. D. Raj (I)	609
6	S. J. Taylor (E)	586
7	B. L. Mooney (A)	562
8	H. Kaur (I)	550
9	S. F. M. Devine (NZ)	534
10	E. J. Villani (A)	531
	M. du Preez (SA)	531

	Bowlers	*Points*
1	H. K. Matthews (WI)	631
2	M. L. Schutt (A)	625
3	A. Mohammed (WI)	609
4	J. L. Jonassen (A)	606
5	D. Hazell (E)	593
6	A. Shrubsole (E)	589
7	L. M. Tahuhu (NZ)	587
8	E. A. Perry (A)	580
9	L. M. Kasperek (NZ)	576
10	M. J. G. Nielsen (NZ)	569

"Some, such as the introduction of the headbutt greeting into the sport's lexicon, were unknown unknowns."

Cricket in the Media in 2017, page 139

WOMEN'S ONE-DAY INTERNATIONAL AVERAGES IN CALENDAR YEAR 2017

BATTING (300 runs)

		M	I	NO	R	HS	100	50	Avge	SR	Ct/St
1	M. M. Lanning (A)	9	9	3	491	152*	2	1	81.83	91.94	5
2	M. D. Raj (I)	19	15	4	783	109	1	9	71.18	76.68	6
3	†A. E. Satterthwaite (NZ)	12	11	4	446	102*	1	2	63.71	72.40	12
4	P. G. Raut (I)	14	14	3	653	109*	2	3	59.36	71.44	1
5	L. Wolvaardt (SA)	15	15	4	643	149	1	5	58.45	64.94	5
6	E. A. Perry (A)	13	12	3	515	71	0	6	57.22	75.29	4
7	A. J. Blackwell (A)	13	10	2	412	90	0	3	51.50	95.37	5
8	H. Kaur (I)	20	15	5	505	171*	1	2	50.50	84.30	5
9	H. C. Knight (E)	12	12	2	503	106	1	3	50.30	81.39	2
10	†D. B. Sharma (I)	20	19	3	787	188	1	7	49.18	70.51	8
11	S. W. Bates (NZ)	12	11	2	432	106*	1	2	48.00	79.70	3
12	S. J. Taylor (E)	12	12	1	525	147	1	3	47.72	95.28	5/5
13	A. Steyn (SA)	8	8	0	361	117	1	3	45.12	68.24	3
14	T. T. Beaumont (E)	12	12	0	516	148	1	2	43.00	75.54	3
15	†B. L. Mooney (A)	11	11	0	458	100	1	4	41.63	77.89	4
16	M. du Preez (SA)	23	21	5	630	79	0	3	39.37	69.45	4
17	N. E. Bolton (A)	14	14	1	509	107*	1	4	39.15	74.30	4
18	†A. M. C. Jayangani (SL)	15	15	1	533	178*	1	2	38.07	76.03	7
19	N. R. Sciver (E)	12	12	1	417	137	2	1	37.90	101.21	8
20	A. J. Healy (A)	14	11	3	303	71	0	3	37.87	113.48	8/7
21	L. Lee (SA)	21	21	1	717	92	0	5	35.85	116.01	15/2
22	Nahida Khan (P)	15	15	0	488	79	0	4	32.53	66.66	4
23	Javeria Khan (P)	14	14	2	385	90*	0	4	32.08	67.30	3
24	†C. L. Tryon (SA)	20	16	3	415	79	0	3	31.92	115.27	2
25	M. A. D. D. Surangika (SL)	15	15	2	390	84	0	3	30.00	58.91	3
26	S. E. Luus (SA)	21	16	4	351	83	0	3	29.25	75.00	5
27	T. Chetty (SA)	18	15	0	407	76	0	3	27.13	72.03	10/6

BOWLING (15 wickets)

		Style	O	M	R	W	BB	4I	Avge	SR	ER
1	D. van Niekerk (SA)	LB	128.5	15	426	31	4-0	3	13.74	24.93	3.30
2	S. S. Pandey (I)	RM	131	18	465	28	4-34	1	16.60	28.07	3.54
3	R. S. Gayakwad (I)	SLA	78.3	7	324	19	5-15	2	17.05	24.78	4.12
4	E. K. Bisht (I)	SLA	147.4	31	501	29	5-8	2	17.27	30.55	3.39
5	H. R. Huddleston (NZ)	RM	64.4	7	271	15	5-35	1	18.06	25.86	4.19
6	Khadija Tul Kobra (B)	OB	81.3	8	348	17	4-33	2	20.47	28.76	4.26
7	J. N. Goswami (I)	RFM	97.4	15	372	18	3-20	0	20.66	32.55	3.80
8	M. Kapp (SA)	RFM	169.4	25	583	28	4-14	1	20.82	36.35	3.43
9	S. E. Luus (SA)	LB	145.5	10	606	29	5-67	1	20.89	30.17	4.15
10	A. C. Kerr (NZ)	LB	104.3	4	432	20	4-51	2	21.60	31.35	4.13
11	M. Schutt (A)	RM	101	11	474	21	4-26	2	22.57	28.85	4.69
12	P. Yadav (I)	LB	138	11	475	20	3-30	0	23.75	41.40	3.44
13	S. Ismail (SA)	RFM	143.1	18	555	23	3-14	0	24.13	37.34	3.87
14	A. Hartley (E)	SLA	98	8	427	16	3-44	0	26.68	36.75	4.35
15	Sadia Yousuf (P)	SLA	103	5	438	16	2-19	0	27.37	38.62	4.25
16	A. Khaka (SA)	RM	157	23	593	21	3-15	0	28.23	44.85	3.77
17	D. B. Sharma (I)	OB	167.2	24	636	22	3-20	0	28.90	45.63	3.80
18	Sana Mir (P)	OB	137.3	9	564	19	4-25	1	29.68	43.42	4.10
19	I. Ranaweera (SL)	SLA	121.4	15	479	16	2-16	0	29.93	45.62	3.93
20	Nashra Sandhu (P)	SLA	121.3	6	561	18	4-26	1	31.16	40.50	4.61
21	J. L. Jonassen (A)	SLA	122	9	558	17	3-33	0	32.82	43.05	4.57
22	A. K. Gardner (A)	OB	112	3	499	15	3-28	0	33.26	44.80	4.45

WOMEN'S BIG BASH LEAGUE IN 2016-17

ADAM COLLINS

1 Sydney Sixers 2 Perth Scorchers

Any concerns that the Women's Big Bash would fall foul of sophomore syndrome proved misplaced. With more games televised and more international talent on show, the second WBBL thrived, epitomised by the 24,547 who turned up for the Melbourne derby on New Year's Day. The competition drew a TV audience of nearly 700,000, while an astonishing 6.9m clicks were registered on live feeds and replays.

The **Sydney Sixers** went one better than the previous year, overcoming the **Perth Scorchers** in a tense final. Ellyse Perry had led the Sixers to the top of the qualifying group, but missed the knockouts with a hamstring strain; Alyssa Healy was an impressive stand-in.

Some unexpected early results meant a tight table by Christmas, after which the favourites pushed ahead. The **Adelaide Strikers** had been among the front-runners, with Sophie Devine clobbering a competition-best 103 in 48 balls on Boxing Day. That afternoon, Australian skipper Meg Lanning hit 97 for the **Melbourne Stars**. Both teams looked set for maiden semi-finals – but that was where their surges ended.

Adelaide didn't win again, not helped by Devine missing two games to play for Wellington in New Zealand domestic cricket. The Stars' over-reliance on Lanning defined their campaign. She was again the leading run-scorer, with 502, but it wasn't enough. In a frantic final-weekend double-header with the **Hobart Hurricanes**, the Stars won the first match by conjuring 12 runs from the last two legitimate balls: the final scheduled delivery was a no-ball, which Jess Cameron hit for four, leaving one required. But they lost the second. The Hurricanes, captained by England's Heather Knight, went on to the semi-finals, but were no match for the Sixers.

Reigning champions **Sydney Thunder** failed to make the most of the class of Indian dynamo Harmanpreet Kaur, though they did come out on top in the most exciting match of the summer, when they defeated the Sixers on a higher boundary count after the super over was tied. The competition's status was underlined when Channel Ten stayed with the climax rather than cut to their news bulletin.

The **Melbourne Renegades** started disastrously, before recovering – but not in time to qualify. They did, however, produce a new international, off-spinner Molly Strano, while all-rounder Sophie Molineux was named Young Cricketer of the Year. Nineteen-year-old Ashleigh Gardner's breakout season netted her 414 runs for Sydney Sixers, and an Australian cap; Healy finished with 479, while Perry (384) and New Zealander Sara McGlashan (343) were also match-winners. The Sixers' Sarah Aley – 32, and an Australian youth representative in 2002-03 – took 28 wickets with her cagey medium-pacers, seven more than Strano, the next-best.

Beth Mooney was Player of the Tournament for her 482 runs, three times helping **Brisbane Heat** over the line with unbeaten scores of 75 or more. But they couldn't match the Scorchers in their semi. Perth had dominated several games thanks to their experienced opening pair of Elyse Villani and Nicole Bolton, who piled up 766 runs between them. Because the Scorchers' men's team had topped the BBL table, the WACA hosted the women's final too, even though the Sixers had led the women's standings. It didn't matter: Sydney's modest total was under threat early on, but Aley's four-wicket burst left Perth eight runs short.

Deference to the men's competition is a teething problem; imports called back for domestic duty another. But taken as a whole, the WBBL established itself in its second season as *the* tournament for the best women players in the world.

WOMEN'S BIG BASH LEAGUE

20-over league plus semi-finals and final

	P	*W*	*L*	*NR*	*Pts*	*NRR*
SYDNEY SIXERS	14	9	5	0	18	0.44
PERTH SCORCHERS	14	8	6	0	16	0.30
BRISBANE HEAT	14	8	6	0	16	0.04
HOBART HURRICANES	14	7	6	1	15	–0.03
Melbourne Stars	14	7	7	0	14	0.25
Sydney Thunder	14	6	7	1	12*	–0.04
Melbourne Renegades	14	6	8	0	11.5*	–0.51
Adelaide Strikers	14	3	9	2	8	–0.54

* *Points deducted for a slow over-rate.*

First semi-final At Perth, January 24, 2017. **Perth Scorchers won by nine wickets. Brisbane Heat 124-5** (20 overs) (K. L. Short 39); ‡**Perth Scorchers 125-1** (15.4 overs) (E. J Villani 52*, N. E. Bolton 36). *PoM:* E. L. King. *The Scorchers made light of a target of 125: Elyse Villani and Nicole Bolton put on 67 before Bolton was run out, then Villani and Suzie Bates (27* from 22 balls) did the rest. Brisbane Heat had been kept in check, with off-spinner Emma King taking 2-17; skipper Kirby Short top-scored with 39, but occupied 49 deliveries.*

Second semi-final At Brisbane, January 25, 2017. **Sydney Sixers won by 103 runs.** ‡**Sydney Sixers 169-6** (20 overs) (A. J. Healy 77, S. J. McGlashan 38, M. Kapp 36*); **Hobart Hurricanes 66** (14.1 overs) (D. van Niekirk 3-15). *PoM:* A. J. Healy. *The Sixers roared to their second successive WBBL final, led by Alyssa Healy's 45-ball 77. The overseas pair of Sara McGlashan and Marizanne Kapp kept up the rate, then Kapp's South African team-mate Dané van Niekirk demolished the Hurricanes' middle order with three wickets and a run-out, to set up a thumping victory.*

FINAL

PERTH SCORCHERS v SYDNEY SIXERS

At Perth, January 28, 2017. Sydney Sixers won by seven runs. Toss: Perth Scorchers.

When the Scorchers, chasing the target they had knocked off with ease in the semi, reached the halfway mark at 60 for one, a home win – and a second successive final defeat for the Sixers – looked on the cards. But Suzie Bates was run out four balls later, and the prolific Nicole Bolton departed two overs after that. The Scorchers succumbed to some fine fielding, and a beguiling spell from the 32-year-old medium-pacer Sarah Aley, whose four wickets took her competition haul to 28. "Some might call me a bottle of red wine – getting better with age," she said. The Sixers won despite being without their captain, Ellyse Perry, who missed the knockouts with a hamstring injury. Alyssa

Healy, the national team's wicketkeeper, took over and led from the front with 40 from 27 balls to set up what turned out to be a large enough target. Local pride was restored later in the day, in the second part of a final double-header, when Perth's men overcame the Sixers to win their trophy.

Player of the Match: S. E. Aley. *Player of the Tournament:* B. L. Mooney (Brisbane Heat).

Sydney Sixers

		B	4/6
1 *†A. J. Healy *c 3 b 9*	40	27	6
2 D. van Niekerk *c 11 b 8*	1	4	0
3 A. K. Gardner *b 3*	21	31	1
4 S. J. McGlashan *c 8 b 5*	8	12	0
5 M. Kapp *not out*	34	28	3
6 A. R. Reakes *b 8*	11	18	0
7 S. E. Aley *not out*	1	1	0
Lb 6, w 1, nb 1	8		
6 overers: 40-1 (20 overs)	124-5		

1/10 2/66 3/70 4/81 5/115

8 K. J. Garth, 9 E. A. Leys, 10 L. E. M. Smith and 11 J. C. Hicks did not bat.

12th woman: C. M. Leeson.

Brunt 3–4–27–0; Shrubsole 4–14–17–2; Cleary 3–9–15–1; King 4–7–32–0; Bates 3–8–15–1; Graham 3–9–12–1.

Perth Scorchers

		B	4/6
1 N. E. Bolton *c 12 b 8*	34	35	4
2 E. J. Villani *c 9 b 7*	23	20	5
3 *S. W. Bates *run out*	7	14	0
4 K. H. Brunt *not out*	35	30	1/1
5 H. L. Graham *b 7*	2	4	0
6 L. K. Ebsary *run out*	1	2	0
7 C. Piparo *b 7*	7	9	0
8 A. Shrubsole *b 7*	0	1	0
9 P. M. Cleary *not out*	5	5	0
Lb 1, w 2	3		
6 overs: 38-1 (20 overs)	117-7		

1/38 2/61 3/75 4/80 5/84 6/100 7/100

10 E. L. King and 11 †E. J. Smith did not bat.

Kapp 4–11–26–0; Gardner 2–7–15–0; Aley 4–10–23–4; Garth 4–12–20–1; van Niekerk 3–6–14–0; Smith 3–6–18–0.

Umpires: S. A. J. Craig and G. J. Davidson. Third umpire: J. D. Ward.
Referee: S. R. Bernard.

KIA SUPER LEAGUE IN 2017

KALIKA MEHTA

1 Western Storm   2 Southern Vipers   3 Surrey Stars

The second edition of the Kia Super League, the UK's first professional domestic competition for women, began less than three weeks after England's thrilling victory over India in the World Cup final, and the biggest question was whether it would be able to harness the tournament's enthusiasm.

The ECB director of women's cricket, Clare Connor, announced that the KSL marketing budget had been doubled. The 2016 competition had been judged a success, though some were puzzled by the decision not to seek television coverage; this time, the first six matches – all double-headers with men's T20 Blast games – and the finals were televised, a first for English domestic women's cricket. After 1.1m tuned in to watch the World Cup final, Connor felt there was no better time to engage with a new audience.

Defending champions **Southern Vipers**, led by former England captain Charlotte Edwards, remained a force to be reckoned with, as did her successor Heather Knight's **Western Storm**, while Nat Sciver's **Surrey Stars** looked a frightening prospect, with five international bowlers. The league opened with a rematch between the Vipers and Storm, the 2016 finalists, but it failed to spark into life. Storm were all out for 70, with New Zealand's Suzie Bates following up two wickets by steering the Vipers to victory with 11 overs to spare. That set the trend: there were few competitive matches. The Stars' bowling quintet – England's Sciver, Alex Hartley and Laura Marsh, South Africa's Marizanne Kapp and Australia's Rene Farrell – swept aside all that came before them, until **Loughborough Lightning** bowled them out for 90 in the last group game.

There had been no centuries in 2016, but this time there were two. Bates smashed an unbeaten 119 – with four sixes – in 72 balls against Lightning, before grabbing three wickets. Her New Zealand team-mate Rachel Priest followed suit, hitting 106 not out off 65 for Storm against **Yorkshire Diamonds**. Boosted by Sri Lanka's Chamari Atapattu Jayangani, the Diamonds looked an improved side, and won two matches, but **Lancashire Thunder** were still the weakest link, losing all five.

The Vipers and the Stars won four games each, but Vipers led on bonus points and advanced straight to the final, while the Stars had to play off against Storm, who clinched third place in their last league game. In front of over 3,000 fans at Hove – more than double the previous finals day attendance – Storm won a low-scoring encounter to set up a repeat of the previous final, and gained their revenge on the Vipers as Priest's 72 helped them stroll to victory.

Afterwards, Edwards announced her retirement from all cricket, aged 37, saying it was time to pass on her knowledge to the next generation. It was also confirmed that the league would expand in 2018, with each side playing ten group games rather than five. The hope was that bigger would mean better.

KIA SUPER LEAGUE IN 2017

20-over league plus play-off and final

	Played	*Won*	*Lost*	*Bonus points*	*Points*	*NRR*
SOUTHERN VIPERS	5	4	1	4	20	2.00
SURREY STARS	5	4	1	2	18	0.29
WESTERN STORM	5	3	2	0	12	–0.88
Loughborough Lightning	5	2	3	2	10	0.66
Yorkshire Diamonds	5	2	3	0	8	–0.31
Lancashire Thunder	5	0	5	0	0	–1.69

Play-off At Hove, September 1. **Western Storm won by three wickets. ‡Surrey Stars 100-7** (20 overs) (S. I. R. Dunkley-Brown 30; A. Shrubsole 3-22); **Western Storm 101-7** (18.5 overs) (S. R. Taylor 37*; M. Kapp 3-11). *PoM:* S. R. Taylor. *Anya Shrubsole took three wickets in the final over of the Stars' innings – and Marizanne Kapp three in her first two as Storm slid to 17-4 in reply. Stafanie Taylor followed up four tight overs costing 17 runs with 37* off 45, the highest score of a game featuring only eight fours on each side – and a single six, by Shrubsole.*

FINAL

SOUTHERN VIPERS v WESTERN STORM

At Hove, September 1 (floodlit). Western Storm won by seven wickets. Toss: Western Storm.

England's World Cup-winning captain Heather Knight raised her second trophy of the summer as Charlotte Edwards announced her retirement, the final confirmation that one era had ended and another begun. Knight had put the Vipers in, and their openers were going well until Stafanie Taylor's off-breaks claimed three wickets in seven deliveries. Edwards struck 20 not out from eight balls in the last innings of her career to raise the target to 146. But Rachel Priest charged to 72 in 36 before she was caught on the midwicket boundary. Taylor, batting with a runner after pulling a hamstring, and Sophie Luff then knocked off 57 in eight overs; with the scores level, Taylor finished the game with a six off 18-year-old left-arm seamer Katie George.

Player of the Match: R. H. Priest.

Southern Vipers

		B	*4/6*
1 S. W. Bates *lbw b 4*	21	24	1/1
2 H. K. Matthews *c and b 4*	31	28	6
3 G. L. Adams *st 1 b 4*	2	4	0
4 D. N. Wyatt *c 6 b 2*	21	15	2/1
5 M. du Preez *c 9 b 11*	31	29	3
6 A. Brindle *not out*	13	13	1
7 *C. M. Edwards *not out*	20	8	4
Lb 1, w 4, nb 1	6		
6 overs: 38-0 (20 overs)	145-5		

1/47 2/58 3/63 4/100 5/117

8 †C. E. Rudd, 9 N. E. Farrant, 10 L. C. N. Smith and 11 K. L. George did not bat.

Nicholas 3–10–20–1; Shrubsole 4–10–30–0; Davies 2–3–19–0; Dibble 4–9–30–0; Taylor 4–8–28–3; Knight 3–7–17–1.

Western Storm

		B	*4/6*
1 †R. H. Priest *c 4 b 11*	72	36	10/3
2 *H. C. Knight *b 10*	6	9	1
3 F. C. Wilson *b 6*	8	11	1
4 S. R. Taylor *not out*	30	29	4/1
5 S. N. Luff *not out*	30	24	5
W 4, nb 1	5		
6 overs: 63-1 (18 overs)	151-3		

1/28 2/80 3/94

6 G. M. Hennessy, 7 A. J. Macleod, 8 A. Shrubsole, 9 J. M. Dibble, 10 F. R. Davies and 11 C. L. Nicholas did not bat.

Farrant 3–8–16–0; Smith 3–9–39–1; Matthews 3–6–27–0; Brindle 4–14–17–1; Bates 2–5–18–0; George 3–6–34–1.

Umpires: D. J. Millns and S. J. O'Shaughnessy. Third umpire: M. J. Saggers.

ENGLISH DOMESTIC CRICKET IN 2017

Lancashire surprised everyone, including themselves, by winning both the Royal London Women's One-Day Cup (the 50-over competition acting as the County Championship) and the NatWest Women's Twenty20 Cup – the first top-level trophies claimed by their women's team. They had won Division Two of the Royal London Cup the previous year – as they had done in 2014, only to go straight back down. At the start of the season, their primary ambition was simply to stay in Division One.

By the end of August, they began to realise they might just do better than that. With two rounds to go, they were joint third, 25 points behind Warwickshire at the top. Victory over Nottinghamshire, however, narrowed the gap; they were now 13 behind the new leaders, Yorkshire, and 12 behind Warwickshire, their opponents in their last match. A maximum-point win put them top – but only as long as Yorkshire failed to beat Nottinghamshire. They had an anxious journey home from Birmingham, until they heard the news they wanted: Yorkshire had lost, and Lancashire were champions by a point. Their star was left-arm spinner Sophie Ecclestone, who took 27 wickets, including a career-best six for 12 in that final game, to earn an Ashes tour. New Zealander Amy Satterthwaite and Eve Jones, who had joined from Staffordshire, greatly strengthened the batting. Meanwhile Kent and Sussex, the teams who had won 13 of the previous 14 County Championships, slid so far down the table that Sussex were relegated, along with Berkshire; Hampshire and Somerset were promoted.

Lancashire had already secured the T20 Cup in July, winning seven of their eight matches; the title was in the bag with one to go, so the seventh victory, over Yorkshire, was the icing on the cake. Nottinghamshire, relegated the previous year, won the second division and thus instant promotion. **Yorkshire** retained the Under-17 County Cup, and took the Under-13 Cup for the fifth year running; **Hampshire** won the Under-15 Cup.

At club level, Midland champions **Walmley** reached the national final of the Regional Leagues for the second year running; this time they won, against a young Newport side. In the semis, Walmley had beaten Yorkshire club Saxton, representing the North, while Finchley Gunns, national club winners a year earlier, were bowled out for 59 by Newport. In 2018, these games were to be replaced by a Twenty20 knockout cup and plate competition, culminating in a finals day for the eight top clubs in June.

NATWEST WOMEN'S TWENTY20 CUP IN 2017

Division One: Lancashire 28pts, Middlesex 20, Sussex 18, Warwickshire 16, Surrey 16, Kent 16, Yorkshire 12, Somerset 6, Berkshire 6.

Division Two: Nottinghamshire 29pts, Worcestershire 20, Hampshire 18, Scotland 16, Wales 14, Durham 12, Derbyshire 12, Staffordshire 10, Essex 5.

Division Three: *Group A:* Gloucestershire 26, Oxfordshire 22, Devon 18, Cornwall 12, Dorset 8, Wiltshire 4; *Group B:* Cheshire 28, Leicestershire 21, Shropshire 17, Northumberland 16, Lincolnshire 12, Cumbria 0; *Group C:* Northamptonshire 28, Hertfordshire 24, Norfolk 20, Suffolk 12, Buckinghamshire 8, Cambridgeshire 4.

ROYAL LONDON WOMEN'S ONE-DAY CUP IN 2017

50-over league

Division One	Played	Won	Lost	NR	Bonus Points Batting	Bonus Points Bowling	Points	Avge pts
Lancashire	7	5	2	0	23	26	99	14.14
Yorkshire	7	5	2	0	23	25	98	14.00
Warwickshire	7	5	2	0	21	25	96	13.71
Nottinghamshire	7	4	3	0	21	27	88	12.57
Middlesex	7	3	4	0	20	26	76	10.85
Kent	7	3	4	0	20	21	71	10.14
Sussex	7	3	4	0	16	19	65	9.28
Berkshire	7	0	7	0	11	12	23	3.28

Division Two	Played	Won	Lost	NR	Bonus Points Batting	Bonus Points Bowling	Points	Avge pts
HAMPSHIRE	7	6	1	0	26	24	110	15.71
SOMERSET	7	5	1	1	22	19	91	15.16
Devon	7	5	2	0	21	25	96	13.71
Surrey	7	4	3	0	23	24	87	12.42
Wales	7	3	4	0	19	23	72	10.28
Derbyshire	7	3	4	0	19	22	71	10.14
Worcestershire	7	1	5	1	14	12	36	6.00
Staffordshire	7	0	7	0	10	13	23	3.28

Division Three

Group A: DURHAM avge pts 15.20, Scotland 10.83, Northumberland 7.80, Cumbria –0.66.

Group B: GLOUCESTERSHIRE avge pts 17.75, Oxfordshire 14.50, Cornwall 9.25, Dorset 6.00, Wiltshire 5.00.

Group C: ESSEX avge pts 17.40, Netherlands 15.20, Shropshire 12.40, Buckinghamshire 8.80, Hertfordshire 6.80, Cambs & Hunts 3.80.

Group D: NORTHAMPTONSHIRE avge pts 16.66, Leicestershire 13.66, Suffolk 10.50, Lincolnshire 10.25, Norfolk 3.25.

Play-offs: Northamptonshire beat Durham by five wickets; Essex beat Gloucestershire by six wickets. Northamptonshire and Essex were promoted to Division Two.

Win = 10pts. Up to four batting and four bowling points are available to each team in each match. Final points are divided by the number of matches played (excluding no results and abandoned games) to calculate the average number of points.

DIVISION ONE AVERAGES

BATTING (145 runs)

	M	I	NO	R	HS	100	50	Avge	SR	Ct/St
K. H. Brunt (*Yorks*)	2	2	1	146	93	0	2	146.00	94.19	0
S. F. M. Devine (*Warwicks*)	4	4	1	159	122	1	0	53.00	135.89	0
†E. Jones (*Lancs*)	6	6	1	218	62	0	1	43.60	59.72	3
S. B. Odedra (*Notts*)	7	7	1	253	86	0	2	42.16	63.40	1
D. N. Wyatt (*Sussex*)	4	4	0	163	67	0	1	40.75	94.21	1
B. L. Morgan (*Middx*)	7	7	0	245	80	0	1	35.00	71.84	1
†A. E. Satterthwaite (*Lancs*)	7	7	0	242	55	0	2	34.57	63.35	3
H. J. Armitage (*Yorks*)	6	6	0	192	55	0	3	32.00	54.54	1
G. M. Hennessy (*Warwicks*)	6	5	0	152	43	0	0	30.40	61.78	0
R. H. Priest (*Berks*)	5	5	0	146	51	0	1	29.20	97.98	0

BOWLING (10 wickets)

	Style	*O*	*M*	*R*	*W*	*BB*	*4I*	*Avge*	*SR*	*ER*
S. Ecclestone (*Lancs*)	SLA	68	13	188	27	6-12	5	6.96	15.11	2.76
E. A. Russell (*Warwicks*)	RM	22	4	75	10	4-12	2	7.50	13.20	3.40
K. A. Levick (*Yorks*)	LB	60	11	161	21	6-28	2	7.66	17.14	2.68
S. I. R. Dunkley-Brown (*Middx*)	LB	36	13	92	11	4-7	1	8.36	19.63	2.55
S. Munro (*Notts*)	RFM	24.1	5	87	10	5-24	2	8.70	14.50	3.60
A. Patel (*Warwicks*)	LB	46.5	9	137	14	6-17	1	9.78	20.07	2.92
E. Walker (*Berks*)	OB	45.2	7	156	11	5-28	1	14.18	24.72	3.44
K. L. Gordon (*Notts*)	SLA	64.2	14	186	13	3-8	0	14.30	29.69	2.89
R. L. Grundy (*Warwicks*)	SLA	54	11	149	10	4-26	2	14.90	32.40	2.75
J. M. Dibble (*Notts*)	SLA	48.3	5	181	12	3-7	0	15.08	24.25	3.73
E. L. Burt (*Sussex*)	RM	55	5	199	10	3-35	0	19.90	33.00	3.61
I. M. G. Westbury (*Middx*)	OB	45	6	219	11	4-19	2	19.90	24.54	4.86

NATIONAL KNOCKOUT CUP REGIONAL LEAGUE FINAL IN 2017

At Bishop's Stortford, September 24. **Walmley won by eight wickets. Newport 132-9** (45 overs) (C. K. Scarborough 30; G. Ballinger 3-11); ‡**Walmley 135-2** (29.2 overs) (M. Kelly 58*, T. F. Brookes 63*). *Walmley had lost the previous final to Finchley, but had the advantage here from the moment they dismissed Newport captain Lauren Parfitt with the game's first ball. Charlotte Scarborough helped Newport reach a respectable total, despite 9–3–11–3 from left-armer Grace Ballinger. But a third-wicket stand of 122* between Marie Kelly and Thea Brookes took Walmley home in style.*

THE UNIVERSITY MATCHES IN 2017

At Cambridge, June 16. **Cambridge University won by nine wickets.** ‡**Oxford University 74-9** (20 overs); **Cambridge University 77-1** (11.4 overs) (F. R. Barber 33*). *Only two Oxford women reached double figures as they were choked by the Cambridge bowlers – especially captain Chloe Allison, who finished with 4–22–3–1. Francesca Barber steered Cambridge to a huge win with 8.2 overs to spare.*

At Lord's (Nursery), June 23. **Oxford University won by seven wickets. Cambridge University 229-4** (50 overs) (C. Allison 82*, H. Fisher 71; H. E. Baxendale 3-39); ‡**Oxford University 230-3** (36.1 overs) (V. M. Picker 37, C. E. Graham 57, S. E. G. Taylor 57*, I. N. Brown 53*). *Allison and Hannah Fisher added 183 for Cambridge's third wicket, though Fisher became one of three victims for Australian seamer Helen Baxendale. But Oxford's top order played forcefully, and a 32-ball 53* from Imogen Brown completed a straightforward victory.*

PART EIGHT

Records and Registers

FEATURES OF 2017

This section covers the calendar year. Some of the features listed occurred in matches reported in *Wisden 2017* and some will be reported in *Wisden 2019*; these items are indicated by W17 or W19.

Double-Hundreds (89)

	Mins	*Balls*	*4*	*6*		
338	511	363	44	2	P. Chopra	Himachal Prad v Punjab at Dharamsala. W19
318	520	408	31	3	S. R. Dickson	Kent v Northamptonshire at Beckenham.
316*	553	435	51	1	M. H. W. Papps	Wellington v Auckland at Wellington. W19
304*	727	494	28	4	M. A. Agarwal	Karnataka v Maharashtra at Pune. W19
303*	550	465	36	1	‡Bahir Shah	Speen Ghar v Boost at Khost. W19
302*	682	456	29	2	G. H. Vihari	Andhra v Odisha at Vizianagram. W19
300*	268	191	35	13	M. Marais	Border v E Province at East London. W19
295	603	510	32	3	Nasir Hossain	Rangpur v Barisal at Rajshahi. W19
278	468	318	36	4	G. J. Maxwell	Victoria v New South Wales at Sydney. W19
267	418	262	32	4	‡Anmolpreet Singh	Punjab v Chhattisgarh at Naya Raipur. W19
265	442	327	28	5	M. C. Henriques	New South Wales v Queensland at Sydney.
265	437	318	25	12	C. Zhuwao	Harare M Eagles v Mid Rhinos at Harare. W19
259*	407	307	30	5	K. Rapulana	North West v N Cape at Potchefstroom. W19
258	366	311	34	7	L. W. P. Wells	Sussex v Durham at Hove.
257*	496	452	23	1	‡S. R. Patel	Nottinghamshire v Gloucestershire at Bristol.
256*	497	417	34	1	‡Bahir Shah	Speen Ghar v Amo at Ghazi Aman Town. W19
252*		318	32	4	‡Anmolpreet Singh	Punjab v Services at Amritsar. W19
251	458	323	28	7	A. P. Agathangelou	Northerns v Northern Cape at Kimberley. W19
247*	538	380	30	1	A. J. Doolan	Tasmania v Victoria at Melbourne. W19
247	425	305	29	2	‡S. R. Patel	Nottinghamshire v Leics at Nottingham.
244*	634	409	27	0	‡A. N. Cook	England v Australia (4th Test) at Melbourne.
244	435	275	25	4	D. J. Vilas	Lancashire v Hampshire at Manchester.
243	588	407	33	0	‡A. N. Cook	England v W Indies (1st Test) at Birmingham.
243	447	287	25	0	‡V. Kohli	India v Sri Lanka (3rd Test) at Delhi.
242	427	302	26	1	Taibur Rahman	Dhaka v Barisal at Sylhet.
239	579	399	30	1	S. P. D. Smith	Australia v England (3rd Test) at Perth.
238	412	293	30	1	Jiwanjot Singh	Punjab v Goa at Porvorim. W19
238	403	301	31	2	M. K. Pandey	Karnataka v Uttar Pradesh at Kanpur. W19
237*	582	370	26	3	D. Elgar	Titans v Dolphins at Pietermaritzburg. W19
237		218	27	1	G. S. N. F. G. Jayasuriya	Chilaw Marians v Bloomfield at Colombo.
232	327	255	37	0	Saad Ali	Utd Bank v Pakistan Television at Sialkot. W19
231*	709	484	21	1	Abid Ali	Islamabad v National Bank at Islamabad. W19
231		256	27	5	S. W. Ambris	Windward Islands v Leeward Is at Basseterre.
228*	513	351	22	3	‡C. T. Bancroft	Western Australia v S Australia at Perth. W19
227	468	320	24	5	J. L. Denly	Kent v Worcestershire at Worcester.
224	438	325	25	4	L. S. Livingstone	Lancashire v Warwickshire at Manchester.
224	501	408	28	0	C. T. Steel	Durham v Leicestershire at Leicester.
221	415	293	17	3	G. M. Thomson	Northerns v Namibia at Centurion.
221	452	384	22	1	N. L. J. Browne	Essex v Middlesex at Chelmsford.
220	453	369	22	3	‡Tushar Imran	South Zone v North Zone at Savar.
219*	603	423	27	1	R. J. Burns	Surrey v Hampshire at The Oval.
219	350	241	26	4	Liton Das	East Zone v Central Zone at Bogra.
218	285	218	38	1	A. D. Hales	Nottinghamshire v Derbyshire at Derby.
217	418	276	31	0	Shakib Al Hasan	Bangladesh v NZ (1st Test) at Wellington. W17
217	452	338	21	0	‡Tushar Imran	South Zone v Central Zone at Savar.
216	512	356	18	2	‡Anamul Haque	Khulna v Rangpur at Khulna. W19
216	536	370	23	1	W. B. Chatterjee	Bengal v Gujarat at Jaipur. W19
216		349	23	5	Naeem Islam	Rangpur v Dhaka at Khulna. W19
215*	485	391	24	3	S. D. Hope	Barbados v Guyana at Bridgetown.
214*		421	27	6	Babar Hayat	Hong Kong v PNG at Sharjah. W19

	Mins	Balls	4	6		
213	386	267	17	2	‡V. Kohli	India v Sri Lanka (2nd Test) at Nagpur.
212	501	386	23	0	E. J. M. Cowan ...	New South Wales v Victoria at Melbourne.
212		319	23	0	F. D. M. Karunaratne	Sri Lanka A v England Lions at Dambulla.
212	394	235	21	5	Israrullah	Peshawar v Islamabad at Islamabad. [W19]
211*	380	323	16	0	Karim Janat	Band-e-Amir v Speen Ghar at G A Town. [W19]
210*		252	23	1	Younas Ahmadzai .	Band-e-Amir v Speen Ghar at G A Town. [W19]
210	616	453	29	1	A. N. Khare	Chhattisgarh v Vidarbha at Nagpur. [W19]
208*	434	288	31	2	J. N. Malan.......	North West v W Prov at Potchefstroom. [W19]
207*	410	298	18	5	Shahriar Nafees ...	South Zone v Central Zone at Savar.
207	347	250	17	9	A. K. Kitchen.....	Otago v Northern Districts at Dunedin.
207		293	21	0	S. C. Serasinghe...	Chilaw Marians v Colombo at Panagoda.
206*	512	393	23	1	‡C. T. Bancroft	Gloucestershire v Kent at Bristol.
206	472	307	31	3	F. Y. Fazal	Vidarbha v Himachal Pradesh at Nagpur. [W19]
205*	437	301	25	0	D. P. Conway.....	Gauteng v Border at Johannesburg.
205*	426	336	23	2	A. Balbirnie	Ireland v Netherlands at Dublin.
204	556	410	20	1	Saif Hasan	Dhaka v Barisal at Sylhet.
204	295	246	24	0	‡V. Kohli	India v Bangladesh (Only Test) at Hyderabad.
204	566	355	28	0	‡C. A. Pujara	Saurashtra v Jharkhand at Rajkot. [W19]
203*	346	272	26	6	W. P. Saha	Rest of India v Gujarat at Mumbai.
203*	491	384	23	0	G. S. Ballance	Yorkshire v Hampshire at Southampton.
203*	331	231	30	0	R. S. Second......	Knights v Cape Cobras at Oudtshoorn. [W19]
203		233	13	9	H. S. M. Zoysa....	Lankan v Kalutara Town at Panagoda.
203	348	237	27	3	V. B. van Jaarsveld	Dolphins v Knights at Kimberley.
203	467	363	19	0	S. M. Ervine......	Hampshire v Warwickshire at Southampton.
203	280	207	31	3	B. D. Schmulian...	C Dists v N Dists at Mount Maunganui. [W19]
202*	327	257	28	2	M. Q. Adams	Northerns v North West at Potchefstroom.
202*	306	210	27	7	S. S. Iyer	India A v Australians at Mumbai.
202*	245	177	22	7	M. H. Wessels	Nottinghamshire v Sussex at Nottingham.
202*	498	332	15	4	J. A. Burns	Queensland v South Australia at Cairns. [W19]
202*		289	17	2	J. K. Silva........	Sinhalese v Bloomfield at Colombo. [W19]
202	672	525	21	0	‡C. A. Pujara	India v Australia (3rd Test) at Ranchi.
202	440	251	23	4	‡Anamul Haque....	Khulna v Dhaka at Savar. [W19]
202	291	203	24	5	A. Gupta.........	Punjab v Himachal Prad at Dharamsala. [W19]
201	430	313	23	2	R. A. Jadeja	Saurashtra v Jammu & Kashmir at Rajkot. [W19]
200*		266	12	10	Alok Kapali	Sylhet v Chittagong at Chittagong.
200*	535	389	15	0	G. J. Bailey	Tasmania v New South Wales at Wollongong.
200*	395	291	25	0	H. G. Kuhn.......	South Africa A v Hampshire at Southampton.
200	435	321	27	0	K. C. Sangakkara..	Surrey v Essex at Chelmsford.
200	349	280	20	6	R. N. B. Indrajith ..	India Red v India Blue at Kanpur. [W19]

‡ *Kohli scored three double-hundreds, while Anamul Haque, Anmolpreet Singh, Bahir Shah, Bancroft, Cook, Patel, Pujara and Tushar Imran each scored two.*

Hundred on First-Class Debut

105	Afif Hossain	East Zone v North Zone at Chittagong.
256*	Bahir Shah	Speen Ghar v Amo at Ghazi Amanullah Town. [W19]
202	A. Gupta.........	Punjab v Himachal Pradesh at Dharamsala. [W19]
102 and 142	Haji Murad.......	Amo v Speen Ghar at Ghazi Amanullah Town. [W19]
111	Imran	Mis Ainak v Band-e-Amir at Kabul. [W19]
121	Navneet Singh	Services v Bengal at Delhi. [W19]
115	N. A. Rathva	Baroda v Odisha at Vadodara. [W19]
203	B. D. Schmulian...	Central Districts v Northern Districts at Mount Maunganui. [W19]
120	P. P. Shaw	Mumbai v Tamil Nadu at Rajkot.
169	Shawkat Zaman ...	Speen Ghar v Amo at Ghazi Amanullah Town. [W19]
104	Zia-ul-Haq	Band-e-Amir v Mis Ainak at Kabul. [W19]

Three or More Hundreds in Successive Innings

K. C. Sangakkara (Surrey)	136	v Lancashire at The Oval.
	105	v Warwickshire at Birmingham.
	114 and 120	v Middlesex at Lord's.
	200	v Essex at Chelmsford.
M. A. Agarwal (Karnataka)	133*	v Uttar Pradesh at Kanpur. W19
	173 and 134	v Railways at Delhi. W19
Asghar Stanikzai (Afghanistan)	145	v Ireland at Greater Noida.
	125	v Hong Kong at Hong Kong.
	114	v United Arab Emirates at Abu Dhabi.
Bahir Shah (Speen Ghar)	111 and 116	v Boost at Kabul. W19
	303*	v Boost at Khost. W19
I. R. Jaggi (Jharkhand)	103*	v Rajasthan at Jaipur. W19
	135	v Haryana at Ranchi. W19
	114	v Saurashtra at Rajkot. W19
V. Kohli (India)	104*	v Sri Lanka (1st Test) at Kolkata.
	213	v Sri Lanka (2nd Test) at Nagpur.
	243	v Sri Lanka (3rd Test) at Delhi.
Mizanur Rahman (Rajasthan)	143	v Sylhet at Bogra. W19
	102	v Chittagong at Bogra. W19
	175	v Dhaka Metro at Chittagong. W19
J. D. Ryder (Central Districts)	109*	v Canterbury at Nelson.
	175 and 106*	v Auckland at Nelson. W19
K. C. Sangakkara (Surrey)	180*	v Yorkshire at Leeds.
	164	v Yorkshire at The Oval.
	157	v Somerset at The Oval.
‡R. S. Second (Free State and Knights)	106*	v Boland at Paarl.
	125	v Dolphins at Kimberley.
	151	v Warriors at Bloemfontein.
S. van Zyl (Cape Cobras)	106	v Knights at Paarl.
	108 and 101*	v Dolphins at Durban.
M. Vijay (Tamil Nadu and India)	140	v Odisha at Cuttack. W19
	128	v Sri Lanka (2nd Test) at Nagpur.
	155	v Sri Lanka (3rd Test) at Delhi.

‡ *Second's first innings was in 2016.*

Hundred in Each Innings of a Match

M. A. Agarwal	173	134	Karnataka v Railways at Delhi. W19
Bahir Shah	111	116	Speen Ghar v Boost at Kabul. W19
G. S. Ballance	108	203*	Yorkshire v Hampshire at Southampton.
J. M. Clarke	142	110*	Worcestershire v Kent at Worcester.
A. R. Easwaran	129	114	Bengal v Gujarat at Jaipur. W19
Haji Murad	102	142	Amo v Speen Ghar at Ghazi Amanullah Town. W19
S. D. Hope	147	118*	West Indies v England (2nd Test) at Leeds.
L. S. Livingstone	105	140*	England Lions v Sri Lanka A at Dambulla.
A. P. Majumdar	119	108*	Bengal v Goa at Kolkata. W19
C. Munro	146	142	Auckland v Central Districts at Auckland.
P. K. Panchal	105	133*	India Red v India Green at Lucknow. W19
Y. K. Pathan	111	136*	Baroda v Madhya Pradesh at Indore. W19
J. D. Ryder	175	106*	Central Districts v Auckland at Nelson. W19
K. C. Sangakkara	114	120	Surrey v Middlesex at Lord's.
D. S. Smith	107*	154	Windward Islands v Jamaica at Gros Islet. W19
S. van Zyl	108	101*	Cape Cobras v Dolphins at Durban.
J. B. Weatherald	152	143	South Australia v Western Australia at Perth. W19
M. S. R. Wijeratne	102	100*	Badureliya v Moors at Colombo.

Carrying Bat through Completed Innings

Abid Ali	231*	Islamabad (416) v National Bank at Islamabad. W19
C. T. Bancroft	206*	Gloucestershire (385) v Kent at Bristol.
C. T. Bancroft	76*	Western Australia (176) v New South Wales at Sydney. W19
D. J. Bell-Drummond	84*	Kent (180) v Nottinghamshire at Nottingham.
R. J. Burns	219*	Surrey (483) v Hampshire at The Oval.
A. N. Cook	244*	England (491) v Australia (4th Test) at Melbourne.
S. C. Cook	70*	South Africa A (177) v India A at Potchefstroom.
T. J. Dean	79*	Victoria (188) v New South Wales at Melbourne.
D. Elgar	113*	Somerset (278) v Lancashire at Manchester.
M. V. Hodge	96*	Leeward Islands (237) v Trinidad & Tobago at Basseterre.
M. D. U. S. Jayasundera	64*	Sri Lanka A (169) v England Lions at Pallekele.
K. K. Jennings	102*	Durham (250) v Nottinghamshire at Chester-le-Street.
W. A. D. P. Madusanka	110*	Badureliya (302) v Saracens at Colombo.
Salman Afridi	126*	Habib Bank (252) v Lahore Blues at Karachi. W19
D. P. Sibley	92*	Warwickshire (188) v Hampshire at Birmingham.
D. S. Smith	119*	Windward Is (259) v Trinidad & Tobago at Port-of-Spain. W19
D. S. Smith	116*	Windward Islands (200) v Jamaica at Kingston. W19

Hundred before Lunch

C. Munro	121*	Auckland v Central Districts at Auckland on day 4.
H. H. Pandya	1* to 108*	India v Sri Lanka (3rd Test) at Pallekele on day 2.
D. A. Warner	100*	Australia v Pakistan (3rd Test) at Sydney on day 1. W17

Fast Double-Hundred and Triple-Hundred

M. Marais (300*)	139 balls and 191 balls	Border v Eastern Province at East London. W19

Most Sixes in an Innings

13	M. Marais (300*)	Border v Eastern Province at East London. W19
13	S. W. Masakadza (140)	Manicaland Mountaineers v Harare Met Eagles at Harare. W19
13	Najeeb Tarakai (153)	Amo v Mis Ainak at Khost. W19
12	C. Zhuwao (265)	Harare Metropolitan Eagles v Midlands Rhinos at Harare. W19
10	Alok Kapali (200*)	Sylhet v Chittagong at Chittagong.
9	S. S. Iyer (138)	Mumbai v Tamil Nadu at Mumbai. W19
9	A. K. Kitchen (207)	Otago v Northern Districts at Dunedin.
9	Shawkat Zaman (169)	Speen Ghar v Amo at Ghazi Amanullah Town. W19
9	H. S. M. Zoysa (203)	Lankan v Kalutara Town at Panagoda.

Most Runs in Boundaries

	4	*6*		
218	35	13	M. Marais (300*)	Border v Eastern Province at East London. W19
210	51	1	M. H. W. Papps (316*)	Wellington v Auckland at Wellington. W19

Longest Innings

Mins		
727	M. A. Agarwal (304*)	Karnataka v Maharashtra at Pune. W19
709	Abid Ali (231*)	Islamabad v National Bank at Islamabad. W19
682	G. H. Vihari (302*)	Andhra v Odisha at Vizianagram. W19
672	C. A. Pujara (202)	India v Australia (3rd Test) at Ranchi.
632	S. R. Ramaswamy (182)	Vidarbha v Bengal at Kalyani. W19

Mins
616 A. N. Khare (210) . . . . Chhattisgarh v Vidarbha at Nagpur. W19
615 Naeem Islam (185). . . . . North Zone v South Zone at Sylhet.
603 R. J. Burns (219*) . . . . Surrey v Hampshire at The Oval.
603 Nasir Hossain (295) . . . . Rangpur v Barisal at Rajshahi. W19

Unusual Dismissals

Obstructing the Field
Ghamai Zadran (45). . . . . . . Mis Ainak v Boost at Ghazi Amanullah Town. W19
Rashid Zadran (23). . . . . Mis Ainak v Band-e-Amir at Kabul. W19
Zia-ur-Rehman (6) . . . . Mis Ainak v Amo at Khost. W19

Timed Out
C. Kunje (0) . . . . Bulawayo Met Tuskers v Manicaland Mountaineers at Bulawayo. W19

First-Wicket Partnership of 100 in Each Innings

241 146 S. D. Robson/N. R. T. Gubbins, Middlesex v Essex at Lord's.
103 109 R. J. Burns/M. D. Stoneman, Surrey v Hampshire at The Oval.

Highest Wicket Partnerships

First Wicket
432 M. H. W. Papps/L. J. Woodcock, Wellington v Auckland at Wellington. W19
373 N. L. J. Browne/A. N. Cook, Essex v Middlesex at Chelmsford.
341 Nazmul Hossain/Mizanur Rahman, Rajshahi v Dhaka Metropolis at Chittagong. W19
333 L. M. Reece/B. A. Godleman, Derbyshire v Northamptonshire at Derby.
305 F. D. M. Karunaratne/J. K. Silva, Sinhalese v Bloomfield at Colombo. W19
299 S. P. Amonkar/S. A. Asnodkar, Goa v Himachal Pradesh at Dharamsala. W19

Second Wicket
382 S. R. Dickson/J. L. Denly, Kent v Northamptonshire at Beckenham.
355 S. Muthusamy/V. B. van Jaarsveld, Dolphins v Knights at Kimberley.
311 Nasir Khan/Bahir Shah, Speen Ghar v Boost at Khost. W19
295 K. D. Petersen/T. B. de Bruyn, Knights v Cape Cobras at Bloemfontein. W19
295 Anamul Haque/Mehedi Hasan, Khulna v Dhaka at Savar. W19

Third Wicket
376 L. W. P. Wells/S. van Zyl, Sussex v Durham at Hove.
308 G. H. Vihari/R. K. Bhui, Andhra v Baroda at Vadodara. W19
292 H. M. Amla/J-P. Duminy, South Africa v Sri Lanka (3rd Test) at Johannesburg. W17
283 M. Vijay/V. Kohli, India v Sri Lanka (3rd Test) at Delhi.

Fourth Wicket
367 J. H. K. Adams/S. M. Ervine, Hampshire v Warwickshire at Southampton.
354 D. Nischal/M. K. Pandey, Karnataka v Uttar Pradesh at Kanpur. W19
315 F. D. M. Karunaratne/W. S. R. Samarawickrama, Sri Lanka A v England Lions at Dambulla.
304 Saif Hasan/Taibur Rahman, Dhaka v Barisal at Sylhet.
291 Bahir Shah/Shawkat Zaman, Speen Ghar v Amo at Ghazi Amanullah Town. W19
281 S. P. Jackson/R. A. Jadeja, Saurashtra v Jammu & Kashmir at Rajkot. W19

Fifth Wicket
428* B. C. Williams/M. Marais, Border v Eastern Province at East London. W19
391 M. C. Henriques/P. M. Nevill, New South Wales v Queensland at Sydney.
368 Nasir Hossain/Ariful Haque, Rangpur v Barisal at Rajshahi. W19
359 Shakib Al Hasan/Mushfiqur Rahim, Bangladesh v New Zealand (1st Test) at Wellington. W17
328* K. Rapulana/W. J. Lubbe, North West v Northern Cape at Potchefstroom. W19
316* C. A. Pujara/W. P. Saha, Rest of India v Gujarat at Mumbai.
301 S. P. D. Smith/M. R. Marsh, Australia v England (3rd Test) at Perth.
287 S. Leelaratne/M. A. D. I. Hemantha, Navy v Panadura at Panadura. W19

Sixth Wicket

288* B. N. Cooper/P. M. Seelaar, Netherlands v Hong Kong at Hong Kong.
285 R. E. van der Merwe/M. P. O'Dowd, Netherlands v Namibia at Dubai. W19
258 W. Coulentianos/M. Arnold, Easterns v Eastern Province at Benoni. W19

Seventh Wicket

246 U. D. Yadav/Saurabh Kumar, Uttar Pradesh v Assam at Guwahati. W19
243 S. Chanderpaul/J. Clark, Lancashire v Surrey at The Oval.
239 A. Gupta/A. Sharma, Punjab v Himachal Pradesh at Dharamsala. W19
227 Nadif Chowdhury/Mosharraf Hossain, Dhaka v Khulna at Chittagong. W19

Eighth Wicket

218 Y. K. Pathan/A. A. Sheth, Baroda v Madhya Pradesh at Indore. W19
212 S. O. Dowrich/J. O. Holder, West Indies v Zimbabwe (2nd Test) at Bulawayo.

Ninth Wicket

157 A. Dananjaya/N. G. R. P. Jayasuriya, Colts v Ragama at Colombo.

Tenth Wicket

178 R. N. B. Indrajith/V. D. Gohil, India Red v India Blue at Kanpur. W19
167 Mohammad Saad/Mohammad Asif, WAPDA v National Bank at Rawalpindi. W19
139 M. J. McClenaghan/R. S. Sandhu, Auckland v Northern Districts at Auckland.
128 R. P. H. D. Ranasinghe/A. M. S. Sahahab, Colts v Bloomfield at Colombo. W19
123 Farhad Reza/Shafiul Islam, Rajshahi v Dhaka Metropolis at Chittagong. W19
122 L. J. Hill/C. F. Parkinson, Leicestershire v Kent at Canterbury.
118 N. A. Dharmasena/R. M. G. K. Sirisoma, Panadura v Kurunegala Youth at Panadura.
111 C. T. Bancroft/M. D. Taylor, Gloucestershire v Kent at Bristol.
110 A. Bramble/G. Motie, Guyana v Leeward Islands at Providence. W19
102 B. A. Godleman/G. S. Sandhu, Derbyshire v Durham at Chesterfield.
101 R. Shreyas Gopal/A. Mithun, Karnataka v Delhi at Alur. W19

Most Wickets in an Innings

9-25	Rumman Raees	United Bank v Lahore Whites at Lahore. W19
9-32	Waqas Maqsood	WAPDA v KRL at Karachi. W19
9-37	J. P. Behrendorff	Western Australia v Victoria at Perth.
9-50	Ahmed Jamal	Sui Southern Gas v Sui Northern Gas at Faisalabad. W19
9-65	R. K. Kleinveldt	Northamptonshire v Nottinghamshire at Northampton.
9-80	Sanjamul Islam	North Zone v Central Zone at Chittagong.
9-95	S. R. Harmer	Essex v Middlesex at Chelmsford.
8-26	P. W. H. de Silva	Colombo v Colts at Colombo. W19
8-32	Tabish Khan	Pakistan Television v KRL at Rawalpindi. W19
8-36	S. R. Harmer	Essex v Warwickshire at Chelmsford.
8-39	Shaheen Shah Afridi	KRL v Rawalpindi at Rawalpindi. W19
8-40	C. T. Gaja	Gujarat v Rajasthan at Surat. W19
8-43	L. C. Norwell	Gloucestershire v Leicestershire at Leicester.
8-50	N. M. Lyon	Australia v India (2nd Test) at Bangalore.
8-50	Kashif Bhatti	Sui Southern Gas v Faisalabad at Faisalabad. W19
8-54	N. O. Miller	Jamaica v Windward Islands at Kingston. W19
8-62	Saad Altaf	Rawalpindi v FATA at Mirpur. W19
8-62	Samiullah Khan	Sui Northern Gas v WAPDA at Karachi. W19
8-70	J. Dawood	Eastern Province v Namibia at Windhoek.
8-73	M. A. Starc	New South Wales v South Australia at Adelaide. W19
8-75	D. I. Stevens	Kent v Leicestershire at Canterbury.
8-76	Raza Hasan	National Bank v Faisalabad at Faisalabad. W19
8-79	S. T. Finn	Middlesex v Lancashire at Lord's.
8-79	Saad Altaf	Rawalpindi v FATA at Mirpur. W19
8-85	J. S. Saxena	Kerala v Rajasthan at Thumba. W19
8-90	G. C. Viljoen	Derbyshire v Sussex at Hove.
8-91	N. M'shangwe	Manicaland Mountaineers v Midlands Rhinos at Mutare.

8-127	P. M. Pushpakumara	Sri Lanka A v England Lions at Dambulla.
8-136	W. E. R. Somerville	New South Wales v Queensland at Sydney.
8-137	T. L. de Soysa	Kurunegala Youth v Navy at Kurunegala. W19
8-148	C. F. Parkinson	Leicestershire v Worcestershire at Worcester.

Most Wickets in a Match

16-141	Saad Altaf	Rawalpindi v FATA at Mirpur. W19
15-170	G. C. Viljoen	Derbyshire v Sussex at Hove.
14-66	R. M. G. K. Sirisoma	Panadura v Kurunegala Youth at Panadura.
14-89	J. P. Behrendorff	Western Australia v Victoria at Perth.
14-102	Kashif Bhatti	Sui Southern Gas v Faisalabad at Faisalabad. W19
14-128	S. R. Harmer	Essex v Warwickshire at Chelmsford.
14-172	S. R. Harmer	Essex v Middlesex at Chelmsford.
13-98	R. K. Kleinveldt	Northamptonshire v Nottinghamshire at Northampton.
13-114	N. O. Miller	Jamaica v Windward Islands at Kingston. W19
13-154	N. M. Lyon	Australia v Bangladesh (2nd Test) at Chittagong.
13-159	J. Dawood	Eastern Province v Namibia at Windhoek.
13-163	Waqar Khan	Band-e-Amir v Speen Ghar at Ghazi Amanullah Town. W19
13-205	P. M. Pushpakumara	Sri Lanka A v England Lions at Dambulla.
13-219	R. M. G. K. Sirisoma	Panadura v Kalutara PCC at Maggona.

Outstanding Innings Analyses

3.4–1–3–4	P. M. Pushpakumara	Chilaw Marians v Colts at Colombo.
10–7–4–4	J. S. Louis	Leeward Islands v Jamaica at Kingston.

Hat-Tricks (8)

C. J. Alexander	KwaZulu-Natal Inland v Eastern Province at Port Elizabeth.
M. M. Ali	England v South Africa (3rd Test) at The Oval.
R. N. Gurbani	Vidarbha v Delhi at Indore. W19
C. Overton	MCC v Middlesex at Abu Dhabi.
M. A. Starc	New South Wales v Western Australia at Sydney (first innings). W19
M. A. Starc	New South Wales v Western Australia at Sydney (second innings). W19
B. M. Tickner	Central Districts v Wellington at Nelson. W19
R. Vinay Kumar	Karnataka v Mumbai at Nagpur. W19

Wicket with First Ball in First-Class Career

Ali Shafiq	KRL v Karachi Whites at Karachi. W19
O. R. Newton	Wellington v Auckland at Wellington. W19

Most Balls Bowled in an Innings

462	77–17–199–3	S. N. J. O'Keefe	Australia v India (3rd Test) at Ranchi.

Match Double (100 runs and 10 wickets)

S. Madanayake	96*, 8; 3-37, 7-70	Police v Kalutara PCC at Colombo.
K. O. Maunze	30, 78; 6-35, 5-46	Harare Metropolitan Eagles v Midlands Rhinos at Kwekwe. W19
J. S. Saxena	79, 105*; 8-85, 2-62	Kerala v Rajasthan at Thumba. W19
Shuvagata Hom	100, 52; 6-91, 4-77	Central Zone v South Zone at Fatullah.
S. von Berg	103, 35*; 4-59, 6-144	Titans v Warriors at Benoni.
M. S. Washington Sundar	88, 42; 5-94, 6-87	India Red v India Blue at Lucknow. W19

Most Wicketkeeping Dismissals in an Innings

7 (5ct, 2st)	Manoj Singh	Chhattisgarh v Punjab at Naya Raipur. [W19]
7 (5ct, 2st)	M. B. Ranasinghe	Sinhalese v Bloomfield at Colombo. [W19]
6 (5ct, 1st)	Ameer Hamza	Lahore Whites v Habib Bank at Karachi. [W19]
6 (6ct)	T. A. Blundell	Wellington v Canterbury at Wellington. [W19]
6 (6ct)	A. L. Davies	Lancashire v Middlesex at Southport.
6 (5ct, 1st)	S. O. Dowrich	West Indians v Derbyshire at Derby.
6 (6ct)	B. I. Louw	South Western Districts v Northern Cape at Oudtshoorn.
6 (6ct)	L. Ronchi	Wellington v Canterbury at Christchurch.
6 (6ct)	Talha Qureshi	Rawalpindi v Lahore Whites at Mirpur. [W19]

Most Wicketkeeping Dismissals in a Match

10 (10ct)	T. A. Blundell	Wellington v Canterbury at Wellington. [W19]
10 (9ct, 1st)	A. L. Davies	Lancashire v Middlesex at Southport.
10 (8ct, 2st)	B. T. Foakes	England Lions v Sri Lanka A at Dambulla.
10 (10ct)	W. P. Saha	Bengal v Himachal Pradesh at Kolkata. [W19]
9 (9ct)	A. Bramble	Guyana v Trinidad & Tobago at Tarouba. [W19]
9 (9ct)	D. C. de Boorder	Otago v Auckland at Auckland. [W19]
9 (9ct)	Farhan Khan	Lahore Blues v Islamabad at Lahore. [W19]
9 (9ct)	T. D. Paine	Tasmania v South Australia at Hobart.
9 (9ct)	L. Ronchi	Wellington v Canterbury at Christchurch.
9 (9ct)	J. A. Simpson	Middlesex v Warwickshire at Lord's.
9 (9ct)	Talha Qureshi	Rawalpindi v Lahore Whites at Mirpur. [W19]

Most Catches in an Innings in the Field

5	H. Z. Finch	Sussex v Worcestershire at Worcester.
5	D. Hooda	Baroda v Tamil Nadu at Vadodara. [W19]
5	P. J. H. S. R. Silva	Army v Ports Authority at Panagoda. [W19]
5	G. M. Thomson	Northerns v Free State at Bloemfontein.

Most Catches in a Match in the Field

7	J. A. Burns	Queensland v Tasmania at Hobart.
6	J. Blackwood	Jamaica v Barbados at Bridgetown.
6	H. Z. Finch	Sussex v Worcestershire at Worcester.
6	D. Hooda	Baroda v Tamil Nadu at Vadodara. [W19]
6	S. C. Serasinghe	Chilaw Marians v Army at Katunayake. [W19]
6	S. S. Tiwary	Jharkhand v Jammu & Kashmir at Jamshedpur. [W19]

No Byes Conceded in Total of 500 or More

A. T. Carey	South Australia v Western Australia (514-7 dec) at Perth. [W19]
D. P. D. N. Dickwella	Sri Lanka v India (536-7 dec) (3rd Test) at Delhi.
S. O. Dowrich	West Indies v England (514-8 dec) (1st Test) at Birmingham.
Haji Murad	Amo v Speen Ghar (635-5 dec) at Ghazi Amanullah Town. [W19]
C. D. Hartley	Queensland v New South Wales (603-6 dec) at Sydney.
L. J. Hill	Leicestershire v Nottinghamshire (548-9 dec) at Nottingham.
M. Mosehle	Lions v Warriors (503-8 dec) at Johannesburg. [W19]
Mushfiqur Rahim	Bangladesh v India (687-6 dec) (Only Test) at Hyderabad.
W. A. S. Niroshan	Moors v Colombo (560) at Colombo.
S. Rawat	Odisha v Andhra (584-5 dec) at Vizianagram. [W19]
R. S. Second	Knights v Dolphins (538-7 dec) at Kimberley.
D. Smit	Derbyshire v Leicestershire (619) at Derby.
Taimur Khan	Pakistan Television v United Bank (504) at Sialkot. [W19]

Highest Innings Totals

749-8 dec	South Zone v Central Zone at Savar.
747-9 dec	Band-e-Amir v Speen Ghar at Ghazi Amanullah Town. W19
729-8 dec	Himachal Pradesh v Punjab at Dharamsala. W19
701-7 dec	Kent v Northamptonshire at Beckenham.
695-6	Bengal v Gujarat at Jaipur. W19
687-6 dec	India v Bangladesh (Only Test) at Hyderabad.
668	Sussex v Durham at Hove.
668	Rajshahi v Dhaka Metropolis at Chittagong. W19
662-9 dec	Australia v England (3rd Test) at Perth.
655	Karnataka v Uttar Pradesh at Kanpur. W19
653-9 dec	Punjab v Chhattisgarh at Naya Raipur. W19
649	Karnataka v Delhi at Alur. W19
648-7 dec	Hampshire v Surrey at The Oval.
648-7 dec	Speen Ghar v Boost at Khost. W19
645-6 dec	Punjab v Services at Amritsar. W19
635-5 dec	Speen Ghar v Amo at Ghazi Amanullah Town. W19
635	Punjab v Goa at Porvorim. W19

Lowest Innings Totals

37	Pakistan Television v KRL at Rawalpindi. W19
39	Colts v Chilaw Marians at Colombo.
44	Namibia v South Western Districts at Oudtshoorn.
55	Assam v Railways at Guwahati. W19
56	Jamaica v Leeward Islands at Kingston.
56	Cambridge MCCU v Lancashire at Cambridge.
56	Jamaica v Windward Islands at Kingstown.
61	Queensland v Victoria at Brisbane.
61	Gloucestershire v Kent at Canterbury.
62	Cambridge MCCU v Lancashire at Cambridge.
62	Auckland v Wellington at Wellington. W19

Highest Fourth-Innings Totals

445-9	Colts v Army at Colombo (set 474).
430-7	Band-e-Amir v Boost at Khost (set 460). W19
401-6	Worcestershire v Kent at Worcester (set 399).

Match Aggregate of 1,500 Runs

1,512 for 31	Punjab (645-6 dec and 94-5) v Services (315 and 458) at Amritsar. W19
1,511 for 30	Bangladesh (595-8 dec and 160) v NZ (539 and 217-3) (1st Test) at Wellington. W17
1,510 for 38	Amo (500 and 277) v Mis Ainak (393 and 340-8) at Khost. W19

Four Individual Hundreds in an Innings

Knights (623-4 dec) v Cape Cobras at Bloemfontein. W19
South Africa (573-4 dec) v Bangladesh (2nd Test) at Bloemfontein.
India (610-6 dec) v Sri Lanka (2nd Test) at Nagpur.

Six Individual Fifties in an Innings

India (687-6 dec) v Bangladesh (Only Test) at Hyderabad.
India (622-9 dec) v Sri Lanka (2nd Test) at Colombo.
England (490-8 dec) v West Indies (2nd Test) at Leeds.
Bengal (552-9 dec) v Services at Delhi. [W19]
Northern Districts (439-5 dec) v Central Districts at Mount Maunganui. [W19]
Band-e-Amir (747-9 dec) v Speen Ghar at Ghazi Amanullah Town. [W19]

Large Margin of Victory

Band-e-Amir (747-9 dec and 265-4 dec) beat Speen Ghar (196 and 279) at Ghazi Amanullah Town by 537 runs. [W19]
Vidarbha (246 and 507-9 dec) beat Kerala (176 and 165) at Surat by 412 runs. [W19]

Win after Following On

Hampshire (254 and 76) lost to Essex (76 and 362) at Southampton by 108 runs.

Tied Matches

Police (235 and 85) v Kalutara PCC (139 and 181) at Colombo.
Windward Islands (117 and 241) v Guyana (194 and 164) at Providence. [W19]
Chilaw Marians (293 and 117) v Burgher (316 and 94) at Katunayake. [W19]
Negombo (221 and 206-8 dec) v Kalutara Town (193 and 234) at Gampaha. [W19]

Eleven Bowlers in an Innings

Central Zone v South Zone (749-8 dec) at Savar.

Most Extras in an Innings

	b	*lb*	*w*	*nb*	
60	8	2	5	45	Kent (370-6 dec) v Leeds/Bradford MCCU at Canterbury.
55	23	13	7	12	Western Province (372-7) v Northerns at Centurion.
51	7	16	15	13	Northern Districts (334) v Auckland at Auckland.
51	21	7	7	16	Cambridge University (417-7 dec) v Oxford University at Cambridge.
50	15	12	1	22	Sussex (458) v South Africa A at Arundel.
50	11	5	10	24	Nottinghamshire (508-9 dec) v Derbyshire at Derby.

Career Aggregate Milestones

25,000 runs	M. E. Trescothick.
20,000 runs	A. N. Cook, K. C. Sangakkara.
15,000 runs	J. C. Hildreth.
10,000 runs	M. M. Ali, T. R. Ambrose, Azhar Ali, J. M. Bairstow, D. Bundela, J. L. Denly, A. B. de Villiers, D. Elgar, F. D. M. Karunaratne, W. L. Madsen, P. A. Patel, S. P. D. Smith, L. R. P. L. Taylor, M. H. Wessels.
1,000 wickets.	H. M. R. K. B. Herath.
500 wickets	T. T. Bresnan, S. T. Finn, M. G. Hogan, V. D. Philander, P. M. Pushpakumara, Samiullah Khan, S. Shillingford, R. M. G. K. Sirisoma, Tabish Khan.
500 dismissals	P. A. Patel.

RECORDS

COMPILED BY PHILIP BAILEY

This section covers

- first-class records to December 31, 2017 (page 1183).
- List A one-day records to December 31, 2017 (page 1211).
- List A Twenty20 records to December 31, 2017 (page 1214).
- Test records to January 27, 2018, the end of the South Africa v India series (page 1216).
- Test records series by series (page 1248).
- one-day international records to December 31, 2017 (page 1291).
- World Cup records (page 1301).
- Twenty20 international records to January 3, 2018 (page 1302).
- miscellaneous other records to December 31, 2017 (page 1307).
- women's Test records, one-day international and Twenty20 international records to December 31, 2017 (page 1311).

The sequence

- Test series records begin with those involving England, arranged in the order their opponents entered Test cricket (Australia, South Africa, West Indies, New Zealand, India, Pakistan, Sri Lanka, Zimbabwe, Bangladesh). Next come all remaining series involving Australia, then South Africa – and so on until Zimbabwe v Bangladesh records appear on page 1287.

Notes

- Unless otherwise stated, all records apply only to first-class cricket. This is considered to have started in 1815, after the Napoleonic War.
- mid-year seasons taking place outside England are given simply as 2016, 2017, etc.
- (E), (A), (SA), (WI), (NZ), (I), (P), (SL), (Z) or (B) indicates the nationality of a player or the country in which a record was made.
- in career records, dates in italic indicate seasons embracing two different years (i.e. non-English seasons). In these cases, only the first year is given, e.g. *2017* for 2017-18.

See also

- up-to-date records on www.wisdenrecords.com.
- Features of 2017 (page 1165).

CONTENTS

FIRST-CLASS RECORDS

BATTING RECORDS

BOWLING RECORDS

ALL-ROUND RECORDS

WICKETKEEPING RECORDS

FIELDING RECORDS

TEAM RECORDS

LIST A ONE-DAY RECORDS

LIST A TWENTY20 RECORDS

TEST RECORDS

BATTING RECORDS

BOWLING RECORDS

ALL-ROUND RECORDS

WICKETKEEPING RECORDS

FIELDING RECORDS

TEAM RECORDS

PLAYERS

UMPIRES

TEST SERIES

ONE-DAY INTERNATIONAL RECORDS

TWENTY20 INTERNATIONAL RECORDS

MISCELLANEOUS RECORDS

WOMEN'S TEST AND OTHER INTERNATIONAL RECORDS

NOTES ON RECORDS

Triumph of the tortoise

ROB SMYTH

Records can be broken by the tortoise as well as the hare. In 2017, most of the notable achievements rewarded longevity and patience. At the age of 39, in his final series before retirement, Younis Khan became the first Pakistani to 10,000 Test runs. Alastair Cook, the only Englishman to reach that milestone, continued to nudge and nurdle his way up the all-time list, overtaking Brian Lara to move into sixth place. Similarly, his mate James Anderson became the first Englishman to take 500 Test wickets, and then moved past Courtney Walsh to fifth on the bowlers' list.

Cook's unbeaten 244 at Melbourne was the highest score by anybody carrying their bat in a Test. By the end of the Ashes, meanwhile, Steve Smith had extended his Test average to a staggering 63, another opportunity to use a phrase – "second only to Don Bradman" – that was becoming common. That phrase has also been used a few times of Kumar Sangakkara: playing for Surrey, he made five consecutive first-class centuries, one short of the all-time record held by Bradman, C. B. Fry and Mike Procter, and averaged 106 in the English season, second to Bradman's 115 in 1938.

During the women's World Cup, India's Mithali Raj overtook Charlotte Edwards as the leading scorer in women's one-day internationals, and in the same innings, against Australia, became the first to reach 6,000. It was a relatively quiet year for Twenty20 milestones, though South Africa's David Miller obliterated the record for the fastest hundred in internationals: he took 35 balls (down from 45) against Bangladesh, equalled two months later by India's Rohit Sharma against Sri Lanka.

In 2018, there is scope for the old-timers to create more records. When Dale Steyn broke down against India in the New Year, he was two short of Shaun Pollock's South African record of 421 Test wickets. If Anderson stays fit, he could overtake Glenn McGrath (563) as the most prolific fast bowler in Test history; and, with 12 Tests scheduled for England, Cook could move up to second on the batting list, behind only Sachin Tendulkar. This may be an age of power-hitting, but there is life in the old tortoise yet.

ROLL OF DISHONOUR

The following players have either been banned after being found guilty of breaching anti-corruption codes, or have admitted to some form of on-field corruption:

Amit Singh (I), Ata-ur-Rehman (P), M. Azharuddin (I), A. Bali (I), G. H. Bodi (SA), A. Chandila (I), A. A. Chavan (I), P. Cleary (A), W. J. Cronje (SA), Danish Kaneria (P), H. H. Gibbs (SA), C. L. Hall (A), Irfan Ahmed (HK), A. Jadeja (I), H. N. K. Jensen (NZ), Khalid Latif (P), J. Logan (A), K. S. Lokuarachchi (SL), P. Matshikwe (SA), N. E. Mbhalati (SA), M. D. Mishra (I), Mohammad Amir (P), Mohammad Ashraful (B), Mohammad Asif (P), Mohammad Irfan (P), Mohammad Nawaz (P), Nasir Jamshed (P), Naved Arif (P), M. O. Odumbe (Ken), A. N. Petersen (SA), M. Prabhakar (I), Salim Malik (P), Salman Butt (P), M. N. Samuels (WI), H. N. Shah (I), Shariful Haque (B), Sharjeel Khan (P), Ajay Sharma (I), S. Sreesanth (I), S. J. Srivastava (I), T. P. Sudhindra (I), J. Symes (SA), S. K. Trivedi (I), T. L. Tsolekile (SA), L. L. Tsotsobe (SA), L. Vincent (NZ), M. S. Westfield (E), H. S. Williams (SA), A. R. Yadav (I).

FIRST-CLASS RECORDS

This section covers first-class cricket to December 31, 2017. Bold type denotes performances in the calendar year 2017 or, in career figures, players who appeared in first-class cricket in that year.

BATTING RECORDS

HIGHEST INDIVIDUAL INNINGS

In all first-class cricket, there have been **220** individual scores of 300 or more. The highest are:

501*	B. C. Lara	Warwickshire v Durham at Birmingham	1994
499	Hanif Mohammad	Karachi v Bahawalpur at Karachi	1958-59
452*	D. G. Bradman	NSW v Queensland at Sydney	1929-30
443*	B. B. Nimbalkar	Maharashtra v Kathiawar at Poona	1948-49
437	W. H. Ponsford	Victoria v Queensland at Melbourne	1927-28
429	W. H. Ponsford	Victoria v Tasmania at Melbourne	1922-23
428	Aftab Baloch	Sind v Baluchistan at Karachi	1973-74
424	A. C. MacLaren	Lancashire v Somerset at Taunton	1895
405*	G. A. Hick	Worcestershire v Somerset at Taunton	1988
400*	B. C. Lara	West Indies v England at St John's	2003-04
394	Naved Latif	Sargodha v Gujranwala at Gujranwala	2000-01
390	S. C. Cook	Lions v Warriors at East London	2009-10
385	B. Sutcliffe	Otago v Canterbury at Christchurch	1952-53
383	C. W. Gregory	NSW v Queensland at Brisbane	1906-07
380	M. L. Hayden	Australia v Zimbabwe at Perth	2003-04
377	S. V. Manjrekar	Bombay v Hyderabad at Bombay	1990-91
375	B. C. Lara	West Indies v England at St John's	1993-94
374	D. P. M. D. Jayawardene	Sri Lanka v South Africa at Colombo (SSC)	2006
369	D. G. Bradman	South Australia v Tasmania at Adelaide	1935-36
366	N. H. Fairbrother	Lancashire v Surrey at The Oval	1990
366	M. V. Sridhar	Hyderabad v Andhra at Secunderabad	1993-94
365*	C. Hill	South Australia v NSW at Adelaide	1900-01
365*	G. S. Sobers	West Indies v Pakistan at Kingston	1957-58
364	L. Hutton	England v Australia at The Oval	1938
359*	V. M. Merchant	Bombay v Maharashtra at Bombay	1943-44
359*	S. B. Gohel	Gujarat v Orissa at Jaipur	2016-17
359	R. B. Simpson	NSW v Queensland at Brisbane	1963-64
357*	R. Abel	Surrey v Somerset at The Oval	1899
357	D. G. Bradman	South Australia v Victoria at Melbourne	1935-36
356	B. A. Richards	South Australia v Western Australia at Perth	1970-71
355*	G. R. Marsh	Western Australia v South Australia at Perth	1989-90
355*	K. P. Pietersen	Surrey v Leicestershire at The Oval	2015
355	B. Sutcliffe	Otago v Auckland at Dunedin	1949-50
353	V. V. S. Laxman	Hyderabad v Karnataka at Bangalore	1999-2000
352	W. H. Ponsford	Victoria v NSW at Melbourne	1926-27
352	C. A. Pujara	Saurashtra v Karnataka at Rajkot	2012-13
351*	S. M. Gugale	Maharashtra v Delhi at Mumbai	2016-17
351	K. D. K. Vithanage	Tamil Union v Air Force at Katunayake	2014-15
350	Rashid Israr	Habib Bank v National Bank at Lahore	1976-77

A fuller list can be found in Wisdens *up to 2011.*

DOUBLE-HUNDRED ON DEBUT

227	T. Marsden	Sheffield & Leicester v Nottingham at Sheffield	1826
207	N. F. Callaway†	New South Wales v Queensland at Sydney	1914-15
240	W. F. E. Marx	Transvaal v Griqualand West at Johannesburg	1920-21
200*	A. Maynard	Trinidad v MCC at Port-of-Spain	1934-35
232*	S. J. E. Loxton	Victoria v Queensland at Melbourne	1946-47

215*	G. H. G. Doggart	Cambridge University v Lancashire at Cambridge	1948
202	J. Hallebone	Victoria v Tasmania at Melbourne	1951-52
230	G. R. Viswanath	Mysore v Andhra at Vijayawada	1967-68
260	A. A. Muzumdar	Bombay v Haryana at Faridabad	1993-94
209*	A. Pandey	Madhya Pradesh v Uttar Pradesh at Bhilai	1995-96
210*	D. J. Sales	Northamptonshire v Worcestershire at Kidderminster	1996
200*	M. J. Powell	Glamorgan v Oxford University at Oxford	1997
201*	M. C. Juneja	Gujarat v Tamil Nadu at Ahmedabad	2011-12
213	Jiwanjot Singh	Punjab v Hyderabad at Mohali	2012-13
202	**A. Gupta**	**Punjab v Himachal Pradesh at Dharamsala**	**2017-18**
256*	**Bahir Shah**	**Speen Ghar v Amo at Ghazi Amanullah Town**	**2017-18**
203	**B. D. Schmulian**	**C. Districts v N. Districts at Mount Maunganui**	**2017-18**

† *In his only first-class innings. He was killed in action in France in 1917.*

TWO SEPARATE HUNDREDS ON DEBUT

148	and 111	A. R. Morris	New South Wales v Queensland at Sydney	1940-41
152	and 102*	N. J. Contractor	Gujarat v Baroda at Baroda	1952-53
132*	and 110	Aamer Malik	Lahore A v Railways at Lahore	1979-80
130	and 100*	Noor Ali	Afghanistan v Zimbabwe XI at Mutare	2009
158	and 103*	K. H. T. Indika	Police v Seeduwa Raddoluwa at Colombo (Police)	2010-11
126	and 112	V. S. Awate	Maharashtra v Vidarbha at Nagpur	2012-13
154*	and 109*	T. J. Dean	Victoria v Queensland at Melbourne	2015-16
102	**and 142**	**Haji Murad**	**Amo v Speen Ghar at Ghazi Amanullah Town**	**2017-18**

TWO DOUBLE-HUNDREDS IN A MATCH

A. E. Fagg	244	202*	Kent v Essex at Colchester	1938

TRIPLE-HUNDRED AND HUNDRED IN A MATCH

G. A. Gooch	333	123	England v India at Lord's	1990
K. C. Sangakkara	319	105	Sri Lanka v Bangladesh at Chittagong	2013-14

DOUBLE-HUNDRED AND HUNDRED IN A MATCH

In addition to Fagg, Gooch and Sangakkara, there have been **62** further instances of a batsman scoring a double-hundred and a hundred in the same first-class match. The most recent are:

C. J. L. Rogers	200	140*	Derbyshire v Surrey at The Oval	2010
M. R. Ramprakash	223	103*	Surrey v Middlesex at The Oval	2010
N. V. Ojha	219*	101*	India A v Australia A at Brisbane	2014
S. D. Robson	231	106	Middlesex v Warwickshire at Lord's	2016
G. S. Ballance	**108**	**203***	**Yorkshire v Hampshire at Southampton**	**2017**

Zaheer Abbas achieved the feat four times, for Gloucestershire between 1976 and 1981, and was not out in all eight innings. M. R. Hallam did it twice for Leicestershire, in 1959 and 1961; N. R. Taylor twice for Kent, in 1990 and 1991; G. A. Gooch for England in 1990 (see above) and Essex in 1994; M. W. Goodwin twice for Sussex, in 2001 and 2007; and C. J. L. Rogers for Northamptonshire in 2006 and for Derbyshire in 2010.

TWO SEPARATE HUNDREDS IN A MATCH MOST TIMES

R. T. Ponting	8	J. B. Hobbs	6	M. L. Hayden	5
Zaheer Abbas	8	G. M. Turner	6	G. A. Hick	5
W. R. Hammond	7	C. B. Fry	5	C. J. L. Rogers	5
M. R. Ramprakash	7	G. A. Gooch	5		

W. Lambert scored 107 and 157 for Sussex v Epsom at Lord's in 1817, a feat not repeated until W. G. Grace's 130 and 102 for South of the Thames v North of the Thames at Canterbury in 1868.*

FIVE HUNDREDS OR MORE IN SUCCESSION

D. G. Bradman (1938-39)	6	B. C. Lara (1993-94–1994)	5
C. B. Fry (1901)	6	P. A. Patel (2007–2007-08)	5
M. J. Procter (1970-71)	6	**K. C. Sangakkara (2017)**	5
M. E. K. Hussey (2003)	5	E. D. Weekes (1955-56)	5

Bradman also scored four hundreds in succession twice, in 1931-32 and 1948–1948-49; W. R. Hammond did it in 1936-37 and 1945–1946, and H. Sutcliffe in 1931 and 1939.

T. W. Hayward (Surrey v Nottinghamshire and Leicestershire), D. W. Hookes (South Australia v Queensland and New South Wales) and V. Sibanda (Zimbabwe XI v Kenya and Mid West v Southern Rocks) are the only players to score two hundreds in each of two successive matches. Hayward scored his in six days, June 4–9, 1906.

The most fifties in consecutive innings is ten – by E. Tyldesley in 1926, by D. G. Bradman in the 1947-48 and 1948 seasons and by R. S. Kaluwitharana in 1994-95.

MOST HUNDREDS IN A SEASON

D. C. S. Compton (1947)	18	W. R. Hammond (1937)	13
J. B. Hobbs (1925)	16	T. W. Hayward (1906)	13
W. R. Hammond (1938)	15	E. H. Hendren (1923)	13
H. Sutcliffe (1932)	14	E. H. Hendren (1927)	13
G. Boycott (1971)	13	E. H. Hendren (1928)	13
D. G. Bradman (1938)	13	C. P. Mead (1928)	13
C. B. Fry (1901)	13	H. Sutcliffe (1928)	13
W. R. Hammond (1933)	13	H. Sutcliffe (1931)	13

Since 1969 (excluding G. Boycott – above)

G. A. Gooch (1990)	12	M. R. Ramprakash (1995)	10
S. J. Cook (1991)	11	M. R. Ramprakash (2007)	10
Zaheer Abbas (1976)	11	G. M. Turner (1970)	10
G. A. Hick (1988)	10	Zaheer Abbas (1981)	10
H. Morris (1990)	10		

The most outside England is nine by V. Sibanda in Zimbabwe (2009-10), followed by eight by D. G. Bradman in Australia (1947-48), D. C. S. Compton (1948-49), R. N. Harvey and A. R. Morris (both 1949-50) all three in South Africa, M. D. Crowe in New Zealand (1986-87), Asif Mujtaba in Pakistan (1995-96), V. V. S. Laxman in India (1999-2000) and M. G. Bevan in Australia (2004-05).

The most double-hundreds in a season is six by D. G. Bradman (1930), five by K. S. Ranjitsinhji (1900) and E. D. Weekes (1950), and four by Arun Lal (1986-87), C. B. Fry (1901), W. R. Hammond (1933 and 1934), E. H. Hendren (1929-30), V. M. Merchant (1944-45), C. A. Pujara (2012-13) and G. M. Turner (1971-72).

MOST DOUBLE-HUNDREDS IN A CAREER

D. G. Bradman	37	W. H. Ponsford	13	A. Sandham	11
W. R. Hammond	36	**K. C. Sangakkara**	**13**	G. Boycott	10
E. H. Hendren	22	J. T. Tyldesley	13	R. Dravid	10
M. R. Ramprakash	17	P. Holmes	12	M. W. Gatting	10
H. Sutcliffe	17	Javed Miandad	12	S. M. Gavaskar	10
C. B. Fry	16	J. L. Langer	12	J. Hardstaff jnr	10
G. A. Hick	16	**C. A. Pujara**	**12**	V. S. Hazare	10
J. B. Hobbs	16	R. B. Simpson	12	B. J. Hodge	10
C. G. Greenidge	14	**Younis Khan**	**12**	D. P. M. D. Jayawardene	10
K. S. Ranjitsinhji	14	J. W. Hearne	11	I. V. A. Richards	10
G. A. Gooch	13	L. Hutton	11	A. Shrewsbury	10
W. G. Grace	13	D. S. Lehmann	11	R. T. Simpson	10
B. C. Lara	13	V. M. Merchant	11	G. M. Turner	10
C. P. Mead	13	C. J. L. Rogers	11	Zaheer Abbas	10

MOST HUNDREDS IN A CAREER

(100 or more)

		Total	Total Inns	100th 100 Season	Inns	400+	300+	200+
1	J. B. Hobbs	197	1,315	1923	821	0	1	16
2	E. H. Hendren	170	1,300	1928-29	740	0	1	22
3	W. R. Hammond	167	1,005	1935	680	0	4	36
4	C. P. Mead	153	1,340	1927	892	0	0	13
5	G. Boycott	151	1,014	1977	645	0	0	10
6	H. Sutcliffe	149	1,088	1932	700	0	1	17
7	F. E. Woolley	145	1,532	1929	1,031	0	1	9
8	G. A. Hick	136	871	1998	574	1	3	16
9	L. Hutton	129	814	1951	619	0	1	11
10	G. A. Gooch	128	990	1992-93	820	0	1	13
11	W. G. Grace	126	1,493	1895	1,113	0	3	13
12	D. C. S. Compton	123	839	1952	552	0	1	9
13	T. W. Graveney	122	1,223	1964	940	0	0	7
14	D. G. Bradman	117	338	1947-48	295	1	6	37
15	I. V. A. Richards	114	796	1988-89	658	0	1	10
	M. R. Ramprakash	114	764	2008	676	0	1	17
17	Zaheer Abbas	108	768	1982-83	658	0	0	10
18	A. Sandham	107	1,000	1935	871	0	1	11
	M. C. Cowdrey	107	1,130	1973	1,035	0	1	3
20	T. W. Hayward	104	1,138	1913	1,076	0	1	8
21	G. M. Turner	103	792	1982	779	0	1	10
	J. H. Edrich	103	979	1977	945	0	1	4
23	L. E. G. Ames	102	951	1950	916	0	0	9
	E. Tyldesley	102	961	1934	919	0	0	7
	D. L. Amiss	102	1,139	1986	1,081	0	0	3

In the above table, 200+, 300+ and 400+ include all scores above those figures.

G. A. Gooch's record includes his century in South Africa in 1981-82, which is no longer accepted by the ICC. Zaheer Abbas and G. Boycott scored their 100th hundreds in Test matches.

Current Players

The following who played in 2017 have scored 40 or more hundreds.

S. Chanderpaul	77	I. R. Bell	51	I. J. L. Trott	43
M. E. Trescothick	65	J. A. Rudolph	51	S. C. Cook	42
K. C. Sangakkara	64	H. M. Amla	50	G. Gambhir	42
A. N. Cook	61	E. C. Joyce	47	J. C. Hildreth	41
Younis Khan	56	C. A. Pujara	44		
Wasim Jaffer	52	Misbah-ul-Haq	43		

MOST RUNS IN A SEASON

	Season	I	NO	R	HS	100	Avge
D. C. S. Compton	1947	50	8	3,816	246	18	90.85
W. J. Edrich	1947	52	8	3,539	267*	12	80.43
T. W. Hayward	1906	61	8	3,518	219	13	66.37
L. Hutton	1949	56	6	3,429	269*	12	68.58
F. E. Woolley	1928	59	4	3,352	198	12	60.94
H. Sutcliffe	1932	52	7	3,336	313	14	74.13
W. R. Hammond	1933	54	5	3,323	264	13	67.81
E. H. Hendren	1928	54	7	3,311	209*	13	70.44
R. Abel	1901	68	8	3,309	247	7	55.15

3,000 in a season has been surpassed on 19 other occasions (a full list can be found in Wisden *1999 and earlier editions). W. R. Hammond, E. H. Hendren and H. Sutcliffe are the only players to achieve the feat three times. K. S. Ranjitsinhji was the first batsman to reach 3,000 in a season, with 3,159 in 1899. M. J. K. Smith (3,245 in 1959) and W. E. Alley (3,019 in 1961) are the only players except those listed above to have reached 3,000 since World War II.*

W. G. Grace scored 2,739 runs in 1871 – the first batsman to reach 2,000 in a season. He made ten hundreds including two double-hundreds, with an average of 78.25 in all first-class matches.

The highest aggregate in a season since the reduction of County Championship matches in 1969 was 2,755 by S. J. Cook (42 innings) in 1991, and the last batsman to achieve 2,000 in England was M. R. Ramprakash (2,026 in 2007); C. A. Pujara scored 2,064 in India in 2016-17.

2,000 RUNS IN A SEASON MOST TIMES

J. B. Hobbs............. 17
E. H. Hendren.......... 15
H. Sutcliffe............. 15
F. E. Woolley........... 13
W. R. Hammond 12
J. G. Langridge......... 11
C. P. Mead............. 11
T. W. Hayward......... 10

Since the reduction of County Championship matches in 1969, G. A. Gooch is the only batsman to have reached 2,000 runs in a season five times.

1,000 RUNS IN A SEASON MOST TIMES

Includes overseas tours and seasons

W. G. Grace........... 28
F. E. Woolley 28
M. C. Cowdrey 27
C. P. Mead............ 27
G. Boycott............ 26
J. B. Hobbs 26
E. H. Hendren 25
D. L. Amiss........... 24
W. G. Quaife.......... 24
H. Sutcliffe 24
A. Jones.............. 23
T. W. Graveney........ 22
W. R. Hammond 22
D. Denton 21
J. H. Edrich 21
G. A. Gooch 21
W. Rhodes............ 21
D. B. Close 20
K. W. R. Fletcher 20
M. W. Gatting......... 20
G. Gunn.............. 20
T. W. Hayward 20
G. A. Hick............ 20
James Langridge 20
J. M. Parks............ 20
M. R. Ramprakash...... 20
A. Sandham........... 20
M. J. K. Smith......... 20
C. Washbrook 20

F. E. Woolley reached 1,000 runs in 28 consecutive seasons (1907–1938), C. P. Mead in 27 (1906–1936).

Outside England, 1,000 runs in a season has been reached most times by D. G. Bradman (in 12 seasons in Australia).

Three batsmen have scored 1,000 runs in a season in each of four different countries: G. S. Sobers in West Indies, England, India and Australia; M. C. Cowdrey and G. Boycott in England, South Africa, West Indies and Australia.

HIGHEST AGGREGATES OUTSIDE ENGLAND

	Season	*I*	*NO*	*R*	*HS*	*100*	*Avge*
In Australia							
D. G. Bradman.............	1928-29	24	6	1,690	340*	7	93.88
In South Africa							
J. R. Reid.................	1961-62	30	2	1,915	203	7	68.39
In West Indies							
E. H. Hendren	1929-30	18	5	1,765	254*	6	135.76
In New Zealand							
M. D. Crowe	1986-87	21	3	1,676	175*	8	93.11
In India							
C. A. Pujara	**2016-17**	**29**	**4**	**2,064**	**256***	**7**	**82.56**

	Season	I	NO	R	HS	100	Avge
In Pakistan							
Saadat Ali	1983-84	27	1	1,649	208	4	63.42
In Sri Lanka							
R. P. Arnold	1995-96	24	3	1,475	217*	5	70.23
In Zimbabwe							
V. Sibanda	2009-10	26	4	1,612	215	9	73.27
In Bangladesh							
Tushar Imran	**2016-17**	**16**	**2**	**1,249**	**220**	**5**	**89.21**
In Afghanistan							
Bahir Shah	**2017-18**	**12**	**3**	**1,096**	**303***	**5**	**121.77**

Excluding Pujara in India (above), the following aggregates of over 2,000 runs have been recorded in more than one country:

M. Amarnath (P/I/WI)	1982-83	34	6	2,234	207	9	79.78
J. R. Reid (SA/A/NZ)	1961-62	40	2	2,188	203	7	57.57
S. M. Gavaskar (I/P)	1978-79	30	6	2,121	205	10	88.37
R. B. Simpson (I/P/A/WI)	1964-65	34	4	2,063	201	8	68.76
M. H. Richardson (Z/SA/NZ)	2000-01	34	3	2,030	306	4	65.48

The only other player to hit ten hundreds in an overseas season was V. V. S. Laxman in India and Australia in 1999-2000.

LEADING BATSMEN IN AN ENGLISH SEASON

(Qualification: 8 completed innings)

Season	Leading scorer	Runs	Avge	Top of averages	Runs	Avge
1946	D. C. S. Compton	2,403	61.61	W. R. Hammond	1,783	84.90
1947	D. C. S. Compton	3,816	90.85	D. C. S. Compton	3,816	90.85
1948	L. Hutton	2,654	64.73	D. G. Bradman	2,428	89.92
1949	L. Hutton	3,429	68.58	J. Hardstaff	2,251	72.61
1950	R. T. Simpson	2,576	62.82	E. D. Weekes	2,310	79.65
1951	J. D. Robertson	2,917	56.09	P. B. H. May	2,339	68.79
1952	L. Hutton	2,567	61.11	D. S. Sheppard	2,262	64.62
1953	W. J. Edrich	2,557	47.35	R. N. Harvey	2,040	65.80
1954	D. Kenyon	2,636	51.68	D. C. S. Compton	1,524	58.61
1955	D. J. Insole	2,427	42.57	D. J. McGlew	1,871	58.46
1956	T. W. Graveney	2,397	49.93	K. Mackay	1,103	52.52
1957	T. W. Graveney	2,361	49.18	P. B. H. May	2,347	61.76
1958	P. B. H. May	2,231	63.74	P. B. H. May	2,231	63.74
1959	M. J. K. Smith	3,245	57.94	V. L. Manjrekar	755	68.63
1960	M. J. K. Smith	2,551	45.55	R. Subba Row	1,503	55.66
1961	W. E. Alley	3,019	56.96	W. M. Lawry	2,019	61.18
1962	J. H. Edrich	2,482	51.70	R. T. Simpson	867	54.18
1963	J. B. Bolus	2,190	41.32	G. S. Sobers	1,333	47.60
1964	T. W. Graveney	2,385	54.20	K. F. Barrington	1,872	62.40
1965	J. H. Edrich	2,319	62.67	M. C. Cowdrey	2,093	63.42
1966	A. R. Lewis	2,198	41.47	G. S. Sobers	1,349	61.31
1967	C. A. Milton	2,089	46.42	K. F. Barrington	2,059	68.63
1968	B. A. Richards	2,395	47.90	G. Boycott	1,487	64.65
1969	J. H. Edrich	2,238	69.93	J. H. Edrich	2,238	69.93
1970	G. M. Turner	2,379	61.00	G. S. Sobers	1,742	75.73
1971	G. Boycott	2,503	100.12	G. Boycott	2,503	100.12
1972	Majid Khan	2,074	61.00	G. Boycott	1,230	72.35
1973	G. M. Turner	2,416	67.11	G. M. Turner	2,416	67.11

Season	Leading scorer	Runs	Avge	Top of averages	Runs	Avge
1974	R. T. Virgin	1,936	56.94	C. H. Lloyd	1,458	63.39
1975	G. Boycott	1,915	73.65	R. B. Kanhai	1,073	82.53
1976	Zaheer Abbas	2,554	75.11	Zaheer Abbas	2,554	75.11
1977	I. V. A. Richards	2,161	65.48	G. Boycott	1,701	68.04
1978	D. L. Amiss	2,030	53.42	C. E. B. Rice	1,871	66.82
1979	K. C. Wessels	1,800	52.94	G. Boycott	1,538	102.53
1980	P. N. Kirsten	1,895	63.16	A. J. Lamb	1,797	66.55
1981	Zaheer Abbas	2,306	88.69	Zaheer Abbas	2,306	88.69
1982	A. I. Kallicharran	2,120	66.25	G. M. Turner	1,171	90.07
1983	K. S. McEwan	2,176	64.00	I. V. A. Richards	1,204	75.25
1984	G. A. Gooch	2,559	67.34	C. G. Greenidge	1,069	82.23
1985	G. A. Gooch	2,208	71.22	I. V. A. Richards	1,836	76.50
1986	C. G. Greenidge	2,035	67.83	C. G. Greenidge	2,035	67.83
1987	G. A. Hick	1,879	52.19	M. D. Crowe	1,627	67.79
1988	G. A. Hick	2,713	77.51	R. A. Harper	622	77.75
1989	S. J. Cook	2,241	60.56	D. M. Jones	1,510	88.82
1990	G. A. Gooch	2,746	101.70	G. A. Gooch	2,746	101.70
1991	S. J. Cook	2,755	81.02	C. L. Hooper	1,501	93.81
1992	P. D. Bowler	2,044	65.93	Salim Malik	1,184	78.93
	M. A. Roseberry	2,044	56.77			
1993	G. A. Gooch	2,023	63.21	D. C. Boon	1,437	75.63
1994	B. C. Lara	2,066	89.82	J. D. Carr	1,543	90.76
1995	M. R. Ramprakash	2,258	77.86	M. R. Ramprakash	2,258	77.86
1996	G. A. Gooch	1,944	67.03	S. C. Ganguly	762	95.25
1997	S. P. James	1,775	68.26	G. A. Hick	1,524	69.27
1998	J. P. Crawley	1,851	74.04	J. P. Crawley	1,851	74.04
1999	S. G. Law	1,833	73.32	S. G. Law	1,833	73.32
2000	D. S. Lehmann	1,477	67.13	M. G. Bevan	1,124	74.93
2001	M. E. K. Hussey	2,055	79.03	D. R. Martyn	942	104.66
2002	I. J. Ward	1,759	62.82	R. Dravid	773	96.62
2003	S. G. Law	1,820	91.00	S. G. Law	1,820	91.00
2004	R. W. T. Key	1,896	79.00	R. W. T. Key	1,896	79.00
2005	O. A. Shah	1,728	66.46	M. E. K. Hussey	1,074	76.71
2006	M. R. Ramprakash	2,278	103.54	M. R. Ramprakash	2,278	103.54
2007	M. R. Ramprakash	2,026	101.30	M. R. Ramprakash	2,026	101.30
2008	S. C. Moore	1,451	55.80	T. Frost	1,003	83.58
2009	M. E. Trescothick	1,817	75.70	M. R. Ramprakash	1,350	90.00
2010	M. R. Ramprakash	1,595	61.34	J. C. Hildreth	1,440	65.45
2011	M. E. Trescothick	1,673	79.66	I. R. Bell	1,091	90.91
2012	N. R. D. Compton	1,494	99.60	N. R. D. Compton	1,494	99.60
2013	C. J. L. Rogers	1,536	51.20	S. M. Katich	1,097	73.13
2014	A. Lyth	1,619	70.39	J. E. Root	1,052	75.14
2015	J. C. Hildreth	1,758	56.70	J. M. Bairstow	1,226	72.11
2016	K. K. Jennings	1,602	64.08	S. A. Northeast	1,402	82.47
2017	**K. C. Sangakkara**	**1,491**	**106.50**	**K. C. Sangakkara**	**1,491**	**106.50**

The highest average recorded in an English season was 115.66 (2,429 runs, 26 innings) by D. G. Bradman in 1938.

In 1953, W. A. Johnston averaged 102.00 from 17 innings, 16 not out.

MOST RUNS

Dates in italics denote the first half of an overseas season; i.e. *1945* denotes the 1945-46 season.

		Career	R	I	NO	HS	100	Avge
1	J. B. Hobbs	1905–1934	61,237	1,315	106	316*	197	50.65
2	F. E. Woolley	1906–1938	58,969	1,532	85	305*	145	40.75
3	E. H. Hendren	1907–1938	57,611	1,300	166	301*	170	50.80
4	C. P. Mead	1905–1936	55,061	1,340	185	280*	153	47.67
5	W. G. Grace	1865–1908	54,896	1,493	105	344	126	39.55

		Career	R	I	NO	HS	100	Avge
6	W. R. Hammond	1920–1951	50,551	1,005	104	336*	167	56.10
7	H. Sutcliffe..........	1919–1945	50,138	1,088	123	313	149	51.95
8	G. Boycott	1962–1986	48,426	1,014	162	261*	151	56.83
9	T. W. Graveney	1948–*1971*	47,793	1,223	159	258	122	44.91
10	G. A. Gooch.........	1973–2000	44,846	990	75	333	128	49.01
11	T. W. Hayward......	1893–1914	43,551	1,138	96	315*	104	41.79
12	D. L. Amiss	1960–1987	43,423	1,139	126	262*	102	42.86
13	M. C. Cowdrey......	1950–1976	42,719	1,130	134	307	107	42.89
14	A. Sandham	1911–*1937*	41,284	1,000	79	325	107	44.82
15	G. A. Hick	*1983*–2008	41,112	871	84	405*	136	52.23
16	L. Hutton	1934–1960	40,140	814	91	364	129	55.51
17	M. J. K. Smith	1951–1975	39,832	1,091	139	204	69	41.84
18	W. Rhodes	1898–1930	39,802	1,528	237	267*	58	30.83
19	J. H. Edrich..........	1956–1978	39,790	979	104	310*	103	45.47
20	R. E. S. Wyatt.......	1923–1957	39,405	1,141	157	232	85	40.04
21	D. C. S. Compton....	1936–1964	38,942	839	88	300	123	51.85
22	E. Tyldesley	1909–1936	38,874	961	106	256*	102	45.46
23	J. T. Tyldesley	1895–1923	37,897	994	62	295*	86	40.66
24	K. W. R. Fletcher....	1962–1988	37,665	1,167	170	228*	63	37.77
25	C. G. Greenidge	1970–1992	37,354	889	75	273*	92	45.88
26	J. W. Hearne.........	1909–1936	37,252	1,025	116	285*	96	40.98
27	L. E. G. Ames.......	1926–1951	37,248	951	95	295	102	43.51
28	D. Kenyon	1946–1967	37,002	1,159	59	259	74	33.63
29	W. J. Edrich	1934–1958	36,965	964	92	267*	86	42.39
30	J. M. Parks	1949–1976	36,673	1,227	172	205*	51	34.76
31	M. W. Gatting	1975–1998	36,549	861	123	258	94	49.52
32	D. Denton...........	1894–1920	36,479	1,163	70	221	69	33.37
33	G. H. Hirst	1891–1929	36,323	1,215	151	341	60	34.13
34	I. V. A. Richards	*1971*–1993	36,212	796	63	322	114	49.40
35	A. Jones	1957–1983	36,049	1,168	72	204*	56	32.89
36	W. G. Quaife	1894–1928	36,012	1,203	185	255*	72	35.37
37	R. E. Marshall	*1945*–1972	35,725	1,053	59	228*	68	35.94
38	M. R. Ramprakash ...	1987–2012	35,659	764	93	301*	114	53.14
39	G. Gunn	1902–1932	35,208	1,061	82	220	62	35.96

Some works of reference provide career figures which differ from those in this list, owing to the exclusion or inclusion of matches recognised or not recognised as first-class by Wisden. *A fuller list can be found in* Wisdens *up to 2011.*

Current Players with 20,000 Runs

	Career	R	I	NO	HS	100	Avge
S. Chanderpaul...........	*1991–2017*	27,192	609	108	303*	77	54.27
M. E. Trescothick.........	1993–2017	25,598	647	36	284	65	41.89
A. N. Cook...............	2003–*2017*	21,491	482	36	294	61	48.18
K. C. Sangakkara.........	*1997*–2017	20,911	430	31	319	64	52.40

HIGHEST CAREER AVERAGE

(Qualification: 10,000 runs)

Avge		Career	I	NO	R	HS	100
95.14	D. G. Bradman	*1927–1948*	338	43	28,067	452*	117
71.22	V. M. Merchant	*1929–1951*	229	43	13,248	359*	44
67.46	Ajay Sharma	*1984–2000*	166	16	10,120	259*	38
65.18	W. H. Ponsford	*1920–1934*	235	23	13,819	437	47
64.99	W. M. Woodfull	*1921–1934*	245	39	13,388	284	49
58.67	**S. P. D. Smith**	***2007–2017***	**199**	**26**	**10,151**	**239**	**37**
58.24	A. L. Hassett	*1932–1953*	322	32	16,890	232	59

Avge		*Career*	*I*	*NO*	*R*	*HS*	*100*
58.19	V. S. Hazare	*1934–1966*	365	45	18,621	316*	60
57.84	S. R. Tendulkar	*1988–2013*	490	51	25,396	248*	81
57.83	D. S. Lehmann	1987–2007	479	33	25,795	339	82
57.46	**C. A. Pujara**	***2005–2017***	**264**	**34**	**13,216**	**352**	**44**
57.32	M. G. Bevan	*1989–2006*	400	66	19,147	216	68
57.22	A. F. Kippax	*1918–1935*	256	33	12,762	315*	43
56.83	G. Boycott	1962–1986	1,014	162	48,426	261*	151
56.55	C. L. Walcott	*1941–1963*	238	29	11,820	314*	40
56.37	K. S. Ranjitsinhji	1893–1920	500	62	24,692	285*	72
56.22	R. B. Simpson	*1952–1977*	436	62	21,029	359	60
56.10	W. R. Hammond	1920–1951	1,005	104	50,551	336*	167
56.02	M. D. Crowe	*1979–1995*	412	62	19,608	299	71
55.90	R. T. Ponting	*1992*–2013	494	62	24,150	257	82
55.51	L. Hutton	1934–1960	814	91	40,140	364	129
55.37	**Fawad Alam**	***2003–2017***	**232**	**38**	**10,742**	**296***	**27**
55.34	E. D. Weekes	*1944*–1964	241	24	12,010	304*	36
55.33	R. Dravid	*1990–2011*	497	67	23,794	270	68
55.11	S. V. Manjrekar	*1984–1997*	217	31	10,252	377	31

G. A. Headley scored 9,921 runs, average 69.86, between 1927-28 and 1954.

FASTEST FIFTIES

Minutes			
11	C. I. J. Smith (66)	Middlesex v Gloucestershire at Bristol	1938
13	Khalid Mahmood (56)	Gujranwala v Sargodha at Gujranwala	2000-01
14	S. J. Pegler (50)	South Africans v Tasmania at Launceston	1910-11
14	F. T. Mann (53)	Middlesex v Nottinghamshire at Lord's	1921
14	H. B. Cameron (56)	Transvaal v Orange Free State at Johannesburg	1934-35
14	C. I. J. Smith (52)	Middlesex v Kent at Maidstone	1935

The number of balls taken to achieve fifties was rarely recorded until recently. C. I. J. Smith's two fifties (above) may have taken only 12 balls each. Khalid Mahmood reached his fifty in 15 balls.

Fifties scored in contrived circumstances and with the bowlers' compliance are excluded from the above list, including the fastest of them all, in 8 minutes (13 balls) by C. C. Inman, Leicestershire v Nottinghamshire at Nottingham, 1965, and 10 minutes by G. Chapple, Lancashire v Glamorgan at Manchester, 1993.

FASTEST HUNDREDS

Minutes			
35	P. G. H. Fender (113*)	Surrey v Northamptonshire at Northampton	1920
40	G. L. Jessop (101)	Gloucestershire v Yorkshire at Harrogate	1897
40	Ahsan-ul-Haq (100*)	Muslims v Sikhs at Lahore	1923-24
42	G. L. Jessop (191)	Gentlemen of South v Players of South at Hastings	1907
43	A. H. Hornby (106)	Lancashire v Somerset at Manchester	1905
43	D. W. Hookes (107)	South Australia v Victoria at Adelaide	1982-83
44	R. N. S. Hobbs (100)	Essex v Australians at Chelmsford	1975

The fastest recorded authentic hundred in terms of balls received was scored off 34 balls by D. W. Hookes (above). Research of the scorebook has shown that P. G. H. Fender scored his hundred from between 40 and 46 balls. He contributed 113 to an unfinished sixth-wicket partnership of 171 in 42 minutes with H. A. Peach.

E. B. Alletson (Nottinghamshire) scored 189 out of 227 runs in 90 minutes against Sussex at Hove in 1911. It has been estimated that his last 139 runs took 37 minutes.

Hundreds scored in contrived circumstances and with the bowlers' compliance are excluded, including the fastest of them all, in 21 minutes (27 balls) by G. Chapple, Lancashire v Glamorgan at Manchester, 1993, 24 minutes (27 balls) by M. L. Pettini, Essex v Leicestershire at Leicester, 2006, and 26 minutes (36 balls) by T. M. Moody, Warwickshire v Glamorgan at Swansea, 1990.

FASTEST DOUBLE-HUNDREDS

Minutes			
113	R. J. Shastri (200*)	Bombay v Baroda at Bombay	1984-85
120	G. L. Jessop (286)	Gloucestershire v Sussex at Hove	1903
120	C. H. Lloyd (201*)	West Indians v Glamorgan at Swansea	1976
130	G. L. Jessop (234)	Gloucestershire v Somerset at Bristol	1905
131	V. T. Trumper (293)	Australians v Canterbury at Christchurch	1913-14

Shastri faced 123 balls, which was matched by A. H. T. Donald for Glamorgan v Derbyshire at Colwyn Bay in 2016.

FASTEST TRIPLE-HUNDREDS

Minutes			
181	D. C. S. Compton (300)	MCC v North Eastern Transvaal at Benoni	1948-49
205	F. E. Woolley (305*)	MCC v Tasmania at Hobart	1911-12
205	C. G. Macartney (345)	Australians v Nottinghamshire at Nottingham	1921
213	D. G. Bradman (369)	South Australia v Tasmania at Adelaide	1935-36

The fastest triple-hundred in terms of balls received was scored off 191 balls by M. Marais for Border v Eastern Province at East London in 2017-18.

MOST RUNS IN A DAY BY ONE BATSMAN

390*	B. C. Lara	Warwickshire v Durham at Birmingham	1994
345	C. G. Macartney	Australians v Nottinghamshire at Nottingham	1921
334	W. H. Ponsford	Victoria v New South Wales at Melbourne	1926-27
333	K. S. Duleepsinhji	Sussex v Northamptonshire at Hove	1930
331*	J. D. Robertson	Middlesex v Worcestershire at Worcester	1949
325*	B. A. Richards	South Australia v Western Australia at Perth	1970-71

These scores do not necessarily represent the complete innings. See page 1183.

*There have been another **14** instances of a batsman scoring 300 in a day, most recently 319 by R. R. Rossouw, Eagles v Titans at Centurion in 2009-10 (see* Wisden *2003, page 278, for full list).*

LONGEST INNINGS

Hrs	Mins			
16	55	R. Nayyar (271)	Himachal Pradesh v Jammu&Kashmir at Chamba	1999-2000
16	10	Hanif Mohammad (337)	Pakistan v West Indies at Bridgetown	1957-58
		Hanif believed he batted 16 hours 39 minutes.		
16	4	S. B. Gohel (359*)	Gujarat v Orissa at Jaipur	2016-17
15	7	V. A. Saxena (257)	Rajasthan v Tamil Nadu at Chennai	2011-12
14	38	G. Kirsten (275)	South Africa v England at Durban	1999-2000
14	32	K. K. Nair (328)	Karnataka v Tamil Nadu at Mumbai	2014-15
13	58	S. C. Cook (390)	Lions v Warriors at East London	2009-10
13	56	A. N. Cook (263)	England v Pakistan at Abu Dhabi	2015-16
13	43	T. Kohli (300*)	Punjab v Jharkhand at Jamshedpur	2012-13
13	41	S. S. Shukla (178*)	Uttar Pradesh v Tamil Nadu at Nagpur	2008-09
13	32	A. Chopra (301*)	Rajasthan v Maharashtra at Nasik	2010-11

1,000 RUNS IN MAY

	Runs	Avge
W. G. Grace, May 9 to May 30, 1895 (22 days)	1,016	112.88
Grace was 46 years old.		
W. R. Hammond, May 7 to May 31, 1927 (25 days)	1,042	74.42
Hammond scored his 1,000th run on May 28, thus equalling Grace's record of 22 days.		
C. Hallows, May 5 to May 31, 1928 (27 days)	1,000	125.00

1,000 RUNS IN APRIL AND MAY

	Runs	Avge
T. W. Hayward, April 16 to May 31, 1900	1,074	97.63
D. G. Bradman, April 30 to May 31, 1930	1,001	143.00
On April 30 Bradman was 75 not out.		
D. G. Bradman, April 30 to May 31, 1938	1,056	150.85
Bradman scored 258 on April 30, and his 1,000th run on May 27.		
W. J. Edrich, April 30 to May 31, 1938	1,010	84.16
Edrich was 21 not out on April 30. All his runs were scored at Lord's.		
G. M. Turner, April 24 to May 31, 1973	1,018	78.30
G. A. Hick, April 17 to May 29, 1988	1,019	101.90
Hick scored a record 410 runs in April, and his 1,000th run on May 28.		

MOST RUNS SCORED OFF AN OVER

(All instances refer to six-ball overs)

36	G. S. Sobers	off M. A. Nash, Nottinghamshire v Glam at Swansea (six sixes)	1968
36	R. J. Shastri	off Tilak Raj, Bombay v Baroda at Bombay (six sixes)	1984-85
34	E. B. Alletson	off E. H. Killick, Notts v Sussex at Hove (46604446 inc 2 nb)	1911
34	F. C. Hayes	off M. A. Nash, Lancashire v Glamorgan at Swansea (646666)	1977
34†	A. Flintoff	off A. J. Tudor, Lancs v Surrey at Manchester (64444660 inc 2 nb)	1998
34	C. M. Spearman	off S. J. P. Moreton, Gloucestershire v Oxford UCCE at Oxford (666646) *Moreton's first over in first-class cricket.*	2005
32	C. C. Smart	off G. Hill, Glamorgan v Hampshire at Cardiff (664664)	1935
32	I. R. Redpath	off N. Rosendorff, Australians v OFS at Bloemfontein (666644)	1969-70
32	P. W. G. Parker	off A. I. Kallicharran, Sussex v Warwicks at Birmingham (466664)	1982
32	I. T. Botham	off I. R. Snook, England XI v C Dists at Palmerston North (466466)	1983-84
32	Khalid Mahmood	off Naved Latif, Gujranwala v Sargodha at Gujranwala (666662)	2000-01

† *Altogether 38 runs were scored off this over, the two no-balls counting for two extra runs each under ECB regulations.*

The following instances have been excluded because of the bowlers' compliance: 34 – M. P. Maynard off S. A. Marsh, Glamorgan v Kent at Swansea, 1992; 34 – G. Chapple off P. A. Cottey, Lancashire v Glamorgan at Manchester, 1993; 34 – F. B. Touzel off F. J. J. Viljoen, Western Province B v Griqualand West at Kimberley, 1993-94. Chapple scored a further 32 off Cottey's next over.

There were 35 runs off an over received by A. T. Reinholds off H. T. Davis, Auckland v Wellington at Auckland 1995-96, but this included 16 extras and only 19 off the bat.

In a match against KwaZulu-Natal at Stellenbosch in 2006-07, W. E. September (Boland) conceded 34 in an over: 27 to M. Bekker, six to K. Smit, plus one no-ball.

In a match against Canterbury at Christchurch in 1989-90, R. H. Vance (Wellington) deliberately conceded 77 runs in an over of full tosses which contained 17 no-balls and, owing to the umpire's understandable miscalculation, only five legitimate deliveries.

The greatest number of runs scored off an eight-ball over is 34 (40446664) by R. M. Edwards off M. C. Carew, Governor-General's XI v West Indians at Auckland, 1968-69.

MOST SIXES IN AN INNINGS

23	C. Munro (281)	Auckland v Central Districts at Napier	2014-15
16	A. Symonds (254*)	Gloucestershire v Glamorgan at Abergavenny	1995
16	G. R. Napier (196)	Essex v Surrey at Croydon	2011
16	J. D. Ryder (175)	New Zealanders v Australia A at Brisbane	2011-12
16	Mukhtar Ali (168)	Rajshahi v Chittagong at Savar	2013-14
15	J. R. Reid (296)	Wellington v Northern Districts at Wellington	1962-63
15	Ziaur Rahman (152*)	South Zone v Central Zone at Mirpur	2012-13
15	H. G. Kumara (200*)	Saracens v Air Force at Katunayake	2014-15
15	K. P. Pietersen (355*)	Surrey v Leicestershire at The Oval	2015
15	A. H. T. Donald (234)	Glamorgan v Derbyshire at Colwyn Bay	2016

There have been ***nine*** *further instances of 14 or more sixes in an innings.*

MOST SIXES IN A MATCH

23	C. Munro (281)	Auckland v Central Districts at Napier	2014-15
21	R. R. Pant (117, 131)	Delhi v Jharkhand at Thumba	2016-17
20	A. Symonds (254*, 76)	Gloucestershire v Glam at Abergavenny	1995
17	W. J. Stewart (155, 125)	Warwickshire v Lancashire at Blackpool	1959
17	K. P. S. P. Karunanayake (52, 150*)	Army v Ports Authority at Colombo (CCC)	2014-15

MOST SIXES IN A SEASON

80	I. T. Botham	1985
66	A. W. Wellard	1935
57	A. W. Wellard	1936
57	A. W. Wellard	1938
51	A. W. Wellard	1933
49	I. V. A. Richards	1985
48	A. W. Carr	1925
48	J. H. Edrich	1965
48	A. Symonds	1995

MOST BOUNDARIES IN AN INNINGS

	4/6			
72	62/10	B. C. Lara (501*)	Warwickshire v Durham at Birmingham	1994
68	68/–	P. A. Perrin (343*)	Essex v Derbyshire at Chesterfield	1904
65	64/1	A. C. MacLaren (424)	Lancashire v Somerset at Taunton	1895
64	64/–	Hanif Mohammad (499)	Karachi v Bahawalpur at Karachi	1958-59
57	52/5	J. H. Edrich (310*)	England v New Zealand at Leeds	1965
57	52/5	Naved Latif (394)	Sargodha v Gujranwala at Gujranwala	2000-01
56	54/2	K. M. Jadhav (327)	Maharashtra v Uttar Pradesh at Pune	2012-13
55	55/–	C. W. Gregory (383)	NSW v Queensland at Brisbane	1906-07
55	53/2	G. R. Marsh (355*)	W. Australia v S. Australia at Perth	1989-90
55	51/3†	S. V. Manjrekar (377)	Bombay v Hyderabad at Bombay	1990-91
55	52/3	D. S. Lehmann (339)	Yorkshire v Durham at Leeds	2006
55	54/1	D. K. H. Mitchell (298)	Worcestershire v Somerset at Taunton	2009
55	54/1	S. C. Cook (390)	Lions v Warriors at East London	2009-10
55	47/8	R. R. Rossouw (319)	Eagles v Titans at Centurion	2009-10

† *Plus one five.* ‡ *Plus three fives.*

PARTNERSHIPS OVER 500

624 for 3rd	K. C. Sangakkara (287)/D. P. M. D. Jayawardene (374), Sri Lanka v South Africa at Colombo (SSC)	2006
594* for 3rd	S. M. Gugale (351*)/A. R. Bawne (258*), Maharashtra v Delhi at Mumbai	2016-17
580 for 2nd	Rafatullah Mohmand (302*)/Aamer Sajjad (289), WAPDA v Sui Southern Gas at Sheikhupura	2009-10
577 for 4th	V. S. Hazare (288)/Gul Mahomed (319), Baroda v Holkar at Baroda	1946-47
576 for 2nd	S. T. Jayasuriya (340)/R. S. Mahanama (225), Sri Lanka v India at Colombo (RPS)	1997-98
574* for 4th	F. M. M. Worrell (255*)/C. L. Walcott (314*), Barbados v Trinidad at Port-of-Spain	1945-46
561 for 1st	Waheed Mirza (324)/Mansoor Akhtar (224*), Karachi Whites v Quetta at Karachi	1976-77
555 for 1st	P. Holmes (224*)/H. Sutcliffe (313), Yorkshire v Essex at Leyton	1932
554 for 1st	J. T. Brown (300)/J. Tunnicliffe (243), Yorks v Derbys at Chesterfield	1898
539 for 3rd	S. D. Jogiyani (282)/R. A. Jadeja (303*), Saurashtra v Gujarat at Surat	2012-13
523 for 3rd	M. A. Carberry (300*)/N. D. McKenzie (237), Hants v Yorks at Southampton	2011
520* for 5th	C. A. Pujara (302*)/R. A. Jadeja (232*), Saurashtra v Orissa at Rajkot	2008-09
503 for 1st	R. G. L. Carters (209)/A. J. Finch (288*), Cricket Australia XI v New Zealanders at Sydney	2015-16
502* for 4th	F. M. M. Worrell (308*)/J. D. C. Goddard (218*), Barbados v Trinidad at Bridgetown	1943-44
501 for 3rd	A. N. Petersen (286)/A. G. Prince (261), Lancs v Glam at Colwyn Bay	2015

HIGHEST PARTNERSHIPS FOR EACH WICKET

First Wicket

561	Waheed Mirza/Mansoor Akhtar, Karachi Whites v Quetta at Karachi	1976-77
555	P. Holmes/H. Sutcliffe, Yorkshire v Essex at Leyton	1932
554	J. T. Brown/J. Tunnicliffe, Yorkshire v Derbyshire at Chesterfield	1898
503	R. G. L. Carters/A. J. Finch, Cricket Australia XI v New Zealanders at Sydney	2015-16
490	E. H. Bowley/J. G. Langridge, Sussex v Middlesex at Hove	1933

Second Wicket

580	Rafatullah Mohmand/Aamer Sajjad, WAPDA v Sui S. Gas at Sheikhupura	2009-10
576	S. T. Jayasuriya/R. S. Mahanama, Sri Lanka v India at Colombo (RPS)	1997-98
480	D. Elgar/R. R. Rossouw, Eagles v Titans at Centurion	2009-10
475	Zahir Alam/L. S. Rajput, Assam v Tripura at Gauhati	1991-92
465*	J. A. Jameson/R. B. Kanhai, Warwicks v Gloucestershire at Birmingham	1974

Third Wicket

624	K. C. Sangakkara/D. P. M. D. Jayawardene, Sri Lanka v SA at Colombo (SSC)	2006
594*	S. M. Gugale/A. R. Bawne, Maharashtra v Delhi at Mumbai	2016-17
539	S. D. Jogiyani/R. A. Jadeja, Saurashtra v Gujarat at Surat	2012-13
523	M. A. Carberry/N. D. McKenzie, Hampshire v Yorks at Southampton	2011
501	A. N. Petersen/A. G. Prince, Lancashire v Glamorgan at Colwyn Bay	2015

Fourth Wicket

577	V. S. Hazare/Gul Mahomed, Baroda v Holkar at Baroda	1946-47
574*	C. L. Walcott/F. M. M. Worrell, Barbados v Trinidad at Port-of-Spain	1945-46
502*	F. M. M. Worrell/J. D. C. Goddard, Barbados v Trinidad at Bridgetown	1943-44
470	A. I. Kallicharran/G. W. Humpage, Warwicks v Lancs at Southport	1982
462*	D. W. Hookes/W. B. Phillips, South Australia v Tasmania at Adelaide	1986-87

Fifth Wicket

520*	C. A. Pujara/R. A. Jadeja, Saurashtra v Orissa at Rajkot	2008-09
494	Marshall Ayub/Mehrab Hossain, Central Zone v East Zone at Bogra	2012-13
479	Misbah-ul-Haq/Usman Arshad, Sui N. Gas v Lahore Shalimar at Lahore	2009-10
464*	M. E. Waugh/S. R. Waugh, New South Wales v Western Australia at Perth	1990-91
428*	**B. C. Williams/M. Marais, Border v Eastern Province at East London**	**2017-18**

Sixth Wicket

487*	G. A. Headley/C. C. Passailaigue, Jamaica v Lord Tennyson's XI at Kingston	1931-32
428	W. W. Armstrong/M. A. Noble, Australians v Sussex at Hove	1902
417	W. P. Saha/L. R. Shukla, Bengal v Assam at Kolkata	2010-11
411	R. M. Poore/E. G. Wynyard, Hampshire v Somerset at Taunton	1899
399	B. A. Stokes/J. M. Bairstow, England v South Africa at Cape Town	2015-16

Seventh Wicket

460	Bhupinder Singh jnr/P. Dharmani, Punjab v Delhi at Delhi	1994-95
371	M. R. Marsh/S. M. Whiteman, Australia A v India A at Brisbane	2014
366*	J. M. Bairstow/T. T. Bresnan, Yorkshire v Durham at Chester-le-Street	2015
347	D. St E. Atkinson/C. C. Depeiza, West Indies v Australia at Bridgetown	1954-55
347	Farhad Reza/Sanjamul Islam, Rajshahi v Chittagong at Savar	2013-14

Eighth Wicket

433	A. Sims and V. T. Trumper, A. Sims' Aust. XI v Canterbury at Christchurch	1913-14
392	A. Mishra/J. Yadav, Haryana v Karnataka at Hubli	2012-13
332	I. J. L. Trott/S. C. J. Broad, England v Pakistan at Lord's	2010
313	Wasim Akram/Saqlain Mushtaq, Pakistan v Zimbabwe at Sheikhupura	1996-97
292	R. Peel/Lord Hawke, Yorkshire v Warwickshire at Birmingham	1896

Ninth Wicket

283	A. Warren/J. Chapman, Derbyshire v Warwickshire at Blackwell	1910
268	J. B. Commins/N. Boje, South Africa A v Mashonaland at Harare	1994-95
261	W. L. Madsen/T. Poynton, Derbyshire v Northants at Northampton	2012
251	J. W. H. T. Douglas/S. N. Hare, Essex v Derbyshire at Leyton	1921
249*†	A. S. Srivastava/K. Seth, Madhya Pradesh v Vidarbha at Indore	2000-01

† *276 unbeaten runs were scored for this wicket in two separate partnerships; after Srivastava retired hurt, Seth and N. D. Hirwani added 27.*

Tenth Wicket

307	A. F. Kippax/J. E. H. Hooker, New South Wales v Victoria at Melbourne	1928-29
249	C. T. Sarwate/S. N. Banerjee, Indians v Surrey at The Oval	1946
239	Aqeel Arshad/Ali Raza, Lahore Whites v Hyderabad at Lahore	2004-05
235	F. E. Woolley/A. Fielder, Kent v Worcestershire at Stourbridge	1909
233	Ajay Sharma/Maninder Singh, Delhi v Bombay at Bombay	1991-92

There have been only 13 last-wicket stands of 200 or more.

UNUSUAL DISMISSALS

Handled the Ball

There have been **63** instances in first-class cricket. The most recent are:

W. S. A. Williams	Canterbury v Otago at Dunedin	2012-13
E. Lewis	Trinidad & Tobago v Leeward Islands at Port-of-Spain	2013-14
C. A. Pujara	Derbyshire v Leicestershire at Derby	2014
I. Khan	Dolphins v Lions at Johannesburg	2014-15
K. Lesporis	Windward Islands v Barbados at Bridgetown	2015-16
S. R. Dickson	Kent v Leicestershire at Leicester	2016
M. Z. Hamza	Cape Cobras v Knights at Bloemfontein	2016-17

Under the 2017 revision of the Laws, Handled the Ball was subsumed under Obstructing the Field.

Obstructing the Field

There have been **29** instances in first-class cricket. T. Straw of Worcestershire was given out for obstruction v Warwickshire in both 1899 and 1901. The most recent are:

Nasir Ahmadzai	Afghanistan v Zimbabwe A at Harare	2014
W. E. Bell	Northern Cape v Border at Kimberley	2015-16
Jahid Ali	Pakistan A v Zimbabwe A at Bulawayo	2016-17
Ghamai Zadran	**Mis Ainak v Boost at Ghazi Amanullah Town**	**2017-18**
Rashid Zadran	**Mis Ainak v Band-e-Amir at Kabul**	**2017-18**
Zia-ur-Rehman	**Mis Ainak v Amo at Khost**	**2017-18**

Hit the Ball Twice

There have been **21** instances in first-class cricket. The last occurrence in England involved J. H. King of Leicestershire v Surrey at The Oval in 1906. The most recent are:

Aziz Malik	Lahore Division v Faisalabad at Sialkot	1984-85
Javed Mohammad	Multan v Karachi Whites at Sahiwal	1986-87
Shahid Pervez	Jammu & Kashmir v Punjab at Srinagar	1986-87
Ali Naqvi	PNSC v National Bank at Faisalabad	1998-99
A. George	Tamil Nadu v Maharashtra at Pune	1998-99
Maqsood Raza	Lahore Division v PNSC at Sheikhupura	1999-2000
D. Mahajan	Jammu & Kashmir v Bihar at Jammu	2005-06

Timed Out

There have been **six** instances in first-class cricket:

A. Jordaan	Eastern Province v Transvaal at Port Elizabeth (SACB match)	1987-88
H. Yadav	Tripura v Orissa at Cuttack	1997-98
V. C. Drakes	Border v Free State at East London	2002-03
A. J. Harris	Nottinghamshire v Durham UCCE at Nottingham	2003
R. A. Austin	Combined Campuses & Colleges v Windward Is at Arnos Vale	2013-14
C. Kunje	**Bulawayo Met Tuskers v Manica Mountaineers at Bulawayo**	**2017-18**

BOWLING RECORDS

TEN WICKETS IN AN INNINGS

In the history of first-class cricket, there have been **80** instances of a bowler taking all ten wickets in an innings, plus a further three instances of ten wickets in 12-a-side matches. Occurrences since the Second World War:

	O	*M*	*R*		
*W. E. Hollies (Warwickshire)	20.4	4	49	v Notts at Birmingham	1946
J. M. Sims (East)	18.4	2	90	v West at Kingston	1948
T. E. Bailey (Essex)	39.4	9	90	v Lancashire at Clacton	1949
J. K. Graveney (Glos.)	18.4	2	66	v Derbyshire at Chesterfield	1949
R. Berry (Lancashire)	36.2	9	102	v Worcestershire at Blackpool	1953
S. P. Gupte (President's XI)	24.2	7	78	v Combined XI at Bombay	1954-55
J. C. Laker (Surrey)	46	18	88	v Australians at The Oval	1956
J. C. Laker (England)	51.2	23	53	v Australia at Manchester	1956
G. A. R. Lock (Surrey)	29.1	18	54	v Kent at Blackheath	1956
K. Smales (Nottinghamshire)	41.3	20	66	v Gloucestershire at Stroud	1956
P. M. Chatterjee (Bengal)	19	11	20	v Assam at Jorhat	1956-57
J. D. Bannister (Warwickshire)	23.3	11	41	v Comb. Services at Birmingham†	1959
A. J. G. Pearson (Cambridge U.)	30.3	8	78	v Leics at Loughborough	1961
N. I. Thomson (Sussex)	34.2	19	49	v Warwickshire at Worthing	1964
P. J. Allan (Queensland)	15.6	3	61	v Victoria at Melbourne	1965-66
I. J. Brayshaw (W. Australia)	17.6	4	44	v Victoria at Perth	1967-68
Shahid Mahmood (Karachi Whites)	25	5	58	v Khairpur at Karachi	1969-70
E. E. Hemmings (International XI)	49.3	14	175	v West Indies XI at Kingston	1982-83
P. Sunderam (Rajasthan)	22	5	78	v Vidarbha at Jodhpur	1985-86
S. T. Jefferies (W. Province)	22.5	7	59	v Orange Free State at Cape Town	1987-88
Imran Adil (Bahawalpur)	22.5	3	92	v Faisalabad at Faisalabad	1989-90
G. P. Wickremasinghe (Sinhalese)	19.2	5	41	v Kalutara PCC at Colombo (SSC)	1991-92
R. L. Johnson (Middlesex)	18.5	6	45	v Derbyshire at Derby	1994
Naeem Akhtar (Rawalpindi B)	21.3	10	28	v Peshawar at Peshawar	1995-96
A. Kumble (India)	26.3	9	74	v Pakistan at Delhi	1998-99

	O	M	R		
D. S. Mohanty (East Zone)	19	5	46	v South Zone at Agartala	2000-01
O. D. Gibson (Durham)	17.3	1	47	v Hampshire at Chester-le-Street	2007
M. W. Olivier (Warriors)	26.3	4	65	v Eagles at Bloemfontein	2007-08
Zulfiqar Babar (Multan)	39.4	3	143	v Islamabad at Multan	2009-10

* *W. E. Hollies bowled seven and had three lbw. The only other instance of a bowler achieving the feat without the direct assistance of a fielder came in 1850 when J. Wisden bowled all ten, for North v South at Lord's.*

† *Mitchells & Butlers Ground.*

OUTSTANDING BOWLING ANALYSES

	O	M	R	W		
H. Verity (Yorkshire)	19.4	16	10	10	v Nottinghamshire at Leeds	1932
G. Elliott (Victoria)	19	17	2	9	v Tasmania at Launceston	1857-58
Ahad Khan (Railways)	6.3	4	7	9	v Dera Ismail Khan at Lahore	1964-65
J. C. Laker (England)	14	12	2	8	v The Rest at Bradford	1950
D. Shackleton (Hampshire)	11.1	7	4	8	v Somerset at Weston-s-Mare	1955
E. Peate (Yorkshire)	16	11	5	8	v Surrey at Holbeck	1883
K. M. Dabengwa (Westerns)	4.4	3	1	7	v Northerns at Harare	2006-07
F. R. Spofforth (Australians)	8.3	6	3	7	v England XI at Birmingham	1884
W. A. Henderson (NE Transvaal)	9.3	7	4	7	v OFS at Bloemfontein	1937-38
Rajinder Goel (Haryana)	7	4	4	7	v Jammu & Kashmir at Chandigarh	1977-78
N. W. Bracken (NSW)	7	5	4	7	v South Australia at Sydney	2004-05
V. I. Smith (South Africans)	4.5	3	1	6	v Derbyshire at Derby	1947
S. Cosstick (Victoria)	21.1	20	1	6	v Tasmania at Melbourne	1868-69
Israr Ali (Bahawalpur)	11	10	1	6	v Dacca U. at Bahawalpur	1957-58
A. D. Pougher (MCC)	3	3	0	5	v Australians at Lord's	1896
G. R. Cox (Sussex)	6	6	0	5	v Somerset at Weston-s-Mare	1921
R. K. Tyldesley (Lancashire)	5	5	0	5	v Leicestershire at Manchester	1924
P. T. Mills (Gloucestershire)	6.4	6	0	5	v Somerset at Bristol	1928

MOST WICKETS IN A MATCH

19-90	J. C. Laker	England v Australia at Manchester	1956
17-48†	C. Blythe	Kent v Northamptonshire at Northampton	1907
17-50	C. T. B. Turner	Australians v England XI at Hastings	1888
17-54	W. P. Howell	Australians v Western Province at Cape Town	1902-03
17-56	C. W. L. Parker	Gloucestershire v Essex at Gloucester	1925
17-67	A. P. Freeman	Kent v Sussex at Hove	1922
17-89	W. G. Grace	Gloucestershire v Nottinghamshire at Cheltenham	1877
17-89	F. C. L. Matthews	Nottinghamshire v Northants at Nottingham	1923
17-91	H. Dean	Lancashire v Yorkshire at Liverpool	1913
17-91†	H. Verity	Yorkshire v Essex at Leyton	1933
17-92	A. P. Freeman	Kent v Warwickshire at Folkestone	1932
17-103	W. Mycroft	Derbyshire v Hampshire at Southampton	1876
17-106	G. R. Cox	Sussex v Warwickshire at Horsham	1926
17-106†	T. W. J. Goddard	Gloucestershire v Kent at Bristol	1939
17-119	W. Mead	Essex v Hampshire at Southampton	1895
17-137	W. Brearley	Lancashire v Somerset at Manchester	1905
17-137	J. M. Davison	Canada v USA at Fort Lauderdale	2004
17-159	S. F. Barnes	England v South Africa at Johannesburg	1913-14
17-201	G. Giffen	South Australia v Victoria at Adelaide	1885-86
17-212	J. C. Clay	Glamorgan v Worcestershire at Swansea	1937

† *Achieved in a single day.*

H. Arkwright took 18-96 for MCC v Gentlemen of Kent in a 12-a-side match at Canterbury in 1861.

*There have been **59** instances of a bowler taking 16 wickets in an 11-a-side match, the most recent being **16-141** by **Saad Altaf** for Rawalpindi v FATA at Mirpur, 2017-18.*

FOUR WICKETS WITH CONSECUTIVE BALLS

There have been **44** instances in first-class cricket. R. J. Crisp achieved the feat twice, for Western Province in 1931-32 and 1933-34. A. E. Trott took four in four balls and another hat-trick in the same innings for Middlesex v Somerset in 1907, his benefit match. Occurrences since 2007:

Tabish Khan	Karachi Whites v ZTBL at Karachi	2009-10
Kamran Hussain	Habib Bank v Lahore Shalimar at Lahore	2009-10
N. Wagner	Otago v Wellington at Queenstown	2010-11
Khalid Usman	Abbottabad v Karachi Blues at Karachi	2011-12
Mahmudullah	Central Zone v North Zone at Savar	2013-14
A. C. Thomas	Somerset v Sussex at Taunton	2014
Taj Wali	Peshawar v Port Qasim Authority at Peshawar	2015-16
N. G. R. P. Jayasuriya	Colts v Badureliya at Maggona	2015-16
K. R. Smuts	Eastern Province v Boland at Paarl	2015-16

In their match with England at The Oval in 1863, Surrey lost four wickets in the course of a four-ball over from G. Bennett.

Sussex lost five wickets in the course of the final (six-ball) over of their match with Surrey at Eastbourne in 1972. P. I. Pocock, who had taken three wickets in his previous over, captured four more, taking in all seven wickets with 11 balls, a feat unique in first-class matches. (The eighth wicket fell to a run-out.)

In 1996, K. D. James took four in four balls for Hampshire against Indians at Southampton and scored a century, a feat later emulated by Mahmudullah and Smuts.

HAT-TRICKS

Double Hat-Trick

Besides Trott's performance, which is mentioned in the preceding section, the following instances are recorded of players having performed the hat-trick twice in the same match, Rao doing so in the same innings.

A. Shaw	Nottinghamshire v Gloucestershire at Nottingham	1884
T. J. Matthews	Australia v South Africa at Manchester	1912
C. W. L. Parker	Gloucestershire v Middlesex at Bristol	1924
R. O. Jenkins	Worcestershire v Surrey at Worcester	1949
J. S. Rao	Services v Northern Punjab at Amritsar	1963-64
Amin Lakhani	Combined XI v Indians at Multan	1978-79
M. A. Starc	**New South Wales v Western Australia at Sydney (Hurstville)**	**2017-18**

Five Wickets in Six Balls

W. H. Copson	Derbyshire v Warwickshire at Derby	1937
W. A. Henderson	NE Transvaal v Orange Free State at Bloemfontein	1937-38
P. I. Pocock	Surrey v Sussex at Eastbourne	1972
Yasir Arafat	Rawalpindi v Faisalabad at Rawalpindi	2004-05
N. Wagner	Otago v Wellington at Queenstown	2010-11

Yasir Arafat's five wickets were spread across two innings and interrupted only by a no-ball. Wagner was the first to take five wickets in a single over.

Most Hat-Tricks

D. V. P. Wright	7
T. W. J. Goddard	6
C. W. L. Parker	6
S. Haigh	5
V. W. C. Jupp	5
A. E. G. Rhodes	5
F. A. Tarrant	5
R. G. Barlow	4
Fazl-e-Akbar	4
A. P. Freeman	4
J. T. Hearne	4
J. C. Laker	4
G. A. R. Lock	4
G. G. Macaulay	4
T. G. Matthews	4
M. J. Procter	4
T. Richardson	4
F. R. Spofforth	4
F. S. Trueman	4

Hat-Trick on Debut

There have been **18** instances in first-class cricket. Occurrences since 2000:

S. M. Harwood	Victoria v Tasmania at Melbourne	2002-03
P. Connell	Ireland v Netherlands at Rotterdam	2008
A. Mithun	Karnataka v Uttar Pradesh at Meerut	2009-10
Zohaib Shera	Karachi Whites v National Bank at Karachi	2009-10

R. R. Phillips (Border) took a hat-trick in his first over in first-class cricket (v Eastern Province at Port Elizabeth, 1939-40) having previously played in four matches without bowling.

250 WICKETS IN A SEASON

	Season	*O*	*M*	*R*	*W*	*Avge*
A. P. Freeman	1928	1,976.1	423	5,489	304	18.05
A. P. Freeman	1933	2,039	651	4,549	298	15.26
T. Richardson	1895‡	1,690.1	463	4,170	290	14.37
C. T. B. Turner	1888†	2,427.2	1,127	3,307	283	11.68
A. P. Freeman	1931	1,618	360	4,307	276	15.60
A. P. Freeman	1930	1,914.3	472	4,632	275	16.84
T. Richardson	1897‡	1,603.4	495	3,945	273	14.45
A. P. Freeman	1929	1,670.5	381	4,879	267	18.27
W. Rhodes	1900	1,553	455	3,606	261	13.81
J. T. Hearne	1896‡	2,003.1	818	3,670	257	14.28
A. P. Freeman	1932	1,565.5	404	4,149	253	16.39
W. Rhodes	1901	1,565	505	3,797	251	15.12

† *Indicates 4-ball overs.* ‡ *5-ball overs.*

In four consecutive seasons (1928–1931), A. P. Freeman took 1,122 wickets, and in eight consecutive seasons (1928–1935), 2,090 wickets. In each of these eight seasons he took over 200 wickets.

T. Richardson took 1,005 wickets in four consecutive seasons (1894–1897).

The earliest date by which any bowler has taken 100 in an English season is June 12, achieved by J. T. Hearne in 1896 and C. W. L. Parker in 1931, when A. P. Freeman did it on June 13.

100 WICKETS IN A SEASON MOST TIMES

(Includes overseas tours and seasons)

W. Rhodes	23	C. W. L. Parker	16	G. H. Hirst	15
D. Shackleton	20	R. T. D. Perks	16	A. S. Kennedy	15
A. P. Freeman	17	F. J. Titmus	16		
T. W. J. Goddard	16	J. T. Hearne	15		

D. Shackleton reached 100 wickets in 20 successive seasons – 1949–1968.

Since the reduction of County Championship matches in 1969, D. L. Underwood (five times) and J. K. Lever (four times) are the only bowlers to have reached 100 wickets in a season more than twice. The highest aggregate in a season since 1969 is 134 by M. D. Marshall in 1982.

The most instances of 200 wickets in a season is eight by A. P. Freeman, who did it in eight successive seasons – 1928 to 1935 – including 304 in 1928. C. W. L. Parker did it five times, T. W. J. Goddard four times, and J. T. Hearne, G. A. Lohmann, W. Rhodes, T. Richardson, M. W. Tate and H. Verity three times each.

The last bowler to reach 200 wickets in a season was G. A. R. Lock (212 in 1957).

An expanded and regularly updated online version of the Records can be found at www.wisdenrecords.com

100 WICKETS IN A SEASON OUTSIDE ENGLAND

W		Season	Country	R	Avge
116	M. W. Tate	1926-27	India/Ceylon	1,599	13.78
113	Kabir Khan	1998-99	Pakistan	1,706	15.09
107	Ijaz Faqih	1985-86	Pakistan	1,719	16.06
106	C. T. B. Turner	1887-88	Australia	1,441	13.59
106	R. Benaud	1957-58	South Africa	2,056	19.39
105	Murtaza Hussain	1995-96	Pakistan	1,882	17.92
104	S. F. Barnes	1913-14	South Africa	1,117	10.74
104	Sajjad Akbar	1989-90	Pakistan	2,328	22.38
103	Abdul Qadir	1982-83	Pakistan	2,367	22.98

LEADING BOWLERS IN AN ENGLISH SEASON

(Qualification: 10 wickets in 10 innings)

Season	Leading wicket-taker	Wkts	Avge	Top of averages	Wkts	Avge
1946	W. E. Hollies	184	15.60	A. Booth	111	11.61
1947	T. W. J. Goddard	238	17.30	J. C. Clay	65	16.44
1948	J. E. Walsh	174	19.56	J. C. Clay	41	14.17
1949	R. O. Jenkins	183	21.19	T. W. J. Goddard	160	19.18
1950	R. Tattersall	193	13.59	R. Tattersall	193	13.59
1951	R. Appleyard	200	14.14	R. Appleyard	200	14.14
1952	J. H. Wardle	177	19.54	F. S. Trueman	61	13.78
1953	B. Dooland	172	16.58	C. J. Knott	38	13.71
1954	B. Dooland	196	15.48	J. B. Statham	92	14.13
1955	G. A. R. Lock	216	14.49	R. Appleyard	85	13.01
1956	D. J. Shepherd	177	15.36	G. A. R. Lock	155	12.46
1957	G. A. R. Lock	212	12.02	G. A. R. Lock	212	12.02
1958	G. A. R. Lock	170	12.08	H. L. Jackson	143	10.99
1959	D. Shackleton	148	21.55	J. B. Statham	139	15.01
1960	F. S. Trueman	175	13.98	J. B. Statham	135	12.31
1961	J. A. Flavell	171	17.79	J. A. Flavell	171	17.79
1962	D. Shackleton	172	20.15	C. Cook	58	17.13
1963	D. Shackleton	146	16.75	C. C. Griffith	119	12.83
1964	D. Shackleton	142	20.40	J. A. Standen	64	13.00
1965	D. Shackleton	144	16.08	H. J. Rhodes	119	11.04
1966	D. L. Underwood	157	13.80	D. L. Underwood	157	13.80
1967	T. W. Cartwright	147	15.52	D. L. Underwood	136	12.39
1968	R. Illingworth	131	14.36	O. S. Wheatley	82	12.95
1969	R. M. H. Cottam	109	21.04	A. Ward	69	14.82
1970	D. J. Shepherd	106	19.16	Majid Khan	11	18.81
1971	L. R. Gibbs	131	18.89	G. G. Arnold	83	17.12
1972	T. W. Cartwright B. Stead	98 98	18.64 20.38	I. M. Chappell	10	10.60
1973	B. S. Bedi	105	17.94	T. W. Cartwright	89	15.84
1974	A. M. E. Roberts	119	13.62	A. M. E. Roberts	119	13.62
1975	P. G. Lee	112	18.45	A. M. E. Roberts	57	15.80
1976	G. A. Cope	93	24.13	M. A. Holding	55	14.38
1977	M. J. Procter	109	18.04	R. A. Woolmer	19	15.21
1978	D. L. Underwood	110	14.49	D. L. Underwood	110	14.49
1979	D. L. Underwood J. K. Lever	106 106	14.85 17.30	J. Garner	55	13.83
1980	R. D. Jackman	121	15.40	J. Garner	49	13.93
1981	R. J. Hadlee	105	14.89	R. J. Hadlee	105	14.89
1982	M. D. Marshall	134	15.73	R. J. Hadlee	61	14.57
1983	J. K. Lever D. L. Underwood	106 106	16.28 19.28	Imran Khan	12	7.16
1984	R. J. Hadlee	117	14.05	R. J. Hadlee	117	14.05

Season	Leading wicket-taker	Wkts	Avge	Top of averages	Wkts	Avge
1985	N. V. Radford	101	24.68	R. M. Ellison	65	17.20
1986	C. A. Walsh	118	18.17	M. D. Marshall	100	15.08
1987	N. V. Radford	109	20.81	R. J. Hadlee	97	12.64
1988	F. D. Stephenson	125	18.31	M. D. Marshall	42	13.16
1989	D. R. Pringle	94	18.64	T. M. Alderman	70	15.64
	S. L. Watkin	94	25.09			
1990	N. A. Foster	94	26.61	I. R. Bishop	59	19.05
1991	Waqar Younis	113	14.65	Waqar Younis	113	14.65
1992	C. A. Walsh	92	15.96	C. A. Walsh	92	15.96
1993	S. L. Watkin	92	22.80	Wasim Akram	59	19.27
1994	M. M. Patel	90	22.86	C. E. L. Ambrose	77	14.45
1995	A. Kumble	105	20.40	A. A. Donald	89	16.07
1996	C. A. Walsh	85	16.84	C. E. L. Ambrose	43	16.67
1997	A. M. Smith	83	17.63	A. A. Donald	60	15.63
1998	C. A. Walsh	106	17.31	V. J. Wells	36	14.27
1999	A. Sheriyar	92	24.70	Saqlain Mushtaq	58	11.37
2000	G. D. McGrath	80	13.21	C. A. Walsh	40	11.42
2001	R. J. Kirtley	75	23.32	G. D. McGrath	40	15.60
2002	M. J. Saggers	83	21.51	C. P. Schofield	18	18.38
	K. J. Dean	83	23.50			
2003	Mushtaq Ahmed	103	24.65	Shoaib Akhtar	34	17.05
2004	Mushtaq Ahmed	84	27.59	D. S. Lehmann	15	17.40
2005	S. K. Warne	87	22.50	M. Muralitharan	36	15.00
2006	Mushtaq Ahmed	102	19.91	Naved-ul-Hasan	35	16.71
2007	Mushtaq Ahmed	90	25.66	Harbhajan Singh	37	18.54
2008	J. A. Tomlinson	67	24.76	M. Davies	41	14.63
2009	Danish Kaneria	75	23.69	G. Onions	69	19.95
2010	A. R. Adams	68	22.17	J. K. H. Naik	35	17.68
2011	D. D. Masters	93	18.13	T. T. Bresnan	29	17.68
2012	G. Onions	72	14.73	G. Onions	72	14.73
2013	G. Onions	73	18.92	T. A. Copeland	45	18.26
2014	M. H. A. Footitt	84	19.19	G. R. Napier	52	15.63
2015	C. Rushworth	90	20.54	R. J. Sidebottom	43	18.09
2016	G. R. Napier	69	22.30	J. M. Anderson	45	17.00
	J. S. Patel	69	24.02			
2017	**J. A. Porter**	**85**	**16.74**	**J. L. Pattinson**	**32**	**12.06**

MOST WICKETS

Dates in italics denote the first half of an overseas season; i.e. *1970* denotes the 1970-71 season.

		Career	W	R	Avge
1	W. Rhodes	1898–1930	4,187	69,993	16.71
2	A. P. Freeman	1914–1936	3,776	69,577	18.42
3	C. W. L. Parker	1903–1935	3,278	63,817	19.46
4	J. T. Hearne	1888–1923	3,061	54,352	17.75
5	T. W. J. Goddard	1922–1952	2,979	59,116	19.84
6	W. G. Grace	1865–1908	2,876	51,545	17.92
7	A. S. Kennedy	1907–1936	2,874	61,034	21.23
8	D. Shackleton	1948–1969	2,857	53,303	18.65
9	G. A. R. Lock	1946–*1970*	2,844	54,709	19.23
10	F. J. Titmus	1949–1982	2,830	63,313	22.37
11	M. W. Tate	1912–1937	2,784	50,571	18.16
12	G. H. Hirst	1891–1929	2,739	51,282	18.72
13	C. Blythe	1899–1914	2,506	42,136	16.81

Some works of reference provide career figures which differ from those in this list, owing to the exclusion or inclusion of matches recognised or not recognised as first-class by Wisden. *A fuller list can be found in* Wisdens *up to 2011.*

Current Players with 750 Wickets

	Career	W	R	Avge
H. M. R. K. B. Herath	1996–2017	1,037	26,039	25.10
D. S. Hettiarachchi	1994–2016	930	21,704	23.33
J. M. Anderson	2002–2017	858	21,953	25.58
S. Weerakoon	1995–2017	811	17,738	21.87
Imran Tahir	1997–2017	784	20,881	26.63
Harbhajan Singh	1997–2017	780	22,652	29.04
R. J. Sidebottom	1997–2017	762	18,138	23.80

ALL-ROUND RECORDS

REMARKABLE ALL-ROUND MATCHES

V. E. Walker	20*	108	10-74	4-17	England v Surrey at The Oval	1859
W. G. Grace	104		2-60	10-49	MCC v Oxford University at Oxford	1886
G. Giffen	271		9-96	7-70	South Australia v Victoria at Adelaide	1891-92
B. J. T. Bosanquet	103	100*	3-75	8-53	Middlesex v Sussex at Lord's	1905
G. H. Hirst	111	117*	6-70	5-45	Yorkshire v Somerset at Bath	1906
F. D. Stephenson	111	117	4-105	7-117	Notts v Yorkshire at Nottingham	1988

E. M. Grace, for MCC v Gentlemen of Kent in a 12-a-side match at Canterbury in 1862, scored 192 and took 5-77 and 10-69.*

HUNDRED AND HAT-TRICK

G. Giffen, Australians v Lancashire at Manchester	1884
*W. E. Roller, Surrey v Sussex at The Oval	1885
W. B. Burns, Worcestershire v Gloucestershire at Worcester	1913
V. W. C. Jupp, Sussex v Essex at Colchester	1921
R. E. S. Wyatt, MCC v Ceylonese at Colombo (Victoria Park)	1926-27
L. N. Constantine, West Indians v Northamptonshire at Northampton	1928
D. E. Davies, Glamorgan v Leicestershire at Leicester	1937
V. M. Merchant, Dr C. R. Pereira's XI v Sir Homi Mehta's XI at Bombay	1946-47
M. J. Procter, Gloucestershire v Essex at Westcliff-on-Sea	1972
M. J. Procter, Gloucestershire v Leicestershire at Bristol	1979
†K. D. James, Hampshire v Indians at Southampton	1996
J. E. C. Franklin, Gloucestershire v Derbyshire at Cheltenham	2009
Sohag Gazi, Barisal v Khulna at Khulna	2012-13
Sohag Gazi, Bangladesh v New Zealand at Chittagong	2013-14
†Mahmudullah, Central Zone v North Zone at Savar	2013-14
†K. R. Smuts, Eastern Province v Boland at Paarl	2015-16

* *W. E. Roller is the only player to combine 200 with a hat-trick.*

† *K. D. James, Mahmudullah and K. R. Smuts all combined 100 with four wickets in four balls (Mahmudullah's split between two innings).*

THE DOUBLE

The double was traditionally regarded as 1,000 runs and 100 wickets in an English season. The feat became exceptionally rare after the reduction of County Championship matches in 1969.

Remarkable Seasons

	Season	R	W		Season	R	W
G. H. Hirst	1906	2,385	208	J. H. Parks	1937	3,003	101

1,000 Runs and 100 Wickets

W. Rhodes	16	W. G. Grace	8	F. J. Titmus	8
G. H. Hirst	14	M. S. Nichols	8	F. E. Woolley	7
V. W. C. Jupp	10	A. E. Relf	8	G. E. Tribe	7
W. E. Astill	9	F. A. Tarrant	8		
T. E. Bailey	8	M. W. Tate	8†		

† *M. W. Tate also scored 1,193 runs and took 116 wickets on the 1926-27 MCC tour of India and Ceylon.*

R. J. Hadlee (1984) and F. D. Stephenson (1988) are the only players to perform the feat since the reduction of County Championship matches in 1969. A complete list of those performing the feat before then may be found on page 202 of the 1982 Wisden. *T. E. Bailey (1959) was the last player to achieve 2,000 runs and 100 wickets in a season; M. W. Tate (1925) the last to reach 1,000 runs and 200 wickets. Full lists may be found in* Wisdens *up to 2003.*

Wicketkeeper's Double

The only wicketkeepers to achieve 1,000 runs and 100 dismissals in a season were L. E. G. Ames (1928, 1929 and 1932, when he scored 2,482 runs) and J. T. Murray (1957).

WICKETKEEPING RECORDS

MOST DISMISSALS IN AN INNINGS

9 (8ct, 1st)	Tahir Rashid	Habib Bank v PACO at Gujranwala	1992-93
9 (7ct, 2st)	W. R. James*	Matabeleland v Mashonaland CD at Bulawayo	1995-96
8 (all ct)	A. T. W. Grout	Queensland v Western Australia at Brisbane	1959-60
8 (all ct)†	D. E. East	Essex v Somerset at Taunton	1985
8 (all ct)	S. A. Marsh‡	Kent v Middlesex at Lord's	1991
8 (6ct, 2st)	T. J. Zoehrer	Australians v Surrey at The Oval	1993
8 (7ct, 1st)	D. S. Berry	Victoria v South Australia at Melbourne	1996-97
8 (7ct, 1st)	Y. S. S. Mendis	Bloomfield v Kurunegala Y at Colombo (Bloomfield)	2000-01
8 (7ct, 1st)	S. Nath§	Assam v Tripura at Guwahati	2001-02
8 (all ct)	J. N. Batty¶	Surrey v Kent at The Oval	2004
8 (all ct)	Golam Mabud	Sylhet v Dhaka at Dhaka	2005-06
8 (all ct)	A. Z. M. Dyili	Eastern Province v Free State at Port Elizabeth	2009-10
8 (all ct)	D. C. de Boorder	Otago v Wellington at Wellington	2009-10
8 (all ct)	R. S. Second	Free State v North West at Bloemfontein	2011-12
8 (all ct)	T. L. Tsolekile	South Africa A v Sri Lanka A at Durban	2012

There have been **107** *further instances of seven dismissals in an innings. R. W. Taylor achieved the feat three times, and G. J. Hopkins, Kamran Akmal, I. Khaleel, S. A. Marsh, K. J. Piper, Shahin Hossain, T. L. Tsolekile and Wasim Bari twice. Khaleel did it twice in the same match. Marsh's and Tsolekile's two instances both included one of eight dismssals – see above. H. Yarnold made six stumpings and one catch in an innings for Worcestershire v Scotland at Dundee in 1951. A fuller list can be found in* Wisdens *before 2004.*

* *W. R. James also scored 99 and 99 not out.*
† *The first eight wickets to fall.*
‡ *S. A. Marsh also scored 108 not out.*
§ *On his only first-class appearance.*
¶ *J. N. Batty also scored 129.*

WICKETKEEPERS' HAT-TRICKS

W. H. Brain, Gloucestershire v Somerset at Cheltenham, 1893 – three stumpings off successive balls from C. L. Townsend.

G. O. Dawkes, Derbyshire v Worcestershire at Kidderminster, 1958 – three catches off successive balls from H. L. Jackson.

R. C. Russell, Gloucestershire v Surrey at The Oval, 1986 – three catches off successive balls from C. A. Walsh and D. V. Lawrence (2).

MOST DISMISSALS IN A MATCH

14 (11ct, 3st)	I. Khaleel	Hyderabad v Assam at Guwahati	2011-12
13 (11ct, 2st)	W. R. James*	Matabeleland v Mashonaland CD at Bulawayo	1995-96
12 (8ct, 4st)	E. Pooley	Surrey v Sussex at The Oval	1868
12 (9ct, 3st)	D. Tallon	Queensland v New South Wales at Sydney	1938-39
12 (9ct, 3st)	H. B. Taber	New South Wales v South Australia at Adelaide	1968-69
12 (all ct)	P. D. McGlashan	Northern Districts v Central Districts at Whangarei	2009-10
12 (11ct, 1st)	T. L. Tsolekile	Lions v Dolphins at Johannesburg	2010-11
12 (all ct)	Kashif Mahmood	Lahore Shalimar v Abbottabad at Abbottabad	2010-11
12 (all ct)	R. S. Second	Free State v North West at Bloemfontein	2011-12

* *W. R. James also scored 99 and 99 not out.*

100 DISMISSALS IN A SEASON

128 (79ct, 49st)	L. E. G. Ames	1929
122 (70ct, 52st)	L. E. G. Ames	1928
110 (63ct, 47st)	H. Yarnold	1949
107 (77ct, 30st)	G. Duckworth	1928
107 (96ct, 11st)	J. G. Binks	1960
104 (40ct, 64st)	L. E. G. Ames	1932
104 (82ct, 22st)	J. T. Murray	1957
102 (69ct, 33st)	F. H. Huish	1913
102 (95ct, 7st)	J. T. Murray	1960
101 (62ct, 39st)	F. H. Huish	1911
101 (85ct, 16st)	R. Booth	1960
100 (91ct, 9st)	R. Booth	1964

L. E. G. Ames achieved the two highest stumping totals in a season: 64 in 1932, and 52 in 1928.

MOST DISMISSALS

Dates in italics denote the first half of an overseas season; i.e. *1914* denotes the 1914-15 season.

			Career	*M*	*Ct*	*St*
1	R. W. Taylor	1,649	1960–1988	639	1,473	176
2	J. T. Murray	1,527	1952–1975	635	1,270	257
3	H. Strudwick	1,497	1902–1927	675	1,242	255
4	A. P. E. Knott	1,344	1964–1985	511	1,211	133
5	R. C. Russell	1,320	1981–2004	465	1,192	128
6	F. H. Huish	1,310	1895–1914	497	933	377
7	B. Taylor	1,294	1949–1973	572	1,083	211
8	S. J. Rhodes	1,263	1981–2004	440	1,139	124
9	D. Hunter	1,253	1888–1909	548	906	347

Current Players with 500 Dismissals

		Career	*M*	*Ct*	*St*
1,104	C. M. W. Read	*1997*–2017	349	1,051	53
883	J. S. Foster	2000–2017	283	823	60
872	Kamran Akmal	*1997–2017*	227	808	64
689	P. Mustard	2002–2017	210	670	19
621	T. R. Ambrose	2001–2017	224	581	40
592	Zulfiqar Jan	*1999–2017*	162	563	29
564	C. D. Hartley	*2003–2016*	131	547	17
530	N. J. O'Brien	2004–2017	171	482	48
518	P. A. Patel	*2001–2017*	179	445	73
516	Adnan Akmal	*2003–2017*	151	485	31

Some of these figures include catches taken in the field.

FIELDING RECORDS
excluding wicketkeepers

MOST CATCHES IN AN INNINGS

7	M. J. Stewart	Surrey v Northamptonshire at Northampton	1957
7	A. S. Brown	Gloucestershire v Nottinghamshire at Nottingham	1966
7	R. Clarke	Warwickshire v Lancashire at Liverpool	2011

MOST CATCHES IN A MATCH

10	W. R. Hammond†	Gloucestershire v Surrey at Cheltenham	1928
9	R. Clarke	Warwickshire v Lancashire at Liverpool	2011
8	W. B. Burns	Worcestershire v Yorkshire at Bradford	1907
8	F. G. Travers	Europeans v Parsees at Bombay	1923-24
8	A. H. Bakewell	Northamptonshire v Essex at Leyton	1928
8	W. R. Hammond	Gloucestershire v Worcestershire at Cheltenham	1932
8	K. J. Grieves	Lancashire v Sussex at Manchester	1951
8	C. A. Milton	Gloucestershire v Sussex at Hove	1952
8	G. A. R. Lock	Surrey v Warwickshire at The Oval	1957
8	J. M. Prodger	Kent v Gloucestershire at Cheltenham	1961
8	P. M. Walker	Glamorgan v Derbyshire at Swansea	1970
8	Masood Anwar	Rawalpindi v Lahore Division at Rawalpindi	1983-84
8	M. C. J. Ball	Gloucestershire v Yorkshire at Cheltenham	1994
8	J. D. Carr	Middlesex v Warwickshire at Birmingham	1995
8	G. A. Hick	Worcestershire v Essex at Chelmsford	2005
8	Naved Yasin	State Bank v Bahawalpur Stags at Bahawalpur	2014-15
8	A. M. Rahane	India v Sri Lanka at Galle	2015-16

† *Hammond also scored a hundred in each innings.*

MOST CATCHES IN A SEASON

78	W. R. Hammond	1928
77	M. J. Stewart	1957
73	P. M. Walker	1961
71	P. J. Sharpe	1962
70	J. Tunnicliffe	1901

The most catches by a fielder since the reduction of County Championship matches in 1969 is 59 by G. R. J. Roope in 1971.

MOST CATCHES

Dates in italics denote the first half of an overseas season; i.e. *1970* denotes the 1970-71 season.

		Career	*M*
1,018	F. E. Woolley	1906–1938	979
887	W. G. Grace	1865–1908	879
830	G. A. R. Lock	1946–*1970*	654
819	W. R. Hammond	1920–1951	634
813	D. B. Close	1949–1986	786
784	J. G. Langridge	1928–1955	574
764	W. Rhodes	1898–1930	1,107
758	C. A. Milton	1948–1974	620
754	E. H. Hendren	1907–1938	833

The most catches by a current player is ***534*** *by* ***M. E. Trescothick*** *between 1993 and 2017 (including two taken while deputising as wicketkeeper).*

TEAM RECORDS

HIGHEST INNINGS TOTALS

1,107	Victoria v New South Wales at Melbourne	1926-27
1,059	Victoria v Tasmania at Melbourne	1922-23
952-6 dec	Sri Lanka v India at Colombo (RPS)	1997-98
951-7 dec	Sind v Baluchistan at Karachi	1973-74
944-6 dec	Hyderabad v Andhra at Secunderabad	1993-94
918	New South Wales v South Australia at Sydney	1900-01
912-8 dec	Holkar v Mysore at Indore	1945-46
912-6 dec†	Tamil Nadu v Goa at Panjim	1988-89
910-6 dec	Railways v Dera Ismail Khan at Lahore	1964-65
903-7 dec	England v Australia at The Oval	1938
900-6 dec	Queensland v Victoria at Brisbane	2005-06

† *Tamil Nadu's total of 912-6 dec included 52 penalty runs from their opponents' failure to meet the required bowling rate.*

The highest total in a team's second innings is 770 by New South Wales v South Australia at Adelaide in 1920-21.

HIGHEST FOURTH-INNINGS TOTALS

654-5	England v South Africa at Durban *After being set 696 to win. The match was left drawn on the tenth day.*	1938-39
604	Maharashtra (*set 959 to win*) v Bombay at Poona	1948-49
576-8	Trinidad (*set 672 to win*) v Barbados at Port-of-Spain	1945-46
572	New South Wales (*set 593 to win*) v South Australia at Sydney	1907-08
541-7	West Zone (*won*) v South Zone at Hyderabad	2009-10
529-9	Combined XI (*set 579 to win*) v South Africans at Perth	1963-64
518	Victoria (*set 753 to win*) v Queensland at Brisbane	1926-27
513-9	Central Province (*won*) v Southern Province at Kandy	2003-04
507-7	Cambridge University (*won*) v MCC and Ground at Lord's	1896
506-6	South Australia (*won*) v Queensland at Adelaide	1991-92
503-4	South Zone (*won*) v England A at Gurgaon	2003-04
502-6	Middlesex (*won*) v Nottinghamshire at Nottingham	1925
502-8	Players (*won*) v Gentlemen at Lord's	1900
500-7	South African Universities (*won*) v Western Province at Stellenbosch	1978-79

MOST RUNS IN A DAY (ONE SIDE)

721	Australians (721) v Essex at Southend (1st day)	1948
651	West Indians (651-2) v Leicestershire at Leicester (1st day)	1950
649	New South Wales (649-7) v Otago at Dunedin (2nd day)	1923-24
645	Surrey (645-4) v Hampshire at The Oval (1st day)	1909
644	Oxford U. (644-8) v H. D. G. Leveson Gower's XI at Eastbourne (1st day)	1921
640	Lancashire (640-8) v Sussex at Hove (1st day)	1937
636	Free Foresters (636-7) v Cambridge U. at Cambridge (1st day)	1938
625	Gloucestershire (625-6) v Worcestershire at Dudley (2nd day)	1934

MOST RUNS IN A DAY (BOTH SIDES)

(excluding the above)

685	North (169-8 and 255-7), South (261-8 dec) at Blackpool (2nd day)	1961
666	Surrey (607-4), Northamptonshire (59-2) at Northampton (2nd day)	1920
665	Rest of South Africa (339), Transvaal (326) at Johannesburg (1st day)	1911-12
663	Middlesex (503-4), Leicestershire (160-2) at Leicester (2nd day)	1947
661	Border (201), Griqualand West (460) at Kimberley (1st day)	1920-21
649	Hampshire (570-8), Somerset (79-3) at Taunton (2nd day)	1901

HIGHEST AGGREGATES IN A MATCH

Runs	Wkts		
2,376	37	Maharashtra v Bombay at Poona	1948-49
2,078	40	Bombay v Holkar at Bombay	1944-45
1,981	35	South Africa v England at Durban	1938-39
1,945	18	Canterbury v Wellington at Christchurch	1994-95
1,929	39	New South Wales v South Australia at Sydney	1925-26
1,911	34	New South Wales v Victoria at Sydney	1908-09
1,905	40	Otago v Wellington at Dunedin	1923-24

In Britain

Runs	Wkts		
1,815	28	Somerset v Surrey at Taunton	2002
1,808	20	Sussex v Essex at Hove	1993
1,795	34	Somerset v Northamptonshire at Taunton	2001
1,723	31	England v Australia at Leeds	1948
1,706	23	Hampshire v Warwickshire at Southampton	1997

LOWEST INNINGS TOTALS

12†	Oxford University v MCC and Ground at Oxford	1877
12	Northamptonshire v Gloucestershire at Gloucester	1907
13	Auckland v Canterbury at Auckland	1877-78
13	Nottinghamshire v Yorkshire at Nottingham	1901
14	Surrey v Essex at Chelmsford	1983
15	MCC v Surrey at Lord's	1839
15†	Victoria v MCC at Melbourne	1903-04
15†	Northamptonshire v Yorkshire at Northampton	1908
15	Hampshire v Warwickshire at Birmingham *Following on, Hampshire scored 521 and won by 155 runs.*	1922
16	MCC and Ground v Surrey at Lord's	1872
16	Derbyshire v Nottinghamshire at Nottingham	1879
16	Surrey v Nottinghamshire at The Oval	1880
16	Warwickshire v Kent at Tonbridge	1913
16	Trinidad v Barbados at Bridgetown	1942-43
16	Border v Natal at East London (first innings)	1959-60
17	Gentlemen of Kent v Gentlemen of England at Lord's	1850
17	Gloucestershire v Australians at Cheltenham	1896
18	The Bs v England at Lord's	1831
18†	Kent v Sussex at Gravesend	1867
18	Tasmania v Victoria at Melbourne	1868-69
18†	Australians v MCC and Ground at Lord's	1896
18	Border v Natal at East London (second innings)	1959-60
18†	Durham MCCU v Durham at Chester-le-Street	2012

† *One man absent.*

At Lord's in 1810, The Bs, with one man absent, were dismissed by England for 6.

LOWEST TOTALS IN A MATCH

34	(16 and 18) Border v Natal at East London	1959-60
42	(27† and 15†) Northamptonshire v Yorkshire at Northampton	1908

† *Northamptonshire batted one man short in each innings.*

LOWEST AGGREGATE IN A COMPLETED MATCH

Runs	*Wkts*		
85	11†	Quetta v Rawalpindi at Islamabad	2008-09
105	31	MCC v Australians at Lord's	1878

† *Both teams forfeited their first innings.*

The lowest aggregate in a match in which the losing team was bowled out twice since 1900 is 157 for 22 wickets, Surrey v Worcestershire at The Oval, 1954.

LARGEST VICTORIES

Largest Innings Victories

Inns and 851 runs	Railways (910-6 dec) v Dera Ismail Khan at Lahore	1964-65
Inns and 666 runs	Victoria (1,059) v Tasmania at Melbourne	1922-23
Inns and 656 runs	Victoria (1,107) v New South Wales at Melbourne	1926-27
Inns and 605 runs	New South Wales (918) v South Australia at Sydney	1900-01
Inns and 579 runs	England (903-7 dec) v Australia at The Oval	1938
Inns and 575 runs	Sind (951-7 dec) v Baluchistan at Karachi	1973-74
Inns and 527 runs	New South Wales (713) v South Australia at Adelaide	1908-09
Inns and 517 runs	Australians (675) v Nottinghamshire at Nottingham	1921

Largest Victories by Runs Margin

685 runs	New South Wales (235 and 761-8 dec) v Queensland at Sydney	1929-30
675 runs	England (521 and 342-8 dec) v Australia at Brisbane	1928-29
638 runs	New South Wales (304 and 770) v South Australia at Adelaide	1920-21
609 runs	Muslim Comm. Bank (575 and 282-0 dec) v WAPDA at Lahore	1977-78

Victory Without Losing a Wicket

Lancashire (166-0 dec and 66-0) beat Leicestershire by ten wickets at Manchester	1956
Karachi A (277-0 dec) beat Sind A by an innings and 77 runs at Karachi	1957-58
Railways (236-0 dec and 16-0) beat Jammu & Kashmir by ten wickets at Srinagar	1960-61
Karnataka (451-0 dec) beat Kerala by an innings and 186 runs at Chikmagalur	1977-78

*There have been **30** wins by an innings and 400 runs or more, the most recent being an innings and 413 runs by Dhaka v Barisal at Mirpur in 2014-15.*

*There have been **23** wins by 500 runs or more, the most recent being 523 runs by Essex v Cambridge MCCU and 517 runs by Nottinghamshire v Cambridge MCCU, both at Cambridge in 2016 in consecutive matches.*

*There have been **33** wins by a team losing only one wicket, the most recent being by KwaZulu-Natal Inland v Namibia at Pietermaritzburg in 2015-16.*

TIED MATCHES

Since 1948, a tie has been recognised only when the scores are level with all the wickets down in the fourth innings. There have been **38** instances since then, including two Tests (see Test record section); Sussex have featured in five of those, Essex and Kent in four each.

The most recent instances are:

Habib Bank v WAPDA at Lahore	2011-12
Border v Boland at East London	2012-13
Police v Kalutara PCC at Colombo (BRC)	**2016-17**
Guyana v Windward Islands at Providence	**2017-18**
Chilaw Marians v Burgher at Katunayake	**2017-18**
Negombo v Kalutara Town at Gampaha	**2017-18**

MATCHES COMPLETED ON FIRST DAY

(Since 1946)

Derbyshire v Somerset at Chesterfield, June 11	1947
Lancashire v Sussex at Manchester, July 12	1950
Surrey v Warwickshire at The Oval, May 16	1953
Somerset v Lancashire at Bath, June 6 (H. F. T. Buse's benefit)	1953
Kent v Worcestershire at Tunbridge Wells, June 15	1960
Griqualand West v Easterns at Kimberley, March 10	2010-11

SHORTEST COMPLETED MATCHES

Balls		
121	Quetta (forfeit and 41) v Rawalpindi (forfeit and 44-1) at Islamabad	2008-09
350	Somerset (35 and 44) v Middlesex (86) at Lord's	1899
352	Victoria (82 and 57) v Tasmania (104 and 37-7) at Launceston	1850-51
372	Victoria (80 and 50) v Tasmania (97 and 35-2) at Launceston	1853-54

LIST A ONE-DAY RECORDS

List A is a concept intended to provide an approximate equivalent in one-day cricket of first-class status. It was introduced by the Association of Cricket Statisticians and Historians and is now recognised by the ICC, with a separate category for Twenty20 cricket. Further details are available at stats.acscricket.com/ListA/Description.html. List A games comprise:

(a) One-day internationals.
(b) Other international matches (e.g. A-team internationals).
(c) Premier domestic one-day tournaments in Test-playing countries.
(d) Official tourist matches against the main first-class teams (e.g. counties, states and Board XIs).

The following matches are excluded:

(a) Matches originally scheduled as less than 40 overs per side (e.g. Twenty20 games).
(b) World Cup warm-up games.
(c) Tourist matches against teams outside the major domestic competitions (e.g. universities).
(d) Festival games and pre-season friendlies.

This section covers one-day cricket to December 31, 2017. Bold type denotes performances in the calendar year 2017 or, in career figures, players who appeared in List A cricket in that year.

BATTING RECORDS

HIGHEST INDIVIDUAL INNINGS

268	A. D. Brown	Surrey v Glamorgan at The Oval	2002
264	R. G. Sharma	India v Sri Lanka at Kolkata	2014-15
248	S. Dhawan	India A v South Africa A at Pretoria	2013
237*	M. J. Guptill	New Zealand v West Indies at Wellington	2014-15
229*	B. R. Dunk	Tasmania v Queensland at Sydney	2014-15
222*	R. G. Pollock	Eastern Province v Border at East London	1974-75
222	J. M. How	Central Districts v Northern Districts at Hamilton	2012-13
220*	B. M. Duckett	England Lions v Sri Lanka A at Canterbury	2016
219	V. Sehwag	India v West Indies at Indore	2011-12
215	C. H. Gayle	West Indies v Zimbabwe at Canberra	2014-15
209	R. G. Sharma	India v Australia at Bangalore	2013-14
208*	**R. G. Sharma**	**India v Sri Lanka at Mohali**	**2017-18**
207	Mohammad Ali	Pakistan Customs v DHA at Sialkot	2004-05
206	A. I. Kallicharran	Warwickshire v Oxfordshire at Birmingham	1984
204*	Khalid Latif	Karachi Dolphins v Quetta Bears at Karachi	2008-09
203	A. D. Brown	Surrey v Hampshire at Guildford	1997
202*	A. Barrow	Natal v SA African XI at Durban	1975-76
202*	P. J. Hughes	Australia A v South Africa A at Darwin	2014
202	T. M. Head	South Australia v Western Australia at Sydney	2015-16
201*	R. S. Bopara	Essex v Leicestershire at Leicester	2008
201	V. J. Wells	Leicestershire v Berkshire at Leicester	1996
200*	S. R. Tendulkar	India v South Africa at Gwalior	2009-10

MOST RUNS

	Career	*M*	*I*	*NO*	*R*	*HS*	*100*	*Avge*
G. A. Gooch	1973–1997	614	601	48	22,211	198*	44	40.16
G. A. Hick	*1983*–2008	651	630	96	22,059	172*	40	41.30
S. R. Tendulkar	*1989–2011*	551	538	55	21,999	200*	60	45.54
K. C. Sangakkara	***1997–2017***	**528**	**500**	**54**	**19,453**	**169**	**39**	**43.61**
I. V. A. Richards	1973–1993	500	466	61	16,995	189*	26	41.96
R. T. Ponting	*1992*–2013	456	445	53	16,363	164	34	41.74
C. G. Greenidge	1970–1992	440	436	33	16,349	186*	33	40.56
S. T. Jayasuriya	*1989–2011*	557	542	25	16,128	189	31	31.19
A. J. Lamb	1972–1995	484	463	63	15,658	132*	19	39.14
D. L. Haynes	1976–1996	419	416	44	15,651	152*	28	42.07

	Career	M	I	NO	R	HS	100	Avge
S. C. Ganguly	*1989–2011*	437	421	43	15,622	183	31	41.32
K. J. Barnett............	1979–2005	527	500	54	15,564	136	17	34.89
D. P. M. D. Jayawardene..	*1995*–2016	546	509	51	15,364	163*	21	33.54
R. Dravid..............	*1992*–2011	449	416	55	15,271	153	21	42.30
M. G. Bevan	*1989–2006*	427	385	124	15,103	157*	13	57.86

HIGHEST PARTNERSHIP FOR EACH WICKET

367*	for 1st	M. N. van Wyk/C. S. Delport, Dolphins v Knights at Bloemfontein	2014-15
372	for 2nd	C. H. Gayle/M. N. Samuels, West Indies v Zimbabwe at Canberra.....	2014-15
309*	for 3rd	T. S. Curtis/T. M. Moody, Worcestershire v Surrey at The Oval.......	1994
276	for 4th	Mominul Haque/A. R. S. Silva, Prime Doleshwar v Abahani at Bogra ..	2013-14
267*	for 5th	Minhazul Abedin/Khaled Mahmud, Bangladeshis v Bahawalpur at Karachi	1997-98
267*	for 6th	G. D. Elliott/L. Ronchi, New Zealand v Sri Lanka at Dunedin.........	2014-15
203*	for 7th	S. H. T. Kandamby/H. M. R. K. B. Herath, Sri Lanka A v South Africa A at Benoni	2008-09
203	for 8th	Shahid Iqbal/Haaris Ayaz, Karachi Whites v Hyderabad at Karachi	1998-99
155	for 9th	C. M. W. Read/A. J. Harris, Notts v Durham at Nottingham	2006
128	for 10th	A. Ashish Reddy/M. Ravi Kiran, Hyderabad v Kerala at Secunderabad .	2014-15

BOWLING RECORDS

BEST BOWLING ANALYSES

8-15	R. L. Sanghvi	Delhi v Himachal Pradesh at Una	1997-98
8-19	W. P. U. J. C. Vaas	Sri Lanka v Zimbabwe at Colombo (SSC).............	2001-02
8-20*	D. T. Kottehewa	Nondescripts v Ragama at Colombo (Moors)	2007-08
8-21	M. A. Holding	Derbyshire v Sussex at Hove.......................	1988
8-26	K. D. Boyce	Essex v Lancashire at Manchester..................	1971
8-30	G. D. R. Eranga	Burgher v Army at Colombo (Colts)................	2007-08
8-31	D. L. Underwood	Kent v Scotland at Edinburgh	1987
8-43	S. W. Tait	South Australia v Tasmania at Adelaide	2003-04
8-52	K. A. Stoute	West Indies A v Lancashire at Manchester	2010
8-66	S. R. G. Francis	Somerset v Derbyshire at Derby	2004

* *Including two hat-tricks.*

MOST WICKETS

	Career	M	B	R	W	BB	4I	Avge
Wasim Akram.......	*1984*–2003	594	29,719	19,303	881	5-10	46	21.91
A. A. Donald........	*1985–2003*	458	22,856	14,942	684	6-15	38	21.84
M. Muralitharan	*1991–2010*	453	23,734	15,270	682	7-30	29	22.39
Waqar Younis.......	*1988–2003*	412	19,841	15,098	675	7-36	44	22.36
J. K. Lever	1968–1990	481	23,208	13,278	674	5-8	34	19.70
J. E. Emburey	1975–2000	536	26,399	16,811	647	5-23	26	25.98
I. T. Botham	1973–1993	470	22,899	15,264	612	5-27	18	24.94

WICKETKEEPING AND FIELDING RECORDS

MOST DISMISSALS IN AN INNINGS

8	(all ct)	D. J. S. Taylor	Somerset v Combined Universities at Taunton ...	1982
8	(5ct, 3st)	S. J. Palframan	Boland v Easterns at Paarl	1997-98
8	(all ct)	D. J. Pipe	Worcestershire v Hertfordshire at Hertford	2001
8	**(6ct, 2st)**	**P. M. Nevill**	**New South Wales v Cricket Aus XI at Sydney..**	**2017-18**
7	(6ct, 1st)	R. W. Taylor	Derbyshire v Lancashire at Manchester.........	1975
7	(4ct, 3st)	Rizwan Umar	Sargodha v Bahawalpur at Sargodha	1991-92

7	(all ct)	A. J. Stewart	Surrey v Glamorgan at Swansea	1994
7	(all ct)	I. Mitchell	Border v Western Province at East London	1998-99
7	(6ct, 1st)	M. K. P. B. Kularatne	Galle v Colts at Colombo (Colts)	2001-02
7	(5ct, 2st)	T. R. Ambrose	Warwickshire v Middlesex at Birmingham	2009
7	(3ct, 4st)	W. A. S. Niroshan	Chilaw Marians v Saracens at Katunayake	2009-10
7	(all ct)	M. Rawat	Railways v Madhya Pradesh at Nagpur	2011-12
7	(all ct)	H. C. Madushan	Badureliya v Colombo at Colombo (CCC)	2013-14
7	(6ct, 1st)	P. A. Patel	West Zone v Central Zone at Visakhapatnam	2013-14
7	(all ct)	D. J. Vilas	Cape Cobras v Knights at Kimberley	2014-15
7	**(5ct, 2st)**	**S. D. Hope**	**Barbados v Leeward Islands at Coolidge**	**2016-17**

MOST CATCHES IN AN INNINGS IN THE FIELD

5	V. J. Marks	Combined Universities v Kent at Oxford	1976
5	J. M. Rice	Hampshire v Warwickshire at Southampton	1978
5	A. J. Kourie	Transvaal v Western Province at Johannesburg	1979-80
5	J. N. Rhodes	South Africa v West Indies at Bombay	1993-94
5	J. W. Wilson	Otago v Auckland at Dunedin	1993-94
5	K. C. Jackson	Boland v Natal at Durban	1995-96
5	Mohammad Ramzan	PNSC v PIA at Karachi	1998-99
5	Amit Sharma	Punjab v Jammu & Kashmir at Ludhiana	1999-2000
5	B. E. Young	South Australia v Tasmania at Launceston	2001-02
5	Hasnain Raza	Bahawalpur v Pakistan Customs at Karachi	2002-03
5	D. J. Sales	Northamptonshire v Essex at Northampton	2007
5	L. N. Mosena	Free State v North West at Bloemfontein	2007-08
5	A. R. McBrine	Ireland v Sri Lanka A at Belfast	2014

TEAM RECORDS

HIGHEST INNINGS TOTALS

496-4	(50 overs)	Surrey v Gloucestershire at The Oval	2007
445-8	(50 overs)	Nottinghamshire v Northamptonshire at Nottingham	2016
444-3	(50 overs)	England v Pakistan at Nottingham	2016
443-9	(50 overs)	Sri Lanka v Netherlands at Amstelveen	2006
439-2	(50 overs)	South Africa v West Indies at Johannesburg	2014-15
438-4	(50 overs)	South Africa v India at Mumbai	2014-15
438-5	(50 overs)	Surrey v Glamorgan at The Oval	2002
438-9	(49.5 overs)	South Africa v Australia at Johannesburg	2005-06
434-4	(50 overs)	Australia v South Africa at Johannesburg	2005-06
434-4	**(50 overs)**	**Jamaica v Trinidad & Tobago at Coolidge**	**2016-17**
433-3	(50 overs)	India A v South Africa A at Pretoria	2013
429-9	**(50 overs)**	**Nottinghamshire v Somerset at Nottingham**	**2017**
429	(49.5 overs)	Glamorgan v Surrey at The Oval	2002

LOWEST INNINGS TOTALS

18	(14.3 overs)	West Indies Under-19 v Barbados at Blairmont	2007-08
19	(10.5 overs)	Saracens v Colts at Colombo (Colts)	2012-13
23	(19.4 overs)	Middlesex v Yorkshire at Leeds	1974
30	(20.4 overs)	Chittagong v Sylhet at Dhaka	2002-03
31	(13.5 overs)	Border v South Western Districts at East London	2007-08
34	(21.1 overs)	Saurashtra v Mumbai at Mumbai	1999-2000
35	(18 overs)	Zimbabwe v Sri Lanka at Harare	2003-04
35	(20.2 overs)	Cricket Coaching School v Abahani at Fatullah	2013-14
35	(15.3 overs)	Rajasthan v Railways at Nagpur	2014-15
36	(25.4 overs)	Leicestershire v Sussex at Leicester	1973
36	(18.4 overs)	Canada v Sri Lanka at Paarl	2002-03

LIST A TWENTY20 RECORDS

This section covers Twenty20 cricket to December 31, 2017. Bold type denotes performances in the calendar year 2017 or, in career figures, players who appeared in Twenty20 cricket in that year.

BATTING RECORDS

HIGHEST INDIVIDUAL INNINGS

175*	C. H. Gayle	RC Bangalore v Pune Warriors at Bangalore	2012-13
162*	H. Masakadza	Mountaineers v Mashonaland Eagles at Bulawayo	2015-16
161	**A. Lyth**	**Yorkshire v Northamptonshire at Leeds**	**2017**
158*	B. B. McCullum	Kolkata Knight Riders v RC Bangalore at Bangalore	2007-08
158*	B. B. McCullum	Warwickshire v Derbyshire at Birmingham	2015
156	A. J. Finch	Australia v England at Southampton	2013
153*	L. J. Wright	Sussex v Essex at Chelmsford	2014
152*	G. R. Napier	Essex v Sussex at Chelmsford	2008
151*	C. H. Gayle	Somerset v Kent at Taunton	2015
150*	**Kamran Akmal**	**Lahore Whites v Islamabad at Rawalpindi**	**2017-18**

MOST RUNS

	Career	*M*	*I*	*NO*	*R*	*HS*	*100*	*Avge*	*SR*
C. H. Gayle	**2005–*2017***	**321**	**315**	**44**	**11,068**	**175***	**20**	**40.84**	**149.02**
B. B. McCullum	***2004–2017***	**313**	**308**	**31**	**8,591**	**158***	**7**	**31.01**	**138.51**
K. A. Pollard	**2006–*2017***	**399**	**359**	**100**	**7,817**	**89***	**0**	**30.18**	**151.40**
D. A. Warner	***2006–2017***	**238**	**237**	**25**	**7,572**	**135***	**6**	**35.71**	**143.35**
Shoaib Malik	***2004–2017***	**293**	**276**	**75**	**7,450**	**95***	**0**	**37.06**	**123.75**
B. J. Hodge	**2003–*2017***	**273**	**259**	**59**	**7,371**	**106**	**2**	**36.85**	**131.20**
D. R. Smith	***2005–2017***	**308**	**301**	**25**	**7,351**	**110***	**5**	**26.63**	**127.97**
V. Kohli	***2006–2017***	**226**	**213**	**40**	**7,068**	**113**	**4**	**40.85**	**133.28**
S. K. Raina	***2006–2017***	**259**	**245**	**40**	**6,872**	**109***	**3**	**33.52**	**139.22**
R. G. Sharma	***2006–2017***	**262**	**250**	**41**	**6,825**	**118**	**4**	**32.65**	**132.44**
L. J. Wright	**2004–*2017***	**284**	**264**	**26**	**6,706**	**153***	**7**	**28.17**	**144.27**
K. C. Sangakkara	***2004–2017***	**254**	**248**	**22**	**6,581**	**94**	**0**	**29.11**	**126.48**

HIGHEST PARTNERSHIP FOR EACH WICKET

209*	**for 1st**	**Kamran Akmal/Salman Butt, Lahore Wh. v Islamabad at Rawalpindi**	**2017-18**
229	for 2nd	V. Kohli/A. B. de Villiers, RC Bangalore v Gujarat Lions at Bangalore	2015-16
162	for 3rd	Abdul Razzaq/Nasir Jamshed, Lahore Lions v Quetta Bears at Lahore	2009
202*	for 4th	M. C. Juneja/A. Malik, Gujarat v Kerala at Indore	2012-13
150	for 5th	H. M. Amla/D. J. Bravo, Trinbago NR v Barb. Tridents at Port-of-Spain	2016
126*	for 6th	C. S. MacLeod/J. W. Hastings, Durham v Northants at Chester-le-Street	2014
107*	for 7th	L. Abeyratne/P. S. R. Anurudhda, Colombo v Chilaw Marians at Colombo	2015-16
120	for 8th	Azhar Mahmood/I. Udana, Wayamba v Uva at Colombo (RPS)	2012
69	**for 9th**	**C. J. Anderson/J. H. Davey, Somerset v Surrey at The Oval**	**2017**
63	for 10th	G. D. Elliott/Zulfiqar Babar, Quetta Glad. v Peshawar Zalmi at Sharjah	2015-16

BOWLING RECORDS

BEST BOWLING ANALYSES

6-5	A. V. Suppiah	Somerset v Glamorgan at Cardiff	2011
6-6	Shakib Al Hasan	Barbados v Trinidad & Tobago at Bridgetown	2013
6-7	S. L. Malinga	Melbourne Stars v Perth Scorchers at Perth	2012-13
6-8	B. A. W. Mendis	Sri Lanka v Zimbabwe at Hambantota	2012-13
6-9	P. Fojela	Border v Easterns at East London	2014-15

6-11	**I. S. Sodhi**	**Adelaide Strikers v Sydney Thunder at Sydney**	**2016-17**
6-14	Sohail Tanvir	Rajasthan Royals v Chennai Superstars at Jaipur	2007-08
6-14	D. Punia	Services v Haryana at Delhi	2014-15
6-15	S. R. Abeywardene	Panadura v Air Force at Colombo (BRC)	2005-06

MOST WICKETS

	Career	*M*	*B*	*R*	*W*	*BB*	*4I*	*Avge*	*ER*
D. J. Bravo	***2005–2017***	**367**	**7,014**	**9,468**	**403**	**5-23**	**11**	**23.49**	**8.09**
S. L. Malinga	***2004–2017***	**247**	**5,434**	**6,239**	**330**	**6-7**	**12**	**18.90**	**6.88**
S. P. Narine	***2010–2017***	**262**	**5,991**	**5,809**	**307**	**5-19**	**11**	**18.92**	**5.81**
Shakib Al Hasan	***2006–2017***	**252**	**5,288**	**5,967**	**292**	**6-6**	**10**	**20.43**	**6.77**
Shahid Afridi	***2004–2017***	**265**	**5,694**	**6,335**	**287**	**5-7**	**11**	**22.07**	**6.67**
Sohail Tanvir	***2004–2017***	**273**	**5,737**	**6,959**	**282**	**6-14**	**7**	**24.67**	**7.27**
Yasir Arafat	*2005–2016*	226	4,702	6,344	281	4-5	10	22.57	8.09
Saeed Ajmal	***2004–2017***	**195**	**4,338**	**4,706**	**271**	**4-14**	**8**	**17.36**	**6.50**
A. C. Thomas	*2003–2015*	225	4,558	5,739	263	5-24	5	21.82	7.55
Azhar Mahmood	2003–2016	230	4,825	6,143	258	5-24	4	23.81	7.63
D. P. Nannes	*2007–2014*	215	4,624	5,719	257	5-31	9	22.25	7.42

WICKETKEEPING AND FIELDING RECORDS

MOST DISMISSALS IN AN INNINGS

7 (all ct)	E. F. M. U. Fernando	Lankan v Moors at Colombo (Bloomfield)	2005-06

MOST CATCHES IN AN INNINGS IN THE FIELD

5	Manzoor Ilahi	Jammu & Kashmir v Delhi at Delhi	2010-11
5	J. M. Vince	Hampshire v Leeward Islands at North Sound	2010-11
5	J. L. Ontong	Cape Cobras v Knights at Cape Town	2014-15
5	A. K. V. Adikari	Chilaw Marians v Bloomfield at Colombo (SSC)	2014-15
5	P. G. Fulton	Canterbury v Northern Districts at Hamilton	2015-16
5	M. W. Machan	Sussex v Glamorgan at Hove	2016

TEAM RECORDS

HIGHEST INNINGS TOTALS

263-3	(20 overs)	Australia v Sri Lanka at Pallekele	2016
263-5	(20 overs)	RC Bangalore v Pune Warriors at Bangalore	2012-13
260-4	**(20 overs)**	**Yorkshire v Northamptonshire at Leeds**	**2017**
260-5	**(20 overs)**	**India v Sri Lanka at Indore**	**2017-18**
260-6	(20 overs)	Sri Lanka v Kenya at Johannesburg	2007-08
254-3	(20 overs)	Gloucestershire v Middlesex at Uxbridge	2011
251-6	(20 overs)	Sinhalese v Saracens at Colombo (Colts)	2015-16
250-3	(20 overs)	Somerset v Gloucestershire at Taunton	2006

LOWEST INNINGS TOTALS

30	(11.1 overs)	Tripura v Jharkhand at Dhanbad	2009-10
39	(10.3 overs)	Netherlands v Sri Lanka at Chittagong	2013-14
44	(12.5 overs)	Leeward Islands v Trinidad & Tobago at North Sound	2011-12
44	(14.4 overs)	Boland v North West at Potchefstroom	2014-15
44	(12.1 overs)	Assam v Delhi at Vadodara	2015-16
44	(10.4 overs)	Khulna Titans v Rangpur Riders at Mirpur	2016-17

TEST RECORDS

This section covers all Tests up to January 27, 2018. Bold type denotes performances since January 1, 2017, or, in career figures, players who have appeared in Test cricket since that date.

BATTING RECORDS

HIGHEST INDIVIDUAL INNINGS

400*	B. C. Lara	West Indies v England at St John's	2003-04
380	M. L. Hayden	Australia v Zimbabwe at Perth	2003-04
375	B. C. Lara	West Indies v England at St John's	1993-94
374	D. P. M. D. Jayawardene	Sri Lanka v South Africa at Colombo (SSC)	2006
365*	G. S. Sobers	West Indies v Pakistan at Kingston	1957-58
364	L. Hutton	England v Australia at The Oval	1938
340	S. T. Jayasuriya	Sri Lanka v India at Colombo (RPS)	1997-98
337	Hanif Mohammad	Pakistan v West Indies at Bridgetown	1957-58
336*	W. R. Hammond	England v New Zealand at Auckland	1932-33
334*	M. A. Taylor	Australia v Pakistan at Peshawar	1998-99
334	D. G. Bradman	Australia v England at Leeds	1930
333	G. A. Gooch	England v India at Lord's	1990
333	C. H. Gayle	West Indies v Sri Lanka at Galle	2010-11
329*	M. J. Clarke	Australia v India at Sydney	2011-12
329	Inzamam-ul-Haq	Pakistan v New Zealand at Lahore	2002
325	A. Sandham	England v West Indies at Kingston	1929-30
319	V. Sehwag	India v South Africa at Chennai	2007-08
319	K. C. Sangakkara	Sri Lanka v Bangladesh at Chittagong	2013-14
317	C. H. Gayle	West Indies v South Africa at St John's	2004-05
313	Younis Khan	Pakistan v Sri Lanka at Karachi	2008-09
311*	H. M. Amla	South Africa v England at The Oval	2012
311	R. B. Simpson	Australia v England at Manchester	1964
310*	J. H. Edrich	England v New Zealand at Leeds	1965
309	V. Sehwag	India v Pakistan at Multan	2003-04
307	R. M. Cowper	Australia v England at Melbourne	1965-66
304	D. G. Bradman	Australia v England at Leeds	1934
303*	K. K. Nair	India v England at Chennai	2016-17
302*	Azhar Ali	Pakistan v West Indies at Dubai	2016-17
302	L. G. Rowe	West Indies v England at Bridgetown	1973-74
302	B. B. McCullum	New Zealand v India at Wellington	2013-14

*There have been **63** further instances of 250 or more runs in a Test innings.*

The highest innings for the countries not mentioned above are:

266	D. L. Houghton	Zimbabwe v Sri Lanka at Bulawayo	1994-95
217	**Shakib Al Hasan**	**Bangladesh v New Zealand at Wellington**	**2016-17**

HUNDRED ON TEST DEBUT

C. Bannerman (165*)	Australia v England at Melbourne	1876-77
W. G. Grace (152)	England v Australia at The Oval	1880
H. Graham (107)	Australia v England at Lord's	1893
†K. S. Ranjitsinhji (154*)	England v Australia at Manchester	1896
†P. F. Warner (132*)	England v South Africa at Johannesburg	1898-99
†R. A. Duff (104)	Australia v England at Melbourne	1901-02
§R. E. Foster (287)	England v Australia at Sydney	1903-04
G. Gunn (119)	England v Australia at Sydney	1907-08
†R. J. Hartigan (116)	Australia v England at Adelaide	1907-08
†H. L. Collins (104)	Australia v England at Sydney	1920-21
W. H. Ponsford (110)	Australia v England at Sydney	1924-25

A. A. Jackson (164)	Australia v England at Adelaide	1928-29
†G. A. Headley (176)	West Indies v England at Bridgetown	1929-30
J. E. Mills (117)	New Zealand v England at Wellington	1929-30
Nawab of Pataudi snr (102)	England v Australia at Sydney	1932-33
B. H. Valentine (136)	England v India at Bombay	1933-34
†L. Amarnath (118)	India v England at Bombay	1933-34
†P. A. Gibb (106)	England v South Africa at Johannesburg	1938-39
S. C. Griffith (140)	England v West Indies at Port-of-Spain	1947-48
A. G. Ganteaume (112)	West Indies v England at Port-of-Spain	1947-48
†J. W. Burke (101*)	Australia v England at Adelaide	1950-51
P. B. H. May (138)	England v South Africa at Leeds	1951
R. H. Shodhan (110)	India v Pakistan at Calcutta	1952-53
B. H. Pairaudeau (115)	West Indies v India at Port-of-Spain	1952-53
†O. G. Smith (104)	West Indies v Australia at Kingston	1954-55
A. G. Kripal Singh (100*)	India v New Zealand at Hyderabad	1955-56
C. C. Hunte (142)	West Indies v Pakistan at Bridgetown	1957-58
C. A. Milton (104*)	England v New Zealand at Leeds	1958
†A. A. Baig (112)	India v England at Manchester	1959
Hanumant Singh (105)	India v England at Delhi	1963-64
Khalid Ibadulla (166)	Pakistan v Australia at Karachi	1964-65
B. R. Taylor (105)	New Zealand v India at Calcutta	1964-65
K. D. Walters (155)	Australia v England at Brisbane	1965-66
J. H. Hampshire (107)	England v West Indies at Lord's	1969
†G. R. Viswanath (137)	India v Australia at Kanpur	1969-70
G. S. Chappell (108)	Australia v England at Perth	1970-71
‡§L. G. Rowe (214, 100*)	West Indies v New Zealand at Kingston	1971-72
A. I. Kallicharran (100*)	West Indies v New Zealand at Georgetown	1971-72
R. E. Redmond (107)	New Zealand v Pakistan at Auckland	1972-73
†F. C. Hayes (106*)	England v West Indies at The Oval	1973
†C. G. Greenidge (107)	West Indies v India at Bangalore	1974-75
†L. Baichan (105*)	West Indies v Pakistan at Lahore	1974-75
G. J. Cosier (109)	Australia v West Indies at Melbourne	1975-76
S. Amarnath (124)	India v New Zealand at Auckland	1975-76
Javed Miandad (163)	Pakistan v New Zealand at Lahore	1976-77
†A. B. Williams (100)	West Indies v Australia at Georgetown	1977-78
†D. M. Wellham (103)	Australia v England at The Oval	1981
†Salim Malik (100*)	Pakistan v Sri Lanka at Karachi	1981-82
K. C. Wessels (162)	Australia v England at Brisbane	1982-83
W. B. Phillips (159)	Australia v Pakistan at Perth	1983-84
¶M. Azharuddin (110)	India v England at Calcutta	1984-85
D. S. B. P. Kuruppu (201*)	Sri Lanka v New Zealand at Colombo (CCC)	1986-87
†M. J. Greatbatch (107*)	New Zealand v England at Auckland	1987-88
M. E. Waugh (138)	Australia v England at Adelaide	1990-91
A. C. Hudson (163)	South Africa v West Indies at Bridgetown	1991-92
R. S. Kaluwitharana (132*)	Sri Lanka v Australia at Colombo (SSC)	1992-93
D. L. Houghton (121)	Zimbabwe v India at Harare	1992-93
P. K. Amre (103)	India v South Africa at Durban	1992-93
†G. P. Thorpe (114*)	England v Australia at Nottingham	1993
G. S. Blewett (102*)	Australia v England at Adelaide	1994-95
S. C. Ganguly (131)	India v England at Lord's	1996
†Mohammad Wasim (109*)	Pakistan v New Zealand at Lahore	1996-97
Ali Naqvi (115)	Pakistan v South Africa at Rawalpindi	1997-98
Azhar Mahmood (128*)	Pakistan v South Africa at Rawalpindi	1997-98
M. S. Sinclair (214)	New Zealand v West Indies at Wellington	1999-2000
†Younis Khan (107)	Pakistan v Sri Lanka at Rawalpindi	1999-2000
Aminul Islam (145)	Bangladesh v India at Dhaka	2000-01
†H. Masakadza (119)	Zimbabwe v West Indies at Harare	2001
T. T. Samaraweera (103*)	Sri Lanka v India at Colombo (SSC)	2001
Taufeeq Umar (104)	Pakistan v Bangladesh at Multan	2001-02
†Mohammad Ashraful (114)	Bangladesh v Sri Lanka at Colombo (SSC)	2001-02
V. Sehwag (105)	India v South Africa at Bloemfontein	2001-02
L. Vincent (104)	New Zealand v Australia at Perth	2001-02
S. B. Styris (107)	New Zealand v West Indies at St George's	2002

J. A. Rudolph (222*)	South Africa v Bangladesh at Chittagong	2003
‡Yasir Hameed (170, 105)	Pakistan v Bangladesh at Karachi	2003
†D. R. Smith (105*)	West Indies v South Africa at Cape Town	2003-04
A. J. Strauss (112)	England v New Zealand at Lord's	2004
M. J. Clarke (151)	Australia v India at Bangalore	2004-05
†A. N. Cook (104*)	England v India at Nagpur	2005-06
M. J. Prior (126*)	England v West Indies at Lord's	2007
M. J. North (117)	Australia v South Africa at Johannesburg	2008-09
†Fawad Alam (168)	Pakistan v Sri Lanka at Colombo (PSS)	2009
†I. J. L. Trott (119)	England v Australia at The Oval	2009
Umar Akmal (129)	Pakistan v New Zealand at Dunedin	2009-10
†A. B. Barath (104)	West Indies v Australia at Brisbane	2009-10
A. N. Petersen (100)	South Africa v India at Kolkata	2009-10
S. K. Raina (120)	India v Sri Lanka at Colombo (SSC)	2010
K. S. Williamson (131)	New Zealand v India at Ahmedabad	2010-11
†K. A. Edwards (110)	West Indies v India at Roseau	2011
S. E. Marsh (141)	Australia v Sri Lanka at Pallekele	2011-12
Abul Hasan (113)	Bangladesh v West Indies at Khulna	2012-13
†F. du Plessis (110*)	South Africa v Australia at Adelaide	2012-13
H. D. Rutherford (171)	New Zealand v England at Dunedin	2012-13
S. Dhawan (187)	India v Australia at Mohali	2012-13
R. G. Sharma (177)	India v West Indies at Kolkata	2013-14
†J. D. S. Neesham (137*)	New Zealand v India at Wellington	2013-14
S. van Zyl (101*)	South Africa v West Indies at Centurion	2014-15
A. C. Voges (130*)	Australia v West Indies at Roseau	2015
S. C. Cook (115)	South Africa v England at Centurion	2015-16
K. K. Jennings (112)	England v India at Mumbai	2016-17
T. A. Blundell (107*)	**New Zealand v West Indies at Wellington**	**2017-18**

† *In his second innings of the match.*
‡ *L. G. Rowe and Yasir Hameed are the only batsmen to score a hundred in each innings on debut.*
§ *R. E. Foster (287, 19) and L. G. Rowe (214, 100*) are the only batsmen to score 300 on debut.*
¶ *M. Azharuddin is the only batsman to score hundreds in each of his first three Tests.*

L. Amarnath and S. Amarnath were father and son.
Ali Naqvi and Azhar Mahmood achieved the feat in the same innings.
Only Bannerman, Houghton and Aminul Islam scored hundreds in their country's first Test.

TWO SEPARATE HUNDREDS IN A TEST

Triple-Hundred and Hundred in a Test

G. A. Gooch (England)	333 and 123 v India at Lord's	1990
K. C. Sangakkara (Sri Lanka)	319 and 105 v Bangladesh at Chittagong	2013-14

The only instances in first-class cricket. M. A. Taylor (Australia) scored 334 and 92 v Pakistan at Peshawar in 1998-99.*

Double-Hundred and Hundred in a Test

K. D. Walters (Australia)	242 and 103 v West Indies at Sydney	1968-69
S. M. Gavaskar (India)	124 and 220 v West Indies at Port-of-Spain	1970-71
†L. G. Rowe (West Indies)	214 and 100* v New Zealand at Kingston	1971-72
G. S. Chappell (Australia)	247* and 133 v New Zealand at Wellington	1973-74
B. C. Lara (West Indies)	221 and 130 v Sri Lanka at Colombo (SSC)	2001-02

† *On Test debut.*

Two Hundreds in a Test

There have been **82** instances of a batsman scoring two separate hundreds in a Test, including the seven listed above. The most recent was by **S. D. Hope for West Indies v England at Leeds in 2017**.

S. M. Gavaskar (India), R. T. Ponting (Australia) and D. A. Warner (Australia) all achieved the feat three times. C. L. Walcott scored twin hundreds twice in one series, for West Indies v Australia in 1954-55. L. G. Rowe and Yasir Hameed both did it on Test debut.

MOST DOUBLE-HUNDREDS

D. G. Bradman (A)	12	M. S. Atapattu (SL)	6	S. R. Tendulkar (I)	6
K. C. Sangakkara (SL)	11	Javed Miandad (P)	6	**Younis Khan (P)**	**6**
B. C. Lara (WI)	9	**V. Kohli (I)**	**6**	**A. N. Cook (E)**	**5**
W. R. Hammond (E)	7	R. T. Ponting (A)	6	R. Dravid (I)	5
D. P. M. D. Jayawardene (SL)	7	V. Sehwag (I)	6	G. C. Smith (SA)	5

M. J. Clarke (Australia) scored four double-hundreds in the calendar year 2012.

MOST HUNDREDS

S. R. Tendulkar (I)	51	M. J. Clarke (A)	28	G. Boycott (E)	22
J. H. Kallis (SA)	45	A. R. Border (A)	27	M. C. Cowdrey (E)	22
R. T. Ponting (A)	41	G. C. Smith (SA)	27	W. R. Hammond (E)	22
K. C. Sangakkara (SL)	38	G. S. Sobers (WI)	26	D. C. Boon (A)	21
R. Dravid (I)	36	Inzamam-ul-Haq (P)	25	**A. B. de Villiers (SA)**	**21**
S. M. Gavaskar (I)	34	G. S. Chappell (A)	24	R. N. Harvey (A)	21
D. P. M. D. Jayawardene (SL)	34	Mohammad Yousuf (P)	24	G. Kirsten (SA)	21
B. C. Lara (WI)	34	I. V. A. Richards (WI)	24	**V. Kohli (I)**	**21**
Younis Khan (P)	**34**	Javed Miandad (P)	23	A. J. Strauss (E)	21
A. N. Cook (E)	**32**	J. L. Langer (A)	23	**D. A. Warner (A)**	**21**
S. R. Waugh (A)	32	K. P. Pietersen (E)	23	K. F. Barrington (E)	20
S. Chanderpaul (WI)	30	V. Sehwag (I)	23	P. A. de Silva (SL)	20
M. L. Hayden (A)	30	**S. P. D. Smith (A)**	**23**	G. A. Gooch (E)	20
D. G. Bradman (A)	29	M. Azharuddin (I)	22	M. E. Waugh (A)	20
H. M. Amla (SA)	**28**	I. R. Bell (E)	22		

*The most hundreds for New Zealand is 17 by M. D. Crowe, the most for Zimbabwe is 12 by A. Flower, and the most for Bangladesh is **8** by **Tamim Iqbal**.*

MOST HUNDREDS AGAINST ONE TEAM

D. G. Bradman	19	Australia v England	K. C. Sangakkara	10	Sri Lanka v Pakistan
S. M. Gavaskar	13	India v West Indies	G. S. Sobers	10	West Indies v England
J. B. Hobbs	12	England v Australia	S. R. Waugh	10	Australia v England
S. R. Tendulkar	11	India v Australia			

MOST DUCKS

	0s	*Inns*		*0s*	*Inns*
C. A. Walsh (WI)	43	185	B. S. Chandrasekhar (I)	23	80
C. S. Martin (NZ)	36	104	M. S. Atapattu (SL)	22	156
G. D. McGrath (A)	35	138	S. R. Waugh (A)	22	260
S. K. Warne (A)	34	199	S. J. Harmison (E/World)	21	86
M. Muralitharan (SL/World)	33	164	M. Ntini (SA)	21	116
Zaheer Khan (I)	29	127	Waqar Younis (P)	21	120
M. Dillon (WI)	26	68	M. S. Panesar (E)	20	68
I. Sharma (I)	**26**	**110**	**M. Morkel (SA)**	**20**	**99**
C. E. L. Ambrose (WI)	26	145	B. S. Bedi (I)	20	101
Danish Kaneria (P)	25	84	**H. M. R. K. B. Herath (SL)**	**20**	**134**
D. K. Morrison (NZ)	24	71	D. L. Vettori (NZ/World)	20	174
S. C. J. Broad (E)	**24**	**164**	M. A. Atherton (E)	20	212
J. M. Anderson (E)	**24**	**186**			

CARRYING BAT THROUGH TEST INNINGS

(Figures in brackets show team's total)

A. B. Tancred	26*	(47)	South Africa v England at Cape Town	1888-89
J. E. Barrett	67*	(176)†	Australia v England at Lord's	1890
R. Abel	132*	(307)	England v Australia at Sydney	1891-92
P. F. Warner	132*	(237)†	England v South Africa at Johannesburg	1898-99
W. W. Armstrong	159*	(309)	Australia v South Africa at Johannesburg	1902-03
J. W. Zulch	43*	(103)	South Africa v England at Cape Town	1909-10
W. Bardsley	193*	(383)	Australia v England at Lord's	1926
W. M. Woodfull	30*	(66)§	Australia v England at Brisbane	1928-29
W. M. Woodfull	73*	(193)‡	Australia v England at Adelaide	1932-33
W. A. Brown	206*	(422)	Australia v England at Lord's	1938
L. Hutton	202*	(344)	England v West Indies at The Oval	1950
L. Hutton	156*	(272)	England v Australia at Adelaide	1950-51
Nazar Mohammad¶	124*	(331)	Pakistan v India at Lucknow	1952-53
F. M. M. Worrell	191*	(372)	West Indies v England at Nottingham	1957
T. L. Goddard	56*	(99)	South Africa v Australia at Cape Town	1957-58
D. J. McGlew	127*	(292)	South Africa v New Zealand at Durban	1961-62
C. C. Hunte	60*	(131)	West Indies v Australia at Port-of-Spain	1964-65
G. M. Turner	43*	(131)	New Zealand v England at Lord's	1969
W. M. Lawry	49*	(107)	Australia v India at Delhi	1969-70
W. M. Lawry	60*	(116)‡	Australia v England at Sydney	1970-71
G. M. Turner	223*	(386)	New Zealand v West Indies at Kingston	1971-72
I. R. Redpath	159*	(346)	Australia v New Zealand at Auckland	1973-74
G. Boycott	99*	(215)	England v Australia at Perth	1979-80
S. M. Gavaskar	127*	(286)	India v Pakistan at Faisalabad	1982-83
Mudassar Nazar¶	152*	(323)	Pakistan v India at Lahore	1982-83
S. Wettimuny	63*	(144)	Sri Lanka v New Zealand at Christchurch	1982-83
D. C. Boon	58*	(103)	Australia v New Zealand at Auckland	1985-86
D. L. Haynes	88*	(211)	West Indies v Pakistan at Karachi	1986-87
G. A. Gooch	154*	(252)	England v West Indies at Leeds	1991
D. L. Haynes	75*	(176)	West Indies v England at The Oval	1991
A. J. Stewart	69*	(175)	England v Pakistan at Lord's	1992
D. L. Haynes	143*	(382)	West Indies v Pakistan at Port-of-Spain	1992-93
M. H. Dekker	68*	(187)	Zimbabwe v Pakistan at Rawalpindi	1993-94
M. A. Atherton	94*	(228)	England v New Zealand at Christchurch	1996-97
G. Kirsten	100*	(239)	South Africa v Pakistan at Faisalabad	1997-98
M. A. Taylor	169*	(350)	Australia v South Africa at Adelaide	1997-98
G. W. Flower	156*	(321)	Zimbabwe v Pakistan at Bulawayo	1997-98
Saeed Anwar	188*	(316)	Pakistan v India at Calcutta	1998-99
M. S. Atapattu	216*	(428)	Sri Lanka v Zimbabwe at Bulawayo	1999-2000
R. P. Arnold	104*	(231)	Sri Lanka v Zimbabwe at Harare	1999-2000
Javed Omar	85*	(168)†‡	Bangladesh v Zimbabwe at Bulawayo	2000-01
V. Sehwag	201*	(329)	India v Sri Lanka at Galle	2008
S. M. Katich	131*	(268)	Australia v New Zealand at Brisbane	2008-09
C. H. Gayle	165*	(317)	West Indies v Australia at Adelaide	2009-10
Imran Farhat	117*	(223)	Pakistan v New Zealand at Napier	2009-10
R. Dravid	146*	(300)	India v England at The Oval	2011
T. M. K. Mawoyo	163*	(412)	Zimbabwe v Pakistan at Bulawayo	2011-12
D. A. Warner	123*	(233)	Australia v New Zealand at Hobart	2011-12
C. A. Pujara	145*	(312)	India v Sri Lanka at Colombo (SSC)	2015-16
D. Elgar	118*	(214)	South Africa v England at Durban	2015-16
K. C. Brathwaite	142*	(337)	West Indies v Pakistan at Sharjah	2016-17
A. N. Cook	**244***	**(491)**	**England v Australia at Melbourne**	**2017-18**
D. Elgar	**86***	**(177)**	**South Africa v India at Johannesburg**	**2017-18**

† *On debut.* ‡ *One man absent.* § *Two men absent.* ¶ *Father and son.*

A. N. Cook (244) holds the record for the highest score by a player carrying his bat in a Test.*

D. L. Haynes, who is alone in achieving this feat on three occasions, also opened the batting and was last man out in each innings for West Indies v New Zealand at Dunedin, 1979-80.

G. M. Turner was the youngest at 22 years 63 days old when he first did it in 1969.

MOST RUNS IN A SERIES

	T	*I*	*NO*	*R*	*HS*	*100*	*Avge*		
D. G. Bradman	5	7	0	974	334	4	139.14	A v E	1930
W. R. Hammond. . .	5	9	1	905	251	4	113.12	E v A	1928-29
M. A. Taylor.	6	11	1	839	219	2	83.90	A v E	1989
R. N. Harvey.	5	9	0	834	205	4	92.66	A v SA	1952-53
I. V. A. Richards. . .	4	7	0	829	291	3	118.42	WI v E	1976
C. L. Walcott	5	10	0	827	155	5	82.70	WI v A	1954-55
G. S. Sobers	5	8	2	824	365*	3	137.33	WI v P	1957-58
D. G. Bradman	5	9	0	810	270	3	90.00	A v E	1936-37
D. G. Bradman	5	5	1	806	299*	4	201.50	A v SA	1931-32

MOST RUNS IN A CALENDAR YEAR

	T	*I*	*NO*	*R*	*HS*	*100*	*Avge*	*Year*
Mohammad Yousuf (P).	11	19	1	1,788	202	9	99.33	2006
I. V. A. Richards (WI).	11	19	0	1,710	291	7	90.00	1976
G. C. Smith (SA).	15	25	2	1,656	232	6	72.00	2008
M. J. Clarke (A).	11	18	3	1,595	329*	5	106.33	2012
S. R. Tendulkar (I).	14	23	3	1,562	214	7	78.10	2010
S. M. Gavaskar (I)	18	27	1	1,555	221	5	59.80	1979
R. T. Ponting (A).	15	28	5	1,544	207	6	67.13	2005
R. T. Ponting (A).	11	18	3	1,503	257	6	100.20	2003

M. Amarnath reached 1,000 runs in 1983 on May 3, in his ninth Test of the year.

The only case of 1,000 in a year before World War II was C. Hill of Australia: 1,060 in 1902.

M. L. Hayden (Australia) scored 1,000 runs in each year from 2001 to 2005.

MOST RUNS

		T	*I*	*NO*	*R*	*HS*	*100*	*Avge*
1	S. R. Tendulkar (India)	200	329	33	15,921	248*	51	53.78
2	R. T. Ponting (Australia).	168	287	29	13,378	257	41	51.85
3	J. H. Kallis (South Africa/World) .	166	280	40	13,289	224	45	55.37
4	R. Dravid (India/World)	164	286	32	13,288	270	36	52.31
5	K. C. Sangakkara (Sri Lanka)	134	233	17	12,400	319	38	57.40
6	**A. N. Cook (England)**	**152**	**275**	**16**	**12,005**	**294**	**32**	**46.35**
7	B. C. Lara (West Indies/World) . .	131	232	6	11,953	400*	34	52.88
8	S. Chanderpaul (West Indies)	164	280	49	11,867	203*	30	51.37
9	D. P. M. D. Jayawardene (SL) . . .	149	252	15	11,814	374	34	49.84
10	A. R. Border (Australia)	156	265	44	11,174	205	27	50.56
11	S. R. Waugh (Australia)	168	260	46	10,927	200	32	51.06
12	S. M. Gavaskar (India)	125	214	16	10,122	236*	34	51.12
13	**Younis Khan (Pakistan)**	**118**	**213**	**19**	**10,099**	**313**	**34**	**52.05**
14	G. C. Smith (South Africa/Wld) . .	117	205	13	9,265	277	27	48.25
15	G. A. Gooch (England)	118	215	6	8,900	333	20	42.58
16	Javed Miandad (Pakistan)	124	189	21	8,832	280*	23	52.57
17	Inzamam-ul-Haq (Pakistan/World)	120	200	22	8,830	329	25	49.60
18	**H. M. Amla (South Africa)**	**113**	**193**	**14**	**8,786**	**311***	**28**	**49.08**
19	V. V. S. Laxman (India)	134	225	34	8,781	281	17	45.97
20	M. J. Clarke (Australia).	115	198	22	8,643	329*	28	49.10
21	M. L. Hayden (Australia)	103	184	14	8,625	380	30	50.73
22	V. Sehwag (India/World)	104	180	6	8,586	319	23	49.34
23	I. V. A. Richards (West Indies). . .	121	182	12	8,540	291	24	50.23
24	A. J. Stewart (England)	133	235	21	8,463	190	15	39.54
25	**A. B. de Villiers (South Africa)** .	**110**	**183**	**16**	**8,338**	**278***	**21**	**49.92**
26	D. I. Gower (England).	117	204	18	8,231	215	18	44.25
27	K. P. Pietersen (England)	104	181	8	8,181	227	23	47.28
28	G. Boycott (England)	108	193	23	8,114	246*	22	47.72
29	G. S. Sobers (West Indies)	93	160	21	8,032	365*	26	57.78

		T	I	NO	R	HS	100	Avge
30	M. E. Waugh (Australia)	128	209	17	8,029	153*	20	41.81
31	M. A. Atherton (England)	115	212	7	7,728	185*	16	37.69
32	I. R. Bell (England)	118	205	24	7,727	235	22	42.69
33	J. L. Langer (Australia)	105	182	12	7,696	250	23	45.27
34	M. C. Cowdrey (England)	114	188	15	7,624	182	22	44.06
35	C. G. Greenidge (West Indies)	108	185	16	7,558	226	19	44.72
36	Mohammad Yousuf (Pakistan)	90	156	12	7,530	223	24	52.29
37	M. A. Taylor (Australia)	104	186	13	7,525	334*	19	43.49
38	C. H. Lloyd (West Indies)	110	175	14	7,515	242*	19	46.67
39	D. L. Haynes (West Indies)	116	202	25	7,487	184	18	42.29
40	D. C. Boon (Australia)	107	190	20	7,422	200	21	43.65
41	G. Kirsten (South Africa)	101	176	15	7,289	275	21	45.27
42	W. R. Hammond (England)	85	140	16	7,249	336*	22	58.45
43	C. H. Gayle (West Indies)	103	182	11	7,214	333	15	42.18
44	S. C. Ganguly (India)	113	188	17	7,212	239	16	42.17
45	S. P. Fleming (New Zealand)	111	189	10	7,172	274*	9	40.06
46	G. S. Chappell (Australia)	87	151	19	7,110	247*	24	53.86
47	A. J. Strauss (England)	100	178	6	7,037	177	21	40.91
48	D. G. Bradman (Australia)	52	80	10	6,996	334	29	99.94
49	S. T. Jayasuriya (Sri Lanka)	110	188	14	6,973	340	14	40.07
50	L. Hutton (England)	79	138	15	6,971	364	19	56.67

MOST RUNS FOR EACH COUNTRY

ENGLAND

A. N. Cook **12,005**
G. A. Gooch 8,900
A. J. Stewart 8,463
D. I. Gower 8,231
K. P. Pietersen 8,181
G. Boycott 8,114

AUSTRALIA

R. T. Ponting 13,378
A. R. Border 11,174
S. R. Waugh 10,927
M. J. Clarke 8,643
M. L. Hayden 8,625
M. E. Waugh 8,029

SOUTH AFRICA

J. H. Kallis† 13,206
G. C. Smith† 9,253
H. M. Amla **8,786**
A. B. de Villiers **8,338**
G. Kirsten 7,289
H. H. Gibbs 6,167

† *J. H. Kallis also scored 44 and 39* and G. C. Smith 12 and 0 for the World XI v Australia (2005-06 Super Series Test).*

WEST INDIES

B. C. Lara† 11,912
S. Chanderpaul 11,867
I. V. A. Richards 8,540
G. S. Sobers 8,032
C. G. Greenidge 7,558
C. H. Lloyd 7,515

† *B. C. Lara also scored 5 and 36 for the World XI v Australia (2005-06 Super Series Test).*

NEW ZEALAND

S. P. Fleming 7,172
B. B. McCullum 6,453
L. R. P. L. Taylor **6,426**
M. D. Crowe 5,444
J. G. Wright 5,334
K. S. Williamson **5,214**

INDIA

S. R. Tendulkar 15,921
R. Dravid† 13,265
S. M. Gavaskar 10,122
V. V. S. Laxman 8,781
V. Sehwag† 8,503
S. C. Ganguly 7,212

† *R. Dravid also scored 0 and 23 and V. Sehwag 76 and 7 for the World XI v Australia (2005-06 Super Series Test).*

PAKISTAN

Younis Khan 10,099	Inzamam-ul-Haq† 8,829	Salim Malik 5,768
Javed Miandad. 8,832	Mohammad Yousuf. . . 7,530	**Misbah-ul-Haq 5,222**

† *Inzamam-ul-Haq also scored 1 and 0 for the World XI v Australia (2005-06 Super Series Test).*

SRI LANKA

K. C. Sangakkara. 12,400	S. T. Jayasuriya 6,973	M. S. Atapattu 5,502
D. P. M. D. Jayawardene . 11,814	P. A. de Silva. 6,973	T. M. Dilshan. 5,492

ZIMBABWE

A. Flower. 4,794	A. D. R. Campbell. . . . 2,858	**H. Masakadza 2,084**
G. W. Flower. 3,457	G. J. Whittall 2,207	H. H. Streak. 1,990

BANGLADESH

Tamim Iqbal 3,886	**Mushfiqur Rahim . . . 3,516**	Mohammad Ashraful . 2,737
Shakib Al Hasan 3,594	Habibul Bashar 3,026	**Mahmudullah. 1,931**

HIGHEST CAREER AVERAGE

(Qualification: 20 innings)

Avge		*T*	*I*	*NO*	*R*	*HS*	*100*
99.94	D. G. Bradman (A)	52	80	10	6,996	334	29
63.75	**S. P. D. Smith (A)**	**61**	**111**	**16**	**6,057**	**239**	**23**
61.87	A. C. Voges (A)	20	31	7	1,485	269*	5
60.97	R. G. Pollock (SA)	23	41	4	2,256	274	7
60.83	G. A. Headley (WI)	22	40	4	2,190	270*	10
60.73	H. Sutcliffe (E)	54	84	9	4,555	194	16
59.23	E. Paynter (E)	20	31	5	1,540	243	4
58.67	K. F. Barrington (E)	82	131	15	6,806	256	20
58.61	E. D. Weekes (WI)	48	81	5	4,455	207	15
58.45	W. R. Hammond (E).	85	140	16	7,249	336*	22
57.78	G. S. Sobers (WI)	93	160	21	8,032	365*	26
57.40	K. C. Sangakkara (SL)	134	233	17	12,400	319	38
56.94	J. B. Hobbs (E)	61	102	7	5,410	211	15
56.68	C. L. Walcott (WI)	44	74	7	3,798	220	15
56.67	L. Hutton (E).	79	138	15	6,971	364	19
55.37	J. H. Kallis (SA/World)	166	280	40	13,289	224	45
55.00	E. Tyldesley (E)	14	20	2	990	122	3

S. G. Barnes (A) scored 1,072 runs at 63.05 from 19 innings.

BEST CAREER STRIKE-RATES

(Runs per 100 balls. Qualification: 1,000 runs)

SR		*T*	*I*	*NO*	*R*	*100*	*Avge*
88.32	**T. G. Southee (NZ)**.	**58**	**88**	**7**	**1,384**	**0**	**17.08**
86.97	Shahid Afridi (P)	27	48	1	1,716	5	36.51
82.22	V. Sehwag (I).	104	180	6	8,586	23	49.34
81.98	A. C. Gilchrist (A).	96	137	20	5,570	17	47.60
76.49	G. P. Swann (E).	60	76	14	1,370	0	22.09

SR		*T*	*I*	*NO*	*R*	*100*	*Avge*
74.73	**D. A. Warner (A)**	**71**	**131**	**5**	**6,146**	**21**	**48.77**
72.48	**Q. de Kock (SA)**	**29**	**47**	**5**	**1,649**	**3**	**39.26**
72.34	**Sarfraz Ahmed (P)**	**38**	**67**	**12**	**2,208**	**3**	**40.14**
70.28	M. Muralitharan (SL)	133	164	56	1,261	0	11.67
68.83	**M. A. Starc (A)**	**40**	**60**	**12**	**1,111**	**0**	**23.14**
67.88	D. J. G. Sammy (WI)	38	63	2	1,323	1	21.68
66.64	**S. Dhawan (I)**	**29**	**49**	**1**	**2,046**	**6**	**42.62**

Comprehensive data on balls faced has been available only in recent decades, and its introduction varied from country to country. Among earlier players for whom partial data is available, Kapil Dev (India) had a strike-rate of 80.91 and I. V. A. Richards (West Indies) 70.19 in those innings which were fully recorded.

HIGHEST PERCENTAGE OF TEAM'S RUNS OVER TEST CAREER

(Qualification: 20 Tests)

	Tests	*Runs*	*Team Runs*	*% of Team Runs*
D. G. Bradman (Australia)	52	6,996	28,810	24.28
G. A. Headley (West Indies)	22	2,190	10,239	21.38
B. C. Lara (West Indies)	131	11,953	63,328	18.87
L. Hutton (England)	79	6,971	38,440	18.13
J. B. Hobbs (England)	61	5,410	30,211	17.90
A. D. Nourse (South Africa)	34	2,960	16,659	17.76
S. P. D. Smith (Australia)	**61**	**6,057**	**34,576**	**17.51**
E. D. Weekes (West Indies)	48	4,455	25,667	17.35
B. Mitchell (South Africa)	42	3,471	20,175	17.20
H. Sutcliffe (England)	54	4,555	26,604	17.12
K. C. Sangakkara (Sri Lanka)	134	12,400	72,779	17.03
B. Sutcliffe (New Zealand)	42	2,727	16,158	16.87

The percentage shows the proportion of a team's runs scored by that player in all Tests in which he played, including team runs in innings in which he did not bat.

FASTEST FIFTIES

Minutes			
24	Misbah-ul-Haq	Pakistan v Australia at Abu Dhabi	2014-15
27	Mohammad Ashraful	Bangladesh v India at Mirpur	2007
28	J. T. Brown	England v Australia at Melbourne	1894-95
29	S. A. Durani	India v England at Kanpur	1963-64
30	E. A. V. Williams	West Indies v England at Bridgetown	1947-48
30	B. R. Taylor	New Zealand v West Indies at Auckland	1968-69

The fastest fifties in terms of balls received (where recorded) are:

Balls			
21	Misbah-ul-Haq	Pakistan v Australia at Abu Dhabi	2014-15
23	**D. A. Warner**	**Australia v Pakistan at Sydney**	**2016-17**
24	J. H. Kallis	South Africa v Zimbabwe at Cape Town	2004-05
25	S. Shillingford	West Indies v New Zealand at Kingston	2014
26	Shahid Afridi	Pakistan v India at Bangalore	2004-05
26	Mohammad Ashraful	Bangladesh v India at Mirpur	2007
26	D. W. Steyn	South Africa v West Indies at Port Elizabeth	2014-15

FASTEST HUNDREDS

Minutes			
70	J. M. Gregory	Australia v South Africa at Johannesburg	1921-22
74	Misbah-ul-Haq	Pakistan v Australia at Abu Dhabi	2014-15
75	G. L. Jessop	England v Australia at The Oval	1902
78	R. Benaud	Australia v West Indies at Kingston	1954-55
80	J. H. Sinclair	South Africa v Australia at Cape Town	1902-03
81	I. V. A. Richards	West Indies v England at St John's	1985-86
86	B. R. Taylor	New Zealand v West Indies at Auckland	1968-69

The fastest hundreds in terms of balls received (where recorded) are:

Balls			
54	B. B. McCullum	New Zealand v Australia at Christchurch	2015-16
56	I. V. A. Richards	West Indies v England at St John's	1985-86
56	Misbah-ul-Haq	Pakistan v Australia at Abu Dhabi	2014-15
57	A. C. Gilchrist	Australia v England at Perth	2006-07
67	J. M. Gregory	Australia v South Africa at Johannesburg	1921-22
69	S. Chanderpaul	West Indies v Australia at Georgetown	2002-03
69	D. A. Warner	Australia v India at Perth	2011-12
70	C. H. Gayle	West Indies v Australia at Perth	2009-10

FASTEST DOUBLE-HUNDREDS

Minutes			
214	D. G. Bradman	Australia v England at Leeds	1930
217	N. J. Astle	New Zealand v England at Christchurch	2001-02
223	S. J. McCabe	Australia v England at Nottingham	1938
226	V. T. Trumper	Australia v South Africa at Adelaide	1910-11
234	D. G. Bradman	Australia v England at Lord's	1930
240	W. R. Hammond	England v New Zealand at Auckland	1932-33

The fastest double-hundreds in terms of balls received (where recorded) are:

Balls			
153	N. J. Astle	New Zealand v England at Christchurch	2001-02
163	B. A. Stokes	England v South Africa at Cape Town	2015-16
168	V. Sehwag	India v Sri Lanka at Mumbai (BS)	2009-10
182	V. Sehwag	India v Pakistan at Lahore	2005-06
186	B. B. McCullum	New Zealand v Pakistan at Sharjah	2014-15
194	V. Sehwag	India v South Africa at Chennai	2007-08

FASTEST TRIPLE-HUNDREDS

Minutes			
288	W. R. Hammond	England v New Zealand at Auckland	1932-33
336	D. G. Bradman	Australia v England at Leeds	1930

The fastest triple-hundred in terms of balls received (where recorded) is:

Balls			
278	V. Sehwag	India v South Africa at Chennai	2007-08

MOST RUNS SCORED OFF AN OVER

28	B. C. Lara (466444)	off R. J. Peterson	WI v SA at Johannesburg	2003-04
28	G. J. Bailey (462466)	off J. M. Anderson	A v E at Perth	2013-14
27	Shahid Afridi (666621)	off Harbhajan Singh	P v I at Lahore	2005-06
26	C. D. McMillan (444464)	off Younis Khan	NZ v P at Hamilton	2000-01
26	B. C. Lara (406664)	off Danish Kaneria	WI v P at Multan	2006-07
26	M. G. Johnson (446066)	off P. L. Harris	A v SA at Johannesburg	2009-10
26	B. B. McCullum (466046)	off R. A. S. Lakmal	NZ v SL at Christchurch	2014-15
26	**H. H. Pandya (446660)**	**off P. M. Pushpakumara**	**I v SL at Pallekele**	**2017**

MOST RUNS IN A DAY

309	D. G. Bradman	Australia v England at Leeds	1930
295	W. R. Hammond	England v New Zealand at Auckland	1932-33
284	V. Sehwag	India v Sri Lanka at Mumbai	2009-10
273	D. C. S. Compton	England v Pakistan at Nottingham	1954
271	D. G. Bradman	Australia v England at Leeds	1934

MOST SIXES IN A CAREER

B. B. McCullum (NZ)	107
A. C. Gilchrist (A)	100
C. H. Gayle (WI)	98
J. H. Kallis (SA/World)	97
V. Sehwag (I/World)	91
B. C. Lara (WI)	88
C. L. Cairns (NZ)	87
I. V. A. Richards (WI)	84
A. Flintoff (E/World)	82
M. L. Hayden (A)	82
Misbah-ul-Haq (P)	**81**
K. P. Pietersen (E)	81
M. S. Dhoni (I)	78
R. T. Ponting (A)	73
C. H. Lloyd (WI)	70
Younis Khan (P)	**70**

SLOWEST INDIVIDUAL BATTING

0	in 101 minutes	G. I. Allott, New Zealand v South Africa at Auckland	1998-99
4*	in 110 minutes	Abdul Razzaq, Pakistan v Australia at Melbourne	2004-05
6	in 137 minutes	S. C. J. Broad, England v New Zealand at Auckland	2012-13
9*	in 184 minutes	Arshad Khan, Pakistan v Sri Lanka at Colombo (SSC)	2000
18	in 194 minutes	W. R. Playle, New Zealand v England at Leeds	1958
19*	in 217 minutes	M. D. Crowe, New Zealand v Sri Lanka at Colombo (SSC)	1983-84
25	in 289 minutes	H. M. Amla, South Africa v India at Delhi	2015-16
35	in 332 minutes	C. J. Tavaré, England v India at Madras	1981-82
43	in 354 minutes	A. B. de Villiers, South Africa v India at Delhi	2015-16
60	in 390 minutes	D. N. Sardesai, India v West Indies at Bridgetown	1961-62
62	in 408 minutes	Ramiz Raja, Pakistan v West Indies at Karachi	1986-87
68	in 458 minutes	T. E. Bailey, England v Australia at Brisbane	1958-59
86	in 474 minutes	Shoaib Mohammad, Pakistan v West Indies at Karachi	1990-91
99	in 505 minutes	M. L. Jaisimha, India v Pakistan at Kanpur	1960-61
104	in 529 minutes	S. V. Manjrekar, India v Zimbabwe at Harare	1992-93
105	in 575 minutes	D. J. McGlew, South Africa v Australia at Durban	1957-58
114	in 591 minutes	Mudassar Nazar, Pakistan v England at Lahore	1977-78
120*	in 609 minutes	J. J. Crowe, New Zealand v Sri Lanka at Colombo (CCC)	1986-87
136*	in 675 minutes	S. Chanderpaul, West Indies v India at St John's	2001-02
163	in 720 minutes	Shoaib Mohammad, Pakistan v New Zealand at Wellington	1988-89
201*	in 777 minutes	D. S. B. P. Kuruppu, Sri Lanka v NZ at Colombo (CCC)	1986-87
275	in 878 minutes	G. Kirsten, South Africa v England at Durban	1999-2000
337	in 970 minutes	Hanif Mohammad, Pakistan v West Indies at Bridgetown	1957-58

SLOWEST HUNDREDS

557 minutes	Mudassar Nazar, Pakistan v England at Lahore	1977-78
545 minutes	D. J. McGlew, South Africa v Australia at Durban	1957-58
535 minutes	A. P. Gurusinha, Sri Lanka v Zimbabwe at Harare	1994-95
516 minutes	J. J. Crowe, New Zealand v Sri Lanka at Colombo (CCC)	1986-87
500 minutes	S. V. Manjrekar, India v Zimbabwe at Harare	1992-93
488 minutes	P. E. Richardson, England v South Africa at Johannesburg	1956-57

The slowest hundred for any Test in England is 458 minutes (329 balls) by K. W. R. Fletcher, England v Pakistan, The Oval, 1974.

The slowest double-hundred in a Test was scored in 777 minutes (548 balls) by D. S. B. P. Kuruppu for Sri Lanka v New Zealand at Colombo (CCC), 1986-87, on his debut.

PARTNERSHIPS OVER 400

624	for 3rd	K. C. Sangakkara (287)/ D. P. M. D. Jayawardene (374)	SL v SA	Colombo (SSC)	2006
576	for 2nd	S. T. Jayasuriya (340)/R. S. Mahanama (225)	SL v I	Colombo (RPS)	1997-98
467	for 3rd	A. H. Jones (186)/M. D. Crowe (299)	NZ v SL	Wellington	1990-91
451	for 2nd	W. H. Ponsford (266)/D. G. Bradman (244)	A v E	The Oval	1934
451	for 3rd	Mudassar Nazar (231)/Javed Miandad (280*)	P v I	Hyderabad	1982-83
449	for 4th	A. C. Voges (269*)/S. E. Marsh (182)	A v WI	Hobart	2015-16
446	for 2nd	C. C. Hunte (260)/G. S. Sobers (365*)	WI v P	Kingston	1957-58
438	for 2nd	M. S. Atapattu (249)/K. C. Sangakkara (270)	SL v Z	Bulawayo	2003-04
437	for 4th	D. P. M. D. Jayawardene (240)/ T. T. Samaraweera (231)	SL v P	Karachi	2008-09
429*	for 3rd	J. A. Rudolph (222*)/H. H. Dippenaar (177*)	SA v B	Chittagong	2003
415	for 1st	N. D. McKenzie (226)/G. C. Smith (232)	SA v B	Chittagong	2007-08
413	for 1st	M. H. Mankad (231)/Pankaj Roy (173)	I v NZ	Madras	1955-56
411	for 4th	P. B. H. May (285*)/M. C. Cowdrey (154)	E v WI	Birmingham	1957
410	for 1st	V. Sehwag (254)/R. Dravid (128*)	I v P	Lahore	2005-06
405	for 5th	S. G. Barnes (234)/D. G. Bradman (234)	A v E	Sydney	1946-47

415 runs were added for the third wicket for India v England at Madras in 1981-82 by D. B. Vengsarkar (retired hurt), G. R. Viswanath and Yashpal Sharma. 408 runs were added for the first wicket for India v Bangladesh at Mirpur in 2007 by K. D. Karthik (retired hurt), Wasim Jaffer (retired hurt), R. Dravid and S. R. Tendulkar.

HIGHEST PARTNERSHIPS FOR EACH WICKET

First Wicket

415	N. D. McKenzie (226)/G. C. Smith (232)	SA v B	Chittagong	2007-08
413	M. H. Mankad (231)/Pankaj Roy (173)	I v NZ	Madras	1955-56
410	V. Sehwag (254)/R. Dravid (128*)	I v P	Lahore	2005-06
387	G. M. Turner (259)/T. W. Jarvis (182)	NZ v WI	Georgetown	1971-72
382	W. M. Lawry (210)/R. B. Simpson (201)	A v WI	Bridgetown	1964-65

Second Wicket

576	S. T. Jayasuriya (340)/R. S. Mahanama (225)	SL v I	Colombo (RPS)	1997-98
451	W. H. Ponsford (266)/D. G. Bradman (244)	A v E	The Oval	1934
446	C. C. Hunte (260)/G. S. Sobers (365*)	WI v P	Kingston	1957-58
438	M. S. Atapattu (249)/K. C. Sangakkara (270)	SL v Z	Bulawayo	2003-04
382	L. Hutton (364)/M. Leyland (187)	E v A	The Oval	1938

Third Wicket

624	K. C. Sangakkara (287)/ D. P. M. D. Jayawardene (374)	SL v SA	Colombo (SSC)	2006
467	A. H. Jones (186)/M. D. Crowe (299)	NZ v SL	Wellington	1990-91
451	Mudassar Nazar (231)/Javed Miandad (280*)	P v I	Hyderabad	1982-83
429*	J. A. Rudolph (222*)/H. H. Dippenaar (177*)	SA v B	Chittagong	2003
397	Qasim Omar (206)/Javed Miandad (203*)	P v SL	Faisalabad	1985-86

Fourth Wicket

449	A. C. Voges (269*)/S. E. Marsh (182)	A v WI	Hobart	2015-16
437	D. P. M. D. Jayawardene (240)/ T. T. Samaraweera (231)	SL v P	Karachi	2008-09
411	P. B. H. May (285*)/M. C. Cowdrey (154)	E v WI	Birmingham	1957
399	G. S. Sobers (226)/F. M. M. Worrell (197*)	WI v E	Bridgetown	1959-60
388	W. H. Ponsford (181)/D. G. Bradman (304)	A v E	Leeds	1934

Fifth Wicket

405	S. G. Barnes (234)/D. G. Bradman (234)	A v E	Sydney	1946-47
385	S. R. Waugh (160)/G. S. Blewett (214)	A v SA	Johannesburg	1996-97
376	V. V. S. Laxman (281)/R. Dravid (180)	I v A	Kolkata	2000-01
359	**Shakib Al Hasan (217)/Mushfiqur Rahim (159)**	**B v NZ**	**Wellington**	**2016-17**
338	G. C. Smith (234)/A. B. de Villiers (164)	SA v P	Dubai	2013-14

Sixth Wicket

399	B. A. Stokes (258)/J. M. Bairstow (150*)	E v SA	Cape Town	2015-16
352	B. B. McCullum (302)/B-J. Watling (124)	NZ v I	Wellington	2013-14
351	D. P. M. D. Jayawardene (275)/ H. A. P. W. Jayawardene (154*)	SL v I	Ahmedabad	2009-10
346	J. H. Fingleton (136)/D. G. Bradman (270)	A v E	Melbourne	1936-37

Seventh Wicket

347	D. St E. Atkinson (219)/C. C. Depeiza (122)	WI v A	Bridgetown	1954-55
308	Waqar Hassan (189)/Imtiaz Ahmed (209)	P v NZ	Lahore	1955-56
280	R. G. Sharma (177)/R. Ashwin (124)	I v WI	Kolkata	2013-14
259*	V. V. S. Laxman (143*)/M. S. Dhoni (132*)	I v SA	Kolkata	2009-10
248	Yousuf Youhana (203)/Saqlain Mushtaq (101*)	P v NZ	Christchurch	2000-01

Eighth Wicket

332	I. J. L. Trott (184)/S. C. J. Broad (169)	E v P	Lord's	2010
313	Wasim Akram (257*)/Saqlain Mushtaq (79)	P v Z	Sheikhupura	1996-97
256	S. P. Fleming (262)/J. E. C. Franklin (122*)	NZ v SA	Cape Town	2005-06
253	N. J. Astle (156*)/A. C. Parore (110)	NZ v A	Perth	2001-02
246	L. E. G. Ames (137)/G. O. B. Allen (122)	E v NZ	Lord's	1931

Ninth Wicket

195	M. V. Boucher (78)/P. L. Symcox (108)	SA v P	Johannesburg	1997-98
190	Asif Iqbal (146)/Intikhab Alam (51)	P v E	The Oval	1967
184	Mahmudullah (76)/Abul Hasan (113)	B v WI	Khulna	2012-13
180	J-P. Duminy (166)/D. W. Steyn (76)	SA v A	Melbourne	2008-09
163*	M. C. Cowdrey (128*)/A. C. Smith (69*)	E v NZ	Wellington	1962-63

Tenth Wicket

198	J. E. Root (154*)/J. M. Anderson (81)	E v I	Nottingham	2014
163	P. J. Hughes (81*)/A. C. Agar (98)	A v E	Nottingham	2013
151	B. F. Hastings (110)/R. O. Collinge (68*)	NZ v P	Auckland	1972-73
151	Azhar Mahmood (128*)/Mushtaq Ahmed (59)	P v SA	Rawalpindi	1997-98
143	D. Ramdin (107*)/T. L. Best (95)	WI v E	Birmingham	2012

HIGHEST PARTNERSHIPS FOR EACH COUNTRY

ENGLAND

359	for 1st	L. Hutton (158)/C. Washbrook (195)	v SA	Johannesburg	1948-49
382	for 2nd	L. Hutton (364)/M. Leyland (187)	v A	The Oval	1938
370	for 3rd	W. J. Edrich (189)/D. C. S. Compton (208)	v SA	Lord's	1947
411	for 4th	P. B. H. May (285*)/M. C. Cowdrey (154)	v WI	Birmingham	1957
254	for 5th	K. W. R. Fletcher (113)/A. W. Greig (148)	v I	Bombay	1972-73
399	for 6th	B. A. Stokes (258)/J. M. Bairstow (150*)	v SA	Cape Town	2015-16
197	for 7th	M. J. K. Smith (96)/J. M. Parks (101*)	v WI	Port-of-Spain	1959-60
332	for 8th	I. J. L. Trott (184)/S. C. J. Broad (169)	v P	Lord's	2010
163*	for 9th	M. C. Cowdrey (128*)/A. C. Smith (69*)	v NZ	Wellington	1962-63
198	for 10th	J. E. Root (154*)/J. M. Anderson (81)	v I	Nottingham	2014

AUSTRALIA

382	for 1st	W. M. Lawry (210)/R. B. Simpson (201)	v WI	Bridgetown	1964-65
451	for 2nd	W. H. Ponsford (266)/D. G. Bradman (244)	v E	The Oval	1934
315	for 3rd	R. T. Ponting (206)/D. S. Lehmann (160)	v WI	Port-of-Spain	2002-03
449	for 4th	A. C. Voges (269*)/S. E. Marsh (182)	v WI	Hobart	2015-16
405	for 5th	S. G. Barnes (234)/D. G. Bradman (234)	v E	Sydney	1946-47
346	for 6th	J. H. Fingleton (136)/D. G. Bradman (270)	v E	Melbourne	1936-37
217	for 7th	K. D. Walters (250)/G. J. Gilmour (101)	v NZ	Christchurch	1976-77
243	for 8th	R. J. Hartigan (116)/C. Hill (160)	v E	Adelaide	1907-08
154	for 9th	S. E. Gregory (201)/J. McC. Blackham (74)	v E	Sydney	1894-95
163	for 10th	P. J. Hughes (81*)/A. C. Agar (98)	v E	Nottingham	2013

SOUTH AFRICA

415	for 1st	N. D. McKenzie (226)/G. C. Smith (232)	v B	Chittagong	2007-08
315*	for 2nd	H. H. Gibbs (211*)/J. H. Kallis (148*)	v NZ	Christchurch	1998-99
429*	for 3rd	J. A. Rudolph (222*)/H. H. Dippenaar (177*)	v B	Chittagong	2003
308	for 4th	H. M. Amla (208)/A. B. de Villiers (152)	v WI	Centurion	2014-15
338	for 5th	G. C. Smith (234)/A. B. de Villiers (164)	v P	Dubai	2013-14
271	for 6th	A. G. Prince (162*)/M. V. Boucher (117)	v B	Centurion	2008-09
246	for 7th	D. J. McGlew (255*)/A. R. A. Murray (109)	v NZ	Wellington	1952-53
150	for 8th	N. D. McKenzie (103)/S. M. Pollock (111)	v SL	Centurion	2000-01
		G. Kirsten (130)/M. Zondeki (59)	v E	Leeds	2003
195	for 9th	M. V. Boucher (78)/P. L. Symcox (108)	v P	Johannesburg	1997-98
107*	for 10th	A. B. de Villiers (278*)/M. Morkel (35*)	v P	Abu Dhabi	2010-11

WEST INDIES

298	for 1st	C. G. Greenidge (149)/D. L. Haynes (167)	v E	St John's	1989-90
446	for 2nd	C. C. Hunte (260)/G. S. Sobers (365*)	v P	Kingston	1957-58
338	for 3rd	E. D. Weekes (206)/F. M. M. Worrell (167)	v E	Port-of-Spain	1953-54
399	for 4th	G. S. Sobers (226)/F. M. M. Worrell (197*)	v E	Bridgetown	1959-60
322	for 5th†	B. C. Lara (213)/J. C. Adams (94)	v A	Kingston	1998-99
282*	for 6th	B. C. Lara (400*)/R. D. Jacobs (107*)	v E	St John's	2003-04
347	for 7th	D. St E. Atkinson (219)/C. C. Depeiza (122)	v A	Bridgetown	1954-55
212	**for 8th**	**S. O. Dowrich (103)/J. O. Holder (110)**	**v Z**	**Bulawayo**	**2017-18**
161	for 9th	C. H. Lloyd (161*)/A. M. E. Roberts (68)	v I	Calcutta	1983-84
143	for 10th	D. Ramdin (107*)/T. L. Best (95)	v E	Birmingham	2012

† *344 runs were added between the fall of the 4th and 5th wickets: P. T. Collins retired hurt when he and Lara had added 22 runs.*

NEW ZEALAND

387	for 1st	G. M. Turner (259)/T. W. Jarvis (182)	v WI	Georgetown	1971-72
297	for 2nd	B. B. McCullum (202)/K. S. Williamson (192)	v P	Sharjah	2014-15
467	for 3rd	A. H. Jones (186)/M. D. Crowe (299)	v SL	Wellington	1990-91
271	for 4th	L. R. P. L. Taylor (151)/J. D. Ryder (201)	v I	Napier	2008-09
222	for 5th	N. J. Astle (141)/C. D. McMillan (142)	v Z	Wellington	2000-01
365*	for 6th	K. S. Williamson (242*)/B-J. Watling (142*)	v SL	Wellington	2014-15
225	for 7th	C. L. Cairns (158)/J. D. P. Oram (90)	v SA	Auckland	2003-04
256	for 8th	S. P. Fleming (262)/J. E. C. Franklin (122*)	v SA	Cape Town	2005-06
136	for 9th	I. D. S. Smith (173)/M. C. Snedden (22)	v I	Auckland	1989-90
151	for 10th	B. F. Hastings (110)/R. O. Collinge (68*)	v P	Auckland	1972-73

INDIA

413	for 1st	M. H. Mankad (231)/Pankaj Roy (173)	v NZ	Madras	1955-56
370	for 2nd	M. Vijay (167)/C. A. Pujara (204)	v A	Hyderabad	2012-13
336	for 3rd†	V. Sehwag (309)/S. R. Tendulkar (194*)	v P	Multan	2003-04
365	for 4th	V. Kohli (211)/A. M. Rahane (188)	v NZ	Indore	2016-17
376	for 5th	V. V. S. Laxman (281)/R. Dravid (180)	v A	Kolkata	2000-01
298*	for 6th	D. B. Vengsarkar (164*)/R. J. Shastri (121*)	v A	Bombay	1986-87
280	for 7th	R. G. Sharma (177)/R. Ashwin (124)	v WI	Kolkata	2013-14
241	for 8th	V. Kohli (235)/J. Yadav (104)	v E	Mumbai	2016-17
149	for 9th	P. G. Joshi (52*)/R. B. Desai (85)	v P	Bombay	1960-61
133	for 10th	S. R. Tendulkar (248*)/Zaheer Khan (75)	v B	Dhaka	2004-05

† *415 runs were scored for India's 3rd wicket v England at Madras in 1981-82, in two partnerships: D. B. Vengsarkar and G. R. Viswanath put on 99 before Vengsarkar retired hurt, then Viswanath and Yashpal Sharma added a further 316.*

PAKISTAN

298	for 1st	Aamir Sohail (160)/Ijaz Ahmed snr (151)	v WI	Karachi	1997-98
291	for 2nd	Zaheer Abbas (274)/Mushtaq Mohammad (100)	v E	Birmingham	1971
451	for 3rd	Mudassar Nazar (231)/Javed Miandad (280*)	v I	Hyderabad	1982-83
350	for 4th	Mushtaq Mohammad (201)/Asif Iqbal (175)	v NZ	Dunedin	1972-73
281	for 5th	Javed Miandad (163)/Asif Iqbal (166)	v NZ	Lahore	1976-77
269	for 6th	Mohammad Yousuf (223)/Kamran Akmal (154)	v E	Lahore	2005-06
308	for 7th	Waqar Hassan (189)/Imtiaz Ahmed (209)	v NZ	Lahore	1955-56
313	for 8th	Wasim Akram (257*)/Saqlain Mushtaq (79)	v Z	Sheikhupura	1996-97
190	for 9th	Asif Iqbal (146)/Intikhab Alam (51)	v E	The Oval	1967
151	for 10th	Azhar Mahmood (128*)/Mushtaq Ahmed (59)	v SA	Rawalpindi	1997-98

SRI LANKA

335	for 1st	M. S. Atapattu (207*)/S. T. Jayasuriya (188)	v P	Kandy	2000
576	for 2nd	S. T. Jayasuriya (340)/R. S. Mahanama (225)	v I	Colombo (RPS)	1997-98
624	for 3rd	K. C. Sangakkara (287)/D. P. M. D. Jayawardene (374)	v SA	Colombo (SSC)	2006
437	for 4th	D. P. M. D. Jayawardene (240)/T. T. Samaraweera (231)	v P	Karachi	2008-09
280	for 5th	T. T. Samaraweera (138)/T. M. Dilshan (168)	v B	Colombo (PSS)	2005-06
351	for 6th	D. P. M. D. Jayawardene (275)/H. A. P. W. Jayawardene (154*)	v I	Ahmedabad	2009-10
223*	for 7th	H. A. P. W. Jayawardene (120*)/W. P. U. J. C. Vaas (100*)	v B	Colombo (SSC)	2007
170	for 8th	D. P. M. D. Jayawardene (237)/W. P. U. J. C. Vaas (69)	v SA	Galle	2004
118	for 9th	T. T. Samaraweera (83)/B. A. W. Mendis (78)	v I	Colombo (PSS)	2010
79	for 10th	W. P. U. J. C. Vaas (68*)/M. Muralitharan (43)	v A	Kandy	2003-04

ZIMBABWE

164	for 1st	D. D. Ebrahim (71)/A. D. R. Campbell (103)	v WI	Bulawayo	2001
160	for 2nd	Sikandar Raza (82)/H. Masakadza (81)	v B	Chittagong	2014-15
194	for 3rd	A. D. R. Campbell (99)/D. L. Houghton (142)	v SL	Harare	1994-95
269	for 4th	G. W. Flower (201*)/A. Flower (156)	v P	Harare	1994-95
277*	for 5th	M. W. Goodwin (166*)/A. Flower (100*)	v P	Bulawayo	1997-98
165	for 6th	D. L. Houghton (121)/A. Flower (59)	v I	Harare	1992-93
154	for 7th	H. H. Streak (83*)/A. M. Blignaut (92)	v WI	Harare	2001
168	for 8th	H. H. Streak (127*)/A. M. Blignaut (91)	v WI	Harare	2003-04
87	for 9th	P. A. Strang (106*)/B. C. Strang (42)	v P	Sheikhupura	1996-97
97*	for 10th	A. Flower (183*)/H. K. Olonga (11*)	v I	Delhi	2000-01

BANGLADESH

312	for 1st	Tamim Iqbal (206)/Imrul Kayes (150)	v P	Khulna	2014-15
232	for 2nd	Shamsur Rahman (106)/Imrul Kayes (115)	v SL	Chittagong	2013-14
157	for 3rd	Tamim Iqbal (70)/Mominul Haque (126*)	v NZ	Mirpur	2013-14
167	for 4th	Naeem Islam (108)/Shakib Al Hasan (89)	v WI	Mirpur	2012-13
359	**for 5th**	**Shakib Al Hasan (217)/ Mushfiqur Rahim (159)**	**v NZ**	**Wellington**	**2016-17**
191	for 6th	Mohammad Ashraful (129*)/ Mushfiqur Rahim (80)	v SL	Colombo (PSS)	2007
145	for 7th	Shakib Al Hasan (87)/Mahmudullah (115)	v NZ	Hamilton	2009-10
113	for 8th	Mushfiqur Rahim (79)/Naeem Islam (38)	v E	Chittagong	2009-10
184	for 9th	Mahmudullah (76)/Abul Hasan (113)	v WI	Khulna	2012-13
69	for 10th	Mohammad Rafique (65)/Shahadat Hossain (3*)	v A	Chittagong	2005-06

UNUSUAL DISMISSALS

Handled the Ball

W. R. Endean	South Africa v England at Cape Town	1956-57
A. M. J. Hilditch	Australia v Pakistan at Perth	1978-79
Mohsin Khan	Pakistan v Australia at Karachi	1982-83
D. L. Haynes	West Indies v India at Bombay	1983-84
G. A. Gooch	England v Australia at Manchester	1993
S. R. Waugh	Australia v India at Chennai	2000-01
M. P. Vaughan	England v India at Bangalore	2001-02

Obstructing the Field

L. Hutton	England v South Africa at The Oval	1951

There have been no cases of Hit the Ball Twice or Timed Out in Test cricket.

BOWLING RECORDS

MOST WICKETS IN AN INNINGS

10-53	J. C. Laker	England v Australia at Manchester	1956
10-74	A. Kumble	India v Pakistan at Delhi	1998-99
9-28	G. A. Lohmann	England v South Africa at Johannesburg	1895-96
9-37	J. C. Laker	England v Australia at Manchester	1956
9-51	M. Muralitharan	Sri Lanka v Zimbabwe at Kandy	2001-02
9-52	R. J. Hadlee	New Zealand v Australia at Brisbane	1985-86
9-56	Abdul Qadir	Pakistan v England at Lahore	1987-88
9-57	D. E. Malcolm	England v South Africa at The Oval	1994
9-65	M. Muralitharan	Sri Lanka v England at The Oval	1998
9-69	J. M. Patel	India v Australia at Kanpur	1959-60
9-83	Kapil Dev	India v West Indies at Ahmedabad	1983-84
9-86	Sarfraz Nawaz	Pakistan v Australia at Melbourne	1978-79
9-95	J. M. Noreiga	West Indies v India at Port-of-Spain	1970-71
9-102	S. P. Gupte	India v West Indies at Kanpur	1958-59
9-103	S. F. Barnes	England v South Africa at Johannesburg	1913-14
9-113	H. J. Tayfield	South Africa v England at Johannesburg	1956-57
9-121	A. A. Mailey	Australia v England at Melbourne	1920-21
9-127	H. M. R. K. B. Herath	Sri Lanka v Pakistan at Colombo (SSC)	2014

*There have been **76** instances of eight wickets in a Test innings.*

The best bowling figures for the countries not mentioned above are:

8-39	Taijul Islam	Bangladesh v Zimbabwe at Mirpur	2014-15
8-109	P. A. Strang	Zimbabwe v New Zealand at Bulawayo	2000-01

OUTSTANDING BOWLING ANALYSES

	O	*M*	*R*	*W*		
J. C. Laker (E)	51.2	23	53	10	v Australia at Manchester	1956
A. Kumble (I)	26.3	9	74	10	v Pakistan at Delhi	1998-99
G. A. Lohmann (E)	14.2	6	28	9	v South Africa at Johannesburg	1895-96
J. C. Laker (E)	16.4	4	37	9	v Australia at Manchester	1956
G. A. Lohmann (E)	9.4	5	7	8	v South Africa at Port Elizabeth	1895-96
J. Briggs (E)	14.2	5	11	8	v South Africa at Cape Town	1888-89
S. C. J. Broad (E)	9.3	5	15	8	v Australia at Nottingham	2015
S. J. Harmison (E)	12.3	8	12	7	v West Indies at Kingston	2003-04
J. Briggs (E)	19.1	11	17	7	v South Africa at Cape Town	1888-89
M. A. Noble (A)	7.4	2	17	7	v England at Melbourne	1901-02
W. Rhodes (E)	11	3	17	7	v Australia at Birmingham	1902

WICKET WITH FIRST BALL IN TEST CRICKET

	Batsman dismissed			
T. P. Horan	W. W. Read	A v E	Sydney	1882-83
A. Coningham	A. C. MacLaren	A v E	Melbourne	1894-95
W. M. Bradley	F. Laver	E v A	Manchester	1899
E. G. Arnold	V. T. Trumper	E v A	Sydney	1903-04
A. E. E. Vogler	E. G. Hayes	SA v E	Johannesburg	1905-06
J. N. Crawford	A. E. E. Vogler	E v SA	Johannesburg	1905-06
G. G. Macaulay	G. A. L. Hearne	E v SA	Cape Town	1922-23
M. W. Tate	M. J. Susskind	E v SA	Birmingham	1924
M. Henderson	E. W. Dawson	NZ v E	Christchurch	1929-30
H. D. Smith	E. Paynter	NZ v E	Christchurch	1932-33
T. F. Johnson	W. W. Keeton	WI v E	The Oval	1939
R. Howorth	D. V. Dyer	E v SA	The Oval	1947
Intikhab Alam	C. C. McDonald	P v A	Karachi	1959-60
R. K. Illingworth	P. V. Simmons	E v WI	Nottingham	1991
N. M. Kulkarni	M. S. Atapattu	I v SL	Colombo (RPS)	1997-98
M. K. G. C. P. Lakshitha	Mohammad Ashraful	SL v B	Colombo (SSC)	2002
N. M. Lyon	K. C. Sangakkara	A v SL	Galle	2011-12
R. M. S. Eranga	S. R. Watson	SL v A	Colombo (SSC)	2011-12
D. L. Piedt	M. A. Vermeulen	SA v Z	Harare	2014-15
G. C. Viljoen	A. N. Cook	SA v E	Johannesburg	2015-16

HAT-TRICKS

Most Hat-Tricks

S. C. J. Broad	**2**	H. Trumble	2
T. J. Matthews†	2	Wasim Akram‡	2

† *T. J. Matthews did the hat-trick in each innings of the same match.*
‡ *Wasim Akram did the hat-trick in successive matches.*

Hat-Tricks

There have been **43** hat-tricks in Tests, including the above. Occurrences since 2007:

R. J. Sidebottom	England v New Zealand at Hamilton	2007-08
P. M. Siddle	Australia v England at Brisbane	2010-11
S. C. J. Broad	England v India at Nottingham	2011
Sohag Gazi†	Bangladesh v New Zealand at Chittagong	2013-14

S. C. J. Broad	England v Sri Lanka at Leeds	2014
H. M. R. K. B. Herath	Sri Lanka v Australia at Galle	2016
M. M. Ali	**England v South Africa at The Oval**	**2017**

† *Sohag Gazi also scored 101 not out.*

M. J. C. Allom, P. J. Petherick and D. W. Fleming did the hat-trick on Test debut. D. N. T. Zoysa took one in the second over of a Test (his first three balls); I. K. Pathan in the first over of a Test.

FOUR WICKETS IN FIVE BALLS

M. J. C. Allom	England v New Zealand at Christchurch *On debut, in his eighth over: W-WWW*	1929-30
C. M. Old	England v Pakistan at Birmingham *Sequence interrupted by a no-ball: WW-WW*	1978
Wasim Akram	Pakistan v West Indies at Lahore (*WW-WW*)	1990-91

MOST WICKETS IN A TEST

19-90	J. C. Laker	England v Australia at Manchester	1956
17-159	S. F. Barnes	England v South Africa at Johannesburg	1913-14
16-136†	N. D. Hirwani	India v West Indies at Madras	1987-88
16-137†	R. A. L. Massie	Australia v England at Lord's	1972
16-220	M. Muralitharan	Sri Lanka v England at The Oval	1998

† *On Test debut.*

There have been 18 further instances of 14 or more wickets in a Test match.

The best bowling figures for the countries not mentioned above are:

15-123	R. J. Hadlee	New Zealand v Australia at Brisbane	1985-86
14-116	Imran Khan	Pakistan v Sri Lanka at Lahore	1981-82
14-149	M. A. Holding	West Indies v England at The Oval	1976
13-132	M. Ntini	South Africa v West Indies at Port-of-Spain	2004-05
12-159	Mehedi Hasan	Bangladesh v England at Mirpur	2016-17
11-255	A. G. Huckle	Zimbabwe v New Zealand at Bulawayo	1997-98

MOST BALLS BOWLED IN A TEST

S. Ramadhin (West Indies) sent down 774 balls in 129 overs against England at Birmingham, 1957, the most delivered by any bowler in a Test, beating H. Verity's 766 for England against South Africa at Durban, 1938-39. In this match Ramadhin also bowled the most balls (588) in any first-class innings, since equalled by Arshad Ayub, Hyderabad v Madhya Pradesh at Secunderabad, 1991-92.

MOST WICKETS IN A SERIES

	T	*R*	*W*	*Avge*		
S. F. Barnes	4	536	49	10.93	England v South Africa	1913-14
J. C. Laker	5	442	46	9.60	England v Australia	1956
C. V. Grimmett	5	642	44	14.59	Australia v South Africa	1935-36
T. M. Alderman	6	893	42	21.26	Australia v England	1981
R. M. Hogg	6	527	41	12.85	Australia v England	1978-79
T. M. Alderman	6	712	41	17.36	Australia v England	1989
Imran Khan	6	558	40	13.95	Pakistan v India	1982-83
S. K. Warne	5	797	40	19.92	Australia v England	2005

The most for South Africa is 37 by H. J. Tayfield against England in 1956-57, for West Indies 35 by M. D. Marshall against England in 1988, for India 35 by B. S. Chandrasekhar against England in 1972-73 (all in five Tests), for New Zealand 33 by R. J. Hadlee against Australia in 1985-86, for Sri Lanka 30 by M. Muralitharan against Zimbabwe in 2001-02, for Zimbabwe 22 by H. H. Streak against Pakistan in 1994-95 (all in three Tests), and for Bangladesh 19 by Mehedi Hasan against England in 2016-17 (two Tests).

MOST WICKETS IN A CALENDAR YEAR

	T	*R*	*W*	*Avge*	*5I*	*10M*	*Year*
S. K. Warne (Australia)	15	2,114	96	22.02	6	2	2005
M. Muralitharan (Sri Lanka)	11	1,521	90	16.89	9	5	2006
D. K. Lillee (Australia)	13	1,781	85	20.95	5	2	1981
A. A. Donald (South Africa)	14	1,571	80	19.63	7	–	1998
M. Muralitharan (Sri Lanka)	12	1,699	80	21.23	7	4	2001
J. Garner (West Indies)	15	1,604	77	20.83	4	–	1984
Kapil Dev (India)	18	1,739	75	23.18	5	1	1983
M. Muralitharan (Sri Lanka)	10	1,463	75	19.50	7	3	2000

MOST WICKETS

		T	*Balls*	*R*	*W*	*Avge*	*5I*	*10M*	*SR*
1	M. Muralitharan (SL/World)	133	44,039	18,180	800	22.72	67	22	55.04
2	S. K. Warne (Australia)	145	40,704	17,995	708	25.41	37	10	57.49
3	A. Kumble (India)	132	40,850	18,355	619	29.65	35	8	65.99
4	G. D. McGrath (Australia)	124	29,248	12,186	563	21.64	29	3	51.95
5	**J. M. Anderson (England)**	**134**	**29,600**	**14,333**	**523**	**27.40**	**25**	**3**	**56.59**
6	C. A. Walsh (West Indies)	132	30,019	12,688	519	24.44	22	3	57.84
7	Kapil Dev (India)	131	27,740	12,867	434	29.64	23	2	63.91
8	R. J. Hadlee (New Zealand)	86	21,918	9,611	431	22.29	36	9	50.85
9	S. M. Pollock (South Africa)	108	24,353	9,733	421	23.11	16	1	57.84
10	**D. W. Steyn (South Africa)**	**86**	**17,391**	**9,354**	**419**	**22.32**	**26**	**5**	**41.50**
11	Harbhajan Singh (India)	103	28,580	13,537	417	32.46	25	5	68.53
12	Wasim Akram (Pakistan)	104	22,627	9,779	414	23.62	25	5	54.65
13	**H. M. R. K. B. Herath (SL)**	**87**	**24,389**	**11,384**	**406**	**28.03**	**33**	**9**	**60.07**
14	C. E. L. Ambrose (WI)	98	22,103	8,501	405	20.99	22	3	54.57
15	**S. C. J. Broad (England)**	**114**	**23,533**	**11,706**	**399**	**29.33**	**15**	**2**	**58.97**
16	M. Ntini (South Africa)	101	20,834	11,242	390	28.82	18	4	53.42
17	I. T. Botham (England)	102	21,815	10,878	383	28.40	27	4	56.95
18	M. D. Marshall (West Indies)	81	17,584	7,876	376	20.94	22	4	46.76
19	Waqar Younis (Pakistan)	87	16,224	8,788	373	23.56	22	5	43.49
20	Imran Khan (Pakistan)	88	19,458	8,258	362	22.81	23	6	53.75
	D. L. Vettori (NZ/World)	113	28,814	12,441	362	34.36	20	3	79.59
22	D. K. Lillee (Australia)	70	18,467	8,493	355	23.92	23	7	52.01
	W. P. U. J. C. Vaas (SL)	111	23,438	10,501	355	29.58	12	2	66.02
24	A. A. Donald (South Africa)	72	15,519	7,344	330	22.25	20	3	47.02
25	R. G. D. Willis (England)	90	17,357	8,190	325	25.20	16	–	53.40
26	M. G. Johnson (Australia)	73	16,001	8,891	313	28.40	12	3	51.12
27	**R. Ashwin (India)**	**57**	**16,515**	**7,951**	**311**	**25.56**	**26**	**7**	**53.10**
	Zaheer Khan (India)	92	18,785	10,247	311	32.94	11	1	60.40
29	B. Lee (Australia)	76	16,531	9,554	310	30.81	10	–	53.32
30	L. R. Gibbs (West Indies)	79	27,115	8,989	309	29.09	18	2	87.75
31	F. S. Trueman (England)	67	15,178	6,625	307	21.57	17	3	49.43

MOST WICKETS FOR EACH COUNTRY

ENGLAND

J. M. Anderson	**523**	I. T. Botham	383	F. S. Trueman	307
S. C. J. Broad	**399**	R. G. D. Willis	325	D. L. Underwood	297

AUSTRALIA

S. K. Warne	708	D. K. Lillee	355	B. Lee	310
G. D. McGrath	563	M. G. Johnson	313	C. J. McDermott	291

SOUTH AFRICA

S. M. Pollock	421	M. Ntini	390	**M. Morkel**	**294**
D. W. Steyn	**419**	A. A. Donald	330	J. H. Kallis†	291

† *J. H. Kallis also took 0-35 and 1-3 for the World XI v Australia (2005-06 Super Series Test).*

WEST INDIES

C. A. Walsh	519	M. D. Marshall	376	J. Garner	259
C. E. L. Ambrose	405	L. R. Gibbs	309	M. A. Holding	249

NEW ZEALAND

R. J. Hadlee	431	C. S. Martin	233	**T. G. Southee**	**208**
D. L. Vettori†	361	C. L. Cairns	218	**T. A. Boult**	**200**

† *D. L. Vettori also took 1-73 and 0-38 for the World XI v Australia (2005-06 Super Series Test).*

INDIA

A. Kumble	619	Harbhajan Singh	417	Zaheer Khan	311
Kapil Dev	434	**R. Ashwin**	**311**	B. S. Bedi	266

PAKISTAN

Wasim Akram	414	Imran Khan	362	Abdul Qadir	236
Waqar Younis	373	Danish Kaneria	261	Saqlain Mushtaq	208

SRI LANKA

M. Muralitharan†	795	W. P. U. J. C. Vaas	355	**M. D. K. Perera**	101
H. M. R. K. B. Herath	**406**	S. L. Malinga	101	C. R. D. Fernando	100

† *M. Muralitharan also took 2-102 and 3-55 for the World XI v Australia (2005-06 Super Series Test).*

ZIMBABWE

H. H. Streak	216	P. A. Strang	70	**A. G. Cremer**	**57**
R. W. Price	80	H. K. Olonga	68	B. C. Strang	56

BANGLADESH

Shakib Al Hasan	**188**	Mashrafe bin Mortaza	78	**Taijul Islam**	**54**
Mohammad Rafique	100	Shahadat Hossain	72	Enamul Haque jnr	44

BEST CAREER AVERAGES

(Qualification: 75 wickets)

Avge		*T*	*W*	*Avge*		*T*	*W*
10.75	G. A. Lohmann (E)	18	112	16.98	R. Peel (E)	20	101
16.43	S. F. Barnes (E)	27	189	17.75	J. Briggs (E)	33	118
16.53	C. T. B. Turner (A)	17	101	18.41	F. R. Spofforth (A)	18	94

Avge		*T*	*W*	*Avge*		*T*	*W*
18.56	F. H. Tyson (E)	17	76	20.94	M. D. Marshall (WI)	81	376
18.63	C. Blythe (E)	19	100	20.97	J. Garner (WI)	58	259
20.39	J. H. Wardle (E)	28	102	20.99	C. E. L. Ambrose (WI)	98	405
20.53	A. K. Davidson (A)	44	186				

BEST CAREER STRIKE-RATES

(Balls per wicket. Qualification: 75 wickets)

SR		*T*	*W*	*SR*		*T*	*W*
34.19	G. A. Lohmann (E)	18	112	45.46	C. Blythe (E)	19	100
38.75	S. E. Bond (NZ)	18	87	45.74	Shoaib Akhtar (P)	46	178
39.73	**K. Rabada (SA)**	**26**	**120**	46.76	M. D. Marshall (WI)	81	376
41.50	**D. W. Steyn (SA)**	**86**	**419**	47.02	A. A. Donald (SA)	72	330
41.65	S. F. Barnes (E)	27	189	**48.56**	**V. D. Philander (SA)**	**50**	**188**
43.49	Waqar Younis (P)	87	373	48.78	Mohammad Asif (P)	23	106
44.52	F. R. Spofforth (A)	18	94	**49.00**	**M. A. Starc (A)**	**40**	**170**
45.12	J. V. Saunders (A)	14	79	49.32	C. E. H. Croft (WI)	27	125
45.18	J. Briggs (E)	33	118	49.43	F. S. Trueman (E)	67	307
45.42	F. H. Tyson (E)	17	76				

BEST CAREER ECONOMY-RATES

(Runs per six balls. Qualification: 75 wickets)

ER		*T*	*W*	*ER*		*T*	*W*
1.64	T. L. Goddard (SA)	41	123	1.94	H. J. Tayfield (SA)	37	170
1.67	R. G. Nadkarni (I)	41	88	1.95	A. L. Valentine (WI)	36	139
1.88	H. Verity (E)	40	144	1.95	F. J. Titmus (E)	53	153
1.88	G. A. Lohmann (E)	18	112	1.97	S. Ramadhin (WI)	43	158
1.89	J. H. Wardle (E)	28	102	1.97	R. Peel (E)	20	101
1.91	R. Illingworth (E)	61	122	1.97	A. K. Davidson (A)	44	186
1.93	C. T. B. Turner (A)	17	101	1.98	L. R. Gibbs (WI)	79	309
1.94	M. W. Tate (E)	39	155				
1.94	W. J. O'Reilly (A)	27	144				

HIGHEST PERCENTAGE OF TEAM'S WICKETS OVER TEST CAREER

(Qualification: 20 Tests)

	Tests	*Wkts*	*Team Wkts*	*% of Team Wkts*
M. Muralitharan (Sri Lanka/World)	133	800	2,070	38.64
S. F. Barnes (England)	27	189	494	38.25
R. J. Hadlee (New Zealand)	86	431	1,255	34.34
Yasir Shah (Pakistan)	**28**	**165**	**481**	**34.30**
C. V. Grimmett (Australia)	37	216	636	33.96
Fazal Mahmood (Pakistan)	34	139	410	33.90
W. J. O'Reilly (Australia)	27	144	446	32.28
S. P. Gupte (India)	36	149	470	31.70
R. Ashwin (India)	**57**	**311**	**992**	**31.35**
Saeed Ajmal (Pakistan)	35	178	575	30.95
Mohammad Rafique (Bangladesh)	33	100	328	30.48
A. V. Bedser (England)	51	236	777	30.37

Excluding the Super Series Test, Muralitharan took 795 out of 2,050 wickets in his 132 Tests for Sri Lanka, a percentage of 38.78.

The percentage shows the proportion of a team's wickets taken by that player in all Tests in which he played, including team wickets in innings in which he did not bowl.

ALL-ROUND RECORDS

HUNDRED AND FIVE WICKETS IN AN INNINGS

England					
A. W. Greig	148	6-164	v West Indies	Bridgetown	1973-74
I. T. Botham	103	5-73	v New Zealand	Christchurch	1977-78
I. T. Botham	108	8-34	v Pakistan	Lord's	1978
I. T. Botham	114	6-58, 7-48	v India	Bombay	1979-80
I. T. Botham	149*	6-95	v Australia	Leeds	1981
I. T. Botham	138	5-59	v New Zealand	Wellington	1983-84
Australia					
C. Kelleway	114	5-33	v South Africa	Manchester	1912
J. M. Gregory	100	7-69	v England	Melbourne	1920-21
K. R. Miller	109	6-107	v West Indies	Kingston	1954-55
R. Benaud	100	5-84	v South Africa	Johannesburg	1957-58
South Africa					
J. H. Sinclair	106	6-26	v England	Cape Town	1898-99
G. A. Faulkner	123	5-120	v England	Johannesburg	1909-10
J. H. Kallis	110	5-90	v West Indies	Cape Town	1998-99
J. H. Kallis	139*	5-21	v Bangladesh	Potchefstroom	2002-03
West Indies					
D. St E. Atkinson	219	5-56	v Australia	Bridgetown	1954-55
O. G. Smith	100	5-90	v India	Delhi	1958-59
G. S. Sobers	104	5-63	v India	Kingston	1961-62
G. S. Sobers	174	5-41	v England	Leeds	1966
R. L. Chase	137*	5-121	v India	Kingston	2016
New Zealand					
B. R. Taylor†	105	5-86	v India	Calcutta	1964-65
India					
M. H. Mankad	184	5-196	v England	Lord's	1952
P. R. Umrigar	172*	5-107	v West Indies	Port-of-Spain	1961-62
R. Ashwin	103	5-156	v West Indies	Mumbai	2011-12
R. Ashwin	113	7-83	v West Indies	North Sound	2016
Pakistan					
Mushtaq Mohammad	201	5-49	v New Zealand	Dunedin	1972-73
Mushtaq Mohammad	121	5-28	v West Indies	Port-of-Spain	1976-77
Imran Khan	117	6-98, 5-82	v India	Faisalabad	1982-83
Wasim Akram	123	5-100	v Australia	Adelaide	1989-90
Zimbabwe					
P. A. Strang	106*	5-212	v Pakistan	Sheikhupura	1996-97
Bangladesh					
Shakib Al Hasan	144	6-82	v Pakistan	Mirpur	2011-12
Sohag Gazi	101*	6-77‡	v New Zealand	Chittagong	2013-14
Shakib Al Hasan	137	5-80, 5-44	v Zimbabwe	Khulna	2014-15

† *On debut.* ‡ *Including a hat-trick; Sohag Gazi is the only player to score a hundred and take a hat-trick in the same Test.*

HUNDRED AND FIVE DISMISSALS IN AN INNINGS

D. T. Lindsay	182	6ct	SA v A	Johannesburg	1966-67
I. D. S. Smith	113*	4ct, 1st	NZ v E	Auckland	1983-84
S. A. R. Silva	111	5ct	SL v I	Colombo (PSS)	1985-86
A. C. Gilchrist	133	4ct, 1st	A v E	Sydney	2002-03
M. J. Prior	118	5ct	E v A	Sydney	2010-11
A. B. de Villiers	103*	6ct and 5ct	SA v P	Johannesburg	2012-13
M. J. Prior	110*	5ct	E v NZ	Auckland	2012-13
B-J. Watling	124	5ct	NZ v I	Wellington	2013-14
B-J. Watling	142*	4ct, 1st	NZ v SL	Wellington	2014-15
J. M. Bairstow	140	5ct	E v SL	Leeds	2016

100 RUNS AND TEN WICKETS IN A TEST

A. K. Davidson	44 80	5-135 6-87	A v WI	Brisbane	1960-61
I. T. Botham	114	6-58 7-48	E v I	Bombay	1979-80
Imran Khan	117	6-98 5-82	P v I	Faisalabad	1982-83
Shakib Al Hasan	137 6	5-80 5-44	B v Z	Khulna	2014-15

Wicketkeeper A. B. de Villiers scored 103 and held 11 catches for South Africa against Pakistan at Johannesburg in 2012-13.*

2,000 RUNS AND 200 WICKETS

	Tests	*Runs*	*Wkts*	*Tests for 1,000/100 Double*
R. Ashwin (India)	**57**	**2,145**	**311**	**24**
R. Benaud (Australia)	63	2,201	248	32
†I. T. Botham (England)	102	5,200	383	21
S. C. J. Broad (England)	**114**	**2,956**	**399**	**35**
C. L. Cairns (New Zealand)	62	3,320	218	33
A. Flintoff (England/World)	79	3,845	226	43
R. J. Hadlee (New Zealand)	86	3,124	431	28
Harbhajan Singh (India)	103	2,224	417	62
Imran Khan (Pakistan)	88	3,807	362	30
M. J. Johnson (Australia)	73	2,065	313	37
†J. H. Kallis (South Africa/World)	166	13,289	292	53
Kapil Dev (India)	131	5,248	434	25
A. Kumble (India)	132	2,506	619	56
S. M. Pollock (South Africa)	108	3,781	421	26
†G. S. Sobers (West Indies)	93	8,032	235	48
W. P. U. J. C. Vaas (Sri Lanka)	111	3,089	355	47
D. L. Vettori (New Zealand/World)	113	4,531	362	47
†S. K. Warne (Australia)	145	3,154	708	58
Wasim Akram (Pakistan)	104	2,898	414	45

H. H. Streak scored 1,990 runs and took 216 wickets in 65 Tests for Zimbabwe.

† *J. H. Kallis also took 200 catches, S. K. Warne 125, I. T. Botham 120 and G. S. Sobers 109. These four and C. L. Hooper (5,762 runs, 114 wickets and 115 catches for West Indies) are the only players to have achieved the treble of 1,000 runs, 100 wickets and 100 catches in Test cricket.*

WICKETKEEPING RECORDS

MOST DISMISSALS IN AN INNINGS

7 (all ct)	Wasim Bari	Pakistan v New Zealand at Auckland	1978-79
7 (all ct)	R. W. Taylor	England v India at Bombay	1979-80
7 (all ct)	I. D. S. Smith	New Zealand v Sri Lanka at Hamilton	1990-91
7 (all ct)	R. D. Jacobs	West Indies v Australia at Melbourne	2000-01

The first instance of seven wicketkeeping dismissals in a Test innings was a joint effort for Pakistan v West Indies at Kingston in 1976-77. Majid Khan made four catches, deputising for the injured wicketkeeper Wasim Bari, who made three more catches on his return.

*There have been **30** instances of players making six dismissals in a Test innings, the most recent being W. P. Saha (5ct, 1st) for India v West Indies at North Sound in 2016.*

MOST STUMPINGS IN AN INNINGS

5	K. S. More	India v West Indies at Madras	1987-88

MOST DISMISSALS IN A TEST

11 (all ct)	R. C. Russell	England v South Africa at Johannesburg	1995-96
11 (all ct)	A. B. de Villiers	South Africa v Pakistan at Johannesburg	2012-13
10 (all ct)	R. W. Taylor	England v India at Bombay	1979-80
10 (all ct)	A. C. Gilchrist	Australia v New Zealand at Hamilton	1999-2000
10 (all ct)	**W. P. Saha**	**India v South Africa at Cape Town**	**2017-18**

*There have been **26** instances of players making nine dismissals in a Test, the most recent being J. M. Bairstow (all ct) for England v Sri Lanka at Leeds in 2016. S. A. R. Silva made 18 in two successive Tests for Sri Lanka against India in 1985-86.*

The most stumpings in a match is 6 by K. S. More for India v West Indies at Madras in 1987-88.

J. J. Kelly (8ct) for Australia v England in 1901-02 and L. E. G. Ames (6ct, 2st) for England v West Indies in 1933 were the only keepers to make eight dismissals in a Test before World War II.

MOST DISMISSALS IN A SERIES

(Played in 5 Tests unless otherwise stated)

29 (all ct)	B. J. Haddin	Australia v England	2013
28 (all ct)	R. W. Marsh	Australia v England	1982-83
27 (25ct, 2st)	R. C. Russell	England v South Africa	1995-96
27 (25ct, 2st)	I. A. Healy	Australia v England (6 Tests)	1997

S. A. R. Silva made 22 dismissals (21ct, 1st) in three Tests for Sri Lanka v India in 1985-86.

H. Strudwick, with 21 (15ct, 6st) for England v South Africa in 1913-14, was the only wicketkeeper to make as many as 20 dismissals in a series before World War II.

MOST DISMISSALS

			T	*Ct*	*St*
1	M. V. Boucher (South Africa/World)	555	147	532	23
2	A. C. Gilchrist (Australia)	416	96	379	37
3	I. A. Healy (Australia)	395	119	366	29
4	R. W. Marsh (Australia)	355	96	343	12
5	M. S. Dhoni (India)	294	90	256	38
6	B. J. Haddin (Australia)	270	66	262	8
6	P. J. L. Dujon (West Indies)	270	79	265	5
8	A. P. E. Knott (England)	269	95	250	19
9	M. J. Prior (England)	256	79	243	13
10	A. J. Stewart (England)	241	82	227	14
11	Wasim Bari (Pakistan)	228	81	201	27
12	R. D. Jacobs (West Indies)	219	65	207	12
12	T. G. Evans (England)	219	91	173	46

			T	Ct	St
14	D. Ramdin (West Indies)	217	74	205	12
15	Kamran Akmal (Pakistan)	206	53	184	22
16	A. C. Parore (New Zealand)	201	67	194	7

The record for P. J. L. Dujon excludes two catches taken in two Tests when not keeping wicket; A. J. Stewart's record likewise excludes 36 catches taken in 51 Tests and A. C. Parore's three in 11 Tests.

Excluding the Super Series Test, M. V. Boucher made 553 dismissals (530ct, 23st in 146 Tests) for South Africa, a national record.

W. A. Oldfield made 52 stumpings, a Test record, in 54 Tests for Australia; he also took 78 catches.

The most dismissals by a wicketkeeper playing for the countries not mentioned above are:

		T	Ct	St
K. C. Sangakkara (Sri Lanka)	151	48	131	20
A. Flower (Zimbabwe)	151	55	142	9
Mushfiqur Rahim (Bangladesh)	**106**	**50**	**93**	**13**

K. C. Sangakkara's record excludes 51 catches taken in 86 matches when not keeping wicket but includes two catches taken as wicketkeeper in a match where he took over when the designated keeper was injured; A. Flower's record excludes nine catches in eight Tests when not keeping wicket, and Mushfiqur Rahim's one catch in eight Tests when not keeping wicket.

FIELDING RECORDS

(Excluding wicketkeepers)

MOST CATCHES IN AN INNINGS

5	V. Y. Richardson	Australia v South Africa at Durban	1935-36
5	Yajurvindra Singh	India v England at Bangalore	1976-77
5	M. Azharuddin	India v Pakistan at Karachi	1989-90
5	K. Srikkanth	India v Australia at Perth	1991-92
5	S. P. Fleming	New Zealand v Zimbabwe at Harare	1997-98
5	G. C. Smith	South Africa v Australia at Perth	2012-13
5	D. J. G. Sammy	West Indies v India at Mumbai	2013-14
5	D. M. Bravo	West Indies v Bangladesh at Arnos Vale	2014-15
5	A. M. Rahane	India v Sri Lanka at Galle	2015-16
5	J. Blackwood	West Indies v Sri Lanka at Colombo (PSO)	2015-16

MOST CATCHES IN A TEST

8	A. M. Rahane	India v Sri Lanka at Galle	2015-16
7	G. S. Chappell	Australia v England at Perth	1974-75
7	Yajurvindra Singh	India v England at Bangalore	1976-77
7	H. P. Tillekeratne	Sri Lanka v New Zealand at Colombo (SSC)	1992-93
7	S. P. Fleming	New Zealand v Zimbabwe at Harare	1997-98
7	M. L. Hayden	Australia v Sri Lanka at Galle	2003-04

*There have been **29** instances of players taking six catches in a Test, the most recent being S. P. D. Smith for Australia v Sri Lanka at Colombo (SSC) in 2016.*

MOST CATCHES IN A SERIES

(Played in 5 Tests unless otherwise stated)

15	J. M. Gregory	Australia v England	1920-21
14	G. S. Chappell	Australia v England (6 Tests)	1974-75
13	R. B. Simpson	Australia v South Africa	1957-58
13	R. B. Simpson	Australia v West Indies	1960-61
13	B. C. Lara	West Indies v England (6 Tests)	1997-98
13	R. Dravid	India v Australia (4 Tests)	2004-05
13	B. C. Lara	West Indies v India (4 Tests)	2005-06

MOST CATCHES

Ct	*T*		*Ct*	*T*	
210	164†	R. Dravid (India/World)	**156**	**152**	**A. N. Cook (England)**
205	149	D. P. M. D. Jayawardene (SL)	156	156	A. R. Border (Australia)
200	166†	J. H. Kallis (SA/World)	**139**	**118**	**Younis Khan (Pakistan)**
196	168	R. T. Ponting (Australia)	135	134	V. V. S. Laxman (India)
181	128	M. E. Waugh (Australia)	134	115	M. J. Clarke (Australia)
171	111	S. P. Fleming (New Zealand)	128	103	M. L. Hayden (Australia)
169	117†	G. C. Smith (SA/World)	**125**	**83**	**L. R. P. L. Taylor (New Zealand)**
164	131†	B. C. Lara (West Indies/World)	125	145	S. K. Warne (Australia)
157	104	M. A. Taylor (Australia)			

† *Excluding the Super Series Test, Dravid made 209 catches in 163 Tests for India, Kallis 196 in 165 Tests for South Africa, and Lara 164 in 130 Tests for West Indies, all national records. G. C. Smith made 166 catches in 116 Tests for South Africa.*

*The most catches in the field for other countries are Zimbabwe 60 in 60 Tests (A. D. R. Campbell); Bangladesh **33** in 35 Tests (**Mahmudullah**).*

TEAM RECORDS

HIGHEST INNINGS TOTALS

952-6 dec	Sri Lanka v India at Colombo (RPS)	1997-98
903-7 dec	England v Australia at The Oval	1938
849	England v West Indies at Kingston	1929-30
790-3 dec	West Indies v Pakistan at Kingston	1957-58
765-6 dec	Pakistan v Sri Lanka at Karachi	2008-09
760-7 dec	Sri Lanka v India at Ahmedabad	2009-10
759-7 dec	India v England at Chennai	2016-17
758-8 dec	Australia v West Indies at Kingston	1954-55
756-5 dec	Sri Lanka v South Africa at Colombo (SSC)	2006
751-5 dec	West Indies v England at St John's	2003-04

The highest innings totals for the countries not mentioned above are:

690	New Zealand v Pakistan at Sharjah	2014-15
682-6 dec	South Africa v England at Lord's	2003
638	Bangladesh v Sri Lanka at Galle	2012-13
563-9 dec	Zimbabwe v West Indies at Harare	2001

HIGHEST FOURTH-INNINGS TOTALS

To win

418-7	West Indies (needing 418) v Australia at St John's	2002-03
414-4	South Africa (needing 414) v Australia at Perth	2008-09
406-4	India (needing 403) v West Indies at Port-of-Spain	1975-76
404-3	Australia (needing 404) v England at Leeds	1948

To tie

347	India v Australia at Madras	1986-87

To draw

654-5	England (needing 696 to win) v South Africa at Durban	1938-39
450-7	South Africa (needing 458 to win) v India at Johannesburg	2013-14
429-8	India (needing 438 to win) v England at The Oval	1979
423-7	South Africa (needing 451 to win) v England at The Oval	1947

To lose

451	New Zealand (lost by 98 runs) v England at Christchurch	2001-02
450	Pakistan (lost by 39 runs) v Australia at Brisbane	2016-17
445	India (lost by 47 runs) v Australia at Adelaide	1977-78
440	New Zealand (lost by 38 runs) v England at Nottingham	1973
431	New Zealand (lost by 121 runs) v England at Napier	2007-08

MOST RUNS IN A DAY (BOTH SIDES)

588	England (398-6), India (190-0) at Manchester (2nd day)	1936
522	England (503-2), South Africa (19-0) at Lord's (2nd day)	1924
509	Sri Lanka (509-9) v Bangladesh at Colombo (PSS) (2nd day)	2002
508	England (221-2), South Africa (287-6) at The Oval (3rd day)	1935

MOST RUNS IN A DAY (ONE SIDE)

509	Sri Lanka (509-9) v Bangladesh at Colombo (PSS) (2nd day)	2002
503	England (503-2) v South Africa at Lord's (2nd day)	1924
494	Australia (494-6) v South Africa at Sydney (1st day)	1910-11
482	Australia (482-5) v South Africa at Adelaide (1st day)	2012-13
475	Australia (475-2) v England at The Oval (1st day)	1934

MOST WICKETS IN A DAY

27	England (18-3 to 53 all out and 62) v Australia (60) at Lord's (2nd day)	1888
25	Australia (112 and 48-5) v England (61) at Melbourne (1st day)	1901-02

HIGHEST AGGREGATES IN A TEST

Runs	*Wkts*			*Days played*
1,981	35	South Africa v England at Durban	1938-39	10†
1,815	34	West Indies v England at Kingston	1929-30	9‡
1,764	39	Australia v West Indies at Adelaide	1968-69	5
1,753	40	Australia v England at Adelaide	1920-21	6
1,747	25	Australia v India at Sydney	2003-04	5
1,723	31	England v Australia at Leeds	1948	5
1,702	28	Pakistan v India at Faisalabad	2005-06	5

† *No play on one day.* ‡ *No play on two days.*

LOWEST INNINGS TOTALS

26	New Zealand v England at Auckland	1954-55
30	South Africa v England at Port Elizabeth	1895-96
30	South Africa v England at Birmingham	1924
35	South Africa v England at Cape Town	1898-99
36	Australia v England at Birmingham	1902
36	South Africa v Australia at Melbourne	1931-32
42	Australia v England at Sydney	1887-88
42	New Zealand v Australia at Wellington	1945-46
42†	India v England at Lord's	1974

43	South Africa v England at Cape Town	1888-89
44	Australia v England at The Oval	1896
45	England v Australia at Sydney	1886-87
45	South Africa v Australia at Melbourne	1931-32
45	New Zealand v South Africa at Cape Town	2012-13

The lowest innings totals for the countries not mentioned above are:

47	West Indies v England at Kingston	2003-04
49	Pakistan v South Africa at Johannesburg	2012-13
51	Zimbabwe v New Zealand at Napier	2011-12
62	Bangladesh v Sri Lanka at Colombo (PSS)	2007
71	Sri Lanka v Pakistan at Kandy	1994-95

FEWEST RUNS IN A FULL DAY'S PLAY

95	Australia (80), Pakistan (15-2) at Karachi (1st day, 5½ hrs)	1956-57
104	Pakistan (0-0 to 104-5) v Australia at Karachi (4th day, 5½ hrs)	1959-60
106	England (92-2 to 198) v Australia at Brisbane (4th day, 5 hrs). *England were dismissed five minutes before the close of play, leaving no time for Australia to start their second innings.*	1958-59
111	S. Africa (48-2 to 130-6 dec), India (29-1) at Cape Town (5th day, 5½ hrs)	1992-93
112	Australia (138-6 to 187), Pakistan (63-1) at Karachi (4th day, 5½ hrs)	1956-57
115	Australia (116-7 to 165 and 66-5 after following on) v Pakistan at Karachi (4th day, 5½ hrs)	1988-89
117	India (117-5) v Australia at Madras (1st day, 5½ hrs)	1956-57
117	New Zealand (6-0 to 123-4) v Sri Lanka at Colombo (SSC) (5th day, 5¾ hrs)	1983-84

In England

151	England (175-2 to 289), New Zealand (37-7) at Lord's (3rd day, 6 hrs)	1978
158	England (211-2 to 369-9) v South Africa at Manchester (5th day, 6 hrs)	1998
159	Pakistan (208-4 to 350), England (17-1) at Leeds (3rd day, 6 hrs)	1971

LOWEST AGGREGATES IN A COMPLETED TEST

Runs	*Wkts*			*Days played*
234	29	Australia v South Africa at Melbourne	1931-32	3†
291	40	England v Australia at Lord's	1888	2
295	28	New Zealand v Australia at Wellington	1945-46	2
309	29	West Indies v England at Bridgetown	1934-35	3
323	30	England v Australia at Manchester	1888	2

† *No play on one day.*

LARGEST VICTORIES

Largest Innings Victories

Inns & 579 runs	England (903-7 dec) v Australia (201 & 123†) at The Oval	1938
Inns & 360 runs	Australia (652-7 dec) v South Africa (159 & 133) at Johannesburg	2001-02
Inns & 336 runs	West Indies (614-5 dec) v India (124 & 154) at Calcutta	1958-59
Inns & 332 runs	Australia (645) v England (141 & 172) at Brisbane	1946-47
Inns & 324 runs	Pakistan (643) v New Zealand (73 & 246) at Lahore	2002
Inns & 322 runs	West Indies (660-5 dec) v New Zealand (216 & 122) at Wellington	1994-95
Inns & 310 runs	West Indies (536) v Bangladesh (139 & 87) at Dhaka	2002-03
Inns & 301 runs	New Zealand (495-7 dec) v Zimbabwe (51 & 143) at Napier	2011-12

† *Two men absent in both Australian innings.*

Largest Victories by Runs Margin

675 runs	England (521 & 342-8 dec) v Australia (122 & 66†) at Brisbane	1928-29
562 runs	Australia (701 & 327) v England (321 & 145‡) at The Oval	1934
530 runs	Australia (328 & 578) v South Africa (205 & 171§) at Melbourne	1910-11
491 runs	Australia (381 & 361-5 dec) v Pakistan (179 & 72) at Perth	2004-05
465 runs	Sri Lanka (384 and 447-6 dec) v Bangladesh (208 and 158) at Chittagong	2008-09
425 runs	West Indies (211 & 411-5 dec) v England (71 & 126) at Manchester	1976
409 runs	Australia (350 & 460-7 dec) v England (215 & 186) at Lord's	1948
408 runs	West Indies (328 & 448) v Australia (203 & 165) at Adelaide	1979-80
405 runs	Australia (566-8 dec & 254-2 dec) v England (312 & 103) at Lord's	2015

† *One man absent in Australia's first innings; two men absent in their second.*
‡ *Two men absent in England's first innings; one man absent in their second.*
§ *One man absent in South Africa's second innings.*

TIED TESTS

West Indies (453 & 284) v Australia (505 & 232) at Brisbane	1960-61
Australia (574-7 dec & 170-5 dec) v India (397 & 347) at Madras	1986-87

MOST CONSECUTIVE TEST VICTORIES

16	Australia	1999-2000 to 2000-01
16	Australia	2005-06 to 2007-08
11	West Indies	1983-84 to 1984-85
9	Sri Lanka	2001 to 2001-02
9	South Africa	2001-02 to 2003
8	Australia	1920-21 to 1921
8	England	2004 to 2004-05

MOST CONSECUTIVE TESTS WITHOUT VICTORY

44	New Zealand	1929-30 to 1955-56
34	Bangladesh	2000-01 to 2004-05
31	India	1981-82 to 1984-85
28	South Africa	1935 to 1949-50
24	India	1932 to 1951-52
24	Bangladesh	2004-05 to 2008-09
23	New Zealand	1962-63 to 1967-68
22	Pakistan	1958-59 to 1964-65
21	Sri Lanka	1985-86 to 1992-93
20	West Indies	1968-69 to 1972-73
20	West Indies	2004-05 to 2007

WHITEWASHES

Teams winning every game in a series of four Tests or more:

Five-Test Series

Australia beat England	1920-21
Australia beat South Africa	1931-32
England beat India	1959
West Indies beat India	1961-62
West Indies beat England	1984
West Indies beat England	1985-86
South Africa beat West Indies	1998-99
Australia beat West Indies	2000-01
Australia beat England	2006-07
Australia beat England	2013-14

Four-Test Series

Australia beat India	1967-68
South Africa beat Australia	1969-70
England beat West Indies	2004
England beat India	2011
Australia beat India	2011-12
India beat Australia	2012-13

The winning team in each instance was at home, except for West Indies in England, 1984.

PLAYERS

YOUNGEST TEST PLAYERS

Years	*Days*			
15	124	Mushtaq Mohammad	Pakistan v West Indies at Lahore	1958-59
16	189	Aqib Javed	Pakistan v New Zealand at Wellington	1988-89
16	205	S. R. Tendulkar	India v Pakistan at Karachi	1989-90

The above table should be treated with caution. All birthdates for Bangladesh and Pakistan (after Partition) must be regarded as questionable because of deficiencies in record-keeping. Hasan Raza was claimed to be 14 years 227 days old when he played for Pakistan against Zimbabwe at Faisalabad in 1996-97; this age was rejected by the Pakistan Cricket Board, although no alternative has been offered. Suggestions that Enamul Haque jnr was 16 years 230 days old when he played for Bangladesh against England in Dhaka in 2003-04 have been discounted by well-informed local observers, who believe he was 18.

The youngest Test players for countries not mentioned above are:

17	122	J. E. D. Sealy	West Indies v England at Bridgetown	1929-30
17	128	Mohammad Sharif	Bangladesh v Zimbabwe at Bulawayo	2000-01
17	189	C. D. U. S. Weerasinghe	Sri Lanka v India at Colombo (PSS)	1985-86
17	239	I. D. Craig	Australia v South Africa at Melbourne	1952-53
17	352	H. Masakadza	Zimbabwe v West Indies at Harare	2001
18	10	D. L. Vettori	New Zealand v England at Wellington	1996-97
18	149	D. B. Close	England v New Zealand at Manchester	1949
18	340	P. R. Adams	South Africa v England at Port Elizabeth	1995-96

OLDEST PLAYERS ON TEST DEBUT

Years	*Days*			
49	119	J. Southerton	England v Australia at Melbourne	1876-77
47	284	Miran Bux	Pakistan v India at Lahore	1954-55
46	253	D. D. Blackie	Australia v England at Sydney	1928-29
46	237	H. Ironmonger	Australia v England at Brisbane	1928-29
42	242	N. Betancourt	West Indies v England at Port-of-Spain	1929-30
41	337	E. R. Wilson	England v Australia at Sydney	1920-21
41	27	R. J. D. Jamshedji	India v England at Bombay	1933-34
40	345	C. A. Wiles	West Indies v England at Manchester	1933
40	295	O. Henry	South Africa v India at Durban	1992-93
40	216	S. P. Kinneir	England v Australia at Sydney	1911-12
40	110	H. W. Lee	England v South Africa at Johannesburg	1930-31
40	56	G. W. A. Chubb	South Africa v England at Nottingham	1951
40	37	C. Ramaswami	India v England at Manchester	1936

The oldest Test player on debut for New Zealand was H. M. McGirr, 38 years 101 days, v England at Auckland, 1929-30; for Sri Lanka, D. S. de Silva, 39 years 251 days, v England at Colombo (PSS), 1981-82; for Zimbabwe, A. C. Waller, 37 years 84 days, v England at Bulawayo, 1996-97; for Bangladesh, Enamul Haque snr, 35 years 58 days, v Zimbabwe at Harare, 2000-01. A. J. Traicos was 45 years 154 days old when he made his debut for Zimbabwe (v India at Harare, 1992-93) having played three Tests for South Africa in 1969-70.

OLDEST TEST PLAYERS

(Age on final day of their last Test match)

Years	*Days*			
52	165	W. Rhodes	England v West Indies at Kingston	1929-30
50	327	H. Ironmonger	Australia v England at Sydney	1932-33
50	320	W. G. Grace	England v Australia at Nottingham	1899
50	303	G. Gunn	England v West Indies at Kingston	1929-30
49	139	J. Southerton	England v Australia at Melbourne	1876-77

Years	Days			
47	302	Miran Bux	Pakistan v India at Peshawar	1954-55
47	249	J. B. Hobbs	England v Australia at The Oval	1930
47	87	F. E. Woolley	England v Australia at The Oval	1934
46	309	D. D. Blackie	Australia v England at Adelaide	1928-29
46	206	A. W. Nourse	South Africa v England at The Oval	1924
46	202	H. Strudwick	England v Australia at The Oval	1926
46	41	E. H. Hendren	England v West Indies at Kingston	1934-35
45	304	A. J. Traicos	Zimbabwe v India at Delhi	1992-93
45	245	G. O. B. Allen	England v West Indies at Kingston	1947-48
45	215	P. Holmes	England v India at Lord's	1932
45	140	D. B. Close	England v West Indies at Manchester	1976

MOST TEST APPEARANCES

200	S. R. Tendulkar (India)
168	R. T. Ponting (Australia)
168	S. R. Waugh (Australia)
166	J. H. Kallis (South Africa/World)
164	S. Chanderpaul (West Indies)
164	R. Dravid (India/World)
156	A. R. Border (Australia)
152	**A. N. Cook (England)**
149	D. P. M. D. Jayawardene (Sri Lanka)
147	M. V. Boucher (South Africa/World)
145	S. K. Warne (Australia)
134	**J. M. Anderson (England)**
134	V. V. S. Laxman (India)
134	K. C. Sangakkara (Sri Lanka)
133	M. Muralitharan (Sri Lanka/World)
133	A. J. Stewart (England)
132	A. Kumble (India)
132	C. A. Walsh (West Indies)
131	Kapil Dev (India)
131	B. C. Lara (West Indies/World)
128	M. E. Waugh (Australia)
125	S. M. Gavaskar (India)
124	Javed Miandad (Pakistan)
124	G. D. McGrath (Australia)
121	I. V. A. Richards (West Indies)
120	Inzamam-ul-Haq (Pakistan/World)

Excluding the Super Series Test, J. H. Kallis has made 165 appearances for South Africa, a national record. The most appearances for New Zealand is 112 by D. L. Vettori; for Zimbabwe, 67 by G. W. Flower; and for Bangladesh 61 by Mohammad Ashraful.

MOST CONSECUTIVE TEST APPEARANCES FOR A COUNTRY

153	A. R. Border (Australia)	March 1979 to March 1994
150	**A. N. Cook (England)**	**May 2006 to January 2018**
107	M. E. Waugh (Australia)	June 1993 to October 2002
106	S. M. Gavaskar (India)	January 1975 to February 1987
101†	B. B. McCullum (New Zealand)	March 2004 to February 2016
98	A. B. de Villiers (South Africa)	December 2004 to January 2015
96†	A. C. Gilchrist (Australia)	November 1999 to January 2008
93	R. Dravid (India)	June 1996 to December 2005
93	D. P. M. D. Jayawardene (Sri Lanka)	November 2002 to January 2013

The most consecutive Test appearances for the countries not mentioned above are:

85	G. S. Sobers (West Indies)	April 1955 to April 1972
56	A. D. R. Campbell (Zimbabwe)	October 1992 to September 2001
53	Javed Miandad (Pakistan)	December 1977 to January 1984
49	**Mushfiqur Rahim (Bangladesh)**	**July 2007 to January 2017**

† *Complete Test career.*

Bold type denotes sequence which was still in progress after January 1, 2017.

MOST TESTS AS CAPTAIN

	P	W	L	D
G. C. Smith (SA/World)	109	53	29*	27
A. R. Border (A)	93	32	22	38†
S. P. Fleming (NZ)	80	28	27	25
R. T. Ponting (A)	77	48	16	13
C. H. Lloyd (WI)	74	36	12	26
M. S. Dhoni (I)	60	27	18	15
A. N. Cook (E)	59	24	22	13
S. R. Waugh (A)	57	41	9	7
Misbah-ul-Haq (P)	**56**	**26**	**19**	**11**
A. Ranatunga (SL)	56	12	19	25
M. A. Atherton (E)	54	13	21	20
W. J. Cronje (SA)	53	27	11	15
M. P. Vaughan (E)	51	26	11	14
I. V. A. Richards (WI)	50	27	8	15
M. A. Taylor (A)	50	26	13	11
A. J. Strauss (E)	50	24	11	15

* *Includes defeat as World XI captain in Super Series Test against Australia.* † *One tie.*

Most Tests as captain of other countries:

	P	W	L	D
Mushfiqur Rahim (B)	**34**	**7**	**18**	**9**
A. D. R. Campbell (Z)	21	2	12	7

A. R. Border captained Australia in 93 consecutive Tests.

W. W. Armstrong (Australia) captained his country in the most Tests without being defeated: ten matches with eight wins and two draws.

Mohammad Ashraful (Bangladesh) captained his country in the most Tests without ever winning: 12 defeats and one draw.

UMPIRES

MOST TESTS

		First Test	Last Test
128	S. A. Bucknor (West Indies)	1988-89	2008-09
117	**Aleem Dar (Pakistan)**	**2003-04**	**2017-18**
108	R. E. Koertzen (South Africa)	1992-93	2010
95	D. J. Harper (Australia)	1998-99	2011
92	D. R. Shepherd (England)	1985	2004-05
84	B. F. Bowden (New Zealand)	1999-2000	2014-15
78	D. B. Hair (Australia)	1991-92	2008
74	S. J. A. Taufel (Australia)	2000-01	2012
73	S. Venkataraghavan (India)	1992-93	2003-04
66	H. D. Bird (England)	1973	1996
64	**I. J. Gould (England)**	**2008-09**	**2017-18**
57	S. J. Davis (Australia)	1997-98	2014-15
57	**R. J. Tucker (Australia)**	**2009-10**	**2017-18**
51	**H. D. P. K. Dharmasena (Sri Lanka)**	**2010-11**	**2017-18**
50	**R. A. Kettleborough (England)**	**2010-11**	**2017-18**

SUMMARY OF TESTS

To January 27, 2018

	Opponents	Tests	Won by E	A	SA	WI	NZ	I	P	SL	Z	B	Wld	Tied	Drawn
England	Australia	**346**	108	144	–	–	–	–	–	–	–	–	–	–	94
	South Africa	**149**	61	–	33	–	–	–	–	–	–	–	–	–	55
	West Indies	**154**	48	–	–	55	–	–	–	–	–	–	–	–	51
	New Zealand	**101**	48	–	–	–	9	–	–	–	–	–	–	–	44
	India	**117**	43	–	–	–	–	25	–	–	–	–	–	–	49
	Pakistan	**81**	24	–	–	–	–	–	20	–	–	–	–	–	37
	Sri Lanka	**31**	12	–	–	–	–	–	–	8	–	–	–	–	11
	Zimbabwe	**6**	3	–	–	–	–	–	–	–	0	–	–	–	3
	Bangladesh	**10**	9	–	–	–	–	–	–	–	–	1	–	–	0
Australia	South Africa	**94**	–	51	23	–	–	–	–	–	–	–	–	–	20
	West Indies	**116**	–	58	–	32	–	–	–	–	–	–	–	1	25
	New Zealand	**57**	–	31	–	–	8	–	–	–	–	–	–	–	18
	India	**94**	–	41	–	–	–	26	–	–	–	–	–	1	26
	Pakistan	**62**	–	31	–	–	–	–	14	–	–	–	–	–	17
	Sri Lanka	**29**	–	17	–	–	–	–	–	4	–	–	–	–	8
	Zimbabwe	**3**	–	3	–	–	–	–	–	–	0	–	–	–	0
	Bangladesh	**6**	–	5	–	–	–	–	–	–	–	1	–	–	0
	ICC World XI	**1**	–	1	–	–	–	–	–	–	–	–	0	–	0
South Africa	West Indies	**28**	–	–	18	3	–	–	–	–	–	–	–	–	7
	New Zealand	**45**	–	–	25	–	4	–	–	–	–	–	–	–	16
	India	**36**	–	–	15	–	–	11	–	–	–	–	–	–	10
	Pakistan	**23**	–	–	12	–	–	–	4	–	–	–	–	–	7
	Sri Lanka	**25**	–	–	14	–	–	–	–	5	–	–	–	–	6
	Zimbabwe	**9**	–	–	8	–	–	–	–	–	0	–	–	–	1
	Bangladesh	**12**	–	–	10	–	–	–	–	–	–	0	–	–	2
West Indies	New Zealand	**47**	–	–	–	13	15	–	–	–	–	–	–	–	19
	India	**94**	–	–	–	30	–	18	–	–	–	–	–	–	46
	Pakistan	**52**	–	–	–	17	–	–	20	–	–	–	–	–	15
	Sri Lanka	**17**	–	–	–	3	–	–	–	8	–	–	–	–	6
	Zimbabwe	**10**	–	–	–	7	–	–	–	–	0	–	–	–	3
	Bangladesh	**12**	–	–	–	8	–	–	–	–	–	2	–	–	2
New Zealand	India	**57**	–	–	–	–	10	21	–	–	–	–	–	–	26
	Pakistan	**55**	–	–	–	–	10	–	24	–	–	–	–	–	21
	Sri Lanka	**32**	–	–	–	–	14	–	–	8	–	–	–	–	10
	Zimbabwe	**17**	–	–	–	–	11	–	–	–	0	–	–	–	6
	Bangladesh	**13**	–	–	–	–	10	–	–	–	–	0	–	–	3
India	Pakistan	**59**	–	–	–	–	–	9	12	–	–	–	–	–	38
	Sri Lanka	**44**	–	–	–	–	–	20	–	7	–	–	–	–	17
	Zimbabwe	**11**	–	–	–	–	–	7	–	–	2	–	–	–	2
	Bangladesh	**9**	–	–	–	–	–	7	–	–	–	0	–	–	2
Pakistan	Sri Lanka	**53**	–	–	–	–	–	–	19	16	–	–	–	–	18
	Zimbabwe	**17**	–	–	–	–	–	–	10	–	3	–	–	–	4
	Bangladesh	**10**	–	–	–	–	–	–	9	–	–	0	–	–	1
Sri Lanka	Zimbabwe	**18**	–	–	–	–	–	–	–	13	0	–	–	–	5
	Bangladesh	**18**	–	–	–	–	–	–	–	15	–	1	–	–	2
Zimbabwe	Bangladesh	**14**	–	–	–	–	–	–	–	–	6	5	–	–	3
		2,294	356	382	158	168	91	144	132	84	11	10	0	2	756

	Tests	Won	Lost	Drawn	Tied	% Won	Toss Won
England	995	356	295	344	–	35.77	484
Australia	808†	382†	216	208	2	47.27	406
South Africa	421	158	139	124	–	37.52	205
West Indies	530	168	187	174	1	31.69	272
New Zealand	424	91	170	163	–	21.46	210
India	521	144	160	216	1	27.63	262
Pakistan	412	132	122	158	–	32.03	196
Sri Lanka	267	84	100	83	–	31.46	146
Zimbabwe	105	11	67	27	–	10.47	60
Bangladesh	104	10	79	15	–	9.61	53
ICC World XI	1	0	1	0	–	0.00	0

† *Includes Super Series Test between Australia and ICC World XI.*

ENGLAND v AUSTRALIA

Season	Captains England	Australia	T	E	A	D
1876-77	James Lillywhite	D. W. Gregory	2	1	1	0
1878-79	Lord Harris	D. W. Gregory	1	0	1	0
1880	Lord Harris	W. L. Murdoch	1	1	0	0
1881-82	A. Shaw	W. L. Murdoch	4	0	2	2
1882	A. N. Hornby	W. L. Murdoch	1	0	1	0

THE ASHES

Season	Captains England	Australia	T	E	A	D	Held by
1882-83	Hon. Ivo Bligh	W. L. Murdoch	4*	2	2	0	E
1884	Lord Harris[1]	W. L. Murdoch	3	1	0	2	E
1884-85	A. Shrewsbury	T. P. Horan[2]	5	3	2	0	E
1886	A. G. Steel	H. J. H. Scott	3	3	0	0	E
1886-87	A. Shrewsbury	P. S. McDonnell	2	2	0	0	E
1887-88	W. W. Read	P. S. McDonnell	1	1	0	0	E
1888	W. G. Grace[3]	P. S. McDonnell	3	2	1	0	E
1890†	W. G. Grace	W. L. Murdoch	2	2	0	0	E
1891-92	W. G. Grace	J. McC. Blackham	3	1	2	0	A
1893	W. G. Grace[4]	J. McC. Blackham	3	1	0	2	E
1894-95	A. E. Stoddart	G. Giffen[5]	5	3	2	0	E
1896	W. G. Grace	G. H. S. Trott	3	2	1	0	E
1897-98	A. E. Stoddart[6]	G. H. S. Trott	5	1	4	0	A
1899	A. C. MacLaren[7]	J. Darling	5	0	1	4	A
1901-02	A. C. MacLaren	J. Darling[8]	5	1	4	0	A
1902	A. C. MacLaren	J. Darling	5	1	2	2	A
1903-04	P. F. Warner	M. A. Noble	5	3	2	0	E
1905	Hon. F. S. Jackson	J. Darling	5	2	0	3	E
1907-08	A. O. Jones[9]	M. A. Noble	5	1	4	0	A
1909	A. C. MacLaren	M. A. Noble	5	1	2	2	A
1911-12	J. W. H. T. Douglas	C. Hill	5	4	1	0	E
1912	C. B. Fry	S. E. Gregory	3	1	0	2	E
1920-21	J. W. H. T. Douglas	W. W. Armstrong	5	0	5	0	A
1921	Hon. L. H. Tennyson[10]	W. W. Armstrong	5	0	3	2	A
1924-25	A. E. R. Gilligan	H. L. Collins	5	1	4	0	A
1926	A. W. Carr[11]	H. L. Collins[12]	5	1	0	4	E
1928-29	A. P. F. Chapman[13]	J. Ryder	5	4	1	0	E
1930	A. P. F. Chapman[14]	W. M. Woodfull	5	1	2	2	A
1932-33	D. R. Jardine	W. M. Woodfull	5	4	1	0	E
1934	R. E. S. Wyatt[15]	W. M. Woodfull	5	1	2	2	A
1936-37	G. O. B. Allen	D. G. Bradman	5	2	3	0	A
1938†	W. R. Hammond	D. G. Bradman	4	1	1	2	A
1946-47	W. R. Hammond[16]	D. G. Bradman	5	0	3	2	A
1948	N. W. D. Yardley	D. G. Bradman	5	0	4	1	A
1950-51	F. R. Brown	A. L. Hassett	5	1	4	0	A
1953	L. Hutton	A. L. Hassett	5	1	0	4	E
1954-55	L. Hutton	I. W. Johnson[17]	5	3	1	1	E
1956	P. B. H. May	I. W. Johnson	5	2	1	2	E
1958-59	P. B. H. May	R. Benaud	5	0	4	1	A
1961	P. B. H. May[18]	R. Benaud[19]	5	1	2	2	A
1962-63	E. R. Dexter	R. Benaud	5	1	1	3	A
1964	E. R. Dexter	R. B. Simpson	5	0	1	4	A
1965-66	M. J. K. Smith	R. B. Simpson[20]	5	1	1	3	A
1968	M. C. Cowdrey[21]	W. M. Lawry[22]	5	1	1	3	A
1970-71†	R. Illingworth	W. M. Lawry[23]	6	2	0	4	E
1972	R. Illingworth	I. M. Chappell	5	2	2	1	E

	Captains						
Season	*England*	*Australia*	*T*	*E*	*A*	*D*	*Held by*
1974-75	M. H. Denness[24]	I. M. Chappell	6	1	4	1	A
1975	A. W. Greig[25]	I. M. Chappell	4	0	1	3	A
1976-77‡	A. W. Greig	G. S. Chappell	1	0	1	0	—
1977	J. M. Brearley	G. S. Chappell	5	3	0	2	E
1978-79	J. M. Brearley	G. N. Yallop	6	5	1	0	E
1979-80‡	J. M. Brearley	G. S. Chappell	3	0	3	0	—
1980‡	I. T. Botham	G. S. Chappell	1	0	0	1	—
1981	J. M. Brearley[26]	K. J. Hughes	6	3	1	2	E
1982-83	R. G. D. Willis	G. S. Chappell	5	1	2	2	A
1985	D. I. Gower	A. R. Border	6	3	1	2	E
1986-87	M. W. Gatting	A. R. Border	5	2	1	2	E
1987-88‡	M. W. Gatting	A. R. Border	1	0	0	1	—
1989	D. I. Gower	A. R. Border	6	0	4	2	A
1990-91	G. A. Gooch[27]	A. R. Border	5	0	3	2	A
1993	G. A. Gooch[28]	A. R. Border	6	1	4	1	A
1994-95	M. A. Atherton	M. A. Taylor	5	1	3	1	A
1997	M. A. Atherton	M. A. Taylor	6	2	3	1	A
1998-99	A. J. Stewart	M. A. Taylor	5	1	3	1	A
2001	N. Hussain[29]	S. R. Waugh[30]	5	1	4	0	A
2002-03	N. Hussain	S. R. Waugh	5	1	4	0	A
2005	M. P. Vaughan	R. T. Ponting	5	2	1	2	E
2006-07	A. Flintoff	R. T. Ponting	5	0	5	0	A
2009	A. J. Strauss	R. T. Ponting	5	2	1	2	E
2010-11	A. J. Strauss	R. T. Ponting[31]	5	3	1	1	E
2013	A. N. Cook	M. J. Clarke	5	3	0	2	E
2013-14	A. N. Cook	M. J. Clarke	5	0	5	0	A
2015	A. N. Cook	M. J. Clarke	5	3	2	0	E
2017-18	**J. E. Root**	**S. P. D. Smith**	**5**	**0**	**4**	**1**	**A**
	In Australia		**180**	**57**	**95**	**28**	
	In England		166	51	49	66	
	Totals		**346**	**108**	**144**	**94**	

* *The Ashes were awarded in 1882-83 after a series of three matches which England won 2–1. A fourth match was played and this was won by Australia.*
† *The matches at Manchester in 1890 and 1938 and at Melbourne (Third Test) in 1970-71 were abandoned without a ball being bowled and are excluded.*
‡ *The Ashes were not at stake in these series.*

The following deputised for the official touring captain or were appointed by the home authority for only a minor proportion of the series:

[1]A. N. Hornby (First). [2]W. L. Murdoch (First), H. H. Massie (Third), J. McC. Blackham (Fourth). [3]A. G. Steel (First). [4]A. E. Stoddart (First). [5]J. McC. Blackham (First). [6]A. C. MacLaren (First, Second and Fifth). [7]W. G. Grace (First). [8]H. Trumble (Fourth and Fifth). [9]F. L. Fane (First, Second and Third). [10]J. W. H. T. Douglas (First and Second). [11]A. P. F. Chapman (Fifth). [12]W. Bardsley (Third and Fourth). [13]J. C. White (Fifth). [14]R. E. S. Wyatt (Fifth). [15]C. F. Walters (First). [16]N. W. D. Yardley (Fifth). [17]A. R. Morris (Second). [18]M. C. Cowdrey (First and Second). [19]R. N. Harvey (Second). [20]B. C. Booth (First and Third). [21]T. W. Graveney (Fourth). [22]B. N. Jarman (Fourth) [23]I. M. Chappell (Seventh). [24]J. H. Edrich (Fourth). [25]M. H. Denness (First). [26]I. T. Botham (First and Second). [27]A. J. Lamb (First). [28]M. A. Atherton (Fifth and Sixth). [29]M. A. Atherton (Second and Third). [30]A. C. Gilchrist (Fourth). [31]M. J. Clarke (Fifth).

HIGHEST INNINGS TOTALS

For England in England: 903-7 dec at The Oval 1938
in Australia: 644 at Sydney 2010-11

For Australia in England: 729-6 dec at Lord's........ 1930
in Australia: 662-9 dec at Perth 2017-18

LOWEST INNINGS TOTALS

For England in England: 52 at The Oval	1948
in Australia: 45 at Sydney	1886-87
For Australia in England: 36 at Birmingham	1902
in Australia: 42 at Sydney	1887-88

DOUBLE-HUNDREDS

For England (14)

364	L. Hutton at The Oval	1938
287	R. E. Foster at Sydney	1903-04
256	K. F. Barrington at Manchester	1964
251	W. R. Hammond at Sydney	1928-29
244*	**A. N. Cook at Melbourne**	**2017-18**
240	W. R. Hammond at Lord's	1938
235*	A. N. Cook at Brisbane	2010-11
231*	W. R. Hammond at Sydney	1936-37
227	K. P. Pietersen at Adelaide	2010-11
216*	E. Paynter at Nottingham	1938
215	D. I. Gower at Birmingham	1985
207	N. Hussain at Birmingham	1997
206	P. D. Collingwood at Adelaide	2006-07
200	W. R. Hammond at Melbourne	1928-29

For Australia (25)

334	D. G. Bradman at Leeds	1930
311	R. B. Simpson at Manchester	1964
307	R. M. Cowper at Melbourne	1965-66
304	D. G. Bradman at Leeds	1934
270	D. G. Bradman at Melbourne	1936-37
266	W. H. Ponsford at The Oval	1934
254	D. G. Bradman at Lord's	1930
250	J. L. Langer at Melbourne	2002-03
244	D. G. Bradman at The Oval	1934
239	**S. P. D. Smith at Perth**	**2017-18**
234	S. G. Barnes at Sydney	1946-47
234	D. G. Bradman at Sydney	1946-47
232	D. G. Bradman at The Oval	1930
232	S. J. McCabe at Nottingham	1938
225	R. B. Simpson at Adelaide	1965-66
219	M. A. Taylor at Nottingham	1989
215	S. P. D. Smith at Lord's	2015
212	D. G. Bradman at Adelaide	1936-37
211	W. L. Murdoch at The Oval	1884
207	K. R. Stackpole at Brisbane	1970-71
206*	W. A. Brown at Lord's	1938
206	A. R. Morris at Adelaide	1950-51
201*	J. Ryder at Adelaide	1924-25
201	S. E. Gregory at Sydney	1894-95
200*	A. R. Border at Leeds	1993

INDIVIDUAL HUNDREDS

In total, England have scored **242** hundreds against Australia, and Australia have scored **313** against England. The players with at least five hundreds are as follows:

For England

12: J. B. Hobbs.
9: D. I. Gower, W. R. Hammond.
8: H. Sutcliffe.
7: G. Boycott, J. H. Edrich, M. Leyland.
5: K. F. Barrington, D. C. S. Compton, **A. N. Cook**, M. C. Cowdrey, L. Hutton, F. S. Jackson, A. C. MacLaren.

For Australia

19: D. G. Bradman.
10: S. R. Waugh.
9: G. S. Chappell.
8: A. R. Border, A. R. Morris, R. T. Ponting, **S. P. D. Smith**.
7: D. C. Boon, M. J. Clarke, W. M. Lawry, M. J. Slater.
6: R. N. Harvey, M. A. Taylor, V. T. Trumper, M. E. Waugh, W. M. Woodfull.
5: M. L. Hayden, J. L. Langer, C. G. Macartney, W. H. Ponsford.

RECORD PARTNERSHIPS FOR EACH WICKET

For England

323 for 1st	J. B. Hobbs and W. Rhodes at Melbourne	1911-12
382 for 2nd†	L. Hutton and M. Leyland at The Oval	1938
262 for 3rd	W. R. Hammond and D. R. Jardine at Adelaide	1928-29
310 for 4th	P. D. Collingwood and K. P. Pietersen at Adelaide	2006-07
237 for 5th	**D. J. Malan and J. M. Bairstow at Perth**	**2017-18**
215 for 6th	L. Hutton and J. Hardstaff jnr at The Oval	1938
	G. Boycott and A. P. E. Knott at Nottingham	1977
143 for 7th	F. E. Woolley and J. Vine at Sydney	1911-12
124 for 8th	E. H. Hendren and H. Larwood at Brisbane	1928-29
151 for 9th	W. H. Scotton and W. W. Read at The Oval	1884
130 for 10th	R. E. Foster and W. Rhodes at Sydney	1903-04

For Australia

329 for 1st	G. R. Marsh and M. A. Taylor at Nottingham	1989
451 for 2nd†	W. H. Ponsford and D. G. Bradman at The Oval	1934
276 for 3rd	D. G. Bradman and A. L. Hassett at Brisbane	1946-47
388 for 4th	W. H. Ponsford and D. G. Bradman at Leeds	1934
405 for 5th‡	S. G. Barnes and D. G. Bradman at Sydney	1946-47
346 for 6th†	J. H. Fingleton and D. G. Bradman at Melbourne	1936-37
165 for 7th	C. Hill and H. Trumble at Melbourne	1897-98
243 for 8th†	R. J. Hartigan and C. Hill at Adelaide	1907-08
154 for 9th†	S. E. Gregory and J. McC. Blackham at Sydney	1894-95
163 for 10th†	P. J. Hughes and A. C. Agar at Nottingham	2013

† *Record partnership against all countries.* ‡ *World record.*

MOST RUNS IN A SERIES

England in England	732 (average 81.33)	D. I. Gower	1985
England in Australia	905 (average 113.12)	W. R. Hammond	1928-29
Australia in England	974 (average 139.14)	D. G. Bradman	1930
Australia in Australia	810 (average 90.00)	D. G. Bradman	1936-37

MOST WICKETS IN A MATCH

In total, England bowlers have taken ten or more wickets in a match **40** times against Australia, and Australian bowlers have done it **43** times against England. The players with at least 12 in a match are as follows:

For England

19-90 (9-37, 10-53)	J. C. Laker at Manchester	1956
15-104 (7-61, 8-43)	H. Verity at Lord's	1934
15-124 (7-56, 8-68)	W. Rhodes at Melbourne	1903-04
14-99 (7-55, 7-44)	A. V. Bedser at Nottingham	1953
14-102 (7-28, 7-74)	W. Bates at Melbourne	1882-83
13-163 (6-42, 7-121)	S. F. Barnes at Melbourne	1901-02
13-244 (7-168, 6-76)	T. Richardson at Manchester	1896
13-256 (5-130, 8-126)	J. C. White at Adelaide	1928-29
12-102 (6-50, 6-52)†	F. Martin at The Oval	1890
12-104 (7-36, 5-68)	G. A. Lohmann at The Oval	1886
12-136 (6-49, 6-87)	J. Briggs at Adelaide	1891-92

There are a further 12 instances of 11 wickets in a match, and 17 instances of ten.

For Australia

16-137 (8-84, 8-53)†	R. A. L. Massie at Lord's	1972
14-90 (7-46, 7-44)	F. R. Spofforth at The Oval	1882
13-77 (7-17, 6-60)	M. A. Noble at Melbourne	1901-02
13-110 (6-48, 7-62)	F. R. Spofforth at Melbourne	1878-79
13-148 (6-97, 7-51)	B. A. Reid at Melbourne	1990-91
13-236 (4-115, 9-121)	A. A. Mailey at Melbourne	1920-21
12-87 (5-44, 7-43)	C. T. B. Turner at Sydney	1887-88
12-89 (6-59, 6-30)	H. Trumble at The Oval	1896
12-107 (5-57, 7-50)	S. C. G. MacGill at Sydney	1998-99
12-173 (8-65, 4-108)	H. Trumble at The Oval	1902
12-175 (5-85, 7-90)†	H. V. Hordern at Sydney	1911-12
12-246 (6-122, 6-124)	S. K. Warne at The Oval	2005

There are a further 13 instances of 11 wickets in a match, and 18 instances of ten.

† *On first appearance in England–Australia Tests.*

A. V. Bedser, J. Briggs, J. C. Laker, T. Richardson, R. M. Hogg, A. A. Mailey, H. Trumble and C. T. B. Turner took ten wickets or more in successive Tests.

MOST WICKETS IN A SERIES

England in England	46 (average 9.60)	J. C. Laker	1956
England in Australia	38 (average 23.18)	M. W. Tate	1924-25
Australia in England	42 (average 21.26)	T. M. Alderman (6 Tests)	1981
Australia in Australia	41 (average 12.85)	R. M. Hogg (6 Tests)	1978-79

WICKETKEEPING – MOST DISMISSALS

	M	*Ct*	*St*	*Total*
†R. W. Marsh (Australia)	42	141	7	148
I. A. Healy (Australia)	33	123	12	135
A. P. E. Knott (England)	34	97	8	105
A. C. Gilchrist (Australia)	20	89	7	96
†W. A. Oldfield (Australia)	38	59	31	90
A. A. Lilley (England)	32	65	19	84
B. J. Haddin (Australia)	20	79	5	84
A. J. Stewart (England)	26	76	2	78
A. T. W. Grout (Australia)	22	69	7	76
T. G. Evans (England)	31	64	12	76

† *The number of catches by R. W. Marsh (141) and stumpings by W. A. Oldfield (31) are respective records in England–Australia Tests.*

Stewart held a further six catches in seven matches when not keeping wicket.

SCORERS OF OVER 2,500 RUNS

	T	*I*	*NO*	*R*	*HS*	*100*	*Avge*
D. G. Bradman (Australia)	37	63	7	5,028	334	19	89.78
J. B. Hobbs (England)	41	71	4	3,636	187	12	54.26
A. R. Border (Australia)	47	82	19	3,548	200*	8	56.31
D. I. Gower (England)	42	77	4	3,269	215	9	44.78
S. R. Waugh (Australia)	46	73	18	3,200	177*	10	58.18
G. Boycott (England)	38	71	9	2,945	191	7	47.50
W. R. Hammond (England)	33	58	3	2,852	251	9	51.85
H. Sutcliffe (England)	27	46	5	2,741	194	8	66.85
C. Hill (Australia)	41	76	1	2,660	188	4	35.46
J. H. Edrich (England)	32	57	3	2,644	175	7	48.96
G. A. Gooch (England)	42	79	0	2,632	196	4	33.31
G. S. Chappell (Australia)	35	65	8	2,619	144	9	45.94

BOWLERS WITH 100 WICKETS

	T	*Balls*	*R*	*W*	*5I*	*10M*	*Avge*
S. K. Warne (Australia)	36	10,757	4,535	195	11	4	23.25
D. K. Lillee (Australia)	29	8,516	3,507	167	11	4	21.00
G. D. McGrath (Australia)	30	7,280	3,286	157	10	0	20.92
I. T. Botham (England)	36	8,479	4,093	148	9	2	27.65
H. Trumble (Australia)	31	7,895	2,945	141	9	3	20.88
R. G. D. Willis (England)	35	7,294	3,346	128	7	0	26.14
M. A. Noble (Australia)	39	6,895	2,860	115	9	2	24.86
R. R. Lindwall (Australia)	29	6,728	2,559	114	6	0	22.44
W. Rhodes (England)	41	5,790	2,616	109	6	1	24.00
S. F. Barnes (England)	20	5,749	2,288	106	12	1	21.58
C. V. Grimmett (Australia)	22	9,224	3,439	106	11	2	32.44
D. L. Underwood (England)	29	8,000	2,770	105	4	2	26.38
A. V. Bedser (England)	21	7,065	2,859	104	7	2	27.49
J. M. Anderson (England)	**31**	**7,027**	**3,594**	**104**	**5**	**1**	**34.55**
G. Giffen (Australia)	31	6,391	2,791	103	7	1	27.09
W. J. O'Reilly (Australia)	19	7,864	2,587	102	8	3	25.36
C. T. B. Turner (Australia)	17	5,179	1,670	101	11	2	16.53
R. Peel (England)	20	5,216	1,715	101	5	1	16.98
T. M. Alderman (Australia)	17	4,717	2,117	100	11	1	21.17
J. R. Thomson (Australia)	21	4,951	2,418	100	5	0	24.18

RESULTS ON EACH GROUND

In England

	Matches	*England wins*	*Australia wins*	*Drawn*
The Oval	37	16	7	14
Manchester	29	7	7	15†
Lord's	36	7	15	14
Nottingham	22	6	7	9
Leeds	24	7	9	8
Birmingham	14	6	3	5
Sheffield	1	0	1	0
Cardiff	2	1	0	1
Chester-le-Street	1	1	0	0

† *Excludes two matches abandoned without a ball bowled.*

In Australia

	Matches	*England wins*	*Australia wins*	*Drawn*
Melbourne	56	20	28	8†
Sydney	56	22	27	7
Adelaide	32	9	18	5
Brisbane				
Exhibition Ground	1	1	0	0
Woolloongabba	21	4	12	5
Perth	14	1	10	3

† *Excludes one match abandoned without a ball bowled.*

ENGLAND v SOUTH AFRICA

	Captains					
Season	*England*	*South Africa*	*T*	*E*	*SA*	*D*
1888-89	C. A. Smith[1]	O. R. Dunell[2]	2	2	0	0
1891-92	W. W. Read	W. H. Milton	1	1	0	0
1895-96	Lord Hawke[3]	E. A. Halliwell[4]	3	3	0	0
1898-99	Lord Hawke	M. Bisset	2	2	0	0

Captains

Season	*England*	*South Africa*	*T*	*E*	*SA*	*D*
1905-06	P. F. Warner	P. W. Sherwell	5	1	4	0
1907	R. E. Foster	P. W. Sherwell	3	1	0	2
1909-10	H. D. G. Leveson Gower[5]	S. J. Snooke	5	2	3	0
1912	C. B. Fry	F. Mitchell[6]	3	3	0	0
1913-14	J. W. H. T. Douglas	H. W. Taylor	5	4	0	1
1922-23	F. T. Mann	H. W. Taylor	5	2	1	2
1924	A. E. R. Gilligan[7]	H. W. Taylor	5	3	0	2
1927-28	R. T. Stanyforth[8]	H. G. Deane	5	2	2	1
1929	J. C. White[9]	H. G. Deane	5	2	0	3
1930-31	A. P. F. Chapman	H. G. Deane[10]	5	0	1	4
1935	R. E. S. Wyatt	H. F. Wade	5	0	1	4
1938-39	W. R. Hammond	A. Melville	5	1	0	4
1947	N. W. D. Yardley	A. Melville	5	3	0	2
1948-49	F. G. Mann	A. D. Nourse	5	2	0	3
1951	F. R. Brown	A. D. Nourse	5	3	1	1
1955	P. B. H. May	J. E. Cheetham[11]	5	3	2	0
1956-57	P. B. H. May	C. B. van Ryneveld[12]	5	2	2	1
1960	M. C. Cowdrey	D. J. McGlew	5	3	0	2
1964-65	M. J. K. Smith	T. L. Goddard	5	1	0	4
1965	M. J. K. Smith	P. L. van der Merwe	3	0	1	2
1994	M. A. Atherton	K. C. Wessels	3	1	1	1
1995-96	M. A. Atherton	W. J. Cronje	5	0	1	4
1998	A. J. Stewart	W. J. Cronje	5	2	1	2
1999-2000	N. Hussain	W. J. Cronje	5	1	2	2
2003	M. P. Vaughan[13]	G. C. Smith	5	2	2	1

THE BASIL D'OLIVEIRA TROPHY

Captains

Season	*England*	*South Africa*	*T*	*E*	*SA*	*D*	*Held by*
2004-05	M. P. Vaughan	G. C. Smith	5	2	1	2	E
2008	M. P. Vaughan[14]	G. C. Smith	4	1	2	1	SA
2009-10	A. J. Strauss	G. C. Smith	4	1	1	2	SA
2012	A. J. Strauss	G. C. Smith	3	0	2	1	SA
2015-16	A. N. Cook	H. M. Amla[15]	4	2	1	1	E
2017	**J. E. Root**	**F. du Plessis[16]**	**4**	**3**	**1**	**0**	**E**
	In South Africa		81	31	19	31	
	In England		**68**	**30**	**14**	**24**	
	Totals		**149**	**61**	**33**	**55**	

The following deputised for the official touring captain or were appointed by the home authority for only a minor proportion of the series:

[1]M. P. Bowden (Second). [2]W. H. Milton (Second). [3]Sir T. C. O'Brien (First). [4]A. R. Richards (Third). [5]F. L. Fane (Fourth and Fifth). [6]L. J. Tancred (Second and Third). [7]J. W. H. T. Douglas (Fourth). [8]G. T. S. Stevens (Fifth). [9]A. W. Carr (Fourth and Fifth). [10]E. P. Nupen (First), H. B. Cameron (Fourth and Fifth). [11]D. J. McGlew (Third and Fourth). [12]D. J. McGlew (Second). [13]N. Hussain (First). [14]K. P. Pietersen (Fourth). [15]A. B. de Villiers (Third and Fourth). [16]D. Elgar (First).

SERIES RECORDS

Highest score	*E*	258	B. A. Stokes at Cape Town	2015-16
	SA	311*	H. M. Amla at The Oval	2012
Best bowling	*E*	9-28	G. A. Lohmann at Johannesburg	1895-96
	SA	9-113	H. J. Tayfield at Johannesburg	1956-57
Highest total	*E*	654-5	at Durban	1938-39
	SA	682-6 dec	at Lord's	2003
Lowest total	*E*	76	at Leeds	1907
	SA	30	at Port Elizabeth	1895-96
		30	at Birmingham	1924

ENGLAND v WEST INDIES

Season	England (Captains)	West Indies (Captains)	T	E	WI	D
1928	A. P. F. Chapman	R. K. Nunes	3	3	0	0
1929-30	Hon. F. S. G. Calthorpe	E. L. G. Hoad[1]	4	1	1	2
1933	D. R. Jardine[2]	G. C. Grant	3	2	0	1
1934-35	R. E. S. Wyatt	G. C. Grant	4	1	2	1
1939	W. R. Hammond	R. S. Grant	3	1	0	2
1947-48	G. O. B. Allen[3]	J. D. C. Goddard[4]	4	0	2	2
1950	N. W. D. Yardley[5]	J. D. C. Goddard	4	1	3	0
1953-54	L. Hutton	J. B. Stollmeyer	5	2	2	1
1957	P. B. H. May	J. D. C. Goddard	5	3	0	2
1959-60	P. B. H. May[6]	F. C. M. Alexander	5	1	0	4

THE WISDEN TROPHY

Season	England (Captains)	West Indies (Captains)	T	E	WI	D	Held by
1963	E. R. Dexter	F. M. M. Worrell	5	1	3	1	WI
1966	M. C. Cowdrey[7]	G. S. Sobers	5	1	3	1	WI
1967-68	M. C. Cowdrey	G. S. Sobers	5	1	0	4	E
1969	R. Illingworth	G. S. Sobers	3	2	0	1	E
1973	R. Illingworth	R. B. Kanhai	3	0	2	1	WI
1973-74	M. H. Denness	R. B. Kanhai	5	1	1	3	WI
1976	A. W. Greig	C. H. Lloyd	5	0	3	2	WI
1980	I. T. Botham	C. H. Lloyd[8]	5	0	1	4	WI
1980-81†	I. T. Botham	C. H. Lloyd	4	0	2	2	WI
1984	D. I. Gower	C. H. Lloyd	5	0	5	0	WI
1985-86	D. I. Gower	I. V. A. Richards	5	0	5	0	WI
1988	J. E. Emburey[9]	I. V. A. Richards	5	0	4	1	WI
1989-90‡	G. A. Gooch[10]	I. V. A. Richards[11]	4	1	2	1	WI
1991	G. A. Gooch	I. V. A. Richards	5	2	2	1	WI
1993-94	M. A. Atherton	R. B. Richardson[12]	5	1	3	1	WI
1995	M. A. Atherton	R. B. Richardson	6	2	2	2	WI
1997-98§	M. A. Atherton	B. C. Lara	6	1	3	2	WI
2000	N. Hussain[13]	J. C. Adams	5	3	1	1	E
2003-04	M. P. Vaughan	B. C. Lara	4	3	0	1	E
2004	M. P. Vaughan	B. C. Lara	4	4	0	0	E
2007	M. P. Vaughan[14]	R. R. Sarwan[15]	4	3	0	1	E
2008-09§	A. J. Strauss	C. H. Gayle	5	0	1	4	WI
2009	A. J. Strauss	C. H. Gayle	2	2	0	0	E
2012	A. J. Strauss	D. J. G. Sammy	3	2	0	1	E
2014-15	A. N. Cook	D. Ramdin	3	1	1	1	E
2017	**J. E. Root**	**J. O. Holder**	**3**	**2**	**1**	**0**	**E**
	In England		**86**	**34**	**30**	**22**	
	In West Indies		68	14	25	29	
	Totals		**154**	**48**	**55**	**51**	

† *The Second Test, at Georgetown, was cancelled owing to political pressure and is excluded.*
‡ *The Second Test, at Georgetown, was abandoned without a ball being bowled and is excluded.*
§ *The First Test at Kingston in 1997-98 and the Second Test at North Sound in 2008-09 were called off on their opening days because of unfit pitches and are shown as draws.*

The following deputised for the official touring captain or were appointed by the home authority for only a minor proportion of the series: [1]N. Betancourt (Second), M. P. Fernandes (Third), R. K. Nunes (Fourth). [2]R. E. S. Wyatt (Third). [3]K. Cranston (First). [4]G. A. Headley (First), G. E. Gomez (Second). [5]F. R. Brown (Fourth). [6]M. C. Cowdrey (Fourth and Fifth). [7]M. J. K. Smith (First), D. B. Close (Fifth). [8]I. V. A. Richards (Fifth). [9]M. W. Gatting (First), C. S. Cowdrey (Fourth), G. A. Gooch (Fifth). [10]A. J. Lamb (Fourth and Fifth). [11]D. L. Haynes (Third). [12]C. A. Walsh (Fifth). [13]A. J. Stewart (Second). [14]A. J. Strauss (First). [15]D. Ganga (Third and Fourth).

SERIES RECORDS

Highest score	*E*	325	A. Sandham at Kingston	1929-30
	WI	400*	B. C. Lara at St John's	2003-04
Best bowling	*E*	8-53	A. R. C. Fraser at Port-of-Spain	1997-98
	WI	8-45	C. E. L. Ambrose at Bridgetown	1989-90
Highest total	*E*	849	at Kingston	1929-30
	WI	751-5 dec	at St John's	2003-04
Lowest total	*E*	46	at Port-of-Spain	1993-94
	WI	47	at Kingston	2003-04

ENGLAND v NEW ZEALAND

	Captains					
Season	*England*	*New Zealand*	*T*	*E*	*NZ*	*D*
1929-30	A. H. H. Gilligan	T. C. Lowry	4	1	0	3
1931	D. R. Jardine	T. C. Lowry	3	1	0	2
1932-33	D. R. Jardine[1]	M. L. Page	2	0	0	2
1937	R. W. V. Robins	M. L. Page	3	1	0	2
1946-47	W. R. Hammond	W. A. Hadlee	1	0	0	1
1949	F. G. Mann[2]	W. A. Hadlee	4	0	0	4
1950-51	F. R. Brown	W. A. Hadlee	2	1	0	1
1954-55	L. Hutton	G. O. Rabone	2	2	0	0
1958	P. B. H. May	J. R. Reid	5	4	0	1
1958-59	P. B. H. May	J. R. Reid	2	1	0	1
1962-63	E. R. Dexter	J. R. Reid	3	3	0	0
1965	M. J. K. Smith	J. R. Reid	3	3	0	0
1965-66	M. J. K. Smith	B. W. Sinclair[3]	3	0	0	3
1969	R. Illingworth	G. T. Dowling	3	2	0	1
1970-71	R. Illingworth	G. T. Dowling	2	1	0	1
1973	R. Illingworth	B. E. Congdon	3	2	0	1
1974-75	M. H. Denness	B. E. Congdon	2	1	0	1
1977-78	G. Boycott	M. G. Burgess	3	1	1	1
1978	J. M. Brearley	M. G. Burgess	3	3	0	0
1983	R. G. D. Willis	G. P. Howarth	4	3	1	0
1983-84	R. G. D. Willis	G. P. Howarth	3	0	1	2
1986	M. W. Gatting	J. V. Coney	3	0	1	2
1987-88	M. W. Gatting	J. J. Crowe[4]	3	0	0	3
1990	G. A. Gooch	J. G. Wright	3	1	0	2
1991-92	G. A. Gooch	M. D. Crowe	3	2	0	1
1994	M. A. Atherton	K. R. Rutherford	3	1	0	2
1996-97	M. A. Atherton	L. K. Germon[5]	3	2	0	1
1999	N. Hussain[6]	S. P. Fleming	4	1	2	1
2001-02	N. Hussain	S. P. Fleming	3	1	1	1
2004	M. P. Vaughan[7]	S. P. Fleming	3	3	0	0
2007-08	M. P. Vaughan	D. L. Vettori	3	2	1	0
2008	M. P. Vaughan	D. L. Vettori	3	2	0	1
2012-13	A. N. Cook	B. B. McCullum	3	0	0	3
2013	A. N. Cook	B. B. McCullum	2	2	0	0
2015	A. N. Cook	B. B. McCullum	2	1	1	0
	In New Zealand		47	18	4	25
	In England		54	30	5	19
	Totals		101	48	9	44

The following deputised for the official touring captain or were appointed by the home authority for only a minor proportion of the series:

[1]R. E. S. Wyatt (Second). [2]F. R. Brown (Third and Fourth). [3]M. E. Chapple (First). [4]J. G. Wright (Third). [5]S. P. Fleming (Third). [6]M. A. Butcher (Third). [7]M. E. Trescothick (First).

SERIES RECORDS

Highest score	*E*	336*	W. R. Hammond at Auckland	1932-33
	NZ	222	N. J. Astle at Christchurch	2001-02
Best bowling	*E*	7-32	D. L. Underwood at Lord's	1969
	NZ	7-74	B. L. Cairns at Leeds	1983
Highest total	*E*	593-6 dec	at Auckland	1974-75
	NZ	551-9 dec	at Lord's	1973
Lowest total	*E*	64	at Wellington	1977-78
	NZ	26	at Auckland	1954-55

ENGLAND v INDIA

Captains

Season	*England*	*India*	*T*	*E*	*I*	*D*
1932	D. R. Jardine	C. K. Nayudu	1	1	0	0
1933-34	D. R. Jardine	C. K. Nayudu	3	2	0	1
1936	G. O. B. Allen	Maharaj of Vizianagram	3	2	0	1
1946	W. R. Hammond	Nawab of Pataudi snr	3	1	0	2
1951-52	N. D. Howard[1]	V. S. Hazare	5	1	1	3
1952	L. Hutton	V. S. Hazare	4	3	0	1
1959	P. B. H. May[2]	D. K. Gaekwad[3]	5	5	0	0
1961-62	E. R. Dexter	N. J. Contractor	5	0	2	3
1963-64	M. J. K. Smith	Nawab of Pataudi jnr	5	0	0	5
1967	D. B. Close	Nawab of Pataudi jnr	3	3	0	0
1971	R. Illingworth	A. L. Wadekar	3	0	1	2
1972-73	A. R. Lewis	A. L. Wadekar	5	1	2	2
1974	M. H. Denness	A. L. Wadekar	3	3	0	0
1976-77	A. W. Greig	B. S. Bedi	5	3	1	1
1979	J. M. Brearley	S. Venkataraghavan	4	1	0	3
1979-80	J. M. Brearley	G. R. Viswanath	1	1	0	0
1981-82	K. W. R. Fletcher	S. M. Gavaskar	6	0	1	5
1982	R. G. D. Willis	S. M. Gavaskar	3	1	0	2
1984-85	D. I. Gower	S. M. Gavaskar	5	2	1	2
1986	M. W. Gatting[4]	Kapil Dev	3	0	2	1
1990	G. A. Gooch	M. Azharuddin	3	1	0	2
1992-93	G. A. Gooch[5]	M. Azharuddin	3	0	3	0
1996	M. A. Atherton	M. Azharuddin	3	1	0	2
2001-02	N. Hussain	S. C. Ganguly	3	0	1	2
2002	N. Hussain	S. C. Ganguly	4	1	1	2
2005-06	A. Flintoff	R. Dravid	3	1	1	1
2007	M. P. Vaughan	R. Dravid	3	0	1	2
2008-09	K. P. Pietersen	M. S. Dhoni	2	0	1	1
2011	A. J. Strauss	M. S. Dhoni	4	4	0	0
2012-13	A. N. Cook	M. S. Dhoni	4	2	1	1
2014	A. N. Cook	M. S. Dhoni	5	3	1	1
2016-17	A. N. Cook	V. Kohli	5	0	4	1
	In England		57	30	6	21
	In India		60	13	19	28
	Totals		117	43	25	49

* *Since 1951-52, series in India have been for the De Mello Trophy. Since 2007, series in England have been for the Pataudi Trophy.*

The following deputised for the official touring captain or were appointed by the home authority for only a minor proportion of the series:

[1]D. B. Carr (Fifth). [2]M. C. Cowdrey (Fourth and Fifth). [3]Pankaj Roy (Second). [4]D. I. Gower (First). [5]A. J. Stewart (Second).

The 1932 Indian touring team was captained by the Maharaj of Porbandar but he did not play in the Test match.

SERIES RECORDS

Highest score	*E*	333	G. A. Gooch at Lord's	1990
	I	303*	K. K. Nair at Chennai	2016-17
Best bowling	*E*	8-31	F. S. Trueman at Manchester	1952
	I	8-55	M. H. Mankad at Madras	1951-52
Highest total	*E*	710-7 dec	at Birmingham	2011
	I	759-7 dec	at Chennai	2016-17
Lowest total	*E*	101	at The Oval	1971
	I	42	at Lord's	1974

ENGLAND v PAKISTAN

	Captains					
Season	*England*	*Pakistan*	*T*	*E*	*P*	*D*
1954	L. Hutton[1]	A. H. Kardar	4	1	1	2
1961-62	E. R. Dexter	Imtiaz Ahmed	3	1	0	2
1962	E. R. Dexter[2]	Javed Burki	5	4	0	1
1967	D. B. Close	Hanif Mohammad	3	2	0	1
1968-69	M. C. Cowdrey	Saeed Ahmed	3	0	0	3
1971	R. Illingworth	Intikhab Alam	3	1	0	2
1972-73	A. R. Lewis	Majid Khan	3	0	0	3
1974	M. H. Denness	Intikhab Alam	3	0	0	3
1977-78	J. M. Brearley[3]	Wasim Bari	3	0	0	3
1978	J. M. Brearley	Wasim Bari	3	2	0	1
1982	R. G. D. Willis[4]	Imran Khan	3	2	1	0
1983-84	R. G. D. Willis[5]	Zaheer Abbas	3	0	1	2
1987	M. W. Gatting	Imran Khan	5	0	1	4
1987-88	M. W. Gatting	Javed Miandad	3	0	1	2
1992	G. A. Gooch	Javed Miandad	5	1	2	2
1996	M. A. Atherton	Wasim Akram	3	0	2	1
2000-01	N. Hussain	Moin Khan	3	1	0	2
2001	N. Hussain[6]	Waqar Younis	2	1	1	0
2005-06	M. P. Vaughan[7]	Inzamam-ul-Haq	3	0	2	1
2006†	A. J. Strauss	Inzamam-ul-Haq	4	3	0	1
2010	A. J. Strauss	Salman Butt	4	3	1	0
2011-12*U*	A. J. Strauss	Misbah-ul-Haq	3	0	3	0
2015-16*U*	A. N. Cook	Misbah-ul-Haq	3	0	2	1
2016	A. N. Cook	Misbah-ul-Haq	4	2	2	0
	In England		51	22	11	18
	In Pakistan		24	2	4	18
	In United Arab Emirates		6	0	5	1
	Totals		81	24	20	37

† *In 2008, the ICC changed the result of the forfeited Oval Test of 2006 from an England win to a draw, in contravention of the Laws of Cricket, only to rescind their decision in January 2009.*

U Played in United Arab Emirates.

The following deputised for the official touring captain or were appointed by the home authority for only a minor proportion of the series:

[1]D. S. Sheppard (Second and Third). [2]M. C. Cowdrey (Third). [3]G. Boycott (Third). [4]D. I. Gower (Second). [5]D. I. Gower (Second and Third). [6]A. J. Stewart (Second). [7]M. E. Trescothick (First).

SERIES RECORDS

Highest score	*E*	278	D. C. S. Compton at Nottingham	1954
	P	274	Zaheer Abbas at Birmingham	1971
Best bowling	*E*	8-34	I. T. Botham at Lord's	1978
	P	9-56	Abdul Qadir at Lahore	1987-88
Highest total	*E*	598-9 dec	at Abu Dhabi	2015-16
	P	708	at The Oval	1987
Lowest total	*E*	72	at Abu Dhabi	2011-12
	P	72	at Birmingham	2010

ENGLAND v SRI LANKA

Season	*Captains* England	Sri Lanka	*T*	*E*	*SL*	*D*
1981-82	K. W. R. Fletcher	B. Warnapura	1	1	0	0
1984	D. I. Gower	L. R. D. Mendis	1	0	0	1
1988	G. A. Gooch	R. S. Madugalle	1	1	0	0
1991	G. A. Gooch	P. A. de Silva	1	1	0	0
1992-93	A. J. Stewart	A. Ranatunga	1	0	1	0
1998	A. J. Stewart	A. Ranatunga	1	0	1	0
2000-01	N. Hussain	S. T. Jayasuriya	3	2	1	0
2002	N. Hussain	S. T. Jayasuriya	3	2	0	1
2003-04	M. P. Vaughan	H. P. Tillekeratne	3	0	1	2
2006	A. Flintoff	D. P. M. D. Jayawardene	3	1	1	1
2007-08	M. P. Vaughan	D. P. M. D. Jayawardene	3	0	1	2
2011	A. J. Strauss	T. M. Dilshan[1]	3	1	0	2
2011-12	A. J. Strauss	D. P. M. D. Jayawardene	2	1	1	0
2014	A. N. Cook	A. D. Mathews	2	0	1	1
2016	A. N. Cook	A. D. Mathews	3	2	0	1
	In England		18	8	3	7
	In Sri Lanka		13	4	5	4
	Totals		31	12	8	11

The following deputised for the official touring captain for only a minor proportion of the series:
[1]K. C. Sangakkara (Third).

SERIES RECORDS

Highest score	*E*	203	I. J. L. Trott at Cardiff	2011
	SL	213*	D. P. M. D. Jayawardene at Galle	2007-08
Best bowling	*E*	7-70	P. A. J. DeFreitas at Lord's	1991
	SL	9-65	M. Muralitharan at The Oval	1998
Highest total	*E*	575-9 dec	at Lord's	2014
	SL	628-8 dec	at Colombo (SSC)	2003-04
Lowest total	*E*	81	at Galle	2007-08
	SL	81	at Colombo (SSC)	2000-01

ENGLAND v ZIMBABWE

Season	*Captains* England	Zimbabwe	*T*	*E*	*Z*	*D*
1996-97	M. A. Atherton	A. D. R. Campbell	2	0	0	2
2000	N. Hussain	A. Flower	2	1	0	1
2003	N. Hussain	H. H. Streak	2	2	0	0
	In England		4	3	0	1
	In Zimbabwe		2	0	0	2
	Totals		6	3	0	3

SERIES RECORDS

Highest score	*E*	137	M. A. Butcher at Lord's	2003
	Z	148*	M. W. Goodwin at Nottingham	2000
Best bowling	*E*	6-33	R. L. Johnson at Chester-le-Street	2003
	Z	6-87	H. H. Streak at Lord's	2000
Highest total	*E*	472	at Lord's	2003
	Z	376	at Bulawayo	1996-97
Lowest total	*E*	147	at Nottingham	2000
	Z	83	at Lord's	2000

ENGLAND v BANGLADESH

Captains

Season	*England*	*Bangladesh*	*T*	*E*	*B*	*D*
2003-04	M. P. Vaughan	Khaled Mahmud	2	2	0	0
2005	M. P. Vaughan	Habibul Bashar	2	2	0	0
2009-10	A. N. Cook	Shakib Al Hasan	2	2	0	0
2010	A. J. Strauss	Shakib Al Hasan	2	2	0	0
2016-17	A. N. Cook	Mushfiqur Rahim	2	1	1	0
	In England		4	4	0	0
	In Bangladesh		6	5	1	0
	Totals		10	9	1	0

SERIES RECORDS

Highest score	*E*	226	I. J. L. Trott at Lord's	2010
	B	108	Tamim Iqbal at Manchester	2010
Best bowling	*E*	5-35	S. J. Harmison at Dhaka	2003-04
	B	6-77	Mehedi Hasan at Mirpur	2016-17
Highest total	*E*	599-6 dec	at Chittagong	2009-10
	B	419	at Mirpur	2009-10
Lowest total	*E*	164	at Mirpur	2016-17
	B	104	at Chester-le-Street	2005

AUSTRALIA v SOUTH AFRICA

Captains

Season	*Australia*	*South Africa*	*T*	*A*	*SA*	*D*
1902-03*S*	J. Darling	H. M. Taberer[1]	3	2	0	1
1910-11*A*	C. Hill	P. W. Sherwell	5	4	1	0
1912*E*	S. E. Gregory	F. Mitchell[2]	3	2	0	1
1921-22*S*	H. L. Collins	H. W. Taylor	3	1	0	2
1931-32*A*	W. M. Woodfull	H. B. Cameron	5	5	0	0
1935-36*S*	V. Y. Richardson	H. F. Wade	5	4	0	1
1949-50*S*	A. L. Hassett	A. D. Nourse	5	4	0	1

Season	Australia	South Africa	T	A	SA	D
	Captains					
1952-53*A*	A. L. Hassett	J. E. Cheetham	5	2	2	1
1957-58*S*	I. D. Craig	C. B. van Ryneveld[3]	5	3	0	2
1963-64*A*	R. B. Simpson[4]	T. L. Goddard	5	1	1	3
1966-67*S*	R. B. Simpson	P. L. van der Merwe	5	1	3	1
1969-70*S*	W. M. Lawry	A. Bacher	4	0	4	0
1993-94*A*	A. R. Border	K. C. Wessels[5]	3	1	1	1
1993-94*S*	A. R. Border	K. C. Wessels	3	1	1	1
1996-97*S*	M. A. Taylor	W. J. Cronje	3	2	1	0
1997-98*A*	M. A. Taylor	W. J. Cronje	3	1	0	2
2001-02*A*	S. R. Waugh	S. M. Pollock	3	3	0	0
2001-02*S*	S. R. Waugh	M. V. Boucher	3	2	1	0
2005-06*A*	R. T. Ponting	G. C. Smith	3	2	0	1
2005-06*S*	R. T. Ponting	G. C. Smith[6]	3	3	0	0
2008-09*A*	R. T. Ponting	G. C. Smith	3	1	2	0
2008-09*S*	R. T. Ponting	G. C. Smith[7]	3	2	1	0
2011-12*S*	M. J. Clarke	G. C. Smith	2	1	1	0
2012-13*A*	M. J. Clarke	G. C. Smith	3	0	1	2
2013-14*S*	M. J. Clarke	G. C. Smith	3	2	1	0
2016-17*A*	S. P. D. Smith	F. du Plessis	3	1	2	0
	In South Africa		50	28	13	9
	In Australia		41	21	10	10
	In England		3	2	0	1
	Totals		94	51	23	20

S Played in South Africa. A Played in Australia. E Played in England.

The following deputised for the official touring captain or were appointed by the home authority for only a minor proportion of the series:

[1]J. H. Anderson (Second), E. A. Halliwell (Third). [2]L. J. Tancred (Third). [3]D. J. McGlew (First). [4]R. Benaud (First). [5]W. J. Cronje (Third). [6]J. H. Kallis (Third). [7]J. H. Kallis (Third).

SERIES RECORDS

Highest score	*A*	299*	D. G. Bradman at Adelaide	1931-32
	SA	274	R. G. Pollock at Durban	1969-70
Best bowling	*A*	8-61	M. G. Johnson at Perth	2008-09
	SA	7-23	H. J. Tayfield at Durban	1949-50
Highest total	*A*	652-7 dec	at Johannesburg	2001-02
	SA	651	at Cape Town	2008-09
Lowest total	*A*	47	at Cape Town	2011-12
	SA	36	at Melbourne	1931-32

AUSTRALIA v WEST INDIES

Season	Australia	West Indies	T	A	WI	T	D
	Captains						
1930-31*A*	W. M. Woodfull	G. C. Grant	5	4	1	0	0
1951-52*A*	A. L. Hassett[1]	J. D. C. Goddard[2]	5	4	1	0	0
1954-55*W*	I. W. Johnson	D. St E. Atkinson[3]	5	3	0	0	2

THE FRANK WORRELL TROPHY

Season	Australia	West Indies	T	A	WI	T	D	Held by
	Captains							
1960-61*A*	R. Benaud	F. M. M. Worrell	5	2	1	1	1	A
1964-65*W*	R. B. Simpson	G. S. Sobers	5	1	2	0	2	WI
1968-69*A*	W. M. Lawry	G. S. Sobers	5	3	1	0	1	A

Season	Australia (Captains)	West Indies (Captains)	T	A	WI	T	D	Held by
1972-73*W*	I. M. Chappell	R. B. Kanhai	5	2	0	0	3	A
1975-76*A*	G. S. Chappell	C. H. Lloyd	6	5	1	0	0	A
1977-78*W*	R. B. Simpson	A. I. Kallicharran[4]	5	1	3	0	1	WI
1979-80*A*	G. S. Chappell	C. H. Lloyd[5]	3	0	2	0	1	WI
1981-82*A*	G. S. Chappell	C. H. Lloyd	3	1	1	0	1	WI
1983-84*W*	K. J. Hughes	C. H. Lloyd[6]	5	0	3	0	2	WI
1984-85*A*	A. R. Border[7]	C. H. Lloyd	5	1	3	0	1	WI
1988-89*A*	A. R. Border	I. V. A. Richards	5	1	3	0	1	WI
1990-91*W*	A. R. Border	I. V. A. Richards	5	1	2	0	2	WI
1992-93*A*	A. R. Border	R. B. Richardson	5	1	2	0	2	WI
1994-95*W*	M. A. Taylor	R. B. Richardson	4	2	1	0	1	A
1996-97*A*	M. A. Taylor	C. A. Walsh	5	3	2	0	0	A
1998-99*W*	S. R. Waugh	B. C. Lara	4	2	2	0	0	A
2000-01*A*	S. R. Waugh[8]	J. C. Adams	5	5	0	0	0	A
2002-03*W*	S. R. Waugh	B. C. Lara	4	3	1	0	0	A
2005-06*A*	R. T. Ponting	S. Chanderpaul	3	3	0	0	0	A
2007-08*W*	R. T. Ponting	R. R. Sarwan[9]	3	2	0	0	1	A
2009-10*A*	R. T. Ponting	C. H. Gayle	3	2	0	0	1	A
2011-12*W*	M. J. Clarke	D. J. G. Sammy	3	2	0	0	1	A
2015*W*	M. J. Clarke	D. Ramdin	2	2	0	0	0	A
2015-16*A*	S. P. D. Smith	J. O. Holder	3	2	0	0	1	A
	In Australia		66	37	18	1	10	
	In West Indies		50	21	14	0	15	
	Totals		116	58	32	1	25	

A *Played in Australia.* *W* *Played in West Indies.*

The following deputised for the official touring captain or were appointed by the home authority for only a minor proportion of the series:

[1]A. R. Morris (Third). [2]J. B. Stollmeyer (Fifth). [3]J. B. Stollmeyer (Second and Third). [4]C. H. Lloyd (First and Second). [5]D. L. Murray (First). [6]I. V. A. Richards (Second). [7]K. J. Hughes (First and Second). [8]A. C. Gilchrist (Third). [9]C. H. Gayle (Third).

SERIES RECORDS

Highest score	*A*	269*	A. C. Voges at Hobart	2015-16
	WI	277	B. C. Lara at Sydney	1992-93
Best bowling	*A*	8-71	G. D. McKenzie at Melbourne	1968-69
	WI	7-25	C. E. L. Ambrose at Perth	1992-93
Highest total	*A*	758-8 dec	at Kingston	1954-55
	WI	616	at Adelaide	1968-69
Lowest total	*A*	76	at Perth	1984-85
	WI	51	at Port-of-Spain	1998-99

AUSTRALIA v NEW ZEALAND

Season	Australia (Captains)	New Zealand (Captains)	T	A	NZ	D
1945-46*N*	W. A. Brown	W. A. Hadlee	1	1	0	0
1973-74*A*	I. M. Chappell	B. E. Congdon	3	2	0	1
1973-74*N*	I. M. Chappell	B. E. Congdon	3	1	1	1
1976-77*N*	G. S. Chappell	G. M. Turner	2	1	0	1
1980-81*A*	G. S. Chappell	G. P. Howarth[1]	3	2	0	1
1981-82*N*	G. S. Chappell	G. P. Howarth	3	1	1	1

TRANS-TASMAN TROPHY

	Captains						
Season	*Australia*	*New Zealand*	*T*	*A*	*NZ*	*D*	*Held by*
1985-86*A*	A. R. Border	J. V. Coney	3	1	2	0	NZ
1985-86*N*	A. R. Border	J. V. Coney	3	0	1	2	NZ
1987-88*A*	A. R. Border	J. J. Crowe	3	1	0	2	A
1989-90*A*	A. R. Border	J. G. Wright	1	0	0	1	A
1989-90*N*	A. R. Border	J. G. Wright	1	0	1	0	NZ
1992-93*N*	A. R. Border	M. D. Crowe	3	1	1	1	NZ
1993-94*A*	A. R. Border	M. D. Crowe[2]	3	2	0	1	A
1997-98*A*	M. A. Taylor	S. P. Fleming	3	2	0	1	A
1999-2000*N*	S. R. Waugh	S. P. Fleming	3	3	0	0	A
2001-02*A*	S. R. Waugh	S. P. Fleming	3	0	0	3	A
2004-05*A*	R. T. Ponting	S. P. Fleming	2	2	0	0	A
2004-05*N*	R. T. Ponting	S. P. Fleming	3	2	0	1	A
2008-09*A*	R. T. Ponting	D. L. Vettori	2	2	0	0	A
2009-10*N*	R. T. Ponting	D. L. Vettori	2	2	0	0	A
2011-12*A*	M. J. Clarke	L. R. P. L. Taylor	2	1	1	0	A
2015-16*A*	S. P. D. Smith	B. B. McCullum	3	2	0	1	A
2015-16*N*	S. P. D. Smith	B. B. McCullum	2	2	0	0	A
	In Australia		31	17	3	11	
	In New Zealand		26	14	5	7	
	Totals		57	31	8	18	

A Played in Australia. N Played in New Zealand.

The following deputised for the official touring captain: [1]M. G. Burgess (Second). [2]K. R. Rutherford (Second and Third).

SERIES RECORDS

Highest score	*A*	253	D. A. Warner at Perth	2015-16
	NZ	290	L. R. P. L. Taylor at Perth	2015-16
Best bowling	*A*	6-31	S. K. Warne at Hobart	1993-94
	NZ	9-52	R. J. Hadlee at Brisbane	1985-86
Highest total	*A*	607-6 dec	at Brisbane	1993-94
	NZ	624	at Perth	2015-16
Lowest total	*A*	103	at Auckland	1985-86
	NZ	42	at Wellington	1945-46

AUSTRALIA v INDIA

	Captains						
Season	*Australia*	*India*	*T*	*A*	*I*	*T*	*D*
1947-48*A*	D. G. Bradman	L. Amarnath	5	4	0	0	1
1956-57*I*	I. W. Johnson[1]	P. R. Umrigar	3	2	0	0	1
1959-60*I*	R. Benaud	G. S. Ramchand	5	2	1	0	2
1964-65*I*	R. B. Simpson	Nawab of Pataudi jnr	3	1	1	0	1
1967-68*A*	R. B. Simpson[2]	Nawab of Pataudi jnr[3]	4	4	0	0	0
1969-70*I*	W. M. Lawry	Nawab of Pataudi jnr	5	3	1	0	1
1977-78*A*	R. B. Simpson	B. S. Bedi	5	3	2	0	0
1979-80*I*	K. J. Hughes	S. M. Gavaskar	6	0	2	0	4
1980-81*A*	G. S. Chappell	S. M. Gavaskar	3	1	1	0	1
1985-86*A*	A. R. Border	Kapil Dev	3	0	0	0	3
1986-87*I*	A. R. Border	Kapil Dev	3	0	0	1	2
1991-92*A*	A. R. Border	M. Azharuddin	5	4	0	0	1

THE BORDER–GAVASKAR TROPHY

Season	Captains: Australia	India	T	A	I	T	D	Held by
1996-97*I*	M. A. Taylor	S. R. Tendulkar	1	0	1	0	0	I
1997-98*I*	M. A. Taylor	M. Azharuddin	3	1	2	0	0	I
1999-2000*A*	S. R. Waugh	S. R. Tendulkar	3	3	0	0	0	A
2000-01*I*	S. R. Waugh	S. C. Ganguly	3	1	2	0	0	I
2003-04*A*	S. R. Waugh	S. C. Ganguly	4	1	1	0	2	I
2004-05*I*	R. T. Ponting[4]	S. C. Ganguly[5]	4	2	1	0	1	A
2007-08*A*	R. T. Ponting	A. Kumble	4	2	1	0	1	A
2008-09*I*	R. T. Ponting	A. Kumble[6]	4	0	2	0	2	I
2010-11*I*	R. T. Ponting	M. S. Dhoni	2	0	2	0	0	I
2011-12*A*	M. J. Clarke	M. S. Dhoni[7]	4	4	0	0	0	A
2012-13*I*	M. J. Clarke[8]	M. S. Dhoni	4	0	4	0	0	I
2014-15*A*	M. J. Clarke[9]	M. S. Dhoni[10]	4	2	0	0	2	A
2016-17*I*	**S. P. D. Smith**	**V. Kohli[11]**	**4**	**1**	**2**	**0**	**1**	**I**
	In Australia		44	28	5	0	11	
	In India		**50**	**13**	**21**	**1**	**15**	
	Totals		**94**	**41**	**26**	**1**	**26**	

A Played in Australia. I Played in India.

The following deputised for the official touring captain or were appointed by the home authority for only a minor proportion of the series:

[1]R. R. Lindwall (Second). [2]W. M. Lawry (Third and Fourth). [3]C. G. Borde (First). [4]A. C. Gilchrist (First, Second and Third). [5]R. Dravid (Third and Fourth). [6]M. S. Dhoni (Second and Fourth). [7]V. Sehwag (Fourth). [8]S. R. Watson (Fourth). [9]S. P. D. Smith (Second, Third and Fourth). [10]V. Kohli (First and Fourth). [11]A. M. Rahane (Fourth).

SERIES RECORDS

Highest score	*A*	329*	M. J. Clarke at Sydney	2011-12
	I	281	V. V. S. Laxman at Kolkata	2000-01
Best bowling	*A*	**8-50**	**N. M. Lyon at Bangalore**	**2016-17**
	I	9-69	J. M. Patel at Kanpur	1959-60
Highest total	*A*	674	at Adelaide	1947-48
	I	705-7 dec	at Sydney	2003-04
Lowest total	*A*	83	at Melbourne	1980-81
	I	58	at Brisbane	1947-48

AUSTRALIA v PAKISTAN

Season	Captains: Australia	Pakistan	T	A	P	D
1956-57*P*	I. W. Johnson	A. H. Kardar	1	0	1	0
1959-60*P*	R. Benaud	Fazal Mahmood[1]	3	2	0	1
1964-65*P*	R. B. Simpson	Hanif Mohammad	1	0	0	1
1964-65*A*	R. B. Simpson	Hanif Mohammad	1	0	0	1
1972-73*A*	I. M. Chappell	Intikhab Alam	3	3	0	0
1976-77*A*	G. S. Chappell	Mushtaq Mohammad	3	1	1	1
1978-79*A*	G. N. Yallop[2]	Mushtaq Mohammad	2	1	1	0
1979-80*P*	G. S. Chappell	Javed Miandad	3	0	1	2
1981-82*A*	G. S. Chappell	Javed Miandad	3	2	1	0
1982-83*P*	K. J. Hughes	Imran Khan	3	0	3	0
1983-84*A*	K. J. Hughes	Imran Khan[3]	5	2	0	3
1988-89*P*	A. R. Border	Javed Miandad	3	0	1	2

Captains

Season	Australia	Pakistan	T	A	P	D
1989-90*A*	A. R. Border	Imran Khan	3	1	0	2
1994-95*P*	M. A. Taylor	Salim Malik	3	0	1	2
1995-96*A*	M. A. Taylor	Wasim Akram	3	2	1	0
1998-99*P*	M. A. Taylor	Aamir Sohail	3	1	0	2
1999-2000*A*	S. R. Waugh	Wasim Akram	3	3	0	0
2002-03*S/U*	S. R. Waugh	Waqar Younis	3	3	0	0
2004-05*A*	R. T. Ponting	Inzamam-ul-Haq[4]	3	3	0	0
2009-10*A*	R. T. Ponting	Mohammad Yousuf	3	3	0	0
2010*E*	R. T. Ponting	Shahid Afridi[5]	2	1	1	0
2014-15*U*	M. J. Clarke	Misbah-ul-Haq	2	0	2	0
2016-17*A*	**S. P. D. Smith**	**Misbah-ul-Haq**	**3**	**3**	**0**	**0**
	In Pakistan		20	3	7	10
	In Australia		**35**	**24**	**4**	**7**
	In Sri Lanka		1	1	0	0
	In United Arab Emirates		4	2	2	0
	In England		2	1	1	0
	Totals		**62**	**31**	**14**	**17**

P Played in Pakistan. A Played in Australia.
S/U First Test played in Sri Lanka, Second and Third Tests in United Arab Emirates.
E Played in England.

The following deputised for the official touring captain or were appointed by the home authority for only a minor proportion of the series:

[1]Imtiaz Ahmed (Second). [2]K. J. Hughes (Second). [3]Zaheer Abbas (First, Second and Third). [4]Yousuf Youhana *later known as Mohammad Yousuf* (Second and Third). [5]Salman Butt (Second).

SERIES RECORDS

Highest score	*A*	334*	M. A. Taylor at Peshawar	1998-99
	P	237	Salim Malik at Rawalpindi	1994-95
Best bowling	*A*	8-24	G. D. McGrath at Perth	2004-05
	P	9-86	Sarfraz Nawaz at Melbourne	1978-79
Highest total	*A*	**624-8 dec**	**at Melbourne**	**2016-17**
	P	624	at Adelaide	1983-84
Lowest total	*A*	80	at Karachi	1956-57
	P	53	at Sharjah	2002-03

AUSTRALIA v SRI LANKA

Captains

Season	Australia	Sri Lanka	T	A	SL	D
1982-83*S*	G. S. Chappell	L. R. D. Mendis	1	1	0	0
1987-88*A*	A. R. Border	R. S. Madugalle	1	1	0	0
1989-90*A*	A. R. Border	A. Ranatunga	2	1	0	1
1992-93*S*	A. R. Border	A. Ranatunga	3	1	0	2
1995-96*A*	M. A. Taylor	A. Ranatunga[1]	3	3	0	0
1999-2000*S*	S. R. Waugh	S. T. Jayasuriya	3	0	1	2
2003-04*S*	R. T. Ponting	H. P. Tillekeratne	3	3	0	0
2004*A*	R. T. Ponting[2]	M. S. Atapattu	2	1	0	1

THE WARNE–MURALITHARAN TROPHY

	Captains						
Season	*Australia*	*Sri Lanka*	*T*	*A*	*SL*	*D*	*Held by*
2007-08*A*	R. T. Ponting	D. P. M. D. Jayawardene	2	2	0	0	A
2011-12*S*	M. J. Clarke	T. M. Dilshan	3	1	0	2	A
2012-13*A*	M. J. Clarke	D. P. M. D. Jayawardene	3	3	0	0	A
2016*S*	S. P. D. Smith	A. D. Mathews	3	0	3	0	SL
	In Australia		13	11	0	2	
	In Sri Lanka		16	6	4	6	
	Totals		29	17	4	8	

A *Played in Australia.* *S* *Played in Sri Lanka.*

The following deputised for the official touring captain or was appointed by the home authority for only a minor proportion of the series:

[1]P. A. de Silva (Third). [2]A. C. Gilchrist (First).

SERIES RECORDS

Highest score	*A*	219	M. J. Slater at Perth	1995-96
	SL	192	K. C. Sangakkara at Hobart	2007-08
Best bowling	*A*	7-39	M. S. Kasprowicz at Darwin	2004
	SL	7-64	H. M. R. K. B. Herath at Colombo (SSC)	2016
Highest total	*A*	617-5 dec	at Perth	1995-96
	SL	547-8 dec	at Colombo (SSC)	1992-93
Lowest total	*A*	106	at Galle	2016
	SL	97	at Darwin	2004

AUSTRALIA v ZIMBABWE

	Captains					
Season	*Australia*	*Zimbabwe*	*T*	*A*	*Z*	*D*
1999-2000*Z*	S. R. Waugh	A. D. R. Campbell	1	1	0	0
2003-04*A*	S. R. Waugh	H. H. Streak	2	2	0	0
	In Australia		2	2	0	0
	In Zimbabwe		1	1	0	0
	Totals		3	3	0	0

A *Played in Australia.* *Z* *Played in Zimbabwe.*

SERIES RECORDS

Highest score	*A*	380	M. L. Hayden at Perth	2003-04
	Z	118	S. V. Carlisle at Sydney	2003-04
Best bowling	*A*	6-65	S. M. Katich at Sydney	2003-04
	Z	6-121	R. W. Price at Sydney	2003-04
Highest total	*A*	735-6 dec	at Perth	2003-04
	Z	321	at Perth	2003-04
Lowest total	*A*	403	at Sydney	2003-04
	Z	194	at Harare	1999-2000

AUSTRALIA v BANGLADESH

Season	Australia (Captains)	Bangladesh	T	A	B	D
2003*A*	S. R. Waugh	Khaled Mahmud	2	2	0	0
2005-06*B*	R. T. Ponting	Habibul Bashar	2	2	0	0
2017-18*B*	**S. P. D. Smith**	**Mushfiqur Rahim**	**2**	**1**	**1**	**0**
	In Australia		2	2	0	0
	In Bangladesh		**4**	**3**	**1**	**0**
	Totals		**6**	**5**	**1**	**0**

A *Played in Australia.* *B* *Played in Bangladesh.*

SERIES RECORDS

Highest score	*A*	201*	J. N. Gillespie at Chittagong	2005-06
	B	138	Shahriar Nafees at Fatullah	2005-06
Best bowling	*A*	8-108	S. C. G. MacGill at Fatullah	2005-06
	B	5-62	Mohammad Rafique at Fatullah	2005-06
Highest total	*A*	581-4 dec	at Chittagong	2005-06
	B	427	at Fatullah	2005-06
Lowest total	*A*	**217**	**at Mirpur**	**2017-18**
	B	97	at Darwin	2003

AUSTRALIA v ICC WORLD XI

Season	Australia	ICC World XI	T	A	ICC	D
2005-06*A*	R. T. Ponting	G. C. Smith	1	1	0	0

A *Played in Australia.*

SERIES RECORDS

Highest score	*A*	111	M. L. Hayden at Sydney	2005-06
	Wld	76	V. Sehwag at Sydney	2005-06
Best bowling	*A*	5-43	S. C. G. MacGill at Sydney	2005-06
	Wld	4-59	A. Flintoff at Sydney	2005-06
Highest total	*A*	345	at Sydney	2005-06
	Wld	190	at Sydney	2005-06
Lowest total	*A*	199	at Sydney	2005-06
	Wld	144	at Sydney	2005-06

SOUTH AFRICA v WEST INDIES

Season	South Africa (Captains)	West Indies	T	SA	WI	D
1991-92*W*	K. C. Wessels	R. B. Richardson	1	0	1	0
1998-99*S*	W. J. Cronje	B. C. Lara	5	5	0	0

SIR VIVIAN RICHARDS TROPHY

Season	*Captains* *South Africa*	*West Indies*	*T*	*SA*	*WI*	*D*	*Held by*
2000-01*W*	S. M. Pollock	C. L. Hooper	5	2	1	2	SA
2003-04*S*	G. C. Smith	B. C. Lara	4	3	0	1	SA
2004-05*W*	G. C. Smith	S. Chanderpaul	4	2	0	2	SA
2007-08 *S*	G. C. Smith	C. H. Gayle[1]	3	2	1	0	SA
2010*W*	G. C. Smith	C. H. Gayle	3	2	0	1	SA
2014-15*S*	H. M. Amla	D. Ramdin	3	2	0	1	SA
	In South Africa		15	12	1	2	
	In West Indies		13	6	2	5	
	Totals		28	18	3	7	

S Played in South Africa. *W Played in West Indies.*

The following deputised for the official touring captain:
[1]D. J. Bravo (Third).

SERIES RECORDS

Highest score	*SA*	208	H. M. Amla at Centurion	2014-15
	WI	317	C. H. Gayle at St John's	2004-05
Best bowling	*SA*	7-37	M. Ntini at Port-of-Spain	2004-05
	WI	7-84	F. A. Rose at Durban	1998-99
Highest total	*SA*	658-9 dec	at Durban	2003-04
	WI	747	at St John's	2004-05
Lowest total	*SA*	141	at Kingston	2000-01
	WI	102	at Port-of-Spain	2010

SOUTH AFRICA v NEW ZEALAND

Season	*Captains* *South Africa*	*New Zealand*	*T*	*SA*	*NZ*	*D*
1931-32*N*	H. B. Cameron	M. L. Page	2	2	0	0
1952-53*N*	J. E. Cheetham	W. M. Wallace	2	1	0	1
1953-54*S*	J. E. Cheetham	G. O. Rabone[1]	5	4	0	1
1961-62*S*	D. J. McGlew	J. R. Reid	5	2	2	1
1963-64*N*	T. L. Goddard	J. R. Reid	3	0	0	3
1994-95*S*	W. J. Cronje	K. R. Rutherford	3	2	1	0
1994-95*N*	W. J. Cronje	K. R. Rutherford	1	1	0	0
1998-99*N*	W. J. Cronje	D. J. Nash	3	1	0	2
2000-01*S*	S. M. Pollock	S. P. Fleming	3	2	0	1
2003-04*N*	G. C. Smith	S. P. Fleming	3	1	1	1
2005-06*S*	G. C. Smith	S. P. Fleming	3	2	0	1
2007-08*S*	G. C. Smith	D. L. Vettori	2	2	0	0
2011-12*N*	G. C. Smith	L. R. P. L. Taylor	3	1	0	2
2012-13*S*	G. C. Smith	B. B. McCullum	2	2	0	0
2016*S*	F. du Plessis	K. S. Williamson	2	1	0	1
2016-17*N*	**F. du Plessis**	**K. S. Williamson**	**3**	**1**	**0**	**2**
	In New Zealand		**20**	**8**	**1**	**11**
	In South Africa		25	17	3	5
	Totals		**45**	**25**	**4**	**16**

N Played in New Zealand. *S Played in South Africa.*

The following deputised for the official touring captain:
[1]B. Sutcliffe (Fourth and Fifth).

SERIES RECORDS

Highest score	*SA*	275*	D. J. Cullinan at Auckland	1998-99
	NZ	262	S. P. Fleming at Cape Town	2005-06
Best bowling	*SA*	8-53	G. B. Lawrence at Johannesburg	1961-62
	NZ	6-60	J. R. Reid at Dunedin	1963-64
Highest total	*SA*	621-5 dec	at Auckland	1998-99
	NZ	595	at Auckland	2003-04
Lowest total	*SA*	148	at Johannesburg	1953-54
	NZ	45	at Cape Town	2012-13

SOUTH AFRICA v INDIA

	Captains					
Season	*South Africa*	*India*	*T*	*SA*	*I*	*D*
1992-93*S*	K. C. Wessels	M. Azharuddin	4	1	0	3
1996-97*I*	W. J. Cronje	S. R. Tendulkar	3	1	2	0
1996-97*S*	W. J. Cronje	S. R. Tendulkar	3	2	0	1
1999-2000*I*	W. J. Cronje	S. R. Tendulkar	2	2	0	0
2001-02*S*†	S. M. Pollock	S. C. Ganguly	2	1	0	1
2004-05*I*	G. C. Smith	S. C. Ganguly	2	0	1	1
2006-07*S*	G. C. Smith	R. Dravid	3	2	1	0
2007-08*I*	G. C. Smith	A. Kumble[1]	3	1	1	1
2009-10*I*	G. C. Smith	M. S. Dhoni	2	1	1	0
2010-11*S*	G. C. Smith	M. S. Dhoni	3	1	1	1
2013-14*S*	G. C. Smith	M. S. Dhoni	2	1	0	1

THE FREEDOM TROPHY

	Captains						
Season	*South Africa*	*India*	*T*	*SA*	*I*	*D*	*Held by*
2015-16*I*	H. M. Amla	V. Kohli	4	0	3	1	I
2017-18*S*	**F. du Plessis**	**V. Kohli**	**3**	**2**	**1**	**0**	**SA**
	In South Africa		**20**	**10**	**3**	**7**	
	In India		16	5	8	3	
	Totals		**36**	**15**	**11**	**10**	

S *Played in South Africa.* *I* *Played in India.*

† *The Third Test at Centurion was stripped of its official status by the ICC after a disciplinary dispute and is excluded.*

The following was appointed by the home authority for only a minor proportion of the series:
[1]M. S. Dhoni (Third).

SERIES RECORDS

Highest score	*SA*	253*	H. M. Amla at Nagpur	2009-10
	I	319	V. Sehwag at Chennai	2007-08
Best bowling	*SA*	8-64	L. Klusener at Calcutta	1996-97
	I	7-66	R. Ashwin at Nagpur	2015-16
Highest total	*SA*	620-4 dec	at Centurion	2010-11
	I	643-6 dec	at Kolkata	2009-10
Lowest total	*SA*	79	at Nagpur	2015-16
	I	66	at Durban	1996-97

SOUTH AFRICA v PAKISTAN

Captains

Season	*South Africa*	*Pakistan*	*T*	*SA*	*P*	*D*
1994-95*S*	W. J. Cronje	Salim Malik	1	1	0	0
1997-98*P*	W. J. Cronje	Saeed Anwar	3	1	0	2
1997-98*S*	W. J. Cronje[1]	Rashid Latif[2]	3	1	1	1
2002-03*S*	S. M. Pollock	Waqar Younis	2	2	0	0
2003-04*P*	G. C. Smith	Inzamam-ul-Haq[3]	2	0	1	1
2006-07*S*	G. C. Smith	Inzamam-ul-Haq	3	2	1	0
2007-08*P*	G. C. Smith	Shoaib Malik	2	1	0	1
2010-11*U*	G. C. Smith	Misbah-ul-Haq	2	0	0	2
2012-13*S*	G. C. Smith	Misbah-ul-Haq	3	3	0	0
2013-14*U*	G. C. Smith	Misbah-ul-Haq	2	1	1	0
	In South Africa		12	9	2	1
	In Pakistan		7	2	1	4
	In United Arab Emirates		4	1	1	2
	Totals		23	12	4	7

S *Played in South Africa.* *P* *Played in Pakistan.* *U* *Played in United Arab Emirates.*

The following deputised for the official touring captain or were appointed by the home authority for only a minor proportion of the series:

[1]G. Kirsten (First). [2]Aamir Sohail (First and Second). [3]Yousuf Youhana *later known as Mohammad Yousuf* (First).

SERIES RECORDS

Highest score	*SA*	278*	A. B. de Villiers at Abu Dhabi	2010-11
	P	146	Khurram Manzoor at Abu Dhabi	2013-14
Best bowling	*SA*	7-29	K. J. Abbott at Centurion	2012-13
	P	6-78	Mushtaq Ahmed at Durban	1997-98
		6-78	Waqar Younis at Port Elizabeth	1997-98
Highest total	*SA*	620-7 dec	at Cape Town	2002-03
	P	456	at Rawalpindi	1997-98
Lowest total	*SA*	124	at Port Elizabeth	2006-07
	P	49	at Johannesburg	2012-13

SOUTH AFRICA v SRI LANKA

Captains

Season	*South Africa*	*Sri Lanka*	*T*	*SA*	*SL*	*D*
1993-94*SL*	K. C. Wessels	A. Ranatunga	3	1	0	2
1997-98*SA*	W. J. Cronje	A. Ranatunga	2	2	0	0
2000*SL*	S. M. Pollock	S. T. Jayasuriya	3	1	1	1
2000-01*SA*	S. M. Pollock	S. T. Jayasuriya	3	2	0	1
2002-03*SA*	S. M. Pollock	S. T. Jayasuriya[1]	2	2	0	0
2004*SL*	G. C. Smith	M. S. Atapattu	2	0	1	1
2006*SL*	A. G. Prince	D. P. M. D. Jayawardene	2	0	2	0
2011-12*SA*	G. C. Smith	T. M. Dilshan	3	2	1	0
2014*SL*	H. M. Amla	A. D. Mathews	2	1	0	1

Season	South Africa	Captains Sri Lanka	T	SA	SL	D
2016-17*SA*	**F. du Plessis**	**A. D. Mathews**	**3**	**3**	**0**	**0**
	In South Africa		**13**	**11**	**1**	**1**
	In Sri Lanka		12	3	4	5
	Totals		**25**	**14**	**5**	**6**

SA *Played in South Africa.* *SL* *Played in Sri Lanka.*

The following deputised for the official captain:
[1]M. S. Atapattu (Second).

SERIES RECORDS

Highest score	*SA*	224	J. H. Kallis at Cape Town	2011-12
	SL	374	D. P. M. D. Jayawardene at Colombo (SSC)	2006
Best bowling	*SA*	7-81	M. de Lange at Durban	2011-12
	SL	7-84	M. Muralitharan at Galle	2000
Highest total	*SA*	580-4 dec	at Cape Town	2011-12
	SL	756-5 dec	at Colombo (SSC)	2006
Lowest total	*SA*	168	at Durban	2011-12
	SL	95	at Cape Town	2000-01

SOUTH AFRICA v ZIMBABWE

Season	South Africa	Captains Zimbabwe	T	SA	Z	D
1995-96*Z*	W. J. Cronje	A. Flower	1	1	0	0
1999-2000*S*	W. J. Cronje	A. D. R. Campbell	1	1	0	0
1999-2000*Z*	W. J. Cronje	A. Flower	1	1	0	0
2001-02*Z*	S. M. Pollock	H. H. Streak	2	1	0	1
2004-05*S*	G. C. Smith	T. Taibu	2	2	0	0
2014-15*Z*	H. M. Amla	B. R. M. Taylor	1	1	0	0
2017-18*S*	**A. B. de Villiers**	**A. G. Cremer**	**1**	**1**	**0**	**0**
	In Zimbabwe		5	4	0	1
	In South Africa		**4**	**4**	**0**	**0**
	Totals		**9**	**8**	**0**	**1**

S *Played in South Africa.* *Z* *Played in Zimbabwe.*

SERIES RECORDS

Highest score	*SA*	220	G. Kirsten at Harare	2001-02
	Z	199*	A. Flower at Harare	2001-02
Best bowling	*SA*	8-71	A. A. Donald at Harare	1995-96
	Z	5-101	B. C. Strang at Harare	1995-96
Highest total	*SA*	600-3 dec	at Harare	2001-02
	Z	419-9 dec	at Bulawayo	2001-02
Lowest total	*SA*	346	at Harare	1995-96
	Z	54	at Cape Town	2004-05

SOUTH AFRICA v BANGLADESH

Season	Captains: South Africa	Captains: Bangladesh	T	SA	B	D
2002-03*S*	S. M. Pollock[1]	Khaled Mashud	2	2	0	0
2003*B*	G. C. Smith	Khaled Mahmud	2	2	0	0
2007-08*B*	G. C. Smith	Mohammad Ashraful	2	2	0	0
2008-09*S*	G. C. Smith	Mohammad Ashraful	2	2	0	0
2015*B*	H. M. Amla	Mushfiqur Rahim	2	0	0	2
2017-18*S*	**F. du Plessis**	**Mushfiqur Rahim**	**2**	**2**	**0**	**0**
	In South Africa		**6**	**6**	**0**	**0**
	In Bangladesh		6	4	0	2
	Totals		**12**	**10**	**0**	**2**

S *Played in South Africa.* *B* *Played in Bangladesh.*

The following deputised for the official captain:
[1]M. V. Boucher (First).

SERIES RECORDS

Highest score	*SA*	232	G. C. Smith at Chittagong	2007-08
	B	**77**	**Mominul Haque at Potchefstroom**	**2017-18**
Best bowling	*SA*	5-19	M. Ntini at East London	2002-03
	B	6-27	Shahadat Hossain at Mirpur	2007-08
Highest total	*SA*	583-7 dec	at Chittagong	2007-08
	B	326	at Chittagong	2015
Lowest total	*SA*	170	at Mirpur	2007-08
	B	**90**	**at Potchefstroom**	**2017-18**

WEST INDIES v NEW ZEALAND

Season	Captains: West Indies	Captains: New Zealand	T	WI	NZ	D
1951-52*N*	J. D. C. Goddard	B. Sutcliffe	2	1	0	1
1955-56*N*	D. St E. Atkinson	J. R. Reid[1]	4	3	1	0
1968-69*N*	G. S. Sobers	G. T. Dowling	3	1	1	1
1971-72*W*	G. S. Sobers	G. T. Dowling[2]	5	0	0	5
1979-80*N*	C. H. Lloyd	G. P. Howarth	3	0	1	2
1984-85*W*	I. V. A. Richards	G. P. Howarth	4	2	0	2
1986-87*N*	I. V. A. Richards	J. V. Coney	3	1	1	1
1994-95*N*	C. A. Walsh	K. R. Rutherford	2	1	0	1
1995-96*W*	C. A. Walsh	L. K. Germon	2	1	0	1
1999-2000*N*	B. C. Lara	S. P. Fleming	2	0	2	0
2002*W*	C. L. Hooper	S. P. Fleming	2	0	1	1
2005-06*N*	S. Chanderpaul	S. P. Fleming	3	0	2	1
2008-09*N*	C. H. Gayle	D. L. Vettori	2	0	0	2
2012*W*	D. J. G. Sammy	L. R. P. L. Taylor	2	2	0	0
2013-14*N*	D. J. G. Sammy	B. B. McCullum	3	0	2	1
2014*W*	D. Ramdin	B. B. McCullum	3	1	2	0

	Captains					
Season	*West Indies*	*New Zealand*	*T*	*WI*	*NZ*	*D*
2017-18*N*	**J. O. Holder**[3]	**K. S. Williamson**	**2**	**0**	**2**	**0**
	In New Zealand		**29**	**7**	**12**	**10**
	In West Indies		18	6	3	9
	Totals		**47**	**13**	**15**	**19**

N Played in New Zealand. *W Played in West Indies.*

The following deputised for the official touring captain or were appointed by the home authority for only a minor proportion of the series:

[1]H. B. Cave (First). [2]B. E. Congdon (Third, Fourth and Fifth). [3]K. C. Brathwaite (Second).

SERIES RECORDS

Highest score	*WI*	258	S. M. Nurse at Christchurch	1968-69
	NZ	259	G. M. Turner at Georgetown	1971-72
Best bowling	*WI*	7-37	C. A. Walsh at Wellington	1994-95
	NZ	7-27	C. L. Cairns at Hamilton	1999-2000
Highest total	*WI*	660-5 dec	at Wellington	1994-95
	NZ	609-9 dec	at Dunedin (University)	2013-14
Lowest total	*WI*	77	at Auckland	1955-56
	NZ	74	at Dunedin	1955-56

WEST INDIES v INDIA

	Captains					
Season	*West Indies*	*India*	*T*	*WI*	*I*	*D*
1948-49*I*	J. D. C. Goddard	L. Amarnath	5	1	0	4
1952-53*W*	J. B. Stollmeyer	V. S. Hazare	5	1	0	4
1958-59*I*	F. C. M. Alexander	Ghulam Ahmed[1]	5	3	0	2
1961-62*W*	F. M. M. Worrell	N. J. Contractor[2]	5	5	0	0
1966-67*I*	G. S. Sobers	Nawab of Pataudi jnr	3	2	0	1
1970-71*W*	G. S. Sobers	A. L. Wadekar	5	0	1	4
1974-75*I*	C. H. Lloyd	Nawab of Pataudi jnr[3]	5	3	2	0
1975-76*W*	C. H. Lloyd	B. S. Bedi	4	2	1	1
1978-79*I*	A. I. Kallicharran	S. M. Gavaskar	6	0	1	5
1982-83*W*	C. H. Lloyd	Kapil Dev	5	2	0	3
1983-84*I*	C. H. Lloyd	Kapil Dev	6	3	0	3
1987-88*I*	I. V. A. Richards	D. B. Vengsarkar[4]	4	1	1	2
1988-89*W*	I. V. A. Richards	D. B. Vengsarkar	4	3	0	1
1994-95*I*	C. A. Walsh	M. Azharuddin	3	1	1	1
1996-97*W*	C. A. Walsh[5]	S. R. Tendulkar	5	1	0	4
2001-02*W*	C. L. Hooper	S. C. Ganguly	5	2	1	2
2002-03*I*	C. L. Hooper	S. C. Ganguly	3	0	2	1
2005-06*W*	B. C. Lara	R. Dravid	4	0	1	3
2011*W*	D. J. G. Sammy	M. S. Dhoni	3	0	1	2
2011-12*I*	D. J. G. Sammy	M. S. Dhoni	3	0	2	1
2013-14*I*	D. J. G. Sammy	M. S. Dhoni	2	0	2	0

	Captains					
Season	*West Indies*	*India*	*T*	*WI*	*I*	*D*
2016*W*	J. O. Holder	V. Kohli	4	0	2	2
	In India		45	14	11	20
	In West Indies		49	16	7	26
	Totals		94	30	18	46

I Played in India. W Played in West Indies.

The following deputised for the official touring captain or were appointed by the home authority for only a minor proportion of the series:

[1]P. R. Umrigar (First), M. H. Mankad (Fourth), H. R. Adhikari (Fifth). [2]Nawab of Pataudi jnr (Third, Fourth and Fifth). [3]S. Venkataraghavan (Second). [4]R. J. Shastri (Fourth). [5]B. C. Lara (Third).

SERIES RECORDS

Highest score	*WI*	256	R. B. Kanhai at Calcutta	1958-59
	I	236*	S. M. Gavaskar at Madras	1983-84
Best bowling	*WI*	9-95	J. M. Noreiga at Port-of-Spain	1970-71
	I	9-83	Kapil Dev at Ahmedabad	1983-84
Highest total	*WI*	644-8 dec	at Delhi	1958-59
	I	644-7 dec	at Kanpur	1978-79
Lowest total	*WI*	103	at Kingston	2005-06
	I	75	at Delhi	1987-88

WEST INDIES v PAKISTAN

	Captains					
Season	*West Indies*	*Pakistan*	*T*	*WI*	*P*	*D*
1957-58*W*	F. C. M. Alexander	A. H. Kardar	5	3	1	1
1958-59*P*	F. C. M. Alexander	Fazal Mahmood	3	1	2	0
1974-75*P*	C. H. Lloyd	Intikhab Alam	2	0	0	2
1976-77*W*	C. H. Lloyd	Mushtaq Mohammad	5	2	1	2
1980-81*P*	C. H. Lloyd	Javed Miandad	4	1	0	3
1986-87*P*	I. V. A. Richards	Imran Khan	3	1	1	1
1987-88*W*	I. V. A. Richards[1]	Imran Khan	3	1	1	1
1990-91*P*	D. L. Haynes	Imran Khan	3	1	1	1
1992-93*W*	R. B. Richardson	Wasim Akram	3	2	0	1
1997-98*P*	C. A. Walsh	Wasim Akram	3	0	3	0
1999-2000*W*	J. C. Adams	Moin Khan	3	1	0	2
2001-02*U*	C. L. Hooper	Waqar Younis	2	0	2	0
2004-05*W*	S. Chanderpaul	Inzamam-ul-Haq[2]	2	1	1	0
2006-07*P*	B. C. Lara	Inzamam-ul-Haq	3	0	2	1
2010-11*W*	D. J. G. Sammy	Misbah-ul-Haq	2	1	1	0
2016-17*U*	J. O. Holder	Misbah-ul-Haq	3	1	2	0
2016-17*W*	**J. O. Holder**	**Misbah-ul-Haq**	**3**	**1**	**2**	**0**
	In West Indies		**26**	**12**	**7**	**7**
	In Pakistan		21	4	9	8
	In United Arab Emirates		5	1	4	0
	Totals		**52**	**17**	**20**	**15**

P Played in Pakistan. W Played in West Indies. U Played in United Arab Emirates.

The following were appointed by the home authority or deputised for the official touring captain for a minor proportion of the series:

[1]C. G. Greenidge (First). [2]Younis Khan (First).

SERIES RECORDS

Highest score	*WI*	365*	G. S. Sobers at Kingston	1957-58
	P	337	Hanif Mohammad at Bridgetown	1957-58
Best bowling	*WI*	8-29	C. E. H. Croft at Port-of-Spain	1976-77
	P	7-80	Imran Khan at Georgetown	1987-88
Highest total	*WI*	790-3 dec	at Kingston	1957-58
	P	657-8 dec	at Bridgetown	1957-58
Lowest total	*WI*	53	at Faisalabad	1986-87
	P	77	at Lahore	1986-87

WEST INDIES v SRI LANKA

Season	*West Indies* (Captains)	*Sri Lanka*	*T*	*WI*	*SL*	*D*
1993-94*S*	R. B. Richardson	A. Ranatunga	1	0	0	1
1996-97*W*	C. A. Walsh	A. Ranatunga	2	1	0	1
2001-02*S*	C. L. Hooper	S. T. Jayasuriya	3	0	3	0
2003*W*	B. C. Lara	H. P. Tillekeratne	2	1	0	1
2005*S*	S. Chanderpaul	M. S. Atapattu	2	0	2	0
2007-08*W*	C. H. Gayle	D. P. M. D. Jayawardene	2	1	1	0
2010-11*S*	D. J. G. Sammy	K. C. Sangakkara	3	0	0	3

THE SOBERS–TISSERA TROPHY

Season	*West Indies* (Captains)	*Sri Lanka*	*T*	*WI*	*SL*	*D*	*Held by*
2015-16*S*	J. O. Holder	A. D. Mathews	2	0	2	0	SL
	In West Indies		6	3	1	2	
	In Sri Lanka		11	0	7	4	
	Totals		17	3	8	6	

W *Played in West Indies.* *S* *Played in Sri Lanka.*

SERIES RECORDS

Highest score	*WI*	333	C. H. Gayle at Galle	2010-11
	SL	204*	H. P. Tillekeratne at Colombo (SSC)	2001-02
Best bowling	*WI*	7-57	C. D. Collymore at Kingston	2003
	SL	8-46	M. Muralitharan at Kandy	2005
Highest total	*WI*	580-9 dec	at Galle	2010-11
	SL	627-9 dec	at Colombo (SSC)	2001-02
Lowest total	*WI*	113	at Colombo (SSC)	2005
	SL	150	at Kandy	2005

WEST INDIES v ZIMBABWE

Season	*West Indies* (Captains)	*Zimbabwe*	*T*	*WI*	*Z*	*D*
1999-2000*W*	J. C. Adams	A. Flower	2	2	0	0

THE CLIVE LLOYD TROPHY

	Captains						
Season	*West Indies*	*Zimbabwe*	*T*	*WI*	*Z*	*D*	*Held by*
2001*Z*	C. L. Hooper	H. H. Streak	2	1	0	1	WI
2003-04*Z*	B. C. Lara	H. H. Streak	2	1	0	1	WI
2012-13*W*	D. J. G. Sammy	B. R. M. Taylor	2	2	0	0	WI
2017-18*Z*	**J. O. Holder**	**A. G. Cremer**	**2**	**1**	**0**	**1**	**WI**
	In West Indies		4	4	0	0	
	In Zimbabwe		**6**	**3**	**0**	**3**	
	Totals		**10**	**7**	**0**	**3**	

W *Played in West Indies.* *Z* *Played in Zimbabwe.*

SERIES RECORDS

Highest score	*WI*	191	B. C. Lara at Bulawayo	2003-04
	Z	**147**	**H. Masakadza at Bulawayo**	**2017-18**
Best bowling	*WI*	6-49	S. Shillingford at Bridgetown	2012-13
	Z	6-73	R. W. Price at Harare	2003-04
Highest total	*WI*	559-6 dec	at Bulawayo	2001
	Z	563-9 dec	at Harare	2001
Lowest total	*WI*	128	at Bulawayo	2003-04
	Z	63	at Port-of-Spain	1999-2000

WEST INDIES v BANGLADESH

	Captains					
Season	*West Indies*	*Bangladesh*	*T*	*WI*	*B*	*D*
2002-03*B*	R. D. Jacobs	Khaled Mashud	2	2	0	0
2003-04*W*	B. C. Lara	Habibul Bashar	2	1	0	1
2009*W*	F. L. Reifer	Mashrafe bin Mortaza[1]	2	0	2	0
2011-12*B*	D. J. G. Sammy	Mushfiqur Rahim	2	1	0	1
2012-13*B*	D. J. G. Sammy	Mushfiqur Rahim	2	2	0	0
2014-15*W*	D. Ramdin	Mushfiqur Rahim	2	2	0	0
	In West Indies		6	3	2	1
	In Bangladesh		6	5	0	1
	Totals		12	8	2	2

B *Played in Bangladesh.* *W* *Played in West Indies.*

The following deputised for the official touring captain for a minor proportion of the series:
[1]Shakib Al Hasan (Second).

SERIES RECORDS

Highest score	*WI*	261*	R. R. Sarwan at Kingston	2003-04
	B	128	Tamim Iqbal at St Vincent	2009
Best bowling	*WI*	6-3	J. J. C. Lawson at Dhaka	2002-03
	B	6-74	Sohag Gazi at Mirpur	2012-13
Highest total	*WI*	648-9 dec	at Khulna	2012-13
	B	556	at Mirpur	2012-13
Lowest total	*WI*	181	at St Vincent	2009
	B	87	at Dhaka	2002-03

NEW ZEALAND v INDIA

Season	Captains: New Zealand	India	T	NZ	I	D
1955-56*I*	H. B. Cave	P. R. Umrigar[1]	5	0	2	3
1964-65*I*	J. R. Reid	Nawab of Pataudi jnr	4	0	1	3
1967-68*N*	G. T. Dowling[2]	Nawab of Pataudi jnr	4	1	3	0
1969-70*I*	G. T. Dowling	Nawab of Pataudi jnr	3	1	1	1
1975-76*N*	G. M. Turner	B. S. Bedi[3]	3	1	1	1
1976-77*I*	G. M. Turner	B. S. Bedi	3	0	2	1
1980-81*N*	G. P. Howarth	S. M. Gavaskar	3	1	0	2
1988-89*I*	J. G. Wright	D. B. Vengsarkar	3	1	2	0
1989-90*N*	J. G. Wright	M. Azharuddin	3	1	0	2
1993-94*N*	K. R. Rutherford	M. Azharuddin	1	0	0	1
1995-96*I*	L. K. Germon	M. Azharuddin	3	0	1	2
1998-99*N*†	S. P. Fleming	M. Azharuddin	2	1	0	1
1999-2000*I*	S. P. Fleming	S. R. Tendulkar	3	0	1	2
2002-03*N*	S. P. Fleming	S. C. Ganguly	2	2	0	0
2003-04*I*	S. P. Fleming	S. C. Ganguly[4]	2	0	0	2
2008-09*N*	D. L. Vettori	M. S. Dhoni[5]	3	0	1	2
2010-11*I*	D. L. Vettori	M. S. Dhoni	3	0	1	2
2012-13*I*	L. R. P. L. Taylor	M. S. Dhoni	2	0	2	0
2013-14*N*	B. B. McCullum	M. S. Dhoni	2	1	0	1
2016-17*I*	K. S. Williamson[6]	V. Kohli	3	0	3	0
	In India		34	2	16	16
	In New Zealand		23	8	5	10
	Totals		57	10	21	26

I Played in India. N Played in New Zealand.

† *The First Test at Dunedin was abandoned without a ball being bowled and is excluded.*

The following deputised for the official touring captain or were appointed by the home authority for a minor proportion of the series:

[1]Ghulam Ahmed (First). [2]B. W. Sinclair (First). [3]S. M. Gavaskar (First). [4]R. Dravid (Second). [5]V. Sehwag (Second). [6]L. R. P. L. Taylor (Second).

SERIES RECORDS

Highest score	*NZ*	302	B. B. McCullum at Wellington	2013-14
	I	231	M. H. Mankad at Madras	1955-56
Best bowling	*NZ*	7-23	R. J. Hadlee at Wellington	1975-76
	I	8-72	S. Venkataraghavan at Delhi	1964-65
Highest total	*NZ*	680-8 dec	at Wellington	2013-14
	I	583-7 dec	at Ahmedabad	1999-2000
Lowest total	*NZ*	94	at Hamilton	2002-03
	I	81	at Wellington	1975-76

NEW ZEALAND v PAKISTAN

Season	Captains: New Zealand	Pakistan	T	NZ	P	D
1955-56*P*	H. B. Cave	A. H. Kardar	3	0	2	1
1964-65*N*	J. R. Reid	Hanif Mohammad	3	0	0	3
1964-65*P*	J. R. Reid	Hanif Mohammad	3	0	2	1
1969-70*P*	G. T. Dowling	Intikhab Alam	3	1	0	2
1972-73*N*	B. E. Congdon	Intikhab Alam	3	0	1	2
1976-77*P*	G. M. Turner[1]	Mushtaq Mohammad	3	0	2	1
1978-79*N*	M. G. Burgess	Mushtaq Mohammad	3	0	1	2

Captains

Season	*New Zealand*	*Pakistan*	*T*	*NZ*	*P*	*D*
1984-85*P*	J. V. Coney	Zaheer Abbas	3	0	2	1
1984-85*N*	G. P. Howarth	Javed Miandad	3	2	0	1
1988-89*N*†	J. G. Wright	Imran Khan	2	0	0	2
1990-91*P*	M. D. Crowe	Javed Miandad	3	0	3	0
1992-93*N*	K. R. Rutherford	Javed Miandad	1	0	1	0
1993-94*N*	K. R. Rutherford	Salim Malik	3	1	2	0
1995-96*N*	L. K. Germon	Wasim Akram	1	0	1	0
1996-97*P*	L. K. Germon	Saeed Anwar	2	1	1	0
2000-01*N*	S. P. Fleming	Moin Khan[2]	3	1	1	1
2002*P*‡	S. P. Fleming	Waqar Younis	1	0	1	0
2003-04*N*	S. P. Fleming	Inzamam-ul-Haq	2	0	1	1
2009-10*N*	D. L. Vettori	Mohammad Yousuf	3	1	1	1
2010-11*N*	D. L. Vettori	Misbah-ul-Haq	2	0	1	1
2014-15*U*	B. B. McCullum	Misbah-ul-Haq	3	1	1	1
2016-17*N*	K. S. Williamson	Misbah-ul-Haq[3]	2	2	0	0
	In Pakistan		21	2	13	6
	In New Zealand		31	7	10	14
	In United Arab Emirates		3	1	1	1
	Totals		55	10	24	21

N *Played in New Zealand.* *P* *Played in Pakistan.* *U* *Played in United Arab Emirates.*

† *The First Test at Dunedin was abandoned without a ball being bowled and is excluded.*
‡ *The Second Test at Karachi was cancelled owing to civil disturbances.*

The following were appointed by the home authority for only a minor proportion of the series or deputised for the official touring captain:
[1]J. M. Parker (Third). [2]Inzamam-ul-Haq (Third). [3]Azhar Ali (Second).

SERIES RECORDS

Highest score	*NZ*	204*	M. S. Sinclair at Christchurch	2000-01
	P	329	Inzamam-ul-Haq at Lahore	2002
Best bowling	*NZ*	7-52	C. Pringle at Faisalabad	1990-91
	P	7-52	Intikhab Alam at Dunedin	1972-73
Highest total	*NZ*	690	at Sharjah	2014-15
	P	643	at Lahore	2002
Lowest total	*NZ*	70	at Dacca	1955-56
	P	102	at Faisalabad	1990-91

NEW ZEALAND v SRI LANKA

Captains

Season	*New Zealand*	*Sri Lanka*	*T*	*NZ*	*SL*	*D*
1982-83*N*	G. P. Howarth	D. S. de Silva	2	2	0	0
1983-84*S*	G. P. Howarth	L. R. D. Mendis	3	2	0	1
1986-87*S*†	J. J. Crowe	L. R. D. Mendis	1	0	0	1
1990-91*N*	M. D. Crowe[1]	A. Ranatunga	3	0	0	3
1992-93*S*	M. D. Crowe	A. Ranatunga	2	0	1	1
1994-95*N*	K. R. Rutherford	A. Ranatunga	2	0	1	1
1996-97*N*	S. P. Fleming	A. Ranatunga	2	2	0	0
1997-98*S*	S. P. Fleming	A. Ranatunga	3	1	2	0
2003*S*	S. P. Fleming	H. P. Tillekeratne	2	0	0	2
2004-05*N*	S. P. Fleming	M. S. Atapattu	2	1	0	1
2006-07*N*	S. P. Fleming	D. P. M. D. Jayawardene	2	1	1	0
2009*S*	D. L. Vettori	K. C. Sangakkara	2	0	2	0
2012-13*S*	L. R. P. L. Taylor	D. P. M. D. Jayawardene	2	1	1	0
2014-15*N*	B. B. McCullum	A. D. Mathews	2	2	0	0

	Captains					
Season	*New Zealand*	*Sri Lanka*	*T*	*NZ*	*SL*	*D*
2015-16*N*	B. B. McCullum	A. D. Mathews	2	2	0	0
	In New Zealand		17	10	2	5
	In Sri Lanka		15	4	6	5
	Totals		32	14	8	10

N Played in New Zealand. S Played in Sri Lanka.

† *The Second and Third Tests were cancelled owing to civil disturbances.*

The following was appointed by the home authority for only a minor proportion of the series:
[1]I. D. S. Smith (Third).

SERIES RECORDS

Highest score	*NZ*	299	M. D. Crowe at Wellington	1990-91
	SL	267	P. A. de Silva at Wellington	1990-91
Best bowling	*NZ*	7-130	D. L. Vettori at Wellington	2006-07
	SL	6-43	H. M. R. K. B. Herath at Galle	2012-13
Highest total	*NZ*	671-4	at Wellington	1990-91
	SL	498	at Napier	2004-05
Lowest total	*NZ*	102	at Colombo (SSC)	1992-93
	SL	93	at Wellington	1982-83

NEW ZEALAND v ZIMBABWE

	Captains					
Season	*New Zealand*	*Zimbabwe*	*T*	*NZ*	*Z*	*D*
1992-93*Z*	M. D. Crowe	D. L. Houghton	2	1	0	1
1995-96*N*	L. K. Germon	A. Flower	2	0	0	2
1997-98*Z*	S. P. Fleming	A. D. R. Campbell	2	0	0	2
1997-98*N*	S. P. Fleming	A. D. R. Campbell	2	2	0	0
2000-01*Z*	S. P. Fleming	H. H. Streak	2	2	0	0
2000-01*N*	S. P. Fleming	H. H. Streak	1	0	0	1
2005-06*Z*	S. P. Fleming	T. Taibu	2	2	0	0
2011-12*Z*	L. R. P. L. Taylor	B. R. M. Taylor	1	1	0	0
2011-12*N*	L. R. P. L. Taylor	B. R. M. Taylor	1	1	0	0
2016*Z*	K. S. Williamson	A. G. Cremer	2	2	0	0
	In New Zealand		6	3	0	3
	In Zimbabwe		11	8	0	3
	Totals		17	11	0	6

N Played in New Zealand. Z Played in Zimbabwe.

SERIES RECORDS

Highest score	*NZ*	173*	L. R. P. L. Taylor at Bulawayo	2016
	Z	203*	G. J. Whittall at Bulawayo	1997-98
Best bowling	*NZ*	6-26	C. S. Martin at Napier	2011-12
	Z	8-109	P. A. Strang at Bulawayo	2000-01
Highest total	*NZ*	582-4 dec	at Bulawayo	2016
	Z	461	at Bulawayo	1997-98
Lowest total	*NZ*	207	at Harare	1997-98
	Z	51	at Napier	2011-12

NEW ZEALAND v BANGLADESH

	Captains					
Season	*New Zealand*	*Bangladesh*	*T*	*NZ*	*B*	*D*
2001-02*N*	S. P. Fleming	Khaled Mashud	2	2	0	0
2004-05*B*	S. P. Fleming	Khaled Mashud	2	2	0	0
2007-08*N*	D. L. Vettori	Mohammad Ashraful	2	2	0	0
2008-09*B*	D. L. Vettori	Mohammad Ashraful	2	1	0	1
2009-10*N*	D. L. Vettori	Shakib Al Hasan	1	1	0	0
2013-14*B*	B. B. McCullum	Mushfiqur Rahim	2	0	0	2
2016-17*N*	**K. S. Williamson**	**Mushfiqur Rahim**[1]	**2**	**2**	**0**	**0**
	In New Zealand		**7**	**7**	**0**	**0**
	In Bangladesh		6	3	0	3
	Totals		**13**	**10**	**0**	**3**

B *Played in Bangladesh.* *N* *Played in New Zealand.*

The following deputised for the official touring captain for only a minor proportion of the series:
[1]Tamim Iqbal (Second).

SERIES RECORDS

Highest score	*NZ*	202	S. P. Fleming at Chittagong	2004-05
	B	**217**	**Shakib Al Hasan at Wellington**	**2016-17**
Best bowling	*NZ*	7-53	C. L. Cairns at Hamilton	2001-02
	B	7-36	Shakib Al Hasan at Chittagong	2008-09
Highest total	*NZ*	553-7 dec	at Hamilton	2009-10
	B	**595-8 dec**	**at Wellington**	**2016-17**
Lowest total	*NZ*	171	at Chittagong	2008-09
	B	108	at Hamilton	2001-02

INDIA v PAKISTAN

	Captains					
Season	*India*	*Pakistan*	*T*	*I*	*P*	*D*
1952-53*I*	L. Amarnath	A. H. Kardar	5	2	1	2
1954-55*P*	M. H. Mankad	A. H. Kardar	5	0	0	5
1960-61*I*	N. J. Contractor	Fazal Mahmood	5	0	0	5
1978-79*P*	B. S. Bedi	Mushtaq Mohammad	3	0	2	1
1979-80*I*	S. M. Gavaskar[1]	Asif Iqbal	6	2	0	4
1982-83*P*	S. M. Gavaskar	Imran Khan	6	0	3	3
1983-84*I*	Kapil Dev	Zaheer Abbas	3	0	0	3
1984-85*P*	S. M. Gavaskar	Zaheer Abbas	2	0	0	2
1986-87*I*	Kapil Dev	Imran Khan	5	0	1	4
1989-90*P*	K. Srikkanth	Imran Khan	4	0	0	4
1998-99*I*	M. Azharuddin	Wasim Akram	2	1	1	0
1998-99*I*†	M. Azharuddin	Wasim Akram	1	0	1	0
2003-04*P*	S. C. Ganguly[2]	Inzamam-ul-Haq	3	2	1	0
2004-05*I*	S. C. Ganguly	Inzamam-ul-Haq	3	1	1	1
2005-06*P*	R. Dravid	Inzamam-ul-Haq[3]	3	0	1	2

Season	Captains: India	Pakistan	T	I	P	D
2007-08*I*	A. Kumble	Shoaib Malik[4]	3	1	0	2
	In India		33	7	5	21
	In Pakistan		26	2	7	17
	Totals		59	9	12	38

I Played in India. P Played in Pakistan.

† *This Test was part of the Asian Test Championship and was not counted as part of the preceding bilateral series.*

The following were appointed by the home authority for only a minor proportion of the series or deputised for the official touring captain:
[1]G. R. Viswanath (Sixth). [2]R. Dravid (First and Second). [3]Younis Khan (Third). [4]Younis Khan (Second and Third).

SERIES RECORDS

Highest score	*I*	309	V. Sehwag at Multan	2003-04
	P	280*	Javed Miandad at Hyderabad	1982-83
Best bowling	*I*	10-74	A. Kumble at Delhi	1998-99
	P	8-60	Imran Khan at Karachi	1982-83
Highest total	*I*	675-5 dec	at Multan	2003-04
	P	699-5	at Lahore	1989-90
Lowest total	*I*	106	at Lucknow	1952-53
	P	116	at Bangalore	1986-87

INDIA v SRI LANKA

Season	Captains: India	Sri Lanka	T	I	SL	D
1982-83*I*	S. M. Gavaskar	B. Warnapura	1	0	0	1
1985-86*S*	Kapil Dev	L. R. D. Mendis	3	0	1	2
1986-87*I*	Kapil Dev	L. R. D. Mendis	3	2	0	1
1990-91*I*	M. Azharuddin	A. Ranatunga	1	1	0	0
1993-94*S*	M. Azharuddin	A. Ranatunga	3	1	0	2
1993-94*I*	M. Azharuddin	A. Ranatunga	3	3	0	0
1997-98*S*	S. R. Tendulkar	A. Ranatunga	2	0	0	2
1997-98*I*	S. R. Tendulkar	A. Ranatunga	3	0	0	3
1998-99*S*†	M. Azharuddin	A. Ranatunga	1	0	0	1
2001*S*	S. C. Ganguly	S. T. Jayasuriya	3	1	2	0
2005-06*I*	R. Dravid[1]	M. S. Atapattu	3	2	0	1
2008*S*	A. Kumble	D. P. M. D. Jayawardene	3	1	2	0
2009-10*I*	M. S. Dhoni	K. C. Sangakkara	3	2	0	1
2010*S*	M. S. Dhoni	K. C. Sangakkara	3	1	1	1
2015-16*S*	V. Kohli	A. D. Mathews	3	2	1	0
2017*S*	**V. Kohli**	**L. D. Chandimal[2]**	**3**	**3**	**0**	**0**
2017-18*I*	**V. Kohli**	**L. D. Chandimal**	**3**	**1**	**0**	**2**
	In India		**20**	**11**	**0**	**9**
	In Sri Lanka		**24**	**9**	**7**	**8**
	Totals		**44**	**20**	**7**	**17**

I Played in India. S Played in Sri Lanka.

† *This Test was part of the Asian Test Championship.*

The following were appointed by the home authority for only a minor proportion of the series:
[1]V. Sehwag (Third). [2]H. M. R. K. B. Herath (First).

SERIES RECORDS

Highest score	*I*	293	V. Sehwag at Mumbai (BS)	2009-10
	SL	340	S. T. Jayasuriya at Colombo (RPS)	1997-98
Best bowling	*I*	7-51	Maninder Singh at Nagpur	1986-87
	SL	8-87	M. Muralitharan at Colombo (SSC)	2001
Highest total	*I*	726-9 dec	at Mumbai (BS)	2009-10
	SL	952-6 dec	at Colombo (RPS)	1997-98
Lowest total	*I*	112	at Galle	2015-16
	SL	82	at Chandigarh	1990-91

INDIA v ZIMBABWE

Season	*India* (Captains)	*Zimbabwe* (Captains)	*T*	*I*	*Z*	*D*
1992-93*Z*	M. Azharuddin	D. L. Houghton	1	0	0	1
1992-93*I*	M. Azharuddin	D. L. Houghton	1	1	0	0
1998-99*Z*	M. Azharuddin	A. D. R. Campbell	1	0	1	0
2000-01*I*	S. C. Ganguly	H. H. Streak	2	1	0	1
2001*Z*	S. C. Ganguly	H. H. Streak	2	1	1	0
2001-02*I*	S. C. Ganguly	S. V. Carlisle	2	2	0	0
2005-06*Z*	S. C. Ganguly	T. Taibu	2	2	0	0
	In India		5	4	0	1
	In Zimbabwe		6	3	2	1
	Totals		11	7	2	2

I *Played in India.* *Z* *Played in Zimbabwe.*

SERIES RECORDS

Highest score	*I*	227	V. G. Kambli at Delhi	1992-93
	Z	232*	A. Flower at Nagpur	2000-01
Best bowling	*I*	7-59	I. K. Pathan at Harare	2005-06
	Z	6-73	H. H. Streak at Harare	2005-06
Highest total	*I*	609-6 dec	at Nagpur	2000-01
	Z	503-6	at Nagpur	2000-01
Lowest total	*I*	173	at Harare	1998-99
	Z	146	at Delhi	2001-02

INDIA v BANGLADESH

Season	*India* (Captains)	*Bangladesh* (Captains)	*T*	*I*	*B*	*D*
2000-01*B*	S. C. Ganguly	Naimur Rahman	1	1	0	0
2004-05*B*	S. C. Ganguly	Habibul Bashar	2	2	0	0
2007*B*	R. Dravid	Habibul Bashar	2	1	0	1
2009-10*B*	M. S. Dhoni[1]	Shakib Al Hasan	2	2	0	0
2015*B*	V. Kohli	Mushfiqur Rahim	1	0	0	1
2016-17*I*	**V. Kohli**	**Mushfiqur Rahim**	**1**	**1**	**0**	**0**
	In Bangladesh		8	6	0	2
	In India		**1**	**1**	**0**	**0**
	Totals		**9**	**7**	**0**	**2**

B *Played in Bangladesh.* *I* *Played in India.*

The following deputised for the official touring captain for a minor proportion of the series:
[1]V. Sehwag (First).

SERIES RECORDS

Highest score	*I*	248*	S. R. Tendulkar at Dhaka	2004-05
	B	158*	Mohammad Ashraful at Chittagong	2004-05
Best bowling	*I*	7-87	Zaheer Khan at Mirpur	2009-10
	B	6-132	Naimur Rahman at Dhaka	2000-01
Highest total	*I*	**687-6 dec**	**at Hyderabad**	**2016-17**
	B	400	at Dhaka	2000-01
Lowest total	*I*	243	at Chittagong	2009-10
	B	91	at Dhaka	2000-01

PAKISTAN v SRI LANKA

	Captains					
Season	*Pakistan*	*Sri Lanka*	*T*	*P*	*SL*	*D*
1981-82*P*	Javed Miandad	B. Warnapura[1]	3	2	0	1
1985-86*P*	Javed Miandad	L. R. D. Mendis	3	2	0	1
1985-86*S*	Imran Khan	L. R. D. Mendis	3	1	1	1
1991-92*P*	Imran Khan	P. A. de Silva	3	1	0	2
1994-95*S*†	Salim Malik	A. Ranatunga	2	2	0	0
1995-96*P*	Ramiz Raja	A. Ranatunga	3	1	2	0
1996-97*S*	Ramiz Raja	A. Ranatunga	2	0	0	2
1998-99*P*‡	Wasim Akram	H. P. Tillekeratne	1	0	0	1
1998-99*B*‡	Wasim Akram	P. A. de Silva	1	1	0	0
1999-2000*P*	Saeed Anwar[2]	S. T. Jayasuriya	3	1	2	0
2000*S*	Moin Khan	S. T. Jayasuriya	3	2	0	1
2001-02*P*‡	Waqar Younis	S. T. Jayasuriya	1	0	1	0
2004-05*P*	Inzamam-ul-Haq	M. S. Atapattu	2	1	1	0
2005-06*S*	Inzamam-ul-Haq	D. P. M. D. Jayawardene	2	1	0	1
2008-09*P*§	Younis Khan	D. P. M. D. Jayawardene	2	0	0	2
2009*S*	Younis Khan	K. C. Sangakkara	3	0	2	1
2011-12*U*	Misbah-ul-Haq	T. M. Dilshan	3	1	0	2
2012*S*	Misbah-ul-Haq[3]	D. P. M. D. Jayawardene	3	0	1	2
2013-14*U*	Misbah-ul-Haq	A. D. Mathews	3	1	1	1
2014*S*	Misbah-ul-Haq	A. D. Mathews	2	0	2	0
2015*S*	Misbah-ul-Haq	A. D. Mathews	3	2	1	0
2017-18*U*	**Sarfraz Ahmed**	**L. D. Chandimal**	**2**	**0**	**2**	**0**
	In Pakistan		21	8	6	7
	In Sri Lanka		23	8	7	8
	In Bangladesh		1	1	0	0
	In United Arab Emirates		**8**	**2**	**3**	**3**
	Totals		**53**	**19**	**16**	**18**

P Played in Pakistan. S Played in Sri Lanka. B Played in Bangladesh.
U Played in United Arab Emirates.

† *One Test was cancelled owing to the threat of civil disturbances following a general election.*
‡ *These Tests were part of the Asian Test Championship.*
§ *The Second Test ended after a terrorist attack on the Sri Lankan team bus on the third day.*

The following deputised for the official touring captain or were appointed by the home authority for only a minor proportion of the series:

[1]L. R. D. Mendis (Second). [2]Moin Khan (Third). [3]Mohammad Hafeez (First).

SERIES RECORDS

Highest score	*P*	313	Younis Khan at Karachi	2008-09
	SL	253	S. T. Jayasuriya at Faisalabad	2004-05
Best bowling	*P*	8-58	Imran Khan at Lahore	1981-82
	SL	9-127	H. M. R. K. B. Herath at Colombo (SSC)	2014
Highest total	*P*	765-6 dec	at Karachi	2008-09
	SL	644-7 dec	at Karachi	2008-09
Lowest total	*P*	90	at Colombo (PSS)	2009
	SL	71	at Kandy	1994-95

PAKISTAN v ZIMBABWE

	Captains					
Season	*Pakistan*	*Zimbabwe*	*T*	*P*	*Z*	*D*
1993-94*P*	Wasim Akram[1]	A. Flower	3	2	0	1
1994-95*Z*	Salim Malik	A. Flower	3	2	1	0
1996-97*P*	Wasim Akram	A. D. R. Campbell	2	1	0	1
1997-98*Z*	Rashid Latif	A. D. R. Campbell	2	1	0	1
1998-99*P*†	Aamir Sohail[2]	A. D. R. Campbell	2	0	1	1
2002-03*Z*	Waqar Younis	A. D. R. Campbell	2	2	0	0
2011-12*Z*	Misbah-ul-Haq	B. R. M. Taylor	1	1	0	0
2013-14*Z*	Misbah-ul-Haq	B. R. M. Taylor[3]	2	1	1	0
	In Pakistan		7	3	1	3
	In Zimbabwe		10	7	2	1
	Totals		17	10	3	4

P *Played in Pakistan.* *Z* *Played in Zimbabwe.*

† *The Third Test at Faisalabad was abandoned without a ball being bowled and is excluded.*

The following were appointed by the home authority for only a minor proportion of the series:
[1]Waqar Younis (First). [2]Moin Khan (Second). [3]H. Masakadza (First).

SERIES RECORDS

Highest score	*P*	257*	Wasim Akram at Sheikhupura	1996-97
	Z	201*	G. W. Flower at Harare	1994-95
Best bowling	*P*	7-66	Saqlain Mushtaq at Bulawayo	2002-03
	Z	6-90	H. H. Streak at Harare	1994-95
Highest total	*P*	553	at Sheikhupura	1996-97
	Z	544-4 dec	at Harare	1994-95
Lowest total	*P*	103	at Peshawar	1998-99
	Z	120	at Harare	2013-14

PAKISTAN v BANGLADESH

	Captains					
Season	*Pakistan*	*Bangladesh*	*T*	*P*	*B*	*D*
2001-02*P*†	Waqar Younis	Naimur Rahman	1	1	0	0
2001-02*B*	Waqar Younis	Khaled Mashud	2	2	0	0
2003-04*P*	Rashid Latif	Khaled Mahmud	3	3	0	0
2011-12*B*	Misbah-ul-Haq	Mushfiqur Rahim	2	2	0	0
2014-15*B*	Misbah-ul-Haq	Mushfiqur Rahim	2	1	0	1
	In Pakistan		4	4	0	0
	In Bangladesh		6	5	0	1
	Totals		10	9	0	1

P *Played in Pakistan.* *B* *Played in Bangladesh.*

† *This Test was part of the Asian Test Championship.*

SERIES RECORDS

Highest score	*P*	226	Azhar Ali at Mirpur	2014-15
	B	206	Tamim Iqbal at Khulna	2014-15
Best bowling	*P*	7-77	Danish Kaneria at Dhaka	2001-02
	B	6-82	Shakib Al Hasan at Mirpur	2011-12
Highest total	*P*	628	at Khulna	2014-15
	B	555-6	at Khulna	2014-15
Lowest total	*P*	175	at Multan	2003-04
	B	96	at Peshawar	2003-04

SRI LANKA v ZIMBABWE

Captains

Season	*Sri Lanka*	*Zimbabwe*	*T*	*SL*	*Z*	*D*
1994-95*Z*	A. Ranatunga	A. Flower	3	0	0	3
1996-97*S*	A. Ranatunga	A. D. R. Campbell	2	2	0	0
1997-98*S*	A. Ranatunga	A. D. R. Campbell	2	2	0	0
1999-2000*Z*	S. T. Jayasuriya	A. Flower	3	1	0	2
2001-02*S*	S. T. Jayasuriya	S. V. Carlisle	3	3	0	0
2003-04*Z*	M. S. Atapattu	T. Taibu	2	2	0	0
2016-17*Z*	H. M. R. K. B. Herath	A. G. Cremer	2	2	0	0
2017*S*	**L. D. Chandimal**	**A. G. Cremer**	**1**	**1**	**0**	**0**
	In Sri Lanka		**8**	**8**	**0**	**0**
	In Zimbabwe		10	5	0	5
	Totals		**18**	**13**	**0**	**5**

S *Played in Sri Lanka.* *Z* *Played in Zimbabwe.*

SERIES RECORDS

Highest score	*SL*	270	K. C. Sangakkara at Bulawayo	2003-04
	Z	266	D. L. Houghton at Bulawayo	1994-95
Best bowling	*SL*	9-51	M. Muralitharan at Kandy	2001-02
	Z	5-106	P. A. Strang at Colombo (RPS)	1996-97
Highest total	*SL*	713-3 dec	at Bulawayo	2003-04
	Z	462-9 dec	at Bulawayo	1994-95
Lowest total	*SL*	218	at Bulawayo	1994-95
	Z	79	at Galle	2001-02

SRI LANKA v BANGLADESH

Captains

Season	*Sri Lanka*	*Bangladesh*	*T*	*SL*	*B*	*D*
2001-02*S*†	S. T. Jayasuriya	Naimur Rahman	1	1	0	0
2002*S*	S. T. Jayasuriya	Khaled Mashud	2	2	0	0
2005-06*S*	M. S. Atapattu	Habibul Bashar	2	2	0	0
2005-06*B*	D. P. M. D. Jayawardene	Habibul Bashar	2	2	0	0
2007*S*	D. P. M. D. Jayawardene	Mohammad Ashraful	3	3	0	0
2008-09*B*	D. P. M. D. Jayawardene	Mohammad Ashraful	2	2	0	0
2012-13*S*	A. D. Mathews	Mushfiqur Rahim	2	1	0	1
2013-14*B*	A. D. Mathews	Mushfiqur Rahim	2	1	0	1
2016-17*S*	**H. M. R. K. B. Herath**	**Mushfiqur Rahim**	**2**	**1**	**1**	**0**
	In Sri Lanka		**12**	**10**	**1**	**1**
	In Bangladesh		6	5	0	1
	Totals		**18**	**15**	**1**	**2**

S *Played in Sri Lanka.* *B* *Played in Bangladesh.*

† *This Test was part of the Asian Test Championship.*

SERIES RECORDS

Highest score	*SL*	319	K. C. Sangakkara at Chittagong	2013-14
	B	200	Mushfiqur Rahim at Galle	2012-13
Best bowling	*SL*	7-89	H. M. R. K. B. Herath at Colombo (RPS)	2012-13
	B	5-70	Shakib Al Hasan at Mirpur	2008-09
Highest total	*SL*	730-6 dec	at Mirpur	2013-14
	B	638	at Galle	2012-13
Lowest total	*SL*	293	at Mirpur	2008-09
	B	62	at Colombo (PSS)	2007

ZIMBABWE v BANGLADESH

	Captains					
Season	*Zimbabwe*	*Bangladesh*	*T*	*Z*	*B*	*D*
2000-01*Z*	H. H. Streak	Naimur Rahman	2	2	0	0
2001-02*B*	B. A. Murphy[1]	Naimur Rahman	2	1	0	1
2003-04*Z*	H. H. Streak	Habibul Bashar	2	1	0	1
2004-05*B*	T. Taibu	Habibul Bashar	2	0	1	1
2011-12*Z*	B. R. M. Taylor	Shakib Al Hasan	1	1	0	0
2012-13*Z*	B. R. M. Taylor	Mushfiqur Rahim	2	1	1	0
2014-15*B*	B. R. M. Taylor	Mushfiqur Rahim	3	0	3	0
	In Zimbabwe		7	5	1	1
	In Bangladesh		7	1	4	2
	Totals		14	6	5	3

Z Played in Zimbabwe. *B Played in Bangladesh.*

The following deputised for the official touring captain:

[1]S. V. Carlisle (Second).

SERIES RECORDS

Highest score	*Z*	171	B. R. M. Taylor at Harare	2012-13
	B	137	Shakib Al Hasan at Khulna	2014-15
Best bowling	*Z*	6-59	D. T. Hondo at Dhaka	2004-05
	B	8-39	Taijul Islam at Mirpur	2014-15
Highest total	*Z*	542-7 dec	at Chittagong	2001-02
	B	503	at Chittagong	2014-15
Lowest total	*Z*	114	at Mirpur	2014-15
	B	107	at Dhaka	2001-02

TEST GROUNDS

in chronological order

	City and Ground	*First Test Match*		*Tests*
1	**Melbourne, Melbourne Cricket Ground**	**March 15, 1877**	**A v E**	**110**
2	**London, Kennington Oval**	**September 6, 1880**	**E v A**	**100**
3	**Sydney, Sydney Cricket Ground (No. 1)**	**February 17, 1882**	**A v E**	**106**
4	**Manchester, Old Trafford**	**July 11, 1884**	**E v A**	**78**
5	**London, Lord's**	**July 21, 1884**	**E v A**	**135**
6	**Adelaide, Adelaide Oval**	**December 12, 1884**	**A v E**	**76**
7	**Port Elizabeth, St George's Park**	**March 12, 1889**	**SA v E**	**28**
8	**Cape Town, Newlands**	**March 25, 1889**	**SA v E**	**55**
9	Johannesburg, Old Wanderers *Now the site of Johannesburg Railway Station.*	March 2, 1896	SA v E	22
10	**Nottingham, Trent Bridge**	**June 1, 1899**	**E v A**	**62**

	City and Ground	*First Test Match*		*Tests*
11	**Leeds, Headingley**	**June 29, 1899**	**E v A**	**76**
12	**Birmingham, Edgbaston**	**May 29, 1902**	**E v A**	**50**
13	Sheffield, Bramall Lane	July 3, 1902	E v A	1
	Sheffield United Football Club have built a stand over the cricket pitch.			
14	Durban, Lord's	January 21, 1910	SA v E	4
	Ground destroyed and built on.			
15	Durban, Kingsmead	January 18, 1923	SA v E	42
16	Brisbane, Exhibition Ground	November 30, 1928	A v E	2
	No longer used for cricket.			
17	Christchurch, Lancaster Park	January 10, 1930	NZ v E	40
	Also known under sponsors' names.			
18	**Bridgetown, Kensington Oval**	**January 11, 1930**	**WI v E**	**52**
19	**Wellington, Basin Reserve**	**January 24, 1930**	**NZ v E**	**61**
20	Port-of-Spain, Queen's Park Oval	February 1, 1930	WI v E	60
21	Auckland, Eden Park	February 14, 1930	NZ v E	49
22	Georgetown, Bourda	February 21, 1930	WI v E	30
23	**Kingston, Sabina Park**	**April 3, 1930**	**WI v E**	**50**
24	**Brisbane, Woolloongabba**	**November 27, 1931**	**A v SA**	**60**
25	Bombay, Gymkhana Ground	December 15, 1933	I v E	1
	No longer used for first-class cricket.			
26	**Calcutta (*now Kolkata*), Eden Gardens**	**January 5, 1934**	**I v E**	**41**
27	Madras (*now Chennai*), Chepauk (Chidambaram Stadium)	February 10, 1934	I v E	32
28	**Delhi, Feroz Shah Kotla**	**November 10, 1948**	**I v WI**	**34**
29	Bombay (*now Mumbai*), Brabourne Stadium	December 9, 1948	I v WI	18
	Rarely used for first-class cricket.			
30	Johannesburg, Ellis Park	December 27, 1948	SA v E	6
	Mainly a football and rugby stadium, no longer used for cricket.			
31	Kanpur, Green Park (Modi Stadium)	January 12, 1952	I v E	22
32	Lucknow, University Ground	October 25, 1952	I v P	1
	Ground destroyed, now partly under a river bed.			
33	Dacca (*now Dhaka*), Dacca (*now Bangabandhu*) Stadium	January 1, 1955	P v I	17
	Originally in East Pakistan, now Bangladesh, no longer used for cricket.			
34	Bahawalpur, Dring (*now Bahawal*) Stadium	January 15, 1955	P v I	1
	Still used for first-class cricket.			
35	Lahore, Lawrence Gardens (Bagh-e-Jinnah)	January 29, 1955	P v I	3
	Still used for club and occasional first-class matches.			
36	Peshawar, Services Ground	February 13, 1955	P v I	1
	Superseded by new stadium.			
37	Karachi, National Stadium	February 26, 1955	P v I	41
38	Dunedin, Carisbrook	March 11, 1955	NZ v E	10
39	Hyderabad, Fateh Maidan (Lal Bahadur Stadium)	November 19, 1955	I v NZ	3
40	Madras, Corporation Stadium	January 6, 1956	I v NZ	9
	Superseded by rebuilt Chepauk Stadium.			
41	**Johannesburg, Wanderers**	**December 24, 1956**	**SA v E**	**38**
42	Lahore, Gaddafi Stadium	November 21, 1959	P v A	40
43	Rawalpindi, Pindi Club Ground	March 27, 1965	P v NZ	1
	Superseded by new stadium.			
44	Nagpur, Vidarbha CA Ground	October 3, 1969	I v NZ	9
	Superseded by new stadium.			
45	**Perth, Western Australian CA Ground**	**December 11, 1970**	**A v E**	**44**
46	Hyderabad, Niaz Stadium	March 16, 1973	P v E	5
47	**Bangalore, Karnataka State CA Ground (Chinnaswamy Stadium)**	**November 22, 1974**	**I v WI**	**22**
48	Bombay (*now Mumbai*), Wankhede Stadium	January 23, 1975	I v WI	25
49	Faisalabad, Iqbal Stadium	October 16, 1978	P v I	24
50	Napier, McLean Park	February 16, 1979	NZ v P	10
51	Multan, Ibn-e-Qasim Bagh Stadium	December 30, 1980	P v WI	1
	Superseded by new stadium.			

	City and Ground	*First Test Match*		*Tests*
52	St John's (Antigua), Recreation Ground	March 27, 1981	WI v E	22
53	**Colombo, P. Saravanamuttu Stadium/ P. Sara Oval**	**February 17, 1982**	**SL v E**	**21**
54	Kandy, Asgiriya Stadium *Superseded by new stadium at Pallekele.*	April 22, 1983	SL v A	21
55	Jullundur, Burlton Park	September 24, 1983	I v P	1
56	Ahmedabad, Sardar Patel (Gujarat) Stadium	November 12, 1983	I v WI	12
57	**Colombo, Sinhalese Sports Club Ground**	**March 16, 1984**	**SL v NZ**	**41**
58	Colombo, Colombo Cricket Club Ground	March 24, 1984	SL v NZ	3
59	Sialkot, Jinnah Stadium	October 27, 1985	P v SL	4
60	Cuttack, Barabati Stadium	January 4, 1987	I v SL	2
61	Jaipur, Sawai Mansingh Stadium	February 21, 1987	I v P	1
62	Hobart, Bellerive Oval	December 16, 1989	A v SL	13
63	Chandigarh, Sector 16 Stadium *Superseded by Mohali ground.*	November 23, 1990	I v SL	1
64	**Hamilton, Seddon Park** *Also known under various sponsors' names.*	**February 22, 1991**	**NZ v SL**	**24**
65	Gujranwala, Municipal Stadium	December 20, 1991	P v SL	1
66	**Colombo, R. Premadasa (Khettarama) Stadium**	**August 28, 1992**	**SL v A**	**9**
67	Moratuwa, Tyronne Fernando Stadium	September 8, 1992	SL v A	4
68	Harare, Harare Sports Club	October 18, 1992	Z v I	34
69	Bulawayo, Bulawayo Athletic Club *Superseded by Queens Sports Club ground.*	November 1, 1992	Z v NZ	1
70	Karachi, Defence Stadium	December 1, 1993	P v Z	1
71	Rawalpindi, Rawalpindi Cricket Stadium	December 9, 1993	P v Z	8
72	Lucknow, K. D. "Babu" Singh Stadium	January 18, 1994	I v SL	1
73	**Bulawayo, Queens Sports Club**	**October 20, 1994**	**Z v SL**	**23**
74	Mohali, Punjab Cricket Association Stadium	December 10, 1994	I v WI	13
75	Peshawar, Arbab Niaz Stadium	September 8, 1995	P v SL	6
76	**Centurion (*ex Verwoerdburg*), Centurion Park**	**November 16, 1995**	**SA v E**	**23**
77	Sheikhupura, Municipal Stadium	October 17, 1996	P v Z	2
78	St Vincent, Arnos Vale	June 20, 1997	WI v SL	3
79	**Galle, International Stadium**	**June 3, 1998**	**SL v NZ**	**30**
80	**Bloemfontein, Springbok Park** *Also known under various sponsors' names.*	**October 29, 1999**	**SA v Z**	**5**
81	Multan, Multan Cricket Stadium	August 29, 2001	P v B	5
82	Chittagong, Chittagong Stadium *Also known as M. A. Aziz Stadium.*	November 15, 2001	B v Z	8
83	Sharjah, Sharjah Cricket Association Stadium	January 31, 2002	P v WI	9
84	St George's, Grenada, Queen's Park New Stadium	June 28, 2002	WI v NZ	3
85	East London, Buffalo Park	October 18, 2002	SA v B	1
86	**Potchefstroom, North West Cricket Stadium** *Now known under sponsor's name.*	**October 25, 2002**	**SA v B**	**2**
87	Chester-le-Street, Riverside Ground *Also known under sponsor's name.*	June 5, 2003	E v Z	6
88	Gros Islet, St Lucia, Beausejour Stadium *Now known as Darren Sammy Stadium.*	June 20, 2003	WI v SL	5
89	Darwin, Marrara Cricket Ground	July 18, 2003	A v B	2
90	Cairns, Cazaly's Football Park *Also known under sponsor's name.*	July 25, 2003	A v B	2
91	**Chittagong, Chittagong Divisional Stadium** *Also known as Bir Shrestha Shahid Ruhul Amin Stadium/Zohur Ahmed Chowdhury Stadium.*	**February 28, 2006**	**B v SL**	**16**
92	Bogra, Shaheed Chandu Stadium	March 8, 2006	B v SL	1
93	Fatullah, Narayanganj Osmani Stadium	April 9, 2006	B v A	2
94	Basseterre, St Kitts, Warner Park	June 22, 2006	WI v I	3
95	**Mirpur (Dhaka), Shere Bangla Natl Stadium**	**May 25, 2007**	**B v I**	**16**
96	**Dunedin, University Oval**	**January 4, 2008**	**NZ v B**	**8**
97	Providence Stadium, Guyana	March 22, 2008	WI v SL	2
98	North Sound, Antigua, Sir Vivian Richards Stadium	May 30, 2008	WI v A	5

	City and Ground	*First Test Match*		*Tests*
99	**Nagpur, Vidarbha CA Stadium, Jamtha**	**November 6, 2008**	**I v A**	**6**
100	Cardiff, Sophia Gardens *Now known under sponsor's name.*	July 8, 2009	E v A	3
101	**Hyderabad, Rajiv Gandhi Intl Stadium**	**November 12, 2010**	**I v NZ**	**4**
102	**Dubai, Dubai Sports City Stadium**	**November 12, 2010**	**P v SA**	**11**
103	**Abu Dhabi, Sheikh Zayed Stadium**	**November 20, 2010**	**P v SA**	**10**
104	**Pallekele, Muttiah Muralitharan Stadium**	**December 1, 2010**	**SL v WI**	**6**
105	Southampton, Rose Bowl	June 16, 2011	E v SL	2
106	**Roseau, Dominica, Windsor Park**	**July 6, 2011**	**WI v I**	**5**
107	Khulna, Khulna Division Stadium *Also known as Bir Shrestha Shahid Flight Lt Motiur Rahman/Shaikh Abu Naser Stadium.*	November 21, 2012	B v WI	3
108	**Christchurch, Hagley Oval**	**December 26, 2014**	**NZ v SL**	**4**
109	Indore, Maharani Usharaje Trust Ground	October 8, 2016	I v NZ	1
110	Rajkot, Saurashtra CA Stadium	November 9, 2016	I v E	1
111	Visakhapatnam, Andhra CA–Visakhapatnam DCA Stadium	November 17, 2016	I v E	1
112	**Pune (Gahunje), Subrata Roy Sahara Stadium**	**February 23, 2017**	**I v A**	**1**
113	**Ranchi, Jharkhand State CA Oval Ground**	**March 16, 2017**	**I v A**	**1**
114	**Dharamsala, Himachal Pradesh CA Stadium**	**March 25, 2017**	**I v A**	**1**

Bold type denotes grounds used for Test cricket since January 1, 2017.

An expanded and regularly updated online version of the Records can be found at www.wisdenrecords.com

ONE-DAY INTERNATIONAL RECORDS

Matches in this section do not have first-class status.

This section covers one-day international cricket to December 31, 2017. Bold type denotes performances since January 1, 2017, or, in career figures, players who have appeared in one-day internationals since that date.

SUMMARY OF ONE-DAY INTERNATIONALS

1970-71 to December 31, 2017

	Opponents	*Matches*	*Won by*														*Tied*	*NR*
			E	*A*	*SA*	*WI*	*NZ*	*I*	*P*	*SL*	*Z*	*B*	*Afg*	*Ire*	*Ass*	*Oth*		
England	Australia	**137**	52	80	–	–	–	–	–	–	–	–	–	–	–	–	2	3
	South Africa	**59**	26	–	29	–	–	–	–	–	–	–	–	–	–	–	1	3
	West Indies	**96**	49	–	–	42	–	–	–	–	–	–	–	–	–	–	–	5
	New Zealand	**84**	37	–	–	–	41	–	–	–	–	–	–	–	–	–	2	4
	India	**96**	39	–	–	–	–	52	–	–	–	–	–	–	–	–	2	3
	Pakistan	**82**	49	–	–	–	–	–	31	–	–	–	–	–	–	–	–	2
	Sri Lanka	**69**	33	–	–	–	–	–	–	34	–	–	–	–	–	–	1	1
	Zimbabwe	**30**	21	–	–	–	–	–	–	–	8	–	–	–	–	–	–	1
	Bangladesh	**20**	16	–	–	–	–	–	–	–	–	4	–	–	–	–	–	–
	Afghanistan	**1**	1	–	–	–	–	–	–	–	–	–	0	–	–	–	–	–
	Ireland	**9**	7	–	–	–	–	–	–	–	–	–	–	1	–	–	–	1
	Associates	**14**	13	–	–	–	–	–	–	–	–	–	–	–	0	–	–	1
Australia	South Africa	**96**	–	47	45	–	–	–	–	–	–	–	–	–	–	–	3	1
	West Indies	**139**	–	73	–	60	–	–	–	–	–	–	–	–	–	–	3	3
	New Zealand	**136**	–	90	–	–	39	–	–	–	–	–	–	–	–	–	–	7
	India	**128**	–	73	–	–	–	45	–	–	–	–	–	–	–	–	–	10
	Pakistan	**98**	–	62	–	–	–	–	32	–	–	–	–	–	–	–	1	3
	Sri Lanka	**96**	–	60	–	–	–	–	–	32	–	–	–	–	–	–	–	4
	Zimbabwe	**30**	–	27	–	–	–	–	–	–	2	–	–	–	–	–	–	1
	Bangladesh	**20**	–	18	–	–	–	–	–	–	–	1	–	–	–	–	–	1
	Afghanistan	**2**	–	2	–	–	–	–	–	–	–	–	0	–	–	–	–	–
	Ireland	**5**	–	4	–	–	–	–	–	–	–	–	–	0	–	–	–	1
	Associates	**16**	–	16	–	–	–	–	–	–	–	–	–	–	0	–	–	–
	ICC World XI	**3**	–	3	–	–	–	–	–	–	–	–	–	–	–	0	–	–
South Africa	West Indies	**61**	–	–	44	15	–	–	–	–	–	–	–	–	–	–	1	1
	New Zealand	**70**	–	–	41	–	24	–	–	–	–	–	–	–	–	–	–	5
	India	**77**	–	–	45	–	–	29	–	–	–	–	–	–	–	–	–	3
	Pakistan	**73**	–	–	47	–	–	–	25	–	–	–	–	–	–	–	–	1
	Sri Lanka	**66**	–	–	35	–	–	–	–	29	–	–	–	–	–	–	1	1
	Zimbabwe	**38**	–	–	35	–	–	–	–	–	2	–	–	–	–	–	–	1
	Bangladesh	**20**	–	–	17	–	–	–	–	–	–	3	–	–	–	–	–	–
	Ireland	**5**	–	–	5	–	–	–	–	–	–	–	–	0	–	–	–	–
	Associates	**18**	–	–	18	–	–	–	–	–	–	–	–	–	0	–	–	–
West Indies	New Zealand	**64**	–	–	–	30	27	–	–	–	–	–	–	–	–	–	–	7
	India	**121**	–	–	–	61	–	56	–	–	–	–	–	–	–	–	1	3
	Pakistan	**133**	–	–	–	70	–	–	60	–	–	–	–	–	–	–	3	–
	Sri Lanka	**56**	–	–	–	28	–	–	–	25	–	–	–	–	–	–	–	3
	Zimbabwe	**47**	–	–	–	35	–	–	–	–	10	–	–	–	–	–	1	1
	Bangladesh	**28**	–	–	–	19	–	–	–	–	–	7	–	–	–	–	–	2
	Afghanistan	**3**	–	–	–	1	–	–	–	–	–	–	1	–	–	–	–	1
	Ireland	**6**	–	–	–	4	–	–	–	–	–	–	–	1	–	–	–	1
	Associates	**16**	–	–	–	15	–	–	–	–	–	–	–	–	1	–	–	–
New Zealand	India	**101**	–	–	–	–	44	51	–	–	–	–	–	–	–	–	1	5
	Pakistan	**98**	–	–	–	–	42	–	53	–	–	–	–	–	–	–	1	2
	Sri Lanka	**95**	–	–	–	–	45	–	–	41	–	–	–	–	–	–	1	8
	Zimbabwe	**38**	–	–	–	–	27	–	–	–	9	–	–	–	–	–	1	1
	Bangladesh	**31**	–	–	–	–	21	–	–	–	–	10	–	–	–	–	–	–
	Afghanistan	**1**	–	–	–	–	1	–	–	–	–	–	0	–	–	–	–	–
	Ireland	**4**	–	–	–	–	4	–	–	–	–	–	–	0	–	–	–	–
	Associates	**12**	–	–	–	–	12	–	–	–	–	–	–	–	0	–	–	–
India	Pakistan	**129**	–	–	–	–	–	52	73	–	–	–	–	–	–	–	–	4
	Sri Lanka	**158**	–	–	–	–	–	90	–	56	–	–	–	–	–	–	1	11
	Zimbabwe	**63**	–	–	–	–	–	51	–	–	10	–	–	–	–	–	2	–
	Bangladesh	**33**	–	–	–	–	–	27	–	–	–	5	–	–	–	–	–	1

	Opponents	*Matches*	*Won by* E	A	SA	WI	NZ	I	P	SL	Z	B	Afg	Ire	Ass	Oth	*Tied*	*NR*
India	Afghanistan	**1**	–	–	–	–	–	1	–	–	–	–	0	–	–	–	–	–
	Ireland	**3**	–	–	–	–	–	3	–	–	–	–	–	0	–	–	–	–
	Associates	**23**	–	–	–	–	–	21	–	–	–	–	–	–	2	–	–	–
Pakistan	Sri Lanka	**153**	–	–	–	–	–	–	90	58	–	–	–	–	–	–	1	4
	Zimbabwe	**54**	–	–	–	–	–	–	47	–	4	–	–	–	–	–	1	2
	Bangladesh	**35**	–	–	–	–	–	–	31	–	–	4	–	–	–	–	–	–
	Afghanistan	**2**	–	–	–	–	–	–	2	–	–	–	0	–	–	–	–	–
	Ireland	**7**	–	–	–	–	–	–	5	–	–	–	–	1	–	–	1	–
	Associates	**20**	–	–	–	–	–	–	20	–	–	–	–	–	0	–	–	–
Sri Lanka	Zimbabwe	**55**	–	–	–	–	–	–	–	43	10	–	–	–	–	–	–	2
	Bangladesh	**41**	–	–	–	–	–	–	–	34	–	5	–	–	–	–	–	2
	Afghanistan	**2**	–	–	–	–	–	–	–	2	–	–	0	–	–	–	–	–
	Ireland	**4**	–	–	–	–	–	–	–	4	–	–	–	0	–	–	–	–
	Associates	**16**	–	–	–	–	–	–	–	15	–	–	–	–	1	–	–	–
Zimbabwe	Bangladesh	**67**	–	–	–	–	–	–	–	–	28	39	–	–	–	–	–	–
	Afghanistan	**19**	–	–	–	–	–	–	–	–	8	–	11	–	–	–	–	–
	Ireland	**9**	–	–	–	–	–	–	–	–	5	–	–	3	–	–	1	–
	Associates	**41**	–	–	–	–	–	–	–	–	33	–	–	–	6	–	–	2
Bangladesh	Afghanistan	**5**	–	–	–	–	–	–	–	–	–	3	2	–	–	–	–	–
	Ireland	**9**	–	–	–	–	–	–	–	–	–	6	–	2	–	–	–	1
	Associates	**26**	–	–	–	–	–	–	–	–	–	18	–	–	8	–	–	–
Afghanistan	Ireland	**16**	–	–	–	–	–	–	–	–	–	–	7	9	–	–	–	–
	Associates	**34**	–	–	–	–	–	–	–	–	–	–	22	–	11	–	–	1
Ireland	Associates	**49**	–	–	–	–	–	–	–	–	–	–	–	36	9	–	1	3
Associates	Associates	**116**	–	–	–	–	–	–	–	–	–	–	–	–	111	–	–	5
Asian CC XI	ICC World XI	**1**	–	–	–	–	–	–	–	–	–	–	–	–	–	1	–	–
	African XI	**6**	–	–	–	–	–	–	–	–	–	–	–	–	–	5	–	1
		3,945	343	555	361	380	327	478	469	373	129	105	43	53	149	6	34	140

Associate and Affiliate Members of ICC who have played one-day internationals are Afghanistan, Bermuda, Canada, East Africa, Hong Kong, Ireland, Kenya, Namibia, Netherlands, Papua New Guinea, Scotland, United Arab Emirates and USA. Sri Lanka, Zimbabwe, Bangladesh, Afghanistan and Ireland played one-day internationals before gaining Test status; these are not counted as Associate results.

RESULTS SUMMARY OF ONE-DAY INTERNATIONALS

1970-71 to December 31, 2017 (3,945 matches)

	Matches	*Won*	*Lost*	*Tied*	*No Result*	*% Won (excl. NR)*
South Africa	583	361	200	6	16	64.19
Australia	906	555	308	9	34	64.16
Pakistan	884	469	389	8	18	54.61
India	933	478	408	7	40	53.91
West Indies	770	380	354	9	27	51.74
England	697	343	322	8	24	51.56
Afghanistan	86	43	41	–	2	51.19
Sri Lanka	811	373	397	5	36	48.45
New Zealand	734	327	362	6	39	47.48
Ireland	126	53	63	3	7	45.79
Bangladesh	335	105	223	–	7	32.01
Zimbabwe	491	129	345	6	11	27.50
Asian Cricket Council XI	7	4	2	–	1	66.66
Hong Kong	20	8	11	–	1	42.10
Netherlands	76	28	44	1	3	39.04
Scotland	95	33	56	–	6	37.07
Papua New Guinea	14	5	9	–	–	35.71
Kenya	154	42	107	–	5	28.18
United Arab Emirates	35	9	26	–	–	25.71
ICC World XI	4	1	3	–	–	25.00
Canada	77	17	58	–	2	22.66
Bermuda	35	7	28	–	–	20.00

	Matches	Won	Lost	Tied	No Result	% Won (excl. NR)
African XI	6	1	4	–	1	20.00
USA	2	–	2	–	–	0.00
East Africa	3	–	3	–	–	0.00
Namibia	6	–	6	–	–	0.00

Matches abandoned without a ball bowled are not included except (from 2004) where the toss took place, in accordance with an ICC ruling. Such matches, like those called off after play began, are now counted as official internationals in their own right, even when replayed on another day. In the percentages of matches won, ties are counted as half a win.

BATTING RECORDS

HIGHEST INDIVIDUAL INNINGS

264	R. G. Sharma	India v Sri Lanka at Kolkata	2014-15
237*	M. J. Guptill	New Zealand v West Indies at Wellington	2014-15
219	V. Sehwag	India v West Indies at Indore	2011-12
215	C. H. Gayle	West Indies v Zimbabwe at Canberra	2014-15
209	R. G. Sharma	India v Australia at Bangalore	2013-14
208*	**R. G. Sharma**	**India v Sri Lanka at Mohali**	**2017-18**
200*	S. R. Tendulkar	India v South Africa at Gwalior	2009-10
194*	C. K. Coventry	Zimbabwe v Bangladesh at Bulawayo	2009
194	Saeed Anwar	Pakistan v India at Chennai	1997-97
189*	I. V. A. Richards	West Indies v England at Manchester	1984
189*	M. J. Guptill	New Zealand v England at Southampton	2013
189	S. T. Jayasuriya	Sri Lanka v India at Sharjah	2000-01
188*	G. Kirsten	South Africa v UAE at Rawalpindi	1995-96
186*	S. R. Tendulkar	India v New Zealand at Hyderabad	1999-2000
185*	S. R. Watson	Australia v Bangladesh at Mirpur	2010-11
185	**F. du Plessis**	**South Africa v Sri Lanka at Cape Town**	**2016-17**
183*	M. S. Dhoni	India v Sri Lanka at Jaipur	2005-06
183	S. C. Ganguly	India v Sri Lanka at Taunton	1999
183	V. Kohli	India v Pakistan at Mirpur	2011-12
181*	M. L. Hayden	Australia v New Zealand at Hamilton	2006-07
181	I. V. A. Richards	West Indies v Sri Lanka at Karachi	1987-88
180*	**M. J. Guptill**	**New Zealand v South Africa at Hamilton**	**2016-17**
179	**D. A. Warner**	**Australia v Pakistan at Adelaide**	**2016-17**
178*	H. Masakadza	Zimbabwe v Kenya at Harare	2009-10
178	D. A. Warner	Australia v Afghanistan at Perth	2014-15
178	Q. de Kock	South Africa v Australia at Centurion	2016-17
177	P. R. Stirling	Ireland v Canada at Toronto	2010
176*	**E. Lewis**	**West Indies v England at The Oval**	**2017**
176	**A. B. de Villiers**	**South Africa v Bangladesh at Paarl**	**2017-18**
175*	Kapil Dev	India v Zimbabwe at Tunbridge Wells	1983
175	H. H. Gibbs	South Africa v Australia at Johannesburg	2005-06
175	S. R. Tendulkar	India v Australia at Hyderabad	2009-10
175	V. Sehwag	India v Bangladesh at Mirpur	2010-11
175	C. S. MacLeod	Scotland v Canada at Christchurch	2013-14

The highest individual scores for other Test countries are:

171	A. D. Hales	England v Pakistan at Nottingham	2016
154	Tamim Iqbal	Bangladesh v Zimbabwe at Bulawayo	2009
131*	Mohammad Shahzad	Afghanistan v Zimbabwe at Sharjah	2015-16

In January 2018, after the deadline for this section, J. J. Roy scored 180 for England v Australia at Melbourne.

MOST HUNDREDS

S. R. Tendulkar (I) 49
V. Kohli (I) **32**
R. T. Ponting (A/World) . . . 30
S. T. Jayasuriya (SL/Asia) . 28
H. M. Amla (SA) **26**
A. B. de Villiers (SA) . . . **25**
K. C. Sangakkara (SL) . . 25
T. M. Dilshan (SL) 22
S. C. Ganguly (I/Asia) . . . 22
C. H. Gayle (WI/World) 22
H. H. Gibbs (SA) 21
Saeed Anwar (P) 20
D. P. M. D. Jayawardene (SL/Asia) 19
B. C. Lara (WI/World) . . 19
M. E. Waugh (A) 18
D. L. Haynes (WI) 17
J. H. Kallis (SA/Wld/Af) . . 17
L. R. P. L. Taylor (NZ) . **17**
N. J. Astle (NZ) 16
A. C. Gilchrist (A/World) . . 16
R. G. Sharma (I) **16**
Mohammad Yousuf (P/As) . 15
V. Sehwag (I/Wld/Asia) . . 15
W. U. Tharanga (SL) . . . **15**

Most hundreds for other Test countries:
M. E. Trescothick (E) . . . 12
W. T. S. Porterfield (Ire) 9
Tamim Iqbal (B) **9**
B. R. M. Taylor (Z) 8
Mohammad Shahzad (Afg) 4

Ponting's total includes one for the World XI, the only hundred for a combined team.

MOST RUNS

		M	*I*	*NO*	*R*	*HS*	*100*	*Avge*
1	S. R. Tendulkar (India)	463	452	41	18,426	200*	49	44.83
2	K. C. Sangakkara (SL/Asia/World)	404	380	41	14,234	169	25	41.98
3	R. T. Ponting (Australia/World)	375	365	39	13,704	164	30	42.03
4	S. T. Jayasuriya (Sri Lanka/Asia)	445	433	18	13,430	189	28	32.36
5	D. P. M. D. Jayawardene (SL/Asia)	448	418	39	12,650	144	19	33.37
6	Inzamam-ul-Haq (Pakistan/Asia)	378	350	53	11,739	137*	10	39.52
7	J. H. Kallis (S. Africa/World/Africa)	328	314	53	11,579	139	17	44.36
8	S. C. Ganguly (India/Asia)	311	300	23	11,363	183	22	41.02
9	R. Dravid (India/World/Asia)	344	318	40	10,889	153	12	39.16
10	B. C. Lara (West Indies/World)	299	289	32	10,405	169	19	40.48
11	T. M. Dilshan (Sri Lanka)	330	303	41	10,290	161*	22	39.27

The leading aggregates for players who have appeared for other Test countries are:

	M	*I*	*NO*	*R*	*HS*	*100*	*Avge*
S. P. Fleming (New Zealand/World)	280	269	21	8,037	134*	8	32.40
A. Flower (Zimbabwe)	213	208	16	6,786	145	4	35.34
E. J. G. Morgan (Ireland/England)	**190**	**177**	**25**	**5,801**	**124***	**11**	**38.16**
Tamim Iqbal (Bangladesh)	**174**	**172**	**4**	**5,766**	**154**	**9**	**34.32**
Mohammad Nabi (Afghanistan)	**86**	**78**	**9**	**1,972**	**116**	**1**	**28.57**

Excluding runs for combined teams, the record aggregate for Sri Lanka is 13,975 in 397 matches by K. C. Sangakkara; for Australia, 13,589 in 374 matches by R. T. Ponting; for Pakistan, 11,701 in 375 matches by Inzamam-ul-Haq; for South Africa, 11,550 in 323 matches by J. H. Kallis; for West Indies, 10,348 in 295 matches by B. C. Lara; for New Zealand, 8,007 in 279 matches by S. P. Fleming; for England, 5,416 in 161 matches by I. R. Bell; and for Ireland, ***3,272*** *in 109 matches by* ***W. T. S. Porterfield.***

BEST CAREER STRIKE-RATES BY BATSMEN

(Runs per 100 balls. Qualification: 1,000 runs)

SR		*Position*	*M*	*I*	*R*	*Avge*
123.93	**G. J. Maxwell (A)**	**5/6**	**80**	**71**	**2,035**	**32.30**
117.93	**J. C. Buttler (E)**	**6/7**	**99**	**83**	**2,505**	**37.38**
117.00	Shahid Afridi (P/World/Asia)	2/7	398	369	8,064	23.57
114.50	**L. Ronchi (A/NZ)**	**7**	**85**	**68**	**1,397**	**23.67**
108.72	**C. J. Anderson (NZ)**	**6**	**49**	**44**	**1,109**	**27.72**
108.35	**N. L. T. C. Perera (SL)**	**7/8**	**128**	**97**	**1,452**	**17.28**
108.29	**M. M. Ali (E)**	**2/7**	**63**	**54**	**1,344**	**29.86**
104.33	V. Sehwag (I/World/Asia)	1/2	251	245	8,273	35.05
104.24	**J. P. Faulkner (A)**	**7/8**	**69**	**52**	**1,032**	**34.40**

SR		*Position*	*M*	*I*	*R*	*Avge*
103.79	**J. J. Roy (E)**	**1**	**48**	**47**	**1,642**	**36.48**
102.26	**D. A. Miller (SA)**	**5/6**	**100**	**88**	**2,396**	**39.27**
101.07	**A. B. de Villiers (SA/Africa)**	**4/5**	**225**	**215**	**9,515**	**54.06**
100.05	D. J. G. Sammy (WI)	7/8	126	105	1,871	24.94

Position means a batsman's most usual position(s) in the batting order.

FASTEST ONE-DAY INTERNATIONAL FIFTIES

Balls			
16	A. B. de Villiers	South Africa v West Indies at Johannesburg	2014-15
17	S. T. Jayasuriya	Sri Lanka v Pakistan at Singapore	1995-96
17	M. D. K. J. Perera	Sri Lanka v Pakistan at Pallekele	2015
17	M. J. Guptill	New Zealand v Sri Lanka at Christchurch	2015-16
18	S. P. O'Donnell	Australia v Sri Lanka at Sharjah	1989-90
18	Shahid Afridi	Pakistan v Sri Lanka at Nairobi	1996-97
18	Shahid Afridi	Pakistan v Netherlands at Colombo (SSC)	2002
18	G. J. Maxwell	Australia v India at Bangalore	2013-14
18	Shahid Afridi	Pakistan v Bangladesh at Mirpur	2013-14
18	B. B. McCullum	New Zealand v England at Wellington	2014-15
18	A. J. Finch	Australia v Sri Lanka at Dambulla	2016

FASTEST ONE-DAY INTERNATIONAL HUNDREDS

Balls			
31	A. B. de Villiers	South Africa v West Indies at Johannesburg	2014-15
36	C. J. Anderson	New Zealand v West Indies at Queenstown	2013-14
37	Shahid Afridi	Pakistan v Sri Lanka at Nairobi	1996-97
44	M. V. Boucher	South Africa v Zimbabwe at Potchefstroom	2006-07
45	B. C. Lara	West Indies v Bangladesh at Dhaka	1999-2000
45	Shahid Afridi	Pakistan v India at Kanpur	2004-05
46	J. D. Ryder	New Zealand v West Indies at Queenstown	2013-14
46	J. C. Buttler	England v Pakistan at Dubai	2015-16
48	S. T. Jayasuriya	Sri Lanka v Pakistan at Singapore	1995-96

HIGHEST PARTNERSHIP FOR EACH WICKET

286	for 1st	W. U. Tharanga/S. T. Jayasuriya	SL v E	Leeds	2006
372	for 2nd	C. H. Gayle/M. N. Samuels	WI v Z	Canberra	2014-15
258	for 3rd	D. M. Bravo/D. Ramdin	WI v B	Basseterre	2014-15
275*	for 4th	M. Azharuddin/A. Jadeja	I v Z	Cuttack	1997-98
256*	for 5th	D. A. Miller/J-P. Duminy	SA v Z	Hamilton	2014-15
267*	for 6th	G. D. Elliott/L. Ronchi	NZ v SL	Dunedin	2014-15
177	for 7th	J. C. Buttler/A. U. Rashid	E v NZ	Birmingham	2015
138*	for 8th	J. M. Kemp/A. J. Hall	SA v I	Cape Town	2006-07
132	for 9th	A. D. Mathews/S. L. Malinga	SL v A	Melbourne	2010-11
106*	for 10th	I. V. A. Richards/M. A. Holding	WI v E	Manchester	1984

BOWLING RECORDS

BEST BOWLING ANALYSES

8-19	W. P. U. J. C. Vaas	Sri Lanka v Zimbabwe at Colombo (SSC)	2001-02
7-12	Shahid Afridi	Pakistan v West Indies at Providence	2013
7-15	G. D. McGrath	Australia v Namibia at Potchefstroom	2002-03
7-18	**Rashid Khan**	**Afghanistan v West Indies at Gros Islet**	**2017**
7-20	A. J. Bichel	Australia v England at Port Elizabeth	2002-03
7-30	M. Muralitharan	Sri Lanka v India at Sharjah	2000-01

7-33	T. G. Southee	New Zealand v England at Wellington	2014-15
7-34	**T. A. Boult**	**New Zealand v West Indies at Christchurch**	**2017-18**
7-36	Waqar Younis	Pakistan v England at Leeds	2001
7-37	Aqib Javed	Pakistan v India at Sharjah	1991-92
7-45	Imran Tahir	South Africa v West Indies at Basseterre	2016
7-51	W. W. Davis	West Indies v Australia at Leeds	1983

The best analyses for other Test countries are:

6-4	S. T. R. Binny	India v Bangladesh at Mirpur	2014
6-19	H. K. Olonga	Zimbabwe v England at Cape Town	1999-2000
6-26	Mashrafe bin Mortaza	Bangladesh v Kenya at Nairobi	2006
6-26	Rubel Hossain	Bangladesh v New Zealand at Mirpur	2013-14
6-31	P. D. Collingwood	England v Bangladesh at Nottingham	2005
6-55	**P. R. Stirling**	**Ireland v Afghanistan at Greater Noida**	**2016-17**

HAT-TRICKS

Four Wickets in Four Balls

S. L. Malinga — Sri Lanka v South Africa at Providence — 2006-07

Four Wickets in Five Balls

Saqlain Mushtaq — Pakistan v Zimbabwe at Peshawar — 1996-97

Most Hat-Tricks

S. L. Malinga	3	W. P. U. J. C. Vaas†	2
Saqlain Mushtaq	2	Wasim Akram	2

† *W. P. U. J. C. Vaas took the second of his two hat-tricks, for Sri Lanka v Bangladesh at Pietermaritzburg in 2002-03, with the first three balls of the match.*

Hat-Tricks

There have been **43** hat-tricks in one-day internationals, including the above. Those since 2015:

K. Rabada	South Africa v Bangladesh at Mirpur	2015
J. P. Faulkner	Australia v Sri Lanka at Colombo (RPS)	2016
Taskin Ahmed	**Bangladesh v Sri Lanka at Dambulla**	**2016-17**
P. W. H. de Silva	**Sri Lanka v Zimbabwe at Galle**	**2017**
K. Yadav	**India v Australia at Kolkata**	**2017-18**

MOST WICKETS

		M	*Balls*	*R*	*W*	*BB*	*4I*	*Avge*
1	M. Muralitharan (SL/World/Asia)	350	18,811	12,326	534	7-30	25	23.08
2	Wasim Akram (Pakistan)	356	18,186	11,812	502	5-15	23	23.52
3	Waqar Younis (Pakistan)	262	12,698	9,919	416	7-36	27	23.84
4	W. P. U. J. C. Vaas (SL/Asia)	322	15,775	11,014	400	8-19	13	27.53
5	Shahid Afridi (Pakistan/World/Asia)	398	17,670	13,635	395	7-12	13	34.51
6	S. M. Pollock (SA/World/Africa)	303	15,712	9,631	393	6-35	17	24.50
7	G. D. McGrath (Australia/World)	250	12,970	8,391	381	7-15	16	22.02
8	B. Lee (Australia)	221	11,185	8,877	380	5-22	23	23.36
9	A. Kumble (India/Asia)	271	14,496	10,412	337	6-12	10	30.89
10	S. T. Jayasuriya (Sri Lanka/Asia)	445	14,874	11,871	323	6-29	12	36.75
11	J. Srinath (India)	229	11,935	8,847	315	5-23	10	28.08
12	D. L. Vettori (New Zealand/World)	295	14,060	9,674	305	5-7	10	31.71
13	**S. L. Malinga (Sri Lanka)**	**204**	**9,830**	**8,705**	**301**	**6-38**	**16**	**28.92**
14	S. K. Warne (Australia/World)	194	10,642	7,541	293	5-33	13	25.73

		M	Balls	R	W	BB	4I	Avge
15	Saqlain Mushtaq (Pakistan)	169	8,770	6,275	288	5-20	17	21.78
	A. B. Agarkar (India)	191	9,484	8,021	288	6-42	12	27.85
17	Zaheer Khan (India/Asia)	200	10,097	8,301	282	5-42	8	29.43
18	J. H. Kallis (S. Africa/World/Africa)	328	10,750	8,680	273	5-30	4	31.79
19	A. A. Donald (South Africa)	164	8,561	5,926	272	6-23	13	21.78
20	J. M. Anderson (England)	194	9,584	7,861	269	5-23	13	29.22
	Abdul Razzaq (Pakistan/Asia)	265	10,941	8,564	269	6-35	11	31.83
	Harbhajan Singh (India/Asia)	236	12,479	8,973	269	5-31	5	33.35
23	M. Ntini (South Africa/World)	173	8,687	6,559	266	6-22	12	24.65
24	Kapil Dev (India)	225	11,202	6,945	253	5-43	4	27.45

The leading aggregates for players who have appeared for other Test countries are:

	M	Balls	R	W	BB	4I	Avge
H. H. Streak (Zimbabwe)	189	9,468	7,129	239	5-32	8	29.82
Mashrafe bin Mortaza (Bangladesh/Asia)	**182**	**9,118**	**7,287**	**232**	**6-26**	**7**	**31.40**
C. A. Walsh (West Indies)	205	10,882	6,918	227	5-1	7	30.47
K. J. O'Brien (Ireland)	**115**	**3,649**	**3,190**	**100**	**4-13**	**4**	**31.90**
Mohammad Nabi (Afghanistan)	**86**	**4,030**	**2,890**	**90**	**4-30**	**2**	**32.11**

Excluding wickets taken for combined teams, the record for Sri Lanka is 523 in 343 matches by M. Muralitharan; for South Africa, 387 in 294 matches by S. M. Pollock; for Australia, 380 in 249 matches by G. D. McGrath; for India, 334 in 269 matches by A. Kumble; for New Zealand, 297 in 291 matches by D. L. Vettori; for Zimbabwe, 237 in 187 matches by H. H. Streak; and for Bangladesh, ***231*** *in 180 matches by* ***Mashrafe bin Mortaza****.*

BEST CAREER STRIKE-RATES BY BOWLERS

(Balls per wicket. Qualification: 1,500 balls)

SR		M	W
22.21	**Rashid Khan (Afg)**	**32**	**70**
25.06	**M. A. Starc (A)**	**68**	**134**
26.95	Mohammed Shami (I)	47	87
27.10	Hamid Hassan (Afg)	32	56
27.22	**M. J. Henry (NZ)**	**34**	**63**
27.22	S. W. Tait (A)	35	62
27.32	B. A. W. Mendis (SL)	87	152
27.74	**Mohammed Shami (I)**	**50**	**91**
28.48	M. J. McClenaghan (NZ)	48	82
28.69	**J. J. Bumrah (I)**	**31**	**56**
28.72	R. N. ten Doeschate (Netherlands)	33	55
29.21	S. E. Bond (NZ)	82	147
29.38	G. I. Allott (NZ)	31	52
29.43	B. Lee (A)	221	380
29.58	L. S. Pascoe (A)	29	53
29.59	**T. A. Boult (NZ)**	**57**	**104**
29.74	**M. Morkel (SA/Africa)**	**112**	**186**
29.95	A. Mishra (I)	36	64

BEST CAREER ECONOMY-RATES

(Runs conceded per six balls. Qualification: 50 wickets)

ER		M	W
3.09	J. Garner (WI)	98	146
3.28	R. G. D. Willis (E)	64	80
3.30	R. J. Hadlee (NZ)	115	158
3.32	M. A. Holding (WI)	102	142
3.40	A. M. E. Roberts (WI)	56	87
3.48	C. E. L. Ambrose (WI)	176	225

WICKETKEEPING AND FIELDING RECORDS

MOST DISMISSALS IN AN INNINGS

6 (all ct)	A. C. Gilchrist	Australia v South Africa at Cape Town	1999-2000
6 (all ct)	A. J. Stewart	England v Zimbabwe at Manchester	2000
6 (5ct, 1st)	R. D. Jacobs	West Indies v Sri Lanka at Colombo (RPS)	2001-02
6 (5ct, 1st)	A. C. Gilchrist	Australia v England at Sydney	2002-03
6 (all ct)	A. C. Gilchrist	Australia v Namibia at Potchefstroom	2002-03
6 (all ct)	A. C. Gilchrist	Australia v Sri Lanka at Colombo (RPS)	2003-04
6 (all ct)	M. V. Boucher	South Africa v Pakistan at Cape Town	2006-07
6 (5ct, 1st)	M. S. Dhoni	India v England at Leeds	2007
6 (all ct)	A. C. Gilchrist	Australia v India at Vadodara	2007-08
6 (5ct, 1st)	A. C. Gilchrist	Australia v India at Sydney	2007-08
6 (all ct)	M. J. Prior	England v South Africa at Nottingham	2008
6 (all ct)	J. C. Buttler	England v South Africa at The Oval	2013
6 (all ct)	M. H. Cross	Scotland v Canada at Christchurch	2013-14
6 (5ct, 1st)	Q. de Kock	S. Africa v N. Zealand at Mount Maunganui	2014-15
6 (all ct)	Sarfraz Ahmed	Pakistan v South Africa at Auckland	2014-15

MOST DISMISSALS

			M	*Ct*	*St*
1	482	K. C. Sangakkara (Sri Lanka/World/Asia)	360	384	98
2	472	A. C. Gilchrist (Australia/World)	282	417	55
3	424	M. V. Boucher (South Africa/Africa)	294	402	22
4	**398**	**M. S. Dhoni (India/Asia)**	**312**	**293**	**105**
5	287	Moin Khan (Pakistan)	219	214	73
6	242	B. B. McCullum (New Zealand)	185	227	15
7	234	I. A. Healy (Australia)	168	195	39
8	220	Rashid Latif (Pakistan)	166	182	38
9	206	R. S. Kaluwitharana (Sri Lanka)	186	131	75
10	204	P. J. L. Dujon (West Indies)	169	183	21

The leading aggregates for players who have appeared for other Test countries are:

		M	*Ct*	*St*
181	**Mushfiqur Rahim (Bangladesh)**	**167**	**141**	**40**
165	A. Flower (Zimbabwe)	186	133	32
163	A. J. Stewart (England)	138	148	15
70	**N. J. O'Brien (Ireland)**	**68**	**59**	**11**
65	**Mohammad Shahzad (Afghanistan)**	**57**	**44**	**21**

Excluding dismissals for combined teams, the most for Sri Lanka is 473 (378ct, 95st) in 353 matches by K. C. Sangakkara; for Australia, 470 (416ct, 54st) in 281 matches by A. C. Gilchrist; for South Africa, 415 (394ct, 21st) in 289 matches by M. V. Boucher; and for India, ***392*** *(290ct, 102st) in 309 matches by* ***M. S. Dhoni****.*

K. C. Sangakkara's list excludes 19 catches taken in 44 one-day internationals when not keeping wicket; M. V. Boucher's record excludes one in one; B. B. McCullum's excludes 35 in 75; R. S. Kaluwitharana's one in three; A. Flower's eight in 27; A. J. Stewart's 11 in 32; Mushfiqur Rahim's two in 12; N. J. O'Brien's eight in 22; and Mohammad Shahzad's one in one. A. C. Gilchrist played five one-day internationals without keeping wicket, but made no catches in those games. R. Dravid (India) made 210 dismissals (196ct, 14st) in 344 one-day internationals but only 86 (72ct, 14st) in 74 as wicketkeeper (including one where he took over during the match).

MOST CATCHES IN AN INNINGS IN THE FIELD

5	J. N. Rhodes	South Africa v West Indies at Bombay	1993-94

There have been ***36*** *instances of four catches in an innings.*

MOST CATCHES

Ct	M	
218	448	D. P. M. D. Jayawardene (SL/Asia)
160	375	R. T. Ponting (Australia/World)
156	334	M. Azharuddin (India)
140	463	S. R. Tendulkar (India)
133	280	S. P. Fleming (New Zealand/World)
131	328	J. H. Kallis (SA/World/Africa)
130	262	Younis Khan (Pakistan)
130	350	M. Muralitharan (SL/World/Asia)
127	273	A. R. Border (Australia)
127	398	Shahid Afridi (Pak/World/Asia)

Most catches for other Test countries:

Ct	M	
120	227	C. L. Hooper (West Indies)
108	197	P. D. Collingwood (England)
86	221	G. W. Flower (Zimbabwe)
56	**182**	**Mashrafe bin Mortaza (Ban/As)**
53	**109**	**W. T. S. Porterfield (Ireland)**
45	**86**	**Mohammad Nabi (Afghanistan)**

*Excluding catches taken for combined teams, the record aggregate for Sri Lanka is 213 in 442 matches by D. P. M. D. Jayawardene; for Australia, 158 in 374 by R. T. Ponting; for New Zealand, 132 in 279 by S. P. Fleming; for South Africa, 131 in 323 by J. H. Kallis; and for Bangladesh, **55** in 180 by **Mashrafe bin Mortaza**.*

Younis Khan's record excludes five catches made in three one-day internationals as wicketkeeper.

TEAM RECORDS

HIGHEST INNINGS TOTALS

444-3	(50 overs)	England v Pakistan at Nottingham	2016
443-9	(50 overs)	Sri Lanka v Netherlands at Amstelveen	2006
439-2	(50 overs)	South Africa v West Indies at Johannesburg	2014-15
438-4	(50 overs)	South Africa v India at Mumbai	2015-16
438-9	(49.5 overs)	South Africa v Australia at Johannesburg	2005-06
434-4	(50 overs)	Australia v South Africa at Johannesburg	2005-06
418-5	(50 overs)	South Africa v Zimbabwe at Potchefstroom	2006-07
418-5	(50 overs)	India v West Indies at Indore	2011-12
417-6	(50 overs)	Australia v Afghanistan at Perth	2014-15
414-7	(50 overs)	India v Sri Lanka at Rajkot	2009-10
413-5	(50 overs)	India v Bermuda at Port-of-Spain	2006-07
411-4	(50 overs)	South Africa v Ireland at Canberra	2014-15
411-8	(50 overs)	Sri Lanka v India at Rajkot	2009-10
408-5	(50 overs)	South Africa v West Indies at Sydney	2014-15
408-9	(50 overs)	England v New Zealand at Birmingham	2015
404-5	(50 overs)	India v Sri Lanka at Kolkata	2014-15
402-2	(50 overs)	New Zealand v Ireland at Aberdeen	2008
401-3	(50 overs)	India v South Africa at Gwalior	2009-10

The highest totals by other Test countries are:

385-7	(50 overs)	Pakistan v Bangladesh at Dambulla	2010
372-2	(50 overs)	West Indies v Zimbabwe at Canberra	2014-15
351-7	(50 overs)	Zimbabwe v Kenya at Mombasa	2008-09
338	**(50 overs)**	**Afghanistan v Ireland at Greater Noida**	**2016-17**
331-8	(50 overs)	Ireland v Zimbabwe at Hobart	2014-15
329-6	(50 overs)	Bangladesh v Pakistan at Mirpur	2014-15

HIGHEST TOTALS BATTING SECOND

438-9	(49.5 overs)	South Africa v Australia at Johannesburg (*Won by 1 wicket*)	2005-06
411-8	(50 overs)	Sri Lanka v India at Rajkot (*Lost by 3 runs*)	2009-10
372-6	(49.2 overs)	South Africa v Australia at Durban (*Won by 4 wickets*)	2016-17
366-8	**(50 overs)**	**England v India at Cuttack** (*Lost by 15 runs*)	**2016-17**
365-9	(45 overs)	England v New Zealand at The Oval (*Lost by 13 runs DLS*)	2015
362-1	(43.3 overs)	India v Australia at Jaipur (*Won by 9 wickets*)	2013-14
356-7	**(48.1 overs)**	**India v England at Pune** (*Won by 3 wickets*)	**2016-17**

351-4	(49.3 overs)	India v Australia at Nagpur (*Won by 6 wickets*)	2013-14
350-3	(44 overs)	England v New Zealand at Nottingham (*Won by 7 wickets*)	2015
350-9	(49.3 overs)	New Zealand v Australia at Hamilton (*Won by 1 wicket*)	2006-07

HIGHEST MATCH AGGREGATES

872-13	(99.5 overs)	South Africa v Australia at Johannesburg	2005-06
825-15	(100 overs)	India v Sri Lanka at Rajkot	2009-10
763-14	(96 overs)	England v New Zealand at The Oval	2015
747-14	**(100 overs)**	**India v England at Cuttack**	**2016-17**
743-12	(99.2 overs)	South Australia v Australia at Durban	2016-17
730-9	(100 overs)	South Africa v West Indies at Johannesburg	2014-15
726-14	(95.1 overs)	New Zealand v India at Christchurch	2008-09
721-6	(93.3 overs)	India v Australia at Jaipur	2013-14

LOWEST INNINGS TOTALS

35	(18 overs)	Zimbabwe v Sri Lanka at Harare	2003-04
36	(18.4 overs)	Canada v Sri Lanka at Paarl	2002-03
38	(15.4 overs)	Zimbabwe v Sri Lanka at Colombo (SSC)	2001-02
43	(19.5 overs)	Pakistan v West Indies at Cape Town	1992-93
43	(20.1 overs)	Sri Lanka v South Africa at Paarl	2011-12
44	(24.5 overs)	Zimbabwe v Bangladesh at Chittagong	2009-10
45	(40.3 overs)	Canada v England at Manchester	1979
45	(14 overs)	Namibia v Australia at Potchefstroom	2002-03

The lowest totals by other Test countries are:

54	(26.3 overs)	India v Sri Lanka at Sharjah	2000-01
54	(23.2 overs)	West Indies v South Africa at Cape Town	2003-04
58	(18.5 overs)	Bangladesh v West Indies at Mirpur	2010-11
58	(17.4 overs)	Bangladesh v India at Mirpur	2014
58	(16.1 overs)	Afghanistan v Zimbabwe at Sharjah	2015-16
64	(35.5 overs)	New Zealand v Pakistan at Sharjah	1985-86
69	(28 overs)	South Africa v Australia at Sydney	1993-94
70	(25.2 overs)	Australia v England at Birmingham	1977
70	(26.3 overs)	Australia v New Zealand at Adelaide	1985-86
77	(27.4 overs)	Ireland v Sri Lanka at St George's	2006-07
86	(32.4 overs)	England v Australia at Manchester	2001

LARGEST VICTORIES

290 runs	New Zealand (402-2 in 50 overs) v Ireland (112 in 28.4 ov) at Aberdeen	2008
275 runs	Australia (417-6 in 50 overs) v Afghanistan (142 in 37.3 overs) at Perth	2014-15
272 runs	South Africa (399-6 in 50 overs) v Zimbabwe (127 in 29 overs) at Benoni	2010-11
258 runs	South Africa (301-8 in 50 overs) v Sri Lanka (43 in 20.1 overs) at Paarl	2011-12
257 runs	India (413-5 in 50 overs) v Bermuda (156 in 43.1 overs) at Port-of-Spain	2006-07
257 runs	South Africa (408-5 in 50 overs) v West Indies (151 in 33.1 overs) at Sydney	2014-15
256 runs	Australia (301-6 in 50 overs) v Namibia (45 in 14 overs) at Potchefstroom	2002-03
256 runs	India (374-4 in 50 overs) v Hong Kong (118 in 36.5 overs) at Karachi	2008
255 runs	Pakistan (337-6 in 47 overs) v Ireland (82 in 23.4 overs) at Dublin	2016

*There have been **51** instances of victory by ten wickets.*

TIED MATCHES

There have been **34** tied one-day internationals. Australia have tied nine matches; Bangladesh are the only Test country never to have tied. The most recent ties are:

India (338 in 49.5 overs) v England (338-8 in 50 overs) at Bangalore	2010-11
India (280-5 in 50 overs) v England (270-8 in 48.5 overs) at Lord's (D/L)	2011
Australia (220 in 49.5 overs) v West Indies (220 in 49.4 overs) at St Vincent	2011-12
Sri Lanka (236-9 in 50 overs) v India (236-9 in 50 overs) at Adelaide	2011-12
South Africa (230-6 in 31 overs) v West Indies (190-6 in 26.1 overs) at Cardiff (D/L)	2013
Ireland (268-5 in 50 overs) v Netherlands (268-9 in 50 overs) at Amstelveen	2013
Pakistan (229-6 in 50 overs) v West Indies (229-9 in 50 overs) at Gros Islet	2013
Pakistan (266-5 in 47 overs) v Ireland (275-5 in 47 overs) at Dublin (D/L)	2013
New Zealand (314 in 50 overs) v India (314-9 in 50 overs) at Auckland	2013-14
Sri Lanka (286-9 in 50 overs) v England (286-8 in 50 overs) at Nottingham	2016
Zimbabwe (257 in 50 overs) v West Indies (257-8 in 50 overs) at Bulawayo	2016-17

OTHER RECORDS

MOST APPEARANCES

463	S. R. Tendulkar (I)	330	T. M. Dilshan (SL)
448	D. P. M. D. Jayawardene (SL/Asia)	328	J. H. Kallis (SA/World/Africa)
445	S. T. Jayasuriya (SL/Asia)	325	S. R. Waugh (A)
404	K. C. Sangakkara (SL/World/Asia)	322	W. P. U. J. C. Vaas (SL/Asia)
398	Shahid Afridi (P/World/Asia)	**312**	**M. S. Dhoni (I/Asia)**
378	Inzamam-ul-Haq (P/Asia)	311	S. C. Ganguly (I/Asia)
375	R. T. Ponting (A/World)	308	P. A. de Silva (SL)
356	Wasim Akram (P)	**304**	**Yuvraj Singh (I/Asia)**
350	M. Muralitharan (SL/World/Asia)	303	S. M. Pollock (SA/World/Africa)
344	R. Dravid (I/World/Asia)	300	T. M. Dilshan (SL)
334	M. Azharuddin (I)		

Excluding appearances for combined teams, the record for Sri Lanka is 441 by S. T. Jayasuriya; for Pakistan, 393 by Shahid Afridi; for Australia, 374 by R. T. Ponting; for South Africa, 323 by J. H. Kallis; for West Indies, 295 by B. C. Lara; for New Zealand, 291 by D. L. Vettori; for Zimbabwe, 221 by G. W. Flower; for England, 197 by P. D. Collingwood; for Bangladesh, 177 by Mohammad Ashraful; for Ireland, ***115*** *by* ***K. J. O'Brien****; and for Afghanistan,* ***86*** *by* ***Mohammad Nabi****.*

MOST MATCHES AS CAPTAIN

	P	*W*	*L*	*T*	*NR*
R. T. Ponting (A/World)	230	165	51	2	12
S. P. Fleming (NZ)	218	98	106	1	13
M. S. Dhoni (I)	199	110	74	4	11
A. Ranatunga (SL)	193	89	95	1	8
A. R. Border (A)	178	107	67	1	3
M. Azharuddin (I)	174	90	76	2	6
G. C. Smith (SA/Af)	150	92	51	1	6

	P	*W*	*L*	*T*	*NR*
S. C. Ganguly (I/Asia)	147	76	66	0	5
Imran Khan (P)	139	75	59	1	4
W. J. Cronje (SA)	138	99	35	1	3
D. P. M. D.	138	99	35	1	3
Jayawardene (SL/As)	129	71	49	1	8
B. C. Lara (WI)	125	59	59	1	7

WORLD CUP FINALS

1975	WEST INDIES (291-8) beat Australia (274) by 17 runs	Lord's
1979	WEST INDIES (286-9) beat England (194) by 92 runs	Lord's
1983	INDIA (183) beat West Indies (140) by 43 runs	Lord's
1987	AUSTRALIA (253-5) beat England (246-8) by seven runs	Calcutta
1992	PAKISTAN (249-6) beat England (227) by 22 runs	Melbourne
1996	SRI LANKA (245-3) beat Australia (241-7) by seven wickets	Lahore
1999	AUSTRALIA (133-2) beat Pakistan (132) by eight wickets	Lord's
2003	AUSTRALIA (359-2) beat India (234) by 125 runs	Johannesburg
2007	AUSTRALIA (281-4) beat Sri Lanka (215-8) by 53 runs (D/L method)	Bridgetown
2011	INDIA (277-4) beat Sri Lanka (274-6) by six wickets	Mumbai
2015	AUSTRALIA (186-3) beat New Zealand (183) by seven wickets	Melbourne

TWENTY20 INTERNATIONAL RECORDS

Matches in this section do not have first-class status.

This section covers Twenty20 international cricket to January 3, 2018. Bold type denotes performances since January 1, 2017, or, in career figures, players who have appeared in Twenty20 internationals since that date.

RESULTS SUMMARY OF TWENTY20 INTERNATIONALS

2004-05 to January 3, 2018 (638 matches)

	Matches	*Won*	*Lost*	*No Result*	*% Won (excl. NR)*
Afghanistan	61	39	22	–	63.93
India	91	56*	33	2	62.92
Pakistan	120	73*	47†	–	60.83
South Africa	100	59	40	1	59.59
New Zealand	103	54†	46‡	3	54.00
West Indies	94	47†	43*	4	52.22
Sri Lanka	102	52*	49	1	51.48
England	96	47*	45	4	51.08
Australia	95	48	46†	1	51.06
Ireland	61	26	29	6	47.27
Bangladesh	69	21	46	2	31.34
Zimbabwe	54	14*	40	–	25.92
Netherlands	45	24	19	2	55.81
Scotland	44	18	23	3	43.90
Hong Kong	24	10	14	–	41.66
United Arab Emirates	26	9	17	–	34.61
Kenya	29	10	19	–	34.48
Papua New Guinea	9	3	6	–	33.33
World XI	3	1	2	–	33.33
Oman	17	5	11	1	31.25
Nepal	11	3	8	–	27.27
Canada	19	4	15*	–	21.05
Bermuda	3	–	3	–	0.00

* *Includes one game settled by a tie-break.* † *Includes two settled by a tie-break.*
‡ *Includes three settled by a tie-break. Ties were decided by bowling contests or one-over eliminators.*

Matches abandoned without a ball bowled are not included except where the toss took place, when they are shown as no result.

BATTING RECORDS

HIGHEST INDIVIDUAL INNINGS

156	A. J. Finch	Australia v England at Southampton	2013
145*	G. J. Maxwell	Australia v Sri Lanka at Pallekele	2016
125*	**E. Lewis**	**West Indies v India at Kingston**	**2017**
124*	S. R. Watson	Australia v India at Sydney	2015-16
123	B. B. McCullum	New Zealand v Bangladesh at Pallekele	2012-13
122	Babar Hayat	Hong Kong v Oman at Fatullah	2015-16
119	F. du Plessis	South Africa v West Indies at Johannesburg	2014-15
118*	Mohammad Shahzad	Afghanistan v Zimbabwe at Sharjah	2015-16
118	**R. G. Sharma**	**India v Sri Lanka at Indore**	**2017-18**
117*	R. E. Levi	South Africa v New Zealand at Hamilton	2011-12
117*	**Shaiman Anwar**	**United Arab Emirates v Papua New Guinea at Abu Dhabi**	**2016-17**

117	C. H. Gayle	West Indies v South Africa at Johannesburg	2007-08
116*	B. B. McCullum	New Zealand v Australia at Christchurch	2009-10
116*	A. D. Hales	England v Sri Lanka at Chittagong	2013-14
114*	M. N. van Wyk	South Africa v West Indies at Durban	2014-15
111*	Ahmed Shehzad	Pakistan v Bangladesh at Mirpur	2013-14
110*	K. L. Rahul	India v West Indies at Lauderhill	2016

MOST RUNS

		M	*I*	*NO*	*R*	*HS*	*100*	*Avge*	*SR*
1	B. B. McCullum (New Zealand)	71	70	10	2,140	123	2	35.66	136.21
2	**V. Kohli (India)**	**55**	**51**	**14**	**1,956**	**90***	**0**	**52.86**	**137.84**
3	**M. J. Guptill (New Zealand)**	**67**	**65**	**7**	**1,926**	**101***	**1**	**33.20**	**130.84**
4	T. M. Dilshan (Sri Lanka)	80	79	12	1,889	104*	1	28.19	120.47
5	**Shoaib Malik (Pakistan)**	**92**	**86**	**24**	**1,821**	**75**	**0**	**29.37**	**117.33**
6	**Mohammad Shahzad (Afghanistan)**	**58**	**58**	**3**	**1,779**	**118***	**1**	**32.34**	**136.84**
7	**J-P. Duminy (South Africa)**	**73**	**67**	**21**	**1,700**	**96***	**0**	**36.95**	**123.90**
8	**D. A. Warner (Australia)**	**65**	**65**	**3**	**1,696**	**90***	**0**	**27.35**	**139.24**
9	Umar Akmal (Pakistan)	82	77	14	1,690	94	0	26.82	122.90
10	**A. B. de Villiers (South Africa)**	**78**	**75**	**11**	**1,672**	**79***	**0**	**26.12**	**135.16**
11	**Mohammad Hafeez (Pakistan)**	**81**	**78**	**5**	**1,658**	**86**	**0**	**22.71**	**113.79**
12	**R. G. Sharma (India)**	**71**	**64**	**12**	**1,647**	**118**	**2**	**31.67**	**135.11**
13	**C. H. Gayle (West Indies)**	**55**	**51**	**4**	**1,589**	**117**	**2**	**33.80**	**145.11**
14	**E. J. G. Morgan (England)**	**70**	**67**	**12**	**1,576**	**85***	**0**	**28.65**	**130.46**
15	D. P. M. D. Jayawardene (Sri Lanka)	55	55	8	1,493	100	1	31.76	133.18
16	**M. N. Samuels (West Indies)**	**60**	**58**	**10**	**1,469**	**89***	**0**	**30.60**	**115.21**
17	S. R. Watson (Australia)	58	56	6	1,462	124*	1	29.24	145.32
18	H. Masakadza (Zimbabwe)	50	50	2	1,413	93*	0	29.43	119.74
19	Shahid Afridi (Pakistan)	98	90	12	1,405	54*	0	18.01	150.75
20	**A. D. Hales (England)**	**48**	**48**	**6**	**1,383**	**116***	**1**	**32.92**	**135.32**
21	K. C. Sangakkara (Sri Lanka)	56	53	9	1,382	78	0	31.40	119.55
22	**M. S. Dhoni (India)**	**86**	**75**	**38**	**1,364**	**56**	**0**	**36.86**	**125.02**
23	**Ahmed Shahzad (Pakistan)**	**53**	**53**	**2**	**1,353**	**111***	**1**	**26.52**	**115.54**

The leading aggregates for players who have appeared for other Test countries are:

Tamim Iqbal (Bangladesh/World)	**59**	**59**	**5**	**1,257**	**103***	**1**	**23.27**	**115.21**
W. T. S. Porterfield (Ireland)	**56**	**54**	**6**	**1,002**	**72**	**0**	**20.87**	**110.96**

Excluding runs for the World XI, the record aggregate for Bangladesh is 1,223 in 61 matches by Shakib Al Hasan.

FASTEST TWENTY20 INTERNATIONAL FIFTIES

Balls			
12	Yuvraj Singh	India v England at Durban	2007-08
14	C. Munro	New Zealand v Sri Lanka at Auckland	2015-16
17	P. R. Stirling	Ireland v Afghanistan at Dubai	2011-12
17	S. J. Myburgh	Netherlands v Ireland at Sylhet	2013-14
17	C. H. Gayle	West Indies v South Africa at Cape Town	2014-15
18	D. A. Warner	Australia v West Indies at Sydney	2009-10
18	G. J. Maxwell	Australia v Pakistan at Mirpur	2013-14
18	G. J. Maxwell	Australia v Sri Lanka at Pallekele	2016
18	**C. Munro**	**New Zealand v West Indies at Mount Maunganui**	**2017-18**

FASTEST TWENTY20 INTERNATIONAL HUNDREDS

Balls			
35	**D. A. Miller**	**South Africa v Bangladesh at Potchefstroom**	**2017-18**
35	**R. G. Sharma**	**India v Sri Lanka at Indore**	**2017-18**
45	R. E. Levi	South Africa v New Zealand at Hamilton	2011-12
46	F. du Plessis	South Africa v West Indies at Johannesburg	2014-15

Balls			
46	K. L. Rahul	India v West Indies at Lauderhill	2016
47	A. J. Finch	Australia v England at Southampton	2013
47	C. H. Gayle	West Indies v England at Mumbai	2015-16
47	**C. Munro**	**New Zealand v West Indies at Mount Maunganui**	**2017-18**
48	E. Lewis	West Indies v India at Lauderhill	2016
49	G. J. Maxwell	Australia v Sri Lanka at Pallekele	2016

HIGHEST PARTNERSHIP FOR EACH WICKET

171*	for 1st	M. J. Guptill/K. S. Williamson	NZ v P	Hamilton	2015-16
166	for 2nd	D. P. M. D. Jayawardene/ K. C. Sangakkara	SL v WI	Bridgetown	2010
152	for 3rd	A. D. Hales/E. J. G. Morgan	E v SL	Chittagong	2013-14
161	for 4th	D. A. Warner/G. J. Maxwell	A v SA	Johannesburg	2015-16
119*	for 5th	Shoaib Malik/Misbah-ul-Haq	P v A	Johannesburg	2007-08
101*	for 6th	C. L. White/M. E. K. Hussey	A v SL	Bridgetown	2010
91	for 7th	P. D. Collingwood/M. H. Yardy	E v WI	The Oval	2007
80	for 8th	P. L. Mommsen/S. M. Sharif	Scot v Neth	Edinburgh	2015
66	for 9th	D. J. Bravo/J. E. Taylor	WI v P	Dubai	2016-17
31*	for 10th	Wahab Riaz/Shoaib Akhtar	P v NZ	Auckland	2010-11

BOWLING RECORDS

BEST BOWLING ANALYSES

6-8	B. A. W. Mendis	Sri Lanka v Zimbabwe at Hambantota	2012-13
6-16	B. A. W. Mendis	Sri Lanka v Australia at Pallekele	2011-12
6-25	**Y. S. Chahal**	**India v England at Bangalore**	**2016-17**
5-3	H. M. R. K. B. Herath	Sri Lanka v New Zealand at Chittagong	2013-14
5-3	**Rashid Khan**	**Afghanistan v Ireland at Greater Noida**	**2016-17**
5-6	Umar Gul	Pakistan v New Zealand at The Oval	2009
5-6	Umar Gul	Pakistan v South Africa at Centurion	2012-13
5-13	Elias Sunny	Bangladesh v Ireland at Belfast	2012
5-13	Samiullah Shenwari	Afghanistan v Kenya at Sharjah	2013-14
5-14	Imad Wasim	Pakistan v West Indies at Dubai	2016-17
5-18	T. G. Southee	New Zealand v Pakistan at Auckland	2010-11
5-19	R. McLaren	South Africa v West Indies at North Sound	2010
5-19	M. A. A. Jamil	Netherlands v South Africa at Chittagong	2013-14
5-20	N. N. Odhiambo	Kenya v Scotland at Nairobi	2009-10

HAT-TRICKS

B. Lee	Australia v Bangladesh at Cape Town	2007-08
J. D. P. Oram	New Zealand v Sri Lanka at Colombo	2009
T. G. Southee	New Zealand v Pakistan at Auckland	2010-11

MOST WICKETS

		M	*B*	*R*	*W*	*BB*	*4I*	*Avge*	*ER*
1	Shahid Afridi (Pakistan)	98	2,144	2,362	97	4-11	3	24.35	6.61
2	**S. L. Malinga (Sri Lanka)**	**68**	**1,451**	**1,780**	**90**	**5-31**	**2**	**19.77**	**7.36**
3	Umar Gul (Pakistan)	60	1,203	1,443	85	5-6	6	16.97	7.19
	Saeed Ajmal (Pakistan)	64	1,430	1,516	85	4-19	4	17.83	6.36
5	**Shakib Al Hasan (Bangladesh)**	**61**	**1,331**	**1,509**	**73**	**4-15**	**3**	**20.67**	**6.80**
6	B. A. W. Mendis (Sri Lanka)	39	885	952	66	6-8	5	14.42	6.45
	K. M. D. N. Kulasekara (Sri Lanka)	**58**	**1,231**	**1,530**	**66**	**4-31**	**2**	**23.18**	**7.45**
8	S. C. J. Broad (England)	56	1,173	1,491	65	4-24	1	22.93	7.62
9	**Mohammad Nabi (Afghanistan)**	**58**	**1,234**	**1,487**	**59**	**4-10**	**3**	**25.20**	**7.23**

		M	B	R	W	BB	4I	Avge	ER
10	D. W. Steyn (South Africa)	42	901	1,009	58	4-9	2	17.39	6.71
	N. L. McCullum (New Zealand)	63	1,123	1,278	58	4-16	2	22.03	6.82
12	**Imran Tahir (South Africa/World)**	**36**	**797**	**904**	**57**	**5-24**	**3**	**15.85**	**6.80**
13	**K. J. O'Brien (Ireland)**	**59**	**837**	**998**	**54**	**4-45**	**1**	**18.48**	**7.15**
	S. Badree (West Indies/World)	**45**	**1,014**	**1,011**	**54**	**4-15**	**1**	**18.72**	**5.98**
	T. G. Southee (New Zealand)	**44**	**921**	**1,343**	**54**	**5-18**	**1**	**24.87**	**8.74**
	Sohail Tanvir (Pakistan)	**57**	**1,214**	**1,454**	**54**	**3-12**	**0**	**26.92**	**7.18**
17	**G. H. Dockrell (Ireland)**	**46**	**856**	**927**	**52**	**4-20**	**1**	**17.82**	**6.49**
	R. Ashwin (India)	**46**	**1,026**	**1,193**	**52**	**4-8**	**2**	**22.94**	**6.97**
	D. J. Bravo (West Indies)	66	1,042	1,470	52	4-28	2	28.26	8.46
20	G. P. Swann (England)	39	810	859	51	3-13	0	16.84	6.36
21	**S. P. Narine (West Indies)**	**48**	**1,030**	**1,034**	**50**	**4-12**	**1**	**20.68**	**6.02**

The leading aggregates for other Test countries are:

	M	B	R	W	BB	4I	Avge	ER
S. R. Watson (Australia)	58	930	1,187	48	4-15	1	24.72	7.65
A. G. Cremer (Zimbabwe)	27	534	622	33	3-11	0	18.84	6.98

*Excluding the World XI, the record aggregate for West Indies is **52** in 43 matches by **S. Badree**.*

WICKETKEEPING AND FIELDING RECORDS

MOST DISMISSALS IN AN INNINGS

5 (3ct, 2st) Mohammad Shahzad Afghanistan v Oman at Abu Dhabi 2015-16

*There have been **18** instances of four dismissals in an innings.*

MOST DISMISSALS

			M	Ct	St
1	**76**	**M. S. Dhoni (India)**	**86**	**47**	**29**
2	**60**	**Kamran Akmal (Pakistan)**	**53**	**28**	**32**
3	**52**	**Mohammad Shahzad (Afghanistan)**	**57**	**25**	**27**
4	51	D. Ramdin (West Indies)	58	32	19
5	**46**	**Mushfiqur Rahim (Bangladesh)**	**57**	**22**	**24**
6	45	K. C. Sangakkara (Sri Lanka)	56	25	20
7	**39**	**Q. de Kock (South Africa)**	**31**	**30**	**9**
8	32	B. B. McCullum (New Zealand)	42	24	8

B. B. McCullum's record excludes 11 catches taken in 28 matches when not keeping wicket, and Mushfiqur Rahim's excludes one catch in four matches when not keeping wicket. Kamran Akmal played five matches and Mohammad Shahzad one in which they did not keep wicket or take a catch.

MOST CATCHES IN AN INNINGS IN THE FIELD

4	D. J. G. Sammy	West Indies v Ireland at Providence	2010
4	Babar Hayat	Hong Kong v Afghanistan at Mirpur	2015-16

MOST CATCHES

Ct	M		Ct	M	
44	**52**	**A. B. de Villiers (South Africa)**	**34**	**65**	**D. A. Warner (Australia)**
43	**74**	**L. R. P. L. Taylor (New Zealand)**	**34**	**73**	**J-P. Duminy (South Africa)**
38	62	Umar Akmal (Pakistan)	**32**	**65**	**S. K. Raina (India)**
37	**57**	**D. A. Miller (South Africa/World)**	**31**	**58**	**Mohammad Nabi (Afghanistan)**
37	**92**	**Shoaib Malik (Pakistan)**	**31**	**68**	**D. J. G. Sammy (West Indies)**
36	**67**	**M. J. Guptill (New Zealand)**	**31**	**70**	**E. J. G. Morgan (England)**
35	66	D. J. Bravo (West Indies)	30	98	Shahid Afridi (Pakistan)

A. B. de Villiers's record excludes 28 dismissals (21ct, 7st) in 26 matches when keeping wicket; Umar Akmal's excludes 13 (11ct, 2st) in 20 matches.

TEAM RECORDS

HIGHEST INNINGS TOTALS

263-3	(20 overs)	Australia v Sri Lanka at Pallekele	2016
260-5	**(20 overs)**	**India v Sri Lanka at Indore**	**2017-18**
260-6	(20 overs)	Sri Lanka v Kenya at Johannesburg	2007-08
248-6	(20 overs)	Australia v England at Southampton	2013
245-6	(20 overs)	West Indies v India at Lauderhill	2016
244-4	(20 overs)	India v West Indies at Lauderhill	2016
243-5	**(20 overs)**	**New Zealand v West Indies at Mount Maunganui**	**2017-18**
241-6	(20 overs)	South Africa v England at Centurion	2009-10
236-6	(19.2 overs)	West Indies v South Africa at Johannesburg	2014-15
233-8	**(20 overs)**	**Afghanistan v Ireland at Greater Noida**	**2016-17**
231-7	(20 overs)	South Africa v West Indies at Johannesburg	2014-15
230-8	(19.4 overs)	England v South Africa at Mumbai	2015-16

LOWEST INNINGS TOTALS

39	(10.3 overs)	Netherlands v Sri Lanka at Chittagong	2013-14
53	(14.3 overs)	Nepal v Ireland at Belfast	2015
56	(18.4 overs)	Kenya v Afghanistan at Sharjah	2013-14
60†	(15.3 overs)	New Zealand v Sri Lanka at Chittagong	2013-14
67	(17.2 overs)	Kenya v Ireland at Belfast	2008
68	(16.4 overs)	Ireland v West Indies at Providence	2010
69	(17 overs)	Hong Kong v Nepal at Chittagong	2013-14
69	(17.4 overs)	Nepal v Netherlands at Amstelveen	2015
70	(20 overs)	Bermuda v Canada at Belfast	2008
70	(15.4 overs)	Bangladesh v New Zealand at Kolkata	2015-16

† *One man absent.*

OTHER RECORDS

MOST APPEARANCES

98	Shahid Afridi (Pakistan)
92	**Shoaib Malik (Pakistan)**
86	**M. S. Dhoni (India)**
82	Umar Akmal (Pakistan)
81	**Mohammad Hafeez (Pakistan)**
80	T. M. Dilshan (Sri Lanka)
78	**A. B. de Villiers (South Africa)**
74	**L. R. P. L. Taylor (New Zealand)**
73	**J-P. Duminy (South Africa)**
71	B. B. McCullum (New Zealand)
71	**A. D. Mathews (Sri Lanka)**
71	**R. G. Sharma (India)**
70	**E. J. G. Morgan (England)**

WORLD TWENTY20 FINALS

2007-08	INDIA (157-5) beat Pakistan (152) by five runs	Johannesburg
2009	PAKISTAN (139-2) beat Sri Lanka (138-6) by eight wickets	Lord's
2010	ENGLAND (148-3) beat Australia (147-6) by seven wickets	Bridgetown
2012-13	WEST INDIES (137-6) beat Sri Lanka (101) by 36 runs	Colombo (RPS)
2013-14	SRI LANKA (134-4) beat India (130-4) by six wickets	Mirpur
2015-16	WEST INDIES (161-6) beat England (155-9) by four wickets	Kolkata

MISCELLANEOUS RECORDS

LARGE ATTENDANCES

Test Series

957,550	Australia v England (5 Tests)	1936-37
In England		
549,650	England v Australia (5 Tests)	1953

Test Matches

†‡465,000	India v Pakistan, Calcutta	1998-99
350,534	Australia v England, Melbourne (Third Test)	1936-37

Attendance at India v England at Calcutta in 1981-82 may have exceeded 350,000.

In England

158,000+	England v Australia, Leeds	1948
140,111	England v India, Lord's	2011
137,915	England v Australia, Lord's	1953

Test Match Day

‡100,000	India v Pakistan, Calcutta (first four days)	1998-99
91,112	Australia v England, Melbourne (Fourth Test, first day)	2013-14
90,800	Australia v West Indies, Melbourne (Fifth Test, second day)	1960-61
89,155	Australia v England, Melbourne (Fourth Test, first day)	2006-07

Other First-Class Matches in England

93,000	England v Australia, Lord's (Fourth Victory Match, 3 days)	1945
80,000+	Surrey v Yorkshire, The Oval (3 days)	1906
78,792	Yorkshire v Lancashire, Leeds (3 days)	1904
76,617	Lancashire v Yorkshire, Manchester (3 days)	1926

One-Day Internationals

‡100,000	India v South Africa, Calcutta	1993-94
‡100,000	India v West Indies, Calcutta	1993-94
‡100,000	India v West Indies, Calcutta	1994-95
‡100,000	India v Sri Lanka, Calcutta (World Cup semi-final)	1995-96
‡100,000	India v Australia, Kolkata	2003-04
93,013	Australia v New Zealand, Melbourne (World Cup final)	2014-15
‡90,000	India v Pakistan, Calcutta	1986-87
‡90,000	India v South Africa, Calcutta	1991-92
87,182	England v Pakistan, Melbourne (World Cup final)	1991-92
86,133	Australia v West Indies, Melbourne	1983-84

Twenty20 International

84,041	Australia v India, Melbourne	2007-08

† *Estimated.*

‡ *No official attendance figures were issued for these games, but capacity at Calcutta (now Kolkata) is believed to have reached 100,000 following rebuilding in 1993.*

LORD'S CRICKET GROUND

Lord's and the Marylebone Cricket Club were founded in London in 1787. The Club has enjoyed an uninterrupted career since that date, but there have been three grounds known as Lord's. The first (1787–1810) was situated where Dorset Square now is; the second (1809–13), at North Bank, had to be abandoned owing to the cutting of the Regent's Canal; and the third, opened in 1814, is the present one at St John's Wood. It was not until 1866 that the freehold of Lord's was secured by MCC. The present pavilion was erected in 1890 at a cost of £21,000.

MINOR CRICKET

HIGHEST INDIVIDUAL SCORES

1,009*	P. P. Dhanawade, K. C. Gandhi English School v Arya Gurukul at Kalyan *Dhanawade faced 327 balls in 6 hours 36 minutes and hit 129 fours and 59 sixes*	2015-16
628*	A. E. J. Collins, Clark's House v North Town at Clifton College. *A junior house match. His innings of 6 hours 50 minutes was spread over four afternoons*	1899
566	C. J. Eady, Break-o'-Day v Wellington at Hobart	1901-02
546	P. P. Shaw, Rizvi Springfield School v St Francis D'Assisi School at Mumbai	2013-14
515	D. R. Havewalla, B. B. and C. I. Railways v St Xavier's at Bombay	1933-34
506*	J. C. Sharp, Melbourne GS v Geelong College at Melbourne	1914-15
502*	Chaman Lal, Mohindra Coll., Patiala v Government Coll., Rupar at Patiala	1956-57
498	Arman Jaffer, Rizvi Springfield School v IES Raja Shivaji School at Mumbai	2010-11
490	**S. Dadswell, North West University v Potchefstroom at Potchefstroom**	**2017-18**
486*	S. Sankruth Sriram, JSS Intl School U16 v Hebron School U16 at Ootacamund	2014-15
485	A. E. Stoddart, Hampstead v Stoics at Hampstead	1886
475*	Mohammad Iqbal, Muslim Model HS v Government HS, Sialkot at Gujranwala	1958-59
473	Arman Jaffer, Rizvi Springfield School v IES VN Sule School at Mumbai	2012-13
466*	G. T. S. Stevens, Beta v Lambda (University College School house match) at Neasden. *Stevens scored his 466 and took 14 wickets on one day*	1919
461*	Ali Zorain Khan, Nagpur Cricket Academy v Reshimbagh Gymkhana at Nagpur	2010-11
459	J. A. Prout, Wesley College v Geelong College at Geelong	1908-09
451*	V. H. Mol, Maharashtra Under-19 v Assam Under-19 at Nasik	2011-12

The highest score in a Minor County match is 323 by F. E. Lacey for Hampshire v Norfolk at Southampton in 1887; the highest in the Minor Counties Championship is 282 by E. Garnett for Berkshire v Wiltshire at Reading in 1908.*

HIGHEST PARTNERSHIPS

721* for 1st	B. Manoj Kumar and M. S. Tumbi, St Peter's High School v St Philip's High School at Secunderabad	2006-07
664* for 3rd	V. G. Kambli and S. R. Tendulkar, Sharadashram Vidyamandir School v St Xavier's High School at Bombay	1987-88

Manoj Kumar and Tumbi reportedly scored 721 in 40 overs in an Under-13 inter-school match; they hit 103 fours between them, but no sixes. Their opponents were all out for 21 in seven overs.

Kambli was 16 years old, Tendulkar 14. Tendulkar made his Test debut 21 months later.

MOST WICKETS WITH CONSECUTIVE BALLS

There are **two** recorded instances of a bowler taking nine wickets with consecutive balls. Both came in school games: Paul Hugo, for Smithfield School v Aliwal North at Smithfield, South Africa, in 1930-31, and Stephen Fleming (not the future Test captain), for Marlborough College A v Bohally School at Blenheim, New Zealand, in 1967-68. There are five further verified instances of eight wickets in eight balls, the most recent by Mike Walters for the Royal Army Educational Corps v Joint Air Transport Establishment at Beaconsfield in 1979.

TEN WICKETS FOR NO RUNS

There are **26** recorded instances of a bowler taking all ten wickets in an innings for no runs, the most recent **Akash Choudhary**, for Disha Cricket Academy v Pearl Academy in the Late Bahwer Singh T20 Tournament in Jaipur 2017-18. When Jennings Tune did it, for the Yorkshire club Cliffe v Eastrington at Cliffe in 1923, all ten of his victims were bowled.

NOUGHT ALL OUT

In minor matches, this is more common than might be imagined. The historian Peter Wynne-Thomas says the first recorded example was in Norfolk, where an Eleven of Fakenham, Walsingham and Hempton were dismissed for nought by an Eleven of Licham, Dunham and Brisley in July 1815.

MOST DISMISSALS IN AN INNINGS

The only recorded instance of a wicketkeeper being involved in all ten dismissals in an innings was by Welihinda Badalge Bennett, for Mahinda College against Richmond College in Ceylon (now Sri Lanka) in 1952-53. His feat comprised six catches and four stumpings. There are three other known instances of nine dismissals in the same innings, one of which – by H. W. P. Middleton for Priory v Mitre in a Repton School house match in 1930 – included eight stumpings. Young Rangers' innings against Bohran Gymkhana in Karachi in 1969-70 included nine run-outs.

The widespread nature – and differing levels of supervision – of minor cricket matches mean that record claims have to be treated with caution. Additions and corrections to the above records for minor cricket will only be considered for inclusion in Wisden *if they are corroborated by independent evidence of the achievement.*

Research: Steven Lynch

RECORD HIT

The Rev. W. Fellows, while at practice on the Christ Church ground at Oxford in 1856, reportedly drove a ball bowled by Charles Rogers 175 yards from hit to pitch; it is claimed that the feat was matched by J. W. Erskine in a match in Galle in 1902.

BIGGEST HIT AT LORD'S

The only known instance of a batsman hitting a ball over the present pavilion at Lord's occurred when A. E. Trott, appearing for MCC against Australians on July 31, August 1, 2, 1899, drove M. A. Noble so far and high that the ball struck a chimney pot and fell behind the building.

THROWING THE CRICKET BALL

140 yards 2 feet	Robert Percival, on the Durham Sands racecourse, Co. Durham	c1882
140 yards 9 inches	Ross Mackenzie, at Toronto	1872
140 yards	"King Billy" the Aborigine, at Clermont, Queensland	1872

Extensive research by David Rayvern Allen has shown that these traditional records are probably authentic, if not necessarily wholly accurate. Modern competitions have failed to produce similar distances although Ian Pont, the Essex all-rounder who also played baseball, was reported to have thrown 138 yards in Cape Town in 1981. There have been speculative reports attributing throws of 150 yards or more to figures as diverse as the South African Test player Colin Bland, the Latvian javelin thrower Janis Lusis, who won a gold medal for the Soviet Union in the 1968 Olympics, and the British sprinter Charley Ransome. The definitive record is still awaited.

COUNTY CHAMPIONSHIP

MOST APPEARANCES

762	W. Rhodes	Yorkshire	1898–1930
707	F. E. Woolley	Kent	1906–1938
668	C. P. Mead	Hampshire	1906–1936
617	N. Gifford	Worcestershire (484), Warwickshire (133)	1960–1988
611	W. G. Quaife	Warwickshire	1895–1928
601	G. H. Hirst	Yorkshire	1891–1921

MOST CONSECUTIVE APPEARANCES

423	K. G. Suttle	Sussex	1954–1969
412	J. G. Binks	Yorkshire	1955–1969

J. Vine made 417 consecutive appearances for Sussex in all first-class matches (399 of them in the Championship) between July 1900 and September 1914.

J. G. Binks did not miss a Championship match for Yorkshire between making his debut in June 1955 and retiring at the end of the 1969 season.

UMPIRES

MOST COUNTY CHAMPIONSHIP APPEARANCES

570	T. W. Spencer	1950–1980
531	F. Chester	1922–1955
523	D. J. Constant	1969–2006
517	H. G. Baldwin	1932–1962
511	A. G. T. Whitehead	1970–2005

MOST SEASONS ON ENGLISH FIRST-CLASS LIST

38	D. J. Constant	1969–2006
36	A. G. T. Whitehead	1970–2005
31	K. E. Palmer	1972–2002
31	T. W. Spencer	1950–1980
30	R. Julian	1972–2001
30	P. B. Wight	1966–1995
29	H. D. Bird	1970–1998
28	F. Chester	1922–1955
28	B. Leadbeater	1981–2008
28	R. Palmer	1980–2007
27	B. Dudleston	1984–2010
27	J. W. Holder	1983–2009
27	J. Moss	1899–1929
26	W. A. J. West	1896–1925
25	H. G. Baldwin	1932–1962
25	A. Jepson	1960–1984
25	J. G. Langridge	1956–1980
25	B. J. Meyer	1973–1997
25	D. R. Shepherd	1981–2005

An expanded and regularly updated online version of the Records can be found at www.wisdenrecords.com

WOMEN'S TEST RECORDS

This section covers all women's Tests to December 31, 2017. Bold type denotes performances in the calendar year 2017 or, in career figures, players who appeared in women's Tests in that year.

BATTING RECORDS

HIGHEST INDIVIDUAL INNINGS

242	Kiran Baluch	Pakistan v West Indies at Karachi	2003-04
214	M. D. Raj	India v England at Taunton	2002
213*	**E. A. Perry**	**Australia v England at North Sydney**	**2017-18**
209*	K. L. Rolton	Australia v England at Leeds	2001
204	K. E. Flavell	New Zealand v England at Scarborough	1996
204	M. A. J. Goszko	Australia v England at Shenley	2001
200	J. Broadbent	Australia v England at Guildford	1998

1,000 RUNS IN A CAREER

R	*T*		*R*	*T*	
1,935	27	J. A. Brittin (England)	1,110	13	S. Agarwal (India)
1,676	23	C. M. Edwards (England)	1,078	12	E. Bakewell (England)
1,594	22	R. Heyhoe-Flint (England)	1,030	15	S. C. Taylor (England)
1,301	19	D. A. Hockley (New Zealand)	1,007	14	M. E. Maclagan (England)
1,164	18	C. A. Hodges (England)	1,002	14	K. L. Rolton (Australia)

BOWLING RECORDS

BEST BOWLING ANALYSES

8-53	N. David	India v England at Jamshedpur	1995-96
7-6	M. B. Duggan	England v Australia at Melbourne	1957-58
7-7	E. R. Wilson	Australia v England at Melbourne	1957-58
7-10	M. E. Maclagan	England v Australia at Brisbane	1934-35
7-18	A. Palmer	Australia v England at Brisbane	1934-35
7-24	L. Johnston	Australia v New Zealand at Melbourne	1971-72
7-34	G. E. McConway	England v India at Worcester	1986
7-41	J. A. Burley	New Zealand v England at The Oval	1966

MOST WICKETS IN A MATCH

13-226	Shaiza Khan	Pakistan v West Indies at Karachi	2003-04

50 WICKETS IN A CAREER

W	*T*		*W*	*T*	
77	17	M. B. Duggan (England)	60	19	S. Kulkarni (India)
68	11	E. R. Wilson (Australia)	57	16	R. H. Thompson (Australia)
63	20	D. F. Edulji (India)	55	15	J. Lord (New Zealand)
60	13	C. L. Fitzpatrick (Australia)	50	12	E. Bakewell (England)
60	14	M. E. Maclagan (England)			

WICKETKEEPING RECORDS

SIX DISMISSALS IN AN INNINGS

8 (6ct, 2st)	L. Nye	England v New Zealand at New Plymouth	1991-92
6 (2ct, 4st)	B. A. Brentnall	New Zealand v South Africa at Johannesburg	1971-72

25 DISMISSALS IN A CAREER

		T	Ct	St
58	C. Matthews (Australia)	20	46	12
43	J. Smit (England)	21	39	4
36	S. A. Hodges (England)	11	19	17
28	B. A. Brentnall (New Zealand)	10	16	12

TEAM RECORDS

HIGHEST INNINGS TOTALS

569-6 dec	Australia v England at Guildford	1998
525	Australia v India at Ahmedabad	1983-84
517-8	New Zealand v England at Scarborough	1996
503-5 dec	England v New Zealand at Christchurch	1934-35

LOWEST INNINGS TOTALS

35	England v Australia at Melbourne	1957-58
38	Australia v England at Melbourne	1957-58
44	New Zealand v England at Christchurch	1934-35
47	Australia v England at Brisbane	1934-35

WOMEN'S ONE-DAY INTERNATIONAL RECORDS

This section covers women's one-day international cricket to December 31, 2017. Bold type denotes performances in the calendar year 2017 or, in career figures, players who appeared in that year.

BATTING RECORDS

HIGHEST INDIVIDUAL INNINGS

229*	B. J. Clark	Australia v Denmark at Mumbai	1997-98
188	**D. B. Sharma**	**India v Ireland at Potchefstroom**	**2017**
178*	**A. M. C. Jayangani**	**Sri Lanka v Australia at Bristol**	**2017**
173*	C. M. Edwards	England v Ireland at Pune	1997-98
171*	**H. Kaur**	**India v Australia at Derby**	**2017**
171	S. R. Taylor	West Indies v Sri Lanka at Mumbai	2012-13
168*	T. T. Beaumont	England v Pakistan at Taunton	2016
168	S. W. Bates	New Zealand v Pakistan at Sydney	2008-09
157	R. H. Priest	New Zealand v Sri Lanka at Lincoln	2015-16
156*	L. M. Keightley	Australia v Pakistan at Melbourne	1996-97
156*	S. C. Taylor	England v India at Lord's	2006
154*	K. L. Rolton	Australia v Sri Lanka at Christchurch	2000-01
153*	J. Logtenberg	South Africa v Netherlands at Deventer	2007
152*	**M. M. Lanning**	**Australia v Sri Lanka at Bristol**	**2017**
151	K. L. Rolton	Australia v Ireland at Dublin	2005

MOST RUNS IN A CAREER

R	M		R	M	
6,190	**186**	**M. D. Raj (India)**	4,064	118	D. A. Hockley (New Zealand)
5,992	191	C. M. Edwards (England)	**4,030**	**108**	**S. R. Taylor (West Indies)**
4,844	118	B. J. Clark (Australia)	**3,807**	**107**	**S. W. Bates (New Zealand)**
4,814	141	K. L. Rolton (Australia)	**3,786**	**113**	**S. J. Taylor (England)**
4,101	126	S. C. Taylor (England)			

BOWLING RECORDS

BEST BOWLING ANALYSES

7-4	Sajjida Shah	Pakistan v Japan at Amsterdam	2003
7-8	J. M. Chamberlain	England v Denmark at Haarlem	1991
7-14	A. Mohammed	West Indies v Pakistan at Mirpur	2011-12
7-24	S. Nitschke	Australia v England at Kidderminster	2005
6-10	J. Lord	New Zealand v India at Auckland	1981-82
6-10	M. Maben	India v Sri Lanka at Kandy	2003-04
6-10	S. Ismail	South Africa v Netherlands at Savar	2011-12

MOST WICKETS IN A CAREER

W	*M*		*W*	*M*	
195	**164**	**J. N. Goswami (India)**	**135**	**142**	**J. L. Gunn (England)**
180	109	C. L. Fitzpatrick (Australia)	**127**	**106**	**K. H. Brunt (England)**
146	125	L. C. Sthalekar (Australia)	**127**	**108**	**S. R. Taylor (West Indies)**
145	**111**	**A. Mohammed (W. Indies)**	**126**	**94**	**E. A. Perry (Australia)**
141	97	N. David (India)	**120**	**85**	**D. van Niekerk (S. Africa)**

WICKETKEEPING RECORDS

MOST DISMISSALS IN AN INNINGS

6 (4ct, 2st)	S. L. Illingworth	New Zealand v Australia at Beckenham	1993
6 (1ct, 5st)	V. Kalpana	India v Denmark at Slough	1993
6 (2ct, 4st)	Batool Fatima	Pakistan v West Indies at Karachi	2003-04
6 (4ct, 2st)	Batool Fatima	Pakistan v Sri Lanka at Colombo (PSO)	2010-11

MOST DISMISSALS IN A CAREER

		M	*Ct*	*St*
137	**T. Chetty (South Africa)**	**98**	**95**	**42**
133	R. J. Rolls (New Zealand)	104	90	43
125	**S. J. Taylor (England)**	**113**	**80**	**45**
114	J. Smit (England)	109	69	45
101	**M. R. Aguilleira (West Indies)**	**106**	**76**	**25**
100	Batool Fatima (Pakistan)	83	54	46
100	J. C. Price (Australia)	84	70	30

Chetty's total includes two catches in two matches, Taylor's and Aguilleira's each include two in eight matches and Batool Fatima's three in 15 while not keeping wicket; Price's includes one taken in the field after giving up the gloves mid-game. Rolls did not keep wicket in three matches and Smit in one; neither took any catches in these games.

TEAM RECORDS

HIGHEST INNINGS TOTALS

455-5	New Zealand v Pakistan at Christchurch	1996-97
412-3	Australia v Denmark at Mumbai	1997-98
397-4	Australia v Pakistan at Melbourne	1996-97
378-5	England v Pakistan at Worcester	2016
377-7	**England v Pakistan at Leicester**	**2017**
376-2	England v Pakistan at Vijayawada	1997-98
375-5	Netherlands v Japan at Schiedam	2003
373-5	**England v South Africa at Bristol**	**2017**
373-7	New Zealand v Pakistan at Sydney	2008-09

LOWEST INNINGS TOTALS

22	Netherlands v West Indies at Deventer	2008
23	Pakistan v Australia at Melbourne	1996-97
24	Scotland v England at Reading	2001
26	India v New Zealand as St Saviour	2002
27	Pakistan v Australia at Hyderabad (India)	1997-98
28	Japan v Pakistan at Amsterdam	2003
29	Netherlands v Australia at Perth	1988-89

WOMEN'S WORLD CUP WINNERS

1973	England	1993	England	2008-09	England
1977-78	Australia	1997-98	Australia	2012-13	Australia
1981-82	Australia	2000-01	New Zealand	2017	England
1988-89	Australia	2004-05	Australia		

WOMEN'S TWENTY20 INTERNATIONAL RECORDS

This section covers women's T20 international cricket to December 31, 2017. Bold type denotes performances in the calendar year 2017 or, in career figures, players who appeared in that year.

BATTING RECORDS

HIGHEST INDIVIDUAL INNINGS

126	M. M. Lanning	Australia v Ireland at Sylhet	2013-14
117*	**B. L. Mooney**	**Australia v England at Canberra**	**2017-18**
116*	S. A. Fritz	South Africa v Netherlands at Potchefstroom	2010-11
112*	D. J. S. Dottin	West Indies v South Africa at Basseterre	2010
112	**D. J. S. Dottin**	**West Indies v Sri Lanka at Coolidge**	**2017-18**
100	**D. N. Wyatt**	**England v Australia at Canberra**	**2017-18**

MOST RUNS IN A CAREER

R	*M*		*R*	*M*	
2,605	95	C. M. Edwards (England)	1,708	63	M. D. Raj (India)
2,474	**80**	**S. R. Taylor (West Indies)**	**1,378**	**78**	**Bismah Maroof (Pakistan)**
2,337	**91**	**S. W. Bates (New Zealand)**	**1,329**	**64**	**S. F. M. Devine (New Zealand)**
2,091	**84**	**S. J. Taylor (England)**	**1,314**	**95**	**A. J. Blackwell (Australia)**
1,959	**94**	**D. J. S. Dottin (West Indies)**	1,223	68	H. Kaur (India)
1,930	**70**	**M. M. Lanning (Australia)**			

BOWLING RECORDS

BEST BOWLING ANALYSES

6-17	A. E. Satterthwaite	New Zealand v England at Taunton	2007
5-8	S. E. Luus	South Africa v Ireland at Chennai	2015-16
5-10	A. Mohammed	West Indies v South Africa at Cape Town	2009-10
5-10	**M. R. Strano**	**Australia v New Zealand at Geelong**	**2016-17**
5-11	J. N. Goswami	India v Australia at Visakhapatnam	2011-12
5-11	A. Shrubsole	England v New Zealand at Wellington	2011-12
5-12	A. Mohammed	West Indies v New Zealand at Bridgetown	2013-14
5-13	**A. S. S. Fletcher**	**West Indies v Sri Lanka at Coolidge**	**2017-18**
5-15	S. F. Daley	West Indies v Sri Lanka at Colombo (RPS)	2012-13

MOST WICKETS IN A CAREER

W	M		W	M	
106	**92**	**A. Mohammed (West Indies)**	**70**	**98**	**J. L. Gunn (England)**
80	**85**	**E. A. Perry (Australia)**	**68**	**49**	**A. Shrubsole (England)**
75	**73**	**D. Hazell (England)**	**68**	**80**	**S. R. Taylor (West Indies)**
72	68	S. F. Daley (West Indies)	**67**	**79**	**Sana Mir (Pakistan)**

WICKETKEEPING RECORDS

MOST DISMISSALS IN AN INNINGS

5 (1ct, 4st)	Kycia A. Knight	West Indies v Sri Lanka at Colombo (RPS)	2012-13
5 (1ct, 4st)	Batool Fatima	Pakistan v Ireland at Dublin	2013
5 (1ct, 4st)	Batool Fatima	Pakistan v Ireland at Dublin (semi-final)	2013

MOST DISMISSALS IN A CAREER

		M	Ct	St
69	**S. J. Taylor (England)**	**84†**	**22**	**47**
68	**R. H. Priest (New Zealand)**	**68†**	**38**	**30**
57	T. Chetty (South Africa)	68	34	23
57	**M. R. Aguilleira (West Indies)**	**84**	**29**	**28**
55*	**J. L. Gunn (England)**	**98**	**55**	
54*	L. S. Greenway (England)	85	54	
50	Batool Fatima (Pakistan)	45	11	39

* *Catches made by non-wicketkeeper in the field.*

† *Taylor's total includes two matches and Priest's one in the field where they made no catches; Aguilleira's total includes ten matches in the field where she made two catches.*

TEAM RECORDS

HIGHEST INNINGS TOTALS

205-1	South Africa v Netherlands at Potchefstroom	2010-11
191-4	West Indies v Netherlands at Potchefstroom	2010-11
191-4	Australia v Ireland at Sylhet	2013-14
188-3	New Zealand v Sri Lanka at Christchurch	2015-16
187-5	England v Pakistan at Bristol	2016
186-1	Australia v Ireland at Dublin	2015
186-7	New Zealand v South Africa at Taunton	2007
185-2	Australia v Pakistan at Sylhet	2013-14

LOWEST INNINGS TOTALS

44	Bangladesh v Pakistan at Bangkok	2016-17
54	Bangladesh v India at Bangkok	2016-17
57	Sri Lanka v Bangladesh at Guanggong	2012-13
60	Pakistan v England at Taunton	2009
60	New Zealand v England at Whangarei	2014-15

WOMEN'S WORLD TWENTY20 WINNERS

2009	England	2012-13	Australia	2015-16	West Indies
2010	Australia	2013-14	Australia		

BIRTHS AND DEATHS

TEST CRICKETERS

Full list from 1876-77 to January 27, 2018

In the Test career column, dates in italics indicate seasons embracing two different years (i.e. non-English seasons). In these cases, only the first year is given, e.g. *1876* for 1876-77. Some non-English series taking place outside the host country's normal season are dated by a single year.

The Test career figures are complete up to January 27, 2018; the one-day international and Twenty20 international totals up to January 3, 2018. Career figures are for one national team only; those players who have appeared for more than one Test team are listed on page 1402, and for more than one one-day international or Twenty20 international team on page 1404.

The forename by which a player is known is underlined if it is not his first name.

Family relationships are indicated by superscript numbers; where the relationship is not immediately apparent from a shared name, see the notes at the end of this section. (*CY 1889*) signifies that the player was a Wisden Cricketer of the Year in the 1889 Almanack. The 5/10 column indicates instances of a player taking five wickets in a Test innings and ten wickets in a match. O/T signifies number of one-day and Twenty20 internationals played.

[1] *Father and son(s).* [2] *Brothers.* [3] *Grandfather, father and son.* [4] *Grandfather and grandson.* [5] *Great-grandfather and great-grandson.*
† *Excludes matches for another Test team.* ‡ *Excludes matches for another ODI or T20I team.*

ENGLAND (683 players)

	Born	*Died*	*Tests*	*Test Career*	*Runs*	*HS*	*100s*	*Avge*	*Wkts*	*BB*	*5/10*	*Avge*	*Ct/St*	*O/T*
Abel Robert (*CY 1890*)	30.11.1857	10.12.1936	13	1888–1902	744	132*	2	37.20	–	–	–/–	–	13	
Absolom Charles Alfred	7.6.1846	30.7.1889	1	*1878*	58	52	0	29.00	–	–	–/–	–	0	
Adams Christopher John (*CY 2004*)	6.5.1970		5	*1999*	104	31	0	13.00	1	1-42	0/0	59.00	6	5
Afzaal Usman	9.6.1977		3	2001	83	54	0	16.60	1	1-49	0/0	49.00	0	
Agnew Jonathan Philip MBE (*CY 1988*)	4.4.1960		3	1984–1985	10	5	0	10.00	4	2-51	0/0	93.25	0	3
Ali Kabir	24.11.1980		1	2003	10	9	0	5.00	5	3-80	0/0	27.20	0	14
Ali Moeen Munir (*CY 2015*)	18.6.1987		49	2014–*2017*	2,467	155*	5	32.89	133	6-53	4/1	40.24	27	63/22
Allen David Arthur	29.10.1935	24.5.2014	39	*1959*–1966	918	88	0	25.50	122	5-30	4/0	30.97	10	
Allen *Sir* George Oswald Browning ("Gubby")	31.7.1902	29.11.1989	25	1930–*1947*	750	122	1	24.19	81	7-80	5/1	29.37	20	
Allom Maurice James Carrick	23.3.1906	8.4.1995	5	*1929–1930*	14	8*	0	14.00	14	5-38	1/0	18.92	0	
Allott Paul John Walter	14.9.1956		13	1981–1985	213	52*	0	14.20	26	6-61	1/0	41.69	4	13
Ambrose Timothy Raymond	1.12.1982		11	*2007–2008*	447	102	1	29.80	–	–	–/–	–	31	5/1
Ames Leslie Ethelbert George CBE (*CY 1929*)	3.12.1905	27.2.1990	47	1929–*1938*	2,434	149	8	40.56	–	–	–/–	–	74/23	

	Born	Died	Tests	Test Career	Runs	HS	100s	Avge	Wkts	BB	5/10	Avge	Ct/St	O/T
Amiss Dennis Leslie MBE (*CY 1975*)	7.4.1943		50	1966–1977	3,612	262*	11	46.30	–	–	–/–	–	24	18
Anderson James Michael (*CY 2009*)	30.7.1982		134	2003–*2017*	1,128	81	0	9.98	523	7-42	25/3	27.40	84	194/19
Andrew Keith Vincent	15.12.1929	27.12.2010	2	*1954*–1963	29	15	0	9.66	–	–	–/–	–	1	
Ansari Zafar Shahaan	10.12.1991		3	*2016*	49	32	0	9.80	5	2-76	0/0	55.00	1	1
Appleyard Robert MBE (*CY 1952*)	27.6.1924	17.3.2015	9	1954–1956	51	19*	0	17.00	31	5-51	1/0	17.87	4	
Archer Alfred German	6.12.1871	15.7.1935	1	*1898*	31	24*	0	31.00	–	–	–/–	–	0	
Armitage Thomas	25.4.1848	21.9.1922	2	*1876*	33	21	0	11.00	0	0-15	0/0	–	0	
Arnold Edward George	7.11.1876	25.10.1942	10	*1903*–1907	160	40	0	13.33	31	5-37	1/0	25.41	8	
Arnold Geoffrey Graham (*CY 1972*)	3.9.1944		34	1967–1975	421	59	0	12.02	115	6-45	6/0	28.29	9	14
Arnold John	30.11.1907	4.4.1984	1	1931	34	34	0	17.00	–	–	–/–	–	0	
Astill William Ewart (*CY 1933*)	1.3.1888	10.2.1948	9	*1927–1929*	190	40	0	12.66	25	4-58	0/0	34.24	7	
Atherton Michael Andrew OBE (*CY 1991*)	23.3.1968		115	1989–2001	7,728	185*	16	37.69	2	1-20	0/0	151.00	83	54
Athey Charles William Jeffrey	27.9.1957		23	1980–1988	919	123	1	22.97	–	–	–/–	–	13	31
Attewell William (*CY 1892*)	12.6.1861	11.6.1927	10	*1884–1891*	150	43*	0	16.66	28	4-42	0/0	22.35	9	
Bailey Robert John	28.10.1963		4	1988–*1989*	119	43	0	14.87	–	–	–/–	–	0	4
Bailey Trevor Edward CBE (*CY 1950*)	3.12.1923	10.2.2011	61	1949–*1958*	2,290	134*	1	29.74	132	7-34	5/1	29.21	32	
[1] **Bairstow** David Leslie	1.9.1951	5.1.1998	4	1979–*1980*	125	59	0	20.83	–	–	–/–	–	12/1	21
[1] **Bairstow** Jonathan Marc (*CY 2016*)	26.9.1989		50	2012–*2017*	3,130	167*	4	39.12	–	–	–/–	–	129/8	32/23
Bakewell Alfred Harry (*CY 1934*)	2.11.1908	23.1.1983	6	1931–1935	409	107	1	45.44	0	0-8	0/0	–	3	
Balderstone John Christopher	16.11.1940	6.3.2000	2	1976	39	35	0	9.75	1	1-80	0/0	80.00	1	
Ball Jacob Timothy	14.3.1991		4	2016–*2017*	67	31	0	8.37	3	1-47	0/0	114.33	1	16
Ballance Gary Simon (*CY 2015*)	22.11.1989		23	*2013*–2017	1,498	156	4	37.45	0	0-0	0/0	–	22	16
Barber Robert William (*1967*)	26.9.1935		28	1960–1968	1,495	185	1	35.59	42	4-132	0/0	43.00	21	
Barber Wilfred	18.4.1901	10.9.1968	2	1935	83	44	0	20.75	1	1-0	0/0	0.00	1	
Barlow Graham Derek	26.3.1950		3	*1976*–1977	17	7*	0	4.25	–	–	–/–	–	0	6
Barlow Richard Gorton	28.5.1851	31.7.1919	17	*1881–1886*	591	62	0	22.73	34	7-40	3/0	22.55	14	
Barnes Sydney Francis (*CY 1910*)	19.4.1873	26.12.1967	27	*1901–1913*	242	38*	0	8.06	189	9-103	24/7	16.43	12	
Barnes William (*CY 1890*)	27.5.1852	24.3.1899	21	1880–1890	725	134	1	23.38	51	6-28	3/0	15.54	19	
Barnett Charles John (*CY 1937*)	3.7.1910	28.5.1993	20	1933–1948	1,098	129	2	35.41	0	0-1	0/0	–	14	
Barnett Kim John (*CY 1989*)	17.7.1960		4	1988–1989	207	80	0	29.57	0	0-32	0/0	–	1	1
Barratt Fred	12.4.1894	29.1.1947	5	1929–*1929*	28	17	0	9.33	5	1-8	0/0	47.00	2	
Barrington Kenneth Frank (*CY 1960*)	24.11.1930	14.3.1981	82	1955–1968	6,806	256	20	58.67	29	3-4	0/0	44.82	58	
Barton Victor Alexander	6.10.1867	23.3.1906	1	*1891*	23	23	0	23.00	–	–	–/–	–	0	
Bates Willie	19.11.1855	8.1.1900	15	*1881–1886*	656	64	0	27.33	50	7-28	4/1	16.42	9	
Batty Gareth Jon	13.10.1977		9	*2003–2016*	149	38	0	14.90	15	3-55	0/0	60.93	3	10/1
Bean George	7.3.1864	16.3.1923	3	*1891*	92	50	0	18.40	–	–	–/–	–	4	

	Born	*Died*	*Tests*	*Test Career*	*Runs*	*HS*	*100s*	*Avge*	*Wkts*	*BB*	*5/10*	*Avge*	*Ct/St*	*O/T*
Bedser *Sir* Alec Victor CBE (*CY 1947*)	4.7.1918	4.4.2010	51	1946–1955	714	79	0	12.75	236	7-44	15/5	24.89	26	
Bell Ian Ronald MBE (*CY 2008*)	11.4.1982		118	2004–*2015*	7,727	235	22	42.69	1	1-33	0/0	76.00	100	161/8
Benjamin Joseph Emmanuel	2.2.1961		1	1994	0	0	0	0.00	4	4-42	0/0	20.00	0	2
Benson Mark Richard	6.7.1958		1	1986	51	30	0	25.50	–	–	–/–	–	0	1
Berry Robert	29.1.1926	2.12.2006	2	1950	6	4*	0	3.00	9	5-63	1/0	25.33	2	
Bicknell Martin Paul (*CY 2001*)	14.1.1969		4	1993–2003	45	15	0	6.42	14	4-84	0/0	38.78	2	7
Binks James Graham (*CY 1969*)	5.10.1935		2	*1963*	91	55	0	22.75	–	–	–/–	–	8	
Bird Morice Carlos	25.3.1888	9.12.1933	10	*1909–1913*	280	61	0	18.66	8	3-11	0/0	15.00	5	
Birkenshaw Jack MBE	13.11.1940		5	*1972–1973*	148	64	0	21.14	13	5-57	1/0	36.07	3	
Blackwell Ian David	10.6.1978		1	*2005*	4	4	0	4.00	0	0-28	0/0	–	0	34
Blakey Richard John	15.1.1967		2	*1992*	7	6	0	1.75	–	–	–/–	–	2	3
Bligh *Hon.* Ivo Francis Walter	13.3.1859	10.4.1927	4	*1882*	62	19	0	10.33	–	–	–/–	–	7	
Blythe Colin (*CY 1904*)	30.5.1879	8.11.1917	19	*1901–1909*	183	27	0	9.63	100	8-59	9/4	18.63	6	
Board John Henry	23.2.1867	15.4.1924	6	*1898–1905*	108	29	0	10.80	–	–	–/–	–	8/3	
Bolus John Brian	31.1.1934		7	1963–*1963*	496	88	0	41.33	0	0-16	0/0	–	2	
Booth Major William (*CY 1914*)	10.12.1886	1.7.1916	2	*1913*	46	32	0	23.00	7	4-49	0/0	18.57	0	
Bopara Ravinder Singh	4.5.1985		13	2007–2012	575	143	3	31.94	1	1-39	0/0	290.00	6	120/38
Borthwick Scott George	19.4.1990		1	*2013*	5	4	0	2.50	4	3-33	0/0	20.50	2	2/1
Bosanquet Bernard James Tindal (*CY 1905*)	13.10.1877	12.10.1936	7	*1903*–1905	147	27	0	13.36	25	8-107	2/0	24.16	9	
Botham *Sir* Ian Terence OBE (*CY 1978*)	24.11.1955		102	1977–1992	5,200	208	14	33.54	383	8-34	27/4	28.40	120	116
Bowden Montague Parker	1.11.1865	19.2.1892	2	*1888*	25	25	0	12.50	–	–	–/–	–	1	
Bowes William Eric (*CY 1932*)	25.7.1908	4.9.1987	15	1932–1946	28	10*	0	4.66	68	6-33	6/0	22.33	2	
Bowley Edward Henry (*CY 1930*)	6.6.1890	9.7.1974	5	1929–*1929*	252	109	1	36.00	0	0-7	0/0	–	2	
Boycott Geoffrey OBE (*CY 1965*)	21.10.1940		108	1964–*1981*	8,114	246*	22	47.72	7	3-47	0/0	54.57	33	36
Bradley Walter Morris	2.1.1875	19.6.1944	2	1899	23	23*	0	23.00	6	5-67	1/0	38.83	0	
Braund Leonard Charles (*CY 1902*)	18.10.1875	23.12.1955	23	*1901–1907*	987	104	3	25.97	47	8-81	3/0	38.51	39	
Brearley John Michael OBE (*CY 1977*)	28.4.1942		39	1976–1981	1,442	91	0	22.88	–	–	–/–	–	52	25
Brearley Walter (*CY 1909*)	11.3.1876	30.1.1937	4	1905–1912	21	11*	0	7.00	17	5-110	1/0	21.11	0	
Brennan Donald Vincent	10.2.1920	9.1.1985	2	1951	16	16	0	8.00	–	–	–/–	–	0/1	
Bresnan Timothy Thomas (*CY 2012*)	28.2.1985		23	2009–*2013*	575	91	0	26.13	72	5-48	1/0	32.73	8	85/34
Briggs John (*CY 1889*)	3.10.1862	11.1.1902	33	*1884*–1899	815	121	1	18.11	118	8-11	9/4	17.75	12	
[1] **Broad** Brian Christopher	29.9.1957		25	1984–1989	1,661	162	6	39.54	0	0-4	0/0	–	10	34
[1] **Broad** Stuart Christopher John MBE (*CY 2010*)	24.6.1986		114	*2007–2017*	2,956	169	1	20.67	399	8-15	15/2	29.33	36	121/56
Brockwell William (*CY 1895*)	21.1.1865	30.6.1935	7	1893–1899	202	49	0	16.83	5	3-33	0/0	61.80	6	
Bromley-Davenport Hugh Richard	18.8.1870	23.5.1954	4	*1895–1898*	128	84	0	21.33	4	2-46	0/0	24.50	1	
Brookes Dennis (*CY 1957*)	29.10.1915	9.3.2006	1	*1947*	17	10	0	8.50	–	–	–/–	–	1	

	Born	Died	Tests	Test Career	Runs	HS	100s	Avge	Wkts	BB	5/10	Avge	Ct/St	O/T
Brown Alan	17.10.1935		2	*1961*	3	3*	0	–	3	3-27	0/0	50.00	1	
Brown David John	30.1.1942		26	1965–1969	342	44*	0	11.79	79	5-42	2/0	28.31	7	
Brown Frederick Richard MBE (*CY 1933*)	16.12.1910	24.7.1991	22	1931–1953	734	79	0	25.31	45	5-49	1/0	31.06	22	
Brown George	6.10.1887	3.12.1964	7	1921–*1922*	299	84	0	29.90	–	–	–/–	–	9/3	
Brown John Thomas (*CY 1895*)	20.8.1869	4.11.1904	8	*1894*–1899	470	140	1	36.15	0	0-22	0/0	–	7	
Brown Simon John Emmerson	29.6.1969		1	1996	11	10*	0	11.00	2	1-60	0/0	69.00	1	
Buckenham Claude Percival	16.1.1876	23.2.1937	4	*1909*	43	17	0	6.14	21	5-115	1/0	28.23	2	
[1] **Butcher** Alan Raymond (*CY 1991*)	7.1.1954		1	1979	34	20	0	17.00	0	0-9	0/0	–	0	1
[1] **Butcher** Mark Alan	23.8.1972		71	1997–*2004*	4,288	173*	8	34.58	15	4-42	0/0	36.06	61	
Butcher Roland Orlando	14.10.1953		3	*1980*	71	32	0	14.20	–	–	–/–	–	3	3
Butler Harold James	12.3.1913	17.7.1991	2	1947–*1947*	15	15*	0	15.00	12	4-34	0/0	17.91	1	
Butt Henry Rigden	27.12.1865	21.12.1928	3	*1895*	22	13	0	7.33	–	–	–/–	–	1/1	
Buttler Joseph Charles	8.9.1990		18	2014–*2016*	784	85	0	31.36	–	–	–/–	–	54	99/57
Caddick Andrew Richard (*CY 2001*)	21.11.1968		62	1993–*2002*	861	49*	0	10.37	234	7-46	13/1	29.91	21	54
Calthorpe *Hon.* Frederick Somerset Gough-	27.5.1892	19.11.1935	4	*1929*	129	49	0	18.42	1	1-38	0/0	91.00	3	
Capel David John	6.2.1963		15	1987–*1989*	374	98	0	15.58	21	3-88	0/0	50.66	6	23
Carberry Michael Alexander	29.9.1980		6	*2009–2013*	345	60	0	28.75	–	–	–/–	–	7	6/1
Carr Arthur William (*CY 1923*)	21.5.1893	7.2.1963	11	*1922*–1929	237	63	0	19.75	–	–	–/–	–	3	
Carr Donald Bryce OBE (*CY 1960*)	28.12.1926	12.6.2016	2	*1951*	135	76	0	33.75	2	2-84	0/0	70.00	0	
Carr Douglas Ward (*CY 1910*)	17.3.1872	23.3.1950	1	1909	0	0	0	0.00	7	5-146	1/0	40.28	0	
Cartwright Thomas William MBE	22.7.1935	30.4.2007	5	1964–1965	26	9	0	5.20	15	6-94	1/0	36.26	2	
Chapman Arthur Percy Frank (*CY 1919*)	3.9.1900	16.9.1961	26	1924–*1930*	925	121	1	28.90	0	0-10	0/0	–	32	
Charlwood Henry Rupert James	19.12.1846	6.6.1888	2	*1876*	63	36	0	15.75	–	–	–/–	–	0	
Chatterton William	27.12.1861	19.3.1913	1	*1891*	48	48	0	48.00	–	–	–/–	–	0	
Childs John Henry (*CY 1987*)	15.8.1951		2	1988	2	2*	0	–	3	1-13	0/0	61.00	1	
Christopherson Stanley	11.11.1861	6.4.1949	1	1884	17	17	0	17.00	1	1-52	0/0	69.00	0	
Clark Edward Winchester	9.8.1902	28.4.1982	8	1929–1934	36	10	0	9.00	32	5-98	1/0	28.09	0	
Clarke Rikki	29.9.1981		2	*2003*	96	55	0	32.00	4	2-7	0/0	15.00	1	20
Clay John Charles	18.3.1898	11.8.1973	1	1935	–	–	–	–	0	0-30	0/0	–	1	
Close Dennis Brian CBE (*CY 1964*)	24.2.1931	14.9.2015	22	1949–1976	887	70	0	25.34	18	4-35	0/0	29.55	24	3
Coldwell Leonard John	10.1.1933	6.8.1996	7	1962–1964	9	6*	0	4.50	22	6-85	1/0	27.72	1	
Collingwood Paul David MBE (*CY 2007*)	26.5.1976		68	*2003–2010*	4,259	206	10	40.56	17	3-23	0/0	59.88	96	197/35‡
[4] **Compton** Denis Charles Scott CBE (*CY 1939*)	23.5.1918	23.4.1997	78	1937–*1956*	5,807	278	17	50.06	25	5-70	1/0	56.40	49	
[4] **Compton** Nicholas Richard Denis (*CY 2013*)	26.6.1983		16	*2012*–2016	775	117	2	28.70	–	–	–/–	–	7	
Cook Alastair Nathan CBE (*CY 2012*)	25.12.1984		152	*2005–2017*	12,005	294	32	46.35	1	1-6	0/0	7.00	156	92/4
Cook Cecil ("Sam")	23.8.1921	5.9.1996	1	1947	4	4	0	2.00	0	0-40	0/0	–	0	

	Born	Died	Tests	Test Career	Runs	HS	100s	Avge	Wkts	BB	5/10	Avge	Ct/St	O/T
Cook Geoffrey	9.10.1951		7	*1981–1982*	203	66	0	15.61	0	0-4	0/0	–	9	6
Cook Nicholas Grant Billson	17.6.1956		15	1983–1989	179	31	0	8.52	52	6-65	4/1	32.48	5	3
Cope Geoffrey Alan	23.2.1947		3	*1977*	40	22	0	13.33	8	3-102	0/0	34.62	1	2
Copson William Henry (*CY 1937*)	27.4.1908	13.9.1971	3	1939–1947	6	6	0	6.00	15	5-85	1/0	19.80	1	
Cork Dominic Gerald (*CY 1996*)	7.8.1971		37	1995–2002	864	59	0	18.00	131	7-43	5/0	29.81	18	32
Cornford Walter Latter	25.12.1900	6.2.1964	4	*1929*	36	18	0	9.00	–	–	–/–	–	5/3	
Cottam Robert Michael Henry	16.10.1944		4	*1968–1972*	27	13	0	6.75	14	4-50	0/0	23.35	2	
Coventry *Hon.* Charles John	26.2.1867	2.6.1929	2	*1888*	13	12	0	13.00	–	–	–/–	–	0	
Cowans Norman George	17.4.1961		19	*1982*–1985	175	36	0	7.95	51	6-77	2/0	39.27	9	23
[1] **Cowdrey** Christopher Stuart	20.10.1957		6	*1984*–1988	101	38	0	14.42	4	2-65	0/0	77.25	5	3
[1] **Cowdrey** *Lord* [Michael Colin] CBE (*CY 1956*)	24.12.1932	4.12.2000	114	*1954–1974*	7,624	182	22	44.06	0	0-1	0/0	–	120	1
Coxon Alexander	18.1.1916	22.1.2006	1	1948	19	19	0	9.50	3	2-90	0/0	57.33	0	
Crane Mason Sidney	18.02.1997		1	*2017*	6	4	0	3.00	1	1-193	0/0	193.00	0	0/2
Cranston James	9.1.1859	10.12.1904	1	1890	31	16	0	15.50	–	–	–/–	–	1	
Cranston Kenneth	20.10.1917	8.1.2007	8	1947–1948	209	45	0	14.92	18	4-12	0/0	25.61	3	
Crapp John Frederick	14.10.1912	13.2.1981	7	1948–*1948*	319	56	0	29.00	–	–	–/–	–	7	
Crawford John Neville (*CY 1907*)	1.12.1886	2.5.1963	12	*1905–1907*	469	74	0	22.33	39	5-48	3/0	29.48	13	
Crawley John Paul	21.9.1971		37	1994–*2002*	1,800	156*	4	34.61	–	–	–/–	–	29	13
Croft Robert Damien Bale MBE	25.5.1970		21	1996–2001	421	37*	0	16.19	49	5-95	1/0	37.24	10	50
Curran Thomas Kevin	12.03.1995		2	*2017*	66	39	0	33.00	2	1-65	0/0	100.00	0	1/3
Curtis Timothy Stephen	15.1.1960		5	1988–1989	140	41	0	15.55	0	0-7	0/0	–	3	
Cuttell Willis Robert (*CY 1898*)	13.9.1863	9.12.1929	2	*1898*	65	21	0	16.25	6	3-17	0/0	12.16	2	
Dawson Edward William	13.2.1904	4.6.1979	5	*1927–1929*	175	55	0	19.44	–	–	–/–	–	0	
Dawson Liam Andrew	1.3.1990		3	*2016*–2017	84	66*	0	21.00	7	2-34	0/0	42.57	2	1/4
Dawson Richard Kevin James	4.8.1980		7	*2001–2002*	114	19*	0	11.40	11	4-134	0/0	61.54	3	
Dean Harry	13.8.1884	12.3.1957	3	1912	10	8	0	5.00	11	4-19	0/0	13.90	2	
DeFreitas Phillip Anthony Jason (*CY 1992*)	18.2.1966		44	*1986*–1995	934	88	0	14.82	140	7-70	4/0	33.57	14	103
Denness Michael Henry OBE (*CY 1975*)	1.12.1940	19.4.2013	28	1969–1975	1,667	188	4	39.69	–	–	–/–	–	28	12
Denton David (*CY 1906*)	4.7.1874	16.2.1950	11	1905–*1909*	424	104	1	20.19	–	–	–/–	–	8	
Dewes John Gordon	11.10.1926	12.5.2015	5	1948–*1950*	121	67	0	12.10	–	–	–/–	–	0	
Dexter Edward Ralph CBE (*CY 1961*)	15.5.1935		62	1958–1968	4,502	205	9	47.89	66	4-10	0/0	34.93	29	
Dilley Graham Roy	18.5.1959	5.10.2011	41	*1979*–1989	521	56	0	13.35	138	6-38	6/0	29.76	10	36
Dipper Alfred Ernest	9.11.1885	7.11.1945	1	1921	51	40	0	25.50	–	–	–/–	–	0	
Doggart George Hubert Graham OBE	18.7.1925	16.2.2018	2	1950	76	29	0	19.00	–	–	–/–	–	3	
D'Oliveira Basil Lewis CBE (*CY 1967*)	4.10.1931	18.11.2011	44	1966–1972	2,484	158	5	40.06	47	3-46	0/0	39.55	29	4
Dollery Horace Edgar ("Tom") (*CY 1952*)	14.10.1914	20.1.1987	4	1947–1950	72	37	0	10.28	–	–	–/–	–	1	

	Born	Died	Tests	Test Career	Runs	HS	100s	Avge	Wkts	BB	5/10	Avge	Ct/St	O/T
Dolphin Arthur	24.12.1885	23.10.1942	1	*1920*	1	1	0	0.50	–	–	–/–	–	1	
Douglas John William Henry Tyler (*CY 1915*)	3.9.1882	19.12.1930	23	*1911–1924*	962	119	1	29.15	45	5-46	1/0	33.02	9	
Downton Paul Rupert	4.4.1957		30	*1980*–1988	785	74	0	19.62	–	–	–/–	–	70/5	28
Druce Norman Frank (*CY 1898*)	1.1.1875	27.10.1954	5	*1897*	252	64	0	28.00	–	–	–/–	–	5	
Ducat Andrew (*CY 1920*)	16.2.1886	23.7.1942	1	1921	5	3	0	2.50	–	–	–/–	–	1	
Duckett Ben Matthew (*CY 2017*)	17.10.1994		4	*2016*	110	56	0	15.71	–	–	–/–	–	1	3
Duckworth George (*CY 1929*)	9.5.1901	5.1.1966	24	1924–1936	234	39*	0	14.62	–	–	–/–	–	45/15	
Duleepsinhji Kumar Shri (*CY 1930*)	13.6.1905	5.12.1959	12	1929–1931	995	173	3	58.52	0	0-7	0/0	–	10	
Durston Frederick John	11.7.1893	8.4.1965	1	1921	8	6*	0	8.00	5	4-102	0/0	27.20	0	
Ealham Mark Alan	27.8.1969		8	1996–1998	210	53*	0	21.00	17	4-21	0/0	28.70	4	64
Edmonds Philippe-Henri	8.3.1951		51	1975–1987	875	64	0	17.50	125	7-66	2/0	34.18	42	29
Edrich John Hugh MBE (*CY 1966*)	21.6.1937		77	1963–1976	5,138	310*	12	43.54	0	0-6	0/0	–	43	7
Edrich William John (*CY 1940*)	26.3.1916	24.4.1986	39	1938–*1954*	2,440	219	6	40.00	41	4-68	0/0	41.29	39	
Elliott Harry	2.11.1891	2.2.1976	4	*1927–1933*	61	37*	0	15.25	–	–	–/–	–	8/3	
Ellison Richard Mark (*CY 1986*)	21.9.1959		11	1984–1986	202	41	0	13.46	35	6-77	3/1	29.94	2	14
Emburey John Ernest (*CY 1984*)	20.8.1952		64	1978–1995	1,713	75	0	22.53	147	7-78	6/0	38.40	34	61
Emmett George Malcolm	2.12.1912	18.12.1976	1	1948	10	10	0	5.00	–	–	–/–	–	0	
Emmett Thomas	3.9.1841	29.6.1904	7	*1876–1881*	160	48	0	13.33	9	7-68	1/0	31.55	9	
Evans Alfred John	1.5.1889	18.9.1960	1	1921	18	14	0	9.00	–	–	–/–	–	0	
Evans Thomas Godfrey CBE (*CY 1951*)	18.8.1920	3.5.1999	91	1946–1959	2,439	104	2	20.49	–	–	–/–	–	173/46	
Fagg Arthur Edward	18.6.1915	13.9.1977	5	1936–1939	150	39	0	18.75	–	–	–/–	–	5	
Fairbrother Neil Harvey	9.9.1963		10	1987–*1992*	219	83	0	15.64	0	0-9	0/0	–	4	75
Fane Frederick Luther	27.4.1875	27.11.1960	14	*1905–1909*	682	143	1	26.23	–	–	–/–	–	6	
Farnes Kenneth (*CY 1939*)	8.7.1911	20.10.1941	15	1934–*1938*	58	20	0	4.83	60	6-96	3/1	28.65	1	
Farrimond William	23.5.1903	15.11.1979	4	*1930*–1935	116	35	0	16.57	–	–	–/–	–	5/2	
Fender Percy George Herbert (*CY 1915*)	22.8.1892	15.6.1985	13	*1920*–1929	380	60	0	19.00	29	5-90	2/0	40.86	14	
Ferris John James	21.5.1867	17.11.1900	1†	*1891*	16	16	0	16.00	13	7-37	2/1	7.00	0	
Fielder Arthur (*CY 1907*)	19.7.1877	30.8.1949	6	*1903–1907*	78	20	0	11.14	26	6-82	1/0	27.34	4	
Finn Steven Thomas	4.4.1989		36	*2009–2016*	279	56	0	11.16	125	6-79	5/0	30.40	8	69/21
Fishlock Laurence Barnard (*CY 1947*)	2.1.1907	25.6.1986	4	1936–*1946*	47	19*	0	11.75	–	–	–/–	–	1	
Flavell John Alfred (*CY 1965*)	15.5.1929	25.2.2004	4	1961–1964	31	14	0	7.75	7	2-65	0/0	52.42	0	
Fletcher Keith William Robert OBE (*CY 1974*)	20.5.1944		59	1968–*1981*	3,272	216	7	39.90	2	1-6	0/0	96.50	54	24
Flintoff Andrew MBE (*CY 2004*)	6.12.1977		78§	1998–2009	3,795	167	5	31.89	219	5-58	3/0	33.34	52	138‡/7
Flowers Wilfred	7.12.1856	1.11.1926	8	*1884*–1893	254	56	0	18.14	14	5-46	1/0	21.14	2	
Ford Francis Gilbertson Justice	14.12.1866	7.2.1940	5	*1894*	168	48	0	18.66	1	1-47	0/0	129.00	5	

§ *Flintoff's figures exclude 50 runs and seven wickets for the ICC World XI v Australia in the Super Series Test in 2005-06.*

	Born	*Died*	*Tests*	*Test Career*	*Runs*	*HS*	*100s*	*Avge*	*Wkts*	*BB*	*5/10*	*Avge*	*Ct/St*	*O/T*
Foster Frank Rowbotham (*CY 1912*)	31.1.1889	3.5.1958	11	*1911*–1912	330	71	0	23.57	45	6-91	4/0	20.57	11	
Foster James Savin	15.4.1980		7	*2001–2002*	226	48	0	25.11	–	–	–/–	–	17/1	11/5
Foster Neil Alan (*CY 1988*)	6.5.1962		29	1983–1993	446	39	0	11.73	88	8-107	5/1	32.85	7	48
Foster Reginald Erskine ("Tip") (*CY 1900*)	16.4.1878	13.5.1914	8	*1903*–1907	602	287	1	46.30	–	–	–/–	–	13	
Fothergill Arnold James	26.8.1854	1.8.1932	2	*1888*	33	32	0	16.50	8	4-19	0/0	11.25	0	
Fowler Graeme	20.4.1957		21	1982–*1984*	1,307	201	3	35.32	0	0-0	0/0	–	10	26
Fraser Angus Robert Charles MBE (*CY 1996*)	8.8.1965		46	1989–*1998*	388	32	0	7.46	177	8-53	13/2	27.32	9	42
Freeman Alfred Percy ("Tich") (*CY 1923*)	17.5.1888	28.1.1965	12	*1924*–1929	154	50*	0	14.00	66	7-71	5/3	25.86	4	
French Bruce Nicholas	13.8.1959		16	1986–*1987*	308	59	0	18.11	–	–	–/–	–	38/1	13
Fry Charles Burgess (*CY 1895*)	25.4.1872	7.9.1956	26	*1895*–1912	1,223	144	2	32.18	0	0-3	0/0	–	17	
Gallian Jason Edward Riche	25.6.1971		3	1995–*1995*	74	28	0	12.33	0	0-6	0/0	–	1	
Gatting Michael William OBE (*CY 1984*)	6.6.1957		79	*1977–1994*	4,409	207	10	35.55	4	1-14	0/0	79.25	59	92
Gay Leslie Hewitt	24.3.1871	1.11.1949	1	*1894*	37	33	0	18.50	–	–	–/–	–	3/1	
Geary George (*CY 1927*)	9.7.1893	6.3.1981	14	1924–1934	249	66	0	15.56	46	7-70	4/1	29.41	13	
Gibb Paul Antony	11.7.1913	7.12.1977	8	*1938–1946*	581	120	2	44.69	–	–	–/–	–	3/1	
Giddins Edward Simon Hunter	20.7.1971		4	1999–2000	10	7	0	2.50	12	5-15	1/0	20.00	0	
Gifford Norman MBE (*CY 1975*)	30.3.1940		15	1964–1973	179	25*	0	16.27	33	5-55	1/0	31.09	8	2
Giles Ashley Fraser MBE (*CY 2005*)	19.3.1973		54	1998–*2006*	1,421	59	0	20.89	143	5-57	5/0	40.60	33	62
[2] **Gilligan** Alfred Herbert Harold	29.6.1896	5.5.1978	4	*1929*	71	32	0	17.75	–	–	–/–	–	0	
[2] **Gilligan** Arthur Edward Robert (*CY 1924*)	23.12.1894	5.9.1976	11	*1922–1924*	209	39*	0	16.07	36	6-7	2/1	29.05	3	
Gimblett Harold (*CY 1953*)	19.10.1914	30.3.1978	3	1936–1939	129	67*	0	32.25	–	–	–/–	–	1	
Gladwin Clifford	3.4.1916	9.4.1988	8	1947–1949	170	51*	0	28.33	15	3-21	0/0	38.06	2	
Goddard Thomas William John (*CY 1938*)	1.10.1900	22.5.1966	8	1930–1939	13	8	0	6.50	22	6-29	1/0	26.72	3	
Gooch Graham Alan OBE (*CY 1980*)	23.7.1953		118	1975–*1994*	8,900	333	20	42.58	23	3-39	0/0	46.47	103	125
Gough Darren (*CY 1999*)	18.9.1970		58	1994–2003	855	65	0	12.57	229	6-42	9/0	28.39	13	158‡/2
Gover Alfred Richard MBE (*CY 1937*)	29.2.1908	7.10.2001	4	1936–1946	2	2*	0	–	8	3-85	0/0	44.87	1	
Gower David Ivon OBE (*CY 1979*)	1.4.1957		117	1978–1992	8,231	215	18	44.25	1	1-1	0/0	20.00	74	114
[2] **Grace** Edward Mills	28.11.1841	20.5.1911	1	1880	36	36	0	18.00	–	–	–/–	–	1	
[2] **Grace** George Frederick	13.12.1850	22.9.1880	1	1880	0	0	0	0.00	–	–	–/–	–	2	
[2] **Grace** William Gilbert (*CY 1896*)	18.7.1848	23.10.1915	22	1880–1899	1,098	170	2	32.29	9	2-12	0/0	26.22	39	
Graveney Thomas William OBE (*CY 1953*)	16.6.1927	3.11.2015	79	1951–1969	4,882	258	11	44.38	1	1-34	0/0	167.00	80	
Greenhough Thomas	9.11.1931	15.9.2009	4	1959–1960	4	2	0	1.33	16	5-35	1/0	22.31	1	
Greenwood Andrew	20.8.1847	12.2.1889	2	*1876*	77	49	0	19.25	–	–	–/–	–	2	
[2] **Greig** Anthony William (*CY 1975*)	6.10.1946	29.12.2012	58	1972–1977	3,599	148	8	40.43	141	8-86	6/2	32.20	87	22
[2] **Greig** Ian Alexander	8.12.1955		2	1982	26	14	0	6.50	4	4-53	0/0	28.50	0	
Grieve Basil Arthur Firebrace	28.5.1864	19.11.1917	2	*1888*	40	14*	0	40.00	–	–	–/–	–	0	

	Born	*Died*	*Tests*	*Test Career*	*Runs*	*HS*	*100s*	*Avge*	*Wkts*	*BB*	*5/10*	*Avge*	*Ct/St*	*O/T*
Griffith Stewart Cathie CBE ("Billy")	16.6.1914	7.4.1993	3	*1947–1948*	157	140	1	31.40	–	–	–/–	–	5	
[2]**Gunn** George (*CY 1914*)	13.6.1879	29.6.1958	15	*1907–1929*	1,120	122*	2	40.00	0	0-8	0/0	–	15	
[2]**Gunn** John Richmond (*CY 1904*)	19.7.1876	21.8.1963	6	*1901*–1905	85	24	0	10.62	18	5-76	1/0	21.50	3	
Gunn William (*CY 1890*)	4.12.1858	29.1.1921	11	*1886*–1899	392	102*	1	21.77	–	–	–/–	–	5	
Habib Aftab	7.2.1972		2	1999	26	19	0	8.66	–	–	–/–	–	0	
Haig Nigel Esmé	12.12.1887	27.10.1966	5	1921–*1929*	126	47	0	14.00	13	3-73	0/0	34.46	4	
Haigh Schofield (*CY 1901*)	19.3.1871	27.2.1921	11	*1898*–1912	113	25	0	7.53	24	6-11	1/0	25.91	8	
Hales Alexander Daniel	3.1.1989		11	*2015*–2016	573	94	0	27.28	0	0-2	0/0	–	8	53/48
Hallows Charles (*CY 1928*)	4.4.1895	10.11.1972	2	1921–1928	42	26	0	42.00	–	–	–/–	–	0	
Hameed Haseeb	17.1.1997		3	*2016*	219	82	0	43.80	–	–	–/–	–	4	
Hamilton Gavin Mark	16.9.1974		1	*1999*	0	0	0	0.00	0	0-63	0/0	–	0	0‡
Hammond Walter Reginald (*CY 1928*)	19.6.1903	1.7.1965	85	*1927–1946*	7,249	336*	22	58.45	83	5-36	2/0	37.80	110	
Hampshire John Harry	10.2.1941	1.3.2017	8	1969–1975	403	107	1	26.86	–	–	–/–	–	9	3
Hardinge Harold Thomas William ("Wally") (*CY 1915*)	25.2.1886	8.5.1965	1	1921	30	25	0	15.00	–	–	–/–	–	0	
[1]**Hardstaff** Joseph snr	9.11.1882	2.4.1947	5	*1907*	311	72	0	31.10	–	–	–/–	–	1	
[1]**Hardstaff** Joseph jnr (*CY 1938*)	3.7.1911	1.1.1990	23	1935–1948	1,636	205*	4	46.74	–	–	–/–	–	9	
Harmison Stephen James MBE (*CY 2005*)	23.10.1978		62§	2002–2009	742	49*	0	12.16	222	7-12	8/1	31.94	7	58/2
Harris *Lord* [George Robert Canning]	3.2.1851	24.3.1932	4	*1878*–1884	145	52	0	29.00	0	0-14	0/0	–	2	
Hartley John Cabourn	15.11.1874	8.3.1963	2	*1905*	15	9	0	3.75	1	1-62	0/0	115.00	2	
Hawke *Lord* [Martin Bladen] (*CY 1909*)	16.8.1860	10.10.1938	5	*1895–1898*	55	30	0	7.85	–	–	–/–	–	3	
Hayes Ernest George (*CY 1907*)	6.11.1876	2.12.1953	5	*1905*–1912	86	35	0	10.75	1	1-28	0/0	52.00	2	
Hayes Frank Charles	6.12.1946		9	1973–1976	244	106*	1	15.25	–	–	–/–	–	7	6
Hayward Thomas Walter (*CY 1895*)	29.3.1871	19.7.1939	35	*1895*–1909	1,999	137	3	34.46	14	4-22	0/0	36.71	19	
[3]**Headley** Dean Warren	27.1.1970		15	1997–1999	186	31	0	8.45	60	6-60	1/0	27.85	7	13
[2]**Hearne** Alec (*CY 1894*)	22.7.1863	16.5.1952	1	*1891*	9	9	0	9.00	–	–	–/–	–	1	
[1,2]**Hearne** Frank	23.11.1858	14.7.1949	2†	*1888*	47	27	0	23.50	–	–	–/–	–	1	
[2]**Hearne** George Gibbons	7.7.1856	13.2.1932	1	*1891*	0	0	0	0.00	–	–	–/–	–	0	
Hearne John Thomas (*CY 1892*)	3.5.1867	17.4.1944	12	*1891*–1899	126	40	0	9.00	49	6-41	4/1	22.08	4	
Hearne John William (*CY 1912*)	11.2.1891	14.9.1965	24	*1911*–1926	806	114	1	26.00	30	5-49	1/0	48.73	13	
Hegg Warren Kevin	23.2.1968		2	*1998*	30	15	0	7.50	–	–	–/–	–	8	
Hemmings Edward Ernest	20.2.1949		16	1982–*1990*	383	95	0	22.52	43	6-58	1/0	42.44	5	33
Hendren Elias Henry ("Patsy") (*CY 1920*)	5.2.1889	4.10.1962	51	*1920–1934*	3,525	205*	7	47.63	1	1-27	0/0	31.00	33	
Hendrick Michael (*CY 1978*)	22.10.1948		30	1974–1981	128	15	0	6.40	87	4-28	0/0	25.83	25	22
Heseltine Christopher	26.11.1869	13.6.1944	2	*1895*	18	18	0	9.00	5	5-38	1/0	16.80	3	

§ *Harmison's figures exclude one run and four wickets for the ICC World XI v Australia in the Super Series Test in 2005-06.*

	Born	*Died*	*Tests*	*Test Career*	*Runs*	*HS*	*100s*	*Avge*	*Wkts*	*BB*	*5/10*	*Avge*	*Ct/St*	*O/T*
Hick Graeme Ashley MBE (*CY 1987*)	23.5.1966		65	1991–*2000*	3,383	178	6	31.32	23	4-126	0/0	56.78	90	120
Higgs Kenneth (*CY 1968*)	14.1.1937	7.9.2016	15	1965–1968	185	63	0	11.56	71	6-91	2/0	20.74	4	
Hill Allen	14.11.1843	28.8.1910	2	*1876*	101	49	0	50.50	7	4-27	0/0	18.57	1	
Hill Arthur James Ledger	26.7.1871	6.9.1950	3	*1895*	251	124	1	62.75	4	4-8	0/0	2.00	1	
Hilton Malcolm Jameson (*CY 1957*)	2.8.1928	8.7.1990	4	1950–*1951*	37	15	0	7.40	14	5-61	1/0	34.07	1	
Hirst George Herbert (*CY 1901*)	7.9.1871	10.5.1954	24	*1897*–1909	790	85	0	22.57	59	5-48	3/0	30.00	18	
Hitch John William (*CY 1914*)	7.5.1886	7.7.1965	7	*1911*–1921	103	51*	0	14.71	7	2-31	0/0	46.42	4	
Hobbs *Sir* John Berry (*CY 1909*)	16.12.1882	21.12.1963	61	*1907*–1930	5,410	211	15	56.94	1	1-19	0/0	165.00	17	
Hobbs Robin Nicholas Stuart	8.5.1942		7	1967–1971	34	15*	0	6.80	12	3-25	0/0	40.08	8	
Hoggard Matthew James MBE (*CY 2006*)	31.12.1976		67	2000–*2007*	473	38	0	7.27	248	7-61	7/1	30.50	24	26
Hollies William Eric (*CY 1955*)	5.6.1912	16.4.1981	13	*1934*–1950	37	18*	0	5.28	44	7-50	5/0	30.27	2	
[2] **Hollioake** Adam John (*CY 2003*)	5.9.1971		4	1997–*1997*	65	45	0	10.83	2	2-31	0/0	33.50	4	35
[2] **Hollioake** Benjamin Caine	11.11.1977	23.3.2002	2	1997–1998	44	28	0	11.00	4	2-105	0/0	49.75	2	20
Holmes Errol Reginald Thorold (*CY 1936*)	21.8.1905	16.8.1960	5	*1934*–1935	114	85*	0	16.28	2	1-10	0/0	38.00	4	
Holmes Percy (*CY 1920*)	25.11.1886	3.9.1971	7	1921–1932	357	88	0	27.46	–	–	–/–	–	3	
Hone Leland	30.1.1853	31.12.1896	1	*1878*	13	7	0	6.50	–	–	–/–	–	2	
Hopwood John Leonard	30.10.1903	15.6.1985	2	1934	12	8	0	6.00	0	0-16	0/0	–	0	
Hornby Albert Neilson ("Monkey")	10.2.1847	17.12.1925	3	*1878*–1884	21	9	0	3.50	1	1-0	0/0	0.00	0	
Horton Martin John	21.4.1934	3.4.2011	2	1959	60	58	0	30.00	2	2-24	0/0	29.50	2	
Howard Nigel David	18.5.1925	31.5.1979	4	*1951*	86	23	0	17.20	–	–	–/–	–	4	
Howell Henry	29.11.1890	9.7.1932	5	*1920*–1924	15	5	0	7.50	7	4-115	0/0	79.85	0	
Howorth Richard	26.4.1909	2.4.1980	5	1947–*1947*	145	45*	0	18.12	19	6-124	1/0	33.42	2	
Humphries Joseph	19.5.1876	7.5.1946	3	*1907*	44	16	0	8.80	–	–	–/–	–	7	
Hunter Joseph	3.8.1855	4.1.1891	5	*1884*	93	39*	0	18.60	–	–	–/–	–	8/3	
Hussain Nasser OBE (*CY 2003*)	28.3.1968		96	*1989*–2004	5,764	207	14	37.18	0	0-15	0/0	–	67	88
Hutchings Kenneth Lotherington (*CY 1907*)	7.12.1882	3.9.1916	7	*1907*–1909	341	126	1	28.41	1	1-5	0/0	81.00	9	
[1] **Hutton** *Sir* Leonard (*CY 1938*)	23.6.1916	6.9.1990	79	1937–*1954*	6,971	364	19	56.67	3	1-2	0/0	77.33	57	
[1] **Hutton** Richard Anthony	6.9.1942		5	1971	219	81	0	36.50	9	3-72	0/0	28.55	9	
Iddon John	8.1.1902	17.4.1946	5	*1934*–1935	170	73	0	28.33	0	0-3	0/0	–	0	
Igglesden Alan Paul	8.10.1964		3	1989–*1993*	6	3*	0	3.00	6	2-91	0/0	54.83	1	4
Ikin John Thomas	7.3.1918	15.9.1984	18	1946–1955	606	60	0	20.89	3	1-38	0/0	118.00	31	
Illingworth Raymond CBE (*CY 1960*)	8.6.1932		61	1958–1973	1,836	113	2	23.24	122	6-29	3/0	31.20	45	3
Illingworth Richard Keith	23.8.1963		9	1991–*1995*	128	28	0	18.28	19	4-96	0/0	32.36	5	25
Ilott Mark Christopher	27.8.1970		5	1993–*1995*	28	15	0	7.00	12	3-48	0/0	45.16	0	
Insole Douglas John CBE (*CY 1956*)	18.4.1926	5.8.2017	9	1950–1957	408	110*	1	27.20	–	–	–/–	–	8	
Irani Ronald Charles	26.10.1971		3	1996–1999	86	41	0	17.20	3	1-22	0/0	37.33	2	31

	Born	Died	Tests	Test Career	Runs	HS	100s	Avge	Wkts	BB	5/10	Avge	Ct/St	O/T
Jackman Robin David (*CY 1981*)	13.8.1945		4	*1980*–1982	42	17	0	7.00	14	4-110	0/0	31.78	0	15
Jackson *Sir* Francis Stanley (*CY 1894*)	21.11.1870	9.3.1947	20	1893–1905	1,415	144*	5	48.79	24	5-52	1/0	33.29	10	
Jackson Herbert Leslie (*CY 1959*)	5.4.1921	25.4.2007	2	1949–1961	15	8	0	15.00	7	2-26	0/0	22.14	1	
James Stephen Peter	7.9.1967		2	1998	71	36	0	17.75	–	–	–/–	–	0	
Jameson John Alexander	30.6.1941		4	1971–*1973*	214	82	0	26.75	1	1-17	0/0	17.00	0	3
Jardine Douglas Robert (*CY 1928*)	23.10.1900	18.6.1958	22	1928–*1933*	1,296	127	1	48.00	0	0-10	0/0	–	26	
Jarvis Paul William	29.6.1965		9	*1987–1992*	132	29*	0	10.15	21	4-107	0/0	45.95	2	16
Jenkins Roland Oliver (*CY 1950*)	24.11.1918	22.7.1995	9	*1948*–1952	198	39	0	18.00	32	5-116	1/0	34.31	4	
Jennings Keaton Kent	19.6.1992		6	*2016*–2017	294	112	1	24.50	0	0-2	0/0	–	3	
Jessop Gilbert Laird (*CY 1898*)	19.5.1874	11.5.1955	18	1899–1912	569	104	1	21.88	10	4-68	0/0	35.40	11	
Johnson Richard Leonard	29.12.1974		3	2003–*2003*	59	26	0	14.75	16	6-33	2/0	17.18	0	10
Jones Arthur Owen	16.8.1872	21.12.1914	12	1899–1909	291	34	0	13.85	3	3-73	0/0	44.33	15	
Jones Geraint Owen MBE	14.7.1976		34	*2003–2006*	1,172	100	1	23.91	–	–	–/–	–	128/5	49‡/2
[1] **Jones** Ivor Jeffrey	10.12.1941		15	*1963–1967*	38	16	0	4.75	44	6-118	1/0	40.20	4	
[1] **Jones** Simon Philip MBE (*CY 2006*)	25.12.1978		18	2002–2005	205	44	0	15.76	59	6-53	3/0	28.23	4	8
Jordan Christopher James	4.10.1988		8	2014–*2014*	180	35	0	18.00	21	4-18	0/0	35.80	14	31/26
Jupp Henry	19.11.1841	8.4.1889	2	*1876*	68	63	0	17.00	–	–	–/–	–	2	
Jupp Vallance William Crisp (*CY 1928*)	27.3.1891	9.7.1960	8	1921–1928	208	38	0	17.33	28	4-37	0/0	22.00	5	
Keeton William Walter (*CY 1940*)	30.4.1905	10.10.1980	2	1934–1939	57	25	0	14.25	–	–	–/–	–	0	
Kennedy Alexander Stuart (*CY 1933*)	24.1.1891	15.11.1959	5	*1922*	93	41*	0	15.50	31	5-76	2/0	19.32	5	
Kenyon Donald	15.5.1924	12.11.1996	8	*1951*–1955	192	87	0	12.80	–	–	–/–	–	5	
Kerrigan Simon Christopher	10.5.1989		1	2013	1	1*	0	–	0	0-53	0/0	–	0	
Key Robert William Trevor (*CY 2005*)	12.5.1979		15	2002–*2004*	775	221	1	31.00	–	–	–/–	–	11	5/1
Khan Amjad	14.10.1980		1	*2008*	–	–	–	–	1	1-111	0/0	122.00	0	0/1
Killick *Rev.* Edgar Thomas	9.5.1907	18.5.1953	2	1929	81	31	0	20.25	–	–	–/–	–	2	
Kilner Roy (*CY 1924*)	17.10.1890	5.4.1928	9	1924–1926	233	74	0	33.28	24	4-51	0/0	30.58	6	
King John Herbert	16.4.1871	18.11.1946	1	1909	64	60	0	32.00	1	1-99	0/0	99.00	0	
Kinneir Septimus Paul (*CY 1912*)	13.5.1871	16.10.1928	1	*1911*	52	30	0	26.00	–	–	–/–	–	0	
Kirtley Robert James	10.1.1975		4	2003–*2003*	32	12	0	5.33	19	6-34	1/0	29.52	3	11/1
Knight Albert Ernest (*CY 1904*)	8.10.1872	25.4.1946	3	*1903*	81	70*	0	16.20	–	–	–/–	–	1	
Knight Barry Rolfe	18.2.1938		29	*1961*–1969	812	127	2	26.19	70	4-38	0/0	31.75	14	
Knight Donald John (*CY 1915*)	12.5.1894	5.1.1960	2	1921	54	38	0	13.50	–	–	–/–	–	1	
Knight Nicholas Verity	28.11.1969		17	1995–2001	719	113	1	23.96	–	–	–/–	–	26	100
Knott Alan Philip Eric (*CY 1970*)	9.4.1946		95	1967–1981	4,389	135	5	32.75	–	–	–/–	–	250/19	20
Knox Neville Alexander (*CY 1907*)	10.10.1884	3.3.1935	2	1907	24	8*	0	8.00	3	2-39	0/0	35.00	0	
Laker James Charles (*CY 1952*)	9.2.1922	23.4.1986	46	*1947–1958*	676	63	0	14.08	193	10-53	9/3	21.24	12	

	Born	*Died*	*Tests*	*Test Career*	*Runs*	*HS*	*100s*	*Avge*	*Wkts*	*BB*	*5/10*	*Avge*	*Ct/St*	*O/T*
Lamb Allan Joseph (*CY 1981*)	20.6.1954		79	1982–1992	4,656	142	14	36.09	1	1-6	0/0	23.00	75	122
Langridge James (*CY 1932*)	10.7.1906	10.9.1966	8	1933–1946	242	70	0	26.88	19	7-56	2/0	21.73	6	
Larkins Wayne	22.11.1953		13	*1979–1990*	493	64	0	20.54	–	–	–/–	–	8	25
Larter John David Frederick	24.4.1940		10	1962–1965	16	10	0	3.20	37	5-57	2/0	25.43	5	
Larwood Harold MBE (*CY 1927*)	14.11.1904	22.7.1995	21	1926–*1932*	485	98	0	19.40	78	6-32	4/1	28.35	15	
Lathwell Mark Nicholas	26.12.1971		2	1993	78	33	0	19.50	–	–	–/–	–	0	
Lawrence David Valentine ("Syd")	28.1.1964		5	1988–*1991*	60	34	0	10.00	18	5-106	1/0	37.55	0	1
Leadbeater Edric	15.8.1927	17.4.2011	2	*1951*	40	38	0	20.00	2	1-38	0/0	109.00	3	
Lee Henry William	26.10.1890	21.4.1981	1	*1930*	19	18	0	9.50	–	–	–/–	–	0	
Lees Walter Scott (*CY 1906*)	25.12.1875	10.9.1924	5	*1905*	66	25*	0	11.00	26	6-78	2/0	17.96	2	
Legge Geoffrey Bevington	26.1.1903	21.11.1940	5	*1927–1929*	299	196	1	49.83	0	0-34	0/0	–	1	
Leslie Charles Frederick Henry	8.12.1861	12.2.1921	4	*1882*	106	54	0	15.14	4	3-31	0/0	11.00	1	
Lever John Kenneth MBE (*CY 1979*)	24.2.1949		21	*1976*–1986	306	53	0	11.76	73	7-46	3/1	26.72	11	22
Lever Peter	17.9.1940		17	*1970*–1975	350	88*	0	21.87	41	6-38	2/0	36.80	11	10
Leveson Gower *Sir* Henry Dudley Gresham	8.5.1873	1.2.1954	3	*1909*	95	31	0	23.75	–	–	–/–	–	1	
Levett William Howard Vincent ("Hopper")	25.1.1908	1.12.1995	1	*1933*	7	5	0	7.00	–	–	–/–	–	3	
Lewis Anthony Robert CBE	6.7.1938		9	*1972*–1973	457	125	1	32.64	–	–	–/–	–	0	
Lewis Clairmonte Christopher	14.2.1968		32	1990–1996	1,105	117	1	23.02	93	6-111	3/0	37.52	25	53
Lewis Jonathan	26.8.1975		1	2006	27	20	0	13.50	3	3-68	0/0	40.66	0	13/2
Leyland Maurice (*CY 1929*)	20.7.1900	1.1.1967	41	1928–1938	2,764	187	9	46.06	6	3-91	0/0	97.50	13	
Lilley Arthur Frederick Augustus ("Dick") (*CY 1897*)	28.11.1866	17.11.1929	35	1896–1909	903	84	0	20.52	1	1-23	0/0	23.00	70/22	
Lillywhite James	23.2.1842	25.10.1929	2	*1876*	16	10	0	8.00	8	4-70	0/0	15.75	1	
Lloyd David	18.3.1947		9	1974–*1974*	552	214*	1	42.46	0	0-4	0/0	–	11	8
Lloyd Timothy Andrew	5.11.1956		1	1984	10	10*	0	–	–	–	–/–	–	0	3
Loader Peter James (*CY 1958*)	25.10.1929	15.3.2011	13	1954–*1958*	76	17	0	5.84	39	6-36	1/0	22.51	2	
Lock Graham Anthony Richard (*CY 1954*)	5.7.1929	30.3.1995	49	1952–*1967*	742	89	0	13.74	174	7-35	9/3	25.58	59	
Lockwood William Henry (*CY 1899*)	25.3.1868	26.4.1932	12	1893–1902	231	52*	0	17.76	43	7-71	5/1	20.53	4	
Lohmann George Alfred (*CY 1889*)	2.6.1865	1.12.1901	18	1886–1896	213	62*	0	8.87	112	9-28	9/5	10.75	28	
Lowson Frank Anderson	1.7.1925	8.9.1984	7	1951–1955	245	68	0	18.84	–	–	–/–	–	5	
Lucas Alfred Perry	20.2.1857	12.10.1923	5	*1878*–1884	157	55	0	19.62	0	0-23	0/0	–	1	
Luckhurst Brian William (*CY 1971*)	5.2.1939	1.3.2005	21	*1970–1974*	1,298	131	4	36.05	1	1-9	0/0	32.00	14	3
Lyth Adam (*CY 2015*)	25.9.1987		7	2015	265	107	1	20.38	0	0-0	0/0	–	8	
Lyttelton *Hon.* Alfred	7.2.1857	5.7.1913	4	1880–1884	94	31	0	15.66	4	4-19	0/0	4.75	2	
Macaulay George Gibson (*CY 1924*)	7.12.1897	13.12.1940	8	*1922*–1933	112	76	0	18.66	24	5-64	1/0	27.58	5	
MacBryan John Crawford William (*CY 1925*)	22.7.1892	14.7.1983	1	1924	–	–	–	–	–	–	–/–	–	0	

	Born	Died	Tests	Test Career	Runs	HS	100s	Avge	Wkts	BB	5/10	Avge	Ct/St	O/T
McCague Martin John	24.5.1969		3	1993–*1994*	21	11	0	4.20	6	4-121	0/0	65.00	1	
McConnon James Edward	21.6.1922	26.1.2003	2	1954	18	11	0	9.00	4	3-19	0/0	18.50	4	
McGahey Charles Percy (*CY 1902*)	12.2.1871	10.1.1935	2	*1901*	38	18	0	9.50	–	–	–/–	–	1	
McGrath Anthony	6.10.1975		4	2003	201	81	0	40.20	4	3-16	0/0	14.00	3	14
MacGregor Gregor (*CY 1891*)	31.8.1869	20.8.1919	8	1890–1893	96	31	0	12.00	–	–	–/–	–	14/3	
McIntyre Arthur John William (*CY 1958*)	14.5.1918	26.12.2009	3	1950–1955	19	7	0	3.16	–	–	–/–	–	8	
MacKinnon Francis Alexander	9.4.1848	27.2.1947	1	*1878*	5	5	0	2.50	–	–	–/–	–	0	
MacLaren Archibald Campbell (*CY 1895*)	1.12.1871	17.11.1944	35	*1894*–1909	1,931	140	5	33.87	–	–	–/–	–	29	
McMaster Joseph Emile Patrick	16.3.1861	7.6.1929	1	*1888*	0	0	0	0.00	–	–	–/–	–	0	
Maddy Darren Lee	23.5.1974		3	1999–*1999*	46	24	0	11.50	0	0-40	0/0	–	4	8/4
Mahmood Sajid Iqbal	21.12.1981		8	2006–*2006*	81	34	0	8.10	20	4-22	0/0	38.10	0	26/4
Makepeace Joseph William Henry	22.8.1881	19.12.1952	4	*1920*	279	117	1	34.87	–	–	–/–	–	0	
Malan Dawid Johannes	03.09.1987		10	2017–*2017*	572	140	1	33.64	0	0-7	0/0	–	4	0/1
Malcolm Devon Eugene (*CY 1995*)	22.2.1963		40	1989–1997	236	29	0	6.05	128	9-57	5/2	37.09	7	10
Mallender Neil Alan	13.8.1961		2	1992	8	4	0	2.66	10	5-50	1/0	21.50	0	
[1] **Mann** Francis George CBE	6.9.1917	8.8.2001	7	*1948*–1949	376	136*	1	37.60	–	–	–/–	–	3	
[1] **Mann** Francis Thomas	3.3.1888	6.10.1964	5	*1922*	281	84	0	35.12	–	–	–/–	–	4	
Marks Victor James	25.6.1955		6	1982–*1983*	249	83	0	27.66	11	3-78	0/0	44.00	0	34
Marriott Charles Stowell ("Father")	14.9.1895	13.10.1966	1	1933	0	0	0	0.00	11	6-59	2/1	8.72	1	
Martin Frederick (*CY 1892*)	12.10.1861	13.12.1921	2	1890–*1891*	14	13	0	7.00	14	6-50	2/1	10.07	2	
Martin John William	16.2.1917	4.1.1987	1	1947	26	26	0	13.00	1	1-111	0/0	129.00	0	
Martin Peter James	15.11.1968		8	1995–1997	115	29	0	8.84	17	4-60	0/0	34.11	6	20
Mason John Richard (*CY 1898*)	26.3.1874	15.10.1958	5	*1897*	129	32	0	12.90	2	1-8	0/0	74.50	3	
Matthews Austin David George	3.5.1904	29.7.1977	1	1937	2	2*	0	–	2	1-13	0/0	32.50	1	
May Peter Barker Howard CBE (*CY 1952*)	31.12.1929	27.12.1994	66	1951–1961	4,537	285*	13	46.77	–	–	–/–	–	42	
Maynard Matthew Peter (*CY 1998*)	21.3.1966		4	1988–*1993*	87	35	0	10.87	–	–	–/–	–	3	14
Mead Charles Philip (*CY 1912*)	9.3.1887	26.3.1958	17	*1911–1928*	1,185	182*	4	49.37	–	–	–/–	–	4	
Mead Walter (*CY 1904*)	1.4.1868	18.3.1954	1	1899	7	7	0	3.50	1	1-91	0/0	91.00	1	
Midwinter William Evans	19.6.1851	3.12.1890	4†	*1881*	95	36	0	13.57	10	4-81	0/0	27.20	5	
Milburn Colin ("Ollie") (*CY 1967*)	23.10.1941	28.2.1990	9	1966–*1968*	654	139	2	46.71	–	–	–/–	–	7	
Miller Audley Montague	19.10.1869	26.6.1959	1	*1895*	24	20*	0	–	–	–	–/–	–	0	
Miller Geoffrey OBE	8.9.1952		34	1976–1984	1,213	98*	0	25.80	60	5-44	1/0	30.98	17	25
Milligan Frank William	19.3.1870	31.3.1900	2	*1898*	58	38	0	14.50	0	0-0	0/0	–	1	
Millman Geoffrey	2.10.1934	6.4.2005	6	*1961*–1962	60	32*	0	12.00	–	–	–/–	–	13/2	
Milton Clement Arthur (*CY 1959*)	10.3.1928	25.4.2007	6	1958–1959	204	104*	1	25.50	0	0-12	0/0	–	5	
Mitchell Arthur	13.9.1902	25.12.1976	6	*1933*–1936	298	72	0	29.80	0	0-4	0/0	–	9	

	Born	*Died*	*Tests*	*Test Career*	*Runs*	*HS*	*100s*	*Avge*	*Wkts*	*BB*	*5/10*	*Avge*	*Ct/St*	*O/T*
Mitchell Frank (*CY 1902*)	13.8.1872	11.10.1935	2†	*1898*	88	41	0	22.00	–	–	–/–	–	2	
Mitchell Thomas Bignall	4.9.1902	27.1.1996	5	*1932*–1935	20	9	0	5.00	8	2-49	0/0	62.25	1	
Mitchell-Innes Norman Stewart ("Mandy")	7.9.1914	28.12.2006	1	1935	5	5	0	5.00	–	–	–/–	–	0	
Mold Arthur Webb (*CY 1892*)	27.5.1863	29.4.1921	3	1893	0	0*	0	0.00	7	3-44	0/0	33.42	1	
Moon Leonard James	9.2.1878	23.11.1916	4	*1905*	182	36	0	22.75	–	–	–/–	–	4	
Morgan Eoin Joseph Gerard (*CY 2011*)	10.9.1986		16	2010–*2011*	700	130	2	30.43	–	–	–/–	–	11	167‡/70
Morley Frederick	16.12.1850	28.9.1884	4	1880–*1882*	6	2*	0	1.50	16	5-56	1/0	18.50	4	
Morris Hugh	5.10.1963		3	1991	115	44	0	19.16	–	–	–/–	–	3	
Morris John Edward	1.4.1964		3	1990	71	32	0	23.66	–	–	–/–	–	3	8
Mortimore John Brian	14.5.1933	13.2.2014	9	*1958*–1964	243	73*	0	24.30	13	3-36	0/0	56.38	3	
Moss Alan Edward	14.11.1930		9	*1953*–1960	61	26	0	10.16	21	4-35	0/0	29.80	1	
Moxon Martyn Douglas (*CY 1993*)	4.5.1960		10	1986–1989	455	99	0	28.43	0	0-3	0/0	–	10	8
Mullally Alan David	12.7.1969		19	1996–2001	127	24	0	5.52	58	5-105	1/0	31.24	6	50
Munton Timothy Alan (*CY 1995*)	30.7.1965		2	1992	25	25*	0	25.00	4	2-22	0/0	50.00	0	
Murdoch William Lloyd	18.10.1854	18.2.1911	1†	*1891*	12	12	0	12.00	–	–	–/–	–	0/1	
Murray John Thomas MBE (*CY 1967*)	1.4.1935		21	1961–1967	506	112	1	22.00	–	–	–/–	–	52/3	
Newham William	12.12.1860	26.6.1944	1	*1887*	26	17	0	13.00	–	–	–/–	–	0	
Newport Philip John	11.10.1962		3	1988–*1990*	110	40*	0	27.50	10	4-87	0/0	41.70	1	
Nichols Morris Stanley (*CY 1934*)	6.10.1900	26.1.1961	14	*1929*–1939	355	78*	0	29.58	41	6-35	2/0	28.09	11	
Oakman Alan Stanley Myles	20.4.1930		2	1956	14	10	0	7.00	0	0-21	0/0	–	7	
O'Brien *Sir* Timothy Carew	5.11.1861	9.12.1948	5	1884–*1895*	59	20	0	7.37	–	–	–/–	–	4	
O'Connor Jack	6.11.1897	22.2.1977	4	1929–*1929*	153	51	0	21.85	1	1-31	0/0	72.00	2	
Old Christopher Middleton (*CY 1979*)	22.12.1948		46	*1972*–1981	845	65	0	14.82	143	7-50	4/0	28.11	22	32
Oldfield Norman	5.5.1911	19.4.1996	1	1939	99	80	0	49.50	–	–	–/–	–	0	
Onions Graham (*CY 2010*)	9.9.1982		9	2009–2012	30	17*	0	10.00	32	5-38	1/0	29.90	0	4
Ormond James	20.8.1977		2	2001–*2001*	38	18	0	12.66	2	1-70	0/0	92.50	0	
Overton Craig	10.04.1994		2	*2017*	62	41*	0	20.66	6	3-105	0/0	37.66	1	
Padgett Douglas Ernest Vernon	20.7.1934		2	1960	51	31	0	12.75	0	0-8	0/0	–	0	
Paine George Alfred Edward (*CY 1935*)	11.6.1908	30.3.1978	4	*1934*	97	49	0	16.16	17	5-168	1/0	27.47	5	
Palairet Lionel Charles Hamilton (*CY 1893*)	27.5.1870	27.3.1933	2	1902	49	20	0	12.25	–	–	–/–	–	2	
Palmer Charles Henry CBE	15.5.1919	31.3.2005	1	*1953*	22	22	0	11.00	0	0-15	0/0	–	0	
Palmer Kenneth Ernest MBE	22.4.1937		1	*1964*	10	10	0	10.00	1	1-113	0/0	189.00	0	
Panesar Mudhsuden Singh ("Monty") (*CY 2007*)	25.4.1982		50	*2005*–*2013*	220	26	0	4.88	167	6-37	12/2	34.71	10	26/1
Parfitt Peter Howard (*CY 1963*)	8.12.1936		37	*1961*–1972	1,882	131*	7	40.91	12	2-5	0/0	47.83	42	
Parker Charles Warrington Leonard (*CY 1923*)	14.10.1882	11.7.1959	1	1921	3	3*	0	–	2	2-32	0/0	16.00	0	
Parker Paul William Giles	15.1.1956		1	1981	13	13	0	6.50	–	–	–/–	–	0	

	Born	Died	Tests	Test Career	Runs	HS	100s	Avge	Wkts	BB	5/10	Avge	Ct/St	O/T
Parkhouse William Gilbert Anthony	12.10.1925	10.8.2000	7	1950–1959	373	78	0	28.69	–	–	–/–	–	3	
Parkin Cecil Harry (*CY 1924*)	18.2.1886	15.6.1943	10	*1920*–1924	160	36	0	12.30	32	5-38	2/0	35.25	3	
[1] **Parks** James Horace (*CY 1938*)	12.5.1903	21.11.1980	1	1937	29	22	0	14.50	3	2-26	0/0	12.00	0	
[1] **Parks** James Michael (*CY 1968*)	21.10.1931		46	1954–*1967*	1,962	108*	2	32.16	1	1-43	0/0	51.00	103/11	
[1] **Pataudi** Iftikhar Ali Khan, Nawab of (*CY 1932*)	16.3.1910	5.1.1952	3†	*1932*–1934	144	102	1	28.80	–	–	–/–	–	0	
Patel Minal Mahesh	7.7.1970		2	1996	45	27	0	22.50	1	1-101	0/0	180.00	2	
Patel Samit Rohit	30.11.1984		6	*2011–2015*	151	42	0	16.77	7	2-27	0/0	60.14	3	36/18
[2] **Pattinson** Darren John	2.8.1979		1	2008	21	13	0	10.50	2	2-95	0/0	48.00	0	
Paynter Edward (*CY 1938*)	5.11.1901	5.2.1979	20	*1931–1939*	1,540	243	4	59.23	–	–	–/–	–	7	
Peate Edmund	2.3.1855	11.3.1900	9	*1881*–1886	70	13	0	11.66	31	6-85	2/0	22.03	2	
Peebles Ian Alexander Ross (*CY 1931*)	20.1.1908	27.2.1980	13	*1927*–1931	98	26	0	10.88	45	6-63	3/0	30.91	5	
Peel Robert (*CY 1889*)	12.2.1857	12.8.1941	20	*1884*–1896	427	83	0	14.72	101	7-31	5/1	16.98	17	
Penn Frank	7.3.1851	26.12.1916	1	1880	50	27*	0	50.00	0	0-2	0/0	–	0	
Perks Reginald Thomas David	4.10.1911	22.11.1977	2	*1938*–1939	3	2*	0	–	11	5-100	2/0	32.27	1	
Philipson Hylton	8.6.1866	4.12.1935	5	*1891–1894*	63	30	0	9.00	–	–	–/–	–	8/3	
Pietersen Kevin Peter MBE (*CY 2006*)	27.6.1980		104	2005–*2013*	8,181	227	23	47.28	10	3-52	0/0	88.60	62	134‡/37
Pigott Anthony Charles Shackleton	4.6.1958		1	*1983*	12	8*	0	12.00	2	2-75	0/0	37.50	0	
Pilling Richard (*CY 1891*)	11.8.1855	28.3.1891	8	*1881*–1888	91	23	0	7.58	–	–	–/–	–	10/4	
Place Winston	7.12.1914	25.1.2002	3	*1947*	144	107	1	28.80	–	–	–/–	–	0	
Plunkett Liam Edward	6.4.1985		13	*2005*–2014	238	55*	0	15.86	41	5-64	1/0	37.46	3	62/14
Pocock Patrick Ian	24.9.1946		25	*1967–1984*	206	33	0	6.24	67	6-79	3/0	44.41	15	1
Pollard Richard	19.6.1912	16.12.1985	4	1946–1948	13	10*	0	13.00	15	5-24	1/0	25.20	3	
Poole Cyril John	13.3.1921	11.2.1996	3	*1951*	161	69*	0	40.25	0	0-9	0/0	–	1	
Pope George Henry	27.1.1911	29.10.1993	1	1947	8	8*	0	–	1	1-49	0/0	85.00	0	
Pougher Arthur Dick	19.4.1865	20.5.1926	1	*1891*	17	17	0	17.00	3	3-26	0/0	8.66	2	
Price John Sidney Ernest	22.7.1937		15	*1963*–1972	66	32	0	7.33	40	5-73	1/0	35.02	7	
Price Wilfred Frederick Frank	25.4.1902	13.1.1969	1	1938	6	6	0	3.00	–	–	–/–	–	2	
Prideaux Roger Malcolm	31.7.1939		3	1968–*1968*	102	64	0	20.40	0	0-0	0/0	–	0	
Pringle Derek Raymond	18.9.1958		30	1982–1992	695	63	0	15.10	70	5-95	3/0	35.97	10	44
Prior Matthew James (*CY 2010*)	26.2.1982		79	2007–2014	4,099	131*	7	40.18	–	–	–/–	–	243/13	68/10
Pullar Geoffrey (*CY 1960*)	1.8.1935	26.12.2014	28	1959–*1962*	1,974	175	4	43.86	1	1-1	0/0	37.00	2	
Quaife William George (*CY 1902*)	17.3.1872	13.10.1951	7	1899–*1901*	228	68	0	19.00	0	0-6	0/0	–	4	
Radford Neal Victor (*CY 1986*)	7.6.1957		3	1986–*1987*	21	12*	0	7.00	4	2-131	0/0	87.75	0	6
Radley Clive Thornton MBE (*CY 1979*)	13.5.1944		8	*1977*–1978	481	158	2	48.10	–	–	–/–	–	4	4
Ramprakash Mark Ravin MBE (*CY 2007*)	5.9.1969		52	1991–*2001*	2,350	154	2	27.32	4	1-2	0/0	119.25	39	18
Randall Derek William (*CY 1980*)	24.2.1951		47	*1976*–1984	2,470	174	7	33.37	0	0-1	0/0	–	31	49

	Born	*Died*	*Tests*	*Test Career*	*Runs*	*HS*	*100s*	*Avge*	*Wkts*	*BB*	*5/10*	*Avge*	*Ct/St*	*O/T*
Ranjitsinhji Kumar Shri (*CY 1897*)	10.9.1872	2.4.1933	15	1896–1902	989	175	2	44.95	1	1-23	0/0	39.00	13	
Rankin William Boyd	5.7.1984		1	*2013*	13	13	0	6.50	1	1-47	0/0	81.00	0	7‡/2‡
Rashid Adil Usman	17.2.1988		10	*2015–2016*	295	61	0	18.43	38	5-64	1/0	42.78	3	54/24
Read Christopher Mark Wells (*CY 2011*)	10.8.1978		15	1999–*2006*	360	55	0	18.94	–	–	–/–	–	48/6	36/1
Read Holcombe Douglas ("Hopper")	28.1.1910	5.1.2000	1	1935	–	–	–	–	6	4-136	0/0	33.33	0	
Read John Maurice (*CY 1890*)	9.2.1859	17.2.1929	17	1882–1893	461	57	0	17.07	–	–	–/–	–	8	
Read Walter William (*CY 1893*)	23.11.1855	6.1.1907	18	*1882–1893*	720	117	1	27.69	0	0-27	0/0	–	16	
Reeve Dermot Alexander OBE (*CY 1996*)	2.4.1963		3	*1991*	124	59	0	24.80	2	1-4	0/0	30.00	1	29
Relf Albert Edward (*CY 1914*)	26.6.1874	26.3.1937	13	*1903–1913*	416	63	0	23.11	25	5-85	1/0	24.96	14	
Rhodes Harold James	22.7.1936		2	1959	0	0*	0	–	9	4-50	0/0	27.11	0	
Rhodes Steven John (*CY 1995*)	17.6.1964		11	1994–*1994*	294	65*	0	24.50	–	–	–/–	–	46/3	9
Rhodes Wilfred (*CY 1899*)	29.10.1877	8.7.1973	58	1899–*1929*	2,325	179	2	30.19	127	8-68	6/1	26.96	60	
Richards Clifton James ("Jack")	10.8.1958		8	*1986*–1988	285	133	1	21.92	–	–	–/–	–	20/1	22
[2] **Richardson** Derek Walter ("Dick")	3.11.1934		1	1957	33	33	0	33.00	–	–	–/–	–	1	
[2] **Richardson** Peter Edward (*CY 1957*)	4.7.1931	16.2.2017	34	1956–1963	2,061	126	5	37.47	3	2-10	0/0	16.00	6	
Richardson Thomas (*CY 1897*)	11.8.1870	2.7.1912	14	1893–*1897*	177	25*	0	11.06	88	8-94	11/4	25.22	5	
Richmond Thomas Leonard	23.6.1890	29.12.1957	1	1921	6	4	0	3.00	2	2-69	0/0	43.00	0	
Ridgway Frederick	10.8.1923	26.9.2015	5	*1951*	49	24	0	8.16	7	4-83	0/0	54.14	3	
Robertson John David Benbow (*CY 1948*)	22.2.1917	12.10.1996	11	1947–*1951*	881	133	2	46.36	2	2-17	0/0	29.00	6	
Robins Robert Walter Vivian (*CY 1930*)	3.6.1906	12.12.1968	19	1929–1937	612	108	1	26.60	64	6-32	1/0	27.46	12	
Robinson Robert Timothy (*CY 1986*)	21.11.1958		29	*1984*–1989	1,601	175	4	36.38	0	0-0	0/0	–	8	26
Robson Samuel David	1.7.1989		7	2014	336	127	1	30.54	–	–	–/–	–	5	
Roland-Jones Tobias Skelton	29.01.1988		4	2017	82	25	0	20.50	17	5-57	1/0	19.64	0	1
Roope Graham Richard James	12.7.1946	26.11.2006	21	*1972*–1978	860	77	0	30.71	0	0-2	0/0	–	35	8
Root Charles Frederick	16.4.1890	20.1.1954	3	1926	–	–	–	–	8	4-84	0/0	24.25	1	
Root Joseph Edward (*CY 2014*)	30.12.1990		65	*2012–2017*	5,701	254	13	53.28	17	2-9	0/0	48.05	76	97/25
Rose Brian Charles (*CY 1980*)	4.6.1950		9	*1977–1980*	358	70	0	25.57	–	–	–/–	–	4	2
Royle Vernon Peter Fanshawe Archer	29.1.1854	21.5.1929	1	*1878*	21	18	0	10.50	0	0-6	0/0	–	2	
Rumsey Frederick Edward	4.12.1935		5	1964–1965	30	21*	0	15.00	17	4-25	0/0	27.11	0	
Russell Albert Charles ("Jack") (*CY 1923*)	7.10.1887	23.3.1961	10	*1920–1922*	910	140	5	56.87	–	–	–/–	–	8	
Russell Robert Charles ("Jack") (*CY 1990*)	15.8.1963		54	1988–*1997*	1,897	128*	2	27.10	–	–	–/–	–	153/12	40
Russell William Eric	3.7.1936		10	*1961*–1967	362	70	0	21.29	0	0-19	0/0	–	4	
Saggers Martin John	23.5.1972		3	*2003*–2004	1	1	0	0.33	7	2-29	0/0	35.28	1	
Salisbury Ian David Kenneth (*CY 1993*)	21.1.1970		15	1992–*2000*	368	50	0	16.72	20	4-163	0/0	76.95	5	4
Sandham Andrew (*CY 1923*)	6.7.1890	20.4.1982	14	1921–*1929*	879	325	2	38.21	–	–	–/–	–	4	
Schofield Christopher Paul	6.10.1978		2	2000	67	57	0	22.33	0	0-73	0/0	–	0	0/4

	Born	Died	Tests	Test Career	Runs	HS	100s	Avge	Wkts	BB	5/10	Avge	Ct/St	O/T
Schultz Sandford Spence	29.8.1857	18.12.1937	1	*1878*	20	20	0	20.00	1	1-16	0/0	26.00	0	
Scotton William Henry	15.1.1856	9.7.1893	15	*1881–1886*	510	90	0	22.17	0	0-20	0/0	–	4	
Selby John	1.7.1849	11.3.1894	6	*1876–1881*	256	70	0	23.27	–	–	–/–	–	1	
Selvey Michael Walter William	25.4.1948		3	1976–*1976*	15	5*	0	7.50	6	4-41	0/0	57.16	1	
Shackleton Derek (*CY 1959*)	12.8.1924	28.9.2007	7	1950–1963	113	42	0	18.83	18	4-72	0/0	42.66	1	
Shah Owais Alam	22.10.1978		6	*2005–2008*	269	88	0	26.90	0	0-12	0/0	–	2	71/17
Shahzad Ajmal	27.7.1985		1	2010	5	5	0	5.00	4	3-45	0/0	15.75	2	11/3
Sharp John	15.2.1878	28.1.1938	3	1909	188	105	1	47.00	3	3-67	0/0	37.00	1	
Sharpe John William (*CY 1892*)	9.12.1866	19.6.1936	3	1890–*1891*	44	26	0	22.00	11	6-84	1/0	27.72	2	
Sharpe Philip John (*CY 1963*)	27.12.1936	19.5.2014	12	1963–1969	786	111	1	46.23	–	–	–/–	–	17	
Shaw Alfred	29.8.1842	16.1.1907	7	*1876–1881*	111	40	0	10.09	12	5-38	1/0	23.75	4	
Sheppard *Rt Rev. Lord* [David Stuart] (*CY 1953*)	6.3.1929	5.3.2005	22	1950–*1962*	1,172	119	3	37.80	–	–	–/–	–	12	
Sherwin Mordecai (*CY 1891*)	26.2.1851	3.7.1910	3	*1886*–1888	30	21*	0	15.00	–	–	–/–	–	5/2	
Shrewsbury Arthur (*CY 1890*)	11.4.1856	19.5.1903	23	*1881*–1893	1,277	164	3	35.47	0	0-2	0/0	–	29	
Shuter John	9.2.1855	5.7.1920	1	1888	28	28	0	28.00	–	–	–/–	–	0	
Shuttleworth Kenneth	13.11.1944		5	*1970*–1971	46	21	0	7.66	12	5-47	1/0	35.58	1	
[1] **Sidebottom** Arnold	1.4.1954		1	1985	2	2	0	2.00	1	1-65	0/0	65.00	0	
[1] **Sidebottom** Ryan Jay (*CY 2008*)	15.1.1978		22	2001–*2009*	313	31	0	15.65	79	7-47	5/1	28.24	5	25/18
Silverwood Christopher Eric Wilfred	5.3.1975		6	*1996–2002*	29	10	0	7.25	11	5-91	1/0	40.36	2	7
Simpson Reginald Thomas (*CY 1950*)	27.2.1920	24.11.2013	27	*1948–1954*	1,401	156*	4	33.35	2	2-4	0/0	11.00	5	
Simpson-Hayward George Hayward Thomas	7.6.1875	2.10.1936	5	*1909*	105	29*	0	15.00	23	6-43	2/0	18.26	1	
Sims James Morton	13.5.1903	27.4.1973	4	1935–*1936*	16	12	0	4.00	11	5-73	1/0	43.63	6	
Sinfield Reginald Albert	24.12.1900	17.3.1988	1	1938	6	6	0	6.00	2	1-51	0/0	61.50	0	
Slack Wilfred Norris	12.12.1954	15.1.1989	3	*1985*–1986	81	52	0	13.50	–	–	–/–	–	3	2
Smailes Thomas Francis	27.3.1910	1.12.1970	1	1946	25	25	0	25.00	3	3-44	0/0	20.66	0	
Small Gladstone Cleophas	18.10.1961		17	1986–*1990*	263	59	0	15.47	55	5-48	2/0	34.01	9	53
Smith Alan Christopher CBE	25.10.1936		6	*1962*	118	69*	0	29.50	–	–	–/–	–	20	
Smith Andrew Michael	1.10.1967		1	1997	4	4*	0	4.00	0	0-89	0/0	–	0	
Smith Cedric Ivan James (*CY 1935*)	25.8.1906	8.2.1979	5	*1934*–1937	102	27	0	10.20	15	5-16	1/0	26.20	1	
Smith *Sir* Charles Aubrey	21.7.1863	20.12.1948	1	*1888*	3	3	0	3.00	7	5-19	1/0	8.71	0	
[2] **Smith** Christopher Lyall (*CY 1984*)	15.10.1958		8	1983–1986	392	91	0	30.15	3	2-31	0/0	13.00	5	4
Smith David Mark	9.1.1956		2	*1985*	80	47	0	20.00	–	–	–/–	–	0	2
Smith David Robert	5.10.1934	17.12.2003	5	*1961*	38	34	0	9.50	6	2-60	0/0	59.83	2	
Smith Denis (*CY 1935*)	24.1.1907	12.9.1979	2	1935	128	57	0	32.00	–	–	–/–	–	1	
Smith Donald Victor	14.6.1923		3	1957	25	16*	0	8.33	1	1-12	0/0	97.00	0	
Smith Edward Thomas	19.7.1977		3	2003	87	64	0	17.40	–	–	–/–	–	5	

	Born	*Died*	*Tests*	*Test Career*	*Runs*	*HS*	*100s*	*Avge*	*Wkts*	*BB*	*5/10*	*Avge*	*Ct/St*	*O/T*
Smith Ernest James ("Tiger")	6.2.1886	31.8.1979	11	*1911–1913*	113	22	0	8.69	–	–	–/–	–	17/3	
Smith Harry	21.5.1891	12.11.1937	1	1928	7	7	0	7.00	–	–	–/–	–	1	
Smith Michael John Knight OBE (*CY 1960*)	30.6.1933		50	1958–1972	2,278	121	3	31.63	1	1-10	0/0	128.00	53	
[2] **Smith** Robin Arnold (*CY 1990*)	13.9.1963		62	1988–*1995*	4,236	175	9	43.67	0	0-6	0/0	–	39	71
Smith Thomas Peter Bromley (*CY 1947*)	30.10.1908	4.8.1967	4	1946–*1946*	33	24	0	6.60	3	2-172	0/0	106.33	1	
Smithson Gerald Arthur	1.11.1926	6.9.1970	2	*1947*	70	35	0	23.33	–	–	–/–	–	0	
Snow John Augustine (*CY 1973*)	13.10.1941		49	1965–1976	772	73	0	13.54	202	7-40	8/1	26.66	16	9
Southerton James	16.11.1827	16.6.1880	2	*1876*	7	6	0	3.50	7	4-46	0/0	15.28	2	
Spooner Reginald Herbert (*CY 1905*)	21.10.1880	2.10.1961	10	1905–1912	481	119	1	32.06	–	–	–/–	–	4	
Spooner Richard Thompson	30.12.1919	20.12.1997	7	*1951*–1955	354	92	0	27.23	–	–	–/–	–	10/2	
Stanyforth Ronald Thomas	30.5.1892	20.2.1964	4	*1927*	13	6*	0	2.60	–	–	–/–	–	7/2	
Staples Samuel James (*CY 1929*)	18.9.1892	4.6.1950	3	*1927*	65	39	0	13.00	15	3-50	0/0	29.00	0	
Statham John Brian CBE (*CY 1955*)	17.6.1930	10.6.2000	70	*1950*–1965	675	38	0	11.44	252	7-39	9/1	24.84	28	
Steel Allan Gibson	24.9.1858	15.6.1914	13	1880–1888	600	148	2	35.29	29	3-27	0/0	20.86	5	
Steele David Stanley OBE (*CY 1976*)	29.9.1941		8	1975–1976	673	106	1	42.06	2	1-1	0/0	19.50	7	1
Stephenson John Patrick	14.3.1965		1	1989	36	25	0	18.00	–	–	–/–	–	0	
Stevens Greville Thomas Scott (*CY 1918*)	7.1.1901	19.9.1970	10	*1922–1929*	263	69	0	15.47	20	5-90	2/1	32.40	9	
Stevenson Graham Barry	16.12.1955	21.1.2014	2	*1979–1980*	28	27*	0	28.00	5	3-111	0/0	36.60	0	4
[1] **Stewart** Alec James OBE (*CY 1993*)	8.4.1963		133	*1989*–2003	8,463	190	15	39.54	0	0-5	0/0	–	263/14	170
[1] **Stewart** Michael James OBE (*CY 1958*)	16.9.1932		8	1962–*1963*	385	87	0	35.00	–	–	–/–	–	6	
Stoddart Andrew Ernest (*CY 1893*)	11.3.1863	3.4.1915	16	*1887–1897*	996	173	2	35.57	2	1-10	0/0	47.00	6	
Stokes Benjamin Andrew (*CY 2016*)	4.6.1991		39	*2013*–2017	2,429	258	6	35.72	95	6-22	4/0	33.93	38	62/21
Stoneman Mark Daniel	26.06.1987		8	2017–*2017*	352	56	0	27.07	–	–	–/–	–	0	
Storer William (*CY 1899*)	25.1.1867	28.2.1912	6	*1897*–1899	215	51	0	19.54	2	1-24	0/0	54.00	11	
Strauss Andrew John OBE (*CY 2005*)	2.3.1977		100	2004–2012	7,037	177	21	40.91	–	–	–/–	–	121	127/4
Street George Benjamin	6.12.1889	24.4.1924	1	*1922*	11	7*	0	11.00	–	–	–/–	–	0/1	
Strudwick Herbert (*CY 1912*)	28.1.1880	14.2.1970	28	*1909*–1926	230	24	0	7.93	–	–	–/–	–	61/12	
[2] **Studd** Charles Thomas	2.12.1860	16.7.1931	5	1882–*1882*	160	48	0	20.00	3	2-35	0/0	32.66	5	
[2] **Studd** George Brown	20.10.1859	13.2.1945	4	*1882*	31	9	0	4.42	–	–	–/–	–	8	
Subba Row Raman CBE (*CY 1961*)	29.1.1932		13	1958–1961	984	137	3	46.85	0	0-2	0/0	–	5	
Such Peter Mark	12.6.1964		11	1993–1999	67	14*	0	6.09	37	6-67	2/0	33.56	4	
Sugg Frank Howe (*CY 1890*)	11.1.1862	29.5.1933	2	1888	55	31	0	27.50	–	–	–/–	–	0	
Sutcliffe Herbert (*CY 1920*)	24.11.1894	22.1.1978	54	1924–1935	4,555	194	16	60.73	–	–	–/–	–	23	
Swann Graeme Peter (*CY 2010*)	24.3.1979		60	*2008–2013*	1,370	85	0	22.09	255	6-65	17/3	29.96	54	79/39
Swetman Roy	25.10.1933		11	*1958–1959*	254	65	0	16.93	–	–	–/–	–	24/2	
[1] **Tate** Frederick William	24.7.1867	24.2.1943	1	1902	9	5*	0	9.00	2	2-7	0/0	25.50	2	

	Born	Died	Tests	Test Career	Runs	HS	100s	Avge	Wkts	BB	5/10	Avge	Ct/St	O/T
[1] **Tate** Maurice William (*CY 1924*)	30.5.1895	18.5.1956	39	1924–1935	1,198	100*	1	25.48	155	6-42	7/1	26.16	11	
Tattersall Roy	17.8.1922	9.12.2011	16	*1950*–1954	50	10*	0	5.00	58	7-52	4/1	26.08	8	
Tavaré Christopher James	27.10.1954		31	1980–1989	1,755	149	2	32.50	0	0-0	0/0	–	20	29
Taylor James William Arthur	6.1.1990		7	2012–*2015*	312	76	0	26.00	–	–	–/–	–	7	27
Taylor Jonathan Paul	8.8.1964		2	*1992*–1994	34	17*	0	17.00	3	1-18	0/0	52.00	0	1
Taylor Kenneth	21.8.1935		3	1959–1964	57	24	0	11.40	0	0-6	0/0	–	1	
Taylor Leslie Brian	25.10.1953		2	1985	1	1*	0	–	4	2-34	0/0	44.50	1	2
Taylor Robert William MBE (*CY 1977*)	17.7.1941		57	*1970–1983*	1,156	97	0	16.28	0	0-6	0/0	–	167/7	27
Tennyson *Lord* Lionel Hallam (*CY 1914*)	7.11.1889	6.6.1951	9	*1913*–1921	345	74*	0	31.36	0	0-1	0/0	–	6	
Terry Vivian Paul	14.1.1959		2	1984	16	8	0	5.33	–	–	–/–	–	2	
Thomas John Gregory	12.8.1960		5	*1985*–1986	83	31*	0	13.83	10	4-70	0/0	50.40	0	3
Thompson George Joseph (*CY 1906*)	27.10.1877	3.3.1943	6	1909–*1909*	273	63	0	30.33	23	4-50	0/0	27.73	5	
Thomson Norman Ian	23.1.1929		5	*1964*	69	39	0	23.00	9	2-55	0/0	63.11	3	
Thorpe Graham Paul MBE (*CY 1998*)	1.8.1969		100	1993–2005	6,744	200*	16	44.66	0	0-0	0/0	–	105	82
Titmus Frederick John MBE (*CY 1963*)	24.11.1932	23.3.2011	53	1955–*1974*	1,449	84*	0	22.29	153	7-79	7/0	32.22	35	2
Tolchard Roger William	15.6.1946		4	*1976*	129	67	0	25.80	–	–	–/–	–	5	1
[1] **Townsend** Charles Lucas (*CY 1899*)	7.11.1876	17.10.1958	2	1899	51	38	0	17.00	3	3-50	0/0	25.00	0	
[1] **Townsend** David Charles Humphery	20.4.1912	27.1.1997	3	*1934*	77	36	0	12.83	0	0-9	0/0	–	1	
Townsend Leslie Fletcher (*CY 1934*)	8.6.1903	17.2.1993	4	*1929–1933*	97	40	0	16.16	6	2-22	0/0	34.16	2	
Tredwell James Cullum	27.2.1982		2	*2009–2014*	45	37	0	22.50	11	4-47	0/0	29.18	2	45/17
[4] **Tremlett** Christopher Timothy	2.9.1981		12	2007–*2013*	113	25*	0	10.27	53	6-48	2/0	27.00	4	15/1
[4] **Tremlett** Maurice Fletcher	5.7.1923	30.7.1984	3	*1947*	20	18*	0	6.66	4	2-98	0/0	56.50	0	
Trescothick Marcus Edward MBE (*CY 2005*)	25.12.1975		76	2000–2006	5,825	219	14	43.79	1	1-34	0/0	155.00	95	123/3
[2] **Trott** Albert Edwin (*CY 1899*)	6.2.1873	30.7.1914	2†	*1898*	23	16	0	5.75	17	5-49	1/0	11.64	0	
Trott Ian Jonathan Leonard (*CY 2011*)	22.4.1981		52	2009–*2014*	3,835	226	9	44.08	5	1-5	0/0	80.00	29	68/7
Trueman Frederick Sewards OBE (*CY 1953*)	6.2.1931	1.7.2006	67	1952–1965	981	39*	0	13.81	307	8-31	17/3	21.57	64	
Tudor Alex Jeremy	23.10.1977		10	*1998–2002*	229	99*	0	19.08	28	5-44	1/0	34.39	3	3
Tufnell Neville Charsley	13.6.1887	3.8.1951	1	*1909*	14	14	0	14.00	–	–	–/–	–	0/1	
Tufnell Philip Clive Roderick	29.4.1966		42	*1990*–2001	153	22*	0	5.10	121	7-47	5/2	37.68	12	20
Turnbull Maurice Joseph Lawson (*CY 1931*)	16.3.1906	5.8.1944	9	*1929*–1936	224	61	0	20.36	–	–	–/–	–	1	
[2] **Tyldesley** [George] Ernest (*CY 1920*)	5.2.1889	5.5.1962	14	1921–*1928*	990	122	3	55.00	0	0-2	0/0	–	2	
[2] **Tyldesley** John Thomas (*CY 1902*)	22.11.1873	27.11.1930	31	*1898*–1909	1,661	138	4	30.75	–	–	–/–	–	16	
Tyldesley Richard Knowles (*CY 1925*)	11.3.1897	17.9.1943	7	1924–1930	47	29	0	7.83	19	3-50	0/0	32.57	1	
Tylecote Edward Ferdinando Sutton	23.6.1849	15.3.1938	6	*1882*–1886	152	66	0	19.00	–	–	–/–	–	5/5	
Tyler Edwin James	13.10.1864	25.1.1917	1	*1895*	0	0	0	0.00	4	3-49	0/0	16.25	0	
Tyson Frank Holmes (*CY 1956*)	6.6.1930	27.9.2015	17	1954–*1958*	230	37*	0	10.95	76	7-27	4/1	18.56	4	

	Born	*Died*	*Tests*	*Test Career*	*Runs*	*HS*	*100s*	*Avge*	*Wkts*	*BB*	*5/10*	*Avge*	*Ct/St*	*O/T*
Udal Shaun David	18.3.1969		4	*2005*	109	33*	0	18.16	8	4-14	0/0	43.00	1	11
Ulyett George	21.10.1851	18.6.1898	25	*1876*–1890	949	149	1	24.33	50	7-36	1/0	20.40	19	
Underwood Derek Leslie MBE (*CY 1969*)	8.6.1945		86	1966–*1981*	937	45*	0	11.56	297	8-51	17/6	25.83	44	26
Valentine Bryan Herbert	17.1.1908	2.2.1983	7	*1933–1938*	454	136	2	64.85	–	–	–/–	–	2	
Vaughan Michael Paul OBE (*CY 2003*)	29.10.1974		82	*1999*–2008	5,719	197	18	41.44	6	2-71	0/0	93.50	44	86/2
Verity Hedley (*CY 1932*)	18.5.1905	31.7.1943	40	1931–1939	669	66*	0	20.90	144	8-43	5/2	24.37	30	
Vernon George Frederick	20.6.1856	10.8.1902	1	*1882*	14	11*	0	14.00	–	–	–/–	–	0	
Vince James Michael	14.3.1991		12	2016–*2017*	454	83	0	22.70	0	0-0	0/0	–	6	5/5
Vine Joseph (*CY 1906*)	15.5.1875	25.4.1946	2	*1911*	46	36	0	46.00	–	–	–/–	–	0	
Voce William (*CY 1933*)	8.8.1909	6.6.1984	27	*1929–1946*	308	66	0	13.39	98	7-70	3/2	27.88	15	
Waddington Abraham	4.2.1893	28.10.1959	2	*1920*	16	7	0	4.00	1	1-35	0/0	119.00	1	
Wainwright Edward (*CY 1894*)	8.4.1865	28.10.1919	5	1893–*1897*	132	49	0	14.66	0	0-11	0/0	–	2	
Walker Peter Michael	17.2.1936		3	1960	128	52	0	32.00	0	0-8	0/0	–	5	
Walters Cyril Frederick (*CY 1934*)	28.8.1905	23.12.1992	11	1933–1934	784	102	1	52.26	–	–	–/–	–	6	
Ward Alan	10.8.1947		5	1969–1976	40	21	0	8.00	14	4-61	0/0	32.35	3	
Ward Albert (*CY 1890*)	21.11.1865	6.1.1939	7	1893–*1894*	487	117	1	37.46	–	–	–/–	–	1	
Ward Ian James	30.9.1972		5	2001	129	39	0	16.12	–	–	–/–	–	1	
Wardle John Henry (*CY 1954*)	8.1.1923	23.7.1985	28	*1947*–1957	653	66	0	19.78	102	7-36	5/1	20.39	12	
Warner *Sir* Pelham Francis (*CY 1904*)	2.10.1873	30.1.1963	15	*1898*–1912	622	132*	1	23.92	–	–	–/–	–	3	
Warr John James	16.7.1927	9.5.2016	2	*1950*	4	4	0	1.00	1	1-76	0/0	281.00	0	
Warren Arnold	2.4.1875	3.9.1951	1	1905	7	7	0	7.00	6	5-57	1/0	18.83	1	
Washbrook Cyril CBE (*CY 1947*)	6.12.1914	27.4.1999	37	1937–1956	2,569	195	6	42.81	1	1-25	0/0	33.00	12	
Watkin Steven Llewellyn (*CY 1994*)	15.9.1964		3	1991–1993	25	13	0	5.00	11	4-65	0/0	27.72	1	4
Watkins Albert John ("Allan")	21.4.1922	3.8.2011	15	1948–1952	810	137*	2	40.50	11	3-20	0/0	50.36	17	
Watkinson Michael	1.8.1961		4	1995–*1995*	167	82*	0	33.40	10	3-64	0/0	34.80	1	1
Watson Willie (*CY 1954*)	7.3.1920	24.4.2004	23	1951–*1958*	879	116	2	25.85	–	–	–/–	–	8	
Webbe Alexander Josiah	16.1.1855	19.2.1941	1	*1878*	4	4	0	2.00	–	–	–/–	–	2	
Wellard Arthur William (*CY 1936*)	8.4.1902	31.12.1980	2	1937–1938	47	38	0	11.75	7	4-81	0/0	33.85	2	
Wells Alan Peter	2.10.1961		1	1995	3	3*	0	3.00	–	–	–/–	–	0	1
Westley Thomas	13.03.1989		5	2017	193	59	0	24.12	0	0-12	0/0	–	1	
Wharton Alan	30.4.1923	26.8.1993	1	1949	20	13	0	10.00	–	–	–/–	–	0	
Whitaker John James (*CY 1987*)	5.5.1962		1	*1986*	11	11	0	11.00	–	–	–/–	–	1	2
White Craig	16.12.1969		30	1994–*2002*	1,052	121	1	24.46	59	5-32	3/0	37.62	14	51
White David William ("Butch")	14.12.1935	1.8.2008	2	*1961*	0	0	0	0.00	4	3-65	0/0	29.75	0	
White John Cornish (*CY 1929*)	19.2.1891	2.5.1961	15	1921–*1930*	239	29	0	18.38	49	8-126	3/1	32.26	6	
Whysall William Wilfrid (*CY 1925*)	31.10.1887	11.11.1930	4	*1924*–1930	209	76	0	29.85	0	0-9	0/0	–	7	

	Born	*Died*	*Tests*	*Test Career*	*Runs*	*HS*	*100s*	*Avge*	*Wkts*	*BB*	*5/10*	*Avge*	*Ct/St*	*O/T*
Wilkinson Leonard Litton	5.11.1916	3.9.2002	3	*1938*	3	2	0	3.00	7	2-12	0/0	38.71	0	
Willey Peter	6.12.1949		26	1976–1986	1,184	102*	2	26.90	7	2-73	0/0	65.14	3	26
Williams Neil FitzGerald	2.7.1962	27.3.2006	1	1990	38	38	0	38.00	2	2-148	0/0	74.00	0	
Willis Robert George Dylan MBE (*CY 1978*)	30.5.1949		90	*1970*–1984	840	28*	0	11.50	325	8-43	16/0	25.20	39	64
[2] **Wilson** Clement Eustace Macro	15.5.1875	8.2.1944	2	*1898*	42	18	0	14.00	–	–	–/–	–	0	
Wilson Donald	7.8.1937	21.7.2012	6	*1963–1970*	75	42	0	12.50	11	2-17	0/0	42.36	1	
[2] **Wilson** Evelyn Rockley	25.3.1879	21.7.1957	1	*1920*	10	5	0	5.00	3	2-28	0/0	12.00	0	
Woakes Christopher Roger (*CY 2017*)	2.3.1989		22	2013–*2017*	789	66	0	28.17	60	6-70	2/1	33.75	9	67/8
Wood Arthur (*CY 1939*)	25.8.1898	1.4.1973	4	1938–1939	80	53	0	20.00	–	–	–/–	–	10/1	
Wood Barry	26.12.1942		12	1972–1978	454	90	0	21.61	0	0-2	0/0	–	6	13
Wood George Edward Charles	22.8.1893	18.3.1971	3	1924	7	6	0	3.50	–	–	–/–	–	5/1	
Wood Henry (*CY 1891*)	14.12.1853	30.4.1919	4	1888–*1891*	204	134*	1	68.00	–	–	–/–	–	2/1	
Wood Mark Andrew	11.1.1990		10	2015–2017	219	32*	0	16.84	26	3-39	0/0	40.65	3	19/2
Wood Reginald	7.3.1860	6.1.1915	1	*1886*	6	6	0	3.00	–	–	–/–	–	0	
Woods Samuel Moses James (*CY 1889*)	13.4.1867	30.4.1931	3†	*1895*	122	53	0	30.50	5	3-28	0/0	25.80	4	
Woolley Frank Edward (*CY 1911*)	27.5.1887	18.10.1978	64	1909–1934	3,283	154	5	36.07	83	7-76	4/1	33.91	64	
Woolmer Robert Andrew (*CY 1976*)	14.5.1948	18.3.2007	19	1975–1981	1,059	149	3	33.09	4	1-8	0/0	74.75	10	6
Worthington Thomas Stanley (*CY 1937*)	21.8.1905	31.8.1973	9	*1929–1936*	321	128	1	29.18	8	2-19	0/0	39.50	8	
Wright Charles William	27.5.1863	10.1.1936	3	*1895*	125	71	0	31.25	–	–	–/–	–	0	
Wright Douglas Vivian Parson (*CY 1940*)	21.8.1914	13.11.1998	34	1938–*1950*	289	45	0	11.11	108	7-105	6/1	39.11	10	
Wyatt Robert Elliott Storey (*CY 1930*)	2.5.1901	20.4.1995	40	*1927–1936*	1,839	149	2	31.70	18	3-4	0/0	35.66	16	
Wynyard Edward George	1.4.1861	30.10.1936	3	1896–*1905*	72	30	0	12.00	0	0-2	0/0	–	0	
Yardley Norman Walter Dransfield (*CY 1948*)	19.3.1915	3.10.1989	20	*1938*–1950	812	99	0	25.37	21	3-67	0/0	33.66	14	
Young Harding Isaac ("Sailor")	5.2.1876	12.12.1964	2	1899	43	43	0	21.50	12	4-30	0/0	21.83	1	
Young John Albert	14.10.1912	5.2.1993	8	1947–1949	28	10*	0	5.60	17	3-65	0/0	44.52	5	
Young Richard Alfred	16.9.1885	1.7.1968	2	*1907*	27	13	0	6.75	–	–	–/–	–	6	

AUSTRALIA (451 players)

	Born	*Died*	*Tests*	*Test Career*	*Runs*	*HS*	*100s*	*Avge*	*Wkts*	*BB*	*5/10*	*Avge*	*Ct/St*	*O/T*
a'Beckett Edward Lambert	11.8.1907	2.6.1989	4	*1928–1931*	143	41	0	20.42	3	1-41	0/0	105.66	4	
Agar Ashton Charles	14.10.1993		4	2013–*2017*	195	98	0	32.50	9	3-46	0/0	45.55	0	4/2
Alderman Terence Michael (*CY 1982*)	12.6.1956		41	1981–*1990*	203	26*	0	6.54	170	6-47	14/1	27.15	27	65
Alexander George	22.4.1851	6.11.1930	2	*1880–1884*	52	33	0	13.00	2	2-69	0/0	46.50	2	
Alexander Harry Houston	9.6.1905	15.4.1993	1	*1932*	17	17*	0	17.00	1	1-129	0/0	154.00	0	

	Born	*Died*	*Tests*	*Test Career*	*Runs*	*HS*	*100s*	*Avge*	*Wkts*	*BB*	*5/10*	*Avge*	*Ct/St*	*O/T*
Allan Francis Erskine	2.12.1849	9.2.1917	1	*1878*	5	5	0	5.00	4	2-30	0/0	20.00	0	
Allan Peter John	31.12.1935		1	*1965*	–	–	–	–	2	2-58	0/0	41.50	0	
Allen Reginald Charles	2.7.1858	2.5.1952	1	*1886*	44	30	0	22.00	–	–	–/–	–	2	
Andrews Thomas James Edwin	26.8.1890	28.1.1970	16	1921–1926	592	94	0	26.90	1	1-23	0/0	116.00	12	
Angel Jo	22.4.1968		4	*1992–1994*	35	11	0	5.83	10	3-54	0/0	46.30	1	3
[2] **Archer** Kenneth Alan	17.1.1928		5	*1950–1951*	234	48	0	26.00	–	–	–/–	–	0	
[2] **Archer** Ronald Graham	25.10.1933	27.5.2007	19	*1952–1956*	713	128	1	24.58	48	5-53	1/0	27.45	20	
Armstrong Warwick Windridge (*CY 1903*)	22.5.1879	13.7.1947	50	*1901*–1921	2,863	159*	6	38.68	87	6-35	3/0	33.59	44	
Badcock Clayvel Lindsay ("Jack")	10.4.1914	13.12.1982	7	*1936*–1938	160	118	1	14.54	–	–	–/–	–	3	
Bailey George John	7.9.1982		5	*2013*	183	53	0	26.14	–	–	–/–	–	10	90/29‡
Bancroft Cameron Timothy	19.11.1992		5	*2017*	179	82*	0	25.57	–	–	–/–	–	5	0/1
[2] **Bannerman** Alexander Chalmers	21.3.1854	19.9.1924	28	*1878*–1893	1,108	94	0	23.08	4	3-111	0/0	40.75	21	
[2] **Bannerman** Charles	23.7.1851	20.8.1930	3	*1876–1878*	239	165*	1	59.75	–	–	–/–	–	0	
Bardsley Warren (*CY 1910*)	6.12.1882	20.1.1954	41	1909–1926	2,469	193*	6	40.47	–	–	–/–	–	12	
Barnes Sidney George	5.6.1916	16.12.1973	13	1938–1948	1,072	234	3	63.05	4	2-25	0/0	54.50	14	
Barnett Benjamin Arthur	23.3.1908	29.6.1979	4	1938	195	57	0	27.85	–	–	–/–	–	3/2	
Barrett John Edward	15.10.1866	6.2.1916	2	1890	80	67*	0	26.66	–	–	–/–	–	1	
Beard Graeme Robert	19.8.1950		3	*1979*	114	49	0	22.80	1	1-26	0/0	109.00	0	2
Beer Michael Anthony	9.6.1984		2	*2010–2011*	6	2*	0	3.00	3	2-56	0/0	59.33	1	
[2] **Benaud** John	11.5.1944		3	*1972*	223	142	1	44.60	2	2-12	0/0	6.00	0	
[2] **Benaud** Richard OBE (*CY 1962*)	6.10.1930	10.4.2015	63	*1951–1963*	2,201	122	3	24.45	248	7-72	16/1	27.03	65	
Bennett Murray John	6.10.1956		3	*1984*–1985	71	23	0	23.66	6	3-79	0/0	54.16	5	8
Bevan Michael Gwyl	8.5.1970		18	*1994–1997*	785	91	0	29.07	29	6-82	1/1	24.24	8	232
Bichel Andrew John	27.8.1970		19	*1996–2003*	355	71	0	16.90	58	5-60	1/0	32.24	16	67
Bird Jackson Munro	11.12.1986		9	*2012–2017*	43	19*	0	14.33	34	5-59	1/0	30.64	2	
Blackham John McCarthy (*CY 1891*)	11.5.1854	28.12.1932	35	*1876–1894*	800	74	0	15.68	–	–	–/–	–	37/24	
Blackie Donald Dearness	5.4.1882	18.4.1955	3	*1928*	24	11*	0	8.00	14	6-94	1/0	31.71	2	
Blewett Gregory Scott	28.10.1971		46	*1994–1999*	2,552	214	4	34.02	14	2-9	0/0	51.42	45	32
Bollinger Douglas Erwin	24.7.1981		12	*2008–2010*	54	21	0	7.71	50	5-28	2/0	25.92	2	39/9
Bonnor George John	25.2.1855	27.6.1912	17	1880–1888	512	128	1	17.06	2	1-5	0/0	42.00	16	
Boon David Clarence MBE (*CY 1994*)	29.12.1960		107	*1984–1995*	7,422	200	21	43.65	0	0-0	0/0	–	99	181
Booth Brian Charles MBE	19.10.1933		29	1961–*1965*	1,773	169	5	42.21	3	2-33	0/0	48.66	17	
Border Allan Robert (*CY 1982*)	27.7.1955		156	*1978–1993*	11,174	205	27	50.56	39	7-46	2/1	39.10	156	273
Boyle Henry Frederick	10.12.1847	21.11.1907	12	*1878–1884*	153	36*	0	12.75	32	6-42	1/0	20.03	10	
Bracken Nathan Wade	12.9.1977		5	*2003–2005*	70	37	0	17.50	12	4-48	0/0	42.08	2	116/19
Bradman *Sir* Donald George AC (*CY 1931*)	27.8.1908	25.2.2001	52	*1928*–1948	6,996	334	29	99.94	2	1-8	0/0	36.00	32	

	Born	Died	Tests	Test Career	Runs	HS	100s	Avge	Wkts	BB	5/10	Avge	Ct/St	O/T
Bright Raymond James	13.7.1954		25	1977–*1986*	445	33	0	14.35	53	7-87	4/1	41.13	13	11
Bromley Ernest Harvey	2.9.1912	1.2.1967	2	*1932*–1934	38	26	0	9.50	0	0-19	0/0	–	2	
Brown William Alfred (*CY 1939*)	31.7.1912	16.3.2008	22	1934–1948	1,592	206*	4	46.82	–	–	–/–	–	14	
Bruce William	22.5.1864	3.8.1925	14	*1884–1894*	702	80	0	29.25	12	3-88	0/0	36.66	12	
Burge Peter John Parnell (*CY 1965*)	17.5.1932	5.10.2001	42	*1954–1965*	2,290	181	4	38.16	–	–	–/–	–	23	
Burke James Wallace (*CY 1957*)	12.6.1930	2.2.1979	24	*1950–1958*	1,280	189	3	34.59	8	4-37	0/0	28.75	18	
Burn Edwin James Kenneth (K. E.)	17.9.1862	20.7.1956	2	1890	41	19	0	10.25	–	–	–/–	–	0	
Burns Joseph Antony	6.9.1989		13	*2014–2016*	873	170	3	37.95	–	–	–/–	–	15	6
Burton Frederick John	2.11.1865	25.8.1929	2	*1886–1887*	4	2*	0	2.00	–	–	–/–	–	1/1	
Callaway Sydney Thomas	6.2.1868	25.11.1923	3	*1891–1894*	87	41	0	17.40	6	5-37	1/0	23.66	0	
Callen Ian Wayne	2.5.1955		1	*1977*	26	22*	0	–	6	3-83	0/0	31.83	1	5
Campbell Gregory Dale	10.3.1964		4	1989–*1989*	10	6	0	2.50	13	3-79	0/0	38.69	1	12
Carkeek William ("Barlow")	17.10.1878	20.2.1937	6	1912	16	6*	0	5.33	–	–	–/–	–	6	
Carlson Phillip Henry	8.8.1951		2	*1978*	23	21	0	5.75	2	2-41	0/0	49.50	2	4
Carter Hanson	15.3.1878	8.6.1948	28	*1907–1921*	873	72	0	22.97	–	–	–/–	–	44/21	
Cartwright Hilton William Raymond	14.2.1992		2	*2016–2017*	55	37	0	27.50	0	0-15	0/0	–	0	2
Casson Beau	7.12.1982		1	*2007*	10	10	0	10.00	3	3-86	0/0	43.00	2	
2, 4 **Chappell** Gregory Stephen MBE (*CY 1973*)	7.8.1948		87	*1970–1983*	7,110	247*	24	53.86	47	5-61	1/0	40.70	122	74
2, 4 **Chappell** Ian Michael (*CY 1976*)	26.9.1943		75	*1964–1979*	5,345	196	14	42.42	20	2-21	0/0	65.80	105	16
2, 4 **Chappell** Trevor Martin	21.10.1952		3	1981	79	27	0	15.80	–	–	–/–	–	2	20
Charlton Percie Chater	9.4.1867	30.9.1954	2	1890	29	11	0	7.25	3	3-18	0/0	8.00	0	
Chipperfield Arthur Gordon	17.11.1905	29.7.1987	14	1934–1938	552	109	1	32.47	5	3-91	0/0	87.40	15	
Clark Stuart Rupert	28.9.1975		24	*2005*–2009	248	39	0	13.05	94	5-32	2/0	23.86	4	39/9
Clark Wayne Maxwell	19.9.1953		10	*1977–1978*	98	33	0	5.76	44	4-46	0/0	28.75	6	2
Clarke Michael John (*CY 2010*)	2.4.1981		115§	*2004*–2015	8,643	329*	28	49.10	31	6-9	2/0	38.19	134	245/34
Colley David John	15.3.1947		3	1972	84	54	0	21.00	6	3-83	0/0	52.00	1	1
Collins Herbert Leslie	21.1.1888	28.5.1959	19	*1920*–1926	1,352	203	4	45.06	4	2-47	0/0	63.00	13	
Coningham Arthur	14.7.1863	13.6.1939	1	*1894*	13	10	0	6.50	2	2-17	0/0	38.00	0	
Connolly Alan Norman	29.6.1939		29	*1963–1970*	260	37	0	10.40	102	6-47	4/0	29.22	17	1
Cook Simon Hewitt	29.1.1972		2	*1997*	3	3*	0	–	7	5-39	1/0	20.28	0	
Cooper Bransby Beauchamp	15.3.1844	7.8.1914	1	*1876*	18	15	0	9.00	–	–	–/–	–	2	
5 **Cooper** William Henry	11.9.1849	5.4.1939	2	*1881–1884*	13	7	0	6.50	9	6-120	1/0	25.11	1	
Copeland Trent Aaron	14.3.1986		3	*2011*	39	23*	0	13.00	6	2-24	0/0	37.83	2	
Corling Grahame Edward	13.7.1941		5	1964	5	3	0	1.66	12	4-60	0/0	37.25	0	
Cosier Gary John	25.4.1953		18	*1975–1978*	897	168	2	28.93	5	2-26	0/0	68.20	14	9

§ *Clarke's figures include 44 runs and one catch for Australia v the ICC World XI in the Super Series Test in 2005-06.*

	Born	*Died*	*Tests*	*Test Career*	*Runs*	*HS*	*100s*	*Avge*	*Wkts*	*BB*	*5/10*	*Avge*	*Ct/St*	*O/T*
Cottam John Thomas	5.9.1867	30.1.1897	1	*1886*	4	3	0	2.00	–	–	–/–	–	1	
Cotter Albert ("Tibby")	3.12.1883	31.10.1917	21	*1903–1911*	457	45	0	13.05	89	7-148	7/0	28.64	8	
Coulthard George	1.8.1856	22.10.1883	1	*1881*	6	6*	0	–	–	–	–/–	–	0	
Cowan Edward James McKenzie	16.6.1982		18	*2011*–2013	1,001	136	1	31.28	–	–	–/–	–	24	
Cowper Robert Maskew	5.10.1940		27	1964–1968	2,061	307	5	46.84	36	4-48	0/0	31.63	21	
Craig Ian David	12.6.1935	16.11.2014	11	*1952–1957*	358	53	0	19.88	–	–	–/–	–	2	
Crawford William Patrick Anthony	3.8.1933	21.1.2009	4	1956–*1956*	53	34	0	17.66	7	3-28	0/0	15.28	1	
Cullen Daniel James	10.4.1984		1	*2005*	–	–	–	–	1	1-25	0/0	54.00	0	5
Cummins Patrick James	8.5.1993		10	*2011–2017*	276	44	0	27.60	44	6-79	1/0	25.00	4	36/18
Dale Adam Craig	30.12.1968		2	*1997–1998*	6	5	0	2.00	6	3-71	0/0	31.16	0	30
Darling Joseph (*CY 1900*)	21.11.1870	2.1.1946	34	*1894*–1905	1,657	178	3	28.56	–	–	–/–	–	27	
Darling Leonard Stuart	14.8.1909	24.6.1992	12	*1932–1936*	474	85	0	27.88	0	0-3	0/0	–	8	
Darling Warrick Maxwell	1.5.1957		14	*1977–1979*	697	91	0	26.80	–	–	–/–	–	5	18
Davidson Alan Keith MBE (*CY 1962*)	14.6.1929		44	1953–*1962*	1,328	80	0	24.59	186	7-93	14/2	20.53	42	
Davis Ian Charles	25.6.1953		15	*1973*–1977	692	105	1	26.61	–	–	–/–	–	9	3
Davis Simon Peter	8.11.1959		1	*1985*	0	0	0	0.00	0	0-70	0/0	–	0	39
De Courcy James Harry	18.4.1927	20.6.2000	3	1953	81	41	0	16.20	–	–	–/–	–	3	
Dell Anthony Ross	6.8.1947		2	*1970–1973*	6	3*	0	–	6	3-65	0/0	26.66	0	
Dodemaide Anthony Ian Christopher	5.10.1963		10	*1987–1992*	202	50	0	22.44	34	6-58	1/0	28.02	6	24
Doherty Xavier John	22.12.1982		4	2010–2012	51	18*	0	12.75	7	3-131	0/0	78.28	2	60/11
Donnan Henry	12.11.1864	13.8.1956	5	*1891*–1896	75	15	0	8.33	0	0-22	0/0	–	2	
Doolan Alexander James	29.11.1985		4	*2013–2014*	191	89	0	23.87	–	–	–/–	–	4	
Dooland Bruce (*CY 1955*)	1.11.1923	8.9.1980	3	*1946–1947*	76	29	0	19.00	9	4-69	0/0	46.55	3	
Duff Reginald Alexander	17.8.1878	13.12.1911	22	*1901*–1905	1,317	146	2	35.59	4	2-43	0/0	21.25	14	
Duncan John Ross Frederick	25.3.1944		1	*1970*	3	3	0	3.00	0	0-30	0/0	–	0	
Dyer Gregory Charles	16.3.1959		6	*1986–1987*	131	60	0	21.83	–	–	–/–	–	22/2	23
Dymock Geoffrey	21.7.1945		21	*1973–1979*	236	31*	0	9.44	78	7-67	5/1	27.12	1	15
Dyson John	11.6.1954		30	*1977–1984*	1,359	127*	2	26.64	–	–	–/–	–	10	29
Eady Charles John	29.10.1870	20.12.1945	2	1896–*1901*	20	10*	0	6.66	7	3-30	0/0	16.00	2	
Eastwood Kenneth Humphrey	23.11.1935		1	*1970*	5	5	0	2.50	1	1-21	0/0	21.00	0	
Ebeling Hans Irvine	1.1.1905	12.1.1980	1	1934	43	41	0	21.50	3	3-74	0/0	29.66	0	
Edwards John Dunlop	12.6.1860	31.7.1911	3	1888	48	26	0	9.60	–	–	–/–	–	1	
Edwards Ross	1.12.1942		20	1972–1975	1,171	170*	2	40.37	0	0-20	0/0	–	7	9
Edwards Walter John	23.12.1949		3	*1974*	68	30	0	11.33	–	–	–/–	–	0	1
Elliott Matthew Thomas Gray (*CY 1998*)	28.9.1971		21	*1996*–2004	1,172	199	3	33.48	0	0-0	0/0	–	14	1
Emery Philip Allen	25.6.1964		1	*1994*	8	8*	0	–	–	–	–/–	–	5/1	1

	Born	Died	Tests	Test Career	Runs	HS	100s	Avge	Wkts	BB	5/10	Avge	Ct/St	O/T
Emery Sidney Hand	15.10.1885	7.1.1967	4	1912	6	5	0	3.00	5	2-46	0/0	49.80	2	
Evans Edwin	26.3.1849	2.7.1921	6	*1881*–1886	82	33	0	10.25	7	3-64	0/0	47.42	5	
Fairfax Alan George	16.6.1906	17.5.1955	10	*1928–1930*	410	65	0	51.25	21	4-31	0/0	30.71	15	
Faulkner James Peter	29.4.1990		1	2013	45	23	0	22.50	6	4-51	0/0	16.33	0	69/24
Favell Leslie Ernest MBE	6.10.1929	14.6.1987	19	*1954–1960*	757	101	1	27.03	–	–	–/–	–	9	
Ferguson Callum James	21.11.1984		1	*2016*	4	3	0	2.00	–	–	–/–	–	0	30/3
Ferris John James (*CY 1889*)	21.5.1867	17.11.1900	8†	*1886*–1890	98	20*	0	8.16	48	5-26	4/0	14.25	4	
Fingleton John Henry Webb OBE	28.4.1908	22.11.1981	18	*1931*–1938	1,189	136	5	42.46	–	–	–/–	–	13	
Fleetwood-Smith Leslie O'Brien ("Chuck")	30.3.1908	16.3.1971	10	*1935*–1938	54	16*	0	9.00	42	6-110	2/1	37.38	0	
Fleming Damien William	24.4.1970		20	*1994–2000*	305	71*	0	19.06	75	5-30	3/0	25.89	9	88
Francis Bruce Colin	18.2.1948		3	1972	52	27	0	10.40	–	–	–/–	–	1	
Freeman Eric Walter	13.7.1944		11	*1967–1969*	345	76	0	19.16	34	4-52	0/0	33.17	5	
Freer Frederick Alfred William	4.12.1915	2.11.1998	1	*1946*	28	28*	0	–	3	2-49	0/0	24.66	0	
Gannon John Bryant ("Sam")	8.2.1947		3	*1977*	3	3*	0	3.00	11	4-77	0/0	32.81	3	
Garrett Thomas William	26.7.1858	6.8.1943	19	*1876–1887*	339	51*	0	12.55	36	6-78	2/0	26.94	7	
Gaunt Ronald Arthur	26.2.1934	30.3.2012	3	*1957–1963*	6	3	0	3.00	7	3-53	0/0	44.28	1	
Gehrs Donald Raeburn Algernon	29.11.1880	25.6.1953	6	*1903–1910*	221	67	0	20.09	0	0-4	0/0	–	6	
George Peter Robert	16.10.1986		1	*2010*	2	2	0	1.00	2	2-48	0/0	38.50	0	
[2] **Giffen** George (*CY 1894*)	27.3.1859	29.11.1927	31	*1881*–1896	1,238	161	1	23.35	103	7-117	7/1	27.09	24	
[2] **Giffen** Walter Frank	20.9.1861	28.6.1949	3	*1886–1891*	11	3	0	1.83	–	–	–/–	–	1	
Gilbert David Robert	29.12.1960		9	1985–*1986*	57	15	0	7.12	16	3-48	0/0	52.68	0	14
Gilchrist Adam Craig (*CY 2002*)	14.11.1971		96§	*1999–2007*	5,570	204*	17	47.60	–	–	–/–	–	379/37	286‡/13
Gillespie Jason Neil (*CY 2002*)	19.4.1975		71	*1996–2005*	1,218	201*	1	18.73	259	7-37	8/0	26.13	27	97/1
Gilmour Gary John	26.6.1951	10.6.2014	15	*1973–1976*	483	101	1	23.00	54	6-85	3/0	26.03	8	5
Gleeson John William	14.3.1938	8.10.2016	29	*1967*–1972	395	45	0	10.39	93	5-61	3/0	36.20	17	
Graham Henry	22.11.1870	7.2.1911	6	1893–1896	301	107	2	30.10	–	–	–/–	–	3	
[2] **Gregory** David William	15.4.1845	4.8.1919	3	*1876–1878*	60	43	0	20.00	0	0-9	0/0	–	0	
[1,2] **Gregory** Edward James	29.5.1839	22.4.1899	1	*1876*	11	11	0	5.50	–	–	–/–	–	1	
Gregory Jack Morrison (*CY 1922*)	14.8.1895	7.8.1973	24	*1920–1928*	1,146	119	2	36.96	85	7-69	4/0	31.15	37	
Gregory Ross Gerald	28.2.1916	10.6.1942	2	*1936*	153	80	0	51.00	0	0-14	0/0	–	1	
[1] **Gregory** Sydney Edward (*CY 1897*)	14.4.1870	31.7.1929	58	1890–1912	2,282	201	4	24.53	0	0-4	0/0	–	25	
Grimmett Clarence Victor (*CY 1931*)	25.12.1891	2.5.1980	37	*1924–1935*	557	50	0	13.92	216	7-40	21/7	24.21	17	
Groube Thomas Underwood	2.9.1857	5.8.1927	1	1880	11	11	0	5.50	–	–	–/–	–	0	
Grout Arthur Theodore Wallace	30.3.1927	9.11.1968	51	*1957–1965*	890	74	0	15.08	–	–	–/–	–	163/24	
Guest Colin Ernest John	7.10.1937		1	*1962*	11	11	0	11.00	0	0-8	0/0	–	0	

§ *Gilchrist's figures include 95 runs, five catches and two stumpings for Australia v the ICC World XI in the Super Series Test in 2005-06.*

	Born	*Died*	*Tests*	*Test Career*	*Runs*	*HS*	*100s*	*Avge*	*Wkts*	*BB*	*5/10*	*Avge*	*Ct/St*	*O/T*
Haddin Bradley James	23.10.1977		66	2007–2015	3,265	169	4	32.97	–	–	–/–	–	262/8	126/34
Hamence Ronald Arthur	25.11.1915	24.3.2010	3	*1946–1947*	81	30*	0	27.00	–	–	–/–	–	1	
Hammond Jeffrey Roy	19.4.1950		5	*1972*	28	19	0	9.33	15	4-38	0/0	32.53	2	1
Handscomb Peter Stephen Patrick	26.4.1991		12	*2016–2017*	805	110	2	47.35	–	–	–/–	–	18	8
Harris Ryan James (*CY 2014*)	11.10.1979		27	*2009–2014*	603	74	0	21.53	113	7-117	5/0	23.52	13	21/3
Harry John	1.8.1857	27.10.1919	1	*1894*	8	6	0	4.00	–	–	–/–	–	1	
Hartigan Roger Joseph	12.12.1879	7.6.1958	2	*1907*	170	116	1	42.50	0	0-7	0/0	–	1	
Hartkopf Albert Ernst Victor	28.12.1889	20.5.1968	1	*1924*	80	80	0	40.00	1	1-120	0/0	134.00	0	
[2] **Harvey** Mervyn Roye	29.4.1918	18.3.1995	1	*1946*	43	31	0	21.50	–	–	–/–	–	0	
[2] **Harvey** Robert Neil MBE (*CY 1954*)	8.10.1928		79	*1947–1962*	6,149	205	21	48.41	3	1-8	0/0	40.00	64	
Hassett Arthur Lindsay MBE (*CY 1949*)	28.8.1913	16.6.1993	43	1938–1953	3,073	198*	10	46.56	0	0-1	0/0	–	30	
Hastings John Wayne	4.11.1985		1	*2012*	52	32	0	26.00	1	1-51	0/0	153.00	1	29/9
Hauritz Nathan Michael	18.10.1981		17	*2004–2010*	426	75	0	25.05	63	5-53	2/0	34.98	3	58/3
Hawke Neil James Napier	27.6.1939	25.12.2000	27	*1962*–1968	365	45*	0	16.59	91	7-105	6/1	29.41	9	
Hayden Matthew Lawrence (*CY 2003*)	29.10.1971		103§	*1993–2008*	8,625	380	30	50.73	0	0-7	0/0	–	128	160‡/9
Hazlewood Josh Reginald	8.1.1991		36	*2014–2017*	274	39	0	11.91	139	6-67	6/0	25.77	15	38/7
Hazlitt Gervys Rignold	4.9.1888	30.10.1915	9	*1907*–1912	89	34*	0	11.12	23	7-25	1/0	27.08	4	
Healy Ian Andrew (*CY 1994*)	30.4.1964		119	*1988–1999*	4,356	161*	4	27.39	–	–	–/–	–	366/29	168
Hendry Hunter Scott Thomas Laurie ("Stork")	24.5.1895	16.12.1988	11	1921–*1928*	335	112	1	20.93	16	3-36	0/0	40.00	10	
Henriques Moises Constantino	1.2.1987		4	*2012*–2016	164	81*	0	23.42	2	1-48	0/0	82.00	1	11/11
Hibbert Paul Anthony	23.7.1952	27.11.2008	1	*1977*	15	13	0	7.50	–	–	–/–	–	1	
Higgs James Donald	11.7.1950		22	*1977–1980*	111	16	0	5.55	66	7-143	2/0	31.16	3	
Hilditch Andrew Mark Jefferson	20.5.1956		18	*1978–1985*	1,073	119	2	31.55	–	–	–/–	–	13	8
Hilfenhaus Benjamin William	15.3.1983		27	*2008–2012*	355	56*	0	13.65	99	5-75	2/0	28.50	7	25/7
Hill Clement (*CY 1900*)	18.3.1877	5.9.1945	49	1896–*1911*	3,412	191	7	39.21	–	–	–/–	–	33	
Hill John Charles	25.6.1923	11.8.1974	3	1953–*1954*	21	8*	0	7.00	8	3-35	0/0	34.12	2	
Hoare Desmond Edward	19.10.1934		1	*1960*	35	35	0	17.50	2	2-68	0/0	78.00	2	
Hodge Bradley John	29.12.1974		6	*2005–2007*	503	203*	1	55.88	0	0-8	0/0	–	9	25/15
Hodges John Robart	11.8.1855	d unknown	2	*1876*	10	8	0	3.33	6	2-7	0/0	14.00	0	
Hogan Tom George	23.9.1956		7	*1982–1983*	205	42*	0	18.63	15	5-66	1/0	47.06	2	16
Hogg George Bradley	6.2.1971		7	*1996–2007*	186	79	0	26.57	17	2-40	0/0	54.88	1	123/15
Hogg Rodney Malcolm	5.3.1951		38	*1978–1984*	439	52	0	9.75	123	6-74	6/2	28.47	7	71
Hohns Trevor Victor	23.1.1954		7	*1988*–1989	136	40	0	22.66	17	3-59	0/0	34.11	3	
Hole Graeme Blake	6.1.1931	14.2.1990	18	*1950–1954*	789	66	0	25.45	3	1-9	0/0	42.00	21	
Holland Jonathan Mark	29.5.1987		2	2016	1	1	0	1.00	5	2-72	0/0	54.80	0	

§ *Hayden's figures include 188 runs and three catches, for Australia v the ICC World XI in the Super Series Test in 2005-06.*

	Born	Died	Tests	Test Career	Runs	HS	100s	Avge	Wkts	BB	5/10	Avge	Ct/St	O/T
Holland Robert George	19.10.1946	17.9.2017	11	*1984–1985*	35	10	0	3.18	34	6-54	3/2	39.76	5	2
Hookes David William	3.5.1955	19.1.2004	23	*1976–1985*	1,306	143*	1	34.36	1	1-4	0/0	41.00	12	39
Hopkins Albert John Young	3.5.1874	25.4.1931	20	*1901*–1909	509	43	0	16.41	26	4-81	0/0	26.76	11	
Horan Thomas Patrick	8.3.1854	16.4.1916	15	*1876–1884*	471	124	1	18.84	11	6-40	1/0	13.00	6	
Hordern Herbert Vivian MBE	10.2.1883	17.6.1938	7	*1910–1911*	254	50	0	23.09	46	7-90	5/2	23.36	6	
Hornibrook Percival Mitchell	27.7.1899	25.8.1976	6	*1928*–1930	60	26	0	10.00	17	7-92	1/0	39.05	7	
Howell William Peter	29.12.1869	14.7.1940	18	*1897–1903*	158	35	0	7.52	49	5-81	1/0	28.71	12	
Hughes Kimberley John (*CY 1981*)	26.1.1954		70	1977–*1984*	4,415	213	9	37.41	0	0-0	0/0	–	50	97
Hughes Mervyn Gregory (*CY 1994*)	23.11.1961		53	*1985–1993*	1,032	72*	0	16.64	212	8-87	7/1	28.38	23	33
Hughes Phillip Joel	30.11.1988	27.11.2014	26	*2008*–2013	1,535	160	3	32.65	–	–	–/–	–	15	25/1
Hunt William Alfred	26.8.1908	30.12.1983	1	*1931*	0	0	0	0.00	0	0-14	0/0	–	1	
Hurst Alan George	15.7.1950		12	*1973–1979*	102	26	0	6.00	43	5-28	2/0	27.90	3	8
Hurwood Alexander	17.6.1902	26.9.1982	2	*1930*	5	5	0	2.50	11	4-22	0/0	15.45	2	
Hussey Michael Edward Killeen	27.5.1975		79	*2005–2012*	6,235	195	19	51.52	7	1-0	0/0	43.71	85	185/38
Inverarity Robert John	31.1.1944		6	1968–1972	174	56	0	17.40	4	3-26	0/0	23.25	4	
Iredale Francis Adams	19.6.1867	15.4.1926	14	*1894*–1899	807	140	2	36.68	0	0-3	0/0	–	16	
Ironmonger Herbert	7.4.1882	31.5.1971	14	*1928–1932*	42	12	0	2.62	74	7-23	4/2	17.97	3	
Iverson John Brian	27.7.1915	24.10.1973	5	*1950*	3	1*	0	0.75	21	6-27	1/0	15.23	2	
Jackson Archibald Alexander	5.9.1909	16.2.1933	8	*1928–1930*	474	164	1	47.40	–	–	–/–	–	7	
Jaques Philip Anthony	3.5.1979		11	*2005–2007*	902	150	3	47.47	–	–	–/–	–	7	6
Jarman Barrington Noel	17.2.1936		19	*1959–1968*	400	78	0	14.81	–	–	–/–	–	50/4	
Jarvis Arthur Harwood	19.10.1860	15.11.1933	11	*1884–1894*	303	82	0	16.83	–	–	–/–	–	9/9	
Jenner Terrence James	8.9.1944	24.5.2011	9	*1970–1975*	208	74	0	23.11	24	5-90	1/0	31.20	5	1
Jennings Claude Burrows	5.6.1884	20.6.1950	6	1912	107	32	0	17.83	–	–	–/–	–	5	
Johnson Ian William Geddes CBE	8.12.1917	9.10.1998	45	*1945–1956*	1,000	77	0	18.51	109	7-44	3/0	29.19	30	
Johnson Leonard Joseph	18.3.1919	20.4.1977	1	*1947*	25	25*	0	–	6	3-8	0/0	12.33	2	
Johnson Mitchell Guy	2.11.1981		73	*2007–2015*	2,065	123*	1	22.20	313	8-61	12/3	28.40	27	153/30
Johnston William Arras (*CY 1949*)	26.2.1922	25.5.2007	40	*1947–1954*	273	29	0	11.37	160	6-44	7/0	23.91	16	
Jones Dean Mervyn (*CY 1990*)	24.3.1961		52	*1983–1992*	3,631	216	11	46.55	1	1-5	0/0	64.00	34	164
Jones Ernest	30.9.1869	23.11.1943	19	*1894–1902*	126	20	0	5.04	64	7-88	3/1	29.01	21	
Jones Samuel Percy	1.8.1861	14.7.1951	12	*1881–1887*	428	87	0	21.40	6	4-47	0/0	18.66	12	
Joslin Leslie Ronald	13.12.1947		1	*1967*	9	7	0	4.50	–	–	–/–	–	0	
Julian Brendon Paul	10.8.1970		7	1993–*1995*	128	56*	0	16.00	15	4-36	0/0	39.93	4	25
Kasprowicz Michael Scott	10.2.1972		38	*1996–2005*	445	25	0	10.59	113	7-36	4/0	32.88	16	43/2
Katich Simon Mathew	21.8.1975		56§	2001–*2010*	4,188	157	10	45.03	21	6-65	1/0	30.23	39	45/3

§ *Katich's figures include two runs and one catch for Australia v the ICC World XI in the Super Series Test in 2005-06.*

	Born	*Died*	*Tests*	*Test Career*	*Runs*	*HS*	*100s*	*Avge*	*Wkts*	*BB*	*5/10*	*Avge*	*Ct/St*	*O/T*
Kelleway Charles	25.4.1886	16.11.1944	26	*1910–1928*	1,422	147	3	37.42	52	5-33	1/0	32.36	24	
Kelly James Joseph (*CY 1903*)	10.5.1867	14.8.1938	36	1896–1905	664	46*	0	17.02	–	–	–/–	–	43/20	
Kelly Thomas Joseph Dart	3.5.1844	20.7.1893	2	*1876–1878*	64	35	0	21.33	–	–	–/–	–	1	
Kendall Thomas Kingston	24.8.1851	17.8.1924	2	*1876*	39	17*	0	13.00	14	7-55	1/0	15.35	2	
Kent Martin Francis	23.11.1953		3	1981	171	54	0	28.50	–	–	–/–	–	6	5
Kerr Robert Byers	16.6.1961		2	*1985*	31	17	0	7.75	–	–	–/–	–	1	4
Khawaja Usman Tariq	18.12.1986		29	*2010–2017*	2,061	174	6	45.80	0	0-1	0/0	–	23	18/9
Kippax Alan Falconer	25.5.1897	5.9.1972	22	*1924*–1934	1,192	146	2	36.12	0	0-2	0/0	–	13	
Kline Lindsay Francis	29.9.1934	2.10.2015	13	*1957–1960*	58	15*	0	8.28	34	7-75	1/0	22.82	9	
Krejza Jason John	14.1.1983		2	*2008*	71	32	0	23.66	13	8-215	1/1	43.23	4	8
Laird Bruce Malcolm	21.11.1950		21	*1979–1982*	1,341	92	0	35.28	0	0-3	0/0	–	16	23
Langer Justin Lee (*CY 2001*)	21.11.1970		105§	*1992–2006*	7,696	250	23	45.27	0	0-3	0/0	–	73	8
Langley Gilbert Roche Andrews (*CY 1957*)	14.9.1919	14.5.2001	26	*1951–1956*	374	53	0	14.96	–	–	–/–	–	83/15	
Laughlin Trevor John	30.1.1951		3	*1977–1978*	87	35	0	17.40	6	5-101	1/0	43.66	3	6
Laver Frank Jonas	7.12.1869	24.9.1919	15	1899–1909	196	45	0	11.52	37	8-31	2/0	26.05	8	
Law Stuart Grant (*CY 1998*)	18.10.1968		1	*1995*	54	54*	0	–	0	0-9	0/0	–	1	54
Lawry William Morris (*CY 1962*)	11.2.1937		67	1961–*1970*	5,234	210	13	47.15	0	0-0	0/0	–	30	1
Lawson Geoffrey Francis	7.12.1957		46	*1980–1989*	894	74	0	15.96	180	8-112	11/2	30.56	10	79
Lee Brett (*CY 2006*)	8.11.1976		76§	*1999–2008*	1,451	64	0	20.15	310	5-30	10/0	30.81	23	221/25
Lee Philip Keith	15.9.1904	9.8.1980	2	*1931–1932*	57	42	0	19.00	5	4-111	0/0	42.40	1	
Lehmann Darren Scott (*CY 2001*)	5.2.1970		27	*1997–2004*	1,798	177	5	44.95	15	3-42	0/0	27.46	11	117
Lillee Dennis Keith MBE (*CY 1973*)	18.7.1949		70	*1970–1983*	905	73*	0	13.71	355	7-83	23/7	23.92	23	63
Lindwall Raymond Russell MBE (*CY 1949*)	3.10.1921	23.6.1996	61	*1945–1959*	1,502	118	2	21.15	228	7-38	12/0	23.03	26	
Love Hampden Stanley Bray	10.8.1895	22.7.1969	1	*1932*	8	5	0	4.00	–	–	–/–	–	3	
Love Martin Lloyd	30.3.1974		5	*2002*–2003	233	100*	1	46.60	–	–	–/–	–	7	
Loxton Samuel John Everett OBE	29.3.1921	3.12.2011	12	*1947–1950*	554	101	1	36.93	8	3-55	0/0	43.62	7	
Lyon Nathan Michael	20.11.1987		74	*2011–2017*	720	40*	0	11.61	290	8-50	12/2	31.64	35	13/1
Lyons John James	21.5.1863	21.7.1927	14	*1886–1897*	731	134	1	27.07	6	5-30	1/0	24.83	3	
McAlister Peter Alexander	11.7.1869	10.5.1938	8	*1903*–1909	252	41	0	16.80	–	–	–/–	–	10	
Macartney Charles George (*CY 1922*)	27.6.1886	9.9.1958	35	*1907*–1926	2,131	170	7	41.78	45	7-58	2/1	27.55	17	
McCabe Stanley Joseph (*CY 1935*)	16.7.1910	25.8.1968	39	1930–1938	2,748	232	6	48.21	36	4-13	0/0	42.86	41	
McCool Colin Leslie	9.12.1916	5.4.1986	14	*1945–1949*	459	104*	1	35.30	36	5-41	3/0	26.61	14	
McCormick Ernest Leslie	16.5.1906	28.6.1991	12	*1935*–1938	54	17*	0	6.00	36	4-101	0/0	29.97	8	
McCosker Richard Bede (*CY 1976*)	11.12.1946		25	*1974–1979*	1,622	127	4	39.56	–	–	–/–	–	21	14
McDermott Craig John (*CY 1986*)	14.4.1965		71	*1984–1995*	940	42*	0	12.20	291	8-97	14/2	28.63	19	138

§ *Langer's figures include 22 runs and one catch, and Lee's four runs, two wickets and one catch for Australia v the ICC World XI in the Super Series Test in 2005-06.*

	Born	Died	Tests	Test Career	Runs	HS	100s	Avge	Wkts	BB	5/10	Avge	Ct/St	O/T
McDonald Andrew Barry	15.6.1981		4	*2008*	107	68	0	21.40	9	3-25	0/0	33.33	2	
McDonald Colin Campbell	17.11.1928		47	*1951*–1961	3,107	170	5	39.32	0	0-3	0/0	–	14	
McDonald Edgar Arthur (*CY 1922*)	6.1.1891	22.7.1937	11	*1920–1921*	116	36	0	16.57	43	5-32	2/0	33.27	3	
McDonnell Percy Stanislaus	13.11.1858	24.9.1896	19	1880–1888	955	147	3	28.93	0	0-11	0/0	–	6	
McGain Bryce Edward	25.3.1972		1	*2008*	2	2	0	1.00	0	0-149	0/0	–	0	
MacGill Stuart Charles Glyndwr	25.2.1971		44§	*1997–2007*	349	43	0	9.69	208	8-108	12/2	29.02	16	3
McGrath Glenn Donald (*CY 1998*)	9.2.1970		124§	*1993–2006*	641	61	0	7.36	563	8-24	29/3	21.64	38	249‡/2
McIlwraith John	7.9.1857	5.7.1938	1	1886	9	7	0	4.50	–	–	–/–	–	1	
McIntyre Peter Edward	27.4.1966		2	*1994–1996*	22	16	0	7.33	5	3-103	0/0	38.80	0	
McKay Clinton James	22.2.1983		1	*2009*	10	10	0	10.00	1	1-56	0/0	101.00	1	59/6
Mackay Kenneth Donald MBE	24.10.1925	13.6.1982	37	1956–*1962*	1,507	89	0	33.48	50	6-42	2/0	34.42	16	
McKenzie Graham Douglas (*CY 1965*)	24.6.1941		60	1961–*1970*	945	76	0	12.27	246	8-71	16/3	29.78	34	1
McKibbin Thomas Robert	10.12.1870	15.12.1939	5	*1894–1897*	88	28*	0	14.66	17	3-35	0/0	29.17	4	
McLaren John William	22.12.1886	17.11.1921	1	*1911*	0	0*	0	–	1	1-23	0/0	70.00	0	
Maclean John Alexander	27.4.1946		4	*1978*	79	33*	0	11.28	–	–	–/–	–	18	2
[2] **McLeod** Charles Edward	24.10.1869	26.11.1918	17	*1894*–1905	573	112	1	23.87	33	5-65	2/0	40.15	9	
[2] **McLeod** Robert William	19.1.1868	14.6.1907	6	*1891*–1893	146	31	0	13.27	12	5-53	1/0	31.83	3	
McShane Patrick George	18.4.1858	11.12.1903	3	*1884–1887*	26	12*	0	5.20	1	1-39	0/0	48.00	2	
Maddinson Nicolas James	21.12.1991		3	*2016*	27	22	0	6.75	0	0-9	0/0	–	2	0/2
Maddocks Leonard Victor	24.5.1926	27.8.2016	7	*1954–1956*	177	69	0	17.70	–	–	–/–	–	19/1	
Maguire John Norman	15.9.1956		3	*1983*	28	15*	0	7.00	10	4-57	0/0	32.30	2	23
Mailey Arthur Alfred	3.1.1886	31.12.1967	21	*1920*–1926	222	46*	0	11.10	99	9-121	6/2	33.91	14	
Mallett Ashley Alexander	13.7.1945		38	1968–1980	430	43*	0	11.62	132	8-59	6/1	29.84	30	9
Malone Michael Francis	9.10.1950		1	1977	46	46	0	46.00	6	5-63	1/0	12.83	0	10
Mann Anthony Longford	8.11.1945		4	*1977*	189	105	1	23.62	4	3-12	0/0	79.00	2	
Manou Graham Allan	23.4.1979		1	2009	21	13*	0	21.00	–	–	–/–	–	3	4
Marr Alfred Percy	28.3.1862	15.3.1940	1	*1884*	5	5	0	2.50	0	0-3	0/0	–	0	
[1] **Marsh** Geoffrey Robert	31.12.1958		50	*1985–1991*	2,854	138	4	33.18	–	–	–/–	–	38	117
[1,2] **Marsh** Mitchell Ross	20.10.1991		24	*2014–2017*	994	181	2	29.23	29	4-61	0/0	42.03	11	48/9
Marsh Rodney William MBE (*CY 1982*)	4.11.1947		96	*1970–1983*	3,633	132	3	26.51	0	0-3	0/0	–	343/12	92
[1,2] **Marsh** Shaun Edward	9.7.1983		28	*2011–2017*	1,921	182	6	40.87	–	–	–/–	–	19	53/15
Martin John Wesley	28.7.1931	16.7.1992	8	*1960–1966*	214	55	0	17.83	17	3-56	0/0	48.94	5	
Martyn Damien Richard (*CY 2002*)	21.10.1971		67	*1992–2006*	4,406	165	13	46.37	2	1-0	0/0	84.00	36	208/4
Massie Hugh Hamon	11.4.1854	12.10.1938	9	*1881–1884*	249	55	0	15.56	–	–	–/–	–	5	
Massie Robert Arnold Lockyer (*CY 1973*)	14.4.1947		6	1972–*1972*	78	42	0	11.14	31	8-53	2/1	20.87	1	3

§ *MacGill's figures include no runs and nine wickets and McGrath's two runs and three wickets for Australia v the ICC World XI in the Super Series Test in 2005-06.*

	Born	*Died*	*Tests*	*Test Career*	*Runs*	*HS*	*100s*	*Avge*	*Wkts*	*BB*	*5/10*	*Avge*	*Ct/St*	*O/T*
Matthews Christopher Darrell	22.9.1962		3	*1986–1988*	54	32	0	10.80	6	3-95	0/0	52.16	1	
Matthews Gregory Richard John	15.12.1959		33	*1983–1992*	1,849	130	4	41.08	61	5-103	2/1	48.22	17	59
Matthews Thomas James	3.4.1884	14.10.1943	8	*1911*–1912	153	53	0	17.00	16	4-29	0/0	26.18	7	
Maxwell Glenn James	14.10.1988		7	*2012–2017*	339	104	1	26.07	8	4-127	0/0	42.62	5	80/38
May Timothy Brian Alexander	26.1.1962		24	*1987–1994*	225	42*	0	14.06	75	5-9	3/0	34.74	6	47
Mayne Edgar Richard	2.7.1882	26.10.1961	4	1912–*1921*	64	25*	0	21.33	0	0-1	0/0	–	2	
Mayne Lawrence Charles	23.1.1942		6	*1964–1969*	76	13	0	9.50	19	4-43	0/0	33.05	3	
Meckiff Ian	6.1.1935		18	*1957–1963*	154	45*	0	11.84	45	6-38	2/0	31.62	9	
Mennie Joe Matthew	24.12.1988		1	*2016*	10	10	0	5.00	1	1-85	0/0	85.00	0	2
Meuleman Kenneth Douglas	5.9.1923	10.9.2004	1	*1945*	0	0	0	0.00	–	–	–/–	–	1	
Midwinter William Evans	19.6.1851	3.12.1890	8†	*1876–1886*	174	37	0	13.38	14	5-78	1/0	23.78	5	
Miller Colin Reid	6.2.1964		18	*1998–2000*	174	43	0	8.28	69	5-32	3/1	26.15	6	
Miller Keith Ross MBE (*CY 1954*)	28.11.1919	11.10.2004	55	*1945–1956*	2,958	147	7	36.97	170	7-60	7/1	22.97	38	
Minnett Roy Baldwin	13.6.1888	21.10.1955	9	*1911*–1912	391	90	0	26.06	11	4-34	0/0	26.36	0	
Misson Francis Michael	19.11.1938		5	*1960*–1961	38	25*	0	19.00	16	4-58	0/0	38.50	6	
Moody Thomas Masson (*CY 2000*)	2.10.1965		8	*1989–1992*	456	106	2	32.57	2	1-17	0/0	73.50	9	76
Moroney John	24.7.1917	1.7.1999	7	*1949–1951*	383	118	2	34.81	–	–	–/–	–	0	
Morris Arthur Robert MBE (*CY 1949*)	19.1.1922	22.8.2015	46	*1946–1954*	3,533	206	12	46.48	2	1-5	0/0	25.00	15	
Morris Samuel	22.6.1855	20.9.1931	1	*1884*	14	10*	0	14.00	2	2-73	0/0	36.50	0	
Moses Henry	13.2.1858	7.12.1938	6	*1886–1894*	198	33	0	19.80	–	–	–/–	–	1	
Moss Jeffrey Kenneth	29.6.1947		1	*1978*	60	38*	0	60.00	–	–	–/–	–	0	1
Moule William Henry	31.1.1858	24.8.1939	1	1880	40	34	0	20.00	3	3-23	0/0	7.66	1	
Muller Scott Andrew	11.7.1971		2	*1999*	6	6*	0	–	7	3-68	0/0	36.85	2	
Murdoch William Lloyd	18.10.1854	18.2.1911	18†	*1876*–1890	896	211	2	32.00	–	–	–/–	–	14	
Musgrove Henry Alfred	27.11.1858	2.11.1931	1	*1884*	13	9	0	6.50	–	–	–/–	–	0	
Nagel Lisle Ernest	6.3.1905	23.11.1971	1	*1932*	21	21*	0	21.00	2	2-110	0/0	55.00	0	
Nash Laurence John	2.5.1910	24.7.1986	2	*1931–1936*	30	17	0	15.00	10	4-18	0/0	12.60	6	
Nevill Peter Michael	13.10.1985		17	2015–*2016*	468	66	0	22.28	–	–	–/–	–	61/2	0/9
Nicholson Matthew James	2.10.1974		1	*1998*	14	9	0	7.00	4	3-56	0/0	28.75	0	
Nitschke Homesdale Carl ("Jack")	14.4.1905	29.9.1982	2	*1931*	53	47	0	26.50	–	–	–/–	–	3	
Noble Montague Alfred (*CY 1900*)	28.1.1873	22.6.1940	42	*1897*–1909	1,997	133	1	30.25	121	7-17	9/2	25.00	26	
Noblet Geffery	14.9.1916	16.8.2006	3	*1949–1952*	22	13*	0	7.33	7	3-21	0/0	26.14	1	
North Marcus James	28.7.1979		21	*2008–2010*	1,171	128	5	35.48	14	6-55	1/0	42.21	17	2/1
Nothling Otto Ernest	1.8.1900	26.9.1965	1	*1928*	52	44	0	26.00	0	0-12	0/0	–	0	
O'Brien Leo Patrick Joseph	2.7.1907	13.3.1997	5	*1932–1936*	211	61	0	26.37	–	–	–/–	–	3	
O'Connor John Denis Alphonsus	9.9.1875	23.8.1941	4	*1907*–1909	86	20	0	12.28	13	5-40	1/0	26.15	3	

	Born	Died	Tests	Test Career	Runs	HS	100s	Avge	Wkts	BB	5/10	Avge	Ct/St	O/T
O'Donnell Simon Patrick	26.1.1963		6	1985–1985	206	48	0	29.42	6	3-37	0/0	84.00	4	87
Ogilvie Alan David	3.6.1951		5	1977	178	47	0	17.80	–	–	–/–	–	5	
O'Keefe Stephen Norman John	9.12.1984		9	2014–2017	86	25	0	9.55	35	6-35	2/1	29.40	0	0/7
O'Keeffe Kerry James	25.11.1949		24	1970–1977	644	85	0	25.76	53	5-101	1/0	38.07	15	2
Oldfield William Albert Stanley MBE (CY 1927)	9.9.1894	10.8.1976	54	1920–1936	1,427	65*	0	22.65	–	–	–/–	–	78/52	
O'Neill Norman Clifford Louis (CY 1962)	19.2.1937	3.3.2008	42	1958–1964	2,779	181	6	45.55	17	4-41	0/0	39.23	21	
O'Reilly William Joseph OBE (CY 1935)	20.12.1905	6.10.1992	27	1931–1945	410	56*	0	12.81	144	7-54	11/3	22.59	7	
Oxenham Ronald Keven	28.7.1891	16.8.1939	7	1928–1931	151	48	0	15.10	14	4-39	0/0	37.28	4	
Paine Timothy David	8.12.1984		9	2010–2017	479	92	0	39.91	–	–	–/–	–	41/2	26/10‡
Palmer George Eugene	22.2.1859	22.8.1910	17	1880–1886	296	48	0	14.09	78	7-65	6/2	21.51	13	
Park Roy Lindsay	30.7.1892	23.1.1947	1	1920	0	0	0	0.00	0	0-9	0/0	–	0	
Pascoe Leonard Stephen	13.2.1950		14	1977–1981	106	30*	0	10.60	64	5-59	1/0	26.06	2	29
[2] **Pattinson** James Lee	3.5.1990		17	2011–2015	332	42	0	27.66	70	5-27	4/0	26.15	4	15/4
Pellew Clarence Everard ("Nip")	21.9.1893	9.5.1981	10	1920–1921	484	116	2	37.23	0	0-3	0/0	–	4	
Phillips Wayne Bentley	1.3.1958		27	1983–1985	1,485	159	2	32.28	–	–	–/–	–	52	48
Phillips Wayne Norman	7.11.1962		1	1991	22	14	0	11.00	–	–	–/–	–	0	
Philpott Peter Ian	21.11.1934		8	1964–1965	93	22	0	10.33	26	5-90	1/0	38.46	5	
Ponsford William Harold MBE (CY 1935)	19.10.1900	6.4.1991	29	1924–1934	2,122	266	7	48.22	–	–	–/–	–	21	
Ponting Ricky Thomas (CY 2006)	19.12.1974		168§	1995–2012	13,378	257	41	51.85	5	1-0	0/0	55.20	196	374‡/17
Pope Roland James	18.2.1864	27.7.1952	1	1884	3	3	0	1.50	–	–	–/–	–	0	
Quiney Robert John	20.8.1982		2	2012	9	9	0	3.00	0	0-3	0/0	–	5	
Rackemann Carl Gray	3.6.1960		12	1982–1990	53	15*	0	5.30	39	6-86	3/1	29.15	2	52
Ransford Vernon Seymour (CY 1910)	20.3.1885	19.3.1958	20	1907–1911	1,211	143*	1	37.84	1	1-9	0/0	28.00	10	
Redpath Ian Ritchie MBE	11.5.1941		66	1963–1975	4,737	171	8	43.45	0	0-0	0/0	–	83	5
Reedman John Cole	9.10.1865	25.3.1924	1	1894	21	17	0	10.50	1	1-12	0/0	24.00	1	
Reid Bruce Anthony	14.3.1963		27	1985–1992	93	13	0	4.65	113	7-51	5/2	24.63	5	61
Reiffel Paul Ronald	19.4.1966		35	1991–1997	955	79*	0	26.52	104	6-71	5/0	26.96	15	92
Renneberg David Alexander	23.9.1942		8	1966–1967	22	9	0	3.66	23	5-39	2/0	36.08	2	
Renshaw Matthew Thomas	28.3.1996		10	2016–2017	623	184	1	36.64	–	–	–/–	–	7	
Richardson Arthur John	24.7.1888	23.12.1973	9	1924–1926	403	100	1	31.00	12	2-20	0/0	43.41	1	
[4] **Richardson** Victor York OBE	7.9.1894	30.10.1969	19	1924–1935	706	138	1	23.53	–	–	–/–	–	24	
Rigg Keith Edward	21.5.1906	28.2.1995	8	1930–1936	401	127	1	33.41	–	–	–/–	–	5	
Ring Douglas Thomas	14.10.1918	23.6.2003	13	1947–1953	426	67	0	22.42	35	6-72	2/0	37.28	5	
Ritchie Gregory Michael	23.1.1960		30	1982–1986	1,690	146	3	35.20	0	0-10	0/0	–	14	44
Rixon Stephen John	25.2.1954		13	1977–1984	394	54	0	18.76	–	–	–/–	–	42/5	6

§ *Ponting's figures include 100 runs and one catch for Australia v the ICC World XI in the Super Series Test in 2005-06.*

	Born	Died	Tests	Test Career	Runs	HS	100s	Avge	Wkts	BB	5/10	Avge	Ct/St	O/T
Robertson Gavin Ron	28.5.1966		4	1997–1998	140	57	0	20.00	13	4-72	0/0	39.61	1	13
Robertson William Roderick	6.10.1861	24.6.1938	1	1884	2	2	0	1.00	0	0-24	0/0	–	0	
Robinson Richard Daryl	8.6.1946		3	1977	100	34	0	16.66	–	–	–/–	–	4	2
Robinson Rayford Harold	26.3.1914	10.8.1965	1	1936	5	3	0	2.50	–	–	–/–	–	1	
Rogers Christopher John Llewellyn (*CY 2014*)	31.8.1977		25	2007–2015	2,015	173	5	42.87	–	–	–/–	–	15	
Rorke Gordon Frederick	27.6.1938		4	1958–1959	9	7	0	4.50	10	3-23	0/0	20.30	1	
Rutherford John Walter	25.9.1929		1	1956	30	30	0	30.00	1	1-11	0/0	15.00	0	
Ryder John	8.8.1889	3.4.1977	20	1920–1928	1,394	201*	3	51.62	17	2-20	0/0	43.70	17	
Saggers Ronald Arthur	15.5.1917	17.3.1987	6	1948–1949	30	14	0	10.00	–	–	–/–	–	16/8	
Saunders John Victor	21.3.1876	21.12.1927	14	1901–1907	39	11*	0	2.29	79	7-34	6/0	22.73	5	
Scott Henry James Herbert	26.12.1858	23.9.1910	8	1884–1886	359	102	1	27.61	0	0-9	0/0	–	8	
Sellers Reginald Hugh Durning	20.8.1940		1	1964	0	0	0	0.00	0	0-17	0/0	–	1	
Serjeant Craig Stanton	1.11.1951		12	1977–1977	522	124	1	23.72	–	–	–/–	–	13	3
[5] **Sheahan** Andrew Paul	30.9.1946		31	1967–1973	1,594	127	2	33.91	–	–	–/–	–	17	3
Shepherd Barry Kenneth	23.4.1937	17.9.2001	9	1962–1964	502	96	0	41.83	0	0-3	0/0	–	2	
Siddle Peter Matthew	25.11.1984		62	2008–2016	1,063	51	0	14.76	211	6-54	8/0	29.92	16	17/2
Sievers Morris William	13.4.1912	10.5.1968	3	1936	67	25*	0	13.40	9	5-21	1/0	17.88	4	
Simpson Robert Baddeley (*CY 1965*)	3.2.1936		62	1957–1977	4,869	311	10	46.81	71	5-57	2/0	42.26	110	2
Sincock David John	1.2.1942		3	1964–1965	80	29	0	26.66	8	3-67	0/0	51.25	2	
Slater Keith Nichol	12.3.1936		1	1958	1	1*	0	–	2	2-40	0/0	50.50	0	
Slater Michael Jonathon	21.2.1970		74	1993–2001	5,312	219	14	42.83	1	1-4	0/0	10.00	33	42
Sleep Peter Raymond	4.5.1957		14	1978–1989	483	90	0	24.15	31	5-72	1/0	45.06	4	
Slight James	20.10.1855	9.12.1930	1	1880	11	11	0	5.50	–	–	–/–	–	0	
Smith David Bertram Miller	14.9.1884	29.7.1963	2	1912	30	24*	0	15.00	–	–	–/–	–	0	
Smith Steven Barry	18.10.1961		3	1983	41	12	0	8.20	–	–	–/–	–	1	28
Smith Steven Peter Devereux (*CY 2016*)	2.6.1989		61	2010–2017	6,057	239	23	63.75	17	3-18	0/0	54.35	89	103/30
Spofforth Frederick Robert	9.9.1853	4.6.1926	18	1876–1886	217	50	0	9.43	94	7-44	7/4	18.41	11	
Stackpole Keith Raymond MBE (*CY 1973*)	10.7.1940		43	1965–1973	2,807	207	7	37.42	15	2-33	0/0	66.73	47	6
Starc Mitchell Aaron	13.1.1990		40	2011–2017	1,111	99	0	23.14	170	6-50	8/1	27.73	19	68/22
Stevens Gavin Byron	29.2.1932		4	1959	112	28	0	16.00	–	–	–/–	–	2	
Symonds Andrew	9.6.1975		26	2003–2008	1,462	162*	2	40.61	24	3-50	0/0	37.33	22	198/14
Taber Hedley Brian	29.4.1940		16	1966–1969	353	48	0	16.04	–	–	–/–	–	56/4	
Tait Shaun William	22.2.1983		3	2005–2007	20	8	0	6.66	5	3-97	0/0	60.40	1	35/21
Tallon Donald (*CY 1949*)	17.2.1916	7.9.1984	21	1945–1953	394	92	0	17.13	–	–	–/–	–	50/8	
Taylor John Morris	10.10.1895	12.5.1971	20	1920–1926	997	108	1	35.60	1	1-25	0/0	45.00	11	
Taylor Mark Anthony (*CY 1990*)	27.10.1964		104	1988–1998	7,525	334*	19	43.49	1	1-11	0/0	26.00	157	113

	Born	Died	Tests	Test Career	Runs	HS	100s	Avge	Wkts	BB	5/10	Avge	Ct/St	O/T
Taylor Peter Laurence	22.8.1956		13	1986–1991	431	87	0	26.93	27	6-78	1/0	39.55	10	83
Thomas Grahame	21.3.1938		8	1964–1965	325	61	0	29.54	–	–	–/–	–	3	
Thoms George Ronald	22.3.1927	29.8.2003	1	1951	44	28	0	22.00	–	–	–/–	–	0	
Thomson Alan Lloyd ("Froggy")	2.12.1945		4	1970	22	12*	0	22.00	12	3-79	0/0	54.50	0	1
Thomson Jeffrey Robert	16.8.1950		51	1972–1985	679	49	0	12.81	200	6-46	8/0	28.00	20	50
Thomson Nathaniel Frampton Davis	29.5.1839	2.9.1896	2	1876	67	41	0	16.75	1	1-14	0/0	31.00	3	
Thurlow Hugh Motley ("Pud")	10.1.1903	3.12.1975	1	1931	0	0	0	0.00	0	0-33	0/0	–	0	
Toohey Peter Michael	20.4.1954		15	1977–1979	893	122	1	31.89	0	0-4	0/0	–	9	5
Toshack Ernest Raymond Herbert	8.12.1914	11.5.2003	12	1945–1948	73	20*	0	14.60	47	6-29	4/1	21.04	4	
Travers Joseph Patrick Francis	10.1.1871	15.9.1942	1	1901	10	9	0	5.00	1	1-14	0/0	14.00	1	
Tribe George Edward (*CY 1955*)	4.10.1920	5.4.2009	3	1946	35	25*	0	17.50	2	2-48	0/0	165.00	0	
[2] **Trott** Albert Edwin (*CY 1899*)	6.2.1873	30.7.1914	3†	1894	205	85*	0	102.50	9	8-43	1/0	21.33	4	
[2] **Trott** George Henry Stevens (*CY 1894*)	5.8.1866	10.11.1917	24	1888–1897	921	143	1	21.92	29	4-71	0/0	35.13	21	
[2] **Trumble** Hugh (*CY 1897*)	12.5.1867	14.8.1938	32	1890–1903	851	70	0	19.79	141	8-65	9/3	21.78	45	
[2] **Trumble** John William	16.9.1863	17.8.1944	7	1884–1886	243	59	0	20.25	10	3-29	0/0	22.20	3	
Trumper Victor Thomas (*CY 1903*)	2.11.1877	28.6.1915	48	1899–1911	3,163	214*	8	39.04	8	3-60	0/0	39.62	31	
Turner Alan	23.7.1950		14	1975–1976	768	136	1	29.53	–	–	–/–	–	15	6
Turner Charles Thomas Biass (*CY 1889*)	16.11.1862	1.1.1944	17	1886–1894	323	29	0	11.53	101	7-43	11/2	16.53	8	
Veivers Thomas Robert	6.4.1937		21	1963–1966	813	88	0	31.26	33	4-68	0/0	41.66	7	
Veletta Michael Robert John	30.10.1963		8	1987–1989	207	39	0	18.81	–	–	–/–	–	12	20
Voges Adam Charles	4.10.1979		20	2015–2016	1,485	269*	5	61.87	0	0-3	0/0	–	15	31/7
Wade Matthew Scott	26.12.1987		22	2011–2017	886	106	2	28.58	0	0-0	0/0	–	63/11	94/26
Waite Mervyn George	7.1.1911	16.12.1985	2	1938	11	8	0	3.66	1	1-150	0/0	190.00	1	
Walker Maxwell Henry Norman	12.9.1948	28.9.2016	34	1972–1977	586	78*	0	19.53	138	8-143	6/0	27.47	12	17
Wall Thomas Welbourn ("Tim")	13.5.1904	26.3.1981	18	1928–1934	121	20	0	6.36	56	5-14	3/0	35.89	11	
Walters Francis Henry	9.2.1860	1.6.1922	1	1884	12	7	0	6.00	–	–	–/–	–	2	
Walters Kevin Douglas MBE	21.12.1945		74	1965–1980	5,357	250	15	48.26	49	5-66	1/0	29.08	43	28
Ward Francis Anthony	23.2.1906	25.3.1974	4	1936–1938	36	18	0	6.00	11	6-102	1/0	52.18	1	
Warne Shane Keith (*CY 1994*)	13.9.1969		145§	1991–2006	3,154	99	0	17.32	708	8-71	37/10	25.41	125	193‡
Warner David Andrew	27.10.1986		71	2011–2017	6,146	253	21	48.77	4	2-45	0/0	67.25	53	101/65
Watkins John Russell	16.4.1943		1	1972	39	36	0	39.00	0	0-21	0/0	–	1	
Watson Graeme Donald	8.3.1945		5	1966–1972	97	50	0	10.77	6	2-67	0/0	42.33	1	2
Watson Shane Robert	17.6.1981		59§	2004–2015	3,731	176	4	35.19	75	6-33	3/0	33.68	45	190/58
Watson William James	31.1.1931		4	1954	106	30	0	17.66	0	0-5	0/0	–	2	
[2] **Waugh** Mark Edward (*CY 1991*)	2.6.1965		128	1990–2002	8,029	153*	20	41.81	59	5-40	1/0	41.16	181	244

§ *Warne's figures include 12 runs and six wickets, and Watson's 34 runs and no wicket, for Australia v the ICC World XI in the Super Series Test in 2005-06.*

	Born	Died	Tests	Test Career	Runs	HS	100s	Avge	Wkts	BB	5/10	Avge	Ct/St	O/T
[2] **Waugh** Stephen Rodger (*CY 1989*)	2.6.1965		168	1985–2003	10,927	200	32	51.06	92	5-28	3/0	37.44	112	325
Wellham Dirk Macdonald	13.3.1959		6	1981–1986	257	103	1	23.36	–	–	–/–	–	5	17
Wessels Kepler Christoffel (*CY 1995*)	14.9.1957		24†	1982–1985	1,761	179	4	42.95	0	0-2	0/0	–	18	54‡
Whatmore Davenell Frederick	16.3.1954		7	1978–1979	293	77	0	22.53	0	0-11	0/0	–	13	1
White Cameron Leon	18.8.1983		4	2008	146	46	0	29.20	5	2-71	0/0	68.40	1	88/47
Whitney Michael Roy	24.2.1959		12	1981–1992	68	13	0	6.18	39	7-27	2/1	33.97	2	38
Whitty William James	15.8.1886	30.1.1974	14	1909–1912	161	39*	0	13.41	65	6-17	3/0	21.12	4	
Wiener Julien Mark	1.5.1955		6	1979	281	93	0	25.54	0	0-19	0/0	–	4	7
Williams Brad Andrew	20.11.1974		4	2003	23	10*	0	7.66	9	4-53	0/0	45.11	4	25
Wilson John William	20.8.1921	13.10.1985	1	1956	–	–	–	–	1	1-25	0/0	64.00	0	
Wilson Paul	12.1.1972		1	1997	0	0*	0	–	0	0-50	0/0	–	0	11
Wood Graeme Malcolm	6.11.1956		59	1977–1988	3,374	172	9	31.83	–	–	–/–	–	41	83
Woodcock Ashley James	27.2.1947		1	1973	27	27	0	27.00	–	–	–/–	–	1	1
Woodfull William Maldon OBE (*CY 1927*)	22.8.1897	11.8.1965	35	1926–1934	2,300	161	7	46.00	–	–	–/–	–	7	
Woods Samuel Moses James (*CY 1889*)	13.4.1867	30.4.1931	3†	1888	32	18	0	5.33	5	2-35	0/0	24.20	1	
Woolley Roger Douglas	16.9.1954		2	1982–1983	21	13	0	10.50	–	–	–/–	–	7	4
Worrall John	20.6.1860	17.11.1937	11	1884–1899	478	76	0	25.15	1	1-97	0/0	127.00	13	
Wright Kevin John	27.12.1953		10	1978–1979	219	55*	0	16.84	–	–	–/–	–	31/4	5
Yallop Graham Neil	7.10.1952		39	1975–1984	2,756	268	8	41.13	1	1-21	0/0	116.00	23	30
Yardley Bruce	5.9.1947		33	1977–1982	978	74	0	19.56	126	7-98	6/1	31.63	31	7
Young Shaun	13.6.1970		1	1997	4	4*	0	4.00	0	0-5	0/0	–	0	
Zoehrer Timothy Joseph	25.9.1961		10	1985–1986	246	52*	0	20.50	–	–	–/–	–	18/1	22

SOUTH AFRICA (334 players)

	Born	Died	Tests	Test Career	Runs	HS	100s	Avge	Wkts	BB	5/10	Avge	Ct/St	O/T
Abbott Kyle John	18.6.1987		11	2012–2016	95	17	0	6.78	39	7-29	3/0	22.71	4	28/21
Ackerman Hylton Deon	14.2.1973		4	1997	161	57	0	20.12	–	–	–/–	–	1	
Adams Paul Regan	20.1.1977		45	1995–2003	360	35	0	9.00	134	7-128	4/1	32.87	29	24
Adcock Neil Amwin Treharne (*CY 1961*)	8.3.1931	6.1.2013	26	1953–1961	146	24	0	5.40	104	6-43	5/0	21.10	4	
Amla Hashim Mahomed (*CY 2013*)	31.3.1983		113	2004–2017	8,786	311*	28	49.08	0	0-4	0/0	–	99	158/40‡
Anderson James Henry	26.4.1874	11.3.1926	1	1902	43	32	0	21.50	–	–	–/–	–	1	
Ashley William Hare	10.2.1862	14.7.1930	1	1888	1	1	0	0.50	7	7-95	1/0	13.57	0	
Bacher Adam Marc	29.10.1973		19	1996–1999	833	96	0	26.03	0	0-4	0/0	–	11	13
Bacher Aron ("Ali")	24.5.1942		12	1965–1969	679	73	0	32.33	–	–	–/–	–	10	

	Born	Died	Tests	Test Career	Runs	HS	100s	Avge	Wkts	BB	5/10	Avge	Ct/St	O/T
Balaskas Xenophon Constantine	15.10.1910	12.5.1994	9	*1930–1938*	174	122*	1	14.50	22	5-49	1/0	36.63	5	
Barlow Edgar John	12.8.1940	30.12.2005	30	*1961–1969*	2,516	201	6	45.74	40	5-85	1/0	34.05	35	
Baumgartner Harold Vane	17.11.1883	8.4.1938	1	*1913*	19	16	0	9.50	2	2-99	0/0	49.50	1	
Bavuma Temba	17.5.1990		27	*2014–2017*	1,259	102*	1	33.13	1	1-29	0/0	51.00	13	2
Beaumont Rolland	4.2.1884	25.5.1958	5	1912–*1913*	70	31	0	7.77	0	0-0	0/0	–	2	
Begbie Denis Warburton	12.12.1914	10.3.2009	5	*1948–1949*	138	48	0	19.71	1	1-38	0/0	130.00	2	
Bell Alexander John	15.4.1906	1.8.1985	16	1929–1935	69	26*	0	6.27	48	6-99	4/0	32.64	6	
Bisset *Sir* Murray	14.4.1876	24.10.1931	3	*1898–1909*	103	35	0	25.75	–	–	–/–	–	2/1	
Bissett George Finlay	5.11.1905	14.11.1965	4	*1927*	38	23	0	19.00	25	7-29	2/0	18.76	0	
Blanckenberg James Manuel	31.12.1892	d unknown	18	*1913*–1924	455	59	0	19.78	60	6-76	4/0	30.28	9	
Bland Kenneth Colin (*CY 1966*)	5.4.1938		21	*1961–1966*	1,669	144*	3	49.08	2	2-16	0/0	62.50	10	
Bock Ernest George	17.9.1908	5.9.1961	1	*1935*	11	9*	0	–	0	0-42	0/0	–	0	
Boje Nico	20.3.1973		43	*1999*–2006	1,312	85	0	25.23	100	5-62	3/0	42.65	18	113‡/1
Bond Gerald Edward	5.4.1909	27.8.1965	1	*1938*	0	0	0	0.00	0	0-16	0/0	–	0	
Bosch Tertius	14.3.1966	14.2.2000	1	*1991*	5	5*	0	–	3	2-61	0/0	34.66	0	2
Botha Johan	2.5.1982		5	2005–*2010*	83	25	0	20.75	17	4-56	0/0	33.70	3	76‡/40
Botten James Thomas ("Jackie")	21.6.1938	14.5.2006	3	1965	65	33	0	10.83	8	2-56	0/0	42.12	1	
Boucher Mark Verdon (*CY 2009*)	3.12.1976		146§	*1997–2011*	5,498	125	5	30.54	1	1-6	0/0	6.00	530/23	290‡/25
Brann William Henry	4.4.1899	22.9.1953	3	*1922*	71	50	0	14.20	–	–	–/–	–	2	
Briscoe Arthur Wellesley ("Dooley")	6.2.1911	22.4.1941	2	*1935–1938*	33	16	0	11.00	–	–	–/–	–	1	
Bromfield Harry Dudley	26.6.1932		9	*1961*–1965	59	21	0	11.80	17	5-88	1/0	35.23	13	
Brown Lennox Sidney	24.11.1910	1.9.1983	2	*1931*	17	8	0	5.66	3	1-30	0/0	63.00	0	
Burger Christopher George de Villiers	12.7.1935	5.6.2014	2	*1957*	62	37*	0	20.66	–	–	–/–	–	1	
Burke Sydney Frank	11.3.1934	3.4.2017	2	*1961–1964*	42	20	0	14.00	11	6-128	2/1	23.36	0	
Buys Isaac Daniel	4.2.1895	d unknown	1	*1922*	4	4*	0	4.00	0	0-20	0/0	–	0	
Cameron Horace Brakenridge ("Jock") (*CY 1936*)	5.7.1905	2.11.1935	26	*1927*–1935	1,239	90	0	30.21	–	–	–/–	–	39/12	
Campbell Thomas	9.2.1882	5.10.1924	5	*1909*–1912	90	48	0	15.00	–	–	–/–	–	7/1	
Carlstein Peter Rudolph	28.10.1938		8	*1957–1963*	190	42	0	14.61	–	–	–/–	–	3	
Carter Claude Pagdett	23.4.1881	8.11.1952	10	1912–1924	181	45	0	18.10	28	6-50	2/0	24.78	2	
Catterall Robert Hector (*CY 1925*)	10.7.1900	3.1.1961	24	*1922–1930*	1,555	120	3	37.92	7	3-15	0/0	23.14	12	
Chapman Horace William	30.6.1890	1.12.1941	2	*1913–1921*	39	17	0	13.00	1	1-51	0/0	104.00	1	
Cheetham John Erskine	26.5.1920	21.8.1980	24	*1948*–1955	883	89	0	23.86	0	0-2	0/0	–	13	
Chevalier Grahame Anton	9.3.1937	14.11.2017	1	*1969*	0	0*	0	0.00	5	3-68	0/0	20.00	1	
Christy James Alexander Joseph	12.12.1904	1.2.1971	10	1929–*1931*	618	103	1	34.33	2	1-15	0/0	46.00	3	

§ *Boucher's figures exclude 17 runs and two catches for the ICC World XI v Australia in the Super Series Test in 2005-06.*

	Born	Died	Tests	Test Career	Runs	HS	100s	Avge	Wkts	BB	5/10	Avge	Ct/St	O/T
Chubb Geoffrey Walter Ashton	12.4.1911	28.8.1982	5	1951	63	15*	0	10.50	21	6-51	2/0	27.47	0	
Cochran John Alexander Kennedy	15.7.1909	15.6.1987	1	*1930*	4	4	0	4.00	0	0-47	0/0	–	0	
Coen Stanley Keppel ("Shunter")	14.10.1902	29.1.1967	2	*1927*	101	41*	0	50.50	0	0-7	0/0	–	1	
Commaille John McIllwaine Moore ("Mick")	21.2.1883	28.7.1956	12	*1909–1927*	355	47	0	16.90	–	–	–/–	–	1	
Commins John Brian	19.2.1965		3	*1994*	125	45	0	25.00	–	–	–/–	–	2	
Conyngham Dalton Parry	10.5.1897	7.7.1979	1	*1922*	6	3*	0	–	2	1-40	0/0	51.50	1	
Cook Frederick James	1870	30.11.1915	1	*1895*	7	7	0	3.50	–	–	–/–	–	0	
[1] **Cook** Stephen Craig	29.11.1982		11	*2015–2016*	632	117	3	33.26	0	0-16	0/0	–	6	
[1] **Cook** Stephen James (*CY 1990*)	31.7.1953		3	*1992–1993*	107	43	0	17.83	–	–	–/–	–	0	4
Cooper Alfred Henry Cecil	2.9.1893	18.7.1963	1	*1913*	6	6	0	3.00	–	–	–/–	–	1	
Cox Joseph Lovell	28.6.1886	4.7.1971	3	*1913*	17	12*	0	3.40	4	2-74	0/0	61.25	1	
Cripps Godfrey	19.10.1865	27.7.1943	1	*1891*	21	18	0	10.50	0	0-23	0/0	–	0	
Crisp Robert James	28.5.1911	2.3.1994	9	1935–*1935*	123	35	0	10.25	20	5-99	1/0	37.35	3	
Cronje Wessel Johannes ("Hansie")	25.9.1969	1.6.2002	68	*1991–1999*	3,714	135	6	36.41	43	3-14	0/0	29.95	33	188
Cullinan Daryll John	4.3.1967		70	*1992–2000*	4,554	275*	14	44.21	2	1-10	0/0	35.50	67	138
Curnow Sydney Harry	16.12.1907	28.7.1986	7	*1930–1931*	168	47	0	12.00	–	–	–/–	–	5	
Dalton Eric Londesbrough	2.12.1906	3.6.1981	15	1929–*1938*	698	117	2	31.72	12	4-59	0/0	40.83	5	
Davies Eric Quail	26.8.1909	11.11.1976	5	*1935–1938*	9	3	0	1.80	7	4-75	0/0	68.71	0	
Dawson Alan Charles	27.11.1969		2	2003	10	10	0	10.00	5	2-20	0/0	23.40	0	19
Dawson Oswald Charles	1.9.1919	22.12.2008	9	1947–*1948*	293	55	0	20.92	10	2-57	0/0	57.80	10	
Deane Hubert Gouvaine ("Nummy")	21.7.1895	21.10.1939	17	1924–*1930*	628	93	0	25.12	–	–	–/–	–	8	
de Bruyn Theunis Booysen	8.10.1992		3	*2016*–2017	72	48	0	12.00	0	0-18	0/0	–	5	0/2
de Bruyn Zander	5.7.1975		3	*2004*	155	83	0	38.75	3	2-32	0/0	30.66	0	
de Kock Quinton	17.12.1992		29	*2013–2017*	1,649	129*	3	39.26	–	–	–/–	–	116/7	88/31
de Lange Marchant	13.10.1990		2	*2011*	9	9	0	4.50	9	7-81	1/0	30.77	1	4/6
de Villiers Abraham Benjamin	17.2.1984		110	*2004–2017*	8,338	278*	21	49.92	2	2-49	0/0	52.00	211/5	220‡/78
de Villiers Petrus Stephanus ("Fanie")	13.10.1964		18	*1993–1997*	359	67*	0	18.89	85	6-23	5/2	24.27	11	83
de Wet Friedel	26.6.1980		2	*2009*	20	20	0	10.00	6	4-55	0/0	31.00	1	
Dippenaar Hendrik Human ("Boeta")	14.6.1977		38	*1999–2006*	1,718	177*	3	30.14	0	0-1	0/0	–	27	101‡/1
Dixon Cecil Donovan	12.2.1891	9.9.1969	1	*1913*	0	0	0	0.00	3	2-62	0/0	39.33	1	
Donald Allan Anthony (*CY 1992*)	20.10.1966		72	*1991–2001*	652	37	0	10.68	330	8-71	20/3	22.25	18	164
Dower Robert Reid	4.6.1876	15.9.1964	1	*1898*	9	9	0	4.50	–	–	–/–	–	2	
Draper Ronald George	24.12.1926		2	*1949*	25	15	0	8.33	–	–	–/–	–	0	
Duckworth Christopher Anthony Russell	22.3.1933	16.5.2014	2	*1956*	28	13	0	7.00	–	–	–/–	–	3	
Dumbrill Richard	19.11.1938		5	1965–*1966*	153	36	0	15.30	9	4-30	0/0	37.33	3	
Duminy Jacobus Petrus	16.12.1897	31.1.1980	3	*1927*–1929	30	12	0	5.00	1	1-17	0/0	39.00	2	

	Born	*Died*	*Tests*	*Test Career*	*Runs*	*HS*	*100s*	*Avge*	*Wkts*	*BB*	*5/10*	*Avge*	*Ct/St*	*O/T*
Duminy Jean-Paul	14.4.1984		46	*2008–2017*	2,103	166	6	32.85	42	4-47	0/0	38.11	38	179/73
Dunell Owen Robert	15.7.1856	21.10.1929	2	*1888*	42	26*	0	14.00	–	–	–/–	–	1	
du Plessis Francois	13.7.1984		48	*2012–2017*	3,022	137	7	45.10	0	0-1	0/0	–	41	116/36‡
du Preez John Harcourt	14.11.1942		2	*1966*	0	0	0	0.00	3	2-22	0/0	17.00	2	
du Toit Jacobus Francois	2.4.1869	10.7.1909	1	*1891*	2	2*	0	–	1	1-47	0/0	47.00	1	
Dyer Dennis Victor	2.5.1914	16.6.1990	3	1947	96	62	0	16.00	–	–	–/–	–	0	
Eksteen Clive Edward	2.12.1966		7	*1993–1999*	91	22	0	10.11	8	3-12	0/0	61.75	5	6
Elgar Dean	11.6.1987		45	*2012–2017*	2,861	199	10	42.07	13	4-22	0/0	44.76	43	6
Elgie Michael Kelsey ("Kim")	6.3.1933		3	*1961*	75	56	0	12.50	0	0-18	0/0	–	4	
Elworthy Steven	23.2.1965		4	1998–*2002*	72	48	0	18.00	13	4-66	0/0	34.15	1	39
Endean William Russell	31.5.1924	28.6.2003	28	1951–*1957*	1,630	162*	3	33.95	–	–	–/–	–	41	
Farrer William Stephen ("Buster")	8.12.1936		6	*1961–1963*	221	40	0	27.62	–	–	–/–	–	2	
Faulkner George Aubrey	17.12.1881	10.9.1930	25	*1905*–1924	1,754	204	4	40.79	82	7-84	4/0	26.58	20	
Fellows-Smith Jonathan Payn	3.2.1932	28.9.2013	4	1960	166	35	0	27.66	0	0-13	0/0	–	2	
Fichardt Charles Gustav	20.3.1870	30.5.1923	2	*1891–1895*	15	10	0	3.75	–	–	–/–	–	2	
Finlason Charles Edward	19.2.1860	31.7.1917	1	*1888*	6	6	0	3.00	0	0-7	0/0	–	0	
Floquet Claude Eugene	3.11.1884	22.11.1963	1	*1909*	12	11*	0	12.00	0	0-24	0/0	–	0	
Francis Howard Henry	26.5.1868	7.1.1936	2	*1898*	39	29	0	9.75	–	–	–/–	–	1	
Francois Cyril Matthew	20.6.1897	26.5.1944	5	*1922*	252	72	0	31.50	6	3-23	0/0	37.50	5	
Frank Charles Newton	27.1.1891	25.12.1961	3	*1921*	236	152	1	39.33	–	–	–/–	–	0	
Frank William Hughes Bowker	23.11.1872	16.2.1945	1	*1895*	7	5	0	3.50	1	1-52	0/0	52.00	0	
Fuller Edward Russell Henry	2.8.1931	19.7.2008	7	*1952–1957*	64	17	0	8.00	22	5-66	1/0	30.36	3	
Fullerton George Murray	8.12.1922	19.11.2002	7	1947–1951	325	88	0	25.00	–	–	–/–	–	10/2	
Funston Kenneth James	3.12.1925	15.4.2005	18	*1952–1957*	824	92	0	25.75	–	–	–/–	–	7	
Gamsy Dennis	17.2.1940		2	*1969*	39	30*	0	19.50	–	–	–/–	–	5	
Gibbs Herschelle Herman	23.2.1974		90	*1996–2007*	6,167	228	14	41.95	0	0-4	0/0	–	94	248/23
Gleeson Robert Anthony	6.12.1873	27.9.1919	1	*1895*	4	3	0	4.00	–	–	–/–	–	2	
Glover George Keyworth	13.5.1870	15.11.1938	1	*1895*	21	18*	0	21.00	1	1-28	0/0	28.00	0	
Goddard Trevor Leslie	1.8.1931	25.11.2016	41	1955–*1969*	2,516	112	1	34.46	123	6-53	5/0	26.22	48	
Gordon Norman	6.8.1911	2.9.2014	5	*1938*	8	7*	0	2.00	20	5-103	2/0	40.35	1	
Graham Robert	16.9.1877	21.4.1946	2	*1898*	6	4	0	1.50	3	2-22	0/0	42.33	2	
Grieveson Ronald Eustace	24.8.1909	24.7.1998	2	*1938*	114	75	0	57.00	–	–	–/–	–	7/3	
Griffin Geoffrey Merton	12.6.1939	16.11.2006	2	1960	25	14	0	6.25	8	4-87	0/0	24.00	0	
Hall Alfred Ewart	23.1.1896	1.1.1964	7	*1922–1930*	11	5	0	1.83	40	7-63	3/1	22.15	4	
Hall Andrew James	31.7.1975		21	*2001–2006*	760	163	1	26.20	45	3-1	0/0	35.93	16	88/2
Hall Glen Gordon	24.5.1938	26.6.1987	1	*1964*	0	0	0	0.00	1	1-94	0/0	94.00	0	

	Born	Died	Tests	Test Career	Runs	HS	100s	Avge	Wkts	BB	5/10	Avge	Ct/St	O/T
Halliwell Ernest Austin (*CY 1905*)	7.9.1864	2.10.1919	8	1891–1902	188	57	0	12.53	–	–	–/–	–	10/2	
Halse Clive Gray	28.2.1935	28.5.2002	3	1963	30	19*	0	–	6	3-50	0/0	43.33	1	
[2] **Hands** Philip Albert Myburgh	18.3.1890	27.4.1951	7	1913–1924	300	83	0	25.00	0	0-1	0/0	–	3	
[2] **Hands** Reginald Harry Myburgh	26.7.1888	20.4.1918	1	1913	7	7	0	3.50	–	–	–/–	–	0	
Hanley Martin Andrew	10.11.1918	2.6.2000	1	1948	0	0	0	0.00	1	1-57	0/0	88.00	0	
Harmer Simon Ross	10.2.1989		5	2014–2015	58	13	0	11.60	20	4-61	0/0	29.40	1	
Harris Paul Lee	2.11.1978		37	2006–2010	460	46	0	10.69	103	6-127	3/0	37.87	16	3
Harris Terence Anthony	27.8.1916	7.3.1993	3	1947–1948	100	60	0	25.00	–	–	–/–	–	1	
Hartigan Gerald Patrick Desmond	30.12.1884	7.1.1955	5	1912–1913	114	51	0	11.40	1	1-72	0/0	141.00	0	
Harvey Robert Lyon	14.9.1911	20.7.2000	2	1935	51	28	0	12.75	–	–	–/–	–	0	
Hathorn Christopher Maitland Howard	7.4.1878	17.5.1920	12	1902–1910	325	102	1	17.10	–	–	–/–	–	5	
Hayward Mornantau ("Nantie")	6.3.1977		16	1999–2004	66	14	0	7.33	54	5-56	1/0	29.79	4	21
[1,2] **Hearne** Frank	23.11.1858	14.7.1949	4†	1891–1895	121	30	0	15.12	2	2-40	0/0	20.00	2	
[1] **Hearne** George Alfred Lawrence	27.3.1888	13.11.1978	3	1922–1924	59	28	0	11.80	–	–	–/–	–	3	
Heine Peter Samuel	28.6.1928	4.2.2005	14	1955–1961	209	31	0	9.95	58	6-58	4/0	25.08	8	
Henderson Claude William	14.6.1972		7	2001–2002	65	30	0	9.28	22	4-116	0/0	42.18	2	4
Henry Omar	23.1.1952		3	1992	53	34	0	17.66	3	2-56	0/0	63.00	2	3
Hime Charles Frederick William	24.10.1869	6.12.1940	1	1895	8	8	0	4.00	1	1-20	0/0	31.00	0	
Hudson Andrew Charles	17.3.1965		35	1991–1997	2,007	163	4	33.45	–	–	–/–	–	36	89
Hutchinson Philip	25.1.1862	30.9.1925	2	1888	14	11	0	3.50	–	–	–/–	–	3	
Imran Tahir	27.3.1979		20	2011–2015	130	29*	0	9.28	57	5-32	2/0	40.24	8	81/33‡
Ironside David Ernest James	2.5.1925	21.8.2005	3	1953	37	13	0	18.50	15	5-51	1/0	18.33	1	
Irvine Brian Lee	9.3.1944		4	1969	353	102	1	50.42	–	–	–/–	–	2	
Jack Steven Douglas	4.8.1970		2	1994	7	7	0	3.50	8	4-69	0/0	24.50	1	2
Johnson Clement Lecky	31.3.1871	31.5.1908	1	1895	10	7	0	5.00	0	0-57	0/0	–	1	
Kallis Jacques Henry (*CY 2013*)	16.10.1975		165§	1995–2013	13,206	224	45	55.25	291	6-54	5/0	32.63	196	323‡/25
Keith Headley James	25.10.1927	17.11.1997	8	1952–1956	318	73	0	21.20	0	0-19	0/0	–	9	
Kemp Justin Miles	2.10.1977		4	2000–2005	80	55	0	13.33	9	3-33	0/0	24.66	3	79‡/8
Kempis Gustav Adolph	4.8.1865	19.5.1890	1	1888	0	0*	0	0.00	4	3-53	0/0	19.00	0	
Khan Imraan	27.4.1984		1	2008	20	20	0	20.00	–	–	–/–	–	1	
[2] **Kirsten** Gary (*CY 2004*)	23.11.1967		101	1993–2003	7,289	275	21	45.27	2	1-0	0/0	71.00	83	185
[2] **Kirsten** Peter Noel	14.5.1955		12	1991–1994	626	104	1	31.30	0	0-5	0/0	–	8	40
Kleinveldt Rory Keith	15.3.1983		4	2012	27	17*	0	9.00	10	3-65	0/0	42.20	2	10/6
Klusener Lance (*CY 2000*)	4.9.1971		49	1996–2004	1,906	174	4	32.86	80	8-64	1/0	37.91	34	171
Kotze Johannes Jacobus ("Kodgee")	7.8.1879	7.7.1931	3	1902–1907	2	2	0	0.40	6	3-64	0/0	40.50	3	

§ *Kallis's figures exclude 83 runs, one wicket and four catches for the ICC World XI v Australia in the Super Series Test in 2005-06.*

	Born	Died	Tests	Test Career	Runs	HS	100s	Avge	Wkts	BB	5/10	Avge	Ct/St	O/T
Kuhn Heino Gunther	1.4.1984		4	2017	113	34	0	14.12	–	–	–/–	–	1	0/7
Kuiper Adrian Paul	24.8.1959		1	1991	34	34	0	17.00	–	–	–/–	–	1	25
Kuys Frederick	21.3.1870	12.9.1953	1	1898	26	26	0	13.00	2	2-31	0/0	15.50	0	
Lance Herbert Roy ("Tiger")	6.6.1940	10.11.2010	13	1961–1969	591	70	0	28.14	12	3-30	0/0	39.91	7	
Langeveldt Charl Kenneth	17.12.1974		6	2004–2005	16	10	0	8.00	16	5-46	1/0	37.06	2	72/9
Langton Arthur Chudleigh Beaumont ("Chud")	2.3.1912	27.11.1942	15	1935–1938	298	73*	0	15.68	40	5-58	1/0	45.67	8	
Lawrence Godfrey Bernard	31.3.1932		5	1961	141	43	0	17.62	28	8-53	2/0	18.28	2	
le Roux Frederick Louis	5.2.1882	22.9.1963	1	1913	1	1	0	0.50	0	0-5	0/0	–	0	
Lewis Percy Tyson	2.10.1884	30.1.1976	1	1913	0	0	0	0.00	–	–	–/–	–	0	
Liebenberg Gerhardus Frederick Johannes	7.4.1972		5	1997–1998	104	45	0	13.00	–	–	–/–	–	0	
[1] **Lindsay** Denis Thomson	4.9.1939	30.11.2005	19	1963–1969	1,130	182	3	37.66	–	–	–/–	–	57/2	
[1] **Lindsay** John Dixon	8.9.1908	31.8.1990	3	1947	21	9*	0	7.00	–	–	–/–	–	4/1	
Lindsay Nevil Vernon	30.7.1886	2.2.1976	1	1921	35	29	0	17.50	–	–	–/–	–	1	
Ling William Victor Stone	3.10.1891	26.9.1960	6	1921–1922	168	38	0	16.80	0	0-20	0/0	–	1	
Llewellyn Charles Bennett (*CY 1911*)	26.9.1876	7.6.1964	15	1895–1912	544	90	0	20.14	48	6-92	4/1	29.60	7	
Lundie Eric Balfour	15.3.1888	12.9.1917	1	1913	1	1	0	1.00	4	4-101	0/0	26.75	0	
Macaulay Michael John	19.4.1939		1	1964	33	21	0	16.50	2	1-10	0/0	36.50	0	
McCarthy Cuan Neil	24.3.1929	14.8.2000	15	1948–1951	28	5	0	3.11	36	6-43	2/0	41.94	6	
McGlew Derrick John ("Jackie") (*CY 1956*)	11.3.1929	9.6.1998	34	1951–1961	2,440	255*	7	42.06	0	0-7	0/0	–	18	
McKenzie Neil Douglas (*CY 2009*)	24.11.1975		58	2000–2008	3,253	226	5	37.39	0	0-1	0/0	–	54	64/2
McKinnon Atholl Henry	20.8.1932	2.12.1983	8	1960–1966	107	27	0	17.83	26	4-128	0/0	35.57	1	
McLaren Ryan	9.2.1983		2	2009–2013	47	33*	0	23.50	3	2-72	0/0	54.00	0	54/12
McLean Roy Alastair (*CY 1961*)	9.7.1930	26.8.2007	40	1951–1964	2,120	142	5	30.28	0	0-1	0/0	–	23	
McMillan Brian Mervin	22.12.1963		38	1992–1998	1,968	113	3	39.36	75	4-65	0/0	33.82	49	78
McMillan Quintin	23.6.1904	3.7.1948	13	1929–1931	306	50*	0	18.00	36	5-66	2/0	34.52	8	
Maharaj Keshav Athmanand	7.2.1990		16	2016–2017	306	41*	0	18.00	57	6-40	3/0	26.78	5	2
Mann Norman Bertram Fleetwood ("Tufty")	28.12.1920	31.7.1952	19	1947–1951	400	52	0	13.33	58	6-59	1/0	33.10	3	
Mansell Percy Neville Frank MBE	16.3.1920	9.5.1995	13	1951–1955	355	90	0	17.75	11	3-58	0/0	66.90	15	
Markham Lawrence Anderson	12.9.1924	5.8.2000	1	1948	20	20	0	20.00	1	1-34	0/0	72.00	0	
Markram Aiden Kyle	4.10.1994		6	2017	520	143	2	52.00	0	0-13	0/0	–	6	1
Marx Waldemar Frederick Eric	4.7.1895	2.6.1974	3	1921	125	36	0	20.83	4	3-85	0/0	36.00	0	
Matthews Craig Russell	15.2.1965		18	1992–1995	348	62*	0	18.31	52	5-42	2/0	28.88	4	56
Meintjes Douglas James	9.6.1890	17.7.1979	2	1922	43	21	0	14.33	6	3-38	0/0	19.16	3	
Melle Michael George	3.6.1930	28.12.2003	7	1949–1952	68	17	0	8.50	26	6-71	2/0	32.73	4	
Melville Alan (*CY 1948*)	19.5.1910	18.4.1983	11	1938–1948	894	189	4	52.58	–	–	–/–	–	8	
Middleton James	30.9.1865	23.12.1913	6	1895–1902	52	22	0	7.42	24	5-51	2/0	18.41	1	

	Born	Died	Tests	Test Career	Runs	HS	100s	Avge	Wkts	BB	5/10	Avge	Ct/St	O/T
Mills Charles Henry	26.11.1867	26.7.1948	1	1891	25	21	0	12.50	2	2-83	0/0	41.50	1	
Milton *Sir* William Henry	3.12.1854	6.3.1930	3	1888–1891	68	21	0	11.33	2	1-5	0/0	24.00	2	
Mitchell Bruce (*CY 1936*)	8.1.1909	1.7.1995	42	1929–1948	3,471	189*	8	48.88	27	5-87	1/0	51.11	56	
Mitchell Frank (*CY 1902*)	13.8.1872	11.10.1935	3†	1912	28	12	0	4.66	–	–	–/–	–	0	
Morkel Denijs Paul Beck	25.1.1906	6.10.1980	16	1927–1931	663	88	0	24.55	18	4-93	0/0	45.61	13	
[2] **Morkel** Johannes Albertus	10.6.1981		1	2008	58	58	0	58.00	1	1-44	0/0	132.00	0	56‡/50
[2] **Morkel** Morne	6.10.1984		83	2006–2017	931	40	0	12.09	294	6-23	7/0	28.08	24	109‡/41‡
Morris Christopher Henry	30.4.1987		4	2015–2017	173	69	0	24.71	12	3-38	0/0	38.25	5	29/14
Murray Anton Ronald Andrew	30.4.1922	17.4.1995	10	1952–1953	289	109	1	22.23	18	4-169	0/0	39.44	3	
Nel Andre	15.7.1977		36	2001–2008	337	34	0	9.91	123	6-32	3/1	31.86	16	79/2
Nel John Desmond	10.7.1928	13.1.2018	6	1949–1957	150	38	0	13.63	–	–	–/–	–	1	
Newberry Claude	1889	1.8.1916	4	1913	62	16	0	7.75	11	4-72	0/0	24.36	3	
Newson Edward Serrurier OBE	2.12.1910	24.4.1988	3	1930–1938	30	16	0	7.50	4	2-58	0/0	66.25	3	
Ngam Mfuneko	29.1.1979		3	2000	0	0*	0	–	11	3-26	0/0	17.18	1	
Ngidi Lungisani True-man	29.03.1996		2	2017	6	4	0	2.00	9	6-39	1/0	17.22	0	0/3
Nicholson Frank	17.9.1909	30.7.1982	4	1935	76	29	0	10.85	–	–	–/–	–	3	
Nicolson John Fairless William	19.7.1899	13.12.1935	3	1927	179	78	0	35.80	0	0-5	0/0	–	0	
Norton Norman Ogilvie	11.5.1881	27.6.1968	1	1909	9	7	0	4.50	4	4-47	0/0	11.75	0	
[1] **Nourse** Arthur Dudley (*CY 1948*)	12.11.1910	14.8.1981	34	1935–1951	2,960	231	9	53.81	0	0-0	0/0	–	12	
[1] **Nourse** Arthur William ("Dave")	25.1.1879	8.7.1948	45	1902–1924	2,234	111	1	29.78	41	4-25	0/0	37.87	43	
Ntini Makhaya	6.7.1977		101	1997–2009	699	32*	0	9.84	390	7-37	18/4	28.82	25	172‡/10
Nupen Eiulf Peter ("Buster")	1.1.1902	29.1.1977	17	1921–1935	348	69	0	14.50	50	6-46	5/1	35.76	9	
Ochse Arthur Edward	11.3.1870	11.4.1918	2	1888	16	8	0	4.00	–	–	–/–	–	0	
Ochse Arthur Lennox	11.10.1899	5.5.1949	3	1927–1929	11	4*	0	3.66	10	4-79	0/0	36.20	1	
O'Linn Sidney	5.5.1927	11.12.2016	7	1960–1961	297	98	0	27.00	–	–	–/–	–	4	
Olivier Duanne	9.5.1992		5	2016–2017	7	4	0	2.33	17	3-38	0/0	23.11	0	
Ontong Justin Lee	4.1.1980		2	2001–2004	57	32	0	19.00	1	1-79	0/0	133.00	1	27‡/14
Owen-Smith Harold Geoffrey ("Tuppy") (*CY 1930*)	18.2.1909	28.2.1990	5	1929	252	129	1	42.00	0	0-3	0/0	–	4	
Palm Archibald William	8.6.1901	17.8.1966	1	1927	15	13	0	7.50	–	–	–/–	–	1	
Parker George Macdonald	27.5.1899	1.5.1969	2	1924	3	2*	0	1.50	8	6-152	1/0	34.12	0	
Parkin Durant Clifford	20.2.1873	20.3.1936	1	1891	6	6	0	3.00	3	3-82	0/0	27.33	1	
Parnell Wayne Dillon	30.7.1989		6	2009–2017	67	23	0	16.75	15	4-51	0/0	27.60	3	65/40
Partridge Joseph Titus	9.12.1932	6.6.1988	11	1963–1964	73	13*	0	10.42	44	7-91	3/0	31.20	6	
Pearse Charles Ormerod Cato	10.10.1884	7.5.1953	3	1910	55	31	0	9.16	3	3-56	0/0	35.33	1	
Pegler Sidney James	28.7.1888	10.9.1972	16	1909–1924	356	35*	0	15.47	47	7-65	2/0	33.44	5	

	Born	Died	Tests	Test Career	Runs	HS	100s	Avge	Wkts	BB	5/10	Avge	Ct/St	O/T
Petersen Alviro Nathan	25.11.1980		36	2009–2014	2,093	182	5	34.88	1	1-2	0/0	62.00	31	21/2
Peterson Robin John	4.8.1979		15	2003–2013	464	84	0	27.29	38	5-33	1/0	37.26	9	79/21
Phehlukwayo Andile Lucky	3.3.1996		4	2017	19	9	0	9.50	11	3-13	0/0	13.36	2	20/9
Philander Vernon Darryl	24.6.1985		50	2011–2017	1,290	74	0	24.33	188	6-42	12/2	21.85	15	30/7
Piedt Dane Lee-Roy	6.3.1990		7	2014–2016	48	19	0	6.85	24	5-153	1/0	36.04	4	
[2] **Pithey** Anthony John	17.7.1933	17.11.2006	17	1956–1964	819	154	1	31.50	0	0-5	0/0	–	3	
[2] **Pithey** David Bartlett	4.10.1936	21.1.2018	8	1963–1966	138	55	0	12.54	12	6-58	1/0	48.08	6	
Plimsoll Jack Bruce	27.10.1917	11.11.1999	1	1947	16	8*	0	16.00	3	3-128	0/0	47.66	0	
[1, 2] **Pollock** Peter Maclean (*CY 1966*)	30.6.1941		28	1961–1969	607	75*	0	21.67	116	6-38	9/1	24.18	9	
[2] **Pollock** Robert Graeme (*CY 1966*)	27.2.1944		23	1963–1969	2,256	274	7	60.97	4	2-50	0/0	51.00	17	
[1] **Pollock** Shaun Maclean (*CY 2003*)	16.7.1973		108	1995–2007	3,781	111	2	32.31	421	7-87	16/1	23.11	72	294‡/12
Poore Robert Montagu (*CY 1900*)	20.3.1866	14.7.1938	3	1895	76	20	0	12.66	1	1-4	0/0	4.00	3	
Pothecary James Edward	6.12.1933	11.5.2016	3	1960	26	12	0	6.50	9	4-58	0/0	39.33	2	
Powell Albert William	18.7.1873	11.9.1948	1	1898	16	11	0	8.00	1	1-10	0/0	10.00	2	
Pretorius Dewald	6.12.1977		4	2001–2003	22	9	0	7.33	6	4-115	0/0	71.66	0	
Prince Ashwell Gavin	28.5.1977		66	2001–2011	3,665	162*	11	41.64	1	1-2	0/0	47.00	47	49‡/1
Prince Charles Frederick Henry	11.9.1874	2.2.1949	1	1898	6	5	0	3.00	–	–	–/–	–	0	
Pringle Meyrick Wayne	22.6.1966		4	1991–1995	67	33	0	16.75	5	2-62	0/0	54.00	0	17
Procter Michael John (*CY 1970*)	15.9.1946		7	1966–1969	226	48	0	25.11	41	6-73	1/0	15.02	4	
Promnitz Henry Louis Ernest	23.2.1904	7.9.1983	2	1927	14	5	0	3.50	8	5-58	1/0	20.12	2	
Quinn Neville Anthony	21.2.1908	5.8.1934	12	1929–1931	90	28	0	6.00	35	6-92	1/0	32.71	1	
Rabada Kagiso	25.5.1995		26	2015–2017	336	34	0	13.44	120	7-112	7/3	22.04	11	43/16
Reid Norman	26.12.1890	6.6.1947	1	1921	17	11	0	8.50	2	2-63	0/0	31.50	0	
Rhodes Jonathan Neil (*CY 1999*)	27.7.1969		52	1992–2000	2,532	117	3	35.66	0	0-0	0/0	–	34	245
[2] **Richards** Alfred Renfrew	14.12.1867	9.1.1904	1	1895	6	6	0	3.00	–	–	–/–	–	0	
Richards Barry Anderson (*CY 1969*)	21.7.1945		4	1969	508	140	2	72.57	1	1-12	0/0	26.00	3	
[2] **Richards** William Henry Matthews	26.3.1862	4.1.1903	1	1888	4	4	0	2.00	–	–	–/–	–	0	
Richardson David John	16.9.1959		42	1991–1997	1,359	109	1	24.26	–	–	–/–	–	150/2	122
Robertson John Benjamin	5.6.1906	5.7.1985	3	1935	51	17	0	10.20	6	3-143	0/0	53.50	2	
Rose-Innes Albert	16.2.1868	22.11.1946	2	1888	14	13	0	3.50	5	5-43	1/0	17.80	2	
Routledge Thomas William	18.4.1867	9.5.1927	4	1891–1895	72	24	0	9.00	–	–	–/–	–	2	
[2] **Rowan** Athol Matthew Burchell	7.2.1921	22.2.1998	15	1947–1951	290	41	0	17.05	54	5-68	4/0	38.59	7	
[2] **Rowan** Eric Alfred Burchell (*CY 1952*)	20.7.1909	30.4.1993	26	1935–1951	1,965	236	3	43.66	0	0-0	0/0	–	14	
Rowe George Alexander	15.6.1874	8.1.1950	5	1895–1902	26	13*	0	4.33	15	5-115	1/0	30.40	4	
Rudolph Jacobus Andries	4.5.1981		48	2003–2012	2,622	222*	6	35.43	4	1-1	0/0	108.00	29	43‡/1
Rushmere Mark Weir	7.1.1965		1	1991	6	3	0	3.00	–	–	–/–	–	0	4

	Born	Died	Tests	Test Career	Runs	HS	100s	Avge	Wkts	BB	5/10	Avge	Ct/St	O/T
Samuelson Sivert Vause	21.11.1883	18.11.1958	1	*1909*	22	15	0	11.00	0	0-64	0/0	–	1	
Schultz Brett Nolan	26.8.1970		9	*1992–1997*	9	6	0	1.50	37	5-48	2/0	20.24	2	1
Schwarz Reginald Oscar (*CY 1908*)	4.5.1875	18.11.1918	20	*1905*–1912	374	61	0	13.85	55	6-47	2/0	25.76	18	
Seccull Arthur William	14.9.1868	20.7.1945	1	*1895*	23	17*	0	23.00	2	2-37	0/0	18.50	1	
Seymour Michael Arthur ("Kelly")	5.6.1936		7	*1963–1969*	84	36	0	12.00	9	3-80	0/0	65.33	2	
Shalders William Alfred	12.2.1880	18.3.1917	12	*1898*–1907	355	42	0	16.13	1	1-6	0/0	6.00	3	
Shamsi Tabraiz	18.2.1990		1	*2016*	18	18*	0	–	2	1-49	0/0	75.00	0	5/2
Shepstone George Harold	9.4.1876	3.7.1940	2	*1895–1898*	38	21	0	9.50	0	0-8	0/0	–	2	
Sherwell Percy William	17.8.1880	17.4.1948	13	*1905–1910*	427	115	1	23.72	–	–	–/–	–	20/16	
Siedle Ivan Julian ("Jack")	11.1.1903	24.8.1982	18	*1927–1935*	977	141	1	28.73	1	1-7	0/0	7.00	7	
Sinclair James Hugh	16.10.1876	23.2.1913	25	*1895–1910*	1,069	106	3	23.23	63	6-26	1/0	31.68	9	
Smith Charles James Edward	25.12.1872	27.3.1947	3	*1902*	106	45	0	21.20	–	–	–/–	–	2	
Smith Frederick William	31.3.1861	17.4.1914	3	*1888–1895*	45	12	0	9.00	–	–	–/–	–	2	
Smith Graeme Craig (*CY 2004*)	1.2.1981		116§	*2001–2013*	9,253	277	27	48.70	8	2-145	0/0	110.62	166	196‡/33
Smith Vivian Ian	23.2.1925	25.8.2015	9	1947–*1957*	39	11*	0	3.90	12	4-143	0/0	64.08	3	
Snell Richard Peter	12.9.1968		5	*1991–1994*	95	48	0	13.57	19	4-74	0/0	28.31	1	42
[2]**Snooke** Sibley John ("Tip")	1.2.1881	14.8.1966	26	*1905–1922*	1,008	103	1	22.40	35	8-70	1/1	20.05	24	
[2]**Snooke** Stanley de la Courtte	11.11.1878	6.4.1959	1	1907	0	0	0	0.00	–	–	–/–	–	2	
Solomon William Rodger Thomson	23.4.1872	13.7.1964	1	*1898*	4	2	0	2.00	–	–	–/–	–	1	
Stewart Robert Burnard	3.9.1856	12.9.1913	1	*1888*	13	9	0	6.50	–	–	–/–	–	2	
Steyn Dale Willem (*CY 2013*)	27.6.1983		86	*2004–2017*	1,178	76	0	14.19	419	7-51	26/5	22.32	23	114‡/42
Steyn Philippus Jeremia Rudolf	30.6.1967		3	*1994*	127	46	0	21.16	–	–	–/–	–	0	1
Stricker Louis Anthony	26.5.1884	5.2.1960	13	*1909*–1912	344	48	0	14.33	1	1-36	0/0	105.00	3	
Strydom Pieter Coenraad	10.6.1969		2	*1999*	35	30	0	11.66	0	0-27	0/0	–	1	10
Susskind Manfred John	8.6.1891	9.7.1957	5	1924	268	65	0	33.50	–	–	–/–	–	1	
Symcox Patrick Leonard	14.4.1960		20	*1993–1998*	741	108	1	28.50	37	4-69	0/0	43.32	5	80
Taberer Henry Melville	7.10.1870	5.6.1932	1	*1902*	2	2	0	2.00	1	1-25	0/0	48.00	0	
[2]**Tancred** Augustus Bernard	20.8.1865	23.11.1911	2	*1888*	87	29	0	29.00	–	–	–/–	–	2	
[2]**Tancred** Louis Joseph	7.10.1876	28.7.1934	14	*1902–1913*	530	97	0	21.20	–	–	–/–	–	3	
[2]**Tancred** Vincent Maximillian	7.7.1875	3.6.1904	1	*1898*	25	18	0	12.50	–	–	–/–	–	0	
[2]**Tapscott** George Lancelot ("Dusty")	7.11.1889	13.12.1940	1	*1913*	5	4	0	2.50	–	–	–/–	–	1	
[2]**Tapscott** Lionel Eric ("Doodles")	18.3.1894	7.7.1934	2	*1922*	58	50*	0	29.00	0	0-2	0/0	–	0	
Tayfield Hugh Joseph (*CY 1956*)	30.1.1929	24.2.1994	37	*1949*– 1960	862	75	0	16.90	170	9-113	14/2	25.91	26	
Taylor Alistair Innes ("Scotch")	25.7.1925	7.2.2004	1	*1956*	18	12	0	9.00	–	–	–/–	–	0	
[2]**Taylor** Daniel	9.1.1887	24.1.1957	2	*1913*	85	36	0	21.25	–	–	–/–	–	0	

§ *G. C. Smith's figures exclude 12 runs and three catches for the ICC World XI v Australia in the Super Series Test in 2005-06.*

	Born	Died	Tests	Test Career	Runs	HS	100s	Avge	Wkts	BB	5/10	Avge	Ct/St	O/T
[2] **Taylor** Herbert Wilfred (*CY 1925*)	5.5.1889	8.2.1973	42	1912–*1931*	2,936	176	7	40.77	5	3-15	0/0	31.20	19	
Terbrugge David John	31.1.1977		7	*1998–2003*	16	4*	0	5.33	20	5-46	1/0	25.85	4	4
Theunissen Nicolaas Hendrik Christiaan de Jong	4.5.1867	9.11.1929	1	*1888*	2	2*	0	2.00	0	0-51	0/0	–	0	
Thornton George	24.12.1867	31.1.1939	1	*1902*	1	1*	0	–	1	1-20	0/0	20.00	1	
Tomlinson Denis Stanley	4.9.1910	11.7.1993	1	1935	9	9	0	9.00	0	0-38	0/0	–	0	
Traicos Athanasios John	17.5.1947		3†	*1969*	8	5*	0	4.00	4	2-70	0/0	51.75	4	0‡
Trimborn Patrick Henry Joseph	18.5.1940		4	*1966–1969*	13	11*	0	6.50	11	3-12	0/0	23.36	7	
Tsolekile Thami Lungisa	9.10.1980		3	*2004*	47	22	0	9.40	–	–	–/–	–	6	
Tsotsobe Lonwabo Lennox	7.3.1984		5	2010–*2010*	19	8*	0	6.33	9	3-43	0/0	49.77	1	61/23
[1] **Tuckett** Lindsay Richard ("Len")	19.4.1885	8.4.1963	1	*1913*	0	0*	0	0.00	0	0-24	0/0	–	2	
[1] **Tuckett** Lindsay Thomas Delville	6.2.1919	5.9.2016	9	1947–*1948*	131	40*	0	11.90	19	5-68	2/0	51.57	9	
Twentyman-Jones Percy Sydney	13.9.1876	8.3.1954	1	*1902*	0	0	0	0.00	–	–	–/–	–	0	
van der Bijl Pieter Gerhard Vintcent	21.10.1907	16.2.1973	5	*1938*	460	125	1	51.11	–	–	–/–	–	1	
van der Merwe Edward Alexander	9.11.1903	26.2.1971	2	1929–*1935*	27	19	0	9.00	–	–	–/–	–	3	
van der Merwe Peter Laurence	14.3.1937	23.1.2013	15	*1963–1966*	533	76	0	25.38	1	1-6	0/0	22.00	11	
van Jaarsveld Martin	18.6.1974		9	*2002–2004*	397	73	0	30.53	0	0-28	0/0	–	11	11
van Ryneveld Clive Berrange	19.3.1928	29.1.2018	19	1951–*1957*	724	83	0	26.81	17	4-67	0/0	39.47	14	
van Zyl Stiaan	19.9.1987		12	*2014*–2016	395	101*	1	26.33	6	3-20	0/0	24.66	6	
Varnals George Derek	24.7.1935		3	*1964*	97	23	0	16.16	0	0-2	0/0	–	0	
Vilas Dane James	10.6.1985		6	2015–*2015*	94	26	0	10.44	–	–	–/–	–	13	0/1
Viljoen G. C. ("Hardus")	6.3.1989		1	*2015*	26	20*	0	26.00	1	1-79	0/0	94.00	0	
Viljoen Kenneth George	14.5.1910	21.1.1974	27	*1930–1948*	1,365	124	2	28.43	0	0-10	0/0	–	5	
Vincent Cyril Leverton	16.2.1902	24.8.1968	25	*1927*–1935	526	60	0	20.23	84	6-51	3/0	31.32	27	
Vintcent Charles Henry	2.9.1866	28.9.1943	3	*1888–1891*	26	9	0	4.33	4	3-88	0/0	48.25	1	
Vogler Albert Edward Ernest (*CY 1908*)	28.11.1876	9.8.1946	15	*1905–1910*	340	65	0	17.00	64	7-94	5/1	22.73	20	
[2] **Wade** Herbert Frederick	14.9.1905	23.11.1980	10	1935–*1935*	327	40*	0	20.43	–	–	–/–	–	4	
[2] **Wade** Walter Wareham ("Billy")	18.6.1914	31.5.2003	11	*1938–1949*	511	125	1	28.38	–	–	–/–	–	15/2	
Waite John Henry Bickford	19.1.1930	22.6.2011	50	1951–*1964*	2,405	134	4	30.44	–	–	–/–	–	124/17	
Walter Kenneth Alexander	5.11.1939	13.9.2003	2	*1961*	11	10	0	3.66	6	4-63	0/0	32.83	3	
Ward Thomas Alfred	2.8.1887	16.2.1936	23	1912–1924	459	64	0	13.90	–	–	–/–	–	19/13	
Watkins John Cecil	10.4.1923		15	*1949–1956*	612	92	0	23.53	29	4-22	0/0	28.13	12	
Wesley Colin	5.9.1937		3	1960	49	35	0	9.80	–	–	–/–	–	1	
Wessels Kepler Christoffel (*CY 1995*)	14.9.1957		16†	*1991*–1994	1,027	118	2	38.03	–	–	–/–	–	12	55‡
Westcott Richard John	19.9.1927	16.1.2013	5	*1953–1957*	166	62	0	18.44	0	0-22	0/0	–	0	
White Gordon Charles	5.2.1882	17.10.1918	17	*1905*–1912	872	147	2	30.06	9	4-47	0/0	33.44	10	
Willoughby Charl Myles	3.12.1974		2	2003	–	–	–	–	1	1-47	0/0	125.00	0	3

	Born	Died	Tests	Test Career	Runs	HS	100s	Avge	Wkts	BB	5/10	Avge	Ct/St	O/T
Willoughby Joseph Thomas	7.11.1874	11.3.1952	2	1895	8	5	0	2.00	6	2-37	0/0	26.50	0	
Wimble Clarence Skelton	22.4.1861	28.1.1930	1	1891	0	0	0	0.00	–	–	–/–	–	0	
Winslow Paul Lyndhurst	21.5.1929	24.5.2011	5	1949–1955	186	108	1	20.66	–	–	–/–	–	1	
Wynne Owen Edgar	1.6.1919	13.7.1975	6	1948–1949	219	50	0	18.25	–	–	–/–	–	3	
Zondeki Monde	25.7.1982		6	2003–2008	82	59	0	16.40	19	6-39	1/0	25.26	1	11‡/1
Zulch Johan Wilhelm	2.1.1886	19.5.1924	16	1909–1921	983	150	2	32.76	0	0-2	0/0	–	4	

WEST INDIES (314 players)

	Born	Died	Tests	Test Career	Runs	HS	100s	Avge	Wkts	BB	5/10	Avge	Ct/St	O/T
Achong Ellis Edgar	16.2.1904	30.8.1986	6	1929–1934	81	22	0	8.10	8	2-64	0/0	47.25	6	
Adams James Clive	9.1.1968		54	1991–2000	3,012	208*	6	41.26	27	5-17	1/0	49.48	48	127
Alexander Franz Copeland Murray ("Gerry")	2.11.1928	16.4.2011	25	1957–1960	961	108	1	30.03	–	–	–/–	–	85/5	
Ali Imtiaz	28.7.1954		1	1975	1	1*	0	–	2	2-37	0/0	44.50	0	
Ali Inshan	25.9.1949	24.6.1995	12	1970–1976	172	25	0	10.75	34	5-59	1/0	47.67	7	
Allan David Walter	5.11.1937		5	1961–1966	75	40*	0	12.50	–	–	–/–	–	15/3	
Allen Ian Basil Alston	6.10.1965		2	1991	5	4*	0	–	5	2-69	0/0	36.00	1	
Ambris Sunil Walford	23.3.1993		2	2017	25	18	0	8.33	–	–	–/–	–	1	1
Ambrose *Sir* Curtly Elconn Lynwall (*CY 1992*)	21.9.1963		98	1987–2000	1,439	53	0	12.40	405	8-45	22/3	20.99	18	176
Arthurton Keith Lloyd Thomas	21.2.1965		33	1988–1995	1,382	157*	2	30.71	1	1-17	0/0	183.00	22	105
Asgarali Nyron Sultan	28.12.1920	5.11.2006	2	1957	62	29	0	15.50	–	–	–/–	–	0	
[2] **Atkinson** Denis St Eval	9.8.1926	9.11.2001	22	1948–1957	922	219	1	31.79	47	7-53	3/0	35.04	11	
[2] **Atkinson** Eric St Eval	6.11.1927	29.5.1998	8	1957–1958	126	37	0	15.75	25	5-42	1/0	23.56	2	
Austin Richard Arkwright	5.9.1954	7.2.2015	2	1977	22	20	0	11.00	0	0-5	0/0	–	2	1
Austin Ryan Anthony	15.11.1981		2	2009	39	19	0	9.75	3	1-29	0/0	51.66	3	
Bacchus Sheik Faoud Ahamul Fasiel	31.1.1954		19	1977–1981	782	250	1	26.06	0	0-3	0/0	–	17	29
Baichan Leonard	12.5.1946		3	1974–1975	184	105*	1	46.00	–	–	–/–	–	2	
Baker Lionel Sionne	6.9.1984		4	2008–2009	23	17	0	11.50	5	2-39	0/0	79.00	1	10/3
Banks Omari Ahmed Clemente	17.7.1982		10	2002–2005	318	50*	0	26.50	28	4-87	0/0	48.82	6	5
Baptiste Eldine Ashworth Elderfield	12.3.1960		10	1983–1989	233	87*	0	23.30	16	3-31	0/0	35.18	2	43
Barath Adrian Boris	14.4.1990		15	2009–2012	657	104	1	23.46	0	0-3	0/0	–	13	14/2
Barrett Arthur George	4.4.1944		6	1970–1974	40	19	0	6.66	13	3-43	0/0	46.38	0	
Barrow Ivanhoe Mordecai	16.1.1911	2.4.1979	11	1929–1939	276	105	1	16.23	–	–	–/–	–	17/5	
Bartlett Edward Lawson	10.3.1906	21.12.1976	5	1928–1930	131	84	0	18.71	–	–	–/–	–	2	
Baugh Carlton Seymour	23.6.1982		21	2002–2011	610	68	0	17.94	–	–	–/–	–	43/5	47/3

	Born	Died	Tests	Test Career	Runs	HS	100s	Avge	Wkts	BB	5/10	Avge	Ct/St	O/T
Benjamin Kenneth Charlie Griffith	8.4.1967		26	1991–1997	222	43*	0	7.92	92	6-66	4/1	30.27	2	26
Benjamin Winston Keithroy Matthew	31.12.1964		21	1987–1994	470	85	0	18.80	61	4-46	0/0	27.01	12	85
Benn Sulieman Jamaal	22.7.1981		26	2007–2014	486	42	0	14.29	87	6-81	6/0	39.10	14	47/24
Bernard David Eddison	19.7.1981		3	2002–2009	202	69	0	40.40	4	2-30	0/0	46.25	0	20/1
Bess Brandon Jeremy	13.12.1987		1	2010	11	11*	0	11.00	1	1-65	0/0	92.00	0	
Best Carlisle Alonza	14.5.1959		8	1985–1990	342	164	1	28.50	0	0-2	0/0	–	8	24
Best Tino la Bertram	26.8.1981		25	2002–2013	401	95	0	12.53	57	6-40	2/0	40.19	6	26/6
Betancourt Nelson	4.6.1887	12.10.1947	1	1929	52	39	0	26.00	–	–	–/–	–	0	
Binns Alfred Phillip	24.7.1929		5	1952–1955	64	27	0	9.14	–	–	–/–	–	14/3	
Birkett Lionel Sydney	14.4.1905	16.1.1998	4	1930	136	64	0	17.00	1	1-16	0/0	71.00	4	
Bishoo Devendra	6.11.1985		28	2010–2017	570	45	0	16.28	102	8-49	4/1	36.01	14	27/5
Bishop Ian Raphael	24.10.1967		43	1988–1997	632	48	0	12.15	161	6-40	6/0	24.27	8	84
Black Marlon Ian	7.6.1975		6	2000–2001	21	6	0	2.62	12	4-83	0/0	49.75	0	5
Blackwood Jermaine	20.11.1991		27	2014–2017	1,324	112*	1	30.09	2	2-14	0/0	97.00	24	2
Boyce Keith David (*CY 1974*)	11.10.1943	11.10.1996	21	1970–1975	657	95*	0	24.33	60	6-77	2/1	30.01	5	8
Bradshaw Ian David Russell	9.7.1974		5	2005	96	33	0	13.71	9	3-73	0/0	60.00	3	62/1
Brathwaite Carlos Ricardo	18.7.1988		3	2015–2016	181	69	0	45.25	1	1-30	0/0	242.00	0	23/25
Brathwaite Kraigg Clairmonte	1.12.1992		44	2010–2017	2,920	212	6	37.43	14	6-29	1/0	59.35	22	10
[2] **Bravo** Dwayne John	7.10.1983		40	2004–2010	2,200	113	3	31.42	86	6-55	2/0	39.83	41	164/66
[2] **Bravo** Darren Michael	6.2.1989		49	2010–2016	3,400	218	8	40.00	0	0-2	0/0	–	47	94/12
Breese Gareth Rohan	9.1.1976		1	2002	5	5	0	2.50	2	2-108	0/0	67.50	1	
Browne Courtney Oswald	7.12.1970		20	1994–2004	387	68	0	16.12	–	–	–/–	–	79/2	46
Browne Cyril Rutherford	8.10.1890	12.1.1964	4	1928–1929	176	70*	0	25.14	6	2-72	0/0	48.00	1	
Butcher Basil Fitzherbert (*CY 1970*)	3.9.1933		44	1958–1969	3,104	209*	7	43.11	5	5-34	1/0	18.00	15	
Butler Lennox Stephen	9.2.1929	1.9.2009	1	1954	16	16	0	16.00	2	2-151	0/0	75.50	0	
Butts Clyde Godfrey	8.7.1957		7	1984–1987	108	38	0	15.42	10	4-73	0/0	59.50	2	
Bynoe Michael Robin	23.2.1941		4	1958–1966	111	48	0	18.50	1	1-5	0/0	5.00	4	
Camacho George Stephen	15.10.1945	2.10.2015	11	1967–1970	640	87	0	29.09	0	0-12	0/0	–	4	
[2] **Cameron** Francis James	22.6.1923	10.6.1994	5	1948	151	75*	0	25.16	3	2-74	0/0	92.66	0	
[2] **Cameron** John Hemsley	8.4.1914	13.2.2000	2	1939	6	5	0	2.00	3	3-66	0/0	29.33	0	
Campbell Sherwin Legay	1.11.1970		52	1994–2001	2,882	208	4	32.38	–	–	–/–	–	47	90
Carew George McDonald	4.6.1910	9.12.1974	4	1934–1948	170	107	1	28.33	0	0-2	0/0	–	1	
Carew Michael Conrad ("Joey")	15.9.1937	8.1.2011	19	1963–1971	1,127	109	1	34.15	8	1-11	0/0	54.62	13	
Challenor George	28.6.1888	30.7.1947	3	1928	101	46	0	16.83	–	–	–/–	–	0	
Chanderpaul Shivnarine (*CY 2008*)	16.8.1974		164	1993–2014	11,867	203*	30	51.37	9	1-2	0/0	98.11	66	268/22
Chandrika Rajindra	8.8.1989		5	2015–2016	140	37	0	14.00	–	–	–/–	–	2	

	Born	*Died*	*Tests*	*Test Career*	*Runs*	*HS*	*100s*	*Avge*	*Wkts*	*BB*	*5/10*	*Avge*	*Ct/St*	*O/T*
Chang Herbert Samuel	2.7.1952		1	*1978*	8	6	0	4.00	–	–	–/–	–	0	
Chase Roston Lamar	22.3.1992		17	2016–*2017*	1,065	137*	3	38.03	31	5-121	1/0	50.16	7	8
Chattergoon Sewnarine	3.4.1981		4	*2007–2008*	127	46	0	18.14	–	–	–/–	–	4	18
[2] **Christiani** Cyril Marcel	28.10.1913	4.4.1938	4	*1934*	98	32*	0	19.60	–	–	–/–	–	6/1	
[2] **Christiani** Robert Julian	19.7.1920	4.1.2005	22	*1947–1953*	896	107	1	26.35	3	3-52	0/0	36.00	19/2	
Clarke Carlos Bertram OBE	7.4.1918	14.10.1993	3	1939	3	2	0	1.00	6	3-59	0/0	43.50	0	
Clarke Sylvester Theophilus	11.12.1954	4.12.1999	11	*1977–1981*	172	35*	0	15.63	42	5-126	1/0	27.85	2	10
[2] **Collins** Pedro Tyrone	12.8.1976		32	*1998–2005*	235	24	0	5.87	106	6-53	3/0	34.63	7	30
Collymore Corey Dalanelo	21.12.1977		30	*1998*–2007	197	16*	0	7.88	93	7-57	4/1	32.30	6	84
Constantine *Lord* [Learie Nicholas] MBE (*CY 1940*)	21.9.1901	1.7.1971	18	1928–1939	635	90	0	19.24	58	5-75	2/0	30.10	28	
Cotterell Sheldon Shane	19.8.1989		2	*2013–2014*	11	5	0	2.75	2	1-72	0/0	98.00	0	4/7
Croft Colin Everton Hunte	15.3.1953		27	*1976–1981*	158	33	0	10.53	125	8-29	3/0	23.30	8	19
Cuffy Cameron Eustace	8.2.1970		15	*1994–2002*	58	15	0	4.14	43	4-82	0/0	33.83	5	41
Cummins Anderson Cleophas	7.5.1966		5	*1992–1994*	98	50	0	19.60	8	4-54	0/0	42.75	1	63‡
Cummins Miguel Lamar	5.9.1990		8	2016–*2017*	69	24*	0	6.90	18	6-48	1/0	39.61	1	11
Da Costa Oscar Constantine	11.9.1907	1.10.1936	5	*1929–1934*	153	39	0	19.12	3	1-14	0/0	58.33	5	
Daniel Wayne Wendell	16.1.1956		10	*1975–1983*	46	11	0	6.57	36	5-39	1/0	25.27	4	18
[2] **Davis** Bryan Allan	2.5.1940		4	*1964*	245	68	0	30.62	–	–	–/–	–	1	
[2] **Davis** Charles Allan	1.1.1944		15	*1968–1972*	1,301	183	4	54.20	2	1-27	0/0	165.00	4	
Davis Winston Walter	18.9.1958		15	*1982–1987*	202	77	0	15.53	45	4-19	0/0	32.71	10	35
De Caires Francis Ignatius	12.5.1909	2.2.1959	3	*1929*	232	80	0	38.66	0	0-9	0/0	–	1	
Deonarine Narsingh	16.8.1983		18	*2004–2013*	725	82	0	25.89	24	4-37	0/0	29.70	16	31/8
Depeiza Cyril Clairmonte	10.10.1928	10.11.1995	5	*1954–1955*	187	122	1	31.16	0	0-3	0/0	–	7/4	
Dewdney David Thomas	23.10.1933		9	*1954–1957*	17	5*	0	2.42	21	5-21	1/0	38.42	0	
Dhanraj Rajindra	6.2.1969		4	*1994–1995*	17	9	0	4.25	8	2-49	0/0	74.37	1	6
Dillon Mervyn	5.6.1974		38	*1996–2003*	549	43	0	8.44	131	5-71	2/0	33.57	16	108
Dowe Uton George	29.3.1949		4	*1970–1972*	8	5*	0	8.00	12	4-69	0/0	44.50	3	
Dowlin Travis Montague	24.2.1977		6	2009–2010	343	95	0	31.18	0	0-3	0/0	–	5	11/2
Dowrich Shane Omari	30.10.1991		18	2015–*2017*	724	103	1	24.13	–	–	–/–	–	40/5	
Drakes Vasbert Conniel	5.8.1969		12	*2002–2003*	386	67	0	21.44	33	5-93	1/0	41.27	2	34
Dujon Peter Jeffrey Leroy (*CY 1989*)	28.5.1956		81	*1981*–1991	3,322	139	5	31.94	–	–	–/–	–	267/5	169
[2] **Edwards** Fidel Henderson	6.2.1982		55	2003–*2012*	394	30	0	6.56	165	7-87	12/0	37.87	10	50/20
Edwards Kirk Anton	3.11.1984		17	2011–*2014*	986	121	2	31.80	0	0-19	0/0	–	15	16
Edwards Richard Martin	3.6.1940		5	*1968*	65	22	0	9.28	18	5-84	1/0	34.77	0	
Ferguson Wilfred	14.12.1917	23.2.1961	8	*1947–1953*	200	75	0	28.57	34	6-92	3/1	34.26	11	

	Born	Died	Tests	Test Career	Runs	HS	100s	Avge	Wkts	BB	5/10	Avge	Ct/St	O/T
Fernandes Maurius Pacheco	12.8.1897	8.5.1981	2	1928–1929	49	22	0	12.25	–	–	–/–	–	0	
Findlay Thaddeus Michael MBE	19.10.1943		10	1969–1972	212	44*	0	16.30	–	–	–/–	–	19/2	
Foster Maurice Linton Churchill	9.5.1943		14	1969–1977	580	125	1	30.52	9	2-41	0/0	66.66	3	2
Francis George Nathaniel	11.12.1897	12.1.1942	10	1928–1933	81	19*	0	5.78	23	4-40	0/0	33.17	7	
Frederick Michael Campbell	6.5.1927	18.6.2014	1	1953	30	30	0	15.00	–	–	–/–	–	0	
Fredericks Roy Clifton (*CY 1974*)	11.11.1942	5.9.2000	59	1968–1976	4,334	169	8	42.49	7	1-12	0/0	78.28	62	12
Fudadin Assad Badyr	1.8.1985		3	2012	122	55	0	30.50	0	0-11	0/0	–	4	
Fuller Richard Livingston	30.1.1913	3.5.1987	1	1934	1	1	0	1.00	0	0-2	0/0	–	0	
Furlonge Hammond Allan	19.6.1934		3	1954–1955	99	64	0	19.80	–	–	–/–	–	0	
Gabriel Shannon Terry	28.4.1988		32	2012–2017	150	20*	0	5.35	83	5-11	2/0	34.27	14	18/2
Ganga Daren	14.1.1979		48	1998–2007	2,160	135	3	25.71	1	1-20	0/0	106.00	30	35/1
Ganteaume Andrew Gordon	22.1.1921	17.2.2016	1	1947	112	112	1	112.00	–	–	–/–	–	0	
Garner Joel MBE (*CY 1980*)	16.12.1952		58	1976–1986	672	60	0	12.44	259	6-56	7/0	20.97	42	98
Garrick Leon Vivian	11.11.1976		1	2000	27	27	0	13.50	–	–	–/–	–	2	3
Gaskin Berkeley Bertram McGarrell	21.3.1908	2.5.1979	2	1947	17	10	0	5.66	2	1-15	0/0	79.00	1	
Gayle Christopher Henry	21.9.1979		103	1999–2014	7,214	333	15	42.18	73	5-34	2/0	42.73	96	272/55
Gibbs Glendon Lionel	27.12.1925	21.2.1979	1	1954	12	12	0	6.00	0	0-2	0/0	–	1	
Gibbs Lancelot Richard (*CY 1972*)	29.9.1934		79	1957–1975	488	25	0	6.97	309	8-38	18/2	29.09	52	3
Gibson Ottis Delroy (*CY 2008*)	16.3.1969		2	1995–1998	93	37	0	23.25	3	2-81	0/0	91.66	0	15
Gilchrist Roy	28.6.1934	18.7.2001	13	1957–1958	60	12	0	5.45	57	6-55	1/0	26.68	4	
Gladstone Morais George	14.1.1901	19.5.1978	1	1929	12	12*	0	–	1	1-139	0/0	189.00	0	
Goddard John Douglas Claude OBE	21.4.1919	26.8.1987	27	1947–1957	859	83*	0	30.67	33	5-31	1/0	31.81	22	
Gomes Hilary Angelo ("Larry") (*CY 1985*)	13.7.1953		60	1976–1986	3,171	143	9	39.63	15	2-20	0/0	62.00	18	83
Gomez Gerald Ethridge	10.10.1919	6.8.1996	29	1939–1953	1,243	101	1	30.31	58	7-55	1/1	27.41	18	
[2] **Grant** George Copeland ("Jackie")	9.5.1907	26.10.1978	12	1930–1934	413	71*	0	25.81	0	0-1	0/0	–	10	
[2] **Grant** Rolph Stewart	15.12.1909	18.10.1977	7	1934–1939	220	77	0	22.00	11	3-68	0/0	32.09	13	
Gray Anthony Hollis	23.5.1963		5	1986	48	12*	0	8.00	22	4-39	0/0	17.13	6	25
Greenidge Alvin Ethelbert	20.8.1956		6	1977–1978	222	69	0	22.20	–	–	–/–	–	5	1
Greenidge Cuthbert Gordon MBE (*CY 1977*)	1.5.1951		108	1974–1990	7,558	226	19	44.72	0	0-0	0/0	–	96	128
Greenidge Geoffrey Alan	26.5.1948		5	1971–1972	209	50	0	29.85	0	0-2	0/0	–	3	
Grell Mervyn George	18.12.1899	11.1.1976	1	1929	34	21	0	17.00	0	0-7	0/0	–	1	
Griffith Adrian Frank Gordon	19.11.1971		14	1996–2000	638	114	1	24.53	–	–	–/–	–	5	9
Griffith Charles Christopher (*CY 1964*)	14.12.1938		28	1959–1968	530	54	0	16.56	94	6-36	5/0	28.54	16	
Griffith Herman Clarence	1.12.1893	18.3.1980	13	1928–1933	91	18	0	5.05	44	6-103	2/0	28.25	4	
Guillen Simpson Clairmonte ("Sammy")	24.9.1924	2.3.2013	5†	1951	104	54	0	26.00	–	–	–/–	–	9/2	
Hall *Sir* Wesley Winfield	12.9.1937		48	1958–1968	818	50*	0	15.73	192	7-69	9/1	26.38	11	

	Born	Died	Tests	Test Career	Runs	HS	100s	Avge	Wkts	BB	5/10	Avge	Ct/St	O/T
Harper Roger Andrew	17.3.1963		25	1983–1993	535	74	0	18.44	46	6-57	1/0	28.06	36	105
Haynes Desmond Leo (*CY 1991*)	15.2.1956		116	1977–1993	7,487	184	18	42.29	1	1-2	0/0	8.00	65	238
[3] **Headley** George Alphonso MBE (*CY 1934*)	30.5.1909	30.11.1983	22	1929–1953	2,190	270*	10	60.83	0	0-0	0/0	–	14	
[3] **Headley** Ronald George Alphonso	29.6.1939		2	1973	62	42	0	15.50	–	–	–/–	–	2	1
Hendriks John Leslie	21.12.1933		20	1961–1969	447	64	0	18.62	–	–	–/–	–	42/5	
Hetmyer Shimron Odilon	26.12.1996		5	2016–2017	218	66	0	21.80	–	–	–/–	–	2	2/2
Hinds Ryan O'Neal	17.2.1981		15	2001–2009	505	84	0	21.04	13	2-45	0/0	66.92	7	14
Hinds Wavell Wayne	7.9.1976		45	1999–2005	2,608	213	5	33.01	16	3-79	0/0	36.87	32	119/5
Hoad Edward Lisle Goldsworthy	29.1.1896	5.3.1986	4	1928–1933	98	36	0	12.25	–	–	–/–	–	1	
Holder Jason Omar	5.11.1991		29	2014–2017	1,218	110	2	29.00	53	5-30	1/0	38.52	18	70/8
Holder Roland Irwin Christopher	22.12.1967		11	1996–1998	380	91	0	25.33	–	–	–/–	–	9	37
Holder Vanburn Alonzo	10.10.1945		40	1969–1978	682	42	0	14.20	109	6-28	3/0	33.27	16	12
Holding Michael Anthony (*CY 1977*)	16.2.1954		60	1975–1986	910	73	0	13.78	249	8-92	13/2	23.68	22	102
Holford David Anthony Jerome	16.4.1940		24	1966–1976	768	105*	1	22.58	51	5-23	1/0	39.39	18	
Holt John Kenneth Constantine	12.8.1923	3.6.1997	17	1953–1958	1,066	166	2	36.75	1	1-20	0/0	20.00	8	
Hooper Carl Llewellyn	15.12.1966		102	1987–2002	5,762	233	13	36.46	114	5-26	4/0	49.42	115	227
[2] **Hope** Kyle Antonio	20.11.1988		5	2017–2017	101	43	0	11.22	–	–	–/–	–	3	7
[2] **Hope** Shai Diego (*CY 2018*)	10.11.1993		17	2014–2017	996	147	2	33.20	–	–	–/–	–	16	26/3
Howard Anthony Bourne	27.8.1946		1	1971	–	–	–	–	2	2-140	0/0	70.00	0	
Hunte *Sir* Conrad Cleophas (*CY 1964*)	9.5.1932	3.12.1999	44	1957–1966	3,245	260	8	45.06	2	1-17	0/0	55.00	16	
Hunte Errol Ashton Clairmore	3.10.1905	26.6.1967	3	1929	166	58	0	33.20	–	–	–/–	–	5	
Hylton Leslie George	29.3.1905	17.5.1955	6	1934–1939	70	19	0	11.66	16	4-27	0/0	26.12	1	
Jacobs Ridley Detamore	26.11.1967		65	1998–2004	2,577	118	3	28.31	–	–	–/–	–	207/12	147
Jaggernauth Amit Sheldon	16.11.1983		1	2007	0	0*	0	0.00	1	1-74	0/0	96.00	0	
Johnson Hophnie Hobah Hines	13.7.1910	24.6.1987	3	1947–1950	38	22	0	9.50	13	5-41	2/1	18.30	0	
Johnson Leon Rayon	8.8.1987		9	2014–2016	403	66	0	25.18	0	0-9	0/0	–	7	6
Johnson Tyrell Fabian	10.1.1917	5.4.1985	1	1939	9	9*	0	–	3	2-53	0/0	43.00	1	
Jones Charles Ernest Llewellyn	3.11.1902	10.12.1959	4	1929–1934	63	19	0	9.00	0	0-2	0/0	–	3	
Jones Prior Erskine Waverley	6.6.1917	21.11.1991	9	1947–1951	47	10*	0	5.22	25	5-85	1/0	30.04	4	
Joseph Alzarri Shaheim	20.11.1996		6	2016–2017	41	8	0	3.72	15	3-53	0/0	38.86	2	14
Joseph David Rolston Emmanuel	15.11.1969		4	1998	141	50	0	20.14	–	–	–/–	–	10	
Joseph Sylvester Cleofoster	5.9.1978		5	2004–2007	147	45	0	14.70	0	0-8	0/0	–	3	13
Julien Bernard Denis	13.3.1950		24	1973–1976	866	121	2	30.92	50	5-57	1/0	37.36	14	12
Jumadeen Raphick Rasif	12.4.1948		12	1971–1978	84	56	0	21.00	29	4-72	0/0	39.34	4	
Kallicharran Alvin Isaac (*CY 1983*)	21.3.1949		66	1971–1980	4,399	187	12	44.43	4	2-16	0/0	39.50	51	31
Kanhai Rohan Bholalall (*CY 1964*)	26.12.1935		79	1957–1973	6,227	256	15	47.53	0	0-1	0/0	–	50	7

	Born	*Died*	*Tests*	*Test Career*	*Runs*	*HS*	*100s*	*Avge*	*Wkts*	*BB*	*5/10*	*Avge*	*Ct/St*	*O/T*
Kentish Esmond Seymour Maurice	21.11.1916	10.6.2011	2	*1947–1953*	1	1*	0	1.00	8	5-49	1/0	22.25	1	
King Collis Llewellyn	11.6.1951		9	1976–1980	418	100*	1	32.15	3	1-30	0/0	94.00	5	18
King Frank McDonald	14.12.1926	23.12.1990	14	*1952–1955*	116	21	0	8.28	29	5-74	1/0	39.96	5	
King Lester Anthony	27.2.1939	9.7.1998	2	*1961–1967*	41	20	0	10.25	9	5-46	1/0	17.11	2	
King Reon Dane	6.10.1975		19	*1998–2004*	66	12*	0	3.47	53	5-51	1/0	32.69	2	50
Lambert Clayton Benjamin	10.2.1962		5	1991–*1998*	284	104	1	31.55	1	1-4	0/0	5.00	8	11‡
Lara Brian Charles (*CY 1995*)	2.5.1969		130§	*1990–2006*	11,912	400*	34	53.17	0	0-0	0/0	–	164	295‡
Lashley Patrick Douglas ("Peter")	11.2.1937		4	*1960*–1966	159	49	0	22.71	1	1-1	0/0	1.00	4	
Lawson Jermaine Jay Charles	13.1.1982		13	*2002–2005*	52	14	0	3.46	51	7-78	2/0	29.64	3	13
Legall Ralph Archibald	1.12.1925	2003	4	*1952*	50	23	0	10.00	–	–	–/–	–	8/1	
Lewis Desmond Michael	21.2.1946		3	*1970*	259	88	0	86.33	–	–	–/–	–	8	
Lewis Rawl Nicholas	5.9.1974		5	*1997–2007*	89	40	0	8.90	4	2-42	0/0	114.00	0	28/1
Lloyd Clive Hubert CBE (*CY 1971*)	31.8.1944		110	*1966–1984*	7,515	242*	19	46.67	10	2-13	0/0	62.20	90	87
Logie Augustine Lawrence	28.9.1960		52	*1982*–1991	2,470	130	2	35.79	0	0-0	0/0	–	57	158
McGarrell Neil Christopher	12.7.1972		4	*2000–2001*	61	33	0	15.25	17	4-23	0/0	26.64	2	17
McLean Nixon Alexei McNamara	20.7.1973		19	*1997–2000*	368	46	0	12.26	44	3-53	0/0	42.56	5	45
McMorris Easton Dudley Ashton St John	4.4.1935		13	*1957*–1966	564	125	1	26.85	–	–	–/–	–	5	
McWatt Clifford Aubrey	1.2.1922	20.7.1997	6	*1953–1954*	202	54	0	28.85	1	1-16	0/0	16.00	9/1	
Madray Ivan Samuel	2.7.1934	23.4.2009	2	*1957*	3	2	0	1.00	0	0-12	0/0	–	2	
Marshall Malcolm Denzil (*CY 1983*)	18.4.1958	4.11.1999	81	*1978*–1991	1,810	92	0	18.85	376	7-22	22/4	20.94	25	136
[2] **Marshall** Norman Edgar	27.2.1924	11.8.2007	1	*1954*	8	8	0	4.00	2	1-22	0/0	31.00	0	
[2] **Marshall** Roy Edwin (*CY 1959*)	25.4.1930	27.10.1992	4	*1951*	143	30	0	20.42	0	0-3	0/0	–	1	
Marshall Xavier Melbourne	27.3.1986		7	2005–*2008*	243	85	0	20.25	0	0-0	0/0	–	7	24/6
Martin Frank Reginald	12.10.1893	23.11.1967	9	1928–*1930*	486	123*	1	28.58	8	3-91	0/0	77.37	2	
Martindale Emmanuel Alfred	25.11.1909	17.3.1972	10	1933–1939	58	22	0	5.27	37	5-22	3/0	21.72	5	
Mattis Everton Hugh	11.4.1957		4	*1980*	145	71	0	29.00	0	0-4	0/0	–	3	2
Mendonca Ivor Leon	13.7.1934	14.6.2014	2	*1961*	81	78	0	40.50	–	–	–/–	–	8/2	
Merry Cyril Arthur	20.1.1911	19.4.1964	2	1933	34	13	0	8.50	–	–	–/–	–	1	
Miller Nikita O'Neil	16.5.1982		1	2009	5	5	0	2.50	0	0-27	0/0	–	0	47/9
Miller Roy	24.12.1924		1	*1952*	23	23	0	23.00	0	0-28	0/0	–	0	
Mohammed Dave	8.10.1979		5	*2003–2006*	225	52	0	32.14	13	3-98	0/0	51.38	1	7
Moodie George Horatio	26.11.1915	8.6.2002	1	*1934*	5	5	0	5.00	3	2-23	0/0	13.33	0	
Morton Runako Shakur	22.7.1978	4.3.2012	15	2005–*2007*	573	70*	0	22.03	0	0-4	0/0	–	20	56/7
Moseley Ezra Alphonsa	5.1.1958		2	*1989*	35	26	0	8.75	6	2-70	0/0	43.50	1	9
[1] **Murray** David Anthony	29.5.1950		19	*1977–1981*	601	84	0	21.46	–	–	–/–	–	57/5	10

§ *Lara's figures exclude 41 runs for the ICC World XI v Australia in the Super Series Test in 2005-06.*

	Born	*Died*	*Tests*	*Test Career*	*Runs*	*HS*	*100s*	*Avge*	*Wkts*	*BB*	*5/10*	*Avge*	*Ct/St*	*O/T*
Murray Deryck Lance	20.5.1943		62	1963–1980	1,993	91	0	22.90	–	–	–/–	–	181/8	26
Murray Junior Randalph	20.1.1968		33	*1992–2001*	918	101*	1	22.39	–	–	–/–	–	99/3	55
Nagamootoo Mahendra Veeren	9.10.1975		5	2000–*2002*	185	68	0	26.42	12	3-119	0/0	53.08	2	24
Nanan Rangy	29.5.1953	23.3.2016	1	*1980*	16	8	0	8.00	4	2-37	0/0	22.75	2	
Narine Sunil Philip	26.5.1988		6	2012–*2013*	40	22*	0	8.00	21	6-91	2/0	40.52	2	65/48
Nash Brendan Paul	14.12.1977		21	*2008*–2011	1,103	114	2	33.42	2	1-21	0/0	123.50	6	9
Neblett James Montague	13.11.1901	28.3.1959	1	*1934*	16	11*	0	16.00	1	1-44	0/0	75.00	0	
Noreiga Jack Mollinson	15.4.1936	8.8.2003	4	*1970*	11	9	0	3.66	17	9-95	2/0	29.00	2	
Nunes Robert Karl	7.6.1894	23.7.1958	4	1928–*1929*	245	92	0	30.62	–	–	–/–	–	2	
Nurse Seymour MacDonald (*CY 1967*)	10.11.1933		29	*1959–1968*	2,523	258	6	47.60	0	0-0	0/0	–	21	
Padmore Albert Leroy	17.12.1946		2	*1975*–1976	8	8*	0	8.00	1	1-36	0/0	135.00	0	
Pagon Donovan Jomo	13.9.1982		2	*2004*	37	35	0	12.33	–	–	–/–	–	0	
Pairaudeau Bruce Hamilton	14.4.1931		13	*1952*–1957	454	115	1	21.61	0	0-3	0/0	–	6	
Parchment Brenton Anthony	24.6.1982		2	*2007*	55	20	0	13.75	–	–	–/–	–	1	7/1
Parry Derick Recaldo	22.12.1954		12	*1977–1979*	381	65	0	22.41	23	5-15	1/0	40.69	4	6
Pascal Nelon Troy	25.4.1987		2	2010–*2010*	12	10	0	6.00	0	0-27	0/0	–	1	1
Passailaigue Charles Clarence	4.8.1901	7.1.1972	1	*1929*	46	44	0	46.00	0	0-15	0/0	–	3	
Patterson Balfour Patrick	15.9.1961		28	*1985–1992*	145	21*	0	6.59	93	5-24	5/0	30.90	5	59
Payne Thelston Rodney O'Neale	13.2.1957		1	*1985*	5	5	0	5.00	–	–	–/–	–	5	7
Permaul Veerasammy	11.8.1989		6	*2012*–2015	98	23*	0	12.25	18	3-32	0/0	43.77	2	7
Perry Nehemiah Odolphus	16.6.1968		4	*1998–1999*	74	26	0	12.33	10	5-70	1/0	44.60	1	21
Peters Keon Kenroy	24.2.1982		1	*2014*	0	0	0	0.00	2	2-69	0/0	34.50	0	
Phillip Norbert	12.6.1948		9	*1977–1978*	297	47	0	29.70	28	4-48	0/0	37.17	5	1
Phillips Omar Jamel	12.10.1986		2	2009	160	94	0	40.00	–	–	–/–	–	1	
Pierre Lancelot Richard	5.6.1921	14.4.1989	1	*1947*	–	–	–	–	0	0-9	0/0	–	0	
Powell Daren Brentlyle	15.4.1978		37	2002–*2008*	407	36*	0	7.82	85	5-25	1/0	47.85	8	55/5
Powell Kieran Omar Akeem	6.3.1990		31	2011–*2017*	1,620	134	3	27.93	0	0-0	0/0	–	28	39/1
Powell Ricardo Lloyd	16.12.1978		2	*1999–2003*	53	30	0	17.66	0	0-13	0/0	–	1	109
Rae Allan Fitzroy	30.9.1922	27.2.2005	15	*1948–1952*	1,016	109	4	46.18	–	–	–/–	–	10	
Ragoonath Suruj	22.3.1968		2	*1998*	13	9	0	4.33	–	–	–/–	–	0	
Ramadhin Sonny (*CY 1951*)	1.5.1929		43	1950–*1960*	361	44	0	8.20	158	7-49	10/1	28.98	9	
Ramdass Ryan Rakesh	3.7.1983		1	2005	26	23	0	13.00	–	–	–/–	–	2	1
Ramdin Denesh	13.3.1985		74	2005–*2015*	2,898	166	4	25.87	–	–	–/–	–	205/12	139/58
Ramnarine Dinanath	4.6.1975		12	*1997–2001*	106	35*	0	6.23	45	5-78	1/0	30.73	8	4
Rampaul Ravindranath	15.10.1984		18	*2009–2012*	335	40*	0	14.56	49	4-48	0/0	34.79	3	92/23
Reifer Floyd Lamonte	23.7.1972		6	*1996*–2009	111	29	0	9.25	–	–	–/–	–	6	8/1

	Born	Died	Tests	Test Career	Runs	HS	100s	Avge	Wkts	BB	5/10	Avge	Ct/St	O/T
Reifer Raymon Anton	11.5.1991		1	2017	52	29	0	52.00	2	1-36	0/0	44.00	0	
Richards Dale Maurice	16.7.1976		3	2009–2010	125	69	0	20.83	–	–	–/–	–	4	8/1
Richards *Sir* Isaac Vivian Alexander (*CY 1977*)	7.3.1952		121	1974–1991	8,540	291	24	50.23	32	2-17	0/0	61.37	122	187
Richardson *Sir* Richard Benjamin (*CY 1992*)	12.1.1962		86	1983–1995	5,949	194	16	44.39	0	0-0	0/0	–	90	224
Rickards Kenneth Roy	22.8.1923	21.8.1995	2	1947–1951	104	67	0	34.66	–	–	–/–	–	0	
Roach Clifford Archibald	13.3.1904	16.4.1988	16	1928–1934	952	209	2	30.70	2	1-18	0/0	51.50	5	
Roach Kemar Andre Jamal	30.6.1988		44	2009–2017	605	41	0	10.25	147	6-48	7/1	29.42	12	67/11
Roberts Alphonso Theodore	18.9.1937	24.7.1996	1	1955	28	28	0	14.00	–	–	–/–	–	0	
Roberts *Sir* Anderson Montgomery Everton CBE (*CY 1975*)	29.1.1951		47	1973–1983	762	68	0	14.94	202	7-54	11/2	25.61	9	56
Roberts Lincoln Abraham	4.9.1974		1	1998	0	0	0	0.00	–	–	–/–	–	0	
Rodriguez William Vicente	25.6.1934		5	1961–1967	96	50	0	13.71	7	3-51	0/0	53.42	3	
Rose Franklyn Albert	1.2.1972		19	1996–2000	344	69	0	13.23	53	7-84	2/0	30.88	4	27
Rowe Lawrence George	8.1.1949		30	1971–1979	2,047	302	7	43.55	0	0-1	0/0	–	17	11
Russell Andre Dwayne	29.4.1988		1	2010	2	2	0	2.00	1	1-73	0/0	104.00	1	51/43
[2] **St Hill** Edwin Lloyd	9.3.1904	21.5.1957	2	1929	18	12	0	4.50	3	2-110	0/0	73.66	0	
[2] **St Hill** Wilton H	6.7.1893	d unknown	3	1928–1929	117	38	0	19.50	0	0-9	0/0	–	1	
Sammy Darren Julius Garvey	20.12.1983		38	2007–2013	1,323	106	1	21.68	84	7-66	4/0	35.79	65	126/66‡
[2] **Samuels** Marlon Nathaniel (*CY 2013*)	5.1.1981		71	2000–2016	3,917	260	7	32.64	41	4-13	0/0	59.63	28	192/60
[2] **Samuels** Robert George	13.3.1971		6	1995–1996	372	125	1	37.20	–	–	–/–	–	8	8
Sanford Adam	12.7.1975		11	2001–2003	72	18*	0	4.80	30	4-132	0/0	43.86	4	
Sarwan Ramnaresh Ronnie	23.6.1980		87	1999–2011	5,842	291	15	40.01	23	4-37	0/0	50.56	53	181/18
Scarlett Reginald Osmond	15.8.1934		3	1959	54	29*	0	18.00	2	1-46	0/0	104.50	2	
[1] **Scott** Alfred Homer Patrick	29.7.1934		1	1952	5	5	0	5.00	0	0-52	0/0	–	0	
[1] **Scott** Oscar Charles ("Tommy")	14.8.1892	15.6.1961	8	1928–1930	171	35	0	17.10	22	5-266	1/0	42.04	0	
Sealey Benjamin James	12.8.1899	12.9.1963	1	1933	41	29	0	20.50	1	1-10	0/0	10.00	0	
Sealy James Edward Derrick	11.9.1912	3.1.1982	11	1929–1939	478	92	0	28.11	3	2-7	0/0	31.33	6/1	
Shepherd John Neil (*CY 1979*)	9.11.1943		5	1969–1970	77	32	0	9.62	19	5-104	1/0	25.21	4	
Shillingford Grayson Cleophas	25.9.1944	23.12.2009	7	1969–1971	57	25	0	8.14	15	3-63	0/0	35.80	2	
Shillingford Irvine Theodore	18.4.1944		4	1976–1977	218	120	1	31.14	–	–	–/–	–	1	2
Shillingford Shane	22.2.1983		16	2010–2014	266	53*	0	13.30	70	6-49	6/2	34.55	9	
Shivnarine Sewdatt	13.5.1952		8	1977–1978	379	63	0	29.15	1	1-13	0/0	167.00	6	1
Simmons Lendl Mark Platter	25.1.1985		8	2008–2011	278	49	0	17.37	1	1-60	0/0	147.00	5	68/45
Simmons Philip Verant (*CY 1997*)	18.4.1963		26	1987–1997	1,002	110	1	22.26	4	2-34	0/0	64.25	26	143
Singh Charran Kamkaran	27.11.1935	19.11.2015	2	1959	11	11	0	3.66	5	2-28	0/0	33.20	2	
Singh Vishaul Anthony	12.1.1989		3	2016	63	32	0	10.50	–	–	–/–	–	2	

	Born	Died	Tests	Test Career	Runs	HS	100s	Avge	Wkts	BB	5/10	Avge	Ct/St	O/T
Small Joseph A.	3.11.1892	26.4.1958	3	1928–1929	79	52	0	13.16	3	2-67	0/0	61.33	3	
Small Milton Aster	12.2.1964		2	1983–1984	3	3*	0	–	4	3-40	0/0	38.25	0	2
Smith Cameron Wilberforce	29.7.1933		5	1960–1961	222	55	0	24.66	–	–	–/–	–	4/1	
Smith Devon Sheldon	21.10.1981		38	2002–2014	1,593	108	1	24.50	0	0-3	0/0	–	30	47/6
Smith Dwayne Romel	12.4.1983		10	2003–2005	320	105*	1	24.61	7	3-71	0/0	49.14	9	105/33
Smith O'Neil Gordon ("Collie") (*CY 1958*)	5.5.1933	9.9.1959	26	1954–1958	1,331	168	4	31.69	48	5-90	1/0	33.85	9	
Sobers *Sir* Garfield St Aubrun (*CY 1964*)	28.7.1936		93	1953–1973	8,032	365*	26	57.78	235	6-73	6/0	34.03	109	1
Solomon Joseph Stanislaus	26.8.1930		27	1958–1964	1,326	100*	1	34.00	4	1-20	0/0	67.00	13	
Stayers Sven Conrad ("Charlie")	9.6.1937	6.1.2005	4	1961	58	35*	0	19.33	9	3-65	0/0	40.44	0	
2 **Stollmeyer** Jeffrey Baxter	11.3.1921	10.9.1989	32	1939–1954	2,159	160	4	42.33	13	3-32	0/0	39.00	20	
2 **Stollmeyer** Victor Humphrey	24.1.1916	21.9.1999	1	1939	96	96	0	96.00	–	–	–/–	–	0	
Stuart Colin Ellsworth Laurie	28.9.1973		6	2000–2001	24	12*	0	3.42	20	3-33	0/0	31.40	2	5
Taylor Jaswick Ossie	3.1.1932	13.11.1999	3	1957–1958	4	4*	0	2.00	10	5-109	1/0	27.30	0	
Taylor Jerome Everton	22.6.1984		46	2003–2015	856	106	1	12.96	130	6-47	4/0	34.46	8	90/30
Thompson Patterson Ian Chesterfield	26.9.1971		2	1995–1996	17	10*	0	8.50	5	2-58	0/0	43.00	0	2
Tonge Gavin Courtney	13.2.1983		1	2009	25	23*	0	25.00	1	1-28	0/0	113.00	0	5/1
Trim John	25.1.1915	12.11.1960	4	1947–1951	21	12	0	5.25	18	5-34	1/0	16.16	2	
Valentine Alfred Louis (*CY 1951*)	28.4.1930	11.5.2004	36	1950–1961	141	14	0	4.70	139	8-104	8/2	30.32	13	
Valentine Vincent Adolphus	4.4.1908	6.7.1972	2	1933	35	19*	0	11.66	1	1-55	0/0	104.00	0	
Walcott *Sir* Clyde Leopold (*CY 1958*)	17.1.1926	26.8.2006	44	1947–1959	3,798	220	15	56.68	11	3-50	0/0	37.09	53/11	
Walcott Leslie Arthur	18.1.1894	27.2.1984	1	1929	40	24	0	40.00	1	1-17	0/0	32.00	0	
Wallace Philo Alphonso	2.8.1970		7	1997–1998	279	92	0	21.46	–	–	–/–	–	9	33
Walsh Courtney Andrew (*CY 1987*)	30.10.1962		132	1984–2000	936	30*	0	7.54	519	7-37	22/3	24.44	29	205
Walton Chadwick Antonio Kirkpatrick	3.7.1985		2	2009	13	10	0	3.25	–	–	–/–	–	10	9/15
Warrican Jomel Andrel	20.5.1992		4	2015	65	21*	0	65.00	11	4-67	0/0	46.27	1	
Washington Dwight Marlon	5.3.1983		1	2004	7	7*	0	–	0	0-20	0/0	–	3	
Watson Chester Donald	1.7.1938		7	1959–1961	12	5	0	2.40	19	4-62	0/0	38.10	1	
1 **Weekes** *Sir* Everton de Courcy (*CY 1951*)	26.2.1925		48	1947–1957	4,455	207	15	58.61	1	1-8	0/0	77.00	49	
Weekes Kenneth Hunnell	24.1.1912	9.2.1998	2	1939	173	137	1	57.66	–	–	–/–	–	0	
White Anthony Wilbur	20.11.1938		2	1964	71	57*	0	23.66	3	2-34	0/0	50.66	1	
Wight Claude Vibart	28.7.1902	4.10.1969	2	1928–1929	67	23	0	22.33	0	0-6	0/0	–	0	
Wight George Leslie	28.5.1929	4.1.2004	1	1952	21	21	0	21.00	–	–	–/–	–	0	
Wiles Charles Archibald	11.8.1892	4.11.1957	1	1933	2	2	0	1.00	–	–	–/–	–	0	
Willett Elquemedo Tonito	1.5.1953		5	1972–1974	74	26	0	14.80	11	3-33	0/0	43.81	0	
Williams Alvadon Basil	21.11.1949	25.10.2015	7	1977–1978	469	111	2	39.08	–	–	–/–	–	5	
Williams David	4.11.1963		11	1991–1997	242	65	0	13.44	–	–	–/–	–	40/2	36

	Born	Died	Tests	Test Career	Runs	HS	100s	Avge	Wkts	BB	5/10	Avge	Ct/St	O/T
Williams Ernest Albert Vivian ("Foffie")	10.4.1914	13.4.1997	4	1939–*1947*	113	72	0	18.83	9	3-51	0/0	26.77	2	
Williams Stuart Clayton	12.8.1969		31	*1993–2001*	1,183	128	1	24.14	0	0-19	0/0	–	27	57
Wishart Kenneth Leslie	28.11.1908	18.10.1972	1	*1934*	52	52	0	26.00	–	–	–/–	–	0	
Worrell *Sir* Frank Mortimer Maglinne (*CY 1951*)	1.8.1924	13.3.1967	51	*1947*–1963	3,860	261	9	49.48	69	7-70	2/0	38.72	43	

NEW ZEALAND (273 players)

	Born	Died	Tests	Test Career	Runs	HS	100s	Avge	Wkts	BB	5/10	Avge	Ct/St	O/T
Adams Andre Ryan	17.7.1975		1	*2001*	18	11	0	9.00	6	3-44	0/0	17.50	1	42/4
Alabaster John Chaloner	11.7.1930		21	*1955–1971*	272	34	0	9.71	49	4-46	0/0	38.02	7	
Allcott Cyril Francis Walter	7.10.1896	19.11.1973	6	*1929–1931*	113	33	0	22.60	6	2-102	0/0	90.16	3	
Allott Geoffrey Ian	24.12.1971		10	*1995–1999*	27	8*	0	3.37	19	4-74	0/0	58.47	2	31
Anderson Corey James	13.12.1990		13	*2013–2015*	683	116	1	32.52	16	3-47	0/0	41.18	7	49/29
[1] **Anderson** Robert Wickham	2.10.1948		9	*1976*–1978	423	92	0	23.50	–	–	–/–	–	1	2
[1] **Anderson** William McDougall	8.10.1919	21.12.1979	1	*1945*	5	4	0	2.50	–	–	–/–	–	1	
Andrews Bryan	4.4.1945		2	*1973*	22	17	0	22.00	2	2-40	0/0	77.00	1	
Arnel Brent John	3.1.1979		6	*2009–2011*	45	8*	0	5.62	9	4-95	0/0	62.88	3	
Astle Nathan John	15.9.1971		81	*1995–2006*	4,702	222	11	37.02	51	3-27	0/0	42.01	70	223/4
Astle Todd Duncan	24.9.1986		2	*2012–2016*	38	35	0	12.66	1	1-56	0/0	109.00	2	3/2
Badcock Frederick Theodore ("Ted")	9.8.1897	19.9.1982	7	*1929–1932*	137	64	0	19.57	16	4-80	0/0	38.12	1	
Barber Richard Trevor	3.6.1925	7.8.2015	1	*1955*	17	12	0	8.50	–	–	–/–	–	1	
Bartlett Gary Alex	3.2.1941		10	*1961–1967*	263	40	0	15.47	24	6-38	1/0	33.00	8	
Barton Paul Thomas	9.10.1935		7	*1961–1962*	285	109	1	20.35	–	–	–/–	–	4	
Beard Donald Derek	14.1.1920	15.7.1982	4	*1951–1955*	101	31	0	20.20	9	3-22	0/0	33.55	2	
Beck John Edward Francis	1.8.1934	23.4.2000	8	*1953–1955*	394	99	0	26.26	–	–	–/–	–	0	
Bell Matthew David	25.2.1977		18	*1998–2007*	729	107	2	24.30	–	–	–/–	–	19	7
Bell William	5.9.1931	23.7.2002	2	*1953*	21	21*	0	–	2	1-54	0/0	117.50	1	
Bennett Hamish Kyle	22.2.1987		1	*2010*	4	4	0	4.00	0	0-47	0/0	–	0	16
Bilby Grahame Paul	7.5.1941		2	*1965*	55	28	0	13.75	–	–	–/–	–	3	
Blain Tony Elston	17.2.1962		11	1986–*1993*	456	78	0	26.82	–	–	–/–	–	19/2	38
Blair Robert William	23.6.1932		19	*1952–1963*	189	64*	0	6.75	43	4-85	0/0	35.23	5	
Blundell Thomas Ackland	1.9.1990		2	*2017*	136	107*	1	68.00	–	–	–/–	–	2	0/1
Blunt Roger Charles (*CY 1928*)	3.11.1900	22.6.1966	9	*1929–1931*	330	96	0	27.50	12	3-17	0/0	39.33	5	
Bolton Bruce Alfred	31.5.1935		2	*1958*	59	33	0	19.66	–	–	–/–	–	1	
Bond Shane Edward	7.6.1975		18	*2001–2009*	168	41*	0	12.92	87	6-51	5/1	22.09	8	82/20

	Born	*Died*	*Tests*	*Test Career*	*Runs*	*HS*	*100s*	*Avge*	*Wkts*	*BB*	*5/10*	*Avge*	*Ct/St*	*O/T*
Boock Stephen Lewis	20.9.1951		30	*1977–1988*	207	37	0	6.27	74	7-87	4/0	34.64	14	14
Boult Trent Alexander	22.7.1989		52	*2011–2017*	529	52*	0	16.03	200	6-40	5/1	28.56	27	57/18
[1, 2] **Bracewell** Brendon Paul	14.9.1959		6	1978–*1984*	24	8	0	2.40	14	3-110	0/0	41.78	1	1
[1] **Bracewell** Douglas Alexander John	28.9.1990		27	*2011*–2016	568	47	0	13.85	72	6-40	2/0	38.83	10	16/17
[2] **Bracewell** John Garry	15.4.1958		41	*1980*–1990	1,001	110	1	20.42	102	6-32	4/1	35.81	31	53
[1] **Bradburn** Grant Eric	26.5.1966		7	*1990–2000*	105	30*	0	13.12	6	3-134	0/0	76.66	6	11
[1] **Bradburn** Wynne Pennell	24.11.1938	25.9.2008	2	*1963*	62	32	0	15.50	–	–	–/–	–	2	
Broom Neil Trevor	20.11.1983		2	*2016*	32	20	0	10.66	–	–	–/–	–	0	39/11
Brown Vaughan Raymond	3.11.1959		2	*1985*	51	36*	0	25.50	1	1-17	0/0	176.00	3	3
Brownlie Dean Graham	30.7.1984		14	*2011*–2013	711	109	1	29.62	1	1-13	0/0	52.00	17	16/5
Burgess Mark Gordon	17.7.1944		50	*1967–1980*	2,684	119*	5	31.20	6	3-23	0/0	35.33	34	26
Burke Cecil	27.3.1914	4.8.1997	1	*1945*	4	3	0	2.00	2	2-30	0/0	15.00	0	
Burtt Thomas Browning	22.1.1915	24.5.1988	10	*1946–1952*	252	42	0	21.00	33	6-162	3/0	35.45	2	
Butler Ian Gareth	24.11.1981		8	*2001–2004*	76	26	0	9.50	24	6-46	1/0	36.83	4	26/19
Butterfield Leonard Arthur	29.8.1913	5.7.1999	1	*1945*	0	0	0	0.00	0	0-24	0/0	–	0	
[1] **Cairns** Bernard Lance	10.10.1949		43	*1973–1985*	928	64	0	16.28	130	7-74	6/1	32.91	30	78
[1] **Cairns** Christopher Lance (*CY 2000*)	13.6.1970		62	*1989*–2004	3,320	158	5	33.53	218	7-27	13/1	29.40	14	214‡/2
Cameron Francis James MBE	1.6.1932		19	*1961*–1965	116	27*	0	11.60	62	5-34	3/0	29.82	1	
Cave Henry Butler	10.10.1922	15.9.1989	19	1949–1958	229	22*	0	8.80	34	4-21	0/0	43.14	8	
Chapple Murray Ernest	25.7.1930	31.7.1985	14	*1952–1965*	497	76	0	19.11	1	1-24	0/0	84.00	10	
Chatfield Ewen John MBE	3.7.1950		43	*1974–1988*	180	21*	0	8.57	123	6-73	3/1	32.17	7	114
Cleverley Donald Charles	23.12.1909	16.2.2004	2	*1931–1945*	19	10*	0	19.00	0	0-51	0/0	–	0	
Collinge Richard Owen	2.4.1946		35	*1964*–1978	533	68*	0	14.40	116	6-63	3/0	29.25	10	15
Colquhoun Ian Alexander	8.6.1924	26.2.2005	2	*1954*	1	1*	0	0.50	–	–	–/–	–	4	
Coney Jeremy Vernon MBE (*CY 1984*)	21.6.1952		52	*1973–1986*	2,668	174*	3	37.57	27	3-28	0/0	35.77	64	88
Congdon Bevan Ernest OBE (*CY 1974*)	11.2.1938	10.2.2018	61	*1964*–1978	3,448	176	7	32.22	59	5-65	1/0	36.50	44	11
Cowie John OBE	30.3.1912	3.6.1994	9	1937–1949	90	45	0	10.00	45	6-40	4/1	21.53	3	
Craig Mark Donald	23.3.1987		15	2014–*2016*	589	67	0	36.81	50	7-94	1/1	46.52	14	
Cresswell George Fenwick	22.3.1915	10.1.1966	3	1949–*1950*	14	12*	0	7.00	13	6-168	1/0	22.46	0	
Cromb Ian Burns	25.6.1905	6.3.1984	5	1931–*1931*	123	51*	0	20.50	8	3-113	0/0	55.25	1	
[2] **Crowe** Jeffrey John	14.9.1958		39	*1982–1989*	1,601	128	3	26.24	0	0-0	0/0	–	41	75
[2] **Crowe** Martin David MBE (*CY 1985*)	22.9.1962	3.3.2016	77	*1981–1995*	5,444	299	17	45.36	14	2-25	0/0	48.28	71	143
Cumming Craig Derek	31.8.1975		11	*2004–2007*	441	74	0	25.94	–	–	–/–	–	3	13
Cunis Robert Smith	5.1.1941	9.8.2008	20	*1963–1971*	295	51	0	12.82	51	6-76	1/0	37.00	1	
D'Arcy John William	23.4.1936		5	1958	136	33	0	13.60	–	–	–/–	–	0	
Davis Heath Te-Ihi-O-Te-Rangi	30.11.1971		5	1994–*1997*	20	8*	0	6.66	17	5-63	1/0	29.35	4	11

	Born	Died	Tests	Test Career	Runs	HS	100s	Avge	Wkts	BB	5/10	Avge	Ct/St	O/T
de Grandhomme Colin	22.7.1986		8	2016–2017	391	105	1	35.54	20	6-41	1/0	26.10	8	12/11
de Groen Richard Paul	5.8.1962		5	1993–1994	45	26	0	7.50	11	3-40	0/0	45.90	0	12
Dempster Charles Stewart (*CY 1932*)	15.11.1903	14.2.1974	10	1929–1932	723	136	2	65.72	0	0-10	0/0	–	2	
Dempster Eric William MBE	25.1.1925	15.8.2011	5	1952–1953	106	47	0	17.66	2	1-24	0/0	109.50	1	
Dick Arthur Edward	10.10.1936		17	1961–1965	370	50*	0	14.23	–	–	–/–	–	47/4	
Dickinson George Ritchie	11.3.1903	17.3.1978	3	1929–1931	31	11	0	6.20	8	3-66	0/0	30.62	3	
Donnelly Martin Paterson (*CY 1948*)	17.10.1917	22.10.1999	7	1937–1949	582	206	1	52.90	0	0-20	0/0	–	7	
Doull Simon Blair	6.8.1969		32	1992–1999	570	46	0	14.61	98	7-65	6/0	29.30	16	42
Dowling Graham Thorne OBE	4.3.1937		39	1961–1971	2,306	239	3	31.16	1	1-19	0/0	19.00	23	
Drum Christopher James	10.7.1974		5	2000–2001	10	4	0	3.33	16	3-36	0/0	30.12	4	5
Dunning John Angus	6.2.1903	24.6.1971	4	1932–1937	38	19	0	7.60	5	2-35	0/0	98.60	2	
Edgar Bruce Adrian	23.11.1956		39	1978–1986	1,958	161	3	30.59	0	0-3	0/0	–	14	64
Edwards Graham Neil ("Jock")	27.5.1955		8	1976–1980	377	55	0	25.13	–	–	–/–	–	7	6
Elliott Grant David	21.3.1979		5	2007–2009	86	25	0	10.75	4	2-8	0/0	35.00	2	83/16‡
Emery Raymond William George	28.3.1915	18.12.1982	2	1951	46	28	0	11.50	2	2-52	0/0	26.00	0	
Fisher Frederick Eric	28.7.1924	19.6.1996	1	1952	23	14	0	11.50	1	1-78	0/0	78.00	0	
Fleming Stephen Paul	1.4.1973		111	1993–2007	7,172	274*	9	40.06	–	–	–/–	–	171	279‡/5
Flynn Daniel Raymond	16.4.1985		24	2008–2012	1,038	95	0	25.95	0	0-0	0/0	–	10	20/5
Foley Henry	28.1.1906	16.10.1948	1	1929	4	2	0	2.00	–	–	–/–	–	0	
Franklin James Edward Charles	7.11.1980		31	2000–2012	808	122*	1	20.71	82	6-119	3/0	33.97	12	110/38
Franklin Trevor John	15.3.1962		21	1983–1990	828	101	1	23.00	–	–	–/–	–	8	3
Freeman Douglas Linford	8.9.1914	31.5.1994	2	1932	2	1	0	1.00	1	1-91	0/0	169.00	0	
Fulton Peter Gordon	1.2.1979		23	2005–2014	967	136	2	25.44	–	–	–/–	–	25	49/12
Gallichan Norman	3.6.1906	25.3.1969	1	1937	32	30	0	16.00	3	3-99	0/0	37.66	0	
Gedye Sidney Graham	2.5.1929	10.8.2014	4	1963–1964	193	55	0	24.12	–	–	–/–	–	0	
Germon Lee Kenneth	4.11.1968		12	1995–1996	382	55	0	21.22	–	–	–/–	–	27/2	37
Gillespie Mark Raymond	17.10.1979		5	2007–2011	76	27	0	10.85	22	6-113	3/0	28.68	1	32/11
Gillespie Stuart Ross	2.3.1957		1	1985	28	28	0	28.00	1	1-79	0/0	79.00	0	19
Gray Evan John	18.11.1954		10	1983–1988	248	50	0	15.50	17	3-73	0/0	52.11	6	10
Greatbatch Mark John	11.12.1963		41	1987–1996	2,021	146*	3	30.62	0	0-0	0/0	–	27	84
Guillen Simpson Clairmonte ("Sammy")	24.9.1924	2.3.2013	3†	1955	98	41	0	16.33	–	–	–/–	–	4/1	
Guptill Martin James	30.9.1986		47	2008–2016	2,586	189	3	29.38	8	3-11	0/0	37.25	50	149/67
Guy John William	29.8.1934		12	1955–1961	440	102	1	20.95	–	–	–/–	–	2	
[1,2] **Hadlee** Dayle Robert	6.1.1948		26	1969–1977	530	56	0	14.32	71	4-30	0/0	33.64	8	11
[1,2] **Hadlee** *Sir* Richard John (*CY 1982*)	3.7.1951		86	1972–1990	3,124	151*	2	27.16	431	9-52	36/9	22.29	39	115
[1] **Hadlee** Walter Arnold CBE	4.6.1915	29.9.2006	11	1937–1950	543	116	1	30.16	–	–	–/–	–	6	

	Born	Died	Tests	Test Career	Runs	HS	100s	Avge	Wkts	BB	5/10	Avge	Ct/St	O/T
Harford Noel Sherwin	30.8.1930	30.3.1981	8	*1955–1958*	229	93	0	15.26	–	–	–/–	–	0	
Harford Roy Ivan	30.5.1936		3	*1967*	7	6	0	2.33	–	–	–/–	–	11	
[1] **Harris** Chris Zinzan	20.11.1969		23	*1992–2002*	777	71	0	20.44	16	2-16	0/0	73.12	14	250
[1] **Harris** Parke Gerald Zinzan	18.7.1927	1.12.1991	9	*1955–1964*	378	101	1	22.23	0	0-14	0/0	–	6	
Harris Roger Meredith	27.7.1933		2	*1958*	31	13	0	10.33	–	–	–/–	–	0	
[2] **Hart** Matthew Norman	16.5.1972		14	*1993–1995*	353	45	0	17.65	29	5-77	1/0	49.58	9	13
[2] **Hart** Robert Garry	2.12.1974		11	2002–*2003*	260	57*	0	16.25	–	–	–/–	–	29/1	2
Hartland Blair Robert	22.10.1966		9	*1991*–1994	303	52	0	16.83	–	–	–/–	–	5	16
Haslam Mark James	26.9.1972		4	*1992–1995*	4	3	0	4.00	2	1-33	0/0	122.50	2	1
Hastings Brian Frederick	23.3.1940		31	*1968–1975*	1,510	117*	4	30.20	0	0-3	0/0	–	23	11
Hayes John Arthur	11.1.1927	25.12.2007	15	*1950*–1958	73	19	0	4.86	30	4-36	0/0	40.56	3	
Henderson Matthew	2.8.1895	17.6.1970	1	*1929*	8	6	0	8.00	2	2-38	0/0	32.00	1	
Henry Matthew James	14.12.1991		9	2015–*2017*	216	66	0	19.63	25	4-93	0/0	46.52	5	34/6
Hopkins Gareth James	24.11.1976		4	2008–*2010*	71	15	0	11.83	–	–	–/–	–	9	25/10
[2] **Horne** Matthew Jeffery	5.12.1970		35	*1996*–2003	1,788	157	4	28.38	0	0-4	0/0	–	17	50
[2] **Horne** Philip Andrew	21.1.1960		4	*1986–1990*	71	27	0	10.14	–	–	–/–	–	3	4
Hough Kenneth William	24.10.1928	20.9.2009	2	*1958*	62	31*	0	62.00	6	3-79	0/0	29.16	1	
How Jamie Michael	19.5.1981		19	*2005–2008*	772	92	0	22.70	0	0-0	0/0	–	18	41/5
[2] **Howarth** Geoffrey Philip OBE	29.3.1951		47	*1974–1984*	2,531	147	6	32.44	3	1-13	0/0	90.33	29	70
[2] **Howarth** Hedley John	25.12.1943	7.11.2008	30	1969–*1976*	291	61	0	12.12	86	5-34	2/0	36.95	33	9
Ingram Peter John	25.10.1978		2	*2009*	61	42	0	15.25	–	–	–/–	–	0	8/3
James Kenneth Cecil	12.3.1904	21.8.1976	11	*1929–1932*	52	14	0	4.72	–	–	–/–	–	11/5	
Jarvis Terrence Wayne	29.7.1944		13	*1964–1972*	625	182	1	29.76	0	0-0	0/0	–	3	
Jones Andrew Howard	9.5.1959		39	*1986–1994*	2,922	186	7	44.27	1	1-40	0/0	194.00	25	87
Jones Richard Andrew	22.10.1973		1	*2003*	23	16	0	11.50	–	–	–/–	–	0	5
Kennedy Robert John	3.6.1972		4	*1995*	28	22	0	7.00	6	3-28	0/0	63.33	2	7
Kerr John Lambert	28.12.1910	27.5.2007	7	1931–1937	212	59	0	19.27	–	–	–/–	–	4	
Kuggeleijn Christopher Mary	10.5.1956		2	*1988*	7	7	0	1.75	1	1-50	0/0	67.00	1	16
Larsen Gavin Rolf	27.9.1962		8	1994–*1995*	127	26*	0	14.11	24	3-57	0/0	28.70	5	121
[1] **Latham** Rodney Terry	12.6.1961		4	*1991–1992*	219	119	1	31.28	0	0-6	0/0	–	5	33
[1] **Latham** Thomas William Maxwell	2.4.1992		34	*2013–2017*	2,295	177	6	38.25	–	–	–/–	–	35	64/13
Lees Warren Kenneth MBE	19.3.1952		21	*1976*–1983	778	152	1	23.57	0	0-4	0/0	–	52/7	31
Leggat Ian Bruce	7.6.1930		1	*1953*	0	0	0	0.00	0	0-6	0/0	–	2	
Leggat John Gordon	27.5.1926	9.3.1973	9	*1951–1955*	351	61	0	21.93	–	–	–/–	–	0	
Lissette Allen Fisher	6.11.1919	24.1.1973	2	*1955*	2	1*	0	1.00	3	2-73	0/0	41.33	1	
Loveridge Greg Riaka	15.1.1975		1	*1995*	4	4*	0	–	–	–	–/–	–	0	

	Born	Died	Tests	Test Career	Runs	HS	100s	Avge	Wkts	BB	5/10	Avge	Ct/St	O/T
Lowry Thomas Coleman	17.2.1898	20.7.1976	7	*1929*–1931	223	80	0	27.87	0	0-0	0/0	–	8	
McCullum Brendon Barrie (*CY 2016*)	27.9.1981		101	*2003–2015*	6,453	302	12	38.64	1	1-1	0/0	88.00	198/11	260/71
McEwan Paul Ernest	19.12.1953		4	*1979–1984*	96	40*	0	16.00	0	0-6	0/0	–	5	17
MacGibbon Anthony Roy	28.8.1924	6.4.2010	26	*1950*–1958	814	66	0	19.85	70	5-64	1/0	30.85	13	
McGirr Herbert Mendelson	5.11.1891	14.4.1964	2	*1929*	51	51	0	51.00	1	1-65	0/0	115.00	0	
McGregor Spencer Noel	18.12.1931	21.11.2007	25	*1954–1964*	892	111	1	19.82	–	–	–/–	–	9	
McIntosh Timothy Gavin	4.12.1979		17	*2008–2010*	854	136	2	27.54	–	–	–/–	–	10	
McKay Andrew John	17.4.1980		1	*2010*	25	20*	0	25.00	1	1-120	0/0	120.00	0	19/2
McLeod Edwin George	14.10.1900	14.9.1989	1	*1929*	18	16	0	18.00	0	0-5	0/0	–	0	
McMahon Trevor George	8.11.1929		5	*1955*	7	4*	0	2.33	–	–	–/–	–	7/1	
McMillan Craig Douglas	13.9.1976		55	*1997–2004*	3,116	142	6	38.46	28	3-48	0/0	44.89	22	197/8
McRae Donald Alexander Noel	25.12.1912	10.8.1986	1	*1945*	8	8	0	4.00	0	0-44	0/0	–	0	
[2] **Marshall** Hamish John Hamilton	15.2.1979		13	*2000–2005*	652	160	2	38.35	0	0-4	0/0	–	1	66/3
[2] **Marshall** James Andrew Hamilton	15.2.1979		7	*2004*–2008	218	52	0	19.81	–	–	–/–	–	5	10/3
Martin Bruce Philip	25.4.1980		5	*2012–2013*	74	41	0	14.80	12	4-43	0/0	53.83	0	
Martin Christopher Stewart	10.12.1974		71	*2000–2012*	123	12*	0	2.36	233	6-26	10/1	33.81	14	20/6
Mason Michael James	27.8.1974		1	*2003*	3	3	0	1.50	0	0-32	0/0	–	0	26/3
Matheson Alexander Malcolm	27.2.1906	31.12.1985	2	*1929*–1931	7	7	0	7.00	2	2-7	0/0	68.00	2	
Meale Trevor	11.11.1928	21.5.2010	2	1958	21	10	0	5.25	–	–	–/–	–	0	
Merritt William Edward	18.8.1908	9.6.1977	6	*1929*–1931	73	19	0	10.42	12	4-104	0/0	51.41	2	
Meuli Edgar Milton	20.2.1926	15.4.2007	1	*1952*	38	23	0	19.00	–	–	–/–	–	0	
Milburn Barry Douglas	24.11.1943		3	*1968*	8	4*	0	8.00	–	–	–/–	–	6/2	
Miller Lawrence Somerville Martin	31.3.1923	17.12.1996	13	*1952*–1958	346	47	0	13.84	0	0-1	0/0	–	1	
Mills John Ernest	3.9.1905	11.12.1972	7	*1929–1932*	241	117	1	26.77	–	–	–/–	–	1	
Mills Kyle David	15.3.1979		19	2004–*2008*	289	57	0	11.56	44	4-16	0/0	33.02	4	170/42
Moir Alexander McKenzie	17.7.1919	17.6.2000	17	*1950–1958*	327	41*	0	14.86	28	6-155	2/0	50.64	2	
Moloney Denis Andrew Robert ("Sonny")	11.8.1910	15.7.1942	3	1937	156	64	0	26.00	0	0-9	0/0	–	3	
Mooney Francis Leonard Hugh	26.5.1921	8.3.2004	14	1949–*1953*	343	46	0	17.15	0	0-0	0/0	–	22/8	
Morgan Ross Winston	12.2.1941		20	*1964–1971*	734	97	0	22.24	5	1-16	0/0	121.80	12	
Morrison Bruce Donald	17.12.1933		1	*1962*	10	10	0	5.00	2	2-129	0/0	64.50	1	
Morrison Daniel Kyle	3.2.1966		48	*1987–1996*	379	42	0	8.42	160	7-89	10/0	34.68	14	96
Morrison John Francis MacLean	27.8.1947		17	*1973–1981*	656	117	1	22.62	2	2-52	0/0	35.50	9	18
Motz Richard Charles (*CY 1966*)	12.1.1940	29.4.2007	32	*1961*–1969	612	60	0	11.54	100	6-63	5/0	31.48	9	
Munro Colin	11.3.1987		1	*2012*	15	15	0	7.50	2	2-40	0/0	20.00	0	30/38
Murray Bruce Alexander Grenfell	18.9.1940		13	*1967–1970*	598	90	0	23.92	1	1-0	0/0	0.00	21	
Murray Darrin James	4.9.1967		8	*1994*	303	52	0	20.20	–	–	–/–	–	6	1

	Born	Died	Tests	Test Career	Runs	HS	100s	Avge	Wkts	BB	5/10	Avge	Ct/St	O/T
Nash Dion Joseph	20.11.1971		32	*1992–2001*	729	89*	0	23.51	93	6-27	3/1	28.48	13	81
Neesham James Douglas Sheehan	17.9.1990		12	*2013–2016*	709	137*	2	33.76	14	3-42	0/0	48.21	12	41/15
Newman *Sir* Jack	3.7.1902	23.9.1996	3	*1931–1932*	33	19	0	8.25	2	2-76	0/0	127.00	0	
Nicholls Henry Michael	15.11.1991		16	*2015–2017*	692	118	1	31.45	–	–	–/–	–	10	17/4
Nicol Robert James	28.5.1983		2	*2011*	28	19	0	7.00	0	0-0	0/0	–	2	22/21
O'Brien Iain Edward	10.7.1976		22	*2004–2009*	219	31	0	7.55	73	6-75	1/0	33.27	7	10/4
O'Connor Shayne Barry	15.11.1973		19	*1997–2001*	103	20	0	5.72	53	5-51	1/0	32.52	6	38
Oram Jacob David Philip	28.7.1978		33	2002–2009	1,780	133	5	36.32	60	4-41	0/0	33.05	15	160/36
O'Sullivan David Robert	16.11.1944		11	*1972–1976*	158	23*	0	9.29	18	5-148	1/0	67.83	2	3
Overton Guy William Fitzroy	8.6.1919	7.9.1993	3	*1953*	8	3*	0	1.60	9	3-65	0/0	28.66	1	
Owens Michael Barry	11.11.1969		8	*1992*–1994	16	8*	0	2.66	17	4-99	0/0	34.41	3	1
Page Milford Laurenson ("Curly")	8.5.1902	13.2.1987	14	*1929*–1937	492	104	1	24.60	5	2-21	0/0	46.20	6	
Papps Michael Hugh William	2.7.1979		8	*2003–2007*	246	86	0	16.40	–	–	–/–	–	11	6
[2] **Parker** John Morton	21.2.1951		36	*1972–1980*	1,498	121	3	24.55	1	1-24	0/0	24.00	30	24
[2] **Parker** Norman Murray	28.8.1948		3	*1976*	89	40	0	14.83	–	–	–/–	–	2	1
Parore Adam Craig	23.1.1971		78	1990–*2001*	2,865	110	2	26.28	–	–	–/–	–	197/7	179
Patel Dipak Narshibhai	25.10.1958		37	*1986–1996*	1,200	99	0	20.68	75	6-50	3/0	42.05	15	75
Patel Jeetan Shashi (*CY 2015*)	7.5.1980		24	*2005–2016*	381	47	0	12.70	65	5-110	1/0	47.35	13	43/11
Petherick Peter James	25.9.1942	7.6.2015	6	*1976*	34	13	0	4.85	16	3-90	0/0	42.81	4	
Petrie Eric Charlton	22.5.1927	14.8.2004	14	*1955–1965*	258	55	0	12.90	–	–	–/–	–	25	
Playle William Rodger	1.12.1938		8	1958–*1962*	151	65	0	10.06	–	–	–/–	–	4	
Pocock Blair Andrew	18.6.1971		15	*1993–1997*	665	85	0	22.93	0	0-10	0/0	–	5	
Pollard Victor	7.9.1945		32	*1964*–1973	1,266	116	2	24.34	40	3-3	0/0	46.32	19	3
Poore Matt Beresford	1.6.1930		14	*1952–1955*	355	45	0	15.43	9	2-28	0/0	40.77	1	
Priest Mark Wellings	12.8.1961		3	1990–*1997*	56	26	0	14.00	3	2-42	0/0	52.66	0	18
Pringle Christopher	26.1.1968		14	*1990–1994*	175	30	0	10.29	30	7-52	1/1	46.30	3	64
Puna Narotam ("Tom")	28.10.1929	7.6.1996	3	*1965*	31	18*	0	15.50	4	2-40	0/0	60.00	1	
Rabone Geoffrey Osborne	6.11.1921	19.1.2006	12	1949–*1954*	562	107	1	31.22	16	6-68	1/0	39.68	5	
Raval Jeet Ashokbhai	22.5.1988		9	*2016–2017*	623	88	0	44.50	–	–	–/–	–	13	
[1] **Redmond** Aaron James	23.9.1979		8	2008–*2013*	325	83	0	21.66	3	2-47	0/0	26.66	5	6/7
[1] **Redmond** Rodney Ernest	29.12.1944		1	*1972*	163	107	1	81.50	–	–	–/–	–	0	2
Reid John Fulton	3.3.1956		19	*1978–1985*	1,296	180	6	46.28	0	0-0	0/0	–	9	25
Reid John Richard OBE (*CY 1959*)	3.6.1928		58	1949–1965	3,428	142	6	33.28	85	6-60	1/0	33.35	43/1	
Richardson Mark Hunter	11.6.1971		38	*2000–2004*	2,776	145	4	44.77	1	1-16	0/0	21.00	26	4
Roberts Albert William	20.8.1909	13.5.1978	5	*1929*–1937	248	66*	0	27.55	7	4-101	0/0	29.85	4	
Roberts Andrew Duncan Glenn	6.5.1947	26.10.1989	7	*1975–1976*	254	84*	0	23.09	4	1-12	0/0	45.50	4	1

	Born	Died	Tests	Test Career	Runs	HS	100s	Avge	Wkts	BB	5/10	Avge	Ct/St	O/T
Robertson Gary Keith	15.7.1960		1	*1985*	12	12	0	12.00	1	1-91	0/0	91.00	0	10
Ronchi Luke	23.4.1981		4	2015–*2016*	319	88	0	39.87	–	–	–/–	–	5	81‡/29‡
Rowe Charles Gordon	30.6.1915	9.6.1995	1	*1945*	0	0	0	0.00	–	–	–/–	–	1	
[1] **Rutherford** Hamish Duncan	27.4.1989		16	*2012–2014*	755	171	1	26.96	0	0-2	0/0	–	11	4/7
[1] **Rutherford** Kenneth Robert	26.10.1965		56	*1984–1994*	2,465	107*	3	27.08	1	1-38	0/0	161.00	32	121
Ryder Jesse Daniel	6.8.1984		18	*2008–2011*	1,269	201	3	40.93	5	2-7	0/0	56.00	12	48/22
Santner Mitchell Josef	5.2.1992		17	*2015–2017*	535	73	0	25.47	34	3-60	0/0	37.05	7	43/20
Scott Roy Hamilton	6.3.1917	5.8.2005	1	*1946*	18	18	0	18.00	1	1-74	0/0	74.00	0	
Scott Verdun John	31.7.1916	2.8.1980	10	*1945–1951*	458	84	0	28.62	0	0-5	0/0	–	7	
Sewell David Graham	20.10.1977		1	*1997*	1	1*	0	–	0	0-9	0/0	–	0	
Shrimpton Michael John Froud	23.6.1940	13.6.2015	10	*1962–1973*	265	46	0	13.94	5	3-35	0/0	31.60	2	
Sinclair Barry Whitley	23.10.1936		21	*1962–1967*	1,148	138	3	29.43	2	2-32	0/0	16.00	8	
Sinclair Ian McKay	1.6.1933		2	*1955*	25	18*	0	8.33	1	1-79	0/0	120.00	1	
Sinclair Mathew Stuart	9.11.1975		33	*1999–2009*	1,635	214	3	32.05	0	0-1	0/0	–	31	54/2
Smith Frank Brunton	13.3.1922	6.7.1997	4	*1946–1951*	237	96	0	47.40	–	–	–/–	–	1	
Smith Horace Dennis	8.1.1913	25.1.1986	1	*1932*	4	4	0	4.00	1	1-113	0/0	113.00	0	
Smith Ian David Stockley MBE	28.2.1957		63	*1980–1991*	1,815	173	2	25.56	0	0-5	0/0	–	168/8	98
Snedden Colin Alexander	7.1.1918	23.4.2011	1	*1946*	–	–	–	–	0	0-46	0/0	–	0	
Snedden Martin Colin	23.11.1958		25	*1980*–1990	327	33*	0	14.86	58	5-68	1/0	37.91	7	93
Sodhi Inderbir Singh ("Ish")	31.10.1992		14	*2013–2016*	365	63	0	22.81	38	4-60	0/0	46.68	8	18/18
Southee Timothy Grant	11.12.1988		58	*2007–2017*	1,384	77*	0	17.08	208	7-64	6/1	31.45	36	123/44
Sparling John Trevor	24.7.1938		11	1958–*1963*	229	50	0	12.72	5	1-9	0/0	65.40	4	
Spearman Craig Murray	4.7.1972		19	*1995–2000*	922	112	1	26.34	–	–	–/–	–	21	51
Stead Gary Raymond	9.1.1972		5	*1998–1999*	278	78	0	34.75	0	0-1	0/0	–	2	
Stirling Derek Alexander	5.10.1961		6	*1984*–1986	108	26	0	15.42	13	4-88	0/0	46.23	1	6
Styris Scott Bernard	10.7.1975		29	2002–*2007*	1,586	170	5	36.04	20	3-28	0/0	50.75	23	188/31
Su'a Murphy Logo	7.11.1966		13	*1991–1994*	165	44	0	12.69	36	5-73	2/0	38.25	8	12
Sutcliffe Bert MBE (*CY 1950*)	17.11.1923	20.4.2001	42	*1946*–1965	2,727	230*	5	40.10	4	2-38	0/0	86.00	20	
Taylor Bruce Richard	12.7.1943		30	*1964*–1973	898	124	2	20.40	111	7-74	4/0	26.60	10	2
Taylor Donald Dougald	2.3.1923	5.12.1980	3	*1946–1955*	159	77	0	31.80	–	–	–/–	–	2	
Taylor Luteru Ross Poutoa Lote	8.3.1984		83	*2007–2017*	6,246	290	17	48.04	2	2-4	0/0	24.00	125	196/74
Thomson Keith	26.2.1941		2	*1967*	94	69	0	31.33	1	1-9	0/0	9.00	0	
Thomson Shane Alexander	27.1.1969		19	*1989–1995*	958	120*	1	30.90	19	3-63	0/0	50.15	7	56
Tindill Eric William Thomas	18.12.1910	1.8.2010	5	1937–*1946*	73	37*	0	9.12	–	–	–/–	–	6/1	
Troup Gary Bertram	3.10.1952		15	*1976–1985*	55	13*	0	4.58	39	6-95	1/1	37.28	2	22
Truscott Peter Bennetts	14.8.1941		1	*1964*	29	26	0	14.50	–	–	–/–	–	1	

	Born	Died	Tests	Test Career	Runs	HS	100s	Avge	Wkts	BB	5/10	Avge	Ct/St	O/T
Tuffey Daryl Raymond	11.6.1978		26	1999–2009	427	80*	0	16.42	77	6-54	2/0	31.75	15	94/3
Turner Glenn Maitland (*CY 1971*)	26.5.1947		41	1968–1982	2,991	259	7	44.64	0	0-5	0/0	–	42	41
Twose Roger Graham	17.4.1968		16	1995–1999	628	94	0	25.12	3	2-36	0/0	43.33	5	87
Vance Robert Howard	31.3.1955		4	1987–1989	207	68	0	29.57	–	–	–/–	–	0	8
Van Wyk Cornelius Francois Kruger	7.2.1980		9	2011–2012	341	71	0	21.31	–	–	–/–	–	23/1	
Vaughan Justin Thomas Caldwell	30.8.1967		6	1992–1996	201	44	0	18.27	11	4-27	0/0	40.90	4	18
Vettori Daniel Luca	27.1.1979		112§	1996–2014	4,523	140	6	30.15	361	7-87	20/3	34.15	58	291‡/34
Vincent Lou	11.11.1978		23	2001–2007	1,332	224	3	34.15	0	0-2	0/0	–	19	102/9
[1] **Vivian** Graham Ellery	28.2.1946		5	1964–1971	110	43	0	18.33	1	1-14	0/0	107.00	3	1
[1] **Vivian** Henry Gifford	4.11.1912	12.8.1983	7	1931–1937	421	100	1	42.10	17	4-58	0/0	37.23	4	
Wadsworth Kenneth John	30.11.1946	19.8.1976	33	1969–1975	1,010	80	0	21.48	–	–	–/–	–	92/4	13
Wagner Neil	13.3.1986		34	2012–2017	402	37	0	12.18	144	7-39	5/0	27.87	8	
Walker Brooke Graeme Keith	25.3.1977		5	2000–2002	118	27*	0	19.66	5	2-92	0/0	79.80	0	11
Wallace Walter Mervyn	19.12.1916	21.3.2008	13	1937–1952	439	66	0	20.90	0	0-5	0/0	–	5	
Walmsley Kerry Peter	23.8.1973		3	1994–2000	13	5	0	2.60	9	3-70	0/0	43.44	0	2
Ward John Thomas	11.3.1937		8	1963–1967	75	35*	0	12.50	–	–	–/–	–	16/1	
Watling Bradley-John	9.7.1985		52	2009–2016	2,702	142*	6	38.05	–	–	–/–	–	171/6	27/5
Watson William	31.8.1965		15	1986–1993	60	11	0	5.00	40	6-78	1/0	34.67	4	61
Watt Leslie	17.9.1924	15.11.1996	1	1954	2	2	0	1.00	–	–	–/–	–	0	
Webb Murray George	22.6.1947		3	1970–1973	12	12	0	6.00	4	2-114	0/0	117.75	0	
Webb Peter Neil	14.7.1957		2	1979	11	5	0	3.66	–	–	–/–	–	2	5
Weir Gordon Lindsay	2.6.1908	31.10.2003	11	1929–1937	416	74*	0	29.71	7	3-38	0/0	29.85	3	
White David John	26.6.1961		2	1990	31	18	0	7.75	0	0-5	0/0	–	0	3
Whitelaw Paul Erskine	10.2.1910	28.8.1988	2	1932	64	30	0	32.00	–	–	–/–	–	0	
Williamson Kane Stuart (*CY 2016*)	8.8.1990		63	2010–2017	5,214	242*	17	50.62	29	4-44	0/0	38.93	56	118/44
Wiseman Paul John	4.5.1970		25	1997–2004	366	36	0	14.07	61	5-82	2/0	47.59	11	15
Wright John Geoffrey MBE	5.7.1954		82	1977–1992	5,334	185	12	37.82	0	0-1	0/0	–	38	149
Young Bryan Andrew	3.11.1964		35	1993–1998	2,034	267*	2	31.78	–	–	–/–	–	54	74
Young Reece Alan	15.9.1979		5	2010–2011	169	57	0	24.14	–	–	–/–	–	8	
Yuile Bryan William	29.10.1941		17	1962–1969	481	64	0	17.81	34	4-43	0/0	35.67	12	

§ *Vettori's figures exclude eight runs and one wicket for the ICC World XI v Australia in the Super Series Test in 2005-06.*

INDIA (290 players)

	Born	Died	Tests	Test Career	Runs	HS	100s	Avge	Wkts	BB	5/10	Avge	Ct/St	O/T
Aaron Varun Raymond	29.10.1989		9	*2011–2015*	35	9	0	3.88	18	3-97	0/0	52.61	1	9
Abid Ali Syed	9.9.1941		29	*1967–1974*	1,018	81	0	20.36	47	6-55	1/0	42.12	32	5
Adhikari Hemchandra Ramachandra	31.7.1919	25.10.2003	21	*1947–1958*	872	114*	1	31.14	3	3-68	0/0	27.33	8	
Agarkar Ajit Bhalchandra	4.12.1977		26	*1998–2005*	571	109*	1	16.79	58	6-41	1/0	47.32	6	191/4
[2] **Amar Singh** Ladha	4.12.1910	21.5.1940	7	1932–1936	292	51	0	22.46	28	7-86	2/0	30.64	3	
[1,2] **Amarnath** Mohinder (*CY 1984*)	24.9.1950		69	*1969–1987*	4,378	138	11	42.50	32	4-63	0/0	55.68	47	85
[1] **Amarnath** Nanik ("Lala")	11.9.1911	5.8.2000	24	*1933–1952*	878	118	1	24.38	45	5-96	2/0	32.91	13	
[1,2] **Amarnath** Surinder	30.12.1948		10	*1975–1978*	550	124	1	30.55	1	1-5	0/0	5.00	4	3
Amir Elahi	1.9.1908	28.12.1980	1†	*1947*	17	13	0	8.50	–	–	–/–	–	0	
Amre Pravin Kalyan	14.8.1968		11	*1992–1993*	425	103	1	42.50	–	–	–/–	–	9	37
Ankola Salil Ashok	1.3.1968		1	*1989*	6	6	0	6.00	2	1-35	0/0	64.00	0	20
[2] **Apte** Arvindrao Laxmanrao	24.10.1934	5.8.2014	1	1959	15	8	0	7.50	–	–	–/–	–	0	
[2] **Apte** Madhavrao Laxmanrao	5.10.1932		7	*1952*	542	163*	1	49.27	0	0-3	0/0	–	2	
Arshad Ayub	2.8.1958		13	*1987–1989*	257	57	0	17.13	41	5-50	3/0	35.07	2	32
Arun Bharathi	14.12.1962		2	*1986*	4	2*	0	4.00	4	3-76	0/0	29.00	2	4
Arun Lal	1.8.1955		16	*1982–1988*	729	93	0	26.03	0	0-0	0/0	–	13	13
Ashwin Ravichandran	17.9.1986		57	*2011–2017*	2,145	124	4	30.64	311	7-59	26/7	25.56	21	111/46
Azad Kirtivardhan	2.1.1959		7	*1980–1983*	135	24	0	11.25	3	2-84	0/0	124.33	3	25
Azharuddin Mohammad (*CY 1991*)	8.2.1963		99	*1984–1999*	6,215	199	22	45.03	0	0-4	0/0	–	105	334
Badani Hemang Kamal	14.11.1976		4	2001	94	38	0	15.66	0	0-17	0/0	–	6	40
Badrinath Subramaniam	30.8.1980		2	*2009*	63	56	0	21.00	–	–	–/–	–	2	7/1
Bahutule Sairaj Vasant	6.1.1973		2	*2000*–2001	39	21*	0	13.00	3	1-32	0/0	67.66	1	8
Baig Abbas Ali	19.3.1939		10	1959–*1966*	428	112	1	23.77	0	0-2	0/0	–	6	
Balaji Lakshmipathy	27.9.1981		8	*2003–2004*	51	31	0	5.66	27	5-76	1/0	37.18	1	30/5
Banerjee Sarobindu Nath ("Shute")	3.10.1911	14.10.1980	1	*1948*	13	8	0	6.50	5	4-54	0/0	25.40	0	
Banerjee Subroto Tara	13.2.1969		1	*1991*	3	3	0	3.00	3	3-47	0/0	15.66	0	6
Banerjee Sudangsu Abinash	1.11.1917	14.9.1992	1	*1948*	0	0	0	0.00	5	4-120	0/0	36.20	3	
Bangar Sanjay Bapusaheb	11.10.1972		12	*2001–2002*	470	100*	1	29.37	7	2-23	0/0	49.00	4	15
Baqa Jilani Mohammad	20.7.1911	2.7.1941	1	1936	16	12	0	16.00	0	0-55	0/0	–	0	
Bedi Bishan Singh	25.9.1946		67	*1966*–1979	656	50*	0	8.98	266	7-98	14/1	28.71	26	10
Bhandari Prakash	27.11.1935		3	*1954–1956*	77	39	0	19.25	0	0-12	0/0	–	1	
Bharadwaj Raghvendrarao Vijay	15.8.1975		3	*1999*	28	22	0	9.33	1	1-26	0/0	107.00	3	10
Bhat Adwai Raghuram	16.4.1958		2	*1983*	6	6	0	3.00	4	2-65	0/0	37.75	0	

	Born	Died	Tests	Test Career	Runs	HS	100s	Avge	Wkts	BB	5/10	Avge	Ct/St	O/T
Bhuvneshwar Kumar	5.2.1990		21	*2012–2017*	552	63*	0	22.08	63	6-82	4/0	26.09	8	81/23
[1] **Binny** Roger Michael Humphrey	19.7.1955		27	*1979–1986*	830	83*	0	23.05	47	6-56	2/0	32.63	11	72
[1] **Binny** Stuart Terence Roger	3.6.1984		6	2014–*2015*	194	78	0	21.55	3	2-24	0/0	86.00	4	14/3
Borde Chandrakant Gulabrao	21.7.1934		55	*1958–1969*	3,061	177*	5	35.59	52	5-88	1/0	46.48	37	
Bumrah Jasprit Jasbirsingh	6.12.1993		3	*2017*	4	2	0	1.00	14	5-54	1/0	25.21	2	31/32
Chandrasekhar Bhagwat Subramanya (*CY 1972*)	17.5.1945		58	*1963*–1979	167	22	0	4.07	242	8-79	16/2	29.74	25	1
Chauhan Chetandra Pratap Singh	21.7.1947		40	*1969–1980*	2,084	97	0	31.57	2	1-4	0/0	53.00	38	7
Chauhan Rajesh Kumar	19.12.1966		21	*1992–1997*	98	23	0	7.00	47	4-48	0/0	39.51	12	35
Chawla Piyush Pramod	24.12.1988		3	*2005–2012*	6	4	0	2.00	7	4-69	0/0	38.57	1	25/7
Chopra Aakash	19.9.1977		10	*2003–2004*	437	60	0	23.00	–	–	–/–	–	15	
Chopra Nikhil	26.12.1973		1	*1999*	7	4	0	3.50	0	0-78	0/0	–	0	39
Chowdhury Nirode Ranjan	23.5.1923	14.12.1979	2	*1948–1951*	3	3*	0	3.00	1	1-130	0/0	205.00	0	
Colah Sorabji Hormasji Munchersha	22.9.1902	11.9.1950	2	1932–*1933*	69	31	0	17.25	–	–	–/–	–	2	
Contractor Nariman Jamshedji	7.3.1934		31	*1955–1961*	1,611	108	1	31.58	1	1-9	0/0	80.00	18	
Dahiya Vijay	10.5.1973		2	*2000*	2	2*	0	–	–	–	–/–	–	6	19
Dani Hemchandra Tukaram	24.5.1933	19.12.1999	1	*1952*	–	–	–	–	1	1-9	0/0	19.00	1	
Das Shiv Sunder	5.11.1977		23	*2000–2001*	1,326	110	2	34.89	0	0-7	0/0	–	34	4
Dasgupta Deep	7.6.1977		8	*2001*	344	100	1	28.66	–	–	–/–	–	13	5
Desai Ramakant Bhikaji	20.6.1939	27.4.1998	28	*1958–1967*	418	85	0	13.48	74	6-56	2/0	37.31	9	
Dhawan Shikhar (*CY 2014*)	5.12.1985		29	*2012–2017*	2,046	190	6	42.62	0	0-0	0/0	–	24	96/28
Dhoni Mahendra Singh	7.7.1981		90	*2005–2014*	4,876	224	6	38.09	0	0-1	0/0	–	256/38	309‡/86
Dighe Sameer Sudhakar	8.10.1968		6	*2000*–2001	141	47	0	15.66	–	–	–/–	–	12/2	23
Dilawar Hussain	19.3.1907	26.8.1967	3	*1933*–1936	254	59	0	42.33	–	–	–/–	–	6/1	
Divecha Ramesh Vithaldas	18.10.1927	11.2.2003	5	*1951–1952*	60	26	0	12.00	11	3-102	0/0	32.81	5	
Doshi Dilip Rasiklal	22.12.1947		33	*1979–1983*	129	20	0	4.60	114	6-102	6/0	30.71	10	15
Dravid Rahul (*CY 2000*)	11.1.1973		163§	1996–*2011*	13,265	270	36	52.63	1	1-18	0/0	39.00	209	340‡/1
Durani Salim Aziz	11.12.1934		29	*1959–1972*	1,202	104	1	25.04	75	6-73	3/1	35.42	14	
Engineer Farokh Maneksha	25.2.1938		46	*1961–1974*	2,611	121	2	31.08	–	–	–/–	–	66/16	5
Gadkari Chandrasekhar Vaman	3.2.1928	11.1.1998	6	*1952–1954*	129	50*	0	21.50	0	0-8	0/0	–	6	
[1] **Gaekwad** Anshuman Dattajirao	23.9.1952		40	*1974–1984*	1,985	201	2	30.07	2	1-4	0/0	93.50	15	15
[1] **Gaekwad** Dattajirao Krishnarao	27.10.1928		11	1952–*1960*	350	52	0	18.42	0	0-4	0/0	–	5	
Gaekwad Hiralal Ghasulal	29.8.1923	2.1.2003	1	*1952*	22	14	0	11.00	0	0-47	0/0	–	0	
Gambhir Gautam	14.10.1981		58	*2004–2016*	4,154	206	9	41.95	0	0-4	0/0	–	38	147/37
Gandhi Devang Jayant	6.9.1971		4	*1999*	204	88	0	34.00	–	–	–/–	–	3	3

§ *Dravid's figures exclude 23 runs and one catch for the ICC World XI v Australia in the Super Series Test in 2005-06.*

	Born	Died	Tests	Test Career	Runs	HS	100s	Avge	Wkts	BB	5/10	Avge	Ct/St	O/T
Gandotra Ashok	24.11.1948		2	1969	54	18	0	13.50	0	0-5	0/0	–	1	
Ganesh Doddanarasiah	30.6.1973		4	1996	25	8	0	6.25	5	2-28	0/0	57.40	0	1
Ganguly Sourav Chandidas	8.7.1972		113	1996–2008	7,212	239	16	42.17	32	3-28	0/0	52.53	71	308‡
Gavaskar Sunil Manohar (*CY 1980*)	10.7.1949		125	1970–1986	10,122	236*	34	51.12	1	1-34	0/0	206.00	108	108
Ghavri Karsan Devjibhai	28.2.1951		39	1974–1980	913	86	0	21.23	109	5-33	4/0	33.54	16	19
Ghorpade Jayasinghrao Mansinghrao	2.10.1930	29.3.1978	8	1952–1959	229	41	0	15.26	0	0-17	0/0	–	4	
Ghulam Ahmed	4.7.1922	28.10.1998	22	1948–1958	192	50	0	8.72	68	7-49	4/1	30.17	11	
Gopalan Morappakam Joysam	6.6.1909	21.12.2003	1	1933	18	11*	0	18.00	1	1-39	0/0	39.00	3	
Gopinath Coimbatarao Doraikannu	1.3.1930		8	1951–1959	242	50*	0	22.00	1	1-11	0/0	11.00	2	
Guard Ghulam Mustafa	12.12.1925	13.3.1978	2	1958–1959	11	7	0	5.50	3	2-69	0/0	60.66	2	
Guha Subrata	31.1.1946	5.11.2003	4	1967–1969	17	6	0	3.40	3	2-55	0/0	103.66	2	
Gul Mahomed	15.10.1921	8.5.1992	8†	1946–1952	166	34	0	11.06	2	2-21	0/0	12.00	3	
[2] **Gupte** Balkrishna Pandharinath	30.8.1934	5.7.2005	3	1960–1964	28	17*	0	28.00	3	1-54	0/0	116.33	0	
[2] **Gupte** Subhashchandra Pandharinath ("Fergie")	11.12.1929	31.5.2002	36	1951–1961	183	21	0	6.31	149	9-102	12/1	29.55	14	
Gursharan Singh	8.3.1963		1	1989	18	18	0	18.00	–	–	–/–	–	2	1
Hafeez Abdul (see Kardar)														
Hanumant Singh	29.3.1939	29.11.2006	14	1963–1969	686	105	1	31.18	0	0-5	0/0	–	11	
Harbhajan Singh	3.7.1980		103	1997–2015	2,224	115	2	18.22	417	8-84	25/5	32.46	42	234‡/28
Hardikar Manohar Shankar	8.2.1936	4.2.1995	2	1958	56	32*	0	18.66	1	1-9	0/0	55.00	3	
Harvinder Singh	23.12.1977		3	1997–2001	6	6	0	2.00	4	2-62	0/0	46.25	0	16
Hazare Vijay Samuel	11.3.1915	18.12.2004	30	1946–1952	2,192	164*	7	47.65	20	4-29	0/0	61.00	11	
Hindlekar Dattaram Dharmaji	1.1.1909	30.3.1949	4	1936–1946	71	26	0	14.20	–	–	–/–	–	3	
Hirwani Narendra Deepchand	18.10.1968		17	1987–1996	54	17	0	5.40	66	8-61	4/1	30.10	5	18
Ibrahim Khanmohammad Cassumbhoy	26.1.1919	12.11.2007	4	1948	169	85	0	21.12	–	–	–/–	–	0	
Indrajitsinhji Kumar Shri	15.6.1937	12.3.2011	4	1964–1969	51	23	0	8.50	–	–	–/–	–	6/3	
Irani Jamshed Khudadad	18.8.1923	25.2.1982	2	1947	3	2*	0	3.00	–	–	–/–	–	2/1	
Jadeja Ajaysinhji	1.2.1971		15	1992–1999	576	96	0	26.18	–	–	–/–	–	5	196
Jadeja Ravindrasinh Anirudhsinh	6.12.1988		35	2012–2017	1,176	90	0	29.40	165	7-48	9/1	23.73	28	136/40
[3] **Jahangir Khan** Mohammad	1.2.1910	23.7.1988	4	1932–1936	39	13	0	5.57	4	4-60	0/0	63.75	4	
Jai Laxmidas Purshottamdas	1.4.1902	29.1.1968	1	1933	19	19	0	9.50	–	–	–/–	–	0	
Jaisimha Motganhalli Laxmanarsu	3.3.1939	6.7.1999	39	1959–1970	2,056	129	3	30.68	9	2-54	0/0	92.11	17	
Jamshedji Rustomji Jamshedji Dorabji	18.11.1892	5.4.1976	1	1933	5	4*	0	–	3	3-137	0/0	45.66	2	
Jayantilal Kenia	13.1.1948		1	1970	5	5	0	5.00	–	–	–/–	–	0	
Johnson David Jude	16.10.1971		2	1996	8	5	0	4.00	3	2-52	0/0	47.66	0	
Joshi Padmanabh Govind	27.10.1926	8.1.1987	12	1951–1960	207	52*	0	10.89	–	–	–/–	–	18/9	
Joshi Sunil Bandacharya	6.6.1969		15	1996–2000	352	92	0	20.70	41	5-142	1/0	35.85	7	69

	Born	Died	Tests	Test Career	Runs	HS	100s	Avge	Wkts	BB	5/10	Avge	Ct/St	O/T
Kaif Mohammad	1.12.1980		13	1999–2005	624	148*	1	32.84	0	0-4	0/0	–	14	125
Kambli Vinod Ganpat	18.1.1972		17	1992–1995	1,084	227	4	54.20	–	–	–/–	–	7	104
[1] **Kanitkar** Hrishikesh Hemant	14.11.1974		2	1999	74	45	0	18.50	0	0-2	0/0	–	0	34
[1] **Kanitkar** Hemant Shamsunder	8.12.1942	9.6.2015	2	1974	111	65	0	27.75	–	–	–/–	–	0	
Kapil Dev (*CY 1983*)	6.1.1959		131	1978–1993	5,248	163	8	31.05	434	9-83	23/2	29.64	64	225
Kapoor Aashish Rakesh	25.3.1971		4	1994–1996	97	42	0	19.40	6	2-19	0/0	42.50	1	17
Kardar Abdul Hafeez	17.1.1925	21.4.1996	3†	1946	80	43	0	16.00	–	–	–/–	–	1	
Karim Syed Saba	14.11.1967		1	2000	15	15	0	15.00	–	–	–/–	–	1	34
Karthik Krishankumar Dinesh	1.6.1985		23	2004–2009	1,000	129	1	27.77	–	–	–/–	–	51/5	79/13
Kartik Murali	11.9.1976		8	1999–2004	88	43	0	9.77	24	4-44	0/0	34.16	2	37/1
Kenny Ramnath Baburao	29.9.1930	21.11.1985	5	1958–1959	245	62	0	27.22	–	–	–/–	–	1	
Kirmani Syed Mujtaba Hussein	29.12.1949		88	1975–1985	2,759	102	2	27.04	1	1-9	0/0	13.00	160/38	49
Kishenchand Gogumal	14.4.1925	16.4.1997	5	1947–1952	89	44	0	8.90	–	–	–/–	–	1	
Kohli Virat	5.11.1988		66	2011–2017	5,554	243	21	53.40	0	0-0	0/0	–	63	202/55
[2] **Kripal Singh** Amritsar Govindsingh	6.8.1933	22.7.1987	14	1955–1964	422	100*	1	28.13	10	3-43	0/0	58.40	4	
Krishnamurthy Pochiah	12.7.1947	28.1.1999	5	1970	33	20	0	5.50	–	–	–/–	–	7/1	1
Kulkarni Nilesh Moreshwar	3.4.1973		3	1997–2000	5	4	0	5.00	2	1-70	0/0	166.00	1	10
Kulkarni Rajiv Ramesh	25.9.1962		3	1986	2	2	0	1.00	5	3-85	0/0	45.40	1	10
Kulkarni Umesh Narayan	7.3.1942		4	1967	13	7	0	4.33	5	2-37	0/0	47.60	0	
Kumar Praveen	2.10.1986		6	2011	149	40	0	14.90	27	5-106	1/0	25.81	2	68/10
Kumar Vaman Viswanath	22.6.1935		2	1960–1961	6	6	0	3.00	7	5-64	1/0	28.85	2	
Kumble Anil (*CY 1996*)	17.10.1970		132	1990–2008	2,506	110*	1	17.77	619	10-74	35/8	29.65	60	269‡
Kunderan Budhisagar Krishnappa	2.10.1939	23.6.2006	18	1959–1967	981	192	2	32.70	0	0-13	0/0	–	23/7	
Kuruvilla Abey	8.8.1968		10	1996–1997	66	35*	0	6.60	25	5-68	1/0	35.68	0	25
Lall Singh	16.12.1909	19.11.1985	1	1932	44	29	0	22.00	–	–	–/–	–	1	
Lamba Raman	2.1.1960	22.2.1998	4	1986–1987	102	53	0	20.40	–	–	–/–	–	5	32
Laxman Vangipurappu Venkata Sai (*CY 2002*)	1.11.1974		134	1996–2011	8,781	281	17	45.97	2	1-2	0/0	63.00	135	86
Madan Lal	20.3.1951		39	1974–1986	1,042	74	0	22.65	71	5-23	4/0	40.08	15	67
Maka Ebrahim Suleman	5.3.1922	7.9.1994	2	1952	2	2*	0	–	–	–	–/–	–	2/1	
Malhotra Ashok Omprakash	26.1.1957		7	1981–1984	226	72*	0	25.11	0	0-0	0/0	–	2	20
Maninder Singh	13.6.1965		35	1982–1992	99	15	0	3.80	88	7-27	3/2	37.36	9	59
[1] **Manjrekar** Sanjay Vijay	12.7.1965		37	1987–1996	2,043	218	4	37.14	0	0-4	0/0	–	25/1	74
[1] **Manjrekar** Vijay Laxman	26.9.1931	18.10.1983	55	1951–1964	3,208	189*	7	39.12	1	1-16	0/0	44.00	19/2	
[1] **Mankad** Ashok Vinoo	12.10.1946	1.8.2008	22	1969–1977	991	97	0	25.41	0	0-0	0/0	–	12	1
[1] **Mankad** Mulvantrai Himmatlal ("Vinoo") (*CY 1947*)	12.4.1917	21.8.1978	44	1946–1958	2,109	231	5	31.47	162	8-52	8/2	32.32	33	

	Born	Died	Tests	Test Career	Runs	HS	100s	Avge	Wkts	BB	5/10	Avge	Ct/St	O/T
Mantri Madhav Krishnaji	1.9.1921	23.5.2014	4	*1951–1954*	67	39	0	9.57	–	–	–/–	–	8/1	
Meherhomji Khershedji Rustomji	9.8.1911	10.2.1982	1	1936	0	0*	0	–	–	–	–/–	–	1	
Mehra Vijay Laxman	12.3.1938	25.8.2006	8	*1955–1963*	329	62	0	25.30	0	0-1	0/0	–	1	
Merchant Vijay Madhavji (*CY 1937*)	12.10.1911	27.10.1987	10	*1933–1951*	859	154	3	47.72	0	0-17	0/0	–	7	
Mhambrey Paras Laxmikant	20.6.1972		2	1996	58	28	0	29.00	2	1-43	0/0	74.00	1	3
[2] **Milkha Singh** Amritsar Govindsingh	31.12.1941	10.11.2017	4	*1959–1961*	92	35	0	15.33	0	0-2	0/0	–	2	
Mishra Amit	24.11.1982		22	*2008–2016*	648	84	0	21.60	76	5-71	1/0	35.72	8	36/10
Mithun Abhimanyu	25.10.1989		4	2010–2011	120	46	0	24.00	9	4-105	0/0	50.66	0	5
Modi Rustomji Sheryar	11.11.1924	17.5.1996	10	1946–*1952*	736	112	1	46.00	0	0-14	0/0	–	3	
Mohammed Shami	3.9.1990		30	*2013–2017*	398	51*	0	14.74	110	5-28	3/0	28.90	6	50/7
Mohanty Debasis Sarbeswar	20.7.1976		2	*1997*	0	0*	0	–	4	4-78	0/0	59.75	0	45
Mongia Nayan Ramlal	19.12.1969		44	*1993–2000*	1,442	152	1	24.03	–	–	–/–	–	99/8	140
More Kiran Shankar	4.9.1962		49	1986–*1993*	1,285	73	0	25.70	0	0-12	0/0	–	110/20	94
Muddiah Venatappa Musandra	8.6.1929	1.10.2009	2	*1959–1960*	11	11	0	5.50	3	2-40	0/0	44.66	0	
Mukund Abhinav	6.1.1990		7	2011–2017	320	81	0	22.85	0	0-14	0/0	–	6	
Mushtaq Ali Syed	17.12.1914	18.6.2005	11	*1933–1951*	612	112	2	32.21	3	1-45	0/0	67.33	7	
Nadkarni Rameshchandra Gangaram ("Bapu")	4.4.1933		41	*1955–1967*	1,414	122*	1	25.70	88	6-43	4/1	29.07	22	
Naik Sudhir Sakharam	21.2.1945		3	1974–*1974*	141	77	0	23.50	–	–	–/–	–	0	2
Nair Karun Kaladharan	6.12.1991		6	*2016*	374	303*	1	62.33	0	0-4	0/0	–	6	2
Naoomal Jeoomal	17.4.1904	28.7.1980	3	1932–*1933*	108	43	0	27.00	2	1-4	0/0	34.00	0	
Narasimha Rao Modireddy Venkateshwar	11.8.1954		4	*1978–1979*	46	20*	0	9.20	3	2-46	0/0	75.66	8	
Navle Janaradan Gyanoba	7.12.1902	7.9.1979	2	1932–*1933*	42	13	0	10.50	–	–	–/–	–	1	
Nayak Surendra Vithal	20.10.1954		2	1982	19	11	0	9.50	1	1-16	0/0	132.00	1	4
[2] **Nayudu** Cottari Kanakaiya (*CY 1933*)	31.10.1895	14.11.1967	7	1932–1936	350	81	0	25.00	9	3-40	0/0	42.88	4	
[2] **Nayudu** Cottari Subbanna	18.4.1914	22.11.2002	11	*1933–1951*	147	36	0	9.18	2	1-19	0/0	179.50	3	
[2] **Nazir Ali** Syed	8.6.1906	18.2.1975	2	1932–*1933*	30	13	0	7.50	4	4-83	0/0	20.75	0	
Nehra Ashish	29.4.1979		17	*1998–2003*	77	19	0	5.50	44	4-72	0/0	42.40	5	117‡/27
Nissar Mohammad	1.8.1910	11.3.1963	6	1932–1936	55	14	0	6.87	25	5-90	3/0	28.28	2	
Nyalchand Sukhlal Shah	14.9.1915	3.1.1997	1	*1952*	7	6*	0	7.00	3	3-97	0/0	32.33	0	
Ojha Naman Vijaykumar	20.7.1983		1	*2015*	56	35	0	28.00	–	–	–/–	–	4/1	1/2
Ojha Pragyan Prayish	5.9.1986		24	*2009–2013*	89	18*	0	8.90	113	6-47	7/1	30.26	10	18/6
Pai Ajit Manohar	28.4.1945		1	*1969*	10	9	0	5.00	2	2-29	0/0	15.50	0	
Palia Phiroze Edulji	5.9.1910	9.9.1981	2	1932–1936	29	16	0	9.66	0	0-2	0/0	–	0	
Pandit Chandrakant Sitaram	30.9.1961		5	1986–*1991*	171	39	0	24.42	–	–	–/–	–	14/2	36
Pandya Hardik Himanshu	11.10.1993		6	2017–*2017*	297	108	1	33.00	7	2-27	0/0	36.71	7	32/27
Pankaj Singh	6.5.1985		2	2014	10	9	0	3.33	2	2-113	0/0	146.00	2	1

	Born	Died	Tests	Test Career	Runs	HS	100s	Avge	Wkts	BB	5/10	Avge	Ct/St	O/T
Parkar Ghulam Ahmed	25.10.1955		1	1982	7	6	0	3.50	–	–	–/–	–	1	10
Parkar Ramnath Dhondu	31.10.1946	11.8.1999	2	1972	80	35	0	20.00	–	–	–/–	–	0	
Parsana Dhiraj Devshibhai	2.12.1947		2	1978	1	1	0	0.50	1	1-32	0/0	50.00	0	
Patankar Chandrakant Trimbak	24.11.1930		1	1955	14	13	0	14.00	–	–	–/–	–	3/1	
[1] **Pataudi** Iftikhar Ali Khan, Nawab of (*CY 1932*)	16.3.1910	5.1.1952	3†	1946	55	22	0	11.00	–	–	–/–	–	0	
[1] **Pataudi** Mansur Ali Khan, Nawab of (*CY 1968*)	5.1.1941	22.9.2011	46	1961–1974	2,793	203*	6	34.91	1	1-10	0/0	88.00	27	
Patel Brijesh Pursuram	24.11.1952		21	1974–1977	972	115*	1	29.45	–	–	–/–	–	17	10
Patel Jasubhai Motibhai	26.11.1924	12.12.1992	7	1954–1959	25	12	0	2.77	29	9-69	2/1	21.96	2	
Patel Munaf Musa	12.7.1983		13	2005–2011	60	15*	0	7.50	35	4-25	0/0	38.54	6	70/3
Patel Parthiv Ajay	9.3.1985		25	2002–2017	934	71	0	31.13	–	–	–/–	–	62/10	38/2
Patel Rashid	1.6.1964		1	1988	0	0	0	0.00	0	0-14	0/0	–	1	1
Pathan Irfan Khan	27.10.1984		29	2003–2007	1,105	102	1	31.57	100	7-59	7/2	32.26	8	120/24
Patiala Maharajah of (Yadavendra Singh)	17.1.1913	17.6.1974	1	1933	84	60	0	42.00	–	–	–/–	–	2	
Patil Sadashiv Raoji	10.10.1933		1	1955	14	14*	0	–	2	1-15	0/0	25.50	1	
Patil Sandeep Madhusudan	18.8.1956		29	1979–1984	1,588	174	4	36.93	9	2-28	0/0	26.66	12	45
Phadkar Dattatraya Gajanan	12.12.1925	17.3.1985	31	1947–1958	1,229	123	2	32.34	62	7-159	3/0	36.85	21	
Powar Ramesh Rajaram	20.5.1978		2	2007	13	7	0	6.50	6	3-33	0/0	19.66	0	31
Prabhakar Manoj	15.4.1963		39	1984–1995	1,600	120	1	32.65	96	6-132	3/0	37.30	20	130
Prasad Bapu Krishnarao Venkatesh	5.8.1969		33	1996–2001	203	30*	0	7.51	96	6-33	7/1	35.00	6	161
Prasad Mannava Sri Kanth	24.4.1975		6	1999	106	19	0	11.77	–	–	–/–	–	15	17
Prasanna Erapalli Anatharao Srinivas	22.5.1940		49	1961–1978	735	37	0	11.48	189	8-76	10/2	30.38	18	
Pujara Cheteshwar Arvind	25.1.1988		57	2010–2017	4,496	206*	14	50.51	0	0-2	0/0	–	40	5
Punjabi Pananmal Hotchand	20.9.1921	4.10.2011	5	1954	164	33	0	16.40	–	–	–/–	–	5	
Rahane Ajinkya Madhukar	6.6.1988		44	2012–2017	2,883	188	9	43.68	–	–	–/–	–	59	84/20
Rahul Kannur Lokesh	18.4.1992		23	2014–2017	1,458	199	4	40.50	–	–	–/–	–	27	10/12
Rai Singh Kanwar	24.2.1922	12.11.1993	1	1947	26	24	0	13.00	–	–	–/–	–	0	
Raina Suresh Kumar	27.11.1986		18	2010–2014	768	120	1	26.48	13	2-1	0/0	46.38	23	223/65
Rajinder Pal	18.11.1937		1	1963	6	3*	0	6.00	0	0-3	0/0	–	0	
Rajindernath Vijay	7.1.1928	22.11.1989	1	1952	–	–	–	–	–	–	–/–	–	0/4	
Rajput Lalchand Sitaram	18.12.1961		2	1985	105	61	0	26.25	–	–	–/–	–	1	4
Raju Sagi Lakshmi Venkatapathy	9.7.1969		28	1989–2000	240	31	0	10.00	93	6-12	5/1	30.72	6	53
Raman Woorkeri Venkat	23.5.1965		11	1987–1996	448	96	0	24.88	2	1-7	0/0	64.50	6	27
Ramaswami Cotar	16.6.1896	1.1990	2	1936	170	60	0	56.66	–	–	–/–	–	0	
Ramchand Gulabrai Sipahimalani	26.7.1927	8.9.2003	33	1952–1959	1,180	109	2	24.58	41	6-49	1/0	46.31	20	
Ramesh Sadagoppan	16.10.1975		19	1998–2001	1,367	143	2	37.97	0	0-5	0/0	–	18	24
[2] **Ramji** Ladha	10.2.1900	20.12.1948	1	1933	1	1	0	0.50	0	0-64	0/0	–	1	

	Born	Died	Tests	Test Career	Runs	HS	100s	Avge	Wkts	BB	5/10	Avge	Ct/St	O/T
Rangachari Commandur Rajagopalachari	14.4.1916	9.10.1993	4	1947–1948	8	8*	0	2.66	9	5-107	1/0	54.77	0	
Rangnekar Khanderao Moreshwar	27.6.1917	11.10.1984	3	1947	33	18	0	5.50	–	–	–/–	–	1	
Ranjane Vasant Baburao	22.7.1937	22.12.2011	7	1958–1964	40	16	0	6.66	19	4-72	0/0	34.15	1	
Rathore Vikram	26.3.1969		6	1996–1996	131	44	0	13.10	–	–	–/–	–	12	7
Ratra Ajay	13.12.1981		6	2001–2002	163	115*	1	18.11	0	0-1	0/0	–	11/2	12
Razdan Vivek	25.8.1969		2	1989	6	6*	0	6.00	5	5-79	1/0	28.20	0	3
Reddy Bharath	12.11.1954		4	1979	38	21	0	9.50	–	–	–/–	–	9/2	3
Rege Madhusudan Ramachandra	18.3.1924	16.12.2013	1	1948	15	15	0	7.50	–	–	–/–	–	1	
Roy Ambar	5.6.1945	19.9.1997	4	1969	91	48	0	13.00	–	–	–/–	–	0	
[1] **Roy** Pankaj	31.5.1928	4.2.2001	43	1951–1960	2,442	173	5	32.56	1	1-6	0/0	66.00	16	
[1] **Roy** Pranab	10.2.1957		2	1981	71	60*	0	35.50	–	–	–/–	–	1	
Saha Wriddhaman Prasanta	24.10.1984		32	2009–2017	1,164	117	3	30.63	–	–	–/–	–	75/10	9
Sandhu Balwinder Singh	3.8.1956		8	1982–1983	214	71	0	30.57	10	3-87	0/0	55.70	1	22
Sanghvi Rahul Laxman	3.9.1974		1	2000	2	2	0	1.00	2	2-67	0/0	39.00	0	10
Sarandeep Singh	21.10.1979		3	2000–2001	43	39*	0	43.00	10	4-136	0/0	34.00	1	5
Sardesai Dilip Narayan	8.8.1940	2.7.2007	30	1961–1972	2,001	212	5	39.23	0	0-3	0/0	–	4	
Sarwate Chandrasekhar Trimbak	22.7.1920	23.12.2003	9	1946–1951	208	37	0	13.00	3	1-16	0/0	124.66	0	
Saxena Ramesh Chandra	20.9.1944	16.8.2011	1	1967	25	16	0	12.50	0	0-11	0/0	–	0	
Sehwag Virender	20.10.1978		103§	2001–2012	8,503	319	23	49.43	40	5-104	1/0	47.35	90	241‡/19
Sekhar Thirumalai Ananthanpillai	28.3.1956		2	1982	0	0*	0	–	0	0-43	0/0	–	0	4
Sen Probir Kumar ("Khokhan")	31.5.1926	27.1.1970	14	1947–1952	165	25	0	11.78	–	–	–/–	–	20/11	
Sen Gupta Apoorva Kumar	3.8.1939	14.9.2013	1	1958	9	8	0	4.50	–	–	–/–	–	0	
Sharma Ajay Kumar	3.4.1964		1	1987	53	30	0	26.50	0	0-9	0/0	–	1	31
Sharma Chetan	3.1.1966		23	1984–1988	396	54	0	22.00	61	6-58	4/1	35.45	7	65
Sharma Gopal	3.8.1960		5	1984–1990	11	10*	0	3.66	10	4-88	0/0	41.80	2	11
Sharma Ishant	2.9.1988		81	2007–2017	572	31*	0	8.41	234	7-74	7/1	35.94	16	80/14
Sharma Karan Vinod	23.10.1987		1	2014	8	4*	0	8.00	4	2-95	0/0	59.50	0	2/1
Sharma Parthasarathy Harishchandra	5.1.1948	20.10.2010	5	1974–1976	187	54	0	18.70	0	0-2	0/0	–	1	2
Sharma Rohit Gurunath	30.4.1987		25	2013–2017	1,479	177	3	39.97	2	1-26	0/0	101.00	24	174/71
Sharma Sanjeev Kumar	25.8.1965		2	1988–1990	56	38	0	28.00	6	3-37	0/0	41.16	1	23
Shastri Ravishankar Jayadritha	27.5.1962		80	1980–1992	3,830	206	11	35.79	151	5-75	2/0	40.96	36	150
Shinde Sadashiv Ganpatrao	18.8.1923	22.6.1955	7	1946–1952	85	14	0	14.16	12	6-91	1/0	59.75	0	
Shodhan Roshan Harshadlal ("Deepak")	18.10.1928	16.5.2016	3	1952	181	110	1	60.33	0	0-1	0/0	–	1	
Shukla Rakesh Chandra	4.2.1948		1	1982	–	–	–	–	2	2-82	0/0	76.00	0	
Siddiqui Iqbal Rashid	26.12.1974		1	2001	29	24	0	29.00	1	1-32	0/0	48.00	1	

§ *Sehwag's figures exclude 83 runs and one catch for the ICC World XI v Australia in the Super Series Test in 2005-06.*

	Born	*Died*	*Tests*	*Test Career*	*Runs*	*HS*	*100s*	*Avge*	*Wkts*	*BB*	*5/10*	*Avge*	*Ct/St*	*O/T*
Sidhu Navjot Singh	20.10.1963		51	*1983–1998*	3,202	201	9	42.13	0	0-9	0/0	–	9	136
Singh Rabindra Ramanarayan ("Robin")	14.9.1963		1	*1998*	27	15	0	13.50	0	0-16	0/0	–	5	136
Singh Robin	1.1.1970		1	*1998*	0	0	0	0.00	3	2-74	0/0	58.66	1	
Singh Rudra Pratap	6.12.1985		14	*2005*–2011	116	30	0	7.25	40	5-59	1/0	42.05	6	58/10
Singh Vikram Rajvir	17.9.1984		5	*2005–2007*	47	29	0	11.75	8	3-48	0/0	53.37	1	2
Sivaramakrishnan Laxman	31.12.1965		9	*1982–1985*	130	25	0	16.25	26	6-64	3/1	44.03	9	16
Sohoni Sriranga Wasudev	5.3.1918	19.5.1993	4	1946–*1951*	83	29*	0	16.60	2	1-16	0/0	101.00	2	
Solkar Eknath Dhondu	18.3.1948	26.6.2005	27	*1969–1976*	1,068	102	1	25.42	18	3-28	0/0	59.44	53	7
Sood Man Mohan	6.7.1939		1	*1959*	3	3	0	1.50	–	–	–/–	–	0	
Sreesanth Shanthakumaran	6.2.1983		27	*2005*–2011	281	35	0	10.40	87	5-40	3/0	37.59	5	53/10
Srikkanth Krishnamachari	21.12.1959		43	*1981–1991*	2,062	123	2	29.88	0	0-1	0/0	–	40	146
Srinath Javagal	31.8.1969		67	*1991–2002*	1,009	76	0	14.21	236	8-86	10/1	30.49	22	229
Srinivasan Thirumalai Echambadi	26.10.1950	6.12.2010	1	*1980*	48	29	0	24.00	–	–	–/–	–	0	2
Subramanya Venkataraman	16.7.1936		9	*1964–1967*	263	75	0	18.78	3	2-32	0/0	67.00	9	
Sunderam Gundibali Rama	29.3.1930	20.6.2010	2	*1955*	3	3*	0	–	3	2-46	0/0	55.33	0	
Surendranath	4.1.1937	5.5.2012	11	*1958–1960*	136	27	0	10.46	26	5-75	2/0	40.50	4	
Surti Rusi Framroze	25.5.1936	13.1.2013	26	*1960–1969*	1,263	99	0	28.70	42	5-74	1/0	46.71	26	
Swamy Venkatraman Narayan	23.5.1924	1.5.1983	1	*1955*	–	–	–	–	0	0-15	0/0	–	0	
Tamhane Narendra Shankar	4.8.1931	19.3.2002	21	*1954–1960*	225	54*	0	10.22	–	–	–/–	–	35/16	
Tarapore Keki Khurshedji	17.12.1910	15.6.1986	1	*1948*	2	2	0	2.00	0	0-72	0/0	–	0	
Tendulkar Sachin Ramesh (*CY 1997*)	24.4.1973		200	*1989–2013*	15,921	248*	51	53.78	46	3-10	0/0	54.17	115	463/1
Umrigar Pahlanji Ratanji ("Polly")	28.3.1926	7.11.2006	59	*1948–1961*	3,631	223	12	42.22	35	6-74	2/0	42.08	33	
Unadkat Jaydev Dipakbhai	18.10.1991		1	*2010*	2	1*	0	2.00	0	0-101	0/0	–	0	7/4
Vengsarkar Dilip Balwant (*CY 1987*)	6.4.1956		116	*1975–1991*	6,868	166	17	42.13	0	0-3	0/0	–	78	129
Venkataraghavan Srinivasaraghavan	21.4.1945		57	*1964–1983*	748	64	0	11.68	156	8-72	3/1	36.11	44	15
Venkataramana Margashayam	24.4.1966		1	*1988*	0	0*	0	–	1	1-10	0/0	58.00	1	1
Vijay Murali	1.4.1984		56	*2008–2017*	3,802	167	11	40.02	1	1-12	0/0	167.00	48	17/9
Vinay Kumar Ranganath	12.2.1984		1	*2011*	11	6	0	5.50	1	1-73	0/0	73.00	0	31/9
Viswanath Gundappa Rangnath	12.2.1949		91	*1969–1982*	6,080	222	14	41.93	1	1-11	0/0	46.00	63	25
Viswanath Sadanand	29.11.1962		3	*1985*	31	20	0	6.20	–	–	–/–	–	11	22
Vizianagram Maharajkumar of (*Sir* Vijaya Anand)	28.12.1905	2.12.1965	3	1936	33	19*	0	8.25	–	–	–/–	–	1	
Wadekar Ajit Laxman	1.4.1941		37	*1966*–1974	2,113	143	1	31.07	0	0-0	0/0	–	46	2
Wasim Jaffer	16.2.1978		31	*1999–2007*	1,944	212	5	34.10	2	2-18	0/0	9.00	27	2
Wassan Atul Satish	23.3.1968		4	*1989*–1990	94	53	0	23.50	10	4-108	0/0	50.40	1	9
[1,2] **Wazir Ali** Syed	15.9.1903	17.6.1950	7	1932–1936	237	42	0	16.92	0	0-0	0/0	–	1	

	Born	Died	Tests	Test Career	Runs	HS	100s	Avge	Wkts	BB	5/10	Avge	Ct/St	O/T
Yadav Jayant	22.1.1990		4	*2016*	228	104	1	45.60	11	3-30	0/0	33.36	1	1
Yadav Kuldeep	14.12.1994		2	*2016–2017*	33	26	0	16.50	9	4-40	0/0	20.77	1	14/8
Yadav Nandlal Shivlal	26.1.1957		35	*1979–1986*	403	43	0	14.39	102	5-76	3/0	35.09	10	7
Yadav Umeshkumar Tilak	25.10.1987		36	*2011–2017*	226	30	0	9.82	99	5-93	1/0	35.90	11	71/1
Yadav Vijay	14.3.1967		1	*1992*	30	30	0	30.00	–	–	–/–	–	1/2	19
Yajurvindra Singh	1.8.1952		4	*1976–1979*	109	43*	0	18.16	0	0-2	0/0	–	11	
Yashpal Sharma	11.8.1954		37	*1979–1983*	1,606	140	2	33.45	1	1-6	0/0	17.00	16	42
[1] **Yograj Singh**	25.3.1958		1	*1980*	10	6	0	5.00	1	1-63	0/0	63.00	0	6
Yohannan Tinu	18.2.1979		3	*2001–2002*	13	8*	0	–	5	2-56	0/0	51.20	1	3
[1] **Yuvraj Singh**	12.12.1981		40	*2003–2012*	1,900	169	3	33.92	9	2-9	0/0	60.77	31	301‡/58
Zaheer Khan (*CY 2008*)	7.10.1978		92	*2000–2013*	1,231	75	0	11.95	311	7-87	11/1	32.94	19	194‡/17

PAKISTAN (230 players)

	Born	Died	Tests	Test Career	Runs	HS	100s	Avge	Wkts	BB	5/10	Avge	Ct/St	O/T
Aamer Malik	3.1.1963		14	*1987–1994*	565	117	2	35.31	1	1-0	0/0	89.00	15/1	24
Aamir Nazir	2.1.1971		6	*1992–1995*	31	11	0	6.20	20	5-46	1/0	29.85	2	9
Aamir Sohail	14.9.1966		47	*1992–1999*	2,823	205	5	35.28	25	4-54	0/0	41.96	36	156
Abdul Kadir	10.5.1944	12.3.2002	4	*1964*	272	95	0	34.00	–	–	–/–	–	0/1	
Abdul Qadir	15.9.1955		67	*1977–1990*	1,029	61	0	15.59	236	9-56	15/5	32.80	15	104
Abdul Razzaq	2.12.1979		46	*1999–2006*	1,946	134	3	28.61	100	5-35	1/0	36.94	15	261‡/32
Abdur Rauf	9.12.1978		3	*2009–2009*	52	31	0	8.66	6	2-59	0/0	46.33	0	4/1
Abdur Rehman	1.3.1980		22	*2007–2014*	395	60	0	14.10	99	6-25	2/0	29.39	8	31/8
[2]**Adnan Akmal**	13.3.1985		21	*2010–2013*	591	64	0	24.62	–	–	–/–	–	66/11	5
Afaq Hussain	31.12.1939	25.2.2002	2	*1961–1964*	66	35*	0	–	1	1-40	0/0	106.00	2	
Aftab Baloch	1.4.1953		2	*1969–1974*	97	60*	0	48.50	0	0-2	0/0	–	0	
Aftab Gul	31.3.1946		6	1968–1971	182	33	0	22.75	0	0-4	0/0	–	3	
Agha Saadat Ali	21.6.1929	25.10.1995	1	*1955*	8	8*	0	–	–	–	–/–	–	3	
Agha Zahid	7.1.1953		1	*1974*	15	14	0	7.50	–	–	–/–	–	0	
Ahmed Shehzad	23.11.1991		13	*2013–2016*	982	176	3	40.91	0	0-8	0/0	–	3	81/53
Aizaz Cheema	5.9.1979		7	*2011*–2012	1	1*	0	–	20	4-24	0/0	31.90	1	14/5
Akram Raza	22.11.1964		9	*1989–1994*	153	32	0	15.30	13	3-46	0/0	56.30	8	49
Ali Hussain Rizvi	6.1.1974		1	*1997*	–	–	–	–	2	2-72	0/0	36.00	0	
Ali Naqvi	19.3.1977		5	*1997*	242	115	1	30.25	0	0-11	0/0	–	1	
Alim-ud-Din	15.12.1930	12.7.2012	25	1954–1962	1,091	109	2	25.37	1	1-17	0/0	75.00	8	

	Born	Died	Tests	Test Career	Runs	HS	100s	Avge	Wkts	BB	5/10	Avge	Ct/St	O/T
Amir Elahi	1.9.1908	28.12.1980	5†	1952	65	47	0	10.83	7	4-134	0/0	35.42	0	
Anil Dalpat	20.9.1963		9	1983–1984	167	52	0	15.18	–	–	–/–	–	22/3	15
Anwar Hussain	16.7.1920	9.10.2002	4	1952	42	17	0	7.00	1	1-25	0/0	29.00	0	
Anwar Khan	24.12.1955		1	1978	15	12	0	15.00	0	0-12	0/0	–	0	
Aqib Javed	5.8.1972		22	1988–1998	101	28*	0	5.05	54	5-84	1/0	34.70	2	163
Arif Butt	17.5.1944	10.7.2007	3	1964	59	20	0	11.80	14	6-89	1/0	20.57	0	
Arshad Khan	22.3.1971		9	1997–2004	31	9*	0	5.16	32	5-38	1/0	30.00	0	58
Asad Shafiq	28.1.1986		58	2010–2017	3,614	137	11	39.71	2	1-7	0/0	63.00	51	60/10
Ashfaq Ahmed	6.6.1973		1	1993	1	1*	0	1.00	2	2-31	0/0	26.50	0	3
Ashraf Ali	22.4.1958		8	1981–1987	229	65	0	45.80	–	–	–/–	–	17/5	16
Asif Iqbal (*CY 1968*)	6.6.1943		58	1964–1979	3,575	175	11	38.85	53	5-48	2/0	28.33	36	10
Asif Masood	23.1.1946		16	1968–1976	93	30*	0	10.33	38	5-111	1/0	41.26	5	7
Asif Mujtaba	4.11.1967		25	1986–1996	928	65*	0	24.42	4	1-0	0/0	75.75	19	66
Asim Kamal	31.5.1976		12	2003–2005	717	99	0	37.73	–	–	–/–	–	10	
Ata-ur-Rehman	28.3.1975		13	1992–1996	76	19	0	8.44	31	4-50	0/0	34.54	2	30
Atif Rauf	3.3.1964		1	1993	25	16	0	12.50	–	–	–/–	–	0	
Atiq-uz-Zaman	20.7.1975		1	1999	26	25	0	13.00	–	–	–/–	–	5	3
Azam Khan	1.3.1969		1	1996	14	14	0	14.00	–	–	–/–	–	0	6
Azeem Hafeez	29.7.1963		18	1983–1984	134	24	0	8.37	63	6-46	4/0	34.98	1	15
Azhar Ali	19.2.1985		62	2010–2017	5,129	302*	14	46.62	8	2-35	0/0	73.62	60	50
Azhar Khan	7.9.1955		1	1979	14	14	0	14.00	1	1-1	0/0	2.00	0	
Azhar Mahmood	28.2.1975		21	1997–2001	900	136	3	30.00	39	4-50	0/0	35.94	14	143
[2] **Azmat Rana**	3.11.1951	30.5.2015	1	1979	49	49	0	49.00	–	–	–/–	–	0	2
Babar Azam	15.10.1994		11	2016–2017	475	90*	0	23.75	–	–	–/–	–	9	36/14
Basit Ali	13.12.1970		19	1992–1995	858	103	1	26.81	0	0-6	0/0	–	6	50
[3] **Bazid Khan**	25.3.1981		1	2004	32	23	0	16.00	–	–	–/–	–	2	5
Bilawal Bhatti	17.9.1991		2	2013	70	32	0	35.00	6	3-65	0/0	48.50	0	10/9
Danish Kaneria	16.12.1980		61	2000–2010	360	29	0	7.05	261	7-77	15/2	34.79	18	18
D'Souza Antao	17.1.1939		6	1958–1962	76	23*	0	38.00	17	5-112	1/0	43.82	3	
Ehsan Adil	15.3.1993		3	2012–2015	21	12	0	5.25	5	2-54	0/0	52.60	0	6
Ehtesham-ud-Din	4.9.1950		5	1979–1982	2	2	0	1.00	16	5-47	1/0	23.43	2	
Faisal Iqbal	30.12.1981		26	2000–2009	1,124	139	1	26.76	0	0-7	0/0	–	22	18
Farhan Adil	25.9.1977		1	2003	33	25	0	16.50	–	–	–/–	–	0	
Farooq Hamid	3.3.1945		1	1964	3	3	0	1.50	1	1-82	0/0	107.00	0	
Farrukh Zaman	2.4.1956		1	1976	–	–	–	–	0	0-7	0/0	–	0	
Fawad Alam	8.10.1985		3	2009–2009	250	168	1	41.66	–	–	–/–	–	3	38/24

	Born	Died	Tests	Test Career	Runs	HS	100s	Avge	Wkts	BB	5/10	Avge	Ct/St	O/T
Fazal Mahmood (*CY 1955*)	18.2.1927	30.5.2005	34	*1952*–1962	620	60	0	14.09	139	7-42	13/4	24.70	11	
Fazl-e-Akbar	20.10.1980		5	*1997–2003*	52	25	0	13.00	11	3-85	0/0	46.45	2	2
Ghazali Mohammad Ebrahim Zainuddin	15.6.1924	26.4.2003	2	1954	32	18	0	8.00	0	0-18	0/0	–	0	
Ghulam Abbas	1.5.1947		1	1967	12	12	0	6.00	–	–	–/–	–	0	
Gul Mahomed	15.10.1921	8.5.1992	1†	*1956*	39	27*	0	39.00	–	–	–/–	–	0	
[1, 2] **Hanif Mohammad** (*CY 1968*)	21.12.1934	11.8.2016	55	*1952–1969*	3,915	337	12	43.98	1	1-1	0/0	95.00	40	
Haris Sohail	9.1.1989		2	*2017*	176	76	0	44.00	5	3-1	0/0	18.60	0	22/4
Haroon Rashid	25.3.1953		23	*1976–1982*	1,217	153	3	34.77	0	0-3	0/0	–	16	12
Hasan Ali	7.2.1994		2	*2016–2017*	60	29	0	30.00	6	3-33	0/0	27.33	1	26/12
Hasan Raza	11.3.1982		7	*1996–2005*	235	68	0	26.11	0	0-1	0/0	–	5	16
Haseeb Ahsan	15.7.1939	8.3.2013	12	*1957–1961*	61	14	0	6.77	27	6-202	2/0	49.25	1	
[2] **Humayun Farhat**	24.1.1981		1	*2000*	54	28	0	27.00	–	–	–/–	–	0	5
Ibadulla Khalid ("Billy")	20.12.1935		4	*1964*–1967	253	166	1	31.62	1	1-42	0/0	99.00	3	
Iftikhar Ahmed	3.9.1990		1	2016	4	4	0	4.00	1	1-1	0/0	13.00	1	2/1
Iftikhar Anjum	1.12.1980		1	*2005*	9	9*	0	–	0	0-8	0/0	–	0	62/2
Ijaz Ahmed snr	20.9.1968		60	*1986–2000*	3,315	211	12	37.67	2	1-9	0/0	38.50	45	250
Ijaz Ahmed jnr	2.2.1969		2	*1995*	29	16	0	9.66	0	0-1	0/0	–	3	2
Ijaz Butt	10.3.1938		8	*1958*–1962	279	58	0	19.92	–	–	–/–	–	5	
Ijaz Faqih	24.3.1956		5	*1980–1987*	183	105	1	26.14	4	1-38	0/0	74.75	0	27
[2] **Imran Farhat**	20.5.1982		40	*2000–2012*	2,400	128	3	32.00	3	2-69	0/0	94.66	40	58/7
Imran Khan (*CY 1983*)	25.11.1952		88	1971–*1991*	3,807	136	6	37.69	362	8-58	23/6	22.81	28	175
Mohammad **Imran Khan**	15.7.1987		9	*2014–2016*	6	6	0	1.00	28	5-58	1/0	30.14	0	
Imran Nazir	16.12.1981		8	*1998–2002*	427	131	2	32.84	–	–	–/–	–	4	79/25
Imtiaz Ahmed	5.1.1928	31.12.2016	41	*1952*–1962	2,079	209	3	29.28	0	0-0	0/0	–	77/16	
Intikhab Alam	28.12.1941		47	*1959–1976*	1,493	138	1	22.28	125	7-52	5/2	35.95	20	4
Inzamam-ul-Haq	3.3.1970		119§	1992–*2007*	8,829	329	25	50.16	0	0-8	0/0	–	81	375‡/1
Iqbal Qasim	6.8.1953		50	*1976–1988*	549	56	0	13.07	171	7-49	8/2	28.11	42	15
Irfan Fazil	2.11.1981		1	*1999*	4	3	0	4.00	2	1-30	0/0	32.50	2	1
Israr Ali	1.5.1927	1.2.2016	4	*1952–1959*	33	10	0	4.71	6	2-29	0/0	27.50	1	
Jalal-ud-Din	12.6.1959		6	*1982–1985*	3	2	0	3.00	11	3-77	0/0	48.81	0	8
Javed Akhtar	21.11.1940	8.7.2016	1	1962	4	2*	0	4.00	0	0-52	0/0	–	0	
Javed Burki	8.5.1938		25	*1960–1969*	1,341	140	3	30.47	0	0-2	0/0	–	7	
Javed Miandad (*CY 1982*)	12.6.1957		124	*1976–1993*	8,832	280*	23	52.57	17	3-74	0/0	40.11	93/1	233
Junaid Khan	24.12.1989		22	*2011*–2015	122	17	0	7.17	71	5-38	5/0	31.73	4	66/9
Kabir Khan	12.4.1974		4	*1994*	24	10	0	8.00	9	3-26	0/0	41.11	1	10

§ *Inzamam-ul-Haq's figures exclude one run for the ICC World XI v Australia in the Super Series Test in 2005-06.*

	Born	Died	Tests	Test Career	Runs	HS	100s	Avge	Wkts	BB	5/10	Avge	Ct/St	O/T
[2] **Kamran Akmal**	13.1.1982		53	*2002–2010*	2,648	158*	6	30.79	–	–	–/–	–	184/22	157/58
Kardar Abdul Hafeez	17.1.1925	21.4.1996	23†	*1952–1957*	847	93	0	24.91	21	3-35	0/0	45.42	15	
Khalid Hassan	14.7.1937	3.12.2013	1	1954	17	10	0	17.00	2	2-116	0/0	58.00	0	
[1] **Khalid Wazir**	27.4.1936		2	1954	14	9*	0	7.00	–	–	–/–	–	0	
Khan Mohammad	1.1.1928	4.7.2009	13	*1952–1957*	100	26*	0	10.00	54	6-21	4/0	23.92	4	
Khurram Manzoor	10.6.1986		16	*2008*–2014	817	146	1	28.17	–	–	–/–	–	8	7/3
Liaqat Ali	21.5.1955		5	*1974–1978*	28	12	0	7.00	6	3-80	0/0	59.83	1	3
Mahmood Hussain	2.4.1932	25.12.1991	27	*1952–1962*	336	35	0	10.18	68	6-67	2/0	38.64	5	
[3] **Majid** Jahangir **Khan** (*CY 1970*)	28.9.1946		63	*1964–1982*	3,931	167	8	38.92	27	4-45	0/0	53.92	70	23
Mansoor Akhtar	25.12.1957		19	*1980–1989*	655	111	1	25.19	–	–	–/–	–	9	41
[2] **Manzoor Elahi**	15.4.1963		6	*1984–1994*	123	52	0	15.37	7	2-38	0/0	27.71	7	54
Maqsood Ahmed	26.3.1925	4.1.1999	16	*1952–1955*	507	99	0	19.50	3	2-12	0/0	63.66	13	
Masood Anwar	12.12.1967		1	*1990*	39	37	0	19.50	3	2-59	0/0	34.00	0	
Mathias Wallis	4.2.1935	1.9.1994	21	*1955–1962*	783	77	0	23.72	0	0-20	0/0	–	22	
Miran Bux	20.4.1907	8.2.1991	2	*1954*	1	1*	0	1.00	2	2-82	0/0	57.50	0	
Misbah-ul-Haq (*CY 2017*)	28.5.1974		75	*2000–2016*	5,222	161*	10	46.62	–	–	–/–	–	50	162/39
Mohammad Abbas	10.3.1990		5	*2016–2017*	11	4	0	3.66	23	5-46	1/0	21.34	1	
Mohammad Akram	10.9.1974		9	*1995–2000*	24	10*	0	2.66	17	5-138	1/0	50.52	4	23
Mohammad Amir (formerly Mohammad Aamer)	13.4.1992		30	2009–*2017*	645	48	0	13.16	95	6-44	4/0	32.87	4	36/32
Mohammad Asif	20.12.1982		23	*2004*–2010	141	29	0	5.64	106	6-41	7/1	24.36	3	35‡/11
Mohammad Aslam Khokhar	5.1.1920	22.1.2011	1	1954	34	18	0	17.00	–	–	–/–	–	0	
Mohammad Ayub	13.9.1979		1	2012	47	25	0	23.50	–	–	–/–	–	1	
Mohammad Farooq	8.4.1938		7	*1960–1964*	85	47	0	17.00	21	4-70	0/0	32.47	1	
Mohammad Hafeez	17.10.1980		50	*2003*–2016	3,452	224	9	39.22	52	4-16	0/0	33.90	43	195/81
Mohammad Hussain	8.10.1976		2	*1996–1998*	18	17	0	6.00	3	2-66	0/0	29.00	1	14
Mohammad Ilyas	19.3.1946		10	*1964–1968*	441	126	1	23.21	0	0-1	0/0	–	6	
Mohammad Irfan	6.6.1982		4	*2012–2013*	28	14	0	5.60	10	3-44	0/0	38.90	0	60/20
Mohammad Khalil	11.11.1982		2	*2004*	9	5	0	3.00	0	0-38	0/0	–	0	3
Mohammad Munaf	2.11.1935		4	*1959–1961*	63	19	0	12.60	11	4-42	0/0	31.00	0	
Mohammad Nawaz	21.3.1994		3	*2016*	50	25	0	12.50	5	2-32	0/0	29.40	2	9/7
Mohammad Nazir	8.3.1946		14	*1969–1983*	144	29*	0	18.00	34	7-99	3/0	33.05	4	4
Mohammad Ramzan	25.12.1970		1	*1997*	36	29	0	18.00	–	–	–/–	–	1	
Mohammad Rizwan	1.6.1992		1	*2016*	13	13*	0	13.00	–	–	–/–	–	1	25/10
Mohammad Salman	7.8.1981		2	*2010*	25	13	0	6.25	–	–	–/–	–	2/1	7/1
Mohammad Sami	24.2.1981		36	*2000*–2012	487	49	0	11.59	85	5-36	2/0	52.74	7	87/13

	Born	Died	Tests	Test Career	Runs	HS	100s	Avge	Wkts	BB	5/10	Avge	Ct/St	O/T
Mohammad Talha	15.10.1988		4	2008–2014	34	19	0	8.50	9	3-65	0/0	56.00	1	3
Mohammad Wasim	8.8.1977		18	1996–2000	783	192	2	30.11	–	–	–/–	–	22/2	25
Mohammad Yousuf (*CY 2007*) (formerly Yousuf Youhana)	27.8.1974		90	1997–2010	7,530	223	24	52.29	0	0-3	0/0	–	65	281‡/3
Mohammad Zahid	2.8.1976		5	1996–2002	7	6*	0	1.40	15	7-66	1/1	33.46	0	11
Mohsin Kamal	16.6.1963		9	1983–1994	37	13*	0	9.25	24	4-116	0/0	34.25	4	19
Mohsin Khan	15.3.1955		48	1977–1986	2,709	200	7	37.10	0	0-0	0/0	–	34	75
[2] **Moin Khan**	23.9.1971		69	1990–2004	2,741	137	4	28.55	–	–	–/–	–	128/20	219
[1] **Mudassar Nazar**	6.4.1956		76	1976–1988	4,114	231	10	38.09	66	6-32	1/0	38.36	48	122
Mufasir-ul-Haq	16.8.1944	27.7.1983	1	1964	8	8*	0	–	3	2-50	0/0	28.00	1	
Munir Malik	10.7.1934	30.11.2012	3	1959–1962	7	4	0	2.33	9	5-128	1/0	39.77	1	
Mushtaq Ahmed (*CY 1997*)	28.6.1970		52	1989–2003	656	59	0	11.71	185	7-56	10/3	32.97	23	144
[2] **Mushtaq Mohammad** (*CY 1963*)	22.11.1943		57	1958–1978	3,643	201	10	39.17	79	5-28	3/0	29.22	42	10
Nadeem Abbasi	15.4.1964		3	1989	46	36	0	23.00	–	–	–/–	–	6	
Nadeem Ghauri	12.10.1962		1	1989	0	0	0	0.00	0	0-20	0/0	–	0	6
[2] **Nadeem Khan**	10.12.1969		2	1992–1998	34	25	0	17.00	2	2-147	0/0	115.00	0	2
Nasim-ul-Ghani	14.5.1941		29	1957–1972	747	101	1	16.60	52	6-67	2/0	37.67	11	1
Nasir Jamshed	6.12.1989		2	2012	51	46	0	12.75	–	–	–/–	–	1	48/18
Naushad Ali	1.10.1943		6	1964	156	39	0	14.18	–	–	–/–	–	9	
Naved Anjum	27.7.1963		2	1989–1990	44	22	0	14.66	4	2-57	0/0	40.50	0	13
Naved Ashraf	4.9.1974		2	1998–1999	64	32	0	21.33	–	–	–/–	–	0	
Naved Latif	21.2.1976		1	2001	20	20	0	10.00	–	–	–/–	–	0	11
Naved-ul-Hasan	28.2.1978		9	2004–2006	239	42*	0	19.91	18	3-30	0/0	58.00	3	74/4
[1] **Nazar Mohammad**	5.3.1921	12.7.1996	5	1952	277	124*	1	39.57	0	0-4	0/0	–	7	
Niaz Ahmed	11.11.1945	12.4.2000	2	1967–1968	17	16*	0	–	3	2-72	0/0	31.33	1	
[2] **Pervez Sajjad**	30.8.1942		19	1964–1972	123	24	0	13.66	59	7-74	3/0	23.89	9	
Qaiser Abbas	7.5.1982		1	2000	2	2	0	2.00	0	0-35	0/0	–	0	
Qasim Omar	9.2.1957		26	1983–1986	1,502	210	3	36.63	0	0-0	0/0	–	15	31
Rahat Ali	12.9.1988		20	2012–2016	136	35*	0	7.55	58	6-127	2/0	37.43	9	14
[2] **Ramiz Raja**	14.8.1962		57	1983–1996	2,833	122	2	31.83	–	–	–/–	–	34	198
Rashid Khan	15.12.1959		4	1981–1984	155	59	0	51.66	8	3-129	0/0	45.00	2	29
Rashid Latif	14.10.1968		37	1992–2003	1,381	150	1	28.77	0	0-10	0/0	–	119/11	166
Rehman Sheikh Fazalur	11.6.1935		1	1957	10	8	0	5.00	1	1-43	0/0	99.00	1	
Riaz Afridi	21.1.1985		1	2004	9	9	0	9.00	2	2-42	0/0	43.50	0	
Rizwan-uz-Zaman	4.9.1961		11	1981–1988	345	60	0	19.16	4	3-26	0/0	11.50	4	3
[2] **Sadiq Mohammad**	3.5.1945		41	1969–1980	2,579	166	5	35.81	0	0-0	0/0	–	28	19

	Born	Died	Tests	Test Career	Runs	HS	100s	Avge	Wkts	BB	5/10	Avge	Ct/St	O/T
[2] **Saeed Ahmed**	1.10.1937		41	*1957–1972*	2,991	172	5	40.41	22	4-64	0/0	36.45	13	
Saeed Ajmal	14.10.1977		35	2009–2014	451	50	0	11.00	178	7-55	10/4	28.10	11	113/64
Saeed Anwar (*CY 1997*)	6.9.1968		55	*1990–2001*	4,052	188*	11	45.52	0	0-0	0/0	–	18	247
Salah-ud-Din	14.2.1947		5	*1964–1969*	117	34*	0	19.50	7	2-36	0/0	26.71	3	
Saleem Jaffer	19.11.1962		14	*1986–1991*	42	10*	0	5.25	36	5-40	1/0	31.63	2	39
Salim Altaf	19.4.1944		21	1967–*1978*	276	53*	0	14.52	46	4-11	0/0	37.17	3	6
[2] **Salim Elahi**	21.11.1976		13	*1995–2002*	436	72	0	18.95	–	–	–/–	–	10/1	48
Salim Malik (*CY 1988*)	16.4.1963		103	*1981–1998*	5,768	237	15	43.69	5	1-3	0/0	82.80	65	283
Salim Yousuf	7.12.1959		32	*1981–1990*	1,055	91*	0	27.05	–	–	–/–	–	91/13	86
Salman Butt	7.10.1984		33	*2003–*2010	1,889	122	3	30.46	1	1-36	0/0	106.00	12	78/24
Sami Aslam	12.12.1995		13	*2014–2017*	758	91	0	31.58	–	–	–/–	–	7	4
Saqlain Mushtaq (*CY 2000*)	29.12.1976		49	*1995–2003*	927	101*	1	14.48	208	8-164	13/3	29.83	15	169
Sarfraz Ahmed	22.5.1987		38	*2009–2017*	2,208	112	3	40.14	–	–	–/–	–	103/18	80/35
Sarfraz Nawaz	1.12.1948		55	*1968–1983*	1,045	90	0	17.71	177	9-86	4/1	32.75	26	45
Shabbir Ahmed	21.4.1976		10	*2003–2005*	88	24*	0	8.80	51	5-48	2/0	23.03	3	32/1
Shadab Kabir	12.11.1977		5	1996–*2001*	148	55	0	21.14	0	0-9	0/0	–	11	3
Shadab Khan	4.10.1998		1	*2016*	17	16	0	8.50	1	1-90	0/0	145.00	0	12/10
Shafiq Ahmed	28.3.1949		6	1974–*1980*	99	27*	0	11.00	0	0-1	0/0	–	0	3
[2] **Shafqat Rana**	10.8.1943		5	*1964–1969*	221	95	0	31.57	1	1-2	0/0	9.00	5	
Shahid Afridi	1.3.1980		27	1998–2010	1,716	156	5	36.51	48	5-52	1/0	35.60	10	393‡/98
Shahid Israr	1.3.1950	29.4.2013	1	*1976*	7	7*	0	–	–	–	–/–	–	2	
Shahid Mahboob	25.8.1962		1	*1989*	–	–	–	–	2	2-131	0/0	65.50	0	10
Shahid Mahmood	17.3.1939		1	1962	25	16	0	12.50	0	0-23	0/0	–	0	
Shahid Nazir	4.12.1977		15	*1996–2006*	194	40	0	12.12	36	5-53	1/0	35.33	5	17
Shahid Saeed	6.1.1966		1	*1989*	12	12	0	12.00	0	0-7	0/0	–	0	10
Shakeel Ahmed snr.	12.2.1966		1	*1998*	1	1	0	1.00	4	4-91	0/0	34.75	1	
Shakeel Ahmed jnr.	12.11.1971		3	*1992–1994*	74	33	0	14.80	–	–	–/–	–	4	2
Shan Masood	14.10.1989		12	*2013–2017*	565	125	1	23.54	0	0-0	0/0	–	10	
Sharjeel Khan	14.8.1989		1	*2016*	44	40	0	22.00	–	–	–/–	–	0	25/15
Sharpe Duncan Albert	3.8.1937		3	*1959*	134	56	0	22.33	–	–	–/–	–	2	
Shoaib Akhtar	13.8.1975		46	*1997–2007*	544	47	0	10.07	178	6-11	12/2	25.69	12	158‡/15
Shoaib Malik	1.2.1982		35	*2001–2015*	1,898	245	3	35.14	32	4-33	0/0	47.46	18	257/92
[1] **Shoaib Mohammad**	8.1.1961		45	*1983–1995*	2,705	203*	7	44.34	5	2-8	0/0	34.00	22	63
Shuja-ud-Din Butt	10.4.1930	7.2.2006	19	1954–*1961*	395	47	0	15.19	20	3-18	0/0	40.05	8	
Sikander Bakht	25.8.1957		26	*1976–1982*	146	22*	0	6.34	67	8-69	3/1	36.00	7	27
Sohail Khan	6.3.1984		9	*2008–2016*	252	65	0	25.20	27	5-68	2/0	41.66	2	13/5

	Born	Died	Tests	Test Career	Runs	HS	100s	Avge	Wkts	BB	5/10	Avge	Ct/St	O/T
Sohail Tanvir	12.12.1984		2	2007	17	13	0	5.66	5	3-83	0/0	63.20	2	62/57
Tahir Naqqash	6.6.1959		15	1981–1984	300	57	0	21.42	34	5-40	2/0	41.11	3	40
Talat Ali Malik	29.5.1950		10	1972–1978	370	61	0	23.12	0	0-1	0/0	–	4	
Tanvir Ahmed	20.12.1978		5	2010–2012	170	57	0	34.00	17	6-120	1/0	26.64	1	2/1
Taslim Arif	1.5.1954	13.3.2008	6	1979–1980	501	210*	1	62.62	1	1-28	0/0	28.00	6/3	2
Taufeeq Umar	20.6.1981		44	2001–2014	2,963	236	7	37.98	0	0-0	0/0	–	48	22
Tauseef Ahmed	10.5.1958		34	1979–1993	318	35*	0	17.66	93	6-45	3/0	31.72	9	70
[2]**Umar Akmal**	26.5.1990		16	2009–2011	1,003	129	1	35.82	–	–	–/–	–	12	116/82
Umar Amin	16.10.1989		4	2010	99	33	0	12.37	3	1-7	0/0	21.00	1	15/11
Umar Gul	14.4.1984		47	2003–2012	577	65*	0	9.94	163	6-135	4/0	34.06	11	130/60
Wahab Riaz	28.6.1985		26	2010–2017	299	39	0	8.30	83	5-63	2/0	33.53	5	79/27
Wajahatullah Wasti	11.11.1974		6	1998–1999	329	133	2	36.55	0	0-0	0/0	–	7	15
[2]**Waqar Hassan**	12.9.1932		21	1952–1959	1,071	189	1	31.50	0	0-10	0/0	–	10	
Waqar Younis (*CY 1992*)	16.11.1971		87	1989–2002	1,010	45	0	10.20	373	7-76	22/5	23.56	18	262
Wasim Akram (*CY 1993*)	3.6.1966		104	1984–2001	2,898	257*	3	22.64	414	7-119	25/5	23.62	44	356
Wasim Bari	23.3.1948		81	1967–1983	1,366	85	0	15.88	0	0-2	0/0	–	201/27	51
[2]**Wasim Raja**	3.7.1952	23.8.2006	57	1972–1984	2,821	125	4	36.16	51	4-50	0/0	35.80	20	54
[2]**Wazir Mohammad**	22.12.1929		20	1952–1959	801	189	2	27.62	0	0-2	0/0	–	5	
Yasir Ali	15.10.1985		1	2003	1	1*	0	–	2	1-12	0/0	27.50	0	
Yasir Arafat	12.3.1982		3	2007–2008	94	50*	0	47.00	9	5-161	1/0	48.66	0	11/13
Yasir Hameed	28.2.1978		25	2003–2010	1,491	170	2	32.41	0	0-0	0/0	–	20	56
Yasir Shah	2.5.1986		28	2014–2017	445	38*	0	12.71	165	7-76	13/2	29.44	18	17/2
[2]**Younis Ahmed**	20.10.1947		4	1969–1986	177	62	0	29.50	0	0-6	0/0	–	0	2
Younis Khan (*CY 2017*)	29.11.1977		118	1999–2016	10,099	313	34	52.05	9	2-23	0/0	54.55	139	265/25
Yousuf Youhana (*see* Mohammad Yousuf)														
Zaheer Abbas (*CY 1972*)	24.7.1947		78	1969–1985	5,062	274	12	44.79	3	2-21	0/0	44.00	34	62
Zahid Fazal	10.11.1973		9	1990–1995	288	78	0	18.00	–	–	–/–	–	5	19
[2]**Zahoor Elahi**	1.3.1971		2	1996	30	22	0	10.00	–	–	–/–	–	1	14
Zakir Khan	3.4.1963		2	1985–1989	9	9*	0	–	5	3-80	0/0	51.80	1	17
Zulfiqar Ahmed	22.11.1926	3.10.2008	9	1952–1956	200	63*	0	33.33	20	6-42	2/1	18.30	5	
Zulfiqar Babar	10.12.1978		15	2013–2016	144	56	0	16.00	54	5-74	2/0	39.42	4	5/7
Zulqarnain	25.5.1962		3	1985	24	13	0	6.00	–	–	–/–	–	8/2	16
Zulqarnain Haider	23.4.1986		1	2010	88	88	0	44.00	–	–	–/–	–	2	4/3

SRI LANKA (144 players)

	Born	Died	Tests	Test Career	Runs	HS	100s	Avge	Wkts	BB	5/10	Avge	Ct/St	O/T
Ahangama Franklyn Saliya	14.9.1959		3	*1985*	11	11	0	5.50	18	5-52	1/0	19.33	1	1
Amalean Kaushik Naginda	7.4.1965		2	*1985–1987*	9	7*	0	9.00	7	4-97	0/0	22.28	1	8
Amerasinghe Amerasinghe Mudalige Jayantha Gamini	2.2.1954		2	*1983*	54	34	0	18.00	3	2-73	0/0	50.00	3	
Amerasinghe Merenna Koralage Don Ishara	5.3.1978		1	*2007*	0	0*	0	–	1	1-62	0/0	105.00	0	8
Anurasiri Sangarange Don	25.2.1966		18	*1985–1997*	91	24	0	5.35	41	4-71	0/0	37.75	4	45
Arnold Russel Premakumaran	25.10.1973		44	*1996*–2004	1,821	123	3	28.01	11	3-76	0/0	54.36	51	180/1
Atapattu Marvan Samson	22.11.1970		90	*1990–2007*	5,502	249	16	39.02	1	1-9	0/0	24.00	58	268/2
Bandara Herath Mudiyanselage Charitha Malinga	31.12.1979		8	*1997–2005*	124	43	0	15.50	16	3-84	0/0	39.56	4	31/4
Bandaratilleke Mapa Rallage Chandima Niroshan	16.5.1975		7	*1997–2001*	93	25	0	11.62	23	5-36	1/0	30.34	0	3
Chameera Pathira Vasan Dushmantha	11.1.1992		6	2015–*2016*	61	19	0	6.10	22	5-47	1/0	33.00	3	17/16
Chandana Umagiliya Durage Upul	7.5.1972		16	*1998–2004*	616	92	0	26.78	37	6-179	3/1	41.48	7	147
Chandimal Lokuge Dinesh	18.11.1989		44	*2011–2017*	3,296	164	10	43.94	–	–	–/–	–	71/10	134/48
Dassanayake Pubudu Bathiya	11.7.1970		11	*1993–1994*	196	36	0	13.06	–	–	–/–	–	19/5	16
de Alwis Ronald Guy	15.2.1959	12.1.2013	11	*1982–1987*	152	28	0	8.00	–	–	–/–	–	21/2	31
de Mel Ashantha Lakdasa Francis	9.5.1959		17	*1981–1986*	326	34	0	14.17	59	6-109	3/0	36.94	9	57
de Saram Samantha Indika	2.9.1973		4	*1999*	117	39	0	23.40	–	–	–/–	–	1	15/1
de Silva Ashley Matthew	3.12.1963		3	*1992–1993*	10	9	0	3.33	–	–	–/–	–	4/1	4
de Silva Dandeniyage Somachandra	11.6.1942		12	*1981*–1984	406	61	0	21.36	37	5-59	1/0	36.40	5	41
de Silva Dhananjaya Maduranga	6.9.1991		11	2016–*2017*	846	129	3	42.30	6	2-91	0/0	67.83	7	17/7
de Silva Ellawalakankanamge Asoka Ranjit	28.3.1956		10	*1985–1990*	185	50	0	15.41	8	2-67	0/0	129.00	4	28
de Silva Ginigalgodage Ramba Ajit	12.12.1952		4	*1981–1982*	41	14	0	8.20	7	2-38	0/0	55.00	0	6
de Silva Karunakalage Sajeewa Chanaka	11.1.1971		8	*1996–1998*	65	27	0	9.28	16	5-85	1/0	55.56	5	38
de Silva Pinnaduwage Aravinda (*CY 1996*)	17.10.1965		93	1984–2002	6,361	267	20	42.97	29	3-30	0/0	41.65	43	308
de Silva Sanjeewa Kumara Lanka	29.7.1975		3	*1997*	36	20*	0	18.00	–	–	–/–	–	1	11
de Silva Weddikkara Ruwan Sujeewa	7.10.1979		3	2002–2007	10	5*	0	10.00	11	4-35	0/0	19.00	1	
Dharmasena Handunnettige Deepthi Priyantha Kumar	24.4.1971		31	*1993–2003*	868	62*	0	19.72	69	6-72	3/0	42.31	14	141
Dias Roy Luke	18.10.1952		20	*1981–1986*	1,285	109	3	36.71	0	0-17	0/0	–	6	58
Dickwella Dickwella Patabandige Dilantha Niroshan	23.6.1993		15	2014–*2017*	917	83	0	33.96	–	–	–/–	–	36/11	32/12
Dilshan Tillekeratne Mudiyanselage	14.10.1976		87	*1999–2012*	5,492	193	16	40.98	39	4-10	0/0	43.87	88	330/80

	Born	Died	Tests	Test Career	Runs	HS	100s	Avge	Wkts	BB	5/10	Avge	Ct/St	O/T
Dunusinghe Chamara Iroshan	19.10.1970		5	1994–1995	160	91	0	16.00	–	–	–/–	–	13/2	1
Eranga Ranaweera Mudiyanselage Shaminda	23.6.1986		19	2011–2016	193	45*	0	12.86	57	4-49	0/0	37.50	5	19/3
Fernando Aththachchi Nuwan Pradeep Roshan	19.10.1986		28	2011–2017	132	17*	0	4.00	70	6-132	1/0	42.90	5	26/5
Fernando Congenige Randhi Dilhara	19.7.1979		40	2000–2012	249	39*	0	8.30	100	5-42	3/0	37.84	10	146‡/18
Fernando Ellekutige Rufus Nemesion Susil	19.12.1955		5	1982–1983	112	46	0	11.20	–	–	–/–	–	0	7
Fernando Kandage Hasantha Ruwan Kumara	14.10.1979		2	2002	38	24	0	9.50	4	3-63	0/0	27.00	1	7
Fernando Kandana Arachchige Dinusha Manoj	10.8.1979		2	2003	56	51*	0	28.00	1	1-29	0/0	107.00	0	1
Fernando Muthuthanthrige Vishwa Thilina	18.9.1991		2	2016–2017	4	4*	0	2.00	3	2-87	0/0	34.33	0	6/1
Fernando Thudellage Charitha Buddhika	22.8.1980		9	2001–2002	132	45	0	26.40	18	4-27	0/0	44.00	4	17
Gallage Indika Sanjeewa	22.11.1975		1	1999	3	3	0	3.00	0	0-24	0/0	–	0	3
Gamage Panagamuwa Lahiru Sampath	5.4.1988		4	2017	3	1*	0	1.00	10	2-38	0/0	46.30	0	9
Goonatillake Hettiarachige Mahes	16.8.1952		5	1981–1982	177	56	0	22.12	–	–	–/–	–	10/3	6
Gunaratne Downdegedara Asela Sampath	8.1.1986		6	2016–2017	455	116	1	56.87	3	2-28	0/0	38.00	6	24/12
Gunasekera Yohan	8.11.1957		2	1982	48	23	0	12.00	–	–	–/–	–	6	3
Gunathilleke Mashtayage Dhanushka	17.03.1991		1	2017	18	16	0	9.00	1	1-16	0/0	57.00	1	31/9
Gunawardene Dihan Avishka	26.5.1977		6	1998–2005	181	43	0	16.45	–	–	–/–	–	2	61
Guneratne Roshan Punyajith Wijesinghe	26.1.1962	21.7.2005	1	1982	0	0*	0	–	0	0-84	0/0	–	0	
Gurusinha Asanka Pradeep	16.9.1966		41	1985–1996	2,452	143	7	38.92	20	2-7	0/0	34.05	33	147
Hathurusinghe Upul Chandika	13.9.1968		26	1990–1998	1,274	83	0	29.62	17	4-66	0/0	46.41	7	35
Herath Herath Mudiyanselage Rangana Keerthi Bandara	19.3.1978		87	1999–2017	1,613	80*	0	15.07	406	9-127	33/9	28.03	22	71/17
Hettiarachchi Dinuka Sulaksana	15.7.1976		1	2000	0	0*	0	0.00	2	2-36	0/0	20.50	0	
Jayasekera Rohan Stanley Amarasiriwardene	7.12.1957		1	1981	2	2	0	1.00	–	–	–/–	–	0	2
Jayasundera Madurawelage Don Udara Supeksha	3.1.1991		2	2015	30	26	0	7.50	0	0-12	0/0	–	2	
Jayasuriya Sanath Teran (*CY 1997*)	30.6.1969		110	1990–2007	6,973	340	14	40.07	98	5-34	2/0	34.34	78	441‡/31
Jayawardene Denagamage Proboth Mahela de Silva (*CY 2007*)	27.5.1977		149	1997–2014	11,814	374	34	49.84	6	2-32	0/0	51.66	205	443‡/55
Jayawardene Hewasandatchige Asiri Prasanna Wishvanath	9.10.1979		58	2000–2014	2,124	154*	4	29.50	–	–	–/–	–	124/32	6
Jeganathan Sridharan	11.7.1951	14.5.1996	2	1982	19	8	0	4.75	0	0-12	0/0	–	0	5
John Vinothen Bede	27.5.1960		6	1982–1984	53	27*	0	10.60	28	5-60	2/0	21.92	2	45
Jurangpathy Baba Roshan	25.6.1967		2	1985–1986	1	1	0	0.25	1	1-69	0/0	93.00	2	
Kalavitigoda Shantha	23.12.1977		1	2004	8	7	0	4.00	–	–	–/–	–	2	
Kalpage Ruwan Senani	19.2.1970		11	1993–1998	294	63	0	18.37	12	2-27	0/0	64.50	10	86
Kaluhalamulla H. K. S. R. (*see* Randiv, Suraj)														

	Born	Died	Tests	Test Career	Runs	HS	100s	Avge	Wkts	BB	5/10	Avge	Ct/St	O/T
[2] **Kaluperuma** Lalith Wasantha Silva	25.6.1949		2	1981	12	11*	0	4.00	0	0-24	0/0	–	2	4
[2] **Kaluperuma** Sanath Mohan Silva	22.10.1961		4	1983–1987	88	23	0	11.00	2	2-17	0/0	62.00	6	2
Kaluwitharana Romesh Shantha	24.11.1969		49	1992–2004	1,933	132*	3	26.12	–	–	–/–	–	93/26	189
Kapugedera Chamara Kantha	24.2.1987		8	2006–2009	418	96	0	34.83	0	0-9	0/0	–	6	102/43
Karunaratne Frank Dimuth Madushanka	28.4.1988		47	2012–2017	3,151	196	7	35.40	1	1-31	0/0	97.00	40	17
Kaushal Paskuwal Handi Tharindu	5.3.1993		7	2014–2015	106	18	0	10.60	25	5-42	2/0	44.20	3	1
Kulasekara Chamith Kosala Bandara	15.7.1985		1	2011	22	15	0	11.00	1	1-65	0/0	80.00	0	4
Kulasekara Kulasekara Mudiyanselage Dinesh Nuwan	22.7.1982		21	2004–2014	391	64	0	14.48	48	4-21	0/0	37.37	8	184/58
Kumara Chandradasa Brahammana Ralalage Lahiru Sudesh	13.2.1997		8	2016–2017	34	10	0	4.85	23	6-122	1/0	45.30	3	4
Kuruppu Don Sardha Brendon Priyantha	5.1.1962		4	1986–1991	320	201*	1	53.33	–	–	-/–	–	1	54
Kuruppuarachchi Ajith Kosala	1.11.1964		2	1985–1986	0	0*	0	–	8	5-44	1/0	18.62	0	
Labrooy Graeme Fredrick	7.6.1964		9	1986–1990	158	70*	0	14.36	27	5-133	1/0	44.22	3	44
Lakmal Ranasinghe Arachchige Suranga	10.3.1987		42	2010–2017	509	42	0	10.82	96	5-63	1/0	44.94	11	70/9
Lakshitha Materba Kanatha Gamage Chamila Premanath	4.1.1979		2	2002–2002	42	40	0	14.00	5	2-33	0/0	31.60	1	7
Liyanage Dulip Kapila	6.6.1972		9	1992–2001	69	23	0	7.66	17	4-56	0/0	39.17	0	16
Lokuarachchi Kaushal Samaraweera	20.5.1982		4	2003–2003	94	28*	0	23.50	5	2-47	0/0	59.00	1	21/2
Madugalle Ranjan Senerath	22.4.1959		21	1981–1988	1,029	103	1	29.40	0	0-0	0/0	–	9	63
Madurasinghe Madurasinghe Arachchige Wijayasiri Ranjith	30.1.1961		3	1988–1992	24	11	0	4.80	3	3-60	0/0	57.33	0	12
Mahanama Roshan Siriwardene	31.5.1966		52	1985–1997	2,576	225	4	29.27	0	0-3	0/0	–	56	213
Maharoof Mohamed Farveez	7.9.1984		22	2003–2011	556	72	0	18.53	25	4-52	0/0	65.24	7	109/8
Malinga Separamadu Lasith	28.8.1983		30	2004–2010	275	64	0	11.45	101	5-50	3/0	33.15	7	204/68
Mathews Angelo Davis (*CY 2015*)	2.6.1987		72	2009–2017	4,914	160	8	44.27	33	4-44	0/0	52.66	55	195/71
Mendis Balapuwaduge Ajantha Winslo	11.3.1985		19	2008–2014	213	78	0	16.38	70	6-99	4/1	34.77	2	87/39
Mendis Balapuwaduge Kusal Gimhan	2.2.1995		22	2015–2017	1,441	194	3	33.51	1	1-10	0/0	41.00	29	39/8
Mendis Louis Rohan Duleep	25.8.1952		24	1981–1988	1,329	124	4	31.64	–	–	–/–	–	9	79
Mirando Magina Thilan Thushara	1.3.1981		10	2003–2010	94	15*	0	8.54	28	5-83	1/0	37.14	3	38/6
Mubarak Jehan	10.1.1981		13	2002–2015	385	49	0	17.50	0	0-1	0/0	–	15	40/16
Muralitharan Muttiah (*CY 1999*)	17.4.1972		132§	1992–2010	1,259	67	0	11.87	795	9-51	67/22	22.67	70	343‡/12
Nawaz Mohamed Naveed	20.9.1973		1	2002	99	78*	0	99.00	–	–	–/–	–	0	3
Nissanka Ratnayake Arachchige Prabath	25.10.1980		4	2003	18	12*	0	6.00	10	5-64	1/0	36.60	0	23
Paranavitana Nishad Tharanga	15.4.1982		32	2008–2012	1,792	111	2	32.58	1	1-26	0/0	86.00	27	

§ *Muralitharan's figures exclude two runs, five wickets and two catches for the ICC World XI v Australia in the Super Series Test in 2005-06.*

	Born	Died	Tests	Test Career	Runs	HS	100s	Avge	Wkts	BB	5/10	Avge	Ct/St	O/T
Perera Anhettige Suresh Asanka	16.2.1978		3	1998–2001	77	43*	0	25.66	1	1-104	0/0	180.00	1	20
Perera Mahawaduge Dilruwan Kamalaneth	22.7.1982		25	*2013–2017*	845	95	0	20.60	101	6-70	5/1	34.47	16	12/3
Perera Mathurage Don Kusal Janith	17.8.1990		10	*2015–2016*	565	110	1	31.38	–	–	–/–	–	16/8	70/30
Perera Narangoda Liyanaarachchilage Tissara Chirantha	3.4.1989		6	2011–2012	203	75	0	20.30	11	4-63	0/0	59.36	1	128/63‡
Perera Panagodage Don Ruchira Laksiri	6.4.1977		8	*1998–2002*	33	11*	0	11.00	17	3-40	0/0	38.88	2	19/2
Prasad Kariyawasam Tirana Gamage Dammika	30.5.1983		25	2008–*2015*	476	47	0	12.86	75	5-50	1/0	35.97	6	24/1
Prasanna Seekkuge	27.6.1985		1	*2011*	5	5	0	5.00	0	0-80	0/0	–	0	38/20
Pushpakumara Karuppiahyage Ravindra	21.7.1975		23	*1994–2001*	166	44	0	8.73	58	7-116	4/0	38.65	10	31
Pushpakumara Paulage Malinda	24.3.1987		2	2017	42	16	0	14.00	5	3-82	0/0	47.60	0	2
Ramanayake Champaka Priyadarshana Hewage	8.1.1965		18	*1987–1993*	143	34*	0	9.53	44	5-82	1/0	42.72	6	62
Ramyakumara Wijekoon Mudiyanselage Gayan	21.12.1976		2	2005	38	14	0	12.66	2	2-49	0/0	33.00	0	0/3
Ranasinghe Anura Nandana	13.10.1956	9.11.1998	2	*1981–1982*	88	77	0	22.00	1	1-23	0/0	69.00	0	9
[2] **Ranatunga** Arjuna (*CY 1999*)	1.12.1963		93	*1981*–2000	5,105	135*	4	35.69	16	2-17	0/0	65.00	47	269
[2] **Ranatunga** Dammika	12.10.1962		2	*1989*	87	45	0	29.00	–	–	–/–	–	0	4
[2] **Ranatunga** Sanjeeva	25.4.1969		9	*1994–1996*	531	118	2	33.18	–	–	–/–	–	2	13
Randiv Suraj (Hewa Kaluhalamullage Suraj Randiv Kaluhalamulla; formerly M. M. M. Suraj)	30.1.1985		12	2010–*2012*	147	39	0	9.18	43	5-82	1/0	37.51	1	31/7
Ratnayake Rumesh Joseph	2.1.1964		23	*1982–1991*	433	56	0	14.43	73	6-66	5/0	35.10	9	70
Ratnayeke Joseph Ravindran	2.5.1960		22	*1981–1989*	807	93	0	25.21	56	8-83	4/0	35.21	1	78
Samarasekera Maitipage Athula Rohitha	5.8.1961		4	1988–*1991*	118	57	0	16.85	3	2-38	0/0	34.66	3	39
[2] **Samaraweera** Dulip Prasanna	12.2.1972		7	*1993–1994*	211	42	0	15.07	–	–	–/–	–	5	5
[2] **Samaraweera** Thilan Thusara	22.9.1976		81	2001–*2012*	5,462	231	14	48.76	15	4-49	0/0	45.93	45	53
Samarawickrama Wedagedara Sadeera Rashen	30.8.1995		4	*2017*	125	38	0	15.62	–	–	–/–	–	4	3/5
Sandakan Paththamperuma Arachchige Don Lakshan Rangika	10.6.1991		8	2016–*2017*	77	19*	0	11.00	25	5-132	1/0	37.20	3	10/3
Sangakkara Kumar Chokshanada (*CY 2012*)	27.10.1977		134	2000–*2015*	12,400	319	38	57.40	0	0-4	0/0	–	182/20	397‡/56
Senanayake Charith Panduka	19.12.1962		3	*1990*	97	64	0	19.40	–	–	–/–	–	2	7
Senanayake Senanayake Mudiyanselage Sachithra Madhushanka	9.2.1985		1	*2013*	5	5	0	5.00	0	0-30	0/0	–	1	49/24
Shanaka Madagamagamage Dasun	9.9.1991		3	2016–*2017*	29	17	0	5.80	9	3-46	0/0	29.00	1	9/18
Silva Athege Roshen Shivanka	17.11.1988		1	*2017*	74	74*	0	74.00	–	–	–/–	–	0	
Silva Jayan Kaushal	27.5.1986		37	*2011–2017*	2,058	139	3	29.40	–	–	–/–	–	33/1	
Silva Kelaniyage Jayantha	2.6.1973		7	*1995–1997*	6	6*	0	2.00	20	4-16	0/0	32.35	1	1

	Born	Died	Tests	Test Career	Runs	HS	100s	Avge	Wkts	BB	5/10	Avge	Ct/St	O/T
Silva Lindamlilage Prageeth Chamara	14.12.1979		11	2006–2007	537	152*	1	33.56	1	1-57	0/0	65.00	7	75/16
Silva Sampathawaduge Amal Rohitha	12.12.1960		9	1982–1988	353	111	2	25.21	–	–	–/–	–	33/1	20
Siriwardene Tissa Appuhamilage Milinda	4.12.1985		5	2015–2016	298	68	0	33.11	11	3-25	0/0	23.36	3	26/22
Tharanga Warushavithana Upul	2.2.1985		31	2005–2017	1,754	165	3	31.89	–	–	–/–	–	24	217‡/20
Thirimanne Hettige Don Rumesh Lahiru	8.9.1989		29	2011–2017	1,153	155*	1	23.06	0	0-5	0/0	–	15	117/26
Tillekeratne Hashan Prasantha	14.7.1967		83	1989–2003	4,545	204*	11	42.87	0	0-0	0/0	–	122/2	200
Upashantha Kalutarage Eric Amila	10.6.1972		2	1998–2002	10	6	0	3.33	4	2-41	0/0	50.00	0	12
Vaas Warnakulasuriya Patabendige Ushantha Joseph Chaminda	27.1.1974		111	1994–2009	3,089	100*	1	24.32	355	7-71	12/2	29.58	31	321‡/6
Vandort Michael Graydon	19.1.1980		20	2001–2008	1,144	140	4	36.90	–	–	–/–	–	6	1
Vithanage Kasun Disi Kithuruwan	26.2.1991		10	2012–2015	370	103*	1	26.42	1	1-73	0/0	133.00	10	6/3
Warnapura Bandula	1.3.1953		4	1981–1982	96	38	0	12.00	0	0-1	0/0	–	2	12
Warnapura Basnayake Shalith Malinda	26.5.1979		14	2007–2009	821	120	2	35.69	0	0-40	0/0	–	14	3
Warnaweera Kahakatchchi Patabandige Jayananda	23.11.1960		10	1985–1994	39	20	0	4.33	32	4-25	0/0	31.90	0	6
Weerasinghe Colombage Don Udesh Sanjeewa	1.3.1968		1	1985	3	3	0	3.00	0	0-8	0/0	–	0	
Welagedara Uda Walawwe Mahim Bandaralage Chanaka Asanka	20.3.1981		21	2007–2014	218	48	0	9.08	55	5-52	2/0	41.32	5	10/2
[2] **Wettimuny** Mithra de Silva	11.6.1951		2	1982	28	17	0	7.00	–	–	–/–	–	2	1
[2] **Wettimuny** Sidath (*CY 1985*)	12.8.1956		23	1981–1986	1,221	190	2	29.07	0	0-16	0/0	–	10	35
Wickremasinghe Anguppulige Gamini Dayantha	27.12.1965		3	1989–1992	17	13*	0	8.50	–	–	–/–	–	9/1	4
Wickremasinghe Gallage Pramodya	14.8.1971		40	1991–2000	555	51	0	9.40	85	6-60	3/0	41.87	18	134
Wijegunawardene Kapila Indaka Weerakkody	23.11.1964		2	1991–1991	14	6*	0	4.66	7	4-51	0/0	21.00	0	26
Wijesuriya Roger Gerard Christopher Ediriweera	18.2.1960		4	1981–1985	22	8	0	4.40	1	1-68	0/0	294.00	1	8
Wijetunge Piyal Kashyapa	6.8.1971		1	1993	10	10	0	5.00	2	1-58	0/0	59.00	0	
Zoysa Demuni Nuwan Tharanga	13.5.1978		30	1996–2004	288	28*	0	8.47	64	5-20	1/0	33.70	4	9

ZIMBABWE (105 players)

	Born	Died	Tests	Test Career	Runs	HS	100s	Avge	Wkts	BB	5/10	Avge	Ct/St	O/T
Arnott Kevin John	8.3.1961		4	*1992*	302	101*	1	43.14	–	–	–/–	–	4	13
Blignaut Arnoldus Mauritius ("Andy")	1.8.1978		19	*2000–2005*	886	92	0	26.84	53	5-73	3/0	37.05	13	54/1
Brain David Hayden	4.10.1964		9	*1992–1994*	115	28	0	10.45	30	5-42	1/0	30.50	1	23
Brandes Eddo André	5.3.1963		10	*1992–1999*	121	39	0	10.08	26	3-45	0/0	36.57	4	59
Brent Gary Bazil	13.1.1976		4	*1999–2001*	35	25	0	5.83	7	3-21	0/0	44.85	1	70/3
Briant Gavin Aubrey	11.4.1969		1	*1992*	17	16	0	8.50	–	–	–/–	–	0	5
Bruk-Jackson Glen Keith	25.4.1969		2	*1993*	39	31	0	9.75	–	–	–/–	–	0	1
Burl Ryan Ponsonby	15.4.1994		1	2017	16	16	0	8.00	–	–	–/–	–	1	9
Burmester Mark Greville	24.1.1968		3	*1992*	54	30*	0	27.00	3	3-78	0/0	75.66	1	8
Butchart Iain Peter	9.5.1960		1	*1994*	23	15	0	11.50	0	0-11	0/0	–	1	20
Campbell Alistair Douglas Ross	23.9.1972		60	*1992–2002*	2,858	103	2	27.21	0	0-1	0/0	–	60	188
Carlisle Stuart Vance	10.5.1972		37	*1994–2005*	1,615	118	2	26.91	–	–	–/–	–	34	111
Chakabva Regis Wiriranai	20.9.1987		12	*2011–2017*	618	101	1	28.09	–	–	–/–	–	14/3	34/5
Chari Brian Bara	14.2.1992		5	*2014–2016*	141	80	0	14.10	0	0-3	0/0	–	5	8
Chatara Tendai Larry	28.2.1991		7	*2012–2014*	82	22	0	6.83	20	5-61	1/0	29.25	0	41/11
Chibhabha Chamunorwa Justice	6.9.1986		3	2016–2017	124	60	0	20.66	1	1-44	0/0	162.00	0	100/30
Chigumbura Elton	14.3.1986		14	*2003–2014*	569	88	0	21.07	21	5-54	1/0	46.00	6	202‡/47
Chinouya Michael Tawanda	9.6.1986		2	2016	1	1	0	0.50	3	1-45	0/0	62.66	0	2
Chisoro Tendai Sam	12.2.1988		1	*2017*	9	9	0	9.00	3	3-113	0/0	37.66	0	12/7
Coventry Charles Kevin	8.3.1983		2	*2005*	88	37	0	22.00	–	–	–/–	–	3	39/13
Cremer Alexander Graeme	19.9.1986		19	*2004–2017*	540	102*	1	16.36	57	5-125	1/0	45.68	12	81/27
Crocker Gary John	16.5.1962		3	*1992*	69	33	0	23.00	3	2-65	0/0	72.33	0	6
Dabengwa Keith Mbusi	17.8.1980		3	*2005*	90	35	0	15.00	5	3-127	0/0	49.80	1	37/8
Dekker Mark Hamilton	5.12.1969		14	*1993–1996*	333	68*	0	15.85	0	0-5	0/0	–	12	23
Duffin Terrence	20.3.1982		2	*2005*	80	56	0	20.00	–	–	–/–	–	1	23
Ebrahim Dion Digby	7.8.1980		29	*2000–2005*	1,226	94	0	22.70	–	–	–/–	–	16	82
[2] **Ervine** Craig Richard	19.8.1985		15	*2011–2017*	941	160	2	33.60	–	–	–/–	–	15	65/16
[2] **Ervine** Sean Michael	6.12.1982		5	*2003–2003*	261	86	0	32.62	9	4-146	0/0	43.11	7	42
Evans Craig Neil	29.11.1969		3	*1996–2003*	52	22	0	8.66	0	0-8	0/0	–	1	53
Ewing Gavin Mackie	21.1.1981		3	*2003–2005*	108	71	0	18.00	2	1-27	0/0	130.00	1	7
Ferreira Neil Robert	3.6.1979		1	*2005*	21	16	0	10.50	–	–	–/–	–	0	
[2] **Flower** Andrew OBE (*CY 2002*)	28.4.1968		63	*1992–2002*	4,794	232*	12	51.54	0	0-0	0/0	–	151/9	213
[2] **Flower** Grant William	20.12.1970		67	*1992–2003*	3,457	201*	6	29.54	25	4-41	0/0	61.48	43	221

	Born	*Died*	*Tests*	*Test Career*	*Runs*	*HS*	*100s*	*Avge*	*Wkts*	*BB*	*5/10*	*Avge*	*Ct/St*	*O/T*
Friend Travis John	7.1.1981		13	2001–2003	447	81	0	29.80	25	5-31	1/0	43.60	2	51
Goodwin Murray William	11.12.1972		19	*1997–2000*	1,414	166*	3	42.84	0	0-3	0/0	–	10	71
Gripper Trevor Raymond	28.12.1975		20	*1999–2003*	809	112	1	21.86	6	2-91	0/0	84.83	14	8
Hondo Douglas Tafadzwa	7.7.1979		9	*2001–2004*	83	19	0	9.22	21	6-59	1/0	36.85	5	56
Houghton David Laud	23.6.1957		22	*1992–1997*	1,464	266	4	43.05	0	0-0	0/0	–	17	63
Huckle Adam George	21.9.1971		8	*1997–1998*	74	28*	0	6.72	25	6-109	2/1	34.88	3	19
James Wayne Robert	27.8.1965		4	*1993–1994*	61	33	0	15.25	–	–	–/–	–	16	11
[1] **Jarvis** Kyle Malcolm	16.2.1989		10	*2011–2017*	111	25*	0	11.10	36	5-54	2/0	30.97	3	24/9
[1] **Jarvis** Malcolm Peter	6.12.1955		5	*1992–1994*	4	2*	0	2.00	11	3-30	0/0	35.72	2	12
Johnson Neil Clarkson	24.1.1970		13	1998–2000	532	107	1	24.18	15	4-77	0/0	39.60	12	48
Kamungozi Tafadzwa Paul	8.6.1987		1	*2014*	5	5	0	2.50	1	1-51	0/0	58.00	0	14/1
Lamb Gregory Arthur	4.3.1980		1	*2011*	46	39	0	23.00	3	3-120	0/0	47.00	2	15/5
Lock Alan Charles Ingram	10.9.1962		1	*1995*	8	8*	0	8.00	5	3-68	0/0	21.00	0	8
Madondo Trevor Nyasha	22.11.1976	11.6.2001	3	*1997–2000*	90	74*	0	30.00	–	–	–/–	–	1	13
Mahwire Ngonidzashe Blessing	31.7.1982		10	*2002–2005*	147	50*	0	13.36	18	4-92	0/0	50.83	1	23
Maregwede Alester	5.8.1981		2	*2003*	74	28	0	18.50	–	–	–/–	–	1	11
Marillier Douglas Anthony	24.4.1978		5	*2000–2001*	185	73	0	30.83	11	4-57	0/0	29.27	2	48
Maruma Timycen	19.4.1988		1	*2012*	20	10	0	10.00	–	–	–/–	–	1	17/10
[2] **Masakadza** Hamilton	9.8.1983		36	2001–2017	2,084	158	5	29.77	16	3-24	0/0	30.12	28	178/50
[2] **Masakadza** Shingirai Winston	4.9.1986		5	*2011–2014*	88	24	0	11.00	16	4-32	0/0	32.18	2	16/7
Masvaure Prince Spencer	7.10.1988		2	2016	55	42	0	13.75	0	0-23	0/0	–	0	
Matambanadzo Everton Zvikomborero	13.4.1976		3	*1996–1999*	17	7	0	4.25	4	2-62	0/0	62.50	0	7
Matsikenyeri Stuart	3.5.1983		8	*2003–2004*	351	57	0	23.40	2	1-58	0/0	172.50	7	113/10
Mawoyo Tinotenda Mbiri Kanayi	8.1.1986		11	*2011–2016*	615	163*	1	29.28	–	–	–/–	–	7	7
Mbangwa Mpumelelo ("Pommie")	26.6.1976		15	*1996–2000*	34	8	0	2.00	32	3-23	0/0	31.43	2	29
Meth Keegan Orry	8.2.1988		2	*2012*	72	31*	0	24.00	4	2-41	0/0	24.50	0	11/2
Mire Solomon Farai	21.8.1989		2	*2017*	78	47	0	19.50	1	1-22	0/0	32.00	0	22
Moor Peter Joseph	2.2.1991		6	2016–2017	374	79	0	31.16	–	–	–/–	–	9/1	26//8
Mpofu Christopher Bobby	27.11.1985		15	*2004–2017*	105	33	0	5.83	29	4-92	0/0	48.00	4	79/20
Mumba Carl Tapfuma	6.5.1995		2	*2016*	14	10*	0	4.66	8	4-50	0/0	37.25	1	2
Mupariwa Tawanda	16.4.1985		1	*2003*	15	14	0	15.00	0	0-136	0/0	–	0	40/4
Murphy Brian Andrew	1.12.1976		11	*1999–2001*	123	30	0	10.25	18	3-32	0/0	61.83	11	31
Musakanda Tarisai Kenneth	31.10.1994		1	2017	6	6	0	3.00	–	–	–/–	–	0	9
Mushangwe Natsai	9.2.1991		2	*2014*	8	8	0	2.00	7	4-82	0/0	62.14	2	6/5
Mutendera David Travolta	25.1.1979		1	*2000*	10	10	0	5.00	0	0-29	0/0	–	0	9
Mutizwa Forster	24.8.1985		1	*2011*	24	18	0	12.00	–	–	–/–	–	0	17/3

	Born	Died	Tests	Test Career	Runs	HS	100s	Avge	Wkts	BB	5/10	Avge	Ct/St	O/T
Mutumbami Richmond	11.6.1989		6	2012–2014	217	43	0	19.72	–	–	–/–	–	17/2	31/14
Muzarabani Blessing	2.10.1996		1	2017	14	10	0	14.00	0	0-48	0/0	–	0	
Mwayenga Waddington	20.6.1984		1	2005	15	14*	0	15.00	1	1-79	0/0	79.00	0	3
Ncube Njabulo	14.10.1989		1	2011	17	14	0	8.50	1	1-80	0/0	121.00	1	1
Nkala Mluleki Luke	1.4.1981		10	2000–2004	187	47	0	14.38	11	3-82	0/0	66.09	4	50/1
Nyumbu John Curtis	1.3.1983		3	2014–2016	38	14	0	7.60	5	5-157	1/0	75.80	2	19
Olonga Henry Khaaba	3.7.1976		30	1994–2002	184	24	0	5.41	68	5-70	2/0	38.52	10	50
Panyangara Tinashe	21.10.1985		9	2003–2014	201	40*	0	16.75	31	5-59	1/0	26.22	3	65/14
Peall Stephen Guy	2.9.1969		4	1993–1994	60	30	0	15.00	4	2-89	0/0	75.75	1	21
Price Raymond William	12.6.1976		22	1999–2012	261	36	0	8.70	80	6-73	5/1	36.06	4	102/16
Pycroft Andrew John	6.6.1956		3	1992	152	60	0	30.40	–	–	–/–	–	2	20
Ranchod Ujesh	17.5.1969		1	1992	8	7	0	4.00	1	1-45	0/0	45.00	0	3
[2] **Rennie** Gavin James	12.1.1976		23	1997–2001	1,023	93	0	22.73	1	1-40	0/0	84.00	13	40
[2] **Rennie** John Alexander	29.7.1970		4	1993–1997	62	22	0	12.40	3	2-22	0/0	97.66	1	44
Rogers Barney Guy	20.8.1982		4	2004	90	29	0	11.25	0	0-17	0/0	–	1	15
Shah Ali Hassimshah	7.8.1959		3	1992–1996	122	62	0	24.40	1	1-46	0/0	125.00	0	28
Sibanda Vusimuzi	10.10.1983		14	2003–2014	591	93	0	21.10	–	–	–/–	–	16	125‡/26
Sikandar Raza	24.4.1986		10	2013–2017	762	127	1	38.10	13	5-99	1/0	58.69	1	70/26
[2] **Strang** Bryan Colin	9.6.1972		26	1994–2001	465	53	0	12.91	56	5-101	1/0	39.33	11	49
[2] **Strang** Paul Andrew	28.7.1970		24	1994–2001	839	106*	1	27.06	70	8-109	4/1	36.02	15	95
Streak Heath Hilton	16.3.1974		65	1993–2005	1,990	127*	1	22.35	216	6-73	7/0	28.14	17	187‡
Taibu Tatenda	14.5.1983		28	2001–2011	1,546	153	1	30.31	1	1-27	0/0	27.00	57/5	149‡/17
Taylor Brendan Ross Murray	6.2.1986		26	2003–2017	1,594	171	4	32.53	0	0-6	0/0	–	25	167/26
Tiripano Donald Tatenda	17.3.1988		6	2014–2017	219	49*	0	24.33	10	3-91	0/0	51.00	2	15/8
Traicos Athanasios John	17.5.1947		4†	1992	11	5	0	2.75	14	5-86	1/0	40.14	4	27
Utseya Prosper	26.3.1985		4	2003–2013	107	45	0	15.28	10	3-60	0/0	41.00	2	164/35
Vermeulen Mark Andrew	2.3.1979		9	2002–2014	449	118	1	24.94	0	0-5	0/0	–	6	43
Viljoen Dirk Peter	11.3.1977		2	1997–2000	57	38	0	14.25	1	1-14	0/0	65.00	1	53
Vitori Brian Vitalis	22.2.1990		4	2011–2013	52	19*	0	10.40	12	5-61	1/0	38.66	2	20/11
[1] **Waller** Andrew Christopher	25.9.1959		2	1996	69	50	0	23.00	–	–	–/–	–	1	39
[1] **Waller** Malcolm Noel	28.9.1984		14	2011–2017	577	72*	0	21.37	8	4-59	0/0	27.25	10	70/28
Watambwa Brighton Tonderai	9.6.1977		6	2000–2001	11	4*	0	3.66	14	4-64	0/0	35.00	0	
Whittall Andrew Richard	28.3.1973		10	1996–1999	114	17	0	7.60	7	3-73	0/0	105.14	8	63
Whittall Guy James	5.9.1972		46	1993–2002	2,207	203*	4	29.42	51	4-18	0/0	40.94	19	147
Williams Sean Colin	26.9.1986		8	2012–2017	421	119	1	26.31	15	3-20	0/0	40.33	8	111/24
Wishart Craig Brian	9.1.1974		27	1995–2005	1,098	114	1	22.40	–	–	–/–	–	15	90

BANGLADESH (86 players)

	Born	Died	Tests	Test Career	Runs	HS	100s	Avge	Wkts	BB	5/10	Avge	Ct/St	O/T
Abdur Razzak	15.6.1982		12	*2005–2013*	245	43	0	17.50	23	3-93	0/0	67.39	4	153/34
Abul Hasan	5.8.1992		3	*2012*	165	113	1	82.50	3	2-80	0/0	123.66	3	6/4
Aftab Ahmed	10.11.1985		16	*2004–2009*	582	82*	0	20.78	5	2-31	0/0	47.40	7	85/11
Akram Khan	1.11.1968		8	2000–2003	259	44	0	16.18	–	–	–/–	–	3	44
Al-Amin Hossain	1.1.1990		6	*2013–2014*	68	32*	0	22.66	6	3-80	0/0	76.66	0	14/25
Al Sahariar	23.4.1978		15	2000–2003	683	71	0	22.76	–	–	–/–	–	10	29
Alamgir Kabir	10.1.1981		3	*2002–2003*	8	4	0	2.00	0	0-39	0/0	–	0	
Alok Kapali	1.1.1984		17	*2002–2005*	584	85	0	17.69	6	3-3	0/0	118.16	5	69/7
Aminul Islam	2.2.1968		13	*2000–2002*	530	145	1	21.20	1	1-66	0/0	149.00	5	39
Anamul Haque	16.12.1992		4	*2012–2014*	73	22	0	9.12	–	–	–/–	–	2	30/13
Anwar Hossain Monir	31.12.1981		3	2003–2005	22	13	0	7.33	0	0-95	0/0	–	0	1
Anwar Hossain Piju	10.12.1983		1	*2002*	14	12	0	7.00	–	–	–/–	–	0	1
Bikash Ranjan Das	14.7.1982		1	*2000*	2	2	0	1.00	1	1-64	0/0	72.00	1	
Ehsanul Haque	1.12.1979		1	2002	7	5	0	3.50	0	0-18	0/0	–	0	6
Elias Sunny	2.8.1986		4	*2011–2012*	38	20*	0	7.60	12	6-94	1/0	43.16	1	4/7
Enamul Haque snr.	27.2.1966		10	2000–2003	180	24*	0	12.00	18	4-136	0/0	57.05	1	29
Enamul Haque jnr.	5.12.1986		15	*2003–2012*	59	13	0	5.90	44	7-95	3/1	40.61	3	10
Fahim Muntasir	1.11.1980		3	*2001*–2002	52	33	0	8.66	5	3-131	0/0	68.40	1	3
Faisal Hossain	26.10.1978		1	*2003*	7	5	0	3.50	–	–	–/–	–	0	6
Habibul Bashar	17.8.1972		50	*2000–2007*	3,026	113	3	30.87	0	0-1	0/0	–	22	111
Hannan Sarkar	1.12.1982		17	2002–*2004*	662	76	0	20.06	–	–	–/–	–	7	20
Hasibul Hossain	3.6.1977		5	*2000–2001*	97	31	0	10.77	6	2-125	0/0	95.16	1	32
Imrul Kayes	2.2.1987		32	*2008–2017*	1,584	150	3	26.40	0	0-1	0/0	–	30	70/14
Jahurul Islam	12.12.1986		7	*2009–2012*	347	48	0	26.69	–	–	–/–	–	7	14/3
Javed Omar Belim	25.11.1976		40	*2000–2007*	1,720	119	1	22.05	0	0-12	0/0	–	10	59
Jubair Hossain	12.9.1995		6	*2014*–2015	13	7*	0	4.33	16	5-96	1/0	30.81	2	3/1
Junaid Siddique	30.10.1987		19	*2007–2012*	969	106	1	26.18	0	0-2	0/0	–	11	54/7
Kamrul Islam	10.12.1991		5	*2016*	44	25*	0	7.33	7	3-87	0/0	56.85	0	
Khaled Mahmud	26.7.1971		12	*2001–2003*	266	45	0	12.09	13	4-37	0/0	64.00	2	77
Khaled Mashud	8.2.1976		44	*2000*–2007	1,409	103*	1	19.04	–	–	–/–	–	78/9	126
Liton Das	13.10.1994		6	2015–*2017*	254	70	0	28.22	–	–	–/–	–	9/1	12/4
Mahbubul Alam	1.12.1983		4	*2008*	5	2	0	1.25	5	2-62	0/0	62.80	0	5
Mahmudullah	4.2.1986		35	2009–*2017*	1,931	115	1	30.17	39	5-51	1/0	46.76	33/1	148/60

	Born	Died	Tests	Test Career	Runs	HS	100s	Avge	Wkts	BB	5/10	Avge	Ct/St	O/T
Manjural Islam	7.11.1979		17	2000–2003	81	21	0	3.68	28	6-81	1/0	57.32	4	34
Manjural Islam Rana	4.5.1984	16.3.2007	6	2003–2004	257	69	0	25.70	5	3-84	0/0	80.20	3	25
Marshall Ayub	5.12.1988		3	2013	125	41	0	20.83	0	0-15	0/0	–	2	
Mashrafe bin Mortaza	5.10.1983		36	2001–2009	797	79	0	12.85	78	4-60	0/0	41.52	9	180‡/54
Mehedi Hasan	25.10.1997		10	2016–2017	281	51	0	16.52	43	6-77	3/1	37.09	9	7/3
Mehrab Hossain snr.	22.9.1978		9	2000–2003	241	71	0	13.38	0	0-5	0/0	–	6	18
Mehrab Hossain jnr.	8.7.1987		7	2007–2008	243	83	0	20.25	4	2-29	0/0	70.25	2	18/2
Mohammad Ashraful	9.9.1984		61	2001–2012	2,737	190	6	24.00	21	2-42	0/0	60.52	25	175‡/23
Mohammad Rafique	5.9.1970		33	2000–2007	1,059	111	1	18.57	100	6-77	7/0	40.76	7	123‡/1
Mohammad Salim	15.10.1981		2	2003	49	26	0	16.33	–	–	–/–	–	3/1	1
Mohammad Shahid	1.11.1988		5	2014–2015	57	25	0	11.40	5	2-23	0/0	57.60	0	1
Mohammad Sharif	12.12.1983		10	2000–2007	122	24*	0	7.17	14	4-98	0/0	79.00	5	9
Mominul Haque	29.9.1991		25	2012–2017	1,840	181	4	43.80	4	3-27	0/0	61.50	18	26/6
Mosaddek Hossain	10.12.1995		1	2016	88	75	0	44.00	0	0-10	0/0	–	2	18/6
Mushfiqur Rahim	1.9.1988		58	2005–2017	3,516	200	5	35.16	–	–	–/–	–	94/13	179/61
Mushfiqur Rahman	1.1.1980		10	2000–2004	232	46*	0	13.64	13	4-65	0/0	63.30	6	28
Mustafizur Rahman	6.9.1995		8	2015–2017	25	10*	0	3.12	20	4-37	0/0	32.00	1	22/17
Naeem Islam	31.12.1986		8	2008–2012	416	108	1	32.00	1	1-11	0/0	303.00	2	59/10
[2] **Nafis Iqbal**	31.1.1985		11	2004–2005	518	121	1	23.54	–	–	–/–	–	2	16
Naimur Rahman	19.9.1974		8	2000–2002	210	48	0	15.00	12	6-132	1/0	59.83	4	29
Nasir Hossain	30.11.1991		19	2011–2017	1,044	100	1	34.80	8	3-52	0/0	55.25	10	61/31
Nazimuddin	1.10.1985		3	2011–2012	125	78	0	20.83	–	–	–/–	–	1	11/7
Nazmul Hossain	5.10.1987		2	2004–2011	16	8*	0	8.00	5	2-61	0/0	38.80	0	38/4
Nazmul Hossain Shanto	25.5.1998		1	2016	30	18	0	15.00	0	0-13	0/0	–	0	
Nurul Hasan	21.11.1993		1	2016	47	47	0	23.50	–	–	–/–	–	2	2/9
Rafiqul Islam	7.11.1977		1	2002	7	6	0	3.50	–	–	–/–	–	0	1
Rajin Saleh	20.11.1983		24	2003–2008	1,141	89	0	25.93	2	1-9	0/0	134.00	15	43
Raqibul Hasan	8.10.1987		9	2008–2011	336	65	0	19.76	1	1-0	0/0	17.00	9	55/5
Robiul Islam	20.10.1986		9	2010–2014	99	33	0	9.00	25	6-71	2/0	39.68	5	3/1
Rubel Hossain	1.1.1990		25	2009–2017	237	45*	0	9.48	33	5-166	1/0	79.00	11	80/16
Sabbir Rahman	20.8.1991		10	2016–2017	480	66	0	26.66	0	0-9	0/0	–	2	46/33
Sajidul Islam	18.1.1988		3	2007–2012	18	6	0	3.00	3	2-71	0/0	77.33	0	0/1
Sanwar Hossain	5.8.1973		9	2001–2003	345	49	0	19.16	5	2-128	0/0	62.00	1	27
Shafiul Islam	6.10.1989		11	2009–2017	211	53	0	10.55	17	3-86	0/0	55.41	2	56/12
Shahadat Hossain	7.8.1986		38	2005–2014	521	40	0	10.01	72	6-27	4/0	51.81	9	51/6
Shahriar Hossain	1.6.1976		3	2000–2003	99	48	0	19.80	–	–	–/–	–	0/1	20

	Born	Died	Tests	Test Career	Runs	HS	100s	Avge	Wkts	BB	5/10	Avge	Ct/St	O/T
Shahriar Nafees	1.5.1985		24	2005–2012	1,267	138	1	26.39	–	–	–/–	–	19	75/1
Shakib Al Hasan	24.3.1987		51	2007–2017	3,594	217	5	40.38	188	7-36	17/2	32.37	19	180/61
Shamsur Rahman	5.6.1988		6	2013–2014	305	106	1	25.41	0	0-5	0/0	–	7	10/9
Shuvagata Hom	11.11.1986		8	2014–2016	244	50	0	22.18	8	2-66	0/0	63.25	8	4/5
Sohag Gazi	5.8.1991		10	2012–2013	325	101*	1	21.66	38	6-74	2/0	42.07	5	20/10
Soumya Sarkar	25.2.1993		10	2014–2017	558	86	0	29.36	1	1-45	0/0	159.00	12	32/26
Subashis Roy	28.11.1988		4	2016–2017	14	12*	0	14.00	9	3-118	0/0	51.66	0	1
Suhrawadi Shuvo	21.11.1988		1	2011	15	15	0	7.50	4	3-73	0/0	36.50	0	17/1
Syed Rasel	3.7.1984		6	2005–2007	37	19	0	4.62	12	4-129	0/0	47.75	0	52/8
Taijul Islam	7.2.1992		16	2014–2017	217	32	0	9.43	54	8-39	3/0	36.77	8	4
Talha Jubair	10.12.1985		7	2002–2004	52	31	0	6.50	14	3-135	0/0	55.07	1	6
[2] **Tamim Iqbal** (*CY 2011*)	20.3.1989		52	2007–2017	3,886	206	8	39.25	0	0-1	0/0	–	13	174/56‡
Tapash Baisya	25.12.1982		21	2002–2005	384	66	0	11.29	36	4-72	0/0	59.36	6	56
Tareq Aziz	4.9.1983		3	2003–2004	22	10*	0	11.00	1	1-76	0/0	261.00	1	10
Taskin Ahmed	3.4.1995		5	2016–2017	68	33	0	6.80	7	2-43	0/0	97.42	1	32/17
Tushar Imran	10.12.1983		5	2002–2007	89	28	0	8.90	0	0-48	0/0	–	1	41
Ziaur Rahman	2.12.1986		1	2012	14	14	0	7.00	4	4-63	0/0	17.75	0	13/14

Notes

Family relationships in the above lists are indicated by superscript numbers; the following list contains only those players whose relationship is not apparent from a shared name.

In one Test, A. and G. G. Hearne played for England; their brother, F. Hearne, for South Africa.
The Waughs and New Zealand's Marshalls are the only instance of Test-playing twins.
Adnan Akmal: brother of Kamran and Umar Akmal.
Amar Singh, L.: brother of L. Ramji.
Azmat Rana: brother of Shafqat Rana.
Bazid Khan (Pakistan): son of Majid Khan (Pakistan) and grandson of M. Jahangir Khan (India).
Bravo, D. J. and D. M.: half-brothers.
Chappell, G. S., I. M. and T. M.: grandsons of V. Y. Richardson.
Collins, P. T.: half-brother of F. H. Edwards.
Cooper, W. H.: great-grandfather of A. P. Sheahan.
Edwards, F. H.: half-brother of P. T. Collins.
Hanif Mohammad: brother of Mushtaq, Sadiq and Wazir Mohammad; father of Shoaib Mohammad.
Headley, D. W (England): son of R. G. A. and grandson of G. A. Headley (both West Indies).
Hearne, F. (England and South Africa): father of G. A. L. Hearne (South Africa).
Jahangir Khan, M. (India): father of Majid Khan and grandfather of Bazid Khan (both Pakistan).
Kamran Akmal: brother of Adnan and Umar Akmal.
Khalid Wazir (Pakistan): son of S. Wazir Ali (India).
Kirsten, G. and P. N.: half-brothers.
Majid Khan (Pakistan): son of M. Jahangir Khan (India) and father of Bazid Khan (Pakistan).
Manzoor Elahi: brother of Salim and Zahoor Elahi.
Moin Khan: brother of Nadeem Khan.
Mudassar Nazar: son of Nazar Mohammad.
Murray, D. A.: son of E. D. Weekes.
Mushtaq Mohammad: brother of Hanif, Sadiq and Wazir Mohammad.
Nadeem Khan: brother of Moin Khan.
Nafis Iqbal: brother of Tamim Iqbal.
Nazar Mohammad: father of Mudassar Nazar.
Nazir Ali, S.: brother of S. Wazir Ali.
Pattinson, D. J. (England): brother of J. L. Pattinson (Australia).
Pervez Sajjad: brother of Waqar Hassan.
Ramiz Raja: brother of Wasim Raja.
Ramji, L.: brother of L. Amar Singh.
Richardson, V. Y.: grandfather of G. S., I. M. and T. M. Chappell.
Sadiq Mohammad: brother of Hanif, Mushtaq and Wazir Mohammad.
Saeed Ahmed: brother of Younis Ahmed.
Salim Elahi: brother of Manzoor and Zahoor Elahi.
Shafqat Rana: brother of Azmat Rana.
Sheahan, A. P.: great-grandson of W. H. Cooper.
Shoaib Mohammad: son of Hanif Mohammad.
Tamim Iqbal: brother of Nafis Iqbal.
Umar Akmal: brother of Adnan and Kamran Akmal.
Waqar Hassan: brother of Pervez Sajjad.
Wasim Raja: brother of Ramiz Raja.
Wazir Ali, S. (India): brother of S. Nazir Ali (India) and father of Khalid Wazir (Pakistan).
Wazir Mohammad: brother of Hanif, Mushtaq and Sadiq Mohammad.
Weekes, E. D.: father of D. A. Murray.
Yograj Singh: father of Yuvraj Singh.
Younis Ahmed: brother of Saeed Ahmed.
Yuvraj Singh: son of Yograj Singh.
Zahoor Elahi: brother of Manzoor and Salim Elahi.

Teams are listed only where relatives played for different sides.

PLAYERS APPEARING FOR MORE THAN ONE TEST TEAM

Fourteen cricketers have appeared for two countries in Test matches, namely:

Amir Elahi (India 1, Pakistan 5)
J. J. Ferris (Australia 8, England 1)
S. C. Guillen (West Indies 5, New Zealand 3)
Gul Mahomed (India 8, Pakistan 1)
F. Hearne (England 2, South Africa 4)
A. H. Kardar (India 3, Pakistan 23)
W. E. Midwinter (England 4, Australia 8)
F. Mitchell (England 2, South Africa 3)
W. L. Murdoch (Australia 18, England 1)
Nawab of Pataudi snr (England 3, India 3)
A. J. Traicos (South Africa 3, Zimbabwe 4)
A. E. Trott (Australia 3, England 2)
K. C. Wessels (Australia 24, South Africa 16)
S. M. J. Woods (Australia 3, England 3)

Wessels also played 54 one-day internationals for Australia and 55 for South Africa.

The following players appeared for the ICC World XI against Australia in the Super Series Test in 2005-06: M. V. Boucher, R. Dravid, A. Flintoff, S. J. Harmison, Inzamam-ul-Haq, J. H. Kallis, B. C. Lara, M. Muralitharan, V. Sehwag, G. C. Smith, D. L. Vettori.

In 1970, England played five first-class matches against the Rest of the World after the cancellation of South Africa's tour. Players were awarded England caps, but the matches are no longer considered to have Test status. Alan Jones (born 4.11.1938) made his only appearance for England in this series, scoring 5 and 0; he did not bowl and took no catches.

ONE-DAY AND TWENTY20 INTERNATIONAL CRICKETERS

The following players had appeared for Test-playing countries (not Afghanistan or Ireland) in one-day or Twenty20 internationals by January 3, 2018, but had not represented their countries in Test matches by January 27, 2018. (Numbers in brackets signify number of ODIs for each player: where a second number appears, e.g. (5/1), it signifies the number of T20Is for that player.)

By January 2018, D. A. Miller (100 ODIs/57 T20Is, including three for the World XI) and K. A. Pollard (101 ODIs/56 T20Is) were the most experienced international players never to have appeared in Test cricket. R. G. Sharma held the record for most international appearances before making his Test debut, with 108 ODIs and 36 T20Is. S. Badree had played a record 45 T20Is (including two for the World XI) without an Test or ODI appearance.

England

M. W. Alleyne (10), I. D. Austin (9), S. W. Billings (13/13), D. R. Briggs (1/7), A. D. Brown (16), D. R. Brown (9), G. Chapple (1), J. W. M. Dalrymple (27/3), S. M. Davies (8/5), J. L. Denly (9/5), J. W. Dernbach (24/34), M. V. Fleming (11), P. J. Franks (1), I. J. Gould (18), A. P. Grayson (2), H. F. Gurney (10/2), G. W. Humpage (3), T. E. Jesty (10), E. C. Joyce (17/2), C. Kieswetter (46/25), L. S. Livingstone (0/2), G. D. Lloyd (6), A. G. R. Loudon (1), J. D. Love (3), M. B. Loye (7), M. J. Lumb (3/27), M. A. Lynch (3), A. D. Mascarenhas (20/14), S. C. Meaker (2/2), T. S. Mills (0/4), P. Mustard (10/2), P. A. Nixon (19/1), S. D. Parry (2/5), J. J. Roy (48/23), M. J. Smith (5), N. M. K. Smith (7), J. N. Snape (10/1), V. S. Solanki (51/3), R. J. W. Topley (10/6), J. O. Troughton (6), C. M. Wells (2), V. J. Wells (9), A. G. Wharf (13), D. J. Willey (31/16), L. J. Wright (50/51), M. H. Yardy (28/14).

D. R. Brown also played 16 ODIs for Scotland, and E. C. Joyce 55 ODIs and 16 T20Is for Ireland.

Australia

S. A. Abbott (1/3), J. P. Behrendorff (0/2), T. R. Birt (0/4), G. A. Bishop (2), S. M. Boland (14/3), C. J. Boyce (0/7), R. J. Campbell (2), D. T. Christian (19/16), M. J. Cosgrove (3), N. M. Coulter-Nile (21/19), B. C. J. Cutting (4/4), M. J. Di Venuto (9), B. R. Dorey (4), B. R. Dunk (0/5), Fawad Ahmed (3/2), A. J. Finch (85/33), P. J. Forrest (15), B. Geeves (2/1), S. F. Graf (11), I. J. Harvey (73), S. M. Harwood (1/3), T. M. Head (30/9), S. D. Heazlett (1), J. R. Hopes (84/12), D. J. Hussey (69/39), M. Klinger (0/3), B. Laughlin (5/3), S. Lee (45), M. L. Lewis (7/2), C. A. Lynn (1/5), R. J. McCurdy (11), K. H. MacLeay (16), J. P. Maher (26), J. M. Muirhead (0/5), D. P. Nannes (1/15), A. A. Noffke (1/2), J. S. Paris (2), L. A. Pomersbach (0/1), G. D. Porter (2), N. J. Reardon (0/2), J. A. Richardson (0/2), K. W. Richardson (15/3), B. J. Rohrer (0/1), L. Ronchi (4/3), G. S. Sandhu (2), J. D. Siddons (1), B. Stanlake (2/1), M. P. Stoinis (8/2), A. M. Stuart (3), C. P. Tremain (4), G. S. Trimble (2), A. J. Turner (0/3), A. J. Tye (0/7), D. J. Worrall (3), B. E. Young (6), A. Zampa (27/12), A. K. Zesers (2).

R. J. Campbell also played three T20Is for Hong Kong, D. P. Nannes two T20Is for the Netherlands, and L. Ronchi four Tests, 72 ODIs and 26 T20Is for New Zealand..

South Africa

Y. A. Abdulla (0/2), S. Abrahams (1), F. Behardien (58/34), D. M. Benkenstein (23), G. H. Bodi (2/1), L. E. Bosman (13/14), R. E. Bryson (7), D. J. Callaghan (29), D. N. Crookes (32), H. Davids (2/9), R. Frylinck (0/2), T. Henderson (0/1), B. E. Hendricks (0/7), R. R. Hendricks (0/9), C. A. Ingram (31/9), J. C. Kent (2), L. J. Koen (5), G. J-P. Kruger (3/1), E. Leie (0/2), R. E. Levi (0/13), J. Louw (3/2), D. A. Miller (100/54), M. Mosehle (0/7), P. V. Mpitsang (2), P. W. A. Mulder (1), S. J. Palframan (7), D. Paterson (3/5), A. M. Phangiso (21/15), N. Pothas (3), D. Pretorius (3), A. G. Puttick (1), C. E. B. Rice (3), M. J. R. Rindel (22), R. R. Rossouw (36/15), D. B. Rundle (2), T. G. Shaw (9), M. Shezi (1), E. O. Simons (23), J. T. Smuts (0/6), E. L. R. Stewart (6), R. Telemachus (37/3), J. Theron (4/9), A. C. Thomas (0/1), T. Tshabalala (4), R. E. van der Merwe (13/13), J. J. van der Wath (10/8), V. B. van Jaarsveld (2/3), M. N. van Wyk (17/8), C. J. P. G. van Zyl (2), D. Wiese (6/20), H. S. Williams (7), M. Yachad (1).

R. E. van der Merwe also played 11 T20Is for the Netherlands.

West Indies

H. A. G. Anthony (3), S. Badree (0/43), C. D. Barnwell (0/6), M. C. Bascombe (0/1), R. R. Beaton (2), N. E. Bonner (0/2), D. Brown (3), B. St A. Browne (4), P. A. Browne (5), H. R. Bryan (15), D. C. Butler (5/1), J. L. Carter (28), J. Charles (48/34), D. O. Christian (0/2), R. T. Crandon (1), R. R. Emrit (2/1), S. E. Findlay (9/2), A. D. S. Fletcher (25/35), R. S. Gabriel (11), R. C. Haynes (8), R. O. Hurley (9), D. P. Hyatt (9/5), K. C. B. Jeremy (6), E. Lewis (25/14), A. Martin (9/1), G. E. Mathurin (0/3), J. N. Mohammed (24/6), A. R. Nurse (26/8), W. K. D. Perkins (0/1), K. A. Pollard (101/56), N. Pooran (0/3), R. Powell (17/10), M. R. Pydanna (3), A. C. L. Richards (1/1), K. Santokie (0/12), K. F. Semple (7), D. C. Thomas (21/3), C. M. Tuckett (1), K. O. K. Williams (6/10), L. R. Williams (15).

New Zealand

G. W. Aldridge (2/1), M. D. Bailey (1), M. D. Bates (2/3), B. R. Blair (14), T. C. Bruce (0/10), C. E. Bulfin (4), T. K. Canning (4), P. G. Coman (3), C. de Grandhomme (1/4), A. P. Devcich (12/4), B. J. Diamanti (1/1), M. W. Douglas (6), A. M. Ellis (15/5), L. H. Ferguson (10/1), B. G. Hadlee (2), L. J. Hamilton (2), R. T. Hart (1), R. L. Hayes (1), R. M. Hira (0/15), P. A. Hitchcock (14/1), L. G. Howell (12), A. K. Kitchen (0/3), S. C. Kuggeleijn (2), M. J. McClenaghan (48/28), N. L. McCullum (84/63), P. D. McGlashan (4/11), B. J. McKechnie (14), E. B. McSweeney (16), A. W. Mathieson (1), J. P. Millmow (5), A. F. Milne (40/19), T. S. Nethula (5), C. J. Nevin (37), A. J. Penn (5), R. G. Petrie (12), G. D. Phillips (0/6), S. H. A. Rance (2/2), R. B. Reid (9), S. J. Roberts (2), S. L. Stewart (4), L. W. Stott (1), G. P. Sulzberger (3), A. R. Tait (5), E. P. Thompson (1/1), M. D. J. Walker (3), R. J. Webb (3), B. M. Wheeler (6/4), J. W. Wilson (6), W. A. Wisneski (3), L. J. Woodcock (4/3), G. H. Worker (7/2).

India

S. Aravind (0/1), P. Awana (0/2), A. C. Bedade (13), A. Bhandari (2), Bhupinder Singh snr (2), G. Bose (1), Y. S. Chahal (17/14), V. B. Chandrasekhar (7), U. Chatterjee (3), N. A. David (4), P. Dharmani (1), R. Dhawan (3/1), A. B. Dinda (13/9), F. Y. Fazal (1), R. S. Gavaskar (11), R. S. Ghai (6), M. S. Gony (2), Gurkeerat Singh (3), S. S. Iyer (3/6), K. M. Jadhav (37/9), Joginder Sharma (4/4), A. V. Kale (1), S. C. Khanna (10), G. K. Khoda (2), A. R. Khurasiya (12), D. S. Kulkarni (12/2), T. Kumaran (8), Mandeep Singh (0/3), J. J. Martin (10), D. Mongia (57/1), S. P. Mukherjee (3), A. M. Nayar (3), P. Negi (0/1), G. K. Pandey (2), M. K. Pandey (22/15), R. R. Pant (0/2), J. V. Paranjpe (4), Parvez Rasool (1/1), A. K. Patel (8), A. R. Patel (38/10), Y. K. Pathan (57/22), Randhir Singh (2), S. S. Raul (2), A. T. Rayudu (34/6), A. M. Salvi (4), S. V. Samson (0/1), M. Sharma (26/8), R. Sharma (4/2), S. Sharma (0/2), L. R. Shukla (3), R. P. Singh (2), M. Siraj (0/2), R. S. Sodhi (18), S. Somasunder (2), B. B. Sran (6/2), S. Sriram (8), Sudhakar Rao (1), S. N. Thakur (2), M. K. Tiwary (12/3), S. S. Tiwary (3), S. Tyagi (4/1), R. V. Uthappa (46/13), P. S. Vaidya (4), Y. Venugopal Rao (16), M. S. Washington Sundar (1/1), Jai P. Yadav (12).

Pakistan

Aamer Hameed (2), Aamer Hanif (5), Aamer Yasin (3/1), Akhtar Sarfraz (4), Anwar Ali (22/16), Arshad Pervez (2), Asad Ali (4/2), Asif Mahmood (2), Awais Zia (0/5), Bilal Asif (3), Fahim Ashraf (3/4), Faisal Athar (1), Fakhar Zaman (9/9), Ghulam Ali (3), Haafiz Shahid (3), Hammad Azam (11/5), Hasan Jamil (6), Imad Wasim (30/25), Imam-ul-Haq (3), Imran Abbas (2), Imran Khan jnr

(0/3), Iqbal Sikandar (4), Irfan Bhatti (1), Javed Qadir (1), Junaid Zia (4), Kamran Hussain (2), Kashif Raza (1), Khalid Latif (5/13), Mahmood Hamid (1), Mansoor Amjad (1/1), Mansoor Rana (2), Manzoor Akhtar (7), Maqsood Rana (1), Masood Iqbal (1), Mohammad Wasim (14/8), Moin-ul-Atiq (5), Mujahid Jamshed (4), Mukhtar Ahmed (0/6), Naeem Ahmed (1), Naeem Ashraf (2), Najaf Shah (1), Naseer Malik (3), Nauman Anwar (0/1), Naumanullah (1), Parvez Mir (3), Rafatullah Mohmand (0/3), Rameez Raja (0/2), Raza Hasan (1/10), Rizwan Ahmed (1), Rumman Raees (4/5), Saad Nasim (3/3), Saadat Ali (8), Saeed Azad (4), Sajid Ali (13), Sajjad Akbar (2), Salim Pervez (1), Samiullah Khan (2), Shahid Anwar (1), Shahzaib Hasan (3/10), Shakeel Ansar (0/2), Shakil Khan (1), Shoaib Khan (0/1), Sohaib Maqsood (26/20), Sohail Fazal (2), Tanvir Mehdi (1), Usman Salahuddin (2), Usman Shinwari (2/6), Wasim Haider (3), Zafar Gohar (1), Zafar Iqbal (8), Zahid Ahmed (2).

Sri Lanka

M. A. Aponso (6), J. R. M. W. S. Bandara (0/8), K. M. C. Bandara (1/1), J. W. H. D. Boteju (2), A. Dananjaya (14/9), D. L. S. de Silva (2), G. N. de Silva (4), P. C. de Silva (7/2), P. W. H. de Silva (7), S. N. T. de Silva (0/3), L. H. D. Dilhara (9/2), A. M. Fernando (1), B. Fernando (0/2), E. R. Fernando (3), T. L. Fernando (1), U. N. K. Fernando (2), W. I. A. Fernando (1), J. C. Gamage (4), W. C. A. Ganegama (4), F. R. M. Goonatilleke (1), P. W. Gunaratne (23), A. A. W. Gunawardene (1), P. D. Heyn (2), W. S. Jayantha (17), P. S. Jayaprakashdaran (1), C. U. Jayasinghe (0/5), S. A. Jayasinghe (2), G. S. N. F. G. Jayasuriya (6/11), S. H. T. Kandamby (39/5), S. H. U. Karnain (19), H. G. J. M. Kulatunga (0/2), L. D. Madushanka (4), B. M. A. J. Mendis (54/16), C. Mendis (1), A. M. N. Munasinghe (5), E. M. D. Y. Munaweera (2/13), H. G. D. Nayanakantha (3), A. R. M. Opatha (5), S. P. Pasqual (2), S. S. Pathirana (18/5), A. K. Perera (4/2), K. G. Perera (1), H. S. M. Pieris (3), S. M. A. Priyanjan (23/3), M. Pushpakumara (3/1), C. A. K. Rajitha (0/3), R. L. B. Rambukwella (0/2), S. K. Ranasinghe (4), N. Ranatunga (2), N. L. K. Ratnayake (2), R. J. M. G. M. Rupasinghe (0/2), A. P. B. Tennekoon (4), M. H. Tissera (3), I. Udana (2/13), M. L. Udawatte (9/8), J. D. F. Vandersay (11/7), D. M. Vonhagt (1), A. P. Weerakkody (1), D. S. Weerakkody (3), S. Weerakoon (2), K. Weeraratne (15/5), S. R. D. Wettimuny (3), R. P. A. H. Wickremaratne (3).

Zimbabwe

R. D. Brown (7), K. M. Curran (11), S. G. Davies (4), K. G. Duers (6), E. A. Essop-Adam (1), D. A. G. Fletcher (6), T. N. Garwe (1), J. G. Heron (6), R. S. Higgins (11), V. R. Hogg (2), A. J. Ireland (26/1), L. M. Jongwe (22/8), R. Kaia (1), F. Kasteni (3), A. J. Mackay (3), N. Madziva (12/9), G. C. Martin (5), W. P. Masakadza (12/7), M. A. Meman (1), T. V. Mufambisi (6), C. T. Mutombodzi (11/5), T. Muzarabani (8/9), R. Ngarava (6), I. A. Nicolson (2), G. A. Paterson (10), G. E. Peckover (3), E. C. Rainsford (39/2), P. W. E. Rawson (10), H. P. Rinke (18), R. W. Sims (3), G. M. Strydom (12), C. Zhuwao (1/5).

Bangladesh

Abu Haider (0/3), Ahmed Kamal (1), Alam Talukdar (2), Aminul Islam jnr (1), Anisur Rahman (2), Arafat Sunny (16/10), Ather Ali Khan (19), Azhar Hussain (7), Dhiman Ghosh (14/1), Dolar Mahmud (7), Farhad Reza (34/13), Faruq Ahmed (7), Gazi Ashraf (7), Ghulam Faruq (5), Ghulam Nausher (9), Hafizur Rahman (2), Harunur Rashid (2), Jahangir Alam (3), Jahangir Badshah (5), Jamaluddin Ahmed (1), Mafizur Rahman (4), Mahbubur Rahman (1), Mazharul Haque (1), Minhazul Abedin (27), Mithun Ali (2/12), Mohammad Saifuddin (1/4), Moniruzzaman (2), Morshed Ali Khan (3), Mosharraf Hossain (5), Mukhtar Ali (0/1), Nadif Chowdhury (0/3), Nasir Ahmed (7), Nazmus Sadat (0/1), Neeyamur Rashid (2), Nurul Abedin (4), Rafiqul Alam (2), Raqibul Hasan snr (2), Rony Talukdar (0/1), Saiful Islam (7), Sajjad Ahmed (2), Samiur Rahman (2), Sanjamul Islam (1), Saqlain Sajib (0/1), Shafiuddin Ahmed (11), Shahidur Rahman (2), Shariful Haq (1), Sheikh Salahuddin (6), Tanveer Haider (2), Wahidul Gani (1), Zahid Razzak (3), Zakir Hassan (2).

PLAYERS APPEARING FOR MORE THAN ONE ONE-DAY/TWENTY20 INTERNATIONAL TEAM

The following players have played ODIs for the **African XI** in addition to their national side:

N. Boje (2), L. E. Bosman (1), J. Botha (2), M. V. Boucher (5), E. Chigumbura (3), A. B. de Villiers (5), H. H. Dippenaar (6), J. H. Kallis (2), J. M. Kemp (6), J. A. Morkel (2), M. Morkel (3), T. M. Odoyo (5), P. J. Ongondo (1), J. L. Ontong (1), S. M. Pollock (6), A. G. Prince (3), J. A. Rudolph (2), V. Sibanda (2), G. C. Smith (1), D. W. Steyn (2), H. H. Streak (2), T. Taibu (1), S. O. Tikolo (4), M. Zondeki (2). (Odoyo, Ongondo and Tikolo played for Kenya, who do not have Test status.)

The following players have played ODIs for the **Asian Cricket Council XI** in addition to their national side:

Abdul Razzaq (4), M. S. Dhoni (3), R. Dravid (1), C. R. D. Fernando (1), S. C. Ganguly (3), Harbhajan Singh (2), Inzamam-ul-Haq (3), S. T. Jayasuriya (4), D. P. M. D. Jayawardene (5), A. Kumble (2), Mashrafe bin Mortaza (2), Mohammad Ashraful (2), Mohammad Asif (3), Mohammad Rafique (2), Mohammad Yousuf (7), M. Muralitharan (4), A. Nehra (3), K. C. Sangakkara (4), V. Sehwag (7), Shahid Afridi (3), Shoaib Akhtar (3), W. U. Tharanga (1), W. P. U. J. C. Vaas (1), Yuvraj Singh (3), Zaheer Khan (6).

The following players have played ODIs for the **ICC World XI** in addition to their national side:

C. L. Cairns (1), R. Dravid (3), S. P. Fleming (1), A. Flintoff (3), C. H. Gayle (3), A. C. Gilchrist (1), D. Gough (1), M. L. Hayden (1), J. H. Kallis (3), B. C. Lara (4), G. D. McGrath (1), M. Muralitharan (3), M. Ntini (1), K. P. Pietersen (2), S. M. Pollock (3), R. T. Ponting (1), K. C. Sangakkara (3), V. Sehwag (3), Shahid Afridi (2), Shoaib Akhtar (2), D. L. Vettori (4), S. K. Warne (1).

The following players have played T20Is for the **World XI** in addition to their national side:

H. M. Amla (3), S. Badree (2), G. J. Bailey (1), P. D. Collingwood (1), B. C. J. Cutting (3), F. du Plessis (3), G. D. Elliott (1), Imran Tahir (3), D. A. Miller (3), M. Morkel (3), T. D. Paine (2), N. L. T. C. Perera (3), D. J. G. Sammy (2), Tamim Iqbal (3).

K. C. Wessels played ODIs (as well as Tests) for both Australia and South Africa. **D. R. Brown** played ODIs for England plus ODIs and T20Is for Scotland. **C. B. Lambert** played Tests and ODIs for West Indies and one ODI for USA. **E. C. Joyce** played ODIs and T20Is for both Ireland and England; **E. J. G. Morgan** ODIs for Ireland and all three formats for England; and **W. B. Rankin** ODIs and T20Is for Ireland and all three formats for England. **A. C. Cummins** played Tests and ODIs for West Indies and ODIs for Canada. **G. M. Hamilton** played Tests for England and ODIs for Scotland. **D. P. Nannes** played ODIs and T20Is for Australia and T20Is for the Netherlands. **L. Ronchi** played ODIs and T20Is for Australia and all three formats for New Zealand. **G. O. Jones** played all three formats for England and ODIs for Papua New Guinea. **R. E. van der Merwe** played ODIs and T20Is for South Africa and T20Is for the Netherlands. **R. J. Campbell** played ODIs for Australia and T20Is for Hong Kong.

ELITE TEST UMPIRES

The following umpires were on the ICC's elite panel in February 2018. The figures for Tests, one-day internationals and Twenty20 internationals and the Test Career dates refer to matches in which they have officiated as on-field umpires (excluding abandoned games). The totals of Tests are complete up to January 27, 2018, the totals of one-day internationals up to December 31, 2017, and Twenty20 internationals up to January 3, 2018.

	Country	*Born*	*Tests*	*Test Career*	*ODIs*	*T20Is*
Aleem Dar	P	6.6.1968	117	*2003–2017*	187	42
Dharmasena Handunnettige Deepthi Priyantha Kumar	SL	24.4.1971	51	*2010–2017*	82	22
Erasmus Marais	SA	27.2.1964	47*	*2009–2017*	74	26
Gaffaney Christopher Blair	NZ	30.11.1975	18	*2014–2017*	54	20
Gould Ian James	E	19.8.1957	64	*2008–2017*	122	37
Illingworth Richard Keith	E	23.8.1963	31*	*2012–2017*	55	16
Kettleborough Richard Allan	E	15.3.1973	50	*2010–2017*	74	22
Llong Nigel James	E	11.2.1969	49	*2007–2017*	112	32
Oxenford Bruce Nicholas James	A	5.3.1960	46	*2010–2017*	83	20
Ravi Sundaram	I	22.4.1966	24	*2013–2017*	33	18
Reiffel Paul Ronald	A	19.4.1966	35	2012–*2017*	54	16
Tucker Rodney James	A	28.8.1964	57	*2009–2017*	72	35

* *Includes one Test where he took over mid-match.*

BIRTHS AND DEATHS

OTHER CRICKETING NOTABLES

The following list shows the births and deaths of cricketers, and people associated with cricket, who have *not* played in men's Test matches.

Criteria for inclusion All non-Test players who have either (1) scored 20,000 first-class runs, or (2) taken 1,500 first-class wickets, or (3) achieved 750 dismissals, or (4) reached both 15,000 runs and 750 wickets. Also included are (5) the leading players who flourished before the start of Test cricket, (6) *Wisden* Cricketers of the Year who did not play Test cricket, and (7) others of merit or interest.

Names Where players were normally known by a name other than their first, this is underlined.

Teams Where only one team is listed, this is normally the one for which the player made most first-class appearances. Additional teams are listed only if the player appeared for them in more than 20 first-class matches, or if they are especially relevant to their career. School and university teams are not given unless especially relevant (e.g. for the schoolboys chosen as wartime Cricketers of the Year in the 1918 and 1919 *Wisdens*).

		Born	*Died*
Adams Percy Webster	Cheltenham College; *CY 1919*	5.9.1900	28.9.1962
Aird Ronald MC	Hampshire; sec. MCC 1953–62, pres. MCC 1968–69	4.5.1902	16.8.1986
Aislabie Benjamin	Surrey, secretary of MCC 1822–42	14.1.1774	2.6.1842
Alcock Charles William	Secretary of Surrey 1872–1907	2.12.1842	26.2.1907
Editor, Cricket *magazine, 1882–1907. Captain of Wanderers and England football teams.*			
Aleem Dar	Umpire in 117 Tests by January 2018	6.6.1968	
Alley William Edward	NSW, Somerset; Test umpire; *CY 1962*	3.2.1919	26.11.2004
Alleyne Mark Wayne	Gloucestershire; *CY 2001*	23.5.1968	
Altham Harry Surtees CBE	Surrey, Hants; historian; pres. MCC 1959–60	30.11.1888	11.3.1965
Arlott Leslie Thomas John OBE	Broadcaster and writer	25.2.1914	14.12.1991
Arthur John Michael	Griq. W, OFS; South Africa coach 2005–10, Australia coach 2011–13, Pakistan coach 2016–	17.5.1968	
Asghar Stanikzai Mohammad	Afghanistan	27.2.1987	
Ashdown William Henry	Kent	27.12.1898	15.9.1979
The only player to appear in English first-class cricket before and after the two world wars.			
Ash Eileen (*née* Whelan)	England women	30.10.1911	
Ashley-Cooper Frederick Samuel	Historian	22.3.1877	31.1.1932
Ashton *Sir* Hubert KBE MC	Cam U, Essex; pres. MCC 1960–61; *CY 1922*	13.2.1898	17.6.1979
Austin *Sir* Harold Bruce Gardiner	Barbados	15.7.1877	27.7.1943
Austin Ian David	Lancashire; *CY 1999*	30.5.1966	
Bailey Jack Arthur	Essex; secretary of MCC 1974–87	22.6.1930	
Bainbridge Philip	Gloucestershire, Durham; *CY 1986*	16.4.1958	
Bakewell Enid (*née* Turton)	England women	16.12.1940	
Bannister John David	Warwickshire; writer and broadcaster	23.8.1930	23.1.2016
Barker Gordon	Essex	6.7.1931	10.2.2006
Bartlett Hugh Tryon	Sussex; *CY 1939*	7.10.1914	26.6.1988
Bates Suzannah Wilson	New Zealand women	16.9.1987	
Bayliss Trevor Harley	NSW; SL coach 2007–11; Eng. coach 2015–	21.12.1962	
Beauclerk *Rev. Lord* Frederick	Middlesex, Surrey, MCC	8.5.1773	22.4.1850
Beldam George William	Middlesex; photographer	1.5.1868	23.11.1937
Beldham William ("Silver Billy")	Hambledon, Surrey	5.2.1766	26.2.1862
Beloff Michael Jacob QC	Head of ICC Code of Conduct Commission	18.4.1942	
Benkenstein Dale Martin	KwaZulu-Natal, Durham; *CY 2009*	9.6.1974	
Berry Anthony Scyld Ivens	Editor of *Wisden* 2008–11	28.4.1954	
Berry Leslie George	Leicestershire	28.4.1906	5.2.1985
Bird Harold Dennis ("Dickie") OBE	Yorkshire, Leics; umpire in 66 Tests	19.4.1933	
Blofeld Henry Calthorpe OBE	Cambridge Univ; broadcaster	23.9.1939	
Bond John David	Lancashire; *CY 1971*	6.5.1932	
Booth Roy	Yorkshire, Worcestershire	1.10.1926	
Bowden Brent Fraser ("Billy")	Umpire in 84 Tests	11.4.1963	
Bowley Frederick Lloyd	Worcestershire	9.11.1873	31.5.1943

		Born	*Died*
Bradshaw Keith	Tasmania; secretary/chief executive MCC 2006–11	2.10.1963	
Brewer Derek Michael	Secretary/chief executive MCC 2012–17	2.4.1958	
Briers Nigel Edwin	Leicestershire; *CY 1993*	15.1.1955	
Brittin Janette Ann MBE	England women	4.7.1959	11.9.2017
Brookes Wilfrid H.	Editor of *Wisden* 1936–39	5.12.1894	28.5.1955
Bryan John Lindsay	Kent; *CY 1922*	26.5.1896	23.4.1985
Buchanan John Marshall	Queensland; Australia coach 1999–2007	5.4.1953	
Bucknor Stephen Anthony	Umpire in a record 128 Tests	31.5.1946	
Bull Frederick George	Essex; *CY 1898*	2.4.1875	16.9.1910
Buller John Sydney MBE	Worcestershire; Test umpire	23.8.1909	7.8.1970
Burnup Cuthbert James	Kent; *CY 1903*	21.11.1875	5.4.1960
Caine Charles Stewart	Editor of *Wisden* 1926–33	28.10.1861	15.4.1933
Calder Harry Lawton	Cranleigh School; *CY 1918*	24.1.1901	15.9.1995
Cardus *Sir* John Frederick Neville	Writer	3.4.1888	27.2.1975
Chalke Stephen Robert	Writer	5.6.1948	
Chapple Glen	Lancashire; *CY 2012*	23.1.1974	
Chester Frank	Worcestershire; Test umpire	20.1.1895	8.4.1957
Stood in 48 Tests between 1924 and 1955, a record that lasted until 1992.			
Clark Belinda Jane	Australia women	10.9.1970	
Clark David Graham	Kent; president MCC 1977–78	27.1.1919	8.10.2013
Clarke Charles Giles CBE	Chairman ECB, 2007–15, pres. ECB, 2015–	29.5.1953	
Clarke William	Nottinghamshire; founded the All-England XI	24.12.1798	25.8.1856
Collier David Gordon OBE	Chief executive of ECB, 2005–14	22.4.1955	
Collins Arthur Edward Jeune	Clifton College	18.8.1885	11.11.1914
Made 628 in a house match in 1899, the highest score in any cricket until 2016.*			
Conan Doyle *Dr Sir* Arthur Ignatius	MCC	22.5.1859	7.7.1930
Creator of Sherlock Holmes; his only victim in first-class cricket was W. G. Grace.			
Connor Clare Joanne CBE	England women; administrator	1.9.1976	
Constant David John	Kent, Leics; first-class umpire 1969–2006	9.11.1941	
Cook Thomas Edwin Reed	Sussex	5.1.1901	15.1.1950
Cox George jnr	Sussex	23.8.1911	30.3.1985
Cox George snr	Sussex	29.11.1873	24.3.1949
Cozier Winston Anthony Lloyd	Broadcaster and writer	10.7.1940	11.5.2016
Dalmiya Jagmohan	Pres. BCCI 2001–04, 2015, pres. ICC 1997–2000	30.5.1940	20.9.2015
Davies Emrys	Glamorgan; Test umpire	27.6.1904	10.11.1975
Davison Brian Fettes	Rhodesia, Leics, Tasmania, Gloucestershire	21.12.1946	
Dawkes George Owen	Leicestershire, Derbyshire	19.7.1920	10.8.2006
Day Arthur Percival	Kent; *CY 1910*	10.4.1885	22.1.1969
de Lisle Timothy John March Phillipps	Editor of *Wisden* 2003	25.6.1962	
Dennett Edward George	Gloucestershire	27.4.1880	14.9.1937
Deutrom Warren Robert	Chief executive, Cricket Ireland 2006–	13.1.1970	
Dhanawade Pranav Prashant	K. C. Gandhi English School	13.5.2000	
Made the highest score in any cricket, 1,009, in a school match in Mumbai in January 2016.*			
Di Venuto Michael James	Tas., Derbys, Durham; Surrey coach 2016–	12.12.1973	
Domingo Russell Craig	South Africa coach 2013–17	30.8.1974	
Eagar Edward Patrick	Photographer	9.3.1944	
Edwards Charlotte Marie CBE	England women; *CY 2014*	17.12.1979	
Ehsan Mani	President of ICC 2003–06	23.3.1945	
Engel Matthew Lewis	Editor of *Wisden* 1993–2000, 2004–07	11.6.1951	
Farbrace Paul	Kent, Middx; SL coach 2014; Eng. asst coach 2014–	7.7.1967	
"Felix" (Nicholas Wanostrocht)	Kent, Surrey, All-England	4.10.1804	3.9.1876
Batsman, artist, author (Felix on the Bat) *and inventor of the Catapulta bowling machine.*			
Ferguson William Henry BEM	Scorer	6.6.1880	22.9.1957
Scorer and baggage-master for five Test teams on 43 tours over 52 years and "never lost a bag".			
Findlay William	Oxford U, Lancs; sec. MCC 1926–36	22.6.1880	19.6.1953
Firth John D'Ewes Evelyn	Winchester College; *CY 1918*	21.2.1900	21.9.1957
Fitzpatrick Cathryn Lorraine	Australia women	4.3.1968	
Fletcher Duncan Andrew Gwynne OBE	Zimbabwe; England coach 1999–2007; India coach 2011–15	27.9.1948	
Ford Graham Xavier	Natal B; South Africa coach 1999–2002; Sri Lanka coach 2012–14, 2016–17	16.11.1960	

		Born	Died
Foster Henry Knollys	Worcestershire; *CY 1911*	30.10.1873	23.6.1950
Frindall William Howard MBE	Statistician	3.3.1939	30.1.2009
Frith David Edward John	Writer	16.3.1937	
Gibbons Harold Harry Ian Haywood	Worcestershire	8.10.1904	16.2.1973
Gibson Clement Herbert	Eton, Cam. U, Sussex, Argentina; *CY 1918*	23.8.1900	31.12.1976
Gibson Norman Alan Stanley	Writer	28.5.1923	10.4.1997
Gore Adrian Clements	Eton College; *CY 1919*	14.5.1900	7.6.1990
Gould Ian James	Middlesex, Sussex; Test umpire	19.8.1957	
Grace *Mrs* Martha	Mother and cricketing mentor of WG	18.7.1812	25.7.1884
Grace William Gilbert jnr	Gloucestershire; son of WG	6.7.1874	2.3.1905
Graveney David Anthony	Gloucestershire, Somerset, Durham	2.1.1953	
Chairman of England selectors 1997–2008.			
Graves Colin James	Chairman of ECB, 2015–	22.1.1948	
Gray James Roy	Hampshire	19.5.1926	31.10.2016
Gray Malcolm Alexander	President of ICC 2000–03	30.5.1940	
Green David Michael	Lancashire, Gloucestershire; *CY 1969*	10.11.1939	19.3.2016
Grieves Kenneth James	New South Wales, Lancashire	27.8.1925	3.1.1992
Griffith Mike Grenville	Sussex, Camb. Univ; president MCC 2012–13	25.11.1943	
Haigh Gideon Clifford Jeffrey Davidson	Writer	29.12.1965	
Hair Darrell Bruce	Umpire in 78 Tests	30.9.1952	
Hall Louis	Yorkshire; *CY 1890*	1.11.1852	19.11.1915
Hallam Albert William	Lancashire, Nottinghamshire; *CY 1908*	12.11.1869	24.7.1940
Hallam Maurice Raymond	Leicestershire	10.9.1931	1.1.2000
Hallows James	Lancashire; *CY 1905*	14.11.1873	20.5.1910
Hamilton Duncan	Writer	24.12.1958	
Harper Daryl John	Umpire in 95 Tests	23.10.1951	
Harrison Tom William	Derbyshire; chief executive of ECB 2015–	11.12.1971	
Hartley Alfred	Lancashire; *CY 1911*	11.4.1879	9.10.1918
Harvey Ian Joseph	Victoria, Gloucestershire; *CY 2004*	10.4.1972	
Hedges Lionel Paget	Tonbridge School, Kent, Glos; *CY 1919*	13.7.1900	12.1.1933
Henderson Robert	Surrey; *CY 1890*	30.3.1865	28.1.1931
Hesson Michael James	New Zealand coach 2012–	30.10.1974	
Hewett Herbert Tremenheere	Somerset; *CY 1893*	25.5.1864	4.3.1921
Heyhoe Flint *Baroness* [Rachael] OBE	England women	11.6.1939	18.1.2017
Hide Mary Edith ("Molly")	England women	24.10.1913	10.9.1995
Hodson Richard Phillip	Cambridge Univ; president MCC 2011–12	26.4.1951	
Horton Henry	Hampshire	18.4.1923	2.11.1998
Howard Cecil Geoffrey	Middlesex; administrator	14.2.1909	8.11.2002
Hughes David Paul	Lancashire; *CY 1988*	13.5.1947	
Huish Frederick Henry	Kent	15.11.1869	16.3.1957
Humpage Geoffrey William	Warwickshire; *CY 1985*	24.4.1954	
Hunter David	Yorkshire	23.2.1860	11.1.1927
Hutchinson James Metcalf	Derbyshire	29.11.1896	7.11.2000
Believed to be the longest-lived first-class cricketer, at 103 years 344 days.			
Ingleby-Mackenzie Alexander Colin David OBE	Hants; pres. MCC 1996–98	15.9.1933	9.3.2006
Iremonger James	Nottinghamshire; *CY 1903*	5.3.1876	25.3.1956
Isaac Alan Raymond	Chair NZC 2008–10; president ICC 2012–14	20.1.1952	
Jackson Victor Edward	NSW, Leicestershire	25.10.1916	30.1.1965
James Cyril Lionel Robert ("Nello")	Writer	4.1.1901	31.5.1989
Jesty Trevor Edward	Hants, Griq W., Surrey, Lancs; umpire; *CY 1983*	2.6.1948	
Johnson Paul	Nottinghamshire	24.4.1965	
Johnston Brian Alexander CBE MC	Broadcaster	24.6.1912	5.1.1994
Jones Alan MBE	Glamorgan; *CY 1978*	4.11.1938	
Played once for England, against Rest of World in 1970, regarded at the time as a Test match.			
Joyce Edmund Christopher	Middlesex, Sussex, England, Ireland	22.9.1978	
Kilburn James Maurice	Writer	8.7.1909	28.8.1993
King John Barton	Philadelphia	19.10.1873	17.10.1965
"Beyond question the greatest all-round cricketer produced by America" – Wisden.			
Knight Heather Clare OBE	England women; *CY 2018*	26.12.1990	

		Born	*Died*
Knight Roger David Verdon OBE	Surrey, Glos, Sussex; sec. MCC 1994–2005, pres. MCC 2015–16	6.9.1946	
Knight W. H.	Editor of *Wisden* 1864–79	29.11.1812	16.8.1879
Koertzen Rudolf Eric	Umpire in 108 Tests	26.3.1949	
Lacey *Sir* Francis Eden	Hants; secretary of MCC 1898–1926	19.10.1859	26.5.1946
Lamb Timothy Michael	Middx, Northants; ECB chief exec 1997–2004	24.3.1953	
Langridge John George MBE	Sussex; Test umpire; *CY 1950*	10.2.1910	27.6.1999
Lanning Meghann Moira	Australia women	25.3.1992	
Lavender Guy William	Secretary/chief executive MCC 2017–	8.7.1967	
Lee Peter Granville	Northamptonshire, Lancashire; *CY 1976*	27.8.1945	
Lillywhite Frederick William	Sussex	13.6.1792	21.8.1854
Long Arnold	Surrey, Sussex	18.12.1940	
Lord Thomas	Middlesex; founder of Lord's	23.11.1755	13.1.1832
Lorgat Haroon	Chief executive of ICC 2008–12	26.5.1960	
Lyon Beverley Hamilton	Gloucestershire; *CY 1931*	19.1.1902	22.6.1970
McEwan Kenneth Scott	Eastern Province, Essex; *CY 1978*	16.7.1952	
McGilvray Alan David MBE	NSW; broadcaster	6.12.1909	17.7.1996
Maclagan Myrtle Ethel	England women	2.4.1911	11.3.1993
MacLaurin *Lord* [Ian Charter]	Chair of ECB 1997–2002, pres. MCC 2017-18	30.3.1937	
Manohar Shashank Vyankatesh	Pres. BCCI 2008–11, 2015–16; ICC chairman 2015–	29.9.1957	
Marlar Robin Geoffrey	Sussex; writer; pres. MCC 2005–06	2.1.1931	
Marshal Alan	Surrey; *CY 1909*	12.6.1883	23.7.1915
Martin-Jenkins Christopher Dennis Alexander MBE	Writer; broadcaster; pres. MCC 2010–11	20.1.1945	1.1.2013
Maxwell James Edward	Commentator	28.7.1950	
Mendis Gehan Dixon	Sussex, Lancashire	20.4.1955	
Mercer John	Sussex, Glamorgan; coach and scorer; *CY 1927*	22.4.1893	31.8.1987
Meyer Rollo John Oliver OBE	Somerset	15.3.1905	9.3.1991
Modi Lalit Kumar	Chairman, Indian Premier League 2008–10	29.11.1963	
Mohammad Nabi Eisakhil	Afghanistan	7.3.1985	
Moles Andrew James	Warwickshire, NZ coach 2008–09	12.2.1961	
Moores Peter	Sussex; England coach 2007–09, 2014–15	18.12.1962	
Moorhouse Geoffrey	Writer	29.11.1931	26.11.2009
Morgan Derek Clifton	Derbyshire	26.2.1929	4.11.2017
Morgan Frederick David OBE	Chair ECB 2003–07, pres. ICC 2008–10, pres. MCC 2014–15	6.10.1937	
Mynn Alfred	Kent, All-England	19.1.1807	1.11.1861
Neale Phillip Anthony	Worcestershire; England manager; *CY 1989*	5.6.1954	
Newman John Alfred	Hampshire	12.11.1884	21.12.1973
Newstead John Thomas	Yorkshire; *CY 1909*	8.9.1877	25.3.1952
Nicholas Mark Charles Jefford	Hampshire; broadcaster	29.9.1957	
Nicholls Ronald Bernard	Gloucestershire	4.12.1933	21.7.1994
Nielsen Timothy John	South Australia; Australia coach 2007–11	5.5.1968	
Nixon Paul Andrew	Leicestershire, Kent	21.10.1970	
Nyren John	Hants; author of *The Young Cricketer's Tutor*, 1833	15.12.1764	28.6.1837
Nyren Richard	Hants; Landlord Bat & Ball Inn, Broadhalfpenny Down	1734	25.4.1797
Ontong Rodney Craig	Border, Glamorgan, N. Transvaal	9.9.1955	
Ormrod Joseph Alan	Worcestershire, Lancashire	22.12.1942	
Pardon Charles Frederick	Editor of *Wisden* 1887–90	28.3.1850	18.4.1890
Pardon Sydney Herbert	Editor of *Wisden* 1891–1925	23.9.1855	20.11.1925
Parks Henry William	Sussex	18.7.1906	7.5.1984
Parr George	Notts, captain/manager of All-England XI	22.5.1826	23.6.1891
Partridge Norman Ernest	Malvern College, Warwickshire; *CY 1919*	10.8.1900	10.3.1982
Pawar Sharadchandra Govindrao	Pres. BCCI 2005–08, ICC 2010–12	12.12.1940	
Payton Wilfred Richard Daniel	Nottinghamshire	13.2.1882	2.5.1943
Pearce Thomas Neill	Essex; administrator	3.11.1905	10.4.1994
Pearson Frederick	Worcestershire	23.9.1880	10.11.1963
Perrin Percival Albert ("Peter")	Essex; *CY 1905*	26.5.1876	20.11.1945

		Born	*Died*
Perry Ellyse Alexandra	Australia women	3.11.1990	
Pilch Fuller	Norfolk, Kent	17.3.1804	1.5.1870
"The best batsman that has ever yet appeared" – Arthur Haygarth, 1862.			
Porter James Alexander	Essex; *CY 2018*	25.5.1993	
Porterfield William Thomas Stuart	Warwicks, Glos, Ireland	6.9.1984	
Preston Hubert	Editor of *Wisden* 1944–51	16.12.1868	6.8.1960
Preston Norman MBE	Editor of *Wisden* 1952–80	18.3.1903	6.3.1980
Pritchard Thomas Leslie	Wellington, Warwickshire, Kent	10.3.1917	22.8.2017
Rait Kerr *Col.* Rowan Scrope	Europeans; sec. MCC 1936–52	13.4.1891	2.4.1961
Raj Mithali Dorai	India women	3.12.1982	
Rashid Khan	Afghanistan	20.9.1998	
Reeves William	Essex; Test umpire	22.1.1875	22.3.1944
Rice Clive Edward Butler	Transvaal, Nottinghamshire; *CY 1981*	23.7.1949	28.7.2015
Richardson Alan	Warwicks, Middx, Worcs; *CY 2012*	6.5.1975	
Robertson-Glasgow Raymond Charles	Somerset; writer	15.7.1901	4.3.1965
Robins Derrick Harold	Warwickshire; tour promoter	27.6.1914	3.5.2004
Robinson Mark Andrew OBE	Northants, Yorkshire, Sussex, coach	23.11.1966	
Robinson Raymond John	Writer	8.7.1905	6.7.1982
Roebuck Peter Michael	Somerset; writer; *CY 1988*	6.3.1956	12.11.2011
Rotherham Gerard Alexander	Rugby School, Warwickshire; *CY 1918*	28.5.1899	31.1.1985
Sainsbury Peter James	Hampshire; *CY 1974*	13.6.1934	12.7.2014
Samson Andrew William	Statistician	17.2.1964	
Sciver Natalie Ruth	England women; *CY 2018*	20.8.1992	
Scott Stanley Winckworth	Middlesex; *CY 1893*	24.3.1854	8.12.1933
Sellers Arthur Brian MBE	Yorkshire; *CY 1940*	5.3.1907	20.2.1981
Seymour James	Kent	25.10.1879	30.9.1930
Shepherd David Robert MBE	Gloucestershire; umpire in 92 Tests	27.12.1940	27.10.2009
Shepherd Donald John	Glamorgan; *CY 1970*	12.8.1927	18.8.2017
Shrubsole Anya MBE	England women; *CY 2018*	7.12.1991	
Silk Dennis Raoul Whitehall CBE	Somerset; pres. MCC 1992–94	8.10.1931	
Simmons Jack MBE	Lancashire, Tasmania; *CY 1985*	28.3.1941	
Skelding Alexander	Leics; first-class umpire 1931–58	5.9.1886	17.4.1960
Smith Sydney Gordon	Northamptonshire; *CY 1915*	15.1.1881	25.10.1963
Smith William Charles ("Razor")	Surrey; *CY 1911*	4.10.1877	15.7.1946
Southerton Sydney James	Editor of *Wisden* 1934–35	7.7.1874	12.3.1935
Speed Malcolm Walter	Chief executive of ICC 2001–08	14.9.1948	
Spencer Thomas William OBE	Kent; Test umpire	22.3.1914	1.11.1995
Srinivasan Narayanaswami	Pres. BCCI 2011–14; ICC chair 2014–15	3.1.1945	
Stephenson Franklyn Dacosta	Nottinghamshire, Sussex; *CY 1989*	8.4.1959	
Stephenson Harold William	Somerset	18.7.1920	23.4.2008
Stephenson Heathfield Harman	Surrey, All-England	3.5.1832	17.12.1896
Captained first English team to Australia, 1861-62; umpired first Test in England, 1880.			
Stephenson *Lt-Col.* John Robin CBE	Secretary of MCC 1987–93	25.2.1931	2.6.2003
Studd *Sir* John Edward Kynaston	Middlesex	26.7.1858	14.1.1944
Lord Mayor of London 1928–29; president of MCC 1930.			
Surridge Walter Stuart	Surrey; *CY 1953*	3.9.1917	13.4.1992
Sutherland James Alexander	Victoria; CEO Cricket Australia 2001–	14.7.1965	
Suttle Kenneth George	Sussex	25.8.1928	25.3.2005
Swanton Ernest William ("Jim") CBE	Middlesex; writer	11.2.1907	22.1.2000
Tarrant Francis Alfred	Victoria, Middlesex; *CY 1908*	11.12.1880	29.1.1951
Taufel Simon James Arnold	Umpire in 74 Tests	21.1.1971	
Taylor Brian ("Tonker")	Essex; *CY 1972*	19.6.1932	12.6.2017
Taylor Samantha Claire MBE	England women; *CY 2009*	25.9.1975	
Taylor Tom Launcelot	Yorkshire; *CY 1901*	25.5.1878	16.3.1960
Thornton Charles Inglis ("Buns")	Middlesex	20.3.1850	10.12.1929
Timms John Edward	Northamptonshire	3.11.1906	18.5.1980
Todd Leslie John	Kent	19.6.1907	20.8.1967
Tunnicliffe John	Yorkshire; *CY 1901*	26.8.1866	11.7.1948
Turner Francis Michael MBE	Leicestershire; administrator	8.8.1934	21.7.2015
Turner Robert Julian	Somerset	25.11.1967	

		Born	*Died*
Ufton Derek Gilbert	Kent	31.5.1928	
van der Bijl Vintcent Adriaan Pieter	Natal, Middx, Transvaal; *CY 1981*	19.3.1948	
Virgin Roy Thomas	Somerset, Northamptonshire; *CY 1971*	26.8.1939	
Ward William	Hampshire	24.7.1787	30.6.1849
Scorer of the first recorded double-century: 278 for MCC v Norfolk, 1820.			
Wass Thomas George	Nottinghamshire; *CY 1908*	26.12.1873	27.10.1953
Watson Frank	Lancashire	17.9.1898	1.2.1976
Webber Roy	Statistician	23.7.1914	14.11.1962
Weigall Gerald John Villiers	Kent; coach	19.10.1870	17.5.1944
West George H.	Editor of *Wisden* 1880–86	1851	6.10.1896
Wheatley Oswald Stephen CBE	Warwickshire, Glamorgan; *CY 1969*	28.5.1935	
Whitaker Edgar Haddon OBE	Editor of *Wisden* 1940–43	30.8.1908	5.1.1982
Wight Peter Bernard	Somerset; umpire	25.6.1930	31.12.2015
Wilson Elizabeth Rebecca ("Betty")	Australia women	21.11.1921	22.1.2010
Wilson John Victor	Yorkshire; *CY 1961*	17.1.1921	5.6.2008
Wisden John	Sussex	5.9.1826	5.4.1884
"The Little Wonder"; founder of Wisden Cricketers' Almanack, *1864.*			
Wood Cecil John Burditt	Leicestershire	21.11.1875	5.6.1960
Woodcock John Charles OBE	Writer; editor of *Wisden* 1981–86	7.8.1926	
Wooller Wilfred	Glamorgan	20.11.1912	10.3.1997
Wright Graeme Alexander	Editor of *Wisden* 1987–92, 2001–02	23.4.1943	
Wright Levi George	Derbyshire; *CY 1906*	15.1.1862	11.1.1953
Young Douglas Martin	Worcestershire, Gloucestershire	15.4.1924	18.6.1993

CRICKETERS OF THE YEAR, 1889–2018

1889 *Six Great Bowlers of the Year:* J. Briggs, J. J. Ferris, G. A. Lohmann, R. Peel, C. T. B. Turner, S. M. J. Woods.
1890 *Nine Great Batsmen of the Year:* R. Abel, W. Barnes, W. Gunn, L. Hall, R. Henderson, J. M. Read, A. Shrewsbury, F. H. Sugg, A. Ward.
1891 *Five Great Wicketkeepers:* J. M. Blackham, G. MacGregor, R. Pilling, M. Sherwin, H. Wood.
1892 *Five Great Bowlers:* W. Attewell, J. T. Hearne, F. Martin, A. W. Mold, J. W. Sharpe.
1893 *Five Batsmen of the Year:* H. T. Hewett, L. C. H. Palairet, W. W. Read, S. W. Scott, A. E. Stoddart.
1894 *Five All-Round Cricketers:* G. Giffen, A. Hearne, F. S. Jackson, G. H. S. Trott, E. Wainwright.
1895 *Five Young Batsmen of the Season:* W. Brockwell, J. T. Brown, C. B. Fry, T. W. Hayward, A. C. MacLaren.
1896 W. G. Grace.
1897 *Five Cricketers of the Season:* S. E. Gregory, A. A. Lilley, K. S. Ranjitsinhji, T. Richardson, H. Trumble.
1898 *Five Cricketers of the Year:* F. G. Bull, W. R. Cuttell, N. F. Druce, G. L. Jessop, J. R. Mason.
1899 *Five Great Players of the Season:* W. H. Lockwood, W. Rhodes, W. Storer, C. L. Townsend, A. E. Trott.
1900 *Five Cricketers of the Season:* J. Darling, C. Hill, A. O. Jones, M. A. Noble, Major R. M. Poore.
1901 *Mr R. E. Foster and Four Yorkshiremen:* R. E. Foster, S. Haigh, G. H. Hirst, T. L. Taylor, J. Tunnicliffe.
1902 L. C. Braund, C. P. McGahey, F. Mitchell, W. G. Quaife, J. T. Tyldesley.
1903 W. W. Armstrong, C. J. Burnup, J. Iremonger, J. J. Kelly, V. T. Trumper.
1904 C. Blythe, J. Gunn, A. E. Knight, W. Mead, P. F. Warner.
1905 B. J. T. Bosanquet, E. A. Halliwell, J. Hallows, P. A. Perrin, R. H. Spooner.
1906 D. Denton, W. S. Lees, G. J. Thompson, J. Vine, L. G. Wright.
1907 J. N. Crawford, A. Fielder, E. G. Hayes, K. L. Hutchings, N. A. Knox.
1908 A. W. Hallam, R. O. Schwarz, F. A. Tarrant, A. E. E. Vogler, T. G. Wass.
1909 *Lord Hawke and Four Cricketers of the Year:* W. Brearley, Lord Hawke, J. B. Hobbs, A. Marshal, J. T. Newstead.
1910 W. Bardsley, S. F. Barnes, D. W. Carr, A. P. Day, V. S. Ransford.
1911 H. K. Foster, A. Hartley, C. B. Llewellyn, W. C. Smith, F. E. Woolley.
1912 *Five Members of MCC's team in Australia:* F. R. Foster, J. W. Hearne, S. P. Kinneir, C. P. Mead, H. Strudwick.
1913 *Special Portrait:* John Wisden.
1914 M. W. Booth, G. Gunn, J. W. Hitch, A. E. Relf, Hon. L. H. Tennyson.
1915 J. W. H. T. Douglas, P. G. H. Fender, H. T. W. Hardinge, D. J. Knight, S. G. Smith.
1916–17 No portraits appeared.
1918 *School Bowlers of the Year:* H. L. Calder, J. D. E. Firth, C. H. Gibson, G. A. Rotherham, G. T. S. Stevens.
1919 *Five Public School Cricketers of the Year:* P. W. Adams, A. P. F. Chapman, A. C. Gore, L. P. Hedges, N. E. Partridge.
1920 *Five Batsmen of the Year:* A. Ducat, E. H. Hendren, P. Holmes, H. Sutcliffe, E. Tyldesley.
1921 *Special Portrait:* P. F. Warner.
1922 H. Ashton, J. L. Bryan, J. M. Gregory, C. G. Macartney, E. A. McDonald.
1923 A. W. Carr, A. P. Freeman, C. W. L. Parker, A. C. Russell, A. Sandham.
1924 *Five Bowlers of the Year:* A. E. R. Gilligan, R. Kilner, G. G. Macaulay, C. H. Parkin, M. W. Tate.
1925 R. H. Catterall, J. C. W. MacBryan, H. W. Taylor, R. K. Tyldesley, W. W. Whysall.
1926 *Special Portrait:* J. B. Hobbs.
1927 G. Geary, H. Larwood, J. Mercer, W. A. Oldfield, W. M. Woodfull.
1928 R. C. Blunt, C. Hallows, W. R. Hammond, D. R. Jardine, V. W. C. Jupp.
1929 L. E. G. Ames, G. Duckworth, M. Leyland, S. J. Staples, J. C. White.
1930 E. H. Bowley, K. S. Duleepsinhji, H. G. Owen-Smith, R. W. V. Robins, R. E. S. Wyatt.
1931 D. G. Bradman, C. V. Grimmett, B. H. Lyon, I. A. R. Peebles, M. J. Turnbull.

1932 W. E. Bowes, C. S. Dempster, James Langridge, Nawab of Pataudi snr, H. Verity.
1933 W. E. Astill, F. R. Brown, A. S. Kennedy, C. K. Nayudu, W. Voce.
1934 A. H. Bakewell, G. A. Headley, M. S. Nichols, L. F. Townsend, C. F. Walters.
1935 S. J. McCabe, W. J. O'Reilly, G. A. E. Paine, W. H. Ponsford, C. I. J. Smith.
1936 H. B. Cameron, E. R. T. Holmes, B. Mitchell, D. Smith, A. W. Wellard.
1937 C. J. Barnett, W. H. Copson, A. R. Gover, V. M. Merchant, T. S. Worthington.
1938 T. W. J. Goddard, J. Hardstaff jnr, L. Hutton, J. H. Parks, E. Paynter.
1939 H. T. Bartlett, W. A. Brown, D. C. S. Compton, K. Farnes, A. Wood.
1940 L. N. Constantine, W. J. Edrich, W. W. Keeton, A. B. Sellers, D. V. P. Wright.
1941–46 No portraits appeared.
1947 A. V. Bedser, L. B. Fishlock, V. (M. H.) Mankad, T. P. B. Smith, C. Washbrook.
1948 M. P. Donnelly, A. Melville, A. D. Nourse, J. D. Robertson, N. W. D. Yardley.
1949 A. L. Hassett, W. A. Johnston, R. R. Lindwall, A. R. Morris, D. Tallon.
1950 T. E. Bailey, R. O. Jenkins, John Langridge, R. T. Simpson, B. Sutcliffe.
1951 T. G. Evans, S. Ramadhin, A. L. Valentine, E. D. Weekes, F. M. M. Worrell.
1952 R. Appleyard, H. E. Dollery, J. C. Laker, P. B. H. May, E. A. B. Rowan.
1953 H. Gimblett, T. W. Graveney, D. S. Sheppard, W. S. Surridge, F. S. Trueman.
1954 R. N. Harvey, G. A. R. Lock, K. R. Miller, J. H. Wardle, W. Watson.
1955 B. Dooland, Fazal Mahmood, W. E. Hollies, J. B. Statham, G. E. Tribe.
1956 M. C. Cowdrey, D. J. Insole, D. J. McGlew, H. J. Tayfield, F. H. Tyson.
1957 D. Brookes, J. W. Burke, M. J. Hilton, G. R. A. Langley, P. E. Richardson.
1958 P. J. Loader, A. J. McIntyre, O. G. Smith, M. J. Stewart, C. L. Walcott.
1959 H. L. Jackson, R. E. Marshall, C. A. Milton, J. R. Reid, D. Shackleton.
1960 K. F. Barrington, D. B. Carr, R. Illingworth, G. Pullar, M. J. K. Smith.
1961 N. A. T. Adcock, E. R. Dexter, R. A. McLean, R. Subba Row, J. V. Wilson.
1962 W. E. Alley, R. Benaud, A. K. Davidson, W. M. Lawry, N. C. O'Neill.
1963 D. Kenyon, Mushtaq Mohammad, P. H. Parfitt, P. J. Sharpe, F. J. Titmus.
1964 D. B. Close, C. C. Griffith, C. C. Hunte, R. B. Kanhai, G. S. Sobers.
1965 G. Boycott, P. J. Burge, J. A. Flavell, G. D. McKenzie, R. B. Simpson.
1966 K. C. Bland, J. H. Edrich, R. C. Motz, P. M. Pollock, R. G. Pollock.
1967 R. W. Barber, B. L. D'Oliveira, C. Milburn, J. T. Murray, S. M. Nurse.
1968 Asif Iqbal, Hanif Mohammad, K. Higgs, J. M. Parks, Nawab of Pataudi jnr.
1969 J. G. Binks, D. M. Green, B. A. Richards, D. L. Underwood, O. S. Wheatley.
1970 B. F. Butcher, A. P. E. Knott, Majid Khan, M. J. Procter, D. J. Shepherd.
1971 J. D. Bond, C. H. Lloyd, B. W. Luckhurst, G. M. Turner, R. T. Virgin.
1972 G. G. Arnold, B. S. Chandrasekhar, L. R. Gibbs, B. Taylor, Zaheer Abbas.
1973 G. S. Chappell, D. K. Lillee, R. A. L. Massie, J. A. Snow, K. R. Stackpole.
1974 K. D. Boyce, B. E. Congdon, K. W. R. Fletcher, R. C. Fredericks, P. J. Sainsbury.
1975 D. L. Amiss, M. H. Denness, N. Gifford, A. W. Greig, A. M. E. Roberts.
1976 I. M. Chappell, P. G. Lee, R. B. McCosker, D. S. Steele, R. A. Woolmer.
1977 J. M. Brearley, C. G. Greenidge, M. A. Holding, I. V. A. Richards, R. W. Taylor.
1978 I. T. Botham, M. Hendrick, A. Jones, K. S. McEwan, R. G. D. Willis.
1979 D. I. Gower, J. K. Lever, C. M. Old, C. T. Radley, J. N. Shepherd.
1980 J. Garner, S. M. Gavaskar, G. A. Gooch, D. W. Randall, B. C. Rose.
1981 K. J. Hughes, R. D. Jackman, A. J. Lamb, C. E. B. Rice, V. A. P. van der Bijl.
1982 T. M. Alderman, A. R. Border, R. J. Hadlee, Javed Miandad, R. W. Marsh.
1983 Imran Khan, T. E. Jesty, A. I. Kallicharran, Kapil Dev, M. D. Marshall.
1984 M. Amarnath, J. V. Coney, J. E. Emburey, M. W. Gatting, C. L. Smith.
1985 M. D. Crowe, H. A. Gomes, G. W. Humpage, J. Simmons, S. Wettimuny.
1986 P. Bainbridge, R. M. Ellison, C. J. McDermott, N. V. Radford, R. T. Robinson.
1987 J. H. Childs, G. A. Hick, D. B. Vengsarkar, C. A. Walsh, J. J. Whitaker.
1988 J. P. Agnew, N. A. Foster, D. P. Hughes, P. M. Roebuck, Salim Malik.
1989 K. J. Barnett, P. J. L. Dujon, P. A. Neale, F. D. Stephenson, S. R. Waugh.
1990 S. J. Cook, D. M. Jones, R. C. Russell, R. A. Smith, M. A. Taylor.
1991 M. A. Atherton, M. Azharuddin, A. R. Butcher, D. L. Haynes, M. E. Waugh.
1992 C. E. L. Ambrose, P. A. J. DeFreitas, A. A. Donald, R. B. Richardson, Waqar Younis.
1993 N. E. Briers, M. D. Moxon, I. D. K. Salisbury, A. J. Stewart, Wasim Akram.
1994 D. C. Boon, I. A. Healy, M. G. Hughes, S. K. Warne, S. L. Watkin.
1995 B. C. Lara, D. E. Malcolm, T. A. Munton, S. J. Rhodes, K. C. Wessels.
1996 D. G. Cork, P. A. de Silva, A. R. C. Fraser, A. Kumble, D. A. Reeve.
1997 S. T. Jayasuriya, Mushtaq Ahmed, Saeed Anwar, P. V. Simmons, S. R. Tendulkar.

1998 M. T. G. Elliott, S. G. Law, G. D. McGrath, M. P. Maynard, G. P. Thorpe.
1999 I. D. Austin, D. Gough, M. Muralitharan, A. Ranatunga, J. N. Rhodes.
2000 C. L. Cairns, R. Dravid, L. Klusener, T. M. Moody, Saqlain Mushtaq.
Cricketers of the Century D. G. Bradman, G. S. Sobers, J. B. Hobbs, S. K. Warne, I. V. A. Richards.
2001 M. W. Alleyne, M. P. Bicknell, A. R. Caddick, J. L. Langer, D. S. Lehmann.
2002 A. Flower, A. C. Gilchrist, J. N. Gillespie, V. V. S. Laxman, D. R. Martyn.
2003 M. L. Hayden, A. J. Hollioake, N. Hussain, S. M. Pollock, M. P. Vaughan.
2004 C. J. Adams, A. Flintoff, I. J. Harvey, G. Kirsten, G. C. Smith.
2005 A. F. Giles, S. J. Harmison, R. W. T. Key, A. J. Strauss, M. E. Trescothick.
2006 M. J. Hoggard, S. P. Jones, B. Lee, K. P. Pietersen, R. T. Ponting.
2007 P. D. Collingwood, D. P. M. D. Jayawardene, Mohammad Yousuf, M. S. Panesar, M. R. Ramprakash.
2008 I. R. Bell, S. Chanderpaul, O. D. Gibson, R. J. Sidebottom, Zaheer Khan.
2009 J. M. Anderson, D. M. Benkenstein, M. V. Boucher, N. D. McKenzie, S. C. Taylor.
2010 S. C. J. Broad, M. J. Clarke, G. Onions, M. J. Prior, G. P. Swann.
2011 E. J. G. Morgan, C. M. W. Read, Tamim Iqbal, I. J. L. Trott.
2012 T. T. Bresnan, G. Chapple, A. N. Cook, A. Richardson, K. C. Sangakkara.
2013 H. M. Amla, N. R. D. Compton, J. H. Kallis, M. N. Samuels, D. W. Steyn.
2014 S. Dhawan, C. M. Edwards, R. J. Harris, C. J. L. Rogers, J. E. Root.
2015 M. M. Ali, G. S. Ballance, A. Lyth, A. D. Mathews, J. S. Patel.
2016 J. M. Bairstow, B. B. McCullum, S. P. D. Smith, B. A. Stokes, K. S. Williamson.
2017 B. M. Duckett, Misbah-ul-Haq, T. S. Roland-Jones, C. R. Woakes, Younis Khan.
2018 S. D. Hope, H. C. Knight, J. A. Porter, N. R. Sciver, A. Shrubsole.

From 2001 to 2003 the award was made on the basis of all cricket round the world, not just the English season. This ended in 2004 with the start of Wisden's *Leading Cricketer in the World award. Sanath Jayasuriya was chosen in 1997 for his influence on the English season, stemming from the 1996 World Cup. In 2011, only four were named after the Lord's spot-fixing scandal made the selection of one of the five unsustainable.*

CRICKETERS OF THE YEAR: AN ANALYSIS

The special portrait of John Wisden in 1913 marked the 50th anniversary of his retirement as a player – and the 50th edition of the Almanack. Wisden died in 1884. The special portraits of P. F. Warner in 1921 and J. B. Hobbs in 1926 were in addition to their earlier selection as a Cricketer of the Year in 1904 and 1909 respectively. These three special portraits and the Cricketers of the Century in 2000 are excluded from the following analysis.

The five players selected to be Cricketers of the Year for 2018 bring the number chosen since selection began in 1889 to 595. They have been chosen from 40 different teams, as follows:

Derbyshire	13	Northants	15	Australians	73	Staffordshire	1
Durham	8	Nottinghamshire	29	South Africans	28	Cheltenham College	1
Essex	25	Somerset	19	West Indians	27	Cranleigh School	1
Glamorgan	12	Surrey	49	New Zealanders	10	Eton College	2
Gloucestershire	17	Sussex	21	Indians	15	Malvern College	1
Hampshire	16	Warwickshire	25	Pakistanis	14	Rugby School	1
Kent	26	Worcestershire	17	Sri Lankans	7	Tonbridge School	1
Lancashire	34	Yorkshire	47	Zimbabweans	1	Univ Coll School	1
Leicestershire	8	Oxford Univ	7	Bangladeshis	1	Uppingham School	1
Middlesex	30	Cambridge Univ	10	England Women	5	Winchester College	1

Schoolboys were chosen in 1918 and 1919 when first-class cricket was suspended due to war. The total of sides comes to 620 because 25 players played regularly for two teams (England excluded) in the year for which they were chosen.

Types of Player

Of the 595 Cricketers of the Year, 296 are best classified as batsmen, 162 as bowlers, 98 as all-rounders and 39 as wicketkeepers or wicketkeeper-batsmen.

Research: Robert Brooke

PART NINE

The Almanack

OFFICIAL BODIES

INTERNATIONAL CRICKET COUNCIL

The ICC are world cricket's governing body. They are responsible for managing the playing conditions and Code of Conduct for international fixtures, expanding the game and organising the major tournaments, including the World Cup and World Twenty20. Their mission statement says the ICC "will lead by providing a world-class environment for international cricket, delivering major events across three formats, providing targeted support to members and promoting the global game".

Twelve national governing bodies are currently Full Members of the ICC; full membership qualifies a nation (or geographic area) to play official Test matches. A candidate for full membership must meet a number of playing and administrative criteria, after which elevation is decided by a vote among existing Full Members. With the former categories of associate and affiliate membership merging in 2017, there are currently 92 Associate Members.

The ICC were founded in 1909 as the Imperial Cricket Conference by three Foundation Members: England, Australia and South Africa. Other countries (or geographic areas) became Full Members and thus acquired Test status as follows: India, New Zealand and West Indies in 1926, Pakistan in 1952, Sri Lanka in 1981, Zimbabwe in 1992, Bangladesh in 2000, and Afghanistan and Ireland in 2017. South Africa ceased to be a member on leaving the Commonwealth in 1961, but were re-elected as a Full Member in 1991.

In 1965, "Imperial" was replaced by "International", and countries from outside the Commonwealth were elected for the first time. The first Associate Members were Ceylon (later Sri Lanka), Fiji and the USA. Foundation Members retained a veto over all resolutions. In 1989, the renamed International Cricket Council (rather than "Conference") adopted revised rules, aimed at producing an organisation which could make a larger number of binding decisions, rather than simply make recommendations to national governing bodies. In 1993, the Council, previously administered by MCC, gained their own secretariat and chief executive. The category of Foundation Member was abolished.

In 1997, the Council became an incorporated body, with an executive board, and a president instead of a chairman. The ICC remained at Lord's, with a commercial base in Monaco, until August 2005, when after 96 years they moved to Dubai in the United Arab Emirates, which offered organisational and tax advantages.

In 2014, the ICC board approved a new structure, under which they were led by a chairman again, while India, Australia and England took permanent places on key committees. But in 2016 the special privileges given to these three were dismantled and, in early 2017, the board agreed to revise the constitution on more egalitarian lines.

Officers

Chairman: S. V. Manohar. *Deputy Chairman:* I. Khwaja. *Chief Executive:* D. J. Richardson.

Chairs of Committees – Chief Executives' Committee: D. J. Richardson. *Cricket:* A. Kumble. *Audit:* E. Quinlan. *Finance and Commercial Affairs:* C. G. Clarke. *Nominations Committee:* S. V. Manohar. *Code of Conduct Commission:* M. J. Beloff QC. *Women's Committee:* C. J. Connor. *Development:* I. Khwaja. *Disputes Resolution Committee:* M. J. Beloff QC. *Membership:* I. Khwaja. *Medical Advisory:* Dr P. Harcourt. *Anti-Corruption Unit:* Sir Ronnie Flanagan. *ICC Ethics Officer:* P. Nicholson.

ICC Board: The chairman and chief executive sit on the board *ex officio*. They are joined by Atif Mashal (Afghanistan), G. J. Barclay (New Zealand), W. O. Cameron (West Indies), A. Choudhary (India), C. G. Clarke (England), F. Erasmus (Namibia), I. Khwaja (Singapore), R. A. McCollum (Ireland), T. Mukuhlani (Zimbabwe), Najam Sethi (Pakistan), Nazmul Hassan (Bangladesh), C. Nenzani (South Africa), D. A. Peever (Australia), T. Sumathipala (Sri Lanka), M. Vallipuram (Malaysia). In June 2018, I. K. Nooyi was to join the board as the ICC's first independent female director.

Chief Executives' Committee: The chief executive, chairman and the chairs of the committee and women's committees sit on this committee *ex officio*. They are joined by the chief executives of the 12 Full Member boards and three Associate Member boards: S. Damodar (Botswana), A. M. de Silva (Sri Lanka), W. Deutrom (Ireland), Faisal Hasnain (Zimbabwe), J. M. Grave (West Indies), T. W. Harrison (England), R. Johri (India), T. Moroe (South Africa), Nizam Uddin Chowdhury (Bangladesh), Shafiq Stanikzai (Afghanistan), N. Speight (Bermuda), Subhan Ahmad (Pakistan), J. A. Sutherland (Australia), B. Timmer (Netherlands), D. J. White (New Zealand).

Cricket Committee: The chief executive and chairman sit on the committee *ex officio*. They are joined by A. Kumble (*chairman*), C. J. Connor, R. Dravid, D. P. M. D. Jayawardene, R. A. Kettleborough, D. S. Lehmann, R. S. Madugalle, T. B. A. May, S. M. Pollock, J. P. Stephenson, A. J. Strauss, D. J. White (with one Associate representative to be nominated).

General Manager – Cricket: G. J. Allardice. *General Manager – Commercial:* D. C. Jamieson. *General Manager – Anti-Corruption Unit:* A. J. Marshall. *General Manager – Strategic Communications:* C. Furlong. *General Manager – Development:* W. Glenwright. *Chief Financial Officer:* A. Khanna. *Chief Operating Officer/General Counsel:* I. Higgins. *Head of Events:* C. M. B. Tetley. *Head of Media Rights, Broadcast & Digital:* A. Dabas. *Head of Media/Communications:* Sami Ul Hasan. *Head of Internal Audit:* Muhammad Ali.

Membership

Full Members (12): Afghanistan, Australia, Bangladesh, England, India, Ireland, New Zealand, Pakistan, South Africa, Sri Lanka, West Indies and Zimbabwe.

Associate Members* (92):

Africa (20): Botswana (2005), Cameroon (2007), Gambia (2002), Ghana (2002), Kenya (1981), Lesotho (2001), Malawi (2003), Mali (2005), Morocco (1999), Mozambique (2003), Namibia (1992), Nigeria (2002), Rwanda (2003), St Helena (2001), Seychelles (2010), Sierra Leone (2002), Swaziland (2007), Tanzania (2001), Uganda (1998), Zambia (2003).

Americas (15): Argentina (1974), Bahamas (1987), Belize (1997), Bermuda (1966), Brazil (2002), Canada (1968), Cayman Islands (2002), Chile (2002), Costa Rica (2002), Falkland Islands (2007), Mexico (2004), Panama (2002), Peru (2007), Suriname (2002), Turks & Caicos Islands (2002).

Asia (16): Bahrain (2001), Bhutan (2001), China (2004), Hong Kong (1969), Iran (2003), Kuwait (2005), Malaysia (1967), Maldives (2001), Myanmar (2006), Nepal (1996), Oman (2000), Qatar (1999), Saudi Arabia (2003), Singapore (1974), Thailand (2005), United Arab Emirates (1990).

East Asia Pacific (9): Cook Islands (2000), Fiji (1965), Indonesia (2001), Japan (2005), Papua New Guinea (1973), Philippines (2000), Samoa (2000), South Korea (2001), Vanuatu (1995).

Europe (32): Austria (1992), Belgium (2005), Bulgaria (2008), Croatia (2001), Cyprus (1999), Czech Republic (2000), Denmark (1966), Estonia (2008), Finland (2000), France (1998), Germany (1999), Gibraltar (1969), Greece (1995), Guernsey (2005), Hungary (2012), Isle of Man (2004), Israel (1974), Italy (1995), Jersey (2007), Luxembourg (1998), Malta (1998), Netherlands (1966), Norway (2000), Portugal (1996), Romania (2013), Russia (2012), Scotland (1994), Serbia (2015), Slovenia (2005), Spain (1992), Sweden (1997), Turkey (2008).

* *Year of election shown in parentheses. Switzerland (1985) were removed in 2012 for failing to comply with the ICC's membership criteria; Cuba (2002) and Tonga (2000) in 2013 for failing to demonstrate a suitable administrative structure; Brunei in 2014; and the USA in 2017. Nepal were suspended in 2016, and the Falkland Islands in 2017.*

Full Members are the governing bodies for cricket of a country recognised by the ICC, or nations associated for cricket purposes, or a geographical area, from which representative teams are qualified to play official Test matches.

Associate Members are the governing bodies for cricket of a country recognised by the ICC, or countries associated for cricket purposes, or a geographical area, which does not qualify as a Full Member, but where cricket is firmly established and organised.

Addresses

ICC Street 69, Dubai Sports City, Sh Mohammed Bin Zayed Road, PO Box 500 070, Dubai, United Arab Emirates (+971 4382 8800; website www.icc-cricket.com; email enquiry@icc-cricket.com).

Afghanistan Afghanistan Cricket Board, Alokozay Kabul International Cricket Stadium, Kabul Nandari, District 8, Kabul (+93 78 813 3144; www.cricket.af; email info@afghancricket.af).

Australia Cricket Australia, 60 Jolimont Street, Jolimont, Victoria 3002 (+61 3 9653 9999; website www.cricket.com.au; email public.enquiries@cricket.com.au).

Bangladesh Bangladesh Cricket Board, Sher-e-Bangla National Cricket Stadium, Mirpur, Dhaka 1216 (+880 2 803 1001; website www.tigercricket.com.bd; email info@tigercricket.com.bd).

England England and Wales Cricket Board (see below).

India Board of Control for Cricket in India, Cricket Centre, 4th Floor, Wankhede Stadium, D Road, Churchgate, Mumbai 400 020 (+91 22 2289 8800; website www.bcci.tv; email office@bcci.tv).

Ireland Cricket Ireland, Unit 22, Grattan Business Park Clonshaugh, Dublin 17 (+353 1 894 7914; website www.cricketireland.ie; email info@cricketireland.ie).

New Zealand New Zealand Cricket, PO Box 8353, Level 4, 8 Nugent Street, Grafton, Auckland 1023 (+64 9 972 0605; website www.nzc.nz; email info@nzcricket.org.nz).

Pakistan Pakistan Cricket Board, Gaddafi Stadium, Ferozpur Road, Lahore 54600 (+92 42 3571 7231; website www.pcb.com.pk; email online@pcb.com.pk).

South Africa Cricket South Africa, PO Box 55009 Northlands 2116; 86, 5th & Glenhove St, Melrose Estate, Johannesburg (+27 11 880 2810; website www.cricket.co.za; email info@cricket.co.za).

Sri Lanka Sri Lanka Cricket, 35 Maitland Place, Colombo 07000 (+94 112 681 601; website www.srilankacricket.lk; email info@srilankacricket.lk).

West Indies West Indies Cricket Board, PO Box 616 W, Factory Road, St John's, Antigua (+1 268 481 2450; website www.windiescricket.com; email wicb@windiescricket.com).

Zimbabwe Zimbabwe Cricket, PO Box 2739, 28 Maiden Drive, Highlands, Harare (+263 4 788 090; website www.zimcricket.org; email info@zimcricket.org).

Associate Members' addresses may be found on the ICC website www.icc-cricket.com

ENGLAND AND WALES CRICKET BOARD

The England and Wales Cricket Board (ECB) are responsible for the administration of all cricket – professional and recreational – in England and Wales. In 1997, they took over the functions of the Cricket Council, the Test and County Cricket Board and the National Cricket Association, which had run the game since 1968. In 2005, a streamlined constitution replaced a Management Board of 18 with a 12-strong Board of Directors, three appointed by the first-class counties, two by the county boards. In 2010, this expanded to 14, and added the ECB's first women directors. It was expected to return to 12, including four independent non-executive directors, after the AGM in May 2018.

Officers

President: C. G. Clarke. *Chairman:* C. J. Graves. *Chief Executive Officer:* T. W. Harrison.

Board of Directors: C. G. Clarke, M. Darlow, M. V. Fleming, C. J. Graves, T. W. Harrison, I. N. Lovett, A. J. Nash, Lord Patel of Bradford, L. C. Pearson, J. Stichbury, R. W. Thompson, J. Wood, P. G. Wright.

Committee Chairs – Executive Committee: T. W. Harrison. *Anti-Corruption Commission for Education, Standards and Security:* J. Stichbury. *Audit, Risk and Governance:* I. N. Lovett. *Cricket:* P. G. Wright. *Discipline:* T. J. G. O'Gorman. *Recreational Assembly:* J. Wood. *Regulatory:* N. I. Coward. *Remuneration:* C. J. Graves.

Chief Operating Officer: G. M. Hollins. *Chief Financial Officer:* S. Smith. *Chief Commercial Officer/MD, T20:* S. Patel. *Chief Strategy Officer:* D. Mahoney. *Director, England Cricket:* A. J. Strauss. *Director, Communications:* C. Haynes. *Managing Director, World Cup 2019:* S. Elworthy. *Director, England Cricket Operations:* J. D. Carr. *Director, England Women's Cricket:* C. J. Connor. *Director, Participation and Growth:* M. Dwyer. *Commercial Director:* R. Calder. *People Director:* R. Ranganathan. *Performance Director:* D. Parsons. *Head of Information Technology:* D. Smith. *National Selector:* J. J. Whitaker. *Other Selectors:* A. R. C. Fraser and M. Newell.

ECB: Lord's Ground, London NW8 8QZ (020 7432 1200; website www.ecb.co.uk).

THE MARYLEBONE CRICKET CLUB

The Marylebone Cricket Club evolved out of the White Conduit Club in 1787, when Thomas Lord laid out his first ground in Dorset Square. Their members revised the Laws in 1788 and gradually took responsibility for cricket throughout the world. However, they relinquished control of the game in the UK in 1968, and the International Cricket Council finally established their own secretariat in 1993. MCC still own Lord's and remain the guardian of the Laws. They call themselves "a private club with a public function" and aim to support cricket everywhere, especially at grassroots level and in countries where the game is least developed.

Patron: HER MAJESTY THE QUEEN

Officers

President: 2017–18 – Lord MacLaurin. *Club Chairman:* G. M. N. Corbett. *Treasurer:* A. B. Elgood. *Trustees:* P. A. B. Beecroft, M. G. Griffith, R. S. Leigh. *Hon. Life Vice-Presidents:* Lord Bramall, E. R. Dexter, C. A. Fry, A. R. Lewis, Sir Oliver Popplewell, D. R. W. Silk, M. O. C. Sturt, J. C. Woodcock.

Chief Executive and Secretary: G. W. Lavender. *Assistant Secretaries – Cricket:* J. P. Stephenson. *Membership and Operations:* J. A. S. Clifford. *Estates:* R. J. Ebdon. *Finance:* A. D. Cameron. *Legal:* H. A. Roper-Curzon. *Commercial:* J. D. Robinson.

MCC Committee: P. R. Carroll, I. S. Duncan, A. R. C. Fraser, W. R. Griffiths, C. M. Gupte, C. J. Guyver, P. L. O. Leaver, H. J. H. Loudon, G. T. E. Monkhouse, J. O. D. Orders, N. M. Peters, N. E. J. Pocock. The president, club chairman, treasurer and committee chairmen are also on the committee.

Chairmen of Committees – Arts and Library: D. J. C. Faber. *Cricket:* M. V. Fleming. *Estates:* D. C. Brooks Wilson. *Finance:* A. B. Elgood. *Membership and General Purposes:* Sir Ian Magee. *World Cricket:* M. W. Gatting.

MCC: The Chief Executive and Secretary, Lord's Ground, London NW8 8QN (020 7616 8500; email reception@mcc.org.uk; website www.lords.org. Tickets 020 7432 1000; email ticketing@mcc.org.uk).

PROFESSIONAL CRICKETERS' ASSOCIATION

The Professional Cricketers' Association were formed in 1967 (as the Cricketers' Association) to be the collective voice of first-class professional players, and enhance and protect their interests. During the 1970s, they succeeded in establishing pension schemes and a minimum wage. In recent years their strong commercial operations and greater funding from the ECB have increased their services to current and past players, including education, legal, financial and benevolent help. In 2011, these services were extended to England's women cricketers.

President: To be announced. *Chairman:* D. K. H. Mitchell. *President – Benevolent Fund:* D. A. Graveney. *Non-Executive Chairman:* M. B. H. Wheeler. *Non-Executive Directors:* I. T. Guha and P. G. Read. *Chief Executive:* D. A. Leatherdale. *Commercial Director:* M. Day. *Financial Director:* P. Garrett. *Business Development Manager:* G. M. Hamilton. *Commercial Manager:* A. Phipps. *Head of Events and Fundraising:* E. Lewis. *Head of Commercial Rights:* E. M. Reid. *Player Rights Manager:* E. Caldwell. *Communications Manager:* L. Reynolds. *Member Services Manager:* A Prosser. *Director of Development and Welfare:* I. J. Thomas.

PCA: *London Office* – The Laker Stand, The Oval, Kennington, London SE11 5SS (0207 449 4226; email communications@thepca.co.uk; website www.thepca.co.uk). *Birmingham Office* – Box 108–9, R. E. S. Wyatt Stand, Warwickshire CCC, Edgbaston, Birmingham B5 7QU.

CRIME AND PUNISHMENT

ICC Code of Conduct – Breaches and Penalties in 2016-17 to 2017-18

C. L. Tryon South Africa v Bangladesh, fourth women's one-day international at Cox's Bazar.
Shook her head and showed bat when lbw. Reprimand/1 demerit pt – G. F. Labrooy (referee).

V. Krishnamurthy India v Sri Lanka, women's World Cup Qualifier at Colombo (PSO).
Made TV referral sign after appeal for catch turned down. Reprimand/1 demerit pt – G. F. Labrooy.

D. P. D. N. Dickwella Sri Lanka v Australia, second Twenty20 international at Geelong.
Dissent when given caught behind. 30% fine/2 demerit pts – J. J. Crowe. Suspended for two games.

T. D. Paine Australia v Sri Lanka, second Twenty20 international at Geelong.
Inappropriate language after Dickwella's dismissal. 15% fine/1 demerit pt – J. J. Crowe.

R. Ngarava Zimbabwe v Afghanistan, third one-day international at Harare.
Inappropriate deliberate physical contact with Rahmat Shah. 50% fine/3 demerit pts – D. T. Jukes.

Rahmat Shah Afghanistan v Zimbabwe, third one-day international at Harare.
Inappropriate deliberate physical contact with Ngarava. 50% fine/3 demerit pts – D. T. Jukes.

Asghar Stanikzai Afghanistan v Zimbabwe, third one-day international at Harare.
Shook his head and pointed at bat when given out. Reprimand/1 demerit pt – D. T. Jukes.

Tamim Iqbal Bangladesh v Sri Lanka, Second Test at Colombo (PSO).
Showed the umpire his bat after lbw appeal. 15% fine/1 demerit pt – A. J. Pycroft.

Imrul Kayes Bangladesh v Sri Lanka, Second Test at Colombo (PSO).
Pointed at his thigh after caught-behind appeal. 15% fine/1 demerit pt – A. J. Pycroft.

S. T. Gabriel West Indies v Pakistan, First Test at Kingston.
Barged into batsman Sarfraz Ahmed. 50% fine/3 demerit pts – B. C. Broad.

S. G. Law (coach) West Indies v Pakistan, Third Test at Roseau.
Entered third umpire's room to question on-field decision. 25% fine/1 demerit pt – B. C. Broad.

Afsar Zazai Afghanistan v West Indies, first one-day international at Gros Islet.
Made TV referral sign after lbw appeal. 15% fine/1 demerit pt – J. J. Crowe.

A. R. Nurse West Indies v Afghanistan, first one-day international at Gros Islet.
Excessive display of disappointment when given lbw. Reprimand/1 demerit pt – J. J. Crowe.

D. P. D. N. Dickwella Sri Lanka v Zimbabwe, first one-day international at Galle.
Stumping attempt after waiting for batsman to leave crease. 30% fine/2 demerit pts – J. J. Crowe.

K. Rabada South Africa v England, First Test at Lord's.
Obscene language after dismissing B. A. Stokes. 15% fine/1 demerit pt – J. J. Crowe.
Suspended for one Test after accumulating four demerit points.

M. A. D. D. Surangika Sri Lanka v West Indies, women's World Cup at Derby.
Given out caught, indicated that the ball had hit her thigh. Reprimand/1 demerit pt – D. T. Jukes.

H. Kaur India v Australia, Women's World Cup semi-final at Derby.
After near run-out, threw her bat to the ground. Reprimand/1 demerit pt – D. T. Jukes.

R. A. Jadeja India v Sri Lanka, Second Test at Colombo (SSC).
Threw the ball towards batsman F. D. M. Karunaratne. 50% fine/3 demerit pts – R. B. Richardson.
Suspended for one Test after accumulating six demerit points.

B. A. Stokes England v West Indies, Second Test at Leeds.
Swore loudly after conceding a boundary off an edge. Reprimand/1 demerit pt – D. C. Boon.

J. O. Holder West Indies v England, Second Test at Leeds.
Swore in frustration during England's second innings. Reprimand/1 demerit pt – D. C. Boon.

Tamim Iqbal Bangladesh v Australia, First Test at Mirpur.
Objected to batsmen changing gloves, made send-off sign. 15% fine/1 demerit pt – J. J. Crowe.

M. L. Schutt Australia v England, third women's one-day international at Coffs Harbour.
Offensive language and gesture on dismissing S. J. Taylor. Reprimand/1 demerit pt – R. W. Stratford.

M. D. Shanaka Sri Lanka v India, Second Test at Nagpur.
Seen on TV picking an area on the ball next to the seam. 75% fine/3 demerit pts – D. C. Boon.

Twenty-six further breaches took place in Associate or Under-19 internationals during this period.

Under ICC regulations on minor over-rate offences, players are fined 10% of their match fee for every over their side fail to bowl in the allotted time, with the captain fined double. There were 13 instances in this period in men's internationals, plus two in women's:

Mashrafe bin Mortaza/Bangladesh v Sri Lanka, 3rd ODI at Colombo (SSC), 40%/20% – A. J. Pycroft.
Mashrafe suspended for one match as it was his second offence within 12 months.

W. U. Tharanga/Sri Lanka v Bangladesh, 1st T20I at Colombo (RPS), 20%/10% – A. J. Pycroft.

J. O. Holder/West Indies v Pakistan, 1st Test at Kingston, 20%/10% – B. C. Broad.

A. B. de Villiers/South Africa v England, 1st ODI at Leeds, 20%/10% – A. J. Pycroft.

W. U. Tharanga/Sri Lanka v South Africa, Champions Trophy, 0%/60% – D. C. Boon.
Tharanga was not fined, but was suspended for two matches.

K. S. Williamson/New Zealand v England, Champions Trophy, 40%/20% – A. J. Pycroft.

Sarfraz Ahmed/Pakistan v Sri Lanka, Champions Trophy, 20%/10% – B. C. Broad.

Sana Mir/Pakistan v England, women's World Cup, Reprimand – R. B. Richardson.

I. Ranaweera/Sri Lanka v India, women's World Cup, Reprimand – R. B. Richardson.

A. G. Cremer/Zimbabwe v Sri Lanka, 4th ODI at Hambantota, 20%/10% – B. C. Broad.

C. R. Brathwaite/West Indies v India, T20I at Kingston, 20%/10% – D. C. Boon.

W. U. Tharanga/Sri Lanka v India, 2nd ODI at Pallekele, 0%/40% – A. J. Pycroft.
Tharanga was not fined, but was suspended for two matches.

J. O. Holder/West Indies v New Zealand, 1st Test at Wellington, 60%/30% – B. C. Broad.
Holder suspended for one Test as it was his second offence within 12 months.

K. C. Brathwaite/West Indies v New Zealand, 2nd Test at Hamilton, 40%/20% – B. C. Broad.

S. P. D. Smith/Australia v England, 3rd ODI at Sydney, 40%/20% – R. S. Madugalle.

There were two further instances in Associate Member internationals.

INTERNATIONAL UMPIRES' PANELS

In 1993, the ICC formed an international umpires' panel, containing at least two officials from each Full Member. A third-country umpire from this panel stood with a home umpire in every Test from 1994 onwards. In 2002, an elite panel was appointed: two elite umpires – both independent – were to stand in all Tests, and at least one in every ODI, where one home umpire was allowed. A supporting panel of international umpires was created to provide cover at peak times in the Test schedule, second umpires in one-day internationals, and third umpires to give rulings from TV replays. The panels are sponsored by Emirates Airlines.

The elite panel at the start of 2018: Aleem Dar (P), H. D. P. K. Dharmasena (SL), M. Erasmus (SA), C. B. Gaffaney (NZ), I. J. Gould (E), R. K. Illingworth (E), R. A. Kettleborough (E), N. J. Llong (E), B. N. J. Oxenford (A), S. Ravi (I), P. R. Reiffel (A), R. J. Tucker (A).

The international panel: G. A. Abood (A), Ahmed Shah Durrani (Afg), Ahmed Shah Pakteen (Afg), Ahmed Shahab (P), Ahsan Raza (P), Anisur Rahman (B), R. J. Bailey (E), Bismillah Shinwari (Afg), R. E. Black (Ire), G. O. Brathwaite (WI), C. M. Brown (NZ), A. K. Chowdhury (I), N. Duguid (WI), S. D. Fry (A), S. George (SA), M. A. Gough (E), S. B. Haig (NZ), M. Hawthorne (Ire), A. T. Holdstock (SA), P. B. Jele (SA), W. R. Knights (NZ), R. E. J. Martinesz (SL), Masudur Rahman (B), T. J. Matibiri (Z), N. N. Menon (I), C. K. Nandan (I), A. J. Neill (Ire), S. J. Nogajski (A), A. Paleker (SA), R. S. A. Palliyaguruge (SL), L. S. Reifer (WI), R. T. Robinson (E), L. Rusere (Z), C. Shamshuddin (I), Sharfuddoula (B), Shozab Raza (P), R. B. Tiffin (Z), A. G. Wharf (E), J. S. Wilson (WI), P. Wilson (A), R. R. Wimalasiri (SL).

ICC development panel: Akbar Ali (UAE), V. R. Angara (Botswana), S. N. Bandekar (USA), R. D'Mello (Kenya), A. J. T. Dowdalls (Scotland), D. A. Haggo (Scotland), C. J. Howard (Hong Kong), Iftikhar Ali (UAE), H. K. G. Jansen (Netherlands), V. K. Jha (Nepal), A. Kapa (PNG), H. E. Kearns (Jersey), A. W. Louw (Namibia), L. Oala (PNG), D. Odhiambo (Kenya), I. O. Oyieko (Kenya), C. A. Polosak (A), B. B. Pradhan (Nepal), S. S. Prasad (Singapore), I. N. Ramage (Scotland), S. Redfern (E), D. N. Subedi (Nepal), Tabarak Dar (Hong Kong), I. A. Thomson (Hong Kong), C. H. Thorburn (Namibia), W. P. M. van Liemt (Netherlands), K. Viswanadan (Malaysia), J. M. Williams (WI).

ICC REFEREES' PANEL

In 1991, the ICC formed a panel of referees to enforce their Code of Conduct for Tests and one-day internationals, to impose penalties for slow over-rates, breaches of the Code and other regulations, and to support the umpires in upholding the game's conduct. In 2002, the ICC launched an elite panel of referees, on full-time contracts, for all international cricket, sponsored by Emirates Airlines. At the start of 2018, it consisted of D. C. Boon (A), B. C. Broad (E), J. J. Crowe (NZ), R. S. Madugalle (SL), A. J. Pycroft (Z), R. B. Richardson (WI), J. Srinath (I).

A further panel of international referees consisted of Akhtar Ahmad (B), Anis Sheikh (P), G. A. V. Baxter (NZ), S. R. Bernard (A), D. Cooke (Ire), E. T. Dube (Z), R. A. Dykes (NZ), K. Gallagher (Ire), D. Govindjee (SA), D. O. Hayles (WI), D. T. Jukes (E), R. D. King (WI), G. F. Labrooy (SL), W. C. Labrooy (SL), Mohammad Javed (P), M. Nayyar (I), Neeyamur Rashid (B), W. M. Noon (E), G. H. Pienaar (SA), C. Sharma (I), R. W. Stratford (A), S. Wadvalla (SA), P. Whitticase (E). Two Afghan referees were also to be appointed.

ENGLISH UMPIRES FOR 2018

First-class: R. J. Bailey, N. L. Bainton, I. D. Blackwell, P. K. Baldwin, M. Burns, N. G. B. Cook, B. J. Debenham, J. H. Evans, M. A. Gough, I. J. Gould, P. J. Hartley, R. K. Illingworth, R. A. Kettleborough, N. J. Llong, G. D. Lloyd, J. W. Lloyds, N. A. Mallender, D. J. Millns, S. J. O'Shaughnessy, P. R. Pollard, R. T. Robinson, M. J. Saggers, B. V. Taylor, R. J. Warren, A. G. Wharf. *Reserves:* T. Lungley, J. D. Middlebrook, M. Newell, I. N. Ramage, C. M. Watts, R. A. White.

Minor Counties: R. G. B. Allen, J. Attridge, J. S. Beckwith, D. Browne, T. Caldicott, G. I. Callaway, S. Cobb, K. Coburn, N. Davies, R. G. Eagleton, D. J. Gower, R. C. Hampshire, A. C. Harris, Hasan Adnan, I. L. Herbert, A. Hicks, C. Johnson, N. Kent, I. P. Laurence, A. Lunn, J. Marshall, P. W. Matten, R. P. Medland, B. Morris, Naeem Ashraf, R. J. Newham, P. D. Nicholls, R. Parker, D. N. Pedley, N. E. Piddock, J. Pitcher, M. Pointer, N. Pratt, D. Price, M. Qureshi, G. M. Roberts, S. J. Ross, S. Shanmugam, P. Smith, M. J. Spenceley, D. M. Warburton, M. D. Watton, A. J. Wheeler.

THE DUCKWORTH/LEWIS/STERN METHOD

In 1997, the ECB's one-day competitions adopted a new method to revise targets in interrupted games, devised by Frank Duckworth of the Royal Statistical Society and Tony Lewis of the University of the West of England. The method was gradually taken up by other countries and, in 1999, the ICC decided to incorporate it into the standard playing conditions for one-day internationals.

The system aims to preserve any advantage that one team have established before the interruption. It uses the idea that teams have two resources from which they make runs – an allocated number of overs, and ten wickets. It also takes into account when the interruption occurs, because of the different scoring-rates typical of different stages of an innings. Traditional run-rate calculations relied only on the overs available, and ignored wickets lost.

It uses one table with 50 rows, covering matches of up to 50 overs, and ten columns, from nought to nine wickets down. Each figure gives the percentage of the total runs that would, on average, be scored with a certain number of overs left and wickets lost. If a match is shortened before it begins, to, say, 33 overs a side, the figure for 33 overs and ten wickets remaining would be the starting point.

If overs are lost, the table is used to calculate the percentage of runs the team would be expected to score in those missing overs. This is obtained by reading the figure for the number of overs left, and wickets down, when play stops, and subtracting the figure for the number of overs left when it resumes. If the delay occurs between innings, and the second team's allocation of overs is reduced, then their target is obtained by calculating the appropriate percentage for the reduced number of overs with all ten wickets standing. For instance, if the second team's innings halves from 50 overs to 25, the table shows that they still have 66.5% of their resources left, so have to beat two-thirds of the first team's total, rather than half. If the first innings is complete and the second innings interrupted or prematurely terminated, the score to beat is reduced by the percentage of the innings lost.

The version known as the "Professional Edition" was introduced into one-day internationals from 2003, and subsequently into most national one-day competitions. Using a more advanced mathematical formula (it is entirely computerised), it adjusts the tables to allow for the different scoring-rates that emerge in matches with above-average first-innings scores. In 2014, analysis by Steven Stern, an Australian professor of statistics who became responsible for the method after Duckworth and Lewis retired, indicated further modification was needed. The Duckworth/Lewis/Stern method is now used in all one-day and Twenty20 internationals, as well as most national competitions. The original "Standard Edition" is used where computers are unavailable, and at lower levels of the game.

The system also covers first-innings interruptions, multiple interruptions and innings ended by rain. The tables are revised slightly every two years, taking account of changing scoring-rates; the average total in a 50-over international is now 252 (up from 225 in 1999).

In the World Cup semi-final between South Africa and New Zealand at Auckland in March 2015, South Africa were 216 for three from 38 overs when seven overs were lost to rain; after the innings resumed, they finished on 281. With three wickets down, the lost overs constituted 14.85% of South Africa's scoring resources, meaning they used only 85.15%. By contrast, New Zealand's 43-over chase constituted 90% of the resources of a full innings. Their revised target was determined by multiplying South Africa's total, 281, by 90% divided by 85.15% and adding one run: 281 x (90/85.15) + 1 = 298. New Zealand scored 299 for six in 42.5 overs to win, with a six off the penultimate delivery. Had South Africa been two down at the interruption, the lost overs would have constituted a higher percentage of their scoring resources; the revised target would have been 301, and New Zealand would have needed two more runs off the final ball.

A similar system, usually known as the VJD method, is used in some domestic matches in India. It was devised by V. Jayadevan, a civil engineer from Kerala.

POWERPLAYS

In one-day and Twenty20 internationals, two semi-circles of 30-yard (27.43 metres) radius are drawn on the field behind each set of stumps, joined by straight lines parallel to the pitch.

At the instant of delivery in the first ten overs of an uninterrupted one-day international innings (the first six overs in a Twenty20 international), only two fielders may be positioned outside this 30-yard area. During the next 30 overs no more than four fielders may be stationed outside the 30-yard area; and in the final ten overs, no more than five. (In Twenty20 internationals, no more than five may be positioned outside the area for the last 14 overs.) In matches affected by the weather, the number of overs in each powerplay stage is reduced in proportion to the overall reduction of overs.

In July 2015, the one-day international requirement for two close fielders in the first ten overs, and the five-over batting powerplay, to be claimed between the 11th and 40th overs, was abolished.

MEETINGS AND DECISIONS IN 2017

ICC BOARD

The ICC Board met in Dubai on February 2–4, 2017, and agreed in principle to changes to the constitution and financial model, with a more equitable distribution of revenues and a revised constitution reflecting good governance and clarifying the ICC's roles and objectives. They also identified their preferred model for all three formats, including a nine-team Test league, a 13-team one-day league and a regional Twenty20 structure. The Chief Executives' Committee agreed to the principle of consistent use of DRS technology across all international cricket, to be fully implemented from October 2017. Further details of this meeting appeared in *Wisden 2017*, page 1475.

The committee agreed that venues and boards should be more accountable for pitches and outfields at international matches: substandard conditions would earn demerit points, similar to those recently introduced for players. A venue accumulating five points over five years would be suspended for 12 months, rising to 24 months for ten points.

The committee authorised ICC management to explore the legal and technical aspects of an amendment to the Anti-Corruption Code permitting the use of cellphone data-extraction equipment. An ICC Medical Advisory Committee was to be introduced, to advise on sports medicine and sports science issues. An update to the ICC's gender recognition policy, bringing it into line with current scientific thinking, was approved.

Giles Clarke reported on his recent visit to Pakistan as chair of the ICC task force, and recommended that members send their own security experts to view the current situation.

Playing conditions for the 2017 Champions Trophy and Women's World Cup were approved; semi-finals and finals would go to a super over in case of a tie.

Afghanistan's Ahmad Shah Abdali regional four-day tournament was awarded first-class status from 2017-18.

ENGLAND TEST CAPTAIN

On February 6, the ECB announced that Alastair Cook had stepped down as England's Test captain. He had led the team in 59 Tests, a national record, winning 24 and losing 22, and won the Ashes in 2013 and 2015.

On February 13, it was confirmed that Joe Root would take over as England's 80th Test captain, with Ben Stokes succeeding him as vice-captain.

ICC CHAIRMAN

On March 15, the ICC said they had received an email from chairman Shashank Manohar tendering his resignation, which followed the BCCI's expression of concern about the proposed new financial model and governance. A board resolution requesting him to remain was passed with overwhelming support and, on March 24, he agreed to defer his resignation at least until the annual conference in June 2017 while he oversaw the reform process. In May, after the ICC Board had provisionally passed the new constitution and finances, it was confirmed that he would continue until the end of his term in June 2018.

ECB ARTICLES OF ASSOCIATION AND T20 COMPETITION

On March 27, the ECB presented proposals for a new Twenty20 competition for eight regional teams, to complement the existing county-based tournaments. It was intended to drive participation in cricket and recruit the next generation of fans. The sides would play 36 games over a 38-day summer window, with an IPL-style play-off system; all fixtures would be televised, with significant free-to-air exposure. Each team would have a squad of 15, including three overseas players, selected through a draft. There would be no overlap with the T20 Blast; though the 18 first-class counties would not take part, each would be paid £1.3m, or 1/19 of net revenues, whichever was higher, with 10% of net revenues going to a participation programme.

The following day, the board agreed to put forward amendments to the ECB Articles of Association to clear the way for the new competition. There would also be a governance review, led by deputy chairman Ian Lovett, looking at board structures and composition, processes, elections and committee selections.

On April 26, the ECB announced that 38 of their 41 members (the chairmen of the 18 first-class counties, 21 county boards, MCC and the Minor Counties Cricket Association) had approved the change to the Articles; Essex and Middlesex were against, with Kent abstaining.

ECB KIT DEAL

On April 5, the ECB announced a five-year deal making sports kit firm New Balance the official supplier of match and training wear to all England teams.

ICC BOARD AND COMMITTEE MEETINGS

The ICC held a series of meetings in Dubai on April 23–27 and agreed the revised financial model and a new constitution to be put before the Full Council in June for adoption.

The new financial model, passed by 13 votes to one (India), was guided by principles of equity, good conscience, common sense, simplicity, transparency, and the recognition that cricket-playing nations need each other; the more strong nations there are, the better for the sport. The proposed revenue distribution for 2016–23 would give $293m to India, $143m to England, $94m to Zimbabwe, and $132m each to the other seven Full Members, with $280m divided between the Associates.

The revised constitution, passed by 12 votes to two (India and Sri Lanka), was intended to reflect good governance and expand on the ICC's role and objectives in providing leadership in international cricket. Further changes included the potential to add Full Members; reducing the membership categories to two (Full and Associate); establishing membership criteria and a Membership Committee to consider applications; the introduction of a deputy chairman, elected by the board, and an independent female director; equally weighted votes for all board members regardless of membership status; and all members to be entitled to attend the AGM. In an effort to support existing Full Members, and sustain and grow the number of members at the top level, the potential for reclassification of Full Membership was removed.

Work on bringing more context to international bilateral cricket continued; the board noted the collective will to resolve calendar congestion and provide a clear framework for all three formats, and endorsed the principles behind a revised global qualification structure for the World T20 tournament in 2020.

Following an ICC delegation to the Pakistan Super League final in Lahore, the board were considering the feasibility of World XI matches from a security and budget perspective.

In women's cricket, the eight teams in the second edition of the Women's Championship (2017–20) would play a fixed set of three ODIs against each of the other seven; the Women's Committee recommended that any additional matches (up to five) should be T20Is. It was agreed to develop a separate rankings system for women's ODI and T20I cricket, with the latter including all T20I teams. The Decision Review System could be used in women's televised bilateral ODIs if the hosts so chose.

After hearing a report on ICC activities in China, the board agreed to develop a detailed China Growth Strategy in consultation with the Asian Cricket Council and Hong Kong Cricket Association.

While the Cricket Association of Nepal remained suspended, the board agreed to pay outstanding salaries to national contracted players.

The board approved the unqualified audited financial statements for the year ending December 31, 2016, and a new Code of Ethics combining the most effective practices from sport and industry.

The Chief Executives' Committee reconfirmed their support for cricket's inclusion in the Olympics.

ICC WOMEN'S CRICKET FORUM

The ICC held their first Women's Cricket Forum in Dubai on April 24. Representatives from all ten Full Members, plus Ireland, the Netherlands and Papua New Guinea, discussed a five-year collaborative strategy to accelerate the growth of the women's game, the opportunities for the sport and the challenges faced by members. Guest speaker Gayatri Yadav of media network Star India talked about how to change perceptions with innovative campaigns that break down cultural stereotypes and present female players as heroes.

USA CRICKET

On May 1, the ICC Board said the Full Council should consider the expulsion of the USA Cricket Association in June. This followed a two-year process attempting to unify the cricket community in the USA, after USACA's third suspension from membership over 12 years. The board believed that, rather than exercising genuine authority over American cricket, USACA presided over a severely fractured community, with most leagues choosing not to join.

The ICC had made significant efforts to identify what changes in USACA's structure would be required to build a sustainable foundation, but they had failed to engage with the process. A Sustainable Foundation Advisory Group had developed a revised governance model built upon best practice in USA sports and the principle of unification, and in February the ICC had asked USACA to put a new constitution to their membership for approval. But in April they had adopted an alternative constitution, including proposals the ICC had specifically rejected as likely to frustrate a successful unification process.

MCC ANNUAL GENERAL MEETING

The 230th AGM of the Marylebone Cricket Club was held at Lord's on May 3, with president Matthew Fleming in the chair. He announced that his successor from October would be Lord MacLaurin of Knebworth, the former chairman and chief executive of Tesco, who had served as chairman of the ECB from 1997 to 2002.

Resolutions were passed increasing members' entrance fees and annual subscriptions; a further resolution to convert the upper tier of the Allen Stand into a new Middlesex Room was withdrawn before the meeting. Members were also formally notified of a new Code of the Laws of Cricket, which had been approved by the MCC committee on March 20 and would come into effect on October 1, 2017.

Membership on December 31, 2016, totalled 23,915, made up of 17,881 full members, 5,536 associate members, 332 honorary members, 49 senior members and 117 out-match members. There were 11,674 candidates awaiting election to full membership; 460 vacancies arose in 2016.

Earlier in the day, the Duke of Edinburgh had opened the new Warner Stand, the first stage of the redevelopment of Lord's. The next day, MCC announced that financial services firm J. P. Morgan had renewed their sponsorship of the Lord's Media Centre, which had just undergone a £4m refurbishment, until the end of 2019.

ECB AGM

The AGM of the England and Wales Cricket Board was held at Lord's on May 10.

The ECB announced that in 2016 it had invested nearly £75m in the professional recreational game, a record, including payments to the first-class counties; a new entry-level participation scheme for recreational and grassroots cricket; and supporting England teams across men's, women's and disability cricket. Overall group reserves were reduced to £35.7m.

The board planned to put forward a package of governance reforms in the autumn, compliant with the Sport England Code and reflecting best practice in sport, which would lead to changes in the board structure.

Law firm CMS had been appointed to advise on the media rights sale for all competitions in 2020–24; an invitation to tender for ECB media rights would be issued shortly.

ICC CRICKET COMMITTEE

At a meeting in London on May 23–24, the ICC Cricket Committee supported plans for a Test competition, to provide context for the future of international cricket, and for cricket's inclusion in the Olympic Games.

The committee also recommended that the Chief Executives' Committee should approve the use of DRS in all Twenty20 internationals, and that teams should not lose a review when an lbw was ruled to be umpire's call, though in that case the 80-over top-up of reviews in Test cricket should be removed.

Having examined the 2017 Code of the Laws of Cricket, they favoured adopting most of MCC's changes, including giving umpires the power to send off players for the most serious misconduct, such as violence on the field; restrictions on bat dimensions (thickness of edges and depth of bat); and the rule that a batsman has made his/her ground when a bat bounces after being grounded behind the crease by a running or diving batsman.

After a presentation on the no-ball trial during England's one-day series with Pakistan in 2016, the committee recommended that the third umpire should call all no-balls in internationals, using instant replays.

They also urged the Chief Executives' Committee to amend the Classification of Official Cricket to allow Members to run a two-year trial on the use of concussion substitutes.

ICC ANNUAL MEETINGS

The ICC annual conference and associated meetings were held at The Oval on June 19–22.

The Full Council confirmed Afghanistan and Ireland as Full Members, eligible to play Test cricket. This followed the unanimous adoption of an extensively revised ICC constitution, which established an objective set of criteria for use in considering membership applications. The category of Affiliate Member was removed, with all existing Affiliates becoming Associate Members.

The revised constitution gave equal votes to every member of the ICC Board – including Full and Associate Member directors, the independent chairman and the independent director – with a two-thirds majority required to approve resolutions. The chairman of the Associate Members should be independent of any member board. The existing Associates chairman, Imran Khwaja (from Singapore), was elected to the new post of deputy chairman, to assume chairman Shashank Manowar's duties when he was unavailable, and a female independent director with full voting rights was to be appointed.

The board agreed a new financial model, reversing the 2014 resolutions, to provide greater equality in distributing ICC income. Based on forecast revenues and costs, the distribution for 2016–23 would give $405m to India, $139m to England, $94m to Zimbabwe, and $128m each to Australia, Bangladesh, New Zealand, Pakistan, South

Africa, Sri Lanka and West Indies. The Associate Members (together with Ireland and Afghanistan) would collectively receive $240m.

The USA Cricket Association, suspended in 2015, were expelled, and the ICC outlined plans for a new governing body. An advisory group of representatives from across the USA and the ICC Americas team would oversee the sport during the transition, and all USA teams would retain their current positions in ICC competitions. An electorate drawn from the whole USA cricket community would vote for a new board in early 2018, and a nominating and governance committee would help identify suitable independent directors.

The Chief Executives' Committee approved the Cricket Committee's recommendations on DRS. It should be used in all Twenty20 internationals. Teams would not lose a review when an lbw came back as umpire's call, but the 80-over top-up of reviews in Test cricket was removed. Minimum standards for DRS in international cricket were agreed, including the mandatory use of accredited ball-tracking and edge-detection technology.

They accepted most of MCC's recent changes to the Laws, to be incorporated into ICC playing conditions from October 1. All ICC Members agreed to implement the umpires' new power to send off players for serious misconduct such as violence, though other offences would continue to be dealt with under the ICC Code of Conduct. Other major changes adopted were the restriction on bat dimensions, and the rule that a batsman has made his/her ground when a bat bounces after being grounded behind the crease.

The Chief Executives' Committee considered plans for a nine-team Test league and a 13-team one-day international league. The board agreed to support the staging of three Twenty20 games between Pakistan and a World XI in Lahore later in 2017.

ECB MEDIA RIGHTS

On June 30, the ECB announced the award of media rights for all domestic and home international matches from 2020 to 2024. New five-year agreements with Sky Sports and the BBC would deliver a combined income of £1.1bn from all audio-visual, digital and audio rights for use in the UK and Ireland, and the ECB planned a partnership with Sky for fuelling grassroots cricket, modelled on their Sky Ride cycling events.

Sky would provide live coverage, highlights and digital clips of men's Tests, ODIs and T20Is, women's internationals, the new Twenty20 competition starting in 2020, the women's T20 league, and the men's County Championship, One-Day Cup and T20 competition. The BBC would broadcast live two men's T20Is and one women's T20I, plus ten matches from the new men's T20 league and eight from the women's league, as well as primetime evening highlights and digital clips for all nine categories. BBC Radio would offer live coverage of all competitions, domestic and international.

On August 9, the ECB announced a further deal with Channel 5, extending their existing contract to provide highlights of all women's home internationals until the end of 2019, including the next women's Ashes series.

On November 20, they announced a six-year media rights deal with BeIN Media Group, allowing them to screen coverage in more than 24 countries in the Middle East and North Africa of all England's home internationals (men and women) and domestic competitions from 2018 to 2024.

MCC WORLD CRICKET COMMITTEE

The MCC World Cricket Committee met at Lord's on July 3–4.

The MCC head of cricket, John Stephenson, thanked outgoing chairman Mike Brearley for his outstanding contribution to the committee; Mike Gatting was to succeed him in October.

The committee were concerned by the imbalance between the richer and poorer cricketing nations. For international cricket to flourish, competitive levels should be close and teams should field their best players, but the spread of privately owned T20 leagues meant that many, especially from countries lacking the funds to pay well, preferred the remuneration of these tournaments to representing their countries. The talk now was of finding a window for international cricket, rather than for domestic T20 leagues. While acknowledging that it might prove too idealistic, the committee asked the richer countries to give up some funding in the long-term interest of cricket as a whole, before the current structure entrenching inequality reached a point of no return.

The committee believed more must be done to protect Test cricket, though they were encouraged by the ICC reviving proposals for a World Test Championship and by experiments with day/night Tests. They felt Tests were still cricket's greatest challenge, the ultimate stage, and mentally the toughest format. Teams and players were celebrated in T20 and 50-over cricket, less so in Test cricket; efforts should be made to reduce the earnings gap between Test players and those on T20 contracts, and between the earnings of Test cricketers in different countries. The committee would form a subgroup, led by Gatting, on what cricket lovers, players and broadcasters most wanted from Test cricket. They strongly favoured retaining five-day Tests, though a minority wanted to try four-day Tests, perhaps in the day/night format.

The committee maintained their strong support for cricket in the Olympic Games, and hoped the ICC would present a unified front in applying to the 2024 host city (Los Angeles or Paris) to include the sport; a direct request to the host was now necessary as the deadline for applying through the International Olympic Committee had passed.

Former England captain Charlotte Edwards, the first woman on the committee, was stepping down after five years, to be succeeded by New Zealand captain Suzie Bates. Edwards outlined the successful evolution of women's cricket over the past few years, with the ICC Women's Championship, the Women's Big Bash League and the Kia Super League among many positive developments.

The committee supported the ICC's recommendation that national governing bodies should be able to experiment with full concussion substitutes. MCC had decided not to alter the Laws of Cricket to allow for concussion to be treated differently from any other injury, because few lower-level matches are overseen by medically trained personnel, and umpires should not be responsible for making a diagnosis; the Laws already allow a replacement with the opposing captain's consent, which in amateur cricket would not normally be withheld after a serious head injury. But, unlike other injuries, a concussed player could not make a rational decision over his/her fitness to play. The committee called for national governing bodies to ensure that players and officials at all levels were educated on the risks, and to take a safety-first attitude. MCC would continue to monitor this area and offer help on framing playing regulations.

The committee supported the ICC Cricket Committee's recent recommendation on DRS that, when a side reviewed an lbw shown to be umpire's call, they should not lose that review.

They were pleased to hear the ICC would incorporate the vast majority of the Law changes into their regulations from October, in particular the new limits on bat sizes and the ability to send a player off for violent conduct.

The committee believed cricket should recognise its impact on the environment and that environmental changes would have a substantial impact on the global game and on cricket-playing nations. They hoped MCC would continue to promote sustainable development and measures to lessen climate change.

MCC SPECIAL GENERAL MEETING

A Special General Meeting of the Marylebone Cricket Club was held in Westminster on September 27 to vote on the updated masterplan for the redevelopment of Lord's Cricket Ground; it was approved by 7,163 votes to 748. The £194m building programme, scheduled for completion in 2032, would include replacements for the Compton and

Edrich Stands, extending the ground's capacity by at least 2,000. It would be funded from MCC's own resources, following the rejection of the alternative Morley plan, which would have included two blocks of flats at the Nursery End.

ENGLAND PLAYER CONTRACTS

The ECB currently award separate contracts for Test and white-ball cricket: players on Test contracts have their salaries paid in full by the ECB, while those on white-ball contracts receive a supplement to their county salary.

On October 6, the ECB awarded eight Test contracts to run for 12 months from October 2017. They went to Moeen Ali, James Anderson, Jonny Bairstow, Stuart Broad, Alastair Cook, Joe Root, Ben Stokes and Chris Woakes. They also awarded 14 white-ball contracts, to Ali, Bairstow, Root, Stokes and Woakes, plus Jake Ball, Jos Buttler, Alex Hales, Eoin Morgan, Liam Plunkett, Adil Rashid, Jason Roy, David Willey and Mark Wood. In addition, Toby Roland-Jones was given an incremental contract.

Compared with the previous year, Steven Finn lost his Test contract; Wood moved to a white-ball contract; Bairstow added a white-ball to his Test contract; Ball and Roland-Jones gained contracts for the first time.

ICC BOARD

The ICC Board met in Auckland in October 11–13 and approved a nine-team Test league and a 13-team ODI league to bring context and meaning to bilateral cricket. In the Test league, to start in 2019, each of the nine top Test sides would play three home and three away series over two years, with a minimum of two five-day Tests and a maximum of five in each series, culminating in a final. The ODI league, to start in 2020, would be a qualifying competition for the World Cup; it would be contested by the 12 Full Members plus the winners of the World Cricket League Championship. In its first edition, each side would play four home and four away series (each comprising three ODIs); in later cycles, all teams would play each other.

The board agreed that members could schedule four-day Tests by bilateral agreement in a trial running until the 2019 World Cup. It was hoped this would provide the new Test countries with more opportunities against experienced opponents.

Zimbabwe would host the next World Cup Qualifier in March 2018, Namibia the World Cricket League Division Two in February 2018, and the Netherlands the Women's World Twenty20 Qualifier 2018.

Player eligibility regulations were revised. On eligibility by residency, the qualification period was standardised at three years for men and women (previously, it was two years for women and four for men, except that Associate teams could pick only two men who had been resident for four years, but any number resident for seven). Once players had qualified and appeared for their new country, they would remain eligible without having to keep proving they met the criteria. The stand-out period for players seeking to transfer to a second country was amended to a flat three years, regardless of membership status and gender. Policies on gender recognition and Under-19 age determination were incorporated.

ECB SPONSORSHIP DEAL

On October 31, the ECB announced that Royal London had renewed their sponsorship of men's and women's domestic and international one-day cricket for a further two years. The deal would include all England's home one-day internationals and the 50-over one-day competition until the end of the 2019 season. Royal London (a life, pensions and investment company) first became an ECB sponsor in 2014.

USA CRICKET

On December 18, the ICC reported that a new constitution for cricket in the USA had been formally approved by the Sustainable Foundation Advisory Group, incorporating minor adjustments based on community feedback or the state law of Colorado, where the new USA Cricket was based. A membership programme, open to individual clubs as well as leagues, was to open in 2018, with elections to follow. The country would be divided into three conferences (Eastern, Central and Western) and six zones (East, Mid-Atlantic, South, South-West, West, Midwest) with services including competitions, high performance camps and education being delivered within each zone.

ECB GOVERNANCE REFORM

On December 19, the ECB announced that their 41 members had unanimously approved significant governance reforms, paving the way for the creation of a fully independent board in 2018.

From the AGM in May, the board would be reduced from 13 directors to 12. There would be three ex-officio directors (the ECB chairman, the chief executive officer and the chief financial officer); five non-executive directors with relevant experience drawn from the wider cricket network (who would be required to stand down from any cricket post creating a potential conflict of interest); and four fully independent non-executive directors, who need not have a close connection to cricket. The chair would serve a single term of up to five years, and the chief executive and chief financial officer for the duration of their tenure; all the non-executive directors would serve for a maximum of three three-year terms. At least 30% of the board should be female.

The new structure exceeded the minimum standard required of national governing bodies in Sport England's recent Code for Sports Governance; they were intended to make the board more representative of the whole game, embracing a more diverse mix of independent voices while drawing on the expertise of those within the cricket network.

DATES IN CRICKET HISTORY

c. 1550 Evidence of cricket being played in Guildford, Surrey.

1610 Reference to "cricketing" between Weald & Upland and North Downs near Chevening, Kent.

1611 Randle Cotgrave's French–English dictionary translates the French word "crosse" as a cricket staff.
Two youths fined for playing cricket at Sidlesham, Sussex.

1624 Jasper Vinall becomes first man known to be killed playing cricket: hit by a bat while trying to catch the ball – at Horsted Green, Sussex.

1676 First reference to cricket being played abroad, by British residents in Aleppo, Syria.

1694 Two shillings and sixpence paid for a "wagger" (wager) about a match at Lewes.

1697 First reference to "a great match" with 11 players a side for 50 guineas, in Sussex.

1700 Cricket match announced on Clapham Common.

1709 First recorded inter-county match: Kent v Surrey.

1710 First reference to cricket at Cambridge University.

1727 Articles of Agreement written governing the conduct of matches between the teams of the Duke of Richmond and Mr Brodrick of Peperharow, Surrey.

1729 Date of earliest surviving bat, belonging to John Chitty, now in the Oval pavilion.

1730 First recorded match at the Artillery Ground, off City Road, central London, still the cricketing home of the Honourable Artillery Company.

1744 Kent beat All-England by one wicket at the Artillery Ground.
First known version of the Laws of Cricket, issued by the London Club, formalising the pitch as 22 yards long.

c. 1767 Foundation of the Hambledon Club in Hampshire, the leading club in England for the next 30 years.

1769 First recorded century, by John Minshull for Duke of Dorset's XI v Wrotham.

1771 Width of bat limited to $4^1/_4$ inches, which it has remained ever since.

1774 Lbw law devised.

1776 Earliest known scorecards, at the Vine Club, Sevenoaks, Kent.

1780 The first six-seamed cricket ball, manufactured by Dukes of Penshurst, Kent.

1787 First match at Thomas Lord's first ground, Dorset Square, Marylebone – White Conduit Club v Middlesex.
Formation of Marylebone Cricket Club by members of the White Conduit Club.

1788 First revision of the Laws of Cricket by MCC.

1794 First recorded inter-school match: Charterhouse v Westminster.

1795 First recorded case of a dismissal "leg before wicket".

1806 First Gentlemen v Players match at Lord's.

1807 First mention of "straight-armed" (i.e. roundarm) bowling: by John Willes of Kent.

1809 Thomas Lord's second ground opened, at North Bank, St John's Wood.

1811 First recorded women's county match: Surrey v Hampshire at Ball's Pond, London.

1814 Lord's third ground opened on its present site, also in St John's Wood.

1827 First Oxford v Cambridge match, at Lord's: a draw.

1828 MCC authorise the bowler to raise his hand level with the elbow.

1833 John Nyren publishes *Young Cricketer's Tutor* and *The Cricketers of My Time.*

1836 First North v South match, for years regarded as the principal fixture of the season.

***c.* 1836** Batting pads invented.

1841 General Lord Hill, commander-in-chief of the British Army, orders that a cricket ground be made an adjunct of every military barracks.

1844 First official international match: Canada v United States.

1845 First match played at The Oval.

1846 The All-England XI, organised by William Clarke, begin playing matches, often against odds, throughout the country.

1849 First Yorkshire v Lancashire match.

***c.* 1850** Wicketkeeping gloves first used.

1850 John Wisden bowls all ten batsmen in an innings for North v South.

1853 First mention of a champion county: Nottinghamshire.

1858 First recorded instance of a hat being awarded to a bowler taking wickets with three consecutive balls.

1859 First touring team to leave England, captained by George Parr, draws enthusiastic crowds in the US and Canada.

1864 "Overhand bowling" authorised by MCC.
John Wisden's *The Cricketer's Almanack* first published.

1868 Team of Australian Aborigines tour England.

1873 W. G. Grace becomes the first player to record 1,000 runs and 100 wickets in a season.
First regulations restricting county qualifications, regarded by some as the official start of the County Championship.

1877 First Test match: Australia beat England by 45 runs at Melbourne.

1880 First Test in England: a five-wicket win against Australia at The Oval.

1882 Following England's first defeat by Australia in England, an "obituary notice" to English cricket in the *Sporting Times* leads to the tradition of the Ashes.

1889 Work begins on present Lord's Pavilion.
South Africa's first Test match.
Declarations first authorised, but only on the third day, or in a one-day match.

1890 County Championship officially constituted.

1895 W. G. Grace scores 1,000 runs in May, and reaches his 100th hundred.

1899 A. E. J. Collins scores 628 not out in a junior house match at Clifton College, the highest recorded individual score in any game – until 2016.
Selectors choose England team for home Tests, instead of host club issuing invitations.

1900 In England, six-ball over becomes the norm, instead of five.

1909 Imperial Cricket Conference (ICC – now the International Cricket Council) set up, with England, Australia and South Africa the original members.

1910 Six runs given for any hit over the boundary, instead of only for a hit out of the ground.

1912 First and only triangular Test series played in England, involving England, Australia and South Africa.

1915 W. G. Grace dies, aged 67.

1926 Victoria score 1,107 v New South Wales at Melbourne, still a first-class record.

1928 West Indies' first Test match.
A. P. Freeman of Kent and England becomes the only player to take more than 300 first-class wickets in a season: 304.

1930 New Zealand's first Test match.
Donald Bradman's first tour of England: he scores 974 runs in five Tests, still a record for any series.

1931 Stumps made higher (28 inches not 27) and wider (nine inches not eight – this was optional until 1947).

1932 India's first Test match.
Hedley Verity of Yorkshire takes ten wickets for ten runs v Nottinghamshire, the best innings analysis in first-class cricket.

1932-33 The Bodyline tour of Australia in which England bowl at batsmen's bodies with a packed leg-side field to neutralise Bradman's scoring.

1934 Jack Hobbs retires, with 197 centuries and 61,237 runs, both records.
First women's Test: Australia v England at Brisbane.

1935 MCC condemn and outlaw Bodyline.

1947 Denis Compton (Middlesex and England) hits a record 3,816 runs in an English season.

1948 First five-day Tests in England.
Bradman concludes Test career with a second-ball duck at The Oval and an average of 99.94 – four runs would have made it 100.

1952 Pakistan's first Test match.

1953 England regain the Ashes after a 19-year gap, the longest ever.

1956 Jim Laker of England takes 19 wickets for 90 v Australia at Manchester, the best match analysis in first-class cricket.

1960 First tied Test: Australia v West Indies at Brisbane.

1963 Distinction between amateurs and professionals abolished in English cricket.
The first major one-day tournament begins in England: the Gillette Cup.

1968 Garry Sobers becomes first man to hit six sixes in an over, for Nottinghamshire against Glamorgan at Swansea.

1969 Limited-over Sunday league inaugurated for first-class counties.

1970 Proposed South African tour of England cancelled; South Africa excluded from international cricket because of their government's apartheid policies.

1971 First one-day international: Australia beat England at Melbourne by five wickets.

1973 First women's World Cup: England are the winners.

1975 First men's World Cup: West Indies beat Australia in final at Lord's.

1976 First women's match at Lord's: England beat Australia by eight wickets.

1977 Centenary Test at Melbourne, with identical result to the first match: Australia beat England by 45 runs.
Australian media tycoon Kerry Packer signs 51 of the world's leading players in defiance of the cricketing authorities.

1978 Graham Yallop of Australia is the first batsman to wear a protective helmet in a Test.

1979 Packer and official cricket agree peace deal.

1981 England beat Australia in Leeds Test, after following on with bookmakers offering odds of 500-1 against them winning.

1982 Sri Lanka's first Test match.

1991 South Africa return, with a one-day international in India.

1992 Zimbabwe's first Test match.
Durham become first county since Glamorgan in 1921 to attain first-class status.

1993 The ICC cease to be administered by MCC, becoming an independent organisation.

1994 Brian Lara becomes the first player to pass 500 in a first-class innings: 501 not out for Warwickshire v Durham.

2000 South Africa's captain Hansie Cronje banned from cricket for life after admitting receiving bribes from bookmakers in match-fixing scandal.
Bangladesh's first Test match.
County Championship split into two divisions, with promotion and relegation.

2001 Sir Donald Bradman dies, aged 92.

2003 First Twenty20 game played, in England.

2004 Lara is the first to score 400 in a Test innings, for West Indies v England in Antigua.

2005 England regain the Ashes after 16 years.

2006 Pakistan become first team to forfeit a Test, for refusing to resume at The Oval.
Shane Warne becomes the first man to take 700 Test wickets.

2007 Australia complete 5–0 Ashes whitewash for the first time since 1920-21.
Australia win the World Cup for the third time running.
India beat Pakistan in the final of the inaugural World Twenty20.

2008 Indian Premier League of 20-over matches launched.
Sachin Tendulkar becomes the leading scorer in Tests, passing Lara.

2009 Terrorists in Lahore attack buses containing Sri Lankan team and match officials.

2010 Tendulkar scores the first double-century in a one-day international, against South Africa; later in the year, he scores his 50th Test century.
Muttiah Muralitharan retires from Test cricket, after taking his 800th wicket.
Pakistan bowl three deliberate no-balls in Lord's Test against England; the ICC ban the three players responsible.

2011 India become the first team to win the World Cup on home soil.
Salman Butt, Mohammad Asif and Mohammad Amir are given custodial sentences of between six and 30 months for their part in the Lord's spot-fix.

2012 Tendulkar scores his 100th international century, in a one-day game against Bangladesh at Mirpur.

2013 150th edition of *Wisden Cricketers' Almanack*.
Tendulkar retires after his 200th Test match, with a record 15,921 runs.

2014 Australia complete only the third 5–0 Ashes whitewash.
India's Rohit Sharma hits 264 in one-day international against Sri Lanka at Kolkata.
Australian batsman Phillip Hughes, 25, dies after being hit on the neck by a bouncer.

2015 Australia win World Cup for fifth time, beating New Zealand in final at Melbourne.

2016 Pranav Dhanawade, 15, makes 1,009 not out – the highest recorded individual score in any match – in a school game in Mumbai.
McCullum hits Test cricket's fastest hundred, from 54 balls, in his final match, against Australia at Christchurch.

2017 Afghanistan and Ireland awarded Test status.
England women beat India by nine runs to win the World Cup at Lord's.
England play their first day/night home Test, against West Indies at Edgbaston.
James Anderson takes his 500th Test wicket, against West Indies at Lord's.
Australia and England play first day/night Ashes Test, at Adelaide.

ANNIVERSARIES IN 2018–19

COMPILED BY STEVEN LYNCH

2018

April 7	Dennis Amiss (Warwickshire) born, 1943. *Long-lasting batsman whose 102 first-class centuries included 11 in Tests.*
April 28	Andy Flower (Zimbabwe) born, 1968. *Averaged 51 in 63 Tests, keeping wicket in most of them; later England's coach.*
May 14	Arthur McIntyre (Surrey) born, 1918. *Wicketkeeper for most of Surrey's seven 1950s Championships; later their coach.*
May 23	Denis Compton (Middlesex) born, 1918. *Charismatic batsman who hit 3,816 runs in 1947, with 18 centuries – both records.*
June 6	Asif Iqbal (Pakistan) born, 1943. *Test all-rounder and captain who also had a long career with Kent.*
July 4	Alec and Eric Bedser (Surrey) born, 1918. *English cricket's most famous twins: Alec took 236 wickets in 51 Tests.*
August 12	Frank Tarrant (Australia) takes all ten wickets in an innings, 1918. *For the Maharaja of Cooch-Behar's XI v Lord Willingdon's team in Poona.*
August 26	Basil D'Oliveira (England) scores 158 at The Oval, 1968. *One of the most famous Test innings, leading to South Africa's isolation.*
August 31	Garry Sobers (Nottinghamshire) hits six sixes in an over, 1968. *First instance in first-class cricket; the bowler was Glamorgan's Malcolm Nash.*
September 26	Ian Chappell (Australia) born, 1943. *Combative batsman and intuitive captain; later a leading TV commentator.*
October 11	Keith Boyce (West Indies) born, 1943, and dies, 1996. *Flamboyant all-rounder for Barbados and Essex; World Cup winner in 1975.*
October 14	Doug Ring (Australia) born, 1918. *Genial leg-spinner; one of Don Bradman's 1948 Invincibles.*
November 18	Reggie Schwarz (South Africa) dies, 1918. *One of a leg-spinning quartet as England were vanquished in 1905-06; died of illness in France.*
November 21	Andrew Caddick (Somerset) born, 1968. *New Zealand-born seamer who took 234 Test wickets for England.*
November 22	Mushtaq Mohammad (Pakistan) born, 1943. *Attractive batsman and underrated leg-spinner; made his Test debut aged 15.*
November 24	Roly Jenkins (Worcestershire) born, 1918. *Leg-spinner who took two hat-tricks against Surrey in 1949; won nine Test caps.*
December 6	Vijay Hazare (India) scores 309 out of 387 in Bombay, 1943. *For The Rest v Hindus, Hazare made 79% of the total. He put on 300 with his brother Vivek, who scored 21.*

2019

February 27	Graeme Pollock (South Africa) born, 1944. *One of the greatest of left-hand batsmen, averaged 60 in 23 Tests.*
March 16	Ottis Gibson (West Indies) born, 1969. *Much-travelled seamer who took all ten for Durham in 2007; became South Africa's coach in 2017.*
March 20	Karen Smithies (East Midlands) born, 1969. *Captained England to victory in the women's World Cup final at Lord's in 1993.*

ONE HUNDRED AND FIFTY YEARS AGO

from WISDEN CRICKETERS' ALMANACK 1869

INDIVIDUAL INNINGS OF 200 OR MORE RUNS by W. H. Knight "404 runs by one man!"... Vast as had unquestionably been the great scores of Alfred Adams, Mr Ward, Marsden, the two Graces, Hayward, and others, they were all outdone and put in the shade by the (numerically) greater scores played in 1868, during which very hot and arid season one innings of 404 runs was hit, and five of more than 200 runs – the six innings giving an aggregate of 1,543 runs. In fact, "the hitters of the period" in 1868 far away outhit the hitters of any other period, as they played the two largest innings – 689 and 630 – ever played by Elevens or any other sides, and they hit the two largest individual scores – 404 and 289 – hit since the game has been played. Mr Tylecote's 404 was made in a Clifton College practice match, and was hit in six hours, or at the rate of about 67 runs per hour, thus: – Mr Tylecote was first man in of his side, played about half-an-hour, and scored 34 runs on the first day (it was an afternoon's match); on the second afternoon he resumed his innings at 2.45, played up to 5.30, and increased the score to 199; and on the third day he was also at the wickets from 2.45 to 5.30, when he carried his bat out for 404 (out of 630). Mr Tylecote's hits were one seven, five fives, 21 fours, 39 threes, 42 twos, and 77 singles, and barring one four (a hit of Mr T's out of the field) *he ran all the runs made by his side*. Mr Batchelor's 289 is by ten runs the second-highest score yet played; it was hit in the highest innings – 689 runs – ever made by a side, and an innings wherein three men hit the astoundingly large number of 555 runs. The others of these innings hit last season were – one of 228 runs by Mr E. P. Ash, one of 211 *not out* by Mr Pauncefote (captain of this year's Oxford Eleven), one of 201 runs by Mr A. N. Hornby, and one of 210 by Mr W. G. Grace (who hit this innings the week following his playing his two great innings of 130 and 102 *not out, in one match* at Canterbury)."

ONE HUNDRED YEARS AGO

From WISDEN CRICKETERS' ALMANACK 1919

OTHER DEATHS IN 1918 GEORGE TUBOW II, King of Tonga. The last of the independent kings in the Pacific. Died April, aged 46. Very fond of cricket, gaining his love of the game while at school in Auckland. His subjects became so devoted to the game that it was necessary to prohibit it on six days of the week in order to avert famine, the plantations being entirely neglected for the cricket field.

NOTES BY THE EDITOR [Sydney Pardon] The long nightmare of the War has come to an end, and in the coming summer first-class cricket will again be in full swing. I have a very strong opinion that a grave mistake has been made in not letting the game alone...

By some evil chance, cricket, alone among our games and pastimes, has since the signing of the Armistice been signalled out for adverse criticism. Racing men, rowing men, golfers, and lawn tennis players were eager to get back as soon as possible to things as they were before the War, but it occurred to some peculiar people that cricket stood in need of drastic alterations. Personally I could not find any sound basis for their arguments. So far as I know the game was flourishing, when in August 1914 the world was suddenly turned upside down. Be this as it may, the resumption of first-class matches was no sooner announced than all the faddists in Great Britain began to fill the newspapers with their ideas of what they were pleased to call reform or reconstruction. Some of the suggestions, such as the penalising of the batting side for every maiden over played, were too preposterous to be worth a moment's consideration. Still, even the most fatuous proposals found supporters. We were advised to play by the clock and, regardless of weather and wicket, to rule a batsman out unless runs came at a certain fixed rate per hour. Then followed a determined agitation to get the boundaries shortened. I confess I was astonished to find among the advocates of this most mischievous proposition the name of F. S. Jackson. Short boundaries are open to three fatal objections. They would inevitably lead to higher scoring, the batsman's task being rendered still easier than it is today; they would kill slow bowling, and they would practically destroy fine out-fielding, the ball getting to the ring too quickly for mortal man to cross it.

As a rule the best cricket I ever see is at The Oval, the reason being that the boundaries are deep enough to make the hits worth the value placed on them. Many people seem to regard cricket purely as a spectacle, never giving a thought to the game itself. They need to be reminded that boundaries are quite outside cricket, being only rendered necessary by the presence of the crowd of spectators. When as a small boy I first went to The Oval, and for years afterwards, the only boundaries were the Pavilion and the refreshment tent. Fieldsmen used to jump over the single row of seats and return the ball from beyond the ring. Batsmen could get five, six, or in rare cases, seven runs for a big drive, but they paid the price in hard running between the wickets. With ten thousand or more people on the ground a return to the old system is impossible, but that is no reason why batsmen should be given increased facilities for getting four runs without moving a yard from the crease.

KENT IN 1918 Designs for the mural tablet in memory of Colin Blythe, to be erected in the parish church of Tonbridge and the County Memorial on the Canterbury ground were approved... The inscription upon the drinking fountain at Canterbury is: "To the memory of Colin Blythe of the Kent eleven, who volunteered for active service upon the outbreak of hostilities in the Great War of 1914-18, and was killed at Ypres on November 8, 1917, aged 39. He was unsurpassed among the famous bowlers of the period, and beloved by his fellow-cricketers. Also of his comrades of the Kent elevens who fell in the service of King and country. This obelisk is raised by the Kent County Cricket Club."

FIFTY YEARS AGO

From WISDEN CRICKETERS' ALMANACK 1969

ENGLAND v AUSTRALIA, FIFTH TEST MATCH, AT THE OVAL, AUGUST 22, 23, 24, 26, 27, 1968 – England won by 226 runs with six minutes to spare and squared the rubber with one victory to each country and three matches drawn, but The Ashes stayed with Australia. Down the years Kennington has generally proved a good place for England and now, after rain had robbed Cowdrey's men at Lord's and Edgbaston, even a storm that flooded the ground at lunch time on the last day could not save Australia. Just before the interval England's final task appeared to be a mere formality with Australia toiling at 85 for five. In half an hour the ground was under water, but the sun reappeared at 2.15pm and the groundsman, Ted Warn, ably assisted by volunteers from the crowd, armed with brooms and blankets, mopped up to such purpose that by 4.45pm the struggle was resumed.

Only 75 minutes remained and even then the deadened pitch gave the England bowlers no encouragement. Inverarity and Jarman stood up nobly to Brown, Snow, Illingworth and Underwood, no matter how Cowdrey switched his attack, with a cordon of ten men close to the bat. Finally, Cowdrey turned to D'Oliveira, who did the trick with the last ball of his second over; it moved from the off and hit the top of the off stump as Jarman reached forward.

Now 35 minutes were left for England to capture the four remaining wickets. Cowdrey promptly whisked D'Oliveira from the Pavilion End and recalled Underwood, who finished the contest by taking those four wickets in 27 deliveries for six runs. The Kent left-arm bowler found the drying pitch ideal for this purpose. He received just enough help to be well nigh unplayable. The ball almost stopped on pitching and lifted to the consternation of the helpless Australians. Underwood had Mallett and McKenzie held by Brown in the leg trap in the first over of his new spell; Gleeson stayed 12 minutes until his off stump was disturbed and to everyone's surprise Inverarity, having defied England for four hours with rare skill, offered no stroke at a straight ball and was leg-before.

So Underwood, with seven wickets for 50 runs, achieved his best bowling analysis in Test cricket and headed the England averages for the series with 20 wickets at 15.10 runs apiece. No praise could be too high for the way he seized his opportunity on this unforgettable day.

MCC IN WEST INDIES, 1967-68, by E. M. Wellings From the English viewpoint the 1967-68 MCC tour of West Indies was a conspicuous success. The team under the captaincy of Cowdrey and the management of Ames went unbeaten through a programme containing 12 first-class matches, and the Test series was won. A team in the full sense of the word played good cricket in most testing circumstances. Neither on nor off the field did they obviously put a foot wrong, despite unpleasant incidents, which might have provoked a group of players less well controlled.

From the West Indies' point of view the season's events were anything but satisfying. The tour focused a spotlight on unpleasant aspects of West Indies cricket. Chief among these were the clearly substandard umpiring and unruly crowds. Such is the pressure from supporters desiring success for the home side that even an efficient umpire is apt to be influenced. Umpiring and crowd behaviour are, therefore, closely associated. Quite the most professional of the umpires was Sang Hue, but he was never so efficient after as before his correct decision against Butcher in the second Test, which sparked a bottle-throwing riot by his fellow Jamaicans.

That riot, the third serious one of its kind in recent West Indies Test history, came when England were winning the match. That was the worst crowd incident of the tour. There was another act of hooliganism in Guyana after the final Test, when England had won the series. There the victorious side were attacked when leaving the ground. Lock was struck on the head by a stone, and Cowdrey was long compelled to wait in the pavilion until he could safely be escorted to his hotel by a police guard. In the previous Test in Trinidad, where England gained the vital victory, Cowdrey was subjected to quite unjustifiable booing by disappointed home supporters. His offences were to have played two superb innings and to have led England much more skilfully than Sobers had led West Indies.

There is no obvious solution to the allied umpiring and crowd behaviour problems. The West Indies authorities, however, must find a way out of their difficulties. In such an inflammatory atmosphere cricket ceases to be worthwhile…

The islands, rich in cricketing talent, have much to contribute to world cricket. It would be a loss to the game if the conditions of their play compelled other countries to cease sending them Test touring teams. It was against this background that M.C.C. triumphed… For the first time England became holders of the Wisden Trophy.

GLAMORGAN v NOTTINGHAMSHIRE, AT SWANSEA, AUGUST 31, SEPTEMBER 1, 2, 1968 Nottinghamshire won by 166 runs… This was the history-making match in which the incredible Garfield Sobers created a new world record by hitting six sixes in a six-ball over. Somehow one sensed that something extraordinary was going to happen when Sobers sauntered to the wicket. With over 300 runs on the board for the loss of only five wickets, he had the right platform from which to launch a spectacular assault, and the manner in which he immediately settled down to score at a fast rate was ominous.

Then came the history-making over by the 23-year-old Malcolm Nash. First crouched like a black panther eager to pounce, Sobers with lightning footwork got into position for a vicious straight-drive or pull. As Tony Lewis, Glamorgan's captain said afterwards, "It was not sheer slogging through strength, but scientific hitting with every movement working in harmony." Twice the ball was slashed out of the ground, and when the last six landed in the street outside it was not recovered until the next day. Then it was presented to Sobers and will have a permanent place in the Trent Bridge Cricket Museum.

Compiled by Christopher Lane

HONOURS AND AWARDS IN 2017-18

In 2017-18, the following were decorated for their services to cricket:

Queen's Birthday Honours, 2017: H. Tulip (services to cricket and community in Northumberland) BEM.

Queen's Birthday Honours (Australia), 2017: K. M. Dixon (Sandgate-Redcliffe DCC; services to cricket in Queensland) OAM; H. D. French (umpire and administrator; services to cricket and community of South Australia) OAM; J. B. Gannon (Western Australia and Australia; services to cricket) OAM; J. W. Hammer (founder of Mid-Year Cricket Association; services to cricket and seniors' sport in Victoria) OAM; J. D. Higgs (Victoria and Australia; services to cricket) OAM; T. J. Lowrey (scorer, South Australia; services to cricket) OAM; G. L. Reilley (Caulfield CC; services to cricket and Australian Rules football) OAM; H. Wooding (Albury and Border CA; services to cricket) OAM.

Queen's Birthday Honours (New Zealand), 2017: C. L. Bull (Canterbury, player and administrator; services to cricket) MNZM; E. A. Watkin (umpire and historian; services to cricket) QSM.

New Year's Honours, 2018: T. T. Beaumont (England women; services to cricket) MBE; C. J. Connor (England women; ECB director of women's cricket; services to cricket) CBE; H. C. Knight (England women; services to cricket) OBE; M. A. Robinson (England women's coach; services to cricket) OBE; A. Shrubsole (England women; services to cricket) MBE.

New Year's Honours (New Zealand), 2018: T. M. Luxton (scorer and administrator in Waitara; services to community and cricket) QSM.

Padma Awards (India), 2018: M. S. Dhoni (Bihar, Jharkhand and India) Padma Bhushan.

Australia Day Honours, 2018: R. J. Allen (North Geelong CC; services to cricket in Victoria) OAM; B. J. Clark (Australia women; services to cricket as player, captain and administrator) AO; P. F. Frawley (Carlton CC; services to cricket and community in Victoria) OAM; R. G. Matthews (Victoria; services to cricket) OAM; G. P. Morrissey (Parkes Junior CA; services to cricket and community in NSW) OAM; R. Sneddon (formerly at Australian Cricket Board; services to sports administration); O. L. Sperling (youth coach; services to cricket in Queensland) OAM.

ICC AWARDS

The ICC's 14th annual awards, selected by a panel of 23, were announced in January 2018.

Cricketer of the Year (Sir Garfield Sobers Trophy)	**Virat Kohli (I)**
Test Player of the Year	**Steve Smith (A)**
One-Day International Player of the Year	**Virat Kohli (I)**
Twenty20 International Performance of the Year	**Yuzvendra Chahal (I)**
Emerging Player of the Year	**Hasan Ali (P)**
Associate Player of the Year	**Rashid Khan (Afg)**
Umpire of the Year (David Shepherd Trophy)	**Marais Erasmus (SA)**
Spirit of Cricket Award	**Anya Shrubsole (E)**
Fans' Moment of the Year	**Pakistan stun India to win the Champions Trophy**

The panel also selected two men's World XIs from the previous 15 months:

ICC World Test team

1 Dean Elgar (SA)
2 David Warner (A)
3 *Virat Kohli (I)
4 Steve Smith (A)
5 Cheteshwar Pujara (I)
6 Ben Stokes (E)
7 †Quinton de Kock (SA)
8 Ravichandran Ashwin (I)
9 Mitchell Starc (A)
10 Kagiso Rabada (SA)
11 James Anderson (E)

ICC World one-day team

1 David Warner (A)
2 Rohit Sharma (I)
3 *Virat Kohli (I)
4 Babar Azam (P)
5 A. B. de Villiers (SA)
6 †Quinton de Kock (SA)
7 Ben Stokes (E)
8 Trent Boult (NZ)
9 Hasan Ali (P)
10 Rashid Khan (Afg)
11 Jasprit Bumrah (I)

Previous Cricketers of the Year were Rahul Dravid (2004), Andrew Flintoff and Jacques Kallis (jointly in 2005), Ricky Ponting (2006 and 2007), Shivnarine Chanderpaul (2008), Mitchell Johnson (2009 and 2014), Sachin Tendulkar (2010), Jonathan Trott (2011), Kumar Sangakkara (2012), Michael Clarke (2013), Steve Smith (2015) and Ravichandran Ashwin (2016).

The women's awards and World XIs, selected by a panel of 15, were announced in December 2017, and included the inaugural Rachael Heyhoe Flint Award for the Women's Cricketer of the Year:

Women's Cricketer of the Year (Rachael Heyhoe Flint Trophy)	**Ellyse Perry (A)**
Women's One-Day International Cricketer of the Year	**Amy Satterthwaite (NZ)**
Women's Twenty20 International Cricketer of the Year	**Beth Mooney (A)**
Women's Emerging Player of the Year	**Beth Mooney (A)**

ICC World Women's one-day team

1 Tammy Beaumont (E)
2 Meg Lanning (A)
3 Mithali Raj (I)
4 Amy Satterthwaite (NZ)
5 Ellyse Perry (A)
6 *Heather Knight (E)
7 †Sarah Taylor (E)
8 Dane van Niekerk (SA)
9 Marizanne Kapp (SA)
10 Ekta Bisht (I)
11 Alex Hartley (E)

ICC World Women's Twenty20 team

1 †Beth Mooney (A)
2 Danni Wyatt (E)
3 Harmanpreet Kaur (I)
4 *Stafanie Taylor (WI)
5 Sophie Devine (NZ)
6 Deandra Dottin (WI)
7 Hayley Matthews (WI)
8 Megan Schutt (A)
9 Amanda-Jade Wellington (A)
10 Lea Tahuhu (NZ)
11 Ekta Bisht (I)

ICC DEVELOPMENT PROGRAMME AWARDS

The ICC announced the global winners of their 2016 Development Programme Awards in April 2017. The Best Overall Cricket Development Programme won \$5,000 plus £5,000 worth of equipment, and the other five won \$2,000 each.

Best Overall Cricket Development Programme	**Malaysia Cricket Association**
Spirit of Cricket Award	**Uganda Cricket Association**
Image of the Year	**Cricket Brazil**
Lifetime Service Award	**Rob Kemming (Netherlands)**
Volunteer of the Year	**Ammar Ashraf (Scotland)**
Women's Cricket Award	**Pauline Njeru (Kenya)**

ALLAN BORDER MEDAL

David Warner retained the Allan Border Medal, for the best Australian international player of the past 12 months, in January 2017. Previous winners were Glenn McGrath, Steve Waugh, Matthew Hayden, Adam Gilchrist, Ricky Ponting (four times), Michael Clarke (four times), Brett Lee, Shane Watson (twice), Mitchell Johnson and Steve Smith. Warner received 269 votes from team-mates, umpires and journalists, 21 ahead of Smith (who was runner-up again), and was also named One-Day International Player of the Year. **Mitchell Starc** was Test Player of the Year and **Shane Watson** Twenty20 International Player of the Year – although he had retired from international cricket in March. **Cameron White** of Victoria was the Men's Domestic Cricketer of the Year, and Western Australia's **Hilton Cartwright** was the Bradman Young Player of the Year. Australia women's captain **Meg Lanning** won her third Belinda Clark Award for the Women's International Cricketer of the Year, as well as the inaugural Female Domestic Player of the Year, while **Sophie Molineux** won the inaugural award for the Betty Wilson Female Young Player of the Year.

SHEFFIELD SHIELD PLAYER OF THE YEAR

The Sheffield Shield Player of the Year Award for 2016-17 was won by **Chadd Sayers**, who took 62 wickets for finalists South Australia, the third-highest total in the competition's history. The award, instituted in 1975-76, is adjudicated by umpires over the season. Australian Capital Territory bowler **Thomas Rogers** won the Toyota Futures League Player of the Year award, and the Lord's

Taverners Indigenous Cricketer of the Year was **Cameron Trask** of Queensland. **Simon Fry** was Umpire of the Year for the fourth year running, while both the Benaud Spirit of Cricket Awards for fair play – men's and women's – were collected by **Tasmania**.

CRICKET SOUTH AFRICA AWARDS

South Africa's wicketkeeper-batsman **Quinton de Kock** won five CSA awards in May 2017: South African Cricketer of the Year, Test Cricketer, One-Day International Cricketer, Players' Player and Fans' Player of the Year. **Imran Tahir** was the Twenty20 International Cricketer of the Year for the second year running. **Kagiso Rabada**, who took six awards the previous year, retained the Delivery of the Year for bowling Usman Khawaja in the Perth Test, and **Temba Bavuma** the Award of Excellence, for his run-out of Australia's David Warner. The Women's Cricketer of the Year was **Sune Luus**, and the Women's Players' Player was **Lizelle Lee**. The International Newcomers of the Year were **Keshav Maharaj** and **Laura Wolvaardt**. In the domestic categories, the Titans collected four awards again: **Henry Davids** was One-Day Cup Cricketer of the Year, **Farhaan Behardien** CSA T20 Challenge Player of the Year, **Aiden Markram** Domestic Newcomer of the Year, and **Mark Boucher** Coach of the Year. **Duanne Olivier** of the Knights was Sunfoil Series Cricketer of the Year. **Colin Ackermann** of the Warriors was the Domestic Players' Player of the Season and the SACA Most Valuable Player. The Africa T20 Cup Player of the Tournament was **Patrick Kruger** of Northern Cape. **Shaun George** was the CSA Umpire of the Year, and the CSA Umpires' Umpire.

PROFESSIONAL CRICKETERS' ASSOCIATION AWARDS

The following awards were announced at the PCA's annual dinner in October 2017.

Reg Hayter Cup (NatWest PCA Player of the Year)	**Samit Patel** (Nottinghamshire)
John Arlott Cup (NatWest PCA Young Player of the Year)	**Jamie Porter** (Essex)
Investec Test Player of the Summer	**James Anderson**
Royal London One-Day International Player of the Summer	**Joe Root**
NatWest Women's Player of the Summer	**Natalie Sciver**
Specsavers County Championship Player of the Year	**Jamie Porter** (Essex)
NatWest T20 Blast Player of the Year	**Wayne Madsen** (Derbyshire)
Royal London One-Day Cup Player of the Year	**Colin Ingram** (Glamorgan)
Greene King PCA England Masters Player of the Year	**Owais Shah**
Harold Goldblatt Award (PCA Umpire of the Year)	**Michael Gough**
ECB Special Award	**Heather Knight and Mark Robinson**
PCA Lifetime Achievement Award	**Fred Rumsey**

PCA Team of the Year: **Alex Hales, Mark Stoneman, Colin Ingram, Kumar Sangakkara, Samit Patel, Darren Stevens, Ben Cox, Kyle Abbott, Craig Overton, Simon Harmer, Jamie Porter.**

CHRISTOPHER MARTIN-JENKINS SPIRIT OF CRICKET AWARDS

MCC and the BBC introduced the Spirit of Cricket awards in 2013 in memory of Christopher Martin-Jenkins, the former MCC president and *Test Match Special* commentator. In September 2017 the Elite Award, for the professional cricketer who made the biggest contribution to the Spirit of Cricket in the English season, went to **Anya Shrubsole**, who hit the winning boundary in the final over of England's semi-final in the women's World Cup, then stopped to console the distraught South African captain, Dane van Niekerk. She was the first woman to win the award.

WALTER LAWRENCE TROPHY

The Walter Lawrence Trophy for the fastest century in 2017 went to **Shahid Afridi**, who reached a hundred in 42 balls for Hampshire against Derbyshire in the T20 Blast quarter-final at Derby in August. He won the trophy plus £3,000. Since 2008, the Trophy has been available for innings in all senior cricket in England; previously, it was reserved for the fastest first-class hundred against authentic bowling (in 2017, Adam Rossington's 66-ball hundred for Northamptonshire v Loughborough MCCU on April 2). For the second year running, **Tammy Beaumont** won the award for the highest score by a woman; she scored 148 to help England beat South Africa at Bristol in the women's World Cup. The MCCU Universities Award went to **Martin Andersson**, who made 185 for Leeds/Bradford MCCU against Durham MCCU at the Racecourse in May. Beaumont and Andersson each received a silver medallion and £500. The award for the highest score by a school batsman against MCC went to **Will Jacks**, who scored 168 in 107 balls, including 14 sixes, for St George's College, Weybridge, in June, and played for England Under-19 against India Under-19 later in the season; he received a medallion and a Gray-Nicolls bat.

CRICKET WRITERS' CLUB AWARDS

In October 2017, the Cricket Writers' Club named **Dan Lawrence** Young Cricketer of the Year, for his role in Essex's Championship-winning campaign, in which he scored 761 runs at 44. His team-mate **Jamie Porter** was County Championship Player of the Year, after finishing as the competition's leading wicket-taker with 75. The second CWC Women's Cricketer of the Year was **Tammy Beaumont**, the leading run-scorer as England won the women's World Cup. The Peter Smith Memorial Award "for services to the presentation of cricket to the public" was made to former chairman of selectors **David Graveney**. The Cricket Book of the Year was **Steve Neal's** biography of Albert Trott, *Over and Out*.

A list of Young Cricketers from 1950 to 2004 appears in Wisden 2005, *page 995. A list of Peter Smith Award winners from 1992 to 2004 appears in* Wisden 2005, *page 745.*

GROUNDSMEN OF THE YEAR

Steve Birks regained the title of ECB Groundsman of the Year, which he last won in 2012, for his four-day pitches at Trent Bridge, and retained the one-day award, which he shared with **Andy Ward** of Grace Road, Leicester. **Lee Fortis** (The Oval) and **Andy Mackay** (Hove) were named as runners-up in the four-day category. **Lee Farquhar** (Arundel) and **Christian Brain** (Cheltenham College) were joint winners of the best outground award. The MCCU groundsman award, which is now the responsibility of MCC, went to **Richard Robinson** of Leeds/Bradford's Weetwood ground.

SPORTS PERSONALITY OF THE YEAR

World Cup winners **England Women** were named Team of the Year at the BBC Sports Personality show in December 2017, when **Anya Shrubsole** was one of the 12 nominees for the main Sports Personality, for her match-winning spell in the final against India. She finished ninth in the public vote, the highest of the four women nominated.

CRICKET SOCIETY AWARDS

Wetherell Award for Leading First-class All-rounder	**Samit Patel** (Nottinghamshire)
Wetherell Award for Leading Schools All-rounder	**Andrew Bramley** (The Leys, Cambridge)
Most Promising Young Male Cricketer	**Dan Lawrence** (Essex)
Most Promising Young Woman Cricketer	**Sophie Ecclestone** (Lancashire and England)
Sir John Hobbs Silver Jubilee Memorial Prize (for Outstanding Under-16 Schoolboy)	**Rishi Wijeratne** (Harrow School)
A. A. Thomson Fielding Prize for Best Schoolboy Fielder	**Eliot Goldthorp** (Ashville College, Harrogate)
Christopher Box-Grainger Memorial Trophy (for schools promoting cricket to the underprivileged)	**Jigsaw School, Cranleigh**
Don Rowan Memorial Trophy (for schools promoting cricket for disabled children)	**The Michael Tippett School, Lambeth**
Ian Jackson Award for Services to Cricket	**Charlotte Edwards**
The Perry-Lewis/Kershaw Trophy (for contribution to the Cricket Society XI)	**Robin Burns**

WOMBWELL CRICKET LOVERS' SOCIETY AWARDS

George Spofforth Cricketer of the Year	**James Anderson** (Lancashire)
Brian Sellers Captain of the Year	**Heather Knight** (England women)
C. B. Fry Young Cricketer of the Year	**Jamie Porter** (Essex)
Arthur Wood Wicketkeeper of the Year	**John Simpson** (Middlesex)
Learie Constantine Fielder of the Year	**Alastair Cook** (Essex/England)
Denis Compton Memorial Award for Flair	**Adam Lyth** (Yorkshire)
Dr Leslie Taylor Award (best Roses performance)	**Ben Coad** (Yorkshire)
Les Bailey Most Promising Young Yorkshire Player	**Ben Coad** (Yorkshire)
Ted Umbers Award – Services to Yorkshire Cricket	**Terry Bentham***
J. M. Kilburn Cricket Writer of the Year	**George Dobell** (ESPNcricinfo)
Jack Fingleton Cricket Commentator of the Year	**Dave Callaghan**

* *For services as an umpire and South Yorkshire Cricket official and administrator.*

ECB COUNTY JOURNALISM AWARDS

The ECB announced the winners of the seventh annual County Cricket Journalism Awards for the coverage of domestic cricket on November 6. **Isabelle Westbury** became the first woman to be named the Christopher Martin-Jenkins County Broadcaster of the Year. **Charlie Taylor**, who broadcast a fortnightly cricket show for BBC Somerset, was the Christopher Martin-Jenkins Young Journalist of the Year, with Will Macpherson (who won in 2016) and Westbury runners-up. The ***Nottingham Post*** was the Regional Newspaper of the Year, and the runners-up were the South-West's *Sunday Independent* and Stuart Rayner, for his coverage of the North-East in *The Journal* and the *Sunday Sun*. ***The Times*** won the award for Outstanding Newspaper Coverage of Domestic Cricket, with the *Daily Mail* commended; **BBC Online** (including Taylor's *BBC Somerset Cricket Show*) took the award for Outstanding Online Coverage of Domestic Cricket, with theguardian.com commended for their County Cricket Live Blog and coverage of the Women's Kia Super League.

ECB BUSINESS OF CRICKET AWARDS

The ECB announced the BOCA awards, designed to celebrate Marketing and PR excellence across domestic and international cricket, in November 2017. The Best International Campaign award was won by **Yorkshire**, who also won the Volunteer Development category, and the Best Domestic Campaign award went to **Derbyshire** for promoting the NatWest T20 Blast campaign; their media marketing manager **Chris Airey** was named Rising Star. **Nottinghamshire** won for Best Growth Strategy and Welcoming Families. MCC took the awards for the Warmest Welcome and for Service Excellence. **Kent** were recognised for the Best Commercial Partnership, **Somerset** for Fan Innovation, **Durham** for Inspiring Fan Loyalty, and **Warwickshire** for Unleashing Cricket, with their community programmes in and around Birmingham.

ECB OSCAs

The ECB presented the 2017 NatWest Outstanding Service to Cricket Awards to volunteers from recreational cricket in October. The winners were:

NatWest CricketForce Award — **Dave Cherry** (Derbyshire)
Organised volunteers at Denby CC to transform old scorebox into women's changing-rooms.

Get the Game On — **Martin Cassidy** (Nottinghamshire)
As chairman and groundsman, has steered Hucknall into the Nottinghamshire Premier League.

Heartbeat of the Club — **Cate Hayes** (Nottinghamshire)
Has served West Bridgfordians as junior co-ordinator, welfare officer, scorer and tea lady.

Leagues and Boards Award — **Andy Hunt** (Nottinghamshire)
Chairman of Nottinghamshire Premier League over the past two years.

Officiating – umpires and scorers — **Albert Pagan** (Durham)
Has just retired from umpiring aged 88 and ran the North Yorks/South Durham umpiring course.

Coach of the Year — **Khushali Patel** (Middlesex)
Runs a girls' team in Harrow and runs the local All Stars project for children.

Young Coach of the Year **Abigail Bates** (Lancashire)

Started girls' team at Shuttleworth College and took her students to watch women's World Cup.

Outstanding Contribution to Coaching **Bruce Storey** (Northumberland)

Benwell Hill coach involved in coach education and youth squads at Northumberland Cricket Board.

Young Volunteer Award (for Under-25s) **Megan Jones** (Staffordshire)

Coaches Under-8s, scores for the second team and promotes the women's game at Audley CC.

Lifetime Achiever **Graham Radford** (Sussex)

President, secretary and development officer at Felbridge & Sunnyside CC; over 45 years, he has captained the team, organised tours, raised funds and built partnerships with local schools.

Outstanding Contribution to Disability Cricket **Richard Hill** (Hertfordshire)

Helped to develop the national championship for disability cricket, and has introduced variations such as walking cricket for over-50s, clock cricket for care homes, and wheelchair cricket.

Under-19 Twenty20 Club of the Year **Ilminster Bears** (Somerset)

Attracted crowds to watch Friday evening matches with music, fancy dress and Prosecco tents.

All Stars Cricket Centre of the Year **Kings Heath CC** (Warwickshire)

Enthused a diverse range of children through social media, marketing and a bursary scheme.

CRICKET COMMUNITY CHAMPION AWARD

MCC and *The Cricketer* introduced a new award in 2017 recognising individuals working to build, maintain and support the game at grassroots level. The inaugural winner, announced in May, was **Julia Farman** from Dunstable in Bedfordshire, a coach and gender equality lead at Cricket Without Boundaries, a UK charity using cricket-related activities to deliver health and social messages in sub-Saharan Africa. She was invited to the one-day international between England and South Africa at Lord's on May 29 to ring the bell that signals the start of play.

ACS STATISTICIAN OF THE YEAR

In March 2018, the Association of Cricket Statisticians and Historians awarded the Brooke–Lambert Statistician of the Year trophy to Melbourne-based statistician **Charles Davis**, who had obtained copies of all surviving Test scorebooks and reconstructed the scores ball by ball, discovering new records in the process.

2018 FIXTURES

Test	Test match
RL ODI	Royal London one-day international
VT20I	Vitality Twenty20 international
RL WODI	Women's one-day-international
WVT20I	Vitality Women's T20 international
SSCC D1/2	Specsavers County Championship Division 1/Division 2
RLODC	Royal London One-Day Cup
VB T20	The Vitality Blast
KSL WT20	Women's Kia Super League
Univs	First-class university match
Univs (nfc)	Non-first-class university match
💡	Day/night or floodlit game

Tue Mar 27–Fri 30	**Friendly**	MCC	v Essex	Barbados	💡
Sun Apr 1–Tue 3	**Univs**	Kent	v Oxford MCCU	Canterbury	
		Warwickshire	v Durham MCCU	Birmingham	
		Cambridge MCCU	v Nottinghamshire	Cambridge	
		Worcestershire	v Leeds/Brad MCCU	Worcester	
		Sussex	v Loughboro MCCU	Hove	
		Gloucestershire	v Cardiff MCCU	Bristol	
Sat Apr 7–Mon 9	**Univs**	Hampshire	v Cardiff MCCU	Southampton	
		Yorkshire	v Leeds/Brad MCCU	Leeds	
		Cambridge MCCU	v Essex	Cambridge	
		Loughboro MCCU	v Lancashire	Loughborough	
		Middlesex	v Durham MCCU	Northwood	
		Oxford MCCU	v Northamptonshire	Oxford	
Fri Apr 13–Mon 16	**SSCC D1**	Hampshire	v Worcestershire	Southampton	
		Kent	v Gloucestershire	Canterbury	
		Warwickshire	v Sussex	Birmingham	
		Yorkshire	v Essex	Leeds	
		Lancashire	v Nottinghamshire	Manchester	
	SSCC D2	Middlesex	v Northamptonshire	Lord's	
Fri Apr 13–Sun 15	**Univs (nfc)**	Durham	v Durham MCCU	Chester-le-Street	
		Surrey	v Cambridge MCCU	The Oval	
		Glamorgan	v Cardiff MCCU	Cardiff	
		Somerset	v Oxford MCCU	Taunton	
		Leicestershire	v Loughboro MCCU	Leicester	
		Leeds/Brad MCCU	v Derbyshire	Weetwood	
Fri Apr 20–Mon 23	**SSCC D1**	Essex	v Lancashire	Chelmsford	
		Yorkshire	v Nottinghamshire	Leeds	
		Surrey	v Hampshire	The Oval	
		Somerset	v Worcestershire	Taunton	
	SSCC D2	Durham	v Kent	Chester-le-Street	
		Northamptonshire	v Warwickshire	Northampton	
		Derbyshire	v Middlesex	Derby	
		Gloucestershire	v Glamorgan	Bristol	
		Leicestershire	v Sussex	Leicester	
Fri Apr 27–Mon 30	**SSCC D1**	Lancashire	v Surrey	Manchester	
		Somerset	v Yorkshire	Taunton	
		Worcestershire	v Nottinghamshire	Worcester	
	SSCC D2	Leicestershire	v Derbyshire	Leicester	
		Middlesex	v Glamorgan	Lord's	
		Northamptonshire	v Durham	Northampton	
		Sussex	v Gloucestershire	Hove	

Sat Apr 28–Tue May 1	**Tour**	Kent	v Pakistanis	Canterbury
Thu May 3–Sun 6	**SSCC D2**	Warwickshire	v Derbyshire	Birmingham
Fri May 4–Mon 7	**SSCC D1**	Essex	v Yorkshire	Chelmsford
		Lancashire	v Somerset	Manchester
		Nottinghamshire	v Hampshire	Trent Bridge
		Surrey	v Worcestershire	The Oval
	SSCC D2	Durham	v Leicestershire	Chester-le-Street
		Glamorgan	v Kent	Cardiff
		Sussex	v Middlesex	Hove
	Tour	Northamptonshire	v Pakistanis	Northampton
Fri May 11–Tue 15	**Test**	**IRELAND**	**v PAKISTAN**	**Malahide**
Fri May 11–Mon 14	**SSCC D1**	Nottinghamshire	v Lancashire	Trent Bridge
		Somerset	v Hampshire	Taunton
		Surrey	v Yorkshire	The Oval
		Worcestershire	v Essex	Worcester
	SSCC D2	Derbyshire	v Durham	Derby
		Kent	v Sussex	Canterbury
		Leicestershire	v Glamorgan	Leicester
		Middlesex	v Gloucestershire	Lord's
		Warwickshire	v Northamptonshire	Birmingham
Thu May 17	**RLODC**	Lancashire	v Nottinghamshire	Manchester
		Middlesex	v Essex	Radlett
		Northamptonshire	v Leicestershire	Northampton
		Sussex	v Kent	Hove
		Warwickshire	v Derbyshire	Birmingham
Fri May 18	**RLODC**	Durham	v Yorkshire	Chester-le-Street
		Glamorgan	v Gloucestershire	Cardiff
		Surrey	v Somerset	The Oval
	Varsity T20	Oxford U	v Cambridge U	Oxford
	W Varsity T20	Oxford U	v Cambridge U	Oxford
Sat May 19	**RLODC**	Sussex	v Hampshire	Hove
		Worcestershire	v Derbyshire	Worcester
Sat May 19-Sun 20	**Tour**	Leicestershire	v Pakistanis	Leicester
Sun May 20	**RLODC**	Gloucestershire	v Essex	Bristol
		Lancashire	v Durham	Manchester
		Middlesex	v Kent	Radlett
		Nottinghamshire	v Northamptonshire	Sookholme
		Somerset	v Glamorgan	Taunton
		Yorkshire	v Warwickshire	Leeds
Mon May 21	**RLODC**	Hampshire	v Surrey	Southampton
Tue May 22	**RLODC**	Somerset	v Sussex	Taunton
Wed May 23	**RLODC**	Derbyshire	v Durham	Derby
		Glamorgan	v Middlesex	Cardiff
		Hampshire	v Essex	Southampton
		Leicestershire	v Nottinghamshire	Leicester
		Northamptonshire	v Lancashire	Northampton
		Surrey	v Gloucestershire	The Oval
		Yorkshire	v Worcestershire	Leeds
Thu May 24–Mon 28	**1st Test**	**ENGLAND**	**v PAKISTAN**	**Lord's**

Fri May 25	**RLODC**	Derbyshire	v	Leicestershire	Derby
		Durham	v	Worcestershire	Gosforth
		Essex	v	Somerset	Chelmsford
		Gloucestershire	v	Hampshire	Bristol
		Kent	v	Glamorgan	Canterbury
		Lancashire	v	Warwickshire	Blackpool
		Sussex	v	Middlesex	Hove
		Yorkshire	v	Nottinghamshire	Leeds
Sun May 27	**RLODC**	Essex	v	Surrey	Chelmsford
		Gloucestershire	v	Sussex	Bristol
		Hampshire	v	Kent	Southampton
		Leicestershire	v	Yorkshire	Leicester
		Northamptonshire	v	Durham	Northampton
		Nottinghamshire	v	Warwickshire	Trent Bridge
		Somerset	v	Middlesex	Taunton
		Worcestershire	v	Lancashire	Worcester
Tue May 29	**RLODC**	Kent	v	Somerset	Canterbury
		Surrey	v	Sussex	The Oval
		Worcestershire	v	Leicestershire	Worcester
Wed May 30	**RLODC**	Derbyshire	v	Yorkshire	Derby
		Essex	v	Glamorgan	Chelmsford
		Middlesex	v	Hampshire	Northwood
		Warwickshire	v	Northamptonshire	Birmingham
Thu May 31	**RLODC**	Leicestershire	v	Lancashire	TBC
Fri Jun 1–Tue 5	**2nd Test**	**ENGLAND**	**v**	**PAKISTAN**	**Leeds**
Fri Jun 1	**RLODC**	Durham	v	Warwickshire	Chester-le-Street
		Glamorgan	v	Sussex	Cardiff
		Kent	v	Surrey	Beckenham
		Northamptonshire	v	Derbyshire	Northampton
		Nottinghamshire	v	Worcestershire	Trent Bridge
		Somerset	v	Gloucestershire	Taunton
Sun Jun 3	**RLODC**	Derbyshire	v	Lancashire	Derby
		Durham	v	Nottinghamshire	Chester-le-Street
		Glamorgan	v	Hampshire	Swansea
		Kent	v	Gloucestershire	Beckenham
		Middlesex	v	Surrey	Lord's
		Sussex	v	Essex	Eastbourne
		Warwickshire	v	Leicestershire	Birmingham
		Worcestershire	v	Northamptonshire	Worcester
Tue Jun 5	**RLODC**	Lancashire	v	Yorkshire	Manchester
Wed Jun 6	**RLODC**	Essex	v	Kent	Chelmsford
		Gloucestershire	v	Middlesex	Bristol
		Hampshire	v	Somerset	Southampton
		Surrey	v	Glamorgan	The Oval
Thu Jun 7	**RLODC**	Leicestershire	v	Durham	Leicester
		Nottinghamshire	v	Derbyshire	Trent Bridge
		Warwickshire	v	Worcestershire	Birmingham
		Yorkshire	v	Northamptonshire	Leeds
Thu Jun 7	**Tour (o-d)**	Sussex	v	Australians	Hove
Sat Jun 9–Tue 12	**SSCC D1**	Hampshire	v	Surrey	Southampton
		Lancashire	v	Essex	Manchester
		Somerset	v	Nottinghamshire	Taunton
	SSCC D2	Durham	v	Derbyshire	Chester-le-Street
		Gloucestershire	v	Kent	Bristol
		Northamptonshire	v	Leicestershire	Northampton
		Warwickshire	v	Glamorgan	Birmingham

Sat Jun 9	**RL WODI**	**ENGLAND WOMEN**	**v SA WOMEN**	**Worcester**
	Tour (o-d)	Middlesex	v Australians	Lord's
Sun Jun 10	**ODI**	**SCOTLAND**	**v ENGLAND**	**Edinburgh**
Tue Jun 12	**RL WODI**	**ENGLAND WOMEN**	**v SA WOMEN**	**Hove**
	T20I	**SCOTLAND**	**v PAKISTAN**	**Edinburgh**
Wed Jun 13	**RL ODI**	**ENGLAND**	**v AUSTRALIA**	**The Oval**
	T20I	**SCOTLAND**	**v PAKISTAN**	**Edinburgh**
Thu Jun 14	**RLODC**	**Quarter-finals**		
Fri Jun 15	**RL WODI**	**ENGLAND WOMEN**	**v SA WOMEN**	**Canterbury**
Sat Jun 16	**RL ODI**	**ENGLAND**	**v AUSTRALIA**	**Cardiff**
Sun Jun 17	**RLODC**	**Semi-final**		
	Tour (o-d)	Warwickshire	v West Indies A	Birmingham
		Yorkshire	v India A	Leeds
Mon Jun 18	**RLODC**	**Semi-final**		
Tue Jun 19	**RL ODI**	**ENGLAND**	**v AUSTRALIA**	**Trent Bridge**
	Tour (o-d)	Leicestershire	v India A	Leicester
		Worcestershire	v West Indies A	Worcester
Wed Jun 20	**WVT20I**	**ENGLAND WOMEN**	**v SA WOMEN**	**Taunton**
	WVT20I	**SA WOMEN**	**v NZ WOMEN**	**Taunton**
Wed Jun 20–Sat 23	**SSCC D1**	Essex	v Nottinghamshire	Chelmsford
		Hampshire	v Yorkshire	Southampton
		Surrey	v Somerset	Guildford
		Worcestershire	v Lancashire	Worcester
	SSCC D2	Glamorgan	v Derbyshire	Swansea
		Kent	v Warwickshire	TBC
		Leicestershire	v Middlesex	Leicester
		Northamptonshire	v Gloucestershire	Northampton
		Sussex	v Durham	Arundel
Thu Jun 21	**RL ODI**	**ENGLAND**	**v AUSTRALIA**	**Chester-le-Street**
Fri Jun 22	**Tour (o-d)**	England Lions	v India A	Derby
	Varsity (o-d)	Oxford U	v Cambridge U	Lord's
	W Varsity (o-d)	Oxford U	v Cambridge U	Lord's (Nursery)
Sat Jun 23	**WVT20I**	**ENGLAND WOMEN**	**v SA WOMEN**	**Taunton**
	WVT20I	**ENGLAND WOMEN**	**v NZ WOMEN**	**Taunton**
	Tour (o-d)	England Lions	v West Indies A	Derby
Sun Jun 24	**RL ODI**	**ENGLAND**	**v AUSTRALIA**	**Manchester**
Mon Jun 25–Thu 28	**SSCC D1**	Essex	v Somerset	Chelmsford
		Lancashire	v Hampshire	Manchester
		Nottinghamshire	v Worcestershire	Trent Bridge
		Yorkshire	v Surrey	Scarborough
	SSCC D2	Derbyshire	v Leicestershire	Derby
		Durham	v Warwickshire	Chester-le-Street
		Glamorgan	v Northamptonshire	Cardiff
		Kent	v Middlesex	Canterbury
Mon Jun 25	**Tour (o-d)**	India A	v West Indies A	Leicester
Tue Jun 26	**Tour (o-d)**	England Lions	v India A	Leicester
Wed Jun 27	**VT20I**	**ENGLAND**	**v AUSTRALIA**	**Birmingham**
	T20I	**IRELAND**	**v INDIA**	**Malahide**

Thu Jun 28	WVT20I	**ENGLAND WOMEN**	**v NZ WOMEN**	**Bristol**
	WVT20I	**SA WOMEN**	**v NZ WOMEN**	**Bristol**
	Tour (o-d)	England Lions	v West Indies A	Northampton
Fri June 29	T20I	**IRELAND**	**v INDIA**	**Malahide**
	Tour (o-d)	India A	v West Indies A	Northampton
Sat Jun 30	RLODC	**Final**		**Lord's**
Sun Jul 1	WVT20I	**Tri-series final**		**Chelmsford**
Mon Jul 2–Thu 5	Varsity	Oxford U	v Cambridge U	Oxford
Mon Jul 2	Tour (o-d)	Lions/A team final		The Oval
Tue Jul 3	VT20I	**ENGLAND**	**v INDIA**	**Manchester**
Wed Jul 4–Sat 7	Tour	India A	v West Indies A	Beckenham
Wed Jul 4	VB T20	Essex	v Sussex	Chelmsford
		Northamptonshire	v Leicestershire	Northampton
		Nottinghamshire	v Warwickshire	Trent Bridge
Thu Jul 5	VB T20	Lancashire	v Worcestershire	Manchester
		Middlesex	v Surrey	Lord's
		Yorkshire	v Durham	Leeds
Fri Jul 6	VT20I	**ENGLAND**	**v INDIA**	**Cardiff**
	VB T20	Derbyshire	v Lancashire	Derby
		Essex	v Middlesex	Chelmsford
		Hampshire	v Glamorgan	Southampton
		Leicestershire	v Durham	Leicester
		Northamptonshire	v Nottinghamshire	Northampton
		Somerset	v Gloucestershire	Taunton
		Surrey	v Kent	The Oval
		Worcestershire	v Warwickshire	Worcester
Sat Jul 7	RL WODI	**ENGLAND WOMEN**	**v NZ WOMEN**	**Leeds**
Sun Jul 8	VT20I	**ENGLAND**	**v INDIA**	**Bristol**
Sun Jul 8–Wed 11	U19 Test	England U19	v South Africa U19	Scarborough
Sun Jul 8	VB T20	Derbyshire	v Worcestershire	Derby
		Glamorgan	v Sussex	Cardiff
		Lancashire	v Northamptonshire	Manchester
		Leicestershire	v Nottinghamshire	Leicester
		Middlesex	v Gloucestershire	Uxbridge
		Somerset	v Kent	Taunton
		Warwickshire	v Yorkshire	Birmingham
Tue Jul 10	RL WODI	**ENGLAND WOMEN**	**v NZ WOMEN**	**Derby**
Tue Jul 10–Fri 13	Tour	India A	v West Indies A	Taunton
Wed Jul 11	VB T20	Gloucestershire	v Kent	Bristol
		Yorkshire	v Derbyshire	Leeds
Thu Jul 12	RL ODI	**ENGLAND**	**v INDIA**	**Trent Bridge**
	VB T20	Hampshire	v Sussex	Southampton
		Surrey	v Essex	The Oval
Fri Jul 13	RL WODI	**ENGLAND WOMEN**	**v NZ WOMEN**	**Leicester**
	VB T20	Derbyshire	v Nottinghamshire	Derby
		Durham	v Yorkshire	Chester-le-Street
		Essex	v Glamorgan	Chelmsford
		Gloucestershire	v Somerset	Bristol
		Kent	v Hampshire	Beckenham
		Sussex	v Surrey	Hove
		Warwickshire	v Leicestershire	Birmingham
		Worcestershire	v Northamptonshire	Worcester

Sat Jul 14	**RL ODI**	**ENGLAND**	**v INDIA**	**Lord's**
	VB T20	Lancashire	v Derbyshire	Manchester
Sun Jul 15	**VB T20**	Warwickshire	v Durham	Birmingham
		Worcestershire	v Yorkshire	Worcester
Mon Jul 16–Thu 19	**SSCC D2**	Gloucestershire	v Sussex	Cheltenham
	Tour	England Lions	v India A	Worcester
	U19 Test	England U19	v South Africa U19	Chester-le-Street
Mon Jul 16–Wed 18	**Tour**	Surrey	v West Indies A	The Oval
Tue Jul 17	**RL ODI**	**ENGLAND**	**v INDIA**	**Leeds**
	VB T20	Nottinghamshire	v Durham	Trent Bridge
Wed Jul 18	**VB T20**	Leicestershire	v Lancashire	Leicester
Thu Jul 19	**VB T20**	Middlesex	v Somerset	Lord's
		Northamptonshire	v Derbyshire	Northampton
Fri Jul 20	**VB T20**	Durham	v Worcestershire	Chester-le-Street
		Glamorgan	v Somerset	Cardiff
		Gloucestershire	v Essex	Cheltenham
		Hampshire	v Middlesex	Southampton
		Kent	v Surrey	Canterbury
		Lancashire	v Yorkshire	Manchester
		Nottinghamshire	v Leicestershire	Trent Bridge
		Warwickshire	v Northamptonshire	Birmingham
Sat Jul 21	**VB T20**	Essex	v Hampshire	Chelmsford
Sun Jul 22–Thu 25	**SSCC D1**	Lancashire	v Yorkshire	Manchester
		Nottinghamshire	v Surrey	Trent Bridge
		Worcestershire	v Somerset	Worcester
	SSCC D2	Derbyshire	v Northamptonshire	Chesterfield
		Gloucestershire	v Durham	Cheltenham
		Kent	v Leicestershire	Canterbury
		Middlesex	v Warwickshire	Lord's
		Sussex	v Glamorgan	Hove
Sun Jul 22	**KSL WT20**	Lancashire T	v Loughboro L	TBC
		Surrey S	v Southern V	Guildford
		Western S	v Yorkshire D	Taunton
Mon Jul 23	**U19 ODI**	England U19	v South Africa U19	Chester-le-Street
Wed Jul 25–Sat 28	**Tour**	Essex	v Indians	Chelmsford
Wed Jul 25	**KSL WT20**	Southern V	v Loughboro L	Southampton
Thu Jul 26	**U19 ODI**	England U19	v South Africa U19	Gosforth
	VB T20	Middlesex	v Hampshire	Lord's
	KSL WT20	Western S	v Surrey S	Cheltenham
Fri Jul 27	**VB T20**	Gloucestershire	v Glamorgan	Cheltenham
		Kent	v Sussex	Canterbury
		Leicestershire	v Derbyshire	Leicester
		Northamptonshire	v Worcestershire	Northampton
		Nottinghamshire	v Lancashire	Trent Bridge
		Surrey	v Somerset	The Oval
		Yorkshire	v Warwickshire	Leeds
	KSL WT20	Yorkshire D	v Lancashire T	Leeds
Sat Jul 28	**VB T20**	Derbyshire	v Yorkshire	Chesterfield
		Durham	v Nottinghamshire	Chester-le-Street

Sun Jul 29	**U19 ODI**	England U19	v South Africa U19	Scarborough
	VB T20	Glamorgan	v Kent	Cardiff
		Somerset	v Middlesex	Taunton
		Sussex	v Hampshire	Hove
		Worcestershire	v Lancashire	Worcester
	KSL WT20	Lancashire T	v Southern V	TBC
		Surrey S	v Yorkshire D	Guildford
		Western S	v Loughboro L	Taunton
Tue Jul 31	**VB T20**	Surrey	v Glamorgan	The Oval
		Yorkshire	v Leicestershire	Leeds
	KSL WT20	Loughboro L	v Yorkshire D	Loughborough
		Southern V	v Western S	Arundel
		Surrey S	v Lancashire T	The Oval
Wed Aug 1–Sun 5	**1st Test**	**ENGLAND**	**v INDIA**	**Birmingham**
Wed Aug 1	**VB T20**	Somerset	v Hampshire	Taunton
		Sussex	v Gloucestershire	Hove
Thu Aug 2	**VB T20**	Durham	v Northamptonshire	Chester-le-Street
		Kent	v Essex	Canterbury
		Leicestershire	v Warwickshire	Leicester
		Nottinghamshire	v Derbyshire	Trent Bridge
		Middlesex	v Sussex	Lord's
	KSL WT20	Loughboro L	v Surrey S	Loughborough
		Yorkshire D	v Southern V	York
Fri Aug 3	**VB T20**	Derbyshire	v Warwickshire	Derby
		Glamorgan	v Gloucestershire	Cardiff
		Hampshire	v Kent	Southampton
		Lancashire	v Leicestershire	Manchester
		Somerset	v Essex	Taunton
		Surrey	v Middlesex	The Oval
		Worcestershire	v Durham	Worcester
		Yorkshire	v Northamptonshire	Leeds
	KSL WT20	Lancashire T	v Western S	Manchester
Sat Aug 4	**VB T20**	Nottinghamshire	v Worcestershire	Trent Bridge
	KSL WT20	Loughboro L	v Southern V	Loughborough
Sun Aug 5	**VB T20**	Essex	v Surrey	Chelmsford
		Kent	v Gloucestershire	Canterbury
		Middlesex	v Glamorgan	Richmond
		Northamptonshire	v Warwickshire	Northampton
		Sussex	v Somerset	Hove
	KSL WT20	Yorkshire D	v Western S	Scarborough
Tue Aug 7	**VB T20**	Glamorgan	v Essex	Cardiff
		Lancashire	v Durham	Manchester
	KSL WT20	Lancashire T	v Surrey S	Manchester
Wed Aug 8	**VB T20**	Derbyshire	v Northamptonshire	Derby
		Durham	v Leicestershire	Chester-le-Street
		Hampshire	v Somerset	Southampton
	KSL WT20	Southern V	v Yorkshire D	Southampton
Thu Aug 9–Mon 13	**2nd Test**	**ENGLAND**	**v INDIA**	**Lord's**
Thu Aug 9	**VB T20**	Gloucestershire	v Middlesex	Bristol
		Surrey	v Sussex	The Oval
		Warwickshire	v Nottinghamshire	Birmingham
		Worcestershire	v Derbyshire	Worcester
		Yorkshire	v Lancashire	Leeds
	KSL WT20	Surrey S	v Loughboro L	Guildford
		Western S	v Lancashire T	Taunton

Fri Aug 10	**VB T20**	Essex	v Gloucestershire	Chelmsford
		Glamorgan	v Hampshire	Cardiff
		Lancashire	v Warwickshire	Manchester
		Leicestershire	v Worcestershire	Leicester
		Northamptonshire	v Durham	Northampton
		Nottinghamshire	v Yorkshire	Trent Bridge
		Somerset	v Surrey	Taunton
		Sussex	v Kent	Hove
Sat Aug 11	**VB T20**	Derbyshire	v Leicestershire	Derby
	KSL WT20	Loughboro L	v Lancashire T	Loughborough
		Western S	v Southern V	Bristol
Sun Aug 12	**VB T20**	Durham	v Lancashire	Chester-le-Street
		Gloucestershire	v Surrey	Bristol
		Hampshire	v Essex	Southampton
		Kent	v Middlesex	Beckenham
		Somerset	v Glamorgan	Taunton
		Worcestershire	v Nottinghamshire	Worcester
	KSL WT20	Yorkshire D	v Surrey S	York
Tue Aug 14	**VB T20**	Sussex	v Glamorgan	Hove
	KSL WT20	Southern V	v Surrey S	Hove
		Lancashire T	v Yorkshire D	Blackpool
Wed Aug 15	**VB T20**	Surrey	v Hampshire	Birmingham
		Warwickshire	v Lancashire	The Oval
	KSL WT20	Loughboro L	v Western S	Birmingham
Thu Aug 16	**VB T20**	Gloucestershire	v Sussex	Bristol
		Kent	v Somerset	Canterbury
		Middlesex	v Essex	Lord's
		Northamptonshire	v Yorkshire	Northampton
Fri Aug 17	**VB T20**	Durham	v Derbyshire	Chester-le-Street
		Essex	v Kent	Chelmsford
		Glamorgan	v Surrey	Cardiff
		Hampshire	v Gloucestershire	Southampton
		Leicestershire	v Northamptonshire	Leicester
		Sussex	v Middlesex	Hove
		Warwickshire	v Worcestershire	Birmingham
		Yorkshire	v Nottinghamshire	Leeds
Sat Aug 18–Wed 22	**3rd Test**	**ENGLAND**	**v INDIA**	**Trent Bridge**
Sat Aug 18	**KSL WT20**	Southern V	v Lancashire T	Southampton
		Surrey S	v Western S	The Oval
		Yorkshire D	v Loughboro L	Leeds
Sun Aug 19–Wed 22	**SSCC D1**	Hampshire	v Nottinghamshire	Southampton
		Somerset	v Essex	Taunton
		Surrey	v Lancashire	The Oval
		Yorkshire	v Worcestershire	Scarborough
	SSCC D2	Glamorgan	v Durham	Cardiff
		Leicestershire	v Kent	Leicester
		Northamptonshire	v Middlesex	Northampton
		Sussex	v Derbyshire	Hove
		Warwickshire	v Gloucestershire	Birmingham
Thu Aug 23	**VB T20**	**Quarter-final**		
Fri Aug 24	**VB T20**	**Quarter-final**		
Sat Aug 25	**VB T20**	**Quarter-final**		
Sun Aug 26	**VB T20**	**Quarter-final**		

Mon Aug 27	**KSL WT20**	**Semi-finals and final**		**Hove**
Wed Aug 29–Sat Sep 1	**SSCC D1**	Essex	v Hampshire	Chelmsford
		Lancashire	v Worcestershire	Southport
		Surrey	v Nottinghamshire	The Oval
		Yorkshire	v Somerset	Leeds
	SSCC D2	Derbyshire	v Kent	Derby
		Durham	v Northamptonshire	Chester-le-Street
		Glamorgan	v Warwickshire	Colwyn Bay
		Gloucestershire	v Leicestershire	Bristol
		Middlesex	v Sussex	Lord's
Thu Aug 30–Mon 1	**4th Test**	**ENGLAND**	**v INDIA**	**Southampton**
Tue Sep 4–Fri 7	**SSCC D1**	Essex	v Surrey	Chelmsford
		Nottinghamshire	v Yorkshire	Trent Bridge
		Somerset	v Lancashire	Taunton
		Worcestershire	v Hampshire	Worcester
	SSCC D2	Derbyshire	v Glamorgan	Derby
		Gloucestershire	v Middlesex	Bristol
		Kent	v Northamptonshire	Canterbury
		Sussex	v Leicestershire	Hove
		Warwickshire	v Durham	Birmingham
Fri Sep 7–Tue 11	**5th Test**	**ENGLAND**	**v INDIA**	**The Oval**
Mon Sep 10–Thu 13	**SSCC D1**	Hampshire	v Somerset	Southampton
		Nottinghamshire	v Essex	Trent Bridge
		Worcestershire	v Surrey	Worcester
		Yorkshire	v Lancashire	Leeds
	SSCC D2	Durham	v Sussex	Chester-le-Street
		Glamorgan	v Gloucestershire	Cardiff
		Leicestershire	v Warwickshire	Leicester
		Middlesex	v Kent	Lord's
		Northamptonshire	v Derbyshire	Northampton
Sat Sep 15	**VB T20**	**Semi-finals and final**		**Birmingham**
Sun Sep 16		Village final		Lord's
Tue Sep 18–Fri 21	**SSCC D1**	Essex	v Worcestershire	Chelmsford
		Somerset	v Surrey	Taunton
		Yorkshire	v Hampshire	Leeds
	SSCC D2	Gloucestershire	v Northamptonshire	Bristol
		Kent	v Glamorgan	Canterbury
		Leicestershire	v Durham	Leicester
		Middlesex	v Derbyshire	Lord's
		Sussex	v Warwickshire	Hove
Sun Sep 23		Clubs final		Bristol
Mon Sep 24–Thu 27	**SSCC D1**	Hampshire	v Lancashire	Southampton
		Nottinghamshire	v Somerset	Trent Bridge
		Surrey	v Essex	The Oval
		Worcestershire	v Yorkshire	Worcester
	SSCC D2	Derbyshire	v Gloucestershire	Derby
		Durham	v Middlesex	Chester-le-Street
		Glamorgan	v Leicestershire	Cardiff
		Northamptonshire	v Sussex	Northampton
		Warwickshire	v Kent	Birmingham

ERRATA

Wisden 1931	Page 268	C. H. Titchmarsh made his Hertfordshire debut in 1900, and played four further games in the Minor Counties Championship in 1901, though he did not reappear until 1906.
Wisden 1938	Pages 147–152	In the first-class averages for 1937, six players' figures mistakenly include a Minor Counties Challenge match between Surrey Second XI and Lancashire Second XI. On p147, W. Place's batting figures should be 20 1 563 137 29.63
		On p150, the bowling figures for R. Parkin and L. L. Wilkinson should be 63 12 200 7 28.57 and 190.4 29 620 22 28.18 respectively.
		On p151, the bowling figures for A. Nutter and F. Berry should be 115.5 26 304 11 27.63 and 91 15 302 12 25.16 respectively.
		On p152, F. Gamble should not appear as he did not play a first-class match in 1937.
	Page 212	In the New Zealanders' second innings, the figures 11–2–31–0 should belong to A. Nutter, not F. Watson.
Wisden 1962	Page 326	In Yorkshire's second innings v MCC, D. Wilson was c Prideaux b Bedford, not the other way round.
Wisden 2000	Page 1560	Donald Shearer did not play football for Ireland, but for the England Amateur International team and the Irish League. He played for Great Britain rather than England in the 1936 Olympics; he scored only one goal against Poland.
Wisden 2016	Page 213	Ken Graveney was Gloucestershire golf champion in 1968 and captain in 1971-72.
Wisden 2017	Page 202	George Ulyett, not Johnny Briggs, scored 1,562 runs without a century in 1883.
	Page 207	Hanif Mohammad scored 3,915 runs in Tests and, as stated, 17,059 in first-class cricket.
	Page 237	Dave Watt died on September 25, 2015 – not 2016, as implied.
	Page 293	T. W. J. Goddard took his comeback 6-29 in 1937, not 1947.
	Page 383	The page reference should be to page 823, the World T20 semi-final.
	Page 455	The Glamorgan attack was missing the rested seamers Graham Wagg, Michael Hogan and Craig Meschede.
	Page 576	It was Burns who dropped Leach at slip in Somerset's match with Surrey.
	Page 717	Leeds/Bradford, not Loughborough, won the 2015 MCC Universities Challenge final.
	Page 789	Scotland's two matches against Hong Kong were one-day internationals, although the first was reduced to 20 overs a side.

"I was leading a different life, because I was playing for England while others were worrying about fake ID."
Five Cricketers of the Year, page 96

Page 831 — Andrew de Boorder and Tim Southee's fifth-wicket stand for New Zealand Under-19 was in 2005-06.

Page 985 — The missing Pakistan bowling averages appear below:

	Style	*O*	*M*	*R*	*W*	*BB*	*5I*	*Avge*
Wahab Riaz	LF	79.1	5	246	10	5-88	1	24.60
Yasir Shah	LB	192.4	38	564	21	6-124	2	26.85
Rahat Ali	LFM	44	10	114	4	3-45	0	28.50
Mohammad Nawaz.	SLA	63.5	12	147	5	2-32	0	29.40
Mohammad Amir.	LFM	79.5	16	231	6	3-63	0	38.50
Zulfiqar Babar	SLA	67	15	149	3	2-51	0	49.66
Sohail Khan	RFM	59	14	157	3	2-35	0	52.33

Page 1020 — David Miller missed the fourth ODI through injury but returned for the fifth.

Page 1043 — Daryn Smit, not Smith, reached 1,000 runs at Pietermaritzburg on March 18–21.

Page 1080 — Garry Sobers combined a century with five wickets in the 1966 Leeds Test, not The Oval.

Page 1101 — Jon-Russ Jaggesar was 29, not 19, for most of the West Indian season.

Page 1138 — In the note on the Quadrangular final at Mackay, David Miller scored 332 not 322.

Page 1140 — In the penultimate game, Kyle Hope was 27 not 17.

Page 1276 — J. M. Anderson had conceded 13,310 runs in Tests up to January 23, 2017.

Page 1480 — Richie Benaud was 84 when he died in 2015.

CHARITIES IN 2017

ARUNDEL CASTLE CRICKET FOUNDATION – more than 300,000 disadvantaged youngsters, many with special needs, mainly from inner-city areas, have received instruction and encouragement at Arundel since 1986. In 2017, there were over 90 days devoted to activities, and 4,500 young people benefited. Donations can be made at www.justgiving.com/arundelcastlecricket. Director of cricket: John Barclay, Arundel Park, Sussex BN18 9LH. Tel: 01903 882602; www.arundelcastlecricketfoundation.co.uk.

THE BRIAN JOHNSTON MEMORIAL TRUST supports cricket for the blind, and aims to ease the financial worries of talented young cricketers through scholarships. The BJMT spin-bowling programme was launched in 2010 to provide expert coaching to the first-class county Academies and the MCCUs. Registered Charity No. 1045946. Trust administrator: Richard Anstey, 178 Manor Drive North, Worcester Park, Surrey KT4 7RU; contact@lordstaverners.org; www.lordstaverners.org/brian-johnston-memorial-trust.

BUNBURY CRICKET CLUB has raised over £17m for national charities and worthwhile causes since 1987. A total of 1,736 boys have played in the Bunbury Festival; 883 have gone on to play first-class cricket, and 85 for England. The 32nd Festival, in August 2018, will be at Monmouth School. The Bunburys also presented the only two Under-15 World Cups (in 1996 and 2000). Further information from Dr David English CBE, 1 Highwood Cottages, Nan Clark's Lane, London NW7 4HJ; davidenglishbunbury@gmail.com; www.bunburycricket.co.uk.

CAPITAL KIDS CRICKET, formed in 1989, aims to improve the physical, social and emotional development of children. It is a fully inclusive organisation providing sporting and social opportunities in the more deprived areas of London, and organises activities in state schools, hospitals, community centres, local parks, and residential centres away from London: the Spirit of Cricket is at the heart of what we do. Around 10,000 young people are involved every year. Chairman: John Challinor, 79 Gore Road, London E9 7HN; johnchallinor@hotmail.com. Chief executive: Shahidul Alam Ratan; 07748 114811; shahidul.alam@capitalkidscricket.org.uk; www.capitalkidscricket.org.uk.

CHANCE TO SHINE is a national children's charity on a mission to spread the power of cricket throughout schools and communities. Since launching in 2005, Chance to Shine has reached over 3.5m children across 14,000 state schools. Contact: The Kia Oval, London SE11 5SW. Tel: 020 7735 2881; www.chancetoshine.org.

THE CHANGE FOUNDATION uses sport to change young lives. In partnership with Investec we use Street20 cricket for the Inner City World Cup in London, and also run the Refugee Cricket Project in partnership with the Refugee Council. Our disability sports programme Hit The Top delivers thriving new clubs and projects. Overseas work has included initiatives in Europe (in partnership with the ICC), Afghanistan, Israel and the West Bank, Brazil, Jamaica, Barbados, Rwanda, Uganda, Sri Lanka, India, Bangladesh, Hong Kong, Ghana and New York. Chief executive: Andy Sellins, The Cricket Centre, Plough Lane, Wallington, Surrey SM6 8JQ. Tel: 020 8669 2177; office@thechangefoundation.org.uk; www.thechangefoundation.org.uk.

CRICKET BUILDS HOPE, formerly the Rwanda Cricket Stadium Foundation, in 2017 successfully completed efforts to raise £1m to build a new cricket facility in Rwanda's capital, Kigali. The charity now plans more cricketing projects. Partnership head: Jon Surtees, The Kia Oval, London SE11 5SS. Tel: 020 7820 5780.

THE CRICKET SOCIETY TRUST aims to support schools and organisations to encourage enjoyment of the game and to develop skills. Particular effort is given to children with special needs, through programmes arranged with the Arundel Castle Cricket Foundation and the Belvoir Castle Cricket Trust. Hon. secretary: Ken Merchant, 16 Louise Road, Rayleigh, Essex SS6 8LW. Tel: 01268 747414; www.cricketsocietytrust.org.uk.

THE DICKIE BIRD FOUNDATION, set up by the former umpire in 2004, helps financially disadvantaged young people under the age of 18 to participate in the sport of their choice. Grants are made towards the cost of equipment and clothing. Trustee: Ted Cowley, 3 The Tower, Tower Drive, Arthington Lane, Pool-in-Wharfedale, Otley, Yorkshire LS21 1NQ. Tel: 07503 641457; www.thedickiebirdfoundation.co.uk.

THE ENGLAND AND WALES CRICKET TRUST was established in 2005 to aid community participation in cricket, with a fund for interest-free loans to amateur cricket clubs. In its last financial year (to January 2017) it spent £10.5m on charitable activities – primarily grants to cricket charities and amateur cricket clubs, and to county boards to support their programmes. Contact: ECB, Lord's Cricket Ground, London NW8 8QZ. Tel: 020 7432 1200; feedback@ecb.co.uk.

THE EVELINA LONDON CHILDREN'S HOSPITAL is the official charity partner of Surrey CCC and The Kia Oval. Ten minutes from the ground, Evelina is one of the country's leading children's hospitals, treating patients from all over south-east England. Partnership head: Jon Surtees, The Kia Oval, London SE11 5SS. Tel: 020 7820 5780; www.kiaoval.com.

FIELDS IN TRUST is the only UK charity protecting and improving green space for future generations to enjoy. We safeguard over 2,700 sites for sport, play and recreation. In the last five years we have added 311 sites where cricket is played. Chief Executive: Helen Griffiths, 36 Woodstock Grove, London W12 8LE. Tel: 020 7427 2110; www.fieldsintrust.org; www.facebook.com/fieldsintrust. Twitter; @FieldsInTrust.

THE HORNSBY PROFESSIONAL CRICKETERS' FUND supports former professional cricketers "in necessitous circumstances", or their dependants, through regular financial help or one-off grants towards healthcare or similar essential needs. Where appropriate it works closely with the PCA and a player's former county. The Trust was established in 1928 from a bequest from the estate of J. H. J. Hornsby (Middlesex, MCC and the Gentlemen), augmented more recently by a bequest from Sir Alec and Eric Bedser, and by a merger with the Walter Hammond Memorial Fund. Secretary: The Rev. Prebendary Mike Vockins OBE, Birchwood Lodge, Birchwood, Storridge, Malvern, Worcestershire WR13 5EZ. Tel: 01886 884366.

THE LEARNING FOR A BETTER WORLD (LBW) TRUST, established in 2006, provides tertiary education to disadvantaged students in the cricket-playing countries of the developing world. In 2017 it assisted over 2,000 students in India, Pakistan, Nepal, Uganda, Afghanistan, Sri Lanka, South Africa, Jamaica, Kenya and Tanzania. Chairman: David Vaux, GPO Box 3029, Sydney, NSW 2000, Australia; www.lbwtrust.com.au.

THE LORD'S TAVERNERS is the UK's leading youth cricket and disability sports charity, dedicated to giving disadvantaged and disabled young people a sporting chance. In 2018, it will donate over £4m to help young people of all abilities and backgrounds to participate in cricket and other sporting activities. Registered Charity No. 306054. The Lord's Taverners, 90 Chancery Lane, London WC2A 1EU. Tel: 020 7025 0000; contact@lordstaverners.org; www.lordstaverners.org.

THE PCA BENEVOLENT FUND is part of the Professional Cricketers' Association's commitment to supporting players and their dependants in need of a helping hand to readjust to a world beyond cricket, as well as current and past players who have fallen on hard times or are in need of specialist advice or assistance. Director of development and welfare: Ian Thomas, PCA, The Kia Oval, Laker Stand, London SE11 5SS. Tel: 07920 575578; www.thepca.co.uk.

THE PRIMARY CLUB provides sporting and recreational facilities for the blind and partially sighted. Membership is nominally restricted to those dismissed first ball in any form of cricket; almost 10,000 belong. In total, the club has raised £3m, helped by sales of its tie, popularised by *Test Match Special.* Andrew Strauss is president of the Primary Club Juniors. Hon. secretary: Chris Larlham, PO Box 12121, Saffron Walden, Essex CB10 2ZF. Tel: 01799 586507; www.primaryclub.org.

THE PRINCE'S TRUST helps disadvantaged young people get their lives on track. Founded by HRH The Prince of Wales in 1976, it supports 13–30-year-olds who are struggling at school or unemployed. The Trust's programmes use a variety of activities, including cricket, to engage young people and help them gain skills, confidence and qualifications. Prince's Trust House, 9 Eldon Street, London EC2M 7LS. Tel: 0800 842842; www.princes-trust.org.uk.

THE TOM MAYNARD TRUST – formed in 2012 after Tom's death – covers three main areas: helping aspiring young professionals with education projects, currently across six sports; running an academy in Spain for young county cricketers on the first rung of the career ladder; and providing grants for sportspeople to help with travel, kit, coaching, training and education. Contact: Mike Fatkin, 67a Radnor Road, Canton, Cardiff CF5 1RA; www.tommaynardtrust.com.

YOUTH TRUSTS – most of the first-class counties operate youth trusts through which donations, legacies and the proceeds of fundraising are channelled for the development of youth cricket and cricket in the community. Information may be obtained from the county chief executives.

CRICKET TRADE DIRECTORY

BOOKSELLERS

AARDVARK BOOKS, 10 Briardene Avenue, Scarborough, North Yorkshire YO12 6PL. Tel: 01723 374072; email: pete@aardvarkcricketbooks.co.uk or **pandlaardvark@btinternet.com**. Peter Taylor specialises in *Wisdens*, including rare hardbacks and early editions. *Wisdens* purchased. Restoration of hardbacks and softbacks, cleaning and gilding undertaken.

BOUNDARY BOOKS, The Haven, West Street, Childrey OX12 9UL. Tel: 01235 751021; email: mike@boundarybooks.com; website: boundarybooks.com. Rare books, cricket antiques, artworks, autographs and memorabilia bought and sold. Please register to receive regular email catalogues. Large Oxfordshire showroom open by appointment. Unusual and scarce items always available.

CHRISTOPHER SAUNDERS, Kingston House, High Street, Newnham-on-Severn, Gloucs GL14 1BB. Tel: 01594 516030; email: chris@cricket-books.com; website: cricket-books.com. Office/bookroom open by appointment. Second-hand/antiquarian cricket books and memorabilia bought and sold. Regular catalogues issued containing selections from over 12,000 items in stock.

GRACE BOOKS AND CARDS (Ted Kirwan), Donkey Cart Cottage, Main Street, Bruntingthorpe, Lutterworth, Leics LE17 5QE. Tel: 0116 247 8417; email: ted@gracecricketana.co.uk. Second-hand and antiquarian cricket books, *Wisdens*, autographed material and cricket ephemera of all kinds. Now also modern postcards of current international cricketers.

JOHN JEFFERS, The Old Mill, Aylesbury Road, Wing, Leighton Buzzard LU7 0PG. Tel: 01296 688543 or 07846 537692; e-mail: edgwarerover@live.co.uk. *Wisden* specialist. Immediate decision and top settlement for purchase of *Wisden* collections. Why wait for the next auction? Why pay the auctioneer's commission anyway?

J. W. McKENZIE, 12 Stoneleigh Park Road, Ewell, Epsom, Surrey KT19 0QT. Tel: 020 8393 7700; email: mckenziecricket@btconnect.com; website: mckenzie-cricket.co.uk. Specialist since 1971. Antiquarian and second-hand cricket books and memorabilia bought and sold. Catalogues issued regularly. Large shop premises open 9–4.30 Monday–Friday. Thirty minutes from London Waterloo. Please phone before visiting.

KEN FAULKNER, 65 Brookside, Wokingham, Berkshire RG41 2ST. Tel: 0118 978 5255; email: kfaulkner@bowmore.demon.co.uk; website: bowmore.demon.co.uk. Bookroom open by appointment. My stall, with a strong *Wisden* content, will be operating at the Cheltenham Cricket Festival in July 2018. We purchase *Wisden* collections which include pre-1946 editions.

ROGER PAGE, 10 Ekari Court, Yallambie, Victoria 3085, Australia. Tel: (+61) 3 9435 6332; email: rpcricketbooks@unite.com.au; website: rpcricketbooks.com. Australia's only full-time dealer in new and second-hand cricket books. Distributor of overseas cricket annuals and magazines. Agent for Association of Cricket Statisticians and Cricket Memorabilia Society.

ST MARY'S BOOKS & PRINTS, 9 St Mary's Hill, Stamford, Lincolnshire PE9 2DP. Tel: 01780 763033; email: info@stmarysbooks.com; website: stmarysbooks.com. Dealers in *Wisdens* 1864–2018, second-hand, rare cricket books and *Vanity Fair* prints. Book-search service offered.

SPORTSPAGES, 7 Finns Business Park, Mill Lane, Farnham, Surrey GU10 5RX. Tel: 01252 851040; email: info@sportspages.com; website: sportspages.com. Large stock of *Wisdens*, fine sports books and sports memorabilia, including cricket, rugby, football and golf. Books and sports memorabilia also purchased, please offer. Visitors welcome to browse by appointment.

TIM BEDDOW, 66 Oak Road, Oldbury, West Midlands B68 0BD. Tel: 0121 421 7117 or 07956 456112; email: wisden1864@hotmail.com. Wanted: any items of sporting memorabilia. Cricket, motor racing, TT, F1, stock cars, speedway, ice hockey, football, rugby, golf, boxing, horse racing, athletics and *all* other sports. Top prices paid for vintage items.

WILLIAM H. ROBERTS, Long Low, 27 Gernhill Avenue, Fixby, Huddersfield, West Yorkshire HD2 2HR. Tel: 01484 654463; email: william@roberts-cricket.co.uk; website: williamroberts-cricket.com. Second-hand/antiquarian cricket books, *Wisdens*, autographs and memorabilia bought and sold. Many thanks for your continued support.

WILLOWS PUBLISHING, 17 The Willows, Stone, Staffs ST15 0DE. Tel: 01785 814700; email: jenkins.willows@ntlworld.com; website: willowsreprints.com. *Wisden* reprints 1864–1946.

WISDEN DIRECT: wisdenalmanack.com/books. Various editions of *Wisden Cricketers' Almanack* since 2001 and other Wisden publications, all at discounted prices.

WISDENS.ORG, Tel: 07793 060706; email: wisdens@cridler.com; website: wisdens.org; Twitter: @Wisdens. The unofficial *Wisden* collectors' website. Valuations, guide, discussion forum, all free to use. *Wisden* prices updated constantly. We also buy and sell *Wisdens* for our members. Email us for free advice about absolutely anything to do with collecting *Wisdens*.

WISDENWORLD.COM, Tel: 01480 819272 or 07966 513171; email: bill.wisden@btinternet.com; website: wisdenworld.com. A unique and friendly service; quality *Wisdens* bought and sold at fair prices, along with free advice on the value of your collection. The UK's largest *Wisden*-only seller; licensed by Wisden.

AUCTIONEERS

CHRISTIE'S, 8 King Street, St. James's, London SW1Y 6QT. Tel: 0207 389 2157; email: jwilson@christies.com; website: christies.com. Christie's sells valuable cricket libraries and sets of *Wisden*. The Books Sale on 11 July 2018 will include *Wisdens* from 1864 to 1878. For valuations of complete collections or single items, contact Julian Wilson, senior books specialist.

DOMINIC WINTER, Specialist Auctioneers & Valuers, Mallard House, Broadway Lane, South Cerney, Gloucestershire GL7 5UQ. Tel: 01285 860006; website: dominicwinter.co.uk. Check our website for forthcoming specialist sales.

GRAHAM BUDD AUCTIONS in association with Sotheby's, PO Box 47519, London N14 6XD. Tel: 020 8366 2525; website: grahambuddauctions.co.uk. Specialist auctioneer of sporting memorabilia.

KNIGHTS WISDEN, Norfolk. Tel: 01263 768488; email: tim@knights.co.uk; website: knightswisden.co.uk. Established and respected auctioneers. World-record *Wisden* prices achieved in 2007. Four major cricket/sporting memorabilia auctions per year including specialist *Wisden* sale in May. Entries invited.

WISDENAUCTION.COM. Tel: 0800 7 999 501; email: wisdenauction@cridler.com; website: wisdenauction.com. A specially designed auction website for buying and selling *Wisdens*. List your spares today and bid live for that missing year. Every original edition for sale including all hardbacks. Built by collectors for collectors, with the best descriptions on the internet. See advert on page 156.

CRICKET DATABASES

CRICKETARCHIVE: cricketarchive.com. The most comprehensive searchable database on the internet with scorecards of all first-class, List A, pro T20 and major women's matches, as well as a wealth of league and friendly matches. The database currently has more than 1.25m players and over 700,000 full and partial scorecards.

CRICVIZ: cricviz.com; email: marketing@cricviz.com. CricViz is the official analytics provider to ICC and operates the largest cricket database, selling predictive modelling and analysis of the sport to broadcasters, teams and media clients, including wisden.com.

CSW DATABASE FOR PCs. Contact Ric Finlay, email: ricf@netspace.net.au; website: tastats.com.au. Men's and women's international, T20, Australian, NZ and English domestic. Full scorecards and 2,500 searches. Suitable for professionals and hobbyists alike.

WISDEN RECORDS: wisdenrecords.com. Up-to-date and in-depth cricket records from *Wisden*.

CRICKET COLLECTING, MEMORABILIA AND MUSEUMS

LORD'S TOURS & MUSEUM, Lord's Cricket Ground, St John's Wood, London NW8 8QN. Tel: 020 7616 8595; email: tours@mcc.org.uk; website: lords.org/tours. A tour of Lord's provides a fascinating behind-the-scenes insight into the world's most famous cricket ground. See the original Ashes urn, plus an outstanding collection of art, cricketing memorabilia and much more.

SIR DONALD BRADMAN'S CHILDHOOD HOME, 52 Shepherd Street, Bowral, NSW 2576, Australia. Tel: (+61) 478 779 642; email: andrewleeming@mac.com; website: 52shepherdstreet.com.au. The house where Don Bradman developed his phenomenal cricketing skills by throwing a golf ball against the base of a tank stand. Open for visits, accommodation, and special events.

WILLOW STAMPS, 10 Mentmore Close, Harrow, Middlesex HA3 0EA. Tel: 020 8907 4200; email: willowstamps@tinyonline.co.uk. Standing order service for new cricket stamp issues, comprehensive back stocks of most earlier issues.

WISDEN COLLECTORS' CLUB: Tel: 01480 819272 or 07966 513171; email: bill.wisden@btinternet.com; website: wisdencollectorsclub.co.uk. Free and completely impartial advice on *Wisdens*. We also offer *Wisdens* and other cricket books to our members, usually at no charge except postage. Quarterly newsletter, discounts on publications and a great website. Licensed by Wisden.

CRICKET EQUIPMENT

ACUMEN BOOKS, Pennyfields, New Road, Bignall End, Stoke-on-Trent ST7 8QF. Tel: 01782 720753; email: wca@acumenbooks.co.uk; website: acumenbooks.co.uk. Everything for umpires, scorers, officials, etc. MCC Lawbooks, open-learning manuals, Tom Smith and other textbooks, Duckworth/Lewis, scorebooks, equipment, over & run counters, gauges, heavy and Hi-Vis bails, etc; import/export.

ALL ROUNDER CRICKET, 39 St Michaels Lane, Headingley, Leeds LS6 3BR. Tel: 0113 203 3679; email: info@allroundercricket.com; website: allroundercricket.com. One of the UK's leading cricket retailers, stocking all the top brands, hand-picked by ex-professionals. Open every day, including our new megastore at the Penistone Road Trading Estate in Hillsborough, Sheffield. Also online with next day delivery available.

BOLA MANUFACTURING LTD, 6 Brookfield Road, Cotham, Bristol BS6 5PQ. Tel: 0117 924 3569; email: info@bola.co.uk; website: bola.co.uk. Manufacturer of bowling machines and ball-throwing machines for all sports. Machines for professional and all recreational levels for sale to the UK and overseas.

CHASE CRICKET, Dummer Down Farm, Basingstoke, Hampshire RG25 2AR. Tel: 01256 397499; email: info@chasecricket.co.uk; website: chasecricket.co.uk. Chase Cricket specialises in handmade bats and hi-tech soft goods. Established 1996. "Support British Manufacturing."

CRICKET SPEAKERS AND SOCIETIES

COUNCIL OF CRICKET SOCIETIES, Secretary: Dave Taylor, 16 Leech Brook Close, Audenshaw, Manchester M34 5PL. Tel: 0161 336 8536; email: taylor_d2@sky.com; website: councilcricketsocieties.com. For cricket lovers in the winter – join a local society and enjoy speaker evenings with fellow enthusiasts for the summer game.

LOOK WHO'S TALKING (Ian Holroyd), 20 Mill Street, Warwick, CV34 4HB. Tel: 01926 494323 or 07831 602131; email: ian@look-whos-talking.co.uk; website: look-whos-talking.co.uk. We specialise in providing first-class public speakers for cricket and other sporting events. Contact us to discuss the event and type of speaker. All budgets catered for.

THE CRICKET SOCIETY, c/o David Wood, Membership Secretary, PO Box 6024, Leighton Buzzard, LU7 2ZS. Email: david.wood@cricketsociety.com; website: cricketsociety.com. A worldwide society which promotes cricket through its awards, acclaimed publications, regular meetings, dinners and special events.

CRICKET TOUR OPERATORS

GULLIVERS SPORTS TRAVEL, Ground Floor, Ashvale 2, Ashchurch Business Centre, Alexandra Way, Tewkesbury, Gloucs GL20 8NB. Tel: 01684 879221; email: gullivers@gulliverstravel.co.uk; website: gulliverstravel.co.uk. The UK's longest-established cricket tour operator offers a great choice of supporter packages for the world's most exciting events – including the Ashes in Australia – and playing tours for schools, clubs, universities and military teams.

SMILE GROUP TRAVEL LTD, Gateway House, Stonehouse Lane, Purfleet, Essex RM19 1NS. Tel: 01708 893250; email: info@smilegrouptravel.com; website: smilegrouptravel.com. Smile are experts in tours for both playing and supporters. We work with many professional clubs, including Hampshire, Northamptonshire and Nottinghamshire. Our tours are defined by their excellence and value for money.

TRAVELBAG. Tel: 0203 139 7074; website: www.travelbag.co.uk. Worldwide tailor-made travel experts. We specialise in creating bespoke holidays to Asia, Australasia, North America, the Middle East, Indian Ocean, Latin America, Caribbean and the Mediterranean.

PITCHES AND GROUND EQUIPMENT

HUCK NETS (UK) LTD, Gore Cross Business Park, Corbin Way, Bradpole, Bridport, Dorset DT6 3UX. Tel: 01308 425100; email: sales@huckcricket.co.uk; website: huckcricket.co.uk. Alongside manufacturing our unique knotless high-quality polypropylene cricket netting, we offer the complete portfolio of ground and club equipment necessary for cricket clubs of all levels.

NOTTS SPORT, Innovation House, Magna Park, Lutterworth LE17 4XH. Tel: 01455 883730; email: info@nottssport.com; website: nottssport.com. Celebrating over 30 years as a leading supplier of ECB-approved, non-turf cricket pitch systems for coaching, practice and matchplay. Also awarded the ECB NTP Code of Practice Accreditation in 2013.

PLUVIUS, Willow Cottage, Canada Lane, Norton Lindsey, Warwick CV35 8JH. Tel: 07966 597203; email: pluviusltd@aol.com; website: pluvius.uk.com. Manufacturers of value-for-money pitch covers and sightscreens, currently used on Test, county, school and club grounds throughout the UK.

CHRONICLE OF 2017

JANUARY

5 South Africa beat Sri Lanka by 282 runs in Second Test at Cape Town; their fast bowler Kyle Abbott signs Kolpak deal with Hampshire. **7** Australia win Third Test at Sydney to complete 3–0 whitewash of Pakistan. **12** Hashim Amla scores a century in his 100th Test, at Johannesburg; South Africa go on to complete 3–0 whitewash of Sri Lanka. **14** Gujarat win India's Ranji Trophy for the first time, 66 years after their only previous final. **16** New Zealand win First Test at Wellington despite Bangladesh's first-innings 595. **18 Former England women's captain Rachael Heyhoe Flint dies, aged 77. 22** England win third ODI at Kolkata, but India take series 2–1. New Zealand beat Bangladesh 2–0 with victory in Second Test in Christchurch. **27** Former Australian batsman Stuart Law appointed coach of West Indies. **28** Perth Scorchers win Australia's T20 Big Bash. **31** Jamaican all-rounder Andre Russell banned for a year after missing three drug tests.

FEBRUARY

1 England lose eight wickets for eight runs in Bangalore as India take Twenty20 series 2–1. **4** ICC approve new constitution reversing many of the "Big Three" changes from 2014. **6 Alastair Cook resigns as England's Test captain after defeat in India; Joe Root later named as successor. 10** South Africa go top of ODI rankings after 5–0 whitewash of Sri Lanka. **13** India win one-off Test against Bangladesh at Hyderabad. **20** Ben Stokes fetches $US2.16m and Tymal Mills $1.8m at IPL auction. **25** Slow left-armer Steve O'Keefe takes six for 35 in each innings as Australia stun India by 333 runs in First Test at Pune. **26** Afghanistan skittle Zimbabwe for 54 in Harare, to win ODI series 3–2.

MARCH

1 Former England batsman and umpire John Hampshire dies, aged 76. **6** Peshawar Zalmi win Pakistan Super League final in Lahore, amid tight security. **7** India win Second Test in Bangalore by 75 runs to square series against Australia. **9 England beat West Indies by 182 runs in Bridgetown to sweep one-day series 3–0. 11** Sri Lanka beat Bangladesh by 259 runs in First Test at Galle. **18** South Africa beat New Zealand by eight wickets in Second Test at Wellington; other two matches are drawn. **19** Sri Lanka win by four wickets in Colombo to beat Bangladesh 2–0. **28** India beat Australia by eight wickets in Fourth Test at Dharamsala to win series 2–1. **29** Fast bowler Mohammad Irfan banned for six months by Pakistan board for failing to report match-fixing approach. **30** Victoria win third successive Sheffield Shield.

APRIL

13 Afghanistan batsman Mohammad Shahzad charged with doping offence by ICC; later banned. **18** Chris Gayle becomes first to reach 10,000 runs in senior Twenty20 cricket, during IPL match for Royal Challengers Bangalore. **23** Younis Khan is the first Pakistani – and, at 39, the oldest from anywhere – to reach 10,000 Test runs. **25** Pakistan beat West Indies by seven wickets in First Test at Kingston. **26 ECB members approve plan to establish eight-team franchise-based Twenty20 tournament in England in 2020.**

MAY

4 West Indies square series with 106-run victory over Pakistan at Brid
first one-day international against England at Lord's ends in 85-run
win Third Test in Dominica with six balls to spare to win serie
Haq and Younis Khan retire. 22 Mumbai Indians win the IPL
scores his 50th first-class century for Somerset, breaking Harold Gir
26 Kumar Sangakkara makes his fifth successive century for Surre

JUNE

1 Champions Trophy starts in England. **9** Afghanistan's 18-year-old leg-spinner Rashid Khan takes seven for 18 in ODI against West Indies in St Lucia. **14** England lose Champions Trophy semi-final to Pakistan in Cardiff. **15** Scotland beat Zimbabwe by 26 runs in Edinburgh, their first ODI victory over a Test-playing nation. **18 Pakistan beat India by 180 runs in Champions Trophy final at The Oval. 20** Anil Kumble resigns as India's coach, saying his partnership with captain Virat Kohli was "untenable". **22 Afghanistan and Ireland elevated to Test status at ICC annual meeting. 24** Women's World Cup starts in England; India beat England at Derby. Graham Ford resigns as Sri Lanka's coach.

JULY

1 Alex Hales hits 187* – a record for a Lord's final – as Nottinghamshire beat Surrey to win the Royal London Cup. **2** Sri Lanka leg-spinner Wanindu Hasaranga de Silva takes a hat-trick on ODI debut against Zimbabwe at Galle. **4** Sean Dickson scores 318 for Kent v Northamptonshire at Beckenham. **9** England win First Test against South Africa at Lord's by 211 runs, after Joe Root makes 190 in first game as captaion. **10** Zimbabwe beat Sri Lanka in Hambantota to take one-day series 3–2; Angelo Mathews resigns as Sri Lanka's captain. **13** Ravi Shastri appointed as India's coach. **17** South Africa square series with 340-run victory in Second Test at Nottingham. **18** Sri Lanka chase 388 to win Test against Zimbabwe in Colombo by four wickets. **23 England beat India by nine runs to win women's World Cup final at Lord's, Anya Shrubsole taking six for 46.** Ross Whiteley hits Karl Carver for six sixes in an over in Worcestershire's T20 Blast game against Yorkshire. **29** India beat Sri Lanka by 304 runs in First Test at Galle. **31** England win Third Test against South Africa by 239 runs; Moeen Ali ends the game with a hat-trick, the first in 100 men's Tests at The Oval.

AUGUST

3 Agreement is reached in long-running pay dispute between Australian board and players. **5** Former England batsman, selector and administrator Doug Insole dies, aged 91. **6** India win Second Test in Colombo. **7** England beat South Africa in Fourth Test at Manchester to win series 3–1. **14** India win Third Test by an innings at Pallekele to complete 3–0 sweep over Sri Lanka. **19 West Indies are trounced by an innings and 209 runs at Birmingham in the first day/night Test in England. 22** Shahid Afridi smashes 42-ball T20 century, the fastest of the English season, for Hampshire. **29** West Indies square series by scoring 322-5 to win the Second Test; Shai Hope becomes the first to score two hundreds in a first-class match at Headingley. Ottis Gibson, England's fast-bowling coach, confirmed as new coach of South Africa, replacing Russell Domingo. **30** Bangladesh beat Australia for the first time in a Test, Shakib Al Hasan taking ten wickets at Mirpur. Pakistan batsman Sharjeel Khan banned for five years for involvement in match-fixing. **31** Championship match between Surrey and Middlesex abandoned after crossbow bolt fired on to the pitch at The Oval.

SEPTEMBER

1 Former England women's captain Charlotte Edwards retires. **2** Nottinghamshire achieve white-ball double by winning T20 Blast. **3** India complete 5–0 whitewash in 50-over series in Sri Lanka. **7** Australia share series in Bangladesh after winning Second Test at Chittagong. **8** James Anderson takes 500th Test wicket at Lord's. **9** England win Third Test to take series against West Indies 2–1. Graham Ford announced as Ireland's new coach, replacing John Bracewell. **9** Trinbago Knight Riders win Caribbean Premier League. **12** World XI, captained by Faf du Plessis, play the first of three Twenty20 internationals in Lahore; Pakistan win 2–1. Jan Brittin, the leading scorer in women's

Tests, dies aged 58. **15** A year after promotion, Essex win first County Championship title since 1992. **16** Sri Lanka Test batsman Chamara Silva banned for two years for manipulating domestic matches. **20** Pakistan batsman Khalid Latif banned for five years for involvement in match-fixing. **25 Ben Stokes arrested after fracas in Bristol; stripped of vice-captaincy and suspended.** **28** Middlesex, the 2016 county champions, are relegated after losing to Somerset. Former ICC chief Haroon Lorgat steps down as CEO of Cricket South Africa. **29** England win ODI series against West Indies 4–0.

OCTOBER

1 New Code of Laws includes provision for umpires to send off unruly players. **2** Sri Lanka beat Pakistan by 21 runs in First Test in Abu Dhabi, Rangana Herath sealing victory with his 400th wicket. At Potchefstroom, South Africa thrash Bangladesh by 333 runs. **8** South Africa lose only four wickets in winning Second Test against Bangladesh at Bloemfontein. **10** Sri Lanka win pink-ball Second Test against Pakistan in Dubai by 68 runs, to claim series 2–0. Planned big-money T20 league in South Africa is cancelled. **13 ICC board approve Test Championship and One-Day League, to start after the 2019 World Cup.** **24** With 316* for Wellington v Auckland, Michael Papps, 38, becomes the oldest first-class triple-centurion since the Second World War. **25** Pune groundsman Pandurang Salgaoncar suspended after offering to manipulate the pitch for India's ODI against New Zealand. **25** West Indies win First Test against Zimbabwe at Bulawayo by 117 runs. **29** South Africa's David Miller reaches century in 35 balls – a T20 international record – against Bangladesh at Potchefstroom. **31** Chris Silverwood resigns as Essex coach to become England's fast-bowling coach.

NOVEMBER

2 West Indies win series in Zimbabwe after Second Test is drawn. **7** Mitchell Starc takes his second hat-trick of the match for NSW against Western Australia in Sydney. **9** Chandika Hathurusinghe resigns as Bangladesh coach; later joins his native Sri Lanka. Worcestershire all-rounder Alex Hepburn charged with rape. **12** Women's Ashes Test at Sydney is drawn; Ellyse Perry scores 213*. **17 Holders Australia retain the women's Ashes, after winning the first T20 international.** **20** Sri Lanka hang on to draw First Test against India at Kolkata. **21** Powered by Danni Wyatt's 56-ball century, England win final T20 international to draw the women's Ashes series, with eight points each overall. **27** Australia win First Ashes Test at Brisbane by ten wickets. India beat Sri Lanka by an innings in Second Test at Nagpur; Virat Kohli scores 213, and Ravichandran Ashwin takes his 300th wicket.

DECEMBER

3 Play in the Third Test in Delhi is held up by smog; the match is eventually drawn, giving India (for whom Kohli made 243) the series 1–0. Ben Stokes plays first of six white-ball matches for Canterbury in New Zealand. **5** New Zealand beat West Indies by five wickets in First Test at Wellington. **6** Australia win day/night Second Test at Adelaide, to go 2–0 up in Ashes. **10** Shakib Al Hasan reappointed Bangladesh's Test captain, in place of Mushfiqur Rahim. **12** Chris Gayle smashes a T20-record 18 sixes in 146* as Rangpur Riders win the BPL final in Bangladesh. New Zealand beat West Indies by 240 runs at Hamilton, to take series 2–0. **14** Steve Rhodes sacked as Worcester … director of cricket. **17** India beat Sri Lanka 3–0, their eighth successive C… **18 Australia win Third Test (England's eighth successive defeat a… the Ashes.** **27** A scheduled four-day Test is over in less than t… skittle Zimbabwe for 68 and 121 at Port Elizabeth. **30** England dra… Alastair Cook's 244* is the highest Test score by a visiting b… **31** Phil Simmons named as Afghanistan's head coach.

The following items were also reported during 2017:

DAILY MIRROR — January 2

County cricketer Laurie Evans had his £25,000 Mercedes stolen by a man posing as a potential purchaser. Evans was trying to sell it before his move from Warwickshire to Sussex. "I started showing the car, as you do," said Evans. "He just drove off." He was particularly upset by the loss of memorabilia signed by his former team-mates – and his best bat.

MUMBAI MIRROR — January 17

Left-arm spinner Sarfaraz Ashraf took six for nought in seven balls in a Karnataka state T20 tournament in Bangalore.

THELADIESFINGER.COM — January 18

The Queer Premier League (QPL), a tournament organised by a lesbian support group in advance of the annual Mumbai Pride march, was played for the third time, with 80 cricketers from the city's LGBTQ+ community taking part. One cheerleader, Sumit, said: "It's especially fun because for once we have women playing on the pitch and men cheerleading."

BBC — January 25

Aled Carey, 29, took six wickets in an over for Golden Point against East Ballarat in Victoria. Carey, unable to take a wicket in his first eight overs, fared dramatically better in the ninth.

WAIKATO TIMES — February 5

Freddy Walker scored an unbeaten 150 off 125 balls at No. 11 for Hamilton against Bay of Plenty. He came in at 189 for nine and shared an unbroken 220-run partnership with the No. 3, Anish Desai. Walker had scored just 54 in six previous innings over three seasons in the competition, which is just below first-class. "They were a little bit unlucky," he said, "but we were due a bit of luck too, and we got it."

AGENCE FRANCE-PRESSE February 6

A 14-year-old cricketer died in Chittagong, Bangladesh, after he was hit by a stump thrown by an angry batsman. Police said Faisal Hossain had been fielding close to the wicket when the batsman was given out and hurled the stump into the air. It hit Hossain in the neck.

THE TIMES February 7

Storms that hit in December 2015 caused over £3.5m worth of damage at 57 cricket clubs, according to an ECB report. Professor Piers Forster, a meteorologist at Leeds University, said: "UK weather will always bowl us the odd googly, but climate change is making them harder to defend against."

TIMES OF INDIA February 8

Delhi cricketer Mohit Ahlawat, 21, scored 300 not out in a local Twenty20 match for the Maavi XI against a Friends XI. The runs came off 72 balls, with 39 sixes and 14 fours. Ahlawat had failed to score in his previous three first-class innings. That night he got a call from IPL team Delhi Daredevils.

WIGAN EVENING POST February 9

An 18-year-old fast bowler from Croston, Lancashire, spent several days on an IV drip after disturbing a red-bellied black snake during a club match in Sydney. Joe Lyth, fielding on the boundary for Pennant Hills, had to collect a six hit into nearby undergrowth when he was bitten on the heel. He told his family at home he had been injured, calculating it would cause less worry.

ESPNCRICINFO February 10

All weekend club matches in New South Wales were cancelled because of extreme heat, with temperatures forecast to reach 40°C. The Sheffield Shield match at the SCG was allowed to go ahead; officials said they did not have the resources to monitor player safety elsewhere.

CANBERRA TIMES February 10

Thomas Perez took six wickets in six balls in Tuggerangong's final two-day game of the summer, against St Edmunds in the Australian Capital Territory's colts competition. Perez had match figures of 12 for 26; he had previously taken four wickets all season.

INDIAN EXPRESS/CRICBUZZ February 21/23

Ranji Trophy cricketer Harmeet Singh caused chaos by driving his car on to the platform of a Mumbai suburban railway station during the morning rush hour. No one was hurt, but Harmeet was charged with endangering the safety of passengers. He claimed to have taken a wrong turning. Early reports suggested the player involved was the better-known Harpreet Singh, who had been hoping to attract bids in the IPL auction that morning. By the time a correction was issued, it was too late (though Harpreet did get a chance as a replacement for Royal Challengers Bangalore).

ASIAN NEWS INTERNATIONAL March 18

Former Pakistan captain Javed Miandad said match-fixers should be executed: "Why don't you take strong measures? You should give death penalty to such people. We must not tolerate such things, not at all." He was supported by his former team-mate Abdul Qadir, who said the practice would have stopped if players involved previously had been hanged.

TIMES OF INDIA March 22

Winners of an annual tournament in Jawhar, Maharashtra, were given edible prizes instead of the customary money. The winning team were awarded a goat, the runners-up five cockerels, and every boundary-hitter a boiled egg. "In the past we have experienced allegations of rigging and fights over prize money. This time, all willingly shared their prizes," said local coach Umesh Tamore.

ABC NEWS April 1

Brayden Hayes, 23, ran 200 miles across Tasmania in his underpants after joking on Facebook that he would do just that if Hobart Hurricanes beat a record run total by Melbourne Renegades in Australia's Twenty20 Big Bash League. They did, and he did, raising nearly $A20,000 for charity.

NEW AGE, DHAKA April 4

A disgruntled team protested to the Bangladesh Cricket Board that electronic scorecards had been manipulated to hide the true number of lbws. Kathal Bagan Green Crescent were relegated after losing to North Bengal Cricket

Academy. Screenshots showed that at various times the number of lbws given had been six, five and four. Kathal Bagan claimed the actual number was seven, implying there had been a cover-up to hide unjust decisions.

THE AGE, MELBOURNE April 4

Cricket Australia announced dramatic plans to increase participation and skills in junior matches, including shorter pitches and boundaries, and smaller teams. Games will be seven a side for Under-11s, and nine for Under-14s. This followed a successful pilot, which showed a big decrease in the number of wides and no-balls, as well as greater involvement by all team members. "Children will no longer have to struggle with playing in conditions suited for adults," said the former Australian captain Belinda Clark.

DHAKA TRIBUNE/REUTERS April 12/May 2

Lalmatia bowler Sujon Mahmud conceded 92 runs in the opening over of an innings in the Dhaka League Second Division. He gave away 65 in wides (from 13 deliveries) and 15 from three no-balls, before opponents Axiom secured a ten-wicket win. Lalmatia were protesting against decisions taken by the umpires when they were all out for 88. Their secretary Adnan Rahman Dipon said the problems began at the toss: "My captain was not allowed to see the coin. We were sent to bat first and, as expected, the umpires' decisions came against us." In a similar incident, Tasnim Hasan of Fear Fighters conceded 69 off seven legitimate balls. The Bangladesh board were unimpressed by the grievances: they banned both bowlers for ten years for "tarnishing the image of Bangladesh cricket"; several club officials were banned for five years, and the teams were suspended from the league indefinitely.

INDIA TODAY April 24

A 12-year-old boy in Howrah, West Bengal, was apparently killed by a friend over a 250 rupee (£3) cricket bet, police said. The victim was reported to have won the bet, but the other boy, also 12, refused to pay, triggering a quarrel which ended with his smashing the other's head with a brick, before hiding the body in jungle.

HERITAGECRAFTS.ORG May 2017

Research into traditional crafts, sponsored by the Radcliffe Trust, lists cricket-ball making as one of four skills now extinct in Britain – along with gold-beating and the manufacture of lacrosse sticks, and of sieves and riddles. Today, no one makes hand-stitched cricket balls in the UK, says the Radcliffe Red List. "In some cases, the raw materials are sent from the UK to the Indian subcontinent for fabrication, and the balls are then finished in the UK." Cricket-bat making is listed as "endangered", but not "critically endangered".

May 2017

HUDDERSFIELD DAILY EXAMINER May 2

Inswing bowler Tony Wilkinson, 40, took six wickets in an over for Holmfirth Seconds against Birkby Rose Hill in the Huddersfield League. He was making his first appearance of the season after a single net session, which he described as "horrendous", and his first ball of the day was smashed into the bowling green for six. Wilkinson finished with 5.4–1–20–8 as the opposition were bowled out for 51. After Holmfirth won by five wickets, Wilkinson said: "It was all a bit of a blur."

INDIAN EXPRESS May 7

A 17-year-old boy, Sundeep Kumar, was killed by his own bat wielded by a 19-year-old market worker in Eluru, Andhra Pradesh, police said. Kumar refused to allow Suravarapu Prasad to join the game outside a local hall. Prasad then snatched the bat and hit him.

CRICKET.COM.AU May 9

Moonee Valley batsman Jatinder Singh's middle stump was sent flying, but the bails remained in place. The incident, in a match against Strathmore Heights in Melbourne, had everyone scratching their heads about how it happened – it remained mysterious – and what the umpire's verdict should be. Singh was eventually given out, correctly under what was then Law 28: "The wicket is put down if a bail is completely removed from the top of the stumps, or a stump is struck out of the ground." Another Australian, Jacobi Unbehaun, was also given out when a similar incident took place in an Under-17 match in Geraldton, even though the stump remained in the ground.

NORWICH EVENING NEWS May 15

John Reynolds, 83, has announced his retirement after 64 years of club cricket in Norfolk because of "worn-out knees". He took 5,811 wickets, including 14 hat-tricks.

TIMES OF INDIA May 16

A farmer died in Amroli, Gujarat, after being struck by a bat for refusing to return a ball that had been hit on to his land, police said. They were hunting for a 20-year-old man.

NEWS & STAR, CARLISLE/DAILY MAIL May 26

Roman remains being excavated at Carlisle CC's Edenside ground have been described as "really stunning" by city council leader Colin Glover. "There are whole rooms, surviving Roman floors, parts of cooking pots, including one with a lion's head through which sauces would be poured out," he said. "We want to work closely with the cricket club to make the best of this exciting discovery." A routine exploratory dig underneath the site of a planned new pavilion revealed the bathhouse used by the Ala Petriana cavalry, the Roman equivalent of the SAS. The pavilion will probably have to be built elsewhere.

DAILY MIRROR May 31

John Hoare, a 67-year-old pub landlord from Tunbridge Wells, took five wickets in five balls for Linden Park against Laughton II in the East Sussex County League. He finished with six for 20.

BALLET NEWS June 2

MCC and the Royal Academy of Dance have launched a pilot scheme in primary schools in an attempt to encourage more boys to try ballet, and girls to try cricket. Alexander Campbell, the Royal Ballet's cricket-loving principal dancer, is acting as the Academy's ambassador for the project.

RADIO AUSTRALIA June 7

The Australian women's team have dropped the name Southern Stars, and will be known as Australia. "Cricket cannot hope to be a sport for all Australians if it does not recognise the power of words, and the respect for women that sits behind such decisions," said Cricket Australia chairman David Peever.

HEREFORD TIMES June 9

A woman angry at being unable to find a parking place near her house drove on to the outfield and stopped play in the match between Dales CC and Luctonians in Leominster, Herefordshire. She got out of the car, locked it, and walked away. Dales asked people at the match to bring their cars inside the ground to free up space, and the woman came back 15 minutes later to remove the obstruction. "We are going to send a letter encouraging people to park inside the ground, as we do want to be good neighbours," said Dales captain Jon Jones.

June 2

HINDUSTAN TIMES June 9

In a phone scan, a 69-year-old man from Kalyan, near Mumbai, who believed he had won 1m rupees (£12,000) in an IPL prediction competition, was instead cheated out of 25,000 (£300).

ALREWAS.PLAY-CRICKET.COM June 10

In the Derbyshire League, Alrewas opening bowler Loz Cousins had figures of 7.3–7–0–9 in a third-team match against Brailsford & Ednaston. Their openers put on 16, but the side were bowled out for 31.

DAILY ECHO, BOURNEMOUTH June 14

Lymington and Bashley played their Hampshire League Division Three South game bowling from only one end after vandals dug holes in the pitch. "Thankfully, the Bashley captain said they wanted to play, and we weren't going to let these hooligans stand in our way," said Lymington captain Chris Tollerfield. (The *Echo's* report began: "Lymington and Bashley are unlikely to receive a mention in *Wisden*...")

DAILY TELEGRAPH June 14

Travellers were accused of leaving a trail of destruction after camping for five days on the outfield of Eight Ash Green CC in Essex. The second-team fixture against West Mersea was called off, and there were fears the pitch would have to be relaid because of damage by vehicles.

DAILY EXPRESS June 16

Ash Tree CC, based in Prestbury, Cheshire, won a match on their annual overseas tour for the first time in 35 years, beating Sir William Hoste CC by two runs on the Croatian island of Vis. Though the club claim a reasonable record at home, their tour results became a standing joke. "We used to share our record with the team we were playing," said chairman Mark Crook. "But they never believed us, and thought it was a ploy." Ash Tree, whose average age is 55, returned to form next day, when they lost the rematch.

TIMES OF INDIA June 20

Mumbai cricket officials are worried about the future of the game on the 25-acre Azad Maidan. One large chunk of land has already been lost to the construction of a new metro line. Now police want to reserve an extra 10,000 square feet to demarcate space for protests.

THE SPIN/TIMES OF INDIA June 21/25

Amnesty International intervened after 19 Pakistan supporters were arrested for celebrating and chanting "Pakistan Zindabad" when India were beaten in the Champions Trophy final. "These arrests are patently absurd," said Amnesty India programme director, Asmita Basu. "Arresting someone for cheering a rival team clearly violates their right to freedom of expression." In the Himalayan city of Roorkee, local lawyers voted unanimously not to represent a man accused of congratulating Pakistan on Facebook.

MACCLESFIELD EXPRESS June 26

A bull stopped play at Kerridge CC, Cheshire, by charging after two fielders and an umpire during a match against Mossley. "At first I just thought 'Hello, what's this?' as it was just plodding around the pitch," said Mossley captain Adam Banks. "But then it took one look at me and started charging." Some people sought refuge in the nearby pub before the bull wandered off. It was recaptured.

DAILY NEWS, COLOMBO JULY 3

Game wardens have been deployed in Sri Lanka to stop wild elephants straying on to the pitch during the three one-day internationals against Zimbabwe at Hambantota. The stadium is next to an elephant sanctuary, and close to a patch of jungle. Elephants have occasionally invaded the pitch at night, but not during a match.

NEW STATESMAN July 6

After being invited to the England–South Africa Test at Lord's, French ambassador Sylvie Bermann thought it was like the Brexit negotiations in Brussels. "Both can be a slow, precise and technical game," she said. "And it can be quite difficult for the uninitiated to understand what is happening. After days of play and exchanges, the match can end in a draw – with each side claiming they've won."

BELFAST TELEGRAPH July 19

Tommy Curlett, 79, has celebrated 55 years as groundsman at Dundrum CC in County Down.

July 6

INDO-ASIAN NEWS SERVICE July 22

A couple were arrested and charged with attempted murder after using a bat and stumps to attack a policeman who stopped their 13-year-old son from playing cricket outside their home in Delhi. Head Constable Satyendra Singh, a neighbour, received multiple head injuries. A police spokesman said the boy was trying to scratch a car with a stump.

DAILY MIRROR July 29

England's cricketers beat the London traffic by taking the Tube to The Oval on the third day of their Test against South Africa.

THE TIMES July 30

Sir Ian Botham announced plans to donate 10,000 pheasants and partridges from his shooting estates to a food charity, along with £40,000 so they can be turned into ready meals for the needy. Sir Ian said he expected criticism: "If everybody out there is a vegetarian or a vegan, well, fine – but they are not. So smell the coffee, try it. We are offering something that has had a wild life, a good life."

SUNDERLAND ECHO/AGENCE FRANCE-PRESSE August 10/11

Luke Robinson, 13, took six wickets in an over, all bowled, in an Under-13 match for Philadelphia CC, County Durham, against Langley Park. "Time stood still, and I thought, 'Is this really happening?'" said the umpire at the bowler's end, Stephen Robinson, who also happened to be the bowler's father. Luke's mother, Helen, was scoring. The opposition were dismissed for 18, and Philadelphia won by 58 runs.

BBC August 13

Needing 35 off the final over, Dorchester-on-Thames scored 40 to win their Oxfordshire Cricket Association match against Swinbrook. Steve McComb, who says he prefers to hit boundaries due to an arthritic ankle, hit 66044666 off Mihai Cucos (there were two no-balls).

AGENCE FRANCE-PRESSE August 21

Geoffrey Boycott apologised for an insulting remark at a Q&A session during the Edgbaston Test against West Indies. He told guests that knighthoods had been showered on West Indian cricketers "like confetti", adding: "Mine's been turned down twice. I'd better black me face."

DAILY EXPRESS August 22

Seagulls prevented play on the opening day of Somerset's Second XI match against Essex at Taunton Vale. They pecked holes in the groundsheets and left the pitch waterlogged. "Once there is a hole in the covers they rip very easily," said Somerset groundsman Rob Hake. "We have just had to spend £12,000 on new covers at our main county ground because they had been damaged by seagulls."

THE SPIN August 22

Cricket clubs across England reported a spate of break-ins in 2017, focused on mowers and ground equipment. They affected not just remote or vulnerable village grounds but also those surrounded by houses. "We have had graffiti in the past, things going missing. But this was something else, it was a professional and clearly planned job," said Paul Hatton, chairman of Oldswinford & Stourbridge CC, Worcestershire. Coldharbour CC in Surrey lost their third generator in three years. No arrests have yet been made, anywhere. The ECB said they were unaware that the problem was worse than before.

PRESS ASSOCIATION/BBC August 24/Sept 28

Residents of a new estate bordering the ground at Feethams, where Darlington CC have played since 1866, objected to a new all-weather practice area, citing the noise from net sessions. They complained about the sound of bat and ball – and also of bowlers grunting. One letter took issue with men "dropping their trousers to remove thigh pads and boxes in their underwear". Councillors agreed training could continue as long as the club reduced their hours, and the sessions were "properly supervised".

BBC August 26

Chris Lintott, presenter of the astronomy programme *The Sky at Night* and a guest on *Test Match Special*, said that working out how a cricket ball behaves was more complicated than understanding the workings of the universe.

BREAKING BELIZE NEWS September 2

A well-known Belize defence lawyer, Leeroy Banner, was ambushed and beaten up at a cricket match in Double Head Cabbage village.

August 26

GAZETTE & HERALD, SWINDON September 4

Jif Wilkins from Wiltshire village club Goatacre had to be carried to the crease when the ninth wicket fell in a crucial match against Cheltenham: the winners would be promoted to the West of England Premier League. Wilkins, who had injured his knee fielding and was unable to move, refused an ambulance "in case it goes down to the wire and I have to bat". He whacked his first ball past cover for four, and worked another away for his runner to scramble the single that tied the scores (and secured promotion). He then hit the winning four. "I don't like to praise him too much," said Goatacre captain Ed Wilkins, "as he's my brother. But it was a great effort."

MANCHESTER EVENING NEWS September 8

Residents in a Cheshire village want to stop a cricket club vacating the site they have occupied for more than a century. Bredbury St Mark's CC want to move to a new, bigger home, financing it by selling the current ground as a 22-house estate. Geoff Mountford of the club's relocation committee said the ground was too small, especially now that modern bats made it so easy to hit sixes. The neighbours prefer the open space.

DAILY MAIL September 10

A vicar was reunited with the cricket ball he lost as a seven-year-old – 38 years before. The Rev. Simon Ward grew up in the rectory at Belton, Norfolk, and when the family moved out he jokingly asked the new occupants to look out for the ball. It resurfaced when work was being done on a pond. "It was brand new, a nice shiny cricket ball, my first one," said Ward. "We barely got the first over finished before it got lost. I remember I cried my eyes out. It's now a shrivelled husk of its former glory, not the red shiny ball I fell in love with. But it was charming to discover it."

TIME.COM September 11

The Sir Vivian Richards Stadium on Antigua was turned into a shelter to house a hundred homeless people after Hurricane Irma devastated the neighbouring island of Barbuda.

PRETORIA NEWS September 14/October 16

Two young coaches were found dead in the pavilion at Laudium CC, Pretoria, and two of their colleagues seriously wounded. Given Nkosi, 24, and Charlson Maseko, 26, died from head injuries. Northerns Cricket said the two men were a valued part of the union's development programme. The four lived at the ground, and the two who survived said they had no idea who had attacked them or why. Nothing was stolen, and a month later police were still baffled.

STAGECC.CO.UK September 17

The 86-year-old actor Brian Jackson (The Man from Del Monte) and 12-year-old John Child – a loan player from the opposition – were both not out at the end of Stage CC's match against Maidenhead & Bray.

THE HINDU September 21

P. Visweswaran, a 12-year-old boy from Sithampoondi, Tamil Nadu, died after being struck on the back of the head by a cricket bat. The accident happened at school when the bat, swung by the boy's teacher, broke in two, leaving the handle in his hands. The boy's family later staged a protest demanding that the teacher, A. Kuppusamy, be arrested. He was charged with "culpable homicide not amounting to murder".

MID-DAY, MUMBAI September 25

An Indian family have sought refuge in Dubai after falling out with their neighbours in a middle-class residential complex in Mumbai: their son, who was playing cricket in a car park, damaged a windscreen wiper. "We couldn't face the harassment and torture any more," said Anil D'Souza, father of 13-year-old Aryan. "We cannot stay in a place where people are jealous and violent, and do not like children."

TELEGRAPH & ARGUS, BRADFORD September 25

Keighley CC have banned all food and drink from changing-rooms after peanuts were found by players. Two members have a severe nut allergy, and the club have also decided to stop selling nuts anywhere in the facilities.

SUNDAY TIMES October 1

Six Afghan refugees who settled nearby have transformed the fortunes of Langton Green CC in Kent. They won every game but two in 2017, having struggled to field a team the previous season. "You couldn't fault these guys," said club stalwart Martin Russell. "They can do it all – bat, bowl, field. It's as if they have been playing English village cricket all their lives."

AGENCE FRANCE-PRESSE October 7

A teenage umpire died after being hit on the chest in an informal match at Balur Math, Dhaka. "He is from a very poor family," said the local police chief. "His father is a rickshaw-puller and mother works as a housemaid. They buried him last night."

CLUBCRICKET.CO.ZA October 10

Club fixture lists in Cape Town and across the Western Cape have been slashed for the second consecutive season because of water restrictions caused by a long-running drought. Most senior leagues have been left untouched, but in some lower divisions the number of games has been halved. This follows the cancellation of 500 matches in 2016-17. "Together, we as an urban family must rise to the challenge during a critical juncture of the city's existence," said Western Province Cricket Association president Beresford Williams.

THE SPIN/KASHMIR OBSERVER October 10

Judges stopped play after 13 overs of the Under-23 match between Jammu & Kashmir and Goa in Srinagar. The regional high court issued an order halting the game after Hashim Saleem, a J&K player who had been dropped from the squad, lodged a petition claiming one of the selectors had unjustly picked his own son instead. The match was rescheduled after the court modified the order.

CRICKET.COM.AU October 16

Josh Dunstan scored 307 – with 40 sixes – for West Augusta in a 35-over match against Central Stirling in Port Augusta, South Australia. West Augusta's total was 354 and, while Dunstan was at the crease, all but 11 runs came from his bat. He shared a seventh-wicket stand of 203 with Ben Russell, who contributed five.

DAILY MAIL AUSTRALIA October 16

A 15-year-old umpire was taken to hospital after allegedly being headbutted by a spectator while officiating in an Under-11 match in the Melbourne suburb of Sunshine North. A witness said he was attacked after telling a group of spectators to stop drinking alcohol during a match between Sunshine and Caroline Springs.

SOMERSET LIVE October 19

The Somerset County Ground has been given Mayfair's place of honour in a Taunton edition of Monopoly.

CRICKET.COM.AU October 21

Nick Gooden of Yallourn North took eight for two in ten balls – including five in five and a separate hat-trick – against Latrobe in a third-grade match in Central Gippsland, Victoria.

INDIAN EXPRESS October 22

The BCCI have banned Dharamveer Pal, who is partially paralysed by polio, from working as a ball boy, as well as all other physically handicapped people. This followed criticism on social media. "Poor advertisement for polio-free India," said one tweet. "I have been cheering the Indian team for years now and will continue to do so," said Dharamveer, who has "Cricket is the reason for my living" tattooed on his arm.

October 19

THE NIGHTWATCHMAN Winter

Eileen Ash (née Whelan), the last survivor of the first women's Test played in England, in 1937, marked her 106th birthday on October 30 by taking a flight in a Tiger Moth over the Norfolk coast. The plane was a mere 76-year-old.

THE STAR, SHEFFIELD November 1

Parkhead CC are considering using urine on the outfield to help deter badgers who have been ripping up the turf.

ESPNCRICINFO November 2

A total of 136 wides were bowled in 65.3 overs during an Under-19 women's championship match in India between Nagaland and Manipur in Dhanbad, India. Manipur bowled 94 of them. "Forget about being accurate, balls were barely reaching the other end," an official said. "The gap in standards between the top sides and the rest is huge in women's cricket." Both states are in north-east India, where cricket is less developed.

DAILY TELEGRAPH/HUFFINGTON POST November 2/8

A racist flyer attacking Indian and Chinese-origin electoral candidates has been distributed in Edison, New Jersey. "The Chinese and Indians are taking over our town. Chinese school! Indian school! Cricket fields! Enough is enough," the flyer said. Next to their pictures was the word "Deport". The two targets, Jerry Shi and Falguni Patel, were both elected.

MANCHESTER EVENING NEWS November 6

Fothergill & Harvey, a predominantly Asian club in Rochdale, may have to fold after the pavilion was burned down on Bonfire Night in an apparently racially motivated attack. A week earlier, the building had been badly vandalised.

SPORTSKEEDA November 8

Akash Choudhary, a 15-year-old left-arm seamer, had figures of 4–4–0–10 in a Twenty20 match for Disha Cricket Academy against Pearl Academy in Jaipur. Choudhary took two wickets in each of his first three overs and four in the last, including a hat-trick. "All luck," he said.

VARIOUS YORKSHIRE NEWSPAPERS November 15/24

Former England captain Andrew Flintoff opened to polite but mixed reviews when *Fat Friends: The Musical*, an adaptation of a TV show about slimming, began its run at the Leeds Grand Theatre prior to a national tour. Lancastrian Flintoff played nice-but-dim Kevin, fiancé of a bride desperate to fit into her wedding dress, in a story set in the unLancastrian suburb of Headingley. Flintoff "proves he can do more than play cricket", said the *Yorkshire Post.* He captured Kevin well and won plenty of laughs, according to the *Huddersfield Daily Examiner*, "but sadly his vocals just weren't up to the task". *The Press*, from York, praised his "warm-toned" singing, but said his movement was "not exactly comfortable".

NEW ZEALAND HERALD November 20

Racist abuse forced the abandonment of a match in Levin, New Zealand. Kapiti Old Boys chose to end the game after a Levin Old Boys batsman insulted a fielder for not signalling a boundary quickly enough. Levin club secretary Daniel Parker said the batsman apologised at once, and the game continued, but eight overs later Kapiti decided to walk off.

ESSEX LIVE November 20

Shenfield CC say they may have to close after nearly 100 years because the borough council are trying to take away their car park, which generates much of the club's income. Shenfield have 200 members, and 250 colts go there for coaching.

SUPERSPORT.COM November 22

On his 20th birthday Shane Dadswell scored 490 off 151 balls, playing for North-West University in Potchefstroom against Potch Dorp CC. He hit 57 sixes and 27 fours, while the team made 677 for three off 50 overs, and won by 387 runs. The previous week Dadswell had scored 126 off 38. He said he was "a bit of an attacking batsman".

INDIAN EXPRESS November 24

The Indian Navy issued a warrant for the arrest of acting petty officer Deepak Punia, who was playing for the Haryana team in the Ranji Trophy without permission. Cricketing members of the armed forces are expected to play for the Services team unless given special dispensation.

THE SPIN November 29

The Nagaland women's Under-19s were bowled out for two by Kerala. Their only runs – a single and a wide – came during the six-over opening partnership. Head coach Hokaito Zhimoni said that Nagaland, a small state in north-east India, had been forced to advertise for players, and had hardly any time to practise. "Now the girls have got a sense of where they stand and where they need to improve," he said.

TIMES OF INDIA November 29

Farmers near Delhi are turning their land into cricket grounds, staging Twenty20 matches for amateur players and charging far more than they ever earned growing wheat or mustard. Some villages now boast several mini-stadiums, complete with canteens and floodlights. With lights, grounds can stage up to five games a day for the city's growing middle classes.

THEREGISTER.CO.UK November 30

Microsoft have announced they will build a cricket pitch as part of a "multi-year campus refresh project" at their HQ outside Seattle. Microsoft CC, who currently play in a nearby park, field four teams in the NorthWest Cricket League.

ALL INDIAN NEWSPAPERS December

Indian captain Virat Kohli married Bollywood actress Anushka Sharma in a private ceremony in Florence on December 11. This was followed by lavish receptions in Delhi and Mumbai. The decision to marry abroad was attacked by Panna Lal Shakya, a BJP assembly member from Madhya Pradesh. "Virat earned money in India, but he didn't find any place to marry in the country," said Shakya. "This proves he is not a patriot." Kohli should have looked to Hindu deities for inspiration, he added: "Lord Rama, Lord Krishna… got married on this land. None of us goes to a foreign country to get married."

MAIL ON SUNDAY December 3

After 18 long-distance walks that have raised more than £30m for charity, Sir Ian Botham, 62, announced he will embark on no more.

RACING POST December 9

Sandow :course are to improve their boundary fences after a steepl ›ed and was found a mile and a half away on the outfield at West C. Mustmeetalady (who, despite his name, is a gelding) was unha s the square.

DAILY TELEGRAPH December 22

›eing replaced by cricket at girls' schools because cricket is seen Re ›ort, whereas rounders is "a leisure activity", according to a London a er. "You can't really represent your country in rounders in quite the ›an at cricket. Where does it lead?" said Carol Chandler-Thompson, Blackheath High School.

e always grateful for contributions from readers, especially stories from or non-UK media. Items from club and school websites are also welcome. ase send newspaper cuttings to Matthew Engel at Fair Oak, Bacton, erefordshire HR2 0AT (always including the paper's name and date) and weblinks to almanack@wisdenalmanack.com.

INDEX OF TEST MATCHES

Ten earlier Test series – India v New Zealand, Pakistan v West Indies, Bangla
Zimbabwe v Sri Lanka, Australia v South Africa, India v England, New Zealand v Pa
v Pakistan, South Africa v Sri Lanka, New Zealand v Bangladesh – appeared in *Wisd*

INDIA v BANGLADESH IN 2016-17

INDIA v AUSTRALIA IN 2016-17

SRI LANKA v BANGLADESH IN 2016-17

NEW ZEALAND v SOUTH AFRICA IN 2016-17

WEST INDIES v PAKISTAN IN 2016-17

ENGLAND v SOUTH AFRICA IN 2017

SRI LANKA v ZIMBABWE IN 2017

SRI LANKA v INDIA IN 2017

INDEX OF UNUSUAL OCCURRENCES

INDEX OF ADVERTISEMENTS

PART TITLES